THE ROYA[L &] ANCIENT

GOLFER'S HANDBOOK

1995

92nd YEAR OF PUBLICATION

EDITOR MICHAEL WILLIAMS

This edition published 1995 by
MACMILLAN REFERENCE BOOKS
18–21 Cavaye Place, London SW10 9PG

British Library Cataloguing in Publication Data
A CIP catalogue record for this book is available from the British Library

ISBN 0–333–626818
ISBN 0–333–626826 (Pbk)

Note
Whilst every care has been taken in compiling the information contained in this book, the Publishers, Editor and Sponsors accept no responsibility for any errors or omissions.

Correspondence
Letters on editorial matters should be addressed to:
The Editor, Royal & Ancient Golfer's Handbook
Macmillan Reference Books
18–21 Cavaye Place
London SW10 9PG

Enquiries about despatch, invoicing and commercial matters should be addressed to:
Customer Services Department
Macmillan Press Limited
Houndmills
Basingstoke
Hampshire RG21 2XS

Advertising
Enquiries about advertising space in this book should be addressed to:
Communications Management International
Chiltern House
120 Eskdale Avenue
Chesham
Buckinghamshire HP5 3BD

Desk editor: Fred Gill

Cover photograph: Nick Price © Phil Sheldon

Typeset by Heronwood Press, Medstead, Hampshire

Printed by BPC Hazell Books, Aylesbury, Bucks

Contents

Part III: Past Tournament Results

Part IV: Who's Who in Golf

Part V: Clubs and Courses in the British Isles and Europe

Part VI: The Government of the Game

Part VII: Golf History

Foreword

Michael Williams

Golf was thrown into some disarray towards the end of 1994 with a surprise announcement by Greg Norman, in conjunction with Rupert Murdoch and the Fox television company, that it was their intention to launch a new World Tour for the best 30 or 40 players in the game. However, it met stern resistance from both the United States PGA Tour and the PGA European Tour, the chief controllers of the professional game.

Norman's proposal was for eight tournaments to be staged, four in America and one each in Canada, the United Kingdom, Spain and Japan for total prize money of $25 million. The feasibility of such an enterprise was quickly deemed impractical by its opponents.

Schedules for 1995 had already been confirmed and there were bound to be breaches of contract with sponsors if the best players were unable to compete because they were otherwise engaged on a World Tour. Certainly there were not enough free weeks in the year to accommodate eight new tournaments and the compromise of staging them at the end of the official season was rejected by the organisers of the splinter group.

Michael Williams

Norman's vision of the best players opposing one another on a more regular basis than at just the major championships had some appeal, though it failed to take into account the fact that the US Open, PGA and Masters are already much more international events than they were, though not yet on the scale of the Open Championship. Furthermore, the immediate proximity of four of the proposed World Tour events to the major championships would clearly be harmful.

Tim Finchem, commissioner of the United States PGA Tour, made it clear that defectors to a World Tour would forfeit their membership of the US Tour and the indications were that the majority of players were not prepared to take such a step, recognising perhaps that any short-term gain would be harmful to the long-term benefit of the game.

There were further signs in 1994 that the United States' domination of the world of golf is a thing of the past. At the conclusion of the season, both in the States and in Europe early in November, only two Americans, Fred Couples and Cory Pavin, were in the top 10 of the Sony world rankings and only seven in the top 20.

For the first time no American won any of the world's four major championships, Nick Price of Zimbabwe taking both the British Open and the US PGA, Ernie Els of South Africa the US Open and José Maria Olazabal of Spain the Masters.

Price is the first player to capture two majors in the same year since Nick Faldo triumphed in the Masters and British Open Championships in 1990. With four other victories on the American tour, which made seven in the year counting an earlier one in South Africa, he accordingly went to the top of the Sony world rankings ahead of Norman, Bernhard Langer, Nick Faldo and Olazabal.

The biggest advance in terms of Sony points was made by Els, a mightily impressive player, who also won the World Matchplay the day before his 25th birthday as well as the Dubai

Desert Classic. He consequently moved from 20th place to seventh. Olazabal jumped from 15th to fifth, Price from fourth to first and Colin Montgomerie, a steadily improving player, from 14th to eighth.

Significant gains were also made by three Americans; Tom Lehman, who moved from 48th to 18th, Fuzzy Zoeller, 46th to 12th and Phil Mickelson, 47th to 19th. Severiano Ballesteros also found much of his old form to advance from 25th to 15th. Mickelson, a left-hander who missed some of the season when he broke his leg skiing, is the most talented of the younger Americans. However, it was a 43-year-old, Mark McCumber, who was the biggest US multiple winner, collecting three tournaments, including the final Tour Championship.

It was a year not totally without international success for the Americans. They won the inaugural President's Cup against an international team which excluded Europeans; Fred Couples and Davis Love won the World Cup for a third successive year, while their women professionals recaptured the Solheim Cup.

Just as Price was again leading money winner in the States, so again was Montgomerie in Europe – the first player to stay at the head of the field since Sandy Lyle in 1980. Montgomerie had three tournament victories and on six other occasions finished fourth or better, a record of remarkable consistency and earning him record prize money of £762,719.

One of the greatest pleasures was nonetheless the revival of Ballesteros, who won twice and in his last eight events had three seconds and a first. It is a tribute to his personality that he was instantly forgiven an ill-conceived campaign against Valderrama, in Spain, getting the 1997 Ryder Cup match, though when he did lose this somewhat messy battle he did so with grace.

There continues to be no shortage of money in professional golf, at the top end of the market anyway. Million-dollar-plus tournaments are, to put it perversely, now two-a-penny and a Five Tours Andersen Consulting World Championship of Golf (itself quite a mouthful) will be worth $3.65 million though since it is to be held in what has become the 'silly season' at the end of the year, there is no guarantee that all the big names will be particularly interested. Money is not everything, particularly when you've got enough of it.

Even so, the European Tour, to keep its upward spiral, has had to spread its wings far beyond Europe with tournaments now in Dubai, the Philippines and South Africa. Equally controversial has been a new alliance with Sky television as a competitor to the BBC. Coverage of tournaments has therefore been considerably more extensive but only for the comparative few as audiences have been very small.

Part of the deal has been to award Sky this year's Ryder Cup in America. Come the time of the match in September when the majority will be deprived of an occasion that is something of a national institution, many friends will be lost. It might be something that should have been borne in mind before the contract was signed.

Though Britain's women professionals lost the Solheim Cup, this was adequately compensated for by Laura Davies, who became the first Briton, and indeed European, to top both the American LPGA money list and the Ping world rankings.

This was an outstanding performance to bear comparison with that of Nick Price in the men's world. Davies won eight times worldwide, three of them on the US Tour, including the McDonald's LPGA title, her second major championship to go with her 1987 US Open. There is no more exciting or more gifted woman golfer in the world today.

The Captain of the Royal & Ancient Golf Club of St Andrews

Gordon Boyd Buchanan Jeffrey, who was nominated by the past captains, drove himself into office as Captain of the Royal & Ancient Golf Club of St Andrews for the year 1994–95 at the club's autumn meeting in September.

He was born in Aberdeen in April 1935 but from a comparatively early age has lived in England, his home now being in Southport, Lancashire.

Mr Jeffrey was educated at Merchant Taylors School, Crosby, and at Liverpool University where he obtained a degree in law.

On leaving university he was awarded a National Service Commission in the Royal Artillery and served with the 17th Gurkha Division in Malaya.

When he returned to civilian life Mr Jeffrey entered the legal profession and has for many years been a partner in Lace Mawer, the well-known firm of Liverpool and Manchester solicitors.

He is a long-standing member of the Royal Birkdale Golf Club where he served on the Council before becoming captain in 1968, the youngest person to hold that office. He remains a trustee of the club.

Mr Jeffrey was elected a member of the Royal & Ancient in 1974 and was a member of the Championship committee before becoming its chairman from 1982–84. His term covered the Open Championship victories by Tom Watson at both Royal Troon and Royal Birkdale and then Severiano Ballesteros at St Andrews. From 1988–91 he became chairman of the Royal & Ancient's General committee and he has also served as joint chairman of the World Amateur Golf Council.

Mr Jeffrey is married and has three sons, all of whom are keen golfers, as is his wife, Jill. A good golfer himself, he reached the fourth round of the 1962 Amateur Championship at Royal Liverpool. His lowest handicap was one and he currently plays off six.

CENTENARY CLUBS 1995

WE WOULD LIKE TO EXTEND OUR WARMEST WISHES TO THE FOLLOWING CLUBS IN THEIR CENTENARY YEAR.

Broadway Golf Club

Willersey Hill, Broadway, Worcestershire WR12 7LG
Tel: (01386) 853683

Broadway Golf Club founded on 18th April 1895 is affiliated to the Gloucestershire Golf Union having moved to its present location in 1911 as a 9-hole course, the 18-holes being completed in 1962. All who play the course have Dr Charles Turner Standring to thank for his foresight in founding the club which is so well thought of. Broadway is not known as a hilly course but has magnificent views over the Vale of Evesham and far beyond.

Abbeydale Golf Club

Twentywell Lane, Dore, Sheffield S17 4QA
Tel: 0114 236 0763 Fax: 0114 236 0762

A mature 18-hole undulating parkland course with a reputation for immaculate condition, Abbeydale is only five miles south-west of Sheffield yet provides extensive views of the Derbyshire moors.

Its well-appointed clubhouse offers wide-ranging catering facilities and a warm welcome to visitors.

The club celebrates its Centenary in 1995

Frinton Golf Club

1 The Esplanade, Frinton on Sea, Essex CO13 9EP. Tel:01255 674618

Golf at Frinton is nearly as old as the town itself. Frinton Golf Club was founded in 1895 and designed by Tom Dunn, on land now occupied by houses in Second and Third Avenue. At 6,265 yards Frinton is not excessively long by modern standards, and at first glance, the absence of trees may indicate an easy test. But this is not the whole story. Fast, firm and undulating greens test the best putters, tidal ditches cross many fairways requiring careful placement of shots and there is usually the wind to consider. It is rare to play in still conditions at Frinton and its open character means that every shot has to be evaluated with both wind strength and direction in mind. A 130yd shot that requires a pitching wedge downwind can often require a long iron when played in the opposite direction.

As the club celebrates its Centenary in 1995, it is able to look back on a distinguished past and looks forward to a successful future in its second century.

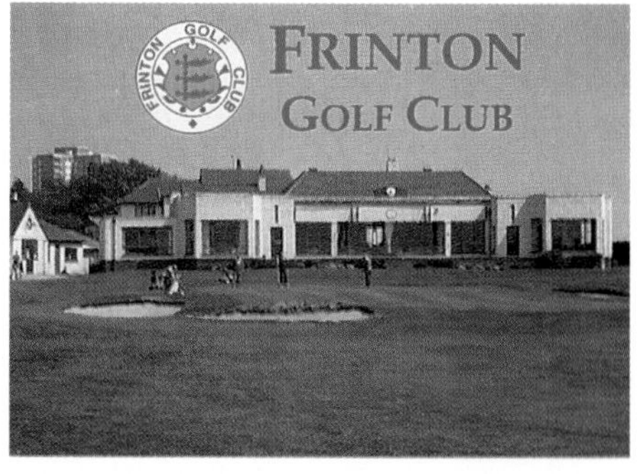

CENTENARY CLUBS 1995

The Edzell Golf Club

High Street, Edzell, Angus DD9 7TF
Tel: (01356) 648235
Fax: (01356) 648094

Play over the same fairways for 100 years shows in the springy turf of this level course with the benefit of sheltering trees revealing fine views of the hills. There is room for the wayward and a challenge for the competent golfer with succour for both in the Clubhouse.

Fairhaven Golf Club Ltd

Lytham Hall Park, Ansdell,
Lytham St Annes FY8 4JU
TEL: (01253) 736741 FAX: (01253) 731461

A course of character which has grown in stature over the years, hosting final Open qualifying competitions, the Roosevelt Nine Nations trophy and in 1995 the Amateur International between England and Spain. On flat terrain the challenge is length and tight bunkering which demands accurate iron play to compile a good score.

Crowborough Beacon Golf Club

Beacon Road, Crowborough, East Sussex
Tel: 01892 667339 Fax: 01892 661511

Crowborough Beacon Golf Club will be celebrating its Centenary in 1995.

Some documentary evidence exists from the early days regarding the result of the efforts of a small group who called a meeting to establish what interest if any there might be in forming a golf club in Crowborough.

As is often the case, minutes of these early meetings are sparse and a hundred years is clearly a long time. Some documents have vanished for ever. Yet enough remains to provide us with a picture, both of the times and the shrewd negotiations which enabled the club to become established; and so it was that originally on only a 25 year lease from Lord Cantelupe (at five shillings a year!) the construction of a golf course began at the Manor of Alchornes.

Golf over the heathland began on 6th October 1895, when Lady Cantelupe struck the first ball on the new, if rather primitive 9 hole course.

The golf club purchased the Manorial Rights of the Manor of Alchornes in 1905 and so, at the time, secured the future of the club and course allowing work to proceed with much more confidence. The now 18 hole course and rebuilt clubhouse stands some 800 feet above sea level, and with views on certain clear days of the Downs, Eastbourne and the sea, it must arguably have one of the finest views around.

STOKE POGES GOLF CLUB

Stoke Poges Golf Club was founded in 1908 and is considered by many to be the finest parkland course in England.

The Stoke Poges course was designed by Harry Shapland Colt, a genius of the twentieth century, who went on to design many of the greatest courses in the world, including the Eden course at St. Andrews.

The original parkland was designed in 1750 by Capability Brown and in 1792 by Humphrey Repton.

In the centre of the superb course is Stoke Park, the Grade One listed Clubhouse. Built in 1795 for the Penn Family, the founders of Pennsylvania, Stoke Park is now the largest Clubhouse in Europe.

Stoke Poges Golf Club welcomes Societies and private visitors to use the excellent entertainment, conferencing and golf facilities. Corporate days and special events can also be easily arranged.

The Club is situated seven miles from Heathrow Airport, and is ideally located for overseas visitors.

Stoke Park, Stoke Poges, Buckinghamshire SL2 4PG
Telephone: (01753) 717171 Facsimile: (01753) 717181

Five Golfers of the Year

Michael Williams

Nick Price

Nick Price was, in every respect, the golfer of the year in 1994. He won both the Open Championship at Turnberry and the American PGA Championship at Southern Hills. The last man to capture two of the major championships in the same year was Nick Faldo in 1990, the Masters and the Open.

For a second consecutive year Price was also leading money winner in America where, altogether, he won five times, his other victories being in the Honda Classic, the Colonial, the Western Open and the Canadian Open. It was the biggest individual haul since Watson triumphed six times in 1980. Hardly surprisingly he consequently jumped from fourth to top of the Sony world rankings.

Price had also won the PGA Championship in 1992 and, at the age of 37, was beginning to be compared to Ben Hogan so firmly was his swing 'in the slot'. From tee to green and then on the green he seemed at times to be unbeatable.

His greatest satisfaction was to win the Open for he had twice been tantalisingly close. In 1982, the year of Watson's double, Price had led by three strokes with six holes to play at Royal Troon but a weak finish was his undoing. Then at Royal Lytham in 1988 he had a second chance but, despite having a 69 when within two strokes of the lead going into the final round, he was eclipsed by a vintage Severiano Ballesteros, who had a 65.

'In 1982', he said in his victory speech at Turnberry, 'I had my left hand on the trophy and in 1988 I had my right hand on it. Now I've got both. And doesn't it feel good.' Indeed it did, right across the board, for there is no more universally popular golfer than Price, whose modesty and unfailing courtesy sets as high a standard off the course as his golf does on it.

Not the least of his advantages is that he is an 'away from home' golfer. Born of British parents in Durban, raised in Zimbabwe, resident now in the United States, he does not, as an overseas player, suffer the pressures that can go with being home-based. As less is perhaps expected of him, he achieves more.

Nick Price with the Open Trophy, 1994

Technically his swing is quick; but it is firm and businesslike and, above all, repeats. Like all champions he also had his moment of luck. With two holes to play in the Open, he did not seem to have a chance. But the long eagle putt he sank at the 17th, just after the Swede, Jesper Parnevik, had dropped an unnecessary stroke at the 18th gave him an opportunity he never looked like missing.

Laura Davies

The achievement of Laura Davies in 1994 of heading both the American LPGA money list and the Ping world rankings was outstanding. She was, in every respect, the most dominant woman player of the year, winning seven times worldwide.

For sheer power and talent, it might be no

Laura Davies swings into action at the Women's British Open at Woburn, 1994

exaggeration to compare her with the late and great Babe Zaharias in the immediate post-war years, though this most gifted of Americans was very much of an all-round athlete, winning 1932 Olympic gold medals and breaking world records in both the hurdles and javelin. She also won the high jump but was disqualified for using an illegal method. Her interest in golf came later and was to prove her last sporting conquest before she died of cancer at the age of 42.

There the comparisons must end. Davies, 31, is not an all-round athlete though her interest and following of other sports is no less avid. 'The Babe' was also an assiduous practiser of golf whereas Davies plays more by natural instinct. She rapidly gets bored on the practice ground.

Altogether Davies won eight times in 1994 worldwide, beginning with the Thailand Open and then, in the States, taking the Standard Register Ping tournament, the Sarah Lee Classic and finally the McDonald's LPGA Championship, her second major title to go alongside her 1987 victory in the US Women's Open. Davies never forsakes her roots however and in her regular visits to Europe, she won both the Irish and Scottish championships. Her final victories in Japan and the Australian Masters made her the first player to win on five tours in the same year.

In 22 American tournaments Davies was in the top 10 on 12 occasions and 42 of her 77 rounds were under par with a stroke average of 70.91, 0.01 worse than Beth Daniel, who was accordingly the LPGA Player of the Year. Altogether Davies had official prize money of $687,201, almost $30,000 ahead of Daniel, who played in three more tournaments. She was also third in the European Tour money list where she won £59,384.

Though self-conscious about her build, Davies has a warmth of personality to go with her natural modesty. Behind it, however, lies rare determination and a power of stroke that draws gasps of wonder from galleries who flock to see her. With her 1-iron she can out-hit almost everyone taking their drivers.

To Davies therefore there is hardly such a thing as a par five, so often and easily can she reach the greens in two. Her one disappointment in an otherwise memorable year will have been to be on a losing European Solheim Cup team.

Ernie Els

Some are born with a sense for a ball. Ernie Els is one of them. If it had not been golf it is just as likely that he would have been successful at tennis or cricket. At 6ft 3in he also has the look of a man who might have been useful in the Springbok lineout. He has however chosen wisely. It may be no exaggeration to say that no greater talent has broken through in golf since Jack Nicklaus.

Time alone will tell but, at just 25 years of age, Els is the schoolboy wonder who is likely to become a giant among men. He had a handicap of scratch in his early teens, was world junior champion at 14, South African Amateur champion at 16, runner-up in the South African Open at 19, champion at 22 and now reigning United States Open champion at 25, having won it at 24.

South Africa has already produced two of the world's greatest golfers in Bobby Locke and Gary Player. Els seems bound to join them, his rise to eminence first being marked as a professional when in 1992, aged 22, he won six tournaments out of 11 on the South African Tour, not only his country's Open but the PGA and Masters titles as well. Only Player had done that before.

His victory in the 1994 US Open at Oakmont, when he beat both Loren Roberts and Colin Montgomerie in a three-man play-off, came in what was only his ninth major championship. Yet already he had made his mark. In his first British Open in 1992 at Muirfield Els finished

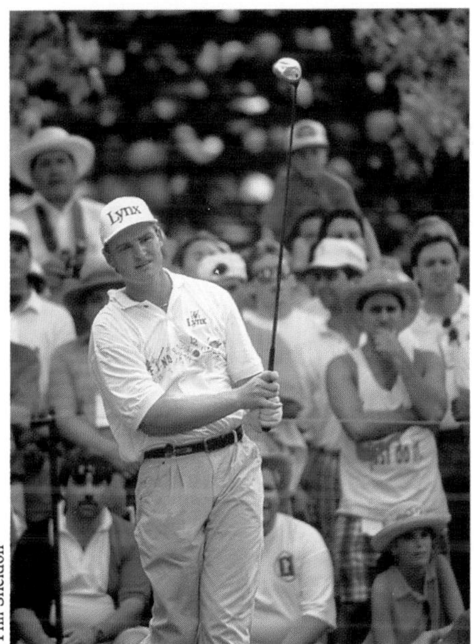

Ernie Els in the US Open at Oakmont, 1994

fifth and a year later at Royal St George's he was sixth, technically the first man to break 70 in all four rounds; though this achievement was followed only an hour or so later by Greg Norman, the winner. In his first US Open at Baltusrol in 1993 he tied seventh and in his first US Masters in 1994 he was eighth.

His first victory outside South Africa came late in 1993 when he won the Japanese Dunlop Phoenix.

He followed this quickly, in early 1994, with his first on the European Tour when, after an opening round of 61, he took the Dubai Desert Classic by six strokes from Greg Norman.

Later that same season he took the World Matchplay title at his first attempt by beating Montgomerie at Wentworth. By the end of the year, he had also triumphed in both the Gene Sarazen World Open and the Johnnie Walker World Championship.

Like many big men, Els has a very delicate touch around the greens but it is his long game that is so impressive. In his hands, a golf club looks no bigger than a riding crop and, with a slow rhythm, he despatches the ball enormous distances with a minimum of apparent effort. Like Severiano Ballesteros in his prime, he appears not so much to hit the ball as to gather it on the clubface before releasing it.

He is by nature level headed and is taking his career one step at a time. His next is in America this year.

José Maria Olazabal

For a number of years José Maria Olazabal, the pretender to the Spanish golfing throne, had been rated the best young player in the world. Now, at the age of 28, he at last reached fulfilment when he won the Masters at Augusta National. Later in the year he added to it the World Series, which he had previously captured in 1990. This does not rank as a major championship but it is certainly one of the six most prestigious in America and attracts, therefore, one of the strongest fields.

In Britain Olazabal also won the Volvo PGA Championship at Wentworth, which is held to be the flagship event on the European Tour, his other victory being in the Mediterranean Open. Such a quartet of successes was ample proof that the high promise he had shown as an amateur was only the beginning to a notable career.

The son of a greenkeeper at the Club de San Sebastian in northern Spain, where his mother also worked, Olazabal was the first player to win the British Boys, Youths and Amateur championships in three consecutive years beginning in 1983. In the final of the 1984 Amateur Championship he beat Colin Montgomerie, now himself a major force in European professional golf and, 10 years on, also one of the five golfers of the year.

José Maria Olazabal in the 1994 US Open

Soon after winning the Youths the following year, Olazabal turned professional and in his first season won the European Masters in Switzerland, finishing second in the order of merit. Only twice since then has he been out of the top 10.

Olazabal has a completely different style to that of Sevé Ballesteros, still the king of Spanish golf. Of shorter and more wiry build, he perhaps lacks some of the grace and balance of the man he will undoubtedly succeed but he is, and always has been, an attacking player – nothing is spared in his shot-making and very little in his practice swings either.

As partners, Olazabal and Ballesteros have proved the greatest European strength in the Ryder Cup, each an inspiration to the other, since first they were paired in 1987. At first, Ballesteros was the guiding hand but these days, it is Olazabal, the younger by nine years, who tends to be the steadying influence.

Olazabal had been very close to winning the Masters once before. In 1991 he took five at the last hole and finished second by a stroke to Ian Woosnam. It was a bitter disappointment to him and he took time to recover. But, when opportunity beckoned again, he made no mistake. After a slow start with a 74 in the first round, he broke 70 each time and won by two from Tom Lehman.

Colin Montgomerie at the B&H International Open at St Mellion in 1994

Colin Montgomerie

Colin Montgomerie became the first player since Sandy Lyle in 1980 to retain the Harry Vardon trophy, which is annually awarded to the leading player in the European order of merit. Had he not done so it would have been the first time he had taken a step backward since he turned professional in 1987.

Seven years of such steady progression in a highly competitive field is outstanding. In 1988, his first full season as a tournament player, Montgomerie finished 52nd. Since then he has progressed to 25th, 14th, fourth, third, first and first again.

Even in 1994 however Montgomerie did not stand still. His advance was further marked by getting into a play-off for the United States Open Championship which, together with Loren Roberts, he lost to Ernie Els, who also beat him in the final of the World Matchplay Championship. His previous best performances in both these events was third in the US Open at Pebble Beach in 1991 and a beaten semi-finalist in the 1993 Matchplay.

His other satisfaction was to win for the first time a tournament in Britain, the Murphy's English Open. His previous five victories, including one earlier in the year in the Spanish Open, had all been on the Continent, as was another subsequently in the German Open.

Though by birth a Scot, Montgomerie was brought up in Yorkshire and finished his education at the Baptist University in Houston where he graduated in Business and Law. As such he considered applying for a position with the Mark McCormack empire. Instead he became a client and a very successful one.

He is a golfer of great consistency and, in the opinion of Nick Faldo, an ideal foursomes partner in the Ryder Cup because he hits the ball so straight, is always therefore in play and putts well. For that reason Montgomerie, with his natural left to right flight of the ball, thinks his best chance of winning a major championship is always likely to be on the tight US Open courses. One third place and one equal second in three attempts rather proves his point, so far anyway.

His one weakness is an occasionally short fuse when things are not going his way. There are also those who believe he carries more weight than is ideal. However, for someone of naturally sturdy build he seldom seems to suffer, flagging though he might have done in that US Open play-off after a week of intense heat. Not doing himself full justice irritates him more than anything.

Britain's Amateurs Trip the Continentals

Raymond Jacobs Golf Correspondent of the *Glasgow Herald*

To the simultaneous arrival of Arnold Palmer, television, and the jet engine has been attributed the explosive development of golf over the last 30 years. That, of course, applied most visibly to professional events in all their forms, but the amateur game, still uniquely among major sports accepted, encouraged, and stabilised as a separate entity, also has developed and expanded its horizons. In 1994, four achievements in particular illustrated that truth.

The precocious and prodigiously talented, 'Tiger' Woods became, at 18, the youngest player to win the US Amateur Championship in its 94-year history; Warren Bennett won the Australian Championship, the first Briton to do so since 1905; Hong Chia-yuh's victory in the Republic of China Open was only the fourth on the Asian Tour by an amateur since 1962; and Stephen Gallacher, nephew of Bernard, Europe's Ryder Cup team captain, took the European individual title to Scotland for the first time.

The greater significance of Woods's triumph than his age was that he became the first black golfer to take his country's national title. The son of a former American army sergeant and a Thai mother, Woods beat Trip Kuehne by two holes in the 36-hole final, having been six down after 13 – the finest recovery ever. The longer-term impact of Woods's victory will be awaited with interest since quite suddenly, it seems, the flow of black American professionals, never more than a trickle, has all but dried up completely.

Subsequently, Woods played his full part in helping the United States win the world amateur team championship from Britain and Ireland by 11 strokes, their tenth victory in the 19 competitions held so far for the Eisenhower Trophy, although their first for 12 years. That, incidentally, was the season's only loss by a combined British side. At senior, youths and boys level the matches against Europe were all won decisively, suggesting that the upsurge of talent from the Continent, although undoubtedly welcome, is not invincible.

Hong, a 20-year-old university student from Taipei, birdied the last two holes of the Taiwan Golf and Country Club to pull off a stunning victory over Boonchu Ruangkit of Thailand, who had appeared set to win, leading by one with two to play. The professional's chagrin was a little assuaged, however, when he inherited the first prize of $50,000 which, of course, Hong had to forego. Facing three more years of study, he was not giving serious thought to playing for pay.

Lee James, Amateur Champion, 1994

Before the year was out Bennett, aged 22 when he beat Jamie McCallum by 2 and 1 at Royal Sydney, would have laid upon him the rather burdensome prediction of Michael Bonallack, secretary of the Royal & Ancient Club, that the willowy Londoner would win the Open Championship within a decade. Bennett certainly looked the part when he later won the Lytham Trophy. He was also runner-up in two other important 72-hole tournaments and was the only amateur to complete four rounds in the Open at Turnberry – foundations well laid.

Ill-health and injury had dogged Gallacher since, at 17, he won the 1992 Scottish championship. But signs of a revival emerged with his cap of the Scottish Youths' title and were confirmed by a record-equalling 65 in the final round of four in the European Championship at Turku, Finland. That score gave Gallacher victory by two strokes over Lee James and Gordon Sherry, by coincidence the winner and runner-up in the Amateur Championship at Nairn. Strange to be thinking of a 19-year-old restoring credibility to his career.

Yet if the current status of the amateur game needed a revealing illustration it emerged in the age-groupings of the last eight of the Scottish Championship – four 20-year-olds, two of 21, and two aged 31 and 41 respectively. A generation gap – two even – was created by the consistent slippage into the inviting, but treacherous, seas of the professional game of players more than willing, though not always ready and able, to cast their bread on those choppy waters.

The father-figure, so to speak was Barclay Howard, who reached his second semi-final of the championship no fewer than 23 years after his first. Almost, Howard upstaged Hugh McKibbin's 39th hole victory (the longest Scottish final) and the revival of a career dogged by personal problems had earlier been confirmed by Howard's winning of the St Andrews Links Trophy against a strong international field, the historic Leven Gold Medal with a record total, and, by a convincing margin the National Order of Merit award.

If Alan Reid had beaten McKibbin he would have become the only other player after Ronnie Shade to win the national, stroke, and boys championships. But Aberdeenshire's Steven Young did become the first to win the Scottish boys' match and stroke play titles in the same year since 1971, when Ewen Murray, the TV commentator, did so. Young nevertheless was the first player for 56 years to retain the match play title. Meanwhile, Charlie Green gained his sixth victory in seven years in the British Seniors' Championship.

In England, too, youth was not wasted on the young. Mark Foster, the 1993 Boys' captain, won the national title and Gary Harris, the British junior captain, took the stroke play title. As if that were not presumption enough Harris, along with another 18-year-old, David Howell, lost in the final of the Sunningdale Foursomes to Anthony Wall and Steven Webster, two other members of the 1993 English boys' side. For good measure, Shaun Webster, aged 17, added the Doug Sanders world boys' title to the Lagonda Trophy.

England translated that strength in depth to a triple-crown victory in the Home International matches. Ireland, less eroded by defections to the professional ranks, offered the most stubborn resistance, but Scotland, unable to hang together in the foursomes, hung separately in the singles, succeeding only in beating Wales, whose usual posture as whipping boys was exacerbated by having had six of the 11 members of the previous side, including four of the six who helped them take the 1993 European Championship, jump ship.

Nevertheless, Wales unearthed another dominant figure in Craig Evans, who won not only the national title but also three major 72-hole events. Ireland's rewards were more extensively spread, even permitting the intrusion of the first English player to win the North Championship, Nick Ludwell, in a way comparable to the punitive expeditions mounted by Cheshire's Jonathon Hodgson, who bearded the Scottish lions in their den to win two of the more important 72-hole competitions.

Elsewhere in Ireland, Padraig Harrington's victory in the West Championship was his first of significance, whereupon he lost two finals in successive weeks, to David Higgins, son of the professional Liam, twice a winner in his first season on the European Seniors tour. He first beat the Walker Cup player in the South Championship and then, having been two down and three to play, won at the 20th for the national title. Meanwhile, Garth McGimpsey, a member of the veteran tendency, won his second East Championship.

How all these results would influence the outcome of events in the season to come could only be speculated on. There seemed, however, a solid basis of achievement and a pause in the stampede among most leading amateurs to turn professional. A team could therefore emerge to give a livelier account of itself in the Walker Cup match, to be played at Royal Porthcawl, the first time this biennial contest with the United States goes to Wales.

Europe's Women Bite the Dust

Lewine Mair

It should have been a glorious double. With Great Britain and Ireland's amateurs having retained the Curtis Cup at Chattanooga, Europe's professionals were level at 5–5 going into the last day of the Solheim Cup at The Greenbrier. Dottie Mochrie, who contributed three points to the American cause but little in the way of sportsmanship, won her single against Catrin Nilsmark by 6 and 5 before Sweden's Helen Alfredsson, playing first, balanced the ledger with a penultimate hole win over Betsy King.

Then, though, everything went badly wrong behind. One by one, Mickey Walker's gallant team of Europeans fell away, with Alison Nicholas the only one to set a win alongside Alfredsson's.

As Laura Davies said, it was simply a case of the Americans having been better on the day. 'It was much the same as at any run-of-the-mill tournament,' sighed a downhearted Davies. 'Whoever plays the best golf on the Sunday gets to win.'

That Davies was not quite at full flow over the three days owed something to a putter which did not wreak its usual magic. She and Nicholas played magnificently in the opening foursomes but lost in the second-day fourballs. When it came to the singles, the former US and British Open champion was up against Brandie Burton in a match which many felt should have been a deal higher in the pecking order than seventh.

Davies maintained she was not remotely upset at being so far down but JoAnne Carner, the American captain, deemed it a mistake: 'I was definitely surprised when Laura wasn't at the top. She's always been up there and I think it becomes a team ritual, sort of. When you move Laura around, it shakes the team atmosphere'.

Though she never uttered a word of complaint to anyone outside team and family, Davies was less than elated at the team uniform. She is more sensitive than most about what she wears and it was not too difficult to detect, from the start, that she was ill at ease in the Marks & Spencer gear. There were some splendid sweaters and slacks in the range but the shirts, in particular, were not for her. They did not begin to fit.

Reverting to her match with Burton, Davies was ahead of the American after holing a long putt at the 14th, but promptly lost the next couple of holes. There was still a chance – admittedly a slight one – of Europe winning the Solheim Cup as she endeavoured to tackle her 117-yard approach to the 16th green. But, at a time when she was in mid-swing and committed to the shot, one of a host of falling leaves cloaked her ball. There was nothing she could do about it.

Janice Moodie chips-in for Britain in the Curtis Cup

Her shot dived into the water and with it the visitors' hopes, though the match was not finally over until that moment when Meg Mallon putted to within inches of the hole at the short 17th to make certain that she could not lose to Scotland's Pam Wright.

JoAnne Carner, with the sun playing on her starred, striped and sequined baseball cap, could not contain her emotions. This larger-than-life captain spoke, amid tears, of how proud she was of her team: 'They wanted to win so bad and so did I. . . .'

Walker was gracious to the last. She was proud of her side and what they had achieved at the last three Solheim Cups. At The Greenbrier, she said, the Americans had played the better golf; our players had not produced the goods when it mattered.

A little later, she reiterated that the Americans, on paper, were always the stronger: 'We have the best golfers in the world but they definitely have more strength in depth. There is no argument with that . . . Any one of the Europeans would agree.'

Hers were comments to leave everyone wondering if a 12-a-side Solheim Cup was asking a bit much for St Pierre in 1996.

It was America's LPGA who had wanted to increase the 10-strong teams, several members of that body, by all accounts, having a preoccupation with bringing the Solheim Cup more in line with the Ryder Cup. Walker rightly made the point that the European Tour, with its extra tournaments, would come on in leaps and bounds over the next couple of years and, in turn, produce more good players. However, what with the Americans having effected alterations after Dalmahoy, where they did not like two of their ten players having to sit out on each of the first two days, there was the thought that it was about time that someone made a change which would be to our advantage.

Oddly enough, the preceding Curtis Cup similarly prompted a deal of chat about matters to do with format. Liz Boatman, the British captain, had been asked in the weeks before the match if she minded playing the singles in front of the foursomes on the first day. It was what the television people wanted and the Americans felt that everything should be done to encourage coverage of the match.

At the time Boatman agreed. But she was quick to change her mind when it came to the match itself, realising that it was not for nothing that foursomes had traditionally been played first. 'Foursomes,' she explained, 'are the perfect vehicle in which to get warmed up and relaxed. They definitely belong in front of the singles.'

Great Britain and Ireland were trailing $2^1/_2$–$3^1/_2$ after the singles, while they were 4–5 behind at the end of the opening day. The following morning, Julie Hall and Lisa Walton, who had had eight birdies in 10 holes on the first day, had the better of McGill and Sarah Ingram on the 17th, while Catriona Matthew and Janice Moodie defeated Wendy Ward and Stephanie Sparks by 3 and 2. Myra McKinlay and Eileen Rose Power started well enough in the other match but faded amid the mounting pressure.

In a situation which would be mirrored at the Solheim Cup, the teams were level going into the closing singles series, and at the end of a tension-packed afternoon on the Honors Course, it was the 21-year-old Janice Moodie, out last against the 45-year-old Carol Semple Thompson, who did most to ensure that Great Britain and Ireland clung to the trophy they won two years before at Hoylake.

For 45 minutes and more, Moodie and Thompson were out there on their own, putting the nerve-jangling, finishing touches to a match which had for long seemed destined to belong to the Americans. With the score at that point 9–8 to the States, Moodie was after a win, Thompson a half.

Moodie, playing in her first Curtis Cup to Thompson's eighth, was one ahead at the 13th, but brought back to square one by a Thompson two at the 14th. The 15th was halved before the American hit her tee shot into water at the short 16th. The Scot seized her chance. She then had the disappointment of seeing an imperial three-wood go to waste as she took three putts from the front of the 17th, but did what had to be done in the perfect setting of the last hole.

Having hit a six-iron to within three feet of the hole, a shot in keeping with the four-iron with which Caroline Hall clinched the 1992 Curtis Cup, Moodie walked up the fairway with the gait of a champion and the glow of a bride. She was thriving on the pressure, loving every minute of it.

With Thompson putting too strongly from the back of the putting surface, Moodie did not have to hole her two-and-a-half-footer. To everyone's disbelief, she was more than a little irritated: 'I dreamed all my life of making a putt like that to win the Curtis Cup . . . It was a bit of a letdown that I wasn't asked to hole it.'

Catriona Matthew and Myra McKinlay, both of whom have now graduated to the professional tour, were the sister Scots who provided the other singles points. One always had the feeling that Matthew would prevail, but what of McKinlay? Up until the Curtis Cup, she had never played anything in the way of competitive golf in the States though, to set against that, there was the fact that she was a lifeguard, one well used to coping in a crisis.

Two up on Wendy Kaupp after the 11th and still two up after the 13th, the West of Scotland golfer missed from four feet to lose the 14th. Then, after a bold birdie at the 15th, she wrapped things up at the next, her holing of a great five-footer having much to do with Kaupp missing from that distance.

For their efforts, the Curtis Cup side and their captain were made honorary members of the lovely Chattanooga club. They also won the *Daily Telegraph* Golfer of the Year award, with Moodie receiving the Joyce Wethered award, a new trophy which will be awarded each year to an upstanding and outstanding amateur under the age of 25.

Another amateur to deserve a mention is Emma Duggleby, who came from nowhere to win the British Women's Championship at

Newport. Each morning, Emma and her mother booked out of their farmhouse accommodation on the grounds that Emma would surely be beaten by the end of the day. To her great credit, she never was, defeating Cecilia Mourgue D'Algue in the final.

On the professional front, there were two things which stopped the tour from finishing on a low note after that Solheim Cup defeat. The first, Terry Coates's success in building up the European circuit to the point where everyone can feel happy about its future, and the second, Laura Davies's extraordinary achievement in winning the LPGA money list.

The player who started her golf in Surrey and went on to play for England, for Britain and for Europe is now, literally and metaphorically, on top of the world.

Quotes of 1994

The Open

In 1982 I had my left hand on the trophy, in 1988 I had my right on it and now I've got both – and doesn't it feel good.
Nick Price on winning the Open Championship

Can I win? I've nothing better to do this weekend.
David Feherty, one of the pre-qualifiers, when challenging for the lead after two rounds

Probably not.
Mark James on being asked if he could stand the hassle of being Open champion

One of the prerequisites to winning the Open Championship is to enter the damned thing.
Tommy Kite on the Americans who stayed away

When you are not hitting your irons well and it is windy, it makes for a long day. That first vodka tonic tasted very good.
Fuzzy Zoeller

Thank God I chose golf as my career.
Gary Player, making his 40th consecutive appearance in the Open

It's nice the R & A do listen.
Severiano Ballesteros when he compared the wider Turnberry fairways to those of 1986

I've lined up a couple of pigeons.
Tom Watson when telephoning Jack Nicklaus to say he had arranged a practice round with Greg Norman and Nick Price

I guess we're all different.
Ernie Els (US Open champion) on being told Nick Faldo spent the month after winning his first Open thinking about it 'every 15 seconds'.

Us Open

My own game is a complete shambles and the trouble is that I have not got the glue any more to repair it.
Arnold Palmer on the eve of his last appearance in a US Open, 41 years after his first

Are the Oakmont greens really as fast as all that? They're faster than all that.
Sam Torrance

Your numbers shrank and mine grew.
Jack Nicklaus when he compared the number of reporters in the interview room after his third-round 77 with those present after his first-round 69

I think I have just played with the next God.
Curtis Strange after witnessing at first hand Ernie Els's third round of 66

She can't understand it when she hears the other wives complain. She says she doesn't have to cook, clean or even make the beds. The tour is OK with her.
Loren Roberts on his wife, Kimberley

The Masters

The strongest thing that ever passes my lips is a glass of whisky after a hard day with the kids.
Nick Faldo on allegations by Mac O'Grady that certain leading players are on beta blockers

All I ever see them take these days is water and bloody bananas.
Dave Musgrove, caddie to Lee Janzen, 1993 US Open champion

My short game is pretty good because when I started playing the game at two years old I wasn't very long.
José Maria Olazabal after collecting his green jacket

I felt like a 20-handicap golfer today compared to the way I played at the Players' Championship.
Greg Norman after his first round of 70

Go out there and be patient. Let the others be nervous.
Severiano Ballesteros's message to Olazabal before the final round

US PGA

I'm just glad it's all over. I was hitting the ball great on the practice ground but when I stood on the first tee I just froze.

Club professional *George Bowman* after missing the cut by 30 strokes

I thought I would never worry about missing a putt again. But when I left one short at the eighth I was angry enough to spit nails.

Paul Azinger

Golf is never going to be the same and you'll never see Americans dominate the game again.

Greg Norman, even before Price's victory to complete a year when for the first time no American won a major

To some players having Squeaky might be a five-stroke penalty

Nick Price on the stroke value of his caddie, Squeaky Medlin

When you do nothing wrong, make no mistakes, the birdies take care of themselves.

Colin Montgomerie after a 67 to share the lead after the first round

Miscellaneous

It is not what you achieve in life, it is what you overcome.

Extract from a letter by *Johnny Miller* to Paul Azinger, who had been diagnosed as suffering from cancer

If this applause goes on much longer we're going to get done for slow play before we even start.

Paul Azinger's caddie on the first tee when he made his return to the US Tour in the Buick Open

The best left arm since Sam Snead.

Peter Thomson after watching Christy O'Connor complete a 68, one under his age, in the Trust House Forte Seniors at Sunningdale

Will the person who bought my two-iron for two dollars at my wife's stall in the Bidwell Street boot sale please call and leave your telephone number. I would like to buy it back and will pay more for it than you did.

Personal ad in a New Hampshire newspaper

1995 Schedule of Events

PGA European Tour

January
19–22 Dubai Desert Classic, Emirates GC, Dubai
26–29 Johnnie Walker Classic, Orchard G&CC, Manila

February
2–5 Madeira Island Open, Campo de Golfe da Madeira
9–12 Turespaña Open de Canarias, Campo de Golf, Gran Canaria
16–19 Lexington SA PGA, Wanderers Club, Johannesburg
23–26 Turespaña Open Mediterrania, Valencia

March
2–5 Turespaña Masters, Islantilla GC
9–12 Moroccan Open, Golf Links-Agadir
16–19 Portuguese Open, Penha Longa, Lisbon
30–2 Open de Extremadura, Golf del Guadiana, Badajoz

April
13–16 Catalan Open (TBA)
20–23 Air France Cannes Open, Mougins
27–30 *Tournoi Perrier de Paris, Saint-Cloud, Paris

May
4–7 Italian Open (TBA)
11–14 Benson and Hedges International, St Mellion, Plymouth
18–21 Peugeot Open, Club de Campo, Madrid
22–23 *Five Tours Andersen Consulting European Qualifier, Golf La Moraleja II, Spain
26–29 Volvo PGA Championship, Wentworth Club, Surrey

June
1–4 Murphy's English Open, Forest of Arden, Warwickshire
8–11 Deutsche Bank Open, Gut Kaden, Hamburg
15–18 Jersey Open, La Moye
22–25 Peugeot Open de France, National GC, Paris
29–2 BMW International Open, St Eurach Land-und, Munich

July
6–9 Murphy's Irish Open, Mount Juliet, Kilkenny
12–15 The Scottish Open, Carnoustie
20–23 Open Championship, St Andrews
24–25 *Five Tours Andersen Consulting European and Rest of World Qualifier, The Oxfordshire
27–30 Heineken Dutch Open, Hilversum

August
3–6 Scandinavian Masters, Barsebacks, Sweden
10–13 Hohe Brücke Open, GC Waldviertel, Austria
17–20 Chemapol Trophy Czech Open, Marianské Lazne GC, Czech Republic
24–27 Volvo German Open, Nippenburg, Stuttgart
31–3 Canon European Masters, Crans-sur-Sierre, Switzerland

September
7–10 Trophée Lancôme, St Nom la Bretèche, Paris
14–17 British Masters, Woburn G&CC, Buckinghamshire
22–24 Ryder Cup, Oak Hill, Rochester, NY
28–1 Smurfit European Open, Kildare CC, Dublin

October
5–8 Mercedes German Masters, Motzener See, Berlin
12–15 *Toyota World Match Play, Wentworth, Surrey
19–22 *Alfred Dunhill Cup, Old Course, St Andrews
26–29 Volvo Masters, Valderrama, Spain

November
9–12 *World Cup, Mission Hills, S. China

December
14–17 *Johnnie Walker World Chp, Tryall, Jamaica
29–31 *Five Tours Andersen Consulting World Championship of Golf, Grayhawk GC, Scottsdale, Arizona

TBA – *To be arranged*
* *Special event*

PGA European Seniors Tour

June
23–25 Northern Electric, Slaley Hall

July
14–16 German Open
27–30 Seniors Open Chp, Royal Portrush

August
2–4 Lawrence Batley Tournament, Huddersfield
11–13 Trust House Forte PGA Chp, Sunningdale
24–26 Collingtree Tnmt, Collingtree

September
1–3 Shell Scottish Open, Royal Aberdeen
8–10 Belton Woods Tnmt, Belton Woods

October
5–7 Zurich Tnmt

United States PGA Tour

January
5–8 Mercedes Chp, La Costa, Carlsbad, CA
12–15 Hawaiian Open, Waialae, Honolulu, HI
19–22 Telecom Open, Nat'l Golf Resort, Tucson, AZ
26–29 Phoenix Open, TPC at Scottsdale, AZ

February
2–5 AT&T Pro-Am, Pebble Beach, CA
9–12 Buick Invitational, Torrey Pines, La Jolla, CA
16–19 Bob Hope Chrysler Classic, Indian Wells, CA
23–26 Nissan Open, Riviera CC, Pacific Palisades, CA

March
2–5 Doral–Ryder Open, Doral, Miami, FL
9–12 Honda Classic, Weston Hills, Ft Lauderdale, FL
16–19 Nestlé Invitational, Bay Hill, Orlando, FL
23–26 Players Chp, TPC at Sawgrass, Ponte Vedra Beach, FL
30–4 Freeport–McMoran Classic, English Turn, New Orleans, LA

April
6–9 The Masters, Augusta National, GA
13–16 Heritage Classic, Harbour Town Golf Links, Hilton Head Island, SC
20–23 Greater Greensboro Open, Forest Oaks, Greensboro, NC
27–30 Houston Open, The Woodlands, TX

May
4–7 BellSouth Classic, Atlanta CC, Marietta, GA
11–14 Byron Nelson Classic, TPC at Las Colinas, Irving, TX
18–21 Buick Classic, Westchester CC, Rye, NY
25–28 Colonial Invitational, Colonial, Ft Worth, TX

June
1–4 Memorial Tournament, Muirfield Village, Dublin, OH
8–11 Kemper Open, TPC at Avenel, Potomac, MD
15–18 US Open, Shinnecock Hills, Southampton, NY
22–25 Greater Hartford Open, TPC at River Highlands, Cromwell, CT
29–2 FedEx St Jude Classic, TPC at Southwind, Memphis, TN

July
6–9 Motorola Western Open, Cog Hill CC, Lemont, IL
13–16 Anheuser–Busch Classic, Kingsmill, Williamsburg, VA
20–23 Deposit Guaranty Classic, Annandale, Madison, MS
27–30 New England Classic, Pleasant Valley, Sutton, MA

August
3–6 Buick Open, Warwick Hills, Grand Blanc, MI
10–13 *PGA Championship, Riviera, Los Angeles, CA
17–20 The International, Castle Pines, Castle Rock, CO
24–27 World Series, Firestone, Akron, OH
31–3 Greater Milwaukee Open, Brown Deer Park, Milwaukee, WI

September
7–10 Canadian Open, Glen Abbey, Oakville, Ontario
14–17 BC Open, En-Joi, Endicott, NY
21–24 Quad Cities Open, Oakwood, Coal Valley, IL
21–24 Ryder Cup, Oak Hill, Rochester, NY
28–1 Buick Southern Open, Callaway Gardens, Pine Mountain, GA

October
5–8 Walt Disney Classic, Magnolia, Orlando, FL
12–15 Las Vegas Invitational, TPC at Summerlin, Las Vegas, NV
19–22 Texas Open, Oak Hills, San Antonio, TX
26–29 The Tour Championship, Southern Hills, Tulsa, OK

* *Special event*

US Senior PGA Tour

January
9–15 Tournament of Champions, Hyatt Dorado Beach, Puerto Rico
30–3 Royal Caribbean Classic, Links at Key Biscayne, FL

February
6–12 IntelliNet Challenge, The Vineyards, Naples, FL
13–19 GTE Suncoast Classic, TPC at Tampa Bay, Tampa, FL
20–26 Chrysler Cup, Tres Vidas, Acapulco, Mexico
27–5 FHP Health Care Classic, Ojai Valley, CA

March
6–12 The Dominion, Dominion CC, San Antonio, TX
13–19 Toshiba Senior Classic, Mesa Verde CC, Costa Mesa, CA
27–2 The Tradition, Desert Mountain, Scottsdale, AZ

April
10–16 *PGA Championship, PGA National, Palm Beach Gardens, FL
17–23 Legends of Golf, PGA West, La Quinta, CA
24–30 Las Vegas Classic, TPC at Summerlin, Las Vegas, NV

May
1–7 PaineWebber Invitational, TPC at Piper Glen, Charlotte, NC
8–14 Cadillac NFL Classic, Upper Montclair CC, Clifton, NJ
15–21 Bell Atlantic Classic, Chester Valley, Malvern, PA
22–28 Quicksilver Classic, Quicksilver CC, Pittsburgh, PA
29–4 Bruno's Memorial Classic, Greystone, Birmingham, AL

June
5–11 BellSouth Classic, Springhouse, Nashville, TN
12–18 Dallas Reunion Pro-Am, Oak Cliff, Dallas, TX
19–25 Nationwide Championship, GC of Georgia, Atlanta, GA

June *continued*
26–2 *US Senior Open, Congressional CC, Bethesda, MD

July
3–9 Kroger Senior Classic, Kings Island, Mason, OH
10–16 Ford Players Championship, TPC of Michigan, Dearborn, MI
17–23 First of America Classic, Egypt Valley, Ada, MI
24–30 Ameritech Senior Open, Stonebridge CC, Chicago, IL

August
1–6 VFW Senior Championship, Loch Lloyd CC, Belton, MO
7–13 Burnet Senior Classic, Bunker Hills, Coon Rapids, MN
14–20 Northville Long Island Classic, Meadow Brook CC, Jericho, NY
21–27 Bank of Boston Classic, Nasawtuc CC, Boston, MA
28–3 Franklin Quest Championship, Park Meadows, Park City, UT

September
4–10 GTE NorthWest Classic, Inglewood CC, Seattle, WA
11–17 Brickyard Crossing Championship, Brickyard Crossing, Indianapolis, IN
18–24 Bank One Classic, Kearney Hill Links, Lexington, KY
25–1 Vantage Championship, Tanglewood Park, Clemmons, NC

October
2–8 The Transamerica, Silverado CC, Napa, CA
9–15 Raley's Senior Gold Rush, Rancho Murieta CC, Sacramento, CA
16–22 Ralph's Senior Classic, Rancho Park, Los Angeles, CA
23–29 Maui Kaanapali Classic, Kaanapali, Maui, HI
30–5 Emerald Coast Classic, The Moors, Pensacola, FL

November
6–12 *Golf Magazine* Championship, The Dunes, Myrtle Beach, SC

Australasian Tour

January
5–8 Canberra Trophy, Royal Canberra
12–15 AMP New Zealand Open, Wellington
18–22 Optus Players' Chp, Kingston Heath

February
2–5 Heineken Classic, The Vines
9–12 Ford Open, Royal Adelaide
16–19 Australian Masters, Huntingdale
23–26 Cannon Challenge, Terrey Hills, Sydney

* *Special event*

Japanese Tour

March
9–12 Token Corporation Cup, Kedoin
16–19 Dydo Drinco Shizuoka Open, Shizuoka
23–26 KSB Selonaikai Open, Kinojo
30–2 Descente Classic Munsingwear Cup, Century Miki

April
13–16 Tsuruya Open, Sports Shinko, Yamanohara
20–23 Dunlop Open, Ibaragi
27–30 The Crowns, Nagoya

May
4–7 Fujisankei Classic, Kawana Hotel
11–14 PGA Championship, Natsudomari
18–21 Pepsi-Ubekosan, Ube
25–28 Mitsubishi Galant, Aso Prince Hotel

June
1–4 JCB Classic Sendai, Omotezao Kokusai
8–11 Sapporo Tokyu Open, Sapporo Kokusai
15–18 Yomiuri Open, Yomiuri
22–25 Mizuno Open, Tokinodai
29–2 PGA Philanthropy, CC Twin Fields

July
6–9 Yonex Open Hiroshima, Hiroshima
13–16 Nikkei Cup Pete Nakamura Memorial, Fuji
27–30 NST Niigata Open, Niigata Sunrise

August
3–6 Sanko Grand Summer Championship, Sanko 72 CC
10–13 Acom International, Seve Ballesteros GC
17–20 Maruman Open, Ranzan CC
24–27 Hisamitsu-KBC Augusta, Keya GC
31–3 PGA Matchplay Championship, Nidom Classic C

September
7–10 Suntory Open, Narashino CC
14–17 ANA Open, Sapporo GC
21–24 Gene Sarazen Junior Classic, Junior Classic CC
28–1 Japan Open, Kasumigaseki

October
5–8 Tokai Classic, Miyoshi
12–15 Golf Digest, Tomei
19–22 Bridgestone Open, Sodegaura
26–29 Philip Morris Championship, ABC GC

November
2–5 Daiwa International, Daiwa Vintage
9–12 Sumitomo VISA Taiheiyo Masters, Taiheiyo, Gotemba
16–19 Dunlop Phoenix, Phoenix CC
23–26 Casio World Open, Ibusuki
30–3 Japan Series Hitachi Cup, Tokyo Yomiuri

December
7–10 Daikyo Open, Daikyo

Asian Tour

February
2–5 Thailand Open, Pinehurst, Bangkok
9–12 Sabah Masters, Sabah, Kota Kinabalu
16–19 Singapore Rolex Masters, Singapore Island
23–26 Philippine Open (TBA)

March
2–5 Indian Open, Delhi
9–12 Malaysian Open, Templer Park, Kuala Lumpur

March *continued*
16–19 Indonesian Open, Pantai Indah, Jakarta
23–26 Bali Open, Bali, Denpasar

April
6–9 Ching Fong ROC Open, Tamsui, Taiwan
13–16 Maekyung Bando Fashion Open, Seoul, Korea
20–23 Dunlop Open, Ibaraki, Japan

South African Tour

January
5–8 Bell's Cup, Fancourt Estate, George
12–15 FNB Players' Chp, Country Club, Durban
19–22 ICL International, Zwartkop, Pretoria
26–29 Royal Swazi Sun Classic, Royal Swazi

February
2–5 South African Masters, Lost City, Sun City
9–12 South African Open, Randpark, Johannesburg
16–19 Lexington PGA Championship, Wanderers, Johannesburg
23–26 Alfred Dunhill Challenge, Houghton, Johannesburg

Women's European Pro Tour

May
11–14 Costa Azul Open, Portugal
18–21 Ford Classic, Chart Hills

June
1–4 Italian Open, Ligano, Venice
7–10 Evian Masters, Royal Evian, France
15–18 OVB Damen Open, Salzburg, Austria
22–25 European Masters, Belgium
28–2 Hennessy Cup, Germany

July
27–30 Guardian Irish Holidays Open, St Margaret's, Dublin

August
3–6 Scottish Open, Dalmahoy
10–13 Welsh Open, St Pierre, Chepstow
17–20 Weetabix British Open, Woburn
25–27 Ford-Stimarol Danish Open, Vejle
31–3 English Open, Oxfordshire

September
8–10 Sens Dutch Open, Rijkvan, Nijmegen
21–24 German Open, Treudelberg, Hamburg

October
5–8 Country Club Hotels Open (TBA)
13–15 Var Open de France, St Endreol, La Motte
19–22 Spanish Open, La Manga

United States LPGA Tour

January
12–15 Chrysler–Plymouth Tournament of Champions, Orlando, FL
20–22 Healthsouth Inaugural, Orlando, FL

February
16–18 Cup Noodles Hawaiian Open, Ewa Beach, Oahu, Hawaii

March
9–12 Ping/Welch's Ch'p, Tucson, AZ
16–19 Standard Register Ping, Phoenix, AZ
23–26 Nabisco Dinah Shore, Rancho Mirage, CA
31–2 Las Vegas Classic, Las Vegas, NV

April
14–16 Pinewild Women's Ch'p, Pinehurst, NC
27–30 Sprint Ch'p, Daytona Beach, FL

May
5–7 Sara Lee Classic, Old Hickory, TN
11–14 McDonald's LPGA Ch'p, Wilmington, DE
19–21 Children's Medical Center LPGA Classic, Dayton, OH
25–28 LPGA Corning Classic, Corning, NY

June
1–4 Oldsmobile Classic, E. Lansing, MI
9–11 Edina Realty LPGA Classic, Brooklyn Park, MN
15–18 Rochester International, Pittsford, NY
23–25 ShopRite LPGA Classic, Somers Point, NJ

June *continued*
30–2 Youngstown–Warren LPGA Classic, Warren, OH

July
7–9 Jamie Farr Toledo Classic, Sylvania, OH
13–16 US Women's Open, Colorado Springs, CO
20–23 JAL Big Apple Classic, New Rochelle, NY

August
3–6 McCall's LPGA Classic, Stratton Mountain, VT
10–13 Ping Welch's Ch'p, Canton, MA
17–20 Chicago Challenge, Naperville, IL
24–27 du Maurier Ltd Classic, Montreal, Canada

September
2–4 State Farm Rail Classic, Springfield, IL
8–10 Ping–Cellular LPGA Golf Ch'p, Portland, OR
14–17 Safeco Classic, Kent, WA
28–1 GHP Heartland Classic, St Louis, MO

October
5–8 Carolina LPGA Classic, Charlotte, NC
12–15 World Chp of Women's Golf, TBA
27–29 Nichirei International, Ibaragi, Japan

November
3–5 Toray Japan Queens Cup, Japan
30–3 JC Penney Classic, Tarpon Springs, FL

December
8–10 Diner's Club Matches, La Quinta, CA

Women's Asian Tour

January
20–22 Malaysia Open, Kuala Lumpur
27–29 Singapore Open, Singapore

February
3–5 Indonesia Open, Jakarta
10–12 Thailand Open, Bangkok
17–19 Republic of China Open, Taipei

* *Special event*

Men's Amateur

April
14–18 West of Ireland Chp, Co. Sligo
15–16 Duncan Putter, Southerndown
22–23 West of England Strokeplay, Saunton

May
6–7 Lytham Trophy, R. Lytham
6–7 Berkshire Trophy, R. Berkshire
13–14 England *v* Spain, Fairhaven
19–21 Brabazon Trophy, Hillside
20–21 Welsh Mid-Amateur, Nefyn
26–28 St Andrews Links Trophy, St Andrews
31–1 Lagonda Trophy, Gog Magog

June
3–5 East of Ireland Chp, Co. Louth
5–10 Amateur Championship, Hoylake
7–9 English Seniors, Copt Heath
9–11 European Mid-Amateur, Estoril, Lisbon
14–15 Welsh Seniors Chp, Aberdovey
15–16 Irish Seniors Chp, Dundalk
17–18 Scottish Strokeplay Chp, Paisley
22–25 Scottish Mid-Amateur, Irvine
23–25 Welsh Strokeplay Chp, Prestatyn

July
4–5 Scottish Seniors, Glasgow
5–9 European Team Chp, R. Antwerp
10–14 North of Ireland Chp, R. Portrush
27–28 Ulster Seniors Chp, Portadown
29–2 South of Ireland Chp, Lahinch
31–5 English Amateur Chp, Hunstanton
31–5 Scottish Amateur Chp, Southerness

August
1–5 Welsh Amateur Chp, R. St David's
9–11 British Seniors Chp, Hankley Common
12–16 Irish Amateur Chp, Lahinch
24–27 European Amateur Chp, El Prat, Barcelona

September
9–10 Walker Cup, R. Porthcawl
20–22 Home Internationals, R. Portrush
24 English County Champions Tnmt, Lindrick
29–1 English County finals, Silloth

Women's Amateur

March
1–5 Spanish Chp, Las Brisas
17 Roehampton Gold Cup, Roehampton
21–24 Sunningdale Foursomes, Sunningdale
22–26 Portuguese Chp, Estoril
28–30 London Foursomes, Chelmsford

April
4–7 Northern Foursomes, Pontefract
8 Mothers & Daughters Foursomes, Royal Mid-Surrey
29–30 Helen Holm Scottish Strokeplay Chp, Royal Troon

May
16–20 Scottish Chp, Portpatrick
21–23 Welsh Chp, Aberdovey
23–27 English Chp, Ipswich

June
3–4 St Rule Trophy, St Andrews
12–14 English Seniors Chp, Tandridge
13–17 British Amateur Chp, Royal Portrush
24–25 Welsh Strokeplay Chp, Newport

July
11–13 South Eastern Chp, Worplesdon
12–16 European Team Chp, Milano, Italy
18–20 Midlands Chp, Trentham
18–21 South Western Chp, Ferndown
25–28 English Girls' Chp, Porters Park
28–29 Vagliano Trophy, Ganton

August
1–3 English Strokeplay Chp, Hallamshire
16–18 English Ladies' Intermediate, Clitheroe
22–25 Burhill Family Foursomes, Burhill
23–25 British Strokeplay Chp, Prince's, Sandwich
31–3 European Amateur Chp, Berlin, Germany

September
6–8 County Finals, Bristol & Clifton
12–13 British Seniors Chp, Blairgowrie
19–21 Northern Chp, Hexham
19–21 Scottish County Finals, Prestonfield
21–22 Welsh Seniors Chp, Tredegar Park

October
4–6 Home Internationals, Wrexham

Juniors

April
10–15 Scottish Boys' Chp, R. Aberdeen
19–20 Peter McEvoy Trophy, Copt Heath

June
3–4 Welsh Youths' Championship, Glamorganshire
11 Welsh Boys' Strokeplay, Portmadog
24–25 Scottish Youths' Chp, Irvine
29–30 Irish Youths' Chp, Ballybunion

July
4–7 Ulster Boys' Chp, Ardglass
4–7 Scottish Girls' Chp, Paisley
5–7 Scottish Boys' Strokeplay, Arbroath
12–16 European Boys' Team Chp, Woodhall Spa
12–16 European Girls' Team Chp, Grand Ducal, Luxembourg

July *continued*
21 South Eastern Girls' Chp, Royal Winchester
23–27 Welsh Girls' Chp, Borth & Ynyslas
25–27 Carris Trophy, Burnham & Berrow
25–28 English Girls' Chp, Porters Park
25–28 Welsh Boys' Chp, Newport

August
8–10 Ulster Youths' Chp, R. County Down
8–11 British Girls' Chp, Northop
10–11 Boys' Internationals, Dunbar
12 GB&I Boys *v* Continent of Europe, Dunbar
14–18 Boys' Championship, Dunbar
15–17 Girls' Home Internationals, Northop
19–20 Doug Sanders World Boys' Chp, Aberdeen
24–25 Irish Boys' Chp, Mullingar

Royal & Ancient Venues and Dates for Championships in 1995–97

	1995	1996	1997
The Amateur Championship			
	12–17 Sept R Liverpool/ Wallasey	**3–8 June** Turnberry	**2–7 June** R. St George's/ R. Cinque Ports
The Open Championship			
Final qualifying competition	**16–17 July** Ladybank Leven Links Lundin Scotscraig	**14–15 July** Fairhavens Formby Southport & Ainsdale St Annes Old Links	**13–14 July** Glasgow (Gailes) Irvine (Bogside) Kilmarnock (Barassie) Western Gailes
Championship	**20–23 July** St Andrews (Old Course)	**18–21 July** Royal Lytham & St Annes	**17–20 July** Royal Troon
The Seniors' Championship			
	9–11 Aug Hankley Common Farnham	**7–9 Aug** Blairgowrie	**6–8 Aug** Frilford Heath
The Walker Cup			
	9–10 Sept Porthcawl		**9–10 Aug** Quaker Ridge GC Scarsdale, NY
The Boys' Championship			
Internationals	**10–12 Aug** Dunbar	**8–10 Aug** Littlestone	**7–9 Aug** Saunton
Championship	**14–18 Aug** Dunbar	**12–16 Aug** Littlestone	**11–15 Aug** Saunton
Mid-Amateur Championship			
Championship	**14–19 Aug** Sunningdale (New)	TBA	TBA

Future Venues and Dates for Other Major Championships

	The Masters	The US Open	USPGA Championship
1995	Augusta National, Augusta, GA	Shinnecock Hills GC, Southampton, Long Island, NY	Riviera CC, Pacific Palisades, Santa Monica, CA
1996	Augusta National, Augusta, GA	South Course, Oakland Hills CC, Birmingham, MI	Valhalla GC, Louisville, Kentucky
1997	Augusta National, Augusta, GA	Congressional CC, Bethesda, Maryland	Winged Foot GC, Mamaroneck, NY
1998	Augusta National, Augusta, GA	The Country Club, Brookline, Boston, MA	Sahalee CC, Redmond, Seattle, Washington
1999	Augusta National, Augusta, GA	Pinehurst No. 2, Pinehurst, NC	
2000	Augusta National, Augusta, GA	Pebble Beach, Monterey CA	

The US Masters begins on the Thursday following the first Sunday in April each year.

The US Open Championship commences on the Thursday following the second Sunday in June each year.

The Open Championship normally commences on the third Thursday in July each year.

The USPGA Championship normally commences on the second Thursday in August each year.

PART I

The Major Championships

(1994 and Past Results)

The Open Golf Championship

123rd Open Championship *at Ailsa Course, Turnberry, Ayrshire* (Par 70)

Entries 1,701. Regional qualifying courses: Blackwell, Glenbervie, Hankley Common, Lanark, Moortown, North Hants, Orsett, Sherwood Forest, South Herts, Sundridge Park, Wilmslow. Final qualifying courses: Glasgow Gailes, Irvine Bogside, Kilmarnock Barassie, Western Gailes. Qualified for final 36 holes: 81 (including 1 amateur).

Pos	Player	Score	Prize Money £
1	Nick Price (Zim)	69-66-67-66—268	110000
2	Jesper Parnevik (Swe)	68-66-68-67—269	88000
3	Fuzzy Zoeller (US)	71-66-64-70—271	74000
4	Anders Forsbrand (Swe)	72-71-66-64—273	50666
	Mark James (GB)	72-67-66-68—273	
	David Feherty (GB)	68-69-66-70—273	
7	Brad Faxon (US)	69-65-67-73—274	36000
8	Nick Faldo (GB)	75-66-70-64—275	30000
	Tom Kite (US)	71-69-66-69—275	
	Colin Montgomerie (GB)	72-69-65-69—275	
11	Russell Claydon (GB)	72-71-68-65—276	19333
	Mark McNulty (Zim)	71-70-68-67—276	
	Frank Nobilo (NZ)	69-67-72-68—276	
	Jonathan Lomas (GB)	66-70-72-68—276	
	Mark Calcavecchia (US)	71-70-67-68—276	
	Greg Norman (Aus)	71-67-69-69—276	
	Larry Mize (US)	73-69-64-70—276	
	Tom Watson (US)	68-65-69-74—276	
	Ronan Rafferty (GB)	71-66-65-74—276	
20	Mark Brooks (US)	74-64-71-68—277	12500
	Vijay Singh (Fiji)	70-68-69-70—277	
	Greg Turner (NZ)	65-71-70-71—277	
	Peter Senior (Aus)	68-71-67-71—277	
24	Bob Estes (US)	72-68-72-66—278	7972
	Terry Price (Aus)	74-65-71-68—278	
	Paul Lawrie (GB)	71-69-70-68—278	
	Jeff Maggert (US)	69-74-67-68—278	
	Tom Lehman (US)	70-69-70-69—278	
	Ernie Els (RSA)	69-69-69-71—278	
	Michael Springer (US)	72-67-68-71—278	
	Loren Roberts (US)	68-69-69-72—278	
	Peter Jacobsen (US)	69-70-67-72—278	
	Craig Stadler (US)	71-69-66-72—278	
	Andrew Coltart (GB)	71-69-66-72—278	
35	Mark Davis (GB)	75-68-69-67—279	6700
	Lee Janzen (US)	74-69-69-67—279	
	Gary Evans (GB)	69-69-73-68—279	
38	David Gilford (GB)	72-68-72-68—280	6100
	Domingo Hospital (Sp)	72-69-71-68—280	
	José-Maria Olazabal (Sp)	72-71-69-68—280	
	Seve Ballesteros (Sp)	70-70-71-69—280	
	Brian Marchbank (GB)	71-70-70-69—280	
	Darren Clarke (GB)	73-68-69-70—280	

Pos	Player	Score	Prize Money £
	Jean Van De Velde (Fr)	68-70-71-71—280	
	Davis Love III (US)	71-67-68-74—280	
	Masashi Ozaki (Jap)	69-71-66-74—280	
47	Jim Gallagher Jnr (US)	73-68-69-71—281	5,450
	David Edwards (US)	68-68-73-72—281	
	Greg Kraft (US)	69-74-66-72—281	
	Howard Twitty (US)	71-72-66-72—281	
51	David Frost (SA)	70-71-71-70—282	4925
	Mats Lanner (Swe)	69-74-69-70—282	
	Katsuyoshi Tomori (Jpn)	69-69-73-71—282	
	Tsukasa Watanabe (Jpn)	72-71-68-71—282	
55	Peter Baker (GB)	71-72-70-70—283	4700
	John Cook (US)	73-67-70-73—283	
	Tommy Nakajima (Jpn)	73-68-69-73—283	
	Brian Watts (US)	68-70-71-74—283	
	Ross McFarlane (GB)	68-74-67-74—283	
60	Gordon Brand Jr (GB)	72-71-73-68—284	4350
	Hajime Meshiai (Jap)	72-71-71-70—284	
	Bernhard Langer (Ger)	72-70-70-72—284	
	Christy O'Connor Jnr (Ire)	71-69-71-73—284	
	Per-Ulrik Johansson (Swe)	73-69-69-73—284	
	Robert Allenby (Aus)	72-69-68-75—284	
	Wayne Grady (Aus)	68-74-67-75—284	
67	Steve Elkington (Aus)	71-72-73-69—285	4050
	Mark Roe (GB)	74-68-73-70—285	
	Lennie Clements (US)	72-71-72-70—285	
	Carl Mason (GB)	69-71-73-72—285	
	Ruben Alvarez (Arg)	70-72-71-72—285	
72	Warren Bennett (Am GB)	72-67-74-73—286	3900
	Wayne Riley (Aus)	77-66-70-73—286	
74	Sandy Lyle (GB)	71-72-72-72—287	3850
75	Craig Ronald (GB)	71-72-72-73—288	3775
	Colin Gillies (GB)	71-70-72-75—288	
77	Ben Crenshaw (US)	70-73-73-73—289	3650
	Craig Parry (Aus)	72-68-73-76—289	
	Joakim Haeggman (Swe)	71-72-69-77—289	
80	Nic Henning (SA)	70-73-70-78—291	3550
81	John Daly (US)	68-72-72-80—292	3500

36-hole cut: 143, three over par. The following players missed the cut (each professional received £600).

Pos	Player	Score
82	K Stables	74-70–144
	H Clark	71-73–144
	J Huston	71-73–144
	P McGinley	71-73–144
	C Gray	69-75–144
	MA Martin	69-75–144
	P Way	73-71–144
	M Krantz	70-74–144
	C Rocca	73-71–144
	DA Weibring	72-72–144
	J Rivero	72-72–144
93	S Robertson	75-70–145
	B Lane	73-72–145
	J Nicklaus	72-73–145
	T Johnstone	75-70–145
	M Campbell	72-73–145
	L James (Am)	75-70–145
	E Romero	73-72–145
	MA Jimenez	71-74–145
	G Player	72-73–145
102	A Bossert	74-72–146
	B Hughes	72-74–146
	S Simpson	73-73–146
	M Clayton	71-75–146
	S Richardson	69-77–146
	P Mitchell	74-72–146
	F Allem	73-73–146
	M Harwood	77-69–146
110	W Westner	73-74–147
	G Hjertstedt	71-76–147
	C Jones	71-76–147
	B Vaughan	69-78–147
	P Curry	73-74–147
	A Magee	67-80–147
	L Trevino	75-72–147
	S Torrance	74-73–147
	K Triplett	71-76–147
	H Goda	71-76–147
120	P Broadhurst	73-75–148
	J McGovern	78-70–148
	G Orr	76-72–148
	F Quinn	77-71–148
	G Emerson	75-73–148
	P Stewart	74-74–148
	K Walker	72-76–148
	J Wright	71-77–148
	S Tinning	75-73–148
	C Franco	72-76–148
	A Oldcorn	77-71–148
131	JM Canizares	80-69–149
	C Evans (Am)	74-75–149
	P Smith	73-76–149
	G Morgan	73-76–149
	J Harris (Am)	73-76–149
	D Smyth	80-69–149
137	F Lindgren	78-72–150
	K Waters	75-75–150
	I Baker-Finch	73-77–150
140	C Beck	76-75–151
	C Pavin	75-76–151
	C Green	75-76–151
143	P Fulke	77-75–152
	I Woosnam	79-73–152
	P Mickelson	78-74–152
	C Cassells	77-75–152
	M Mouland	76-76–152
148	B Charles	74-79–153
	R Davis	77-76–153
	A Gillner	74-79–153
151	P Eales	76-78–154
	J Higgins	78-76–154
153	S Pullan (Am)	81-74–155
	E Herrera	77-79–156
	A George	74-83–157
	L Fickling	80-80–160

1993 at Royal St George's

Prize money: £1,017,000. Entries 1,827. Regional qualifying courses: Beau Desert, Blackwell, Coxmoor, Hankley Park, Lanark, Langley Park, North Hants, Orsett, Sherwood Forest, South Herts, Sundridge Park, Wilmslow. Final qualifying courses: Littlestone, North Foreland, Prince's and Royal Cinque Ports. Qualified for final 36 holes: 78 (77 professionals, 1 amateur). Non-qualifiers after 36 holes: 78 (73 professionals, 5 amateurs) with scores of 144 and above.

Pos	Name	Score	Prize £
1	G Norman (Aus)	66-68-69-64—267	100000
2	N Faldo (GB)	69-63-70-67—269	80000
3	B Langer (Ger)	67-66-70-67—270	67000
4	C Pavin (US)	68-66-68-70—272	50500
	P Senior (Aus)	66-69-70-67—272	50500
6	N Price (Zim)	68-70-67-69—274	33166
	E Els (SA)	68-69-69-68—274	33166
	P Lawrie (GB)	72-68-69-65—274	33166
9	W Grady (Aus)	74-68-64-69—275	25500
	F Couples (US)	68-66-72-69—275	25500
	S Simpson (US)	68-70-71-66—275	25500
12	P Stewart (US)	71-72-70-63—276	21500
13	B Lane (GB)	70-68-71-68—277	20500
14	J Daly (US)	71-66-70-71—278	15214
	F Zoeller (US)	66-70-71-71—278	15214
	G Morgan (US)	70-68-70-70—278	15214
	J Rivero (Spa)	68-73-67-70—278	15214
	M McNulty (Zim)	67-71-71-69—278	15214
	M Calcavecchia (US)	66-73-71-68—278	15214
	T Kite (US)	72-70-68-68—278	15214
21	H Clark (GB)	67-72-70-70—279	10000
	J Parnevik (Swe)	68-74-68-69—279	10000
	P Baker (GB)	70-67-74-68—279	10000
24	R Davis (Aus)	68-71-71-70—280	8400
	D Frost (SA)	69-73-70-68—280	8400
	M Roe (GB)	70-71-73-66—280	8400
27	L Mize (US)	67-69-74-71—281	7225
	S Ballesteros (Spa)	68-73-69-71—281	7225
	M James (GB)	70-70-70-71—281	7225
	D Smyth (Ire)	67-74-70-70—281	7225
	Y Mizumaki (Jap)	69-69-73-70—281	7225
	M Mackenzie (GB)	72-71-71-67—281	7225
	I Pyman (Am) (GB)	68-72-70-71—281	
34	H Twitty (US)	71-71-67-73—282	6180
	R Floyd (US)	70-72-67-73—282	6180
	W Westner (SA)	67-73-72-70—282	6180
	P Broadhurst (GB)	71-69-74-68—282	6180
	J Van de Velde (Fr)	75-67-73-67—282	6180

Other Totals: D Clarke (GB), C O'Connor Jr (Ire), A Sorensen (Den), D Waldorf (US), P Moloney (Aus), G Turner (NZ), C Mason (GB), A Magee (US), R Mediate (US) 283; L Janzen (US), S Elkington (Aus), J Huston (US) 284; J Sewell (GB), M Pinero (Spa), F Nobilo (NZ), S Torrance (GB), MA Jimenez (Spa), I Woosnam (GB), S Ames (T&T), I Garbutt (GB) 285; C Parry (Aus), T Lehman (US), V Singh (Fiji), P Azinger (US) 286; J Spence (GB), O Karlsson (Swe), R Drummond (GB) 287; T Pernice (US), W Guy (GB), James Cook (GB), M Sunesson (Swe) 288; I Baker-Finch (Aus), T Purtzer (US), M Miller (GB) 289; M Harwood (Aus), P Mitchell (GB), P Fowler (Aus), D Forsman (US) 290; M Krantz (Swe) 292; R Willison (GB) 293.

1992 at Muirfield

Prize money: £950,000. Entries 1,666. Regional qualifying courses: Beau Desert, Blackwell, Coxmoor, Glenbervie, Lanark, North Hants, Orsett, Sherwood Forest, South Herts, Sundridge Park, Wilmslow. Final qualifying courses: Dunbar, Gullane, Luffness New, North Berwick. Qualified for final 36 holes: 75 (74 Professionals, 1 Amateur). Non-qualifiers after 36 holes: 81 (77 Professionals, 4 Amateurs) with scores of 143 and above.

Pos	Name	Score	Prize £
1	N Faldo (GB)	66-64-69-73—272	95000
2	J Cook (US)	66-67-70-70—273	75000
3	JM Olazabal (Spa)	70-67-69-68—274	64000
4	S Pate (US)	64-70-69-73—276	53000
5	D Hammond (US)	70-65-70-74—279	30071
	A Magee (US)	67-72-70-70—279	30071
	E Els (SA)	66-69-70-74—279	30071
	I Woosnam (GB)	65-73-70-71—279	30071
	G Brand Jr (GB)	65-68-72-74—279	30071
	M Mackenzie (Chile)	71-67-70-71—279	30071
	R Karlsson (Swe)	70-68-70-71—279	30071
12	J Spence (GB)	71-68-70-71—280	17383
	C Beck (US)	71-68-67-74—280	17383
	R Floyd (US)	64-71-73-72—280	17383
	A Lyle (GB)	68-70-70-72—280	17383
	M O'Meara (US)	71-68-72-69—280	17383
	L Rinker (US)	69-68-70-73—280	17383
18	G Norman (Aus)	71-72-70-68—281	13200
19	H Irwin (US)	70-73-67-72—282	11066
19	I Baker-Finch (Aus)	71-71-72-68—282	11066
	T Kite (US)	70-69-71-72—282	11066
22	P Mitchell (GB)	69-71-72-71—283	8950
	P Lawrie (GB)	70-72-68-73—283	8950
	T Purtzer (US)	68-69-75-71—283	8950
25	B Andrade (US)	69-71-70-74—284	7700
	D Waldorf (US)	69-70-73-72—284	7700
	P Senior (Aus)	70-69-70-75—284	7700
28	M Calcavecchia (US)	69-71-73-72—285	6658
	M McNulty (Zim)	71-70-70-74—285	6658
	J Mudd (US)	71-69-74-71—285	6658
	C Parry (Aus)	67-71-76-71—285	6658
	R Cochran (US)	71-68-72-74—285	6658
	M Lanner (Swe)	72-68-71-74—285	6658
34	A Forsbrand (Swe)	70-72-70-74—286	5760
	C Pavin (US)	69-74-73-70—286	5760
	P Stewart (US)	70-73-71-72—286	5760
	S Elkington (Aus)	68-70-75-73—286	5760
	T Johnstone (Zim)	72-71-74-69—286	5760

Other Totals: DW Basson (SA), L Janzen (US), L Trevino (US), S Richardson (GB), W Grady (Aus), R Rafferty (Ire) 287; M Harwood (Aus), L Wadkins (US), J Coceres (Arg), R Mediate (US), C Mann (Aus), B Marchbank (GB) 288; R Mackay (Aus), V Singh (Fiji), N Price (Zim), B Lane (GB) 289; C Rocca (Ita), D Feherty (Ire), M Brooks (US), O Vincent III (US) 290; P Azinger (US), B Langer (Ger), W Riley (Aus), W Guy (GB), M Clayton (Aus) 291; C Stadler (US), R Chapman (GB), D Mijovic (Can), H Buhrmann (SA) 292; P-U Johansson (Swe), P O'Malley (Aus), A Sherbourne (GB), J Robson (GB), D Lee (GB) 293; F Funk (US) 294; P Mayo (GB) 295; J Daly (US) 298.

1991 at R Birkdale

Prize money: £900,000. Entries 1,496. Regional Qualifying Courses: Beau Desert, Blackwell, Deer Park, Hankley Common, Langley Park, Ormskirk, Orsett, Sherwood Forest, South Herts. Final Qualifying Courses: Hesketh, Hillside, Southport & Ainsdale, West Lancashire. Qualified for final 36 holes: 113 (111 Professionals, 2 Amateurs). Non-qualifiers after 36 holes: 43 (37 Professionals, 6 Amateurs) with scores of 149 and above.

Pos	Name	Score	Prize £
1	I Baker-Finch (Aus)	71-71-64-66—272	90000
2	M Harwood (Aus)	68-70-69-67—274	70000
3	M O'Meara (US)	71-68-67-69—275	55000
	F Couples (US)	72-69-70-64—275	55000
5	J Mudd (US)	72-70-72-63—277	34166
	E Darcy (Ire)	73-68-66-70—277	34166
	B Tway (US)	75-66-70-66—277	34166
8	C Parry (Aus)	71-70-69-68—278	27500
9	G Norman (Aus)	74-68-71-66—279	22833
	B Langer (Ger)	71-71-70-67—279	22833
	S Ballesteros (Spa)	66-73-69-71—279	22833
12	M Sunesson (Swe)	72-73-68-67—280	17100
	D Williams (GB)	74-71-68-67—280	17100
	V Singh (Fij)	71-69-69-71—280	17100
	R Davis (Aus)	70-71-73-66—280	17100
	R Chapman (GB)	74-66-71-69—280	17100
17	L Trevino (US)	71-72-71-67—281	10055
	B Lane (GB)	68-72-71-70—281	10055
	N Faldo (GB)	68-75-70-68—281	10055
17	C Beck (US)	67-78-70-66—281	10055
	I Woosnam (GB)	70-72-69-70—281	10055
	P Broadhurst (GB)	71-73-68-69—281	10055
	M Mouland (GB)	68-74-68-71—281	10055
	A Sherborne (GB)	73-70-68-70—281	10055
	P Senior (Aus)	74-67-71-69—281	10055
26	C Montgomerie (GB)	71-69-71-71—282	6750
	M Reid (US)	68-71-70-73—282	6750
	W Grady (Aus)	69-70-73-70—282	6750
	T Watson (US)	69-72-72-69—282	6750
	E Romero (Arg)	70-73-68-71—282	6750
	M James (GB)	72-68-70-72—282	6750
32	G Hallberg (US)	68-70-73-72—283	5633
	P Stewart (US)	72-72-71-68—283	5633
	S Richardson (GB)	74-70-72-67—283	5633
	G Brand Jr (GB)	71-72-69-71—283	5633
	M Miller (GB)	73-74-67-69—283	5633
	C O'Connor Jr (Ire)	72-71-71-69—283	5633

Other Totals: C Strange (US), A Forsbrand (Swe), P O'Malley (Aus), N Henke (US), M Poxon (GB), J Payne (Am) (GB) 284; G Marsh (Aus), R Gamez (US), T Kite (US), S Elkington (Aus), F Allem (SA), S Torrance (GB), C Rocca (Ita), D Love III (US), D Smyth (Ire), J Spence (GB), J Nicklaus (US), N Price (Zim), D Hammond (US) 285; G Levenson (SA), A Magee (US), H Irwin (US), S Simpson (US), T Simpson (US), J Rivero (Spa), G Player (SA) 286; MA Martin (Spa), JD Blake (US), M McLean (GB), A Oldcorn (GB), M McNulty (Zim), S Jones (US), S Pate (US), G Morgan (US), D Clarke (Ire) 287.

1990 at St Andrews

Prize money: £825,000. Entries 1,707. Regional Qualifying Courses: Blackwell, Deer Park, Hankley Common, Langley Park, Ormskirk, Orsett, Sherwood Forest, South Herts. Final Qualifying Courses: Ladybank, Leven Links, Lundin, Panmure, Scotscraig. Qualified for final 36 holes: 72 (72 Professionals, No Amateurs). Non-qualifiers after 36 holes: 84 (80 Professionals and 4 Amateurs) with scores of 144 and above.

Pos	Name	Score	Prize £
1	N Faldo (GB)	67-65-67-71—270	85000
2	M McNulty (Zim)	74-68-68-65—275	60000
	P Stewart (US)	68-68-68-71—275	60000
4	I Woosnam (GB)	68-69-70-69—276	40000
	J Mudd (US)	72-66-72-66—276	40000
6	I Baker-Finch (Aus)	68-72-64-73—277	28500
	G Norman (Aus)	66-66-76-69—277	28500
8	S Pate (US)	70-68-72-69—279	22000
	C Pavin (US)	71-69-68-71—279	22000
	D Hammond (US)	70-71-68-70—279	22000
	D Graham (Aus)	72-71-70-66—279	22000
12	V Singh (Fij)	70-69-72-69—280	16375
	T Simpson (US)	70-69-69-72—280	16375
	R Gamez (US)	70-72-67-71—280	16375
	P Broadhurst (GB)	74-69-63-74—280	16375
16	M Roe (GB)	71-70-72-68—281	11150
	S Jones (US)	72-67-72-70—281	11150
	A Lyle (GB)	72-70-67-72—281	11150
	JM Olazabal (Spa)	71-67-71-72—281	11150
16	P Jacobsen (US)	68-70-70-73—281	11150
	F Nobilo (NZ)	72-67-68-74—281	11150
22	E Darcy (Ire)	71-71-72-68—282	7933
	C Parry (Aus)	68-68-69-77—282	7933
	J Spence (GB)	72-65-73-72—282	7933
25	N Price (Zim)	70-67-71-75—283	6383
	F Couples (US)	71-70-70-72—283	6383
	C O'Connor Jr (Ire)	68-72-71-72—283	6383
	L Trevino (US)	69-70-73-71—283	6383
	J Rivero (Spa)	70-70-70-73—283	6383
	J Sluman (US)	72-70-70-71—283	6383
31	B Norton (US)	71-72-68-73—284	5125
	L Mize (US)	71-72-70-71—284	5125
	R Rafferty (N Ire)	70-71-73-70—284	5125
	B Crenshaw (US)	74-69-68-73—284	5125
	M McCumber (US)	69-74-69-72—284	5125
	M James (GB)	73-69-70-72—284	5125
	V Fernandez (Arg)	72-67-69-76—284	5125
	G Powers (US)	74-69-69-72—284	5125

Other Totals: D Cooper (GB), N Ozaki (Jpn), D Pooley (US), M Hulbert (US), M Reid (US), A North (US), S Simpson (US), R Floyd (US), S Torrance (GB) 285; M O'Meara (US), C Montgomerie (GB), B Langer (Ger), P Fowler (Aus), P Azinger (US) 286; H Irwin (US), E Romero (Arg), J Bland (SA), M Allen (US) 287; D Ray (GB), A Sorensen (Den), B McCallister (US), J Rutledge (Can), D Mijovic (US), M Clayton (Aus) 288; M Poxon (GB), P Baker (GB), J Nicklaus (US), R Chapman (GB), D Canipe (US) 289; J Berendt (Arg), D Feherty (GB) 290; A Saavedra (Arg) 291; M Mackenzie (GB) 292; JM Canizares (Spa) 296.

1989 at R Troon

Prize money: £750,000. Entries 1,481. Regional Qualifying Courses: Glenbervie, Hankley Common, Langley Park, Lindrick, Little Aston, Ormskirk, Porters Park, South Herts. Final Qualifying Courses: Glasgow Gailes, Irvine (Bogside), Kilmarnock (Barassie), Western Gailes. Qualified for final 36 holes: 80 (78 Professionals, 2 Amateurs). Non-qualifiers after 36 holes: 76 (68 Professionals, 8 Amateurs) with scores of 147 and above.

Pos	Name	Score	Prize £
1	M Calcavecchia (US)	71-68-68-68—275	80000
2	W Grady (Aus)	68-67-69-71—275	55000
	G Norman (Aus)	69-70-72-64—275	55000
	(Calcavecchia won 4-hole play-off)		
4	T Watson (US)	69-68-68-72—277	40000
5	J Mudd (US)	73-67-68-70—278	30000
6	F Couples (US)	68-71-68-72—279	26000
	D Feherty (GB)	71-67-69-72—279	26000
8	E Romero (Arg)	68-70-75-67—280	21000
	P Azinger (US)	68-73-67-72—280	21000
	P Stewart (US)	72-65-69-74—280	21000
11	N Faldo (GB)	71-71-70-69—281	17000
	M McNulty (Zim)	75-70-70-66—281	17000
13	P Walton (Ire)	69-74-69-70—282	13000
	H Clark (GB)	72-68-72-70—282	13000
	S Pate(US)	69-70-70-73—282	13000
	R Chapman (GB)	76-68-67-71—282	13000
	M James (GB)	69-70-71-72—282	13000
	C Stadler (US)	73-69-69-71—282	13000
19	L Mize (US)	71-74-66-72—283	8575
19	D Cooper (GB)	69-70-76-68—283	8575
	T Kite (US)	70-74-67-72—283	8575
	D Pooley (US)	73-70-69-71—283	8575
23	V Singh (Fiji)	71-73-69-71—284	6733
	D Love III (US)	72-70-73-69—284	6733
	JM Olazabal (Spa)	68-72-69-75—284	6733
26	S Bennett (GB)	75-69-68-73—285	5800
	L Wadkins (US)	72-70-69-74—285	5800
	C Beck (US)	75-69-68-73—285	5800
	S Simpson (US)	73-66-72-74—285	5800
30	J Hawkes (SA)	75-67-69-75—286	4711
	G Koch (US)	72-71-74-69—286	4711
	J Nicklaus (US)	74-71-71-70—286	4711
	P Jacobsen (US)	71-74-71-70—286	4711
	B Marchbank (GB)	69-74-73-70—286	4711
	M Martin (Spa)	68-73-73-72—286	4711
	I Baker-Finch (Aus)	72-69-70-75—286	4711
	M Ozaki (Jpn)	71-73-70-72—286	4711
	M Davis (GB)	77-68-67-74—286	4711

Other Totals: M Harwood (Aus), T Armour III (US), J Woodland (Aus) 287; M O'Meara (US), L Trevino (US), R Floyd (US), J Rivero (Spa) 288; M McCumber (US), A Lyle (GB), N Ozaki (Jpn) 289; J Miller (US), I Woosnam (GB), C O'Connor Jr (Ire) 290; B Ogle (Aus), M Roe (GB), T Ozaki (Jpn), M Allen (US), T Johnstone (Zim), E Dussart (Fra), R Boxall (GB), G Sauers (US), B Crenshaw (US) 291; C Strange (US), D Graham (Aus), K Green (US), P Hoad (GB), B Tway (US), R Rafferty (Ire), M Reid (US), W Stephens (GB) 292; L Carbonetti (Arg), A Stephen (GB), R Claydon (Am) (GB) 293; C Gillies (GB) 294; B Faxon (US), P Teravainen (US) 295; E Aubrey (US) 296; M Sludds (Ire) 297; S Ballesteros (Spa), R Karlsson (Am) (Swe) 299; G Levenson (SA) 301; B Langer (W Ger) 309.

1988 at R Lytham & St Annes

Prize money: £700,000. Entries 1,393. Regional Qualifying Courses: Beau Desert, Camberley Heath, Glenbervie, Hankley Common, Langley Park, Lindrick, Little Aston, Ormskirk, Porters Park. Final Qualifying Courses: Blackpool North Shore, Fairhaven, Lytham Green Drive, St Annes Old Links. Qualified for final 36 holes: 71 (70 Professionals, 1 Amateur). Non-qualifiers after 36 holes: 83 (76 Professionals, 7 Amateurs) with scores of 149 and above.

Pos	Name	Score	Prize £
1	S Ballesteros (Spa)	67-71-70-65—273	80000
2	N Price (Zim)	70-67-69-69—275	60000
3	N Faldo (GB)	71-69-68-71—279	47000
4	F Couples (US)	73-69-71-68—281	33500
	G Koch (US)	71-72-70-68—281	33500
6	P Senior (Aus)	70-73-70-69—282	27000
7	I Aoki (Jpn)	72-71-73-67—283	21000
	P Stewart (US)	73-75-68-67—283	21000
	D Frost (SA)	71-75-69-68—283	21000
	A Lyle (GB)	73-69-67-74—283	21000
11	D Russell (GB)	71-74-69-70—284	16500
	B Faxon (US)	69-74-70-71—284	16500
13	C Strange (US)	79-69-69-68—285	14000
	E Romero (Arg)	72-71-69-73—285	14000
	L Nelson (US)	73-71-68-73—285	14000
16	J Rivero (Spa)	75-69-70-72—286	10500
	B Crenshaw (US)	73-73-68-72—286	10500
	A Bean (US)	71-70-71-74—286	10500
	D Pooley (US)	70-73-69-74—286	10500
20	T Kite (US)	75-71-73-68—287	7000
	R Davis (Aus)	76-71-72-68—287	7000
	G Brand Jr (GB)	72-76-68-71—287	7000
	B Tway (US)	71-71-72-73—287	7000
	R Charles (NZ)	71-74-69-73—287	7000
25	J Nicklaus (US)	75-70-75-68—288	5500
	I Woosnam (GB)	76-71-72-69—288	5500
27	M O'Meara (US)	75-69-75-70—289	5200
28	H Clark (Eng)	71-72-75-72—290	4600
	M McNulty (Zim)	73-73-72-72—290	4600
	T Watson (US)	74-72-72-72—290	4600
	C Beck (US)	72-71-74-73—290	4600
	T Armour III (US)	73-72-72-73—290	4600
	J Benepe III (US)	75-72-70-73—290	4600
34	W Riley (Aus)	72-71-72-76—291	4150
	L Wadkins (US)	73-71-71-76—291	4150
36	G Brand (GB)	73-74-72-73—292	3950
	JM Olazabal (Spa)	73-71-73-75—292	3950

Other Totals: J Haas (US), N Ratcliffe (GB), B Marchbank (GB), R Rafferty (Ire), G March (Aus), C Pavin (US), D Russell (GB), W Grady (Aus), K Brown (GB) 293; P Kent (GB), S Torrance (GB), P Azinger (US), A North (US), M McCumber (US) 294; P Fowler (Aus), F Zoeller (US), P Walton (GB), H Green (US), J Miller (US) 295; M Smith (GB), C Mason (GB), P Broadhurst (Am.) (GB) 296; C Stadler (US), G Player (SA) 297; M James (GB), S Bishop (GB), A Sherborne (GB) 298; M Pinero (Spa) 299; P Carman 301; G Bruckner, C-H Hsieh 302; B Langer (W Ger) 303; G Stafford 305; P Mitchell 308.

1987 at Muirfield

Prize money: £650,000. Entries 1,407. Regional Qualifying Courses: Glenbervie, Haggs Castle, Hankley Common, Langley Park, Lindrick, Little Aston, Ormskirk, Porters Park. Final Qualifying Courses: Gullane No 1, Longniddry, Luffness New, North Berwick. Qualified for final 36 holes: 78 (76 Professionals, 2 Amateurs). Non-qualifiers after 36 holes: 75 (65 Professionals, 10 Amateurs) with scores of 147 and above.

Pos	Name	Score	Prize £
1	N Faldo (GB)	68-69-71-71—279	75000
2	R Davis (Aus)	64-73-74-69—280	49500
	P Azinger (US)	68-68-71-73—280	49500
4	B Crenshaw (US)	73-68-72-68—281	31000
	P Stewart (US)	71-66-72-72—281	31000
6	D Frost (SA)	70-68-70-74—282	26000
7	T Watson (US)	69-69-71-74—283	23000
8	I Woosnam (GB)	71-69-72-72—284	18666
	N Price (Zim)	68-71-72-73—284	18666
	C Stadler (US)	69-69-71-75—284	18666
11	M McNulty (Zim)	71-69-75-70—285	13500
	H Sutton (US)	71-70-73-71—285	13500
	JM Olazabal (Spa)	70-73-70-72—285	13500
	M Ozaki (Jpn)	69-72-71-73—285	13500
11	M Calcavecchia (US)	69-70-72-74—285	13500
	G Marsh (Aus)	69-70-72-74—285	13500
17	W Grady (Aus)	70-71-76-69—286	7450
	A Lyle (GB)	76-69-71-70—286	7450
	E Darcy (Ire)	74-69-72-71—286	7450
	B Langer (W Ger)	69-69-76-72—286	7450
	L Trevino (US)	67-74-73-72—286	7450
	M Roe (GB)	74-68-72-72—286	7450
	K Brown (GB)	69-73-70-74—286	7450
	R Floyd (US)	72-68-70-76—286	7450
25	G Taylor (Aus)	69-68-75-75—287	5300
26	D Feherty (Ire)	74-70-77-67—288	4933
	G Brand Jr (GB)	73-70-75-70—288	4933
	L Mize (US)	68-71-76-73—288	4933

Other Totals: L Wadkins (US), F Zoeller (US), K Green (US), D Edwards (US), A Forsbrand (Swe) 289; D Graham (Aus) 290; R Drummond (GB), M Calero (Spa), J Haas (US), G Norman (Aus), R Tway (US) 291; D Cooper (GB), F Couples (US), A Bean (US), GJ Brand (GB) 292; F Allem (SA), B Marshbank (GB), O Moore (Aus), C Mason (GB), L Nelson (US), J Slaughter (US) 294; M Lanner (Swe), S Torrance (GB), S Ballesteros (Spa), P Walton (Ire) 295; J O'Leary (Ire), R Chapman (GB), W Andrade (US) 296; O Sellberg (Swe), P Mayo (GB) 297; B Jones (Aus), W McColl (GB), T Nakajima (Jpn) 298; S Simpson (US), N Hansen (GB), H Clark (GB), M Martin (Spa) 299; M O'Meara (US), G Player (SA), T Ozaki (Jpn), H Baiocchi (SA), B Chamblee (US) 300; W Westner (SA) 301; J Nicklaus (US), T Kite (US) 302; J Hawkes (SA) 303; R Willison (GB) 305; C Moody (GB) 306; D Jones (Ire) 307; A Stevens (GB) 312.

1986 at Turnberry

Prize money: £600,000. Entries 1,347. Regional Qualifying Courses: Glenbervie, Haggs Castle, Hankley Common, Langley Park, Lindrick, Little Aston, Ormskirk, Porters Park. Final Qualifying Courses: Glasgow Gailes, Kilmarnock (Barassie), Prestwick St Nicholas, Western Gailes. Qualified for final 36 holes: 77 Professionals. Non-qualifiers after 36 holes: 74 (71 Professionals, 3 Amateurs) with scores of 152 and above.
Other Totals: I Stanley (Aus), J Mahaffey (US), M Karamoto (Jpn), DA Weibring (US), A Lyle (GB) 295;

Pos	Name	Score	Prize £
1	G Norman (Aus)	74-63-74-69—280	70000
2	GJ Brand (GB)	71-68-75-71—285	50000
3	B Langer (W Ger)	72-70-76-68—286	35000
	I Woosnam (GB)	70-74-70-72—286	35000
5	N Faldo (GB)	71-70-76-70—287	25000
6	S Ballesteros (Spa)	76-75-73-64—288	25000
	G Koch (US)	73-72-72-71—288	25000
8	F Zoeller (US)	75-73-72-69—289	17333
	B Marchbank (GB)	78-70-72-69—289	17333
	T Nakajima (Jpn)	74-67-71-77—289	17333
11	C O'Connor Jr (Ire)	75-71-75-69—290	14000
	D Graham (Aus)	75-73-70-72—290	14000
	JM Canizares (Spa)	76-68-73-73—290	14000
14	C Strange (US)	79-69-74-69—291	11500
	A Bean (US)	74-73-73-71—291	11500
16	A Forsbrand (Swe)	71-73-77-71—292	9000
	JM Olazabal (Spa)	78-69-72-73—292	9000
	R Floyd (US)	78-67-73-74—292	9000
19	R Charles (NZ)	76-72-73-72—293	7250
	M Pinero (Spa)	78-71-70-74—293	7250
21	R Rafferty (N Ire)	75-74-75-70—294	5022
	D Cooper (GB)	72-79-72-71—294	5022
	V Somers (Aus)	73-77-72-72—294	5022
	B Crenshaw (US)	77-69-75-73—294	5022
	R Lee (GB)	71-75-75-73—294	5022
	P Parkin (GB)	78-70-72-74—294	5022
	D Edwards (US)	77-73-70-74—294	5022
	V Fernandez (Arg)	78-70-71-75—294	5022
	S Torrance (GB)	78-69-71-76—294	5022

T Watson (US), R Chapman (GB), A Brooks (GB), R Commans (US), M James (GB), P Stewart (US), G Player (SA), G Turner (NZ) 296; R Maltbie (US), M O'Meara (US), HM Chung (Tai) 297; J Nicklaus (US), M O'Grady (US), T Charnley (GB), F Couples (US), M Clayton (Aus), L Mize (US), J Hawkes (SA), LS Chuen (Tai), R Tway (US), T Armour III (US) 298; S Randolph (US), G Marsh (Aus), C Mason (GB) 300; M McNulty (Zim), M Mackenzie (GB), L Trevino (US), E Darcy (Ire), T Lamore (US), F Nobilo (NZ) 301; A Chandler (GB), J Heggarty (GB), M Gray (GB), D Hammond (US), S Simpson (US) 302; O Moore (Aus), P Fowler (Aus) 303; D Jones (GB), R Drummond (GB) 305; T Horton (GB) 306; G Weir (GB) 307; K Moe (US) 314; H Green (US) ret'd.

1985 at Sandwich, R St George's

Prize money: £530,000. Entries 1,361. Regional Qualifying Courses: Camberley Heath, Glenbervie, Lindrick, Little Aston, Pleasington, Porters Park, Wildernesse. Final Qualifying Courses: Royal Cinque Ports Deal, Littlestone, North Foreland. Qualified for final 36 holes: 85 (83 Professionals, 2 Amateurs) with scores of 149 and below. Qualified for final 18 holes: 60 (59 Professionals, 1 Amateur) with scores of 221 and below.

Pos	Name	Score	Prize £
1	A Lyle (GB)	68-71-73-70—282	65000
2	P Stewart (US)	70-75-70-68—283	40000
3	J Rivero (Spa)	74-72-70-68—284	23600
	C O'Connor Jr (Ire)	64-76-72-72—284	23600
	M O'Meara (US)	70-72-70-72—284	23600
	D Graham (Aus)	68-71-70-75—284	23600
	B Langer (W Ger)	72-69-68-75—284	23600
8	A Forsbrand (Swe)	70-70-69-70—285	15566
	DA Weibring (US)	69-71-74-71—285	15566
	T Kite (US)	73-73-67-72—285	15566
11	E Darcy (Ire)	76-68-74-68—286	11400
	G Koch (US)	75-72-70-69—286	11400
	J-M Canizares (Sp)	72-75-70-69—286	11400
	F Zoeller (US)	69-76-70-71—286	11400
	P Jacobsen (US)	71-74-68-73—286	11400
16	S Bishop (GB)	71-75-72-69—287	7900
16	S Torrance (GB)	74-74-69-70—287	7900
	G Norman (Aus)	71-72-71-73—287	7900
	I Woosnam (GB)	70-71-71-75—287	7900
20	I Baker-Finch (Aus)	71-73-74-70—288	5260
	J Gonzales (Bra)	72-72-73-71—288	5260
	L Trevino (US)	73-76-68-71—288	5260
	G Marsh (Aus)	71-75-69-73—288	5260
	M James (GB)	71-78-66-73—288	5260
25	P Parkin (GB)	68-76-77-68—289	3742
	K Moe (US)	70-76-73-70—289	3742
	JM Olazabal (Am Sp)	72-76-71-70—289	3742
	M Cahill (Aus)	72-74-71-72—289	3742
	D Frost (SA	70-74-73-72—289	3742
	GJ Brand (GB)	73-72-72-72—289	3742
	M Pinero (Sp)	71-73-72-73—289	3742
	R Lee (GB)	68-73-74-74—289	3742

Other Totals: O Sellberg (Swe), W Riley (Aus) 290; H Baiocchi (SA), B Crenshaw (US), A Bean (US), R Shearer (Aus) 291; A Johnstone (Zim), M Parsson (Swe), J Pinsent (GB), S Ballesteros (Spa), C Pavin (US) 292; P Senior (Aus), R Rafferty (N Ire), D Russell (GB) 293; D Watson (SA), M Mouland (GB), G Brand, Jr (GB), B Gallacher (GB), H Clark (GB), T Watson (US) 294; N Faldo (GB), E Rodriguez (Spa) 295; L Nelson (US), P Fowler (Aus) 296; D Whelan (GB) 298; D Williams (GB) 300; V Somers (Aus) 301; R Charles (NZ) retired.

The Belt

Year	Winner	Score	Venue	Entrants
1860	W Park, Musselburgh	174	Prestwick	8
1861	T Morris, Sr, Prestwick	163	Prestwick	12
1862	T Morris, Sr, Prestwick	163	Prestwick	6
1863	W Park, Musselburgh	168	Prestwick	14
1864	T Morris, Sr, Prestwick	167	Prestwick	6
1865	A Strath, St Andrews	162	Prestwick	10
1866	W Park, Musselburgh	169	Prestwick	12
1867	T Morris, Sr, St Andrews	170	Prestwick	10
1868	T Morris, Jr, St Andrews	157	Prestwick	10
1869	T Morris, Jr, St Andrews	154	Prestwick	8
1870	T Morris, Jr, St Andrews	149	Prestwick	17

Having been won thrice in succession by young Tom Morris, the Belt became his property. The Championship was held in abeyance for one year. From 1872 the present cup was offered for yearly competition.

The Cup

Year	Winner	Score	Venue	Entrants
1872	T Morris, Jr, St Andrews	166	Prestwick	8
1873	T Kidd, St Andrews	179	St Andrews	26
1874	M Park, Musselburgh	159	Musselburgh	32
1875	W Park, Musselburgh	166	Prestwick	18
1876	B Martin, St Andrews	176	St Andrews	34
(D Strath tied but refused to play off)				
1877	J Anderson, St Andrews	160	Musselburgh	24
1878	J Anderson, St Andrews	157	Prestwick	26
1879	J Anderson, St Andrews	169	St Andrews	46
1880	B Ferguson, Musselburgh	162	Musselburgh	30
1881	B Ferguson, Musselburgh	170	Prestwick	22
1882	B Ferguson, Musselburgh	171	St Andrews	40
1883	W Fernie, Dumfries	159	Musselburgh	41
After a tie with B Ferguson, Musselburgh				
1884	J Simpson, Carnoustie	160	Prestwick	30

Year	Winner	Score	Venue	Entrants
1885	B Martin, St Andrews	171	St Andrews	51
1886	D Brown, Musselburgh	157	Musselburgh	46
1887	W Park, Jr, Musselburgh	161	Prestwick	36
1888	J Burns, Warwick	171	St Andrews	53
1889	W Park, Jr, Musselburgh	155	Musselburgh	42
After a tie with A Kirkaldy				
1890	J Ball, Royal Liverpool (Am)	164	Prestwick	40
1891	H Kirkaldy, St Andrews	166	St Andrews	82
After 1891 the competition was extended to 72 holes and for the first time entry money was imposed				
1892	H Hilton, Royal Liverpool (Am)	305	Muirfield	66
1893	W Auchterlonie, St Andrews	322	Prestwick	72
1894	J Taylor, Winchester	326	Sandwich, R St George's	94
1895	J Taylor, Winchester	322	St Andrews	73
1896	H Vardon, Ganton	316	Muirfield	64
After a tie with J Taylor. Play-off scores for 36 holes: H Vardon 157; Taylor 161				
1897	H Hilton, Royal Liverpool (Am)	314	Hoylake, R Liverpool	86
1898	H Vardon, Ganton	307	Prestwick	78
1899	H Vardon, Ganton	310	Sandwich, R St George's	98
1900	J Taylor, Mid-Surrey	309	St Andrews	81
1901	J Braid, Romford	309	Muirfield	101
1902	A Herd, Huddersfield	307	Hoylake, R Liverpool	112
1903	H Vardon, Totteridge	300	Prestwick	127
1904	J White, Sunningdale	296	Sandwich, R St George's	144
1905	J Braid, Walton Heath	318	St Andrews	152
1906	J Braid, Walton Heath	300	Muirfield	183
1907	A Massy, La Boulie	312	Hoylake, R Liverpool	193

Year	Winner	Score	Venue	Qual	Ents
1908	J Braid, Walton Heath	291	Prestwick	180	
1909	J Taylor, Mid-Surrey	295	Deal, R Cinque Ports	204	
1910	J Braid, Walton Heath	299	St Andrews	210	
1911	H Vardon, Totteridge	303	Sandwich, R St George's	226	
After a tie with A Massy. The tie was over 36 holes, but Massy picked up at the 35th hole before holing out. He had taken 148 for 34 holes, and when Vardon holed out at the 35th hole his score was 143.					
1912	E Ray, Oxhey	295	Muirfield	215	
1913	J Taylor, Mid-Surrey	304	Hoylake, R Liverpool	269	
1914	H Vardon, Totteridge	306	Prestwick	194	
1915–19	*No Championship owing to the Great War*				
1920	G Duncan, Hanger Hill	303	Deal, R Cinque Ports	81	190
1921	J Hutchison, Glenview, Chicago	296	St Andrews	85	158
After a tie with R Wethered (Am). Royal and Ancient-Play-off scores: Hutchison 150; Wethered 159.					
1922	W Hagen, Detroit, USA	300	Sandwich, R St George's	80	225
1923	A Havers, Coombe Hill	295	Troon	88	222
1924	W Hagen, Detroit, USA	301	Hoylake, R Liverpool	86	277
1925	J Barnes, USA	300	Prestwick	83	200
1926	R Jones, USA (Am)	291	R Lytham and St Annes	117	293
1927	R Jones, USA (Am)	285	St Andrews	108	207
1928	W Hagen, USA	292	Sandwich, R St George's	113	271
1929	W Hagen, USA	292	Muirfield	109	242
1930	R Jones, USA (Am)	291	Hoylake, R Liverpool	112	296
1931	T Armour, USA	296	Carnoustie	109	215
1932	G Sarazen, USA	283	Sandwich, Prince's	110	224
1933	D Shute, USA	292	St Andrews	117	287
After a tie with C Wood, USA-Play-off scores: Shute 149; Wood 154.					
1934	T Cotton, Waterloo, Belgium	283	Sandwich, R St George's	101	312
1935	A Perry, Leatherhead	283	Muirfield	109	264
1936	A Padgham, Sundridge Park	287	Hoylake, R Liverpool	107	286
1937	T Cotton, Ashridge	290	Carnoustie	141	258
1938	R Whitcombe, Parkstone	295	Sandwich, R St George's	120	268
1939	R Burton, Sale	290	St Andrews	129	254
1940–45	*No Championship owing to Second World War*				
1946	S Snead, USA	290	St Andrews	100	225
1947	F Daly, Balmoral	293	Hoylake, R Liverpool	100	263
1948	T Cotton, Royal Mid-Surrey	284	Muirfield	97	272
1949	A Locke, South Africa	283	Sandwich, R St George's	96	224
After a tie with H Bradshaw, Kilcroney-Play-off scores: Locke 135; Bradshaw 147.					
1950	A Locke, South Africa	279	Troon	93	262
1951	M Faulkner, GB	285	R Portrush	98	180
1952	A Locke, South Africa	287	R Lytham and St Annes	96	275
1953	B Hogan, USA	282	Carnoustie	91	196

Open Championship *continued*

Year	Winner	Score	Venue	Qual	Ents
1954	P Thomson, Australia	283	Birkdale	97	349
1955	P Thomson, Australia	281	St Andrews	94	301
1956	P Thomson, Australia	286	Hoylake, R Liverpool	96	360
1957	A Locke, South Africa	279	St Andrews	96	282
1958	P Thomson, Australia	278	R Lytham and St Annes	96	362
After a tie with D Thomas, Sudbury-Play-off scores: Thomson 139; Thomas 143.					
1959	G Player, South Africa	284	Muirfield	90	285
1960	K Nagle, Australia	278	St Andrews	74	410
1961	A Palmer, USA	284	Birkdale	101	364
1962	A Palmer, USA	276	Troon	119	379
1963	R Charles, New Zealand	277	R Lytham and St Annes	119	261
After a tie with P Rodgers, USA-Play-off scores: Charles 140; Rodgers 148					
1964	T Lema, USA	279	St Andrews	119	327
1965	P Thomson, Australia	285	R Birkdale	130	372
1966	J Nicklaus, USA	282	Muirfield	130	310
1967	R De Vicenzo, Argentina	278	Hoylake, R Liverpool	130	326
1968	G Player, South Africa	289	Carnoustie	130	309
1969	A Jacklin, GB	280	R Lytham and St Annes	129	424
1970	J Nicklaus USA	283	St Andrews	134	468
After a tie with Doug Sanders, USA-Play-off scores: Nicklaus 72; Sanders 73.					
1971	L Trevino, USA	278	R Birkdale	150	528
1972	L Trevino, USA	278	Muirfield	150	570
1973	T Weiskopf, USA	276	Troon	150	569
1974	G Player, South Africa	282	R Lytham and St Annes	150	679
1975	T Watson, USA	279	Carnoustie	150	629
After a tie with J Newton. Australia-Play-off scores: Watson 71; Newton 72.					
1976	J Miller, USA	279	R Birkdale	150	719
1977	T Watson, USA	268	Turnberry	150	730
1978	J Nicklaus, USA	281	St Andrews	150	788
1979	S Ballesteros, Spain	283	R Lytham and St Annes	150	885
1980	T Watson, USA	271	Muirfield	151	994
1981	B Rogers, USA	276	Sandwich, R St George's	153	971
1982	T Watson, USA	284	R Troon	176	1,121
1983	T Watson, USA	275	R Birkdale	151	1,107
1984	S Ballesteros, Spain	276	St Andrews		1,413
1985	A Lyle, GB	282	Sandwich, R St George's	149	1,361
1986	G Norman, Australia	280	Turnberry	152	1,347
1987	N Faldo, GB	279	Muirfield	153	1,407
1988	S Ballesteros, Spain	273	R Lytham and St Annes	153	1,393
1989	M Calcavecchia, USA	275	R Troon	156	1,481
After a tie with W Grady,. Australia, and G Norman, Australia-Calcavecchia won a 4-hole play-off.					
1990	N Faldo, GB	270	St Andrews	152	1,707
1991	I Baker-Finch, Australia	272	R Birkdale	156	1,496
1992	N Faldo, GB	272	Muirfield	156	1,666
1993	G Norman, Australia	267	Sandwich, R St George's	156	1,827
1994	N Price, Zimbabwe	268	Turnberry	156	1,701

US Open

94th US Open *at Oakmont, Pennsylvania*

36-hole cut: 147, five over par; 65 players qualified

Pos	Player	Score	Prize Money $
1	E Els (SA)	69-71-66-73—279	320000
2	L Roberts (US)	76-69-64-70—279	141828
	C Montgomerie (GB)	71-65-73-70—279	141828
(18-hole play-off scores: Els 74, Roberts 74, Montgomerie 78. Els beat Roberts at 2nd hole of sudden death play-off)			
4	C Strange (US)	70-70-70-70—280	75728
5	J Cook (US)	73-65-73-71—282	61318
6	C Dennis (US)	71-71-70-71—283	49485
	G Norman (Aus)	71-71-69-72—283	49485
	T Watson (US)	68-73-68-74—283	49485
9	D Waldorf (US)	74-68-73-69—284	37179
	J Maggert (US)	71-68-75-70—284	37179
	J Sluman (US)	72-69-72-71—284	37179
	F Nobilo (NZ)	69-71-68-76—284	37179
13	J McGovern (US)	73-69-74-69—285	29767
	S Hoch (US)	72-72-70-71—285	29767
	D Edwards (US)	73-65-75-72—285	29767
16	F Couples (US)	72-71-69-74—286	25899
	S Lowery (US)	71-71-68-76—286	25899
18	S Verplank (US)	70-72-75-70—287	22477
	S Ballesteros (Sp)	72-72-70-73—287	22477
	H Irwin (US)	69-69-71-78—287	22477
21	S Torrance (GB)	72-71-76-69—288	19464
	S Pate (US)	74-66-71-77—288	19464
23	B Langer (Ger)	72-72-73-72—289	17223
	K Triplett (US)	70-71-71-77—289	17223
25	M Springer (US)	74-72-73-71—290	14705
	C Parry (Aus)	78-68-71-73—290	14705
	C Beck (US)	73-73-70-74—290	14705
28	D Love III (US)	74-72-74-72—292	11514
	J Furyk (US)	74-69-74-75—292	11514
	L Clements (US)	73-71-73-75—292	11514
	J Nicklaus (US)	69-70-77-76—292	11514
	M Ozaki (Jpn)	70-73-69-80—292	11514
33	M Carnevale (US)	75-72-76-70—293	9578
	T Lehman (US)	77-68-73-75—293	9578
	F Allen (US)	73-70-74-76—293	9578
	T Kite (US)	73-71-72-77—293	9578
	B Crenshaw (US)	71-74-70-78—293	9578
	B Faxon (US)	73-69-71-80—293	9578
39	B Hughes (US)	71-72-77-74—294	8005
	P Baker (GB)	73-73-73-75—294	8005
	G Brand Jr (GB)	73-71-73-77—294	8005
	B Jobe (US)	72-74-68-80—294	8005

Pos	Player	Score	Prize Money $
43	F Quinn Jr (US)	75-72-73-75—295	7222
44	P Goydos (US)	74-72-79-71—296	6595
	F Funk (US)	74-71-74-77—296	6595
	D Walsworth (US)	71-75-73-77—296	6595
47	T Dunlavey (US)	76-70-78-73—297	5105
	O Browne (US)	74-73-77-73—297	5105
	B Lane (GB)	77-70-76-74—297	5105
	M Emery (US)	74-73-75-75—297	5105
	D Bergano (US)	73-72-76-76—297	5105
	J Gallagher Jr (US)	74-68-77-78—297	5105
	W Levi (US)	76-70-73-78—297	5105
	P Mickelson (US)	75-70-73-79—297	5105
55	T Armour III (US)	73-73-79-73—298	4324
	H Royer III (US)	72-71-77-78—298	4324
	S Simpson (US)	74-73-73-78—298	4324
58	S Richardson (GB)	74-73-76-76—299	4105
	F Zoeller (US)	76-70-76-77—299	4105
60	D Rummells (US)	71-74-82-74—301	3967
	D Martin (US)	76-70-74-81—301	3967
62	E Humenik (US)	74-72-81-75—302	3800
	M Smith (US)	74-73-78-77—302	3800
	M Aubrey (US)	72-69-81-80—302	3800

The following players missed the cut

65	Brad Bryant	76-72—148
	K Green	76-72—148
	C Perry	78-70—148
	M Brooks	75-73—148
	L Janzen	77-71—148
	J Mahaffey	78-70—148
	M Meshiai	71-77—148
	L Nelson	75-73—148
	J Maas	75-73—148
	N Price	76-72—148
	N Faldo	73-75—148
	M O'Meara	72-76—148
	M Calcavecchia	71-77—148
	B Britton	76-72—148
	M Wurtz	71-77—148
	S Flesch	74-74—148
81	B Mayfair	76-73—149
	M Hulbert	74-75—149
	D Frost	72-77—149
	L Mize	77-72—149
	W Grady	75-74—149
	J Green	74-75—149
	B Maddera	75-74—149
	M Bradley	74-75—149
	M Sullivan	75-74—149
	H Taylor	76-73—149
	M Lye	73-76—149
	B Alexander†	75-74—149
	JD Blake	79-70—149
	B Tway	78-71—149
	P Stewart	74-75—149
	E Johnson	77-72—149
97	J Adams	75-75—150
	JM Olazabal	76-74—150
	J Haeggman	77-73—150
	B Studer	76-74—150
	P Stankowski	75-75—150
102	S Randolph	74-77—151
	J Thorpe	71-80—151
	R Fehr	78-73—151
	C Rocca	77-74—151
	G Day	75-76—151
	J Ferenz	75-76—151
	R Friend	78-73—151
	M Kuramoto	79-72—151
	D Ogrin	74-77—151
	C Pavin	78-73—151
	A North	78-73—151
	R Gamez	76-75—151
	J Stacey	78-73—151
115	T Simpson	79-73—152
	J Huston	76-76—152
	I Woosnam	77-75—152
	C Stadler	78-74—152
	J Morse	77-75—152
	T Dodds	77-75—152
	G Morgan	79-73—152
122	N Henke	75-78—153
	D Clarke	78-75—153
	T Barranger	76-77—153
	M Schiene	74-79—153
	W Burnitz	79-74—153
	H Twitty	78-75—153
	M Small	77-76—153
	A Knoll	77-76—153
130	B Craig	73-81—154
	M Soli	78-76—154
	J Daly	81-73—154
	M Mielke	80-74—154
134	PH Horgan III	79-76—155
	B Kamm	79-76—155
	F Lickliter Jr	79-76—155
137	J Harris†	79-77—156
	G Hallberg	78-78—156
	M Grant	80-76—156
	C Haarlow	82-74—156
	D Delcher†	78-78—156
142	I Baker-Finch	83-74—157
	R Sonnier†	82-75—157
	J Miller	81-76—157
145	A Palmer	77-81—158
	D Duchateau	79-79—158
	Bart Bryant	76-82—158
	P Dewitt	81-77—158
149	J Sanchez	79-80—159
	M Mason	82-77—159
151	C Barlow†	80-80—160
	T Garner	79-81—160
153	S Medlin	79-82—161
	J Ferrari†	82-79—161
155	M Weeks	83-83—166

Wdn: C Patton; D Lundstrom – 80; R Mediate 76-70-79.
Dsq: M Allen 77-82

† *Denotes amateur*

1993 US Open

at Baltusrol, Springfield, NJ

Prize money: $1,600,000

Pos	Name	Score	Prize $
1	L Janzen (US)	67-67-69-69—272	290000
2	P Stewart (US)	70-66-68-70—274	145000
3	C Parry (Aus)	66-74-69-68—277	78556
	P Azinger (US)	71-68-69-69—277	78556
5	S Hoch (US)	66-72-72-68—278	48730
	T Watson (US)	70-66-73-69—278	48730
7	E Els (SA)	71-73-68-67—279	35481
	R Floyd (US)	68-73-70-68—279	35481
	N Henke (US)	72-71-67-69—279	35481
	F Funk (US)	70-72-67-70—279	35481

1992 US Open

at Pebble Beach, Monterey, California

Prize money: $1,500,000

Pos	Name	Score	Prize $
1	T Kite (US)	71-72-70-72—285	275000
2	J Sluman (US)	73-74-69-71—287	137500
3	C Montgomerie (GB)	70-71-77-70—288	84245
4	N Faldo (GB)	70-76-68-77—291	54924
	N Price (Zim)	71-72-77-71—291	54924
6	I Woosnam (GB)	72-72-69-79—292	32315
6	JD Blake (US)	70-74-75-73—292	32315
	B Gilder (US)	73-70-75-74—292	32315
	B Andrade (US)	72-74-72-74—292	32315
	M Hulbert (US)	74-73-70-75—292	32315
	T Lehman (US)	69-74-72-77—292	32315
	J Sindelar (US)	74-72-68-78—292	32315

1991 US Open

at Hazeltine National, Chaska, Minnesota

Prize money: $1,300,000

Pos	Name	Score	Prize $
1	P Stewart (US)*	67-70-73-72—282	235000
2	S Simpson (US)	70-68-72-72—282	117500
3	L Nelson (US)	73-72-72-68—285	62574
	F Couples (US)	70-70-75-70—285	62574
5	F Zoeller (US)	72-73-74-67—286	41542
6	S Hoch (US)	69-71-74-73—287	36090
7	N Henke (US)	67-71-77-73—288	32176
8	R Floyd (US)	73-72-76-68—289	26958
	JM Olazabal (Spa)	73-71-75-70—289	26958
	C Pavin (US)	71-67-79-72—289	26958

1990 US Open

at Medinah, Chicago, Illinois

Prize money: $1,200,000

Pos	Name	Score	Prize $
1	H Irwin (US)*	69-70-74-67—280	180000
2	M Donald (US)	67-70-72-71—280	108000
3	N Faldo (GB)	72-72-68-69—281	56878
	BR Brown (US)	69-71-69-72—281	56878
5	G Norman (Aus)	72-73-69-69—283	33271
	T Simpson (US)	66-69-75-73—283	33271
	M Brooks (US)	68-70-72-73—283	33271
8	S Jones (US)	67-76-74-67—284	22236
	C Stadler (US)	71-70-72-71—284	22236
	S Hoch (US)	70-73-69-72—284	22236
	T Sieckmann (US)	70-74-68-72—284	22236
	JM Olazabal (Sp)	73-69-69-73—284	22236
	F Zoeller (US)	73-70-68-73—284	22236

1989 US Open

at Oak Hill, Rochester, New York

Prize money: $1,100,000

Pos	Name	Score	Prize $
1	C Strange (US)	71-64-73-70—278	200000
2	I Woosnam (GB)	70-68-73-68—279	67823
	M McCumber (US)	70-68-72-69—279	67823
	C Beck (US)	71-69-71-68—279	67823
5	B Claar (US)	71-72-68-69—280	34345
6	S Simpson (US)	67-70-69-75—281	28220
6	J Ozaki (Jap)	70-71-68-72—281	28220
8	P Jacobsen (US)	71-70-71-70—282	24307
9	JM Olazabal (Sp)	69-72-70-72—283	19968
	T Kite (US)	67-69-69-78—283	19968
	H Green (US)	69-72-74-68—283	19968
	P Azinger (US)	71-72-70-70—283	19968

* *Winner after play-off*

United States Open Championship

Year	Winner	Runner-up	Venue	By
1894	W Dunn	W Campbell	St Andrews, NY	2 holes

After 1894 decided by stroke play

Year	Winner	Venue	Score
1895	HJ Rawlins	Newport	173
1896	J Foulis	Southampton	152
1897	J Lloyd	Wheaton, Ill	162
1898	F Herd	Shinnecock Hills	328
72 holes played from 1898			
1899	W Smith	Baltimore	315
1900	H Vardon (GB)	Wheaton, Ill	313
1901	W Anderson	Myopia, Mass	315
1902	L Auchterlonie	Garden City	305
1903	W Anderson	Baltusrol	307
1904	W Anderson	Glenview	304
1905	W Anderson	Myopia, Mass	335
1906	A Smith	Onwentsia	291
1907	A Ross	Chestnut Hill, Pa	302
1908	F McLeod	Myopia, Mass	322
1909	G Sargent	Englewood, NJ	290
1910	A Smith	Philadelphia	289
(After a tie with J McDermott and M Smith)			
1911	J McDermott	Wheaton, Ill	307
1912	J McDermott	Buffalo, NY	294
1913	F Ouimet (Am)	Brookline, Mass	304
(After a tie with H Vardon and E Ray)			
1914	W Hagen	Midlothian	297
1915	J Travers (Am)	Baltusrol	290
1916	C Evans (Am)	Minneapolis	286
1917-18	No Championship		
1919	W Hagen	Braeburn	301
1920	E Ray (GB)	Inverness	295
1921	J Barnes	Washington	289
1922	G Sarazen	Glencoe	288
1923	R Jones, Jr (Am)	Inwood, LI	295
(After a tie with R Cruikshank. Play-off: 76; Cruikshank 78)			
1924	C Walker	Oakland Hills	297
1925	W MacFarlane	Worcester	291
1926	R Jones, Jr (Am)	Scioto	293
1927	T Armour	Oakmont	301
(After a tie with H Cooper. Play-off: Armour 76; Cooper 79)			
1928	J Farrell	Olympia Fields	294
(After a tie with R Jones, Jr. Play-off: Farrell 143; Jones 144)			
1929	R Jones, Jr (Am)	Winged Foot, NY	294
(After a tie with A Espinosa. Play-off: Jones 141; Espinosa 164)			
1930	R Jones, Jr (Am)	Interlachen	287
1931	B Burke	Inverness	292
(After a tie with G von Elm. Play-off: Burke 149-148; von Elm 149-149)			
1932	G Sarazen	Fresh Meadow	286
1933	J Goodman (Am)	North Shore	287
1934	O Dutra	Merion	293
1935	S Parks	Oakmont	299
1936	T Manero	Springfield	282
1937	R Guldahl	Oakland Hills	281
1938	R Guldahl	Cherry Hills	284
1939	B Nelson	Philadelphia	284
(After a tie with C Wood and D Shute)			
1940	W Lawson Little	Canterbury, Ohio	287
(After a tie with G Sarazen. Tie scores: Little 70; Sarazen 73)			
1941	Craig Wood	Fort Worth, Texas	284
1942–45	*No Championship*		
1946	L Mangrum	Canterbury	284
(After a tie with B Nelson and V Ghezzie)			
1947	L Worsham	St Louis	282
(After a tie with S Snead. Replay scores: Worsham 69; Snead 70)			
1948*	B Hogan	Los Angeles	276
1949	Dr C Middlecoff	Medinah, Ill	286
1950	B Hogan	Merion, Pa	287
(After a tie with L Mangrum and G Fazio. Replay scores: Hogan 69; Mangrum 73; Fazio 75)			
1951	B Hogan	Oakland Hills, Mich	287
1952	J Boros	Dallas, Texas	281
1953	B Hogan	Oakmont	283
1954	E Furgol	Baltusrol	284
1955	J Fleck	San Francisco	287
(After a tie with B Hogan. Replay scores: Fleck 69; Hogan 72)			
1956	Dr C Middlecoff	Rochester	281
1957	D Mayer	Inverness	282
(After a tie with Dr C Middlecoff. Tie scores: Mayer 72; Middlecoff 79)			
1958	T Bolt	Tulsa, Okla	283
1959	W Casper	Winged Foot, NY	282
1960	A Palmer	Denver, Col	280
1961	G Littler	Birmingham, Mich	281
1962	J Nicklaus	Oakmont	283
(After a tie with A Palmer: Nicklaus 71; Palmer 74)			
1963	J Boros	Brookline, Mass	293
(After a tie. Play-off: J Boros 70; J Cupit 73, A Palmer 76)			
1964	K Venturi	Washington	278
1965	G Player (SA)	St Louis, Mo	282
(After a tie with K Nagle (Aus). Replay scores: Player 71; Nagle 74)			
1966	W Casper	San Francisco	278
(After a tie with A Palmer. Replay scores: Casper 69; Palmer 73)			
1967	J Nicklaus	Baltusrol	275
1968	L Trevino	Rochester	275
1969	O Moody	Houston, Texas	281
1970	A Jacklin (GB)	Hazeltine, Minn	281
1971	L Trevino	Merion, Pa	280
(After a tie with J Nicklaus. Play-off: Trevino 68; Nicklaus 71)			
1972	J Nicklaus	Pebble Beach	290
1973	J Miller	Oakmont, Pa	279
1974	H Irwin	Winged Foot, NY	287
1975	L Graham	Medinah, Ill	287
(After a tie with Mahaffey. Play-off: Graham 71; Mahaffey 73)			
1976	J Pate	Atlanta, Georgia	277
1977	H Green	Southern Hills, Tulsa	278
1978	A North	Cherry Hills	285
1979	H Irwin	Inverness, Ohio	284
1980	J Nicklaus	Baltusrol	272
1981	D Graham (Aus)	Merion, Pa	273
1982	T Watson	Pebble Beach	282
1983	L Nelson	Oakmont, Pa	280
1984	F Zoeller	Winged Foot	276
(After a tie with G Norman. Play-off: Zoeller 67; Norman 75)			
1985	A North	Oakland Hills, Mich	279
1986	R Floyd	Shinnecock Hills, NY	279
1987	S Simpson	Olympic, San Francisco	277
1988	C Strange	Brookline, Mass.	278
(After a tie with N Faldo (GB). Play-off Strange 71, Faldo 75)			
1989	C Strange	Rochester, NY	278
1990	H Irwin	Medinah	280
(After a tie with M Donald, at 1st extra hole after 18-hole play-off tie)			
1991	P Stewart	Hazeltine, Minn	282
1992	T Kite	Pebble Beach	285
1993	L Janzen	Baltusrol	272
1994	E Els	Oakmont, Pa	279

US Masters

58th US Masters

at Augusta National GC, Georgia

Pos	Player	Score	Prize Money $
1	JM Olazabal (Sp)	74-67-69-69—279	360000
2	T Lehman (US)	70-70-69-72—281	216000
3	L Mize (US)	68-71-72-71—282	136000
4	T Kite (US)	69-72-71-71—283	96000
5	J Haas (US)	72-72-72-69—285	73000
	J McGovern (US)	72-70-71-72—285	73000
	L Roberts (US)	75-68-72-70—285	73000
8	E Els (SA)	74-67-74-71—286	60000
	C Pavin (US)	71-72-73-70—286	60000
10	I Baker-Finch (Aus)	71-71-71-74—287	50000
	R Floyd (US)	70-74-71-72—287	50000
	J Huston (US)	72-72-74-69—287	50000
13	T Watson (US)	70-71-73-74—288	42000
14	D Forsman (US)	74-66-76-73—289	38000
15	C Beck (US)	71-71-75-74—291	34000
	B Faxon (US)	71-73-73-74—291	34000
	M O'Meara (US)	75-70-76-70—291	34000
18	S Ballesteros (Sp)	70-76-75-71—292	24343
	B Crenshaw (US)	74-73-73-72—292	24343
	D Edwards (US)	73-72-73-74—292	24343
	B Glasson (US)	72-73-75-72—292	24343
	H Irwin (US)	73-68-79-72—292	24343
	G Norman (Aus)	70-70-75-77—292	24343
	L Wadkins (US)	73-74-73-72—292	24343
25	B Langer (Ger)	74-74-72-73—293	16800
	J Sluman (US)	74-75-71-73—293	16800
27	S Simpson (US)	74-74-73-73—294	14800
	V Singh (Fiji)	70-75-74-75—294	14800
	C Strange (US)	74-70-75-75—294	14800
30	L Janzen (US)	75-71-76-73—295	13300
	C Parry (Aus)	75-74-73-73—295	13300
32	N Faldo (GB)	76-73-73-74—296	12400
33	R Cochran (US)	71-74-74-78—297	11500
	S Torrance (GB)	76-73-74-74—297	11500
35	D Frost (SA)	74-71-75-78—298	10300
	N Price (Zim)	74-73-74-77—298	10300
	F Zoeller (US)	74-72-74-78—298	10300
38	F Allem (SA)	69-77-76-77—299	9000
	F Funk (US)	79-70-75-75—299	9000
	S Lyle (GB)	75-73-78-73—299	9000
41	W Grady (Aus)	74-73-73-80—300	7400
	A Magee (US)	74-74-76-76—300	7400
	H Meshiai (Jpn)	71-71-80-78—300	7400
	C Rocca (Ita)	79-70-78-73—300	7400

Pos	Player	Score	Prize Money $
41T	M Standly (US)	77-69-79-75—300	7400
46	J Cook (US)	77-72-77-75—301	6000
	I Woosnam (GB)	76-73-77-75—301	6000
48	J Daly (US)	76-73-77-78—304	5250
	H Twitty (US)	73-76-74-81—304	5250
50	J Maggert (US)	75-73-82-75—305	5000
	J Harris (US Am)	72-76-80-77—305	

(The following players missed the cut)

Pos	Player	Score
52	M Calcavecchia (US)	75-75—150
	R Fehr (US)	77-73—150
	N Henke (US)	77-73—150
	J Miller (US)	77-73—150
	C Montgomerie (GB)	77-73—150
	G Morgan (US)	74-76—150
	J Ozaki (Jpn)	76-74—150
	G Player (SA)	71-79—150
	C Stadler (US)	76-74—150
61	J Gallagher Jr (US)	74-77—151
	D Hart (US)	76-75—151
	B Mayfair (US)	74-77—151
	B Ogle (Aus)	74-77—151
65	D Ellis (USA Am)	78-74—152
	J Inman (US)	76-76—152
	J Nicklaus (US)	78-74—152
	G Waite (NZ)	74-78—152
69	P Baker (GB)	78-75—153
	B Estes (US)	77-76—153
71	J Adams (US)	76-78—154
	B Casper (US)	77-77—154
	C Coody (US)	80-74—154
	A Forsbrand (Swe)	80-74—154
	S Hoch (US)	75-79—154
	D Love III (US)	76-78—154
77	S Elkington (Aus)	81-74—155
	A Palmer (US)	78-77—155
79	T Aaron (US)	76-80—156
	P Stewart (US)	78-78—156
	J Thomas (US Am)	78-78—156
82	B McAllister (US)	79-78—157
83	B Lane (GB)	76-82—158
84	I Pyman (GB Am)	82-79—161
85	G Brewer (US)	84-79—163
86	D Ford (US)	85——Wdn

1993 US Masters

Prize money: $1,705,700

Pos	Name	Score	Prize $
1	B Langer (Ger)	68-70-69-70—277	306000
2	C Beck (US)	72-67-72-70—281	183600
3	T Lehman (US)	67-75-73-68—283	81600
	J Daly (US)	70-71-73-69—283	81600
	S Elkington (Aus)	71-70-71-71—283	81600
3=	L Wadkins (US)	69-72-71-71—283	81600
7	JM Olazabal (Spa)	70-72-74-68—284	54850
	D Forsman (US)	69-69-73-73—284	54850
9	P Stewart (US)	74-70-72-69—285	47600
	B Faxon (US)	71-70-72-72—285	47600

1992 US Masters

Prize money: $1,500,000

Pos	Name	Score	Prize $
1	F Couples (US)	69-67-69-70—275	270000
2	R Floyd (US)	69-68-69-71—277	162000
3	C Pavin (US)	72-71-68-67—278	102000
4	J Sluman (US)	65-74-70-71—280	66000
	M O'Meara (US)	74-67-69-70—280	66000
6	S Pate (US)	73-71-70-67—281	43829
6	N Henke (US)	70-71-70-70—281	43829
	I Baker-Finch (Aus)	70-69-68-74—281	43829
	N Price (Zim)	70-71-67-73—281	43829
	G Norman (Aus)	70-70-73-68—281	43829
	L Mize (US)	73-69-71-68—281	43829
	T Schulz (US)	68-69-72-72—281	43829

1991 US Masters

Prize money: $1,347,700

Pos	Name	Score	Prize $
1	I Woosnam (GB)	72-66-67-72—277	243000
2	JM Olazabal (Sp)	68-71-69-70—278	145800
3	T Watson (US)	68-68-70-73—279	64800
	S Pate (US)	72-73-69-65—279	64800
	B Crenshaw (US)	70-73-68-68—279	64800
	L Wadkins (US)	67-71-70-71—279	64800
7	J Mudd (US)	70-70-71-69—280	42100
	I Baker-Finch (Aus)	71-70-69-70—280	42100
	A Magee (US)	70-72-68-70—280	42100
10	H Irwin (US)	70-70-75-66—281	35150
	T Nakajima (Jpn)	74-71-67-69—281	35150

1990 US Masters

Prize money: $1,237,300

Pos	Name	Score	Prize $
1	N Faldo (GB)*	71-72-66-69—278	225000
2	R Floyd (US)	70-68-68-72—278	135000
3	J Huston (US)	66-74-68-75—283	72500
	L Wadkins (US)	72-73-70-68—283	72500
5	F Couples (US)	74-69-72-69—284	50000
6	J Nicklaus (US)	72-70-69-74—285	45000
7	S Ballesteros (Spa)	74-73-68-71—286	35150
	B Britton (US)	68-74-71-73—286	35150
	B Langer (Ger)	70-73-69-74—286	35150
	S Simpson (US)	74-71-68-73—286	35150
	C Strange (US)	70-73-71-72—286	35150
	T Watson (US)	77-71-67-71—286	35150

1989 US Masters

Prize money: $1,109,600

Pos	Name	Score	Prize $
1	N Faldo (GB)*	68-73-77-65—283	200000
2	S Hoch (US)	69-74-71-69—283	120000
3	G Norman (Aus)	74-75-68-67—284	64450
	B Crenshaw (US)	74-75-68-67—284	64450
5	S Ballesteros (Sp)	71-72-73-69—285	44400
6	M Reid (US)	72-71-71-72—286	40000
7	J Mudd (US)	73-76-72-66—287	37200
8	J Sluman (US)	74-72-74-68—288	32200
	JM Olazabal (Spa)	77-73-70-68—288	32200
	C Beck (US)	74-76-70-68—288	32200

US Masters

at Augusta National Golf Course, Augusta, Georgia

Year	Winner	Score
1934	H Smith	284
1935	G Sarazen	282
1936	H Smith	285
1937	B Nelson	283
1938	H Picard	285
1939	R Guldahl	279
1940	J Demaret	280
1941	C Wood	280
1942	B Nelson*	280
1946	H Keiser	282
1947	J Demaret	281
1948	C Harmon	279
1949	S Snead	283
1950	J Demaret	282
1951	B Hogan	280
1952	S Snead*	286
1953	B Hogan	274
1954	S Snead	289
1955	C Middlecoff	279
1956	J Burke	289
1957	D Ford	283
1958	A Palmer	284
1959	A Wall	284
1960	A Palmer	282
1961	G Player (SA)	280
1962	A Palmer*	280
1963	J Nicklaus	286
1964	A Palmer	276
1965	J Nicklaus	271
1966	J Nicklaus	288
1967	G Brewer	280
1968	R Goalby	277
1969	G Archer	281
1970	W Casper*	279
1971	C Coody	279
1972	J Nicklaus	286
1973	T Aaron	283
1974	G Player (SA)	278
1975	J Nicklaus	276
1976	R Floyd	271
1977	T Watson	276
1978	G Player (SA)	277
1979	F Zoeller*	280
1980	S Ballesteros (Sp)	275
1981	T Watson	280
1982	C Stadler*	284
1983	S Ballesteros (Sp)	280
1984	B Crenshaw	277
1985	B Langer (WGer)	282
1986	J Nicklaus	279
1987	L Mize*	285
1988	A Lyle (GB)	281
1989	N Faldo (GB)*	283
1990	N Faldo (GB)*	278
1991	I Woosnam (GB)	277
1992	F Couples	275
1993	B Langer (Ger)	277
1994	JM Olazabal (Sp)	279

* *Winner after play-off*

US PGA Championship

76th US PGA Championship

at Southern Hills, Tulsa, Oklahoma

36-hole cut: 145, five over par; 76 players qualified

Pos	Player	Score	Prize Money $
1	N Price (Zim)	67-65-70-67—269	310000
2	C Pavin (US)	70-67-69-69—275	160000
3	P Mickelson (US)	68-71-67-70—276	110000
4	N Faldo (GB)	73-67-71-66—277	76666
	G Norman (Aus)	71-69-67-70—277	76666
	J Cook (US)	71-67-69-70—277	76666
7	S Elkington (Aus)	73-70-66-69—278	57500
	JM Olazabal (Spa)	72-66-70-70—278	57500
9	I Woosnam (GB)	68-72-73-66—279	41000
	T Kite (US)	72-68-69-70—279	41000
	T Watson (US)	69-72-67-71—279	41000
	L Roberts (US)	69-72-67-71—279	41000
	B Crenshaw (US)	70-67-70-72—279	41000
14	J Haas (US)	71-66-68-75—280	32000
15	K Triplett (US)	71-69-71-70—281	27000
	L Mize (US)	72-72-67-70—281	27000
	M McNulty (Zim)	72-68-70-71—281	27000
	G Day (US)	70-69-70-72—281	27000
19	C Stadler (US)	70-70-74-68—282	18666
	M McCumber (US)	73-70-71-68—282	18666
	F Zoeller (US)	69-71-72-70—282	18666
	B Glasson (US)	71-73-68-70—282	18666
	C Strange (US)	73-71-68-70—282	18666
	C Parry (Aus)	70-69-70-73—282	18666
25	B Lane (GB)	70-73-68-72—283	13000
	B Langer (Ger)	73-71-67-72—283	13000
	D Frost (SA)	70-71-69-73—283	13000
	E Els (SA)	68-71-69-75—283	13000
	J Sluman (US)	70-72-66-75—283	13000
30	B Faxon (US)	72-73-73-66—284	8458
	W Grady (Aus)	75-68-71-70—284	8458
	B Boyd (US)	72-71-70-71—284	8458
	L Clements (US)	74-70-69-71—284	8458
	S Torrance (GB)	69-75-69-71—284	8458
	R Zokol (Can)	77-67-67-73—284	8458
36	C Beck (US)	72-70-72-71—285	7000
	B McAllister (US)	74-64-75-72—285	7000
	C Montgomerie (GB)	67-76-70-72—285	7000
39	F Couples (US)	68-74-75-69—286	6030
	B Mayfair (US)	73-72-71-70—286	6030
	G Morgan (US)	71-68-73-74—286	6030
	T Lehman (US)	73-71-68-74—286	6030

* *Winner after play-off*

Pos	Player	Score	Prize Money $
	H Irwin (US)	75-69-68-74—286	6030
44	N Lancaster (US)	73-72-72-70—287	5200
	D Edwards (US)	72-70-74-71—287	5200
	D Gilford (GB)	69-73-73-72—287	5200
47	B Andrade (US)	71-71-78-68—288	4112
	F Allem (SA)	74-67-74-73—288	4112
	B Estes (US)	72-71-72-73—288	4112
	A Magee (US)	70-74-71-73—288	4112
	F Nobilo (NZ)	72-67-74-75—288	4112
	G Kraft (US)	74-69-70-75—288	4112
	J Ozaki (Jpn)	71-69-72-76—288	4112
	DA Weibring (US)	69-73-70-76—288	4112
55	D Hart (US)	72-71-75-71—289	3158
	F Funk (US)	76-69-72-72—289	3158
	H Sutton (US)	76-69-72-72—289	3158
	T Dolby (US)	73-68-75-73—289	3158
	K Perry (US)	78-67-70-74—289	3158
	M Springer (US)	77-66-69-77—289	3158
61	R Floyd (US)	69-76-73-72—290	2800
	T Nakajima (Jpn)	73-71-74-72—290	2800
	R McDougal (US)	76-69-72-73—290	2800
	L Wadkins (US)	69-73-73-75—290	2800
	B Fleisher (US)	75-68-72-75—290	2800
66	L Janzen (US)	73-71-73-74—291	2600
	JD Blake (US)	72-71-74-74—291	2600
	P Stewart (US)	72-73-72-74—291	2600
	J Inman (US)	70-72-73-76—291	2600
	T Smith (US)	74-69-71-77—291	2600
71	D Hammond (US)	74-69-76-73—292	2512
	P Senior (Aus)	74-71-70-77—292	2512
73	S Lyle (GB)	75-70-76-76—297	2462
	D Pride (US)	75-69-73-80—297	2462
75	B Henninger (US)	77-65-78-78—298	2412
	H Meshiai (Jpn)	74-71-74-79—298	2412

The following players missed the cut.

Pos	Player	Score
77	B Bryant (US)	76-70–146
	J Daly (US)	73-73–146
	J Mahaffey (US)	72-74–146
	T Johnstone (Zim)	75-71–146
	D Love III (US)	73-73–146
	B Ackerman (US)	72-74–146
	J Roth (US)	73-73–146
	L Nelson (US)	75-71–146
	J Gallagher Jr (US)	77-69–146
	M Calcavecchia (US)	74-72–146
87	N Henke (US)	72-75–147
	S Hoch (US)	74-73–147
	M Gove (US)	72-75–147
	D Kestner (US)	73-74–147
	J Haeggman (Swe)	72-75–147
	T Tryba (US)	74-73–147
	D Barr (Can)	71-76–147
	J McGovern (US)	73-74–147
	M James (GB)	71-76–147
	P Baker (GB)	76-71–147
	A Forsbrand (Swe)	73-74–147
98	S Simpson (US)	75-73–148
	I Baker-Finch (Aus)	74-74–148
	M Heinen (US)	75-73–148
	G Hallberg (US)	70-78–148
	M Brooks (US)	78-70–148
103	R Philo Jr (US)	76-73–149
	S Lowery (US)	72-77–149
	B Tway (US)	77-72–149
	V Singh (Fiji)	70-79–149
	J White (US)	81-68–149
	P Azinger (US)	75-74–149
	D Graham (Aus)	75-74–149
	J DeForest (US)	74-75–149
111	W Chapman (US)	75-75–150
	B Lohr (US)	77-73–150
	W Smith (US)	72-78–150
	C Rocca (Ita)	73-77–150
	J Nicklaus (US)	79-71–150
	R Cochran (US)	72-78–150
	R Fehr (US)	71-79–150
	G Jones (US)	71-79–150
	R Hoyt (US)	76-74–150
	J Bermel (US)	72-78–150
	L Nielsen (US)	73-77–150
122	M Baum (US)	77-74–151
	J Huston (US)	78-73–151
	J Lee (US)	77-74–151
	J Wisz (US)	74-77–151
	B Ogle (Aus)	75-76–151
	D Hepler (US)	77-74–151
	R Nuckolls (US)	74-77–151
129	B Redmond (US)	77-75–152
	R Action (US)	76-76–152
	J Parnevik (Swe)	79-73–152
	B Zabriski (US)	78-74–152
133	A Palmer (US)	79-74–153
	B Sherfy (US)	79-74–153
	P Oakley (US)	77-76–153
	P O'Brien (US)	76-77–153
	J Maggert (US)	78-75–153
	T Gray (US)	75-78–153
139	W Frantz (US)	78-76–154
	S Ballesteros (Sp)	78-76–154
	K Cashman (US)	75-79–154
	JL Lewis (US)	77-77–154
143	S Steger (US)	81-74–155
144	S Smitha (US)	83-74–157
	T Cleaver (US)	77-80–157
	E Terasa (US)	78-79–157
147	S Williams (US)	77-81–158
	M Biamon (US)	82-76–158
	S Mahlberg (US)	79-79–158
150	G Bowman (US)	87-88–175
	J Ozaki (Jpn)	–wdn

1993 US PGA *at Inverness, Toledo, Ohio*

Prize money: $1,700,000

Pos	Name	Score	Prize $
1	P Azinger (US)*	69-66-69-68—272	300000
2	G Norman (Aus)	68-68-67-69—272	155000
3	N Faldo (GB)	68-68-69-68—273	105000
4	V Singh (Fiji)	68-63-73-70—274	90000
5	T Watson (US)	69-65-70-72—276	75000
6	S Hoch (US)	74-68-68-67—277	47812
	N Henke (US)	72-70-67-68—277	47812
	P Mickelson (US)	67-71-69-70—277	47812
	J Cook (US)	72-66-68-71—277	47812
	S Simpson (US)	64-70-71-72—277	47812
	D Hart (US)	66-68-71-72—277	47812
	B Estes (US)	69-66-69-73—277	47812
	H Irwin (US)	68-69-67-73—277	47812

1992 US PGA *at Bellerive, St Louis, Missouri*

Prize money: $1,400,000

Pos	Name	Score	Prize $
1	N Price (Zim)	70-70-68-70—278	280000
2	N Faldo (GB)	68-70-76-67—281	101250
	J Gallagher Jr (US)	72-66-72-71—281	101250
	J Cook (US)	71-72-67-71—281	101250
	G Sauers (US)	67-69-70-75—281	101250
6	J Maggert (US)	71-72-65-74—282	60000
7	R Cochran (US)	69-69-76-69—283	52500
	D Forsman (US)	70-73-70-70—283	52500
9	D Waldorf (US)	74-73-68-69—284	40000
	A Forsbrand (Swe)	73-71-70-70—284	40000
	B Claar (US)	68-73-73-70—284	40000

1991 US PGA *at Crooked Stick, Carmel, Indiana*

Prize money: $1,400,000

Pos	Name	Score	Prize $
1	J Daly (US)	69-67-69-71—276	230000
2	B Lietzke (US)	68-69-72-70—279	140000
3	J Gallagher Jr (US)	70-72-72-67—281	95000
4	K Knox (US)	67-71-70-74—282	75000
5	S Richardson (GB)	70-72-72-69—283	60000
	B Gilder (US)	73-70-67-73—283	60000
7	D Feherty (Ire)	71-74-71-68—284	38000
	R Floyd (US)	69-74-72-69—284	38000
	S Pate (US)	70-75-70-69—284	38000
	H Sutton (US)	74-67-72-71—284	38000
	J Huston (US)	70-72-70-72—284	38000
	C Stadler (US)	68-71-69-76—284	38000

1990 US PGA *at Shoal Creek, Birmingham, Alabama*

Prize money: $1,350,000

Pos	Name	Score	Prize $
1	W Grady (Aus)	72-67-72-71—282	225000
2	F Couples (US)	69-71-73-72—285	135000
3	G Morgan (US)	77-72-65-72—286	90000
4	B Britton (US)	72-74-72-71—289	73500
5	C Beck (US)	71-70-78-71—290	51666
	B Mayfair (US)	70-71-75-74—290	51666
5	L Roberts (US)	73-71-70-76—290	51666
8	M McNulty (Zim)	74-72-75-71—292	34375
	D Pooley (US)	75-74-71-72—292	34375
	T Simpson (US)	71-73-75-73—292	34375
	P Stewart (US)	71-72-70-69—292	34375

1989 US PGA *at Kemper Lakes, Illinois*

Prize money: $1,200,000

Pos	Name	Score	Prize $
1	P Stewart (US)	74-66-69-67—276	200000
2	A Bean (US)	70-67-74-66—277	83333
	M Reid (US)	66-67-70-74—277	83333
	C Strange (US)	70-68-70-69—277	83333
5	D Rummells (US)	68-69-69-72—278	45000
6	I Woosnam (GB)	68-70-70-71—279	40000
7	C Stadler (US)	71-64-72-73—280	36250
	S Hoch (US)	69-69-69-73—280	36250
9	T Watson (US)	67-69-74-71—281	30000
	E Fiori (US)	70-67-75-69—281	30000
	N Faldo (GB)	70-73-69-69—281	30000

* *Winner after play-off*

United States PGA Championship

Year	Winner	Runner-up	Venue	By
1916	J Barnes	J Hutchison	Siwanoy	1 hole
1919	J Barnes	F McLeod	Engineers' Club	6 and 5
1920	J Hutchison	D Edgar	Flossmoor	1 hole
1921	W Hagen	J Barnes	Inwood Club	3 and 2
1922	G Sarazen	E French	Oakmont	4 and 3
1923	G Sarazen	W Hagen	Pelham	38th hole
1924	W Hagen	J Barnes	French Lick	2 holes
1925	W Hagen	W Mehlhorn	Olympic Fields	6 and 4
1926	W Hagen	L Diegel	Salisbury	4 and 3
1927	W Hagen	J Turnesa	Dallas, Texas	1 hole
1928	L Diegel	A Espinosa	Five Farms	6 and 5
1929	L Diegel	J Farrell	Hill Crest	6 and 4
1930	T Armour	G Sarazen	Fresh Meadow	1 hole
1931	T Creavy	D Shute	Wannamoisett	2 and 1
1932	O Dutra	F Walsh	St Paul, Minnesota	4 and 3
1933	G Sarazen	W Goggin	Milwaukee	5 and 4
1934	P Runyan	C Wood	Buffalo	38th hole
1935	J Revolta	T Armour	Oklahoma	5 and 4
1936	D Shute	J Thomson	Pinehurst	3 and 2
1937	D Shute	H McSpaden	Pittsburgh	37th hole
1938	P Runyan	S Snead	Shawnee	8 and 7
1939	H Picard	B Nelson	Pomonok	37th hole
1940	B Nelson	S Snead	Hershey, Pa	1 hole
1941	V Ghezzie	B Nelson	Denver, Colo	38th hole
1942	S Snead	J Turnesa	Atlantic City	2 and 1
1943	*No Championship*			
1944	B Hamilton	B Nelson	Spokane, Wash	1 hole
1945	B Nelson	S Byrd	Dayton, Ohio	4 and 3
1946	B Hogan	E Oliver	Portland	6 and 4
1947	J Ferrier	C Harbert	Detroit	2 and 1
1948	B Hogan	M Turnesa	Norwood Hills	7 and 6
1949	S Snead	J Palmer	Richmond, Va	3 and 2
1950	C Harper	H Williams	Scioto, Ohio	4 and 3
1951	S Snead	W Burkemo	Oakmont, Pa	7 and 6
1952	J Turnesa	C Harbert	Big Spring, Louisville	1 hole
1953	W Burkemo	F Lorza	Birmingham, Michigan	2 and 1
1954	C Harbert	W Burkemo	St Paul, Minnesota	4 and 3
1955	D Ford	C Middlecoff	Detroit	4 and 3
1956	J Burke	T Kroll	Boston	3 and 2
1957	L Hebert	D Finsterwald	Miami Valley, Dayton	3 and 1

Changed to stroke play

Year	Winner	Venue	Score
1958	D Finsterwald	Llanerch, PA	276
1959	B Rosburg	Minneapolis, MN	277
1960	J Hebert	Firestone, Akron, OH	281
1961	J Barber*	Olympia Fields, IL	277
1962	G Player	Aronimink, PA	278
1963	J Nicklaus	Dallas, TX	279
1964	B Nichols	Columbus, OH	271
1965	D Marr	Laurel Valley, PA	280
1966	A Geiberger	Firestone, Akron, OH	280
1967	D January*	Columbine, CO	281
1968	J Boros	Pecan Valley, TX	281
1969	R Floyd	Dayton, OH	276
1970	D Stockton	Southern Hills, OK	279
1971	J Nicklaus	PGA National, FL	281
1972	G Player	Oakland Hills, MI	281
1973	J Nicklaus	Canterbury, OH	277
1974	L Trevino	Tanglewood, NC	276
1975	J Nicklaus	Firestone, Akron, OH	276
1976	D Stockton	Congressional, MD	281
1977	L Wadkins*	Pebble Beach, CA	287
1978	J Mahaffey*	Oakmont, PA	276
1979	D Graham*	Oakland Hills, MI	272
1980	J Nicklaus	Oak Hill, NY	274
1981	L Nelson	Atlanta, GA	273
1982	R Floyd	Southern Hills, OK	272
1983	H Sutton	Pacific Palisades, CA	274
1984	L Trevino	Shoal Creek, AL	273
1985	H Green	Cherry Hills, Denver, CO	278
1986	R Tway	Inverness, Toledo, OH	276
1987	L Nelson*	PGA National, FL	287
1988	J Sluman	Oaktree, OK	272
1989	P Stewart	Kemper Lakes, IL	276
1990	W Grady	Shoal Creek, AL	282
1991	J Daly	Crooked Stick, IN	276
1992	N Price	Bellerive, MS	278
1993	P Azinger*	Inverness, Toledo, OH	272
1994	N Price	Southern Hills, OK	269

* *Winner after play-off*

Ladies' Major Championships

Weetabix Ladies' British Open Championship

Year	Winner	Club/Country	Venue	Score	
1976	J Lee Smith	Gosforth Park	Fulford	299	
1977	V Saunders	Tyrrells Wood	Lindrick	306	
1978	J Melville	Furness	Foxhills	310	
1979	A Sheard	South Africa	Southport and Ainsdale	301	
1980	D Massey	USA	Wentworth (East)	294	
1981	D Massey	USA	Northumberland	295	
1982	Figueras-Dotti	Spain	R Birkdale	296	
1983	*Not played*				
1984	A Okamoto	Japan	Woburn	289	
1985	B King	USA	Moor Park	300	
1986	L Davies	GB	R Birkdale	283	
1987	A Nicholas	GB	St Mellion	296	
1988T	C Dibnah*	Australia	Lindrick	296	
	S Little	South Africa			
1989	J Geddes	USA	Ferndown	274	
1990	H Alfredsson	Sweden	Woburn	288	
1991	P Grice-Whittaker	GB	Woburn	284	
1992	P Sheehan	USA	Woburn	207	*(Reduced to 54 holes by rain)*
1993	K Lunn	Australia	Woburn	275	
1994	L Neumann	Sweden	Woburn	280	

United States Ladies' Open Championship

Winners are American unless stated

Year	Winner	Venue	By
1946	P Berg	Spokane	5 and 4

Changed to stroke play

Year	Winner	Venue	Score
1947	B Jamieson	Greensboro	300
1948	B Zaharias	Atlantic City	300
1949	L Suggs	Maryland	291
1950	B Zaharias	Wichita	291
1951	B Rawls	Atlanta	294
1952	L Suggs	Bala, Philadelphia	284
1953	B Rawls	Rochester, NY	302 *(after a tie with J Pung)*
1954	B Zaharias	Peabody, Mass	291
1955	F Crocker	Wichita	299
1956	K Cornelius	Duluth	302 *(after a tie with B McIntire)*
1957	B Rawls	Mamaroneck	299
1958	M Wright	Bloomfield Hills, Mich	290
1959	M Wright	Pittsburgh, Pa	287
1960	B Rawls	Worchester, Mass	292
1961	M Wright	Springfield, NJ	293
1962	M Lindstrom	Myrtle Beach	301
1963	M Mills	Kenwood	289
1964	M Wright	San Diego	290 *(after a tie with R Jessen, Seattle)*
1965	C Mann	Northfield, NJ	290
1966	S Spuzich	Hazeltine Nat'l GC, Minn	297

* *Winner after play-off*

Year	Winner	Venue	Score
1967	C Lacoste (Fr)	Hot Springs, Virginia	294
1968	S Berning	Moselem Springs, Pa	289
1969	D Caponi	Scenic-Hills	294
1970	D Caponi	Muskogee, Okla	287
1971	J Gunderson-Carner	Erie, Pa	288
1972	S Berning	Mamaroneck, NY	299
1973	S Berning	Rochester, NY	290
1974	S Haynie	La Grange, Ill	295
1975	S Palmer	Northfield, NJ	295
1976	J Carner	Springfield, Pa	292 *(after a tie with S Palmer)*
1977	H Stacy	Hazeltine, Minn	292
1978	H Stacy	Indianapolis	299
1979	J Britz	Brooklawn, Conn	284
1980	A Alcott	Richland, Tenn	280
1981	P Bradley	La Grange, Illinois	279
1982	J Alex	Del Paso, Sacramento	283
1983	J Stephenson (Aus)	Broken Arrow, Oklahoma	290
1984	H Stacy	Salem, Mass	290
1985	K Baker	Baltusrol, NJ	280
1986	J Geddes	NCR	287
1987	L Davies (GB)	Plainfield	285
(After a tie with J Carner and A Akamoto (Jpn))			
1988	L Neumann (Swe)	Baltimore	277
1989	B King	Indianwood, MI	278
1990	B King	Atlanta Athletic Club, GA	284
1991	M Mallon	Colonial, TX	283
1992	P Sheehan	Oakmont, PA	280*(after a tie with J Inkster)*
1993	L Merton	Crooked Stick	280
1994	P Sheehan	Indianwood, MI	277

McDonald's LPGA Championship

(Formerly: LPGA Championship 1955–87; Mazda LPGA 1988–93)

Year	Winner	Venue	Score
1955	B Hanson	Orchard Ridge	4 & 3
1956	M Hagg	Forest Lake	291 *(after a tie with P Berg)*
1957	L Suggs	Churchill Valley	285
1958	M Wright	Churchill CC	288
1959	B Rawls	Churchill CC	288
1960	M Wright	French Lick	292
1961	M Wright	Stardust	287
1962	J Kimball	Stardust	282
1963	M Wright	Stardust	294
1964	M Mills	Stardust	278
1965	S Haynie	Stardust	279
1966	G Ehret	Stardust	282
1967	K Whitworth	Pleasant Valley	284
1968	S Post	Pleasant Valley	294 *(after a tie with K Whitworth)*
1969	B Rawls	Concord	293
1970	S Englehorn	Pleasant Valley	285 *(after a tie with K Whitworth)*
1971	K Whitworth	Pleasant Valley	288
1972	K Ahern	Pleasant Valley	293
1973	M Mills	Pleasant Valley	288
1974	S Haynie	Pleasant Valley	288
1875	K Whitworth	Pine Ridge	288
1976	B Burfeindt	Pine Ridge	287
1977	C Higuchi (Jpn)	Bay Tree	279
1978	N Lopez	Kings Island	275
1979	D Caponi	Kings Island	279
1980	S Little (SA)	Kings Island	285
1981	D Caponi	Kings Island	280
1982	J Stephenson (Aus)	Kings Island	279
1983	P Sheehan	Kings Island	279
1984	P Sheehan	Kings Island	272
1985	N Lopez	Kings Island	273

continued

McDonald's LPGA Championship *continued*

Year	Winner	Venue	Score
1986	P Bradley	Kings Island	277
1987	J Geddes	Kings Island	275
1988	S Turner	Kings Island	281
1989	N Lopez	Kings Island	274
1990	B Daniel	Bethesda	280
1991	M Mallon	Bethesda	274
1992	B King	Bethesda	267
1993	P Sheehan	Bethesda	275
1994	L Davies (GB)	Wilmington	275

Nabisco Dinah Shore

(Designated major championship 1983)

Year	Winner	Venue	Score
1983	A Alcott	Mission Hills	282
1984	J Inkster	Mission Hills	280 *(after a tie with P Bradley)*
1985	A Miller	Mission Hills	278
1986	P Bradley	Mission Hills	280
1987	B King	Mission Hills	283 *(after a tie with P Sheehan)*
1988	A Alcott	Mission Hills	274
1989	J Inkster	Mission Hills	279
1990	B King	Mission Hills	283
1991	A Alcott	Mission Hills	273
1992	D Mochrie	Mission Hills	279 *(after a tie with J Inkster)*
1993	H Alfredson (Swe)	Mission Hills	284
1994	D Andrews	Mission Hills	276

Du Maurier Classic

(Designated major championship 1979)

Year	Winner	Venue	Score
1979	A Alcott	Richelieu Valley	285
1980	P Bradley	St George's	277
1981	J Stephenson (Aus)	Summerlea	278
1982	S Haynie	St George's	280
1983	H Stacy	Beaconsfield	277
1984	J Inkster	St. George's	279
1985	P Bradley	Montreal	278
1986	P Bradley	Board of Trade	276 *(after a tie with A Okamoto)*
1987	J Rosenthal	Islesmere	272
1988	S Little (SA)	Vancouver	279
1989	T Green	Beaconsfield	279
1990	C Johnston	Westmount	276
1991	N Scranton	Vancouver	279
1992	S Steinhauer	St Charles	277
1993	B Burton	London Hunt	277 *(after a tie with B King)*
1994	M Nause	Ottawa Hunt	279

Major Championship League Tables

Major Championship Leaders – Men

	US Open	British Open	PGA	Masters	US Amateur	British Amateur	Total Titles
Jack Nicklaus	4	3	5	6	2	0	20
Bobby Jones	4	3	0	0	5	1	13
Walter Hagen	2	4	5	0	0	0	11
John Ball	0	1	0	0	0	8	9
Ben Hogan	4	1	2	2	0	0	9
Gary Player	1	3	2	3	0	0	9
Arnold Palmer	1	2	0	4	1	0	8
Tom Watson	1	5	0	2	0	0	8
Harold Hilton	0	2	0	0	1	4	7
Gene Sarazen	2	1	3	1	0	0	7
Sam Snead	0	1	3	3	0	0	7
Harry Vardon	1	6	0	0	0	0	7
Lee Trevino	2	2	2	0	0	0	6

Major Championship Leaders – Women

	US Open	LPGA	Du Maurier*	Nabisco Dinah Shore†	US Amateur	British Amateur	Total Titles
Mickey Wright	4	4	0	0	0	0	8
JoAnne Carner	2	0	0	0	5	0	7
Pat Bradley	1	1	3	1	0	0	6
Betsy Rawls	4	2	0	0	0	0	6
Glenna Collett Vare	0	0	0	0	6	0	6
Juli Inkster	0	0	1	2	3	0	6
Louise Suggs	2	1	0	0	1	1	5
Babe Zaharias	3	0	0	0	1	1	5
Amy Alcott	1	0	1	3	0	0	5
Betsy King	2	1	0	2	0	0	5

* Designated a major championship in 1979
† Designated a major championship in 1983

PART II

1994 Season

(Compiled by Judy Williams)

Sony World Rankings, 1994

Pos	Name	Circuit		Points
1	Nick Price	Afr	1	21.19
2	Greg Norman	ANZ	1	20.57
3	Nick Faldo	Eur	1	16.93
4	Bernhard Langer	Eur	2	15.32
5	José Maria Olazabal	Eur	3	15.18
6	Ernie Els	Afr	2	14.70
7	Fred Couples	USA	1	12.86
8	Colin Montgomerie	Eur	4	12.19
9	Masashi Ozaki	Jpn	1	11.39
10	Corey Pavin	USA	2	10.87
11	David Frost	Afr	3	9.88
12	Fuzzy Zoeller	USA	3	9.73
13	Tom Kite	USA	4	9.03
14	Severiano Ballesteros	Eur	5	8.96
15	Vijay Singh	Asa	1	8.49
16	Ian Woosnam	Eur	6	8.46
17	Tom Lehman	USA	5	8.13
18	Mark McNulty	Afr	4	8.01
19	Mark McCumber	USA	6	7.68
20	Loren Roberts	USA	7	7.46
21	Paul Azinger	USA	8	7.25
22	Phil Mickelson	USA	9	7.24
23	Tom Watson	USA	10	6.82
24	John Cook	USA	11	6.67
25	Davis Love III	USA	12	6.53
26	Brad Faxon	USA	13	6.43
27	Jeff Maggert	USA	14	6.20
28	Larry Mize	USA	15	6.14
29	Hale Irwin	USA	16	5.96
30	Scott Hoch	USA	17	5.91
31	Frank Nobilo	ANZ	2	5.74
32	Lee Janzen	USA	18	5.68
33	David Gilford	Eur	7	5.59
34	Ben Crenshaw	USA	19	5.58
35	Barry Lane	Eur	8	5.48
36	Bill Glasson	USA	20	5.47
37	Bob Estes	USA	21	5.36
38	Sam Torrance	Eur	9	5.23
39	Jesper Parnevik	Eur	10	5.23
40	John Huston	USA	22	5.22
41	Bruce Lietzke	USA	23	5.22
42	Miguel Angel Jimenez	Eur	11	5.20
43	Steve Elkington	ANZ	3	5.18
44	Craig Parry	ANZ	4	5.14
45	David Edwards	USA	24	5.07
46	Tsun'ki Nakajima	Jpn	2	5.00
47	Jay Haas	USA	25	4.99
48	Robert Allenby	ANZ	5	4.94
49	Mark Calcavecchia	USA	26	4.92
50	Rick Fehr	USA	27	4.82
51	Mark Roe	Eur	12	4.68
52	Eduardo Romero	SAm	1	4.67
53	Peter Senior	ANZ	6	4.60
54	Payne Stewart	USA	28	4.59
55	Mark James	Eur	13	4.54
56	Joakim Haeggman	Eur	14	4.42
57	Scott Simpson	USA	29	4.41
58	Curtis Strange	USA	30	4.33
59	Craig Stadler	USA	31	4.32
60	Gordon Brand Jr	Eur	15	4.30
61	Brian Watts	USA	32	4.30
62	Chip Beck	USA	33	4.18
63	Costantino Rocca	Eur	16	4.11
64	Tony Johnstone	Afr	5	4.09
65	Jim Gallagher Jr	USA	34	4.07
66	Gil Morgan	USA	35	4.01
67	Brett Ogle	ANZ	7	3.93
68	Per-Ulrik Johansson	Eur	17	3.90
69	Steve Lowery	USA	36	3.85
70	Naomichi Ozaki	Jpn	3	3.83
71	Anders Forsbrand	Eur	18	3.77
72	John Daly	USA	37	3.67
73	Wayne Westner	Afr	6	3.65
74	Darren Clarke	Eur	19	3.61
75	Howard Clark	Eur	20	3.49
76	Raymond Floyd	USA	38	3.48
77	Mike Springer	USA	39	3.43
78	Duffy Waldorf	USA	40	3.37
79	Andrew Magee	USA	41	3.30
80	Todd Hamilton	USA	42	3.24
81	Rodger Davis	ANZ	8	3.24
82	Peter Baker	Eur	21	3.22
83T	Mark O'Meara	USA	43	3.12
	Carl Mason	Eur	22	3.12
85	Dan Forsman	USA	44	3.11
86	Nolan Henke	USA	45	3.11
87	Greg Turner	ANZ	9	3.08
88	Robert Gamez	USA	46	3.06
89	David Feherty	Eur	23	3.02
90	Jeff Sluman	USA	47	2.99
91	Billy Andrade	USA	48	2.95
92	Ronan Rafferty	Eur	24	2.92
93	Sandy Lyle	Eur	25	2.91
94	Roger Mackay	ANZ	10	2.88
95	Lennie Clements	USA	49	2.79
96	David Ishii	USA	50	2.78
97	Fulton Allem	Afr	7	2.78
98	Brad Bryant	USA	51	2.77
99	Kirk Triplett	USA	52	2.76
100	Retief Goosen	Afr	8	2.73

PGA European Tour, 1994

(including Volvo Tour and Approved Special Events)

Volvo Order of Merit

Pos	Name	Prize Money £
1	Colin Montgomerie (Scot)	762719
2	Bernhard Langer (Ger)	635483
3	Seve Ballesteros (Sp)	590101
4	José Maria Olazabal (Sp)	516107
5	Miguel Angel Jiménez (Sp)	437403
6	Vijay Singh (Fiji)	364313
7	David Gilford (Eng)	326629
8	Nick Faldo (Eng)	321256
9	Mark Roe (Eng)	312539
10	Ernie Els (SA)	311849
11	Barry Lane (Eng)	277362
12	Ian Woosnam (Wal)	273264
13	Mark McNulty (Zim)	270349
14	Eduardo Romero (Arg)	269422
15	Per-Ulrik Johansson (Swe)	259952
16	Howard Clark (Eng)	247865
17	Robert Allenby (Aus)	240174
18	Peter Mitchell (Eng)	231332
19	Carl Mason (Eng)	205112
20	Frank Nobilo (NZ)	191583
21	Anders Forsbrand (Swe)	191235
22	Sam Torrance (Scot)	186043
23	Pierre Fulke (Swe)	178842
24	Gordon Brand Jr (Scot)	171602
25	Joakim Haeggman (Swe)	170989
26	Jesper Parnevik (Swe)	169633
27	Greg Turner (NZ)	168136
28	Russell Claydon (Eng)	167328
29	Mark James (Eng)	166434
30	Costantino Rocca (It)	165121
31	Mark Davis (Eng)	164885
32	Jonathan Lomas (Eng)	162715
33	Paul Curry (Eng)	161633
34	Phillip Price (Wal)	158756
35	Paul Eales (Eng)	151977
36	Peter Hedblom (Swe)	151441
37	Darren Clarke (N. Ire)	148685
38	Gabriel Hjerstedt (Swe)	142805
39	Retief Goosen (SA)	140820
40	Gary Orr (Scot)	138575
41	Sven Strüver (Ger)	137682
42	Andrew Coltart (Sco)	136357
43	Lee Westwood (Eng)	122322
44	Miguel Angel Martin (Sp)	121592
45	Klas Eriksson (Swe)	121437
46	Paul McGinley (Ire)	121020
47	José Rivero (Sp)	120723
48	Rodger Davis (Aus)	117262
49	Philip Walton (Ire)	115352
50	Wayne Westner (SA)	114569
51	Mike Clayton (Aus)	110185
52	Jean Van de Velde (Fr)	109067
53	Wayne Riley (Aus)	107300
54	Mike Harwood (Aus)	99883
55	Peter Baker (Eng)	99660
56	Robert Karlsson (Swe)	98482
57	Richard Boxall (Eng)	96521
58	Stephen Ames (T&T)	95905
59	Jim Payne (Eng)	94742
60	Des Smyth (Ire)	94090
61	Sandy Lyle (Scot)	93695
62	John Bland (SA)	91499
63	Ignacio Garrido (Sp)	90088
64	Ronan Rafferty (N.Ire)	86179
65	Andrew Sherborne (Eng)	86098
66	Ross McFarlane (Eng)	84279
67	Andrew Murray (Eng)	81190
68	José Coceres (Arg)	81146
69	Adam Hunter (Scot)	80813
70	Mats Lanner (Swe)	79811
71	Silvio Grappasonni (It)	73407
72	Tony Johnstone (Zim)	73278
73	Domingo Hospital (Sp)	73004
74	Steven Richardson (Eng)	72252
75	André Bossert (Swi)	72239
76	Paul Lawrie (Scot)	71975
77	David Feherty (N.Ire)	71475
78	Jeremy Robinson (Eng)	71300
79	Santiago Luna (Sp)	70912
80	Michel Besanceney (Fr)	70301
81	Peter Teravainen (US)	67886
82	Gordon J Brand (Eng)	67058
83	Alberto Binaghi (It)	66735
84	Martin Gates (Eng)	62715
85	Peter O'Malley (Aus)	59723
86	Mathias Grönberg (Swe)	59542
87	Gary Evans (Eng)	59513
88	Thomas Levet (Fr)	58375
89	Fredrik Lindgren (Swe)	58292
90	Eoghan O'Connell (Ire)	58123
91	Steen Tinning (Den)	58120
92	Jamie Spence (Eng)	57283
93	Pedro Linhart (Sp)	57164
94	Andrew Oldcorn (Eng)	55893
95	Derrick Cooper (Eng)	55674
96	Ross Drummond (Sco)	54600
97	Malcolm Mackenzie (Eng)	53236
98	Craig Cassells (Eng)	53048
99	Terry Price (Aus)	52614
100	Jay Townsend (US)	51689

Tour results

Air France Cannes Open

at Cannes Mougins

1	I Woosnam	72-70-63-66—271	£50000
2	C Montgomerie	70-69-67-70—276	33330
3	J Van de Velde	73-71-68-65—277	16890
	W Riley	69-69-73-76—277	16890

Alfred Dunhill Belgian Open

at Royal Zoute, Knokke-le-Zoute

1	N Faldo*	67-74-67-71—279	£100000
2	J Haeggman	73-68-66-72—279	66660
3	P Hedblom	69-73-65-73—280	30986
	B Langer	69-68-68-75—280	30986
	C Montgomerie	67-70-66-70—280	30986

Bell's Scottish Open

at King's Course, Gleneagles

1	C Mason	67-69-61-68—265	£100000
2	P Mitchell	67-64-65-70—266	66660
3	J Parnevik	70-65-64-68—267	37560

Benson and Hedges International Open

at Nicklaus Course, St Mellion, Cornwall

1	S Ballesteros	69-70-72-70—281	£108330
2	N Faldo	75-69-70-70—284	72210
3	J Lomas	74-70-69-72—285	36595
	G Orr	70-70-70-75—285	36595

BMW International Open

at St Eurach Land-und GC, Munich

1	M McNulty	70-71-68-65—274	£87500
2	S Ballesteros	69-68-72-66—275	58250
3	M Roe	68-71-68-69—276	32750

Canon European Masters – Swiss Open

at Crans-sur-Sierre

1	E Romero	64-68-66-68—266	111290
2	P Fulke	70-65-65-67—267	74150
3	J Van de Velde	68-68-67-66—269	34513
	B Lane	67-69-66-67—269	34513
	S Torrance	67-65-69-68—269	34513

* *Winner after play-off*

Czech Open – Chemapol Trophy

at Marianske, Czech Republic

1	P-U Johansson	61-56-54-66—237	£83330
2	K Eriksson	59-58-56-67—240	55550
3	R Claydon	56-61-57-67—241	28150
	F Nobilo	54-59-57-71—241	28150

Reduced to 63 holes: holes 11, 13 and 14 unplayable for first three rounds due to frost

Dubai Desert Classic

at Emirates, Dubai, Arab Emirates

1	E Els	61-69-67-71—268	£75000
2	G Norman	68-69-68-69—274	50000
3	W Westner	70-68-69-68—275	28170

Dunhill British Masters

at Duke's Course, Woburn G&CC

1	I Woosnam	71-70-63-67—271	£108330
2	S Ballesteros	69-65-69-72—275	72210
3	C Montgomerie	72-66-70-68—276	36595
	B Langer	71-69-65-71—276	36595

European Open

at East Course, East Sussex National, Uckfield

1	D Gilford	70-68-70-67—275	£100000
2	C Rocca	68-72-70-70—280	52110
	JM Olazabal	68-74-69-69—280	52110

Extremadura Open

at Golf del Guadiana, Badajoz, Spain

1	P Eales	72-69-69-71—281	£41660
2	P Hedblom	72-69-71-70—282	27770
3	A Coltart	68-74-71-70—283	14075
	JM Canizares	70-73-68-72—283	14075

Heineken Dutch Open

at Hilversum, The Netherlands

1	MA Jimenez	65-68-67-70—270	£108330
2	H Clark	67-67-71-67—272	72210
3	P Mitchell	65-67-70-71—273	40690

Heineken Open Catalonia

at Pals, Girona, Spain

1	J Coceres	70-69-67-69—275	£50000
2	JL Guepy	67-68-72-71—278	33330
3	R Claydon	72-73-69-65—279	18780

Höhe Brücke Austrian Open

at GC Waldviertel, Litschau, Austria

1	M Davis	68-69-69-64—270	£41660
2	P Walton	68-65-69-70—272	27770
3	R Goosen	68-72-66-67—273	15650

Honda Open

at Gut Kaden, Hamburg, Germany

1	R Allenby*	72-67-68-69—276	£83330
2	MA Jimenez	70-71-65-70—276	55550
3	R Davis	66-68-76-68—278	31300

Jersey European Airways Open

at La Moye, Jersey

1	P Curry	73-62-68-63—266	£58330
2	M James	69-63-68-69—269	38880
3	I Pyman	66-67-68-70—271	21910

Johnnie Walker Classic

at Blue Canyon CC, Phuket, Thailand

1	G Norman	75-70-64-68—277	£100000
2	F Couples	66-72-70-70—278	66660
3	B Langer	68-70-71-70—279	37560

Johnnie Walker World Championship

at Tryall, Jamaica

1	E Els	64-64-71-69—268	$550000
2	M McCumber	67-70-70-67—274	250000
	N Faldo	67-67-73-67—274	250000
4	B Faxon	72-70-69-64—275	106666
	P Azinger	71-74-62-68—275	106666
	I Woosnam	70-68-69-68—275	106666

Madeira Island Open

at Campo de Golfe da Madeira, Santa da Serra, Madeira

1	M Lanner	70-67-69—206	£41660
2	M Gronberg	69-70-69—208	18640
	P Hedblom	69-69-70—208	18640
	H Clark	68-67-73—208	18640

Mercedes German Masters

at Motzener See, Berlin

1	S Ballesteros*	68-70-65-67—270	£104125
	E Els	63-64-70-73—270	54250
	JM Olazabal	67-67-66-70—270	54250

* *Winner after play-off*

Moroccan Open

at Golf Royale de Agadir, Morocco

1	A Forsbrand	70-68-69-69—276	£58330
2	H Clark	68-67-72-73—280	38880
3	R Karlsson	68-72-70-71—281	21910

Murphy's English Open

at Forest of Arden, Warwickshire

1	C Montgomerie	70-67-68-69—274	£100000
2	B Lane	66-69-72-68—275	66660
3	R Goosen	72-72-65-67—276	37560

Murphy's Irish Open

at Mount Juliet, Co. Kilkenny

1	B Langer	70-68-70-67—275	£98766
2	R Allenby	68-68-68-72—276	51466
	J Daly	70-68-73-65—276	51466

Open V33 du Grand Lyon

at Terrain des Sangliers, Lyon

1	S Ames	70-67-71-74—282	£37500
2	P Linhart	72-68-72-72—284	19535
	G Hjertstedt	68-68-71-77—284	19535

Perrier Fourball Tournament

at St Cloud, Paris

1	P Baker and DJ Russell	58-68-65-69—260	£35000 each
2	M Mouland and J Spence	62-69-66-64—261	25000
3	R Claydon and P Eales	60-66-71-66—263	15000
	S Ballesteros and JM Olazabal	63-67-67-66—263	15000

Peugeot Open de France

at Le Golf National, Paris

1	M Roe	70-71-67-66—274	£91660
2	G Hjertstedt	67-70-68-70—275	61100
3	JM Olazabal	68-72-69-69—278	34430

Peugeot Open de España

at Club de Campo, Madrid

1	C Montgomerie	70-71-66-70—277	£83330
2	R Boxall	69-69-70-70—278	37283
	M Roe	70-68-69-71—278	37283
	M McNulty	68-69-70-71—278	37283

* *Winner after play-off*

Portuguese Open

at Penha Longa, Sintra

1	P Price	64-71-71-72—278	£50000
2	D Gilford	71-69-69-73—282	22370
	P Eales	66-71-72-73—282	22370
	R Goosen	69-66-73-74—282	22370

Scandinavian Masters

at Drottningholms, Stockholm

1	V Singh	68-67-69-64—268	£108330
2	M McNulty	67-69-69-66—271	72210
3	J Parnevik	69-71-65-67—272	33573
	M Davis	64-72-65-71—272	33573
	P Haugsrud	70-66-68-68—272	33573

Tisettanta Italian Open

at Marco Simone, Rome

1	E Romero	69-67-69-67—272	£75000
2	G Turner	69-69-70-65—273	50000
3	F Lindgren	71-64-69-71—275	28170

Toyota World Match Play Championship

at Wentworth Club (West Course), Surrey

Total prize fund: £600000

First Round
V Singh (Fiji) beat J Parnevik (Swe) 4 and 3
C Montgomerie (Sco) beat Y Mizumaki (Jpn) 2 and 1
S Ballesteros (Sp) beat D Frost (SA) 8 and 7
B Faxon (US) beat I Woosnam (Wal) 1 hole
(Each loser received £25000)

Second Round
V Singh beat C Pavin (US) at 37th
C Montgomerie beat N Faldo (Eng) 1 hole
E Els (SA) beat S Ballesteros 2 and 1
JM Olazabal (Sp) beat B Faxon 6 and 4
(Each loser received £35000)

Semi-Finals
C Montgomerie beat V Singh 1 hole
E Els beat JM Olazabal 2 and 1

Play-off for 3rd and 4th places
JM Olazabal beat V Singh 2 and 1
(*Olazabal received £60000, Singh received £50000*)

Final
E Els beat C Montgomerie 4 and 2
(*Els received £160000, Montgomerie received £90000*)

Trophée Lancôme

at St Nom-la-Bretèche, Versailles, Paris

1	V Singh	65-63-69-66—263	£100000
2	MA Jimenez	67-64-66-67—264	66000
3	S Ballesteros	65-69-66-65—265	37000

Turespana Masters – Open de Andalucia

at Montecastillo, Jerez, Spain

1	C Mason	67-70-71-70—278	£50535
2	JM Olazabal	69-68-71-72—280	33670
3	G Brand Jr	71-69-69-72—281	18988

Turespana Open de Baleares

at Son Vida, Majorca

1	B Lane	64-70-66-69—269	£41616
2	J Payne	67-68-70-66—271	27727
3	W Westner	68-70-67-68—273	15637

Turespana–Iberia Open de Canarias

at Golf del Sur, Tenerife

1	D. Gilford	72-70-66-70—278	£41660
2	W Riley	68-71-70-71—280	18640
	A Murray	73-67-68-72—280	18640
	J Quiros	70-68-67-75—280	18640

Turespana Open Mediterrania

at Villamartin, Torrevieja, Spain

1	JM Olazabal*	70-65-71-70—276	£50000
2	P McGinley	70-68-68-70—276	33330
3	P Baker	73-71-65-69—278	16890
	GJ Brand	68-66-70-74—278	16890

Volvo German Open

at Hubbelrath, Dusseldorf

1	C Montgomerie	65-68-66-70—269	£108330
2	B Langer	69-68-65-68—270	72210
3	P Price	65-67-67-72—271	40690

Volvo Masters

at Valderrama, Sotogrande, Spain

1	B Langer	71-62-73-70—276	£125000
2	V Singh	71-70-70-66—277	65175
	S Ballesteros	69-67-68-73—277	65175
4	MA Jimenez	65-70-72-71—278	34800
	C Montgomerie	69-65-72-72—278	34800
6	M McNulty	70-69-69-71—279	26800
7	C Rocca	69-72-67-73—281	23000
8	JM Olazabal	70-70-71-71—282	18250
	I Woosnam	68-69-73-72—282	18250
10	F Nobilo	70-69-73-71—283	15500

* *Winner after play-off*

Volvo PGA Championship

at Wentworth Club (West Course), Surrey

1	JM Olazabal	67-68-71-65—271	£133330
2	E Els	66-66-71-69—272	88880
3	B Langer	69-70-67-68—274	50070
4	J Haeggman	69-69-70-68—276	36940
	MA Jimenez	68-66-72-70—276	36940
6	S Ballesteros	73-66-70-68—277	28000
7	M James	68-72-71-67—278	24000
8	A Hunter	71-65-72-71—279	20000
9	S Lyle	68-71-70-71—280	17840
10	M Mackenzie	73-70-69-69—281	14340
	F Nobilo	73-66-69-73—281	14340
	P Hedblom	69-69-71-72—281	14340
	K Stables	71-71-71-68—281	14340
14	J Lomas	74-68-69-71—282	11280
	C Rocca	67-70-72-73—282	11280
	E Romero	69-72-68-73—282	11280
	H Clark	73-69-70-70—282	11280
	P Lawrie	69-70-71-72—282	11280
19	V Singh	72-69-70-72—283	9760
	P Baker	73-67-73-70—283	9760
21	L Westwood	75-70-67-72—284	8520
	M Roe	71-70-68-75—284	8520
	P Way	72-72-71-69—284	8520
	B Lane	70-70-73-71—284	8520
	MA Martin	71-74-71-68—284	8520
	M Clayton	70-73-72-69—284	8520
	M Lanner	70-70-69-75—284	8520
	N Faldo	72-70-70-72—284	8520

Tour Statistics, 1994 *(provided by Philips CD-Interactive)*

Stroke Average

1	Vijay Singh	69.55
2	Colin Montgomerie	69.60
3	Bernhard Langer	69.63
4	Ernie Els	69.70
5	José Maria Olazabal	69.80
6	Nick Faldo	69.81
7	Severiano Ballesteros	69.95
8	Ian Woosnam	70.52
9	Howard Clark	70.57
10	Mark McNulty	70.71

Birdie Leaders

1	Russell Claydon	383
2	Peter Mitchell	372
3	Miguel Angel Jiménez	354
4	Colin Montgomerie	333
5	Gary Orr	332
6	Barry Lane	327
7	Pierre Fulke	326
	Miguel Angel Martin	326
9	Andrew Sherborne	323
10	Mark Davis	321
	Michel Besanceney	321

Eagle Leaders

1	Eduardo Romero	13
	Anders Forsbrand	13
	Alberto Binaghi	13
	Lee Westwood	13
5	Barry Lane	12
	Colin Montgomerie	12
	Greg Turner	12
8	Thomas Gögele	11
	Sandy Lyle	11
	Miguel Angel Jiménez	11
	Peter Hedblom	11

Driving Accuracy

		%
1	Nick Godin	84.09
2	Tony Johnstone	83.14
3	Jeff Hawkes	82.01
4	John Bland	81.33
5	Gavin Levenson	80.81
6	Eduardo Romero	79.85
7	Colin Montgomerie	79.80
8	Pierre Fulke	78.03
9	André Bossert	77.68
10	Keith Waters	77.43

Greens in Regulation

		%
1	Thomas Levet	78.04
2	Mikael Piltz	76.30
3	Ricky Willison	75.28
4	Scott Watson	75.21
5	Paul McGinley	73.20
6	John Bland	73.11
7	David Williams	72.22
8	Colin Montgomerie	72.03
9	Ian Woosnam	70.88
10	Glenn Ralph	70.49

Sand Saves

		%
1	Anders Sorensen	72.35
2	Tony Johnstone	70.33
3	Glenn Ralph	69.79
4	Rodger Davis	60.00
5	Brian Nelson	58.73
6	Johan Ryström	58.33
	Paul Moloney	58.33
8	David R Jones	56.33
9	Manuel Piñero	56.22
10	Nick Godin	54.39

Putts per Greens in Regulation

		Avg
1	Mark Davis	1.717
2	Ronan Rafferty	1.719
3	José Maria Olazabal	1.724
4	Anders Forsbrand	1.728
5	Wayne Westner	1.730
6	Darren Clarke	1.736
7	Olle Nordberg	1.737
8	David Gilford	1.743
9	Paul Curry	1.743
10	Gary Orr	1.747

PGA European Tour Qualifying School

at La Grande Motte and Golf Massane, Montpellier, France

Pos	Name	Score
1	David Carter (Eng)	72-69-64-68—273
2	Christian Cevaer (Fr)	72-72-66-68—278
3	Oyvind Rojahn (Nor)	74-65-69-73—281
4	David Ray (Eng)	72-72-67-71—282
5	Liam White (Eng)	68-73-70-71—282
6	Anders Gillner (Swe)	73-69-70-71—283
7	Fredrik Andersson (Swe)	69-70-70-74—283
8	Phil Golding (Eng)	76-70-71-68—285
9	Paul Richard Simpson (Eng)	71-75-70-69—285
10	George Ryall (Eng)	71-66-73-75—285
11	Carl Suneson (Eng)	73-70-75-68—286
12	Martyn Roberts (Aus)	72-71-74-69—286
13	Philip Talbot (Eng)	72-71-72-71—286
14	Ian Spencer (Eng)	72-71-72-71—286
15	Rolf Muntz (Neth)	72-70-73-71—286
16	Glenn Ralph (Eng)	72-68-74-72—286
17	John Mellor (Eng)	75-68-70-73—286
18	Anders Sorensen (Den)	71-70-72-73—286
19	Craig Ronald (Sco)	71-73-73-70—287
20	Mark Nichols (Eng)	73-72-71-71—287
21	Joakim Gronhagen (Swe)	69-72-75-71—287
22	Fredrik Jacobson (Swe)	70-70-76-71—287
23	Stephen Dodd (Wal)	76-69-69-73—287
24	Emanuele Canonica (Ita)	71-72-71-73—287
25	Paolo Quirici (Swi)	70-73-71-73—287
26	Mark Litton (Wal)	72-70-71-74—287
27	Adam Mednick (Swe)	71-71-71-74—287
28	Antoine Lebouc (Fra)	70-69-73-75—287
29	Gary Emerson (Eng)	74-74-70-70—288
30	John Hawksworth (Eng)	72-73-73-70—288
31	Kenny Cross (Swe)	77-71-68-72—288
32	José Manuel Carriles (Sp)	71-74-68-75—288
33	Carlos Larrain (Ven)	73-72-75-69—289
34	Jonathan Wilshire (Eng)	75-72-72-70—289
35	Olle Karlsson (Swe)	72-71-74-72—289
36	Michael Jonzon (Swe)	73-75-68-73—289
37	Keith Waters (Eng)	69-73-74-73—289
38	Fabrice Tarnaud (Fr)	71-70-73-75—289
39	Dean Robertson* (Sco)	72-73-74-71—290
40	Jesus Maria Arruti (Sp)	71-76-70-73—290

* *After play-off*

PGA European Challenge Tour Order of Merit, 1994

Pos	Name	Prize Money £
1	Raymond Burns (N. Ire)	43583
2	Jon Robson (Eng)	38334
3	Michael Campbell (NZ)	29707
4	Michael Archer (Eng)	29673
5	Neal Briggs (Eng)	29626
6	John Bickerton (Eng)	25933
7	Mats Hallberg (Swe)	25663
8	Stuart Cage (Eng)	25529
9	Jarmo Sandelin (Swe)	24630
10	Daniel Westermark (Swe)	24341
11	Stuart Little (Eng)	23162
12	Daniel Chopra (Swe)	22568
13	Rolf Muntz (Neth)	21976
14	Raymond Russell (Sco)	20833
15	Jesus Maria Arruti (Sp)	20410
16	Frederik Andersson (Swe)	19672
17	Liam White (Eng)	18722
18	Mark Litton (Wal)	18243
19	Jean Francois Remesy (Fr)	16858
20	Eric Giraud (Fr)	16460
21	Giuseppe Cali (Ita)	16395
22	Stephen Dodd (Wal)	15835
23	Philip Talbot (Eng)	15586
24	Paolo Quirici (Swi)	15311
25	Miles Tunnicliff (Eng)	14925
26	Christian Cevaer (Fr)	14682
27	Carl Watts (Eng)	13881
28	Per Nyman (Swe)	13792
29	Marcello Santi (Ita)	13505
30	Kenny Cross (Swe)	12843
31	Dennis Edlund (Swe)	12806
32	Andrew Sandywell (Eng)	12794
33	Michael Jonzon (Swe)	12264
34	Nicholas Leconte (Eng)	11888
35	Joakim Gronhagen (Swe)	11667
36	Fernando Roca (Sp)	11642
37	Stephen Bennett (Eng)	11270
38	Robert Huxtable (US)	11125
39	John Metcalfe (Eng)	11048
40	Ricky Willison (Eng)	10956

PGA European Challenge Tour, 1994

* *Winner after play-off*
† *Invitational event*
(c) *closed national event*

Tournament	Venue	Winner
Tunisia Open	Tunisia	J Robson (Eng)
El Corte Ingles Open	Spain	J Pinero (Sp)
Tessali Open	Italy	M Archer (Eng)
Open Jezequel	France	C Watts (Eng)
Stockley Park Challenge	England	R Willison (Eng)
Centenario Copa Palmer	Gran Canaria	D Westermark (Swe)
American Express Trophy (c)	Germany	T Giedeon (Ger)
Scottish Professional Championship (c)	Scotland	A Coltart (Sco)
Club Med	Italy	R Burns (Ire)
Ramlosa Open	Sweden	E Carlberg (Swe Am)
Challenge AGF	France	J Robson (Eng)
SIAB Open	Sweden	P Haugsrud (Nor)
Italian Native Open (c)	Italy	G Cali (Ita)
Himmerland Open	Denmark	M Archer (Eng)
Championnat de France Pro (c)	France	JC Cambon (Fr)
PGA Spanish Championship (c)	Spain	J Pinero (Sp)
Nedcar Open (c)	The Netherlands	R Muntz (Neth)
Memorial Olivier Barras	Switzerland	M Campbell (NZ)*
Bank Austria Open	Austria	M Campbell (NZ)
Vasteras Open	Sweden	J Gronhagen (Swe)
Neuchatel Open SBS Trophy	Switzerland	R Muntz (Neth)
Open Divonne	France	S Cage (Eng)

Tournament	Venue	Winner
Volvo Finnish Open	Finland	M Piltz (Fin)
Open des Volcans	France	E Giraud (Fr)
Interlaken Open	Switzerland	N Briggs (Eng)*
Jamtland Open	Sweden	D Chopra (Swe)
Rolex Pro-Am†	Switzerland	S Little (Eng)
SM Matchplay	Sweden	P Nyman (Swe)
Audi Quattro Trophy	Germany	M Campbell (NZ)
Esbjerg Pro-Am (c)	Denmark	B Tinning (Den)
Norwegian Challenge	Norway	R Burns (Ire)
Gore-Tex Challenge	Scotland	J Bickerton (Eng)
Toyota Danish PGA	Denmark	A Overbring (Swe)
Open de Dijon Bourgogne	France	M Santi (Ita)
Compaq Open	Sweden	A Mednick (Swe)
Dutch Challenge	The Netherlands	J Remesy (Fr)
Challenge Novotel	France	J Sandelin (Swe)
Diners Club Championship (c)	Austria	G Manson (Sco)
Perrier European Pro-Am	Belgium	A Sandywell (Eng)
Team Erhverv Danish Open	Denmark	L White (Eng)
Challenge Chargeurs	France	D Chopra (Swe)
Biarritz International Pro-Am	France	M Litton (Wal)

Professional Men's Internationals, 1994

Alfred Dunhill Cup *at The Old Course, St Andrews*

Day One

Group 1
USA beat Japan 2–1
New Zealand beat Ireland 2–1

Group 2
England beat Spain 3–0
Australia beat France 2–1

Group 3
South Africa beat Republic of China 2–1
Scotland beat Paraguay 2–1

Group 4
Sweden beat Canada 2–1
Zimbabwe beat Germany 2–1

Day Two

Group 1
Japan beat New Zealand 2–1
Ireland beat USA 2–1

Group 2
Australia beat Spain 2–1
England beat France 3–0

Group 3
Scotland beat Republic of China 3–0
South Africa beat Paraguay 2–1

Group 4
Germany beat Sweden 2–1
Canada beat Zimbabwe 2–1

Day Three

Group 1
USA beat New Zealand 3–0
Ireland beat Japan 2–1

Group 2
France beat Spain 2–1
England beat Australia 3–0

Group 3
Republic of China beat Paraguay 2–1
South Africa beat Scotland 2–1

Group 4
Canada beat Germany 2–1
Zimbabwe beat Sweden 2–1

Semi-Finals

USA beat England 3–0
T Kite (69) beat M Roe (70)
F Couples (68) beat H Clark (74)
C Strange (70) beat B Lane (71)

Canada beat South Africa 2–1
R Stewart (70) beat D Frost (75)
R Gibson (70) beat W Westner (74)
D Barr (72) lost to E Els (68)

Final

Canada beat USA 2–1
D Barr (70) beat T Kite (71)
R Gibson (74) lost to C Strange (67)
R Stewart (71) beat F Couples (72)

	Prize Money £ Team	Player	Total
Group 1			
USA			
Ireland	45000	15000	
Japan	25500	8500	
New Zealand	19500	6500	90000
Group 2			
England			
Australia	45000	15000	
France	25500	8500	
Spain	19500	6500	90000
Group 3			
South Africa			
Scotland	45000	15000	
R. of China	25500	8500	
Paraguay	19500	6500	90000
Group 4			
Canada			
Zimbabwe	45000	15000	
Germany	25500	8500	
Sweden	19500	6500	90000
Losing Semi-Finalists			
England	95000	31666	
South Africa	95000	31666	190000
Runners-up			
USA	150000	50000	150000
Winners			
Canada	300000	100000	300000
Total			1000000

The President's Cup

United States *v* International Team Inaugural Match

at Robert Trent Jones GC, Lake Manassas, Washington

Day One

Fourballs

C Pavin and J Maggert beat S Elkington and Vijay Singh 2 and 1
J Haas and S Hoch beat F Allem and D Frost 6 and 5
D Love III and F Couples beat N Price and B Hughes 1 up
J Huston and J Gallagher beat C Parry and R Allenby 4 and 2
T Lehman and P Mickelson beat F Nobilo and P Senior 3 and 2

US 5, International 0

Foursomes

H Irwin and L Roberts beat D Frost and F Allem 3 and 1
J Haas and S Hoch beat C Parry and T Watanabe 4 and 3
C Pavin and J Maggert lost to F Nobilo and R Allenby 2 and 1
P Mickelson and T Lehman lost to S Elkington and V Singh 2 and 1
D Love III and J Gallagher halved with N Price and M McNulty

US 2½, International 2½

Day Two

Fourballs

J Gallagher and J Huston lost to F Allem and M McNulty 4 and 3
J Haas and S Hoch lost to T Watanabe and V Singh 3 and 1
L Roberts and T Lehman lost to C Parry and B Hughes 4 and 3
F Couples and D Love III beat F Nobilo and R Allenby 2 up
P Mickelson and C Pavin halved with N Price and S Elkington

US 1½, International 3½

Foursomes

H Irwin and J Haas lost to D Frost and P Senior 6 and 5
C Pavin and L Roberts beat C Parry and F Allem 1 up
J Maggert and J Huston lost to V Singh and S Elkington 3 and 2
D Love III and J Gallagher beat F Nobilo and R Allenby 7 and 5
P Mickelson and T Lehman beat B Hughes and M McNulty 3 and 2

US 3, International 2

continued

The President's Cup *continued*

Day Three

Singles
J Haas beat M McNulty 4 and 3
J Gallagher beat T Watanabe 4 and 3
H Irwin beat R Allenby 1 up
J Huston lost to P Senior 3 and 2
J Maggert beat B Hughes 2 and 1
F Couples beat N Price 1 up
P Mickelson halved with F Allem
T Lehman halved with V Singh
S Hoch halved with D Frost
L Roberts halved with F Nobilo
D Love III beat S Elkington 1 up
C Pavin lost to C Parry 1 up

US 8, International 4

Match result: US 20; International 12.

PGA Cup

United States Club Professionals *v* European Club Professionals

at Palm Beach Gardens, Florida

Day 1

Foursomes

USA	Matches	Europe	Matches
R Acton and T Smith (6 and 4)	1	D Jones and R Mann	0
JL Lewis and P Oakley	0	N Job and C Hall (2 and 1)	1
W Chapman and G Bowman	0	J Harrison and J Higgins (3 and 2)	1
J Roth and R McDougal	0	R Weir and C Maltman (5 and 4)	1
	1		3

Fourball

USA	Matches	Europe	Matches
R Acton and T Smith (2 and 1)	1	A Baguley and H Stott	0
T Cleaver and J Lee (1 hole)	1	N Job and C Hall	0
JL Lewis and P Oakley (1 hole)	1	J Harrison and J Higgins	0
J Roth and R McDougal (3 and 2)	1	R Weir and C Maltman	0
	4		0

Day Two

Foursomes

USA	Matches	Europe	Matches
R Acton and T Smith	0	C Maltman and R Weir (4 and 3)	1
JL Lewis and J Lee (3 and 2)	1	C Hall and N Job	0
G Bowman and P Oakley	0	J Harrison and J Higgins (1 hole)	1
J Roth and R McDougal	0	D Jones and H Stott (3 and 1)	1
	1		3

Fourball

USA	Matches	Europe	Matches
R Acton and T Smith (4 and 3)	1	A Baguley and R Mann	0
JL Lewis and J Lee (4 and 3)	1	C Hall and N Job	0
W Chapman and T Cleaver	0	J Harrison and R Weir (3 and 1)	1
J Roth and R McDougal (3 and 1)	1	D Jones and H Stott	0
	3		1

USA		**Europe**	
Day Three			
Singles			
R Acton (3 and 2)	1	D Jones	0
T Smith	0	C Hall (2 and 1)	1
JL Lewis (1 hole)	1	R Mann	0
R McDougal	0	C Maltman (2 and 1)	1
J Roth	0	A Baguley (3 and 2)	1
J Lee (2 and 1)	1	H Stott	0
P Oakley (6 and 5)	1	J Harrison	0
G Bowman	0	J Higgins (5 and 4)	1
W Chapman (4 and 3)	1	R Weir	0
T Cleaver (1 hole)	1	N Job	0
	6		4

Result: USA 15, Europe 11.

World Cup of Golf by Heineken

at Dorado Beach GC, Puerto Rico

1	USA (536)	Fred Couples	65-63-68-69—265	£92966 each
		Davis Love III	67-66-69-69—271	
2	Zimbabwe (550)	Mark McNulty	68-67-67-70—272	£46483 each
		Tony Johnstone	67-72-66-73—278	
3	Sweden (551)	Jesper Parnevik	69-69-70-67—275	£30989 each
		Joakim Haeggman	71-65-70-70—276	
4	New Zealand (553)	Frank Nobilo	70-66-67-69—272	£23241 each
		Greg J Turner	72-70-68-71—281	
5T	Scotland (557)	Gordon Brand Jr	73-69-72-64—279	£14151 each
		Andrew Coltart	71-68-69-70—278	
	Paraguay (557)	Pedro Roddolfo Martinez	71-69-69-69—278	£14151 each
		Angel Unsulino Franco	69-68-72-70—279	
	Japan (557)	Masayuki Kawamura	71-67-65-73—276	£14151 each
		Toru Suzuki	75-68-66-72—281	
8	Germany (558)	Bernhard Langer	71-71-65-69—276	£7437 each
		Sven Strüver	71-69-73-69—282	
9T	Australia (559)	Steve Elkington	69-68-71-66—274	£5578 each
		Mike Clayton	75-65-75-70—285	
	Italy (559)	Costantino Rocca	68-66-68-68—270	£5578 each
		Silvio Grappasonni	69-71-75-74—289	
	Malaysia (559)	P Gunasegaran	73-69-71-73—286	£5578 each
		Marimuthu Ramayah	66-64-69-74—273	

Individual Results

1	Fred Couples (US)	265	£61977
2	Costantino Rocca (Ita)	270	30989
3	Davis Love III (US)	271	15494
4T	Frank Nobilo (NZ)	272	4648
	Mark McNulty (Zim)	272	4648

Miscellaneous Professional Tournaments

Alfred Dunhill Masters
at Bali, Indonesia

1	J Kay	73-66-66-72—277	Aus$83918
2	P Burke	68-70-70-70—278	47554
3	V Singh	75-70-67-67—279	31469

Lord Derby Assistants' Tournament
at Bolton

1	C Tyson	69-68—137	£1000
2	C Phillips	70-68—138	687
	S Raybould	72-66—138	687

Glenmuir Club Professional Championship
at North Berwick

1	D Jones	74-69-69-66—278
2	N Job	79-64-67-70—280
	R Mann	74-69-70-67—280
	H Stott	76-69-68-67—280

The Grand Match (Past Ryder Cup players *v* Past Walker Cup players)
at Royal Cinque Ports, Deal, Kent

(Ex-Walker Cup names given first)

Morning Foursomes
B Critchley and M Christmas beat P Alliss and H Boyle 7 and 6
R Willison and P Hedges beat P Butler and B Waites 6 and 5
G Godwin and P Benka beat B Hunt and C Clark 5 and 4
I Hutcheon and C Dalgleish beat B Barnes and L Platts 3 and 2

Afternoon Foursomes
B Critchley and G Godwin lost to P Alliss and B Hunt 5 and 4
M Christmas and P Benka beat C Clark and H Boyle 2 and 1
C Dalgleish and P Hedges beat B Waites and L Platts 3 and 2
R Willison and I Hutcheon halved with B Barnes and P Butler

Result: Bruce Critchley's Players 6½, Peter Alliss's Gentlemen 1½.

Grand Slam
at Kauai, Hawaii

1	G Norman	70-66—136	$400000
2	N Price	70-69—139	250000
3	E Els	72-71—143	175000
4	JM Olazabal	74-70—144	150000

Hassan II Trophy

at Royal Dar-es-Salaam, Rabat, Morocco

1	M Gates	68-67-75-69—279	$93000
2	R Karlsson	70-72-68-72—282	49500
3	S Gump	69-72-74-71—286	29500

Howson Futures Tour

Event No. 1 *at Wildwood, Cranleigh, Surrey*

1	M Nichols	72-70—142	£2300
2	D Tapping	78-67—145	815
	J Higgins	73-72—145	815
	P Simpson	73-72—145	815
	A Tillman	71-74—145	815

Event No. 2 *at Manor of Groves, Sawbridgeworth, Hertfordshire*

1	P Page*	69-70—139	£2300
2	P Simpson	71-68—139	1100
3	A Rogers	67-73—140	775
	D Carter	72-68—140	775

Event No. 3 *at Slaley Hall, Northumberland*

1	R Russell	67-72—139	£2100
2	C Watts	74-72—146	1000
3	J Metcalfe	73-74—147	750

Event No. 4 *at Mill Ride, Ascot*

1	G Pooley*	70-72—142	£2300
2	S Robertson	71-71—142	900
	P Parkin	71-71—142	900

Event No. 5 *at Mill Ride, Ascot*

1	P Simpson	69-71—140	£2300
2	N Briggs	69-72—141	1050
3	P Talbot	71-71—142	750

Event No. 6 *at Wildwood, Alfold, Surrey*

1	J Hawksworth	71-65—136	£2225
2	M McGuire	69-68—137	1050

Event No. 7 *at Mill Ride, Ascot*

1	G Hanrahan	70-70—140	£2350
2	A Tillman	68-73—141	895
	J Langmead	70-71—141	895

Event No. 8 *at The Warwickshire*

1	M Nichols	70-68—138	£5000
2	G Emerson	73-66—139	2100
3	A Hare	71-69—140	1400

Howson Futures Tour Final Order of Merit

Pos	Player	Prize Money
1	M Nichols	£8094
2	P Simpson	5917
3	J Hawksworth	3571
4	G Hanrahan	3378
5	G Emerson	3282

Midland Open Championship

at Kilworth Springs, Leicestershire

1	S Webster	68-68-69—205
2	S Bennett	68-68-70—206
3	F Clark	68-71-68—207

Midland PGA Championship

at The Warwickshire, Little Wooton

1	P Baker	74-69—143
2	J King	72-73—145
	D Eddiford	68-77—145

* *Winner after play-off*

Million Dollar Challenge

at Sun City, Bophuthatswana

1	N Faldo	66-64-73-69—272	$1000000
2	N Price	71-66-70-68—275	250000
3	E Els	68-70-67-72—277	187500
	D Frost	73-67-71-66—277	187500

North Region PGA Championship

at Mottram Hall, Cheshire

1	P Wesselingh	70-68-70—208	£2500
2	J Harrison	74-66-70—210	1900
3	T Rastall	72-73-66—211	1300
	G Vickers	73-71-67—211	1300

PGA Assistants' Championship

at Foxhills

1	M Plummer	69-70-70-69—278
2	M Deal	72-68-72-67—279
3	C Smellie	75-73-69-69—286

Gene Sarazen World Open Championship

at The Legends at Chateau Elan, Atlanta Georgia

1	E Els	67-73-68-65—273	$350000
2	F Funk	69-69-66-72—276	200000
3	M Calcavecchia	69-73-68-70—280	106400
	T Siekmann	67-69-71-73—280	106400

Scottish Assistants' Championship

at Newmachar, Aberdeen

1	S Henderson	68-74-71-70—283	£800
2	E McIntosh	73-71-72-68—284	587
3	B Moffat	74-73-68-71—286	460

Scottish Professional Championship

at Dalmahoy, Edinburgh

1	A Coltart*	73-71-69-68—281	£10000
2	G Orr	74-66-68-73—281	7000
3	D Robertson	70-69-72-72—283	4250
	C Elliott	70-70-70-73—283	4250

Southern Professional Championship

at Slinfold Park, Sussex

1	R Edwards	69-66-65—200
2	D Williams	65-70-69—204
3	M Nichols	65-68-73—206

* *Winner after play-off*

South West PGA Championship

at Manor House, Moretonhampstead

1	G Emerson	63-69—129	£825
2	M Wiggett	68-66—134	700
3	M Plummer	68-67—135	550
	G Ryall	69-66—135	550

Sunderland of Scotland Masters

at Westerwood, Cumbernauld, Dunbarton

1	R Weir	76-68-71-67—282
2	R Dinsdale	76-69-68-70—283
3	C Gillies	74-73-71-67—285

Sunningdale Foursomes

at Sunningdale

Semi-Finals

D Howell and G Harris beat M King and J Healey 5 and 3
S Webster and A Wall beat J Bunch and J Farmer 1 hole

Final

S Webster and A Wall beat D Howell and G Harris 2 holes

Welsh Professional Championship

at Northop, Clwyd

1	M Plummer	68-65—133
2	P Price	69-66—135
3	M Litton	67-70—137
	B Rimmer	67-70—137

West of England PGA Championship

at Lanhydrock and St Mellion, Cornwall

1	M Stanford	63-73—136	£1000
2	R Troake	70-68—138	675
	S Hurley	67-71—138	675

West Region PGA Championship

at Puckrup Hall, Tewkesbury

1	S Little	70-68-67—205
2	D Ray	71-64-71—206
3	K Aitken	69-70-70—209
	M Stanford	70-67-72—209

PGA European Seniors Tour, 1994

Final Order of Merit

Pos	Name	Prize Money £
1	John Morgan (Eng)	57209
2	Brian Huggett (Wal)	48678
3	Tommy Horton (Eng)	45716
4	Malcolm Gregson (Eng)	41189
5	Antonio Garrido (Sp)	41102
6	Liam Higgins (Ire)	37470
7	Renato Campagnoli (Ita)†	32590
8	Brian Waites (Eng)	28943
9	Neil Coles (Eng)	25415
10	Doug Dalziel (US)	23083
11	David Snell (Eng)	19654
12	Alberto Croce (Ita)†	17102
13	John Fourie (SA)	15570
14	David Butler (Eng)	15415
15	Bernard Hunt (Eng)	15361
16	Bobby Verwey (SA)	15099
17	José Maria Roca (Sp)	13904
18	Peter Butler (Eng)	13822
19	David Jimenez (US)	12670
20	Vincent Tshabalala (SA)	11887
21	David Creamer (Eng)	11217
22	Tony Grubb (Eng)	10805
23	Chick Evans (US)	10480
24	Michael Murphy (Ire)	9787
25	Phil Ferranti (US)	9358
26	Roger Fidler (Eng)	9074
27	Bryan Carter (Eng)	8559
28	Terry Squires (Eng)†	8504
29	Norman Drew (N. Ire)	8055
30	David Huish (Sco)	7788
31	Ramon Sota (Sp)	7772
32	Joe Carr (US)	7709
33	Francisco Abreu (Sp)	7613
34	Hugh Boyle (Ire)	7590
35	Rafe Botts (US)	7525
36	Tony Coveney (Ire)	6615
37	Hedley Muscroft (Eng)	6578
38	David Talbot (Eng)	6557
39	Hugh Inggs (SA)	6556
40	Michael Damiano (Fr)	6450

Tour Results

Senior British Open Championship
at Royal Lytham & St Annes

1	T Wargo	73-68-68-71—280	£36650
2	B Charles	70-69-72-71—282	18950
	D Dalziel	75-66-71-70—282	18950
4	G Player	73-69-71-74—287	10165
	B Huggett	78-68-70-71—287	10165
6	J Morgan	71-73-71-73—288	7150
	A Palmer	69-74-71-74—288	7150
8	T Horton	71-72-71-75—289	5500
9	B Dunk	73-69-74-74—290	4665
	L Higgins	69-75-76-70—290	4665

†*Denotes 1994 Qualifying School Graduate*

Lawrence Batley Seniors

at Woodsome Hall, Huddersfield

1	J Morgan	67-65-70—202	£10170
2	JM Roca	69-69-68—206	6800
3	T Horton	69-68-70—207	3445
	P Butler	71-64-72—207	3445

Belfast Telegraph Irish Seniors Masters

at Malone GC, Belfast

1	T Horton*	68-71-69—208	£9665
2	R Campagnoli	67-70-71—208	6430
3	M Gregson	70-69-72—211	2790
	L Higgins	70-70-71—211	2790
	P Butler	73-69-69—211	2790
	A Garrido	73-70-68—211	2790

D-Day Seniors Open

at Omaha Beach, Normandy, France

1	B Waites	69-66-71—206	£8330
2	A Garrido	72-69-71—212	5550
3	T Horton	72-73-68—213	2815
	T Grubb	71-69-73—213	2815

Forte PGA Seniors Championship

at Old Course, Sunningdale

1	J Morgan	68-68-67—203	£12500
2	D Creamer	70-66-69—205	8330
3	R Campagnoli	72-69-65—206	4700

La Manga Club Spanish Seniors Open

at La Manga, Spain

1	B Huggett*	72-74-69—215	£16660
2	D Snell	69-78-68—215	8680
	M Gregson	73-77-65—215	8680

Joe Powell Memorial Seniors Classic

at Collingtree Park, Northants

1	L Higgins	70-70-70—210	£8330
2	M Gregson	71-71-72—214	5550
3	N Coles	69-72-75—216	3130

Northern Electric Seniors

at Slaley Hall, Northumberland

1	J Morgan*	74-71-74—219	£8330
2	B Hunt	70-76-73—219	5550
3	T Horton	76-72-72—220	2815
	L Higgins	73-71-76—220	2815

* *Winner after play-off*

St Pierre Seniors Classic

at St Pierre, Chepstow

1	T Horton	71-71-70—212	£8330
2	B Huggett	73-70-72—215	5550
3	N Coles	71-71-74—216	3130

Shell Scottish Seniors Open

at Royal Aberdeen

1	A Garrido	66-68-67—201	£16660
2	N Coles	73-65-68—206	8680
	R Campagnoli	72-68-66—206	8680

The Tandem Open

at Stockley Park, Heathrow

1	M Gregson	69-67-69—205	£8330
2	J Morgan	71-70-65—206	4340
	L Higgins	70-67-69—206	4340

Zurich Senior Pro-Am Lexus Trophy

at Breitenloo, Zurich, Switzerland

1	L Higgins	67-66-67—200	£7850
2	A Garrido	68-64-71—203	5200
3	N Coles	67-68-71—206	3000

US PGA Tour, 1994

Money List

Pos	Name	Prize Money $	Pos	Name	Prize Money $
1	Nick Price	1499927	51	Jim Gallagher Jr	325976
2	Greg Norman	1330307	52	Vijay Singh	325959
3	Mark McCumber	1208209	53	Dave Barr	314885
4	Tom Lehman	1031144	54	Gil Morgan	309690
5	Fuzzy Zoeller	1016804	55	Jay Don Blake	309351
6	Loren Roberts	1015671	56	Scott Simpson	307884
7	José Maria Olazabal	969900	57	Dicky Pride	305769
8	Cory Pavin	906305	58	Neal Lancaster	305038
9	Jeff Maggert	814475	59	Jeff Sluman	301178
10	Hale Irwin	814436	60	Mike Sullivan	298586
11	Scott Hoch	804559	61	Donnie Hammond	295436
12	Steve Lowery	794048	62	Steve Elkington	294943
13	Mike Springer	770717	63	Brian Henninger	294075
14	Bob Estes	765360	64	Steve Pate	291651
15	Phil Mickelson	748316	65	Clark Dennis	289065
16	John Huston	731499	66	Brett Ogle	284495
17	Bill Glasson	689110	67	Fred Funk	281905
18	Brad Bryant	687803	68	Chip Beck	281131
19	Ernie Els	684440	69	Greg Kraft	279901
20	David Frost	671683	70	Nolan Henke	278419
21	Ben Crenshaw	659252	71	Duffy Waldorf	274971
22	Tom Kite	658689	72	DA Weibring	255757
23	Fred Couples	625654	73	Gene Sauers	250654
24	Brad Faxon	612847	74	Ted Tryba	246481
25	Jay Haas	593386	75	Paul Goydos	241107
26	Kenny Perry	585941	76	Guy Boros	240775
27	Rick Fehr	573963	77	Russ Cochran	239827
28	Bruce Lietzke	564926	78	Jim Furyk	236603
29	Hal Sutton	540162	79	Jim McGovern	227764
30	Mark Calcavecchia	533201	80	Bob Lohr	225048
31	Mark Brooks	523285	81	Johnny Miller	225000
32	Craig Stadler	474831	82	Gary Hallberg	224965
33	Davis Love III	474219	83	Nick Faldo	221146
34	David Edwards	458845	84	Mike Hulbert	221007
35	Lee Janzen	442588	85	Chris Dimarco	216839
36	Andrew Magee	431041	86	Mark O'Meara	214070
37	John Cook	429725	87	Colin Montgomerie	213828
38	Kirk Triplett	422171	88	Peter Jacobsen	211762
39	Lennie Clements	416880	89	Bobby Wadkins	208358
40	Mike Heinen	390963	90	Keith Clearwater	203549
41	Curtis Strange	390881	91	Wayne Levi	200476
42	Larry Mize	386029	92	David Ogrin	199199
43	Tom Watson	380378	93	Mark Carnevale	192653
44	Robert Gamez	380353	94	Tom Purtzer	187307
45	Glen Day	357236	95	Jim Thorpe	185714
46	Craig Parry	354602	96	Dave Stockton Jr	185209
47	Blaine McCallister	351554	97	Scott Verplank	183015
48	Billy Andrade	342208	98	Brian Kamm	181884
49	John Daly	340034	99	Mike Standly	179850
50	Steve Stricker	334409	100	David Feherty	178501

Tour Results

Anheuser-Busch Classic

at Kingsmill G&CC, Williamsburg, Virginia

1	M McCumber	67-69-65-66—267	$193000
2	G Day	64-68-72-66—270	118800
3	J Leonard	67-69-67-69—272	74800

AT&T National Pro-Am

at Pebble Beach, Spyglass Hill, Poppy Hills, California

1	J Miller	68-72-67-74—281	$225000
2	J Maggert	68-72-72-70—282	82500
	C Pavin	69-71-71-71—282	82500
	K Triplett	69-74-67-72—282	82500
	T Watson	69-67-72-74—282	82500

BC Open

at En-Joie GC, Endicott, New York

1	M Sullivan	65-67-68-66—266	$162000
2	J Sluman	63-68-67-72—270	97200
3	B Claar	68-68-65-71—272	52200
	M Hulbert	67-67-68-70—272	52200

BellSouth Classic

at Atlanta CC, Marietta, Georgia

1	J Daly	69-64-69-72—274	$216000
2	N Henke	70-67-69-69—275	105600
	B Henninger	68-67-69-71—275	105600

Bob Hope Chrysler Classic

at Bermuda Dunes, California

1	S Hoch	66-62-70-66-70—334	$198000
2	F Zoeller	70-67-66-68-66—337	82133
	I Clements	67-69-61-72-68—337	82133
	J Gallagher Jr	66-67-74-62-68—337	82133

Buick Classic

at Westchester CC, Harrison, New York

1	L Janzen	69-69-64-66—268	$216000
2	E Els	68-66-69-68—271	129600
3	B Faxon	70-68-70-66—274	69600
	J Haas	68-70-69-67—274	69600

Buick Invitational

at Torrey Pines, San Diego, California

1	C Stadler	67-67-68-66—268	$198000
2	S Lowery	67-68-66-68—269	118800
3	P Mickelson	68-69-69-64—270	74800

Buick Open

at Warwick Hills G&CC, Grand Blanc, Michigan

1	F Couples	72-65-65-68—270	$198000
2	C Pavin	66-65-70-71—272	118800
3	G Kraft	71-72-67-66—276	57200
	C Strange	71-70-67-68—276	57200
	S Pate	71-67-69-69—276	57200

Buick Southern Open

at Pine Mountain, Georgia

1	S Elkington	66-66-68—200	$144000
2	S Rintoul	70-65-70—205	86400
3	B Bryant	70-68-69—207	54400

Canadian Open

at Glen Abbey GC, Oakville, Ontario

1	N Price	67-72-68-68—275	234000
2	M Calcavecchia	67-71-71-67—276	140400
3	T Lehman	69-69-70-69—277	88400

Canon Greater Hartford Open

at TPC at River Highlands, Cromwell, Connecticut

1	D Frost	65-68-66-69—268	$216000
2	G Norman	69-65-66-69—269	129600
3	D Barr	68-70-68-65—271	57600
	C Pavin	65-73-66-67—271	57600
	D Stockton Jr	66-66-67-72—271	57600
	S Stricker	70-67-67-67—271	57600

Deposit Guaranty Classic

at Annandale, Madison, Mississippi

1	B Henninger*	67-68—135	$126000
2	D Sullivan	66-69—135	75600
3	G Boros	69-67—136	31570
	S Hoch	69-67—136	31570
	C Dimarco	70-66—136	31570
	D Stockton Jr	69-67—136	31570
	T Armour III	71-65—136	31570

Reduced to two rounds due to bad weather

Doral Ryder Open

at Doral Resort & CC, Miami, Florida

1	J Huston	70-68-70-66—274	$252000
2	B Andrade	70-68-66-73—277	123200
	B Bryant	70-69-69-69—277	123200

Federal Express St Jude Classic

at TPC at Southwind, Memphis, Tennessee

1	D Pride*	66-67-67-67—267	$225000
	H Sutton	67-68-68-64—267	110000
	G Sauers	67-66-68-66—267	110000

* *Winner after play-off*

Freeport–McMoran Classic

at English Turn, New Orleans, Louisiana

1	B Crenshaw	69-68-68-68—273	$216000
2	JM Olazabal	63-74-70-69—276	129600
3	S Torrance	67-71-67-73—278	81600

Greater Milwaukee Open

at Brown Deer GC, Milwaukee, Wisconsin

1	M Springer	69-67-65-67—268	$180000
2	L Roberts	70-63-68-68—269	108000
3	T Purtzer	70-69-67-64—270	48000
	J Sindelar	67-68-66-69—270	48000
	B Estes	67-66-65-72—270	48000
	M Calcavecchia	67-68-64-71—270	48000

GTE Byron Nelson Classic

at TPC at Las Colinas, Irving, Texas

1	N Lancaster*	67-65—132	$216000
	T Byrum	68-64—132	72000
	M Carnevale	65-67—132	72000
	D Edwards	67-65—132	72000
	Y Mizumaki	66-66—132	72000
	D Ogrin	64-68—132	72000

Reduced to 36 holes due to bad weather

Hardee's Classic

at Oakwood CC, Coal Valley, Illinois

1	M McCumber	66-67-65-67—265	$180000
2	K Perry	67-66-65-68—266	108000
3	M Donald	70-66-64-67—267	58000
	D Frost	68-67-67-65—267	58000

HEB Texas Open

at Oak Hills, San Antonio, Texas

1	B Estes	62-65-68-70—265	$180000
2	G Morgan	66-68-65-67—266	108000
3	D Pooley	69-65-65-68—267	48000

Honda Classic

at Weston Hills, Fort Lauderdale, Florida

1	N Price	70-67-73-66—276	198000
2	C Parry	68-73-69-67—277	118800
3	B Chamblee	67-68-72-71—278	74800

* *Winner after play-off*

The International

at Castle Pines GC, Castle Pines, Colorado

Format: Modified Stableford with points awarded as follows – albatross +8; eagle +5; birdie +2; par 0; bogey –1; double bogey or worse –3

1	S Lowery*	7-14-5-9—35	$252000
2	R Fehr	10-5-9-11—35	151200
3	D Waldorf	7-6-8-13—34	95200

Kemper Open

at TPC at Avenal, Potomac, Maryland

1	M Brooks	65-68-69-69—271	$234000
2	DA Weibring	70-68-68-68—274	114400
	B Wadkins	68-67-65-74—274	114400

K-Mart Greater Greensboro Open

at Forest Oaks CC, Greensboro, North Carolina

1	M Springer	64-69-70-72—275	$270000
2	E Humenik	72-65-73-68—278	112000
	H Irwin	65-73-71-69—278	112000
	B Bryant	68-71-68-71—278	112000

Las Vegas Invitational

at Summerlin, Las Vegas

1	B Lietzke	66-67-68-66-65—332	$270000
2	R Gamez	66-70-64-69-64—333	162000
3	P Mickelson	70-66-66-70-63—335	87000
	B Andrade	66-68-67-67-67—335	87000

Lincoln–Mercury Kapalua International

at Kapalua, Maui, Hawaii

1	F Couples	66-71-72-70—279	$180000
2	B Gilder	70-67-71-73—281	104000
3	T Lehman	66-69-76-72—283	65000

MCI Heritage Classic

at Harbour Town, Hilton Head, South Carolina

1	H Irwin	68-65-65-68—266	$225000
2	G Norman	67-66-67-68—268	135000
3	L Roberts	69-70-68-62—269	85000

Memorial Tournament

at Muirfield Village, Dublin, Ohio

1	T Lehman	67-67-67-67—268	$270000
2	G Norman	70-69-70-64—273	162000
3	J Cook	67-69-69-71—276	102000

* *Winner after play-off*

Mercedes Championship

(Formerly Tournament of Champions)
at La Costa, Carlsbad, California

1	P Mickelson*	70-68-70-68—276	$180000
2	F Couples	69-70-69-68—276	120000
3	T Kite	73-68-69-68—278	80000

Motorola Western Open

at Cog Hill, Lemont, Illinois

1	N Price	67-67-72-71—277	$216000
2	G Kraft	67-70-68-73—278	129600
3	S Hoch	67-69-73-70—279	62400
	M Calcavecchia	67-70-72-70—279	62400
	B Glasson	66-70-72-71—279	62400

NEC World Series of Golf

at Firestone CC, Akron, Ohio

1	JM Olazabal	66-67-69-67—269	$360000
2	S Hoch	71-64-65-70—270	216000
3	B Faxon	69-68-65-69—271	116000
	S Lowery	67-66-66-72—271	116000

The Nestlé Invitational

at Bay Hill, Orlando, Florida

1	L Roberts	70-70-68-67—275	$216000
2	N Price	66-72-68-70—276	89600
	V Singh	68-69-68-71—276	89600
	F Zoeller	72-68-67-69—276	89600

New England Classic

at Pleasant Valley CC, Sutton, Massachusetts

1	K Perry	67-66-70-65—268	$180000
2	D Feherty	65-69-68-67—269	108000
3	E Fiori	66-66-70-70—272	68000

Nissan Los Angeles Open

at Riviera GC, Pacific Palisades, California

1	C Pavin	67-64-72-68—271	$180000
2	F Couples	67-67-68-71—273	108000
3	C Beck	66-71-72-68—277	68000

Northern Telecom Open

at Tucson National and Starr Pass, Tucson, Arizona

1	A Magee	69-67-67-67—270	$198000
2	JD Blake	68-69-67-68—272	72600
	L Roberts	68-68-72-64—272	72600
	V Singh	67-68-72-65—272	72600
	S Stricker	68-69-68-67—272	72600

Phoenix Open
at TPC Scottsdale, Phoenix, Arizona

1	B Glasson	68-68-68-64—268	$216000
2	B Estes	66-68-69-68—271	129600
3	J Maggert	70-68-69-65—272	62400
	B McCallister	67-69-69-67—272	62400
	M Springer	68-68-71-65—272	62400

The Players Championship
at TPC at Sawgrass, Ponte Vedra, Florida

1	G Norman	63-67-67-67—264	$450000
2	F Zoeller	66-67-68-67—268	270000
3	J Maggert	65-69-69-68—271	170000
4	H Irwin	67-70-70-69—276	120000
5	N Faldo	67-69-68-73—277	100000

Shell Houston Open
at The Woodlands, Texas

1	M Heinen	67-68-69-68—272	$234000
2	J Maggert	70-66-68-71—275	97066
	H Sutton	68-70-68-69—275	97066
	T Kite	68-65-71-71—275	97066

Southwestern Bell Colonial
at Colonial CC, Fort Worth, Texas

1	N Price*	65-70-67-64—266	$252000
2	S Simpson	66-65-64-71—266	151600
3	H Irwin	64-70-68-65—267	95200

Tour Championship
at The Olympic Club, San Francisco

1	M McCumber	66-71-69-68—274	$540000
2	F Zoeller	71-69-66-68—274	324000
3	B Bryant	72-68-67-68—275	207000

United Airlines Hawaiian Open
at Waialae CC, Honolulu

1	B Ogle	66-66-69-68—269	$216000
2	D Love III	68-60-71-71—270	129600
3	J Huston	70-68-67-67—272	81600

Walt Disney World Oldsmobile Classic
at Lake Buena Vista, Florida

1	R Fehr	63-70-68-68—269	$198000
2	C Stadler	68-66-67-70—271	96800
	F Zoeller	66-70-69-66—271	96800

* *Winner after play-off*

Official Tour Statistics, 1994

Scoring Leaders

		Rds	Avg
1	Greg Norman	63	68.81
2	Fred Couples	51	69.28
3	Nick Price	60	69.39
4	Tom Lehman	81	69.46
5	Mark McCumber	76	69.56
6	Loren Roberts	77	69.61
7	Corey Pavin	68	69.63
8	Phil Mickelson	65	69.66
9	Hale Irwin	74	69.72
10	Bob Estes	95	69.78

Putting Leaders

		Rds	Avg
1	Loren Roberts	77	1.737
2	Ben Crenshaw	86	1.739
3	David Frost	78	1.742
4	Phil Mickelson	65	1.744
	Mark Wurtz	81	1.744
6	Greg Norman	63	1.747
7	Corey Pavin	68	1.749
8	Blaine McCallister	95	1.750
9	Greg Kraft	86	1.751
10	Steve Stricker	93	1.752

Greens in Regulation

		Rds	%
1	Bill Glasson	75	73.0
2	Fuzzy Zoeller	73	72.8
3	Hal Sutton	97	72.2
4	Mark McCumber	76	71.3
5	Dan Forsman	68	71.2
6	Dave Barr	94	70.9
	Bob Estes	95	70.9
8	Tom Lehman	81	70.8
9	Three players tied with		70.6

Sand Saves

		Rds	%
1	Corey Pavin	68	65.4
2	Ben Crenshaw	86	63.1
3	Stan Utley	73	62.8
4	Kirk Triplett	90	61.6
5	Brian Kamm	94	61.4
6	Bob Estes	95	60.4
	Payne Stewart	76	60.4
8	Scott Hoch	94	60.3
	Richard Zokol	74	60.3
10	John Inman	101	59.9

Driving Distance

		Rds	Yds
1	Davis Love III	91	283.8
2	Dennis Paulson	77	283.0
3	Fred Couples	51	279.9
4	Todd Barranger	67	279.1
5	Robert Gamez	76	278.4
6	Kelly Gibson	93	277.5
	Nick Price	60	277.5
8	Bill Glasson	75	277.1
	Greg Norman	63	277.1
10	Mike Heinen	79	275.3

Driving Accuracy

		Rds	%
1	David Edwards	82	81.6
2	Fred Funk	105	80.1
3	John Mahaffey	75	79.0
	Doug Tewell	84	79.0
5	Larry Mize	75	78.8
6	Hale Irwin	74	78.0
7	David Ogrin	90	77.9
8	Bruce Fleisher	82	77.7
	Tom Garner	56	77.7
10	DA Weibring	63	77.6

US Senior PGA Tour, 1994

Money List

Pos	Name	Prize Money $	Pos	Name	Prize Money $
1	Dave Stockton	1402519	51	Dick Lotz	167152
2	Ray Floyd	1382762	52	Rives McBee	166177
3	Jim Albus	1237128	53	Dick Hendrickson	153155
4	Lee Trevino	1202369	54	Gay Brewer	151314
5	Jim Colbert	1012115	55	Don January	147976
6	Tom Wargo	1005344	56	Don Bies	137185
7	Jim Dent	950891	57	Larry Mowry	135923
8	Bob Murphy	855862	58	Bobby Nichols	131695
9	Larry Gilbert	848544	59	Harold Henning	126894
10	George Archer	717578	60	Miller Barber	126327
11	Simon Hobday	634721	61	Bill Hall	125352
12	Jay Sigel	634130	62	Bob Smith	123957
13	Isao Aoki	632975	63	Jim Ferree	119963
14	Jimmy Powell	588378	64	Marion Heck	110097
15	JC Snead	584864	65	Bruce Crampton	103860
16	Mike Hill	580621	66	Joe Jiménez	103106
17	Chi Chi Rodriguez	571598	67	Robert Zimmerman	82882
18	Dale Douglass	543886	68	Robert Gaona	74873
19	Kermit Zarley	538274	69	Al Geiberger	72729
20	Dave Eichelberger	535087	70	Randy Petri	70669
21	Jack Kiefer	532467	71	Babe Hiskey	68720
22	Rocky Thompson	529073	72	Gene Littler	66592
23	Bob Charles	511737	73	Richard Bassett	62869
24	Graham Marsh	492402	74	Mike Joyce	58155
25	Jerry McGee	398219	75	Dave Hill	57757
26	Tommy Aaron	397515	76	Rod Curl	57176
27	Gibby Gilbert	352342	77	Fred Ruiz	52986
28	Dewitt Weaver	318387	78	George Shortridge	50014
29	Tom Weiskopf	315024	79	Bob Carson	45528
30	Gary Player	309776	80	Bob Reith	45078
31	John Paul Cain	291868	81	Ken Still	44991
32	Bob Dickson	254532	82	Bob Goalby	44904
33	Walter Zembriski	246412	83	Billy Casper	43970
34	Jack Nicklaus	239278	84	Bob Betley	42683
35	Tom Shaw	229119	85	Lee Elder	42070
36	Terry Dill	224885	86	Bob Wynn	40523
37	Tony Jacklin	221384	87	Bruce Devlin	40224
38	Larry Laoretti	220001	88	Al Kelley	39304
39	Charles Coody	219295	89	Bob Panasik	39020
40	Tommy Aycock	212660	90	Charles Sifford	35325
41	Richard Rhyan	210183	91	Arnold Palmer	34471
42	Orville Moody	208490	92	Ed Sneed	30256
43	Harry Toscano	207508	93	Walter Morgan	27444
44	Dick Goetz	202657	94	Lou Graham	24153
45	Homero Blancas	193550	95	Don Massengale	23595
46	Larry Ziegler	185644	96	Bruce Summerhays	20711
47	Bob Brue	184693	97	Ron Skiles*	18926
48	Ben Smith	180943	98	Tommy Horton	18119
49	Butch Baird	177031	99	Bob Irving	16958
50	Calvin Peete	175432	100	Gene Borek	16475

* *Non-Tour Member*

Tour Results

15th US Senior Open

at Pinehurst No 2, North Carolina

1	S Hobday	66-67-66-75—274	$145000
2	J Albus	66-69-66-74—275	63418
	G Marsh	68-68-69-70—275	63418

Ameritech Senior Open

at Stonebridge, Aurora, Illinois

1	JP Cain	66-67-69—202	$112500
2	S Hobday	66-69-68—203	60000
	J Colbert	67-67-69—203	60000

Bank of Boston Senior Classic

at Nashawutuc, Boston, Massachusetts

1	J Albus	67-66-70—203	$112500
2	B Brue	67-73-65—205	60000
	R Floyd	69-67-69—205	60000

Bank One Senior Classic

at Kierney Hills, Lexington

1	I Aoki	69-64-69—202	$82500
2	CC Rodriguez	71-68-66—205	48400
3	J Dent	69-72-66—207	33000
	G Brewer	68-69-70—207	33000
	J Kiefer	69-67-71—207	33000

Bell Atlantic Classic

at Chester Valley, Philadelphia

1	L Trevino	71-67-68—206	$105000
2	M Hill	69-71-68—208	61600
3	T Aaron	71-68-71—210	50400

BellSouth Senior Classic at Opryland

at Springhouse, Nashville, Tennessee

1	L Trevino	67-65-67—199	$157500
2	D Stockton	62-69-69—200	84000
	J Albus	66-68-66—200	84000

Brickyard Crossing Championship

at Brickyard Crossing, Indianapolis

1	I Aoki	66-67—133	$105000
2	J Powell	68-66—134	56000
	T Wargo	68-66—134	56000

Reduced to two rounds due to bad weather

Bruno's Memorial Classic
at Greystone, Birmingham, Alabama

1	J Dent	66-68-67—201	$150000
2	L Gilbert	67-66-70—203	73333
	B Charles	66-66-71—203	73333
	K Zarley	67-68-68—203	73333

Burnet Senior Classic
at Bunker Hills, Minneapolis

1	D Stockton	68-66-69—203	$167000
2	J Albus	69-66-69—204	92400
3	G Archer	67-69-73—209	53760
	J Dent	68-72-69—209	53760
	D Eichelberger	71-72-68—209	53760
	L Gilbert	69-73-67—209	53760
	CC Rodriguez	73-67-69—209	53760

Cadillac NFL Classic
at Upper Montclair, Clifton, New Jersey

1	R Floyd	64-68-74—207	$135000
2	B Murphy	70-69-68—207	72000
	G Player	71-67-69—207	72000

Chrysler Cup
(United States *v* Internationals Team Match)
at TPC Prestancia, Sarasota, Florida

Team
United States 1024 (-56), International 1022 (-58)

Individual

1	G Archer*	68-63-72—203	$55000
2	S Hobday	67-67-69—203	39000
3	B Charles	67-70-69—205	26000
	T Weiskopf	71-67-67—205	26000

Doug Sanders Celebrity Classic
at Deerwood, Kingswood, Texas

1	T Wargo	71-66-72—209	$75000
2	B Murphy	75-69-66—210	45000
3	CC Rodriguez	69-69-73—211	37000

First of America Classic
at ADA, Michigan

1	T Jacklin	68-68—136	$97500
2	D Stockton	67-70—137	57200
3	L Trevino	72-66—138	42900
	J Albus	66-72—138	42900

* *Winner after play-off*

Ford Senior Players Championship
at TPC at Dearborn, Michigan

1	D Stockton	66-66-71-68—271	$210000
2	J Albus	67-69-72-69—277	123200
3	I Aoki	67-70-73-68—278	84000
	R Floyd	72-68-71-67—278	84000
	L Trevino	66-69-74-69—278	84000

Franklin Quest Championship
at Park Meadows, Utah

1	T Weiskopf*	68-67-69—204	$75000
2	D Stockton	68-66-70—204	44000
3	J Kiefer	68-69-68—205	33000
	B Murphy	69-66-70—205	33000

GTE Northwest Classic
at Inglewood, Kenmore, Washington

1	S Hobday*	70-69-70—209	$82500
2	J Albus	66-75-68—209	48400
3	L Laoretti	72-70-69—211	33000
	T Jacklin	67-73-71—211	33000
	J Sigel	72-68-71—211	33000

GTE Suncoast Senior Classic
at TPC at Tampa Bay, Lutz, Florida

1	R Thompson	73-67-61—201	$105000
2	R Floyd	70-66-66—202	61600
3	L Trevino	69-68-66—203	50400

GTE West Classic
at Ojai Valley Inn, California

1	J Sigel*	70-66-62—198	$82500
2	J Colbert	62-64-72—198	48400
3	L Laoretti	65-68-66—199	36300
	B Murphy	67-66-66—199	36300

Intellinet Challenge
at The Vineyards, Naples, Florida

1	M Hill	69-69-63—201	$75000
2	T Wargo	71-65-68—204	44000
3	G Archer	67-67-71—205	30000

Kaanapali Classic
at North Course, Royal Kaanapali, Maui, Hawaii

1	B Murphy	62-67-66—195	$82500
2	J Kiefer	66-66-65—197	48400
3	D Douglass	68-66-65—199	39600

* *Winner after play-off*

Kroger Senior Classic
at The Golf Centre, Kings Island

1	J Colbert	66-64-69—199	£127500
2	R Floyd	68-68-65—201	74800
3	M Hill	68-70-67—205	46750
	R Thompson	66-70-69—205	46750
	D Weaver	65-71-69—205	46750
	B Murphy	71-65-69—205	46750

Las Vegas Senior Classic
at TPC Las Vegas, Nevada

1	R Floyd	68-70-65—203	$135000
2	T Wargo	71-67-68—206	80100
3	J Dent	70-66-71—207	65700

Liberty Mutual Legends of Golf
at Barton Creek, Austin, Texas

1	D Douglass and C Coody	63-61-64—188	$200000 per team
2	CC Rodriguez and J Dent	63-63-63—189	82500
	B Murphy and J Colbert	65-61-63—189	82500

Mercedes Championship
at La Costa, Carlsbad, California

1	J Nicklaus	73-69-69-68—279	$100000
2	B Murphy	71-70-67-72—280	60000
3	D Stockton	67-72-69-75—283	48000

Nationwide Championship
at CC of the South, Apharetta, Georgia

1	D Stockton	67-63-68—198	$172500
2	B Murphy	67-64-68—199	101200
3	J Albus	66-73-64—203	75900
	J Dent	72-64-67—203	75900

Northville Long Island Classic
at Meadow Brook, Jericho, New York

1	L Trevino	66-69-65—200	$97500
2	J Colbert	70-72-65—207	57200
3	J Sigel	68-68-72—208	46800

Painewebber Invitational
at TPC at Piper Glen, Charlotte, North Carolina

1	L Trevino	70-65-68—203	$112500
2	J Colbert	68-70-66—204	60000
	J Powell	69-66-69—204	60000

Quicksilver Classic

at Quicksilver, Pittsburgh, Pennsylvania

1	D Eichelberger	71-67-71—209	$157500
2	H Blancas	71-71-69—211	84000
	R Floyd	69-72-70—211	84000

Raley's Senior Gold Rush

at Rancho Murieta CC, Sacramento, California

1	B Murphy*	69-71-68—208	$97500
2	D Eichelberger	68-69-71—208	57200
3	JC Snead	71-76-63—210	42900
	J Albus	69-72-69—210	42900

Ralphs Senior Classic

at Rancho Park, Los Angeles, California

1	J Kiefer	69-65-63—197	$112500
2	D Douglass	70-67-61—198	66000
3	J Colbert	68-67-66—201	54000

Royal Caribbean Senior Classic

at The Links, Key Biscayne, Florida

1	L Trevino*	66-73-66—205	$120000
2	K Zarley	71-66-68—205	70400
3	JC Snead	71-66-70—207	52800
	B Charles	70-67-70—207	52800

Senior Tour Championship

at Dunes Golf & Beach Club, Myrtle Beach, South Carolina

1	R Floyd*	67-73-67-66—273	$240000
2	J Albus	64-71-66-72—273	141000
3	J Sigel	69-72-71-63—275	115000

Southwestern Bell Classic

at Loch Lloyd, Belton, Missouri

1	J Colbert	68-63-65—196	$105000
2	I Aoki	69-64-65—198	56000
	L Gilbert	67-66-65—198	56000

The Tradition at Desert Mountain

at Desert Mountain, Scottsdale, Arizona

1	R Floyd*	65-70-68-68—271	$127500
2	D Douglass	68-68-69-66—271	74800
3	J Colbert	70-66-68-70—274	61200

* *Winner after play-off*

Transamerica Senior Championship

at Silverado, Napa, California

1	K Zarley*	70-68-66—204	$90000
2	I Aoki	69-72-63—204	52000
3	JC Snead	71-69-66—206	36000
	D Stockton	71-69-66—206	36000
	G Player	68-68-70—206	36000

US PGA Seniors' Championship

at PGA National, Palm Beach Gardens, Florida

1	L Trevino	70-69-70-70—279	$115000
2	J Colbert	68-71-74-67—280	85000
3	R Floyd	69-69-69-75—282	57500
	D Stockton	70-69-71-72—282	57500

The Vantage

at The Dominion CC, San Antonio, Texas

1	J Albus	68-67-73—208	$97500
2	L Trevino	71-69-69—209	47666
	G Marsh	72-67-70—209	47666
	G Archer	69-69-71—209	47666

Vantage Championship

at Tanglewood, Clemmons, North Carolina

1	L Gilbert	66-66-66—198	$225000
2	R Floyd	70-64-65—199	132000
3	D Stockton	63-74-64—201	99000
	J Dent	66-66-69—201	99000

Official Tour Statistics, 1994

Scoring Leaders

		Avg
1	Ray Floyd	69.08
2	Dave Stockton	69.41
3	Lee Trevino	69.55
4	Jim Albus	69.85
5	Tom Wargo	69.88
6	George Archer	69.96
7	Isao Aoki	70.03
8	Jim Dent	70.12
9	Jim Colbert	70.15
	Bob Murphy	70.15

Greens in Regulation

		%
1	Ray Floyd	76.0
2	Larry Gilbert	74.9
3	Dave Stockton	74.6
4	Jim Albus	74.4
	Bob Charles	74.4
6	Bob Murphy	74.2
7	Isao Aoki	73.8
8	Tom Weiskopf	73.6
9	Dale Douglass	73.2
10	Jay Sigel	72.9

* *Winner after play-off*

Driving Distance

		Yds
1	Jim Dent	275.5
2	Tom Weiskopf	273.3
3	Jay Sigel	272.0
4	Terry Dill	271.7
5	Rocky Thompson	267.8
6	Ray Floyd	267.1
7	Tommy Aycock	266.6
8	Bob Carson	266.3
9	Jim Albus	265.7
10	JC Snead	264.4

Driving Accuracy

		%
1	Calvin Peete	84.1
2	Charles Sifford	81.8
3	John Paul Cain	81.5
4	Howie Johnson	79.1
5	Walter Zembriski	77.8
6	Bob Charles	77.7
7	Lee Elder	77.4
8	Bob Murphy	77.3
9	Robert Zimmerman	77.2
10	Graham Marsh	77.1

Putting Leaders

		Avg
1	Dave Stockton	1.730
2	Ray Floyd	1.734
3	Jim Colbert	1.739
4	Lee Trevino	1.741
5	Jim Dent	1.744
6	Isao Aoki	1.753
	George Archer	1.753
8	Jim Albus	1.757
9	Tom Wargo	1.758
10	Mike Hill	1.765

Sand Saves

		%
1	Lee Trevino	62.9
2	Chi Chi Rodriguez	61.4
3	Dale Douglass	58.8
4	Tom Weiskopf	58.3
5	Dave Stockton	57.1
6	Bob Murphy	56.6
7	Tommy Aaron	54.7
8	Jim Colbert	54.3
9	Kermit Zarley	54.1
	Simon Hobday	54.1

Australasian Tour, 1994

Heineken Australian Open
at Royal Sydney

1	R Allenby	70-70-70-70—280	Aus $153000
2	B Ogle	69-68-70-74—281	86700
3	P Baker	70-71-68-73—282	57375

Australian Masters
at Huntingdale, Melbourne

1	C Parry	74-70-70-68—282	Aus $135000
2	E Els	70-70-72-73—285	76500
3	P Senior	73-71-74-68—286	43312
	P Teravainen	71-70-75-70—286	43312

New Zealand Open
at Remuera, Auckland

1	C Jones	69-71-65-72—277	NZ $54000
2	F Nobilo	68-68-72-70—278	30600
3	S Conran	70-69-70-71—280	15550
	T Maloney	68-70-70-72—280	15550
	Z Zorkic	67-66-73-74—280	15550

Other Tournaments

Tournament	**Winner**	**Score**	**Prize Aus $**
Air New Zealand Shell Open	S Robinson	70-64-69-71—274	43929
Alfred Dunhill Masters – Bali	J Kay	73-66-66-72—277	83918
Australian PGA Championship, NSW	A Coltart	67-67-77-70—281	36000
Canon Challenge	P Senior	68-67-72-69—276	54000
Coolum Classic, Queensland	M Clayton	69-73-66-69—277	36000
Epson Singapore Open	KH Han	67-69-68-71—275	98287
Floodlink Queensland Open	L Parsons	66-72-75-69—282	36000
Heineken Classic	M Clayton	67-71-71-70—279	54000
Greg Norman's Holden Classic	A Gilligan	71-66-70-67—274	126000
Optus Players' Championship	P Burke	69-67-72-72—280	54000
Victoria Open	P Burke	73-70-68-67—278	36000

Final Order of Merit, 1994

Pos	Player	Prize Aus $
1	Robert Allenby	199645
2	Craig Parry	185920
3	Patrick Burke (US)	182571
4	Michael Clayton	177663
5	Anthony Gilligan	136327
6	Wayne Grady	128896
7	Peter Senior	125531
8	Lucas Parsons	103828
9	Paul Moloney	99397
10	André Stolz	91525
11	Chris Gray	91156
12	Jack Kay (Can)	89716
13	Robert Willis	88104
14	Terry Price	84754
15	Paul Devenport (NZ)	79217
16	Michael Harwood	70420
17	Michael Campbell (NZ)	65132
18	Craig Jones	59105
19	Jack O'Keefe (US)	58274
20	Shane Robinson	57868
21	Peter Teravainen (US)	56412
22	Peter O'Malley	49296
23	Simon Owen (NZ)	48798
24	Peter Fowler	47870
25	Bradley Hughes	46984
26	Steven Conran	43892
27	Grant Moorhead (NZ)	43583
28	Leith Wastle	41371
29	Don Fardon	40211
30	Glenn Joyner	38441
31	Rob Whitlock	38120
32	David Iwasaki-Smith	35740
33	Anthony Painter	34299
34	Richard Green	34028
35	Russell Swanson	33265
36	Tim Elliott	31991
37	Stuart Appleby	31747
38	Lyndsay Stephen	31690
39	Stephen Leaney	30735
40	David Ecob	29106
41	Ossie Moore	26970
42	Max Stevens	26540
43	David McKenzie	26170
44	David Podlich	25970
45	Evan Droop	25302
46	Jeffrey Wagner	25208
47	Grant Kenny	25009
48	Matthew King	23773
49	Robert Farley	23328
50	John Senden	23112

Japan Tour, 1994

Japan Open

at Biwako, Shiga Prefecture

1	M Ozaki	68-66-69-67—270	¥18000000
2	D Ishii	70-74-69-70—283	8600000
	H Kase	71-67-71-74—283	8600000

Other Tournaments

Tournament	**Winner**	**Score**	**Prize Yen**
Touken Corporation Cup	C Warren	70-68-70—208	13500000
Daidodrinko Shizuoka Open	T Nakajima*	71-71-69-69—280	18000000
KSB Setonaikai Open	K Takami	70-71-67-73—281	12600000
Descente Classic	B Watts	67-71-69-73—280	14400000
Pocari Sweat Open	Y Mizumaki	72-65-66—203	10800000
Tsuruya Open	T Nakajima*	68-70-70-71—279	18000000
Dunlop Open	M Ozaki	67-68-70-69—274	18000000
Chunichi Crowns	R Mackay	64-67-67-71—269	21600000
Fuji–Sankei Classic	K Muroja	69-70-73-72—284	21600000
PGA Championship	H Goda	66-73-67-73—279	18000000
Pepsi Ube-kosan	T Nakajima	65-67-67-69—268	14440000
Mitsubishi Galant	K Tomori	69-66-70—205	13500000
JCB Classic Sendai	H Kuramoto	71-65-67-68—271	18000000
Sapporo Tokyu Open	Y Mizumaki	65-70-68-74—277	18000000
Yomiuri Sapporo Beer Open	T Watanabe	68-64-67-71—270	18000000
Mizuno Open	B Watts	68-68-73-71—280	18000000
PGA Philanthropy	T Hamilton	74-69-68-67—278	12600000
Yonex Open Hiroshima	M Ozaki	68-74-67-65—274	14000000
Nikkei Cup Pete Nakamura Memorial	T Suzuki	72-67-65-64—268	14400000
NST Niigata Open	P Izumikawa	67-70-70-69—276	10800000
Acom International	N Ozaki	14-2-12-13—+41pts	18000000
Maruman Open	D Ishii	69-71-67-72—279	21600000
KBC Augusta	B Watts	66-67-71-67—271	18000000
PGA Matchplay Chp Unisys Cup	T Hamilton		14400000
Suntory Open	D Ishii	72-68-69-68—277	18000000
Ana Open	M Ozaki	68-68-63-69—268	18000000
Junior Classic	C Franco	65-67-68-72—272	19800000
Tokai Classic	C Pavin	68-69-68-72—277	19800000
Bridgestone Open	B Watts	68-67-67-72—274	21600000
Philip Morris Championship	B Watts	71-66-71-68—276	36000000
Daiwa International	M Ozaki	65-72-70-63—270	30600000
Sumitomo Visa Taiheiyo	M Ozaki	66-69-68-67—270	27000000
Dunlop Phoenix	M Ozaki	66-69-65—201	27000000
Casio World Open	R Gamez	68-66-68-69—271	27000000
Golf Japan Series Hitachi Cup	H Sasaki	68-66-70-66—270	30000000
Daikyo Open	H Kase	69-66-66-67—268	21600000

* *Winner after play-off*

Final Order of Merit

Pos	Player	Prize Yen
1	Masashi Ozaki	215468000
2	Brian Watts	139052710
3	Tsuneyuki Nakajima	115771280
4	Naomichi Ozaki	91685057
5	David Ishii	87271410
6	Todd Hamilton	86960890
7	Eiji Mizoguchi	79771083
8	Hisayuki Sasaki	77077194
9	Nobuo Serizawa	69619200
10	Tsukasa Watanabe	65455698
11	Kiyoshi Murota	63222505
12	Masahiro Kuramoto	62655316
13	Hideki Kase	59781084
14	Yoshinori Mizumaki	56076556
15	Katsuyoshi Tomori	54921414
16	Yoshinori Kaneko	53695686
17	Masayuki Kawamura	52867173
18	Roger Mackay	49896904
19	Hsieh Chin-Sheng	49243852
20	Hiroshi Ueda	44524800

Asian Tour, 1994

Tour Results

Tournament	Winner	Score	Prize Money
Manila Southwoods Philippine Open	C Franco	72-69-68-71—280	$51646
Hong Kong Open	D Frost*	69-69-69-67—274	$49980
Classic Indian Open	E Aubrey	69-70-76-70—285	$33320
Thailand Open	B Jobe	65-72-69-70—276	$49980
Benson and Hedges Malaysian Open	J Haeggman	71-67-72-69—279	$41650
Sampoerna Indonesian Open	F Nobilo	69-67-68-69—273	$41650
Republic of China Open	H Chia-yuh (Am)	70-65-73-68—276	
Maekyung Open	K Jong-Duck*	74-72-70-68—284	$49980
Dunlop Open	M Ozaki	67-68-70-69—274	¥18000000
Sabah Masters, Malaysia	C McClellan*	75-71-71-67—284	$43316

Asia Golf Circuit Order of Merit

Pos	Player	Pts
1	Carlos Franco	827
2	Brandt Jobe	708
3	Jim Rutledge	686
4	Lee Porter	683
5	Emlyn Aubrey	663
6	Mike Tschetter	617
7	Jerry Smith	577
8	Steve Flesch	512
9	Philip Jonas	494
10	Don Walsworth	491

* *Winner after play-off*

South African PGA Tour, 1993–94

Tour Results

South Africa Open Championship
at Durban CC

1	T Johnstone	64-69-69-65—267	R90850
2	E Els	66-70-68-70—274	66125
3	B Fouchee	69-69-69-69—276	34011
	W Westner	69-72-69-66—276	34011

Other Tournaments

Tournament	Winner	Score	Prize Rand
FNB Players Championship	M McNulty	69-68-70-66—273	90850
Zimbabwe Open	T Johnstone	71-68-65-68—273	94800
Bell's Cup	T Johnstone	65-68-68-70—271	82950
Lexington PGA	D Frost	64-67-65-63—259	90850
ICL International	N Price	61-69-65-72—267	79000
South African Masters	C Davison	69-74-68-70—281	79000
Hollard Insurance Royal Swazi Sun Classic	O Uresti	65-73-68-68—274	63200
Mount Edgecombe Trophy	B Vaughan	72-70-70-63—275	79000

Final Order of Merit

Pos	Player	Prize Rand
1	T Johnstone	297358
2	B Vaughan	189452
3	E Els	160410
4	C Davison	156219
5	R Wessels	135517
6	W Westner	127423
7	B Fouchee	107612
8	J Bland	87781
9	I Leggatt	78404
10	O Uresti	76675
11	J Kingston	75737
12	A Pitts	65957
13	H Baiocchi	64556
14	I Hutchings	61181
15	R Goosen	56245

1995 Ping Leaderboard World Rankings

Pos		Name	Nat	Points
1	(5)	Laura Davies	(GB)	338.32
2	(24)	Liselotte Neumann	(Swe)	216.65
3	(30)	Beth Daniel	(US)	189.58
4	(11)	Donna Andrews	(US)	176.42
5	(2)	Betsy King	(US)	175.05
6	(4)	Dottie Mochrie	(US)	171.45
7	(6)	Helen Alfredsson	(Swe)	164.55
8	(1)	Patty Sheehan	(US)	160.17
9	(10)	Tammie Green	(US)	157.98
10	(3)	Brandie Burton	(US)	125.88
11	(13)	Jane Geddes	(US)	121.53
12	(8)	Meg Mallon	(US)	119.53
13	(45)	Kelly Robbins	(US)	118.78
14	(20)	Mayumi Hirase	(Jpn)	114.05
15	(15)	Sherri Steinhauer	(US)	113.91
16	(69)	Elaine Crosby	(US)	103 70
17	(19)	Hiromi Kobayashi	(Jpn)	99.09
18	(18)	Lauri Merten	(US)	96.78
19	(23)	Michelle McGann	(US)	93.21
20	(28)	Deb Richard	(US)	92.05
21	(149)	Jae-Sook Won	(Kor)	89.60
22	(17)	Dawn Coe-Jones	(Can)	89.40
23	(12)	Ayako Okamoto	(Jpn)	84.18
24	(31)	Michiko Hattori	(Jpn)	84.13
25	(39)	Annika Sorenstam	(Swe)	77.38
26	(40)	Pat Bradley	(US)	76.99
27	(59)	Ikuyo Shiotani	(Jpn)	76.20
28	(9)	Trish Johnson	(GB)	76.02
29	(26)	Judy Dickinson	(US)	75.69
30	(78)	Val Skinner	(US)	74.65
31	(72)	Akiko Fukushima	(Jpn)	72.10
32	(7)	Nancy Lopez	(US)	71.82
33	(32)	Toshimi Kimura	(Jpn)	70.95
34	(46)	Kumiko Hiyoshi	(Jpn)	69.30
35	(41)	Corinne Dibnah	(Aus)	67.75
36	(25)	Mayyumi Murai	(Jpn)	62.60
37	(61)	Yuko Moriguchi	(Jpn)	61.70
38	(21)	Rosie Jones	(US)	56.63
39	(236)	Martha Nause	(US)	55.82
40	(76)	Missie McGeorge	(US)	55.68
41	(119)	Nancy Ramsbottom	(US)	55.32
42	(184)	Lisa Kiggens	(US)	55.30
43	(109)	Aiko Hashimoto	(Jpn)	53.25
44	(89)	Chris Johnson	(US)	51.50
45	(57)	Alice Ritzman	(US)	50.59
46	(66)	Lora Fairclough	(GB)	50.50
47	(51)	Marie Laure de Lorenzi	(Fra)	50.25
48	(16)	Juli Inkster	(US)	48.90
49	(—)	Tracy Hanson	(US)	48.60
50	(74)	Young-Me Lee	(Kor)	47.70

Women's Professional Golf European Tour, 1994

Money List

Pos	Name	Prize Money £	Pos	Name	Prize Money £
1	Liselotte Neumann (Swe)	102750	51	Valerie Michaud (Fr)	9777
2	Helen Alfredsson (Swe)	63315	52	Laurette Maritz-Atkins (SA)	9227
3	Laura Davies (Eng)	59384	53	Diane Barnard (Eng)	8893
4	Annika Sorenstam (Swe)	58360	54	Maureen Madill (Ire)	8706
5	Corinne Dibnah (Aus)	57040	55	Jennifer Allmark (Swe)	7643
6	Lora Fairclough (Eng)	44585	56	Allison Shapcott (Eng)	7482
7	Tracy Hanson (US)	44205	57	Debbie Petrizzi (US)	7217
8	Helen Wadsworth (Wal)	41979	58	Rachel Hetherington (Aus)	7198
9	Alison Nicholas (Eng)	38550	59	Sarah Nicklin (Eng)	7111
10	Karina Orum (Den)	34613	60	Mette Hageman (Neth)	7083
11	Sarah Gautrey (Aus)	34547	61	Shoko Yamamoto (Jpn)	6998
12	Florence Descampe (Fr)	31862	62	Isabella Maconi (Ita)	6878
13	Dale Reid (Sco)	31792	63	Mardi Lunn (Aus)	6850
14	Marie Laure De Lorenzi (Fr)	31593	64	Regine Lautens (Swi)	6394
15	Trish Johnson (Eng)	31309	65	Veronique Palli (Fr)	6381
16	Catrin Nilsmark (Swe)	29956	66	Malin Burstrom (Swe)	6370
17	Joanne Morley (Eng)	26636	67	Corinne Soules (Fr)	6095
18	Sofia Gronberg Whitmore (Swe)	26543	68	Petra Rigby (Swe)	5849
19	Kristal Parker (US)	24613	69	Janet Soulsby (Eng)	5731
20	Laura Navarro (Sp)	22870	70	Franca Fehlauer (Ger)	5543
21	Loraine Lambert (Aus)	22393	71	Asa Gottmo (Swe)	5123
22	Susan Moon (US)	22348	72	Catherine Panton-Lewis (Sco)	5116
23	Sandrine Mendiburu (Fr)	22136	73	Karen Davies (Wal)	4916
24	Sally Prosser (Eng)	21969	74	Jean Bartholomew (US)	4865
25	Julie Forbes (Sco)	21379	75	Sara Robinson (Eng)	4811
26	Patricia Maunier (Fr)	20005	76	Maria Bertilskold (Swe)	4593
27	Gillian Stewart (Sco)	19846	77	Sarah Bennett (Eng)	4570
28	Shani Waugh (Aus)	19528	78	Laree Sugg (US)	4539
29	Federica Dassu (Ita)	18700	79	Helen Hopkins (Aus)	4219
30	Penny Grice-Whittaker (Eng)	18557	80	Nicola Moult (Eng)	4081
31	Suzanne Strudwick (Eng)	18156	81	Claire Duffy (Eng)	3965
32	Karine Espinasse (Fr)	16861	82	Tracy Hammond (Eng)	3963
33	Evelyn Orley (Swi)	16422	83	Pernilla Sterner (Swe)	3833
34	Estefanta Knuth (Sp)	16116	84	Marjan De Boer (Neth)	3785
35	Carin Hjalmarsson (Swe)	15675	85	Lara Tadiotto (Bel)	3779
36	Susan Hodge (Eng)	15225	86	Kitrina Douglas (Eng)	3557
37	Caroline Hall (Eng)	15148	87	Rae Hast (SA)	3541
38	Amaia Arruti (Sp)	15054	88	Natascha Fink (Aust)	3464
39	Liz Weima (Neth)	14844	89	Wendy Dicks (Eng)	3304
40	Debbie Dowling (Eng)	14672	90	Tina Yarwood (Eng)	3272
41	Lisa Hackney (Eng)	14381	91	Joanne Furby (Eng)	3213
42	Pamela Wright (Sco)	13504	92	Rica Comstock (US)	3190
43	Janice Arnold (NZ)	13226	93	Alison Brighouse (Eng)	3101
44	Cindy Figg-Currier (US)	12789	94	Kimberley Cayce (US)	3054
45	Kathryn Marshall (Sco)	12675	95	Tracey Craik (Sco)	2469
46	Karen Pearce (Aus)	12629	96	Diane Patterson (US)	2207
47	Xonia Wunsch-Ruiz (Sp)	10736	97	Myra McKinlay (Sco)	2160
48	Wendy Doolan (Aus)	10684	98	Susan Ginter (US)	2135
49	Karen Lunn (Aus)	10157	99	Heidi Person (US)	2122
50	Patti Rizzo (US)	9895	100	Emma-Jane Smith (Eng)	1983

Solheim Cup Europe *v* United States *At the Greenbriar, West Virginia*

Day One Foursomes

United States		Europe	
B Burton and D Mochrie (3 and 2)	1	H Alfredsson and L Neumann	0
B Daniel and M Mallon	0	C Nilsmark and A Sorenstam (1 hole)	1
T Green and K Robbins	0	L Fairclough and D Reid (2 and 1)	1
D Andrews and B King	0	L Davies and A Nicholas (2 and 1)	1
P Sheehan and S Steinauer (2 holes)	1	T Johnson and P Wright	0
	2		3

Day Two Fourballs

United States		Europe	
B Burton and D Mochrie (2 and 1)	1	L Davies and A Nicholas	0
B Daniel and M Mallon (7 and 5)	1	C Nilsmark and A Sorenstam	0
T Green and K Robbins	0	L Fairclough and D Reid (5 and 3)	1
D Andrews and B King (3 and 2)	1	T Johnson and P Wright	0
P Sheehan and S Steinhauer	0	H Alfredsson and L Neumann (1 hole)	1
	3		2

Day Three Singles

United States		Europe	
B King	0	H Alfredsson (2 and 1)	1
D Mochrie (6 and 5)	1	C Nilsmark	0
B Daniel (2 holes)	1	T Johnson	0
K Robbins (4 and 2)	1	L Fairclough	0
M Mallon (2 holes)	1	P Wright	0
P Sheehan	0	A Nicholas (3 and 2)	1
B Burton (2 holes)	1	L Davies	0
T Green (3 and 2)	1	A Sorenstam	0
S Steinhauer (2 holes)	1	D Reid	0
D Andrews (3 and 2)	1	L Neumann	0
	8		2

Final Score: United States 13, Europe 7

Tour results

Weetabix Women's British Open

at Duke's Course, Woburn G&CC

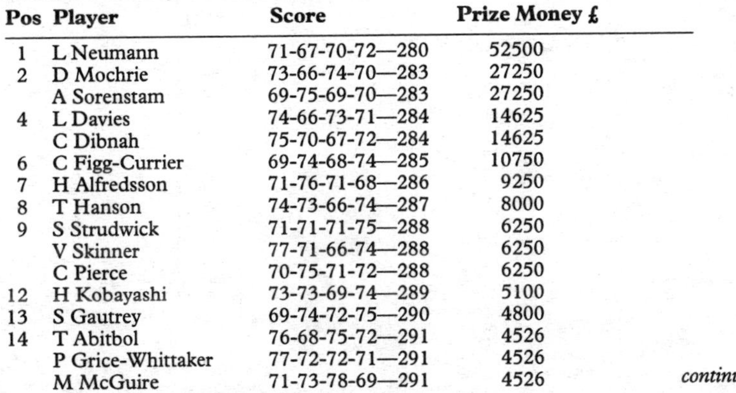

Pos	Player	Score	Prize Money £
1	L Neumann	71-67-70-72—280	52500
2	D Mochrie	73-66-74-70—283	27250
	A Sorenstam	69-75-69-70—283	27250
4	L Davies	74-66-73-71—284	14625
	C Dibnah	75-70-67-72—284	14625
6	C Figg-Currier	69-74-68-74—285	10750
7	H Alfredsson	71-76-71-68—286	9250
8	T Hanson	74-73-66-74—287	8000
9	S Strudwick	71-71-71-75—288	6250
	V Skinner	77-71-66-74—288	6250
	C Pierce	70-75-71-72—288	6250
12	H Kobayashi	73-73-69-74—289	5100
13	S Gautrey	69-74-72-75—290	4800
14	T Abitbol	76-68-75-72—291	4526
	P Grice-Whittaker	77-72-72-71—291	4526
	M McGuire	71-73-78-69—291	4526

continued

Weetabix Women's British Open *continued*

Pos	Player	Score	Prize Money £
17	S Gronberg-Whitmore	71-69-74-78—292	4100
	L Wen-Lin	73-70-73-76—292	4100
	J Geddes	74-72-72-74—292	4100
	E Knuth	78-69-72-73—292	4100
21	P Wright	68-75-78-72—293	3740
	K Pearce	70-74-75-74—293	3740
	K Tschetter	68-76-75-74—293	3740
24	K Cockrill	71-77-73-73—294	3425
	A Alcott	74-74-75-71—294	3425
	B King	73-74-69-78—294	3425
	A Ritzman	69-76-75-74—294	3425
28	S Moon	72-78-74-71—295	2930
	A Nicholas	72-73-70-80—295	2930
	D Reid	76-72-75-72—295	2930
	M Lunn	73-75-75-72—295	2930
	K Marshall	76-72-75-72—295	2930
	L Fairclough	75-72-72-76—295	2930
	S Redman	74-71-76-74—295	2930
35	T Johnson	75-75-72-74—296	2480
	E Orley	73-76-74-73—296	2480
	K Albers	75-67-78-76—296	2480
	L A Mills	72-76-73-76—297	2122
	H Person	75-74-72-76—297	2122
	C Hall	71-77-77-72—297	2122
	L Navarro	74-76-76-71—297	2122
	L West	77-73-74-73—297	2122
43	T Barrett	78-71-73-76—298	1870
44	M Figueras-Dotti	74-73-76-76—299	1685
	K Orum	73-75-76-75—299	1685
	W Doolan	75-76-73-75—299	1685
	M Fischer (Am)	71-78-76-74—299	
	J Forbes	73-75-75-76—299	1685
49	ML De Lorenzi	74-76-73-77—300	1440
	C Hjalmarsson	75-74-75-76—300	1440
	I Maconi	72-74-75-79—300	1440
52	X Wunsch-Ruiz	78-73-76-74—301	1230
	L Sugg	76-74-76-75—301	1230
	K Noble	75-73-72-81—301	1230
55	F Dassu	78-70-78-76—302	820
	MD Boer	76-75-75-76—302	820
	G Stewart	74-77-74-77—302	820
	F Descampe	76-75-78-73—302	820
	C Nilsmark	74-76-75-77—302	820
	S Prosser	74-72-76-80—302	820
	M Spencer-Devlin	73-74-79-76—302	820
	S Waugh	76-74-75-77—302	820
	H Wadsworth	73-78-78-73—302	820
	S Mendiburu	72-77-81-72—302	820
	S Robinson	73-76-74-79—302	820
66	N Scranton	80-70-73-80—303	650
67	D Barnard	75-74-77-78—304	630
	L Hackney	76-75-77-76—304	630
	E Crosby	76-73-77-78—304	630
70	M Hageman	73-77-76-80—306	610
71	B New	76-74-82-75—307	450
	M Burstrom	72-76-80-79—307	450
	N Moult	77-73-77-80—307	450
	ML Wengler	76-74-77-80—307	450
75	J Lawrence	74-77-77-81—309	400
	S Gustafson	76-75-83-75—309	400

The following players missed the cut:
E Duggleby; J Kinloch; S Bennett; A Gottmo; M Estuesta; P Rizzo; D Dowling; T Yarwood; S Hodge; K Parker; S Sharpe (Am); L Percival; T Craik; A Arruti; A Brighouse; S Croce; K Davies; K Lunn; D Petrizzi; V Michaud; A Shapcott; J Allmark; L Cowan; J Morley; D Hanna; L Lambert; J Mills; S Van Wyk; L Maritz-Atkins; K Egford (Am); C Scholefield-McConnel; J Furby; S Lambert (Am); B Salmon; P Rigby; C Duffy; B Helbig; R Hast; J Soulsby; MC Navarro-Corbacho; C Soules; J Arnold; N Buxton; E Farquharson-Black; H Reid; L Tadiotto; S Maynor; L Jensen; E Rundle; K Espinasse; C Panton-Lewis; T Eakin (Am): L Copeman; P Sterner; R Bolas; K Shepherd (Am); M Sutton (Am); M Landehag; V Palli; C Keggi; M Wright; B Pestana; R Lautens; A Johns. Retired: T Loveys; N Way; H Dobson.

BMW European Masters

at Golf de Bercuit, Brussels, Belgium

1	H Wadsworth*	69-66-70-73—278	£24000
2	T Hanson	69-69-70-73—281	16240
3	L Davies	69-70-72-72—283	9920
	A Sorenstam	71-70-71-71—283	9920

BMW Italian Open

at Lignano, Sabbiadoro, Italy

1	C Dibnah*	73-67-71-66—277	£10500
2	D Reid	73-68-79-66—277	7105
3	S Moon	70-69-72-67—278	6900

Costa Azul Open

at Aroeira, Lisbon, Portugal

1	S Mendiburu	70-70—140	£7500
2	L Fairclough	70-71—141	5075

Reduced to 36 holes due to bad weather

Evian Masters

at Royal Evian, France

1	H Alfredsson	71-73-73-70—287	£34875
2	S Gautrey	73-71-77-69—290	19936
	L Fairclough	68-72-77-73—290	19936

Ford Classic

at Duchess Course, Woburn G&CC

1	C Nilsmark	73-68-73-70—284	£15000
2	T Johnson	74-70-73-71—288	8575
	J Morley	73-69-77-69—288	8575

Hennessy Cup

at Refrath, Cologne, Germany

1	L Neumann*	69-71-72-65—277	£33000
2	A Nicholas	69-71-67-71—278	22300
3	K Parker	70-72-68-69—279	15400

* *Winner after play-off*

Irish Holidays Open *at St Margaret's, Dublin*

1	L Davies	70-72-69-71—282	£10500
2	C Hjalmarsson	72-75-70-73—290	6002
	H Wadsworth	72-71-75-72—290	6002

New Scoda Scottish Open *at Dalmahoy*

1	L Davies	69-69-68-72—278	£11250
2	K Orum	68-70-71-70—279	7610
	L Navarro	73-69-70-68—280	4650
	J Geddes	71-68-71-70—280	4650

OVB Austria Open *at Zell-am-See, Austria*

1	F Descampe*	70-70-69-68—277	£15000
2	T Hanson	70-69-66-72—277	10150
3	L Lambert	71-64-71-73—279	7000

Sens Ladies Netherlands Open
at Rijk van Nijmegen, Groesbeek

1	L Weima	74-68-72—214	£8250
2	S Gronberg-Whitmore	72-74-70—216	5580
3	J Arnold	74-72-72—218	2768
	R Hetherington	73-75-70—218	2768
	J Morley	73-74-71—218	2768
	C Matthew	74-71-73—218	2768

Spanish Open *at La Manga, Spain*

1	ML de Lorenzi*	71-72-68-71—282	£9000
2	S Gronberg-Whitmore	68-69-73-72—282	6090
3	K Orum	70-72-70-72—284	4200

Trygg Hansa Open
at Haninge, Stockholm, Sweden

1	L Neumann	69-67-71-67—274	£15000
2	C Dibnah	71-70-69-68—278	10150
3	A Sorenstam	73-73-72-66—284	7000

Var Open de France
at St Endreol, The Var, France

1	J Forbes*	73-70-70—213	£8250
2	D Reid	72-69-72—213	4715
	S Strudwick	73-66-74—213	4715

Waterford Dairies English Open
at The Tytherington, Macclesfield, Cheshire

1	P Meunier	73-74-70-71—288	£9000
2	ML de Lorenzi	78-69-72-71—290	5145
	C Dibnah	75-73-67-75—290	5145
3	L Fairclough	73-71-71-76—291	3240

* *Winner after play-off*

US Ladies' PGA Tour, 1994

Money Winners

Pos	Name	Prize Money $
1	Laura Davies	687201
2	Beth Daniel	659426
3	Liselotte Neumann	505701
4	Dottie Mochrie	472728
5	Donna Andrews	429015
6	Tammie Green	418969
7	Sherri Steinhauer	413398
8	Kelly Robbins	396778
9	Betsy King	390239
10	Meg Mallon	353385
11	Elaine Crosby	344735
12	Val Skinner	328021
13	Patty Sheehan	323562
14	Helen Alfredsson	277971
15	Jane Geddes	273600
16	Michelle McGann	269936
17	Deb Richard	256960
18	Judy Dickinson	246879
19	Hiromi Kobayashi	242323
20	Pat Bradley	236274
21	Dawn Coe-Jones	230388
22	Martha Nause	212130
23	Chris Johnson	208228
24	Lauri Merten	202002
25	Nancy Lopez	197952
26	Alicia Dibos	192132
27	Nancy Ramsbottom	187842
28	Alice Ritzman	186715
29	Lisa Kiggens	183279
30	Missie McGeorge	181281
31	Brandie Burton	172821
32	Barb Bunkowsky	167039
33	Dale Eggeling	158501
34	Michelle Estill	155667
35	Amy Alcott	154183
36	Barb Mucha	152685
37	Colleen Walker	141200
38	Kristi Albers	136834
39	Annika Sorenstam	127451
40	Gail Graham	124551
41	Amy Benz	124189
42	Rosie Jones	123683
43	Marta Figueras-Dotti	123513
44	Missie Berteotti	123161
45	Julie Larsen	121402
46	Carolyn Hill	120060
47	Joan Pitcock	114735
48	Michele Redman	113918
49	Juli Inkster	113829
50	Kris Tschetter	112229
51	Vicki Fergon	109635
52	Sherri Turner	108282
53	Robin Walton	104421
54	Dana Dormann	101715
55	Jan Stephenson	99766
56	Sally Little	98115
57	Kim Shipman	97024
58	Hollis Stacy	96124
59	Katie Peterson-Parker	95684
60	Pearl Sinn	91499
61	Nanci Bowen	88302
62	Maggie Will	87307
63	Tina Barrett	86034
64	Caroline Pierce	84756
65	Tracy Kerdyk	84145
66	Cindy Rarick	82848
67	Marianne Morris	78630
68	Jenny Lidback	75036
69	Tania Abitbol	72586
70	Stephanie Farwig	72454
71	Cindy Figg-Currier	72158
72	Shelley Hamlin	71864
73	Lisa Walters	71732
74	Allison Finney	69132
75	Jane Crafter	65730
76	Danielle Ammaccapane	61964
77	Suzanne Strudwick	61951
78	Kim Williams	61703
79	Karen Lunn	61152
80	Muffin Spencer-Devlin	59294
81	Janice Gibson	58156
82	Vicki Goetze	57311
83	Terry-Jo Myers	57053
84	Lori West	56594
85	Ellie Gibson	56279
86	JoAnne Carner	55474
87	Page Dunlap	55048
88	Cathy Johnston-Forbes	53950
89	Susie Redman	53168
90	Florence Descampe	53020
91	Dina Ammaccapane	52453
92	Kris Monaghan	51847
93	Kim Saiki	50817
94	Alice Miller	50563
95	Jill Briles-Hinton	50532
96	Denise Baldwin	46246
97	Nancy Scranton	45413
98	Cindy Schreyer	44994
99	Melissa McNamara	43337
100	Leigh Ann Mills	43286

Tour results

49th US Women's Open

at Indianwood, Lake Orion, Michigan

Pos	Player	Score	Prize Money $
1	Patty Sheehan	66-71-69-71—277	155000
2	Tammie Green	66-72-69-71—278	85000
3	Liselotte Neumann	69-72-71-69—281	47752
4	Tania Abitbol	72-68-73-70—283	31132
	Alicia Dibos	69-68-73-73—283	31132
6	Meg Mallon	70-72-73-69—284	21486
	Amy Alcott	71-67-77-69—284	21486
	Betsy King	69-71-72-72—284	21486
9	Kelly Robbins	71-72-70-72—285	16445
	Donna Andrews	67-72-70-76—285	16445
	Helen Alfredsson	63-69-76-77—285	16445
12	Lauri Merten	74-68-75-69—286	12805
	Dottie Mochrie	72-72-71-71—286	12805
	Lisa Grimes	72-73-69-72—286	12805
	Judy Dickinson	66-73-73-74—286	12805
	Michelle Estil	69-68-75-74—286	12805
	Laura Davies	68-68-75-75—286	12805

Atlanta Women's Championship

at Eagle's Landing, Stockbridge, Georgia

Pos	Player	Score	Prize Money $
1	V Skinner	70-68-68—206	$97500
2	L Neumann	69-67-71—207	60510
3	B Daniel	69-70-70—209	44156

Big Apple Classic

at New Rochelle, New York

Pos	Player	Score	Prize Money $
1	B Daniel*	70-69-66-71—276	$97500
2	L Davies	71-69-60-66—276	60510
3	N Ramsbottom	67-74-72-65—278	39250
	N Bowen	68-70-72-68—278	39250

Children's Medical Centre Classic

at CC of the North, Dayton, Ohio

Pos	Player	Score	Prize Money $
1	M Will*	70-70-70—210	$52500
2	J Briles-Hinton	68-72-70—210	28179
	A Dibos	67-72-71—210	28179

Chicago Challenge

at White Eagle, Illinois

Pos	Player	Score	Prize Money $
1	J Geddes	68-69-68-67—272	$75000
2	R Walton	72-70-68-65—275	40256
	D Eggeling	70-67-71-67—275	40256

* *Winner after play-off*

Corning Classic

at Corning CC, Corning, New York

1	B Daniel	67-71-71-68—278	$75000
2	S Farwig	68-71-69-71—279	40256
	N Ramsbottom	64-71-71-73—279	40256

Chrysler–Plymouth Tournament of Champions

at Grand Cypress Resort, Orlando, Florida

1	D Mochrie	72-75-71-69—287	$115000
2	L Merten	71-78-70-70—289	62250
	N Lopez	75-72-69-73—289	62250

du Maurier Classic

at Ottawa Hunt, Ontario, Canada

1	M Nause	65-71-72-71—279	$120000
2	M McGann	66-71-71-72—280	74474
3	L Neumann	70-67-71-73—281	54346

Hawaiian Ladies' Open

at Ko Olina, Ewa Beach, Hawaii

1	M Figueras-Dotti	68-70-71—209	$75000
2	J Geddes	69-70-71—210	46546
3	V Fergon	69-74-69—212	27256

Healthsouth Palm Beach Classic

at Wycliff, Lake Worth, Florida

1	D Coe-Jones	67-69-65—201	$60000
2	L Merten	71-67-64—202	37237
3	L Davies	69-65-69—203	27173

Heartland Classic

at Forest Hill, St Louis, Missouri

1	L Neumann	70-71-67-70—278	$75000
2	E Crosby	71-71-69-70—281	40256
	P Sinn	67-70-72-72—281	40256

Jamie Farr Toledo Classic

at Highland Meadows GC, Sylvania, Ohio

1	K Robbins*	69-70-65—204	$75000
2	T Green	66-71-67—204	46546
3	M Mallon	67-70-69—206	33966

Lady Keystone Open

at Hershey CC, Hershey, Pennsylvania

1	E Crosby	69-72-70—211	$60000
2	L Davies	70-71-71—212	37237
3	V Skinner	70-71-72—213	24253
	B King	70-70-73—213	24253

* *Winner after play-off*

McCall's LPGA Classic
at Stratton Mountain, Vermont

1	C Hill	69-72-65-69—275	$75000
2	N Ramsbottom	69-69-70-70—278	46546
3	P Bradley	73-73-71-66—283	27256
	D Richard	71-69-74-69—283	27256
	J Pitcock	73-68-68-74—283	27256

McDonald's LPGA Championship
at Du Pont CC, Wilmington, Delaware

1	L Davies	70-72-69-68—279	$165000
2	A Ritzman	68-73-71-70—282	102402
3	E Crosby	76-71-69-67—283	54660
	P Bradley	73-73-70-67—283	54660
	H Kobayashi	72-73-71-67—283	54660
	L Neumann	74-73-67-69—283	54660

Minnesota LPGA Classic
at Edinburgh, Brooklyn Park, Minnesota

1	L Neumann	68-71-66—205	$75000
2	H Kobayashi	72-70-65—207	46546
3	S Steinhauer	72-70-66—208	33966

Nabisco Dinah Shore
at Mission Hills CC, Palm Springs, California

1	D Andrews	70-69-67-70—276	$105000
	L Davies	70-68-69-70—277	65165
	T Green	70-72-69-68—279	47553

Nichirei International
at Ami GC, Ibaragi-ken, Japan

US 22½, Japan 13½

Oldsmobile Classic
at Walnut Hills, East Lansing, Michigan

1	B Daniel	67-63-70-68—268	$90000
2	L Kiggens	68-69-67-68—272	55855
3	A Benz	68-67-70-68—273	40759

Ping-Cellular One Championship
at Columbia Edgewater CC, Portland, Oregon

1	M McGeorge	72-69-66—207	$75000
2	B King	71-70-69—210	46546
3	C Rarick	72-71-68—211	30192
	A Finney	71-69-71—211	30192

Ping/Welch's Championship
at Blue Hill CC, Canton, Massachusetts

1	H Alfredsson	70-68-70-66—274	$67500
2	P Bradley	67-71-72-68—278	36230
	J Inkster	68-69-72-69—278	36230

Ping/Welch's Championship
at Randolph Park North, Tucson, Arizona

1	D Andrews	66-68-69-73—276	$63750
2	J Dickinson	71-71-69-68—279	34217
	B Burton	69-68-69-73—279	34217

Rochester International
at Locust Hill CC, Pittsford, New York

1	L Kiggens	67-69-71-66—273	$75000
2	D Coe-Jones	69-67-71-67—274	46546
3	B King	66-68-72-69—275	33966

Safeco Classic
at Meridian Valley, Seattle, Washington

1	D Richard	71-68-70-67—276	$75000
2	T Green	72-69-69-67—277	32079
	R Jones	70-69-70-68—277	32079
	M Estill	68-70-69-70—277	32079
	C Johnson	68-71-67-71—277	32079

Sara Lee Classic
at Hermitage GC, Old Hickory, Tennessee

1	L Davies	65-70-68—203	$78750
2	M Mallon	65-70-69—204	48873
3	D Richard	71-71-64—206	35664

Shoprite Classic
at Greate Bay, Somers Point, New Jersey

1	D Andrews	67-66-74—207	$75000
2	M Estill	67-77-65—209	46546
3	C Pierce	70-69-71—210	24845
	K Saiki	68-71-71—210	24845
	D Mochrie	69-68-73—210	24845
	B Bunkowsky	67-69-74—210	24845

Sprint Challenge
at Indigo Lakes, Daytona, Florida

1	S Steinhauer	68-68-67-70—273	$180000
2	K Robbins	68-68-70-68—274	111711
3	B Bunkowsky	68-72-68-70—278	81519

Standard Register Ping Tournament

at Moon Valley CC, Phoenix, Arizona

1	L Davies	69-72-66-70—277	$105000
2	B Daniel	71-71-70-69—281	56359
	E Crosby	73-69-66-73—281	56359

State Farm Rail Classic

at Rail Golf Club, Illinois

1	B Mucha	67-69-67—203	$78750
2	K Shipman	68-67-69—204	48873
3	G Graham	70-66-69—205	31701
	S Strudwick	69-66-70—205	31701

Toray Japan Queens Cup

at Oak Hills, Chiba, Japan

1	W-S Ko	65-71-70—206	$105000
2	B King	67-67-72—206	65165
3	N Lopez	67-71-69—207	47553
4	V Skinner	70-68-70—208	30527
	H Alfredsson	70-68-70—208	30527
	J Larsen	66-72-70—208	30527
7	H Kobayashi	72-68-69—209	19549
	L Davies	67-69-73—209	19549
9	J Geddes	68-68-74—210	16555
10	S Steinhauer	70-68-74—212	14794

World Championship of Women's Golf

at Naples National, Florida

1	B Daniel	68-70-71-65—274	$105000
2	E Crosby	70-66-69-72—277	55000
3	L Davies	68-73-67-71—279	35000

Youngstown-Warren Classic

at Avalon Lakes, Warren, Ohio

1	T Green	67-69-70—206	$82500
2	C Walker	68-69-71—208	51201
3	K Shipman	69-69-71—209	33211
	D Mochrie	68-70-71—209	33211

Women's Asian Tour, 1994

Thailand Open

at Thana City G&CC, Bangkok, Thailand

1	L Davies	70-70-66—206	$13500
2	M Lunn	72-71-70—213	9000
3	Y-M Lee	74-71-70—215	6750

Indonesia Ladies Open

at Bali Handara Kosaido, Bali, Indonesia

1	T Hanson*	71-70-71—212	$12000
2	J-S Won	75-69-68—212	7000
	S Prosser	73-66-73—212	7000

Malaysian Ladies Open

at Bukit Jambul, Penang, Malaya

1	J-S Won	75-75-70—220	$12750
2	T Hanson	75-73-74—222	8500
3	J-M Lee	77-76-72—225	5737
	K Weiss	77-74-74—225	5737

Republic of China Ladies Open

at Chang Goog, Taipei

1	K Weiss	74-71-68—213	$16500
2	C Hjalmarsson	78-72-64—214	11000
3	Tsai Li-Hsiang	77-69-69—215	8250

Final Order of Merit

Pos	Player	Prize Money $
1	Karen Weiss (USA)	24352
2	Tracy Hanson (USA)	22994
3	Loo Young-Mi (Kor)	20117
4	Won Jac-Sook (Kor)	19750
5	Carin Hjalmarsson (Swe)	17518
6	Laura Davies (GB)	13500
7	Mardi Lunn (Aus)	13118
8	Lora Fairclough (GB)	12835
9	Sally Prosser (GB)	11421
10	Helen Wadsworth (GB)	9365

* *Winner after play-off*

Men's Amateur Tournaments

The Amateur Championship *at Nairn and Nairn Dunbar, Scotland*

Starting field of 288. There were 68 qualifiers on 155 or better for match play stage, after a 36-hole stroke play competition. Players from 18 nations competed.

First Round

S Drummond beat A Emery 5 and 4
S Griffith (US) beat S Thomas (US) 2 and 1
S Burnell beat R Bland 2 holes
G Marsden beat A Crombie 3 and 2
M Beveridge beat P Williams 3 and 1
G Homewood beat C Nowicki 1 hole
S Allen (Aus) beat G Paterson 6 and 5
Y Taylor beat M Thomson 4 and 3

Second Round

M Blackey beat S Gallacher at 20th
M Erlandsson (Swe) beat
G Wolstenholme 4 and 3
B Collier beat D Summers 3 and 2
B Howard beat D Watson 6 and 4
H McKibbin beat R Goodey 2 and 1
A Turnbull beat T Havemann (Den) 7 and 5
M Welch beat N Zitny (Austria) 3 and 2
P Nelson beat P Streeter 1 hole
S Griffiths beat M Backhausen (Den) 3 and 2
L James beat T Milford 5 and 3
F McGuirk beat A Print 1 hole
D Howell beat S Knowles 3 and 2
J Harris beat G Clark 3 and 1
C Watson beat C Fort 3 and 2
B Dredge beat R Beames 1 hole
D Berridge beat W Bennett 1 hole
D Park beat S Taylor 4 and 3
I Hardy beat E Power 2 and 1
G Sherry beat G Harris 1 hole
D Whittaker beat G Houston at 19th
S Green beat J Taylor (US) 1 hole
R Shiels beat K Miller 1 hole
S Davis beat S East 2 and 1
D Downie beat J Barnes 2 and 1
P Harrington beat S Hurd 3 and 2
C Duke beat G Shaw 4 and 3
S Drummond beat F Poppmeier (Austria) at 20th
S Griffith (US) beat J Hodgson 2 holes
K Brink (Swe) beat S Burnell 1 hole
G Marsden beat M Beveridge 3 and 2
G Homewood beat S Allan 5 and 4
M Wilcox beat Y Taylor 1 hole

Third Round

M Erlandsson (Swe) beat M Blackey 1 hole
B Howard beat B Collier 2 and 1
A Turnbull beat H McKibbin 3 and 2
M Welch beat P Nelson at 19th
L James beat S Griffiths 4 and 3
D Howell beat F McGuirk 2 and 1
C Watson beat J Harris 2 holes
B Dredge beat D Berridge 3 and 2
I Hardy beat D Park 1 hole
G Sherry beat D Whittaker 2 and 1
R Shiels beat S Green 2 and 1
S Davis beat D Downie 3 and 1
C Duke beat P Harrington 3 and 2
S Griffith (US) beat S Drummond 1 hole
K Brink (Swe) beat G Marsden 5 and 4
G Homewood beat M Wilcox 1 hole

Fourth Round

M Erlandsson (Swe) beat B Howard 1 hole
A Turnbull beat M Welch 3 and 2
L James beat D Howell 3 and 2
C Watson beat B Dredge at 23rd
G Sherry beat I Hardy 3 and 1
R Shiels beat S Davis at 19th
C Duke beat S Griffith (US) 1 hole
K Brink (Swe) beat C Homewood 8 and 6

Fifth Round

A Turnbull beat M Erlandsson (Swe) at 19th
L James beat C Watson 5 and 4
G Sherry beat R Shiels 2 and 1
K Brink (Swe) beat C Duke at 19th

Semi-finals

L James beat A Turnbull 2 and 1
G Sherry beat K Brink (Swe) 4 and 3

Final (36 holes)

L James beat G Sherry 2 and 1

US Amateur Championship *at TPC Sawgrass*

Semi-finals
T Woods beat E Frishette 5 and 3
T Kuehne beat K Cox 1 up

Final
T Woods beat T Kuehne 2 holes

World Amateur Team Championship for the Eisenhower Trophy

at Golf National, Paris

Leading team scores (Discarded scores in brackets)

1	UNITED STATES	208	214	207	209—838
	T Woods	70	75	67	72—284
	A Doyle	68	70	69	70—277
	J Harris	70	(77)	(72)	67—286
	T Dempsey	(72)	69	71	(80)—292
2	GB & I	213	208	209	219—849
	W Bennett	72	68	67	74—281
	S Gallacher	(73)	(75)	70	74—292
	L James	69	66	72	(75)—282
	G Sherry	72	74	(75)	71—292
3	SWEDEN	210	221	213	211—855
	K Brink	(76)	(79)	72	68—295
	E Carlberg	75	76	(76)	73—300
	F Jacobson	67	73	73	70—283
	M Lundberg	68	72	68	(77)—285

Leading individual scores

A Doyle (USA)	277
W Bennett (GB&I)	281
L James (GB&I)	282
F Jacobson (Swe)	283
M Brown (NZ)	283
T Woods (USA)	284
F Cea (Sp)	285
M Lundberg (Swe)	285
J Dawes (Aus)	285

St Andrew's Trophy *at Chantilly, France*

Great Britain and Ireland		Continent of Europe	
***First Day* – Foursomes**			
L James and B Dredge (3 and 2)	1	K Brink and L Westerberg	0
W Bennett and G Wolstenholme (2 and 1)	1	J Kjaerbye and N Zitny	0
B Howard and G Sherry (2 and 1)	1	F Valera and C Hannell	0
P Harrington and R Johnson (3 and 2)	1	D Dupin and N Van Hootegem	0
	4		0
Singles			
L James	1/2	L Westerberg	1/2
W Bennett (6 and 5)	1	N Van Hootegem	0
G Sherry	1/2	C Hannell	1/2
R Johnson	0	M Backhausen (5 and 4)	1
D Fisher	1/2	F Valera	1/2
B Dredge	0	D Dupin (2 and 1)	1
P Harrington (1 hole)	1	K Brink	0
G Wolstenholme (4 and 3)	1	J Kjaerbye	0
	4 1/2		3 1/2

continued

St Andrew's Trophy *continued*

***Second Day* – Foursomes**

L James and B Dredge	0	K Brink and L Westerberg (3 and 2)	1
W Bennett and G Wolstenholme (1 hole)	1	F Valera and C Hannell	0
B Howard and G Sherry	0	D Dupin and N Van Hootegem	1
P Harrington and R Johnson	1/2	M Backhausen and N Zitny	1/2
	1 1/2		2 1/2

Singles

W Bennett (1 hole)	1	M Backhausen	0
L James (2 and 1)	1	L Westerberg	0
G Sherry (5 and 4)	1	N Van Hootegem	0
D Fisher	0	F Valera (3 and 2)	1
R Johnson (1 hole)	1	K Brink	0
B Howard	0	D Dupin (2 and 1)	1
P Harrington	0	N Zitny (4 and 2)	1
G Wolstenholme	0	C Hannell (5 and 4)	1
	4		4

Result: Great Britain and Ireland 14; Continent of Europe 10.

Amateur Inaugural Centenary International Team Championship

at The Australian, Sydney, Australia

ENGLAND 596

W Bennett	75-75-71-73—294
C Edwards	74-77-73-78—302

European Amateur Championship

at Aura, Turku, Finland

1	S Gallacher (Sco)	69-73-71-65—278
2	G Sherry (Sco)	73-72-70-65—280
	L James (Eng)	65-74-71-70—280

European Club Championship

at Vilamoura III, Portugal

1 Kilmarnock, Scotland 585
A Reid, RL Crawford, G Sherry

2 GC de Nîmes Campagne, France 588
D Dupin, I Goroneskoul, M Dolisie

Other Scores

7 Sand Moor, England 608
ML Pullan, A Frontalgay, G Harland

9 Monmouthshire GC, Wales 612
R Price, D Phillips, S Lewis

10 Shandon Park, Ireland 614
P Purdy, G Lynas, B Wilson

Individual Scores

G Sherry (Sco)	71-69-70-70—280
D Dupin (Fr)	73-72-74-71—290
F de Pablo (Sp)	77-69-72-72—290
S Kjeldsen (Den)	73-71-75-75—294

Men's Home Internationals *at Ashburnham, Dyfed*

England beat Scotland	9½–5½
Ireland beat Wales	10½–4½
England beat Wales	10–5
Ireland beat Scotland	11–4
Scotland beat Wales	8–7
England beat Ireland	9–6

Result: England 3, Ireland 2, Scotland 1, Wales 0

British Seniors' Open Amateur Championship
at Formby and Southport & Ainsdale

1	C Green	72-77-74—223
2	I Fisher	76-77-74—227
	C Wagner	78-77-72—227

English Amateur Championship *at Moortown, Leeds*

Quarter Finals
A Johnson beat M Keeling at 20th
C Poxon beat A Emery 1 hole
G Homewood beat A Wall 5 and 3
M Foster beat J Loosemore 5 and 3

Semi-Finals
A Johnson beat C Poxon 3 and 2
M Foster beat G Homewood 2 and 1

Final (36 holes)
M Foster beat A Johnson 8 and 7

Scottish Amateur Championship *at Renfrew*

Quarter Finals
H McKibbin beat M Urquhart at 23rd
G Sherry beat B Collier 3 and 2
A Reid beat D Downie 1 hole
B Howard beat N Shillinglaw 5 and 3

Semi-Finals
H McKibbin beat G Sherry 3 and 2
A Reid beat B Howard 3 and 2

Final
H McKibbin beat A Reid at 39th

Irish Amateur Championship *at Portmarnock*

Quarter Finals
J Fanagan beat J Langan 3 and 2
D Higgins beat R Conway 2 holes
P Harrington beat P Errity 3 and 2
J Morris beat G Spring at 20th

Semi-Finals
D Higgins beat J Fanagan 3 and 1
P Harrington beat J Morris 3 and 2

Final
D Higgins beat P Harrington at 20th

Welsh Amateur Championship

at Royal Porthcawl, Glamorgan

Quarter Finals
B Dredge beat A Cooper 2 and 1
M Smith beat D Park 5 and 4
R Price beat C Platt 6 and 4
C Evans beat A Hall 5 and 4

Semi-Finals
M Smith beat B Dredge 2 and 1
C Evans beat R Price 1 hole

Final (36 holes)
C Evans beat M Smith 5 and 4

English Open Amateur Stroke Play Championship (for the Brabazon Trophy)

at Little Aston, Birmingham

1	G Harris	72-70-64-74—280
2	W Bennett	69-74-70-73—286
3	S Burnell	74-75-69-70—288
	F Valera	71-76-71-70—288
	R Bland	73-72-71-72—288

Scottish Stroke Play Championship

at Letham Grange, Angus

1	D Downie	69-69-74-76—288
2	N Van Hootegem	67-74-73-75—289
3	B Howard	68-76-76-71—291

Welsh Open Stroke Play Championship

at St Pierre, Gwent

1	N Van Hootegem*	75-76-69-70—290
2	G Houston	74-72-72-72—290
3	S Allan	74-75-77-71—297
	P Edwards	76-76-73-72—297

Aberconwy Trophy

at Conwy/Llandudno (Maesdu), Gwynedd

1	G Marsden	73-76-75-74—298
2	S Andrew	75-76-75-74—300
	M Smith	72-79-74-75—300

The Antlers

at Royal Mid-Surrey

1	D Cowap and J Brant	72-70—142
2	C Rodgers and N Reilly	75-68—143
	G Maly and P Wilkins	73-70—143

* *Winner after play-off*

Berkhamsted Trophy

at Berkhamsted, Hertfordshire

1	M Treleaven	70-70—140
2	D Watson	72-71—143
	G Wolstenholme	73-70—143

The Berkshire Trophy

at The Berkshire GC

1	J Knight	68-72-66-68—274
	A Marshall	67-69-74-64—274
2	B Sandry	70-71-66-69—276

(Knight and Marshall share trophy)

Burhill Family Foursomes

at Burhill, Surrey

Semi-Finals

M Toole and Miss SJ Toole beat Mrs P Legg and G Legg 1 hole
Mrs A Croft and M Croft beat Mrs R Earnshaw and H Deane 2 and 1

Final

M Toole and Miss SJ Toole beat Mrs A Croft and M Croft 1 hole

Cameron Corbett Vase

at Haggs Castle, Glasgow

1	J Hodgson*	66-72-71-71—280
2	G Rankin	68-68-76-68—280
3	M Brooks	72-70-70-70—282

Central England Open Men's Foursomes

at Woodhall Spa

Semi-Finals

C Banks and J Hemphrey beat W Hopkinson and I Houldsworth 3 and 2
M Jones and C Jones beat R Cole and R Beekie at 19th

Final

C Banks and J Hemphrey beat M Jones and C Jones 1 hole

County Champions Tournament

at Rye

1	G Wolstenholme (Glos)	71-64—135
2	S Webster (Warwicks)	69-67—136
3	C Edwards (Somerset)	69-68—137

Craigmillar Park Open

at Craigmillar Park, Edinburgh

1	B Collier	71-67-70-71—279
2	J Hodgson	71-68-71-71—281
3	S Gallacher	72-73-73-64—282

* *Winner after play-off*

Duncan Putter

at Southerndown, Bridgend, Glamorgan

1	G Wolstenholme	78-74-74—226
2	B Dredge	76-77-75—228
	M Foster	75-72-81—228
	D Park	78-75-75—228

Reduced to 54 holes due to bad weather

East of Ireland Amateur Open Championship

at Co. Louth, Baltry

1	G McGimpsey	72-71-76-71—290
2	N Beirth	72-74-74-73—293
3	J Fanagan	75-74-70-78—297

East of Scotland Open Amateur Stroke Play Championship

at Lundin Links

1	A Reid	66-70-66-76—278
2	S Mackenzie	70-71-68-72—281
3	G Davidson	71-71-69-71—282
	D Downie	72-70-68-72—282

English Champion Club Championship

at Coxmoor, Notts

1	Sand Moor		287
	S Pullan	72-68	
	M Pullan	74-73	
	G Harland	(77)-(74)	
2	Sittingbourne & Milton Regis		288
	T Milford	70-71	
	P Stuart	73-74	
	P Newman	(77)-(77)	

(Discarded scores in brackets)

English County Finals

at Moor Park

Day One

Gloucestershire	5	Lincolnshire	4
Middlesex	4½	Lancashire	4½

Day Two

Gloucestershire	4	Middlesex	5
Lincolnshire	5	Lancashire	$

Day Three

Gloucestershire	5½	Lancashire	3½
Middlesex	5	Lincolnshire	4

Result

Middlesex 5 pts, Gloucestershire 4 pts, Lincolnshire 2 pts, Lancashire 1 pt

English Open Mid-amateur Championship for the Logan Trophy

at Trentham

1	I Richardson	76-73-68—217
	A McLure	75-70-72—217
2	A Mew	75-73-70—218

Richardson and McLure share trophy

English Seniors' Championship

at Parkstone & Broadstone, Dorset

1	G Steel	72
	F Jones	72
2	G Edwards	73

Reduced to one round due to bad weather. Steel and Jones share trophy.

Fathers and Sons Foursomes

at West Hill, Surrey

Semi-Finals

RJ and P Hill beat MRW and J Attoe 4 and 3
A and R Guest-Gornall beat RA and D Wood 1 hole

Final

RJ and P Hill beat A and R Guest-Gornall 4 and 3

Frame Trophy

at Worplesdon, Surrey

1	D Lane	77-73-72—222
2	J Caplan	76-74-73—223
3	M Kirby	78-78-70—226

Golf Illustrated Gold Vase

at Walton Heath, Surrey

		Old	New
1	S Burnell	71	69—140
2	A Raitt	73	68—141
3	G Clark	72	71—143
	C Rotheroe	70	73—143

Hampshire Hog

at North Hants

1	B Ingleby	69-67—136
2	L Cox	70-69—139
3	S Griffiths	72-68—140

Irish Seniors Amateur Open Championship

at Tramore, Waterford

1	B Buckley	73-78—151
2	T O'Donoghue	80-75—155
3	F Boswell	81-78—159

John Cross Bowl

at Worplesdon

1	P Benka*	73-69—142
2	A Wall	68-74—142
3	J Collier	74-70—144
	P Alabaster	71-73—144
	D Boxall	70-74—144
	L Jackson	68-76—144
	J Jones	68-76—144

King George V Coronation Cup

at Porters Park, Hertfordshire

1	S Webster*	72-74—146
	D Hamilton	73-73—146
	P Wilkins	70-76—146
	D Howell	73-73—146

Lagonda Trophy

at Gog Magog, Cambridge

1	S Webster	71-76-71-68—276
2	J Hodgson	68-72-68-71—279
	W Bladon	67-68-71-73—279
	A Emery	70-68-67-74—279

Leven Gold Medal

at Leven Links, Fife

1	B Howard	67-66-66-66—265
2	S Meiklejohn	67-66-67-68—268
3	J Hodgson	66-66-70-71—273

Lytham Trophy

at Royal Lytham & St Annes and Fairhaven

1	W Bennett	70-67-77-71—285
2	S Drummond	72-70-69-75—286
3	A Emery	70-73-72-73—288

Midland Open Amateur Championship

at Little Aston and Sutton Coldfield

1	D Howell*	74-74-70-67—285
2	S Burnell	71-71-71-72—285
3	M Blackey	77-70-70-70—287

* *Winner after play-off*

North of Ireland Championship

at Royal Portrush

Semi-Finals
J Fanagan beat D Baker 2 and 1
N Ludwell beat P Harrington 2 and 1

Final
N Ludwell beat J Fanagan 3 and 1

North of Scotland Open Championship

at Elgin, Morayshire

1	E Forbes *	74-72-70-67—283
	P Haggerty	72-71-71-69—283
	A Turnbull	73-69-70-71—283

Oxford *v* Cambridge Varsity Match

at Rye, Sussex

Foursomes: Oxford beat Cambridge 5–0
Singles: Oxford beat Cambridge 8–2

Result: Oxford beat Cambridge 13–2

Oxford and Cambridge Society – President's Putter

at Rye

Fifth Round
I Smith beat C Weight 2 and 1
S Seman beat A Mangeot 2 and 1
M Benka beat R Kelly 6 and 5
R Sanders beat S Ellis 2 and 1
J Webster beat R Devlin 3 and 2
P Hill beat N Peplow 4 and 3
C Dale beat R Lawson 5 and 4
A Holmes beat S Sharpe 5 and 4

Sixth Round
S Seman beat I Smith 1 hole
R Sanders beat M Benka at 19th hole
P Hill beat J Webster 1 hole
A Holmes beat C Dale 5 and 4

Semi-Finals
S Seman beat R Sanders 1 hole
P Hill beat A Holmes 2 holes

Final
S Seman beat P Hill 4 and 3

Pringle Champion of Champions Tournament

at Muirfield, East Lothian

1	D Park	73-73—146
2	G Waters	75-74—149
3	J Pounder	75-75—150
	M Welch	74-76—150

* *Winner after play-off*

St Andrews Links Trophy

at Old Course, St Andrews

1	B Howard	78-74-72-70—294
2	W Bennett	77-74-72-72—295
	G Houston	74-74-74-73—295
3	N Van Hootegem	76-78-73-70—297

St David's Gold Cross

at Royal St David's, Harlech

1	C Evans	73-68-71-69—281
2	M Ellis	71-72-71-70—284
	D Park	72-76-65-71—284

Scottish Champion of Champions

at Leven Links, Fife

1	G Sherry	73-72-71-65—281
2	A Reid	73-69-73-71—286
3	S Mackenzie	70-75-71-71—287

Selborne Salver

at Blackmoor

1	W Bennett*	68-68—136
2	M Blackey	65-71—136
3	J Healey	74-65—139

South of Ireland Championship

at Lahinch

Semi-Finals
P Harrington beat K Kearney 1 hole
D Higgins beat B O'Melia 5 and 4

Final
D Higgins beat P Harrington 1 hole

Tennant Cup

at Glasgow Gailes and Killermont

1	G Rankin	71-70-64-66—271
2	G Lawrie	70-73-68-69—280
3	S Mackenzie	74-73-70-68—285

Trubshaw Cup

at Ashburnham and Tenby, Dyfed

1	C Evans	70-71-73-79—293
2	D Park	72-72-76-77—297
3	M Peet	72-71-77-79—299

* *Winner after play-off*

Welsh Inter-Counties Championship

at Borth and Ynyslas, Dyfed

1	Glamorgan	376
2	Denbighshire	280
3	Anglesey	282

Reduced to one round due to bad weather

Welsh Over-35 Championship

at Cardigan GC

1	CJ Davies (Llandrindod Wells)	72-78-74—224
2	JS Hogg (Llantrisant & Pontyclun)	76-77-77—230
3	A Jones (Copt Heath)	81-78-73—232

Welsh Seniors Championship

at Aberdovey, Gwynedd

1	G Perks	83-74—157
	I Hughes	79-78—157
	A Prytherch	75-82—157

Title shared three ways

Welsh Amateur Team Championship

at Carmarthen GC

Semi-Finals

Monmouthshire beat South Pembrokeshire 4–1
Whitchurch beat Wrexham 3½–1½

Final

Monmouthshire beat Whitchurch 3½–1½

Welsh Brewers Champion of Champions

at Cradoc, Brecon

1	B Dredge	67-67-71-71—276
2	RW Price	72-75-71-68—286
	M Smith	69-72-74-71—286

West of England Stroke Play Championship

at Royal North Devon, Westward Ho!, Devon

1	C Nowicki	70-76-74-74—294
2	P Streeter	75-75-76-70—296
3	M Treleaven	75-77-74-71—297

West of Ireland Championship

at Rosses Point, Co Sligo

Semi-Finals

P Harrington beat S McParland 1 hole
K Kearney beat J Fanagan 4 and 3

Final

P Harrington beat K Kearney 2 holes

West of Scotland Open Championship

at Bothwell Castle, Lanarkshire

1	J Hodgson	67-71-65-70—273
2	C Hislop	67-70-68-69—274
3	S Gallacher	73-71-64-69—277
	C Watson	73-69-69-66—277
	B Howard	68-70-67-72—277

Wolsey La Manga Masters (Inaugural)

at La Manga, Spain

1	P Page (Dartford)	76-69-73-69—287
2	G Harris (Broome Manor)	76-68-75-69—288
3	R Roper (Catterick Garrison)	76-77-68-70—291

Worplesdon Scratch Mixed Foursomes

at Worplesdon

Semi-Finals

C Titcombe and C Rotheroe beat A and F Edmonds 3 and 2
C and K Quinn beat H Wheeler and A Inglis 1 hole

Final

Mr and Mrs K Quinn beat C Titcombe and C Rotheroe 3 and 2

Women's Amateur Tournaments

Curtis Cup

at The Honors Course, Ooltewah, Chattanooga, Tennessee, on 30–31 July 1994

Great Britain & Ireland		United States	
Day One			
Singles			
J Hall	½	J McGill	½
J Moodie	0	E Klein (3 and 2)	1
L Walton (1 hole)	1	W Ward	0
M McKinlay	0	C Semple Thompson (2 and 1)	1
M McKay	0	E Port (2 and 1)	1
C Matthew (1 hole)	1	S Sparks	0
	2½		3½
Foursomes			
C Matthew and J Moodie	½	J McGill and S LeBrun Ingram	½
M McKay and K Speak	0	C Semple Thompson and E Klein (7 and 5)	1
J Hall and L Walton (6 and 5)	1	W Kaupp and E Port	0
	1½		1½
Day Two			
Foursomes			
J Hall and L Walton (2 and 1)	1	J McGill and S LeBrun Ingram	0
M McKinlay and ER Power	0	C Semple Thompson and E Klein (4 and 2)	1
C Matthew and J Moodie (3 and 2)	1	W Ward and S Sparks	0
	2		1
Singles			
J Hall	0	J McGill (4 and 3)	1
C Matthew (2 and 1)	1	E Klein	0
M McKay	0	E Port (7 and 5)	1
M McKinlay (3 and 2)	1	W Kaupp	0
L Walton	0	W Ward (4 and 3)	1
J Moodie (2 holes)	1	C Semple Thompson	0
	3		3

Result: Great Britain and Ireland 9, United States 9

Women's World Amateur Team Championship for the Espirito Santo Trophy

at Golf National, Paris, France

Leading team scores (Discarded scores in brackets)

1	UNITED STATES	141	141	141	146—569
	S Ingram	72	73	(78)	72
	C Thompson	(76)	(77)	74	(78)
	W Ward	69	68	67	74
2	KOREA	141	146	146	140—573
	MH Kim	(72)	73	75	75
	OY Kwon	70	73	71	(80)
	SR Pak	71	(74)	(76)	65
3	SWEDEN	147	143	146	138—574
	S Eriksson	74	(78)	72	(73)
	M Hjorth	(75)	69	(78)	69
	A-C Jonasson	73	74	74	69
4	SPAIN	140	148	143	144—575
	M Arruti	70	76	75	74
	MJ Pons	(72)	(79)	(76)	(78)
	S Beautell	70	72	68	70
5	AUSTRALIA	140	144	147	146—577
	A-M Knight	69	76	71	73
	K Webb	71	68	76	73
	S Williams	(73)	(76)	(80)	(75)
6	SOUTH AMERICA	149	148	146	138—581
	M Adamson	74	76	(77)	68
	S Marais	75	72	75	(74)
	B Plant	(77)	(78)	71	70
7	FRANCE	141	145	146	150—582
	S Dallongeville	69	(73)	72	74
	C Mourgue d'Algue	72	74	74	76
	A Vincent	(81)	72	(79)	(79)
8	GERMANY	150	147	145	147—589
	M Fischer	(77)	72	71	72
	H Klump	74	75	(75)	(78)
	M Koch	76	(78)	74	75
	GB & I	156	146	144	143—589
	J Hall	(80)	70	71	74
	K Speak	78	76	(80)	(76)
	L Walton	78	(76)	73	69
	NEW ZEALAND	146	145	153	145—589
	L Brooky	(76)	(76)	76	72
	S Farron	75	73	77	(78)
	K Starr	71	72	(77)	73

Leading individual scores

W Ward (US)	278
S Beautell (Spa)	280
SR Pak (Kor)	286
K Webb (Aus)	288
S Dallongeville (Fr)	288
A-M Knight (Aus)	289
A-C Jonasson (Swe)	290
L Freund (Bel)	290
M Hjorth (Swe)	291
M Fischer (Ger)	292

Women's British Amateur Championship

at Newport, Gwent

Quarter Finals
C Matthew beat J Hall 2 and 1
C Mourge d'Algue beat K Egford 2 and 1
AJ Adamson beat M Alsuguren 2 holes
E Duggleby beat K Stupples at 19th

Semi-Finals
C Mourge d'Algue beat C Matthew at 20th
E Duggleby beat A-J Adamson 2 and 1

Final
E Duggleby beat C Mourgue d'Algue 3 and 1

British Women's Open Stroke Play Championship

at Woodhall Spa

1	K Speak	72-77-75-73—297
2	ER Power	75-76-74-74—299
3	M Arruti	71-76-75-78—300
	T McKinnon	74-72-75-79—300

European Women's Amateur Championship

at Bastad GC, Sweden

1	M Fischer (Ger)	73-71-73-71—288
2	T McKinnon (Aus)	76-74-69-70—289
3	S Dallongeville (Fr)	72-74-71-73—290

European Women's Team Championship

at Colony CC, Himberg, Vienna

Semi-Finals
Sweden beat Scotland 5–2
France beat Spain 5–2

Final
Sweden beat France 5½–1½

Women's Home Internationals

at Huddersfield

England beat Ireland	6½–2½
Scotland beat Wales	8½–½
England beat Wales	8–1
Scotland halved with Ireland	4½–4½
England beat Scotland	6–3
Ireland beat Wales	5½–3½

Result: England 3; Scotland 1½; Ireland 1½; Wales 0

Senior Women's British Open Amateur Championship

at Nottingham

1	D Williams	79-75—154
2	J Thornhill	79-76—155
3	H Kaye	80-78—158

English Women's Amateur Championship

at The Berkshire

Semi-Finals

J Hall beat K Tebbet 5 and 4
S Sharpe beat A Murray 1 hole

Final

J Hall beat S Sharpe 1 hole

English Women's Stroke Play Championship

at Ferndown, Bournemouth

1	F Brown	71-74-72-72—289
2	S Morgan	73-73-73-74—293
	K Egford	71-74-73-75—293

English Women's Intermediate Championship

at Beaconsfield

Semi-Finals

J Oliver beat S Morgan at 19th
E Fields beat R Bailey 3 and 2

Final

J Oliver beat E Fields 2 up

English Women's Seniors Championship

at Littlestone

1	S Bassindale (Holme Hall	78-85—163
2	A Duck (Northants Co)	86-82—168
3	H Bristow (Ashford)	87-82—169
	V Morgan (Rhyl Ashdown Forest)	86-83—169
	A Uzielli (The Berkshire)	82-87—169

English Women's Senior Match Play Championship

at Whitting Heath, Staffordshire

Semi-Finals

S Bassindale beat H Kay 3 and 1
E Annison beat C Bailey 1 hole

Final

E Annison beat S Bassindale 4 and 3

English Women's County Championship Finals

at Stratford-on-Avon

Day One
Sussex beat Glamorgan 6½–2½
Staffordshire beat Lancashire 8–1

Day Two
Lancashire beat Glamorgan 6½–2½
Staffordshire halved with Sussex 4½–4½

Day Three
Sussex beat Lancashire 5–4
Staffordshire beat Glamorgan 7–2

Final Positions
Staffordshire 19½; Sussex 16; Lancashire 11½; Glamorgan 7

Irish Women's Championship

at Rosses Point, Co. Sligo

Semi-Finals
L Webb beat P Gorman 4 and 3
H Kavanagh beat A Rogers 3 and 2

Final
L Webb beat H Kavanagh at 20th

Irish Women's Open Stroke Play Championship

at Milltown, Dublin

1	H Kavanagh	73-70-73-70—286
2	T Eakin	77-70-75-71—293
3	D Mahon	71-75-74-76—296

Irish Women's Senior Championship

at Athlone

1	G Costello	80 *(won on countback)*
2	V Butler	80
3	M O'Connor	84

Pringle Champion of Champions Tournament

at Muirfield, East Lothian

1	E Duggleby	77
2	K Tebbet	79
3	A Gemmill	80
	A Greenfield	80

Scottish Women's Championship

at Gullane, East Lothian

Semi-Finals
C Matthew beat F Anderson 6 and 5
F Melvin beat J Ford 1 hole

Final
C Matthew beat F Melvin 1 hole

Scottish Women's Junior (Under-21) Open Stroke Play Championship

at Dumfries and County GC

1	C Agnew	75-72-72—219
2	V Melvin	74-76-72—222
3	H Stirling	81-70-73—224

US Women's Amateur Championship

at Hot Springs, Virginia

Semi-Finals
W Ward beat A Baxter 7 and 5
J McGill beat C Klein 1 hole

Final
W Ward beat J McGill 2 and 1

Welsh Women's Championship

at Royal Porthcawl

Semi-Finals
L Dermott beat J Thomas 3 and 2
V Thomas beat L Isherwood 2 and 1

Final
V Thomas beat L Dermott at 19th

Welsh Women's Champion of Champions

at Glamorgan

1	V Thomas	79-74—153
2	J Thomas	80-74—154
3	J Edwards	81-79—160
	V McKenzie	81-79—160
	D Richards	79-81—160

Welsh Women's Open Stroke Play Championship

at Newport, Gwent

1	A Rose	68-73-76—217
2	E Fields	75-68-75—218
3	L Dermott	73-73-76—222

Welsh Women's Seniors Championship

at Llandudno

1	C Thomas	88-75—163
2	P Morgan	84-89—173
3	B Burnell	86-89—175

Welsh Women's Team Championship

at Portmadoc

Semi-Finals
Pennard beat Holyhead
St Pierre beat Llandudno (Maesdu)

Final
St Pierre beat Pennard

Astor Salvor

at The Berkshire

1	S Lambert	74-68—142
	J Head	73-69—142
	M Sutton	69-73—142

The Bridget Jackson Bowl

at Handsworth, Birmingham

1	K Speak	70-74—144
2	S Burnell	71-74—145
3	S Gallaher	75-71—146

Hampshire Rose

at North Hants

1	K Shepherd*	70-71—141
	K Egford	68-73—141
3	C Quinn	73-71—144
	C Hourihane	72-72—144
	R Nugent	70-74—144

Helen Holm Trophy

at Royal Troon, Ayrshire

1	K Tebbet	71-72-80—223
2	M McKinlay	76-76-74—226
3	J Hall	70-79-79—228

London Women's Foursomes

at Tandridge

Semi-Finals
Knebworth beat Porters Park 1 hole
Chelmsford beat Rochester & Cobham 2 and 1

Final
Knebworth beat Chelmsford 5 and 4

Midland Women's Championship

at Royal Cromer

Semi-Finals
J Morris beat S Sharpe 3 and 2
S Morgan beat R Bailey 4 and 3

Final
J Morris beat S Morgan 1 hole

* *Winner after play-off*

Mid-Wales Women's Championship

at Aberdovey

Semi-Finals
G Gibb beat A Hubbard 2 and 1
P Morgan beat T Gittins 5 and 3

Final
G Gibb beat P Morgan 1 hole

Mothers and Daughters Foursomes

at Royal Mid-Surrey

1	Mrs P Carrick and Mrs A Uzielli*	121
2	Mrs P Huntley and Miss J Huntley	121

Northern Women's Championship

at Wilmslow

Semi-Finals
G Nutter beat J Walley 8 and 6
R Hughes beat N Evans 3 and 1

Final
G Nutter beat R Hughes 3 and 1

Northern Women's Counties Championship

First Series

Cumbria	6	Durham	3
Northumberland	2	Lancashire	7
Yorkshire	6	Cheshire	3

Second Series

Northumberland	3	Yorkshire	6
Cumbria	1½	Lancashire	7½
Cheshire	5	Durham	4

Third Series

Lancashire	5½	Cheshire	3½
Durham	2	Yorkshire	7
Northumberland	8	Cumbria	1

Fourth Series

Durham	2	Northumberland	7
Cumbria	3	Cheshire	6
Yorkshire	3½	Lancashire	5½

Fifth Series

Yorkshire	8	Cumbria	1
Cheshire	7	Northumberland	2
Lancashire	6	Durham	3

Final Positions

Lancashire	5
Yorkshire	4
Cheshire	3
Northumberland	2
Cumbria	1
Durham	0

* *Winners on countback*

Northern Women's Open Foursomes

at Haydock Park

Semi-Finals

K Speak and K Rostron beat N Paton and J Theyton 5 and 4
N Buxton and G Simpson beat S Harper and J Walsh 5 and 4

Final

K Speak and K Rostron beat N Buxton and G Simpson 3 and 2

St Rule Trophy

at St Andrews

1	C Matthew	71-74-72—217
2	C McMaster	76-77-74—227
	A Rose	77-76-74—227
	K Speak	77-72-78—227

Scottish Women's County Championship

at Cawder, Lanarkshire

Day One

East Lothian beat Dunbarton & Argyll	6–3
Northern Counties beat Dumfriesshire	7½–1½

Day Two

East Lothian beat Northern Counties	7½–1½
Dunbarton & Argyll beat Dumfriesshire	8½–½

Day Three

East Lothian beat Dumfriesshire	8½–½
Northern Counties beat Dunbarton & Argyll	5–4

Final Positions

1 East Lothian
2 Northern Counties
3 Dunbarton & Argyll
4 Dumfriesshire

South-East Women's Championship

at Newbury and Crookham

Semi-Finals

K Egford beat S Lambert 2 and 1
C Quinn beat C Titcombe 1 hole

Final

K Egford beat C Quinn 3 and 2

South-West Women's Championship

at Ross-on-Wye

Semi-Finals

E Fields beat J Clingen 1 up
R Morgan beat V Thomas 1 up

Final

R Morgan beat E Fields 3 and 1

West of Scotland Women's Championship

at Hilton Park, Glasgow

1	V Melvin	72-74—146
2	M McKinley	74-77—151
3	D Jackson	78-75—153

Juniors and Youths

Youths and Boys

Boys' Amateur Championship *at Little Aston*

Quarter Finals
C Rodgers beat R Leonard 3 and 1
C Duke beat P Huggett 5 and 4
J Torines beat S Webster 3 and 2
C Smith beat S Garcia 7 and 5

Semi-Finals
C Rodgers beat C Duke 3 and 1
C Smith beat J Torines 2 and 1

Final
C Smith beat C Rodgers 2 and 1

Boys' Home Internationals *at Little Aston*

England *v* Scotland

Foursomes	England	2	Scotland	3
Singles	England	8	Scotland	2
Total	England	10	Scotland	5

Ireland *v* Wales

Foursomes	Ireland	4½	Wales	½
Singles	Ireland	4	Wales	6
Total	Ireland	8½	Wales	6½

England *v* Ireland

Foursomes	England	3	Ireland	2
Singles	England	8½	Ireland	1/2
Total	England	11½	Ireland	3½

Scotland *v* Wales

Foursomes	Scotland	4	Wales	1
Singles	Scotland	8½	Wales	1½
Total	Scotland	12½	Wales	2½

Result: 1st England, 2nd Ireland, 3rd Scotland, 4th Wales

Great Britain & Ireland *v* Continent of Europe

Foursomes	GB & I	4½	Continent of Europe	½
Singles	GB & I	8	Continent of Europe	2
Total	GB & I	12½	Continent of Europe	2½

Youths' Championship *at Royal St David's*

1	F Jacobson	66-67-71-73—277
2	S Hurd	69-68-68-74—279
3	R Tate	70-71-67-72—280
	S Davis	68-67-73-72—280

Scotland *v* England Youths' International

at Royal St Davids

England		Scotland	
Foursomes			
M Foster and S Drummond	0	G Sherry and D Downie (3 and 2)	1
A Wall and S Webster	0	A Reid and H McKibbin (2 and 1)	1
S Davis and J Healey (2 holes)	1	C Hislop and G Davidson	0
D Lynn and D Howell	0	B Collier and M Urquhart (3 and 1)	1
R Bland and L James	0	S Gallacher and D Summers (7 and 5)	1
	1		4
Singles			
M Foster	0	H McKibbin (2 and 1)	1
S Drummond (3 and 2)	1	S Gallacher	0
S Griffiths	0	G Sherry (1 hole)	1
A Wall	0	A Reid (1 hole)	1
S Webster (2 and 1)	1	A Macdonald	0
S Davis	0	M Urquhart (5 and 4)	1
D Lynn (3 and 2)	1	S Summers	0
D Howell (3 and 2)	1	C Hislop	0
R Bland	1/2	D Downie	1/2
L James	0	B Collier (2 and 1)	1
	4 1/2		5 1/2

Result: Scotland 9 1/2, England 5 1/2

Great Britain and Ireland *v* Continent of Europe Boys for the Jacques L'Eglise Trophy

at Little Aston

Great Britain & Ireland		Continent of Europe	
Foursomes			
G Harris and S Craig (6 and 5)	1	JM Lara and JA Viscaya	0
J Harris and S Webster	1/2	M Vildhoj and M Zaretti	1/2
A Forsyth and C Heap (2 holes)	1	D Smolin and M Thannhauser	0
S Raybould and C McMonagle (2 holes)	1	P Davidson and H Ingemarsson	0
J Little and C Duke (3 and 2)	1	H Stenson and J Torines	0
	4 1/2		1/2
Singles			
G Harris (4 and 3)	1	M Thannhauser	0
S Craig	0	M Vildhoj (4 and 2)	1
J Harris (1 hole)	1	P Davidson	0
A Forsyth (1 hole)	1	M Zaretti	0
C Heap (4 and 2)	1	D Smolin	0
S Raybould (2 holes)	1	H Ingemarsson	0
C McMonagle	0	JM Lara (5 and 4)	1
J Little (2 and 1)	1	H Stenson	0
C Duke (5 and 4)	1	JA Viscaya	0
S Webster (4 and 3)	1	J Torines	0
	8		2

Result: Great Britain & Ireland 12 1/2, Continent of Europe 2 1/2

Great Britain and Ireland *v* Continent of Europe Youths for the EGA Trophy

at Golf de Pan, Holland

First Day

Foursomes

Continent of Europe		Great Britain and Ireland	
K Brink and M Lundbers	0	L James and B Dredge (2 and 1)	1
N Zitny and M Lehtinen	1/2	G Sherry and D Downie	1/2
E Carlberg and V Gustafsson	0	S Gallacher and R Bland (3 and 1)	1
F Cea and D Dupin	1/2	R Coughlan and K Nolan	1/2
	1		3

Singles

Continent of Europe		Great Britain and Ireland	
M Lehtinen (2 and 1)	1	L James	0
N Zitny	0	G Sherry (3 and 2)	1
M Hagen	0	D Downie (1 up)	1
V Gustafsson	0	S Gallacher (7 and 6)	1
D Diego	1/2	R Bland	1/2
K Brink (2 and 1)	1	S Drummond	0
F Cea	0	R Coughlan (6 and 5)	1
E Carlberg	1/2	B Dredge	1/2
	3		5

Second Day

Foursomes

Continent of Europe		Great Britain and Ireland	
E Carlberg and M Hagen	0	S Gallacher and R Bland	1
M Lundberg and K Brink	0	L James and B Dredge (1 up)	1
N Zitny and M Lehtinen	0	R Coughlan and K Nolan (1 up)	1
D Dupin and F Cea	0	G Sherry and D Downie (1 up)	1
	0		4

Singles

Continent of Europe		Great Britain and Ireland	
V Gustafsson	0	S Gallacher (1 up)	1
F Cea	0	L James (1 up)	1
M Lehtinen	0	G Sherry (4 and 2)	1
N Zitny	0	K Nolan (3 and 2)	1
M Lundberg (3 and 2)	1	S Drummond	0
D Dupin (1 up)	1	R Coughlan	0
E Carlberg	0	D Downie (3 and 2)	1
K Brink	0	B Dredge (1 up)	1
	2		6

Result: Great Britain & Ireland 18, Continent of Europe 6

European Boys' Team Championship

at Vilamoura, Portugal

Semi-Finals

England beat Spain 4–3
Sweden beat Germany 5–2

Final

England beat Sweden 4–3

European Youths' Team Championship

at Esbjerg, Denmark

Quarter Finals
Sweden beat Denmark 6–1
England beat France 5½–1½
Ireland beat Finland 4–3
Spain beat Scotland 5–2

Semi-Finals
Sweden beat England 5–2
Ireland beat Spain 4½–2½

Play-off for 3rd and 4th places
England beat Spain 6–1

Final
Ireland beat Sweden 4–3

English Boys' Stroke Play Championship for the Carris Trophy

at Northamptonshire County Club

1	R Duck	72-73-65-70—280
2	S Nightingale	72-72-70-68—282
	B Barham	74-71-70-67—282
	J Harris	71-73-67-71—282

English Boys' Under-16 Championship

at Radcliffe-on-Trent, Notts

1	G Storm	74-75-73-69—291
2	D Kirton	73-75-74-71—293
3	P Rowe	74-74-75-71—294
	S Walker	72-71-76-75—294

English Boys' County Finals

at The Hallamshire

Sussex beat Cornwall 6½–2½
Yorkshire beat Warwickshire 5½–3½
Sussex beat Yorkshire 5–4
Cornwall beat Warwickshire 5½–3½
Yorkshire beat Cornwall 5½–3½
Sussex beat Warwickshire 8–1

Result: 1 Sussex 6 pts
2 Yorkshire 4 pts
3 Cornwall 2 pts
4 Warwickshire 0 pts

Irish Boys' Championship

at Nenagh, Tipperary

1	P Byrne	67-71-71—209
2	R Leonard	72-75-66—213
	A Thomas	70-71-72—213

Irish Youths' Championship
at Tullamore

1	B Omelia	69-66-69-68—272
2	C Hislop	71-71-69-68—279
	R Coughlan	70-75-65-69—279

Scottish Boys' Championship
at Dunbar, East Lothian

Quarter Finals
S Young beat G Fox 3 and 2
S McGavin beat A Forsyth 1 hole
E Little beat C Kelly 4 and 3
C Lee beat E McCluskey 5 and 3

Semi-Finals
S Young beat S McGavin 5 and 3
E Little beat C Lee 7 and 5

Final
S Young beat E Little 2 and 1

Scottish Boys' Stroke Play Championship
at Drumpellier, Strathclyde

1	S Young	76-76-67-69—288
2	A Forsyth	77-69-74-71—291
3	C Davidson	77-72-74-71—293

Scottish Boys' Under-16 Stroke Play Championship
at Crieff, Perthshire

1	S Fraser	67-75—142
2	M Loftus	72-72—144
3	K Ferrie	74-71—145

Scottish Youths' Open Stroke Play Championship
at Crieff, Perthshire

1	S Gallacher	71-64-68-72—275
2	K Nolan	71-68-68-69—276
3	R Coughlan	72-70-65-70—277

Welsh Boys' Championship
at Abergele and Pensarn, Clwyd

Semi-Finals
K Sullivan beat C Williams 1 hole
R Peet beat M Palmer 2 and 1

Final
R Peet beat K Sullivan 7 and 6

Welsh Boys' Under-15 Championship

at Aberystwyth

1	A Smith	83-76—159
2	T Williams	78-82—160
3	G Taylor	81-80—161

Welsh Youths' Championship

at Vale of Llangollen, Clwyd

1	D Quinney	69-69-76-76—290
2	P Hunt	74-73-73-76—296
3	R Price	77-71-73-77—298

Peter McEvoy Trophy

at Copt Heath

1	J Harris	73-75-75-77—300
2	G Harris	74-77-77-74—302
	J Little	77-72-73-80—302

Doug Sanders World Junior Championship

at Deeside

1	S Webster (Eng)	72-67-72-64—275
2	D Gleeson (Aust)	71-69-66-70—276
3	C Aronsen (Nor)	66-64-76-71—277
	A Ochoa (US)	66-72-71-68—277

Girls

British Girls' Open Championship

at Gog Magog, Cambridge

Semi-Finals

R Hudson beat E Esterl at 23rd

A Vincent beat MJ Pons 1 up

Final

A Vincent beat R Hudson 1 up

European Junior Girls' Team Championship

at Gutenhof, Austria

Semi-Finals

Sweden beat Scotland 5–2

France beat Spain 5–2

Final

Sweden beat France 5½–1½

Girls' Home International Championship for the Stroyan Cup

at Gog Magog, Cambridge

England beat Wales	7–2
Ireland halved with Scotland	$4^1/2$–$4^1/2$
England beat Ireland	5–4
Scotland beat Wales	7–2
Ireland beat Wales	7–2
Scotland beat England	7–2

Final placings
1st Scotland $2^1/2$, 2nd England 2, 3rd Ireland $1^1/2$, 4th Wales 0

English Girls' Championship

at Whitley Bay, Tyne & Wear

Quarter Finals
L Wixon beat N Bracey 4 and 3
K Hamilton beat G Nutter 1 hole
S Coverley beat D Rushworth 2 and 1
S Forster beat G Scase 5 and 4

Semi-Finals
K Hamilton beat L Wixon at 20th
S Forster beat S Coverley 5 and 4

Final
K Hamilton beat S Forster 3 and 2

Irish Girls' Championship

at Mullingar, Co. Westmeath

Semi-Finals
A Doyle beat M McGreevey at 19th
A O'Leary beat P Murphy 3 and 1

Final
A O'Leary beat D Doyle at 23rd

Scottish Girls' Championship

at Deeside, Aberdeen

Semi-Finals
L Moffat beat F Lockhart 5 and 4
L Nicholson beat C Agnew 3 and 2

Final
L Nicholson beat L Moffat 2 and 1

Welsh Girls' Championship

at Wrexham, Clwyd

Semi-Finals
K Stark beat E Pilgrim at 19th
J Evans beat J Nicholson 1 hole

Final
K Stark beat J Evans 4 and 3

Golf Foundation Tournament Winners

Team Championship for Schools 1994

International Final at St Andrews

1st France

Lycée Bellevue, Toulouse

Georges Plumet	74-75—149
Olivier David	74-77—151
Gregory Havret	77-82—159
	459

2nd New Zealand

Otago Boys' High School

Mahal Pearce	71-76—147
Phillip Rust	80-72—152
Jason Hughes	85-85—170
	469

3rd Australia

International School

Jonathan Riley	75-70—145
Peter Smith	77-88—165
Shannon Bridger	85-79—164
	474

4th Netherlands

Kennemer Lyceum

Joppe de Vries	83-83—166
Rolf Exalto	81-78—159
Matthys Spaans	77-77—154
	479

5th Scotland

Dumfries Academy

Clark Riddick	78-80—158
Craig Smith	76-79—155
Mark Nicoll	85-84—169
	482

6th Germany

Goethe Gymnasium

David Smolin	77-78—155
Pascale Zillmer*	80-80—160
Victoria Smolin*	88-84—172
	487

7th Ireland

Coleraine Academical Institute

Richard Elliott	78-82—160
Christopher Brown	85-81—166
Mark Hemphill	79-83—162
	488

8th England

Millfield School

Brian Caulfield	84-80—164
Alex Hodges	80-77—157
Tom Rawlings	86-82—168
	489

9th Iceland

Akranes College

Birgir L Hafthorsson	75-76—151
Helgi Dan Steinsson	88-81—169
Gunnar O Helgason	90-87—177
	497

10th Wales

Neath College

Mark Selby	83-85—168
Darren Williams	87-81—168
James Doble	87-82—169
	505

11th Sweden

Dergarden Gymnasium

Claes Nilsson	85-80—165
Carl Ekener	81-93—174
Johanna Marciniak*	89-88—177
	516

PGA European Tour Trophy

Jonathan Riley, Australia 75-70—145

* Girls

Golf Foundation/Weetabix Age Group Championships

at Patshull Park, Shropshire

Under 16

Boys

Alex Smith (Rhondda)	73-73—146
Mark Wood (Rawdon)	74-74—148
Lee Rogers (Royston)	77-72—149
Simon Young (Seascale)	75-74—149
Matthew Naylor (Cotgrave Place)	76-74—150
Mark Cameron (Alyth)	76-75—151

Girls

Lisa Meredith (Wentworth)	73-76—149
Rebecca Hudson (Wheatley)	77-75—152
Fiona Prior (Cawder)	77-87—164
Kathryn Fallows (Clitheroe)	82-86—168
Jill de Villiers (Rushcliffe)	82-87—169
Sara Garbutt (Knaresborough)	90-82—172
Ailbhe Farrell (Roscommon)	83-89—172

Under 15

Boys

Tony Hilton (Lewes)	77-73—150
Ross Hadley (Canons Brook)	77-77—154
John Cockroft (Nelson)	82-76—158
Paul Heppenstall (Worlebury)	80-78—158
Mark Prue (Hillside)	81-78—159
Philip McIlvaney (Bellshill)	84-76—160
Michael Jones (Heswall)	80-80—160
Mark Campbell (Stackstown)	76-84—160

Girls

Laura Moffat (West Kilbride)	80-75—155
Lisa Walters (Ormonde Fields)	81-79—160
Kate Stark (Brynhill)	80-84—164
Helen Marriott (Sherwood Forest)	80-88—168
Ellie Brede (Whitehill)	88-86—174
Suzanne Cross (Hazel Grove)	86-91—177

Under 14

Boys

Andrew Smith (Enville)	72-77—149
James Shilton (Rawdon)	81-74—155
Simon Robinson (Seaton Carew)	76-81—157
Andrew Richards (Stanmore)	77-81—158
Gavin Legg (Enmore Park)	80-80—160
Mark King (Bawburgh)	79-84—163

Girls

Vikki Laing (Musselburgh)	78-83—161
Fame More (Chesterfield)	78-87—165
Kamilla Lawton (Tytherington)	86-86—172
Michele Fossett (Broome Manor)	88-85—173
Ellen Gaines (Ashburnham)	98-88—186
Julie Ross (Wallsend)	98-92—190

Under 13

Boys

David Tarbotton (Hull)	76-80—156
David Porter (Wellow)	77-80—157
Sandeep Grewal (Prenton)	78-80—158
David Addison (West Berkshire)	76-82—158
Peter Wheatcroft (Worksop)	79-80—159
Tom Dawson (Rookery Park)	82-80—162

Duke of York Trophy winners

Alex Smith (Rhondda) 146 and Lisa Meredith (Wentworth) 149

Golf Foundation Team Championship for Schools for the R&A Trophy

Year	Winner	Country	Venue
1987	Klippans Gymnasieskola	Sweden	Foxhills
1988	Klippans Gymnasieskola	Sweden	Sunningdale
1989	Marks Gymnasium	Sweden	St Andrews
1990	Lycée Bellevue	France	St Andrews
1991	Lycée Bellevue	France	Sunningdale
1992	Lycée Bellevue	France	St Andrews
1993	Lycée Bellevue	France	Gleneagles
1994	Lycée Bellevue	France	St Andrews

Golf Foundation Award Winners

Year	Winner	Club
1982	Lindsey Anderson	Tain
1983	Nigel Osborne Clarke	Shirehampton
1984	Wayne Henry	Redbourn
1985	David Grantham	Hull
1986	Matthew Stanford	Saltford
1987	Jane Marchant	Whittington Barracks
1988	*Boys:* Ian Garbutt	Wheatley
	Girls: Lisa Dermott	St Melyd
1989	*Boys:* Lee Westwood	Worksop
	Girls: Lynn McCool	Strabane
1990	*Boys:* Keith Law	Forfar
	Girls: Mhairi McKay	Turnberry
1991	*Boys:* Gary Harris	Broome Manor
	Girls: Nicola Buxton	Woodsome Hall
1992	*Boys:* Shaun Devenney	Strabane
	Girls: Mhairi McKay	Turnberry
1993	*Boys:* Craig Williams	Greigiau
	Girls: Georgina Simpson	Cleckheaton & Dist
1994	*Boys:* Denny Lucas (Worksop)	
	Girls: Rebecca Hudson (Wheatley)	

Awards

Association of Golf Writers' Trophy

Awarded to the man or woman who, in the opinion of Golf Writers, has done most for golf during the year

1951 Max Faulkner
1952 Miss Elizabeth Price
1953 Joe Carr
1954 Mrs Roy Smith (Miss Frances Stephens)
1955 Ladies' Golf Union's Touring Team
1956 John Beharrell
1957 Dai Rees
1958 Harry Bradshaw
1959 Eric Brown
1960 Sir Stuart Goodwin (sponsor of international golf)
1961 Commdr Charles Roe (ex-hon secretary, PGA)
1962 Mrs Marley Spearman, British Ladies' Champion 1961–1962
1963 Michael Lunt, Amateur Champion, 1963
1964 Great Britain & Ireland Eisenhower Trophy Team
1965 Gerald Micklem, golf administrator, President, English Golf Union
1966 Ronnie Shade
1967 John Panton
1968 Michael Bonallack
1969 Tony Jacklin
1970 Tony Jacklin
1971 Great Britain & Ireland Walker Cup Team
1972 Miss Michelle Walker
1973 Peter Oosterhuis
1974 Peter Oosterhuis
1975 Golf Foundation
1976 Great Britain & Ireland Eisenhower Trophy Team
1977 Christy O'Connor
1978 Peter McEvoy
1979 Severiano Ballesteros
1980 Sandy Lyle
1981 Bernhard Langer
1982 Gordon Brand Jr
1983 Nick Faldo
1984 Severiano Ballesteros
1985 European Ryder Cup Team
1986 Great Britain and Ireland Curtis Cup Team
1987 European Ryder Cup Team
1988 Sandy Lyle
1989 Great Britain & Ireland Walker Cup Team
1990 Nick Faldo
1991 Severiano Ballesteros
1992 European Solheim Cup Team
1993 Bernhard Langer
1994 Laura Davies

Harry Vardon Trophy

Currently awarded to the PGA member heading the Order of Merit at the end of the season

1937	Charles Whitcombe
1938	Henry Cotton
1939	Roger Whitcombe
1940–45	*In abeyance*
1946	Bobby Locke
1947	Norman Von Nida
1948	Charlie Ward
1949	Charlie Ward
1950	Bobby Locke
1951	John Panton
1952	Harry Weetman
1953	Flory van Donck
1954	Bobby Locke
1955	Dai Rees
1956	Harry Weetman
1957	Eric Brown
1958	Bernard Hunt
1959	Dai Rees
1960	Bernard Hunt
1961	Christy O'Connor
1962	Christy O'Connor
1963	Neil Coles
1964	Peter Alliss
1965	Bernard Hunt
1966	Peter Alliss
1967	Malcolm Gregson
1968	Brian Huggett
1969	Bernard Gallacher
1970	Neil Coles
1971	Peter Oosterhuis
1972	Peter Oosterhuis
1973	Peter Oosterhuis
1974	Peter Oosterhuis
1975	Dale Hayes
1976	Severiano Ballesteros
1977	Severiano Ballesteros
1978	Severiano Ballesteros
1979	Sandy Lyle
1980	Sandy Lyle
1981	Bernhard Langer
1982	Greg Norman
1983	Nick Faldo
1984	Bernhard Langer
1985	Sandy Lyle
1986	Severiano Ballesteros
1987	Ian Woosnam
1988	Severiano Ballesteros
1989	Ronan Rafferty
1990	Ian Woosnam
1991	Severiano Ballesteros
1992	Nick Faldo
1993	Colin Montgomerie
1994	Colin Montgomerie

Rookie of the Year

1960	Tommy Goodwin	1978	Sandy Lyle
1961	Alex Caygill	1979	Mike Miller
1962	*No Award*	1980	Paul Hoad
1963	Tony Jacklin	1981	Jeremy Bennett
1964	*No Award*	1982	Gordon Brand Jr
1966	Robin Liddle	1983	Grant Turner
1967	*No Award*	1984	Philip Parkin
1968	Bernard Gallacher	1985	Paul Thomas
1969	Peter Oosterhuis	1986	José Maria Olazabal
1970	Stuart Brown	1987	Peter Baker
1971	David Llewellyn	1988	Colin Montgomerie
1972	Sam Torrance	1989	Paul Broadhurst
1973	Philip Elson	1990	Russell Claydon
1974	Carl Mason	1991	Per-Ulrik Johansson
1975	*No Award*	1992	Jim Payne
1976	Mark James	1993	Gary Orr
1977	Nick Faldo	1994	Jonathan Lomas

Daily Telegraph Woman Golfer of the Year *(Formerly The Avia Award)*

1982	Jane Connachan
1983	Jill Thornhill
1984	Gillian Stewart and Claire Waite
1985	Belle Robertson
1986	Great Britain and Ireland Curtis Cup Team
1987	Linda Bayman
1988	Great Britain and Ireland Curtis Cup Team
1989	Helen Dobson
1990	Angela Uzielli
1991	Joanne Morley
1992	Great Britain and Ireland Curtis Cup Team, Captain Liz Boatman
1993	Catriona Lambert and Julie Hall
1994	Great Britain and Ireland Curtis Cup Team, Captain Liz Boatman

Bobby Jones Award

Awarded by USGA for distinguished sportsmanship in golf

1955	Francis Ouimet	1977	Joseph C Dey
1956	Bill Campbell	1978	Bob Hope and Bing Crosby
1957	Babe Zaharias	1979	Tom Kite
1958	Margaret Curtis	1980	Charles Yates
1959	Findlay Douglas	1981	Mrs JoAnne Carner
1960	Charles Evans Jr	1982	Billy Joe Patton
1961	Joe Carr	1983	Mrs Maureen Garrett
1962	Horton-Smith	1984	Jay Sigel
1963	Patty Berg	1985	Fuzzy Zoeller
1964	Charles Coe	1986	Jess W Sweetser
1965	Mrs Edwin Vare	1987	Tom Watson
1966	Gary Player	1988	Isaac B Grainger
1967	Richard Tufts	1989	Chi-Chi Rodriquez
1968	Robert Dickson	1990	Peggy Kirk Bell
1969	Gerald Micklem	1991	Ben Grenshaw
1970	Roberto De Vicenzo	1992	Gene Sarazen
1971	Arnold Palmer	1993	PJ Boatwright Jr
1972	Michael Bonallack	1994	Lewis Oehmig
1973	Gene Littler	1995	Herbert Warren Wind
1974	Byron Nelson		
1975	Jack Nicklaus		
1976	Ben Hogan		

The US Vardon Trophy

The award is made to the member of the US PGA who completes 60 rounds or more, with the lowest scoring average over the calendar year.

1948	Ben Hogan	1972	Lee Trevino
1949	Sam Snead	1973	Bruce Crampton
1950	Sam Snead	1974	Lee Trevino
1951	Lloyd Mangrum	1975	Bruce Crampton
1952	Jack Burke	1976	Don January
1953	Lloyd Mangrum	1977	Tom Watson
1954	Ed Harrison	1978	Tom Watson
1955	Sam Snead	1979	Tom Watson
1956	Cary Middlecoff	1980	Lee Trevino
1957	Dow Finsterwald	1981	Tom Kite
1958	Bob Rosburg	1982	Tom Kite
1959	Art Wall	1983	Ray Floyd
1960	Billy Casper	1984	Calvin Peete
1961	Arnold Palmer	1985	Don Pooley
1962	Arnold Palmer	1986	Scott Hoch
1963	Billy Casper	1987	Dan Pohl
1964	Arnold Palmer	1988	Chip Beck
1965	Billy Casper	1989	Greg Norman
1966	Billy Casper	1990	Greg Norman
1967	Arnold Palmer	1991	Fred Couples
1968	Billy Casper	1992	Fred Couples
1969	Dave Hill	1993	Nick Price
1970	Lee Trevino	1994	Greg Norman
1971	Lee Trevino		

US PGA Player of the Year Award

1948	Ben Hogan	1972	Jack Nicklaus
1949	Sam Snead	1973	Jack Nicklaus
1950	Ben Hogan	1974	Johnny Miller
1951	Ben Hogan	1975	Jack Nicklaus
1952	Julius Boros	1976	Jack Nicklaus
1953	Ben Hogan	1977	Tom Watson
1954	Ed Furgol	1978	Tom Watson
1955	Doug Ford	1979	Tom Watson
1956	Jack Burke	1980	Tom Watson
1957	Dick Mayer	1981	Bill Rogers
1958	Dow Finsterwald	1982	Tom Watson
1959	Art Wall	1983	Hal Sutton
1960	Arnold Palmer	1984	Tom Watson
1961	Jerry Barner	1985	Lanny Wadkins
1962	Arnold Palmer	1986	Bob Tway
1963	Julius Boros	1987	Paul Azinger
1964	Ken Venturi	1988	Curtis Strange
1965	Dave Marr	1989	Tom Kite
1966	Billy Casper	1990	Nick Faldo
1967	Jack Nicklaus	1991	Corey Pavin
1968	*not awarded*	1992	Fred Couples
1969	Orville Moody	1993	Nick Price
1970	Billy Casper	1994	Nick Price
1971	Lee Trevino		

Arnold Palmer

Awarded to the US PGA Tour leading money-winner

1981	Tom Kite	1988	Curtis Strange
1982	Craig Stadler	1989	Tom Kite
1983	Hal Sutton	1990	Greg Norman
1984	Tom Watson	1991	Corey Pavin
1985	Curtis Strange	1992	Fred Couples
1986	Greg Norman	1993	Nick Price
1987	Paul Azinger	1994	Nick Price

US PGA Tour Player of the Year

1990	Wayne Levi
1991	Fred Couples
1992	Fred Couples
1993	Nick Price
1994	Nick Price

US LPGA Rolex Player of the Year

1980	Beth Daniel	1988	Nancy Lopez
1981	JoAnne Carner	1989	Betsy King
1982	JoAnne Carner	1990	Beth Daniel
1983	Patty Sheehan	1991	Pat Bradley
1984	Betsy King	1992	Dottie Mochrie
1985	Nancy Lopez	1993	Betsy King
1986	Pat Bradley	1994	Beth Daniel
1987	Ayako Okamoto		

US LPGA Vare Trophy

		Scoring average
1980	Amy Alcott	71.51
1981	JoAnne Carner	71.75
1982	JoAnne Carner	71.49
1983	JoAnne Carner	71.41
1984	Patty Sheehan	71.40
1985	Nancy Lopez	70.73
1986	Pat Bradley	71.10
1987	Betsy King	71.14
1988	Colleen Walker	71.26
1989	Beth Daniel	70.38
1990	Beth Daniel	70.54
1991	Pat Bradley	70.66
1992	Dottie Mochrie	70.80
1993	Nancy Lopez	70.83
1994	Beth Daniel	70.90

US LPGA Gatorade Rookie of the Year

1980	Myra Van Hoose
1981	Patty Sheehan
1982	Patti Rizzo
1983	Stephanie Farwig
1984	Juli Inkster
1985	Penny Hammel
1986	Jody Rosenthal
1987	Tammie Green
1988	Liselotte Neumann (Swi)
1989	Pamela Wright (GB)
1990	Hiromi Kobayashi (Jap)
1991	Brandie Burton
1992	Helen Alfredsson (Swe)
1993	Suzanne Strudwick (GB)
1994	Annika Sorenstam (Swe)

Vivien Saunders Trophy

Awarded to the Women Professional Golfers' European Tour winner of the stroke play averages

1992	Laura Davies
1993	Laura Davies
1994	Liselotte Neumann

Joyce Wethered Trophy

Awarded to the outstanding amateur under the age of 25

1994	Janice Moodie

PART III

Past Tournament Results

British and Irish National Championships

Amateur Championship

Year	Winner	Runner-up	Venue	By	Ent
1885	A MacFie	H Hutchinson	Hoylake, R Liverpool	7 and 6	44
1886	H Hutchinson	H Lamb	St Andrews	7 and 6	42
1887	H Hutchinson	J Ball	Hoylake, R Liverpool	1 hole	33
1888	J Ball	J Laidlay	Prestwick	5 and 4	38
1889	J Laidlay	L Melville	St Andrews	2 and 1	40
1890	J Ball	J Laidlay	Hoylake, R Liverpool	4 and 3	44
1891	J Laidlay	H Hilton	St Andrews	20th hole	50
1892	J Ball	H Hilton	Sandwich, R St George's	3 and 1	45
1893	P Anderson	J Laidlay	Prestwick	1 hole	44
1894	J Ball	S Fergusson	Hoylake, R Liverpool	1 hole	64
1895	L Melville	J Ball	St Andrews	19th hole	68
1896*	F Tait	H Hilton	Sandwich, R St George's	8 and 7	64
**36 holes played on and after this date*					
1897	A Allan	J Robb	Muirfield	4 and 2	74
1898	F Tait	S Fergusson	Hoylake, R Liverpool	7 and 5	77
1899	J Ball	F Tait	Prestwick	37th hole	101
1900	H Hilton	J Robb	Sandwich, R St George's	8 and 7	68
1901	H Hilton	J Low	St Andrews	1 hole	116
1902	C Hutchings	S Fry	Hoylake, R Liverpool	1 hole	114
1903	R Maxwell	H Hutchinson	Muirfield	7 and 5	142
1904	W Travis (USA)	E Blackwell	Sandwich, R St George's	4 and 3	104
1905	A Barry	Hon O Scott	Prestwick	3 and 2	148
1906	J Robb	C Lingen	Hoylake, R Liverpool	4 and 3	166
1907	J Ball	C Palmer	St Andrews	6 and 4	200
1908	E Lassen	H Taylor	Sandwich, R St George's	7 and 6	197
1909	R Maxwell	Capt C Hutchison	Muirfield	1 hole	170
1910	J Ball	C Aylmer	Hoylake, R Liverpool	10 and 9	160
1911	H Hilton	E Lassen	Prestwick	4 and 3	146
1912	J Ball	A Mitchell	Westward Ho!, R North Devon	38th hole	134
1913	H Hilton	R Harris	St Andrews	6 and 5	198
1914	J Jenkins	C Hezlet	Sandwich, R St George's	3 and 2	232
1915–19	*No Championship owing to the Great War*				
1920	C Tolley	R Gardner (USA)	Muirfield	37th hole	165
1921	W Hunter	A Graham	Hoylake, R Liverpool	12 and 11	223
1922	E Holderness	J Caven	Prestwick	1 hole	252
1923	R Wethered	R Harris	Deal, R Cinque Ports	7 and 6	209
1924	E Holderness	E Storey	St Andrews	3 and 2	201
1925	R Harris	K Fradgley	Westward Ho!, R North Devon	13 and 12	151
1926	J Sweetser (USA)	A Simpson	Muirfield	6 and 5	216
1927	Dr W Tweddell	D Landale	Hoylake, R Liverpool	7 and 6	197
1928	T Perkins	R Wethered	Prestwick	6 and 4	220
1929	C Tolley	J Smith	Sandwich, R St George's	4 and 3	253
1930	R Jones (USA)	R Wethered	St Andrews	7 and 6	271
1931	E Smith	J De Forest	Westward Ho!, R North Devon	1 hole	171
1932	J De Forest	E Fiddian	Muirfield	3 and 1	235
1933	Hon M Scott	T Bourn	Hoylake, R Liverpool	4 and 3	269
1934	W Lawson Little (USA)	J Wallace	Prestwick	14 and 13	225
1935	W Lawson Little (USA)	Dr W Tweddell	R Lytham and St Annes	1 hole	232
1936	H Thomson	J Ferrier (Aus)	St Andrews	2 holes	283
1937	R Sweeney, Jr (USA)	L Munn	Sandwich, R St George's	3 and 2	223
1938	C Yates (USA)	R Ewing	Troon	3 and 2	241
1939	A Kyle	A Duncan	Hoylake, R Liverpool	2 and 1	167
1940–45	*Suspended during Second World War*				
1946	J Bruen	R Sweeny (USA)	Birkdale	4 and 3	263
1947	W Turnesa (USA)	R Chapman (USA)	Carnoustie	3 and 2	200

Year	Winner	Runner-up	Venue	By	Ent
1948	F Stranahan (USA)	C Stowe	Sandwich, R St George's	5 and 4	168
1949	S McCready	W Turnesa (USA)	Portmarnock	2 and 1	204
1950	F Stranahan (USA)	R Chapman (USA)	St Andrews	8 and 6	324
1951	R Chapman (USA)	C Coe (USA)	R Porthcawl	5 and 4	192
1952	E Ward (USA)	F Stranahan (USA)	Prestwick	6 and 5	286
1953	J Carr	E Harvie Ward (USA)	Hoylake, R Liverpool	2 holes	279
1954	D Bachli (Aus)	W Campbell (USA)	Muirfield	2 and 1	286
1955	J Conrad (USA)	A Slater	R Lytham and St Annes	3 and 2	240
1956	J Beharrell	L Taylor	Troon	5 and 4	200
1957	R Reid Jack	H Ridgley (USA)	Formby	2 and 1	200
In 1956 and 1957 the Quarter Finals, Semi-Finals and Final were played over 36 holes					
1958	J Carr	A Thirlwell	St Andrews	3 and 2	488
In 1958, Semi-Finals and Final only were played over 36 holes					
1959	D Beman (USA)	W Hyndman (USA)	Sandwich, R St George's	3 and 2	362
1960	J Carr	R Cochran (USA)	R Portrush	8 and 7	183
1961	M Bonallack	J Walker	Turnberry	6 and 4	250
1962	R Davies (USA)	J Povall	Hoylake, R Liverpool	1 hole	256
1963	M Lunt	J Blackwell	St Andrews	2 and 1	256
1964	G Clark	M Lunt	Ganton	39th hole	220
1965	M Bonallack	C Clark	R Porthcawl	2 and 1	176
1966	R Cole (SA)	R Shade	Carnoustie (18 holes)	3 and 2	206
1967	R Dickson (USA)	R Cerrudo (USA)	Formby	2 and 1	
1968	M Bonallack	J Carr	Troon	7 and 6	249
1969	M Bonallack	W Hyndman (USA)	Hoylake, R Liverpool	3 and 2	245
1970	M Bonallack	W Hyndman (USA)	Newcastle, R Co Down	8 and 7	256
1971	S Melnyk (USA)	J Simons (USA)	Carnoustie	3 and 2	256
1972	T Homer	A Thirlwell	Sandwich, R St George's	4 and 3	253
1973	R Siderowf (USA)	P Moody	R Porthcawl	5 and 3	222
1974	T Homer	J Gabrielsen (USA)	Muirfield	2 holes	330
1975	M Giles (USA)	M James	Hoylake, R Liverpool	8 and 7	206
1976	R Siderowf (USA)	J Davies	St Andrews	37th hole	289
1977	P McEvoy	H Campbell	Ganton	5 and 4	235
1978	P McEvoy	P McKellar	R Troon	4 and 3	353
1979	J Sigel (USA)	S Hoch (USA)	Hillside	3 and 2	285
1980	D Evans	D Suddards (SA)	R Porthcawl	4 and 3	265
1981	P Ploujoux (Fra)	J Hirsch (USA)	St Andrews	4 and 2	256
1982	M Thompson	A Stubbs	Deal, R Cinque Ports	4 and 3	245
1983	A Parkin	J Holtgrieve (USA)	Turnberry	5 and 4	288
1984	JM Olazabal (Spa)	C Montgomerie	Formby	5 and 4	291
1985	G McGimpsey	G Homewood	R Dornoch	8 and 7	457
1986	D Curry	G Birtwell	R Lytham and St Annes	11 and 9	427
1987	P Mayo	P McEvoy	Prestwick	3 and 1	373
1988	C Hardin (Swe)	B Fouchee (SA)	R Porthcawl	1 hole	391
1989	S Dodd	C Cassells	R. Birkdale	5 and 3	378
1990	R Muntz (Neth)	A Macara	Muirfield	7 and 6	510
1991	G Wolstenholme	B May (USA)	Ganton	8 and 6	345
1992	S Dundas	B Dredge	Carnoustie	7 and 6	364
1993	I Pyman	P Page	R Portrush	37th hole	279
1994	L James	G Sherry	Nairn	2 and 1	288

Senior Open Amateur Championship

Year	Winner	Venue	Score
1969	R Pattinson	Formby	154
1970	K Bamber	Prestwick	150
1971	GH Pickard	Deal, R Cinque Ports; Sandwich, R St George's	150
1972	TC Hartley	St Andrews	147
1973	JT Jones	Longniddry	142
1974	MA Ivor-Jones	Moortown	149
1975	HJ Roberts	Turnberry	138
1976	WM Crichton	Berkshire	149
1977	Dr TE Donaldson	Panmure	228
1978	RJ White	Formby	225
1979	RJ White	Harlech, R St David's	226
1980	JM Cannon	Prestwick St Nicholas	218
1981	T Branton	Hoylake, R Liverpool	227
1982	RL Glading	Blairgowrie	218
1983	AJ Swann (USA)	Walton Heath	222
1984	JC Owens (USA)	Western Gailes	222

continued

Senior Open Amateur Championship *continued*

Year	Winner	Venue	Score
1985	D Morey (USA)	Hesketh	223
1986	AN Sturrock	Panmure	229
1987	B Soyars (USA)	Deal, R Cinque Ports	226
1988	CW Green	Barnton, Edinburgh	221
1989	CW Green	Moortown and Alwoodley	226
1990	CW Green	The Berkshire	207
1991	CW Green	Prestwick	219
1992	C Hartland	Purdis Heath	221
1993	CW Green	R Aberdeen and Murcar	150
1994	CW Green	Formby, Southport & Ainsdale	223

Ladies' British Open Amateur Championship

Year	Winner	Runner-up	Venue	By
1893	Lady Margaret Scott	Miss I Pearson	St Annes	7 and 5
1894	Lady Margaret Scott	Miss I Pearson	Littlestone	3 and 2
1895	Lady Margaret Scott	Miss E Lythgoe	Portrush	5 and 4
1896	Miss Pascoe	Miss L Thomson	Hoylake, R Liverpool	3 and 2
1897	Miss EC Orr	Miss Orr	Gullane	4 and 2
1898	Miss L Thomson	Miss EC Neville	Yarmouth	7 and 5
1899	Miss M Hezlet	Miss Magill	Newcastle Co Down	2 and 1
1900	Miss Adair	Miss Neville	Westward Ho!, R North Devon	6 and 5
1901	Miss Graham	Miss Adair	Aberdovey	3 and 1
1902	Miss M Hezlet	Miss E Neville	Deal	19th hole
1903	Miss Adair	Miss F Walker-Leigh	Portrush	4 and 3
1904	Miss L Dod	Miss M Hezlet	Troon	1 hole
1905	Miss B Thompson	Miss ME Stuart	Cromer	3 and 2
1906	Mrs Kennon	Miss B Thompson	Burnham	4 and 3
1907	Miss M Hezlet	Miss F Hezlet	Newcastle Co Down	2 and 1
1908	Miss M Titterton	Miss D Campbell	St Andrews	19th hole
1909	Miss D Campbell	Miss F Hezlet	Birkdale	4 and 3
1910	Miss Grant Suttie	Miss L Moore	Westward Ho!, R North Devon	6 and 4
1911	Miss D Campbell	Miss V Hezlet	Portrush	3 and 2
1912	Miss G Ravenscroft	Miss S Temple	Turnberry	3 and 2
(Final played over 36 holes after 1912)				
1913	Miss M Dodd	Miss Chubb	St Annes	8 and 6
1914	Miss C Leitch	Miss G Ravenscroft	Hunstanton	2 and 1
1915–18	*No Championship owing to the Great War*			
1919	*Should have been played at Burnham in October, but abandoned owing to Railway Strike*			
1920	Miss C Leitch	Miss M Griffiths	Newcastle Co Down	7 and 6
1921	Miss C Leitch	Miss J Wethered	Turnberry	4 and 3
1922	Miss J Wethered	Miss C Leitch	Prince's, Sandwich, R St George's	9 and 7
1923	Miss D Chambers	Miss A Macbeth	Burnham, Somerset	2 holes
1924	Miss J Wethered	Mrs Cautley	Portrush	7 and 6
1925	Miss J Wethered	Miss C Leitch	Troon	37th hole
1926	Miss C Leitch	Mrs Garon	Harlech	8 and 7
1927	Miss Thion de la Chaume (Fra)	Miss Pearson	Newcastle Co Down	5 and 4
1928	Miss N Le Blan (Fra)	Miss S Marshall	Hunstanton	3 and 2
1929	Miss J Wethered	Miss G Collett (USA)	St Andrews	3 and 1
1930	Miss D Fishwick	Miss G Collett (USA)	Formby	4 and 3
1931	Miss E Wilson	Miss W Morgan	Portmarnock	7 and 6
1932	Miss E Wilson	Miss CPR Montgomery	Saunton	7 and 6
1933	Miss E Wilson	Miss D Plumpton	Gleneagles	5 and 4
1934	Mrs AM Holm	Miss P Barton	Porthcawl	6 and 5
1935	Miss W Morgan	Miss P Barton	Newcastle Co Down	3 and 2
1936	Miss P Barton	Miss B Newell	Southport and Ainsdale	5 and 3
1937	Miss J Anderson	Miss D Park	Turnberry	6 and 4
1938	Mrs AM Holm	Miss E Corlett	Burnham	4 and 3
1939	Miss P Barton	Mrs T Marks	Portrush	2 and 1
1940–45	*No Championship owing to Second World War*			
1946	GW Hetherington	P Garvey	Hunstanton	1 hole
1947	B Zaharias (USA)	J Gordon	Gullane	5 and 4
1948	L Suggs (USA)	J Donald	Lytham St Annes	1 hole
1949	F Stephens	V Reddan	Harlech	5 and 4
1950	Vicomtesse de Saint Sauveur (Fra)	J Valentine	Newcastle Co Down	3 and 2
1951	PJ MacCann	F Stephens	Broadstone	4 and 3
1952	M Paterson	F Stephens	Troon	39th hole

Year	Winner	Runner-up	Venue	By
1953	M Stewart (Can)	P Garvey	Porthcawl	7 and 6
1954	F Stephens	E Price	Ganton	4 and 3
1955	J Valentine	B Romack (USA)	Portrush	7 and 6
1956	M Smith (USA)	M Janssen (USA)	Sunningdale	8 and 7
1957	P Garvey	J Valentine	Gleneagles	4 and 3
1958	J Valentine	E Price	Hunstanton	1 hole
1959	E Price	B McCorkindale	Ascot	37th hole
1960	B McIntyre (USA)	P Garvey	Harlech	4 and 2
1961	M Spearman	DJ Robb	Carnoustie	7 and 6
1962	M Spearman	A Bonallack	Birkdale	1 hole
1963	B Varangot (Fra)	P Garvey	Newcastle Co Down	3 and 1
1964	C Sorenson (USA)	BAB Jackson	Sandwich, Prince's, R St George's	37th hole
1965	B Varangot (Fra)	IC Robertson	St Andrews	4 and 3
1966	E Chadwick	V Saunders	Ganton	3 and 2
1967	E Chadwick	M Everard	Harlech	1 hole
1968	B Varangot (Fra)	C Rubin (Fra)	Walton Heath	20th hole
1969	C Lacoste (Fra)	A Irvin	Portrush	1 hole
1970	D Oxley	IC Robertson	Gullane	1 hole
1971	M Walker	B Huke	Alwoodley	3 and 1
1972	M Walker	C Rubin (Fra)	Hunstanton	2 holes
1973	A Irvin	M Walker	Carnoustie	3 and 2
1974	C Semple (USA)	A Bonallack	Porthcawl	2 and 1
1975	N Syms (USA)	S Cadden	St Andrews	3 and 2
1976	C Panton	A Sheard	Silloth	1 hole
1977	A Uzielli	V Marvin	Hillside	6 and 5
1978	E Kennedy (Aus)	J Greenhalgh	Notts	1 hole
1979	M Madill	J Lock (Aus)	Nairn	2 and 1
1980	A Quast (USA)	L Wollin (Swe)	Woodhall Spa	3 and 1
1981	IC Robertson	W Aitken	Conway	20th hole
1982	K Douglas	G Stewart	Walton Heath	4 and 2
1983	J Thornhill	R Lautens (Switz)	Silloth	4 and 2
1984	J Rosenthal (USA)	J Brown	Royal Troon	4 and 3
1985	L Beman (Ire)	C Waite	Ganton	1 hole
1986	McGuire (NZ)	L Briars (Aus)	West Sussex	2 and 1
1987	J Collingham	S Shapcott	Harlech	19th hole
1988	J Furby	J Wade	Deal	4 and 3
1989	H Dobson	E Farquharson	Hoylake, R Liverpool	6 and 5
1990	J Hall	H Wadsworth	Dunbar	3 and 2
1991	V Michaud (Fra)	W Doolan (Aus)	Pannal	3 and 2
1992	P Pedersen (Den)	J Morley	Saunton	1 hole
1993	C Lambert	K Speak	R Lytham	3 and 2
1994	E Duggleby	C Mourgue d'Algue	Newport	3 and 1

Ladies' British Open Amateur Stroke Play Championship

Year	Winner	Club	Venue	Score
1969	A Irvin	R Lytham and St Annes	Gosforth Park	295
1970	M Everard	Hallamshire	Birkdale	313
1971	IC Robertson	Dunaverty	Ayr Belleisle	302
1972	IC Robertson	Dunaverty	Silloth	296
1973	A Stant	Beau Desert	Purdis Heath	298
1974	J Greenhalgh	Pleasington	Seaton Carew	302
1975	J Greenhalgh	Pleasington	Gosforth Park	298
1976*	J Lee Smith	Gosforth Park	Fulford	299
1977*	M Everard	Hallamshire	Lindrick	306
1978*	J Melville	Furness	Foxhills	310
1979	M McKenna	Donabate	Moseley	305
1980	M Mahill	Portstewart	Brancepeth Castle	304
1981	J Soulsby	Prudhoe	Norwich	300
1982	J Connachan	Musselburgh	Downfield	294
1983	A Nicholas		Moortown	292
1984	C Waite	Swindon	Caernarvonshire	295
1985	IC Robertson	Dunaverty	Formby	300
1986	C Hourihane		Blairgowrie	291
1987	L Bayman	Princes	Ipswich	297
1988	K Mitchell	Worthing	Porthcawl	317
1989	H Dobson	Seacroft	Southerness	298
1990	V Thomas	Pennard	Strathaven	287
1991	J Morley	Sale	Long Ashton	297

continued

* *Played concurrently with Ladies' British Open Championship*

Ladies' British Open Amateur Stroke Play Championship *continued*

Year	Winner	Club	Venue	Score
1992	J Hockley	Felixstowe	Frilford Heath	287
1993	J Hall	Felixstowe Ferry	Gullane	290
1994	K Speak	Clitheroe	Woodhall Spa	297

Senior Ladies' British Open Amateur Stroke Play Championship

Year	Winner	Club	Venue	Score
1981	BM King	Pleasington	Formby	159
1982	P Riddiford	Royal Ashdown Forest	Ilkley	161
1983	M Birtwistle		Troon Portland	167
1984	O Semelaigne	France	Woodbridge	152
1985	Dr G Costello	Formby Ladies	Prestatyn	158
1986	P Riddiford	Royal Ashdown Forest	Longniddry	154
1987	O Semelaigne	France	Copt Heath	152
1988	C Bailey	Tandridge	Littlestone	156
1989	C Bailey	Tandridge	Wrexham	149
1990	A Uzielli	The Berkshire	Harrogate	153
1991	A Uzielli	The Berkshire	Ladybank	154
1992	A Uzielli	The Berkshire	Stratford-upon-Avon	148
1993	J Thornhill	Walton Heath	Ashburnham	151
1994	D Williams	Calgary	Nottingham	154

English Amateur Championship

Year	Winner	Runner-up	Venue	By
1925	TF Ellison	S Robinson	Hoylake, R Liverpool	1 hole
1926	TF Ellison	Sq Ldr CH Hayward	Walton Heath	6 and 4
1927	TP Perkins	JB Beddard	Little Aston	2 and 1
1928	JA Stout	TP Perkins	R Lytham and St Annes	3 and 2
1929	W Sutton	EB Tipping	Northumberland	3 and 2
1930	TA Bourn	CE Hardman	Burhham	3 and 2
1931	LG Crawley	W Sutton	Hunstanton	1 hole
1932	EW Fiddian	AS Bradshaw	Sandwich, R St George's	1 hole
1933	J Woollam	TA Bourn	Ganton	4 and 3
1934	S Lunt	LG Crawley	Formby	37th hole
1935	J Woollam	EW Fiddian	Hollinwell	2 and 1
1936	HG Bentley	JDA Langley	Deal	5 and 4
1937	JJ Pennink	LG Crawley	Saunton	6 and 5
1938	JJ Pennink	SE Banks	Moortown	2 and 1
1939	AL Bentley	W Sutton	R Birkdale	5 and 4
1946	IR Patey	K Thom	Mid-Surrey	5 and 4
1947	GH Micklem	C Stow	Ganton	1 hole
1948	AGB Helm	HJR Roberts	Little Aston	2 and 1
1949	RJ White	C Stowe	Formby	5 and 4
1950	JDA Langley	IR Patey	Deal	1 hole
1951	GP Roberts	H Bennett	Hunstanton	39th hole
1952	E Millward	TJ Shorrock	Burnham and Berrow	2 holes
1953	GH Micklem	RJ White	R Birkdale	2 and 1
1954	A Thirlwell	HG Bentley	Sandwich, R St George's	2 and 1
1955	A Thirlwell	M Burgess	Ganton	7 and 6
1956	GB Wolstenholme	H Bennett	R Lytham and St Annes	1 hole
1957	A Walker	G Whitehead	Hoylake, R Liverpool	4 and 3
1958	DN Sewell	DA Procter	Walton Heath	8 and 7
1959	GB Wolstenholme	MF Bonallack	Formby	1 hole
1960	DN Sewell	MJ Christmas	Hunstanton	41st hole
1961	I Caldwell	GJ Clark	Wentworth	37th hole
1962	MF Bonallack	MSR Lunt	Moortown	2 and 1
1963	MF Bonallack	A Thirlwell	Burnham and Berrow	4 and 3
1964	Dr D Marsh	R Foster	Hollinwell	1 hole
1965	MF Bonallack	CA Clark	Berkshire	3 and 2
1966	MSR Lunt	DJ Millensted	R Lytham and St Annes	3 and 2
1967	MF Bonallack	GE Hyde	Woodhall Spa	4 and 2
1968	MF Bonallack	PD Kelley	Ganton	12 and 11
1969	JH Cook	P Dawson	Sandwich, R St George's	6 and 4

Year	Winner	Runner-up	Venue	By
1970	Dr D Marsh	SG Birtwell	R Birkdale	6 and 4
1971	W Humphreys	JC Davies	Burnham and Berrow	9 and 8
1972	H Ashby	R Revell	Northumberland	5 and 4
1973	H Ashby	SC Mason	Formby	5 and 4
1974	M James	JA Watts	Woodhall Spa	6 and 5
1975	N Faldo	D Eccleston	R Lytham and St Annes	6 and 4
1976	P Deeble	JC Davies	Ganton	3 and 1
1977	TR Shingler	J Mayell	Walton Heath	4 and 3
1978	P Downes	P Hoad	R Birkdale	1 hole
1979	R Chapman	A Carman	Sandwich, R St George's	6 and 5
1980	P Deeble	P McEvoy	Moortown	4 and 3
1981	D Blakeman	A Stubbs	Burnham and Berrow	3 and 1
1982	A Oldcorn	I Bradshaw	Hoylake, R Liverpool	4 and 3
1983	G Laurence	A Brewer	Wentworth	7 and 6
1984	D Gilford	M Gerrard	Woodhall Spa	4 and 3
1985	R Winchester	P Robinson	Little Aston	1 hole
1986	J Langmead	B White	Hillside	2 and 1
1987	K Weeks	R Eggo	Frilford Heath	37th hole
1988	R Claydon	D Curry	R Birkdale	38th hole
1989	S Richardson	R Eggo	Sandwich, R St George's	2 and 1
1990	I Garbutt	G Evans	Woodhall Spa	8 and 7
1991	R Willison	M Pullan	Formby	10 and 8
1992	S Cage	R Hutt	Deal	3 and 2
1993	D Fisher	R Bland	Saunton	3 and 1
1994	M Foster	A Johnson	Moortown	8 and 7

English Open Amateur Stroke Play Championship for the Brabazon Trophy

Year	Winner	Club	Venue	Score
1957	D Sewell	Hook Heath	Moortown	287
1958	AH Perowne	Norwich	Birkdale	289
1959	D Sewell	Hook Heath	Hollinwell	300
1960	GB Wolstenholme	Sunningdale	Ganton	286
1961	RDBM Shade	Duddingston	Hoylake, R Liverpool	284
1962	A Slater	Wakefield	Woodhall Spa	209
1963	RDBM Shade	Duddingston	R Birkdale	306
1964	MF Bonallack	Thorpe Hall	Deal, R Cinque Ports	290
1965 T	CA Clark	Ganton	Formby	289
	DJ Millensted	Wentworth		
	MJ Burgess	West Sussex		
1966	PM Townsend	Porters Park	Hunstanton	282
1967	RDBM Shade	Duddingston	Saunton	299
1968	MF Bonallack	Thorpe Hall	Walton Heath	210
1969 T	R Foster	Bradford	Moortown	290
	MF Bonallack	Thorpe Hall		
1970	R Foster	Bradford	Little Aston	287
1971	MF Bonallack	Thorpe Hall	Hillside	294
1972	PH Moody	Notts	Hoylake, R Liverpool	296
1973	R Revell	Farnham	Hunstanton	294
1974	N Sundelson	South Africa	Moortown	291
1975	A Lyle	Hawkstone Park	Hollinwell	298
1976	P Hedges	Langley Park	Saunton	294
1977	A Lyle	Hawkstone Park	Hoylake, R Liverpool	293
1978	G Brand, Jr	Knowle	Woodhall Spa	289
1979	D Long	Shandon Park	Little Aston	291
1980 T	R Rafferty	Warrenpoint	Hunstanton	293
	P McEvoy	Copt Heath		
1981	P Way	Neville	Hillside	292
1982	P Downes	Coventry	Woburn	299
1983	C Banks	Stanton-on-the-Wolds	Hollinwell	294
1984	M Davis	Thorndon Park	Deal, R Cinque Ports	286
1985 T	R Roper	Catterick Garrison	Seaton Carew	296
	P Baker	Lillieshall Park		
1986	R Kaplan	South Africa	Sunningdale	286
1987	JG Robinson	Woodhall Spa	Ganton	287
1988	R Eggo	L'Ancresse	Saunton	289
1989 T	C Rivett		Hoylake, R Liverpool	293
	RN Roderick			

continued

English Open Amateur Stroke Play Championship *continued*

Year	Winner	Club	Venue	Score
1990 T	O Edmond	Fontainbleau	Burnham and Berrow	287
	G Evans	Worthing		
1991	G Evans	Worthing	Hunstanton	284
	M Pullan	Sand Moor		
1992	I Garrido	Spain	Notts	280
1993	D Fisher	Stoke Poges	Stoneham	227 *(54 holes only)*
1994	G Harris	Broome Manor	Little Aston	280

English Seniors Championship

Year	Winner	Venue	Score
1981	CR Spalding	Copt Heath	152
1982	JL Whitworth	Lindrick	152
1983	B Cawthray	Ross-on-Wye	154
1984	RL Glading	Thetford	150
1985	JR Marriott	Bristol and Clifton	153
1986	R Hiatt	Northants County	153
1987	I Caldwell	North Hants, Fleet	72 *(Curtailed due to storm)*
1988	G Edwards	Bromborough	222
1989	G Clark	West Sussex	212
1990	N Paul	Enville and Bridgnorth	217
1991	W Williams	Gerrards Cross and Denham	217
1992	B Cawthray	Fulford	223
1993	G Edwards	John O'Gaunt	221
1994T	G Steel	Parkstone & Broadstone	72 *(Bad weather)*
	F Jones		

English Open Mid-Amateur Championship for the Logan Trophy

Year	Winner	Venue	Score
1988	P McEvoy	Little Aston	284
1989	A Mew	Moortown	290
1990	A Mew	Wentworth	214
1991	I Richardson	West Lancashire	223
1992	A Mew	King's Lynn	222
1993	R Godley	Southport & Ainsdale	210
1994T	I Richardson	Trentham	217
	A McLure		

English Club Champions

Year	Winner	Venue	Score
1989	Ealing	Southport and Ainsdale	289
1990	Ealing	Goring and Streatley	277
1991	Trentham	Porters Park	279
1992	Bristol & Clifton	South Staffs	294
1993	Worksop	Rotherham	276
1994	Sandmoor	Coxmoor	287

English County Championship (Men)

Year	Winner	Year	Winner	Year	Winner
1928	Warwickshire	1955	Yorkshire	1976	Warwickshire
1929	Lancashire	1956	Staffordshire	1977	Warwickshire
1930	Lancashire	1957	Surrey	1978	Kent
1931	Yorkshire	1958	Surrey	1979	Gloucestershire
1932	Surrey	1959	Northumberland	1980	Surrey
1933	Yorkshire	1961	Lancashire	1981	Surrey
1934	Worcestershire	1962	Northumberland	1982	Yorkshire
1935	Worcestershire	1963	Yorkshire	1983	Berks, Bucks, Oxon
1936	Surrey	1964	Northumberland	1984	Yorkshire
1937	Lancashire	1965	Northumberland	1985 T	Devon
1938	Staffordshire	1966	Surrey		Hertfordshire
1939	Worcestershire	1967	Lancashire	1986	Hertfordshire
1947	Staffordshire	1968	Surrey	1987	Yorkshire
1848	Staffordshire	1969	Berks, Bucks, Oxon	1988	Warwickshire
1949	Lancashire	1970	Gloucestershire	1989	Middlesex
1950	*Not played*	1971	Staffordshire	1990	Warwickshire
1951	Lancashire	1972	Berks, Bucks, Oxon	1991	Middlesex
1952	Yorkshire	1973	Yorkshire	1992	Dorset
1953	Yorkshire	1974	Lincolnshire	1993	Yorkshire
1954	Cheshire	1975	Staffordshire	1994	Middlesex

English Ladies' Amateur Championship

Year	Winner	Runner-up	Venue	By
1960	M Nichol	A Bonallack	Burnham	3 and 1
1961	R Porter	P Reece	Littlestone	2 holes
1962	J Roberts	A Bonallack	Woodhall Spa	3 and 1
1963	A Bonallack	E Chadwick	Liphook	7 and 6
1964	M Spearman	M Everard	R Lytham and St Annes	6 and 5
1965	R Porter	C Cheetham	Whittington Barracks	6 and 5
1966	J Greenhalgh	JC Holmes	Hayling Island	3 and 1
1967	A Irwin	A Pickard	Alwoodley	3 and 2
1968	S Barber	D Oxley	Hunstanton	5 and 4
1969	B Dixon	M Wenyon	Burnham and Berrow	6 and 4
1970	D Oxley	S Barber	Rye	3 and 2
1971	D Oxley	S Barber	Hoylake	5 and 4
1972	M Everard	A Bonallack	Woodhall Spa	2 and 1
1973	M Walker	C Le Feuvre	Broadstone	6 and 5
1974	A Irvin	J Thornhill	Sunningdale	1 hole
1975	B Huke	L Harrold	R Birkdale	2 and 1
1976	L Harrold	A Uzielli	Hollinwell	3 and 2
1977	V Marvin	M Everard	Burnham and Berrow	1 hole
1978	V Marvin	R Porter	West Sussex	2 and 1
1979	J Greenhalgh	S Hedges	Hoylake	2 and 1
1980	B New	J Walker	Aldeburgh	3 and 2
1981	D Christison	S Cohen	Cotswold Hills	2 holes
1982	J Walter	C Nelson	Brancepeth Castle	4 and 3
1983	L Bayman	C Mackintosh	Hayling Island	4 and 3
1984	C Waite	L Bayman	Hunstanton	3 and 2
1985	P Johnson	L Bayman	Ferndown	1 hole
1986	J Thornhill	S Shapcott	Sandwich, Princes	3 and 1
1987	J Furby	M King	Alwoodley	4 and 3
1988	J Wade	S Shapcott	Little Aston	19th hole
1989	H Dobson	S Morgan	Burnham and Berrow	4 and 3
1990	A Uzielli	L Fletcher	Rye	2 and 1
1991	N Buxton	K Stupples	Sheringham	2 holes
1992	C Hall	J Hockley	St Annes Old Links	1 hole
1993	N Buxton	S Burnell	St Enodoc	2 and 1
1994	J Hall	S Sharpe	The Berkshire	1 hole

English Ladies' Under-23 Championship

Year	Winner	Venue	Score
1978	S Bamford	Caldy	228
1979	B Cooper	Coxmoor	223
1980	B Cooper	Porters Park	226
1981	J Soulsby	Willesley Park	220
1982	M Gallagher	High Post	221
1983	P Grice	Hallamshire	219
1984	P Johnson	Moor Park	300
1985	P Johnson	Northants County	301
1986	S Shapcott	Broadstone	301
1987	J Wade	Northumberland	296
1988	J Wade	Wentworth	299
1989	A Shapcott	Notts Ladies	302
1990	K Tebbet	Saunton	299
1991	J Hockley	Saunton	303
1992	N Buxton	Littlestone	292
1993	R Millington	King's Norton	302
1994	F Brown	Ferndown	289

English Ladies' Seniors Championship

Year	Winner	Venue	Score
1988	A Thompson	Wentworth	158
1989	C Bailey	Notts Ladies	163
1990	A Thompson	Fairhaven	162
1991	C Bailey	Burnham and Berrow	155
1992	A Thompson	Pleasington	154
1993	A Uzielli	Hunstanton	150
1994	S Bassindale	Littlestone	163

English Ladies' Stroke Play Championship

Year	Winner	Venue	Score
1984	P Grice	Moor Park	300
1985	P Johnson	Northants County	301
1986	S Shapcott	Broadstone	301
1987	J Wade	Northumberland	296
1988	S Prosser	Wentworth	297
1989	S Robinson	Notts	302
1990	K Tebbet	Saunton	299
1991	J Morley	Ganton	301
1992	J Morley	Littlestone	289
1993	J Hall	King's Norton	298
1994	F Brown	Ferndown	289

English Ladies' Intermediate Championship

Year	Winner	Venue	Score
1982	J Rhodes	Headingley	19th hole
1983	L Davies	Worksop	2 and 1
1984	P Grice	Whittington Barracks	3 and 2
1985	S Lowe	Caldy	2 and 1
1986	S Moorcroft	Hexham	6 and 5
1987	J Wade	Sheringham	2 and 1
1988	S Morgan	Enville, Staffs	20th hole
1989	L Fairclough	Warrington	4 and 3
1990	L Fletcher	Whitley Bay	7 and 6
1991	J Morley	West Lancashire	6 and 5
1992	K Speak	South Staffs	3 and 1
1993	K Speak	Seascale	2 and 1
1994	J Oliver	Beaconsfield	2 up

England and Wales (Ladies') County Championship

Year	Winner	Year	Winner	Year	Winner
1908	Lancashire	1947	Surrey	1972	Kent
1909	Surrey	1948	Yorkshire	1973	Northumberland
1910	Cheshire	1949	Surrey	1974	Surrey
1911	Cheshire	1950	Yorkshire	1975	Glamorgan
1912	Cheshire	1951	Lancashire	1976	Staffordshire
1913	Surrey	1952	Lancashire	1977	Essex
1920	Middlesex	1953	Surrey	1978	Glamorgan
1921	Surrey	1954	Warwickshire	1979	Essex
1922	Surrey	1955	Surrey	1980	Lancashire
1923	Surrey	1956	Kent	1981	Glamorgan
1924	Surrey	1957	Middlesex	1982	Surrey
1925	Surrey	1958	Lancashire	1983	Surrey
1926	Surrey	1959	Middlesex	1984	Surrey/Yorkshire
1927	Yorkshire	1960	Lancashire	1985	Surrey
1928	Cheshire	1961	Middlesex	1986	Glamorgan
1929	Yorkshire	1962	Staffordshire	1987	Lancashire
1930	Surrey	1963	Warwickshire	1988	Surrey
1931	Middlesex	1964	Lancashire	1989	Cheshire
1932	Cheshire	1965	Staffordshire	1990	Cheshire
1933	Yorkshire	1966	Lancashire	1991	Glamorgan
1934	Surrey	1967	Lancashire	1992	Hampshire
1935	Essex	1968	Surrey	1993	Lancashire
1936	Surrey	1969	Lancashire	1994	Staffordshire
1937	Surrey	1970	Yorkshire		
1938	Lancashire	1971	Kent		

Irish National Professional Championship

Year	Winner	Club	Venue	Score
1960	C O'Connor	Royal Dublin	Warrenpoint	271
1961	C O'Connor	Royal Dublin	Lahinch	280
1962	C O'Connor	Royal Dublin	Bangor	264
1963	C O'Connor	Royal Dublin	Little Island	271
1964	E Jones	Bangor	Knock	279
1965	C O'Connor	Royal Dublin	Mullingar	283
1966	C O'Connor	Royal Dublin	Warrenpoint	269
1967	H Boyle	Jacobs Golf Centre	Tullamore (3 rounds)	214
1968	C Greene	Mill Town	Knock	282
1969	J Martin	Unattached	Dundalk	268
1970	H Jackson	Knockbracken	Massareene	283
1971	C O'Connor	Royal Dublin	Galway	278
1972	J Kinsella	Castle	Bundoran	289
1973	J Kinsella	Castle	Limerick	284
1974	E Polland	Balmoral	Portstewart	277
1975	C O'Connor	Royal Dublin	Carlow	275
1976	P McGuirk	Co Louth	Waterville	291
1977	P Skerritt	St Annes	Woodbrook	281
1978	C O'Connor	Royal Dublin	Dollymount	286
1979	D Smyth	Bettystown	Dollymount	215 *(54 holes)*
1980	D Feherty	Balmoral	Dollymount	283
1981	D Jones	Bangor	Woodbrook	283
1982	D Feherty	Balmoral	Woodbrook	287
1983	L Higgins	Waterville	Woodbrook	275
1984	M Sludds	—	Skerries	277
1985	D Smyth	—	Co Louth	204 *(54 holes due to bad weather)*
1986	D Smyth	—	Waterville	282
1987	P Walton	Malahide	Co Louth	144 *(36 holes due to bad weather)*
1988	E Darcy	Delgany	Castle, Dublin	269
1989	P Walton	Malahide	Castle, Dublin	266
1990	D Smyth	—	Woodbrook	271
1991	P Walton	—	Woodbrook	277
1992	E Darcy	—	K Club	285
1993	M Sludds	—	K Club	285
1994	D Clarke	Mount Juliet	Galway Bay	285

Irish Amateur Championship

Year	Winner	Runner-up	Venue	By
1960	M Edwards	N Fogarty	Portstewart	6 and 5
1961	D Sheahan	J Brown	Rosses Point	5 and 4
1962	M Edwards	J Harrington	Baltray	42nd hole
1963	JB Carr	EC O'Brien	Killarney	2 and 1
1964	JB Carr	A McDade	Co Down	6 and 5
1965	JB Carr	T Craddock	Rosses Point	3 and 2
1966	D Sheahan	J Faith	Dollymount	3 and 2
1967	JB Carr	PD Flaherty	Lahinch	1 hole
1968	M O'Brien	F McCarroll	Portrush	2 and 1
1969	V Nevin	J O'Leary	Co Sligo	1 hole
1970	D Sheahan	M Bloom	Grange	2 holes
1971	P Kane	M O'Brien	Ballybunion	3 and 2
1972	K Stevenson	B Hoey	Co Down	2 and 1
1973	RKM Pollin	RM Staunton	Rosses Point	1 hole
1974	R Kane	M Gannon	Portmarnock	5 and 4
1975	MD O'Brien	JA Bryan	Cork	5 and 4
1976	D Brannigan	D O'Sullivan	Portrush	2 holes
1977	M Gannon	A Hayes	Westport	19th hole
1978	M Morris	T Cleary	Carlow	1 hole
1979	J Harrington	MA Gannon	Ballybunion	2 and 1
1980	R Rafferty	MJ Bannon	Co Down	8 and 7
1981	D Brannigan	E McMenamin	Co Sligo	19th hole
1982	P Walton	B Smyth	Woodbrook	7 and 6
1983	T Corridan	E Power	Killarney	2 holes
1984	CB Hoey	L McNamara	Malone	20th hole
1985	D O'Sullivan	D Branigan	Westport	1 hole
1986	J McHenry	P Rayfus	Dublin	4 and 3
1987	E Power	JP Fitzgerald	Tranmore	2 holes
1988	G McGimpsey	D Mulholland	Portrush	2 and 1
1989	P McGinley	N Goulding	Rosses Point	3 and 2
1990	D Clarke	P Harrington	Baltray	3 and 2
1991	G McNeill	N Goulding	Ballybunion	3 and 1
1992	G Murphy	JP Fitzgerald	Portstewart	2 and 1
1993	E Power	D Higgins	Enniscrome	3 and 2
1994	D Higgins	P Harrington	Portmarnock	20th hole

Irish Seniors' Open Amateur Championship

Year	Winner	Venue	Score
1980	GN Fogarty	Galway	144
1981	GN Fogarty	Bundoran	149
1982	J Murray	Douglas	141
1983	F Sharpe	Courtown	153
1984	J Boston	Connemara	147
1985	J Boston	Newcastle	155
1986	J Coey	Waterford	141
1987	J Murray	Castleroy	150
1988	WB Buckley	Westport	154
1989	B McCrea	Royal Belfast	150
1990	C Hartland	Cork	149
1991	C Hartland	Mullingar	147
1992	C Hartland	Athlone	145
1993	P Breen	Bangor	147
1994	B Buckley	Tramore	151

Irish Ladies' Amateur Championship

Year	Winner	Runner-up	Venue	By
1960	P Garvey	PG McGann	Cork	5 and 3
1961	K McCann	A Sweeney	Newcastle	5 and 3
1962	P Garvey	M Earner	Baltray	7 and 6
1963	P Garvey	E Barnett	Killarney	9 and 7
1964	Z Fallon	P O'Sullivan	Portrush	37th hole
1965	E Purcell	P O'Sullivan	Mullingar	3 and 2

Year	Winner	Runner-up	Venue	By
1966	E Bradshaw	P O'Sullivan	Rosslare	3 and 2
1967	G Brandom	P O'Sullivan	Castlerock	3 and 2
1968	E Bradshaw	M McKenna	Lahinch	3 and 2
1969	M McKenna	C Hickey	Ballybunion	3 and 2
1970	P Garvey	M Earner	Portrush	2 and 1
1971	E Bradshaw	M Mooney	Baltray	3 and 1
1972	M McKenna	I Butler	Killarney	5 and 4
1973	M Mooney	M McKenna	Bundoran	2 and 1
1974	M McKenna	V Singleton	Lahinch	3 and 2
1975	M Gorry	E Bradshaw	Tramore	1 hole
1976	C Nesbitt	M McKenna	Rosses Point	20th hole
1977	M McKenna	R Hegarty	Ballybunion	2 holes
1978	M Gorry	I Butler	Grange	4 and 3
1979	M McKenna	C Nesbitt	Donegal	6 and 5
1980	C Nesbitt	C Hourihane	Lahinch	1 hole
1981	M McKenna	M Kenny	Laytown & Bettystown	1 hole
1982	M McKenna	M Madill	Portrush	2 and 1
1983	C Hourihane	V Hassett	Cork	6 and 4
1984	C Hourihane	M Madill	Rosses Point	19th hole
1985	C Hourihane	M McKenna	Waterville	4 and 3
1986	T O'Reilly	E Higgins	Castlerock	4 and 3
1987	C Hourihane	C Hickey	Lahinch	5 and 4
1988	L Bolton	E Higgins	Tramore	2 and 1
1989	M McKenna	C Wickham	West Port	19th hole
1990	ER McDaid	L Callan	The Island	2 and 1
1991	C Hourihane	E McDaid	Ballybunion	1 hole
1992	ER Power	C Hourihane	Co. Louth	1 hole
1993	E Higgins	A Rogers	R Belfast	2 and 1
1994	L Webb	H Kavanagh	Rosses Point	20th hole

Scottish Amateur Championship

Year	Winner	Runner-up	Venue	By
1922	J Wilson	E Blackwell	St Andrews	19th hole
1923	TM Burrell	Dr A McCallum	Troon	1 hole
1924	WW Mackenzie	W Tulloch	Aberdeen	3 and 2
1925	JT Dobson	W Mackenzie	Muirfield	3 and 2
1926	WJ Guild	SO Shepherd	Leven	2 and 1
1927	A Jamieson, Jr	Rev D Rutherford	Gailes	22nd hole
1928	WW Mackenzie	W Dodds	Muirfield	5 and 3
1929	JT Bookless	J Dawson	Aberdeen	5 and 4
1930	K Greig	T Wallace	Carnoustie	9 and 8
1931	J Wilson	A Jamieson, Jr	Prestwick	2 and 1
1932	J McLean	K Greig	Dunbar	5 and 4
1933	J McLean	KC Forbes	Aberdeen	6 and 4
1934	J McLean	W Campbell	Western Gailes	3 and 1
1935	H Thomson	J McLean	St Andrews	2 and 1
1936	ED Hamilton	R Neill	Carnoustie	1 hole
1937	H McInally	K Patrick	Barassie	6 and 5
1938	ED Hamilton	R Rutherford	Muirfield	4 and 2
1939	H McInally	H Thomson	Prestwick	6 and 5
1946	EC Brown	R Rutherford	Carnoustie	3 and 2
1947	H McInally	J Pressley	Glasgow Gailes	10 and 8
1948	AS Flockhart	G Taylor	Balgownie, Aberdeen	7 and 6
1949	R Wright	H McInally	Muirfield	1 hole
1950	WC Gibson	D Blair	Prestwick	2 and 1
1951	JM Dykes	J Wilson	St Andrews	4 and 2
1952	FG Dewar	J Wilson	Carnoustie	4 and 3
1953	DA Blair	J McKay	Western Gailes	3 and 1
1954	JW Draper	W Gray	Nairn	4 and 3
1955	RR Jack	AC Miller	Muirfield	2 and 1
1956	Dr FWG Deighton	A MacGregor	Troon	8 and 7
1957	JS Montgomerie	J Burnside	Balgownie	2 and 1
1958	WD Smith	I Harris	Prestwick	6 and 5
1959	Dr FWG Deighton	R Murray	St Andrews	6 and 5
1960	JR Young	S Saddler	Carnoustie	5 and 3
1961	J Walker	ST Murray	Western Gailes	4 and 3
1962	SWT Murray	R Shade	Muirfield	2 and 1
1963	RDBM Shade	N Henderson	Troon	4 and 3

continued

Scottish Amateur Championship *continued*

Year	Winner	Runner-up	Venue	By
1964	RDBM Shade	J McBeath	Nairn	8 and 7
1965	RDBM Shade	G Cosh	St Andrews	4 and 2
1966	RDBM Shade	C Strachan	Western Gailes	9 and 8
1967	RDBM Shade	A Murphy	Carnoustie	5 and 4
1968	GB Cosh	R Renfrew	Muirfield	4 and 3
1969	JM Cannon	A Hall	Troon	6 and 4
1970	CW Green	H Stewart	Balgownie, Aberdeen	1 hole
1971	S Stephen	C Green	St Andrews	3 and 2
1972	HB Stuart	A Pirie	Prestwick	3 and 1
1973	IC Hutcheon	A Brodie	Carnoustie	3 and 2
1974	GH Murray	A Pirie	Western Gailes	2 and 1
1975	D Greig	G Murray	Montrose	7 and 6
1976	GH Murray	H Stuart	St Andrews	6 and 5
1977	A Brodie	P McKellar	Troon	1 hole
1978	IA Carslaw	J Cuddihy	Downfield	7 and 6
1979	K Macintosh	P McKellar	Prestwick	5 and 4
1980	D Jamieson	C Green	Balgownie, Aberdeen	2 and 1 *(18 holes)*
1981	C Dalgleish	A Thomson	Western Gailes	7 and 6
1982	CW Green	G McGregor	Carnoustie	1 hole
1983	CW Green	J Huggan	Gullane	1 hole
1984	A Moir	K Buchan	Renfrew	3 and 3
1985	D Carrick	D James	Southerness	4 and 2
1986	C Brooks	A Thomson	Monifieth	3 and 2
1987	C Montgomerie	A Watt	Nairn	9 and 8
1988	J Milligan	A Colthart	Barassie	1 hole
1989	A Thomson	A Tait	Moray	1 hole
1990	C Everett	M Thomson	Gullane	7 and 5
1991	G Lowson	L Salariya	Downfield	4 and 3
1992	S Gallacher	D Kirkpatrick	Glasgow Gailes	37th hole
1993	D Robertson	R Russell	R Dornoch	2 holes
1994	M McKibben	A Reid	Renfrew	39th hole

Scottish Open Amateur Stroke Play Championship

Year	Winner	Club	Venue	Score
1967	BJ Gallacher	Bathgate	Muirfield and Gullane	291
1968	RDBM Shade	Duddingston	Prestwick and Prestwick St Nicholas	282
1969	JS Macdonald	Dalmahoy	Carnoustie and Monifieth	288
1970	D Hayes	South Africa	Glasgow Gailes and Barassie	275
1971	IC Hutcheon	Monifieth	Leven and Lundin Links	277
1972	BN Nicholas	Nairn	Dalmahoy and Ratho Park	290
1973 T	DM Robertson	Dunbar	Dunbar and	
	GJ Clark	Whitley Bay	North Berwick	284
1974	IC Hutcheon	Monifieth	Blairgowrie and Alyth	283
1975	CW Green	Dumbarton	Nairn and Nairn Dunbar	295
1976	S Martin	Downfield	Monifieth and Carnoustie	299
1977	PJ McKellar	East Renfrewshire	Muirfield and Gullane	299
1978	AR Taylor	East Kilbride	Keir and Cawder	281
1979	IC Hutcheon	Monifieth	Lansdowne and Rosemount	286
1980	G Brand Jr	Knowle	Musselburgh and R Musselburgh	207 *(54 holes)*
1981	F Walton	Malahide	Erskine and Renfrew	287
1982	C Macgregor	Glencourse	Downfield and Camperdown	287
1983	C Murray	Fereneze	Irvine	291
1984	CW Green	Dumbarton	Blairgowrie	287
1985	C Montgomerie	Royal Troon	Dunbar	274
1986	KH Walker	Royal Burgess	Carnoustie	289
1987	D Carrick	Douglas Park	Lundin Links	282
1988	S Easingwood	Dunbar	Cathkin Braes	277
1989	F Illouz	France	Blairgowrie	281
1990	G Hay	Hilton Park	R Aberdeen	133 *(36 holes)*
1991	A Coltart	Thornhill	Renfrew	291
1992	D Robertson	Cochrane Castle	Mortonhall	281
1993	A Reid	Kilmarnock Barassie	St Andrews	289
1994	D Downie	Ladybank	Letham Grange	288

Scottish Open Amateur Seniors' Championship

Year	Winner	Club	Venue	Score
1978 T	JM Cannon	Irvine	Glasgow Killermont	149
	GR Carmichael	Ladybank		
1979	A Sinclair	Drumpellier	Glasgow Killermont	143
1980	JM Cannon	Irvine	Royal Burgess	149
1981 T	IR Harris	Royal Troon	Glasgow Killermont	146
	Dr J Hastings	Royal Troon		
	AN Sturrock	Royal Troon		
1982 T	JM Cannon	Irvine	Royal Burgess	143
	J Niven	Newbury & Crookham		
1983	WD Smith	Prestwick	Glasgow Killermont	145
1984	A Sinclair	Drumpellier	Royal Burgess	148
1985	AN Sturrock	Prestwick	Glasgow Killermont	143
1986	RL Glading	Mitcham	Royal Burgess	153
1987	I Hornsby	Ponteland	Glasgow Killermont	145
1988	J Hayes	Gosforth	Royal Burgess	143
1989	AS Mayer	Torwoodlee	Glasgow Killermont	
1990	G Hartland	Huddersfield	Royal Burgess	146
1991	CW Green	Dumbarton	Glasgow Killermont	140
1992	G Clark	Whitley Bay	Royal Burgess	148
1993	J Maclean	Bathgate	Glasgow Killermont	141
1994	DM Laurie	St Andrews New	Ladybank	149

Scottish Ladies' Amateur Championship

Year	Winner	Runner-up	Venue	By
1960	JS Robertson	DT Sommerville	Turnberry	2 and 1
1961	JS Wright (née Robertson)	AM Lurie	St Andrews	1 hole
1962	JB Lawrence	C Draper	R Dornoch	5 and 4
1963	JB Lawrence	IC Robertson	Troon	2 and 1
1964	JB Lawrence	SM Reid	Gullane	5 and 3
1965	IC Robertson	JB Lawrence	Nairn	5 and 4
1966	IC Robertson	M Fowler	Machrihanish	2 and 1
1967	J Hastings	A Laing	North Berwick	5 and 3
1968	J Smith	J Rennie	Carnoustie	10 and 9
1969	JH Anderson	K Lackie	West Kilbride	5 and 4
1970	A Laing	IC Robertson	Dunbar	1 hole
1971	IC Robertson	A Ferguson	R Dornoch	3 and 2
1972	IC Robertson	CJ Lugton	Machrihanish	5 and 3
1973	I Wright	Dr AJ Wilson	St Andrews	2 holes
1974	Dr AJ Wilson	K Lackie	Nairn	22nd hole
1975	LA Hope	JW Smith	Elie	1 hole
1976	S Needham	T Walker	Machrihanish	3 and 2
1977	CJ Lugton	M Thomson	R Dornoch	1 hole
1978	IC Robertson	JW Smith	Prestwick	2 holes
1979	G Stewart	LA Hope	Gullane	2 and 1
1980	IC Robertson	F Anderson	Carnoustie	1 hole
1981	A Gemmill	W Aitken	Stranraer	2 and 1
1982	J Connachan	P Wright	R Troon	19th hole
1983	G Stewart	F Anderson	North Berwick	3 and 1
1984	G Stewart	A Gemmill	R Dornoch	3 and 2
1985	A Gemmill	D Thomson	Barassie	2 and 1
1986	IC Robertson	L Hope	St Andrews	3 and 2
1987	F Anderson	C Middleton	Nairn	4 and 3
1988	S Lawson	F Anderson	Southerness	3 and 1
1989	J Huggon	L Anderson	Lossiemouth	5 and 4
1990	E Farquharson	S Huggan	Machrihanish	3 and 2
1991	C Lambert	F Anderson	Carnoustie	3 and 2
1992	J Moody	E Farquharson	R Aberdeen	2 and 1
1993	C Lambert	M McKay	Prestwick St Nicholas	5 and 4
1994	C Matthew	V Melvin	Gullane	1 hole

Welsh Amateur Championship

Year	Winner	Runner-up	Venue	By
1934	SB Roberts	GS Noon	Prestatyn	4 and 3
1935	R Chapman	GS Noon	Tenby	1 hole
1936	RM de Lloyd	G Wallis	Aberdovey	1 hole
1937	DH Lewis	R Glossop	Porthcawl	2 holes
1938	AA Duncan	SB Roberts	Rhyl	2 and 1
1946	JV Moody	A Marshman	Porthcawl	9 and 8
1947	SB Roberts	G Breen Turner	Harlech	8 and 7
1948	AA Duncan	SB Roberts	Porthcawl	2 and 1
1949	AD Evans	MA Jones	Aberdovey	2 and 1
1950	JL Morgan	DJ Bonnell	Southerndown	9 and 7
1951	JL Morgan	WI Tucker	Harlech	3 and 2
1952	AA Duncan	JL Morgan	Ashburnham	4 and 3
1953	SB Roberts	D Pearson	Prestatyn	5 and 3
1954	AA Duncan	K Thomas	Tenby	6 and 5
1955	TJ Davies	P Dunn	Harlech	38th hole
1956	A Lockley	WI Tucker	Southerndown	2 and 1
1957	ES Mills	H Griffiths	Harlech	2 and 1
1958	HC Squirrell	AD Lake	Conway	4 and 3
1959	HC Squirrell	N Rees	Porthcawl	8 and 7
1960	HC Squirrell	P Richards	Aberdovey	2 and 1
1961	AD Evans	J Toye	Ashburnham	3 and 2
1962	J Povall	HC Squirrell	Harlech	3 and 2
1963	WI Tucker	J Povall	Southerndown	4 and 3
1964	HC Squirrell	WI Tucker	Harlech	1 hole
1965	HC Squirrell	G Clay	Porthcawl	6 and 4
1966	WI Tucker	EN Davies	Aberdovey	6 and 5
1967	JK Povall	WI Tucker	Asburnham	3 and 2
1968	J Buckley	J Povall	Conway	8 and 7
1969	JL Toye	EN Davies	Porthcawl	1 hole
1970	EN Davies	J Povall	Harlech	1 hole
1971	CT Brown	HC Squirrell	Southerndown	6 and 5
1972	EN Davies	JL Toye	Prestatyn	40th hole
1973	D McLean	T Holder	Ashburnham	6 and 4
1974	S Cox	EN Davies	Caernarvonshire	3 and 2
1975	JL Toye	WI Tucker	Porthcawl	5 and 4
1976	MPD Adams	WI Tucker	Harlech	6 and 5
1977	D Stevens	JKD Povall	Southerndown	3 and 2
1978	D McLean	A Ingram	Caernarvonshire	11 and 10
1979	TJ Melia	MS Roper	Ashburnham	5 and 4
1980	DL Stevens	G Clement	Prestatyn	10 and 9
1981	S Jones	C Davies	Porthcawl	5 and 3
1982	D Wood	C Davies	Harlech	8 and 7
1983	JR Jones	AP Parkin	Southerndown	2 holes
1984	JR Jones	A Llyr	Prestatyn	1 hole
1985	ED Jones	MA Macara	Ashburnham	2 and 1
1986	C Rees	B Knight	Conwy	1 hole
1987	PM Mayo	DK Wood	Porthcawl	2 holes
1988	K Jones	RN Roderick	Harlech	40th hole
1989	S Dodd	K Jones	Tenby	2 and 1
1990	A Barnett	A Jones	Prestatyn	1 hole
1991	S Pardoe	S Jones	Ashburnham	7 and 5
1992	H Roberts	R Johnson	Pyle and Kenfig	3 and 2
1993	B Dredge	M Ellis	Southerndown	3 and 1
1994	C Evans	M Smith	Royal Porthcawl	5 and 4

Welsh Amateur Stroke Play Championship

Year	Winner	Club	Venue	Score
1967	EN Davies	Llantrisant	Harlech	295
1968	JA Buckley	Rhos-on-Sea	Harlech	294
1969	DL Stevens	Llantrisant	Tenby	288
1970	JK Povall	Whitchurch	Newport	292
1971 T	EN Davies	Llantrisant	Harlech	296
	JL Toye	Radyr		
1972	JR Jones	Wrexham	Pyle and Kenfig	299
1973	JR Jones	Caernarvonshire	Llandudno (Maesdu)	300
1974	JL Toye	Radyr	Tenby	307
1975	D McLean	Holyhead	Wrexham	288

Year	Winner	Club	Venue	Score
1976	WI Tucker	Monmouthshire	Newport	282
1977	JA Buckley	Abergele and Pensarn	Prestatyn	302
1978	HJ Evans	Llangland Bay	Pyle and Kenfig	300
1979	D McLean	Holyhead	Holyhead	289
1980	TJ Melia	Cardiff	Tenby	291
1981	D Evans	Leek	Wrexham	270
1982	JR Jones	Langland Bay	Cradoc	287
1983	G Davies	Pontypool	Aberdovey	287
1984	RN Roderick	Portardawe	Newport	292
1985	MA Macara	Llandudno	Harlech	291
1986	M Calvert	Aberystwyth	Pyle and Kenfig	299
1987	MA Macara	Llandudno	Llandudno (Maesdu)	290
1988	RN Roderick	Portardawe	Tenby	283
1989	SC Dodd	Brynhill	Conwy	304
Open event since 1990				
1990	G Houston	Flint	Pyle and Kenfig	288
1991	A Jones	Wrexham	R Porthcawl	290
1992	AJ Barnett	R St David's	R St David's	278
1993	M Macara	Maesdu	Maesdu	280
1994	N Van Hootegem	Belgium	St Pierre	290

Welsh Seniors' Amateur Championship

Year	Winner	Club	Venue	Score
1975	A Marshman	Brecon	Aberdovey	77 (18 holes)
1976	AD Evans	Ross on Wye	Aberdovey	156
1977	AE Lockley	Swansea Bay	Aberdovey	154
1978	AE Lockley	Swansea Bay	Aberdovey	75 (18 holes)
1979	CR Morgan	Monmouthshire	Aberdovey	158
1980	ES Mills	Llandudno (Maesdu)	Aberdovey	152
1981	T Branton	Newport	Aberdovey	153
1982	WI Tucker	Monmouthshire	Aberdovey	147
1983	WS Gronow	East Berks	Aberdovey	153
1984	WI Tucker	Monmouthshire	Aberdovey	150
1985	NA Lycett	Aberdovey	Aberdovey	149
1986	E Mills	Aberdovey	Aberdovey	154
1987	WS Gronow	East Berks	Aberdovey	146
1988	NA Lycett	Aberdovey	Aberdovey	150
1989	WI Tucker	Monmouthshire	Aberdovey	160
1990	I Hughes	Abergele and Pensarn	Aberdovey	159
1991	RO Ward	Abersoch	Aberdovey	155
1992	I Hughes	Abergele and Pensarn	Aberdovey	150
1993	G Perks	Baron Hill	Aberdovey	149
1994T	G Perks	Baron Hill	Aberdovey	157
	I Hughes	Abergele & Pensarn		
	A Prytherch	Borth & Ynyslas		

Welsh Ladies' Amateur Championship

Year	Winner	Runner-up	Venue	By
1960	M Barron	E Brown	Tenby	8 and 6
1961	M Oliver	N Sneddon	Aberdovey	5 and 4
1962	M Oliver	P Roberts	Radyr	4 and 2
1963	P Roberts	N Sneddon	Harlech	7 and 5
1964	M Oliver	M Wright	Southerndown	1 hole
1965	M Wright	E Brown	Prestatyn	3 and 2
1966	A Hughes	P Roberts	Ashburnham	5 and 4
1967	M Wright	C Phipps	Harlech	21st hole
1968	S Hales	M Wright	Porthcawl	3 and 2
1969	P Roberts	A Hughes	Caernarvonshire	3 and 2
1970	A Briggs	J Morris	Newport	19th hole
1971	A Briggs	EN Davies	Harlech	2 and 1
1972	A Hughes	J Rogers	Tenby	3 and 2
1973	A Briggs	J John	Holyhead	3 and 2
1974	A Briggs	Dr H Lyall	Ashburnham	3 and 2
1975	A Johnson (*née* Hughes)	K Rawlings	Prestatyn	1 hole
1976	T Perkins	A Johnson	Porthcawl	4 and 2

continued

Welsh Ladies' Amateur Championship *continued*

Year	Winner	Runner-up	Venue	By
1977	T Perkins	P Whitley	Aberdovey	5 and 4
1978	P Light	A Briggs	Newport	2 and 1
1979	V Rawlings	A Briggs	Caernarvonshire	2 holes
1980	M Rawlings	A Briggs	Tenby	2 and 1
1981	M Rawlings	A Briggs	Harlech	5 and 3
1982	V Thomas (*née* Rawlings)	M Rawlings	Ashburnham	7 and 6
1983	V Thomas	T Thomas (*née* Perkins)	Llandudno	1 hole
1984	S Roberts	K Davies	Newport	5 and 4
1985	V Thomas	S Jump	Prestatyn	1 hole
1986	V Thomas	L Isherwood	Porthcawl	7 and 6
1987	V Thomas	S Roberts	Aberdovey	3 and 1
1988	S Roberts	F Connor	Tenby	4 and 2
1989	H Lawson	V Thomas	Conwy	2 and 1
1990	S Roberts	H Wadsworth	Ashburnham	3 and 2
1991	V Thomas	H Lawson	R St David's	4 and 3
1992	J Foster	S Boyes	Newport	4 and 3
1993	A Donne	V Thomas	Abergele & Pensarn	19th hole
1994	V Thomas	L Dermott	Royal Porthcawl	19th hole

Welsh Ladies' Open Amateur Stroke Play Championship

Year	Winner	Club	Venue	Score
1981	V Thomas	Pennard	Aberdovey	224
1982	V Thomas	Pennard	Aberdovey	225
1983	J Thornhill	Walton Heath	Aberdovey	239
1984	L Davies	West Byfleet	Aberdovey	230
1985	C Swallow		Aberdovey	219
1986	H Wadsworth	Princes	Aberdovey	223
1987	S Shapcott	Knowle	Newport	225
1988	S Shapcott	Knowle	Newport	218
1989	V Thomas	Pennard	Newport	220
1990	L Hackney	Trentham	Newport	218
1991	M Sutton	R Blackheath	R Porthcawl	224
1992	C Lambert	Stirling University	R Porthcawl	218
1993	J Hall	Felixstowe Ferry	Newport	221
1994	A Rose	Stirling	Newport	217

Welsh Ladies' Senior Championship

Year	Winner	Club	Venue	Score
1990	E Higgs	Wrexham	Vale of Llangollen	171
1991	H Lyall	R St David's	Pyle and Kenfig	160
1992	P Morgan	St Giles	Cardigan	83
1993	P Morgan	St Giles	Pwllheli	157
1994	C Thomas	Holyhead	Llandudno	163

Overseas National Championships

(Excluding PGA European Tour Events)

Argentine Open Championship

Year	Winner	Year	Winner
1985	V Fernandez	1990	V Fernandez
1986	V Fernandez	1991	JD Blake (USA)
1987	M Fernandez	1992	C Stadler
1988	M Fernandez	1993	M Calcavecchia
1989	E Romero	1994	M O'Meara

Australian Open Championship

Year	Winner	Score
1975	J Nicklaus	279
1976	J Nicklaus	286
1977	D Graham	284
1978	J Nicklaus	284
1979	J Newton	288
1980	G Norman	284
1981	W Rogers	282
1982	B Shearer	287
1983	P Fowler	285
1984	T Watson	281
1985	G Norman	212 *(54 holes only – rain)*
1986	R Davis	278
1987	G Norman	273
1988	M Calcavecchia	269
1989	P Senior	271
1990	J Morse	283
1991	W Riley	285
1992	S Elkington	280
1993	B Faxon	275
1994	R Allenby	280

Australian Professional Championship

Year	Winner	Year	Winner
1985	G Norman	1990	B Ogle
1986	M Harwood	1991	W Grady
1987	R Mackay	1992	C Parry
1988	W Grady	1993	I Baker-Finch
1989	P Senior	1994	A Coltart

Australian Amateur Championship

Year	Winner	Year	Winner
1985	B Ruangkit	1990	C Gray
1986	D Ecob	1991	L Parsons
1987	B Johns	1992	M Campbell
1988	S Bouvier	1993	GJ Chalmers
1989	S Conran	1994	W Bennett

Australian Ladies' Amateur Championship

Year	Winner	Year	Winner
1985	H Greenwood	1990	J Shearwood
1986	E Kennedy	1991	L Briers
1987	E Cavill	1992	J Leary
1988	C Bourtayre	1993	A-M Knight
1989	J Higgins	1994	T McKinnon

Austrian Amateur Open Championship

Year	Winner	Year	Winner
1985	C-S Hsieh	1990	A Peterskovsky
1986	D Carrick	1991	D Vanbegin
1987	Y-S Chen	1992	H-C Winkler
1988	L Peterson	1993	N Zitny
1989	U Zilg	1994	J-J Wolff

Austrian Ladies' Open Championship

Year	Winner	Year	Winner
1985	P Peter	1990	A Rast
1986	W-L Li	1991	L Navarro
1987	Y-S Chen	1992	K Poppmeier
1988	H-F Tseng	1993	N Fink
1989	K Poppmeier	1994	F Descampe

BMW European Ladies' Masters *(Formerly Belgian Ladies' Open Championship)*

Year	Winner	Year	Winner
1986	P Grice-Whittaker	1991	C Dibnah
1987	ML de Lorenzi	1992	K Douglas
1988	K Lunn	1993	H Dobson
1989	K Douglas	1994	H Wadsworth
1990	K Lunn		

Canadian Open Championship

Year	Winner	Year	Winner
1975	T Weiskopf	1985	C Strange
1976	J Pate	1986	B Murphy
1977	L Trevino	1987	C Strange
1978	B Lietzke	1988	K Green
1979	L Trevino	1989	S Jones
1980	B Gilder	1990	W Levi
1981	P Oosterhuis	1991	N Price
1982	B Lietzke	1992	G Norman
1983	J Cook	1993	D Frost
1984	G Norman	1994	N Price

Canadian Amateur Championship

Year	Winner	Year	Winner
1985	B Franklin	1990	W Sye
1986	B Franklin	1991	J Kraemer
1987	B Franklin	1992	D Ritchie
1988	D Roxburgh	1993	G Simpson
1989	P Major	1994	W Sye

Canadian Ladies' Open Amateur Championship

Year	Winner	Year	Winner
1985	K Williams	1990	S Lebrun
1986	M O'Connor	1991	A Moore
1987	T Kerdyk	1992	MJ Rouleau
1988	M Hattori	1993	MA Lapointe
1989	C Damphouse	1994	A Robertson

Czechoslovak Open Amateur Championship

Year	Winner	Year	Winner
1985	J Juhaniak	1990	J Janda
1986	D Kraljic	1991	J Kunšta
1987	G Nikitaidis	1992	R Chudoba
1988	M Brtek	1993	R Pientka
1989	A Krag	1994	F Mansson

Czechoslovak Ladies' Open Amateur Championship

Year	Winner	Year	Winner
1985	L Křenková	1990	A Kugelmüller
1986	L Křenková	1991	L Křenková
1987	A Hudcovă	1992	L Křenková
1988	A Hudcovă	1993	H Dvorská
1989	A Kugelmüller	1994	L Křenková

Danish Amateur Stroke Play Championship

Year	Winner	Year	Winner
1985	A Sørensen	1991	T Svendsen
1986	P Digebjerg	1992	AR Hansen
1987	M Brodersen	1993	N Rorbaek-Peterson
1988	B Tinning		
1989	R Budde	1994	AR Hansen
1990	T Bjørn		

Danish Ladies' Stroke Play Championship

Year	Winner	Year	Winner
1985	M Meiland	1990	P Carlson
1986	M Meiland	1991	I Tinning
1987	A Peitersen	1992	I Tinning
1988	J Kragh	1993	A Östberg
1989	M Brandt Anderson	1994	C Faaborg

French Amateur Championship

Year	Winner	Year	Winner
1985	J-F Remesy	1990	O Edmond
1986	J Van de Velde	1991	F Cupillard
1987	G Brizay	1992	N Joakimides
1988	P Barquez	1993	M Dieu
1989	C Cevaer	1994	L Pargade

French Ladies' Open Championship

Year	Winner
1987	L Neumann
1988	ML de Lorenzi
1989	S Strudwick
1990	*Not played*
1991	S Strudwick
1992	*Not played*
1993	*Not played*
1994	J Forbes

French Ladies' Amateur Championship

Year	Winner	Year	Winner
1985	V Pamard	1990	C Bourson
1986	ML de Lorenzi	1991	V Michaud
1987	S Louapre	1992	P Mennier
1988	C Marty	1993	S Louapre-Pfeiffer
1989	C Bourtayre	1994	C Mourgue d'Algue

German PGA Championship

Year	Winner	Year	Winner
1985	H-P Thül	1990	S Strüver
1986	S Vollrath	1991	T Giedeon
1987	H-P Thül	1992	M Pyatt
1988	T Giedeon	1993	W Linnenfelser
1989	T Giedeon	1994	S Yates

German Ladies' Open Championship *(1993 – Hennessy Cup)*

Year	Winner	Year	Winner
1985	J Brown	1990	A Okamoto
1986	L Neumann	1991	F Descampe
1987	ML de Lorenzi	1992	*Not played*
1988	L Neumann	1993	L Neumann
1989	A Nicholas	1994	L Neumann

German Ladies' PGA Close Championship

Year	Winner	Year	Winner
1986	S Eckrodt	1991	S Lehmeier
1987	S Eckrodt	1992	S Lehmeier
1988	D Franz	1993	S Lehmeier
1989	D Franz	1994	F Fehlauer
1990	D Franz		

Hong Kong Open Championship

Year	Winner	Year	Winner
1985	M Aebli	1990	K Green
1986	S Kanai	1991	B Langer
1987	I Woosnam	1992	T Watson
1988	H Chin-sheng	1993	B Watts
1989	B Claar	1994	D Frost

India Open Championship

Year	Winner	Year	Winner
1985	A Grimes	1990	A Debusk
1986	L Hsi-Chuen	1991	A Sher
1987	B Tennyson	1992	S Ginn
1988	L Chien-Soon	1993	A Sher
1989	R Bouchard	1994	E Aubrey

Italian Professional Championship

Year	Winner	Year	Winner
1985	G Cali	1990	M Mannelli
1986	M Mannelli	1991	A Canessa
1987	G Cali	1992	M Reale
1988	A Canessa	1993	G Cali
1989	C Rocca	1994	G Cali

Italian Open Amateur Championship

Year	Winner	Year	Winner
1985	JM Olazabal	1990	M Tadini
1986	A Binaghi	1991	D Borrego
1987	P Quirici	1992	*Not played*
1988	E Giraud	1993	J Kjaerbye
1989	R Victor	1994	D Dupin

Italian Close Amateur Championship

Year	Winner	Year	Winner
1985	E Nistri	1990	M Aragnetti
1986	A Binaghi	1991	M Santi
1987	M Grabau	1992	F Pustetto
1988	M de Rossi	1993	F Crotti
1989	G Ferrero	1994	N Bisazza

Italian Ladies' Open Championship

Year	Winner	Year	Winner
1985	R Lautens	1990	F Descampe
1986	S Moorcroft	1991	C Dibnah
1987	R Lautens	1992	L Davies
1988	L Davies	1993	F Stensrud
1989	X Wunsch-Ruiz	1994	K Speak

Japan Open Championship

Year	Winner	Year	Winner
1985	T Nakajima	1990	T Nakajima
1986	T Nakajima	1991	T Nakajima
1987	I Aoki	1992	M Ozaki
1988	M Ozaki	1993	S Okuda
1989	M Ozaki	1994	M Ozaki

Japan Professional Championship

Year	Winner	Year	Winner
1985	T Ozaki	1990	H Kase
1986	I Aoki	1991	O Masashi
1987	D Ishii	1992	M Kuramoto
1988	T Ozaki	1993	M Ozaki
1989	M Ozaki	1994	H Goda

Japan Amateur Championship

Year	Winner	Year	Winner
1985	T Nakagawa	1990	Y Kuramoto
1986	Y Ito	1991	K Miyamoto
1987	T Suzuki	1992	K Yonekura
1988	R Kawagishi	1993	K Yonekura
1989	K Oie	1994	S Sugimoto

Kenya Open Championship

Year	Winner	Year	Winner
1985	G Harvey	1990	C O'Connor Jr
1986	I Woosnam	1991	J Robinson
1987	C Mason	1992	A Bossert
1988	C Platts	1993	C Maltman
1989	D Jones	1994	P Carman

Korea Open Championship

Year	Winner	Year	Winner
1985	Cho Ho Sang	1990	L Kang-Sun
1986	Choi Yoon Soo	1991	Choi Sang Ho
1987	K Lang-Sun	1992	T Hamilton
1988	Kwak Yu Hyun	1993	Y Kun Han
1989	Chul Sang Cho	1994	M Cunning

Malaysian Open Championship

Year	Winner	Year	Winner
1985	T Gale	1990	G Day
1986	S Ginn	1991	R Gibson
1987	T Gale	1992	V Singh
1988	T Tyner	1993	G Norquist
1989	J Maggert	1994	J Haeggman

Malaysian Women's Open Championship

Year	Winner	Year	Winner
1987	I Shiotani	1991	C Nishida
1988	B New	1992	C Nishida
1989	N Terazawa	1993	S Prosser
1990	C Nishida	1994	J-S Won

Mexican Open Championship

Year	Winner
1993	T Sieckmann
1994	C Perry

New Zealand Open Championship

Year	Winner	Year	Winner
1985	C Pavin	1990	*Not played*
1986	R Davis	1991	R Davis
1987	R Rafferty	1992	G Waite
1988	I Stanley	1993	P Fowler
1989	G Turner	1994	C Jones

New Zealand Amateur Championship

Year	Winner	Year	Winner
1985	G Power	1990	M Long
1986	P O'Malley	1991	L Parsons
1987	O Kendall	1992	R Lee
1988	B Hughes	1993	P Tataurangi
1989	L Peterson	1994	P Fitzgibbon

New Zealand Ladies' Amateur Championship

Year	Winner	Year	Winner
1985	E Kennedy	1990	L Brooky
1986	A Kita	1991	A Stott
1987	J Wyatt	1992	L Lambert
1988	E Cavill	1993	L Brooky
1989	W Sook	1994	JA Atkin

Nigerian Open Championship

Year	Winner	Year	Winner
1985	B Longmuir	1990	W Stephens
1986	GJ Brand	1991	J Lebbie
1987	*Not played*	1992	J Lebbie
1988	V Singh	1993	G Manson
1989	V Singh	1994	

Nordic Amateur Championship *(Team event since 1993; previously Scandinavian Amateur Open)*

Year	Winner	Year	Winner
1985	C Härdin	1990	P Magnebrandt
1986	J Ryström	1991	M Olander
1987	P Hedblom	1992	P Sterner
1988	H Simonsen	1993	Sweden
1989	P-U Johansson	1994	*Not played*

Nordic Ladies' Amateur Championship *(Previously Scandinavian Ladies's Amateur Open. Became a team event in 1993)*

Year	Winner	Year	Winner
1985	M Meiland	1990	A Dönnestad
1986	A Öquist	1991	K Larsson
1987	H Anderssen	1992	C Norvang
1988	M Binau	1993	Sweden
1989	K Orum	1994	*Not played*

Pakistan Open Championship

Year	Winner	Year	Winner
1985	G Muhammad	1990	F Qureshi
1986	M Ali	1991	
1987	T Hassan	1992	M Ahmed
1988	G Nabi	1993	I Hussain
1989	F Minosa	1994	

Polish Open Championship

Year	Winner
1994	G Marks

Portuguese Open Amateur Championship

Year	Winner	Year	Winner
1985	M Grabbau	1990	R Oliveira
1986	R Nissen	1991	*Not played*
1987	S Struven	1992	K Ekjord
1988	C Waesberg	1993	A Townhill
1989	S Bjorn	1994	M Backhausen

Portuguese Close Amateur Championship

Year	Winner	Year	Winner
1985	C Marta	1990	J Grahja
1986	JS Melo	1991	G Carvalhosa
1987	D Silva	1992	A Castelo
1988	R Uliveira	1993	J Pedro
1989	A Castelo	1994	J Correia

Portuguese Ladies' Open Amateur Championship

Year	Winner	Year	Winner
1985	T Abitbol	1990	S Navarro
1986	MC Navarizo	1991	T Abecassis
1987	MC Navarizo	1992	L Navarro
1988	H Andersson	1993	M Arruti
1989	S Clauset	1994	S Dallongeville

Singapore Open Championship

Year	Winner	Year	Winner
1985	CT Ming	1990	A Fernando
1986	G Turner	1991	J Kay
1987	P Fowler	1992	B Israelson
1988	G Bruckner	1993	P Maloney
1989	C-S Lu	1994	KH Han

South African Open Championship

Year	Winner	Year	Winner
1985	G Levenson	1990	T Dodds
1986	D Frost	1991	W Westner
1987	M McNulty	1992	E Els
1988	W Westner	1993	C Whitelaw
1989	F Wadsworth	1994	T Johnstone

South African Masters

Year	Winner	Year	Winner
1985	M McNulty	1990	H Baiocchi
1986	M McNulty	1991	F Allem
1987	D Frost	1992	E Els
1988	J Bland	1993	T Johnstone
1989	H Baiocchi	1994	C Davison

South African PGA Championship

Year	Winner	Year	Winner
1985	C Williams	1990	F Allem
1986	B Cole	1991	R Wessels
1987	F Allem	1992	E Els
1988	D Feherty	1993	M McNulty
1989	A Johnstone	1994	D Frost

South African Amateur Championship

Year	Winner	Year	Winner
1985	N Clarke	1990	R Goosen
1986	E Els	1991	D Botes
1987	B Fouchee	1992	B Davison
1988	N Clarke	1993	L Chitengwa
1989	C Rivett	1994	B Vaughn

South African Amateur Stroke Play Championship

Year	Winner	Year	Winner
1985	D van Staden	1990	P Pascoe
1986	C-S Hsieh	1991	N Henning
1987	B Fouchee	1992	J Nelson
1988	N Clarke	1993	D Kinnear
1989	E Els	1994	N Homann

South African Ladies' Championship

Year	Winner	Year	Winner
1985	W Warrington	1990	G Tebbutt
1986	W Warrington	1991	B Lunsford
1987	C Louw	1992	M Adamson
1988	G Tebbutt	1993	M Adamson
1989	L Rose	1994	S Marais

Spanish Open Amateur Championship

Year	Winner	Year	Winner
1985	BQ de Llano	1990	D Clarke
1986	A Haglund	1991	TJ Muñoz
1987	M Quirke	1992	M Stanford
1988	S Atako	1993	F Stolear
1989	E Giraud	1994	J Healey

Spanish Amateur Close Championship

Year	Winner	Year	Winner
1985	L Garbarda	1990	G de la Riva
1986	BQ de Llano	1991	D Borrego
1987	JM Arruti	1992	A Prat
1988	T Muñoz	1993	JA Vizcaya
1989	T Muñoz	1994	F Valera

Spanish Ladies' Open Amateur Championship

Year	Winner	Year	Winner
1985	C Espinasse	1990	D Bourson
1986	R Lautens	1991	C Quintarelli
1987	C Hourihane	1992	J Hall
1988	I Calogero	1993	C Lambert
1989	I Calogero	1994	AC Jonasson

Spanish Ladies' Amateur Close Championship

Year	Winner	Year	Winner
1985	C Navarro	1990	E Valera
1986	C Navarro	1991	A Arruti
1987	C Navarro	1992	E Knuth
1988	S Navarro	1993	E Knuth
1989	S Navarro	1994	M Arruti

Swedish Professional Championship

Year	Winner	Year	Winner
1985	P Brostedt	1990	A Mednick
1986	M Persson	1991	J Ryström
1987	C-M Strömberg	1992	S Bottomley
1988	V Singh	1993	N Fasth
1989	L Hederström	1994	A Mednick

Swedish Open International Stroke Play Championship

(Amateur before 1984)

Year	Winner	Year	Winner
1985	Y Nilsson	1990	J Parnevik
1986	M Lanner	1991	J Sewell
1987	M Pendaries	1992	J Haeggman
1988	P Haugsrud	1993	D Chopra
1989	A Gillner	1994	E Carlberg

Swedish Open Championship

(Amateur before 1984; Close 1984–9)

Year	Winner	Year	Winner
1985	Y Nilsson	1990	E O'Connell
1986	M Grankvist	1991	M Gronberg
1987	C-M Strömberg	1992	J Cantero
1988	M Krantz	1993	P Haugsrud
1989	M Grankvist	1994	P Nyman

Swedish Ladies' International Open Stroke Play Championship

(Amateur before 1984)

Year	Winner	Year	Winner
1985	K Espinasse	1990	M Bjurö
1986	P Nilsson	1991	A Sörenstam
1987	M Hattori	1992	C Sörenstam
1988	H Alfredsson	1993	D Reid
1989	S Norberg	1994	P Rigby

Swedish Ladies' Open Championship

(Close before 1989)

Year	Winner	Year	Winner
1985	S Gronberg	1990	J Allmark
1986	H Alfredsson	1991	L Ericsson
1987	H Alfredsson	1992	C Hjalmarsson
1988	H Alfredsson	1993	M Hjorth
1989	P Nilsson	1994	L Neumann

Swiss Open Amateur Championship

Year	Winner	Year	Winner
1985	T Hubner	1990	M Santi
1986	A Binaghi	1991	J Wade
1987	M Durante	1992	T Gottstein
1988	A Bossert	1993	N Zitny
1989	M Frank	1994	M Brier

Swiss Close Amateur Championship

Year	Winner	Year	Winner
1985	M Gottstein	1990	T Gottstein
1986	M Frank	1991	M Frank
1987	M Frank	1992	J Ciola
1988	A Bossert	1993	J Ciola
1989	M Frank	1994	M Chatelain

Swiss Ladies' Open Amateur Championship

Year	Winner	Year	Winner
1985	M Koch	1990	M Hagemann
1986	M Koch	1991	M Hagemann
1987	R Lautens	1992	M Alsuguren
1988	M Koch	1993	N Fink
1989	V Pamard	1994	A Nistri

Swiss Ladies' Close Amateur Championship

Year	Winner	Year	Winner
1985	E Orley	1990	C Vannini
1986	E Orley	1991	S Ducrey
1987	E Orley	1992	S Ducrey
1988	E Orley	1993	L Schaufelberger
1989	C Vannini	1994	S Storjohann

United States Amateur Championship

Year	Winner	Runner-up	Venue	By
1946	SE Bishop	S Quick	Baltusrol	37th hole
1947	RH Riegel	J Dawson	Pebble Beach	2 and 1
1948	WP Turnesa	R Billows	Memphis	2 and 1
1949	C Coe	R King	Rochester	11 and 10
1950	S Urzetta	FR Stranahan	Minneapolis	39th hole
1951	WJ Maxwell	J Cagliardi	Saucon Valley, Pa	4 and 3
1952	J Westland	A Mengert	Seattle	3 and 2
1953	G Littler	D Morey	Oklahoma City	1 hole
1954	A Palmer	R Sweeney	Detroit	1 hole
1955	E Harvie Ward	W Hyndman	Richmond, Va	9 and 8
1956	E Harvie Ward	C Kocsis	Lake Forest, Ill	5 and 4
1957	H Robbins	Dr F Taylor	Brookline	5 and 4
1958	C Coe	T Aaron	San Francisco	5 and 4
1959	J Nicklaus	C Coe	Broadmoor	1 hole
1960	DR Beman	R Gardner	St Louis, Mo	6 and 4
1961	J Nicklaus	D Wysong	Pebble Beach	8 and 6
1962	LE Harris, Jr	D Gray	Pinehurst	1 hole
1963	DR Beman	D Sikes	Des Moines	2 and 1
1964	W Campbell	E Tutweiler	Canterbury, Ohio	1 hole
Changed to stroke play				
1965	R Murphy		Tulsa, Okla	291
1966	G Cowan		Ardmore, Penn	285
1967	R Dickson		Colorado	285
1968	B Fleisher		Columbus	284
1969	S Melnyk		Oakmont	286
1970	L Wadkins		Portland	280
1971	G Cowan		Wilmington	280
1972	M Giles		Charlotte, NC	285
Reverted to match play				
1973	C Stadler	D Strawn	Inverness, Ohio	6 and 5
1974	J Pate	J Grace	Ridgewood, NJ	2 and 1
1975	F Ridley	K Fergus	Richmond, Va	2 holes
1976	B Sander	P Moore	Bel-Air	8 and 6
1977	J Fought	D Fischesser	Aronimonk, Pa	9 and 8
1978	J Cook	S Hoch	Plainfield, NJ	5 and 4
1979	M O'Meara	J Cook	Canterbury, Ohio	8 and 7
1980	H Sutton	B Lewis	North Carolina	9 and 8
1981	N Crosby	B Lyndley	San Francisco	37th hole
1982	J Sigel	D Tolley	The Country Club, Brookline	8 and 7
1983	J Sigel	C Perry	North Shore, Chicago	8 and 7
1984	S Verplank	S Randolph	Oak Tree, Okla	4 and 3

continued

Year	Winner	Runner-up	Venue	By
1985	S Randolph	P Persons	Montclair, NJ	1 hole
1986	S Alexander	C Kite	Shoal Creek	5 and 3
1987	W Mayfair	E Rebmann	Jupiter Hills, Fl	4 and 3
1988	E Meeks	D Yates	Hot Springs, VA	7 and 6
1989	C Patton	D Green	Merion, PA	3 and 1
1990	P Mickelson	M Zerman	Cherry Hills, CO	5 and 4
1991	M Voges	M Zerman	Honours Course, TN	7 and 6
1992	J Leonard	T Scherrer	Muirfield Village, OH	8 and 7
1993	J Harris	D Ellis	Champions, Houston	5 and 3
1994	T Woods	T Kuehne	Sawgrass	2 holes

United States Ladies' Amateur Championship

Year	Winner	Runner-up	Venue	By
1960	J Gunderson	J Ashley	Tulsa, Okla	6 and 5
1961	A Quast	P Preuss	Tacoma	14 and 13
1962	J Gunderson	A Baker	Rochester, NY	9 and 8
1963	A Quast	P Conley	Williamstown	2 and 1
1964	B McIntyre	J Gunderson	Prairie Dunes, Kansas	3 and 2
1965	J Ashley	A Quast	Denver	5 and 4
1966	J Carner (*née* Gunderson)	JD Streit	Pittsburgh	41st hole
1967	L Dill	J Ashley	Annandale, Pasadena	5 and 4
1968	J Carner	A Quast	Birmingham, Mich	5 and 4
1969	C Lacoste (Fra)	S Hamlin	Las Colinas, Texas	3 and 2
1970	M Wilkinson	C Hill	Darien, Conn	3 and 2
1971	L Baugh	B Barry	Atlanta	1 hole
1972	M Budke	C Hill	St Louis, Mo	5 and 4
1973	C Semple	A Quast	Montclair, NJ	1 hole
1974	C Hill	C Semple	Broadmoor, Seattle	5 and 4
1975	B Daniel	D Horton	Brae Burn, Mass	3 and 2
1976	D Horton	M Bretton	Del Paso, California	2 and 1
1977	B Daniel	C Sherk	Cincinnati	3 and 1
1978	C Sherk	J Oliver	Sunnybrook, Pa	4 and 3
1979	C Hill	P Sheehan	Memphis	7 and 6
1980	J Inkster	P Rizzo	Prairie Dunes, Kansas	2 holes
1981	J Inkster	L Coggan (Aus)	Portland, Oregon	1 hole
1982	J Inkster	C Hanton	Colorado Springs	4 and 3
1983	J Pacillo	S Quinlan	Canoe Brook, NJ	2 and 1
1984	D Richard	K Williams	Broadmoor, Seattle	37th hole
1985	M Hattori (Jpn.)	C Stacy	Pittsburgh, PA	5 and 4
1986	K Cockerill	K McCarthy	Pasatiempo, California	9 and 7
1987	K Cockerill	T Kerdyk	Barrington, RI	3 and 2
1988	P Sinn	K Noble	Minikahde, MN	6 and 5
1989	V Goetze	B Burton	Pinehurst, NC	4 and 3
1990	P Hurst	S Davis	Canoe Brook, NJ	37th hole
1991	A Fruhwirth	H Voorhees	Prairie Dunes	5 and 4
1992	V Goetze	A Sörenstam	Kemper Lakes	1 hole
1993	J McGill	S Ingram	San Diego	1 hole
1994	W Ward	J McGill	Hot Springs, Va	2 and 1

Zambian Open Championship

Year	Winner	Year	Winner
1985	I Woosnam	1990	GJ Brand
1986	G Cullen	1991	DR Jones
1987	P Carrigill	1992	J Robinson
1988	D Llewellyn	1993	P Harrison
1989	C Maltman	1994	

PGA European Tour

Asian Classic

Year	Winner	Score
1992	I Palmer	268
1993	N Faldo	269
1994	G Norman	277

Austrian Open

Year	Winner	Score
1990	B Langer	271
1991	B Davis	269
1992	P Mitchell	271
1993	R Rafferty	274
1994	M Davis	270

Belgian Open

Year	Winner	Venue	Score
1987	E Darcy	Royal Waterloo	200 *(3 rounds only – rain)*
1988	JM Olazabal	Bercuit	269
1989	GJ Brand	Royal Waterloo	273
1990	O Sellberg	Royal Waterloo	272
1991	P-U Johansson	Royal Waterloo	276
1992	MA Jimenez	Royal Zoute	274
1993	D Clarke	Royal Zoute	270
1994	N Faldo	Royal Zoute	279

Benson and Hedges International Open

Year	Winner	Score
1985	A Lyle	274
1986	M James	274
1987	N Ratcliffe	275
1988	P Baker	271
1989	G Brand, Jr	272
1990	JM Olazabal	279
1991	B Langer	286
1992	P Senior	287
1993	P Broadhurst	276
1994	S Ballesteros	281

BMW International Open

Year	Winner	Score
1989	D Feherty	269
1990	P Azinger	277
1991	A Lyle	268
1992	P Azinger	266
1993	P Fowler	267
1994	M McNulty	274

British Masters

Year	Winner	Club/Country	Venue	Score
1982	G Norman	Australia	St Pierre	267
1983	I Woosnam	Wales	St Pierre	269
1984	*Not played*			
1985	L Trevino	USA	Woburn	278
1986	S Ballesteros	Spain	Woburn	275
1987	M McNulty	Zimbabwe	Woburn	274
1988	A Lyle	Scotland	Woburn	273
1989	N Faldo	England	Woburn	267
1990	M James	England	Woburn	270
1991	S Ballesteros	Spain	Woburn	275
1992	C O'Connor Jr	Ireland	Woburn	270
1993	P Baker	England	Woburn	266
1994	I Woosnam	Wales	Woburn	271

Cannes Open

Year	Winner	Score	Year	Winner	Score
1985	R Lee	280	1990	M McNulty	280
1986	J Bland	276	1991	D Feherty	275
1987	S Ballesteros	275	1992	A Forsbrand	273
1988	M McNulty	279	1993	R Davis	271
1989	P Broadhurst	207 *(54 holes)*	1994	I Woosnam	271

Open Catalonia

Year	Winner	Score
1991	JM Olazabal	271
1992	J Rivero	280
1993	S Torrance	201 *(54 holes only)*
1994	J Coceres	275

Czech Open

Year	Winner	Score
1994	P-U Johansson	237

Dubai Desert Classic

Year	Winner	Score	Year	Winner	Score
1989	M James	277	1992	S Ballesteros	272
1990	E Darcy	276	1993	W Westner	274
1991	*Not played*		1994	E Els	268

Dutch Open

Year	Winner	Score	Year	Winner	Score
1985	G Marsh	282	1990	S McAllister	274
1986	S Ballesteros	271 *(70 holes)*	1991	P Stewart	267
1987	G Brand, Jr	272	1992	B Langer	277
1988	M Mouland	274	1993	C Montgomerie	281
1989	JM Olazabal	277	1994	MA Jimenez	270

English Open

Year	Winner	Venue	Score	Year	Winner	Venue	Score
1988	H Clark	R Birkdale	279	1992	V Fernandez	The Belfry	283
1989	M James	The Belfry	279	1993	I Woosnam	Forest of Arden	269
1990	M James	The Belfry	284	1994	C Montgomerie	Forest of Arden	274
1991	D Gilford	The Belfry	278				

European Masters – Swiss Open

Year	Winner	Score	Year	Winner	Score
1985	C Stadler	267	1990	R Rafferty	267
1986	JM Olazabal	262	1991	J Hawkes	268
1987	A Forsbrand	263	1992	J Spence	271
1988	C Moody	268	1993	B Lane	270
1989	S Ballesteros	266	1994	E Romero	266

European Open

Year	Winner	Venue	Score	Year	Winner	Venue	Score
1979	A Lyle	Turnberry	275	1987	P Way	Walton Heath	279
1980	T Kite	Walton Heath	284	1988	I Woosnam	Sunningdale	260
1981	G Marsh	Liverpool	275	1989	A Murray	Walton Heath	277
1982	M Pinero	Sunningdale	266	1990	P Senior	Sunningdale	267
1983	I Aoki	Sunningdale	274	1991	M Harwood	Walton Heath	277
1984	G Brand, Jr	Sunningdale	270	1992	N Faldo	Sunningdale	262
1985	B Langer	Sunningdale	269	1993	G Brand Jr	East Sussex National	275
1986	G Norman	Sunningdale	269	1994	D Gilford	East Sussex National	275

Extremadura Open

Year	Winner	Score
1994	P Eales	281

French Open

Year	Winner	Score	Year	Winner	Score
1985	S Ballesteros	263	1990	P Walton	275
1986	S Ballesteros	269	1991	E Romero	281
1987	J Rivero	269	1992	MA Martin	276
1988	N Faldo	274	1993	C Rocca	273
1989	N Faldo	273	1994	M Roe	274

German Masters

Year	Winner	Score	Year	Winner	Score
1987	A Lyle	278	1991	B Langer	275
1988	JM Olazabal	279	1992	B Lane	272
1989	B Langer	276	1993	S Richardson	271
1990	S Torrance	272	1994	S Ballesteros	270

German Open

Year	Winner	Score	Year	Winner	Score
1985	B Langer	183 *(54 holes)*	1990	M McNulty	270
1986	B Langer	273	1991	M McNulty	273
1987	M McNulty	259	1992	V Singh	262
1988	S Ballesteros	263	1993	B Langer	269
1989	C Parry	266	1994	C Montgomerie	269

Honda Open

Year	Winner	Score
1992	B Langer	273
1993	S Torrance	278
1994	R Allenby	276

Irish Open

Year	Winner	Club/Country	Venue	Score
1982	J O'Leary	Unattached	Portmarnock	287
1983	S Ballesteros	Spain	R Dublin	271
1984	B Langer	Germany	R Dublin	267
1985	S Ballesteros	Spain	R Dublin	278
1986	S Ballesteros	Spain	Portmarnock	285
1987	B Langer	Germany	Portmarnock	269
1988	I Woosnam	Wales	Portmarnock	278
1989	I Woosnam	Wales	Portmarnock	278
1990	JM Olazabal	Spain	Portmarnock	282
1991	N Faldo	England	Killarney	283
1992	N Faldo	England	Killarney	274
1993	N Faldo	England	Mount Juliet	276
1994	B Langer	Germany	Mount Juliet	275

Italian Open

Year	Winner	Score	Year	Winner	Score
1985	M Pinero	267	1990	R Boxall	267
1986	D Feherty	270	1991	C Parry	279
1987	S Torrance	271	1992	A Lyle	270
1988	G Norman	270	1993	G Turner	267
1989	R Rafferty	273	1994	E Romero	272

Jersey Open

Year	Winner	Score	Year	Winner	Score
1985	H Clark	279	1990	*Not played*	
1986	J Morgan	275	1991	S Torrance	279
1987	I Woosnam	279	1992	D Silva	277
1988	D Smyth	273	1993	I Palmer	268
1989	C O'Connor Jr	281	1994	P Curry	266

Lyon Open

Year	Winner	Score
1992	DJ Russell	267
1993	C Rocca	267
1994	S Ames	282

Madeira Island Open

Year	Winner	Score
1993	M James	281
1994	M Lanner	206

Madrid Open

Year	Winner	Score	Year	Winner	Score
1985	M Pinero	278	1990	B Langer	270
1986	H Clark	274	1991	A Sherborne	272
1987	I Woosnam	269	1992	D Feherty	272
1988	D Cooper	275	1993	D Smyth	272
1989	S Ballesteros	272	1994	*Not played*	

Moroccan Open

Year	Winner	Score
1992	D Gilford	287
1993	D Gilford	279
1994	A Forsbrand	276

Portuguese Open Championship

Year	Winner	Score	Year	Winner	Score
1985	W Humphreys	279	1990	M McLean	274
1986	M McNulty	270	1991	S Richardson	283
1987	R Lee	195 *(54 holes)*	1992	R Rafferty	273
1988	M Harwood	280	1993	D Gilford	275
1989	C Montgomerie	264	1994	P Price	278

Roma Masters

Year	Winner	Score
1992	B Langer	273
1993	J Van de Velde	281
1994	*Not played*	

Scandinavian Masters

Year	Winner	Score
1991	C Montgomerie	270
1992	N Faldo	277
1993	P Baker	278
1994	V Singh	268

Scottish Open

Year	Winner	Venue	Score	Year	Winner	Venue	Score
1985	H Clark	Haggs Castle	274	1990	I Woosnam	Gleneagles	269
1986	D Feherty	Haggs Castle	270	1991	C Parry	Gleneagles	268
1987	I Woosnam	Gleneagles	264	1992	P O'Malley	Gleneagles	262
1988	B Lane	Gleneagles	271	1993	J Parnevik	Gleneagles	271
1989	M Allen	Gleneagles	272	1994	C Mason	Gleneagles	265

Spanish Open

Year	Winner	Score	Year	Winner	Score
1985	S Ballesteros	266	1990	R Davis	277
1986	H Clark	272	1991	E Romero	275
1987	N Faldo	286	1992	A Sherborne	271
1988	M James	262	1993	J Haeggman	275
1989	B Langer	281	1994	C Montgomerie	277

Trophée Lancôme

Year	Winner	Score	Year	Winner	Score
1985	N Price	275	1990	JM Olazabal	269
1986T	S Ballesteros	274	1991	F Nobilo	267
	B Langer		1992	M Roe	267
1987	I Woosnam	264	1993	I Woosnam	267
1988	S Ballesteros	269	1994	V Singh	263
1989	E Romero	266			

Turespaña Open de Andalucia

Year	Winner	Score
1992	V Singh	277
1993	A Oldcorn	285
1994	C Mason	278

Turespaña Open de Baleares

Year	Winner	Score	Year	Winner	Score
1988	S Ballesteros	272	1992	S Ballesteros	277
1989	O Sellberg	279	1993	J Payne	277
1990	S Ballesteros	269	1994	B Lane	269
1991	G Levenson	282			

Turespaña Open de Canarias

Year	Winner	Score
1993	M James	275
1994	D Gilford	278

Turespaña Open de Mediterranea

Year	Winner	Venue	Score
1990	I Woosnam	Las Brisas	210 *(54 holes)*
1991	I Woosnam	Golf d'Esterel	279
1992	JM Olazabal	El Bosque	276
1993	F Nobilo	El Saler	279
1994	JM Olazabal	Vilamartin	276

Volvo PGA Championship (Until 1966 restricted to UK and Irish Pros. In 1967 and 1968 PGA 'open' and 'closed' were contested. From 1969 Championship has been open)

Year	Winner	Venue	Score	Year	Winner	Venue	Score
1955	K Bousfield	Pannal	277	1976	NC Coles	Sandwich, R St George's	280
1956	C Ward	Maesdu	282	1977	M Pinero	Sandwich, R St George's	283
1957	P Alliss	Maesdu	286	1978	N Faldo	R Birkdale	278
1958	H Bradshaw	Llandudno	287	1979	V Fernandez	St Andrews	288
1959	D Rees	Ashburnham	283	1980	N Faldo	Sandwich, R St George's	283
1960	A Stickley	Coventry *(63 holes)*	247	1981	N Faldo	Ganton	274
1961	B Bamford	R Mid-Surrey	266	1982	A Jacklin	Hillside	284
1962	P Alliss	Little Aston	287	1983	S Ballesteros	Sandwich, R St George's	278
1963	P Butler	R Birkdale	306	1984†	H Clark	Wentworth	204
1964	A Grubb	Western Gailes	287	1985	P Way	Wentworth	282
1965	P Alliss	Sandwich, Prince's	286	1986	R Davis	Wentworth	281
1966	G Wostenholme	Saunton	278	1987	B Langer	Wentworth	270
1967	M Gregson	Hunstanton	275	1988	I Woosnam	Wentworth	274
1968	D Talbot	Dunbar	276	1989	N Faldo	Wentworth	272
1969	B Gallacher	Ashburnham	291	1990	M Harwood	Wentworth	271
1970–71	*Not played*			1991	S Ballesteros	Wentworth	271
1972	A Jacklin	Wentworth	279	1992	T Johnstone	Wentworth	272
1973	P Oosterhuis	Wentworth	280	1993	B Langer	Wentworth	274
1974	M Bembridge	Wentworth	278	1994	JM Olazabal	Wentworth	271
1975	A Palmer	Sandwich, R St George's	285				

† *(3 rounds only due to weather)*

Volvo Masters

Year	Winner	Score	Year	Winner	Score
1988	N Faldo	284	1992	A Lyle	287
1989	R Rafferty	282	1993	C Montgomerie	274
1990	M Harwood	286	1994	B Langer	276
1991	R Davis	280			

World Match Play

Year	Winner	Runner-up	By	Year	Winner	Runner-up	By
1964	A Palmer	N Coles	2 and 1	1980	G Norman	A Lyle	1 hole
1965	G Player	P Thomson	3 and 2	1981	S Ballesteros	B Crenshaw	1 hole
1966	G Player	J Nicklaus	6 and 4	1982	S Ballesteros	A Lyle	37th hole
1967	A Palmer	P Thomson	1 hole	1983	G Norman	N Faldo	3 and 2
1968	G Player	R Charles	1 hole	1984	S Ballesteros	B Langer	2 and 1
1969	R Charles	G Littler	37th hole	1985	S Ballesteros	B Langer	6 and 5
1970	J Nicklaus	L Trevino	2 and 1	1986	G Norman	A Lyle	2 and 1
1971	G Player	J Nicklaus	5 and 4	1987	I Woosnam	A Lyle	1 hole
1972	T Weiskopf	L Trevino	4 and 3	1988	A Lyle	N Faldo	2 and 1
1973	G Player	G Marsh	40th hole	1989	N Faldo	I Woosnam	1 hole
1974	H Irwin	G Player	3 and 1	1990	I Woosnam	M McNulty	4 and 2
1975	H Irwin	A Geiberger	4 and 2	1991	S Ballesteros	N Price	3 and 2
1976	D Graham	H Irwin	38th hole	1992	N Faldo	J Sluman	8 and 7
1977	G Marsh	R Floyd	5 and 3	1993	C Pavin	N Faldo	1 hole
1978	I Aoki	S Owen	3 and 2	1994	E Els	C Montgomerie	4 and 2
1979	W Rogers	I Aoki	1 hole				

Seniors

Senior British Open Championship

Year	Winner	Score	Year	Winner	Score
1987	N Coles	279	1991	B Verwey	285
1988	G Player	272	1992	J Fourie	282
1989	R Charles	269	1993	B Charles	291
1990	G Player	280	1994	T Wargo	280

Other Men's Professional Tournaments

PGA Seniors Championship *(Sponsored by Forte since 1983)*

Year	Winner	Club/Country	Venue	Score
1970	M Faulkner	Ifield	Longniddry	288
1971	K Nagle	Australia	Elie	269
1972	K Bousfield	Coombe Hill	Longniddry	291
1973	K Nagle	Australia	Elie	270
1974	E Lester	Astbury	Lundin	282
1975	K Nagle	Australia	Longniddry	268
1976	C O'Connor	Royal Dublin	Cambridgeshire Hotel	284
1977	C O'Connor	Royal Dublin	Cambridgeshire Hotel	288
1978	P Skerritt	St Annes, Dublin	Cambridgeshire Hotel	288
1979	C O'Connor	Royal Dublin	Cambridgeshire Hotel	280
1980	P Skerritt	St Annes, Dublin	Gleneagles Hotel	286
1981	C O'Connor	Royal Dublin	North Berwick	287
1982	C O'Connor	Royal Dublin	Longniddry	285
1983	C O'Connor	Royal Dublin	Burnham and Berrow	277
1984	E Jones	Royal Co Down	Stratford-upon-Avon	280
1985	N Coles	Expotel	Pannal, Harrogate	284
1986	N Coles	Expotel	Mere, Cheshire	276
1987	N Coles	Expotel	Turnberry	279
1988	P Thomson	Australia	North Berwick	287
1989	N Coles	Expotel	West Hill	277
1990	B Waites	Notts	Brough	269
1991	B Waites	Notts	Wollaton Park	277
1992	T Horton	R Jersey	R Dublin	290
1993	B Huggett	Wales	Sunningdale	204 *(54 holes)*
1994	J Morgan	England	Sunningdale	203

Club Professionals' Championship

Year	Winner	Club	Venue	Score
1973	DN Sewell	Ferndown	Calcot Park	276
1974	WB Murray	Coombe Wood	Calcot Park	275
1975	DN Sewell	Ferndown	Calcot Park	276
1976	WJ Ferguson	Ilkley	Moortown	283
1977	D Huish	North Berwick	Notts	284
1978	D Jones	Bangor	Pannal	281
1979	D Jones	Bangor	Pannal	278
1980	D Jagger	Selby	Turnberry	286
1981	M Steadman	Cleeve Hill Mun	Woburn	289
1982	D Durnian	Northenden	Hill Valley	285
1983	J Farmer		Heaton Park	270
1984	D Durnian		Bolton Old Links	278
1985	R Mann	Thorpeness	The Belfry	291
1986	D Huish	North Berwick	R Birkdale	278
1987	R Weir		Sandiway	273
1988	R Weir		Harlech	269
1989	B Barnes	W Chiltington	Sandwich, Prince's	280
1990	A Webster	Edzell	Carnoustie	292
1991	W McGill	Northenden	King's Lynn	285
1992	J Hoskison	W Surrey	St Pierre	275
1993	C Hall	Bulwell Forest	Coventry	274
1994	D Jones	Knockbracken	North Berwick	278

Assistants' Scottish Championship

Year	Winner	Club	Venue	Score
1980	F Mann	Banchory	Dunbar	294
1981	M Brown	Strathclyde	West Kilbride	290
1982	R Collinson	Windyhill	West Kilbride	294
1983	A Webster	Edzell	Stirling	285
1984	C Elliott	Falkirk Tryst	Stirling	285
1985	C Elliott	Falkirk Tryst	Falkirk Tryst	284
1986	P Helsby	Hilton Park	Erskine	295
1987	C Innes	Turnberry	Hilton Park	284
1988	G Collinson	Windyhill	Turnberry	289
1989	C Brooks	Grangemouth	Windyhill	282
1990	P Lawrie	Banchory	Cruden Bay	279
1991	G Hume	Clydebank	Kilmarnock Barassie	299
1992	E McIntosh	Turnhouse	Turnberry Hotel	266
1993	J Wither	Paisley	Alloa	280
1994	S Henderson	Kings Links	Newmachar	283

PGA Assistants' Championship

Year	Winner	Venue	Score
1984	G Weir	Coombe Hill	286
1985	G Coles	Coombe Hill	284
1986	J Brennand	Sand Moor	280
1987	J Hawksworth	Coombe Hill	282
1988	J Oates	Coventry	284
1989	C Brooks	Hillside	291
1990	A Ashton	Hillside	213 (54 holes)
1991	S Wood	Wentworth	288
1992	P Mayo	E Sussex National	285
1993	C Everett	Oaklands	280
1994	M Plummer	Burnham & Berrow	278

Scottish Professional Championship

Year	Winner	Club/Attachment	Venue	Score
1960	EC Brown	Buchanan Castle	West Kilbride	278
1961	RT Walker	Downfield, Dundee	Forres	271
1962	EC Brown	Unattached	Dunbar	283
1963	WM Miller	Cardross	Crieff	284
1964	RT Walker	Downfield, Dundee	Machrihanish	277
1965	EC Brown	Cruden Bay	Forfar	271
1966 T	EC Brown	Cruden Bay	Cruden Bay	137 *(36 holes)*
	J Panton	Glenbervie		
1967	H Bannerman	Aberdeen	Montrose	279
1968	EC Brown	Cruden Bay	Monktonhall	286
1969	G Cunningham	Troon Municipal	Machrihanish	284
1970	RDBM Shade	Duddingston	Montrose	276
1971	NJ Gallacher	Wentworth	Lundin Links	282
1972	H Bannerman	Banchory	Strathaven	268
1973	BJ Gallacher	Wentworth	Kings Links, Aberdeen	276
1974	BJ Gallacher	Wentworth	Drumpellier	276
1975	D Huish	North Berwick	Duddingston	279
1976	J Chillas	Crow Wood	Haggs Castle	286
1977	BJ Gallacher	Wentworth	Barnton	282
1978	S Torrance	Caledonian Hotel	Strathaven	269
1979	AWB Lyle	Hawkstone Park	Glasgow Gailes	274
1980	S Torrance	Caledonian Hotel	East Kilbride	273
1981	B Barnes	Caledonian Hotel	Dalmahoy	275
1982	B Barnes	Caledonian Hotel	Dalmahoy	286
1983	B Gallacher	Wentworth	Dalmahoy	276
1984	I Young	Dalmahoy	Dalmahoy	276
1985	S Torrance	Unattached	Dalmahoy	277
1986	R Drummond	Strathclyde Hardware	Glenbervie	270
1987	R Drummond	Strathclyde Hardware	Glenbervie	268
1988	S Stephen	Stephen Architects	Haggs Castle	283

continued

Scottish Professional Championship *continued*

Year	Winner	Club/Attachment	Venue	Score
1989	R Drummond	Continental Airlines	Monktonhall	274
1990	R Drummond	Continental Airlines	Deer Park	278
1991	S Torrance	La Duquesa	Erskine	274
1992	P Lawrie	King's Links	Cardross	273
1993	S Torrance	Unattached	Dalmahoy	269
1994	A Coltart	Thornhill	Dalmahoy	281

Welsh Professional Championship

Year	Winner	Club/Attachment	Venue	Score
1960	RH Kemp, Jr	Unattached	Llandudno	288
1961	S Mouland	Glamorganshire	Southerndown	286
1962	S Mouland	Glamorganshire	Porthcawl	302
1963	H Gould	Southerndown	Wrexham	291
1964	B Bielby	Portmadoc	Tenby	297
1965	S Mouland	Glamorganshire	Penarth	281
1966	S Mouland	Glamorganshire	Conway	281
1967	S Mouland	Glamorganshire	Pyle and Kenfig	219 *(54 holes, fog)*
1968	RJ Davies	South Herts	Southerndown	292
1969	S Mouland	Glamorganshire	Llandudno	277
1970	W Evans	Pennard	Tredegar Park	289
1971	J Buckley	North Wales	St Pierre	291
1972	J Buckley	Rhos-on-Sea	Porthcawl	298
1973	A Griffiths	Wrexham	Newport	289
1974	M Hughes	Aberystwyth	Cardiff	284
1975	C DeFoy	Bryn Meadows	Whitchurch	285
1976	S Cox	Wenvoe Castle	Radyr	284
1977	C DeFoy	Calcot Park	Glamorganshire	135
1978	BCC Huggett	Cambridgeshire Hotel	Whitchurch	145
1979 *Cancelled*				
1980	A Griffiths	Llanymynech	Cardiff	139
1981	C DeFoy	Coombe Hill	Cardiff	139
1982	C DeFoy	Coombe Hill	Cardiff	137
1983	S Cox	Wenvoe Castle	Cardiff	136
1984	K Jones	Caldy	Cardiff	135
1985	D Llewellyn	Thirsk	Whitchurch	132
1986	P Parkin	Blue Arrow	Whitchurch	142
1987	A Dodman	St Pierre	Cardiff	132
1988	I Woosnam	Wang	Cardiff	137
1989	K Jones	Caldy	Royal Porthcawl	140
1990	P Mayo	Powell Duffryn	Fairwood Park	136
1991	P Mayo	BIG Batteries	Fairwood Park	138
1992	C Evans	Prince's	Asburnham	142
1993	P Price	Pontypridd	Caerphilly	138
1994	M Plummer	Burnham & Berrow	Northop	133

Million Dollar Challenge

at Gary Player CC, Sun City, Bophuthatswana

Year	Winner	Score
1982	J Miller	277
1983	R Floyd	280
1984	S Ballesteros	274
1985	S Ballesteros	279
1986	B Langer	278
1987	M McNulty	282
1988	I Woosnam	274
1989	D Frost	276
1990	D Frost	284
1991	B Langer	272
1992	D Frost	276
1993	N Price	264
1994	N Faldo	272

Men's Professional Internationals

Great Britain & Ireland (Europe from 1979) *v* USA

Year		Great Britain & Ireland		USA		Venue
1921 (June 6)	Foursomes	4	10½	1	4½	Gleneagles
	Singles	6½		3½		
1926 (June 4–5)	Foursomes	5	13½	0	1½	Wentworth
	Singles	8½		1½		

The Ryder Cup

Instituted 1927

Year		Great Britain & Ireland		USA		Venue
1927 (June 3–4)	Foursomes	1	2½	3	9½	Worcester, Mass
	Singles	1½		6½		
1929 (May 26–27)	Foursomes	1½	7	2½	5	Moortown
	Singles	5½		2½		
1931 (June 26–27)	Foursomes	1	3	3	9	Columbus, Ohio
	Singles	2		6		
1933 (June 26–27)	Foursomes	2½	6½	1½	5½	Southport and Ainsdale
	Singles	4		4		
1935 (Sept 28–29)	Foursomes	1	3	3	9	Ridgewood, NJ
	Singles	2		6		
1937 (June 29–30)	Foursomes	1½	4	2½	8	Southport and Ainsdale
	Singles	2½		5½		
1947 (Nov 1–2)	Foursomes	0	1	4	11	Portland, Oregon
	Singles	1		7		
1949 (Sept 16–17)	Foursomes	3	5	1	7	Ganton
	Singles	2		6		
1951 (Nov 2 and 4)	Foursomes	1	2½	3	9½	Pinehurst, N Carolina
	Singles	1½		6½		
1953 (Oct 2–3)	Foursomes	1	5½	3	6½	Wentworth
	Singles	4½		3½		
1955 (Nov 5–6)	Foursomes	1	4	3	8	Palm Springs, California
	Singles	3		5		
1957 (Oct 4–5)	Foursomes	1	7½	3	4½	Lindrick
	Singles	6½		1½		
1959 (Nov 6–7)	Foursomes	1½	3½	2½	8½	Eldorado, California
	Singles	2		6		
1961 (Oct 13–14)	Foursomes	2	9½	6	14½	R Lytham and St Annes
	Singles	7½		8½		
1963 (Oct 11–13)	Foursomes	2		6		
	Four-ball	2	9	6	23	Atlanta, Ga.
	Singles	5		11		
1965 (Oct 7–9)	Foursomes	4		4		
	Fourball	3	12½	5	19½	R Birkdale
	Singles	5½		10½		

continued

The Ryder Cup *continued*

Year		Great Britain & Ireland		USA		Venue
1967	Foursomes	2½		5½		
(Oct 20–22)	Fourball	½	8½	7½	23½	Houston, Tex.
	Singles	5½		10½		
1969	Foursomes	4½		3½		
(Oct 18–20)	Fourball	3½	16	4½	16	R Birkdale
	Singles	8		8		
1971	Foursomes	4½		3½		
(Sept 16–18)	Fourball	1½	13½	6½	18½	St Louis, Missouri
	Singles	7½		8½		
1973	Foursomes	4½		3½		
(Sept 20–22)	Fourball	3½	13	4½	19	Muirfield
	Singles	5		11		
1975	Foursomes	1		7		
(Sept 19–21)	Fourball	2½	11	5½	21	Laurel Valley, Pa.
	Singles	7½		8½		
1977	Foursomes	1½		3½		
(Sept 15–17)	Fourball	1	7½	4	12½	R Lytham and St Annes
	Singles	5		5		

From 1979 players from the Continent of Europe became available for selection in addition to those from Great Britain and Ireland

Year						Venue
1979	Foursomes	4½		3½		
(Sept 14–16)	Four-ball	3	11	5	17	Greenbrier, WVa
	Singles	3½		8½		
1981	Foursomes	2		6		
(Sept 18–20)	Four-ball	3½	9½	4½	18½	Walton Heath
	Singles	4		8		
1983	Foursomes	4		4		
(Oct 14–16)	Four-ball	4	13½	4	14½	PGA National, Florida
	Singles	5½		6½		

At The Belfry, Sutton Coldfield, on 13th, 14th and 15th September, 1985

Europe / USA

First Day – Foursomes

Europe	Matches	USA	Matches
S Ballesteros and M Pinero (2 and 1)	1	C Strange and M O'Meara	0
B Langer and N Faldo	0	C Peete and T Kite (3 and 2)	1
A Lyle and K Brown	0	L Wadkins and R Floyd (4 and 3)	1
H Clark and S Torrance	0	C Stadler and H Sutton (3 and 2)	1
	1		3

Four–ball

Europe	Matches	USA	Matches
P Way and I Woosnam (1 hole)	1	F Zoeller and H Green	0
S Ballesteros and M Pinero (2 and 1)	1	A North and P Jacobsen	0
B Langer and JM Canizares (halved)	½	C Stadler and H Sutton (halved)	½
S Torrance and H Clark	0	R Floyd and L Wadkins (1 hole)	1
	2½		1½

Second Day – Fourball

Europe	Matches	USA	Matches
S Torrance and H Clark (2 and 1)	1	T Kite and A North	0
P Way and I Woosnam (4 and 3)	1	H Green and F Zoeller	0
S Ballesteros and M Pinero	0	M O'Meara and L Wadkins (3 and 2)	1
B Langer and A Lyle (halved)	½	C Stadler and C Strange (halved)	½
	2½		1½

Foursomes

Europe	Matches	USA	Matches
JM Canizares and J Rivero (7 and 5)	1	T Kite and C Peete	0
S Ballesteros and M Pinero (5 and 4)	1	C Stadler and H Sutton	0
P Way and I Woosnam	0	C Strange and P Jacobsen (4 and 2)	1
B Langer and K Brown (3 and 2)	1	R Floyd and L Wadkins	0
	3		1

***Third Day* – Singles**

M Pinero (3 and 1)	1	L Wadkins	0
I Woosnam	0	C Stadler (2 and1)	1
P Way (2 holes)	1	R Floyd	0
S Ballesteros (halved)	1/2	T Kite (halved)	1/2
A Lyle (3 and 2)	1	P Jacobsen	0
B Langer (5 and 4)	1	H Sutton	0
S Torrance (1 hole)	1	A North	0
H Clark (1 hole)	1	M O'Meara	0
N Faldo	0	H Green (3 and 1)	1
J Rivero	0	C Peete (1 hole)	1
JM Canizares (2 holes)	1	F Zoeller	0
K Brown	0	C Strange (4 and 2)	1
	7 1/2		4 1/2

Match Aggregate: Europe 16 1/2; USA 11 1/2. Non-playing Captains: A Jacklin, Europe; L Trevino, USA.

At Muirfield Village, Ohio, 25th, 26th and 27th September, 1987

Europe / **USA**

***First Day* – Foursomes**

Europe	Matches	USA	Matches
S Torrance and H Clark	0	C Strange and T Kite (4 and 2)	1
K Brown and B Langer	0	H Sutton and D Pohl (2 and 1)	1
N Faldo and I Woosnam (2 holes)	1	L Wadkins and L Mize	0
S Ballesteros and JM Olazabal (1 hole)	1	L Nelson and P Stewart	0
	2		2

Fourball

G Brand Jr and J Rivero (3 and 2)	1	B Crenshaw and S Simpson	0
A Lyle and B Langer (1 hole)	1	A Bean and M Calcavecchia	0
N Faldo and I Woosnam (2 and 1)	1	H Sutton and D Pohl	0
S Ballesteros and JM Olazabal (2 and 1)	1	C Strange and T Kite	0
	4		0

***Second Day* – Foursomes**

J Rivero and G Brand Jr	0	C Strange and T Kite (3 and 1)	1
N Faldo and I Woosnam (halved)	1/2	H Sutton and L Mize (halved)	1/2
S Ballesteros and JM Olazabal (1 hole)	1	B Crenshaw and P Stewart	0
A Lyle and B Langer (2 and 1)	1	L Wadkins and L Nelson	0
	2 1/2		1 1/2

Fourball

I Woosnam and N Faldo (5 and 4)	1	T Kite and C Strange	0
E Darcy and G Brand Jr	0	A Bean and P Stewart (3 and 2)	1
S Ballesteros and JM Olazabal	0	H Sutton and L Mize (2 and 1)	1
A Lyle and B Langer (1 hole)	1	L Wadkins and L Nelson	0
	2		2

***Third Day* – Singles**

I Woosnam	0	A Bean (1 hole)	1
H Clark (1 hole)	1	D Pohl	0
S Torrance (halved)	1/2	L Mize (halved)	1/2
N Faldo	0	M Calcavecchia (1 hole)	1
JM Olazabal	0	P Stewart (2 holes)	1
E Darcy (1 hole)	1	B Crenshaw	0
J Rivero	0	S Simpson (2 and 1)	1
B Langer (halved)	1/2	L Nelson (halved)	1/2
A Lyle	0	T Kite (3 and 2)	1
S Ballesteros (2 and 1)	1	C Strange	0
G Brand Jr (halved)	1/2	H Sutton (halved)	1/2
K Brown	0	L Wadkins (3 and 2)	1
	4 1/2		7 1/2

Match Aggregate: USA 13; Europe 15. Non-playing Captains: J Nicklaus, USA; A Jacklin, Europe.

The Ryder Cup *continued*

At The Belfry, Sutton Coldfield, on 22nd, 23rd and 24th September, 1989

Europe | **USA**

First Day – Foursomes

Europe	Matches	USA	Matches
N Faldo and I Woosnam (halved)	1/2	T Kite and C Strange (halved)	1/2
H Clark and M James	0	L Wadkins and P Stewart (1 hole)	1
S Ballesteros and JM Olazabal (halved)	1/2	T Watson and C Beck (halved)	1/2
B Langer and R Rafferty	0	M Calcavecchia and K Green (2 and 1)	1
	1		3

Fourball

Europe	Matches	USA	Matches
S Torrance and G Brand Jr (1 hole)	1	C Strange and P Azinger	0
H Clark and M James (3 and 2)	1	F Couples and L Wadkins	0
N Faldo and I Woosnam (2 holes)	1	M Calcavecchia and M McCumber	0
S Ballesteros and JM Olazabal (6 and 5)	1	T Watson and M O'Meara	0
	4		0

Second Day – Foursomes

Europe	Matches	USA	Matches
I Woosnam and N Faldo (3 and 2)	1	L Wadkins and P Stewart	0
G Brand Jr and S Torrance	0	C Beck and P Azinger (4 and 3)	1
C O'Connor Jr and R Rafferty	0	M Calcavecchia and K Green (3 and 2)	1
S Ballesteros and JM Olazabal (1 hole)	1	T Kite and C Strange	0
	2		2

Fourball

Europe	Matches	USA	Matches
N Faldo and I Woosnam	0	C Beck and P Azinger (2 and 1)	1
B Langer and JM Canizares	0	T Kite and M McCumber (2 and 1)	1
H Clark and M James (1 hole)	1	P Stewart and C Strange	0
S Ballesteros and JM Olazabal (4 and 2)	1	M Calcavecchia and K Green	0
	2		2

Third Day – Singles

Europe	Matches	USA	Matches
S Ballesteros	0	P Azinger (1 hole)	1
B Langer	0	C Beck (3 and 2)	1
JM Olazabal (1 hole)	1	P Stewart	0
R Rafferty (1 hole)	1	M Calcavecchia	0
H Clark	0	T Kite (8 and 7)	1
M James (3 and 2)	1	M O'Meara	0
C O'Connor Jr (1 hole)	1	F Couples	0
JM Canizares (1 hole)	1	K Green	0
G Brand Jr	0	M McCumber (1 hole)	1
S Torrance	0	T Watson (3 and 2)	1
N Faldo	0	L Wadkins (1 hole)	1
I Woosnam	0	C Strange (2 holes)	1
	5		7

Match Aggregate: Europe 14; USA 14. Non-playing Captains: A Jacklin, Europe; R Floyd, USA.

At Kiawah Island, South Carolina, on 27th, 28th and 29th September, 1991

Europe | **USA**

First Day – Foursomes

Europe	Matches	USA	Matches
S Ballesteros and JM Olazabal (2 and 1)	1	P Azinger and C Beck	0
B Langer and M James	0	R Floyd and F Couples (2 and 1)	1
D Gilford and C Montgomerie	0	L Wadkins and H Irwin (4 and 2)	1
N Faldo and I Woosnam	0	P Stewart and M Calcavecchia (1 hole)	1
	1		3

Fourball

Europe	Matches	USA	Matches
S Torrance and D Feherty	1/2	L Wadkins and M O'Meara	1/2
S Ballesteros and JM Olazabal (2 and 1)	1	P Azinger and C Beck	0
S Richardson and M James (5 and 4)	1	C Pavin and M Calcavecchia	0
N Faldo and I Woosnam	0	R Floyd and F Couples (5 and 3)	1
	2 1/2		1 1/2

Second Day – Foursomes

S Torrance and D Feherty	0	H Irwin and L Wadkins (4 and 2)	1
M James and S Richardson	0	M Calcavecchia and P Stewart (1 hole)	1
N Faldo and D Gilford	0	P Azinger and M O'Meara (7 and 6)	1
S Ballesteros and JM Olazabal (3 and 2)	1	F Couples and R Floyd	0
	1		3

Fourball

I Woosnam and P Broadhurst (2 and 1)	1	P Azinger and H Irwin	0
B Langer and C Montgomerie (2 and 1)	1	S Pate and C Pavin	0
M James and S Richardson (3 and 1)	1	L Wadkins and W Levi	0
S Ballesteros and JM Olazabal	1/2	F Couples and P Stewart	1/2
	3 1/2		1/2

Third Day – Singles

N Faldo (2 holes)	1	R Floyd	0
D Feherty (2 and 1)	1	P Stewart	0
C Montgomerie	1/2	M Calcavecchia	1/2
JM Olazabal	0	P Azinger (2 holes)	1
S Richardson	0	C Pavin (2 and 1)	1
S Ballesteros (3 and 2)	1	W Levi	0
I Woosnam	0	C Beck (3 and 1)	1
P Broadhurst (3 and 1)	1	M O'Meara	0
S Torrance	0	F Couples (3 and 2)	1
M James	0	L Wadkins (3 and 2)	1
B Langer	1/2	H Irwin	1/2
D Gilford (withdrawn at start of day)	1/2	S Pate (withdrawn at start of day)	1/2
	5 1/2		6 1/2

Match Aggregate: USA 14 1/2; Europe 13 1/2. Non-playing Captains: D Stockton, USA; B Gallacher, Europe.

At The Belfry, Sutton Coldfield, on 24th, 25th and 26th September, 1993

First Day – Foursomes

Europe	Matches	USA	Matches
S Torrance and M James	0	L Wadkins and C Pavin (4 and 3)	1
I Woosnam and B Langer (7 and 5)	1	P Azinger and P Stewart	0
S Ballesteros and JM Olazabal	0	T Kite and D Love III (2 and 1)	1
N Faldo and C Montgomerie (4 and 3)	1	R Floyd and F Couples	0
	2		2

Fourball

I Woosnam and P Baker (1 hole)	1	J Gallagher Jr and L Janzen	0
B Lane and B Langer	0	L Wadkins and C Pavin (4 and 2)	1
N Faldo and C Montgomerie	1/2	P Azinger and F Couples	1/2
S Ballesteros and JM Olazabal (4 and 3)	1	T Kite and D Love III	0
	2 1/2		1 1/2

Second Day – Foursomes

N Faldo and C Montgomerie (3 and 2)	1	L Wadkins and C Pavin	0
B Langer and I Woosnam (2 and 1)	1	F Couples and P Azinger	0
P Baker and B Lane	0	R Floyd and P Stewart (3 and 2)	1
S Ballesteros and JM Olazabal (2 and 1)	1	T Kite and D Love III	0
	3		1

Fourball

N Faldo and C Montgomerie	0	C Beck and J Cook (2 holes)	1
M James and C Rocca	0	C Pavin and J Gallagher Jr (5 and 4)	1
I Woosnam and P Baker (6 and 5)	1	F Couples and P Azinger	0
JM Olazabal and J Haeggman	0	R Floyd and P Stewart (2 and 1)	1
	1		3

continued

The Ryder Cup 1993 *continued*

Third Day – Singles

Europe		USA	
I Woosnam	½	F Couples	½
B Lane	0	C Beck (1 hole)	1
C Montgomerie (1 hole)	1	L Janzen	0
P Baker (2 holes)	1	C Pavin	0
J Haeggman (1 hole)	1	J Cook	0
S Torrance *(withdrawn at start of day)*	½	L Wadkins *(withdrawn at start of day)*	½
M James	0	P Stewart (3 and 2)	1
C Rocca	0	D Love III (1 hole)	1
S Ballesteros	0	J Gallagher Jr (3 and 2)	1
JM Olazabal	0	R Floyd (2 holes)	1
B Langer	0	T Kite (5 and 3)	1
N Faldo	½	P Azinger	½
	4½		7½

Match Aggregate: Europe 13; USA 15. Non-playing Captains: B Gallacher, Europe; T Watson, USA.

INDIVIDUAL RECORDS

Matches were contested as Great Britain v USA from 1927–71; as Great Britain and Ireland from 1973–7; and as Europe v USA from 1979. Bold type indicates captain; in brackets – did not play.

Europe

Name	Year	Played	Won	Lost	Halved
Jimmy Adams	*1939-47-49-51-53	7	2	5	0
Percy Alliss	1929-33-35-37	6	3	2	1
Peter Alliss	1953-57-59-61-63-65-67-69	30	10	15	5
Laurie Ayton	1949	0	0	0	0
Peter Baker	1993	4	3	1	0
Severiano Ballesteros	1979-83-85-87-89-91-93	34	19	10	5
Harry Bannerman	1971	5	2	2	1
Brian Barnes	1969-71-73-75-77-79	25	10	14	1
Maurice Bembridge	1969-71-73-75	16	5	8	3
Aubrey Boomer	1927-29	4	2	2	0
Ken Bousfield	1949-51-55-57-59-61	10	5	5	0
Hugh Boyle	1967	3	0	3	0
Harry Bradshaw	1953-55-57	5	2	2	1
Gordon J Brand	1983	1	0	1	0
Gordon Brand Jr	1987-89	7	2	4	1
Paul Broadhurst	1991	2	2	0	0
Eric Brown	1953-55-57-59-**(69)**-**(71)**	8	4	4	0
Ken Brown	1977-79-83-85-87	13	4	9	0
Stewart Burns	1929	0	0	0	0
Dick Burton	1935-37-*39-49	5	2	3	0
Jack Busson	1935	2	0	2	0
Peter Butler	1965-69-71-73	14	3	9	2
José Maria Canizares	1981-83-85-89	11	5	4	2
Alex Caygill	1969	1	0	0	1
Clive Clark	1973	1	0	1	0
Howard Clark	1977-81-85-87-89	13	6	6	1
Neil Coles	1961-63-65-67-69-71-73-77	40	12	21	7
Archie Compston	1927-29-31	6	1	4	1
Henry Cotton	1929-37-*39-**47**-**(53)**	6	2	4	0
Bill Cox	1935-37	3	0	2	1
Allan Dailey	1933	0	0	0	0
Fred Daly	1947-49-51-53	8	3	4	1
Eamonn Darcy	1975-77-81-87	11	1	8	2
William Davies	1931-33	4	2	2	0
Peter Dawson	1977	3	1	2	0
Norman Drew	1959	1	0	0	1
George Duncan	1927-**29**-31	5	2	3	0
Syd Easterbrook	1931-33	3	2	1	0
Nick Faldo	1977-79-81-83-85-87-89-91-93	36	19	13	4
John Fallon	1955-**(63)**	1	1	0	0
Max Faulkner	1947-49-51-53-57	8	1	7	0
David Feherty	1991	3	1	1	1
George Gadd	1927	0	0	0	0
Bernard Gallacher	1969-71-73-75-77-79-81-83-**(91)**-**(93)**	31	13	13	5
John Garner	1971-73	1	0	1	0

* Great Britain named eight members of their 1939 side, but the match was not played because of the Second World War.

Name	Year	Played	Won	Lost	Halved
Antonio Garrido	1979	5	1	4	0
David Gilford	1991	2	0	2	0
Eric Green	1947	0	0	0	0
Malcolm Gregson	1967	4	0	4	0
Joakim Haeggman	1993	2	1	1	0
Tom Haliburton	1961-63	6	0	6	0
Jack Hargreaves	1951	0	0	0	0
Arthur Havers	1927-31-33	6	3	3	0
Jimmy Hitchcock	1965	3	0	3	0
Bert Hodson	1931	1	0	1	0
Reg Horne	1947	0	0	0	0
Tommy Horton	1975-77	8	1	6	1
Brian Huggett	1963-67-69-71-73-75-(77)	25	9	10	6
Bernard Hunt	1953-57-59-61-63-65-67-69-(73)-(75)	28	6	16	6
Geoffrey Hunt	1963	3	0	3	0
Guy Hunt	1975	3	0	2	1
Tony Jacklin	1967-69-71-73-75-77-79-(83)-(85)-(87)-(89)	35	13	14	8
John Jacobs	1955-(79)-(81)	2	2	0	0
Mark James	1977-79-81-89-91-93	22	7	14	1
Edward Jarman	1935	1	0	1	0
Herbert Jolly	1927	2	0	2	0
Michael King	1979	1	0	1	0
Sam King	1937-*39-47-49	5	1	3	1
Arthur Lacey	1933-37-(51)	3	0	3	0
Barry Lane	1993	3	0	3	0
Bernhard Langer	1981-83-85-87-89-91-93	29	13	11	5
Arthur Lees	1947-49-51-55	8	4	4	0
Sandy Lyle	1979-81-83-85-87	18	7	9	2
Jimmy Martin	1965	1	0	1	0
Peter Mills	1957-59	1	1	0	0
Abe Mitchell	1929-31-33	6	4	2	0
Ralph Moffitt	1961	1	0	1	0
Colin Montgomerie	1991-93	8	3	2	2
Christy O'Connor, Jr	1975-89	4	1	3	0
Christy O'Connor, Sr	1955-57-59-61-63-65-67-69-71-73	36	11	21	4
José Maria Olazabal	1987-89-91-93	20	12	6	2
John O'Leary	1975	4	0	4	0
Peter Oosterhuis	1971-73-75-77-79-81	28	14	11	3
Alf Padgham	1933-35-37-*39	6	0	6	0
John Panton	1951-53-61	5	0	5	0
Alf Perry	1933-35-37	4	0	3	1
Manuel Pinero	1981-85	9	6	3	0
Lionel Platts	1965	5	1	2	2
Eddie Polland	1973	2	0	2	0
Ronan Rafferty	1989	3	1	2	0
Ted Ray	1927	2	0	2	0
Dai Rees	1937-*39-47-49-51-53-55-57-59-61-(67)	18	7	10	1
Steven Richardson	1991	4	2	2	0
Jose Rivero	1985-87	5	2	3	0
Fred Robson	1927-29-31	6	2	4	0
Costantino Rocca	1993	2	0	2	0
Syd Scott	1955	2	0	2	0
Des Smyth	1979-81	7	2	5	0
Dave Thomas	1959-63-65-67	18	3	10	5
Sam Torrance	1981-83-85-87-89-91-93	22	4	13	5
Peter Townsend	1969-71	11	3	8	0
Brian Waites	1983	4	1	3	0
Charlie Ward	1947-49-51	6	1	5	0
Paul Way	1983-85	9	6	2	1
Harry Weetman	1951-53-55-57-59-61-63-(65)	15	2	11	2
Charles Whitcombe	1927-29-31-33-35-37-*39-(49)	9	3	2	4
Ernest Whitcombe	1929-31-35	6	1	4	1
Reg Whitcombe	1935-*39	1	0	1	0
George Will	1963-65-67	15	2	11	2
Norman Wood	1975	3	1	2	0
Ian Woosnam	1983-85-87-89-91-93	26	12	10	4

United States of America

Name	Year	Played	Won	Lost	Halved
Tommy Aaron	1969-73	6	1	4	1
Skip Alexander	1949-51	2	1	1	0
Paul Azinger	1989-91-93	14	5	7	2

* Great Britain named eight members of their 1939 side, but the match was not played because of the Second World War.

Name	Year	Played	Won	Lost	Halved
Jerry Barber	1955-61	5	1	4	0
Miller Barber	1969-71	7	1	4	2
Herman Barron	1947	1	1	0	0
Andy Bean	1979-87	6	4	2	0
Frank Beard	1969-71	8	2	3	3
Chip Beck	1989-91-93	9	6	2	1
Homero Blancas	1973	4	2	1	1
Tommy Bolt	1955-57	4	3	1	0
Julius Boros	1959-63-65-67	16	9	3	4
Gay Brewer	1967-73	9	5	3	1
Billy Burke	1931-33	3	3	0	0
Jack Burke	1951-53-55-57-59-(73)	8	7	1	0
Walter Burkemo	1953	1	0	1	0
Mark Calcavecchia	1987-89-91	11	5	5	1
Billy Casper	1961-63-65-67-69-71-73-75-(79)	37	20	10	7
Bill Collins	1961	3	1	2	0
Charles Coody	1971	3	0	2	1
John Cook	1993	2	1	1	0
Fred Couples	1989-91-93	12	3	6	3
Wilfred Cox	1931	2	2	0	0
Ben Crenshaw	1981-83-87	9	3	5	1
Jimmy Demaret	**1941-47-49-51	6	6	0	0
Gardner Dickinson	1967-71	10	9	1	0
Leo Diegel	1927-29-31-33	6	3	3	0
Dale Douglass	1969	2	0	2	0
Dave Douglas	1953	2	1	0	1
Ed Dudley	1929-33-37	4	3	1	0
Olin Dutra	1933-35	4	1	3	0
Lee Elder	1979	4	1	3	0
Al Espinosa	1927-29-31	4	2	1	1
Johnny Farrell	1927-29-31	6	3	2	1
Dow Finsterwald	1957-59-61-63-(77)	13	9	3	1
Ray Floyd	1969-75-77-81-83-85-(89)-91-93	31	12	16	3
Doug Ford	1955-57-59-61	9	4	4	1
Ed Furgol	1957	1	0	1	0
Marty Furgol	1955	1	0	1	0
Jim Gallagher Jr	1993	3	2	1	0
Al Geiberger	1967-75	9	5	1	3
Vic Ghezzi	*1939-**41	0	0	0	0
Bob Gilder	1983	4	2	2	0
Bob Goalby	1963	5	3	1	1
Johnny Golden	1927-29	3	3	0	0
Lou Graham	1973-75-77	9	5	3	1
Hubert Green	1977-79-85	7	4	3	0
Ken Green	1989	4	2	2	0
Ralph Guldahl	1937-*39	2	2	0	0
Fred Haas, Jr	1953	1	0	1	0
Jay Haas	1983	4	2	1	1
Walter Hagen	1927-29-31-33-35-(37)	9	7	1	1
Bob Hamilton	1949	2	0	2	0
Chick Harbert	1949-55	2	2	0	0
Chandler Harper	1955	1	0	1	0
Dutch (EJ) Harrison	1947-49-51	3	2	1	0
Fred Hawkins	1957	2	1	1	0
Mark Hayes	1979	3	1	2	0
Clayton Heafner	1949-51	4	3	0	1
Jay Hebert	1959-61-(71)	4	2	1	1
Lionel Hebert	1957	1	0	1	0
Dave Hill	1969-73-77	9	6	3	0
Jimmy Hines	*1939	0	0	0	0
Ben Hogan	**1941-47-(49)-51-(67)	3	3	0	0
Hale Irwin	1975-77-79-81-91	20	13	5	2
Tommy Jacobs	1965	4	3	1	0
Peter Jacobsen	1985	3	1	2	0
Don January	1965-77	7	2	3	2
Lee Janzen	1993	2	0	2	0
Herman Keiser	1947	1	0	1	0
Tom Kite	1979-81-83-85-87-89-93	28	15	9	4
Ted Kroll	1953-55-57	4	3	1	0
Ky Laffoon	1935	1	0	1	0
Tony Lema	1963-65	11	8	1	2
Wayne Levi	1991	2	0	2	0
Bruce Lietzke	1981	3	0	2	1

US teams were selected in 1939 (*) and 1941 (**), but the matches were not played because of the Second World War.

Name	Year	Played	Won	Lost	Halved
Gene Littler	1961-63-65-67-69-71-75	27	14	5	8
Davis Love III	1993	4	2	2	0
John Mahaffey	1979	3	1	2	0
Mark McCumber	1989	3	2	1	0
Jerry McGee	1977	2	1	1	0
Harold McSpaden	*1939-**41	0	0	0	0
Tony Manero	1937	2	1	1	0
Lloyd Mangrum	**1941-47-49-51-53	8	6	2	0
Dave Marr	1965-(81)	6	4	2	0
Billy Maxwell	1963	4	4	0	0
Dick Mayer	1957	2	1	0	1
Bill Mehlhorn	1927	2	1	1	0
Dick Metz	*1939	0	0	0	0
Cary Middlecoff	1953-55-59	6	2	3	1
Johnny Miller	1975-81	6	2	2	2
Larry Mize	1987	4	1	1	2
Gil Morgan	1979-83	6	1	2	3
Bob Murphy	1975	4	2	1	1
Byron Nelson	1937-*39-**41-47-(65)	4	3	1	0
Larry Nelson	1979-81-87	13	9	3	1
Bobby Nichols	1967	5	4	0	1
Jack Nicklaus	1969-71-73-75-77-81-(83)-(87)	28	17	8	3
Andy North	1985	3	0	3	0
Ed Oliver	1947-51-53	5	3	2	0
Mark O'Meara	1985-89-91	8	2	5	1
Arnold Palmer	1961-63-65-67-71-73-(75)	32	22	8	2
Johnny Palmer	1949	2	0	2	0
Sam Parks	1935	1	0	0	1
Jerry Pate	1981	4	2	2	0
Steve Pate	1991	1	0	1	0
Corey Pavin	1991-93	3	1	2	0
Calvin Peete	1983-85	7	4	2	1
Henry Picard	1935-37-*39	4	3	1	0
Dan Pohl	1987	3	1	2	0
Johnny Pott	1963-65-67	7	5	2	0
Dave Ragan	1963	4	2	1	1
Henry Ransom	1951	1	0	1	0
Johnny Revolta	1935-37	3	2	1	0
Chi Chi Rodriguez	1973	2	0	1	1
Bill Rogers	1981	4	1	2	1
Bob Rosburg	1959	2	2	0	0
Mason Rudolph	1971	3	1	1	1
Paul Runyan	1933-35-*39	4	2	2	0
Doug Sanders	1967	5	2	3	0
Gene Sarazen	1927-29-31-33-35-37-**41	12	7	2	3
Densmore Shute	1931-33-37	6	2	2	2
Dan Sikes	1969	3	2	1	0
Scott Simpson	1987	2	1	1	0
Horton Smith	1929-31-33-35-37-*39-**41	4	3	0	1
JC Snead	1971-73-75	11	9	2	0
Sam Snead	1937-*39-**41-47-49-51-53-55-59-(69)	13	10	2	1
Ed Sneed	1977	2	1	0	1
Mike Souchak	1959-61	6	5	1	0
Craig Stadler	1983-85	8	4	2	2
Payne Stewart	1987-89-91-93	16	7	8	1
Ken Still	1969	3	1	2	0
Dave Stockton	1971-77-(91)	5	3	1	1
Curtis Strange	1983-85-87-89	17	6	9	2
Hal Sutton	1985-87	9	3	3	3
Lee Trevino	1969-71-73-75-79-81-(85)	30	17	7	6
Jim Turnesa	1953	1	1	0	0
Joe Turnesa	1927-29	4	1	2	1
Ken Venturi	1965	4	1	3	0
Lanny Wadkins	1977-79-83-85-87-89-91-93	33	20	11	2
Art Wall, Jnr	1957-59-61	6	4	2	0
Al Watrous	1927-29	3	2	1	0
Tom Watson	1977-81-83-89-(93)	15	10	4	1
Tom Weiskopf	1973-75	10	7	2	1
Craig Wood	1931-33-35-**41	4	1	3	0
Lew Worsham	1947	2	2	0	0
Fuzzy Zoeller	1979-83-85	10	1	8	1

US teams were selected in 1939 (*) and 1941 (**), but the matches were not played because of the Second World War.

Alfred Dunhill Cup *(Instituted 1985)*

at St Andrews

Year	Winner	Runner-up	Year	Winner	Runner-up
1985	Australia	USA	1990	Ireland	England
1986	Australia	Japan	1991	Sweden	South Africa
1987	England	Scotland	1992	England	Scotland
1988	Ireland	Australia	1993	USA	England
1989	USA	Japan	1994	Canada	USA

PGA Cup *(Instituted 1973)*

Year	Winner	Venue	Result
1973	USA	Pinehurst, USA	13–3
1974	USA	Pinehurst, USA	11½–4½
1975	USA	Hillside	9½–6½
1976	USA	Moortown	9½–6½
1977	Halved	Miss Hills, USA	8½–8½
1978	GB & I	St Mellion	10½–6½
1979	GB&I	Castletown	12½–4½
1980	USA	Oak Tree	15–6
1981	Halved	Turnberry, Isle	10½–10½
1982	USA	Knoxville, Tennessee	13–7
1983	GB & I	Muirfield	14½–6½
1984	GB & I	Turnberry	12½–8½
Played alternate years from 1984			
1986	USA	Knollwood	16–9
1988	USA	The Belfry	15½–10½
1990	USA	Kiawah Island, S Carolina	19–7
1992	USA	K Club, Ireland	15–11
1994	USA	Palm Beach, Florida	15–11

World Cup of Golf *(Called Canada Cup until 1966)*

Year	Winner	Runners-up	Venue	Score
1953	Argentina (A Cerda and R De Vincenzo)	Canada (S Leonard and B Kerr)	Montreal	287
	(Individual: A Cerda, Argentina, 140)			
1954	Australia (P Thomson and K Nagle)	Argentina (A Cerda and R De Vincenzo)	Laval-Sur-Lac	556
1955	United States (C Harbert and E Furgol)	Australia (P Thomson and K Nagle)	Washington	560
	(Individual: E Furgol, USA, after a play-off with P Thomson and F van Donck, 279)			
1956	United States (B Hogan and S Snead)	South Africa (A Locke and G Player)	Wentworth	567
	(Individual: B Hogan, USA, 277)			
1957	Japan (T Nakamura and K Ono)	United States (S Snead and J Demaret)	Tokyo	557
	(Individual: T Nakamura, Japan, 274)			
1958	Ireland (H Bradshaw and C O'Connor)	Spain (A Miguel and S Miguel)	Mexico City	579
	(Individual: A Miguel, Spain, after a play-off with H Bradshaw, 286)			
1959	Australia (P Thomson and K Nagle)	United States (S Snead and C Middlecoff)	Melbourne	563
	(Individual: S Leonard, Canada, 275, after a tie with P Thomson, Australia)			
1960	United States (S Snead and A Palmer)	England (H Weetman and B Hunt)	Portmarnock	565
	(Individual: F van Donck, Belgium, 279)			
1961	United States (S Snead and J Demaret)	Australia (P Thomson and K Nagle)	Puerto Rico	560
	(Individual: S Snead, USA, 272)			
1962	United States (S Snead and A Palmer)	Argentina (F de Luca and R De Vicenzo)	Buenos Aires	557
	(Individual: R De Vincenzo, Argentina, 276)			
1963	United States (A Palmer and J Nicklaus)	Spain (S Miguel and R Sota)	St Nom-La-Breteche	482
	(Individual: J Nicklaus, USA, 237 [63 holes])			

continued

World Cup of Golf *continued*

Year	Winner	Runners-up	Venue	Score
1964	United States (A Palmer and J Nicklaus)	Argentina (R De Vicenzo and L Ruiz)	Maui, Hawaii	554
	(Individual: J Nicklaus, USA, 276)			
1965	South Africa (G Player and H Henning)	Spain (A Miguel and R Sota)	Madrid	571
	(Individual: G Player, South Africa, 281)			
1966	United States (J Nicklaus and A Palmer)	South Africa (G Player and H Henning)	Tokyo	548
	(Individual: G Knudson, Canada, and H Sugimoto, Japan, each 272; Knudson won play-off)			
1967	United States (J Nicklaus and A Palmer)	New Zealand (R Charles and W Godfrey)	Mexico City	557
	(Individual: A Palmer, USA, 276)			
1968	Canada (A Balding and G Knudson)	United States (J Boros and L Trevino)	Olgiata, Rome	569
	(Individual: A Balding, Canada, 274)			
1969	United States (O Moody and L Trevino)	Japan (T Kono and H Yasuda)	Singapore	552
	(Individual: L Trevino, USA, 275)			
1970	Australia (B Devlin and D Graham)	Argentina (R De Vicenzo and V Fernandez)	Buenos Aires	545
	(Individual: R De Vicenzo, Argentina, 269)			
1971	United States (J Nicklaus and L Trevino)	South Africa (H Henning and G Player)	Palm Beach, Florida	555
	(Individual: J Nicklaus, USA, 271)			
1972	Taiwan (H Min-Nan and LL Huan)	Japan (T Kono and T Murakami)	Melbourne	438
	(Individual: H Min-Nan, Taiwan, 217 [3 rounds only])			
1973	United States (J Nicklaus and J Miller)	South Africa (G Player and H Baiocchi)	Marbella, Spain	558
	(Individual: J Miller, USA, 277)			
1974	South Africa (R Cole and D Hayes)	Japan (I Aoki and M Ozaki)	Caracas	554
	(Individual: R Cole, South Africa, 271)			
1975	United States (J Miller and L Graham)	Taiwan (H Min-Nan and KC Hsiung)	Bangkok	554
	(Individual: J Miller, USA, 275)			
1976	Spain (S Ballesteros and M Pinero)	United States (J Pate and D Stockton)	Palm Springs	574
	(Individual: EP Acosta, Mexico, 282)			
1977	Spain (S Ballesteros and A Garrido)	Philippines (R Lavares and B Arda)	Manilla, Philippines	591
	(Individual: G Player, South Africa, 289)			
1978	United States (J Mahaffey and A North)	Australia (G Norman and W Grady)	Hawaii	564
	(Individual: J Mahaffey, USA, 281)			
1979	United States (J Mahaffey and H Irwin)	Scotland (A Lyle and K Brown)	Glyfada, Greece	575
	(Individual: H Irwin, USA, 285)			
1980	Canada (D Halldorson and J Nelford)	Scotland (A Lyle and S Martin)	Bogota	572
	(Individual: A Lyle, Scotland, 282)			
1981	*Not played*			
1982	Spain (M Pinero and JM Canizares)	United States (B Gilder and B Clampett)	Acapulco	563
	(Individual: M Pinero, Spain, 281)			
1983	United States (R Caldwell and J Cook)	Canada (D Barr and J Anderson)	Pondok Inah, Jakarta	565
	(Individual: D Barr, Canada, 276)			
1984	Spain (JM Canizares and J Rivero)	Scotland (S Torrance and G Brand, Jr)	Olgiata, Rome	414
	(Individual: JM Canizares, Spain, 205. Played over 54 holes due to storm)			
1985	Canada (D Halidorson and D Barr)	England (H Clark and P Way)	La Quinta, Calif.	559
	(Individual: H Clark, England, 272)			
1986	*Not played*			
1987	Wales (won play-off) (I Woosnam and D Llewelyn)	Scotland (S Torrance and A Lyle)	Kapalua, Hawaii	574
	(Individual: I Woosnam, Wales, 274)			
1988	United States (B Crenshaw and M McCumber)	Japan (T Ozaki and M Ozaki)	Royal Melbourne, Australia	560
	(Individual: B Crenshaw, USA, 275)			

World Cup of Golf *continued*

Year	Winner	Runners-up	Venue	Score
1989	Australia (P Fowler and W Grady)	Spain (JM Olazabal and JM Canizares)	Las Brisas, Spain	
	(Individual: P Fowler. Played over 36 holes due to storms.)			
1990	Germany (B Langer andT Giedeon)	England (M James andR Boxall) } tie Ireland (R Rafferty and D Feherty) } tie	Grand Cypress Resort, Orlando, Florida	556
	(Individual: P Stewart, USA, 271)			
1991	Sweden (A Forsbrand and P-U Johansson)	Wales (I Woosnam and P Price)	La Querce, Rome	563
	(Individual: I Woosnam, Wales, 273)			
1992	USA (F Couples and D Love III)	Sweden (A Forsbrand and P-U Johansson)	La Moraleja II, Madrid, Spain	548
	(Individual: B Ogle, Australia, 270 after a tie with I Woosnam, Wales)			
1993	USA (F Couples and D Love III)	Zimbabwe (N Price and M McNulty)	Lake Nona, Orlando, FL	556
	(Individual: B Langer, Germany, 272)			
1994	USA (F Couples and D Love III)	Zimbabwe (M McNulty and T Johnstone)	Dorado Beach, Puerto Rico	
	(Individual: F Couples, USA, 265)			

Men's Amateur Tournaments

Berkhamsted Trophy

Year	Winner	Score	Year	Winner	Score	Year	Winner	Score
1970	R Hunter	145	1978	JC Davies	146	1987	F George	141
1971	A Millar	144	1979	JC Davies	147	1988	J Cowgill	146
1971	A Millar	144	1980	R Knott	143	1989	J Payne	142
1972	C Cieslewicz	148	1981	P Dennett	146	1990	J Barnes	144
1973	SC Mason	141	1982	DG Lane	148	1991	G Homewood	141
1974	P Fisher	144	1983	J Hawksworth	146	1992	P Page	141
1975	P Deeble	147	1984	R Willison	139	1993	S Burnell	143
1976	J Davies	144	1985	F George	144	1994	M Treleaven	140
1977	A Lyle	144	1986	P McEvoy	144			

Berkshire Trophy

Year	Winner	Score	Year	Winner	Score	Year	Winner	Score
1970	MF Bonallack	274	1979	D Williams	274	1989	J Metcalfe	
1971 T	MF Bonallack	277	1980	P Downes	280	1990	J O'Shea	271
	J Davies		1981	D Blakeman	280	1991	J Bickerton	280
1972	DP Davidson	280	1982	S Keppler	278	1992	V Phillips	274
1973	P Hedges	278	1983	S Hamer	288	1993	V Phillips	271
1974	J Downie	280	1984	JL Plaxton	276	1994T	J Knight	274
1975	N Faldo	281	1985	P McEvoy	279		A Marshall	
1976	P Hedges	284	1986	R Muscroft	280			
1977	A Lyle	279	1987	J Robinson	275			
1978	P Hedges	281	1988	R Claydon	276			

Duncan Putter

Year	Winner	Score	Year	Winner	Score
1985	P McEvoy	299	1990	R Willison	311
1986	D Wood	300	1991	R Willison	267
1987	P McEvoy	278	1992	R Dinsdale	213
1988	S Dodd	290	1993	M Thomson	289
1989	RN Roderick	280	1994	G Wolstenholme	226

Frame Trophy *at Worplesdon*

Year	Winner	Score	Year	Winner	Score
1986	DW Frame	220	1991	DB Sheahan	223
1987	JRW Walkinshaw	225	1992	D Frame	223
1988	DW Frame	229	1993	D Frame	216
1989	JRW Walkinshaw	219	1994	D Lane	222
1990	WJ Williams	224			

Golf Illustrated Gold Vase

Year	Winner	Year	Winner	Year	Winner
1948	RD Chapman	1965	C Clark	1979	KJ Miller
1949	RJ White	1966	PM Townsend	1980	G Brand, Jr
1950	AW Whyte	1967 T	RA Durrant	1981	P Garner
1951	JB Carr		MF Bonallack	1982	I Carslaw
1952	JDA Langley	1968	MF Bonallack	1983	S Keppler
1953	JDA Langley	1969 T	MF Bonallack	1984	JV Marks
1954	H Ridgeley		J Hayes	1985	M Davis
1955	Major DA Blair	1970	D Harrison	1986	R Eggo
1956	Major DA Blair	1971	MF Bonallack	1987	D Lane
1957	G Wolstenholme		H Ashby	1988	M Turner
1958	M Lunt	1972 T	DP Davidson	1989	G Wolstenholme
1959	A Bussell		R Hunter	1990	A Rogers
1960	D Sewell	1973	J Davies	1991	R Scott
1961 T	DJ Harrison	1974	P Hedges	1992	P Page
	MF Bonallack	1975	MF Bonallack	1993T	C Challen
1962	BHG Chapman	1976	A Brodie		V Phillips
1963	RH Mummery	1977	J Davies	1994	S Burnell
1964	D Moffat	1978	P Thomas		

Grafton Morrish Trophy *Public Schools Old Boys' Golf Association*

Year	Winner	Year	Winner	Year	Winner
1963	Tonbridge	1974	Millfield	1985	Warwick
1964	Tonbridge	1975	Oundle	1986	Tonbridge
1965	Charterhouse	1976	Charterhouse	1987	Harrow
1966	Charterhouse	1977	Haileybury	1988	Robert Gordon's
1967	Charterhouse	1978	Charterhouse	1989	Tonbridge
1968	Wellington	1979	Harrow	1990	Clifton
1969	Sedbergh	1980	Charterhouse	1991	Repton
1970	Sedbergh	1981	Charterhouse	1992	Charterhouse
1971	Dulwich	1982	Marlborough	1993	Malvern
1972	Sedbergh	1983	Wellington	1994	George Heriot's
1973	Pangbourne	1984	Sedbergh		

Halford-Hewitt Challenge Cup *Public Schools Old Boys' Tournament*

Year	Winner	Year	Winner	Year	Winner
1947	Harrow	1963	Repton	1979	Stowe
1948	Winchester	1964	Fettes	1980	Shrewsbury
1949	Charterhouse	1965	Rugby	1981	Watsons
1950	Rugby	1966	Charterhouse	1982	Charterhouse
1951	Rugby	1967	Eton	1983	Charterhouse
1952	Harrow	1968	Eton	1984	Charterhouse
1953	Harrow	1969	Eton	1985	Harrow
1954	Rugby	1970	Merchiston	1986	Repton
1955	Eton	1971	Charterhouse	1987	Merchiston
1956	Eton	1972	Marlborough	1988	Stowe
1957	Watsons	1973	Rossall	1989	Eton
1958	Harrow	1974	Charterhouse	1990	Tonbridge
1959	Wellington	1975	Harrow	1991	Shrewsbury
1960	Rossall	1976	Merchiston	1992	Tonbridge
1961	Rossall	1977	Watsons	1993	Shrewsbury
1962	Oundle	1978	Harrow	1994	Tonbridge

Hampshire Hog *at North Hants*

Year	Winner	Year	Winner
1985	A Clapp	1990	J Metcalfe
1986	R Eggo	1991	M Welch
1987	A Rogers	1992	S Graham
1988	S Richardson	1993	D Hamilton
1989	P McEvoy	1994	B Ingleby

The Lagonda Trophy

Year	Winner	Year	Winner
1985	J Robinson	1990	L Parsons
1986	D Gilford	1991	J Cook
1987	DG Lane	1992	L Westwood
1988	R Claydon	1993	L James
1989	T Spence	1994	S Webster

Leven Amateur Championship Gold Medal

Year	Winner	Year	Winner
1985	A Turnball	1990	C Everett
1986	P-U Johansson	1991	A Graham Lowson
1987	G Macgregor	1992	D Robertson
1988	CE Everett	1993	L Westwood
1989	AJ Coltart	1994	B Howard

The Lytham Trophy *at Royal Lytham and St Annes*

Year	Winner	Score	Year	Winner	Score	Year	Winner	Score
1965T	MF Bonallack	295	1973 T	MG King	292	1984	J Hawksworth	289
	CA Clark			SG Birtwell		1985	L Macnamara	144
1966	PM Townsend	290	1974	CW Green	291	1986	S McKenna	297
1967	R Foster	296	1975	G Macgregor	299	1987	D Wood	293
1968	R Foster	286	1976	MJ Kelley	292	1988	P Broadhurst	296
1969T	T Craddock	290	1977	P Deeble	296	1989	N Williamson	286
	SG Birtwell		1978	B Marchbank	288	1990	G Evans	291
1970T	JC Farmer	296	1979	P McEvoy	279	1991	G Evans	284
	CW Green		1980	IC Hutcheon	293	1992	S Cage	294
	GC Marks		1981	R Chapman	221	1993	T McLure	292
1971	W Humphreys	292	1982	MF Sludds	306	1994	W Bennett	285
1972	MF Bonallack	281	1983	S McAllister	299			

One-armed Championship

Year	Winner	Year	Winner
1985	A Robinson	1990	D Parsons
1986	M O'Grady	1991	Q Talbot
1987	J Cann	1992	B Crombie
1988	Q Talbot	1993	M Benning
1989	A Robinson	1994	M Benning

Oxford *v* Cambridge

Year	Winner	Venue	Year	Winner	Venue
1946	Cambridge	R Lytham and St Annes	1971	Oxford	Rye
1947	Oxford	Rye	1972	Cambridge	Formby
1948	Oxford	Sandwich, R St George's	1973	Oxford	Saunton
1949	Cambridge	Hoylake	1974	Cambridge	Ganton
1950	Oxford	R Lytham and St Annes	1975	Cambridge	Hoylake
1951	Cambridge	Rye	1976	Cambridge	Woodhall Spa
1952	Cambridge	Rye	1977	Cambridge	Porthcawl
1953	Cambridge	Rye	1978	Oxford	Rye
1954	Cambridge	Rye	1979	Oxford	Harlech
1955	Cambridge	Rye	1980	Oxford	Hoylake
1956	Oxford	Formby	1981	Cambridge	Formby
1957	Oxford	Sandwich, R St George's	1982	Cambridge	Hunstanton
1958	Cambridge	Rye	1983	Cambridge	Sandwich, R St George's
1959	Cambridge	Burnham & Berrow	1984	Cambridge	Sunningdale
1960	Cambridge	R Lytham and St Annes	1985	Oxford	Rye
1961	Oxford	Sandwich, R St George's	1986	Oxford	Ganton
1962	Halved	Hunstanton	1987	Cambridge	Formby
1963	Cambridge	R Birkdale	1988	Cambridge	Royal Porthcawl
1964	Oxford	Rye	1989	Cambridge	Rye
1965	Cambridge	Sandwich, R St George's	1990	Cambridge	Muirfield
1966	Cambridge	Hunstanton	1991	Cambridge	Sandwich, R St George's
1967	Cambridge	Rye	1992	Oxford	R Cinque Ports
1968	Cambridge	Porthcawl	1993	Oxford	Royal Liverpool
1969	Cambridge	Formby	1994	Oxford	Rye
1970	Halved	Sandwich, R St George's			

Oxford and Cambridge Golfing Society's President's Putter

Year	Winner	Year	Winner	Year	Winner
1947	LG Crawley	1963	JG Blackwell	1981	AWJ Holmes
1948	Major AA Duncan	1964	DMA Steel	1982	DMA Steel
1949	PB Lucas	1965	WI Uzielli	1983	ER Dexter
1950	DHR Martin	1966	MF Attenborough	1984	A Edmond
1951	LG Crawley	1969	P Moody	1985	ER Dexter
1952	LG Crawley	1970	DMA Steel	1986	J Caplan
1953	GH Micklem	1971	GT Duncan	1987	CD Meacher
1954	G Huddy	1972	P Moody	1988	G Woollett
1955	G Huddy	1973	AD Swanston	1967	JR Midgley
1956	GT Duncan	1974	R Biggs	1989	M Froggatt
1957	AE Shepperson	1975	CJ Weight	1968	AWJ Holmes
1958	Lt-Col AA Duncan	1976	MJ Reece	1990	G Woollett
1959	ID Wheater	1977	AWJ Holmes	1991	B Ingleby
1960	JME Anderson	1978	MJ Reece	1992	M Cox
1961	ID Wheater	1979	*Cancelled due to snow*	1993	C Weight
1962	MF Attenborough	1980	S Melville	1994	S Seman

HRH Prince of Wales Challenge Cup *at Deal*

Year	Winner	Score	Year	Winner	Score
1985	RJ Tickner	141	1990 T	G Homewood	145
1986	JM Baldwin	149		BS Ingleby	
1987	S Finch	148	1991	S Pardoe	152
1988	MP Palmer	144	1992	L Westwood	160
1989 T	T Lloyd	146	1993	ML Welch	143
	NA Farrell		1994	I Hardy	149

Rosebery Challenge Cup *at Ashridge*

Year	Winner	Year	Winner
1985	P Wharton	1990	C Tingey
1986 T	JE Ambridge	1991	M Thompson
	RY Mitchell – won play-off)	1992	R Harris
1987	HA Wilkerson	1993	M Hooper
1988	N Leconte	1994	P Wilkins
1989	C Slattery		

St David's Gold Cross *at Royal St David's, Harlech*

Year	Winner	Year	Winner
1985	KH Williams	1990	M Macara
1986	RN Roderick	1991	RJ Dinsdale
1987	SR Andrew	1992	B Dredge
1988	MW Calvert	1993	B Dredge
1989	AJ Barnett	1994	C Evans

Grand Challenge Cup

at Royal St George's, Sandwich

Year	Winner	Year	Winner
1985	SJ Wood	1990	P Sullivan
1986	R Claydon	1991	D Fisher
1987	MR Goodin	1992	L Westwood
1988	T Ryan	1993	P Sefton
1989	S Green	1994	M Welch

Selborne Salver *at Blackmoor GC, Hampshire*

Year	Winner	Year	Winner
1985	SM Bottomley	1990	J Metcalfe
1986	TE Clarke	1991	J Payne
1987	AJ Clapp	1992	M Treleaven
1988	N Holman	1993	M Welch
1989	M Stanford	1994	W Bennett

Sunningdale Foursomes

Year	Winners
1970	R Barrell and Miss A Willard beat R Hunter and Miss M Everard, 2 and 1
1971	A Bird and H Flatman beat J Putt and Miss K Phillips, 3 and 2
1972	JC Davies and MG King beat JK Tullis and AJ Howard, 6 and 5
1973	JA Putt and Miss M Everard beat H Clark and SC Mason, 6 and 5
1974	PJ Butler and C Clark beat HK Clark and DN Brunyard, 1 hole
1975	*Cancelled due to snow*
1976	C Clark and M Hughesdon beat BJ Hunt and IM Stungo, 2 and 1
1977	GN Hunt and D Matthew beat D Huish and G Logan, 3 and 2
1978	GA Caygill and Miss J Greenhalgh beat A Stickley and Mrs C Caldwell, 5 and 4
1979	G Will and R Chapman beat NC Coles and D McClelland, 3 and 2
1980	NC Coles and D McClelland beat SC Mason and J O'Leary, 2 and 1
1981	A Lyddon and G Brand beat MG King and MH Dixon, 1 hole
1982	Miss MA McKenna and Miss M Madill beat Miss C Langford and Miss M Walker, 1 hole
1983	J Davies and M Devetta beat M Hughesdon and Mrs L Bayman, 4 and 3
1984	Miss M McKenna and Miss M Madill beat Miss M Walker and Miss C Langford
1985	J O'Leary and S Torrance beat B Gallacher and P Garner at 25th
1986	R Rafferty and R Chapman beat Mrs M Garner and Miss M McKenna, 1 hole
1987	I Mosey and W Humphries beat Miss G Stewart and D Huish, 3 and 2
1988	C Mason and A Chandler beat Miss M McKenna and Mrs J Garner, 5 and 3
1989	A Hare and R Claydon beat Miss V Thomas and Miss J Wade, 4 and 3
1990	Miss D Reid and Miss C Dibnah beat Miss T Craik and P Hughes, 7 and 6
1991	J Robinson and W Henry beat B Critchley and R Hunter 4 and 3
1992	R Boxall and D Cooper beat P Sherman and P Page 3 and 2
1993	A Beal and L James beat L Warwick and D Wood 2 and 1
1994	S Webster and A Wall beat D Howell and G Harris 2 holes

Tennant Cup

This trophy was presented by Sir Charles Tennant to the Glasgow Club in 1880. It is the oldest open amateur stroke play competition in the world. It has been a 72-hole competition since 1986.

Year	Winner	Year	Winner	Year	Winner
1970	CW Green	1979	G Hay	1988	C Dalgleish
1971	Andrew Brodie	1980	Allan Brodie	1989	DG Carrick
1972	Allan Brodie	1981	G MacDonald	1990	C Everett
1973	PJ Smith	1982	LS Mann	1991	C Everett
1974	D McCart	1983	C Dalgleish	1992	D Robertson
1975	CW Green	1984	E Wilson	1993	D Robertson
1976	IC Hutcheon	1985	CJ Brooks	1994	G Rankin
1977	S Martin	1986	PG Irvan		
1978	IA Carslaw	1987	J Rasmussen		

The Tillman Trophy *at Royal St George's, Sandwich*

Year	Winner	Year	Winner
1985	P Baker	1990	M Wiggett
1986	P Baker	1991	A Tillman
1987	R Morris	1992	D Probert
1988	E Els	1993	C Nowicki
1989	J Cook	1994	*Not played*

West of England Open Amateur Championship

at Burnham & Berrow

Year	Winner	Year	Winner
1985	AC Nash	1990	I West
1986	J Bennett	1991	S Amor
1987	D Rosier	1992	K Baker
1988	N Holman	1993	D Haines
1989	N Holman	1994	A Emery

West of England Open Amateur Stroke Play Championship

Year	Winner	Year	Winner
1985	P McEvoy	1990	I West
1986	P Baker	1991	S Amor
1987	G Wolstenholme	1992	M Stanford
1988	M Evans	1993	P Trew
1989	AD Hare	1994	C Nowicki

West of Scotland Open Amateur Championship

Year	Winner	Year	Winner
1985	JA Thomson	1990	ST Knowles
1986	C Brooks	1991	A Coltart
1987	R Jenkins	1992	S Henderson
1988	S Savage	1993	B Howard
1989	AJ Elliott	1994	J Hodgson

Worplesdon Mixed Foursomes

Year	Winners
1980	L Bayman and I Boyd beat L Davies and R Hurst, 1 hole
1981	J Nicholsen and MN Stern beat S Birley and RL Glading, 2 and 1
1982	B New and K Dobson beat S Cohen and J Tarbuck, 2 and 1
1983	B New and K Dobson beat N McCormack and N Briggs at 19th
1984	L Bayman and MC Hughesdon beat N McCormack and N Briggs, 5 and 4
1985	H Kaye and D Longmuir beat J Collingham and GS Melville, 5 and 3
1986	P Johnson and RN Roderick beat C Duffy and L Hawkins, 2 and 1
1987	J Nicholsen and B White beat T Craik and P Hughes, 4 and 3
1988	Mme A Larrezac and JJ Caplan beat S Bennett and BK Turner, 4 and 3
1989	J Kershaw and M Kershaw beat H Kaye and D Longmuir, 2 and 1
1990	S Keogh and A Rogers beat J Rhodes and C Banks, 3 and 1
1991	J Rhodes and C Banks beat S Ledger and J Brant, 1 hole
1992	D Henson and B Turner beat S Lambert and J Tarbuck 4 and 2
1993	A Macdonald and S Skeldon beat Mr and Mrs KM Quinn 3 and 2
1994	Mr and Mrs K Quinn beat C Titcombe and C Rotheroe 3 and 2

Amateur International Tournaments and Matches

United States *v* Great Britain & Ireland

Unofficial

Year		Great Britain		USA		Venue
1921	Foursomes	0	3	4	9	
(May 21)	Singles	3		5		Hoylake

The Walker Cup

Instituted 1922

Year		Great Britain & Ireland		USA		Venue
1922	Foursomes	1	4	3	8	Long Island, NY
(August 29)	Singles	3		5		
1923	Foursomes	3	5½	1	6½	St Andrews
(May 18–19)	Singles	2½		5½		
1924	Foursomes	1	3	3	9	Garden City, NY
(Sept 12–13)	Singles	2		6		
1926	Foursomes	1	5½	3	6½	St Andrews
(June 2–3)	Singles	4½		3½		
1928	Foursomes	0	1	4	11	Chicago
(Aug 30–31)	Singles	1		7		
1930	Foursomes	1	2	3	10	Sandwich
(May 15–16)	Singles	1		7		
1932	Foursomes	0	2½	4	9½	Brookline, Massachusetts
(Sept 1–2)	Singles	2½		5½		
1934	Foursomes	1	2½	3	9½	St Andrews
(May 11–12)	Singles	1½		6½		
1936	Foursomes	1	1½	3	10½	Pine Valley, NJ
(Sept 2–3)	Singles	0½		7½		
1938	Foursomes	2½	7½	1½	4½	St Andrews
(June 3–4)	Singles	5		3		
1947	Foursomes	2	4	2	8	St Andrews
(May 16–17)	Singles	2		6		
1949	Foursomes	1	2	3	10	Winged Foot, NY
(Aug 19–20)	Singles	1		7		
1951	Foursomes	1	4½	3	7½	Royal Birkdale
(May 11–12)	Singles	3½		4½		
1953	Foursomes	1	3	3	9	Kittansett, Massachusetts
(Sept 4–5)	Singles	2		6		
1955	Foursomes	0	2	4	10	St Andrews
(May 20–21)	Singles	2		6		
1957	Foursomes	1½	3½	2½	8½	Minikahda
(Sept 1–2)	Singles	2		6		
1959	Foursomes	0	3	4	9	Muirfield
(May 15–16)	Singles	3		5		
1961	Foursomes	0	1	4	11	Seattle, Washington
(Sept 1–2)	Singles	1		7		

continued

The Walker Cup *continued*

From 1963 Foursomes and Singles matches were played on both days, each match over 18 holes.

Year		Great Britain & Ireland		USA		Venue
1963 (May 24–25)	Foursomes Singles	1 7	8	6 6	12	Turnberry
1965 (Sept 3–4)	Foursomes Singles	4 7	11	3 8	11	Baltimore, Maryland
1967 (May 15–20)	Foursomes Singles	3 4	7	4 9	13	Sandwich
1969 (Aug 22–23)	Foursomes Singles	3 5	8	3 7	10	Milwaukee, Wisconsin
1971 (May 26–27)	Foursomes Singles	5½ 7½	13	2½ 8½	11	St Andrews
1973 (Aug 24–25)	Foursomes Singles	1 9	10	7 7	14	Brookline, Massachusetts
1975 (May 28–29)	Foursomes Singles	3 5½	8½	5 10½	15½	St Andrews
1977 (Aug 26–27)	Foursomes Singles	3 5	8	5 11	16	Shinnecock Hills, NY
1979 (May 30–31)	Foursomes Singles	4 4½	8½	4 11½	15½	Muirfield
1981 (Aug 28–29)	Foursomes Singles	4 5	9	4 11	15	Cypress Point
1983 (May 25–26)	Foursomes Singles	4½ 6	10½	3½ 10	13½	Hoylake

At Pine Valley, New Jersey, on 21st and 22nd August, 1985

First Day – Foursomes

Great Britain and Ireland	Matches	USA	Matches
C Montgomerie and G Macgregor	0	S Verplank and J Sigel (1 hole)	1
J Hawksworth and G McGimpsey (4 and 3)	1	D Waldorf and S Randolph	0
P Baker and P McEvoy (6 and 5)	1	R Sonnier and J Haas	0
C Bloice and S Stephen	½	M Podolak and D Love	½
	2½		1½

Singles

Great Britain and Ireland	Matches	USA	Matches
G McGimpsey	0	S Verplank (2 and 1)	1
P Mayo	0	S Randolph (5 and 4)	1
J Hawksworth	½	R Sonnier	½
C Montgomerie	0	J Sigel (5 and 4)	1
P McEvoy (2 and 1)	1	B Lewis	0
G Macgregor (2 holes)	1	C Burroughs	0
D Gilford	0	D Waldorf (4 and 2)	1
S Stephen (2 and 1)	1	J Haas	0
	3½		4½

First day's aggregate: Great Britain and Ireland, 6; USA, 6.

Second Day – Foursomes

Great Britain and Ireland	Matches	USA	Matches
P Mayo and C Montgomerie	½	S Verplank and J Sigel	½
J Hawksworth and G McGimpsey	0	S Randolph and J Hass (3 and 2)	1
P Baker and P McEvoy	0	B Lewis and C Burroughs (2 and 1)	1
C Bloice and S Stephen	0	M Podolak and D Love (3 and 2)	1
	½		3½

continued

Great Britain & Ireland / **USA**

***Second Day* – Singles**

Great Britain & Ireland	Matches	USA	Matches
G McGimpsey	$^1/_2$	S Randolph	$^1/_2$
C Montgomerie	0	S Verplank (1 hole)	1
J Hawksworth (4 and 3)	1	J Sigel	0
P McEvoy	0	D Love (5 and 3)	1
P Baker (5 and 4)	1	R Sonnier	0
G Macgregor (3 and 2)	1	C Burroughs	0
C Bloice	0	B Lewis (4 and 3)	1
S Stephen (2 and 1)	1	D Waldorf	0
	$4^1/_2$		$3^1/_2$

Second day's aggregate: Great Britain and Ireland, 5; USA, 7.

Grand Match aggregate: Great Britain and Ireland, 11; USA, 13.

At Sunningdale, Berkshire, 27th and 28th May, 1987

Great Britain and Ireland / **USA**

***First Day* – Foursomes**

Great Britain and Ireland	Matches	USA	Matches
C Montgomerie and G Shaw	0	B Alexander and B Mayfair (5 and 4)	1
D Curry and P Mayo	0	C Kite and L Mattice (2 and 1)	1
G Macgregor and J Robinson	0	B Lewis and B Loeffler (2 and 1)	1
J McHenry and P Girvan	0	J Sigel and B. Andrade (3 and 2)	1
	0		4

Singles

Great Britain and Ireland	Matches	USA	Matches
D Curry (2 holes)	1	B Alexander	0
J Robinson	0	B Andrade (7 and 5)	1
C Montgomerie (3 and 2)	1	J Sorenson	0
R Eggo	0	J Sigel (3 and 2)	1
J McHenry	0	B Montgomery (1 hole)	1
P Girvan	0	B Lewis (3 and 2)	1
D Carrick	0	B Mayfair (2 holes)	1
G Shaw (1 hole)	1	C Kite	0
	3		5

First day's aggregate: Great Britain and Ireland, 3; USA, 9.

***Second Day* – Foursomes**

Great Britain and Ireland	Matches	USA	Matches
D Curry and D Carrick	0	B Lewis and B Loeffler (4 and 3)	1
C Montgomerie and G Shaw	0	C Kite and L Mattice (5 and 3)	1
P Mayo and G Macgregor	0	J Sorenson and B Montgomery (4 and 3)	1
J McHenry and J Robinson (4 and 2)	1	J Sigel and B Andrade	0
	1		3

Singles

Great Britain and Ireland	Matches	USA	Matches
D Curry	0	B Alexander (5 and 4)	1
C Montgomerie (4 and 2)	1	B Andrade	0
J McHenry (3 and 2)	1	B Loeffler	0
G Shaw (half)	$^1/_2$	J Sorenson (half)	$^1/_2$
J Robinson (1 hole)	1	L Mattice	0
D Carrick	0	B Lewis (3 and 2)	1
R Eggo	0	B Mayfair (1 hole)	1
P Girvan	0	J Sigel (6 and 5)	1
	$3^1/_2$		$4^1/_2$

Second day's aggregate: Great Britain and Ireland, $4^1/_2$; USA, $7^1/_2$.

Grand Match aggregate: Great Britain and Ireland, $7^1/_2$; USA, $16^1/_2$.

The Walker Cup *continued*

At Peachtree, Atlanta, 16th and 17th August, 1989

Great Britain and Ireland — **USA**

***First Day* – Foursomes**

Great Britain and Ireland	Matches	USA	Matches
R Claydon and D Prosser	0	R Gamez and D Martin (3 and 2)	1
S Dodd and G McGimpsey	$^1/_2$	D Yates and P Mickelson	$^1/_2$
P McEvoy and E O'Connell (6 and 5)	1	G Lesher and J Sigel	0
J Milligan and A Hare (2 and 1)	1	D Eger and K Johnson	0
	$2^1/_2$		$1^1/_2$

Singles

Great Britain and Ireland	Matches	USA	Matches
J Milligan	0	R Gamez (7 and 6)	1
R Claydon (5 and 4)	1	D Martin	0
S Dodd	$^1/_2$	E Meeks	$^1/_2$
E O'Connell (5 and 4)	1	R Howe	0
P McEvoy (2 and 1)	1	D Yates	0
G McGimpsey	0	P Mickelson (4 and 2)	1
C Cassells (1 hole)	1	G Lesher	0
RN Roderick	$^1/_2$	J Sigel	$^1/_2$
	5		3

First day's aggregate: Great Britain and Ireland, $7^1/_2$; USA, $4^1/_2$.

***Second Day* – Foursomes**

Great Britain and Ireland	Matches	USA	Matches
P McEvoy and E O'Connell	$^1/_2$	R Gamez and D Martin	$^1/_2$
R Claydon and C Cassells (3 and 2)	1	J Sigel and G Lesher	0
J Milligan and A Hare (2 and 1)	1	D Eger and K Johnson	0
G McGimpsey and S Dodd (2 and 1)	1	P Mickelson and D Yates	0
	$3^1/_2$		$3^1/_2$

Singles

Great Britain and Ireland	Matches	USA	Matches
S Dodd	0	R Gamez (1 hole)	1
A Hare	$^1/_2$	D Martin	$^1/_2$
R Claydon	0	G Lesher (3 and 2)	1
P McEvoy	0	D Yates (4 and 3)	1
E O'Connell	$^1/_2$	P Mickelson	$^1/_2$
RN Roderick	0	D Eger (4 and 2)	1
C Cassells	0	GK Johnson (4 and 2)	1
J Milligan	$^1/_2$	J Sigel	$^1/_2$
	$1^1/_2$		$6^1/_2$

Second day's aggregate: Great Britain and Ireland, 5; USA, 7.

Grand Match aggregate: Great Britain and Ireland, $12^1/_2$; USA, $11^1/_2$.

At Portmarnock, Dublin, 5th and 6th September, 1991

Great Britain and Ireland — **USA**

***First Day* – Foursomes**

Great Britain and Ireland	Matches	USA	Matches
J Milligan and G Hay	0	P Mickelson and B May (5 and 3)	1
J Payne and G Evans	0	D Duval and M Sposa (1 hole)	1
G McGimpsey and R Willison	0	M Voges and D Eger (1hole)	1
P McGinley and P Harrington	0	J Sigel and A Doyle (2 and 1)	1
	0		4

Singles

Great Britain and Ireland	Matches	USA	Matches
A Coltart	0	P Mickelson (4 and 3)	1
J Payne (2 and 1)	1	F Langham	0
G Evans (2 and 1)	1	D Duval	0
R Willison	0	B May (2 and 1)	1
G McGimpsey (1 hole)	1	M Sposa	0
P McGinley	0	A Doyle (6 and 4)	1
G Hay (1 hole)	1	T Scherrer	0
L White	0	J Sigel (4 and 3)	1
	4		4

First day's aggregate: Great Britain and Ireland 4; USA, 8.

continued

***Second Day* – Foursomes**

	Matches		Matches
J Milligan and G McGimpsey (2 and 1)	1	M Voges and D Eger	0
J Payne and R Willison	0	D Duval and M Sposa (1 hole)	1
G Evans and A Coltart (4 and 3)	1	F Langham and T Scherrer	0
L White and P McGinley (1 hole)	1	P Mickelson and B May	0
	3		1

Singles

J Milligan	0	P Mickelson (1 hole)	1
J Payne (3 and 1)	1	A Doyle	0
G Evans	0	F Langham (4 and 2)	1
A Coltart (1 hole)	1	J Sigel	0
R Willison (3 and 2)	1	T Scherrer	0
P Harrington	0	D Eger (3 and 2)	1
G McGimpsey	0	B May (4 and 3)	1
G Hay	0	M Voges (3 and 1)	1
	3		5

Second day's aggregate: Great Britain and Ireland 6; USA, 6.

Grand Match aggregate: Great Britain and Ireland 10; USA 14.

At Interlachen, Edina, Minnesota, on 18th and 19th August, 1993

Great Britain and Ireland — **USA**

***First Day* – Singles**

	Matches		Matches
I Pyman	0	A Doyle (1 hole)	1
M Stanford (3 and 2)	1	D Berganio	0
D Robertson (3 and 2)	1	J Sigel	0
S Cage	1/2	K Mitchum	1/2
P Harrington	0	T Herron (1 hole)	1
P Page	0	D Yates (2 and 1)	1
R Russell	0	T Demsey (2 and 1)	1
R Burns	0	J Leonard (4 and 3)	1
V Phillips (2 and 1)	1	B Gay	0
B Dredge	0	J Harris (4 and 3)	1
	3 1/2		6 1/2

First day's aggregate: Great Britain and Ireland, 3 1/2; USA, 6 1/2.

***Second Day* – Foursomes**

I Pyman and S Cage	0	A Doyle and J Leonard (4 and 3)	1
M Stanford and P Harrington	0	D Berganio and T Demsey (3 and 2)	1
B Dredge and V Phillips	0	J Sigel and K Mitchum (3 and 2)	1
R Russsell and D Robertson	0	J Harris and T Herron (1 hole)	1
	0		4

Singles

D Robertson	0	A Doyle (4 and 3)	1
I Pyman	0	J Harris (3 and 2)	1
S Cage	0	D Yates (2 and 1)	1
P Harrington	1/2	B Gay	1/2
P Page	0	J Sigel (5 and 4)	1
V Phillips	0	T Herron (3 and 2)	1
R Russell	0	K Mitchum (4 and 2)	1
R Burns (1 hole)	1	D Berganio	0
B Dredge	0	T Demsey (3 and 2)	1
M Stanford	0	J Leonard (5 and 4)	1
	1 1/2		8 1/2

Second day's aggregate: Great Britain and Ireland, 1 1/2; USA, 12 1/2.

Grand Match aggregate: Great Britain and Ireland, 5; USA, 19.

INDIVIDUAL RECORDS

Great Britain and Ireland

Notes: Bold type indicates captain; in brackets, did not play.
*Players who have also played in the Ryder Cup.

Name		Year	Played	Won	Lost	Halved
MF Attenborough	Eng	1967	2	0	2	0
CC Aylmer	Eng	1922	2	1	1	0
*P Baker	Eng	1985	3	2	1	0
JB Beck	Eng	1928-(**38**)-(**47**)	1	0	1	0
PJ Benka	Eng	1969	4	2	1	1
HG Bentley	Eng	1934-36-38	4	0	2	2
DA Blair	Scot	1955-61	4	1	3	0
C Bloice	Scot	1985	3	0	2	1
MF Bonallack	Eng	1957-59-61-63-65-67-**69-71-73**	25	8	14	3
*G Brand	Scot	1979	3	0	3	0
OC Bristowe	Eng	(1923)-24	1	0	1	0
A Brodie	Scot	1977-79	8	5	2	1
A Brooks	Scot	1969	3	2	0	1
Hon WGE Brownlow	Eng	1926	2	0	2	0
J Bruen	Ire	1938-49-51	5	0	4	1
JA Buckley	Wales	1979	1	0	1	0
J Burke	Ire	1932	2	0	1	1
R Burns	Ire	1993	2	1	1	0
AF Bussell	Scot	1957	2	1	1	0
S Cage	Eng	1993	3	0	2	1
I Caldwell	Eng	1951-55	4	1	2	1
W Campbell	Scot	1930	2	0	2	0
JB Carr	Ire	1947-49-51-53-55-57-59-61-63-**(65)-67**	20	5	14	1
RJ Carr	Ire	1971	4	3	0	1
DG Carrick	Scot	1983-87	5	0	5	0
IA Carslaw	Scot	1979	3	1	1	1
C Cassells	Eng	1989	3	2	1	0
JR Cater	Scot	1955	1	0	1	0
J Caven	Scot	1922	2	0	2	0
BHG Chapman	Eng	1961	1	0	1	0
R Chapman	Eng	1981	4	3	1	0
MJ Christmas	Eng	1961-63	3	1	2	0
*CA Clark	Eng	1965	4	2	0	2
GJ Clark	Eng	1965	1	0	1	0
*HK Clark	Eng	1973	3	1	1	1
R Claydon	Eng	1989	4	2	2	0
A Coltart	Scot	1991	3	2	1	0
GB Cosh	Scot	1965	4	3	1	0
T Craddock	Ire	1967-69	6	2	3	1
LG Crawley	Eng	1932-34-38-47	6	3	3	0
B Critchley	Eng	1969	4	1	1	2
D Curry	Eng	1987	4	1	3	0
CR Dalgleish	Scot	1981	3	1	2	0
B Darwin	Eng	1922	2	1	1	0
JC Davies	Eng	1973-75-77-79	13	3	8	2
P Deeble	Eng	1977-81	5	1	4	0
FWG Deighton	Scot	(1951)-57	2	0	2	0
SC Dodd	Wales	1989	4	1	1	2
B Dredge	Wales	1993	3	0	3	0
*NV Drew	Ire	1953	1	0	1	0
AA Duncan	Wales	**(1953)**	0	0	0	0
JM Dykes	Scot	1936	2	0	1	1
R Eggo	Eng	1987	2	0	2	0
D Evans	Wales	1981	3	1	1	1
G Evans	Eng	1991	4	2	2	0
RC Ewing	Ire	1936-38-47-49-51-55	10	1	7	2
GRD Eyles	Eng	1975	4	2	2	0
EW Fiddian	Eng	1932-34	4	0	4	0
J de Forest	Eng	1932	1	0	1	0
R Foster	Eng	1965-67-69-71-73-(**79**)-(**81**)	17	2	13	2
DW Frame	Eng	1961	1	0	1	0
*D Gilford	Eng	1985	1	0	1	0
P Girvan	Scot	1987	3	0	3	0
G Godwin	Eng	1979-81	7	2	4	1
CW Green	Scot	1963-69-71-73-75-(**83**)-(**85**)	17	4	10	3
RH Hardman	Eng	1928	1	0	1	0

Name		Year	Played	Won	Lost	Halved
A Hare	Eng	1989	3	2	2	0
P Harrington	Ire	1991-93	5	0	4	1
R Harris	Scot	**(1922)-23-26**	4	1	3	0
RW Hartley	Eng	1930-32	4	0	4	0
WL Hartley	Eng	1932	2	0	2	0
J Hawksworth	Eng	1985	4	2	1	1
G Hay	Scot	1991	3	1	2	0
P Hedges	Eng	1973-75	5	0	2	3
CO Hezlet	Ire	1924-26-28	6	0	5	1
GA Hill	Eng	1936-(**55**)	2	0	1	1
Sir EWE Holderness	Eng	1923-26-30	6	2	4	0
TWB Homer	Eng	1973	3	0	3	0
CVL Hooman	Eng	1922-23	3	†1	2	†0
WL Hope	Scot	1923-24-28	5	1	4	0
G Huddy	Eng	1961	1	0	1	0
W Humphreys	Eng	1971	3	2	1	0
IC Hutcheon	Scot	1975-77-79-81	15	5	8	2
RR Jack	Scot	1957-59	4	2	2	0
*M James	Eng	1975	4	3	1	0
A Jamieson, Jr	Scot	1926	2	1	1	0
MJ Kelley	Eng	1977-79	7	3	3	1
SD Keppler	Eng	1983	4	0	3	1
*MG King	Eng	1969-73	7	1	5	1
AT Kyle	Scot	1938-47-51	5	2	3	0
DH Kyle	Scot	1924	1	0	1	0
JA Lang	Scot	(1930)	0	0	0	0
JDA Langley	Eng	1936-51-53	6	0	5	1
CD Lawrie	Scot	(**1961**)-(**63**)	0	0	0	0
ME Lewis	Eng	1983	1	0	1	0
PB Lucas	Eng	(1936)-47-(**49**)	2	1	1	0
MSR Lunt	Eng	1959-61-63-65	11	2	8	1
*AWB Lyle	Scot	1977	3	0	3	0
AR McCallum	Scot	1928	1	0	1	0
SM McCready	Ire	1949-51	3	0	3	0
JS Macdonald	Scot	1971	3	1	1	1
P McEvoy	Eng	1977-79-81-85-89	18	5	11	2
G McGimpsey	Ire	1985-89-91	11	4	5	2
P McGinley	Ire	1991	3	1	2	0
G Macgregor	Scot	1971-75-83-85-87	14	5	8	1
RC MacGregor	Scot	1953	2	0	2	0
J McHenry	Ire	1987	4	2	2	0
P McKellar	Scot	1977	1	0	1	0
WW Mackenzie	Scot	1922-23	3	1	2	0
SL McKinlay	Scot	1934	2	0	2	0
J McLean	Scot	1934-36	4	1	3	0
EA McRuvie	Scot	1932-34	4	1	2	1
JFD Madeley	Ire	1963	2	0	1	1
LS Mann	Scot	1983	4	2	1	1
B Marchbank	Scot	1979	4	2	2	0
GC Marks	Eng	1969-71-(**87**)-(**89**)	6	2	4	0
DM Marsh	Eng	(1959)-71-(**73**)-(**75**)	3	2	1	0
GNC Martin	Ire	1928	1	0	1	0
S Martin	Scot	1977	4	2	2	0
P Mayo	Wales	1985-87	4	0	3	1
GH Micklem	Eng	1947-49-53-55-(**57**)-(**59**)	6	1	5	0
DJ Millensted	Eng	1967	2	1	1	0
JW Milligan	Scot	1989-91	7	3	3	1
EB Millward	Eng	(1949)-55	2	0	2	0
WTG Milne	Scot	1973	4	2	2	0
*CS Montgomerie	Scot	1985-87	8	2	5	1
JL Morgan	Wales	1951-53-55	6	2	4	0
P Mulcare	Ire	1975	3	2	1	0
GH Murray	Scot	1977	2	1	1	0
SWT Murray	Scot	1963	4	2	2	0
WA Murray	Scot	1923-24-(26)	4	1	3	0
E O'Connell	Ire	1989	4	2	0	2
A Oldcorn	Eng	1983	4	4	0	0
*PA Oosterhuis	Eng	1967	4	1	2	1
R Oppenheimer	Eng	(**1951**)	0	0	0	0
P Page	Eng	1993	2	0	2	0
P Parkin	Wales	1983	3	2	1	0
J Payne	Eng	1991	4	2	2	0

† CVL Hooman and J Sweetser in 1922 were all square after 36 holes; instructions to the contrary not being readily available, they played on and Hooman won at the 37th. On all other occasions halved matches have counted as such.

Name		Year	Played	Won	Lost	Halved
JJF Pennink	Eng	1938	2	1	1	0
TP Perkins	Eng	1928	2	0	2	0
AH Perowne	Eng	1949-53-59	4	0	4	0
GB Peters	Scot	1936-38	4	2	1	1
V Phillips	Eng	1993	3	1	2	0
AD Pierse	Ire	1983	3	0	2	1
AK Pirie	Scot	1967	3	0	2	1
MA Poxon	Eng	1975	2	0	2	0
D Prosser	Eng	1989	1	0	1	2
I Pyman	Eng	1993	3	0	3	0
*R Rafferty	Ire	1981	4	2	2	0
D Robertson	Scot	1993	3	1	2	0
J Robinson	Eng	1987	4	2	2	0
RN Roderick	Wales	1989	2	0	1	1
R Russell	Scot	1993	3	0	3	0
AC Saddler	Scot	1963-65-67-(77)	10	3	5	2
Hon M Scott	Eng	1924-34	4	2	2	0
R Scott, Jr	Scot	1924	1	1	0	0
PF Scrutton	Eng	1955-57	3	0	3	0
DN Sewell	Eng	1957-59	4	1	3	0
RDBM Shade	Scot	1961-63-65-67	14	6	6	2
G Shaw	Scot	1987	4	1	2	1
DB Sheahan	Ire	1963	4	2	2	0
AE Shepperson	Eng	1957-59	3	1	1	1
AF Simpson	Scot	(1926)	0	0	0	0
JN Smith	Scot	1930	2	0	2	0
WD Smith	Scot	1959	1	0	1	0
M Stanford	Eng	1993	3	1	2	0
AR Stephen	Scot	1985	4	2	1	1
EF Storey	Eng	1924-26-28	6	1	5	0
JA Stout	Eng	1930-32	4	0	3	1
C Stowe	Eng	1938-47	4	2	2	0
HB Stuart	Scot	1971-73-75	10	4	6	0
A Thirlwell	Eng	1957	1	0	1	0
KG Thom	Eng	1949	2	0	2	0
MS Thompson	Eng	1983	3	1	2	0
H Thomson	Scot	1936-38	4	2	2	0
CJH Tolley	Eng	1922-23-24-26-30-34	12	4	8	0
TA Torrance	Scot	1924-28-30-32-34	9	3	5	1
WB Torrance	Scot	1922	2	0	2	0
*PM Townsend	Eng	1965	4	3	1	0
LP Tupling	Eng	1969	2	1	1	0
W Tweddell	Eng	1928-(36)	2	0	2	0
J Walker	Scot	1961	2	0	2	0
P Walton	Ire	1981-83	8	6	2	0
*P Way	Eng	1981	4	2	2	0
RH Wethered	Eng	1922-23-26-30-34	9	5	3	1
L White	Eng	1991	2	1	1	0
RJ White	Eng	1947-49-51-53-55	10	6	3	1
R Willison	Eng	1991	4	1	3	0
J Wilson	Scot	1923	2	2	0	0
JC Wilson	Scot	1947-53	4	0	4	0
GB Wolstenholme	Eng	1957-59	4	1	2	1

United States of America

Name	Year	Played	Won	Lost	Halved
*TD Aaron	1959	2	1	1	0
B Alexander	1987	3	2	1	0
DC Allen	1965-67	6	0	4	2
B Andrade	1987	4	2	2	0
ES Andrews	1961	1	1	0	0
D Ballenger	1973	1	1	0	0
R Baxter, jr	1957	2	2	0	0
DR Beman	1959-61-63-65	11	7	2	2
D Berganio	1993	3	1	2	0
RE Billows	1938-49	4	2	2	0
SE Bishop	1947-49	3	2	1	0
AS Blum	1957	1	0	1	0
J Bohmann	1969	3	1	2	0

Name	Year	Played	Won	Lost	Halved
M Brannan	1977	3	1	2	0
GF Burns	1975	3	2	1	0
C Burroughs	1985	3	1	2	0
AE Campbell	1936	2	2	0	0
JE Campbell	1957	1	0	1	0
WC Campbell	1951-53-(55)-57-65-67-71-75	18	11	4	3
RJ Cerrudo	1967	4	1	1	2
RD Chapman	1947-51-53	5	3	2	0
D Cherry	1953-55-61	5	5	0	0
D Clarke	1979	3	2	0	1
RE Cochran	1961	1	1	0	0
CR Coe	1949-51-53-(57)-59-61-63	13	7	4	2
R Commans	1981	3	1	1	1
JW Conrad	1955	2	1	1	0
N Crosby	1983	2	1	1	0
BH Cudd	1955	2	2	0	0
RD Davies	1963	2	0	2	0
JW Dawson	1949	2	2	0	0
T Demsey	1993	3	3	0	0
RB Dickson	1967	3	3	0	0
A Doyle	1991-93	6	5	1	0
GT Dunlap Jr	1932-34-36	5	3	1	1
D Duval	1991	3	2	1	0
D Edwards	1973	4	4	0	0
HC Egan	1934	1	1	0	0
D Eger	1991	3	2	1	0
HC Eger	1989	3	1	2	0
D Eichelberger	1965	3	1	2	0
J Ellis	1973	3	2	1	0
W Emery	1936	2	1	0	1
C Evans Jr	1922-24-28	5	3	2	0
J Farquhar	1971	3	1	2	0
B Faxon	1983	4	3	1	0
R Fehr	1983	4	2	1	1
JW Fischer	1934-36-38-(65)	4	3	0	1
D Fischesser	1979	3	1	2	0
MA Fleckman	1967	2	0	2	0
B Fleisher	1969	4	0	2	2
J Fought	1977	4	4	0	0
WC Fownes Jr	1922-24	3	1	2	0
F Fuhrer	1981	3	2	1	0
JR Gabrielsen	1977-(81)-(91)	3	1	2	0
R Gamez	1989	4	3	0	1
RA Gardner	1922-23-24-26	8	6	2	0
RW Gardner	1961-63	5	4	0	1
B Gay	1993	2	0	1	1
M Giles	1969-71-73-75	15	8	2	5
HL Givan	1936	1	0	0	1
JG Goodman	1934-36-38	6	4	2	0
M Gove	1979	3	2	1	0
J Grace	1975	3	2	1	0
JA Grant	1967	2	2	0	0
AD Gray Jr	1963-65-67	12	5	6	1
JP Guilford	1922-24-26	6	4	2	0
W Gunn	1926-28	4	4	0	0
*F Haas Jr	1938	2	0	2	0
*J Haas	1975	3	3	0	0
J Haas	1985	3	1	2	0
G Hallberg	1977	3	1	2	0
GS Hamer Jr	(1947)	0	0	0	0
J Harris	1993	3	3	0	0
LE Harris Jr	1963	4	3	1	0
V Heafner	1977	3	3	0	0
SD Herron	1923	2	0	2	0
T Herron	1993	3	3	0	0
S Hoch	1979	4	4	0	0
W Hoffer	1983	2	1	1	0
J Holtgrieve	1979-81-83	10	6	4	0
JM Hopkins	1965	3	0	2	1
R Howe	1989	1	0	1	0
W Howell	1932	1	1	0	0
W Hyndman	1957-59-61-69-71	9	6	1	2

Name	Year	Played	Won	Lost	Halved
J Inman	1969	2	2	0	0
JG Jackson	1953-55	3	3	0	0
K Johnson	1989	3	1	2	0
HR Johnston	1923-24-28-30	6	5	1	0
RT Jones Jr	1922-24-26-**28-30**	10	9	1	0
AF Kammer	1947	2	1	1	0
M Killian	1973	3	1	2	0
C Kite	1987	3	2	1	0
*TO Kite	1971	4	2	1	1
RE Knepper	(1922)	0	0	0	0
RW Knowles	1951	1	1	0	0
G Koch	1973-75	7	4	1	2
CR Kocsis	1938-49-57	5	2	2	1
F Langham	1991	3	1	2	0
J Leonard	1993	3	3	0	0
G Lesher	1989	4	1	3	0
B Lewis Jr	1981-83-85-87	14	10	4	0
JW Lewis	1967	4	3	1	0
WL Little Jr	1934	2	2	0	0
*GA Littler	1953	2	2	0	0
B Loeffler	1987	3	2	1	0
*D Love	1985	3	2	0	1
MJ McCarthy Jr	(1928)-32	1	1	0	0
BN McCormick	1949	1	1	0	0
JB McHale	1949-51	3	2	0	1
RR Mackenzie	1926-28-30	6	5	1	0
MR Marston	1922-23-24-34	8	5	3	0
D Martin	1989	4	1	1	2
L Mattiace	1987	3	2	1	0
R May	1991	4	3	1	0
B Mayfair	1987	3	3	0	0
E Meeks	1989	1	0	0	1
SN Melnyk	1969-71	7	3	3	1
P Mickelson	1989-91	8	4	2	2
AL Miller	1969-71	8	4	3	1
L Miller	1977	4	4	0	0
K Mitchum	1993	3	2	0	1
DK Moe	1930-32	3	3	0	0
B Montgomery	1987	2	2	0	0
G Moody	1979	3	1	2	0
GT Moreland	1932-34	4	4	0	0
D Morey	1955-65	4	1	3	0
J Mudd	1981	3	3	0	0
*RJ Murphy	1967	4	1	2	1
JF Neville	1923	1	0	1	0
*JW Nicklaus	1959-61	4	4	0	0
LW Oehmig	(1977)	0	0	0	0
FD Ouimet	1922-23-24-26-30-**32-34**-(**36**)-(**38**)-(**47**)-(**49**)	16	9	5	2
HD Paddock Jr	1951	1	0	0	1
*J Pate	1975	4	0	4	0
WJ Patton	1955-57-59-63-65-(**69**)	14	11	3	0
*C Pavin	1981	3	2	0	1
M Peck	1979	3	1	1	1
M Pfeil	1973	4	2	1	1
M Podolak	1985	2	1	0	1
SL Quick	1947	2	1	1	0
S Randolph	1985	4	2	1	1
J Rassett	1981	3	3	0	0
F Ridley	1977-(**87**)-(**89**)	3	2	1	0
RH Riegel	1947-49	4	4	0	0
H Robbins Jr	1957	2	0	1	1
*W Rogers	1973	2	1	1	0
GV Rotan	1923	2	1	1	0
*EM Rudolph	1957	2	1	0	1
B Sander	1977	3	0	3	0
T Scherrer	1991	3	0	3	0
CH Seaver	1932	2	2	0	0
RL Siderowf	1969-73-75-77-(**79**)	14	4	8	2
J Sigel	1977-79-81-**83**-85-87-89-91-93	33	18	10	5
RH Sikes	1963	3	1	2	0
JB Simons	1971	2	0	2	0
*S Simpson	1977	3	3	0	0

Name	Year	Played	Won	Lost	Halved
CB Smith	1961-63	2	0	1	1
R Smith	1936-38	4	2	2	0
R Sonnier	1985	3	0	2	1
J Sorensen	1987	3	1	1	1
M Sposa	1991	3	2	1	0
*C Stadler	1975	3	3	0	0
FR Stranahan	1947-49-51	6	3	2	1
*C Strange	1975	4	3	0	1
*H Sutton	1979-81	7	2	4	1
JW Sweetser	1922-23-24-26-28-32-(**67**)-(73)	12	7	†4	†1
FM Taylor	1957-59-61	4	4	0	0
D Tentis	1983	2	0	1	1
RS Tufts	(**1963**)	0	0	0	0
WP Turnesa	1947-49-**51**	6	3	3	0
B Tuten	1983	2	1	1	0
EM Tutweiler	1965-67	6	5	1	0
ER Updegraff	1963-65-69-(**75**)	7	3	3	1
S Urzetta	1951-53	4	4	0	0
K Venturi	1953	2	2	0	0
S Verplank	1985	4	3	0	1
M Voges	1991	3	2	1	0
GJ Voigt	1930-32-36	5	2	2	1
G Von Elm	1926-28-30	6	4	1	1
D von Tacky	1981	3	1	2	0
*JL Wadkins	1969-71	7	3	4	0
D Waldorf	1985	3	1	2	0
EH Ward	1953-55-59	6	6	0	0
MH Ward	1938-47	4	2	2	0
M West	1973-79	6	2	3	1
J Westland	1932-34-53-(**61**)	5	3	0	2
HW Wettlaufer	1959	2	2	0	0
E White	1936	2	2	0	0
OF Willing	1923-24-30	4	4	0	0
JM Winters Jr	(**1971**)	0	0	0	0
W Wood	1983	4	1	2	1
FJ Wright	1923	1	1	0	0
CR Yates	1936-38-(**53**)	4	3	0	1
D Yates	1989-93	6	3	2	1
RL Yost	1955	2	2	0	0

Eisenhower Trophy (World Amateur Team Championship)

Year	Winners	Runners-up	Venue	Score
1958	Australia	United States	St Andrews	918
(After a tie, Australia won the play-off by two strokes: Australia 222, United States 224)				
1960	United States	Australia	Ardmore, USA	834
1962	United States	Canada	Kawana, Japan	854
1964	Great Britain & Ireland	Canada	Olgiata, Rome	895
1966	Australia	United States	Mexico City	877
1968	United States	Great Britain & Ireland	Melbourne	868
1970	United States	New Zealand	Madrid	857
1972	United States	Australia	Buenos Aires	865
1974	United States	Japan	Dominican Rep.	888
1976	Great Britain & Ireland	Japan	Penina, Portugal	892
1978	United States	Canada	Fiji	873
1980	United States	South Africa	Pinehurst, USA	848
1982	United States	Sweden	Lausanne	859
1984	Japan	United States	Hong Kong	870
1986	Canada	United States	Caracas, Venezuela	860
1988	Great Britain & Ireland	United States	Ullva, Sweden	882
1990	Sweden	New Zealand	Christchurch, New Zealand	879
1992	New Zealand	United States	Capilano, Canada	823
1994	United States	Great Britain & Ireland	Paris, France	838

† CVL Hooman and J Sweetser in 1922 were all square after 36 holes; instructions to the contrary not being readily available, they played on and Hooman won at the 37th. On all other occasions halved matches have counted as such.

European Amateur Team Championship

Year	Winner	Second	Venue
1959	Sweden		
1961	Sweden	England	Brussels, Belgium
1963	England	Sweden	Falsterbo, Sweden
1965	Ireland	Scotland	St George's, England
1967	Ireland	France	Turin, Italy
1969	England	W Germany	Hamburg, W Germany
1971	England	Scotland	Lausanne, Switzerland
1973	England	Scotland	Penina, Portugal
1975	Scotland	Italy	Killarney, Ireland
1977	Scotland	Sweden	The Haagsche, Holland
1979	England	Wales	Esbjerg, Denmark
1981	England	Scotland	St Andrews, Scotland
1983	Ireland	Spain	Chantilly, France
1985	Scotland	Sweden	Halmstad, Sweden
1987	Ireland	England	Murhof, Austria
1989	England	Scotland	Royal Porthcawl
1991	England	Italy	Puerta de Hierro
1993	Wales	England	Marianske Lasne, Czech Republic

Home Internationals

Year	Winner	Year	Winner	Year	Winner
1932	Scotland	1956	Scotland	1971	Scotland
1933	Scotland	1957	England	1972 T	Scotland and England
1934	Scotland	1958	England	1973	England
1935 T	England, Scotland and Ireland	1959 T	England, Ireland and Scotland	1974	England
				1975	Scotland
1936	Scotland	1960	England	1976	Scotland
1937	Scotland	1961	Scotland	1977	England
1938	England	1962T	England, Ireland and Scotland	1978	England
1939–46	No Internationals held			1979	No Internationals held
1947	England	1963 T	England, Ireland and Scotland	1980	England
1948	England			1981	Scotland
1949	England	1964	England	1982	Scotland
1950	Ireland	1965	England	1983	Ireland
1951 T	Ireland and Scotland	1966	England	1984	England
1952	Scotland	1967	Scotland	1985	England
1953	Scotland	1968	England	1986	Scotland
1954	England	1969	England		
1955	Ireland	1970	Scotland		

1987

at Lahinch

First day foursomes were abandoned due to bad weather, singles only were played.

Ireland beat England	6 matches to 4
Ireland beat Scotland	$10^1/_2$ matches to $4^1/_2$
Ireland beat Wales	8 matches to 7
England beat Scotland	9 matches to 6
England halved with Wales	7 matches each
Scotland beat Wales	$6^1/_2$ matches to $3^1/_2$

Winners: Ireland

1988

at Muirfield

England beat Wales	11 matches to 4
England beat Scotland	9 matches to 6
England beat Ireland	8 matches to 7
Ireland halved with Wales	$7^1/_2$ matches each
Ireland beat Scotland	10 matches to 5
Wales beat Scotland	8 matches to 7

Winners: England

1989

at Ganton

England beat Ireland	8 matches to 7
England beat Scotland	9 matches to 6
England beat Wales	12 matches to 3
Ireland beat Wales	11 matches to 4
Scotland beat Wales	8 matches to 7
Scotland beat Ireland	$8^1/_2$ matches to $6^1/_2$

Winners: England

1990

at Conwy

England beat Wales	10 matches to 5
Ireland beat Scotland	9 matches to 6
Scotland beat England	$9^1/_2$ matches to $5^1/_2$
Ireland beat Wales	11 matches to 4
Wales beat Scotland	8 matches to 7
Ireland beat England	8 matches to 7

Winners: Ireland

1991

at Rosses Point

Ireland halved with Wales	$7^1/_2$ matches each
Scotland beat England	$9^1/_2$ matches to $5^1/_2$
Ireland beat England	11 matches to 4
Wales beat Scotland	8 matches to 7
England beat Wales	9 matches to 6
Ireland beat Scotland	10 matches to 5

Winners: Ireland

1992

at Prestwick

Ireland halved with England	$7^1/_2$ matches each
Scotland beat Wales	8 matches to 7
Ireland beat Wales	11 matches to 4
England beat Scotland	$11^1/_2$ matches to $3^1/_2$
England beat Wales	$8^1/_2$ matches to $6^1/_2$
Ireland beat Scotland	$12^1/_2$ matches to $2^1/_2$

Winners: England and Ireland tied

1993

at Hoylake

England beat Scotland	8 matches to 7
Wales beat Ireland	$8^1/_2$ matches to $6^1/_2$
England beat Ireland	$9^1/_2$ matches to $5^1/_2$
Wales halved with Scotland	$7^1/_2$ matches each
Ireland beat Scotland	$8^1/_2$ matches to $6^1/_2$
England halved with Wales	$7^1/_2$ matches each

Winners: England

1994

at Ashburnham, Dyfed

England beat Scotland	$9^1/_2$ matches to $5^1/_2$
Ireland beat Wales	$10^1/_2$ matches to $4^1/_2$
England beat Wales	10 matches to 5
Ireland beat Scotland	11 matches to 4
Scotland beat Wales	8 matches to 7
England beat Ireland	9 matches to 6

Winners: England

St Andrews Trophy (Great Britain and Ireland *v* Continent of Europe)

Match instituted 1956, trophy presented 1962

Year	Winner	Venue	Result
1956	Great Britain & Ireland	Wentworth	$12^1/_2$–$2^1/_2$
1958	Great Britain & Ireland	St Cloud, France	10–5
1960	Great Britain & Ireland	Walton Heath	13–5
1962	Great Britain & Ireland	Halmstead, Sweden	18–12
1964	Great Britain & Ireland	Muirfield	23–7
1966	Great Britain & Ireland	Bilbao, Spain	$19^1/_2$–$10^1/_2$
1968	Great Britain & Ireland	Portmarnock	20–10
1970	Great Britain & Ireland	La Zoute, Belgium	$17^1/_2$–$12^1/_2$
1972	Great Britain & Ireland	Berkshire	$19^1/_2$–$10^1/_2$
1974	Continent of Europe	Punta Ala, Italy	16–14
1976	Great Britain & Ireland	St Andrews	$18^1/_2$–$11^1/_2$
1978	Great Britain & Ireland	Bremen, Germany	$20^1/_2$–$9^1/_2$
1980	Great Britain & Ireland	Sandwich, R St George's	$19^1/_2$–$10^1/_2$
1982	Continent of Europe	Rosendaelsche, Netherlands	14–10
1984	Great Britain & Ireland	Taunton, Devon	13–11
1986	Great Britain & Ireland	Halmstead, Sweden	$14^1/_2$–$9^1/_2$
1988	Great Britain & Ireland	St Andrews	$15^1/_2$–$8^1/_2$
1990	Great Britain & Ireland	El Saler, Spain	13–11
1992	Great Britain & Ireland	R Cinque Ports	14–10
1994	Great Britain & Ireland	Chantilly, France	14–10

Women's Professional Internationals

Solheim Cup

At Lake Nona GC, Florida, 16th, 17th and 18th November, 1990

Foursomes

Europe	Matches	USA	Matches
L Davies and A Nicholas (2 and 1)	1	P Bradley and N Lopez	0
P Wright and L Neumann	0	C Gerring and D Mochrie (6 and 5)	1
D Reid and H Alfredsson	0	P Sheehan and R Jones (6 and 5)	1
T Johnson and ML de Lorenzi	0	B Daniel and B King (5 and 4)	1
	1		3

Four-balls

Europe	Matches	USA	Matches
T Johnson and ML de Lorenzi	0	P Sheehan and R Jones (2 and 1)	1
D Reid and H Alfredsson	0	P Bradley and N Lopez (2 and 1)	1
L Davies and A Nicholas	0	B King and B Daniel (4 and 3)	1
L Neumann and P Wright (4 and 2)	1	C Gerring and D Mochrie	0
	1		3

Singles

Europe	Matches	USA	Matches
H Alfredsson	0	C Gerring (4 and 3)	1
L Davies (3 and 2)	1	R Jones	0
A Nicholas	0	N Lopez (6 and 4)	1
P Wright	$^1/_2$	B King	$^1/_2$
L Neumann	0	B Daniel (7 and 6)	1
D Reid (2 and 1)	1	P Sheehan	0
ML de Lorenzi	0	D Mochrie (4 and 2)	1
T Johnson	0	P Bradley (8 and 7)	1
	$2^1/_2$		$5^1/_2$

Result: USA $11^1/_2$; Europe $4^1/_2$

At Dalmahoy on 2nd, 3rd and 4th October, 1992

***First Day* – Foursomes**

Europe	Matches	USA	Matches
L Davies and A Nicholas (1hole)	1	B King and B Daniel	0
L Neumann and H Alfredsson (2 and 1)	1	P Bradley and D Mochrie	0
F Descampe and T Johnson	0	A Ammaccapane and M Mallon (1hole)	1
D Reid and P Wright	$^1/_2$	P Sheehan and J Inkster	$^1/_2$
	$2^1/_2$		$1^1/_2$

***Second Day* – Fourball**

Europe	Matches	USA	Matches
L Davies and A Nicholas (1 hole)	1	P Sheehan and J Inkster	0
T Johnson and F Descampe	$^1/_2$	B Burton and D Richard	$^1/_2$
P Wright and D Reid	0	M Mallon and B King (1 hole)	1
H Alfredsson and L Neumann	$^1/_2$	P Bradley and D Mochrie	$^1/_2$
	2		2

continued

Third Day – Singles

L Davies (4 and 2)	1	B Burton	0
H Alfredsson (4 and 3)	1	D Ammaccapane	0
T Johnson (2 and 1)	1	P Sheehan	0
A Nicholas	0	J Inkster (3 and 2)	1
F Descampe	0	B Daniel (2 and 1)	1
P Wright (4 and 3)	1	P Bradley	0
C Nilsmark (3 and 2)	1	M Mallon	0
K Douglas	0	D Richard (7 and 6)	1
L Neumann (2 and 1)	1	B King	0
D Reid (3 and 2)	1	D Mochrie	0
	7		3

Match Aggregate: Europe 11½, United States 6½.

At the Greenbrier, West Virginia, 21st, 22nd and 23rd October, 1994

First Day – Foursomes

USA	Matches	Europe	Matches
B Burton and DMochrie (3 and 2)	1	H Alfredsson and L Neumann	0
B Daniel and M Mallon	0	C Nilsmark and A Sorenstam (1 hole)	1
T Green and K Robbins	0	L Fairclough and D Reid (2 and 1)	1
D Andrews and B King	0	L Davies and A Nicholas (2 and 1)	1
P Sheehan and S Steinhauer (2 holes)	1	T Johnson and P Wright	0
	2		3

Second Day – Fourball

B Burton and D Mochrie (2 and 1)	1	L Davies and A Nicholas	0
B Daniel and M Mallon (7 and 5)	1	C Nilsmark and A Sorenstam	0
T Green and K Robbins	0	L Fairclough and D Reid (5 and 3)	1
D Andrews and B King (3 and 2)	1	T Johnson and P Wright	0
P Sheehan and S Steinhauer	0	H Alfredsson and L Neumann (1 hole)	1
	3		2

Third Day – Singles

B King	0	H Alfredsson (2 and 1)	1
D Mochrie (6 and 5)	1	C Nilsmark	0
B Daniel (2 holes)	1	T Johnson	0
K Robbins (4 and 2)	1	L Fairclough	0
M Mallon (2 holes)	1	P Wright	0
P Sheehan	0	A Nicholas (3 and 2)	1
B Burton (2 holes)	1	L Davies	0
T Green (3 and 2)	1	A Sorenstam	0
S Steinhauer (2 holes)	1	D Reid	0
D Andrews (3 and 2)	1	L Neumann	0
	8		2

Match Aggregate: United States 13, Europe 7

INDIVIDUAL RECORDS

Brackets indicate non-playing captain

Europe

Name		Year	Played	Won	Lost	Halved
Helen Alfredsson	Swe	1990-92-94	9	4	4	1
Laura Davies	Eng	1990-92-94	9	6	3	0
Florence Descampe	Bel	1992	3	0	2	1
Kitrina Douglas	Eng	1992	1	0	1	0
Lora Fairclough	Eng	1994	3	2	1	0
Trish Johnson	Eng	1990-92-94	9	1	7	1
Marie-Laure de Lorenzi	Fra	1990	3	0	3	0
Liselotte Neumann	Swe	1990-92-94	9	4	4	1
Alison Nicholas	Eng	1990-92-94	9	5	4	0
Catrin Nilsmark	Swe	1992-94	4	2	2	0

Name		Year	Played	Won	Lost	Halved
Dale Reid	Sco	1990-92-94	9	4	4	1
Annika Sorenstam	Swe	1994	3	1	2	0
Mickey Walker	Eng	(1990)-(92)-(94)	0	0	0	0
Pam Wright	Sco	1990-92-94	6	1	4	1

United States

Name	Year	Played	Won	Lost	Halved
Danielle Ammacapane	1992	2	1	1	0
Donna Andrews	1994	3	2	1	0
Pat Bradley	1990-92	6	2	3	1
Brandie Burton	1992-94	5	3	1	1
JoAnne Carner	(1994)	0	0	0	0
Beth Daniel	1990-92-94	8	6	2	0
Cathy Gerring	1990	3	2	1	0
Tammie Green	1994	3	1	2	0
Juli Inkster	1992	3	1	1	1
Rosie Jones	1990	3	2	1	0
Betsy King	1990-92-94	9	4	4	1
Nancy Lopez	1990	3	2	1	0
Meg Mallon	1992-94	6	4	2	0
Alice Miller	(1992)*	0	0	0	0
Dottie Mochrie	1990-92-94	9	5	3	1
Deb Richard	1992	2	1	0	1
Kelly Robbins	1994	3	1	2	0
Patty Sheehan	1990-92-94	9	3	5	1
Sherri Steinhauer	1994	3	2	1	0
Kathy Whitworth	(1990)-(92)*	0	0	0	0

* Kathy Whitworth had to return home because of a bereavement; Alice Miller took over the captaincy.

Ladies' Amateur Tournaments

Astor Salver *at The Berkshire*

Year	Winner	Score	Year	Winner	Score
1985	H Wadsworth	138	1991	EJ Smith	145
1986	C Pierce	144	1992	L Walton	139
1987	V Thomas	145	1993	S Lambert	141
1988	J Thornhill	136	1994	S Lambert	142
1989	S Sutton	140			
1990T	J Hall	144			
	J Morley				

Hampshire Rose *at North Hants*

Year	Winner	Year	Winner
1985	A Uzielli	1991	K Egford
1986	C Hourihane	1992	A Uzielli
1987	J Thornhill	1993	C Hourihane
1988	J Thornhill	1994T	K Shepherd
1989	A MacDonald		K Egford
1990	S Keogh		

Helen Holm Trophy

Year	Winner	Year	Winner
1985	P Wright	1990	C Lambert
1986	IC Robertson	1991	J Hall
1987	E Farquharson	1992	M McKay
1988	E Farquharson	1993	J Hall
1989	S Robinson	1994	K Tebbet

London Ladies' Foursomes

Year	Winner	Year	Winner
1985	Harpenden	1990	Stoke Poges
1986	Thorndon Park	1991	Stoke Poges
1987	Nevill	1992	Chelmsford
1988	Harpenden	1993	Knebworth
1989	Walton Heath	1994	Knebworth

Ladies' Amateur International Tournaments and Matches

Great Britain & Ireland *v* USA (Ladies) Curtis Cup

Year		Great Britain & Ireland		USA		Venue
1932	Foursomes	0	3½	3	5½	Wentworth
	Singles	3½		2½		
1934	Foursomes	1½	2½	1½	6½	Chevy Chase
	Singles	1		5		
1936	Foursomes	1½	4½	1½	4½	Gleneagles
	Singles	3		3		
1938	Foursomes	2½	3½	½	5½	Essex County Club
	Singles	1		5		
1948	Foursomes	1	2½	2	6½	Birkdale
	Singles	1½		4½		
1950	Foursomes	1	1½	2	7½	Buffalo
	Singles	½		5½		
1952	Foursomes	2	5	1	4	Muirfield
	Singles	3		3		
1954	Foursomes	0	3	3	6	Merion
	Singles	3		3		
1956	Foursomes	1	5	2	4	Sandwich, Prince's
	Singles	4		2		
1958	Foursomes	2	4½	1	4½	Brae Burn GC
	Singles	2½		3½		
1960	Foursomes	1	2½	2	6½	Lindrick
	Singles	1½		4½		
1962	Foursomes	0	1	3	8	Colorado Springs
	Singles	1		5		
1964	Foursomes	3½	7½	2½	10½	Porthcawl
	Singles	4		8		
1966	Foursomes	1½	5	4½	13	Hot Springs
	Singles	3½		8½		
1968	Foursomes	2½	7½	3½	10½	Newcastle, Co Down
	Singles	5		7		
1970	Foursomes	2½	6½	3½	11½	Brae Burn, USA
	Singles	4		8		
1972	Foursomes	3½	8	2½	10	Western Gailes
	Singles	4½		7½		
1974	Foursomes	2½	5	3½	13	San Francisco, California
	Singles	2½		9½		
1976	Foursomes	2	6½	4	11½	R Lytham and St Annes
	Singles	4½		7½		
1978	Foursomes	2½	6	3½	12	Apawamis, NY
	Singles	3½		8½		
1980	Foursomes	1	5	5	13	St Pierre
	Singles	4		8		
1982	Foursomes	1½	3½	4½	14½	Denver, Colorado
	Singles	2		10		
1984	Foursomes	3	8½	3	9½	Muirfield
	Singles	5½		6½		

At Prairie Dunes, Kansas, on 1st and 2nd August, 1986

Great Britain and Ireland | **USA**

First Day – Foursomes

Great Britain and Ireland	Matches	USA	Matches
L Behan and J Thornhill (7 and 6)	1	K Kessler and C Schreyer	0
P Johnson and K Davies (2 and 1)	1	D Ammaccapane and D Mochrie	0
IC Robertson and M McKenna (1 hole)	1	K Gardner and K McCarthy	0
	3		0

Singles

Great Britain and Ireland	Matches	USA	Matches
P Johnson (1 hole)	1	L Shannon	0
J Thornhill (4 and 3)	1	K Williams	0
L Behan (4 and 3)	1	D Ammaccapane	0
V Thomas	0	K Kessler (3 and 2)	1
K Davies	½	D Mochrie	½
C Hourihane	0	C Schreyer (2 and 1)	1
	3½		2½

Second Day – Foursomes

Great Britain and Ireland	Matches	USA	Matches
P Johnson and K Davies (1 hole)	1	D Ammaccapane and D Mochrie	0
L Behan and J Thornhill (5 and 3)	1	L Shannon and K Williams	0
IC Robertson and M McKenna	½	K Gardner and K McCarthy	½
	2½		½

Singles

Great Britain and Ireland	Matches	USA	Matches
J Thornhill	½	L Shannon	½
P Johnson (5 and 3)	1	K McCarthy	0
L Behan	0	K Gardner (1 hole)	1
V Thomas (4 and 3)	1	K Williams	0
K Davies	½	K Kessler	½
C Hourihane (5 and 3)	1	C Schreyer	0
	4		2

Aggregate: Great Britain and Ireland 13, United States 5

At Royal St George's on 10th and 11th June, 1988

Great Britain and Ireland | **USA**

First Day – Foursomes

Great Britain and Ireland	Matches	USA	Matches
L Bayman and J Wade (2 and 1)	1	T Kerdyk and K Scrivner	0
S Shapcott and K Davies (5 and 4)	1	C Scholefield and C Thompson	0
J Thornhill and V Thomas	½	L Shannon and C Keggi	½
	2½		½

Singles

Great Britain and Ireland	Matches	USA	Matches
L Bayman	½	T Kerdyk	1/2
J Wade (2 holes)	1	C Scholefield	0
S Shapcott	0	C Thompson (1 hole)	1
K Davies	0	P Sinn (4 and 3)	1
S Lawson (1 hole)	1	P Cornett	0
J Thornhill (3 and 2)	1	L Shannon	0
	3½		2½

Second Day – Foursomes

Great Britain and Ireland	Matches	USA	Matches
L Bayman and J Wade	0	T Kerdyk and K Scrivner (1 hole)	1
S Shapcott and K Davies (2 holes)	1	L Shannon and C Keggi	0
J Thornhill and V Thomas (6 and 5)	1	C Scholefield and C Thompson	0
	2		1

Singles

Great Britain and Ireland	Matches	USA	Matches
J Wade	0	T Kerdyk (2 and 1)	1
S Shapcott (3 and 2)	1	C Keggi	0
S Lawson	0	K Scrivner (4 and 3)	1
V Thomas (5 and 3)	1	P Cornett	0
L Bayman (1 hole)	1	P Sinn	0
J Thornhill	0	C Thompson (3 and 2)	1
	3		3

Aggregate: Great Britain and Ireland 11, United States 7

Curtis Cup *at Somerset Hills, New Jersey, on 28th and 29th July, 1990*

First Day – Foursomes

Great Britain and Ireland	Matches	USA	Matches
H Dobson and C Lambert	0	V Goetze and A Sander (4 and 3)	1
J Hall and K Imrie (2 and 1)	1	K Noble and M Platt	0
E Farquharson and H Wadsworth	0	C Semple-Thompson and R Weiss (3 and 1)	1
	1		2

Singles

Great Britain and Ireland	Matches	USA	Matches
J Hall (2 and 1)	1	V Goetze	0
K Imrie	0	K Peterson (3 and 2)	1
E Farquharson	0	B Burton (3 and 1)	1
L Fletcher	0	R Weiss (4 and 3)	1
C Lambert	0	K Noble (1 hole)	1
V Thomas (1 hole)	1	C Semple-Thompson	0
	2		4

Second Day – Foursomes

Great Britain and Ireland	Matches	USA	Matches
J Hall and K Imrie	0	V Goetze and A Sander (4 and 3)	1
C Lambert and H Dobson (1 hole)	1	K Noble and M Platt	0
E Farquharson and H Wadsworth	0	K Peterson and B Burton (5 and 4)	1
	1		2

Singles

Great Britain and Ireland	Matches	USA	Matches
H Dobson	0	V Goetze (4 and 3)	1
C Lambert	0	B Burton (4 and 3)	1
K Imrie	0	K Peterson (1 hole)	1
J Hall	0	K Noble (2 holes)	1
E Farquharson	0	R Weiss (2 and 1)	1
V Thomas	0	C Semple-Thompson (3 and 1)	1
	0		6

Aggregate: United States 14; Great Britain and Ireland 4

At Royal Liverpool, Hoylake, on 5th and 6th June, 1992

First Day – Foursomes

Great Britain and Ireland	Matches	USA	Matches
J Hall and C Hall	1/2	A Fruhwirth and V Goetze	1/2
V Thomas and C Lambert (2 and 1)	1	L Shannon and S Le Brun Ingram	0
J Morley and C Hourihane (2 and 1)	1	T Hanson and C Semple Thompson	0
	2 1/2		1/2

Singles

Great Britain and Ireland	Matches	USA	Matches
J Morley	1/2	A Fruhwirth	1/2
J Hall	0	V Goetze (3 and 2)	1
E Farquharson (2 and 1)	1	R Weiss	0
N Buxton	0	M Lang (2 holes)	1
C Lambert (3 and 2)	1	C Semple Thompson	0
C Hall (6 and 5)	1	L Shannon	0
	3 1/2		2 1/2

Second Day – Foursomes

Great Britain and Ireland	Matches	USA	Matches
J Hall and C Hall	1/2	A Fruhwirth and V Goetze	1/2
C Hourihane and J Morley	1/2	M Lang and R Weiss	1/2
C Lambert and V Thomas	0	T Hanson and C Semple Thompson (3 and 2)	1
	1		2

Singles

Great Britain and Ireland	Matches	USA	Matches
J Morley (2 and 1)	1	A Fruhwirth	0
C Lambert (6 and 5)	1	T Hanson	0
E Farquharson	0	S Le Brun Ingram (2 and 1)	1
V Thomas	0	L Shannon (2 and 1)	1
C Hourihane	0	M Lang (2 and1)	1
C Hall (1 hole)	1	V Goetze	0
	3		3

Result: Great Britain and Ireland 10, United States 8

At The Honors Course, Ooltewah, Chattanooga, Tennessee, on 30–31 July 1994

Great Britain and Ireland	Matches	USA	Matches
***First Day* – Singles**			
J Hall	1/2	J McGill	1/2
J Moodie	0	E Klein (3 and 2)	1
L Walton (1 hole)	1	W Ward	0
M McKinlay	0	C Semple Thompson (2 and 1)	1
M McKay	0	E Port (2 and 1)	1
C Matthew (1 hole)	1	S Sparks	0
	2 1/2		3 1/2
Foursomes			
C Matthew and J Moodie	1/2	J McGill and S LeBrun Ingram	1/2
M McKay and K Speak	0	C Semple Thompson and E Klein (7 and 5)	1
J Hall and L Walton (6 and 5)	1	W Kaupp and E Port	0
	1 1/2		1 1/2
***Second Day* – Foursomes**			
J Hall and L Walton (2 and 1)	1	J McGill and S LeBrun Ingram	0
M McKinlay and ER Power	0	C Semple Thompson and E Klein (4 and 2)	1
C Matthew and J Moodie (3 and 2)	1	W Ward and S Sparks	0
	2		1
Singles			
J Hall	0	J McGill (4 and 3)	1
C Matthew (2 and 1)	1	E Klein	0
M McKay	0	E Port (7 and 5)	1
M McKinlay (3 and 2)	1	W Kaupp	0
L Walton	0	W Ward (4 and 3)	1
J Moodie (2 holes)	1	C Semple Thompson	0
	3		3

Result: Great Britain and Ireland 9, United States 9

INDIVIDUAL RECORDS

Great Britain and Ireland

Bold print: captain; bold print in brackets: non-playing captain
Maiden name in parentheses, former surname in square brackets

Name		Year	Played	Won	Lost	Halved
Jean Anderson (Donald)	Scot	1948	6	3	3	0
Diane Bailey [Frearson] (Robb)	Eng	1962-72-**(84)**-**(86)**-**(88)**	5	2	2	1
Sally Barber (Bonallack)	Eng	1962	1	0	1	0
Pam Barton	Eng	1934-36	4	0	3	1
Linda Bayman	Eng	1988	4	2	1	1
Baba Beck (Pym)	Ire	**(1954)**	0	0	0	0
Charlotte Beddows [Watson] (Stevenson)	Scot	1932	1	0	1	0
Lilian Behan	Ire	1986	4	3	1	0
Veronica Beharrell (Anstey)	Eng	1956	1	0	1	0
Pam Benka (Tredinnick)	Eng	1966-68	4	0	3	1
Jeanne Bisgood	Eng	1950-52-54-**(70)**	4	1	3	0
Elizabeth Boatman (Collis)	Eng	**(1992)**-**(94)**	0	0	0	0
Zara Bolton (Davis)	Eng	1948-**(56)**-**(66)**-**(68)**	2	0	2	0
Angela Bonallack (Ward)	Eng	1956-58-60-62-64-66	15	6	8	1
Ita Butler (Burke)	Ire	1966	3	2	1	0
Nicola Buxton	Eng	1992	1	0	1	0
Lady Katherine Cairns	Eng	(1952)	0	0	0	0
Carole Caldwell (Redford)	Eng	1978-80	5	0	3	2
Doris Chambers	Eng	**(1934)**-**(36)**-**(48)**	0	0	0	0
Carol Comboy (Grott)	Eng	**(1978)**-**(80)**	0	0	0	0
Jane Connachan	Scot	1980-82	5	0	5	0
Elsie Corlett	Eng	1932-38-**(64)**	3	1	2	0
Diana Critchley (Fishwick)	Eng	1932-34-**(50)**	3	1	2	0
Karen Davies	Wales	1986-88	7	4	1	2

Name		Year	Played	Won	Lost	Halved
Laura Davies	Eng	1984	2	1	1	0
Helen Dobson	Eng	1990	3	1	2	0
Kitrina Douglas	Eng	1982	4	0	3	1
Marjorie Draper [Peel] (Thomas)	Scot	1954	1	0	1	0
Mary Everard	Eng	1970-72-74-78	15	6	7	2
Elaine Farquharson	Scot	1990-92	6	1	5	0
Daisy Ferguson	Ire	**(1958)**	0	0	0	0
Marjory Ferguson (Fowler)	Scot	1966	1	0	1	0
Elizabeth Price Fisher (Price)	Eng	1950-52-54-56-58-60	12	7	4	1
Linzi Fletcher	Eng	1990	1	0	1	0
Maureen Garner (Madill)	Ire	1980	4	0	3	1
Marjorie Ross Garon	Eng	1936	2	1	0	1
Maureen Garrett (Ruttle)	Eng	1948-(**60**)	2	0	2	0
Philomena Garvey	Ire	1948-50-52-54-56-60	11	2	8	1
Carol Gibbs (Le Feuvre)	Eng	1974	3	0	3	0
Jacqueline Gordon	Eng	1948	2	1	1	0
Molly Gourlay	Eng	1932-34	4	0	2	2
Julia Greenhalgh	Eng	1964-70-74-76-78	17	6	7	4
Penny Grice-Whittaker (Grice)	Eng	1984	4	2	1	1
Caroline Hall	Eng	1992	4	2	0	2
Julie Hall (Wade)	Eng	1988-90-92-94	15	6	6	3
Marley Harris [Spearman] (Baker)	Eng	1960-62-64	6	2	2	2
Dorothea Hastings (Sommerville)	Scot	1958	0	0	0	0
Lady Heathcoat-Amory (Joyce Wethered)	Eng	**1932**	2	1	1	0
Dinah Henson (Oxley)	Eng	1968-70-72-76	11	3	6	2
Helen Holm (Gray)	Scot	1936-38-48	5	3	2	0
Claire Hourihane	Ire	1984-86-88-90-92	8	3	3	2
Ann Howard (Phillips)	Eng	1956-68	2	0	2	0
Beverley Huke	Eng	1972	2	0	2	0
Kathryn Imrie	Scot	1990	4	1	3	0
Ann Irvin	Eng	1962-68-70-76	12	4	7	1
Bridget Jackson	Eng	1958-64-68	8	1	6	1
Patricia Johnson	Eng	1986	4	4	0	0
Susan Langridge (Armitage)	Eng	1964-66	6	0	5	1
Joan Lawrence	Scot	1964	2	0	2	0
Shirley Lawson	Scot	1988	2	1	1	0
Wilma Leburn (Aitken)	Scot	1982	2	0	2	0
Jenny Lee Smith	Eng	1974-76	3	0	3	0
Kathryn Lumb (Phillips)	Eng	1970-72	2	1	1	0
Mhairi McKay	Scot	1994	3	0	3	0
Mary McKenna	Ire	1970-72-74-76-78-80-82-84-86	30	10	16	4
Myra McKinlay	Scot	1994	3	1	2	0
Suzanne McMahon (Cadden)	Scot	1976	4	0	4	0
Sheila Maher (Vaughan)	Eng	1962-64	4	1	2	1
Vanessa Marvin	Eng	1978	3	1	2	0
Catriona Matthew (Lambert)	Scot	1990-92-94	12	7	4	1
Moira Milton (Paterson)	Scot	1952	2	1	1	0
Janice Moodie	Scot	1994	4	2	1	1
Wanda Morgan	Eng	1932-34-36	6	0	5	1
Joanne Morley	Eng	1992	4	2	0	2
Beverley New	Eng	1984	4	1	3	0
Maire O'Donnell	Ire	**(1982)**	0	0	0	0
Margaret Pickard (Nichol)	Eng	1968-70	5	2	3	0
Diana Plumpton	Eng	1934	2	1	1	0
Elizabeth Pook (Chadwick)	Eng	1966	4	1	3	0
Doris Porter (Park)	Scot	1932	1	0	1	0
Eileen Rose Power (McDaid)	Ire	1994	1	0	1	0
Clarrie Reddan (Tiernan)	Ire	1938-48	3	2	1	0
Joan Rennie (Hastings)	Scot	1966	2	0	1	1
Maureen Richmond (Walker)	Scot	1974	4	2	2	0
Jean Roberts	Eng	1962	1	0	1	0
Belle Robertson (McCorkindale)	Scot	1960-66-68-70-72-(**74**)-(**76**)-82-86	24	5	12	7
Claire Robinson (Nesbitt)	Ire	1980	3	0	1	2
Vivien Saunders	Eng	1968	4	1	2	1
Susan Shapcott	Eng	1988	4	3	1	0
Linda Simpson (Moore)	Eng	1980	3	1	1	1
Ruth Slark (Porter)	Eng	1960-62-64	7	3	3	1
Anne Smith [Stant] (Willard)	Eng	1976	1	0	1	0
Frances Smith (Stephens)	Eng	1950-52-54-56-58-60-(**62**)-(**72**)	11	7	3	1
Janet Soulsby	Eng	1982	4	1	2	1
Kirsty Speak	Eng	1994	1	0	1	0
Gillian Stewart	Scot	1980-82	4	1	3	0

Name		Year	Played	Won	Lost	Halved
Tegwen Thomas (Perkins)	Wales	1974-76-78-80	14	4	8	2
Vicki Thomas (Rawlings)	Wales	1982-84-86-88-90-92	13	6	5	2
Muriel Thomson	Scot	1978	3	2	1	0
Jill Thornhill	Eng	1984-86-88	12	6	2	4
Angela Uzielli (Carrick)	Eng	1978	1	0	1	0
Jessie Valentine (Anderson)	Scot	1936-38-50-52-54-56-58	13	4	9	0
Helen Wadsworth	Wales	1990	2	0	2	0
Claire Waite	Eng	1984	4	2	2	0
Mickey Walker	Eng	1972	4	3	0	1
Pat Walker	Ire	1934-36-38	6	2	3	1
Verona Wallace- Williamson	Scot	**(1938)**	0	0	0	0
Lisa Walton	Eng	1994	4	3	1	0
Nan Wardlaw (Baird)	Scot	1938	1	0	1	0
Enid Wilson	Eng	1932	2	1	1	0
Janette Wright (Robertson)	Scot	1954-56-58-60	8	3	5	0
Phyllis Wylie (Wade)	Eng	1938	1	0	0	1

United States of America

Name	Year	Played	Won	Lost	Halved
Roberta Albers	1968	2	1	0	1
Danielle Ammaccapane	1986	3	0	3	0
Kathy Baker	1982	4	3	0	1
Barbara Barrow	1976	2	1	0	1
Beth Barry	1972-74	5	3	1	1
Larua Baugh	1972	4	2	1	1
Judy Bell	1960-62-**(86)**-**(88)**	2	1	1	0
Peggy Kirk Bell (Kirk)	1950	2	1	1	0
Amy Benz	1982	3	2	1	0
Patty Berg	1936-38	4	1	2	1
Barbara Fay Boddie (White)	1964-66	8	7	0	1
Jane Booth (Bastanchury)	1970-72-74	12	9	3	0
Mary Budke	1974	3	2	1	0
Brandie Burton	1990	3	3	0	0
JoAnne Carner (Gunderson)	1958-60-62-64	10	6	3	1
Lori Castillo	1980	3	2	1	0
Leona Cheney (Pressler)	1932-34-36	6	5	1	0
Sis Choate	**(1974)**	0	0	0	0
Peggy Conley	1964-68	6	3	1	2
Mary Ann Cook (Downey)	1956	2	1	1	0
Patricia Cornett	1978-88	4	1	2	1
Jean Crawford (Ashley)	1962-66-68-**(72)**	8	6	2	0
Clifford Ann Creed	1962	2	2	0	0
Grace Cronin (Lenczyk)	1948-50	3	2	1	0
Carolyn Cudone	1956-**(70)**	1	1	0	0
Beth Daniel	1976-78	8	7	1	0
Virginia Dennehy	**(1958)**	0	0	0	0
Mary Lou Dill	1968	3	1	1	1
Alice Dye	1970	2	1	0	1
Heather Farr	1984	3	2	1	0
Jane Fassinger	1970	1	0	1	0
Mary Lena Faulk	1954	2	1	1	0
Carol Sorensen Flenniken (Sorensen)	1964-66	8	6	1	1
Edith Flippin (Quier)	**(1954)**-**(56)**	0	0	0	0
Amy Fruhwirth	1992	4	0	1	3
Kim Gardner	1986	3	1	1	1
Charlotte Glutting	1934-36-38	5	3	1	1
Vicki Goetze	1990-92	8	4	2	2
Brenda Goldsmith	1978-80	4	2	2	0
Aniela Goldthwaite	1934-**(52)**	1	0	1	0
Joanne Goodwin	1960	2	1	1	0
Mary Hafeman	1980	2	1	0	1
Shelley Hamkin	1968-70	8	3	3	2
Penny Hammel	1984	3	1	1	1
Nancy Hammer (Hager)	1970	2	1	1	0
Cathy Hanlon	1982	3	2	1	0
Beverley Hanson	1950	2	2	0	0
Tracy Hanson	1992	3	1	2	0
Patricia Harbottle (Lesser)	1954-56	3	2	1	0
Helen Hawes	**(1964)**	0	0	0	0
Kathryn Hemphill	1938	1	0	0	1

Name	Year	Played	Won	Lost	Halved
Helen Hicks	1932	2	1	1	0
Carolyn Hill	1978	2	0	0	2
Cindy Hill	1970-74-76-78	14	5	6	3
Opel Hill	1932-34-36	6	2	3	1
Marion Hollins	(**1932**)	0	0	0	0
Dana Howe	1984	3	1	1	1
Juli Inkster	1982	4	4	0	0
Ann Casey Johnstone	1958-60-62	4	3	1	0
Mae Murray Jones (Murray)	1952	1	0	1	0
Wendy Kaupp	1994	2	0	2	0
Caroline Keggi	1988	3	0	2	1
Tracy Kerdyk	1988	4	2	1	1
Kandi Kessler	1986	3	1	1	1
Dorothy Kielty	1948-50	4	4	0	0
Dorothy Kirby	1948-50-52-54	7	4	3	0
Martha Kirouac (Wilkinson)	1970-72	8	5	3	0
Emilee Klein	1994	4	3	1	0
Nancy Knight (Lopez)	1976	2	2	0	0
Martha Lang	1992	3	2	0	1
Bonnie Lauer	1974	4	2	2	0
Sarah Le Brun Ingram	1992-94	4	1	2	1
Marjorie Lindsay	1952	2	1	1	0
Patricia Lucey (O'Sullivan)	1952	1	0	1	0
Mari McDougall	1982	2	2	0	0
Jill McGill	1994	4	1	1	2
Barbara McIntire	1958-60-62-64-66-72-(**76**)	16	6	6	4
Lucile Mann (Robinson)	1934	1	0	1	0
Debbie Massey	1974-76	5	5	0	0
Marion Miley	1938	2	1	0	1
Dottie Mochrie (Pepper)	1986	3	0	2	1
Evelyn Monsted	(**1968**)	0	0	0	0
Terri Moody	1980	2	1	0	1
Karen Noble	1990	4	2	2	0
Judith Oliver	1978-80-82-(**92**)	8	5	1	2
Maureen Orcutt	1932-34-36-38	8	5	3	0
Joanne Pacillo	1984	3	1	1	1
Estelle Page (Lawson)	1938-48	4	3	1	0
Katie Peterson	1990	3	3	0	0
Margaret Platt	1990	2	0	2	0
Frances Pond (Stebbins)	(**1938**)	0	0	0	0
Ellen Port	1994	3	2	1	0
Dorothy Germain Porter	1950-(**66**)	2	1	0	1
Phyllis Preuss	1962-64-66-68-70-(**84**)	15	10	4	1
Betty Probasco	(**1982**)	0	0	0	0
Mildred Prunaret	(**1960**)	0	0	0	0
Polly Riley	1948-50-52-54-56-58-(**62**)	10	5	5	0
Barbara Romack	1954-56-58	5	3	2	0
Jody Rosenthal	1984	3	2	0	1
Anne Sander [Welts] [Decker] (Quast)	1958-60-62-66-68-74-84-90	22	11	7	4
Cindy Scholefield	1988	3	0	3	0
Cindy Schreyer	1986	3	1	2	0
Kathleen McCarthy Scrivner (McCarthy)	1986-88	6	2	3	1
Carol Semple Thompson	1974-76-80-82-90-92-94	24	13	9	2
Leslie Shannon	1986-88-90-92	9	1	6	2
Patty Sheehan	1980	4	4	0	0
Pearl Sinn	1988	2	1	1	0
Grace De Moss Smith (De Moss)	1952-54	3	1	2	0
Lancy Smith	1972-78-80-82-84-(**94**)	16	7	5	4
Margaret Smith	1956	2	2	0	0
Stephanie Sparks	1994	2	0	2	0
Hollis Stacy	1972	2	0	1	1
Claire Stancik (Doran)	1952-54	4	4	0	0
Judy Street (Eller)	1960	2	2	0	0
Louise Suggs	1948	2	0	1	1
Nancy Roth Syms (Roth)	1964-66-76-(**80**)	9	3	5	1
Noreen Uihlein	1978	3	1	1	1
Virginia Van Wie	1932-34	4	3	0	1
Glenna Collett Vare (Collett)	1932-(**34**)-**36**-38-**48**-(**50**)	7	4	2	1
Wendy Ward	1994	3	1	2	0
Jane Weiss (Nelson)	1956	1	0	1	0
Robin Weiss	1990-92	5	3	1	1
Donna White (Horton)	1976	2	2	0	0
Mary Anne Widman	1984	3	2	1	0

Name	Year	Played	Won	Lost	Halved
Kimberley Williams	1986	3	0	3	0
Helen Sigel Wilson (Sigel)	1950-66-(78)	2	0	2	0
Joyce Ziske	1954	1	0	1	0

Commonwealth Tournament (Ladies)

Year	Winner	Venue
1959	Great Britain	St Andrews
1963	Great Britain	Royal Melbourne, Australia
1967	Great Britain	Ancaster, Ontario, Canada
1971	Great Britain	Hamilton, New Zealand
1975	Great Britain	Ganton, England
1979	Canada	Lake Karrinup, Perth, Australia
1983	Australia	Glendale, Edmonton, Canada
1987	Canada	Christchurch, New Zealand
1991	Great Britain	Northumberland, England

European Ladies' Amateur Team Championship

Year	Winner	Second	Venue
1967	England	France	Penina, Portugal
1969	France	England	Tylosand, Sweden
1971	England	France	Ganton, England
1973	England	France	Brussels, Belgium
1975	France	Spain	Paris, France
1977	England	Spain	Sotogrande, Spain
1979	Ireland	Germany	Hermitage, Ireland
1981	Sweden	France	Troia, Portugal
1983	Ireland	England	Waterloo, Belgium
1985	England	Italy	Stavanger, Norway
1987	Sweden	Wales	Turnberry, Scotland
1989	France	England	Pals, Spain
1991	England	Sweden	Wentworth, England
1993	England	Spain	Royal Haagshe

Vagliano Trophy – Great Britain & Ireland *v* Europe (Ladies)

Played for biennially between teams of women amateur golfers representing the British Isles and Europe. (From 1947 to 1957 was between the British Isles and France.)

Year	Winner	Result	Venue
1959	Great Britain & Ireland	12–3	Wentworth
1961	Great Britain & Ireland	8–7	Villa d'Este
1963	Great Britain & Ireland	20–10	Muirfield
1965	Continent of Europe	17–13	Cologne
1967	Continent of Europe	15½–14½	R Lytham and St Anne's
1969	Continent of Europe	16–14	Chantilly
1971	Great Britain & Ireland	17½–12½	Worplesdon
1973	Great Britain & Ireland	20–10	Eindhoven
1975	Great Britain & Ireland	13½–10½	Muirfield
1977	Great Britain & Ireland	15½–8½	Malmo
1979	Halved	12–12	R Porthcawl
1981	Continent of Europe	14–10	P de Hierro
1983	Great Britain & Ireland	14–10	Woodhall Spa
1985	Great Britain & Ireland	14–10	Hamburg
1987	Great Britain & Ireland	15–9	The Berkshire
1989	Great Britain & Ireland	14½–9½	Venice
1991	Great Britain & Ireland	13½–10½	Nairn
1993	Great Britain & Ireland	13½–10½	Morfontaine

Women's Home Internationals

Year	Winner	Venue
1948	England	R Lytham and St Annes
1949	Scotland	Harlech
1950	Scotland	Newcastle Co Down
1951	Scotland	Broadstone
1952	Scotland	Troon
1953	England	Porthcawl
1954	England	Ganton
1955T	England Scotland	Western Gailes
1956	Scotland	Sunningdale
1957	Scotland	Troon
1958	England	Hunstanton
1959	England	Hoylake
1960	England	Gullane
1961	Scotland	Portmarnock
1962	Scotland	Porthcawl
1963	England	Formby
1964	England	Troon
1965	England	Portrush
1966	England	Woodhall Spa
1967	England	Sunningdale
1968	England	Porthcawl
1969T	England Scotland	Western Gailes
1970	England	Killarney
1971	England	Longniddry
1972	England	R Lytham and St Annes
1973	England	Harlech
1974T	England Scotland Ireland	Sandwich, Princes
1975	England	Newport
1976	England	Troon
1977	England	Cork
1978	England	Moortown
1979T	Scotland Ireland	Harlech
1980	Ireland	Cruden Bay
1981	Scotland	Portmarnock
1982	England	Burnham and Barrow
1983	*Matches abandoned due to weather*	
1984	England	Gullane
1985	England	Waterville
1986	Ireland	Whittington Barracks
1987	England	Ashburnham
1988	Scotland	Barassie

1989
at Westport, Ireland

Scotland beat Ireland	7 matches to 2
England beat Wales	$6^1/_2$ matches to $2^1/_2$
Scotland beat Wales	5 matches to 4
England beat Ireland	$5^1/_2$ matches to $3^1/_2$
England beat Scotland	8 matches to 1
Ireland beat Wales	6 matches to 3

Result: England 3; Scotland 2; Ireland 1; Wales 0

1990
at Hunstanton, Norfolk

England halved with Ireland	4 matches each
Scotland beat Wales	5 matches to 4
Scotland beat Ireland	5 matches to 4
England beat Wales	6 matches to 3
Ireland halved with Wales	4 matches each
Scotland beat England	6 matches to 3

Result: Scotland 3; England 1; Ireland 1; Wales 0

1991
at Aberdovey, Wales

England beat Wales	7 matches to 2
Scotland beat Ireland	6 matches to 3
Wales halved with Ireland	41/2 matches each
Scotland beat England	5 matches to 4
Scotland beat Wales	6 matches to 3
England beat Ireland	7 matches to 2

Result: Scotland 3; England 2; Ireland $^1/_2$; Wales $^1/_2$

1992
at Hamilton, Lanarkshire

Ireland beat Wales	$5^1/_2$ matches to $2^1/_2$
England halved with Scotland	4 matches each
Scotland beat Wales	6 matches to 3
England beat Ireland	8 matches to 1
Scotland beat Ireland	6 matches to 3
England beat Wales	$7^1/_2$ matches to $1^1/_2$

Result: England $2^1/_2$; Scotland $2^1/_2$; Ireland 1; Wales 0

1993
at Hermitage, Dublin

England beat Wales	7 matches to 2
Scotland beat Ireland	5 matches to 4
England beat Ireland	$5^1/_2$ matches to $3^1/_2$
Scotland beat Wales	7 matches to 2
England beat Scotland	$5^1/_2$ matches to $3^1/_2$
Ireland beat Wales	7 matches to 2

Result: England 3; Scotland 2; Ireland 1; Wales 0

1994
at Huddersfield, Yorkshire

England beat Ireland	$6^1/_2$ matches to $2^1/_2$
Scotland beat Wales	$8^1/_2$ matches to $^1/_2$
England beat Wales	8 matches to 1
Scotland halved with Ireland	$4^1/_2$ matches to $4^1/_2$
England beat Scotland	6 matches to 3
Ireland beat Wales	$5^1/_2$ matches to $3^1/_2$

Result: England 3; Scotland $1^1/_2$; Ireland $1^1/_2$; Wales 0

Women's World Amateur Team Championship (Espirito Santo Trophy)

Year	Winners	Runners-up	Venue	Score
1964	France	United States	St Germain	588
1966	United States	Canada	Mexico	580
1968	United States	Australia	Melbourne	616
1970	United States	France	Madrid	598
1972	United States	France	Buenos Aires	583
1974	United States	GB & I, South Africa	Dominican Republic	620
1976	United States	France	Vilamoura, Portugal	605
1978	Australia	Canada	Fiji	596
1980	United States	Australia	Pinehurst, USA	588
1982	United States	New Zealand	Geneva, Switzerland	579
1984	United States	France	Hong Kong	585
1986	Spain	France	Caracas, Venezuela	580
1988	United States	Sweden	Drottningholm, Sweden	587
1990	United States	New Zealand	Christchurch, New Zealand	585
1992	Spain	GB & I	Vancouver, Canada	588
1994	United States	Korea	Paris, France	569

Juniors and Youths

Boys' Amateur Championship

Year	Winner	Runner-up	Venue	By
1921	ADD Mathieson	GH Lintott	Ascot	37th hole
1922	HS Mitchell	W Greenfield	Ascot	4 and 2
1923	ADD Mathieson	HS Mitchell	Dunbar	3 and 2
1924	RW Peattie	P Manuevrier	Coombe Hill	2 holes
1925	RW Peattie	A McNair	Barnton	4 and 3
1926	EA McRuvie	CW Timmis	Coombe Hill	1 hole
1927	EW Fiddian	K Forbes	Barnton	4 and 2
1928	S Scheftel	A Dobbie	Formby	6 and 5
1929	J Lindsay	J Scott-Riddell	Barnton	6 and 4
1930	J Lindsay	J Todd	Fulwell	9 and 8
1931	H Thomson	F McGloin	Killermont	5 and 4
1932	IS MacDonald	LA Hardie	R Lytham and St Annes	2 and 1
1933	PB Lucas	W McLachlan	Carnoustie	3 and 2
1934	RS Burles	FB Allpass	Moortown	12 and 10
1935	JDA Langley	R Norris	Balgownie, Aberdeen	6 and 5
1936	J Bruen	W Innes	Birkdale	11 and 9
1937	IM Roberts	J Stewart	Bruntsfield	8 and 7
1938	W Smeaton	T Snowball	Moor Park	3 and 2
1939	SB Williamson	KG Thom	Carnoustie	4 and 2
1940-45	*Suspended during War*			
1946	AFD MacGregor	DF Dunstan	Bruntsfield	7 and 5
1947	J Armour	I Caldwell	Hoylake	5 and 4
1948	JD Pritchett	DH Reid	Barasssie	37th hole
1949	H MacAnespie	NV Drew	St Andrews	3 and 2
1950	J Glover	I Young	R Lytham and St Annes	2 and 1
1951	N Dunn	MSR Lunt	Prestwick	6 and 5
1952	M Bonallack	AE Shepperson	Formby	37th hole
1953	AE Shepperson	AT Booth	Dunbar	6 and 4
1954	AF Bussell	K Warren	Hoylake	38th hole
1955	SC Wilson	BJK Aitken	Barassie	39th hole
1956	JF Ferguson	CW Cole	Sunningdale	2 and 1
1957	D Ball	J Wilson	Carnoustie	2 and 1
1958	R Braddon	IM Stungo	Moortown	4 and 3
1959	AR Murphy	EM Shamash	Pollok	3 and 1
1960	P Cros	PO Green	Olton	5 and 3
1961	FS Morris	C Clark	Dalmahoy	3 and 2
1962	PM Townsend	DC Penman	R Mid-Surrey	1 hole
1963	AHC Soutar	DI Rigby	Prestwick	2 and 1
1964	PM Townsend	RD Gray	Formby	9 and 8
1965	GR Milne	DK Midgley	Gullane	4 and 2
1966	A Phillips	A Muller	Moortown	12 and 11
1967	LP Tupling	SC Evans	Western Gailes	4 and 2
1968	SC Evans	K Dabson	St Annes Old Links	3 and 2
1969	M Foster	M Gray	Dunbar	37th hole
1970	ID Gradwell	JE Murray	Hillside	1 hole
1971	H Clark	G Harvey	Barassie	6 and 5
1972	G Harvey	R Newsome	Moortown	7 and 5
1973	DM Robertson	S Betti	Blairgowrie	5 and 3
1974	TR Shannon	A Lyle	Hoylake	10 and 9
1975	B Marchbank	A Lyle	Bruntsfield	1 hole
1976	M Mouland	G Hargreaves	Sunningdale	6 and 5
1977	I Ford	CR Dalgleish	Downfield	1 hole
1978	S Keppler	M Stokes	Seaton Carew	3 and 2
1979	R Rafferty	D Ray	Barassie	6 and 5
1980	D Muscroft	A Llyr	Formby	7 and 6

continued

Year	Winner	Runner-up	Venue	By
1981	J Lopez	R Weedon	Gullane	4 and 3
1982	M Grieve	G Hickman	Burnham and Barrow	37th hole
1983	JM Olazabal	M Pendaries	Glenbervie	6 and 5
1984	L Vannett	A Mednick	Royal Porthcawl	2 and 1
1985	J Cook	W Henry	Barnton	5 and 4
1986	L Walker	G King	Seaton Carew	5 and 4
1987	C O'Carrol	P Olsson	Barassie	3 and 1
1988	S Pardoe	D Haines	Formby	3 and 2
1989	C Watts	C Fraser	Nairn	5 and 3
1990	M Welch	M Ellis	Hunstanton	3 and 1
1991	F Valera	R Walton	Montrose	4 and 3
1992	L Westerberg	T Biermann	R Mid-Surrey	3 and 2
1993	D Howell	V Gustavsson	Glenbervie	3 and 1
1994	C Smith	C Rodgers	Little Aston	2 and 1

Boys' Internationals

England *v* Scotland

Year	Winner	Result	Venue
1946	England	$8\frac{1}{2}$–$3\frac{1}{2}$	Bruntsfield
1947	England	7–5	Hoylake
1948	England	9–3	Barassie
1949	Scotland	8–4	St Andrews
1950	Scotland	$8\frac{1}{2}$–$3\frac{1}{2}$	R Lytham and St Annes
1951	England	7–5	Prestwick
1952	England	$6\frac{1}{2}$–$5\frac{1}{2}$	Formby
1953	Scotland	7–5	Dunbar
1954	England	$6\frac{1}{2}$–$5\frac{1}{2}$	Hoylake
1955	Scotland	9–3	Barassie
1956	England	$7\frac{1}{2}$–$4\frac{1}{2}$	Sunningdale
1957	Scotland	$7\frac{1}{2}$–$4\frac{1}{2}$	Carnoustie
1958	England	7–5	Moortown
1959	England	$8\frac{1}{2}$–$3\frac{1}{2}$	Pollok
1960	England	10–2	Olton
1961	Scotland	7–5	Dalmahoy
1962	England	$6\frac{1}{2}$–$5\frac{1}{2}$	R Mid-Surrey
1963	Scotland	9–3	Prestwick
1964	England	9–3	Formby
1965	England	10–5	Gullane
1966	England	12–3	Moortown
1967	Scotland	8–7	Western Gailes
1968	England	10–5	St Annes Old Links
1969	England	12–3	Dunbar
1970	England	12–3	Hillside
1971	Halved	$7\frac{1}{2}$–$7\frac{1}{2}$	Barassie
1972	England	$13\frac{1}{2}$–$1\frac{1}{2}$	Moortown
1973	England	9–6	Blairgowrie
1974	England	11–4	Liverpool
1975	England	$9\frac{1}{2}$–$5\frac{1}{2}$	Bruntsfield
1976	Scotland	8–7	Sunningdale
1977	England	8–7	Downfield
1978	Scotland	$8\frac{1}{2}$–$6\frac{1}{2}$	Seaton Carew
1979	England	11–4	Barassie
1980	England	9–6	Formby
1981	Halved	$7\frac{1}{2}$–$7\frac{1}{2}$	Gullane
1982	England	8–7	Burnham & Berrow
1983	England	8–7	Glenbervie
1984	England	$9\frac{1}{2}$–$5\frac{1}{2}$	Porthcawl
1985	England	10–5	Barnton
1986	Scotland	$8\frac{1}{2}$–$6\frac{1}{2}$	Seaton Carew
1987	Scotland	8–7	Barassie
1988	England	11–4	Formby
1989	England	8–7	Nairn
1990	Scotland	$10\frac{1}{2}$–$4\frac{1}{2}$	Hunstanton
1991	England	10–5	Montrose
1992	Scotland	10–5	R Mid-Surrey
1993	England	8–7	Glenbervie
1994	England	10–5	Little Aston

Wales *v* Ireland

Year	Winner	Result	Venue
1972	Ireland	5–4	Moortown
1973	Ireland	$5\frac{1}{2}$–$3\frac{1}{2}$	Blairgowrie
1974	Wales	5–4	Hoylake
1975	Wales	$6\frac{1}{2}$–$2\frac{1}{2}$	Bruntsfield
1976	Wales	71/2–$1\frac{1}{2}$	Sunningdale
1977	Ireland	61/2–51/2	Downfield
1978	Wales	8–4	Seaton Carew
1979	Ireland	$9\frac{1}{2}$–$2\frac{1}{2}$	Barassie
1980	Wales	$6\frac{1}{2}$–$5\frac{1}{2}$	Formby
1981	Ireland	8–4	Gullane
1982	Wales	9–3	Burnham & Berrow
1983	Ireland	7–5	Glenbervie
1984	Wales	$6\frac{1}{2}$–$5\frac{1}{2}$	Porthcawl
1985	Ireland	$11\frac{1}{2}$–$3\frac{1}{2}$	Barnton
1986	Ireland	$8\frac{1}{2}$–$6\frac{1}{2}$	Seaton Carew
1987	Wales	$10\frac{1}{2}$–$4\frac{1}{2}$	Barassie
1988	Wales	8–7	Formby
1989	Wales	$10\frac{1}{2}$–$4\frac{1}{2}$	Nairn
1990	Ireland	$8\frac{1}{2}$–$6\frac{1}{2}$	Hunstanton
1991	Wales	10–5	Montrose
1992	Wales	9–6	R Mid-Surrey
1993	Ireland	11–4	Glenbervie
1994	Ireland	$8\frac{1}{2}$–$6\frac{1}{2}$	Little Aston

R & A Trophy

This trophy is played between the winners of the England *v* Scotland and Wales *v* Ireland International Matches and was introduced in 1985.

Year	Winner	Result	Venue
1985 T	England Ireland	$7^1/_2$–$7^1/_2$	Barnton
1986	Ireland	$8^1/_2$–$6^1/_2$	Seaton Carew
1987	Scotland	$10^1/_2$–$4^1/_2$	Barassie
1988	England	14–1	Formby
1989	England	$11^1/_2$–$^1/_2$	Nairn
1990	Scotland	$12^1/_2$–$2^1/_2$	Hunstanton
1991	England	12–3	Montrose
1992 T	Wales Scotland	$7^1/_2$–$7^1/_2$	R Mid-Surrey
1993	England	11–4	Glenbervie
1994	England	$11^1/_2$–$3^1/_2$	Little Aston

British Youths' Open Amateur Championship

Year	Winner	Club/Country	Venue	Score
1954	JS More	Swanston, Edinburgh	Erskine	287
1955	B Stockdale	Royal Lytham St Annes	Pannal	297
1956	AF Bussell	Coxmoor	Barnton	287
1957	G Will	St Andrews	Pannal	290
1958	RH Kemp	Glamorganshire	Dumfries and County	281
1959	RA Jowle	Moseley	Pannal	286
1960	GA Caygill	Sunningdale	Pannal	279
1961	JS Martin	Kilbirnie Place	Bruntsfield	284
1962	GA Caygill	Sunningdale	Pannal	287
1963	AJ Low	St Andrews University	Pollok	283
1964	BW Barnes	Burnham and Berrow	Pannal	290
1965	PM Townsend	Porters Park	Cosforth Park	281
1966	PA Oosterhuis	Dulwich and Sydenham	Dalmahoy	219 *(54 holes)*
1967	PJ Benka	Addington	Copt Heath	278
1968	PJ Benka	Addington	Ayr Belleisle	281
1969	JH Cook	Calcot Park	Lindrick	289
1970	B Dassu	Italy	Barnton	276
1971	P Elson	Coventry	Northamptonshire	277
1972	AH Chandler	Regent Park	Glasgow Gailes	281
1973	SC Mason	Goring and Streatley	Southport and Ainsdale	284
1974	DM Robertson	Dunbar	Downfield	284
1975	N Faldo	Welwyn Garden City	Pannal	278
1976	ME Lewis	Henbury	Gullane	277
1977	A Lyle	Hawkstone Park	Moor Park	285
1978	B Marchbank	Auchterarder	East Renfrewshire	278
1979	G Brand Jr	Knowle	Woodhall Spa	291
1980	G Hay	Hilton Park	Troon	303
1981	T Antevik	Sweden	West Lancashire	290
1982	AP Parkin	Newtown	St Andrews New	280
1983	P Mayo	Newport	Sunningdale	290
1984	R Morris	Padeswick and Buckley	Blairgowrie	281
1985	JM Olazabal	Spain	Ganton	281
1986	D Gilford	GB	Carnoustie	283
1987 T	J Cook* O Nordberg	GB Sweden	Hollinwell	283
1988 T	C Cassells C Cevaer*	Murcar France	Royal Aberdeen	275
1989 T	M Smith* A Coltart	Brokenhurst Manor Thornhill	Ashburnham	285
1990	M Gronberg	Sweden	Southerness	275
1991	J Payne	Sandilands	Woodhall Spa	287
1992	W Bennett	Ruislip	Northumberland	282
1993	L Westwood	Worksop	Glasgow Gailes	278
1994	F Jacobson	Sweden	Royal St David's	277

* *Winner after play-off*

Youths' Internationals **England *v* Scotland**

Year	Winner	Result	Venue
1955	England	13–5	Pannal
1956	Scotland	+17 holes	Burgess
1957	*Not played*		
1958	England	+4 holes	Dumfries & County
1959	Scotland	12–6	Pannal
1960	Scotland	11½–6½	Pannal
1961	England	11½–6½	Bruntsfield
1962	England	9½–8½	Pannal
1963	Scotland	9–6	Pollok
1964	Scotland	9–6	Pannal
1965	Scotland	10½–3½	Northumberland
1966	England	9½–5½	Dalmahoy
1967	Halved	7½–7½	Copt Heath
1968	Scotland	8½–6½	Ayr Belleisle
1969	England	8½–6½	Lindrick
1970	Scotland	8½–6½	Barnton
1971	England	11–4	Northampton County
1972	England	11–4	Glasgow Gailes
1973	England	10–5	Southport & Ainsdale
1974	England	9–6	Downfield
1975	Scotland	11–4	Pannal
1976	England	8½–6½	Gullane
1977	Scotland	9½–5½	Moor Park
1978	Scotland	8½–6½	East Renfrewshire
1979	Halved	7½–7½	Woodhall Spa
1980	Scotland	9–6	Troon
1981	Scotland	8–7	West Lancs
1982	Halved	7½–7½	St Andrews New
1983	Scotland	8½–6½	Sunningdale
1984	Scotland	9–6	Blairgowrie
1985	Halved	7½–7½	Ganton
1986	Scotland	8–7	Carnoustie
1987	England	9½–5½	Hollinwell
1988	England	10–5	R. Aberdeen
1989	England	9–6	Ashburnham
1990	Scotland	9–6	Southerness
1991T	England Scotland	7½–7½	Woodhall Spa
1992	Scotland	10–5	Northumberland
1993	England	8–7	Glasgow Gailes
1994	Scotland	9½–5½	Royal St David's

Great Britain & Ireland *v* Continent of Europe, Youths (EGA Trophy)

Year	Winner	Result	Venue
1967	GB&I	8–7	Copt Heath
1968	GB&I	11–4	Ayr Belleisle
1969	GB&I	13½–1½	Lindrick
1970	GB&I	10½–4½	Barnton
1971	GB&I	10–5	Northampton County
1972	GB&I	11½–3½	Glasgow Gailes
1973	GB&I	10–5	Southport & Ainsdale
1974	GB&I	10–5	Downfield
1975	GB&I	9–6	Pannal
1976	GB&I	17–13	Chantilly
1977	GB&I	11½–3½	Moor Park
1978	GB&I	12½–2½	East Renfrewshire
1979	GB&I	12–3	Woodhall Spa
1980	Europe	13–11	Lunds Akademiska
1981	GB&I	7½–4½	West Lancs
1982	GB&I	7½–4½	St Andrews New
1983	GB&I	11–13	Punta Ala, Italy
1984	Halved	6–6	Blairgowrie
1985	GB&I	8–4	Ganton
1986	GB&I	13½–10½	Bilbao, Spain
1987	Europe	7–5	Hollinwell
1988	GB&I	13½–10½	Copenhagen
1989	GB&I	8½–3½	Ashburnham
1990	GB&I	14½–9½	Oporto, Portugal
1991	GB&I	14½–9½	Dalmahoy
1992	Europe	14–10	Bremen, Germany
1993	GB&I	16–8	Royal Troon
1994	GB&I	18–6	Golf de Pan, Holland

(Singles curtailed owing to weather)

English Boys' Amateur Open Stroke Play Championship

(Formerly Carris Trophy)

Year	Winner	Score
1935	R Upex	75
1936	JDA Langley	152
1937	RJ White	149
1938	IP Garrow	147
1939	CW Warren	149
1946	AH Perowne	158
1947	I Caldwell	159
1948	I Caldwell	152
1949	PB Hine	148
1950	J Glover	144
1951	I Young	154
1952	N Thygesen	150
1953	N Johnson	148
1954	K Warren	149
1955	ID Wheater	151
1956	G Maisey	141
1957	G Maisey	145
1958	J Hamilton	149
1959	RT Walker	152
1960	PM Baxter	150
1961	DJ Miller	143
1962	FS Morris	145
1963	EJ Threlfall	147
1964	PM Townsend	148
1965	G McKay	145
1966	A Black	151
1967	RF Brown	147
1968	P Dawson	149
1969	ID Gradwell	150
1970	MF Foster	146
1971	RJ Evans	146
1972	L Donovan	143
1973	S Hadfield	148
1974	KJ Brown	304
1975	A Lyle	270
1976	H Stott	285
1977	R Mugglestone	293
1978	J Plaxton	144
1979	P Hammond	288
1980	MP McLean	290
1981	D Gilford	290
1982	M Jarvis	298
1983	P Baker	288
1984	J Coe	283
1985	P Baker	286
1986	G Evans	292
1987	D Bathgate	289
1988	P Page	284
1989	I Garbutt	285
1990	M Welch	276
1991	I Pyman	284
1992	M Foster	286
1993	J Harris	285
1994	R Duck	280

Peter McEvoy Trophy *at Copt Heath*

Year	Winner	Year	Winner
1985	A Morley	1990	P Sherman
1986	C Mitchell	1991	L Westwood
1987	W Henry	1992	B Davis
1988	P Sefton	1993	S Webster
1989	D Bathgate	1994	J Harris

Scottish Boys' Championship

Year	Winner	Runner-up	Venue	By
1960	L Carver	S Wilson	North Berwick	6 and 5
1961	K Thomson	G Wilson	North Berwick	10 and 8
1962	HF Urquhart	S MacDonald	North Berwick	3 and 2
1963	FS Morris	I Clark	North Berwick	9 and 8
1964	WR Lockie	MD Cleghorn	North Berwick	1 hole
1965	RL Penman	J Wood	North Berwick	9 and 8
1966	J McTear	DG Greig	North Berwick	4 and 3
1967	DG Greig	I Cannon	North Berwick	2 and 1
1968	RD Weir	M Grubb	North Berwick	6 and 4
1969	RP Fyfe	IP Doig	North Berwick	4 and 2
1970	S Stephen	M Henry	North Berwick	38th hole
1971	JE Murray	AA Mackay	North Berwick	4 and 3
1972	DM Robertson	G Cairns	North Berwick	9 and 8
1973	R Watson	H Alexander	North Berwick	8 and 7
1974	DM Robertson	J Cuddihy	North Berwick	6 and 5
1975	A Brown	J Cuddihy	North Berwick	6 and 4
1976	B Marchbank	J Cuddihy	Dunbar	2 and 1
1977	JS Taylor	GJ Webster	Dunbar	3 and 2
1978	J Huggan	KW Stables	Dunbar	2 and 1
1979	DR Weir	S Morrison	West Kilbride	5 and 3
1980	R Gregan	AJ Currie	Dunbar	2 and 1
1981	C Stewart	G Mellon	Dunbar	3 and 2
1982	A Smith	J White	Dunbar	39th hole
1983	C Gillies	C Innes	Dunbar	38th hole
1984	K Buchan	L Vannet	Dunbar	2 and 1
1985	AD McQueen	FJ McCulloch	Dunbar	1 hole
1986	AG Tait	EA McIntosh	Dunbar	6 and 5
1987	AJ Coltart	SJ Bannerman	Dunbar	37th hole
1988	CA Fraser	F Clark	Dunbar	9 and 8
1989	M King	D Brolls	Dunbar	8 and 7
1990	B Collier	D Keeney	West Kilbride	2 and 1
1991	C Hislop	R Thorton	West Kilbride	11 and 9
1992	A Reid	A Forsyth	West Kilbride	2 and 1
1993	S Young	A Campbell	West Kilbride	4 and 2
1994	S Young	E Little	Dunbar	2 and 1

Scottish Boys' Open Amateur Stroke Play Championship

Year	Winner	Club	Venue	Score
1970	D Chillas	R Aberdeen	Carnoustie	298
1971	JE Murray	Baberton	Lanark	274
1972	S Martin	Downfield	Montrose	280
1973	S Martin	Carnoustie	Barnton	284
1974	PW Gallacher	Peebles	Lundin Links	290
1975	A Webster	Edzell	Kilmarnock Barassie	286
1976	A Webster	Edzell	Forfar	292
1977T	J Huggan	Winterfield	Renfrew	303
	L Mann			
1978	R Fraser	Hilton Park	Arbroath	283
1979	L Mann	Carnoustie	Stirling	289
1980	ASK Glen	Ormesson (France)	Forfar	288
1981	J Gullen	Tillicoultry	Bellshill	296
1982	D Purdie	Turriff	Monifieth	296
1983	L Vannet	Carnoustie	Barassie	286
1984	K Walker	Royal Burgess	Carnoustie	280
1985	G Matthew	Melrose	Baberton	297

continued

Year	Winner	Club	Venue	Score
1986	G Cassells	Cruden Bay	Edzell	294
1987	C Ronald	Torrance House	Lanark	287
1988	M Urquhart	Inverness	Dumfries and County	280
1989	C Fraser	Burntisland	Stirling	282
1990	N Archibald	Kingsknowe	Monifieth	292
1991	S Gallacher	Ratho Park	Crieff	280
1992	S Gallacher	Bathgate	Monifieth	288
1993	J Bunch	St Andrews, New	Powfoot	292
1994	S Young	Inverallochy	Drumpellier	288

Welsh Boys' Championship

Year	Winner	Runner–up	Venue	By
1960	C Gilford	JL Toye	Llandrindod Wells	5 and 4
1961	AR Porter	JL Toye	Llandrindod Wells	3 and 2
1962	RC Waddilove	W Wadrup	Harlech	20th hole
1963	G Matthews	R Witchell	Penarth	6 and 5
1964	D Lloyd	M Walters	Conway	2 and 1
1965	G Matthews	DG Lloyd	Wenvoe Castle	7 and 6
1966	J Buckley	DP Owen	Holyhead	4 and 2
1967	J Buckley	DL Stevens	Glamorganshire	2 and 1
1968	J Buckley	C Brown	Maesdu	1 hole
1969	K Dabson	P Light	Glamorganshire	5 and 3
1970	P Tadman	A Morgan	Conway	2 and 1
1971	R Jenkins	TJ Melia	Ashburnham	3 and 2
1972	MG Chugg	RM Jones	Wrexham	3 and 2
1973	R Tate	N Duncan	Penarth	2 and 1
1974	D Williams	S Lewis	Llandudno	5 and 4
1975	G Davies	PG Garrett	Glamorganshire	20th hole
1976	JM Morrow	MG Mouland	Caernarvonshire	1 hole
1977	JM Morrow	MG Mouland	Glamorganshire	2 and 1
1978	JM Morrow	A Laking	Harlech	2 and 1
1979	P Mayo	M Hayward	Penarth	24th hole
1980	A Llyr	DK Wood	Llandudno (Maesdu)	2 and 1
1981	M Evans	P Webborn	Pontypool	5 and 4
1982	CM Rees	KH Williams	Prestatyn	2 holes
1983	MA Macara	RN Roderick	Radyr	1 hole
1984	GA Macara	D Bagg	Llandudno	1 hole
1985	B Macfarlane	R Herbert	Cardiff	1 hole
1986	C O'Carroll	GA Macara	Rhuddlan	1 hole
1987	SJ Edwards	A Herbert	Abergavenny	19th hole
1988	C Platt	P Murphy	Holyhead	2 and 1
1989	R Johnson	RL Evans	Southerndown	2 holes
1990	M Ellis	C Sheppard	Llandudno (Maesdu)	3 and 2
1991	B Dredge	A Cooper	Tenby	2 and 1
1992	Y Taylor	J Pugh	Wrexham	1 hole
1993	R Davies	S Raybould	Pyle and Kenfig	3 and 2
1994	R Peet	K Sullivan	Abergele & Pensarn	7 and 6

European Boys' Team Championship

Year	Winner	Venue
1980	Spain	El Prat Golf Club, Barcelona
1981	England	Olgiata Golf Club, Rome
1982	Italy	Frankfurt Golf Club, West Germany
1983	Sweden	Helsinki Golf Club, Finland
1984	Scotland	Royal St George's Golf Club, England
1985	England	Troia Golf Club, Portugal
1986	England	Turin Golf Club, Italy
1987	Scotland	Chantilly Golf Club, France
1988	France	Renfrew Golf Club, Scotland
1989	England	Lyckoma, Sweden
1990	Spain	Reykjavik, Iceland
1991	Sweden	Oslo, Norway
1992	Scotland	Conwy, Wales
1993	Sweden	Ascona, Switzerland
1994	England	Vilamoura, Portugal

Great Britain and Ireland *v* Continent of Europe, Boys (Jacques Leglise Trophy)

Year	Winner	Result	Venue
1958	GB&I	$11^1/_2$–$^1/_2$	Moortown
1959	GB&I	7–2	Pollok
1960	GB&I	8–7	Olton
1961	GB&I	11–4	Dalmahoy
1962	GB&I	11–4	Mid-Surrey
1963	GB&I	12–3	Prestwick
1964	GB&I	12–1	Formby
1965	GB&I	12–1	Gullane
1966	GB&I	10–2	Moortown
1967–76	*Not played*		
1977	Europe	7–6	Downfield
1978	Europe	7–6	Seaton Carew
1979	GB&I	$9^1/_2$–$2^1/_2$	Barassie
1980	GB&I	7–5	Formby
1981	GB&I	8–4	Gullane
1982	GB&I	11–1	Burnham & Berrow
1983	GB&I	$6^1/_2$–$5^1/_2$	Glenbervie
1984	GB&I	$6^1/_2$–$5^1/_2$	Porthcawl
1985	GB&I	$7^1/_2$–$4^1/_2$	Barnton
1986	Europe	$8^1/_2$–$3^1/_2$	Seaton Carew
1987	GB&I	$7^1/_2$–$4^1/_2$	Barassie
1988	GB&I	$5^1/_2$–$2^1/_2$	Formby
1989	GB&I	$7^1/_2$–$4^1/_2$	Nairn
1990	GB&I	10–2	Hunstanton
1991	GB&I	$6^1/_2$–$5^1/_2$	Montrose
1992	GB&I	8–7	Royal Mid-Surrey
1993	GB&I	8–7	Glenbervie
1994	GB&I	$12^1/_2$–$2^1/_2$	Little Aston

Girls' British Open Amateur Championship

Year	Winner	Runner-up	Venue	By
1960	S Clarke	AL Irvin	Barassie	2 and 1
1961	D Robb	J Roberts	Beaconsfield	3 and 2
1962	S McLaren-Smith	A Murphy	Foxton Hall	2 and 1
1963	D Oxley	B Whitehead	Gullane	2 and 1
1964	P Tredinnick	K Cumming	Camberley Heath	2 and 1
1965	A Willard	A Ward	Formby	3 and 2
1966	J Hutton	D Oxley	Troon Portland	20th hole
1967	P Burrows	J Hutton	Liphook	2 and 1
1968	C Wallace	C Reybroeck	Leven	4 and 3
1969	J de Witt Puyt	C Reybroeck	Ilkley	2 and 1
1970	C Le Feuvre	Michelle Walker	North Wales	2 and 1
1971	J Mark	Maureen Walker	North Berwick	4 and 3
1972	Maureen Walker	S Cadden	Norwich	2 and 1
1973	AM Palli	N Jeanson	Northamptonshire	2 and 1
1974	R Barry	T Perkins	Dunbar	1 hole
1975	S Cadden	L Isherwood	Henbury	4 and 3
1976	G Stewart	S Rowlands	Pyle and Kenfig	5 and 4
1977	W Aitken	S Bamford	Formby Ladies	2 and 1
1978	M L de Lorenzi	D Glenn	Largs	2 and 1
1979	S Lapaire	P Smilie	Edgbaston	19th hole
1980	J Connachan	L Bolton	Wrexham	2 holes
1981	J Connachan	P Grice	Woodbridge	20th hole
1982	C Waite	M Mackie	Edzell	6 and 5
1983	E Orley	A Walters	Leeds	7 and 6
1984	C Swallow	E Farquharson	Maesdu	1 hole
1985	S Shapcott	E Farquharson	Hesketh	3 and 1
1986	S Croce	S Bennett	West Kilbride	5 and 4
1987	H Dobson	S Croce	Barnham Broom	19th hole
1988	A Macdonald	J Posener	Pyle and Kenfig	3 and 2
1989	M McKinlay	S Eriksson	Carlisle	19th hole
1990	S Cavalleri	E Valera	Penrith	5 and 4
1991	M Hjorth	J Moodie	Whitchurch	3 and 2
1992	M McKay	L Navarro	Northamptonshire	2 holes
1993	M McKay	A Vincent	Helensburgh	4 and 3
1994	A Vincent	R Hudson	Gog Magog	1 up

English Girls' Championship

Year	Winner	Runner-up	Venue	By
1964	S Ward	P Tredinnick	Wollaton Park	2 and 1
1965	D Oxley	A Payne	Edgbaston	2 holes
1966	B Whitehead	D Oxley	Woodbridge	1 hole
1967	A Willard	G Holloway	Burhill	1 hole
1968	K Phillips	C le Feuvre	Harrogate	6 and 5
1969	C le Feuvre	K Phillips	Hawkstone Park	2 and 1
1970	C le Feuvre	M Walker	High Post	2 and 1
1971	C Eckersley	J Stevens	Liphook	4 and 3
1972	C Barker	R Kelly	Trentham	4 and 3
1973	S Parker	S Thurston	Lincoln	19th hole
1974	C Langford	L Harrold	Knowle	2 and 1
1975	M Burton	R Barry	Formby	6 and 5
1976	H Latham	D Park	Moseley	3 and 2
1977	S Bamford	S Jolly	Chelmsford	21st hole
1978	P Smillie	J Smith	Willesley Park	3 and 2
1979	L Moore	P Barry	Cirencester	1 hole
1980	P Smillie	J Soulsby	Kedleston Park	3 and 2
1981	J Soulsby	C Waite	Worksop	7 and 5
1982	C Waite	P Grice	Wilmslow	3 and 2
1983	P Grice	K Mitchell	West Surrey	2 and 1
1984	C Swallow	S Duhig	Bath	3 and 1
1985	L Fairclough	K Mitchell	Coventry	6 and 5
1986	S Shapcott	N Way	Huddersfield	7 and 6
1987	S Shapcott	S Morgan	Sandy Lodge	1 hole
1988	H Dobson	S Shapcott	Long Ashton	1 hole
1989	H Dobson	A MacDonald	Edgbaston	3 and 1
1990	C Hall	J Hockley	Bolton Old Links	20th hole
1991	N Buxton	C Hall	Knole Park	2 and 1
1992	F Brown	L Nicholson	Finham Park	2 and 1
1993	G Simpson	L Wixon	Cotswold Hills	7 and 5
1994	K Hamilton	S Forster	Whitley Bay	3 and 2

Irish Girls' Championship

Year	Winner	Runner-up	Venue	By
1961	M Coburn	C McAuley	Portrush	6 and 5
1962	P Boyd	P Atkinson	Elm Park	4 and 3
1963	P Atkinson	C Scarlett	Donaghadee	8 and 7
1964	C Scarlett	A Maher	Milltown	6 and 5
1965	V Singleton	P McKenzie	Ballycastle	7 and 6
1966	M McConnell	D Hulme	Dun Laoghaire	3 and 2
1967	M McConnell	C Wallace	Portrush	6 and 5
1968	C Wallace	A McCoy	Louth	3 and 1
1969	EA McGregor	M Sheenan	Knock	6 and 5
1970	EA McGregor	J Mark	Greystones	3 and 2
1971	J Mark	C Nesbitt	Belfast	3 and 2
1972	P Smyth	M Governey	Elm Park	1 hole
1973	M Governey	R Hegarty	Mullingar	3 and 1
1974	R Hegarty	M Irvine	Castletroy	2 holes
1975	M Irvine	P Wickham	Carlow	2 and 1
1976	P Wickham	R Hegarty	Castle	5 and 3
1977	A Ferguson	R Walsh	Birr	3 and 2
1978	C Wickham	B Gleeson	Killarney	1 hole
1979	L Bolton	B Gleeson	Milltown	3 and 2
1980	B Gleeson	L Bolton	Kilkenny	5 and 3
1981	B Gleeson	E Lynn	Donegal	1 hole
1982	D Langan	S Lynn	Headfort	5 and 4
1983	E McDaid	S Lynn	Ennis	20th hole
1984	S Sheehan	L Tormey	Thurles	6 and 4
1985	S Sheehan	D Hanna	Laytown/Bettystown	5 and 4
1986	D Mahon	T Eakin	Mallow	4 and 3
1987	V Greevy	B Ryan	Galway	8 and 7
1988	L McCool	P Gorman	Courtown	3 and 2
1989	A Rogers	R MacGuigan	Athlone	2 and 1
1990	G Doran	L McCool	Royal Portrush	3 and 1
1991	A Rogers	D Powell	Mallow	2 and 1
1992	M McGreevy	N Gorman	Kilkenny	2 and 1
1993	M McGreevy	E Dowdall	Strandhill	2 and 1
1994	A O'Leary	D Doyle	Mullingar	23rd hole

Scottish Girls' Open Stroke Play Championship

Year	Winner	Venue
1960	J Greenhalgh	Ranfurly Castle
1961	D Robb	Whitecraigs
1962	S Armitage	Dalmahoy
1963	A Irvin	Dumfries
1964	M Nuttall	Dalmahoy
1965	I Wylie	Carnoustie
1966	J Smith	Douglas Park
1967	J Bourassa	Dunbar
1968	K Phillips	Dumfries
1969	K Phillips	Prestonfield
1970	B Huke	Leven
1971	B Huke	Dalmahoy
1972	L Hope	Troon, Portland
1973	G Cadden	Edzell
1974	S Lambie	Stranraer
1975	S Cadden	Lanark
1976	S Cadden	Prestonfield
1977	S Cadden	Edzell

Year	Winner	Venue
1978	J Connachan	Peebles
1979	A Gemmill	Troon, Portland
1980	J Connachan	Kirkcaldy
1981	K Douglas	Downfield
1982	J Rhodes	Dumfries & Galloway
1983	S Lawson	Largs
1984	S Lawson	Dunbar
1985	K Imrie	Ballater
1986	K Imrie	Dumfries and County
1987	K Imrie	Douglas Park
1988	C Lambert	Baberton
1989	C Lambert	Dunblane New
1990	J Moodie	Royal Troon
1991	C Macdonald	Alyth
1992	L McCool	North Berwick
1993	J Moodie	Dumfries and County
1994	C Agnew	Dumfries and County

Scottish Girls' Close Amateur Championship

Year	Winner	Runner-up	Venue	By
1960	J Hastings	A Lurie	Kilmacolm	6 and 4
1961	I Wylie	W Clark	Murrayfield	3 and 1
1962	I Wylie	U Burnet	West Kilbride	3 and 1
1963	M Norval	S MacDonald	Carnoustie	6 and 4
1964	JW Smith	C Workman	West Kilbride	2 and 1
1965	JW Smith	I Walker	Leven	7 and 5
1966	J Hutton	F Jamieson	Arbroath	2 holes
1967	J Hutton	K Lackie	West Kilbride	4 and 2
1968	M Dewar	J Crawford	Dalmahoy	2 holes
1969	C Panton	A Coutts	Edzell	23rd hole
1970	M Walker	L Bennett	Largs	3 and 2
1971	M Walker	S Kennedy	Edzell	1 hole
1972	G Cadden	C Panton	Stirling	3 and 2
1973	M Walker	M Thomson	Cowal, Dunoon	1 hole
1974	S Cadden	D Reid	Arbroath	3 and 1
1975	W Aitken	S Cadden	Leven	1 hole
1976	S Cadden	D Mitchell	Dumfries and County	4 and 2
1977	W Aitken	G Wilson	West Kilbride	2 holes
1978	J Connachan	D Mitchell	Stirling	7 and 5
1979	J Connachan	G Wilson	Dunbar	3 and 1
1980	J Connachan	P Wright	Dumfries and County	21st hole
1981	D Thomson	P Wright	Barassie	2 and 1
1982	S Lawson	D Thomson	Montrose	1 hole
1983	K Imrie	D Martin	Leven	2 and 1
1984	T Craik	D Jackson	Peebles	3 and 2
1985	E Farquharson	E Moffat	West Kilbride	2 holes
1986	C Lambert	F McKay	Nairn	4 and 3
1987	S Little	L Moretti	Stirling	3 and 2
1988	J Jenkins	F McKay	Dumfries and County	4 and 3
1989	J Moodie	V Melvin	Kilmacolm	19th hole
1990	M McKay	J Moodie	Duff House Royal	3 and 2
1991	J Moodie	M McKay	Leven Links	5 and 4
1992	M McKay	L Nicholson	Powfoot	2 and 1
1993	C Agnew	H Stirling	Baberton	19th hole
1994	C Nicholson	L Moffat	Deeside	3 and 1

Welsh Girls' Amateur Championship

Year	Winner	Runner-up	Venue	By
1960	A Hughes	D Wilson	Llandrindod Wells	6 and 4
1961	J Morris	S Kelly	North Wales	3 and 2
1962	J Morris	P Morgan	Southerndown	4 and 3
1963	A Hughes	A Brown	Conway	8 and 7

Year	Winner	Runner–up	Venue	By
1964	A Hughes	M Leigh	Holyhead	5 and 3
1965	A Hughes	A Reardon-Hughes	Swansea Bay	19th hole
1966	S Hales	J Rogers	Prestatyn	1 hole
1967	E Wilkie	L Humphreys	Pyle and Kenfig	1 hole
1968	L Morris	J Rogers	Portmadoc	1 hole
1969	L Morris	L Humphreys	Wenvoe Castle	5 and 3
1970	T Perkins	P Light	Rhuddlan	2 and 1
1971	P Light	P Whitley	Glamorganshire	4 and 3
1972	P Whitley	P Light	Llandudno (Maesdu)	2 and 1
1973	V Rawlings	T Perkins	Whitchurch	19th hole
1974	L Isherwood	S Rowlands	Wrexham	4 and 3
1975	L Isherwood	S Rowlands	Swansea Bay	1 hole
1976	K Rawlings	C Parry	Rhuddlan	5 and 4
1977	S Rowlands	D Taylor	Clyne	7 and 5
1978	S Rowlands	G Rees	Abergele	3 and 2
1979	M Rawlings	J Richards	St Mellons	19th hole
1980	K Davies	M Rawlings	Vale of Llangollen	19th hole
1981	M Rawlings	F Connor	Radyr	4 and 3
1982	K Davies	K Beckett	Wrexham	6 and 5
1983	N Wesley	J Foster	Whitchurch	4 and 2
1984	J Foster	J Evans	Pwllheli	6 and 5
1985	J Foster	S Caley	Langland Bay	6 and 5
1986	J Foster	L Dermott	Holyhead	3 and 2
1987	J Lloyd	S Bibbs	Cardiff	2 and 1
1988	L Dermott	A Perriam	Builth Wells	2 holes
1989	L Dermott	N Stroud	Carmarthen	4 and 2
1990	L Dermott	N Stroud	Padeswood and Buckley	6 and 4
1991	S Boyes	R Morgan	Clyne	3 and 1
1992	B Jones	S Musto	Rhuddlan	2 and 1
1993	K Stark	S Tudor-Jones	Radyr	3 and 2
1994	K Stark	J Evans	Wrexham	4 and 3

European Girls' Team Championship

Year	Winner	Second	Venue
1990	Sweden	England	Shannon, Ireland
1992	Spain	Sweden	St Nom–la–Breteche, France
1994	Sweden	France	Gutenhof, Vienna, Austria

Girls' Home Internationals: Stroyan Cup

Year	Winner	Venue
1966	Scotland	Troon (Portland)
1967	England	Liphook
1968	England	Leven
1969	England	Ilkley
1970	England	North Wales
1971	England	North Berwick
1972	Scotland	Royal Norwich
1973	Scotland	Northamptonshire County
1974	England	Dunbar
1975	England	Henbury
1976	Scotland	Pyle and Kenfig
1977	England	Formby Ladies
1978	England	Largs
1979	England	Edgbaston
1980	England	Wrexham
1981	England	Woodbridge
1982	England	Edzell
1983	England	Alwoodley
1984	Scotland	Llandudno (Maesdu)
1985	England	Hesketh GC
1986	England	West Kilbride
1987	England	Barnham Broom
1988	England	Pyle and Kenfig

1989
at Carlisle

Ireland beat Scotland	$4^1/_2$–$2^1/_2$
England beat Wales	4–3
Ireland beat Wales	$4^1/_2$–$2^1/_2$
England beat Scotland	5–2
Scotland beat Wales	4–3
England beat Ireland	$4^1/_2$–$2^1/_2$

Result: England 3; Ireland 2; Scotland 1; Wales 0

1990
at Penrith

England beat Wales	7–2
Ireland beat Scotland	6–3
England beat Scotland	8–1
Ireland beat Wales	9–0
England beat Ireland	$7^1/_2$–$1^1/_2$
Scotland beat Wales	7–2

Result: England 3; Ireland 2; Scotland 1; Wales 0

Girls' Home Internationals: Stroyan Cup *continued*

1991
at Whitchurch

Scotland halved with England	4½–4½
Ireland beat Wales	5½–3½
Wales halved with Scotland	4½–4½
England beat Ireland	7½–1½
England beat Wales	8–1
Ireland beat Scotland	5½–3½

Result: England 2½; Ireland 2; Scotland 1; Wales ½

1992
at Moseley

Scotland beat Ireland	6½–2½
England beat Wales	6½–2½
Scotland beat Wales	8½–½
England beat Ireland	7½–1½
Ireland beat Wales	7–2
Scotland beat England	5–4

Result: Scotland 3; England 2; Ireland 1; Wales 0

1993
at Helensburgh

Scotland beat Wales	8–1
England beat Ireland	7½–1½
Ireland beat Wales	9–0
Scotland beat England	7½–1½
Scotland beat Ireland	6–3
England beat Wales	9–0

Result: Scotland 3; England 2; Ireland 1; Wales 0

1994
at Gog Magog

England beat Wales	7–2
Scotland halved with Ireland	4½–4½
England beat Ireland	5–4
Scotland beat Wales	7–2
Ireland beat Wales	7–2
Scotland beat England	7–2

Result: Scotland 2½; England 2; Ireland 1½; Wales 0

Irish Youths' Open Amateur Championship

Year	Winner	Venue	Score
1980	J McHenry	Clandeboye	296
1981	J McHenry	Westport	303
1982	K O'Donnell	Mullingar	286
1983	P Murphy	Cork	287
1984	JC Morris	Bangor	292
1985	J McHenry	Co Sligo	287
1986	JC Morris	Carlow	280
1987	C Everett	Killarney	300
1988	P McGinley	Malone	283
1989	A Mathers	Athlone	280
1990	D Errity	Dundalk	293
1991	R Coughlan	Lahinch	288
1992	K Nolan	Clandeboye	275
1993	CD Hislop	Co Sligo	279
1994	B O'Melia	Tullamore	272

Scottish Youths' Open Amateur Stroke Play Championship

Year	Winner	Venue	Score
1979	A Oldcorn	Dalmahoy	217
1980	G Brand, Jr	Monifieth and Ashludie	281
1981	S Campbell	Cawder and Keir	279
1982	LS Mann	Leven and Scoonie	270
1983	A Moir	Mortonhall	284
1984	B Shields	Eastwood, Renfrew	280
1985	H Kemp	East Kilbride	282
1986	A Mednick	Cawder	282
1987	K Walker	Bogside	291
1988	P McGinley	Ladybank & Glenrothes	281
1989	J Mackenzie	Longniddry	281
1990	S Bannerman	Portpatrick and Stranraer	213 *(54 holes)*
1991	D Robertson	Hilton Park	273
1992	R Russell	Nairn	296
1993	CD Hislop	West Kilbride	284
1994	S Gallacher	Crieff	275

Ulster Youths' Open Amateur Championship

Year	Winner
1985	J Carvill
1986	DA Mulholland
1987	J Carvill
1988	G McAllister
1989	G Moore
1990	N Crawford
1991	P Russell
1992	C Feenan
1993	P Collins
1994	A McCormick

European Youths' Team Championship

Year	Winner	Second	Venue
1990	Italy	Sweden	Turin, Italy
1992	Sweden	England	Helsinki, Finland
1994	Ireland	Sweden	Esbjerg, Denmark

Golf Foundation Age Group Championships

Under 16

Year	Boys	Girls
1987	I Garbutt (Wheatley)	L Walton (Calcot Park)
1988	L Westwood (Worksop)	V Melvin (Clydebank & District)
1989	K Harrison (Cottesmore)	S Boyes (Wenvoe Castle)
1990	C Lane (Kingsthorpe)	T Poulton (Boyce Hill)
1991	G Harris (Broome Manor)	G Simpson (Cleckheaton & District)
1992	C Leach (Gillingham)	H Stirling (Bridge of Allan)
1993	K Godfrey (St Enodoc)	K Wrigglesworth (Hornsea)
1994	A Smith (Rhondda)	L Meredith (Wentworth)

Under 15

Year	Boys	Girls
1987	L Westwood (Worksop)	N Buxton (Woodsome Hall)
1988	B Collier (Callander)	J Williamson (Hadley Wood)
1989	C Lane (Kingsthorpe)	N Gorman (Balmoral)
1990	G Harris (Broome Manor)	V Hanks (Broome Manor)
1991	C Richardson (Burghley Park)	D Doyle (Lahinch)
1992	S Walker (Walmley)	G Nutter (Prestwich)
1993	S Young (Seascale)	R Hudson (Wheatley)
1994	T Hilton (Lewes)	L Moffat (W. Kilbride)

Under 14

Year	Boys	Girls
1987	N Heron (Ashridge)	L Tupholme (Northcliffe)
1988	S Pigott (West Malling)	M McKay (Turnberry)
1989	G Harris (Broome Manor)	V Hanks (Broome Manor)
1990	P Collier (Limerick)	K Wrigglesworth (Hornsea)
1991	J Bajcer (Church Stretton)	E Wilcock (Sherwood Forest)
1992	D Kirton (Worksop)	R Hudson (Wheatley)
1993	J Rose (North Hants)	L Walters (Ormonde Fields)
1994	A Smith (Enville)	V Laing (Musselburgh)

Under 13

Year	Boys	Girls
1987	M Neil (Stirling)	M McKay (Turnberry)
1988	P Drew (Worthing)	
1989	A Cooper (Taymouth Castle)	
1990	S Walker (Boldmere)	
1991	N Rossin (John O'Gaunt)	
1992	D Main (Moray)	
1993	S Godfrey (St Enodoc)	
1994	D Tarbotton (Hull)	

County and District Championships

Aberdeenshire Ladies' Championship

Year	Winner	Year	Winner
1985	P Wright	1990	E Farquharson
1986	E Farquharson	1991	C Middleton
1987	E Farquharson	1992	R MacLennan
1988	L Urquhart	1993	G Penny
1989	J Forbes	1994	C Hunter

Anglesey Amateur Championship

Year	Winner	Year	Winner
1985	I Furlong	1990	D McLean
1986	M Perdue	1991	J Campbell
1987	S Owen	1992	D McLean
1988	EO Jones	1993	M Perdue
1989	M Robinson	1994	J Campbell

Angus Amateur Championship

Year	Winner	Year	Winner
1988	D Downie	1992	D Downie
1989	T Peebles	1993	G Dough
1990	D Leith	1994	J Ray
1991	W Taylor		

Angus Ladies' Championship

Year	Winner	Year	Winner
1985	M Mackie	1990	K Sutherland
1986	F Farquharson	1991	M Summers
1987	F Farquharson	1992	M Summers
1988	C Hay	1993	M Summers
1989	C Hope	1994	M Summers

Argyll and Bute Amateur Championship

Year	Winner	Year	Winner
1985	G Reynolds	1990	G Reynolds
1986	G Tyre	1991	G Bolton
1987	S Campbell	1992	G Bolton
1988	G Bolton	1993	G Tyre-Cole
1989	G Tyre	1994	G Bolton

Ayrshire Amateur Championship

Year	Winner	Year	Winner
1985	P Girvan	1990	R Crawford
1986	G Armstrong	1991	JA Thomson
1987	B Gemmell	1992	G Lawrie
1988	G Blair	1993	G Sherry
1989	D Hawthorn	1994	G Lawrie

Ayrshire Ladies' Championship

Year	Winner	Year	Winner
1985	J Leishman	1990	C Gibson
1986	A Gemmill	1991	A Gemmill
1987	A Gemmill	1992	C Gibson
1988	M Wilson	1993	M Wilson
1989	A Gemmill	1994	A Gemmill

Bedfordshire Amateur Championship

Year	Winner	Year	Winner
1985	R Harris	1990	D Charlton
1986	M Wharton	1991	M Wharton
1987	P Wharton	1992	L Watcham
1988	P Wharton	1993	C Beard
1989	C Staroscik	1994	J Kemp

Bedfordshire Ladies' Championship

Year	Winner	Year	Winner
1985	S White	1990	C Cummings
1986	C Westgate	1991	E James
1987	S White	1992	S Cormack
1988	S Cormack	1993	S Cormack
1989	T Gale	1994	T Gale

Berks, Bucks and Oxfordshire Amateur Championship

Year	Winner	Year	Winner
1985	M Rapley	1990	S Barwick
1986	D Lane	1991	VL Phillips
1987	F George	1992	VL Phillips
1988	F George	1993	R Walton
1989	H Bareham	1994	D Fisher

Berkshire Ladies' Championship

Year	Winner	Year	Winner
1985	A Uzielli	1990	A Uzielli
1986	A Uzielli	1991	A Uzielli
1987	A Uzielli	1992	J Guntrip
1988	T Smith	1993	A Uzielli
1989	L Walton	1994	J Guntrip

Border Counties Ladies' Championship

Year	Winner	Year	Winner
1985	S Gallacher	1990	J Anderson
1986	S Gallacher	1991	J Anderson
1987	S Simpson	1992	J Anderson
1988	A Hunter	1993	D Turnbull
1989	A Fleming	1994	W Wells

Border Golfers' Association Amateur Championship

Year	Winner	Year	Winner
1985	L Wallace	1990	M Thomson
1986	L Wallace	1991	A Turnbull
1987	D Ballantyne	1992	M Thomson
1988	W Renwick	1993	D Valentine
1989	A Turnbull	1994	M Thomson

Bucks Ladies' Championship

Year	Winner	Year	Winner
1985	E Franklin	1990	C Watson
1986	A Tyreman	1991	C Watson
1987	C Watson	1992	C Watson
1988	C Hourihane	1993	C Watson
1989	C Hourihane	1994	P Williamson

Caernarfonshire and District Amateur Championship

Year	Winner	Year	Winner
1985	M Macara	1990	D McLean
1986	R Roberts	1991	J Dabecki
1987	D McLean	1992	D McLean
1988	D McLean	1993	E Jones
1989	W Jones	1994	D McLean

Caernarfonshire Amateur Championship Cup

Year	Winner	Year	Winner
1989	M Sheppard	1992	MA Macara
1990	I Jones	1993	L Harpin
1991	R Williams	1994	J Dabecki

Caernarvonshire and Anglesey Ladies' Championship

Year	Winner	Year	Winner
1985	A Lewis	1990	S Roberts
1986	S Turner	1991	*Not played*
1987	S Roberts	1992	S Turner
1988	S Turner	1993	A Lewis
1989	S Roberts	1994	C Thomas

Cambridge Area GU Amateur Championship

Year	Winner	Year	Winner
1985	D Wood	1990	G Stevenson
1986	J Miller	1991	M Seaton
1987	R Claydon	1992	LG Yearn
1988	R Claydon	1993	LG Yearn
1989	B Jackson	1994	A Emery

Cambridgeshire and Hunts Ladies' Championship

Year	Winner	Year	Winner
1985	J Walter	1990	J Walter
1986	J Walter	1991	J Walter
1987	R Farrow	1992	T Eakin
1988	S Meadows	1993	T Eakin
1989	J Hatcher	1994	T Eakin

Channel Islands Amateur Championship

Year	Winner	Year	Winner
1985	DJ Warr	1990	TA Gray
1986	ND Le Noury	1991	R Eggo
1987	J McGarragle	1992	C Chevalier
1988	DA Rowlinson	1993	B Eggo
1989	TA Gray	1994	C Chevalier

Channel Islands Ladies' Championship

Year	Winner	Year	Winner
1985	L Cummins	1990	L Cummins
1986	V Bougourd	1991	L Cummins
1987	L Cummins	1992	V Bougourd
1988	L Cummins	1993	L Cummins
1989	L Cummins	1994	L Cummins

Cheshire Amateur Championship

Year	Winner	Year	Winner
1985	C Harrison	1990	J Berry
1986	P Bailey	1991	D Bathgate
1987	P Jones	1992	A Hill
1988	P Bailey	1993	J Hodgson
1989	P Bailey	1994	J Hodgson

Cheshire Ladies' Championship

Year	Winner	Year	Winner
1985	L Percival	1990	J Morley
1986	J Hill	1991	F Brown
1987	S Robinson	1992	J Morley
1988	J Morley	1993	J Morley
1989	J Morley	1994	F Brown

Clackmannanshire Amateur Championship

Year	Winner	Year	Winner
1988	R Stewart	1992	G Kennedy
1989	J Gullen	1993	S Horne
1990	P MacLeod	1994	P McLeod
1991	AJ Watson		

Cornwall Amateur Championship

Year	Winner	Year	Winner
1985	C Phillips	1990	M Edmunds
1986	R Simmons	1991	I Veale
1987	P Clayton	1992	P Clayton
1988	P Clayton	1993	C Phillips
1989	C Phillips	1994	R Binney

Cornwall Ladies' Championship

Year	Winner	Year	Winner
1985	J Fern	1990	S Currie
1986	J Ryder	1991	S Currie
1987	J Ryder	1992	G Fields
1988	S Currie	1993	J Ryder
1989	S Currie	1994	E Fields

County Champions' Tournament (England)

(Formerly President's Bowl)

Year	Winner
1962 T	G Edwards, Cheshire A Thirwell, Northumberland
1963 T	M Burgess, Sussex R Foster, Yorks
1964	M Attenborough, Kent
1965	M Lees, Lincs
1966	R Stephenson, Middx
1967	P Benka, Surrey
1968	G Hyde, Sussex
1969	A Holmes, Herts
1970	M King, Berks, Bucks and Oxon
1971	M Lee, Yorks
1972	P Berry, Glos
1973	A Chandler, Lancs
1974 T	G Hyde, Sussex A Lyle, Shrops & Hereford
1975	N Faldo, Herts
1976	R Brown, Devon
1977	M Walls, Cumbria
1978	I Simpson, Notts
1979	N Burch, Essex
1980	D Lane, Berks, Bucks and Oxon
1981	M Kelly, Yorks
1982	P Deeble, Northumberland
1983	N Chesses, Warwickshire
1984 T	N Briggs, Herts P McEvoy, Warwickshire
1985	P Robinson, Herts
1986	A Gelsthorpe, Yorks
1987 T	F George, Berks, Bucks & Oxon D Fay, Surrey
1988	R Claydon, Cambridge
1989	R Willison, Middlesex
1990 T	P Streeter, Lincs R Sloman, Kent
1991	T Allen, Warwickshire
1992	L Westwood, Notts
1993	R Walker, Durham
1994	G Wolstenholme, Glos

Cumbria Amateur Championship *(Formerly Cumberland and Westmorland Amateur Championship)*

Year	Winner	Year	Winner
1985	J Longcake	1990	G Winter
1986	M Ruddick	1991	G Winter
1987	J Longcake	1992	A Greenbank
1988	G Waters	1993	R Secular
1989	G Winter	1994	B Story

Cumbria Ladies' Championship

Year	Winner	Year	Winner
1985	J Currie	1990	S Tuck
1986	H Porter	1991	J Currie
1987	J McColl	1992	J Currie
1988	D Thomson	1993	J Currie
1989	S Tuck	1994	J Currie

Denbighshire and Flintshire Ladies' Championship

Year	Winner	Year	Winner
1985	E Davies	1990	L Dermott
1986	S Thomas	1991	B Jones
1987	S Thomas	1992	B Jones
1988	S Thomas	1993	S Lovatt
1989	S Thomas	1994	A Donne

Derbyshire Amateur Championship

Year	Winner	Year	Winner
1985	R Davenport	1990	R Fletcher
1986	J Feeney	1991	J Feeney
1987	R Green	1992	J Feeney
1988	N Wylde	1993	G Shaw
1989	P Eastwood	1994	J Feeney

Derbyshire Ladies' Championship

Year	Winner	Year	Winner
1985	L Holmes	1990	D Andrews
1986	E Robinson	1991	L Holmes
1987	E Clark	1992	L Holmes
1988	A Howe	1993	L Holmes
1989	D Andrews	1994	L Walters

Derbyshire Match Play Championship

Year	Winner	Year	Winner
1985	C Ibbotson	1990	R Fletcher
1986	J Feeney (Am)	1991	S Davis
1987	G Shaw	1992	G Shaw
1988	M Higgins	1993	G Shaw
1989	G Shaw	1994	G Shaw

Derbyshire Open Championship

Year	Winner	Year	Winner
1985	M McLean	1990	M Deeley
1986	N Furniss (Am)	1991	J Feeney (Am)
1987	S Smith	1992	J Feeney (Am)
1988	G Shaw	1993	J Feeney (Am)
1989	D Clark (Am)	1994	D Thompson

Derbyshire Professional Championship

Year	Winner	Year	Winner
1985	J Turnbull	1990	M Deeley
1986	J Lower	1991	W Bird
1987	A Skingle	1992	J Proctor
1988	M McLean	1993	K Cross
1989	N Hallam	1994	D Stafford

Devon Amateur Championship

Year	Winner	Year	Winner
1985	J Langmead	1990	G Milne
1986	P Newcombe	1991	A Richards
1987	J Langmead	1992	D Lewis
1988	J Langmead	1993	R Goodey
1989	R Barrow	1994	M Crossfield

Devon Ladies' Championship

Year	Winner	Year	Winner
1985	L Lines	1990	V Holloway
1986	J Hurley	1991	K Tebbet
1987	G Jenkinson	1992	K Tebbet
1988	J Hurley	1993	K Tebbet
1989	S Germain	1994	K Tebbet

Devon Open Championship

Year	Winner	Year	Winner
1985	A MacDonald	1991	R Troake
1986	P Newcombe	1992	R Troake
1987	G Milne	1993T	D Sheppard
1988	D Sheppard		T McSherry
1989	D Sheppard	1994	I Higgins
1990	G Tomkinson		

Dorset Amateur Championship

Year	Winner	Year	Winner
1985	J Bloxham	1990	P McMullen
1986	A Lawrence	1991	A Lawrence
1987	A Lawrence	1992	L James
1988	A Lawrence	1993	A Lawrence
1989	A Lawrence	1994	M Davies

Dorset Ladies' Championship

Year	Winner	Year	Winner
1985	S Lowe	1990	T Loveys
1986	H Delew	1991	H Davidson
1987	J Sugden	1992	S Lowe
1988	H Delew	1993	S Sanderson
1989	T Loveys	1994	W Russell

Dumfriesshire Ladies' Championship

Year	Winner	Year	Winner
1985	R Morrison	1990	L Armstrong
1986	M McKerrow	1991	M Morrison
1987	M McKerrow	1992	D Douglas
1988	D Douglas	1993	G Adamson
1989	D Douglas	1994	F Watson

Dunbartonshire Amateur Championship

Year	Winner	Year	Winner
1985	S Miller	1990	J Kinloch
1986	D Carrick	1991	T McKeown
1987	D Shaw	1992	D Shaw
1988	J Laird	1993	F Jardine
1989	D Shaw	1994	D Carrick

Dunbartonshire Amateur Match Play Championship

Year	Winner	Year	Winner
1985	D Carrick	1990	D Shaw
1986	W Thom	1991	F Jardine
1987	A Brodie	1992	R Blair
1988	R Blair	1993	F Jardine
1989	C Stewart	1994	F Hutchison

Dunbartonshire and Argyll Ladies' Championship

Year	Winner	Year	Winner
1985	V McAlister	1990	M McKinlay
1986	J Kinloch	1991	M McKinlay
1987	S McDonald	1992	J Moodie
1988	V McAlister	1993	M McKinlay
1989	M McKinlay	1994	V Melvin

Durham Amateur Championship

Year	Winner	Year	Winner
1985	A Robertson	1990	R Walker
1986	H Ashby	1991	C Kilgour
1987	P Highmoor	1992	A McLure
1988	J Ellwood	1993	R Walker
1989	G Bell	1994	J Kennedy

Durham Ladies' Championship

Year	Winner	Year	Winner
1985	M Scullan	1990	B Mansfield
1986	L Chesterton	1991	P Dobson
1987	B Mansfield	1992	L Still
1988	L Chesterton	1993	L Keers
1989	L Still	1994	P Dobson

East Anglian Ladies' Championship

Year	Winner	Year	Winner
1986	J Walter	1991	J Walter
1987	J Walter	1992	T Eakin
1988	R Farrow	1993	T Eakin
1989	W Fryer	1994	T Eakin
1990	J Sheldrick		

East Anglian Open Championship

Year	Winner	Year	Winner
1985	C Platts	1990	N Wichelow
1986	M Stokes	1991	M Mackenzie
1987	*Not played*	1992	L Fickling
1988	P Kent	1993	A George
1989	R Mitchell	1994	R Mann

East Lothian Ladies' Championship

Year	Winner	Year	Winner
1985	M Ferguson	1990	C Lambert
1986	P Lees	1991	S Spiewak
1987	J Ford	1992	C Lambert
1988	C Lugton	1993	S McMester
1989	C Lugton	1994	C Matthew

East of Ireland Open Amateur Championship

Year	Winner	Year	Winner
1985	F Ronan	1990	D O'Sullivan
1986	P Hogan	1991	P Hogan
1987	P Rayfus	1992	R Burns
1988	G McGimpsey	1993	R Burns
1989	D Clarke	1994	G McGimpsey

Eastern Division Ladies' Championship (Scotland)

Year	Winner	Year	Winner
1985	L Bennett	1990	A Hendry
1986	J Harrison	1991	C Lambert
1987	A Rose	1992	J Ford
1988	J Ford	1993	A Rose
1989	H Rose	1994	J Ford

East of Scotland Open Amateur Stroke Play

Year	Winner	Year	Winner
1985	A McQueen	1990	G Lawrie
1986	S Knowles	1991	R Clark
1987	T Cochrane	1992	ST Knowles
1988	C Everett	1993	S Meiklejohn
1989	K Hird	1994	A Reid

Essex Amateur Championship

Year	Winner	Year	Winner
1985	D Wood	1990	*Null and void*
1986	M Davis	1991	D Lee
1987	V Cox	1992	D Lee
1988	R Scott	1993	R Coles
1989	V Cox	1994	R Coles

Essex Ladies' Championship

Year	Winner	Year	Winner
1985	S Barber	1990	S Bennett
1986	S Moorcroft	1991	M King
1987	M King	1992	F Edmond
1988	W Dicks	1993	T Poulton
1989	A MacDonald	1994	T Wilson

Essex Open Championship

Year	Winner	Year	Winner
1985	L Platts	1990	G Burrows
1986	G Burrows	1991	R Joyce
1987	S Cipa	1992	C Platts
1988	H Flatman	1993	A Blackburn
1989	H Flatman	1994	D Jones

Essex Professional Championship

Year	Winner	Year	Winner
1985	S Levermore	1990	C Cox
1986	C Tucker	1991	S Cipa
1987	H Flatman	1992	P Barham
1988	K Ashdown	1993	T Wheals
1989	C Williams	1994	V Cox

Fife Amateur Championship

Year	Winner	Year	Winner
1985	D Weir	1990	D Spriddle
1986	D Spriddle	1991	GD McNab
1987	S Meiklejohn	1992	N Urquhart
1988	A Mathers	1993	DA Paton
1989	D Spriddle	1994	C MacDougall

Fife County Ladies' Championship

Year	Winner	Year	Winner
1985	L Bennett	1990	J Lawrence
1986	L Bennett	1991	C McDonald
1987	L Bennett	1992	A Watson
1988	J Lawrence	1993	K Milne
1989	J Ford	1994	L Bennett

Galloway Ladies' Championship

Year	Winner	Year	Winner
1985	M Wright	1990	F Rennie
1986	M Wright	1991	M Wright
1987	M Wright	1992	C Meldrum
1988	M Wright	1993	H Nesbit
1989	F Rennie	1994	C Meldrum

Glamorgan Amateur Championship

Year	Winner	Year	Winner
1985	R Brown	1990	P Bloomfield
1986	L Price	1991	R Maliphant
1987	RN Roderick	1992	CM Rees
1988	I Booth	1993	M Stimson
1989	B Knight	1994	N Edwards

Glamorgan County Ladies' Championship

Year	Winner	Year	Winner
1985	P Johnson	1990	A Perriam
1986	P Johnson	1991	V Thomas
1987	V Thomas	1992	J Foster
1988	V Thomas	1993	V Thomas
1989	V Thomas	1994	V Thomas

Glasgow Match Play Championship

Year	Winner	Year	Winner
1985	S Savage	1990	C Barrowman
1986	G Shaw	1991	C Barrowman
1987	S Dixon	1992	C Barrowman
1988	J Finnigan	1993	M Pairman
1989	L McLaughlin	1994	C Kelly

Glasgow Stroke Play Championship

Year	Winner	Year	Winner
1985	I Carslaw	1990	H Kemp
1986	A Maclaine	1991	C Barrowman
1987	S Machin	1992	G Crawford
1988	D Martin	1993	CE Watson
1989	G Shaw	1994	G Crawford

Gloucestershire Amateur Championship

Year	Winner	Year	Winner
1985	D Carroll	1990	D Hares
1986	R Broad	1991	J Webber
1987	M Bessell	1992	G Wolstenholme
1988	J Webber	1993	G Wolstenholme
1989	R Broad	1994	G Wolstenholme

Gloucestershire Ladies' Championship

Year	Winner	Year	Winner
1985	C Griffiths	1990	M Mayes
1986	S Shapcott	1991	C Hall
1987	R Page	1992	C Hall
1988	S Elliott	1993	C Hamilton
1989	S Elliott	1994	K Hamilton

Gwent Amateur Championship

(Formerly Monmouthshire Amateur Championship)

Year	Winner	Year	Winner
1985	M Brimble	1990	M Hayward
1986	G Hughes	1991	E Foster
1987	M Bearcroft	1992	CN Evans
1988	A Williams	1993	A Harray
1989	P Glyn	1994	B Dredge

Hampshire, Isle of Wight and Channel Islands Amateur Championship

Year	Winner	Year	Winner
1985	R Alker	1990	M Wiggett
1986	R Eggo	1991	AD Mew
1987	A Mew	1992	C Chevalier
1988	S Richardson	1993	M Blackey
1989	M Smith	1994	R Bland

Hampshire, Isle of Wight and Channel Islands Open Championship

Year	Winner	Year	Winner
1985	I Young	1990	R Watkins
1986	M Desmond	1991	R Adams
1987	T Healey	1992	I Benson
1988	K Bowden	1993	R Bland
1989	J Coles	1994	R Bland

Hampshire Ladies' Championship

Year	Winner	Year	Winner
1985	C Stirling	1990	A MacDonald
1986	C Hayllar	1991	H Wheeler
1987	C Stirling	1992	A MacDonald
1988	C Stirling	1993	K Egford
1989	S Pickles	1994	K Egford

Hampshire Professional Match Play Championship

Year	Winner	Year	Winner
1985	P Dawson	1990	K Bowden
1986	K Bowden	1991	S Ward
1987	M Desmond	1992	J Hay
1988	K Bowden	1993	K Saunders
1989	I Young	1994	M Wheeler

Hampshire PGA Championship

Year	Winner	Year	Winner
1985	T Healy	1990	S Watson
1986	M Desmond	1991	J Hay
1987	T Healy	1992	I Benson
1988	G Stubbington	1993	R Edwards
1989	J Coles	1994	G Hughes

Herts Amateur Championship

Year	Winner	Year	Winner
1985	P Robinson	1990	N Leconte
1986	P Cherry	1991	M Peake
1987	A Clark	1992	S Burnell
1988	J Ambridge	1993	S Burnell
1989	S Hankin	1994	G Maly

Herts Ladies' Championship

Year	Winner	Year	Winner
1985	H Kaye	1990	S Alison
1986	T Jeary	1991	A Magee
1987	H Kaye	1992	S Alison
1988	T Jeary	1993	C Hawkes
1989	H Kaye	1994	J Oliver

Herts Professional Championship

Year	Winner	Year	Winner
1985	J Fowler	1991	L Jones
1986	J Fowler	1992	P Cherry
1987	N Brown	1993	L Jones
1988	N Brown	1994T	N Brown
1989	N Lawrence		D Tapping
1990	N Brown		

Isle of Wight Ladies' Championship

Year	Winner	Year	Winner
1985	G Wright	1990	M Ankers
1986	M Ankers	1991	M Ankers
1987	M Ankers	1992	G Fahy
1988	M Butler	1993	M Ankers
1989	M Ankers	1994	J Hurd

Kent Amateur Championship

Year	Winner	Year	Winner
1985	J Simmance	1990	R Sloman
1986	M Lawrence	1991	P Oliver
1987	L Batchelor	1992	P Sherman
1988	W Hodkin	1993	G Brown
1989	S Green	1994	B Barham

Kent Ladies' Championship

Year	Winner	Year	Winner
1985	L Bayman	1990	H Wadsworth
1986	C Caldwell	1991	H Wadsworth
1987	L Bayman	1992	C Caldwell
1988	C Caldwell	1993	M Sutton
1989	S Sutton	1994	M Sutton

Kent Open Championship

Year	Winner	Year	Winner
1985	G Will	1990	S Barr
1986	J Bennett	1991	S Wood
1987	M Goodin	1992	S Barr
1988	J Bennett	1993	N Haynes
1989	R Cameron	1994	T Berry

Kent Professional Championship

Year	Winner	Year	Winner
1985	J Bennett	1990	R Cameron
1986	P Mitchell	1991	R Cameron
1987	S Barr	1992	M Lawrence
1988	R Cameron	1993	R Cameron
1989	P Lyons	1994	M Lawrence

Lanarkshire Amateur Championship

Year	Winner	Year	Winner
1985	J Reid	1990	G Shanks
1986	W Bryson	1991	D Blair
1987	S Henderson	1992	W Bryson
1988	G Jones	1993	D Brown
1989	J Taylor	1994	W Bryson

Lanarkshire Ladies' County Championship

Year	Winner	Year	Winner
1985	P Hutton	1990	A Hendry
1986	J Scott	1991	A Hendry
1987	A Hendry	1992	F McKay
1988	F McKay (*née* Needham)	1993	M Hughes
1989	K Dallas	1994	J Gardner

Lancashire Amateur Championship

Year	Winner	Year	Winner
1985	R Bardsley	1990	T Foster
1986	M Wild	1991	GS Lacy
1987	T Foster	1992	R Hutt
1988	M Kingsley	1993	G Helsby
1989	R Bardsley	1994	K Wallbank

Lancashire Ladies' Championship

Year	Winner	Year	Winner
1985	A Bromilow	1990	L Fairclough
1986	J Collingham	1991	A Baines
1987	J Collingham	1992	J Collingham
1988	L Fairclough	1993	K Rostron
1989	C Blackshaw	1994	G Nutter

Lancashire Open Championship

Year	Winner	Year	Winner
1985	R Green	1990	P Allan
1986	T Foster (Am)	1991	G Furey
1987	S Hamer (Am)	1992	S Townend
1988	P Wesselingh	1993	L Edwards
1989	M Jones	1994	A Lancaster

Leicestershire and Rutland Amateur Championship

Year	Winner	Year	Winner
1985	E Hammond	1990	D Gibson
1986	I Middleton	1991	D Gibson
1987	G Marshall	1992	D Gibson
1988	A Martinez	1993	P Frith
1989	J Cayless	1994	I Lyner

Leicestershire and Rutland Ladies' Championship

Year	Winner	Year	Winner
1985	A Waters	1990	R Reed
1986	V Davis	1991	A Jenno
1987	M Page	1992	H Summ
1988	A Walters	1993	M Page
1989	M Page	1994	M Page

Leicestershire and Rutland Open Championship

Year	Winner	Year	Winner
1985	R Adams	1990	R Larratt
1986	R Stephenson	1991	CM Harries
1987	*Not played*	1992	*Not played*
1988	D Gibson	1993	P Frith
1989	R Adams	1994	J Herbert

Lincolnshire Amateur Championship

Year	Winner	Year	Winner
1985	J Robinson	1990	P Streeter
1986	J Purdy	1991	J Payne
1987	P Stenton	1992	P Streeter
1988	P Streeter	1993	J Crampton
1989	J Payne	1994	J Crampton

Lincolnshire Ladies' Championship

Year	Winner	Year	Winner
1985	H Dobson	1990	A Johns
1986	A Johns	1991	A Thompson
1987	H Dobson	1992	R Jones
1988	H Dobson	1993	R Broughton
1989	H Dobson	1994	S Brook

Lincolnshire Open Championship

Year	Winner	Year	Winner
1985	A Carter	1990	A Butler (Am)
1986	G Stafford	1991	J Payne (Am)
1987	S Dickinson (Am)	1992	P Streeter (Am)
1988	J Heib	1993	S Bennett
1989	A Hare	1994	S Brewer

Lothians Amateur Championship

Year	Winner	Year	Winner
1985	S Easingwood	1990	S Middleton
1986	S Smith	1991	C MacPhail
1987	D Kirkpatrick	1992	C MacPhail
1988	B Shields	1993	S Smith
1989	K Hastings	1994	S Smith

Manx Amateur Championship

Year	Winner	Year	Winner
1985	J Sutton	1990	M Pugh
1986	A Cain	1991	GK Gelling
1987	J Sutton	1992	G Wilson
1988	G Kelly	1993	G Wilson
1989	G Ashe	1994	R Sayle

Middlesex Amateur Championship

Year	Winner	Year	Winner
1985	R Willison	1990	A Rogers
1986	A Rogers	1991	J O'Shea
1987	R Willison	1992	WJ Bennett
1988	A Rogers	1993	GAF Homewood
1989	R Willison	1994	W Bennett

Middlesex Ladies' Championship

Year	Winner	Year	Winner
1985	C Nelson	1990	S Keogh
1986	A Gems	1991	J Dannhauser
1987	A Gems	1992	J Sadler
1988	S Keogh	1993	L Housman
1989	S Keogh	1994	M Henderson

Middlesex Open Championship

Year	Winner	Year	Winner
1985	P Golding	1990	R Willison (Am)
1986	*Not played*	1991	R Willison (Am)
1987	L Fickling	1992	GA Homewood
1988	L Fickling	1993	GA Homewood
1989	L Fickling	1994	N Wichelow

Midland Close Amateur Championship

Year	Winner	Year	Winner
1985	M Hassall	1990	J Bickerton
1986	G Wolstenholme	1991	P Streeter
1987	C Suneson	1992	I Richardson
1988	A Hare	1993	M Roberts
1989	J Cook	1994	M Foster

Midland Open Amateur Championship

Year	Winner	Year	Winner
1985	MC Hassall	1990	J Bickerton
1986	G Wolstenholme	1991	P Sefton
1987	C Suneson	1992	M McGuire
1988	R Winchester	1993	N Williamson
1989	J Cook	1994	D Howell

Midland Masters

Year	Winner	Year	Winner
1988	B Waites	1992	C Hall
1989	C Haycock	1993	*Not played*
1990	J King	1994	C Hall
1991	S Rose		

Midland Ladies' Championship

Year	Winner	Year	Winner
1985	L Waring	1990	J Hockley
1986	J Collingham	1991	R Millington
1987	S Roberts	1992	R Bolas
1988	S Roberts	1993	R Bolas
1989	R Bolas	1994	J Morris

Midland Professional Match Play Championship

Year	Winner	Year	Winner
1985	D Ridley	1990	G Farr
1986	J Higgins	1991	B Waites
1987	K Hayward	1992	J Higgins
1988	J Higgins	1993	C Clark
1989	K Hayward	1994	N Turley

Midland Professional Stroke Play Championship

Year	Winner	Year	Winner
1985	K Hayward	1990	G Stafford
1986	A Skingle	1991	K Dickens
1987	M Mouland	1992	J Higgins
1988	G Farr	1993	P Baker
1989	J Higgins	1994	P Baker

The Midland Boys' Amateur Championship

Year	Winner	Year	Winner
1985	D Prosser	1990	ML Welch
1986	J Payne	1991	S Drummond
1987	S Prestcote	1992	S Drummond
1988	AJ Salt	1993	S Webster
1989	M Wilson	1994	R Duck

Midland Senior Championship

Year	Winner	Year	Winner
1985	JL Whitworth	1990	A Harrison
1986	RG Hiatt	1991	DS Kirkland
1987	JC Thomas	1992	A Guest
1988	TE Kelsall	1993	J Humphries
1989	RG Hiatt	1994	G Pope

Midlothian Ladies' Championship

Year	Winner	Year	Winner
1985	F de Vries	1990	E Jack
1986	J Marshall	1991	E Bruce
1987	M Stavert	1992	K Marshall
1988	M Stavert	1993	E Bruce
1989	E Bruce	1994	E Bruce

Mid-Wales Ladies' Championship

Year	Winner	Year	Winner
1987	A Hubbard	1991	T Gittens
1988	S James	1992	P Morgan
1989	S Wilson	1993	A Owen
1990	P Morgan	1994	G Gibb

Monmouthshire Ladies' Championship

Year	Winner	Year	Winner
1985	P Lord	1990	W Wood
1986	H Buckley	1991	W Wood
1987	H Buckley	1992	R Morgan
1988	H Armstrong	1993	S Musto
1989	B Chambers	1994	E Pilgrim

Norfolk Amateur Championship

Year	Winner	Year	Winner
1985	C Lamb	1990	P Little
1986	I Sperrin	1991	CJ Lamb
1987	N Williamson	1992	A Marshall
1988	N Williamson	1993	DA Edwards
1989	N Williamson	1994	J Durrant

Norfolk Ladies' Championship

Year	Winner	Year	Winner
1985	M Whybrow	1990	T Ireland
1986	N Clarke	1991	T Williamson
1987	A Davies	1992	T Williamson
1988	L Elliott	1993	T Williamson
1989	T Keeley	1994	J Wilkerson

Norfolk Open Championship

Year	Winner	Year	Winner
1985	T Hurrell	1990	A Brydon
1986	M Spooner	1991	I Hardy
1987	M Elsworthy	1992	C Green
1988	M Few	1993	A Collison
1989	M Few	1994	J Hill

Norfolk Professional Championship

Year	Winner	Year	Winner
1985	M Spooner	1990	M Few
1986	M Spooner	1991	A Collison
1987	M Elsworthy	1992	A Collison
1988	M Few	1993	A Collison
1989	M Few	1994	A Collison

Northamptonshire Amateur Championship

Year	Winner	Year	Winner
1985	M McNally	1990	A Print
1986	M Scott	1991	S McDonald
1987	D Jones	1992	AJ Wilson
1988	D Ellson	1993	S McIlwain
1989	N Goodman	1994	A Print

Northamptonshire Ladies' Championship

Year	Winner	Year	Winner
1985	A Duck	1990	C Gibbs
1986	P Le Vai	1991	C Gibbs
1987	J Kendrick	1992	G Gibbs
1988	A Duck	1993	S Sharpe
1989	C Gibbs	1994	S Sharpe

Northern (England) Professional Championship

Year	Winner	Year	Winner
1985	A Murray	1990	J Morgan
1986	D Stirling	1991	H Selby-Green
1987	D Jagger	1992	P Cowen
1988	K Waters	1993	C Smiley
1989	S Bottomley	1994	P Wesselingh

Northern Counties (Scotland) Ladies' Championship

Year	Winner	Year	Winner
1985	A Shannon	1990	F McKay
1986	F McKay	1991	M Vass
1987	I McIntosh	1992	I Shannon
1988	I McIntosh	1993	S Alexander
1989	E Fiskin	1994	L Roxburgh

North of Ireland Open Amateur Championship

Year	Winner	Year	Winner
1985	I Elliott	1990	D Clarke
1986	D Ballantine	1991	G McGimpsey
1987	A Pierse	1992	G McGimpsey
1988	N Anderson	1993	G McGimpsey
1989	N Anderson	1994	N Ludwell

Northern Open Championship

Year	Winner	Year	Winner
1985	B Barnes	1990	C Brooks
1986	R Weir	1991	C Cassells
1987	A Hunter	1992	P Smith
1988	D Huish	1993	K Stables
1989	C Brooks	1994	K Stables

Northern Women's Championship

Year	Winner	Year	Winner
1985	C Hall	1990	L Fairclough
1986	L Fairclough	1991	C White
1987	S Robinson	1992	G Simpson
1988	K Tebbet	1993	A Brighouse
1989	L Fletcher	1994	G Nutter

Northumberland Amateur Championship

Year	Winner	Year	Winner
1985	D Faulder	1990	K Fairbairn
1986	D Martin	1991	K Fairbairn
1987	K Fairbairn	1992	S Philipson
1988	J Metcalfe	1993	P Taylor
1989	J Metcalfe	1994	S Twynholm

Northumberland Ladies' Championship

Year	Winner	Year	Winner
1985	C Hall	1990	L Fletcher
1986	C Hall	1991	C Hall
1987	C Breckon	1992	C Hall
1988	D Glenn	1993	H Wilson
1989	D Glenn	1994	D Glenn

Northern Division Ladies' Championship (Scotland)

Year	Winner	Year	Winner
1985	A Shannon	1990	K Imrie
1986	C Middleton	1991	C Middleton
1987	A Murray (*née* Shannon)	1992	S Alexander
1988	K Imrie	1993	S Alexander
1989	S Wood	1994	J Matthews

North of Scotland Open Amateur Stroke Play Championship

Year	Winner	Year	Winner
1985	J Macdonald	1990	S McIntosh
1986	S Cruickshank	1991	S Henderson
1987	S McIntosh	1992	K Buchan
1988	K Hird	1993	D Downie
1989	G Hickman	1994	E Forbes

Nottinghamshire Amateur Championship

Year	Winner	Year	Winner
1985	M Scothern	1990	L White
1986	G Krause	1991	L White
1987	R Sallis	1992	L Westwood
1988	C Banks	1993	L Westwood
1989	P Shaw	1994	D Lucas

Nottinghamshire Ladies' Championship

Year	Winner	Year	Winner
1985	K Horberry	1990	L Broughton
1986	C Palmer	1991	L Broughton
1987	M Elswood	1992	S Bishop
1988	A Ferguson	1993	L Rayner
1989	A Peters	1994	G Palmer

Nottinghamshire Open Championship

Year	Winner	Year	Winner
1985	C Jepson	1990	C Hall
1986	B Waites	1991	C Jepson
1987	C Hall	1992	J King
1988	C Banks (Am)	1993	J King
1989	P Hinton	1994	J King

Oxfordshire Ladies' Championship

Year	Winner	Year	Winner
1985	N Sparks	1990	N Sparks
1986	T Craik	1991	L King
1987	T Craik	1992	L King
1988	T Craik	1993	N Sparks
1989	L King	1994	L King

Perth and Kinross Amateur Stroke Play Championship

Year	Winner	Year	Winner
1985	G Lowson	1990	G Smith
1986	C Bloice	1991	D Robertson
1987	B Grieve	1992	B Grieve
1988	E Lindsay	1993	T McLevy
1989	A Campbell	1994	E Lindsay

Perth and Kinross Ladies' Championship

Year	Winner	Year	Winner
1985	A Guthrie	1990	S Mailer
1986	I Shannon	1991	I Shannon
1987	F Anderson	1992	S Mailer
1988	V Pringle	1993	E Wilson
1989	A Sharp	1994	C Dunbar

Renfrewshire Amateur Championship

Year	Winner	Year	Winner
1985	J McDonald	1990	R Clark
1986	I Riddell	1991	R Clark
1987	D Howard	1992	G Urquhart
1988	E Grey	1993	R Clark
1989	R Clark	1994	M Carmichael

Renfrewshire County Ladies' Championship

Year	Winner	Year	Winner
1985	S Lawson	1990	D Jackson
1986	S Lawson	1991	D Jackson
1987	S Lawson	1992	D Jackson
1988	S Lawson	1993	K Fitzgerald
1989	D Jackson	1994	C Agnew

Scottish Area Team Championship

Year	Winner	Year	Winner
1985	Lothians	1990	North East
1986	Ayrshire	1991	Glasgow
1987	Lothians	1992	North East
1988	Lothians	1993	Lothians
1989	Lanarkshire	1994	Lothians

Scottish Champion of Champions

Year	Winner	Year	Winner
1970	A Horne	1983	D Carrick
1971	D Black	1984	S Stephen
1972	R Strachan	1985	I Brotherston
1973	*Not held*	1986	I Hutcheon
1974	M Niven	1987	G Shaw
1975	A Brodie	1988	I Hutcheon
1976	A Brodie	1989	J Milligan
1977	V Reid	1990	J Milligan
1978	D Greig	1991	G Hay
1979	B Marchbank	1992	D Robertson
1980	I Hutcheon	1993	R Russell
1981	I Hutcheon	1994	G Sherry
1982	G Macgregor		

Scottish Foursomes Tournament – *Glasgow Evening Times* Trophy

Year	Winner	Year	Winner
1985	East Renfrewshire	1990	Dunblane New
1986	Hamilton	1991	Irvine Ravenspark
1987	Drumpellier	1992	Cochrane Castle
1988	Irvine Ravenspark	1993	Baberton
1989	Cochrane Leith	1994	Standard Life

Scottish Ladies' County Championship

Year	Winner	Year	Winner
1985	East Lothian	1991	East Lothian
1986	Aberdeenshire	1992	Dunbartonshire & Argyll
1987	Renfrewshire	1993	Gullane
1988	Lanarkshire	1994	East Lothian
1989	Lanarkshire		
1990	East Lothian		

Scottish Ladies' Foursomes

Year	Winner	Year	Winner
1985	*No championship*	1991	West of Scotland Girls' Golf Association
1986	Blairgowrie	1992	Haggs Castle
1987	Baberton	1993	North Berwick
1988	Gullane	1994	Turnberry
1989	Gullane		
1990	Gullane		

Shropshire and Herefordshire Amateur Championship

Year	Winner	Year	Winner
1985	P Baker	1990	M Welch
1986	C Bufton	1991	M Welch
1987	R Dixon	1992	M Welch
1988	S Thomas	1993	M Welch
1989	M Welch	1994	M Welch

Shropshire Ladies' Championship

Year	Winner	Year	Winner
1985	A Johnson	1990	J Marvell
1986	S Pidgeon	1991	A Johnson
1987	S Pidgeon	1992	A Johnson
1988	A Jackson	1993	A Johnson
1989	C Gauge	1994	A Johnson

Somerset Amateur Championship

Year	Winner	Year	Winner
1985	P Hare	1990	C Edwards
1986	C Edwards	1991	C Edwards
1987	G Hickman	1992	C Edwards
1988	C Edwards	1993	C Edwards
1989	C Edwards	1994	C Edwards

Somerset Ladies' Championship

Year	Winner	Year	Winner
1985	K Nicholls	1990	K Nicholls
1986	K Nicholls	1991	S Whiting
1987	K Nicholls	1992	C Whiting
1988	C Whiting	1993	R Murr
1989	K Nicholls	1994	S Burnell

South-Eastern Ladies' Championship

Year	Winner	Year	Winner
1985	J Thornhill	1990	A MacDonald
1986	S Moorcroft	1991	K Egford
1987	N Way	1992	A MacDonald
1988	C Stirling	1993	K Smith
1989	A MacDonald	1994	K Egford

South Professional Championship

Year	Winner	Year	Winner
1985	C Mason	1990	*Not played*
1986	P Mitchell	1991	J Hoskison
1987	*Not played*	1992	J Hoskison
1988	P Harrison	1993	G Smith
1989	W Grant	1994	R Edwards

Southern Assistants Championship

Year	Winner	Year	Winner
1985	C Platts	1990	*Not played*
1986	N Brown	1991	G Orr
1987	H Francis	1992	G Orr
1988	J Sewell	1993	R Edwards
1989	J Sewell	1994	M Wheeler

Southern Assistants Match Play Championship

Year	Winner	Year	Winner
1985	H Francis	1990	G Orr
1986	H Francis	1991	I Roper
1987	M Sludds	1992	G McQuitty
1988	*Not played*	1993	N Gorman
1989	*Not played*	1994	M Groombridge

South of Ireland Open Amateur Championship

Year	Winner	Year	Winner
1985	P O'Rourke	1990	D Clarke
1986	J McHenry	1991	P McGinley
1987	B Reddan	1992	L MacNamara
1988	MA Gannon	1993	P Sheehan
1989	S Keenan	1994	D Higgins

South of Scotland Championship

Year	Winner	Year	Winner
1985	I Brotherston	1990	B Kerr
1986	I Semple	1991	J Power
1987	I Brotherston	1992	J Wright
1988	A Coltart	1993	D Wallis
1989	V Reid	1994	I Reid

Southern Division Ladies' Championship (Scotland)

Year	Winner	Year	Winner
1985	S Simpson	1990	F Rennie
1986	M Wright	1991	J Anderson
1987	M Wright	1992	D Douglas
1988	S Simpson	1993	C Meldrum
1989	F Rennie	1994	D Douglas

South of Scotland Ladies' Championship

Year	Winner	Year	Winner
1985	F Rennie	1990	M Wright
1986	F Rennie	1991	F Rennie
1987	S McDonald	1992	M Wilson
1988	M Wright	1993	D Douglas
1989	M Wright	1994	F Rennie

South-Western Ladies' Championship

Year	Winner	Year	Winner
1985	S Shapcott	1990	V Thomas
1986	K Nicholls	1991	V Thomas
1987	J Fernley	1992	C Hall
1988	V Thomas	1993	E Fields
1989	C Hall	1994	R Morgan

South-Western Counties Amateur Championship

Year	Winner	Year	Winner
1985	C Phillips	1990	S Amor
1986	C Phillips	1991	P McMullen
1987	P Newcombe	1992	S Edgley
1988	J Langmead	1993	B Sandry
1989	K Jones	1994	A Lawrence

Staffordshire Amateur Championship

Year	Winner	Year	Winner
1985	M Hassall	1990	P Sweetsur
1986	M Scarrett	1991	M McGuire
1987	M Hassall	1992	M McGuire
1988	P Sweetsur	1993	C Poxon
1989	C Poxon	1994	R Mayfield

Staffordshire Ladies' Championship

Year	Winner	Year	Winner
1985	L Hackney	1990	R Bolas
1986	A Booth	1991	R Bolas
1987	D Christison	1992	P Hale
1988	D Boyd	1993	R Bolas
1989	R Bolas	1994	S Gallagher

Staffordshire Open Championship

Year	Winner	Year	Winner
1985	J Annable	1990	J Rhodes
1986	J Higgins	1991	M McGuire
1987	J Annable	1992	J Rhodes
1988	J Rhodes	1993	M McGuire
1989	M Passmore	1994	D Scott

Staffordshire and Shropshire Stroke Play Championship

Year	Winner	Year	Winner
1985	A Stubbs	1990	G Farr
1986	A Minshall	1991	M Knight
1987	J Higgins	1992	S Russell
1988	J Annable	1993	J Rhodes
1989	J Higgins	1994	J Rhodes

Stirlingshire Amateur Championship

Year	Winner	Year	Winner
1985	W Fleming	1990	K Goodwin
1986	R Godfrey	1991	K Goodwin
1987	S Lee	1992	H Anderson
1988	H Anderson	1993	D Smith
1989	S Russell	1994	K McArthur

Stirling and Clackmannan County Ladies' Championship

Year	Winner	Year	Winner
1985	S Michie	1990	A Rose
1986	S Michie	1991	A Rose
1987	J Harrison	1992	A Rose
1988	J Harrison	1993	H Stirling
1989	J Abernethy	1994	H Stirling

Suffolk Amateur Championship

Year	Winner	Year	Winner
1985	R Barrell	1990	J Booth
1986	M Clark	1991	N Meadows
1987	C Coulton	1992	P Buckle
1988	J Whitby	1993	J Maddock
1989	M Turner	1994	J Maddock

Suffolk Ladies' Championship

Year	Winner	Year	Winner
1985	Dr J Gibson	1990	J Hall
1986	J Wade	1991	J Hall
1987	W Day	1992	J Hall
1988	S Dawson	1993	J Hall
1989	J Hall	1994	J Hockley

Suffolk Open Championship

Year	Winner	Year	Winner
1985	K Preston	1990	S Crosby (Am)
1986	S Beckham	1991	R Mann
1987	M Turner	1992	R Mann
1988	J Maddock	1993	R Mann
1989	M Elsworthy	1994	L Patterson

Suffolk Professional Championship

Year	Winner	Year	Winner
1985	S Beckham	1990	R Mann
1986	R Mann	1991	K Golding
1987	S Beckham	1992	R Mann
1988	S Whymark	1993	K Golding
1989	S Whymark	1994	L Patterson

Surrey Amateur Championship

Year	Winner	Year	Winner
1985	G Walmsley	1990	J Good
1986	B White	1991	A Tillman
1987	J Paramor	1992	A Wall
1988	A Carter	1993	A Raitt
1989	T Lloyd	1994	M Ellis

Surrey Ladies' Championship

Year	Winner	Year	Winner
1985	J Nicolson	1990	W Wooldridge
1986	S Prosser	1991	J Thornhill
1987	W Wooldridge	1992	J Thornhill
1988	C Bailey	1993	S Lambert
1989	J Thornhill	1994	S Lambert

Sussex Amateur Championship

Year	Winner	Year	Winner
1985	M Jarvis	1990	D Arnold
1986	A Schofield	1991	R Lowles
1987	D Fay	1992	M Galway
1988	D Alderson	1993	M Galway
1989	P Hurring	1994	P Clevely

Sussex Ladies' Championship

Year	Winner	Year	Winner
1985	N Way	1990	M Cornelius
1986	M Cornelius	1991	K Mitchell
1987	K Mitchell	1992	J Head
1988	M Cornelius	1993	C Titcomb
1989	M Cornelius	1994	J Head

Sussex Open Championship

Year	Winner	Year	Winner
1985	J Spence (Am)	1990	*Not played*
1986	C Giddins	1991	J Pinsent
1987	B Barnes	1992	P Harrison
1988	S Rolley	1993	N Burke
1989	M Groombridge (Am)	1994	K Hinton

Ulster Professional Championship

Year	Winner	Year	Winner
1985	D Jones	1990	J Heggarty
1986	W Todd	1991	D Carson
1987	W Todd	1992	D Clarke
1988	J Heggarty	1993	D Jones
1989	D Feherty	1994	P Russell

Warwickshire Ladies' Championship

Year	Winner	Year	Winner
1985	S Seville	1990	S Morgan
1986	T Hammond	1991	S Morgan
1987	M Button	1992	N Moutt
1988	S Morgan	1993	S Morgan
1989	S Morgan	1994	S Westhall

Warwickshire Amateur Championship

Year	Winner	Year	Winner
1985	C Suneson	1990	J Cook
1986	P Downes	1991	A Allen
1987	W Bladon	1992	G Lord
1988	A Allen	1993	G Marston
1989	J Cook	1994	N Connolly

Warwickshire Stroke Play Championship

Year	Winner	Year	Winner
1985	P Elson	1990	N McEwan
1986	P Elson	1991	M Jennings
1987	P Elson	1992	A Allen
1988	C Wicketts	1993	G Marston
1989	T Rouse	1994	S Webster

Warwickshire Open Championship

Year	Winner	Year	Winner
1985	J Gould	1990	M Biddle (Am)
1986	P Weaver	1991	A Allen (Am)
1987	P Weaver	1992	P Chalkley
1988	A Allen (Am)	1993	A Bownes
1989	A Allen (Am)	1994	D White

Warwickshire Professional Championship

Year	Winner	Year	Winner
1985	P Elson	1990	N McEwan
1986	P Elson	1991	D Quinn
1987	P Elson	1992	C Harrison
1988	C Wicketts	1993	A Bands
1989	T Rouse	1994	C Wicketts

Welsh Team Championship

Year	Winner	Year	Winner
1985	Whitchurch	1990	Whitchurch
1986	Pontnewydd	1991	Wrexham
1987	Llandudno (Maesdu)	1992	Llanwern
		1993	Morriston
1988	Ashburnham	1994	Monmouthshire
1989	Cardiff		

Welsh Ladies' Team Championship

Year	Winner	Year	Winner
1985	Llandudno (Maesdu)	1990	Llandudno (Maesdu)
1986	Porthcawl	1991	Wenvoe Castle
1987	Whitchurch	1992	Whitchurch
1988	Pennard	1993	Pennard
1989	Llandudno (Maesdu)	1994	St Pierre

West of Ireland Open Amateur Championship

Year	Winner	Year	Winner
1985	J Feeney	1990	N Goulding
1986	P Rayfus	1991	N Goulding
1987	N McGrane	1992	K Kearney
1988	G McGimpsey	1993	G McGimpsey
1989	P McInerney	1994	P Harrington

West of Scotland Close Amateur Championship

Year	Winner	Year	Winner
1985	S Savage	1990	B Smith
1986	S Savage	1991	W Bryson
1987	R Jenkins	1992	D Robertson
1988	G King	1993	R Weir
1989	G Lawrie	1994	A Forsyth

West of Scotland Open Amateur Championship

Year	Winner	Year	Winner
1985	J Thomson	1990	S Knowles
1986	C Brooks	1991	A Coltart
1987	K Hird	1992	S Henderson
1988	S Savage	1993	B Howard
1989	A Elliot	1994	J Hodgson

Western Division Ladies' Championship (Scotland)

Year	Winner	Year	Winner
1985	I Robertson	1990	S Spiewak
1986	S Lawson	1991	J Moodie
1987	A Hendry	1992	M McKinlay
1988	S Lawson	1993	J Moodie
1989	K Dallas	1994	V Melvin

West Region PGA Championship

(Previously West of England Professional Championship)

Year	Winner	Year	Winner
1985	D Sheppard	1990	P Price
1986	S Little	1991	S Dodd
1987	A Sherborne	1992	M Thomas
1988	M Thomas	1993	P Mayo
1989	G Laing	1994	S Little

Wigtownshire Championship

Year	Winner	Year	Winner
1985	M Gibson	1990	R Burns
1986	A Cunningham	1991	G Sharp
1987	J Burns	1992	R O'Keefe
1988	K Hardie	1993	K Hardie
1989	D Taylor	1994	K Hardie

Wiltshire Amateur Championship

Year	Winner	Year	Winner
1985	S Amor	1990	N Williams
1986	G Clough	1991	R White
1987	RE Searle	1992	D Howell
1988	G Clough	1993	RE Searle
1989	A Burch	1994	R Searle

Wiltshire Ladies' Championship

Year	Winner	Year	Winner
1985	C Waite	1990	M Johnston
1986	S Marks	1991	S Sutton
1987	J Lawrence	1992	S Sutton
1988	S Sutton	1993	V Hanks
1989	J Lawrence	1994	S Sutton

Wiltshire Professional Championship

(Now known as the 'Hills' Wiltshire Pro Champ)

Year	Winner	Year	Winner
1985	G Laing	1991	A Beal
1986	B Sandry	1992	G Emerson
1987	G Laing	1993T	G Emerson
1988	R Emery		D Ray
1989	G Emerson	1994	S Robertson
1990	G Clough		

Worcestershire Amateur Championship

Year	Winner	Year	Winner
1985	S Pimley	1990	D Eddiford
1986	D Eddiford	1991	J Bickerton
1987	D Prosser	1992	M Reynard
1988	D Prosser	1993	M Reynard
1989	S Braithwaite	1994	R Sadler

Worcestershire Ladies' Championship

Year	Winner	Year	Winner
1985	L Waring	1990	J Deeley
1986	K Cheetham	1991	L Jones
1987	L Waring	1992	L Montgomery
1988	J Blaymire	1993	L Jones
1989	L Waring	1994	N Lawrenson

Worcestershire Open Championship

Year	Winner	Year	Winner
1985	D Eddiford	1990	J Bickerton
1986	W Painter (Am)	1991	MC Reynard
1987	K Hayward	1992	A Robinson
1988	D Eddiford	1993	P Scarrett
1989	K Hayward	1994	S Edwards

Worcestershire Professional Stroke Play Championship

Year	Winner	Year	Winner
1985	D Dunk	1990	K Hayward
1986	K Hayward	1991	L Bashford
1987	G Mercer	1992	R Cameron
1988	C Haycock	1993	F Clark
1989	K Hayward	1994	C Clark

Yorkshire Amateur Championship

Year	Winner	Year	Winner
1985	S Field	1990	P Wood
1986	A Gelsthorpe	1991	ML Pullan
1987	R Roper	1992	ID Pyman
1988	S Field	1993	J Healey
1989	G Harland	1994	P Wood

Yorkshire Amateur Stroke Play Championship

Year	Winner	Year	Winner
1986	P Hall	1990	L Walker
1987T	P Hall	1991	D Delaney
	RM Roper	1992	J Docker
1988	C Rawson	1993	J Roberts
1989	S East	1994	N Ludwell

Yorkshire Ladies' Championship

Year	Winner	Year	Winner
1985	A Farmery	1990	N Buxton
1986	P Smillie	1991	N Buxton
1987	J Copley	1992	N Buxton
1988	J Furby	1993	N Buxton
1989	K Firth	1994	N Buxton

Yorkshire Professional Championship

Year	Winner	Year	Winner
1985	B Jagger	1990	D Stirling
1986	M Ingham	1991	S Elliott
1987	D Stirling	1992	L Turner
1988	M Higginbottom	1993	A Nicholson
1989	D Stirling	1994	L Turner

PART IV

Who's Who in Golf

Compiled by Alan Elliott

British Isles Players

Abbreviations used

Cls Club membership
Maj The Open, US Open, USPGA, US Masters (men) Ladies British Open, US Women's Open, USLPGA (ladies)
Chp Amateur Championship or Ladies British Open Amateur (or, within text, any championship)
Nat The player's national championship
Trn Tournament(s)
Oth Other national championship or tournament
Reg Regional tournaments
Int International team appearances
Eur European Tour or general European tournament(s)
US Tournament(s) in United States or Canada
RoW Tournament(s) in the rest of the world
Sen Senior
Jun Junior
Mis Miscellaneous information
r/u runner up
s/f semi-finalist
tied A lost play-off after first place tie
Eur(L) T Ch European (Ladies) Amateur Team Championship

Captaincy is indicated by the year printed in bold type; years in bold type within brackets indicate non-playing captain.

Aitken, Wilma *See* Leburn

Alliss, Peter
Born Berlin on 28th February, 1931. Turned Professional 1946
PROFESSIONAL
Eur Spanish Open 1956-58. Italian Open, Portuguese Open 1958.
Trn Daks 1954; Dunlop 1955; PGA Close 1957; Dunlop 1959; Sprite 1960 (shared). PGA Close 1962; Daks 1963 (shared); Swallow-Penfold, Esso Golden 1964; PGA Close, Jeyes 1965; Martini (shared), Rediffusion 1966; Agfa-Gevaert 1967; Piccadilly 1969; Sunningdale Foursomes 1958-61; Wentworth Pro-Am Foursomes 1959
Oth British Assistants 1952
RoW Brazilian Open 1961
Reg West of England Open Professional 1956-58-62-66
Int Ryder Cup 1953-57-59-61-63-65-67-69; UK v Europe 1954-55-56; England in World Cup 1954-55-57-58-59-61-62-64-66-67; Home International **1967**
Mis Vardon Trophy 1964-66; PGA Captain 1962-87; Author, TV commentator. Golf course architect.
AMATEUR
Jun Int England Boys 1946

Anderson, Fiona
Born Perth on 24th August, 1954
Cls Blairgowrie
Nat Scottish Ladies Amateur 1987. r/u 1980-83-88
Reg North of Scotland Ladies 1977. Scottish Universities Champion 1975
Int Vagliano Trophy 1987. (Scotland) Home Int 1977-79-80-81-83-84-86-87-88-89-90-91-92; (Eur(L) T Ch) 1979-83-87-91

Anderson, Jessie *See* Valentine

Anstey, Veronica *See* Beharrell

Armitage, Susan *See* Langridge

Attenborough, Michael F

Born Britford, nr Salisbury in October, 1939

Cls Chislehurst, Royal St George's, Royal & Ancient
Oth Scandinavian Amateur 1965
Trn Hampshire Hog 1960. President's Putter 1962-66. County Champion of Champions 1964. Duncan Putter 1966. Prince of Wales Challenge Cup 1969
Reg Kent Amateur 1963-64-65
Int Walker Cup 1967. GB v Europe 1966-68. England (Home Int) 1964-66-67-68; (Eur T Ch) 1967
Mis Captain of Royal & Ancient 1989/90

Bailey, Diane, MBE [Frearson], (*née* Robb)

Born Wolverhampton on 31st August, 1943

Cls Enville (Hon), Reigate Heath, Betchworth Park
Chp British Ladies Amateur r/u 1961
Trn Worplesdon Mixed Foursomes 1971. Avia Foursomes 1972
Reg Staffordshire Ladies 1961. Lincolnshire Ladies 1966-67. Midland Ladies 1966
Int Curtis Cup 1962-72-(**84**)-(**86**)-(**88**). Vagliano Trophy 1961-(**83**)-(**85**). Espirito Santo 1968. England (Home Int) 1961-62-71. Commonwealth Team Ch (**1983**).
Mis Surrey Ladies County Captain 1981-2
Jun British Girls 1961. Scottish Girls Open Stroke Play 1959-61
Int England Girls 1957-61

Baker, Peter

Born Shifnal on 7th October, 1967. Turned Professional 1986

PROFESSIONAL
Eur Benson & Hedges International 1988; Dunhill British Masters, Scandinavian Masters 1993
Oth UAP U25 European Open 1990; Midland Professional Chp 1993-94; Tournoi Perrier de Paris 1994
Int Ryder Cup 1993; England in Dunhill Cup 1993 (r/u)
Mis Rookie of the Year 1987
AMATEUR
Nat English Open Amateur Stroke Play 1985 (shared)
Reg Shropshire & Herefordshire Amateur 1983-84-85
Trn Tillman Trophy 1985
Int Walker Cup 1985; GBI v Europe 1986; England (Home Int) 1985
Jun Carris Trophy 1983-85

Bannerman, Harry

Born Aberdeen on 5th March, 1942. Turned Professional 1965

PROFESSIONAL
Oth Scottish Professional 1967-72. Northern Scottish Open 1967-69-72. East of Scotland PGA Match Play 1969. Scottish Coca Cola 1976
Int Ryder Cup 1971. Scotland in World Cup 1967-72; in Double Diamond 1972-74
Mis Frank Moran Trophy 1972
AMATEUR
Reg North of Scotland Stroke Play 1962; North-East Scotland Stroke Play 1963-64-65
Jun Int Scottish Boys 1959

Barber, Sally (*née* Bonallack)

Born Chigwell, Essex on 9th April, 1938. Turned Professional 1979. Reinstated Amateur 1982

AMATEUR
Cls Thorpe Hall, Thorndon Park, Hunstanton (Hon), Killarney (Hon)
Nat English Ladies Amateur 1968; r/u 1970-71
Oth German Ladies 1958
Trn Astor Salver 1972; Avia Foursomes 1976
Reg Essex Ladies 1958-59-60-61-62-63-66-67-70-71; London Foursomes 1984
Int Curtis Cup 1962; Vagliano Trophy 1961-69; England (Home Int) 1960-61-62-63-68-70-72-77-(**78**) (Eur(L) T Ch) 1969-71

Barnes, Brian

Born Addington, Surrey on 3rd June, 1945. Turned Professional 1964

PROFESSIONAL
Eur Agfacolor 1969; Martini International 1972; Dutch Open 1974; French Open 1975; Sun Alliance PGA Match Play 1976; Spanish Open, Greater Manchester Open 1978; Italian Open, Portuguese Open 1979; Tournament Players Chp 1981
Oth Scottish Professional 1981-82; Coca Cola Young Professionals 1969; East of Scotland Professional 1975; Northern Scottish Open 1978; PGA Club Professional Chp 1989
RoW Flame Lily (Rhodesia) 1967; Australian Masters 1970; Zambian Open 1979-81; Kenya Open 1981
Int Ryder Cup 1969-71-73-75-77-79; Hennessy–Cognac Cup 1974-76-78-80; v South Africa; Scotland in World Cup 1974-75-76-77; in Double Diamond 1972-73-74-75-76-77; in PGA Cup 1990
AMATEUR
Reg Somerset Amateur 1964; South Western Counties Amateur 1964
Jun British Youths 1964
Int English Youths 1964

Bayman, Linda (*née* Denison-Pender)

Born 10th June, 1948

Nat English Ladies Amateur 1983; Ladies British Amateur Stroke Play 1987
Trn Avia Foursomes 1969-71-73-79-80; Worplesdon Mixed Foursomes 1980-84; Astor Salver 1983-84; Critchley Salver 1984
Reg Kent Ladies 1968-72-73-78
Int Curtis Cup 1988; Vagliano Trophy 1971-73-85-87; Espirito Santo 1988; England (Home Int) 1971-72-73-83-84-85-87-88; Eur(L) T Ch 1983-85-87
Jun Kent Girls 1966
Mis Avia Woman Golfer of the Year 1987; Doris Chambers Trophy 1987-88-89; Angus Trophy 1987-89

Behan, Lillian

Born Co Kildare on 12th January, 1965. Turned Professional 1986

AMATEUR
Chp Ladies British Open Amateur 1985
Trn The Curragh Scratch Cup 1986
Int Curtis Cup 1986; Vagliano Trophy 1985; Ireland (Home Int) 1984-85-86; (Eur(L) T Ch) 1985

Beharrell, John Charles

Born Solihull, Warwickshire on 2nd May, 1938

Cls Royal & Ancient, Edgbaston, Aldeburgh. Hon member of Little Aston, Blackwell, Handsworth
Chp Amateur Champion 1956
Trn Antlers Royal Mid-Surrey 1960.
Reg Central England Mixed Foursomes 1956-57-75
Int GB v Europe 1956; v Professionals 1956. England (Home Int) 1956
Jun Int English Boy 1955

Beharrell, Veronica (*née* Anstey)

Born Birmingham on 14th January, 1935

Cls Edgbaston (Hon), Little Aston
Oth Australian Ladies, New Zealand Ladies 1955; Victoria Ladies Open 1955
Reg Warwickshire Ladies 1955-56-57-58-60-71-72-75; Central England Mixed Foursomes 1957-75
Int Curtis Cup 1956. England (Home Int) 1955-56-58-(61)
Jun Int English Girls 1953

Benka, Peter

Born London on 18th September, 1946

Cls Addington, West Sussex
Nat Scottish Open Amateur Stroke Play r/u 1969
Oth Dutch Amateur 1972
Trn County Champion of Champions 1967; Sunningdale Foursomes 1969; St George's Challenge Cup 1969. Mullingar Trophy 1970; St George's Hill Trophy 1971-75; John Cross Bowl 1994
Reg Surrey Amateur 1967-68
Int Walker Cup 1969; GBI v Europe 1970; England (Home Int) 1967-68-69-70; (Eur T Ch) 1969
Jun British Youths 1967-68.
Int Boys 1964; Youths 1966-67-68

Bennett, Warren

Born Ruislip on 20th August, 1971. Turned Professional 1994

Cls Ruislip
Maj Open: leading amateur 1994
Nat English Open Amateur Stroke Play (Brabazon) r/u 1994
Oth Australian Centennial Amateur 1994; International Team Chp Sydney
Trn St Andrews Links Trophy r/u 1994. Selborne Salver; Lytham Trophy 1994.
Reg Middlesex Chp 1994
Int GBI *v* Europe 1994; Eisenhower Trophy 1994; England (Home Int) 1992-93-94; *v* France 1994
Jun Int English Youths 1991-92; British Youths 1992

Bentley, Arnold Lewis

Born Southport on 11th June, 1911

Cls Royal & Ancient, Hesketh (Hon), Royal Birkdale
Nat English Amateur 1939
Int England (Home Int) 1936-37; v France 1937-39
Mis Played for British Seniors 1969
Jun Int Boys 1928

Bisgood, Jeanne, CBE

Born Richmond, Surrey on 11th August, 1923

Cls Parkstone (Hon)
Nat English Ladies 1951-53-57
Oth Swedish Ladies 1952; Italian Ladies, German Ladies 1953; Portuguese Ladies 1954; Norwegian Ladies 1955.
Trn Astor Salver 1951-52-53; Roehampton Gold Cup 1951-52-53. Daily Graphic Cup 1945-51
Reg South Eastern Ladies 1950-52; Surrey Ladies 1951-53-69
Int Curtis Cup 1950-52-54-(**70**); England (Home Int) 1949-50-51-52-53-54-56-58

Boatman, Elizabeth (*née* Collis)

Born 7th April, 1944

Nat English Ladies s/f 1974
Reg Essex Ladies 1964-65-69-80-83
Int England (Home Int) 1974-80-(**84**)-(**85**)-(**90**)-(**91**); (Eur(L) T Ch) (**1985**)-(**87**)-(91); (GBI) Commonwealth Trn (1987)-(91); Vagliano Trophy (**1987**); Curtis Cup (**1992**)-(**94**)
Mis Chairman ELGA 1989

Bonallack, Michael Francis, OBE

Born Chigwell on 31st December, 1934

Cls Thorpe Hall, Pine Valley, Elie.
Maj Leading Amateur in Open 1968-71
Chp Amateur Champion 1961-65-68-69-70; s/f 1958-72-77
Nat English Amateur 1962-63-65-67-68; r/u 1959; English Open Amateur Stroke Play 1964-68-69 (tied)-71; r/u 1959-66-67
Trn Berkshire Trophy 1957-61-65-68-70-71 (shared); Hampshire Hog 1957-79; Worplesdon Mixed Foursomes 1958; Sunningdale Foursomes 1959; Golf Illustrated Golf Vase 1961 (shared)-67 (shared)-68-69 (shared)-71-75; Scrutton Jug 1961-64-66-68-70-71; Lytham Trophy 1965 (shared)-72; Antlers Royal Mid-Surrey 1964; St George's Challenge Cup 1965-68-81; Prince of Wales Challenge Cup 1967
Reg Essex Amateur 1954-57-59-60-61-63-64-68-69-70-72; Essex Open 1969; East Anglian Open 1973
Int Walker Cup 1957-59-61-63-65-67-**69**-**71**-73; GB Commonwealth Team 1959-63-**67**-**71**-(**75**); Eisenhower Trophy 1960-62-64-66-**68** (individual winner, shared)-**70**-**72**; v Professionals 1957-58-59-60; v Europe 1958-60-62-64-66-68-70-72. England (Home Int) 1957 to 72-74 (**1962 to 67**); (Eur T Ch) 1959-61-63-65-67-69-71
Jun British Boys 1952
Mis AGW Trophy 1968; Bobby Jones Award 1972; PGA Chairman 1976 to 1981; Chairman Golf Foundation 1977; President English Golf Union 1982. Best equal individual score Eisenhower Trophy 1968. Chairman Royal & Ancient Selection Committee 1975 to 1979. Donald Ross Award 1991. Gerald Micklem Award 1991. Secretary to Royal & Ancient since 1983

Bonallack, Angela (*née* Ward)

Born Birchington on 7th April, 1937

Cls Prince's, Thorpe Hall, St Rule
Chp Ladies British Open Amateur r/u 1962-74

Nat English Ladies 1958-63, r/u 1960-62-72. British Ladies r/u 1962-74
Oth Swedish Ladies, German Ladies 1955; Scandinavian Ladies 1956; Portuguese Ladies 1957
Trn Astor Salver 1957-58-60-61-66; Worplesdon Mixed Foursomes 1958; Kayser-Bondor Foursomes 1958 (shared); Astor Prince's 1968; Avia Foursomes 1976; Roehampton Gold Cup 1980.
Reg Essex Ladies 1968-69-73-74-76-77-78-82; South East Ladies 1957-65; Kent Ladies' 1955-56-58
Int Curtis Cup 1956-58-60-62-64-66. Vagliano Trophy 1959-61-63. England (Home Int) 1956 to 1964; 1966-72
Jun British Girls 1955
Mis Leading amateur Colgate European Ladies' Open 1975-76

Bousfield, Kenneth

Born Marston Moor on 2nd October, 1919. Turned Professional 1938

Eur German Open 1955-59. Swiss Open, Belgian Open 1958; Portuguese Open 1960-61
Trn News Chronicle 1951; PGA Match Play 1955. PGA Close 1955; Yorkshire Evening News 1956 (shared); Dunlop 1957. Sprite 1959. Irish Hospitals 1960 (shared); Swallow-Penfold 1961. Maritime Foursomes (with G Low) 1957; Lord Derby Trn (Formby) 1959; Ryder Cup Re-Union Foursomes (A Caygill) 1964.
Oth Gleneagles Pro-Am 1964. Surrey Open 1951, 1975; Surrey Match Play 1967
Reg Southern England Professional 1951-57-74. Pringle Seniors 1972
Int Ryder Cup 1949-51-55-57-59-61; England in World Cup 1956-57

Brand, Gordon J

Born Cambridge on 6th August, 1955. Turned Professional 1976

PROFESSIONAL
Maj Open r/u 1986
Eur Volvo Belgian Open 1989
RoW Ivory Coast Open 1981; Nigerian Open 1983; Nigerian Open, Ivory Coast Open 1986; Zimbabwe Open 1987; Ivory Coast Open 1988; Zambian Open 1990
Int Ryder Cup 1983; Nissan Cup 1986; England in World Cup 1983; Dunhill Cup 1986-87 (winners)
Mis Tooting Bec Cup 1981-86; Braid-Taylor Memorial Medal 1986; Headed Safari Tour Order of Merit 1983, 1986, 1987
AMATEUR
Int GBI v Europe 1976; England (Home Int) 1976

Brand, Gordon Jr

Born Burntisland, Fife on 19th August, 1958. Turned Professional 1981

Cls Hon member of Woodhall Spa, Knowle
PROFESSIONAL
Eur Coral Classic, Bob Hope British Classic 1982; Celtic International, Panasonic European Open 1984; KLM Dutch Open, Scandinavian Enterprise Open 1987; Benson & Hedges International 1989; GA European Open 1993
RoW South Australian Open 1988
Oth PGA Qualifying School winner 1981
Int Ryder Cup 1987-89; Nissan Cup 1985; Kirin Cup 1988; Four Tours World Chp 1989; Scotland in World Cup 1984-85-88-89-90-92-94; in Dunhill Cup 1985-86-87 (r/u)-88-89-91-92(r/u)-93-94.
Mis Rookie of the Year 1982; AGW Trophy 1982
AMATEUR
Nat English Open Amateur Stroke Play 1978; Scottish Open Amateur Stroke Play 1980
Oth Swedish Open Amateur Stroke Play 1979; Portuguese Amateur 1981
Trn Golf Illustrated Gold Vase 1980; Sunningdale Foursomes 1981
Reg Gloucestershire Amateur 1977; South-Western Counties Amateur 1977-78
Int Walker Cup 1979; Eisenhower Trophy 1978-80; GB v Europe 1978-80; Scotland (Home Int) 1978-80; v England 1979; v Italy 1979; v France 1980-81; v Belgium 1980; (Eur T Ch) 1979
Jun British Youths 1979; Scottish Youths 1980
Int Youths 1977-78-79

Briggs, Audrey (*née* Brown)

Born Kent on 31st January, 1945

Cls Royal Liverpool
Nat Welsh Ladies 1970-71-73-74, r/u 1978-79-80-81
Reg Sussex Ladies 1969. Cheshire Ladies 1971-73-76-80-81. North of England Ladies 1976
Int Vagliano Trophy 1971-73. Wales (Home Int) 1969 to 84, (Eur(L) T Ch) 1969-71-73-75-77-79-81-83; Fiat Trophy 1978-79-80

Broadhurst, Paul

Born Staffordshire on 14th August, 1965. Turned Professional 1988

Maj Leading amateur in Open 1988
PROFESSIONAL
Eur Crédit Lyonnais Cannes Open 1989; Motorola Classic 1990; European Pro-Celebrity 1991; B&H International Open 1993
Int Ryder Cup 1991. England in Dunhill Cup 1991. Four Tours World Chp 1991
Mis Rookie of the Year 1989; Tooting Bec Cup 1990
AMATEUR
Trn Lytham Trophy 1988
Int (GBI) v Europe 1988. England (Home Int) 1986-87.

Brodie, Allan

Born Glasgow on 25th September, 1947

Cls Balmore (Hon), Glasgow
Chp Amateur s/f 1976
Nat Scottish Amateur 1977; r/u 1973. Scottish Open Amateur Stroke Play r/u 1970
Trn Tennant Cup 1972-80; Golf Illustrated Gold Vase 1976
Reg West of Scotland Open Amateur 1974; Dunbartonshire Amateur Stroke Play 1975-76
Int Walker Cup 1977-79; Eisenhower Trophy 1978; GBI v Europe 1974-76-78-80; Scotland (Home Int) 1970-72-73-74-75-76-77-78-80; (Eur T Ch) 1973-77-79; v Belgium, Spain 1977; v France 1978; v England, Italy 1979
Jun Int Youths 1966-67

Brown, Audrey *See* Briggs

Brown, Kenneth

Born Harpenden, Herts on 9th January, 1957. Turned Professional 1974

Eur Carrolls Irish Open 1978; KLM Dutch Open 1983; Glasgow Classic 1984; Four Stars Pro-Celebrity 1985
US Southern Open 1987
RoW Kenya Open 1983
Oth Hertfordshire Open 1975
Int Ryder Cup 1977-79-83-85-87; Hennessy-Cognac Cup 1978-84; Kirin Cup 1987. Scotland: Double Diamond 1977; World Cup 1977-78-79-83
Mis Tooting Bec Cup 1980
Jun Carris Trophy 1974
Int Boys 1974

Burke, Ita *See* Butler

Bussell, Alan Francis

Born Glasgow on 25th February, 1937

Cls Whitecraigs (Hon), Coxmoor (Hon), Chevin
Chp Amateur s/f 1957
Trn Antlers Royal Mid-Surrey 1956. Golf Illustrated Gold Vase 1959
Reg Nottinghamshire Amateur 1959-60-62-63-64-68-69. Nottinghamshire Open 1960-62. Nottinghamshire Match Play 1960-62. Renfrewshire Amateur 1955
Int Walker Cup 1957. GB v Europe 1956-62; v Professionals 1956-57-59. Scotland (Home Int) 1956-57-58-61; v Scandinavia 1956-60
Jun British Boys 1954. Boy International 1954. British Youths 1956. Youth International 1954-55-56

Butler, Ita (*née* Burke)

Born Nenagh, Co Tipperary

Cls Hon member of Elm Park, Killarney, Woodbrook, Nenagh
Nat Irish Ladies r/u 1972-78
Reg Leinster Ladies three times. Munster and Midland Ladies twice
Int Curtis Cup 1966. World Team Championship 1966. Vagliano Trophy 1965-(91)-(93). Ireland (World Cup) 1964; (Home Int) 1962-63-64-65-66-68-71-72-73-76-77-78-79; (Eur T Ch) 1967; Fiat Trophy 1978

Butler, Peter J

Born Birmingham on 25th March, 1932. Turned Professional 1948

Tls French Open 1968. Colombian Open 1975
Trn Swallow-Penfold 1959. Yorkshire Evening News 1962; PGA Close 1963. Bowmaker 1963-67. Cox Moore 1964. PGA Match Play r/u 1964-75. Martini 1965. Piccadilly 1965-67. Penfold, Wills 1968. RTV 1969. Classic International 1971. Sumrie 1974 Evian International 1963. Grand Bahama Invitation Open 1971-72
Reg Midland Open 1956-58-60-65-69. Midland Professional 1961.
Sen Lawrence Batley Seniors 1993
Oth Gleneagles Pro-Am 1963. Sunningdale Foursomes 1974
Int Ryder Cup 1965-69-71-73. England in World Cup. 1969-70-73. England in Double Diamond 1971-72-76. GBI v Europe 1976. PGA Cup 1978-79-81-82-84
Mis Equal lowest round in British events of 61. Second in Order of Merit 1968. PGA Captain 1972

Buxton, Nicola

Born 9th March, 1973

Cls Woodsome Hall
Nat English Ladies 1991-93; English Ladies Stroke Play r/u 1992; English U-23 and U-21 Stroke Play 1992
Oth Portuguese Women's Open r/u 1994
Trn Critchley Salver 1991
Reg Yorkshire Ladies 1989-90-91
Int Curtis Cup 1992; Vagliano Trophy 1991-93; England (Home Int) 1991-92-93; (Eur(L) T Ch) 1991
Jun English Girls 1991

Cadden, Suzanne *See* McMahon

Cage, Stuart

Born 16th July, 1973. Turned Professional 1993

PROFESSIONAL
Oth Open Divonne 1994
AMATEUR
Nat English Amateur 1992
Trn Lytham Trophy 1992
Int (GBI) Walker Cup 1993. England (Home Int) 1993
Jun Int (England) Boys 1991; Youths 1992

Caldwell, Ian

Born Streatham on 17th May, 1930

Cls Royal & Ancient, Sunningdale, Walton Heath
Nat English Amateur 1961
Trn Prince of Wales Challenge Cup 1950-51-52. Boyd Quaich 1954.
Reg Surrey Amateur 1961
Int Walker Cup 1951-55. GB Commonwealth Team 1954. GBI v Europe 1955. England (Home Int) 1950-51-52-53-54-55-56-57-61
Jun Carris Trophy 1947-48

Caldwell, Carole (*née* Redford)

Born Kingston, Surrey on 23rd April, 1949

Cls Canterbury (Hon)
Trn Newmark-Avia International 1973. Roehampton Gold Cup 1973-75-78; Hampshire Rose 1973, 1984; Avia Foursomes 1974; Critchley Salver 1974; Canadian Ladies Foursomes 1978; London Foursomes 1984
Oth Portuguese Ladies 1980
Reg South Eastern Ladies 1973-78. Kent Ladies 1970-75-77-86. Berkshire Ladies 1982
Int Curtis Cup 1978-80; Vagliano Trophy 1973; England (Home Int) 1973-78-79-80
Mis Playing captain of LGU U-23 team to tour Canada 1973. Lost at 27th hole in first round of American Ladies Amateur 1978

Carr, Joseph B

Born Dublin on 18th February, 1922

Cls Sutton (Hon)
Maj Leading Amateur in Open 1956-58

Chp Amateur Champion 1953-58-60, r/u 1968 s/f 1952-54.
Nat Irish Amateur 1954-57-63-64-65-67, r/u 1951-59. Irish Open Amateur 1946-50-54-56, r/u 1947-48-51; US Amateur s/f 1961
Trn Golf Illustrated Gold Vase 1951. Gleneagles Saxone 1955. Berkshire Trophy 1959. Formby Hare 1962. Mullingar Trophy 1963. Antlers Royal Mid-Surrey 1970
Reg South of Ireland Open Amateur 1948-66-69. East of Ireland Open Amateur 1941-43-45-46-48-56-57-58-60-61-64-69. West of Ireland Open Amateur 1946-47-48-51-53-54-56-58-60-61-62-66.
Int Walker Cup 1947-49-51-53-55-57-59-61-**63**-(**65**)-67. GBI v Europe 1954-56-**64**-**66**-68. Eisenhower Trophy 1958-60-(**64**)-(**66**). Ireland (Home Int) 1947 to 1969 (Eur T Ch) 1965-67-69
Mis AGW Trophy 1953. Bobby Jones Award 1961. Walter Hagen Award 1967. Captain of Royal & Ancient 1991/92

Carrick, David

Born Glasgow on 28th January, 1957
Nat Scottish Amateur 1985. Scottish Open Amateur Stroke Play 1987
Trn Scottish Champion of Champions 1983. Glasgow Amateur 1980-81
Reg Dunbartonshire Amateur 1979-80-82-83
Int Walker Cup 1983-87. GBI v Europe 1986. Scotland (Home Int) 1981 to 1989; v Italy 1988; v France 1989; (Eur T Ch) 1989; v West Germany 1987
Mis Braid Panton Trophy 1987

Carslaw, Iain Alexander

Born Glasgow on 4th October, 1949
Cls Williamwood (Hon), Walton Heath
Chp Amateur s/f 1976
Nat Scottish Amateur 1978
Trn Tennant Cup 1978. *Golf Illustrated* Gold Vase 1982
Reg Glasgow County Match Play 1977-78-79-80. Glasgow Amateur 1978
Int Walker Cup 1979. GB v Europe 1978. Scotland (Home Int) 1976-77-78-80-81; (Eur T Ch) 1977-79; v Spain 1977; v Belgium 1978; v France 1978-83; in Fiat Trophy 1978; v Italy 1979; v England 1979; in Moroccan International 1979
Jun Int Boys 1967. Youths 1971

Cassells, Craig

Born Newcastle on 9th May, 1969. Turned Professional 1990
PROFESSIONAL
Eur Northern Open 1991; Quietwaters Challenge 1992
Oth Scottish U-25 Open 1991
AMATEUR
Chp Amateur r/u 1989; s/f 1990
Reg South-East of Scotland Amateur 1989
Int Walker Cup 1989; England (Home Int) 1989; GBI v Europe 1990
Jun Int Youths 1987-88-89

Cater, John Robert

Born Edinburgh, 1919
Cls Williamwood (Hon), Royal & Ancient, Elie
Chp Amateur s/f 1952
Trn Gleneagles Silver Tassie 1952
Reg West of Scotland Amateur 1951-55. Glasgow County 1957
Int Walker Cup 1955. Scotland (Home Int) 1952-53-54-55-56; v South Africa 1954; v Scandinavia 1956
Mis Captain of Royal & Ancient 1986/87

Chadwick, Elizabeth *See* Pook

Chapman, Roger

Born in Nakuru, Kenya on 1st May, 1959. Turned Professional 1981
PROFESSIONAL
RoW Zimbabwe Open 1988
Trn Sunningdale Open Foursomes 1986
Mis Tooting Bec Cup 1991(shared)
AMATEUR
Nat English Amateur 1979
Trn Duncan Putter (shared), Lytham Trophy 1981; Sunningdale Open Foursomes 1979
Int Walker Cup 1981; GBI v Europe 1980; England (Home Int) 1980-81; (Eur T Ch) 1981

Christmas, Martin J

Born 1939
Cls West Sussex, Addington
Chp Amateur s/f 1961-64-65
Nat English Amateur r/u 1960. English Open Amateur Stroke Play r/u 1960
Trn Gleneagles Pro-Am 1961. Wentworth Pro-Am Foursomes 1962
Oth Belgian Open Amateur 1976
Reg Sussex Amateur 1962
Int Walker Cup 1961-63. Eisenhower Trophy 1962. GB v Europe 1960-62-64. England (Home Int) 1960-61-62-63-64

Clark, Clive Anthony

Born Winchester, Hants on 27th June, 1945. Turned Professional 1965
PROFESSIONAL
Maj Open (tied) 3rd 1967 (leading British player)
Tls Danish Open 1966; Bowmaker Agfa-Gevaert 1968; John Player Trophy 1970; Sumrie 1974
AMATEUR
Chp Amateur r/u 1965
Nat English Amateur r/u 1965. English Open Amateur Stroke Play 1965 (tied)
Trn Lytham Trophy 1965 (tied). Golf Illustrated Gold Vase, Scrutton Jug 1965
Oth Sunningdale Foursomes 1974-76
Int Walker Cup 1965. GBI v Europe 1964. England (Home Int) 1964-65. Ryder Cup 1973
Mis Braid-Taylor Memorial Medal 1967; TV commentator. Golf course architect

Clark, Howard K

Born Leeds on 26th August, 1954. Turned Professional October 1973

PROFESSIONAL

Eur Portuguese Open, Madrid Open 1978; Cepsa Madrid Open, Whyte & Mackay PGA Chp 1984; Jersey Open, Glasgow Open 1985; Cepsa Madrid Open, Peugeot Spanish Open 1986; Moroccan Open, PLM Open 1987; English Open 1988

Oth U-25 TPD 1976

Int Ryder Cup 1977-81-85-87-89; Nissan Cup 1985-86; Hennessy-Cognac Cup 1978-84; England in World Cup 1978-84-85 (individual winner)-87; Dunhill Cup 1985-86-87 (winners)-89-90(r/u)-94

AMATEUR

Chp Amateur s/f 1973

Reg Yorkshire Amateur 1973

Int Walker Cup 1973; England (Home Int) 1973

Jun British Boys 1971

Int Boys 1969-71; Youths 1971-72-73

Claydon, Russell

Born on 19th November 1965. Turned Professional 1989

Maj Leading amateur in Open 1989

PROFESSIONAL

Mis Rookie of the Year 1990

AMATEUR

Nat English Amateur 1988

RoW Australian Masters r/u 1989

Trn St George's Challenge Cup 1986; Berkshire Trophy, County Champion of Champions 1988; St Andrews Links Trophy 1989; Sunningdale Open Foursomes 1989

Reg Cambridge Amateur 1987-88

Oth UAP U-25 European Open r/u 1988

Int Walker Cup 1989; England (Home Int) 1988 (Eur T Ch) 1989

Coles, Neil, MBE

Born London on 26th September, 1934. Turned Professional 1950

Maj Open 3rd 1961; r/u 1973; leading British player 1975 (7th)

Eur German Open 1971. Spanish Open 1973

Trn Ballantine 1961. Senior Service 1962. Daks 1963 (tied)-64-70-71 (tied). Martini 1963 (tied). Engadine Open 1963. Bowmaker 1964-70. PGA Match Play 1964-65-73, r/u 1966-72-78. Carrolls 1965-71. Pringle, Dunlop Masters 1966. Sumrie 1970-73. Shell BP Italy, Walworth Aloyco Italy 1970; Penfold 1971. Sunbeam 1972. Wills 1974. Penfold PGA 1976. Tournament Players' Championship 1977. Sanyo Open 1982

Oth British Assistants 1956. Sunningdale Foursomes 1962-67-80. Wentworth Pro-Am Foursomes 1963-70. Southern England Professionals 1970

Int Ryder Cup 1961-63-65-67-69-71-73-77. England in World Cup 1963-68. England in Double Diamond 1971-73-75-76-77. Hennessy-Cognac Cup 1974-76-78-80

Sen Seniors British Open 1987. PGA Seniors Chp 1985-86-87-89. Geneva Seniors Open 1991. Collingtree Homes Senior Classic 1992. Gary Player Seniors Classic 1993

Mis Harry Vardon Trophy 1963-70. Second in Order of Merit 1987. Chairman PGA European Tour. Golf course architect.

Collingham, Janet (*née* Melville)

Born Barrow-in-Furness on 16th March, 1958

Cls Notts Ladies

Chp Ladies British Open Amateur 1987

Nat Ladies British Open Amateur Stroke Play 1978

Trn Worplesdon Mixed Foursomes 1979. Northern Foursomes 1977-78. Mary McCalley Trophy 1980

Reg Highland Open 1978. Midland Ladies 1986. Lancashire Champion 1983-86

Int Vagliano Trophy 1979-87. England (Home Int) 1978-79-81-84-86-87-92; (Eur(L) T Ch) 1979. Girls International 1976-(81)

Mis Varsity Athlete in golf at Florida International University 1980-81; Duncan Salver 1978

Collis, Elizabeth *See* Boatman

Coltart, Andrew John

Born Dumfries on 12th May, 1970. Turned Professional 1991

Cls Thornhill

PROFESSIONAL

RoW Australian PGA 1994

Oth Scottish Professional 1994

Int Scotland: Dunhill Cup 1994, World Cup 1994

AMATEUR

Nat Scottish Amateur r/u 1988; Scottish Open Amateur Stroke Play 1991

Trn Leven Gold Medal 1989

Reg West of Scotland 1991

Int Walker Cup 1991. World Cup (Eisenhower) 1990; GBI v Europe 1990. Scotland (Home Int) 1988-89-90; (Eur T Ch) 1989-91; Nixdorf Nations Cup 1990; v Sweden, Italy 1990

Oth Leone de San Marco 1990

Jun British Youths r/u 1989-90; Scottish Boys 1987

Cosh, Gordon B

Born Glasgow on 26th March, 1939

Cls Troon, Royal Aberdeen, Bruntsfield Links. Hon member of Cowglen, Killarney

Nat Scottish Amateur 1968, r/u 1965. Scottish Open Amateur Stroke Play r/u 1968

Trn Newlands Trophy 1980

Reg West of Scotland Amateur 1961-64-65-66. Glasgow County Match Play 1965-66. Glasgow Amateur 1969. Glasgow County Stroke Play 1972-74

Int Walker Cup 1965. Eisenhower Trophy 1966-68. GB Commonwealth Team 1967. GBI v Europe 1966-68. Scotland (Home Int) 1964-65-66-67-68-69; (Eur T Ch) 1965-69

Jun Int Youths 1959-60

Craddock, Tom

Born Malahide on 16th December, 1931

Cls Malahide, Donabate, Sutton, The Island Malahide, Malone, Woodbrook, Mullingar, Carlow, Howth, Tara, Killarney

Nat Irish Amateur 1959, r/u 1965. Irish Open Amateur 1958

Trn Lytham Trophy 1969

Reg East of Ireland Open Amateur 1959-65-66

Int Walker Cup 1967-69. Ireland (Home Int) 1955-56-57-58-59-60-65-66-67-69; (Eur T Ch) 1967-71

Critchley, Bruce

Born 9th December, 1942

Cls Sunningdale, Killarney (Hon)
Chp Amateur s/f 1970
Trn Worplesdon Mixed Foursomes 1961. Sunningdale Foursomes 1964. Hampshire Hog 1969. Antlers Royal Mid-Surrey 1974
Reg Surrey Amateur 1969
Int Walker Cup 1969. GBI v Europe 1970. England (Home Int) 1962-69-70; (Eur T Ch) 1969
Mis TV commentator. Co-founder annual match between former Ryder Cup v Walker Cup Players

Critchley, Diana Lesley (*née* Fishwick)

Born London on 12th April, 1911

Cls North Foreland, Bramley, Canterbury, Sunningdale, Sunningdale Ladies
Chp British Ladies 1930.
Nat English Ladies 1932-49, r/u 1929
Oth French Ladies 1932. German Ladies 1936-38. Belgian Ladies 1938. Dutch Ladies 1946. Florida (USA) West Coast 1933
Trn Sunningdale Foursomes 1934
Reg Kent Ladies 1934. Surrey Ladies 1936-46
Int Curtis Cup 1932-34-(**50**). GBI v France 1931-32-33-34-(**48**); v Canada 1934-50. England (Home Int) 1930-31-32-33-35-36-47
Jun British Girls 1927-28
Mis Chairman of ELGA Selection Committee 1967-68-69-70. LGU International Selector 1970-71-72-73. Member LGU Team to tour South Africa 1933

Curry, David H

Born 6th July, 1963. Turned Professional 1988

Chp Amateur Champion 1986
Trn Selborne Salver 1984
Int England (Home Int) 1984-86-87. v France 1988. (GBI) v Europe 1986-88. Walker Cup 1987

Dalgleish, Colin R

Born Glasgow on 24th September, 1960

Cls Helensburgh (Hon), Millstone Mills (Hon)
Nat Scottish Amateur 1981
Trn Tennant Cup 1983-88
RoW East of India Amateur 1981. Indian Amateur r/u 1981. Lake Macquarie International Stroke-Play Champion (Australia) 1983
Oth Scottish Universities Champion 1983
Int Walker Cup 1981. Scotland (Home Int) 1981-82-83; v France 1982; (Eur T Ch) 1981-83. GB v Europe 1982. Europe v South America 1982
Jun International Junior Masters 1977. Belgian Junior Championship 1980. British Boys r/u 1977. British Youths r/u 1979-82. Boy International 1976-77-78. Youth International 1979-80-81-82

Darcy, Eamonn

Born Delgany on 7th August, 1952. Turned Professional 1969

Eur Spanish Open 1983; Belgian Open 1987; Desert Classic 1990
Trn Sumrie 1976-78. Greater Manchester Open 1977
RoW Air New Zealand Open 1980. Cock o' the North Open 1981. Kenya Open 1982. Mufulira Open 1984. West Lakes Classic (Aus) 1981
Oth Irish Dunlop 1976. Cacharel World Under-25 1976. Irish Match Play 1981
Int Ryder Cup 1975-77-81-87. Ireland in Double Diamond 1975-76-77. Ireland in World Cup 1976-77-83-84-85-87-91. GBI v Europe 1976; v South Africa 1976. Hennessy-Cognac Cup 1976-84. Dunhill Cup 1987-88 (winners)-91
Mis Second in Order of Merit 1976; Tooting Bec Cup 1980(shared)-1991(shared); Braid Taylor Memorial Medal 1991

Davies, John C

Born London on 14th February, 1948

Cls Mid-Surrey, Sunningdale, Royal Cinque Ports, Killarney
Chp Amateur r/u 1976.
Nat English Amateur r/u 1971-76. English Open Amateur Stroke Play r/u 1977
Trn Berkshire Trophy 1969-71 (tied). Royal St George's Challenge Cup 1972-73-74-75-76-77. Sunningdale Foursomes 1968-72. Antlers Royal Mid-Surrey 1969-75-77. Golf Illustrated Gold Vase 1973-77. Prince of Wales Cup 1975. Berkhamsted Trophy 1976-78-79
Oth Second equal in South African Open Amateur Stroke Play 1974
Reg Surrey Amateur 1971-72-77
Int Walker Cup 1973-75-77-79. Eisenhower Trophy 1974-76 (winners). GBI v Europe 1972-74-76-78; England (Home Int) 1969-70-71-72-73-74-78; (Eur T Ch) 1973-75-77
Mis Member of European Team to tour South Africa 1974

Davies, Karen L

Born 19th June, 1965. Turned Professional 1988

PROFESSIONAL
Int Sunrise Cup 1992
AMATEUR
Oth Florida State Tournament 1985. South-Eastern USA Championship 1985
Int Curtis Cup 1986-88. Wales (Home Int) 1981-82-83 (Eur L U-22) 1981-82-83-84-85-86; (Eur(L) T Ch) 1987, Commonwealth Team 1987
Jun Welsh Girls 1980-82

Davies, Laura

Born Coventry on 5th October, 1963. Turned Professional 1985

Maj Ladies British Open 1986; r/u 1987. US Women's Open 1987; McDonald's LPGA 1994
PROFESSIONAL
Eur Belgian Ladies Open 1985; McEwan's Wirral Classic, Greater Manchester Tournament, Ladies Spanish Open 1986; Italian Open 1987; Italian Open, Ford Ladies Classic, Biarritz Ladies Open 1988; Laing Charity Ladies Classic 1989; AGF Biarritz Ladies Open 1990; Valextra Classic 1991; European Ladies Open, Ladies English Open, BMW Ladies Italian Open 1992; Ladies English Open 1993; Ladies Irish Open, Ladies Scottish Open 1994
US Tucson Open, Toledo Classic 1988; Lady Keystone Open 1989; Inamori Classic 1991; McDonald's Chp 1993; Standard Register Ping, Sara Lee Classic 1994

RoW Australian Ladies' Masters, Thailand Open 1993; Itoen Ladies (Jpn) 1994
Int Solheim Cup 1990-92-94; Sunrise Cup 1992; (for LPGA) Nichirei International 1993
Mis Rookie of the Year 1985. Order of Merit winner 1985-86-92. Hon. Member of WPGET 1993. Top of LPGA Money List 1994. Ping No. 1 1994
AMATEUR
Nat Welsh Open Stroke Play 1984
Oth English Intermediate 1983
Trn London Foursomes 1981.
Reg South-Eastern Champion 1983-84
Int Curtis Cup 1984; Vilmorin Cup 1984; England (Home Int) 1983-84
Jun Surrey Girls 1982

De Bendern, Count John (John de Forest)

Born 1907

Cls Royal & Ancient, Sunningdale, Addington, Lausanne
Chp Amateur Champion 1932, r/u 1931
Oth Austrian Amateur 1937. Czechoslovakian Amateur 1937
Reg Surrey Amateur 1931-49
Int Walker Cup 1932. England (Home Int) 1931

Deeble, Peter George

Born Alnwick on 27th February, 1954

Cls Alnmouth, Alnwick, Hon member of Ponteland, Hexham, Rothbury, Washington, Tynedale
Nat English Amateur 1976-80
Trn Antlers Royal Mid-Surrey 1976. Lytham Trophy 1977. Berkhamsted Trophy 1975. County Champion of Champions 1982
Reg Northumberland Amateur 1975-82-83. Northumberland Stroke Play 1973-75-77-78-79. Northumberland and Durham Open 1976
Int Walker Cup 1977-81. GBI v Europe 1978. Europe v South America 1980. GB in Colombian International 1978. England (Home Int) 1975-76-77-78-80-81-83; (Eur T Ch) 1979-81; v Scotland 1979; v France 1982. England in Fiat Trophy 1980
Jun Int Boys 1970-71. Youths 1973-75-76

Deighton, Dr FWG

Born Glasgow on 21st May, 1927

Cls Royal & Ancient, Western Gailes, Elie, Glasgow, Hilton Park (Hon), North Hants
Nat Scottish Amateur 1956-59
Trn Edward Trophy 1954. Gleneagles Silver Tassie 1956. Tennant Cup 1958-60-64
Oth Boyd Quaich 1947 (tied). Royal & Ancient Silver Cross 1953-60-63-70-73. Royal Medal 1956-59-61-63-66-73. Glennie Medal 1956-58-59-60-66-70-73
Reg West of Scotland Amateur 1959. Dunbartonshire Amateur 1949-50-53-54. Glasgow Amateur 1951-55
Int Walker Cup 1951-57. GB Commonwealth Team 1954-59. GBI v Professionals 1956-57. Scotland (Home Int) 1950-52-53-56-58-59-60; v South Africa 1954; v New Zealand 1954; v Scandinavia 1956
Mis Member of British Touring Team to South Africa 1952

Dobson, Helen

Born Skegness on 25th February, 1971. Turned Professional 1990

PROFESSIONAL
Eur BMW European Masters 1993
US LPGA: State Farm Rail Classic 1993
Int Union Cup 1994
AMATEUR
Chp Ladies British Open Amateur 1989
Nat Ladies British Open Amateur Stroke Play 1989; English Ladies 1989
Trn Wentworth Scratch Trophy, Bridget Jackson Bowl 1989
Oth World Fourball (with Elaine Farquharson) 1989
Int Curtis Cup 1990; Vagliano Trophy 1989; England (Home Int) 1987-88-89; (Eur(L) T Ch) 1989
Jun British Girls 1987; English Girls 1988-89
Jun Int English Girls 1988
Mis Duncan Salver 1989. Avia Woman Golfer of the Year 1989.

Dodd, Stephen

Born Cardiff on 15th July, 1966. TurnedProfessional 1990

PROFESSIONAL
Eur Memorial Olivier Barras 1991; Bank of Austria Open 1992
Reg West Region PGA 1991
AMATEUR
Chp Amateur Champion 1989
Nat Welsh Amateur 1989
Trn Silver Dragon, WI Tucker Trophy 1987; Duncan Putter, Carad Trophy, Cardiff Feathers, Golden Lamp 1988
Int Walker Cup 1989; Wales (Home Int) 1985-87-88-89, (Eur T Ch) 1987

Douglas, Kitrina

Born Bristol on 6th September, 1960. Turned Professional 1984

Maj Ladies British Open 3rd 1990
PROFESSIONAL
Eur Ford Classic, Swedish Ladies Open, Rookie of the Year 1984; Mitsubishi Colt Cars, Jersey Open 1986; Hennessy-Cognac Ladies Cup 1987; St Moritz Ladies Classic, Godiva European Masters 1989; English Open 1991; BMW European Masters 1992
Int Solheim Cup 1992
Mis Rookie of the Year 1984
AMATEUR
Chp British Ladies 1982
Oth Portuguese Champion 1983
Trn Critchley Salver 1983
Reg Gloucestershire Champion 1980-81-82-83-84
Int Curtis Cup 1982. Vagliano Trophy 1983. England (Home Int) 1981-82. Eur(L) T Ch 1983
Jun Scottish Girls Stroke-Play 1981

Dowling, Deborah

Born Wimbledon on 26th July, 1962. Turned Professional 1981

PROFESSIONAL
Eur Jersey Open, Woodhall Hills Trn 1983; Portuguese Ladies Open 1985; Eastleigh Classic, Laing Ladies Classic 1986; Bloor Homes Eastleigh Classic 1989

Int Union Cup 1994
AMATEUR
Reg Surrey Champion 1980
Int England (Home Int) 1981 (Eur(L) T Ch) 1981

Dredge, Bradley

Born Gwent, Wales on 6th July, 1973.

Cls Bryn Meadows
Chp Amateur r/u 1992
Nat European Amateur r/u 1992
Trn St David's Gold Cross 1992; Welsh Trn of Champions 1994
Int World Cup 1992; (Wales) Home Int 1992-93; (GBI) Walker Cup 1993; *v* Europe 1994
Jun Welsh Boys 1991

Drew, Norman Vico

Born Belfast on 25th May, 1932. Turned Professional 1958

PROFESSIONAL
Trn Yorkshire Evening News, Irish Dunlop 1959
Oth Irish Professional 1959; Ulster Professional 1966-72
Int Ryder Cup 1959; Ireland in World Cup 1960-61
AMATEUR
Nat Irish Open Amateur 1952-53
Reg North of Ireland Open Amateur 1950-52; East of Ireland Open Amateur 1952
Int Walker Cup 1953; Ireland (Home Int) 1952-53

Duncan, Colonel Anthony Arthur, OBE

Born Cardiff on 10th December, 1914

Cls Royal & Ancient, Southerndown, Hindhead, Royal Porthcawl
Chp Amateur r/u 1939.
Nat Welsh Amateur 1938-48-52-54, r/u 1933
Trn Worplesdon Mixed Foursomes 1946-47. Hampshire Hog 1959. President's Putter 1948-58
Int Walker Cup **1953**. Wales (Home Int) 1933-34-36-38-47-48-**49**-50-51-52-53-54-55-56-57-**58**-59
Mis Chairman Walker Cup Selection Committee 1954-55. Won all six matches in 1956 Home Internationals. President Oxford and Cambridge Golfing Society 1979-83

Dundas, Stephen

Born Glasgow on 20th December, 1973

Cls Haggs Castle
Chp Amateur Champion 1992
Nat Scottish Amateur s/f 1992
Int Scotland Boys **1989**
Jun Glasgow Boys Stroke Play, Match Play 1988-89; West of Scotland Boys 1988

Evans, Albert David

Born Newton, Brecon, Wales on 28th August, 1911

Cls Royal & Ancient, Royal Porthcawl. Hon member of Brecon, Ross-on-Wye, Hereford, Worcestershire, Builth Wells, Pennard, Monmouth, Killarney
Chp Welsh Amateur 1949-61
Reg Herefordshire Amateur 1938-46-49-51-53-54-55-59-60-61-62. Breconshire Amateur 1929-31-32-33-34-37
Int Wales (Home Int) 1931-32-33-34-35-38-39-47-48-49-50-51-52-53-54-55-56-**60-61-62-63-64-65**; v Australia 1954
Mis Walker Cup Selector 1964-75

Evans, Duncan

Born Crewe on 23rd January, 1959

Cls Hon member of Leek, Conway, Holyhead, Royal Porthcawl, Westwood
Chp Amateur Champion 1980.
Nat Welsh Amateur Stroke Play Championship 1981, r/u 1980
Reg Staffordshire Amateur 1979. Aberconwy Trophy 1981
Int GBI v Europe. Europe v South America 1980. Wales (Home Int) 1978-80; v Ireland 1979; in Fiat Trophy 1980. Walker Cup 1981; (Eur T Ch) 1981
Jun Int Youths 1980

Evans, Gary

Born Rustington on 22nd February, 1969. Turned Professional 1991

Cls Worthing
Nat English Amateur r/u 1990; English Open Amateur Stroke Play 1990-91
Trn Lytham Trophy 1990-91; St Andrews Trophy r/u 1991
Int Walker Cup 1991; World Cup (Eisenhower) 1990; England (Home Int) 1990; (Eur T Ch) 1991
Jun Int British Youths 1989; English Youths 1989; English Boys 1986

Everard, Mrs D Mary

Born Sheffield on 8th October, 1942

Cls Hallamshire (Hon), Woodhall Spa (Hon), Kilton Forest (Hon), Lindrick
Maj Ladies British Open r/u 1977
Chp Ladies British Open Amateur r/u 1967
Nat Ladies British Open Amateur Stroke Play 1970-77, r/u 1971-73; English Ladies 1972, r/u 1964-77
Trn Astor Salver 1967-68-78. Hovis Ladies 1967. Roehampton Gold Cup 1970. Sunningdale Foursomes 1973. Hoylake Mixed Foursomes 1965-67-71-76. Avia Foursomes 1978
Reg North of England Ladies 1972. Yorkshire Ladies 1964-67-72-73-77
Int Curtis Cup 1970-72-74-78. Vagliano Trophy 1967-69-71-73. GB Commonwealth Team 1971. World Team Championship 1968-72-78, England (Home Int) 1964-67-70-72-73-77-78; (Eur(L) T Ch) 1967-71-73-77
Mis Member of British team to tour Australia 1973. Captain English team to tour Kenya 1973

Everett, Craig

Born Glasgow on 31st January, 1968. Turned Professional 1991

Cls Cambuslang
Nat Scottish Amateur 1990
Trn Cameron Corbett Vase 1988; Leven Gold Medal 1988
Reg East of Scotland Open Amateur 1988
Int Scotland (Home Int) 1988-89-90; v Italy 1988-90; v France 1989; (Eur T Ch) 1989-91; Nixdorf Nations Cup 1989; v Sweden 1990

Jun Irish Youths Open 1987; Scottish Boys Stroke Play r/u 1985
Int Scottish Boys 1985; Scottish Youths 1987-88; British Boys 1985; British Youth 1988

Faldo, Nicholas Alexander, MBE

Born Welwyn Garden City on 18th July, 1957. Turned Professional 1976

PROFESSIONAL
Maj Open Champion 1987-90-92, r/u 1993; 3rd 1988; US Open r/u 1988 (tied) 3rd 1990; US Masters 1989-90; US PGA r/u 1992; 3rd 1993
Eur Colgate PGA 1978; Sun Alliance PGA 1980; Sun Alliance 1981; Haig Whisky TPC 1982; French Open, Martini Int'l, Lawrence Batley Int'l, Car Care Plan Int'l, Ebel Swiss Open European Masters 1983; Car Care Plan Int'l 1984; Peugeot Spanish Open 1987; Peugeot French Open, Volvo Masters 1988; Volvo PGA, Dunhill British Masters, Peugeot French Open, Suntory World Match Play 1989; Carrolls Irish Open 1991; Carrolls Irish Open, Scandinavian Masters, GA European Open, Toyota World Match Play 1992; Johnnie Walker Classic, Carrolls Irish Open 1993; Alfred Dunhill Open 1994
US Heritage Classic 1984
RoW ICL Int'l 1979; Johnnie Walker Asian Classic 1990; Johnnie Walker World Chp 1992; Million Dollar Challenge 1994
Oth Skol Lager 1977
Int Ryder Cup 1977-79-81-83-85-87-89-91-93; Nissan Cup 1986; Kirin Cup 1987-88; Hennessy-Cognac Cup 1978-80-82-84; England in World Cup 1977-91; in Double Diamond 1977; in Dunhill Cup 1985-86-87 (winners)-88-90-91-93(r/u); Four Tours Chp 1990
Mis Rookie of the Year 1977; Harry Vardon Trophy 1983-92; AGW Trophy 1983-90; Braid-Taylor Memorial Medal 1983-84-87-88-90; BBC Sports Personality of the Year 1989; US PGA Player of the Year 1990; Tooting Bec Cup 1992
AMATEUR
Nat English Amateur 1975
Trn Berkshire Trophy, Scrutton Jug, County Champion of Champions 1975
Reg Hertfordshire Amateur 1975
Oth South African GU Special Stroke Chp 1975
Int GB Commonwealth Trn 1975; England (Home Int) 1975
Jun British Youths 1975
Int Boys 1974; Youths 1975

Farquharson-Black, Elaine

Born Aberdeen on 21st March, 1968. Turned Professional 1992

Cls Deeside
PROFESSIONAL
Int Union Cup 1994
AMATEUR
Chp Ladies British Open Amateur r/u 1989
Nat Scottish Ladies 1990
Oth World Fourball (with Helen Dobson) 1989
Trn Helen Holm Trophy 1987
Reg Aberdeenshire Ladies 1983-86-87
Int Curtis Cup 1990-92; Vagliano Trophy 1989-91; Commonwealth Trn 1991; Scotland (Home Int) 1987-88-89-90-91; (Eur(L) T Ch) 1989-91
Jun British Girls r/u 1984-85; Scottish Girls 1985
Int Scottish Girls 1982-84-85; Eur Jun(L) T Ch 1986-88

Faulkner, Max

Born Bexhill, Sussex on 29th July, 1916. Turned Professional June 1933

Maj Open Champion 1951
Eur Spanish Open 1952-53-57. Portuguese Open 1968
Trn Dunlop Southport 1946. Dunlop 1949-52. Penfold Foursomes 1949. Lotus 1949. Dunlop Masters 1951. PGA Match Play 1953. Irish Hospitals 1959
Reg West of England Open Professional 1947. Southern England Professional 1964.
Oth Sunningdale Open Foursomes 1964; Pringle Seniors 1968-70
Int Ryder Cup 1947-49-51-53-57; PGA Cup 1975

Feherty, David

Born in Bangor, NI on 13th August, 1958. Turned Professional 1976

Eur Italian Open, Bells Scottish Open 1986; BMW International Open 1989; Cannes Open 1991; Iberia Madrid Open 1992
RoW ICL International 1984; Lexington PGA 1988; Bells Cup (SA) 1992
Int Ryder Cup 1991. Ireland: Dunhill Cup 1986-90 (winners) -91-93; World Cup 1990; Four Tours World Chp 1990-91
Mis Braid-Taylor Memorial Medal 1989

Ferguson, Marjory (*née* Fowler)

Born North Berwick on 15th May, 1937

Cls North Berwick, Gullane, Killarney (Hon)
Nat Scottish Ladies r/u 1966-71
Oth Portuguese Ladies 1960
Reg East of Scotland Ladies 1959-60-62-75. East Lothian Ladies 1957-58-59-60-61-62-63-64-66-67-69-74-81
Int Curtis Cup 1966. Vagliano Trophy 1965. Scotland (Home Int) 1959-62-63-64-65-66-67-69-70; (Eur(L) T Ch) 1965-67-71

Le Feuvre, Carol *See* Gibbs

Fiddian, Eric Westwood

Born Stourbridge on 28th March, 1910

Cls Stourbridge, Handsworth, Lindrick
Chp Amateur r/u 1932.
Nat English Amateur 1932, r/u 1935. Irish Open Amateur r/u 1933
Reg Worcestershire Amateur 1928-30-50. Midland Counties 1931
Int Walker Cup 1932-34. England (Home Int) 1929-30-31-32-33-34-35
Jun Boys 1927.
Int English Boys 1926-27
Mis Had two holes-in-one in the Final of 1933 Irish Open Amateur

Fishwick, Diana Lesley *See* Critchley

Fletcher, Linzi

Born on 21st January, 1968

Cls Alnmouth
Nat English Ladies r/u 1990; English Womens Intermediate 1990

Trn Critchley Salver 1989; Wentworth Scratch Trophy 1990
Int Curtis Cup 1990; GB Commonwealth Trn 1991; England (Home Int) 1989-90; (Eur(L) T Ch) 1991

Foster, Rodney
Born Shipley, Yorkshire on 13th October, 1941
Cls Royal & Ancient, Hon member of Bradford, Halifax, Leeds, West Bowling, Ilkley, East Bierley
Chp Amateur s/f 1962-65
Nat English Amateur r/u 1964. English Open Amateur Stroke Play 1969 (tied)-70, r/u 1965
Trn Berkshire Trophy 1964. Lytham Trophy 1967-68. County Champion of Champions 1963 (tied)
Reg Yorkshire Amateur 1963-64-65-67-70
Int Walker Cup 1965-67-69-71-73-(**79**). GBI v Europe 1964-66-68-70-(**80**). Eisenhower Trophy 1964-70-(**80**). GB Commonwealth Team 1967-71. England (Home Int) 1963-64-66-67-68-69-70-71-72-(**76**)-(**77**)-(**78**); (Eur T Ch) 1963-65-67-69-71-73-(**77**)
Jun Int Boys 1958. Youths 1959

Fowler, Marjory *See* Ferguson

Frearson, Diane *See* Bailey

Furby, Joanne
Born Ripon on 13th May, 1969. Turned Professional 1989
Cls Masham
Chp British Ladies 1988
Nat English Ladies 1987.
Reg Yorkshire Ladies 1988
Int England (Home Int) 1987-88; (Eur(L) T Ch) 1987

Gallacher, Bernard
Born Bathgate on 9th February, 1949. Turned Professional 1967
PROFESSIONAL
Eur Spanish Open 1977; French Open 1979
Trn Schweppes, Wills 1969; Martini International 1971; Carrolls International, Dunlop Masters 1974; Dunlop Masters 1975; Tournament Players Chp 1980; Greater Manchester Open 1981; Martini International; Jersey Open 1982; Jersey Open 1984
Oth Scottish Professional 1971-73-74-77; Coca-Cola Young Professionals 1973
RoW Zambia Eagle Open, Zambia Cock o' the North 1969; Mufulira Open 1970
Int Ryder Cup 1969-71-73-75-77-79-81-83-(**91**)-(**93**)-(95); Hennessy-Cognac Cup 1974-78-82-84; Scotland in World Cup 1969-71-74-82-83; in Double Diamond 1971-72-73-74-75-76-77; v South Africa 1976
Mis Rookie of the Year 1968; Harry Vardon Trophy 1969 (then youngest winner); Scottish Sportsman of the Year 1969; Frank Moran Trophy 1973
AMATEUR
Nat Scottish Open Amateur Stroke Play 1967
Int Scotland (Home Int) 1967
Jun Int Boys 1965-66

Gallacher, Stephen
Born Dechmont on 1 November 1974
Cls Bathgate
Chp Amateur: leading qualifier 1994
Nat Scottish Amateur 1992; European Individual Amateur 1994
Reg Lothians Stroke Play 1992
Int Eisenhower Trophy 1994; Scotland (Home Int) 1992-93-94; *v* Italy, *v* Spain 1994; (Eur T Ch) 1993
Jun Scottish Boys Chp 1991-92; Scottish Youths Chp 1994
Jun Int Scottish Boys 1991-92; British Boys 1992; Scottish Youths 1992-93-94; British Youths 1994

Garrett, Maureen (*née* Ruttle)
Born 22nd August, 1922
Oth French Ladies 1964
Int Curtis Cup **1960**. England (Home Int) **1960**. Vagliano Trophy **1961**
Mis LGU President 1982-85. Bobby Jones Award 1983

Garvey, Philomena K
Born Drogheda, Co Louth on 26th April, 1927. Turned Professional 1964, subsequently reinstated Amateur
Cls Co Down, Co Louth, Portrush, Milltown
Chp British Ladies 1957, r/u 1946-53-60-63.
Nat Irish Ladies 1946-47-48-50-51-53-54-55-57-58-59-60-62-63-70
Trn Worplesdon Mixed Foursomes 1955
Reg Munster Ladies 1951
Int Curtis Cup 1948-50-52-54-56-60. GBI v France 1949-51-53-55; v Belgium 1951-53. Vagliano Trophy 1959-63. Ireland (Home Int) 1947-48-49-50-51-52-53-54-55-56-59-60-61-62-63-69; v Australia 1950
Mis Quarter-finalist US Ladies 1950.

Gibbs, Carol (*née* Le Feuvre)
Born Jersey on 18th October, 1951
Cls Jersey, Lee-on-the-Solent
Nat English Ladies r/u 1973
Oth Dutch Ladies 1972
Trn Avia Foursomes 1974
Reg Jersey Ladies 1966-67-68. Hampshire Ladies 1970-71-72-73-74-76. South-Eastern Ladies 1974
Int Curtis Cup 1974. Vagliano Trophy 1973. England (Home Int) 1971-72-73-74; (Eur(L) T Ch) 1973
Jun English Girls 1969-70. British Girls 1970.
Int English Girls 1968-69-70
Mis Member of LGU Team to tour Australia 1973, and Under-25 team to tour Canada 1973

Gilford, David
Born 14th September, 1965. Turned Professional 1986
PROFESSIONAL
Eur Johnnie Walker International 1990; English Open 1991; Moroccan Open 1992-93; Portuguese Open 1993; Open de Tenerife, European Open 1994

RoW Tobago International 1992
Oth Silvermere Satellite Trophy 1987
Int Ryder Cup 1991. (England) Dunhill Cup 1992(winners). World Cup 1992-93
AMATEUR
Nat English Amateur 1984
Trn Lagonda Trophy 1986
Int Walker Cup 1985. GBI v Europe 1986. England (Home Int) 1983-84-85
Jun British Youths 1986. Carris Trophy 1981

Glover, John

Born Belfast on 3rd March, 1933

Cls Killarney (Hon), New Club, St Andrews
Trn Formby Hare 1963
Oth British Universities 1954-55
Reg Lancashire Amateur 1970
Int Ireland (Home Int) 1951-52-53-55-59-60-62-70
Jun Boy Champion 1950. Carris Trophy 1950
Mis Secretary Royal & Ancient Rules of Golf Committee

Green, Charles Wilson

Born Dumbarton on 2nd August, 1932

Cls Dumbarton, Cardross, Helensburgh
Maj Leading amateur in Open 1962
Nat Scottish Amateur 1970-82-83, r/u 1971-80. Scottish Open Amateur Stroke Play 1975, 1984, r/u 1967-83. British Seniors 1988-89-90-91-92(r/u)-93-94. Scottish Seniors 1991
Trn Lytham Trophy 1970 (tied)-74. Eden Tournament 1959. Tennant Cup 1968-70-75. Edward Trophy 1968-73-74-75
Reg West of Scotland Amateur 1962-70-79. Dunbartonshire Amateur 1960-67-68-73-77. Dunbartonshire Match Play 1965-67-69-71-74. Glasgow Amateur 1979
Int Walker Cup 1963-69-71-73-75-(**83**)-(**85**); GBI v Scandinavia 1962; v Europe 1962-66-68-70-72-74-76. Eisenhower Trophy 1970-**72**-84-86. GB Commonwealth Team 1971. Scotland (Home Int) 1961to 1965; 1967 to 1978; **1980**; v Australia 1964, (Eur T Ch) 1965-67-69-71-73-75-77-79-81-83; v Belgium 1973-75-77-78; v Spain 1977; v Italy 1979; v England 1979
Mis Frank Moran Trophy 1974. British Selector 1980. Scottish Sports Photographer Award 1983

Greenhalgh, Julia *See* Merrill

Gregson, Malcolm Edward

Born Leicester on 15th August, 1943. Turned Professional 1961

Trn Schweppes 1967. RTV 1967. Daks 1967-68. Martini 1967 (tied). Sumrie 1972
RoW Zambia Cock o' the North 1974. Gambian Open 1981
Oth Pannal Foursomes 1964. British Assistants 1964
Int Ryder Cup 1967. England in World Cup 1967. GBI v France 1966. Sumrie 1972 England in Double Diamond 1975
Mis Harry Vardon Trophy 1967
Am Boy International 1959-60

Grice-Whittaker, Penny

Born Sheffield on 11th September, 1964. Turned Professional 1985

PROFESSIONAL
Maj Women's British Open 1991
Eur Belgian Open 1986; Longines Classic 1991
AMATEUR
Nat English Intermediate Champion 1984; English Stroke Play 1984; English Ladies U-23 Chp 1983
Reg Yorkshire Champion 1981-82-83. Northern Foursomes 1984
Int Curtis Cup 1984. England (Home Int) 1983-84. (Eur(L) T Ch) 1983. Vilmorin Trophy 1984. Espirito Santo 1984
Jun English Girls 1983

Hall, Caroline

Born on 4th November, 1973. Turned Professional 1992

Cls Filton
PROFESSIONAL
Int Union Cup 1994
AMATEUR
Chp Ladies British Open Amateur s/f 1991
Nat English Ladies Under-18 Stroke Play 1991; English Ladies 1992
Trn Frilford Heath Scratch Cup 1990; Cotswold Hills Gold Vase 1990-91
Reg Gloucestershire Ladies 1991
Int Curtis Cup 1992; Vagliano Trophy 1991; England (Home Int) 1991-92; (Eur(L) T Ch) 1991
Jun English Girls 1990, r/u 1991

Hall, Julie (*née* Wade)

Born on 10th March, 1967

Cls Felixstowe Ferry
Chp Ladies British Open Amateur 1990
Nat English Ladies Stroke Play 1987-93; English Ladies 1988-94; British Ladies Amateur Stroke Play 1988(r/u)-94; Welsh Women's Open Stroke Play 1993
Oth World Fourball Chp (with Helen Wadsworth) 1987
Trn Astor Salver 1990; Helen Holm Trophy 1991-93; Wentworth Scratch Cup 1993
Int Curtis Cup 1988-90-92-94; England (Home Int) 1987-88-89-90-91-92-93, (Eur(L) T Ch) 1987-89-91-93; GBI Espirito Santo 1988-90-94, Vagliano Trophy 1989-91-93; Commonwealth Trn 1991
Mis Winner of the Doris Chambers Trophy, the Angus Trophy and *The Daily Telegraph* Woman Golfer of the Year Trophy (shared) in 1993

Hargreaves, Jack

Born Fleetwood on 12th February, 1914. Turned Professional 1930

Maj Open 3rd 1948
Trn Spalding 1951. Swallow-Harrogate 1953. Goodwin Foursomes 1953
Reg Midland Professional 1952-60
Int Ryder Cup 1951
Mis Secretary Midland PGA. Captain PGA 1977

Harrington, Padraig

Born Dublin on 31st August, 1971

Cls Stackstown
Nat Irish Close Amateur r/u 1990-94
Oth Sherry Cup 1991
Int Walker Cup 1991-93. Ireland (Home Int) 1990-91-92; (Eur T Ch) 1991. GBI v Europe 1992-94
Jun Int GBI Youths 1990-91; Boys 1988-89; Ireland Youths 1990-91; Boys 1987-88-89

Harris, Marley [Spearman]

Born on 11th January, 1928

Cls Sudbury
Chp British Ladies 1961-62.
Nat English Ladies 1964
Trn Spalding Ladies 1956; Worplesdon Mixed Foursomes r/u 1956-64; Kayser-Bondor Foursomes 1958 (tied); London Ladies Foursomes 1960; Astor Salver 1964-65; Astor Princes' Trophy 1964-65; Sunningdale Foursomes, Casa Pupo Foursomes, Roehampton Gold Cup, Hovis Ladies 1965
RoW New Zealand Ladies Stroke Play 1963
Reg Middlesex Ladies 1955-56-57-58-59-61-64-65. South-East Ladies 1956-58-61
Int Curtis Cup 1960-62-64. Vagliano Trophy 1959-61. GB Commonwealth Team 1959-63. England (Home Int) 1955 to 65
Mis AGW Trophy 1962. Non-playing captain English Team European Team Championship 1971

Hay, Garry

Born Perth on 27th August, 1959

Cls Hilton Park, Downfield
Nat Scottish Amateur Stroke Play 1990, r/u 1980
Trn Tennant Cup 1979. Scottish Champion of Champions 1991; St Andrews Links Trophy 1993
Int Walker Cup 1991. Scotland (Home Int) 1980-88-90-91-92; *v* England 1979; *v* Belgium 1980; *v* France 1980-82-89-91-93; *v* Italy 1988-92-94; *v* Sweden 1992; *v* Spain 1994. GBI *v* Europe 1980
Jun British Youths 1980

Heathcoat-Amory, Lady (*née* Joyce Wethered)

Born 17th November, 1901

Cls Worplesdon
Chp British Ladies 1922-24-25-29, r/u 1921.
Nat English Ladies 1920-21-22-23-24
Trn Worplesdon Mixed Foursomes 1922-23-27-28-31-32-33-36. Sunningdale Foursomes 1935-36
Reg Surrey Ladies 1921-22-24-29-32
Int Curtis Cup 1932. GBI v France 1931. England (Home Int) 1921-22-23-24-25-29
Mis Forfeited Amateur status and toured USA in 1935. Reinstated as Amateur after the war

Hedges, Peter J

Born 30th March, 1947

Cls Langley Park (Hon), Royal Cinque Ports, Addington, Wildernesse, Royal & Ancient
Nat English Open Amateur Stroke Play 1976
Trn Royal St George's Challenge Cup 1970. Prince of Wales Challenge Cup 1972-73-74-77. Berkshire Trophy 1973-76-78. Golf Illustrated Gold Vase 1974. Scrutton Jug 1976
Reg Kent Amateur 1968-71-79. Kent Open 1970-74
Int Walker Cup 1973-75. GBI v Europe 1974-76 Eisenhower Trophy 1974. England (Home Int) 1970-73-74-75-76-77-78-82; (Eur T Ch) 1973-75-77
Jun Youth International 1968
Mis Member of European Team to tour South Africa 1974

Henson, Dinah (*née* Oxley)

Born Dorking on 17th October, 1948

Cls Hon member of West Byfleet, Killarney, Fairfield, USA
Chp British Ladies 1970.
Nat English Ladies 1970-71, r/u 1968. British Ladies Stroke Play r/u 1969
Trn Wills Ladies 1969-70-71. Worplesdon Mixed Foursomes 1968-77. Newmark International 1975 (tied)-77
Reg Surrey Ladies 1967-70-71-76
Int Curtis Cup 1968-70-72-76. Vagliano Trophy 1967-69-71. World Team 1970. GB Commonwealth Team 1967-71. England (Home Int) 1967-68-69-70-75-76-77-78; (Eur(L) T Ch) 1971-77
Jun British Girls 1963. English Girls 1965. French Girls 1969. Girl International 1964-65-66
Mis Daks Woman Golfer of the Year 1970. Leading Amateur Colgate European Ladies Open 1974

Hetherington, Jean (*née* McClure) See Holmes

Holmes, Jean [Hetherington] (*née* McClure)

Born Wanstead, Essex on 17th August, 1923

Cls Wanstead, Hunstanton, Thorndon Park
Chp British Ladies 1946, r/u 1958.
Nat English Ladies r/u 1966
Reg Nottinghamshire Ladies 1949-50-51. Essex Ladies 1956-57
Int England (Home Int) 1957-66-(67)

Homer, Trevor Walter Brian

Born Bloxwich on 8th September, 1943. Turned Professional July 1974. Reinstated as Amateur in 1978

Chp Amateur Champion 1972-74
Trn Leicestershire Fox 1972. Harlech Gold Cross 1970
Int Walker Cup 1973. Eisenhower Trophy 1972. GBI v Europe 1972. England (Home Int) 1972-73; (Eur T Ch) 1973

Horton, Tommy

Born St Helens, on 16th June, 1941. Turned Professional 1957

Trn RTV 1968. PGA Match Play 1970. Gallaher Ulster 1971. Piccadilly 1972. Penfold 1974. Uniroyal International 1976. Dunlop Masters 1978

RoW South African Open 1970. Nigerian Open 1973. Zambian Open 1977. Tobago Open 1975. Gambian Open 1975
Sen Forte PGA Senior Chp 1992; Shell Scottish Seniors, Collingtree Seniors, Zurich Lexus Trophy 1993; Irish Seniors Masters 1994
Int Ryder Cup 1975-77. GBI v France 1966. England in World Cup 1976. England in Double Diamond 1971-74-75-76-77. GBI v Europe 1974-76
Mis Second in Order of Merit 1967. PGA Captain 1978; Braid-Taylor Memorial Medal 1976-77; Seniors Order of Merit winner 1993

Hourihane, Claire

Born 18th February, 1958

Cls Woodbrook
Nat Irish Ladies 1983-84-85-87-91; r/u 1980. British Ladies Stroke Play 1986; r/u 1990
Trn South Atlantic (USA) 1983; Hampshire Rose 1986; Critchley Salver 1990
Reg South Ireland Cup 1977; Leinster Ladies 1980
Int Curtis Cup 1984-86-88-90-92; Vagliano Trophy 1981-83-85-87-89-91; Espirito Santo 1986-90; Ireland (Home Int) 1979 to 1992; (Eur(L) T Ch) 1981-83-85-87-89.

Howard, Ann (*née* Phillips)

Born Prestwich on 22nd October, 1934

Cls Whitefield (Hon), Royal Birkdale, Castletown
Oth Danish Ladies 1955
Reg Lancashire Ladies 1957. Manx Ladies 1977-78
Int Curtis Cup 1956-68. GBI v France and Belgium 1955-57. England (Home Int) 1953-54-55-56-(79)-(**80**). Senior European (**1981**)
Jun British Girls 1952

Huggan, Shirley Margaret (*née* Lawson)

Born Glasgow on 16th September, 1964

Cls Eastwood, Rock Ridge, USA
Nat Scottish Ladies Amateur 1988-89 r/u 1990; Taunton Trophy 1987
Reg West of Scotland Ladies 1986-88; Renfrewshire Ladies 1985-86-87-88
Int Curtis Cup 1988; Scotland (Home Int) 1985-86-87-88-89; (Eur(L) T Ch) 1985-87-89; GBI Vagliano Trophy 1989
Jun Scottish Girls 1982; Scottish Girls Stroke Play 1983-84; r/u 1982-85
Int Girls 1980-81-82

Huggett, Brian George Charles, MBE

Born Porthcawl on 18th November, 1936. Turned Professional 1951

Maj Open r/u 1965. 3rd 1962
Eur Dutch Open 1962. German Open 1963. Portuguese Open 1974
Trn Cox-Moore 1963. Smart-Weston 1965. Sumrie 1968-72. PGA Close 1967. Martini 1967 (tied)-68. Shell Winter Tournament 1967-68. PGA Match Play 1968, r/u 1977. Daks 1969-71 (tied). Bowmaker 1969 (tied). Carrolls 1970. Dunlop Masters 1970. British Airways-Avis 1978
RoW Singapore International 1962. Algarve Open 1970
Sen Anvil Seniors Classic, Northern Electric Seniors 1992; Northern Electric Seniors, Forte PGA Seniors 1993
Oth Sunningdale Foursomes 1957. British Assistants 1958. Gleneagles Pro-Am 1961-65. Turnberry Pro-Am 1968. Welsh Professional 1978
Reg East Anglian Open 1962-67
Int Ryder Cup 1963-67-69-71-73-75-(77). Wales in World Cup 1963-64-65-68-69-70-71-76-79. Wales in Double Diamond 1971-72-73-74-75-76-77. GBI v Europe 1974-**78**
Mis Vardon Trophy 1968. 1972

Huke, Beverly Joan Mary

Born Great Yarmouth on 10th May, 1951. Turned Professional 1978

Cls Cotswold Hills (Hon), Windmill Hill (Hon), Leighton Buzzard, Panmure Barry
Chp British Ladies r/u 1971.
Nat English Ladies 1975
Eur Carlsberg (Ballater) 1979. Carlsberg (Rosemount) 1980. NABS Pro-Am 1st Pro Individual 1981. Brickendon Grange and Stourbridge Pro-Am 1983; Lark Valley Classic 1983 (shared); White Horse Whisky Challenge Trophy 1983. Trusthouse Forte Classic 1985. German Ladies Open 1984. Wester Volkswagen Classic 1986
Trn Roehampton Gold Cup 1971. Renfrew Rose Bowl 1976-77-78. Helen Holm Trophy 1977
Reg Gloucestershire Ladies 1972. Angus Ladies 1976
Int Curtis Cup 1972. Vagliano Trophy 1971-75. England (Home Int) 1971-72-75-76-77; (Eur(L) T Ch) 1975-77
Jun Scottish Girls Open Stroke Play 1970-71. Girl International 1966-67-68
Mis Chairman WPGET 1988

Hunt, Bernard John, MBE

Born Atherstone on 2nd February, 1930. Turned Professional 1946

Maj Open 3rd 1960; leading British player (4th) 1964
Eur Belgian Open 1957; German Open 1961; French Open 1967
Trn Spalding, Goodwin Foursomes, Gleneagles-Saxone 1953; Goodwin Foursomes 1954; Irish Hospitals 1956; Bowmaker 1958 (shared); Martini, Daks 1961; Carrolls, Swallow-Penfold, Smart-Weston, Gevacolour, Dunlop Masters 1963; Rediffusion 1964; Dunlop Masters, Gallaher Ulster 1965; Piccadilly 1966; Gallaher Ulster 1967; Penfold, Sumrie, Agfacolor 1970; Wills 1971; Sumrie 1973
Reg Southern England Professional 1959-60-62-67; West of England Open Professional 1960-61
Oth British Assistants 1953; Algarve Open, BP Italy 1969
RoW Egyptian Open 1956; Brazilian Open 1962
Int Ryder Cup 1953-57-59-61-63-65-67-69-(**73**)-(**75**); England in World Cup 1958-59-60-62-63-64-68; in Double Diamond 1971-72-73
Mis Harry Vardon Trophy 1958-60-65. PGA Captain 1966

Hutcheon, Ian C

Born Monifieth, Angus on 22nd February, 1942

Cls Monifieth (Hon), Grange and Dundee (Hon)
Nat Scottish Amateur 1973. Scottish Open Amateur Stroke Play 1971-74-79
Trn Tennant Cup 1976; Lytham Trophy 1980; Scottish Champion of Champions 1980-81-86-88; Leven Gold Medal 1981-82

Oth North of Spain Stroke Play 1972
Reg Scottish Central District Amateur 1972. Angus Match Play 1965-70-72. Angus Stroke Play 1968-71-72-74. North of Scotland District Amateur Stroke Play 1975-76-82
Int GBI v Europe 1974-76. Eisenhower Trophy 1974-76 (winners and joint winning individual)-80. Scotland (Home Int) 1971-72-73-74-75-76-77-78-80; (Eur T Ch) 1973-75-77-79-81; v Spain 1972-77; v Belgium 1973-75-77-78-80; v France 1978-80-81; v Italy 1979; in Fiat Trophy 1979. GBI in Dominican International 1973. Walker Cup 1975-77-79-81. GBI in Colombian International 1975. GB Commonwealth Team 1975
Mis Frank Moran Trophy 1976

Imrie, Kathryn *See* Marshall

Irvin, Ann Lesley

Born 11th April, 1943

Cls Lytham (Hon), Lytham Green Drive (Hon)
Chp British Ladies 1973, r/u 1969.
Nat English Ladies 1967-74. British Ladies Stroke Play 1969.
Trn Roehampton Gold Cup 1967-68-69-72-76. Hovis Ladies 1966-68-70. Avia Foursomes 1968
Reg Northern Ladies 1963-64. Lancashire Ladies 1965-67-69-71-72-74. Northern Foursomes Championship 1973
Int Curtis Cup 1962-68-70-76. Vagliano Trophy 1961-63-65-67-69-71-73-75. GB Commonwealth Team 1967-75. England (Home Int) 1962-63-65-67-68-69-70-71-72-73-75; (Eur(L) T Ch) 1965-67-69-71-73-75
Jun French Girls 1963.
Int Girls 1960-61; British Girls 1961
Mis Daks Woman Golfer of the Year 1968-69. Captain of British Team to tour Australia 1973. Lancashire 1981. County Captain 1979. England Junior Captain. 1981-82. International Selector 1981-82. England Selector 1981-82. County Selector and Junior Organiser

Jack, Robert Reid

Born Cumbernauld on 17th January, 1924

Cls Dullatur
Maj Leading Amateur in Open 1959
Chp Amateur Champion 1957
Nat Scottish Amateur 1955
Trn Edward Trophy 1959. Tennant Cup 1961
Oth Royal & Ancient Royal Medal 1965-67. Silver Cross 1956-66. Glennie Medal 1965
Reg Glasgow Amateur 1953-54-58. Dunbartonshire Match Play 1949
Int Walker Cup 1957-59. Eisenhower Trophy 1958. GB Commonwealth Team 1959. GBI v Europe 1956. Scotland (Home Int) 1950-51-54-55-56-57-58-59-61; v Scandinavia 1956-58

Jacklin, Tony, CBE

Born Scunthorpe on 7th July, 1944. Turned Professional 1962

PROFESSIONAL

Maj Open 1969, 3rd 1971-72; US Open 1970
Eur Blaxnit 1966; Pringle, Dunlop Masters 1967; Wills, Lancôme Trophy 1970; Benson & Hedges Festival 1971; Viyella PGA Close 1972; Dunlop Masters, Italian Open 1973; Scandinavian Enterprise Open 1974; Kerrygold International Classic 1976; German Open 1979; Jersey Open 1981; Sun Alliance PGA 1982
Oth British Assistants 1964; English Professional 1977
US Greater Jacksonville Open 1968-72
RoW Kimberley 1966 (shared); Forest Products, New Zealand, New Zealand PGA 1967; Dunlop International Australia 1972; Los Lagartos Open 1973-74; Venezuelan Open 1979
Sen US Tour: First of America Classic 1994
Int Ryder Cup 1967-69-71-73-75-77-79-(**83**)-(**85**)-(**87**)-(**89**); Hennessy-Cognac 1976; England in World Cup 1966-70-71-72; in Double Diamond 1972-73-74-76-77
Mis Rookie of the Year 1963; Hon Life President PGA; first British player since Harry Vardon to hold Open and US Open simultaneously; Braid-Taylor Memorial Medal 1969-70-71-72

AMATEUR

Reg Lincolnshire Open 1961

Jackson, Barbara Amy Bridget

Born Birmingham on 10th July, 1936

Cls Royal St David's, Edgbaston. Hon member of Handsworth, Hunstanton, Killarney
Chp British Ladies r/u 1964.
Nat English Ladies 1956, r/u 1958
Trn Fairway and Hazard Foursomes 1954. Kayser Bondor Foursomes 1962. Avia Foursomes 1967. Worplesdon Mixed Foursomes 1960. Astor Prince's 1963
Oth German Ladies 1956. Canadian Ladies 1967
Reg Midland Ladies 1954-56-57-58-59-60-69. Staffordshire Ladies 1954-56-57-58-59-63-64-67-69-76
Int Curtis Cup 1958-64-68. Vagliano Trophy 1959-63-65-67-(**73**)-(**75**). GB Commonwealth Team 1959-67. GBI v Belgium 1957; v France 1957. World Team Championship 1964. England (Home Int) 1955-56-57-58-59-63-64-65-66-(**73**)-(**74**); (Eur(L) T Ch) (**1975**), v France 1964-66
Jun British Girls 1954
Mis LGU International Selector 1983. English and GBI Selector 1983 to 1988. Chairman of English Ladies Association 1970-71

Jacobs, John Robert Maurice

Born Lindrick, Yorkshire on 14th March, 1925. Turned Professional 1947

Eur Dutch Open 1957
RoW South African Match Play 1957
Int Ryder Cup 1955-(**79**)-(**81**). GBI v Continent 1954-55-58
Mis Former PGA Tournament Director-General. TV commentator. Coach to many international teams

James, Lee

Born Poole on 27th January, 1973

Cls Broadstone
Chp Amateur Champion 1994
Nat European Amateur r/u 1994
Int GBI *v* Europe 1994; Eisenhower Trophy 1994; England (Home Int) 1993-94; *v* France 1994

James, Mark H

Born Manchester on 28th October, 1953. Turned Professional 1975

PROFESSIONAL

Maj Open 3rd 1981
Eur Sun Alliance Match Play 1978; Welsh Classic, Carroll's Irish Open 1979; Carroll's Irish Open, Italian Open 1980; Tunisian Open 1983; GSI Open 1985; Benson & Hedges International 1986; Peugeot Spanish Open 1988; Karl Litten Desert Classic, AGF Open, NM English Open 1989; Dunhill British Masters, English Open 1990; Madeira Island Open, Open de Canarias 1993
RoW Lusaka Open 1977; Sao Paulo Open 1981; South African TPC 1988
Int Ryder Cup 1977-79-81-89-91-93; Hennessy-Cognac 1976-78-80-82 (individual winner)-84; World Cup 1978-79-82-84-87-88-90-93; Dunhill Cup 1988-89-90(r/u)-93(r/u); Kirin Cup 1988; Four Tours World Chp 1989-90
Mis Tooting Bec Cup 1976; Braid-Taylor Memorial Medal 1976-79-81; Rookie of the Year 1976

AMATEUR

Chp Amateur r/u 1975
Nat English Amateur 1974
Trn Leicestershire Fox 1974
Int Walker Cup 1975; England (Home Int) 1974-75; (Eur T Ch) 1975
Jun Int (England) Boys 1971; Youths 1974-75

Johnson, Patricia (Trish)

Born Bristol on 17th January, 1966. Turned Professional 1987

PROFESSIONAL

Eur McEwan's Wirral Classic, Bloor Homes Eastleigh Classic, Woolmark Match Play 1987; Hennessy Cup, Bloor Homes Eastleigh Classic, European Open, Longines Classic 1990; Spanish Classic 1992
US LPGA Qualifying School 1987; Las Vegas LPGA, Atlanta Women's Chp 1993
Int Solheim Cup 1990-92; Sunrise Cup 1992 (individual winner); (for LPGA) Nichirei International 1993
Mis Rookie of the Year 1987. Woolmark Order of Merit leader 1990

AMATEUR

Nat English Ladies 1985. English Ladies Stroke Play 1985
Trn Roehampton Gold Cup 1986
Reg South-Western Ladies 1984
Int Curtis Cup 1986; England (Home Int) 1984-85
Jun Devon Girls 1982

Jones, John Roger

Born Old Colwyn, Denbighshire on 14th June, 1944

Cls Langland Bay (Hon)
Nat Welsh Amateur Stroke Play 1972-73-82, r/u 1983. Welsh Amateur 1983
Trn Harlech Gold Cross 1976
Reg Denbighshire Amateur 1969-71. Caernarfonshire and Anglesey Amateur 1970 (tied)-72-74-75. Glamorgan Amateur 1977-79. North Wales Amateur 1976. Carmarthenshire Amateur 1979-80. Landsdowne Trophy (Channel League) Stroke Play 1979-80-83
Int Wales (Home Int) 1970-72-73-77-78-80-81-82-83; (Eur T Ch) 1973-79-81-83; v Denmark 1976-80; v Ireland 1979; v Switzerland 1980; v Spain 1980; in Asian Team Championship 1979

Kelley, Michael John

Born Scarborough on 6th February, 1945

Cls Ganton, Hon member of Scarborough North Cliff, Bridlington, Bradford
Trn Lytham Trophy 1976. Antlers Royal Mid-Surrey 1972
Reg Yorkshire Amateur 1969-74-81. Yorkshire Open 1969-75. Champion of Champions 1981
Int Walker Cup 1977-79. Eisenhower Trophy 1976 (winners). GBI v Europe 1976-78-82; GBI in Colombian International 1978. England (Home Int) 1974-75-76-77-78-80-81-82-88; (Eur T Ch) 1977-79; v France 1982
Jun Int Boys 1962. Youths 1965-66

King, Michael

Born London on 15th February, 1950. Turned Professional 1974

PROFESSIONAL

Eur Tournament Players Chp 1979
Int Ryder Cup 1979; England in World Cup 1979

AMATEUR

Trn St George's Hill Trophy 1970; County Champion of Champions 1970; Sunningdale Foursomes 1972; Lytham Trophy 1973 (shared)
Reg Berks, Bucks & Oxon Amateur 1968-69-70-73-74; Berks, Bucks & Oxon Open 1968-73
Int Walker Cup 1969-73; GB Commonwealth Trn 1971; v Europe 1972; England (Home Int) 1971-72-73; (Eur T Ch) 1971-73

King, Samuel Leonard

Born Sevenoaks, Kent on 27th March, 1911

Maj Open 3rd 1939
Trn Daily Mail 1937. Yorkshire Evening News 1944-49
Oth British Assistants 1933. Dunlop-Southern 1936-37. Sunningdale Foursomes 1948. Teachers Senior 1961-62
Int Ryder Cup 1937-47-49. England 1934-36-37-38

Lambert, Catriona *See* Matthew

Lane, Barry

Born Hayes, Middlesex on 21st June, 1960. Turned Professional 1976

Eur Equity & Law Challenge 1987; Scottish Open 1988; Mercedes German Masters 1992; European Masters 1993; Open de Baleares 1994
RoW Jamaica Open 1983
Int Ryder Cup 1993; (England) Dunhill Cup 1988; World Cup 1988

Langley, John DA

Born Northwood, Middlesex on 25th April, 1918.

Cls Sunningdale, Burnham (Hon), Swinley Forest, Fulwell (Hon), Metropolitan (Aus)
Nat English Amateur 1950, r/u 1936
Trn Golf Illustrated Gold Vase 1952-53. St George's Hill Trophy 1952
Int Walker Cup 1936-51-53. England (Home Int) 1950-51-52-53; v France 1950-52

Jun British Boys 1935. Carris Trophy 1936
Int Boys 1932-33-34-35
Mis Chairman Royal & Ancient Selection Committee 1967 to 1969

Langridge, Susan (*née* Armitage)

Born Huddersfield on 5th April, 1943

Cls Walsall, Whittington Barracks (Hon)
Reg Midland Ladies 1961-65
Int Curtis Cup 1964-66. Vagliano Trophy 1963-65-67. England (Home Int) 1963-64-65-66-67
Jun Scottish Girls Open Stroke Play 1962

Lawrence, Joan B

Born Kinghorn, Fife on 20th April, 1930

Cls Hon. mem. of Dunfermline, Aberdour, Killarney
Chp Scottish Ladies 1962-63-64, r/u 1965. Scottish Veteran Ladies Champion 1982
Reg East of Scotland Ladies 1971-72. Fife Ladies fifteen times winner 1953-90
Int Curtis Cup 1964. World Team Champion 1964. GB Commonwealth Team **1971**. Vagliano Trophy 1963-65. Scotland (Home Int) 1959 to 70-(77); (Eur(L) T Ch) 1965-67-**69**-71-(77)
Jun Girl International 1949
Mis LGU International Selector 1973-74-75-76-80-81-82-83. Treasurer Scottish Ladies Golfing Association from 1980. Chairman LGU Executive 1989

Leburn, Wilma (*née* Aitken)

Born 24th January, 1959

Trn Helen Holm Trophy 1978-80-82. Avia Foursomes 1982
Reg West of Scotland 1978-80-81. Renfrewshire Champion 1978-79-80-81-82
Int Curtis Cup 1982. Vagliano Trophy 1981-83. Scotland (Home Int) 1978-79-80-81-82-83. Vilmorin Cup 1979. (Eur(L) T Ch) 1979-81-83.
Jun Scottish Girls 1975-77. West of Scotland Girls 1977. British Girls 1977
Int Scottish Girls 1975-77-78

Lee-Smith, Jenny

Born Newcastle-upon-Tyne on 2nd December, 1948. Turned Professional 1977

Maj Ladies British Open 1976 (as amateur)

PROFESSIONAL

Eur Carlsberg 1979; Carlsberg, Robert Windsor Trn, Volvo Swedish International, Manchester Evening News Classic 1980; Sports Space Trn, McEwan's Lager Welsh Classic, Lambert & Butler Match Play 1981; Ford Classic 1982; British Olivetti 1984
Mis Order of Merit winner 1981-82

AMATEUR

Nat Ladies British Open Amateur Stroke Play 1976
Trn Wills Match Play 1974; Newmark 1976; Hoylake Mixed Foursomes 1969
Reg Northumberland Ladies 1972-73-74
Int Curtis Cup 1974-76; Espirito Santo 1976; GB Commonwealth Trn 1975; Colombian International 1975; England (Home Int) 1973-74-75-76; (Eur(L) T Ch) 1975
Mis Daks Woman Golfer of the Year 1976

Lucas, Percy Belgrave, CBE, DSO, DFC

Born Sandwich Bay, Kent on 2nd September, 1915

Cls Sandy Lodge, Walton Heath, Prince's, Royal West Norfolk
Trs Berkshire Trophy 1947-49. St George's Challenge Cup 1947. Prince of Wales Challenge Cup 1947. President's Putter 1949
Reg Herts Amateur 1946-47
Int Walker Cup 1936-47-(**49**). GBI v Professionals 1935. England (Home Int) 1936-48-**49**; v France 1936-47
Jun British Boys 1933.
Int Boys 1930-31-32-33
Mis President Golf Foundation 1963 to 1966. President National Golf Clubs Advisory Association 1963 to 1969. President Association of Golf Club Secretaries 1968 to 1974. Member UK Sports Council 1971 to 1983. Author.

Lumb, Kathryn (*née* Phillips)

Born Bradford on 24th February, 1952

Cls Hon member of Bradford, West Bowling, Killarney, Filton
Reg Central England Mixed Foursomes 1966-70. Yorkshire Ladies 1968-69
Int Curtis Cup 1970-72. Vagliano Trophy 1969-71. England (Home Int) 1968-69-70-71; (Eur(L) T Ch) 1969
Jun English Girls 1968. Scottish Girls Open Stroke Play 1968-69. French Girls 1970.
Int Girls 1967-68-69

Lunt, Michael Stanley Randle

Born Birmingham on 20th May, 1935

Cls Royal & Ancient, Walton Heath, St Enodoc, Hon. mem. of Blackwell, Royal St David's, Moseley, Edgbaston, Stourbridge, Willesley Park, Kibworth, Handsworth, King's Norton, Dudley
Chp Amateur Champion 1963, r/u 1964
Nat English Amateur 1966, r/u 1962. English Open Amateur Stroke Play r/u 1961
Trn Golf Illustrated Gold Vase 1958, Harlech Gold Cross 1959-61-64-65-66-67. Leicestershire Fox 1966
Reg Midland Counties Amateur 1960-62
Int Walker Cup 1959-61-62-65. Eisenhower Trophy 1964 GB Commonwealth Team 1963. England (Home Int) 1956-57-58-59-60-62-63-64-66-(72)-(73)-(74)-(75). (Eur T Ch) (**1973**)-(75)
Jun Boy International 1949-50-51-52
Mis AGW Trophy 1963. President Midland Counties Golf Association 1978 to 1980

Lyle, Alexander Walter Barr (Sandy), MBE

Born Shrewsbury on 9th February, 1958. Turned Professional 1977

PROFESSIONAL

Maj Open Champion 1985. US Masters 1988
Eur Jersey Open, Scandinavian Enterprise Open, European Open 1979; Coral Classic 1980; French Open, Lawrence Batley International 1981; Lawrence Batley International 1982; Madrid Open 1983; Italian Open, Lancôme Trophy 1984; Benson & Hedges International 1985; German Masters 1987; Dunhill British

Masters, Suntory World Match Play 1988; BMW International Open 1991; Italian Open, Volvo Masters 1992
US Greater Greensboro Open 1986; Tournament Players Championship 1987; Phoenix Open, Greater Greensboro Open 1988
Oth PGA Qualifying School winner 1977; Scottish Professional Chp 1979
RoW Nigerian Open 1978; Casio World Open, Kapalua International (Hawaii) 1984
Int Ryder Cup 1979-81-83-85-87; Nissan Cup 1985-86, Kirin Cup 1987-88; Hennessy-Cognac Cup 1980-84; Scotland in World Cup 1979-80 (Individual Winner) -87(r/u); Dunhill Cup 1985-86-87 (r/u)-88-89-90-92(r/u)
Mis Rookie of the Year 1978; Harry Vardon Trophy 1979-80-85; AGW Trophy 1980-88; Tooting Bec Cup 1982-88; Braid-Taylor Memorial Medal 1985; Frank Moran Trophy 1985

AMATEUR
Nat English Open Amateur Stroke Play 1975-77
Trn County Champion of Champions 1974; Hampshire Hog, Berkshire Trophy, Scrutton Jug, Berkhamsted Trophy 1977
Reg Midland Amateur, Shropshire & Herefordshire Amateur 1974; Midland Open 1975; Shropshire & Herefordshire Amateur 1976
Int Walker Cup 1977; GB Commonwealth Trn 1975; GBI v Europe 1976; England (Home Int) 1975-76-77, (Eur T Ch) 1977
Jun Carris Trophy 1975; British Youths 1977; r/u British Boys 1974-75
Int Boys 1972-73-74-75
Mis In 1975 represented England in Boy, Youth and Full Internationals.

McCann, Catherine (*née* Smye)

Born Clonmel, Co Tipperary in 1922
Cls Tullamore
Chp British Ladies 1951.
Nat Irish Ladies 1949-61, r/u 1947-52-57-60
Reg Munster Ladies 1958, Irish Midland Ladies 1952-57-58
Int Curtis Cup 1952. Ireland (Home Int) 1947-48-49-50-51-52-53-54-56-57-58-60-61-62; v New Zealand 1953; v Canada 1953

McClure, Jean *See* Holmes

McCorkindale, Isabella *See* Robertson

Macdonald, JS

Born St Andrews on 9th July, 1944
Cls Elgin, Baberton, Hon. mem. Killarney, Frigate Bay
Nat Scottish Amateur Open Stroke Play 1969. English Open Amateur Stroke Play r/u 1970-71.
Oth Kuwait Open Champion 1977
Trn Boyd Quaich 1963-65. British Universities 1965
Reg South East Scotland Amateur 1969-71. North of Scotland Open Amateur Stroke Play 1984-85
Int Walker Cup 1971. GBI v Europe 1970. Scotland (Home Int) 1969-70-71-72; (Eur T Ch) 1971; v Belgium 1973
Jun Int Boys 1961. Youths 1962-64-65

McEvoy, Peter

Born London on 22nd March, 1953
Cls Copt Heath (Hon), R&A
Maj Open leading amateur 1978-79
Chp Amateur Champion 1977-78, r/u 1987
Nat English Open Amateur Stroke Play 1980 (tied), r/u 1978. English Amateur r/u 1980
Trn Duncan Putter 1978-80-87; Scrutton Jug 1978-80-85; Lytham Trophy 1978; Selborne Salver 1979-80; Leicestershire Fox 1976; Lagonda Trophy 1980; Berkshire Trophy 1985; County Champion of Champions 1984 (shared); Berkhamsted Trophy 1986; Hampshire Hog 1989
Oth British Universities Stroke Play 1973
Reg Warwickshire Match Play 1973-75-81; Warwickshire Amateur 1974-76-77-80-84; Warwickshire Open 1973-74; West of England Open Amateur Stroke Play 1977-80-83-85; Midland Open Amateur Stroke Play 1978; Midland Scratch Cup (Ireland) 1982-83-84-88
Int Walker Cup 1977-79-81-85-89; Eisenhower Trophy 1978-80-84-86-88 (winners) (leading individual); GBI v Europe 1978-80-82-84-86-88; England (Home Int) 1976-77-78-80-81-82-83-84-85-86-87-88-89-91; v Scotland 1979; (Eur T Ch) 1977-79-81-83-85-87-89; in Fiat Trophy 1980; v France 1982-84-86-88-90; v Spain 1985-87-89
Jun Youth International 1974
Mis Only British amateur to complete 72 holes in US Masters (1978); AGW Trophy 1978; most capped England player

McGimpsey, Garth M

Born 17th July, 1955
Cls Bangor, Royal Portrush, Royal Co Down
Chp Amateur Champion 1985, s/f 1989
Nat Irish Amateur 1985-88
Reg North of Ireland 1978-84-91-92, West of Ireland 1984-88, East of Ireland 1988-94, r/u 1979-80
Int Walker Cup 1985-89-91. GBI v Europe 1984-86-88-92. Eisenhower Trophy 1984-86-88 (winners). Ireland (Home Int) 1978; 1980 to 1994. (Eur T Ch) 1981-89-91
Mis Irish long-driving champion 1977; UK long-driving champion 1979

McGinley, Paul

Born Dublin on 16th December, 1966. Turned Professional 1991

PROFESSIONAL
Oth UAP U-25 European Open 1991
Int (Ireland) Dunhill Cup 1993; World Cup 1993

AMATEUR
Nat Irish Amateur 1989
Reg South of Ireland 1991
Oth Long Beach Open 1990
Int Walker Cup 1991; Ireland (Home Int) 1989-90
Jun Irish Youths, Scottish Youths 1988

Macgregor, George

Born Edinburgh on 19th August, 1944
Cls Glencorse, Killarney (Hon), West Linton (Hon)
Nat Scottish Open Amateur Stroke Play 1982 r/u 1975-79-80
Trn Lytham Trophy 1975. Leven Gold Medal 1987

Reg Lothians Amateur 1968. South-East Scotland Amateur 1972-75-79-80-81. East of Scotland Open Amateur 1979-82
Int Walker Cup 1971-75-83-85-87-(91). Eisenhower 1982. GBI v Europe 1970-74-84. GB Commonwealth Team 1971-75. Scotland (Home Int) 1969-70-71-72-73-74-75-76-80-81-82-83-84-85-86-87; (Eur T Ch) 1971-73-75-81-83-85-87; v Belgium 1973-75-80; v England 1979; v France 1981-82; Scotland v Sweden 1983
Jun Int Youths 1964-65-66
Mis Leading Amateur Wills PGA Open 1970-71

McKay, Mhairi

Born on 18th April, 1975

Cls Turnberry
Nat British Ladies Stroke Play U-23 (Duncan Salver), U-21 (Dinwiddy Trophy) 1993; Scottish Ladies 1993(r/u); Scottish U-21 Stroke Play 1991(r/u)-92-93
Trn Mackie Bowl 1991-93; Helen Holm Trophy 1992; Riccarton Rosebowl 1993
Int Curtis Cup 1994; Vagliano Trophy 1993; Scotland (Home Int) 1991-92-93-94; (Eur L T Ch) 1993
Jun British Girls 1992-93; Scottish Girls 1990-91(r/u)-92; Belgian Junior 1992
Jun Int Scottish Girls 1989-90-91-92-93
Mis *Daily Telegraph* Junior Golfer of the Year 1991

McKenna, Mary A

Born Dublin on 29th April, 1949

Cls Donabate
Nat British Ladies Open Amateur Stroke Play 1979, r/u 1976. Irish Ladies 1969-72-74-77-79-81-82-89, r/u 1968-73-76. Irish Women's Close Ch 1981
Trn Dorothy Grey Stroke Play 1970-71-73. Players No 6 Cup 1971-72-74. Avia Foursomes 1977-84-86. Hermitage Scratch Cup 1975-79
Reg South of Ireland Scratch Cup 1973-74-76-79
Int Curtis Cup 1970-72-74-76-78-80-82-84-86. Vagliano Trophy 1969-71-73-75-77-79-81-85-87. World Team Chp 1970-74-76-**86**; Espirito Santo (1993); Ireland (Home Int) 1968 to 1991; (Eur(L) T Ch) 1969-71-73-75-77-79-81-83-85-87; in Fiat Trophy 1979
Mis S/f US Women's Western 1972, Broadmoor Tournament 1972 and US Women's Amateur 1980. Captain of LGU Touring Team to South Africa 1974. Leading Amateur Colgate European LPGA 1977 (tied)-79. Daks Woman Golfer of the Year 1979. Smyth Salver 1984. Taunton Trophy 1976

McLean, David

Born Holyhead on 30th January, 1947

Cls Holyhead, Baron Hill, Killarney
Nat Welsh Amateur 1973-78. Welsh Amateur Stroke Play 1975-79
Trn Duncan Putter 1982
Reg North Wales Amateur 1971-75-77-81. Caernarfonshire Amateur 1966-68-69-70 (tied)-77-79-81-82. Anglesey Amateur 1965-67-68-69-70-72-73-74-76-78-79-80-81-82
Int Wales (Home Int) 1968-69-70-71-72-73-74-75-76-77-78-80-81-82-83-85-86-88; (Eur T Ch) 1975-77-79-81-83; v France 1975-76; v Denmark 1976-80-82; v Ireland 1979; v Spain 1980; v Austria 1982; v Switzerland 1980-82; in Fiat Trophy 1978-79; in Asian Team Championship 1979

McMahon, Suzanne (*née* Cadden)

Born Old Kilpatrick, Dunbartonshire on 8th October, 1957

Cls Troon
Chp British Ladies r/u 1975. British Ladies Stroke Play r/u 1975
Nat Scottish Ladies Foursomes 1972
Reg Dunbartonshire Ladies 1976-77-79
Int Curtis Cup 1976. Vagliano Trophy 1975. Scotland (Home Int) 1974-75-76-77-79; (Eur(L) T Ch) 1975
Jun Scottish Girls 1974-76. Scottish Girls Open Stroke Play 1976-77. British Girls 1975. Girl International 1972-73-74-75-76. World Junior Championship 1973
Mis Daks Woman Golfer of the Year 1975

Madill, Maureen

Born Coleraine, Co Derry on 1st February, 1958. Turned Professional 1986

Cls Hon member of Portstewart, Royal Portrush, Milltown, Co Down, Brancepeth Castle, Delamere Forest
Chp Ladies British Amateur 1979
Nat Ladies British Open Amateur Stroke Play 1980. Irish Foursomes 1980
Maj Avia Foursomes 1980-85.
Reg North-West Scratch Cup 1978. Ulster Ladies 1980
Int Curtis Cup 1980. Vagliano Trophy 1979-81-85. GB Commonwealth Team 1979. World Team Championship 1980. Ireland (Home Int) 1978-79-80-81-82-83; (Eur(L) T Ch) 1979-81-83
Jun Int Girls 1972-73-74-75-76

Maher, Sheila (*née* Vaughan)

Born Whiston, Liverpool on 9th March, 1942

Cls Huyton and Prescot
Reg Lancashire Ladies 1958-63-64
Int Curtis Cup 1962-64. Vagliano Trophy 1961-65. GB Commonwealth Team 1963. England (Home Int) 1960-61-62-63-64
Jun British Girls 1959.
Jun Int England Girls 1956-57-58-59
Mis In 1963 member of GB Commonwealth Team on tour of Australasia, tied first in Australian Ladies Foursomes, New Zealand Ladies Foursomes, New Zealand Junior Stroke Play

Marchbank, Brian

Born Perth on 20th April, 1958. TurnedProfessional 1979

PROFESSIONAL
Eur Equity & Law Challenge 1990-91
AMATEUR
Nat English Open Amateur Stroke Play r/u 1979
Trn Lytham Trophy 1978. Scottish Champion of Champions 1979
Int Walker Cup 1979. GBI v Europe 1976-78. Eisenhower Trophy 1978. Scotland (Home Int) 1978; (Eur T Ch) 1979; v Italy 1979

Jun British Boys 1975. Scottish Boys 1976. British Youths 1978.
Jun Int Boys 1973-74-75. Youths 1976-77-78-79

Marks, Geoffrey C

Born Hanley, Stoke-on-Trent, in November, 1938

Cls Hon member of Trentham, Trentham Park, Greenway Hall, Killarney, Walsall, Newcastle, Trevose, Stone. Royal & Ancient
Chp Amateur s/f 1968-75
Nat English Open Amateur Stroke Play r/u 1973-75
Trn Scrutton Jug 1967. Prince of Wales Challenge Cup 1968. Leicestershire Fox 1968. Lytham Trophy 1970 (tied). Harlech Gold Cup 1974. Homer Salver 1977
Reg Midland Amateur 1967. Staffordshire Amateur1959-60-63-66-67-68-69-73
Int Walker Cup 1969-71-**87**. Eisenhower Trophy 1970. GBI v Europe 1968-70. England (Home Int) 1963-67-68-69-70-71-74-75-(**80**)-(**81**)-(**82**)-(**83**); (Eur T Ch) 1967-69-71-75. GB Commonwealth Team 1975. GBI in Colombian International 1975
Jun Int Boys 1955-56. Youths 1957-58-59-60
Mis England Selector 1980-81-82-83 (chairman); R&A Selection Committee (chairman) 1989-93

Marsh, Dr David Max

Born Southport on 29th April, 1934

Cls Royal & Ancient, Hon member of Southport and Ainsdale, Ormskirk, West Lancashire, Worlington and Newmarket, Hillside, Clitheroe, Whalley
Nat English Amateur 1964-70
Trn Antlers Royal Mid-Surrey 1964-66. Formby Hare 1968. Boyd Quaich 1957
Int Walker Cup 1959-71-(**73**)-(**75**); GBI v Europe 1958-(**72**)-(**74**). GBI v Professionals 1959. England (Home Int) 1956-57-58-59-60-64-65-66-**68**-**69**-**70**-**71**-72; (Eur T Ch) 1971
Jun Int Boys 1951
Mis EGU Selector 1974. British Selector 1975. Chairman Royal & Ancient Selection Committee 1979-83. President EGU 1987. Captain of Royal & Ancient 1990/91

Marshall, Kathryn (*née* Imrie)

Born Southend on 8th June, 1967. Turned Professional 1990

Cls Monifieth
Maj Ladies British Open 3rd1993; leading amateur 1988 (Smyth Salver)
Trn St Rule Trophy 1985; Riccarton Rosebowl 1985; Roehampton Gold Cup 1990
Reg Highland Open 1985; North of Scotland Ladies Amateur 1988-90; Northern Counties Ladies Open Stroke Play 1986-87-88-89; Angus Ladies 1982-83-84-85
Int Curtis Cup 1990; Vagliano Trophy 1989; Scotland (Home Int) 1984-88-89; (Eur(L) T Ch) 1987-89
Mis Taunton Trophy 1986; winner of two NCAA events whilst at University of Arizona (1985-89); Doris Chambers Trophy, Angus Trophy 1990
Jun Scottish Girls Open Stroke Play 1985-86-87

Marvin, Vanessa Price

Born Cosford on 30th December, 1954. Turned Professional 1978

Cls Easingwold (Hon)
PROFESSIONAL
Eur Carlsberg Trn 1979
AMATEUR
Chp British Ladies Amateur r/u 1977
Nat English Ladies Amateur 1977-78.
Trn Hampshire Rose 1975-78 (tied). Roehampton Gold Cup 1976. Newmark-Avia 1978
Reg Yorkshire Ladies 1975-78. North of England Ladies 1975
Int Curtis Cup 1978. Vagliano Trophy 1977. England (Home Int) 1977-78; (Eur(L) T Ch) 1977; in Fiat Trophy 1978
Mis Leading amateur Colgate European LPGA 1977. Daks Woman Golfer of the Year 1978.

Matthew, Catriona (*née* Lambert)

Born on 25th August, 1969. Turned Professional 1994

Cls North Berwick
Chp British Ladies 1993
Nat Scottish Ladies 1991-93-94. Welsh Women's Open Stroke Play 1992
Trn Roehampton Gold Cup 1989; Helen Holm Trophy 1990; British Universities Women's Chp 1990; St Rule Trophy, Ness Trophy 1993; Astor Salver 1994
Int Curtis Cup 1990-92-94; Espirito Santo 1992; Vagliano Trophy 1989-91-93; Commonwealth Trn 1991; Scotland (Home Int) 1989-90-91-92-93; (Eur(L) T Ch) 1989-91
Jun Scottish Girls 1986; Scottish Girls Open Stroke Play 1988-89, r/u 1987

Matthews, Tegwen [Thomas] (*née* Perkins)

Born Cardiff on 2nd October, 1955

Cls Wenvoe Castle, Porthcawl, Pennard
Nat Welsh Ladies Amateur 1976-77. Welsh Ladies Open Amateur Stroke Play 1980. British Ladies Amateur Stroke Play r/u 1974
Trn Wills Match Play 1973. Avia Foursomes 1977. Worplesdon Mixed Foursomes 1973-78
Reg South-Western Ladies 1973-74-76. Glamorganshire Ladies 1972-74-75-77-78-80-81-83
Int Curtis Cup 1974-76-78-80. Vagliano Trophy 1973-75-77-79. World Team Chp 1974. GBCommonwealth Team 1975-79. GBI: Colombian Int. 1977-79. Wales (Home Int) 1972 to 84; (Eur(L) T Ch) 1975-77-79-81-83; in Fiat Trophy 1978.
Jun Welsh Girls 1970.
Int Girls 1970-71-72-73
Mis Dinwiddy Trophy 1973-74. 1974: in LGU Team touring SA; first Welsh player in Curtis Cup team; Taunton Trophy. 1976: first Welsh woman player to win all matches in Home Ints; Daks Woman Golfer of the Year (joint). Duncan Salver 1974-76.

Mayo, Paul M

Born Newport, Gwent on 6th January, 1963. Turned Professional 1988

PROFESSIONAL
Nat Welsh PGA 1990-91
Int Wales Dunhill Cup 1993
AMATEUR
Maj Leading Amateur in Open 1987

Chp Amateur Champion 1987
Nat Welsh Amateur 1987
Reg Gwent Amateur 1982
Int Walker Cup 1985-87; GBI v Europe 1986; Wales (Home Int) 1982-87
Jun British Youths 1983; Welsh Boys 1979

Merrill, Julia (*née* Greenhalgh)

Born Bolton on 6th January, 1941

Cls Hon member of Pleasington, Killarney, Ganton, Hermitage
Chp Ladies British Open Amateur r/u 1978
Nat British Ladies Stroke Play 1974-75. Runner-up British English Ladies 1966-79. Welsh Ladies Open Amateur Stroke Play 1977
Trn Astor Salver 1969-79. Hermitage Cup, Hampshire Rose 1977. Sunningdale Foursomes 1978
Oth New Zealand Ladies 1963
Reg Lancashire Ladies 1961-62-66-68-73-75-76-77-78; Northern Ladies 1961-62
Int Curtis Cup 1964-70-74-76-78. Vagliano Trophy 1961-65-75-77. GB Commonwealth Team 1963-75. World Team 1970-74-78. England (Home Int) 1960-61-63-66-69-70-71-76-77-78; (Eur(L) T Ch) 1971-75-77-79
Jun Scottish Girls Open Stroke Play 1960. Girl International 1957-58-59
Mis Leading Amateur (4th) in Australian Wills Ladies Open Stroke Play 1974. Daks Woman Golfer of the Year 1974. Taunton Trophy 1975-77. Doris Chambers Trophy 1977

Milligan, James W

Born Irvine on 15th June, 1963

Cls Kilmarnock (Barassie)
Nat Scottish Amateur 1988
Trn Scottish Champion of Champions 1989-90
Int Walker Cup 1989-91; Scotland (Home Int) 1986-87-88-89-90-91-92; v West Germany 1987; v Italy 1988-90; v Sweden 1990-92; (Eur T Ch) 1989-91; GBI v Europe 1988-90-92; World Cup (Eisenhower) 1988 (winners)-90
Jun Scottish Youths 1984

Milton, Moira (*née* Paterson)

Born 18th December, 1923

Cls Turnhouse, Hon Member of Gullane, Lenzie, Maccauvlei
Chp British Ladies 1952.
Nat Scottish Ladies r/u 1951
Reg Dunbartonshire Ladies 1949. Midlothian Ladies 1962
Int Curtis Cup 1952. GBI v France 1949-50; v Belgium 1950; Scotland (Home Int) 1949-50-51-52; v Australia 1951; v South Africa 1951; (Eur(L) T Ch) (**1973**)
Mis Member of LGU Team to South Africa 1951.

Montgomerie, Colin S

Born Glasgow on 23rd June, 1963. Turned Professional 1987

PROFESSIONAL

Maj US Open r/u 1994, 3rd 1992
Eur Portuguese Open 1989; Scandinavian Masters 1991; Dutch Open, Volvo Masters 1993; Open de España, English Open, German Open 1994
Int Ryder Cup 1991-93; Scotland in Dunhill Cup 1988-91-92(r/u)-93; in World Cup 1988-91-92-93; Four Tours World Chp 1991
Mis Rookie of the Year 1988; Harry Vardon Trophy 1993-94

AMATEUR

Chp Amateur r/u 1984
Nat Scottish Open Amateur Stroke Play 1985; Scottish Amateur 1987
Int Walker Cup 1985-87; Eisenhower Trophy 1984-86; GBI v Europe 1986; Scotland (Home Int) 1984-85-86 (Eur T Ch) 1985; v Sweden 1984-86; v France 1985

Montgomerie, John Speir

Born Cambuslang on 7th August, 1913

Cls Royal & Ancient, Cambuslang, Kilmarnock (Barassie), Pollok
Nat Scottish Amateur 1957
Reg Lanarkshire Amateur 1951-54
Int Scotland (Home Int) 1957-(**62**)-(**63**); v Scandinavia 1958
Mis Non-playing captain Scottish Team (Eur T Ch) 1965. Walker Cup Selector 1957 to 1965. President Scottish Golf Union 1965-66

Moodie, Janice

Born on 31st May, 1973

Cls Windyhill
Nat British Ladies Stroke Play r/u 1991; winner U-23 (Duncan Salver) and U-21 (Dinwiddy Trophy) 1990-91; Scottish Ladies 1992; Scottish U-21 Stroke Play 1990-93
Trn Munross Trophy, Mary McCallay Trophy; Inverness Stroke Play 1993
Reg West of Scotland Ladies 1991
Int Curtis Cup 1994; Vagliano Trophy 1993; Espirito Santo 1994; Scotland (Home Int) 1990-91-92; (Eur L T Ch) 1991-93
Jun Scottish Girls 1990(r/u)-91; British Girls s/f 1989-91
Jun Int Scottish Girls 1989-90-91; (Eur Jun L T Ch) 1990-92
Mis Doris Chambers Trophy, Angus Trophy 1993; Wilson PGA Junior Chp 1990. Currently a golf scholar at San José State University.

Morley, Joanne

Born on 30th December 1966. Turned Professional 1994

Cls Sale
Maj Leading Amateur in Women's British Open (Smyth Salver) 1989-93

PROFESSIONAL

Eur Ford Golf Classic r/u 1994
Int Union Cup 1994

AMATEUR

Nat Ladies British Amateur r/u 1992; Ladies British Amateur Stroke Play 1991; English Ladies Close Amateur Stroke Play 1991-92, r/u 1990; English Intermediate 1991
Trn St Rule Trophy 1987; Wentworth Scratch Cup 1988(tied); Avia Foursomes (with L Fairclough) 1989; Astor Salver 1990
Int Curtis Cup 1992; Vagliano Trophy 1991-93; Espirito Santo 1992; England (Home Int) 1990-91-92-93; (Eur(L) T Ch) 1991
Mis Taunton Trophy 1991; Daily Telegraph Woman Golfer of the Year 1991

Murray, Gordon H

Born Paisley on 19th December, 1936

Cls Fereneze (Hon)
Nat Scottish Amateur 1974-76, r/u 1975; Scottish Stroke Play 1983
Reg West of Scotland Amateur 1971-73-76-78
Int Walker Cup 1977. GBI v Europe 1978. Scotland (Home Int) 1973-74-75-76-77-78-83 (Eur T Ch) 1975-77; v Spain 1974-77; v Belgium 1975-77

Nesbitt, Claire *See* Robinson

New, Beverley Jayne

Born Bristol on 30th July, 1960. Turned Professional 1984

PROFESSIONAL
Eur Broadway Group Wirral Classic 1988
RoW Thailand Ladies Open 1987; Malaysian Ladies Open 1988
AMATEUR
Nat English Ladies 1980; Welsh Ladies Stroke Play r/u 1979
Trn Hampshire Rose 1980; WPGA United Friendly Insurance Trn, Worplesdon Mixed Foursomes 1982; Roehampton Gold Cup, Worplesdon Mixed Foursomes, Martin Bowl 1983
Reg Somerset Ladies 1979-80-81-82-83; Bristol & District Open 1983
Int Curtis Cup 1984; Vagliano Trophy 1983; England (Home Int) 1980-81-82-83; (Eur(L) T Ch) 1981-83; Fiat Trophy 1980
Mis Doris Chambers Trophy 1983

Nichol, Margaret *See* Pickard

Nicholas, Alison

Born Gibraltar on 6th March, 1962. Turned Professional 1984

PROFESSIONAL
Maj Ladies British Open 1987, 3rd 1988
Eur Laing Charity Classic 1987; Variety Club Classic, British Olivetti, Guernsey Open 1988; Lufthansa German Open, Gislaved Open 1989; Variety Club Classic 1990; Open de Paris 1992
RoW Malaysian Open, Western Open (Aus) 1992
Int Solheim Cup 1990-92
AMATEUR
Nat Ladies British Open Amateur Stroke Play 1983
Reg Yorkshire Ladies 1984; Northern Foursomes 1983
Jun North of England Girls 1982-83
Mis Taunton Trophy 1983; Duncan Salver 1983

O'Connell, Eoghan

Turned Professional 1990

PROFESSIONAL
Eur Swedish Match Play, Torras Hostench-El Prat 1990
AMATEUR
Int Walker Cup 1989; Eisenhower Trophy 1988 (winners); GBI v Europe 1988; Ireland (Home Int) 1985; (Eur T Ch) 1989

O'Connor, Christy

Born Galway on 21st December, 1924

Maj Open r/u 1965, 3rd 1958-61.
Trn Swallow-Penfold 1955. Dunlop Masters 1956-59. Spalding 1956 (tied). PGA Match Play 1957. Daks 1959. Ballantine 1960. Irish Hospitals 1960-62. Carling-Caledonian 1961. Martini 1963 (tied)-64. Jeyes 1964. Carrolls 1964-66-67-72. Senior Service 1965; Gallaher Ulster 1966-68-69. Alcan International 1968 (tied). Bowmaker 1970. John Player Classic 1970.
Oth Ulster Professional 1953-54. Irish Professional 1958-60-61-62-63-65-66-71-75-77. Irish Dunlop 1962-65-66-67. Gleneagles Pro-Am 1962. Southern Ireland Professional 1969-76. Sean Connery Pro-Am 1970.
Sen PGA Seniors 1976-77-79-81-82-83. World Seniors 1976-77
Int Ryder Cup 1955-57-59-61-63-65-67-69-71-73. GBI v Commonwealth 1956. Ireland in World Cup 1956-57-58 (winners) -59-60-61-62-63-64-66-67-68-69-71-75. Ireland in Double Diamond 1971-72-73-74-75-76-77
Mis Harry Vardon Trophy 1961-62. Second in order of Merit 1964 (equal)-65-66-69-70. AGW Trophy 1977

O'Connor, Christy, Jr

Born Galway on 19th August, 1948. Turned Professional 1965

Maj Open 3rd 1985
Eur Martini 1975 (tied). Carrolls Irish Open 1975. Sumrie 1976-78. Jersey European Airways Open 1989. Dunhill British Masters 1992
Oth Irish Dunlop 1974. Carrolls Irish Match Play 1975-77
RoW Zambian Open 1974. Kenya Open 1990
Int Ryder Cup 1975-89. Ireland in Double Diamond 1972-74-76-77. Ireland in World Cup 1974-75-78-85-89-92. Hennessy-Cognac 1974-84. GBI v South Africa 1976. Dunhill Cup 1985-89-92
Mis Braid Taylor Memorial Medal 1976-83. Tooting Bec Cup 1985

O'Leary, John E

Born Dublin on 19th August, 1949. Turned Professional 1970

PROFESSIONAL
Trn Sumrie 1975. Greater Manchester Open 1976. Carrolls Irish Open 1982; Irish Dunlop 1972
RoW Holiday Inns (Swaziland) 1975
Int Ryder Cup 1975; Ireland in World Cup 1972-80-82.;Ireland in Double Diamond 1972-73-74-75-76-77; GBI v Europe 1976-78-82
AMATEUR
Reg South of Ireland Amateur 1970.
Int Ireland (Home Int) 1969-70; (Eur T Ch) 1969
Jun Int Youths 1970

Oosterhuis, Peter A

Born London on 3rd May, 1948. Turned Professional November 1968

PROFESSIONAL
Maj Open r/u 1974-82; leading British player 1975 (7th), 1978 (6th) US Masters 3rd 1973
Eur Agfacolor, Sunbeam Pro-Am, Piccadilly 1971; Penfold 1972; French Open, Piccadilly, Viyella

PGA 1973; French Open, Italian Open 1974
US Canadian Open 1981
RoW General Motors South Africa 1970; Transvaal Open, Schoeman Park, Rhodesian Dunlop Masters 1971; Glen Anil Classic 1972; Rothman's Match Play South Africa, Maracaibo Open 1973; El Paraiso Open 1974
Oth Sunningdale Foursomes 1969; Coca-Cola Young Professionals 1970-72
Reg Southern England Professional 1971
Int Ryder Cup 1971-73-75-77-79-81; Hennessy-Cognac 1974; England in World Cup 1971-73, in Double Diamond 1973-74
Mis Rookie of the Year 1969; Harry Vardon Trophy 1971-72-73-74; AGW Trophy 1973-74
AMATEUR
Trn Berkshire Trophy 1966
Int Walker Cup 1967; Eisenhower Trophy 1968; England (Home Int) 1966-67-68
Jun British Youths 1966
Int Boys 1964-65; Youths 1966-67-68

O'Sullivan, Dr William M

Born Killarney on 13th March, 1911
Cls Waterville, Hon member of Killarney, Dooks, Tralee, Muskerry, Cork, Ballybunion
Chp Irish Open Amateur 1949, r/u 1936-53. Irish Amateur r/u 1940
Int Ireland (Home Int) 1934-35-36-37-38-47-48-49-50-51-53-54. President Golfing Union of Ireland 1959-60

Oxley, Dinah *See* Henson

Panton-Lewis, Catherine Rita

Born Bridge of Allan, Stirlingshire on 14th June, 1955. Turned Professional 1978
Cls Glenbervie (Hon), Pitlochry (Hon), Silloth (Hon), South Herts
PROFESSIONAL
Eur Carlsberg Tournament 1979. State Express Ladies Championship 1979. Elizabeth Ann Classic 1980. European Ladies Champion 1981. Moben Kitchens Classic 1982. Qualified for USLPGA Tour, January 1983. Smirnoff Irish Classic, UBM Northern Classic 1983, Dunham Forest Pro-Am 1983. McEwans Wirral Caldy Classic 1985. Delsjö Open 1985. Portuguese Open 1986-87. Scottish Open 1988
Int Union Cup 1994
Mis Order of Merit winner 1979
AMATEUR
Chp Ladies British Open Amateur 1976
Reg East of Scotland Ladies 1976
Int World Team Championship 1976. Vagliano Trophy 1977. Scotland (Home Int) 1972-73-76-77-78; (Eur(L) T Ch) 1973-77
Jun Scottish Girls 1969. Girl Int 1969-70-71-72-73
Mis Scottish Sportswoman of the Year 1976. Member of LGU under-25 team to tour Canada 1973

Panton, John, MBE

Born Pitlochry, Perthshire on 9th October, 1916. Turned Professional 1935
Maj Leading British player in 1956 Open (5th)
Trn Silver King 1950. Daks 1951. North-British-Harrogate 1952. Goodwin Foursomes 1952. Yorkshire Evening News 1954. PGA Match Play 1956, r/u 1968
Eur Woodlawn Invitation Open (Germany) 1958-59-60
Oth West of Scotland Professional 1947-48-52-54-55-61-63. Scottish Professional 1948-49-50-51-54-55-59-66 (tied). Northern Open 1948-51-52-56-59-60-62. West of Scotland PGA Match Play 1954-55-56-64. Goodwin Foursomes 1952. Gleneagles-Saxone 1956.
Sen Pringle Seniors 1967-69. World Seniors 1967
Int Ryder Cup 1951-53-61. Scotland in World Cup 1955-56-57-58-59-60-62-63-64-65-66-68
Mis Harry Vardon Trophy 1951. AGW Trophy 1967. Hon Professional to Royal & Ancient from 1988

Parkin, Philip

Born Doncaster on 12th December, 1961. Turned Professional 1984
PROFESSIONAL
Reg Welsh PGA 1986
Int Wales in World Cup 1984-89; Dunhill Cup 1985-86-87-89-90-91; Hennessy-Cognac Cup 1984
Mis Rookie of the Year 1984
AMATEUR
Chp Amateur Champion 1983
Int Walker Cup 1983. Wales (Home Int) 1980-81-82.
Jun British Youths 1982

Paterson, Moira *See* Milton

Payne, Jim

Born Louth, Lincolnshire on 17th April, 1970. Turned Professional 1991
PROFESSIONAL
Maj Leading Amateur in Open 1991
Eur Open de Baleares 1993
AMATEUR
Oth European Amateur 1991
Trn Berkhamsted Trophy 1989; Selborne Salver 1991
Reg West of England Stroke Play 1990
Oth Greek Amateur 1989
Int Walker Cup 1991; England (Home Int) 1989-90; (Eur T Ch) 1991; GBI v Europe 1990
Jun British Youths 1991
Int English Youths 1989-90-91
Mis PGA European Rookie of the Year 1992

Perkins, Tegwen *See* Matthews

Perowne, Arthur Herbert

Born Norwich on 21st February, 1930
Cls Royal Norwich, Hunstanton, West Norfolk
Chp English Open Amateur Stroke Play 1958
Oth Swedish Amateur 1974
Trn Berkshire Trophy 1958 (tied)
Reg East Anglia Open 1952. Norfolk Amateur 1948-51-52-53-54-55-56-57-58-60-61. Norfolk Open 1964
Int Walker Cup 1949-53-59. Eisenhower Trophy 1958. GBI v Denmark 1955; v Professionals 1956-58. England (Home Int) 1947-48-49-50-51-53-54-55-57; v France 1950-54-56-59; v Sweden 1947; v Denmark 1947
Jun Carris Trophy 1946
Int Boys 1946

Phillips, Ann *See* Howard

Phillips, Kathryn *See* Lumb

Pickard, Margaret (*née* Nichol)
Born on 25th April, 1938
Cls Alnmouth (Hon)
Nat English Ladies 1960, r/u 1957-67
Reg Northern Ladies 1957-58. Northumberland Ladies 1956-57-58-61-62-64-65-66-67-69-70-71-76-77-82
Int Curtis Cup 1968-70. Vagliano Trophy 1959-61-67. England (Home Int) 1957-58-59-60-61-67-69-(**83**). (Eur(L) T Ch) (**1983**)

Pirie, Alex Kemp
Born Aberdeen on 21st June, 1942
Cls Hazelhead (Hon), Cruden Bay
Nat Scottish Amateur r/u 1972-74
Trn Eden Tournament 1963.
Reg Northern Scottish Open 1970. West of Scotland Open Amateur 1972. East of Scotland Open Amateur Stroke Play 1975. North East Scotland Match Play 1964-66-67-68-71-73. Aberdeenshire Stroke Play 1966-68
Int Walker Cup 1967. GBI v Europe 1970. Scotland (Home Int) 1966-67-68-69-70-71-72-73-74-75; (Eur T Ch) 1967-69; v Belgium 1973-75; v Spain 1974

Pook, Elizabeth (*née* Chadwick)
Born Inverness on 4th April, 1943
Cls Bramall Park (Hon), Anglesey (Rhosneigr)
Chp British Ladies 1966-67.
Nat English Ladies r/u 1963. Italian Ladies r/u 1967
Reg Central England Mixed Foursomes 1962-63-64 North of England Ladies 1965-66-67. Cheshire Ladies 1963-64-65-66-67
Trn Avia Foursomes (with C Lacoste) r/u 1967
Int Curtis Cup 1966. GB Commonwealth 1967. GBI v Europe 1963-67. England (Home Int) 1963-65-66-67; (Eur(L) T Ch) 1967; v France 1965
Jun Girl International 1961

Porter, Ruth *See* Slark

Price Fisher, Elizabeth
Born London on 17th January, 1923. Turned Professional 1968, reinstated as Amateur 1971
Cls Hankley Common, Farnham, Berkshire
Chp British Ladies 1959, r/u 1954-58.
Nat English Ladies r/u 1947-54-55
Oth Danish Ladies 1952. Portuguese Ladies 1964
Trn Spalding Ladies 1955-59. Astor Salver 1955-56-59. Fairway and Hazard Foursomes 1954-60. Kayser Bondor Foursomes 1958 (tied). Roehampton Gold Cup 1960. Central England Mixed Foursomes 1971-76-82
Reg South Eastern Ladies 1955-59-60-69. Surrey Ladies 1954-55-56-57-58-59-60
Int Curtis Cup 1950-52-54-56-58-60. Vagliano Trophy 1959. GBI v Canada 1950-54-58; v France 1953-55-57; v Belgium 1953-55-57. GB Commonwealth Team 1955-59. England (Home Int) 1948-51-52-53-54-55-56-57-58-59-60
Mis AGW Trophy 1952.

Pyman, Iain
Born Whitby on 3rd March, 1973
Cls Sand Moor
Maj Open Chp 1993; leading amateur 1993
Chp Amateur Champion 1993
Trn Formby Hare 1992
Oth Top amateur in NSW Open (Aus)
Reg Yorkshire champion 1992
Int GBI Walker Cup 1993; England (Home Int) 1993
Jun Carris Trophy 1991; Yorkshire Youths 1993
Jun Int GBI Boys 1991; England Boys 1991

Rafferty, Ronan
Born Newry on 13th January, 1964. Turned Professional 1981
PROFESSIONAL
Eur Equity & Law Challenge 1988; Lancia Italian Open, Scandinavian Enterprise Open, Volvo Masters 1989; PLM Open, Swiss Open 1990; Portuguese Open 1992; Austrian Open 1993
RoW Venezuelan Open 1982; South Australian Open, New Zealand Open 1987; Australian Match Play 1988; Coca-Cola Classic (Aus) 1990; Daikyo Palm Meadow (Aus) 1992
Int Ryder Cup 1989; Kirin Cup 1988; Four Tours World Chp 1989-90-91; GBI v Australia 1988; Hennessy-Cognac 1984; Ireland in World Cup 1983-84-87-88-91-92-93; Dunhill Cup 1986-87-88(winners)-89-90(winners)-91-92-93
Mis Harry Vardon Trophy 1989
AMATEUR
Nat Irish Amateur 1980; English Amateur Open Stroke Play 1980(tied)
Int Walker Cup 1981; Eisenhower Trophy 1980; GBI v Europe 1980; Ireland (Home Int) 1980; v Wales 1979; v France, Germany, Sweden 1980; Fiat Trophy 1980; (Eur T Ch) 1981
Jun British Boys 1979; Irish Youths 1979; Ulster Youths 1979
Int Boys 1978-79; Youths 1979-80

Rawlings, Vicki *See* Thomas

Reddan, Clarrie (*née* Tiernan)
Born Drogheda on 3rd July, 1916
Cls Co Louth
Chp British Ladies r/u 1949
Nat Irish Ladies 1936, r/u 1946-48.
US New Jersey State Ladies 1937. Canadian Ladies r/u 1938
Int Curtis Cup 1938-48. GBI v Canada 1938. Ireland (Home Int) 1935-36-37-38-39-47-48-49

Redford, Carole *See* Caldwell

Reid, Dale
Born Ladybank, Fife on 20th March, 1959. Turned Professional 1979
PROFESSIONAL
Eur Carlsberg (Coventry) 1980. Carlsberg (Gleneagles), Moben Kitchens 1981. Guernsey Open 1982. United Friendly, International Classic 1983. Caldy Classic 1983. UBM Classic, JS Bloor Classic 1984. Ulster Volkswagen Classic, Brend Hotels International 1985. British Olivetti 1986. Volmac Open, European Open,

Bowring Scottish Ladies Open, Volkswagen Classic 1987. European Open, Toshiba Players Chp 1988. Haninge Ladies Open 1990. Ford Ladies Classic, Eastleigh Classic 1991
Oth Sunningdale Foursomes (with C. Dibnah) 1990
Int Solheim Cup 1990-92-94; Sunrise Cup 1992; Union Cup 1994
Mis Order of Merit winner 1984-87; first Honorary Member of WPGET 1991
AMATEUR
Int Scotland (Home Int) 1978
Jun Fife Girls 1973-75
Jun Int Scottish Girls International 1974-75-76-77

Richardson, Steven

Born Windsor on 24th July, 1966. Turned Professional 1989

PROFESSIONAL
Eur Girona Open, Portuguese Open 1991; German Masters 1993
Int Ryder Cup 1991; England in Dunhill Cup 1991-92(winners); World Cup 1991-92; Four Tours World Chp 1991
AMATEUR
Nat English Amateur 1989
Int England (Home Int) 1986-87-88

Robb, Diane *See* Bailey

Robertson, Dean

Born Sarnia, Canada on 11th July, 1970. Turned Professional 1993

Cls Cochrane Castle
PROFESSIONAL
Trn HIS Assistants 1994
AMATEUR
Nat Scottish Amateur Stroke Play 1993, r/u 1993
Trn Scottish Champion of Champions 1992; Tennant Cup 1992-93; Leven Gold Medal 1992
Int GBI Walker Cup 1993; v Europe 1992; World Cup 1992; Scotland (Home Int) 1991-92-93; v Sweden 1992, v Italy 1992
Mis Scottish Golfer of the Year 1992

Robertson, Isabella (Belle), MBE

Born Southend, Argyll, on 11th April, 1936

Cls Dunaverty (Hon)
Maj Ladies British Open: leading amateur (Smyth Salver); r/u 1980-81
Chp Ladies British Open Amateur 1981; r/u 1959-65-70
Nat Ladies British Open Amateur Stroke Play 1971-72-85; Scottish Ladies 1965-66-71-72-78-80; r/u 1959-63-70
Oth New Zealand Ladies Match Play 1971
Trn Sunningdale Foursomes 1960; Avia Foursomes 1972-81-84-86; Helen Holm Trophy 1973-79-86; Players No 6 Cup 1973-76; Roehampton Gold Cup 1978 (tied)-79-81-82
Reg West of Scotland Ladies 1957-64-66-69; Dunbartonshire Ladies 1958 to 1963, 1965-66-68-69-78
Sen US Women's Amateur Seniors r/u 1991
Int Curtis Cup 1960-66-68-70-72-(74)-(76)-82-86; Vagliano Trophy 1959-63-65-69-71-81; Espirito Santo 1964-66-**68**-72-80-82; GB Commonwealth Team 1971-(**75**); Scotland (Home Int) 1958 to 1966, 69-72-73-78-80-81-82 (Eur(L) T Ch) 1965-**67**-69-71-73-81-83; Fiat Trophy 1978-80
Mis Daks Woman Golfer of the Year 1971-81; Frank Moran Trophy 1971; leading qualifier US Ladies Amateur 1978; Scottish Sportswoman of the Year 1968-71-78-81; Avia Woman Golfer of the Year 1985

Robertson, Janette *See* Wright

Robinson, Jeremy

Born 21st January, 1966. Turned Professional 1987

PROFESSIONAL
Eur Old Links Satellite 1989; Open Dijon Bourgogne 1992
RoW Kenya Open 1991; Zambian Open 1992
AMATEUR
Nat English Amateur Stroke Play (Brabazon Trophy) 1987
Trn Lagonda Trophy 1985
Int Walker Cup 1987. England (Home Int) 1986

Roderick, R Neil

Born Swansea on 8th March, 1966. Turned Professional 1990

PROFESSIONAL
Trn Cawder Challenge 1991
AMATEUR
Nat Welsh Amateur Stroke Play 1984-88. English Open Amateur Stroke Play 1989
Trn Tenby Eagle 1988. Harlech Gold Cross 1986. Southerndown Silver Ram 1984-85-86. Worplesdon Mixed Foursomes 1986. Duncan Putter 1989
Int Walker Cup 1989. Wales (Home Int) 1983-84-85-86-87-88. GBI v Europe 1988
Jun Welsh Boys 1982-83

Roe, Mark

Born Sheffield on 20th February, 1963. Turned Professional 1981

Eur Catalan Open 1989; Trophée Lancôme 1992; Open de France 1994
Int England in World Cup 1989-94; Dunhill Cup 1994

Saddler, AC

Born Forfar, Angus on 11th August, 1935

Cls Forfar, Carnoustie
Nat Scottish Amateur r/u 1960
Trn Berkshire Trophy 1962
Int Walker Cup 1963-65-67-(77) Eisenhower Trophy 1962-(**76**) (winners)-78. GB Commonwealth Team 1959-63-67; v Europe 1960-62-66-(**76**)-(**78**); v Professionals 1959-61. Scotland (Home Int) 1959-60-61-62-63-65-(**74**)-(**75**)-(**76**)-(**77**); (Eur T Ch) (**1975**)-(**77**)

Saunders, Vivien Inez

Born Sutton on 24th November, 1946. Turned Professional 1969

PROFESSIONAL
Maj Ladies British Open 1977
Trn Avia Foursomes 1978; Keighley Trophy 1981; British Car Auctions 1980

US 1969 First European to qualify for LPGA tour
RoW Schweppes-Tarax Open (Australia), Chrysler Open (Australia) 1973
Mis Founder WPGA & Chairman 1978-79
AMATEUR
Chp Ladies British Open Amateur r/u 1966
Trn Avia Foursomes 1967
Int Curtis Cup 1968; Vagliano Trophy 1967; GB Commonwealth Team 1967; England (Home Int) 1967-68 (Eur(L) T Ch) 1967; v France 1966-67
Jun Int Girls 1964-65-66-67

Sewell, Douglas

Born Woking on 19th November, 1929. Turned Professional 1960

PROFESSIONAL
Trn Martini International 1970 (shared); Wentworth Pro-Am Foursomes 1968
Reg West of England Open Professional 1968-70
Int PGA Cup 1973-74-75
AMATEUR
Nat English Amateur 1958-60; English Open Amateur Stroke-Play 1957-59
Trn Scrutton Jug 1959; Golf Illustrated Gold Vase 1960; Sunningdale Foursomes 1959
Reg Surrey Amateur 1954-56-58
Int Walker Cup 1957-59; Eisenhower Trophy 1960; GB Commonwealth Team 1959; England (Home Int) 1956-57-58-59-60

Sheahan, Dr David B

Born Southsea, England on 25th February, 1940

Cls Grange
Nat Irish Amateur 1961-66-70
Trn Jeyes Professional 1962 (as an Amateur); Frame Trophy 1991
Oth Boyd Quaich 1962
Int Walker Cup 1963. GBI v Europe 1962-64. Ireland (Home Int) 1961-62-63-64-65-66-67-70; (Eur T Ch) 1965-67 (winners both times)

Shepperson, AE

Born Sutton-in-Ashfield on 8th April, 1936

Cls Coxmoor (Hon), Notts
Nat English Open Amateur Stroke Play r/u 1958-62
Trn President's Putter 1957
Reg Nottinghamshire Amateur 1955-58-61-65. Nottinghamshire Open 1955-58
Int Walker Cup 1957-59. England (Home Int) 1956-57-58-59-60-62
Jun British Boys 1953

Sinclair, Alexander, OBE

Born West Kilbride, Ayrshire on 6th July, 1920

Cls Royal & Ancient, Hon member of West Kilbride, Drumpellier, Bothwell Castle, Royal Troon
Trn Newlands Trophy 1950
Oth Royal & Ancient Silver Cross 1972. Royal Medal 1977. Scottish Open Amateur Seniors 1979
Reg West of Scotland Amateur 1950. Lanarkshire Amateur 1952-59-61. Glasgow Amateur 1961
Int Scotland (Home Int) 1950-(**66**)-(**67**). (Eur T Ch) (**1967**)
Mis Chairman R & A Selection Committee from 1969 to 1975. Leading Amateur (joint second) in Northern Open 1948. President Scottish Golf Union 1976-78. Frank Moran Trophy 1978. Chairman R & A Amateur Status Committee 1979-81. President European Golf Association 1981-82-83. Captain of R&A 1988/89. President of Golf Foundation from 1990

Slark, Ruth (*née* Porter)

Born Chesterfield on 6th May, 1939

Cls Long Ashton (Hon), Bath, Burnham and Berrow, Reigate Heath, Walton Heath
Nat English Ladies 1959-61-65, r/u 1978
Oth Australian Ladies r/u 1963
Trn Astor Prince's 1961. Fairway and Hazard Foursomes 1958. Roehampton Gold Cup 1963. Astor Salver 1962-63. Hovis Ladies 1966 (tied). Avia Foursomes 1968
Reg South Western Ladies 1956-57-60-61-62-64-65-66-67-69-72-77-79. Gloucestershire Ladies 1957-59-61-62-63-64-66-67-69-73-74-75-76-77
Int Curtis Cup 1960-62-64. Vagliano Trophy 1959-61-65. GB Commonwealth Team 1963. World Team Ch 1964-66. England (Home Int) 1959-60-61-62-64-65-66-68-75-78; (Eur(L) T Ch) 1965
Jun British Girls 1956. Scottish Girls Open Stroke Play 1958. Girls International 1955-56-57
Mis Taunton Trophy 1978

Smith, William Dickson

Born Glasgow on 2nd February, 1918

Cls Prestwick (Hon), Royal & Ancient, Royal Troon, Selkirk (Hon), Southerness, Gullane
Maj Leading amateur (5th) in Open 1957
Nat Scottish Amateur 1958. Scottish Senior Open Amateur 1983
Oth Indian Open Amateur 1945. Portuguese Open Amateur 1967-70.
Trn Worplesdon Mixed Foursomes 1957. Royal & Ancient Royal Medal 1971
Reg Border Amateur 1949-51-57-63. Dumfriesshire Amateur 1956
Int Walker Cup 1959. GBI v Europe 1958. Scotland (Home Int) 1957-58-59-60-63-(83); v Scandinavia 1958-60

Smye, Catherine *See* McCann

Smyth, Des

Born Drogheda on 12th February, 1953. Turned Professional 1973

PROFESSIONAL
Trn PGA Match Play 1979. Newcastle Brown 900, Greater Manchester Open 1980. Coral Classic 1981. Sanyo Open 1983. Jersey Open 1988. Madrid Open 1993
Oth Irish PGA 1979-90. Carrolls Irish Match Play, Irish Dunlop 1980. Irish Masters 1994.
Int Ryder Cup 1979-81. Ireland in World Cup 1979-80-82-83-88-89. Hennessy-Cognac Cup 1980-82-84. Dunhill Cup 1985-86-87-88 (winners)
AMATEUR
Int Ireland (Home Int) 1972-73; (Eur T Ch) 1973

Speak, Kirsty

Born on 18th June, 1971

Cls Clitheroe
Chp British Ladies r/u 1993

Nat English Intermediate 1990(r/u)-92-93; British Ladies Stroke Play 1994
Trn Pleasington Putter 1990; Bridget Jackson Bowl 1994; Wentworth Scratch 1994
Oth World Student Chp 1992
Int Curtis Cup 1994; Vagliano Trophy 1993; Espirito Santo 1994; England (Home Int) 1993-94; (Eur L T Ch) 1993

Spearman, Marley See **Harris**

Squirrell, Hew Crawford

Born Cardiff on 15th August, 1932

Cls Hon member of Cardiff, Moseley, Killarney
Nat Welsh Amateur 1958-59-60-64-65, r/u 1962-71
Trn Antlers Royal Mid-Surrey 1959-61. Hampshire Hog 1961. Berkhamsted Trophy 1960-63. Boyd Quaich 1955
Reg Glamorgan Amateur 1959-65. Herts Amateur 1963-73
Int Wales (Home Int) 1955-56-57-58-59-60-61-62-63-64-65-66-67-68-69-70-71-73-74-75; (Eur T Ch) 1965-67-69-71-75; v France 1975
Mis Deputy-Director Golf Foundation

Stanford, Mathew

Born Pontypool on 14th July, 1969. Turned Professional 1993

Cls Saltford
PROFESSIONAL
Reg West of England PGA 1994
AMATEUR
Chp Amateur Chp s/f 1992
Nat Spanish Amateur 1992
Trn Selborne Salver 1989
Reg West of England Stroke Play 1992
Int GBI Walker Cup 1993; World Cup 1992; England (Home Int) 1991-92-93; *v* France 1992

Stephen, Alexander R (Sandy)

Born St Andrews on 8th January, 1954. Turned Professional 1985

Cls Lundin (Hon), Muckhart (Hon), Broomieknowe
PROFESSIONAL
Trn Scottish Professional Chp 1988
AMATEUR
Nat Scottish Amateur 1971
Trn Scottish Champion of Champions 1984. Leven Gold Medal 1984
Reg North of Scotland Open Amateur 1972-77. Fife Amateur 1973. Lothians Amateur 1978; East of Scotland Open Amateur 1974-77-83-84. West of Scotland Open Amateur 1975.
Int Walker Cup 1985. GBI v Europe 1972. Scotland (Home Int) 1971-72-73-74-75-76-77-84-85; (Eur T Ch) 1975-85; v Spain 1974; v Belgium 1975-77-78.
Jun Scottish Boys 1970.
Int Boys 1970-71. Youths 1972-73-74-75
Mis Finished third in World Boys International Trophy (USA) 1970

Stewart, Gillian

Born Inverness on 21st October, 1958. Turned Professional 1985

Cls Inverness (Hon), Nairn
PROFESSIONAL
Eur IBM European Open 1984 (as amateur). Ford Ladies Classic 1985-87
Int Union Cup 1994
AMATEUR
Nat Scottish Ladies 1979-83-84. Ladies British Open Amateur r/u 1982
Trn Helen Holm Trophy 1981-84
Reg Northern Counties Ladies 1976-78-82. North of Scotland Ladies 1975-78-80-82-83.
Int Curtis Cup 1980-82. GB Commonwealth Team 1979-83. Vagliano Trophy 1979-81-83. World Cup 1982-84. Scotland (Home Int) 1979-80-81-82-83-84; (Eur(L) T Ch) 1979-81-83.
Jun British Girls 1976. Scottish U-19 Stroke Play Champion 1975
Int Girls 1975-76-77
Mis Member of Scottish team which won the 1980 European Junior Team Championship. Avia Woman Golfer of the Year 1984.

Stuart, Hugh Bannerman

Born Forres on 27th June, 1942

Cls Forres (Hon), Murcar (Hon)
Chp Amateur s/f 1974
Nat Scottish Amateur 1972, r/u 1970-76
Reg North of Scotland Amateur 1967-74. Moray Amateur 1960. Nairnshire Amateur 1966
Int Walker Cup 1971-73-75. GB Commonwealth Team 1971. Eisenhower Trophy 1972. GBI v Europe 1968-72-74. Scotland (Home Int) 1967-68-70-71-72-73-74-76; (Eur T Ch) 1969-71-73-75; v Belgium 1973-75
Jun Scottish Boys 1959.
Int Boys 1959
Mis Won all his matches in 1971 Walker Cup. In European Team touring South Africa 1974

Thirlwell, Alan

Born 8th August, 1928

Cls Gosforth, Formby
Chp Amateur r/u 1958-72.
Nat English Amateur 1954-55, r/u 1963. English Open Amateur Stroke Play r/u 1964
Trn County Champion of Champions 1962. Wentworth Pro-Am Foursomes 1960-61-68
Reg Northumberland Amateur 1952-55-62-64. Northumberland and Durham Open 1960
Int Walker Cup 1957. GB Commonwealth Team 1954-63. GBI v Europe 1956-58; v Denmark 1955; v Professionals 1963. England (Home Int) 1951-52-54-55-56-57-58-59-63-64; v France 1954-56-59
Mis Canadian Amateur s/f 1957. EGU Selector 1974 to 1977. Secretary CONGU

Thomas, David C

Born Newcastle-upon-Tyne on 16th August, 1934. Turned Professional 1949

Maj Open r/u 1958 (tied), r/u 1966
Eur Belgian Open 1955. Dutch Open 1958. French Open 1959
Trn Esso Golden 1961 (tied)-62-66. PGA Match Play, Olgiata Trophy (Rome) 1963. Silentnight 1965 (tied). Penfold-Swallow, Jeyes 1966. Penfold 1968 (tied). Graham Textiles 1969. Pains-Wessex 1969

RoW Caltex (NZ) 1958-59.
Oth British Assistants 1955. Wentworth Pro-Am Foursomes 1960-61
Int Ryder Cup 1959-63-65-67. Wales in World Cup 1957-58-59-60-61-62-63-66-67-69-70. Wales in Double Diamond 1972-73
Mis Won qualifying competition for US Open 1964

Thomas, Vicki (*née* Rawlings)

Born Northampton on 27th October, 1954

Cls Pennard
Maj Leading Amateur in Women's British Open (Smyth Salver) 1986
Nat Welsh Ladies Amateur 1979-82-83-85-86-87-91-94; British Ladies Amateur Stroke Play 1990, r/u 1979. Welsh Ladies Open Stroke Play 1981-82-89, r/u 1980
Trn Roehampton Gold Cup 1983-85. Cotswold Gold Vase 1983. Keithley Trophy 1983. Sunningdale Foursomes 1989. Welsh Trn of Champions 1991-94
Reg Glamorganshire Ladies 1970-71-79; Women's South-West Chp 1991
Oth Women's Greek Amateur Stroke Play 1991
Int Curtis Cup 1982-84-86-88-90-92; GB Commonwealth Trn 1979-83-87-91; Vagliano Trophy 1979-83-85-87-89-91; Espirito Santo 1990; Wales (Home Int) 1971 to 1992; (Eur(L) T Ch) 1973-75-77-79-81-83-87-91
Jun Welsh Girls 1973.
Int Girls 1969-70-71-72-73
Mis Taunton Trophy 1979

Thomson, James Allan

Born Prestwick on 2nd May 1958

Cls Ayr Belleisle
Nat Scottish Amateur 1989; r/u 1981-86; s/f 1983-88
Reg West of Scotland Amateur 1985
Int Scotland (Home Int) 1981-82-83-84-85-86-87-88-89-90-91; v West Germany 1987; v Italy 1988-90; v Sweden 1990

Thomson, Muriel

Born Aberdeen on 12th December, 1954. Turned Professional 1979

PROFESSIONAL
Eur Carlsberg, Viscount Double Glazing, Barnham Broom 1980; Elizabeth Ann Classic 1981; Guernsey Open, Sands International 1984; Laing Ladies Classic 1985; Irish Open, Ford Ladies Classic 1986
Mis Order of Merit winner 1980-83; Frank Moran Trophy 1981
AMATEUR
Nat Scottish Ladies r/u 1977
Trn Helen Holm Trophy 1975-76; Canadian Ladies Foursomes 1978
Reg North of Scotland Ladies 1973-74; Aberdeenshire Ladies 1977
Int Curtis Cup 1978; Vagliano Trophy 1977; Espirito Santo 1978; GBI in Colombian International 1979; Scotland (Home Int) 1974-75-76-77-78; (Eur(L) T Ch) 1975-77

Thornhill, Jill

Born 18th August, 1942

Cls Walton Heath, Silloth-on-Solway
Chp Ladies British Open Amateur 1983
Nat English Ladies 1986, r/u 1974. Ladies British Open Amateur Stroke Play r/u 1987
Trn Avia Foursomes 1970-83. Astor Salver 1972-75. Newmark International 1974. Worplesdon Mixed Foursomes 1975. Hampshire Rose 1982-87
Eur Belgian Ladies 1967
Reg South Eastern Ladies 1964-64-85. Surrey Ladies 1962-64-65-73-74-77-78-81-82-83-84
Int Curtis Cup 1984-86-88-(**90**). Vagliano Trophy 1965-83-85-87-(**90**). England (Home Int) 1964-65-74-82-83-84-85-86 -87-88. Commonwealth Team Ch 1983; (Eur(L) T Ch) 1983.
Mis Doris Chambers Trophy 1986. Avia Woman Golfer of the Year 1983

Tiernan, Clarrie *See* Reddan

Torrance, Sam

Born Largs, Ayrshire on 24th August, 1953. Turned Professional 1970

PROFESSIONAL
Eur Piccadilly Medal, Martini International 1976; Carrolls Irish Open 1981; Spanish Open, Portuguese Open 1982; Scandinavian Enterprise Open, Portuguese Open 1983; Tunisian Open, Benson & Hedges International, Sanyo Open 1984; Monte Carlo Open 1985; Lancia Italian Open 1987; German Masters 1990; Jersey Open 1991; Kronenbourg Open, Catalan Open, Honda Open 1993
Oth U-25 Match Play 1972; Scottish Uniroyal 1975; Scottish Professional 1978-80-91-93
RoW Zambian Open 1975; Colombian Open 1979; Australian PGA 1980
Int Ryder Cup 1981-83-85-87-89-91-93; Hennessy-Cognac Cup 1976-80-82-84; Nissan Cup 1985; Four Tours World Chp 1991; Scotland in World Cup 1976-78-82-84-85-87-89-90-91-93; Double Diamond 1973-76-77; Dunhill Cup 1985-86-87-89-90-91-93
Mis Rookie of the Year 1972; Tooting Bec Cup 1984
AMATEUR
Jun Int Scottish Boys 1970

Townsend, Peter Michael Paul

Born Cambridge on 16th September, 1946. Turned Professional 1966

PROFESSIONAL
Eur Dutch Open 1967; Swiss Open, Carrolls Irish Match Play 1971; Carrolls Irish Match Play 1976; Irish Dunlop 1977
Oth PGA Close, Coca-Cola Young Professionals 1968
US Chesterfield 1968
RoW Western Australia Open 1968; Caracas Open 1969; Walworth Aloyco 1971; Los Lagaratos Open 1972; ICL International (South Africa) 1975; Moroccan Grand Prix, Los Lagaratos Open, Caribbean Open, Zambian Open 1978; Laurent Perrier 1981
Int Ryder Cup 1969-71; Hennessy-Cognac 1974; England in World Cup 1969-74; in Double Diamond 1971-72-74

AMATEUR
Nat English Open Amateur Stroke Play 1966
Trn Duncan Putter 1965; Mullingar Trophy 1965-66; Lytham Trophy 1966; *Golf Illustrated* Golf Vase 1966; Prince of Wales Challenge Cup 1966; St George's Challenge Cup 1966; Berkhamsted Trophy 1966
Reg Herts Amateur 1964
Int Walker Cup 1965; Eisenhower Trophy 1966; GBI v Europe 1966; England (Home Int) 1965-66
Jun British Boys 1962-64; British Youths 1965
Int Boys 1961-62-63-64; Youths 1965
Mis Captain PGA 1984

Tucker, William Iestyn

Born Nantyglo, Monmouth on 9th December, 1926

Cls Monmouthshire, Brecon, Killarney, Morlais Castle, Tredegar and Rhymney, Pontynewydd, Llantrisant, Radyr, Whitehall
Nat Welsh Amateur 1933-36, r/u 1951-56-64-67-75-76. Welsh Amateur Stroke Play 1976
Trn Duncan Putter 1960-61 (tied)-63-69-76
Reg Monmouthshire Amateur 1949, 1952 to 63, 1967-69-74. Gwent Amateur 1976
Int Wales (Home Int) 1949 to 72, 1974-75; (Eur T Ch) 1965-67-69-75; v Australia 1953; v France 1975. Captain Welsh Team 1966-67-68

Uzielli, Angela (*née* Carrick)

Born Swanton Morley, Norfolk on 1st February, 1940

Cls Berkshire (Hon),
Chp British Ladies Open Amateur 1977.
Nat English Ladies 1990, r/u 1976
Trn Astor Salver 1971-73 (tied)-77-81. Roehampton Gold Cup 1977. Avia Foursomes 1982. Hampshire Rose 1985
Reg Berkshire Ladies 1976-77-78-79-80-81-83
Int Curtis Cup 1978. Vagliano Trophy 1977. England (Home Int) 1976-77-78-90; (Eur(L) T Ch) 1977
Sen British Ladies Seniors 1990-91-92
Mis Daks Woman Golfer of the Year 1977; Daily Telegraph Woman Golfer of the Year 1990

Valentine, Jessie, MBE (*née* Anderson)

Born Perth on 18th March, 1915. Turned Professional 1960

Cls Hon member of Craigie Hill, St Rule, Hunstanton, Blairgowrie, Murrayshall
Chp British Ladies 1937-55-58, r/u 1950-57.
Nat Scottish Ladies 1938-39-51-53-55-56, r/u 1934-54
Oth New Zealand Ladies 1935. French Ladies 1936
Trn Spalding Ladies 1957. Kayser Bondor Foursomes 1959-61. Worplesdon Mixed Foursomes 1963-64-65
Reg East of Scotland Ladies 1936-38-39-50
Int Curtis Cup 1936-38-50-52-54-56-58. GBI v France 1935-36-38-39-47-49-51-55; v Belgium 1949-51-54-55; v Canada 1938-50. GB Commonwealth Team 1953-55-(59). Scotland (Home Int) 1934-35-36-37-38-39-47-49-50-51-52-53-54-55-56-57-58
Jun British Girls 1933
Mis Canadian Ladies s/f 1938. Member of LGU Team to Australia and New Zealand 1935. Frank Moran Trophy 1967

Vaughan, Sheila *See* Maher

Wade, Julie *See* Hall

Wadsworth, Helen Elizabeth

Born on the Gower, Swansea on 7th April, 1964. Turned Professional 1991

PROFESSIONAL
Int Sunrise Cup 1992
Mis Rookie of the Year 1991
AMATEUR
Chp British Ladies Open Amateur r/u 1990 s/f 1988
Nat Welsh Ladies Open Amateur Stroke Play 1986. Welsh Ladies r/u 1990
Oth World Fourball Chp with Julie Hall 1987
Trn Astor Salver, Wentworth Scratch Trophy1985.
Reg Kent Ladies 1990
Int Curtis Cup 1990. Wales (Home Int) 1987-88-89-90; (Eur(L) T Ch) 1985-87-89
Jun South-East Girls 1981
Int Wales (Jun Eur T Ch) 1983
Mis Leading amateur, Ladies European Open 1990. Taunton Trophy 1990

Waite, Claire

Born Marlborough on 4th November, 1964. Turned Professional 1985

Nat English Ladies 1984. British Ladies Stroke Play 1984
Oth Australian Stroke Play Team 1982. South Atlantic (USA) 1984. Trans National (USA) 1984
Reg Wiltshire Ladies 1980-81-83
Int Curtis Cup 1984. Vagliano Trophy 1983. Commonwealth Trn 1983. Espirito Santo 1984. England (Home Int) 1981-82-83. (Eur(L) T Ch) 1983.
Jun British Girls 1982.
Int English Girls 1982
Mis Avia Woman Golfer of the Year 1984

Waites, Brian J

Born Bolton on 1st March, 1940. Turned Professional 1957

Eur Tournament Players' Championship 1978. Car Care Plan International 1982
RoW Kenya Open 1980. Mufulira Open (Zambia) 1980-82. Cock o' the North (Zambia) Open 1985
Oth National ProAm Chp 1979
Reg Midland Open 1971-76-81. Midland Professional Stroke Play 1972-77-78-79. Midland Professional Match Play 1972-73-74.
Int Ryder Cup 1983; PGA Cup 1973-75-76-77-78-90; GBI v Europe 1980; Hennessy-Cognac Cup 1984; England in World Cup 1980-82-83
Sen PGA Seniors 1990-91; D-Day Sen Open 1994

Walker, Carole Michelle (Mickey)

Born Alwoodley, nr Leeds on 17th December, 1952. Turned Professional 1973

PROFESSIONAL
Maj Ladies British Open r/u 1979
Eur Carlsberg 1979; Lambert & Butler Match Play 1980; Carlsberg 1981; Sands International 1983; Baume-Mercier Classic, Lorne Stewart Match Play 1984

Oth Sunningdale Foursomes 1982
Int Solheim Cup **(1990)**-**(92)**-**(94)**
AMATEUR
Chp Ladies British Open Amateur 1971-72; r/u 1973
Nat Ladies British Open Amateur Stroke Play r/u 1972; English Ladies 1973
Oth Portuguese Ladies Amateur, US Trans-Mississippi 1972; Spanish Ladies Amateur 1973
Trn Hovis Ladies 1972
Int Curtis Cup 1972; GB Commonwealth Team 1971; Espirito Santo 1972; Vagliano Trophy 1971; England (Home Int) 1970-72 (Eur(L) T Ch) 1971-73
Jun French Girls U-22 Open 1971
Int English Girls 1969-70-71
Mis AGW Trophy 1972; Daks Women Golfer of the Year 1972; Duncan Salver 1972

Walker, James

Born Bartonholme, by Irvine, on 11th February, 1921
Cls Irvine Bogside
Chp Amateur Championship r/u 1961
Nat Scottish Amateur 1961
Reg West of Scotland Amateur 1954. Ayrshire Amateur 1956 (tied)
Int Walker Cup 1961. GBI v Europe 1958-60; v Professionals 1958-60. Scotland (Home Int) 1954-55-57-58-60-61-62-63

Walton, Philip

Born Dublin on 28th March, 1962. Turned Professional 1983
PROFESSIONAL
Eur French Open 1990
Trn Irish Professional 1989-91
Int Dunhill Cup 1989-90 (winners)-92
AMATEUR
Nat Scottish Open Amateur Stroke Play 1981. Irish Amateur 1982
Int Walker Cup 1981-83. Ireland (Home Int) 1980-81; (Eur T Ch) 1981

Ward, Angela *See* Bonallack

Ward, Charles Harold

Born Birmingham on 16th September, 1911
Maj Open 3rd 1948-51, leading British player (4th) 1946
Trn Daily Mail Victory 1945. Silver King (tied), Yorkshire Evening News 1948. Spalding, North British-Harrogate, Dunlop Masters 1949. Daily Mail 1950. Dunlop, Lotus 1951. PGA Close 1956
Oth West of England Open Professional 1937. Daily Telegraph Pro-Am 1947-48. Midland Professional 1933-34-50-53-55-63. Midland Open 1949-51-52-54-57
Int Ryder Cup 1947-49-51
Mis Vardon Trophy 1948-49

Way, Paul

Born Kingsbury, Middlesex on 12th March, 1963. Turned Professional 1981
PROFESSIONAL
Eur KLM Dutch Open 1982. Whyte & McKay PGA 1985. European Open 1987
RoW South African Charity Classic 1985
Int Ryder Cup 1983-85. England in World Cup 1985. Dunhill Cup 1985
AMATEUR
Nat English Open Amateur Stroke Play 1981
Int Walker Cup 1981

Wethered, Joyce *See* Lady Heathcoat-Amory

White, Ronald James

Born Wallasey on 9th April, 1921
Cls Hon member of Royal Birkdale, Woolton, Buxton and High Peak, Killarney
Nat English Amateur 1949 r/u, 1953. English Open Amateur Stroke Play 1950-51
Trn Golf Illustrated Gold Vase 1949. Daily Telegraph Pro-Am 1947-49
Sen British Seniors Open Amateur 1978-79
Reg Lancashire Amateur 1948
Int Walker Cup 1947-49-51-53-55. England (Home Int) 1947-48-49-53; France 1947-48
Jun Carris Trophy 1937
Int Boys 1936-37-38

Whitlock, Susan *See* Hedges

Willison, Ricky Brian

Born Ruislip on 30th July, 1959. Turned Professional 1991
PROFESSIONAL
Oth Stockley Park Challenge 1994
AMATEUR
Nat English Amateur 1991, s/f 1988
Trn St George's Challenge Cup 1983; Berkhamsted Trophy 1984; Duncan Putter 1990-91; St Andrews Links Trophy 1991
Reg English Champion of Champions 1989
Oth Lake McQuarie Open (Aus), Greek Amateur Stroke Play 1990
Int Walker Cup 1991; England (Home Int) 1988-89-90; (Eur T Ch) 1989-91. GBI v Europe 1990; World Cup (Eisenhower) 1990
Mis Scrutton Jug 1991

Wilson, Enid

Born Stonebroom, nr Alfreton, Derbyshire on 15th March, 1910
Cls Hon member of Notts, Sherwood Forest, Chesterfield, Bramley, Sandy Lodge, Knole Park, North Hants, Crowborough
Chp British Ladies 1931-32-33.
Nat English Ladies 1928-30, r/u 1927; US Ladies Amateur s/f 1931-33
Trn Roehampton Gold Cup 1930
Reg Midland Ladies 1926-28-29-30. Derbyshire Ladies 1925-26. Cheshire Ladies 1933
Int Curtis Cup 1932. England (Home Int) 1928-29-30
Jun British Girls 1925

Wolstenholme, Gary Peter

Born Egham, Surrey on 21st August, 1960
Cls Bristol & Clifton

Chp Amateur Champion 1991
Nat English Amateur 1991; English Open Amateur Stroke Play 1992
Oth European Amateur Stroke Play 1991; Chinese Amateur 1994
Trn Bristol Open, Ashton Vase 1990; Leicestershire Fox 1984-85-89; Fraser Trophy 1986; *Golf Illustrated* Gold Vase 1989; Ealing Scratch Open 1990; Failand Cup 1989-90-91; Cameron Trophy 1984-86-89; Duncan Putter 1994; English County Champions Trn 1994
Reg Midland Amateur 1986; West Midland Amateur, West of England Amateur 1987; Leicestershire Match Play 1984-85-86-88; Gloucestershire Chp 1992
Int GBI v Europe 1994; England (Home Int) 1988-89-90-91-92; v France 1988-90-92; v Spain 1989-91
Mis Duchess Salver 1990

Woosnam, Ian, MBE

Born Oswestry on 2nd March, 1958. Turned Professional 1976

PROFESSIONAL
Maj Open 3rd 1986; US Open r/u 1989; US Masters 1991
Eur Swiss Open 1982; Silk Cut Masters 1983; Scandinavian Enterprise Open 1984; Lawrence Batley TPC 1986; Jersey Open, Cepsa Madrid Open, Bell's Scottish Open, Lancôme Trophy, Suntory World Match Play 1987; Volvo PGA, Carrolls Irish Open, Panasonic European Open 1988; Carrolls Irish Open 1989; Mediterranean Open, Monte Carlo Open, Bell's Scottish Open, Suntory World Match Play, Epson Grand Prix 1990; Mediterranean Open, Monte Carlo Open 1991; Monte Carlo Open 1992; English Open, Lancôme Trophy 1993; Cannes Open, Dunhill British Masters 1994
US USF&G Classic, Grand Slam of Golf 1991
Oth News of the World U-23 Match Play 1979; Cacharel U-25 Chp 1982
RoW Zambian Open 1985; Kenya Open 1986; Hong Kong Open 1987
Reg Welsh PGA 1988
Int Ryder Cup 1983-85-87-89-91-93; Nissan Cup 1985-86; Kirin Cup 1987; Four Tours World Chp 1989-90; GBI v Australia 1988; Hennessy-Cognac Cup 1982-84; Wales in World Cup 1980-82-83-84-85-87 (winners; also individual winner)-90-91 (r/u; individual winner)-92-93; in Dunhill Cup 1985-86-87-88-89-90-91-93
Mis Harry Vardon Trophy 1987-90

AMATEUR
Reg Shropshire & Herefordshire Amateur 1975

Wright, Janette (*née* Robertson)

Born Glasgow on 7th January, 1935

Cls Hon member of Lenzie, Troon, Cruden Bay, Aboyne, St Rule
Nat Scottish Ladies 1959-60-61-73, r/u 1958
Trn Kayser Bondor Foursomes 1958 (tied)-61. Worplesdon Mixed Foursomes 1959
Reg North of Scotland Ladies 1970. Lanarkshire Ladies 1954-55-56-57-58-59. West of Scotland Ladies 1956-58-59
Int Curtis Cup 1954-56-58-60. Vagliano Trophy 1959-61. GBI v France 1957; v Belgium 1957; v Canada 1954. GB Commonwealth Team 1959. Scotland (Home Int) 1952-53-54-55-56-57-58-59-60-61-63-65-66-67-73-(78)-(79)-(80). (Eur(L) T Ch) 1965-73-(79)
Jun British Girls 1950.
Int Girls 1950-51-52-53

Wright, Pamela

Born Aboyne on 26th June, 1964. Turned Professional 1988

PROFESSIONAL
Int Europe Solheim Cup 1990-92-94; Scotland Sunrise Cup 1992
Mis Gatorade Rookie of the Year 1989

AMATEUR
Nat British U-18 Stroke Play 1981; British Ladies Stroke Play r/u 1981; Scottish Ladies Junior Stroke Play r/u 1980; Scottish Ladies r/u 1982; Scottish Ladies Stroke Play 1985
Reg North of Scotland Ladies 1984
Int GBI Vagliano 1981; Scotland (Home Int) 1981 to 1984; (Eur(L) T Ch) 1987
Jun Scottish Girls r/u 1980-81
Mis All-American 1987-88; Collegiate Player of the Year 1988

Overseas Players

See page 274 for list of abbreviations

Aaron, Tommy

Born Gainesville, Georgia, USA on 22nd February, 1937. Turned Professional 1961

PROFESSIONAL

Maj US Masters 1973; USPGA r/u 1972
Eur Lancôme Trophy 1972
US Canadian Open 1969; Georgia-Pacific Atlanta Golf Classic 1970
Sen Kaanapali Classic 1992
Int Ryder Cup 1969-73

AMATEUR

Nat US Amateur r/u 1958
Int Walker Cup 1959

Alcott, Amy

Born Kansas City, Missouri, USA on 22nd February, 1956. Turned Professional 1975

PROFESSIONAL

Maj US Women's Open 1980, 3rd 1984-91; USLPGA r/u 1988
US 29 LPGA wins 1975 to 1992
Mis Gatorade Rookie of the Year 1975; Vare Trophy, Golf Magazine Player of the Year 1980; Founders Cup 1986

AMATEUR

Jun USGA Girls 1973

Alfredsson, Helen

Born Göteborg on 9th April, 1965. Turned Professional 1989

Maj Ladies British Open 1990, r/u 1991; US Women's Open, 3rd 1993

PROFESSIONAL

Eur Hennessy Ladies Cup, Trophée Coconut Skol, Benson & Hedges Trophy (with A Forsbrand 1991; Hennessy Ladies Cup 1992; Evian Masters 1994
US Nabisco Dinah Shore 1993
RoW Queensland Women's Open, Ellair Open (Japan) 1991; Itoki Classic 1992
Int Solheim Cup 1990-92-94; Sunrise Cup 1990 (winners)-92(winners) (for LPGA) Nichirei International 1993
Mis Rookie of the Year 1989; Gatorade Rookie of the Year 1992

AMATEUR

Nat Swedish Ladies 1986-87-88; Swedish Ladies Open Stroke Play 1988
Int Sweden (Eur(L) T Ch) 1983-85-87 (winners) Espirito Santo 1988(r/u)

Allem, Fulton Peter

Born Kroonstad, South Africa on 15th September, 1957. Turned Professional 1976

US Independent Insurance Agent Open 1991; South-western Bell Colonial, NEC World Series 1993
RoW SA PGA 11 wins 1976-91; SA PGA 1987-90; SA Masters 1991
Oth Sun City Challenge 1993
Int South Africa Dunhill Cup 1993; President's Cup 1994

Aoki, Isao

Born Abiko, Chiba, Japan on 31st August, 1942. Turned Professional 1964

Eur World Match Play Chp 1978. European Open 1983
US Hawaiian Open 1983
RoW Japan PGA 1973-81-86; Japan Open 1983-87; Dunlop Jap International 1987; Tokai Classic, Casio World Open, Coca Cola Classic (Aust) 1989; Mitsubishi Gallant 1990-92; Casio World Open 1992
Sen US Tour Nationwide Chp 1992; Bank One Senior Classic, Brickyard Crossing Chp 1994
Int Japan v US 1982-83-84. Dunhill Cup 1985. Nissan Cup 1985. Kirin Cup 1987-88

Azinger, Paul William

Born Holyoke Massachusetts, USA on 6th January, 1960. Turned Professional 1981

Maj Open r/u 1987; US Open 3rd 1993; USPGA 1993, r/u 1988
Eur BMW International Open 1990-92
US 1987-three; 1988-one; 1989-one; 1990-one; 1991-one; 1992-one (Tour Chp); 1993-two (Memorial Trn, New England Classic)
Int Ryder Cup 1989-91-93. World Cup 1989
Mis USPGA Player of the Year 1987

Baiocchi, Hugh

Born Johannesburg, South Africa on 17th August, 1946. Turned Professional 1971

PROFESSIONAL

Eur Swiss Open 1973; Dutch Open 1975; Scandinavian Enterprise Open 1976; PGA Match Play 1977; Swiss Open 1979; State Express Classic 1983
RoW South African Open 1978; South African PGA 1980; Western Province Open, SA International

Classic 1973; Transvaal Open 1974-76; Rhodesian Dunlop Masters, Swaziland Holiday Inns, 1976; Zimbabwe Open, Vaal Reefs Open 1980; Twee Jongegezellen Masters 1989
Int South Africa in World Cup 1973-77-79; Hennessy-Cognac Cup 1982
Mis Captain SA PGA 1978-79
AMATEUR
Nat South African Amateur 1970
Oth Brazilian Amateur 1968

Baker, Kathy

Born Albany, New York, USA on 20th March, 1961. Turned Professional 1983.

PROFESSIONAL
Maj US Women's Open 1985
AMATEUR
Int Curtis Cup 1982; Espirito Santo 1982 (winners)

Baker-Finch, Ian

Born Nambour, Queensland, Australia on 24th October, 1960. Turned Professional 1979

Maj Open Champion 1991
Eur Scandinavian Open 1985
US Colonial National Invitation 1989
RoW New Zealand Open 1983; Australian Match Play 1987; Australian Masters 1988; Western Australian Open, NSW Open, Queensland PGA 1984; Victoria Open 1985; Golf Digest 1987; Pocarisweat Open 1988; Vines Classic 1992; Australian PGA 1993
Int Nissan Cup 1986; Kirin Cup 1987-88; Four Tours World Chp 1990(winners) -91; Dunhill Cup 1992

Ballesteros, Severiano

Born Pedreña, Spain on 9th April, 1957. Turned Professional 1974

Maj Open Champion 1979-84-88; r/u 1976. US Open 3rd 1987. US Masters 1980-83 r/u 1985-87; 3rd 1982
Eur Dutch Open, Lancôme Trophy 1976; French Open, Uniroyal International, Swiss Open 1977; Martini International, German Open, Scandinavian Enterprise Open, Swiss Open 1978; English Classic 1979; Madrid Open, Martini International, Dutch Open 1980; Scandinavian Enterprise Open, Spanish Open, Suntory World Match Play 1981; Madrid Open, French Open, Suntory World Match Play 1982; Sun Alliance PGA, Irish Open, Lancôme Trophy 1983. Suntory World Match Play 1984; Irish Open, French Open, Sanyo Open, Spanish Open, Suntory World Match Play 1985; British Masters, Irish Open, Monte Carlo Open, French Open, Dutch Open, Lancôme Trophy (tied) 1986; Suze Open 1987; Open de Baleares, Scandinavian Enterprise Open, German Open, Lancôme Trophy 1988. Cepsa Madrid Open; Epson Grand Prix; Ebel European Masters-Swiss Open 1989; Open de Baleares 1990. Volvo PGA, Dunhill British Masters, Toyota World Match Play 1991; Dubai Desert Classic, Open de Baleares 1992; Benson & Hedges International Open, German Masters 1994
US Greater Greensboro Open 1978; Westchester Classic 1983; USF&G Classic 1985; Westchester Classic 1988
RoW Japanese Open, Dunlop Phoenix , Otago Classic 1977; Japanese Open, Kenya Open 1978; Dunlop Phoenix, Australian PGA 1981; Visa Taiheiyo Masters 1988; Chunichi Crowns 1991
Int Ryder Cup 1979-83-85-87-89-91-93; Hennessy-Cognac Cup 1976-78; Spain in World Cup 1975-76(winners)-77(winners)-91; Dunhill Cup 1985-86-88
Mis Harry Vardon Trophy 1976-77-78-86-88-91; AGW Trophy 1979-84-91; Ritz Club Golfer of the Year 1988-91

Barber, Miller

Born Shreveport, Louisiana, USA on 31st March, 1931. Turned Professional 1958

US 11 wins 1964 to 1978
Sen US Seniors PGA 1981. US Seniors Open 1982-84-85.US Sen Tour 24 wins 1981-89
Int Ryder Cup 1969-71

Bean, Andy

Born Lafayette, Georgia on 13th March, 1953. Turned Professional 1975

Maj Open r/u 1983, USPGA r/u 1980-89, 3rd 1985
US 11 wins 1977 to 1986
Int Ryder Cup 1979-87

Beck, Chip

Born Fayetteville, North Carolina, USA on 12th September, 1956. Turned Professional 1978

Maj US Open r/u 1986-89; US Masters r/u 1993
US Los Angeles Open, USF & G Classic 1988; Buick Open 1990; Freeport Classic 1992
Int Ryder Cup 1989-91-93, Dunhill Cup 1988
Mis Vardon Trophy 1988

Beman, Deane R

Born Washington, DC, USA on 22nd April, 1938. Turned Professional 1987

Maj US Open r/u 1969, leading amateur 1962
PROFESSIONAL
US Texas Open 1969; Greater Milwaukee Open; Quad Cities Open 1972; Shrine-Robinson Classic 1973
Mis Commissioner of US PGA Tour since 1974; Herb Graffis Award 1987
AMATEUR
Chp Amateur Champion 1959
Nat US Amateur 1960-63, r/u 1966
Reg Eastern Amateur 1960-61-63-64
Int Walker Cup 1959-61-63-65; Eisenhower Trophy 1960(winners)-62(winners)-64-66(r/u)

Berg, Patty

Born Minneapolis, USA on 13th February, 1918. Turned Professional 1940 (Founder member of LPGA)

PROFESSIONAL
Maj US Women's Open 1946, r/u 1957
US 57 LPGA wins 1941-62 Western Open 1941-48-51-55-57-58; Titleholders Chp 1948-53-55-57)
Mis Leading money winner 1954-55-57; Bobby Jones Award 1963; Ben Hogan Award 1975; first President of USLPGA; LPGA Hall of Fame 1951; World Golf Hall of Fame 1974; Founder's Cup 1981; Old Tom Morris Award 1986

AMATEUR
Nat US Ladies Amateur 1938
Reg Western Amateur 1938
Trn 29 amateur wins 1934-40
Int Curtis Cup 1936-38

Bevione, Isa *See* Goldschmid

Bradley, Pat

Born Westford, Massachusetts, USA on 24th March, 1951. Turned Professional 1974

Maj US Women's Open 1981, r/u 1991, 3rd 1989; USLPGA 1986 r/u 1991, 3rd 1984-85
US 31 LPGA wins 1976 to 1992
RoW Colgate Far East Open 1975; JC Penney Classic 1978-89
Int Solheim Cup 1990-92
Mis Rolex Player of the Year 1986-91; Vare Trophy 1986-91; Mazda-LPGA Series 1983-86; Golf Magazine Player of the Year 1986; Ben Hogan, Powell Award 1991; LPGA Hall of Fame 1991

Burke, Jack, Jr

Born Fort Worth, Texas, USA in January, 1923. Turned Professional 1940

Maj USPGA 1956; US Masters 1956, r/u 1952
US 15 wins 1950 to 1963
Int Ryder Cup 1951-53-55-57-59-(**73**)
Mis USPGA Player of the Year 1956

Calcavecchia, Mark

Born Laurel, Nebraska, USA on 12th June, 1960. Turned Professional 1981

Maj Open Champion 1989; US Masters r/u 1988
US WSW Golf Classic 1986 Honda Classic 1987, Bank of Boston Classic 1988; Phoenix Open, Nissan Los Angeles Open, Spalding Invitational Pro-Am 1989; Phoenix Open 1992
RoW Australian Open 1988
Int Ryder Cup 1987-89-91; Dunhill Cup 1989 (winners) -90; Kirin Cup 1987; Four Tours World Chp 1990

Campbell, William Cammack

Born West Virginia, USA on 5th May, 1923

Chp Amateur r/u 1954
Nat US Amateur 1964
Oth Canadian Amateur r/u 1952-54-65; Mexican Amateur 1956
Reg North & South Amateur 1950-53-57-67. Tam O'Shanter World Amateur 1948-49. Ontario Amateur 1967
Sen USGA Seniors 1979-80. US Seniors Open r/u 1980
Int Walker Cup 1951-53-55-57-65-67-71-75. Eisenhower Trophy 1964-(**68**)
Mis Bobby Jones Award 1956. President USGA 1983. Captain R&A 1987/88. Old Tom Morris Award 1991; World Golf Hall of Fame 1990

Canizares, José Maria

Born Madrid on 18th February, 1947. Turned Professional 1967

Eur Lancia D'Oro 1972; Avis Jersey Open; Bob Hope British Classic 1980; Italian Open 1981; Bob Hope British Classic 1983; Benson & Hedges Trophy (with Tania Abitbol) 1990; Roma Masters 1992
RoW Kenya Open 1984
Int Ryder Cup 1981-83-85-89; Hennessy-Cognac Cup 1974-76-78-80-82-84; Spain in World Cup 1974-80-82(winners)-83-84(winners; individual winner)-85-87-89; Dunhill Cup 1985-87-89-90; Double Diamond 1974

Caponi, Donna

Born Detroit, Michigan, USA on 29th January, 1945. Turned Professional 1965

Maj US Women's Open 1969-70. USLPGA 1979-81
Eur Colgate European Open 1975
US 24 LPGA wins 1969 to 1981
Mis LA Times Woman Golfer of the Year 1970

Carner, JoAnne (*née* Gunderson)

Born Kirkland, Washington, USA on 4th April, 1939. Turned Professional 1970

PROFESSIONAL
Maj US Women's Open 1971-76, r/u 1975-78-82-83-87 (tied); USLPGA r/u 1974-82
US 42 LPGA wins 1970 to 85
RoW Australian Ladies Open 1975
Int Solheim Cup (**1994**)
Mis Rolex Player of the Year 1974-81-82; Vare Trophy 1974-75-81-82-83; Gatorade Rookie of the Year 1970; Golf Magazine Player of the Year 1974-81-82; LPGA Hall of Fame 1982; World Golf Hall of Fame 1985; Bobby Jones Award 1981

AMATEUR
Nat US Ladies Amateur 1957-60-62-66-68, r/u 1956-64
Trn LPGA Burdine's Invitational 1969 (as amateur)
Reg Western Ladies Open Amateur 1959
Int Curtis Cup 1958-60-62-64
Jun US Girls 1956

Casper, Billy

Born in San Diego, California, USA on 24th June, 1931. Turned Professional 1954

Maj US Open 1959-66; USPGA r/u 1958-65-71; US Masters 1970, r/u 1969
Eur Lancôme Trophy 1974; Italian Open 1975
Oth Lancia D'Oro 1974
US 51 wins 1956 to 1975; Canadian Open 1967
RoW Moroccan Grand Prix 1973-75; Mexican Open 1977
Sen Arizona Classic 1987
Int Ryder Cup 1961-63-65-67-69-71-73-75-(**79**)
Mis Vardon Trophy 1960-63-65-66-68; leading money winner 1966-68. USPGA Player of the Year 1966-70; Byron Nelson Award 1966-68-70. World Golf Hall of Fame 1978; USPGA Hall of Fame 1982

Charles, Robert J (Bob)

Born Carterton, New Zealand on 14th March, 1936. Turned Profesional 1960

PROFESSIONAL
Maj Open Champion 1963, r/u 1968-69; US Open 3rd 1964-70; USPGA r/u 1968

Eur Bowmaker 1961; Engadine Open, Swiss Open, Daks 1962; Piccadilly World Match Play 1969, r/u 1968; John Player Classic, Dunlop Masters 1972; Scandinavian Enterprise Open 1973; Swiss Open 1974
US 4 wins 1963 to 1974; Canadian Open 1968
RoW New Zealand Open 1954 (as amateur)-66-70-73, r/u 1974; New Zealand Professional 1961-79-80; 17 other trn wins in New Zealand 1961-78; South African Open 1973
Sen Volvo Seniors British Open 1989-93; US Sen Tour 22 wins 1986-94; Japan Sen 3 wins
Int New Zealand in World Cup 1962 to 1968, 1971-72; Dunhill Cup 1985-86
Mis First New Zealander and first left-handed player to win the Open
AMATEUR
Int Eisenhower Trophy 1960

Coe, Charles R

Born Oklahoma City, USA on 26th October, 1923

Maj US Masters r/u 1961
Chp Amateur r/u 1951
Nat US Amateur 1949-58; r/u 1959
Reg Western Amateur 1950
Int Walker Cup 1949-51-53-(57)-59-61-63. Eisenhower Trophy 1960
Mis Bobby Jones Award 1964

Cole, Robert

Born Springs, South Africa on 11th May, 1948. Turned Professional 1966

PROFESSIONAL
Maj Open 3rd 1975
US Buick Open 1977
RoW South African Open 1974-80; Dunlop Masters (SA) 1969; Natal Open 1969-70-72; Cape Classic 1970; Transvaal Open 1972; Rhodesian Masters 1972; Vavasseur (SA) 1974
Int South Africa in World Cup 1969-74 (winners; individual winner)-76
AMATEUR
Chp Amateur 1966
Nat English Open Amateur Stroke Play r/u 1966
Trn *Golf Illustrated* Gold Vase 1966 (shared)
Int Eisenhower Trophy 1966

Cook, John

Born Toledo, Ohio, USA on 2nd October, 1957. Turned Professional 1979

PROFESSIONAL
Maj Open r/u 1992; USPGA r/u 1992
US Bing Crosby National ProAm 1981; Canadian Open 1983; The International 1987; Bob Hope Chrysler Classic, Hawaiian Open, Las Vegas Invitational 1992
RoW Sao Paulo–Brazilian Open 1982
Int Ryder Cup 1993; World Cup 1983
AMATEUR
Nat US Amateur 1978
Int US World Cup 1979
Jun World Juniors 1974
Mis All-American 1977-78-79

Couples, Fred

Born Seattle, Washington, USA on 3rd October, 1959. Turned Professional 1980

Maj Open 3rd 1991; US Open leading amateur 1978, 3rd 1991; US Masters 1992; USPGA r/u 1990, 3rd 1982
US 12 wins 1983-94 (Buick Open, Kapalua Int'l 1994)
RoW Tournoi Perrier de Paris, Johnnie Walker World Chp 1991
Int Ryder Cup 1989-91-93; Four Tours World Chp 1990(individual winner)-91; Dunhill Cup 1991-92-93(winners)-94(r/u); World Cup 1992(winners)-93(winners)-94(winners; individual winner); President's Cup 1994
Mis Vardon Trophy 1991-92; USPGA Player of the Year 1991-92; Arnold Palmer Award 1992

Crenshaw, Ben

Born Austin, Texas, USA on 11th January, 1952. Turned Professional 1973

PROFESSIONAL
Maj Open r/u 1978-79, 3rd 1980; US Open leading amateur 1970, 3rd 1975; USPGA r/u 1979; US Masters 1984, r/u 1976-83, 3rd 1989-91
Eur Carrolls Irish Open 1976
US 18 wins 1973 to 1994 (Freeport–McMoRan Classic 1994)
RoW Australian Open r/u 1978; Mexican Open 1982
Int Ryder Cup 1981-83-87; US in World Cup 1972-87-88(winners; individual winner); Kirin Cup 1988
Mis Rookie of the Year 1974; Byron Nelson Award 1976; William Richardson Award 1989; Bobby Jones Award 1991
AMATEUR
Trn NCAA Chp 1971-72(shared)-73
Int Eisenhower Trophy 1972(winners)

Daly, John

Born Sacramento, California, USA on 28th April, 1966. Turned Professional 1984

Maj USPGA 1991; US Masters 3rd 1993
PROFESSIONAL
US BC Open 1992; BellSouth Classic 1994
Oth Ben Hogan Utah Classic 1990; Missouri Open 1987
Int Dunhill Cup 1993(winners)
Mis USPGA Rookie of the Year 1991
AMATEUR
Reg Missouri and Arkansas State Amateur 1983-84

Daniel, Beth

Born Charleston, South Carolina, USA on 14th October, 1956. Turned Professional October, 1978

Maj USLPGA 1990, r/u 1984
PROFESSIONAL
US 31 LPGA wins 1979 to 1994
RoW World Ladies Championship (Japan) 1979
Mis USLPGA Rookie of the Year 1979. USLPGA leading money winner 1980. Rolex Player of the Year 1980-90-94. Vare Trophy 1989-90-94. Order of Merit winner 1990
Int Solheim Cup 1990-92-94
AMATEUR
Nat US Ladies' Amateur 1975-77
Int Curtis Cup 1976-78

Davies, Richard

Born USA on 29th October, 1930

Maj US Open leading amateur 1963
Chp Amateur Champion 1962
Int Walker Cup 1963

Davis, Rodger

Born Sydney, New South Wales, Australia on 18th May, 1951. Turned Professional 1974

Maj Open r/u 1987
Eur State Express Classic 1981; Whyte & Mackay PGA 1986; Wang Four Stars 1988; Spanish Open, Wang Four Stars 1990; Volvo Masters 1991; Cannes Open 1993
RoW Australian Open 1986; New Zealand Open 1986-91; South Australia Open 1978; Victoria Open 1979; New South Wales Open 1989; Palm Meadows Cup 1990; Sanctuary Cove Classic 1991-92
Int World Cup 1985-87-91-93; Dunhill Cup 1986 (winners)-87-88-90-92; Nissan Cup 1986; Kirin Cup 1987-88, Four Tours World Chp 1990 (winners)-91

Decker, Anne *See* Sander

Descampe, Florence

Born Belgium on 1st June, 1969. Turned Professional 1988

PROFESSIONAL
Eur Danish Ladies Open 1988; Valextra Classic, Italian Open, Woolmark Ladies Match Play 1990; Ladies German Open 1991; Ladies Austrian Open 1994
US McCall's LPGA Classic 1992
Int Solheim Cup 1992
AMATEUR
Nat European Amateur 1988; Belgian Ladies Match Play 1987
Jun Belgian Junior Champion 1987

Dibnah, Corinne

Born Brisbane, Australia on 29th July, 1962. Turned Professional 1984

Maj Women's British Open 1988, r/u 1992
PROFESSIONAL
Eur 12 WPGET wins 1986-92 (Ladies Italian Open 1994)
Oth Sunningdale Foursomes (with Dale Reid) 1990
Int Sunrise Cup 1992
Mis Woolmark Order of Merit winner 1991
AMATEUR
Nat Australian Ladies 1981. New Zealand Ladies' 1983
Int Commonwealth Tournament 1983 (winners)

Dickson, Robert B

Born McAlester, Oklahoma, USA on 25th January, 1944. Turned Professional 1968

PROFESSIONAL
US 2 wins 1968-73
AMATEUR
Chp Amateur Champion 1967
Nat US Amateur 1967
Int Walker Cup 1967
Mis One of only four to win British and US Amateur titles in the same year. Bobby Jones Award 1968.

Elkington, Steve

Born Inverell, Australia on 8th December, 1962. Turned Professional 1985

PROFESSIONAL
Maj US Masters 3rd 1993
US Greater Greensboro Open 1990; Trn Players Chp 1991; Infiniti Trn of Champions 1992; Buick Southern Open 1994; Mercedes Chp 1995
RoW Australian Open 1992
Int President's Cup, World Cup, Dunhill Cup 1994
AMATEUR
Nat Australia-New Zealand Amateur 1980; Australian Amateur 1981
Jun Doug Sanders Jun World Chp 1981
Mis All-American 1984-85

Els, Ernie

Born Johannesburg on 17th October, 1969. Turned Professional 1989

PROFESSIONAL
Maj US Open 1994
Eur Dubai Desert Classic, Toyota World Match Play Chp 1994
US Sarazen World Open 1994
RoW SA Open, SA Masters (Jpn), SAPGA, Swazi Sun Classic, Goodyear Classic, SA Trn Players Chp 1992; Dunlop Phoenix 1993; Johnnie Walker World Chp 1994; SA Bells Cup 1995
Int SA Dunhill Cup 1992-93-94; World Cup 1992-93
Mis USPGA Rookie of the Year 1994
AMATEUR
Nat SA Amateur 1986; SA Amateur Stroke Play 1989
Trn Tillman Trophy 1988

Fernandez, Vicente

Born Corrientes, Argentina on 5th May, 1946. Turned Professional 1964

Eur Dutch Open 1970; Benson & Hedges 1975; Colgate PGA 1979; Tenerife Open 1990; English Open 1992
RoW Argentine Open 1968-69-81-90; Maracaibo Open 1972; Brazil Open 1977-83-84
Int World Cup 1970-72-78-84-85. Dunhill Cup 1986-88-89

Finsterwald, Dow

Born Athens, Ohio, USA on 6th September, 1929. Turned Professional 1951

Maj US Open 3rd 1960; USPGA 1958; r/u 1957; US Masters r/u 1962 (tied), 3rd, 1960
US 11 wins 1955 to 1963; Canadian Open 1956
Int Ryder Cup 1957-59-61-63-(77)
Mis Vardon Trophy 1957; USPGA Player of the Year 1958

Floyd, Ray

Born Fort Bragg, North Carolina, USA on 4th September, 1942. Turned Professional 1961

Maj Open r/u 1978; 3rd 1981; US Open 1986; US Masters 1976, r/u 1985-90-92; USPGA 1969-82, r/u 1976
US 22 wins 1963 to 1994
RoW Brazilian Open 1978; Daiwa KBC Augusta Open (Japan) 1991

Sen US Tour 7 wins 1992-94 (Senior Tour Chp 1992-94)
Int Ryder Cup 1969-75-77-83-(89)-91-93. Dunhill Cup 1985-86. Nissan Cup 1985
Mis Rookie of the Year 1963. Vardon Trophy 1983. World Golf Hall of Fame 1989.

Ford, Doug

Born West Haven, Connecticut, USA on 6th August, 1922. Turned Professional 1949

Maj US Masters 1957; r/u 1958. USPGA 1955
US 15 wins 1955 to 1962; Canadian Open 1959-63
Sen 1987-one
Int Ryder Cup 1955-57-59-61
Mis USPGA Player of the Year 1955

Forsbrand, Anders

Born Filipstad, Sweden on 1st April, 1961. Turned Professional 1981

PROFESSIONAL
Eur Ebel European Masters–Swiss Open 1987; Open di Firenze, Benson & Hedges Trophy (with H Alfredsson) 1991; Open di Firenze, Cannes Open, Equity & Law Challenge 1992; Moroccan Open 1994
Oth Swedish PGA 1982
Int Hennessy-Cognac Cup 1984; Kirin Cup 1984; World Cup 1984-85-88-91(winners)-92-93; Dunhill Cup 1985-86-87-88-91(winners)-92-94

Frost, David

Born Cape Town, South Africa on 11th September, 1959

Eur Cannes Open 1984
RoW South African Open 1986; Million Dollar Challenge 1989-90-92; Dunlop Phoenix Open 1992; Lexington PGA, Hong Kong Open 1994
US 1988-two; 1989-one (NEC World Series); 1990-one (USF & G Classic); 1992-one (Buick Classic); 1993-two (Canadian Open, Hardee's Classic); 1994-one (Greater Hartford Open)
Int South Africa in Dunhill Cup 1991(r/u)-92-94; President's Cup 1994

Garrido, Antonio

Born Madrid on 2nd February, 1944. Turned Professional 1961

Eur Benson & Hedges International 1977. Standard Four Stars National 1986. Madrid Open 1977. Spanish Open 1972. Tunisian Open 1982
Int Ryder Cup 1979. Spain in World Cup 1977(winners)-78-79. Hennessy-Cognac Cup 1976-78-80-82-84. Double Diamond 1976

Geddes, Jane

Born Huntingdon, New York, USA on 5th February, 1960. Turned Professional 1983

Maj Ladies British Open 1989; US Women's Open 1986; USLPGA 1987
US Boston Five Classic 1986; Women's Kemper Open, GNA Glendale Federal Classic, Toledo Classic, Boston Five Classic 1987; Jamaica Classic, Atlantic City Classic 1991; Oldsmobile Classic 1993; Chicago Challenge 1994
RoW Australian Women's Masters 1990-92
Int Sunrise Cup 1992; Nichirei Int 1993

Giles, Marvin

Maj US Open leading amateur 1973
Chp Amateur Champion 1975
Nat US Amateur Champion 1972, r/u 1967-68-69
Int Walker Cup 1969-71-73-75. Eisenhower Trophy (winners) 1968-70-72

Goldschmid, Isa (*née* Bevione)

Born Italy

Nat Italian Ladies' Close 1947-51-53-54-55-56-57-58-59-60-61-62-63-64-65-66-67-69-71-73-74. Italian Ladies' Open 1952-57-58-60-61-63-64-67-68-69
Oth Spanish Ladies 1952. French Ladies 1975
Trn Kayser Bondor 1963
Int Vagliano Trophy 1959-61-63-65-67-69-71-73-(77) Eur v United States 1968. Italy in Espirito Santo 1964-66-68-70-72

Grady, Wayne

Born Brisbane, Queensland, Australia on 26th July, 1957. Turned Professional 1978

Maj Open r/u 1989 (tied); USPGA 1990
Eur German Open 1984
US Westchester Classic 1989
RoW Australia PGA 1991; West Lakes Classic (Aus) 1978
Int Australia in World Cup 1978-83-89 (winners); Nissan Cup 1985; Four Tours Chp 1990 (winners); Dunhill Cup 1989-90-91

Graham, David

Born Windsor, Tasmania on 23rd May, 1946. Turned Professional 1962

Maj Open 3rd 1985; US Open 1981; USPGA 1979
Eur French Open 1970; Piccadilly World Match Play 1976; Lancôme Trophy 1982
US 6 wins 1972-83
RoW Australian Open 1977, r/u 1972; Australian Wills Masters 1975; Thailand Open, Victoria Open, Tasmanian Open, Yomiuri Open 1970; Caracas Open, Japanese Airlines 1971; Chunichi Crowns (Japan) 1976; West Lakes Classic (Aust), New Zealand Open 1979; Queensland Open 1987
Int President's Cup 1994

Graham, Lou

Born Nashville, Tennessee, USA on 7th January, 1938. Turned Professional 1962

Maj US Open 1975; r/u 1977
US 1967-one. 1972-one. 1979-three.
Int Ryder Cup 1973-75-77. World Cup 1975(winners)

Green, Hubert

Born Birmingham, Alabama, USA on 18th December, 1946. Turned Professional 1970

Maj US Open 1977. US Masters r/u 1978. US PGA 1985
Eur Carrolls Irish Open 1977
US 16 wins 1971 to 1984
RoW Dunlop Phoenix (Japan) 1975
Int Ryder Cup 1977-79-85. USA in World Cup 1977
Mis Rookie of the Year 1971

Green, Ken

Born Danbury, Connecticut, USA on 23rd July 1958. Turned Professional 1979

US Buick Open 1985; The International 1986; Canadian Open, Greater Milwaukee Open 1988; Greater Greensboro Open 1989
RoW Hong Kong Open 1990
Int Ryder Cup 1989

Guadagnino, Kathy *See* Baker

Gunderson, JoAnne *See* Carner

Haeggman, Joakim

Born Kalmar, Sweden on 28th August, 1969. Turned Professional 1989

Eur Peugeot Open d'España 1993
RoW Malaysian Open 1994
Oth Wermland Open 1990; St Compaq Open 1992
Int Ryder Cup (Sweden), Dunhill Cup, World Cup 1993-94
Mis First Swede to play for Europe in Ryder Cup

Harper, Chandler

Born Portsmouth, Virginia, USA on 10th March, 1914. Turned Professional 1934

Maj USPGA 1950
US Won over 20 tournaments. Ten times Virginia Open Champion.
Sen National Seniors 1965 World Senior Professional, USPGA Seniors 1968.
Int Ryder Cup 1955
Mis Elected to USPGA Hall of Fame 1969. In 1941 scored round of 58 (29-29) on 6100 yards, Portsmouth, Virginia

Harwood, Mike

Born Sydney, NSW, Australia on 8th January, 1959 Turned Professional 1979

Maj Open r/u 1991
Eur Portuguese Open 1988; PLM Open 1989; Volvo PGA, Volvo Masters 1990; European Open 1991
RoW Australian PGA 1986; Fijian Open, Pacific Harbour Open 1984; South Australian Open 1990.
Int Australia in World Cup1984; Dunhill Cup 1991; Four Tours World Chp 1991

Hayes, Dale

Born Pretoria, South Africa on 1st July, 1952. Turned Professional 1970

PROFESSIONAL
Eur Spanish Open 1971; Swiss Open 1975; Italian Open, French Open 1978; Spanish Open 1979
Oth Coca-Cola Young Professionals 1974; PGA U-25 1975
RoW South African Open 1976, leading amateur 1969; South African PGA 1974-75-76; 12 wins in Southern Africa 1970-76; Brazilian Open 1970; Bogota Open 1979
Int South Africa in World Cup 1974(winners)-76
Mis Accles & Pollock Award 1973; Harry Vardon Trophy 1975

AMATEUR
Nat South African Amateur Stroke Play 1969-70
Oth English Open Amateur Stroke Play r/u 1969; German Amateur 1969; Scottish Open Amateur Stroke Play 1970
Trn Golf Illustrated Gold Vase 1969 (shared)
Int Eisenhower Trophy 1970(r/u individual)
Jun World Junior Chp 1969

Haynie, Sandra

Born Fort Worth, Texas, USA on 4th June 1943. Turned Professional 1961

Maj US Open 1965-74, r/u 1963-70-82; USLPGA 1974, r/u 1975-83
US 42 LPGA wins 1962-82
Mis Rolex Player of the Year 1970; LPGA Hall of Fame 1977

Henning, Harold

Born Johannesburg, South Africa on 3rd October, 1934. Turned Professional 1953

Maj Open 3rd 1960-70.
Trn Daks 1958 (tied). Yorkshire Evening News 1958 (tied). Spalding 1959 (tied). Sprite 1960. Pringle 1964
Nat South African Open 1957-62. South African PGA 1965-66-67-72
Eur Italian Open 1957. Swiss Open 1960-64. Danish Open 1960-64-65. German Open 1965.
RoW Malaysian Open 1966
US 2 wins 1966-70
Sen US Liberty Mutual Legends 1993
Oth Transvaal Open 1957. Natal Open 1957. Western Province Open 1957-59. Cock o' the North 1959. Engadine Open 1966. South African International Classic 1972. ICL International (SA) 1980
Int South Africa in World Cup 1957-58-59-61-65 (winners)-66-67-69-70-71

Hogan, Ben W

Born Dublin, Texas, USA on 13th August, 1912. Turned Professional 1929

Maj Open Champion 1953; US Open 1948-50-51-53; r/u 1955-56. USPGA 1946-48. US Masters 1951-53; r/u 1942-46-54-55
US 57 wins 1938 to 1959
Int Ryder Cup **1947-49**-51-(**67**). World Cup 1956 (winners and individual winner)-58
Mis USPGA Player of the Year 1948-50-51-53. US leading money winner 1940-41-42-46-48. Sportsman of the Decade Award 1946-56. Had a serious car crash in 1949 which seemed likely to prevent him playing golf again but returned to win more major victories. In 1965 was named the greatest professional of all time by US golf writers. Bobby Jones Award 1976

Hyndman, William III

Born 25th December, 1915

Chp Amateur r/u 1959-69-70
Nat US Amateur r/u 1955
Sen US Seniors 1973
Int Walker Cup 1957-59-61-71. Eisenhower Trophy 1958-**60**

Inkster, Juli

Born Santa Cruz, California, USA on 24th June, 1960. Turned Professional 1983

PROFESSIONAL

Maj US Women's Open r/u 1992; USLPGA 3rd 1986
US 15 wins 1983 to 1992 (JAL Big Apple Classic, 1992)
Int Solheim Cup 1992
Mis Gatorade Rookie of the Year 1984

AMATEUR

Nat US Ladies Amateur 1980-81-82
Int Curtis Cup 1982; World Cup 1980-82

Irwin, Hale

Born Joplin, Montana, USA on 3rd June, 1945. Turned Professional 1968

Maj Open r/u 1983; US Open 1974-79-90, 3rd 1975
Eur Piccadilly World Match Play 1974-75
US 20 wins 1971 to 1994 (MCI Heritage Classic 1994)
RoW Australian PGA 1978. South African PGA 1978. Bridgestone 1981
Int Ryder Cup 1975-77-79-81-91. USA in World Cup 1974-79 (winners and individual winner); President's Cup 1994
Mis World Golf Hall of Fame 1992

January, Don

Born Plainview, Texas, USA on 20th November, 1929. Turned Professional 1955

Maj USPGA 1967; r/u 1961-76
US 11 wins 1956 to 1976
Sen US Sen Tour 22 wins 1980-87
Int Ryder Cup 1965-67

Janzen, Lee

Born Austin, MN, USA on 28th August, 1964. Turned Professional 1986

Maj US Open 1993
US Northern Telecom Open 1992; Phoenix Open 1993; Buick Classic 1994
Int Ryder Cup 1993
Mis All-American 1985-86

Johansson, Per-Ulrik

Born Uppsala, Sweden on 6th December, 1966. Turned Professional 1990

PROFESSIONAL

Eur Renault Belgian Open 1991; Czech Open 1994
Int World Cup 1991(winners); Dunhill Cup 1991(winners)-92
Mis Sir Henry Cotton Rookie of the Year 1991

AMATEUR

Trn Leven Gold Medal 1986
Mis Arizona State University Team 1990

Kennedy, Edwina

Born 10th June, 1959

Nat Ladies British Amateur 1978.
Oth Canadian Ladies Amateur 1980. New Zealand Ladies' 1985
Int World Cup 1978 (winners) 80-84-86. Commonwealth Tournament 1979-83-87-91

King, Betsy

Born Reading, Pennsylvania, USA on 13th August, 1955. Turned Professional 1977

Maj Ladies British Open 1985, r/u 1984; US Woman's Open 1989-90, 3rd 1986; USLPGA 1992, r/u 1987
US 29 LPGA wins 1984 to 1993 (JC Penny Classic, Toray Queen's Classic 1993)
Int Solheim Cup 1990-92-94
Mis Golf Magazine Player of the Year 1984-89; Founder's Cup 1989; Rolex Player of the Year 1984-89-93; Vare Trophy 1987

Kite, Tom

Born Austin, Texas, USA on 9th December, 1949. Turned Professional 1972

PROFESSIONAL

Maj Open r/u 1978; US Open 1992; US Masters r/u 1983-86, 3rd 1977
US 19 wins 1976 to 1993 (Bob Hope Classic, Los Angeles Open 1993)
RoW Auckland Classic (NZ) 1974
Int Ryder Cup 1979-81-83-85-87-89-93; Kirin Cup 1987(individual winner); Dunhill Cup 1989(winners)-90-92-94(r/u); World Cup 1984-85
Mis Rookie of the Year 1973; Vardon Trophy 1981-82; Arnold Palmer Award 1981-89; Bobby Jones Award 1979; Golf Writers Player of the Year 1981; USPGA Player of the Year 1989

AMATEUR

Chp Amateur s/f 1971
Nat US Amateur r/u 1970
Trn NCAA Chp 1972(shared)
Int Walker Cup 1971; Eisenhower Trophy 1970 (winners)

Knight, Nancy *See* Lopez

Lacoste, Catherine *See* Prado

Langer, Bernhard

Born Anhausen, Germany on 27th August, 1957. Turned Professional 1972

Maj Open r/u 1981-84, 3rd 1985-86-93; US Masters 1985-93
Eur Dunlop Masters 1980; German Open, Bob Hope Classic 1981; German Open 1982; Italian Open, Glasgow Golf Classic, St Mellion TPC 1983; French Open, Dutch Open, Irish Open, Spanish Open 1984; German Open, European Open 1985; Lancôme Trophy(shared), German Open 1986; Whyte & Mackay PGA, Irish Open 1987; Epson Grand Prix 1988; Peugeot Spanish Open, German Masters 1989; Cepsa Madrid Open, Austrian Open 1990; B&H International Open, German Masters 1991; Dutch Open, Honda Open 1992; Volvo PGA, German Open 1993; Murphy's Irish Open, Volvo Masters 1994
Oth German Close Professional, Cacherel U-25 Chp 1979; Belgian Classic 1987
US Sea Pines Heritage Classic 1985
RoW Colombian Open 1980; Johnnie Walker Tournament, Casio World Open 1983; Australian Masters 1985; Hong Kong Open, Million Dollar Challenge 1991

Int Ryder Cup 1981-83-85-87-89-91-93; Hennessy-Cognac Cup 1976-78-80-**82**; Germany in World Cup 1976-77-78-79-80-90 (winners)-91-92-93 (individual winner)-94; Four Tours World Chp 1989-90; Nissan Cup 1985-86; Kirin Cup 1987; Dunhill Cup 1992-94
Mis Harry Vardon Trophy 1981-84; AGW Trophy 1981-93. Ritz Club Trophy 1985; PGAET Golfer of the Year 1993

Lewis, Bob

Nat US Amateur r/u 1980
Int Walker Cup 1981-83-85-87. Eisenhower Trophy (winners) 1982

Littler, Gene

Born San Diego, California, USA on 21st July, 1930. Turned Professional 1954

PROFESSIONAL
Maj US Open 1961, r/u 1954; USPGA r/u 1977; US Masters r/u 1970(tied)
US 26 wins 1955 to 1977; Canadian Open 1965
RoW Taiheiyo Pacific Masters 1974-75; Australian Masters 1980; Yellow Pages (SA) 1977
Sen 1987-two
Int Ryder Cup 1961-63-65-67-69-71-75
Mis Byron Nelson Award 1959; Bobby Jones Award, Ben Hogan Award 1973; USPGA Hall of Fame 1982; World Golf Hall of Fame 1990
AMATEUR
Nat US Amateur 1953
Int Walker Cup 1953

Lopez, Nancy

Born Torrance, California, USA on 6th January, 1957. Turned Professional July, 1977

Maj US Women's Open r/u 1975(leading amateur)-77-89; USLPGA 1978-85-89
PROFESSIONAL
Eur Colgate European 1978-79
US 46 LPGA wins 1978 to 1993 (Youngstown-Warren Classic 1993)
RoW Colgate Far East 1978
Int Solheim Cup 1990
Mis Rolex Player of the Year 1978-79-85-88; Vare Trophy 1978-79-85; Mazda-LPGA Series 1985; Gatorade Rookie of the Year 1978; Powell Award 1987; Golf Magazine Player of the Year 1978-79-85; LPGA Hall of Fame 1987; World Golf Hall of Fame 1989
AMATEUR
Oth Mexican Ladies Amateur 1975
Int Curtis Cup 1976; Espirito Santo 1976(winners)
Jun US Girls 1972-74

de Lorenzi, Marie-Laure

Born Biarritz, France on 21st January, 1961. Turned Professional 1986

PROFESSIONAL
Maj Women's British Open 3rd 1989-92
Eur BMW Ladies German Open, Belgian Ladies Godiva Open 1987; French Open, Volmac Open, Hennessy Ladies Cup, Gothenburg Ladies Open, Laing Charity Classic, Woolmark Match Play Chp, Qualitair Ladies Spanish Open, Benson & Hedges Trophy (with M McNulty) 1988; Ford Ladies Classic, Hennessy Ladies Cup, BMW Ladies Classic 1989; Ford Ladies Classic 1990; Var Open de France Féminin 1993; Spanish Open 1994
Int Solheim Cup 1990; Sunrise Cup 1992
Mis Woolmark Order of Merit winner 1988-89
AMATEUR
Nat French Close Chp 1983
Oth Spanish Ladies 1978-80-83; South African Ladies', South African Ladies' Stroke Play 1981
Int France (Eur(L) T Ch) 1977-83; Vagliano Trophy 1983
Jun French Girls 1976; British Girls 1978
Mis Doris Chambers Trophy 1982-85; Angus Trophy 1980

Love III, Davis

Born Charlotte, NC, USA on 13th April, 1964. Turned Professional 1985

PROFESSIONAL
US Heritage Classic 1987-91-92; The International 1990; Trn Players Chp, Greater Greensboro Open, Kapalua International 1992; Infiniti Trn of Champions, Las Vegas Invitational 1993
Int (US) Ryder Cup 1993; Dunhill Cup 1992-93; World Cup 1992(winners)-93(winners)-94(winners); President's Cup 1994
AMATEUR
Int Walker Cup 1985

Lunn, Karen

Born Sydney, Australia on 21st March, 1966. Turned Professional 1985

PROFESSIONAL
Maj Ladies British Open 1993
Eur Borlange Ladies Open 1986; European Masters 1988-90; Slovenian Open 1992
RoW Thailand Ladies Open 1988; Daikyo Challenge 1990
Mis Spalding Order of Merit winner 1993
AMATEUR
Reg Queensland Ladies Amateur, Victoria Ladies Match Play, South Australian Ladies Stroke Play 1984
Jun NSW Junior, Australian Schoolgirls 1982; Queensland Junior 1984
Int NSW Juniors 1981-85

McGuire, Marnie

Born New Zealand

Nat Ladies British Amateur 1986

McIntire, Barbara

Maj US Women's Open r/u 1956
Chp Ladies British Amateur 1960
Nat US Ladies Amateur 1959-64
Int Curtis Cup 1958-60-62-64-66-72

McNulty, Mark

Born Zimbabwe on 25th October, 1953. Turned Professional 1977

Maj Open r/u 1990
Eur Greater Manchester Open 1979; German Open 1980; Portuguese Open 1986; German Open, 4 Stars Pro-Celebrity, Dunhill Masters 1987; Cannes Open, Benson & Hedges Trophy (with

Marie-Laure de Lorenzi) 1988; Torres Monte Carlo Open 1989; Cannes Open, German Open 1990; German Open 1991, BMW Int'l Open 1994
RoW SA Open 1987, SA Masters 1982-86; 20 wins 1980 to 1993; Malay Open 1980; Zimbabwe Open 1992
Int (Zimbabwe) Dunhill Cup 1993-94; World Cup 1993(r/u)-94(r/u); President's Cup 1994

Mahaffey, John Drayton

Born Kerrville, Texas, USA on 9th May, 1948. Turned Professional 1971

PROFESSIONAL
Maj US Open leading Amateur 1970, r/u 1975; USPGA 1978
US 8 wins 1973 to 1986; St Jude Classic 1989
Int Ryder Cup 1979, US in World Cup 1978 (winners; individual winner) 1979 (winners)
AMATEUR
Trn NCAA Champion 1970

Mallon, Meg

Born Natick, Maryland, USA on 14th April, 1963. Turned Professional 1986.

Maj US Women's Open 1991; USLPGA 1991
PROFESSIONAL
US Oldsmobile Classic, Trophée-Urban-World Chp 1991; Ping Welch's Chp, Sara Lee Classic 1993
RoW Daikyo World Chp 1991
Int Solheim Cup 1992; Sunrise Cup 1992
AMATEUR
Oth Michigan Ladies Amateur 1983

Marsh, Graham, MBE

Born Kalgoorlie, Western Australia on 14th January, 1944. Turned Professional 1968

Eur Swiss Open 1970; German Open 1972; Sunbeam Electric 1973; Benson & Hedges International 1976; Colgate World Match Play, Lancôme Trophy 1977; Dutch Open, Dunlop Masters 1979; Benson & Hedges International 1980; European Open 1981; Dutch Open 1985
US 1977-one
RoW Watties Open (NZ) 1970; Indian Open, Spalding Masters (NZ) 1971; Indian Open, Thailand Open 1973; Malaysian Open 1974; Malaysian Open 1975; Western Australian Open 1976; 17 wins in Japan 1972-81; Sapporo-Tokyu Open (Jpn) 1989; Tokai Classic 1990
Int Dunhill Cup 1985(winners); Nissan Cup 1986; Kirin Cup 1987; Four Tours World Chp 1991
Mis USPGA Rookie of the Year 1977; Australian Sportsman of the Year 1977

Massey, Debbie

Born Grosse Pointe, Michigan, USA on 5th November, 1950. Turned Professional 1977.

Maj Ladies British Open 1980-81; US Women's Open leading amateur 1974; USLPGA 3rd 1983
PROFESSIONAL
US Mizuno Japan Classic 1977; Wheeling Classic 1979; Mazda Japan Classic 1990
Mis Gatorade Rookie of the Year 1977
AMATEUR
Oth Canadian Ladies Amateur 1974-75-76

Reg Western Amateur 1972-75; Eastern Amateur 1975
Int Curtis Cup 1974-76; Espirito Santo 1976
Mis Doris Chambers Trophy, Angus Trophy 1976

Melnyk, Steve

Born Brunswick, Georgia, USA on 26th February, 1947. Turned Professional 1971

AMATEUR
Maj Leading amateur Open and US Masters 1970
Chp Amateur Champion 1971
Nat US Amateur 1969
Reg Western Amateur 1969. Eastern Amateur 1970
Int Walker Cup 1969-71
Mis US Amateur Golfer of the Year 1969

Mickelson, Phil

Born Arizona, USA. Turned Professional 1991

Maj Leading amateur in US Open 1991, US Masters 1991; USPGA 3rd 1994
PROFESSIONAL
US Tucson Open 1991 (as amateur); Buick Invitational of California, The International 1993; Mercedes Chp 1994
Int President's Cup 1994
AMATEUR
Nat US Amateur 1990
Oth NCAA Chp 1989-90-92
Int Walker Cup 1989-91
Mis Plays left-handed

Middlecoff, Cary

Born Halls, Tennessee, USA on 6th January, 1921. Turned Professional 1947

Maj US Open 1949-56, r/u 1957; USPGA r/u 1955; US Masters 1955, r/u 1948
US 37 wins 194 to 19-61
Int Ryder Cup 1953-55-59; World Cup 1959
Mis Byron Nelson Award 1955; Vardon Trophy 1956; USPGA Hall of Fame 1974; World Golf Hall of Fame 1986

Miller, Johnny Lawrence

Born San Francisco, USA on 29th April, 1947. Turned Professional 1969

Maj Open Champion 1976, r/u 1973, 3rd 1975; US Open 1973, leading amateur 1966; US Masters r/u 1971-75
Eur Lancôme Trophy 1973-79
US 24 wins 1971 to 1994 (AT&T Pebble Beach 1994)
RoW Dunlop Phoenix International (Jpn) 1974. Otago Classic (NZ) 1972
Int Ryder Cup 1975-81; World Cup 1973 (winners; individual winner)-75 (winners; individual winner)-80; v Japan 1983
Mis USPGA Player of the Year 1974. US leading money winner 1974

Mize, Larry Hogan

Born Augusta, Georgia, USA on 23rd September, 1958. Turned Professional 1980

Maj US Masters 1987; 3rd 1994
US Memphis Classic 1983; Northern Telecom Open, Buick Open 1993
RoW Casio World Open (Jpn) 1988; Dunlop Phoenix Open 1989-90; Johnnie Walker World Chp 1993
Int Ryder Cup 1987

Mochrie, Dottie

Born Saratoga Springs, NY on 17th August, 1965. Turned Professional 1987

PROFESSIONAL

US Oldsmobile LPGA Classic 1989; Crestar Classic 1990; Nabisco Dinah Shore, Sega Women's Chp, Welch's Classic, Sun Times Challenge 1992; World Chp of Women's Golf 1993; Chrysler–Plymouth Trn of Champions 1994
RoW Tokyo Ladies Open (Jpn) 1989
Oth JC Penney Classic, Wendy's Three-Tour Challenge 1992
Int Solheim Cup 1990-92-94
Mis Rolex Player of the Year 1992; Vare Trophy 1992

AMATEUR

Reg New York State Champion 1981

Muntz, Rolf

Born Voorschoten, Netherlands on 26th March, 1969. Turned Professional 1993

Cls Toxandria

PROFESSIONAL

Oth Nedcar Open, Neuchatel Open 1994

AMATEUR

Chp Amateur Champion 1990
Nat Dutch Open Amateur 1989
Trn Lancôme Trophy 1988-89
Int Europe v GBI 1990-92; Dutch National Team 1989-90
Jun Dutch Junior Match Play, Dutch Junior Stroke Play 1989; Dutch International Junior Open 1989
Int Dutch Boys 1986-87

Nagle, Kelvin DG

Born North Sydney, Australia on 21st December, 1920. Turned Professional 1946

Maj Open Champion 1960, r/u 1962; US Open r/u 1965 (tied)
Eur Irish Hospitals, Dunlop, French Open 1961. Bowmaker 1962-65. Esso Golden 1963-67
US Canadian Open 1964
RoW Australian Open 1959. Australian Professional 1949-54-58-59-65-68. New Zealand Professional 1957-58-60-70-73-74-75. New Zealand Open 1957-58-62-64-67-68-69. In New Zealand BP 1968; Caltex 1969, Garden City, 1969, Otago Charity Classic 1970-76. Stars Travel 1970. In Australia: West End 1968-72-74, New South Wales Open 1968. Victoria Open 1969, NBN Newcastle 1970, New South Wales Professional 1971, South Coast Open 1975, Western Australia PGA 1977
Sen World Seniors 1971-75; British Seniors 1971-73-75(winners)
Int Australia in World Cup 1954(winners) 55-58-59-(winners)-60-61-62-65-66
Mis Honorary Member of Royal & Ancient.

Nakajima, Tsuneyuki

Born Kiryu City, Gumma, Japan on 20th October, 1954. Turned Professional 1975

Maj USPGA 3rd 1988
RoW Japan Amateur 1973. Japan Open 1985-86-90-91. Japan PGA 1983-84-86-92; 22 wins 1984 to 1994
Int Dunhill Cup 1986. Nissan Cup 1986(individual winner). Kirin Cup 1987-88.

Nelson, Byron

Born Fort Worth, Texas, USA on 4th February, 1912. Turned Professional 1932

Maj US Open 1939; r/u 1946; USPGA 1940-45, r/u 1939-41-44; US Masters 1937-42, r/u 1941-47
Eur French Open 1955
US 54 wins 1935-one 1936-one 1937-two 1938-two 1939-three 1940-two 1941-three 1942-three 1944-six 1945-fifteen 1946-five
Int Ryder Cup 1937-47
Mis Vardon Trophy 1939; leading money winner 1944-45; USPGA Hall of Fame 1953; World Golf Hall of Fame 1974; Bobby Jones Award 1974; 11 consecutive tour wins March-August 1945, and 18 for the year.

Nelson, Larry Gene

Born Fort Payne, Alabama, USA on 10th September, 1947. Turned Professional 1971

Maj US Open 1983, 3rd 1991. USPGA 1981-87.
US 4 wins 1979 to 1988
RoW Suntory Open (Japan) 1989; Dunlop Phoenix Open (Japan) 1991
Int Ryder Cup 1979-81-87

Neumann, Liselotte

Born Finspang, Sweden on 20th May, 1966. Turned Professional 1985

PROFESSIONAL

Maj Weetabix Women's British Open 1994; US Women's Open 1988; USLPGA r/u 1986-92
Eur 9 wins 1985 to 1994 (Hennessy Cup, Trygg Hansa Open 1994)
US Mazda Japan Classic 1991; Minnesota LPGA Classic, GHP Heartland Classic 1994
RoW Singapore Open 1987; Takara Invitational (Jpn) 1993
Int Solheim Cup 1990-92-94; Sunrise Cup 1992(winners) (individual winner)
Mis Gatorade Rookie of the Year 1988.

AMATEUR

Nat Swedish Ladies Open 1982-83; Swedish Ladies Match Play 1983
Int Sweden (Eur(L) T Ch) 1983. Espirito Santo 1982-84; Vagliano Trophy 1983

Newton, Jack

Born Sydney, Australia on 30th January, 1950. Turned Professional 1969

Maj Open r/u 1975 (tied); US Masters r/u 1980
Nat Australian Open 1979
Eur Benson & Hedges Festival 1972. Benson & Hedges PGA Match Play 1974. Sumrie 1975. Dutch Open 1972
US 1978-one
RoW City of Auckland Classic (NZ) 1972. Amoco Forbes (Aust) 1972. Nigerian Open 1974. Cock o' the North (Zambia) 1976. Mufulira Open 1976. New South Wales Open 1976-79
Mis Seriously injured on tarmac by aeroplane propeller accident 1983

Nicklaus, Jack William

Born Columbus, Ohio, USA on 21st January, 1940. Turned Professional 1961

Maj Open Champion 1966-70-78, r/u 1964-67-72-76-79, 3rd 1963-74-75; US Open 1962-67-72-80, r/u 1960 (leading am)-68-71(tied)-82, leading am (4th) 1961; USPGA 1963-71-73-75-80, r/u 1964-65-74-83, 3rd 1967-77; US Masters 1963-65-66-72-75-86, r/u 1964-71-77-81, 3rd 1973-76

PROFESSIONAL

Eur Piccadilly World Match Play 1970, r/u 1966-71

US 71 wins 1962-84; World Series 1962-63-67-70-76

RoW Australian Open 1964-68-71-75-76-78; Dunlop International (Aust) 1971; Indonesian Open 1994

Sen US Sen Tour 2 wins 1990; US Seniors Open, USPGA Seniors, Tradition 1991; US Seniors Open 1993

Int Ryder Cup 1969-71-73-75-77-81-(**83**)-(**87**); World Cup 1963(winners; individual winner)-64(winners; individual winner)-65-66(winners)-67(winners)-71(winners; individual winner)-73(winners)

Mis Rookie of the Year 1962; USPGA Player of the Year 1967-72-73-75-76; leading money winner 1964-65-67-71-72-73-75-76; Byron Nelson Award 1964-65-67-72-73; Bobby Jones Award 1975; Walter Hagen Award 1980; World Golf Hall of Fame 1974; US Sportsman of the Year 1978; Card Walker Award 1983; Honorary Member of Royal & Ancient

AMATEUR

Nat US Amateur 1959-61

Trn NCAA Chp 1961

Int Walker Cup 1959-61; Eisenhower Trophy 1960(winners; individual winner)

Nobilo, Frank

Born Auckland, New Zealand on 14th May, 1960. Turned Professional 1979

PROFESSIONAL

Eur PLM Open 1988; Lancôme Trophy 1991; Open Mediterrania 1993

RoW New South Wales PGA 1982; New Zealand PGA 1985-87; Indonesian Open 1994

Oth New Zealand U-25 Stroke Play 1979

Int New Zealand in World Cup 1982-87-88-90-93-94; Dunhill Cup 1985-86-87-89-90-92-94; President's Cup 1994

Mis Rookie of the Year 1981

AMATEUR

Nat New Zealand Amateur 1978

Norman, Greg

Born Mt Isa, Queensland, Australia on 10th February, 1955. Turned Professional 1976

Maj Open Champion 1986-93, r/u 1989(tied); US Open r/u 1984(tied); USPGA 1986(r/u)-93(tied); US Masters r/u 1986-1987(tied), 3rd 1989

Eur Martini 1977; Martini 1979; Scandinavian Enterprise Open, French Open, Suntory World Match Play 1980; Martini, Dunlop Masters 1981; Dunlop Masters, Benson & Hedges Int'l, State Express Classic 1982; Suntory World Match Play 1983; European Open, Suntory World Match Play 1986; Italian Open 1988; Johnnie Walker Classic 1994

US Kemper Open, Canadian Open 1984; Panasonic-Las Vegas Invitational, Kemper Open 1986; MCI Heritage Classic 1988; The International, Greater Milwaukee Open 1989; Doral Ryder Open 1990; Canadian Open 1992; Doral Ryder Open 1993; The Players Chp 1994

RoW Australian Open 1980-85; Australian Masters 1984-87-89-90; Australian PGA 1984-85; Australian TPC 1988-89; West Lakes Classic (Aus) 1976; South Seas Classic (Fiji), NSW Open 1978; Hong Kong Open 1979; NSW Open, Hong Kong Open 1983; Victoria Open 1984; NSW Open, Queensland Open, South Australian Open, Western Australian Open 1986; ESP Open, Palm Meadows Cup 1988; Chunichi Crowns 1989; Taiheiyo Masters 1993

Int Australia in World Cup 1976-78; Dunhill Cup 1985(winners)-1986(winners)-87-88-89-90-92-94; Nissan Cup 1985-86, Kirin Cup 1987; test match v GBI 1988

Mis Harry Vardon Trophy 1982; Arnold Palmer Award 1986-90; Mary Bea Porter Award 1988; Vardon Trophy 1989-90-94

North, Andy

Born Thorp, Wisconsin, USA on 9th March, 1950. Turned Professional 1972

Maj US Open 1978-85

US 1 win 1977

Int US in World Cup 1978

Okamoto, Ayako

Born Hiroshima, Japan on 2nd April, 1951. Turned Professional 1976

Maj Ladies British Open 1984; US Women's Open r/u 1987 (tied), 3rd 1986; USLPGA r/u 1989-91, 3rd 1986-87-88

Eur German Open 1990

US 17 wins 1982 to 1992

RoW Japan Women's Open, Itoen Ladies (Jpn) 1993

Mis Rolex Player of the Year 1987; Mazda-LPGA Series 1984-87

Olazabal, José Maria

Born Fuenterrabia, Spain on 5th February, 1966. Turned Professional 1985

Maj Open 3rd 1992; US Masters 1994, 1991(r/u)

PROFESSIONAL

Eur Ebel European Masters -Swiss Open, Sanyo Open 1986; Volvo Belgian Open, German Masters 1988; Tenerife Open, KLM Dutch Open 1989; Benson & Hedges International, Carrolls Irish Open, Lancôme Trophy 1990; Catalonia Open, Epson Grand Prix 1991; Open de Tenerife, Open Mediterrania 1992; Turespaña Open Mediterrania, Volvo PGA Chp 1994

US NEC World Series 1990-94; Wild Coast Skins Game 1990; The International 1991

RoW Japanese Masters 1989

Int Ryder Cup 1987-89-91-93; Kirin Cup 1987; Spain in Dunhill Cup 1986-87-88-89-92; Four Tours World Chp 1989; World Cup 1989.

Mis PGA Qualifying School winner 1985

AMATEUR

Chp Amateur Champion 1984

Nat Spanish Open Amateur 1983

Oth Italian Open Amateur 1983

Jun British Boys 1983; Belgian International Youths Chp 1984; British Youths 1985

O'Meara, Mark

Born Goldsboro, North Carolina, USA on 13th January, 1957. Turned Professional 1980

PROFESSIONAL
Maj Open 3rd 1985-91; US Open 3rd 1988
Eur Lawrence Batley International 1987
US Greater Milwaukee Open 1984; Bing Crosby Pro-Am, Hawaiian Open 1985; AT&T Pebble Beach National Pro-Am 1989-90; Texas Open 1990; Walt Disney World Classic 1991; AT&T Pebble Beach National Pro-Am 1992
RoW Kapalua International, Fuji Sankei Classic (Jap) 1985; Australian Masters 1986
Int Ryder Cup 1985-89-91; Nissan Cup 1985; Dunhill Cup 1985-86-87; US v Japan 1984
Mis Rookie of the Year 1981
AMATEUR
Nat US Amateur 1979
Oth Mexican Amateur 1979

Ozaki, Masashi 'Jumbo'

Born Kaiman Town, Tokushima, Japan on 24th January, 1947. Turned Professional 1980

RoW Japan Open 1974-88-89-94; Japan PGA 1971-74-89-91-93; Japan Match Play 1989; Japan Tour 39 wins 1984 to 1994
Oth Dunlop International Open (Asa) 1992
Int Nissan Cup 1986; Kirin Cup 1987; Four Tours World Chp 1989

Palmer, Arnold

Born Latrobe, Pennsylvania, USA on 10th September, 1929. Turned Professional 1954

PROFESSIONAL
Maj Open Champion 1961-62, r/u 1960; US Open 1960, r/u 1962-63(tied)-66(tied)-67, 3rd 1972; USPGA r/u 1964-68-70; US Masters 1958-60-62-64, r/u 1961-65, 3rd 1959
Eur Piccadilly World Match Play 1964-67; Lancôme Trophy 1971; Penfold PGA, Spanish Open 1975
US 61 wins 1956-four 1957-four 1958-two 1959-three 1960-six 1961-five 1962-six 1963-seven 1964-one 1965-one 1966-four 1967-four 1968-two 1969-two 1970-one 1971-four 1973-one. Canadian Open 1955; Canadian PGA 1980
RoW Australian Open 1966
Int Ryder Cup 1961-63-65-67-71-73-(75); World Cup 1960-62-63-64-66-67 (winners each year; individual winner 1967)
Mis USPGA Player of the Year 1960-62; Vardon Trophy 1961-62-64-67; leading money winner 1958-60-62-63; Byron Nelson Award 1957-60-61-62-63; World Golf Hall of Fame 1974; USPGA Hall of Fame 1980; Bobby Jones Award 1971; William Richardson Award 1970; Walter Hagen Award 1981; Old Tom Morris Award 1983; Honorary Member of Royal & Ancient
AMATEUR
Nat US Amateur 1954

Parry, Craig

Born Sunshine, Victoria, Australia on 12th January, 1966. Turned Professional 1985

Maj US Open 3rd 1993
Eur Wang Four Stars National Pro-Celebrity, German Open 1989; Italian Open, Scottish Open 1991
US Canadian TPC 1987
RoW Australian Masters, Australian PGA 1992; NSW Open, South Australian PGA 1987; Bridgestone Open 1989; NSW Open 1992; Australian Masters 1994
Int Kirin Cup 1988; Four Tours World Chp 1990(winners)-91; Dunhill Cup 1991-93; President's Cup 1994

Pate, Jerry

Born Macon, Georgia, USA on 16th September, 1953. Turned Professional 1975

PROFESSIONAL
Maj US Open 1976; r/u 1979; USPGA 1978; US Masters 3rd 1982
US 4 wins 1977 to 1982; Canadian Open 1976
RoW Taiheiyo Pacific Masters 1976; Brazilian Open 1980
Int Ryder Cup 1981; USA in World Cup 1976
Mis Rookie of the Year 1976
AMATEUR
Nat US Amateur 1974
Int Walker Cup 1975

Pate, Steve

Born Ventura, California, USA on 26th May, 1961. Turned Professional 1983

Maj US Masters 3rd 1991
US Southwest Classic 1987; Tournament of Champions, Andy Williams Open 1988; Honda Classic 1991; Buick Invitational of California 1992
Int Ryder Cup 1991; US in Kirin Cup 1988; Dunhill Cup 1991

Pavin, Corey

Born Oxnard, California, USA on 16th November, 1959. Turned Professional 1981

PROFESSIONAL
Maj US Masters 3rd 1992; USPGA r/u 1994
Eur German Open 1983; Toyota World Match Play 1993
US 11 wins 1984 to 1994 (Los Angeles Open 1994)
RoW SA PGA 1983; Tokai Classic (Jpn) 1994
Int Ryder Cup 1991-93; Nissan Cup 1985; President's Cup 1994
Mis USPGA Player of the Year 1991; Arnold Palmer Award 1991
AMATEUR
Int Walker Cup 1981

Peete, Calvin

Born Detroit, USA on 18th July, 1943. Turned Professional 1971

Maj USPGA 3rd 1982
US 12 wins 1979 to 1986
Int Ryder Cup 1983-85-93; Nissan Cup 1985-86
Mis Ben Hogan Award, Vardon Trophy 1984

Pinero, Manuel

Born Badajoz, Spain on 1st September, 1952. Turned Professional 1968

Eur Madrid Open 1974; Swiss Open 1976; Penfold PGA 1977; English Classic 1980; Madrid Open, Swiss Open 1981; European Open 1982; Cepsa Madrid Open, Italian Open 1985

Oth Spanish Professional 1972-73
Int Ryder Cup 1981-85; Hennessy-Cognac Cup 1974-76-78-80-82; Spain in World Cup 1974-76(winners)-78-79-80-82(winners; individual winner)-83-85-88; Dunhill Cup 1985

Player, Gary

Born Johannesburg, South Africa on 1st November, 1935. Turned Professional 1953

Maj Open Champion 1959-68-74, 3rd 1967; US Open 1965, r/u 1958-79; USPGA 1962-72, r/u 1969; US Masters 1961-74-78, r/u 1962(tied)-65, 3rd 1970
Eur Dunlop 1956; Piccadilly World Match Play 1965-66-68-71-73; Ibergolf European Chp 1974; Lancôme Trophy 1975
US 21 wins 1958-78; World Series 1965-68-72
RoW South African Open 1956-60-65-66-67-68-69-72-75-76-77-79-81; South African PGA 1968-79-81; South African Masters 1959-60-64-67-71-72-73-74-76-76(2)-79; Australian Open 1958-62-63-65-69-70-74; Australian PGA 1957; Brazilian Open 1972-74; Chile Open 1980; Ivory Coast Open 1980; Transvaal Open 1959-60-62-66; Natal Open 1958-60-66-68; Western Province Open 1968-71-72; General Motors (SA) 1971-75-76; Rothmans Match Play (SA) 1973; Int'l Classic (SA) 1974; ICL Int'l (SA) 1977; Johannesburg Int'l, Sun City Classic 1979; Wills Masters (Aust) 1968; Dunlop Int'l (Aus) 1970; Japan Airlines Open 1972
Sen USGA Senior Open 1987-88; Senior TPC 1987; Volvo Seniors British Open 1988-90; US Sen Tour 16 wins 1985-91
Int South Africa in World Cup 1956-57-58-59-60-62-63-64-65(winners; individual winner) -66-67-68-71-72-73-77(individual winner); Dunhill Cup 1991 (r/u)
Mis US leading money winner 1961; Bobby Jones Award 1966; World Golf Hall of Fame 1974; William Richardson Award 1976; SA PGA captain 1977, president 1978; Honorary Member Royal & Ancient

Ploujoux, Philippe

Born La Bouille, Seine Maritime, France on 20th February, 1955

Chp Amateur Champion 1981
Nat French Amateur Close Match Play 1977
Oth International Moroccan Stroke Play 1977
Int Continental Team (St Andrews Trophy) five times (including winners 1982) Continental Youth Team four times. Represented France more than fiftytimes
Jun French Youths Match Play 1972-73-74-75-76. French Boys 1969-70

Prado, Catherine (*née* Lacoste)

Born Paris on 27th June, 1945

Maj US Women's Open 1967
Chp Ladies British Open Amateur 1969
Nat French Ladies Open Amateur 1967-69-70-72. French Ladies Close Amateur 1968-69
Oth US Ladies' Amateur 1969; Spanish Ladies Amateur 1969-72-76
Reg Western Ladies Amateur 1968
Trn Astor Princes' 1966; Worplesdon Foursomes 1967; Hovis 1969
Int Espirito Santo 1964 (winners; individual winner)-68 (individual winner)
Mis Doris Chambers Trophy 1967-69; First amateur, first non-American and youngest player at that time to win the US Women's Open

Price, Nick

Born Durban, South Africa on 28th January, 1957. Turned Professional 1977

Maj Open Champion 1994, r/u 1982-1988; US PGA 1992-94
Eur Swiss Open 1980; Lancôme Trophy 1985
US World Series 1983; Byron Nelson Classic, Canadian Open 1991; Texas Open 1992; Players Chp, Greater Hartford Open, Sprint Western Open, St Jude Classic 1993; Honda Classic, SouthWestern Bell Colonial, Motorola Western Open, Canadian Open 1994
RoW South African Masters 1980; Vaal Reefs Open (SA) 1982; ICL International (SA) 1985-93; South Australian Open 1989
Int Zimbabwe in Dunhill Cup 1993-94; World Cup 1993 (r/u); President's Cup 1994
Mis Arnold Palmer Award and USPGA Player of the Year 1993-94; Vardon Trophy 1993; Sony Ranking No. 1 1994

Quast, Anne *See* Sander

Rawls, Betsy

Born Spartanburg, South Carolina, USA on 4th May, 1928. Turned Professional 1951

Maj US Women's Open 1951-53-57-60, r/u 50(as amateur)-61; USLPGA 1959-69
US 55 LPGA wins 1951 to 1972 (incl Western Open 1952-59)
Mis Vare Trophy 1959; LPGA Hall of Fame 1960; World Golf Hall of Fame 1987; Patty Berg Award 1980

Rivero, José

Born Spain on 20th September, 1955. Turned Professional 1973

Eur Lawrence Batley International 1984. French Open 1987. Monte Carlo Open 1988. Open de Catalonia 1992
Int Ryder Cup 1985-87. World Cup 1984 (winners)-87-88-90-91-93-94. Dunhill Cup 1986-87-88-90-91-92-94 Kirin Cup 1988

Rocca, Costantino

Born Bergamo, Italy on 4th December, 1956. Turned Professional 1981

Eur Open du Grand Lyon, Peugeot Open de France 1993
Oth Rolex ProAm (Swi) 1988
Int Ryder Cup 1993; Italy in World Cup 1993-94
Mis First Italian to play for Europe in the Ryder Cup

Rogers, William Charles (Bill)

Born Waco, Texas, USA on 10th September, 1951. Turned Professional 1974

PROFESSIONAL

Maj Open Champion 1981; US Open r/u 1981, 3rd 1982
Eur Suntory World Match Play 1979

US 1978-one, 1981-three, 1983-one
Oth Pacific Masters 1977
RoW Suntory Open (Jap) 1980; NSW Open, Australian Open, Suntory Open (Jap) 1981
Int Ryder Cup 1981
Mis USPGA Player of the Year 1981
AMATEUR
Int Walker Cup 1973

Romero, Eduardo

Born Cordoba, Argentina on 12th July, 1954. Turned Professional 1982

Eur Lancôme Trophy 1989; Volvo Open de Firenze 1990; Spanish Open, French Open 1991; Italian Open, European Masters 1994
RoW Argentine Open 1989; Argentine PGA 1983-86; Chile Open 1984-86
Int Argentine in Dunhill Cup 1988-89-90; World Cup 1983-84-87-88-91-93-94

Rosenthal, Jody

Born Minneapolis, Minnesota, USA on 18th October, 1962. Turned Professional 1985

PROFESSIONAL
US United Virginia Bank Classic, du Maurier Classic 1987
Mis Gatorade Rookie of the Year 1986
AMATEUR
Chp Ladies British Open Amateur 1984
Int Curtis Cup 1984; Espirito Santo 1984(winners)

St Sauveur, Vicomtesse de *See* Segard

Sander, Anne [Welts] [Decker] (*née* Quast)

Chp Ladies British Open Amateur 1980.
Nat US Ladies Amateur 1958-61-63, r/u 1965-68-73
Int Curtis Cup 1958-60-62-66-68-74-84-90; Espirito Santo 1966(winners)-68(winners)
Mis Doris Chambers Trophy 1973-74; Angus Trophy 1974

Sarazen, Gene

Born Harrison, New York, USA on 27th February, 1902. Turned Professional 1920

Maj Open Champion 1932, r/u 1928, 3rd 1931-33; US Open 1922-32, r/u 1934-40; USPGA 1922-23-33, r/u 1930; US Masters 1935
Eur North of England Professional 1923
US 1922-one 1925-one 1927-two 1928-two 1930-two 1935-one 1936-one 1937-two 1938-one 1939-one 1941-one; USPGA Seniors 1954-58
RoW Australian Open 1936
Int Ryder Cup 1927-29-31-33-35-37
Mis PGA Hall of Fame 1940; World Golf Hall of Fame 1974; William Richardson Award 1966; Old Tom Morris Award 1988; Bobby Jones Award 1992; one of the few to win the Open and the US Open in the same year; Honorary Member of the Royal & Ancient

Segard, Mme Patrick [De St Sauveur] (*née* Lally Vagliano)

Chp British Ladies 1950.
Trn Worplesdon Foursomes 1962. Avia Foursomes 1966. Kayser-Bondor Foursomes 1960
Nat French Ladies' Open 1948-50-51-52. French Ladies' Close 1939-46-49-50-51-54
Oth Swiss Ladies 1949-65. Luxembourg Ladies 1949. Italian Ladies 1949-51. Spanish Ladies 1951
Int France 1937-38-39-47-48-49-50-51-52-53-54-55-56-57-58-59-60-61-62-63-64-65-70. Vagliano Trophy **1959-61**-63-65-(75)
Jun British Girls 1937
Mis Chairman of The Women's Committee of World Amateur Golf Council 1964 to 1972

Semple Thompson, Carol

Chp British Ladies 1974.
Nat US Ladies' Amateur 1973
Trn Newmark International 1975 (tied), r/u 1974
Int Curtis Cup 1974-77-80-82-90-94. World Team Championship 1974(winners)-80 (winners)

Senior, Peter

Born Singapore on 31st July, 1959. Turned Professional 1978

Eur PLM Open 1986; Monte Carlo Open 1987; Panasonic European Open 1990; Benson & Hedges International Open 1992
RoW New South Wales PGA, Rich River Classic, (South Australian Open) 1979; Queensland Open, New South Wales PGA 1984; Queensland PGA 1987; Australian Open, Australian PGA 1989; Johnnie Walker Classic 1989-91; Australian Masters 1991; Bridgestone Open (Jpn) 1992; Vines Classic, Chunichi Crowns (Jpn) 1993; Canon Challenge 1994
Int Australia in Dunhill Cup 1987. Kirin Cup 1987; World Cup 1988-90. Four Tours World Chp 1990 (winners); President's Cup 1994

Sheehan, Patty

Born Middlebury, Vermont, USA on 27th October, 1956. Turned Professional 1980

PROFESSIONAL
Maj Women's British Open 1992-94; US Women's Open 1992-94, r/u 1983-88-90; USLPGA 1983-84-93, r/u 1986
US 30 LPGA wins 1981 to 1994
Int Solheim Cup 1990-92-94
Mis Gatorade Rookie of the Year 1981; Rolex Player of the Year 1983; Vare Trophy 1984; Founders Cup 1985; LPGA Hall of Fame 1993
AMATEUR
Nat US Ladies' Amateur r/u 1979
Int Curtis Cup 1980

Siderowf, Dick

Maj US Open leading amateur 1968
Chp Amateur Champion 1973-76
Oth Canadian Amateur 1971
Int Walker Cup 1969-73-75-77-(79). Eisenhower Trophy 1968-76

Sigel, Jay

Born Narberth, PA, USA on 13th November, 1943. Turned Professional 1993

PROFESSIONAL
Sen US Tour GTE West Classic 1994

AMATEUR
Maj US Open leading amateur 1984; US Masters leading amateur 1981-82-88
Chp Amateur Champion 1979
Nat US Amateur 1982-83
Int Walker Cup 1977-79-81-**83**-85-87-89-91-93
Mis Most wins (18) in Walker Cup matches; Bobby Jones Award 1984

Simpson, Scott William

Born San Diego, California, USA on 17th September, 1955. Turned Professional 1977

PROFESSIONAL
Maj US Open 1987, r/u 1991 (tied)
US 1980-one. 1984-one. 1987-one (Greater Greensboro Open); Bell South Atlanta Classic 1989
RoW 1984-two (Chunichi Crowns, Dunlop Phoenix)
Int Ryder Cup 1987. Kirin Cup 1987
AMATEUR
Trn NCAA Chp 1976-77

Singh, Vijay

Born Lautoka, Fiji on 22nd February, 1963. Turned Professional 1982

Eur Volvo Open 1989; El Bosque Open 1990; Open de Andalucia, German Open 1992; Scandinavian Masters, Trophée Lancôme 1994
US Buick Classic 1993
RoW Malay PGA 1984; Nigerian Open, Swedish PGA 1988; Zimbabwe Open, Nigerian Open, Ivory Coast Open 1989; Hassan Trophy (Morocco) 1991; Malaysian Open 1992; Bell's Cup (SA) 1993; President's Cup 1994
Mis USPGA Rookie of the Year 1993

Snead, Samuel Jackson

Born Hot Springs, Virginia, USA on 27th May, 1912. Turned Professional 1934

Maj Open Champion 1946; US Open r/u 1937-47-49-53; USPGA 1942-49-51, r/u 1938-40, 3rd 1974; US Masters 1949-52-54, r/u 1939-57
US 84 wins 1936 to 1965; Canadian Open 1938-40-41
Sen USPGA Seniors 1964-65-67-70-72-73 World Senior Professional 1964-65-70-72-73
Int Ryder Cup 1937-47-49-**51**-53-55-59-(**69**); USA in World Cup 1954-56-57-58-59-60-61-62; (winners 56-60-61-62; individual winner 1961)
Mis US leading money winner 1938-49-50. USPGA Player of the Year 1949. Oldest professional to win a Tour event 1965. Unofficially credited with 164 victories (including 84 official USPGA trns) in his long career of which full details are not available. Finished 2nd equal in a 1974 USPGA tournament aged 61 and 3rd equal in 1974 USPGA Chp aged 62. 24 holes-in-one

Somerville, Charles Ross

Born London, Ontario, Canada on 4th May, 1903

Nat Canadian Amateur 1926-28-30-31-35-37; r/u 1924-25-34-38
Oth US Amateur 1932
Reg Ontario Amateur 1927-28-29-37. Manitoba Amateur 1926. Canadian Seniors 1960-61 (tied)-65-66 (tied)
Mis President Royal Canadian Golf Association 1957

Stacy, Hollis

Born Savannah, Georgia, USA on 16th March, 1954. Turned Professional 1974

PROFESSIONAL
Maj US Women's Open 1977-78-84; r/u 1980
US 14 wins 1977 to 1985
AMATEUR
Int Curtis Cup 1972
Jun US Girls 1969-70-71

Stadler, Craig

Born San Diego, California, USA on 2nd June, 1953. Turned Professional 1975

PROFESSIONAL
Maj US Masters 1982, 3rd 1988
Eur Scandinavian Enterprise Open 1990
US 11 wins 1980-94 (Buick Invitational of CA 1994)
RoW Argentine Open 1992
Int Ryder Cup 1983-85
Mis Arnold Palmer Award 1982
AMATEUR
Nat US Amateur 1973
Int Walker Cup 1975

Stephenson, Jan

Born Sydney, NSW, Australia on 22nd December, 1951. Turned Professional 1973

Chp US Women's Open 1983. LPGA 1982
Nat Australian Ladies Open 1973-77
US 13 wins 1976 to 1986; 1987-two
Int Sunrise Cup 1992
Mis Gatorade Rookie of the Year 1974

Stewart, Payne

Born Springfield, Missouri, USA on 30th January, 1957. Turned Professional 1979

Maj Open r/u 1985-90; US Open 1991, r/u 1993; USPGA 1989
Eur Dutch Open 1991
US 1982-two 1983-one; 1987-on;e 1989-one;1990-two (MCI Heritage Classic, Byron Nelson Classic)
RoW Indian Open, Indonesian Open 1981; Tweed Head Classic (Aust) 1982; Jun Classic (Jap) 1985
Int Ryder Cup 1987-89-91-93; Nissan Cup 1986; Kirin Cup 1988; Four Tours World Chp 1990; World Cup 1990 (individual winner); Dunhill Cup 1993 (winners)

Stockton, Dave

Born San Bernardino, California, USA on 2nd November, 1941. Turned Professional 1964

Maj US Open r/u 1978. USPGA 1970-76. US Masters r/u 1974.
US 1967-two. 1968-two. 1971-one. 1973-one. 1974-three 9 wins 1967 to 1974
Sen 8 wins 1991-94; US Senior Players Chp 1992
Int Ryder Cup 1971-77-(**91**). World Cup 1970-76

Stranahan, Frank R

Born Toledo, Ohio, USA on 5th August, 1922. Turned Professional 1954

PROFESSIONAL
Maj Open r/u 1947-53, leading amateur 1947-49-50-51-53

US 1955-one 1958-one
AMATEUR
Chp Amateur 1948-50, r/u 1952
Nat US Amateur r/u 1950
Oth Mexican Amateur 1946-48-51; Canadian Amateur 1947-48
Reg North & South Amateur 1946-49-52; Western Amateur 1946-49-51-53; Tam o' Shanter All-American Amateur 1948-49-50-51-52-53; Tam o' Shanter World Amateur 1950-51-52-53-54
Int Walker Cup 1947-49-51

Strange, Curtis

Born Norfolk, Virginia, USA on 20th January, 1955. Turned Professional 1976

PROFESSIONAL
Maj US Open 1988-89, 3rd 1984; USPGA r/u 1989; US Masters r/u 1985
Oth Canadian Open 1985-87
US 14 wins 1979 to 1988
RoW Palm Meadows Cup (Aus) 1989
Int Ryder Cup 1983-85-87-89. Dunhill Cup 1985-87-88-89 (winners)-90-91-94(r/u). Nissan Cup 1985. Kirin Cup 1987-88
Mis Arnold Palmer Award 1985-87. USPGA Player of the Year 1988
AMATEUR
Int Walker Cup 1975; Eisenhower Trophy 1974

Streit, Marlene Stewart

Born Cereal, Alberta, Canada on 9th March, 1934

Chp Ladies British Amateur 1953
Nat Canadian Ladies' Open 1951-54-55-56-58-59-63-68-72-73. Canadian Ladies' Close 1951 to 1957, 1963-68
Oth US Ladies Amateur 1956; r/u 1966. Australian Ladies 1963
Reg Ontario Provincial 1951-56-57-58. US North and South Ladies 1956
Int Canadian Commonwealth Team 1959-63-79
Mis Canadian Athlete of the Year 1951-53-56. Canadian Woman Athlete of the Year 1951-53-56-60-63

Suggs, Louise

Born Atlanta, Georgia, USA on 7th September, 1923. Turned Professional 1948

PROFESSIONAL
Maj US Women's Open 1949-52, r/u 1951-55-58-59-63; USLPGA 1957, r/u 1955-60-61-63
US 50 LPGA wins 1949 to 1962 (incl Titleholders Chp 1946(as amateur)-54-56-59; Western Open 1946-47(both as amateur)-49-53
Mis Leading money winner 1953-60; Vare Trophy 1957; LPGA Hall of Fame 1951; World Golf Hall of Fame 1979. Founder Member of LPGA
AMATEUR
Chp British Ladies 1948
Nat US Ladies Amateur 1947
Int Curtis Cup 1948

Sutton, Hal

Born Shreveport, Louisiana, USA on 28th April, 1958. Turned Professional 1981

Maj USPGA 1983
US 1982-one 1983-one 1985-two 1986-two
Int Ryder Cup 1985-87; Nissan Cup 1986; v Japan 1983
Mis Arnold Palmer Award 1983; Golf Writers Player of the Year 1983; USPGA Player of the Year 1983
AMATEUR
Nat US Amateur 1980
Int Walker Cup 1979-81

Thomson, Peter W, CBE

Born Melbourne, Australia on 23rd August, 1929. Turned Professional 1949

Maj Open Champion 1954-55-56-58-65, r/u 1952-53-57. 3rd 1969
Eur PGA Match Play 1954; Yorkshire Evening News 1957; Dunlop, Daks(shared) 1958; Italian Open, Spanish Open 1959; German Open, Yorkshire Evening News, Bowmaker, Daks 1960; PGA Match Play, Yorkshire Evening News, Esso Golden(shared), Dunlop Masters 1961; Martini International, Piccadilly 1962; Daks 1965; PGA Match Play 1966; Alcan International, PGA Match Play, Esso Golden(tied) 1967; Dunlop Masters 1968; Martini International 1970(shared); Wills 1972
US 1956-one 1957-one
RoW Australian Open 1951-67-72, r/u 1950, leading amateur 1948; Australian Professional 1967; New Zealand Open 1950-51-53-55-59-60-61-65-71; New Zealand Professional 1953; Hong Kong Open 1960-65-67; India Open 1963-76; Philippines Open 1964; New Zealand Caltex 1967; Victorian Open 1973
Sen PGA Seniors Chp 1988
Int Australia in World Cup 1953-54(winners)-55-56-67-59(winners)-60-61-62-65-69
Mis World Golf Hall of Fame 1988. Honorary Member of Royal & Ancient

Trevino, Lee

Born Dallas, Texas, USA on 1st December, 1939. Turned Professional 1961

Maj Open Champion 1971-72, r/u 1980, 3rd 1970; US Open 1968-71; USPGA 1974-84, r/u 1985
Eur Benson & Hedges International, Lancôme Trophy 1978; Lancôme Trophy 1980; Dunhill British Masters 1985
US 27 wins 1968-one 1969-one 1970-two 1971-three 1972-three 1973-two 1974-one 1975-one 1976-one 1978-one 1980-three 1981-one; World Series 1974; Canadian Open 1971-77-79; Canadian PGA 1979-83
RoW Chrysler Classic (Aust) 1973; Mexican Open 1975; Moroccan Grand Prix 1977
Sen US Sen Tour 24 wins 1990 to 1994; USPGA Senior Open 1990; USPGA Seniors Chp 1992-94; Fuji Electric Grand Slam (Jpn) 1993
Int Ryder Cup 1969-71-73-75-79-81-(85); World Cup 1968-69(winners; individual winner) -70-71(winners) -74
Mis Rookie of the Year 1967; leading money winner 1970; USPGA Player of the Year 1971; Vardon Trophy 1970-71-72-74-80; Byron Nelson Award 1971; Ben Hogan Award 1981; World Golf Hall of Fame 1981; William Richardson Award 1985

Vagliano, Lally *See* **Segard**

Varangot, Brigitte

Born Biarritz, France on 1st May, 1940

Chp Ladies British Open Amateur 1963-65-68
Nat French Ladies Open Amateur 1961-62-64-65-66-73, r/u 1960-63-67-70; French Ladies Close Amateur 1959-61-63-70
Oth Italian Ladies 1970
Trn Kayser-Bondor Foursomes; Casa Pupo Foursomes 1965; Avia Foursomes 1966-73
Int France in Vagliano Trophy 1959-61-63-65-69-71; Espirito Santo 1964(winners)-66-68-70-72-74

De Vicenzo, Roberto

Born Buenos Aires, Argentina on 14th April, 1923. Turned Professional 1938

Maj Open Champion 1967, r/u 1950, 3rd 1948-49-56-60-64-69; US Masters r/u 1968
Eur Belgian Open, Dutch Open, French Open 1950; French Open 1960; French Open, German Open 1964; Spanish Open 1966
US 1951-two 1953-one 1957-two 1966-one
RoW Argentine Open 1944-49-51-52-58-65-67-70-74; Argentine Professional 1944-45-47-48-49-51-52; Chile Open 1946; Colombia Open 1947; Uruguay Open 1949; Mexican Open 1951; Panama Open 1952; Mexican Open 1953; Jamaican Open 1956; Brazilian Open, Jamaican Open 1957; Brazilian Open 1960-63-64; Bogota Open 1969; Panama Open, Brazilian Open, Caracas Open 1973; Panama Open 1974
Sen USPGA Seniors 1974; World Senior Professional 1974; Legends of Golf 1979; US Senior Open 1980
Int Argentina in World Cup 1953(winners) -54-55-62(individual winner) -63-64-65-66-68-69-70 (individual winner) -71-72-73-74; Mexico in World Cup 1956-59-60-61
Mis Bobby Jones Award 1970; William Richardson Award 1971; Walter Hagen Award 1979; USPGA Hall of Fame 1979; World Golf Hall of Fame 1989; Honorary Member of the Royal & Ancient.

Wadkins, Lanny

Born Richmond, Virginia, USA on 5th December, 1949. Turned Professional 1971

PROFESSIONAL
Maj US Open r/u 1986; USPGA 1977, r/u 1982-84-87, 3rd 1973; US Masters 3rd 1990-91-93
US 20 wins 1972 to 1991; World Series 1977, r/u 1990; Greater Hartford Open 1992
RoW Victoria PGA (Aust) 1978
Int Ryder Cup 1977-79-83-85-87-89-91-93; World Cup 1977-84-85; v Japan 1982-83; Nissan Cup 1985; Kirin Cup 1987; Four Tours World Chp 1991
Mis USPGA Player of the Year 1985; Rookie of the Year 1972

AMATEUR
Nat US Amateur 1970
Reg Western Amateur 1970; Southern Amateur 1968-70; Eastern Amateur 1969
Int Walker Cup 1969-71; Eisenhower Trophy 1970(winners)

Ward, Harvie

Born Tarboro, North Carolina, USA in 1926. Turned Professional 1973

Chp Amateur Champion 1952; r/u 1953
Nat US Amateur 1955-56
Oth Canadian Amateur 1964
Trn NCAA Chp 1949
Reg North and South Amateur 1948
Int Walker Cup 1953-55-59

Watson, Tom

Born Kansas City, Missouri, USA on 4th September, 1949. Turned Professional 1971

Maj Open Champion 1975-77-80-82-83, r/u 1984; US Open 1982, r/u 1983-87, 3rd 1980; USPGA r/u 1978; US Masters 1977-81, r/u 1978-79-84, 3rd 1991
US 32 wins 1974-one 1975-one 1977-three 1978-five 1979-five 1980-five 1981-four 1982-two 1984-three 1987-one; World Series 1975-80
RoW Phoenix Open (Jap) 1980; Hong Kong Open 1992
Int Ryder Cup 1977-81-83-89-(93); v Japan 1982-84
Mis Vardon Trophy 1977-78-79; leading money winner 1977-78-79-80-84; USPGA Player of the Year 1977-78-79-80-82-84; Bobby Jones Award 1986; World Golf Hall of Fame 1988; William Richardson Award 1991; Old Tom Morris Award 1991

Weiskopf, Tom

Born Massillon, Ohio, USA on 9th November, 1942. Turned Professional 1964

Maj Open Champion 1973; US Open r/u 1976; 3rd 1973-77; USPGA 3rd 1975; US Masters r/u 1969-72-74-75
Eur Piccadilly World Match Play 1972
US 1968-two 1971-two 1972-one 1973-three 1975-one 1977-one 1978-one 1982-one World Series 1973; Canadian Open 1973-75
RoW South African PGA 1973; Argentine Open 1979
Sen US Tour Franklin Quest Chp 1994
Int Ryder Cup 1973-75; USA in World Cup 1972

Welts, Anne *See* Sander

Whitworth, Kathy

Born Monahans, Texas, USA on 27th September, 1939. Turned Professional 1959

Maj US Open r/u 1971; USLPGA 1967-71-75, r/u 1968-70
US 88 LPGA wins 1962-85 (incl Titleholder's Chp 1965-66; Western Open 1967)
Int Solheim Cup (1990)-(92)
Mis Rolex Player of the Year 1966-67-68-69-71-72-73. Vare Trophy 1965-66-67-69-70-71-72. William Richardson Award 1986; Woman Athlete of the Year 1965-66; LPGA Hall of Fame; World Golf Hall of Fame 1982; Powell Award 1986; Patty Berg Award 1987

Woods, Eldrick 'Tiger'

Born Cypress, CA, USA on 30th December, 1975

Nat US amateur 1994
Reg Western amateur, Pacific North West amateur 1994
Int Eisenhower Trophy 1994
Jun USGA Junior National Chp 1991-92-93
Int Rolex Junior All American 1990-91-92-93
Mis Nine holes in 48 at age 3; won Junior World Trns in 1984-85-88-89; Golf Digest Player of the Year 1991-92; Golf World Player of the Year 1993. Entered Stanford University 1994

Wright, Mary Kathryn (Mickey)

Born San Diego, California, USA on 14th February, 1935. Turned Professional 1954

Maj US Open 1958-59-61-64, r/u 1968, leading amateur 1954; USLPGA 1958-60-61-63, r/u 1964-66
US 82 LPGA wins 1956-73 (incl Titleholders Chp 1961-62; Western Open 1962-63-66; 13 wins in 1963)
Mis Leading money winner 1961-62-63-64; Vare Trophy 1960-61-62-63-64; LPGA Hall of Fame 1964; World Golf Hall of Fame 1976; Woman Athlete of the Year 1963-64

Yates, Charles Richard

Born Atlanta, Georgia, USA on 9th September, 1913

Maj US Masters leading amateur 1934-39-40
Chp Amateur Champion 1938
Reg Western Amateur 1935.
Int Walker Cup 1936-38-(53)
Mis Bobby Jones Award 1980

Zoeller, Frank Urban (Fuzzy)

Born New Albany, Indiana, USA on 11th November, 1951. Turned Professional 1973

Maj US Open 1984, 3rd 1994; USPGA r/u 1981; US Masters 1979
US 1979-two 1983-two 1985-one 1986-three
Int Ryder Cup 1979-83-85
Mis Bobby Jones Award 1985. Ben Hogan Award 1986

British Isles International Players, Professional Men

Since 1979 the 'Great Britain and Ireland' team format for the Ryder Cup match against the United States has been widened to include professionals from the Continent of Europe

Adams, J
(Scotland): *v* England 1932-33-34-35-36-37-38; *v* Wales 1937-38; *v* Ireland 1937-38. (GBI): Ryder Cup 1947-49-51-53

Ainslie, T
(Scotland): *v* Ireland 1936

Alliss, Percy
(England): *v* Scotland 1932-33-34-35-36-37; *v* Ireland 1932-38; *v* Wales 1938. (GBI): *v* France 1929; Ryder Cup 1929-31-33-35-37

Alliss, Peter
(England): Canada Cup 1954-55-57-58-59-61-62-64-66; World Cup 1967. (GBI): Ryder Cup 1953-57-59-61-63-65-67-69

Anderson, Joe
(Scotland): *v* Ireland 1932

Anderson, W
(Scotland): *v* Ireland 1936; *v* England 1937; *v* Wales 1937

Ayton, LB
(Scotland): *v* England 1910-12-13-33-34

Ayton, JB, jr
(Scotland): *v* England 1937. (GBI): Ryder Cup 1949

Baker, P
(England): Dunhill Cup 1993 (r/u). (Eur): Ryder Cup 1993

Ballantine, J
(Scotland): *v* England 1932-36

Ballingall, J
(Scotland): *v* England 1938; Ireland 1938; *v* Wales 1938

Bamford, BJ
(England): Canada Cup 1961

Bannerman, H
(Scotland): World Cup 1967-72. (GBI): Ryder Cup 1971

Barber, T
(England): *v* Ireland 1932-33

Barnes, BW
(Scotland): World Cup 1974-75-76-77. (GBI): Ryder Cup 1969-71-73-75-77-79; *v* Europe 1974-76-78-80; *v* South Africa 1976

Batley, JB
(England): *v* Scotland 1912

Beck, AG
(England): *v* Wales 1938; *v* Ireland 1938

Bembridge, M
(England): World Cup 1974-75. (GBI): Ryder Cup 1969-71-73-75; *v* South Africa 1976

Boomer, A
(England): (GBI): *v* America 1926; Ryder Cup 1927-29

Bousfield, K
(England): Canada Cup 1956-57. (GBI): Ryder Cup 1949-51-55-57-59-61

Boxall, R
(England): Dunhill Cup 1990; World Cup 1990

Boyle, HF
(Ireland): World Cup 1967. (GBI): Ryder Cup 1967

Bradshaw, H
(Ireland): Canada Cup 1954-55-56-57-58-59; *v* Scotland 1937-38; *v* Wales 1937; *v* England 1938. (GBI): Ryder Cup 1953-55-57

Braid, J
(Scotland): *v* England 1903-04-05-06-07-09-10-12. (GBI): *v* America 1921

Branch, WJ
(England): *v* Scotland 1936

Brand, G, jr
(Scotland): World Cup 1984-85-88-89-90-92-94; Dunhill Cup 1985-86-87-88-89-91-92-93-94; (Eur): Nissan Cup 1985; Kirin Cup 1988; Four Tours World Chp 1989; (GBI): Ryder Cup 1987-89; *v* Australia 1988

Brand, GJ
(England): World Cup 1983; Dunhill Cup 1986-87 (winners). (GBI): Ryder Cup 1983; (Eur) Nissan Cup 1986

Broadhurst, P
(England): Dunhill Cup 1991. (Eur) Ryder Cup 1991; Four Tours World Chp 1991

Brown, EC
(Scotland): Canada Cup 1954-55-56-57-58-59-60-61-62-65-66; World Cup 1987-68. (GBI): Ryder Cup 1953-55-57-59

Brown, K
(Scotland): World Cup 1977-78-79-83. (GBI): Ryder Cup 1977-79-83-85-87; *v* Europe 1978; (Eur) Kirin Cup 1987

Burns, S
(Scotland): *v* England 1932. (GBI): Ryder Cup 1929

Burton, J
(England): *v* Ireland 1933

Burton, R
(England): *v* Scotland 1935-36-37-38; *v* Ireland 1938; *v* Wales 1938. (GBI): Ryder Cup 1935-37-49

Busson, JH
(England): *v* Scotland 1938

Busson, JJ
(England): *v* Scotland 1934-35-36-37. (GBI): Ryder Cup 1935

Butler, PJ
(England): World Cup 1969-70-73. (GBI): Ryder Cup 1965-69-71-73; *v* Europe 1976

Callum, WS
(Scotland): *v* Ireland 1935

Campbell, J
(Scotland): *v* Ireland 1936

Carrol, LJ
(Ireland): *v* Scotland 1937-38; *v* Wales 1937; *v* England 1938

Cassidy, D
(Ireland): *v* Scotland 1936-37; *v* Wales 1937

Cassidy, J
(Ireland): *v* England 1933; *v* Scotland 1934-35

Cawsey, GH
(England): *v* Scotland 1906-07

Caygill, GA
(England): (GBI): Ryder Cup 1969

Clark, C
(England): (GBI): Ryder Cup 1973

Clark, HK
(England): World Cup 1978-84-85-87; Dunhill Cup 1985-86-87 (winners)-89-90(r/u)-94. (GBI): Ryder Cup 1977-81-85-87-89; *v* Australia 1988; *v* Europe 1978-84. (Eur): Nissan Cup 1985

Clarke, D
(Ireland): Dunhill Cup 1994; World Cup 1994

Coles, NC
(England): Canada Cup 1963; World Cup 1968. (GBI): Ryder Cup 1961-63-65-67-69-71-73-77; *v* Europe 1974-76-78-80

Collinge, T
(England): *v* Scotland 1937

Collins, JF
(England): *v* Scotland 1903-04

Coltart, A
(Scotland): Dunhill Cup 1994; World Cup 1994

Coltart, F
(Scotland): *v* England 1909

Compston, A
(England): *v* Scotland 1932-35; *v* Ireland 1932. (GBI): *v* America 1926, Ryder Cup 1927-29-31; *v* France 1929

Cotton, TH
(England): (GBI): Ryder Cup 1929-37-47; *v* France 1929

Cox, S
(Wales): World Cup 1975

Cox, WJ
(England): *v* Scotland 1935-36-37. (GBI): Ryder Cup 1935-37

Curtis, D
(England): *v* Scotland 1934-38; *v* Ireland 1938; *v* Wales 1938

Dabson, K
(Wales): World Cup 1972

Dailey, A
(Scotland): *v* England 1932-33-34-35-36-38; *v* Ireland 1938; *v* Wales 1938. (GBI): Ryder Cup 1933

Daly, F
(Ireland): *v* Scotland 1936-37-38; *v* England 1938; *v* Wales 1937; Canada Cup 1954-55. (GBI): Ryder Cup 1947-49-51-53

Darcy, E
(Ireland): World Cup 1976-77-83-84-85-87; Dunhill Cup 1987-88(winners) -91. (GBI): Ryder Cup 1975-77-81-87; *v* Europe 1976-84; *v* South Africa 1976

Davies, R
(Wales): World Cup 1968

Davies, WH
(England): *v* Scotland 1932-33; *v* Ireland 1932-33. (GBI): Ryder Cup 1931-33

Davis, W
(Scotland): *v* Ireland 1933-34-35-36-37-38; *v* England 1937-38; *v* Wales 1937-38

Dawson, P
(England): World Cup 1977. (GBI): Ryder Cup 1977

De Foy, CB
(Wales): World Cup 1971-73-74-75-76-77-78

Denny, CS
(England): *v* Scotland 1936

Dobson, T
(Scotland): *v* England 1932-33-34-35-36-37; *v* Ireland 1932-33-34-35-36-37-38; *v* Wales 1937-38

Don, W
(Scotland): *v* Ireland 1935-36

Donaldson, J
(Scotland): *v* England 1932-35-38; *v* Ireland 1937; *v* Wales 1937

Dornan, R
(Scotland): *v* Ireland 1932

Drew, NV
(Ireland): Canada Cup 1960-61. (GBI): Ryder Cup 1959

Duncan, G
(Scotland): *v* England 1906-07-09-10-12-13-32-34-35-36-37. (GBI): *v* America 1921-26, Ryder Cup 1927-29-31

Durnian, D
(England): World Cup 1989; Dunhill Cup 1989

Durward, JG
(Scotland): *v* Ireland 1934; *v* England 1937

Easterbrook, S
(England): *v* Scotland 1932-33-34-35-38; *v* Ireland 1933. (GBI): Ryder Cup 1931-33

Edgar, J
(Ireland): *v* Scotland 1938

Fairweather, S
(Ireland): *v* England 1932; *v* Scotland 1933. (Scotland): *v* England 1933-35-36; *v* Ireland 1938; *v* Wales 1938

Faldo, NA
(England): World Cup 1977-91; Dunhill Cup 1985-86-87 (winners) -88-91-93 (r/u). (GBI): Ryder Cup 1977-79-81-83-85-87-89-91-93; *v* Europe 1978-80-82-84; *v* Rest of World 1982. (Eur) Nissan Cup 1986. Kirin Cup 1987; Four Tours World Chp 1990

Fallon, J
(Scotland): *v* England 1936-37-38; *v* Ireland 1937-38; *v* Wales 1937-38. (GBI): Ryder Cup 1955

Faulkner, M
(England): (GBI): Ryder Cup 1947-49-51-53-57

Feherty, D
(Ireland): World Cup 1990; Dunhill Cup 1985-86-90(winners) -91-93; (Eur): Ryder Cup 1991; Four Tours World Chp 1990-91

Fenton, WB
(Scotland): *v* England 1932; *v* Ireland 1932-33

Fernie, TR
(Scotland): *v* England 1910-12-13-33

Foster, M
(England): World Cup 1976. (GBI): *v* Europe 1976

Gadd, B
(England): *v* Scotland 1933-35-38; *v* Ireland 1933-38; *v* Wales 1938

Gadd, G
(England): (GBI): *v* America 1926, Ryder Cup 1927

Gallacher, BJ
(Scotland): World Cup 1969-71-74-82-83. (GBI): Ryder Cup 1969-71-73-75-77-79-81-83-91 (Captain) - 93(Captain); *v* Europe 1974-78-82-84; *v* South Africa 1976; *v* Rest of World 1982

Garner, JR
(England): (GBI): Ryder Cup 1971-73

Gaudin, PJ
(England): *v* Scotland 1905-06-07-09-12-13

Gilford, D
(England): World Cup 1992-93; Dunhill Cup 1992(winners); (Eur): Ryder Cup 1991

Good, G
(Scotland): *v* England 1934-36

Gould, H
(Wales): Canada Cup 1954-55

Gow, A
(Scotland): *v* England 1912

Grabham, C
(Wales): *v* England 1938; *v* Scotland 1938

Grant, T
(Scotland): *v* England 1913

Gray, E
(England): *v* Scotland 1904-05-07

Green, E
(England): (GBI): Ryder Cup 1947

Green, T
(England): *v* Scotland 1935. (Wales): *v* Scotland 1937-38; *v* Ireland 1937; *v* England 1938

Greene, C
(Ireland): Canada Cup 1965

Gregson, M
(England): World Cup 1967. (GBI): Ryder Cup 1967

Haliburton, TB
(Scotland): *v* Ireland 1935-36-38; *v* England 1938; *v* Wales 1938; Canada Cup 1954. (GBI): Ryder Cup 1961-63

Hamill, J
(Ireland): *v* Scotland 1933-34-35; *v* England 1932-33

Hargreaves, J
(England): (GBI): Ryder Cup 1951

Hastings, W
(Scotland): England 1937-38; *v* Wales 1937-38; *v* Ireland 1937-38

Havers, AG
(England): *v* Scotland 1932-33-34; *v* Ireland 1932-33. (GBI): *v* America 1921-26, Ryder Cup 1927-31-33; *v* France 1929

Healing, SF
(Wales): *v* Scotland 1938

Hepburn, J
(Scotland): *v* England 1903-05-06-07-09-10-12-13

Herd, A
(Scotland): *v* England 1903-04-05-06-09-10-12-13-32

Hill, EF
(Wales): *v* Scotland 1937-38; *v* Ireland 1937; *v* England 1938

Hitchcock, J
(England): (GBI): Ryder Cup 1965

Hodson, B
(England): *v* Ireland 1933. (Wales): *v* Scotland 1937-38; *v* Ireland 1937; *v* England 1938. (GBI): Ryder Cup 1931

Holley, W
(Ireland): *v* Scotland 1933-34-35-36-38; *v* England 1932-33-38

Horne, R
(England): (GBI): Ryder Cup 1947

Horton, T
(England): World Cup 1976. (GBI): *v* Europe 1974-76; Ryder Cup 1975-77

Houston, D
(Scotland): *v* Ireland 1934

Huggett, BGC
(Wales): Canada Cup 1963-64-65; World Cup 1968-69-70-71-76-79. (GBI): Ryder Cup 1963-67-69-71-73-75; *v* Europe 1974-78

Huish, D
(Scotland): World Cup 1973

Hunt, BJ
(England): Canada Cup 1958-59-60-62-63-64; World Cup 1968. (GBI): Ryder Cup 1953-57-59-61-63-65-67-69

Hunt, GL
(England): World Cup 1972-75. (GBI): *v* Europe 1974; Ryder Cup 1975

Hunt, Geoffrey M
(England): (GBI): Ryder Cup 1963

Hunter, W
(Scotland): *v* England 1906-07-09-10

Hutton, GC
(Scotland): *v* Ireland 1936-37; *v* England 1937-38; *v* Wales 1937

Ingram, D
(Scotland): World Cup 1973

Jacklin, A
(England): Canada Cup 1966; World Cup 1970-71-72. (GBI): Ryder Cup 1967-69-71-73-75-77-79-83(captain) -85(captain) -87(captain) -89(captain); *v* Europe 1976-82; *v* Rest of World 1982

Jackson, H
(Ireland): World Cup 1970-71

Jacobs, JRM
(England): (GBI): Ryder Cup 1955

Jagger, D
(England): (GBI): *v* Europe 1976

James, G
(Wales): *v* Scotland 1937; *v* Ireland 1937

James, MH
(England): World Cup 1978-79-82-84-87-88-93; Dunhill Cup 1988-89-90(r/u)-93(r/u). (GBI): Ryder Cup 1977-79-81-89-91-93; *v* Europe 1978-80-82; *v* Rest of World 1982; *v* Australia 1988; (Eur): Kirin Cup 1988; Four Tours World Chp 1989-90

Jarman, EW
(England): *v* Scotland 1935. (GBI): Ryder Cup 1935

Job, N
(England): (GBI): *v* Europe 1980

Jolly, HC
(England): (GBI): *v* America 1926, Ryder Cup 1927; *v* France 1929

Jones, DC
(Wales): *v* Scotland 1937-38; *v* Ireland 1937; *v* England 1938

Jones, E
(Ireland): Canada Cup 1965

Jones, R
(England): *v* Scotland 1903-04-05-06-07-09-10-12-13

Jones, T
(Wales): *v* Scotland 1936; *v* Ireland 1937; *v* England 1938

Kenyon, EWH
(England): *v* Scotland 1932; *v* Ireland 1932

King, M
(England): World Cup 1979. (GBI): Ryder Cup 1979

King, SL
(England): *v* Scotland 1934-36-37-38; *v* Wales 1938; *v* Ireland 1938. (GBI): Ryder Cup 1937-47-49

Kinsella, J
(Ireland): World Cup 1968-69-72-73

Kinsella, W
(Ireland): *v* Scotland 1937-38; *v* England 1938

Knight, G
(Scotland): *v* England 1937

Lacey, AJ
(England): *v* Scotland 1932-33-34-36-37-38; *v* Ireland 1932-33-38; *v* Wales 1938. (GBI): Ryder Cup 1933-37

Laidlaw, W
(Scotland): *v* England 1935-36-38; *v* Ireland 1937; *v* Wales 1937

Lane, B
(England): World Cup 1988-94; Dunhill Cup 1988-94. (Eur): Ryder Cup 1993

Lees, A
(England): *v* Scotland 1938; *v* Wales 1938; *v* Ireland 1938. (GBI): Ryder Cup 1947-49-51-55

Llewellyn, D
(Wales): World Cup 1974-85-87 (winners)-88; Dunhill Cup 1985-88. (GBI): *v* Europe 1984

Lloyd, F
(Wales): *v* Scotland 1937-38; *v* Ireland 1937; *v* England 1938

Lockhart, G
(Scotland): *v* Ireland 1934-35

Lyle, AWB
(Scotland): World Cup 1979-80-87; Dunhill Cup 1985-86-87-88-89-90-92. (GBI): Ryder Cup 1979-81-83-85-87; *v* Europe 1980-82-84; *v* Rest of World 1982; *v* Australia 1988. (Eur): Nissan Cup 1985-86; Kirin Cup 1987.

McCartney, J
(Ireland): *v* Scotland 1932-33-34-35-36-37-38; *v* England 1932-33-38; *v* Wales 1937

McCulloch, D
(Scotland): *v* England 1932-33-34-35-36-37; *v* Ireland 1932-33-34-35

McDermott, M
(Ireland): *v* England 1932; *v* Scotland 1932

McDowall, J
(Scotland): *v* England 1932-33-34-35-36; *v* Ireland 1933-34-35-36

McEwan, P
(Scotland): *v* England 1907

McGinley, P
(Ireland): Dunhill Cup 1993-94, World Cup 1993-94

McIntosh, G
(Scotland): *v* England 1938; *v* Ireland 1938; *v* Wales 1938

McKenna, J
(Ireland): *v* Scotland 1936-37-38; *v* Wales 1937-38; *v* England 1938

McKenna, R
(Ireland): *v* Scotland 1933-35; *v* England 1933

McMillan, J
(Scotland): *v* England 1933-34-35; *v* Ireland 1933-34

McMinn, W
(Scotland): *v* England 1932-33-34

McNeill, H
(Ireland): *v* England 1932

Mahon, PJ
(Ireland): *v* Scotland 1932-33-34-35-36-37-38; *v* Wales 1937-38; *v* England 1932-33-38

Martin, J
(Ireland): Canada Cup 1962-63-64-66; World Cup 1970. (GBI): Ryder Cup 1965

Martin, S
(Scotland): World Cup 1980

Mason, SC
(England): World Cup 1980. (GBI): *v* Europe 1980

Mayo, CH
(England): *v* Scotland 1907-09-10-12-13

Mayo, P
(Wales): Dunhill Cup 1993

Mills, RP
(England): (GBI): Ryder Cup 1957

Mitchell, A
(England): *v* Scotland 1932-33-34. (GBI): *v* America 1921-26, Ryder Cup 1929-31-33

Moffitt, R
(England): (GBI): Ryder Cup 1961

Montgomerie, C
(Scotland): World Cup 1988-91-92-93; Dunhill Cup 1988-91-92-93-94. (Eur): Ryder Cup 1991-93; Four Tours World Chp 1991

Mouland, M
(Wales): World Cup 1988-89-90-92-93; Dunhill Cup 1986-87-88-89-93. (Eur): Kirin Cup 1988.

Mouland, S
(Wales): Canada Cup 1965-66; World Cup 1967

O'Brien, W
(Ireland): *v* Scotland 1934-36-37; *v* Wales 1937

Ockenden, J
(England): (GBI): *v* America 1921

O'Connor, C
(Ireland): Canada Cup 1956-57-58-59-60-61-62-63-64-66; World Cup 1967-68-69-71-73. (GBI): Ryder Cup 1955-57-59-61-63-65-67-69-71-73

O'Connor, C, jr
(Ireland): World Cup 1974-75-78-85-89-92; Dunhill Cup 1985-89-92. (GBI): *v* Europe 1974-84; Ryder Cup 1975-89; *v* South Africa 1976

O'Connor, P
(Ireland): *v* Scotland 1932-33-34-35-36; *v* England 1932-33

Oke, WG
(England): *v* Scotland 1932

O'Leary, JE
(Ireland): World Cup 1972-80-82. (GBI): Ryder Cup 1975; *v* Europe 1976-78-82; *v* Rest of World 1982

O'Neill, J
(Ireland): *v* England 1933

O'Neill, M
(Ireland): *v* Scotland 1933-34; *v* England 1933

Oosterhuis, PA
(England): World Cup 1971. (GBI): Ryder Cup 1971-73-75-77-79-81; *v* Europe 1974

Padgham, AH
(England): *v* Scotland 1932-33-34-35-36-37-38; *v* Ireland 1932-33-38; *v* Wales 1938. (GBI): Ryder Cup 1933-35-37

Panton, J
(Scotland): Canada Cup 1955-56-57-58-59-60-61-62-63-64-65-66; World Cup 1968. (GBI): Ryder Cup 1951-53-61

Park, J
(Scotland): *v* England 1909

Parkin, P
(Wales): World Cup 1984-89; Dunhill Cup 1985-86-87-89-90-91. (GBI): *v* Europe 1984

Patterson, E
(Ireland): *v* Scotland 1933-34-35-36; *v* England 1933; *v* Wales 1937

Perry, A
(England); *v* Ireland 1932; *v* Scotland 1933-36-38. (GBI): Ryder Cup 1933-35-37

Pickett, C
(Wales): *v* Scotland 1937-38; *v* Ireland 1937; *v* England 1938

Platts, L
(Wales): (GBI): Ryder Cup 1965

Polland, E
(Ireland): World Cup 1973-74-76-77-78-79. (GBI): Ryder Cup 1973; *v* Europe 1974-76-78-80; *v* South Ryder Cup 1976

Pope, CW
(Ireland): *v* England 1932; *v* Scotland 1932

Price, P
(Wales): Dunhill Cup 1991; World Cup 1994

Rafferty, R
(Ireland): World Cup 1983-84-87-88-90-91-92-93; Dunhill Cup 1986-87-88(winners)-89-90(winners)-91-92-93. (GBI): *v* Europe 1984; *v* Australia 1988. (Eur): Ryder Cup 1989; Kirin Cup 1988; Four Tours World Chp 1989-90-91

Rainford, P
(England): *v* Scotland 1903-07

Ray, E
(England): *v* Scotland 1903-04-05-06-07-09-10-12-13. (GBI): *v* America 1921-26, Ryder Cup 1927

Rees, DJ
(Wales): *v* Scotland 1937-38; *v* Ireland 1937; England 1938; Canada Cup 1954-56-57-58-59-60-61-62-64. (GBI): Ryder Cup 1937-47-49-51-53-55-57-59-61

Reid, W
(England): *v* Scotland 1906-07

Renouf, TG
(England): *v* Scotland 1903-04-05-10-13

Richardson, S
(England): Dunhill Cup 1991-92(winners); World Cup 1992. (Eur): Ryder Cup 1991; Four Tours World Chp 1991

Ritchie, WL
(Scotland): *v* England 1913

Robertson, F
(Scotland): *v* Ireland 1933; *v* England 1938

Robertson, P
(Scotland): *v* England 1932; *v* Ireland 1932-34

Robson, F
(England): *v* Scotland 1909-10. (GBI): *v* America 1926, Ryder Cup 1927-29-31

Roe, M
(England): World Cup 1989-94; Dunhill Cup 1994

Rowe, AJ
(England): *v* Scotland 1903-06-07

Sayers, B, jr
(Scotland): *v* England 1906-07-09

Scott, SS
(England): (GBI): Ryder Cup 1955

Seymour, M
(England): *v* Scotland 1932-33; *v* Ireland 1932-33. (Scotland): *v* Ireland 1932

Shade, RDBM
(Scotland): World Cup 1970-71-72

Sherlock, JG
(England): *v* Scotland 1903-04-05-06-07-09-10-12-13. (GBI): *v* America 1921

Simpson, A
(Scotland): *v* England 1904

Smalldon, D
(Wales): Canada Cup 1955-56

Smith, CR
(Scotland): *v* England 1903-04-07-09-13

Smith, GE
(Scotland): *v* Ireland 1932

Smyth, D
(Ireland): World Cup 1979-80-82-83-88-89; Dunhill Cup 1985-86-87-88 (winners). (GBI): Ryder Cup 1979-81; *v* Europe 1980-82-84; *v* Rest of World 1982

Snell, D
(England): Canada Cup 1965

Spark, W
(Scotland): *v* Ireland 1933-35-37; *v* England 1935; *v* Wales 1937

Spence, J
(England): Dunhill Cup 1992 (winners)

Stevenson, P
(Ireland): *v* Scotland 1933-34-35-36-38; *v* England 1933-38

Sutton, M
(England): Canada Cup 1955

Taylor, JH
(England): *v* Scotland 1903-04-05-06-07-09-10-12-13 (GBI): *v* America 1921

Taylor, JJ
(England): *v* Scotland 1937

Taylor, Josh
(England): *v* Scotland 1913. (GBI): *v* America 1921

Thomas, DC
(Wales): Canada Cup 1957-58-59-60-61-62-63-66; World Cup 1967-69-70. (GBI): Ryder Cup 1959-63-65-67

Thompson, R
(Scotland): *v* England 1903-04-05-06-07-09-10-12

Tingey, A
(England): *v* Scotland 1903-05

Torrance, S
(Scotland): World Cup 1976-78-82-84-85-87-89-90-93; Dunhill Cup 1985-86-87-89-90-91-93. (GBI): *v* Europe 1976-78-80-82-84; Ryder Cup 1981-83-85-87-89-91-93; *v* Rest of World 1982. (Eur): Nissan Cup 1985; Four Tours World Chp 1991

Townsend, P
(England): World Cup 1969-74. (GBI): Ryder Cup 1969-71; *v* Europe 1974

Twine, WT
(England): *v* Ireland 1932

Vardon, H
(England): (GBI): *v* America 1921

Vaughan, DI
(Wales): World Cup 1972-73-77-78-79-80

Waites, BJ
(England): World Cup 1980-82-83. (GBI): *v* Europe 1980-82-84; *v* Rest of World 1982; Ryder Cup 1983

Walker, RT
(Scotland): Canada Cup 1964

Wallace, L
(Ireland): *v* England 1932; *v* Scotland 1932

Walton P
(Ireland): Dunhill Cup 1989-90 (winners)-92-94

Ward, CH
(England): *v* Ireland 1932. (GBI): Ryder Cup 1947-49-51

Watt, T
(Scotland): *v* England 1907

Watt, W
(Scotland): *v* England 1912-13

Way, P
(England): Dunhill Cup 1985; World Cup 1985. (GBI): Ryder Cup 1983-85

Weetman, H
(England): Canada Cup 1954-56-60. (GBI): Ryder Cup 1951-53-55-57-59-61-63

Whitcombe, CA
(England): *v* Scotland 1932-33-34-35-36-37-38; *v* Ireland 1933. (GBI): Ryder Cup 1927-29-31-33-35-37; *v* France 1929

Whitcombe, EE
(England): *v* Scotland 1938; *v* Wales 1938; *v* Ireland 1938

Whitcombe, ER
(England): *v* Scotland 1932; *v* Ireland 1933. (GBI): *v* America 1926, Ryder Cup 1929-31-35; *v* France 1929

Whitcombe, RA
(England): *v* Scotland 1933-34-35-36-37-38. (GBI): Ryder Cup 1935

White, J
(Scotland): *v* England 1903-04-05-06-07-09-12-13

Wilcock, P
(England): World Cup 1973

Will, G
(Scotland): Canada Cup 1963; World Cup 1969-70. (GBI): Ryder Cup 1963-65-67

Williams, K
(Wales): *v* Scotland 1937-38; *v* Ireland 1937; *v* England 1938

Williamson, T
(England): *v* Scotland 1904-05-06-07-09-10-12-13

Wilson, RG
(England): *v* Scotland 1913

Wilson, T
(Scotland): *v* England 1933-34; *v* Ireland 1932-33-34

Wolstenholme, GB
(England): Canada Cup 1965

Wood, N
(Scotland): World Cup 1975. (GBI): Ryder Cup 1975

Woosnam, I
(Wales): World Cup 1980-82-83-84-85-87 (winners)-90-91-92-93-94; Dunhill Cup 1985-86-87-88-89-90-91-93. (GBI): *v* Europe 1982-84; *v* Rest of World 1982; Ryder Cup 1983-85-87-89-91-93; *v* Australia 1988. (Eur): Nissan Cup 1985-86. Kirin Cup 1987; Four Tours World Chp 1989-90

British Isles International Players, Amateur Men

Abbreviations:

CW	Commonwealth Tournament
Eur T Ch	played in European Team Championship for home country
Home Int	played in Home International matches

Adams, MPD
(Wales): Home Int 1969-70-71-72-75-76-77; Eur T Ch 1971

Aitken, AR
(Scotland): *v* England 1906-07-08

Alexander, DW
(Scotland): Home Int 1958; *v* Scandinavia 1958

Allison, A
(Ireland): *v* England 1928; *v* Scotland 1929

Anderson, N
(Ireland): Home Int 1985-86-87-88-89-90-93. Eur T Ch 1989. (GBI): *v* Europe 1988

Anderson, RB
(Scotland): *v* Scandinavia 1960-62; Home Int 1962-63

Andrew, R
(Scotland): *v* England 1905-06-07-08-09-10

Armour, A
(Scotland): *v* England 1922

Armour, TD
(GBI): *v* America 1921

Ashby, H
(England): Home Int 1972-73-74. (GBI): Dominican Int 1973. (GBI): *v* Europe 1974

Atkinson, HN
(Wales): *v* Ireland 1913

Attenborough, M
(England): Home Int 1964-66-67-68; Eur T Ch 1967. (GBI): Walker Cup 1967; *v* Europe 1966-68

Aylmer, CC
(England): *v* Scotland 1911-22-23-24. (GBI): *v* America 1921, Walker Cup 1922

Babington, A
(Ireland): *v* Wales 1913

Baker, P
(England): Home Int 1985. (GBI): Walker Cup 1985; *v* Europe 1986

Baker, RN
(Ireland): Home Int 1975

Ball, J
(England): *v* Scotland 1902-03-04-05-06-07-08-09-10-11-12

Bamford, JL
(Ireland): Home Int 1954-56

Banks, C
(England): Home Int 1983

Banks, SE
(England): Home Int 1934-38

Bannerman, SJ
(Scotland): Home Int 1988; *v* Sweden 1990

Bardsley, R
(England): Home Int 1987; *v* France 1988

Barker, HH
(England): *v* Scotland 1907

Barnett, A
(Wales): Home Int 1989-90-91; Eur T Chp 1991

Barrie, GC
(Scotland): Home Int 1981-83; *v* Sweden 1983

Barry, AG
(England): *v* Scotland 1906-07

Bathgate, D
(England): Home Int 1990

Bayliss, RP
(England): *v* Ireland 1929; Home Int 1933-34

Bayne, PWGA
(Wales): Home Int 1949

Beamish, CH
(Ireland): Home Int 1950-51-53-56

Beck, JB
(England): *v* Scotland 1926-30; Home Int 1933. (GBI): Walker Cup 1928-38 (Captain) -47 (Captain)

Beddard, JB
(England): *v* Wales/Ireland 1925; *v* Ireland 1929; *v* Scotland 1927-28-29

Beharrell, JC
(England): Home Int 1956

Bell, HE
(Ireland): *v* Wales 1930; Home Int 1932

Bell, RK
(England): Home Int 1947

Benka, PJ
(England): Home Int 1967-68-69-70: Eur T Ch 1969. (GBI): Walker Cup 1969; *v* Europe 1970

Bennett, H
(England): Home Int 1948-49-51

Bennett, S
(England): *v* Scotland 1979

Bennett, W
(England): Home Int 1992-93-94; *v* France 1994. (GBI) *v* Europe 1994; World Team Ch 1994

Bentley, AL
(England): Home Int 1936-37; *v* France 1937-39

Bentley, HG
(England): *v* Ireland 1931; *v* Scotland 1931. Home Int 1932-33-34-35-36-37-38-47; *v* France 1934-35-36-37-39-54. (GBI): Walker Cup 1934-36-38

Berry, P
(England): Home Int 1972. (GBI): *v* Europe 1972

Bevan, RJ
(Wales): Home Int 1964-65-66-67-73-74

Beveridge, HW
(Scotland): *v* England 1908

Birnie, J
(Scotland): *v* Ireland 1927

Birtwell, SG
(England): Home Int 1968-70-73

Black, D
(Scotland): Home Int 1966-67

Black, FC
(Scotland): Home Int 1962-64-65-66-68; *v* Scandinavia 1962; Eur T Ch 1965-67. (GBI): *v* Europe 1966

Black, GT
(Scotland): Home Int 1952-53; *v* South Africa 1954

Black, JL
(Wales): Home Int 1932-33-34-35-36

Black, WC
(Scotland): Home Int 1964-65

Blackey, M
(England): *v* France 1994

Blackwell, EBH
(Scotland): *v* England 1902-04-05-06-07-09-10-12-23-24-25

Blair, DA
(Scotland): Home Int 1948-49-51-52-53-55-56-57; *v* Scandinavia 1956-58-62. (GBI): Walker Cup 1955-61; CW 1954

Blakeman, D
(England): Home Int 1981; *v* France 1982

Bland, R
(England): Home Int 1994

Bloice, C
(Scotland): Home Int 1985-86; *v* France 1985; Eur T Ch 1985; *v* Italy 1986; *v* Sweden 1986. (GBI): Walker Cup 1985

Bloxham, JA
(England): Home Int 1966

Blyth, AD
(Scotland): *v* England 1904

Bonallack,MF
(England): Home Int 1957-58-59-60-61-62-63-64-65-66-67-68-69-70-71-72-73-74; Eur T Ch 1969-71. (GBI): Walker Cup 1957-59-61-63-65-67-69 (Captain) -71 (Captain) -73; *v* Europe 1958-62-64-66-68-70-72; CW 1959-63-67-71; World Team Ch 1960-62-64-66-68-70-72

Bonnell, DJ
(Wales): Home Int 1949-50-51

Bookless, JT
(Scotland): *v* England 1930-31; *v* Ireland 1930; *v* Wales 1931

Bottomley, S
(England): Home Int 1986

Bourn, TA
(England): *v* Ireland 1928; *v* Scotland 1930; Home Int 1933-34; *v* France 1934. (GBI): *v* Australia 1934

Bowen, J
(Ireland): Home Int 1961

Bowman, TH
(England): Home Int 1932

Boxall, R
(England): Home Int 1980-81-82; *v* France 1982

Boyd, HA
(Ireland): *v* Wales 1913-23

Bradshaw, AS
(England): Home Int 1932

Bradshaw, EI
(England): *v* Scotland 1979; Eur T Ch 1979

Braid, H
(Scotland): *v* England 1922-23

Bramston, JAT
(England): *v* Scotland 1902

Brand, GJ
(England): Home Int 1976. (GBI) *v* Europe 1976

Brand Jr, G
(Scotland): Home Int 1978-80; *v* England 1979; Eur T Ch 1979; *v* Italy 1979; *v* Belgium 1980; *v* France 1980-81. (GBI): Walker Cup 1979; *v* Europe 1978-80; World Team Ch 1978-80

Branigan, D
(Ireland): Home Int 1975-76-77-80-81-82-86; Eur T Ch 1977-81; *v* West Germany, France, Sweden 1976

Bretherton, CF
(England): *v* Scotland 1922-23-24-25; *v* Wales/Ireland 1925

Briscoe, A
(Ireland): *v* England 1928-29-30-31; *v* Scotland 1929-30-31; *v* Wales 1929-30-31; Home Int 1932-33-38

Bristowe, OC
(GBI): Walker Cup 1923-24

Broad, RD
(Wales): *v* Ireland 1979; Home Int 1980-81-82-84; Eur T Ch 1981

Broadhurst, P
(England): Home Int 1986-87; *v* France 1988. (GBI) *v* Europe 1988

Brock, J
(Scotland) *v* Ireland 1929; Home Int 1932

Brodie, Allan
(Scotland): Home Int 1970-72-73-74-75-76-77-78-80; Eur T Ch 1973-77-79; *v* England 1979; *v* Italy 1979; *v* Belgium 1977; *v* Spain 1977; *v* France 1978. (GBI): Walker Cup 1977-79; *v* Europe 1974-76-78-80; World Team Ch 1978

Brodie, Andrew
(Scotland): Home Int 1968-69; *v* Spain 1974

Bromley-Davenport, E
(England): Home Int 1938-51

Brooks, A
(Scotland): Home Int 1968-69; Eur T Ch 1969. (GBI): Walker Cup 1969

Brooks, CJ
(Scotland): Home Int 1984-85; *v* Sweden 1984-86; *v* Italy 1986. (GBI): *v* Europe 1986

Brooks, M
(Scotland): *v* Austria 1994

Brotherston, IR
(Scotland): Home Int 1984-85; *v* France 1985; Eur T Ch 1985

Brough, S
(England): Home Int 1952-55-59-60; *v* France 1952-60. (GBI): *v* Europe 1960

Brown, CT
(Wales): Home Int 1970-71-72-73-74-75-77-78-80-88 (captain); Eur T Ch 1973; *v* Denmark 1977-80; *v* Ireland 1979; *v* Switzerland, Spain 1980

Brown, D
(Wales): *v* Ireland 1923-30-31; *v* England 1925; *v* Scotland 1931

Brown, JC
(Ireland): Home Int 1933-34-35-36-37-38-48-52-53

Brownlow, Hon WGE
(GBI): Walker Cup 1926

Bruen, J
(Ireland): Home Int 1937-38-49-50. (GBI): Walker Cup 1938-49-51

Bryson, WS
(Scotland): Home Int 1991-92-93; *v* Sweden 1992; *v* Italy 1992; *v* France 1993; *v* Spain 1994

Bucher, AMM
(Scotland): Home Int 1954-55-56; *v* Scandinavia 1956

Buckley, JA
(Wales): Home Int 1967-68-69-76-77-78; Eur T Ch 1967-69; *v* Denmark 1976-77. (GBI): Walker Cup 1979

Burch, N
(England): Home Int 1974

Burgess, MJ
(England): Home Int 1963-64-67; Eur T Ch 1967

Burke, J
(Ireland): *v* England 1929-30-31; *v* Wales 1929-30-31; *v* Scotland 1930-31; Home Int 1932-33-34-35-36-37-38-47-48-49. (GBI): Walker Cup 1932

Burns, M
(Ireland): Home Int 1973-75-83

Burns, R
(Ireland): Home Int 1991-92. (GBI): Walker Cup 1993; *v* Europe 1992; World Cup 1992

Burnside, J
(Scotland): Home Int 1956-57

Burrell, TM
(Scotland): *v* England 1924

Bussell, AF
(Scotland): Home Int 1956-57-58-61; *v* Scandinavia 1956-60. (GBI): Walker Cup 1957; *v* Europe 1956-62

Butterworth, JR
(England): *v* France 1954

Cage, S
(England): Home Int 1992. (GBI): Walker Cup 1993

Cairnes, HM
(Ireland): *v* Wales 1913-25; *v* England 1904; *v* Scotland 1904-27

Caldwell, I
(England): Home Int 1950-51-52-53-54-55-56-57-58-59-61; *v* France 1950. (GBI): Walker Cup 1951-55

Calvert, M
(Wales): Home Int 1983-84-86-87-89-91

Cameron, D
(Scotland): Home Int 1938-51

Campbell, Bart, Sir Guy C
(Scotland): *v* England 1909-10-11

Campbell, HM
(Scotland): Home Int 1962-64-68; *v* Scandinavia 1962; *v* Australia 1964; Eur T Ch 1965-79 (Captain). (GBI): *v* Europe 1964

Campbell, JGS
(Scotland): Home Int 1947-48

Campbell, W
(Scotland): *v* Ireland 1927-28-29-30-31; *v* England 1928-29-30-31; *v* Wales 1931; Home Int 1933-34-35-36. (GBI): Walker Cup 1930

Cannon, JHS
(England): *v* Ireland/Wales 1925

Cannon, JM
(Scotland): Home Int 1969; *v* Spain 1974

Carman, A
(England): *v* Scotland 1979; Home Int 1980

Carr, FC
(England): *v* Scotland 1911

Carr, JB
(Ireland): Home Int 1947-48-49-50-51-52-53-54-55-56-57-58-59-60-61-62-63-64-65-66-67-68-69; Eur T Ch 1965-67-69. (GBI): Walker Cup 1947-49-51-53-55-57-59-61-63-65 (Captain) -67 (Captain); *v* Europe 1954-56-64-66-68; World Team Ch 1958-60

Carr, JJ
(Ireland): Home Int 1981-82-83

Carr, JP
(Wales): *v* Ireland 1913

Carr, JR
(Ireland): *v* Wales 1930-31; *v* England 1931; Home Int 1933

Carr, R
(Ireland): Home Int 1970-71; Eur T Ch 1971; (GBI): Walker Cup 1971

Carrgill, PM
(England): Home Int 1978

Carrick, DG
(Scotland): Home Int 1981-82-83-84-85-86-87-88-89; *v* West Germany 1987; *v* Italy 1984-86-88; *v* France 1987-89; *v* Sweden 1983-84-86; Eur T Ch 1987-89-91 (Captain). (GBI): Walker Cup 1983-87; *v* Europe 1986

Carroll, CA
(Ireland): *v* Wales 1924

Carroll, JP
(Ireland): Home Int 1948-49-50-51-62

Carroll, W
(Ireland): *v* Wales 1913-23-24-25; *v* England 1925; *v* Scotland 1929; Home Int 1932

Carslaw, IA
(Scotland): Home Int 1976-77-78-80-81; Eur T Ch 1977-79; *v* England 1979; *v* Italy 1979; *v* Spain 1977; *v* Belgium 1978; *v* France 1978-83. (GBI): Walker Cup 1979; *v* Europe 1978

Carvill, J
(Ireland): Home Int 1989; Eur T Ch 1989. (GBI): *v* Europe 1990

Cashell, BG
(Ireland): Home Int 1978; *v* France, West Germany, Sweden 1978

Cassells, C
(England): Home Int 1989

Castle, H
(England): *v* Scotland 1903-04

Cater, JR
(Scotland): Home Int 1952-53-54-55-56; *v* South Africa 1954; *v* Scandinavia 1956. (GBI): Walker Cup 1955

Caul, P
(Ireland): Home Int 1968-69-71-72-73-74-75

Caven, J
(Scotland): *v* England 1926. (GBI): Walker Cup 1922

Chapman, BHG
(England): Home Int 1961-62. (GBI): Walker Cup 1961; *v* Europe 1962

Chapman, JA
(Wales): *v* Ireland 1923-29-30-31; *v* Scotland 1931; *v* England 1925

Chapman, R
(Wales): *v* Ireland 1929; Home Int 1932-34-35-36

Chapman, R
(England): *v* Scotland 1979; Home Int 1980-81; Eur T Ch 1981. (GBI): Walker Cup 1981; *v* Europe 1980

Charles, WB
(Wales): *v* Ireland 1924

Chillas, D
(Scotland): Home Int 1971

Christmas, MJ
(England): Home Int 1960-61-62-63-64. (GBI): Walker Cup 1961-63; *v* Europe 1962-64; World Team Ch 1962

Clark, CA
(England): Home Int 1964. (GBI): Walker Cup 1965; *v* Europe 1964

Clark, D
(Ireland): Home Int 1987-89; (GBI): *v* Europe 1990

Clark, GJ
(England): Home Int 1961-64-66-67-68-71. (GBI): Walker Cup 1965; *v* Europe 1964-66.

Clark, HK
(England): Home Int 1973. (GBI): Walker Cup 1973

Clark, MD
(Wales): *v* Ireland 1947

Clay, G
(Wales): Home Int 1962

Claydon, R
(England): Home Int 1988; Eur T Ch 1989: (GBI): Walker Cup 1989

Cleary, T
(Ireland): Home Int 1976-77-78-82-83-84-85-86; *v* Wales 1979; *v* France, West Germany, Sweden 1976

Clement, G
(Wales): *v* Ireland 1979

Cochran, JS
(Scotland): Home Int 1966

Collier, B
(Scotland): Home Int 1994; *v* Austria 1994

Colt, HS
(England): *v* Scotland 1908

Coltart, A
(Scotland): Home Int 1988-89-90; Eur T Ch 1989-91; *v* Sweden 1990; *v* Italy 1990; Nixdorf Nations Cup 1990; *v* France 1991. (GBI): Walker Cup 1991; *v* Europe 1990; World Team Ch 1990

Cook, J
(England): Home Int 1989-90

Cook, JH
(England): Home Int 1969

Corcoran, DK
(Ireland): Home Int 1972-73; Eur T Ch 1973

Corridan, T
(Ireland): Home Int 1983-84-91-92

Cosh, GB
(Scotland): Home Int 1964-65-66-67-68-69; Eur T Ch 1965-69. (GBI): Walker Cup 1965; *v* Europe 1966-68; CW 1967; World Team Ch 1966-68

Coughlan, R
(Ireland): Home Int 1991-94

Coulter, JG
(Wales): Home Int 1951-52

Coutts, FJ
(Scotland): Home Int 1980-81-82; Eur T Ch 1981-83; *v* France 1981-82-83

Cox, S
(Wales): Home Int 1970-71-72-73-74; Eur T Ch 1971-73

Crabbe, JL
(Ireland): *v* Wales 1925; *v* Scotland 1927-28

Craddock, T
(Ireland): Home Int 1955-56-57-58-59-60-67-68-69-70; Eur T Ch 1971. (GBI): Walker Cup 1967-69

Craigan, RM
(Ireland): Home Int 1963-64

Crawford, DR
(Scotland): Home Int 1990-91; Eur T Ch 1991; *v* France 1991

Crawley, LG
(England): *v* Ireland 1931; *v* Scotland 1931; Home Int 1932-33-34-36-37-38-47-48-49-54-55; *v* France 1936-37-38-49. (GBI): Walker Cup 1932-34-38-47

Critchley, B
(England): Home Int 1962-69-70; Eur T Ch 1969. (GBI): Walker Cup 1969; *v* Europe 1970

Crosbie, GF
(Ireland): Home Int 1953-55-56-57-88 (captain)

Crowley, M
(Ireland): *v* England 1928-29-30-31; *v* Wales 1929-31; *v* Scotland 1929-30-31; Home Int 1932

Cuddihy, J
(Scotland): Home Int 1977-78

Curry, DH
(England): Home Int 1984-86-87; *v* France 1988. (GBI): Walker Cup 1987; *v* Europe 1986-88

Dalgleish, CR
(Scotland): Home Int 1981-82-83-89; *v* France 1982; Eur T Ch 1981-83; Nixdorf Nations Cup 1989. (GBI): Walker Cup 1981; *v* Europe 1982

Darwin, B
(England): *v* Scotland 1902-04-05-08-09-10-23-24. (GBI): Walker Cup 1922

Davies, EN
(Wales): Home Int 1959-60-61-62-63-64-65-66-67-68-69-70-71-72-73-74; Eur T Ch 1969-71-73

Davies, JC
(England) Home Int 1969-71-72-73-74-78; Eur T Ch 1973-75-77. (GBI): Walker Cup 1973-75-77-79; *v* Europe 1972-74-76-78; World Team Ch 1974-76

Davies, FE
(Ireland): *v* Wales 1923

Davies, G
(Wales): *v* Denmark 1977; Home Int 1981-82-83

Davies, HE
(Wales): Home Int 1933-34-36

Davies, M
(England): Home Int 1984-85

Davies, TJ
(Wales): Home Int 1954-55-56-57-58-58-60

Davison, C
(England): Home Int 1989

Dawson, JE
(Scotland): *v* Ireland 1927-29-30-31; *v* England 1930-31; *v* Wales 1931; Home Int 1932-33-34-37

Dawson, M
(Scotland): Home Int 1963-65-66

Dawson, P
(England): Home Int 1969

Deboys, A
(Scotland): Home Int 1956-59-60; *v* Scandinavia 1960

Deeble, P
(England): Home Int 1975-76-77-78-80-81-83-84; *v* France 1982; *v* Scotland 1979; Eur T Ch 1979-81. (GBI): Walker Cup 1977-81; *v* Europe 1978; Colombian Int 1978

Deighton, FWG
(Scotland): Home Int 1950-52-53-56-57-58-59-60; *v* South Africa 1954; *v* New Zealand 1954; *v* Scandinavia 1956. (GBI): Walker Cup 1951-57; CW 1954-59

Denholm, RB
(Scotland): *v* Ireland 1927-29-31; *v* Wales 1931; *v* England 1931; Home Int 1932-33-34

Dewar, FG
(Scotland): Home Int 1952-53-55; *v* South Africa 1954; Eur T Ch 1971 (Captain)-73 (Captain)

Dick, CE
(Scotland): *v* England 1902-03-04-05-09-12

Dickson, HM
(Scotland): *v* Ireland 1929-31

Dickson, JR
(Ireland): Eur T Ch 1977; Home Int 1980

Dinsdale, R
(Wales): Home Int 1991-92-93

Disley, A
(Wales): Home Int 1976-77-78; *v* Denmark 1977; *v* Ireland 1979

Dodd, SC
(Wales):Home Int 1985-87-88-89. (GBI): Walker Cup 1989

Donellan, B
(Ireland): Home Int 1952

Dowie, A
(Scotland): Home Int 1949

Downes, P
(England): Home Int 1976-77-78-80-81-82; Eur T Ch 1977-79-81. (GBI): *v* Europe 1980

Downie, D
(Scotland): Home Int 1993-94; *v* Italy 1994; *v* Spain 1994

Downie, JJ
(England): Home Int 1974

Draper, JW
(Scotland): Home Int 1954

Dredge, B
(Wales): Home Int 1992-93-94. (GBI): Walker Cup 1993; World Cup 1992; *v* Europe 1994

Drew, NV
(Ireland): Home Int 1952-53. (GBI): Walker Cup 1953

Duffy, I
(Wales): Home Int 1975

Duncan, AA
(Wales): Home Int 1933-34-36-38-47-48-49-50-51-52-53-54-55-56-57-58-59. (GBI): Walker Cup (Captain) 1953

Duncan, GT
(Wales): Home Int 1952-53-54-55-56-57-58

Duncan, J, jr
(Wales): *v* Ireland 1913

Duncan, J
(Ireland): Home Int 1959-60-61

Dundas, S
(Scotland): Home Int 1992-93

Dunn, NW
(England): *v* Ireland 1928

Dunn, P
(Wales): Home Int 1957-58-59-60-61-62-63-65-66

Dunne, E
(Ireland): Home Int 1973-74-76-77; *v* Wales 1979; Eur T Ch 1975

Durrant, RA
(England): Home Int 1967; Eur T Ch 1967

Dykes, JM
(Scotland): Home Int 1934-35-36-48-49-51. (GBI): Walker Cup 1936

Easingwood, SR
(Scotland): Home Int 1986-87-88-90; *v* Italy 1988-90; *v* France 1987-89; Eur T Ch 1989

Eaves, CH
(Wales): Home Int 1935-36-38-47-48-49

Edwards, B
(Ireland): Home Int 1961-62-64-65-66-67-68-69-73

Edwards, C
(England): Home Int 1991-92-93-94; *v* France 1992-94

Edwards, M
(Ireland): Home Int 1956-57-58-60-61-62

Edwards, S
(Wales): Home Int 1992

Edwards, TH
(Wales): Home Int 1947

Egan, TW
(Ireland): Home Int 1952-53-59-60-62-67-68; Eur T Ch 1967-69

Eggo, R
(England): Home Int 1986-87-88-89-90; *v* France 1988. (GBI): Walker Cup 1987; *v* Europe 1988

Elliot, A
(Scotland): Home Int 1989; *v* France 1989; Eur T Ch 1989

Elliot, C
(Scotland): Home Int 1982; *v* France 1983

Elliot, IA
(Ireland): Home Int 1975-77-78; Eur T Ch 1975, *v* France, West Germany, Sweden 1978

Ellis, HC
(England): *v* Scotland 1902-12

Ellis, M
(Wales): Home Int 1992-93-94

Ellison, TF
(England): *v* Scotland 1922-25-26-27

Emerson, T
(Wales): Home Int 1932

Emery, G
(Wales): *v* Ireland 1925; Home Int 1933-36-38

Errity, D
(Ireland): Home Int 1990

Evans, AD
(Wales): *v* Scotland 1931-35; *v* Ireland 1931; Home Int 1932-33-34-35-38-47-49-50-51-52-53-54-55-56-61

Evans, C
(Wales): Home Int 1990-91-92-93-94

Evans, Duncan
(Wales): Home Int 1978-80-81; *v* Ireland 1979; Eur T Ch 1981. (GBI) Walker Cup 1981; *v* Europe 1980

Evans, G
(England): Home Int 1961

Evans, G
(England): Home Int 1990; Eur T Ch 1991. (GBI) Walker Cup 1991; World Cup 1990

Evans, HJ
(Wales): Home Int 1976-77-78-80-81-84-85-87-88; *v* France 1976; *v* Denmark 1977-80; *v* Ireland 1979; Eur T Ch 1979-81; *v* Switzerland, Spain 1980

Evans, M Gear
(Wales): *v* Ireland 1930-31; *v* Scotland 1931

Everett, C
(Scotland): Home Int 1988-89-90; *v* Italy 1988-90; *v* France 1988-89-91; Eur T Ch 1989-91; Nixdorf Nations Cup 1989-90; *v* Sweden 1990

Ewing, RC
(Ireland): Home Int 1934-35-36-37-38-47-48-49-50-51-53-54-55-56-57-58. (GBI): Walker Cup 1936-38-47-49-51-55

Eyles, GR
(England): Home Int 1974-75; Eur T Ch 1975. (GBI): Walker Cup 1975; *v* Europe 1974; World Team Ch 1974

Fairbairn, KA
(England): Home Int 1988

Fairchild, CEL
(Wales): *v* Ireland 1923; *v* England 1925

Fairchild, LJ
(Wales): *v* Ireland 1924

Fairlie, WE
(Scotland): *v* England 1912

Faldo, N
(England): Home Int 1975. (GBI): CW 1975

Fanagan, J
(Ireland): Home Int 1989-90-91-92-93-94. (GBI): *v* Europe 1992

Farmer, JC
(Scotland): Home Int 1970

Ferguson, M
(Ireland): Home Int 1952

Ferguson, WJ
(Ireland): Home Int 1952-54-55-58-59-61

Fergusson, S Mure
(Scotland): *v* England 1902-03-04

Ffrench, WF
(Ireland): *v* Scotland 1929; Home Int 1932

Fiddian, EW
(England): *v* Scotland 1929-30-31; *v* Ireland 1929-30-31; Home Int 1932-33-34-35; *v* France 1934. (GBI): Walker Cup 1932-34

Fisher, D
(England): Home Int 1993-94; *v* France 1994. (GBI): *v* Europe 1994

Fitzgibbon, JF
(Ireland): Home Int 1955-56-57

Fitzsimmons, J
(Ireland): Home Int 1938-47-48

Flaherty, JA
(Ireland): Home Int 1934-35-36-37

Flaherty, PD
(Ireland): Home Int 1967; Eur T Ch 1967-69

Fleming, J
(Scotland): Home Int 1987

Fleury, RA
(Ireland): Home Int 1974

Flockhart, AS
(Scotland): Home Int 1948-49

Fogarty, GN
(Ireland): Home Int 1956-58-63-64-67

Fogg, HN
(England): Home Int 1933

Forest, J de (now **Count J de Bendern**)
(England): *v* Ireland 1931; *v* Scotland 1931. (GBI): Walker Cup 1932

Foster, M
(England): Home Int 1994

Foster, MF
(England): Home Int 1973

Foster, R
(England): Home Int 1963-64-66-67-68-69-70-71-72; Eur T Ch 1967-69-71-73. (GBI): Walker Cup 1965-67-69-71-73-79 (Captain) - 81 (Captain); *v* Europe 1964-66-68-70; CW 1967-71; World Team Ch 1964-70

Fowler, WH
(England): *v* Scotland 1903-04-05

Fox, SJ
(England): Home Int 1956-57-58

Frame, DW
(England): Home Int 1958-59-60-61-62-63.
(GBI): Walker Cup 1961

Francis, F
(England): Home Int 1936; *v* France 1935-36

Frazier, K
(England): Home Int 1938

Froggatt, P
(Ireland): Home Int 1957

Fry, SH
(England): *v* Scotland 1902-03-04-05-06-07-09

Gairdner, JR
(Scotland): *v* England 1902

Gallacher, BJ
(Scotland): Home Int 1967

Gallacher, S
(Scotland): Home Int 1992-93-94; *v* Italy 1994; *v* Spain 1994; Eur T Ch 1993. (GBI): World Team Ch 1994

Galloway, RF
(Scotland): Home Int 1957-58-59; *v* Scandinavia 1958

Gannon, MA
(Ireland): Home Int 1973-74-77-78-80-81-83-84-87-88-89-90; *v* France, West Germany, Sweden 1978-80; Eur T Ch 1979-81-89. (GBI): *v* Europe 1974-78

Garbutt, I
(England): Home Int 1990-91-92; Eur T Ch 1991; *v* France 1992. (GBI): *v* Europe 1992

Garner, PF
(England): Home Int 1977-78-80; *v* Scotland 1979

Garnet, LG
(England): *v* France 1934. (GBI): *v* Australia 1934

Garson, R
(Scotland): *v* Ireland 1927-28-29

Gent, J
(England): *v* Ireland 1930; Home Int 1938

Gibb, C
(Scotland): *v* England 1927; *v* Ireland 1928

Gibson, WC
(Scotland): Home Int 1950-51

Gilford, CF
(Wales): Home Int 1963-64-65-66-67

Gilford, D
(England): Home Int 1983-84-85. (GBI): Walker Cup 1985; *v* Europe 1986

Gill, WJ
(Ireland): *v* Wales 1931; Home Int 1932-33-34-35-36-37

Gillies, HD
(England): *v* Scotland 1908-25-26-27

Girvan, P
(Scotland): Home Int 1986; West Germany 1987; Eur T Ch 1987. (GBI): Walker Cup 1987

Glossop, R
(Wales): Home Int 1935-37-38-47

Glover, J
(Ireland): Home Int 1951-52-53-55-59-60-70

Godwin, G
(England): Home Int 1976-77-78-80-81; *v* Scotland 1979; *v* France 1982; Eur T Ch 1979-81. (GBI): Walker Cup 1979-81

Goulding, N
(Ireland): Home Int 1988-89-90-91-92; Eur T Ch 1991

Graham, AJ
(Scotland): *v* England 1925

Graham, J
(Scotland): *v* England 1902-03-04-05-06-07-08-09-10-11

Graham, JSS
(Ireland): Home Int 1938-50-51

Gray, CD
(England): Home Int 1932

Green, CW
(Scotland): Home Int 1961 to 1978; Eur T Ch 1965-67-69-71-73-75-77-79-81 (Captain)-83 (Captain); *v* Scandinavia 1962; *v* Australia 1964; *v* Belgium 1973-75-77-78; *v* Spain 1977; *v* Italy 1979; *v* England 1979. (GBI): Walker Cup 1963-69-71-73-75-83 (Captain) -85 (Captain); *v* Europe 1962-66-68-70-72-74-76; CW 1971; World Team Ch 1970-72-84 (Captain)-86 (Captain)

Green, HB
(England): *v* Scotland 1979

Green, PO
(England): Home Int 1961-62-63. (GBI): CW 1963

Greene, R
(Ireland): Home Int 1933

Greig, DG
(Scotland): Home Int 1972-73-75. (GBI): CW 1975

Greig, K
(Scotland): Home Int 1933

Griffiths, HGB
(Wales): *v* Ireland 1923-24-25

Griffiths, HS
(Wales): *v* England 1958

Griffiths, JA
(Wales): Home Int 1933

Guerin, M
(Ireland): Home Int 1961-62-63

Guild, WJ
(Scotland): *v* England 1925-27-28; *v* Ireland 1927-28

Hales, JP
(Wales): *v* Scotland 1963

Hall, A
(Wales): Home Int 1994

Hall, AH
(Scotland): Home Int 1962-66-69

Hall, D
(Wales): Home Int 1932-37

Hall, K
(Wales): Home Int 1955-59

Hambro, AV
(England): *v* Scotland 1905-08-09-10-22

Hamilton, CJ
(Wales): *v* Ireland 1913

Hamilton, ED
(Scotland): Home Int 1936-37-38

Hamer, S
(England): Home Int 1983-84

Hanway, M
(Ireland): Home Int 1971-74

Hardman, RH
(England): *v* Scotland 1927-28. (GBI): Walker Cup 1928

Hare, A
(England): Home Int 1988; Eur T Ch 1989. (GBI) Walker Cup 1989

Hare, WCD
(Scotland): Home Int 1953; *v* New Zealand 1954

Harrhy, A
(Wales): Home Int 1988-89

Harrington, J
(Ireland): Home Int 1960-61-74-75-76; Eur T Ch 1975; *v* Wales 1979

Harrington, P
(Ireland): Home Int 1990-91-92-93-94; Eur T Ch 1991. (GBI): Walker Cup 1991-93; *v* Europe 1992-94

Harris, G
(England): Home Int 1994

Harris, IR
(Scotland): Home Int 1955-56-58-59

Harris, R
(Scotland): *v* England 1905-08-10-11-12-22-23-24-25-26-27-28 (GBI): Walker Cup 1922 (Captain) -23 (Captain) -26 (Captain)

Harrison, JW
(Wales): Home Int 1937-50

Hartley, RW
(England): *v* Scotland 1926-27-28-29-30-31; *v* Ireland 1928-29-30-31; Home Int 1933-34-35. (GBI): Walker Cup 1930-32

Hartley, WL
(England): *v* Ireland/Wales 1925; *v* Scotland 1927-31;*v* Ireland 1928-31; Home Int 1932-33; *v* France 1935.(GBI): Walker Cup 1932

Hassall, JE
(England): *v* Scotland 1923; *v* Ireland/Wales 1925

Hastings, JL
(Scotland): Home Int 1957-58; *v* Scandinavia 1958

Hawksworth, J
(England): Home Int 1984-85. (GBI): Walker Cup 1985

Hay, G
(Scotland): *v* England 1979; Home Int 1980-88-90-91-92; *v* Belgium 1980; *v* France 1980-82-89-91-93; *v* Italy 1988-92-94; *v* Sweden 1992; *v* Spain 1994; Eur T Ch 1991-93. (GBI): *v* Europe 1980; Walker Cup 1991

Hay, J
(Scotland): Home Int 1972

Hayes, JA
(Ireland): Home Int 1977

Hayward, CH
(England): *v* Scotland 1925; *v* Ireland 1928

Healy, TM
(Ireland): *v* Scotland 1931; *v* England 1931

Heather, D
(Ireland): Home Int 1976; *v* France, West Germany, Sweden 1976

Hedges, PJ
(England): Home Int 1970-73-74-75-76-77-78-82-83; Eur T Ch 1973-75-77. (GBI): Walker Cup 1973-75; *v* Europe 1974-76; World Team Ch 1974

Hegarty, J
(Ireland): Home Int 1975

Hegarty, TD
(Ireland): Home Int 1957

Helm, AGB
(England): Home Int 1948

Henderson, J
(Ireland): *v* Wales 1923

Henderson, N
(Scotland): Home Int 1963-64

Henriques, GLQ
(England): *v* Ireland 1930

Henry, W
(England): Home Int 1987; *v* France 1988

Herlihy, B
(Ireland): Home Int 1950

Herne, KTC
(Wales): *v* Ireland 1913

Heverin, AJ
(Ireland): Home Int 1978; *v* France, West Germany, Sweden 1978

Hezlet, CO
(Ireland): *v* Wales 1923-25-27-29-31; *v* Scotland 1927-28-29-30-31; *v* England 1929-30-31. (GBI): Walker Cup 1924-26-28; *v* South Africa 1927

Higgins, D
(Ireland): Home Int 1993-94

Higgins, L
(Ireland): Home Int 1968-70-71

Hill, GA
(England): Home Int 1936-37. (GBI): Walker Cup 1936-55 (Captain)

Hilton, HH
(England): *v* Scotland 1902-03-04-05-06-07-09-10-11-12

Hird, K
(Scotland): Home Int 1987-88-89; Nixdorf Nations Cup 1989; *v* Italy 1990

Hislop, C
(Scotland): Home Int 1994; *v* Austria 1994

Hoad, PGJ
(England): Home Int 1978; *v* Scotland 1979

Hodgson, C
(England): *v* Scotland 1924

Hodgson, J
(England): Home Int 1994

Hoey, TBC
(Ireland): Home Int 1970-71-72-73-77-84; Eur T Ch 1971-77

Hogan, P
(Ireland): Home Int 1985-86-87-88; Eur T Ch 1991

Holderness, Sir EWE
(England): *v* Scotland 1922-23-24-25-26-28. (GBI): *v* America 1921, Walker Cup 1923-26-30

Holmes, AW
(England): Home Int 1962

Homer, TWB
(England): Home Int 1972-73; Eur T Ch 1973. (GBI): Walker Cup 1973; *v* Europe 1972; World Team Ch 1972

Homewood, G
(England): Home Int 1985-91; Eur T Ch 1991

Hooman, CVL
(England): *v* Scotland 1910-22. (GBI): Walker Cup 1922-23

Hope, WL
(Scotland): *v* England 1923-25-26-27-28-29. (GBI): Walker Cup 1923-24-28

Horne, A
(Scotland): Home Int 1971

Hosie, JR
(Scotland): Home Int 1936

Houston, G
(Wales): Home Int 1990-91-92-93-94; Eur T Ch 1991

Howard, DB
(Scotland): *v* England 1979; Home Int 1980-81-82-83-93-94; *v* Belgium 1980; *v* France 1980-81-83; *v* Italy 1984-94; *v* Spain 1994. Eur T Ch 1981; (GBI): *v* Europe 1980-94.

Howell, D
(England): Home Int 1994

Howell, HR
(Wales): *v* Ireland 1923-24-25-29-30-31; *v* England 1925; *v* Scotland 1931; Home Int 1932-34-35-36-37-38-47

Howell, H Logan
(Wales): *v* Ireland 1925

Huddy, G
(England): Home Int 1960-61-62. (GBI): Walker Cup 1961

Huggan, J
(Scotland): Home Int 1981-82-83-84; *v* France 1982-83; *v* Sweden 1983; *v* Italy 1984; Eur T Ch 1981

Hughes, I
(Wales): Home Int 1954-55-56

Hulme, WJ
(Ireland): Home Int 1955-56-57

Humphrey, JG
(Wales): *v* Ireland 1925

Humphreys, AR
(Ireland): *v* England 1957

Humphreys, DI
(Wales): Home Int 1972

Humphreys, W
(England): Home Int 1970-71; Eur T Ch 1971. (GBI): Walker Cup 1971; *v* Europe 1970

Hunter, NM
(Scotland): *v* England 1903-12

Hunter, WI
(Scotland): *v* England 1922

Hutcheon, I
(Scotland): Home Int 1971-72-73-74-75-76-77-78-80; *v* Belgium 1973-75-77-78-80; *v* Spain 1977; *v* France 1978-80-81; *v* Italy 1979; *v* Sweden 1983; Eur T Ch 1973-75-77-79-81. (GBI): Walker Cup 1975-77-79-81; *v* Europe 1974-76; World Team Ch 1974-76-80; CW 1975; Dominican Int 1973; Colombian Int 1975

Hutchings, C
(England): *v* Scotland 1902

Hutchinson, HG
(England): *v* Scotland 1902-03-04-06-07-09

Hutchison, CK
(Scotland): *v* England 1904-05-06-07-08-09-10-11-12

Hutt, R
(England): Home Int 1991-92-93

Hutton, R
(Ireland): Home Int 1991

Hyde, GE
(England): Home Int 1967-68

Illingworth, G
(England): *v* Scotland 1929; *v* France 1937

Inglis, MJ
(England): Home Int 1977

Isitt, GH
(Wales): *v* Ireland 1923

Jack, RR
(Scotland): Home Int 1950-51-54-55-56-57-58-59-61; *v* New Zealand 1954; *v* Scandinavia 1956-58. (GBI): Walker Cup 1957-59; *v* Europe 1956; World Team Ch 1958; CW 1959

Jack, WS
(Scotland): Home Int 1955

Jacob, NE
(Wales): Home Int 1932-33-34-35-36

James, D
(Scotland): Home Int 1985

James, L
(England): Home Int 1993-94; *v* France 1994. (GBI): *v* Europe 1994; World Team Ch 1994

James, M
(England): Home Int 1974-75; Eur T Ch 1975. (GBI): Walker Cup 1975

James, RD
(England): Home Int 1974-75

Jameson, JF
(Ireland): *v* Wales 1913-24

Jamieson, A, jr
(Scotland): *v* England 1927-28-31; *v* Ireland 1928-31; *v* Wales 1931; Home Int 1932-33-36-37. (GBI): Walker Cup 1926

Jamieson, D
(Scotland): Home Int 1980

Jenkins, JLC
(Scotland): *v* England 1908-12-22-24-26-28; *v* Ireland 1928. (GBI): *v* America 1921

Jermine, JG
(Wales): Home Int 1972-73-74-75-76-82; Eur T Ch 1975-77; *v* France 1975

Jobson, RH
(England): *v* Ireland 1928

Johnson, R
(Wales): Home Int 1990-92-93-94; Eur T Ch 1991. (GBI) *v* Europe 1994

Johnson, TWG
(Ireland): *v* England 1929

Johnstone, JW
(Scotland): Home Int 1970-71

Jones, A
(Wales): Home Int 1989-90; Eur T Ch 1991

Jones, DK
(Wales): Home Int 1973

Jones, EO
(Wales): Home Int 1983-85-86

Jones, JG Parry
(Wales): Home Int 1959-60

Jones, JL
(Wales): Home Int 1933-34-36

Jones, JR
(Wales): Home Int 1970-72-73-77-78-80-81-82-83-84-85; Eur T Ch 1973-79-81; *v* Denmark 1976-80; *v* Ireland 1979; *v* Switzerland, Spain 1980; *v* Ireland 1979

Jones, JW
(England): Home Int 1948-49-50-51-52-54-55

Jones, KG
(Wales): Home Int 1988

Jones, MA
(Wales): Home Int 1947-48-49-50-51-53-54-57

Jones, Malcolm F
(Wales): Home Int 1933

Jones, SP
(Wales): Home Int 1981-82-83-84-85-86-88-89-91-93

Kane, RM
(Ireland): Home Int 1967-68-71-72-74-78; Eur T Ch 1971-79; *v* Wales 1979. (GBI): *v* Europe 1974

Kearney, K
(Ireland): Home Int 1988-89-90-92-94

Keenan, S
(Ireland): Home Int 1989

Kelleher, WA
(Ireland): Home Int 1962

Kelley, MJ
(England): Home Int 1974-75-76-77-78-80-81-82-88(Captain); *v* France 1982; Eur T Ch 1977-79. (GBI): Walker Cup 1977-79; *v* Europe 1976-78; World Team Ch 1976; Colombian Int 1978

Kelley, PD
(England): Home Int 1965-66-68

Kelly, NS
(Ireland): Home Int 1966

Keppler, SD
(England): Home Int 1982-83; *v* France 1982. (GBI): Walker Cup 1983

Kilduff, AJ
(Ireland): *v* Scotland 1928

Killey, GC
(Scotland): *v* Ireland 1928

King, M
(England): Home Int 1969-70-71-72-73; Eur T Ch 1971-73 (GBI): Walker Cup 1969-73; *v* Europe 1970-72; CW 1971

Kirkpatrick, D
(Scotland): Home Int 1992; *v* France 1993; Eur T Ch 1993

Kissock, B
(Ireland): Home Int 1961-62-74-76; *v* France, West Germany, Sweden 1978

Kitchin, JE
(England): *v* France 1949

Knight, B
(Wales): Home Int 1986

Knipe, RG
(Wales): Home Int 1953-54-55-56

Knowles, ST
(Scotland): Home Int 1990-91-92; *v* France 1991

Knowles, WR
(Wales): *v* England 1948

Kyle, AT
(Scotland): Home Int 1938-47-49-50-51-52-53. (GBI): Walker Cup 1938-47-51; *v* South Africa 1952

Kyle, DH
(Scotland): *v* England 1924-30. (GBI): Walker Cup 1924

Kyle, EP
(Scotland): *v* England 1925

Laidlay, JE
(Scotland): *v* England 1902-03-04-05-06-07-08-09-10-11

Lake, AD
(Wales): Home Int 1958

Lang, JA
(Scotland): *v* England 1929-31; *v* Ireland 1929-30-31; *v* Wales 1931. (GBI): Walker Cup 1930

Langley, JDA
(England): Home Int 1950-51-52-53; *v* France 1950. (GBI): Walker Cup 1936-51-53

Langmead, J
(England): Home Int 1986

Lassen, EA
(England): *v* Scotland 1909-10-11-12

Last, CN
(Wales): Home Int 1975

Laurence, C
(England): Home Int 1983-84-85

Lawrie, CD
(Scotland): Home Int 1949-50-55-56-57-58; *v* Sweden 1950; *v* Scandinavia 1956-58. (GBI): Walker Cup 1961 (Captain) -63 (Captain); *v* South Africa 1952; *v* Europe 1960 (Captain)-62 (Captain); World Team Ch 1960 (Captain)-62 (Captain)

Lawrie, GA
(Scotland): Home Int 1990-91; Eur T Ch 1991

Layton, EN
(England): *v* Scotland 1922-23-26; *v* Ireland/Wales 1925

Lee, IGF
(Scotland): Home Int 1958-59-60-61-62; *v* Scandinavia 1960

Lee, JN
(Wales): Home Int 1988-89; Eur T Ch 1991

Lee, M
(England): Home Int 1950

Lee, MG
(England): Home Int 1965

Lehane, N
(Ireland): Home Int 1976; *v* France, West Germany, Sweden 1976

Lewis, DH
(Wales): Home Int 1935-36-37-38

Lewis, DR
(Wales): *v* Ireland 1925-29-30-31; *v* Scotland 1931; Home Int 1932-34

Lewis, ME
(England): Home Int 1980-81-82; *v* France 1982. (GBI): Walker Cup 1983

Lewis, R Cofe
(Wales): *v* Ireland 1925

Leyden, PJ
(Ireland): Home Int 1953-55-56-57-59

Lincoln, AC
(England): *v* Scotland 1907

Lindsay, J
(Scotland): Home Int 1933-34-35-36

Lloyd, HM
(Wales): *v* Ireland 1913

Lloyd, RM de
(Wales): *v* Scotland 1931; *v* Ireland 1931; Home Int 1932-33-34-35-36-37-38-47-48

Llyr, A
(Wales): Home Int 1984-85

Lockhart, G
(Scotland): *v* England 1911-12

Lockley, AE
(Wales): Home Int 1956-57-58-62

Logan, GW
(England): Home Int 1973

Long, D
(Ireland): Home Int 1973-74-80-81-82-83-84; *v* Wales 1979; Eur T Ch 1979

Low, AJ
(Scotland): Home Int 1964-65; Eur T Ch 1965; *v* Australia 1964

Low, JL
(Scotland): *v* England 1904

Lowdon, CJ
(Scotland): *v* Ireland 1927

Lowe, A
(Ireland): *v* Wales 1924; *v* England 1925-28; *v* Scotland 1927-28

Lowson, AG
(Scotland): Home Int 1989-90-91; *v* Sweden 1990-92; *v* Italy 1992

Lucas, PB
(England): Home Int 1936-48-49; *v* France 1936. (GBI): Walker Cup 1936-47-49 (Captain)

Ludwell, N
(England): Home Int 1991; *v* France 1992

Lunt, MSR
(England): Home Int 1956-57-58-59-60-62-63-64-66. (GBI): Walker Cup 1959-61-63-65; *v* Europe 1964; CW 1963; World Team Ch 1964

Lunt, S
(England): Home Int 1932-33-34-35; *v* France 1934-35-39

Lygate, M
(Scotland): Home Int 1970-75-88 (Captain); Eur T Ch 1971-85 (Captain)-87 (Captain)

Lyle, AWB
(England): Home Int 1975-76-77; Eur T Ch 1977. (GBI): Walker Cup 1977; CW 1975; *v* Europe 1976

Lyon, JS
(England): Home Int 1937-38

Lyons, P
(Ireland): Home Int 1986

McAllister, SD
(Scotland): Home Int 1983; *v* Sweden 1983; Eur T Ch 1983

Macara, MA
(Wales): Home Int 1983-84-85-87-89-90-91-92-93

McArthur, W
(Scotland): Home Int 1952-54; *v* South Africa 1954

McBeath, J
(Scotland): Home Int 1964

McBride, D
(Scotland): Home Int 1932

McCallum, AR
(Scotland): *v* England 1929. (GBI): Walker Cup 1928

McCarrol, F
(Ireland): Home Int 1968-69

McCart, DM
(Scotland): Home Int 1977-78; *v* Belgium 1978; *v* France 1978

McCarthy, L
(Ireland): Home Int 1953-54-55-56

McConnell, FP
(Ireland): *v* Wales 1929-30-31; *v* England 1929-30-31;*v* Scotland 1930-31; Home Int 1934

McConnell, RM
(Ireland): *v* Wales 1924-25-29-30-31; *v* England 1925-28-29-30-31; *v* Scotland 1927-28-29-31; Home Int 1934-35-36-37

McConnell, WG
(Ireland): *v* England 1925

McCormack, JD
(Ireland): *v* Wales 1913-24; *v* England 1928, Home Int 1932-33-34-35-36-37

McCrea, WE
(Ireland): Home Int 1965-66-67; Eur T Ch 1965

McCready, SM
(Ireland): Home Int 1947-49-50-52-54. (GBI): Walker Cup 1949-51

McDaid, B
(Ireland): *v* Wales 1979

MacDonald, GK
(Scotland): Home Int 1978-81-82; *v* England 1979; *v* France 1981-82-83

McDonald, H
(Scotland): Home Int 1970

Macdonald, JS
(Scotland): Home Int 1969-70-71-72; *v* Belgium 1973; Eur T Ch 1971. (GBI): Walker Cup 1971; *v* Europe 1970

McEvoy, P
(England): Home Int 1976-77-78-80-81-83-84-85-86-87-88-89-91-94 (Captain); *v* Scotland 1979; *v* France 1982-88-92; Eur T Ch 1977-79-81-89; (GBI): Walker Cup 1977-79-81-85-89; *v* Europe 1978-80-86-88; World Cup 1978-80-88 (winners)

Macfarlane, CB
(Scotland): *v* England 1912

McGimpsey, G
(Ireland): Home Int 1978 and 1980 to 1994; *v* Wales 1979; Eur T Ch 1981-89-91. (GBI): Walker Cup 1985-89-91; *v* Europe 1986-88-90-92; World Cup 1988 (winners)

McGinley, P
(Ireland): Home Int 1989-90; Eur T Ch 1991. (GBI): Walker Cup 1991

Macgregor, A
(Scotland): *v* Scandinavia 1956

Macgregor, G
(Scotland): Home Int 1969-70-71-72-73-74-75-76-80-81-82-83- 84-

85-86-87; *v* Belgium 1973-75-80; *v* England 1979; *v* Sweden 1983-84-86; *v* Italy 1984-86; *v* France 1981-82-85-87; Eur T Ch 1971-73-75-81-83-85-87. (GBI): Walker Cup 1971-75-83-85-87-91 (Captain)-93 (Captain); *v* Europe 1970-74-84; CW 1971-75; World Team Ch 1982;

MacGregor, RC
(Scotland): Home Int 1951-52-53-54; *v* New Zealand 1954. (GBI): Walker Cup 1953

McGuire, M
(England): Home Int 1992

McHenry, J
(Ireland): Home Int 1985-86. (GBI): Walker Cup 1987

McInally, H
(Scotland): Home Int 1937-47-48

McInally, RH
(Ireland): Home Int 1949-51

McIntosh, EA
(Scotland): Home Int 1989

Macintosh, KW
(Scotland): *v* England 1979; Home Int 1980; *v* France 1980; *v* Belgium 1980. (GBI): *v* Europe 1980

McKay, G
(Scotland): Home Int 1969

McKay, JR
(Scotland): Home Int 1950-51-52-54; *v* New Zealand 1954

McKellar, PJ
(Scotland): Home Int 1976-77-78; *v* Belgium 1978; *v* France 1978; *v* England 1979. (GBI): Walker Cup 1977; *v* Europe 1978

Mackenzie, F
(Scotland): *v* England 1902-03

MacKenzie, S
(Scotland): Home Int 1990-93-94; *v* Italy 1994; *v* Spain 1994

Mackenzie, WW
(Scotland): *v* England 1923-26-27-29; *v* Ireland 1930. (GBI): Walker Cup 1922-23

Mackeown, HN
(Ireland): Home Int 1973; Eur T Ch 1973

McKibbin, H
(Scotland): Home Int 1994

Mackie, GW
(Scotland): Home Int 1948-50

McKinlay, SL
(Scotland): *v* England 1929-30-31; *v* Ireland 1930; *v* Wales 1931; Home Int 1932-33-35-37-47. (GBI): Walker Cup 1934

McKinna, RA
(Scotland): Home Int 1938

McKinnon, A
(Scotland): Home Int 1947-52

McLean, D
(Wales): Home Int 1968-69-70-71-72-73-74-75-76-77-78-80-81-82-83-85-86-88-90; Eur T Ch 1975-77-79-81; *v* France 1975-76; *v* Denmark 1976-80; *v* Ireland 1979; *v* Switzerland, Spain 1980

McLean, J
(Scotland): Home Int 1932-33-34-35-36. (GBI): Walker Cup 1934-36; *v* Australia 1934

McLeod, AE
(Scotland): Home Int 1937-38

McLeod, WS
(Scotland): Home Int 1935-37-38-47-48-49-50-51; *v* Sweden 1950

McMenamin, E
(Ireland): Home Int 1981

McMullan, C
(Ireland): Home Int 1933-34-35

McNair, AA
(Scotland): *v* Ireland 1929

MacNamara, L
(Ireland): Home Int 1977-83-84-85-86-87-88-89-90-91-92; Eur T Ch 1977-91

McNeill, G
(Ireland): Home Int 1991-93

McRuvie, EA
(Scotland): *v* England 1929-30-31; *v* Ireland 1930-31; *v* Wales 1931; Home Int 1932-33-34-35-36. (GBI): Walker Cup 1932-34

McTear, J
(Scotland): Home Int 1971

Madeley, JFD
(Ireland): Home Int 1959-60-61-62-63-64. (GBI): Walker Cup 1963; *v* Europe 1962

Mahon, RJ
(Ireland): Home Int 1938-52-54-55

Maliphant, FR
(Wales): Home Int 1932

Malone, B
(Ireland): Home Int 1959-64-69-71-75; Eur T Ch 1971-75

Manford, GC
(Scotland): *v* England 1922-23

Manley, N
(Ireland): *v* Wales 1924; *v* England 1928; *v* Scotland 1927-28

Mann, LS
(Scotland): Home Int 1982-83; *v* Sweden 1983; Eur T Ch 1983. (GBI): Walker Cup 1983

Marchbank, B
(Scotland): Home Int 1978; *v* Italy 1979; Eur T Ch 1979. (GBI): Walker Cup 1979; *v* Europe 1976-78; World Team Ch 1978

Marks, GC
(England): Home Int 1963-67-68-69-70-71-74-75-82; Eur T Ch 1967-69-71-75; *v* France 1982 (Captain). (GBI): Walker Cup 1969-71-87 (Captain)-89 (Captain); *v* Europe 1968-70; World Team Ch 1970; CW 1975; Colombian Int 1975.

Marren, JM
(Ireland): *v* Wales 1925

Marsden, G
(Wales): Home Int 1994

Marsh, DM
(England): Home Int 1956-57-58-59-60-64-66-68-69-70-71-72; Eur T Ch 1971. (GBI): Walker Cup 1959-71-73 (Captain) -75 (Captain); *v* Europe 1958

Marshman, A
(Wales): Home Int 1952

Marston, CC
(Wales): *v* Ireland 1929-30-31; *v* Scotland 1931

Martin, DHR
(England): Home Int 1938; *v* France 1934-49

Martin, GNC
(Ireland): *v* Wales 1923-29; *v* Scotland 1928-29-30; *v* England 1929-30. (GBI): Walker Cup 1928

Martin, S
(Scotland): Home Int 1975-76-77; Eur T Ch 1977; *v* Belgium 1977; *v* Spain 1977. (GBI): Walker Cup 1977; *v* Europe 1976; World Team Ch 1976

Mason, SC
(England): Home Int 1973

Mathias-Thomas, FEL
(Wales): *v* Ireland 1924-25

Matthews, RL
(Wales): Home Int 1935-37

Maxwell, R
(Scotland): *v* England 1902-03-04-05-06-07-09-10

Mayo, PM
(Wales): Home Int 1982-87. (GBI): Walker Cup 1985-87

Meharg, W
(Ireland): Home Int 1957

Melia, TJ
(Wales): Home Int 1976-77-78-80-81-82; *v* Ireland 1979; Eur T Ch 1977-79; *v* Denmark 1976-80; *v* Switzerland, Spain 1980

Mellin, GL
(England): *v* Scotland 1922

Melville, LM Balfour
(Scotland): *v* England 1902-03

Melville, TE
(Scotland): Home Int 1974

Menzies, A
(Scotland): *v* England 1925

Metcalfe, J
(England): Home Int 1989. (GBI) *v* Europe 1990

Micklem, GH
(England): Home Int 1947-48-49-50-51-52-53-54-55. (GBI): Walker Cup 1947-49-53-55-57 (Captain) -59 (Captain); World Team 1958

Mill, JW
(Scotland): Home Int 1953-54

Millensted, DJ
(England): Home Int 1966; Eur T Ch 1967. (GBI): Walker Cup 1967; CW 1967

Miller, AC
(Scotland): Home Int 1954-55

Miller, MJ
(Scotland): Home Int 1974-75-77-78; *v* Belgium 1978; *v* France 1978

Milligan, JW
(Scotland): Home Int 1986-87-88-89-90-91-92; *v* West Germany 1987; *v* Italy 1988-90-92; *v* France 1987-89-91; Eur T Ch 1987-89-91; Nixdorf Nations Cup 1989; *v* Sweden 1990-92. (GBI): Walker Cup 1989-91; World Cup 1988 (winners)-90; *v* Europe 1988-92

Mills, ES
(Wales): Home Int 1957

Millward, EB
(England): Home Int 1950-52-53-54-55. (GBI): Walker Cup 1949-55

Milne, WTG
(Scotland): Home Int 1972-73; Eur T Ch 1973; *v* Belgium 1973. (GBI): Walker Cup 1973

Mitchell, A
(England): *v* Scotland 1910-11-12

Mitchell, CS
(England): Home Int 1975-76-78

Mitchell, FH
(England): *v* Scotland 1906-07-08

Mitchell, JWH
(Wales): Home Int 1964-65-66

Moffat, DM
(England): Home Int 1961-63-67; *v* France 1959-60

Moir, A
(Scotland): Home Int 1983-84; *v* Europe 1984; Eur T Ch 1985

Montgomerie, CS
(Scotland): Home Int 1984-85-86; *v* West Germany 1987; *v* Sweden 1984-86; *v* Italy 1984; *v* France 1985; Eur T Ch 1985-87. (GBI): Walker Cup 1985-87; *v* Europe 1986; World Team Ch 1984-86

Montgomerie, JS
(Scotland): Home Int 1957; *v* Scandinavia 1958; Eur T Ch 1965

Montmorency, RH de
(England): *v* Scotland 1908; *v* Wales/Ireland 1925; *v* South Africa 1927. (GBI): *v* America 1921

Moody, JV
(West): Home Int 1947-48-49-51-56-58-59-60-61

Moody, PH
(England): Home Int 1971-72. (GBI): *v* Europe 1972

Moore, GJ
(Ireland): *v* England 1928; *v* Wales 1929

Morgan, JL
(Wales): 1948-49-50-51-52-53-54-55-56-57-58-59-60-61-62-64-68. (GBI): Walker Cup 1951-53-55

Morris, FS
(Scotland): Home Int 1963

Morris, J
(Ireland): Home Int 1993-94

Morris, MF
(Ireland): Home Int 1978-80-82-83-84; *v* Wales 1979; Eur T Ch 1979; *v* France, West Germany, Sweden 1980

Morris, R
(Wales): Home Int 1983-86-87

Morris, TS
(Wales): *v* Ireland 1924-29-30

Morrison, JH
(Scotland): *v* Scandinavia 1960

Morrison, JSF
(England): *v* Ireland 1930

Morrow, AJC
(Ireland): Home Int 1975-83-92-93

Morrow, JM
(Wales): *v* Ireland 1979; Home Int 1980-81; Eur T Ch 1979-81; *v* Denmark, Switzerland, Spain 1980

Mosey, IJ
(England): Home Int 1971

Moss, AV
(Wales): Home Int 1965-66-68

Mouland, MG
(Wales): Home Int 1978-81; *v* Ireland 1979; Eur T Ch 1979

Moxon, GA
(Wales): *v* Ireland 1929-30

Mulcare, P
(Ireland): Home Int 1968-69-70-71-72-74-78-80; *v* France, West Germany, Sweden 1978-80; Eur T Ch 1975-79. (GBI): Walker Cup 1975; *v* Europe 1972

Mulholland, D
(Ireland): Home Int 1988

Munn, E
(Ireland): *v* Wales 1913-23-24; *v* Scotland 1927

Munn, L
(Ireland): *v* Wales 1913-23-24; Home Int 1936-37

Munro, RAG
(Scotland): Home Int 1960

Murdoch, D
(Scotland): Home Int 1964

Murphy, AR
(Scotland): Home Int 1961-67

Murphy, G
(Ireland): Home Int 1992-93-94

Murphy, P
(Ireland): Home Int 1985-86

Murray, GH
(Scotland): Home Int 1973-74-75-76-77-78-83; *v* Spain 1974-77; *v* Belgium 1975-77; Eur T Ch 1975-77. (GBI): Walker Cup 1977; *v* Europe 1978

Murray, SWT
(Scotland): Home Int 1959-60-61-62-63; *v* Scandinavia 1960. (GBI): Walker Cup 1963; *v* Europe 1958-62

Murray, WA
(Scotland): *v* England 1923-24-25-26-27. (GBI): Walker Cup 1923-24

Murray, WB
(Scotland): Home Int 1967-68-69; Eur T Ch 1969

Muscroft, R
(England): Home Int 1986

Nash A
(England): Home Int 1988-89

Neech, DG
(England): Home Int 1961

Neill, JH
(Ireland): Home Int 1938-47-48-49

Neill, R
(Scotland): Home Int 1936

Nestor, JM
(Ireland): Home Int 1962-63-64

Nevin, V
(Ireland): Home Int 1960-63-65-67-69-72; Eur T Ch 1967-69-73

Newey, AS
(England): Home Int 1932

Newman, JE
(Wales): Home Int 1932

Newton, H
(Wales): *v* Ireland 1929

Nicholson, J
(Ireland): Home Int 1932

Nolan, K
(Ireland): Home Int 1992-93-94

Noon, GS
(Wales): Home Int 1935-36-37

Noon, J
(Scotland): Home Int 1987

O'Boyle, P
(Ireland): Eur T Ch 1977

O'Brien, MD
(Ireland): Home Int 1968-69-70-71-72-75-76-77; Eur T Ch 1971; *v* France, West Germany, Sweden 1976

O'Carroll, C
(Wales): Home Int 1989-90-91-92-93; Eur T Ch 1991

O'Connell, A
(Ireland): Home Int 1967-70-71

O'Connell, E
(Ireland): Home Int 1985; Eur T Ch 1989. (GBI): Walker Cup 1989; *v* Europe 1988; World Cup 1988 (winners)

O'Leary, JE
(Ireland): Home Int 1969-70; Eur T Ch 1969

O'Neill, JJ
(Ireland): Home Int 1968

O'Rourke, P
(Ireland): Home Int 1980-81-82-84-85

O'Sullivan, DF
(Ireland): Home Int 1976-85-86-87-91; Eur T Ch 1977

O'Sullivan, WM
(Ireland): Home Int 1934-35-36-37-38-47-48-49-50-51-53-54

Oldcorn, A
(England): Home Int 1982-83. (GBI): Walker Cup 1983

Omelia, B
(Ireland): Home Int 1994

Oosterhuis, PA
(England): Home Int 1966-67-68. (GBI): Walker Cup 1967; *v* Europe 1968; World Team Ch 1968

Oppenheimer, RH
(England): *v* Ireland 1928-29-30; *v* Scotland 1930. (GBI): Walker Cup 1957 (Captain)

Osgood, TH
(Scotland): *v* England 1925

Owen, JB
(Wales): Home Int 1971

Owens, GF
(Wales): Home Int 1960-61

Ownes, GH
(Ireland): Home Int 1935-37-38-47

Page, P
(England): Home Int 1993. (GBI): Walker Cup 1993

Palferman, H
(Wales): Home Int 1950-53

Palmer, DJ
(England): Home Int 1962-63

Pardoe, S
(Wales): Home Int 1991

Parfitt, RWM
(Wales): *v* Ireland 1924

Park, D
(Wales): Home Int 1994

Parkin, AP
(Wales): Home Int 1980-81-82. (GBI): Walker Cup 1983

Parry, JR
(Wales): Home Int 1966-75-76-77; *v* France 1976

Patey, IR
(England): Home Int 1952; *v* France 1948-49-50

Paton, DA
(Scotland): Home Int 1991

Patrick, KG
(Scotland): Home Int 1937

Patterson, AH
(Ireland): *v* Wales 1913

Pattinson, R
(England): Home Int 1949

Payne, J
(England): Home Int 1950-51

Payne, J
(England): Home Int 1989-90; Eur T Ch 1991. (GBI): Walker Cup 1991; *v* Europe 1990

Pearson, AG
(GBI): *v* South Africa 1927

Pearson, MJ
(England): Home Int 1951-52

Pease, JWB (*later* **Lord Wardington)**
(England): *v* Scotland 1903-04-05-06

Pennink, JJF
(England): Home Int 1937-38-47; *v* France 1937-38-39. (GBI): Walker Cup 1938

Perkins, TP
(England): *v* Scotland 1927-28-29. (GBI): Walker Cup 1928

Perowne, AH
(England): Home Int 1947-48-49-50-51-53-54-55-57. (GBI): Walker Cup 1949-53-59; World Team Ch 1958

Peters, GB
(Scotland): Home Int 1934-35-36-37-38. (GBI): Walker Cup 1936-38

Peters, JL
(Wales): Home Int 1987-88-89

Phillips, LA
(Wales): *v* Ireland 1913

Phillips, V
(GBI): Walker Cup 1993

Pierse, AD
(Ireland): Home Int 1976-77-78-80-81-82-83-84-85-87-88; *v* Wales 1979; *v* France, West Germany, Sweden 1980; Eur T Ch 1981. (GBI): Walker Cup 1983; *v* Europe 1980

Pinch, AG
(Wales): Home Int 1969

Pirie, AK
(Scotland): Home Int 1966-67-68-69-70-71-72-73-74-75; Eur T Ch 1967-69; *v* Belgium 1973-75; *v* Spain 1974.
(GBI): Walker Cup 1967; *v* Europe 1970

Plaxton, J
(England): Home Int 1983-84

Pollin, RKM
(Ireland): Home Int 1971; Eur T Ch 1973

Pollock, VA
(England): *v* Scotland 1908

Povall, J
(Wales): Home Int 1960-61-62-63-65-66-67-68-69-70-71-72-73-74-75-76-77; Eur T Ch 1967-69-71-73-75-77; *v* France 1975-76; *v* Denmark 1976. (GBI): *v* Europe 1962

Powell, WA
(England): *v* Scotland 1923-24; *v* Wales/Ireland 1925

Power, E
(Ireland): Home Int 1987-88-93-94

Power, M
(Ireland): Home Int 1947-48-49-50-51-52-54

Poxon, MA
(England): Home Int 1975-76; Eur T Ch 1975. (GBI): Walker Cup 1975

Pressdee, RNG
(Wales): Home Int 1958-59-60-61-62

Pressley, J
(Scotland): Home Int 1947-48-49

Price, JP
(Wales): Home Int 1986-87-88

Price, R
(Wales): Home Int 1994

Prosser, D
(England): Eur T Ch 1989

Pugh, RS
(Wales): *v* Ireland 1923-24-29

Pullan, M
(England): Home Int 1991-92

Purcell, J
(Ireland): Home Int 1973

Pyman, I
(England): Home Int 1993. (GBI): Walker Cup 1993

Raeside, A
(Scotland): *v* Ireland 1929

Rafferty, R
(Ireland): *v* Wales 1979; Home Int 1980-81; *v* France, West Germany, Sweden 1980; Eur T Ch 1981.
(GBI): Walker Cup 1981; *v* Europe 1980; World Team Ch 1980

Rainey, WHE
(Ireland): Home Int 1962

Rankin, G
(Scotland): Home Int 1994

Rawlinson, D
(England): Home Int 1949-50-52-53

Ray, D
(England): Home Int 1982; *v* France 1982

Rayfus, P
(Ireland): Home Int 1986-87-88

Reade, HE
(Ireland): *v* Wales 1913

Reddan, B
(Ireland): Home Int 1987

Rees, CN
(Wales): Home Int 1986-88-89-91-92-94

Rees, DA
(Wales): Home Int 1961-62-63-64

Reid, A
(Scotland): Home Int 1993-94; Eur T Ch 1993; *v* Spain 1994; *v* Italy 1994

Renfrew, RL
(Scotland): Home Int 1964

Renwick, G, jr
(Wales): *v* Ireland 1923

Revell, RP
(England): Home Int 1972-73; Eur T Ch 1973

Ricardo, W
(Wales); *v* Ireland 1930-31; *v* Scotland 1931

Rice, JH
(Ireland): Home Int 1947-52

Rice-Jones, L
(Wales): *v* Ireland 1924

Richards, PM
(Wales): Home Int 1960-61-62-63-71

Richardson, S
(England): Home Int 1986-87-88

Risdon, PWL
(England): Home Int 1935-36

Robb, J, jr
(Scotland): *v* England 1902-03-05-06-07

Robb, WM
(Scotland): Home Int 1935

Roberts, AT
(Scotland): *v* Ireland 1931

Roberts, G
(Scotland): Home Int 1937-38

Roberts, GP
(England): Home Int 1951-53; *v* France 1949

Roberts, H
(Wales): Home Int 1992-93

Roberts, HJ
(England): Home Int 1947-48-53

Roberts, J
(Wales): Home Int 1937

Roberts, SB
(Wales): Home Int 1932-33-34-35-37-38-47-48-49-50-51-52-53-54

Roberts, WJ
(Wales): Home Int 1948-49-50-51-52-53-54

Robertson, A
(England): Home Int 1986-87; *v* France 1988

Robertson, CW
(Ireland): *v* Wales 1930; *v* Scotland 1930

Robertson, D
(Scotland): Home Int 1991-92-93; *v* Sweden 1992; *v* Italy 1992; *v* France 1993; Eur T Ch 1993.
(GBI): Walker Cup 1993; *v* Europe 1992; World Team Ch 1992

Robertson, DM
(Scotland): Home Int 1973-74; *v* Spain 1974

Robertson-Durham, JA
(Scotland): *v* England 1911

Robinson, J
(England): *v* Ireland 1928

Robinson, J
(England): Home Int 1986.
(GBI): Walker Cup 1987

Robinson, S
(England): *v* Scotland 1925; *v* Ireland 1928-29-30

Roderick, RN
(Wales): Home Int 1983-84-85-86-87-88. (GBI) *v* Europe 1988.
(GBI): Walker Cup 1989

Rogers, A
(England): Home Int 1991; *v* France 1992

Rolfe, B
(Wales): Home Int 1963-65

Roobottom, EL
(Wales): Home Int 1967

Roper, HS
(England): *v* Ireland 1931; *v* Scotland 1931

Roper, MS
(Wales): *v* Ireland 1979

Roper, R
(England): Home Int 1984-85-86-87

Rothwell, J
(England): Home Int 1947-48

Russell, R
(Scotland): Home Int 1992-93; *v* France 1993; Eur T Ch 1993. (GBI): Walker Cup, 1993

Rutherford, DS
(Scotland): *v* Ireland 1929

Rutherford, R
(Scotland): Home Int 1938-47

Saddler, AC
(Scotland): Home Int 1959-60-61-62-63-64-66; *v* Scandinavia 1962; Eur T Ch 1965-67-(75)-(77). (GBI): Walker Cup 1963-65-67-77 (Captain); *v* Europe 1960-62-64-66; CW 1959-63-67; World Team Ch 1962

Sandywell, A
(England): Home Int 1990; Eur T Ch 1991

Scannel, BJ
(Ireland): Home Int 1947-48-49-50-51-53-54

Scott, KB
(England): Home Int 1937-38; *v* France 1938

Scott, Hon M
(England): *v* Scotland 1911-12-23-24-25-26. (GBI): Walker Cup 1924-34 (Captain); *v* Australia 1934

Scott, Hon O
(England): *v* Scotland 1902-05-06

Scott, R, jr
(Scotland): *v* England 1924-28. (GBI): Walker Cup 1924

Scott, WGF
(Scotland): *v* Ireland 1927

Scratton, EWHB
(England): *v* Scotland 1912

Scroggie: FH
(Scotland): *v* England 1910

Scrutton, PF
(England): Home Int 1950-55. (GBI): Walker Cup 1955-57

Sewell, D
(England): Home Int 1956-57-58-59-60. (GBI): Walker Cup 1957-59; CW 1959; World Team Ch 1960

Shade, RDBM
(Scotland): Home Int 1957-60-61-62-63-64-65-66-67-68; *v* Scandinavia 1960-62; Eur T Ch 1965-67. (GBI): Walker Cup 1961-63-65-67; *v* Europe 1962-64-66-68; World Team Ch 1962-64-66-68; CW 1963-67

Shaw, G
(Scotland): Home Int 1984-86-87-88-90; *v* West Germany 1987; *v* Sweden 1984; *v* France 1987; Eur T Ch 1987. (GBI): Walker Cup 1987

Sheals, HS
(Ireland): *v* Wales 1929; *v* England 1929-30-31; *v* Scotland 1930; Home Int 1932-33

Sheahan, D
(Ireland): Home Int 1961-62-63-64-65-66-67-70. (GBI): Walker Cup 1963; *v* Europe 1962-64-67

Sheppard, M
(Wales): Home Int 1990

Shepperson, AE
(England): Home Int 1956-57-58-59-60-62. (GBI): Walker Cup 1957-59

Sherborne, A
(England): Home Int 1982-83-84

Sherry, G
(Scotland): Home Int 1993-94; *v* France 1993; *v* Spain 1994. (GBI): *v* Europe 1994; World Team Ch 1994

Shields, B
(Scotland):Home Int 1986

Shingler, TR
(England): Home Int 1977

Shorrock, TJ
(England): *v* France 1952

Simcox, R
(Ireland): *v* Wales 1930-31; *v* Scotland 1930-31; *v* England 1931; Home Int 1932-33-34-35-36-38

Simpson, AF
(Scotland): *v* Ireland 1928; *v* England 1927

Simpson, JG
(Scotland): *v* England 1906-07-08-09-11-12-22-24-26. (GBI): *v* America 1921

Sinclair, A
(Scotland): Home Int 1950

Slark, WA
(England): Home Int 1957

Slater, A
(England): Home Int 1955-62

Slattery, B
(Ireland): Home Int 1947-48

Sludds, MF
(Ireland): Home Int 1982

Smith, Eric M
(England): *v* Ireland 1931; *v* Scotland 1931

Smith, Everard
(England): *v* Scotland 1908-09-10-12

Smith, GF
(England): *v* Scotland 1902-03

Smith, JN
(Scotland): *v* Ireland 1928-30-31; *v* England 1929-30-31; *v* Wales 1931; Home Int 1932-33-34. (GBI): Walker Cup 1930

Smith, JR
(England): Home Int 1932

Smith, LOM
(England): Home Int 1963

Smith, M
(Wales): Home Int 1993-94

Smith, S
(Scotland): *v* Austria 1994

Smith, VH
(Wales): *v* Ireland 1924-25

Smith, W
(England): Home Int 1972. (GBI): *v* Europe 1972

Smith, WD
(Scotland): Home Int 1957-58-59-60-63; *v* Scandinavia 1958-60. (GBI): Walker Cup 1959; *v* Europe 1958

Smyth, D
(Ireland): Home Int 1972-73; Eur T Ch 1973

Smyth, DW
(Ireland): *v* Wales 1923-30; *v* England 1930; *v* Scotland 1931; Home Int 1933

Smyth, HB
(Ireland): Home Int 1974-75-76-78; Eur T Ch 1975-79; *v* France, West Germany, Sweden 1976. (GBI): *v* Europe 1976

Smyth, V
(Ireland): Home Int 1981-82

Snowdon, J
(England): Home Int 1934

Soulby, DEB
(Ireland): *v* Wales 1929-30; *v* England 1929-30; *v* Scotland 1929-30

Spiller, EF
(Ireland): *v* Wales 1924; *v* England 1928; *v* Scotland 1928-29

Squirrell, HC
(Wales): Home Int 1955-56-57-58-59-60-61-62-63-64-65-66-67-68-69-70-71-73-74-75; Eur T Ch 1967-69-71-75; *v* France 1975

Stanford, M
(England): Home Int 1991-92-93; *v* France 1992. (GBI): Walker Cup 1993; *v* Europe 1992; World Team Ch 1992

Staunton, R
(Ireland): Home Int 1964-65-72; Eur T Ch 1973

Steel, DMA
(England): Home Int 1970

Stephen, AR
(Scotland): Home Int 1971-72-73-74-75-76-77-84-85; Eur T Ch 1975-85; *v* France 1985; *v* Spain 1974; *v* Belgium 1975-77-78. (GBI): Walker Cup 1985; *v* Europe 1972

Stevens, DI
(Wales): Home Int 1968-69-70-74-75-76-77-78-80-82; Eur T Ch 1969-77; *v* France 1976; *v* Denmark 1977

Stevens, LB
(England): *v* Scotland 1912

Stevenson, A
(Scotland): Home Int 1949

Stevenson, JB
(Scotland): *v* Ireland 1931; Home Int 1932-38-47-49-50-51

Stevenson, JF
(Ireland): *v* Wales 1923-24; *v* England 1925

Stevenson, K
(Ireland): Home Int 1972

Stockdale, B
(England): Home Int 1964-65

Stoker, K
(Wales): *v* Ireland 1923-24

Stokoe, GC
(Wales): *v* England 1925; *v* Ireland 1929-30

Storey, EF
(England): *v* Scotland 1924-25-26-27-28-30; Home Int 1936; *v* France 1936. (GBI): Walker Cup 1924-26-28

Stott, HAN
(England): Home Int 1976-77

Stout, JA
(England): *v* Scotland 1928-29-30-31; *v* Ireland 1929-31. (GBI): Walker Cup 1930-32

Stowe, C
(England): Home Int 1935-36-37-38-47-49-54; *v* France 1938-39-49. (GBI): Walker Cup 1938-47

Strachan, CJL
(Scotland): Home Int 1965-66-67; Eur T Ch 1967

Straker, R
(England): Home Int 1932

Streeter, P
(England): Home Int 1992; *v* France 1994

Stuart, HB
(Scotland): Home Int 1967-68-69-70-71-72-73-74-76; Eur T Ch 1969-71-73-75; *v* Belgium 1973-75. (GBI): Walker Cup 1971-73-75; *v* Europe 1968-72-74; CW 1971; World Team Ch 1972

Stuart, JE
(Scotland): Home Int 1959

Stubbs, AK
(England): Home Int 1982

Suneson, C
(England): Home Int 1988; Eur T Ch 1989

Sutherland, DMG
(England): Home Int 1947

Sutton, W
(England): *v* Scotland 1929-31; *v* Ireland 1929-30-31

Symonds, A
(Wales): *v* Ireland 1925

Taggart, J
(Ireland): Home Int 1953

Tait, AG
(Scotland): Home Int 1987-88-89; Nixdorf Nations Cup 1989

Tate, JK
(England): Home Int 1954-55-56

Taylor, GN
(Scotland): Home Int 1948

Taylor, HE
(England): *v* Scotland 1911

Taylor, JS
(Scotland): *v* England 1979; Home Int 1980; *v* Belgium 1980; *v* France 1980

Taylor, LG
(Scotland): Home Int 1955-56

Taylor, TPD
(Wales): Home Int 1963

Thirlwell, A
(England): Home Int 1951-52-54-55-56-57-58-63-64. (GBI): Walker Cup 1957; *v* Europe 1956-58-64; CW 1953-64

Thirsk, TJ
(England): *v* Ireland 1929; Home Int 1933-34-35-36-37-38; *v* France 1935-36-37-38-39

Thom, KG
(England): Home Int 1947-48-49-53. (GBI): Walker Cup 1949

Thomas, I
(England): Home Int 1933

Thomas, KR
(Wales): Home Int 1951-52

Thompson, ASG
(England): Home Int 1935-37

Thompson, MS
(England): Home Int 1982. (GBI): Walker Cup 1983

Thomson, AP
(Scotland): Home Int 1970; Eur T Ch 1971

Thomson, H
(Scotland): Home Int 1934-35-36-37-38. (GBI): Walker Cup 1936-38

Thomson, JA
(Scotland): Home Int 1981-82-83-84-85-86-87-88-89-91-92; Eur T Ch 1983; *v* West Germany 1987; *v* Italy 1984-86-88-90; *v* Sweden 1990

Thorburn, K
(Scotland): *v* England 1928; *v* Ireland 1927

Timbey, JC
(Ireland): *v* Scotland 1928-31; *v* Wales 1931

Timmis, CW
(England): *v* Ireland 1930; Home Int. 1936-37

Tipping, EB
(England): *v* Ireland 1930

Tipple, ER
(England): *v* Ireland 1928-29; Home Int 1932

Tolley, CJH
(England): *v* Scotland 1922-23-24-25-26-27-28-29-30; Home Int 1936-37-38; *v* Ireland/Wales 1925; *v* France 1938. (GBI): *v* America 1921, Walker Cup 1922-23-24 (Captain) -26-30-34; *v* South Africa 1927

Tooth, EA
(Wales): *v* Ireland 1913

Torrance, TA
(Scotland): *v* England 1922-23-25-26-28-29-30; Home Int 1933. (GBI): Walker Cup 1924-28-30-32 (Captain) -34

Torrance, WB
(Scotland): *v* England 1922-23-24-26-27-28-30; *v* Ireland 1928-29-30. (GBI): Walker Cup 1922

Townsend, PM
(England): Home Int 1965-66. (GBI): Walker Cup 1965; *v* Europe 1966; World Team Ch 1966

Toye, JL
(Wales): Home Int 1963-64-65-66-67-69-70-71-72-73-74-76-78; Eur T Ch 1971-73-75-77; *v* France 1975

Tredinnick, SV
(England): Home Int 1950

Tucker, WI
(Wales): Home Int 1949-50-51-52-53-54-55-56-57-58-59-60-61-62-63-64-65-66-67-68-69-70-71-72-74-75; Eur T Ch 1967-69-75; *v* France 1975

Tulloch, W
(Scotland): *v* England 1927-29-30-31; *v* Ireland 1930-31; *v* Wales 1931; Home Int 1932

Tupling, LP
(England): Home Int 1969; Eur T Ch 1969. (GBI): Walker Cup 1969

Turnbull, CH
(Wales): *v* Ireland 1913-25

Turner, A
(England): Home Int 1952

Turner, GB
(Wales): Home Int 1947-48-49-50-51-52-55-56

Tweddell, W
(England): *v* Scotland 1928-29-30; Home Int 1935.(GBI): Walker Cup 1928 (Captain) -36 (Captain)

Twynholm, S
(Scotland): Home Int 1990. Nixdorf Nations Cup 1990

Urquhart, M
(Scotland): Home Int 1993

Vannet, L
(Scotland): Home Int 1984

Waddell, G
(Ireland): *v* Wales 1925

Walker, J
(Scotland): Home Int 1954-55-57-58-60-61-62-63; *v* Scandinavia 1958-62. (GBI): Walker Cup 1961; *v* Europe 1958-60

Walker, KH
(Scotland): Home Int 1985-86

Walker, MS
(England): *v* Ireland/Wales 1925

Walker, RS
(Scotland): Home Int 1935-36

Wallis, G
(Wales): Home Int 1934-36-37-38

Walls, MPD
(England): Home Int 1980-81-85

Walters, EM
(Wales): Home Int 1967-68-69; Eur T Ch 1969

Walton, AR
(England): Home Int 1934-35

Walton, P
(Ireland): *v* Wales 1979: Home Int 1980-81; *v* France, Germany, Sweden 1980; Eur T Ch 1981. (GBI): Walker Cup 1981-83

Warren, KT
(England): Home Int 1962

Watson, CR
(Scotland): Home Int 1991-92-94; *v* Sweden 1992; *v* Italy 1992; *v* Austria 1994

Watt, AW
(Scotland): Home Int 1987

Watts, C
(England): Home Int 1991-92; *v* France 1992

Way, P
(England): Home Int 1981; Eur T Ch 1981. (GBI): Walker Cup 1981.

Webster, A
(Scotland): Home Int 1978

Webster, F
(Ireland): Home Int 1949

Weeks, K
(England): Home Int 1987-88; *v* France 1988

Welch, L
(Ireland): Home Int 1936

Welch, M
(England): Home Int 1993-94; *v* France 1994

Wemyss, DS
(Scotland): Home Int 1937

Werner, LE
(Ireland): *v* Wales 1925

West, CH
(Ireland): *v* England 1928; Home Int 1932

Westwood, L
(England): Home Int 1993

Wethered, RH
(England): *v* Scotland 1922-23-24-25-26-27-28-29-30.(GBI): *v* America 1921, Walker Cup 1922-23-26-30 (Captain) -34

White, L
(England): Home Int 1990; Eur T Ch 1991. (GBI): Walker Cup 1991

White, RJ
(England): Home Int 1947-48-49-53-54. (GBI): Walker Cup 1947-49-51-53-55

Whyte, AW
(Scotland): Home Int 1934

Wiggett, M
(England): Home Int 1990

Wilkie, DF
(Scotland): Home Int 1962-63-65-67-68

Wilkie, G
(Scotland): *v* England 1911

Wilkie, GT
(Wales): Home Int 1938

Wilkinson, S
(Wales): Home Int 1990-91

Willcox, FS
(Wales): *v* Scotland 1931; *v* Ireland 1931

Williams, DF
(England): *v* Scotland 1979

Williams KH
(Wales): Home Int 1983-84-85-86-87

Williams, PG
(Wales): *v* Ireland 1925

Williamson, SB
(Scotland): Home Int 1947-48-49-51-52

Willison, R
(England): Home Int 1988-89-90; Eur T Ch 1989-91. (GBI): Walker Cup 1991; *v* Europe 1990. World Cup 1990

Wills, M
(Wales): Home Int 1990

Wilson, E
(Scotland): Home Int 1985

Wilson, J
(Scotland): *v* England 1922-23-24-26; *v* Ireland 1932. (GBI): Walker Cup 1923

Wilson, JC
(Scotland): Home Int 1947-48-49-51-52-53; *v* Sweden 1950; *v* New Zealand 1954. (GBI): Walker Cup 1947-53; *v* South Africa 1954; CW 1954

Wilson, P
(Scotland): Home Int 1976; Belgium 1977

Winchester, R
(England): Home Int 1985-87-89

Winfield, HB
(Wales): *v* Ireland 1913

Winter, G
(England): Home Int 1991

Wise, WS
(England): Home Int 1947

Wolstenholme, GB
(England): Home Int 1953-55-56-57-58-59-60 (GBI): Walker Cup 1957-59; World Team Ch 1958-60; CW 1959

Wolstenholme, GP
(England): Home Int 1988-89-90-91-92-93-94; *v* France 1988-92-94. (GBI): *v* Europe 1992-94

Wood, DK
(Wales): Home Int 1982-83-84-85-86-87

Woollam, J
(England): Home Int 1933-34-35; *v* France 1935

Woolley, FA
(England): *v* Scotland 1910-11-12

Woosnam, I
(Wales): *v* France 1976

Worthington, JS
(England): *v* Scotland 1905

Wright, I
(Scotland): Home Int 1958-59-60-61; *v* Scandinavia 1960-62

Yeo, J
(England): Home 1971

Young, D
(Ireland): Home Int 1969-70-77

Young, ID
(Scotland): Home Int 1981-82; *v* France 1982. (GBI): *v* Europe 1982

Young, JR
(Scotland): Home Int 1960-61-65; *v* Scandinavia 1960. (GB): *v* Europe 1960

Zacharias, JP
(England): Home Int 1935

Zoete, HW de
(England): *v* Scotland 1903-04-06-07

British Isles International Players, Amateur Ladies

Abbreviations

Eur L T Ch played in European Ladies Amateur Team Championship
Home Int played in Home International matches
Previous surnames are shown in brackets.

Aitken, E (Young)
(Scotland): Home Int 1954

Alexander, M
(Ireland): Home Int 1920-21-22-30

Allen, F
(England): Home Int 1952

Allington Hughes, Miss
(Wales): Home Int 1908-09-10-12-14-22-25

Anderson, E
(Scotland): Home Int 1910-11-12-21-25

Anderson, F
(Scotland): Home Int 1977-79-80-81-83-84-86-87-88-89-90-91-92; Eur L T Ch 1979-83-87-91. (GBI): Vagliano Trophy 1987

Anderson, H
(Scotland): Home Int 1964-65-68-69-70-71; Eur L T Ch 1969. (GBI): Vagliano Trophy 1969

Anderson, J (Donald)
(Scotland): Home Int 1947-48-49-50-51-52-53. (GBI): Curtis Cup 1948-50-52

Anderson, L.
(Scotland): Home Int 1986-87-88-89; Eur L T Ch 1987-89

Anderson, VH
(Scotland): Home Int 1907

Arbuthnot, M
(Ireland): Home Int 1921

Archer, A (Rampton)
(England): Home Int 1968 (Captain)

Armstrong, M
(Ireland): Home Int 1906

Ashcombe, Lady
(Wales): Home Int 1950-51-52-53-54

Aubertin, Mrs
(Wales): Home Int 1908-09-10

Bailey, D [Frearson] (Robb)
(England): Home Int 1961-62-71; Eur L T Ch 1968-93 (Captain). (GBI): Curtis Cup 1962-72-84 (Captain)-86 (Captain)-88(Captain); Vagliano Trophy 1961-83(Captain) -85 (Captain); CW 1983

Baker, J
(Wales): Home Int 1990

Bald, J
(Scotland): Home Int 1968-69-71; Eur L T Ch 1969

Barber, S (Bonallack)
(England): Home Int 1960-61-62-68-70-72-77-78 (Captain); Eur L T Ch 1969-71. (GBI): Curtis Cup 1962; Vagliano Trophy 1961-63-69

Barclay, C (Brisbane)
(Scotland): Home Int 1953-61-68

Bargh Etherington, B (Whitehead)
(England): Home Int 1974

Barlow, Mrs
(Ireland): Home Int 1921

Barron, M
(Wales): Home Int 1929-30-31-34-35-36-37-38-39-47-48-49-50-51-52-53-54-55-56-57-58-60-61-62-63

Barry, L
(England): Home Int 1911-12-13-14

Barry, P
(England): Home Int 1982

Barton, P
(England): Home Int 1935-36-37-38-39. (GBI): Curtis Cup 1934-36

Bastin, G
(England): Home Int 1920-21-22-23-24-25

Bayliss, Mrs
(Wales): Home Int 1921

Bayman, L (Denison Pender)
(England): Home Int 1971-72-73-83-84-85-87-88; Eur L T Ch 1985-87-89. (GBI) Curtis Cup 1988; Vagliano Trophy 1971-85-87; Espirito Santo 1988

Baynes, Mrs CE
(Scotland): Home Int 1921-22

Beck, B (Pim)
(Ireland): Home Int 1930-31-32-33-34-36-37-47-48-49-50-51-52-53-54-55-56-58-59-61

Beckett, J
(Ireland): Home Int 1962-66-67-68: Eur L T Ch 1967

Beddows, C [Watson] (Stevenson)
(Scotland): Home Int 1913-14-21-22-23-27-29-30-31-32-33-34-35-36-37-39-47-48-49-50-51. (GBI): Curtis Cup 1932

Behan, L
(Ireland): Home Int 1984-85-86. (GBI): Curtis Cup 1986; Vagliano Trophy 1985

Beharrell, V (Anstey)
(England): Home Int 1955-56-57-61 (Captain). (GBI): Curtis Cup 1956

Benka, P (Tredinnick)
(England): Home Int 1967. (GBI): Curtis Cup 1966-68; Vagliano Trophy 1967

Bennett, L
(Scotland): Home Int 1977-80-81

Benton, MH
(Scotland): Home Int 1914

Birmingham, M
(Ireland): Home Int 1967(Captain)

Bisgood, J
(England) Home Int 1949-50-51-52-53-54-56-58. (GBI): Curtis Cup 1950-52-54-70(Captain)

Blair, N (Menzies)
(Scotland): Home Int 1955

Blake, Miss
(Ireland): Home Int 1931-32-34-35-36

Blaymire, J
(England): Home Int 1971-88-89(Captain)

Bloodworth, D (Lewis)
(Wales): Home Int 1954-55-56-57-60

Boatman, EA (Collis)
(England): Home Int 1974-80-84 (Captain)-85 (Captain)-90 (Captain)-91 (Captain); Eur L T Ch 1985 (Captain)-87 (Captain). (GBI): Curtis Cup 1992 (Captain)-94 (Captain); CW 1987 (Captain)-91 (Captain)

Bolas, R
(England): Home Int 1992

Bolton, Z (Bonner Davis)
(England): Home Int 1939-48-49-50-51-55-(Captain)-56. (GBI): Curtis Cup 1948-56(Captain)-66(Captain)-68(Captain)-94 (Captain); CW 1967

Bonallack, A (Ward)
(England): Home Int 1956-57-58-59-60-61-62-63-64-65 (Captain)-66-72. (GBI): Curtis Cup 1956-58-60-62-64-66; Vagliano Trophy 1959-61-63

Bostock, M
(England): Home Int 1954 (Captain)

Bourn, Mrs
(England): Home Int 1909-12

Bowhill, M (Robertson-Durham)
(Scotland): Home Int 1936-37-38

Boyd, J
(Ireland): Home Int 1912-13-14

Boyes, S
(Wales): Home Int 1992

Bradley, K (Rawlings)
(Wales): Home Int 1975-76-77-78-79-82-83

Bradshaw, E
(Ireland): Home Int 1964-66-67-68-69-70-71-74-75-80 (Captain)-81(Captain); Eur L T Ch 1969-71-75. (GBI): Vagliano Trophy 1969-71

Brandom, G
(Ireland): Home Int 1965-66-67-68; Eur L T Ch 1967. (GBI): Vagliano Trophy 1967

Brearley, M
(Wales): Home Int 1937-38

Brennan, R (Hegarty)
(Ireland): Home Int 1974-75-76-77-78-79-81

Brice, Mrs
(Ireland): Home Int 1948

Bridges, Mrs
(Wales): Home Int 1933-38-39

Briggs, A (Brown)
(Wales): Home Int 1969-70-71-72-73-74-75-76-77-78-79-80-81 (Captain) -82 (Captain)-83 (Captain) -84-93 (Captain); Eur L T Ch 1971-75. (GBI): Vagliano Trophy 1971-75

Brinton, Mrs
(Ireland): Home Int 1922

Bromley-Davenport, I (Rieben)
(Wales): Home Int 1932-33-34-35-36-48-50-51-52-53-54-55-56

Brook, D
(Wales): Home Int 1913

Brooks, E
(Ireland): Home Int 1953-54-56

Broun, JG
(Scotland): Home Int 1905-06-07-21

Brown, B
(Ireland): Home Int 1960

Brown, E (Jones)
(Wales): Home Int 1947-48-49-50-52-53-57-58-59-60-61-62-63-64-65-66-68-69-70

Brown, F
(England): Home Int 1994

Brown, Mrs FW (Gilroy)
(Scotland): Home Int 1905-06-07-08-09-10-11-13-21

Brown, J
(Wales): Home Int 1960-61-62-64-65; Eur L T Ch 1965-69

Brown, J
(England): Home Int 1984

Brown, TWL
(Scotland): Home Int 1924-25

Brown, Mrs
(Wales): Home Int 1924-25-27

Brownlow, Miss
(Ireland): Home Int 1923

Bryan-Smith, S
(Wales): Home Int 1947-48-49-50-51-52-56

Burnell, S
(England): Home Int 1993; Eur L T Ch 1993

Burrell, Mrs
(Wales): Home Int 1939

Burton, H (Mitchell)
(Scotland): Home Int 1931-55-56-59(Captain). (GBI): Vagliano Trophy 1961

Burton, M
(England): Home Int 1975-76

Butler, I (Burke)
(Ireland): Home Int 1962-63-64-65-66-68-70-71-72-73-76-77-78-79-86(Captain)-87(Captain): Eur L T Ch 1967. (GBI): Curtis Cup 1966; Vagliano Trophy 1965; Espirito Santo 1964-66

Buxton, N
(England): Home Int 1991-92-93; Eur LT Ch 1991-93. (GBI): Curtis Cup 1992; Vagliano Trophy 1991-93

Byrne, A (Sweeney)
(Ireland): Home Int 1959-60-61-62-63-90(Captain)-91(Captain)

Cadden, G
(Scotland): Home Int 1974-75

Cairns, Lady Katherine
(England): Home Int 1947-48-50-51-52-53-54. (GBI): Curtis Cup 1952(Captain)

Caldwell, C (Redford)
(England): Home Int 1973-78-79-80. (GBI): Curtis Cup 1978-80; Vagliano Trophy 1973

Callen, L
(Ireland): Home Int 1990

Campbell, J (Burnett)
(Scotland): Home Int 1960

Cann, M (Nuttall)
(England): Home Int 1966

Carrick, P (Bullard)
(England): Home Int 1939-47

Caryl, M
(Wales): Home Int 1929

Casement, M (Harrison)
(Ireland): Home Int 1909-10-11-12-13-14

Cassidy, Y
(Ireland): Home Int 1994

Cautley, B (Hawtrey)
(England): Home Int 1912-13-14-22-23-24-25-27

Chambers, D
(England): Home Int 1906-07-09-10-11-12-20-24-25. (GBI): Curtis Cup 1934 (Captain)-36 (Captain)-38 (Captain)

Christison, D
(England): Home Int 1981

Chugg, P (Light)
(Wales): Home Int 1973-74-75-76-77-78-86-87-78; Eur L T Ch 1975-87

Clark, G (Atkinson)
(England): Home Int 1955

Clarke, Mrs ML
(England): Home Int 1933-35

Clarke, P
(England): Home Int 1981

Clarke, Mrs
(Ireland): Home Int 1922

Clarkson, H (Reynolds)
(Wales): Home Int 1935-38-39

Clay, E
(Wales): Home Int 1912

Clement, V
(England): Home Int 1932-34-35

Close, M (Wenyon)
(England): Home Int 1968-69; Eur L T Ch 1969. (GBI): Vagliano Trophy 1969

Coats, Mrs G
(Scotland): Home Int 1931-32-33-34

Cochrane, K
(Scotland): Home Int 1924-25-28-29-30

Collett, P
(England): Home Int 1910

Collingham, J (Melville)
(England): Home Int 1978-79-81-84-86-87-92; Eur L T Ch 1989. (GBI): Vagliano Trophy 1979-87; CW 1987

Colquhoun, H
(Ireland): Home Int 1959-60-61-63

Comboy, C (Grott)
(England): Home Int 1975 (Captain) -76 (Captain). (GBI): Curtis Cup 1978 (Captain)-80 (Captain); Vagliano Trophy 1977 (Captain) - 1979 (Captain); Espirito Santo 1978 (Captain); CW 1979

Connachan, J
(Scotland): Home Int 1979-80-81-82-83. (GBI): Curtis Cup 1980-82; Vagliano Trophy 1981-83; Espirito Santo 1980-82; CW 1983

Coote, Miss
(Ireland): Home Int 1925-28-29

Copley, K (Lackie)
(Scotland): Home Int 1974-75

Corlett, E
(England): Home Int 1927-29-30-31-32-33-35-36-37-38-39. (GBI): Curtis Cup 1932-38-64 (Captain)

Costello, G
(Ireland): Home Int 1973-84(Captain)-85(Captain)

Cotton, S (German)
(England): Home Int 1967-68; Eur L T Ch 1967. (GBI): Vagliano Trophy 1967

Couper, M
(Scotland): Home Int 1929-34-35-36-37-39-56

Cowley, Lady
(Wales): Home Int 1907-09

Cox, Margaret
(Wales): Home Int 1924-25

Cox, Nell
(Wales): Home Int 1954

Craik, T
(Scotland): Home Int 1988

Cramsie, F (Hezlet)
(Ireland): Home Int 1905-06-07-08-09-10-13-20-24

Crawford, I (Wylie)
(Scotland): Home Int 1970-71-72

Cresswell, K (Stuart)
(Scotland): Home Int 1909-10-11-12-14

Critchley, D (Fishwick)
(England): Home Int 1930-31-32-33-35-36-47. (GBI): Curtis Cup 1932-34-50 (Captain)

Croft, A
(England): Home Int 1927

Cross, M
(Wales): Home Int 1922

Cruickshank, DM (Jenkins)
(Scotland): Home Int 1910-11-12

Crummack, Miss
(England): Home Int 1909

Cuming, Mrs
(Ireland): Home Int 1910

Cunninghame, S
(Wales): Home Int 1922-25-29-31

Cuthell, R (Adair)
(Ireland): Home Int 1908

Dampney, S
(Wales): Home Int 1924-25-27-28-29-30

David, Mrs
(Wales): Home Int 1908

Davidson, B (Inglis)
(Scotland): Home Int 1928

Davies, K
(Wales): Home Int 1981-82-83; Eur L T Ch 1987. (GBI): Curtis Cup 1986-88; Vagliano Trophy 1987; CW 1987

Davies, L
(England): Home Int 1983-84. (GBI): Curtis Cup 1984; CW 1987

Davies, P (Griffiths)
(Wales): Home Int 1965-66-67-68-70-71-73; Eur L T Ch 1971

Deacon, Mrs
(Wales): Home Int 1912-14

Denny, A (Barrett)
(England): Home Int 1951

Dering, Mrs
(Ireland): Home Int 1923

Dermott, L
(Wales): Home Int 1987-88-89-91-92-93-94; Eur L T Ch 1991-93

Dickson, M
(Ireland): Home Int 1909

Dobson, H
(England): Home Int 1987-88-89; Eur L T Ch 1989. (GBI): Curtis Cup 1990; Vagliano Trophy 1989

Dod, L
(England): Home Int 1905

Donne, A
(Wales): Home Int 1993-94; Eur L T Ch 1993

Douglas, K
(England): Home Int 1981-82-83. (GBI): Curtis Cup 1982; Vagliano Trophy 1983

Dowling, D
(England): Home Int 1979

Draper, M [Peel] (Thomas)
(Scotland): Home Int 1929-34-38-49-50-51-52-53-54(Captain)-55 (Captain)-56-57-58-61 (Captain)-62. (GBI): Curtis Cup 1954; Vagliano Trophy 1963 (Captain)

Duggleby, E
(England): Home Int 1994

Duncan, B
(Wales): Home Int 1907-08-09-10-12

Duncan, M
(Wales): Home Int 1922-23-28-34

Duncan, MJ (Wood)
(Scotland): Home Int 1925-27-28-39

Durlacher, Mrs
(Ireland): Home Int 1905-06-07-08-09-10-14

Durrant, B [Green] (Lowe)
(England): Home Int 1954

Dwyer, Mrs
(Ireland): 1928

Eakin, P (James)
(Ireland): Home Int 1967

Eakin, T
(Ireland): Home Int 1990-91-92-93-94; Eur L T Ch 1993

Earner, M
(Ireland): Home Int 1960-61-62-63-70

Edmond, F
(England): Home Int 1991; Eur LT Ch 1991. (GBI): Vagliano Trophy 1991

Edwards, E
(Wales): Home Int 1949-50

Edwards, J
(Wales): Home Int 1932-33-34-36-37

Edwards, J (Morris)
(Wales): Home Int 1962-63-66-67-68-69-70-77(Captain)-78(Captain) -79 (Captain); Eur L T Ch 1967-69-93(Captain)

Egford, K
(England): Home Int 1992-94

Ellis, E
(Ireland): Home Int 1932-35-37-38

Ellis Griffiths (Mrs)
(Wales): Home Int 1907-08-09-12-13

Emery, MJ
(Wales): Home Int 1928-29-30-31-32-33-34-35-36-37-38-47

Evans, H
(England): Home Int 1908

Evans, N
(Wales): Home Int 1908-09-10-13

Everard, M
(England): Home Int 1964-67-69-70-72-73-77-78; Eur L T Ch 1967-71-77. (GBI): Curtis Cup 1970-72-74-78; Vagliano Trophy 1967-69-71-73; Espirito Santo 1968-72-78; CW 1971

Fairclough, L
(England): Home Int 1988-89-90; Eur L T Ch 1989. (GBI): Vagliano Trophy 1989

Falconer, V (Lamb)
(Scotland): Home Int 1932-36-37-47-48-49-50-51-52-53-54-55-56

Fallon, Gaynor, Z
(Ireland): Home Int 1952-53-54-55-56-57-58-59-60-61-62-63-64-65-68-69-70-72 (Captain). (GBI): Espirito Santo 1964

Farie-Anderson, J
(Scotland): Home Int 1924

Farquharson-Black, E
(Scotland): Home Int 1987-88-89-90-91; Eur L T Ch 1989-91. (GBI): Curtis Cup 1990-92; Vagliano Trophy 1989-91; CW 1991

Ferguson, A
(Ireland): Home Int 1989

Ferguson, D
(Ireland): Home Int 1927-28-29-30-31-32-34-35-36-37-38-61 (Captain). (GBI): Curtis Cup 1958(Captain)

Ferguson, M (Fowler)
(Scotland): Home Int 1959-62-63-64-65-66-67-69-70-85; Eur L T Ch 1965-67-71. (GBI): Curtis Cup 1966; Vagliano Trophy 1965

Ferguson R (Ogden)
(England): Home Int 1957

Fitzgibbon, M
(Ireland): Home Int 1920-21-29-30-31-32-33

FitzPatrick, O (Heskin)
(Ireland): Home Int 1967

Fletcher, L
(England): Home Int 1989-90; Eur LT Ch 1991. (GBI): Curtis Cup 1990; CW 1991

Fletcher, P (Sherlock)
(Ireland): Home Int 1932-34-35-36-38-39-54-55-66 (Captain)

Forbes, J
(Scotland): Home Int 1985-86-87-88-89; Eur L T Ch 1987-89

Ford, J
(Scotland): Home Int 1993-94

Foster, C
(England): Home Int 1905-06-09

Foster, J
(Wales): Home Int 1984-85-86-87-92; Eur L T Ch 1987-91

Fowler, J
(England): Home Int 1928

Franklin Thomas, E
(Wales): Home Int 1909

Freeguard, C
(Wales): Home Int 1927

Furby, J
(England): Home Int 1987-88; Eur L T Ch 1987

Fyshe, M
(England): Home Int 1938

Gallagher, S
(Scotland): Home Int 1983-84

Gardiner, A
(Ireland): Home Int 1927-29

Garfield Evans, PR (Whittaker)
(Wales): Home Int 1948-49-50-51-52-53-54-55(Captain)-56(Captain) -57 (Captain)-58(Captain)

Garon, MR
(England): Home Int 1927-28-32-33-34-36-37-38. (GBI); Curtis Cup 1936

Garrett, M (Ruttle)
(England): Home Int 1947-48-50-53-59(Captain)-60(Captain)-63(Captain). (GBI): Curtis Cup 1948-60(Captain); Vagliano Trophy 1959

Garvey, P
(Ireland): Home Int 1947-48-49-50-51-52-53-54(Captain)-56-57 (Captain) -58(Captain)-59(Captain) -60(Captain)-61-62-63-68-69. (GBI): Curtis Cup 1948-50-52-54-56-60; Vagliano Trophy 1959-63

Gear Evans, A
(Wales): Home Int 1932-33-34

Gee, Hon. J (Hives)
(England): Home Int 1950-51-52

Gemmill, A
(Scotland): Home Int 1981-82-84-85-86-87-88-89-91

Gethin Griffith, S
(Wales): Home Int 1914-22-23-24-28-29-30-31-35

Gibb, M (Titterton)
(England): Home Int 1906-07-08-10-12

Gibbs, C (Le Feuvre)
(England): Home Int 1971-72-73-74. (GBI): Curtis Cup 1974; Vagliano Trophy 1973

Gibbs, S
(Wales): Home Int 1933-34-39

Gildea, Miss
(Ireland): Home Int 1936-37-38-39

Glendinning, D
(Ireland): Home Int 1937-54

Glennie, H
(Scotland): Home Int 1959

Glover, A
(Scotland): Home Int 1905-06-08-09-12

Gold, N
(England): Home Int 1929-31-32

Gordon, J
352(England): Home Int 1947-48-49-52-53. (GBI): Curtis Cup 1948

Gorman, S
(Ireland): Home Int 1976-79-80-81-82-92(Captain)-93(Captain); Eur L T Ch 1993(Captain)

Gorry, Mary
(Ireland): Home Int 1971-72-73-74-75-76-77-78-79-80-88-89 (Captain); Eur L T Ch 1971-75. (GBI): Vagliano Trophy 1977

Gotto, Mrs C
(Ireland): Home Int 1923

Gotto, Mrs L
(Ireland): Home Int 1920

Gourlay, M
(England): Home Int 1923-24-27-28-29-30-32-33-34-38-57(Captain). (GBI): Curtis Cup 1932-34

Gow, J
(Scotland): Home Int 1923-24-27-28

Graham, MA
(Scotland): Home Int 1905-06

Graham, N
(Ireland): Home Int 1908-09-10-12

Granger Harrison, Mrs
(Scotland): Home Int 1922

Grant-Suttie, E
(Scotland): Home Int 1908-10-11-14-22-23

Grant-Suttie, R
(Scotland): Home Int 1914

Green, B (Pockett)
(England): Home Int 1939

Grice-Whittaker, P (Grice)
(England): Home Int 1983-84. (GBI): Curtis Cup 1984; Espirito Santo 1984

Griffith, W
(Wales): Home Int 1981

Griffiths, M
(England): Home Int 1920-21

Greenlees, E
(Scotland): Home Int 1924

Greenlees, Y
(Scotland): Home Int 1928-30-31-33-34-35-38

Guadella, E (Leitch)
(England): Home Int 1908-10-20-21-22-27-28-29-30-33

Gubbins, Miss
(Ireland): Home Int 1905

Hackett, B
(Ireland): Home Int 1993-94

Hackney, L
(England): Home Int 1990

Haig, J (Mathias Thomas)
(Wales): Home Int 1938-39

Hall, C
(England): Home Int 1991-92; Eur LT Ch 1991. (GBI): Curtis Cup 1992; Vagliano Trophy 1991

Hall, CM
(England): Home Int 1985

Hall, J (Wade)
(England): Home Int 1987-88-89-90-91-92-93-94; Eur L T Ch 1987-89-91-93. (GBI): Curtis Cup 1988-90-92-94; Espirito Santo 1988-90-94; Vagliano Trophy 1989-91-93; CW 1991

Hall, Mrs
(Ireland): Home Int 1927-30

Hamilton, S (McKinven)
(Scotland): Home Int 1965

Hambro, W (Martin Smith)
(England): Home Int 1914

Hamilton, J
(England): Home Int 1937-38-39

Hammond, T
(England): Home Int 1985

Hampson, M
(England): Home Int 1954

Hanna, D
(Ireland): Home Int 1987-88

Harrington, D
(Ireland): Home Int 1923

Harris, M [Spearman]
(England): Home Int 1955-56-57-58-59-60-61-62-63-64-65; Eur L T Ch 1965-71. (GBI): Curtis Cup 1960-62-64; Vagliano Trophy 1959-61-65; Espirito Santo 1964

Harrold, L
(England): Home Int 1974-75-76

Hartill, D
(England): Home Int 1923

Hartley, E
(England): Home Int 1964(Captain)

Hartley, R
(Wales): Home Int 1958-59-62

Hastings, D (Sommerville)
(Scotland): Home Int 1955-56-57-58-59-60-61-62-63. (GBI): Curtis Cup 1958; Vagliano Trophy 1963

Hay, J (Pelham Burn)
(Scotland): Home Int 1959

Hayter, J (Yuille)
(England): Home Int 1956

Hazlett, VP
(Ireland): Home Int 1956(Captain)

Healy, B (Gleeson)
(Ireland): Home Int 1980-82

Heathcoat-Amory, Lady (Joyce Wethered)
(England): Home Int 1921-22-23-24-25-29. (GBI): Curtis Cup 1932(Captain)

Hedges, S (Whitlock)
(England): Home Int 1979. (GBI): Vagliano Trophy 1979; CW 1979

Hedley Hill, Miss
(Wales): Home Int 1922

Hegarty, G
(Ireland): Home Int 1955-56-64(Captain)

Helme, E
(England): Home Int 1911-12-13-20

Heming Johnson, G
(England): Home Int 1909-11-13

Henson, D (Oxley)
(England): Home Int 1967-68-69-70-75-76-77-78; Eur L T Ch 1971-77. (GBI): Curtis Cup 1968-70-72-76; Vagliano Trophy 1967-69-71; Espirito Santo 1970; CW 1967-71

Heskin, A
(Ireland): Home Int 1968-69-70-72-75-77-82(Captain)-83(Captain)

Hetherington, Mrs (Gittens)
(England): Home Int 1909

Hewett, G
(Ireland): Home Int 1923-24

Hezlet, Mrs
(Ireland): Home Int 1910

Hickey, C
(Ireland): Home Int 1969-75 (Captain)-76(Captain)

Higgins, E
(Ireland): Home Int 1981-82-83-84-85-86-87-88-91-92-93-94; Eur L T Ch 1987-93

Hill, J
(England): Home Int 1986

Hill, Mrs
(Wales): Home Int 1924

Hockley, J
(England): Home Int 1991-92-93. (GBI): Espirito Santo 1992; Vagliano Trophy 1993

Hodgson, M
(England): Home Int 1939

Holland, I (Hurst)
(Ireland): Home Int 1958

Holm, H (Gray)
(Scotland): Home Int 1932-33-34-35-36-37-38-47-48-50-51-55-57. (GBI): Curtis Cup 1936-38-48

Holmes, A
(England): Home Int 1931

Holmes, J [Hetherington] (McClure)
(England): Home Int 1957-66-67(Captain)

Hooman, EM [Gavin]
(England): Home Int 1910-11

Hope, LA
(Scotland): Home Int 1975-76-80-84-85-86-87-88(Captain)-89 (Captain)-90 (Captain)

Hort, K
(Wales): Home Int 1929

Hourihane, C
(Ireland): Home Int 1979 to 1992; Eur L T Ch 1981-83-85-87-89. (GBI):Curtis Cup 1984-86-88-90-92; Vagliano Trophy 1981-83-85-87-89-91; Espirito Santo 1986-90

Howard, A (Phillips)
(England): Home Int 1953-54-55-56-57-58-79(Captain)-80(Captain). (GBI): Curtis Cup 1956-58

Huggan, S (Lawson)
(Scotland): Home Int 1985-86-87-88-89; Eur L T Ch 1985-87-89. (GBI): Curtis Cup 1988, Vagliano Trophy 1989

Hughes, J
(Wales): Home Int 1967-71-88-89(Captain); Eur L T Ch 1971

Hughes, Miss
(Wales): Home Int 1907

Huke, B
(England): Home Int 1971-72-75-76-77. (GBI): Curtis Cup 1972; Vagliano Trophy 1975

Hulton, V (Hezlet)
(Ireland): Home Int 1905-07-09-10-11-12-20-21

Humphreys, A (Coulman)
(Wales): Home Int 1969-70-71

Humphreys, D (Forster)
(Ireland): Home Int 1951-52-53-55-57

Hunter, D (Tucker)
(England): Home Int 1905

Hurd, D [Howe] (Campbell)
(Scotland): Home Int 1905-06-08-09-11-28-30

Hurst, Mrs
(Wales): Home Int 1921-22-23-25-27-28

Hyland, B
(Ireland): Home Int 1964-65-66

Inghram, E (Lever)
(Wales): Home Int 1947-48-49-50-51-52-53-54-55-56-57-58-64-65

Irvin, A
(England): Home Int 1962-63-65-67-68-69-70-71-72-73-75; Eur L T Ch 1965-67-69-71. (GBI): Curtis Cup 1962-68-70-76; Vagliano Trophy 1961-63-65-67-69-71-73-75; Espirito Santo 1982(Captain); CW 1967-75

Irvine, Miss
(Wales): Home Int 1930

Isaac, Mrs
(Wales): Home Int 1924

Isherwood, L
(Wales): Home Int 1972-76-77-78-80-86-88-89-90-91

Jack, E (Philip)
(Scotland): Home Int 1962-63-64-81(Captain)-82(Captain)

Jackson, B
(Ireland): Home Int 1937-38-39-50

Jackson, B
(England): Home Int 1955-56-57-58-59-63-64-65-66-73(Captain)-74(Captain). (GBI): Curtis Cup 1958-64-68; Vagliano Trophy 1959-63-65-67-73(Captain)-75(Captain); Espirito Santo 1964; CW 1959-67

Jackson, D
(Scotland): Home Int 1990

Jackson, Mrs H
(Ireland): Home Int 1921

Jackson, J
(Ireland): Home Int 1912-13-14-20-21-22-23-24-25-27-28-29-30

Jackson, Mrs L
(Ireland): Home Int 1910-12-14-20-22-25

Jameson, S (Tobin)
(Ireland): Home Int 1913-14-20-24-25-27

Jenkin, B
(Wales): Home Int 1959

Jenkins, J (Owen)
(Wales): Home Int 1953-56

John, J
(Wales): Home Int 1974

Johns, A
(England): Home Int 1987-88-89

Johnson, A (Hughes)
(Wales): Home Int 1964-66-67-68-69-70-71-72-73-74-75-76-78-79-85; Eur L T Ch 1965-67-69-71

Johnson, J (Roberts)
(Wales): Home Int 1955

Johnson, M
(England): Home Int 1934-35

Johnson, R
(Wales): Home Int 1955

Johnson, T
(England): Home Int 1984-85-86; Eur L T Ch 1985. (GBI): Curtis Cup 1986; Vagliano Trophy 1985; Espirito Santo 1986

Jones, A (Gwyther)
(Wales): Home Int 1959

Jones, B
(Wales): Home Int 1994; Eur L T Ch 1993

Jones, K
(Wales): Home Int 1959(Captain)-1960(Captain)-61(Captain)

Jones, M (De Lloyd)
(Wales): Home Int 1951

Jones, Mrs
(Wales): Home Int 1932-35

Justice, M
(Wales): Home Int 1931-32

Kavanagh, H
(Ireland): Home Int 1993-94

Kaye, H (Williamson)
(England): Home Int 1986 (Captain) -87(Captain)

Keenan, D
(Ireland): Home Int 1989

Keiller, G [Style]
(England): Home Int 1948-49-52

Kelway Bamber, Mrs
(Scotland): Home Int 1923-27-33

Kennedy, D (Fowler)
(England): Home Int 1923-24-25-27-28-29

Kennion, Mrs (Kenyon Stow)
(England) Home Int 1910

Kerr, J
(Scotland): Home Int 1947-48-49-54

Kidd, Mrs
(Ireland): Home Int 1934-37

King Mrs
(Ireland): Home Int 1923-25-27-29

Kinloch, Miss
(Scotland): Home Int 1913-14

Kirkwood, Mrs
(Ireland): Home Int 1955

Knight, Mrs
(Scotland): Home Int 1922

Kyle, B [Rhodes] (Norris)
(England): Home Int 1937-38-39-48-49

Kyle, E
(Scotland): Home Int 1909-10

Laing, A
(Scotland): Home Int 1966-67-70-71-73(Captain)-74(Captain); Eur L T Ch 1967. (GBI): Vagliano Trophy 1967

Lambert, S (Cohen)
(England): Home Int 1979-80-93-94. (GBI): Vagliano Trophy 1979

Lambie, S
(Scotland): Home Int 1976

Laming Evans, Mrs
(Wales): Home Int 1922-23

Langford, Mrs
(Wales): Home Int 1937

Langridge, S (Armitage)
(England): Home Int 1963-64-65-66; Eur L T Ch 1965. (GBI): Curtis Cup 1964-66; Vagliano Trophy 1963-65

Large, P (Davies)
(England): Home Int 1951-52-81(Captain)-82(Captain)

Larkin, C (McAuley)
(Ireland): Home Int 1966-67-68-69-70-71-72; Eur L T Ch 1971

Latchford, B
(Ireland): Home Int 1931-33

Latham Hall, E (Chubb)
(England): Home Int 1928

Lauder, G
(Ireland): Home Int 1911

Lauder, R
(Ireland): Home Int 1911

Lawrence, JB
(Scotland): Home Int 1959-60-61-62-63-64-65-66-67-68-69-70-77(Captain); Eur L T Ch 1965-67-69-71. (GBI): Curtis Cup 1964; Vagliano Trophy 1963-65; Espirito Santo 1964; CW 1971

Lawson, H
(Wales): Home Int 1989-90-91-92; Eur L T Ch 1991-93

Lebrun, W (Aitken)
(Scotland): Home Int 1978-79-80-81-82-83-85. (GBI): Curtis Cup 1982; Vagliano Trophy 1981-83

Leaver, B
(Wales): Home Int 1912-14-21

Lee Smith, J
(England): Home Int 1973-74-75-76. (GBI): Curtis Cup 1974-76; Espirito Santo 1976; CW 1975

Leete, Mrs IG
(Scotland): Home Int 1933

Leitch, C
(England): Home Int 1910-11-12-13-14-20-21-22-24-25-27-28

Leitch, M
(England): Home Int 1912-14

Little, S
(Scotland): Home Int 1993

Llewellyn, Miss
(Wales): Home Int 1912-13-14-21-22-23

Lloyd, J
(Wales): Home Int 1988

Lloyd, P
(Wales): Home Int 1935-36

Lloyd Davies, VH
(Wales): Home Int 1913

Lloyd Roberts, V
(Wales): Home Int 1907-08-10

Lloyd Williams, Miss
(Wales): Home Int 1909-10-12-14

Lobbett, P
(England): Home Int 1922-24-27-29-30

Lovatt, S
(Wales): Home Int 1994

Lowry, Mrs
(Ireland): Home Int 1947

Luckin, B (Cooper)
(England): Home Int 1980

Lugton, C
(Scotland): Home Int 1968-72-73-75(Captain)-76(Captain)-77-78-80

Lumb, K (Phillips)
(England): Home Int 1968-69-70-71; Eur L T Ch 1969. (GBI): Curtis Cup 1972; Vagliano Trophy 1969-71

Lyons, T (Ross Steen)
(England): Home Int 1959. (GBI): Vagliano Trophy 1959

MacAndrew, F
(Scotland): Home Int 1913-14

Macbeth, M (Dodd)
(England): Home Int 1913-14-20-21-22-23-24-25

MacCann, K
(Ireland): Home Int 1984-85-86

MacCann, K (Smye)
(Ireland): Home Int 1947-48-49-50-51-52-53-54-56-57-58-60-61-62-64-65(Captain)

McCarthy, A
(Ireland): Home Int 1951-52

McCarthy, D
(Ireland): Home Int 1988-90-91; Eur L T Ch 1993

McCool, L
(Ireland): Home Int 1993

McCulloch, J
(Scotland): Home Int 1921-22-23-24-27-29-30-31-32-33-35-60(Captain)

McDaid, E (O'Grady)
(Ireland): Home Int 1959

Macdonald, F
(England): Home Int 1990

Macdonald, K
(Scotland): Home Int 1928-29

MacGeach, C
(Ireland): Home Int 1938-39-48-49-50

McGreevy, V
(Ireland): Home Int 1987-90-92

McIntosh, B (Dixon)
(England): Home Int 1969-70; Eur L T Ch 1969. (GBI): Vagliano Trophy 1969

MacIntosh, I
(Scotland): Home Int 1991(Captain)-92(Captain)-93(Captain); Eur L T Ch 1993(Captain)

McIntyre, J
(England): Home Int 1949-54

McKay, F
(Scotland): Home Int 1992-93-94; Eur L T Ch 1993

McKay, M
(Scotland): Home Int 1991-93-94; Eur L T Ch 1993. (GBI): Curtis Cup 1994; Vagliano Trophy 1993

MacKean, Mrs
(Wales): Home Int 1938-39-47

McKenna, M
(Ireland): Home Int 1968 to 1991-93; Eur L T Ch 1969-71-75-87. (GBI): Curtis Cup 1970-72-74-76-78-80-82-84-86; Vagliano Trophy 1969-71-73-75-77-79-81-85-87; Espirito Santo 1970-74-76-86(Captain)-90(Captain)

Mackenzie, A
(Scotland): Home Int 1921

McKinlay, M
(Scotland): Home Int 1990-92-93; Eur L T Ch 1993. (GBI): Curtis Cup 1994

McLarty, E
(Scotland): Home Int 1966 (Captain) -67(Captain)-68(Captain)

McMahon, S (Cadden)
(Scotland): Home Int 1974-75-76-77-79. (GBI): Curtis Cup 1976; Vagliano Trophy 1975

McMaster, S
(Scotland): Home Int 1994

McNair, W
(England): Home Int 1921

McNeil, K
(Scotland): Home Int 1969(Captain)-70(Captain)

McNeile, CL
(Ireland): Home Int 1906

McQuillan, Y
(Ireland): Home Int 1985-86

MacTier, Mrs
(Wales): Home Int 1927

Madeley, M (Coburn)
(Ireland): Home Int 1964-69; Eur L T Ch 1969

Madill, M
(Ireland): Home Int 1978-79-80-81-82-83-84-85. (GBI): Curtis Cup 1980; Vagliano Trophy 1979-81-85; Espirito Santo 1980; CW 1979

Madill, Mrs
(Ireland): Home Int 1920-24-25-27-28-29-33

Magee, A-M
(Wales): Home Int 1991-92-93-94

Magill, J
(Ireland): Home Int 1907-11-13

Maher, S (Vaughan)
(England): Home Int 1960-61-62-63-64. (GBI): Curtis Cup 1962-64; Vagliano Trophy 1961; CW 1963

Mahon, D
(Ireland): Home Int 1989-90

Main, M (Farquhar)
(Scotland): Home Int 1950-51

Maitland, M
(Scotland): Home Int 1905-06-08-12-13

Mallam, Mrs S
(Ireland): Home Int 1922-23

Marks, Mrs T
(Ireland): Home Int 1950

Marks, Mrs
(Ireland): Home Int 1930-31-33-35

Marley, MV
(Wales): Home Int 1921-22-23-30-37

Marr, H (Cameron)
(Scotland): Home Int 1927-28-29-30-31

Marshall, K (Imrie)
(Scotland): Home Int 1984-85-89. Eur L T Ch 1987-89 (GBI): Curtis Cup 1990; Vagliano Trophy 1989

Martin, P [Whitworth Jones] (Low)
(Wales): Home Int 1948-50-56-59-60-61

Marvin, V
(England): Home Int 1977-78; Eur L T Ch 1977. (GBI): Curtis Cup 1978; Vagliano Trophy 1977

Mason, Mrs
(Wales): Home Int 1923

Mather, H
(Scotland): Home Int 1905-09-12-13-14

Matthew, C (Lambert)
(Scotland): Home Int 1989-90-91-92-93; Eur L T Ch 1989-91-93. (GBI): Curtis Cup 1990-92-94; Vagliano Trophy 1989-91-93; Espirito Santo 1992; CW 1991

Matthews, T [Thomas] (Perkins)
(Wales): Home Int 1972-73-74-75-76-77-78-79-80-81-82-83-84; Eur L T Ch 1975. (GBI): Curtis Cup 1974-76-78-80; Vagliano Trophy 1973-75-77-79; Espirito Santo 1979; CW 1975-79

Mellis, Mrs
(Scotland): Home Int 1924-27

Melvin, V
(Scotland): Home Int 1994

Menton, D
(Ireland): Home Int 1949

Menzies, M
(Scotland): Home Int 1962 (Captain)

Merrill, J (Greenhalgh)
(England): Home Int 1960-61-63-66-69-70-71-75-76-77-78; Eur L T Ch 1971-77. (GBI): Curtis Cup 1964-70-74-76-78; Vagliano Trophy 1961-65-75-77; Espirito Santo 1970-74(Captain)-78; CW 1963

Millar, D
(Ireland): Home Int 1928

Milligan, J (Mark)
(Ireland): Home Int 1971-72-73

Mills, I
(Wales): Home Int 1935-36-37-39-47-48

Milton, M (Paterson)
(Scotland): Home Int 1948-49-50-51-52. (GBI): Curtis Cup 1952

Mitchell, J
(Ireland): Home Int 1930

Moodie, J
(Scotland): Home Int 1990-91-92; Eur L T Ch 1991-93. (GBI): Curtis Cup 1994; Vagliano Trophy 1993; Espirito Santo 1994

Mooney, M
(Ireland): Home Int 1972-73; Eur L T Ch 1971. (GBI): Vagliano Trophy 1973

Moorcroft, S
(England): Home Int 1985-86; Eur L T Ch 1985-87

Moore, S
(Ireland): Home Int 1937-38-39-47-48-49-68(Captain)

Moran, V (Singleton)
(Ireland): Home Int 1970-71-73-74-75; Eur L T Ch 1971-75

Morant, E
(England): Home Int 1906-10

Morgan, S
(England): Home Int 1989; Eur L T Ch 1989

Morgan, W
(England): Home Int 1931-32-33-34-35-36-37. (GBI): Curtis Cup 32-34-36

Morgan, Miss
(Wales): Home Int 1912-13-14

Moriarty, M (Irvine)
(Ireland): Home Int 1979

Morley, J
(England): Home Int 1990-91-92-93; Eur L T Ch 1991-93. (GBI): Curtis Cup 1992; Vagliano Trophy 1991-93; Espirito Santo 1992

Morris, L (Moore)
(England): Home Int 1912-13

Morris, Mrs de B
(Ireland): Home Int 1933

Morrison, G (Cheetham)
(England): Home Int 1965-69(Captain). (GBI): Vagliano Trophy 1965

Morrison, G (Cradock-Hartopp)
(England): Home Int 1936

Mountford, S
(Wales): Home Int 1989-90-91-92; Eur L T Ch 1991

Murray, Rachel
(Ireland): Home Int 1952

Murray, S (Jolly)
(England): Home Int 1976

Musgrove, Mrs
(Wales): Home Int 1923-24

Myles, M
(Scotland): Home Int 1955-57-59-60-67

Neill-Fraser, M
(Scotland): Home Int 1905-06-07-08-09-10-11-12-13-14

Nes, K (Garnham)
(England): Home Int 1931-32-33-36-37-38-39

Nevile, E
(England): Home Int 1905-06-08-10

New, B
(England): Home Int 1980-81-82-83. (GBI): Curtis Cup 1984; Vagliano Trophy 1983

Newell, B
(England): Home Int 1936

Newman, L
(Wales): Home Int 1927-31

Newton, B (Brown)
(England): Home Int 1930-33-34-35-36-37

Nicholls, M
(Wales): Home Int 1962(Captain)

Nicholson, J (Hutton)
(Scotland): Home Int 1969-70; Eur L T Ch 1971. (GBI): CW 1971

Nicholson, L
(Scotland): Home Int 1994

Nicholson, Mrs WH
(Scotland): Home Int 1910-13

Nimmo, H
(Scotland): Home Int 1936-38-39

Norris, J (Smith)
(Scotland): Home Int 1966-67-68-69-70-71-72-75-76-77-78-79-83(Captain)-84(Captain)-84(Captain); Eur L T Ch 1971. (GBI): Vagliano Trophy 1977

Norwell, I (Watt)
(Scotland): Home Int 1954

Nutting, P (Jameson)
(Ireland): Home Int 1927-28

O'Brien, A
(Ireland): Home Int 1969

O'Brien Kenney, S
(Ireland): Home Int 1977-78-83-84-85-86

O'Donnell, M
(Ireland): Home Int 1974-77 (Captain) -78(Captain)-79 (Captain); Eur L T Ch 1980 (Captain). (GBI): Curtis Cup 1982; Vagliano Trophy 1981 (Captain)

O'Donohoe, A
(Ireland): Home Int 1948-49-50-51-53-73(Captain)-74 (Captain)

O'Hare, S
(Ireland): Home Int 1921-22

O'Reilly, T (Moran)
(Ireland): Home Int 1977-78-86-88; Eur L T Ch 1987

O'Sullivan, A
(Ireland): Home Int 1982-83-84-92-94; Eur L T Ch 1993

O'Sullivan, P
(Ireland): Home Int 1950-51-52-53-54-55-56-57-58-59-60-63-64-65-66-67-69 (Captain)-70(Captain) -71(Captain); Eur L T Ch 1971(Captain)

Oliver, M (Jones)
(Wales): Home Int 1955-60-61-62-63-64-65-66. (GBI): Espirito Santo 1964

Ormsby, Miss
(Ireland): Home Int 1909-10-11

Orr, P (Boyd)
(Ireland): Home Int 1971

Orr, Mrs
(Wales): Home Int 1924

Owen, E
(Wales): Home Int 1947

Panton-Lewis, C (Panton)
(Scotland): Home Int 1972-73-76-77-78. (GBI): Vagliano Trophy 1977; Espirito Santo 1976

Park, Mrs
(Scotland): Home Int 1952

Parker, S
(England): Home Int 1973

Patey, Mrs
(Scotland): Home Int 1922-23

Pearson, D
(England): Home Int 1928-29-30-31-32-34

Percy, G (Mitchell)
(Scotland): Home Int 1927-28-30-31

Perriam, A
(Wales): Home Int 1988-90-91-92; Eur L T Ch 1991

Phelips, M
(Wales): Home Int 1913-14-21

Phillips, ME
(England): Home Int 1905

Phillips, Mrs
(Wales): Home Int 1921

Pickard, M (Nichol)
(England): Home Int 1958-59-60-61-67-69-83(Captain). (GBI): Curtis Cup 1968-70; Vagliano Trophy 1959-61-67

Pim, Mrs
(Ireland): Home Int 1908

Pook, E (Chadwick)
(England): Home Int 1963-65-66-67; Eur L T Ch 1967.(GBI): Curtis Cup 1966; Vagliano Trophy 1963-67; CW 1967

Porter, D (Park)
(Scotland): Home Int 1922-25-27-29-30-31-32-33-34-35-37-38-47-48. (GBI): Curtis Cup 1932

Porter, M (Lazenby)
(England): Home Int 1931-32

Powell, M
(Wales): Home Int 1908-09-10-12

Power, ER (McDaid)
(Ireland): Home Int 1987-88-89-90-91-92-93-94; Eur L T Ch 1987-93. (GBI): Curtis Cup 1994

Price, M (Greaves)
(England): Home Int 1956(Captain)

Price Fisher, E (Price)
(England): Home Int 1948-51-52-53-54-55-56-57-58-59-60. (GBI): Curtis Cup 1950-52-54-56-58-60; Vagliano Trophy 1959; CW 1959

Proctor, Mrs
(Wales): Home Int 1907

Provis, I (Kyle)
(Scotland): Home Int 1910-11

Purcell, E
(Ireland): Home Int 1965-66-67-72-73

Purvis-Russell-Montgomery, C
(Scotland): Home Int 1921-22-23-25-28-29-30-31-32-33-34-35-36-37-38-39-47-48-49-50-52

Pyman, B
(Wales): Home Int 1925-28-29-30-32-33-34-35-36-37-38

Rabbidge, R
(England): Home Int 1931

Rawlings, M
(Wales): Home Int 1979-80-81-83-84-85-86-87. (GBI): Vagliano Trophy 1981

Rawlinson, T (Walker)
(Scotland): Home Int 1970-71-73-76. (GBI): Vagliano Trophy 1973

Read, P
(England): Home Int 1922

Reddan, C (Tiernan)
(Ireland): Home Int 1935-36-38-39-47-48-49. (GBI): Curtis Cup 1938-48

Reddan, MV
(Ireland): Home Int 1955

Reece, P (Millington)
(England): Home Int 1966(Captain)

Rees, G
(Wales): Home Int 1981

Rees, MB
(Wales): Home Int 1927-31

Reid, A (Lurie)
(Scotland) Home Int 1960-61-62-63-64-66. (GBI): Vagliano Trophy 1961

Reid, A (Kyle)
(Scotland): Home Int 1923-24-25

Reid, D
(Scotland): Home Int 1978-79

Remer, H
(England): Home Int 1909

Rennie, J (Hastings)
(Scotland): Home Int 1961-65-66-67-71-72; Eur L T Ch 1967. (GBI): Curtis Cup 1966; Vagliano Trophy 1961-67

Rhys, J
(Wales): Home Int 1979

Rice, J
(Ireland): Home Int 1924-27-29

Richards, D
(Wales): Home Int 1994

Richards, J
(Wales): Home Int 1980-82-83-85

Richards, S
(Wales): Home Int 1967

Richardson, Mrs
(England): Home Int 1907-09

Richmond, M (Walker)
(Scotland): Home Int 1972-73-74-75-77-78. (GBI): Curtis Cup 1974; Vagliano Trophy 1975

Rieben, Mrs
(Wales): Home Int 1927-28-29-30-31-32-33

Rigby, F (Macbeth)
(Scotland): Home Int 1912-13

Ritchie, C (Park)
(Scotland): Home Int 1939-47-48-51-52-53-64(Captain)

Roberts, B
(Wales): Home Int 1984(Captain)-85(Captain)-86(Captain)

Roberts, E (Pentony)
(Ireland): Home Int 1932-33-34-35-36-39

Roberts, E (Barnett)
(Ireland): Home Int 1961-62-63-64-65; Eur L T Ch 1964

Roberts, G
(Wales): Home Int 1949-52-53-54

Roberts, M (Brown)
(Scotland): Home Int 1965(Captain). (GBI): Espirito Santo 1964

Roberts, P
(Wales): Home Int 1950-51-53-55-56-57-58-59-60-61-62-63-64 (Captain) -65 (Captain)-66 (Captain) -67 (Captain)-68-69-70; Eur L T Ch 1965-67-69. (GBI): Espirito Santo 1964

Roberts, S
(Wales): Home Int 1983-84-85-86-87-88-89-90; Eur L T Ch 1983-87

Robertson, B (McCorkindale)
(Scotland): Home Int 1958-59-60-61-62-63-64-65-66-69-72-73-78-80-81-82-84 -85-86; Eur L T Ch 1965-67(Captain)-69-71(Captain). (GBI): Curtis Cup 1960-66-68-70-72-74(Captain)-76(Captain)-82-86; Vagliano Trophy 1959-63-69-71-81-85; Espirito Santo 1959-63-69-71-81-85; CW 1971-75(Captain)

Robertson, D
(Scotland): Home Int 1907

Robertson, E
(Scotland): Home Int 1924

Robertson, G
(Scotland): Home Int 1907-08-09

Robinson, C (Nesbitt)
(Ireland): Home Int 1974-75-76-77-78-79-80-81. (GBI): Curtis Cup 1980; Vagliano Trophy 1979

Robinson, R (Bayly)
(Ireland): Home Int 1947-56-57

Robinson, S
(England): Home Int 1989

Roche, Mrs
(Ireland): Home Int 1922

Rogers, A
(Ireland): Home Int 1992-93; Eur L T Ch 1993

Rogers, J
(Wales): Home Int 1972

Rose, A
(Scotland): Home Int 1990-91-92-93-94; Eur L T Ch 1991-93

Roskrow, M
(England): Home Int 1948-50

Ross, M (Hezlet)
(Ireland): Home Int 1905-06-07-08-11-12

Roxburgh, L
(Scotland): Home Int 1993-94

Roy, S (Needham)
(Scotland): Home Int 1969-71-72-73-74-75-76-83. (GBI): Vagliano Trophy 1973-75

Rudgard, G
(England): Home Int 1931-32-50-51-52

Rusack, J
(Scotland): Home Int 1908

Sabine, D (Plumpton)
(England): Home Int 1934-35. (GBI): Curtis Cup 1934

Saunders, V
(England): Home Int 1967-68; Eur L T Ch 1967. (GBI): Curtis Cup 1968; Vagliano Trophy 1967; CW 1967

Scott Chard, Mrs
(Wales) Home Int 1928-30

Seddon, N
(Wales): Home Int 1962-63-74 (Captain)-75(Captain)-76 (Captain)

Selkirk, H
(Wales): Home Int 1925-28

Shapcott, A
(England): Home Int 1989

Shapcott, S
(England): Home Int 1986-88; Eur L T Ch 1987. (GBI): Curtis Cup 1988; Vagliano Trophy 1987; CW 1987; Espirito Santo 1988

Shaw, P
(Wales): Home Int 1913

Sheldon, A
(Wales): Home Int 1981

Sheppard, E (Pears)
(England): Home Int 1947

Simpson, L (Moore)
(England): Home Int 1979-80

Singleton, B (Henderson)
(Scotland): Home Int 1939-52-53-54-55-56-57-58-60-61-62-63-64-65

Slade, Lady
(Ireland): Home Int 1906

Slark, R (Porter)
(England): Home Int 1959-60-61-62-64-65-66-68-78; Eur L T Ch 1965. (GBI): Curtis Cup 1960-62-64; Vagliano Trophy 1959-61-65; Espirito Santo 1964-66(Captain); CW 1963

Slocombe, E (Davies)
(Wales): Home Int 1974-75

Smalley, Mrs A
(Wales): Home Int 1924-25-31-32-33-34

Smillie, P
(England): Home Int 1985-86

Smith, A [Stant] (Willard)
(England): Home Int 1974-75-76. (GBI): Curtis Cup 1976; Vagliano Trophy 1975; CW 1959-63

Smith, E
(England): Home Int 1991

Smith, F (Stephens)
(England): Home Int 1947-48-49-50-51-52-53-54-55-59-62 (Captain)-71(Captain) -72 (Captain). (GBI): Curtis Cup 1950-52-54-56-58-60-62(non-playing Captain)-72(non-playing Captain); Vagliano Trophy 1959-71; CW 1959-63

Smith, Mrs L
(Ireland): Home Int 1913-14-21-22-23-25

Smythe, M
(Ireland): Home Int 1947-48-49-50-51-52-53-54-55-56-58-59-62(Captain)

Sowter, Mrs
(Wales): Home Int 1923

Speak, K
(England): Home Int 1993-94; Eur L T Ch 1993. (GBI): Curtis Cup 1994; Vagliano Trophy 1993; Espirito Santo 1994

Speir, M
(Scotland): Home Int 1957-64-68-71(Captain)-72(Captain)

Starrett, L (Malone)
(Ireland): Home Int 1975-76-77-78-80

Stavert, M
(Scotland): Home Int 1979

Steel, Mrs DC
(Scotland): Home Int 1925

Steel, E
(England): Home Int 1905-06-07-08-11

Stewart, G
(Scotland): Home Int 1979-80-81-82-83-84; Eur L T Ch 1982-84. (GBI): Curtis Cup 1980-82; Vagliano Trophy 1979-81-83; CW 1979-83

Stewart, L (Scraggie)
(Scotland): Home Int 1921-22-23

Stocker, J
(England): Home Int 1922-23

Stockton, Mrs
(Wales): Home Int 1949

Storry, Mrs
(Wales): Home Int 1910-14

Stroud, N
(Wales): Home Int 1989

Stuart, M
(Ireland): Home Int 1905-07-08

Stuart-French, Miss
(Ireland): Home Int 1922

Sugden, J (Machin)
(England): Home Int 1953-54-55

Summers, M (Mackie)
(Scotland): Home Int 1986

Sumpter, Mrs
(England): Home Int 1907-08-12-14-24

Sutherland Pilch, R (Barton)
(England): Home Int 1947-49-50-58(Captain)

Swallow, C
(England): Home Int 1985; Eur L T Ch 1985

Sweeney, L
(Ireland): Home Int 1991

Tamworth, Mrs
(England): Home Int 1908

Taylor, I
(Ireland): Home Int 1930

Teacher, F
(Scotland): Home Int 1908-09-11-12-13

Tebbet, K
(England): Home Int 1990-94

Temple, S
(England): Home Int 1913-14

Temple Dobell, G (Ravenscroft)
(England): Home Int 1911-12-13-14-20-21-25-30

Thomas, C (Phipps)
(Wales): Home Int 1959-63-64-65-66-67-68-69-70-71-72-73-76-77-80

Thomas, I
(Wales): Home Int 1910

Thomas, J
(Wales): Home Int 1993; Eur L T Ch 1993

Thomas, O
(Wales): Home Int 1921

Thomas, S (Rowlands)
(Wales): Home Int 1977-82-84-85

Thomas, V (Rawlings)
(Wales): Home Int 1971 to 1994; Eur L T Ch 1975-87-91-93. (GBI): Curtis Cup 1982-84-86-88-90; Vagliano Trophy 1979-83 -85-87-89-91; CW 1979-83-87-91. Espirito Santo 1990

Thompson, M
(Wales): Home Int 1937-38-39

Thompson, M (Wallis)
(England): Home Int 1948-49

Thompson, M
(Scotland): Home Int 1949

Thomson, D
(Scotland): Home Int 1982-83-85-87

Thomson, M
(Scotland): Home Int 1907

Thomson, M
(Scotland): Home Int 1974-75-76-77-78; Eur L T Ch 1978. (GBI): Curtis Cup 1978; Vagliano Trophy 1977

Thornhill, J (Woodside)
(England): Home Int 1965-74-82-83-84-85-86-87-88; Eur L T Ch 1965-85-87. (GBI): Curtis Cup 1984-86-88; Vagliano Trophy 1965-83-85-87-89(Captain); CW 1983-87

Thornhill, Miss
(Ireland): Home Int 1924-25

Thornton, Mrs
(Ireland): Home Int 1924

Todd, Mrs
(Ireland): Home Int 1931-32-34-35-36

Thomlinson, J [Evans] (Roberts)
(England): Home Int 1962-64. (GBI): Curtis Cup 1962; Vagliano Trophy 1963

Treharne, A [Mills]
(Wales): Home Int 1952-61

Turner, B
(England): Home Int 1908

Turner, S (Jump)
(Wales): Home Int 1982-84-85-86-91-93

Tynte, V
(Ireland): Home Int 1905-06-08-09-11-12-13-14

Uzielli, A (Carrick)
(England): Home Int 1976-77-78-90-92(Captain)-93(Captain); Eur L T Ch 1977. (GBI): Curtis Cup 1978; Vagliano Trophy 1977

Valentine, J (Anderson)
(Scotland): Home Int 1934-35-36-37-38-39-47-49-50-51-52-53-54-55-56 (Captain)-57-58. (GBI): Curtis Cup 1938-48-50-52-54-56-58; CW 1959

Valentine, P (Whitley)
(Wales): Home Int 1973-74-75-77-78-79-80-90 (Captain)

Veitch, F
(Scotland): Home Int 1912

Wadsworth, H
(Wales): Home Int 1987-88-89-90; Eur L T Ch 1987-90. (GBI): Curtis Cup 1990

Waite, C
(England): Home Int 1981-82-83-84, Eur L T Ch 1985. (GBI): Curtis Cup 1984; Vagliano Trophy 1983; Espirito Santo 1984; CW 1983

Wakelin, H
(Wales): Home Int 1955

Walker, B (Thompson)
(England): Home Int 1905-06-07-08-09-11

Walker, M
(England): Home Int 1970-72; Eur L T Ch 1971. (GBI): Curtis Cup 1972; Vagliano Trophy 1971; CW 1971

Walker, P
(Ireland): Home Int 1928-29-30-31-32-33-34-35-36-37-38-39-48. (GBI): Curtis Cup 1934-36-38

Walker-Leigh, F
(Ireland): Home Int 1907-08-09-11-12-13-14

Wallace-Williamson, V
(Scotland): Home Int 1932. (GBI): Curtis Cup 1938 (Captain)

Walsh, R
(Ireland): Home Int 1987

Walter, J
(England): Home Int 1974-79-80-82-86

Walton, L
(England): Home Int 1991-94; Eur L T Ch 1993. (GBI): Curtis Cup 1994; Vagliano Trophy 1993

Wardlaw, N (Baird)
(Scotland): Home Int 1932-35-36-37-38-39-47-48. (GBI): Curtis Cup 1938

Watson, C (Nelson)
(England): Home Int 1982

Webb, L (Bolton)
(Ireland): Home Int 1981-82-88-89-91-92-94

Webster, S (Hales)
(Wales): Home Int 1968-69-72-91(Captain)

Wesley, N
(Wales): Home Int 1986

Westall, S (Maudsley)
(England): Home Int 1973

Weston, R
(Wales): Home Int 1927

Whieldon, Miss
(Wales): Home Int 1908

Wickham, C
(Ireland): Home Int 1983-89

Wickham, P
(Ireland): Home Int 1976-83-87; Eur L T Ch 1987

Williams, M
(Wales): Home Int 1936

Williamson, C (Barker)
(England): Home Int 1979-80-81

Willock-Pollen, G
(England): Home Int 1907

Wilson, A
(Scotland): Home Int 1973-74-85 (Captain)

Wilson, E
(England): Home Int 1928-29-30. (GBI): Curtis Cup 1932

Wilson, Mrs
(Ireland): Home Int 1931

Wilson Jones, D
(Wales): Home Int 1952

Winn, J
(England): Home Int 1920-21-23-25

Wooldridge, W (Shaw)
(Scotland): Home Int 1982

Wragg, M
(England): Home Int 1929

Wright, J (Robertson)
(Scotland): Home Int 1952-53-54-55-56-57-58-59-60-61-63-65-67-73-78 (Captain)-79(Captain)-80(Captain)-86(Captain); Eur L T Ch 1965. (GBI): Curtis Cup 1954-56-58-60; Vagliano Trophy 1959-61-63; CW 1959

Wright, M
(Scotland): Home Int 1990-91-92; Eur L T Ch 1991

Wright, N (Cook)
(Wales): Home Int 1938-47-48-49-51-52-53-54-57-58-59-60-62-63-64-66-67-68-71 (Captain)-72(Captain) -73(Captain); Eur L T Ch 1965-71 (Captain). (GBI): Espirito Santo 1964

Wright, P
(Scotland): Home Int 1981-82-83-84; Eur L T Ch 1987. (GBI): Vagliano Trophy 1981

Wylie, P (Wade)
(England): Home Int 1934-35-36-37-38-47. (GBI): Curtis Cup 1938

Association of Golf Writers

(L) = Life member
(H) = Honorary member

Andrew, Harry H

(L) Baker, John E

Ballantine, John

Bisher, Firman
Atlanta Journal, Constitution

Blackstock, Dixon
Sunday Mail, Glasgow

Blighton, Bill

Blomqvist, Jan
Golf Digest Sverige

Bolze, Gerd A

Booth, Alan

Bowden, Ken

Britten, Mike

(H) Butler, Frank

Callander, Colin
Golf Monthly

Campbell, John G

Campbell, Malcolm

Carter, Jane
Women and Golf

Chancellor, Matthew
Golf Illustrated Weekly

Chapman, Jeremy
The Sporting Life

Clark, Bill
Sunday Mirror, Belfast

Clough, Frank

Creighton, Brian
Reuters

Crockett, Scott

Dabell, Norman

Davies, Bob
Shropshire Star

Davies, David
The Guardian

Davies, Patricia

Dobereiner, Peter

Dodd, Richard

Donald, Peter

Ebbinge, Jan B

(L) Edwards, Leslie

Elliott, Bill
The Daily Star

Ellison, Stanley
Turf Management

Farquharson, Colin
Press and Journal, Aberdeen

Farrell, Andrew
Golf Weekly

(H) Fenton, John

Ferrie, Kevin
Dundee Courier

Ferrier, Bob

Figar, Jose
Adesport, Madrid

Frederick, Adrian

Garrod, Mark
Press Association

Gilleece, Dermot
The Irish Times

Glover, Tim
The Independent

Goodner, Ross
Golf Digest, USA

Green, Bob
The Associated Press, New York

Green, Robert
Golf World

Grimsley, Will

Hamilton, David
Golf Weekly

Hamilton, Eddie

Hardy, Martin

Haslam, Peter
Golf World

Hedley, Alan
The Journal, Newcastle-upon-Tyne

Hennessy, John

Hermann, Philippe
Tribune de Geneva

Herron, Allan
The People

Higgs, Peter
Mail on Sunday

Hopkins, John
The Times

Howard, Jock
Golf World

(L) Huggins, Percy

Ingham, John

Jacobs, Raymond
Glasgow Herald

Jenkins, Bob

Jenkins, Dan
Golf Digest, USA

Johnson, Bill

Kahn, Elizabeth

Kelly, Jeff
Andalucia Golf

Lafaurie, André-Jean
Golf European, Paris

Laidlaw, Renton
Evening Standard, London

Lawrenson, Derek

(L) Lincoln, Stanley

McDonnell, Michael
Daily Mail

(H) McKinlay, S L

Macniven, Ian

MacVicar, Jock
Daily Express

Mackie, Keith

Magowan, Jack
Belfast Telegraph

Mair, Norman

Mair, Lewine
Daily Telegraph

Maitland, Bobby

Mancinelli, Piero
Parliamo di Golf, Milan

Masters, Peter
Golf World

Mearing, Paddy

Moody, John

Mossop, James
Sunday Express

Mulqueen, Charles
Cork Examiner

Nicol, Alister

Oakley, John

Ortega, Jesús Ruiz
Golf, Madrid

Ostermann, Ted

Pargeter, John

Pastor, Nuria
La Vanguardia, Barcelona

Pinner, John

(H) Place, Tom

Platts, Mitchell
PGA European Tour

Plumridge, Chris

Potter, Bryan

Price Fisher, Elizabeth

Ramsey, Tom
News Limited Australia

Redmond, John
Irish Press

Reece, John K

Reid, Philip
Irish Press

Riach, Ian
Scottish Sunday Express

Richardson, Gordon

Robertson, Bill
Today's Golfer

Robertson, Jack
Evening Times, Glasgow

Rodrigo, Robert (Bob Rodney)

Roseforte, Tim
Sports Illustrated

Ross, John M
American Golf Magazine

Ruddy, Pat
Golfers Companion

(L) Ryde, Peter

St John, Lauren

(L) Scatchard, Charles

Seitz, Nick
Golf Digest/Tennis, USA

Severino, Dick
Golf Features Service, San Diego

Simpson, Gordon

Skelton, Ronald
Dundee Courier

Smart, Chris
Mid-Glamorgan Press Agency

Smith, Colm
Independent Newspapers, Dublin

Somers, Robert

Spander, Art
San Francisco Examiner

Spink, Alex
Today

(L) Steel, Donald

Stobbs, John
Golf and Greenkeeping

Tait, Alistair
Golf Monthly

Taylor, Dick

(H) Thornberry, Henry W

(H) Ullyett, Roy

Van Esbeck, Edmund
The Irish Times

Ward, Barry E

Webb, Mel

Whitbread, John S
Surrey Herald Newspapers

White, Gordon S

Williams, Michael
The Daily Telegraph, also Editor, *Royal & Ancient Golfer's Handbook*

(L) Wilson, Enid

Wilson, Mark
PGA European Tour

Wind, Herbert Warren

Wood, Ian
The Scotsman

Wright, Ben

Zachrisson, Goran

Golfing Hotel Compendium

The Golfing Hotel Compendium is a comprehensive source of information for golfers wishing to find the most comfortable place to stay at or close to some of the finest courses in the country. This section has been compiled from the premier hotels in the British Isles which include golf among their many attractions.

If readers wish especially to recommend an establishment which is not listed in this section of the Royal & Ancient Golfer's Handbook the editors will be happy to be advised.

ENGLAND

South West

The Broadsands Links Hotel

Bascombe Road, Churston Ferrers,
Brixham, Devon TQ5 0JJ.
Tel (01803) 842360

Overlooking Torbay with unrivalled sea views our hotel offers a warm welcome to our guests. All 30 bedrooms have tea and coffee-making facilities, colour TV, beautifully appointed en suite bathrooms. Enjoy our excellent food and wine. Marvellous Churston Golf Course, 6,238 yards par 70, is adacent to the hotel.

Burn Court Hotel

Bude, Cornwall EX23 8DB.
Tel/Fax (01288) 352872

Situated on edge of town overlooking golf course with easy access to beach, close to town centre. Extensive à la carte and vegetarian menu. 32 bedrooms, 22 en suite. BB from £25 per person per night. DBB from £37 per person per night.

Burnham & Berrow Golf Club

St Cristopher's Way, Burnham-on-Sea,
Somerset TA8 2PE.
Tel (01278) 785760

18-hole championship links golf course and 9-hole course. (See advertisement page 23 for further details.)

Chedington Court

Chedington,
Beaminster,
Dorset DT8 3HY.
Tel (01935) 891265

Jacobean-style country house hotel of distinctive informality. Spectacular views from all the well furnished and spacious rooms. Renowned for good food and wines. Own 18-hole course nearby on parkland in beautiful wooded surroundings.

Commodore Hotel AA/RAC 3-Star

Beach Road,
Sand Bay, Kewstoke,
Weston-Super-Mare,
Somerset BS22 9UZ.
Tel (01934) 415778 Fax (01934) 636483

Peaceful and stylish haven dedicated to fine food and service. Reduced green fees at both Weston/Worlebury clubs. Special break/party rates. AA/RAC awards for cuisine and service.

Commonwood Manor Hotel

St Martins Road,
East Looe,
Cornwall PL13 1LP.
Tel (01503) 262929

Family run AA/RAC 2-Star hotel. 11 bedrooms, two luxury cottages and heated pool in six acre grounds. Spectacular views overlooking river valley yet only ten minutes' walk to Looe. A perfect base for Cornwall's finest courses.

Elfordleigh Hotel & Country Club

Colebrook,
Plympton,
Plymouth, Devon PL7 5EB.
Tel (01752) 336428

The hotel has 18 bedrooms situated in the picturesque Plym Valley offering an attractive 9-hole 68 par golf course. Extensive leisure facilities including two heated swimming pools, jacuzzi, steam room, sauna, sun beds, gym, squash, tennis, snooker and croquet.

Gloucester Hotel & Country Club

Robinswood Hill,
Matson Lane,
Gloucester GL4 9EA.
Tel (01452) 525653

Extensive leisure facilities including indoor swimming pool, sauna, gymnasium, solarium. Squash courts, tennis courts, snooker, pool, skittles. Championship dry ski slopes. Full 18-hole and 9-hole par 3 courses.

Heron House Hotel

Thurlestone Sands,
Nr Salcombe,
South Devon TQ7 3JY.
Tel (01548) 561308/600 Fax (01548) 560180

Beautifully appointed hotel. Situated in tranquil surroundings at sea's edge. Views over two excellent 18-hole courses and one 9-hole course (concession available). Excellent cuisine and wine. (See advertisement page 367 for further details.)

Holbrook Country House Hotel

Holbrook,
Nr Wincanton,
Somerset BA9 8BS.
Tel (01963) 32377

Delightful country house set in its own grounds. Ideal centre for golf courses in Somerset, Dorset, Wiltshire. Outdoor pool, tennis, squash, croquet. Restaurant and lounge bar open to non-residents. Special rates for two day breaks. Open all year.

Holne Chase Hotel

Ashburton,
Devon TQ13 7NS.
Tel (01364) 631471

A secluded country house central for eighteen golf courses within an hour's drive. Reduced green fees at Wrangaton and Hele Park. The proprietor views the golf courses like whisky - some very much better than others. Ask for his notes.

Home Farm Country Hotel

Wilmington,
Honiton, Devon EX14 9JR.
Tel (01404) 831278 Fax (01404) 831411

16th century farmhouse in five acres of garden. Friendly and relaxed atmosphere. With 14 en suite rooms, attractive bar serving light meals, lunch and dinner. Table d'hôte or à la carte in restaurant. Six golf courses within fifteen miles.

Littlecourt Hotel

Seafield Road,
Sidmouth,
Devon EX10 8HF.
Tel (01395) 515279

Amazingly four golf courses within half an hour's drive, including one on our doorstep. Beautifully run, quiet, warm Regency hotel offering the best of West country dishes. Private parking. Some non-smoking bedrooms. AA/RAC awards. Visa/Access. Super short breaks.

Lostwithiel Golf & Country Club

Lower Polscoe,
Lostwithiel,
Cornwall PL22 0HQ.
Tel (01208) 873550 Fax (01208) 873479

A hotel, golf and country club of great charm and character. The 18-hole course with its two distinctive nines provides pleasurable golf for the low handicap player and less experienced golfer alike. Set amid the valley of the river Fowey.

The Manor House Hotel

Castle Combe,
Chippenham, Wiltshire SN14 7HR.
Tel (01249) 782206 Fax (01249) 782159

Nestling in sixteen acres of gardens and parkland, the 15th century Manor House Hotel is one of Britain's most idyllically set country house hotels. 36 luxurious bedrooms, award winning cusine and first class service. Spectacular and challenging 18-hole 6,340 yard par 73 championship golf course set in 200 acres. Golfing breaks available all year. (See advertisement page 379 for further details).

Marine Hotel

Cliff Road, Salcombe,
South Devon TQ8 8JH.
(01548) 844444

The quiet Devon sailing resort of Salcombe enjoys a mild Mediterranean climate throughout the year. In this tranquil setting directly on the Kingsbridge estuary, the Marine Hotel welcomes golfers of all abilities!

The Maypool Park Hotel

Maypool, Galmpton,
Nr Brixham,
Devon TQ5 0ET.
Tel (01803) 842442 Fax (01803) 845782

Peace, quiet, spectacular views of the river Dart and gourmet food. 10 luxury en suite rooms with all facilities from £35. Nearest golf two miles - ten courses within 35 mile radius. Parking. 100% non-smoking. ETB 4-Crowns.

The Old Manor

Dunster,
Somerset TA24 6PJ.
Tel (01643) 821216

Peaceful accommodation situated in lovely grounds. Five minutes' walk from the 9th hole. Minehead Golf Course only five minutes by car to the clubhouse. Resident proprietors.

Orchard Hill Hotel

Bideford,
North Devon EX39 2QY.
Tel (01237) 472872

AA 2-Star country style hotel. Extensive grounds and car park. All bedrooms en suite, superb restaurant. Minutes from the Royal North Devon and another six excellent courses within a short driving distance.

Penhallow Manor

Altarnun,
Nr Launceston,
Cornwall PL15 7SJ.
Tel (01566) 86206 Fax (01566) 86179

Exclusive country hotel, centrally situated for both north and south coasts. At least twelve courses within twenty mile radius providing wonderful varied golf in most beautiful countryside. We guarantee excellent value and service. Noted cuisine and wine list. Small parties and functions a speciality. (See advertisement page 377 for further details.)

Penventon Hotel
AA/RAC 3-Star Rosette

Redruth,
Cornwall.
Tel (01209) 214141 Fax (01209) 219164

Large country house hotel, parkland setting, central for six courses. Superior restaurant, resident pianists, three bars, nightclub, indoor pool complex, sauna, jacuzzi, robes provided, masseuse, hairdresser. Special bargain rates all year. Colour brochures. A Cornish welcome awaits you. Open all year.

Pines Hotel

Burlington Road, Swanage,
Dorset BH19 1LT.
Tel (01929) 425211

50-bedroom family run 3-Star hotel. All bedrooms have private bathroom, telephone and colour TV. One and a half miles from Isle of Purbeck Golf Club. Within easy reach of all Dorset courses.

Port Gaverne Hotel

Nr Port Isaac, Cornwall PL29 3SQ.
Tel (01208) 880244 Fax (01208) 880151

Courses within easy reach of hotel are St Enodoc, Bowood Park, St Mellion, Lanhydrock and Looe. Freephone 0500 657867.

Riversford Hotel

Limers Lane, Bideford, Devon EX39 2RG.
Tel (01237) 474239

Peace and tranquility in gardens beside the river Torridge. A relaxing retreat after a day on the fairways of North Devon. Excellent food, a flexible lounge bar and comfortable en suite bedrooms. Concessionary golf at North Devon only five minutes from hotel.

Royal Beacon Hotel

The Beacon, Exmouth, Devon EX8 2AF.
Tel (01395) 264886 Fax (01395) 268890

Magnificently situated south facing hotel directly overlooking the sea. 30 en suite bedrooms with radio, colour TV and video 'Film of the Day' system, hairdryer, trouser press and direct dial telephone. Games and snooker room, Fennels restaurant and Eccentrics bar. Unlimited golf on Woodbury Park championship course (6,707 yards), Nigel Mansell golf complex planned for 1995.

Royal Clarence Hotel

31 The Esplanade, Burnham-on-Sea,
Somerset TA8 1BQ.
Tel (01278) 783138 Fax (01278) 792965

Sea front hotel ideal for Berrow and Brean golf courses. Great selection of real ales. Good food. AA/RAC 2-Star hotel ETB 4-Crown.

Royal Oak Hotel

Duke Street, Lostwithiel,
Cornwall PL22 1AO.
Tel (01208) 872552

Family run country inn famous for its range of real ales and superb restaurant food. Centrally situated with twelve courses within 25 miles radius. Bedrooms with en suite facilities, TV etc.

Springfield Country Hotel & Leisure Club

Grange Road, Wareham, Dorset BH20 5AL.
Tel (01929) 552177

Country setting in six acres of gardens. 32 bedrooms en suite with colour TV, radio, direct dial telephone. Large new leisure complex, two swimming pools, two saunas, steam room, spa, solarium, gymnasium, snooker, two squash courts, games room, tennis. Three golf courses nearby.

St Mellion Lodges & Hotel St Mellion Golf & Country Club

St Mellion, Saltash, Cornwall PL12 6SD.
Tel (01579) 50101 Fax (01579) 50116

Gold Award luxury lodges nestled in the heart of Nicklaus championship and Old Course. AA/RAC 3-star hotel and full range of sport, personal fitness and leisure facilities.

Tewkesbury Park Hotel Country Club Resort

Lincoln Green Lane, Tewkesbury, Gloucestershire GL20 7DN.
Tel (01684) 295405 Fax (01684) 292386

This 78-bedroom hotel with modern facilities is surrounded by its own 18-hole golf course. It also offers heated indoor pool, sauna, jacuzzi, solarium, health and beauty salon, snooker, squash/floodlit tennis courts, steam room and fitness centre. (Part of the Country Club Hotels Group, see page 4.)

Trevose Golf & Country Club

Constantine Bay, Padstow, North Cornwall PL28 8JB.
Tel (01841) 520208 Fax (01841) 521057

Trevose offers not only great golf (championship 18-hole course, a 9-hole full length (3,100 yards) par 35 plus a 9-hole short course) but also a first class clubhouse and restaurant, three hard all-weather tennis courts, a heated outdoor swimming pool in the summer, a games room for the kids and a boutique. Accommodation is available in bungalows, chalets, luxury flats and dormy suites. Send for our detailed full colour

Watergate Bay Hotel

Watergate Bay, Cornwall TR8 4AA.
Tel (01637) 860543 Fax (01637) 860333

On its own beach between Trevose and Newquay, this family run hotel offers old fashioned service, good food/good living with entertainment most evenings. Warm indoor/outdoor pools, sports hall. SuperBreak bargains - compare our golf terms before you book. (See advertisement page 367 for further details.)

Welbeck Manor & Sparkwell Golf Course

Blacklands, Sparkwell, Plymouth, Devon PL7 5DF.
Tel/Fax (01752) 837219

A testing 9-hole pay as you play course and also a par 3 course, set in 60 acres of parkland. Facilities include a well equipped golf shop, excellent hotel accommodation, restaurant and bar. Open to the public. Golf societies welcome.

Westberry Hotel

Rhind Street, Bodmin, Cornwall PL31 2EL.
Tel (01208) 72772

The hotel has 22 bedrooms mostly en suite. Situated close to Lanhydrock Golf Club and central for many other courses. Good food and service with a comfortable bar lounge and snooker room.

White Hart Hotel

Broad Street, Launceston, Cornwall PL15 8AA.
Tel (01566) 772013 Fax (01566) 773668

Old coaching inn two miles from Cornwall Devon border. Breaks available with choice of seven courses within twenty miles. Golf arranged for you. 27 en suite rooms with colour TV, telephone and tea and coffee-making facilities. Excellent menu available Residents' lounge with full size snooker table and Sky TV.

Whitsand Bay Hotel Golf & Country Club

Portwrinkle, Crafthole, By Torpoint, Cornwall PL11 3BU.
Tel (01503) 30276

Spectacularly sited *own 18-hole golf course*, overlooking the ocean in Cornish fishing hamlet, with 1st tee 100 yards from front door. Leisure complex, heated indoor swimming pool, sauna, solarium, massage/beauty salons.

Yeoldon House Hotel

Durrant Lane,
Northam,
Bideford, Devon EX39 2RL.
Tel (01237) 474400 Fax (01237) 476618

Play the oldest course in England: Royal North Devon. We take pride in our excellent cuisine and fine wines. Our rooms are comfortable and perfect to rest those well golfed bones. Societies and parties of any number welcome. ETB 4-Crown Highly Commended. (See advertisement page 367 for further details.)

South East

Ashdown Forest Hotel

Chapel Lane,
Forest Row, East Sussex.
Tel (01342) 824866 Fax (01342) 824869

Royal Ashdown New Course. Family owned and run hotel offering comfortable accommodation and good food and wines. Royal Ashdown Forest New Course operated by hotel exclusively for residents and visitors. (See advertisement page 367 for further details.)

The Berystede

Bagshot Road,
Sunninghill,
Ascot,
Berkshire SL5 9JH.
Tel (01344) 23311

Supplement the enjoyment of your golf by staying at The Berystede Hotel. Within a short distance of many excellent courses, just 30 minutes from Heathrow, three miles from M3, six miles from M2/M4. Special golf breaks available.

The Blakemore Thistle Hotel

Blakemore End Road,
Little Wymondley,
Nr Hitchin,
Hertfordshire SG4 7JJ.
Tel (01438) 355821 Fax (01438) 742114

A secluded comfortable hotel set in over six acres of attractive landscaped grounds, with 82 en suite bedrooms and outdoor swimming pool. Only two minutes from Chesfield Downs Golf Centre an 18-hole golf course (01462) 482929.

Boship Farm Hotel

A22, Lower Dicker, Nr Hailsham,
East Sussex.
Tel (01323) 844826

Set within seventeen acres, with health suite including jacuzzi and sauna. Outdoor heated pool and tennis court. Bedrooms have full facilities. Ten golf courses within half an hour, including East Sussex National. Teeing-off times booked.

Botley Park Hotel & Country Club

Winchester Road, Boorley Green, Botley,
Hampshire SO3 2UA.
Tel (01489) 780888 Fax (01489) 789242

Set in 176 acres of rolling Hampshire countryside, this 4-star hotel has 100 en suite bedrooms, superb restaurant, extensive leisure facilities and its own picturesque and challenging 18-hole par 70 golf course and driving range. (See advertisement page 377 for further details).

The Boxley House Hotel

Boxley Village, Maidstone,
Kent ME14 3DZ.
Tel (01622) 692269

Set in twenty acres of parkland, this beautiful Georgian house with 18 en suite rooms offers friendly service, excellent menus, comfortable bar. Easy access to the best of Kent's golf courses and motorways.

Chewton Glen Hotel
Health & Country Club

New Milton, Hampshire BH25 6QS.
Tel (01425) 275341

Renowned for outstanding cuisine, extensive wine list and its health club with magnificent indoor pool, gymnasium, indoor tennis. Uncrowded 9-hole par 3 golf course which is free for residents. Tuition available. Many interesting and beautiful courses nearby including Ferndown, Brockenhurst, Broadstone, Isle of Purbeck and Parkstone.

Cottesmore Country Club

Buchan Hill, Pease Pottage, Crawley,
Sussex RH11 9AT.
Tel (01293) 528256 Fax (01293) 522819

11 en suite bedrooms overlooking quiet undulating Sussex countryside. Guests can enjoy two full 18-hole mature golf courses, tennis, squash, indoor pool, spa bath, steam, sauna and fitness rooms. Fifteen minutes from Gatwick, one mile from Pease Pottage exit off M23.

The Crest Hotel - Swindon

Oxford Road,
Stratton St Margaret,
Swindon, Wiltshire SN3 4TL.
Tel (01793) 831333

A modern 91-bedroomed hotel on the outskirts of Swindon. All rooms with full en suite facilities. The Laurels restaurant and bar offer comfortable surroundings to enjoy good food and drink. Fifteen major courses within twelve miles of the hotel, with 9-18 holes from £5.50 to £40.00.

Crown Inn

(The Famous Cherry Brandy House)
Ramsgate Road,
Sarre,
Nr Birchington, Kent CT7 0LF.
Tel (01843) 847808 Fax (01843) 847914

Close to the famous courses at Deal, Sandwich and Broadstairs. All 12 rooms en suite. Excellent restaurant and bar meals, fine wine. Traditional locally blended ales. Warm informal atmosphere. Private parking for 40. BB or bargain break rates available year round. 3-Crown Commended. Log fires...gleaming horse brasses...oak beams...

Dale Hill Hotel

Ticehurst,
Wadhurst,
East Sussex TN5 7DQ.
Tel (01580) 200112

4-star 5-crown highly commended award winning luxurious new hotel situated in an area of outstanding national beauty, with elegant health club and highly acclaimed 18-hole golf course. An additional 18-hole course under construction.

Five Lakes Hotel
Golf & Country Club

Colchester Road,
Whitehouse Hill,
Tolleshunt Knights,
Maldon, Essex CM9 8HX.
Tel (01621) 868888 Fax (01621) 869696

Luxury hotel and country club nestling in 320 acres of Essex countryside, close to the Roman town of Colchester and 'Constable Country'. Extensive facilities include a deluxe hotel, indoor and outdoor tennis, squash courts, health centre and indoor pool. Golf packages, incentive and leisure breaks available upon request.

Flackley Ash Hotel

Peasmarsh, Rye, East Sussex TN31 6YH.
Tel (01797) 230651

3-star Georgian country house hotel set in five acres with croquet lawn. Indoor swimming pool, whirlpool spa, saunas, mini-gym and 'beautique'. Extensive wine list, a friendly welcome and an AA Rosette for our food.

Gatton Manor Hotel
Golf & Country Club Ltd

Ockley, Nr Dorking, Surrey RH5 5PQ.
Tel (01306) 627555/7

Set amidst its own 18-hole golf course in 200 acres of parklands and lakes, situated between London and the south coast, in the heart of the Surrey countryside. Superb all en suite accommodation overlooking the golf course and grounds. À la carte restaurants, large lounge bar, sport pursuits and conference suites.

Goodwood Park Hotel
Country Club Resort

Goodwood, Nr Chichester,
West Sussex PO18 0QB.
Tel (01243) 775987 Fax (01243) 533802

Country club hotel set in the 12,000 acre Goodwood Estate with a testing 18-hole golf course and superb leisure facilities including golf range, practice area, putting green and fully equipped sports shop. (Part of the Country Club Hotels group see page 4.)

Holiday Inn Crowne Plaza - London Heathrow

Stockley Road, West Drayton,
Middlesex UB7 9NA.
Tel (01895) 445555

4-Star Deluxe hotel: 375 Executive bedrooms with minibar, satellite TV, tea and coffee-making facilities. 24-hour room service available to all rooms. 24-hour lounge service. Two restaurants, two bars. 33 conference rooms. Superb health and leisure facilities. Indoor pool, spa bath, sauna, solarium, gym and 9-hole golf course. Helipad and free parking to residents.

Hope Anchor Hotel

Watch Bell Street, Rye,
East Sussex TN31 7HA.
Tel (01797) 222216 Fax (01797) 223796

Family run hotel with a super restaurant. We cater for golfers' needs, ie. early morning calls and breakfasts, and drying out facilities. Golf societies welcome. Other activities in our area, wind surfing, tennis, squash and swimming all close by.

Kennel Holt Hotel

Goldhurst Road,
Cranbrook,
Kent TN17 2PF.
Tel (01580) 712032

A tranquil Elizabethan manor house in the heart of the Kentish Weald golfing area - Lamberhurst, Tunbridge Wells, Cranbrook, Benenden. Eight double bedrooms en suite, wonderful gardens. Our restaurant serves fresh ingredients imaginatively cooked.

The Langham Hotel

Royal Parade,
Eastbourne,
East Sussex BN22 7AH.
Tel (01323) 731451

Play 72 holes over three days staying half board at family run 4-crown hotel. 87 en suite bedrooms with entertainment during season. £140 per player, £60 non-playing partner. Small groups and societies welcome.

Lansdowne Hotel

King Edward's Parade,
Eastbourne,
East Sussex BN21 4EE.
Tel (01323) 725174 Fax (01323) 739721

Play 36 holes a day on choice of seven courses; we book your tee-off time. Two nights with green fees, light lunch at club and use of our drying room. 15 January to 28 February, £134; 1 to 31 March, £144; 1 April to 31 May, £146; 1 June to 30 September, £150; 1 October to 31 December, £144. Extra days pro rata. (See advertisement page 377 for further details.

The Lawns Hotel

Station Road,
Holt, Norfolk NR25 6BS.
Tel (01263) 713390

An outstanding Georgian hotel. Highly acclaimed cuisine. ETB 3-Crown Commended. We will be pleased to organise your golfing tour. Small groups and couples catered for. Bargain breaks.

Lyndhurst Park Hotel

High Street,
Lyndhurst,
Hampshire SO43 7NL.
Tel (01703) 283923

59-bedroomed hotel set in its own grounds. Ten minutes' walk from the New Forest Golf Club and within easy driving distance of Brockenhurst and Burley golf clubs. Ample free parking.

Manor of Groves Golf & Country Club

High Wych,
Sawbridgeworth, Hertfordshire CM21 0LA.
Tel (01279) 722333 Fax (01279) 726972

This superb 18-hole golf course set around its own Geogian manor house offers the ideal setting for that break away. Along with its special rated packages, and golf school, the clubhouse facilities include superb cuisine, bar, and a function room suitable for all occasions.

Meon Valley Hotel Country Club Resort

Sandy Lane,
Shedfield,
Nr Southampton, Hampshire SO32 2HQ.
Tel (01329) 833455 Fax (01329) 834411

Set in 225 acres of Hampshire parkland, Meon Valley Hotel offers a challenging 18-hole golf course and an equally testing 9-hole course. The hotel also offers extensive leisure and conference facilities. (Part of the Country Club Hotels group see page 4.)

Pennyhill Park Hotel & Country Club

London Road,
Bagshot, Surrey GU19 5ET.
Tel (01276) 471774

An exceptional country house hotel with international reputation for its restaurant, bedrooms and grounds. 9-hole par 4 golf, shooting lodge, tennis, swimming, fishing and horse riding from own stables. Wentworth, Sunningdale, Ascot, Smiths Lawn all within ten minutes.

Royal Berkshire Hotel

London Road,
Sunninghill,
Ascot, Berkshire.
Tel (01344) 23322

Superb Queen Anne country house hotel, set in fifteen acres of gardens. Excellent leisure facilities. Award winning restaurant.

Selsdon Park Hotel

Sanderstead,
South Croydon, Surrey CR2 8YA.
Tel 0181-657 8811 Fax 0181-651 6171

Traditional country house set in 200 acres of parkland with an 18-hole championship course. Green fee players welcome. Exclusive tropical leisure club. Touring golf professional - Sam Torrance.

Tudor Park Hotel Country Club Resort
Ashford Road, Bearsted, Maidstone, Kent ME14 4NQ.
Tel (01622) 734334 Fax (01622) 735360

Situated in the Garden of England, Tudor Park is set in a 220 acre former deer park. Its superb golf course is designed by Donald Steel. The hotel also offers excellent accommodation, leisure and conference facilities. (Part of the Country Club Hotels Group see page 4.)

Whitehaven Hotel
34 Willbury Road, Hove, Brighton, Sussex.
Tel (01273) 778355 Fax (01273) 731177

Independent small hotel offering personal service and friendly atmosphere. 4-Crown and Egon Ronay recommended. All rooms en suite. Golfing details and green fees provided on enquiry. Golfing mini breaks available on request.

The Woolpack Inn
High Street, Chilham, Canterbury, Kent CT4 8DL.
Tel (01227) 730351 Fax (01227) 731053

Close to several excellent golf courses five miles from Canterbuy. 13 en suite rooms. Oak beamed restaurant, inglenook bar. Private parking. BB or bargain break rates available all year round. 3-Crown Commended. Log fires...gleaming horse brasses...oak beams. Award winning locally brewed ales.

East Anglia

Abbotsley Golf Hotel
Eynesbury Hardwicke, St Neots, Cambridgeshire PE19 4XN.
Tel (01480) 474000 Fax (01480) 471018

Luxurious moated country house amidst picturesque golf course. Delightful bedrooms and galleried dining room. Surrounding courtyard of award winning gardens. Internationally renowned golf schools with Vivien Saunders. Squash and golf range.

Barnham Broom Hotel Golf & Leisure Centre
Honingham Road, Barnham Broom, Norwich, Norfolk NR9 4DD.
Tel (01603) 759393 Fax (01603) 758224

East Anglia's finest conference and leisure centre lies in 250 acres of countryside. 52 fully equipped bedrooms include family rooms, served by Flints restaurant and sports snack bar. Four squash courts, snooker, heated indoor swimming pool and spa jets, tennis and 36-hole golf. Golfing Getaway £164. (See advertisement page 379 for further details.)

Beaumaris Hotel
15 South Street, Sheringham, Norfolk NR26 8LL.
Tel (01263) 822370

Established and run by the same family for almost fifty years with a reputation for personal service and excellent English cuisine. 24 en suite bedrooms. AA 2-Star Ashley Courtenay recommended. Three minutes' walk Sheringham's exhilarating cliff top golf course.

Crown & Castle Hotel
Orford, Nr Woodbridge, Suffolk IP12 2LJ.
Tel (01394) 450205 Fax (01394) 450176

A warm welcome awaits you at our privately owned 20-bedroom Tudor hotel. AA, Tourist Board and Les Routiers recommended. Six excellent courses within a fifteen mile radius. Special rates for party bookings and midweek breaks.

The Linksway Hotel
Golf Course Road, Old Hunstanton, Norfolk PE36 6JE.
Tel (01485) 532209

Set in secluded gardens, overlooking stanton's 1st fairway - The ideal location. *'Good Food'*, *'Good Wine'* and a *'Hearty'* welcome. All rooms fully en suite. Cocktail bar. Heated indoor swimming pool and spa pool.

Riverside Hotel & Restaurant
Mill Street, Mildenhall, Bury St Edmunds, Suffolk IP28 7DP.
Tel (01638) 717274

Family run 24-bedroom hotel (AA/RAC 3-Star) on edge of busy market town, two minutes' walk from centre. Nine courses and driving range within twelve miles including Royal Worlington. Super food, warm atmosphere, amenable insomniac hosts!

Thorpeness Golf Club Hotel
Thorpeness, Nr Leiston, Suffolk IP16 4NH.
Tel (01728) 452176 Fax (01728) 453868

Modern luxury hotel adjoining the clubhouse on one of East Anglia's finest 18-hole courses. Situated on the lovely, unspoiled Suffolk coast. Ideal too for non-golfers. (See advertisement page 373 for further details.)

Ufford Park Hotel Golf & Leisure

Yarmouth Road, Ufford, Woodbridge, Suffolk IP12 1QW.
Tel (01394) 383555 Fax (01394) 383582

Challenging 18-hole par 70 golf course set in historic parkland. Accommodation, restaurant, bars, leisure facilities inclusive of indoor heated pool, gym, fitness studio, sauna, solarium and beauty salon. Competitive rates. (See advertisement page 373 for further details.)

Wentworth Hotel

Wentworth Road, Aldeburgh, Suffolk IP15 5BD.
Tel (01728) 452312 Fax (01728) 454343

Country house hotel with sea views. 38 bedrooms all with colour TV, radio and tea-maker. Two comfortable lounges, cosy bar, log fires and antique furniture. Our restaurant specialises in local fresh produce and seafood.

White Horse Hotel

Station Road, Leiston, Suffolk IP16 4HD.
Tel (01728) 830694 Fax (01728) 833105

Close to three excellent courses in the heart of Suffolk heritage coast. Friendly bars, excellent food, 12 rooms, 11 en suite, all with TV and telephone. Bargain weekend breaks all year.

East Midlands

Belton Woods Hotel

Belton, Nr Grantham, Lincolnshire NG32 2LN.
Tel (01476) 593200

A magnificent hotel, golf and leisure development set in 475 acres of glorious countryside. Two challenging 18-hole golf courses, 9-hole course, driving range, putting green and extensive leisure facilities. 136 bedrooms. (Part of the De Vere Hotels Group.)

Breadsall Priory Hotel Country Club Resort

Moor Road, Morley, Nr Derby, Derbyshire DE7 6DL.
Tel (01332) 832235 Fax (01332) 833509

Based on a 13th century mansion set in 400 acres of stunning parkland, Breadsall Priory offers two superb golf courses, excellent accommodation and comprehensive leisure and conference facilities. (Part of the Country Club Hotels Group see page 4.)

West Midlands

The Belfry

Wishaw, North Warwickshire B76 9PR.
Tel (01675) 470 301

The Belfry, set in 370 acres of beautiful parkland, offers the Brabazon Golf Course, venue for the Ryder Cup and the Derby Course - a challenge for the amateur golfer. The luxury hotel itself has a superb leisure centre and a fine selection of restaurants and bars. (Part of The De Vere Hotels Group.)

Farthingstone Hotel Golf & Leisure Centre

Farthingstone, Towcester, Northamptonshire NN12 8HA.
Tel (01327) 361291 Fax (01327) 361645

Set in glorious wooded countryside, just 90 minutes outside London. Farthingstone Hotel offers 16 superb en suite rooms, a challenging 18-hole golf course, squash courts, full size snooker tables, and a carvery restaurant. Highly competitve tariffs.

Forest of Arden Hotel Country Club Resort

Maxstoke Lane, Meriden, Warwickshire CV7 7HR.
Tel (01676) 522335 Fax (01676) 523711

Set in 10,000 acres of Warwickshire countryside, the Forest of Arden in 1995, host to the Murphy's English Open for the third year running, offers some of Britain's best golfing alongside first class accommodation, leisure and conference facilities. (Part of the Country Club Hotels Group see page 4.)

Patshull Park Hotel Golf & Country Club

Pattingham, Shropshire WV6 7HR.
Tel (01902) 700100 Fax (01902) 700874

Parkland, lakeside 18-hole championship John Jacobs' designed course in grounds of the Earl of Dartmouth estate. Corporate, society and residential packages. 49 en suite bedrooms, swimming pool, leisure centre, gymnasium, snooker room, fishing. Restaurant and Bunkers coffee shop.

The Redfern Hotel

Cleobury Mortimer, Shropshire DY14 8AA.
Tel (01299) 270395

Family run 2-Star 4-Crown Commended hotel with AA Rosette and RAC Merit award for food. Fifteen golf courses within a short drive. Reasonable inclusive prices with unlimited golf available.

Telford Golf & Country Club Moat House

Great Hay, Sutton Hill, Telford, Shropshire TF7 4DT.
Tel (01952) 585642

Overlooking the Ironbridge Gorge, this recently extended and refurbished hotel offers its own 18-hole championship course, 9-hole par 3 course, driving range and practice areas. The extensive leisure facilities include squash courts, swimming pool, gymnasium, snooker, whirlpool, sauna and steam rooms. There is a resident masseur. (See advertisement page 379 for further details.)

Welcombe Hotel & Golf Course

Warwick Road, Stratford-upon-Avon, Warwickshire CV37 0NR.
Tel (01789) 295252 Fax (01789) 414666

A 4-star Jacobean-style mansion set within its own 6,217 yards private golf course. A newly created clubhouse and pro shop within the hotel's 157 acres enhance the parkland course.

Ye Olde Dog & Partridge Hotel

High Street, Tutbury, Nr Burton-on-Trent, Staffordshire DE13 9LS.
Tel (01283) 813030

Situated centre of village of Tutbury, 15th-century inn of historic interest. 17 bedrooms, carvery, grand piano nightly. Branston Golf Club six miles away owned by parent company. Several other courses close by.

Yorkshire & Humberside

Aldwark Manor Golf Hotel

Aldwark, Alne, York, Yorkshire YO6 2NF.
Tel (01347) 838146 (Hotel)
Tel (01347) 838353 (Golf)
Fax (01347) 838867

This fully restored Victorian manor offers its guests all modern facilities with superb food, wine and country location to complement the 18-hole par 71 parkland course, which holds many surprises for our visitors. Open all year round to non-residents. Twelve miles from York and Harrogate on the river Ure. (See advertisement page 381 for further details.)

Bay Horse Inn

Burnt Yates,
Harrogate,
South Yorkshire HG3 3EJ.
Tel (01423) 770230

Join a list of golfing parties who have enjoyed the warm welcome and very good food at this renowned old inn ideally situated for all your golfing needs. Also local race meetings Ripon, Thirsk, York, Wetherby.

Cave Castle Golf Hotel

South Cave,
Brough,
East Yorkshire HU15 2EU.
Tel (01430) 421286

An ancient manor house hotel in 160 acres at the foot of the Wolds. 18 holes, 6,409 yards sss 71. À la carte, banqueting and conference facilities. Situated at the end of the M62 and easily accessible. Societies and non-members welcome.

The Flaneburg Hotel

North Marine Road,
Flamborough,
Nr Bridlington, East Yorkshire.
Tel/Fax (01850) 284 0262

Situated on Flamborough Headland the Flaneburg is an ideal base for golfers to the East Yorkshire coast. Eight good courses to choose from - all very affordable. Hotel has 14 rooms (9 en suite) upto 20 singles. Licensed. AA/ETB 3-Crowns.

The Harewood Arms Hotel

Harrogate Road,
Harewood,
Nr Leeds,
West Yorkshire LS17 9LH.
Tel 0113 288 6566 Fax 0113 288 6064

Ideally located for businessmen and tourists. Seven miles from the commercial centre of Leeds and seven miles from the spa town of Harrogate. The hotel is conveniently situated for discovering the charm of the Yorkshire Dales, with an abundance of things to see and do. (See advertisement page 373 for further details.)

The Jarvis Bankfield Hotel

Bradford Road,
Bingley,
Bradford BD16 1TU.
Tel (01274) 567123

A warm Yorkshire welcome to this 103-bedroomed hotel. Set in its own grounds within easy reach of four courses, Bingley St Ives, Shipley, Northcliffe and Bradford. Room and breakfast from £32.00 per person.

Millers House Hotel

Middleham,
Wensleydale,
North Yorkshire.
Tel (01969) 622630

Hotel of the Year runner-up YHTB, winner of AA Red Rosette and 4-Crown Highly Commended. Elegant Georgian country house in historic, peaceful village. Four golf courses nearby plus fishing and horse racing. Golfing house parties.

Park View Hotel

6 Grosvenor Crescent,
Scarborough,
North Yorkshire.
Tel 01723 364280

Park View Hotel is a family run hotel offering a warm welcome from Anne and Derek Menary. Conveniently situated for easy access to all golf courses in the Scarborough area.

North West

Alma Lodge

149 Buxton Road,
Stockport,
Greater Manchester.
Tel 0161-483 4431

Located on the southern edge of Stockport, within easy access to M63, M56, M6 and M62. 52 bedrooms with one suite, all rooms have radio, colour TV, direct dial telephone, hairdryer, tea and coffee-making facilities etc. Extensive car park. Seven miles from Manchester Airport.

The Borrowdale Hotel

Borrowdale,
Keswick, Cumbria CA12 5UY.
Tel (017687) 77224

Traditional lakeland hotel set amidst beautiful scenery. All rooms have modern facilities. Excellent reputation for food, service and wine. Four poster beds available! Free golf at Keswick Golf Club, a challenging 18-hole moorland course, Monday to Friday. (See advertisement page 381 for further details.)

Brabyns Hotel

Shaftesbury Avenue,
Blackpool,
Lancashire FY2 9QQ.
Tel (01253) 354263 Fax (01253) 352915

2-Star hotel open all year. Appointed to high standard. Restaurant offers excellent and varied menus including vegetarian dishes. Choice of several golf courses including Royal Lytham. Easy access from M55. Car park. Near Blackpool North Shore Golf Club.

Bramhall Moat House Hotel

Bramhall Lane South,
Bramhall, Cheshire SK7 2EB.
Tel 0161-439 8116

In the heart of Bramhall lies this 65-bedroomed modern hotel. Situated close to more than ten golf courses, including Bramhall Park and Prestbury. Competitive prices. Full restaurant and bar facilities. Ample free car parking.

Broomhaugh Hotel

Ridingmill,
Northumberland NE44 6EG.
Tel (01434) 682256

Peacefully situated next to the village cricket ground, our family run licensed country house hotel is close to many golf courses, including Slaley Hall. All the recently refurbished bedrooms are spacious with en suites and colour TV.

Calder House Private Hotel

The Banks,
Seascale, Cumbria CA20 1QP.
Tel (01946) 728538 Fax (01946) 728265

Hotel is adjacent to the 6,416 yards links Seascale championship courses, and 100 yards from the beach. Fully centrally heated, double glazed, TV, tea and coffee-making facilities, radio/clock/alarm, direct dial telephone. Fax facilities. Fully licensed. Special golf breaks. (See advertisement page 381 for further details.)

The Dormy

Lancaster Golf & Country Club
Ashton Hall,
Ashton-with-Stodday,
Lancaster LA2 0AJ.
Tel (01524) 751247 Fax (01524) 752135

Ideal for small parties of up to eighteen persons. For terms and reservations please apply to the secretary. (See advertisement page 22 for further details.)

The Dormy House

Royal Lytham & St Anne's Golf Club
Links Gate,
Lytham St Anne's,
Lancashire FY8 3LQ.
Tel (01253) 724206 Fax (01253) 780946

Ideal for small parties wishing to play the championship course. Accommodation for men only. Apply to the secretary. (See advertisement page 20 for further details.)

The George Hotel

Devonshire Street,
Penrith,
Cumbria CA11 7SU.
Tel (01768) 862696 Fax (01768) 868223

Privately owned hotel. All rooms with private facilities, TV, direct dial telephone, hospitality tray, radio and baby listening system. Private car park. Double or twin room from £53.00. Single room from £38.95 inclusive of VAT and full English breakfast.

Lord Crewe Arms Hotel

Front Street,
Bamburgh,
Northumberland NE69 7BL.
Tel (01668) 214243 Fax (01668) 214273

Charming old country inn situated below the castle and close to the famous golf course. RAC/AA 2-Star. Ideally placed to take advantage of the other eight first class courses within a fifteen mile radius.

Metropole Hotel

3 Portland Street,
Southport,
Merseyside PR8 1LL.
Tel (01704) 536836 Fax (01704) 549041

RAC/AA 2-Star hotel. Centrally situated and close to Royal Birkdale and other championship courses. Fully licensed - late bar facilities for residents. Full size snooker table. Reduced rates for golfers. Golfing proprietors will assist with tee reservations.

Mottram Hall Hotel

Wilmslow Road,
Mottram St Andrew,
Prestbury, Cheshire SK10 4QT.
Tel (01625) 828135

An 18th-century Georgian manor house set in 270 acres of parkland with a magnificent 18-hole championship length golf course. 133 bedrooms and extensive leisure facilities afford the utmost comfort to every guest. Part of the De Vere Hotels Group.

The Prince of Wales Hotel

Lord Street, Southport PR8 1JS.
Tel (01704) 536688 Fax (01704) 543488

Less than an hour's drive from twelve top class golf courses. 104 bedrooms, nine suites, one restaurant and famous clubhouse bar. The hotel offers an ideal venue for golfing parties from two to 100 or more. (See advertisement page 373 for further details.)

Shrigley Hall Hotel Golf & Country Club

Shrigley Park, Pott Shrigley,
Nr Macclesfield, Cheshire SK10 5SB.
Tel (01625) 575757 Fax (01625) 573323

4-star country house on the edge of the Peak District, with magnificent views over the 18-hole championship course to the Cheshire Plain below. Adjoining leisure club has swimming pool, squash, snooker, tennis, steam, sauna and solaria. (See advertisement page 381 for further details.)

Tree Tops Country House Hotel

Southport Old Road, Formby, Southport,
Merseyside L37 0AB.
Tel/Fax (01704) 879651

Outstanding restaurant and hotel set in five acres close to ten golf courses, six at championship level. Truly friendly and efficient staff. Superb renowned restaurant and very attractive package deals ensure a pleasurable stay.

Whitworth Falls Hotel

16 Lathom Road, Southport PR9 0JH.
Tel (01704) 530074

Personally run private detached Victorian family hotel welcomes golfers. En suite facilities. Large comfortable separate bar. Extensive forecourt. Close to promenade entertainments. Easy travelling to championship golf courses. Larger parties can have sole use of hotel.

Isle of Man

Castletown Golf Links Hotel

Derbyhaven, Castletown, Isle of Man.
Tel (01624) 822201 Fax (01624) 625535

Situated on our own peninsula, our championship golf course of 6,700 yards, with all holes having sea views, is a real test of links golf. The hotel facilities are of a luxurious 3-Star standard.

North East

Washington Moat House Hotel

Stone Cellar Road, Washington,
Tyne & Wear NE37 1PH.
Tel 0191-417 2626

Everything for the golfer, championship 18-hole course, 9-hole par 3 course, 21-bay floodlit driving range and well stocked pro shop. Hotel accommodation offers superbly appointed bedrooms, restaurant and bars. Snooker, squash and leisure centre with pool.

SCOTLAND

Scottish Borders

The Black Bull Hotel

3 Market Place, Lauder,
Berwickshire TD2 6SR.
Tel/Fax (01578) 722208

This comfortable 11-bedroomed hotel offers a traditional Scottish welcome to all guests. Recently refurbished suite is available for the family. Enjoy excellent fresh imaginative cuisine in our restaurant. Lauder Golf Course close by and several other challenging courses within a ten minutes' drive. Full parking facilities.

Hillside Hotel & Restaurant

3 Queen's Road, Dunbar,
East Lothian EH42 1LA.
Tel (01368) 862071

'We Keep a Welcome in the Hillside Hotel and Restaurant'. Situated in the fishing port of Dunbar on the south east coast close to two golf courses (one championship). Eighteen other courses within twenty minutes' drive. Golf parties DBB £28.50 per person. Excellent restaurant and steak house. (See advertisement page 395 for further details.)

Marine Hotel

Cromwell Road, North Berwick,
East Lothian EH39 4LZ.
Tel (01620) 892406 Fax (01620) 894480

A superb 80-bedroomed sporting hotel with bars, snooker, tennis, swimming and gardens. Famed for its friendly service and value for money holidays. Ask for our leisure breaks or stay five nights for the price of three mid-September to late April. (See advertisement page 395 for further details.)

Moreig Hotel

67 Annan Road, Dumfries DG1 3EG.
Tel (01387) 55524

9-bedroomed family hotel with excellent facilities, central heating and colour TV in all rooms. Two links courses and numerous inland courses within close proximity of Dumfries. Reservations can be arranged.

South

Balmoral Hotel

High Street, Moffat,
Dumfriesshire DG10 9DL.
Tel (01683) 20288 Fax (01683) 20451

A dozen courses within 45 minutes' drive, including the town's own hill course two minutes away, makes the Balmoral Hotel ideally situated for your golfing break in Dumfries and Galloway and the Borders.

Clonyard House Hotel

Colvend, Dalbeattie, Kirkshire DG5 4QW.
Tel (01556) 630372 Fax (01556) 630422

Family run country hotel in quiet grounds. Excellent restaurant, also informal meals in our lively bar. Ground floor rooms with facilities including direct dial telephone. Five golf courses within a ten mile radius, including Southerness.

Johnstounburn House Hotel

Humbie, Nr Edinburgh,
East Lothian EH36 5PL.
Tel (01875) 833696 Fax (01875) 83362

Magnificent 17th-century country house set on its own estate. 20 bedrooms each with private facilities. 30 minutes from East Lothian's championship courses, Edinburgh City centre and airport. STB 4-Crown Commended. Thistle Hotel Group. (See advertisement page 383 for further details.)

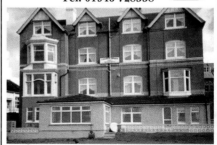

Central & East

Altamount House Hotel

Coupar Angus Road, Blairgowrie, Perthshire.
Tel (01250) 873512/873814
Fax (01250) 876200

Delightful Georgian manor house situated in six acres of well kept garden, grounds and paddocks. Resident owners provide excellent accommodation and cuisine. Rosemount Golf Course is only a few minutes from the hotel.

Balbirnie House Hotel

Balbirnie Park, Markinch, by Glenrothes, Fife KY7 6NE.
Tel (01592) 610066

Balbirnie is an elegant 18th-century mansion in a 416 acre park. AA/RAC 4-Star 5-Crown Deluxe STB with 30 rooms/suites. Ideally located for Ladybank, St Andrews, Carnoustie and Balbirnie Park golf courses on our doorstep.

Balcomie Links Hotel

Balcomie Road, Crail, Fife KY10 3TN.
Tel (01333) 450237 Fax (01333) 450540

AA 2-star STB 3-crown family run hotel, located on the edge of this lovely fishing village. All bedrooms are en suite, some have sea view. We serve good traditional home cooking both in our *'Links Dining Room'* or in Balcomie lounge bar. Full size snooker table for guests' use.

Balgeddie House Hotel

Balgeddie Way, Glenrothes North, Fife KY6 3ET.
Tel (01592) 742511 Fax (01590) 681702

Beautifully situated in immaculate gardens in the heart of some of the country's finest golf courses. All bedrooms have private bathroom, satellite TV, telephone, radio, tea-making facilities. Elegant cocktail bar/restaurant - table d'hôte/à la carte menus. Golf packages arranged. AA/RAC 3-Star STB 4-Crown.

The Barnton

Queensferry Road, Edinburgh EH4 6AS.
Tel 0131-339 1144

Situated four miles from the centre of Edinburgh. Within walking distance of the Royal Burgess Golfing Society and a short distance from Lothian's numerous golf courses. 50 bedrooms all en suite. Restaurant and three bars.

The Bein Inn Hotel

Glenfarg, Perthshire PH2 9PY.
Tel (01557) 830216 Fax (01557) 830211

Excellent facilities in beautiful surroundings. Eight miles from Perth and within 35 minutes of Carnoustie, Gleneagles, St Andrews, Downfield and Ladybank. Under new experienced ownership since October 1993. Egon Ronay AA 2-Star STB 3-Star. (See advertisement page 386 for further details.)

Bell Craig Guest House

8 Murray Park, St Andrews, Fife KY16 9AW.
Tel (01334) 472962

A small comfortable guest house catering for individual and small golfing parties. 400 metres from lst tee of the 'Old Course'. Open all year, budget prices. AA and RAC acclaimed. Credit cards accepted.

Brown's Hotel

1 West Road, Haddington, East Lothian EH41 3RD.
Tel/Fax (01620) 822254

Georgian country house hotel with open outlook towards Lammermuir Hills. Furnished in a sympathetic manner with contemporary Scottish art. The restaurant has an excellent local reputation dinner being served every evening and lunch available on Sundays. (See advertisement page 383 for further details.)

Carmelite House Hotel

Low Street, Banff AB45 1AY.
Tel (01261) 812152

Carmelite House is a small family run hotel in Banff, within walking distance of Duff House Royal Golf Course, and two miles from Royal Tarlair at Macduff. Discount on green fees at Duff House Royal.

Castleton House Hotel

By Glamis, Forfar, Angus DD8 1SJ.
Tel (01307) 840340 Fax (01307) 840506

Country house hotel situated in the heart of the Angus countryside. First class cuisine and accommodation. Many excellent golf courses within easy reach including Rosemount and Carnoustie. Special golf packages available.

Crusoe Hotel

2 Main Street,
Lower Largo, Fife KY8 6BT.
Tel (01333) 320759 Fax (01333) 320865

Crusoe Hotel is situated at Watersedge and has 12 en suite bedrooms and a suite. High tea, à la carte and table d'hôte meals are served in the Castaway restaurant, seafood and flambée dishes a speciality. 10% discount given for groups of eight plus.

Cullen Bay Hotel

Cullen,
Banffshire AB56 2XA.
Tel (01542) 40432 Fax (01542) 40900

Panoramic views over Cullen Bay and Cullen Links Course. Special ticket for one or two rounds on each of ten local courses. All rooms en suite, bar, good food and friendly atmosphere. In family ownership.

Dalhousie Castle Hotel & Restaurant

Bonnyrigg,
Edinburgh EH19 3JB.
Tel (01875) 820153

25-bedroom luxury castle, located seven miles south of Edinburgh. Superb cuisine in barrel-vaulted Dungeon restaurant. Library bar (golfers' 19th hole!). Special golfing rates on application. Muirfield, Dalmahoy, St Andrews and more all within easy reach.

Dalmahoy Hotel Country Club Resort

Kirknewton,
Midlothian EH27 8EB.
Tel 0131-333 1845

Swimming pool (18m x 10m), steam room, sauna, two solariums, fitness studio, health and beauty salon, two squash courts, two outdoor tennis courts, snooker room. Two golf courses. 4-Star hotel with 116 bedrooms. (Part of the Country Club Hotels Group see page 4.)

Dalmunzie House Hotel

Spittal O'Glenshee,
Blairgowrie, Perthshire PH10 7QG.
Tel (01250) 885224 Fax (01250) 885225

Set in the Highlands with our own 9-hole course. The highest in Britain. This friendly country house offers an ideal base for a golfing holiday with excellent local courses at Blairgowrie, Pitlochry, Alyth and many more. (See advertisement page 385 for further details.)

Dupplin Castle

By Perth,
Perthshire PH2 0PY.
Tel (01738) 623224 Fax (01738) 444140

Dupplin is not a hotel but a private house of the highest quality with all the sophistication and relaxed informality of an old fashioned house party. Ideally situated in the heart of golf countryside, Gleneagles, St Andrews, Rosemount at Blairgowrie and Carnoustie. (See advertisement page 386 for further details.)

Eden House Hotel

2 Pitscottie Road,
Cupar, Fife.
Tel/Fax (01334) 652510

Eden House is just eight miles from the world famous Home of Golf St Andrews, a must for any golfer. There are 54 courses within one hour, some used for qualifying in the Open Championship. Your hosts will give every help with itineraries, tee times and transport. Eden House Hotel centre of a golfing paradise.

The Forest Hills Hotel

The Square,
Auchtermuchty,
Fife KY14 7AP.
Tel (01337) 828318

Traditional inn located in the square of this pleasant old Royal Burgh which was once a busy weaving centre. Surrounding forest and hills once favoured deer and boar hunting. Nearby is Falkland Palace, one time hunting seat of Scottish monarchs. Well furnished, bright bedrooms, restaurant, bistro, cocktail bar. STB 3-Crown Commended. (See advertisement page 395 for further details.)

Gleddoch House

Langbank,
Renfrewshire PA14 6YE.
Tel (01475) 540711

Country house hotel overlooking the river Clyde within easy reach of Glasgow and airport. Own golf course (par 72, 6,300 yards). Pro shop, clubhouse with own restaurant, bar, sauna, squash and horse riding.

Glencoe Hotel

Links Parade,
Carnoustie, Angus DD7 7JF.
Tel (01241) 853273 Fax (01241) 853319

THE golf hotel in Carnoustie, directly opposite the 18th green of the championship golf course. Family run hotel, offering excellent cuisine and accommodation. Golf parties welcome.

Golf Hotel

Main Street,
Aberlady,
East Lothian EH32 0RF.
Tel (01875) 870503 Fax (01875) 870209

Family run hotel specialising in golfing packages. All rooms with full en suite facilities and TV. Traditional bar and comfortable restaurant. Fourteen golf courses situated within fourteen miles' drive of hotel including Muirfield. Telephone for brochure.

Green Craigs

Aberlady,
East Lothian EH32 0PY.
Tel (01875) 870301 Fax (01875) 870440

The white house set on the bay overlooking Edinburgh is the Green Craigs Hotel, Restaurant and Bistro. All 6 rooms en suite, colour TV, tea and coffee-making facilities, with toiletries, mineral water and fresh fruit as added extras. Exceptionally good food and wines. Sixteen golf courses within the county with Muirfield only five minutes away. Courtesy bus and limo service for diners.

Hazelbank Hotel

28 The Scores,
St Andrews, Fife KY16 9AS.
Tel (01334) 72466

Situated 400 yards from R&A Clubhouse overlooking St Andrews Bay this family run hotel offers quality accommodation (STB 3-Crown Commended) at affordable prices. All rooms en suite. Rates 1995 £25 - £38 per person bed and breakfast.

Hotel Seaforth

Dundee Road,
Arbroath, Angus.
Tel (01241) 872232 Fax (01241) 877473

20 en suite bedrooms. On the seafront a short drive from many fine courses. Hotel's facilities include lounge bar, restaurant and leisure centre with indoor pool, jacuzzi and sun bed. Snooker tables. Large car park.

The Kenmore Hotel

Kenmore,
Perthshire PH15 2NU.
Tel (01887) 830205 Fax (01887) 830262

Scotland's oldest inn is uniquely situated on the banks of the river and Loch Tay. We offer modern, comfortable rooms, exciting menus, a fine cellar and our own 18-hole par 69 Taymouth Castle Golf Course. (See advertisement page 395 for further details).

Kinloch House Hotel

By Blairgowrie,
Perthshire PH10 6SG.
Tel (01250) 884237

Kinloch House offers an almost unique proposition for golfers. 35 courses within an hour's drive, planning of rounds and booking of tee times, sportsman's room with every facility and the best of Scottish hospitality. AA 3-Star 2-Red Rosettes.

Kintrae House Hotel

Balmoral Road,
Blairgowrie, Perthshire PH10 7AH.
Tel (01250) 872106

Small family run 3-star hotel, serving excellent food and real ale. Spacious en suite bedrooms. Small parties catered for - breakfast arranged to suit golf. Close to Rosemount with twelve other courses within a twenty mile radius.

The Lake Hotel

Port of Menteith,
Perthshire FK8 3RA.
Tel (01877) 358258 Fax (01877) 358671

Outstanding situation on the shore of the lake of Menteith. Refurbished under new ownership and management in 1990. All rooms with en suite facilities. Our cuisine emulates the restaurant with its spectacular lakeside setting. STB 4-Crown Highly Commended.

Lathones Hotel

By Largoward, St Andrews, Fife.
Tel (01334) 84494

A small country hotel situated five miles south of St Andrews. Formerly a coaching inn it has been tastefully converted to provide 14 en suite bedrooms in two chalet blocks. Fifteen golf courses within six miles of hotel.

Letham Grange

Colliston, by Arbroath DD11 4RL.
Tel (01241) 890373 Fax (01241) 890414

20-bedroom Victorian mansion, with 36-holes of superb golf. First class facilities set in the heartland of golf. Company/society golf outings/ breaks welcome. (See advertisement page 383 for further details.)

Lochearnhead Hotel

Lochearnhead, Perthshire FK19 8PU.
Tel (01567) 830229

Play five 9-hole courses for £40. Central to several excellent 18-holers, also ideal centre for water sports, hill walking, fishing and general touring. Five day breaks and packages available.

The Log Cabin Hotel

Kirkmichael, Perthshire PH10 7NB.
Tel (01250) 881288 Fax (01250) 881402

A unique log building equidistant between Pitlochry and Blairgowrie. 42 courses within two hours' drive through stunning scenery. Freshly prepared cuisine served in our award winning restaurant. Relax in the well stocked bar around the log fire and sample some of the malt whiskies - over 100 to choose from. AA/ RAC 2-Star STB 3-Crown Commended Taste of Scotland.

The Lomond Hills Hotel

Freuchie, Nr Glenrothes, Fife KY7 7EY.
Tel/Fax (01337) 857329/498 & 858180

Lying at the foot of the Lomond Hills, this old inn is an ideal base for a visit to Fife. The hotel is close to many golf courses and has comfortable bedrooms with TV, radio and private facilities. There is a candlelit restaurant, wine bar and leisure centre. Contact the proprietor, Mr E L Van Beusekom on (01337) 857329. STB 4-Crown Commended. (See advertisement page 395 for further details.)

The Lundin Links Hotel

Leven Road, Lundin Links,
(Nr St Andrews), Fife KY8 6AP.
Tel (01333) 320201

Golfing packages of every description from championship courses to tuition breaks. Everything arranged. Groups and societies welcome. Only yards from Fife's finest links course. Superb, friendly hotel with excellent rooms and food.

Murrayshall Country House Hotel & Golf Course

Scone, Perthshire PH2 7PH.
Tel (01738) 551171 Pro Shop (01738)552784

Murrayshall is a Scottish country house set in 300 acres of parkland. Of the 19 bedrooms many have scenic views over the course and picturesque Perthshire countryside. Adjacent is the 18-hole golf course with its own clubhouse, ideal for hosting company golf events and societies. Indoor golf school facilities.

The Park Hotel

John Street, Montrose, Angus DD10 8RJ.
Tel (01674) 673415 Fax (01674) 677091

A short distance from Montrose Medal Course. Privately owned hotel, 59 bedrooms all with colour TV and most with private bathroom. (See advertisement page 385 for further details.)

Point Garry Hotel

20 West Bay Road,
North Berwick,
East Lothian.
Tel (01620) 892380

100 yards from 1st tee North Berwick West Championship Course. Twelve courses within twelve miles. Golf course booking service, packages available. Good food, wine, comfortable bar, billiard room. Edinburgh 35 minutes by train. Personal attention at all times. (See advertisement page 396 for further details).

Queens Hotel

Main Street,
Gullane, East Lothian EH31 2AS.
Tel (01620) 842275 Fax (01620) 842970

Family run, good home cooking, friendly atmosphere. Sixteen golf courses within radius of sixteen miles which includes open golf championship course 'Muirfield' eighteen miles from Edinburgh. Most rooms en suite/shower, tea-makers, TV, telephone.

Radnor Park Hotel

Kilbow Road,
Clydebank,
Glasgow, Dunbartonshire G81 2AP.
Tel 0141-952 3427 Fax 0141-952 0167

Comfortable friendly run 12-bedroomed hotel. All rooms en suite, colour TV, tea and coffee-making facilities. Enjoy good food at our carvery and relax in the Terrace bar with other golfers. Live entertainment including quiz nights and discos.

Rescobie Hotel

Leslie,
Fife KY6 3BQ.
Tel (01592) 742143 Fax (01592) 620231

A small country house hotel with 10 fully equipped bedrooms and an AA Rosette for its excellent food. Positioned centrally between Carnoustie, Dalmahoy, Gleneagles and St Andrews. Over 100 golf courses are within easy driving range

The Royal George Hotel

Tay Street,
Perth PH1 5LD.
Tel (01738) 624455

Set overlooking the river Tay and a short drive to St Andrews, Carnoustie, Gleneagles and many other fine courses. The hotel guarantees a warm welcome, good food and excellent facilities.

Rusacks Hotel

Pilmour Links,
St Andrews, Fife KY16 9JQ.
Tel (01334) 474321 Fax (01334) 477896

Rusacks Hotel offers the first and last word in facilities for golfers. Our car jockey and golf steward are at your disposal. Lockers and changing facilities for ladies and gentlemen, plus sauna, solarium and well stocked golf shop. Voted one of the top ten golf hotels in the world. STB 4-Crown. (See advertisement page 385 for further details.)

Russell Hotel

The Scores,
St Andrews, Fife KY16 9AS.
Tel (01334) 473447 Fax (01334) 478279

STB 3-Crown Commended AA 2-Star. Two minutes' walk from 'Old Course' overlooking the bay. Full facility bedrooms, restaurant serving delicious food and wine, cosy Victorian bar with coal fire. All combine to offer a warm welcome. Golf parties welcome. Please call.

The Scores Hotel

St Andrews,
Fife, KY16 9BB
Tel (01334) 472451 Fax (01334) 473947

Overlooking St Andrews Bay and the Royal & Ancient clubhouse, this famous 3-star hotel is only yards from the 1st tee of the Old Course and a short stroll from the historic town centre. 30 en suite rooms, noted restaurant, parking.

The Seafield Arms Hotel

Seafield Street,
Cullen, Banffshire.
Tel (01542) 840791 Fax (01542) 840736

Situated in the centre of the coastal town of Cullen with its beautiful beaches and scenery. This hotel has open fire lounge bar, restaurant and 25 en suite bedrooms. Eighteen golf courses within a twenty mile radius.

St Andrews Golf Hotel

St Andrews,
Fife KY16 9AS.
Tel (01334) 472611 Fax (01334) 472188

AA 3-Star and Rossette STB 4-Crown Highly Commended. Most comfortable, traditional Scottish hotel (all bedrooms en suite). Fine restaurant. Extensive cellar. On the seafront 220 yards from the 'Old Course'. Let us arrange your golf in Scotland.

St Andrews Old Course Hotel

St Andrews, Fife KY16 9SP.
Tel (01334) 474371 Fax (01334) 477668

This luxury 125-bedroom hotel overlooks the 17th Road Hole of the Old Course and is a five minute walk to the beach and town. Facilities include health spa with swimming pool, whirlpool, fitness room and full range of massage and beauty treatments. Construction completed of our own 18-hole championship standard golf course on land surrounding Craigtoun Park, two miles inland. Anticipated opening by Spring 1996.

The Tayside Hotel

Mill Street, Stanley, Nr Perth PH1 4NL.
Tel (01738) 828249 Fax (01738) 827216

The hotel arranges inclusive golfing holidays using a variety of heath, links and parkland courses for individual or party bookings. Based in the village of Stanley on the river Tay this is a traditional Edwardian hotel, AA 2-star rosette award, RAC 2-star STB 3-crown commended with en suite accommodation, TV, tea and coffee-making facilities. Moderately priced. Menus feature fresh local produce and Scottish specialities. (See advertisement page 396 for further details.)

The Waverley Hotel

7 James Square, Crieff,
Perthshire PH7 3HX.
Tel/Fax (01764) 652652

Friendly family run hotel in centre of Crieff with 6 en suite bedrooms. STB 3-Crown Commended. Play five Perthshire highland courses for £40. Twenty courses within twenty miles. £22 per person bed and breakfast.

Westerwood Hotel Golf & Country Club

St Andrews Drive, Cumbernauld,
Glasgow G68 0EW.
Tel (01236) 457171
Tee-off Times (01236) 452772

Westerwood Hotel, Golf and Country Club is located twenty minutes from Glasgow and boasts an 18-hole championship golf course designed by Seve Ballesteros and Dave Thomas. A range of golfing breaks and society packages are available including residential golf schools using our indoor golfing facility. The venue is ideal for hosting company golf days. The country club offers a range of other sporting activities. Indoor golf school facilities.

POINT GARRY
AA★★ HOTEL

20 West Bay Road, North Berwick, East Lothian EH39 4AW
Tel (01620) 892380 Fax (01620) 892848

100 yards from 1st tee North Berwick West Championship Course.
12 courses within twelve miles.
Let us arrange your golf - Golf packages available
After a day of golf come back to the comfort of the Point Garry and enjoy good food and wine. Personal attention guaranteed. Full sized Billiard table
35 minutes by train from Edinburgh.

THE TAYSIDE HOTEL

Stanley, Nr Perth PH1 4NL.
Tel: 01738 828249 Fax: 01738 827216

Golfing in Perthshire

Play Golf on a variety of links and inland courses

BROCHURE WITH GOLF COURSES
available on request
INDIVIDUAL AND PARTY BOOKINGS

Inclusive Quotation for Golfing Breaks, Courses Booked with Tee-off Times

AA ★★

AA ROSETTE
STB 3 crowns Commended

THE BOAT HOTEL
Master Classes & Tee Breaks

AA ★★★ RAC

Situated overlooking the beautiful but challenging Boat of Garten Golf Course - the 'Gleneagles' of the Highlands - The Boat Hotel offers you both Master Classes with our resident Professional, or, the superb value Tee Break holidays with golf on any of six local courses.

Please contact: Golf Desk, The Boat Hotel, Boat of Garten, Inverness-shire PH24 3BH
Telephone 01479 831258 Fax 01479 831414

Craigard House Hotel

Overlooking Boat of Garten Golf Course

Kinchurdy Road, Boat of Garten, Inverness-shire PH24 3BP Tel: (01479) 831206 Fax: (01479) 831423

An elegantly restored Victorian Shooting Lodge that offers traditional Highland Hospitality, excellent Scottish Cuisine and Fine Wines together with over 80 Malt Whiskies in Braids Bar.

Many top quality 18-hole courses within easy access, including the championship courses at Nairn and Royal Dornoch as well as the beautiful yet heartbreaking Boat of Garten which abuts our grounds.

Attractive Golf Packages • Starting Times arranged
Secure club storeroom • Transport can be arranged to and from courses

The style and comfort of Country House living

The Woodside Hotel RAC 3-Star

High Street, Aberdour, Fife KY3 0SW.
Tel (01383) 860328 Fax (01383) 860920

You will enjoy our warm hospitality and excellent food. BB from £26.50 (each sharing) £44.50 (single). You must visit our unique bar - taken from the RMS Orontes. Edinburgh and St Andrews golf courses within easy driving distance. Enjoy free golf when you stay with us! Book your tee time with the hotel for Aberdour's scenic 18-hole course. Telephone for brochure and tariff.

Highlands, Islands & North

Altens Skean Dhu Hotel

Souterhead Road, Altens,
Aberdeen AB1 4LF.
Tel/Fax (01224) 877000

5-Crown STB Commended modern hotel with 221 bedrooms. Within a fifteen mile radius we have a choice of fifteen different golf courses from parkland to championship size links courses. (Part of the Thistle & Mount Charlotte Hotel Group.)

Ben Mhor Hotel

High Street, Grantown on Spey,
Morayshire PH26 3ES.
Tel (01479) 872056 Fax (01479) 873537

Centrally situated, three minutes from the course, with large car park and drying room, the Ben Mhor puts you within reach of twelve courses, links and inland making up a varied challenge for the dedicated golfer.

The Boat Hotel

Boat of Garten,
Inverness-shire PH24 3BH.
Tel (01479) 831258 Fax (01479) 831414

Overlooking the beautiful but challenging 18-hole Boat of Garten Golf Course, The Boat Hotel offers a high standard of food and accommodation (32 rooms) within a traditional Highland hotel. Our golf desk will take care of all your requirements. (See advertisement page 396 for further details.)

Bogroy Inn

Kirkhill, Inverness IV5 7PX.
Tel/Fax (01463) 831296

Friendly 2-star 4-crown commended family run hotel in the country, seven miles from Inverness. We offer good clean comfortable accommodation with all facilities, and have an enviable reputation for particularly good food. Easy access to around fifteen golf courses in the locality. Attractive weekend and small group rates.

Burghfield House Hotel

Dornoch, Sutherland IV25 3HN.
Tel (01862) 810212 Fax (01862) 810404

4-crown commended 36-bedroom country house hotel extensively refurbished 1991. A few minutes from the golf course. Superb restaurant. Golf packages on Royal Dornoch and nearby courses.

Castle Hotel

Huntly, Aberdeenshire AB54 4SH.
(01466) 792696

In our own grounds above Huntly Golf Course this family run hotel offers peace and tranquility for the individual or groups. Ideally situated for numerous courses in the north east, all within easy *'driving'* range.

Charleston Hotel

Ballater Road, Aboyne,
Aberdeenshire AB34 5HY.
Tel (01339) 886475

Access to 18-hole golf course, fishing, shooting, hunting, gliding, leisure centre, hill walking and ski-ing. Facilities in hotel include en suite bedrooms with ramp access and a delightful self-contained cottage for six. Disabled and handicapped persons very welcome.

Clifton House

Nairn IV12 4HW.
Tel (01667) 453119 Fax (01667) 452836

Having been 'home' to the owner for sixty years, Clifton has a high standard to maintain and welcomes all those who appreciate good food and wines. It is small, elegant, charming and very personal. (See advertisement page 387 for further details.)

Covenanters' Inn

Auldearn, Nairn IV12 5TG.
Tel (01667) 452456 Fax (01667) 453583

Olde Worlde country inn central to fifteen courses, (two championship within three miles, Royal Dornoch within an hour's drive). 8 en suite rooms, TV, tea and coffee-making facilities and phone. Excellent menu - specialists in seafood and game. (On booking mention the R&A Golfer's Handbook for a 10% accommodation discount).

Craigard House Hotel

Kingchurdy Road, Boat of Garten, Inverness-shire PH24 3BP.
Tel (01479) 831206 Fax (01479) 831423

Traditional Highland welcome awaits you at this elegantly restored Victorian shooting lodge overlooking Boat of Garten Golf Course. Excellent Scottish cuisine and fine wines with over 80 malt whiskies. Many top quality 18-hole courses within easy reach. All inclusive golf packages, starting times arranged and transport if required. (See advertisement page 396 for further details.)

Craigellachie Hotel

Craigellachie, Speyside, Banffshire AB38 9SR.
Tel (01340) 881204 Fax (01340) 881253

Ideally located for enjoying the best of golf in Scotland with many golf courses within one hour's drive including links, parkland, championship moorland. The Craigellachie is fully refurbished providing true Highland hospitality. Call for brochure today. (See advertisement page 387 for further details.)

The Craighaar Hotel

Waterton Road, Bucksburn, Aberdeen AB2 9HS.
Tel (01224) 712275

A warm and friendly welcome awaits you at the Craighaar Hotel, which boasts a reputation for the best seafood in the north east. A variety of leisure and sports facilities are close at hand, curling, skating and of course GOLF.

Dornoch Castle

Dornoch, Sutherland IV25 3SD.
Tel (01862) 810216 Fax (01862) 810981

Formerly a bishop's palace, the hotel has 17 bedrooms. The panelled cocktail bar, elegant lounge and Bishop's Room restaurant overlook historic Dornoch Cathedral. AA, RAC, STB Commended 4-Crowns. (See advertisement page 386 for further details.)

Golf Links

Church Street, Golspie, Sutherland KW10 6TT.
Tel (01408) 633408

Predominantly a golfing hotel adjacent to the beach and 18-hole golf course. Family run, 9 double bedrooms all en suite. Good food and friendly atmosphere. Also three self-catering chalets.

Holiday Inn Crowne Plaza - Aberdeen

Oldmeldrum Road, Bucksburn, Aberdeen AB2 9LN.
Tel (01224) 713911

Quality 4-star hotel with 144 spacious bedrooms with a fully equipped luxurious leisure club. Within a ten minute radius we can offer a choice of fifteen excellent golf courses from public to championship size.

Kingsmills Hotel

Culcabock Road, Inverness IV2 3LP.
Tel (01463) 237166

Overlooking Inverness Golf Course, the hotel has large luxurious rooms. Purpose built *GOLF VILLAS*, extensive leisure complex with pool and sauna. 3-hole pitch and putt course. Special golf holidays avaiable in spring and autumn.

Kinloch Hotel

Blackwaterfoot, Isle of Arran KA27 8ET.
Tel (01770) 860444

Beside the world's only 12-hole golf course. Breathtaking test of links skill. Six other courses nearby. Swimming pool, tennis, sauna, squash court, solarium. Full en suite facilities. Special golfers' rates.

Loch Ness House Hotel

Glenurquhart Road, Inverness IV3 6JL.
Tel (0146) 3231248

19th century family run AA/RAC 3-Star hotel. All rooms en suite. Excellent cuisine. Weekend ceilidhs. Surrounded by Torvean golf courses and Caledonian canal. One and a half miles from town centre. Ideal base for touring Highlands.

Mackay's Hotel

Union Street, Wick, Caithness.
Tel (01955) 602323

Your room is warm, clean and comfortable. Whatever, whenever you need, our friendly helpful staff are at your service. The family run centrally situated hotel offers the atmosphere you'll enjoy especially the *free golf!!* Unlimited free golf on a choice of three courses.

Mansion House Hotel

The Haugh,
Elgin, Moray IV30 1AW.
Tel (01343) 548811

The Mansion House Hotel offers luxurious accommodation in an imposing mansion close by to many of the region's finest courses. With our gym, swimming pool etc. we offer a relaxing base for your golfing holiday.

Moorfield House Private Hotel

Deshar Road,
Boat of Garten,
Inverness-shire PH24 3BN.
Tel (01479) 831646

Victorian house situated minutes from golf course. STB 3-Crown Commended AA/RAC acclaimed. 4 bedrooms all with private facilities, tea and coffee-making and TV. BB £18 per person per night.

Morangie House Hotel

Morangie Road,
Tain, Ross-shire IV19 1PY.
Tel (01862) 892281

Family run mansion house hotel with outstanding reputation for award winning cuisine. Discounted golf at Tain. Ten minutes' drive from Dornoch and other superb golf courses. AA/RAC 3-Star STB and Taste of Scotland 4-Crown Commended. Discount available for small groups. (See advertisement page 387 for further details.)

The Palm Court Hotel

81 Seafield Road,
Aberdeen AB1 7YU.
Tel (01224) 310351

There are 25 beautiful golf courses all within a short drive from the Palm Court Hotel, three of which are virtually on our doorstep. Staying at the Palm Court hotel is the perfect way to enjoy the many attractions of Aberdeen and the Highlands.

Priory Hotel

The Square,
Beauly,
Inverness-shire IV4 7BX.
Tel (01463) 782309 Fax (01463) 782531

Bustling local hotel offering excellent accommodation, friendly efficient staff and a reputation for particularly good food. Easy access to at least fifteen golf courses in the surrounding area. Attractive weekend and small group tariff.

Ramleh Hotel & Fingal's Restaurant

2 Academy Street, Nairn,
Inverness IV12 4RJ.
Tel (01667) 453551 Fax (01667) 456577

1994 Les Routiers British Restaurant of the Year. George and Carol Woodhouse offer a warm welcome to their 10-bedroomed hotel and renowned restaurant. Close to both of Nairn's championship courses, many more within 30 miles. Beautiful beaches, whisky and castle trails.

Ramnee Hotel

Victoria Road, Forres,
Morayshire IV36 0BN.
Tel (01309) 672410

Ramnee is a charming country house hotel renowned for traditional highland hospitality, excellent service and superb cuisine. Ideally situated to take advantage of the inexpensive quality golf available at Forres, Nairn, Elgin, Lossiemouth and Grantown.

West

Ardenslate House

James Street, Hunters Quay, Dunoon.
Tel (01369) 2068

Small friendly hotel commanding unsurpassed views over the Firth of Clyde. Near Cowal Golf Course but transport can be arranged. All rooms have tea and coffee-making facilities, TV and private facilities.

Balcary Bay Hotel

The Shore Road, Auchencairn, Nr Castle Douglas, Kirkcudbrightshire DG7 1QZ.
Tel (01556) 640217

AA/RAC 3-star restaurant award, STB 4-crown highly commended country house in delightful and peaceful situation on the shores of the bay. Ideal for golfing, walking, bird watching and touring. Good food and wine.

Barons Craig Hotel

Rockcliffe, By Dalbeattie,
Kirkcudbrightshire DG5 4QF.
Tel (01556) 630225

This imposing granite structured hotel dated 1880 is situated in nine acres of wooded area with lush lawns and gardens overlooking the Solway and Rough Firth. Excellent 18-hole golf course and three golf courses within easy reach.

Cairndale Hotel & Leisure Club

English Street, Dumfries DG1 2DF.
Tel (01387) 254111 Fax (01387) 250555

Golf available on a choice of local courses, links and parkland, from 9-hole courses to the Southerness championship course. Groups welcome from £57.50 per person per night. Hotel has full leisure facilities including 14-metre heated pool.

Caledonian Hotel

Dalblair Road, Ayr KA7 1UG.
Tel (01292) 269331

Town centre hotel, with private facilities. Restaurants, bars, swimming pool and leisure club. Try our golf packages with guaranteed starting times on any of our eight local courses. Just call for details. STB 5-Crown Commended. (See advertisement page 389 for further details.)

Craiglea Hotel

78-80 South Beach, Troon, Ayrshire KA10 6EG.
Tel/Fax (01292) 311366

Situated on the seafront, in the midst of Ayrshire golfing country, this comfortable family owned and run 2-star AA/RAC hotel is central for up to twenty courses including Royal Troon, Prestwick, and Turnberry. Special rates for golf parties, rooms en suite, fully licensed, bar and restaurant meals. Open all year.

Douglas Hotel

Brodick, Isle of Arran, Ayrshire KA27 8AW.
Tel (01770) 302155

Seven golf courses within a fifteen mile radius of the hotel. Accommodation consists of 30 bedrooms, 15 en suite, all with TV, direct dial telephone and tea-making facilities. The hotel is situated within spacious grounds, directly opposite the ferry terminal. Extensive Indian and European menu. Special rates for group bookings from £15 per person. (See advertisement page 383 for further details.)

Downshire Arms Hotel

10-14 Main Street, Portpatrick, Wigtownshire.
Tel (01776) 810300

400 yards from golf course. TV and tea-making facilities in all rooms. Most rooms have direct dial telephone and en suite facilities. Pony trekking and sea angling can be arranged. (See advertisement page 389 for further details.)

Dunduff House

Dunduff Farm, Dunure, Ayr KA7 4LH.
Tel (01292) 50225

Situated on the edge of Dunure overlooking Arran and Firth of Clyde. Golf courses include Royal Troon, Turnberry and many more interesting courses. All rooms have TV, radio, tea-making facilities, wash hand basin. Two double rooms have en suite facilities. STB Highly Commended 2-Crowns AA Selected 4Qs. Self-catering cottage available sleeps six.

The Fernhill Hotel

Heugh Road, Portpatrick, Nr Stranraer DG9 8TD.
STB 4-Crown Highly Commended Member of Scotland's Commended
Tel (01776) 810220 Fax (01776) 810596

Golf package holidays available throughout the year. Family run 3-Star AA/RAC hotel. Concession golf at the scenic Portpatrick, championship Stranraer and improving county club at Glenluce. Highly recommended by *Golf World* and *Golf Illustrated Weekly*.

Malin Court Hotel & Restaurant

Turnberry, Ayrshire KA26 9PB.
Tel (01655) 331457 Fax (01655) 331072

Situated in the heart of Burns' country on the beautiful Ayrshire coast, overlooking Turnberry's famous golf course. There are 17 well appointed bedrooms. The best of modern Scottish food is served, complemented by an extensive wine list. Golf can be arranged locally on twelve courses.

Manor Park Hotel

Monkton, By Prestwick Airport, Ayrshire KA9 2RJ.
Tel (01292) 79365

Practice net in grounds. All rooms have private facilities, telephone, TV and tea and coffee-makers. We are fifteen minutes from twelve golf courses, three of which are championship. Our restaurant is 'Above Par'.

Montgreenan Mansion House Hotel

Montgreenan Estate, Torranyard, Kilwinning, Ayrshire KA13 7QZ.
Tel (01294) 557733 Fax (01294) 850397

Montgreenan Mansion is situated in the heart of Ayrshire and is surrounded by 30 quality golf courses including Royal Troon, Turnberry and Old Prestwick. The hotel is of a high 3-star standard and has a fine restaurant, snooker, tennis and golf practice area.

Portpatrick Hotel

Portpatrick, Nr Stranraer, Wigtownshire DG9 8TA.
Tel (01776) 810333 Fax (01776) 810457

This majestic hotel commands one of the most spectacular sea views in Britain. Four excellent golf courses including Portpatrick and Stranraer where special golf packages are available from £50.00. Dinner, bed and breakfast per person including free weekday golf. (Mount Charlotte Thistle Hotel Group.)

Tarbert Hotel

Harbour Street, Tarbert, Loch Fyne, Argyll PA29 6UB.
Tel (01880) 820264 Fax (01880) 820847

Traditional family hotel. A delightful base to visit courses on the Isles of Islay, Gigha and Arran or down the Mull of Kintyre to Machrahanish, returning to dine on local seafood or Kintyre beef and lamb.

Turnberry Hotel Golf Courses & Spa

Ayrshire KA26 9LT.
Tel (01655) 331000 Fax (01655) 331706

One of the world's finest luxury hotel, golf and spa resorts. Edwardian country house overlooking its own Ailsa and Arran championship courses. The Ailsa is ranked 16th in the world and was the venue for the 1994 Open Championship.

WALES

Welsh Borders

Belmont Lodge & Golf Course

Belmont, Hereford HR2 9SA.
Tel (01432) 352666 Fax (01432) 358090

18-hole golf course running along the beautiful Wye Valley with a 30-bedroomed hotel on-site. Other facilities include bar, restaurant, fishing, bowling, tennis and snooker. Only a mile and a half from Hereford City centre. (See advertisement page 389 for further details.)

The Chase Hotel

Gloucester Road, Ross-on-Wye, Herefordshire HR9 5LH.
Tel (01989) 763161 Fax (01989) 768330

Outstanding country house hotel, standing in eleven acres of grounds yet close to the town centre. 39 bedrooms all en suite, with satellite TV, radio and hospitality tray. Six uncrowded courses within twenty minutes' drive. Special rates available for parties.

Hill Valley Golf Hotel & Country Club

Terrick Road, Whitchurch, Shropshire SY13 4JZ.
Tel (01948) 663584

The complex has twin-bedded motel accommodation. All rooms have bathroom en suite, colour TV, tea and coffee-making facilities. Two golf courses, tennis and snooker.

Maes Manor Hotel

- Incorporating Savvas Country Club & Seasons Restaurant
Blackwood, Gwent NP2 0AG.
Tel (01495) 220011 Fax (01495) 228217

Beautiful accommodation, magnificent surroundings, excellent cuisine. Situated in the centre of the Welsh valleys in nine acres of beautiful grounds. Only minutes away from Blackwood Golf Course and Bryn Meadow Golf Club and Course.

Pengwern Sports Hotel

Longden Road, Shrewsbury SY3 7JE.
Tel (01743) 343871 Fax (01743) 365387

Two to seven day inclusive holidays in sportsman owned all en suite hotel. Choose from 25 courses within 30 minutes' drive including Hawkstone, Hill Valley, Oswestry and Llanymynech. Discounts from October to March. Quality food, late bars, weekend entertainment. Freephone 0500 182738.

Rossett Hall Hotel

Chester Road, Rossett, Nr Chester, Clwyd LL12 0DE.
Tel (01244) 571000

Fifteen golf courses within fifteen minutes' drive of the hotel. Many more within one hour's drive. Relax in the superb comfort of Rossett Hall with its award winning restaurant and friendly staff. Contact Dave Craven - golfing partner.

[T]he Talbot Hotel
[W]est Street,
[L]eominster,
[H]erefordshire HR6 8EP.
[T]el (01568) 616347

[A]n old coaching house with parts dating from [1]5th-century, situated in the small ancient [m]arket town of Leominster. Beamed bars, log [fi]re and friendly staff all help to make your [b]reak enjoyable. Golfing arranged at nearby [c]ourses: Kington, Leominster, Wormsley, [L]udlow, Upper Sapey and Hereford.

[C]entral

[T]he Harbour Hotel
[A]berdovey,
[G]wynedd LL35 0EB.
[T]el (01654) 767250

[A] small, family run, seafront hotel of [o]utstanding quality. In the prime waterfront [s]ituation in the picturesque seaside village of [A]berdovey and only two minutes from the golf [c]lub. Golf parties a speciality. Tailor-made quotations on request.

South & South West

The Baverstock Hotel
Heads of the Valleys Road,
Aberdare,
Mid Glamorgan CF44 0LX.
Tel (01685) 386221

3-Star hotel on the edge of the beautiful Brecon Beacons National Park. Excellent cuisine and well appointed en suite rooms. Group bookings welcome. The perfect base for South Wales' golf courses. Local clubs: Mountain Ash, Morlais, Aberdare and Merthyr.

Carlton Hotel & Restaurant
654-656 Mumbles Road,
Mumbles,
Nr Swansea SA3 4EA.
Tel/Fax (01792) 360450

Very friendly 3-Crown hotel near five golf courses. Perfect for parties of golfers. Private bar. All rooms, mostly en suite, have TV, telephone and tea and coffee-making facilities. Excellent restaurant. In the heart of Mumbles with panoramic views.

Cliff Hotel (Gwbert) Ltd
Gwbert-on-Sea,
Cardigan, Dyfed.
Tel (01239) 613241 Fax (01239) 615391

AA/RAC 3-star hotel with its many leisure facilities is surrounded by its own 9-hole course on cliffs overlooking Cardigan Bay. The 18-hole Cardigan Golf Course is only half a mile away. (See advertisement page 389 for further details.)

The Dolphin Hotel
Whitewalls,
Swansea SA1 3AB.
Tel (01792) 650011 Fax (01792) 642871

The Dolphin Hotel ideally situated in the Swansea City centre close to the unrivalled beauty of the Gower Peninsula. Five courses within ten miles. 66 bedrooms, all with private bathroom, satellite TV, hairdryer, trouser press and welcome tray.

Giltar Hotel
The Esplanade,
Tenby, Pembrokeshire,
Dyfed SA70 7DV.
Tel (01834) 842507

Five minutes' walk from golf club. Seafront facing two mile south beach. All rooms private facilities, tea-making and TV. Late bar and entertainment including Welsh choir concerts weekly. Noted good food and hospitality.

The Mill At Glynhir
Llandybie,
Nr Ammanford,
Dyfed SA18 2TE.
Tel (01269) 850672

17th-century flour mill now converted to a small secluded country house hotel. Beautiful views and golf inclusive packages. All rooms are en suite with spa baths and colour TV. Also heated pool.

Nicholaston House Hotel
Nicholaston,
Penmaen, Gower,
West Glamorgan SA3 2HL.
Tel (01792) 371317

Tranquil country house hotel with magnificent sea views. 12 rooms all en suite, colour TV, tea and coffee-making facilities. Extensive à la carte menu. Full size snooker table. Safe car parking. Four golf courses within fifteen minutes' drive.

Penally Abbey
Penally,
Nr Tenby,
South Pembrokeshire, Dyfed.
Tel (01834) 843033 Fax (01834) 844714

We overlook Tenby's 18-hole championship course and are 30 minutes from three other courses. 12 rooms en suite. (See advertisement page 401 for further details.)

Queens Hotel
19 Bridge Street,
Newport,
Gwent NP9 4RN.
Tel (01633) 262992

Victorian city centre hotel with 43 en suite bedrooms with telephone, coffee and tea-making facilities and colour TV. Close to all public transport. Two minutes from M4 with three friendly bars and restaurant.

St Pierre Hotel Country Club Resort
St Pierre Park,
Chepstow, Gwent NP6 6YA.
Tel (01291) 625261 Fax (01291) 629975

St Pierre has recently undergone a multi-million pound refurbishment. Set in 400 acres of exceptional parkland, the hotel offers two superb golf courses, including the Old Course, host to the 1996 Solheim Cup and extensive leisure and conference facilities. (Part of the Country Club Hotels Group see page 4.)

North

The Beach Hotel
Trearddur Bay,
Anglesey,
Gwynedd LL65 2YT.
Tel (01407) 860332 Fax (01407) 861140

3-star hotel complex offering à la carte restaurant, pub and bistro leisure complex with swim spa, snooker club. One mile from Holyhead Golf Club. Two more 18-hole courses within easy reach. Holyhead ferry port two miles. (See advertisement page 390 for further details).

Castle Bank Hotel
Mount Pleasant, Conwy,
Gwynedd LL32 8NY.
Tel (01492) 593888

Family run 9-bedroom hotel within easy reach of three championship courses. Cosy bar, ample parking. Totally non-smoking. AA Rosette for our high culinary standards.

Deganwy Castle Hotel
Deganwy, Conwy, Gwynedd LL31 9DA.
Tel (01492) 583555

Situated within two miles of Conwy, North Wales and Maesdu courses. The hotel has 32 en suite rooms and a first class reputation for its food and bars. Special golfing breaks available. RAC 2-Star WTB 3-Crown Highly Commended.

Esplanade Hotel
Glan-Y-Mor Parade, Promenade,
Llandudno, Gwynedd LL30 2LL.
Tel (01492) 860300 Fax (01492) 860418

Premier seafront position. Ideally situated for town and leisure facilities. 60 rooms all en suite, tea and coffee-making facilities, colour TV, radio, intercom and baby listening service. Direct dial telephone. Central heating. Car park. Fully licensed. Lift. Small ballroom. Open all year. Christmas and New Year festivities, spring and autumn breaks. (See advertisement page 390 for details.)

The Hand Hotel
Church Street, Chirk, Clwyd LL14 5EY.
Tel (01691) 773472 Fax (01691) 772479

This 16th-century coaching inn stands in the centre of five golf courses and works in conjunction with Chirk Golf and Country Club to provide excellent two day breaks at affordable prices. (See advertisement page 401 for further details.)

Headlands Hotel
Hill Terrace, Llandudno,
Gwynedd LL30 2CS.
Tel (01492) 877485

Situated in a superb position giving views of Llandudno Bay, the Conwy estuary and the mountains of Snowdonia. Three golf courses within five miles. AA/RAC 2-Star and recommended by Ashley Courteny and Les Routiers. Three days DBB for £86.

Imperial Hotel
The Promenade, Llandudno,
Gwynedd LL30 1AP.
Tel (01492) 877466 Fax (01492) 878043

100-bedroomed hotel with extensive leisure facilities including 45' indoor swimming pool. Ideally situated for all North Wales' golf courses. Award winning restaurant and private dining room for up to 30 available.

The Linksway Hotel
Morfa Nefyn,
Pwllelhi, Gwynedd.
Tel (01758) 720258 Fax (01758) 721456

26 bedrooms. Situated at the entrance to private golf road, 200 yards from clubhouse of Morfa Nefyn Golf Club. Specialising in golfing and conference breaks and within half an hour of provincial airport. Telephone for further details.

Lyndale Hotel
Abergele Road,
Colwyn Bay,
Clwyd LL29 9AB.
Tel (01492) 515429 Fax (01492) 518805

Centrally located on the beautiful North Wales coast, in the village of Old Colwyn. Within easy distance of the many excellent local courses. Inclusive breaks. Group discounts from £17.50 BB. Course fees arranged on request.

St Margarets Hotel
Princes Drive,
Colwyn Bay,
Clwyd LL29 8RP.
Tel (01492) 532718

RAC 1-Star hotel with Merit Awards for 'Hospitality, Comfort and Service'. All 10 bedrooms are en suite, with TV, radio and beverage tray. Special rates for groups of ten or more. Eight golf courses within easy reach.

Trearddur Bay Hotel
Trearddur Bay,
Holyhead, Anglesey LL65 2UN.
Tel (01407) 860301 Fax (01407) 861181

AA 3-Star 73% and WTB 4-Crown Highly Commended. Excellent facilities at this prestigious hotel with indoor heated swimming pool and superb '19th hole' in the residents' bar with over 80 malts and blended whiskies. Holyhead course one mile away plus three other golf courses within fifteen miles. Golf packages available.

Trefeddian Hotel
Aberdovey, Gwynedd LL35 0SB.
Tel (01654) 767213

3-star hotel with 46 rooms all with bath or shower en suite, central heating, telephone and colour TV. Indoor pool, putting green, tennis court. Games room with snooker. Overlooks the golf links and sea. Reduced golfer's green fee. Details and hotel colour brochure sent on request. No societies. (See advertisement page 401 for further details.)

CHANNEL ISLANDS

La Grande Mare Hotel Golf & Country Club
Vazon Bay,
Castel,
Guernsey.
Tel (01481) 56576 Fax (01481) 56532

Beautifully appointed RAC 4-star hotel with 18-hole golf course playing off 14 greens. Professional shop and tuition on-site. Gourmet restaurant awarded 2 AA Rosettes. There is also a 9-hole pitch and putt course ideal for the family. Beachside location. Golfing breaks catered for.

Les Arches Hotel
Archirondel,
Gorey,
St Martin,
Jersey JE3 6DR.
Tel (01534) 853839 Fax (01534) 856660

Overlooking France. Private access to beach. All rooms en suite with satellite TV. One and a half miles from Royal Jersey Golf Club. Swimming pool, garden, tennis court, golf net, night club, sauna, mini-gym and bars. Restaurant. Bed and breakfast rates from £29. Special discount for golfers.

Pembroke Bay Hotel
Vale,
Guernsey GY3 5BY.
Tel (01481) 47573 Fax (01481) 48838

4-crown fully refurbished family run hotel situated between superb beach and golf course (100 yards). Two restaurants (AA Rosette 1994), heated outdoor pool, bitmac tennis court, surf and sailing school and mountain bike hire.

The St Pierre Park Hotel
Rohais,
St Peter Port,
Guernsey GY1 1FD.
Tel (01481) 728282

This 4-star hotel offers extensive leisure facilities including a 9-hole, par 3, golf course designed by Tony Jacklin, three tennis courts and a health suite with heated indoor swimming pool, spa bath, saunas, steam rooms, solaria and exercise room.

NORTHERN IRELAND

The Antrim Arms Hotel

75 Castle Street,
Ballycastle,
Co Antrim BT54 6AS.
Tel (01265) 762284 Fax (01265) 763876

Centrally located in Ballycastle, this 250 year old hotel is one of the north's oldest posting inns. It has 16 bedrooms and golfing parties are a speciality. Famous for food, value, good service and hospitality.

EIRE

Aghadoe Heights Hotel

Killarney,
Co Kerry.
Tel +353 64 31766 Fax +353 64 31345.

Stunning panoramic views, comfort, good food and personal service are the keynotes of this luxury 4-star hotel, with its rooftop restaurant and superb indoor leisure facilities. Perfectly located for playing Ireland's premier golf courses including Killarney, Tralee, Ballybunion and Waterville.

Forte Crest - Dublin

Dublin Airport,
Co Dublin.
Tel +353 1 8444211

A stay at the Forte Crest places the golfing enthusiast within easy reach of some of Dublin's premier golf courses, Portmarnock, Royal Dublin, St Margaret's and Malahide.

Hunter's Hotel

Rathnew,
Co Wicklow.
Tel +353 404 40106 Fax +353 404 40338

270 year old coaching inn run by the same family for the past 170 years. Ideal centre for golf holidays. Eight 18-hole courses within half an hour, nearest three minute's drive away.

The Kildare Hotel & Country Club

At Straffan, Co Kildare.
Tel +353 1 627 3333 Fax +353 1 627 3312

Situated 40 minutes from Dublin. Arnold Palmer designed 18-hole championship golf course with clubhouse including restaurant and bar. Practice area and driving range. Resident golf professional Ernie Jones. Hotel AA 5-Star with 45 luxurious bedrooms. Health club and sports centre. River and coarse fishing and other activities. (See advertisement page 390 for further details.)

Marine Links Hotel

Ballybunion,
Co Kerry.
Tel (01686) 27139

The Marine Links is just one mile from Ballybunion Golf Club. All our en suite bedrooms have been refurbished, multi-channel TV, telephone and tea and coffee-making facilities. Our seafood restaurant is renowned. Concession green fees.

Mount Falcon Castle

Ballina,
Co Mayo.
Tel +353 96 70811

Mount Falcon Castle offers tranquility and the quiet comfort of log fires and superb cuisine in a country house atmosphere. Within easy reach of three magnificent courses all situated in areas of outstanding natural beauty in the wild and wonderful West of Ireland.

Mount Juliet

Thomastown,
Co Kilkenny.
Tel +353 56 24455

Deluxe accommodation in the elegant Mount Juliet House or the informal Hunters Yard. Ireland's premier sporting estate offers guests on-site fishing, shooting, archery, horse riding, tennis, stylish leisure centre, golf academy. Home of the Irish Open, '93 & '94.

Golf Club Facilities

This section, included for the first time in 1992, lists clubs which can offer hotel accommodation, and provision for society or corporate days together with driving ranges and leisure complexes offering an extensive range of other sports and leisure activities.

Abbotsley Golf Hotel

Eynesbury Hardwicke, St Neots, Cambridgeshire PE19 4XN.
Tel (01480) 474000 Fax (01480) 471018

Luxurious moated country house amidst picturesque golf course. Delightful bedrooms and galleried dining room. Surrounding courtyard of award winning gardens. Internationally renowned golf schools with Vivien Saunders. Squash and golf range.

Aldwark Manor Golf Club

Aldwark, Alne, York, Yorkshire YO6 2NF.
Tel (01347) 838353 (Golf) 838146 (Hotel)

Aldwark Manor extends a warm welcome to everyone. Situated in the Vale of York is a 6,171 yard par 71 golf course, laid out in easy walking parkland with the river Ure meandering beside a number of fairways. The ideal venue for your society or company golf day. (See advertisement page 381 for further details.)

Ashdown Forest Hotel

Chapel Lane, Forest Row, East Sussex.
Tel (01342) 824866 Fax (01342) 824869

Royal Ashdown New Course. Family owned and run hotel offering comfortable accommodation and good food and wines. Royal Ashdown Forest New Course operated by hotel exclusively for residents and visitors. (See advertisement page 367 for further details.)

Barnham Broom Hotel Golf & Leisure Centre

Honingham Road, Barnham Broom, Norwich, Norfolk NR9 4DD.
Tel (01603) 759393 Fax (01603) 758224

East Anglia's finest conference and leisure centre lies in 250 acres of countryside. 52 fully equipped bedrooms include family rooms, served by Flints restaurant and sports snack bar. Four squash courts, snooker, heated indoor swimming pool and spa jets, tennis and 36-hole golf. Golfing Getaway £164. (See advertisement page 379 for further details.)

The Belfry

Wishaw,
North Warwickshire B76 9PR.
Tel (01675) 470 301

The Belfry, set in 370 acres of beautiful parkland, offers the Brabazon Golf Course, venue for the Ryder Cup and the Derby Course - a challenge for the amateur golfer. The luxury hotel itself has a superb leisure centre and a fine selection of restaurants and bars. (Part of The De Vere Hotels Group.)

Belmont Lodge & Golf Course

Belmont,
Hereford HR2 9SA.
Tel (01432) 352666 Fax (01432) 358090

18-hole golf course running along the beautiful Wye Valley with a 30-bedroomed hotel on-site. Other facilities include bar, restaurant, fishing, bowling, tennis and snooker. Only a mile and a half from Hereford City centre. (See advertisement page 389 for further details.)

Boothferry Golf Club

Spaldington Lane,
Howden, Goole,
North Humberside DN14 7NG.
Tel (01430) 430364 Fax (01430) 430567

A pleasant meadowland course on the Vale of York is situated two and a half miles from Junction 37 on the M62 on the B1228 Howden to Bubwith Road. 18-hole course, practice area, putting green, clubhouse facilities, restaurant and bar.

Botley Park Hotel & Country Club

Winchester Road,
Boorley Green, Botley,
Hampshire SO3 2UA.
Tel (01489) 780888 Fax (01489) 789242

Set in 176 acres of rolling Hampshire countryside, this 4-star hotel has 100 en suite bedrooms, superb restaurant, extensive leisure facilities and its own picturesque and challenging 18-hole par 70 golf course and driving range. (See advertisement page 377 for further details).

Burnham & Berrow Golf Club

St Cristopher's Way,
Burnham-on-Sea,
Somerset TA8 2PE.
Tel (01278) 785760

18-hole championship links golf course and 9-hole course. (See advertisement page 23 for further details.)

Bushey Hall Golf Club

Bushey Hill Drive,
Bushey,
Hertfordshire WD2 2EP.
Tel (01923) 222253 Fax (01923) 229759

Established 1890 Bushey Hall Golf Club has one of the oldest and best established courses in Hertfordshire. Pro Ken Wickham, fully equipped pro shop, practice net, clubhouse restaurant and bar. Open for membership. Pay as you play operated. (See advertisement page 21 for further details.)

Castletown Golf Links Hotel

Derbyhaven, Castletown,
Isle of Man.
Tel (01624) 822201 Fax (01624) 625535

Situated on our own peninsula, our championship golf course of 6,700 yards, with all holes having sea views, is a real test of links golf. The hotel facilities are of a luxurious 3-star standard.

Cottesmore Country Club

Buchan Hill, Pease Pottage,
Crawley,
Sussex RH11 9AT.
Tel (01293) 528256 Fax (01293) 522819

11 en suite bedrooms overlooking quiet undulating Sussex countryside. Guests can enjoy two full 18-hole mature golf courses, tennis, squash, indoor pool, spa bath, steam, sauna and fitness rooms. Fifteen minutes from Gatwick, one mile from Pease Pottage exit off M23.

Dale Hill Hotel

Ticehurst, Wadhurst,
East Sussex TN5 7DQ.
Tel (01580) 200112

4-star 5-Crown highly commended award winning luxurious new hotel situated in an area of outstanding national beauty with elegant health club and highly acclaimed 18-hole golf course. An additional 18-hole course under construction.

Dalmahoy Hotel Country Club Resort

Kirknewton,
Nr Edinburgh,
Midlothian EH27 8EB.
Tel 0131-333 1845

Swimming pool (18m x 10m), steam room, sauna, two solariums, fitness studio, health and beauty salon, two squash courts, two outdoor tennis courts, snooker room. Two golf courses. 4-star hotel with 116 bedrooms. (Part of the Country Club Hotels group.)

Dewlands Manor Golf Course

Rotherfield,
East Sussex TN6 3JN.
Tel (01892) 852266

20 minute tee times. Wonderful views. Course maintained to very high standard. Converted 15th-century malthouse clubroom provides perfect location for small business/golf meetings. Club bar, buggies, light snacks. Pro-shop stockists for Joe Powell, Callaway, Reebok.

Farthingstone Hotel Golf & Leisure Centre

Farthingstone,
Towcester,
Northamptonshire NN12 8HA.
Tel (01327) 361291 Fax (01327) 361645

Set in glorious wooded countryside, just 90 minutes outside London. Farthingstone Hotel offers 16 superb en suite rooms, a challenging 18-hole golf course, squash courts, full size snooker tables, and a carvery restaurant. Highly competitve tariffs.

Five Lakes Hotel Golf & Country Club

Colchester Road,
Whitehouse Hill,
Tolleshunt Knights,
Maldon, Essex CM9 8HX.
Tel (01621) 868888 Fax (01621) 869696

Luxury hotel and country club nestling in 320 acres of Essex countryside, close to the Roman town of Colchester and 'Constable Country'. Extensive facilities include a deluxe hotel, indoor and outdoor tennis, squash courts, health centre and indoor pool. Golf packages, incentive and leisure breaks available upon request.

Gatton Manor Hotel Golf & Country Club Ltd

Ockley,
Nr Dorking,
Surrey RH5 5PQ.
Tel (01306) 627555/7

Set amidst its own 18-hole golf course in 200 acres of parklands and lakes, situated between London and the south coast, in the heart of the Surrey countryside. Superb all en suite accommodation overlooking the golf course and grounds. A la carte restaurants, large lounge bar, sport pursuits and conference suites.

Gleddoch House

Langbank,
Renfrewshire PA14 6YE.
Tel (01475) 540711

Country house hotel overlooking the river Clyde within easy reach of Glasgow and airport. Own golf course (par 72, 6,300 yards). Pro shop, clubhouse with own restaurant, bar, sauna, squash and horse riding.

Goodwood Park Hotel Country Club Resort

Goodwood,
Nr Chichester,
West Sussex PO18 0QB.
Tel (01243) 775987 Fax (01243) 533802

Country club hotel set in the 12,000 acre Goodwood Estate with a testing 18-hole golf course and superb leisure facilities including golf range, practice area, putting green and fully equipped sports shop. (Part of the Country Club Hotels Group.)

Hill Valley Golf Hotel & Country Club

Terrick Road, Whitchurch,
Shropshire SY13 4JZ.
Tel (01948) 663584

The complex has twin-bedded motel accommodation. All rooms have bathroom en suite, colour TV, tea and coffee-making facilities. Two golf courses, tennis and snooker.

Horam Park Golf Club

Chiddingly Road, Horam,
East Sussex TN21 0JJ.
Tel (01435) 81 3477 Fax (01435) 81 3677

9-hole golf course 18 tee positions, pitch 'n' putt course, 16-bay driving range open 8am to 10pm seven days. Extensive pro shop, bar, restaurant, PGA qualified teaching professionals. Societies and visitors welcome. Specialises in corporate days.

The Kenmore Hotel

Kenmore, Perthshire PH15 2NU.
Tel (01887) 830205 Fax (01887) 830262

Scotland's oldest inn is uniquely situated on the banks of the river and Loch Tay. We offer modern, comfortable rooms, exciting menus, a fine cellar and our own 18-hole par 69 Taymouth Castle Golf Course. (See advertisement page 395 for further details.)

The Kildare Hotel & Country Club

At Straffan, Co Kildare.
Tel +353 1 627 3333 Fax +353 1 627 3312

Situated 40 minutes from Dublin. Arnold Palmer designed 18-hole championship golf course with clubhouse including restaurant and bar. Practice area and driving range. Resident golf professional Ernie Jones. Hotel AA 5-Star with 45 luxurious bedrooms. Health club and sports centre. River and coarse fishing and other activities. (See advertisement page 390 for further details.)

La Grande Mare Hotel Golf & Country Club

Vazon Bay, Castel, Guernsey.
Tel (01481) 56576 Fax (01481) 56532

Beautifully appointed RAC 4-star hotel with 18-hole golf course playing off 14 greens. Professional shop and tuition on-site. Gourmet restaurant awarded 2 AA Rosettes. There is also a 9-hole pitch and putt course ideal for the family. Beachside location. Golfing breaks catered for.

Lancaster Golf & Country Club

The Dormy, Ashton Hall,
Ashton-with-Stodday,
Lancaster LA2 0AJ.
Tel (01524) 751247 Fax (01524) 752135

Ideal for small parties of up to eighteen persons. For terms and reservations please apply to the secretary. (See advertisement page 22 for further details.)

Letham Grange

Colliston,
by Arbroath DD11 4RL.
Tel (01241) 890373 Fax (01241) 890414

20-bedroom Victorian mansion, with 36-holes of superb golf. First class facilities set in the heartland of golf. Company/society golf outings/ breaks welcome. (See advertisement page 383 for further details.)

Lostwithiel Golf & Country Club

Lower Polscoe,
Lostwithiel,
Cornwall PL22 0HQ.
Tel (01208) 873550 Fax (01208) 873479

A hotel, golf and country club of great charm and character. The 18-hole course with its two distinctive nines provides pleasurable golf for the low handicap player and less experienced golfer alike. Set amid the valley of the river Fowey.

The Manor of Groves Golf & Country Club

High Wych,
Sawbridgeworth,
Hertfordshire CM21 0LA.
Tel (01279) 722333 Fax (01279) 726972

This superb 18-hole golf course set around its own Geogian manor house offers the ideal setting for that break away. Along with its special rated packages, and golf school, the clubhouse facilities include superb cuisine, bar, and a function room suitable for all occasions.

Mentmore Golf & Country Club

Mentmore,
Nr Leighton Buzzard,
Bedfordshire LU7 0UA.
Tel (01296) 662020 Fax (01296) 662592

Two 18-hole championship golf courses. Rothschild Course par 72, 6,763 yards. Rosebery Course par 72, 6,777 yards. Practice range. Restaurant, swimming pool, sauna, jacuzzi and steam room.

Mount Juliet

Thomastown,
Co Kilkenny,
Eire.
Tel +353 56 24455

Deluxe accommodation in the elegant Mount Juliet House or the informal Hunters Yard. Ireland's premier sporting estate offers guests on-site fishing, shooting, archery, horse riding, tennis, stylish leisure centre, golf academy. Home of the Irish Open, '93 & '94.

Murrayshall Country House Hotel & Golf Course

Scone,
Perthshire PH2 7PH.
Tel (01738) 551171
Pro Shop (01738) 552784

Murrayshall is a Scottish country house set in 300 acres of parkland. Of the 19 bedrooms many have scenic views over the course and picturesque Perthshire countryside. Adjacent is the 18-hole golf course with its own clubhouse, ideal for hosting company golf events and societies. Indoor golf school facilities.

Patshull Park Hotel Golf & Country Club

Pattingham,
Shropshire WV6 7HR.
Tel (01902) 700100 Fax (01902) 700874

Parkland, lakeside 18-hole championship John Jacobs' designed course in grounds of the Earl of Dartmouth estate. Corporate, society and residential packages. 49 en suite bedrooms, swimming pool, leisure centre, gymnasium, snooker room, fishing. Restaurant and Bunkers coffee shop.

Praa Sands Golf Club

Germoe Cross Road,
Penzance,
Cornwall TR20 9QT.
Tel (01736) 763445 (01736) 763399

Situated on the main A394 Helston to Penzance holiday route, our club offers a warm welcome to everyone, in an informal friendly environment. The 9-hole course offers outstanding views and a deceptively challenging par 60. After playing, relax in the licensed bar and enjoy a quiet meal or snack with your family. (See advertisement page 20 for further details.)

Rodway Hill Golf Course

Newent Road,
Highnam,
Gloucestershire GL2 8DN.
Tel (01452) 384222 Fax (01989) 766450

An 18-hole pay and play par 68 course two miles south west of Gloucester, with panoramic views of the Cotswolds. It has a well stocked shop, practice and teaching facilities. Hire kit available. Societies welcome.

Royal Lytham & St Anne's Golf Club

The Dormy House,
Links Gate,
Lytham St Annes,
Lancashire FY8 3LQ.
Tel (01253) 724206 Fax (01253) 780946

Ideal for small parties wishing to play the championship course. Accommodation for men only. Apply to the secretary. (See advertisement page 20 for further details.)

Seaford Golf Club

Dormy House,
East Blatchington,
Seaford, East Sussex BN25 2JD.
Tel (01323) 892442

The Dormy House provides comfortable accommodation for eighteen guests in 6 single and 6 twin-bedded rooms, the bedrooms being on the first floor of the clubhouse. For latest brochure ring 01323 892442.

Sedlescombe Golf Club

Kent Street,
Sedlescombe, East Sussex.
Tel (01424) 870898

9-hole golf course, pitch and putt course. 24-bay floodlit driving range. Bar and restaurant, facilities. All facilities open to the public. Societies and corporate days welcome.

Selsdon Park Hotel

Sanderstead,
South Croydon,
Surrey CR2 8YA.
Tel 0181-657 8811 Fax 0181-651 6171

Traditional country house set in 200 acres of parkland with an 18-hole championship course. Green fee players welcome. Exclusive tropical leisure club. Touring golf professional - Sam Torrance.

Shrigley Hall Hotel Golf & Country Club

Shrigley Park,
Pott Shrigley,
Nr Macclesfield, Cheshire SK10 5SB.
Tel (01625) 575757 Fax (01625) 573323

4-star country house on the edge of the Peak District, with magnificent views over the 18-hole championship course to the Cheshire Plain below. Adjoining leisure club has swimming pool, squash, snooker, tennis, steam, sauna and solaria. (See advertisement page 381 for further details.)

St Mellion Lodges & Hotel St Mellion Golf & Country Club

St Mellion,
Saltash,
Cornwall PL12 6SD.
Tel (01579) 50101 Fax (01579) 50116

Gold Award luxury lodges nestled in the heart of Nicklaus championship and Old Course. AA/RAC 3-star hotel and full range of sport, personal fitness and leisure facilities.

Telford Golf & Country Club Moat House

Great Hay,
Sutton Hill,
Telford, Shropshire TF7 4DT.
Tel (01952) 585642

Overlooking the Ironbridge Gorge, this recently extended and refurbished hotel offers its own 18-hole championship course, 9-hole par 3 course, driving range and practice areas. The extensive leisure facilities include squash courts, swimming pool, gymnasium, snooker, whirlpool, sauna and steam rooms. There is a resident masseur. (See advertisement page 379 for further details.)

Tewkesbury Park Hotel Country Club Resort

Lincoln Green Lane,
Tewkesbury,
Gloucestershire GL20 7DN.
Tel (01684) 295405

This 78-bedroom hotel with modern facilities is surrounded by its own 18-hole golf course. It also offers heated indoor pool, sauna, jacuzzi, solarium, health and beauty salon, snooker, squash/floodlit tennis courts, steam room and fitness centre. (Part of the Country Club Hotels group.)

Thorpeness Golf Club Hotel

Thorpeness, Nr Leiston, Suffolk IP16 4NH.
Tel (01728) 452176 Fax (01728) 453868

Modern luxury hotel adjoining the clubhouse on one of East Anglia's finest 18-hole courses. Situated on the lovely, unspoiled Suffolk coast. Ideal too for non-golfers. (See advertisement page 373 for further details.)

Trevose Golf & Country Club

Constantine Bay, Padstow,
North Cornwall PL28 8JB.
Tel (01841) 520208 Fax (01841) 521057

Trevose offers not only great golf (championship 18-hole course, a 9-hole full length (3,100 yards) par 35 plus a 9-hole short course) but also a first class clubhouse and restaurant, three hard all-weather tennis courts, a heated outdoor swimming pool in the summer, a games room for the kids and a boutique. Accommodation is available in bungalows, chalets, luxury flats and dormy suites. Send for our detailed full colour

Turnberry Hotel Golf Courses & Spa

Ayrshire KA26 9LT.
Tel (01655) 331000 Fax (01655) 331706

One of the world's finest luxury hotel, golf and spa resorts. Edwardian country house overlooking its own Ailsa and Arran championship courses. The Ailsa is ranked 16th in the world and was the venue for the 1994 Open.

Ufford Park Hotel Golf & Leisure

Yarmouth Road, Ufford, Woodbridge,
Suffolk IP12 1QW.
Tel (01394) 383555 Fax (01394) 383582

Challenging 18-hole, par 70 golf course set in historic parkland. Accommodation, restaurant, bars, leisure facilities inclusive of indoor heated pool, gym, fitness studio, sauna, solarium and beauty salon. Competitive rates. (See advertisement page 373 for further details.)

Welbeck Manor & Sparkwell Golf Course

Blacklands, Sparkwell, Plymouth,
Devon PL7 5DF.
Tel/Fax (01752) 837219

A testing 9-hole pay as you play course and also a par 3 course, set in 60 acres of parkland. Facilities include a well equipped golf shop, excellent hotel accommodation, restaurant and bar. Open to the public. Golf societies welcome.

Welcombe Hotel & Golf Course

Warwick Road,
Stratford-upon-Avon,
Warwickshire CV37 0NR.
Tel (01789) 295252 Fax (01789) 414666

A 4-star Jacobean-style mansion set within its own 6,217 yards private golf course. A newly created clubhouse and pro shop within the hotel's 157 acres enhance the parkland course.

Westerwood Hotel Golf & Country Club

St Andrews Drive,
Cumbernauld,
Glasgow G68 0EW.
Tee-off Times (01236) 452772
Tel (01236) 457171

Westerwood Hotel, Golf and Country Club is located twenty minutes from Glasgow and boasts an 18-hole championship golf course designed by Seve Ballesteros and Dave Thomas. A range of golfing breaks and society packages are available including residential golf schools using our indoor golfing facility. The venue is ideal for hosting company golf days. The country club offers a range of other sporting activities. Indoor golf school facilities.

Whitsand Bay Hotel Golf & Country Club

Portwrinkle,
Crafthole,
By Torpoint, Cornwall PL11 3BU.
Tel (01503) 30276

Spectacularly sited *own 18-hole golf course*, overlooking the ocean in Cornish fishing hamlet, with 1st tee 100 yards from front door. Leisure complex, heated indoor swimming pool, sauna, solarium, massage/beauty salons.

Wyre Forest Golf Centre

Zortech Avenue,
Kidderminster,
Worcestershire DY11 7NY.
Tel (01299) 822682 Fax (01299) 879433

18-hole 6,000 yards par 70 course. 32-bay floodlit driving range. Set in rolling countryside we have a clubhouse with fully stocked pro shop. Golf societies welcome. We offer a warm welcome to visitors and golf societies as well as promoting a growing membership. (See advertisement page 21 for further details.)

DRIVING RANGES, PRACTICE GROUNDS & LEISURE SERVICES

Colnbrook Golf Range

Gallymead Road, Colnbrook, Berkshire SL3 0EN.
Tel (01753) 682670

A busy well equipped range with PGA staff on hand for first class tuition and advice on all golfers requisites. Also a members' club (only £10.00 per year) serving a very wide selection of drinks and first class food. Ideal for Heathrow Airport. M25 Jct 14, one mile. M4 Jct 4 or 5, one mile.

Drayton Park Golf Course & Driving Range

Steventon Road, Drayton Village, Oxfordshire OX14 2RR.
Tel (01235) 550607

18-hole pay and play scenic parkland course and 9-hole par 3 course, 21-bay floodlit range and professional shop.

Gosforth Park Golfing Complex Ltd

(Parklands Golf Course) High Gosforth Park, Newcastle-upon-Tyne NE3 5HQ.
Tel 0191-236 4480

The complex has an 18-hole golf course, 45-bay two tier floodlit driving range, 9-hole pitch and putt course and putting green. Also pro shop, bar and restaurant. Open to non-members.

Kyle & Carrick Leisure Services

30 Miller Road, Ayr KA7 2AY.
Tel (01292) 282842

Excellent courses on Scotland's golf coast, including championship courses at Ayr (Belleisle) and Troon (Lochgreen and Darley). Other courses at Ayr, Troon, Girvan and Maybole. Open all year. Special rates for playing more than one day. (See advertisement page 23 for further details.)

Rudding Park Golf

Rudding Park, Harrogate, North Yorkshire HG3 1DJ.
Tel (01423) 872100 Fax: (01423) 873011

Superb 18-bay covered driving range and golf academy. Complete the golf expereience on our outstanding 18-hole, par 72 parkland course. Corporate and society bookings welcome. (See advertisement page 21 for further details.)

Telford Golf & Country Club Moat House

Great Hay, Sutton Hill, Telford, Shropshire TF7 4DT.
Tel (01952) 585642

Overlooking the Ironbridge Gorge, this recently extended and refurbished hotel offers its own 18-hole championship course, 9-hole par 3 course, driving range and practice areas. The extensive leisure facilities include squash courts, swimming pool, gymnasium, snooker, whirlpool, sauna and steam rooms. There is a resident masseur. (See advertisement page 379 for further details.)

Buyer's Guide to Good Golfing and Golf Course Maintenance

This compact but informative guide to manufacturers and organisations offering services to golf clubs and individual golfers includes a wide number of categories, from personal accessories and golfing equipment to golf course maintenance.
The editors do not necessarily endorse the information supplied.

ARCHITECTS, CONSTRUCTORS & CONSULTANTS

British Institute of Golf Course Architects

The Pheasantry, Godstone Road,
Oxted, Surrey RH8 9NQ.
Tel (01883) 712072 Fax (01883) 730376

Professional institute of qualified golf course architects officially recognised by the Royal & Ancient and English Golf Union.

Golf Landscapes Ltd

Ashwells Road, Bentley,
Brentwood, Essex CM15 9SR.
Tel (01277) 373720 Fax (01277) 374834

The country's leading specialists in golf course construction, drainage and contract maintenance, working throughout Europe with leading international golf course architects. (See advertisement page 391 for further details.)

Hamilton Stutt & Co

12 Bingham Avenue,
Poole, Dorset BH14 8NE.
Tel (01202) 708406

Fellow and founder member of the British Institute of Golf Course Architects. One of Europe's most experienced golf course architects. Personal attention throughout to each new project.

Hawtree
5 Oxford Street,
Woodstock, Oxford OX20 1TQ.
Tel (01993) 811976 Fax (01993) 812448

Hawtree celebrates 82 years of golf architectural service throughout the world. (See advertisement page 425 for further details.)

Maxel Golf Ltd
Manor Cottage, 1 Front Street, Whickham,
Newcastle-upon-Tyne NE16 4HF.
Tel 0191-496 0312 Fax 0191-496 0084

Golf Course Constructors.

AWARDS & PRIZES

Derek Burridge Trophies
5-11 Hanbury Road,
Acton, London W3 8RF.
Tel 0181-992 5948/7313 Fax 0181-993 4814

The country's leading suppliers of golf prizes. We offer a vast range of silverplate, crystal, china, clocks, leather goods and sporting trophies, all at trade prices. Glass and silverplate in-house engraving service. Next day delivery throughout the UK. Call for brochure. (See advertisement page 391 for further details).

Majestic Crystal
The Old Chapel, Main Street,
Martin, Lincolnshire LN4 3QY.
Tel (01526) 378676 Fax (01526) 378633

Wholesale suppliers and engravers of fine crystal. All of our artwork and engraving is undertaken in-house enabling us to provide rapid turnaround and probably the best engraving in the country! If you wish we can call and discuss your particular requirements, and can provide a free sample of your artwork. (See advertisement page 392 for further details.)

BAG TAGS

H.M.T. Plastics Ltd
PO Box 195, Haywards Heath,
West Sussex RH16 1FQ.
Tel/Fax (01444) 416088

Bag tags supplied in nine colours either round, pear shaped or sunrise to accommodate club logo, from a choice of six print colours. Adhesive date discs available annually in choice of seven colours and sold separately. (See advertisement page 421 for further details.)

CARTS, TROLLEYS & BUGGIES

Blackweld Ltd
Malthouse Road, Tipton,
West Midlands DY4 9AE.
Tel 0121-520 4786 Fax 0121-557 3680

Manufacturer of the superior 'Kaddy' range of pull carts, including the 'Nu-Lite' and 'Kaddy Kub' models.

Fraser Products Ltd
Brockhill Works, Windsor Road,
Redditch, Worcestershire B97 6DJ.
Tel (01527) 64126

Manufacturers of Fraser Foldaway powered trolleys and Fraser Fairway pull trolleys. Fraser products also distribute the world's foremost remote controlled Lectronic Kaddy, already sold in over 26 countries and backed by over six years' experience.

The Green Family (Green Drive International Ltd)
Hollywood Works, Valley Road,
Cinderford, Gloucestershire GL14 2PD.
Tel (01594) 827800 Fax (01594) 827133

We offer a larger range than any trolley manufacturer. Three wheeled trolleys to a four wheeled ride-on. We have 26 years combined experience of manufacturing. It is the choice of the world's No 1 lady golfer.

Kinbag Golf Equipment
Micron House, Baird Close,
Drayton Fields, Daventry,
Northamptonshire NN11 5RY.
Tel (01327) 300340

The sales and service of the most practical golf bag in the world consisting of a combination golf bag and trolley and in addition all the necessary ancillary equipment, ie, travel cover, rain cover and brolly.

CLOTHING/GOLF WEAR

Belding Sports (UK)
Unit 4, 46 Croydon Road,
Reigate, Surrey RH2 0NH.
Tel (01737) 221196 Fax (01737) 226606

Sole distributors for Belding Sports California. Superbly designed golf bags and travel accessories of peerless quality. Also golf clothing new for 1995. Logo embroidery and custom design specialist. Largest range in the world. Available through good pro shops.

Belle Golf

2 Ghyll Industrial Estate, Ghyll Road, Heathfield, East Sussex TN21 8AW.
Tel (01435) 866449 Fax (01435) 866914

Exclusive distributor in Europe for the American manufacturers Marcia Originals, Lily's of Beverly Hills and Leon Levin of their fashionable ladies' golf wear. The ranges emphasise colour co-ordination, quality, easy care and originality. Sold almost exclusively through the golf professional shops, supporting the industry in the growing market area of ladies' fashionable golf wear.

Braxus LeisureWear Ltd

Unit 3, Park Works, Kingsley, Bordon, Hampshire GU35 9LX.
Tel (01420) 487171 Fax (01420) 487144

British company offering understated designs, visible quality and meticulous care in their exciting range of golf wear. Polo shirts in the new Tactel Aquator fabric, complementary styles of trousers and cotton cable crew neck sweaters and matching V-neck slipovers. Send for brochure of our complete collection.

Head Sportswear

Lui e Lei Sportswear Ltd
Unit 5, Parkside, Avenue 2, Station Lane, Witney, Oxon OX8 6YF.
Tel (01993) 778020 Fax (01993) 776798

Suppliers of both mens' and ladies' clothing to the golf trade. Fully co-ordinating collections of shirts, sweaters and trousers. Also available from Head Sportswear are the popular Gore-Windstopper sweaters in various designs and colours.

Jayros Golf

Shannon Street, Leeds LS9 8SS.
Tel 0113 240 2662

Jayros the brand leading golf trouser in the UK. Our comprehensive range including plus twos and fours uses the best materials from pure wool to cotton. Whatever your preference there's a Jayros garment to suit you.

CLUB CONSULTANTS & TRAINING COURSES

Club Management Services

50 Town Street, Duffield, Belper, Derbyshire DE56 4GG.
Tel (01332) 840075

Provision of training courses in golf club management. Existing correspondence courses for secretary/managers and stewards. Management consultancy and staff recruitment for golf clubs in Great Britain and in Europe. Expert golf club advisory service.

COMPUTER SYSTEMS

Euro Systems Projects

Europa House,
8 Kimpton Link Business Park,
Kimpton Road,
Sutton,
Surrey SM3 9PF.
Tel 0181-641 7216

ESP is universally recognised as the UK's market leader for integrated point of sale and management systems. *Golfmaster* has been specifically designed for both the golf professional and the golf club, and encompasses all aspects encountered when running a successful and profitable golf operation.

DISTRIBUTORS & WHOLESALERS

Aldila UK

12 Heather Road,
Binley Woods,
Coventry CV3 2DE.
Tel/Fax (01203) 545651

Aldila Golf equipment distributors: Diamond Golf Ltd, 4/5 Rudford Industrial Estate, Ford Road, Arundel BN18 0BS Tel (01903) 726999 Fax (01903) 726998; Golfsmith (Europe) Ltd, Leewood Business Park, Upton Road, Huntingdon PE17 5XQ Tel (01480) 891909 Fax (01480) 891836; Gratex Golf, Golf House, Broad Lane, Bradford, West Yorkshire Tel (01274) 664289 Fax (01274) 656040.

Belle Golf

2 Ghyll Industrial Estate,
Ghyll Road,
Heathfield,
East Sussex TN21 8AW.
Tel (01435) 866449 Fax (01435) 866914

Exclusive distributor in Europe for the American manufacturers Marcia Originals, Lily's of Beverly Hills and Leon Levin of their fashionable ladies' golf wear. The ranges emphasise colour co-ordination, quality, easy care and originality. Sold almost exclusively through the golf professional shops, supporting the industry in the growing market area of ladies' fashionable golf wear.

Cleveland Golf UK

Unit 1, The Griffin Centre,
Staines Road,
Feltham, Middlesex TW14 0HS.
Tel 0181-893 2218 Fax 0181-893 1770

Cleveland Golf, pioneers in golf club technology offer a range of VAS (Vibration Absorbing System) woods, irons and putters. With patents on both the VAS system and inset hosel Cleveland boast the most advanced and stable clubs available. Cleveland also manufacture a range of speciality wedges used by most of the top tour players around the world.

ESTUSA

C T Sport, PO Box 57,
Falmouth, Cornwall TR11 3XP.
Tel (01326) 212000

ESTUSA - The brand name of one of the world's premier manufacturers of sports equipment, your assurance of quality, performance, value. Guaranteed to improve your game or your money back. Contact us through your golf shop. (See page 421.)

Yonex UK Ltd

74 Wood Lane,
White City,
London W12 7RH.
Tel 0181-742 9777 Fax 0181-749 9612

Importer and distributor of Yonex golf, tennis and badminton products in the United Kingdom. Professionals like Liselotte Neumann and Phil Mickelson use Yonex golf products, and 80% of badminton professionals use Yonex rackets.

DRIVING RANGE EQUIPMENT

Amalgamated Golf & Recreation Ltd

Brook Bend,
Weston Subedge,
Nr Chipping Campden,
Gloucestershire GL55 6QH.
Tel (01386) 840435

Manufacturers and installers of sand filled turf for golf tees, pathways and other recreational areas, driving range mats a speciality. Spike-proof carpets to suit all needs including personal designs together with one of the most comprehensive collections of all types of floor covering.

European Golf Machinery

Street Garage,
Bucklesham,
Ipswich,
Suffolk IP10 0DN.
Tel (01473) 659815 Fax (01473) 659045

Manufacturers of various collectors including lightweight plastic collectors, golf ball dispensers and washers. Motocol motorised ball collector. Kawasaki ATV and Mule distributors. (See advertisement page 427 for further details).

Golf Equip (GB) Ltd

Gladonian Road,
Littlehampton,
West Sussex BN17 6JW.
Tel (01903) 724500 Fax (01903) 716184

British manufacturers and specialists in all golf range requirements since 1979 including winter and alternative tee mats. Equipment suppliers and management of the R&A Open Championship professionals' practice grounds since 1984. Free advisory service. (See advertisement page 421 for further details.)

H Pattisson & Co Ltd

342 Selbourne Road,
Luton,
Bedfordshire LU4 8NU.
Tel (01582) 597262 Fax (01582) 505241

1994 saw the new Pattisson's emerge, with many innovative quality products for all course furnishing requirements. The new brochure for Driving Range gives the customer a complete 'one stop shop' for their practice ground and with the direct delivery service it offers the customer that traditional service in the modern manner. (See advertisement page 417 for further details.)

Heritage Fairway Ltd

1 St Johns Road,
Hove,
East Sussex BN3 2FB.
Tel (01273) 220116 Fax (01273) 571621

UK manufacturers of golf range equipment including manual and electronic ball dispensers. Acadamy ball washers and washing systems, ball conveyors and ball collectors. Also suppliers of ancillary equipment: Range mats, winter tee mats, range balls, baskets, target nets and range markers. (See advertisement page 391 for further details.)

Standard Golf (UK) Ltd

Maxwell Hart Business Centre,
PO Box 297, Lightwater GU18 5HJ.
Tel (0325) 125398 Fax (01276) 452616

UK sole distributor for Standard Golf, the world's leading manufacturer of golf course furniture. The widest choice available. Also manufacturers of golf mats for ranges and courses. Full range of driving range equipment available. (See advertisement page 417 for further details.)

Tildenet Ltd

Longbrook House,
Ashton Vale Road, Bristol BS3 2HA.
Tel 0117 966 9684

Netting manufacturers and suppliers to the golf industry. Products include perimeter safety netting (with an installation facility); a range of practice nets to cater for professionals, advanced players and beginners; anti-ball plugging net; target and chipping nets and anti-dazzle netting.

GOLF BALL MANUFACTURERS

Spalding Sports UK Ltd

16 Trafalgar Way,
Bar Hill, Cambridge CB3 8SQ.
Tel (01945) 781672

Spalding Sports UK Ltd is the UK distributor of the world's largest general sports company. We supply all major golf professionals with a complete range of golfing equipment under the Top Flite brands.

GOLF CLUB MANUFACTURERS

Aero Golf

Winsport House, Leicester Road,
Lutterworth, Leicestershire LE17 4PL.
Tel (01455) 556073 Fax (01455) 209298

'Aero' range of British manufactured, hi-tech game improvement, graphite golf clubs, including unique custom weighted woods featuring the world record holding (365 yards carry) 'Zapper' driver with its range of six, two-piece synchronised shafts to match swing speeds from 50-10 mph. Available 1995: 'Zapper' 385 W 'Zapper' irons and lightweight pocketed 'Zapper' bag. 'Redfern & Jones' range of British quality leather golf shoes, leather trimmed golf bags, holdalls and small leathergoods. We offer club/corporate customisation/design service.

Aldila UK

12 Heather Road,
Binley Woods, Coventry CV3 2DE.
Tel/Fax (01203) 545651

World's leading manufacturers of graphite golf shafts, including the low tongue, HM Line, filament wound and Superlite range. For Aldila distributors see under Distributors and Wholesalers.

Bronty Golf Co Ltd

81 Bradford Road, Stanningley,
Pudsey, West Yorkshire LS28 6AT.
Tel 0113 257 7266 Fax 0113 257 0771

Manufacturers of high quality British made custom golf clubs, putters and specialist clubs. Authentic replicas and hickory shafted putters etc. (See advertisement page 425 for further details.)

Cleveland Golf UK

Unit 1, The Griffin Centre, Staines Road,
Feltham, Middlesex TW14 0HS.
Tel 0181-893 2218 Fax 0181-893 1770

Cleveland Golf, pioneers in golf club technology offer a range of VAS (Vibration Absorbing System) woods, irons and putters. With patents on both the VAS system and inset hosel Cleveland boast the most advanced and stable clubs available. Cleveland also manufacture a range of speciality wedges used by most of the top tour players around the world.

ESTUSA

C T Sport, PO Box 57,
Falmouth, Cornwall TR11 3XP.
Tel (01326) 212000

ESTUSA - The brand name of one of the world's premier manufacturers of sports equipment, your assurance of quality, performance, value. Guaranteed to improve your game or your money back. Contact us through your golf shop. (See page 421.)

Golden Eagle International Putters

The Beeches, Borrowdale Drive,
Burnley, Lancashire BB10 2QL.
Tel/Fax (01282) 423762

Exclusive hand made *'Limited Edition'* putters in hallmarked precious metals. Platinum, 18ct gold and silver, all in handcrafted leather presentation cases with matching headcover. Perfect presentation for corporate, retirement and special occasions where *only the best is good enough.*

J B Halley & Co Ltd

New Pixmore Centre, Pixmore Avenue, Letchworth, Hertfordshire SG6 1JG.
Tel (01462) 483398 Fax (01462) 483404

Manufacturers of golf clubs and accessories for over 100 years. Over 90% of our equipment is British made and we supply 60 countries throughout the world. St Andrews factory: Tel (01334) 472833 Fax (01334) 477971.

Spalding Sports UK Ltd

16 Trafalgar Way,
Bar Hill, Cambridge CB3 8SQ.
Tel (01945) 781672

Spalding Sports UK Ltd is the UK distributor of the world's largest general sports company. We supply all major golf professionals with a complete range of golfing equipment under the Top Flite brands.

Swilken Golf Company Ltd

Argyll Business Park, Largo Road,
St Andrews, Fife KY16 8PJ.
Tel (01334) 472266 Fax (01334) 475037

A dedicated Scottish manufacturer which has established itself as a producer of quality golf clubs: Alta, Icon and Tournament G1 in the game improvement range, plus the new TF 270 classic blades and Rossa ladies' irons.

Yonex UK Ltd

74 Wood Lane,
White City, London W12 7RH.
Tel 0181-742 9777 Fax 0181-749 9612

Importer and distributor of Yonex golf, tennis and badminton products in the United Kingdom. Professionals like Liselotte Neumann and Phil Mickelson use Yonex golf products, and 80% of badminton professionals use Yonex rackets.

GOLF COURSE FURNISHINGS

Amalgamated Golf & Recreation Ltd

Brook Bend, Weston Subedge,
Nr Chipping Campden,
Gloucestershire GL55 6QH.
Tel (01386) 840435

Manufacturers and installers of sand filled turf for golf tees, pathways and other recreational areas, driving range mats a speciality. Spike-proof carpets to suit all needs including personal designs together with one of the most comprehensive collections of all types of floor covering.

H Pattisson & Co Ltd

342 Selbourne Road,
Luton,
Bedfordshire LU4 8NU.
Tel (01582) 597262 Fax (01582) 505241

1994 saw the new Pattisson's emerge, with many innovative quality products for all course furnishing requirements. The new brochure for Driving Range gives the customer a complete 'one stop shop' for their practice ground and with the direct delivery service it offers the customer that traditional service in the modern manner. (See advertisement page 417 for further details.)

Standard Golf (UK) Ltd

Maxwell Hart Business Centre,
PO Box 297,
Lightwater GU18 5HJ.
Tel (0325) 125398 Fax (01276) 452616

UK sole distributor for Standard Golf, the world's leading manufacturer of golf course furniture. The widest choice available. Also manufacturers of golf mats for ranges and courses. Full range of driving range equipment available. (See advertisement page 417 for further details.)

GOLF COURSE MAINTENANCE

Claymore Grass Machinery

Waterloo Road,
Waterloo Industrial Estate,
Bidford-on-Avon,
Warwickshire B50 4JH.
Tel (01789) 490177 Fax (01789) 490170

High quality grass cutting machinery for all types of terrain is available from Claymore. Distributors for Roberine and Bolens mowers with sales and service centres throughout the UK. From ride-on diesel hydrostatic cylinder mowers to lawn tractors. The accent is on comfort, ease and efficiency. Claymore are distributors for the Columbia Par Car range of golf cars, utility vehicles and people movers.

Golf Landscapes Ltd

Ashwells Road,
Bentley,
Brentwood, Essex CM15 9SR.
Tel (01277) 373720 Fax (01277) 374834

The country's leading specialists in golf course construction, drainage and contract maintenance, working throughout Europe with leading international golf course architects. (See advertisement page 391 for further details.)

GOLF GRIPS

Avon Golf Grips

Bath Road,
Melksham,
Wiltshire SN12 8AA.
Tel (01225) 791947 Fax (01225) 700828

Manufacture a comprehensive range of premium quality all-weather golf grips. Models include Chamois aircusion, Nexus, New Nexus 820 with its unique fibre filled compound. Avon, the official grip of the PGA of Europe, quality approved to ISO 9001. (See advertisement page 417 for further details).

Eaton Ltd - Golf Pride Grips

Units 1 & 2 Stirling Centre,
Northfields Industrial Estate,
Market Deeping,
Nr Peterborough PE6 8LB.
Tel (01778) 341555

Manufacturers of golf grips for over 45 years, they have been the leader in golf grip technology and the leader in rubber and cord grip sales for both professional and amateur players alike.

GOLF HOLIDAYS

HF Holidays Ltd

Imperial House,
Edgware Road,
London NW9 5AL.
Tel 0181-905 9556

Range of fully inclusive holidays from beginner to more experienced - many with professional tuition. Friendly competition with small group sizes, all organised by your experienced leader. Full board from £329 per person for seven nights.

Personal Holidays Scotland

PO Box 89,
Perth PH2 0YW.
Tel (01764) 684 410 Fax (01738) 827 216

We arrange golfing itineraries and inclusive holidays throughout Scotland. Different courses will be booked with tee-off times for each day of your holiday. Hotel accommodation, and travel arrangements will be booked and other special interests will be incorporated in the itinerary. We also arrange for salmon and trout fishing and visits taking in Scotland's heritage. (See advertisement page 396 for further details.)

The Scottish National Sports Centre - Inverclyde

Burnside Road, Largs,
Ayrshire KA30 8RW.
Tel (01475) 674666

Residential tuition courses for all abilities using the purpose built SGU golf facility. Top PGA teaching professionals. Driving bays, video playback swing analysis, training bunkers and variety of types of green.

GOLF INDUSTRY ACCOUNTANTS

S H Landes & Co

2 Milford House,
7 Queen Anne Street, London W1M 9FD.
Tel 0171-323 5757

S H Landes & Co are accountants specialising in golf club advisory work. Services provided include audit, accountancy, tax and VAT planning, advice on the sale, purchase and financing of golf developments, and the design of membership schemes including share/ debenture arrangements.

GOLF RANGE, PRACTICE GROUND EQUIPMENT

Range Servant UK Ltd

4 Arden Close,
Bovingdon,
Hertfordshire HP3 0QS.

Manufacture and market golf range and practice ground equipment. Golf ball dispensers; golf ball washers; golf ball collectors; play mats for ranges and practice grounds - winter tee mats a speciality; range balls and baskets.

IRRIGATION EQUIPMENT INSTALLATION

S G I Sales

6 Stuart Road,
Market Harborough,
Leicestershire LE16 9PQ.
Tel (01858) 463153 (4 lines)
Fax (01858) 410085

S G I Sales are authorised distributors of Hunter sprinklers. We specialise in golf course irrigation products for the European market.

Watermation Ltd

Tongham Road,
Aldershot,
Hampshire GU12 4AA.
Tel (01252) 336838

Manufacturers and installers of top quality golf course irrigation equipment including computer controllers and heavy duty pop-up sprinklers. Installations on hundreds of top quality courses around the UK, mainland Europe and worldwide.

LOCKER MANUFACTURERS

I M P Ltd (Improving Merchandise Presentation)

DEC House,
143/145 Cardiff Road,
Reading, Berkshire RG1 8JF.
Tel (01734) 560763 Fax (01734) 583619

Shopfitters and manufacturers of merchandisers, lockers and display accessories. IMP can help through the design stages providing ideas and sound advice. Our skilled fitters complete the service. Why not call us! (See advertisement page 425 for further details.)

NETTING

Tildenet Ltd

Longbrook House,
Ashton Vale Road, Bristol BS3 2HA.
Tel 0117 966 9684

Netting manufacturers and suppliers to the golf industry. Products include perimeter safety netting (with an installation facility); a range of practice nets to cater for professionals, advanced players and beginners; anti-ball plugging net; target and chipping nets and anti-dazzle netting.

PERSONAL ACCESSORIES & SUPPLIERS

Belding Sports (UK)

Unit 4, 46 Croydon Road,
Reigate, Surrey RH2 0NH.
Tel (01737) 221196 Fax (01737) 226606

Sole distributors for Belding Sports California. Superbly designed golf bags and travel accessories of peerless quality. Also golf clothing new for 1995. Logo embroidery and custom design specialist. Largest range in the world. Available through good pro shops.

Cleveland Golf UK

Unit 1, The Griffin Centre,
Staines Road,
Feltham, Middlesex TW14 0HS.
Tel 0181-893 2218 Fax 0181-893 1770

Cleveland Golf, pioneers in golf club technology offer a range of VAS (Vibration Absorbing System) woods, irons and putters. With patents on both the VAS system and inset hosel Cleveland boast the most advanced and stable clubs available. Cleveland also manufacture a range of speciality wedges used by most of the top tour players around the world.

Danestyle A/S

194 High Road,
Broxbourne, Hertfordshire EN10 6QF.
Tel (01992) 471300 Fax (01992) 471400

European manufacturer of Fairway Fruit Club covers and Walt Disney golfing accessories, including: headcovers, towels, cleanclubs, balls and bags. The headcovers available as puppets or with a knitted sleeve for graphites.

J B Halley & Co Ltd

New Pixmore Centre, Pixmore Avenue,
Letchworth, Hertfordshire SG6 1JG.
Tel (01462) 483398 Fax (01462) 483404

Manufacturers of golf clubs and accessories for over 100 years. Over 90% of our equipment is British made and we supply 60 countries throughout the world. St Andrews factory Tel (01334) 472833 Fax (01334) 477971.

Kinbag Golf Equipment

Micron House, Baird Close,
Drayton Fields, Daventry,
Northamptonshire NN11 5RY.
Tel (01327) 300340

The sales and service of the most practical golf bag in the world consisting of a combination golf bag and trolley and in addition all the necessary ancillary equipment, ie. travel cover, rain cover and brolly.

N S Pyramid Ltd

Unit 5, Ashburton Industrial Estate,
Ross-on-Wye, Herefordshire HR9 7BW.
Tel (01989) 767676 Fax (01989) 766450

Actual manufacturers of British made top quality golf accessories and personalised on-course merchandise for golf days, societies and tournaments. Support British Industry.

Spalding Sports UK Ltd

16 Trafalgar Way,
Bar Hill, Cambridge CB3 8SQ.
Tel (01945) 781672

Spalding Sports UK Ltd is the UK distributor of the world's largest general sports company. We supply all major golf professionals with a complete range of golfing equipment under the Top Flite brands.

Wilson Sporting Goods Co Ltd

The Harlequin Centre,
Southall Lane,
Southall, Middlesex UB2 5LY.
Tel 0181-893 0400 Fax 0181-893 0500

Full range supplier of golf equipment for all types of golfer. Specialising in the staff range of clubs, ultra range of balls and gloves and a leading name on the European Tour via Bernhard Langer.

PERSONALISED PRODUCTS

Belding Sports (UK)

Unit 4, 46 Croydon Road,
Reigate, Surrey RH2 0NH.
Tel (01737) 221196 Fax (01737) 226606

Sole distributors for Belding Sports California. Superbly designed golf bags and travel accessories of peerless quality. Also golf clothing new for 1995. Logo embroidery and custom design specialist. Largest range in the world. Available through good pro shops.

Hatton Towel Company

47 Marsh Green Road,
Marsh Barton Industrial Estate,
Exeter, Devon EX2 8PN.
Tel (01392) 412061 Fax (01392) 425141

Manufacturers of the Sir Christopher Hatton golf towel collection. Our 100% cotton jacquards are famous for quality and design and used by many of the world's leading courses and resorts. Custom towels from 160 pieces or stock ranges with no minimums.

The Highland Connection Ltd

38 Watt Road, Glasgow G52 4RW.
Tel 0141-882 8340

The Highland Connection supply the golf professionals at the best known golf clubs throughout the UK with their own distinctive woven golf towels made in Glasgow, Scotland. Embroidered towels in various quantities also available.

PLUS TWOS & FOURS

Jayros Golf

Shannon Street,
Leeds LS9 8SS.
Tel 0113 240 2662

Jayros the brand leading golf trouser in the UK. Our comprehensive range including plus twos and fours uses the best materials from pure wool to cotton. Whatever your preference there's a Jayros garment to suit you.

PRACTICE EQUIPMENT SUPPLIERS

Golftek (UK) Ltd

1a St Barnabas Road,
Sutton,
Surrey SM1 4NJ.
Tel 0181-643 7712 Fax 0181-643 7828

Distributor of the world's best golf swing and club fitting analyser as well as the most advanced three dimensional golf simulator. Manufacturer of golf mats, portarange nets and cage nets.

Standard Golf (UK) Ltd

Maxwell Hart Business Centre,
PO Box 297,
Lightwater GU18 5HJ.
Tel (0325) 125398 Fax (01276) 452616

UK sole distributor for Standard Golf, the world's leading manufacturer of golf course furniture. The widest choice available. Also manufacturers of golf mats for ranges and courses. Full range of driving range equipment available. (See advertisement page 417 for further details.)

PROFESSIONAL BODIES

The Golf Club Great Britain

3 Sage Yard,
Off Douglas Road,
Surbiton,
Surrey KT6 7TS.
Tel 0181-390 3113 Fax 0181-399 9371

The organisation for all golfers whether club members or not. Own handicap scheme based on CONGU rules plus tournaments, rules and etiquette, directory of clubs, informative newsletter, etc. Working together with private golf clubs. (See advertisement page 421 for further details.)

PROMOTION & PUBLICITY

The Highland Connection Ltd

38 Watt Road,
Glasgow G52 4RW.
Tel 0141-882 8340

The Highland Connection supply the golf professionals at the best known golf clubs throughout the UK with their own distinctive woven golf towels made in Glasgow, Scotland. Embroidered towels in various quantities also available.

N S Pyramid Ltd

Unit 5,
Ashburton Industrial Estate,
Ross-on-Wye,
Herefordshire HR9 7BW.
Tel (01989) 767676 Fax (01989) 766450

Actual manufacturers of British made top quality golf accessories and personalised on-course merchandise for golf days, societies and tournaments. Support British Industry.

PROPERTY CONSULTANTS

Edward Symmons & Partners

2 Southwark Street,
London Bridge,
London SE1 1RQ.
Tel 0171-407 8454

Consultant surveyors, valuers and auctioneers providing professional property advice to the golf and leisure industry on valuations, acquisitions, disposals, development appraisals, feasibility studies and management agreements in the UK and overseas. (See advertisement page 392 for further details.)

PUBLISHERS & BOOKSELLERS

Rhod McEwan Golf Books

Glengarden,
Ballater,
Aberdeenshire AB35 5UB.
Tel (01339) 755429 Fax (01339) 755995

Rare and out of print golf books. Catalogue available on request. Also stock paintings of Scottish championship courses by leading contemporary artists. We are always looking to purchase golf books in any quantity. (See advertisement page 427 for further details.)

RECRUITMENT CONSULTANTS

Golf Personnel UK

Roundabouts,
Haven Lane,
Bucks Green, Horsham,
West Sussex RH12 3JH.
Tel (01403) 823828

Recruitment Consultants specialising in the golf industry. Providing a fast, cost effective, confidential and professional service for clubs/ organisations when recruiting staff. Providing access to a unique database of quality candidates actively looking for positions in the industry eg. Club Professionals/Managers, Sales & Marketing Managers/Representatives, Club Secretaries/Directors, Greenkeepers, Course Managers.

SHOES

Aero Golf

Winsport House,
Leicester Road,
Lutterworth,
Leicestershire LE17 4PL.
Tel (01455) 556073 Fax (01455) 209298

'Aero' range of British manufactured, hi-tech game improvement, graphite golf clubs, including unique custom weighted woods featuring the world record holding (365 yards carry) 'Zapper' driver with its range of six, two-piece synchronised shafts to match swing speeds from 50 - 10 mph. Available 1995: 'Zapper' 385 W 'Zapper' irons and lightweight pocketed 'Zapper' bag. 'Redfern & Jones' range of British quality leather golf shoes, leather trimmed golf bags, holdalls and small leathergoods. We offer club/corporate customisation/design service.

Special Purpose Footwear Ltd

31 Bedford Square,
London WC1B 3SG.
Tel 0171-314 1504 Fax 0171-631 4659

Orthopaedic golf shoes. Low pressure over instep made possible by unique design. High stability despite low pressure. Designed for golfers with foot problems; even an alternative for golfers without foot problems who desire greater comfort resulting from less pressure. (See advertisement page 17 for further details.)

SHOPFITTING & RETAIL DISPLAY

I M P Ltd (Improving Merchandise Presentation)

DEC House,
143/145 Cardiff Road,
Reading,
Berkshire RG1 8JF.
Tel (01734) 560763 Fax (01734) 583619

Shopfitters and manufacturers of merchandisers, lockers and display accessories. IMP can help through the design stages providing ideas and sound advice. Our skilled fitters complete the service. Why not call us! (See advertisement page 425 for further details.)

THERMAL WEAR

Mycoal Warm Packs Ltd

Unit 1,
Imperial Park,
Empress Road,
Southampton SO14 0JW.
Tel (01703) 211068 Fax (01703) 231398

Suppliers and manufacturers of the ever popular handwarmers and thermo-mittens. All enquiries welcomed. Nothing too small or too large.

TOWELS

Danestyle A/S

194 High Road,
Broxbourne,
Hertfordshire EN10 6QF.
Tel (01992) 471300 Fax (01992) 471400

European manufacturer of Fairway Fruit Club covers and Walt Disney golfing accessories, including: headcovers, towels, cleanclubs, balls and bags. The headcovers available as puppets or with a knitted sleeve for graphites.

Hatton Towel Company

47 Marsh Green Road,
Marsh Barton Industrial Estate,
Exeter,
Devon EX2 8PN.
Tel (01392) 412061 Fax (01392) 425141

Manufacturers of the Sir Christopher Hatton golf towel collection. Our 100% cotton jacquards are famous for quality and design and used by many of the world's leading courses and resorts. Custom towels from 160 pieces or stock ranges with no minimums.

The Highland Connection Ltd

38 Watt Road,
Glasgow G52 4RW.
Tel 0141-882 8340

The Highland Connection supply the golf professionals at the best known golf clubs throughout the UK with their own distinctive woven golf towels made in Glasgow, Scotland. Embroidered towels in various quantities also available.

TUITION

Rodway Hill Golf Course

Newent Road,
Highnam, Gloucestershire GL2 8DN.
Tel (01452) 384222 Fax (01989) 766450

An 18-hole pay and play par 68 course two miles south west of Gloucester, with panoramic views of the Cotswolds. It has a well stocked shop, practice and teaching facilities. Hire kit available. Societies welcome.

The Scottish National Sports Centre - Inverclyde

Burnside Road,
Largs, Ayrshire KA30 8RW.
Tel (01475) 674666

Residential tuition courses for all abilities using the purpose built SGU golf facility. Top PGA teaching professionals. Driving bays, video playback swing analysis, training bunkers and variety of types of green.

WEATHER/RAINWEAR

Aquavis

99 Bancroft, Hitchin, Herts SG5 1NQ.
Tel/Fax (01462) 441168

Rain visor for bespectacled golfers eliminates the handicap of rain on the inside and outside of the lenses. No restriction of vision. Has own case for storage, lightweight. Wear with or without hat.

Belding Sports (UK)

Unit 4, 46 Croydon Road,
Reigate, Surrey RH2 0NH.
Tel (01737) 221196 Fax (01737) 226606

Sole distributors for Belding Sports California. Superbly designed golf bags and travel accessories of peerless quality. Also golf clothing new for 1995. Logo embroidery and custom design specialist. Largest range in the world. Available through good pro shops.

Head Sportswear

Lui e Lei Sportswear Ltd
Unit 5, Parkside,
Avenue 2,
Station Lane,
Witney, Oxon OX8 6YF.
Tel (01993) 778020 Fax (01993) 776798

Suppliers of both mens' and ladies' clothing to the golf trade. Fully co-ordinating collections of shirts, sweaters and trousers. Also available from Head Sportswear are the popular Gore-Windstopper sweaters in various designs and colours.

Sunderland of Scotland Ltd

PO Box 14,
Glasgow G2 1ER.
Tel 0141-552 3261 Fax 0141-552 8518

Sunderland of Scotland manufacture high quality golf rainwear in Scotland, all rainsuits are tour tested and guaranteed waterproof and breathable, a variety of fabrics including Goretex being used. Sunderlands also manufacture the famous Sunderland Original Weatherbeater and Classic Windproof Pullover. Official supplier to PGA, LPGA, R&A and St Andrews Links Tour.

Walrus Waterproofs Ltd

Mersey Street,
Bulwell,
Nottingham NG6 8JA.
Tel 0115 927 7736 Fax 0115 977 0283

Walrus Waterproofs make a range of golfwear in supple breathable fabrics which are 100% waterproof. Attractive print trim styles are complemented by matching waterproof windcheaters and a full range of co-ordinating accessories.

WINTER TEE MATS

Golf Equip (GB) Ltd

Gladonian Road,
Littlehampton,
West Sussex BN17 6JW.
Tel (01903) 724500 Fax (01903) 716184

British manufacturers and specialists in all golf range requirements since 1979 including winter and alternative tee mats. Equipment suppliers and management of the R&A Open Championship professionals' practice grounds since 1984. Free advisory service. (See advertisement page 421 for further details.)

Heritage Fairway Ltd

1 St Johns Road, Hove,
East Sussex BN3 2FB.
Tel (01273) 220116 Fax (01273) 571621

UK manufacturers of golf range equipment including manual and electronic ball dispensers. Acadamy ball washers and washing systems, ball conveyors and ball collectors. Also suppliers of ancillary equipment: Range mats, winter tee mats, range balls, baskets, target nets and range markers. (See advertisement page 391 for further details.)

Range Servant UK Ltd

4 Arden Close,
Bovingdon,
Hertfordshire HP3 0QS.

Manufacture and market golf range and practice ground equipment. Golf ball dispensers; golf ball washers; golf ball collectors; play mats for ranges and practice grounds - winter tee mats a speciality; range balls and baskets.

Index of Advertisers

PART V

Clubs and courses in the British Isles and Europe

Compiled by Jan Bennett

Centenary Clubs

The following clubs celebrate their centenary in 1995:

England

Abbeydale, South Yorkshire
Broadway, Gloucestershire
Bush Hill Park, Middlesex
Cosby, Leicestershire
Crowborough Beacon, East Sussex
Exeter, Devon
Fairhaven, Lancashire
Flempton, Suffolk
Frinton, Essex
Goring & Streatley, Berkshire
Halifax, West Yorkshire
Handsworth, West Midlands
Herne Bay, Kent
Home Park, Surrey
Horwich, Greater Manchester
Ipswich, Suffolk
Mullion, Cornwall
New Zealand, Surrey
Peacehaven, East Sussex
Peel, Isle of Man
Reigate Heath, Surrey
Rowany, Isle of Man
RLGC Village Play, Merseyside
Sandwell Park, West Midlands
Seacroft, Lincolnshire
Settle, North Yorkshire
Sherwood Forest, Nottinghamshire
Staddon Heights, Devon
Surbiton, Surrey
Ulverston, Cumbria
Wrangaton, Devon

Ireland

Abbey Leix, Co. Laois
Ballinrobe, Co. Mayo
Galway, Co. Galway
Greystones, Co. Wicklow
Malone, Belfast
Massereene, Co. Antrim
The Knock, Belfast

Scotland

Aberfeldy, Perthshire
Biggar, Lanarkshire
Bridge of Allan, Stirlingshire
Campsie, Stirlingshire
Cardross, Dunbarton
Cathcart, Renfrewshire
Cochrane Castle, Rentrewshire
Craigmillar Park, Midlothian
Duddingston, Midlothian
Edzell, Angus
Helmsdale, Sutherland
Kirkintilloch, Dunbarton
Milngavie, Dunbarton
Northern, Aberdeen
Paisley, Renfewshire
Port Glasgow, Renfewshire
Pumpherston, West Lothian
Shotts, Larnarkshire
Torwoodlee, Selkirkshire
Uphall, West Lothian
Whiting Bay, Arran, Bute

Wales

Baron Hill, Anglesey

Golf Clubs and Courses in the British Isles

How to use this section

1. Geographical divisions

In England, Ireland and Wales clubs are listed in alphabetical order within counties. Listing is generally under geographical county, and not the county of affiliation.

In Scotland, counties are grouped under the recognised administrative regions.

European clubs are listed in alphabetical order by country, and grouped under regional headings.

In some areas only 18-hole courses are included.

All clubs and courses are listed in the general index at the back of the book.

2. Club dctails

After the name of the club is the date of foundation (where available).

Courses are private unless otherwise stated. Many public courses have members' clubs which play over them; information on these clubs can be obtained from the course concerned.

The address is the postal address of each club or course. If the postal county is different from the one under which the club or course is listed, it will be shown in the address.

Tel: club telephone number general use.

Mem: total number of playing members. The number of lady members (L) and juniors (J) are sometimes shown separately.

Sec/Pro: telephone numbers for Secretaries and Professionals are shown if different from the club telephone number.

Holes: course length refers to medal tee yardages whenever possible.

Recs: Professional, Amateur and Ladies' Course Records.

Vtors: playing opportunities and restrictions for unaccompanied visitors.

Fees: green fees are quoted for visitors if they are permitted to play unaccompanied by a member. The basic cost per round or per day (D) is shown first, then in brackets, the cost of a weekend and/or Bank Holiday round. Weekly (W) and monthly (M) are sometimes shown. *Green fees quoted are the most up to date supplied by each club.*

Loc: general location of course.

Mis: other facilities/useful information.

Arch: Course architect/designer.

3. Abbreviations

WD Weekdays
WE Weekends
BH Bank Holidays
U Unrestricted.
M With a member, ie casual visitors are not allowed. Only visitors playing with a member are permitted on the days stated.
H Handicap cerificate required.
I Introduction, ie visitors are permitted on the days stated if they have a letter of introduction from their own club or their own club's membership card.
XL No ladies allowed on the days stated.
NA No visitors allowed.
SOC Recognised Golfing Societies welcome if previous arrangements made with secretary.

The following information is as up to date as possible at the time of going to press. For the accuracy of this information we are indebted to the club secretaries who supply the details, but we are always grateful to be notified of any inaccuracies.

Great Britain and Ireland County Index

England

Ireland

Scotland

Wales

List of new entries in 1995

England

Bedfordshire
Pavenham Park

Buckinghamshire
Chalfont Park

Cambridgeshire
Cambridge Meridian
Heydon Grange

Cheshire
Pryor Hayes

Devon
Hele Park Golf Centre
Sparkwell

Essex
Crondon Park
Epping Forest
Essex Golf Complex
Weald Park

Gloucestershire
Rodway
Sherdons Golf Centre

Hampshire
Paultons Golf Centre
Tournerbury Golf Centre
Worldham Park

Hereford & Worcester
South Herefordshire
Wyre Forest Golf Centre

Hertfordshire
Aldwickbury Park

Isle of Man
Mount Murray

Lancashire
Hurlston Hall

Leicestershire
Park Hill

Northamptonshire
Overstone Park

Nottinghamshire
College Pines
Trent Lock Golf Centre

Oxfordshire
Banbury
Carswell CC
Rye Hill
Witney Golf Centre

Shropshire
Chesterton Valley
Cleobury Mortimer
Worfield

Somerset
Cannington
Frome Golf Centre

Staffordshire
Izaak Walton
St Thomas's Priory

Suffolk
Brett Vale

Surrey
Chobham
Hazelwood Golf Centre
Windlesham

Sussex (West)
Burgess Hill

Warwickshire
Crocketts Manor

West Midlands
Tidbury Green

Wiltshire
Cumberwell Park

Yorkshire (North)
Drax
Forest of Galtres
Rudding Park

Yorkshire (West)
Leeds Golf Centre
Willow Valley

Ireland

Co Dublin
Hollywood Lakes

Co Kerry
Beaufort
Killorglin

Co Kildare
Castlewarden

Co Louth
Seapoint

Co Tipperary
Ballykisleen

Co Wicklow
Glenmalure
Kilcoole

Scotland

Dumfries & Galloway Region
Gretna (Dumfriesshire)
Hoddom Castle (Dumfriesshire)

Grampian Region
Peterculter (Aberdeenshire)
Rosehearty (Aberdeenshire)

Strathclyde Region
Inveraray (Argyll)
Loch Lomond (Dunbartonshire)

Wales

Clwyd
Kinmel Park
Northop Country Park

Mid Glamorgan
Virginia Park

South Glamorgan
Peterstone

West Glamorgan
Earlswood

England

Avon

Bath (1880)

Sham Castle, North Road, Bath BA2 6JG

Tel **(01225) 425182**
Mem 750
Sec PE Ware (01225) 463834
Pro P Hancox (01225) 466953
Holes 18 L 6369 yds SSS 70
Recs Am–65 CS Edwards (1989)
Pro–68 G Brand (1982)
V'tors H SOC
Fees £25 (£30)
Loc 1½ miles SE of Bath, off A36

Bristol & Clifton (1891)

Beggar Bush Lane, Failand, Clifton, Bristol BS8 3TH

Tel **(01275) 393474/393117**
Mem 800
Sec J Lafford (01275) 393474
Pro P Mawson (01275) 393031
Holes 18 L 6294 yds SSS 70
Recs Am–65 G Wolstenholme
Pro–64 P Oosterhuis
V'tors WD–UH WE/BH–MH
Fees On request
Loc 2 miles W of suspension bridge. 4 miles S of M5 Junction 19

Chipping Sodbury

Chipping Sodbury, Bristol BS17 6PU

Tel **(01454) 312024 (Members), (01454) 315822 Catering**
Fax **(01454) 319042**
Mem 750
Sec KG Starr (01454) 319042
Pro M Watts (01454) 314087
Holes New 18 L 6912 yds SSS 73
Old 9 L 6194 yds SSS 69
Recs New Am–66 D Wood (1988)
Pro–65 B Austin (1993)
V'tors WD–U WE–pm only Sat/Sun am–XL SOC
Fees New £20 (£25) Old £4 (£5)
Loc 12 miles NE of Bristol. M4 Junction 18, 5 miles. M5 Junction 14, 9 miles.
Arch Fred Hawtree

Clevedon (1891)

Castle Road, Clevedon BS21 7AA

Tel **(01275) 873140**
Fax **(01275) 341228**
Mem 700
Sec M Sullivan (01275) 874057
Pro M Heggie (01275) 874704
Holes 18 L 5998 yds SSS 69
Recs Am–63 J Woodward (1992)
Pro–67 G Ryall (1987)
V'tors WD–U H exc Wed am–NA WE/BH–H I NA before 11am SOC–Mon & Tues
Fees £22 (£35)
Loc Off Holly Lane, Walton. M5 Junction 19 or 20

Entry Hill (1985)

Public

Entry Hill, Bath BA2 5NA

Tel **(01225) 834248**
Sec J Sercombe
Pro T Tapley
Holes 9 L 4206 yds SSS 61
Recs Am–63 I Hulley (1992)
V'tors WD/WE–booking only
Fees 18 holes–£7.25 (£8.30)
9 holes–£4.55 (£5.20)
Loc 1 mile S of Bath, off A367

Farrington (1992)

Marsh Lane, Farrington Gurney, Bristol BS18 5TS

Tel **(01761) 241274**
Fax **(01761) 241274**
Mem 320
Sec Mrs PM Thompson
Pro P Thompson
Holes 9 hole Par 3 course
V'tors U–booking required
Fees 9 holes–£5 (£6)
18 holes–£9 (£10)
Loc 12 miles S of Bristol (A37)
10 miles S of Bath (A39)
Mis Floodlit driving range. Further 18 holes open Sept 1995
Arch Peter Thompson

Filton (1909)

Golf Course Lane, Bristol BS12 7QS

Tel **(0117) 969 2021**
Fax **(0117) 931 4359**
Mem 800
Sec M Burns (0117) 969 4169
Pro JCN Lumb (0117) 969 4158
Holes 18 L 6264 yds SSS 70
Recs Am–68 RH Evans
Pro–66 RH White
V'tors WD–U WE/BH–M SOC–WD
Fees £20 D–£25
Loc 4 miles N of Bristol
Arch Hawtree

Fosseway CC (1970)

Charlton Lane, Midsomer Norton, Bath BA3 4BD

Tel **(01761) 412214**
Fax **(01761) 418357**
Mem 438
Sec RF Jones (Mgr)
Holes 9 L 4608 yds SSS 65
Recs Am–55 M Chedgy (1985)
V'tors WD–U exc Wed–M after 5pm WE–NA before 1.30pm
Fees £10 (£15)
Loc 10 miles SW of Bath on A367

Henbury (1891)

Westbury-on-Trym, Bristol BS10 7QB

Tel **(0117) 950 0660**
Mem 698
Sec RH White (0117) 950 0044
Pro N Riley (0117) 950 2121
Holes 18 L 6039 yds SSS 70
Recs Am–62 G Wolstenholme
Pro–67 B Sandry
V'tors WD–H WE–M SOC–Tues & Fri
Fees £21
Loc 3 miles N of Bristol. M5 Junction 17

Knowle (1905)

Fairway, West Town Lane, Brislington, Bristol BS4 5DF

Tel **(0117) 977 6341**
Mem 700
Sec Mrs JD King (0117) 977 0660
Pro GM Brand (0117) 977 9193
Holes 18 L 6016 yds SSS 69
Recs Am–61 MR Jeffery (1994)
Pro–64 S Brown
V'tors WD exc Thurs–H WE/BH–H SOC–Thurs
Fees £22 D–£27 (£27 D–£32)
Loc Brislington Hill, 3 miles S of Bristol, off A4
Arch JH Taylor

Lansdown (1894)

Lansdown, Bath BA1 9BT

Tel **(01225) 425007**
Fax **(01225) 339252**
Mem 750
Sec RW Smith (01225) 422138
Pro T Mercer (01225) 420242
Holes 18 L 6316 yds SSS 70
Recs Am–66 VL Phillips (1992)
Pro–65 D Ray (1987)
V'tors WD/WE–H SOC
Fees £18 (£30)
Loc 2 miles NW of Bath, by racecourse. M4 Junction 18, 6 miles
Arch HS Colt

Long Ashton (1893)

Long Ashton, Bristol BS18 9DW

Tel **(01275) 392229**
Fax **(01275) 394395**
Mem 750
Sec BJG Manning (01275) 392316
Pro DP Scanlan (01275) 392265
Holes 18 L 6077 yds SSS 70
Recs Am–66 G Wolstenholme
Pro–66 K Aitken
V'tors WD–U H WE/BH–I H SOC–Wed
Fees £26 (£35)
Loc 3 miles S of Bristol on B3128
Arch JH Taylor

Mangotsfield (1975)

Carsons Road, Mangotsfield, Bristol BS17 3LW

Tel **(0117) 956 5501**
Mem 600
Sec C Main
Pro C Trewin
Holes 18 L 5337 yds SSS 66
Recs Am–63 N Pillinger (1990)
Ladies–77 P Chapman (1988)
V'tors U
Fees £8 (£10)
Loc 6 miles NE of Bristol

Mendip Spring (1992)

Honeyhall Lane, Congresbury BS19 5JT

Tel **(01934) 853337/852322**
Fax **(01934) 853465**
Mem 300
Sec L Lovell
Pro J Blackburn
Holes 18 L 6328 yds SSS 71
9 L 2287 yds SSS 65
Recs Am–70 D Thomas
V'tors U
Fees 18 hole:£15; 9 hole:£5
Loc Congresbury. M5 Junction 21.
Mis Driving range
Arch Langholt

Puxton Park (1992)

Pay and play
Puxton, Weston-super-Mare BS24 6TA

Tel **(01934) 876942**
Pro C Ancsell
Holes 18 L 6600 yds Par 72
V'tors U SOC
Fees £8 (£10)
Loc A370, 2 miles E of M5 Junction 21

Saltford (1904)

Golf Club Lane, Saltford, Bristol BS18 3AA

Tel **(01225) 873220**
Fax **(01225) 873525**
Mem 650
Sec V Radnedge (01225) 873513
Pro D Millensted (01225) 872043
Holes 18 L 6081 yds SSS 69
Recs Am–64 D Young
Pro–63 S Little
V'tors U SOC–Mon & Thurs
Fees £22 (£28)
Loc 7 miles SE of Bristol

Shirehampton Park (1907)

Park Hill, Shirehampton, Bristol BS11 0UL

Tel **(0117) 982 3059**
Mem 600
Sec PAC Drew-Wilkinson (0117) 982 2083
Pro B Ellis (0117) 982 2488
Holes 18 L 5521 yds SSS 67
Recs Am–64 R Bullock (1993)
V'tors WD–U H WE–M
Fees £18 (£25)
Loc 2 miles E of M5 Junction 18, on B4018

Stockwood Vale (1991)

Public
Stockwood Lane, Keynsham, Bristol BS18 2ER

Tel **(0117) 986 6505**
Mem 150
Sec J Wade
Pro D Holder
Holes 9 L 2005 yds SSS 61
V'tors U SOC
Fees £9 (£11)
Loc 1 mile SE of Bristol, off A4174
Mis Driving range
Arch Wade/Ramsay

Tall Pines (1991)

Public
Cooks Bridle Path, Downside, Backwell, Bristol BS19 3DS

Tel **(01275) 472076**
Fax **(01275) 472076**
Sec T Murray
Pro G Coombe
Holes 18 L 5827yds SSS 68
V'tors U SOC
Fees £10 (£12.50)
Loc 8 miles SW of Bristol (A470)

Thornbury Golf Centre (1992)

Bristol Road, Thornbury

Tel **(01454) 281144**
Fax **(01454) 281177**
Mem 400
Sec I Gibson
Pro S Baker
Holes 18 L 6154 yds SSS 69 Par 71
18 L 2195 yds Par 54
Recs Am–73 J Moody (1994)
Pro–68 G Orr (1994)
V'tors U SOC–WD
Fees £12
Loc 10 miles N of Bristol, off A38
Mis Driving range
Arch Hawtree

Tickenham Golf Centre (1991)

Clevedon Road, Tickenham, Bristol BS21 6SB

Tel **(01275) 856626**
Pro A Sutcliffe
Holes 9 L 2000 yds
V'tors U SOC
Fees 18 holes–£9
Loc 2 miles E of M5 Junction 20 on B3130, nr Nailsea
Mis Driving range
Arch Andrew Sutcliffe

Tracy Park (1976)

Tracy Park, Bath Road, Wick, Bristol BS15 5RN

Tel **(0117) 937 2251**
Fax **(0117) 937 4288**
Mem 950
Sec PA Murphy
Pro R Berry (0117) 937 3521
Holes 27 holes:
Avon L 6834 yds SSS 73
Bristol L 6861 yds SSS 73
Cotswold L 6203 yds SSS 70
Recs Am–65 S Pugh
Pro–64 P Pring
V'tors WD/WE–phone first SOC
Fees £20 (£30)
Loc 10 miles NW of Bath, off A420. M4 Junction 18

Weston-super-Mare (1892)

Uphill Road North, Weston-super-Mare BS23 4NQ

Tel **(01934) 621360**
Fax **(01934) 626968**
Mem 752
Sec J Keight (01934) 626968
Pro P Barrington (01934) 633360
Holes 18 L 6251 yds SSS 70
Recs Am–64 B Porter, S Martin
Pro–69 A Lees, WJ Branch
V'tors H SOC
Fees £20 (£28) W–£60
Loc Weston-super-Mare
Arch T Dunn

Woodlands G & CC (1989)

Pay and play
Woodlands Lane, Almondsbury, Bristol BS12 4JZ

Tel **(01454) 201856**
Holes 18 L 6100 yds SSS 70
V'tors U SOC
Fees £10 (£12)
Loc Nr M5 Junction 16

Worlebury (1908)

Monks Hill, Worlebury, Weston-super-Mare BS22 9SX

Tel **(01934) 623214**
Fax **(01934) 625789**
Mem 640
Sec MW Penny (01934) 625789
Pro G Marks (01934) 418473
Holes 18 L 5963 yds SSS 69
Recs Am–67 I Heppenstall, P Simmonds (1992)
Pro–66 G Marks (1992)
V'tors U SOC–WD
Fees £20 (£30)
Loc 2 miles NE of Weston, off A370
Arch Hawtree

Bedfordshire

Aspley Guise & Woburn Sands (1914)

West Hill, Aspley Guise, Milton Keynes MK17 8DX

Tel **(01908) 582264**
Mem 560
Sec MA Beadle (01908) 583596
Pro T Hill (01908) 582974
Holes 18 L 6135 yds SSS 70

Recs Am–67 M Wharton
Pro–68 P Webster
V'tors WD–H WE/BH–MH
SOC–Wed & Fri
Fees £22 D–£27
Loc 2 miles W of M1 Junction 13
Arch Herd/Sandow

Aylesbury Vale (1991)

Wing, Leighton Buzzard LU7 0UJ
Tel **(01525) 240196**
Sec C Wright (Sec/Mgr)
Pro L Scarbrow
Holes 18 L 6622 yds SSS 72
V'tors U H SOC
Fees £12 (£18.50)
Loc 3 miles W of Leighton Buzzard on A418
Mis Driving range
Arch Sq Ldr Don Wright

Beadlow Manor Hotel G & CC (1973)

Beadlow, Shefford SG17 5PH
Tel **(01525) 860800**
Mem 700
Pro (0525) 61292
Holes 18 L 6238 yds SSS 71
18 L 6042 yds SSS 70
Recs Am–71 C Skinner
Pro–66 L Fickling
V'tors U H SOC
Fees £14 (£17)
Loc 2 miles W of Shefford on A507
Mis Driving range

Bedford & County (1912)

Green Lane, Clapham, Bedford MK41 6ET
Tel **(01234) 352617**
Fax **(01234) 357195**
Mem 600
Sec E Bullock (Mgr)
Pro E Bullock (01234) 359189
Holes 18 L 6347 yds SSS 70
Recs Am–66 C Allen (1980), SD Folbigg (1990)
Pro–66 M King (1978)
V'tors WD–U H WE–M SOC
Fees WD–£27.50
Loc 2 miles NW of Bedford on A6

Bedfordshire (1891)

Bromham Rd, Biddenham, Bedford MK40 4AF
Tel **(01234) 353241**
Mem 600
Sec JK White (Mgr) (01234) 261669
Pro G Buckle (01234) 353653
Holes 18 L 6185 yds SSS 69
Recs Am–63 JC Kemp
Pro–65 K Warren
V'tors WD–U (phone first) WE–M before noon SOC–WD
Fees On application
Loc 2 miles NW of Bedford (A428)

Colmworth (1992)

New Road, Colmworth MK44 2NV
Tel **(01234) 378181**
Fax **(01234) 376235**
Mem 350
Sec P Whatmough (01234) 266636
Pro J MacFarlane (01234) 378181
Holes 18 L 6420 yds SSS 71 Par 70
V'tors U SOC
Fees £10 (£15)
Loc 6 miles N of Bedford, off Kimbolton road
Arch John Glasgow

Colworth (1985)

Unilever Research, Sharnbrook, Bedford MK44 1LQ
Tel **(01234) 781781**
Mem 350
Sec S Granger
Holes 9 L 2500 yds SSS 64
V'tors M
Loc 10 miles N of Bedford, off A6

Dunstable Downs (1907)

Whipsnade Road, Dunstable LU6 2NB
Tel **(01582) 604472**
Fax **(01582) 478700**
Mem 604
Sec CD Alexander
Pro M Weldon (01582) 662806
Holes 18 L 6255 yds SSS 70
Recs Am–64 J Todd (1989)
Pro–64 K Golding (1992)
V'tors WD–H WE–M SOC–Tues & Thurs
Fees On application
Loc 2 miles SW of Dunstable on B4541. M1 Junction 11
Arch James Braid

Griffin (1985)

Chaul End Road, Caddington LU1 4AX
Tel **(01582) 415573**
Mem 450
Sec Mrs J Johnson
Holes 18 L 6161 yds Par 71
Recs Am–63 M Ecart (1993)
V'tors WD–U before 3pm WE/BH–M (exc Sun before 2pm) SOC
Fees D–£10
Loc 3 miles W of Luton on A505 between Dunstable and Caddington. M1 Junction 11

Henlow (1985)

Henlow Camp, Henlow SG16 6DN
Tel **(01462) 851515** Ext 7083
Fax **(01462) 851515** Ext 7687
Mem 320
Sec JV Foster (01462) 851515 (Ext 7873)
Holes 9 L 5618 yds SSS 67
Recs Am–69 T Dobbins (1993)
V'tors M
Fees D–£6
Loc 3 miles SE of Shefford on A600

John O'Gaunt (1948)

Sutton Park, Sandy, Biggleswade SG19 2LY
Tel **(01767) 260360**
Fax **(01767) 261381**
Mem 1450
Sec IM Simpson
Pro P Round (01767) 260094
Holes John O'Gaunt 18 L 6513 yds SSS 71
Carthagena 18 L 5869 yds SSS 69
Recs Am–64 N Wharton
Pro–67 SC Evans
V'tors H–phone first SOC–WD
Fees £42 (£50)
Loc 3 miles NE of Biggleswade on B1040
Arch Hawtree

Leighton Buzzard (1925)

Plantation Road, Leighton Buzzard LU7 7JF
Tel **(01525) 373811/373812**
Mem 600
Sec J Burchell (01525) 373811
Pro LJ Muncey (01525) 372143
Holes 18 L 6101 yds SSS 70
Recs Am–66 S Wells (1993)
V'tors WD exc Tues–U H WE/BH–MH
Fees £18 D–£25
Loc Heath and Reach, 1 mile N of Leighton Buzzard. M1 Junction 12

Millbrook (1980)

Millbrook, Bedford MK45 2JB
Tel **(01525) 840252**
Mem 520
Sec Gael Sutherland
Pro T Devine (01525) 402269
Holes 18 L 6530 yds SSS 71
V'tors WD–U exc Thurs WE–NA
Fees £20 (D–£45)
Loc 4 miles from M1 Junctions 12 or 13 on B507
Arch W Sutherland

Mount Pleasant (1992)

Pay and play
Station Road, Lower Stondon, Henlow SG16 6JL
Tel **(01462) 850999**
Mem 350
Sec D Simkins (Prop)
Pro Z Thompson
Holes 9 L 6172 yds SSS 69 Par 72
V'tors U SOC–WD
Fees 9 holes–£5 (£7)
18 holes–£9 (£13)
Loc 4 miles N of Hitchin, off A600
Arch Derek Young

Mowsbury (1975)

Public
Kimbolton Road, Bedford MK41 8DQ
Tel **(01234) 216374/771041**
Mem 850
Sec LW Allan

For list of abbreviations see page 435

Pro M Summers
Holes 18 L 6514 yds SSS 71
Pro–66
V'tors U
Fees £5 (£8)
Loc 2 miles N of Bedford on B660
Mis Driving range
Arch Hawtree

Pavenham Park (1994)

Pay and play
Pavenham, Bedford MK43 7PE
Tel **(01234) 822202**
Fax **(01234) 826602**
Sec Sue Tearle
Pro ZL Thompson
Holes 18 L 6353 yds SSS 71
V'tors WD–U WE–M SOC–WD
Fees £12 (£18)
Loc 4 miles NW of Bedford on A6
Arch Zac Thompson

South Beds (1892)

Warden Hill Road, Luton LU2 7AA
Tel **(01582) 575201**
Mem 750
Sec (01582) 591500
Pro E Cogle (01582) 591209
Holes Galley 18 L 6332 yds SSS 71
Warden 9 L 4954 yds SSS 64
Recs Am–64 I Tottingham (1993)
V'tors Galley WD–U (Ladies Day–Tues) WE/BH–H exc comp days–NA SOC
Warden–U
Fees 18 hole:£18 D–£27 (£25 D–£36) 9 hole:£8.50 (£11.50)
Loc 3 miles N of Luton, E of A6

Stockwood Park (1973)

Public
Stockwood Park, London Rd, Luton LU1 4LX
Tel **(01582) 413704**
Fax **(01582) 481001**
Mem 800
Sec Mrs B McMillan
Pro G McCarthy
Holes 18 L 6049 yds SSS 69
Recs Am–67 D Smith (1993)
Pro–66 T Minshall
V'tors U
Fees £7.30 (£9.60)
Loc 1 mile S of Luton on A6. M1 Junction 10
Mis Driving range

Tilsworth (1972)

Public
Dunstable Rd, Tilsworth, Dunstable
Tel **(01525) 210721/210722**
Pro N Webb (Mgr)
Holes 18 L 5303 yds SSS 66
V'tors U
Fees £8 (£10)
Loc 2 miles N of Dunstable (A5)
Mis Driving range

Wyboston Lakes (1978)

Public
Wyboston Lakes, Wyboston MK44 3AL
Tel **(01480) 212501**
Fax **(01480) 216652**
Mem 300
Sec B Chinn (Mgr)
Pro P Ashwell (01480) 212501
Holes 18 L 5721 yds SSS 69
Recs Am–69
V'tors WD–U WE–booking SOC
Fees £10 (£14)
Loc S of St Neots, off A1 and St Neots by-pass
Mis Driving range
Arch Neil Ockden

Berkshire

Bearwood (1986)

Mole Road, Sindlesham, Wokingham RG11 5DB
Tel **(01734) 761330**
Fax **(01734) 772687**
Mem 570
Sec HM Barker (01734) 760060
Pro M Griffiths (01734) 760156
Holes 9 L 5614 yds SSS 68
Recs Am–69 JB Tustin, R Donald, G Daniels
Pro–68 AF Smith (1991)
V'tors WD–H before 4pm –M after 4pm WE/BH–M
Fees 18 holes–£15 9 holes–£8
Loc 1 mile SW of Winnersh, on B3030. M4 Junction 10
Mis 9 hole pitch & putt

The Berkshire (1928)

Swinley Road, Ascot SL5 8AY
Tel **(01344) 21495**
Mem 935
Sec Maj PD Clarke (01344) 21496
Pro P Anderson (01344) 22351
Holes Red 18 L 6369 yds SSS 71
Blue 18 L 6260 yds SSS 71
V'tors WD–I WE/BH–M
Fees On application
Loc 3 miles from Ascot on A332
Arch Herbert Fowler

Bird Hills (1985)

Public
Drift Road, Hawthorn Hill, Maidenhead SL6 3ST
Tel **(01628) 771030/75588/26035**
Fax **(01628) 31023**
Sec A Kibblewhite
Pro S Kelly, C Cowie
Holes 18 L 6212 yds SSS 69
Pro–65 S Kelly (1988)
V'tors U SOC–WD
Fees £12 (£15)
Loc 4 miles S of Maidenhead on A330
Mis Floodlit driving range

Blue Mountain Golf Centre (1993)

Pay and play
Wood Lane, Binfield RG12 5EY
Tel **(01344) 300200**
Fax **(01344) 360039**
Mem 1200
Pro N Dainton
Holes 18 L 6097 yds SSS 70
Recs Am–69 C Challen (1993)
Pro–63 P Simpson
V'tors U SOC
Fees £14 (£18)
Loc 1 mile W of Bracknell on B3408. M4 Junction 10
Mis Driving range. Golf Academy

Calcot Park (1930)

Bath Road, Calcot, Reading RG3 5RN
Tel **(01734) 427124**
Fax **(01734) 453373**
Mem 750
Sec AL Bray
Pro A Mackenzie (01734) 427797
Holes 18 L 6283 yds SSS 70
Recs Am–65 R Walton (1994)
Pro–63 C Defoy (1983)
Ladies–69 L Walton (1992)
V'tors WD–U WE/BH–M
Fees On application
Loc 3 miles W of Reading on A4. M4 Junction 12
Arch HS Colt

Datchet (1890)

Buccleuch Road, Datchet SL3 9BP
Tel **(01753) 543887**
Mem 210 50(L) 25(J)
Sec Ms A Perkins (01753) 541872
Pro B Mainwaring (01753) 542755
Holes 9 L 5978 yds SSS 69
Recs Am–66 R Blyfield
Pro–63 N Wood
V'tors WD–U before 3pm –M after 3pm WE–M
Fees £18 D–£25
Loc Slough, Windsor 2 miles

Donnington Valley (1985)

Old Oxford Road, Donnington, Newbury RG16 9AG
Tel **(01635) 32488**
Mem 500
Sec LC Storey
Pro N Mitchell
Holes 18 L 4002 yds SSS 60
V'tors U
Fees On application
Loc N of Newbury, off Old Oxford road

Downshire (1973)

Public
Easthampstead Park, Wokingham RG11 3DH
Tel **(01344) 302030**
Fax **(01344) 301020**
Sec P Watson (Golf Dir)
Pro P Watson

Holes 18 L 6382 yds SSS 70
Recs Am–67 T Smith
Pro–66 M King
V'tors U SOC
Fees Summer–£11 (£13)
Winter–£9 (£11)
Loc Off Nine Mile Ride
Mis Driving range. Pitch & putt

East Berkshire (1903)

Ravenswood Ave, Crowthorne RG11 6BD
Tel **(01344) 772041**
Fax **(01344) 777378**
Mem 700
Sec WH Short
Pro A Roe (01344) 774112
Holes 18 L 6345 yds SSS 70
Recs Am–64 J Brant (1992)
V'tors WD–H WE/BH–M SOC
Fees £35
Loc Nr Crowthorne Station
Arch P Paxton

Goring & Streatley (1895)

Rectory Road, Streatley-on-Thames RG8 9QA
Tel **(01491) 872688**
Fax **(01491) 875224**
Mem 740 115(L) 50(J)
Sec J Menzies (01491) 873229
Pro R Mason (01491) 873715
Holes 18 L 6320 yds SSS 70
Recs Am–65 DG Lane
Pro–62 P Simpson
V'tors WD–U WE/BH–M SOC–WD
Fees £28 After noon–£19
Loc 10 miles NW of Reading on A417
Arch Tom Dunne

Hennerton (1992)

Crazies Hill Road, Wargrave RG10 8LT
Tel **(01734) 401000/404778**
Fax **(01734) 401042**
Mem 530
Sec PJ Hearn
Pro W Farrow (01734) 404778
Holes 9 L 2730 yds SSS 34
Recs Am–66 C Pilbrow (1994)
V'tors WD–U WE–pm only SOC
Fees 18 holes–£12 (£18)
9 holes–£9 (£14)
Loc Between Maidenhead and Reading (A4/A321)
Mis Driving range
Arch Dion Beard

Hurst (1979)

Public
Sandford Lane, Hurst, Wokingham RG10 0SQ
Tel **(01734) 344355**
Sec AG Poncia (Hon)
Pro P Watson
Holes 9 L 3015 yds SSS 70
Fees On application
Loc Reading 5 miles. Wokingham 3 miles

Maidenhead (1896)

Shoppenhangers Road, Maidenhead SL6 2PZ
Tel **(01628) 24693**
Mem 600
Sec IG Lindsay
Pro S Geary (01628) 24067
Holes 18 L 6360 yds SSS 70
Recs Am–S Maynard (1992)
Pro–64 AN Walker, G Wolstenholme
V'tors WD–H Fri–M after noon WE–M
Fees D–£27
Loc Off A308, nr Station

Mapledurham (1992)

Mapledurham, Reading RG4 7UD
Tel **(01734) 463353**
Fax **(01734) 463363**
Mem 650
Sec N Wootten
Pro D Burton
Holes 18 L 5625 yds SSS 69
V'tors U
Fees £14 (£17)
Loc 4 miles NW of Reading, off A4074
Arch MRM Sandow

Mill Ride (1990)

Mill Ride, Ascot SL5 8LT
Tel **(01344) 886777**
Fax **(01344) 886820**
Mem 300
Sec CR Freemantle
Pro G Marks
Holes 18 L 6690 yds SSS 72
Recs Am–68 G Weeks (1992)
Pro–68 B Lane
V'tors H SOC
Fees £35 D–£50 (£50)
Loc 2 miles W of Ascot
Arch Donald Steel

Newbury & Crookham (1873)

Bury's Bank Road, Greenham Common, Newbury RG15 8BZ
Tel **(01635) 40035**
Mem 626
Sec Mrs JR Hearsey
Pro DW Harris (01635) 31201
Holes 18 L 5880 yds SSS 68
Recs Am–63 D Rosier (1984)
Pro–61 M Howell (1986)
V'tors WD–U H WE–M (recognised club members)
Fees £25
Loc 2 miles SE of Newbury

Pincents Manor (1992)

Pincents Lane, Calcot, Reading RG3 5OQ
Tel **(01734) 323511**
Mem 150
Sec W Longstaff
Holes 9 L 4882 yds SSS 63
V'tors U SOC
Fees 9 holes–£6.50
Loc M4 Junction 12, 1 mile

Reading (1910)

17 Kidmore End Road, Emmer Green, Reading RG4 8SG
Tel **(01734) 472169**
Mem 725
Sec (01734) 472909
Pro AR Wild (01734) 476115
Holes 18 L 6212 yds SSS 70
Recs Am–67 LK Pearce
Pro–64 TP Morrison
V'tors Mon–Thurs–UH
Fri/WE/BH–M
SOC–Tues–Thurs
Fees £27
Loc 2 miles N of Reading, off Peppard Road (B481)

Royal Ascot (1887)

Winkfield Road, Ascot SL5 7LJ
Tel **(01344) 25175**
Fax **(01344) 872330**
Mem 600
Sec DD Simmonds
Pro G Malia (01344) 24656
Holes 18 L 5716 yds SSS 68
Recs Am–65 M Milne, G Woodman
Pro–67 B Lane
V'tors M SOC
Fees On application
Loc On Ascot Heath, inside Ascot racecourse. Windsor 4 miles
Arch JH Taylor

The Royal Household (1901)

Buckingham Palace, London SW1A 1AA
Tel **(0171) 930 4832**
Fax **(0171) 839 5950**
Mem 200
Sec A Jarred
Holes 9 L 4560 yds SSS 62
V'tors Strictly by invitation
Loc Home Park, Windsor Castle
Arch Muir Ferguson

Sand Martins (1993)

Finchampstead Road, Wokingham RG11 3RQ
Tel **(01734) 792711**
Fax **(01734) 770282**
Mem 870
Sec P Watkin
Pro W Milne (01734) 770265
Holes 18 L 6297 yds SSS 70
Recs Am–71 D Price
V'tors WD–U WE–NA SOC
Fees £25
Loc 1 mile S of Wokingham. M4 Junction 10
Arch ET Fox

Sonning (1914)

Duffield Road, Sonning-on-Thames RG4 0GJ
Tel **(01734) 693332**
Fax **(01734) 448409**
Mem 700
Sec PF Williams

Pro RT McDougall (01734) 692910
Holes 18 L 6366 yds SSS 70
Recs Am–65 J Lush
Pro–65 B Lane
V'tors WD–U WE–M
Fees On application
Loc 1½miles E of A329(M). S of A4, nr Sonning

Swinley Forest (1909)
Coronation Road, Ascot SL9 5LE
Tel **(01344) 20197**
Mem 310
Sec IL Pearce
Pro RC Parker
Holes 18 L 5952 yds SSS 69
Recs Am–65 IL Pearce
Pro–64 P Alliss
V'tors M
Fees £50 (£60)
Loc S of Ascot
Arch HS Colt

Temple (1909)
Henley Road, Hurley, Maidenhead SL6 5LH
Tel **(01628) 824248**
Fax **(01628) 828119**
Mem 600
Sec Lt Col JCF Hunt (01628) 824795
Pro (01628) 824254
Holes 18 L 6206 yds SSS 70
Recs Am–63 S Hodsdon
V'tors WD–H WE/BH–M SOC
Fees £25 (£45)
Loc Between Maidenhead and Henley on A4130. M4 Junction 8/9. M40 Junction 4
Arch Willie Park Jr

West Berkshire (1975)
Chaddleworth, Newbury RG16 0HS
Tel **(01488) 638574**
Mem 700
Sec Mrs CM Clayton
Pro W Grant (01488) 638851
Holes 18 L 7059 yds SSS 74
Recs Am–71 D Murphy (1993)
Pro–65 W Grant (1994)
Ladies–79 N Williams (1992)
V'tors WD–U WE–M SOC–WD
Fees £24
Loc On A338 to Wantage. M4 Junction 14

Winter Hill (1976)
Grange Lane, Cookham SL6 9RP
Tel **(01628) 527613**
Fax **(01628) 527613**
Mem 800
Sec GB Charters-Rowe
Pro D Hart (01628) 527610
Holes 18 L 6408 yds SSS 71
Recs Am–70 M Hunt (1983), C Bell (1985), K Boulter (1988), DR Hobbs (1992)
V'tors WD–U WE–M SOC
Fees £24
Loc Maidenhead 3 miles
Arch Charles Lawrie

Buckinghamshire

Abbey Hill (1975)
Monks Way, Two Mile Ash, Milton Keynes MK8 8AA
Tel **(01908) 563845**
Sec C Clingan (Golf Mgr)
Pro S Harlock
Holes 18 L 6193 yds SSS 69
Recs Am–67 T Mernagh
Pro–67 H Stott
V'tors U
Fees On application
Loc 2 miles S of Stony Stratford

Aylesbury Golf Centre (1992)
Public
Hulcott Lane, Bierton HP22 5GA
Tel **(01296) 393644**
Sec K Partington (Mgr)
Pro AR Taylor
Holes 9 L 5488 yds SSS 68
V'tors U
Fees £9 (£10)
Loc 1 mile N of Aylesbury on A418
Mis Driving range
Arch AR Taylor

Beaconsfield (1914)
Seer Green, Beaconsfield HP9 2UR
Tel **(01494) 676545**
Fax **(01494) 681148**
Mem 862
Sec PI Anderson
Pro M Brothers (01494) 676616
Holes 18 L 6487 yds SSS 71
Recs Am–66 D Haines
Pro–63 E Murray
V'tors WD–H WE–NA
Fees £36
Loc 2 miles E of Beaconsfield. M40 Junction 2
Arch HS Colt

Buckingham (1914)
Tingewick Road, Buckingham MK18 4AE
Tel **(01280) 813282 (Clubhouse)**
Fax **(01280) 815566**
Mem 680
Sec D Rolph (01280) 815566
Pro T Gates (01280) 815210
Holes 18 L 6082 yds SSS 69
Recs Am–67 S Impey (1993)
Pro–67 S Watson (1990)
V'tors WD–U WE–M SOC–Tues & Thurs
Fees £28
Loc 2 miles SW of Buckingham on A421

Buckinghamshire (1992)
Denham Court, Denham Court Drive, Denham UB9 5BG
Tel **(01895) 835777**
Fax **(01895) 835210**
Mem 650
Sec KN Munt (Mgr)
Pro J O'Leary
Holes 18 L 6880 yds SSS 72
Recs Am–72 P Kilgour
Pro–70 G Lee
V'tors I or M SOC–WD exc Fri
Fees £35.25 (£47)
Loc Off A40(M). M25 Junction 16b/M40 Junction 1
Mis Driving range (Members)
Arch John Jacobs

Burnham Beeches (1891)
Green Lane, Burnham, Slough SL1 8EG
Tel **(01628) 661150**
Mem 670
Sec AJ Buckner (Mgr) (01628) 661448
Pro T Buckner (01628) 661661
Holes 18 L 6463 yds SSS 71
Recs Am–67 M Orris
Pro–64 H Flatman
V'tors WD–I WE/BH–M
Fees £25 D–£37.50
Loc 4 miles W of Slough

Chalfont Park (1994)
Three Households, Chalfont St Giles HP8 4LW
Tel **(01494) 876293**
Mem 450
Sec G Harvey (Golf Dir)
Pro D Hawes
Holes 9 L 3000 yds SSS 68
V'tors U SOC
Fees 18 holes–£10.50 (£12.50)
9 holes–£6 (£8)
Loc 3 miles N of M40 Junction 2
Mis Further 9 holes under construction
Arch Jonathan Gaunt

Chartridge Park (1989)
Chartridge, Chesham HP5 2TF
Tel **(01494) 791772**
Fax **(01494) 786462**
Mem 700
Sec Mr & Mrs P Gibbins
Pro P Gibbins
Holes 18 L 5516 yds SSS 66
Recs Am–71 R Garrood (1994)
Pro–68 P Gibbins (1990)
V'tors U SOC
Fees £20 (£25)
Loc 2 miles NW of Chesham. 9 miles W of M25 Junction 18
Arch John Jacobs

Chesham & Ley Hill (1919)
Ley Hill, Chesham HP5 1UZ
Tel **(01494) 784541**
Mem 384
Sec K Brown (Mgr)
Holes 9 L 5240 yds SSS 66
Recs Am–64 GA Knowes
Pro–65 M Lovegrove
V'tors Mon & Thurs–U Wed–U after noon Fri–U before 1pm –M after 1pm Tues–M after 3pm WE/BH–M SOC–Thurs only
Fees On application
Loc Chesham 2 miles
Mis Course closed Sun after 2pm from 1st Apr-30th Sept

Chiltern Forest

Aston Hill, Halton, Aylesbury HP22 5NQ

Tel **(01296) 630899**
Mem 600
Sec LEA Clark (01296) 631267
Pro C Skeet (01296) 631817
Holes 18 L 5765 yds SSS 70
Recs Am–68 R Conway-Lye (1992)
V'tors WD–U WE–M SOC
Fees D–£22 (1994)
Loc 5 miles SE of Aylesbury, off A4011

Denham (1910)

Tilehouse Lane, Denham UB9 5DE

Tel **(01895) 832022**
Fax **(01895) 835340**
Mem 550
Sec Wg Cdr D Graham
Pro J Sheridan (01895) 832801
Holes 18 L 6439 yds SSS 71
Recs Am–66 DMA Steel
Pro–68 J Sheridan
V'tors Mon–Thurs–I H
Fri–Sun/BH–M
Fees £32 D–£48
Loc 3 miles NW of Uxbridge
Arch HS Colt

Ellesborough (1906)

Butlers Cross, Aylesbury HP17 0TZ

Tel **(01296) 622375**
Mem 780
Sec KM Flint (01296) 622114
Pro P Warner (01296) 623126
Holes 18 L 6276 yds SSS 71
Recs Am–66 N Lucas, NM Allen, P Stevens
Pro–68 G Will
V'tors WE/BH–M WD–I or H SOC–Wed & Thurs only
Fees On application
Loc 1 mile W of Wendover

Farnham Park (1974)

Public

Park Road, Stoke Poges, Slough SL2 4PJ

Tel **(01753) 643332**
Mem 800
Sec Mrs M Brooker (01753) 647065
Pro P Harrison
Holes 18 L 6172 yds SSS 71
Recs Am–69 N Harrison, D Ivall
Pro–68 T Bowers
V'tors U
Fees £8 (£11)
Loc 2 miles N of Slough
Arch Hawtree

Flackwell Heath (1905)

Treadaway Road, Flackwell Heath, High Wycombe HP10 9PE

Tel **(01628) 520027**
Mem 750
Sec PN Jeans (01628) 520929
Pro S Bryan (01628) 523017
Holes 18 L 6207 yds SSS 70
Recs Am–63 PJ Collett
Pro–65 J Hoskison, E Murray
V'tors WD–H WE–M SOC–Wed & Thurs
Fees £27
Loc Between High Wycombe and Beaconsfield, off A40. M40 Junction 3/4

Gerrards Cross (1934)

Chalfont Park, Gerrards Cross SL9 0QA

Tel **(01753) 883263**
Fax **(01753) 883593**
Mem 825
Sec PH Fisher
Pro M Barr (01753) 885300
Holes 18 L 6295 yds SSS 70
Recs Am–65 JB Berney, D Messias
Pro–63 AP Barr
V'tors WD–H WE/BH–M SOC
Fees £29 D–£36
Loc 1 mile from Station, off A413

Harewood Downs (1908)

Cokes Lane, Chalfont St Giles HP8 4TA

Tel **(01494) 762308**
Mem 700
Sec Wg Cdr MR Cannon (01494) 762184
Pro GC Morris (01494) 764102
Holes 18 L 5958 yds SSS 69
Recs Am–65 AL Parsons
Pro–65 JM Hume
V'tors WD–H WE/BH–H XL before noon SOC
Fees £22 (£30)
Loc 2 miles E of Amersham, off A413

Hazlemere G & CC (1982)

Penn Road, Hazlemere, High Wycombe HP15 7LR

Tel **(01494) 714722**
Mem 950
Sec DE Hudson
Pro SR Morvell (01494) 718298
Holes 18 L 5855 yds SSS 68
Recs Am–66 D Taylor (1994)
Pro–62 M Booth (1994)
V'tors WD–U WE–booking req SOC–WD
Fees £25 (£34)
Loc 3 miles NE of High Wycombe on B474
Arch Terry Murray

Iver (1983)

Hollow Hill Lane, Iver SL0 0JJ

Tel **(01753) 655615**
Mem 500
Sec T Notley
Pro T Notley
Holes 9 L 5988 yds SSS 69
Recs Am–68 D Sargood (1990)
Pro–71 T Notley (1989)
V'tors U SOC
Fees On application
Loc 1/2 mile from Langley station, off Langley Park Road. M4 Junction 5, 2 miles

Ivinghoe (1967)

Wellcroft, Ivinghoe, Leighton Buzzard LU7 9EF

Tel **(01296) 668696**
Fax **(01296) 662755**
Mem 250
Sec Mrs SE Garrad (0296) 662478
Pro PW Garrad
Holes 9 L 4508 yds SSS 62
Recs Am–61 J Dillon (1984)
Pro–60 R Garrad (1967)
V'tors WD–U WE–U after 8am SOC
Fees £7 (£8)
Loc 3 miles N of Tring.
M1 Junction 11, 5 miles
Arch R Garrad

Lambourne (1992)

Dropmore Road, Burnham SL1 8NF

Tel **(01628) 666755**
Fax **(01628) 663301**
Mem 600
Sec CJ Lumley
Pro RA Newman (Golf Dir) (01628) 662936
Holes 18 L 6783 yds SSS 72
V'tors H or I
Fees £30 (£40)
Loc 1 mile N of Burnham. M40 Junction 2. M4 Junction 7
Arch Donald Steel

Little Chalfont (1981)

Lodge Lane, Little Chalfont, Amersham

Tel **(01494) 764877**
Mem 400
Sec JM Dunne
Pro B Woodhouse (01494) 762942
Holes 9 L 5852 yds SSS 68
Recs Am–76 D Brown
Pro–65 S Parker
V'tors U SOC
Fees £10 (£12)
Loc Station 1/2mile

Mentmore G & CC (1992)

Mentmore, Leighton Buzzard LU7 0UA

Tel **(01296) 662020**
Fax **(01296) 662592**
Mem 850
Sec P Elson (Mgr)
Pro P Elson, Claire Waite
Holes Rothschild 18 L 6777 yds SSS 72; Rosebery 18 L 6763 yds SSS 72
V'tors WD–H WE/BH–H by appointment SOC
Fees £25 (£25)
Loc 4 miles S of Leighton Buzzard
Mis Driving range
Arch Bob Sandow

Princes Risborough (1990)

Lee Road, Saunderton Lee, Princes Risborough HP27 9NX

Tel **(01844) 346989 (Clubhouse)**
Mem 400
Sec JF Tubb (Man Dir)

Pro P Dougan (01844) 274567
Holes 9 L 5017 yds SSS 66 Par 68
V'tors U SOC
Fees £12 (£16)
Loc 7 miles NW of High Wycombe on A4010
Arch Guy Hunt

Silverstone (1992)

Pay and play
Silverstone Road, Stowe, Buckingham MK18 5LH
Tel **(01280) 850005**
Fax **(01280) 850080**
Mem 670
Sec D Mears, J Faulkner (Props)
Pro R Holt
Holes 18 L 6164 yds SSS 70
V'tors U–booking advisable SOC–WD
Fees £8 (£12)
Loc Opposite Silverstone Race Circuit, N of Buckingham
Mis Driving range
Arch David Snell

Stoke Poges (1908)

Park Road, Stoke Poges SL2 4PG
Tel **(01753) 717171**
Fax **(01753) 717172**
Mem 700
Sec RC Pickering
Pro T Morrison
Holes 18 L 6654 yds SSS 71
Recs Am–65 BA Price, V Phillips, D Fisher
Pro–65 J Hudson
V'tors WD–I or H WE/BH–M
Fees £35 D–£50
Loc 2 miles N of Slough
Arch HS Colt

Stowe (1974)

Stowe, Buckingham MK18 5EH
Mem 300
Sec Mrs CM Shaw (01280) 813650
Holes 9 L 4573 yds SSS 63
V'tors WD/WE 8am–1pm & after 7pm–M; School holidays–M SOC
Fees On application
Loc M1 Junction 16. 4 miles NW of Buckingham

Thorney Park (1992)

Thorney Mill Lane, Iver SL0 9AL
Tel **(01895) 422095**
Fax **(01895) 431307**
Mem 175
Holes 9 L 3000 yds SSS 34
V'tors WD–U WE/BH–NA before noon SOC
Fees 9 holes–£5 (£8)
18 holes–£8 (£12)
Loc 3 miles N of M4 Junction 5 (B470)
Arch S Adby

Three Locks (1992)

Great Brickhill, Milton Keynes MK17 9BH
Tel **(01525) 270050**
Mem 250
Sec P Critchley (01525) 270470
Pro J Lamble (01525) 270050
Holes 9 L 6654 yds Par 70 SSS 73
Recs Am–67 M Ecart
V'tors U SOC exc Sun
Fees 9 holes–£5.50 (£7.50)
18 holes–£8.50 (£10)
Loc N of Leighton Buzzard on A4146. M1 Junction 14
Mis Extension to 18 holes ready in 1995
Arch MRM Sandow

Wavendon Golf Centre (1990)

Lower End Road, Wavendon, Milton Keynes MK17 8DA
Tel **(01908) 281811**
Fax **(01908) 281257**
Mem 250
Sec Mrs C Cheney
Pro G Iron
Holes 18 L 5800 yds SSS 66
9 hole Par 3 course
V'tors U
Fees £9 (£12)
Loc 2 miles W of M1 Junction 13
Mis Floodlit driving range

Weston Turville (1974)

New Road, Weston Turville, Aylesbury HP22 5QT
Tel **(01296) 24084**
Fax **(01296) 395376**
Mem 600
Sec BJ Hill
Pro T Jones (01296) 25949
Holes 18 L 6100 yds SSS 69
Recs Am–71 S Allder
V'tors U
Fees £15 (£20)
Loc 1½ miles SE of Aylesbury

Wexham Park (1979)

Pay and play
Wexham Street, Wexham, Slough SL3 6NB
Tel **(01753) 663271**
Fax **(01753) 663210**
Mem 850
Sec PJ Gale
Pro D Morgan (01753) 663425
Holes 18 L 5390 yds SSS 66
Green 9 L 2383 yds SSS 32
Red 9 L 2585 yds SSS 34
V'tors U SOC–WD/Sat pm
Fees 18 hole:£8.50 (£12)
9 hole:£5 (£6.50)
Loc 2 miles N of Slough
Mis Driving range
Arch David Morgan

Whiteleaf (1904)

Whiteleaf, Aylesbury HP27 0LY
Tel **(01844) 343097/274058**
Mem 300
Sec Mrs BA Parsley
Pro KS Ward (01844) 345472
Holes 9 L 2756 yds SSS 66
Recs Am–66 GE Oates
Pro–63 MM Caines
V'tors WD–U WE–M SOC
Fees £18
Loc Princes Risborough 2 miles

Windmill Hill (1972)

Public
Tattenhoe Lane, Bletchley, Milton Keynes MK3 7RB
Tel **(01908) 378623**
Fax **(01908) 271478**
Mem 535
Sec Mrs PM Long
Pro C Clingan
Holes 18 L 6773 yds SSS 72
Recs Am–69 RJ Long
Pro–66 C Defoy
V'tors U SOC
Fees £6.10 (£9)
Loc 4 miles from M1 Junction 14, on A421
Mis Floodlit driving range
Arch Henry Cotton

Woburn (1976)

Bow Brickhill, Milton Keynes MK17 9LJ
Tel **(01908) 370756**
Sec A Hay (Man Dir)
Pro A Hay (01908) 647987
Holes Duke's 18 L 6940 yds SSS 74
Duchess 18 L 6641 yds SSS 72
Recs Duke's Pro–63 P Baker
Ladies Pro–64 J Geddes
Duchess Ladies Pro–67 S Waugh
V'tors WD–H (by arrangement) WE–M
Fees By arrangement
Loc 4 miles W of M1 Junction 13
Arch Charles Lawrie (Duke's)

Wycombe Heights (1991)

Public
Rayners Avenue, Loudwater, High Wycombe HP10 9SW
Tel **(01494) 816686**
Fax **(01494) 816728**
Mem 1200
Sec P Talbot (01494) 813185
Pro D Marsden (01494) 812862
Holes 18 L 6300 yds SSS 72
18 hole Par 3 course
V'tors U SOC
Fees £10.50 (£13.50)
Loc ½ mile from M40 Junction 3, on A40 to Wycombe
Mis Driving range
Arch John Jacobs

For list of abbreviations see page 435

Cambridgeshire

Abbotsley (1986)

Eynesbury Hardwicke, St Neots PE19 4XN

Tel **(01480) 474000**
Fax **(01480) 471018**
Mem 700
Sec J Wisson
Pro Vivien Saunders
Holes 18 L 6150 yds SSS 71
Recs Am–72 J Morrow (1987)
Pro–69 S Whymark (1984)
V'tors WD/BH–U WE–M before 10am –U after 10am SOC
Fees £18 (£25)
Loc 2 miles SE of St Neots on B1046. M11 Junction 13 (A45)
Mis Floodlit driving range

Bourn (1991)

Toft Road, Bourn, Cambridge CB3 7TT

Tel **(01954) 718057**
Sec Fiona Ellis
Pro D Germany (01954) 718958
Holes 18 L 6275 yds SSS 70
V'tors U SOC–WD
Fees On application
Loc 8 miles W of Cambridge, off B1046. M11 Junction 12

Brampton Park (1990)

Buckden Road, Brampton, Huntingdon PE18 8NF

Tel **(01480) 434700**
Fax **(01480) 434705**
Mem 500
Sec M Staveley
Pro A Currie (01480) 434705
Holes 18 L 6403 yds SSS 73
Recs Am–72 JR Prout (1992)
Pro–67 N Brown (1992)
V'tors U
Fees £18 D–£24 (D–£36)
Loc 3 miles W of Huntingdon, off A1/A604
Arch Simon Gidman

Cambridge Meridian

Comberton Road, Toft, Cambridge CB3 7RY

Tel **(01223) 264700**
Fax **(01223) 264701**
Mem 400
Sec P Lloyd (Golf Dir)
Pro N Harvey (01223) 264702
Holes 18 L 6227 yds Par 73 SSS 72
Recs Am–72 G Hopkinson (1994)
V'tors U SOC
Fees £15 (£18)
Loc 3 miles SW of Cambridge on B1046. M11 Junction 12
Arch Alliss/Clark

Cambridgeshire Moat House (1974)

Bar Hill, Cambridge CB3 8EU

Tel **(01954) 780555**
Fax **(01954) 780010**
Mem 550
Sec D Hefferland
Pro D Vernon (01954) 780098
Holes 18 L 6734 yds SSS 72
Recs Am–68 P Way
Pro–68 P Townsend
V'tors U SOC
Fees £15 D–£25 (£30)
Loc 5 miles NW of Cambridge on A14

Elton Furze (1993)

Bullock Road, Haddon, Peterborough PE7 3TT

Tel **(01733) 280189**
Mem 380
Sec P Vaughan
Pro F Kiddie
Holes 18 L 6289 yds SSS 70
Recs Am–71 S Carr (1993)
Pro–69 F Kiddie (1994)
V'tors Tues & Thurs–U Mon/Wed/Fri–M WE/BH–NA SOC
Fees On application
Loc 4 miles W of Peterborough on old A605
Arch Roger Fitton

Ely City (1961)

Cambridge Road, Ely CB7 4HX

Tel **(01353) 662751**
Fax **(01353) 668636**
Mem 950
Sec MS Hoare (Mgr)
Pro A George (01353) 663317 (Touring Pro H Baiocchi)
Holes 18 L 6602 yds SSS 72
Recs Am–66 L Yearn
Pro–66 L Trevino
Ladies Am–71 K Miller
Ladies Pro–68 B Lunsford
V'tors WD–H WE–H SOC–Tues–Fri
Fees £24 (£30)
Loc 12 miles N of Cambridge
Arch Henry Cotton

Girton (1936)

Dodford Lane, Girton CB3 0QE

Tel **(01223) 276169**
Fax **(01223) 277150**
Mem 800
Sec Mrs MA Cornwell
Pro S Thomson (01223) 276991
Holes 18 L 6085 yds SSS 69
Recs Am–67 C Sherriff (1993)
V'tors WD–U WE/BH–M SOC
Fees £18 D–£20
Loc 3 miles N of Cambridge (A604)

The Gog Magog (1901)

Shelford Bottom, Cambridge CB2 4AB

Tel **(01223) 247626**
Fax **(01223) 414990**
Mem 1050
Sec I Skellern
Pro I Bamborough (01223) 246058
Holes Old 18 L 6386 yds SSS 70
New 9 L 5833 yds SSS 68
Recs Am–64 RW Guy, MT Seaton, DWG Woods, R Claydon
Pro–64 G Wolstenholme, PJ Butler
Ladies–69 J Hockley
V'tors WD–I or H WE/BH–M SOC–Tues & Thurs
Fees Old–£30 D–£37.50 New–£19
Loc 2 miles S of Cambridge on A1307 (A604)

Hemingford Abbots (1991)

New Farm Lodge, Cambridge Road, Hemingford Abbots PE18 9HQ

Tel **(01480) 495000**
Fax **(01480) 496149**
Mem 410
Sec BJ Smith
Pro B Mylward (01480) 492939
Holes 9 L 5468 yds SSS 68
V'tors WD–U WE–M before 1pm –U after 1pm
Fees On application
Loc 2 miles S of Huntingdon on A604
Mis Floodlit driving range

Heydon Grange G & CC (1994)

Heydon, Royston SG8 7NS

Tel **(01763) 208988**
Fax **(01763) 208926**
Mem 200
Sec J Riches
Pro S Bonham
Holes 18 L 6512 yds SSS 71
9 L 3249 yds SSS 71
V'tors U SOC
Fees £15 (£20)
Loc 4 miles E of Royston on A505. M11 Junction 10
Arch Walker/Young

Lakeside Lodge (1992)

Fen Road, Pidley, Huntingdon PE17 3DD

Tel **(01487) 740540**
Fax **(01487) 740852**
Mem 250
Sec Mrs J Hopkins
Pro A Headley (01487) 741541
Holes 18 L 6821 yds SSS 73
9 hole Par 3 course
V'tors U SOC
Fees £9 (£15)
Loc 4 miles N of St Ives on B1040
Mis Driving range
Arch A Headley

March (1922)

Frogs Abbey, Grange Rd, March PE15 0YH

Tel **(01354) 52364**
Mem 400
Sec JB Clapham
Pro N Pickerell
Holes 9 L 6210 yds SSS 70
Recs Am–68 JW Kisby
V'tors H SOC–WD
Fees £15
Loc 18 miles E of Peterborough on A141

Old Nene G & CC (1992)

Muchwood Lane, Bodsey, Ramsey PE17 1XQ

Tel **(01487) 813519**
Mem 200
Sec PB Cade (Golf Dir)
Pro M Webber (01487) 710122
Holes 9 L 5524 yds SSS 67
Recs Am–68 S Willis (1994)
V'tors U SOC
Fees 18 holes–£10 (£12)
9 holes–£7 (£10)
Loc 1 mile N of Ramsey, towards Ramsey Mereside
Mis Driving range
Arch Richard Edrich

Orton Meadows (1987)

Public
Ham Lane, Peterborough PE2 0UU

Tel **(01733) 237478**
Mem 450
Sec K Boyer
Pro J Mitchell
Holes 18 L 5800 yds SSS 68
Recs Am–70 A Emery (1991)
Pro–67 R Mann, A Dow, A Headley (1987)
V'tors U–phone Pro
Fees £8.50 (£11)
Loc 2 miles SW of Peterborough on old A605
Mis 12 hole pitch & putt

Peterborough Milton (1937)

Milton Ferry, Peterborough PE6 7AG

Tel **(01733) 380204**
Fax **(01733) 380489**
Mem 800
Sec Mrs D Adams (01733) 380489
Pro M Gallagher (01733) 380793
Holes 18 L 6462 yds SSS 72
Recs Am–69 JR Ellis (1991)
Pro–66 J Higgins (1992)
V'tors WD–U WE–M SOC
Fees £20 (£25)
Loc 4 miles W of Peterborough on A47
Arch James Braid

Ramsey (1964)

4 Abbey Terrace, Ramsey, Huntingdon PE17 1DD

Tel **(01487) 813573**
Fax **(01487) 815746**
Mem 750
Sec R Muirhead (01487) 812600
Pro S Scott (01487) 813022
Holes 18 L 6123 yds SSS 70
Recs Am–66 DP Smith (1987)
Pro–66 R Robertson (1994)
V'tors WD–H WE/BH–M SOC
Fees £20
Loc 12 miles SE of Peterborough
Arch J Hamilton Stutt

St Ives (1923)

St Ives, Huntingdon PE17 4RS

Tel **(01480) 64459**
Mem 320
Sec BE Dunn (01480) 468392
Pro D Glasby (01480) 66067
Holes 9 L 6100 yds SSS 69
Recs Am–67 Fl-Lt CJB Murdoch
Pro–61 P Alliss
V'tors WD–U H WE–M
Fees £20
Loc 5 miles E of Huntingdon

St Neot's (1890)

Crosshall Road, St Neot's PE19 4AE

Tel **(01480) 474311**
Fax **(01480) 472363**
Mem 600
Sec RJ Marsden (01480) 472363
Pro G Bithrey (01480) 476513
Holes 18 L 6027 yds SSS 69
Recs Am–64 J Boast
Pro–65 M Gallagher, H Flatman
V'tors WD–H WE–M
Fees On application
Loc 1 mile W of St Neot's on B645

Thorney Golf Centre (1991)

Public
English Drove, Thorney, Peterborough PE6 0TJ

Tel **(01733) 270570**
Sec Jane Hind
Pro M Templeman
Holes 18 L 6104 yds SSS 69
9 hole Par 3 course
Recs Am–71 M Perkins (1992)
Pro–66 M Templeman (1993)
V'tors U SOC
Fees £5 (£7)
Loc 8 miles E of Peterborough, off A47
Mis Floodlit driving range
Arch A Dow

Thorpe Wood (1975)

Public
Nene Parkway, Peterborough PE3 6SE

Tel **(01733) 267701**
Fax **(01733) 332774**
Sec R Palmer
Pro D Fitton, R Fitton
Holes 18 L 7086 yds SSS 74
Recs Am–71 J Frankum (1992)
Pro–71 R Fitton
Ladies–72 S Sharpe (1992)
V'tors U–booking required SOC–WD
Fees £8 (£11)
Loc 3 miles W of Peterborough, on A47
Arch Alliss/Thomas

Channel Islands

Alderney (1969)

Route des Carrieres, Alderney

Tel **(01481) 822835**
Fax **(01481) 823609**
Mem 320
Sec A Albuery (Mgr)
Holes 9 L 2528 yds SSS 33
Recs Am–29 M Hugman
Pro–28 PL Cunningham
V'tors U
Fees £15 (£20)
Loc 1 mile E of St Anne

La Grande Mare (1994)

Vazon Bay, Castel, Guernsey

Tel **(01481) 55313**
Fax **(01481) 55194**
Mem 169
Sec D Russell (01481) 53544
Pro P Sykes (01481) 53432
Holes 18 L 5026 yds SSS 66
V'tors U–booking necessary SOC
Fees D–£20
Loc Vazon Bay, W coast of Guernsey
Mis 9 hole pitch & putt course
Arch Hawtree

Les Mielles G & CC (1994)

Public
The Mount, Val de la Mare, St Ouens, Jersey

Tel **(01534) 482787**
Fax **(01534) 485414**
Mem 1500
Sec J Le Brun (Mgr)
Pro J Phillips
Holes 18 L 5610 yds Par 70
V'tors H or Green Card
Fees £18
Loc Five Mile Road, St Ouens Bay
Mis Driving range

La Moye (1902)

La Moye, St Brelade, Jersey

Tel **(01534) 42701**
Fax **(01534) 47289**
Mem 1350
Sec CHM Greetham (01534) 43401
Pro M Deeley (01534) 43130
Holes 18 L 6741 yds SSS 72
Recs Am–69 K O'Toole (1993)
Pro–62 G Brand Jr
V'tors I H SOC–9.30–11am and 2.30–4pm WE–after 2.30pm
Fees £35 D–£55 (inc lunch) W–£160
Loc 6 miles W of St Helier
Mis Driving range

Royal Guernsey (1890)

L'Ancresse, Guernsey

Tel **(01481) 47022**
Fax **(01481) 43960**
Mem 1520
Sec M de Laune (Club Mgr)
R Eggo (Golf Mgr)

Pro N Wood (01481) 45070
Holes 18 L 6206 yds SSS 70
Recs Am–64 R Eggo (1986)
Pro–64 P Cunningham
V'tors WD–H WE–NA
Fees £26
Loc 3 miles N of St Peter Port
Mis Driving range

Royal Jersey (1878)
Grouville, Jersey
Tel **(01534) 854416**
Fax **(01534) 854684**
Mem 1300
Sec RC Leader
Pro T Horton (01534) 852234
Holes 18 L 6059 yds SSS 70
Recs Am–64 R Harrop (1989)
Pro–64 P Le Chevalier (1988)
V'tors WD–H after 10am WE/BH–H after 2.30pm
Fees £30 (£35)
Loc 4 miles E of St Helier

St Clements (1925)
Public
St Clements, Jersey JE2 6QN
Tel **(01534) 821938**
Pro R Marks
Holes 9 L 3972 yds SSS 61
Recs Am–61 T Gray, B McCarthy
V'tors U exc Sun am–NA
Fees £12
Loc 1 mile E of St Helier

St Pierre Park Par Three
Rohais, St Peter Port, Guernsey
Tel **(01481) 727039**
Mem 290
Pro R Corbet (Mgr)
Holes 9 hole Par 3 course
V'tors U SOC
Fees 18 holes–£15 (£17)
9 holes–£10 (£12)
Loc 1 mile W of St Peter Port
Mis Driving range
Arch Tony Jacklin

Cheshire

Alder Root (1993)
Alder Root Lane, Winwick, Warrington WA2 8RZ
Tel **(01925) 291919**
Fax **(01925) 291919**
Mem 450
Sec Mrs K Young
Pro T Yarwood (01925) 291932
Holes 9 L 5761 yds Par 69 SSS 68
Recs Am–71 I Abbott (1994)
V'tors WD–U SOC
Fees £16 (£18)
Loc 4 miles N of Warrington (A49). M6 Junction 22. M62 Junction 9
Arch Millington/Lander

Alderley Edge (1907)
Brook Lane, Alderley Edge SK9 7RU
Tel **(01625) 585583**
Mem 212 90(L) 40(J) 40(5)
Sec JBD Page
Pro P Rowe (01625) 584493
Holes 9 L 5823 yds SSS 68
Recs Am–62 RF Brindle (1993)
Pro–63 MJ Slater (1994)
V'tors M or H
Fees £18 (£22)
Loc 12 miles S of Manchester

Astbury (1922)
Peel Lane, Astbury, Congleton CW12 4RE
Tel **(01260) 272772**
Mem 700
Sec JH Williams
Pro A Salt
Holes 18 L 6403 yds SSS 72
Recs Am–65 AJA Hurst (1983)
Pro–69 I Mosey (1979)
V'tors WD–H or M WE–M SOC–Thurs only
Fees £25 SOC–£20
Loc 1 mile S of Congleton, off A34

Birchwood (1979)
Kelvin Close, Birchwood, Warrington WA3 7PB
Tel **(01925) 818819**
Fax **(01925) 822403**
Mem 1069
Sec A Harper
Pro D Cooper
Holes 18 L 6808 yds SSS 73
Recs Am–68 P McEwan
Pro–65 P Affleck
V'tors U SOC–Mon/Wed/Thurs
Fees On application
Loc M62 Junction 11, 2 miles. Signs to 'Science Park North'

Carden Park (1993)
Carden, Tilston, Chester CH3 9DQ
Tel **(01829) 250325**
Fax **(01829) 250539**
Holes 18 L 6828 yds SSS 70
9 hole Par 3 course
V'tors H SOC
Fees £25 D–£30
Loc 10 miles S of Chester on A534
Mis Golf Academy. Driving range

Chester (1900)
Curzon Park, Chester CH4 8AR
Tel **(01244) 675130**
Mem 840
Sec VFC Wood (01244) 677760
Pro G Parton (01244) 671185
Holes 18 L 6508 yds SSS 71
Recs Am–66 R Howell
Pro–66 D Screeton
V'tors U H SOC
Fees £21 (£26)
Loc Chester 1 mile

Congleton (1897)
Biddulph Road, Congleton CW12 3LZ
Tel **(01260) 273540**
Mem 425
Sec FT Pegg
Pro JA Colclough (01260) 271083
Holes 12 L 5103 yds Par 68 SSS 65
Recs Am–60 M Griffiths (1989)
Pro–59 N Coles (1968)
V'tors U
Fees £14 (£20)
Loc 1½ miles E of Congleton on A527

Crewe (1911)
Fields Road, Haslington, Crewe CW1 1TB
Tel **(01270) 584227 (Steward)**
Fax **(01270) 584099**
Mem 628
Sec Ms PM Stratton (01270) 584099
Pro C Smith (01270) 585032
Holes 18 L 6259 yds SSS 70
Recs Am–66 CR Smethurst (1993)
Pro–65 M Brunton (1994)
V'tors WD–U WE/BH–M SOC
Fees £27 After 1pm–£22
Loc 2 miles NE of Crewe Station, off A534. 5 miles W of M6 Junction 17

Davenport (1913)
Worth Hall, Middlewood Road, Poynton, Stockport SK12 1TS
Tel **(01625) 877321**
Mem 600
Sec DW Scott (01625) 876951
Pro W Harris (01625) 877319
Holes 18 L 6065 yds SSS 69
Recs Am–64 R Lauder
Pro–67 B Evans
V'tors U exc Sat–NA SOC–Tues & Thurs
Fees £24 (£30)
Loc 5 miles S of Stockport

Delamere Forest (1910)
Station Road, Delamere, Northwich CW8 2JE
Tel **(01606) 883264**
Mem 400
Sec RH Allardice (01606) 883800
Pro EB Jones (01606) 883307
Holes 18 L 6305 yds SSS 70
Recs Am–65 J Brown
Pro–63 M Bembridge
V'tors WD–U WE–2 ball only SOC
Fees £25 D–£35 (£30)
Loc 10 miles E of Chester, off B5152
Arch Herbert Fowler

Eaton (1965)
Guy Lane, Waverton, Chester CH3 7PH
Tel **(01244) 335885**
Fax **(01244) 335782**
Mem 550

Sec GC Parry
Pro A Mitchell (01244) 335826
Holes 18 L 6562 yds SSS 71
Recs Am–69 M Picton (1994)
V'tors H SOC–WD
Fees On application
Loc 3 miles SE of Chester, off A41
Arch Donald Steel

Ellesmere Port (1971)

Public
Chester Road, Childer Thornton, South Wirral L66 1QF
Tel **(0151) 339 7689**
Mem 350
Sec S Hough
Pro D Yates
Holes 18 L 6432 yds SSS 71
Recs Am–66 A Waterhouse
Pro–67 B Evans, A Caygill
V'tors WD–U WE–arrange with Pro SOC–WD
Fees £5 (£6.30)
Loc 9 miles N of Chester on A41

Frodsham (1990)

Simons Lane, Frodsham WA6 6HE
Tel **(01928) 732159**
Mem 550
Sec EI Roylance
Pro G Tonge (01928) 739442
Holes 18 L 6289 yds SSS 70
V'tors WD–U WE/BH–M SOC
Fees £18 (£25)
Loc 9 miles NE of Chester (A56). M56 Junction 12, 3 miles

Helsby (1902)

Tower's Lane, Helsby, Warrington WA6 0JB
Tel **(01928) 722021**
Mem 600
Sec GA Johnson
Pro I Wright (01928) 725457
Holes 18 L 6229 yds SSS 70
Recs Am–69 D Stallard
Pro–68 I Wright
V'tors H WE–NA SOC–Tues & Thurs
Fees £20
Loc 1 mile SE of M56 Junction 14, off Primrose Lane
Arch James Braid

Heyrose (1990)

Budworth Road, Tabley, Knutsford WA16 0HY
Tel **(01565) 733664/733623**
Fax **(01565) 734267**
Mem 700
Sec CN Bridge
Pro M Redrup (01565) 734267
Holes 18 L 6510 yds SSS 71
Pro–68
V'tors U SOC
Fees £18.50 (£24)
Loc 3 miles W of Knutsford, off Pickmere Lane. M6 Junction 19

Knights Grange (1983)

Public
Grange Lane, Winsford CW7 2PT
Tel **(01606) 552780**
Pro G Moore (01606) 75476
Holes 9 L 5720 yds SSS 68
V'tors U SOC
Fees 18 holes–£3.50 (£5.10)
9 holes–£2.70 (£3.95)
Loc Knights Grange Sports Complex

Knutsford (1891)

Mereheath Lane, Knutsford WA16 6HS
Tel **(01565) 633355**
Mem 250
Sec D Francis
Pro A Gillies
Holes 9 L 6288 yds SSS 70
Recs Am–65 B Stockdale
Pro–65 D Cooper
V'tors H exc Wed–NA SOC
Fees £18 (£25)
Loc Knutsford 1/2 mile

Leigh (1906)

Kenyon Hall, Culcheth, Warrington WA3 4BG
Tel **(01925) 763130**
Mem 700
Sec GD Riley (01925) 762943
Pro A Baguley (01925) 762013
Holes 18 L 5892 yds SSS 68
Recs Am–64 J Critchley (1980)
Pro–64 M Sludds (1994)
V'tors U H SOC
Fees £25 (£32) (1994)
Loc 5 miles NE of Warrington
Arch James Braid

Lymm (1907)

Whitbarrow Road, Lymm WA13 9AN
Tel **(01925) 752177**
Mem 400 100(L) 75(J) 50(5)
Sec JM Pearson (01925) 755020
Pro S McCarthy (01925) 755054
Holes 18 L 6304 yds SSS 70
Recs Am–68 CN Brown (1987)
Pro–69 S Lyle (1987)
V'tors WD–H WE–M SOC–Wed
Fees £20
Loc 5 miles SE of Warrington. M6 Junction 20

Macclesfield (1889)

The Hollins, Macclesfield SK11 7EA
Tel **(01625) 423227**
Fax **(01625) 615845**
Mem 600
Sec NH Edwards (01625) 615845
Pro T Taylor (01625) 616952
Holes 18 L 5625 yds SSS 67
Recs Am–69 D Brereton
V'tors WD/BH–H WE–M SOC–WD
Fees £17 (£20)
Loc SE edge of Macclesfield
Arch Hawtree

Malkins Bank (1980)

Public
Malkins Bank, Sandbach
Tel **(01270) 765931**
Pro D Wheeler
Holes 18 L 6071 yds SSS 69
Recs Am–65 J Parry (1994)
V'tors U SOC
Fees £5.50 (£6.60) (1994)
Loc 2 miles S of Sandbach via A534/A533. M6 Junction 17

Mere G & CC (1934)

Chester Road, Mere, Knutsford WA16 6LJ
Tel **(01565) 830155**
Fax **(01565) 830713**
Mem 375 200(L) 10(J)
Sec WG Squires, Karen Bucksey
Pro P Eyre (01565) 830219
Holes 18 L 6817 yds SSS 73
Recs Am–66 J Gallagher (1994)
Pro–64 P McGinley (1992)
V'tors WE/BH–M Wed & Fri–M Mon/Tues/Thurs–H SOC
Fees D–£50
Loc 1 mile E of M6 Junction 19
Mis Driving range-members and green fees only
Arch James Braid

Mottram Hall Hotel (1991)

Pay and play
Wilmslow Road, Mottram St Andrew, Prestbury SK10 4QT
Tel **(01625) 828135**
Fax **(01625) 829284**
Mem 500
Sec DE Crawford
Pro T Rastall
Holes 18 L 7006 yds SSS 74
Recs Pro–66 J Matthews (1991)
V'tors U H
Fees £32 (£37)
Loc 4 miles SE of Wilmslow
Arch Dave Thomas

New Mills (1907)

Shaw Marsh, New Mills, Stockport SK12 4QE
Tel **(01663) 743485**
Mem 350
Sec R Tuson (01663) 747205
Pro S James (01663) 746161
Holes 9 L 5633 yds SSS 67
Recs Am–66 N Coverley
Pro–64 E Litchfield
V'tors WD–U WE–M SOC
Fees On application
Loc 8 miles SE of Stockport

Oaklands G & CC (1990)

Forest Road, Tarporley CW6 0JA
Tel **(01829) 733884**
Fax **(01829) 733666**
Mem 630
Sec P Burroughes
Pro Miss J Statham (0829) 733703
Holes 18 L 6508 yds SSS 71
V'tors U SOC–WD

For list of abbreviations see page 435

Fees £16 (£21)
Loc 1 mile N of Tarporley on A49 Warrington road
Arch Tim Rouse

Portal G & CC (1992)

Cobblers Cross Lane, Tarporley CW6 0DJ
Tel **(01829) 733933**
Fax **(01829) 733928**
Mem 100
Pro D Clare, D Wills (Golf Dirs)
Holes 18 L 7145 yds SSS 73 Pro–67 D Cooper, D Wills, D Clare
V'tors U H SOC
Fees Summer–£30 Winter–£20
Loc 11 miles SE of Chester on A51. M6 Junctions 16 or 19
Arch Donald Steel

Poulton Park (1980)

Dig Lane, Cinnamon Brow
Tel **(01925) 812034**
Mem 360
Sec DJ Coleman
Pro D Newing (01925) 825220
Holes 9 L 4918 metres SSS 66
Recs Am–66 S Bennett
V'tors WD–NA 5–6pm WE–NA 12–2pm
Fees £16 (£18)
Loc Off Crab Lane, Fearnhead

Prestbury (1920)

Macclesfield Road, Prestbury, Macclesfield SK10 4BJ
Tel **(01625) 829388**
Fax **(01625) 828241**
Mem 725
Sec J Wright (01625) 828241
Pro Dianne Bradley (01625) 828242
Holes 18 L 6359 yds SSS 71
Recs Am–64 P Bolton Pro–68 M Faulkener
V'tors WD–I WE–M SOC–Thurs
Fees £30
Loc 2 miles NW of Macclesfield

Pryor Hayes (1993)

Willingdon Road, Oscroft, Tarvin CH3 8NL
Tel **(01829) 740140**
Fax **(01829) 741250**
Mem 550
Sec I Chilton
Pro N Rothe
Holes 18 L 5923 yds SSS 69
V'tors U SOC
Fees £15 (£20)
Loc 5 miles E of Chester
Arch Wundke/Day

Queens Park (1985)

Public
Queens Park Drive, Crewe CW2 7SB
Tel **(01270) 666724**
Mem 250
Sec KF Lear
Pro R Johnson
Holes 9 L 4920 yds SSS 64
Recs Am–67 A Jennings (1994)
V'tors WD–U WE–U after 12 noon SOC
Fees £4.60 (£6.10)
Loc 2 miles from Crewe, off Victoria Avenue

Reaseheath (1987)

Reaseheath College, Reaseheath, Nantwich CW5 6DF
Tel **(01270) 625131**
Fax **(01270) 625665**
Mem 120
Sec D Mortram (Hon)
Holes 9 L 3334 yds SSS 54
V'tors M SOC–WD
Fees £3
Loc 2 miles NW of Nantwich on College campus

Runcorn (1909)

Clifton Road, Runcorn WA7 4SU
Tel **(01928) 572093 (Members)**
Mem 375 80(L) 80(J)
Sec WB Reading (01928) 574214
Pro S Dooley (01928) 564791
Holes 18 L 6035 yds SSS 69
Recs Am–67 I Rockliffe
V'tors WD–U H exc comp days WE–M SOC
Fees £17
Loc Runcorn (A557). M56 Junction 12

Sandbach (1923)

Middlewich Road, Sandbach CW11 9EA
Tel **(01270) 762117**
Mem 230 110(L) 50(J)
Sec AF Pearson
Holes 9 L 5397 yds SSS 67
Recs Am–64 K Brooks
V'tors WD–U WE/BH–M
Fees D–£16
Loc 1 mile W of Sandbach (A533). M6 Junction 17

Sandiway (1921)

Chester Road, Sandiway CW8 2DJ
Tel **(01606) 882606**
Fax **(01606) 888548**
Mem 300
Sec MC Gilyeat (01606) 883247
Pro W Laird (01606) 883180
Holes 18 L 6435 yds SSS 72
Recs Am–67 AE Hill Pro–65 D Huish
V'tors I H
Fees £30 (£35)
Loc 15 miles E of Chester on A556
Arch Ted Ray

Shrigley Hall (1990)

Shrigley Park, Pott Shrigley, Macclesfield SK10 5SB
Tel **(01625) 575755**
Fax **(01625) 576957**
Mem 540
Sec Mrs S Major
Pro G Ogden (01625) 575626
Holes 18 L 6305 yds SSS 71
Recs Am–73 N Green (1990) Pro–68 G Ogden (1989)
V'tors H SOC
Fees £22 (£28)
Loc 5 miles NE of Macclesfield, off A523. M6 Junction 18
Arch Donald Steel

St Michaels Jubilee (1977)

Public
Dundalk Road, Widnes WA8 8BS
Tel **(0151) 424 6230**
Mem 200
Sec KB Stevenson
Pro R Bilton (01295) 65241
Holes 18 L 5612 yds SSS 67
Recs Am–67 I O'Connor (1989)
V'tors U
Fees On application

The Tytherington Club (1986)

Macclesfield SK10 2JP
Tel **(01625) 434562**
Fax **(01625) 430882**
Mem 700
Sec A Thorp (Mgr)
Pro To be appointed
Holes 18 L 6737 yds SSS 73
Recs Am–68 J Hodgson Pro–71 P Affleck, L Turner Ladies Pro–63 L Davies
V'tors U H SOC–WD
Fees £25 D–£35 (£30 D–£40)
Loc N of Macclesfield (A523)
Mis Driving range
Arch Thomas/Dawson

Upton-by-Chester (1934)

Upton Lane, Chester CH2 1EE
Tel **(01244) 381183**
Mem 750
Sec JB Durban
Pro PA Gardner (01244) 381333
Holes 18 L 5875 yds SSS 68
Recs Am–62 J Davies Pro–66 A Perry
V'tors U SOC–WD
Fees £20 (£25)
Loc Off Liverpool road, near 'Frog' PH

Vicars Cross (1939)

Tarvin Road, Great Barrow, Chester CH3 7HN
Tel **(01244) 335174**
Mem 800
Sec A Rogers
Pro JA Forsythe (01244) 335595
Holes 18 L 6243 yds SSS 70
V'tors Mon–Thurs–U Fri/WE/BH–M SOC–Tues and Thurs
Fees £20 After 4pm–£14
Loc 3 miles E of Chester on A51
Arch E Parr

Walton Hall (1972)

Public
Warrington Road, Higher Walton, Warrington WA4 5LU
Tel **(01925) 266775**
Sec R Davies
Pro P Maton (01925) 263061

For list of abbreviations see page 435

Holes 18 L 6843 yds SSS 73
Recs Am–70 R Davies (1988)
V'tors U SOC
Fees £6.50 (£8)
Loc 2 miles S of Warrington. M56 Junctions 10/11
Arch Dave Thomas

Warrington (1903)
Hill Warren, Appleton WA4 5HR
Tel **(01925) 261620**
Mem 875
Sec NF Morrall (01925) 261775
Pro R Mackay (01925) 265431
Holes 18 L 6305 yds SSS 70
Recs Am–66 JR Bennett
Pro–65 EG Lester
V'tors U SOC–Wed
Fees On application
Loc 3 miles S of Warrington

Widnes (1924)
Highfield Road, Widnes WA8 7DT
Tel **(0151) 424 2440**
Fax **(0151) 495 2849**
Mem 800
Sec MM Cresswell (0151) 424 2995
Pro N Parr (0151) 420 7467
Holes 18 L 5719 yds SSS 68
Recs Am–64 F Whitfield (1990)
Pro–64 A Murray (1976)
V'tors WD–U WE–NA on comp days SOC–Wed
Fees £20 (£30)
Loc Station ½ mile

Wilmslow (1889)
Great Warford, Mobberley, Knutsford WA16 7AY
Tel **(01565) 872148**
Mem 770
Sec A Laurence
Pro J Nowicki (01565) 873620
Holes 18 L 6607 yds SSS 72
Recs Am–67 C Nowicki (1994)
Pro–62 C Corrigan (1994)
V'tors U H exc Wed–NA before 3pm
Fees £30 (£40)
Loc 3 miles W of Alderley Edge

Cleveland

Billingham (1967)
Sandy Lane, Billingham TS22 5NA
Tel **(01642) 554494/533816**
Mem 850
Sec EI Douglas (01642) 533816
Pro P Bradley (01642) 557060
Holes 18 L 6430 yds SSS 71
Recs Am–66 S Twynholm (1993)
Pro–63 M Maith (1993)
V'tors WD–H after 9am WE/BH–H after 10am SOC
Fees D–£20 (£33)
Loc W boundary of Billingham by A19, E of bypass
Arch Frank Pennink

Castle Eden & Peterlee (1927)
Castle Eden, Hartlepool TS27 4SS
Tel **(01429) 836220**
Mem 650
Sec P Robinson
Pro G Laidlaw (01429) 836689
Holes 18 L 6262 yds SSS 70
Recs Am–66 G Border (1987)
V'tors U
Fees £20
Loc 2 miles S of Peterlee
Arch Henry Cotton

Cleveland (1887)
Queen Street, Redcar TS10 1BT
Tel **(01642) 483693**
Fax **(01642) 471798**
Mem 800
Sec LR Manley (01642) 471798
Pro S Wynn (01642) 483462
Holes 18 L 6707 yds SSS 72
Recs Am–67 A McClure (1994)
Pro–70 B Hardcastle (1976)
V'tors WD–U after 9.30am WE/BH–no parties SOC
Fees £18 (£27)
Loc S bank of River Tees

Eaglescliffe (1914)
Yarm Road, Eaglescliffe, Stockton-on-Tees TS16 0DQ
Tel **(01642) 780098**
Mem 835
Sec AH Painter (01642) 780238
Pro N Gilks (01642) 790122
Holes 18 L 6275 yds SSS 70
Recs Am–63 CM Hoggart (1993)
Pro–65 N Gilkes (1993)
V'tors U SOC
Fees £22 (£28)
Loc 3 miles S of Stockton-on-Tees on A135

Hartlepool (1906)
Hart Warren, Hartlepool TS24 9QF
Tel **(01429) 274398**
Mem 600
Sec WE Storrow (01429) 870282
Pro ME Cole (01429) 267473
Holes 18 L 6255 yds SSS 70
Recs Am–63 G Bell (1990)
Pro–65 J Harrison, D Curry
V'tors WD–U SOC
Fees £18 (£24)
Loc N boundary of Hartlepool

Hunley Hall (1993)
Brotton, Saltburn TS12 2QQ
Tel **(01287) 676216**
Fax **(01287) 678250**
Mem 500
Sec E Lillie
Pro A Brook (0287) 77444
Holes 18 L 6918 yds SSS 73
Recs Am–74 J Jackson (1994)
V'tors U SOC
Fees £18 (£25)
Loc 15 miles SE of Middlesbrough on A174
Mis Floodlit driving range
Arch John Morgan

Knotty Hill Golf Centre (1992)
Pay and play
Sedgefield, Stockton-on-Tees TS21 2BB
Tel **(01740) 620320**
Fax **(01740) 620320**
Mem 1200
Sec D Craggs (Mgr)
Pro N Todd
Holes 18 L 6517 yds Par 72 SSS 71
V'tors U SOC
Fees £12 (£12)
Loc 1 mile N of Sedgefield on A177. A1(M) Junction 60, 2 miles
Mis Driving range
Arch Chris Stanton

Middlesbrough (1908)
Brass Castle Lane, Marton, Middlesbrough TS8 9EE
Tel **(01642) 316430**
Fax **(01642) 319607**
Mem 950
Sec BC Hunt (01642) 311515
Pro DJ Jones (01642) 311766
Holes 18 L 6167 yds SSS 70
Recs Am–65 S Taylor (1993)
Pro–65 D Padgett (1993)
V'tors U
Fees D–£26 (£32)
Loc 3 miles S of Middlesbrough

Middlesbrough Municipal (1977)
Public
Ladgate Lane, Middlesbrough TS5 7YZ
Tel **(01642) 315533**
Fax **(01642) 300726**
Mem 625
Sec J Dilworth (Hon)
Pro A Hope (01642) 300720
Holes 18 L 6314 yds SSS 70
Recs Am–68 M Wright (1992)
Pro–67 B Gallagher (1981)
V'tors U
Fees £7.50 (£9.50)
Loc 2 miles S of Middlesbrough on A174
Mis Floodlit driving range

Norton (1989)
Pay and play
Junction Road, Norton, Stockton-on-tees TS20 1SU
Tel **(01642) 676385**
Fax **(01642) 608647**
Holes 18 L 5870 yds SSS 71
V'tors U SOC–WD
Fees £8.50
Loc 1 mile E of A177 on B1274
Arch Tim Harper

For list of abbreviations see page 435

Saltburn (1894)
Hob Hill, Saltburn-by-the-Sea TS12 1NJ
Tel **(01287) 622812**
Mem 900
Sec D Becker
Pro D Forsythe (01287) 624653
Holes 18 L 5846 yds SSS 68
Recs Am–66
Pro–62 D Rees
V'tors H SOC
Fees £19 (£22)
Loc 1 mile S of Saltburn

Seaton Carew (1874)
Tees Road, Hartlepool TS25 1DE
Tel **(01429) 266249/261040**
Mem 650
Sec PR Wilson (01429) 261473
Pro W Hector
Holes Old 18 L 6613 yds SSS 72
Brabazon 18 L 6855 yds SSS 73
Recs Old Am–66 MJ Kelley, B Popple.
Pro–66 N Bell
Brabazon Am–66 ID Garbutt
V'tors U SOC
Fees £26 (£36)
Loc Hartlepool 2 miles
Arch Dr A Mackenzie

Tees-side (1901)
Acklam Road, Thornaby TS17 7JS
Tel **(01642) 676249**
Mem 600
Sec MS Higgins (01642) 616516
Pro K Hall (01642) 673822
Holes 18 L 6505 yds SSS 71
V'tors WD–U before 4.30pm WE–U after 11am BH–M before 11am SOC
Fees D–£20 (£26)
Loc 2 miles S of Stockton on A1130. 1/2 mile from A19 on A1130

Wilton (1952)
Wilton, Redcar TS10 4QY
Tel **(01642) 465265**
Mem 863
Sec JCP Elder (Sec/Mgr)
Pro Pat Smillie
Holes 18 L 6145 yds SSS 69
Recs Am–64 BM Christie (1991)
Pro–68 S Hunt
Ladies–75 V Duncan (1984)
V'tors WD–U after 10am Sat–NA Sun/BH–U after 10am SOC–WD exc Tues
Fees D–£18 (D–£24)
Loc 3 miles W of Redcar on A174 – signs to Wilton Castle

Cornwall

Bowood (1992)
Valley Truckle, Lanteglos, Camelford PL32 9RT
Tel **(01840) 213017**
Mem 300
Sec T Japes
Pro B Patterson
Holes 18 L 6692 yds SSS 72
V'tors H (phone first) SOC
Fees £23 (£25)
Loc 2 miles SW of Camelford (A39 and B3266)
Mis Driving range

Bude & North Cornwall (1891)
Burn View, Bude EX23 8DA
Tel **(01288) 352006**
Fax **(01288) 356855**
Mem 500 220(L) 60(J)
Sec PK Brown
Pro J Yeo
Holes 18 L 6202 yds SSS 70
Recs Am–65 S Rickard
Pro–67 B Austin
Ladies–73 S Currie
V'tors WD–H 9.30–12.30pm, 2–5pm and after 6.30pm WE–restricted SOC
Fees D–£20 (D–£25)
Loc Bude town centre

Budock Vean Hotel (1922)
Falmouth TR11 5LG
Tel **(01326) 250288**
Fax **(01326) 250892**
Mem 250
Sec E Duncan
Pro A Ramsden (Golf Mgr)
Holes 9 L 5153 yds SSS 65
Recs Am–61 RJ Sadler
Pro–64 D Short
V'tors H
Fees D–£14 (D–£18)
Loc Falmouth 5 miles

Cape Cornwall G & CC (1990)
St Just, Penzance TR19 7NL
Tel **(01736) 788611**
Mem 450
Sec RA Doe
Pro R Hamilton
Holes 18 L 5650 yds SSS 68
V'tors WD/Sat–U Sun–NA before noon SOC
Fees £16
Loc 1 mile W of St Just. 8 miles W of Penzance, off A3071
Arch R Hamilton

Carlyon Bay (1926)
Carlyon Bay, St Austell PL25 3RD
Tel **(01726) 814250**
Mem 600
Sec P Clemo
Pro NJ Sears (01726) 814228
Holes 18 L 6510 yds SSS 71
Recs Am–68 A Nash
Pro–65 N Coles
V'tors U–book with Pro
Fees £20
Loc 2 miles E of St Austell
Arch J Hamilton Stutt

China Fleet CC (1991)
Saltash PL12 6LJ
Tel **(01752) 848668**
Fax **(01752) 848456**
Mem 600
Sec DW O'Sullivan
Pro RA Moore
Holes 18 L 6551 yds SSS 72
Recs Am–69 I Ashenden (1993)
V'tors H–by arrangement SOC
Fees On application
Loc 1 mile from Tamar Bridge, off A38
Mis Floodlit driving range
Arch Hawtree

Culdrose
Royal Naval Air Station, Culdrose
Tel **(01326) 574121** Ext 2413
Mem 175
Sec G Faraway (Ext 7512)
Holes 14 L 6214 yds SSS 71
V'tors M
Loc Culdrose

Falmouth (1894)
Swanpool Road, Falmouth TR11 5BQ
Tel **(01326) 314296**
Mem 600
Sec Mrs CM Patterson
Pro B Patterson (Golf Dir) (01326) 311262
Holes 18 L 5680 yds SSS 68
Recs Am–61 GM Bawden (1992)
Pro–65 G Brand Jr (1981)
Ladies–65 K Wells (1991)
V'tors U H SOC
Fees £20 D–£25
Loc 1/4 mile W of Swanpool Beach

Isles of Scilly (1904)
St Mary's, Isles of Scilly TR21 0NF
Tel **(01720) 422692**
Mem 130
Sec S Watt
Holes 9 L 6001 yds SSS 69
Recs Am–70 M Twynham
Pro–66 G Ryall, P Evans
V'tors WD–U Sun–M
Fees £15
Loc Hughtown 1 1/2 miles
Arch Horace Hutchinson

Killiow Golf Park (1987)
Killiow, Kea, Truro TR3 6AG
Tel **(01872) 70246**
Fax **(01872) 40915**
Sec J Penrose
Pro J Penrose
Holes 18 L 3500 yds Par 60
V'tors WD–U WE–NA before 10.30am
Fees £10
Loc 2 1/2 miles S of Truro, off A39

Lanhydrock (1991)
Lostwithiel Road, Bodmin PL30 5AQ
Tel **(01208) 73600**
Fax **(01208) 77325**
Mem 300
Sec G Bond (Dir)
Pro J Broadway
Holes 18 L 6185 yds SSS 71
V'tors U
Fees On application
Loc 1 mile S of Bodmin, off B3268
Mis Driving range
Arch J Hamilton Stutt

Launceston (1928)
St Stephen, Launceston PL15 8HF
Tel **(01566) 773442**
Mem 900
Sec BJ Grant
Pro J Tozer
Holes 18 L 6407 yds SSS 71
Recs Am–67 C Phillips (1987)
Pro–64 S Little (1989)
V'tors WD–U H WE–NA SOC
Fees £20
Loc 1 mile N of Launceston, off Bude road
Arch J Hamilton Stutt

Looe (1933)
Bin Down, Looe PL13 1PX
Tel **(015034) 239**
Fax **(015034) 239**
Mem 600
Sec G Bond (Gen Mgr)
Pro A MacDonald
Holes 18 L 5940 yds SSS 68
Recs Am–64 I Veale (1993)
V'tors U
Fees On application
Loc 3 miles E of Looe
Arch Harry Vardon

Lostwithiel G & CC (1990)
Lower Polscoe, Lostwithiel PL22 0HQ
Tel **(01208) 873550**
Fax **(01208) 873479**
Mem 281
Sec D Higman
Pro M Hammond (01208) 873822
Holes 18 L 6098 yds Par 72
Pro–70 M Hammond (1990)
V'tors WD–H WE–restricted SOC
Fees £15 (£19)
Loc 1 mile E of Lostwithiel, off A390
Mis Driving range
Arch Stuart Wood

Merlin (1991)
Mawganporth, Newquay TR8 4AD
Tel **(01841) 540222**
Holes 18 L 5600 yds SSS 68
V'tors U SOC
Fees £9
Loc 2 miles N of Newquay
Mis Driving range
Arch Ross Oliver

Mullion (1895)
Cury, Helston TR12 7BP
Tel **(01326) 240276**
Mem 760
Sec D Watts (01326) 240685
Pro R Goodway (01326) 241176
Holes 18 L 6022 yds SSS 69
V'tors H (restricted comp days and open days) SOC–WD
Fees £20 W–£70
Loc 6 miles S of Helston

Newquay (1890)
Tower Road, Newquay TR7 1LT
Tel **(01637) 872091**
Fax **(01637) 874354**
Mem 600
Sec G Binney (01637) 874354
Pro P Muscroft (01637) 874830
Holes 18 L 6140 yds SSS 69
Recs Am–63 P Clayton (1989)
Pro–69 PJ Yeo
V'tors WD/Sat–H Sun–H SOC
Fees £20 (£20) W–£80
Loc Newquay town centre
Arch HS Colt

Perranporth (1927)
Budnic Hill, Perranporth TR6 0AB
Tel **(01872) 572454**
Mem 600
Sec PDR Barnes (01872) 573701
Pro DC Mitchell (01872) 572317
Holes 18 L 6286 yds SSS 72
Recs Am–62 P Trew (1993)
Pro–68
V'tors WD–U WE–H SOC
Fees D–£20 (D–£25)
Loc 1/2 mile NW of Perranporth
Arch James Braid

Praa Sands (1971)
Praa Sands, Germoe Cross Roads, Penzance TR20 9TQ
Tel **(01736) 763445**
Fax **(01736) 763399**
Mem 300
Sec D & K Phillips (Props)
Pro M Singleton
Holes 9 L 4104 yds SSS 60
Recs Am–59 P Lorys (1981)
V'tors U exc Sun am–NA
Fees £14 W–£84
Loc 7 miles E of Penzance on A394 Penzance-Helston road

St Austell (1912)
Tregongeeves, St Austell PL26 7DS
Tel **(01726) 74756**
Mem 780
Sec SH Davey
Pro M Rowe (01726) 68621
Holes 18 L 5981 yds SSS 69
Recs Am–67 AC Nash
Pro–64 AC Nash (1993)
V'tors SOC exc comp days
Fees On application
Loc 1 1/2 miles W of St Austell

St Enodoc (1890)
Rock, Wadebridge PL27 6LB
Tel **(01208) 863216**
Mem 1050
Sec Col L Guy OBE
Pro NJ Williams (01208) 862402
Holes Church 18 L 6207 yds SSS 70
Holywell 18 L 4165 yds SSS 61
Recs Am–65 K Jones
Pro–67 Dai Rees
V'tors Church H–max 24 SOC
Holywell–U
Fees Church £22 W–£123
Holywell £12 W–£56
Loc 6 miles NW of Wadebridge
Arch James Braid

St Kew (1993)
Pay and play
St Kew Highway, Bodmin PL30 3EF
Tel **(01208) 841500**
Fax **(01208) 841500**
Mem 240
Sec MC Cole
Pro T Pitts
Holes 9 L 2204 yds SSS 62
V'tors U SOC
Fees 9 holes–£7 18 holes–£11
Loc 2 1/2 miles N of Wadebridge on A39
Mis Driving range
Arch David Derry

St Mellion (1976)
St Mellion, Saltash PL12 6SD
Tel **(01579) 50101**
Fax **(01579) 50116**
Mem 800
Sec PJ Flavin, DM Webb (Golf Dirs)
Pro J Garner
Holes Old 18 L 5782 yds SSS 68
Nicklaus 18 L 6651 yds SSS 72
Recs Nicklaus Am–70 C Eichstedt
Nicklaus Pro–65 A Oldcorn, K Trimble, R Chapman, P Lawrie, R Karlsson
V'tors H SOC
Fees On application
Loc Tamar Bridge, 5 miles NW of Saltash
Mis Driving range for members and visitors
Arch Hamilton Stutt/Nicklaus

Tehidy Park (1922)
Camborne TR14 0HH
Tel **(01209) 842208**
Mem 1000
Sec J Prosser
Pro J Dumbreck (01209) 842914
Holes 18 L 6241 yds SSS 70
Recs Am–67 N Rogers (1989)
Pro–68 J Langmead (1990)
V'tors H
Fees £21 (£27)
Loc 3 miles N of Camborne

For list of abbreviations see page 435

Tregenna Castle Hotel (1982)
St Ives TR26 2DE
Tel **(01736) 795254 Ext 121**
Mem 297
Sec J Goodman
Holes 18 L 3549 yds SSS 57
Recs Am–62 G Thomas (1989)
Pro–54 L Knapp (1986)
V'tors U SOC
Fees On application
Loc St Ives 1 mile, off A3074

Treloy (1991)
Treloy, Newquay TR7 4JN
Tel **(01637) 878554**
Mem 145
Sec J Reid
Holes 9 L 2143 yds SSS 31
V'tors U SOC
Fees 18 holes–£11.50
9 holes–£7.50
Loc Newquay 2 miles
Arch MRM Sandow

Trevose (1924)
Constantine Bay, Padstow PL28 8JB
Tel **(01841) 520208**
Fax **(01841) 521057**
Mem 960
Sec P Gammon (Prop)
GL Grindley (Sec/Mgr)
Pro G Alliss (01841) 520261
Holes 18 L 6608 yds SSS 72
9 L 3031 yds SSS 35
9 L 1367 yds SSS 29
Recs Am–67 C Phillips
Pro–66 N Burch
V'tors H SOC
Fees On application
Loc 4 miles W of Padstow
Mis 3 & 4 ball times restricted (phone first)
Arch HS Colt

Truro (1937)
Treliske, Truro TR1 3LG
Tel **(01872) 72640**
Mem 900
Sec BE Heggie (01872) 78684
Pro NK Bicknell (01872) 76595
Holes 18 L 5347 yds SSS 66
Recs Am–61 AJ Ring
Pro–63 M Hoyle
V'tors U H SOC
Fees £18 (£22)
Loc 2 miles W of Truro on A390

West Cornwall (1889)
Lelant, St Ives TR26 3DZ
Tel **(01736) 753401**
Mem 825
Sec MC Lack
Pro P Atherton (01736) 753177
Holes 18 L 5884 yds SSS 69
Recs Am–65 MC Edmunds, P Darlington
Pro–64 G Emerson
V'tors H
Fees £20 (£25)
Loc 2 miles E of St Ives

Whitsand Bay Hotel (1909)
Portwrinkle, Torpoint PL11 3BU
Tel **(01503) 30276**
Fax **(01503) 30329**
Mem 500
Sec GG Dyer (01503) 30418
Pro S Poole (01503) 30778
Holes 18 L 5800 yds SSS 69
Recs Am–62 GG Dyer (1981)
Pro–62 M Faulkner (1948)
V'tors U SOC
Fees £15 (£16.50)
Loc 6 miles W of Plymouth
Arch Willie Fernie

Cumbria

Alston Moor (1906)
The Hermitage, Alston CA9 3DB
Tel **(01434) 381675**
Mem 170
Sec H Robinson (01434) 381354
Holes 10 L 5380 yds SSS 66
Recs Am–70 R Rutherford, R Green
V'tors U SOC
Fees £8 (£10)
Loc 2 miles S of Alston on B6277

Appleby (1903)
Brackenber Moor, Appleby CA16 6LP
Tel **(017683) 51432**
Mem 834
Sec Maj BW Rimmer (Hon)
Holes 18 L 5901 yds SSS 68
Recs Am–63 K Bush
Pro–69 SS Scott
V'tors U
Fees £12 (£16)
Loc 2 miles NE of Appleby. ½ mile N of A66
Arch Willie Fernie

Barrow (1921)
Rakesmoor Lane, Hawcoat, Barrow-in-Furness LA14 4QB
Tel **(01229) 825444**
Mem 506 117(L) 80(J)
Sec J Slater (Hon)
Pro N Hyde (01229) 832121
Holes 18 L 6209 yds SSS 70
Recs Am–66 NL Brooks, P McNulty (1994)
Ladies–68 J McCall (1984)
V'tors U H Ladies Day–Fri
Fees £15 (£25) W–£60
Loc 2 miles E of Barrow, off A590

Brampton (Talkin Tarn) (1907)
Brampton CA8 1HN
Tel **(0169) 772255**
Mem 750
Sec IJ Meldrum (01228) 23155
Pro S Harrison (0169) 772000
Holes 18 L 6420 yds SSS 71
Recs Am–66 R Secular (1993)
Ladies–71 L Fletcher (1989)
V'tors U
Fees D–£16 (D–£20) W–£50
Loc B6413, 1 mile SE of Brampton
Arch James Braid

Brayton Park (1986)
Pay and play
Lakeside Inn, Brayton Park, Aspatria CA5 3TD
Tel **(016973) 20840**
Mem 110
Sec D MacLaren
Holes 9 L 2521 yds SSS 65
V'tors U
Fees 9 holes–£5 (£6)
18 holes–£7 (£8)
Loc 1 mile N of Aspatria. 10 miles N of Cockermouth
Mis Driving range

Carlisle (1908)
Aglionby, Carlisle CA4 8AG
Tel **(01228) 513303**
Fax **(01228) 513303**
Mem 735
Sec HM Rowell
Pro JS More (01228) 513241
Holes 18 L 6278 yds SSS 70
Recs Am–65 M Ruddick (1989)
Pro–63 M Archer (1993)
V'tors WD–U after 9.30am & 1.30pm Tues pm/comp days–NA Sat–M after 10am Sun–U SOC–Mon/Wed/Fri
Fees £20 D–£27.50 (D–£35)
Loc E of M6 Junction 43, on A69

Casterton
Sedbergh Road, Casterton, Carnforth LA6 2LA
Tel **(015242) 71592**
Mem 300
Sec J & E Makinson (Props)
Pro R Williamson
Holes 9 L 3015 yds Par 35
V'tors U
Fees £8 (£10)
Loc 1 mile NE of Kirkby Lonsdale on A683. M6 Junction 36, 6 miles
Arch Will Adamson

Cockermouth (1896)
Embleton, Cockermouth CA13 9SG
Tel **(017687) 76223**
Mem 539
Sec RD Pollard (01900) 822650
Holes 18 L 5496 yds SSS 67
Recs Am–65 S Gabb
V'tors WD–U before 5pm exc Wed Sun–NA before 11am and 2–3.15pm SOC
Fees £15 (£20)
Loc 4 miles E of Cockermouth
Arch James Braid

Dalston Hall (1990)
Dalston Hall, Dalston, Carlisle CA5 7JX
Tel **(01228) 710165**
Mem 270
Sec Jane Simpson

Holes 9 L 2647 yds SSS 67
V'tors U
Fees 9 holes–£5 (£6)
18 holes–£8 (£10)
Loc 5 miles SW of Carlisle on B5299. 6 miles W of M6 Junction 42

The Dunnerholme (1905)
Duddon Road, Askam-in-Furness LA16 7AW
Tel **(01229) 462675**
Mem 440
Sec Mrs ME Tyson (01229) 581400
Holes 10 L 6162 yds SSS 69
Recs Am–68 H Bayliff
Pro–70 JB Ball
V'tors U
Fees £10 (£15)
Loc 6 miles N of Barrow on A595

Eden (1992)
Crosby-on-Eden, Carlisle CA6 4RA
Tel **(01228) 573003**
Fax **(01228) 818435**
Mem 550
Sec A Wannop, D Willey
Pro P Harrison (01228) 573003
Holes 18 L 6368 yds SSS 72
Recs Am–71 RA Whitaker (1994)
Pro–74 G Key
V'tors U SOC
Fees £15 (£20)
Loc 5 miles NE of Carlisle, off A689. M6 Junction 44
Mis Driving range

Furness (1872)
Walney Island, Barrow-in-Furness LA14 3LN
Tel **(01229) 471232**
Mem 700
Sec WT French
Holes 18 L 6363 yds SSS 71
Recs Am–67 A Miles (1986)
Pro–65 A Chandler, GJ Brand (1984)
V'tors U H SOC
Fees £15 (£15)

Grange Fell (1952)
Fell Road, Grange-over-Sands LA11 6HB
Tel **(015395) 32536**
Mem 300
Sec JB Asplin (015395) 32021
Holes 9 L 4826 metres SSS 66
Recs Am–67 FWW Foster (1992)
Pro–66 F Robinson
V'tors U
Fees £10 (£15)
Loc W of Grange-over-Sands, towards Cartmel

Grange-over-Sands (1919)
Meathop Road, Grange-over-Sands LA11 6QX
Tel **(015395) 33180**
Mem 415 145(L) 35(J)
Sec JR Green (015395) 33754
Pro S Sumner-Roberts (015395) 35937
Holes 18 L 5938 yds SSS 69
Recs Am–64 S McMillan
Pro–67 G Cuthbert
V'tors H SOC
Fees £15 D–£20 (£20 D–£25)
Loc E of Grange, off B5277

Kendal (1891)
The Heights, Kendal LA9 4PQ
Tel **(01539) 724079 (Clubhouse)**
Mem 575
Sec D Leake, R Maunder (Sec/Mgr) (0539) 733708
Pro D Turner (0539) 723499
Holes 18 L 5515 yds SSS 67
Recs Am–57 P Millar
Pro–63 P Tupling, GC Norton
V'tors U H SOC
Fees £16 (£20)
Loc 1 mile NW of Kendal

Keswick (1978)
Threlkeld Hall, Keswick CA12 4SX
Tel **(017687) 79324**
Fax **(01768) 65367**
Mem 900
Sec R Bell
Pro C Hamilton (017687) 79010
Holes 18 L 6225 yds SSS 72
Recs Am–69 P Lourie (1994)
Pro–69 I Clark (1984)
V'tors U–book with Pro SOC
Fees D–£15 (D–£20)
Loc 4 miles E of Keswick (A66)
Arch E Brown

Kirkby Lonsdale
Scaleber Lane, Barbon, Carnforth LA6 2LE
Mem 500 50(L) 40(J)
Sec P Jackson (015242) 76365
Pro R Williams (015242) 76366
Holes 18 L 6286 yds SSS 70
V'tors U SOC
Fees £16 (£20)
Loc 2 miles N of Kirkby Lonsdale, off A683

Maryport (1905)
Bankend, Maryport CA15 6PA
Tel **(01900) 812605**
Mem 380
Sec A Carlton (01900) 822680
Holes 18 L 6088 yds SSS 70
Recs Am–70 D Roberts (1989)
V'tors U SOC
Fees D–£15 (£20)
Loc 1 mile N of Maryport, off B5300

Penrith (1890)
Salkeld Road, Penrith CA11 8SG
Tel **(01768) 891919/65429**
Mem 750
Sec D Noble (01768) 891919
Pro CB Thomson (01768) 891919
Holes 18 L 6026 yds SSS 69
Recs Am–63 JD Dockar
Pro–65 K Bousfield
V'tors WD–H WE/BH–H 10.06–11.30am & after 3pm
Fees £20 D–£25 (£25 D–£30)
Loc ½ mile E of Penrith

St Bees (1931)
Rhoda Grove, Rheda, Frizington CA26 3TE
Tel **(01946) 812105**
Mem 350
Sec JB Campbell
Holes 9 L 5122 yds SSS 65
Recs Am–65 P Hanratty, M Pink (1992)
V'tors U
Fees On application
Loc 4 miles S of Whitehaven

Seascale (1893)
The Banks, Seascale CA20 1QL
Tel **(019467) 28202/28800**
Fax **(019467) 28202**
Mem 650
Sec C Taylor (019467) 28202
Pro G Key
Holes 18 L 6416 yds SSS 71
Recs Am–67 D Weston, ID Stavert, G Shuttleworth (1987)
Pro–65 MF Studds (1992)
V'tors U SOC
Fees D–£19 (D–£23)
Loc 15 miles S of Whitehaven

Sedbergh (1896)
Catholes-Abbot Holme, Sedbergh LA10 5SS
Tel **(015396) 21551**
Fax **(015396) 20993**
Mem 350
Sec AD Lord (015396) 20993
Pro J Garner
Holes 9 L 5588 yds Par 70 SSS 68
Recs Am–71 A Pickering (1994)
Pro–70 N Taylor (1994)
V'tors U–phone in advance SOC H
Fees £12 D–£18 (£15 D–£21)
Loc 1 mile S of Sedbergh on Dent road. M6 Junction 37, 5 miles
Arch WG Squires

Silecroft (1903)
Silecroft, Millom LA18 4AG
Tel **(01229) 774250**
Mem 320
Sec DLA MacLardie (01229) 774342
Holes 9 L 5877 yds SSS 68
Recs Am–67 D Lloyd (1994)
V'tors WD–U WE/BH–restricted before 5.30pm SOC
Fees £10 (£15)
Loc 3 miles W of Millom

Silloth-on-Solway (1892)
Silloth, Carlisle CA5 4AD
Tel **(016973) 31304**
Fax **(016973) 31782**
Mem 800
Sec JG Proudlock
Pro J Burns (016973) 32404
Holes 18 L 6445 yds SSS 72

For list of abbreviations see page 435

Recs Am–66 C Wallace, DL Watson
V'tors U H–booking advisable SOC
Fees £25 D–£35 (£30)
Loc 22 miles W of Carlisle (B5302). M6 Junction 43
Arch Willie Park Jr

Silverdale (1906)

Red Bridge Lane, Silverdale, Carnforth LA5 0SP
Tel **(01524) 701300**
Mem 513
Sec PJ Watts (01524) 701307
Pro S Sumner Roberts
Holes 12 L 5417 yds SSS 67
Recs Am–66
V'tors U exc Sun (Summer)–M
Fees £12 (£17)
Loc 3 miles NW of Carnforth, by Silverdale Station

Stoneyholme (1974)

Public
St Aidan's Road, Carlisle CA7 1LS
Tel **(01228) 34856**
Pro S Ling
Holes 18 L 5775 yds SSS 68
Recs Am–64
V'tors U SOC
Fees On application
Loc 1 mile E of Carlisle, off A69. M6 Junction 43
Arch Frank Pennink

Ulverston (1895)

Bardsea Park, Ulverston LA12 9QJ
Tel **(01229) 582824**
Mem 745
Sec P Wedgwood (01229) 587806
Pro MR Smith (01229) 582806
Holes 18 L 6122 yds SSS 70
Recs Am–65 AJ Edwards (1991)
Pro–71 JA Raisbeck
V'tors H or I SOC
Fees £20 (£25) Summer
£14 (£18) Winter
Loc 1½ miles SW of Ulverston on A5087
Arch Herd/Colt

Windermere (1891)

Cleabarrow, Windermere LA23 3NB
Tel **(015394) 43123**
Mem 965
Sec KR Moffat
Pro WSM Rooke (015394) 43550
Holes 18 L 5006 yds SSS 65
Recs Am–58 P Chapman (1988)
Pro–58 D Cooper (1990)
Ladies–71 J Blaydes (1994)
V'tors H SOC
Fees £23 (£28)
Loc 1½ miles E of Bowness
Arch George Lowe

Workington (1893)

Branthwaite Road, Workington CA14 4SS
Tel **(01900) 603460**
Mem 500 125(L) 100(J)
Sec MWStG Addison
Pro A Drabble
Holes 18 L 6252 yds SSS 70
Recs Am–65 A Drabble
V'tors H SOC
Fees £17 (£22)
Loc 2 miles SE of Workington
Arch James Braid

Derbyshire

Alfreton (1892)

Oakerthorpe, Alfreton DE55 7DH
Tel **(01773) 832070**
Mem 300
Sec T McKenzie
Pro N Hallam (01773) 831901
Holes 9 L 5074 yds SSS 65
Recs Am–62 S Kyte
Pro–65 J Smith
V'tors WD–U H before 4.30pm –M after 4.30pm WE–M SOC H
Fees £13 (£17)
Loc Alfreton

Allestree Park (1949)

Public
Allestree Hall, Allestree, Derby
Tel **(01332) 550616**
Sec G Rawson (01332) 552971
Pro A Carnell
Holes 18 L 5749 yds SSS 68
Recs Am–66 A Oates
V'tors WD–U WE–booking req SOC
Fees £7.60
Loc 2 miles N of Derby on A6

Ashbourne (1910)

Clifton, Ashbourne DE6 4BN
Tel **(01335) 342078**
Mem 400
Sec NPA James (01335) 342077
Holes 9 L 5388 yds SSS 66
V'tors U SOC
Fees £14 (£18)
Loc 2 miles W of Ashbourne on A515
Arch Frank Pennink

Bakewell (1899)

Station Road, Bakewell DE4 1GB
Tel **(01629) 812307**
Mem 205 67(L) 40(J)
Sec T Turner
Pro TE Jones
Holes 9 L 5840 yds SSS 68
Recs Am–63 W Hudson
V'tors WD–U WE/BH–M
Fees £12
Loc ½ mile NE of Bakewell and A6

Blue Circle (1985)

Cement Works, Hope S30 2RP
Tel **(01433) 620317**
Mem 146
Sec DS Smith
Holes 9 L 5350 yds SSS 66
Recs Am–69 B Harper
V'tors M
Loc Hope Valley

Breadsall Priory Hotel G & CC (1976)

Moor Road, Morley, Derby DE7 6DL
Tel **(01332) 832235**
Fax **(01332) 833509**
Mem 782
Sec A Busman (Gen Mgr)
Pro A Smith (01332) 834425
Holes 18 L 6201 yds SSS 70
18 L 6028 yds SSS 69
Recs Am–66 A Thomas
Pro–66 M Glynn, DJ Russell
V'tors WD–U SOC–WD only
Fees £23 (£26)
Loc Morley, 5 miles N of Derby (A61)

Burton-on-Trent (1894)

43 Ashby Road East, Burton-on-Trent DE15 0PS
Tel **(01283) 568708 (Clubhouse)**
Mem 600
Sec D Hartley (01283) 544551
Pro G Stafford (01283) 562240
Holes 18 L 6555 yds SSS 71
Recs Am–67 DI Clarke, M Grundy
Pro–65 C Hall (1994)
V'tors M or I WD–NA before 9am or 1–2pm SOC
Fees £22 (£27)
Loc 3 miles E of Burton on A50
Arch HS Colt

Buxton & High Peak (1887)

Townend, Buxton SK17 7JB
Tel **(01298) 23453**
Mem 450
Sec JM Williams
Pro A Hoyles (01298) 23112
Holes 18 L 5954 yds SSS 69
Recs Am–66 P Anderson, P Norton
Pro–63 N Hallam
V'tors U
Fees £20 (£25)
Loc NE boundary of Buxton (A6)

Carsington Water (1994)

Pay and play
Carsington, Wirksworth
Tel **(01629) 85650**
Mem 300
Sec GWR Coleman (Mgr)
(01403) 784864
Pro To be appointed
Holes 9 L 6000yds SSS
V'tors U SOC
Fees On application
Loc 8 miles NE of Ashbourne, off B5035
Arch John Ludlow

Cavendish (1925)

Gadley Lane, Buxton SK17 6XD
Tel **(01298) 23494**
Mem 600
Sec JA Lockley
Pro P Hunstone (01298) 25052
Holes 18 L 5833 yds SSS 68
Recs Am–64 I Menzies (1992)
Pro–63 I Buckley (1988)

V'tors U H SOC–by prior arrangement with Pro
Fees £22 (£33)
Loc ¾mile W of Buxton Station. St John's Road (A53)
Arch Dr A Mackenzie

Chapel-en-le-Frith (1905)

The Cockyard, Manchester Road, Chapel-en-le-Frith, Stockport SK12 6UH
Tel **(01298) 812118**
Fax **(01298) 813943**
Mem 604
Sec JW Dranfield (01298) 813943
Pro DJ Cullen (01298) 812118
Holes 18 L 6035 yds SSS 69
V'tors U
Fees £20 (£30)
Loc 13 miles SE of Stockport, off A6 (B5470)

Chesterfield (1897)

Walton, Chesterfield S42 7LA
Tel **(01246) 279256**
Mem 590
Sec K Bradshaw
Pro M McLean (01246) 276297
Holes 18 L 6247 yds SSS 70
Recs Am–65 I Wyatt
Pro–66 K Nagle, B Hutchison
V'tors WD–U H WE–M SOC
Fees £22–£30
Loc 2 miles SW of Chesterfield on A263

Chesterfield Municipal (1934)

Public
Murray House, Crow Lane, Chesterfield S41 0EQ
Tel **(01246) 273887, (01246) 239500 (Bookings)**
Sec J Hearnshaw
Pro C Weatherhead (01246) 203960
Holes 18 L 6013 yds SSS 69
9 hole course
Pro–71 K Moss
V'tors U
Fees On application
Loc ¼mile past Chesterfield station
Mis Pitch & putt

Chevin (1894)

Duffield, Derby DE56 4EE
Tel **(01332) 841864**
Mem 500 100(L) 80(J) 70(5D)
Sec CP Elliott
Pro W Bird (01332) 841112
Holes 18 L 6057 yds SSS 69
Recs Am–65 C Radford (1987), ME Rawson (1991)
Pro–64 A Hare (1991)
V'tors WD–U WE–M SOC–WD
Fees £27
Loc 5 miles N of Derby on A6

Derby Sinfin (1923)

Public
Wilmore Road, Sinfin, Derby DE24 9HD
Tel **(01332) 766323**
Sec P Davidson
Pro A Carnell (01332) 766462
Holes 18 L 6153 yds SSS 69
Recs Am–66 R Mosley
Pro–68 C Henderson
V'tors U SOC
Fees On application
Loc 1 mile S of Derby, off A52

Erewash Valley (1905)

Stanton-by-Dale, Ilkeston DE7 4QR
Tel **(0115) 932 3258**
Fax **(0115) 932 2984**
Mem 575
Sec JA Beckett (0115) 932 2984
Pro MJ Ronan (0115) 932 4667
Holes 18 L 6492 yds SSS 71
Recs Am–67 R Claydon (1988), A Dalton (1993)
Pro–68 MJ Ronan (1981)
V'tors WE/BH–NA before noon SOC–WD
Fees £22 D–£27 (D–£27)
Loc 10 miles E of Derby, off A52. M1 Junction 25, 3 miles

Glossop & District (1894)

Sheffield Road, Glossop SK13 9PU
Tel **(01457) 865247 (Clubhouse)**
Mem 250
Sec DM Pridham
Pro G Brown (01457) 853117
Holes 11 L 5800 yds SSS 68
Recs Am–64 MA Boothroyd
Pro–68 S Sewgolum
V'tors U SOC
Fees £15 (£20)
Loc 1 mile E of Glossop, off A57

Grassmoor Golf Centre

Pay and play
North Wingfield Road, Grassmoor, Chesterfield S42 5EA
Tel **(01246) 856044**
Fax **(01246) 856200**
Mem 500
Sec M Shattock
Pro J Gallagher
Holes 18 L 5721 yds Par 69
V'tors U SOC
Fees £7.50 (£10)
Loc 2 miles S of Chesterfield on B6038. M1 Junction 29, 3 miles
Mis Floodlit driving range

Horsley Lodge (1992)

Smalley Mill Road, Horsley DE2 5BL
Tel **(01332) 780838**
Fax **(01332) 781118**
Mem 580
Sec G Johnson
Pro S Berry (01332) 781400
Holes 18 L 6400 yds SSS 71
Recs Am–71 S Hughes (1994)
V'tors U H
Fees £17 (£17)
Loc 4 miles NE of Derby. M1 Junction 28
Mis Driving range
Arch GM White

Ilkeston (1929)

Public
Peewit West End Drive, Ilkeston DE7 5GH
Tel **(0115) 930 4550**
Holes 9 L 4116 yds SSS 60
V'tors U SOC–WD
Fees £6
Loc ½ mile E of Ilkeston

Kedleston Park (1947)

Kedleston, Quarndon, Derby DE22 5JD
Tel **(01332) 840035**
Mem 797
Sec K Wilson
Pro J Hetherington (01332) 841685
Holes 18 L 6585 yds SSS 71
Recs Am–65 M Betteridge
Pro–65 K Waters
V'tors U
Fees £25 (£35)
Loc 4 miles N of Derby. National Trust signs to Kedleston Hall

Matlock (1907)

Chesterfield Road, Matlock DE4 5LF
Tel **(01629) 582191**
Mem 382 69(L) 60(J)
Sec AJ Box
Pro M Whithorn (01629) 584934
Holes 18 L 5801 yds SSS 68
Recs Am–64 N Furniss
Pro–65 W Bird
V'tors WD–U exc 12.30–1.30pm–NA WE/BH–M SOC–WD
Fees D–£25 W–£100
Loc 1½ miles NE of Matlock (A632)

Maywood (1990)

Rushy Lane, Risley, Derby DE7 3ST
Tel **(0115) 939 2306**
Mem 500
Sec P Moon (Prop)
Pro None
Holes 18 L 6424 yds SSS 71
Recs Am–76 M Long (1992)
V'tors WD–U before 4pm WE–NA SOC
Fees £15 (£20)
Loc Between Nottingham and Derby. M1 Junction 25

Mickleover (1923)

Uttoxeter Road, Mickleover DE3 5AD
Tel **(01332) 513339 (Clubhouse)**
Mem 760
Sec D Rodgers (01332) 512092
Pro T Coxon (01332) 518662
Holes 18 L 5708 yds SSS 68
Recs Am–64 CRJ Ibbotson
Pro–63 A Skingle
V'tors U SOC–Tues & Thurs
Fees £20 (£25)
Loc 3 miles W of Derby on A516/B5020

For list of abbreviations see page 435

Ormonde Fields (1906)
Nottingham Road, Codnor, Ripley DE5 9RG
Tel **(01773) 742987**
Mem 660
Sec RN Walters
Pro P Buttifant
Holes 18 L 6011 yds SSS 69
V'tors U SOC
Fees On application
Loc A610 Ripley to Nottingham road. M1 Junction 26, 5 miles

Pastures (1969)
Pastures Hospital, Mickleover DE3 5DQ
Tel **(01332) 513921 Ext 348**
Mem 320
Sec S McWilliams
Holes 9 L 5005 yds SSS 64
Recs Am–62 C Whyatt (1989)
V'tors M SOC–WD
Loc 4 miles W of Derby

Shirland (1977)
Lower Delves, Shirland DE5 6AU
Tel **(01773) 834935**
Mem 350
Sec G Brassington (01246) 852816
Pro NB Hallam (01773) 834935
Holes 18 L 6072 yds SSS 70
Recs Am–67 R Skingle (1990) Pro–71 NB Hallam (1987)
V'tors WD–U WE–U after 3pm SOC
Fees £15 (£20) (1994)
Loc 1 mile N of Alfreton, off A61 by Shirland Church

Sickleholme (1898)
Bamford, Sheffield S30 2BH
Tel **(01433) 651306**
Mem 250 100(L) 72(J)
Sec PH Taylor (Mgr)
Pro PH Taylor
Holes 18 L 6064 yds SSS 69
Recs Am–63 IL Fletcher, DRM Kinsey Pro–65 AP Highfield
V'tors U exc Wed am
Fees £22 (£30)
Loc W of Sheffield, between Hathersage and Hope (A625)

Stanedge (1934)
Walton Hay Farm, Chesterfield S45 0LW
Tel **(01246) 566156**
Mem 300
Sec W Tyzack (01246) 276568
Holes 9 L 4867 yds SSS 64
Recs Am–64 W Steel Jr (1982), J Weston-Taylor (1991) Pro–65 A Skingle (1987)
V'tors WD–U before 2pm –M after 2pm Sat–M Sun–NA before 4pm –M after 4pm
Fees £15
Loc 5 miles SW of Chesterfield, off B5057

Devon

Ashbury (1991)
Fowley Cross, Okehampton EX20 4NL
Tel **(01837) 55453**
Fax **(01837) 55468**
Mem 100
Sec DJ Fensom
Holes 18 L 5839 yds SSS 68 18 hole Par 3 course
V'tors U
Fees £12 (£15) Par 3–£6 (£8)
Loc 4 miles W of Okehampton, off A3079

Axe Cliff (1894)
Squires Lane, Axmouth, Seaton EX12 4AB
Tel **(01297) 24371**
Mem 400
Sec Mrs D Rogers
Pro M Dack
Holes 18 L 5057 yds SSS 65
Recs Am–65 P Cricard
V'tors U H SOC
Fees £18 (£22)
Loc Nr Yacht Club at Axmouth Bridge

Bigbury (1923)
Bigbury, Kingsbridge TQ7 4BB
Tel **(01548) 810207**
Mem 850
Sec BJ Perry (01548) 810557
Pro S Lloyd (01548) 810412
Holes 18 L 6076 yds SSS 69
Recs Am–65 CS Yeoman Pro–65 R Tuddenham, S Little
V'tors I H SOC
Fees D–£20 (£24)
Loc 15 miles SE of Plymouth

Chulmleigh (1976)
Leigh Road, Chulmleigh EX18 7BL
Tel **(01769) 580519**
Fax **(01769) 580519**
Mem 150
Sec PN Callow
Holes Summer 18 L 1450 yds SSS 54 Winter 9 L 2372 yds SSS 56
Recs Am–52 H Gillibrand (1989), P Cook (1991)
V'tors U
Fees £5.50 D–£10
Loc 1 mile N of Chulmleigh, off A377
Arch John Goodban

Churston (1890)
Churston, Brixham TQ5 0LA
Tel **(01803) 842218**
Fax **(01803) 845738**
Mem 640
Sec DG Daniell (01803) 842751
Pro R Penfold
Holes 18 L 6201 yds SSS 70
Recs Am–64 RHP Knott Pro–67 JM Green
V'tors H exc Tues am–NA
Fees £22 (£27)
Loc 5 miles S of Torquay
Arch HS Colt

Clovelly G & CC (1991)
East Yagland, Wolsery, Bideford EX39 5RA
Tel **(01237) 431442**
Fax **(01237) 431734**
Mem 130
Sec AMJ Dando
Holes 9 L 5641 yds SSS 67
V'tors U SOC
Fees On application
Loc 6 miles S of Clovelly, off A39
Arch John Hepplewhite

Dainton Park (1992)
Totnes Road, Ipplepen, Newton Abbot TQ12 5TN
Tel **(01803) 813812**
Mem 500
Sec D Wood
Pro R Jessop
Holes 18 L 6210 yds SSS 70
V'tors U SOC
Fees £12 (£15)
Loc 2 miles S of Newton Abbot on A381
Mis Driving range
Arch Adrian Stiff

Dartmouth G & CC (1992)
Blackawton, Totnes TQ9 7DG
Tel **(01803) 712686**
Fax **(01803) 712628**
Sec C Dale (Gen Mgr)
Pro P Laugher (Golf Dir) (01803) 712650
Holes Ch'ship 18 L 7191 yds SSS 74 Club 9 L 2583 yds SSS 33
V'tors WD–U phone first WE–H SOC
Fees Ch'ship £26 (£32) Club £10 (£15)
Loc 4 miles NE of Dartmouth on A3122
Mis Driving range
Arch Jeremy Pern

Dinnaton (1989)
Ivybridge PL21 9HU
Tel **(01752) 892512/892452**
Fax **(01752) 698334**
Mem 300
Sec B Rimes
Pro D Ridyard (01752) 691288
Holes 9 L 4100 yds SSS 59 9 hole course
V'tors U SOC
Fees D–£10 (D–£12.50)
Loc 12 miles SE of Plymouth, off A38/B3213
Mis Floodlit driving range
Arch Pink/Cotton

Downes Crediton (1976)
Hookway, Crediton EX17 3PT
Tel **(01363) 773991**
Mem 720
Sec Mrs P Humphries (01363) 773025
Pro H Finch (01363) 774464

Holes 18 L 5958 yds SSS 69
V'tors H SOC
Fees £16 (£22)
Loc 2 miles S of Crediton, off A377

East Devon (1902)

North View Road, Budleigh Salterton EX9 6DQ

Tel **(01395) 443370**
Mem 850
Sec JC Tebbet (01395) 443370
Pro T Underwood (01395) 445195
Holes 18 L 6214 yds SSS 70
Recs Am–65 R Winchester (1987), R Martin (1992)
Pro–64 G Ryall (1990)
V'tors H SOC–Thurs only
Fees £25 (£30)
Loc 12 miles SE of Exeter

Elfordleigh Hotel G & CC (1932)

Colebrook, Plympton, Plymouth PL7 5EB

Tel **(01752) 336428**
Fax **(01752) 344581**
Mem 300
Sec Mrs P Parfitt (01752) 348425
Pro A Rickard
Holes 9 L 5664 yds SSS 67
Recs Am–65 A Moon (1992)
Ladies–78 E McLarty (1991)
V'tors WD–U WE–phone first
Fees £15 (£20)
Loc 4 miles E of Plymouth

Exeter G & CC (1895)

Countess Wear, Exeter EX2 7AE

Tel **(01392) 874139**
Fax **(01392) 874139**
Mem 850
Sec KJ Ham
Pro M Rowett (01392) 875028
Holes 18 L 6000 yds SSS 69
Recs Am–63 G Milne (1988)
Pro–62 I Sparks (1990)
V'tors WD–U WE–I SOC–Thurs
Fees £22
Loc 4 miles SE of Exeter
Arch James Braid

Fingle Glen (1992)

Tedburn St Mary, Exeter EX6 6AF

Tel **(01647) 61817**
Fax **(01647) 61135**
Mem 450
Pro S Gould
Holes 9 L 2466 yds SSS 63
Recs Am–65 J Breading (1994)
Pro–63 R Troake (1992)
V'tors U SOC
Fees 18 holes–£10 (£14)
9 holes–£7 (£8)
Loc 5 miles W of Exeter on A30
Mis Driving range

Hele Park Golf Centre

Pay and play

Ashburton Road, Newton Abbot TQ12 6JN

Tel **(01626) 336060**
Pro J Langmead
Holes 9 L 2469 yds SSS 65
V'tors U
Fees £8.50 (£11.50)
Loc W of Newton Abbot on A383
Mis Driving range

Holsworthy (1937)

Kilatree, Holsworthy EX22 6XU

Tel **(01409) 253177**
Mem 650
Sec B Megson
Pro (01409) 254771
Holes 18 L 6062 yds SSS 69
Recs Am–69 D Vanstone (1994)
Pro–67 G Ryall, R Troake (1987)
V'tors WD–U Sun–U after 2.30pm
Fees £15 (£20)
Loc 1 mile W of Holsworthy. 7 miles E of Bude

Honiton (1896)

Middlehills, Honiton EX14 8TR

Tel **(01404) 44422**
Fax **(01404) 42943**
Mem 800
Sec JL Carter
Pro A Cave (01404) 42943
Holes 18 L 5940 yds SSS 68
Recs Am–67 A March (1992)
Pro–67 D Sheppard, T McSherry (1993)
Ladies–75 A Davies (1990)
V'tors U (recognised club member) SOC
Fees On application
Loc 2 miles S of Honiton

Hurdwick (1990)

Tavistock Hamlets, Tavistock PL19 8PZ

Tel **(01822) 612746**
Mem 175
Sec Maj RW Cullen (Mgr)
Holes 18 L 4861 yds Par 67
V'tors U SOC
Fees £14 D–£20 (£16 D–£25)
Loc 1 mile N of Tavistock, on Brentor Church road
Arch Hawtree/Bartlett

Ilfracombe (1892)

Hele Bay, Ilfracombe EX34 9RT

Tel **(01271) 862176**
Fax **(01271) 867731**
Mem 648
Sec RC Beer
Pro D Hoare (01271) 863328
Holes 18 L 5893 yds SSS 69
Recs Am–66 PA Boot (1993)
V'tors H SOC WD–NA 12–2pm WE/BH–U after 10am –NA 12–2pm
Fees £17 (£20) 5D–£75
Loc 2 miles E of Ilfracombe, towards Combe Martin
Arch TK Weir

Libbaton (1990)

High Bickington, Umberleigh EX37 9BS

Tel **(01769) 60269**
Mem 475
Sec JH Brough
Pro JN Phillips (01769) 60167
Holes 18 L 5812 yds SSS 68
V'tors U SOC
Fees £12 (£15)
Loc 1 mile S of High Bickington on B3217. M5 Junction 27
Mis Floodlit driving range

Manor House Hotel (1929)

Moretonhampstead TQ13 8RE

Tel **(01647) 40355**
Fax **(01647) 40961**
Mem 250
Sec R Lewis
Pro R Lewis
Holes 18 L 6016 yds SSS 69
Recs Am–68 G Milne (1989)
Pro–65 G Emerson (1985)
V'tors U H SOC
Fees £22.50 (£28)
Loc 15 miles SW of Exeter on B3212. M5 Junction 31
Mis Driving range
Arch JF Abercromby

Mortehoe & Woolacombe (1992)

Easewell, Mortehoe, Ilfracombe

Tel **(01271) 870225**
Holes 9 L 4852 yds SSS 64
V'tors U
Fees 9 holes–£6 18 holes–£10
Loc E of Mortehoe village

Newton Abbot (1930)

Newton Abbot TQ12 6QQ

Tel **(01626) 52460**
Mem 886
Sec R Smith
Pro M Craig (01626) 62078
Holes 18 L 5899 yds SSS 68
Recs Am–63 M Pym (1989)
Pro–67 B Barnes (1977)
V'tors H SOC–Thurs
Fees D–£22
Loc Stover, 3 miles N of Newton Abbot on A382
Arch James Braid

Okehampton (1913)

Okehampton EX20 1EF

Tel **(01837) 52113**
Mem 500
Sec CS Hicks
Pro P Blundell (01837) 53541
Holes 18 L 5300 yds SSS 67
Recs Am–65 M Moore
Pro–H Finch
V'tors H SOC
Fees On application
Loc S boundary of Okehampton

Padbrook Park (1992)

Pay and play
Cullompton EX15 1RU
Tel **(01884) 38286**
Fax **(01804) 34359**
Mem 450
Sec R Chard (Mgr)
Pro S Adwick (01884) 820805
Holes 9 L 6108 yds SSS 70
V'tors U SOC–WD
Fees 18 holes–£10 (£16)
9 holes–£7 (£8)
Loc 10 miles W of Exeter. M5 Junction 28, 1 mile
Arch Bob Sandow

Royal North Devon (1864)

Golf Links Road, Westward Ho! EX39 1HD
Tel **(01237) 473824**
Fax **(01237) 423456**
Mem 1000
Sec JE Linaker (Gen Mgr) (01237) 473817
Pro G Johnston (01237) 477598
Holes 18 L 6662 yds SSS 72
Recs Am–66 D Boughey
Pro–66 P Dawson, KDG Nagle, MF Foster
Ladies–69 P Johnson
V'tors U H
Fees £22 D–£26
Loc 2 miles N of Bideford (A39)
Arch Tom Morris

Saunton (1897)

Saunton, Braunton EX33 1LG
Tel **(01271) 812436**
Fax **(01271) 814241**
Mem 1160
Sec PR Stevens
Pro JA McGhee (01271) 812013
Holes East 18 L 6708 yds SSS 73
West 18 L 6356 yds SSS 71
Recs East Am–65 M Treleaven (1993)
Pro–69 B Huggett
West Am–68 PH Watts (1991)
Pro–69 P Berry
V'tors U H
Fees D–£28 (D–£33) (1994)
Loc 6 miles W of Barnstaple
Arch Fowler/Pennink

Sidmouth (1889)

Cotmaton Road, Sidmouth EX10 8SX
Tel **(01395) 513023**
Mem 850
Sec IM Smith (0395) 513451
Pro M Kemp (0395) 516407
Holes 18 L 5109 yds SSS 65
Recs Am–59 N Winchester
Pro–62 J Robinson
V'tors U SOC
Fees £18
Loc 1/2 mile W of Sidmouth. 12 miles SE of M5 Junction 30

Sparkwell (1993)

Pay and play
Sparkwell, Plymouth PL7 5DF
Tel **(01752) 837219**
Fax **(01752) 837219**
Mem 60
Sec G Axworthy
Holes 9 L 5772 yds SSS 68
V'tors U SOC
Fees 18 holes–£8 (£10)
9 holes–£5 (£6)
Loc 8 miles NE of Plymouth. A38 Plympton Junction
Mis 9 hole pitch & putt
Arch J Gabb

Staddon Heights (1904)

Plymstock, Plymouth PL9 9SP
Tel **(01752) 402475**
Mem 740
Sec MG Holliday
Pro (01752) 492630
Holes 18 L 5861 yds SSS 68
Recs Am–64 R Clark, D Roberts
Pro–67 J Langmead
V'tors WE–H SOC–WD
Fees D–£15 (D–£20)
Loc SE Plymouth

Tavistock (1890)

Down Road, Tavistock PL19 9AQ
Tel **(01822) 612049**
Fax **(01822) 612344**
Mem 700
Sec BG Steer (01822) 612344
Pro R Cade (01822) 612316
Holes 18 L 6250 yds SSS 70
Recs Am–66 MG Symons (1981)
Pro–69 S Chadwick, N Bicknell
Ladies–72 D Gosling (1989), E Fields (1991)
V'tors U SOC–WD
Fees £18 (£23)
Loc Whitchurch Down

Teignmouth (1924)

Teignmouth TQ14 9NY
Tel **(01626) 773614**
Mem 900
Sec D Holloway (01626) 774194
Pro P Ward (01626) 772894
Holes 18 L 6227 yds SSS 70
Recs Am–65 JH Laidler (1980)
Pro–66 P Millhouse (1987)
V'tors WD–H (recognised club member) WE–by appointment SOC–WD
Fees £22 (£25)
Loc 2 miles N of Teignmouth on B3192
Arch Dr A Mackenzie

Thurlestone (1897)

Thurlestone, Kingsbridge TQ7 3NZ
Tel **(01548) 560405**
Mem 700
Sec R Marston
Pro N Whitley (01548) 560715
Holes 18 L 6340 yds Par 71 SSS 70
Recs Am–66 RP Knott
Pro–67 PJ Yeo
V'tors I or H
Fees £24 W–£90 (1994)
Loc 5 miles W of Kingsbridge, off A379

Tiverton (1932)

Post Hill, Tiverton EX16 4NE
Tel **(01884) 252114 (Clubhouse)**
Mem 475 130(L) 45(J)
Sec MJ Lowry (Sec/Mgr) (01884) 252187
Pro D Sheppard (01884) 254836
Holes 18 L 6236 yds SSS 71
Recs Am–65 SC Waddington
Pro–70 A Moore
Ladies–70 C Trew (1977)
V'tors H
Fees On application
Loc 5 miles W of M5 Junction 27. 1 1/2 miles E of Tiverton on B3391
Arch Braid/Cotton

Torquay (1910)

Petitor Road, St Marychurch, Torquay TQ1 4QF
Tel **(01803) 314591**
Fax **(01803) 316116**
Mem 800
Sec BG Long
Pro M Ruth (01803) 329113
Holes 18 L 6198 yds SSS 70
Recs Am–66 M Pougiouros (1990)
Pro–65 G Emerson (1992)
V'tors H SOC
Fees £20 (£25)
Loc 2 miles N of Torquay

Torrington (1895)

Weare Trees, Torrington EX38 7EZ
Tel **(01805) 622229**
Mem 440
Sec GSC Green (Hon)
Holes 9 L 4419 yds Par 64 SSS 62
Recs Am–58 DL George
V'tors U exc Sun am–NA SOC
Fees £10 (£10)
Loc 1 mile W of Torrington on Weare Gifford road

Warren (1892)

Dawlish EX7 0NF
Tel **(01626) 862255**
Mem 650
Sec PG Tomlinson
Pro AJ Naldrett (01626) 864002
Holes 18 L 5968 yds SSS 69
Recs Am–65 J Langmead (1987)
V'tors H SOC
Fees £21 (£24) W–£100
Loc 1 1/2 miles E of Dawlish

Woodbury Park (1992)

Woodbury Castle, Woodbury EX5 1JJ
Tel **(01395) 233382**
Fax **(01395) 233384**
Mem 340
Sec B Warren
Pro A Richards

For list of abbreviations see page 435

Holes 18 L 6707 yds SSS 72
9 L 4582 yds SSS 62
Pro–69 A Richards,
J Langmead, B Keatch,
H Barrell, S Little (1993)
V'tors U
Fees 18 hole:£20 (£25)
9 hole:£8 (£9)
Loc 10 miles E of Exeter on A3052. M5 Junction 30, 6 miles
Mis Driving range
Arch J Hamilton Stutt

Wrangaton (1895)

Golf Links Road, Wrangaton, South Brent TQ10 9HJ
Tel **(01364) 73229**
Mem 600
Sec B Cooke
Pro A Whitehead (01364) 72161
Holes 18 L 6040 yds SSS 69
Recs Am–66 D Marsh (1994)
V'tors H SOC
Fees £16 (£20)
Loc Dartmoor, 10 miles SW of Ashburton
Arch Donald Steel

Yelverton (1904)

Golf Links Road, Yelverton PL20 6BN
Tel **(01822) 853618**
Mem 700
Sec RJ Tibbs (01822) 852824
Pro T McSherry (01822) 853593
Holes 18 L 6363 yds SSS 70
Recs Am–65 DWJ Wright (1990)
V'tors H SOC
Fees D–£20
Loc 6 miles N of Plymouth on A386
Arch Herbert Fowler

Dorset

The Ashley Wood (1896)

Tarrant Rawston, Blandford Forum DT11 9HN
Tel **(01258) 452253**
Fax **(01258) 452253**
Mem 570
Sec P Lillford
Pro S Taylor (01258) 480379
Holes 18 L 6230 yds Par 71 SSS 70
Recs Am–69 R Pullen (1994)
Pro–70 S Taylor (1994)
V'tors U SOC
Fees £17 (£25)
Loc 1½ miles SE of Blandford
Arch Patrick Tallack

Bournemouth & Meyrick Park (1890)

Pay and play
Central Drive, Meyrick Park, Bournemouth BH2 6LH
Tel **(01202) 290307, (01202) 290862 (Bookings)**
Mem 400
Sec Maj (Rtd) JR Wood
Pro W Butcher
Holes 18 L 5637 yds Par 68
Recs Am–63
Pro–62 D Ray (1994)
V'tors U
Fees £10 (£11)
Loc ½mile behind Town Hall, Bournemouth
Arch Dunn(1894)/Colt(1925)

Bridport & West Dorset (1891)

East Cliff, West Bay, Bridport DT6 4EP
Tel **(01308) 422597**
Mem 700
Sec PJ Ridler (01308) 421095
Pro D Parsons (01308) 421491
Holes 18 L 5246 yds SSS 66
Recs Am–61 M Rees (1990)
Pro–66 S Bishop (1980),
R Crockford (1983)
V'tors WD/Sat–U after 9.30am
Sun–U after noon SOC
Fees £18 After 2pm–£12
Loc 1½ miles S of Bridport at West Bay
Mis 9 hole pitch & putt course (summer)

Broadstone (1898)

Wentworth Drive, Broadstone BH18 8DQ
Tel **(01202) 692595**
Fax **(01202) 692595**
Mem 700
Sec C Robinson
Pro N Tokely (01202) 692835
Holes 18 L 6315 yds SSS 70
Recs Am–66 JH Nash (1988),
LS James (1992)
Pro–66 R Davies (1992),
J Langmead (1994)
V'tors WD–H after 9.30am
WE/BH–restricted SOC–WD
Fees £27 D–£33
Loc 4 miles N of Poole
Arch Dunn(1898)/Colt(1925)

Bulbury Woods (1989)

Halls Road, Lytchett Matravers, Poole BH16 6EP
Tel **(01929) 459574**
Fax **(01929) 459000**
Mem 600
Sec P Dickinson (Sec/Mgr)
Pro J Sharkey (Golf Dir)
Holes 18 L 6020 yds SSS 69
Pro–63 D Read (1991)
V'tors U SOC–WD
Fees £15 D–£25 (£18 D–£30)
Loc 3 miles NW of Poole, off A35 to Bere Regis
Arch John Sharkey

Came Down (1896)

Came Down, Dorchester DT2 8NR
Tel **(01305) 812531**
Fax **(01305) 813494**
Mem 700
Sec DE Matthews (Mgr)
(01305) 813494
Pro B Preston (01305) 812670
Holes 18 L 6244 yds SSS 71
Recs Am–66 A Louden (1993)
Pro–68 M McKenna (1975)
V'tors H Sun am–NA SOC
Fees £20 (£25)
Loc 2 miles S of Dorchester
Arch Taylor/Colt

Canford School

Canford School, Wimborne BH21 3AD
Tel **(01202) 841254**
Fax **(01202) 881009**
Mem 300
Sec C Jervis BEd
Holes 9 L 5918 yds SSS 68
V'tors M SOC
Fees £8
Loc 2 miles SE of Wimborne, off A341

Chedington Court (1991)

South Perrott, Beaminster DT8 3HU
Tel **(01935) 891413**
Fax **(01935) 891442**
Mem 275
Sec JPH Chapman (Mgr),
R Gudge (Sec)
Pro J Bloxham
Holes 9 L 6754 yds SSS 72
Recs Am–73 S Fussell (1994)
V'tors U SOC
Fees 18 holes–£11 (£13)
9 holes–£6.50 (£8)
Loc 4 miles SE of Crewkerne on A356
Mis Extension to 18 holes June 1995
Arch Chapman/Hemstock

Christchurch (1977)

Barrack Road, Iford, Christchurch BH23 2BA
Tel **(01202) 473817**
Mem 300
Sec J Lucas
Pro PL Troth
Holes 9 L 4330 yds SSS 61
Recs Am–63 P Holbert
V'tors U
Fees £5.40 (£6.10)
Loc Bournemouth/Christchurch boundary
Mis Driving range

Crane Valley (1992)

The Clubhouse, Verwood BH31 7LE
Tel **(01202) 814088**
Fax **(01202) 813407**
Mem 500
Sec M Wilson (Man Dir),
A Blackwell (Mgr)
Pro A Egford
Holes 18 L 6421 yds SSS 71
9 L 2030 yds SSS 60
Recs Am–72 B McCarthy (1993)
Pro–72 G Emerson (1993)
V'tors H SOC 9 hole–U
Fees 18 hole:£17 (£22)
9 hole:£5.50 (£6.50)
Loc Off B3081 Cranborne road
Mis Floodlit driving range
Arch Donald Steel

Dudsbury (1992)

Christchurch Road, Ferndown BH22 8ST

Tel **(01202) 593499**
Fax **(01202) 594555**
Sec K Legg
Pro K Spurgeon (01202) 594488
Holes 18 L 6650 yds SSS 72
V'tors U
Fees On application
Loc 3 miles N of Bournemouth (B3073)
Mis Driving range. Academy course
Arch Donald Steel

East Dorset (1978)

Hyde, Wareham BH20 7NT

Tel **(01929) 472244/472272** (Bookings)
Fax **(01929) 471294**
Mem 730
Sec BR Lee (Gen Mgr)
Pro K Thomas (01929) 472272
Holes Lakeland 18 L 7027 yds SSS 75; Woodland 18 L 4887 yds SSS 64
Recs Am–71 L James (1992)
V'tors U H SOC
Fees Lakeland–£20 (£25) Woodland–£14 (£18)
Loc 5 miles S of Bere Regis, off Puddletown road
Mis Driving range
Arch Martin Hawtree

Ferndown (1923)

119 Golf Links Road, Ferndown BH22 8BU

Tel **(01202) 874602**
Fax **(01202) 873926**
Mem 700
Sec E Robertson (Mgr) (01202) 874602
Pro IAB Parker (01202) 873825
Holes 18 L 6452 yds SSS 71
9 L 5604 yds SSS 68
Recs Old Am–66 JHA Leggett
Pro–68 DN Sewell
New Am–67 G Howell
Pro–68 DN Sewell
V'tors WD–I H after 9.30am SOC–Tues & Fri
Fees Old £35 (£40) New £15 (£20)
Loc 6 miles N of Bournemouth
Arch Harold Hilton

Halstock (1988)

Pay and play
Common Lane, Halstock BA22 9SF

Tel **(01935) 891689**
Mem 200
Sec LR Church (Mgr)
Pro T Lovegrove
Holes 18 L 4351 yds Par 65 SSS 63
Recs Am–65 H Stallard (1994)
V'tors U SOC
Fees £9.50 (£11.50)
Loc 6 miles S of Yeovil, off A37
Mis Driving range

Highcliffe Castle (1913)

107 Lymington Road, Highcliffe-on-Sea, Christchurch BH23 4LA

Tel **(01425) 272953**
Mem 350 100(L) 50(J)
Sec DA Chidley (01425) 272210
Pro R Crockford (01425) 276640
Holes 18 L 4686 yds SSS 63
Recs Am–58 S Jenkins (1986)
Pro–59 M Butcher (1988)
V'tors H SOC
Fees £18 (£27)
Loc 8 miles E of Bournemouth

Isle of Purbeck (1892)

Studland BH19 3AB

Tel **(01929) 44361**
Fax **(01929) 44501**
Mem 600
Sec Mrs J Robinson (Man Dir)
Pro K Spurgeon (01929) 44354
Holes 18 L 6283 yds SSS 71
9 L 2022 yds SSS 30
Recs Am–67 N Holman
Pro–72 K Sparkes
V'tors U H SOC
Fees On application
Loc 3 miles N of Swanage on B3351

Knighton Heath (1976)

Francis Avenue, West Howe, Bournemouth BH11 8NX

Tel **(01202) 572633**
Fax **(01202) 590774**
Mem 700
Sec R Bestwick
Pro Miss J Miles (01202) 578275
Holes 18 L 5987 yds SSS 69
Recs Am–64 H McCann (1990), N Tanswell (1991)
Pro–64 A Beal (1990)
Ladies–69 J Brown (1990)
V'tors WD–H after 9.30am WE–M
Fees On application
Loc 3 miles N of Poole, at junction of A348/A3049

Lyme Regis (1893)

Timber Hill, Lyme Regis DT7 3HQ

Tel **(01297) 442963, (01297) 442043 (Steward)**
Mem 750
Sec RG Fry (01297) 442963
Pro A Black (01297) 443822
Holes 18 L 6220 yds SSS 70
Recs Am–66 MR Searle, R Clapp (1994)
Pro–65 D Driver (1991)
V'tors H WD–U after 9.30am (1.30pm Thurs) Sun–U after noon SOC
Fees £24 After 2pm–£20
Loc Between Lyme Regis and Charmouth, off A3502/A35

Lyons Gate (1991)

Lyons Gate Farm, Lyons Gate, Dorchester DT2 7AZ

Tel **(01300) 345239**
Mem 125
Sec TH Wood
Pro T Lovegrove
Holes 9 L 2100 yds SSS 60
V'tors U SOC
Fees 18 holes–£7.50 9 holes–£4.50
Loc Middle Marsh, 12 miles N of Dorchester (A352)
Arch Ken Abel

The Mid Dorset (1990)

Belchalwell, Blandford Forum DT11 0EG

Tel **(01258) 861386**
Fax **(01258) 860656**
Mem 350
Sec D Astill (Mgr)
Holes 18 L 6500 yds SSS 71
V'tors U SOC
Fees £18 (£25)
Loc Between Okeford Fitzpaine and Ibberton
Arch D Astill

Moors Valley (1989)

Public
Horton Road, Ringwood BH24 2ET

Tel **(01425) 479776**
Fax **(01425) 472057**
Sec K Hockey (Golf Dir)
Holes 18 L 6270 yds SSS 70
V'tors U
Fees £8 (£10.50)
Loc 4 miles SW of Ringwood, off A31
Mis Driving range
Arch Martin Hawtree

Parkstone (1910)

Links Road, Parkstone, Poole BH14 9JU

Tel **(01202) 707138**
Fax **(01202) 707138**
Mem 500 160(L) 50(J)
Sec AS Kinnear
Pro M Thomas (01202) 708092
Holes 18 L 6250 yds SSS 70
Recs Am–65 RA Latham, T Spence
Pro–63 P Alliss
V'tors H WD–NA before 9.30am and 12.30–2.10pm WE–NA before 9.45am and 12.30–2.30pm
Fees £25 D–£34 (£30 D–£40)
Loc 3 miles W of Bournemouth, off A35
Mis Driving range
Arch W Park Jr/Braid

Queens Park (1905)

Public
Queens Park West Drive, Queens Park, Bournemouth BH8 9BY

Tel **(01202) 302611/396198** (Bookings)
Mem 490
Sec MJ Poole
Pro R Hill
Holes 18 L 6072 yds SSS 72
Recs Am–69 M Butcher
Pro–66 A Caygill, H Boyle
V'tors U SOC
Fees £11.40
Loc 2 miles NE of Bournemouth
Mis Closed Sun pm

For list of abbreviations see page 435

Riversmeet Par Three

Stony Lane South, Christchurch BH23 1HW

Tel **(01202) 473912/477987**
Holes 18 L 1650 yds Par 27
V'tors U
Fees On application
Loc 2 miles W of Bournemouth

Sherborne (1894)

Clatcombe, Sherborne DT9 4RN

Tel **(01935) 812475**
Fax **(01935) 814431**
Sec Mrs JMC Guy (01935) 814431
Pro S Wright (01935) 812274
Holes 18 L 5949 yds SSS 68
Recs Am–63 AW Lawrence (1994)
Pro–63 M Thomas
V'tors H
Fees £20 (£25)
Loc 1 mile N of Sherborne

Solent Meads Par Three

Public
Rolls Drive, Hengistbury Head, Bournemouth

Tel **(01202) 420795**
Holes 18 L 2325 yds Par 54
V'tors U
Fees On application
Loc Hengistbury Head, S of Christchurch
Mis Driving range

Sturminster Marshall (1992)

Pay and play
Moor Lane, Sturminster Marshall BH21 4AH

Tel **(01258) 858444**
Mem 530
Sec K Iball
Pro R Tuddenham
Holes 9 L 4650 yds SSS 63
V'tors U SOC
Fees 18 holes–£8 9 holes–£5
Loc 8 miles N of Poole, off A31

Wareham (1924)

Sandford Road, Wareham BH20 4DH

Tel **(01929) 554147**
Mem 600
Sec Maj JL Holloway
Pro None
Holes 18 L 5603 yds SSS 67
Recs Am–66 K Knott (1993)
V'tors WD–H 9.30am–5pm WE–M SOC
Fees D–£15
Loc 1 mile NE of Wareham, on A351
Arch C Whitcombe

Weymouth (1909)

Links Road, Weymouth DT4 0PF

Tel **(01305) 773981**
Mem 750
Sec DA Frost
Pro D Lochrie (01305) 773997
Holes 18 L 6035 yds SSS 69
Recs Am–63 MJ Watson (1987)
Pro–60 G Emerson (1993)
Ladies–72 T Loveys (1988)
V'tors H SOC–Tues & Thurs
Fees £20 (£26)
Loc A354, off Manor roundabout
Arch Braid/Hamilton Stutt

Durham

Barnard Castle (1898)

Harmire Road, Barnard Castle DL12 8QN

Tel **(01833) 38355**
Mem 700
Pro D Pearce (01833) 31980
Holes 18 L 5838 yds SSS 68
Recs Am–65 M Porter (1984), J Egglestone, R Beadle (1990)
Pro–63 P Harrison (1990)
V'tors U SOC
Fees £15 D–£18 (£24)
Loc N boundary of Barnard Castle on B6278

Beamish Park (1950)

Beamish, Stanley DH9 0RH

Tel **(0191) 370 1382**
Mem 520
Sec L Gilbert (0191) 370 1382
Pro C Cole (0191) 370 1984
Holes 18 L 6205 yds SSS 70
Recs Am–67 A Stewart
V'tors WD/Sat–U before 4pm Sun–NA SOC
Fees £16 (£24)
Loc Beamish, nr Stanley

Bishop Auckland (1894)

High Plains, Durham Road, Bishop Auckland DL14 8DL

Tel **(01388) 602198**
Mem 840
Sec G Thatcher (01388) 663648
Pro D Skiffington (01388) 661618
Holes 18 L 6420 yds SSS 71
Recs Am–64 G Border (1994)
Pro–65 P Harrison
V'tors H (closed Good Friday and Christmas Day)
Fees £20 D–£24 (£26)
Loc 1/2 mile NE of Bishop Auckland

Blackwell Grange (1930)

Briar Close, Blackwell, Darlington DL3 8QX

Tel **(01325) 464464**
Mem 650
Sec F Hewitson (Hon) (01325) 464458
Pro R Givens (01325) 462088
Holes 18 L 5621 yds SSS 67
Recs Am–65 L McCavanagh
Pro–63 M Gregson
V'tors U exc Wed 11am–2.30pm–NA Sat–booking only. Sun–comps in progress SOC
Fees £16 D–£22 (£20)
Loc 1 mile S of Darlington on A66
Arch Frank Pennink

Brancepeth Castle (1924)

Brancepeth Village, Durham DH7 8EA

Tel **(0191) 378 0075**
Fax **(0191) 378 3835**
Mem 768 118(L) 74(J)
Sec JT Ross
Pro D Howdon (0191) 378 0183
Holes 18 L 6415 yds SSS 71
Recs Am–64 G Boardman (1992)
Pro–64 B Rumney (1990)
V'tors SOC–WD WE–NA
Fees £24 (£30)
Loc 5 miles W of Durham on A690
Arch HS Colt

Chester-Le-Street (1909)

Lumley Park, Chester-Le-Street DH3 4NS

Tel **(0191) 388 3218**
Mem 400 130(L) 90(J)
Sec WB Dodds
Pro A Hartley (0191) 389 0157
Holes 18 L 6437 yds SSS 71
Recs Am–67 SJ Watson, DH Foreman
V'tors WD–H after 9.30am –NA 12–1.30pm WE–NA before 10.30am or 12–2pm
Fees £20 (£25)
Loc E of Chester-Le-Street
Arch JH Taylor

Consett & District (1911)

Elmfield Road, Consett DH8 5NN

Tel **(01207) 502186**
Mem 650
Sec J Horrill (01207) 562261
Pro S Corbally (01207) 580210
Holes 18 L 6001 yds SSS 69
Recs Am–62 NC Raine
V'tors WD–U SOC–exc Sat
Fees £15 (£22)
Loc 12 miles NW of Durham on A691
Arch Harry Vardon

Crook (1919)

Low Job's Hill, Crook DL15 9AA

Tel **(01388) 762429**
Mem 450
Sec PN Willis
Pro None
Holes 18 L 6102 yds SSS 70
Recs Am–66 N Tweddle
V'tors U SOC
Fees £12 (£20)
Loc 1/2 mile E of Crook (A689)

Darlington (1908)

Haughton Grange, Darlington DL1 3JD

Tel **(01325) 355324**
Mem 410 87(L) 110(J)
Sec N Adair
Pro (01325) 484198
Holes 18 L 6272 yds SSS 70
Recs Am–64 H Teschner
Pro–67 M Gallacher

V'tors WD–U 10–12 & 2–4pm WE–M SOC
Fees D–£22
Loc Off Salters Lane, NE of Darlington

Dinsdale Spa (1910)

Middleton St George, Darlington DL2 1DW
Tel **(01325) 332222**
Mem 875
Sec PJ Wright (01325) 332297
Pro C Imlah (01325) 332515
Holes 18 L 6090 yds Par 71 SSS 69
Recs Am–67 I Liddle (1994)
Pro–66 D Pearce (1994)
V'tors WD–U exc Tues–NA WE–M
Fees £16 D–£20
Loc 5 miles SE of Darlington

Durham City (1887)

Littleburn, Langley Moor, Durham DH7 8HL
Tel **(0191) 378 0069**
Mem 750
Sec LTI Wilson (0191) 386 0200
Pro S Corbally (0191) 378 0029
Holes 18 L 6326 yds SSS 70
V'tors WD–U SOC
Fees £18 (£24)
Loc 1½ miles W of Durham, off A690
Arch CC Stanton

Hobson Municipal (1978)

Public
Hobson, Burnopfield, Newcastle-upon-Tyne
Tel **(01207) 71605**
Sec RJ Handrick
Pro J Ord
Holes 18 L 6403 yds SSS 71
V'tors U SOC
Fees £8 (£11.50)
Loc Between Gateshead and Consett on A692

Mount Oswald (1924)

South Road, Durham City DH1 3TQ
Tel **(0191) 386 7527**
Fax **(0191) 386 0975**
Mem 120
Sec SE Reeve
Holes 18 L 6009 yds SSS 69
Recs Am–64 J Mee (1986)
Pro–66 J Mathews (1984)
V'tors U SOC
Fees £10 D–£17 (£12 D–£20)
Loc SW of Durham on A177

Oakleaf Golf Complex (1993)

Pay and play
School Aycliffe Lane, Newton Aycliffe DL5 6QZ
Tel **(01325) 310820**
Fax **(01325) 300873**
Sec A Bailey (Mgr) (01325) 300700
Pro C Burgess
Holes 18 L 5334 yds SSS 66
V'tors WD–U WE–booking required
Fees £6 (£7)
Loc 1 mile W of Aycliffe on A6072, from A68
Mis Floodlit driving range

Roseberry Grange (1986)

Public
Grange Villa, Chester-Le-Street DH2 3NF
Tel **(0191) 370 0670**
Mem 500
Sec R McDermott (Hon)
Pro A Hartley (0191) 370 0660
Holes 18 L 5892 yds SSS 68
Recs Am–66 D Brolls (1989), D Matthews (1994)
Pro–65 B Rumney (1988)
V'tors U SOC
Fees £8.60 (£12)
Loc 3 miles W of Chester-Le-Street on A693
Mis Driving range

Ryhope (1992)

Leechmere Way, Hollycarrside, Ryhope, Sunderland SR2 0DH
Tel **(0191) 521 3811/523 7333**
Fax **(0191) 521 3811**
Mem 500
Sec BL Johnson (0191) 521 3811
Pro None
Holes 9 L 6000 yds SSS 69
V'tors U
Fees £6 (£9)
Loc 2 miles SW of Sunderland, off A1018
Arch Jonathan Gaunt

Seaham (1911)

Shrewsbury Street, Dawdon, Seaham SR7 7RD
Tel **(0191) 581 2354**
Mem 550
Sec V Smith (0191) 581 1268
Pro D Patterson (0191) 513 0837
Holes 18 L 5972 yds SSS 69
Recs Am–64 J Sanderson Jr (1984)
V'tors U SOC
Fees On application
Loc Dawdon, 2 miles NE of A19

South Moor (1923)

The Middles, Craghead, Stanley DH9 6AG
Tel **(01207) 232848/283525**
Mem 650
Sec B Davison (0191) 388 4523
Pro S Cowell (01207) 283525
Holes 18 L 6445 yds SSS 71
Recs Am–66 G Wearmouth (1991)
Pro–67 LP Tupling (1980)
Ladies–70 PA Dobson (1987)
V'tors WD–H WE/BH–M SOC–WD/Sat
Fees £14 (£25)
Loc 8 miles NW of Durham
Arch Dr A Mackenzie

Stressholme (1976)

Public
Snipe Lane, Darlington DL2 2SA
Tel **(01325) 461002**
Fax **(01325) 351826**
Sec R Lister (Mgr)
Pro R Lister
Holes 18 L 6511 yds SSS 71
Recs Am–69 S Aitken
Pro–64 N Coles
V'tors U
Fees On application
Loc 2 miles S of Darlington on A66
Mis Floodlit driving range

Woodham G & CC (1983)

Burnhill Way, Newton Aycliffe DH5 4PM
Tel **(01325) 318346**
Mem 610
Sec HJ Stafford
Pro P Lunson
Holes 18 L 6770 yds SSS 72
Recs Am–71 R McGhan, D Burnham
Pro–67 M Ure
V'tors WD–U WE/BH–booking SOC
Fees On application
Loc 1 mile N of Newton Aycliffe
Arch J Hamilton Stutt

Essex

Abridge G & CC (1964)

Epping Lane, Stapleford Tawney RM4 1ST
Tel **(01708) 688388**
Fax **(01708) 688550**
Mem 650
Sec PG Pelling (Mgr) (01708) 688396
Pro M Herbert (01708) 688333
Holes 18 L 6703 yds SSS 72
Recs Am–68 NK Burch
Pro–68 D Feherty
V'tors WD–H WE/BH–NA
Fees £30
Loc Theydon Bois/Epping Stations 3 miles
Arch Henry Cotton

Ballards Gore (1980)

Gore Road, Canewdon, Rochford SS4 2DA
Tel **(01702) 258917**
Mem 600
Sec NG Patient
Pro IP Marshall (01702) 258924
Holes 18 L 7062 yds SSS 74
V'tors WD–U WE–M after 12.30pm (summer) 11.30am (winter) SOC
Fees £16 D–£22
Loc 1½ miles NE of Rochford

Basildon (1967)

Public
Clayhill Lane, Sparrow's Hearne, Basildon SS16 5HL

Tel **(01268) 533297**
Fax **(01268) 533849**
Sec AM Burch
Pro W Paterson (01268) 533532
Holes 18 L 6153 yds SSS 69
Pro–66 R Mann, W Longmuir
V'tors U SOC
Fees £8.70 (£14.50)
Loc 1 mile S of Basildon, off A176 at Kingswood roundabout

Belfairs (1926)

Public
Eastwood Road North, Leigh-on-Sea SS9 4LR

Tel **(01702) 525345 (Starter)**
Pro R Foreman (01702) 520202
Holes 18 L 5802 yds SSS 68
V'tors WD–U exc Thurs am WE/BH–booking
Fees £11 (£16)
Loc Between A127 and A13

Belhus Park (1972)

Pay and play
Belhus Park, South Ockendon RM15 4QR

Tel **(01708) 854260**
Mem 280
Sec DA Faust
Pro G Lunn
Holes 18 L 5188 yds SSS 66
Recs Am–67 M Jennings, J Bearman
Pro–63 R Joyce
V'tors U
Fees £7 (£10)
Loc 1 mile N of A13/M25 Dartford Tunnel
Mis Floodlit driving range

Bentley G & CC (1972)

Ongar Road, Brentwood CM15 9SS

Tel **(01277) 373179**
Mem 550
Sec JA Vivers
Pro N Garrett (01277) 372933
Holes 18 L 6709 yds SSS 72
Recs Am–71 J Moody (1987)
Pro–69 S Cipa (1988), B Smith (1988)
V'tors WD–UH WE–M after noon BH–after 11am SOC–WD
Fees £20 D–£26
Loc 18 miles E of London. M25 Junction 28, 3 miles

Benton Hall (1993)

Wickham Hill, Witham CM8 3LH

Tel **(01376) 502454**
Fax **(01376) 521050**
Mem 300
Sec PS Holmes (Mgr)
Pro M Watt
Holes 18 L 6520 yds SSS 71
9 hole Par 3 course
V'tors U SOC–WD
Fees £16 (£20)
Loc Witham, 8 miles NE of Chelmsford, off A12
Mis Driving range

Birch Grove (1970)

Layer Road, Colchester CO2 0HS

Tel **(01206) 734276**
Mem 250
Sec Mrs M Marston
Holes 9 L 4108 yds SSS 60
Recs Am–58 A Green (1993)
V'tors WD/BH–U Sat–XL before 11am Sun–U after 1pm SOC
Fees £10 (£12)
Loc 3 miles S of Colchester on B1026

Boyce Hill (1921)

Vicarage Hill, Benfleet SS7 1PD

Tel **(01268) 793625**
Fax **(01268) 750497**
Mem 600
Sec JE Atkins
Pro G Burroughs (01268) 752565
Holes 18 L 5882 yds SSS 68
Recs Am–64 N Perrin
Pro–61 G Burroughs
V'tors WD–UH WE/BH–MH SOC–Thurs only
Fees D–£25
Loc 4 miles W of Southend
Arch James Braid

Braintree (1891)

Kings Lane, Stisted, Braintree CM7 8DA

Tel **(01376) 346079**
Fax **(01376) 331216**
Mem 700
Sec MND Robinson
Pro T Parcell (01376) 343465
Holes 18 L 6161 yds SSS 69
Recs Am–65 M Hawes, M Davis
Pro–65 P Golding
V'tors WD–U exc Fri–H Sat/BH–H Sun–NA SOC
Fees £25 (£40)
Loc 1 mile E of Braintree, off A120 towards Stisted
Arch Hawtree

Bunsay Downs (1982)

Public
Little Baddow Road, Woodham Walter, Maldon CM9 6RW

Tel **(01245) 412648/412369**
Sec MFL Durham
Pro Mickey Walker (01245) 414662
Holes 9 L 2913 yds SSS 68
9 hole Par 3 course
V'tors WD–U WE/BH–book in advance SOC–WD
Fees On application
Loc 7 miles E of Chelmsford, off A414
Mis Indoor driving range

Burnham-on-Crouch (1923)

Ferry Road, Creeksea, Burnham-on-Crouch CM0 8PQ

Tel **(01621) 782282/785508**
Mem 485
Sec WF Miller
Holes 18 L 6056 yds SSS 69
Recs Am–66 D Clarke (1966)
Pro–64 FJ Winser
V'tors WD–H WE/BH–M
Fees £20
Loc 1½ miles W of Burnham

Canons Brook (1962)

Elizabeth Way, Harlow CM19 5BE

Tel **(01279) 421482**
Mem 800
Sec AF Reid
Pro A McGinn (01279) 418357
Holes 18 L 6728 yds SSS 73
Recs Am–68 H Cornick
Pro–65 G Burroughs
V'tors WD–U WE/BH–M
Fees D–£25
Loc 25 miles N of London
Arch Henry Cotton

Castle Point (1988)

Public
Waterside Farm, Somnes Avenue, Canvey Island SS8 9FG

Tel **(01268) 510830**
Mem 300
Sec VW Russell (01268) 698909
Pro J Hudson (01268) 510830
Holes 18 L 5627 yds SSS 69
V'tors U SOC
Fees £8 (£12)
Loc On A130 to Canvey Island, off A13 Eastbound
Mis Driving range
Arch Golf Landscapes

Channels (1974)

Belsteads Farm Lane, Little Waltham, Chelmsford CM3 3PT

Tel **(01245) 440005**
Fax **(01245) 442032**
Mem 650
Sec AM Squire
Pro IB Sinclair (01245) 441056
Holes 18 L 6272 yds SSS 71
18 L 4779 yds Par 67 SSS 63
V'tors WD–U WE–M SOC
Fees £15 D–£28
Loc 3 miles NE of Chelmsford on A130
Mis Pitch & putt course. Driving range

Chelmsford (1893)

Widford, Chelmsford CM2 9AP

Tel **(01245) 250555**
Mem 650
Sec A Johnson (01245) 256483
Pro GD Bailey (01245) 257079
Holes 18 L 5944 yds SSS 68
Recs Am–67 G Turner
Pro–65 C Platts

For list of abbreviations see page 435

V'tors WD–H WE/BH–M SOC
Fees £25 D–£35
Loc Off A1016 at Widford roundabout

Chigwell (1925)
High Road, Chigwell IG7 5BH
Tel **(0181) 500 2059**
Fax **(0181) 501 3410**
Mem 700
Sec RH Danzey
Pro R Beard (0181) 500 2384
Holes 18 L 6279 yds SSS 70
Recs Am–66 AM Ronald, JM Bint (1991)
Pro–66 H Flatman
V'tors WD–H WE/BH–M
Fees £28 D–£35
Loc 13 miles NE of London (A113)

Clacton (1892)
West Road, Clacton-on-Sea CO15 1AJ
Tel **(01255) 424331**
Mem 650
Sec H Lucas (01255) 421919
Pro SJ Levermore (01255) 426304
Holes 18 L 6243 yds SSS 71
Recs Am–68 D Lee, A Wenn, D Robertson
Pro–66 L Fickling
V'tors H WE/BH–H after 11am SOC
Fees £20 (£30)
Loc On sea front

Colchester (1909)
Braiswick, Colchester CO4 5AU
Tel **(01206) 852946**
Fax **(01206) 852698**
Mem 330 90(L) 70(J)
Sec Mrs J Boorman (01206) 853396
Pro M Angel (01206) 853920
Holes 18 L 6319 yds SS 70
Recs Am–63 B Booth
Pro–68 A Parcell
V'tors WD–H WE/BH–NA SOC
Fees D–£22 (£30)
Loc 3/4 mile NW of Colchester North Station, towards West Bergholt
Arch James Braid

Colne Valley (1991)
Station Road, Earls Colne CO6 2LT
Tel **(01787) 224233/224343**
Fax **(01787) 224452**
Mem 250
Sec MG Gage (Mgr) (01787) 224343
Pro Mrs K Martin (01787) 224233
Holes 18 L 6272 yds SSS 70
V'tors WD–U H WE/BH–after 10.30am SOC–WD
Fees On application
Loc 12 miles W of Colchester (A604)
Arch Howard Swann

Crondon Park (1994)
Stock Road, Stock CM4 9DP
Tel **(01277) 841115**
Fax **(01277) 841356**
Mem 875
Sec Lt Cdr J Lewes
Pro P Wernham
Holes 18 L 6585 yds SSS 71
9 hole course
V'tors WD–U WE–M SOC–WD
Fees £15 (£20)
Loc 5 miles S of Chelmsford on B1007. M25 Junction 28
Mis Driving range
Arch Martin Gillett

Earls Colne (1990)
Public
Earls Colne, Colchester CO6 2NS
Tel **(01787) 224466**
Fax **(01787) 224410**
Sec Sally Blackwell (Mgr)
Pro O McKenna
Holes 18 L 6842 yds SSS 72
9 hole course Par 30
Pro–70 SJ Smith (1992)
V'tors U SOC–WD
Fees £12 (£15)
Loc 2 miles N of A120 at Coggeshall on B1024
Mis Floodlit driving range.
Arch Reg Plumridge

Epping Forest G & CC (1994)
Woolston Manor, Abridge Road, Chigwell IG7 6BX
Tel **(0181) 500 2549**
Fax **(0181) 501 5452**
Mem 750
Sec T Peck
Pro D St.John Jones
Holes 18 L 6408 yds SSS 71
V'tors M
Loc Chigwell, 1/2 mile from M11 Junction 5
Mis Floodlit driving range
Arch Neil Coles

The Essex Golf Complex (1993)
Pay and play
Garon Park, Eastern Avenue, Southend-on-Sea SS9 4PT
Tel **(01702) 601701**
Fax **(01702) 601033**
Mem 700
Sec S Hodson (Mgr)
Holes 18 L 6237 yds SSS 70
9 hole Par 3 course
V'tors U SOC
Fees £12 (£16)
Loc E side of Southend-on-Sea. M25 Junction 29
Mis Floodlit driving range
Arch Walker/Cox

Fairlop Waters (1987)
Public
Forest Road, Barkingside, Ilford IG6 3JA
Tel **(0181) 500 9911**
Pro A Bowers (0181) 501 1881
Holes 18 L 6288 yds SSS 72
9 hole Par 3 course
V'tors U
Fees £7.50 (£11)
Loc 2 miles from S end of M11, by Fairlop underground station
Mis Driving range

Five Lakes (1974)
Colchester Road, Tolleshunt Knights, Maldon CM9 8HX
Tel **(01621) 868888**
Fax **(01621) 869696**
Mem 500
Sec PD Keeble (Golf Dir)
Holes Links 18 L 6250 yds SSS 70
Lakes 18 L 6765 yds SSS 72
Recs Links Am–68 D Wilks (1991)
Pro–68 K Ashdown (1988)
Lakes Pro–63 E Dussart (1992)
V'tors U BH–U after 1pm SOC
Fees Links £18 (£22.50)
Lakes £30 (£30)
Loc 8 miles S of Colchester, off B1026

Forrester Park (1975)
Beckingham Road, Great Totham, Maldon CM9 8AE
Tel **(01621) 891406**
Mem 900
Sec T Forrester-Muir
Pro G Pike
Holes 18 L 6073 yds SSS 69
Recs Am–70 S Roast (1992)
V'tors WD–U WE–NA before 1pm SOC–WD
Fees £15 (£20)
Loc 3 miles NE of Maldon on B1022
Arch Everett/Forrester-Muir

Frinton (1895)
1 The Esplanade, Frinton-on-Sea CO13 9EP
Tel **(01255) 674618**
Fax **(01255) 674618**
Mem 900
Sec Lt Col RW Attrill
Pro P Taggart (01255) 671618
Holes 18 L 6259 yds SS 70
9 L 2508 yds SSS 33
Recs Am–67 IA Quick
Pro–66 CS Denny
V'tors 18 hole:H WE/BH–NA before 11.30am SOC
Fees 18 hole:D–£22 9 hole:£7.50
Loc 18 miles E of Colchester

Gosfield Lake (1986)
The Manor House, Gosfield, Halstead CO9 1SE
Tel **(01787) 474747**
Fax **(01787) 476044**
Mem 830
Sec JA O'Shea (Sec/Mgr)
Pro R Wheeler (01787) 474488

Holes Lakes 18 L 6707 yds SSS 72
Meadows 9 L 4180 yds Par 66
Recs Lakes Am–68 S Bearman (1993)
V'tors WD–H WE(pm)–H by arrangement SOC
Fees Lakes D–£25
Meadows D–£10
Loc 7 miles N of Braintree (A1017)
Arch Cotton/Swann

Hainault Forest (1912)
Public
Chigwell Row, Hainault Forest
Tel **(0181) 500 2097**
Sec DK Cope (0181) 500 0385
Pro T Dungate (0181) 500 2131
Holes No 1 18 L 5754 yds SSS 67
No 2 18 L 6600 yds SSS 71
Recs No 1 Am–65 TG Patmore
Pro–65 A Frost
No 2 Am–68 S Middleton
Pro–68 AE Frost Jr
V'tors U
Fees On application
Loc Hog Hill, Redbridge

Hanover G & CC (1991)
Hullbridge Road, Rayleigh SS6 9QS
Tel **(01702) 232377**
Fax **(01702) 231811**
Mem 700
Sec G Harrold
Pro A Blackburn
Holes Georgian 18 L 6669 yds SSS 72; Regency 18 L 3700 yds SSS 58
Recs Am–71 D Twyman (1992)
Pro–65 A Blackburn (1993)
V'tors Georgian:WD–H WE–M SOC
Regency:U SOC
Fees Georgian £25 D–£35
Regency £11.75 (£14.10)
Loc 3 miles NW of Southend
Arch Reg Plumbridge

Hartswood (1967)
Public
King George's Playing Fields, Brentwood CM14 5AE
Tel **(01277) 214830** (Bookings)
Sec M Freeman (01227) 218850
Pro M Siggens (01277) 218714
Holes 18 L 6238 yds SSS 70
Recs Am–70 A Cornell
Pro–64 M Sharman
V'tors U SOC
Fees On application
Loc E of Brentwood on A128

Harwich & Dovercourt (1906)
Station Road, Parkeston, Harwich CO12 4NZ
Tel **(01255) 503616**
Mem 400
Sec BQ Dunham
Holes 9 L 2950 yds SSS 69
V'tors WD–U SOC
Fees On application
Loc A120 to r'bout to Parkeston Quay, entrance 20 yds on left

Ilford (1907)
Wanstead Park Road, Ilford IG1 3TR
Tel **(0181) 554 2930**
Mem 618
Sec PH Newson
Pro S Dowsett (0181) 554 0094
Holes 18 L 5251 yds SSS 66
Recs Am–60 P Happe (1990)
Pro–64 B Huggett, A Campbell
V'tors WD–U WE–phone Pro
Fees £13.50 (£16)
Loc S end of M11, off A406

Langdon Hills (1991)
Lower Dunton Road, Bulphan RM14 3TY
Tel **(01268) 548444/544300**
Fax **(01268) 490084**
Mem 700
Pro A Lavers
Holes 18 L 6485 yds SSS 71
9 hole course
V'tors H SOC
Fees 18 hole:£12.50 (£15.50)
9 hole:£6 (£7.50)
Loc SW of Basildon between A127 and A13. M25 Junction 29, 8 miles
Mis Floodlit driving range
Arch MRM Sandow

Loughton (1981)
Public
Clays Lane, Debden Green, Loughton IG10 2RZ
Tel **(0181) 502 2923**
Mem 190
Sec A Day
Pro S Layton
Holes 9 L 4735 yds SSS 62
V'tors U–booking required SOC
Fees 18 holes–£8 (£10)
9 holes–£5 (£6)
Loc M25 Junction 26

Maldon (1891)
Beeleigh Langford, Maldon CM9 6LL
Tel **(01621) 853212**
Mem 480
Sec GR Bezant
Holes 9 L 6197 yds SSS 69
Recs Am–71 R Byford
Pro–67 S Levermore
V'tors WD–U H WE–M SOC
Fees £15 D–£20
Loc 3 miles NW of Maldon on B1019

Maylands (1936)
Harold Park, Romford RM3 0AZ
Tel **(017083) 42055**
Mem 600
Sec (017083) 73080
Pro JS Hopkin (017083) 46466
Holes 18 L 6351 yds SSS 70
Recs Am–67 G Johnson
Pro–67 H Flatman
V'tors WD–I WE/BH–M SOC
Fees £20 (£30)
Loc 2 miles E of Romford on A12. M25 Junction 28, 1 mile

Nazeing (1992)
Middle Street, Nazeing EN9 2LW
Tel **(01992) 893798/893915**
Fax **(01992) 893882**
Mem 300
Sec D Sharpe (Mgr) (01992) 893915
Pro R Green (01992) 893798
Holes 18 L 6598 yds SSS 71
Recs Am–68 M Hales (1994)
V'tors WD–H WE/BH–H after 11am SOC
Fees £20 (£28)
Loc 3 miles SW of Harlow. M11 Junction 7
Mis Open air driving range
Arch Martin Gillett

Orsett (1899)
Brentwood Road, Orsett RM16 3DS
Tel **(01375) 891352**
Fax **(01375) 892471**
Mem 900
Pro R Newberry (01375) 891797
Holes 18 L 6614 yds SSS 72
Recs Am–68 A Pollock, I Quick
Pro–68 K Lunt
V'tors WD–H SOC–Mon–Wed only
Fees £30
Loc 4 miles NE of Grays on A128. M25 Junction 30/31

Risebridge (1972)
Pay and play
Risebridge Chase, Lower Bedfords Road, Romford RM1 4DG
Tel **(01708) 741429**
Mem 275
Sec J Alexander
Pro P Jennings
Holes 18 L 6280 yds SSS 70
9 hole Par 3
Recs Am–67 B Reeve (1979), D Girdlestone (1985)
V'tors U
Fees £8.45 (£10.50)
Loc 2 miles from M25 Junction 28, off A12
Arch F Hawtree

Rochford Hundred (1893)
Rochford Hall, Hall Road, Rochford SS4 1NW
Tel **(01702) 544302**
Mem 340 150(L) 60(J)
Sec AH Bondfield
Pro GS Hill
Holes 18 L 6256 yds SSS 70
Recs Am–65 DK Wood
Pro–65 C Tucker
V'tors WD–U H WE–M
Fees On application
Loc 4 miles N of Southend-on-Sea
Arch James Braid

Romford (1894)
Heath Drive, Gidea Park, Romford RM2 5QB
Tel **(01708) 740007** (Members)
Fax **(01708) 752157**
Mem 542

Sec Mrs H Robinson (01708) 740986
Pro H Flatman (01708) 749393
Holes 18 L 6395 yds SSS 70
Recs Am–66 D Girdlestone
Pro–66 D Jones
Ladies–72 M Knights
V'tors WD–I WE–NA SOC
Fees £23 D–£30
Loc 1 mile E of Romford. 3 miles W of M25 Junction 29
Arch HS Colt

Royal Epping Forest (1888)

Public
Forest Approach, Station Road, Chingford, London E4 7AZ
Tel **(0181) 529 6407**
Fax **(0181) 559 4664**
Mem 300 50(L) 25(J)
Sec Mrs P Runciman (0181) 529 2195
Pro R Gowers (0181) 529 5708
Holes 18 L 6220 yds SSS 70
Recs Am–68 A Johns
Pro–65 R Gowers
V'tors U–booking necessary SOC
Fees £9 (£12.50)
Loc Nr Chingford station
Mis Red coats or trousers compulsory

Saffron Walden (1919)

Windmill Hill, Saffron Walden CB10 1BX
Tel **(01799) 522689**
Fax **(01799) 522786**
Mem 950
Sec DH Smith (Mgr) (01799) 522786
Pro P Davis (01799) 527728
Holes 18 L 6608 yds SSS 72
Recs Am–67 AD Emery (1988)
Pro–63 L Fickling (1991)
V'tors WD–U H WE/BH–M SOC
Fees £30
Loc Saffron Walden, on B184

Stapleford Abbotts (1989)

Horseman's Side, Tysea Hill, Stapleford Abbotts RM4 1JU
Tel **(01708) 381108**
Fax **(01708) 386345**
Mem 800
Sec K Fletcher
Pro D Eagle (01708 381278)
Holes Abbotts 18 L 6487 yds SSS 71
Priors 18 L 5965 yds SSS 69
Friars 9 L 1140 yds
Recs Am–70 P Daykin (1994)
Pro–66 D Eagle (1994)
V'tors WD–U H WE–M SOC
Fees £15–£40
Loc 3 miles N of Romford. M25 Junction 28
Mis Tee reservations:(01708) 370040/(01277) 373344
Arch Howard Swann

Stock Brook Manor (1992)

Queen's Park Avenue, Stock, Billericay CM12 0SP
Tel **(01277) 653616**
Sec K Roe (Dir)
Pro K Merry
Holes 18 L 6725 yds SSS 71
9 L 2977 yds SSS 69
V'tors H–booking necessary
Fees £25 (£30)
Loc 5 miles S of Chelmsford on B1007
Mis Driving range. Par 3 course
Arch Martin Gillett

Theydon Bois (1897)

Theydon Bois, Epping CM16 4EH
Tel **(01992) 813054**
Fax **(01992) 813054**
Mem 600
Sec DT Jones
Pro RJ Hall (01992) 812460
Holes 18 L 5480 yds SSS 68
Recs Am–64 T Moncur (1993)
Pro–64 R Joyce (1989)
V'tors Thurs am–restricted H SOC WE–M
Fees £23 After 2pm–£20
Loc 1 mile S of Epping. M25 Junction 26
Arch James Braid

Thorndon Park (1920)

Ingrave, Brentwood CM13 3RH
Tel **(01277) 811666**
Mem 300 140(L) 60(J)
Sec JE Leggitt (01277) 810345
Pro BV White (01277) 810736
Holes 18 L 6481 yds SSS 71
Recs Am–66 MES Davis
Pro–65 BJ Hunt, B Waites
V'tors WD–I WE/BH–M
Fees £25 D–£40
Loc 2 miles SE of Brentwood on A128

Thorpe Hall (1907)

Thorpe Hall Avenue, Thorpe Bay SS1 3AT
Tel **(01702) 582205**
Mem 1000
Sec GRG Winckless
Pro WJ McColl (01702) 588195
Holes 18 L 6286 yds SSS 71
Recs Am–66 R Jeffs (1993)
Pro–66 C Laurence (1993)
V'tors WD–H
Fees On application
Loc E of Southend-on-Sea

Three Rivers (1973)

Stow Road, Purleigh, Chelmsford CM3 6RR
Tel **(01621) 828631**
Fax **(01621) 828060**
Mem 600
Sec G Packer (Golf Dir)
Pro G Packer
Holes 18 L 6609 yds Par 73 SSS 71
9 hole Par 3 course
V'tors WD–U WE/BH–U after 10.30am SOC–WD
Fees £19 (£22)
Loc Cold Norton, 5 miles S of Maldon
Arch Hawtree

Toot Hill (1991)

School Road, Toot Hill, Ongar CM5 9PU
Tel **(01277) 365747**
Mem 400
Sec Mrs Cameron
Pro G Bacon
Holes 18 L 6013 yds SSS 70
V'tors H SOC–WD
Fees £25
Loc 2 miles W of Ongar
Mis Practice range
Arch Martin Gillett

Top Meadow (1986)

Fen Lane, North Ockendon RM14 3PR
Tel **(01708) 852239** (Clubhouse)
Sec G Bourton
Pro P King (01708) 859545
Holes 18 L 5500 yds SSS 69
9 L 1633 yds Par 30
V'tors WD–U WE–NA SOC
Fees £12
Loc N Ockendon, off B186
Mis Driving range

Towerlands (1985)

Panfield Road, Braintree CM7 5BJ
Tel **(01376) 552487/326802**
Mem 325
Sec K Cooper
Pro R Taylor
Holes 9 L 2703 yds SSS 66
V'tors WD–U WE–U after 2pm SOC–WD
Fees 18 holes–£10.50 (£12.50)
9 holes–£8.50
Loc 1 mile NW of Braintree
Mis Driving range

Upminster (1928)

114 Hall Lane, Upminster RM14 1AU
Tel **(01708) 222788**
Mem 930
Sec K Moyse
Pro N Carr (01708) 220000
Holes 18 L 6076 yds SSS 69
Recs Am–66 A Emery, N Leonard
V'tors WD–U H exc Tues am Ladies Day WE/BH–NA SOC
Fees £25 D–£30
Loc Station 3/4 mile

Wanstead (1893)

Wanstead, London E11 2LW
Tel **(0181) 989 0604**
Fax **(0181) 532 9138**
Mem 650
Sec K Jones (0181) 989 3938
Pro D Hawkins (0181) 989 9876
Holes 18 L 6262 yds SSS 69
Recs Am–62 P Sullivan
Pro–64 N Coles, P Brown

V'tors WD–H WE/BH–M
Fees D–£25
Loc Off A12, nr Wanstead station

Warley Park (1975)
Magpie Lane, Little Warley, Brentwood CM13 3DX
Tel **(01277) 224891**
Fax **(01277) 200679**
Mem 800
Sec K Regan
Pro P O'Conner (01277) 212552
Holes 27 hole course
Recs Am–68 N Smith (1994)
V'tors WD–H
Fees £24
Loc 2 miles S of Brentwood. M25 Junction 29
Arch Reg Plumbridge

Warren (1932)
Woodham Walter, Maldon CM9 6RW
Tel **(01245) 223258/223198**
Fax **(01245) 223989**
Mem 840
Sec MFL Durham (01245) 223258
Pro Mickey Walker OBE (01245) 224662
Holes 18 L 6211 yds SSS 69
Recs Am–65 M Robarts (1990) Pro–66 H Flatman
V'tors WD–H WE–M SOC
Fees £28 D–£35
Loc 7 miles E of Chelmsford, off A414
Mis Golf Academy (01245) 223198

Weald Park
Coxtie Green Road, South Weald, Brentwood CM14 5RJ
Tel **(01277) 375101**
Mem 400
Sec June Harrison
Pro P Barham (01277) 372246
Holes 18 L 6308 yds SSS 71
Recs Am–70 D Mackison (1994) Pro–65 P Barham (1994)
V'tors WD–H SOC
Fees £25
Loc 3 miles from M25 Junction 28 (A1023)
Arch Reg Plumbridge

West Essex (1900)
Bury Road, Sewardstonebury, Chingford, London E4 7QL
Tel **(0181) 529 7558**
Fax **(0181) 524 7870**
Mem 654
Sec To be appointed
Pro (081) 529 4367
Holes 18 L 6289 yds SSS 70
Recs Am–66 S Parrish, RCR Woods Pro–65 D Jones
V'tors WD–U H WE/BH–M H SOC–Mon/Wed/Fri
Fees £25 D–£30
Loc 2 miles N of Chingford BR station. M25 Junction 26

Woodford (1890)
2, Sunset Avenue, Woodford Green IG8 0ST
Tel **(0181) 504 0553/4254**
Mem 460
Sec GJ Cousins (0181) 504 3330
Pro A Johns (0181) 504 4254
Holes 9 L 5806 yds SSS 68
Recs Am–69 M Everitt, R Piper, P Blaxill Pro–66 C Platts, L Jones
V'tors WD–U exc Tues am–NA Sat–M Sun–NA before noon SOC
Fees £10–£15
Loc 11 miles NE of London
Mis Major item of red clothing to be worn on course
Arch Tom Dunn

Gloucestershire

Broadway (1895)
Willersey Hill, Broadway, Worcs WR12 7LG
Tel **(01386) 858997**
Fax **(01386) 858643**
Mem 500 160(L) 70(J)
Sec B Carnie (Sec/Mgr) (01386) 853683
Pro M Freeman (01386) 853275
Holes 18 L 6216 yds SSS 70
Recs Am–65 M Dove Pro–66 D Steele, R Adams
V'tors H exc Sat–M SOC
Fees £25 (£32)
Loc 1½ miles E of Broadway (A44)
Arch James Braid

Cirencester (1893)
Cheltenham Road, Bagendon, Cirencester GL7 7BH
Tel **(01285) 653939**
Fax **(01285) 650665**
Mem 800
Sec ND Jones (01285) 652465
Pro G Robbins (01285) 656124
Holes 18 L 6021 yds Par 70 SSS 69
Recs Am–64 D Rollo Pro–67 DJ Rees
V'tors H SOC–WD
Fees £20 (£25)
Loc 1½ miles N of Cirencester on A435
Arch James Braid

Cleeve Hill (1976)
Pay and play
Cleeve Hill, Cheltenham GL52 3PW
Tel **(01242) 672025**
Sec S Gilman (Mgr)
Pro (01242) 672592
Holes 18 L 6444 yds SSS 71
V'tors U exc Sat 11–3pm/Sun am–NA SOC
Fees £8 (£10)
Loc 3 miles N of Cheltenham on A46 to Winchcombe
Mis Tee booking 7 days in advance

Cotswold Edge (1980)
Upper Rushmire, Wotton-under-Edge GL12 7PT
Tel **(01453) 844167**
Mem 800
Sec NJ Newman
Pro DJ Gosling (01453) 844398
Holes 18 L 6170 yds SSS 69
Recs Am–68 J Lathom-Sharp (1989) Pro–66 J Loughnane (1994) Ladies–71 M Mayes (1992)
V'tors WD–U WE–M SOC
Fees £15
Loc 2 miles NE of Wotton-under-Edge on B4058 Tetbury road. M5 Junction 14

Cotswold Hills (1902)
Ullenwood, Cheltenham GL53 9QT
Tel **(01242) 522421**
Mem 750
Sec A O'Reilly (01242) 515264
Pro N Boland (01242) 515263
Holes 18 L 6716 yds SSS 72
Recs Am–67 G Wolstenholme (1992) Pro–67 J Loughnane, S Little (1992)
V'tors I (recognised club members) SOC
Fees £21 (£26)
Loc 3 miles S of Cheltenham

Forest Hills (1992)
Mile End Road, Coleford
Tel **(01594) 810620**
Mem 500
Sec N Anstice (01594) 810620
Holes 18 L 5988 yds SSS 68
V'tors U SOC
Fees £13 (£15)
Loc 1 mile W of Coleford (B4028)
Mis Driving range
Arch Adrian Stiff

Forest of Dean (1974)
Lords Hill, Coleford GL16 8BD
Tel **(01594) 832583**
Fax **(01594) 832584**
Mem 500
Sec Charlotte Clifford (Mgr)
Pro J Nicol (01594) 833689
Holes 18 L 5682 yds SSS 67
V'tors U SOC
Fees £14 (£16)
Loc ½ mile SE of Coleford on Parkend road. M50, 10 miles
Arch John Day

Gloucester Hotel (1976)
Matson Lane, Gloucester GL4 9EA
Tel **(01452) 525653**
Mem 750
Sec R Jewell
Pro R Jewell (01452) 411311
Holes 18 L 6127 yds SSS 69 9 L 1980 yds SSS 27
Recs Am–68 J Wallace Pro–65 P Darnell

V'tors U
Fees £19 (£25)
Loc 2 miles S of Gloucester, off Painswick road. M5 Junction 11
Mis Driving range

Lilley Brook (1922)

Cirencester Road, Charlton Kings, Cheltenham GL53 8EG

Tel **(01242) 526785**
Mem 700
Sec K Skeen
Pro F Hadden (01242) 525201
Holes 18 L 6226 yds SSS 70
Recs Am–64 B Mitten (1987) Pro–63 I Sparkes (1990)
V'tors WD–H or I (recognised club members) WE–M SOC–WD
Fees D–£20
Loc 3 miles SE of Cheltenham on A435

Lydney (1909)

Lakeside Avenue, Lydney GL15 5QA

Tel **(01594) 842614**
Mem 300
Sec L Ellerington (01594) 841561
Holes 9 L 5382 yds SSS 66
Recs Am–63 MA Barnard (1988) Pro–68 F Goulding
V'tors WD–U WE/BH–M SOC
Fees £12 W–£35
Loc 20 miles SW of Gloucester, off A48

Minchinhampton (1889)

Minchinhampton, Stroud GL6 9BE

Tel **(01453) 832642 (Old), (01453) 833866 (New)**
Mem 1881
Sec DR Vickers (01453) 833866
Pro C Steele (01453) 833860
Holes Old 18 L 6295 yds SSS 70; New-Avening 18 L 6244 yds SSS 70; New-Cherington 18 L 6270 yds SSS 71
Recs Old Am–67 PH Fisher, L Scott Pro–67 RA Brown
V'tors H–restricted SOC
Fees Old–£10 (£13) New–£24 (£30)
Loc Old-3 miles E of Stroud. New-5 miles E of Stroud
Arch Old:R Wilson. New–Avening: F Hawtree Cherington–M Hawtree

Naunton Downs (1993)

Naunton, Cheltenham GL54 3AE

Tel **(01451) 850090**
Fax **(01451) 850091**
Sec Miss CA Eager
Pro ND Powell (Golf Dir) (01451) 850092
Holes 18 L 6174 yds SSS
Recs Am–76 C Wood
V'tors U–by arrangement
Fees £19.95
Loc 5 miles SW of Stow-on-the-Wold, off B4068
Arch Jacob Pott

Painswick (1891)

Painswick, Stroud GL6 6TL

Tel **(01452) 812180**
Mem 430
Sec AR Green
Pro None
Holes 18 L 4780 yds SSS 65
Recs Am–61 B Hill
V'tors WD/Sat–U Sun–M SOC
Fees £10 Sat–£15
Loc 1/2 mile N of Painswick on A46
Arch David Brown

Puckrup Hall Hotel (1992)

Puckrup, Tewkesbury GL20 6EL

Tel **(01684) 296200**
Fax **(01684) 850788**
Pro K Pickett
Holes 18 L 6431 yds SSS 71
V'tors WD–H SOC WE–residents
Fees £25
Loc 2 miles N of Tewkesbury on A38. M50 Junction 1. M5 Junction 8
Arch S Gidman

Rodway (1991)

Pay and play
Highnam GL2 8DN

Tel **(01452) 384222**
Fax **(01989) 766450**
Mem 450
Sec S Williams
Pro T Grubb
Holes 18 L 5860 yds SSS 68
V'tors U SOC
Fees 18 holes–£9 (£11) 9 holes–££5 (£6)
Loc 2 miles SW of Gloucester (B4215)
Arch J Gabb

Sherdons Golf Centre (1993)

Pay and play
Manor Farm, Tredington, Tewkesbury

Tel **(01684) 274782**
Pro P Clark
Holes 9 L 2654 yds Par 34
V'tors U
Fees 18 holes–£9 (£12) 9 holes–£5.50 (£7.50)
Loc 2 miles S of Tewkesbury, off A38
Mis Driving range

Stinchcombe Hill (1889)

Stinchcombe Hill, Dursley GL11 6AQ

Tel **(01453) 542015**
Mem 550
Sec JR Clarke (Hon)
Pro B Wynne (01453) 543878
Holes 18 L 5734 yds SSS 68
Recs Am–63 TP Smith (1992) Pro–64 I Bolt (1984)
V'tors WD–U WE/BH–NA before 10.30am SOC
Fees £12.50 D–£20 (£25) W–£50
Loc 1 mile W of Dursley

Streamleaze (1982)

Bradley, Wotton-under-Edge

Tel **(01453) 843128**
Mem 200
Sec J Hewlett
Pro I Watts
Holes 9 L 4582 yds SSS 63
V'tors U
Fees D–£6 Sat–£7 Sun–£8
Loc 3 miles E of M5 Junction 14, off B4058

Tewkesbury Park Hotel (1976)

Lincoln Green Lane, Tewkesbury GL20 7DN

Tel **(01684) 295405**
Mem 550
Sec RS Nichol (01684) 299452
Pro R Taylor (01684) 294892
Holes 18 L 6533 yds SSS 72 6 hole Par 3 course
Recs Am–69 B Wilson Pro–68 N Job
V'tors WD–U H SOC–WD WE–residential SOC only
Fees £25 (£30)
Loc 1/2 mile S of Tewkesbury on A38. M5 Junction 9, 2 miles

Westonbirt (1971)

Westonbirt, Tetbury GL8 8QG

Tel **(01666) 880242**
Mem 200
Sec Bursar, Westonbirt School
Holes 9 L 4504 yds SSS 61
Recs Am–62 S Dunlop
V'tors U SOC–WD
Fees On application
Loc 3 miles S of Tetbury, off A433

Hampshire

Alresford (1890)

Cheriton Road, Alresford SO24 0PN

Tel **(01962) 733746**
Fax **(01962) 736040**
Mem 670
Sec P Kingston
Pro M Scott (01962) 733998
Holes 18 L 5905 yds Par 69 SSS 68
Recs Am–67 G Richardson Pro–65 R Edwards
V'tors U H WE–after noon SOC
Fees £15 D–£25 (£30)
Loc 1 mile S of Alresford on B3046
Arch Scott Webb Young

Alton (1908)

Old Odiham Road, Alton GU34 4BU

Tel **(01420) 84774**
Mem 370
Sec WJ Cleveland
Pro P Brown (01420) 86518
Holes 9 L 5744 yds SSS 68
Recs Am–64 R Lamport (1993) Pro–62 R Edwards (1993)

V'tors WD–U WE–H or M SOC–WD
Fees £9 (£12 D–£16)
Loc 2 miles N of Alton. 6 miles S of Odiham, off B3349
Arch James Braid

Ampfield Par Three (1963)

Winchester Road, Ampfield, Romsey SO51 9BQ
Tel **(01794) 368480**
Mem 500
Sec Mrs S Baker
Pro R Benfield (01794) 368750
Holes 18 L 2478 yds SSS 53
Recs Am–49 R Bailey
Pro–49 A Timms
V'tors WD–U WE/BH–H (phone first) SOC
Fees £9 (£15.50)
Loc 5 miles E of Romsey on A31
Arch Henry Cotton

Andover (1907)

51 Winchester Road, Andover SP10 2EF
Tel **(01264) 323980**
Mem 460 70(L) 35(J)
Sec DA Fairweather (01264) 358040
Pro A Timms (01264) 324151
Holes 9 L 5933 yds SSS 68
Recs Am–65 V Rusher (1993)
Pro–64 I Young (1991)
V'tors WD–U WE/BH–NA before noon SOC
Fees £10 (£22)
Loc ½ mile S of Andover on A3057
Arch JH Taylor

Army (1883)

Laffans Road, Aldershot GU11 2HF
Tel **(01252) 541104**
Fax **(01252) 376562**
Mem 800
Sec RT Crabb(Sec/Mgr) (01252) 540638
Pro N Turner (01252) 547232
Holes 18 L 6579 yds SSS 71
Recs Am–67 M Rollason
Pro–69 I Young
V'tors WD–H–contact Sec/Mgr SOC
Fees Special rates for Forces
Loc Between Aldershot and Farnborough

Barton-on-Sea (1897)

Milford Road, New Milton BH25 5PP
Tel **(01425) 615308**
Fax **(01425) 621457**
Mem 440 115(L) 50(J)
Sec N Hallam-Jones
Pro P Coombs (01425) 611210
Holes 27 L 6289-6505 yds Par 72
V'tors H NA before 9am SOC–WD exc Tues
Fees D–£25 (D–£30)
Loc 1 mile from New Milton, off B3058. M27 Junction 1
Arch J Hamilton Stutt

Basingstoke (1928)

Kempshott Park, Basingstoke RG23 7LL
Tel **(01256) 465990**
Fax **(01256) 465990**
Mem 700
Sec G Hogg
Pro I Hayes (01256) 51332
Holes 18 L 6350 yds SSS 70
Recs Am–69 C Humphrey (1994)
Pro–68 I Hayes (1994)
V'tors WD–H WE–M SOC–Wed & Thurs
Fees £20 D–£30
Loc 3 miles W of Basingstoke on A30. M3 Junction 7

Bishopswood (1978)

Bishopswood Lane, Tadley, Basingstoke RG26 6AT
Tel **(01734) 815213**
Mem 520
Sec MW Phillips (Mgr) (01734) 812200
Pro S Ward
Holes 9 L 6474 yds SSS 71
Recs Am–69 C Wilkins (1987)
Pro–66 P Bryden (1992)
V'tors WD–U WE–M
Fees £13
Loc 6 miles N of Basingstoke, off A340
Mis Floodlit driving range

Blackmoor (1913)

Whitehill, Bordon GU35 9EH
Tel **(01420) 472775**
Fax **(01420) 487666**
Mem 680 100(L) 70(J)
Sec TH Glover
Pro S Clay (01420) 472345
Holes 18 L 6213 yds SSS 70
Recs Am–66 NE Holman (1988)
Pro–64 R Dickman (1990)
V'tors H WE–NA
Fees £27 D–£36
Loc ½ mile W of Whitehill on A325
Arch HS Colt

Blacknest (1993)

Frith End, Binsted GU34 4QL
Tel **(01420) 22888**
Fax **(01420) 22001**
Mem 250
Sec GD Lawson
Pro I Benson
Holes 9 L 6726 yds SSS 72
9 hole Par 3 course
V'tors U SOC
Fees 18 holes–£13 (£15)
9 holes–£7 (£8.50)
Loc 7 miles SW of Farnham, off A325
Mis Driving range
Arch Dr Peter Nicholson

Botley Park Hotel & CC (1989)

Winchester Road, Boorley Green, Botley SO3 2UA
Tel **(01489) 780888 Ext 444**
Fax **(01489) 789242**
Mem 700
Sec Miss A Gardiner
Pro T Barter (01489) 789771
Holes 18 L 6026 yds SSS 70
V'tors H SOC
Fees £30
Loc 6 miles E of Southampton on B3354. M27 Junction 7. 8 miles SE of M3
Mis Driving range
Arch Potterton/Murray

Bramshaw (1880)

Brook, Lyndhurst SO43 7HE
Tel **(01703) 813433**
Fax **(01703) 813958**
Mem 1400
Sec RD Tingey
Pro C Bonner (01703) 813434
Holes Forest 18 L 5774 yds SSS 68
Manor 18 L 6257 yds SSS 70
Recs Forest Am–67 G Hill
Pro–65 R Tuddenham
Manor Am–66 M LeMesurier
Pro–66 G Stubbington
V'tors WD–U H WE–M
Fees £20 (£30)
Loc 10 miles SW of Southampton. M27 Junction 1, 1 mile

Brokenhurst Manor (1919)

Sway Road, Brockenhurst SO42 7SG
Tel **(01590) 623332**
Fax **(01590) 624140**
Mem 800
Sec AS Craven
Pro J Lovell (01590) 623092
Holes 18 L 6222 yds SSS 70
Recs Am–64 K Weeks
Pro–64 N Tokely
V'tors WD–H after 9.30am NA–Tues–Ladies' Day SOC
Fees D–£25 D–£30 (£35)
Loc 1 mile SW of Brockenhurst on B3055
Arch HS Colt

Burley (1905)

Burley, Ringwood BH24 4BB
Tel **(01425) 402431**
Mem 520
Sec GR Kendall
Holes 9 L 3135 yds SSS 69
Recs Am–68 AS Elliott (1991)
V'tors H
Fees £14 (£16) W–£40
Loc 4 miles SE of Ringwood

Chilworth Golf Centre (1989)

Pay and play
Main Road, Chilworth, Southampton SO16 7JP
Tel **(01703) 740544**
Fax **(01703) 733166**
Sec Mrs E Garner
Pro M Butcher, L Blake
Holes Manor 18 L 5740 yds SSS 69
Pro–68 M Butcher (1994)
V'tors U

For list of abbreviations see page 435

Fees 9 holes–£5 (£7.50)
Loc Between Romsey and Southampton on A27
Mis Driving range

Corhampton (1891)

Sheeps Pond Lane, Droxford, Southampton SO3 1QZ
Tel **(01489) 877279**
Fax **(01489) 877680**
Mem 750
Sec R Easson
Pro G Stubbington (01489) 877638
Holes 18 L 6088 yds SSS 69
Recs Am–66 R Edwards (1988), A Clotworthy (1992)
Pro–64 MD Jarvis (1991), G Stubbington (1992)
V'tors WD–U H WE/BH–M SOC–Mons & Thurs
Fees £20 D–£30
Loc 9 miles S of Winchester

Dibden (1974)

Public
Main Road, Dibden, Southampton SO4 5TB
Tel **(01703) 845596**
Fax **(01703) 845596**
Mem 700
Sec Mrs J Lock (Hon) (01703) 843943
Pro A Bridge
Holes 18 L 6206 yds SSS 70
9 hole course
Recs Am–63 R Bland (1992)
Pro–63 I Young (1988)
V'tors U
Fees £7.25 (£10.50)
Loc 10 miles W of Southampton, off A326 at Dibden r'bout
Mis Floodlit driving range

Dummer (1993)

Dummer, Basingstoke RG25 2AR
Tel **(01256) 397888**
Fax **(01256) 397889**
Mem 750
Sec M Reeves
Pro M Reeves
Holes 18 hole course SSS 72
V'tors U
Fees £20
Loc 7 miles SW of Basingstoke. M3 Junction 7
Arch Alliss/Clark

Dunwood Manor (1969)

Shootash Hill, Romsey SO5 10GF
Tel **(01794) 340549**
Fax **(01794) 341215**
Mem 700
Sec Mrs H Johnson
Pro J Simpson (01794) 340663
Holes 18 L 5885 yds SSS 69
Recs Am–69 D Harris
Pro–61 G Stubbington
V'tors WE/BH–restricted SOC–WD
Fees £20 (£30)
Loc Romsey 4 miles, off A27

Fleetlands (1961)

Fareham Road, Gosport PO13 0AW
Tel **(01705) 822351**
Mem 120
Sec A Eade (Ext 44384)
Holes 9 L 4852 yds SSS 64
Recs Am–67 M Squibb, D Edmunds
Pro–68 K Jackson
V'tors M at all times
Loc 2 miles S of Fareham on A32 Gosport road. M27 Junction 12

Fleming Park (1973)

Public
Fleming Park, Magpie Lane, Eastleigh SO5 3LH
Tel **(01703) 612797**
Sec D Ainsworth-Lay
Pro C Strickett
Holes 18 L 4436 yds SSS 62
Recs Am–62 D Cox (1989)
Pro–61 J Hay
V'tors U SOC–WD
Fees £5.95 (£8.65) (1993)
Loc 6 miles N of Southampton

Furzeley (1993)

Pay and play
Furzeley, Denmead PO7 6TX
Tel **(01705) 231180**
Fax **(01705) 231180**
Pro D Brown
Holes 9 L 1858 yds SSS 29
Recs Am–28 M Jeune (1993)
V'tors U SOC
Fees 9 holes–£5 (£6)
Loc 2 miles NW of Waterlooville

Gosport & Stokes Bay (1885)

Fort Road, Haslar, Gosport PO12 2AT
Tel **(01705) 581625**
Fax **(01705) 527941**
Mem 450
Sec AP Chubb (01705) 527941
Holes 9 L 5668 yds SSS 69
Recs Am–69 M Stubley (1986)
Pro–65 P Dawson (1985)
V'tors U exc Sun–NA
Fees £15 (£20)
Loc S boundary of Gosport

Great Salterns (1914)

Public
Portsmouth Golf Centre, Burrfields Road, Portsmouth PO3 5HH
Tel **(01705) 664549/699519**
Fax **(01705) 650525**
Pro T Healy
Holes 18 L 5970 yds SSS 68
V'tors U SOC
Fees £9
Loc 1 mile off M27 on A2030
Mis Driving range

Hartley Wintney (1891)

London Road, Hartley Wintney, Basingstoke RG27 8PT
Tel **(01252) 842214**
Mem 410
Sec BD Powell (01252) 844211
Pro M Smith (01252) 843779
Holes 9 L 6096 yds SSS 69
Recs Am–70 M Wild
Pro–63 R Lewington
V'tors Wed–Ladies Day
WE/BH–restricted SOC–Tues & Thurs
Fees £17 (£20)
Loc A30 between Camberley and Basingstoke
Mis Extension to 18 holes 1996/7

Hayling (1883)

Links Lane, Hayling Island PO11 0BX
Tel **(01705) 463712/463777**
Mem 800
Sec Cdr D Harrison (01705) 464446
Pro R Gadd (01705) 464491
Holes 18 L 6521 yds SSS 71
Recs Am–65 EJ Tambling (1993)
Pro–66 F Gilbride
V'tors H WE/BH–after 11.30am SOC
Fees £28 (£34)
Loc 5 miles S of Havant on A3023
Arch Taylor (1905)/Simpson (1933)

Hockley (1915)

Twyford, Winchester SO21 1PL
Tel **(01962) 713165**
Mem 750
Sec A Heron
Pro T Lane (01962) 713678
Holes 18 L 6296 yds SSS 70
V'tors WD–U WE/BH–M
Fees On application
Loc 2 miles S of Winchester on B3335
Arch James Braid

Leckford & Longstock (1929)

Leckford, Stockbridge SO20 6JS
Tel **(01264) 810320**
Mem 200
Sec J Wood
Pro LG Lucas
Holes 9 L 3251 yds SSS 71
V'tors M
Loc 5 miles W of Andover

Lee-on-the-Solent (1905)

Brune Lane, Lee-on-the-Solent PO13 9PB
Tel **(01705) 550207**
Mem 715
Sec P Clash (Mgr) (01705) 551170
Pro J Richardson (01705) 551181
Holes 18 L 5959 yds SSS 69
Recs Am–66 S Richardson
Pro–63 R Edwards (1993)
V'tors WD–U H WE–M H SOC–Thurs
Fees D–£25 (£30)
Loc 3 miles S of Fareham. M27 Junction 11

For list of abbreviations see page 435

Liphook (1922)
Liphook GU30 7EH
Tel **(01428) 723271**
Fax **(01428) 724853**
Mem 700
Sec Maj JB Morgan MBE (01428) 723785
Pro I Large
Holes 18 L 6207 yds SSS 70
Recs Am–67 A Thomson, N Clemens, M Bolsover
Pro–66 TR Pinner
V'tors I H (max 24) Sun–NA before 1pm SOC
Fees £25 D–£35 (£35 D–£45)
Loc 1 mile S of Liphook on old A3 Portsmouth road
Arch ACG Groome

Meon Valley Hotel (1977)
Sandy Lane, Shedfield, Southampton SO32 2HQ
Tel **(01329) 833455**
Fax **(01329) 834411**
Mem 750
Sec T Hussey (Gen Mgr)
GF McMenemy (Sec)
Pro P Green
Holes 18 L 6519 yds SSS 71
9 L 2885 yds SSS 68
Recs Am–69 T Page (1991)
Pro–67 J Garner (1987)
V'tors H SOC
Fees 18 hole:£30 (£40) 9 hole:£15
Loc 2 miles NW of Wickham. N off A334
Arch J Hamilton Stutt

New Forest (1888)
Southampton Road, Lyndhurst SO43 7BU
Tel **(01703) 282752**
Mem 900
Sec Mrs W Swann
Pro K Gilhespy
Holes 18 L 5742 yds SS 68
Recs Am–63 J Longford (1993)
Pro–67 S Clay, R Brown
V'tors U exc Sun am
Fees £12 (£14)
Loc 8 miles W of Southampton on A35

North Hants (1904)
Minley Road, Fleet GU13 8RE
Tel **(01252) 616443**
Fax **(01252) 811627**
Mem 550
Sec IR Goodliffe
Pro S Porter (01252) 616655
Holes 18 L 6257 yds Par 69 SSS 70
Recs Am–66 MC Hughesdon (1976), J Dodds, JS Cheetham (1988), G Evans (1990)
Pro–65 LR Booth, GM Hughes (1994)
Ladies–65 A MacDonald, C Caldwell (1990)
V'tors WD–H by prior arrangement WE/BH–MH SOC–Tues & Wed
Fees On application
Loc 3 miles W of Farnborough on B3013. M3 Junction 4A
Arch James Braid

Old Thorns (1982)
Pay and play
Longmoor Road, Griggs Green, Liphook GU30 7PE
Tel **(01428) 724555**
Fax **(01428) 725322**
Sec GM Jones (Gen Mgr)
Pro P Loxley
Holes 18 L 6533 yds SSS 71
Pro–69 I Aoki (1982)
V'tors U SOC
Fees £25 (£35)
Loc Griggs Green exit off A3
Mis Driving range
Arch Cdr John Harris

Paultons Golf Centre (1993)
Pay and play
Old Salisbury Road, Ower, Romsey SO51 6AN
Tel **(01703) 813992**
Fax **(01703) 813993**
Sec J Smith (Golf Dir)
Pro J Cave, H Teschner (01703) 814626
Holes 18 L 6238 yds SSS 71
9 hole Academy course
V'tors U SOC
Fees 18 holes–£17.50 (£18.50)
9 holes–£6.50
Loc Nr M27 Junction 2, at Ower
Mis Driving range

Petersfield (1892)
Heath Road, Petersfield GU31 4EJ
Tel **(01730) 263725**
Mem 521 108(L) 79(J)
Sec RR Hine (01730) 262386
Pro G Hughes (01730) 267732
Holes 18 L 5603 yds SSS 67
Recs Am–67 J Britton
Pro–65 G Hughes
V'tors WD–U WE/BH–NA before noon SOC–Wed/Thurs/Fri
Fees £15 D–£21 (£21 D–£30)
Loc ½ mile E of Petersfield

Portsmouth (1926)
Public
Crookhorn Lane, Widley, Portsmouth PO7 5QL
Tel **(01705) 372210/372299**
Fax **(01705) 200766**
Mem 750
Sec D Houlihan
Pro I Roper (01705) 372210
Holes 18 L 6139 yds SSS 69
V'tors U SOC–arrange with Pro
Fees £7.25–£9.90
Loc 1 mile N of Portsmouth, on B2177

Romsey (1900)
Nursling, Southampton SO1 9XW
Tel **(01703) 732218**
Fax **(01703) 741036**
Mem 825
Sec P Hargraves (01703) 734637
Pro M Desmond (01703) 736673
Holes 18 L 5752 yds SSS 68
Recs Am–65 J Archer (1990)
Pro–64 J Slade (1985)
V'tors WD–H WE/BH–M H
Fees £19.50 D–£24
Loc 2 miles SE of Romsey on A3057. M27/M271 Junction 3

Rowlands Castle (1902)
Links Lane, Rowlands Castle PO9 6AE
Tel **(01705) 412216**
Mem 710 150(L) 60(J)
Sec KD Fisher (01705) 412784
Pro P Klepacz (01705) 412785
Holes 18 L 6627 yds SSS 72
Recs Am–70 N Cole, C Anderson, I McLeod
Pro–66 M Gregson
Ladies–73 A Wheble
V'tors WD–U H exc Wed am–restricted WE–phone first Sat–M SOC–Tues & Thurs
Fees £22 (£27)
Loc 9 miles S of Petersfield, off A3(M). 3 miles N of Havant

Royal Winchester (1888)
Sarum Road, Winchester SO22 5QE
Tel **(01962) 852462**
Fax **(01962) 865048**
Mem 700
Sec AD Bluck (Mgr)
Pro S Hunter (01962) 862473
Holes 18 L 6218 yds SSS 70
Recs Am–67 J Curren, P Driver, D Driver
Pro–67 B Lane, D Feherty, K Bowden, I Roper
V'tors WD–U H WE/BH–M SOC–Mon–Wed
Fees On application
Loc W of Winchester, off A31

Sandford Springs (1988)
Wolverton, Basingstoke RG26 5RT
Tel **(01635) 297881**
Fax **(01635) 298065**
Mem 700
Sec G Tipple
Pro K Brake, G Edmunds (01635) 297883
Holes 27 L 6100 yds SSS 70
V'tors WD–prior booking WE–M SOC
Fees £23 D–£29
Loc 8 miles NW of Basingstoke on A339
Arch Hawtree

South Winchester
Pitt, Winchester SO22 5QW
Tel **(01962) 877800**
Fax **(01962) 877900**
Sec S Wright (Gen Mgr)
Pro R Adams (01962) 840469
Holes 18 L 7086 yds SSS 74
V'tors M
Loc S side of Winchester on Romsey road
Mis Driving range
Arch Thomas/Alliss

Southampton Municipal (1935)

Public
Golf Course Road, Bassett, Southampton
Tel **(01703) 768407**
Pro J Cave
Holes 18 L 6218 yds SSS 70
9 L 2391 yds SSS 33
Recs Am–64 P Dedman
Pro–62 SW Murray
V'tors U
Fees On application
Loc 2 miles N of Southampton

Southwick Park (1977)

Pinsley Drive, Southwick PO17 6EL
Tel **(01705) 380131**
Mem 650 80(L)
Sec NW Price
Pro J Green (01705) 380442
Holes 18 L 5972 yds SSS 69
Recs Am–67 R Edwards, R Berry
Pro–64 G Hughes
V'tors WD–U before 11am only
SOC–Tues
Fees On application. Royal Navy Personnel reduced rate
Loc 5 miles N of Portsmouth, off B2177

Southwood (1977)

Public
Ively Road, Farnborough GU14 0LJ
Tel **(01252) 548700**
Sec R Hammond
Pro R Hammond
Holes 18 L 5738 yds SSS 68
Recs Am–67 (1991)
Pro–61 R Edwards
V'tors U
Fees £11.50 (£14)
Loc 1 mile W of Farnborough, off A325
Arch M Hawtree

Stoneham (1908)

Monks Wood Close, Bassett, Southampton SO16 3TT
Tel **(01703) 768151**
Fax **(01703) 766320**
Mem 800
Sec AGM Bennett
(01703) 769272
Pro I Young (01703) 768397
Holes 18 L 6310 yds SSS 70
Recs Am–63 M Blackey
Pro–63 J Martin
V'tors WD–U SOC–Mon/Thurs/Fri
Fees £27 (£30)
Loc 2 miles N of Southampton on A27
Arch Willie Park

Test Valley (1992)

Micheldever Road, Overton, Basingstoke RG25 3DS
Tel **(01256) 771737**
Mem 400
Sec T Notley (Sec/Mgr)
Pro T Notley
Holes 18 L 6811 yds SSS 73
V'tors U SOC
Fees £14 (£20)
Loc 2 miles S of Overton on Micheldever road. M3 Junction 8
Arch Wright/Darcy

Tournerbury Golf Centre (1993)

Pay and play
Tournerbury Road, Hayling Island PO11 9DL
Tel **(01705) 462266**
Pro R Brown
Holes 9 L 2956 yds SSS 35
V'tors U SOC
Fees 9 holes–£6.80 (£7.80)
Loc E coast of Hayling Island. 3 miles S of Havant
Mis Driving range

Tylney Park (1973)

Rotherwick, Basingstoke RG27 9AY
Tel **(01256) 762079**
Mem 700
Sec AD Bewley
Pro C de Bruin (Mgr)
Holes 18 L 6108 yds SSS 69
Recs Am–65 J Shaw
Pro–68 S Watson (1988)
V'tors WD–U WE–M or H SOC
Fees £20 (£28)
Loc 2 miles NW of Hook. M3 Junction 5

Waterlooville (1907)

Cherry Tree Ave, Cowplain, Waterlooville PO8 8AP
Mem 700
Sec C Chamberlain
(01705) 263388
Pro J Hay (01705) 256911
Holes 18 L 6647 yds SSS 72
Recs Am–68 D Hickman (1987), NF Borrow (1994)
Pro–66 H Stott (1988), R Edwards (1993)
Ladies–71 K Smith (1992)
V'tors WD/WE–M H (Sun am–XL) SOC
Fees £20 D–£30
Loc 10 miles N of Portsmouth on A3
Arch Henry Cotton

Wellow (1991)

Ryedown Lane, East Wellow, Romsey SO51 6BD
Tel **(01794) 322872**
Mem 400
Sec Mrs C Gurd
Pro N Bratley (01794) 323833
Holes 18 L 5966 yds SSS 69
Recs Am–68 A Hemington (1994)
V'tors U SOC–WD
Fees £15 (£20)
Loc 2 miles W of Romsey. M27 Junction 2
Arch W Wiltshire

Weybrook Park (1971)

Aldermaston Road, Sherborne St John, Basingstoke RG24 9ND
Tel **(01256) 20347**
Mem 400
Sec GE Carpenter
Holes 18 L 6100 yds SSS 70
V'tors WD–U WE–contact Mgr SOC
Fees £12 (£14)
Loc 1½ miles N of Basingstoke

Worldham Park (1993)

Pay and play
Cakers Lane, Worldham, Alton GU34 3AG
Tel **(01420) 543151**
Mem 500
Sec R Buss (Hon)
Pro C Troth (01420) 544606
Holes 18 L 5836 yds SSS 68
V'tors WD–U WE–U after 11 am
SOC–WD
Fees £8 (£10)
Loc ½ mile E of Alton on B3004 to Bordon
Mis Driving range
Arch Troth/Widborne

Hereford & Worcester

Abbey Park G & CC (1985)

Dagnell End Road, Redditch B98 7BD
Tel **(01527) 63918**
Fax **(01527) 65872**
Mem 1200
Sec ME Bradley
Pro RK Cameron (01527) 68006
Holes 18 L 6411 yds SSS 71
V'tors WD–U SOC
Fees £10 (£12.50)
Loc B4101, off A441 Birmingham road
Mis Driving range
Arch Donald Steel

Bank House Hotel G & CC (1992)

Bransford, Worcester WR6 5JD
Tel **(01886) 833551**
Fax **(01886) 832461**
Sec PAD Holmes
Pro G Hawkings
Holes 18 L 6101 yds SSS 69
V'tors U SOC
Fees £20 (£25)
Loc 3 miles SW of Worcester on A4103 Hereford road. M5 Junction 7
Mis Driving range
Arch Bob Sandow

Belmont Lodge (1983)

Belmont, Hereford HR2 9SA
Tel **(01432) 352666**
Fax **(01432) 358090**
Mem 500

Pro M Welsh (01432) 352717
Holes 18 L 6480 yds SSS 71
Recs Am–74 R Hemmings
Pro–70 A Griffiths, J Lomas
V'tors U SOC
Fees On application
Loc 1½ miles S of Hereford on A465

Blackwell (1893)

Blackwell, Bromsgrove B60 1PY
Tel **(0121) 445 1781**
Fax **(0121) 445 1994**
Mem 300 100(L) 20(J)
Sec RWA Burns (0121) 445 1994
Pro N Blake (0121) 445 3113
Holes 18 L 6202 yds SSS 71
Recs Am–65 M Reynard (1994)
Pro–63 W Stephens (1994)
V'tors WD–U H WE/BH–M
Fees £45
Loc 3 miles E of Bromsgrove. M42 Junction 1 (South)

Burghill Valley (1991)

Tillington Road, Burghill, Hereford HR4 7RW
Tel **(01432) 760456**
Sec K Smith (Mgr)
Holes 18 L 6239 yds SSS 70
V'tors U SOC
Fees £14 (£16)
Loc 3 miles N of Hereford, off A4110

Cadmore Lodge (1990)

Pay and play
Berrington Green, Tenbury Wells, Worcester WR15 8TQ
Tel **(01584) 810044**
Mem 150
Sec RV Farr
Pro None
Holes 9 L 5129 yds Par 68 SSS 65
V'tors U
Fees D–£7 (D–£10)
Loc 2 miles S of Tenbury Wells on A4112

Churchill & Blakedown (1926)

Churchill Lane, Blakedown, Kidderminster DY10 3NB
Tel **(01562) 700018**
Mem 350
Sec B Pendry
Pro K Wheeler
Holes 9 L 6472 yds SSS 71
V'tors WD–U WE–M
Fees £17.50
Loc 3 miles N of Kidderminster on A456

Droitwich G & CC (1897)

Ford Lane, Droitwich WR9 0BQ
Tel **(01905) 770129**
Fax **(01905) 797290**
Mem 782
Sec MJ Taylor (01905) 774344
Pro CS Thompson (01905) 770207
Holes 18 L 6058 yds SSS 69
Recs Am–63 J Bickerton
V'tors WD–U WE/BH–M
SOC–Wed & Fri
Fees £24
Loc 1 mile N of Droitwich, off A38. M5 Junction 5

Evesham (1894)

Craycombe Links, Fladbury, Pershore WR10 2QS
Tel **(01386) 860395**
Mem 340
Sec FG Vincent (Hon)
(01386) 552373
Pro C Haynes (01386) 861144
Holes 9 L 6415 yds SSS 71
V'tors WD–H WE–M NA on comp/match days SOC
Fees D–£15
Loc Fladbury, 4 miles W of Evesham (B4084)

Fulford Heath (1933)

Tanners Green Lane, Wythall, Birmingham B47 6BH
Tel **(01564) 822806 (Clubhouse)**
Fax **(01564) 822629**
Mem 700
Sec RG Bowen (01564) 824758
Pro D Down (01564) 822930
Holes 18 L 6216 yds SSS 70
Recs Am–70 A Hill
Pro–S Leahy
V'tors WD–H WE/BH–M SOC
Fees £25
Loc 8 miles S of Birmingham

Habberley (1924)

Trimpley Road, Kidderminster DY11 5RG
Tel **(01562) 745756**
Mem 400
Sec DB Lloyd
Holes 9 L 5440 yds SSS 67
Recs Am–65 P Hopkins
V'tors WD–U WE–M SOC
Fees £10
Loc 3 miles NW of Kidderminster

Hereford Municipal (1983)

Public
Holmer Road, Hereford HR4 9UD
Tel **(01432) 278178**
Fax **(01432) 266281**
Sec S Chalk (Mgr)
Pro S Ward
Holes 9 L 3060 yds SSS 69
V'tors U SOC
Fees 18 holes–£5.20 (£7)
9 holes–£3.20 (£4.40)
Loc Hereford Leisure Centre (A49)

Herefordshire (1896)

Raven's Causeway, Wormsley, Hereford HR4 8LY
Tel **(01432) 830219**
Mem 500 75(L) 85(J)
Sec WJ Bullock (Hon)
Pro D Hemming (01432) 830465
Holes 18 L 6069 yds SSS 69
Recs Am–63 D Park (1993)
Pro–61 B Barnes
V'tors U–phone first SOC
Fees £14 D–£20 (£18 D–£26)
Loc 6 miles NW of Hereford

Kidderminster (1909)

Russell Road, Kidderminster DY10 3HT
Tel **(01562) 822303**
Fax **(01562) 862041**
Mem 800
Sec AD Biggs
Pro NP Underwood
(01562) 740090
Holes 18 L 6405 yds SSS 71
Recs Am–67 MJ Houghton (1986)
Pro–67 D Blakeman (1987)
Ladies–71 K Greenfield (1991)
V'tors WD–H WE–M SOC–Thurs
Fees £22
Loc Signposted off A449 Wolverhampton–Worcester

King's Norton (1892)

Brockhill Lane, Weatheroak, Alvechurch, Birmingham B48 7ED
Tel **(01564) 826789**
Fax **(01564) 826955**
Mem 950
Sec LNW Prince (Sec/Mgr)
Pro K Hayward (01564) 822822
Holes 18 L 7057 yds SSS 74
9 L 3300 yds SSS 36
Recs Am–J Kemp (1993)
V'tors WD–U WE–NA SOC
Fees £27 D–£29.50
Loc 8 miles S of Birmingham. M42 Junction 3, 2 miles
Mis 12 hole short course
Arch Fred Hawtree

Kington (1926)

Bradnor Hill, Kington HR5 3RE
Tel **(01544) 230340**
Fax **(01544) 340270**
Mem 500
Sec GR Wictome (01544) 340270
Pro D Oliver (01544) 231320
Holes 18 L 5840 yds SSS 68
Recs Am–65 K Alexander
V'tors WE–NA before 10.15am –restricted 1.30–2.45pm SOC
Fees £13 D–£16 (£16 D–£20)
Loc 1 mile N of Kington
Arch CK Hutchinson

Leominster (1967)

Ford Bridge, Leominster HR6 0LE
Tel **(01568) 612863**
Mem 650
Sec JA Ashcroft (01432) 880493
Pro G Bebb (01568) 611402
Holes 18 L 6029 yds SSS 69
Recs Am–69 D Francis (1992)
Pro–71 F Clark (1992)
V'tors I or H SOC
Fees £12.50 D–£17 (£21)
Loc 3 miles S of Leominster on A49 (Leominster By-pass)
Arch R Sandow

Little Lakes (1975)

Lye Head, Bewdley, Worcester DY12 2UZ

Tel **(01299) 266385**
Mem 400 50(L)
Sec T Norris (01562) 67495
Pro M Laing
Holes 9 L 6247 yds SSS 72
Recs Am–70 R Dean (1990)
Pro–70 R Lane (1986)
V'tors WD–U WE–NA SOC
Fees £12 D–£15
Loc 3 miles W of Bewdley, off A456

Ombersley (1991)

Bishopswood Road, Ombersley, Droitwich WR9 0LE

Tel **(01905) 620747**
Fax **(01905) 620047**
Mem 700
Sec G Glenister (Mgr)
Pro G Glenister
Holes 18 L 6139 yds SSS 69
V'tors U
Fees £9.60 (£12.80)
Loc 6 miles N of Worcester, off A449
Mis Driving range
Arch David Morgan

Perdiswell Municipal

Pay and play
Bilford Road, Worcester WR3 8DX

Tel **(01905) 754668**
Sec HA Ward
Holes 9 L 6004 yds SSS 69
V'tors U
Fees On application

Pitcheroak (1973)

Public
Plymouth Road, Redditch B97 4PB

Tel **(01527) 541054**
Pro D Stewart
Holes 9 L 4584 yds SSS 62
V'tors U
Fees On application
Loc Redditch

Redditch (1913)

Lower Grinsty, Green Lane, Callow Hill, Redditch B97 5PJ

Tel **(01527) 543309**
Mem 883
Sec C Holman
Pro F Powell (01527) 546372
Holes 18 L 6671 yds SSS 72
Pro–68 G Mercer (1991)
V'tors WD–U SOC
Fees £27.50
Loc 3 miles SW of Redditch, off A441
Arch F Pennink

Ross-on-Wye (1903)

Two Park, Gorsley, Ross-on-Wye HR9 7UT

Tel **(01989) 720267**
Fax **(01989) 720212**
Mem 760
Sec GH Cason
Pro N Catchpole (01989) 720439
Holes 18 L 6500 yds SSS 73
Recs Am–69 D Powell (1994)
Pro–68 J Peters (1994)
Ladies–69 E Fields (1994)
V'tors U SOC–Wed–Fri (min 20 players)
Fees £30 D–£35
Loc 5 miles N of Ross-on-Wye, by M50 Junction 3
Arch CK Cotton

Sapey (1991)

Upper Sapey, Worcester WR6 6XT

Tel **(01886) 853288**
Fax **(01886) 853485**
Mem 50
Sec Miss L Stevenson
Pro C Knowles
Holes 18 L 5885 yds SSS 69
Recs Am–64 E Deasey (1994)
Pro–63 K Craggs (1994)
V'tors WD–U WE–NA before 10am SOC
Fees £15 D–£22 (£20 D–£25)
Loc 6 miles N of Bromyard on B4203. M5 Junction 5
Mis Driving range

South Herefordshire (1992)

Twin Lakes, Hartleton, Upton Bishop, Ross-on-Wye HR9 7UA

Tel **(01989) 780535**
Fax **(01989) 740611**
Mem 150
Sec RLA Lee (Mgr)
(01989) 740612
Holes 18 L 6672 yds Par 71 SSS 72
9 hole Par 3 course
Recs Am–71 M Wilson (1993)
V'tors U
Fees £15 (£17)
Loc 3 miles NE of Ross-on-Wye. M50 Junction 4
Mis Driving range
Arch John Day

Tolladine (1898)

The Fairway, Tolladine Road, Worcester WR4 9BA

Tel **(01905) 21074 (Clubhouse)**
Mem 350
Pro (01905) 726180
Holes 9 L 5174 yds SSS 67
Recs Am–65 T Sanders (1992)
Ladies–71 C George (1991)
V'tors WD–U before 4pm –M after 4pm WE/BH–M SOC
Fees £15
Loc M5 Junction 6, 1 mile

The Vale G & CC (1991)

Bishampton, Pershore WR10 2LZ

Tel **(01386) 82781**
Fax **(01386) 82597**
Mem 500
Sec R Gardner (Golf Dir) (01386) 82520 R Harrison (Mgr) (01386) 82597
Pro Caroline Griffiths, R Gardner
Holes 18 L 7041 yds SSS 73
9 L 2950 yds SSS 70
V'tors U–phone Pro SOC
Fees On application
Loc 6 miles NW of Evesham, off B4084. M5 Junction 6, 8 miles
Mis Driving range

Wharton Park (1992)

Long Bank, Bewdley DY12 2QW

Tel **(01299) 405222**
Fax **(01299) 405121**
Mem 500
Sec CJ Price
Pro A Hoare (01299) 405163
Holes 18 L 6600 yds SSS 72
Recs Am–69 D Healing (1993)
Pro–67 C Clark (1993)
V'tors U SOC
Fees £15 (£20)
Loc Bewdley By-pass on A456
Mis Driving range. Academy

Worcester G & CC (1898)

Boughton Park, Worcester WR2 4EZ

Tel **(01905) 422555**
Mem 1100
Sec JM Kennedy
Pro C Colenso (01905) 422044
Holes 18 L 6154 yds SSS 69
V'tors WD–H WE–M SOC
Fees £23
Loc 1 mile W of Worcester on A4103
Arch Dr A Mackenzie

Worcestershire (1879)

Wood Farm, Malvern Wells WR14 4PP

Tel **(01684) 573905**
Mem 770
Sec GR Scott (01684) 575992
Pro GM Harris (01684) 564428
Holes 18 L 6449 yds SSS 71
Recs Am–67 PM Guest, MC Reynard, S Braithwaite
Pro–66 R Larratt
V'tors WD–H WE–H after 10am
Fees £25 (£30) W–£87
Loc 2 miles S of Gt Malvern, off A449/B4209

Wyre Forest Golf Centre

Pay and play
Birchen Coppice Farm, Zortech Avenue, Kidderminster DY11 7EX

Tel **(01299) 822682**
Fax **(01299) 379433**
Mem 125
Sec Elaine Fincher
Pro S Barker
Holes 18 L 5790 yds Par 70 SSS 68
V'tors U SOC
Fees £7.50 (£10)
Loc 18 miles S of Birmingham on A451, between Kidderminster and Stourport
Mis Floodlit driving range

Hertfordshire

Aldenham G & CC (1975)

Church Lane, Aldenham WD2 8AL

Tel **(01923) 853929**
Fax **(01923) 858472**
Mem 560
Sec DW Phillips
Pro A McKay (01923) 857889
Holes 18 L 6500 yds SSS 71
9 L 2350 yds
Recs Am–67 P Wharton (1987)
Pro–69 B Charles (1982)
V'tors U
Fees £20 (£28)
Loc 3 miles E of Watford, off B462. M1 Junction 5

Aldwickbury Park (1995)

Piggottshill Lane, Wheathampstead Road, Harpenden AL5 1AB

Tel **(01582) 765112**
Fax **(01582) 760113**
Sec J Connell
Pro (01582) 760112
Holes 18 L 6333 yds Par 71 SSS 69
9 hole Par 3 course
V'tors WD–U booking necessary WE–NA before 1pm SOC
Fees £18.50 (£25)
Loc E of Harpenden on Wheathampstead road. M1 Junction 9. A1(M) Junction 4
Mis Course opening May/June 1995
Arch Gillett/Brown

Arkley (1909)

Rowley Green Road, Barnet EN5 3HL

Tel **(0181) 449 0394**
Mem 350
Sec GD Taylor
Pro M Squire (0181) 440 8473
Holes 9 L 6045 yds SSS 69
Recs Am–67 SN McWilliams
Pro–63 LV Baker
V'tors WD–U WE–M SOC–Wed–Fri
Fees £15
Loc NW of Barnet, off A1(M)
Arch James Braid

Ashridge (1932)

Little Gaddesden, Berkhamsted HP4 1LY

Tel **(01442) 842244**
Fax **(01442) 843770**
Mem 730
Sec Mrs MA West
Pro G Pook (01442) 842307
Holes 18 L 6547 yds SSS 71
Recs Am–64 C Slattery
Pro–66 JRM Jacobs
V'tors WD only–phone Sec
Fees On application
Loc 5 miles N of Berkhamsted on B4506
Arch Campbell/Hutchison/Hotchkin

Batchwood Hall (1935)

Pay and play

Batchwood Drive, St Albans AL3 5XA

Tel **(01727) 833349**
Fax **(01582) 793215**
Mem 425
Sec BR Mercer
Pro J Thomson
Holes 18 L 6487 yds SSS 71
Recs Am–67 D Tapping (1991)
Pro–62 PP Wynne
V'tors WD–U WE–NA before 10am
Fees £9 (£11)
Loc NW of St Albans on A5081. 5 miles S of M1 Junction 9
Arch JH Taylor

Berkhamsted (1890)

The Common, Berkhamsted HP4 2QB

Tel **(01442) 863730**
Mem 300 120(L) 50(J)
Sec CD Hextall (01442) 865832
Pro BJ Proudfoot (01442) 865851
Holes 18 L 6605 yds SSS 72
Recs Am–64 N Leconte (1986)
Pro–69 S Proudfoot (1987)
V'tors U H WE–M before 11.30am SOC–Wed & Fri
Fees £20 (£35)
Loc 1 mile N of Berkhamsted
Arch HS Colt/James Braid

Bishop's Stortford (1910)

Dunmow Road, Bishop's Stortford CM23 5HP

Tel **(01279) 654027 (Clubhouse)**
Fax **(01279) 655215**
Mem 850
Sec B Hunt (01279) 654715
Pro V Duncan (01279) 651324
Holes 18 L 6440 yds SSS 71
Recs Am–63 N Quin
Pro–65 J Reynolds
Ladies–70 T Jeary
V'tors WD–U WE–M SOC–WD exc Tues
Fees £21
Loc E of Bishop's Stortford on A1250. M11 Junction 8

Boxmoor (1890)

18 Box Lane, Hemel Hempstead HP3 0DJ

Tel **(01442) 242434 (Clubhouse)**
Mem 290
Sec CG Witney (01442) 259439
Pro None
Holes 9 L 4854 yds SSS 64
Recs Am–62 D Boyd
V'tors U exc Sun–NA
Fees £10 Sat–£15
Loc 1 mile W of Hemel Hempstead on B4505 to Chesham

Brickendon Grange (1964)

Brickendon, Hertford SG13 8PD

Tel **(01992) 511228**
Fax **(01992) 511411**
Mem 650
Sec CT MacDonald
(01992) 511258
Pro J Hamilton (01992) 511218
Holes 18 L 6325 yds SSS 70
Recs Am–66 S Burnell (1991)
Pro–67 S James, K Robson (1985)
V'tors WD–U H WE/BH–M SOC
Fees On application
Loc Bayford, 3 miles S of Hertford

Briggens House Hotel (1988)

Briggens Park, Stanstead Road, Stanstead Abbotts SG12 8LD

Tel **(01279) 793742**
Fax **(01279) 793685**
Mem 200
Sec P Warwick
Pro J O'Leary
Holes 9 L 5825 yds SSS 72
V'tors U
Fees On application
Loc 4 miles E of Hertford, off A414

Brockett Hall (1992)

Welwyn AL8 7XG

Tel **(01707) 390055**
Fax **(01707) 390052**
Mem 315
Sec Miss K Hills
Pro K Wood (01707) 390063
Holes 18 L 6584 yds SSS 72
Recs Am–68 Ujlaki (1994)
Pro–65 K Wood (1994)
V'tors M H
Fees £40 (£50)
Loc On B653 to Wheathampstead. A1(M) Junction 4
Arch Alliss/Clark

Brookmans Park (1930)

Brookmans Park, Hatfield AL9 7AT

Tel **(01707) 652487**
Fax **(01707) 661851**
Mem 780
Sec PA Gill
Pro I Jelley (01707) 652468
Holes 18 L 6459 yds SSS 71
Recs Am–66 P Embleton (1990)
Pro–66 I Jelley (1990)
V'tors WD–UH WE/BH–M SOC
Fees £27
Loc 3 miles S of Hatfield, off A1000
Arch Hawtree/Taylor

Bushey G & CC (1980)

High Street, Bushey WD2 1BJ

Tel **(0181) 950 2283**
Fax **(0181) 386 1181**
Mem 600
Sec D Hourihan
Pro M Lovegrove
(0181) 950 2215
Holes 9 L 3000 yds SSS 69
Pro–67
V'tors WD–before 6pm WE/BH–after 2pm Wed–closed SOC–WD exc Wed
Fees 18 holes–£10 (14)
9 holes–£7 (£9)
Loc 2 miles S of Watford on A4008
Mis Driving range

Bushey Hall (1890)

Pay and play
Bushey Hall Drive, Bushey WD2 2EP
Tel **(01923) 222253**
Fax **(01923) 229759**
Mem 350
Sec JK Smith
Pro K Wickham (01923) 225802
Holes 18 L 6099 yds SSS 69
Recs Am–66 M Bowen (1990), S Clement (1992)
Pro–65 N Brown (1992), J Pinsent (1994)
V'tors U SOC–WD
Fees £7 (£15)
Loc 1 mile SE of Watford. M1 Junction 5

Chadwell Springs (1974)

Hertford Road, Ware SG12 9LE
Tel **(01920) 463647**
Mem 350
Sec D Evans (01920) 461447
Pro AN Shearn (01920) 462075
Holes 9 L 3021 yds SSS 69
V'tors WD–U WE–M
Fees £20
Loc Between Ware and Hertford on A119

Chesfield Downs Golf Centre (1991)

Pay and play
Jack's Hill, Graveley, Stevenage SG4 7EQ
Tel **(01462) 482929**
Fax **(01462) 482930**
Mem 550
Sec P McCullough
Pro Beverly Huke
Holes 18 L 6630 yds SSS 72
9 holes Par 3 course
V'tors U SOC
Fees 18 hole:£13.25 (£19.25)
9 hole:£2 (£3)
Loc B197, N of Stevenage. A1(M) Junctions 8 or 9
Mis Driving range
Arch Jonathan Gaunt

Cheshunt (1976)

Public
Park Lane, Cheshunt EN7 6QD
Tel **(01992) 29777**
Mem 480
Sec JG Duncan
Pro C Newton (01992) 24009
Holes 18 L 6608 yds SSS 71
Recs Am–65 S Blight (1986)
V'tors U–booking required
Fees £9 (£11.50)
Loc Off A10 at Church Lane, Cheshunt. M25 Junction 25, 3 miles
Arch Hawtree

Chorleywood (1890)

Common Road, Chorleywood WD3 5LN
Tel **(01923) 282009**
Mem 200 55(L) 40(J)
Sec RM Lennard
Holes 9 L 2838 yds SSS 67
Recs Am–65 N Leconte (1990)
Pro–61 M Squires (1990)
V'tors WD–U exc Tues & Thurs am WE–Sat pm only SOC
Fees £14 (£17.50)
Loc 3 miles W of Rickmansworth, off A404. M25 Junction 18

Danesbury Park (1992)

Codicote Road, Welwyn AL6 9SD
Tel **(01438) 840100**
Fax **(01727) 46109**
Mem 300
Sec D Snowdon
Pro G Aris
Holes 9 L 4150 yds SSS 60
V'tors M SOC–WD
Loc ¾ mile from A1(M) Junction 6 on B656 Hitchin road
Arch Derek Snowdon

Dyrham Park CC (1963)

Galley Lane, Barnet EN5 4RA
Tel **(0181) 440 3361**
Fax **(0181) 441 9836**
Mem 300
Sec P Court
Pro W Large (0181) 440 3904
Holes 18 L 6369 yds SSS 70
V'tors M SOC–Wed
Loc 10 miles N of London, W off A1
Arch CK Cotton

East Herts (1898)

Hamels Park, Buntingford SG9 9NA
Tel **(01920) 821923**
Mem 700
Sec GN Taylor (01920) 821978
Pro J Hamilton (01920) 821922
Holes 18 L 6455 yds SSS 71
Recs Am–66 D Hamilton
Pro–64 R Joyce
V'tors WD–H exc Wed–NA before 1pm WE–M
Fees On application
Loc ¼ mile N of Puckeridge on A10

Elstree (1984)

Watling Street, Elstree WD6 3AA
Tel **(0181) 953 6115**
Fax **(0181) 207 6390**
Mem 600
Sec K Ellis
Pro M Warwick
Holes 18 L 6100 yds SSS 69
Recs Am–68 C Woodcock (1987)
V'tors U SOC
Fees On application
Loc A5183, 1 mile N of Elstree. M1 Junction 4
Mis Floodlit driving range

Great Hadham (1993)

Great Hadham Road, Much Hadham SG10 6JE
Tel **(01279) 843558**
Fax **(01279) 842122**
Mem 700
Sec To be appointed
Pro K Lunt
Holes 18 L 6854 yds SSS 73
V'tors WD–U WE/BH–M SOC
Fees £16 (£22)
Loc 3 miles SW of Bishops Stortford (B1004). M11 Junction 8
Mis Driving range

Hadley Wood (1922)

Beech Hill, Hadley Wood, Barnet EN4 0JJ
Tel **(0181) 449 4486**
Fax **(0181) 364 8633**
Mem 600
Sec PS Bryan (0181) 449 4328
Pro P Jones (0181) 449 3285
Holes 18 L 6457 yds SSS 71
Recs Am–67 CC Holton (1983), N Leconte (1989)
Pro–67 PP Elson (1980)
V'tors WD–H or I WE/BH–M SOC
Fees On application
Loc 10 miles N of London, off A111 between Potters Bar and Cockfosters. 2 miles S of M25 Junction 24
Arch Dr A Mackenzie

Hanbury Manor (1990)

Ware SG12 0SD
Tel **(01920) 487722**
Fax **(01920) 487692**
Mem 600
Sec D MacLaren
Pro P Blaze
Holes 18 L 7016 yds SSS 74
V'tors M H
Loc 8 miles N of M25 Junction 25 on A10
Arch Jack Nicklaus Jr

Harpenden (1894)

Hammonds End, Harpenden AL5 2AX
Tel **(01582) 712580**
Fax **(01582) 712725**
Mem 800
Sec J Newton
Pro DH Smith (01582) 767124
Holes 18 L 6381 yds SSS 70
Recs Am–67 B Bulmer (1987)
Pro–65 J Sewell (1994)
V'tors WD–U exc Thurs WE/BH–M SOC–WD exc Thurs
Fees £20 D–£30
Loc 6 miles N of St Albans on B487
Arch Hawtree/Taylor

Harpenden Common (1931)

East Common, Harpenden AL5 1BL
Tel **(01582) 712856**
Fax **(01582) 715959**
Mem 865
Sec RD Parry (01582) 715959
Pro B Puttick (01582) 460655
Holes 18 L 5664 yds SSS 67
Recs Am–59 M Mulkerrin (1994)
Pro–63 N Brown, M Squires (1989)

For list of abbreviations see page 435

V'tors WD–U H WE–M SOC
Fees £20
Loc 5 miles N of St Albans, on A1081

Hartsbourne G & CC (1946)

Hartsbourne Avenue, Bushey Heath WD2 1JW
Tel **(0181) 950 1133**
Fax **(0181) 950 5357**
Mem 750
Sec DJ Woodman
Pro G Hunt (0181) 950 2836
Holes 18 L 6305 yds SSS 70
9 L 5432 yds SSS 66
Recs Am–67 E Silver
Pro–62 P Oosterhuis
V'tors NA SOC
Loc 5 miles SE of Watford, off A4008
Arch Hawtree/Taylor

Hatfield London CC (1976)

Bedwell Park, Essendon, Hatfield AL9 6JA
Tel **(01707) 642624**
Fax **(01707) 646187**
Mem 735
Sec T Takizawa
Pro N Greer (01707) 650431
Holes 18 L 6854 yds SSS 73
V'tors U
Fees £16 (£32)
Loc 5 miles E of Hatfield on B158. A1(M) Junction 4
Arch Fred Hawtree

Kingsway Golf Centre (1991)

Cambridge Road, Melbourn, Royston SG8 6EY
Tel **(01763) 262727**
Fax **(01763) 263298**
Mem 450
Sec Mrs AJ Tinston
Pro D Armor, Miss D Hastings
Holes 9 L 2500 yds Par 33
9 hole Par 3
V'tors U SOC
Fees £5 (£6)
Loc N of Royston on A10
Mis Driving range

Knebworth (1908)

Deards End Lane, Knebworth SG3 6NL
Tel **(01438) 814681 (Clubhouse)**
Fax **(01438) 815216**
Mem 1000
Sec M Parsons MBE
(01438) 812752
Pro G Parker (01438) 812757
Holes 18 L 6492 yds SSS 71
Recs Am–68 G Maly (1994)
Pro–66 L Jones (1991)
V'tors WD–U H WE–M
SOC–Mon/Tues/Thurs
Fees £29
Loc 1 mile S of Stevenage on B197
Arch Willie Park

Letchworth (1905)

Letchworth SG6 3NQ
Tel **(01462) 683203**
Fax **(01462) 484567**
Mem 900
Sec AR Bailey
Pro SJ Mutimer (01462) 682713
Holes 18 L 6181 yds SSS 69
Recs Am–67 J Dickens
Pro–66 NC Coles
V'tors WD–U WE–M
SOC–Wed–Fri
Fees £23.50
Loc S of Letchworth, off A505. A1(M) Junction 9
Arch Harry Vardon

Little Hay Golf Complex (1977)

Pay and play
Box Lane, Bovingdon, Hemel Hempstead HP3 0DQ
Tel **(01442) 833798**
Pro D Johnson (Golf Dir)
Holes 18 L 6610 yds SSS 72
Pro–69
V'tors U SOC
Fees £7.50 (£11.25)
Loc 2 miles W of Hemel Hempstead, on B4505 to Chesham
Mis Driving range
Arch Hawtree

Manor of Groves G & CC (1991)

High Wych, Sawbridgeworth CM21 0LA
Tel **(01279) 722333**
Fax **(01279) 726972**
Mem 350
Pro L Jones
Holes 18 L 6250 yds SSS 70
V'tors U SOC
Fees £16 (£20)
Loc 1 mile N of Harlow
Arch S Sharer

Mid Herts (1892)

Gustard Wood, Wheathampstead AL4 8RS
Tel **(01582) 832242**
Fax **(01582) 832242**
Mem 500(M) 125(L)
Sec RJH Jourdan
Pro N Brown (01582) 832788
Holes 18 L 6060 yds SSS 69
Recs Am–68 P Mayles (1987)
Pro–63 P Winston (1992)
V'tors WD–UH exc Tues & Wed pm
WE/BH–M SOC
Fees On application
Loc 6 miles N of St Albans on B651

Moor Park (1923)

Rickmansworth WD3 1QN
Tel **(01923) 773146**
Fax **(01923) 777109**
Mem 1700
Sec JA Davies
Pro L Farmer
Holes High 18 L 6713 yds SSS 72
West 18 L 5823 yds SSS 68
Recs High Am–65 G Harris (1993)
Pro–63 B Gallacher (1969)
West Am–62 AJ Eisner (1984)
Pro–63 AD Locke, A Lees, EE Whitcombe
V'tors WD–H WE/BH–M SOC
Fees On application
Loc 1 mile SE of Rickmansworth, off Batchworth roundabout (A4145). M25 Junction 18, 2 miles
Arch HS Colt

Old Fold Manor (1910)

Hadley Green, Barnet EN5 4QN
Tel **(0181) 440 9185**
Mem 520
Sec AW Dickens (Mgr)
Pro D Fitzsimmons
(0181) 440 7488
Holes 18 L 6471 yds SSS 71
Recs Am–66 A Clark
Pro–68 SL King
V'tors WD–H WE–M
Fees £27 D–£30
Loc 1 mile N of Barnet on A1000

Oxhey Park

Prestwick Road, South Oxhey, Watford WD1 6DT
Tel **(01923) 248312**
Mem 210
Sec D McFadden (Mgr)
Holes 9 L 1637 yds Par 58
V'tors U
Fees 9 holes–£6 18 holes–£8
Loc 2 miles SW of Watford. M1 Junction 5
Mis Driving range

Panshanger (1976)

Public
Old Herns Lane, Welwyn Garden City AL7 2ED
Tel **(01707) 339507**
Mem 352
Pro B Lewis, M Corlass
Holes 18 L 6626 metres SSS 72
Recs Am–71 S Walton (1987)
Pro–70 R Green
V'tors U
Fees On application
Loc 2 miles off A1, via B1000 to Hertford

Porters Park (1899)

Shenley Hill, Radlett WD7 7AZ
Tel **(01923) 854127**
Mem 650
Sec JH Roberts (Mgr)
Pro D Gleeson (01923) 854366
Holes 18 L 6313 yds SSS 70
Recs Am–65 CC Boal (1990)
Pro–64 P Townsend
V'tors WD–H (phone first)
WE/BH–M SOC–Wed & Thurs
Fees £28–£42
Loc E of Radlett on Shenley road

For list of abbreviations see page 435

Potters Bar (1923)
Darkes Lane, Potters Bar EN6 1DE
Tel **(01707) 652020**
Fax **(01707) 655051**
Mem 550
Sec A Williams (Mgr)
Pro G Carver (01707) 652987
Holes 18 L 6279 yds SSS 70
Recs Am–66 RR Davis
Pro–65 D McClelland
V'tors WD–H WE/BH–M
SOC–Mon/Tues/Fri
Fees £18.50 (1994)
Loc 1 mile N of M25 Junction 24, off A1000
Arch James Braid

Redbourn (1970)
Kinsbourne Green Lane, Redbourn, St Albans AL3 7QA
Tel **(01582) 793493**
Fax **(01582) 794362**
Sec CAI Gyford
Pro W Street
Holes 18 L 6407 yds SSS 71
9 hole Par 3 course
Recs Am–67 P Wilkins, T Stafford
V'tors WD–U booking necessary
WE/BH–H SOC–WD
Fees 18 hole:£14 (£18)
9 hole:£4.20
Loc 4 miles N of St Albans, off A5. 1 mile S of M1 Junction 9
Mis Target golf range

Rickmansworth (1937)
Public
Moor Lane, Rickmansworth WD3 1QL
Tel **(01923) 775278**
Mem 250
Sec I Duncan
Pro I Duncan
Holes 18 L 4493 yds SSS 62
Recs Am–63 JC Jackson (1991)
V'tors U
Fees £8.50 (£12)
Loc ½ mile SE of Rickmansworth, off Batchworth roundabout (A4145). M25 Junction 18, 2 miles
Mis 9 hole pitch & putt course

Royston (1892)
Baldock Road, Royston SG8 5BG
Tel **(01763) 242177 (Members)**
Fax **(01763) 242696**
Mem 750
Sec DH Mear (01763) 242696
Pro M Hatcher (01763) 243476
Holes 18 L 6032 yds SSS 69
Recs Am–65 GA Hainsworth
Pro–63 B Waites
V'tors WD–U WE/BH–M SOC
Fees £20
Loc SW of Royston on A505

Sandy Lodge (1910)
Sandy Lodge Lane, Northwood, Middx HA6 2JD
Tel **(01923) 825429**
Fax **(01923) 824319**
Mem 700
Sec JN Blair
Pro J Pinsent (01923) 825321
Holes 18 L 6340 yds SSS 71
Recs Am–66 DG Scammell (1990)
Pro–64 A Jacklin (1977)
V'tors H or M SOC
Fees On application
Loc Adjacent Moor Park Station
Arch Harry Vardon

Shendish Manor (1988)
Pay and play
Shendish House, Apsley, Hemel Hempstead HP3 0AA
Tel **(01442) 232220**
Holes 9 L 6076 yds SSS 69
Recs Am–69 K Swatman (1991)
V'tors WD–U WE–NA before noon SOC
Fees £10 (£14)
Loc S of Hemel Hempstead, off A41. M25 Junction 20
Arch Cotton/Steel

South Herts (1899)
Links Drive, Totteridge, London N20 8QU
Tel **(0181) 445 0117**
Fax **(0181) 445 7569**
Mem 850
Sec PF Wise (0181) 445 2035
Pro RY Mitchell (0181) 445 4633
Holes 18 L 6470 yds SSS 71
9 L 1581 yds
Recs Am–67 R Neil (1964)
Pro–66 D Thomas (1966)
V'tors WD–IH WE/BH–M
Fees On application
Loc Totteridge Lane
Arch Harry Vardon

Stevenage (1980)
Public
Aston Lane, Stevenage SG2 7EL
Tel **(01438) 880424**
Mem 580
Sec JM Ryder (01438) 880322
Pro K Bond
Holes 18 L 6451 yds SSS 71
9 hole Par 3 course
Recs Am–69 T Carter (1990), C Elwin (1992)
Pro–65 R Green (1989)
V'tors U
Fees £9 (£11)
Loc Off A602 to Hertford. A1(M) Junction 7
Mis Driving range
Arch John Jacobs

Stocks Hotel & CC (1993)
Stocks Road, Aldbury, Tring HP23 5RX
Tel **(01442) 851341**
Fax **(01442) 851253**
Mem 500
Sec PN Waters
Pro PJ Lane (Ext 308)
Holes 18 L 7016 yds SSS 73
V'tors H SOC
Fees £30 (£40)
Loc Aldbury, 2 miles E of Tring. A41(T), 2 miles
Arch M Billcliffe

Verulam (1905)
London Road, St Albans AL1 1JG
Tel **(01727) 853327**
Fax **(01727) 812201**
Mem 640
Sec A Crichton-Smith
Pro N Burch (01727) 861401
Holes 18 L 6457 yds SSS 71
Recs Am–67 DCN Longmuir (1991)
Pro–65 R Mitchell (1986)
V'tors WD–H exc Mon–U
WE/BH–M
SOC–Tues/Thurs/Fri
Fees £25 (Mon–£13)
Loc 1 mile SE of St Albans on A1081
Arch Braid/Steel

Welwyn Garden City (1922)
Mannicotts, High Oaks Road, Welwyn Garden City AL8 7BP
Tel **(01707) 322722**
Fax **(01707) 393213**
Mem 700
Sec MP Flint (Gen Mgr)
(01707) 325243
Pro R May (01707) 325525
Holes 18 L 6100 yds SSS 69
Recs Am–64 MJ Deal (1991)
Pro–63 N Faldo (1988)
V'tors WD–H WE/BH–NA
Fees On application
Loc 1 mile N of Hatfield. A1(M) Junction 4 - B197 to Valley Road
Arch Hawtree

West Herts (1890)
Cassiobury Park, Watford WD1 7SL
Tel **(01923) 224264**
Fax **(01923) 222300**
Mem 700
Sec CM Brown (01923) 236484
Pro CS Gough (01923) 220352
Holes 18 L 6488 yds SSS 71
Recs Am–67 JE Ambridge (1994)
Pro–66 N Brown (1994)
Ladies–73 F Smith (1992)
V'tors WD–H WE/BH–M H
SOC–Wed & Fri
Fees £20
Loc Off A412, between Watford and Rickmansworth
Arch Morris/Mackenzie

Whipsnade Park (1974)
Studham Lane, Dagnall HP4 1RH
Tel **(01442) 842330**
Mem 400
Sec D Whalley
Pro M Lewendon
Holes 18 L 6812 yds SSS 72
Recs Am–71 A Calder
Pro–66 A Clapp

For list of abbreviations see page 435

V'tors WD–U WE–M SOC–WD
Fees £21 D–31
Loc 8 miles N of Hemel Hempstead, off A4146

Whitehill (1990)
Dane End, Ware SG12 0JS
Tel **(01920) 438495**
Fax **(01920) 438891**
Mem 700
Sec Mr & Mrs A Smith (Props)
Pro D Ling
Holes 18 L 6636 yds SSS 72
V'tors H–booking necessary
Fees £15 (£18)
Loc 6 miles N of Ware (A10)
Mis Floodlit driving range

Humberside

Beverley & East Riding (1889)
The Westwood, Beverley HU17 8RG
Tel **(01482) 867190**
Mem 460
Sec B Granville (01482) 868757
Pro I Mackie (01482) 869519
Holes 18 L 6127 yds SSS 69
Recs Am–65 N Burnley (1994)
V'tors U SOC–WD
Fees £11 (£15)
Loc Beverley-Walkington road (B1230)

Boothferry (1982)
Public
Spaldington Lane, Spaldington, Goole DN14 7NG
Tel **(01430) 430364**
Pro S Wilkinson
Holes 18 L 6593 yds SSS 72
Recs Am–70 R Giles (1988)
Pro–70 M Ingham (1984)
S Rolley (1987)
V'tors U SOC
Fees On application
Loc 3 miles N of Howden on B1288. M62 Junction 37, 2 miles
Arch Donald Steel

Bridlington (1905)
Belvedere Road, Bridlington YO15 3NA
Tel **(01262) 672092/606367**
Mem 623
Sec C Wilson (01262) 674679
Pro ARA Howarth (01262) 674721
Holes 18 L 6491 yds SSS 71
Recs Am–66 SPP Drum (1993)
V'tors U exc Sun–after 11.15am
Fees £12 D–£18 (£20 D–£25)
Loc 1½ miles S of Bridlington, off A165
Arch James Braid

Brough (1893)
Cave Road, Brough HU15 1HB
Tel **(01482) 667374**
Fax **(01482) 667291**
Mem 800
Sec WG Burleigh (01482) 667291
Pro G Townhill (01482) 667483
Holes 18 L 6183 yds SSS 69
Recs Am–64 PWJ Greenhough
Pro–64 B Thompson
V'tors WD–U exc Wed–NA
Fees £25
Loc 10 miles W of Hull on A63

Cave Castle Hotel (1989)
South Cave, N Humberside HU15 2EU
Tel **(01430) 421286/422245 (Hotel)**
Fax **(01430) 421118**
Sec JR Bean
Pro C Gray (01430) 421286
Holes 18 L 6409 yds SSS 71
V'tors U
Fees £12.50 (£18)
Loc 10 miles W of Hull. Junction of A63/M62

Cleethorpes (1894)
Kings Road, Cleethorpes DN35 0PN
Tel **(01472) 814060**
Mem 750
Sec GB Standaloft
Pro P Davies
Holes 18 L 6360 yds SSS 70
Recs Am–69 D Burchill (1994)
V'tors WD–U exc Wed pm–NA Sat pm/Sun am–XL
Fees £18 (£22)
Loc 1 mile S of Cleethorpes

Driffield (1934)
Sunderlandwick, Driffield YO25 9AD
Tel **(01377) 253116** (Clubhouse), **(01377) 240599** (Office)
Fax **(01377) 240599**
Mem 634
Sec M Winn (Hon)
Pro (01377) 240448
Holes 18 L 6212 yds SSS 70
Recs Am–67 G Drewery (1985), KA Gray (1994)
V'tors H I SOC
Fees D–£18 (D–£25)
Loc S of Driffield on A164

Elsham (1900)
Barton Road, Elsham, Brigg DN20 0LS
Tel **(01652) 688382**
Mem 650
Sec BP Nazer (Mgr) (01652) 680291
Pro S Brewer (01652) 680432
Holes 18 L 6411 yds SSS 71
Recs Am–67 DJ Bush
Pro–69 MT Hoyle
V'tors WE–M SOC–WD
Fees £20
Loc 5 miles N of Brigg. M180 Junction 5

Flamborough Head (1932)
Lighthouse Road, Flamborough, Bridlington YO15 1AR
Tel **(01262) 850333**
Mem 400
Sec WR Scarle (01262) 676494
Pro G Hutchinson
Holes 18 L 5438 yds SSS 66
Recs Am–63 GR Allen
Pro–63 P Dawson
V'tors U
Fees £14 (£18) W–£56
Loc 5 miles NE of Bridlington

Ganstead Park (1976)
Longdales Lane, Coniston, Hull HU11 4LB
Tel **(01482) 811280 (Steward)**
Mem 700
Sec J Kirby (01482) 874754
Pro M Smee (01482) 811121
Holes 18 L 6801 yds SSS 73
V'tors U H WE–NA before noon SOC
Fees On application
Loc 5 miles E of Hull on A165

Grange Park (1992)
Pay and play
Butterwick Road, Messingham, Scunthorpe DN17 3PP
Tel **(01724) 762945**
Sec I Cannon (Mgr)
Holes 9 L 2970 yds SSS 35
9 hole Par 3 course
V'tors U
Fees £5 (£8)
Loc 5 miles from Messingham. M180 Junction 3
Mis Floodlit driving range
Arch RW Price

Grimsby (1922)
Littlecoates Road, Grimsby DN34 4LU
Tel **(01472) 342823 (Clubhouse)**
Mem 720 150(L) 70(J)
Sec BJ Hoggett (01472) 342630
Pro R Smith (01472) 356981
Holes 18 L 6068 yds Par 70 SSS 69
Recs Am–66 M James
Pro–66 BJ Hunt
V'tors WD–U Sat pm/Sun am–XL
Fees £18 D–£25 (£25)
Loc 1 mile W of Grimsby

Hainsworth Park (1983)
Brandesburton, Driffield YO25 8RT
Tel **(01964) 542362**
Fax **(01964) 542362**
Mem 450
Sec Maj R Kilpatrick (Mgr)
BW Atkin (Prop)
Holes 18 L 6003 yds SSS 69
V'tors U SOC
Fees £10 (£15)
Loc 6 miles N of Beverley on A165

For list of abbreviations see page 435

Hessle (1898)

Westfield Road, Cottingham HU16 5YL

Tel **(01482) 650171**
Fax **(01482) 652679**
Mem 669
Sec RL Dorsey
Pro G Fieldsend (01482) 650190
Holes 18 L 6638 yds SSS 72
Recs Am–65 NMP Robinson (1994)
Pro–69 B Thompson (1980)
Ladies–72 E Duggleby (1994)
V'tors WD–U exc Tues 9am–1pm
WE–NA before 11am
Fees £18 (£25)
Loc 3 miles SW of Cottingham
Arch Thomas/Alliss

Holme Hall (1908)

Holme Lane, Bottesford, Scunthorpe DN16 3RF

Tel **(01724) 282053 (Caterer)**
Mem 470 90(L) 50(J)
Sec G Smith (01724) 862078
Pro R McKiernan (01724) 851816
Holes 18 L 6475 yds SSS 71
Recs Am–67 S Steele, A Thain, K Blow, FW Wood
Pro–66 B Thompson
V'tors WD–U WE–M H SOC–WD
Fees D–£20
Loc 4 miles SE of Scunthorpe. M180 Junction 4

Hornsea (1898)

Rolston Road, Hornsea HU18 1XG

Tel **(01964) 535488**
Fax **(01964) 534989**
Mem 600
Sec BW Kirton (01964) 532020
Pro B Thompson (01964) 534989
Holes 18 L 6685 yds SSS 72
Recs Am–68 CJ Waite (1994)
Pro–66 G Brown (1991)
V'tors WD–U WE–restricted SOC
Fees £18 D–£25
Loc 300 yds past Hornsea Pottery
Arch Dr A Mackenzie/James Braid

Hull (1921)

The Hall, 27 Packman Lane, Kirk Ella, Hull HU10 7JT

Tel **(01482) 653026**
Mem 756
Sec R Toothill (Gen Mgr)
(01482) 658919
Pro D Jagger (01482) 653074
Holes 18 L 6242 yds SSS 70
Recs Am–64 JD Dockar, R Roper
Pro–66 D Dunk, N Hunt, S Smith, D Jagger
V'tors WD–U WE–NA
Fees £20 D–£25
Loc 5 miles W of Hull

Immingham (1975)

Church Lane, Immingham, Grimsby DN40 2EU

Tel **(01469) 575298**
Mem 650
Pro G Norton (01469) 575493
Holes 18 L 6161 yds SSS 69
Recs Am–65 P Wall (1992)
V'tors WD–U WE–M Sun–NA before noon SOC–WD
Fees £15 (£20)
Loc N of St Andrew's Church, Immingham
Arch Hawtree/Pennink

Kingsway (1971)

Public

Kingsway, Scunthorpe DN15 7ER

Tel **(01724) 840945**
Sec C Mann
Pro C Mann
Holes 9 L 1915 yds SSS 59
V'tors U
Fees £3 (£3.50)
Loc ¾ mile W of Scunthorpe, off A18

Links at Bridlington Bay (1993)

Pay and play

Flamborough Road, Marton, Bridlington YO15 1DW

Tel **(01262) 401584**
Fax **(01262) 401702**
Mem 200
Sec K Stenton
Pro D Edwards
Holes 18 L 6720 yds SSS 72
9 hole course
Recs Am–71 C Clarkson
V'tors U
Fees £12.50 (£15)
Loc 2 miles N of Bridlington on B1255
Mis Driving range. 3 Academy holes
Arch Howard Swann

Manor (1992)

Laceby Manor, Laceby, Grimsby DN37 7EA

Tel **(01472) 873468**
Fax **(01472) 276706**
Mem 450
Sec Mrs J Mackay, G Mackay (Mgr)
Pro M Davenport
Holes 9 L 3127 yds SSS 70
V'tors U SOC
Fees 9 holes–£6 (£7)
18 holes–£9 (£11)
Loc 5 miles W of Grimsby at Barton Street (A18)
Mis Extension to 18 holes 1995
Arch Nicholson/Rushton

Normanby Hall (1978)

Public

Normanby Park, Scunthorpe DN15 9HU

Tel **(01724) 280444 Ext 852 (Bookings)**
Mem 800
Sec NJ Over
Pro C Mann (01724) 720226
Holes 18 L 6548 yds SSS 71
Recs Am–68
Pro–68 N Bundy
V'tors U SOC–WD
Fees £10 D–£15 (£12)
Loc 5 miles N of Scunthorpe
Arch Hawtree

Scunthorpe (1936)

Ashby Decoy, Burringham Road, Scunthorpe DN17 2AB

Tel **(01724) 842913**
Fax **(01724) 271708**
Mem 520 130(L) 65(J)
Sec KR Ford (01724) 866561
Pro A Lawson (01724) 868972
Holes 18 L 6281 yds SSS 71
Recs Am–67 J Payne
Pro–67 K Waters
V'tors WD–H Sat–M SOC
Fees £16 (£20)
Loc 2 miles SW of Scunthorpe

Springhead Park (1930)

Public

Willerby Road, Hull HU5 5JE

Tel **(01482) 656309**
Sec A Farr (Hon)
Pro B Herrington
Holes 18 L 6402 yds SSS 71
Recs Am–69 AD Hill, A Wright
Pro–65 S Rolley
V'tors U
Fees £5.20 (£6.75)
Loc 4 miles W of Hull

Sutton Park (1935)

Public

Salthouse Road, Hull HU8 9HF

Tel **(01482) 374242**
Mem 400
Sec JR Allen (Hon)
Pro P Rushworth
(01482) 711450
Holes 18 L 6251 yds SSS 70
Recs Am–67 A Wright
Pro–64 L Herrington
V'tors U
Fees £5.50 (£6.75)
Loc 3 miles E of Hull on A165

Withernsea (1907)

Chestnut Avenue, Withernsea HU19 2PG

Tel **(01964) 612258** (Clubhouse)
Mem 329 55(L) 40(J)
Sec B Williams (01964) 612078
Pro G Harrison (01482) 492720
Holes 9 L 5112 yds SSS 64 Par 66
Recs Am–62 SH Kellet
Pro–63 G Townhill
V'tors WD–U WE/BH–M before 3pm SOC
Fees £10
Loc 17 miles E of Hull on A1033. S side of Withernsea

For list of abbreviations see page 435

Isle of Man

Castletown (1892)
Fort Island, Derbyhaven
Tel **(01624) 822201 (Hotel)**
Fax **(01624) 824633**
Mem 400
Sec JM Fowlds
Pro M Crowe (01624) 822211
Holes 18 L 6716 yds SSS 72
Recs Am–68 WR Ennett
Pro–65 D Dunk
V'tors U SOC
Fees £25 Hotel residents–£20
Loc 1 mile E of Castletown
Arch Mackenzie Ross

Douglas Municipal (1927)
Public
Pulrose Park, Douglas
Tel **(01624) 661558**
Pro K Parry
Holes 18 L 5922 yds SSS 68
Recs Am–63
V'tors U
Fees On application
Loc Douglas Pier 2 miles
Arch Dr A Mackenzie

King Edward Bay (1893)
Groudle Road, Onchan
Tel **(01624) 620430/673821**
Fax **(01624) 676794**
Mem 400
Sec RG Cowley (01624) 861430
Pro D Jones (01624) 672709
Holes 18 L 5457 yds SSS 66
Recs Am–63
V'tors U SOC
Fees £10 (£12)
Loc 1 mile N of Douglas
Arch Tom Morris (1893 course)

Mount Murray G & CC (1994)
Santon IM4 2HT
Tel **(01624) 661111**
Fax **(01624) 611116**
Mem 300
Sec RG Jackson (Ext 597)
Pro AD Dyson (Ext 489)
Holes 18 L 6709 yds SSS 72
V'tors U H SOC
Fees £18 (£24) Hotel guests–£9
Loc 3 miles S of Douglas
Mis Driving range

Peel (1895)
Rheast Lane, Peel
Tel **(01624) 842227**
Mem 600
Sec TP Kissack
(01624) 843456(am)
Holes 18 L 5914 yds SSS 68
Recs Am–64 J Sutton
V'tors WD–U WE/BH–NA before
10.30am SOC
Fees £15 (£18)
Loc 10 miles W of Douglas
Arch James Braid

Port St Mary (1936)
Public
Kallow Road, Port St Mary
Tel **(01624) 834932**
Holes 9 L 2711 yds SSS 66
Recs Am–62 A Cain (1994)
V'tors WD–U WE–NA before
10.30am SOC
Fees On application
Loc Port St Mary, nr sea shore

Ramsey (1891)
Brookfield, Ramsey
Tel **(01624) 813365/812244**
Mem 812
Sec Maj B Hodgson
(01624) 812244
Pro C Wilson (01624) 814736
Holes 18 L 6019 yds SSS 69
Recs Am–65 S Boyd
Pro–64 D Wills
V'tors WD–U after 10am WE–M
SOC
Fees £15 (£18)
Loc W boundary of Ramsey
Arch James Braid

Rowany (1895)
Port Erin
Tel **(01624) 834108**
Mem 600
Sec AJ Laine (Mgr)
(01624) 834072
Holes 18 L 5840 yds SSS 69
Recs Am–68 A Cain
V'tors U H SOC
Fees £12.50 (£17)
Loc 6 miles W of Castletown

Isle of Wight

Cowes (1908)
Crossfield Avenue, Cowes PO31 8HN
Tel **(01983) 292303**
Mem 300
Sec D Weaver
Holes 9 L 5934 yds SSS 68
Recs Am–66 M Leek
V'tors H Thurs–NA before 3pm
(Ladies Day) Fri–NA after
5pm Sun am–NA
Fees £15 (£18)
Loc Nr Cowes High School
Arch J Hamilton Stutt

Freshwater Bay (1894)
Afton Down, Freshwater PO40 9TZ
Tel **(01983) 752955**
Fax **(01983) 752955**
Mem 500
Sec G Smith MBE
Holes 18 L 5725 yds SSS 68
Recs Am–64 J Greenhill (1990)
Pro–66 T Underwood (1981)
V'tors H SOC
Fees £18 (£22)
Loc 400 yds off Military Road

Newport (1896)
St George's Down, Shide, Newport PO30 3BA
Tel **(01983) 525076**
Mem 350
Sec PJ Mills
Holes 9 L 5704 yds SSS 68
Recs Am–65 J Burton (1987)
V'tors WD–U Sat–NA before
3.30pm Sun–NA before noon
Fees £15 (£17.50)
Loc 1 mile SE of Newport
Arch Guy Hunt

Osborne (1903)
Club House, Osborne, East Cowes PO32 6JX
Tel **(01983) 295421**
Mem 260 90(L)
Sec RS Jones
Pro A Scullion (01983) 295649
Holes 9 L 6276 yds SSS 70
Recs Am–66 MC Crosskey (1990)
Pro–64 A Scullion (1994)
Ladies–72 J Cotton (1993)
V'tors WD–U exc Ladies Day (Tues)
9am–1pm–NA WE–NA
before noon SOC
Fees £16 (£19) 5D–£60
Loc S of East Cowes in grounds of
Osborne House

Ryde (1921)
Binstead Road, Ryde PO33 3NF
Tel **(01983) 614809**
Mem 450
Sec ARJ Goodall
Holes 9 L 5287 yds SSS 66
Recs Am–65 J Thorp
V'tors WD–U exc Wed pm Sun–NA
before noon
Fees £15 (£20)
Loc On main Ryde/Newport road

Shanklin & Sandown (1900)
Fairway Lake, Sandown PO36 9PR
Tel **(01983) 403217**
Mem 700
Sec GA Wormald
Pro P Hammond (01983) 404424
Holes 18 L 6063 yds SSS 69
Recs Am–65 D McToldridge
Pro–65 R Wynn
V'tors WD–U WE–NA before
3pm(summer) noon (winter)
SOC–WD
Fees £21 (£25) 3D–£50
Loc Sandown
Arch Cowper/James Braid

Ventnor (1892)
Steephill Down Road, Ventnor
Tel **(01983) 853326**
Mem 250
Sec R Hose (01983) 853198
Holes 9 L 5752 yds SSS 68
Recs Am–73 IH Guy
V'tors WD–U exc Ladies Day–Fri
Sun–NA before 1pm SOC
Fees On application
Loc NW boundary of Ventnor

For list of abbreviations see page 435

Kent

Aquarius (1913)
Marmora Rd, Honor Oak, London SE22 0RY
Tel **(0181) 693 1626**
Mem 400
Sec Mrs ML Moss
Pro F Private
Holes 9 L 5246 yds SSS 66
Recs Am–62 R Hare
Pro–63 F Private
V'tors M

Ashford (1904)
Sandyhurst Lane, Ashford TN25 4NT
Tel **(01233) 620180**
Mem 650
Sec AH Story (01233) 622655
Pro H Sherman (01233) 629644
Holes 18 L 6246 yds SSS 70
Recs Am–66 SM Green
Pro–63 RS Fidler
V'tors WD–H WE/BH–H SOC
Fees £20 (£42)
Loc Ashford 1½ miles (A20)

Austin Lodge (1991)
Eynsford, Swanley DA4 0HU
Tel **(01322) 863000**
Fax **(01322) 862406**
Mem 600
Sec S Bevan
Pro N Willis
Holes 18 L 6600 yds Par 73 SSS 71
Pro–67 N Willis (1994)
V'tors WD–U WE–NA before noon SOC
Fees £15 (£21)
Loc Off A225, nr Eynsford Station. M25 Junction 3, 3 miles
Mis Driving range for members and guests
Arch Peter Bevan

Barnehurst (1903)
Public
Mayplace Road East, Bexley Heath DA7 6JU
Tel **(01322) 523746**
Fax **(01322) 554612**
Mem 300
Sec B Davies (01322) 552952
Pro P Tallack (01322) 552952
Holes 9 L 5448 yds SSS 69
Pro–63 S Barr
V'tors U SOC
Fees £5.70 (£9.20)
Loc Between Crayford and Bexleyheath
Arch James Braid

Bearsted (1895)
Ware Street, Bearsted, Maidstone ME14 4PQ
Tel **(01622) 738389**
Mem 700
Sec Mrs LM Siems (01622) 738198
Pro T Simpson (01622) 738024
Holes 18 L 6253 yds SSS 70
Recs Am–68 D Jenner (1987)
Pro–68 T Britz, R Tinworth (1991)
V'tors WD–I H WE–H M (recognised GC members) SOC
Fees £24 D–£32
Loc 2½ miles E of Maidstone

Beckenham Place Park (1907)
Public
Beckenham Hill Road, Beckenham BR3 2BP
Tel **(0181) 650 2292**
Fax **(0181) 663 1201**
Pro H Davies-Thomas
Holes 18 L 5722 yds SSS 68
Recs Am–62 S Champion
Pro–65 T Cotton
V'tors U
Fees £7.60 (£12.40) WE–booking fee
Loc Off A21 on A222

Bexleyheath (1907)
Mount Road, Bexleyheath BR8 7RJ
Tel **(0181) 303 6951**
Mem 350
Sec SE Squires
Holes 9 L 5239 yds SSS 66
Recs Am–65 D Fillary
V'tors WD–H before 4pm
Fees £20
Loc Station 1 mile

Birchwood Park (1990)
Birchwood Road, Wilmington, Dartford DA2 7HJ
Tel **(01322) 660554**
Fax **(01322) 667283**
Mem 360
Sec G Gibson (01322) 662038
Pro M Hirst (01322) 660554
Holes 18 L 6364 yds SSS 70
9 hole course
V'tors U SOC
Fees £18 (£23)
Loc 2 miles S of A2/A2018 Junction
Mis Driving range. Indoor teaching centre
Arch Howard Swann

Boughton (1993)
Pay and play
Brickfield Lane, Boughton, Faversham ME13 9AJ
Tel **(01227) 752277**
Fax **(01227) 752361**
Mem 800
Sec P Sparks
Pro P Sparks
Holes 18 L 6452 yds SSS 71
Pro–70 T Berry, C Evans
V'tors U SOC–WD
Fees £16 (£21)
Loc NE of Boughton, nr M2/A2 interchange. 6 miles W of Canterbury
Mis Driving range
Arch Philip Sparks

Broke Hill (1993)
Sevenoaks Road, Halstead TN14 7HR
Tel **(01959) 533225**
Fax **(01959) 532880**
Sec T Collingwood
Pro C Gillick (01959) 533810
Holes 18 L 6454 yds Par 72 SSS 71
V'tors WD–U before 5pm WE–NA
Fees £25
Loc 4 miles S of Bromley on A21. M25 Junction 4
Arch David Williams

Bromley (1948)
Public
Magpie Hall Lane, Bromley BR2 8JF
Tel **(0181) 462 7014**
Pro A Hodgson
Holes 9 L 5538 yds SSS 66
Recs Am–66 HE Harding, KW Miles
V'tors U
Fees On application
Loc Off Bromley Common (A21)

Broome Park (1981)
Broome Park Estate, Barham, Canterbury CT4 6QX
Tel **(01227) 831701**
Fax **(01227) 831973**
Mem 600
Sec JW Cowling (Ext 263)
Pro T Britz (01227) 831126
Holes 18 L 6610 yds SSS 72
Recs Am–68 B Ingleby
Pro–66 B Impett (1984)
V'tors H WE–NA before noon SOC–WD
Fees £26 (£30)
Loc M2/A2-A260 Folkestone road, 1½ miles on RH side
Mis Driving range
Arch Donald Steel

Canterbury (1927)
Scotland Hills, Littlebourne Road, Canterbury CT1 1TW
Tel **(01227) 453532**
Mem 650
Sec J Lucas
Pro P Everard (01227) 462865
Holes 18 L 6249 yds SSS 70
Recs Am–65 SP Blake
Pro–64 K Redford
V'tors WD–U H WE–NA before 3pm SOC–Tues & Thurs
Fees £27 D–£36 (£36)
Loc 1 mile E of Canterbury on A257
Arch HS Colt

Chart Hills (1993)
Weeks Lane, Biddenden TN27 8JX
Tel **(01580) 292222**
Sec R Hyder (Golf Dir)
Pro R Hyder (01580) 292148
Holes 18 L 7086 yds SSS 74
V'tors H
Fees £45 (£48)
Loc 12 miles W of Ashford (A262)
Mis David Leadbetter Golf Academy
Arch Nick Faldo

Chelsfield Lakes Golf Centre (1992)

Pay and play
Court Road, Orpington BR6 9BX
Tel **(01689) 896266**
Fax **(01689) 824577**
Mem 650
Sec DT Howe (Mgr)
Pro N Lee, D Clark
Holes 18 L 6077 yds Par 71 SSS 69
9 hole Par 3 course
V'tors U–booking required SOC
Fees £14 (£17)
Loc 1 mile from M25 Junction 4 (A224)
Mis Target golf range
Arch MRM Sandow

Cherry Lodge (1969)

Jail Lane, Biggin Hill, Westerham TN16 3AX
Tel **(01959) 572250**
Fax **(01959) 540672**
Mem 650
Sec AA Kemsley
Pro N Child (01959) 572989
Holes 18 L 6652 yds SSS 73
Recs Am–71 N French (1992)
Pro–69 S Barr (1992)
V'tors WD–U WE–M
Fees £18 D–£23
Loc 3 miles N of Westerham, off A233
Arch John Day

Chestfield (1925)

103 Chestfield Road, Whitstable CT5 3LU
Tel **(01227) 794411**
Mem 692
Sec MA Sutcliffe
Pro J Brotherton (01227) 793563
Holes 18 L 6181 yds SSS 70
Recs Am–64 G Pini
Pro–66 M Campos
V'tors WD–H
Fees On application
Loc 1 mile S of A299 and Chestfield Station

Chislehurst (1894)

Camden Place, Chislehurst BR7 5HJ
Tel **(0181) 467 3055**
Fax **(0181) 295 0874**
Mem 740
Sec NE Pearson (0181) 467 2782
Pro M Lawrence (0181) 467 6798
Holes 18 L 5128 yds SSS 65
Recs Am–61 J Murray (1993)
Pro–61 J Bennett
V'tors WD–H WE–M
Fees D–£25
Loc M25 Junction 3/A20/A222

Cobtree Manor Park (1984)

Public
Chatham Road, Boxley, Maidstone ME14 3AZ
Tel **(01622) 753276**
Sec A Ferras
Holes 18 L 5716 yds SSS 68
Recs Am–67 M White (1991)
V'tors WD–U WE/BH–(book 1 wk in advance) SOC–WD
Fees £8.50 (£13.25)
Loc 3 miles N of Maidstone on A229
Arch F Hawtree

Corinthian (1987)

Gay Dawn Farm, Fawkham, Dartford DA3 8LZ
Tel **(01474) 707559**
Mem 400
Sec M Harris
Pro D Private
Holes 9 L 6045 yds SSS 70
Recs Am–77 G Hesketh (1993)
V'tors WD–U H WE/BH–NA before noon SOC
Fees D–£12.50
Loc 4 miles S of Dartford Tunnel. E of Brands Hatch along Fawkham Valley road

Cranbrook (1969)

Benenden Road, Cranbrook TN17 4AL
Tel **(01580) 712833**
Fax **(01580) 714274**
Mem 500
Pro A Gillard
Holes 18 L 6351 yds SSS 70
Recs Am–67 S Coulter
Pro–70 S Barr
V'tors WD–U WE/BH–restricted SOC
Fees £19 (£27.50)
Loc 15 miles S of Maidstone. Sissinghurst 1 mile
Arch Cdr J Harris

Cray Valley (1972)

Sandy Lane, St Paul's Cray, Orpington BR5 3HY
Tel **(01689) 831927**
Mem 700
Sec R Hill (01689) 839677
Pro J Gregory (01689) 837909
Holes 18 L 5624 yds SSS 67
9 L 2100 yds SSS 60
V'tors WD–U WE–H
Fees £10 (£16)
Loc 1 mile S of Chislehurst

Darenth Valley (1973)

Pay and play
Station Road, Shoreham, Sevenoaks TN14 7SA
Tel **(01959) 522944 (Clubhouse)**
Fax **(01959) 525089**
Sec N Morgan (Mgr)
Pro S Fotheringham (01959) 522922
Holes 18 L 6327 yds Par 72 SSS 71
Recs Am–69 W Leo
Pro–65 S Wood
V'tors U–booking required SOC
Fees £12 (£16)
Loc 3 miles N of Sevenoaks, off A225

Dartford (1897)

Dartford Heath, Dartford DA1 2TN
Tel **(01322) 223616**
Mem 600
Sec Mrs MM Gronow
Pro G Cooke (01322) 226409
Holes 18 L 5914 yds SSS 69
Recs Am–65 N Buttery (1992)
Pro–65 N Burke (1988)
V'tors WD–I WE–M H
Fees £28
Loc Dartford 2 miles

Deangate Ridge (1972)

Public
Duxcourt Road, Hoo, Rochester ME3 8RZ
Tel **(01634) 250537**
Mem 800
Sec JH Orr
Pro R Fox (01634) 251180
Holes 18 L 6300 yds SSS 70
Recs Am–67 L Brookwell (1994)
Pro–65 N Allen (1990)
V'tors U SOC
Fees £9.95 (£12.30)
Loc 7 miles NE of Rochester on A228. M2, 5 miles

Edenbridge G & CC (1973)

Crouch House Road, Edenbridge TN8 5LQ
Tel **(01732) 867381**
Fax **(01732) 867029**
Mem 800
Sec Mrs J Scully
Pro (01732) 865202
Holes 18 L 6604 yds SSS 72
18 L 5671 yds SSS 67
9 hole course
Recs Am–66 ACI Cox
V'tors WD/WE–booking necessary
Fees £15 (£18)
Loc 2 miles W of Edenbridge. M25 Junction 6
Mis Floodlit driving range. 9 hole pitch & putt course

Eltham Warren (1890)

Bexley Road, Eltham, London SE9 2PE
Tel **(0181) 850 1166**
Mem 400
Sec DJ Clare (0181) 850 4477
Pro RV Taylor (0181) 859 7909
Holes 9 L 5840 yds SSS 68
Recs Am–66 G Janes, D Holmes
Pro–67 T Spence
V'tors WD–I WE/BH–M
SOC–Thurs only
Fees £25
Loc 1/2 mile from Eltham station on A210

Faversham (1910)

Belmont Park, Faversham ME13 0HB
Tel **(01795) 890251**
Fax **(01795) 890760**
Mem 750
Sec FW Prescott (Mgr) (01795) 890561

Pro S Rokes (01795) 890275
Holes 18 L 6021 yds SSS 69
Recs Am–65 R Chapman
Pro–67 D Place
V'tors WD–I or H WE–M SOC
Fees £25
Loc Faversham and M2, 2 miles

Gillingham (1908)

Woodlands Road, Gillingham ME27 2AP
Tel **(01634) 850999**
Fax **(01634) 574749**
Mem 450 100(L) 50(J)
Sec LP O'Grady (01634) 853017
Pro B Impett (01634) 855862
Holes 18 L 5911 yds SSS 68
Recs Am–65 T Williamson
Pro–64 P Clark
V'tors WD–I H WE/BH–M
Fees D–£22
Loc A2/M2, 2 miles
Arch James Braid

Hawkhurst (1968)

High Street, Hawkhurst TN18 4JS
Tel **(01580) 752396**
Mem 450
Sec A Shipley
Pro T Collins (01580) 753600
Holes 9 L 5709 yds SSS 68
Recs Am–63 R Gerrard
Pro–68 R Cameron
V'tors WD–U WE–M SOC
Fees 18 holes–£15 9 holes–£9
Loc 14 miles S of Tunbridge Wells on A268

Herne Bay (1895)

Eddington, Herne Bay CT6 7PG
Tel **(01227) 374097**
Mem 480
Sec B Warren (01227) 373964
Pro D Lambert (01227) 374727
Holes 18 L 5466 yds SSS 66
Recs Am–60 SJ Wood
Pro–65 C Clark
V'tors WD–U WE/BH–H after noon SOC–WD
Fees £18 D–£25 (£25)
Loc A291 Canterbury road

Hever (1993)

Hever TN8 7NG
Tel **(01732) 700771**
Mem 560
Sec G Bushby
Pro J Powell (01732) 700785
Holes 18 L 7002 yds SSS 74
V'tors H SOC
Fees £26 D–£39 (£39 D–£55)
Loc 2 miles E of Edenbridge
Arch Peter Nicholson

High Elms (1969)

Public
High Elms Road, Downe, Orpington
Tel **(01689) 858175**
Sec Mrs P O'Keeffe (Hon)
Pro A Hodgson
Holes 18 L 6210 yds SSS 70
Recs Am–68 I Farman
Pro–A Hodgson
V'tors U
Fees On application
Loc Off A21 via Shire Lane

Hythe Imperial (1950)

Prince's Parade, Hythe CT21 6AE
Tel **(01303) 267441**
Mem 445
Sec R Barrett (01303) 267554
Pro G Ritchie (01303) 267441
Holes 9 L 5560 yds SSS 67
Recs Am–63 PI Kaye
Pro–63 G Ritchie
V'tors H SOC
Fees £20
Loc On coast, 4 miles W of Folkestone

Knole Park (1924)

Seal Hollow Road, Sevenoaks TN15 0HJ
Tel **(01732) 452709**
Mem 700
Sec DJL Hoppe (01732) 452150
Pro PE Gill (01732) 451740
Holes 18 L 6249 yds SSS 70
Recs Am–64 RW Seamer
V'tors WD–restricted WE/BH–M H SOC
Fees £27 D–£38
Loc ½mile from Sevenoaks centre
Arch JF Abercromby

Lamberhurst (1890)

Church Road, Lamberhurst TN3 8DT
Tel **(01892) 890241**
Fax **(01892) 891140**
Mem 700
Sec P Gleeson (01892) 890591
Pro M Travers (01892) 890552
Holes 18 L 6232 yds SSS 70
Recs Am–69 R Groves, G Coldwell
Pro–65 A Lavers
V'tors WD–U H WE–NA before noon
Fees £20 D–£30 (£36)
Loc 5 miles SE of Tunbridge Wells, off A21

Langley Park (1910)

Barnfield Wood Road, Beckenham BR3 2SZ
Tel **(0181) 650 2090**
Mem 650
Sec JL Smart (0181) 658 6849
Pro C Staff (0181) 650 1663
Holes 18 L 6488 yds SSS 71
Recs Am–66 T Trodd
Pro–65 P Mitchell (1987), GT Ritchie (1991)
V'tors WD–H WE–M SOC–WD
Fees £35
Loc Bromley South Station 1 mile
Arch JH Taylor

Leeds Castle (1928)

Public
Leeds Castle, Hollingbourne, Maidstone ME17 1PL
Tel **(01622) 880467/765400**
Sec Mrs A Knowlden
Pro None
Holes 9 L 2880 yds Par 34
Pro–32 A Jacklin
V'tors U SOC–WD
Fees 9 holes–£9
Loc 10 miles E of Maidstone (A20). M20, 1 mile
Mis 6-day advance booking

Littlestone (1888)

St Andrews Road, Littlestone, New Romney TN28 8RB
Tel **(01797) 362310**
Mem 550
Sec JD Lewis (01797) 363355
Pro S Watkins (01797) 362231
Holes 18 L 6460 yds SSS 72
Recs Am–67 G Godmon (1984), S Wood (1988)
Pro–65 P Eales, D Clark, R Green, (1993)
V'tors WD–H WE–by arrangement SOC
Fees £26 (£32)
Loc 2 miles E of New Romney. 15 miles SE of Ashford
Arch W Laidlaw Purves/ Dr A Mackenzie

The London Golf Club (1993)

Stansted Lane, Ash Green, Sevenoaks TN15 7EN
Tel **(01474) 879899**
Pro P Fosten
Holes Heritage 18 L 7208 yds SSS 74 Par 72; International 18 L 7005 yds Par 72 SSS 74
V'tors M
Fees N/A
Loc Off A20, nr Brands Hatch
Arch Nicklaus/Kirby

Lullingstone Park (1967)

Public
Parkgate Road, Chelsfield, Orpington BR6 7PX
Tel **(01959) 533793**
Pro D Cornford
Holes 18 L 6779 yds SSS 72
9 L 2445 yds Par 33
Recs Am–71
Pro–69
V'tors U
Fees On application
Loc Off Orpington by-pass (A224) towards Well Hill. M25 Junction 4

Mid Kent (1909)

Singlewell Road, Gravesend DA11 7RB
Tel **(01474) 568035**
Fax **(01474) 564218**
Mem 1050

Sec T Potter
Pro N Hansen (01474) 332810
Holes 18 L 6199 yds SSS 69
Pro–60 K McDonald (1993)
V'tors WD–H WE–M
Fees On application
Loc SE of Gravesend, nr A2
Arch Frank Pennink

Moatlands (1993)

Watermans Lane, Brenchley, Tonbridge TN12 6ND
Tel **(01892) 724400**
Fax **(01892) 723300**
Mem 800
Sec T Kusaba (Gen Mgr)
Pro (01892) 724252
Holes 18 L 7060 yds Par 72 SSS 74
V'tors WD–U H WE–NA before noon SOC
Fees £27 (£37)
Loc Between Matfield and Paddock Wood, off A21
Mis Driving range
Arch T Saito

Nizels (1992)

Nizels Lane, Hildenborough, Tonbridge TN11 8NX
Tel **(01732) 833138**
Fax **(01732) 833764**
Mem 700
Sec JH Bellamy
Pro N Way (01732) 838926
Holes 18 L 6408 yds SSS 71
Recs Am–67 R Edwards
V'tors WD–U SOC
Fees £25 D–£35
Loc 4 miles from M25 on B245. A21 Tonbridge North Junction
Arch Lennan/Purnell

North Foreland (1903)

Kingsgate, Broadstairs, Thanet CT10 3PU
Tel **(01843) 862140**
Fax **(01843) 862140**
Mem 800
Sec BJ Preston
Pro (01843) 869628
Holes 18 L 6430 yds SSS 71
Recs Am–66 P Walton
Pro–65 M Lawrence
V'tors WD–H WE–NA am –H pm
Fees £25 (£35)
Loc B2052, 1½ miles N of Broadstairs
Mis 18 hole pitch & putt course

Oastpark (1993)

Malling Road, Snodland ME6 5LG
Tel **(01634) 242661**
Mem 600
Sec Valerie Hagger
Pro T Cullen
Holes 18 L 6200 yds SSS 69
Recs Am–71 D Porthouse (1993)
V'tors U SOC
Fees £10 (£13)
Loc 1 mile E of M20 Junction 4

Poult Wood (1974)

Public
Higham Lane, Tonbridge TN11 9QR
Tel **(01732) 364039** (Bookings), **(01732) 366180** (Clubhouse)
Sec A Hope (Mgr)
Pro C Miller
Holes 18 L 5569 yds SSS 67
V'tors U–booking required SOC–WD
Fees £8.40 (£12.60)
Loc 1 mile N of Tonbridge, off A227
Arch Hawtree

Prince's (1904)

Sandwich Bay, Sandwich CT13 9QB
Tel **(01304) 611118**
Fax **(01304) 612000**
Mem 350
Sec WM Howie(Gen Mgr)
Pro C Evans (01304) 613797
Holes 27 hole course (3 x 9 holes): Dunes/Himalayas/Shore Length 6238-6947 yds Par 71-72 SSS 70-73
Recs Himalayas/Shore
Am–67 M Goodin
Pro–69 M Mannelli
Dunes/Himalayas Am–69 S Wood
V'tors U SOC–WD/WE (book with M Stone)
Fees £32.50 D–£38 (£37 Sat–£43 Sun–£49)
Loc Sandwich Bay (A258)
Mis Driving range
Arch Morrison/Campbell

The Ridge (1993)

Chartway Street, East Sutton, Maidstone ME17 3DL
Tel **(01622) 844382**
Fax **(01622) 844168**
Mem 650
Sec G Sones
Pro A Robertson (01622) 844243
Holes 18 L 6254 yds SSS 70
V'tors H SOC–Tues & Thurs
Fees £25 (£30)
Loc 3 miles E of Maidstone, off A274. M20 Junction 8
Mis Driving range
Arch Patrick Dawson

Rochester & Cobham Park (1891)

Park Pale, by Rochester ME2 3UL
Tel **(01474) 823411**
Fax **(01474) 824446**
Mem 720
Sec Maj JW Irvine (Mgr)
Pro J Blair (01474) 823658
Holes 18 L 6467 yds SSS 71
Recs Am–66 A Aram (1990)
Pro–66 P Mitchell (1991)
V'tors WD–U H WE–M before 5pm SOC–Tues & Thurs
Fees £26
Loc 3 miles E of Gravesend exit (A2)

Romney Warren (1993)

Pay and play
St Andrews Road, Littlestone, New Romney TN28 8RB
Tel **(01797) 362231**
Mem 420
Sec JD Lewis
Pro S Watkins
Holes 18 L 5126 yds SSS 65
V'tors U SOC
Fees £10 (£15)
Loc 2 miles E of New Romney. 15 miles SE of Ashford
Arch Evans/Lewis

Royal Blackheath (1608)

Court Road, Eltham, London SE9 5AF
Tel **(0181) 850 1795**
Fax **(0181) 859 0150**
Mem 700
Sec Wg Cdr R Barriball RAF (Rtd)
Pro I McGregor (0181) 850 1763
Holes 18 L 6219 yds SSS 70
Recs Am–68 M Harris (1994)
Pro–66 M Lawrence, B Cameron (1993)
V'tors WD–I or H WE/BH–M SOC
Fees £30
Loc 5 miles W of M25 Junction 3
Mis Golf museum
Arch James Braid

Royal Cinque Ports (1892)

Golf Road, Deal CT14 6RF
Tel **(01304) 374328** (Clubhouse), **(01304) 374007** (Office)
Fax **(01304) 379530**
Mem 1000+
Sec CC Hammond (01304) 367856
Pro A Reynolds (01304) 374170
Holes 18 L 6406 yds SSS 71
Recs Am–65 MF Bonallack (1964)
Pro–63 GD Manson (1981)
V'tors WD–I H
Fees On application
Loc A258, N of Deal

Royal St George's (1887)

Sandwich CT13 9PB
Tel **(01304) 613090**
Fax **(01304) 611245**
Mem 675
Sec GE Watts
Pro N Cameron (01304) 615236
Holes 18 L 6565 yds SSS 72
Recs Am–67 H Berwick (1954)
Pro–63 N Faldo, P Stewart (1993)
V'tors WD–I H WE–M SOC–WD
Fees £50 D–£70 (1994)
Loc 1 mile E of Sandwich

Ruxley Park (1975)

Pay and play
Sandy Lane, St Paul's Cray, Orpington BR5 3HY
Tel **(01689) 871490**
Fax **(01689) 891428**
Mem 520
Sec PW Davis
Pro R Pilbury
Holes 18 L 6027 yds SSS 69
V'tors U SOC
Fees £10.30 (£15.50)
Loc Off A20 Ruxley roundabout at Sidcup
Mis Floodlit driving range

Sene Valley (1888)

Sene, Folkestone CT18 8BL
Mem 650
Sec RW Leaver (01303) 268513
Pro P Moger (01303) 268514
Holes 18 L 6287 yds SSS 69
Recs Am–65 J Hamilton
Pro–69 G Will
V'tors H SOC
Fees £20 (£30)
Loc 2 miles N of Hythe on B2065
Arch Henry Cotton

Sheerness (1906)

Power Station Road, Sheerness ME12 3AE
Tel **(01795) 662585**
Mem 550
Sec R Pearce
Pro W Evans (01795) 666840
Holes 18 L 6460 yds SSS 71
Recs Am–67 JD Simmance (1993)
V'tors WD–U WE–M SOC
Fees £15
Loc 9 miles N of Sittingbourne. M20, M2 or A2 to A249

Shooter's Hill (1903)

Lowood, Eaglesfield Road, London SE18 3DA
Tel **(0181) 854 1216**
Fax **(0181) 854 0469**
Mem 310 60(L) 31(J)
Sec BR Adams (0181) 854 6368
Pro M Ridge (0181) 854 0073
Holes 18 L 5721 yds SSS 68
Recs Am–63 M Holland (1984)
Pro–62 M Parker (1990)
V'tors WD–I WE/BH–M SOC–Tues & Thurs only
Fees £24 D–£30
Loc Off A207 nr Blackheath

Shortlands (1894)

Meadow Road, Shortlands, Bromley BR2 0PB
Tel **(0181) 460 2471**
Mem 525
Sec PW Smeeth
Pro J Bates (0181) 464 6182
Holes 9 L 5261 yds SSS 66
Recs Am–59 T Coulstock (1990)
Pro–62 P Lyons (1989)
V'tors M
Loc Ravensbourne Ave, Shortlands

Sidcup (1891)

Hurst Road, Sidcup DA15 9AE
Tel **(0181) 300 2864**
Mem 350
Sec S Watt (0181) 300 2150
Pro N Terry (0181) 309 0679
Holes 9 L 5722 yds SSS 68
Recs Am–65 M Bennett
Pro–64 D Webb
V'tors WD–H WE/BH–M SOC–WD before 2pm
Fees £18
Loc On A222. A2/A20, 2 miles

Sittingbourne & Milton Regis (1929)

Wormdale, Newington, Sittingbourne ME9 7PX
Tel **(01795) 842261**
Mem 325 100(L) 50(J)
Sec HDG Wylie
Pro JR Hearn (01795) 842775
Holes 18 L 6251 yds SSS 70
Recs Am–Am–64 TW Milford (1994)
V'tors WD–H Sat–NA Sun–M SOC–Tues & Thurs
Fees £20
Loc 1 mile N of M2 Junction 5 (A249)

St Augustines (1907)

Cottington Road, Cliffsend, Ramsgate CT12 5JN
Tel **(01843) 590333**
Mem 525 55(J)
Sec LP Dyke
Pro DB Scott (01843) 590222
Holes 18 L 5197 yds SS 65
Recs Am–64 AD Setterfield
Pro–61 P Mitchell
V'tors H SOC–WD
Fees £20 (£22) W–£62 M–£185
Loc 2 miles SW of Ramsgate from A253 or A256. Signs to St Augustines Cross

Sundridge Park (1902)

Garden Road, Bromley BR1 3NE
Tel **(0181) 460 1822**
Fax **(0181) 466 1072**
Mem 1200
Sec D Lowton (0181) 460 0278
Pro B Cameron (0181) 460 5540
Holes East 18 L 6490 yds SSS 71
West 18 L 6007 yds SSS 69
Recs East Am–65 W Hodkin (1988)
Pro–63 R Cameron
West Am–64 R Hurd (1993)
Pro–65 R Fidler
V'tors H SOC–WD
Fees £36
Loc 1 mile N of Bromley, by Sundridge Park Station. M25 Junctions 3/4

Sweetwoods Park (1994)

Pay and play
Cowden, Edenbridge TN8 7JN
Tel **(01342) 850729**
Fax **(01342) 850866**
Mem 900
Sec P Strand (Mgr)
Pro K Kelsall
Holes 18 L 6400 yds Par 72
Recs Am -66 S Randall
Pro–65 K Kelsall
V'tors U SOC
Fees £14 (£24)
Loc 5 miles E of E Grinstead on A264
Mis Practice range

Tenterden (1905)

Woodchurch Road, Tenterden TN30 7DR
Tel **(01580) 763987**
Mem 650
Sec JB Shaw
Pro D Lewis (01580) 762409
Holes 18 L 6050 yds Par 70 SSS 69
Recs Am–69 R Murley (1992)
Pro–65 R Cameron (1991)
V'tors WD–U WE/BH–M Sun–NA before noon
Fees On application
Loc 1 mile E of Tenterden on B2067

Tudor Park Hotel (1988)

Ashford Road, Bearsted, Maidstone ME14 4NQ
Tel **(01622) 734334**
Fax **(01622) 735360**
Mem 750
Sec J Ladbrook
Pro J Slinger (01622) 739412
Holes 18 L 6041yds SSS 69
Recs Am–64 D Jessop (1992)
Pro–65 N Haynes (1993)
V'tors H SOC
Fees £25 (£30)
Loc 3 miles E of Maidstone on A20. M20 Junction 8
Arch Donald Steel

Tunbridge Wells (1889)

Langton Road, Tunbridge Wells TN4 8XH
Tel **(01892) 523034**
Mem 360 86(L) 45(J)
Sec PF Janes (01892) 536918
Pro K Smithson (01892) 541386
Holes 9 L 4684 yds SSS 62
Recs Am–59 EC Chapman
Pro–59 J Humphrey
V'tors WD–U H SOC
Fees £22 D–£29.50
Loc Tunbridge Wells, by Spa Hotel

Upchurch River Valley (1991)

Pay and play
Oak Lane, Upchurch, Sittingbourne ME9 7AY
Tel **(01634) 360626**
Fax **(01634) 387784**
Mem 700
Sec AJ New (Hon)
Pro MR Daniels (01634) 379592
Holes 18 L 6181 yds SSS 69
9 hole Par 3 course

For list of abbreviations see page 435

V'tors U SOC–WD
Fees 18 hole:£9.95 (£12.95)
9 hole:£5.95 (£6.95)
Loc 3 miles NE of Rainham, off A2. M2 Junction 4
Mis Floodlit driving range
Arch David Smart

Walmer & Kingsdown (1909)

The Leas, Kingsdown, Deal CT14 8EP
Tel **(01304) 373256**
Mem 620
Sec BW Cockerill
Pro I Coleman (01304) 363017
Holes 18 L 6437 yds SSS 71
Recs Am–69 A Randall
Pro–70 M Lee
V'tors WD–H WE–after noon SOC
Fees D–£22 (£24)
Loc 2½ miles S of Deal on clifftop
Arch James Braid

Weald of Kent (1992)

Pay and play
Maidstone Road, Headcorn TN27 9PT
Tel **(01622) 890866**
Mem 1000
Sec J Millen (Mgr)
Pro N McNally (01622) 863163
Holes 18 L 6169 yds SSS 69
V'tors U–booking 3 days in advance SOC
Fees £14 (£18.50)
Loc 5 miles S of Maidstone on A274. M20 Junction 8
Arch John Millen

West Kent (1916)

West Hill, Downe, Orpington BR6 7JJ
Tel **(01689) 851323**
Fax **(01689) 851323**
Mem 750
Sec AJ Messing
Pro RS Fidler (01689) 856863
Holes 18 L 6399 yds SSS 70
Recs Am–62 DC Smith (1984)
Pro–65 H Baiocchi (1985)
V'tors WD–H or I–phone to arrange WE/BH–M
Fees On application
Loc 5 miles S of Orpington

West Malling (1974)

Addington, Maidstone ME19 5AR
Tel **(01732) 844785**
Mem 900
Sec MR Ellis
Pro J Foss
Holes Spitfire 18 L 6142 yds Par 70
Hurricane 18 L 6240 yds Par 70
Recs Spitfire Am–67 S Pigott
Pro–67 H Baiocchi
Hurricane Am–69 S Pigott
V'tors WD–U WE–U H after noon
Fees £20 (£30)
Loc 12 miles W of Maidstone (A20)

Westgate & Birchington (1893)

176, Canterbury Road, Westgate-on-Sea CT8 8LT
Tel **(01843) 831115/833905**
Mem 325
Sec JM Wood
Pro R Game
Holes 18 L 4926 yds SSS 64
Pro–60 J Hickman
Ladies–60 W Morgan
V'tors H or I WD–NA before 10am
WE–NA before 11am SOC
Fees £12 (£15)
After 2pm–£10 (£10)
Loc 1 mile W of Westgate (A28)

Whitstable & Seasalter (1910)

Collingwood Road, Whitstable CT5 1EB
Tel **(01227) 272020**
Mem 300
Sec GA Hodson (01227) 273589
Holes 9 L 5284 yds SSS 63
V'tors WD–U WE–M
Fees On application
Loc 1 mile W of Whitstable

Wildernesse (1890)

Seal, Sevenoaks TN15 0JE
Tel **(01732) 761526**
Mem 750
Sec RA Foster (01732) 761199
Pro W Dawson (01732) 761527
Holes 18 L 6438 yds SSS 72
Recs Am–64 AD Tillman (1991)
Pro–65 I Grant (1980)
V'tors WD–I H SOC–Mon & Thurs
Fees £27 D–£38
Loc 2 miles E of Sevenoaks (A25). M25 Junction 5

Woodlands Manor (1928)

Woodlands, Tinkerpot Lane, Sevenoaks TN15 6AB
Tel **(01959) 523805**
Mem 650
Sec EF Newman (01959) 523806
Pro A Brooks (01959) 524161
Holes 18 L 6000 yds SSS 68
Recs Am–65 N Sherman
Pro–65 N Coles
V'tors WD–U WE–H NA before noon SOC–WD
Fees On application
Loc 4 miles S of M25 Junction 3. Off A20 between West Kingsdown and Otford
Arch Coles/Lyons

Wrotham Heath (1906)

Seven Mile Lane Comp, Sevenoaks TN15 8QZ
Tel **(01732) 884800**
Mem 424 75(L) 50(J)
Sec LJ Byrne
Pro H Dearden (01732) 883854
Holes 18 L 5954 yds SSS 69
V'tors WD–H WE/BH–M
SOC–Thurs & Fri
Fees £22 D–£32
Loc 8 miles W of Maidstone on B2016. M26/A20 Junction, 1 mile
Arch Donald Steel

Lancashire

Accrington & District (1893)

West End, Oswaldtwistle, Accrington BB5 4LS
Tel **(01254) 232734**
Mem 350
Sec JE Pilkington (01254) 235070
Pro W Harling (01254) 231091
Holes 18 L 5954 yds SSS 69
Recs Am–64 J Rothwell
V'tors WD/WE–U SOC
Fees On application
Loc 3 miles SW of Accrington

Ashton & Lea (1913)

Tudor Ave, Blackpool Rd, Lea, Preston PR4 0XA
Tel **(01772) 726480**
Fax **(01772) 735762**
Mem 850
Sec MG Gibbs (01772) 735282
Pro M Greenough (01772) 720374
Holes 18 L 6346 yds SSS 70
Recs Am–65 K Wallbank (1989)
Pro–66 J Hawksworth (1988), S Townend (1992)
Ladies–72 L Fairclough (1985)
V'tors U SOC
Fees £23 (£25)
Loc 3 miles W of Preston, off A5085
Arch J Steer

Bacup (1912)

Maden Road, Bacup OL13 8HY
Tel **(01706) 873170**
Mem 395
Sec J Garvey (01706) 874485
Holes 9 L 6008 yds SSS 69
Recs Am–72 M Butcher
V'tors U
Fees On application
Loc Bankside Lane

Baxenden & District (1913)

Top o' th' Meadow, Baxenden, Accrington BB5 2EA
Tel **(01254) 234555**
Mem 350
Sec L Howard (01706) 213394
Holes 9 L 5702 yds SSS 68
Recs Am–68 W Horvath
Pro–66 C Tobin
V'tors WD–U WE/BH–M
Fees £13
Loc 2 miles SE of Accrington

Blackburn (1894)
Beardwood Brow, Blackburn BB2 7AX
Tel **(01254) 51122**
Fax **(01254) 665578**
Mem 440 90(L) 90(J)
Sec PD Haydock
Pro A Rodwell (01254) 55942
Holes 18 L 6144 yds SSS 70
Recs Am–63 JS Reed (1991)
Pro–66 M Foster
Ladies–68 CD Blackshaw (1994)
V'tors U SOC–WD
WE/BH–restricted
Fees £19 (£22)
Loc 1 mile NW of Blackburn (A677). M6 Junction 31

Blackpool North Shore (1904)
Devonshire Road, Blackpool FY2 0RD
Tel **(01253) 351017**
Fax **(01253) 591240**
Mem 980
Sec R Yates (01253) 352054
Pro B Ward (01253) 354640
Holes 18 L 6443 yds SSS 71
Recs Am–67 T Foster (1988), ID Hill (1990)
Pro–63 C O'Connor
V'tors WD–U WE–restricted SOC
Fees £23 (£28)
Loc 1/2 mile E of Queens Promenade (B5124)

Blackpool Park (1925)
Public
North Park Drive, Blackpool FY3 8LS
Mem 650
Sec DP Woodman (01253) 397916
Pro B Purdie (01253) 391004
Holes 18 L 6192 yds SSS 69
Recs Am–65 AV Moss
Pro–68 D Lewis
V'tors U–no telephone booking
Fees £9 (£10.50)
Loc 2 miles E of Blackpool, signposted off M55
Mis Tee reservations:Blackpool Borough Council, Stanley Park Offices, West Park Drive, Blackpool
Arch Dr A Mackenzie

Burnley (1905)
Glen View, Burnley BB11 3RW
Tel **(01282) 421045**
Mem 700
Sec GJ Butterfield (01282) 451281
Pro WP Tye (01282) 455266
Holes 18 L 5899 yds SSS 69
Recs Am–65 ID Gradwell, L Samuels, DA Brown
GD Haworth, P Preston
Pro–66 JS Steer
V'tors U SOC
Fees £20 (£25)
Loc Via Manchester Road to Glen View Road

Chorley (1897)
Hall o' th' Hill, Heath Charnock, Chorley PR6 9HX
Tel **(01257) 480263**
Mem 550
Sec AK Tyrer
Pro M Tomlinson (01257) 481245
Holes 18 L 6307 yds SSS 70
Recs Am–64 WG Bromilow
Pro–65 RN Giles
V'tors WD–I or H WE–NA SOC
Fees On application
Loc 1 mile S of Chorley at junction A6/A673
Arch JA Steer

Clitheroe (1891)
Whalley Road, Clitheroe BB7 1PP
Tel **(01200) 22618 (Clubhouse)**
Mem 725 120(L) 60(J)
Sec G Roberts JP (01200) 22292
Pro J Twissell (01200) 24242
Holes 18 L 6326 yds SSS 71
Recs Am–67 J Cartmell
V'tors WD–U H SOC
Fees £25 (£30)
Loc 2 miles S of Clitheroe
Arch James Braid

Colne (1901)
Law Farm, Skipton Old Road, Colne BB8 7EB
Tel **(01282) 863391**
Mem 310
Sec JT Duerden (Hon)
Pro None
Holes 9 L 5961 yds SSS 69
Recs Am–63 M Brooks
Ladies–66 M Birtwistle
V'tors U exc comp days SOC–WD
Fees £14 (£18)
Loc 1 1/2 miles N of Colne. From end of M65, signs to Keighley and then Lothersdale

Darwen (1893)
Winter Hill, Darwen BB3 0LB
Tel **(01254) 701287**
Mem 375 70(L) 60(J)
Sec J Kenyon (01254) 704367
Pro W Lennon (01254) 776370
Holes 18 L 5752 yds SSS 68
Recs Am–63 J Grimshaw (1994)
Pro–65
V'tors U
Fees £15 (£20)
Loc Darwen 1 1/2 miles

Dean Wood (1922)
Lafford Lane, Up Holland, Skelmersdale WN8 0QZ
Tel **(01695) 622980**
Mem 850
Sec A McGregor (01695) 622219
Pro AB Coop
Holes 18 L 6137 yds SSS 70
V'tors WD–U WE/BH–M SOC
Fees £24 (£30)
Loc 4 miles W of Wigan (A577)
Arch James Braid

Duxbury Park (1975)
Public
Duxbury Hall Road, Duxbury Park, Chorley PR7 4AS
Tel **(01257) 265380**
Fax **(01257) 241378**
Sec R Blease
Pro D Clarke
Holes 18 L 6270 yds SSS 70
Recs Am–74 A Jones
Pro–66 J Anglada
V'tors U
Fees £6.25 (£8.50)
Loc 1 1/2 miles S of Chorley, off Wigan Lane

Fairhaven (1895)
Lytham Hall Park, Ansdell, Lytham St Annes FY8 4JU
Tel **(01253) 736741**
Fax **(01253) 731461**
Mem 900
Pro (01253) 736976
Holes 18 L 6883 yds SSS 73
Recs Am–65 SG Birtwell
Pro–65 R Commans
V'tors WD–U WE–NA before 9am SOC–WD
Fees £27 (£30)
Loc Lytham 2 miles. St Annes 2 miles. M55 Junction 4

Fishwick Hall (1912)
Glenluce Drive, Farringdon Park, Preston PR1 5TD
Tel **(01772) 798300**
Mem 750
Sec RR Gearing
Pro S Bence (01772) 795870
Holes 18 L 6092 yds SSS 69
Recs Am–66 C Cross
V'tors Apply to Sec SOC
Fees £20 (£25)
Loc 1 mile E of Preston, nr junction of A59 and M6 Junction 31

Fleetwood (1932)
Golf House, Princes Way, Fleetwood FY7 8AF
Tel **(01253) 873114**
Mem 548
Sec H Fielding (01253) 773573
Pro CT Burgess (01253) 873661
Holes L 18 L 6723 yds SSS 72
Recs Am–69 JC Roberts
Pro–70 S Bennett
V'tors U SOC
Fees £20 (£25)
Loc 1 mile W of Fleetwood

Ghyll (1907)
Ghyll Brow, Barnoldswick, Colne BB8 6JQ
Tel **(01282) 842466**
Mem 310
Sec JL Gill (01756) 798592
Holes 9 L 5708 yds SSS 68
Recs Am–64 M Boardman (1989)
V'tors U exc Sun–NA
Fees £14 (£16)
Loc 7 miles N of Colne, off A56

Great Harwood (1896)

Harwood Bar, Great Harwood BB6 7TE

Tel **(01254) 884391**
Mem 175 60(L) 45(J)
Sec A Garraway (01254) 886802
Holes 9 L 6413 yds SSS 71
Recs Am–68 J Aspinall
Pro–64 AH Padgham
V'tors U SOC
Fees £13 (£16)
Loc 5 miles NE of Blackburn

Green Haworth (1914)

Green Haworth, Accrington BB5 3SL

Tel **(01254) 237580**
Mem 225
Sec JKS Allan
Holes 9 L 5513 yds SSS 68
Recs Am–67 S Ormerod (1992)
V'tors WD–U exc Wed–Ladies only after 5pm WE/BH–M SOC
Fees On application
Loc Willows Lane

Herons Reach (1993)

Pay and play

Village Hotel & Leisure Club, East Park Drive, Blackpool FY3 8LL

Tel **(01253) 838866**
Fax **(01253) 798800**
Mem 500
Sec D Hughes (Mgr)
Pro R Hudson
Holes 18 L 6416 yds SSS 71
V'tors U H SOC
Fees £20 (£30)
Loc M55 Junction 4. Follow signs to Blackpool Zoo
Mis Floodlit driving range
Arch Alliss/Clark

Heysham (1910)

Trumacar Park, Middleton Road, Heysham, Morecambe LA3 3JH

Tel **(01524) 851011**
Mem 685
Sec FA Bland (Sec/Mgr)
Pro S Fletcher (01524) 852000
Holes 18 L 6258 yds SSS 70
Recs Am–64 M Murray (1994)
Pro–64 P Walker (1990)
V'tors U H SOC
Fees £19 D–£24 (£29)
Loc 2 miles S of Morecambe. M6 Junction 34, 5 miles
Arch A Herd

Hurlston Hall (1994)

Hurlston Lane, Southport Road, Scarisbrick L40 8JD

Tel **(01704) 840400**
Fax **(01704) 841404**
Mem 600
Sec Hilary Griffiths (Admin)
Pro G Bond (01704) 841120
Holes 18 L 6746 yds SSS 72
V'tors H SOC
Fees £25 (£30)
Loc 2 miles NW of Ormskirk (A570). M58 Junction 3
Mis Floodlit driving range
Arch Donald Steel

Ingol (1981)

Tanterton Hall Road, Ingol, Preston PR2 7BY

Tel **(01772) 734556**
Mem 700
Sec H Parker
Pro S Laycock
Holes 18 L 5868 yds SSS 68
Recs Am–68
Pro–67
V'tors U SOC–WD
Fees £15 (£25)
Loc 1½ miles NW of Preston (A6). M6 Junction 32

Knott End (1911)

Wyreside, Knott End on Sea, Blackpool FY6 0AA

Tel **(01253) 810254 (Clubhouse)**
Fax **(01253) 810576**
Mem 660
Sec KE Butcher (01253) 810576
Pro P Walker (01253) 811365
Holes 18 L 5789 yds SSS 68
Recs Am–58 M Davies (1994)
Pro–66 P Harrison (1978)
V'tors WD–U WE/BH–by arrangement SOC–WD
Fees D–£20 (£24)
Loc Over Wyre, 12 miles NE of Blackpool (A588)

Lancaster G & CC (1932)

Ashton Hall, Ashton-with-Stodday, Lancaster LA2 0AJ

Tel **(01524) 752090**
Fax **(01524) 752135**
Mem 525 165(L) 125(J)
Sec DDJ Palmer (01524) 751247
Pro DE Sutcliffe (01524) 751802
Holes 18 L 6465 yds SSS 71
Recs Am–66 S Andrew
V'tors WD–H SOC–WD
Fees £28
Loc 2 miles S of Lancaster (A588)
Arch James Braid

Lansil (1947)

Caton Road, Lancaster LA4 3PD

Tel **(01524) 39269**
Mem 450
Sec J McIntyre (01524) 823732
Holes 9 L 5608 yds SSS 67
Recs Am–68 DC Whiteway
V'tors WD–U WE–U after 1pm
Fees £12 (£12)
Loc A683, 2 miles E of Lancaster

Leyland (1923)

Wigan Road, Leyland PR5 2UD

Tel **(01772) 421359**
Fax **(01772) 436457**
Mem 750
Sec J Ross (01772) 436457
Pro C Burgess (01772) 423425
Holes 18 L 6123 yds SSS 69
Recs Am–62 J Mann (1991)
Pro–66 T Hastings (1993)
V'tors WD–U WE–M SOC–WD
Fees £25 (1994)
Loc M6 Junction 28, ½mile

Lobden (1888)

Whitworth, Rochdale OL12 8XJ

Tel **(01706) 343228**
Mem 220
Sec N Danby (01706) 43241
Holes 9 L 5770 yds SSS 68
Recs Am–67 C Turner
V'tors U
Fees £10 (£12)
Loc 4 miles N of Rochdale

Longridge (1877)

Fell Barn, Jeffrey Hill, Longridge, Preston PR3 2TU

Tel **(01772) 783291**
Mem 650
Sec DS Helm (01772) 202373
Pro NS James (01772) 783291
Holes 18 L 5766 yds SSS 68
Recs Am–66 A Taylor (1990)
V'tors U
Fees £18 (£21)
Loc 8 miles NE of Preston, off B6243

Lytham Green Drive (1922)

Ballam Road, Lytham FY8 4LE

Tel **(01253) 734782**
Fax **(01253) 731350**
Mem 700
Sec R Kershaw (01253) 737390
Pro A Lancaster (01253) 737379
Holes 18 L 6175 yds SSS 69
Recs Am–64 C Rymer (1988)
Pro–64 E Romero (1988)
V'tors WD–U H WE–NA SOC–WD
Fees £23 (£35)
Loc Lytham St Annes

Marsden Park (1969)

Public

Townhouse Road, Nelson BB9 8DG

Tel **(01282) 67525**
Pro N Brown
Holes 18 L 5806 yds SSS 68
Recs Am–66 A Skelton (1987)
Pro–74 T Gillett
V'tors U SOC
Fees On application
Loc Signposted Walton Lane

Morecambe (1904)

Bare, Morecambe LA4 6AJ

Tel **(01524) 418050**
Fax **(01524) 418050**
Mem 1071
Sec MJ Potts (01524) 412841
Pro P de Valle (01524) 415596
Holes 18 L 5770 yds SSS 68
Recs Am–64 J Swallow, DP Carney
Pro–63 B Gallacher, P Oosterhuis
V'tors U H SOC
Fees £17 (£21)
Loc On coast road towards Carnforth (A5105)

Nelson (1902)

Kings Causeway, Brierfield, Nelson BB9 0EU

Tel **(01282) 614583**
Mem 550
Sec DT Ingham
Pro N Sumner (01282) 617000
Holes 18 L 5967 yds SSS 69
Recs Am–64 I Greenwood (1994)
Pro–68 H Shoesmith
V'tors WD–U H exc Thurs–NA
WE–U exc Sat before 4pm
SOC
Fees £25 (£25)
Loc 2 miles N of Burnley

Ormskirk (1899)

Cranes Lane, Lathom, Ormskirk L40 5UJ

Tel **(01695) 572112**
Mem 300
Sec PD Dromgoole
(01695) 572227
Pro J Hammond (01695) 572074
Holes 18 L 6358 yds SSS 70
Recs Am–63 DJ Eccleston
Pro–67 MJ Slater
V'tors I exc Sat–NA SOC
Fees £25 Wed–£30 Sun–£30
D–£35
Loc 2 miles E of Ormskirk

Penwortham (1908)

Blundell Lane, Penwortham, Preston PR1 0AX

Tel **(01772) 743207**
Mem 700
Sec J Parkinson (01772) 744630
Pro J Wright (01772) 742345
Holes 18 L 5915 yds SSS 68
Recs Am–62 A Gillespie
Pro–66 W Fletcher
V'tors WD–U WE–no parties
Fees £22 (£28)
Loc 1½ miles W of Preston (A59)

Pleasington (1891)

Pleasington, Blackburn BB2 5JF

Tel **(01254) 202177**
Fax **(01254) 201028**
Mem 520
Sec AA Cook
Pro GJ Furey (01254) 201630
Holes 18 L 6445 yds SSS 71
Recs Am–64 SG Birtwell (1983)
Pro–66 S Holden (1988)
V'tors H
Fees £30 (£35)
Loc 3 miles SW of Blackburn

Poulton-le-Fylde (1982)

Public

Myrtle Farm, Breck Road, Poulton, Blackpool

Tel **(01253) 892444**
Mem 250
Sec KG Avdis
Pro D Spencer
Holes 9 L 2979 yds SSS 69
Recs Am–72 R Walker,
L Chenery (1992)
Pro–74 C Mawdesley
V'tors U
Fees On application
Loc 3 miles NE of Blackpool
Mis Driving range

Preston (1892)

Fulwood Hall Lane, Fulwood, Preston PR2 4DD

Tel **(01772) 700436/794234**
(Clubhouse)
Mem 800
Sec JR Spedding (01772) 700011
Pro PA Wells (01772) 700022
Holes 18 L 6233 yds SSS 70
Recs Am–65 MA Holmes, J Wright
Pro–66 JM Hulme
V'tors U H SOC–WD
Fees £22 D–£27
Loc 1½ miles W of M6 Junction
32
Arch James Braid

Rishton (1927)

Eachill Links, Hawthorn Drive, Rishton BB1 4HG

Tel **(01254) 884442**
Mem 250
Sec P Chesterton (Hon)
Holes 9 L 6097 yds SSS 69
Recs Am–66 G Walmsley
Pro–68 J Matthews
V'tors WD–U WE–M
Fees £12
Loc 3 miles E of Blackburn

Rossendale (1903)

Ewood Lane, Head Haslingden, Rossendale BB4 6LH

Tel **(01706) 213056**
Mem 682
Sec JR Swain (01706)
831339/214968
Pro SJ Nicholls (01706) 213616
Holes 18 L 6293 yds SSS 70
Recs Am–67 A Siddle
Pro–67 D Screeton
V'tors WD/Sun–U Sat–M
Fees £22.50 (£27.50)
Loc 7 miles N of Bury, nr end of
M66

Royal Lytham & St Annes (1886)

Links Gate, Lytham St Annes FY8 3LQ

Tel **(01253) 724206**
Fax **(01253) 780946**
Mem 600
Sec LB Goodwin FCA
Pro E Birchenough
(01253) 720094
Holes 18 L 6685 yds SSS 73
Recs Am–66 R Foster,
T Craddock
Pro–65 C O'Connor,
BGC Huggett, W Longmuir,
S Ballesteros
V'tors WD–I H
Fees £60 D–£80 (incl lunch)
Loc St Annes 1 mile (A584)

Shaw Hill Hotel G & CC (1925)

Preston Road, Whittle-le-Woods, Chorley PR6 7PP

Tel **(01257) 269221**
Fax **(01257) 261223**
Mem 500
Sec F Wharton
Pro D Clarke (01257) 279222
Holes 18 L 6405 yds SSS 71
Recs Am–66 N Hopwood (1991)
Pro–69 I Evans (1984)
V'tors WD–U H SOC
Fees On application
Loc A6, 1½ miles N of Chorley.
M61 Junction 8.
M6 Junction 28

St Annes Old Links (1901)

Highbury Road, Lytham St Annes FY8 2LD

Tel **(01253) 723597**
Fax **(01253) 781506**
Mem 975
Sec PW Ray
Pro GG Hardiman
(01253) 722432
Holes 18 L 6647 yds SSS 72
Recs Am–66 RD Squire, AC Nash
Pro–66 AD Sowa, T Webber,
GL Parslow
V'tors WD–NA before 9.15am and
12–2pm WE/BH–arrange with
Sec SOC
Fees £28 (£35)
Loc Between St Annes and
Blackpool, off A584

Stonyhurst Park (1980)

Stonyhurst, Hurst Green, Blackburn BB6 9QB

Tel **(01254) 826478**
Mem 315
Sec TA Cooke (01200) 23089
Holes 9 L 5529 yds SSS 66
V'tors WD–phone first WE–M
Fees £12
Loc 5 miles SW of Clitheroe
(B6243)
Mis Green fees payable at Bayley
Arms, Hurst Green

Towneley (1932)

Public

Towneley Park, Todmorden Road, Burnley BB11 3ED

Tel **(01282) 451636**
Mem 300
Sec I Kippax
Pro (01282) 38473
Holes 18 L 5862 yds SSS 68
9 hole course
Recs Am–67 T Foster (1990)
Pro–65 D Whittaker (1985)
V'tors U
Fees £5 (£6)
Loc 1½ miles E of Burnley

For list of abbreviations see page 435

Whalley (1912)
Long Leese Barn, Clerkhill, Whalley, Blackburn BB7 9DR
Tel **(01254) 822236**
Mem 475
Sec R Bolsover (01254) 824259
Pro H Smith
Holes 9 L 6258 yds Par 72 SSS 70
Recs Am–67 G Richards
V'tors U exc Sat (Apr–Oct) SOC–WD
Fees £15 (£20)
Loc 7 miles NE of Blackburn

Wilpshire (1890)
72 Whalley Road, Wilpshire, Blackburn BB1 9LF
Tel **(01254) 248260/249691**
Mem 650
Pro W Slaven (01254) 249558
Holes 18 L 5911 yds SSS 68
Recs Am–64 H Green (1975), MJ Savage (1978), PC Livesey (1990)
Pro–61 J Hawkesworth (1989)
V'tors WD–U WE/BH–on request
Fees £25 (£30)
Loc 3 miles NE of Blackburn, off A666

Leicestershire

Birstall (1901)
Station Road, Birstall, Leicester LE4 3BB
Tel **(0116) 267 4450**
Mem 360 107(L) 50(J)
Sec Mrs SE Chilton (0116) 267 4322
Pro D Clark (0116) 267 5245
Holes 18 L 6222 yds SSS 70
Recs Am–63 PA Frith, DE Gibson
Pro–62 RS Larratt
V'tors Mon/Wed/Fri–I Other days–M SOC
Fees £25
Loc 3 miles N of Leicester (A6)

Blaby (1991)
Pay and play
Lutterworth Road, Blaby LE8 3DB
Tel **(0116) 278 4804**
Pro B Morris
Holes 9 L 2600 yds SSS 68
V'tors U
Fees 18 holes–£6 (£8)
Loc S of Blaby village
Mis Driving range

Breedon Priory (1990)
Wilson, Derby DE73 1AT
Tel **(01332) 863081**
Fax **(01332) 863081**
Mem 850
Sec D Ashton
Pro D Ashton
Holes 18 L 5700 yds Par 68
Recs Am–66 J Carter (1993)
Pro–68 T Coxon (1992)
V'tors WD–U WE–NA before 2pm (phone first) SOC–WD
Fees £13 (£15)
Loc 3½ miles W of M1 Junction 23A on A453
Arch Snell/Ashton

Charnwood Forest (1890)
Breakback Road, Woodhouse Eaves, Loughborough LE12 8TA
Tel **(01509) 890259**
Mem 330
Sec J Clarke (01530) 835579
Holes 9 L 5960 yds SSS 69
Recs Am–64 C Radford (1992)
V'tors WD–H WE/BH–NA SOC
Fees £20 (£30)
Loc M1 Junction 23, 3 miles

Cosby (1895)
Chapel Lane, Broughton Road, Cosby, Leicester LE9 1RG
Tel **(0116) 286 4759**
Fax **(0116) 286 4484**
Mem 690
Sec MD Riddle
Pro M Wing (0116) 284 8275
Holes 18 L 6417 yds SSS 71
Recs Am–68 A Allen (1986)
Pro–65 C Harries (1991)
V'tors WD–U before 4pm WE/BH–M SOC–WD–H
Fees £22 D–£24
Loc ½ mile S of Cosby. 7 miles S of Leicester

Enderby (1986)
Public
Mill Lane, Enderby, Leicester LE9 5NW
Tel **(0116) 284 9388**
Sec LJ Speake (0116) 284 1133
Pro C D'Araujo
Holes 9 L 4356 yds SSS 61
V'tors U
Fees 18 holes–£4.75 (£6.75)
Loc Enderby 2 miles. M1 Junction 21

Glen Gorse (1933)
Glen Road, Oadby, Leicester LE2 4RF
Tel **(0116) 271 2226/271 4159**
Fax **(0116) 271 4159**
Mem 360 110(L) 60(J)
Sec M Goodson (0116) 271 4159
Pro R Larratt (0116) 271 3748
Holes 18 L 6603 yds SSS 72
Recs Am–65 AD Hare (1989)
Pro–66 DT Steele (1980), N Turley (1992)
Ladies–70 M Page (1992)
V'tors WD–U WE/BH–M SOC–WD
Fees £22 D–£25
Loc 3 miles S of Leicester on A6

Greetham Valley (1992)
Greetham, Oakham LE15 7RG
Tel **(01780) 460444**
Fax **(01780) 460623**
Mem 700
Sec FE Hinch
Pro M Cunningham (01780) 460666
Holes 18 hole course SSS 71
9 hole Par 3 course
Recs Am–70 G Shelton (1993)
Pro–68 J Higgins (1992)
V'tors U SOC–WD
Fees £15 (£25)
Loc 5 miles NE of Oakham (B668)
Mis Floodlit driving range

Hinckley (1983)
Leicester Road, Hinckley LE10 3DR
Tel **(01455) 615124**
Mem 650
Sec J Toon
Pro R Jones (01455) 615014
Holes 18 L 6517 yds SSS 71
Recs Am–66 JJ Herbert (1990)
Pro–67 K Dickens (1987)
V'tors WD–U exc Tues Sat–NA before 4pm Sun–M after 11am SOC
Fees £23
Loc NE of Hinckley on A47

Humberstone Heights (1978)
Public
Gipsy Lane, Leicester LE5 0TB
Tel **(0116) 276 1905**
Sec S Day
Pro P Highfield (0116) 276 4674
Holes 18 L 6444 yds SSS 71
Recs Am–69 D Butler (1987)
Pro–67 R Adams (1985)
V'tors U SOC–WD
Fees On application
Loc 3 miles E of Leicester, off A47
Mis Pitch & putt course

Kibworth (1905)
Weir Road, Kibworth Beauchamp, Leicester LE8 0LP
Tel **(0116) 279 2301**
Mem 700
Sec Mrs A Towers
Pro (0116) 279 2283
Holes 18 L 6312 yds SSS 70
Recs Am–67 EE Feasey, C Noble (1991)
Pro–64 P Broadhurst (1991)
V'tors WD–U WE–M SOC–WD
Fees £21
Loc 9 miles SE of Leicester on A6
Mis Driving range

Kilworth Springs (1993)
South Kilworth Road, North Kilworth, Lutterworth LE17 6HJ
Tel **(01858) 575082**
Fax **(01858) 575078**
Mem 514
Sec K Mattock
Pro N Melvin
Holes 18 L 6718 yds SSS 72
V'tors U SOC
Fees £17 (£21)
Loc 4 miles E of M1 Junction 20
Mis Driving range

For list of abbreviations see page 435

Kirby Muxloe (1893)
Station Road, Kirby Muxloe, Leicester LE9 2EP
Tel **(0116) 239 3107**
Mem 425
Sec SF Aldwinckle (0116) 239 3457
Pro RT Stephenson (0116) 239 2813
Holes 18 L 6303 yds SSS 70
Recs Am–66 P Bosworth, J Coulthurst (1994) Pro–62 J Higgins (1993)
V'tors WD–U before 3.45pm exc Tues–NA WE–Captain's permission only SOC–H
Fees £20 D–£25
Loc 3 miles W of Leicester
Mis Driving range for members and green fees only

Langton International (1992)
Langton Hall, Leicester LE16 7TY
Tel **(01858) 84374**
Fax **(01858) 84358**
Mem 500
Sec R Cripps
Holes 18 L 6965 yds SSS 72
V'tors H or I SOC
Fees On application
Loc 12 miles SE of Leicester, off A6. 2 miles N of Market Harborough
Mis Driving range
Arch Hawtree

Leicestershire (1890)
Evington Lane, Leicester LE5 6DJ
Tel **(0116) 273 6035**
Fax **(0116) 273 8825**
Mem 750
Sec JL Adams (0116) 273 8825
Pro JR Turnbull (0116) 273 6730
Holes 18 L 6330 yds SSS 70
Recs Am–64 IR Lyner, DJ Bush Pro–63 H Henning, I Mosey, S Sherratt
V'tors U H SOC
Fees £23 (£29)
Loc 2 miles E of Leicester

Leicestershire Forest (1991)
Markfield Lane, Botcheston LE9 9FJ
Tel **(01455) 824800**
Mem 460
Sec M Fixter
Pro M Wing
Holes 18 L 6111 yds SSS 69
V'tors U–phone first
Fees £9 (£13)
Loc 6 miles W of Leicester. M1 Junction 22, 4 miles
Mis Driving range
Arch York/Fixter

Lingdale (1967)
Joe Moore's Lane, Woodhouse Eaves, Loughborough LE12 8TF
Tel **(01509) 890703**
Mem 609
Sec M Green
Pro P Sellears (01509) 890684
Holes 18 L 6545 yds SSS 71
Recs Am–68 R Walker (1994) Pro–70 R Larratt (1992)
V'tors U SOC
Fees D–£18 (£20)
Loc 6 miles S of Loughborough. M1 Junction 23, 4 miles

Longcliffe (1905)
Snells Nook Lane, Nanpantan, Loughborough LE11 3YA
Tel **(01509) 216321**
Mem 550
Sec G Harle (01509) 239129
Pro I Bailey (01509) 231450
Holes 18 L 6551 yds SSS 71
Recs Am–69 M Wilson Pro–68 M Reay
V'tors WD–H WE–M
Fees £22
Loc 3 miles SW of Loughborough. M1 Junction 23

Luffenham Heath (1911)
Ketton, Stamford, Lincs PE9 3UU
Tel **(01780) 720205**
Mem 555
Sec IF Davenport
Pro ISC Burnett (01780) 720298
Holes 18 L 6273 yds SSS 70
Recs Am–64 M Welch Pro–67 PJ Butler, RL Moffitt
V'tors U H SOC–WD
Fees £30 (£35)
Loc 5 miles W of Stamford on A6121
Arch James Braid

Lutterworth (1904)
Lutterworth, Leicester LE17 5HN
Tel **(01455) 552532**
Mem 670
Sec JD Jaynes
Pro R Tisdall
Holes 18 L 5570 yds SSS 67
Recs Am–67 M Moore Pro–71 M Faulkner
V'tors WD–U WE–M SOC
Fees £16 D–£22
Loc By M1 Junction 20

Market Harborough (1898)
Great Oxendon Road, Market Harborough LE16 8NF
Tel **(01858) 463684**
Mem 560
Sec JR Ingleby
Pro FJ Baxter
Holes 18 L 6022 yds Par 70 SSS 69
Recs Am–68 R Williams (1993) Pro–63 FJ Baxter (1994)
V'tors WD–U WE–M SOC–WD
Fees £16 D–£22
Loc 1 mile S of Mkt Harborough on A508
Arch Howard Swann

Melton Mowbray (1925)
Waltham Rd, Thorpe Arnold, Melton Mowbray LE14 4SD
Tel **(01664) 62118**
Mem 620
Sec Mrs EA Sallis
Pro T Westwood (01664) 69629
Holes 18 L 6222 yds SSS 70
V'tors U H before 3pm –M after 3pm SOC
Fees £18 (£25)
Loc 2 miles NE of Melton Mowbray on A607

Oadby (1974)
Public
Leicester Road Racecourse, Oadby, Leicester LE2 4AB
Tel **(0116) 270 9052/270 0215**
Pro S Ward (0116) 270 9052
Holes 18 L 6376 yds Par 72 SSS 70
Recs Am–65 S Davis (1988) Pro–73 C O'Connor Jr
V'tors WD–U WE/BH–book with Pro SOC–WD
Fees £6 (£9)
Loc 2 miles SE of Leicester (A6)

Park Hill (1994)
Park Hill, Seagrave LE12 7NG
Tel **(01509) 815454**
Fax **(01509) 816062**
Mem 220
Sec SG Winterton
Pro DC Mee
Holes 9 hole course
V'tors U SOC
Fees £12 D–£16 (£18 D–£22)
Loc 6 miles N of Leicester on A46
Mis Extension to 18 holes Sept 1995

RAF Cottesmore (1982)
Oakham, Leicester LE15 7BL
Tel **(01572) 812241** Ext 429
Mem 195
Sec PA Cuttle
Holes 9 L 5622 yds SSS 67
Recs Am–64 P Holiday (1993)
V'tors M
Fees £5

RAF North Luffenham (1975)
RAF North Luffenham, Oakham LE15 8RL
Tel **(01780) 720041 Ext 7216**
Mem 350 62(L) 25(J)
Sec JA Anderson
Holes 9 L 6006 yds Par 70 SSS 69
Recs Am–71 KP Hickman
V'tors U SOC
Loc 1/2 mile from S shore of Rutland Water

Rothley Park (1911)
Westfield Lane, Rothley, Leicester LE7 7LH
Tel **(0116) 230 2019**
Sec BS Durham (0116) 230 2809

Pro PJ Dolan (0116) 230 3023
Holes 18 L 6487 yds SSS 71
Recs Am–67 EE Feasey
Pro–68 PJ Dolan
V'tors WD–H exc Tues–NA
WE/BH–NA SOC
Fees £25 D–£30
Loc 6 miles N of Leicester, W of A6

Rutland County (1991)
Great Casterton, Stamford PE9 4AQ
Tel **(01780) 460239**
Fax **(01780) 460330**
Sec S Lowe (Golf Dir)
Pro J Darroch
Holes 18 L 6189 yds SSS 69
9 hole Par 3 course
Pro–64 J Darroch (1993)
V'tors U H SOC
Fees £15 (£20)
Loc 3 miles N of Stamford on A1
Mis Driving range
Arch Cameron Sinclair

Scraptoft (1928)
Beeby Road, Scraptoft, Leicester LE7 9SJ
Tel **(0116) 241 9000**
Mem 535
Sec AM Robertson
(0116) 241 8863
Pro S Sherratt (0116) 241 9138
Holes 18 L 6166 yds SSS 69
Recs Am–66 D Gibson,
CM Harries
Pro–A Bownes
V'tors WD–U WE–M SOC–WD
Fees £20.50 (£25.50)
Loc 3 miles E of Leicester

Ullesthorpe Court Hotel (1976)
Frolesworth Road, Ullesthorpe, Lutterworth
Tel **(01455) 209023**
Fax **(01455) 202537**
Mem 600
Sec PE Woolley
Pro D Bowring (01455) 209150
Holes 18 L 6650 yds SSS 72
Recs Am–70 M Hodgson
Pro–68
V'tors U SOC–WD
Fees £12.50 D–£20
Loc 3 miles NW of Lutterworth, off B577

Western Park (1920)
Public
Scudamore Road, Leicester LE3 1UQ
Tel **(0116) 287 2339/287 6158**
Pro BN Whipham
(0116) 287 2339
Holes 18 L 6532 yds SSS 71
Recs Am–68 DE Gibson
V'tors U
Fees On application
Loc 4 miles W of Leicester. M1 Junction 21, 3 miles

Whetstone (1965)
Cambridge Road, Cosby, Leicester LE9 5SH
Tel **(0116) 286 1424**
Fax **(0116) 286 1424**
Mem 600
Sec J Collins
Pro N Leatherland, D Raitt
Holes 18 L 5795 yds SSS 68
Recs Am–68 R Fines (1994)
Pro–64 D Raitt (1989)
V'tors U SOC
Fees £10 (£13)
Loc S boundary of Leicester
Mis Driving range
Arch E Callaway

Willesley Park (1921)
Measham Road, Ashby-de-la-Zouch LE65 2PF
Tel **(01530) 411532**
Mem 600 99(L) 38(J)
Sec (01530) 414596
Pro C Hancock (01530) 414820
Holes 18 L 6304 yds SSS 70
Recs Am–64 P Frith, M McGuire (1993)
Pro–65 L Jones (1990)
V'tors WD–H WE/BH–H after 9.30am SOC
Fees £27.50 (£32.50)
Loc 2 miles S of Ashby on B5006. M1 Junctions 22/23/24. A42(M) Junction 12

Lincolnshire

Belton Park (1890)
Belton Lane, Londonthorpe Road, Grantham NG31 9SH
Tel **(01476) 67399**
Fax **(01476) 592078**
Mem 950
Sec RM O'Hara (Mgr)
Pro B McKee (01476) 63911
Holes 27 holes:
Brownlow L 6412 yds SSS71
Ancaster L 6109 yds SSS 69
Belmont L 5857 yds SSS 68
Recs Am–66 AR Midgley (1991)
Pro–65 S Bennett (1984)
V'tors U H SOC–WD exc Tues
Fees £20 D–£25
Loc 2 miles N of Grantham

Belton Woods Hotel (1991)
Belton, Grantham NG32 2LN
Tel **(01476) 593200**
Fax **(01476) 74547**
Mem 800
Pro T Roberts
Holes Lakes 18 hole course
Woodside 18 hole course
9 hole course
V'tors H
Fees £20 D–£30 (£25 D–£35)
Loc 2 miles N of Grantham on A607
Mis Driving range
Arch Cayford

Blankney (1903)
Blankney, Lincoln LN4 3AZ
Tel **(01526) 320263**
Fax **(01526) 322521**
Mem 664 138(L) 40(J)
Sec DA Priest
Pro G Bradley (01526) 320202
Holes 18 L 6419 yds SSS 71
Recs Am–69 A Bradley (1994)
Pro–69 G Bradley (1994)
V'tors U H SOC
Fees £17 (£25)
Loc 10 miles SE of Lincoln on B1188
Mis Indoor teaching facilities
Arch Cameron Sinclair

Boston (1962)
Cowbridge, Horncastle Road, Boston PE22 7EL
Tel **(01205) 362306**
Fax **(01205) 350589**
Mem 650 115L) 60(J)
Sec DE Smith (01205) 350589
Pro TR Squires (01205) 362306
Holes 18 L 6483 yds SSS 71
Recs Am–73 J Woodcock (1993)
Pro–69 C Jepson (1994)
V'tors WD–U WE/BH–H
Fees £15 (£20)
Loc 2 miles N of Boston on B1183

Burghley Park (1890)
St Martin's, Stamford PE9 3JX
Tel **(01780) 53789**
Mem 560 140(L) 100(J)
Sec PH Mulligan
Pro G Davies (01780) 62100
Holes 18 L 6236 yds SSS 70
Recs Am–64 I Richardson (1992)
Pro–70 B Thomson (1990)
V'tors WD–I or H WE/BH–M SOC–WD
Fees £20
Loc 1 mile S of Stamford, off A1 at roundabout
Arch Rev JD Day

Canwick Park (1893)
Canwick Park, Washingborough Road, Lincoln LN4 1EF
Tel **(01522) 522166**
Mem 576
Sec J Arnold (01522) 690810
Pro S Williamson (01522) 536870
Holes 18 L 6257 yds SSS 70
Recs Am–66 J Shelton
V'tors WD–U WE–M
Fees £13.50 D–£19.50 (£17 D–£23) Mon–£7.50 D–£15
Loc 1 mile SE of Lincoln

Carholme (1906)
Carholme Road, Lincoln LN1 1SE
Tel **(01522) 523725**
Mem 700
Sec RD Motts
Pro G Leslie (01522) 536811
Holes 18 L 6114 yds SSS 69
Recs Am–69 RJ Taylor (1988)
Ladies–77 J Edmondson (1993)

V'tors WD–U WE–M SOC
Fees On application
Loc Lincoln 1 mile (A57)

Gainsborough (1894)

Thonock, Gainsborough DN21 1PZ
Tel **(01427) 613088**
Fax **(01427) 810172**
Mem 470
Sec DJ Garrison (Mgr)
Pro S Cooper
Holes 18 L 6551 yds SSS 71
Recs Am–66
V'tors WD–U H WE/BH–M SOC–WD
Fees £20 D–£25
Loc N of Gainsborough
Mis Floodlit driving range

Gedney Hill (1991)

Public
West Drove, Gedney End Hill PE12 0NT
Tel **(01406) 330922**
Mem 400
Sec S McGregor
Pro D Creek
Holes 18 L 5450 yds SSS 66
Recs Am–71 A Cook
Pro–66 D Creek (1991)
V'tors U SOC–WD
Fees £5.75 (£9.75)
Loc 4 miles from A47 on B1166
Mis Driving range
Arch C Britton

Horncastle (1990)

West Ashby, Horncastle LN9 5PP
Tel **(01507) 526800**
Mem 300
Sec RC Chantry
Pro EC Wright
Holes 18 L 5782 yds SSS 70
Recs Am–71 J Page
V'tors U SOC
Fees £10 D–£15
Loc 1 mile N of Horncastle, off A158
Mis Floodlit driving range
Arch EC Wright

Kenwick Park (1992)

Kenwick Hall, Louth LN11 8NY
Tel **(01507) 605134**
Sec M Dredge
Pro E Sharp (01507) 607161
Holes 18 L 6815 yds Par 72 SSS 73
V'tors I SOC
Fees D–£25
Loc 1 mile SE of Louth
Arch Patrick Tallack

Kirton Holme (1992)

Pay and play
Holme Road, Kirton Holme, Boston PE20 1SY
Tel **(01205) 290669**
Fax **(01205) 290385**
Mem 360
Sec Mrs T Welberry
(01205) 290560
Pro Alison Johns (01205) 369948
Holes 9 L 2884 yds SSS 68
V'tors U SOC–WD
Fees 9 holes–£4 (£5) D–£7 (£8)
Loc 3 miles W of Boston, off A52
Arch DW Welberry

Lincoln (1891)

Torksey, Lincoln LN1 2EG
Tel **(01427) 718721**
Mem 600
Sec MA Colls
Pro A Carter (01427) 718273
Holes 18 L 6438 yds SSS 71
Recs Am–66 A Thain, P Taylor
Pro–65 M James
V'tors WD–H WE–by appointment
Fees £20 D–£25
Loc 12 miles NW of Lincoln, off A156

Louth (1965)

Crowtree Lane, Louth LN11 9LJ
Tel **(01507) 602554**
Fax **(01507) 603681**
Mem 750
Sec M Covey (Mgr),
Mrs TL Covey (01507) 603681
Pro AJ Blundell (01507) 604648
Holes 18 L 6477 yds SSS 71
Recs Am–64 D Smith (1991)
Pro–69 C Hall (1989)
V'tors U SOC–WD
Fees £16 D–£20 (£25 D–£30)
Loc W side of Louth

Market Rasen (1922)

Legsby Road, Market Rasen LN8 3DZ
Tel **(01673) 842319**
Mem 550
Sec JA Brown
Pro AM Chester (01673) 842416
Holes 18 L 6043 yds SSS 69
Recs Am–66 C Osbourne (1990)
Pro–65 S Bennett (1989)
V'tors WD–I WE/BH–M SOC
Fees £16 D–£24
Loc 1 mile E of Market Rasen

Millfield (1985)

Public
Laughterton, Lincoln LN1 2LB
Tel **(01427) 718255/718473**
Mem 600
Sec PG Guthrie
Holes 18 L 5973 yds SSS 69
15 L 4300 yds
9 hole Par 3 course
V'tors U
Fees £7
Loc 9 miles W of Lincoln
Mis Driving range

North Shore (1910)

North Shore Road, Skegness PE25 1DN
Tel **(01754) 763298**
Fax **(01754) 761902**
Mem 450
Sec B Howard (01754) 763298
Pro J Cornelius (01754) 764822
Holes 18 L 6254 yds SSS 71
Recs Am–71 G Hunter (1989)
V'tors H SOC–WD
Fees On application
Loc 1 mile N of Skegness
Arch James Braid

RAF Waddington

Waddington, Lincoln LN5 9NB
Tel **(01522) 720271** Ext 7958
Mem 90
Sec D Bennett
Holes 9 L 5519 yds SSS 69
Recs Am–68 T Graham (1987)
V'tors By prior arrangement
Fees On application
Loc 4 miles S of Lincoln (A607)

Sandilands (1900)

Sandilands, Sutton-on-Sea LN12 2RJ
Tel **(01507) 441432**
Mem 400
Sec D Mumby (01507) 441617
Pro D Vernon (01507) 441600
Holes 18 L 5995 yds SSS 69
Recs Am–66 JR Payne
Pro–63 FG Allott
V'tors U SOC
Fees £12 D–£18 (£18)
Loc 1 mile S of Sutton-on-Sea, off A52

Seacroft (1895)

Seacroft, Skegness PE25 3AU
Tel **(01754) 763020**
Mem 340 190(L) 90(J)
Sec HK Brader (Mgr)
Pro R Lawie (01754) 69624
Holes 18 L 6501 yds SSS 71
Recs Am–67 DR Rose
Pro–67 J Heib (1988)
V'tors WD–U WE–XL before 11am
Fees £25 (£30)
Loc S boundary of Skegness

Sleaford (1905)

Willoughby Road, South Rauceby, Sleaford NG34 8PL
Tel **(01529) 488273**
Mem 650
Sec TGE Churms
(01529) 488644/488207
Pro J Wilson (01529) 488644
Holes 18 L 6443 yds SSS 71
Recs Am–65 A Hare (1988)
V'tors U H exc Sun–NA (Winter) SOC–WD
Fees £21 (£29)
Loc 1 mile W of Sleaford on A153
Arch Tom Wlliamson

South Kyme (1990)

Skinners Lane, South Kyme, Lincoln LN4 4AT
Tel **(01526) 861113**
Sec A Maplethorpe
Pro P Chamberlain
Holes 18 L 6597 yds SSS 71
Recs Am–72 R Sanderson
Pro–67 A Hare

For list of abbreviations see page 435

V'tors U SOC
Fees £10 (£12)
Loc 2 miles from A17 on B1395
Mis 6 hole practice course
Arch Graham Bradley

Spalding (1908)

Surfleet, Spalding PE11 4EA
Tel **(01775) 680234**
Mem 750
Sec BW Walker (01775) 680386
Pro J Spencer (01775) 680474
Holes 18 L 6478 yds SSS 71
Recs Am–64 J Ronson, R Brotherton
Pro–65 J Spencer
V'tors U H SOC–Tues after 2pm & Thurs
Fees On application
Loc 4 miles N of Spalding, off A16
Arch Spencer/Ward/Price

Stoke Rochford (1924)

Great North Rd, Grantham NG33 5EW
Tel **(01476) 683275**
Mem 515
Sec JM Butler
Pro A Dow (01476) 683218
Holes 18 L 6252 yds SSS 70
Recs Am–65 A Hare, J Payne, M Wilson
Pro–65 A Dow
V'tors WD–U WE/BH–U after 10.30am
Fees On application
Loc 6 miles S of Grantham (A1)

Sudbrook Moor (1991)

Public
Charity Lane, Carlton Scroop, Grantham NG32 3AT
Tel **(01400) 250876 (Clubhouse)**
Pro T Hutton (01400) 250796
Holes 9 L 4712 yds SSS 63
V'tors U
Fees D–£5 (D–£7)
Loc 8 miles N of Grantham (A607)
Arch Tim Hutton

Sutton Bridge (1914)

New Road, Sutton Bridge
Tel **(01406) 350323 (Clubhouse)**
Mem 340
Sec KC Buckle (01945) 870455
Pro R Wood (01406) 351080
Holes 9 L 5820 yds SSS 68
Pro–62 CJ Norton
V'tors WD–H WE–NA
Fees £15
Loc 8 miles N of Wisbech (A17)

Woodhall Spa (1905)

Woodhall Spa LN10 6PU
Tel **(01526) 352511**
Fax **(01526) 352778**
Mem 450
Sec BH Fawcett
Pro CC Elliot (01526) 353229
Holes 18 L 6907 yds SSS 73
Recs Am–68 R Hutt, D Robertson
Pro–68 EB Williamson
V'tors H–booking essential SOC
Fees £28 D–£45 (£32 D–50)
Loc 19 miles SE of Lincoln (B1191)
Mis Max h'cap Men-20 Ladies-30

Woodthorpe Hall (1986)

Woodthorpe, Alford LN13 0DD
Tel **(01507) 450294**
Fax **(01507) 463664**
Mem 400
Sec PC Bell (01507) 463664
Holes 18 L 5222 yds SSS 66
V'tors U SOC
Fees D–£10
Loc 3 miles N of Alford, off B1371. 8 miles SE of Louth

London

Aquarius (Kent)
Beckenham (Kent)
Brent Valley (Middlesex)
Bush Hill Park (Middlesex)
Chingford (Essex)
Dulwich & Sydenham Hill (Surrey)
Eltham Warren (Kent)
Finchley (Middlesex)
Hampstead (Middlesex)
Hendon (Middlesex)
Highgate (Middlesex)
London Scottish (Surrey)
Mill Hill (Middlesex)
Muswell Hill (Middlesex)
North Middlesex (Middlesex)
Picketts Lock (Middlesex)
Richmond Park (Surrey)
Roehampton (Surrey)
Royal Blackheath (Kent)
Royal Epping Forest (Essex)
Royal Wimbledon (Surrey)
Shooter's Hill (Kent)
South Herts (Hertfordshire)
Springfield Park (Surrey)
Trent Park (Middlesex)
Wanstead (Essex)
West Essex (Essex)
Wimbledon Common (Surrey)
Wimbledon Park (Surrey)

Manchester (Greater)

Altrincham Municipal (1935)

Public
Stockport Road, Timperley, Altrincham WA15
Tel **(0161) 928 0761**
Pro R West
Holes 18 L 6204 yds SSS 69
Recs Am–67
Pro–67
V'tors U
Fees On application
Loc 1 mile W of Altrincham (A560)

Ashton-in-Makerfield (1902)

Garswood Park, Liverpool Road, Ashton-in-Makerfield, Wigan WN4 0YT
Tel **(01942) 727267**
Mem 500
Sec JR Hay (01942) 719330
Pro P Allan (01942) 724229
Holes 18 L 6120 yds SSS 69
Recs Am–66 GS Lacy
V'tors WD–U exc Wed WE/BH–M SOC
Fees £21
Loc 1 mile W of Ashton-in-Makerfield on A58. M6 Junction 23/24

Ashton-on-Mersey (1897)

Church Lane, Sale M33 5QQ
Tel **(0161) 973 3220**
Mem 180 70(L) 40(J)
Sec D Singleton (0161) 976 4390
Pro MJ Williams (0161) 962 3727
Holes 9 L 3073 yds SSS 69
Recs Am–68 B Armitage, M Gleave
Pro–67 R Williamson, D Cooper, MJ Williams
V'tors WD–U H exc Tues–NA before 3pm WE–M
Fees £20
Loc 5 miles W of Manchester

Ashton-under-Lyne (1913)

Gorsey Way, Hurst, Ashton-under-Lyne OL6 9HT
Tel **(0161) 330 1537**
Mem 450
Sec KJ Clayton (0161) 330 6406
Pro C Boyle (0161) 308 2095
Holes 18 L 6209 yds SSS 70
Recs Am–67 S Hamer (1992)
V'tors WD–U WE/BH–M SOC
Fees £20
Loc 8 miles E of Manchester

Beacon Park (1982)

Public
Beacon Lane, Dalton, Up Holland WN8 7RU
Tel **(01695) 622700**
Mem 300
Sec S Clayton

Pro R Peters
Holes 18 L 5927 yds SSS 69
Recs Am–68 D Parkin, I Donaldson
V'tors U–book 6 days in advance SOC
Fees On application
Loc Nr Ashurst Beacon and M58/M6 Junction 26
Mis Driving range

Blackley (1907)

Victoria Avenue, Manchester M9 6HW
Tel (0161) 643 2980
Mem 750
Sec CB Leggott (0161) 654 7770
Pro M Barton (0161) 643 3912
Holes 18 L 6235 yds SSS 70
Recs Am–65 D Royle
Pro–66 J Nixon
V'tors WD–U WE–M SOC–WD exc Thurs
Fees £18
Loc North Manchester

Bolton (1891)

Lostock Park, Bolton BL6 4AJ
Tel (01204) 843278
Mem 600
Sec H Cook (01204) 843067
Pro R Longworth (01204) 843073
Holes 18 L 6215 yds SSS 70
Recs Am–66 JB Hope, DE Roocroft
Pro–64 J Wright
V'tors U SOC
Fees WD exc Wed–£26 D–£30
Wed/WE/BH –£30 D–£35
Loc 3 miles W of Bolton. M61 Junction 6, 2 miles

Bolton Old Links (1891)

Chorley Old Road, Montserrat, Bolton BL1 5SU
Tel (01204) 840050
Fax (01204) 842307
Mem 750
Sec KG Jennions (01204) 842307
Pro P Horridge (01204) 843089
Holes 18 L 6406 yds SSS 72
Recs Am–66 L Mooney (1981)
Pro–64 J Cheetham (1990)
V'tors U H exc comp Sats SOC
Fees £25 (£30)
Loc 3 miles NW of Bolton on B6226
Arch Dr A Mackenzie

Brackley Municipal (1977)

Public
Bullows Road, Little Hulton, Worsley M38 9TR
Tel (0161) 790 6076
Pro S Lomax (Mgr)
Holes 9 L 3003 yds SSS 69
V'tors U
Fees £3
Loc 2 miles NW of Walkden, off A6

Bramall Park (1894)

20 Manor Road, Bramhall, Stockport SK7 6NW
Tel (0161) 485 3119 (Clubhouse)
Mem 715
Sec JC O'Shea (0161) 485 7101
Pro M Proffit (0161) 485 2205
Holes 18 L 6214 yds SSS 70
Recs Am–65 SM Hughes (1993)
Pro–63 D Cooper (1984)
V'tors I
Fees £25 (£35)
Loc 8 miles S of Manchester (A5102)

Bramhall (1905)

Ladythorn Road, Bramhall, Stockport SK7 2EY
Tel (0161) 439 4057
Mem 300 155(L) 85(J)
Sec JG Lee (Hon) (0161) 439 6092
Pro R Green (0161) 439 1171
Holes 18 L 6300 yds SSS 70
Recs Am–63 G Bradley (1994)
Pro–66 I Higby (1987)
V'tors U exc Thurs SOC–Wed
Fees D–£25 (D–£35)
Loc S of Stockport, off A5102

Breightmet (1911)

Red Bridge, Ainsworth, Bolton BL2 5PA
Tel (01204) 27381
Mem 200
Sec R Weir
Holes 9 L 6416 yds SSS 71
Recs Am–71 M Durham (1992))
Pro–68 P Alliss (1971)
V'tors WD–H WE–NA SOC–WD
Fees £15 (£18)
Loc 3 miles E of Bolton

Brookdale (1905)

Woodhouses, Failsworth M35 9WS
Tel (0161) 681 4534
Mem 650
Sec T Warren (0161) 681 8996
Pro J Spibey (0161) 681 2655
Holes 18 L 5841 yds SSS 68
Recs Am–65 G Lever
V'tors U SOC–WD
Fees £20 (£23)
Loc 5 miles N of Manchester

Bury (1890)

Unsworth Hall, Blackford Bridge, Bury BL9 9TJ
Tel (0161) 766 4897
Mem 725
Sec AN Burkey
Pro S Crake
Holes 18 L 5961 yds SSS 69
Recs Am–64 PD Hilton
Pro–PWT Evans
V'tors H SOC
Fees £22 (£28.50)
Loc A56, 5 miles N of Manchester. 3 miles N of M62 Junction 17

Castle Hawk (1975)

Heywood Road, Castleton, Rochdale OL11 3BY
Tel (01706) 40841
Fax (01706) 860587
Mem 200
Sec J Saxon
Pro M Vipond
Holes 18 L 5398 yds SSS 68
9 L 3158 yds SSS 55
Recs Am–68 S Tyrell
Pro–66 M Vipond
V'tors U SOC
Fees D–£6 (D–£8)
Loc Castleton Station 1 mile. M62 Junction 20

Cheadle (1885)

Shiers Drive, Cheadle SK8 1HW
Tel (0161) 428 2160
Mem 350
Sec PP Webster (0161) 491 4452
Pro GJ Norcott (0161) 428 9878
Holes 9 L 5006 yds SSS 65
Recs Am–63 PS Griffiths (1991)
V'tors H or I exc Tues & Sat–NA SOC
Fees D–£15 (£23)
Loc 1 mile S of Cheadle. M63 Junction 11, 2 miles

Chorlton-cum-Hardy (1903)

Barlow Hall, Barlow Hall Road, Manchester M21 7JJ
Tel (0161) 881 3139
Fax (0161) 881 3139
Mem 650
Sec Mrs HM Stuart (0161) 881 5830
Pro D Screeton (0161) 881 9911
Holes 18 L 5980 yds SSS 69
Recs Am–63 JR Berry
Pro–65 FS Boobyer
V'tors U H SOC–Thurs
Fees £20 (£25)
Loc 4 miles S of Manchester (A5103/A5145)

Crompton & Royton (1913)

High Barn, Royton, Oldham OL2 6RW
Tel (0161) 624 2154
Mem 620
Sec TR Jones (0161) 624 0986
Pro DA Melling
Holes 18 L 6222 yds SSS 70
Recs Am–65 JA Osbaldeston
Pro–65 D Durnian
V'tors U SOC–WD
Fees £24 (£30)
Loc 3 miles NW of Oldham

Davyhulme Park (1910)

Gleneagles Road, Davyhulme, Manchester M41 8SA
Tel (0161) 748 2856 (Clubhouse)
Mem 600
Sec HA Langworthy (0161) 748 2260
Pro D Butler (0161) 748 3931

Holes 18 L 6237 yds SSS 70
Recs Am–67 TF Sharp, B Connor, D Dunwoodie
Pro–68 KG Geddes, D Rees
V'tors WD–H exc Wed–NA Sat–NA Sun–M
SOC–Mon/Tues/Thurs
Fees £22 (£26)
Loc 7 miles SW of Manchester

Deane (1906)

Off Junction Road, Deane, Bolton BL3 4NB
Tel **(01204) 61944**
Mem 490
Sec P Flaxman (01204) 651808
Pro D Martindale
Holes 18 L 5583 yds SSS 67
Recs Am–64 N Hazzleton
V'tors WD–U WE–restricted SOC–Tues/Thurs/Fri
Fees £18 (£22.50)
Loc 2 miles W of Bolton. M61 Junction 5, 1 mile

Denton (1909)

Manchester Road, Denton, Manchester M34 2NU
Tel **(0161) 336 3218**
Mem 590
Sec R Wickham
Pro R Vere (0161) 336 2070
Holes 18 L 6541 yds SSS 71
Recs Am–66 R Bardsley (1993)
Pro–68 D Cooper, S Scanlon, D Durnian
V'tors WD–U WE/BH–NA before 3pm SOC
Fees £20 (£25)
Loc Off A57, nr M66 Junction 11

Didsbury (1891)

Ford Lane, Northenden, Manchester M22 4NQ
Tel **(0161) 998 9278**
Mem 760
Sec CB Turnbull (Sec/Mgr)
Pro P Barber (061) 998 2811
Holes 18 L 6273 yds SSS 70
Recs Am–66 PR Dalby (1991)
Pro–64 N Walton (1994)
V'tors WD–U H exc 9–10am & 12–1.30pm–NA WE–U H 10.30–11.30am & after 4pm
Fees £22 (£25)
Loc 6 miles S of Manchester. M63 Junction 9

Disley (1889)

Stanley Hall Lane, Disley, Stockport SK12 2JX
Tel **(01663) 762071**
Mem 500
Sec D English
Pro AG Esplin (01663) 762884
Holes 18 L 6015 yds SSS 69
Recs Am–67 P Leadbetter
Pro–63 B Charles
V'tors U SOC
Fees D–£25
Loc 6 miles S of Stockport (A6)

Dukinfield (1913)

Yew Tree Lane, Dukinfield SK16 5DB
Tel **(0161) 338 2340**
Mem 225 70(L) 45(J)
Sec KP Parker (0161) 338 2669
Pro J Peel
Holes 18 L 5203 yds SSS 66
Recs Am–7 C Kenworthy
V'tors WD–U exc Wed pm WE–M SOC
Fees £16.50
Loc 6 miles E of Manchester

Dunham Forest G & CC (1961)

Oldfield Lane, Altrincham WA14 4TY
Tel **(0161) 928 2605**
Fax **(0161) 929 8975**
Mem 600
Sec Mrs S Klaus
Pro I Wrigley (0161) 928 2727
Holes 18 L 6636 yds SSS 72
V'tors WD–U WE/BH–M SOC exc 12.30–1.30pm
Fees £25 (£30)
Loc 1 mile SW of Altrincham

Dunscar (1908)

Longworth Lane, Bromley Cross, Bolton BL7 2NB
Tel **(01204) 303321**
Mem 600
Sec TM Yates (01204) 301090
Pro G Treadgold (01204) 592992
Holes 18 L 6085 yds SSS 69
Recs Am–66 I Bond
Pro–66 W Slater
V'tors WD–U WE–restricted SOC
Fees £20 (£30)
Loc 3 miles N of Bolton, off A666

Ellesmere (1913)

Old Clough Lane, Worsley, Manchester M28 7HZ
Tel **(0161) 790 2122**
Mem 350 80(L) 75(J)
Sec AC Kay
Pro T Morley (0161) 790 8591
Holes 18 L 5957 yds SSS 69
Recs Am–67 BA Toone
Pro–66 G Weir
V'tors U exc comp days (recognised club members, check with Pro) SOC–WD
Fees £18 (£22)
Loc 6 miles W of Manchester, nr junction of M62/A580

Fairfield Golf & Sailing Club (1892)

Booth Road, Audenshaw, Manchester M34 5GA
Tel **(0161) 370 1641**
Mem 550
Sec J Humphries (0161) 336 3950
Pro N Harding (0161) 370 2292
Holes 18 L 5664 yds SSS 68
Recs Am–65 PW Wrigley, ARS Pownell
V'tors WD–U WE–NA before noon SOC–WD
Fees £17 (£23)
Loc 5 miles E of Manchester on A635

Flixton (1893)

Church Road, Flixton, Manchester M41 6EP
Tel **(0161) 748 2116**
Mem 400
Sec JG Frankland (0161) 747 0296
Pro R Ling (0161) 746 7160
Holes 9 L 6410 yds SSS 71
Recs Am–63 MJ Wallwork (1988)
Pro–65 P Reeves (1985)
V'tors WD–U exc Wed SOC
Fees £17.50
Loc 6 miles SW of Manchester on B5213

Gathurst (1913)

Miles Lane, Shevington, Wigan WN6 8EW
Tel **(01257) 252861**
Mem 500
Sec J Clarke (01257) 252432
Pro D Clarke (01257) 254909
Holes 12 L 6308 yds SSS 70
Recs Am–66 S Ainscough
Pro–66 D Clarke
V'tors WD–U before 5pm WE/BH/Wed–M SOC–WD
Fees £20
Loc 4 miles W of Wigan. 1 mile S of M6 Junction 27
Mis Extension to 18 holes 1996

Gatley (1911)

Waterfall Farm, Styal Road, Heald Green, Cheadle SK8 3TW
Tel **(0161) 437 2091**
Mem 400
Sec P Hannam
Pro AJ Ayre (0161) 436 2830
Holes 9 L 5934 yds SSS 68
Recs Am–67 M Hoyland
Pro–63 C Timperley
V'tors WD exc Tues–arrange with Sec WE/Tues–NA
Fees £20
Loc 7 miles S of Manchester. Manchester Airport 2 miles

Great Lever & Farnworth (1911)

Lever Edge Lane, Bolton BL3 3EN
Tel **(01204) 62582**
Mem 500
Sec MJ Ivill (01204) 656137
Pro D Stirling
Holes 18 L 5859 yds SSS 69
Recs Am–67 D Barr (1989)
Ladies–B Hill (1974)
V'tors WD–H WE–NA SOC–WD
Fees £15 (£25)
Loc 1½ miles S of Bolton

Greenmount (1920)
Greenmount, Bury BL8 4LH
Tel **(01204) 883712**
Mem 200
Sec GJ Lowe
Pro G Pearson
Holes 9 L 4920 yds SSS 64
Recs Am–62 G Dalziel
V'tors WD–U exc Tues WE–M
Fees £12
Loc 3 miles N of Bury

Haigh Hall (1972)
Public
Haigh Hall Country Park, Haigh, Wigan WN2 1PE
Tel **(01942) 833337 (Clubhouse)**
Mem 300
Sec W Fleetwood
Pro I Lee (01942) 831107
Holes 18 L 6423 yds SSS 71
Recs Am–65 G Lacy (1992)
Pro–66 K Waters (1988)
V'tors U
Fees £5.95 (£8.50)
Loc 2 miles NW of Wigan. M6 Junction 27. M61 Junction 6

Hale (1903)
Rappax Road, Hale WA15 0NU
Tel **(0161) 980 4225**
Mem 300
Sec JW Hughes
Pro J Jackson (0161) 904 0835
Holes 9 L 5780 yds SSS 68
Recs Am–66 PF Veitch
Pro–65 D Durnian
V'tors WD–U exc Thurs–NA before 5pm WE/BH–M SOC
Fees D–£20
Loc 2 miles SE of Altrincham

Harwood (1926)
Springfield, Roading Brook Road, Bolton BL2 4JD
Tel **(01204) 22878**
Mem 480
Sec D Bamber
Pro M Grey
Holes 9 L 5960 yds SSS 69
Recs Am–67 PM Lay, N Stirling
V'tors WD–U WE–M SOC
Fees £15
Loc 4 miles NE of Bolton (B6391)

Hazel Grove (1912)
Hazel Grove, Stockport SK7 6LU
Tel **(0161) 483 3217**
Mem 550
Sec HAG Carlisle (0161) 483 3978
Pro ME Hill (0161) 483 7272
Holes 18 L 6310 yds SSS 71
Recs Am–65 D Parkin
Pro–67 M Slater
V'tors U
Fees £22.50 (£27.50)
Loc 3 miles S of Stockport (A6)

Heaton Moor (1892)
Mauldeth Road, Heaton Mersey, Stockport SK4 3NX
Tel **(0161) 432 2134**
Mem 550
Sec AD Townsend (0161) 432 7235
Pro CR Loydall (0161) 432 0846
Holes 18 L 5876 yds SSS 68
Recs Am–66 D Howarth
Pro–66 D Cooper
V'tors U SOC
Fees £23 (£31)
Loc 2 miles from M63 Junction 12, off A5145

Heaton Park (1912)
Public
Heaton Park, Prestwich, Manchester M25 5SW
Tel **(0161) 798 0295**
Sec FW Lewis
Pro J Pennington
Holes 18 L 5849 yds SSS 68
Recs Am–66 J Griffiths (1986), S Pilling (1988)
Pro–65 AP Thomson, B Evans, I Collins, M Gray
V'tors U SOC
Fees £5.50 (£6.50)
Loc North Manchester, via M62 and M66 to Middleton Road

Hindley Hall (1905)
Hall Lane, Hindley, Wigan WN2 2SQ
Tel **(01942) 55131/523116**
Mem 430
Sec R Bell (01942) 55131, GW Gooch (Admin)
Pro N Brazell (01942) 55991
Holes 18 L 5904 yds SSS 68
Recs Am–63 JB Dickinson
Pro–65
V'tors I SOC
Fees £20 (£27)
Loc 2 miles S of Wigan. M61 Junction 6

Horwich (1895)
Victoria Road, Horwich BL6 5PH
Tel **(01204) 696980**
Mem 200
Sec C Sherborne
Holes 9 L 5404 yds SSS 67
Recs Am–65 J Farrimond
V'tors M SOC–WD
Loc 5 miles W of Bolton

Houldsworth (1910)
Houldsworth Park, Houldsworth Street, Reddish, Stockport SK5 6BN
Tel **(0161) 442 9611**
Mem 580
Sec SW Zielinski (0161) 442 1712
Pro D Naylor (0161) 442 1714
Holes 18 L 6209 yds Par 71 SSS 70
Recs Am–67 R Arnold
Pro–63 D Vaughan
V'tors U SOC
Fees £20 (£25)
Loc 4 miles S of Manchester

Lowes Park (1914)
Hill Top, Lowes Road, Bury BL9 6SU
Tel **(0161) 764 1231**
Mem 300
Sec J Entwistle
Holes 9 L 6043 yds Par 70 SSS 69
Recs Am–67 MJ Bailey (1991)
V'tors WD–U exc Wed–NA WE/BH–by appointment
Fees £15 (£22)
Loc 2 miles NE of Bury, off A56

Manchester (1882)
Hopwood Cottage, Rochdale Road, Middleton, Manchester M24 2QP
Tel **(0161) 643 2718, (0161) 643 0023 (Bookings)**
Fax **(0161) 643 9174**
Mem 700
Sec KG Flett (0161) 643 3202
Pro B Connor (0161) 643 2638
Holes 18 L 6450 yds SSS 72
Recs Am–66 RE Tattersall, M Russell, RB Smities
Pro–65 I Mosey, D Cooper, P Magnebrant, P Bates
V'tors WD–H WE–NA SOC
Fees D–£26 (£30)
Loc 7 miles N of Manchester. M62 Junction 20
Mis Driving range-members and green fees only
Arch HS Colt

Marland (1928)
Public
Springfield Park, Rochdale
Tel **(01706) 49801**
Fax **(01706) 49801**
Mem 300
Sec B Wynn
Pro D Wills
Holes 18 L 5237 yds SSS 66
Recs Am–67 C Thornsby (1993)
Pro–67 ME Hill
V'tors WD–U WE–booking necessary
Fees £5.20 (£6.70)
Loc W of Rochdale (A58). M62 Junctions 19/20, 2 miles

Marple (1892)
Barnsfold Road, Hawk Green, Marple, Stockport SK6 7EL
Tel **(0161) 427 2311**
Mem 335 100(L) 60(J) 50(5)
Sec FW Ogden (0161) 480 4903
Pro N Hamilton (0161) 449 0690
Holes 18 L 5506 yds SSS 67
Recs Am–66 T Christie (1984)
V'tors WD–U exc Thurs–NA WE/BH–M SOC
Fees £20 (£30)
Loc 2 miles from High Lane North, off A6

Mellor & Townscliffe (1894)
Tarden, Gibb Lane, Mellor, Stockport SK6 5NA
Tel **(0161) 427 2208**
Mem 700
Sec DA Ogden

Pro G Broadley (0161) 427 5759
Holes 18 L 5925 yds SSS 69
Recs Am–68 GD Williams (1988), MG Senior, AJH Ellis (1992)
Pro–64 MJ Slater (1977)
V'tors WD–U WE–M SOC
Fees £20 (£27.50)
Loc 7 miles SE of Stockport, off A626

North Manchester (1894)

Rhodes House, Manchester Old Road, Middleton, Manchester M24 4PE
Tel **(0161) 643 2941**
Mem 300 60(L) 38(J)
Sec JB O'Loughlin (0161) 643 9033
Pro PJ Lunt (0161) 643 7094
Holes 18 L 6542 yds SSS 72
Recs Am–66 J Cheetham
Pro–66 G Furey
V'tors U
Fees £22 (£22)
Loc 5 miles N of Manchester. M62 Junction 18

Northenden (1913)

Palatine Road, Manchester M22 4FR
Tel **(0161) 998 4738**
Fax **(0161) 945 5592**
Mem 700
Sec RN Kemp (Sec/Mgr)
Pro (0161) 945 3386
Holes 18 L 6435 yds SSS 71
Recs Am–67 JEB Waddell
Pro–64 D Durnian
V'tors U SOC
Fees £25 (£27.50)
Loc 5 miles S of Manchester. M63 Junction 9

Old Manchester (1818)

Tel **(0161) 766 4157**
Sec PT Goodall, 9 Ashbourne Grove, Whitefield M45 7NJ
Holes Club without a course

Oldham (1892)

Lees New Road, Oldham OL4 5EN
Tel **(0161) 624 4986**
Mem 300 45(L) 35(J)
Pro A Laverty (0161) 626 8346
Holes 18 L 5045 yds SSS 65
Recs Am–66 D Maloney (1987)
Pro–65 E Smith
V'tors U SOC–WD
Fees On application
Loc Off Oldham-Stalybridge road

Pike Fold (1909)

Cooper Lane, Victoria Avenue, Blackley, Manchester M9 2QQ
Tel **(0161) 740 1136**
Mem 200
Sec H Adams
Pro None
Holes 9 L 5789 yds SSS 68
Recs Am–66 P Bradley (1989)
Pro–66 JE Wiggett
V'tors WD–U WE/BH–M SOC
Fees D–£12
Loc 5 miles N of Manchester. M62 Junction 18, 2 miles

Prestwich (1908)

Hilton Lane, Prestwich M25 9XB
Tel **(0161) 773 2544**
Mem 500
Sec WV Trees (0161) 773 4578
Pro A Sproston
Holes 18 L 4086 yds SSS 63
Recs Am–60 J Liwosz
V'tors WD–H WE–NA before 3pm SOC
Fees £16 (£18)
Loc 2½ miles N of Manchester, off A56. M63 Junction 17

Reddish Vale (1912)

Southcliffe Road, Reddish, Stockport SK5 7EE
Tel **(0161) 480 2359**
Mem 600
Sec JL Blakey
Pro RA Brown (0161) 480 3824
Holes 18 L 6086 yds SSS 69
Recs Am–64 KR Gorton, D Young
Pro–67 R Williamson, P Cheetham, D Fletcher
V'tors WD–U exc 12.30–1.30pm–M WE–M SOC–WD
Fees £22
Loc 1 mile NNE of Stockport
Arch Dr A Mackenzie

Regent Park (Bolton) (1931)

Public
Links Road, Chorley New Road, Bolton BL6 4AF
Tel **(01204) 844170**
Mem 260
Sec K Taylor (01204) 652882
Pro B Longworth (01204) 842336
Holes 18 L 6450yds SSS 70
Recs Am–67 PK Abbott
Pro–68 L Alamby
V'tors U SOC–WD
Fees £4.50 (£6.75)
Loc A673, 3 miles W of Bolton. M61 Junction 6

Ringway (1909)

Hale Mount, Hale Barns, Altrincham WA15 8SW
Tel **(0161) 904 9609**
Mem 345 165(L) 41(J)
Sec D Wright (0161) 980 2630
Pro N Ryan (0161) 980 8432
Holes 18 L 6494 yds SSS 71
Recs Am–67 RE Preston
V'tors Tues–NA before 3pm Fri–M Sun–NA before 11am SOC
Fees £28 (£34)
Loc 8 miles S of Manchester, off M56 Junction 6 (A538)

Rochdale (1888)

Edenfield Road, Bagslate, Rochdale OL11 5YR
Tel **(01706) 46024** (Clubhouse)
Mem 750
Sec (01706) 43818
Pro A Laverty (01706) 522104
Holes 18 L 6031 yds SSS 69
Recs Am–65 SM Lord (1992)
Pro–65 G Hammond (1989)
V'tors U
Fees £21 (£25)
Loc 3 miles from M62 Junction 20 on A680

Romiley (1897)

Goosehouse Green, Romiley, Stockport SK6 4LJ
Tel **(0161) 430 2392**
Mem 700
Sec P Trafford (0161) 430 7257
Pro G Butler (0161) 430 7122
Holes 18 L 6421 yds Par 70 SSS 71
Recs Am–67 CC Harrison
Pro–67 D Roberts
V'tors U SOC
Fees £22 (£33)
Loc Station ¾ mile (B6104)

Saddleworth (1904)

Mountain Ash, Uppermill, Oldham OL3 6AT
Tel **(01457) 873653**
Mem 700
Sec HA Morgan
Pro ET Shard
Holes 18 L 5976 yds SSS 69
Recs Am–64 RC Hughes
Pro–69 M Melling, A Gillies
V'tors U
Fees £22 (£25)
Loc 5 miles E of Oldham

Sale (1913)

Sale Lodge, Golf Road, Sale M33 2LU
Tel **(0161) 973 3404**
Fax **(0161) 962 4217**
Mem 600
Sec JH Prow (0161) 973 1638
Pro M Stewart (0161) 973 1730
Holes 18 L 6351 yds SSS 70
Recs Am–66 RW Kill
V'tors U SOC–WD
Fees £24 (£30)
Loc N boundary of Sale. M63 Junction 8

Stamford (1900)

Oakfield House, Huddersfield Road, Stalybridge SK15 3PY
Tel **(01457) 832126**
Mem 500
Sec FE Rowles
Pro B Badger (01457) 834829
Holes 18 L 5701 yds SSS 68
Recs Am–68 A Derry
V'tors WD–U WE comp days–after 2.30pm SOC–WD
Fees On application
Loc NE boundary of Stalybridge on B6175

Stand (1904)
The Dales, Ashbourne Grove, Whitefield, Manchester M45 7NL
Tel **(0161) 766 2388**
Fax **(0161) 796 3234**
Mem 700
Sec EB Taylor (0161) 766 3197
Pro M Dance (0161) 766 2214
Holes 18 L 6411 yds SSS 71
Recs Am–67 J Seddon (1990)
Pro–67 PM Eales
V'tors U SOC–WD
Fees £25 (£30)
Loc 5 miles N of Manchester. M62 Junction 17
Arch Alex Herd

Stockport (1906)
Offerton Road, Offerton, Stockport SK2 5HL
Tel **(0161) 427 2001 (Members)**
Fax **(0161) 427 8369**
Mem 495
Sec P Moorhead (0161) 427 8369
Pro M Peel (0161) 427 2421
Holes 18 L 6326 yds SSS 71
Recs Am–67 JR Whittaker
Pro–66 E Lester
Ladies–68 RA Hughes
V'tors SOC–WD
Fees £30 (£40)
Loc 4 miles SE of Stockport on A627

Swinton Park (1926)
East Lancashire Road, Swinton, Manchester M27 5LX
Tel **(0161) 794 1785**
Mem 450 120(L) 50(J)
Sec F Slater (0161) 794 0861
Pro J Wilson (0161) 793 8077
Holes 18 L 6712 yds SSS 72
Recs Am–66 J Thornley (1984)
Pro–65 D Wheeler (1992)
V'tors WD–U WE–M SOC–Tues
Fees On application
Loc On A580, 5 miles NW of Manchester

Tunshill (1901)
Kiln Lane, Milnrow, Rochdale
Tel **(01706) 342095**
Mem 180
Sec D Norbury
Holes 9 L 5742 yds SSS 68
Recs Am–66 D Williams (1994)
V'tors WD–U WE–M SOC
Fees On application
Loc 2 miles E of Rochdale. M62 Junction 21

Turton (1908)
Woodend Farm, Bromley Cross, Bolton BL7 9QH
Tel **(01204) 852235**
Mem 340 60(L) 17(J)
Sec B Stanley (01204) 306881
Holes 18 L 5901 yds Par 69 SSS 68
V'tors WD–U exc Wed–NA 11.30–2.30pm WE/BH–M
Fees £15
Loc 3½ miles N of Bolton

Walmersley (1906)
Garrett's Close, Walmersley, Bury BL9 6TE
Tel **(0161) 764 1429**
Mem 350
Sec C Stock (0161) 764 5057
Holes 9 L 5588 metres SSS 70
Recs Am–66 JW Senogles
V'tors WD–U exc Tues–NA Sat–NA Sun–M SOC–Wed–Fri
Fees D–£15
Loc 2 miles N of Bury (A56). S of M66 Junction 1
Mis Extension to 18 holes 1995
Arch SG Marnoch

Werneth (1909)
Green Lane Garden Suburb, Oldham OL8 3AZ
Tel **(0161) 624 1190**
Mem 400
Sec JH Barlow
Pro R Penny
Holes 18 L 5363 yds SSS 66
Recs Am–62 LA Lawton
Pro–63 S Holden
V'tors WD–U WE–M SOC
Fees £16.50
Loc 2 miles S of Oldham

Werneth Low (1912)
Werneth Low Road, Gee Cross, Hyde SK14 3AF
Tel **(0161) 368 2503**
Mem 315 60(L) 40(J)
Sec R Clapham (0161) 366 0837
Pro T Bacchus
Holes 11 L 6113 yds Par 70 SSS 69
Recs Am–67 S Madden
Pro–57 D Cooper
V'tors U exc Sun–NA Sat/BH–M SOC
Fees £15
Loc 2 miles SE of Hyde, nr Gee Cross. M67 Junction 4
Arch Peter Campbell

Westhoughton (1929)
Long Island, Westhoughton, Bolton BL5 2BR
Tel **(01942) 811085**
Mem 200
Sec DJ Kinsella
Pro A Franklin
Holes 9 L 5834 yds SSS 68
Recs Am–64 T Woodward
V'tors WD–U WE/BH–M
Fees £12
Loc 4 miles SW of Bolton on A58

Whitefield (1932)
Higher Lane, Whitefield, Manchester M45 7EZ
Tel **(0161) 766 2728**
Mem 500
Sec Miss S Addleman (0161) 766 2904
Pro P Reeves (0161) 766 3096
Holes 18 L 6045 yds SSS 69
18 L 5755 yds SSS 68
V'tors U SOC–WD
Fees £25 (£30)
Loc 4 miles N of Manchester. M62 Junction 17

Whittaker (1906)
Littleborough OL5 0LH
Tel **(01706) 378310**
Mem 120
Sec GA Smith (01484) 428546
Holes 9 L 5576 yds SSS 67
Recs Am–61 D Kernick
Pro–65 MT Hoyle
V'tors WD/Sat–U Sun–NA
Fees £10 (£12)
Loc 1½ miles N of Littleborough, off A58
Arch NP Stott

Wigan (1898)
Arley Hall, Haigh, Wigan WN1 2UH
Tel **(01257) 421360**
Mem 280
Sec E Walmsley
Holes 9 L 6058 yds SSS 69
Recs Am–68 RM Hodson
V'tors U exc Tues & Sat
Fees £25 (£30)
Loc 4 miles N of Wigan, off A5106/B5239. M6 Junction 27

William Wroe (1973)
Public
Pennybridge Lane, Flixton, Manchester M31 3DL
Tel **(0161) 748 8680**
Pro B Parkinson
Holes 18 L 4395 yds SSS 61
Recs Am–60 C Meadows, D Dunwoodie
V'tors U–booking necessary
Fees £5 (£7)
Loc 6 miles SW of Manchester, by M63 Junction 4

Withington (1892)
243 Palatine Road, West Didsbury, Manchester M20 8UD
Tel **(0161) 445 3912**
Mem 340 97(L) 38(J)
Sec A Larsen (0161) 445 9544
Pro RJ Ling (0161) 445 4861
Holes 18 L 6410 yds SSS 71
Recs Am–68 C Webb (1989)
Pro–67 D Scholes
V'tors WD–H exc Thurs SOC
Fees On application
Loc 6 miles S of Manchester on B5166

Worsley (1894)
Stableford Avenue, Monton Green, Eccles, Manchester M30 8AP
Tel **(0161) 789 4202**
Mem 625
Sec R Pizzey MBE
Pro C Cousins
Holes 18 L 6217 yds SSS 70
Recs Am–65 D Harding (1994)
V'tors I NA–9–9.45am & 12.15–1.30pm
Fees £20
Loc 5 miles W of Manchester

For list of abbreviations see page 435

Merseyside

Allerton Municipal (1934)

Public
Allerton Road, Liverpool 18
Tel **(0151) 428 1046**
Pro B Large
Holes 18 L 5494 yds SSS 65
9 hole course
V'tors U SOC
Fees On application
Loc 5 miles S of Liverpool

Arrowe Park (1931)

Public
Arrowe Park, Woodchurch, Birkenhead, Wirral L49 5LW
Tel **(0151) 677 1527**
Sec K Finlay
Pro C Scanlon
Holes 18 L 6377 yds SSS 70
Recs Am–68
V'tors U
Fees £6 (£6)
Loc 3 miles S of Birkenhead on A552. M53 Junction 3, 1 mile

Bidston (1913)

Bidston Link Road, Wallasey L44 2HR
Tel **(0151) 638 3412**
Mem 500
Sec JJ Gleeson
Pro S Hubbard (0151) 630 6650
Holes 18 L 6207 yds SSS 70
Recs Am–64 S Earnden (1993)
Pro–68 JM Hume
V'tors WD–U WE–M SOC
Fees On application
Loc Off Bidston Link Road

Bootle (1934)

Dunnings Bridge Road, Litherland L30 2PP
Tel **(0151) 928 6196**
Mem 400
Sec J Morgan (Hon)
Pro A Bradshaw (0151) 928 1371
Holes 18 L 6362 yds SSS 70
Recs Am–64 S Ashcroft
Pro–69 R Boobyer
V'tors U–book by phone SOC
Fees £3.65 (£5.05)
Loc 5 miles N of Liverpool (A565)

Bowring (1913)

Public
Bowring Park, Roby Road, Huyton L36 4HD
Tel **(0151) 489 1901**
Pro D Weston
Holes 9 L 5592 yds SSS 66
Recs Am–67 G Spurrier
V'tors U
Fees £4
Loc 6 miles N of Liverpool. M62 Junction 5

Brackenwood (1933)

Public
Brackenwood Lane, Bebington, Wirral L63 2LY
Tel **(0151) 608 3093**
Pro C Disbury
Holes 18 L 6131 yds SSS 69
Recs Am–67 D Charlton
Pro–64 C Disbury
V'tors U SOC
Fees On application
Loc Nr M53 Junction 4

Bromborough (1904)

Raby Hall Road, Bromborough L63 0NW
Tel **(0151) 334 2155**
Mem 600
Sec JT Barraclough
(0151) 334 2978
Pro G Berry (0151) 334 4499
Holes 18 L 6650 yds SSS 73
Recs Am–67 J Berry, GM Edwards, GJ Bradley
V'tors U–contact Pro in advance
Fees £26 (£30)
Loc Mid Wirral, M53 Junction 4

Caldy (1908)

Links Hey Road, Caldy, Wirral L48 1NB
Tel **(0151) 625 5660**
Fax **(0151) 625 7394**
Mem 875
Sec TDM Bacon
Pro K Jones (0151) 625 1818
Holes 18 L 6675 yds SSS 73
Recs Am–67 JR Berry
V'tors WD–U exc before 9.30am and from 1–2pm (booking necessary) SOC
Fees On application
Loc 1½ miles S of West Kirby

Childwall (1913)

Naylor's Road, Gateacre, Liverpool L27 2YB
Tel **(0151) 487 0654**
Mem 650
Sec L Upton
Pro N Parr (0151) 487 9871
Holes 18 L 6425 yds SSS 71
Recs Am–66 M Gamble
V'tors WE/BH/Tues–restricted
Fees £22
Loc 7 miles E of Liverpool. M62 Junction 6, 2 miles
Arch James Braid

Eastham Lodge (1973)

117 Ferry Road, Eastham, Wirral L62 0AP
Tel **(0151) 327 1483**
Mem 570
Sec CS Camden (0151) 327 3003
Pro R Boobyer (0151) 327 3008
Holes 15 L 5813 yds SSS 68
Recs Am–67 PA Knight (1991)
Pro–66 I Jones
V'tors WD–U WE/BH–M SOC–Tues
Fees £22
Loc 6 miles S of Birkenhead, off A41. M53 Junction 5. Signs to Eastham Country Park

Formby (1884)

Golf Road, Formby, Liverpool L37 1LQ
Tel **(01704) 874273**
Fax **(01704) 833028**
Mem 600
Sec RIF Dixon (01704) 872164
Pro C Harrison (01704) 873090
Holes 18 L 6701 yds SSS 73
Recs Am–66 I Pyman, MJC Hudson
Pro–65 NC Coles
V'tors WD–I H WE/BH–I
Fees £45
Loc By Freshfield Station
Arch Willie Park

Formby Ladies' (1896)

Formby, Liverpool L37 1YL
Tel **(01704) 874127**
Sec Mrs V Bailey (01704) 873493
Pro C Harrison (01704) 873090
Holes 18 L 5426 yds SSS 71
Recs Am–60 CD Lee
V'tors U–phone first SOC
Fees £25 (£31)
Loc Formby, off A565

Grange Park (1891)

Prescot Road, St Helens WA10 3AD
Tel **(01744) 22980 (Members)**
Fax **(01744) 26318**
Mem 730
Sec DA Wood (01744) 26318
Pro P Roberts (01744) 28785
Holes 18 L 6480 yds SSS 71
Recs Am–65 G Boardman (1989)
Pro–66 R Ellis (1986)
V'tors I SOC–WD exc Tues
Fees £21 (£26)
Loc 1½ miles W of St Helens on A58

Haydock Park (1877)

Golborne Park, Newton Lane, Newton-le-Willows WA12 0HX
Tel **(01925) 224389**
Mem 390 120(L)
Sec G Tait (01925) 228525
Pro PE Kenwright
(01925) 226944
Holes 18 L 6043 yds SSS 69
Recs Am–65 D Pilkington, P Boydell, K Sargent, P Eckersley
V'tors H or I SOC–WD exc Tues
Fees £24
Loc 1 mile E of M6 Junction 23

Hesketh (1885)

Cockle Dick's Lane, Cambridge Road, Southport PR9 9QQ
Tel **(01704) 530226**
Fax **(01704) 539250**
Mem 580
Sec PB Seal (01704) 536897
Pro J Donoghue (01704) 530050

Holes 18 L 6407 yds SSS 72
Recs Am–66 MP Thorpe
Pro–64 D Hayes
V'tors WD–U WE/BH–restricted SOC
Fees £25 D–£35 (£40)
Loc 1 mile N of Southport (A565)

Heswall (1901)

Cottage Lane, Gayton, Heswall, Wirral L60 8PB
Tel **(0151) 342 1237**
Fax **(0151) 342 1237**
Mem 902
Sec RJ Butler
Pro AE Thompson (0151) 342 7431
Holes 18 L 6472 yds SSS 72
Recs Am–62 CJ Sands (1994)
Pro–66 AE Thompson (1990)
V'tors U H BH–NA SOC–Wed & Fri
Fees D–£30 (D–£35)
Loc 8 miles NW of Chester off A540. M53 Junction 4

Hillside (1909)

Hastings Road, Hillside, Southport PR8 2LU
Tel **(01704) 569902**
Fax **(01704) 563192**
Mem 800
Sec JG Graham (01704) 567169
Pro B Seddon (01704) 568360
Holes 18 L 6850 yds SSS 74
Recs Am–67 I Garbutt, J Payne
Pro–66 M O'Grady, R Craig
V'tors By arrangement with Sec
Fees D–£35 (£45)
Loc Southport

Hoylake Municipal (1933)

Public
Carr Lane, Hoylake, Wirral L47 4BQ
Tel **(0151) 632 2956/4883 (Bookings)**
Sec A Peacock
Pro S Hooton
Holes 18 L 6330 yds SSS 70
Recs Am–67 T Manning (1989)
Pro–64 T Bennett (1982)
V'tors WD–U WE–phone booking 1 week in advance SOC
Fees £6
Loc 4 miles W of Birkenhead
Arch James Braid

Huyton & Prescot (1905)

Hurst Park, Huyton, Liverpool L36 1UA
Tel **(0151) 489 1138**
Mem 700
Sec Mrs E Holmes (0151) 489 3948
Pro R Pottage (0151) 489 2022
Holes 18 L 5738 yds SSS 68
Recs Am–67
V'tors WD–U WE–M SOC–WD
Fees On application
Loc 7 miles E of Liverpool. 1 mile S of Prescot (A57)

Leasowe (1891)

Leasowe Road, Moreton, Wirral L46 3RD
Tel **(0151) 677 5852**
Mem 610
Sec CPR Calvert
Pro N Sweeney (0151) 678 5460
Holes 18 L 6204 yds SSS 71
Recs Am–63 J Maddocks
V'tors U SOC–H
Fees D–£20 (D–£25)
Loc 1 mile N of Queensway Tunnel. M53 Junction 1
Arch John Ball Jr

Lee Park (1954)

Childwall Valley Road, Gateacre, Liverpool L27 3YA
Tel **(0151) 487 9861 (Clubhouse)**
Mem 550
Sec Mrs D Barr (0151) 487 3882
Holes 18 L 6024 yds SSS 69
V'tors SOC
Fees On application
Loc 7 miles SE of Liverpool (B5171)

Liverpool Municipal (1967)

Public
Ingoe Lane, Kirkby, Liverpool L32 4SS
Tel **(0151) 546 5435**
Pro D Weston
Holes 18 L 6571 yds SSS 71
Recs Am–70 J Paton (1986)
Pro–70
V'tors U WE–booking required SOC
Fees £5.50
Loc M57 Junction 6 to B5192

Prenton (1905)

Golf Links Road, Prenton, Birkenhead L42 8LW
Tel **(0151) 608 1461**
Mem 360 100(L) 60(J)
Sec WFW Disley (0151) 608 1053
Pro R Thompson (0151) 608 1636
Holes 18 L 6411 yds SSS 71
Recs Am–65 P Langford (1993)
V'tors U SOC–Wed & Fri
Fees £23 (£25)
Loc Outskirts of Birkenhead. M53 Junction 3

RLGC Village Play (1895)

Hoylake, Wirral L47 4AL
Mem 40
Sec CJ Peddie (0151) 625 1587
Holes Play over Royal Liverpool

Royal Birkdale (1889)

Waterloo Road, Birkdale, Southport PR8 2LX
Tel **(01704) 569913**
Fax **(01704) 562327**
Sec NT Crewe (01704) 567920
Pro RN Bradbeer (01704) 568857
Holes 18 L 6703 yds SSS 73
Recs Am–68 C Cassells (1989)
Pro–63 J Mudd (1991 Open)
V'tors I H SOC
Fees £50 D–£70 (£70)
Loc 1½ miles S of Southport (A565)
Arch George Lowe

Royal Liverpool (1869)

Meols Drive, Hoylake L47 4AL
Tel **(0151) 632 3101/3102**
Fax **(0151) 632 6737**
Mem 810
Sec Gp Capt CT Moore CBE
Pro J Heggarty (0151) 632 5868
Holes 18 L 6821 yds SSS 74
Recs Am–67 C Nowicki (1993)
Pro–64 B Waites
V'tors H SOC
Fees £45 (£60)
Loc On A553 from M53 Junction 2

Sherdley Park Municipal

Public
Sherdley Park, St Helens
Tel **(01744) 813149**
Sec B Collins (Mgr)
Pro PR Parkinson
Holes 18 L 5974 yds SSS 69
Recs Am–68 J Greenough
V'tors U
Fees £5.50 (£6.60)
Loc 2 miles E of St Helens (A570). M62 Junction 7, 2 miles
Mis Driving range

Southport & Ainsdale (1907)

Bradshaws Lane, Ainsdale, Southport PR8 3LG
Tel **(01704) 578092**
Fax **(01704) 570896**
Mem 390 110(L) 78(J)
Sec IF Sproule (01704) 578000
Pro M Houghton (01704) 577316
Holes 18 L 6612 yds SSS 73
Recs Am–66 RAR Hutt (1991)
Pro–62 C Moody (1991)
V'tors WD–I H before 4pm –M after 4pm WE/BH–M
Fees £30 D–£40 (£45)
Loc 3 miles S of Southport on A565
Arch James Braid

Southport Municipal (1914)

Public
Park Road West, Southport PR9 0JS
Tel **(01704) 535286**
Pro W Fletcher
Holes 18 L 6253 yds SSS 69
Pro–67 W Fletcher (1986)
V'tors U SOC
Fees On application
Loc N end of Southport promenade

Southport Old Links (1926)

Moss Lane, Southport PR9 7QS

Tel **(01704) 24294/28207**
Mem 390
Sec GM Rimington
Holes 9 L 6486 yds SSS 71
Recs Am–68 J Robinson
V'tors U exc WE comp days/BH–NA SOC–WD
Fees £15 (£20) W–£40
Loc Churchtown, 3 miles NE of Southport

Wallasey (1891)

Bayswater Road, Wallasey L45 8LA

Tel **(0151) 639 3630**
Mem 350 90(L) 50(J)
Sec Mrs LM Dolman (0151) 691 1024
Pro M Adams (0151) 638 3888
Holes 18 L 6607 yds SSS 73
Recs Am–68 P Morgan
Pro–66 P Barber
V'tors H SOC
Fees On application
Loc M53-signs to New Brighton
Arch Tom Morris

Warren (1911)

Public
Grove Road, Wallasey, Wirral

Tel **(0151) 639 8323** (Clubhouse)
Pro K Lamb (051) 639 5730
Holes 9 L 5914 yds SSS 68
Recs Am–66 J Hayes
Pro–66 JA MacLachlan
V'tors U
Fees On application
Loc Wallasey

West Derby (1896)

Yew Tree Lane, Liverpool L12 9HQ

Tel **(0151) 228 1540**
Mem 556
Sec S Young (0151) 254 1034
Pro N Brace (0151) 220 5478
Holes 18 L 6346 yds SSS 70
Recs Am–66 M Gamble
Pro–67 AC Coop
V'tors SOC–WD after 9.30am
Fees £22.50 (£30)
Loc 2 miles E of Liverpool, off A580-West Derby Junction

West Lancashire (1873)

Blundellsands, Crosby, Liverpool L23 8SZ

Tel **(0151) 924 4115**
Fax **(0151) 931 4448**
Mem 700
Sec DE Bell (0151) 924 1076
Pro D Lloyd (0151) 924 5662
Holes 18 L 6767 yds SSS 73
Recs Am–68 J Payne
Pro–66 C Mason
V'tors H SOC
Fees £25 D–£35 (£40)
Loc Between Liverpool and Southport, off A565
Arch CK Cotton

Wirral Ladies (1894)

93 Bidston Road, Birkenhead, Wirral L43 6TS

Tel **(0151) 652 1255**
Fax **(0151) 653 4323**
Mem 450
Sec Mrs C Piper
Pro (0151) 652 2468
Holes 18 L 4966 yds SSS 70 (Ladies)
18 L 5170 yds SSS 66 (Men)
Recs Am–71 Miss H Lyall
V'tors U H SOC
Fees On application
Loc Birkenhead 1/2 mile. M53, 2 miles

Woolton (1901)

Doe Park, Speke Road, Woolton, Liverpool L25 7TZ

Tel **(0151) 486 1601**
Fax **(0151) 486 1664**
Mem 750
Sec (0151) 486 2298
Pro A Gibson (0151) 486 1298
Holes 18 L 5706 yds SSS 68
Recs Am–63 J Edwards
Pro–66 DJ Rees
V'tors U exc comp days
Fees £20 (£28)
Loc SE Liverpool

Middlesex

Airlinks (1984)

Public
Southall Lane, Hounslow TW5 9PE

Tel **(0181) 561 1418**
Fax **(0181) 813 6284**
Sec B Mylward (Mgr)
Pro B Mylward
Holes 18 L 6001 yds SSS 69
Recs Am–60 K Dempster
V'tors WD–U Sat am–NA
Fees £10.40 (£13)
Loc Just off M4 Junction 3
Mis Floodlit driving range
Arch Alliss/Taylor

Ashford Manor (1898)

Fordbridge Road, Ashford TW15 3RT

Tel **(01784) 252049**
Fax **(01784) 420355**
Mem 800
Sec BJ Duffy (01784) 257687
Pro M Finney (01784) 255940
Holes 18 L 6372 yds SSS 70
Recs Am–65 GA Homewood (1989)
Pro–64 D Talbot
V'tors H
Fees £25 (£30)
Loc Ashford, off A308

Brent Valley (1938)

Public
Church Road, Hanwell, London W7

Tel **(0181) 567 1287 (Bookings)**
Sec P Bryant
Pro P Bryant
Holes 18 L 5426 yds SSS 66
Recs Am–65 S Harper (1985)
Pro–61 R Green (1988)
V'tors U SOC
Fees On application

Bush Hill Park (1895)

Bush Hill, Winchmore Hill, London N21 2BU

Tel **(0181) 360 5738**
Fax **(0181) 360 5583**
Mem 665
Sec M Burnand
Pro (0181) 360 4103
Holes 18 L 5825 yds SSS 68
Recs Am–63 PD Lawrence
Pro–64 L Farmer
V'tors WD–H WE–M SOC
Fees £22 (£30)
Loc S of Enfield

C & L Country Club (1991)

West End Road, Northolt UB5 6RD

Tel **(0181) 845 5662**
Holes 9 L 4440 yds SSS 62
V'tors U SOC
Fees £10
Loc A40, opp Northolt Airport
Arch Patrick Tallack

Crews Hill (1920)

Cattlegate Road, Crews Hill, Enfield EN2 8AZ

Tel **(0181) 363 0787**
Mem 600
Sec EJ Hunt (0181) 363 6674
Pro J Reynolds (0181) 366 7422
Holes 18 L 6208 yds SSS 70
Recs Am–68 S Bishop
Pro–65 H Flatman
V'tors WD–I H WE/BH–M SOC
Fees On application
Loc 2 1/2 miles N of Enfield. M25 Junction 24
Arch HS Colt

Ealing (1898)

Perivale Lane, Greenford UB6 8SS

Mem 600
Sec MR Gibson (Gen Mgr) (0181) 997 0937
Pro A Stickley (0181) 997 3959
Holes 18 L 6216 yds SSS 70
Recs Am–64 R Neill, C Challens
Pro–64 R Verwey
V'tors WD–U H WE/BH–M
Fees On application
Loc Marble Arch 6 miles on A40
Arch HS Colt

Enfield (1893)

Old Park Road South, Enfield EN2 7DA

Tel **(0181) 363 3970**
Fax **(0181) 342 0381**
Mem 625
Sec NA Challis (0181) 342 0313
Pro L Fickling (0181) 366 4492
Holes 18 L 6154 yds SSS 70
Recs Am–62 T Greenwood
Pro–66 L Fickling

For list of abbreviations see page 435

V'tors WD–H WE/BH–M SOC–WD
Fees £20 D–£30
Loc 1 mile NE of Enfield. M25 Junction 24-A1005
Arch James Braid

Finchley (1929)
Nether Court, Frith Lane, London NW7 1PU
Tel **(0181) 346 2436**
Fax **(0181) 343 4205**
Mem 550
Sec KL Monk
Pro DM Brown (0181) 346 5086
Holes 18 L 6411 yds SSS 71
Recs Am–65 D Chatterton
Pro–67 T Moore
V'tors WD–U WE–pm only SOC
Fees On application
Loc M1 Junction 2
Arch James Braid

Fulwell (1904)
Wellington Road, Hampton Hill TW12 1JY
Tel **(0181) 977 3188**
Fax **(0181) 977 7732**
Mem 750
Sec PF Butcher (0181) 977 2733
Pro D Haslam (0181) 977 3844
Holes 18 L 6544 yds SSS 71
Recs Am–65 P Wharton
Pro–63 P Buchan
V'tors WD–I WE–M SOC
Fees £30 (£35)
Loc Opposite Fulwell Station

Grim's Dyke (1910)
Oxhey Lane, Hatch End, Pinner HA5 4AL
Tel **(0181) 428 4093**
Mem 575
Sec PH Payne (0181) 428 4539
Pro J Rule (0181) 428 7484
Holes 18 L 5600 yds SSS 67
Recs Am–65 J Thornton (1988)
Pro–64 BJ Hunt (1978)
V'tors WD–U H WE–M SOC
Fees £20 D–£25
Loc 2 miles W of Harrow (A4008)
Arch James Braid

Hampstead (1893)
Winnington Road, London N2 0TU
Tel **(0181) 455 0203**
Mem 435
Sec KF Young
Pro PJ Brown (0181) 455 7089
Holes 9 L 5812 yds SSS 68
Recs Am–66 RDA Smith
Pro–65 D Stevenson
V'tors Phone Pro first SOC
Fees £23 D–£28 (£30)
Loc 1 mile from Hampstead by Spaniards Inn

Harrow School (1978)
High Street, Harrow-on-the-Hill HA1 3HW
Mem 440 100(L) 40(J)
Sec PG Dunbar (0181) 869 1253
Holes 9 L 3690 yds SSS 57
Recs Am–58
V'tors M
Loc Harrow School
Arch Donald Steel

Haste Hill (1933)
Public
The Drive, Northwood HA6 1HN
Tel **(01895) 638835**
Fax **(01923) 822877**
Sec T Le Brocq (Mgr)
Pro T Le Brocq
Holes 18 L 5794 yds SSS 68
Recs Am–68 J Joyce
V'tors U SOC
Fees £10 (£12.50–£15)
Loc Northwood-Hillingdon

Hendon (1903)
Sanders Lane, Devonshire Road, London NW7 1DG
Tel **(0181) 346 6023**
Fax **(0181) 343 1974**
Mem 560
Sec DE Cooper
Pro S Murray (0181) 346 8990
Holes 18 L 6266 yds SSS 70
Recs Am–68 AL MacLeod
Pro–66 SWT Murray
V'tors WD–U WE/BH–bookings SOC
Fees £25 D–£30 (£35)
Loc M1 Junction 2
Arch HS Colt

Highgate (1904)
Denewood Road, Highgate, London N6 4AH
Tel **(0181) 340 1906 (Clubhouse)**
Fax **(0181) 348 9152**
Mem 700
Sec JG Wilson (0181) 340 3745
Pro R Turner (0181) 340 5467
Holes 18 L 5964 yds SSS 69
Recs Am–66 D Kingsman, P Bax, G Clarke, CR Lloyd
Pro–66 I Martin (1987)
V'tors WD–U exc Wed–NA WE/BH–M SOC
Fees £27
Loc Off Sheldon Avenue

Hillingdon (1892)
18 Dorset Way, Hillingdon, Uxbridge UB10 0JR
Tel **(01895) 239810**
Fax **(01895) 233956**
Mem 375
Sec Mrs AM Cooper (01895) 233956
Pro N Wichelow (01895) 251980
Holes 9 L 5459 yds SSS 67
Recs Am–62 J Hall
Pro–61 N Wichelow
V'tors WD–U exc Thurs 12–4pm WE pm–M H SOC–WD
Fees 18 holes–£18 D–£25
Loc Off Uxbridge Road, opposite St John's Church

Holiday (1975)
Stockley Road, West Drayton
Mem 180
Sec J O'Loughlin (Prop) (01895) 444232
Holes 9 L 3800 yds SSS 62
Recs Am–65 P Moor (1994)
V'tors U SOC
Fees 18 holes–£5.50 (£6.50)
Loc Holiday Inn, Heathrow

Horsenden Hill (1935)
Public
Woodland Rise, Greenford UB6 0RD
Tel **(0181) 902 4555**
Pro T Martin
Holes 9 L 3264 yds SSS 56
V'tors U
Fees On application
Loc Greenford

Hounslow Heath (1979)
Public
Staines Road, Hounslow TW4 5DS
Tel **(0181) 570 5271**
Holes 18 L 5901 yds SSS 68
V'tors WD–U WE–booking essential
Fees £7.30 (£10.20)
Loc Opposite Green Lane, Staines Road (A315)
Arch Fraser

Lee Valley (1973)
Pay and play
Lee Valley Leisure, Picketts Lock Lane, Edmonton, London N9 0AS
Tel **(0181) 803 3611**
Pro RG Gerken
Holes 18 L 4902 yds SSS 64
V'tors WD–U WE–booking advisable
Fees £8.50 (£11.50)
Loc 1 mile N of north Circular Road, Edmonton on Meridian Way
Mis Floodlit driving range

London Golf Centre (1984)
Public
Ruislip Road, Northolt UB5 6QZ
Tel **(0181) 841 6162/845 2332**
Fax **(0181) 842 2097**
Sec JP Clifford (Gen Mgr), N Sturgess
Pro G Newall (0181) 845 3180
Holes 9 L 5838 yds SSS 69
Recs Am–71 D Clark (1990)
Pro–67 J Livesley (1990)
V'tors U SOC
Fees 9 holes–£5 18 holes–£9
Loc Off A40, nr Polish war memorial
Mis Driving range

Mill Hill (1925)
100 Barnet Way, Mill Hill, London NW7 3AL
Tel **(0181) 959 2282**
Fax **(0181) 906 0731**

For list of abbreviations see page 435

Mem 450
Sec FH Scott (0181) 959 2339
Pro G Harvey (0181) 959 7261
Holes 18 L 6309 yds SSS 70
Recs Am–65 H Aarons
Pro–67 J Hudson
V'tors WD–U H WE/BH–U H after 11.30am SOC–Mon/Wed/Fri
Fees £20 (£30)
Loc 3/4 mile N of Apex Corner, nr A1/A41 junction
Arch Abercromby/Colt

Muswell Hill (1893)

Rhodes Avenue, Wood Green, London N22 4UT
Tel **(0181) 888 2044**
Fax **(0181) 889 9380**
Mem 500
Sec DE Beer (0181) 888 1764
Pro IB Roberts (0181) 888 8046
Holes 18 L 6474 yds SSS 71
Recs Am–67 PJ Montague
Pro–65 H Weetman
V'tors WD–U WE–book with Pro SOC
Fees £23 D–£33 (£35)
Loc 1 mile from Bounds Green Station

North Middlesex (1928)

The Manor House, Friern Barnet Lane, Whetstone, London N20 0NL
Tel **(0181) 445 1732**
Mem 600
Sec MCN Reding (Mgr) (0181) 445 1604
Pro ASR Roberts (081) 445 3060
Holes 18 L 5625 yds SSS 67
Recs Am–65 M Cohen
Pro–64 S Levermore
V'tors WE/BH–restricted SOC–WD
Fees £22 (£30)
Loc 5 miles S of M25 Junction 23, between Barnet and Finchley
Arch Willie Park Jr

Northwood (1891)

Rickmansworth Road, Northwood HA6 2QW
Tel **(01923) 825329**
Mem 560
Sec RA Bond
Pro CJ Holdsworth (01923) 820112
Holes 18 L 6553 yds SSS 71
Recs Am–68 BE Marsden(1987)
Pro–67 J Bland (1977)
V'tors WD–H WE/BH–NA SOC
Fees £22
Loc 3 miles SE of Rickmansworth (A404)
Arch James Braid

Perivale Park (1932)

Public
Stockdove Way, Argyle Road, Greenford UB6 8EN
Sec GC Taylor
Pro P Bryant (0181) 575 7116
Holes 9 L 5296 yds SSS 65
Recs Am–63 W McWilliams
Pro–63
V'tors U
Fees 9 holes–£3.95 (£5.95)
18 holes–£11.50
Loc 1 mile E of Greenford, off A40

Pinner Hill (1927)

Southview Road, Pinner Hill HA5 3YA
Tel **(0181) 866 0963**
Fax **(0181) 868 4817**
Mem 770
Sec JP Devitt
Pro M Grieve (0181) 866 2109
Holes 18 L 6266 yds SSS 70
Recs Am–63 SR Warrin
Pro–67 TH Cotton, G Player, T Wilkes, G Low, J Warren
V'tors WD–H exc Wed & Thurs–U Sun/BH–M SOC
Fees £25 (£32) exc Wed & Thurs–£8.10 D–£11.15
Loc 1 mile from West Pinner Green
Arch JH Taylor

Rectory Park (1991)

Pay and play
Huxley Close, Northolt UB5 5UL
Tel **(0181) 841 5550**
Sec C White (Mgr)
Pro D Morgan, C White
Holes 9 hole course Par 56 SSS 52
V'tors U SOC
Fees £3.95 (£4.95)
Loc Nr M40 Target roundabout
Arch Morgan/White

Ruislip (1936)

Public
Ickenham Road, Ruislip HA4 7DQ
Tel **(01895) 638835**
Fax **(01923) 822877**
Sec S Dunlop (01895) 635780
Pro G Lloyd
Holes 18 L 5702 yds SSS 68
Recs Am–64 W Bennet
Pro–65 A George
V'tors U SOC
Fees £10 (£12.50–£15)
Loc W Ruislip BR/LTE Station
Mis Driving range
Arch A Herd

Stanmore (1893)

29 Gordon Avenue, Stanmore HA7 2RL
Tel **(0181) 954 4661**
Mem 590
Sec LJ Pertwee (0181) 954 2599
Pro VR Law (0181) 954 2646
Holes 18 L 5860 yds SSS 68
Recs Am–64 P Hardy (1994)
Pro–62 V Law (1984)
V'tors WD–H WE/BH–M SOC–Wed & Thurs
Fees £25
Loc Between Stanmore and Belmont, off Old Church Lane

Stockley Park (1993)

Pay and play
The Clubhouse, Stockley Park, Uxbridge UB11 1AQ
Tel **(0181) 813 5700** (Enquiries), **(0181) 569 2939** (Bookings)
Fax **(0181) 813 5655**
Mem 1000
Sec Mrs S Hubbard
Pro S Hubbard
Holes 18 L 6548 yds SSS 71
V'tors U
Fees £25 (£30)
Loc Heathrow Airport, 2 miles. M4 Junction 4, 1 mile
Arch Robert Trent Jones Sr

Strawberry Hill (1900)

Wellesley Road, Strawberry Hill, Twickenham TW2 5SD
Tel **(0181) 894 1246**
Mem 350
Sec DW Seward (0181) 894 0165
Pro P Buchan (0181) 898 2082
Holes 9 L 2381 yds Par 64 SSS 62
Recs Am–61 RE Heryet
Pro–59 H Fullicks, R Gerken, K Bousfield
V'tors WD–U WE–M XL
Fees £18
Loc Strawberry Hill Station
Arch JH Taylor

Sudbury (1920)

Bridgewater Road, Wembley HA0 1AL
Tel **(0181) 902 3713**
Fax **(0181) 903 2966**
Mem 640
Sec AJ Poole (Gen Mgr)
Pro N Jordan (0181) 902 7910
Holes 18 L 6282 yds SSS 70
Recs Am–63 T Greenwood, L White
Pro–65 J Gill
V'tors WD–H WE–M SOC
Fees On application
Loc Junction of A4005/A4090

Sunbury (1993)

Charlton Lane, Shepperton TW17 8QA
Tel **(01932) 772898**
Fax **(01932) 866120**
Mem 450
Sec P Davison
Pro A Hardaway
Holes 9 L 3105 yds SSS 70
V'tors U
Fees £6.50 (£15)
Loc M3 Junction 1, 1 mile
Mis Floodlit driving range

Trent Park (1973)

Public
Bramley Road, Southgate, London N14
Tel **(0181) 366 7432**
Pro G Harris
Holes 18 L 6008 yds SSS 69
Recs Am–65 M Skinner (1989)
Pro–64 V Law (1979)
V'tors WD–U SOC WE–NA before 11am
Fees £8.50 (£10.50)
Loc Nr Oakwood Tube station

For list of abbreviations see page 435

Twickenham Park (1977)
Public
Staines Road, Twickenham TW2 5JD
Tel **(0181) 783 1698**
Fax **(0181) 941 9134**
Pro S Lloyd (0181) 783 1698
Holes 9 L 6014 yds SSS 69
V'tors U
Fees £5 (£6)
Loc 2 miles NW of Hampton Court, nr end of M3
Mis Floodlit driving range

Uxbridge (1947)
Public
The Drive, Harefield Place, Uxbridge UB10 8PA
Tel **(01895) 231169**
Fax **(01895) 810262**
Pro P Howard (01895) 237287
Holes 18 L 5711 yds SSS 68
Recs Am–65 A Schyns (1988)
Pro–64 P Smith (1994)
V'tors U SOC
Fees £10 (£15)
Loc 2 miles N of Uxbridge. B467 off A40 towards Ruislip

West Middlesex (1891)
Greenford Road, Southall UB1 3EE
Tel **(0181) 574 3450**
Mem 700
Sec PJ Furness
Pro IP Harris (0181) 574 1800
Holes 18 L 6242 yds SSS 70
Recs Am–65 J Walsh
Pro–64 L Farmer
V'tors WD–U WE–NA
Fees Tues/Thurs/Fri–£15.50 (£27.50) Mon & Wed–£10
Loc Junction of Uxbridge Road and Greenford Road
Arch James Braid

Whitewebbs (1932)
Public
Beggars Hollow, Clay Hill, Enfield EN2 9JN
Tel **(0181) 363 4454**
Mem 230
Sec V van Grann
Pro D Lewis (0181) 363 4454
Holes 18 L 5863 yds SSS 68
Recs Am–61 C Smith
Pro–68 D Lewis
V'tors U
Fees £10 (£12)
Loc 1 mile N of Enfield

Wyke Green (1928)
Syon Lane, Isleworth TW7 5PT
Tel **(0181) 560 8777**
Mem 700
Sec D Wentworth-Pollock
Pro DA Holmes (0181) 847 0685
Holes 18 L 6242 yds SSS 70
Recs Am–65 MR Johnson
Pro–64 C DeFoy
V'tors WD–U WE/BH–NA before 3pm SOC
Fees £28 (£42)
Loc 1/2 mile from Gillettes Corner (A4)

Norfolk

Barnham Broom Hotel (1977)
Barnham Broom, Norwich NR9 4DD
Tel **(01605) 45393**
Fax **(01605) 458224**
Mem 600
Sec A Long (Man Dir),
P Ballingall (Golf Dir)
Pro S Beckham
Holes Valley 18 L 6470 yds SSS 71
Hill 18 L 6628 yds SSS 72
Recs Valley Am–69 A Elliot
Pro–65 J Higgins
Hill Am–71 A Marshall
V'tors I or H WE/BH–NA (exc hotel residents) SOC
Fees £25 Residents–£17.50
Loc 8 miles SW of Norwich, off A47. 4 miles NW of Wymondham, off A11

Bawburgh (1978)
Long Lane, Bawburgh, Norwich NR9 3LX
Tel **(01603) 746390**
Fax **(01603) 812429/811110**
Mem 800
Sec F Black
Pro C Potter (01603) 742323
Holes 18 L 6066 yds SSS 69
V'tors U–phone first SOC
Fees £14 (£20)
Loc 2 miles W of Norwich, off A47 Norwich Southern Bypass
Mis Floodlit driving range

Costessey Park (1983)
Costessey Park, Costessey, Norwich NR8 5AL
Tel **(01603) 746333**
Mem 500
Sec CL House
Pro S Cook (01603) 747085
Holes 18 L 6104 yds Par 72 SSS 69
V'tors U SOC–WD
Fees On application
Loc 3 miles W of Norwich, off A47 at Round Well PH

Dereham (1934)
Quebec Road, Dereham NR19 2DS
Tel **(01362) 695900**
Mem 480
Sec J Holland
Pro G Kitley (01362) 695631
Holes 9 L 6225 yds SSS 70
Recs Am–66 AC Marshall (1992)
Pro–65 M Elsworthy (1986)
V'tors H WE–M
Fees £16
Loc Dereham 1/2 mile

Dunham (1987)
Little Dunham, King's Lynn PE32 2DF
Tel **(01328) 701718**
Fax **(01328) 701906**
Mem 250
Sec J Glencross
Pro J Laing (01485) 520076
Holes 9 L 2269 yds SSS 62
V'tors U SOC
Fees £9 (£12)
Loc 4 miles NE of Swaffham, off A47. Signs from Necton
Arch Cecil Denny

Dunston Hall (1994)
Pay and play
Ipswich Road, Dunston, Norwich NR14 8PQ
Tel **(01508) 470444**
Fax **(01508) 471499**
Mem 65
Sec G Robertson-Burnett
Pro P Briggs
Holes 10 L 6050 yds Par 71 SSS 69
V'tors U
Fees £15 (£18)
Loc 5 miles S of Norwich on A140
Mis Driving range
Arch John Glasgow

Eagles (1990)
School Road, Tilney All Saints, Kings Lynn PE34 4RS
Tel **(01553) 827147**
Mem 300
Sec D Horn
Pro K Worby
Holes 9 L 2142 yds SSS 61
Par 3 course
V'tors U
Fees 9 holes–£ 5.50 (£6.50)
Loc 5 miles W of Kings Lynn on A47
Mis Driving range
Arch David Horn

Eaton (1910)
Newmarket Road, Norwich NR4 6SF
Tel **(01603) 452881**
Fax **(01603) 451686**
Mem 640 135(L) 70(J)
Sec DLP Sochon (01603) 451686
Pro N Bundy (01603) 452478
Holes 18 L 6135 yds SSS 69
Recs Am–64 AK Nichols (1990)
Pro–65 M Spooner (1988)
V'tors H WE–NA before noon SOC
Fees £28 (£35)
Loc S Norwich, off A11

Fakenham (1973)
The Race Course, Fakenham
Tel **(01328) 862867**
Mem 510
Sec G Cocker (01328) 855665
Pro C Williams (01328) 863534
Holes 9 L 5988 yds SSS 69
Recs Am–67 D Futter (1991)
Pro–65 K Golding (1991)
V'tors WD–U WE–NA before 3pm SOC
Fees £14 (£18)
Loc Fakenham racecourse

Feltwell (1976)

Thor Ave, Wilton Road, Feltwell IP26 9XX

Tel **(01842) 827644**
Mem 400
Sec PJ Jessop
Holes 9 L 6260 yds SSS 70
Recs Am–68 S Dupe (1994)
Pro–67 M Snazell (1992)
V'tors U SOC–WD
Fees £12 (£20)
Loc 1 mile S of Feltwell on B1112
Mis Former Feltwell aerodrome

Gorleston (1906)

Warren Road, Gorleston, Gt Yarmouth NR31 6JT

Tel **(01493) 661911**
Mem 900
Sec NP Longbottom (01493) 661911
Pro N Brown (01493) 662103
Holes 18 L 6400 yds SSS 71
Recs Am–68 J Maddock (1981)
Pro–66 R Mann (1991)
V'tors U H SOC
Fees D–£20 (D–£25) W–£60
Loc S of Gorleston, off A12
Arch JH Taylor

Great Yarmouth & Caister (1882)

Beach House, Caister-on-Sea, Gt Yarmouth NR30 5TD

Tel **(01493) 720421**
Mem 700
Sec HJ Harvey (01493) 728699
Pro R Foster
Holes 18 L 6330 yds SSS 70
Recs Am–65 C Green
Pro–66 E Murray
V'tors WE–NA before noon SOC
Fees £23.50 (£28)
Loc Caister-on-Sea

Hunstanton (1891)

Golf Course Road, Old Hunstanton PE36 6QJ

Tel **(01485) 532811**
Fax **(01485) 532319**
Mem 650 250(L) 60(J)
Sec M Whybrow
Pro J Carter (01485) 532751
Holes 18 L 6670 yds SSS 72
Recs Am–65 S Robertson (1989)
Pro–65 ME Gregson (1967)
V'tors WD–H after 9.30am WE–H after 10.30am SOC
Fees D–£34 (D–£40)
Loc ½mile NE of Hunstanton
Arch George Fernie

King's Lynn (1923)

Castle Rising, King's Lynn PE31 6BD

Tel **(01553) 631656**
Fax **(01553) 631036**
Mem 980
Sec GJ Higgins (01553) 631654
Pro C Hanlon (01553) 631655
Holes 18 L 6646 yds SSS 72
Recs Am–68 J Jones (1993)
Pro–64 P Hinton (1991)
Ladies–75 W Fryer (1989)
V'tors WD–U H WE/BH–NA SOC
Fees £30 (£38)
Loc 4 miles NE of King's Lynn, off A149
Arch Alliss/Thomas

Links Country Park Hotel

West Runton, Cromer NR27 9QH

Tel **(01263) 838383**
Fax **(01263) 838264**
Mem 300
Sec CL Savage (Hon)
Pro M Jubb (01263) 838215
Holes 9 L 4814 yds SSS 64
Recs Am–64 CJ Lamb (1988)
Pro–65 R Mann, GR Harvey (1987)
V'tors U
Fees £19 (£23)
Loc 3 miles W of Cromer (A149)
Arch JH Taylor

Mattishall (1990)

South Green, Mattishall, Dereham

Tel **(01362) 850464**
Mem 300
Sec Miss B Todd
Holes 9 L 6218 yds SSS 70
V'tors WD–U WE–U before noon SOC
Fees £8 (£10)
Loc 6 miles E of Dereham (B1063)
Mis 9 hole pitch & putt
Arch BC Todd

Middleton Hall G & CC (1989)

Middleton, King's Lynn PE32 1RH

Tel **(01553) 841800**
Mem 342
Sec MP Quince
Pro F Scott
Holes 9 L 5570 yds SSS 67
Recs Am–69 M Easey, S Littlefair
V'tors U SOC–WD exc Tues & Thurs am
Fees £12 (£14)
Loc 2 miles SE of King's Lynn on A47
Mis Driving range

Mundesley (1903)

Links Road, Mundesley NR11 8ES

Tel **(01263) 720279**
Mem 400
Sec P Hampel (Sec/Mgr) (01263) 720095
Pro TG Symmons (01831) 455461
Holes 9 L 5377 yds SSS 66
V'tors WD–U exc Wed 12–3pm WE–NA before 11.30am
Fees On application
Loc 7 miles SE of Cromer

RAF Marham (1974)

RAF Marham, Kings Lynn PE33 9NP

Mem 300
Sec HM Jones (01760) 337261 (Ext 7560)
Holes 9 L 5244 yds SSS 66
Recs Am–71
V'tors By prior arrangement–U exc Sun am
Fees £5 (£7)
Loc 11 miles SE of King's Lynn, nr Narborough
Mis Course situated on MOD land, and may be closed without prior notice

Reymerston (1993)

Hingham Road, Reymerston, Norwich NR9 4QQ

Tel **(01362) 850297**
Fax **(01362) 850614**
Mem 350
Sec RR Wright
Pro Alison Sheard (01362) 850778
Holes 18 L 6603 yds SSS 72
Recs Am–74 G Head (1994)
V'tors WD–U before 4pm –M after 4pm WE/BH–NA before noon SOC
Fees £20 (£25)
Loc 14 miles W of Norwich, off B1135
Mis 9 hole pitch & putt course

Richmond Park (1990)

Saham Road, Watton IP25 6EA

Tel **(01953) 881803**
Fax **(01953) 881817**
Mem 600
Sec Gp Capt E Durham RAF Rtd
Pro A Hemsley
Holes 18 L 6300 yds SSS 70
Recs Am–71 D Glenn (1994)
Pro–70 C Green (1994)
V'tors WD–U WE–H before noon SOC
Fees D–£15 (D–£20)
Loc ½ mile NW of Watton
Mis Driving range
Arch Scott/Jessup

Royal Cromer (1888)

Overstrand Road, Cromer NR27 0JH

Tel **(01263) 512884**
Mem 700
Sec BA Howson
Pro RJ Page (01263) 512267
Holes 18 L 6508 yds SSS 71
Recs Am–67 T Hurrell (1993)
Pro–69 C Williams, R Waugh (1991)
V'tors H SOC–WD
Fees £25 (£30)
Loc 1 mile E of Cromer on B1159

For list of abbreviations see page 435

Royal Norwich (1893)
Drayton High Road, Hellesdon, Norwich NR6 5AH
Tel **(01603) 425712**
Mem 780
Sec J Meggy (01603) 429928
Pro G Potter (01603) 408459
Holes 18 L 6603 yds SSS 72
Recs Am–67 A Barker
Pro–66 HJ Boyle
V'tors WE/BH–restricted SOC
Fees D–£26 (£30)
Loc 1/2 mile W of Norwich ring road, on Fakenham road

Royal West Norfolk (1892)
Brancaster, King's Lynn PE31 8AX
Tel **(01485) 210223**
Fax **(01485) 210087**
Mem 760
Sec Major NA Carrington Smith (01485) 210087
Pro RE Kimber (01485) 210616
Holes 18 L 6428 yds SSS 71
Recs Am–67 AH Perowne
Pro–66 M Elsworthy
V'tors M No four balls allowed Mid July–mid Sept WE–NA before 10am SOC
Fees £32 (£42.50)
Loc 7 miles E of Hunstanton on A419
Arch Holcombe Ingleby

Ryston Park (1932)
Ely Road, Denver, Downham Market PE38 0HH
Tel **(01366) 382133**
Mem 320
Sec WJ Flogdell (01366) 383834
Pro None
Holes 9 L 6292 yds SSS 70
Recs Am–66 JP Alflatt (1975)
V'tors WD–H WE–M BH–NA
Fees £20
Loc 1 mile S of Downham Market on A10

Sheringham (1891)
Sheringham NR26 8HG
Tel **(01263) 822038**
Fax **(01263) 825189**
Mem 700
Sec MJ Garrett (10263) 823488
Pro RH Emery (01263) 822980
Holes 18 L 6464 yds SSS 71
Recs Am–68 PR Little (1993)
Pro–66 R Mann (1991)
V'tors WD–U H after 9.15am SOC
Fees £30 (£35)
Loc 1/2 mile W of Sheringham (A149)
Arch Tom Dunn

Sprowston Park (1980)
Pay and play
Wroxham Road, Sprowston, Norwich NR9 8RP
Tel **(01603) 410657**
Fax **(01603) 788884**
Mem 650
Sec G Porter
Pro P Grice (01603) 417264
Holes 18 L 5982 yds SSS 70
Recs Am–66 R Marett
Pro–65 N Catchpole
V'tors U SOC
Fees £12 (£15)
Loc 2 miles NE of Norwich on A1151
Mis Floodlit driving range

Swaffham (1922)
Cley Road, Swaffham PE37 8AE
Tel **(01760) 721611**
Mem 500
Sec R Joslin
Pro P Field
Holes 9 L 6252 yds SSS 70
Recs Am–68 G Head
Pro–64 CJ Norton
V'tors WD–U WE–M exc Sun am–NA
Fees £18
Loc 1 1/2 miles SW of Swaffham

Thetford (1912)
Brandon Road, Thetford IP24 3NE
Tel **(01842) 752258**
Mem 700
Sec RJ Ferguson (01842) 752169
Pro N Arthur (01842) 752662
Holes 18 L 6879 yds SSS 73
Recs Am–72 S Torrington
Pro–70 C Green
V'tors H SOC–Wed–Fri
Fees £26
Loc 2 miles W of Thetford (B1107), off A11 By-pass

Wensum Valley (1990)
Beech Avenue, Taverham, Norwich NR8 6HP
Tel **(01603) 261012**
Mem 850
Sec Miss B Todd
Pro T Varney
Holes 18 L 6000 yds SSS 69
18 L 4862 yds SSS 66
Recs Am–69 P Robson (1993)
Pro–67 M Spooner (1990)
V'tors WD–U H WE–NA before noon SOC
Fees £15 (£18)
Loc 4 miles NW of Norwich on A1067
Mis Floodlit driving range
Arch BC Todd

Weston Park (1993)
Weston Longville, Norwich NR9 5JW
Tel **(01603) 872363**
Mem 120
Sec Sue Warnes (01603) 870245
Pro MR Few (01603) 872998
Holes 9 L 3132 yds SSS 70
V'tors WD–U H
Fees £17 (£22)
Loc 7 miles NW of Norwich, off A1067
Arch John Glasgow

Northamptonshire

Cold Ashby (1974)
Stanford Road, Cold Ashby, Northampton NN6 6EP
Tel **(01604) 740548**
Fax **(01604) 740548**
Mem 600 40(L) 40(J)
Sec DA Croxton (Prop)
Pro S Rose (01604) 740099
Holes 27 L 6007 yds Par 70 SSS 69
Recs Am–68 S Keir (1993)
Pro–63 G Stafford (1991), S Edwards (1993)
V'tors WD–U WE–U after 2pm (if booked) SOC
Fees £14 (£20)
Loc 11 miles N of Northampton, nr A50/A14 Junction. 7 miles E of M1 Junction 18
Arch John Day

Collingtree Park (1989)
Windingbrook Lane, Northampton NN4 0XN
Tel **(01604) 700000**
Fax **(01604) 702600**
Mem 1200
Sec Miss J Byrne
Pro J Cook
Holes 18 L 6821 yds SSS 73
Recs Am–67 S Bottomley (1993)
Pro–66 M Persson (1994)
Ladies Pro–69 J Hill (1994)
V'tors H SOC
Fees £20 (£30)
Loc 1/2 mile E of M1 Junction 15
Mis Floodlit driving range
Arch Johnny Miller

Corby (1965)
Public
Stamford Road, Weldon, Corby
Tel **(01536) 260756**
Fax **(01536) 260756**
Pro G Brown
Holes 18 L 6677 yds SSS 72
Recs Am–75 R Beekie, M Scott, WF Kearney
Pro–70 RH Kemp
V'tors U SOC–WD
Fees On application
Loc 4 miles E of Corby (A43)

Daventry & District (1922)
Norton Road, Daventry NN11 5LS
Tel **(01327) 702829**
Mem 450
Sec F Higham (01327) 703204
Pro M Higgins
Holes 9 L 5812 yds Par 69 SSS 68
V'tors WD–U Sun–NA before 11am SOC–phone Pro
Fees £8 (£10)
Loc 2 miles E of Daventry

Delapre (1976)

Public
Eagle Drive, Nene Valley Way, Northampton NN4 0DU
Tel **(01604) 764036/763957**
Fax **(01604) 763957**
Sec JS Corby (01604) 763957
Pro J Corby, J Cuddihy (01604) 764036
Holes 18 L 6293 yds SSS 70
9 L 2146 yds SSS 32
2 x 9 holes Par 3 courses
Recs Am–66 M McNally
V'tors U SOC
Fees £7.30 (£9.50)
Loc 3 miles from M1 Junction 15, on A508/A45
Mis Pitch & putt. Driving range
Arch Jacobs/Corby

Embankment (1975)

The Embankment, Wellingborough NN8 1LD
Tel **(01933) 228465**
Mem 175
Sec JB Andrew, F Smith (Mgr)
Holes 9 L 3374 yds SSS 55
Recs Am–60
V'tors WD–M
Fees £2
Loc 1 mile SE of Wellingborough
Arch TH Neal

Farthingstone Hotel (1974)

Farthingstone, Towcester NN12 8HA
Tel **(01327) 136291**
Fax **(01327) 136645**
Mem 650
Sec DC Donaldson (Prop/Mgr)
Pro (01327) 136533
Holes 18 L 6248 yds SSS 71
Recs Am–68 K Leason (1989)
Pro–66 D Thorp (1984), M Gallagher (1985), K Dickens (1989)
V'tors U SOC
Fees £10 D–£15 (£15 D–£20) SOC–from £10
Loc 4 miles W of A5 on Farthingstone-Everdon road. M1 Junction 16, 6 miles

Hellidon Lakes Hotel & CC (1991)

Hellidon, Daventry NN11 6LN
Tel **(01327) 62550**
Fax **(01327) 62559**
Mem 500
Sec J Nicoll
Pro J Kennedy (01327) 62551
Holes 18 L 6700 yds SSS 72
Recs Am–73 C Woodhouse (1991)
V'tors U H SOC
Fees £15 (£20)
Loc 7 miles SW of Daventry, via A361.
Mis Driving range. Further 9 holes open 1995
Arch David Snell

Kettering (1891)

Headlands, Kettering NN15 6XA
Tel **(01536) 512074**
Mem 380 100(L) 50(J)
Sec DG Buckby (01536) 511104
Pro K Theobald (01536) 81014
Holes 18 L 6087 yds SSS 69
Recs Am–65 A Draper (1992)
Pro–64 P Smith (1991)
V'tors WD–U WE/BH–M SOC
Fees £22
Loc S boundary of Kettering
Arch Tom Morris

Kingsthorpe (1908)

Kingsley Road, Northampton NN2 7BU
Tel **(01604) 711173**
Mem 600
Sec PL Voke (01604) 710610
Pro P Armstrong (01604) 719602
Holes 18 L 6006 yds SSS 69
Recs Am–63 S McDonald
Pro–64 B Larratt
V'tors WD–U WE/BH–M H SOC–WD
Fees D–£25
Loc 2 miles N of Northampton, off A508

Northampton (1893)

Harlestone, Northampton NN7 4EF
Tel **(01604) 845102**
Fax **(01604) 820262**
Mem 500 100(L) 70(J)
Sec IMC Kirkwood (01604) 845155
Pro M Chamberlain (01604) 845167
Holes 18 L 6534 yds SSS 71
V'tors WD–U H WE–M SOC
Fees £25
Loc 4 miles NW of Northampton, on A428 beyond Harlestone
Arch Donald Steel

Northamptonshire County (1909)

Church Brampton, Northampton NN6 8AZ
Tel **(01604) 842170**
Mem 650
Sec ME Wadley (01604) 843025
Pro T Rouse (01604) 842226
Holes 18 L 6503 yds SSS 71
Recs Am–65 R Duck (1994)
Pro–64 J Higgins (1990)
V'tors WD–H WE–H XL before 3.30pm Sat/11.15am Sun
Fees Summer–£37.50 (£37.50)
Winter–£27.50 (£27.50)
Loc 5 miles NW of Northampton, off A50
Arch HS Colt

Oundle (1893)

Benefield Road, Oundle PE8 4EZ
Tel **(01832) 273267**
Mem 600
Sec AJ Dobson (Gen Mgr)
Pro R Keys (01832) 272273
Holes 18 L 5507 yds SSS 67
Recs Am–68
Pro–67
V'tors WD–U WE–M before 10.30am –U after 10.30am SOC
Fees £20 (£30)
Loc 1½ miles W of Oundle on A427

Overstone Park (1994)

Watermark Leisure, Billing Lane, Northampton NN6 0AP
Tel **(01604) 647666**
Fax **(01604) 642635**
Mem 700
Sec A McLundie
Pro B Mudge (01604) 643555
Holes 18 L 6602 yds SSS 72
V'tors M
Loc 4 miles E of Northampton, off A45. M1 Junction 15
Arch Donald Steel

Rushden (1919)

Kimbolton Road, Chelveston, Wellingborough NN9 6AN
Tel **(01933) 312581**
Mem 350
Sec E Richardson (01933) 314910
Holes 10 L 6335 yds Par 71 SSS 70
Recs Am–69
V'tors WD–U exc Wed pm WE/BH–M SOC
Fees £15
Loc On A45, 2 miles E of Higham Ferrers

Staverton Park (1977)

Staverton Park, Staverton, Daventry NN11 6JT
Tel **(01327) 705911**
Fax **(01327) 311428**
Sec S Essex (Gen Mgr), NJ Lucas (Sec)
Pro R Mudge (01327) 705506
Holes 18 L 6634 yds SSS 72
Recs Am–67
Pro–64
V'tors H SOC
Fees On application
Loc 1 mile SW of Daventry, off A425. M1 Junctions 16/18. M40 Junction 11

Wellingborough (1893)

Harrowden Hall, Great Harrowden, Wellingborough NN9 5AD
Tel **(01933) 677234/673022**
Fax **(01933) 679379**
Mem 850
Sec R Tomlin (01933) 677234
Pro D Clifford (01933) 678752
Holes 18 L 6620 yds SSS 72
Recs Am–69 J Campbell (1993)
Pro–68 M Gallagher (1993)
V'tors WD–U H exc Tues WE–M SOC–WD exc Tues
Fees £25 D–£30
Loc 2 miles N of Wellingborough on A509
Arch Hawtree

For list of abbreviations see page 435

West Park G & CC (1992)
Whittlebury, Towcester NN12 8XW
Tel **(01327) 858092**
Fax **(01327) 858009**
Mem 450
Sec RL Jones
Pro S Murdoch (01327) 858588
Holes 36 holes: 5000-7000 yds SSS 66-72
V'tors U H SOC
Fees £20 D–£30 (£25 D–£35)
Loc 4 miles S of Towcester on A413
Mis Driving range. Indoor golf centre
Arch Cameron Sinclair

Northumberland

Allendale (1906)
High Studdon, Allenheads Road, Allendale, Hexham NE47 9DQ
Mem 140 30(L) 9(J)
Sec JC Hall (Hon) (0191) 267 5875
Holes 9 L 5044 yds SSS 65
V'tors U BH–NA before 2pm SOC
Fees £8 (£10)
Loc 1½ miles S of Allendale on B6295

Alnmouth (1869)
Foxton Hall, Alnmouth NE66 3BE
Tel **(01665) 830231**
Fax **(01665) 830922**
Mem 800
Sec C Jobson
Holes 18 L 6484 yds SSS 71
Recs Am–65 P Deeble (1973)
V'tors Mon/Tues/Thurs–H (restricted) SOC
Fees D–£25
Loc 5 miles SE of Alnwick
Mis Dormy House accommodation

Alnmouth Village (1869)
Marine Road, Alnmouth NE66 2RZ
Tel **(01665) 830370**
Mem 340
Sec W Maclean (01665) 602096
Holes 9 L 6020 yds SSS 70
Recs Am–63 D Weddell
V'tors H
Fees £10 (£15)

Alnwick (1907)
Swansfield Park, Alnwick
Tel **(01665) 602632**
Mem 400
Sec LE Stewart (01665) 602499
Holes 18 L 6250 yds SSS 70
Recs Am–62 P Deeble (1988) Ladies–72 C Malone (1991)
V'tors U
Fees D–£15 (D–£20)
Loc Alnwick, off A1
Mis Extension to 18 holes open May 1995
Arch Rochester/Rae

Arcot Hall (1909)
Dudley, Cramlington NE23 7QP
Mem 660
Sec JM Forteath QGM (0191) 236 2794
Pro GM Cant (0191) 236 2147
Holes 18 L 6389 yds SSS 70
Recs Am–65 G Pickup (1990) Pro–65 P Walker (1990)
V'tors WD–H WE/BH–M SOC
Fees D–£25 (£28) After 3pm–£20
Loc 7 miles N of Newcastle, off A1
Arch James Braid

Bamburgh Castle (1896)
The Club House, 40 The Wynding, Bamburgh NE69 7DE
Tel **(01668) 214378**
Mem 650
Sec TC Osborne (01668) 214321
Holes 18 L 5621 yds SSS 67
Recs Am–64 M Dawson (1994)
V'tors WD–U H WE/BH–M SOC
Fees D–£23 (£30 D–£35)
Loc 7 miles E of A1, via B1341 or B1342
Arch George Rochester

Bedlingtonshire (1972)
Public
Acorn Bank, Bedlington
Tel **(01670) 822457**
Mem 931
Sec AJ Gray
Pro M Webb (01670) 822087
Holes 18 L 6224 metres SSS 73
Recs Am–68 D Gray Pro–65 K Waters
V'tors U
Fees £14 D–£20 (£16 D–£22)
Loc 12 miles N of Newcastle (A1068)
Arch Frank Pennink

Belford (1993)
South Road, Belford NE70 7HY
Tel **(01668) 213433**
Mem 300
Sec AM Gilhome
Pro None
Holes 9 L 6304 yds SSS 70
Recs Am–73 M Williamson (1994)
V'tors U SOC
Fees 9 holes–£9 (£10)
Loc 15 miles N of Alnwick, off A1
Mis Driving range
Arch Nigel Williams

Bellingham (1893)
Boggle Hole, Bellingham NE48 2DT
Tel **(01434) 220530**
Mem 400
Sec P Cordiner (01434) 220182
Holes 9 L 5245 yds SSS 66
Recs Am–63 I Wilson (1978)
V'tors U exc comp days SOC
Fees £10 (£15)
Loc 15 miles N of Hexham, off B6320

Berwick-upon-Tweed (Goswick) (1890)
Goswick Beal, Berwick-upon-Tweed TD15 2RW
Tel **(01289) 387256**
Mem 550
Sec AE French
Pro P Terras (01289) 387380
Holes 18 L 6449 yds SSS 71
Recs Am–64 A Cotton Pro–69 GJ Brand
V'tors WD–U WE–U 10–12 and after 2.30pm SOC
Fees £18 D–£24 (£24 D–£32)
Loc 5 miles S of Berwick, off A1
Arch James Braid

Blyth (1905)
New Delaval, Blyth NE24 4DB
Tel **(01670) 367728**
Mem 580 120(L) 120(J)
Sec J Tate
Pro P Chapman (01670) 356514
Holes 18 L 6498 yds SSS 71
Recs Am–66 P Simpson (1989) Ladies–K Ferguson
V'tors WD–U WE–M BH–NA SOC–WD
Fees £16 D–£18
Loc W end of Plessey Road, Blyth

Burgham Park G & CC (1994)
Felton, Morpeth NE65 8QP
Tel **(01670) 787898**
Fax **(01670) 787164**
Mem 500
Sec J Carr
Pro S McNally
Holes 18 L 6751 yds SSS 72
V'tors U SOC
Fees £13.50 (£16)
Loc 7 miles N of Morpeth on A1
Arch Andrew Mair

Close House (1968)
Close House, Heddon-on-the-Wall, Newcastle-upon-Tyne NE15 0HT
Tel **(01661) 852953**
Mem 1000
Sec J Pearson
Holes 18 L 5587 yds SSS 67
Recs Am–66 W Parker (1984), R Ingham (1986)
V'tors M SOC–WD
Fees D–£15
Loc 9 miles W of Newcastle on A69

Dunstanburgh Castle (1900)
Embleton, Alnwick NE66 3XQ
Tel **(01665) 576562**
Mem 374
Sec PFC Gilbert (Mgr)
Holes 18 L 6298 yds SSS 70
Recs Am–69
V'tors U
Fees £15 (£18)
Loc 7 miles NE of Alnwick on B1339
Arch James Braid

Haltwhistle

Banktop, Greenhead, Haltwhistle

Tel **(016977) 47367**
Mem 300
Sec WE Barnes (Hon)
Pro J Metcalf
Holes 12 5968 yds SSS 69
V'tors U SOC
Fees D–£10
Loc 3 miles W of Haltwhistle on A69
Mis Extending to 18 holes
Arch Andrew Mair

Hexham (1892)

Spital Park, Hexham NE46 3RZ

Tel **(01434) 602057**
Fax **(01434) 601865**
Mem 700
Sec JC Oates (01434) 603072
Pro MW Forster (01434) 604904
Holes 18 L 6272 yds SSS 70
Recs Am–64 JP Arnott (1994)
Pro–67 I Waugh
V'tors U
Fees £22 (£28) W–£100
Loc 21 miles W of Newcastle (A69)

Magdalene Fields (1903)

Pay and play

Magdalene Fields, Berwick-upon-Tweed

Tel **(01289) 306384**
Sec PJ Rae (01289) 304452
Holes 18 L 6407 yds SSS 71
Recs Am–66 J Blackie (1994)
V'tors U SOC
Fees £14 (£16)
Loc Berwick-upon-Tweed 1 mile
Arch Park/Jefferson/Thompson

Matfen Hall (1994)

Matfen, Hexham

Tel **(01661) 886500**
Mem 300
Sec J Harrison
Pro J Harrison
Holes 18 L 6732 yds Par 72
V'tors U
Fees £15 (£20)
Loc 12 miles W of Newcastle, off B6318
Arch Andrew Mair

Morpeth (1907)

The Common, Morpeth NE61 2BT

Tel **(01670) 519980**
Fax **(01670) 504918**
Mem 700
Sec G Hogg (01670) 504942
Pro MR Jackson (01670) 515675
Holes 18 L 5671 metres SSS 70
Recs Am–67 K Brown (1983)
Pro–68 T Horton (1976)
V'tors H SOC
Fees £20 (£25)
Loc 1 mile S of Morpeth on A197

Newbiggin (1884)

Newbiggin-by-the-Sea NE64 6DW

Tel **(01670) 817344 (Clubhouse)**
Mem 500
Sec D Lyall
Pro D Fletcher (01670) 817833
Holes 18 L 6452 yds SSS 71
Recs Am–67 B Bennett, SE Philipson
Pro–68 K Saint
V'tors U after 10am exc Comp days–NA SOC
Fees On application
Loc Newbiggin, nr Church Point

Ponteland (1927)

53 Bell Villas, Ponteland, Newcastle-upon-Tyne NE20 9BD

Tel **(01661) 822689**
Mem 460 150(L) 80(J)
Sec J Hillyer
Pro A Crosby
Holes 18 L 6524 yds SSS 71
Recs Am–66 J Hayes, WMM Jenkins, DG Potter (1987)
Pro–63 B Rumney (1994)
V'tors WD–U WE/BH–M
Fees £22.50
Loc 6 miles NW of Newcastle on A696, nr Airport

Prudhoe (1930)

Eastwood Park, Prudhoe-on-Tyne NE42 5DX

Tel **(01661) 832466**
Mem 450
Sec GB Garratt
Pro J Crawford (01661) 836188
Holes 18 L 5862 yds SSS 68
Recs Am–63 CN Hunter
Pro–65 A Crosby
V'tors WD–U
Fees £20 (£25)
Loc 15 miles W of Newcastle (A695)

Rothbury (1891)

Old Race Course, Rothbury, Morpeth NE65 7TR

Tel **(01669) 621271**
Mem 410
Sec WT Bathgate (01669) 620718
Holes 9 L 5560 yds SSS 67
Recs Am–64 S Twynholm
V'tors WD–U exc Tues pm WE–NA exc by arrangement
Fees D–£11 (D–£16)
Loc 15 miles N of Morpeth on A697. W side of Rothbury

Seahouses (1913)

Beadnell Road, Seahouses NE68 7XT

Tel **(01665) 720794**
Mem 600
Sec JA Stevens (01665) 720809
Holes 18 L 5462 yds SSS 67
Recs Am–64 K Johnston (1993)
V'tors U SOC
Fees £15 (£20)
Loc 14 miles N of Alnwick. 9 miles E of A1 on B1340

Slaley Hall G & CC (1988)

Slaley, Hexham NE47 0BY

Tel **(01434) 673350**
Fax **(01434) 673735**
Pro S Brown (Golf Dir)
Holes 18 L 7021 yds SSS 74
Recs Am–74 S Twynholme
Pro–70 P Mitchell
V'tors U H SOC
Fees £22.50 D–£35 (£25 D–£40)
Loc 16 miles W of Newcastle. 7 miles S of Corbridge, off A68
Mis Driving range

Stocksfield (1913)

New Ridley, Stocksfield NE43 7RE

Tel **(01661) 843041**
Mem 410 100(L) 70(J)
Sec W Martin
Pro S McKenna
Holes 18 L 5594 yds SSS 68
Recs Am–68 TGW Dinning
Pro–66 P Harrison
V'tors U SOC
Fees £15 (£20)
Loc 2 miles S of Stocksfield. 3 miles E of A68

Swarland Hall (1993)

Coast View, Swarland, Morpeth NE65 9JG

Tel **(01670) 787010**
Sec K Rutter
Pro D Fletcher
Holes 18 L 6628 yds SSS 72
V'tors WD–U SOC–WD
Fees £10 (£20)
Loc 8 miles S of Alnwick, W of A1

Tynedale (1908)

Public

Tyne Green, Hexham

Tel **(01434) 608154**
Sec J McDiarmid
Pro Mrs C Brown
Holes 9 L 5706 yds SSS 68
Recs Am–63
V'tors U exc Sun–booking necessary
Fees £10 (£12) (1993)
Loc S side of Hexham

Warkworth (1891)

The Links, Warkworth, Morpeth NE65 0SW

Tel **(01665) 711596**
Mem 400
Sec JW Anderson (01665) 575608
Holes 9 L 5817 yds SSS 68
Recs Am–65 B Nattrass
V'tors U SOC
Fees D–£12 (D–£20)
Loc 9 miles SE of Alnwick (A1068)
Arch Tom Morris

Wooler (1975)

Doddington, Wooler NE71 6EA

Mem 250
Sec JH Curry (01668) 81956
Holes 9 L 6353 yds SSS 70
Recs Am–72 K Fairbairn, C Renton, M Thompson (1992)

For list of abbreviations see page 435

V'tors U SOC
Fees D–£10 (D–£15) (1993)
Loc 3 miles N of Wooler on B6525

Nottinghamshire

Beeston Fields (1923)

Beeston, Nottingham NG9 3DD
Tel **(0115) 925 7062**
Mem 450 160(L) 52(J)
Sec J Lewis
Pro A Wardle (0115) 922 0872
Holes 18 L 6404 yds SSS 71
Recs Am–66 P Benson
V'tors U SOC
Fees £20 (£25)
Loc 4 miles W of Nottingham. M1 Junction 25

Bulwell Forest (1902)

Public
Hucknall Road, Bulwell, Nottingham NG6 9LQ
Tel **(0115) 977 0576**
Fax **(0115) 977 1229**
Mem 400
Sec D Stubbs (Hon)
Pro CD Hall (0115) 976 3172
Holes 18 L 5746 yds SSS 68
Recs Am–63 J Worthy
Pro–62 CD Hall
V'tors U
Fees £8 (£10)
Loc 4 miles N of Nottingham. M1 Junction 26, 3 miles

Chilwell Manor (1906)

Meadow Lane, Chilwell, Nottingham NG9 5AE
Tel **(0115) 925 8958**
Mem 700
Sec To be appointed
Pro P Wilson (0115) 925 8993
Holes 18 L 6379 yds SSS 69
18 L 5438 yds SSS 67
Recs Am–67 C Gray
Pro–66 B Waites
V'tors SOC–WD
Fees £18
Loc 4 miles W of Nottingham on A6005

College Pines (1993)

Worksop College Drive, Sparken Hill, Worksop S80 3AP
Tel **(01909) 501431**
Mem 550
Sec C Snell (Golf Dir)
Pro C Snell
Holes 18 L 6663 yds SSS 72
Recs Am–71 W Beeston (1994)
Pro–69 B Hunt (1994)
V'tors U–phone first SOC
Fees £12 (£18)
Loc 1 mile SE of Worksop on B6034, off Worksop Bypass
Mis Driving range
Arch David Snell

Cotgrave Place G & CC (1991)

Stragglethorpe NG12 3HB
Tel **(0115) 933 3344/933 5500**
Mem 400
Sec DE Roberts
Pro G Towne (0115) 933 4686
Holes 27 L 6560 yds SSS 71-72
V'tors U
Fees £15 (£25)
Loc 4 miles SE of Nottingham, off A52
Mis Driving range
Arch Small/Glasgow

Coxmoor (1913)

Coxmoor Road, Sutton-in-Ashfield NG17 5LF
Tel **(01623) 557359**
Fax **(01623) 559854**
Mem 650
Sec I McDonald
Pro D Ridley (01623) 559906
Holes 18 L 6501 yds SSS 72
Recs Am–67 M Nunn
Pro–65 B Waites
V'tors H exc Ladies Day–Tues WE–NA SOC
Fees D–£24
Loc 1½ miles S of Mansfield. 3 miles NE of M1 Junction 27 on A611

Edwalton (1982)

Public
Edwalton, Nottingham
Tel **(0115) 923 4775**
Sec EM Watts (Hon)
Pro J Staples
Holes 9 L 3336 yds SSS 36
9 hole Par 3 course
Recs Am–73 Pro–72
V'tors U
Fees £4. Par 3 course–£2.20
Loc 2 miles S of Nottingham (A606)
Mis Driving range

Kilton Forest (1978)

Public
Blyth Road, Worksop S81 0TL
Tel **(01909) 472488**
Sec G Lawman (Hon) (01909) 485994
Pro PW Foster (01909) 486563
Holes 18 L 6344 yds SSS 71
Recs Am–68 B Hurt (1993)
Pro–72 DJ Ridley (1988)
V'tors WD–U WE–booking necessary SOC
Fees £6.50 (£8.80)
Loc 1 mile NE of Worksop on B6045

Mansfield Woodhouse (1973)

Public
Mansfield Woodhouse NG19 9EU
Tel **(01623) 23521**
Sec T Mason
Pro L Highfield Jr
Holes 9 L 2411 yds SSS 65
Recs Am–67 S Fisher
Pro–L Highfield Jr
V'tors U
Fees £2
Loc 2 miles N of Mansfield (A60)

Mapperley (1913)

Central Avenue, Plains Road, Mapperley, Nottingham NG3 5RH
Tel **(0115) 926 5611**
Mem 650
Sec A Newton
Pro P Richmond (0115) 920 2227
Holes 18 L 6224 yds SSS 70
Recs Am–68 P Benson (1991)
Pro–69 D Ridley (1990)
V'tors U SOC
Fees £15.50 (£17.50)
Loc 3 miles NE of Nottingham, off B684

Newark (1901)

Kelwick, Coddington, Newark NG24 2QX
Tel **(01636) 626241**
Fax **(01636) 626282**
Mem 600
Sec AW Morgans (01636) 626282
Pro HA Bennett (01636) 626492
Holes 18 L 6421 yds SSS 71
Recs Am–67 AD Allen
Pro–68 C Hall
Ladies–73 M Clayton
V'tors H SOC
Fees £21 (£26)
Loc 4 miles E of Newark on A17

Nottingham City (1910)

Public
Lawton Drive, Bulwell, Nottingham NG6 8BL
Tel **(0115) 927 8021**
Mem 460
Sec WL Whyte (0115) 927 6916
Pro CR Jepson (0115) 927 2767
Holes 18 L 6218 yds SSS 70
Recs Am–65 D Weir (1994)
Pro–66 T Smart
V'tors WD–U WE–NA before noon SOC
Fees £8 (£10)
Loc 5 miles N of Nottingham. M1 Junction 26

Notts (1887)

Hollinwell, Kirby-in-Ashfield NG17 7QR
Tel **(01623) 752042/753225**
Fax **(01623) 753655**
Mem 500
Sec SFC Goldie (01623) 753225
Pro BJ Waites (01623) 753087
Holes 18 L 7030 yds SSS 74
Recs Am–66 AR Gelsthorpe
Pro–64 J Bland
V'tors WD–H WE/BH–M
Fees On application
Loc 4 miles S of Mansfield on A611. M1 Junction 27
Mis Driving range-green fees only
Arch Willie Park Jr

Oakmere Park (1974)

Oaks Lane, Oxton NG25 0RH

Tel **(0115) 965 3545**
Fax **(0115) 965 5628**
Mem 450
Sec J Wright (Dir)
Pro S Meade (0115) 965 5553
Holes 18 L 6617 yds SSS 72
9 L 3495 yds SSS 37
Recs Am–69 J Vaughan
Pro–65 J Mellor
V'tors WD–U WE/BH–arrange times with Mgr SOC
Fees 18 hole:£16 (£20)
9 hole:£6 (£8)
Loc 8 miles NE of Nottingham on A614
Mis Floodlit driving range
Arch F Pennink

Radcliffe-on-Trent (1909)

Dewberry Lane, Cropwell Road, Radcliffe-on-Trent NG12 2JH

Tel **(0115) 933 3000**
Fax **(0115) 933 2396**
Mem 670
Sec L Wake (0115) 933 3000
Pro R Ellis (0115) 933 2396
Holes 18 L 6381 yds Par 70 SSS 71
Recs Am–64 M Harris (1994)
Pro–67 P Hilton (1979)
Ladies–72 G Harris (1983)
V'tors H SOC–Wed only
Fees £21 (£26)
Loc 6 miles E of Nottingham, off A52
Arch Tom Williamson

Ramsdale Park Golf Centre (1992)

Pay and play
Oxton Road, Calverton NG14 6NU

Tel **(0115) 965 5600**
Fax **(0115) 965 4105**
Sec B Jenkinson (Mgr)
Pro R Macey
Holes 18 L 6546 yds SSS 71
18 hole Par 3 course
Recs Pro–69 G Orr (1993)
V'tors U SOC–WD
Fees 18 hole:£12 9 hole:£6.50
Loc 5 miles NE of Nottingham on B6386
Mis Floodlit driving range
Arch Hawtree

Retford (1921)

Brecks Road, Ordsall, Retford DN22 7UA

Tel **(01777) 703733**
Mem 700
Sec A Harrison (01777) 860682
Pro S Betteridge
Holes 18 L 6301 yds SSS 70
Recs Am–67 PJ Grout (1993)
V'tors WD–U WE–M SOC–WD
Fees £18 D–£22
Loc 2 miles SW of Retford, off A638 or A620. M1 Junction 30

Ruddington Grange (1988)

Wilford Road, Ruddington, Nottingham NG11 6NB

Tel **(0115) 984 6141**
Fax **(0115) 940 5165**
Mem 600
Sec DJT Johnson (Mgr), AR Dessaur
Pro R Daibell (0115) 921 1951
Holes 18 L 6490 yds SSS 72
Recs Am–71 DJT Johnson (1988)
Pro–68 C Hall (1990)
V'tors U H BH–U exc comp days SOC
Fees D–£15
Loc 3 miles S of Nottingham

Rushcliffe (1910)

Stocking Lane, East Leake, Loughborough LE12 5RL

Tel **(01509) 852959**
Mem 600
Sec DJ Barnes
Pro T Smart (01509) 852701
Holes 18 L 6090 yds SSS 69
V'tors SOC–WD
Fees D–£22
Loc 9 miles S of Nottingham. M1 Junction 24

Serlby Park (1905)

Serlby, Doncaster DN10 6BA

Tel **(01777) 818268**
Mem 250
Sec R Wilkinson (01302) 536336
Holes 9 L 5370 yds SSS 66
Recs Am–63 A Pugsley (1988)
Pro–65 M Bembridge (1965)
V'tors M
Loc 12 miles S of Doncaster, between A614 and A638

Sherwood Forest (1895)

Eakring Road, Mansfield NG18 3EW

Tel **(01623) 23327**
Fax **(01623) 26689**
Mem 648
Sec K Hall (01623) 26689
Pro K Hall (01623) 27403
Holes 18 L 6714 yds SSS 73
Recs Am–68 J Payne
Pro–68 C Gray, G Stafford
V'tors H SOC–WD
Fees On application
Loc 2 miles E of Mansfield (A617)
Arch Colt/Braid

Southwell (1993)

Southwell Racecourse, Rolleston, Newark NG25 0TS

Tel **(01636) 814481**
Mem 200
Sec R Stevenson
Pro R Stevenson
Holes 9 L 5500 yds SSS 66
Recs Am–70 A Cook
Pro–64 R Stevenson
V'tors U SOC
Fees £10 (£15)
Loc 6 miles W of Newark on A617. Course on racetrack
Arch Ron Muddle

Springwater (1990)

Pay and play
Moor Lane, Calverton, Nottingham NG14 6FZ

Tel **(0115) 965 2129**
Mem 287
Sec PJ Hallam
Pro M Lawrence (0115) 965 3634
Holes 9 L 3203 yds SSS 71
Recs Am–71 D Richardson (1993)
V'tors U SOC
Fees £11 (£11)
Loc Off A6097 between Lowdham and Oxton
Mis Floodlit driving range
Arch ADAS/McEvoy

Stanton-on-the-Wolds (1906)

Stanton Lane, Keyworth NG12 5BH

Tel **(0115) 937 2044**
Mem 500 167(L) 100(J)
Sec HG Gray FCA (0115) 937 2006
Pro N Hernon ((0115) 937 2390
Holes 18 L 6437 yds SSS 71
Recs Am–67 CA Banks, PJ Whitt
Pro–68 N Turley
V'tors WD–U exc comp days WE–M SOC
Fees D–£20 SOC–£25–£30
Loc 9 miles S of Nottingham

Trent Lock Golf Centre (1991)

Lock Lane, Sawley, Long Eaton NG10 3DD

Tel **(0115) 946 4398**
Fax **(0115) 946 1183**
Mem 425
Sec E McCausland (Golf Dir)
Pro M Taylor
Holes 18 hole course Par 72 SSS 70
V'tors U SOC
Fees £8.50
Loc S of Long Eaton. M1 Junction 25
Mis Driving range

Wollaton Park (1927)

Wollaton Park, Nottingham NG8 1BT

Tel **(0115) 978 7574**
Fax **(0115) 978 7574**
Mem 700
Sec OB Kirk
Pro J Lower (0115) 978 4834
Holes 18 L 6494 yds SSS 71
Recs Am–65 L White
Pro–64 L White
V'tors U SOC
Fees On application
Loc 2 miles SW of Nottingham
Arch T Williamson

Worksop (1914)
Windmill Lane, Worksop S80 2SQ
Tel **(01909) 472696**
Mem 500
Sec PG Jordan (01909) 477731
Pro JR King (01909) 477732
Holes 18 L 6651 yds SSS 72
Recs Am–70 D Bagshaw
Pro–69 A Carter
V'tors WD–U H (phone first) WE/BH–M SOC
Fees On application
Loc 1 mile SE of Worksop, off A6009 via by-pass (A57). M1 Junction 30, 9 miles

Oxfordshire

Aspect Park (1989)
Remenham Hill, Henley-on-Thames RG9 3EH
Tel **(01491) 578306**
Fax **(01491) 578306**
Mem 600
Sec T Winsland
Pro R Frost (01491) 577562
Holes 18 L 6369 yds Par 71
V'tors H WE–restricted SOC
Fees £18 (£20)
Loc 1 mile E of Henley. M40 Junction 4, 8 miles
Mis Driving range
Arch T Winsland

Badgemore Park (1972)
Henley-on-Thames RG9 4UR
Tel **(01491) 573667** (Clubhouse)
Fax **(01491) 576899**
Mem 850
Sec M Morley (Mgr) (01491) 572206
Pro J Dunn (01491) 574175
Holes 18 L 6112 yds SSS 69
Recs Am–67 SJ Mann
Pro–65 M Howell
V'tors WD–U WE–H SOC–WD
Fees £27
Loc 3/4 mile W of Henley on B290

Banbury (1994)
Aynho Road, Adderbury, Banbury OX17 3NT
Tel **(01295) 810419**
Fax **(01295) 810056**
Mem 70
Sec MA Reed (Prop)
AT Rathbone (Mgr)
Holes 18 L 6333 yds Par 71 SSS 70
Pro–72 G Wills
V'tors U
Fees £6 (£8)
Loc 6 miles S of Banbury on B4100. M40 Junction 10 or 11
Mis Further 9 holes under construction

Brailes (1992)
Sutton Lane, Brailes, Banbury OX15 5BB
Tel **(01608) 685336**
Mem 430
Sec RAS Malir
Pro M Bendall (01608) 685633
Holes 18 L 6270 yds SSS 70
V'tors WD–U WE/BH–M SOC–WD
Fees £15 (£21)
Loc 3 miles E of Shipston-on-Stour on B4035. M40 Junction 11, 10 miles
Arch BA Hull

Burford (1936)
Burford OX18 4JG
Tel **(01993) 822149**
Mem 680
Sec R Cane (01993) 822583
Pro N Allen (01993) 822344
Holes 18 L 6405 yds SSS 71
Recs Am–67 DE Giles
Pro–67 H Weetman
V'tors WD–H SOC
Fees On application
Loc 19 miles W of Oxford on A40

Carswell CC (1993)
Carswell, Faringdon SN7 8PU
Tel **(01367) 87422**
Mem 300
Sec G Lisi (Prop)
Pro J Nicholas
Holes 18 L 6133 yds Par 72
Recs Am–73 I Lewis (1994)
Pro–68 S Defoy (1993), J Nicholas, M Booth (1994)
V'tors U SOC
Fees £12 (£15)
Loc 12 miles W of Oxford on A420
Mis Floodlit driving range

Cherwell Edge (1980)
Chacombe, Banbury OX17 2EN
Tel **(01295) 711591**
Fax **(01295) 712404**
Mem 623
Sec RA Beare
Pro R Jefferies
Holes 18 L 5925 yds SSS 68
Recs Am–67 C Lowe (1993)
Ladies–76 J Lane (1990)
V'tors U SOC–WD
Fees £9.50 (£13)
Loc 3 miles E of Banbury on B4525
Mis Driving range

Chesterton (1973)
Chesterton, Bicester OX6 8TE
Tel **(01869) 241204**
Mem 750
Sec BT Carter
Pro JW Wilkshire (01869) 242023
Holes 18 L 6224 yds SSS 70
Recs Am–68 D Grant (1994)
Pro–68 B Lane (1983)
V'tors U SOC–WD
Fees £12 (£18)
Loc 2 miles SW of Bicester. M40 Junction 9

Chipping Norton (1890)
Southcombe, Chipping Norton OX7 5QH
Tel **(01608) 642383**
Mem 900
Sec AJB Norman
Pro R Gould (01608) 643356
Holes 18 L 6280 yds SSS 70
Recs Am–67 A Perrie, J Morewood, A Jones
Pro–69 M Nichols, M Parker (1990)
V'tors WD–U WE–M
Fees £15
Loc 1 mile E of Chipping Norton

Drayton Park (1992)
Pay and play
Steventon Road, Drayton, Abingdon OX14 2RR
Tel **(01235) 550607**
Fax **(01235) 525731**
Mem 600
Sec T Williams, Dinah Masey (Golf Dirs)
Pro T Williams, Dinah Masey
Holes 18 L 6000 yds SSS 67
Par 3 course
Recs Am–67 GA Johnson (1993)
V'tors U SOC
Fees £12 (£15)
Loc 5 miles S of Oxford on A34. M4 Junction 13
Mis Floodlit driving range
Arch Hawtree

Frilford Heath (1908)
Frilford Heath, Abingdon OX13 5NW
Tel **(01865) 390864**
Fax **(01865) 390823**
Mem 900 190(L)
Sec JW Kleynhans
Pro DC Craik (01865) 390887
Holes Red 18 L 6768 yds SSS 73
Green 18 L 6006 yds SSS 69
Blue 18 L 6726 yds SSS 73
Recs Red Am–71 L Jackson (1994)
Green Am–64 DP King (1994)
Blue Am–69 DP King (1994)
V'tors WD–I H WE/BH–M SOC
Fees D–£43 (D–£53)
Loc 3 miles W of Abingdon on A338
Arch Blue-Simon Gidman

Hadden Hill (1990)
Pay and play
Wallingford Road, Didcot OX11 9BJ
Tel **(01235) 510410**
Fax **(01235) 510410**
Mem 320 62(L)
Sec MV Morley

Pro D Halford, A Waters
Holes 18 L 6563 yds SSS 71
Recs Am–68 M Greenwood (1992)
V'tors WD–U SOC–WD
Fees £12 (£15)
Loc E of Didcot on A4130
Mis Driving range
Arch MV Morley

Henley (1908)

Harpsden, Henley-on-Thames
RG9 4HG
Tel **(01491) 573304**
Fax **(01491) 575742**
Mem 750
Sec AM Chaundy (01491) 575742
Pro M Howell (01491) 575710
Holes 18 L 6329 yds SSS 70
Recs Am–65 D Griffin (1989)
Pro–64 P Harrison (1989)
V'tors WD–H WE–M SOC
Fees D–£30
Loc 1 mile S of Henley (A4155)
Arch James Braid

Huntercombe (1901)

Nuffield, Henley-on-Thames
RG9 5SL
Tel **(01491) 641207**
Fax **(01491) 642060**
Mem 700
Sec Lt Col TJ Hutchison
Pro JB Draycott (01491) 641241
Holes 18 L 6261 yds SSS 70
Recs Am–64 MH Dixon
Pro–63 J Morris
V'tors H–by appointment only
SOC–WD
Fees D–£35
Loc 6 miles W of Henley on
A4130
Mis Foursomes and singles only
Arch Willie Park Jr

Lyneham (1992)

Lyneham, Chipping Norton
OX7 6QQ
Tel **(01993) 831841**
Fax **(01993) 831775**
Mem 700
Sec CJT Howkins
Pro M Stancer
Holes 18 L 6669 yds SSS 72
Pro–67 M Stancer,
P Simpson (1993)
V'tors U SOC
Fees £13 (£16)
Loc 4 miles W of Chipping
Norton, off A361
Mis Driving range
Arch D Carpenter

North Oxford (1907)

Banbury Road, Oxford OX2 8EZ
Tel **(01865) 54415**
Fax **(01865) 515921**
Mem 701
Sec GW Pullin (01865) 54924
Pro R Harris (01865) 53977
Holes 18 L 5805 yds SSS 67
Recs Am–64 S Donaghey
Pro–M Faulkner
V'tors WD–U WE–M
SOC–Wed–Fri
Fees On application
Loc 4 miles N of Oxford, off
A4260 to Kidlington

The Oxfordshire (1993)

Rycote Lane, Milton Common, Thame
OX9 2PU
Tel **(01844) 278300**
Fax **(01844) 278003**
Mem 650
Sec A McMillan
Pro I Mosey
Holes 18 L 7187 yds SSS 74
V'tors M I
Fees On application
Loc 1½ miles W of Thame on
A329. M40 Junction 7,
2 miles
Mis Driving range
Arch Rees Jones

RAF Benson (1975)

Royal Air Force, Benson
Tel **(01491) 37766**
Mem 200
Sec Flt Lt JW Williams RAF
(01491) 35376
Holes 9 L 4395 yds SSS 61
Recs Am–63 R Mills (1991)
V'tors M
Loc 3½ miles NE of Wallingford

Rye Hill

Barn Farm, Milcombe, Banbury
OX15 4RU
Tel **(01295) 721818**
Fax **(01295) 267779**
Pro R Davies
Holes 18 L 6569 yds Par 71
V'tors WD–U WE–Booking
necessary
Fees £8 (£10)
Loc 5 miles SW of Banbury, off
A361. M40 Junction 11
Mis Academy holes

Southfield (1875)

Hill Top Road, Oxford OX4 1PF
Tel **(01865) 242158**
Mem 700
Sec AG Hopcraft
Pro A Rees (01865) 244258
Holes 18 L 6230 yds SSS 70
Recs Am–66 CM Barrett,
GL Morley
Pro–61 A Rees
V'tors WD–U WE/BH–M H SOC
Fees £24
Loc 2 miles E of Oxford

Tadmarton Heath (1922)

Wigginton, Banbury OX15 5HL
Tel **(01608) 737278**
Mem 600
Sec RE Wackrill
Pro L Bond (01608) 730047
Holes 18 L 5917 yds SSS 69
Recs Am–65 RJ Stroud
Pro–63 G Smith
V'tors WD–H by appointment
WE–M SOC–WD
Fees £26 After 2pm–£18
Loc 5 miles SW of Banbury, off
B4035
Arch Maj CJ Hutchison

Waterstock (1994)

Pay and play
Thame Road, Waterstock, Oxford
OX33 1HT
Tel **(01844) 338093**
Fax **(01844) 338036**
Mem 470
Sec AJ Wyatt
Pro A Wyatt
Holes 18 L 6482 yds Par 72
Recs Am–69 M Hornsey
V'tors U
Fees £12 (£16)
Loc E of Oxford on A418.
M40 Junction 8
Mis Floodlit driving range
Arch Donald Steel

Witney Golf Centre (1994)

Pay and play
Downs Road, Witney OX8 5SY
Tel **(01993) 779000**
Fax **(01993) 778866**
Mem 400
Sec M Bennett (Mgr)
Pro P Sowerby
Holes 18 L 6460 yds SSS 71
Recs Pro–72 S Richardson (1994)
V'tors U
Fees £12 (£15)
Loc 2 miles W of Witney on
B4047
Mis Floodlit driving range
Arch Simon Gidman

Shropshire

Arscott (1992)

Arscott, Pontesbury, Shrewsbury
SY5 0XP
Tel **(01743) 860114**
Mem 550
Sec B Harper
(01743) 262342
Pro G Sawyer
(01743) 860881
Holes 18 L 6112 yds SSS 69
Recs Am–72 R Edwards (1993)
V'tors WD–U WE/BH–M before
noon SOC
Fees £15.50 (£20.50)
Loc 5 miles SW of Shrewsbury, off
A488
Arch Martin Hamer

For list of abbreviations see page 435

Bridgnorth (1889)

Stanley Lane, Bridgnorth WV16 4SF

Tel **(01746) 763315**
Mem 690
Sec KD Cole (01746) 764179
Pro P Hinton (01746) 762045
Holes 18 L 6638 yds SSS 72
Recs Am–67 C Banks (1985)
Pro–66 P Hinton (1989)
V'tors U SOC
Fees £18 (£25)
Loc 1 mile N of Bridgnorth

Chesterton Valley

Chesterton, Worfield, Bridgnorth

Tel **(01476) 783682**
Mem 250
Sec P Hinton
Pro P Hinton
Holes 9 L 3392 yds Par 74 SSS 72
V'tors U–phone first
Fees £6 (£6)
Loc 10 miles W of Wolverhampton on B4176

Church Stretton (1898)

Trevor Hill, Church Stretton SY6 6JH

Tel **(01694) 722281**
Mem 470
Sec R Broughton (01694) 722633
Holes 18 L 5008 yds SSS 66
Recs Am–62 NJ Evans (1993)
V'tors H WE–NA before 10.30am SOC
Fees £12 (£18)
Loc ½ mile W of Church Stretton, off A49
Arch James Braid

Cleobury Mortimer (1993)

Wyre Common, Cleobury Mortimer DY14 8HQ

Tel **(01299) 271320** (Clubhouse)
Fax **(01299) 271112**
Mem 350
Sec G Pain (01299) 271112
Pro G Farr (01299) 271112
Holes 9 L 6256 yds SSS 70
Recs Am–69 F Lee (1994)
V'tors WD–U H WE–M H SOC
Fees 18 holes–£7.50 (£10)
Loc 10 miles SW of Kidderminster on A4117
Mis Driving range. Extension to 18 holes Sept 1995

Hawkstone Park (1921)

Weston-under-Redcastle, Shrewsbury SY4 5UY

Tel **(01939) 200611**
Fax **(01939) 200311**
Mem 615
Sec RE Thomas
Pro K Williams
Holes Hawkstone 18 L 6465 yds SSS 71; Windmill 18 L 6655 yds SSS 72
Recs Am–67 AWB Lyle, MA Smith
Pro–65 A Jacklin
Ladies–71 S Parker
V'tors U after 10.35am SOC–H
Fees £25 (£31)
Loc 7 miles S of Whitchurch. 14 miles N of Shrewsbury on A49

Hill Valley G & CC (1975)

Terrick Road, Whitchurch SY13 4JZ

Tel **(01948) 663584**
Fax **(01948) 665927**
Mem 600
Sec RB Walker
Pro AR Minshall (01948) 663032
Holes Main 18 L 6517 yds SSS 71
No 2 18 L 5285 yds SSS 66
Recs Am–67 M Welch
Pro–64 W Milne
V'tors U
Fees Main–£19 (£25)
No 2–£6 (£9)
Loc 1 mile N of Whitchurch, off A41/A49 Bypass
Arch Alliss/Thomas

Lilleshall Hall (1937)

Abbey Road, Lilleshall, Newport TF10 9AS

Tel **(01952) 603840**
Mem 600
Sec BG Weaver (01952) 604776
Pro NW Bramall (01952) 604104
Holes 18 L 5906 yds SSS 68
Recs Am–65 P Baker
Pro–70 J Anderson
Ladies–76 S Hall
V'tors WD–U WE–M SOC
Fees £18 (BH+day after–£30)
Loc 3 miles S of Newport between Lilleshall and Sheriffhales. M54 Junction 4
Arch HS Colt

Llanymynech (1933)

Pant, Oswestry SY10 8LB

Tel **(01691) 830542**
Mem 760
Sec DR Thomas (01691) 830983
Pro A Griffiths (01691) 830879
Holes 18 L 6114 yds Par 70 SSS 69
Recs Am–66 M Evans (1984)
Pro–65 I Woosnam (1983)
V'tors U before 4.30pm –M after 4.30pm SOC–WD
Fees £14 (£20)
Loc 5 miles S of Oswestry on A483

Ludlow (1889)

Bromfield, Ludlow SY8 2BT

Tel **(01584) 77285**
Mem 550
Sec CR Vane Percy (Admin)
WR Spanner
Pro R Price (01584) 77366
Holes 18 L 6240 yds SSS 70
Recs Am–67 T Clare
Pro–65 PA Brookes
V'tors H SOC–WD
Fees D–£18 (D–£24)
Loc A49, 2 miles N of Ludlow

Market Drayton (1925)

Sutton, Market Drayton TF9 1LX

Tel **(01630) 652266**
Fax **(01630) 657496**
Mem 500
Sec PC Price (01630) 657496
Pro R Clewes
Holes 18 L 6225 yds SSS 70
Recs Am–70 S Thomas (1991)
V'tors WD–U WE–NA
Fees £20
Loc 1 mile S of Market Drayton

Meole Brace (1976)

Public

Meole Brace, Shrewsbury SY2 6QQ

Tel **(01743) 364050**
Fax **(01743) 364050**
Pro I Doran
Holes 9 L 2915 yds SSS 68
Recs Am–68 J Mansell
Pro–68 R Cockcroft
V'tors WD–U WE–book in advance
Fees On application
Loc 1 mile S of Shrewsbury. Junction A5/A49

Mile End (1992)

Mile End, Oswestry SY11 4JE

Tel **(01691) 670580**
Sec R Thompson
Pro S Carpenter (01691) 671246
Holes 9 L 6130 yds SSS 69
V'tors H SOC–WD
Fees £10 D–£14 (£14 D–£18)
Loc 1 mile from Oswestry, off A5
Mis Driving range. Extension to 18 holes mid 1995
Arch Price/Gough

Oswestry (1930)

Aston Park, Oswestry SY11 4JJ

Tel **(01691) 610221**
Mem 800
Sec A Jennings (01691) 610535
Pro D Skelton (01691) 610448
Holes 18 L 6038 yds SSS 69
Recs Am–62 AL Strange
Pro–68 JW Walker
V'tors M or H SOC–WD
Fees £18 (£25)
Loc 3 miles E of Oswestry on A5
Arch James Braid

Severn Meadows (1989)

Pay and play

Highley, Bridgenorth WV16 6HZ

Tel **(01746) 862212**
Mem 190
Sec C Harrison
Pro None
Holes 9 L 2520 yds SSS 65
V'tors WD–U WE–booking required
Fees £8 (£12)
Loc 8 miles S of Bridgenorth on B4555

Shifnal (1929)
Decker Hill, Shifnal TF11 8QL
Tel **(01952) 460467/460330**
Mem 500
Sec PW Holden (01952) 460330
Pro J Flanaghan (01952) 460457
Holes 18 L 6422 yds SSS 71
Recs Am–65 C Watts
Pro–64 P Baker
V'tors WD–phone first WE/BH–M
Fees On application
Loc 1 mile NE of Shifnal. M54 Junction 4, 2 miles

Shrewsbury (1891)
Condover, Shrewsbury SY5 7BL
Tel **(01743) 872976**
Fax **(01743) 874647**
Mem 529 184(L) 70(J)
Sec Mrs SM Kenny (01743) 872977
Pro P Seal (01743) 873751
Holes 18 L 6212 yds SSS 70
Recs Am–60 JR Burn
V'tors H SOC
Fees £15 (£20)
Loc 4 miles S of Shrewsbury

The Shropshire (1992)
Pay and play
Muxton Grange, Muxton, Telford TF2 8PQ
Tel **(01952) 677866**
Fax **(01952) 677844**
Mem 500
Pro K Craggs
Holes 27 holes:
9 L 3286 yds; 9 L 3303 yds;
9 L 3334 yds SSS 70-72
V'tors U SOC
Fees £10 (£17) (1994)
Loc 4 miles NW of Telford (B5060). M54 Junction 4
Mis Floodlit driving range. Pitch & putt course
Arch Martin Hawtree

Telford Hotel G & CC (1981)
Great Hay, Sutton Hill, Telford TF7 4DT
Tel **(01952) 585642**
Fax **(01952) 586602**
Mem 500
Sec DA Paterson (Ext 274)
Pro G Farr (01952) 586052
Holes 18 L 6766 yds SSS 72
9 hole Par 3 course
Recs Am–66 C Bufton (1986)
Pro–62 D Thorpe (1983)
V'tors H SOC
Fees £25 (£30)
Loc 4 miles SE of Telford, off A442
Mis Driving range
Arch John Harris

Worfield (1991)
Worfield, Bridgnorth WV15 5HE
Tel **(01746) 716541**
Mem 350
Sec W Weaver (Gen Mgr) (01746) 716372
Pro S Russell
Holes 18 L 6801 yds SSS 73
Recs Am–73 M Phillips (1993)
Pro–71 D Prosser (1994)
V'tors U SOC
Fees £15 (£20)
Loc 7 miles W of Wolverhampton on A454
Arch Gough/Williams

Wrekin (1905)
Wellington, Telford TF6 5BX
Tel **(01952) 244032**
Mem 400 100(L) 90(J)
Sec S Leys
Pro K Housden (01952) 223101
Holes 18 L 5657 yds SSS 67
Recs Am–64 S Price, AJ Ford (1993), A Stephenson (1994)
Pro–67 C Holmes
V'tors WD–U before 5pm –M after 5pm SOC
Fees £18 (£25)
Loc Wellington, off B5061

Somerset

Brean (1973)
Coast Road, Brean, Burnham-on-Sea TA8 2RT
Tel **(01278) 751595**
Fax **(01278) 751595**
Mem 400
Sec WS Martin (Hon)
Pro Sue Spencer (01278) 751570
Holes 18 L 5714 yds SSS 68
Recs Am–67 C Clarke (1987)
V'tors WD–U H WE–pm only SOC–WD
Fees On application
Loc 4 miles N of Burnham-on-Sea. M5 Junction 22, 6 miles

Burnham & Berrow (1890)
St Christopher's Way, Burnham-on-Sea TA8 2PE
Tel **(01278) 783137**
Mem 800
Sec Mrs EL Sloman (01278) 785760
Pro M Crowther-Smith (01278) 784545
Holes 18 L 6668 yds SSS 73
9 L 6332 yds SSS 72
Recs Medal Am–68 SJ Martin
C'ship Am–66 DG Haines (1993)
V'tors I SOC
Fees £32 (£44). 9 hole: £8
Loc 1 mile N of Burnham-on-Sea on B3140

Cannington (1993)
Pay and play
Cannington College, Bridgwater TA5 2LS
Tel **(01278) 652394**
Mem 150
Pro R Macrow
Holes 9 L 2929 yds SSS 68
V'tors H
Fees £10 (£12)
Loc 4 miles NW of Bridgwater on A39. M5 Junction 24
Arch Hawtree

Enmore Park (1906)
Enmore, Bridgwater TA5 2AN
Tel **(01278) 671244 (Members)**
Fax **(01278) 671481**
Mem 780
Sec D Weston (01278) 671481
Pro N Wixon (01278) 671519
Holes 18 L 6406 yds SSS 71
Recs Am–66 T Lawrence (1990), D Dixon Jr (1994)
Pro–64 R Davis (1994)
Ladies–70 K Nicholls (1989)
V'tors U SOC–WD
Fees £18 (£25)
Loc 3 miles W of Bridgwater, off Durleigh road. M5 Junctions 23/24
Arch Hawtree

Frome Golf Centre
Pay and play
Critchill Manor, Frome BA11 4LJ
Tel **(01373) 453410**
Sec Mrs S Austin
Pro A Wright
Holes 18 hole course Par 62 SSS 60
Pro–53 A Wright
V'tors U
Fees £7.50 (£8.50)
Loc 12 miles S of Bath
Mis Driving range

Isle of Wedmore (1992)
Lineage, Lascots Hill, Wedmore BS28 4QT
Tel **(01934) 712452**
Mem 500
Sec AC Edwards
Pro G Coombe
Holes 18 L 5850 yds SSS 68
V'tors U SOC–WD
Fees £12 (£15)
Loc 3/4 mile N of Wedmore. M5 Junction 22
Arch Terry Murray

Kingweston (1983)
(Sec) Mead Run, Compton Street, Compton Dundon, Somerton TA11 6PP
Tel **(01458) 43921**
Mem 200
Sec JG Willetts
Holes 9 L 4516 yds SSS 62
V'tors M exc Wed & Sat 2–5pm–NA
Fees NA
Loc 1 mile SE of Butleigh. 2 miles SE of Glastonbury

Long Sutton (1991)
Pay and play
Long Load, Langport TA10 9JU
Tel **(01458) 241017**
Mem 500
Sec GC Bennett

For list of abbreviations see page 435

Pro M Blackwell
Holes 18 L 6367 yds SSS 71
Recs Am–70 B Parker
V'tors WD–U WE–booking required SOC
Fees £12 (£16)
Loc 3 miles E of Langport
Mis Driving range
Arch Patrick Dawson

Mendip (1908)
Gurney Slade, Bath BA3 4UT
Tel **(01749) 840570**
Fax **(01749) 841439**
Mem 700
Sec Mrs JP Howe
Pro RF Lee (01749) 840793
Holes 18 L 6033 yds SSS 70
Recs Am–65 M Stephens (1992)
Pro–64 N Blenkarne (1987)
V'tors WD–U WE–H SOC–WD
Fees £20 (£30)
Loc 3 miles N of Shepton Mallet (A37)

Minehead & West Somerset (1882)
The Warren, Warren Road, Minehead TA24 5SJ
Tel **(01643) 702057**
Fax **(01643) 702057**
Mem 604
Sec LS Harper
Pro I Read (01643) 704378
Holes 18 L 6228 yds SSS 71
Recs Am–66 M Luckett
Pro–66 BJ Hunt
V'tors U after 9.15am SOC
Fees £19.50 (£23) W–£70
Loc E end of sea front

Oake Manor (1993)
Pay and play
Oake, Taunton TA4 1BA
Tel **(01823) 461993**
Fax **(01823) 461995**
Sec R Gardner (Mgr)
Pro R Gardner
Holes 18 L 6109 yds Par 70 SSS 69
V'tors U (phone first) SOC
Fees £12 (£15)
Loc 4 miles W of Taunton, off B3227. M5 Junctions 25/26
Mis Driving range
Arch Adrian Stiff

Taunton & Pickeridge (1892)
Corfe, Taunton TA3 7BY
Tel **(01823) 421240**
Fax **(01823) 421742**
Mem 630
Sec GW Sayers (01823) 421537
Pro G Milne (01823) 421790
Holes 18 L 5927 yds SSS 68
Recs Am–63 SN Richards (1992)
Pro–61 M Plummer (1994)
V'tors H SOC
Fees On application
Loc 5 miles S of Taunton on B3170

Taunton Vale (1992)
Creech Heathfield, Taunton TA3 5EY
Tel **(01823) 412220**
Fax **(01823) 413583**
Mem 640
Sec Mrs JA Thomas
Pro M Keitch (01823) 412880
Holes 18 L 6072 yds SSS 69
9 L 2004 yds SSS 60
Recs Am–70 D Land (1992)
Pro–66 J Palmer (1994)
V'tors U SOC
Fees 18 hole:£14 (£17.50)
9 hole:£7 (£8.75)
Loc 3 miles N of Taunton, off A361. M5 Junctions 24/25
Mis Floodlit driving range
Arch John Pyne

Vivary Park (1928)
Public
Taunton
Tel **(01823) 289274 (Clubhouse)**
Mem 500
Sec G Potter
Pro J Wright (01823) 333875
Holes 18 L 4620 yds SSS 63
V'tors U SOC–WD
Fees £7.50
Loc Centre of Taunton
Arch Herbert Fowler

Wells (1893)
East Horrington Road, Wells BA5 3DS
Tel **(01749) 672868**
Mem 800
Sec GE Ellis (Sec/Mgr)
(01749) 675005
Pro A Bishop (01749) 679059
Holes 18 L 6015 yds SSS 69
Recs Am–66 M Stevens (1993)
V'tors WD–U WE–H SOC–WD
Fees £16 (£20) Mon–Fri £55
Loc 1½ miles E of Wells, off Radstock road

Wheathill (1993)
Pay and play
Wheathill, Somerton TA11 7HG
Tel **(01963) 240667**
Fax **(01963) 240230**
Mem 200
Sec A Lyddon (Sec/Mgr)
Pro A England
Holes 18 L 5362 yds SSS 66
V'tors U SOC
Fees £9 (£11)
Loc 3 miles W of Castle Cary on B3153

Windwhistle G & CC (1932)
Cricket St Thomas, Chard TA20 4DG
Tel **(01460) 30231**
Fax **(01460) 30055**
Mem 550
Sec IN Dodd
Pro I Yard
Holes 18 L 6500 yds SSS 71
Recs Am–69
V'tors U–phone first SOC
Fees On application
Loc Windwhistle, 3 miles E of Chard on A30, opp Wildlife Park. M5 Junction 25, 12 miles
Arch JH Taylor/Fisher

Yeovil (1919)
Sherborne Road, Yeovil BA21 5BW
Tel **(01935) 75949 (Clubhouse)**
Fax **(01935) 411283**
Mem 685 165(L) 70(J)
Sec J Riley (01935) 22965
Pro G Kite (01935) 73763
Holes 18 L 6144 yds SSS 70
9 L 4876 yds SSS 65
Recs Am–64 J Pounder (1991)
Pro–65 G Laing (1987), R Troake (1989)
S Little, G Hampshire (1991)
V'tors WD–U H WE/BH–H (WD/WE–phone Pro) SOC
Fees 18 hole:£20 (£25)
9 hole:£12 (£15)
Loc 1 mile from Yeovil on A30 to Sherborne
Arch Fowler/Alison

Staffordshire

Alsager G & CC (1977)
Audley Road, Alsager, Stoke-on-Trent ST7 2UR
Tel **(01270) 875700**
Fax **(01270) 882207**
Mem 640
Sec G Williams
Pro P Preston (01270) 877432
Holes 18 L 6193 yds SSS 70
Recs Am–68 K Statham (1991)
V'tors WD–U before 5pm –M after 5pm WE/BH–M SOC
Fees £21
Loc 5 miles W of Crewe. M6 Junction 16

Barlaston (1987)
Meaford Road, Stone ST15 8UX
Tel **(01782) 372795**
Mem 600
Sec MJ Degg (01782) 372867
Pro I Rogers
Holes 18 L 5800 yds SSS 68
Recs Am–68 T Newton (1991)
V'tors WD–U WE–NA before 10am
Fees On application
Loc ½ mile S of Barlaston

Beau Desert (1921)
Hazel Slade, Cannock WS12 5PJ
Tel **(01543) 422626/422773**
Mem 500
Sec AJR Fairfield (01543) 422626
Pro B Stevens (01543) 422492
Holes 18 L 6279 yds SSS 71
Recs Am–67 P Broadhurst (1986)
Pro–64 T Minshall
V'tors WD–U WE–phone in advance BH–NA SOC
Fees £30
Loc 4 miles NE of Cannock, off A460

For list of abbreviations see page 435

Branston G & CC (1975)

Burton Road, Branston, Burton-on-Trent DE14 3DP

Tel **(01283) 543207**
Fax **(01283) 566984**
Mem 800
Sec DP Norris
Pro N Hirst
Holes 18 L 6541 yds SSS 71
Recs Am–69 T Bailey (1987)
Pro–67 P Kent
V'tors WD–U WE–M before noon SOC
Fees £19 (£23)
Loc ½ mile S of Burton (A38)
Mis Driving range

Brocton Hall (1894)

Brocton, Stafford ST17 0TH

Tel **(01785) 662627**
Mem 500
Sec WR Lanyon (01785) 661901
Pro R Johnson (01785) 661485
Holes 18 L 6095 yds SSS 69
Recs Am–67 WB Taylor
V'tors I H SOC
Fees £25 (£30)
Loc 4 miles SE of Stafford, off A34
Arch Harry Vardon

Burslem (1907)

Wood Farm, High Lane, Stoke-on-Trent ST6 7JT

Tel **(01782) 837006**
Mem 300
Sec F Askey (01782) 835141
Holes 9 L 5354 yds SSS 66
Recs Am–64 M Keeling (1988)
Pro–66 T Williamson
V'tors WD–U WE–NA
Fees £15
Loc Burslem 2 miles

Cannock Park (1993)

Public
Stafford Road, Cannock WS11 2AL

Tel **(01543) 578850**
Fax **(01543) 578850**
Sec EG Jones
Pro D Dunk
Holes 18 L 5048 yds SSS 65
V'tors U SOC–WD
Fees £6 (£7.50)
Loc ½ mile N of Cannock on A34. M6 Junction 11, 2 miles
Arch John Mainland

Craythorne (1972)

Craythorne Road, Stretton, Burton-on-Trent DE13 0AZ

Tel **(01283) 564329**
Fax **(01283) 511908**
Mem 500
Sec AA Wright (Man Dir)
Pro S Hadfield (05283) 533745
Holes 18 L 5255 yds Par 68 SSS 67
V'tors WD–U SOC
Fees £13 (£17)
Loc Stretton, 1½ miles N of Burton. A38/A5121 Junction
Mis Floodlit driving range. Pitch & putt course

Drayton Park (1897)

Drayton Park, Tamworth B78 3TN

Tel **(01827) 251139**
Fax **(01827) 284035**
Mem 450
Sec AO Rammell JP
Pro MW Passmore (01827) 251478
Holes 18 L 6414 yds SSS 71
Recs Am–62 M McGuire (1993)
Pro–65 DJ Russell (1987)
V'tors WD–H WE/BH–NA SOC–Tues & Thurs
Fees D–£27
Loc 2 miles S of Tamworth (A4091)
Arch James Braid

Goldenhill (1983)

Public
Mobberley Road, Goldenhill, Stoke-on-Trent ST6 5SS

Tel **(01782) 784715**
Fax **(01782) 775940**
Mem 600
Sec P Jones
Pro A Clingan
Holes 18 L 5957 yds SSS 68
V'tors U SOC–book with Pro
Fees £6 (£7)
Loc Between Tunstall and Kidsgrove, off A50

Greenway Hall (1908)

Stockton Brook, Stoke-on-Trent ST9 9LI

Tel **(01782) 503158**
Mem 450
Sec EH Jones (Mgr)
Holes 18 L 5676 yds SSS 67
Recs Am–65 A Bailey, A Dathan
V'tors WD–U SOC
Fees £14
Loc 5 miles N of Stoke, off A53

Ingestre Park (1977)

Ingestre, Stafford ST18 0RE

Tel **(01889) 270061**
Mem 740
Sec DD Humphries (Mgr) (01889) 270845
Pro D Scullion (01889) 270304
Holes 18 L 6334 yds SSS 70
Recs Am–67 D Hughes (1990)
Pro–68 D Scullion (1982)
Ladies–73 K Edwards (1994)
V'tors WD–H before 3.30pm WE/BH–M SOC–WD exc Wed
Fees £20 D–£25
Loc 6 miles E of Stafford, off Tixall Road. M6 Junctions 13/14
Arch Hawtree

Izaak Walton

Cold Norton, Stone ST15 0NS

Tel **(01785) 760900**
Mem 250
Sec To be appointed
Pro J Brown
Holes 18 L 6281 yds SSS 72
Recs Am–73 D Evans (1994)
V'tors U H SOC–WD
Fees £10 (£15)
Loc 7 miles NW of Stafford on B2056. M6 Junction 14

Lakeside (1969)

Rugeley Power Station, Rugeley WS15 1PR

Tel **(01889) 575667**
Fax **(01889) 576412**
Mem 450
Sec EG Jones
Holes 18 L 5534 yds SSS 68
Recs Am–69 D Glenn (1990)
V'tors M
Loc 2 miles SE of Rugeley on A513

Leek (1892)

Big Birchall, Leek ST13 5RE

Tel **(01538) 385889**
Mem 500 100(L) 45(J)
Sec F Cutts (01538) 384779
Pro P Stubbs (01538) 384767
Holes 18 L 6240 yds SSS 70
Recs Am–63 D Evans
Pro–65 P Baker
V'tors U H before 3pm –M after 3pm SOC–Wed only
Fees £24 (£30)
Loc ½ mile S of Leek on A520

Manor (Kingstone) (1991)

Leese Hill, Kingstone, Uttoxeter ST14 8QT

Tel **(01889) 563234**
Mem 280
Sec A Campbell
Holes 9 hole course
V'tors U
Fees £10 (£15)
Loc 4 miles W of Uttoxeter
Mis Driving range. Extension to 18 holes 1995
Arch E Anderson

Newcastle Municipal (1973)

Public
Keele Road, Newcastle-under-Lyme ST5 5AB

Tel **(01782) 627596**
Pro GA Bytheway
Holes 18 L 5822 metres SSS 70
Recs Am–70 P Rowe
Pro–68 P Rowe
V'tors U
Fees £6.50 (£8.40)
Loc 2 miles W of Newcastle on A525, opposite University. M6 Junction 15
Mis Driving range

For list of abbreviations see page 435

Newcastle-under-Lyme (1908)

Whitmore Road, Newcastle-under-Lyme ST5 2QB

Tel **(01782) 616583**
Fax **(01782) 617006**
Mem 575
Sec KP Geddes (Sec/Mgr) (01782) 617006
Pro P Symonds (01782) 618526
Holes 18 L 6450 yds SSS 71
Recs Am–64 MC Keates (1989) Pro–68 A Pauly (1988)
V'tors WD–U H WE/BH–M SOC
Fees On application
Loc 2 miles SW of Newcastle-under-Lyme on A53

Onneley (1968)

Onneley, Crewe, Cheshire CW3 5QF

Tel **(01782) 750577**
Mem 410
Sec D Whittick (01630) 647022
Holes 9 L 5584 yds SSS 67
Recs Am–67 D Davenport
V'tors WD–U Sat/BH–M Sun–NA SOC–Tues–Thurs
Fees £15
Loc 8 miles W of Newcastle, off A51

Parkhall (1989)

Public
Hulme Road, Weston Coyney, Stoke-on-Trent ST3 5BH

Tel **(01782) 599584**
Sec N Worrall (Mgr) (01831) 456409
Pro A Clingan
Holes 18 L 2335 yds Par 54
Recs Am–53 N Worrall (1991)
V'tors WE–booking necessary SOC
Fees £4 (£4.50)
Loc 3 miles E of Stoke. Longton 1 mile

Seedy Mill (1991)

Elmhurst, Lichfield WS13 3HE

Tel **(01543) 417333**
Fax **(01543) 418098**
Mem 1100
Sec S Lloyd (Gen Mgr)
Pro A Bolton
Holes 18 L 6247 yds SSS 70 9 hole Par 3 course
V'tors U H SOC
Fees On application
Loc 2 miles N of Lichfield on A515
Mis Floodlit driving range
Arch Hawtree

St Thomas's Priory (1995)

Armitage Lane, Armitage, Lichfield WS15 1ED

Tel **(01543) 491116**
Fax **(01543) 492244**
Mem 500
Sec J Bissell
Pro B Rimmer
Holes 18 L 6637 yds SSS 72
V'tors M
Loc 1 mile SE of Rugeley on A513, opp Ash Tree Inn
Mis Course open June 1995
Arch Paul Mulholland

Stafford Castle (1907)

Newport Road, Stafford ST16 1BP

Tel **(01785) 223821**
Mem 400
Sec DH Fellowes
Holes 9 L 6462 yds SSS 71
Recs Am–68 J Campion (1992)
V'tors WD–U WE–after 1pm
Fees £14 (£18)
Loc 1/2 mile W of Stafford

Stone (1896)

Filleybrooks, Stone ST15 0NB

Tel **(01785) 813103**
Mem 317
Sec MG Pharaoh (01889) 508224
Holes 9 L 6299 yds Par 71 SSS 70
Recs Am–68 A Hurst (1991)
V'tors WD–U WE/BH–M SOC–WD
Fees £15
Loc 1/2 mile W of Stone on A34

Tamworth (1978)

Public
Eagle Drive, Amington, Tamworth B77 4EG

Tel **(01827) 53850**
Sec BN Jones (01827) 53858
Pro BN Jones
Holes 18 L 6695 yds SSS 72
Recs Am–67 CJ Christison Pro–65 BN Jones
V'tors U SOC–WD
Fees On application
Loc 2 1/2 miles E of Tamworth on B5000. M42, 3 miles

Trentham (1894)

14 Barlaston Old Road, Trentham, Stoke-on-Trent ST4 8HB

Tel **(01782) 642347**
Mem 680
Sec RB Irving (01782) 658109
Pro M Budz (01782) 657309
Holes 18 L 6644 yds SSS 72
Recs Am–66 DJ Boughey (1987) Pro–68 D Gilford (1991)
V'tors WD–U H WE/BH–M (or enquire Sec) SOC–WD
Fees £30
Loc 3 miles S of Newcastle, off A34. M6 Junction 15

Trentham Park (1936)

Trentham Park, Stoke-on-Trent ST4 8AE

Tel **(01782) 642245**
Mem 500 100(L) 50(J)
Sec RN Portas (01782) 658800
Pro J McLeod (01782) 642125
Holes 18 L 6403 yds SSS 71
Recs Am–67 S Clarke Pro–68 D Gilford, R Rafferty
V'tors H SOC–Wed & Fri
Fees £22.50 (£30)
Loc 4 miles S of Newcastle on A34. M6 Junction 15, 1 mile

Uttoxeter (1970)

Wood Lane, Uttoxeter ST14 8JR

Tel **(01889) 565108**
Mem 780
Sec Mrs G Davies (01889) 566552
Pro J Pearsall (01889) 564884
Holes 18 L 5468 yds SSS 68
Recs Am–64 B Belcher (1992)
V'tors WD–U WE–by arrangement SOC
Fees £13 D–£20 (£17)
Loc Uttoxeter racecourse 1/2 mile

Westwood (1923)

Newcastle Road, Wallbridge, Leek ST13 7AA

Tel **(01538) 398385**
Mem 550
Sec J Mitchell (Admin Asst)
Pro C Smith
Holes 18 L 6156 yds SSS 69
Recs Am–68 M Ball
V'tors WD–U Sat–M BH–H SOC–Mon & Tues
Fees WD–£18
Loc W boundary of Leek on A53

Whiston Hall (1971)

Whiston, Cheadle ST10 2HZ

Tel **(01538) 266260, (01850) 903815**
Fax **(01538) 383600**
Mem 400
Sec HL Wainscott (Mgr)
Holes 18 L 5742 yds SSS 69
V'tors U SOC
Fees £10 (£14)
Loc 8 miles NE of Stoke-on-Trent on A52, nr Alton Towers

Whittington Heath (1886)

Tamworth Road, Lichfield WS14 9PW

Tel **(01543) 432317 (Admin), (01543) 432212 (Steward)**
Mem 670
Sec NA Spence (Admin), DWJ Macalester (Golf Sec)
Pro AR Sadler (01543) 432261
Holes 18 L 6448 yds SSS 71
V'tors WD–H or I WE/BH + day after–M SOC–Wed & Thurs
Fees D–£32
Loc 2 1/2 miles E of Lichfield on Tamworth road (A51)

Wolstanton (1904)

Dimsdale Old Hall, Hassam Parade, Wolstanton, Newcastle ST5 9DR

Tel **(01782) 616995**
Mem 625
Sec MA Staniforth (01782) 622413
Pro (01782) 622718
Holes 18 L 5807 yds SSS 68
Recs Am–63 P Sweetsur Pro–66 CH Ward

V'tors WD–H WE–M SOC–WD
Fees £18
Loc 1½ miles NW of Newcastle (A34)

Suffolk

Aldeburgh (1884)

Aldeburgh IP15 5PE
Tel **(01728) 452408**
Fax **(01728) 452937**
Mem 831
Sec RC Van de Velde (01728) 452890
Pro K Preston (01728) 453309
Holes 18 L 6330 yds SSS 71
9 L 2114 yds SSS 64
Recs Am–65 J Lloyd
Pro–67 JM Johnson
V'tors H SOC–WD
Fees On application
Loc 6 miles E of A12 (A1094)

Brett Vale

Noakes Road, Raydon IP7 5LR
Tel **(01473) 310718**
Fax **(01473) 824482**
Sec LJ Morrison
Pro A Boulter
Holes 18 L 5808 yds Par 70
V'tors U–booking advisable
Fees £15 (£17.50)
Loc 10 miles SW of Ipswich, off A12 (B1070)

Bungay & Waveney Valley (1889)

Outney Common, Bungay NR35 1DS
Tel **(01986) 892337**
Mem 695
Sec WJ Stevens
Pro N Whyte
Holes 18 L 6063 yds SSS 69
Recs Am–67 R Kidd
Pro–64 T Spurgeon
V'tors WD–U WE–M SOC–WD
Fees D–£18
Loc ½ mile W of Bungay, on N side of A143
Arch James Braid

Bury St Edmunds (1922)

Tut Hill, Bury St Edmunds IP28 6LG
Tel **(01284) 755979**
Fax **(01284) 763288**
Mem 650 180(L)
Sec JC Sayer
Pro M Jillings (01284) 755978
Holes 18 L 6615 yds SSS 72
9 L 4664 yds SSS 63
Recs Am–69 S Goodman, A Currie, J Maddock
Pro–67 K Golding
V'tors WD/BH–U WE–M SOC–WD
Fees 18 hole:£24 9 hole:£11 (£12)
Loc 2 miles W of Bury St Edmunds on B1106, off A14
Arch Ted Ray

Cretingham (1984)

Grove Farm, Cretingham, Woodbridge IP13 7BA
Tel **(01728) 685275**
Fax **(01728) 685037**
Mem 300
Sec C Jenkins (Prop)
Pro C Jenkins
Holes 9 L 2260 yds Par 33
Pro–61 T Johnson (1994)
V'tors U
Fees 18 holes–£7 (£10)
Loc 2 miles SE of Earl Soham. 11 miles N of Ipswich
Mis Practice range. Pitch & putt course
Arch J Austin

Diss (1903)

Stuston Common, Diss IP22 3JB
Tel **(01379) 642847**
Mem 700
Sec J Bell (01379) 641025
Pro N Taylor (01379) 644399
Holes 18 L 6238 yds SSS 70
Recs Am–72 S Brawn (1993)
Pro–67 R Curtis (1993)
V'tors WD only
Fees £20
Loc 1 mile SE of Diss, off A140

Felixstowe Ferry (1880)

Ferry Road, Felixstowe IP4 9RY
Tel **(01394) 286834**
Mem 750
Sec IH Kimber
Pro I Macpherson (01394) 283975
Holes 18 L 6308 yds SSS 70
Recs Am–67 S Macpherson (1993)
Pro–65 I Richardson (1979), L Paterson
V'tors U H WE–M before 10.30am SOC
Fees £21 (£24)
Loc 2 miles NE of Felixstowe, towards Felixstowe Ferry

Flempton (1895)

Bury St Edmunds IP28 6HQ
Tel **(01284) 728291**
Mem 250
Sec JF Taylor
Pro M Jillings
Holes 9 L 6240 yds SSS 70
Recs Am–67 Lt J Reynolds
Pro–69 J Arbon
V'tors WD–H WE/BH–M
Fees £18.50 D–£24
Loc 4 miles NW of Bury St Edmunds on A1101
Arch JH Taylor

Fornham Park G & CC (1974)

St John's Hill Plantation, The Street, Fornham All Saints, Bury St Edmunds IP28 6JQ
Tel **(01284) 706777**
Fax **(01284) 706721**
Mem 700
Sec S Clark
Pro S Clark
Holes 18 L 6209 yds SSS 70
Recs Am–69 R Nicholson (1992)
Pro–67 S Clark (1991)
V'tors WD–U WE–NA before 1pm SOC
Fees £15 (£20)
Loc 2 miles NW of Bury St Edmunds, off B1106

Fynn Valley (1992)

Witnesham, Ipswich IP6 9JA
Tel **(01473) 785267**
Fax **(01473) 785632**
Mem 650
Sec T Tyrrell
Pro R Mann
Holes 18 L 5700 yds SSS 69
Par 3 course
Recs Am–68 M Millett
Pro–62 R Mann (1992)
V'tors U exc Sun am–NA SOC
Fees £15 (£18)
Loc 2 miles N of Ipswich on B1077
Mis Driving range
Arch Tony Tyrrell

Haverhill (1974)

Coupals Road, Haverhill CB9 7UW
Tel **(01440) 61951**
Fax **(01440) 714883 (Pro)**
Mem 490
Sec Mrs J Edwards
Pro S Mayfield (01440) 712628
Holes 9 L 5707 yds SSS 68
Recs Am–66 A Carter (1991), R Cramsie (1993)
Pro–66 C Cook
V'tors U SOC–Tues & Thurs
Fees £10 (£15)
Loc 1 mile E of Haverhill, off A604. Signs to Calford Green
Arch Charles Lawrie

Hintlesham Hall (1991)

Hintlesham, Ipswich IP8 3NS
Tel **(01473) 652761**
Fax **(01473) 652750**
Mem 200
Sec A Spink (Sec/Mgr)
Pro A Spink
Holes 18 L 6638 yds SSS 72
V'tors U SOC
Fees £26 (£45)
Loc 4 miles W of Ipswich
Arch Hawtree

Ipswich (Purdis Heath) (1895)

Purdis Heath, Bucklesham Road, Ipswich IP3 8UQ
Tel **(01473) 727474 (Steward)**
Fax **(01473) 715236**
Mem 850
Sec Brig AP Wright MBE (01473) 728941
Pro SJ Whymark (01473) 724017
Holes 18 L 6405 yds SSS 71
9 L 1950 yds Par 31
Recs Am–64 JVT Marks
Pro–67 RA Knight

For list of abbreviations see page 435

V'tors 18 hole:H SOC 9 hole:U
Fees 18 hole:£32 (£36) 9 hole:£8 (£10)
Loc 3 miles E of Ipswich
Arch James Braid

Links (Newmarket) (1902)

Cambridge Road, Newmarket CB8 0TG
Tel **(01638) 662708**
Mem 685
Sec Lt Cdr DM Baird RN (01638) 663000
Pro J Sharkey (01638) 662395
Holes 18 L 6424 yds SSS 71
Recs Am–66 R Wiseman
Pro–67 L Jones
Ladies–68 T Eakin
V'tors WD–H WE/BH–H exc Sun–MH before 11.30am SOC
Fees £24 (£28)
Loc 1 mile S of Newmarket

Newton Green (1907)

Newton Green, Sudbury
Tel **(01787) 77501**
Mem 500
Sec G Bright (01787) 77217
Pro K Lovelock (01787) 313215
Holes 18 L 5488 yds SSS 67
Recs Am–59 K Burton
Pro–29 A Davey (9 holes)
V'tors WD–U WE–M
Fees £12
Loc 4 miles E of Sudbury

Rookery Park (1891)

Carlton Colville, Lowestoft NR33 8HJ
Tel **(01502) 560380**
Mem 750
Sec SR Cooper
Pro M Elsworthy (01502) 515103
Holes 18 L 6649 yds SSS 72
9 hole Par 3 course
Recs Am–71 G Long (1985)
Pro–69 P Kent (1985)
V'tors WD–U Sat/BH–after 11am Sun–NA SOC
Fees £20 (£25)
Loc 3 miles W of Lowestoft (A146)

Royal Worlington & Newmarket (1893)

Golf Links Road, Worlington, Bury St Edmunds IP28 8SD
Tel **(01638) 712216**
Mem 310
Sec Maj GWM Hipkin
Pro M Hawkins (01638) 715224
Holes 9 L 6210 yds SSS 70
Recs Am–67 DJ Millensted
Pro–66 EE Beverley
V'tors I or H–phone first WE–NA
Fees D–£32 After 2pm–£21
Loc 6 miles NE of Newmarket, off A11
Arch HS Colt

Rushmere (1927)

Rushmere Heath, Ipswich IP4 5QQ
Tel **(01473) 727109**
Mem 800
Sec PL Coles (01473) 725648
Pro NTJ McNeill (01473) 728076
Holes 18 L 6263 yds SSS 70
Recs Am–66 F Knights (1989), M Turner (1990)
Pro–67 NTJ McNeill(1984), S Beckham (1985)
V'tors WD–H WE/BH–H after 2.30pm
Fees On application
Loc 3 miles E of Ipswich, off Woodbridge road (A1214)

Seckford (1991)

Pay and play
Seckford Hall Road, Great Bealings, Woodbridge IP13 6NT
Tel **(01394) 388000**
Fax **(01394) 382818**
Mem 225
Sec T Pennock (Golf Dir)
Pro T Pennock
Holes 18 L 5088 yds SSS 65
Recs Am–63 S Jay
Pro–63 J Skinner
V'tors U SOC
Fees D–£12 9 holes–£7.50
Loc SW of Woodbridge, off A12
Arch J Johnson

Southwold (1884)

The Common, Southwold IP18 6TB
Tel **(01502) 723234**
Mem 450
Sec DF Randall (01502) 723248
Pro B Allen (01502) 723790
Holes 9 L 6050 yds SSS 69
Recs Am–67 S Fitzgerald
Pro–65 R Mann
V'tors U (subject to fixtures)
Fees £14 (£18)
Loc 35 miles NE of Ipswich

St Helena (1990)

Bramfield Road, Halesworth IP19 9XA
Tel **(01986) 875567**
Fax **(01986) 874565**
Mem 600
Sec Mrs RK Ward
Pro PM Heil
Holes 18 L 6580 yds SSS 72
9 hole course SSS 36
Recs Am–71 G Lay (1994)
Pro–68 PM Heil (1994)
V'tors H SOC
Fees 18 hole:£15 D–£19 (£21)
9 hole:£7.50
Loc 1 mile S of Halesworth, off A144
Mis Floodlit driving range
Arch JW Johnson

Stoke-by-Nayland (1972)

Keepers Lane, Leavenheath, Colchester CO6 4PZ
Tel **(01206) 262836**
Fax **(01206) 263356**
Mem 1600
Sec J Loshak
Pro K Lovelock (01206) 262769
Holes Gainsborough 18 L 6516 yds SSS 71; Constable 18 L 6544 yds SSS 71
Recs Gainsborough:
Am–63 M Parry (1994)
Pro–66 R Mann (1987)
Constable:
Am–68 M Clark (1991)
Pro–70 J Hudson, H Flatman (1990)
V'tors WD–U WE/BH–H after 10am SOC
Fees £24 (£29)
Loc Off A134 Colchester-Sudbury road on B1068
Mis Driving range

Stowmarket (1962)

Lower Road, Onehouse, Stowmarket IP14 3DA
Tel **(01449) 736392**
Mem 600
Sec J Edwards-Hayes (01449) 736473
Pro C Aldred
Holes 18 L 6119 yds SSS 69
Recs Am–67 I Oakes
Pro–66 H Flatman
V'tors H SOC–Thurs & Fri
Fees £24 (£33)
Loc 2½ miles SW of Stowmarket
Mis Driving range

Thorpeness Golf Hotel (1923)

Thorpeness, Leiston IP16 4NH
Tel **(01728) 452176**
Fax **(01728) 453868**
Mem 400
Sec NW Griffin
Pro (01728) 454926
Holes 18 L 6241 yds SSS 71
Recs Am–66 J Marks
Pro–67 K McDonald
V'tors U
Fees On application
Loc 2 miles N of Aldeburgh
Arch James Braid

Ufford Park Hotel (1992)

Yarmouth Road, Ufford, Woodbridge IP12 1QW
Tel **(01394) 382836**
Fax **(01394) 383582**
Mem 260
Sec D Cotton
Pro S Robertson
Holes 18 L 6335 yds SSS 70
Recs Am–67 J Maddock
Pro–67
V'tors U SOC
Fees £12 (£15)
Loc 2 miles N of Woodbridge, off A12
Arch P Pilgrim

Waldringfield Heath (1983)

Newbourne Road, Waldringfield, Woodbridge IP12 4PT

Tel **(01473) 736768**
Mem 640
Sec LJ McWade
Pro A Dobson (01473) 736417
Holes 18 L 6153 yds SSS 69
Pro–64 A Dobson (1990)
V'tors WD–U WE/BH–M before noon SOC–WD
Fees On application
Loc 3 miles E of Ipswich, off A12

Wood Valley (1899)

The Common, Beccles NR34 9BX

Tel **(01502) 712244**
Mem 200
Sec Mrs LW Allen (01502) 712479
Holes 9 L 2696 yds SSS 67
Recs Am–65 S Shulver
V'tors WD–U Sun–M SOC
Fees £11 (£13)
Loc 10 miles W of Lowestoft (A146)

Woodbridge (1893)

Bromeswell Heath, Woodbridge IP12 2PF

Tel **(01394) 382038**
Fax **(01394) 382392**
Mem 930
Sec Capt LA Harpum RN
Pro LA Jones (01394) 383213
Holes 18 L 6314 yds SSS 70
9 L 2243 yds SSS 31
Recs Am–64 JVT Marks (1983)
Pro–65 F Sunderland (1970)
V'tors WD–H WE/BH–M SOC
Fees £27
Loc 2 miles E of Woodbridge on A1152 towards Orford
Arch F Hawtree

Surrey

The Addington (1913)

Shirley Church Road, Croydon CR50 5AB

Tel **(0181) 777 1055**
Sec JW Beale
Pro E Campbell (0181) 777 1701
Holes 18 L 6242 yds SSS 71
Recs Am–66 P Benka
Pro–68 F Robson
V'tors H SOC–WD
Fees On application
Loc E Croydon 2½ miles
Arch JF Abercromby

Addington Court (1931)

Public

Featherbed Lane, Addington, Croydon CR0 9AA

Tel **(0181) 657 0281/2/3**
Fax **(0181) 651 0282**
Sec G Cotton
Pro G Cotton
Holes Old 18 L 5577 yds SSS 67
New 18 L 5513 yds SSS 66
Lower 9 L 1812 yds SSS 62
Recs Am–62 S Griffiths (1994)
Pro–60 W Grant, C DeFoy (1992)
V'tors U
Fees Old:£12.50 New:£11.50
9 hole:£7
Loc 3 miles E of Croydon
Mis 18 hole pitch & putt course
Arch F Hawtree Sr

Addington Palace (1923)

Addington Park, Gravel Hill, Addington CR0 5BB

Tel **(0181) 654 3061**
Mem 700
Sec LM Dennis-Smither
Pro R Williams (0181) 654 1786
Holes 18 L 6410 yds SSS 71
Recs Am–63 R Glading
Pro–65 AD Locke
V'tors WD–H WE/BH–M
Fees £30
Loc 2 miles E of Croydon Station

Banstead Downs (1890)

Burdon Lane, Belmont, Sutton SM2 7DD

Tel **(0181) 642 2284**
Fax **(0181) 642 5252**
Mem 650
Sec RHA Steele
Pro R Dickman (0181) 642 6884
Holes 18 L 6168 yds SSS 69
Recs Am–64 P Brittain (1992)
Pro–65 RAF Lewis (1992)
V'tors WD–H WE/BH–M SOC–Thurs
Fees £30. After 12 noon–£20
Loc 1 mile S of Sutton

Barrow Hills (1970)

Longcross, Chertsey KT16 0DS

Mem 350
Sec RW Routley (01932) 848117
Holes 18 L 3090 yds SSS 53
Recs Am–58 EJ Sewell (1979)
V'tors M
Fees On application
Loc 4 miles W of Chertsey

Betchworth Park (1913)

Reigate Road, Dorking RH4 1NZ

Tel **(01306) 882052**
Fax **(01306) 877462**
Mem 725
Sec DAS Bradney
Pro R Blackie (01306) 884334
Holes 18 L 6266 yds SSS 70
Recs Am–66 J Robson, M Osborne (1993)
Pro–65 NC Coles
V'tors WD–by arrangement exc Tues & Wed am–NA WE–NA exc Sun pm
Fees £31 (£43)
Loc 1 mile E of Dorking on A25
Arch HS Colt

Bletchingley (1993)

Church Lane, Bletchingley RH1 4LP

Tel **(01883) 744666**
Fax **(01883) 744284**
Mem 450
Sec CT Manktelow (Mgr)
Pro P Webster (01883) 744848
Holes 18 L 6504 yds SSS 71
V'tors WD–U WE–M
Fees £20
Loc 1 mile S of M25 Junction 6 on A25

Bramley (1913)

Bramley, Guildford GU5 0AL

Tel **(01483) 893042**
Fax **(01483) 894673**
Mem 800
Sec Ms M Lambert (01483) 892696
Pro G Peddie (01483) 893685
Holes 18 L 5990 yds SSS 69
Recs Am–65 J Jones (1993)
Pro–63 P Hughes (1994)
V'tors WD–U WE–M SOC–WD
Fees £25 D–£30 (1994)
Loc 3 miles S of Guildford on A281
Mis Driving range-members and green fees only
Arch Mayo/Braid

Burhill (1907)

Walton-on-Thames KT12 4BL

Tel **(01932) 227345**
Mem 1100
Sec MB Richards
Pro L Johnson (01932) 221729
Holes 18 L 6224 yds SSS 70
Recs Am–64 RJ Pollitt (1991)
Pro–65 G Orr (1988)
V'tors WD–H WE/BH–M
Fees On application
Loc Between Walton-on-Thames and Cobham, off Burwood road
Arch Willie Park

Camberley Heath (1913)

Golf Drive, Camberley GU15 1JG

Tel **(01276) 23258**
Fax **(01276) 692505**
Mem 725
Sec J Greenwood
Pro G Smith (01276) 27905
Holes 18 L 6337 yds SSS 70
V'tors WD–H WE–M SOC H
Fees On application
Loc 1½ miles S of Camberley on A325
Arch HS Colt

Chessington Golf Centre (1983)

Pay and play

Garrison Lane, Chessington KT9 2LW

Tel **(0181) 391 0948**
Fax **(0181) 974 1705**
Mem 250
Sec A Maxted (Mgr) (0181) 974 1705
Holes 9 L 1400 yds Par 54 SSS 50

For list of abbreviations see page 435

Recs Am–60 N Murphy
Pro–54 R Hunter
V'tors WD–U WE–NA before noon
Fees £3.75 (£4.50)
Loc Off A243, opp Chessington South Station. M25 Junction 9
Mis Driving range

Chipstead (1906)

How Lane, Chipstead, Coulsdon CR5 3PR
Tel **(01737) 551053**
Fax **(01737) 555404**
Mem 600
Sec SLD Spencer-Skeen (01737) 555781
Pro G Torbett (01737) 554939
Holes 18 L 5450 yds SSS 67
Recs Am–64 R Mullane (1991)
Pro–63 J Morgan, R Mullane (1993)
V'tors WD–U WE/BH–M
Fees £25 After 2pm–£20
Loc Nr Chipstead Station

Chobham (1994)

Chobham Road, Knaphill, Woking GU2 1TU
Tel **(01276) 855584**
Fax **(01276) 855663**
Mem 750
Sec D Cross
Pro P Young
Holes 18 L 5821 yds Par 69 SSS 68
Recs Pro–67 C Montgomerie, S Richardson (1994)
V'tors M H–restricted SOC
Fees £24 (£30)
Loc 3 miles E of M3 Junction 3 between Chobham and Knaphill (A3046)
Arch Alliss/Clark

Coombe Hill (1911)

Golf Club Drive, Coombe Lane West, Kingston KT2 7DG
Tel **(0181) 942 2284**
Fax **(0181) 949 5815**
Mem 565
Sec CA Fereday
Pro C De Foy (0181) 949 3713
Holes 18 L 6303 yds SSS 71
Recs Am–66 C Boal
Pro–67 B Gallagher
V'tors WD–I or H WE–NA SOC
Fees D–£45
Loc 1 mile W of New Malden on A238
Arch JF Abercromby

Coombe Wood (1904)

George Road, Kingston Hill, Kingston-upon-Thames KT2 7NS
Tel **(0181) 942 3828 (Clubhouse)**
Fax **(0181) 942 0388**
Mem 620
Sec PM Urwin (0181) 942 0388
Pro D Butler (0181) 942 6764
Holes 18 L 5210 yds SSS 66
Recs Am–62 FJ Cocker
Pro–60 D Butler (1987)
V'tors WD–U H after 9am
WE/BH–M SOC–WD
Fees On application
Loc 1 mile N of Kingston-upon-Thames, off A3 at Robin Hood roundabout

Coulsdon Manor (1937)

Pay and play
Coulsdon Court Road, Croydon CR5 2LL
Tel **(0181) 660 0468**
Fax **(0181) 668 3118**
Pro (0181) 660 6083
Holes 18 L 6037 yds SSS 70
Recs Am–66 K Smale
Pro–66 G Ralph
V'tors U
Fees £12 (£15)
Loc 5 miles S of Croydon on B2030. M25 Junction 6 or 7

Croham Hurst (1911)

Croham Road, South Croydon CR2 7HJ
Tel **(0181) 657 5581**
Mem 314 110(L) 80(J)
Sec R Passingham (Mgr)
Pro E Stillwell (0181) 657 7705
Holes 18 L 6286 yds SSS 70
Recs Am–64 CF Staroscik (1991)
Pro–66 B Firkins
V'tors WD–I WE/BH–M
Fees £32 (£42)
Loc 1 mile from S Croydon. M25 Junction 6-A22-B270-B269

Cuddington (1929)

Banstead Road, Banstead SM7 1RD
Tel **(0181) 393 0952**
Fax **(0181) 786 7025**
Mem 620
Sec DM Scott
Pro M Warner (0181) 393 5850
Holes 18 L 6394 yds SSS 70
Recs Am–69 S Nunn
Pro–61 J Spence
V'tors WD–I WE–M
Fees £30 (£35)
Loc Nr Banstead Station
Arch HS Colt

Dorking (1897)

Chart Park, Dorking RH5 4BX
Tel **(01306) 886917**
Mem 420
Sec JB Hawkins
Pro P Napier
Holes 9 L 5120 yds SSS 65
Recs Am–65 J Houston
Pro–62 A King
V'tors WD–U WE/BH–M SOC–WD
Fees £16
Loc 1 mile S of Dorking on A24
Arch James Braid

Drift (1976)

The Drift, East Horsley KT24 5HD
Tel **(01483) 284641**
Fax **(01483) 284642**
Mem 700
Sec C Rose
Pro J Hagen (01483) 284772
Holes 18 L 6425 yds SSS 72
Recs Am–71 B Rowan
Pro–71 J Bennett
V'tors WD–U SOC
Fees £30 After 1pm–£20
Loc 2 miles off A3 (B2039). M25 Junction 10

Dulwich & Sydenham Hill (1894)

Grange Lane, College Road, London SE21 7LH
Tel **(0181) 693 3961**
Mem 850
Sec Mrs S Alexander
Pro D Baillie (0181) 693 8491
Holes 18 L 6051 yds SSS 69
Recs Am–64 J Piner
Pro–63 LF Rowe
V'tors WD–I WE/BH–M SOC
Fees £25

Dunsfold Aerodrome (1965)

Dunsfold Aerodrome, Godalming GU8 4BS
Tel **(01483) 265472**
Mem 270
Sec RG Grout (01483) 276118
Holes 9 L 6090 yds Par 70 SSS 69
Recs Am–70 R Arkwright (1991)
V'tors M
Fees £3 (£3)
Loc 10 miles S of Guildford, off A281
Arch Sharkey/Hayward

Effingham (1927)

Effingham Crossroads, Effingham KT24 5PZ
Tel **(01372) 452203**
Fax **(01372) 459959**
Mem 980
Sec Col SC Manning OBE
Pro S Hoatson (01372) 452606
Holes 18 L 6516 yds SSS 71
Recs Am–66 J Vardy (1987)
Pro–65 B Barnes (1984)
V'tors WD–H WE/BH–M
Fees £35 After 2pm–£27.50
Loc 8 miles N of Guildford on A246
Arch HS Colt

Epsom (1889)

Longdown Lane South, Epsom Downs, Epsom KT17 4JR
Tel **(01372) 721666**
Fax **(01372) 729233**
Mem 800
Sec JH Carter FCA
Pro R Goudie (01372) 741867
Holes 18 L 5701 yds SSS 68
Recs Am–68 D Barnett (1994)
Pro–66 D Butler (1992)
V'tors WD–U exc Tues am
WE/BH–NA before noon SOC
Fees £16 (£18)
Loc ¾ mile NE of Epsom Racecourse

For list of abbreviations see page 435

Farnham (1896)

The Sands, Farnham GU10 1PX

Tel **(01252) 783163**
Mem 750
Sec J Pevalin (01252) 782109
Pro G Cowlishaw (01252) 782198
Holes 18 L 6313 yds SSS 70
Recs Am–67 G Walmsley (1988)
Pro–67 J Bennett (1990), P Simpson (1991)
V'tors WD–H WE–M SOC–Wed & Thurs
Fees £27 D–£32
Loc 1 mile E of Farnham, off A31

Farnham Park Par Three (1966)

Pay and play

Farnham Park, Farnham GU9 0AU

Tel **(01252) 715216**
Sec P Chapman
Pro P Chapman
Holes 9 L 1163 yds Par 54
Recs Am–61 JA Pike (1966)
Pro–56 G Wheeler (1966)
V'tors U
Fees £3.50 (£4)
Loc By Farnham Castle
Arch Henry Cotton

Fernfell G & CC (1985)

Barhatch Lane, Cranleigh GU6 7NG

Tel **(01483) 268855**
Fax **(01483) 267251**
Mem 850
Sec M Hale
Pro T Longmuir (01483) 277188
Holes 18 L 5599 yds SSS 67
Recs Am–69 R Ford (1992)
Pro–65 R Dickman (1991)
V'tors WD–U WE/BH–pm only SOC–WD
Fees £20 (£25)
Loc 1 mile from Cranleigh, off A281

Foxhills (1975)

Stonehill Road, Ottershaw KT16 0EL

Tel **(01932) 872050**
Fax **(01932) 874762**
Mem 975
Sec A Laking (Mgr)
Pro A Good (01932) 873961
Holes 18 L 6680 yds SSS 73
18 L 6547 yds SSS 72
9 hole course
Pro–65 P Dawson
V'tors WD–U WE–NA before noon
Fees £45 D–£65 (£55)
Loc 2 miles SW of Chertsey on B386
Mis Driving range
Arch FW Hawtree

Gatton Manor Hotel G & CC (1969)

Standon Lane, Ockley, Dorking RH5 5PQ

Tel **(01306) 627555**
Fax **(01306) 627713**
Mem 250
Sec DG Heath
Pro R Sargent (01306) 627557
Holes 18 L 6913 yds SSS 74
Recs Am–72 J McLaren (1985)
Pro–73 R Sargent (1985)
V'tors U exc Sun before 1 pm–NA SOC–WD
Fees £18 (£25)
Loc 1½ miles SW of Ockley, off A29. M25 Junction 9, S on A24
Mis Driving range

Goal Farm Par Three (1977)

Public

Gole Road, Pirbright GU24 OP2

Tel **(01483) 473183/473205**
Sec R & J Church (Props)
Pro K Warne
Holes 9 hole Par 3 course
Recs Am–45 P Wakefield (1991)
V'tors Sat/Thurs am–restricted SOC–WD
Fees £6.50 (£7)
Loc 7 miles NW of Guildford

Guildford (1886)

High Path Road, Merrow, Guildford GU1 2HL

Tel **(01483) 63941**
Fax **(01483) 453228**
Mem 600
Sec RE Thomas (01483) 63941
Pro PG Hollington (01483) 66765
Holes 18 L 6090 yds SSS 70
Recs Am–64 DG Lintott (1989)
Pro–67 PG Hollington (1987)
V'tors WD–U WE–M SOC–WD
Fees £25
Loc 2 miles E of Guildford on A246

Hankley Common (1896)

Tilford, Farnham GU10 2DD

Tel **(01252) 792493**
Fax **(01252) 795699**
Mem 700
Sec JKA O'Brien
Pro P Stow (01252) 793761
Holes 18 L 6465 yds SSS 71
Recs Am–66 J Lee (1987)
Pro–62 H Stott (1988)
V'tors WD–I WE–discretion of Sec
Fees £28 D–£35
Loc 3 miles SE of Farnham on Tilford road

Hazelwood Golf Centre

Pay and play

Croysdale Avenue, Green Street, Sunbury-on-Thames TW16 6QU

Tel **(01932) 770932**
Fax **(01932) 770933**
Sec C Patey
Pro C Patey
Holes 9 hole course Par 35
Recs Am–69 C Stones (1994)
V'tors U SOC
Fees £7 (£8.50)
Loc S of M3 Junction 1
Mis Driving range
Arch Jonathan Gaunt

Hindhead (1904)

Churt Road, Hindhead GU26 6HX

Tel **(01428) 604614**
Fax **(01428) 604614**
Mem 350 50(L) 100(J)
Sec Miss A McMenemy
Pro N Ogilvy (01428) 604458
Holes 18 L 6373 yds SSS 70
Recs Am–64 M Lassam
Pro–63 A Tillman
V'tors WD–U WE–by arrangement SOC–Wed & Thurs
Fees £35 (£42)
Loc 1½ miles N of Hindhead on A287

Hoebridge Golf Centre (1982)

Public

Old Woking Road, Old Woking GU22 8JH

Tel **(01483) 722611**
Fax **(01483) 740369**
Mem 480
Sec P Gaylor (Mgr)
Pro TD Powell
Holes 18 L 6587 yds SSS 71
Inter 9 L 2294 yds Par 33
18 hole Par 3 course
V'tors U
Fees 18 hole:£13 Inter:£7
Par 3:£6.50
Loc Between Old Woking and West Byfleet on B382
Mis Floodlit driving range
Arch Jacobs/Hawtree

Home Park (1895)

Hampton Wick, Kingston-upon-Thames KT1 4AD

Tel **(0181) 977 6645**
Fax **(0181) 977 4414**
Mem 500
Sec BW O'Farrell (0181) 977 2423
Pro L Roberts (081) 977 2658
Holes 18 L 6610 yds SSS 71
V'tors U
Fees £15 (£26)
Loc 1 mile W of Kingston

Horton Park CC (1993)

Hook Road, Epsom KT19 8QG

Tel **(0181) 393 8400** (Enquiries), **(0181) 394 2626** (Bookings)
Fax **(0181) 394 1369**
Mem 510
Sec P Hart (Gen Mgr) (0181) 393 8400
Pro J Robson, G Clements (0181) 394 2626
Holes 18 L 5197 yds SSS 66
V'tors U SOC
Fees £11 (£13)
Loc 1 mile from A3, W of Ewell. M25 Junction 9
Mis Driving range
Arch Patrick Tallack

Hurtmore (1991)
Pay and play
Hurtmore Road, Hurtmore, Godalming GU7 2RN
Tel **(01483) 426492**
Fax **(01483) 426121**
Mem 200
Sec N Spinney
Pro T White
Holes 18 L 5444 yds SSS 66
V'tors WD–U WE–booking advisable SOC
Fees £12 (£15)
Loc 3 miles S of Guildford on A3. M25 Junction 10
Arch Alliss/Clark

Kingswood (1928)
Sandy Lane, Kingswood, Tadworth KT20 6NE
Tel **(01737) 832188**
Fax **(01737) 833920**
Mem 640
Sec L Thompson (Admin)
Pro M Platts (01737) 832334
Holes 18 L 6880 yds SSS 72
Recs Am–70 P Stanford
Pro–67 R Blackie
V'tors H SOC
Fees £30 (£45)
Loc 5 miles S of Sutton on A217. M25 Junction 8, 2 miles
Arch James Braid

Laleham (1907)
Laleham Reach, Chertsey KT16 8RP
Tel **(01932) 564211**
Mem 600
Sec RR Fry
Holes 18 L 6203 yds SSS 70
Recs Am–68 C Poulton
Pro–66 R Mandeville, J Hitchcock
V'tors WD–U 9.30–4.30pm WE–M SOC–Mon/Wed/Fri
Fees £16.50 D–£25
Loc 2 miles S of Staines, opp Thorpe Park

Leatherhead (1903)
Kingston Road, Leatherhead KT22 0EE
Tel **(01372) 843966**
Fax **(01372) 842241**
Mem 600
Sec L Laithwaite (Mgr)
Pro R Hurst (01372) 843956
Holes 18 L 6157 yds SSS 69
Recs Am–67 T Paterson (1990)
Pro–69 J Sewell (1992), S Norman (1993)
V'tors U SOC
Fees £25 (£35)
Loc On A243 to Chessington. M25 Junction 9

Limpsfield Chart (1889)
Westerham Road, Limpsfield RH8 0SL
Tel **(01883) 723405**
Mem 395
Sec DS Adams
Holes 9 L 5718 yds SSS 68
Recs Am–67 N Simmons
Pro–64 B Huggett
V'tors WD–U exc Thurs (Ladies Day) WE–M or by appointment SOC
Fees £18 (£20)
Loc 2 miles E of Oxted

Lingfield Park (1987)
Racecourse Road, Lingfield RH7 6PQ
Tel **(01342) 834602**
Fax **(01342) 832833**
Mem 700
Sec Ms G Milne
Pro C Morley (01342) 832659
Holes 18 L 6500 yds SSS 72
Pro–67 E Stillwell (1987)
V'tors WD–U WE/BH–M SOC–WD
Fees £25 (£35)
Loc Next to Lingfield racecourse. M25 Junction 6
Mis Driving range

London Scottish (1865)
Windmill Enclosure, Wimbledon Common, London SW19 5NQ
Tel **(0181) 788 0135**
Mem 250
Sec J Johnson (0181) 789 7517
Pro M Barr (0181) 789 1207
Holes 18 L 5438 yds SSS 66
Recs Am–64 A Glickberg (1975)
Pro–63 D Butler (1970), A King (1975)
V'tors WE/BH–NA SOC
Fees On application
Loc Wimbledon Common
Mis Club has joint use of Wimbledon Common course
Arch Willie Dunn/Tom Dunn

Malden (1893)
Traps Lane, New Malden KT3 4RS
Tel **(0181) 942 0654**
Fax **(0181) 336 2219**
Mem 800
Sec PG Fletcher
Pro R Hunter (0181) 942 6009
Holes 18 L 6295 yds SSS 70
Recs Am–65 G Lashford
Pro–63 P Talbot
V'tors WD–U WE–restricted SOC–Wed–Fri
Fees On application
Loc Off A3, between Wimbledon and Kingston

Mitcham (1897)
Carshalton Road, Mitcham Junction CR4 4HN
Tel **(0181) 648 1508**
Mem 450
Sec CA McGahan (0181) 648 4197
Pro JA Godfrey (0181) 640 4280
Holes 18 L 5931 yds SSS 68
Recs Am–D Wilde
V'tors WD–U WE–NA before 2pm SOC
Fees £10 (£10)
Loc Mitcham Junction Station

Moore Place (1926)
Public
Portsmouth Road, Esher KT10 9LN
Tel **(01372) 463533**
Mem 160
Sec D Allen (Mgr)
Pro D Allen
Holes 9 L 4216 yds SSS 58
Recs Am–29 W Cavanagh
Pro–25 P Loxley
V'tors U
Fees £5.40 (£7.25)
Loc Centre of Esher
Arch D Allen

New Zealand (1895)
Woodham Lane, Addlestone KT15 3QD
Tel **(01932) 345049**
Fax **(01932) 342891**
Mem 300
Sec J Manley (01932) 342891
Pro VR Elvidge (01932) 349619
Holes 18 L 6012 yds SSS 69
Recs Am–66 P Cannings
Pro–72 A Herd
V'tors By request
Fees On application
Loc Woking 3 miles. West Byfleet 1 mile. Weybridge 5 miles

North Downs (1899)
Northdown Road, Woldingham CR3 7AA
Tel **(01883) 653397**
Fax **(01883) 652832**
Mem 650
Sec JAL Smith (Mgr) (01883) 652057
Pro M Homewood (01883) 653004
Holes 18 L 5843 yds SSS 68
Recs Am–66 M Smallcorn (1989)
Pro–65 W Humphreys (1987)
V'tors WD–U WE–M SOC–Tues/Wed/Fri
Fees £28 (1994)
Loc 3 miles E of Caterham. M25 Junction 6

Oak Park (1984)
Heath Lane, Crondall, Farnham GU10 5PB
Tel **(01252) 850880**
Fax **(01252) 850851**
Mem 500
Sec Mrs R Smythe (Prop)
Pro S Coaker (01252) 850066
Holes 18 L 6437 yds SSS 71
Recs Am–71 A Wheeler (1994)
Pro–69 R Edwards (1994)
V'tors U SOC
Fees £16 (£22.50)
Loc Off A287 Farnham-Odiham road. M3 Junction 5, 4 miles
Mis Floodlit driving range
Arch Patrick Dawson

Oaks Sports Centre (1973)
Public
Woodmansterne Road, Carshalton SM5 4AN
Tel **(0181) 643 8363**

For list of abbreviations see page 435

Mem 1000
Pro G Horley
Holes 18 L 6033 yds SSS 69
9 hole course
Recs Pro–66 G Horley
V'tors U
Fees 18 hole:£10.50 (£12.50)
9 hole:£5 (£6)
Loc 2 miles from Sutton on B278
Mis Floodlit driving range

Pachesham Golf Centre (1990)

Pay and play
Oaklawn Road, Leatherhead KT22 0BT
Tel **(01372) 843453**
Fax **(01372) 844076**
Mem 350
Sec P Taylor
Pro P Taylor
Holes 9 L 2750 yds Par 35
V'tors U SOC
Fees 9 holes–£6.50 (£7.50)
Loc NW of Leatherhead, off A244. M25 Junction 9
Mis Driving range
Arch P Taylor

Pine Ridge (1992)

Pay and play
Old Bisley Road, Frimley, Camberley GU16 5NX
Tel **(01276) 20770**
Fax **(01276) 678837**
Pro A Kelso
Holes 18 L 6458 yds SSS 71
Recs Am–65 V Phillips (1993)
Pro–67 C Montgomerie (1993)
V'tors U
Fees £16 (£20)
Loc Off the Maultway, between Lightwater and Frimley. M3 Junction 3, 2 miles
Mis Floodlit driving range
Arch Clive D Smith

Purley Downs (1894)

106 Purley Downs Road, South Croydon CR2 0RB
Tel **(0181) 657 8347**
Fax **(0181) 651 5044**
Mem 700
Sec PC Gallienne
Pro G Wilson (0181) 651 0819
Holes 18 L 6212 yds SSS 70
Recs Am–66 AJ Glover
Pro–64 R Blackie
V'tors WD–I WE–M
Fees On application
Loc 3 miles S of Croydon (A235)

Puttenham (1894)

Puttenham, Guildford GU3 1AL
Tel **(01483) 810498**
Fax **(01483) 810988**
Mem 500
Sec G Simmons
Pro G Simmons (01483) 810277
Holes 18 L 6200 yds SSS 70
Recs Am–69 M Bolsover
V'tors WD–H by prior appointment WE/BH–M SOC–Wed & Thurs
Fees On application
Loc Midway between Guildford and Farnham on Hog's Back

Pyrford (1993)

Warren Lane, Pyrford GU22 8XR
Tel **(01483) 723555**
Fax **(01483) 729777**
Sec D Renton
Pro J Bennett (01483) 751070
Holes 18 L 6201 yds SSS 70
V'tors H SOC
Fees £35 (£50)
Loc 2 miles from A3 at Ripley
Arch Alliss/Clark

RAC Country Club (1913)

Woodcote Park, Epsom KT18 7EW
Tel **(01372) 276311**
Fax **(01372) 276117**
Sec K Symons
Pro I Howieson (01372) 279514
Holes Old 18 L 6709 yds SSS 72
Coronation 18 L 5598 yds SSS 67
Recs Old Am–68 GW Nielsen (1994)
V'tors M SOC
Loc Epsom Station 1 3/4 miles
Arch Fowler/Myddleton

Redhill & Reigate (1887)

Clarence Lodge, Pendleton Road, Redhill RH1 6LB
Tel **(01737) 244626/244433**
Mem 500
Sec FR Cole (01737) 240777
Pro B Davies (01737) 244433
Holes 18 L 5238 yds SSS 66
V'tors WD–U WE–phone first Sun–NA (June–Sept) SOC
Fees £10 (£15)
Loc 1 mile S of Redhill on A23

Reigate Heath (1895)

The Club House, Reigate Heath RH2 8QR
Tel **(01737) 242610**
Mem 350 90(L) 50(J)
Sec RJ Perkins (01737) 226793
Pro G Gow (01737) 243077
Holes 9 L 5658 yds SSS 67
Recs Am–67 R Vauqulin (1993)
Pro–65 P Loxley (1977)
V'tors WD–U Sun/BH–M SOC–Wed & Thurs
Fees On application
Loc W boundary of Reigate Heath

Richmond (1891)

Sudbrook Park, Richmond TW10 7AS
Tel **(0181) 940 1463**
Mem 500
Sec RL Wilkins (0181) 940 4351
Pro N Job (0181) 940 7792
Holes 18 L 6007 yds SSS 69
Recs Am–63 A Riley, T Cowgill
Pro–63 N Price
V'tors WD–H
Fees £38
Loc Between Richmond and Kingston-upon-Thames

Richmond Park (1923)

Public
Roehampton Gate, Richmond Park, London SW15 5JR
Tel **(0181) 876 3205/1795**
Pro J Slinger
Holes Dukes 18 L 5940 yds SSS 68
Princes 18 L 5969 yds SSS 68
V'tors WD–U WE–booking necessary SOC–WD
Fees £9 (£12.50)
Loc In Richmond Park
Mis Driving range
Arch Hawtree

Roehampton (1901)

Roehampton Lane, London SW15 5LR
Tel **(0181) 876 1621**
Fax **(0181) 392 2386**
Mem 900
Sec M Yates (0181) 876 5505
Pro AL Scott (0181) 876 3858
Holes 18 L 6046 yds SSS 69
Recs Am–67 AL Scott
Pro–62 H Stott
V'tors WD–Introduced by member WE–M
Loc 1 mile W of Putney, off South Circular

Roker Park (1993)

Pay and play
Holly Lane, Aldershot Road, Guildford GU3 3PB
Tel **(01483) 236677**
Mem 200
Sec M Bedlow
Pro K Warn
Holes 9 L 3037 yds SSS 70
V'tors U SOC
Fees £6.50 (£7.50)
Loc 2 miles W of Guildford on A323
Arch Alan Helling

Royal Mid-Surrey (1892)

Old Deer Park, Richmond TW9 2SB
Tel **(0181) 940 1894**
Fax **(0181) 332 2957**
Mem 1250
Sec MSR Lunt
Pro D Talbot (0181) 940 0459
Holes Outer 18 L 6385 yds SSS 70
Inner 18 L 5446 yds SSS 67
Recs Outer Am–65 D Cotton
Pro–64 R Charles, B Gallacher
V'tors WD–H or M WE/BH–M SOC
Fees £45
Loc Nr Richmond roundabout, off A316
Arch JH Taylor

For list of abbreviations see page 435

Royal Wimbledon (1865)
29 Camp Road, Wimbledon, London SW19 4UW
Tel **(0181) 946 2125**
Mem 800
Sec Maj. GE Jones
Pro H Boyle (0181) 946 4606
Holes 18 L 6343 yds SSS 70
Recs Am–66 JFM Connolly
Pro–71 R Burton
V'tors NA
Arch HS Colt

Rusper (1992)
Pay and play
Rusper Road, Newdigate RH5 5BX
Tel **(01293) 871456**
Fax **(01293) 871987**
Mem 280
Sec G Hems
Pro K Spurrier (01293) 871871
Holes 9 L 6069 yds SSS 69
Recs Pro–67 R Dickman
V'tors WD–U WE–by arrangement SOC
Fees 18 holes–£11.50 (£15.50) 9 holes–£7 (£8.50)
Loc 5 miles S of Dorking, off A24
Mis Driving range
Arch S Hood

Sandown Park (1970)
Public
More Lane, Esher KT10 8AN
Tel **(01372) 463340**
Sec P Barriball (Mgr)
Pro N Bedward
Holes 9 L 5658 yds SSS 67
9 hole Par 3 course
Recs Am–68 M Mabbott (1993)
V'tors U–closed on race days
Fees £5.25 (£7)
Loc Sandown Park Racecourse
Mis Floodlit driving range
Arch John Jacobs

Selsdon Park Hotel (1929)
Addington Road, Sanderstead, South Croydon CR2 8YA
Tel **(0181) 657 8811**
Fax **(0181) 651 6171**
Pro T O'Keefe, S Torrance (Touring Pro) (0181) 657 4129
Holes 18 L 6407 yds SSS 71
Recs Am–68 M Welch
V'tors U SOC (min 12 golfers)
Fees £20 (£30)
Loc 3 miles S of Croydon on A2022 Purley-Addington road
Mis Driving range
Arch JH Taylor

Shillinglee Park (1980)
Pay and play
Chiddingfold, Godalming GU8 4TA
Tel **(01428) 653237**
Fax **(01428) 644391**
Mem 400
Sec R Mace (Prop)
Pro R Mace
Holes 9 L 2500 yds Par 32
V'tors U SOC
Fees £11 D–£12.50 (£13 D–£16) 9 holes–£7.50
Loc 2½ miles SE of Chiddingfold
Mis Pitch & putt course
Arch Roger Mace

Shirley Park (1914)
194 Addiscombe Road, Croydon CR0 7LB
Tel **(0181) 654 1143**
Mem 600
Sec A Baird
Pro N Allen (0181) 654 8767
Holes 18 L 6210 yds SSS 70
Recs Am–66 J Good
Pro–65 J Bennett
V'tors WD–U WE/BH–M SOC
Fees £29
Loc On A232, 1 mile E of East Croydon Station

Silvermere (1976)
Pay and play
Redhill Road, Cobham KT11 1EF
Tel **(01932) 867275**
Mem 900
Sec Mrs P Devereux
Pro D McClelland
Holes 18 L 6333 yds SSS 71
Pro–65 S Rolley (1986)
V'tors WD–U WE–NA before 1pm SOC
Fees £18.50 (£25)
Loc ½ mile from M25 Junction 10 on B366 to Byfleet
Mis Floodlit driving range

Springfield Park (1992)
Public
Burntwood Lane, Wandsworth, London SW17 0AT
Tel **(0181) 871 2468**
Fax **(0181) 871 2221**
Mem 320
Sec B Davies (0181) 874 8510
Pro P Tallack
Holes 9 L 4658 yds SSS 62
V'tors WD–U WE–NA before 12 noon SOC
Fees £5–£6.50 (£8.50)
Loc Off Burntwood Lane SW17
Arch Patrick Tallack

St George's Hill (1912)
Golf Club Road, St George's Hill, Weybridge KT13 0NL
Tel **(01932) 847758**
Fax **(01932) 821564**
Mem 600
Sec J Robinson
Pro AC Rattue (01932) 843523
Holes 27 L 6097-6569 yds SSS 69-71
Recs Am–65 D Swanston
Pro–65 M Faulkner
V'tors WD–I H WE/BH–M SOC–Wed–Fri
Fees £40 D–£50
Loc 2 miles N of M25/A3 Junction, on B374
Arch HS Colt

Sunningdale (1901)
Ridgemount Road, Sunningdale SL5 9RW
Tel **(01344) 21681**
Fax **(01344) 24154**
Mem 800
Sec S Zuill
Pro K Maxwell (01344) 20128
Holes Old 18 L 6609 yds SSS 72
New 18 L 6703 yds SSS 72
Recs Old Am–66 MC Hughesdon
Pro–62 N Faldo
New Am–62 C Challen
Pro–64 GJ Player
V'tors Mon–Thurs–I Fri/WE–M
Fees £84
Loc Sunningdale Station ¼ mile on A30
Arch Willie Park/HS Colt

Sunningdale Ladies (1902)
Cross Road, Sunningdale SL5 9RX
Tel **(01344) 20507**
Mem 400
Sec JF Darroch
Holes 18 L 3622 yds SSS 60
V'tors WD/WE–by appointment. No 3 or 4 balls before 11am
Fees D–Ladies £17 (£19) Men £22 (£27)
Loc Sunningdale Station ¼ mile

Surbiton (1895)
Woodstock Lane, Chessington KT9 1UG
Tel **(0181) 398 3101**
Fax **(0181) 339 0992**
Mem 750
Sec GA Keith MBE
Pro P Milton (0181) 398 6619
Holes 18 L 6055 yds SSS 69
Recs Am–63 N Reilly
Pro–65 C de Foy, H Stott
V'tors WD–H WE/BH–M
Fees £27 D–£40.50
Loc 2 miles E of Esher

Tandridge (1925)
Oxted RH8 9NQ
Tel **(01883) 712273 (Clubhouse)**
Fax **(01883) 730537**
Mem 750
Sec AS Furnival (01883) 712274
Pro A Farquhar (01883) 713701
Holes 18 L 6250 yds SSS 70
Recs Am–68 JC Robson
Pro–69 BGC Huggett
V'tors Mon/Wed/Thurs only–H SOC–Mon/Wed/Thurs
Fees On application
Loc 5 miles E of Redhill, off A25. M25 Junction 6
Arch HS Colt

Thames Ditton & Esher

(1892)

Portsmouth Road, Esher KT10 9AL

Tel **(0181) 398 1551**
Mem 300
Sec D Kaye
Pro R Hutton
Holes 9 L 5419 yds SSS 65
Recs Am–61 T Petitt
Pro–61 D Regan
V'tors WD–U WE–by arrangement
Fees £10 (£12)

Tyrrells Wood (1924)

Tyrrells Wood, Leatherhead KT22 8QP

Tel **(01372) 376025 (2 lines)**
Fax **(01372) 360836**
Mem 744
Sec CGR Kydd
Pro M Taylor (01372) 375200
Holes 18 L 6234 yds SSS 70
Recs Am–67 P Earl (1988)
Pro–65 P Hoad (1988)
V'tors WD–I BH/Sat–NA Sun–NA before noon SOC
Fees £32 (£42)
Loc 2 miles SE of Leatherhead, off A24 nr Headley. M25 Junction 9, 1 mile

Walton Heath (1903)

Deans Lane, Walton-on-the-Hill, Tadworth KT20 7TP

Tel **(01737) 812060**
Fax **(01737) 814225**
Mem 900
Sec Gp Capt GR James (01737) 812380
Pro K Macpherson (01737) 812152
Holes Old 18 L 6801 yds SSS 73
New 18 L 6609 yds SSS 72
Recs Old Am–68 R Revell
Pro–65 P Townsend
New Am–67 JK Tate, AJ Wells
Pro–64 C Clark
Ch'ship Pro–64 I Woosnam (1987), M Harwood (1991)
V'tors WD–I H WE/BH–M SOC
Fees £60
Loc 18 miles S of London on A217/B2032. 2 miles N of M25 Junction 8
Arch WH Fowler

The Wentworth Club

(1924)

Wentworth Drive, Virginia Water GU25 4LS

Tel **(01344) 842201**
Fax **(01344) 842804**
Mem 2335
Sec N Flanagan (Admin)
Pro B Gallacher (01344) 843353
Holes West 18 L 6945 yds SSS 74
East 18 L 6176 yds SSS 70
Edinburgh 18 L 6979 yds SSS 73
Executive 9 L 1902 yds Par 27
Recs West Am–72 P McEvoy
Pro–63 W Riley
East Am–65 GB Wolstenholme
Pro–62 DN Sewell, G Will
Edinburgh Pro–67 G Orr
V'tors WD–H by prior arrangement WE–M SOC–WD
Fees On application
Loc 21 miles SW of London at A30/A329 junction. M25 Junction 13, 8 miles
Mis Driving range
Arch HS Colt (East/West). Jacobs/Player (Edinburgh)

West Byfleet (1922)

Sheerwater Road, West Byfleet KT14 6AA

Tel **(01932) 345230**
Fax **(01932) 343433**
Mem 550
Sec DG Lee (01932) 343433
Pro D Regan (01932) 346584
Holes 18 L 6211 yds SSS 70
Recs Am–66 W Calderwood
Pro–65 R Dickman, N Gorman (1994)
V'tors WD–U WE/BH–NA SOC
Fees £27 D–£33
Loc West Byfleet 1/2 mile on A245. M25 Junction 10

West Hill (1909)

Bagshot Road, Brookwood GU24 0BH

Tel **(01483) 474365/472110**
Fax **(01483) 474252**
Mem 550
Sec MC Swatton
Pro JA Clements (01483) 473172
Holes 18 L 6368 yds SSS 70
Recs Am–65 A Carter
Pro–66 N Coles
V'tors WD–H WE–M SOC
Fees £32 D–£42
Loc 5 miles W of Woking on A322

West Surrey (1910)

Enton Green, Godalming GU8 5AF

Tel **(01483) 421275**
Mem 750
Sec RS Fanshawe
Pro J Hoskison (01483) 417278
Holes 18 L 6259 yds SSS 70
Recs Am–66 SD Cook
Pro–65 G Orr
V'tors H SOC–WD
Fees £25 (£41)
Loc 1/2 mile SE of Milford Station
Arch Herbert Fowler

Wildwood (1992)

Horsham Road, Afold GU6 8JE

Tel **(01403) 753255**
Fax **(01403) 752005**
Sec A Hill
Pro N Parfrement
Holes 18 L 6650 yds SSS 72
Pro–67 H Stott (1993)
V'tors H SOC–WD
Fees D–£25 (£37.50)
Loc 10 miles S of Guildford on A281
Mis Driving range
Arch Hawtree

Wimbledon Common

(1908)

19 Camp Road, Wimbledon Common, London SW19 4UW

Tel **(0181) 946 0294**
Mem 250
Sec BK Cox (0181) 946 7571
Pro JS Jukes
Holes 18 L 5438 yds SSS 66
Recs Am–63 MA Woodward, TP Standish
Pro–64 JS Jukes
V'tors WD–U WE–M Sun pm BH–NA
Fees £13.50
Mis Pillarbox red outer garment must be worn. London Scottish play here

Wimbledon Park (1898)

Home Park Road, London SW19 7HR

Tel **(0181) 946 1002**
Fax **(0181) 944 8688**
Mem 650
Sec MK Hale (0181) 946 1250
Pro D Wingrove (0181) 946 4053
Holes 18 L 5492 yds SSS 66
Recs Am–61 SJ Bennett, B King
Pro–60 M Gerrard
V'tors WD–H I WE/BH–after 3pm SOC
Fees D–£25 (£25)
Loc Opp All England Lawn Tennis Club

Windlemere (1978)

Pay and play

Windlesham Road, West End, Woking GU24 9QL

Tel **(01276) 858727**
Fax **(01276) 678837**
Sec CD Smith
Pro D Thomas
Holes 9 L 5346 yds SSS 66
V'tors U
Fees 9 holes–£7.50 (£9)
Loc A319 at Lightwater/West End
Mis Floodlit driving range
Arch Clive D Smith

Windlesham (1994)

Grove End, Bagshot GU19 5HY

Tel **(01276) 452220**
Fax **(01276) 452290**
Mem 800
Sec P Watts
Pro A Barber (01276) 472323
Holes 18 L 6515 yds SSS 71
V'tors H–phone first SOC–WD
Fees £30 (£40)
Loc 1/2 mile N of M3 Junction 3, off A30
Arch Tommy Horton

The Wisley (1991)

Ripley, Woking GU23 6QU
Tel **(01483) 211022**
Fax **(01483) 211662**
Mem 750
Sec JR Arthur OBE
Pro W Reid (01483) 211213
Holes 27 holes SSS 73:
Church 9 L 3355 yds;
Garden 9 L 3385 yds;
Mill 9 L 3473 yds
V'tors M
Loc 1 mile S of M25 Junction 10
Arch Robert Trent Jones Jr

Woking (1893)

Pond Road, Hook Heath, Woking GU22 0JZ
Tel **(01483) 760053**
Fax **(01483) 772441**
Mem 500
Sec Lt Col IJ Holmes
Pro J Thorne (01483) 769582
Holes 18 L 6340 yds SSS 70
Recs Am–65 PJ Benka (1968)
V'tors WD–I H WE/BH–M
Fees £30
Loc W of Woking in St John's/Hook Heath area
Arch Tom Dunn

Woodcote Park (1912)

Meadow Hill, Bridle Way, Coulsdon CR5 2QQ
Tel **(0181) 660 0176**
Fax **(0181) 668 2788**
Mem 630
Sec TJ Fensom (0181) 668 2788
Pro D Hudspith (0181) 668 1843
Holes 18 L 6669 yds SSS 72
Recs Am–66 S Keppler
Pro–66 C Bonner
V'tors WD–U WE–M
Fees £20
Loc Purley 2 miles

Worplesdon (1908)

Heath House Road, Woking GU22 0RA
Tel **(01483) 489876** (Steward)
Fax **(01483) 473303**
Mem 560
Sec Maj REE Jones (01483) 472277
Pro J Christine (01483) 473287
Holes 18 L 6440 yds SSS 71
Recs Am–64 KG Jones (1988), AD Tillman (1991)
Pro–62
Ladies–67 W Wooldridge
V'tors WD–H WE–M
Fees On application
Loc E of Woking, off A322. 6 miles S of M3 Junction 3

Sussex (East)

Aldershaw (1990)

Kent Street, Sedlescombe TN33 0SD
Tel **(01424) 870898**
Mem 380
Sec R George
Pro M Palmer
Holes 18 L 6218 yds Par 72
V'tors WD–H WE–M
Fees On application
Loc 5 miles N of Hastings

Ashdown Forest Hotel

Chapel Lane, Forest Row RH18 5BB
Tel **(01342) 824866** (Hotel)
Fax **(01342) 824869**
Mem 150
Sec AJ Riddick/RL Pratt (Hotel Proprietors)
Pro M Landsborough (01342) 822247
Holes 18 L 5510 yds SSS 67
V'tors U SOC
Fees On application
Loc 4 miles S of E Grinstead, off A22

Brighton & Hove (1887)

Dyke Road, Brighton BN1 8YJ
Tel **(01273) 556482**
Mem 350
Sec SC Cawkwell
Pro C Burgess (01273) 540560
Holes 9 L 5722 yds SSS 68
Recs Am–65
V'tors U SOC Sun–NA before noon
Fees £12.50 (£21)
Loc 4 miles N of Brighton
Arch James Braid

Cooden Beach (1912)

Cooden Beach, Bexhill-on-Sea TN39 4TR
Tel **(01424) 842040**
Mem 700
Sec TE Hawes
Pro J Sim (01424) 843938
Holes 18 L 6470 yds SSS 71
Recs Am–67 G Burton, CM Skinner, Sir H Birkmyre
Pro–65 AG Harrison
V'tors H SOC
Fees £26 (£33) (1994)
Loc W boundary of Bexhill
Arch Herbert Fowler

Crowborough Beacon (1895)

Beacon Road, Crowborough TN6 1UJ
Tel **(01892) 661511**
Fax **(01892) 667339**
Mem 700
Sec Mrs V Harwood (01892) 661511
Pro D Newnham (01892) 653877
Holes 18 L 6279 yds SSS 70
Recs Am–67 GCD Carter, SF Robson, I McKellow (1993)
Pro–66 D Geal (1992)
V'tors I H WE/BH–M
Fees £22.50–£34
Loc 9 miles S of Tunbridge Wells on A26

Dale Hill Hotel (1973)

Ticehurst, Wadhurst TN5 7DQ
Tel **(01580) 200112**
Fax **(01580) 201249**
Mem 640
Sec M Ruellan (Sec/Mgr)
Pro L Greasley (01580) 201090
Holes 18 L 6150 yds SSS 69
Pro–68 K MacDonald
V'tors WD–U WE/BH–H (phone first) SOC
Fees £20 (£35)
Loc B2087, off A21 at Flimwell

Dewlands Manor (1992)

Pay and play
Cottage Hill, Rotherfield TN6 3JN
Tel **(01892) 852266**
Fax **(01892) 853015**
Sec R Page
Pro N Godin
Holes 9 L 3186 yds Par 36
V'tors U–phone first
Fees 9 holes–£12.50 (£14.50)
18 holes–£23 (£27)
Loc 1/2 mile S of Rotherfield, off A267/B2101. 10 miles S of Tunbridge Wells. M25 Junction 5
Arch Reg Godin

The Dyke (1906)

Dyke Road, Brighton BN1 8YJ
Tel **(01273) 857296**
Mem 750
Sec TR White
Pro M Ross (01273) 857260
Holes 18 L 6611 yds SSS 72
Recs Am–68 S Crooks
Pro–66 I Dryden
V'tors U exc Sun–NA
Fees £21 D–£31 (£31)
Loc 4 miles N of Brighton

East Brighton (1893)

Roedean Road, Brighton BN2 5RA
Tel **(01273) 604838**
Mem 650
Sec CP Simpson
Pro WH Street (01273) 603989
Holes 18 L 6346 yds SSS 70
Recs Am–68 AW Schofield (1992)
Pro–63 S King (Old course)
V'tors WD–U H after 9am WE–NA before 11am SOC
Fees £16 D–£21 (£20 D–£30)
Loc 1 1/2 miles E of Town Centre, overlooking Marina
Arch James Braid

East Sussex National
(1989)
Little Horsted, Uckfield TN22 5ES
Tel **(01825) 880088**
Fax **(01825) 880066**
Mem 500
Pro G Dukart (Golf Dir)
Holes East 18 L 7138 yds SSS 74
West 18 L 7154 yds SSS 74
Recs Am–68 M Watson (1993)
Pro–65 G Brand Jr (1993)
V'tors U on one course
Fees £60 D–£80
Loc 2 miles S of Uckfield, on A22
Mis Driving range. Golf academy
Arch Bob Cupp

Eastbourne Downs (1907)
East Dean Road, Eastbourne BN20 8ES
Tel **(01323) 720827**
Mem 700
Sec DJ Eldrett
Pro T Marshall (01323) 732264
Holes 18 L 6635 yds SSS 72
Recs Am–67 J Collison (1988)
Pro–70 B Gallacher
V'tors U exc Sun–NA before 1pm
Fees £18
Loc 1 mile W of Eastbourne on A259
Arch JH Taylor

Eastbourne Golfing Park
(1992)
Pay and play
Lottbridge Drove, Eastbourne BN23 6QJ
Tel **(01323) 520400**
Fax **(01323) 504134**
Mem 250
Sec C Packham
Pro B Finch
Holes 9 L 5046 yds SSS 65
Recs Am–64 G Murray (1994)
V'tors U
Fees £10 (£12)
Loc ½ mile S of Hampden Park
Mis Floodlit driving range
Arch David Ashton

Hastings (1973)
Public
Beauport Park, Battle Road, St Leonards-on-Sea TN38 0TA
Tel **(01424) 852977**
Sec R Thomson
Pro M Barton (01424) 852981
Holes 18 L 6248 yds SSS 71
Recs Am–69 V Massarella (1981)
Pro–72 S Hall (1987)
V'tors U–booking necessary SOC
Fees On application
Loc 3 miles N of Hastings, off A2100 Battle road
Mis Driving range

Highwoods (1925)
Ellerslie Lane, Bexhill-on-Sea TN39 4LJ
Tel **(01424) 212625**
Mem 800
Sec JE Osborough
Pro MJ Andrews (01424) 212770
Holes 18 L 6218 yds SSS 70
Recs Am–65 S Graham (1990)
Pro–68 C Clark (1976)
V'tors WD/Sat–H Sun am–M Sun pm–H
Fees £22 (£28)
Loc 2 miles N of Bexhill
Arch JH Taylor

Hollingbury Park (1911)
Public
Ditching Road, Brighton BN1 7HS
Tel **(01273) 552010**
Mem 300
Sec J Walling
Pro P Brown (01273) 500086
Holes 18 L 6415 yds SSS 71
Recs Am–68 G Derkson (1988)
Pro–65 J Spence (1989)
V'tors U SOC
Fees £12 D–£17 (£14)
Loc 1 mile NE of Brighton

Holtye (1893)
Holtye, Cowden, Edenbridge TN8 7ED
Tel **(01342) 850635**
Mem 480
Sec JP Holmes (01342) 850576
Pro K Hinton (01342) 850957
Holes 9 L 5325 yds SSS 66
Recs Am–65 PD Scarles, JA Couling, BD Clarke
Pro–64 S Frost
V'tors WD–U exc Thurs am–NA
WE–NA before noon
SOC–Tues & Fri
Fees D–£15 (£18)
Loc 4 miles E of E Grinstead on A264

Horam Park (1985)
Pay and play
Chiddingly Road, Horam TN21 0JJ
Tel **(014353) 3477**
Fax **(014353) 3677**
Mem 400
Sec Mrs G Hewitt
Pro M Jarvis
Holes 9 L 5864 yds SSS 70
Pro–64 J Pinsent (1988)
V'tors U exc Sat–M before 4pm SOC
Fees 18 holes–£10.50 D–£12
9 holes–£7.50 D–£9
Loc ½ mile S of Horam towards Chiddingley. 12 miles N of Eastbourne on A267
Mis Floodlit driving range
Arch Glen Johnson

Lewes (1896)
Chapel Hill, Lewes BN7 2BB
Tel **(01273) 473245**
Mem 700
Sec PG White (01273) 483474
Pro P Dobson (01273) 483823
Holes 18 L 6218 yds Par 71 SSS 70
Recs Am–68 D Cosham (1994)
Pro–67 CA Burgess (1988)
V'tors WD–U WE–NA before 2pm SOC
Fees £16.50 (£27)
Loc ½ mile from Lewes at E end of Cliffe High Street

Nevill (1914)
Benhall Mill Road, Tunbridge Wells TN2 5JW
Tel **(01892) 525818**
Fax **(01892) 517861**
Mem 579 152(L) 55(J)
Sec Miss KNR Pudner
Pro P Huggett (01892) 532941
Holes 18 L 6336 yds SSS 70
Recs Am–64 J Harris (1994)
Pro–66 M Warner (1988)
V'tors WD–H WE/BH–M
Fees £33
Loc Tunbridge Wells 1 mile

Peacehaven (1895)
Brighton Road, Newhaven BN9 9UH
Tel **(01273) 514049**
Mem 290
Sec LM Dennis-Smither (01273) 512571
Pro G Williams (01273) 512602
Holes 9 L 5235 yds SSS 66
Recs Am–65 J Harris (1993)
V'tors WD–U WE/BH–after 11am SOC
Fees £10 (£16)
Loc 8 miles E of Brighton on A259
Arch James Braid

Piltdown (1904)
Piltdown, Uckfield TN22 3XB
Tel **(01825) 722033**
Mem 400
Sec JC Duncan (Hon)
Pro J Amos (01825) 722389
Holes 18 L 6070 yds SSS 69
Recs Am–67 A Smith (1988)
Pro–69 S Frost, P Lovesey
V'tors I or H exc BH/Tues am/Thurs am/Sun am
Fees £27.50
Loc 1 mile W of Maresfield, off A272 towards Isfield

Royal Ashdown Forest
(1888)
Chapel Lane, Forest Row, East Grinstead RH18 5LR
Tel **(01342) 822018**
Fax **(01342) 825211**
Mem 450
Sec DJ Scrivens
Pro MA Landsborough (01342) 822247
Holes Old 18 L 6477 yds SSS 71
New 18 L 5586 yds SSS 67
Recs Am–67 RA Darlington
Pro–62 HA Padgham
V'tors On application (phone first)
Fees £28 (£36) (1994)
Loc 4 miles S of E Grinstead on B2100 Hartfield road. M25 Junction 6

Royal Eastbourne (1887)

Paradise Drive, Eastbourne BN20 8BP

Tel **(01323) 729738**
Fax **(01323) 736986**
Mem 850
Sec P Robins
Pro R Wooller (01323) 736986
Holes 18 L 6109 yds SSS 69
9 L 2147 yds SSS 32
Recs Am–62 J Beland (1991)
Pro–62 J Pinsent (1987)
V'tors U H SOC
Fees 18 hole:£20 (£25)
9 hole:£8 (£10)
Loc 1/2 mile from Town Hall

Rye (1894)

Camber, Rye TN31 7QS

Tel **(01797) 225241**
Fax **(01797) 225460**
Mem 800 105(L) 110(J)
Sec CJW Gilbert
Pro P Marsh, MP Lee
(01797) 225218
Holes 18 L 6301 yds SSS 71
9 L 6625 yds SSS 72
Recs Am–64 P Hurring (1988),
G Wolstenholme (1994)
Pro–63 G Ralph (1994)
V'tors M
Loc 3 miles E of Rye on B2075
Arch HS Colt

Seaford (1887)

East Blatchington, Seaford BN25 2JD

Tel **(01323) 892442**
Mem 420 110(L) 37(J)
Pro P Stevens (01323) 894160
Holes 18 L 6233 yds SSS 70
Recs Am–66 EA Snow, A Flygt
Pro–67 H Weetman
V'tors WD–U after 9.30am exc Wed
WE–M SOC
Fees £20 D–£30
Loc 1 mile N of Seaford (A259)
Arch JH Taylor

Seaford Head (1907)

Public

Southdown Road, Seaford BN25 4JS

Tel **(01323) 890139**
Sec D Strickland
Pro AJ Lowles
Holes 18 L 5812 yds SSS 68
Recs Am–65 D Hills
Pro–66 M Andrews
V'tors U
Fees £10 D–£14.90 (£12.10
D–£17.10)
Loc 8 miles W of Eastbourne.
3/4 mile S of A259

Waterhall (1923)

Public

Devils Dyke Road, Brighton BN1 8YN

Tel **(01273) 508658**
Sec PV Verner (Hon)
Pro P Charman
Holes 18 L 5775 yds SSS 68
Recs Am–66 R Vance
V'tors WD–U WE–U after 8am
Fees £10.50 (£14.50)
Loc 3 miles N of Brighton between
A23 and A27. 1 mile N of
A2308

Wellshurst G & CC (1992)

North Street, Hellingly BN27 4EE

Tel **(01435) 813636**
Fax **(01435) 812444**
Mem 300
Sec M Adams (Man Dir)
Pro M Barton (01435) 813456
Holes 18 L 5717 yds SSS 68
V'tors U SOC
Fees £16 D–£26
Loc 2 miles N of Hailsham on
A267
Mis Driving range

West Hove (1910)

Church Farm, Hangleton, Hove BN3 8AN

Tel **(01273) 413411** (Clubhouse)
Fax **(01273) 439988**
Sec NG Hill (Mgr)
(01273) 419738
Pro D Mills (01273) 413494
Holes 18 L 6201 yds SSS 70 Par 70
Pro–70 G McWhitty
V'tors U–phone first SOC
Fees On application
Loc N of Brighton By-pass. 2nd
junction W from A23 flyover
Mis Practice driving range
Arch Hawtree

Willingdon (1898)

Southdown Road, Eastbourne BN20 9AA

Tel **(01323) 410983**
Mem 550
Sec B Kirby (01323) 410981
Pro JN Debenham
(01323) 410984
Holes 18 L 6049 yds SSS 69
Recs Am–64 DM Sewell (1986)
Pro–62 J Sewell (1990)
V'tors WD–U H WE–MH exc Sun
am–NA SOC–H
Fees D–£24 (£27)
Loc 1/2 mile N of Eastbourne, off
A22
Arch JH Taylor/Dr A Mackenzie

Sussex (West)

Avisford Park (1993)

Walberton, Arundel BH18 0LS

Tel **(01243) 554611**
Fax **(01243) 555580**
Mem 75
Sec J Beach
Pro R Beach
Holes 9 L 3009 yds SSS 70
Pro–68 R Beach
V'tors U SOC
Fees £10–£12 (£13–£15)
Loc 4 miles W of Arundel on A27

Bognor Regis (1892)

Downview Road, Felpham, Bognor Regis PO22 8JD

Tel **(01243) 865867**
Fax **(01243) 860719**
Mem 650
Sec BD Poston (01243) 821929
Pro AP Barr (01243) 865209
Holes 18 L 6238 yds SSS 70
Recs Am–65 G Evans (1989),
M Galway (1991/4)
Pro–64 JR Day (1992)
V'tors WD–H after 9.30am
WE/BH–M (Apr–Sept)
SOC
Fees £25 (£30)
Loc 2 miles E of Bognor Regis
Arch James Braid

Burgess Hill

Cuckfield Road, Burgess Hill

Tel **(01444) 870615**
Sec L Green (Mgr)
Pro P Tallack
Holes 9 L 4433 yds SSS 62
V'tors U
Fees On application
Loc N of Burgess Hill
Mis Floodlit driving range

Chichester Golf Centre (1990)

Hunston Village, Chichester PO20 6AX

Tel **(01243) 533833**
Fax **(01243) 539922**
Mem 300
Sec MJ Doyle (01243) 536666
Pro C Rota
Holes Cathedral 18 L 6461 yds
SSS 71
Tower 18 L 6174 yds SSS 69
9 hole Par 3 course
Recs Cathedral Am–70 S Kirkland
Tower Pro–67 C Rota
V'tors U SOC
Fees Tower–£14 (£19.50)
Cathedral–£20 (£28)
Loc 3 miles S of A27 on B2145 to
Selsey
Mis Driving range
Arch Phillip Sanders

Copthorne (1892)

Borers Arm Road, Copthorne RH10 3LL

Tel **(01342) 712508**
Fax **(01342) 717682**
Mem 565
Sec IJ Evans
Pro J Burrell (01342) 712405
Holes 18 L 6505 yds SSS 71
Recs Am–68 D Arnold,
M Logan
Pro–66 K MacDonald
V'tors WD–U WE/BH–after 1pm
SOC
Fees £25 (£30)
Loc 1 mile E of M23 Junction 10,
on A264
Arch James Braid

Cottesmore (1974)

Buchan Hill, Crawley RH11 9AT

Tel **(01293) 528256**
Fax **(01293) 522819**
Mem 1200
Sec M Topper
Pro A Prior (01293) 535399
Holes Old 18 L 6280 yds SSS 70
New 18 L 5489 yds SSS 68
Recs Old Am–66 S Pardoe
Pro–67 R Tinworth
V'tors WD–U WE–NA before 11am
SOC–Mon/Wed/Fri
Fees Old–£30 (£40)
New–£20 (£26)
Loc 4 miles S of Crawley, off M23
Arch MD Rogerson

Cowdray Park (1949)

Petworth Road, Midhurst GU29 0BB

Tel **(01730) 812088**
Mem 700
Sec JK McIver (01730) 813599
Pro S Hall (01730) 812091
Holes 18 L 6212 yds SSS 70
Recs Am–67 S Brown (1994)
Pro–66 G Ralph (1989)
V'tors I or H WD–NA before 9am
Sat–NA before 10am
Sun/BH–NA before 3pm SOC
Fees £20 (£25)
Loc 1 mile E of Midhurst on A272

Effingham Park (1980)

West Park Road, Copthorne RH10 3EU

Tel **(01342) 716528**
Fax **(01342) 716039**
Mem 400
Sec J O'Donovan (Mgr)
(01342) 712138
Pro I Dryden
Holes 9 L 1749 yds Par 30
Recs Am–29
Pro–26
V'tors WD–U WE–M before noon
–U after noon
Fees £8 D–£11.50 (£9 D–£13.50)
Loc B2028/B2039. M23 Junction
10
Mis Golf academy
Arch Francisco Escario

Foxbridge (1993)

Foxbridge Lane, Plaistow RH14 0LB

Tel **(01403) 753303/753343**
(Bookings)
Fax **(01403) 753433**
Mem 300
Sec Miss K Harridge
Pro S Hall (01403) 753343
Holes 9 L 3015 yds SSS 69
V'tors M SOC
Loc 15 miles S of Guildford, off
B2133
Arch Paul Clark

Gatwick Manor (1975)

London Road, Lowfield Heath, Crawley RH10 2ST

Tel **(01293) 538587**
Pro C Jenkins
Holes 9 L 1246 yds SSS 28
Pro–24 C Jenkins (1991)
V'tors U SOC
Fees 9 holes–£3
Loc A23 to Crawley, 1 mile past
Gatwick Airport
Arch Patrick Tallack

Goodwood (1892)

Goodwood, Chichester PO18 0PN

Tel **(01243) 785012 (Members)**
Fax **(01243) 536650**
Mem 900
Sec CAR Pickup (01243) 774968
Pro K MacDonald (01243) 774994
Holes 18 L 6401 yds SSS 71
Recs Am–67 C Fogden (1993)
Pro–64 G Orr (1992)
V'tors WD–H after 9am WE–H after
10am SOC–Wed & Thurs
Fees £28 (£38)
Loc 3 miles NE of Chichester, on
road to racecourse
Arch James Braid

Goodwood Park G & CC (1989)

Goodwood, Chichester PO18 0QB

Tel **(01243) 775987**
Mem 750
Sec B Geoghegan (Sec/Mgr)
Pro A Wratting
Holes 18 L 6530 yds SSS 72
V'tors WD–H WE/BH–NA before
noon H SOC
Fees £30 (£40)
Loc 4 miles N of Chichester
Arch Donald Steel

Ham Manor (1936)

West Drive, Angmering, Littlehampton BN16 4JE

Tel **(01903) 783288**
Mem 860
Sec PH Saubergue
Pro S Buckley (01903) 783732
Holes 18 L 6216 yds SSS 70
Recs Am–64 F Wieland (1987)
Pro–62 TA Horton
V'tors WD/WE–H
Fees On application
Loc Between Worthing and
Littlehampton
Arch HS Colt

Haywards Heath (1924)

High Beech Lane, Haywards Heath RH16 1SL

Tel **(01444) 414310**
Fax **(01444) 458319**
Mem 625
Sec JE Jarman (01444) 414457
Pro M Henning (01444) 414866
Holes 18 L 6204 yds SSS 70
Recs Am–69 G Batt-Rawden,
R Arnold, S Hoskins
V'tors WD/WE–H–restricted
SOC–Wed & Thurs
Fees £22 (£30)
Loc 2 miles N of Haywards Heath,
off B2112

Hill Barn (1935)

Public

Hill Barn Lane, Worthing BN14 9QE

Tel **(01903) 237301**
Pro AP Higgins
Holes 18 L 6224 yds SSS 70
Recs Am–66 H Francis, B Roberts
Pro–63 J Kinsella
V'tors U
Fees £10.80 (£12.85)
Loc NE of A27 at Warren Road
roundabout
Arch Hawtree

Horsham Golf Park (1993)

Pay and play

Worthing Road, Horsham RH13 7AX

Tel **(01403) 271525**
Fax **(01403) 274528**
Mem 190
Sec J Ellwood (01403) 271525
Pro N Burke (Mgr)
Holes 9 L 2061 yds Par 33 SSS 30
Recs Am–63 J Ellwood (1994)
Pro–55 J Spence (1993)
V'tors U SOC
Fees 9 holes–£6 (£7)
Loc 1 mile S of Horsham, off A24

Ifield (1927)

Rusper Road, Ifield, Crawley RH11 0LN

Tel **(01293) 520222**
Fax **(01293) 612973**
Mem 875
Sec B Gazzard
Pro J Earl (01293) 523088
Holes 18 L 6314 yds SSS 70
Recs Am–67 C Paterson
Pro–65 G Cowlishaw,
P Mitchell
V'tors WD–H WE–M SOC
Fees £27
Loc W of Crawley.
M23 Junction 11

Littlehampton (1889)

170 Rope Walk, Littlehampton BN17 5DL

Tel **(01903) 717170**
Fax **(01903) 726629**
Mem 650
Sec KR Palmer (Sec/Mgr)
Pro G McQuitty (01903) 716369
Holes 18 L 6244 yds SSS 70
Recs Am–66 J Jones
Pro–66 G Ralph
V'tors WD–U after 9.30am
WE/BH–NA before noon SOC
Fees £24 (£30)
Loc W bank of River Arun,
Littlehampton

Mannings Heath (1908)

Goldings Lane, Mannings Heath, Horsham RH13 6JU

Tel **(01403) 210228**
Fax **(01403) 270974**
Mem 657
Sec D Pecorelli
Pro P Harrison (01403) 210228

For list of abbreviations see page 435

Holes 18 L 6404 yds SSS 71
Recs Am–66 JM Dodds
Pro–64 G Ralph
V'tors WD–H SOC
Fees £27 (£35)
Loc 3 miles SE of Horsham (A281)

Osiers Farm (1991)
Osiers Farm, Petworth GU28 9LX
Tel **(01798) 344097**
Mem 100
Sec Mrs S Drake
Holes 18 L 6191 yds Par 71 SSS 66
V'tors U SOC
Fees 18 holes–£9 9 holes–£7
Loc 1½ miles N of Petworth on A285
Arch C & T Duncton

Paxhill Park (1990)
East Mascalls Lane, Lindfield RH16 2QN
Tel **(01444) 484467**
Fax **(01444) 482709**
Mem 540
Sec RS Bainbridge
Pro S Dunkley
Holes 18 L 6196 yds SSS 68
Recs Am–67 E Pagden (1993)
V'tors WD–U WE–pm only
Fees £15 (£20)
Loc 1 mile N of Lindfield, off B2028. 4 miles NE of Haywards Heath
Arch Patrick Tallack

Pease Pottage (1986)
Horsham Road, Pease Pottage, Crawley RH11 9AP
Tel **(01293) 521706**
Mem 56
Sec A Venn
Pro M Root
Holes 9 L 3511 yds SSS 57
Recs Am–63 M Bolton Smith (1992)
Pro–58 S Mantel (1992)
V'tors U
Fees £8 (£11)
Loc S of Crawley, off A23
Mis Driving range

Pyecombe (1894)
Pyecombe, Brighton BN45 7FF
Tel **(01273) 845372**
Mem 650
Sec WM Wise MA
Pro CR White (01273) 845398
Holes 18 L 6234 yds SSS 70
Recs Am–67 TM Greenfield
Pro–66 JA Brown
Ladies–68 A Greenfield
V'tors WD–U exc Tues after 9.15am WE–U after 2pm SOC–WD exc Tues
Fees £16 (£25)
Loc 5 miles N of Brighton on A273

Selsey (1906)
Golf Links Lane, Selsey PO20 9DR
Tel **(01243) 602203**
Mem 400
Sec BG Keen (01243) 605176
Pro P Grindley
Holes 9 L 5834 yds SSS 68
Recs Am–66 A Kelly, K Terry
V'tors U
Fees £10 (£15)
Loc 7 miles S of Chichester

Singing Hills (1992)
Pay and play
Albourne, Brighton BN6 9EB
Tel **(01273) 835353**
Fax **(01273) 835444**
Mem 500
Sec CA Pluck
Holes 27 holes SSS 69-71:
River 9 L 2826 yds
Valley 9 L 3348 yds
Lakes 9 L 3253 yds
Recs Am–67 B Anderson (1992)
Pro–66 R Frost (1993)
V'tors U H SOC
Fees £20 (£25)
Loc 6 miles N of Brighton, off B2117
Mis Driving range
Arch MRM Sandow

Slinfold Park (1993)
Stane Street, Slinfold, Horsham RH13 7RE
Tel **(01403) 791154**
Pro G McKay (01403) 791555
Holes 18 L 6450 yds SSS 71
9 hole course
V'tors U SOC
Fees £20 (£25)
Loc 3 miles W of Horsham (A29)
Mis Driving range
Arch John Fortune

Tilgate Forest (1982)
Public
Titmus Drive, Tilgate, Crawley RH10 5EU
Tel **(01293) 530103**
Fax **(01293) 523478**
Pro S Trussell, D McClelland
Holes 18 L 6359 yds SSS 70
9 hole Par 3 course
Recs Am–74 M Hearn (1988)
Pro–68 J Hodgkinson (1986)
V'tors U SOC–Mon–Thurs
Fees 18 hole: £12 (£16)
9 hole: £4 (£5.30)
Loc 1½ miles SE of Crawley. M23 Junction 11
Mis Driving range

West Chiltington (1988)
Pay and play
Broadford Bridge Road, West Chiltington RH20 2YA
Tel **(01798) 813574**
Fax **(01798) 812631**
Mem 700
Sec SE Coulson
Pro G Downer (01798) 812115
Holes 18 L 5969 yds Par 70 SSS 69
9 hole Par 3 course
Recs Am–68 P Monks (1992)
Pro–62 B Barnes (1991)
V'tors U SOC
Fees £12.50 (£15)
Loc 2 miles E of Pulborough
Mis Driving range
Arch Faulkner/Barnes

West Sussex (1930)
Hurston Lane, Pulborough RH20 2EN
Tel **(01798) 872563**
Mem 800
Sec GR Martindale
Pro T Packham (01798) 872426
Holes 18 L 6221 yds SSS 70
Recs Am–61 G Evans
V'tors WD–I H after 9.30am exc Fri–M SOC–Wed & Thurs
Fees On application
Loc 1½ miles E of Pulborough on A283

Worthing (1905)
Links Road, Worthing BN14 9QZ
Tel **(01903) 260801**
Fax **(01903) 694664**
Mem 1000
Sec D Browse
Pro S Rolley (01903) 260718
Holes Lower 18 L 6530 yds SSS 72
Upper 18 L 5243 yds SSS 66
Recs Lower Am–62 P Drew (1994)
Pro–66 P Harrison (1992)
V'tors WD–U H WE–confirm in advance with Pro
Fees On application
Loc Central Station 1½ miles (A27), nr A24 Junction
Arch HS Colt

Tyne & Wear

Backworth (1937)
The Hall, Backworth, Shiremoor, Newcastle-upon-Tyne ME27 0AH
Tel **(0191) 268 1048**
Mem 400
Holes 9 L 5930 yds SSS 69
Recs Am–66
V'tors Mon & Fri–U Tues–Thurs–M after 5pm WE–after 12.30pm exc comp Sats–after 6pm
Fees On application
Loc Off Tyne Tunnel link road, Holystone roundabout

Birtley (1922)
Birtley Lane, Birtley DH3 2LR
Tel **(0191) 410 2207**
Mem 220
Sec T Stobbart
Holes 9 L 5660 yds SSS 67
Recs Am–63 I McEntee
V'tors WD–U exc Fri pm–M WE/BH–M SOC
Fees £12
Loc 3 miles from Birtley service area on A1(M)

Boldon (1912)

Dipe Lane, East Boldon NE36 0PQ

Tel **(0191) 536 4182 (Clubhouse)**
Mem 700
Sec RE Jobes (0191) 536 5360
Pro Phipps Golf (0191) 536 5835
Holes 18 L 6348 yds SSS 70
Recs Am–67 GR Simpson (1987)
Pro–66 M Archer (1993)
V'tors WD–U WE/BH–NA before 3.30pm
Fees On application
Loc 8 miles SE of Newcastle

City of Newcastle (1891)

Three Mile Bridge, Gosforth, Newcastle-upon-Tyne NE3 2DR

Tel **(0191) 285 1775**
Mem 400 110(L) 60(J)
Sec AJ Matthew
Pro AJ Matthew (0191) 285 5481
Holes 18 L 6508 yds SSS 71
Recs Am–67 M Blackburn (1989), B Simpson (1991), R Hayhoe (1992), K Ferrie (1994)
Pro–67 W Tyrie (1988)
V'tors U exc comp days–NA
Fees £19 (£21)
Loc B1318, 3 miles N of Newcastle
Arch Harry Vardon

Garesfield (1922)

Chopwell NE17 7AP

Tel **(01207) 561278/561309**
Mem 440
Sec JR Peart
Pro D Race (01207) 563082
Holes 18 L 6196 yds SSS 70
Recs Am–68 I Turner (1991)
Pro–70 D Dunk (1978)
V'tors WD–U WE/BH–NA before 4.30pm SOC
Fees On application
Loc 7 miles SW of Newcastle, between High Spen and Chopwell

Gosforth (1906)

Broadway East, Gosforth, Newcastle-upon-Tyne NE3 5ER

Tel **(0191) 285 6710**
Mem 370 100(L) 50(J)
Sec P Keady (0191) 285 3495
Pro G Garland (0191) 285 0553
Holes 18 L 6024 yds SSS 69
Recs Am–65 I Potter (1992)
V'tors WD–U WE–M before 4pm –U after 4pm SOC
Fees £20
Loc 3 miles N of Newcastle, off A6125

Heworth (1911)

Gingling Gate, Heworth, Gateshead NE10 8XY

Tel **(0191) 469 2137**
Mem 600
Sec G Holbrow (0191) 469 9832
Holes 18 L 6462 yds SSS 71
Recs Am–65 D Moralee
Pro–69 P Highmoor
V'tors WD–U WE–NA before noon
Fees £13 (£13)
Loc SE boundary of Gateshead

Houghton-le-Spring (1908)

Copt Hill, Houghton-le-Spring DH5 8LU

Tel **(0191) 584 1198**
Mem 600
Sec N Wales (0191) 584 0048
Pro (0191) 584 7421
Holes 18 L 6416 yds SSS 71
Recs Am–66 J Ellison
V'tors U SOC
Fees £17 (£22)
Loc 3 miles SW of Sunderland

Newcastle United (1892)

Ponteland Road, Cowgate, Newcastle-upon-Tyne NE5 3JW

Tel **(0191) 286 4693 (Clubhouse)**
Mem 500
Sec J Simpson
Pro (0191) 286 9998
Holes 18 L 6573 yds SSS 71
Recs Am–64 G Grant (1993)
V'tors WD–U WE/BH–M
Fees On application
Loc Nuns Moor, 2 miles W of city centre

Northumberland (1898)

High Gosforth Park, Newcastle-upon-Tyne NE3 5HT

Tel **(0191) 236 2009**
Fax **(0191) 236 2498**
Mem 500
Sec SC Owram (0191) 236 2498
Holes 18 L 6629 yds SSS 72
Recs Am–67 W Bennett, PH Coulthard
Pro–65 A Jacklin, T Horton
V'tors WD–I BH–M
Fees £30–£35
Loc 5 miles N of Newcastle
Arch HS Colt/James Braid

Parklands (1971)

High Gosforth Park, Newcastle-upon-Tyne NE3 5HQ

Tel **(0191) 236 4480/4867**
Mem 750
Sec B Woof
Pro B Rumney
Holes 18 L 6060 yds SSS 69
Recs Am–66 S Johnston, G Hewitt
Pro–65 B Rumney
V'tors U
Fees £13 (£15)
Loc 5 miles N of Newcastle
Mis 9 hole pitch & putt course. Driving range

Ravensworth (1906)

Moss Heaps, Wrekenton, Gateshead NE9 7UU

Tel **(0191) 487 6014/2843**
Mem 550
Sec L Winter (0191) 488 7549
Pro D Race (0191) 491 3475
Holes 18 L 5872 yds SSS 68
Recs Am–63 K Kelly
Pro–64 T Horton
V'tors U H SOC
Fees £17 (£25)
Loc 3 miles S of Newcastle on B1296

Ryton (1891)

Doctor Stanners, Clara Vale, Ryton NE40 3TD

Tel **(0191) 413 3737**
Mem 600
Sec FR Creed
Holes 18 L 6300 yds SSS 69
Recs Am–69 P Brougham
V'tors WD–U WE–M SOC
Fees £12 (£16)
Loc 7 miles W of Newcastle, off A695

South Shields (1893)

Cleadon Hills, South Shields NE34 8EG

Tel **(0191) 456 0475**
Mem 700
Sec WH Loades (0191) 456 8942
Pro G Parsons (0191) 456 0110
Holes 18 L 6264 yds SSS 70
Recs Am–64 J Dryden (1993)
Pro–64 M Gregson (1978)
V'tors U SOC
Fees On application
Loc Cleadon Hills

Tynemouth (1913)

Spital Dene, Tynemouth, North Shields NE30 2ER

Tel **(0191) 257 4578**
Mem 824
Sec W Storey (0191) 257 3381
Pro J McKenna (0191) 258 0728
Holes 18 L 6403 yds SSS 71
Recs Am–65 CS Hill
Pro–64 J Ord
V'tors WD–U 9.30am–5pm –NA before 9.30am and after 5pm WE/BH–M
Fees £20
Loc 8 miles E of Newcastle
Arch Willie Park

Tyneside (1879)

Westfield Lane, Ryton NE40 3QE

Tel **(0191) 413 2177**
Mem 660
Sec JR Watkin (0191) 413 2742
Pro M Gunn (0191) 413 1600
Holes 18 L 6042 yds SSS 69
Recs Am–65 CW Philipson
Pro–65 JR Harrison
V'tors WD–U (exc 11.30–1.30pm) WE–NA before 3pm SOC
Fees £18 (£28)
Loc 7 miles W of Newcastle. S of river, off A695
Arch HS Colt

For list of abbreviations see page 435

Wallsend (1973)

Public
Rheydt Avenue, Bigges Main, Wallsend NE28 8SU
Tel **(0191) 262 1973**
Sec D Souter
Pro K Phillips (0191) 262 4231
Holes 18 L 6608 yds SSS 72
Recs Am–68 G Pickup (1986)
V'tors U
Fees £10 (£12)
Loc Between Newcastle and Wallsend on coast road
Mis Driving range
Arch G Showball

Washington Moat House (1980)

Stone Cellar Road, Usworth, District 12, Washington NE37 1PH
Tel **(0191) 417 2626**
Fax **(0191) 415 1166**
Sec B Wardle (Mgr)
Pro W Marshall (0191) 417 8346
Holes 18 L 6604 yds SSS 72
Recs Am–69 G Taylor (1993)
Pro–64 P Harrison (1991)
V'tors U SOC
Fees £16 (£23)
Loc Off A1(M), on A195
Mis Driving range. 9 hole pitch & putt

Wearside (1892)

Coxgreen, Sunderland SR4 9JT
Tel **(0191) 534 2518**
Mem 650
Sec N Hildrew
Pro D Brolls (0191) 534 4269
Holes 18 L 6315 yds SSS 70
Par 3 course
Recs Am–64 R Walker
Pro–68 A Bickerdike
V'tors H SOC
Fees £24 (£30)
Loc 2 miles W of Sunderland, off A183, by A19

Westerhope (1941)

Whorlton Grange, Westerhope, Newcastle-upon-Tyne NE5 1PP
Tel **(0191) 286 9125**
Mem 778
Sec JW Hedley (0191) 286 7636
Pro N Brown (0191) 286 0594
Holes 18 L 6407 yds SSS 71
Recs Am–64 R Roper
Pro–67 D Russell
V'tors WD–U
Fees £16
Loc 5 miles W of Newcastle

Whickham (1911)

Hollinside Park, Whickham, Newcastle-upon-Tyne NE16 5BE
Tel **(0191) 488 7309**
Fax **(0191) 488 1576**
Mem 500
Sec MJ Musto (0191) 488 1576
Pro B Ridley (0191) 488 8591
Holes 18 L 6129 yds SSS 68
Recs Am–61 AJ McClure
V'tors U
Fees £20 (£25)
Loc 5 miles SW of Newcastle

Whitburn (1931)

Lizard Lane, South Shields NE34 7AF
Tel **(0191) 529 2144**
Mem 380 73(L) 61(J)
Sec Mrs V Atkinson
(0191) 529 4944
Pro D Stephenson
(0191) 529 4210
Holes 18 L 5773 yds Par 69 SSS 68
Recs Am–64 M Samak (1994)
V'tors U SOC–WD exc Tues
Fees £15 (£20)
Loc 2 miles N of Sunderland on coast

Whitley Bay (1890)

Claremont Road, Whitley Bay NE26 3UF
Tel **(0191) 252 0180**
Mem 700
Sec B Dockar
Pro G Shipley (0191) 252 5688
Holes 18 L 6614 yds SSS 72
Recs Am–68 GJ Clark
Pro–66 J Fourie
V'tors WD–U WE–M
Fees £18 D–£25
Loc 10 miles E of Newcastle

Warwickshire

Ansty (1992)

Brinklow Road, Ansty, Coventry CV7 9JH
Tel **(01203) 621341/621305**
Fax **(01203) 602671**
Mem 350
Sec R Challis
Pro J Reay
Holes 18 L 5823 yds SSS 68
V'tors U SOC
Fees £9 (£11)
Loc Between Ansty and Brinklow (B4029). M6 Junction 2, 1 mile.
Mis Driving range
Arch D Morgan

Atherstone (1894)

The Outwoods, Coleshill Road, Atherstone CV9 2RL
Tel **(01827) 713110**
Mem 400 40(L) 40(J)
Sec VA Walton (01827) 892568
Holes 18 L 6239 yds SSS 70
18 L 6006 yds SSS 71
V'tors WD–H WE–M SOC–WD
Fees D–£17 BH–£20
Loc 1/4 mile from Atherstone on Coleshill road

Bidford Grange (1992)

Stratford Road, Bidford-on-Avon B50 4LY
Tel **(01789) 490319**
Fax **(01789) 778184**
Mem 270
Sec D Hemming (Mgr)
Pro G Hale (01527) 892721
Holes 18 L 7233 yds Par 72 SSS 74
Recs Am–66 D Webber
Pro–71 M Dove
V'tors U
Fees £12 (£15)
Loc 5 miles W of Stratford-on-Avon on B439
Arch Swann/Tillman/Granger

City of Coventry (Brandon Wood) (1977)

Public
Brandon Lane, Coventry CV8 3GQ
Tel **(01203) 543141**
Fax **(01203) 545108**
Sec C Gledhill
Pro C Gledhill
Holes 18 L 6610 yds SSS 72
Pro–68 AR Sadler
V'tors U SOC
Fees On application
Loc 6 miles SE of Coventry, off A45(S)
Mis Floodlit driving range

Crocketts Manor G & CC (1994)

Henley-in-Arden B95 5QA
Tel **(01564) 793715**
Fax **(01564) 795754**
Mem 600
Sec S Edwin (Golf Mgr)
Pro S Edwin
Holes 18 L 6933 yds SSS 73
9 hole Par 3 course
V'tors U–booking required SOC
Fees £20 D–£25 (£25 D–£30)
Loc N of Stratford-on-Avon on A3400. M40 Junction 16, 3 miles
Mis Driving range. Golf Academy
Arch N Selwyn-Smith

Ingon Manor (1993)

Ingon Lane, Snitterfield, Stratford-on-Avon CV37 0QE
Tel **(01789) 731857**
Mem 300
Pro M Reay
Holes 18 L 6554 yds Par 72 SSS 71
Recs Am–74 J Webber (1993)
Pro–74 P Broadhurst (1993)
V'tors H SOC
Fees £12 (£25)
Loc 3 miles N of Stratford-on-Avon, off A461. M40 Junction 15
Arch David Hemstock

Kenilworth (1889)

Crewe Lane, Kenilworth CV8 2EA
Tel **(01926) 54296**
Fax **(01926) 864453**
Mem 1010

Sec JH McTavish (01926) 58517
Pro S Yates (01926) 512732
Holes 18 L 6413 yds SSS 71
Recs Am–67 J Herbert, A Allen (1992)
V'tors U H BH–M SOC
Fees £26 (£37)
Loc 1½ miles E of Kenilworth. 5 miles S of Coventry

Ladbrook Park (1908)

Poolhead Lane, Tanworth-in-Arden, Solihull B94 5ED
Tel **(01564) 742264**
Fax **(01564) 742909**
Mem 760
Sec JR Basford
Pro S Harrison (01564) 742581
Holes 18 L 6427 yds SSS 71
Recs Am–67 PJ Sant
Pro–65 RDS Livingston
V'tors WD–U H WE/BH–M H
Fees On application
Loc 12 miles S of Birmingham. M42 Junction 3
Arch HS Colt

Leamington & County (1908)

Golf Lane, Whitnash, Leamington Spa CV31 2QA
Tel **(01926) 425961**
Mem 650
Sec SM Cooknell
Pro I Grant (01926) 428014
Holes 18 L 6430 yds SSS 71
Recs Am–65 RG Hiatt
Pro–66 D Thomas
V'tors U SOC
Fees £25 (£37)
Loc 1½ miles S of Leamington Spa
Arch HS Colt

Maxstoke Park (1896)

Castle Lane, Coleshill, Birmingham B46 2RD
Tel **(01675) 466743**
Fax **(01675) 466743**
Mem 600
Sec D Haywood (Hon)
Pro N McEwan (01675) 464915
Holes 18 L 6442 yds SSS 71
Recs Am–64 AM Allen
Pro–65 C O'Connor Jr
V'tors WD–U WE–M
Fees £25
Loc 3 miles SE of Coleshill

Newbold Comyn (1973)

Public
Newbold Terrace East, Leamington Spa
Tel **(01926) 421157**
Sec AA Pierce
Pro D Knight
Holes 18 L 6221 yds SSS 70
Recs Am–70 G Knight
Pro–S Hutchinson (1987)
V'tors WD–U WE–booking 1 week in advance SOC
Fees £6.50 (£8)
Loc Off Willes Road (B4099)

Nuneaton (1906)

Golf Drive, Whitestone, Nuneaton
Tel **(01203) 347810**
Fax **(01203) 347810**
Mem 650
Sec G Pinder
Pro J Reay Golf (01203) 340201
Holes 18 L 6412 yds SSS 71
Recs Am–67 P Broadhurst
Pro–67 C Holmes
V'tors WD–U H WE–M SOC
Fees £22
Loc 2 miles S of Nuneaton

Purley Chase (1980)

Pipers Lane, Ridge Lane, Nuneaton CV10 0RB
Tel **(01203) 393118**
Mem 600
Sec RG Place
Pro D Llewelyn (01203) 395348
Holes 18 L 6604 yds SSS 72
Recs Am–72 P Broadhurst
Pro–64 P Elson
V'tors WD/BH–U WE–U after 2.30pm SOC
Fees On application
Loc 4 miles WNW of Nuneaton on B4114 (A47) A5 Mancetter Island
Mis Driving range

Rugby (1891)

Clifton Road, Rugby CV21 3RD
Tel **(01788) 542306**
Mem 550
Sec R Scott
Pro A Peach (01788) 575134
Holes 18 L 5457 yds SSS 67
Recs Am–62 A Stephenson, P Godding
Pro–68 D Sutherland
V'tors WD–U WE/BH–M SOC
Fees On application
Loc 1 mile N of Rugby on B5414

Stoneleigh Deer Park (1992)

The Old Deer Park, Coventry Road, Stoneleigh CV8 3DR
Tel **(01203) 639991**
Fax **(01203) 692471**
Mem 900
Sec AJ Sledger
Pro S Mouland
Holes 18 L 6083 yds SSS 71
9 hole Par 3 course
V'tors WD–U WE–NA before noon SOC–WD
Fees On application
Loc ½ mile E of Stoneleigh
Arch K Harrison

Stratford Oaks (1991)

Bearley Road, Snitterfield, Stratford-on-Avon CV37 0EZ
Tel **(01789) 731571**
Fax **(01789) 731700**
Mem 600
Sec P Davison
Pro F Leek
Holes 18 L 6100 yds SSS 71
Recs Am–67 S Millington (1992)
Pro–66 D Eddiford (1992)
V'tors WD–U WE–booking necessary
Fees £12 (£15)
Loc 4 miles NE of Stratford-on-Avon
Mis Driving range
Arch Howard Swann

Stratford-on-Avon (1894)

Tiddington Road, Stratford-on-Avon CV37 7BA
Tel **(01789) 297296**
Mem 770
Sec (01789) 205749
Pro D Sutherland (01789) 205677
Holes 18 L 6311 yds SSS 70
Recs Am–63 I Roberts
Pro–64 M Gallagher
V'tors U H SOC
Fees On application
Loc ½ mile E of Stratford-on-Avon on B4086

Warwick (1971)

Public
Warwick Racecourse, Warwick CV34 6HW
Tel **(01926) 494316**
Sec Mrs R Dunkley
Pro J Nixon (01926) 491284
Holes 9 L 2682 yds SSS 66
Recs Am–67 R Buckingham
Pro–70 P Sharp
V'tors U exc while racing in progress
Fees £3.80 (£5.50)
Loc Centre of Warwick racecourse
Mis Driving range

The Warwickshire (1993)

Leek Wootton, Warwick CV35 7QT
Tel **(01926) 409409**
Fax **(01926) 408409**
Mem 800
Sec PA Chubb (Mgr)
Holes 18 L 7178 yds SSS 74
18 L 7154 yds SSS 74
9 hole Par 3 course
Recs Pro–68 P Baker (1993)
V'tors U
Fees £35 (£35)
Loc 1 mile N of Warwick, off A46. M40 Junction 15
Mis Driving range
Arch Karl Litton

Welcombe Hotel (1980)

Warwick Road, Stratford-on-Avon CV37 0NR
Tel **(01789) 299012**
Fax **(01789) 414666**
Mem 425
Sec PJ Day (Golf Mgr) (01789) 295252
Holes 18 L 6217 yds SSS 70
Recs Am–67 R Fletcher
V'tors WD–U H WE/BH–U H after noon
Fees £40 (£45)
Loc 1½ miles NE of Stratford-on-Avon on A439 to Warwick

For list of abbreviations see page 435

Whitefields Hotel Golf Complex (1992)

Coventry Road, Thurlaston, Rugby CV23 9JR

Tel **(01788) 521800**
Fax **(01788) 521695**
Mem 650
Sec B Coleman (01788) 522393
Holes 18 L 6433 yds SSS 71
V'tors U SOC
Fees £16 (£20)
Loc 3 miles SW of Rugby at A45/M45 Junction
Mis Driving range

West Midlands

The Belfry (1977)

Public
Lichfield Road, Wishaw B76 9PR

Tel **(01675) 470301**
Fax **(01675) 470178**
Sec R Maxfield
Pro P McGovern
Holes Brabazon 18 L 7177 yds SSS 72; Derby 18 L 6186 yds SSS 69
V'tors H SOC
Fees Brabazon–£50
Derby–£25
Loc 2 miles N of M42 Junction 9, off A446
Mis Driving range
Arch Alliss/Thomas

Bloxwich (1924)

Stafford Road, Bloxwich WS3 3PQ

Tel **(01922) 405724**
Mem 500
Sec Mrs JN Loveridge (01922) 476593
Pro G Broadbent
Holes 18 L 6277 yds SSS 70
Recs Am–67 JPG Windsor
Pro–65 J Rhodes
V'tors WD–U WE–M SOC
Fees On application
Loc N of Walsall on A34

Boldmere (1936)

Public
Monmouth Drive, Sutton Coldfield, Birmingham BJ3 6JR

Tel **(0121) 354 3379**
Mem 300
Sec I Furlong
Pro T Short
Holes 18 L 4463 yds SSS 62
Recs Am–57 G Marston (1987)
Pro–57 P Weaver (1987)
V'tors U
Fees £7.80
Loc By Sutton Park, 1 mile W of Sutton Coldfield

Brandhall (1946)

Public
Heron Road, Oldbury, Warley B68 8AQ

Tel **(0121) 552 2195**
Mem 320
Sec WH Rushton
Holes 18 L 5813 yds SSS 68
Recs Am–63 M Daw
V'tors U exc first 2 hrs Sat/Sun
Fees £5.50 (£8)
Loc 6 miles NW of Birmingham. M5 Junction 2, 1½ miles

Bromsgrove Golf Centre (1992) Pay and play

Stratford Road, Bromsgrove B60 1LD

Tel **(01527) 570505**
Mem 500
Sec D Went (01527) 877224
Pro G Long (01527) 575886
Holes 9 L 3159 yds SSS 70
V'tors U SOC–WD
Fees 9 holes–£6 (£7)
18 holes–£10 (£12)
Loc Junction of A38/A448. M42 Junction 1
Mis Driving range. Extension to 18 holes Spring 1996
Arch Hawtree

Calderfields (1983)

Aldridge Road, Walsall WS4 2JS

Tel **(01922) 640540** (Clubhouse), **(01922) 32243** (Bookings)
Fax **(01922) 38787**
Mem 550
Sec JE Hampshire
Holes 18 L 6636 yds SSS 72
V'tors U SOC
Fees £10
Loc 1 mile N of Walsall (A454). M6 Junction 10
Mis Floodlit driving range

Cocks Moor Woods (1926)

Public
Alcester Road, South King's Heath, Birmingham BK1 6ER

Tel **(0121) 444 3584**
Pro S Ellis
Holes 18 L 5742 yds SSS 67
Recs Am–65 V Pailing
Pro–71 B Jones, K Dodsworth
V'tors U
Fees On application
Loc 6 miles S of B'ham (A435)

Copt Heath (1907)

1220 Warwick Road, Knowle, Solihull B93 9LN

Tel **(01564) 772650**
Fax **(01564) 771022**
Mem 700
Sec W Lenton
Pro BJ Barton (01564) 776155
Holes 18 L 6500 yds SSS 71
Recs Am–67 JMH Mayell
Pro–67 D Stokes
V'tors WD–H WE/BH–M SOC
Fees £35
Loc 2 miles S of Solihull on A4141

Coventry (1887)

Finham Park, Coventry CV3 6PJ

Tel **(01203) 411123**
Fax **(01203) 690131**
Mem 750
Sec B Fox (01203) 414152
Pro P Weaver (01203) 411298
Holes 18 L 6613 yds SSS 72
Recs Am–66 P Downes
Pro–64 C Hall, A Webster (1993)
Ladies Pro–62 J Arnold (1990)
V'tors WD–H
Fees £30
Loc 2 miles S of Coventry on A444/4113

Coventry Hearsall (1894)

Beechwood Avenue, Coventry CV5 6DF

Tel **(01203) 713470**
Mem 450
Sec WG Doughty
Pro J Sawyer (01203) 713156
Holes 18 L 5983 yds SSS 69
Recs Am–64 W Nicolson (1992)
Pro–66 B Morris (1987)
V'tors WD–U WE–M
Fees D–£23
Loc 1½ miles S of Coventry off A45

Dartmouth (1910)

Vale Street, West Bromwich B71 4DW

Tel **(0121) 588 2131**
Mem 350
Sec M Morton
Pro C Yates
Holes 9 L 6060 yds SSS 70
Recs Am–66 T Cheese (1991)
Pro–70 P Lester
V'tors WD–U WE–M SOC
Fees D–£16.50
Loc 1 mile from W Bromwich, behind Churchfields High School. Junction M5/M6

Druids Heath (1974)

Stonnall Road, Aldridge WS9 8JZ

Tel **(01922) 55595**
Mem 578 65(L) 64(J)
Sec PJ Bradford
Pro S Elliott (01922) 59523
Holes 18 L 6914 yds SSS 73
Recs Am–69 M Pearce
V'tors WD–U WE–M
Fees £25 (£32)
Loc 6 miles NW of Sutton Coldfield, off A452

Dudley (1893)

Turners Hill, Rowley Regis, Warley B65 9DP

Tel **(01384) 253719**
Mem 320
Sec RP Fortune (01384) 233877
Pro P Taylor (01384) 254020
Holes 18 L 5715 yds SSS 67
Recs Am–66 AA Davies
Pro–63 R Livingstone
V'tors WD–U WE–M
Fees £18
Loc 2 miles S of Dudley

Edgbaston (1896)

Church Road, Edgbaston, Birmingham B15 3TB

Tel **(0121) 454 1736**
Mem 653
Sec AD Mollett

Pro AH Bownes (0121) 454 3226
Holes 18 L 6118 yds SSS 69
Recs Am–66 J Cook (1990)
Pro–65 J Rhodes
V'tors H SOC
Fees £35 (£45) (1994)
Loc 1½ miles S of Birmingham, off A38
Arch HS Colt

Enville (1935)

Highgate Common, Enville, Stourbridge DY7 5BN
Tel **(01384) 872551**
Fax **(01384) 872074**
Mem 900
Sec RJ Bannister (Sec/Mgr) (01384) 872074
Pro S Power (01384) 872585
Holes Highgate 18 L 6556 yds SSS 72; Lodge 18 L 6217 yds SSS 70
Recs Highgate Am–67 PJ Randle (1991)
Pro–65 J Stafford (1991)
Lodge Am–65 M McGuire (1992)
V'tors WD–U WE/BH–M H SOC
Fees £22 D–£32
Loc 6 miles W of Stourbridge

Forest of Arden Hotel G & CC (1970)

Maxstoke Lane, Meriden, Coventry CV7 7HR
Tel **(01676) 522335**
Fax **(01676) 523711**
Mem 700
Sec SJ Clarke (Golf Mgr)
Pro M Tarn (01676) 522118
Holes Arden 18 L 7100 yds SSS 71
Aylesford 18 L 6525 yds SSS 69
V'tors WD–U SOC–WD
Fees Arden–£50 Aylesford–£28
Loc 9 miles W of Coventry, off A45. M6 Junction 4
Arch Donald Steel

Gay Hill (1913)

Hollywood Lane, Birmingham B47 5PP
Tel **(0121) 430 6523/7077**
Fax **(0121) 436 7796**
Mem 700
Sec Mrs EK Devitt (0121) 430 8544
Pro A Hill (0121) 474 6001
Holes 18 L 6532 yds SSS 71
Recs Am–64 P Johnson (1993)
Pro–66 R Livingston
V'tors WD–U H WE–M SOC
Fees £28.50
Loc 7 miles S of Birmingham on A435. M42 Junction 3, 3 miles

GPT (formerly Grange GC)

Copsewood, Coventry CV3 1HS
Tel **(01203) 451465**
Mem 350
Sec E Soutar (Hon)
Holes 9 L 6002 yds SSS 69
Recs Am–70
V'tors WD–U before 2.30pm
Sat–NA Sun–NA before noon
Fees £10 Sun–£15
Loc 2½ miles E of Coventry on A428
Arch TJ McAuley

Great Barr (1961)

Chapel Lane, Birmingham B43 7BA
Tel **(0121) 357 1232**
Mem 600
Sec Mrs JS Pembridge (0121) 358 4376
Pro R Spragg (0121) 357 5270
Holes 18 L 6545 yds SSS 72
Recs Am–67 CM Lambert
Pro–71 J Higgins
V'tors WD–U WE–I (h'cap max 18) SOC
Fees £25
Loc 6 miles NW of Birmingham. M6 Junction 7

Hagley (1980)

Wassell Grove, Hagley, Stourbridge DY9 9JW
Tel **(01562) 883701**
Mem 670
Sec GF Yardley
Pro I Clark (01562) 883852
Holes 18 L 6353 yds SSS 72
Recs Am–71 S Carpenter (1993)
Pro–69 I Clark (1990)
V'tors WD–U exc Wed NA before 1.30pm WE–M after 10am SOC–WD
Fees £20 D–£25
Loc 5 miles SW of Birmingham on A456. M5 Junction 3

Halesowen (1909)

The Leasowes, Halesowen B62 8QF
Tel **(0121) 550 1041**
Mem 600
Sec Mrs M Bateman (0121) 501 3606
Pro S Fanning (0121) 503 0593
Holes 18 L 5754 yds SSS 68
Recs Am–65 D Henn
Pro–66
V'tors WD–U WE–M SOC–WD exc Wed
Fees £16 D–£23
Loc M5 Junction 3, 2 miles

Handsworth (1895)

Sunningdale Close, Handsworth Wood, Birmingham B20 1NP
Tel **(0121) 554 3387**
Mem 850
Sec PS Hodnett (Hon)
Pro L Bashford (0121) 523 3594
Holes 18 L 6297 yds SSS 70
Recs Am–65 P Johnson (1994)
Pro–71 HF Boyce
V'tors WD–U WE/BH–M SOC
Fees £30
Loc 3 miles NW of Birmingham. M5 Junction 1. M6 Junction 7

Harborne (1893)

40 Tennal Road, Harborne, Birmingham B32 2JE
Tel **(0121) 427 1728**
Mem 600
Sec EJ Humphreys (0121) 427 3058 (mornings)
Pro A Quarterman (0121) 427 3512
Holes 18 L 6235 yds SSS 70
Recs Am–65 JA Fisher, R Ellis
Pro–65 E Cogle
V'tors WD–U WE/BH–M SOC
Fees £30 D–£35
Loc 3 miles SW of Birmingham. M5 Junction 3
Arch HS Colt

Harborne Church Farm (1926) Public

Vicarage Road, Harborne, Birmingham B17 0SN
Tel **(0121) 427 1204**
Fax **(0121) 427 1204**
Mem 236
Sec B Flanagan
Pro M Hampton
Holes 9 L 4914 yds SSS 62
Recs Am–62 J McAllister
V'tors U
Fees 18 holes–£7.20. 9 holes–£4.20
Loc 3 miles SW of Birmingham

Hatchford Brook (1969)

Public
Coventry Road, Sheldon, Birmingham B26 3PY
Tel **(0121) 743 9821**
Sec D Williams
Pro P Smith
Holes 18 L 6164 yds SSS 69
Recs Am–69 A Allen (1987)
Pro–68 P Smith (1988)
V'tors U SOC–WD
Fees On application
Loc City boundary close to airport. A45/M42 Junction

Hilltop (1979)

Public
Park Lane, Handsworth, Birmingham B21 8LJ
Tel **(0121) 554 4463**
Pro K Highfield
Holes 18 L 6114 yds SSS 69
Recs Am–66 H Ali
Pro–65 BN Jones
V'tors U
Fees On application
Loc Sandwell Valley. M5 Junction 1

Himley Hall (1980)

Public
Himley Hall Park, Dudley DY3 4DF
Tel **(01902) 895207**
Mem 300
Sec M Harris
Holes 9 L 3145 yds SSS 36
9 hole short course
Recs Am–69 K Baker
V'tors WD–U WE/BH–restricted

Fees 18 holes–£6 (£6.50)
9 holes–£4.30 (£4.50)
Loc Grounds of Himley Hall Park. B4176, off A449
Arch A & K Baker

Lickey Hills (1927)

Public
Lickey Hills, Rednal, Birmingham B45 8RR
Tel **(0121) 453 3159**
Sec MR Billingham
Pro MS March
Holes 18 L 6010 yds SSS 69
Recs Am–66 S Green
Pro–72 R Livingston
V'tors U
Fees £6.50
Loc 10 miles SW of Birmingham. M5 Junction 4

Little Aston (1908)

Streetly, Sutton Coldfield B74 3AN
Tel **(0121) 353 2066**
Mem 250
Sec NH Russell (0121) 353 2942
Pro J Anderson (0121) 353 2942
Holes 18 L 6670 yds SSS 73
Recs Am–64 Pro–68
V'tors H–by arrangement WE–XL
Fees On application
Loc 4 miles NW of Sutton Coldfield, off A454
Arch Harry Vardon

Moor Hall (1932)

Moor Hall Drive, Four Oaks, Sutton Coldfield B75 6LN
Tel **(0121) 308 6130**
Mem 628
Sec RV Wood
Pro A Partridge (0121) 308 5106
Holes 18 L 6249 yds SSS 70
Recs Am–65 J Cook
Pro–66 P Broadhurst
V'tors WD–U H exc Thurs–U after 1pm WE/BH–M
Fees £25 D–£35
Loc 1 mile E of Sutton Coldfield

Moseley (1892)

Springfield Road, Kings Heath, Birmingham B14 7DX
Tel **(0121) 444 2115**
Fax **(0121) 441 4662**
Mem 600
Sec RA Jowle (0121) 444 4957
Pro G Edge (0121) 444 2063
Holes 18 L 6285 yds SSS 70
Recs Am–64 C Norman (1992)
Pro–67 G Edge (1992)
Ladies–72 J Thorne (1976)
V'tors I H or M
Fees £37
Loc South Birmingham

North Warwickshire (1894)

Hampton Lane, Meriden, Coventry CV7 7LL
Tel **(01676) 522259**
Mem 400
Sec EG Barnes (Hon)
Pro D Ingram
Holes 9 L 6362 yds SSS 70
Recs Am–64 A Allen (1993)
V'tors WD–U WE/BH–M SOC
Fees £18
Loc 6 miles W of Coventry, off A45

North Worcestershire (1907)

Frankley Beeches Road, Northfield, Birmingham B31 5LP
Tel **(0121) 475 1047**
Mem 550
Sec BC Lediard
Pro K Jones (0121) 475 5721
Holes 18 L 5907 yds SSS 69
Recs Am–64 DJ Russell
Pro–63 K Dickens (1988)
V'tors WD–U WE/BH–M
Fees £19.50 D–£29.50
Loc 7 miles SW of Birmingham, off A38
Arch James Braid

Olton (1893)

Mirfield Road, Solihull B91 1JH
Tel **(0121) 705 1083**
Fax **(0121) 711 2010**
Mem 600
Sec MA Perry (0121) 704 1936 (am) (01564) 777953 (pm)
Pro MP Daubney (0121) 705 7296
Holes 18 L 6229 yds SSS 71
Recs Am–63 J Berry
Pro–64 I Clark
V'tors WD–U exc Wed am WE–M
Fees £30
Loc 7 miles SE of Birmingham (A41)

Oxley Park (1914)

Stafford Road, Bushbury, Wolverhampton WV10 6DE
Tel **(01902) 20506**
Mem 550
Sec Mrs K Mann (01902) 25892
Pro LA Burlison (01902) 25445
Holes 18 L 6168 yds SSS 69
Recs Am–62 R Weaver (1994)
Pro–65 P Weaver (1987)
V'tors U SOC
Fees £20
Loc 1 mile N of Wolverhampton, off A449

Patshull Park Hotel G & CC (1980)

Pattingham, Wolverhampton WV6 7HR
Tel **(01902) 700100/700342**
Fax **(01902) 700874**
Mem 440
Sec T Sharples
Pro D Thorp
Holes 18 L 6412 yds SSS 71
Recs Am–67 S Weir
Pro–63 J Higgins
V'tors U SOC
Fees £20 D–£35 (£25 D–£40)
Loc 7 miles W of Wolverhampton, off A41. M54 Junction 3, 5 miles
Arch John Jacobs

Penn (1908)

Penn Common, Wolverhampton WV4 5JN
Tel **(01902) 341142**
Mem 650
Sec PW Thorrington
Pro A Briscoe (01902) 330472
Holes 18 L 6462 yds SSS 71
Recs Am–67 C Upton
Pro–70 J Rhodes, R Cameron
V'tors WD–U WE–M SOC
Fees £20 (Nov–Feb £15)
Loc 2 miles SW of Wolverhampton, off A449

Perton Park (1990)

Wrottesley Park Road, Perton, Wolverhampton WV6 7HL
Tel **(01902) 380103/380073**
Fax **(01902) 326219**
Mem 300
Sec E Greenway (Mgr)
Holes 18 L 7007 yds SSS 71
V'tors U SOC
Fees £7 (£15)
Loc 6 miles W of Wolverhampton, off A454
Mis Driving range

Pype Hayes (1932)

Public
Eachelhurst Road, Walmley, Sutton Coldfield B76 8EP
Tel **(0121) 351 1014**
Sec K Haden
Pro JF Bayliss
Holes 18 L 5067 yds SSS 68
Recs Am–62 L Jacks (1985)
Pro–59 J Cawsey (1954)
V'tors U
Fees On application
Loc 5 miles NE of Birmingham

Robin Hood (1893)

St Bernards Road, Solihull B92 7DJ
Tel **(0121) 706 0159**
Mem 650
Sec AJ Hanson (0121) 706 0061
Pro A Harvey (0121) 706 0806
Holes 18 L 6635 yds SSS 72
Recs Am–68 J Draper (1988), GW Barton (1993)
V'tors WD–U WE/BH–M SOC–WD
Fees £29 D–£35
Loc 7 miles S of Birmingham
Arch HS Colt

Sandwell Park (1897)

Birmingham Road, West Bromwich B71 4JJ
Tel **(0121) 553 4384**
Mem 600
Sec JB Mawby (0121) 553 4637
Pro N Wylie (0121) 553 4384
Holes 18 L 6470 yds SSS 72

Recs Am–67 T Allen (1988)
Pro–67 F Clarke
V'tors WD–U WE–MH SOC–WD
Fees D–£32.50
Loc West Bromwich/Birmingham boundary. By M5 Junction 1

Sedgley (1992)

Pay and play
Sandyfields Road, Sedgley, Dudley DY3 3DL
Tel **(01902) 880503**
Mem 150
Sec JA Cox
Pro D Fereday (01384) 287996
Holes 9 L 3150 yds SSS 71
V'tors WD–U WE–booking required
Fees 9 holes–£4 (£4.50)
18 holes–£6 (£6.50)
Loc 1/2 mile from Sedgley, off A463 between Dudley and Wolverhampton
Mis Driving range
Arch WG Cox

Shirley (1956)

Stratford Road, Monkspath, Shirley, Solihull B90 4EW
Tel **(0121) 744 6001**
Fax **(0121) 745 4979**
Mem 450
Sec AJ Phillips
Pro C Wicketts (0121) 745 4979
Holes 18 L 6510 yds SSS 71
Recs Am–67 N Burdekin
Pro–68
V'tors WD–U WE–M
Fees £25 D–£35
Loc 8 miles S of Birmingham, nr M42 Junction 4

South Staffordshire (1892)

Danescourt Road, Tettenhall, Wolverhampton WV6 9BQ
Tel **(01902) 751065**
Mem 600
Sec JA Macklin
Pro J Rhodes (01902) 754816
Holes 18 L 6513 yds SSS 71
Recs Am–68 GA Moore (1991)
Pro–67 D Gilford (1984)
Ladies–73 A Bullock (1994)
V'tors WD–U WE/BH–M SOC
Fees £30 D–£35 (£40)
Loc 3 miles W of Wolverhampton, off A41
Arch Harry Vardon

Sphinx (1948)

Sphinx Drive, Coventry CV3 1WA
Tel **(01203) 451361**
Mem 300
Sec GE Brownbridge (01203) 597731
Holes 9 L 4262 yds SSS 60
Recs Am–61 G Mason (1994)
V'tors Fri/WE–M after 4.30pm SOC
Fees £8 (£10)
Loc Nr Binley Road, Coventry

Stourbridge (1892)

Worcester Lane, Pedmore, Stourbridge DY8 2RB
Tel **(01384) 393062**
Mem 720
Sec Ms MA Cooper (01384) 395566
Pro WH Firkins (01384) 393129
Holes 18 L 6231 yds SSS 70
Recs Am–65 J Fisher
Pro–63 WH Firkins
V'tors WD–U exc Wed before 4pm–M WE/BH–M
Fees £25
Loc 1 mile S of Stourbridge on Worcester road

Sutton Coldfield (1889)

110 Thornhill Road, Sutton Coldfield B74 3ER
Tel **(0121) 353 2014**
Fax **(0121) 353 5503**
Mem 600
Sec RF Fletcher, Mrs T Thomas (0121) 353 9633
Pro JK Hayes (0121) 353 9633
Holes 18 L 6541 yds SSS 71
Recs Am–65 L Jacks (1986)
Pro–64 PA Elson (1978)
V'tors U H SOC
Fees £30 (£30)
Loc 9 miles N of Birmingham, off B4138

Swindon (1986)

Bridgnorth Road, Swindon, Dudley DY3 4PU
Tel **(01902) 897031**
Fax **(01902) 326219**
Mem 500
Sec E Greenway (Mgr)
Pro P Lester (01902) 896191
Holes 18 L 6081 yds SSS 69
9 hole Par 3 course
Recs Am–68 N Bennett (1990)
V'tors U SOC–WD
Fees £15 (£25)
Loc 5 miles SW of Wolverhampton on B4176
Mis Driving range

Tidbury Green (1994)

Tilehouse Lane, Shirley, Solihull B90 1HP
Tel **(01564) 824460**
Sec Lucy Broadhurst
Pro R Thompson, S Evans
Holes 9 L 2473 yds Par 34
V'tors U
Fees 18 holes–£8 (£8)
9 holes–£5 (£5)
Loc 2 miles from M42 Junction 4, nr Earlswood lakes
Mis Driving range
Arch Derek Stevenson

Walmley (1902)

Brooks Road, Wylde Green, Sutton Coldfield B72 1HR
Tel **(0121) 377 7272**
Fax **(0121) 377 7272**
Mem 700
Sec MJ Roberts
Pro MJ Skerritt (0121) 373 7103
Holes 18 L 6537 yds SSS 72
Recs Am–68 JT Hemphill (1994)
Pro–67 C Hall (1992)
V'tors WD–U WE–M SOC
Fees £25 D–£30
Loc N boundary of Birmingham

Walsall (1907)

Broadway, Walsall WS1 3EY
Tel **(01922) 613512**
Fax **(01922) 616460**
Mem 700
Sec E Murray (01922) 613512
Pro R Lambert (01922) 26766
Holes 18 L 6232 yds SSS 70
Recs Am–66 RG Hiatt, D Blakeman
Pro–66 N Brunyard
V'tors WD–U WE–M SOC
Fees £33
Loc 1 mile S of Walsall, off A34. M6 Junction 7

Warley (1921)

Public
Lightwoods Hill, Warley B67 5EO
Tel **(0121) 429 2440**
Pro D Owen
Holes 9 L 2606 yds SSS 64
Recs Am–62 M Daw
Pro–58 B Fereday
V'tors U
Fees On application
Loc 5 miles W of Birmingham, off A456

Wergs (1990)

Pay and play
Keepers Lane, Tettenhall WV6 8UA
Tel **(01902) 742225**
Fax **(01902) 744748**
Mem 255
Sec Mrs G Parsons
Pro M Moseley
Holes 18 L 6949 yds SSS 73
Recs Am–74 T Mathers (1991)
Pro–74 D Prosser (1990)
V'tors U
Fees D–£12.50 (D–£15)
Loc 3 miles W of Wolverhampton on A41
Arch CW Moseley

Widney Manor (1993)

Pay and play
Saintbury Drive, Widney Manor, Solihull B91 3SZ
Tel **(0121) 711 3646**
Fax **(0121) 711 3691**
Mem 530
Sec T Atkinson (Sec/Mgr)
Pro T Atkinson
Holes 18 L 4709 yds Par 68
V'tors U–booking 2 days in advance SOC
Fees £7 (£10)
Loc 3 miles from M42 Junction 4, off A34

Windmill Village (1990)
Birmingham Road, Allesley, Coventry CV5 9AL
Tel **(01203) 407241**
Fax **(01203) 407016**
Mem 500
Sec M Harrhy
Pro R Hunter
Holes 18 L 5129 yds Par 70
Recs Am–71 Pro–69
V'tors U SOC
Fees £9.50 (£11.95)
Loc 3 miles W of Coventry, off A45

Wiltshire

Bowood G & CC (1992)
Derry Hill, Calne SN11 9PQ
Tel **(01249) 822228**
Fax **(01249) 822218**
Mem 250
Sec J Bavington
Pro N Blenkarne (Golf Dir)
Holes 18 L 7317 yds SSS 74
Recs Am–69 C Edwards (1994)
Pro–67 N Brown (1994)
V'tors U–booking required WE–M before noon SOC
Fees £27 (£32)
Loc 3 miles SE of Chippenham on A342. M4 Junction 17
Mis Driving range. 3 Academy holes
Arch David Thomas

Bradford-on-Avon (1991)
Trowbridge Road, Bradford-on-Avon
Tel **(01225) 868268**
Pro G Sawyer
Holes 9 L 2100 metres SSS 61
V'tors WD–U WE–pm only
Fees 9 holes–£6.50. 18 holes–£10
Loc SE of Bradford, nr River Avon

Brinkworth (1984)
Longmans Farm, Brinkworth, Chippenham SN15 5DG
Tel **(01666) 510277**
Mem 250
Sec J Sheppard
Holes 18 L 5900 yds SSS 69
V'tors U SOC
Fees On application
Loc 2 miles from Brinkworth (B4042). 12 miles NE of Chippenham

Broome Manor (1976)
Public
Pipers Way, Swindon SN3 1RG
Tel **(01793) 532403**
Mem 1000
Sec T Watt (Mgr)(01793) 495761
Pro B Sandry (01793) 532403
Holes 18 L 6283 yds SSS 70
9 L 2690 yds SSS 67
Recs Am–62 G Harris
Pro–66 M Bevan
V'tors U
Fees 18 hole:£8 (£9.80)
9 hole:£4.80 (£5.90)
Loc Swindon 2 miles
Mis Floodlit driving range
Arch F Hawtree

Chippenham (1896)
Malmesbury Road, Chippenham SN15 5LT
Tel **(01249) 652040**
Fax **(01249) 446681**
Mem 650
Sec D Maddison
Pro W Creamer (01249) 655519
Holes 18 L 5540 yds SSS 67
Recs Am–64 RE Searle (1993)
Pro–64 B Sandry
V'tors U WE–M SOC
Fees £20 (£25)
Loc 1 mile N of Chippenham, off A350. M4 Junction 17

Cricklade Hotel (1992)
Common Hill, Cricklade SN6 6HA
Tel **(01793) 750751**
Mem 140
Sec T Hooley
Pro I Bolt
Holes 9 L 1830 yds SSS 57
V'tors WD–U SOC–WD
Fees £16 D–£25
Loc 1/2 mile W of Cricklade on B4040. M4 Junctions 15/16
Arch Bolt/Smith

Cumberwell Park (1994)
Bradford-on-Avon BA15 2PQ
Tel **(01225) 863322**
Fax **(01225) 868160**
Mem 600
Sec R Smith (Mgr)
Pro J Jacobs
Holes 18 L 6807 yds SSS 73
V'tors U SOC
Fees £18 (£25)
Loc Between Bradford-on-Avon and Bath on A363. M4 Junction 18
Arch Adrain Stiff

Erlestoke Sands (1992)
Erlestoke, Devizes SN10 5UA
Tel **(01380) 831069**
Fax **(01380) 831069**
Mem 740
Sec R Hampton
Pro A Valentine (01380) 831027
Holes 18 L 6649 yds SSS 72
Recs Am–71 P Oakey (1993)
V'tors U–book with Pro SOC
Fees £12 (£16)
Loc 6 miles E of Westbury on B3098
Mis Driving area. 3 Academy holes
Arch Adrian Stiff

Hamptworth G & CC (1994)
Elmtree Farmhouse, Hamptworth Road, Landford SP5 2DU
Tel **(01794) 390155**
Fax **(01794) 390022**
Sec M Pierson (Mgr)
Holes 18 L 6516 yds SSS
V'tors WD–H or M WE–H
Fees £17.50 (£22.50)
Loc 10 miles SE of Salisbury, off A36/B3079. M27 Junction 2, 6 miles

High Post (1922)
Great Durnford, Salisbury SP4 6AT
Tel **(01722) 782231**
Mem 600
Sec WWR Goodwin
(01722) 782356
Pro AJ Harman (01722) 782219
Holes 18 L 6297 yds SSS 70
Recs Am–64 K Weeks, RE Searle
Pro–65 P Alliss, N Sutton
V'tors WD–U WE/BH–H SOC
Fees £20 D–£25 (£30) SOC–£30
Loc 4 miles N of Salisbury on A345

Highworth (1990)
Swindon Road, Highworth SN6 7SJ
Tel **(01793) 766014**
Pro M Toombs
Holes 9 L 3220 yds SSS 70
V'tors U SOC
Fees £4.50 (£5)
Loc 5 miles N of Swindon (A361)
Mis 9 hole pitch & putt

Kingsdown (1880)
Kingsdown, Corsham SN14 9BS
Tel **(01225) 742530**
Mem 505 105(L) 45(J)
Sec SH Phipps (01225) 743472
Pro A Butler (01225) 742634
Holes 18 L 6445 yds SSS 71
Recs Am–66 S Hodges (1991)
Pro–64 M Wiggett (1993)
V'tors WD–H WE–M
Fees £22
Loc 5 miles E of Bath

Manor House (Castle Combe) (1992)
Castle Combe SN14 7PL
Tel **(01249) 782982**
Fax **(01249) 782992**
Mem 300
Sec P Ware
Pro C Smith (Golf Dir)
Holes 18 L 6340 yds SSS 71
V'tors U H–booking necessary SOC
Fees £25
Loc N of Castle Combe, off B4039
Mis Driving range
Arch Alliss/Clarke

Marlborough (1888)
The Common, Marlborough SN8 1DU
Tel **(01672) 512147**
Mem 710
Sec L Ross (Mgr), S Lynch (Admin)
Pro L Ross (01672) 512493
Holes 18 L 6526 yds SSS 71

Recs Am–61 G Harris
Pro–63 B Sandry
V'tors WD/WE–H SOC
Fees £21 D–£32 (£40)
Loc 1 mile N of Marlborough (A345)

Monkton Park Par Three (1975)

Pay and play
Chippenham SN15 3PP
Tel **(01249) 653928**
Fax **(01249) 653928**
Mem 100
Sec MR & BJ Dawson (Props)
Holes 9 hole Par 3 course
Recs Am–23 J Dawson (1991)
V'tors U
Fees 18 holes–£4 (£5)
9 holes–£2.75 (£3)
Loc Centre of Chippenham. M4 Junction 17
Arch M Dawson

North Wilts (1890)

Bishops' Cannings, Devizes SN10 2LP
Tel **(01380) 860257**
Fax **(01380) 860061**
Mem 600 96(L) 90(J)
Sec SA Musgrove (01380) 860627
Pro GJ Laing (01380) 860330
Holes 18 L 6322 yds SSS 71
Recs Am–69 N Williams (1994)
Pro–67 GJ Laing
Ladies–73 L Moore (1982)
V'tors WE–NA before 10am (–M Xmas Day–Mar 31) SOC
Fees £18 (£30)
Loc 1 mile from A4, E of Calne

Oaksey Park (1991)

Pay and play
Oaksey, Malmesbury SN16 9SB
Tel **(01666) 577995**
Fax **(01666) 577174**
Holes 9 L 2900 yds SSS 68
V'tors U SOC
Fees £10 (£15)
Loc 8 miles NE of Malmesbury, off A429
Mis Driving range
Arch Chapman/Warren

Ogbourne Downs (1907)

Ogbourne St George, Marlborough SN8 1TB
Tel **(01672) 841217**
Mem 700
Sec DJ Knight (01672) 841327
Pro C Harraway (01672) 841287
Holes 18 L 6226 yds SSS 70
Recs Am–66 RJ Binsted, S Robertson
Pro–65 I Bolt, G Wraith
V'tors WD–H WE–M SOC–WD
Fees £20 (£30)
Loc 5 miles S of M4 Junction 15, on A345

RMCS Shrivenham (1953)

RMCS Shrivenham, Swindon SN6 8LA
Tel **(01793) 785725**
Mem 500
Sec R Humphrey (Mgr)
Pro S Jefferies
Holes 12 L 5547 yds SSS 69
V'tors M SOC
Fees £8 (£10)
Loc Grounds of Royal Military College of Science. Entry must be arranged with Mgr

Salisbury & South Wilts (1888)

Netherhampton, Salisbury SP2 8PR
Tel **(01722) 742645**
Fax **(01722) 742645**
Mem 1100
Sec J Newcomb (Sec/Mgr)
Pro G Emerson (01722) 742929
Holes 18 L 6528 yds SSS 71
9 hole course
Recs Am–65 D Hutton
Pro–63 G Emerson
V'tors WD–U WE–H SOC–WD
Fees £25 (£40)
Loc Wilton, 3 miles SW of Salisbury on A3094
Arch JH Taylor

Shrivenham Park (1967)

Pay and play
Penny Hooks, Shrivenham, Swindon SN6 8EX
Tel **(01793) 783853**
Fax **(01793) 782999**
Sec G Johnson (Golf Dir)
Pro S Jeffries
Holes 18 L 5989 yds SSS 68
V'tors U SOC
Fees £10.50 (£13.50)
Loc 4 miles E of Swindon, off A420

Thoulstone Park (1992)

Chapmanslade, Westbury BA13 4AQ
Tel **(01373) 832825**
Fax **(01373) 832821**
Mem 550
Sec MD Sagar
Pro D Thomson (01373) 832808
Holes 18 L 6300 yds Par 71 SSS 70
Recs Am–69 S Wilson (1994)
Pro–67 T Nash (1992)
V'tors U SOC–WD
Fees £12 (£18)
Loc 12 miles S of Bath, off A36
Mis Driving range
Arch MRM Sandow

Tidworth Garrison (1908)

Bulford Road, Tidworth SP9 7AF
Tel **(01980) 42321 (Steward)**
Mem 800
Sec Lt Col DFT Tucker (Mgr) (01980) 42301
Pro T Godsen (01980) 42393
Holes 18 L 6075 yds SSS 69
Recs Am–66 C Akrill (1992)
Pro–64
V'tors SOC–Tues & Thurs
Fees £18
Loc 1 mile SW of Tidworth on Bulford road

Upavon (RAF) (1918)

Douglas Avenue, Upavon SN9 6BQ
Tel **(01980) 630787**
Fax **(01980) 630787**
Mem 400
Sec L Mitchell
Pro R Blake (01980) 630281
Holes 9 L 5589 yds SSS 67
Recs Am–66 RB Duckett (1982), S Wootton (1993)
V'tors WD–U WE–H –M before 11am SOC–WD
Fees £10 D–£16 (£24)
Loc 2 miles SE of Upavon on A342

West Wilts (1891)

Elm Hill, Warminster BA12 0AU
Tel **(01985) 212702**
Mem 520 70(L) 70(J)
Sec ID Wheater (01985) 213133
Pro AJ Lamb (01985) 212110
Holes 18 L 5709 yds SSS 68
Recs Am–62 CG Burton (1989)
Pro–64 R Emery (1985)
V'tors WD–U H WE–U H after noon –NA before noon
Fees £24 (£35)
Loc Off A350, on Westbury road
Arch JH Taylor

Wootton Bassett (1993)

Wootton Bassett, Swindon SN4 7PB
Tel **(01793) 849999**
Fax **(01793) 849988**
Mem 680
Sec N Comper (Gen Mgr)
Pro B McAdams
Holes 18 L 6496 yds SSS 72
Recs Am–69 D Rigby (1992)
Pro–70 S Little (1992)
V'tors U H SOC–WD
Fees £25 D–£30 (£30 D–£35)
Loc 1 mile S of Wootton Bassett. M4 Junction 16
Arch Alliss/Clark

Wrag Barn (1990)

Shrivenham Road, Highworth, Swindon SN6 7QQ
Tel **(01793) 861327**
Fax **(01793) 861325**
Mem 462
Sec Mrs S Manners
Pro B Loughrey (01793) 766027
Holes 18 L 6548 yds SSS 72
Recs Am–71 P Poulton (1993)
Pro–66 G Clough (1992)
V'tors WD–U WE–NA before noon SOC–WD
Fees £15 (£22)
Loc 6 miles NE of Swindon on B4000. M4 Junction 15, 8 miles
Mis Driving range
Arch Hawtree

Yorkshire (North)

Aldwark Manor (1978)

Aldwark Manor, Aldwark Alne, York YO6 2NF

Tel **(01347) 838353**
Fax **(01347) 838867**
Sec GF Platt (Golf Dir)
Pro GM Platt
Holes 18 L 6171 yds SSS 69
Recs Am–70 RW Smart (1994)
Pro–69 N Squire (1992)
V'tors U SOC
Fees £16 D–£20 (£20 D–£24)
Loc 5 miles SE of Boroughbridge, off A1. 13 miles NW of York, off A19

Ampleforth College (1962)

56 High Street, Helmsley, York YO6 5AE

Mem 175
Sec JE Atkinson (01439) 770678
Holes 10 L 4018 yds SSS 63
V'tors U exc WD 2–4pm SOC–WD
Fees £8 (£12)
Loc Driveway of Gilling Castle. 18 miles N of York (B1363)
Mis Green fees payable at Fairfax Arms, Gilling East
Arch Rev Jerome Lambert OSB

Bedale (1894)

Leyburn Road, Bedale DL8 1EZ

Tel **(01677) 422568**
Mem 600 60(J)
Sec GA Shepherdson (01677) 422451
Pro AD Johnson (01677) 422443
Holes 18 L 6565 yds SSS 71
Recs Am–68 R Lawson (1994)
Pro–76 N Walton (1992)
V'tors U SOC
Fees £18 (£24)
Loc N boundary of Bedale

Bentham (1922)

Robin Lane, Bentham, Lancaster LA2 7AG

Tel **(015242) 61018**
Mem 450
Sec JM Philipson (015242) 62455
Holes 9 L 5760 yds SSS 69
Recs Am–67 CJ Carter (1992)
V'tors U SOC
Fees £14 (£20) W–£56
Loc NE of Lancaster on B6480 towards Settle. 13 miles E of M6 Junction 34

Catterick Garrison (1930)

Leyburn Road, Catterick Garrison DL9 3QE

Tel **(01748) 833401**
Fax **(01748) 833263**
Mem 730
Sec JK Mayberry (01748) 833268
Pro A Marshall (01748) 833671
Holes 18 L 6331 yds SSS 70
Recs Am–65 CS Carveth
Pro–69 D Edwards
V'tors U H SOC
Fees £18 (£25)
Loc 6 miles SW of Scotch Corner, via A1
Arch Arthur Day

Cocksford (1992)

Stutton, Tadcaster LS24 9NG

Tel **(01937) 834253**
Fax **(01937) 834253**
Sec Gill Coxon
Pro G Thompson
Holes 18 L 5570 yds SSS 68
V'tors WD–U WE–by arrangement SOC
Fees £15 D–£20 (£20 D–25)
Loc 1½miles S of Tadcaster
Mis Further 9 holes open 1995

Crimple Valley (1976)

Hookstone Wood Road, Harrogate HG2 8PN

Tel **(01423) 883485**
Mem 200
Sec R Lumb
Pro R Lumb
Holes 9 L 2500 yds SSS 33
V'tors U
Fees On application
Loc By Yorkshire Fairground

Drax (1989)

Drax, Selby YO8 8PQ

Mem 465
Sec J Clough (01405) 860533
Holes 9 L 5510 yds Par 68 SSS 67
Recs Am–70 A Dick (1993)
V'tors M
Fees £5 (£7)
Loc 5 miles S of Selby, off A1041
Arch JM Scott

Easingwold (1930)

Stillington Road, Easingwold, York YO6 3ET

Tel **(01347) 821486**
Mem 625
Sec KC Hudson
Pro J Hughes (01347) 821964
Holes 18 L 6285 yds SSS 70
Recs Am–67 JP Miller
Pro–65 G Brown
V'tors U
Fees D–£25 (£30)
Loc 12 miles N of York on A19. S end of Easingwold

Filey (1897)

West Ave, Filey YO14 9BQ

Tel **(01723) 513293**
Fax **(01723) 513293**
Mem 937
Sec TM Thompson
Pro D England (01723) 513134
Holes 18 L 6112 yds SSS 69
Recs Am–67 AS Roberts, S Pybus (1993)
Pro–64 AS Murray
V'tors U H BH–no visiting parties SOC
Fees £20 (£25) Summer
£14 (£18) Winter
Loc 1 mile S of Filey centre

Forest of Galtres (1994)

Wide Open Farm, Skelton Lane YO3 3RF

Tel **(01904) 766198**
Mem 380
Sec TW Procter (Prop) (01904) 769280
Pro N Suckling
Holes 18 L 6312 yds Par 72 SSS 70
V'tors U SOC
Fees £22.50 (£25)
Loc Skelton, 4 miles N of York, off A19
Arch Simon Gidman

Forest Park (1991)

Stockton-on Forest, York YO3 9UW

Tel **(01904) 400425**
Mem 650
Sec N Crossley (01904) 400688
Pro None
Holes 18 L 6521 yds SSS 71
9 L 3084 yds Par
V'tors U SOC
Fees £14.50 D–£20 (£20 D–£24)
Loc 1½ miles from E end of A64 York By-pass
Mis Driving range

Fulford (1906)

Heslington Lane, York YO1 5DY

Tel **(01904) 413579**
Fax **(01904) 416918**
Mem 650
Sec R Bramley BEM MIMgt
Pro B Hessay (01904) 412882
Holes 18 L 6775 yds SSS 72
Recs Am–66 G Harland (1989)
Pro–62 I Woosnam (1985)
V'tors By arrangement with Sec SOC
Fees £26 D–£35 (£40)
Loc 2 miles S of York (A64)

Ganton (1891)

Station Road, Ganton, Scarborough YO12 4PA

Tel **(01944) 710329**
Mem 600
Sec Maj RG Woolsey
Pro G Brown (01944) 710260
Holes 18 L 6720 yds SSS 74
Recs Am–67 G Boardman
Pro–65 N Coles
V'tors By prior arrangement
Fees On application
Loc 11 miles SW of Scarborough on A64
Arch Dunn/Vardon/Braid/Colt

Harrogate (1892)

Forest Lane Head, Harrogate HG2 7TF

Tel **(01423) 863158 (Clubhouse)**
Mem 700
Sec PH Ince (01423) 862999
Pro P Johnson (01423) 862547

Holes 18 L 6241 yds SSS 70
Recs Am–66 P Wood (1993)
Pro–63 P Scott (1994)
Ladies–69 R Scaife (1993)
V'tors WD–U WE/BH–enquire first SOC–WD exc Tues
Fees £26 D–£30 (£40)
Loc 2 miles E of Harrogate on Knaresborough road (A59)
Arch Sandy Herd

Heworth (1911)

Muncaster House, Muncastergate, York YO3 9JX
Tel **(01904) 424618**
Mem 245 80(L) 50(J)
Sec JR Richards (01904) 426156
Pro G Roberts (01904) 422389
Holes 11 L 6141 yds SSS 69
V'tors U
Fees £10 (£14)
Loc NE boundary of York (A1036)

Kirkbymoorside (1951)

Manor Vale, Kirkbymoorside, York YO6 6EG
Tel **(01751) 431525**
Mem 650
Sec DG Saunders
Holes 18 L 6017 yds SSS 69
Recs Am–A Holmes (1992)
Ladies–69 J Brown
V'tors U between 9.30–12.30 and after 1.30pm
Fees £17 (£25)
Loc A170 between Helmsley and Pickering

Knaresborough (1919)

Boroughbridge Road, Knaresborough HG5 0QQ
Tel **(01423) 863219**
Mem 795
Sec Gp Capt JI Barrow (Mgr) (01423) 862690
Pro GJ Vickers (01423) 864865
Holes 18 L 6481 yds SSS 71
Pro–69 A Miller (1994)
V'tors U
Fees £18.50 (£25)
Loc 1½ miles N of Knaresborough

Malton & Norton (1910)

Welham Park, Welham Road, Norton, Malton YO17 9QE
Tel **(01653) 692959**
Fax **(01653) 697912**
Mem 820
Sec WG Wade (01653) 697912
Pro SI Robinson (01653) 693882
Holes 27 holes:
Welham L 6456 yds SSS 71
Park L 6231 yds SSS 70
Derwent L 6267 yds SSS 70
V'tors WD–U WE–restricted on match days H SOC
Fees £20 (£25)
Loc 18 miles NE of York (A64)

Masham (1895)

Burnholme, Swinton Road, Masham, Ripon HG4 4HT
Tel **(01765) 689379**
Mem 305
Sec Mrs MA Willis (01765) 689491
Holes 9 L 5308 yds SSS 66
Recs Am–68 M Edwards
V'tors WD–U before 5pm WE–M BH–NA
Fees £15
Loc 10 miles N of Ripon

Oakdale (1914)

Oakdale, Harrogate HG1 2LN
Tel **(01423) 567162**
Mem 775
Sec FR Hindmarsh
Pro C Dell (01423) 560510
Holes 18 L 6456 yds SSS 71
Recs Am–66 G Cuthbert (1989)
Pro–66 P Hall (1989)
V'tors WD–U 9.30–12.30 and after 2pm SOC–WD
Fees £25 D–£30
Loc ½ mile NE of Royal Hall, Harrogate
Arch Dr A Mackenzie

Pannal (1906)

Follifoot Road, Pannal, Harrogate HG3 1ES
Tel **(01423) 871641**
Fax **(01423) 870043**
Mem 780
Sec TB Davey (01423) 872628
Pro M Burgess (01423) 872620
Holes 18 L 6659 yds SSS 72
Recs Am–62 SR Macfarlane (1984)
Pro–65 A Nicholson (1993)
V'tors WD–H 9.30–12 and after 1.30pm WE–H 11–12 and after 2.30pm SOC
Fees £29 D–£36 (£36)
Loc 2½ miles S of Harrogate, on A61

Pike Hills (1920)

Tadcaster Road, Askham Bryan, York YO2 3UW
Tel **(01904) 706566**
Mem 800
Sec G Rawlings
Pro I Gradwell (01904) 708756
Holes 18 L 6121 yds SSS 69
Recs Am–68 S Banks (1992)
V'tors WD–U H before 4.30pm –M after 4.30pm SOC–WD
Fees Summer–£15 D–£20
Winter–£12 D–£15
Loc 3 miles SW of York on A64

Richmond (1892)

Bend Hagg, Richmond DL10 5EX
Tel **(01748) 825319**
Mem 600
Sec BD Aston (01748) 823231
Pro P Jackson (01748) 822457
Holes 18 L 5769 yds SSS 68
Recs Am–AP Jackson
Pro–64 J Harrison, P Harrison
V'tors U
Fees £16 (£25)
Loc 3 miles SW of Scotch Corner
Arch Frank Pennink

Ripon City (1905)

Palace Road, Ripon HG4 3HH
Tel **(01765) 603640**
Mem 650 100(L) 45(J)
Sec B Denbigh-White
Pro T Davis (01765) 600411
Holes 18 L 6120 yds SSS 69
Recs Am–63
V'tors U SOC
Fees £18 (£25)
Loc 1 mile N of Ripon on A6108
Arch ADAS

Romanby (1993)

Pay and play
Yafforth Road, Northallerton DL7 0PE
Tel **(01609) 779988**
Fax **(01609) 779084**
Mem 450
Sec G McDonnell (01609) 778855
Pro F Thorpe
Holes 18 L 6663 yds SSS 72
V'tors U SOC
Fees £10.50 (£14)
Loc 1 mile W of Northallerton on B6271
Mis Floodlit driving range
Arch Will Adamson

Rudding Park (1995)

Pay and play
Rudding Park, Harrogate HG3 1DJ
Tel **(01423) 872100**
Fax **(01423) 873011**
Sec Cathryn Kilgarriff (Sec/Mgr)
Pro S Footman (01423) 873400
Holes 18 L 6871 yds SSS 72
V'tors U H SOC
Fees £20 (£25) Summer
£15 (£20) Winter
Loc 2 miles S of Harrogate (A658)
Mis Driving range. Golf Academy
Arch Hawtree

Scarborough North Cliff (1927)

North Cliff Avenue, Burniston Road, Scarborough YO12 6PP
Tel **(01723) 360786**
Mem 860
Sec JR Freeman
Pro SN Deller (01723) 365920
Holes 18 L 6425 yds SSS 71
Recs Am–66 F Andersson
V'tors U exc Sun before 10am and comp days H SOC
Fees £25 (£30)
Loc 2 miles N of Scarborough on coast road
Arch James Braid

Scarborough South Cliff (1903)

Deepdale Avenue, Scarborough YO11 2UE

Tel **(01723) 360522**
Fax **(01723) 374737**
Mem 565
Sec CE Lee (01723) 374737
Pro AR Skingle (01723) 365150
Holes 18 L 6039 yds SSS 69
Recs Am–64 J Smith (1994)
Pro–66 MJ Slater (1987)
V'tors U H
Fees £20 D–£25 (£27.50 D–£35)
Loc 1 mile S of Scarborough

Selby (1907)

Mill Lane, Brayton, Selby YO8 9LD

Tel **(01757) 228622**
Mem 749
Sec BLC Moore
Pro A Smith (01757) 228785
Holes 18 L 6246 yds SSS 70
Recs Am–65 L Walker
Pro–64 D Matthew
V'tors WD–H WE–NA
SOC–Wed–Fri
Fees £15 D–£18
Loc 3 miles SW of Selby, off A19 at Brayton. 5 miles N of M62 Junction 34

Settle (1895)

Giggleswick, Settle BD24

Tel **(01729) 825288**
Mem 250
Sec RG Bannier
Holes 9 L 2276 yds SSS 31
Recs Am–62 P Robinson
V'tors U exc Sun–restricted SOC
Fees D–£10
Loc 1 mile N of Settle on A65
Arch Tom Vardon

Skipton (1893)

Off NW Bypass, Skipton BD23 1LL

Tel **(01756) 795657**
Mem 720
Sec D Farnsworth (Sec/Mgr)
Pro P Robinson (01756) 793257
Holes 18 L 6087 yds SSS 70
Recs Am–68 BJ Mallinson (1994)
V'tors U SOC
Fees £20 (£25)
Loc Skipton 1 mile

Thirsk & Northallerton (1914)

Thornton-le-Street, Thirsk YO7 4AB

Tel **(01845) 522170**
Mem 400
Sec JS Weatherall (01845) 525115
Pro (01845) 526216
Holes 9 L 6257 yds SSS 70
Recs Am–69 R Cable
Pro–67 M Ure
V'tors WD/Sat–U H Sun–M SOC
Fees £15 D–£20 Sat/BH–£25
Loc 2 miles N of Thirsk, nr A19 and A168 roundabout

Whitby (1892)

Sandsend Road, Low Straggleton, Whitby YO21 3SR

Tel **(01947) 602768**
Mem 900
Sec A Dyson (01947) 600660
Pro B English (01947) 602719
Holes 18 L 6134 yds SSS 70
Recs Am–67 Pro–68
V'tors U H SOC
Fees £18 (£25)
Loc 2 miles N of Whitby on A174

York (1890)

Lords Moor Lane, Strensall, York YO3 5XF

Tel **(01904) 491840**
Fax **(01904) 491852**
Mem 380 123(L) 100(J)
Sec F Appleyard
Pro A Mason (01904) 490304
Holes 18 L 6312 yds SSS 70
Recs Am–66 D Oxley (1990)
Pro–66 P Fowler
V'tors U–phone Sec SOC–WD
Fees £26 (£28)
Loc 3 miles N of York ring road (A1237)
Arch JH Taylor

Yorkshire (South)

Abbeydale (1895)

Twentywell Lane, Dore, Sheffield S17 4QA

Tel **(0114) 236 0763**
Fax **(0114) 236 0762**
Mem 700
Sec Mrs KM Johnston
Pro N Perry (0114) 236 5633
Holes 18 L 6419 yds SSS 71
V'tors U SOC–Tues & Fri
Fees £30 (£35)
Loc 5 miles S of Sheffield, off A621

Austerfield Park (1974)

Cross Lane, Austerfield, Bawtry, Doncaster DN10 6RF

Tel **(01302) 710841**
Fax **(01302) 710841**
Mem 370 45(L) 35(J)
Sec A Bradley (01709) 540928
Pro P Rothery (01302) 710850
Holes 18 L 6824 yds SSS 73
Recs Am–71 M Hayward (1990)
Pro–67 J Brennand (1988)
V'tors WD–U WE–after 10am SOC
Fees £17 (£21)
Loc 2 miles NE of Bawtry, off A614
Mis Driving range. Pitch & putt course

Barnsley (1925)

Public

Wakefield Road, Staincross, Barnsley S75 6JZ

Tel **(01226) 382856**
Sec L Lammas
Pro M Melling (01226) 382954
Holes 18 L 6042 yds SSS 69
Recs Am–64 RI Shaw (1988)
Pro–62 M Melling (1986)
V'tors U
Fees £7 (£8)
Loc 4 miles N of Barnsley on A61

Beauchief Municipal (1925)

Public

Beauchief, Abbey Lane, Sheffield S8 0DB

Tel **(0114) 236 7274/262 0040**
Mem 450
Sec JG Pearson (0114) 230 6720
Pro A Highfield
Holes 18 L 5452 yds SSS 66
Recs Am–65 PW Hickinson
Pro–63 P Tupling
V'tors U
Fees £8
Loc A621 Sheffield

Birley Wood (1974)

Public

Birley Lane, Sheffield S12 3BP

Tel **(0114) 264 7262**
Mem 294
Sec M Hollis
Pro P Ball
Holes 18 L 5483 yds SSS 67
Recs Am–66 S Pearson (1991)
Pro–67 D Muscroft (1990)
V'tors U
Fees £7 (£8)
Loc 4 miles S of Sheffield on A616. M1 Junction 30

Concord Park (1952)

Public

Shiregreen Lane, Sheffield S5 6AE

Tel **(0114) 257 0274/257 0053**
Sec B Shepherd
Pro None
Holes 18 L 4321 yds SSS 62
Recs Am–56 S Ridal (1991)
V'tors U
Fees £5.20
Loc M1 Junction 34, 1 mile

Crookhill Park (1973)

Public

Conisborough, Doncaster DN12 2AH

Tel **(01709) 862979**
Mem 500
Sec M Belk
Pro R Swaine
Holes 18 L 5839 yds SSS 68
Recs Am–67 R Jones
Pro–70
V'tors U
Fees £8.50 (£9)
Loc 3 miles W of Doncaster (A630)

Doncaster (1894)

Bawtry Road, Bessacarr, Doncaster DN4 7PD

Tel **(01302) 868316**
Fax **(01302) 865994**
Mem 375

For list of abbreviations see page 435

Sec R Collingwood (01302) 865632
Pro G Bailey (01302) 868404
Holes 18 L 6230 yds SSS 70
Recs Am–66 H Green
Pro–66 H Clark
V'tors WD–U H WE/BH–NA before 11.30am SOC–WD
Fees £24 (£30)
Loc 4½ miles S of Doncaster on A638

Doncaster Town Moor (1895)

Bawtry Road, Bellevue, Doncaster DN4 5HU
Tel **(01302) 533778**
Mem 545
Sec G Sampson
Pro SC Poole (01302) 535286
Holes 18 L 6094 yds SSS 69
Recs Am–67 JM Laszkowicz (1992)
Pro–68 SC Poole (1992)
V'tors U exc Sun–NA before 11.30am SOC
Fees £14 (£16)
Loc Inside racecourse. Clubhouse on A638

Dore & Totley (1913)

Bradway Road, Bradway, Sheffield S17 4QR
Tel **(0114) 236 0492**
Mem 580
Sec Mrs C Ward (0114) 236 9872
Pro N Cheetham (0114) 236 6844
Holes 18 L 6265 yds SSS 70
Recs Am–65 NM Parkinson
Pro–64 P Cowen
V'tors WD–U H WE/BH–M H
Fees £25
Loc 5 miles SW of Sheffield off A61

Grange Park (1972)

Public
Upper Wortley Road, Kimberworth, Rotherham S61 2SJ
Tel **(01709) 559497**
Sec R Charity (01709) 583400
Pro E Clark (01709) 559497
Holes 18 L 6461 yds SSS 71
Recs Am–67 D Leng
Pro–68 G Tickell
V'tors U
Fees £8.50 (£9.50)
Loc 2 miles W of Rotherham on A629

Hallamshire (1897)

Sandygate, Sheffield S10 4LA
Tel **(0114) 230 1007**
Mem 600
Sec K Sharrocks (0114) 230 2153
Pro G Tickell (0114) 230 5222
Holes 18 L 6359 yds SSS 71
Recs Am–66 W Bremner
Pro–63 JW Wilkinson
V'tors H SOC–WD
Fees £27 (£32)
Loc W boundary of Sheffield

Hallowes (1892)

Dronfield, Sheffield S18 6UA
Tel **(01246) 413734**
Mem 508
Sec LF Smith
Pro P Dunn (01246) 411196
Holes 18 L 6342 yds SSS 70
Recs Am–66 S Priest (1989)
Pro–64 PL Cowen (1991)
V'tors WD–U WE–M
Fees £20 D–£27
Loc 6 miles S of Sheffield on B6057

Hickleton (1909)

Hickleton, Doncaster DN5 7BE
Tel **(01709) 892496** (Clubhouse)
Mem 525
Sec (01709) 896081
Pro P Shepherd (01709) 895170/ 888436
Holes 18 L 6403 yds SSS 71
Recs Am–69 P Goodwin (1988)
V'tors U exc Sun am SOC
Fees £18 (£25)
Loc 6 miles W of Doncaster on A635
Arch Huggett/Coles

Hillsborough (1920)

Worrall Road, Sheffield S6 4BE
Tel **(0114) 234 3608**
Mem 533
Sec KA Dungey (0114) 234 9151
Pro G Walker (0114) 233 2666
Holes 18 L 6035 yds SSS 70
Recs Am–64 JE Laycock (1987), MI Mackenzie (1992)
Pro–63 CW Gray (1987)
V'tors H SOC
Fees £28 (£35)
Loc Wadsley, Sheffield

Lees Hall (1907)

Hemsworth Road, Norton, Sheffield S8 8LL
Tel **(0114) 255 4402**
Mem 550
Sec JW Poulson (0114) 255 2900
Pro S Mackinder
Holes 18 L 6137 yds SSS 69
Recs Am–65 AR Gellsthorpe
Pro–63 B Hutchinson
V'tors U SOC
Fees £18 (£30)
Loc 3 miles S of Sheffield. E of A61

Lindrick (1891)

Lindrick Common, Worksop, Notts S81 8BH
Tel **(01909) 485802**
Fax **(01909) 488685**
Mem 500
Sec Lt Cdr RJM Jack RN
Pro P Cowen (01909) 475820
Holes 18 L 6615 yds SSS 72
Recs Am–65 DF Livingston
Pro–65 G Bond, J Morgan
V'tors U H–by prior arrangement exc Tues am–NA SOC–WD
Fees £40 (£45)
Loc 4 miles W of Worksop on A57. M1 Junction 31

Owston Park (1988)

Public
Owston Hall, Owston, Doncaster DN6 9JF
Tel **(01302) 330821**
Pro M Parker
Holes 9 L 6148 yds SSS 71
V'tors U
Fees On application
Loc 5 miles N of Doncaster on A19
Arch Michael Parker

Phoenix (1932)

Pavilion Lane, Brinsworth, Rotherham S60 5PA
Tel **(01709) 363788**
Fax **(01709) 363788**
Mem 700
Sec J Burrows (01709) 370759
Pro A Limb (01709) 382624
Holes 18 L 6145 yds SSS 69
Recs Am–65
V'tors U
Fees D–£21
Loc 2 miles S of Rotherham. M1 Junction 34

Renishaw Park (1911)

Golf House, Renishaw, Sheffield S31 9UZ
Tel **(01246) 432044**
Mem 450
Sec LT Hughes
Pro S Elliott (01246) 435484
Holes 18 L 6253 yds SSS 70
Recs Am–64 CS Bright
Pro–66 D Dunk
V'tors H SOC
Fees £22 D–£28 Sun–D–£33
Loc 7 miles SE of Sheffield. 2 miles W of M1 Junction 30

Rotherham (1903)

Thrybergh Park, Rotherham S65 4NU
Tel **(01709) 850466**
Mem 400
Sec G Smalley (01709) 850812
Pro S Thornhill (01709) 850480
Holes 18 L 6324 yds SSS 70
Recs Am–65 ID Garbutt (1992)
Pro–66 B Hutchison
V'tors WD–U SOC
Fees £26.50 (£31.50)
Loc 4 miles E of Rotherham on A630

Roundwood (1976)

Green Lane, Rawmarsh, Rotherham S62 6LA
Tel **(01709) 523471**
Mem 400
Sec D Abel (01709) 826134
Holes 9 L 5646 yds SSS 67
V'tors WE–NA before 4.30pm on comp days SOC–WD
Fees £12 (£15)
Loc 2 miles N of Rotherham on A633

Sandhill (1993)

Pay and play
Little Houghton, Barnsley S72 0HW
Tel **(01226) 753444**
Mem 275
Sec GD Bell
Holes 18 L 6214 yds SSS 70
Recs Am–69 P Kelly (1994)
V'tors U SOC
Fees £8 (£10)
Loc 6 miles E of Barnsley, off A635
Mis Driving range
Arch John Royston

Sheffield Transport (1923)

Meadow Head, Sheffield S8 7RE
Tel **(0114) 237 3216**
Mem 125
Sec AE Mason
Holes 18 L 3966 yds SSS 62
Recs Am–62 VR Hutton, E Tonks, PR Pemberton
V'tors M
Loc S of Sheffield on A61

Silkstone (1893)

Field Head, Elmhirst Lane, Silkstone, Barnsley S75 4LD
Tel **(01226) 790328**
Fax **(01226) 388080**
Mem 450
Sec L Depledge
Pro K Guy (01226) 790128
Holes 18 L 6059 yds SSS 70
Recs Am–66 PA Truelove (1994)
V'tors WD–U SOC–WD
Fees D–£23 SOC(12+)–£34
Loc 1 mile W of M1 Junction 37 on A628

Sitwell Park (1913)

Shrogs Wood Road, Rotherham S60 4BY
Tel **(01709) 541046**
Mem 500
Sec G Simmonite
Pro N Taylor (01709) 540961
Holes 18 L 6250 yds SSS 70
Recs Am–67 RN Portas (1983), G Lewis (1991)
V'tors WD–U Sat–M Sun–NA before 12.30pm SOC
Fees £20 D–£24 (£24)
Loc 2½ miles E of Rotherham on A631. M18 Junction 1

Stocksbridge & District (1924)

30 Royd Lane, Townend, Deepcar, Sheffield S30 5RZ
Tel **(0114) 288 2003**
Mem 300
Sec S Lee (0114) 288 2408
Holes 18 L 5200 yds SSS 65
Recs Am–61 CR Dale (1977)
Pro–61 TJ Brookes (1986)
V'tors U SOC
Fees £15 (£24)
Loc 9 miles W of Sheffield (A616)

Tankersley Park (1907)

High Green, Sheffield S30 4LG
Tel **(0114) 246 8247**
Mem 574
Sec PA Bagshaw
Pro I Kirk (0114) 245 5583
Holes 18 L 6212 yds Par 69 SSS 70
Recs Am–65 D Platts
Pro–69 W Atkinson
V'tors WD–U WE–M SOC–WD
Fees £19.50 D–£24.50 (£24.50)
Loc Chapeltown, 7 miles N of Sheffield. M1 Junctions 35A/36
Arch Hawtree

Thorne (1980)

Kirton Lane, Thorne, Doncaster DN8 5RJ
Tel **(01405) 812054**
Sec P Kitteridge (01302) 813827
Pro RD Highfield
Holes 18 L 5366 yds SSS 65
V'tors U
Fees £7.60 (£8.60)
Loc 10 miles NE of Doncaster. M18 Junction 5/6
Arch RD Highfield

Tinsley Park (1920)

Public
High Hazel Park, Darnell, Sheffield S9
Tel **(0114) 256 0237**
Mem 560
Sec SP Edwards
Pro AP Highfield
Holes 18 L 6103 yds SSS 69
Recs Am–68 SJ Thorpe
Pro–66 D Snell
V'tors U
Fees £7.50
Loc M1 Junction 32, 1 mile

Wath-upon-Dearne (1904)

Abdy Rawmarsh, Rotherham S62 7SJ
Tel **(01709) 872149**
Mem 600
Sec AM Buckler (01709) 878609
Pro C Bassett (01709) 878677
Holes 18 L 5857 yds SSS 68
V'tors WD–U WE/BH–M SOC
Fees £16
Loc Abdy Farm, 1½ miles S of Wath-upon-Dearne

Wheatley (1913)

Armthorpe Road, Doncaster DN2 5QB
Tel **(01302) 831655**
Mem 385 100(L) 50(J)
Sec TAD Crumpton
Pro S Fox (01302) 834085
Holes 18 L 6405 yds SSS 71
Recs Am–67 M Haddock
Pro–67 G Walker
V'tors U SOC
Fees £19 (£24)
Loc 3 miles NE of Doncaster

Wombwell Hillies (1989)

Public
Wentworth View, Wombwell, Barnsley S73 0LA
Tel **(01226) 754433**
Sec S Rolbiecki (Mgr)
Holes 9 L 2095 yds SSS 60
V'tors U
Fees £6 (£7.50)
Loc 4 miles SE of Barnsley

Wortley (1894)

Hermit Hill Lane, Wortley, Sheffield S30 7DF
Tel **(0114) 288 8469**
Mem 320
Sec AK McCririck
Pro J Tilson (0114) 288 6490
Holes 18 L 6033 yds SSS 69
Recs Am–65 Pro–64
V'tors WD–U WE–NA before 10am SOC
Fees £21 (£25)
Loc 2 miles W of M1 Junction 36, off A629

Yorkshire (West)

Alwoodley (1908)

Wigton Lane, Alwoodley, Leeds LS17 8SA
Tel **(0113) 268 1680**
Mem 450
Sec RCW Banks
Pro J Green
Holes 18 L 6686 yds SSS 72
Recs Am–67 SJM Peel
Pro–68 D Fitton
V'tors SOC–WD
Fees On application
Loc 5 miles N of Leeds on A61
Arch Dr A Mackenzie

Baildon (1898)

Moorgate, Baildon, Shipley BD17 5PP
Tel **(01274) 584266**
Mem 900
Sec E Northard (01274) 582428
Pro R Masters (01274) 595162
Holes 18 L 6225 yds SSS 70
Recs Am–66 D Farnsworth
Pro–64 G Brand, D Durnian
V'tors WD–U before 5pm (restricted Tues) WE/BH–restricted
Fees £10 (£15)
Loc 5 miles N of Bradford, off A6038

Ben Rhydding (1947)

High Wood, Ben Rhydding, Ilkley LS9 8SB
Tel **(01943) 608759**
Mem 185 60(L) 36(J)
Sec JDB Watts
Holes 9 L 4711 yds SSS 64
Recs Am–64 H Barker
Pro–64 GJ Brand
V'tors WD–U exc Wed–M WE–M
Fees £10
Loc 2 miles SE of Ilkley

For list of abbreviations see page 435

Bingley St Ives (1931)

St Ives Estate, Bingley BD16 1AT

Tel **(01274) 562436**
Fax **(01274) 511788**
Sec Mrs M Welch
Pro R Firth (01274) 562506
Holes 18 L 6480 yds SSS 71
Recs Am–66 M Foster
Pro–62 N Faldo
Ladies–71 H Butterfield
V'tors WD–U before 4pm
Fees £22 D–£27
Loc 6 miles NW of Bradford, off A650

Bradford (1891)

Hawksworth Lane, Guiseley, Leeds LS20 8NP

Tel **(01943) 875570**
Fax **(01943) 875570**
Mem 550
Sec P Atkinson
Pro S Weldon (01943) 873719
Holes 18 L 6259 yds SSS 71
Recs Am–66 WJ Dowswell
V'tors WD–U WE–NA before noon SOC–WD
Fees On application
Loc 8 miles N of Bradford, off A6038

Bradford Moor (1907)

Scarr Hall, Pollard Lane, Bradford BD2 4RW

Tel **(01274) 638313**
Mem 350
Sec CP Bedford
Pro R Hughes (01274) 626107
Holes 9 L 5854 yds SSS 68
Recs Am–67 P Sutcliffe (1994)
Pro–69 H Waller
V'tors U
Fees £12
Loc 2 miles N of Bradford

Bradley Park (1978)

Public

Bradley Road, Huddersfield HD2 1PZ

Tel **(01484) 539988**
Mem 300
Sec DW Miller
Pro PE Reilly
Holes 18 L 6202 yds SSS 70
9 hole Par 3 course
Recs Am–69 R Hall
Pro–64 P Carman
V'tors U SOC
Fees £9 (£11)
Loc 2 miles N of Huddersfield, off A6107, M62 Junction 25
Mis Floodlit driving range

Branshaw (1912)

Branshaw Moor, Oakworth, Keighley BD22 7ES

Tel **(01535) 643235**
Mem 525
Sec J Woolridge (01274) 565843
Pro S Bassil (01535) 647441
Holes 18 L 5858 yds SSS 69
Recs Am–65 D Eeles (1990)
V'tors WD–U SOC
Fees £15 (£20)
Loc 2 miles SW of Keighley on B6143
Arch James Braid/Dr A Mackenzie

Calverley (1984)

Woodhall Lane, Pudsey LS28 5JX

Tel **(0113) 256 9244**
Mem 700
Sec WW Gardner
Pro D Johnson
Holes 18 L 5527 yds SSS 67
9 hole course
Recs Am–68 R Hall
V'tors WD–U WE–pm only
Fees 18 hole–£12 (£17); 9 hole–£6
Loc 4 miles NE of Bradford
Mis Driving range

Castle Fields (1900)

Rastrick Common, Brighouse

Mem 140
Sec P Bentley (01484) 712108
Holes 6 L 2406 yds SSS 50
Recs Am–54
V'tors M
Loc 1 mile S of Brighouse

City of Wakefield (1936)

Public

Lupset Park, Horbury Road, Wakefield WF2 8QS

Tel **(01924) 367442**
Sec Mrs P Ambler
Pro R Holland (01924) 360282
Holes 18 L 6299 yds SSS 70
Recs Am–66 PE Monaghan, DA Ware, DJ Oxley
Pro–67 P Cowen
Ladies–73 R Wilkinson
V'tors U SOC–WD
Fees On application
Loc A642, 2 miles W of Wakefield. 2 miles E of M1 Junction 39/40
Arch JSF Morrison

Clayton (1906)

Thornton View Road, Clayton, Bradford BD14 6JX

Tel **(01274) 880047**
Mem 210 35(L) 35(J)
Sec FV Wood (01274) 574203
Holes 9 L 5515 yds SSS 67
Recs Am–65 ND Hawkins
V'tors WD–U Sat–U Sun–after 4pm
Fees £10 D–£12 (£12)
Loc 3 miles W of Bradford, off A647

Cleckheaton & District (1900)

483 Bradford Road, Cleckheaton BD19 6BU

Tel **(01274) 874118 (Clubhouse)**
Mem 550
Sec H Thornton (01274) 851266
Pro M Ingham (01274) 851267
Holes 18 L 5860 yds SSS 69
Recs Am–62 CA Bloice (1985)
Pro–E Wilson (1989)
V'tors U SOC
Fees £22 (£28)
Loc Nr M62 Junction 26-A638

Crosland Heath (1914)

Crosland Heath, Huddersfield HD4 7AF

Tel **(01484) 653216**
Mem 320
Sec D Walker (01484) 653262
Pro C Gaunt (01484) 653877
Holes 18 L 5972 yds SSS 70
Recs Am–66 AR Busfield (1991), S Ellis (1992)
Pro–63 G Walker (1994)
V'tors U SOC
Fees On application
Loc 3 miles W of Huddersfield, off A62

Dewsbury District (1891)

The Pinnacle, Sands Lane, Mirfield WF14 8HJ

Tel **(01924) 492399**
Mem 650
Sec CB Rhodes
Pro N Hirst (01924) 496030
Holes 18 L 6248 yds SSS 71
Recs Am–68 M Colcombe (1985)
Pro–64 S Elliott (1991)
V'tors WD–U WE–U after 4pm SOC
Fees £18 (£18)
Loc 2 miles W of Dewsbury, off A644

East Bierley (1928)

South View Road, Bierley, Bradford

Tel **(01274) 681023**
Mem 156 47(L) 30(J)
Sec RJ Welch (01274) 683666
Holes 9 L 4692 yds SSS 63
Recs Am–59 R Watts
Pro–62 B Hill
V'tors U exc Mon–NA after 4pm Sun–NA
Fees £10 (£12.50)
Loc 4 miles SE of Bradford

Elland (1910)

Hammerstones Leach Lane, Hullen Edge, Elland HD5 0TA

Tel **(01422) 372505**
Mem 265
Sec AD Blackburn (01422) 372014
Pro N Bell (01422) 374886
Holes 9 L 2763 yds SSS 66
Recs Am–64 C Hartland
V'tors U
Fees £12 (£20)
Loc Elland 1 mile. M62 Junction 24, signpost Blackley

Ferrybridge 'C' (1976)

PO Box 39, Stranglands Lane, Knottingley WF11 8SQ

Tel **(01977) 674188**
Mem 340
Sec NE Pugh (01977) 793884

Holes 9 L 5138 yds SSS 65
Recs Am–67 R MacDonald (1989)
V'tors M
Fees D–£5 (D–£6)
Loc 1/2 mile off A1, on B6136
Arch NE Pugh

Fulneck (1892)

Fulneck, Pudsey LS28 8NT
Tel **(0113) 256 5191**
Mem 273
Sec J Brogden (0113) 257 4049
Holes 9 L 5564 yds SSS 67
Recs Am–64 I Holdsworth
V'tors WD–U WE/BH–M SOC
Fees £12
Loc 5 miles W of Leeds

Garforth (1913)

Long Lane, Garforth, Leeds LS25 2DS
Tel **(0113) 286 2021**
Fax **(0113) 286 2063**
Mem 550
Sec FA Readman (0113) 286 3308
Pro K Findlater (0113) 286 2063
Holes 18 L 6327 yds SSS 70
Recs Am–63 AR Gelsthorpe
V'tors WD–U H WE/BH–M SOC
Fees £21 D–£26
Loc 9 miles E of Leeds, between Garforth and Barwick-in-Elmet, off A642

Gotts Park (1933)

Public
Armley Ridge Road, Armley, Leeds LS12 2QX
Tel **(0113) 234 2019**
Mem 300
Sec M Gill (0113) 256 2994
Pro JK Simpson
Holes 18 L 4960 yds SSS 64
V'tors U
Fees On application
Loc 2 miles W of Leeds

Halifax (1895)

Union Lane, Ogden, Halifax HX2 8XR
Tel **(01422) 244171**
Mem 450
Sec JP Clark
Pro SA Foster (01422) 240047
Holes 18 L 6038 yds SSS 70
Recs Am–66 J Robinson, AMA Bagott, J Rushworth
Pro–65 PW Good
V'tors U WE–parties welcome SOC
Fees On application
Loc 4 miles N of Halifax on A629

Halifax Bradley Hall (1907)

Holywell Green, Halifax HX4 9AN
Tel **(01422) 374108**
Mem 608
Sec PM Pitchforth (01422) 376626
Pro P Wood (01422) 370231
Holes 18 L 6213 yds SSS 70
Recs Am–65 AR Whitworth
V'tors U SOC
Fees £18 (£28)
Loc S of Halifax on A6112

Halifax West End (1913)

Paddock Lane, Highroad Well, Halifax HX2 0NT
Tel **(01422) 353608**
Mem 340 110(L) 60(J)
Sec BR Thomas (01422) 341878
Pro D Rishworth (01422) 363293
Holes 18 L 5951 yds SSS 69
Recs Am–64 SC Ingham
Pro–64 AJ Bickerdike
V'tors U SOC
Fees £17 (£20) (1994)
Loc 2 miles NW of Halifax

Hanging Heaton (1922)

Whitecross Road, Bennett Lane, Dewsbury WF12 7DT
Tel **(01924) 461606**
Mem 550
Sec SM Simpson (01924) 461729
Pro (01924) 467077
Holes 9 L 2868 yds SSS 67
Recs Am–67 J Allott (1993)
Pro–65 M Pearson (1988)
V'tors WD–U WE–M
Fees £12
Loc Dewsbury 3/4 mile (A653)

Headingley (1892)

Back Church Lane, Adel, Leeds LS16 8DW
Tel **(0113) 267 3052**
Mem 640
Sec RW Hellawell (0113) 267 9573
Pro SA Foster (0113) 267 5100
Holes 18 L 6298 yds SSS 70
Recs Am–67 S Pullan (1987)
Pro–64 S Field (1990)
V'tors U SOC
Fees £25 D–£30 (£36)
Loc 5 miles NW of Leeds, off A660

Headley (1907)

Headley Lane, Thornton, Bradford BD13 3LX
Tel **(01274) 833481**
Fax **(01274) 670398**
Mem 270 35(L) 35(J)
Sec K Allan (01274) 670398
Holes 9 L 4914 yds SSS 64
Recs Am–61 A Cording (1985)
Pro–66 M Ingham (1982)
V'tors WD–U WE–M SOC
Fees On application
Loc 5 miles W of Bradford (B6145)

Hebden Bridge (1930)

Wadsworth, Hebden Bridge HX7 8PH
Tel **(01422) 842896**
Mem 300
Sec Miss S Greenwood (01422) 842732
Holes 9 L 5064 yds SSS 65
Recs Am–63 IS Marsland (1978), PJ Richardson (1989), IR Powell (1994)
Pro–63 M Ingham (1974)
V'tors U
Fees £10 (£15)
Loc 1 mile N of Hebden Bridge

Horsforth (1907)

Layton Rise, Layton Road, Horsforth, Leeds LS18 5EX
Tel **(0113) 258 6819**
Mem 365 90(L) 85(J)
Sec B Brown
Pro P Scott (0113) 258 5200
Holes 18 L 6293 yds SSS 70
Recs Am–66 SG Hurd
Pro–67 HW Muscroft
V'tors U SOC
Fees D–£24 (£30)
Loc 6 miles NW of Leeds

Howley Hall (1900)

Scotchman Lane, Morley, Leeds LS27 0NX
Tel **(01924) 472432**
Mem 465
Sec Mrs A Pepper (01924) 478417
Pro SA Spinks (01924) 473852
Holes 18 L 6029 yds SSS 69
Recs Am–66 JD Roberts (1994)
V'tors U
Fees £21 D–£25 (D–£30)
Loc 4 miles SW of Leeds on B6123

Huddersfield (1891)

Fixby Hall, Lightridge Road, Huddersfield HD2 2EP
Tel **(01484) 420110**
Fax **(01484) 424623**
Mem 576
Sec DL Bennett (Gen Mgr), Mrs D Lockett (01484) 426203
Pro P Carman (01484) 426463
Holes 18 L 6432 yds SSS 71
Recs Am–64 S Hurd (1994)
Pro–64 D Padgett (1991)
V'tors U SOC–WD
Fees £30 D–£40 (£40 D–£50)
Loc 2 miles N of Huddersfield, off A6107. M62 Junction 24

Ilkley (1890)

Myddleton, Ilkley LS29 0BE
Tel **(01943) 607277**
Mem 530
Sec AK Hatfield (01943) 600214
Pro JL Hammond (01943) 607463
Holes 18 L 6260 yds SSS 70
Recs Am–65 AC Flather (1984)
Pro–66 CS Montgomerie (1990)
V'tors U
Fees £30 (£35)
Loc NW of Ilkley, off A65

Keighley (1904)

Howden Park, Utley, Keighley BD20 6DH

Tel **(01535) 603179**
Fax **(01535) 604778**
Mem 600
Sec CL Hodge (01535) 604778
Pro M Bradley (01535) 665370
Holes 18 L 6141 yds SSS 70
Recs Am–65 PI Wood (1991)
Pro–65 J Holchaks
V'tors WD–U ex Tues Sat–NA
Sun/BH–NA before 2pm
Fees £21 D–£25 (£23 D–£27)
Loc 1 mile W of Keighley

Leeds (1896)

Elmete Road, Roundhay, Leeds LS8 2LJ

Tel **(0113) 265 8775**
Mem 480
Sec GW Backhouse
(0113) 265 9203
Pro S Longster (0113) 265 8786
Holes 18 L 6097 yds SSS 69
Recs Am–64 J Whiteley
Pro–63 P Hall
V'tors WD–U WE–M
Fees £19 D–£25
Loc 4 miles NE of Leeds, off A58

Leeds Golf Centre (1994)

Pay and play
Wike Ridge Lane, Shadwell, Leeds LS17 9JW

Tel **(0113) 288 6000**
Fax **(0113) 288 6185**
Mem 400
Sec CJ Brocklebank
Pro J Clapham
Holes 18 L 6800 yds SSS 72
9 hole Par 3 course
V'tors U SOC
Fees £12.50 (£12.50)
Loc NE of Leeds, between A58 and A61
Mis Driving range. Golf Academy
Arch Donald Steel

Lightcliffe (1907)

Knowle Top Road, Lightcliffe HX3 8SW

Tel **(01422) 202459**
Mem 145 92(L) 87(J)
Sec TH Gooder (01422) 201051
Pro W Lockett
Holes 9 L 5368 metres SSS 68
Recs Am–66 JR Denham,
CRC Denham
V'tors U H–exc comp days Sun am–M SOC
Fees £15 (£20)
Loc 3 miles E of Halifax (A58)

Longley Park (1911)

Maple Street, Huddersfield HD5 9AX

Tel **(01484) 426932**
Mem 400
Sec D Palliser
Pro P Middleton (01484) 422304
Holes 9 L 5269 yds SSS 66
Recs Am–63 J Beaumont (1993)
Pro–65 PW Booth
V'tors WD–U exc Thurs
WE–restricted
Fees £13.50 (£16)
Loc Huddersfield ½ mile

Low Laithes (1925)

Parkmill Lane, Flushdyke, Ossett WF5 9AP

Tel **(01924) 273275**
Mem 575
Sec D Wilford (01924) 378363
Pro P Browning (01924) 274667
Holes 18 L 6468 yds SSS 71
Recs Am–67
Pro–68
V'tors U WE–no parties SOC–WD
Fees £18 D–£22 (£30)
Loc 2 miles W of Wakefield. M1 Junction 40
Arch Dr A Mackenzie

Marsden (1921)

Hemplow, Marsden, Huddersfield HD7 6NN

Tel **(01484) 844253**
Mem 200 49(L) 22(J)
Sec D Horncastle
Pro AJ Bickerdike
Holes 9 L 5702 yds SSS 68
Recs Am–63 AJ Bickerdike
Pro–A Bickerdike
V'tors WD–U Sat–NA before 4pm
Sun–M SOC
Fees £10
Loc 8 miles W of Huddersfield, off A62
Arch Dr A Mackenzie

Meltham (1908)

Thick Hollins Hall, Meltham, Huddersfield HD7 3DQ

Tel **(01484) 850227**
Mem 450
Sec J Holdsworth (Hon)
Pro PF Davies (01484) 851521
Holes 18 L 6145 yds SSS 70
Recs Am–65 A Sheard
Pro–69 W Casper
V'tors H
Fees £20 (£25)
Loc 5 miles SW of Huddersfield (B6107)

Mid Yorkshire (1993)

Havercroft Lane, Darrington, Pontefract WF8 3BP

Tel **(01977) 704522**
Fax **(01977) 600823**
Mem 600
Sec IM Collins (Mgr)
Pro W Heywood (01977) 600844
Holes 18 L 6340 yds SSS 71
V'tors U H SOC
Fees £15 (£25)
Loc Nr A1/M62 junction
Mis Floodlit driving range
Arch Steve Marnoch

Middleton Park (1933)

Public
Ring Road, Beeston Park, Middleton LS10 3TN

Tel **(0113) 270 9506**
Mem 310
Sec F Ramsey (0113) 253 3993
Pro D Bulmer
Holes 18 L 5233 yds SSS 66
Recs Am–63 S Nicholson
V'tors U
Fees On application
Loc 3 miles S of Leeds

Moor Allerton (1923)

Coal Road, Wike, Leeds LS17 9NH

Tel **(0113) 266 1154**
Mem 400
Sec S Mack (Hon)
Pro R Lane (0113) 266 5209
Holes 27 holes:
6470-6843 yds SSS 73-74
Recs Am–65 K Wallbank (1994)
Pro–65
V'tors WD/Sat–U Sun–NA SOC
Fees £36 (£50)
Loc 5½ miles N of Leeds, off A61

Moortown (1909)

Harrogate Road, Leeds LS17 7DB

Tel **(0113) 268 6521**
Fax **(0113) 268 0986**
Mem 580
Sec T Hughes
Pro B Hutchinson
(0113) 268 3636
Holes 18 L 6826 yds SSS 74
Recs Am–69 C Turner
Pro–68 K Waters
V'tors H
Fees £35 D–£40 (£40 D–£45)
Loc 5½ miles N of Leeds on A61
Arch Dr A Mackenzie

Normanton (1903)

Snydale Road, Normanton, Wakefield WF6 1PA

Tel **(01924) 892943**
Mem 300
Sec J McElhinney
Pro M Evans (01924) 220134
Holes 9 L 5323 yds SSS 66
Recs Am–65 R Booth (1992)
Pro–65 A Wright (1991)
Ladies–69 D Evans (1992)
V'tors U exc Sun–NA
Fees £8 Sat/BH–£14
Loc 1 mile from M62 Junction 31. A655 towards Wakefield

Northcliffe (1921)

High Bank Lane, Shipley, Bradford BD18 4LJ

Tel **(01274) 584085**
Mem 660
Sec HR Archer
Pro M Hillas (01274) 587193
Holes 18 L 6104 yds SSS 69
Recs Am–65 R Bell (1991)
Pro–67 M James

V'tors U SOC
Fees £20 (£25)
Loc 3 miles NW of Bradford, off A650 Keighley road
Arch James Braid

Otley (1906)

West Busk Lane, Otley LS21 3NG
Tel **(01943) 461015**
Mem 700
Sec Mrs P Bates (01943) 465329
Pro S Poot (01943) 463403
Holes 18 L 6235 yds SSS 70
Recs Am–66 J Blears (1989)
Pro–62 GJ Brand (1988)
V'tors U exc Sat–NA SOC
Fees £23 (£28)
Loc Off Bradford road, Otley

Oulton Park (1990)

Public
Oulton, Rothwell, Leeds LS26 8EX
Tel **(0113) 282 3152**
Fax **(0113) 282 6290**
Mem 390
Sec Lyn Robb (Mgr)
Pro S Gromett
Holes 18 L 6500 yds SSS 71
9 L 3299 yds SSS 35
Recs Am–68 G Fish (1993)
V'tors U SOC
Fees 18 hole:£6.80 (£7.40)
9 hole:£4.40
Loc 5 miles SE of Leeds, off A642. N of M62 Junction 30
Mis Driving range
Arch Alliss/Thomas

Outlane (1906)

Slack Lane, Outlane, Huddersfield HD3 3YL
Tel **(01422) 374762**
Mem 500
Sec JS Donnelly
Pro D Chapman
Holes 18 L 6003 yds SSS 69
Recs Am–67 NJ Nuttall
V'tors U SOC
Fees £18 (£30)
Loc 4 miles W of Huddersfield, off A640. M62 Junction 23

Painthorpe House (1961)

Painthorpe Lane, Crigglestone, Wakefield WF4 3HE
Tel **(01924) 255083**
Fax **(01924) 252022**
Mem 180
Sec H Kershaw (01924) 274527
Holes 9 L 4520 yds SSS 62
Recs Am–64 J Turner,
J Whitehouse (1986)
V'tors U exc Sun–NA
Fees £6 Sat–£10
Loc 1 mile SE of M1 Junction 39

Phoenix Park (1922)

Phoenix Park, Thornbury, Bradford 3
Tel **(01274) 667573**
Mem 180
Sec B Mitchell (01274) 667669
Pro B Ferguson
Holes 9 L 4982 yds SSS 64
Recs Am–66 C Lally
V'tors WD/BH–U WE–NA
Fees On application
Loc Thornbury Roundabout (A647)

Pontefract & District (1900)

Park Lane, Pontefract WF8 4QS
Tel **(01977) 792241**
Mem 800
Sec WT Smith (01977) 792115
Pro NJ Newman (01977) 706806
Holes 18 L 6227 yds SSS 70
Recs Am–63 DC Rooke
Pro–67 GW Townhill
V'tors I SOC–Tues/Thurs/Fri
Fees £25 (£32)
Loc Pontefract 1 mile on B6134. M62 Junction 32

Pontefract Park (1973)

Public
Park Road, Pontefract
Tel **(01977) 702799**
Holes 18 L 4068 yds SSS 62
V'tors U
Fees On application
Loc Between Pontefract and M62 roundabout, nr racecourse

Queensbury (1923)

Brighouse Road, Queensbury, Bradford BD13 1QF
Tel **(01274) 882155**
Mem 230 55(L) 40(J)
Sec H Andrew
Pro G Howard (01274) 816864
Holes 9 L 5102 yds SSS 65
Recs Am–64 S Rogers,
H Wilkerson
Pro–63 P Cowan
V'tors U
Fees £10 (£20)
Loc 4 miles SW of Bradford (A647)

Rawdon (1896)

Buckstone Drive, Micklefield Lane, Rawdon LS19 6BD
Tel **(0113) 250 6040**
Mem 220 55(L) 50(J)
Sec RA Adams (0113) 250 6064
Pro (0113) 250 5017
Holes 9 L 5982 yds SSS 69
Recs Am–64 A Coverdale
V'tors WD–H WE/BH–M SOC
Fees £16
Loc 6 miles NW of Leeds nr A65/A658 junction

Riddlesden (1927)

Howden Rough, Riddlesden, Keighley
Tel **(01535) 602148**
Mem 250
Sec Mrs KM Brooksbank (01535) 607646
Holes 18 L 4295 yds Par 63 SSS 61
Recs Am–60 M Mitchell (1987)
Pro–59 P Cowan (1983)
V'tors U exc Sun–NA before 2pm
Fees £10 (£15)
Loc 1 mile from Riddlesden, off Scott Lane West. 3 miles N of Keighley, off A650

Roundhay (1923)

Public
Park Lane, Leeds LS8 2EJ
Tel **(0113) 266 2695**
Pro JA Pape (0113) 266 1686
Holes 9 L 5322 yds SSS 65
Recs Am–62 AR White
Pro–62 M Bembridge
V'tors U
Fees On application
Loc N of Leeds, off Moortown Ring Road

Ryburn (1910)

Norland, Sowerby Bridge, Halifax
Tel **(01422) 831355**
Mem 200
Sec J Hoyle (01422) 843070
Holes 9 L 4907 yds SSS 64
Recs Am–64 DS Lumb (1987)
Pro–61 M Pearson (1987)
V'tors U
Fees £15 (£20)
Loc 3 miles S of Halifax

Sand Moor (1926)

Alwoodley Lane, Leeds LS17 7DJ
Tel **(0113) 268 1685**
Mem 540
Sec BF Precious (0113) 268 5180
Pro P Tupling (0113) 268 3925
Holes 18 L 6429 yds SSS 71
Recs Am–63 SR Cage (1993)
Pro–62 S Holden (1991)
V'tors WD–H by arrangement WE–NA
Fees £28 (£35)
Loc 5 miles N of Leeds, off A61

Scarcroft (1937)

Syke Lane, Leeds LS14 3BQ
Tel **(0113) 289 2263**
Mem 540
Sec RD Barwell (0113) 289 2311
Pro D Tear (0113) 289 2780
Holes 18 L 6426 yds SSS 71
Recs Am–67 E Shaw
Pro–65 D Padgett
V'tors WD–U WE/BH–M or by arrangement SOC–WD exc Mon
Fees £25 (£35)
Loc 7 miles N of Leeds, off A58

Shipley (1896)

Beckfoot Lane, Cottingley Bridge, Bingley BD16 1LX
Tel **(01274) 563212**
Mem 600
Sec GM Shaw (01274) 568652
Pro JR Parry (01274) 563674

Holes 18 L 6218 yds SSS 70
Recs Am–66 GM Shaw (1975), IC Bottomley (1991), I Pyman (1993) Pro–64 M Ingham (1987)
V'tors WD–U exc Tues–NA before 2pm Sat–NA before 4pm
Fees £27 (£36)
Loc 6 miles N of Bradford on A650

Silsden (1913)

Brunthwaite, Silsden, Keighley BD20 0HN
Tel **(01535) 652998**
Mem 300
Sec G Davey
Holes 14 L 4870 yds SSS 64
Recs Am–61
V'tors Sat–restricted Sun–U after 1pm
Fees £10 (£15)
Loc 5 miles N of Keighley, off A6034

South Bradford (1906)

Pearson Road, Odsal, Bradford BD6 1BH
Tel **(01274) 679195**
Mem 200
Sec DW Clow
Pro I Marshall (01274) 673346
Holes 9 L 6004 yds SSS 69
Recs Am–65 GM Yarnold Pro–67 S Miguel, A Caygill
V'tors WD–U WE–M
Fees On application
Loc Bradford 2 miles, nr Odsal Stadium

South Leeds (1914)

Gipsy Lane, Ring Road, Beeston, Leeds LS11 5TU
Tel **(0113) 270 0479**
Mem 600
Sec J Neal (0113) 277 1676
Pro M Lewis (0113) 270 2598
Holes 18 L 5835 yds SSS 68
Recs Am–65 R Lister Pro–68 B Waites
V'tors WD–U WE–M SOC
Fees £18 (£25)
Loc 4 miles S of Leeds. 2 miles from M62 and M1

Temple Newsam (1923)

Public
Temple Newsam Road, Halton, Leeds LS15 0LN
Tel **(0113) 264 5624**
Mem 500
Sec G Gower
Pro D Bulmer (0113) 264 7362
Holes Lord Irwin 18 L 6448 yds SSS 71; Lady Dorothy Wood 18 L 6029 yds SSS 70
V'tors U SOC
Fees £6.80 (£7.40)
Loc 5 miles E of Leeds, off A63

Todmorden (1894)

Rive Rocks, Cross Stone, Todmorden, Lancs 0L14 8RD
Tel **(01706) 812986**
Mem 180 40(L) 30(J)
Sec PH Eastwood
Holes 9 L 5878 yds SSS 68
Recs Am–67 G Morgan, J May Pro–68 B Hunt
V'tors WD/BH–U WE–M SOC–WD
Fees £15 (£20)
Loc 1 mile N of Todmorden, off A646

Wakefield (1891)

28 Woodthorpe Lane, Sandal, Wakefield WF2 6JH
Tel **(01924) 255104**
Mem 500
Sec RE Guiver (01924) 258778
Pro IM Wright (01924) 255380
Holes 18 L 6613 yds SSS 72
Recs Am–66 S Cage (1992) Pro–68 HW Muscroft (1982)
V'tors U SOC–Wed–Fri
Fees £25
Loc 3 miles S of Wakefield on A61. M1 Junction 39

West Bowling (1898)

Newall Hall, Rooley Lane, West Bowling, Bradford BD5 8LB
Tel **(01274) 724449**
Mem 500
Sec MEL Lynn (01274) 393207
Pro AP Swaine (01274) 728036
Holes 18 L 5657 yds SSS 67
Recs Am–65 M Evans Pro–66 G Brand
V'tors WD–U H WE–U after 3.30pm SOC
Fees £26 (£30)
Loc Junction of M606 and Bradford Ring Road East

West Bradford (1900)

Chellow Grange, Haworth Road, Bradford BD9 6NP
Tel **(01274) 542767**
Mem 450
Sec D Ingham (Hon)
Pro NM Barber (01274) 542102
Holes 18 L 5777 yds SSS 68
Recs Am–63 RJ Ellis (1984) Pro–66
V'tors U
Fees £16 (£22)
Loc 3 miles W of Bradford (B6269)

Wetherby (1910)

Linton Lane, Linton, Wetherby LS22 4JF
Tel **(01937) 580089**
Mem 630
Sec JR Nicholson
Pro D Padgett (01937) 583375
Holes 18 L 6235 yds SSS 70
Recs Am–67 N Robinson (1991), J Mountford (1992) Pro–66 MB Ingham (1985)
V'tors WE–U after 10am SOC–Mon pm/Wed–Fri
Fees £23 (£34)
Loc 3/4 mile W of Wetherby. A1 Wetherby roundabout

Whitwood (1987)

Public
Altofts Lane, Whitwood, Castleford WF10 5PZ
Tel **(01977) 512835**
Sec S Hicks (Hon)
Pro R Holland
Holes 9 L 6176 yds SSS 69
V'tors WD–U WE–booking necessary
Fees On application
Loc 2 miles SW of Castleford (A655). M62 Junction 31

Willow Valley (1994)

Pay and play
Clifton, Brighouse HD6 4JB
Tel **(01274) 878624**
Mem 100
Sec G Selway
Holes 9 hole course
V'tors U
Fees 9 holes–£5. 18 holes–£9
Loc SW of Leeds, M62 Junction 25
Mis Driving range
Arch Jonathan Gaunt

Woodhall Hills (1905)

Woodhall Road, Calverley, Pudsey LS28 5UN
Tel **(0113) 256 4771/255 4594**
Mem 315
Sec D Harkness
Pro D Tear (0113) 256 2857
Holes 18 L 6102 yds SSS 69
Recs Am–66 PA Crosby Pro–66 M Ingham
V'tors WD–U Sat–U after 4.30pm Sun–U after 10.30am
Fees D–£20.50 (D–£25.50)
Loc 4 miles E of Bradford, off A647-signposted Calverley

Woodsome Hall (1922)

Woodsome Hall, Fenay Bridge, Huddersfield HD8 0LQ
Tel **(01484) 602971**
Mem 394 194(L) 103(J)
Sec WDN Woodhouse (Hon)
Pro M Higginbottom (01484) 602034
Holes 18 L 6080 yds SSS 69
Recs Am–65 M Broadbent Pro–65 D Jagger
V'tors U H exc Tues–NA before 4pm SOC
Fees £25 (£30)
Loc 6 miles SE of Huddersfield on A629 Penistone road

Ireland

Co Antrim

Ballycastle (1890)
Cushendall Road, Ballycastle BT64 6QP
Tel **(012657) 62536**
Mem 920
Sec HA Fraser (Hon)
Pro I McLaughlin (012657) 62506
Holes 18 L 5882 yds SSS 69
Recs Am–66 F Fleming (1962), J McAleese, RJ McCoy, E Hughes
Pro–64 F Daly
V'tors U H SOC
Fees £15 (£20) W–£65
Loc Between Portrush and Cushendall (A2)

Ballyclare (1923)
25 Springvale Road, Ballyclare BT39 9JW
Tel **(01960) 342352/324542**
Mem 440
Sec H McConnell (01960) 322696
Holes 18 L 5840 yds SSS 71
Recs Am–69 J Foster
Pro–69 S Hamill
V'tors WD–U WE–NA before 4pm
Fees £14 (£20)
Loc 1½ miles N of Ballyclare. 14 miles N of Belfast

Ballymena (1902)
128 Raceview Road, Ballymena BT42 4HY
Tel **(01266) 861207/861487**
Mem 824
Sec C McAuley (Hon)
Pro J Gallagher (01266) 861652
Holes 18 L 5245 metres SSS 67
Recs Am–62 D Cunning
V'tors WD/Sun–U SOC
Fees £12 (£15)
Loc 2 miles E of Ballymena on A42

Bushfoot (1890)
Bushfoot Road, Portballintrae B57 8RR
Tel **(012657) 31317**
Mem 660
Sec J Knox Thompson (Sec/Mgr)
Holes 9 L 5812 yds SSS 67
Recs Am–63 A McIlroy (1990)
V'tors U Sat–NA after noon SOC
Fees £12 (£15)
Loc 1 mile N of Bushmills. 4 miles E of Portrush

Cairndhu (1928)
192 Coast Road, Ballygally, Larne BT40 2QC
Tel **(01574) 583248**
Fax **(01574) 583324**
Mem 875
Sec Mrs J Robinson (01574) 583324
Pro R Walker (01574) 583417
Holes 18 L 6112 yds SSS 69
Recs Am–64 B McMillen, R Houston
Pro–64 D Jones, P Townsend
V'tors U exc Sat–NA
Fees £12 (£20)
Loc 4 miles N of Larne
Arch JSF Morrison

Carrickfergus (1926)
35 North Road, Carrickfergus BT38 8LP
Tel **(019603) 63713**
Mem 800
Sec RJ Campbell (Sec/Mgr)
Pro R Stevenson (019603) 51803
Holes 18 L 5752 yds SSS 68
Recs Am–62 G Parkhill
Pro–64 N Drew
V'tors U
Fees £13 (£18)
Loc 8 miles E of Belfast, off A2

Cushendall (1937)
21 Shore Road, Cushendall BT44 0QQ
Tel **(012667) 71318**
Mem 715
Sec S McLaughlin (012667) 58366
Holes 9 L 4678 yds SSS 63
Recs Am–61 S McKillop (1993)
V'tors WE–restricted SOC
Fees £8 (£10) M–£60
Loc 25 miles N of Larne

Greenisland (1894)
156 Upper Road, Greenisland, Carrickfergus BT38 8RW
Tel **(01232) 862236**
Mem 510
Sec J Wyness (01232) 864583
Holes 9 L 5536 metres SSS 69
Recs Am–65
V'tors WD–U Sat–NA before 5pm SOC–exc Sat
Fees £10 (£15)
Loc 9 miles NE of Belfast
Arch H Middleton

Lambeg (1986)
Bells Lane, Lambeg, Lisburn
Tel **(01846) 662738**
Mem 200
Sec T Burrell
Pro I Murdock
Holes 9 L 4383 metres SSS 65
Recs Am–64 A Mason (1993)
V'tors U SOC
Fees £6 (£6.50)
Loc SW of Belfast, off Lisburn road

Larne (1894)
54 Ferris Bay Road, Islandmagee, Larne BT40 3RT
Tel **(01960) 382228**
Mem 420
Sec JB Stewart (01960) 372043
Holes 9 L 6114 yds SSS 69
Recs Am–66 IA Nesbitt, BR Hobson
Pro–68 N Drew
V'tors WD–U WE–M after 5pm SOC–WD/Sun
Fees £8 (£15)
Loc 6 miles N of Whitehead on Browns Bay road
Arch George Baillie

Lisburn (1891)
68 Eglantine Road, Lisburn BT27 5RQ
Tel **(01846) 677216**
Fax **(01846) 603608**
Mem 961
Sec G Graham (Sec/Mgr)
Pro BR Campbell (01846) 677217
Holes 18 L 6647 yds SSS 72
Recs Am–65 P Grant
Pro–64 D Feherty (1989)
V'tors WD–U WE–M SOC–Mon/Thurs/Fri
Fees £25 (£30)
Loc 3 miles S of Lisburn on A3
Arch Hawtree

Massereene (1895)
51 Lough Road, Antrim BT41 4DQ
Tel **(01849) 429293**
Mem 850
Sec Mrs M Agnew (01849) 428096
Pro J Smyth (01849) 464074
Holes 18 L 6614 yds SSS 71
Recs Am–68 J O'Meekin
V'tors U SOC
Fees £18 (£23)
Loc 1 mile S of Antrim

Royal Portrush (1888)
Dunluce Road, Portrush BT56 8JQ
Tel **(01265) 822311**
Fax **(01265) 823139**
Mem 1042 256(L)
Sec Miss W Erskine
Pro DA Stevenson (01265) 823335
Holes Dunluce 18 L 6772 yds SSS 73
Valley 18 L 6273 yds SSS 70
9 hole short course
Recs Dunluce Am–67 G McGimpsey
Pro–66 J Hargreaves
Valley Am–65 MJC Hoey
V'tors WD–U H Sat–NA before 2.30pm Sun–NA before 10am SOC
Fees Dunluce D–£43 (D–£50)
Valley D–£18 (D–£25)
Loc Portrush Coastal Rd ½ mile
Arch HS Colt

Whitehead (1904)
McCrae's Brae, Whitehead, Carrickfergus BT38 9NZ
Tel **(01960) 353792**
Mem 850
Sec J Niblock, R Patrick (01960) 353631
Pro T Loughran (01960) 353118
Holes 18 L 6426 yds SSS 71
Recs Am–68 A Hope
V'tors WD–U Sun–M Sat SOC–exc Sat
Fees £11 (£17)
Loc ½ mile from Whitehead, off road to Island Magee

Co Armagh

Ashfield (1990)
Freeduff, Cullyhanna
Tel **(01693) 868180**
Mem 150
Sec J Quinn (Sec/Mgr)
Pro E Maney
Holes 18 L 6540 yds SSS 69
V'tors U
Fees On application
Loc 6 miles S of Newtownhamilton (B135)
Mis Driving range
Arch Frank Ainsworth

County Armagh (1893)
Newry Road, Armagh BT60 1EN
Tel **(01861) 522501**
Mem 900
Sec P Reid (01861) 525861
Pro A Rankin (01861) 525864
Holes 18 L 6184 yds SSS 69
V'tors U SOC–WD
Fees £10 (£15)
Loc 40 miles SW of Belfast by M1

Lurgan (1893)
The Demesne, Lurgan BT67 9BN
Tel **(01762) 325306 (Clubhouse)**
Fax **(01762) 325306**
Mem 874
Sec Mrs G Turkington (01762) 322087
Pro D Paul (01762) 321068
Holes 18 L 5836 metres SSS 70
Recs Am–65 T Cummins (1990) Pro–65 B Todd
V'tors U SOC–Mon/Thurs/Fri am/Sun am
Fees £15 (£20)
Loc Nr Brownlow Castle, Lurgan
Arch Frank Pennink

Portadown (1906)
Carrickblacker, Portadown BT63 5LF
Tel **(01762) 355356**
Mem 1066
Sec Mrs ME Holloway
Pro P Stevenson (01762) 334655
Holes 18 L 6119 yds SSS 70
Recs Am–S Paul (1990) Pro–63
V'tors WD–U exc Tues
Fees £16 (£20)
Loc 3 miles S of Portadown, towards Gilford

Silverwood (1983)
Public
Turmoyra Lane, Silverwood, Lurgan
Tel **(01762) 326606**
Mem 180
Sec V McCorry (Sec/Mgr)
Holes 18 L 6496 yds SSS 72
V'tors U
Fees £7 (£10)
Loc Lurgan 1 mile. M1 Junction 10
Mis Floodlit driving range

Tandragee (1922)
Markethill Road, Tandragee BT26 2ER
Tel **(01762) 840727 (Steward)**
Fax **(01762) 841272**
Mem 1085
Sec H McCready (01762) 841272
Pro E Maney (01762) 841761
Holes 18 L 6084 yds SSS 69
Recs Am–62 P Topley Pro–65 W Sullivan (1983)
V'tors U SOC
Fees £10 (£15)
Loc 8 miles S of Portadown on A27
Arch F Hawtree

Belfast

Ballyearl Golf Centre
Public
585 Doagh Road, Newtownabbey BT36 8RZ
Tel **(01232) 848287**
Sec A Bevan
Holes 9 L 2362 yds Par 3 course
V'tors U
Fees £3 (£4)
Loc N of Mossley on B59
Mis Driving range
Arch A Bevan

Balmoral (1914)
518 Lisburn Road, Belfast BT9 6GX
Tel **(01232) 381514**
Fax **(01232) 669505**
Mem 1002
Sec RC McConkey (Mgr)
Pro G Bleakley (01232) 667747
Holes 18 L 5909 metres SSS 70
Recs Am–66 M Wilson Pro–64 D Jones
V'tors U exc Sat SOC–Mon & Thurs
Fees £20 Wed–£24 (£30)
Loc 2 miles S of Belfast by Kings Hall

Belvoir Park (1927)
Church Road, Newtownbreda, Belfast BT8 4AN
Tel **(01232) 491693**
Fax **(01232) 646113**
Mem 1100
Sec KH Graham (01232) 491693
Pro GM Kelly (01232) 646714
Holes 18 L 6501 yds SSS 71
Recs Am–66 TS Anderson, JN Browne Pro–66 P Alliss, EC Brown
V'tors U exc Sat–NA
Fees £30 (£35)
Loc 3 miles S of Belfast, off Newcastle road
Arch HS Colt

Cliftonville (1911)
Westland Road, Belfast BT14 6NH
Tel **(01232) 744158/746595**
Mem 429
Sec JM Henderson (Hon)
Holes 9 L 6242 yds SSS 70
Recs Am–66 WRA Tennant, IA Nesbitt, B Doherty Jr Pro–67 S Hamill
V'tors U exc Sat
Fees £12 (£15)
Loc Belfast

Dunmurry (1905)
91 Dunmurry Lane, Dunmurry, Belfast BT17 9JS
Tel **(01232) 610834**
Mem 493 127(L) 117(J)
Sec A Taylor (Sec/Mgr)
Pro P Leonard (01232) 621314
Holes 18 L 5348 metres SSS 68
Recs Am–68 J Johnston Pro–67 P Leonard
V'tors Tues & Thurs–NA after 5pm Sat–NA before 5pm SOC
Fees £14 (£20) SOC–£13 (£18)
Loc Belfast 5 miles

Fortwilliam (1891)
Downview Avenue, Belfast B15 4EZ
Tel **(01232) 370770**
Fax **(01232) 781891**
Mem 1100
Sec M Purdy
Pro P Hanna (01232) 770980
Holes 18 L 5973 yds SSS 69
Recs Am-67 A O'Neill Pro-65 P Leonard
V'tors U SOC
Fees £16 (£21)
Loc 2 miles N of Belfast on A2

Gilnahirk (1983)
Public
Manns Corner, Upper Braniel Road, Belfast
Tel **(01232) 448477**
Mem 200
Sec K Gray (Mgr)
Pro K Gray
Holes 9 L 2699 metres SSS 68
Recs Am–65 T McIver (1993)
V'tors U
Fees On application
Loc 3 miles SE of Belfast, off A23

The Knock Club (1895)

Summerfield, Dundonald, Belfast BT16 0QX

Tel **(01232) 482249**
Fax **(01232) 483251**
Mem 870
Sec SG Managh (01232) 483251
Pro G Fairweather (01232) 483825
Holes 18 L 6407 yds SSS 71
Recs Am–67 KH Graham
Pro–69 PR McGuirk
V'tors U SOC–Mon & Thurs
Fees D–£20 (£25)
Loc 4 miles E of Belfast on the Upper Newtownards Road
Arch Colt/Mackenzie/Alison

Malone (1895)

240 Upper Malone Road, Dunmurry, Belfast BT17 9LB

Tel **(01232) 612695**
Mem 759 379(L) 211(J)
Sec TH Young (01232) 612758
Pro M McGee (01232) 614917
Holes 18 L 6499 yds SSS 71
9 L 2895 yds SSS 34
Pro–68 E Jones
V'tors Wed–NA after 2pm Sat–NA before 5pm SOC–Mon & Thurs
Fees £23 (£26)
Loc 6 miles S of Belfast

Mount Ober G & CC

Ballymaconaghy Road, Knockbracken, Belfast BT8 4SB

Tel **(01232) 792108 (Bookings)**
Mem 600
Sec P Laverty (Hon)
Pro D Jones (01232) 401811
Holes 18 L 5312 yds SSS 68
Recs Am–66
Pro–68
V'tors WD–U Sat–U after 11am SOC
Fees £10 (£12)
Loc 2 miles SW of Belfast, nr Four Winds
Mis Floodlit driving range

Ormeau (1893)

50 Park Road, Belfast BT7 2EX

Tel **(01232) 641069 (Members)**
Mem 260 50(L) 25(J)
Sec GE McVeigh (01232) 640700
Pro (01232) 640999
Holes 9 L 5308 yds SSS 65
Recs Am–61 M Fleming (1989)
V'tors U SOC
Fees £9 (£11)
Loc 2 miles S of Belfast

Shandon Park (1926)

73 Shandon Park, Belfast BT5 6NY

Tel **(01232) 793730**
Fax **(01232) 402773**
Mem 1100
Sec MG Corsar (Mgr)
(01232) 401856
Pro B Wilson (01232) 797859
Holes 18 L 6261 yds SSS 70
Recs Am–64 N Anderson
Pro–68 CP Posnett
V'tors WD–U Sat–NA before 5pm SOC
Fees £22 (£27)
Loc 3 miles E of Belfast on the Knock road

Co Carlow

Borris (1908)

Deerpark, Borris

Tel **(0503) 73143**
Mem 350
Sec E Lennon (Hon)
Holes 9 L 6026 yds SSS 69
Recs Am–66 J Joyce (1990)
V'tors WD–U Sun–M SOC–WD/Sat
Fees £10

Carlow (1899)

Deer Park, Dublin Road, Carlow

Tel **(0503) 31695**
Fax **(0503) 40065**
Mem 970
Sec Mrs M Meaney
Pro A Gilbert (0503) 41745
Holes 18 L 5844 metres SSS 71
Recs Am–64 J Kavanagh
Pro–68 C O'Connor
V'tors U SOC
Fees £20 (£25) SOC–£18 (£22)
Loc 2 miles N of Carlow. 52 miles S of Dublin (N7)
Arch Tom Simpson

Co Cavan

Belturbet (1950)

Erne Hill, Belturbet

Tel **(049) 22287**
Mem 175
Sec PF Coffey
Holes 9 L 5347 yds SSS 65
Recs Am–64 J Costello (1982)
V'tors U SOC
Fees £7 (£8)
Loc 1 mile E of Belturbet

Blacklion (1962)

Toam, Blacklion, via Sligo

Tel **(072) 53024**
Mem 220
Sec R Thompson (Hon)
Holes 9 L 5544 metres SSS 69
V'tors U SOC
Fees £5 (£8)
Loc 12 miles SW of Enniskillen on A4
Arch Eddie Hackett

Cabra Castle (1978)

Kingscourt

Mem 130
Holes 9 L 5308 metres SSS 68
V'tors U exc Sun–NA SOC
Fees D–£9
Loc 2 miles E of Kingscourt

County Cavan (1894)

Arnmore House, Drumelis, Cavan

Tel **(049) 31283**
Mem 760
Sec J Sheridan (049) 32045
Holes 18 L 5519 metres SSS 69
Recs Am–66 A Cafferty
Pro–65 J Purcell (1987)
V'tors Mon/Tues/Thurs–U
Fees IR£10 (IR£12)
Loc 2 miles W of Cavan on Killeshandra road

Slieve Russell (1994)

Ballyconnell

Tel **(049) 26444**
Fax **(049) 26474**
Mem 150
Sec A Mawhinney (Golf Dir)
Pro L McCool (049) 26458
Holes 18 L 6413 metres Par 72 SSS 74
9 hole Par 3 course
V'tors U SOC
Fees £35 Sat–£33
Loc 15 miles N of Cavan Town
Arch Paddy Merrigan

Virginia (1946)

Park Hotel, Virginia

Tel **(049) 47235**
Mem 307
Sec V Nesbitt (Hon)
Holes 9 L 4900 metres SSS 62
Recs Am–64 P Gallagher
V'tors U
Fees £8
Loc 35 miles SE of Cavan, nr Lough Ramor (N3)

Co Clare

Drumoland Castle (1964)

Newmarket-on-Fergus

Tel **(061) 368144/368444**
Fax **(061) 363355**
Mem 400
Sec J O'Halloran (061) 368444
Pro P Murphy
Holes 18 L 6098 yds SSS 71
Recs Am–74 Dr C Hackett (1986)
V'tors U SOC
Fees D–£20 (£25)
Loc 18 miles NW of Limerick. Shannon Airport 4 miles

Ennis (1907)

Drumbiggle Road, Ennis

Tel **(065) 24074**
Fax **(065) 41848**
Mem 482
Sec M Walshe
Pro M Ward (065) 20690
Holes 18 L 5358 metres SSS 68
Recs Am–65 R Hennessy
Pro–66 P Skerritt
V'tors U exc Sun SOC
Fees £15 SOC–£12
Loc ½ mile NW of Ennis, off N18

Kilkee (1896)
East End, Kilkee
Tel **(065) 56048**
Fax **(065) 56041**
Mem 579
Sec T Lillis
Holes 18 L 5690 metres Par 72 SSS 71
Recs Am–68 D Nagle, N Cotter
V'tors U SOC
Fees £15
Loc 10 miles NW of Kilrush
Arch Eddie Hackett

Kilrush (1934)
Parknamoney, Kilrush
Tel **(065) 51138**
Mem 237
Holes 9 L 2739 yds SSS 67
Recs Am–64 DF Nagle
V'tors U SOC
Fees On application
Loc 25 miles SW of Ennis

Lahinch (1892)
Lahinch
Tel **(065) 81003**
Fax **(065) 81592**
Mem 1250
Sec A Reardon (Sec/Mgr)
Pro R McCavery (065) 81408
Holes Old 18 L 6699 yds SSS 73
Castle 18 L 5620 yds SSS 69
V'tors WD–U WE–NA 9–10.30am and 1–2pm SOC
Fees Old–£30 Castle–£18
Loc 20 miles NW of Ennis on T69
Arch Old Tom Morris/Gibson/ Mackenzie

Shannon (1966)
Shannon Airport
Tel **(061) 471020**
Fax **(061) 471507**
Mem 800
Sec DJ Lempriere (061) 471849
Pro A Pyke (061) 471551
Holes 18 L 6854 yds SSS 72
Recs Am–63 J Purcell
Pro–65 D Durnian
V'tors WD–U SOC
Fees £20 (£25)
Loc Shannon Airport

Spanish Point (1915)
Spanish Point, Miltown Malbay
Tel **(065) 84198**
Mem 100
Sec G O'Loughlin
Holes 9 L 3820 yds SSS 58
Recs Am–27 D Twomey
Pro–23 P Skerritt
V'tors U
Fees £10
Loc 2 mile S of Miltown Malbay (N67). 20 miles W of Ennis

Co Cork

Bandon (1910)
Castlebernard, Bandon
Tel **(023) 41111/44544**
Fax **(023) 44690**
Mem 520
Sec B O'Neill (Hon)
Pro P O'Boyle (023) 42224
Holes 18 L 5663 metres Par 70 SSS 69
Recs Am–66 J Carroll
V'tors U
Fees £12 (£15)
Loc Bandon 1½ miles. 18 miles SW of Cork

Bantry Park (1975)
Donemark, Bantry
Tel **(027) 50579**
Mem 280
Sec M Milner (Hon)
Holes 9 L 6436 yds SSS 70
Recs Am–P Dalton
Pro–66 C O'Connor Jr
V'tors U
Fees £10
Loc 1 mile N of Bantry on Glengarriff road

Berehaven (1902)
Millcove, Castletownbere
Tel **(027) 70700**
Mem 118
Sec Mrs A Harrington (Sec/Mgr)
Holes 9 L 2605 yds SSS 66
Recs Am–65 T Harrington (1990)
V'tors U SOC
Fees £8 (£10)
Loc 2 miles E of Castletownbere on Glengarriff road

Charleville (1909)
Smiths Road, Ardmore, Charleville
Tel **(063) 81257**
Fax **(063) 81274**
Mem 650
Sec M Keane (Sec/Mgr)
Holes 18 L 6430 yds SSS 69
Recs Am–68 J Murphy
Ladies–68 S Keane
V'tors WD–U WE–book in advance SOC
Fees £12 (£15) SOC–£12
Loc 35 miles N of Cork on Limerick road

Cobh (1987)
Ballywilliam, Cobh
Tel **(021) 812399**
Mem 120
Holes 9 L 4366 metres SSS 63
Recs Am–65 G Mellerick
Pro–64 C O'Connor Sr
V'tors WD–U WE/BH–NA before noon
Fees £8 (£9)
Loc 1 mile N of Cobh. 16 miles SE of Cork
Arch Eddie Hackett

Cork (1888)
Little Island, Cork
Tel **(021) 353451/353037**
Fax **(021) 353410**
Mem 350 160 (L)
Sec M Sands (021) 353451
Pro T Higgins (021) 353421
Holes 18 L 6065 metres SSS 72
Recs Am–66 P Murphy
V'tors WD–U H exc 12–2pm –M after 4pm Thurs–(Ladies Day)–phone in advance WE–NA before 2.30pm H
Fees £23 (£26)
Loc 5 miles E of Cork, off Cobh road
Arch Dr A Mackenzie

Doneraile (1927)
Doneraile
Tel **(022) 24137**
Mem 152
Holes 9 L 5528 yds SSS 67
V'tors U
Fees On application
Loc 8 miles NW of Mallow

Douglas (1909)
Douglas, Cork
Tel **(021) 891086**
Fax **(021) 895297**
Mem 839
Sec B Barrett (Mgr) (021) 895297
Pro GS Nicholson (021) 362055
Holes 18 L 5664 metres SSS 69
Recs Am–66 D O'Herlihy
Pro–64 E Darcy
V'tors WD–U exc Tues WE–NA before 11.30am SOC–WD
Fees IR£18 (IR£20)
Loc Cork 3 miles

Dunmore (1967)
Dunmore House, Muckross, Clonakilty
Tel **(023) 33352**
Mem 163
Sec G O'Sullivan (Hon)
Holes 9 L 4464 yds SSS 61
Recs Am–65
Pro–62
V'tors U exc Sun–NA SOC
Fees £10
Loc 3 miles S of Clonakilty
Arch Eddie Hackett

East Cork (1971)
Gortacrue, Midleton
Tel **(021) 631687**
Fax **(021) 631273**
Mem 600
Sec M Moloney (Sec/Mgr)
Holes 18 L 5207 metres SSS 67
Recs Am–66 B O'Regan (1983)
V'tors WD–U WE–NA before noon BH–U
Fees £12
Loc 2 miles N of Midleton on L35
Arch Eddie Hackett

For list of abbreviations see page 435

Fermoy (1893)
Corrin, Fermoy
Tel **(025) 31472**
Mem 645
Holes 18 L 5825 metres SSS 70
V'tors U SOC
Fees £12 (£15)
Loc 2 miles S of Fermoy, off N8

Fota Island (1993)
Carrigtwohill, Cork
Tel **(021) 883710**
Fax **(021) 883713**
Mem 200
Sec K Mulcahy (Sec/Mgr)
Pro K Morris
Holes 18 L 6886 yds SSS 74
V'tors U H
Fees £27 (£30)
Loc 8 miles E of Cork on N25
Mis Driving range
Arch O'Connor Jr/McEvoy

Glengarriff (1935)
Glengarriff
Tel **(027) 63150**
Mem 120
Sec J Brooks (Hon)
Holes 9 L 4094 metres SSS 66
V'tors U
Fees £10.
Loc 1 mile E of Glengarriff (N71)

Harbour Point (1991)
Clash, Little Island
Tel **(021) 353094**
Mem 270
Sec Ms N O'Connell (Sec/Mgr)
Holes 18 L 6063 yds SSS 72
V'tors U SOC
Fees £20
Loc 5 miles E of Cork
Mis Floodlit driving range
Arch Paddy Merrigan

Kanturk (1971)
Fairy Hill, Kanturk
Tel **(029) 50534**
Mem 350
Sec D Fitzgerald (Hon)
Holes 9 L 5508 metres SSS 69
Recs Am–72 D O'Riordan, M Arsdeacon (1987), J O'Connor (1989)
V'tors U
Fees £10
Loc 2 miles SW of Kanturk (R579)

Kinsale (1912)
Ringenane, Belgooly, Kinsale
Tel **(021) 772197**
Mem 400
Sec JJ Murphy (Hon)
Holes 9 L 5332 metres SSS 68
Recs Am–63 K McCarthy
V'tors WD–U WE–NA SOC
Fees £12
Loc 2 miles N of Kinsale. 16 miles S of Cork

Lee Valley G & CC (1993)
Clashanure, Ovens, Cork
Tel **(021) 331721**
Fax **(021) 331695**
Mem 350
Sec B O'Connell
Pro B McDaid
Holes 18 L 6800 yds SSS 72
Recs Am–71 D McFarlane (1993)
Pro–68 F Couples (1993)
V'tors U H
Fees £20
Loc 8 miles W of Cork (N22)
Mis Floodlit driving range
Arch C O'Connor Jr

Macroom (1924)
Lackaduve, Macroom
Tel **(026) 41072**
Mem 485
Sec G McKay
Holes 18 L 5598 metres SSS 70
Recs Am–66 J Mills
V'tors U H SOC
Fees D–IR£12
Loc Macroom Town, through Castle Arch. 25 miles W of Cork

Mahon (1980)
Cloverhill, Blackrock, Cork
Tel **(021) 362480**
Mem 250
Holes 18 L 4818 metres SSS 66
V'tors U
Fees £9 (£9.50)
Loc SE of Cork City

Mallow (1948)
Balleyellis, Mallow
Tel **(022) 21145**
Fax **(022) 42122**
Mem 1500
Sec M O'Sullivan (Hon)
Pro S Conway
Holes 18 L 6559 yds SSS 71
Recs Am–66 J Murphy (1982)
V'tors WD–U before 5pm SOC
Fees £15 (£18)
Loc 2 miles SE of Mallow Bridge on Killavullen road
Arch J Harris

Mitchelstown (1908)
Mitchelstown
Tel **(025) 24072**
Mem 500
Sec D Nolan
Holes 15 L 5057 metres SSS 67
Recs Am–68 W Coughlan
V'tors U SOC
Fees £10 (£10)
Loc 30 miles NE of Cork
Arch David Jones

Monkstown (1908)
Parkgarriffe, Monkstown
Tel **(021) 841376**
Fax **(021) 841376**
Mem 900
Sec GA Finn
Pro B Murphy (021) 841686
Holes 18 L 5669 metres SSS 69
Recs Am–66 J Morris Jr (1988)
Pro–67 K Morris (1992)
V'tors U H SOC
Fees £20 (£23)
Loc 7 miles SE of Cork

Muskerry (1897)
Carrigrohane
Tel **(021) 385297**
Fax **(021) 385297**
Mem 722
Sec JJ Moynihan
Pro WM Lehane (021) 381445
Holes 18 L 5786 metres SSS 71
Recs Am–64 K Bornemann
Pro–66 J Hegerty
V'tors Mon/Tues–U
Wed–Fri/WE–phone first
SOC
Fees £17
Loc 7 miles NW of Cork

Raffeen Creek (1989)
Ringaskiddy
Tel **(021) 378430**
Mem 450
Sec P Farry (Mgr)
Holes 9 L 5800 yds SSS 68
Recs Am–67 J Hornibrook (1993)
Pro–71 C O'Connor Sr (1989)
V'tors WD–U WE–U after noon
Fees IR£10 (IR£13)
Loc 1 mile from Ringaskiddy Ferryport
Arch Eddie Hackett

Skibbereen (1931)
Licknavar, Skibbereen
Tel **(028) 21227/22340**
Mem 376
Sec Brenda O'Driscoll (Hon)
Pro None
Holes 18 L 5900 metres Par 70 SSS 68
Recs Am–68 J Kenneally (1993)
V'tors U SOC–Sat
Fees £12 (£15)
Loc 1 mile W of Skibbereen. 52 miles SW of Cork
Mis Driving range
Arch Eddie Hackett

Youghal (1898)
Knockaverry, Youghal
Tel **(024) 92787**
Fax **(024) 92641**
Mem 640
Sec Margaret O'Sullivan
Pro L Burns (024) 92590
Holes 18 L 5664 metres SSS 70
Recs Am–63 T Kenefick (1992)
V'tors U
Fees D–IR£14
Loc 30 miles E of Cork on N25 from Rosslare
Arch Cdr Harris

Co Donegal

Ballybofey & Stranorlar
(1957)
Stranorlar, Ballybofey
Tel **(074) 31093**
Mem 450
Sec P Carr (074) 31104
Holes 18 L 5922 yds SSS 68
Recs Am–64 E McMenamin (1992)
V'tors U SOC
Fees £12 SOC–£10
Loc Stranorlar ¼ mile
Arch PC Carr

Ballyliffin (1947)
Ballyliffin, Clonmany
Tel **(077) 76119**
Fax **(077) 76672**
Mem 590
Sec T Hands (Sec/Mgr)
KJ O'Doherty (Hon)
Holes 18 L 6611 yds SSS 72
Recs Am–67 G Doherty
V'tors U SOC–WD
Fees IR£8 (IR£14)
Loc 8 miles N of Buncrana.
15 miles N of Londonderry

Buncrana (1951)
Public
Buncrana
Tel **(077) 62279**
Mem 175
Pro NS Doherty
Holes 9 L 4250 metres SSS 62
V'tors U
Fees £6
Loc 1 mile S of Buncrana, off R238

Bundoran (1894)
Bundoran
Tel **(072) 41302**
Mem 400
Sec L McDevitt (Hon)
Pro D Robinson
Holes 18 L 6159 yds SSS 70
V'tors WD–U WE–restricted SOC
Fees £12 (£14)
Loc E boundary of Bundoran.
20 miles S of Donegal
Arch H Vardon

Cruit Island (1985)
Kincasslagh, Dunglow
Tel **(075) 43296**
Mem 190
Pro None
Holes 9 L 5297 yds SSS 66
V'tors U SOC
Fees £7 (£9)
Loc 5 miles N of Dunglow, off R259

Donegal (1960)
Murvagh, Laghey
Tel **(073) 34054**
Fax **(073) 34377**
Mem 590
Sec J Nixon (073) 22166
J McBride (Admin)
Holes 18 L 7271 yds SSS 73
Recs Am–68 M Gannon
V'tors H SOC–exc Sun
Fees £15 (£18)
Loc 7 miles S of Donegal on N18
Arch Eddie Hackett

Dunfanaghy (1903)
Dunfanaghy, Letterkenny
Tel **(074) 36335**
Mem 300
Sec M McGinley (074) 35238
Holes 18 L 5066 metres SSS 66
Recs Am–64 J Brogan
Pro–66 L Wallace
V'tors U SOC
Fees IR£10 (IR£12)
Loc 25 miles NW of Letterkenny on N56

Greencastle (1892)
Via Lifford, Greencastle
Tel **(077) 81013**
Mem 600
Sec B Gormley (077) 82280
Holes 18 L 5211 metres SSS 67
Recs Am–67 F McCarroll (1993)
V'tors WD–U WE–restricted SOC
Fees £10 (£15)
Loc 21 miles NE of Londonderry, nr Moville
Arch Eddie Hackett

Gweedore (1926)
Magheragallon, Derrybeg, Letterkenny
Tel **(075) 31140**
Mem 145
Holes 9 L 6230 yds SSS 69
Recs Am–64 S Murphy
V'tors U
Fees £7 (£8)
Loc 3 miles N of Gweedore, off R257
Arch Eddie Hackett

Letterkenny (1913)
Barnhill, Letterkenny
Tel **(074) 21150**
Mem 490
Pro N McCole
Holes 18 L 6299 yds SSS 71
Recs Am–67 P Shiels
Pro–68 J Gallagher
V'tors U SOC
Fees £10 SOC–£6
Loc 1 mile E of Letterkenny
Arch Eddie Hackett

Narin & Portnoo (1931)
Narin, Portnoo
Tel **(075) 45107**
Mem 400
Sec M Naughton
Holes 18 L 5950 yds SSS 68
Recs Am–64 B McBride
Pro–62 R Browne
V'tors WD–U H Sat–restricted 9.30–11.30am & 1–2.30pm Sun–restricted SOC
Fees £10 (£13) SOC–£10
Loc 6 miles N of Ardara, West Donegal

North West (1891)
Lisfannon, Fahan
Tel **(077) 61027**
Mem 400
Sec S Doherty (Hon)
Pro S McBriarty
Holes 18 L 6203 yds SSS 69
Recs Am–65 F Friel
Pro–64 M Doherty
V'tors U
Fees IR£10 (IR£15)
Loc 2 miles S of Buncrana.
12 miles N of Londonderry

Otway (1893)
Saltpans, Rathmullan, Letterkenny
Tel **(074) 58319**
Mem 85
Sec H Gallagher (Hon)
Holes 9 L 4234 yds SSS 60
Recs Am–29 F Friel
V'tors U
Fees £5
Loc 15 miles NE of Letterkenny, by Lough Swilly

Portsalon (1891)
Portsalon, Letterkenny
Tel **(074) 59459**
Mem 300
Sec C Toland (Hon)
Holes 18 L 5878 yds Par 69 SSS 68
Recs Am–66 K McLaughlin (1994)
Pro–71 J Henderson
V'tors U
Fees £10 (£12)
Loc 20 miles N of Letterkenny

Redcastle (1983)
Redcastle, Moville
Tel **(077) 82073**
Mem 120
Holes 9 L 6046 yds SSS 70
V'tors U
Fees £9 (£10)
Loc 15 miles NE of Londonderry, by Lough Foyle (R238)

Rosapenna (1894)
Downings, Rosapenna
Tel **(074) 55301**
Fax **(074) 55128**
Mem 300
Sec MJ Gallagher (Hon)
Pro D Patterson
Holes 18 L 6254 yds SSS 71
Recs Am–M McGinley, D Boyce
Pro–68 F Daly
V'tors U
Fees IR£15
Loc 20 miles N of Letterkenny
Mis Golf academy
Arch Morris/Vardon/Braid

Co Down

Ardglass (1896)

Castle Place, Ardglass BT30 7TP

Tel **(01396) 841219**
Fax **(01396) 841841**
Mem 841
Sec A Cannon (Sec/Mgr)
Pro K Whitson (01396) 841022
Holes 18 L 5498 metres SSS 69
Recs Am–66 J Milligan
Pro–64 K Morris
V'tors U
Fees £15 (£20)
Loc 7 miles SE of Downpatrick on B1

Banbridge (1913)

Huntly Road, Banbridge BT32 3UR

Tel **(018206) 62342**
Mem 650
Sec TF Fee (Sec/Mgr) (018206) 62211
Holes 18 L 5376 metres SSS 68
Recs Am–66 S McVey
V'tors U SOC
Fees £7 (£12)
Loc 1 mile N of Banbridge

Bangor (1903)

Broadway, Bangor BT20 4RH

Tel **(01247) 270922**
Mem 1100
Sec T Russell (Sec/Mgr)
Pro N Drew (01247) 462164
Holes 18 L 6424 yds SSS 71
Recs Am–64 P Barry
Pro–66 C O'Connor
V'tors WD–U exc –M 1–2pm
Wed–U before 4.45pm
Sat–NA SOC–Mon & Wed
Fees £17 (£23)
Loc 1 mile S of Bangor, off Donaghadee road
Arch James Braid

Bright Castle (1970)

14 Coniamstown Road, Bright, Downpatrick BT30 8LU

Tel **(01396) 841319**
Mem 54
Holes 18 L 6730 yds SSS 74
Recs Am–70 A Ennis
V'tors U SOC
Fees £10 (£12)
Loc 5 miles S of Downpatrick, off Killough road (B176)

Carnalea (1927)

Station Road, Bangor BT19 1EZ

Tel **(01247) 465004**
Mem 800
Sec JH Crozier (01247) 270368
Holes 18 L 5584 yds SSS 67
Recs Am–63 A Robinson (1991)
V'tors U SOC–WD
Fees £11 (£15)
Loc By Carnalea Station, Bangor

Clandeboye (1933)

Conlig, Newtownards BT23 3PN

Tel **(01247) 271767/473706**
Mem 1291
Sec TI Marks (01247) 271767
Pro P Gregory (01247) 271750
Holes Dufferin 18 L 5915 metres SSS 71;
Ava 18 L 5172 metres SSS 68
Recs Am–65 S King
Pro–68 J Heggarty, D Jones, D Feherty
V'tors WD–U WE–M
Fees Dufferin–£21 Ava–£17
Loc Conlig, off A21 Bangor–Newtownards road

Donaghadee (1899)

Warren Road, Donaghadee BT21 0PQ

Tel **(01247) 883624**
Fax **(01247) 888891**
Mem 1250
Sec ME Dilley
Pro G Drew (01247) 882392
Holes 18 L 5576 metres Par 71
Recs Am–65 J Nelson
Pro–69 E Clarke
V'tors U exc Sat–NA
SOC–Mon/Wed/Fri
Fees £14 (£18)
Loc 18 miles E of Belfast on A2

Downpatrick (1932)

Saul Road, Downpatrick BT30 6PA

Tel **(01396) 612152/615947**
Mem 800
Sec JP McCoubrey (01396) 615947
Pro (01396) 615167
Holes 18 L 5702 metres SSS 69
Recs Am–64 D Baker (1990)
V'tors U SOC
Fees £14 (£18)
Loc 25 miles SE of Belfast (A1). Downpatrick 1½ miles
Arch Hawtree

Helen's Bay (1896)

Golf Road, Helen's Bay, Bangor BT19 1TL

Tel **(01247) 852601 (Clubhouse)**
Fax **(01247) 852815**
Mem 784
Sec LWL Mann (01247) 852815
Holes 9 L 5176 metres SSS 67
Recs Am–67 JR Longmore
Pro–67 L Esdale
V'tors WD exc Tues–M after 2.30pm Sat/BH–M Sun–U
SOC–WD exc Tues
Fees On application
Loc 9 miles E of Belfast, off A2

Holywood (1904)

Nuns Walk, Demesne Road, Holywood BT18 9LE

Tel **(01232) 422138**
Fax **(01232) 425040**
Mem 800
Sec D Jenkins (01232) 423135
Pro M Bannon (01232) 425503
Holes 18 L 5885 yds SSS 68
Recs Am–61 J Watts
Pro–64 M Bannon
V'tors WD–U exc 1.30–2.15pm
Sat–after 5pm
Fees £15 (£21)
Loc 5 miles E of Belfast on Bangor road

Kilkeel (1948)

Mourne Park, Ballyardle, Kilkeel BT34 4LB

Tel **(016937) 62296/65095**
Mem 672
Sec SC McBride (016937) 63787
Holes 18 L 6625 yds SSS 72
V'tors U SOC–exc BH/Sat
Fees £16 (£18)
Loc 3 miles W of Kilkeel on Newry road
Arch Eddie Hackett

Kirkistown Castle (1902)

142 Main Road, Cloughey, Newtownards BT22 1JH

Tel **(012477) 71233/71353**
Fax **(012477) 71699**
Mem 924
Sec DJ Ryan
Pro J Peden
Holes 18 L 5628 metres SSS 70
Recs Am–68 Jas Brown
Pro–71 RJ Polley, C O'Connor
V'tors WD–U WE/BH–NA 1st tee 9.30–10.30am and 12–1.30pm SOC
Fees £13 (£25)
Loc 25 miles SE of Belfast
Arch James Braid

Mahee Island (1930)

Comber, Belfast BT23 6ET

Tel **(01238) 541234**
Mem 500
Sec J McMillen (Hon)
Pro A McCracken
Holes 9 L 2790 yds SSS 67
Recs Am–65 C Boyd
Pro–65 N Drew
V'tors U exc Sat–NA before 5pm
SOC–WD exc Mon
Fees £10 (£15)
Loc Strangford Lough, 14 miles SE of Belfast

Mourne (1946)

36 Golf Links Road, Newcastle BT33 0AN

Tel **(013967) 23218**
Mem 275
Sec EJ Kane (Sec/Mgr) N McCready (Hon)
Holes Play over Royal Co Down

Royal Belfast (1881)

Holywood, Craigavad BT19 0BP

Tel **(01232) 428165**
Mem 1200

For list of abbreviations see page 435

Sec IM Piggot
Pro D Carson
Holes 18 L 6184 yds SSS 70
Recs Am–69 B Purdy (1991)
Pro–65 D Clark (1992)
V'tors I Sat–NA before 4.30pm
Fees £30 (£35)
Loc E of Belfast on A2

Royal County Down (1889)

Newcastle BT33 0AN

Tel **(013967) 23314**
Fax **(013967) 26281**
Mem 450
Sec PE Rolph
Pro KJ Whitson (013967) 22419
Holes C'ship 18 L 6969 yds SSS 73
No 2 18 L 4100 yds SSS 60
Recs C'ship Am–66 J Bruen, JM Jamison, HB Smyth
Pro–67 A Compston, B Gadd
V'tors Contact Sec
Fees Summer–£43 (£55)
Winter–£32 (£43)
Loc 30 miles S of Belfast
Arch Tom Morris

Scrabo (1907)

233 Scrabo Road, Newtownards BT23 4SL

Tel **(01247) 812355**
Fax **(01247) 822919**
Mem 750
Sec J Fraser (Sec/Mgr)
Pro G Fairweather (01247) 817848
Holes 18 L 5699 metres SSS 71
Recs Am–65 J Rea (1991)
Pro–67 N Drew (1987)
V'tors WD–U WE–after 5pm SOC
Fees £8 (£15)
Loc 2 miles W of Newtownards, by Scrabo Tower

The Spa (1907)

Grove Road, Ballynahinch BT24 8BR

Tel **(01238) 562365**
Mem 895
Holes 18 L 5938 metres SSS 72
Recs Am–67 R Wallace
V'tors U exc Wed–NA after 3pm Sat–NA
Fees £11.50 (£16.50)
Loc 1 mile S of Ballynahinch. 15 miles S of Belfast

Warrenpoint (1893)

Lower Dromore Rd, Warrenpoint BT34 3LN

Tel **(016937) 52219**
Fax **(016937) 52918**
Mem 1066
Sec J McMahon (016937) 53695
Pro N Shaw (016937) 52371
Holes 18 L 5628 metres SSS 70
Recs Am–67 S McParland
Pro–69 S Hamill
V'tors U SOC
Fees £15 (£21)
Loc 5 miles S of Newry

Co Dublin

Balbriggan (1945)

Blackhall, Balbriggan

Tel **(01) 841 2229**
Mem 600
Sec M O'Halloran (Sec/Mgr)
Holes 18 L 5881 metres SSS 71
V'tors WD–U WE–M SOC
Fees £14 (£18)
Loc 2 miles S of Balbriggan on N1. 18 miles N of Dublin
Arch Paramour/Stillwell

Balcarrick (1972)

Corballis, Donabate

Tel **(01) 843 6228**
Fax **(01) 843 6957**
Mem 224
Sec J King (Hon)
Holes 9 L 5167 metres SSS 71
V'tors WD–U Sat–NA before 10am Sun–NA SOC
Fees £10
Loc 2 miles E of Donabate. 18 miles N of Dublin

Ballinascorney (1971)

Ballinascorney, Tallaght, Dublin

Tel **(01) 512516/512082**
Mem 500
Holes 18 L 5464 yds SSS 67
V'tors WD–U
Fees £10 (£16)
Loc 8 miles SW of Dublin

Beaverstown (1985)

Beaverstown, Donabate

Tel **(01) 843 6439**
Fax **(01) 843 6721**
Mem 800
Sec E Smyth (Sec/Mgr)
Holes 18 L 5855 metres SSS 71
Recs Am–72 M Perry (1987)
V'tors WD–U WE/BH–M SOC
Fees £12 (£20)
Loc 4 miles N of Dublin Airport
Arch Eddie Hackett

Beech Park (1983)

Johnstown, Rathcoole

Tel **(01) 580522/580100**
Fax **(01) 588365**
Mem 500
Sec J Deally (Sec/Mgr)
Holes 18 L 5730 metres SSS 70
Recs Am–71 P Stapleton (1990)
Pro–67 B Todd (1989)
V'tors WD–U exc Tues/Wed–M WE–M BH–NA
Fees £17
Loc Rathcoole 1 mile on Kilteel road. SW of Dublin
Arch Eddie Hackett

Donabate (1925)

Balcarrick, Donabate

Tel **(01) 843 6059/6346/6001**
Sec Nancy Campion (01) 843 6346
Pro H Jackson
Holes 18 L 6187 yds SSS 69
Recs Am–67 AJ Coughlan
Pro–65 M Murphy
V'tors WE/BH–NA
Fees On application
Loc Dublin Airport 8 miles

Dun Laoghaire (1910)

Eglinton Park, Dun Loaghaire

Tel **(01) 280 1055**
Mem 972
Sec T Stewart (01) 280 3916
Pro O Mulhall (01) 280 1694
Holes 18 L 5478 metres SSS 69
Recs Am–66 P McCormack Jr
Pro–65 P Skerritt
V'tors WD–U exc 12.30–2pm SOC
Fees IR£25
Loc 7 miles S of Dublin
Arch HS Colt

Forrest Little (1972)

Forest little, Cloghran

Tel **(01) 840 1183/840 1763**
Fax **(01) 840 1000**
Mem 900
Sec T Greany (Sec/Mgr)
Pro T Judd
Holes 18 L 5865 metres SSS 70
Recs Am–67 T Judd (1984)
Pro–65 C O'Connor Jr (1984)
V'tors WD–U WE–NA
Fees IR£18
Loc Nr Dublin Airport
Arch F Hawtree

Hermitage (1905)

Lucan

Tel **(01) 626 5396**
Mem 1153
Sec Kay Russell (01) 626 8491
Pro C Carroll (01) 626 8072
Holes 18 L 6032 metres SSS 71
Recs Am–65 T Moran
Pro–65 R Davis
V'tors U SOC–WD
Fees £25 (£35)
Loc Lucan 2 miles. 8 miles W of Dublin

Hollywood Lakes (1992)

Ballyboughal

Tel **(01) 843 3406**
Fax **(01) 843 3002**
Mem 350
Sec BP Judd (Sec/Mgr)
Holes 18 L 6834 yds Par 72
Recs Am–69 M Hogan (1993)
V'tors WD–U WE/BH–U after noon
Fees £12 (£15)
Loc 10 miles N of Dublin Airport
Arch Mel Flanaghan

The Island (1890)

Corballis, Donabate

Tel **(01) 843 6104**
Fax **(01) 843 6860**
Mem 600
Sec LA O'Connor (01) 843 6205

Holes 18 L 6053 metres SSS 72
Recs Am–B Moore, B Byrne
V'tors WD–U WE–NA
Fees £27
Loc 14 miles N of Dublin
Arch Hawtree

Killiney (1903)

Ballinclea Road, Killiney
Tel **(01) 851983**
Mem 520
Sec H Keegan (Sec/Mgr)
Pro P O'Boyle
Holes 9 L 6201 yds SSS 69
Recs Am–72 N Duke
Pro–65 H Bradshaw
V'tors U
Fees D–£17 (£20)
Loc 8 miles S of Dublin

Kilternan (1987)

Enniskerry Road, Kilternan
Tel **(01) 295 5559**
Fax **(01) 295 5670**
Mem 730
Sec J Kinsella
Holes 18 L 5413 yds SSS 67
Recs Am–69 S Foley (1991)
V'tors U SOC
Fees £12 (£16)
Loc 5 miles S of Dublin
Arch Eddie Hackett

Lucan (1897)

Celbridge Road, Lucan
Tel **(01) 628 0246**
Fax **(01) 628 2929**
Mem 740
Sec G Long (Sec/Mgr)
(01) 628 2106
Holes 18 L 5958 metres SSS 71
Recs Am–73 T Gough
V'tors WD–U WE/BH–M SOC–WD exc Thurs
Fees £16
Loc 14 miles W of Dublin, nr Lucan

Malahide (1892)

Beechwood, The Grange, Malahide
Tel **(01) 846 1611**
Mem 850
Sec AC Brogan (Sec/Mgr)
Pro D Barton
Holes 27 holes:
6257-6619 yds SSS 70-71
Recs Am–70 PA Hearne Jr
V'tors WD–U WE–by arrangement SOC
Fees £21 (£31)
Loc 1½ miles S of Malahide. 10 miles N of Dublin, nr Airport
Arch Eddie Hackett

Old Conna (1987)

Ferndale Road, Bray
Tel **(01) 282 6055**
Fax **(01) 282 5611**
Mem 750
Sec D Diviney (Sec/Mgr)
Pro N Murray (01) 282 0822
Holes 18 L 6551 yds SSS 71
V'tors WD–U before 4pm
WE/BH–NA SOC
Fees £20
Loc 2 miles N of Bray. 12 miles S of Dublin
Arch Eddie Hackett

Portmarnock (1894)

Portmarnock
Tel **(01) 846 2968**
Fax **(01) 846 2601**
Mem 971
Sec JJ Quigley
Pro J Purcell (01) 846 2634
Holes 27 holes: 6361–6497 metres SSS 74–75
Recs Am–68 JB Carr
Pro–64 S Lyle (1989)
V'tors I WE–XL
Fees IR£40 (IR£50) Ladies–IR£30 WD
Loc 8 miles NE of Dublin

Rush (1943)

Rush
Tel **(01) 843 7548**
Mem 360
Sec BJ Clear (Sec/Mgr)
(01) 843 8177
Holes 9 L 5598 metres SSS 69
Recs Am–68 PJ Dolan
V'tors WD–U WE–M
Fees £14
Loc 16 miles N of Dublin, off R127

Skerries (1906)

Skerries
Tel **(01) 849 1204** (Clubhouse)
Fax **(01) 849 1591**
Mem 908
Sec A Burns (01) 849 1567
Pro J Kinsella (01) 849 1567
Holes 18 L 6113 metres SSS 72
V'tors U SOC
Fees IR£17 (IR£22)
Loc 20 miles N of Dublin

Slade Valley (1970)

Lynch Park, Brittas
Tel **(01) 582739**
Mem 800
Sec P Maguire (01) 582183
Pro J Dignam
Holes 18 L 5337 metres SSS 68
Recs Am–65
Pro–64
V'tors WD–U am WE–M
Fees £15
Loc 8 miles W of Dublin, off N4

St Margaret's G & CC (1993)

St Margaret's, Dublin
Tel **(01) 864 0400**
Fax **(01) 864 0289**
Mem 200
Sec D Kane (Gen Mgr)
Pro (01) 864 0416
Holes 18 L 6900 yds SSS 73
Pro–69 C Monaghan (1993)
V'tors U SOC
Fees £30 (£35)
Loc 3 miles NW of Dublin Airport, between N1/N2
Mis Driving range
Arch Craddock/Ruddy

Westmanstown (1988)

Clonsilla, Dublin 15
Tel **(01) 820 5817**
Mem 950
Holes 18 L 5819 metres SSS 70
V'tors U SOC
Fees £15 (£20)
Loc 15 miles W of Dublin, nr Lucan
Arch Eddie Hackett

Woodbrook (1921)

Dublin Road, Bray
Tel **(01) 282 4799**
Fax **(01) 282 1950**
Mem 950
Sec D Smyth
Pro W Kinsella
Holes 18 L 6007 metres SSS 71
Recs Am–L Macnamara
Pro–D Smyth, J McHenry
Ladies Pro–L Davies
V'tors WD–U WE–phone Sec SOC
Fees £25 (£35)
Loc 11 miles SE of Dublin on N11

Dublin City

Carrickmines (1900)

Golf Lane, Carrickmines, Dublin 18
Tel **(01) 295 5972**
Mem 500
Sec JNS Pickering (Hon)
Holes 9 L 6103 yds SSS 69
Recs Am–68
Pro–68
V'tors M
Fees £15 Sun–£18 Sat–NA
Loc 6 miles S of Dublin

Castle (1913)

Woodside Drive, Rathfarnham, Dublin 14
Tel **(01) 490 4207**
Fax **(01) 492 0264**
Mem 800
Sec LF Blackburne (Sec/Mgr)
Pro D Kinsella (01) 492 0272
Holes 18 L 6168 metres SSS 69
Recs Am–67 J Pender
Pro–63 P Townsend
V'tors Mon/Thurs/Fri–U Wed–U before 12.30pm WE/BH–M SOC
Fees £25
Loc 5 miles S of Dublin

For list of abbreviations see page 435

Clontarf (1912)

Donnycarney House, Malahide Road, Dublin 3

Tel **(01) 833 1520**
Fax **(01) 833 1933**
Mem 1035
Sec D Gilroy (01) 833 1892
Pro J Craddock (01) 833 1877
Holes 18 L 5447 metres SSS 68
Recs Am–66 R Murray
Pro–64 H Bradshaw
V'tors WD–U WE–M SOC
Fees £21
Loc 2 miles NE of Dublin
Arch HS Colt

Deer Park (1974)

Deer Park Hotel, Howth Castle, Howth

Tel **(01) 832 2624**
Fax **(01) 839 2405**
Mem 250
Sec JP Doran (Hon)
Holes 18 L 6752 yds Par 72 SSS 71
18 L 6475 yds Par 72 SSS 70
12 hole Par 3 course
Recs Am–71 P Coldrick
V'tors U
Fees £10
Loc 8 miles NE of Dublin
Arch F Hawtree

Edmondstown (1944)

Rathfarnham, Dublin 16

Tel **(01) 493 2461**
Fax **(01) 493 3152**
Mem 600
Sec S Davies (01) 493 1082
Pro A Crofton (01) 494 1049
Holes 18 L 5663 metres SSS 69
Recs Am–68 A Bernstein
V'tors WD–U SOC
Fees £20 (£25) Summer
£15 (£20) Winter
Loc 5 miles S of Dublin

Elm Park G & SC (1927)

Nutley House, Donnybrook, Dublin 4

Tel **(01) 269 3438/269 3014**
Fax **(01) 269 4505**
Mem 1750
Sec A McCormack (01) 269 3438
Pro S Green (01) 269 2650
Holes 18 L 5353 metres SSS 68
Recs Am–63 PF Hogan
Pro–63 P Townsend
V'tors U–phone Pro
Fees £30 (£35)
Loc 3 miles S of Dublin

Foxrock (1893)

Torquay Road, Foxrock, Dublin 18

Tel **(01) 289 5668**
Fax **(01) 289 4943**
Mem 550
Sec WM Daly (01) 289 3992
Pro D Walker (01) 289 3414
Holes 9 L 5667 metres SSS 69
Recs Am–68 D Campbell,
M Sludds
Pro–66 M Murphy
V'tors WD/BH/Sun–M Tues &
Sat–NA
Fees £20
Loc 5 miles S of Dublin

Grange (1911)

Whitechurch Road, Rathfarnham, Dublin 16

Tel **(01) 493 2832**
Fax **(01) 493 9490**
Mem 1050 235(L) 210(J)
Sec JA O'Donoghue
(01) 493 2889
Pro B Hamill (01) 493 2299
Holes 18 L 5517 metres SSS 69
Recs Am–64 WB Buckley
Pro–62 C O'Connor Jr
V'tors WD–U exc Tues/Wed
pm–NA WE–M
Fees £25 (£28)
Loc Rathfarnham, 5 miles from
centre of Dublin

Hazel Grove (1988)

Mount Seskin Road, Jobstown, Tallaght, Dublin 24

Tel **(01) 520911**
Mem 300 175(L)
Sec J Whelan (Sec/Mgr)
Holes 9 L 5300 metres SSS 67
V'tors Mon/Wed/Fri–U Sun–NA
Tues/Thurs/Sat–restricted
Fees £9
Loc 3 miles from Tallaght, off
Blessington road
Mis Extension to 18 holes 1995
Arch Eddie Hackett

Howth (1916)

Carrickbrack Road, Sutton, Dublin 13

Tel **(01) 832 3055**
Fax **(01) 832 1793**
Mem 1200
Sec Ms A MacNeice
Pro JF McGuirk (01) 839 3895
Holes 18 L 5618 metres SSS 69
Recs Am–66 M Roe
Pro–71
V'tors WD–U exc Wed WE–M
Fees £16 Fri–£18
Loc 9 miles NE of Dublin,
nr Sutton Cross

Milltown (1907)

Lower Churchtown Road, Milltown, Dublin 14

Tel **(01) 977060/976090**
Fax **(01) 976008**
Mem 1296
Sec JB Cassidy (Sec/Mgr)
Pro J Hamett (01) 977072
Holes 18 L 5638 metres SSS 69
Recs Am–67 J O'Brien
Pro–64 C Greene
V'tors WD–U exc Tues
Fees £30
Loc 4 miles S of Dublin

Newlands (1926)

Clondalkin, Dublin 22

Tel **(01) 459 2903**
Fax **(01) 459 3498**
Mem 1086
Sec AT O'Neill (01) 459 3157
Pro K O'Donnell (01) 459 3538
Holes 18 L 6184 yds SSS 69
Recs Am–66 R Burdon,
P Hanley Jr
Pro–68 C O'Connor
V'tors Tues/Wed pm–NA WD–NA
1.30–2.30pm WE/BH–NA
SOC
Fees IR£25
Loc 6 miles SW of Dublin at
Newlands Cross (N7)
Arch James Braid

Rathfarnham (1896)

Newtown, Dublin 16

Tel **(01) 931201/931561**
Mem 561
Sec DO Tipping (01) 931201
Pro B O'Hara
Holes 9 L 5787 metres SSS 70
Recs Am–70 C O'Carrol,
N Hynes, T O'Donnell
V'tors WD–U exc Tues WE–NA
Fees £20
Loc 6 miles S of Dublin
Arch John Jacobs

Royal Dublin (1885)

North Bull Island, Dollymount, Dublin 3

Tel **(01) 833 6346**
Fax **(01) 833 6504**
Mem 877
Sec JA Lambe (01) 833 1262
Pro L Owens (01) 833 6477
(Touring Pro C O'Connor Sr)
Holes 18 L 6850 yds SSS 71
Recs Am–67 G O'Donovan (1984)
Pro–63 B Langer,
G Cullen (1985)
V'tors U H exc Wed & Sat
SOC–WD
Fees £35 (£45)
Loc 3 miles NE of Dublin, on
coast road to Howth
Mis Practice range
Arch HS Colt

St Anne's (1921)

North Bull Island, Dollymount, Dublin 5

Tel **(01) 833 2797/6471**
Fax **(01) 833 6471**
Mem 520
Sec J Carberry (01) 336471
Pro P Skerritt
Holes 18 L 5797 metres Par 70
SSS 69
Recs Am–67 S Rodgers
Pro–64 P Skerritt
V'tors WE/BH–NA SOC
Fees £20 (£25)
Loc Dublin 5 miles
Arch Eddie Hackett

For list of abbreviations see page 435

Stackstown (1975)
Kellystown Road, Rathfarnham, Dublin 16
Tel **(01) 942338/941993**
Mem 1120
Sec K Lawlor (Sec/Mgr)
Pro M Kavanagh (01) 944561
Holes 18 L 5952 metres SSS 72
Recs Am–70 P Harrington
V'tors WD–U SOC
Fees £12 (£15)
Loc 7 miles SE of Dublin

Sutton (1890)
Cush Point, Burrow Road, Sutton, Dublin 13
Tel **(01) 323013**
Fax **(01) 321603**
Mem 221 185(L) 63(J)
Sec H O'Neill
Pro N Lynch
Holes 9 L 5522 yds SSS 67
Recs Am–64 M Hanway
Pro–64 L Owens (1987)
V'tors Tues–NA Sat–NA before 5.30pm
Fees £15 (£20)
Loc 7 miles E of Dublin

Co Fermanagh

Enniskillen (1896)
Castlecoole, Enniskillen BT&4 6HZ
Tel **(01365) 25250**
Mem 600
Sec WJ Hamilton
Pro None
Holes 18 L 5574 metres SSS 70
Recs Am–67 D Robinson (1992)
V'tors U SOC
Fees D–£10 (£12)
Loc 1 mile SE of Enniskillen, on Castlecoole Estate
Arch TJ McAuley

Co Galway

Athenry (1902)
Palmerstown, Oranmore
Tel **(091) 94466**
Mem 600
Sec P Burkitt (091) 94681
Holes 18 L 6100 yds SSS 69
Recs Am–70 M Waters
V'tors WD/Sat–U Sun–M
Fees £12 Sun–NA
Loc 10 miles E of Galway on Athenry road
Arch Eddie Hackett

Ballinasloe (1894)
Rossgloss, Ballinasloe
Tel **(0905) 42126**
Fax **(0905) 42538**
Mem 800
Sec M Uniacke (0905) 42904
Holes 18 L 5889 metres SSS 70
Recs Am–64 M Quinn
Pro–66 C O'Connor
Ladies–68 M Madden
V'tors U SOC
Fees £10 (£12)
Loc Ballinasloe 2 miles
Arch Eddie Hackett

Connemara (1973)
Aillebrack, Ballyconnelly, Clifden
Tel **(095) 23502**
Fax **(095) 23662**
Mem 480
Sec J McLaughlin (Sec/Mgr)
Holes 18 L 6560 metres SSS 72
V'tors U H SOC
Fees £16–£18
Loc 8 miles SW of Clifden
Arch Eddie Hackett

Galway (1895)
Blackrock, Salthill, Galway
Tel **(091) 22169/27622**
Fax **(091) 22169**
Mem 1020
Sec P Fahy (091) 22033
Pro D Wallace (091) 23038
Holes 18 L 5828 metres SSS 70
V'tors Restricted Tues & Sun
Fees £15
Loc 3 miles W of Galway City

Gort (1924)
Laughtyshaughnessy, Gort
Tel **(091) 31336**
Mem 320
Sec S Devlin (Hon)
Pro None
Holes 9 L 5174 metres SSS 67
Recs Am–67 SO Boyle
Pro–66 C O'Connor
V'tors U exc Sun am SOC
Fees £8
Loc Gort 1 mile on Tubber road. 20 miles S of Galway
Mis 18 holes open 1996

Loughrea (1924)
Graigue, Loughrea
Tel **(091) 41049**
Mem 400
Sec C McGuinness (Hon)
Holes 18 L 5613 yds SSS 68
Recs Am–67 S Glynn
V'tors U SOC
Fees On application
Loc 1 mile N of Loughrea, off Dublin-Galway road. 20 miles E of Galway
Arch Eddie Hackett

Mountbellew (1929)
Mountbellew, Ballinasloe
Tel **(0905) 79259**
Mem 300
Holes 9 L 5564 yds SSS 66
Recs Am–68 I Hayden
V'tors U SOC
Fees On application
Loc 50km NE of Galway on N63

Oughterard (1973)
Gortreevagh, Oughterard
Tel **(091) 82131**
Fax **(091) 82733**
Mem 800
Sec J Waters (Hon)
Pro M Ryan
Holes 18 L 6150 yds SSS 69
Recs Am–69 D Forde (1990)
V'tors U
Fees £13 (£14)
Loc 15 miles NW of Galway
Arch Harris

Portumna (1907)
Ennis Road, Portumna
Tel **(0509) 41059**
Mem 450
Sec G Ryan (Hon)
Holes 18 L 6776 yds SSS 67
Recs Am–66 M Harney (1982)
Pro–63 H Bradshaw
V'tors U SOC
Fees £10
Loc 40 miles SE of Galway on Lough Derg

Tuam (1907)
Barnacurragh, Tuam
Tel **(093) 28993**
Mem 700
Sec Mary Tierney (Sec/Mgr)
Pro H Reynolds (093) 24091
Holes 18 L 5944 metres SSS 71
Recs Am–69 DJ McGrath
Pro–68 R Rafferty (1983)
V'tors Sun–NA SOC–WD
Fees £10
Loc 20 miles N of Galway

Co Kerry

Ballybunion (1893)
Sandhill Road, Ballybunion
Tel **(068) 27146**
Fax **(068) 27387**
Mem 648
Sec J McKenna (Sec/Mgr)
Pro T Higgins
Holes Old 18 L 6542 yds SSS 72
Cashen 18 L 6477 yds SSS 70
Recs Am–67 P Mulcare
V'tors U SOC
Fees Old–£35 New–£25 Old+New D–£50
Loc 2 miles S of Ballybunion. 50 miles W of Limerick, via Tarbert

Beaufort (1994)
Churchtown, Beaufort, Killarney
Tel **(064) 44440**
Fax **(064) 44752**
Mem 65
Sec C Kelly
Holes 18 L 6605 yds Par 71 SSS 72
V'tors WD–H SOC
Fees £25 (£28)
Loc 7 miles W of Killarney, off R562
Arch Dr Arthur Spring

For list of abbreviations see page 435

Castlegregory
Stradbally, Castlegregory
Tel **(066) 39444**
Mem 150
Sec M Moloney (Sec/Mgr)
Holes 9 L 5340 metres SSS 68
V'tors U SOC
Fees £10 (£10)
Loc 18 miles W of Tralee
Arch Arthur Spring

Ceann Sibeal (1924)
Ballyferriter
Tel **(066) 56255/56408**
Fax **(066) 56409**
Mem 306
Sec G Partington (Sec/Mgr)
Pro D O'Connor
Holes 18 L 6560 yds SSS 71
V'tors U SOC
Fees D–£18 (£20) W–£90 SOC–£13
Loc Dingle Peninsula, W of Tralee
Arch Hackett/O'Connor Jr

Dooks (1889)
Glenbeigh
Tel **(066) 68205/68200**
Fax **(066) 68476**
Mem 585
Sec M Shanahan (Sec/Mgr) (066) 67370
Holes 18 L 5346 metres SSS 68
Recs Am–72 MI McGillicuddy (1992)
V'tors WD–U H before 5pm WE/BH–phone first SOC
Fees £16
Loc 3 miles N of Glenbeigh, on Ring of Kerry

Kenmare (1903)
Kenmare
Tel **(064) 41291**
Fax **(064) 42061**
Mem 349
Sec M MacGearailt
Holes 18 L 5441 metres SSS 69
Recs Am–64 B Mulcahy
V'tors U SOC
Fees £12.50
Loc 20 miles S of Killarney on Cork road
Arch Eddie Hackett

Killarney (1893)
Mahoney's Point, Killarney
Tel **(064) 31034**
Fax **(064) 33065**
Mem 1500
Sec T Prendergast
Pro T Coveney (064) 31615
Holes Mahoney's Point 18 L 6164 metres SSS 72; Killeen 18 L 6475 metres SSS 73
Recs Mahoney's Point Am–68 S Coyne (1968)
Killeen Am–73 DF O'Sullivan
Pro–65 D Feherty
V'tors H SOC
Fees £28
Loc 3 miles W of Killarney
Arch Longhurst/Campbell

Killorglin (1992)
Steelroe, Killorglin
Tel **(066) 61979**
Fax **(066) 61437**
Mem 175
Sec B Harman
Pro None
Holes 18 L 6464 yds SSS 72
V'tors U SOC
Fees IR£12 (IR£14)
Loc 1 mile from Killorglin on Tralee road (N70)
Arch Eddie Hackett

Parknasilla (1974)
Parknasilla, Sneem
Tel **(064) 45122**
Fax **(064) 45323**
Mem 70
Sec M Walsh
Pro C McCarthy
Holes 9 L 4834 yds SSS 65
V'tors U
Fees £10
Loc Great Southern Hotel, 2 miles E of Sneem on Ring of Kerry

Tralee (1896)
West Barrow, Ardfert
Tel **(066) 36379**
Fax **(066) 36008**
Mem 1000
Pro None
Holes 18 L 6252 metres SSS 71
Recs Am–66 G O'Sullivan (1987)
V'tors WD–U H before 4.30pm exc Wed–restricted WE/BH–NA exc 11–12.30–H SOC–WD
Fees £25 (£30)
Loc 8 miles NW of Tralee on Spa/Fenit road
Arch Arnold Palmer

Waterville (1889)
Ring of Kerry, Waterville
Tel **(0667) 4102/4545**
Fax **(0667) 4482**
Mem 252
Sec N Cronin (0667) 4545
Pro L Higgins (0667) 4237
Holes 18 L 7184 yds SSS 74
Pro–65 L Higgins
V'tors U H SOC
Fees £35
Loc 2 miles N of Waterville on Ring of Kerry

Co Kildare

Athy (1906)
Geraldine, Athy
Tel **(0507) 31729**
Mem 350
Holes 18 L 6308 yds SSS 70
V'tors WD–U Sat–M SOC
Fees £10 (£15)
Loc 1 mile N of Athy on Kildare road

Bodenstown (1983)
Bodenstown, Sallins
Tel **(045) 97096**
Mem 650
Sec Mrs B Curtin (Sec/Mgr)
Holes Old 18 L 6132 metres SSS 71
Ladyhill 18 L 5278 metres SSS 68
Recs Am–71 J Gray (1991)
V'tors U exc WE–NA (Old course)
Fees Old–£9 Ladyhill–£7
Loc 4 miles N of Naas on Clane road. 18 miles W of Dublin, off N7

Castlewarden G & CC (1989)
Straffan
Tel **(01) 458 9254**
Fax **(01) 458 9838**
Mem 520 200(L)
Sec J Ferriter (Hon)
Pro G Egan (01) 458 8219
Holes 18 L 6008 yds SSS 71
V'tors WD–U WE–M SOC
Fees £12 (£14)
Loc 18 miles W of Dublin, off N4
Arch Halpin/Browne

Cill Dara (1920)
Little Curragh, Kildare Town
Tel **(045) 21433/21295**
Mem 400
Sec J Watters (Hon)
Pro J Bolger
Holes 9 L 5842 metres SSS 70
Recs Am–67 T Royce, P Doyle (1989)
V'tors WD–U before 2pm Sat–NA after noon Sun/BH–NA SOC
Fees £10 (£12)
Loc 1 mile W of Kildare town

Curragh (1883)
Curragh
Tel **(045) 41238/41714**
Mem 500 160(L)
Sec Ann Culleton
Pro P Lawlor
Holes 18 L 6001 metres SSS 71
Recs Am–68 L Walker (1990)
Pro–69 A Whitson
V'tors WD–check with Sec
Fees IR£14 (IR£17)
Loc 3 miles S of Newbridge

Highfield (1992)
Highfield House, Carbury
Tel **(0405) 31021**
Fax **(0405) 31021**
Mem 150
Sec P Duggan (Sec/Mgr)
Pro None
Holes 18 L 5707 m SSS 70
V'tors WD–U WE–U after 9.30am
Fees £6 (£8)
Loc 32 miles W of Dublin on N4
Mis Further 9 holes open Spring 1995
Arch Alan Duggan

The K Club (1991)
Kildare Hotel & CC, Straffan
Tel **(01) 627 3987**
Fax **(01) 627 3990**
Mem 278
Sec K Greene (Golf Dir)
Pro E Jones
Holes 18 L 7200 yds SSS 72
Pro–69 D Smyth (1994)
V'tors U H SOC–WD
Fees IR£85
Loc 18 miles SW of Dublin (N7)
Mis Driving range
Arch Arnold Palmer

Killeen (1986)
Killeenbeg, Kill
Tel **(045) 66003**
Fax **(045) 75881**
Mem 300
Sec P Carey
Holes 18 L 5011 metres SSS 66
Recs Am–70 P O'Keefe
V'tors WD–U WE–NA before 10am
Fees £11 (£13)
Loc 2 miles off N7 on Sallins road

Knockanally (1985)
Donadea, North Kildare
Tel **(045) 69322**
Fax **(045) 69322**
Mem 475
Sec N Lyons
Pro P Hickey
Holes 18 L 6424 yds SSS 72
Recs Pro–66 K O'Donnell, D James (1988)
V'tors U
Fees £15 (£20)
Loc 20 miles W of Dublin on Galway road (N4)
Arch N Lyons

Naas (1896)
Kerdiffstown, Naas
Tel **(045) 97509/74644**
Mem 514
Sec K Dermody
Holes 18 L 5660 metres SSS 70
V'tors U SOC
Fees £12 (£15)
Loc 2 miles N of Naas
Arch Arthur Spring

Co Kilkenny

Callan (1929)
Geraldine, Callan
Tel **(056) 25136**
Mem 350
Sec M Duggan (Hon)
Holes 9 L 5844 yds SSS 68
Recs Am–70 J Madden
Pro–71 M Kavanagh
V'tors U SOC
Fees £8
Loc 1 mile SE of Callan. 10 miles SW of Kilkenny

Castlecomer (1935)
Dromgoole, Castlecomer
Tel **(056) 41139**
Mem 425
Sec M Doheny (Hon)
Holes 9 L 5923 metres SSS 71
Recs Am–69 K Kenny (1994)
V'tors U
Fees £8 (£10)
Loc 11 miles N of Kilkenny

Kilkenny (1896)
Glendine, Kilkenny
Tel **(056) 22125/65400**
Mem 950
Sec S O'Neill (056) 65400
Pro N Leahy (056) 61730
Holes 18 L 6409 yds SSS 70
Recs Am–65 J White, D McDonald
Pro–68 B Todd
V'tors U
Fees £16 (£18)
Loc 1 mile N of Kilkenny

Mount Juliet (1991)
Thomastown
Tel **(056) 24725**
Fax **(056) 24828**
Sec Katherine MacCann (Golf Dir)
Pro N Bradley
Holes 18 L 7143 yds SSS 74
Recs Pro–65 N Faldo (1993)
V'tors U
Fees £65 (£70)
Loc 10 miles S of Kilkenny, off Dublin-Waterford road.
Mis Driving range-residents and green fees. Golf Academy
Arch Jack Nicklaus

Co Laois

Abbeyleix (1895)
Rathmoyle, Abbeyleix
Tel **(0502) 31450**
Mem 230
Sec AJ Nolan (Hon)
Holes 9 L 5680 yds SSS 68
V'tors WD–U WE–NA SOC–WD/Sat
Fees £6 (£8)
Loc 10 miles S of Portlaoise. 60 miles SW of Dublin on Cork road

Heath (Portlaoise) (1930)
The Heath, Portlaoise
Tel **(0502) 46533**
Mem 540
Sec P Malone (0502) 21074
Pro E Doyle (0502) 46622
Holes 18 L 6247 yds SSS 70
Recs Am–67 T Tyrrell (1983)
V'tors U
Fees On application
Loc 4 miles E of Portlaoise
Mis Floodlit driving range

Mountrath (1929)
Knockanina, Mountrath
Mem 350
Sec T O'Grady (0502) 32558
Holes 9 L 5300 yds SSS 66
Recs Am–67 S Carter
V'tors U
Fees £5
Loc 10 miles W of Portlaoise. Mountrath 2 miles

Portarlington (1909)
Garryhinch, Portarlington
Tel **(0502) 23115**
Mem 385
Sec MJ Turley (Hon)
Holes 18 L 5749 metres SSS 70
Recs Am–65
V'tors WE–restricted
Fees £10 (£12)
Loc Between Portarlington and Mountmellick on L116

Rathdowney (1931)
Coulnaboul West, Rathdowney
Tel **(0505) 46170**
Mem 181
Sec S Pyne (Hon)
Holes 9 L 6086 yds SSS 69
Recs Am–71 J O'Malley
V'tors U SOC
Fees On application
Loc 1 mile S of Rathdowney. 20 miles SW of Portlaoise

Co Leitrim

Ballinamore (1941)
Creevy, Ballinamore
Tel **(078) 44346**
Mem 86
Sec P Duignan (Hon)
Holes 9 L 5204 yds SSS 66
Recs Am–68 D Gannon
V'tors U SOC
Fees D–£5
Loc 2 miles N of Ballinamore. 20 miles NE of Carrick-on-Shannon

Carrick-on-Shannon (1910)
Woodbrook, Carrick-on-Shannon
Tel **(079) 67015**
Mem 210
Sec A McNally (Sec/Mgr)
Holes 9 L 5584 yds SSS 68
V'tors U
Fees IR£10
Loc 4 miles W of Carrick-on-Shannon on N4

For list of abbreviations see page 435

Co Limerick

Adare Manor (1900)

Adare

Tel **(061) 396204**
Mem 580
Sec TR Healy (Hon)
Holes 18 L 5396 metres SSS 69
V'tors WD–U WE–M
Fees D–£15
Loc 10 miles SW of Limerick

Castletroy (1937)

Castletroy, Limerick

Tel **(061) 335261**
Fax **(061) 335373**
Mem 940
Sec L Hayes (061) 335753
Pro N Cassidy (061) 338283
Holes 18 L 5793 metres SSS 71
V'tors WD–U Sat am–U Sat pm/Sun–M SOC–Mon/Wed/Fri
Fees £20 (£20)
Loc 2 miles N of Limerick on Dublin road

Limerick (1891)

Ballyclough, Limerick

Tel **(061) 414083**
Mem 1205
Sec D McDonogh (061) 415146
Pro J Cassidy (061) 412492
Holes 18 L 6479 yds SSS 71
Recs Am–68 M Morrissey (1994) Pro–69 N Hanson (1990)
V'tors WD–U before 5pm exc Tues WE–M SOC–WD
Fees £20
Loc 3 miles S of Limerick

Newcastle West (1938)

Ardagh

Tel **(069) 76500**
Fax **(069) 76511**
Mem 450
Sec P Lyons (069) 72142
Holes 18 L 5905 metres SSS 73
V'tors U exc Sun–U after 4pm SOC
Fees £15
Loc 6 miles N of Newcastle West, off Limerick-Killarney road (N21)
Mis Driving range
Arch Arthur Spring

Co Londonderry

Benone Par Three

53 Benone Avenue, Benone, Limavady BT49 0LQ

Tel **(015047) 50555**
Sec CL Smith
Holes 9 L 1427 yds Par 3 course
V'tors U
Fees On application
Loc 12 miles N of Limavady on A2 coast road

Brown Trout (1984)

209 Agivey Road, Aghadowey, Coleraine

Tel **(01265) 868209**
Mem 210
Sec R Engall (Sec/Mgr)
Pro K Revie
Holes 9 L 2800 yds SSS 68
V'tors U SOC
Fees £8 (£12)
Loc 8 miles S of Coleraine at junction of A54/B66
Arch W O'Hara Sr

Castlerock (1901)

Circular Road, Castlerock BT51 4TJ

Tel **(01265) 848314**
Fax **(01265) 848314**
Mem 920
Sec RG McBride
Pro R Kelly
Holes 18 L 6121 metres SSS 72 9 L 2457 metres SSS 34
Recs Am–68 G Forbes
V'tors WD–U exc Fri (Ladies preference) SOC
Fees £15 (£25) 9 hole–£7 (£10)
Loc 5 miles W of Coleraine on A2
Arch Ben Sayers

City of Derry (1912)

49 Victoria Road, Londonderry BT47 2PU

Tel **(01504) 311610/46369**
Mem 692
Sec PJ Doherty
Pro M Doherty (01504) 311496
Holes Prehen 18 L 6487 yds SSS 71 Dunhugh 9 L 4708 yds SSS 63
Recs Am–68 D Ballentine
V'tors WD–U before 4pm –M after 4pm WE–U H SOC
Fees Prehen £11 (£13) Dunhugh £5
Loc 3 miles from E end of Craigavon Bridge towards Strabane

Kilrea (1920)

Drumagarner Road, Kilrea

Tel **(012665) 41316**
Fax **(012665) 40277**
Mem 240
Sec RT Moore
Holes 9 L 4326 yds SSS 62
Recs Am–61 R Rees (1982), T Moore (1989)
V'tors Tues & Wed–NA after 5pm Sat–NA before 4pm
Fees £10
Loc Nr Kilrea on Maghera road. 15 miles S of Coleraine

Moyola Park (1976)

Shanemullagh, Castledawson, Magherafelt BT45 8DG

Tel **(01648) 468468**
Mem 901
Sec LWP Hastings (Hon)
Pro V Teague (01648) 468830
Holes 18 L 6517 yds SSS 71
Recs Am–70 R Hogg, R Evans Pro–70 D Smyth
V'tors U SOC exc Sat
Fees £12 (£22)
Loc 40 miles NW of Belfast by M2. 35 miles S of Coleraine
Arch Don Patterson

Portstewart (1894)

117 Strand Road, Portstewart BT55 7PG

Tel **(01265) 832015**
Fax **(01265) 834097**
Mem 1431
Sec M Moss BA (01265) 833839
Pro A Hunter (01265) 832601
Holes Strand 18 L 6784 yds SSS 73 Riverside 9 L 2662 yds Par 32 Town 18 L 4733 yds SSS 62
Recs Strand Am–68 F Howley (1992)
V'tors SOC–by arrangement
Fees Strand–£25 (£35) Riverside–£10 (£15) Town £8 (£12)
Loc W boundary of Portstewart. N of Coleraine

Co Longford

County Longford (1900)

Glack, Dublin Road, Longford

Tel **(043) 46310**
Mem 327
Holes 18 L 6008 yds SSS 69
V'tors U SOC
Fees On application
Loc Longford 1/2 mile on Dublin road
Arch Eddie Hackett

Co Louth

Ardee (1911)

Townparks, Ardee

Tel **(041) 53227/56283**
Fax **(041) 56137**
Mem 650
Sec S Kelly (Sec/Mgr) (041) 53227
Holes 18 L 6046 yds SSS 69
Recs Am–67 J Carroll Pro–70 C O'Connor
V'tors U SOC
Fees £15 (£15)
Loc 1/2 mile N of Ardee
Arch Eddie Hackett

County Louth (1892)

Baltray, Drogheda

Tel **(041) 22327**
Fax **(041) 22969**
Mem 1055
Sec M Delany (041) 22329
Pro P McGuirk (041) 22444
Holes 18 L 6783 yds SSS 72
Recs Am–66 R Burns Pro–65 J Heggarty
V'tors By prior arrangement
Fees On request
Loc 3 miles NE of Drogheda
Arch Tom Simpson

For list of abbreviations see page 435

Dundalk (1905)
Blackrock, Dundalk
Tel **(042) 21731**
Fax **(042) 22022**
Mem 850
Sec J Carroll (042) 21731
Pro J Cassidy (042) 22102
Holes 18 L 6115 metres SSS 72
V'tors U SOC
Fees £16 (£20)
Loc 3 miles S of Dundalk

Greenore (1896)
Greenore
Tel **(042) 73212**
Fax **(042) 73678**
Mem 500
Sec B Rafferty (Sec/Mgr)
Holes 18 L 6506 yds SSS 71
Recs Am–68 E McCarten
Pro–68 A Cardwell
V'tors WD–U before 5pm
WE/BH–by arrangement SOC
Fees £12 (£18)
Loc 15 miles E of Dundalk on Carlingford Lough
Arch Eddie Hackett

Killinbeg (1991)
Killin Park, Dundalk
Tel **(042) 39303**
Mem 100
Sec D Bell (Sec/Mgr)
Pro None
Holes 12 L 3322 yds SSS 69
V'tors U SOC
Fees £7 (£10)
Loc 2 miles NW of Dundalk on Castletown road

Seapoint (1993)
Termonfeckin, Drogheda
Tel **(041) 22333**
Fax **(041) 22331**
Mem 250
Sec Amelia Smith
Pro D Carroll
Holes 18 L 5900 metres SSS 71
Recs Am–72 D Branigan (1993)
V'tors U SOC
Fees £20 (£25)
Loc 10 miles NE of Drogheda (R166)
Arch Des Smyth

Co Mayo

Achill Island (1951)
Keel, Achill
Tel **(098) 43456**
Mem 100
Sec P Lavelle (Hon)
Holes 9 L 2723 yds SSS 66
Recs Am–69 J Lawlor (1990)
V'tors U H SOC
Fees £4
Loc 50 miles NW of Westport, on Achill Island

Ballina (1910)
Mossgrove, Shanaghy, Ballina
Tel **(096) 21050**
Mem 448
Sec V Frawley (096) 21795
Holes 9 L 5700 yds SSS 67
Recs Am–64 J Corcoran (1984)
Pro–66 C O'Connor
V'tors WD–U Sun–NA before noon SOC–WD
Fees £10 (£10) W–£30
Loc 1 mile E of Ballina

Ballinrobe (1895)
Castlebar Road, Ballinrobe
Tel **(092) 41448**
Mem 300
Sec P Holian (092) 41659
Holes 9 L 5790 yds SSS 68
Recs Am–67 B Finlay
V'tors U exc Sun–NA SOC
Fees D–£10 W–£40
Loc 2 miles NW of Ballinrobe

Ballyhaunis (1929)
Coolnaha, Ballyhaunis
Tel **(0907) 30014**
Mem 185
Sec JG Forde (Hon)
Holes 9 L 5393 metres SSS 68
Recs Am–70 D Charlton Jr (1990)
V'tors U exc Thurs (Ladies Day)–M Sun–NA SOC–WD
Fees £8
Loc 2 miles N of Ballyhaunis

Belmullet (1925)
Carne, Belmullet
Tel **(097) 82292/81051**
Fax **(097) 81477**
Mem 150
Sec L McAndrew (097) 81051
Holes 18 L 6016 metres SSS 72
V'tors U SOC
Fees £15 W–£75
Loc 2 miles W of Belmullet. 40 miles W of Ballina
Arch Eddie Hackett

Castlebar (1910)
Rocklands, Castlebar
Tel **(094) 21649**
Mem 450
Sec AA Ryan (094) 32232
Holes 18 L 6229 yds SSS 69
Recs Am–67 D Kelly
V'tors U exc Sun
Fees £2 (£15)
Loc 1 mile S of Castlebar, on Galway road

Claremorris (1917)
Castlemagarrett, Claremorris
Tel **(094) 71527**
Fax **(094) 62137**
Mem 279
Sec P Killeen (Hon)
Holes 9 L 6454 yds SSS 69
Recs Am–66 P Killeen
Pro–63 C O'Connor
V'tors U
Fees £8
Loc 2 miles S of Claremorris

Mulrany (1968)
Mulrany, Westport
Tel **(098) 36262**
Mem 22
Sec D Nevin (Hon)
Holes 9 L 6380 yds SSS 70
V'tors U
Fees £6
Loc 20 miles NW of Castlebar

Swinford (1922)
Brabazon Park, Swinford
Tel **(094) 51378**
Mem 300
Holes 9 L 5901 yds SSS 68
Recs Am–70 B Finlay (1991)
V'tors U
Fees D–£5 (£12) W–£25
Loc S of Swinford, off Kiltimagh road

Westport (1908)
Carowholly, Westport
Tel **(098) 25113/27070**
Fax **(098) 27217**
Mem 700
Pro A Mealia
Holes 18 L 6667 yds SSS 73
Recs Am–65 L Gibbons (1984)
V'tors U SOC
Fees £18 (£22)
Loc 2 miles W of Westport
Arch F Hawtree

Co Meath

The Black Bush (1987)
Thomastown, Dunshaughlin
Tel **(01) 825 0021**
Mem 900
Sec I Yorston
Pro None
Holes 18 L 6930 yds SSS 73
9 L 2800 yds SSS 35
V'tors WD–U WE–NA before 4pm SOC
Fees On application
Loc 1 mile E of Dunshaughlin, off N3. 20 miles NW of Dublin
Mis Driving range for members and green fees
Arch Robert J Browne

Gormanston College (1961)
Franciscan College, Gormanston
Tel **(01) 8412203**
Mem 160
Sec Br Laurence Brady
Pro B Browne
Holes 9 L 1973 metres
Recs Am–60 G Ormsby (1972)
V'tors NA
Loc 22 miles N of Dublin

Headfort (1928)
Kells
Tel **(046) 40857**
Mem 882
Pro B McGovern (046) 40639
Holes 18 L 6543 yds SSS 70
Recs Am–67 D McGrane (1990)
Pro–64 D Smyth (1973)
V'tors U SOC
Fees £15 (£18)
Loc Kells ½ mile

Kilcock (1985)
Gallow, Kilcock
Tel **(01) 628 7283**
Mem 230
Sec F Reid (Hon)
Holes 9 L 5364 metres SSS 68
V'tors U
Fees £7 (£9)
Loc 20 miles W of Dublin (N4)

Laytown & Bettystown (1909)
Bettystown
Tel **(041) 27170/27534**
Fax **(041) 27170**
Mem 850
Sec Stella Garvey-Hoey
Pro RJ Browne (041) 27563
Holes 18 L 6254 yds SSS 69
V'tors U SOC–WD
Fees On application
Loc 25 miles N of Dublin

Royal Tara (1923)
Bellinter, Navan
Tel **(046) 25244/25508/25584**
Fax **(046) 25508**
Mem 900
Sec P O'Brien
Pro A Whiston
Holes 18 L 5757 yds Par 71
9 L 3184 yds Par 35
Recs Am–66 M McQuaid
V'tors U
Fees £14 (£18)
Loc 25 miles N of Dublin, off N3

Trim (1898)
Newtownmoynagh, Trim
Tel **(046) 31463**
Mem 450
Sec PJ Darby (046) 31438
Holes 18 L 6720 yds SSS 72
Recs Am–72 S Corrigan
V'tors WD–U exc Ladies day
WE–restricted SOC–exc Sun
Fees £13 (£15)
Loc 2 miles SW of Trim. 25 miles NW of Dublin
Arch Eddie Hackett

Co Monaghan

Castleblayney (1985)
Muckno Park, Castleblayney
Mem 175
Sec D McGlynn (042) 40197
Holes 9 L 2678 yds SSS 66
Recs Am–70 J McCarthy (1987)
V'tors U SOC
Fees £5 (£8)
Loc Castleblayney town centre. 18 miles SE of Monaghan

Clones (1913)
Hilton Park, Clones
Tel **(049) 56017**
Mem 245
Holes 9 L 5790 yds SSS 68
Recs Am–64 D McGuigan
V'tors WD–U Sun–NA before noon
Fees £6 (£10)
Loc Hilton Park, 2½ miles from Clones

Nuremore (1964)
Nuremore, Carrickmacross
Tel **(042) 61438**
Mem 220
Pro M Cassidy
Holes 18 L 6246 yds SSS 74
V'tors U
Fees On application
Loc 1 mile S of Carrickmacross on Dublin road
Arch Eddie Hackett

Rossmore (1916)
Rossmore Park, Monaghan
Tel **(047) 81316**
Mem 325
Sec J McKenna (Hon)
Holes 18 L 6082 yds Par 70 SSS 68
Recs Am–64 R Berry
V'tors WD–U WE/BH–U exc comp days SOC
Fees £8 (£10)
Loc 2 miles S of Monaghan on Cootehill road
Arch Des Smyth

Co Offaly

Birr (1893)
The Glenns, Birr
Tel **(0509) 20082**
Mem 500
Sec E Connolly (Hon)
Holes 18 L 6216 yds SSS 70
Recs Am–64 R Coughlan
Pro–68 RJ Browne
V'tors U SOC–exc Sun–NA 11.30–12 noon
Fees £10 (£12)
Loc 2 miles W of Birr

Edenderry (1910)
Kishavanna, Edenderry
Tel **(0405) 31072**
Mem 550
Sec V Allen (0405) 31826
Holes 18 L 6121 yds Par 73 SSS 72
Recs Am–64 J Brady (1990)
V'tors WD–U exc Thurs (Ladies Day) WE–NA SOC
Fees £10
Loc 1 mile E of Edenderry
Arch Havers/Hackett

Tullamore (1896)
Brookfield, Tullamore
Tel **(0506) 21439**
Mem 993
Sec A Marsden (Hon)
Pro D McArdle (0506) 51757
Holes 18 L 6322 yds SSS 70
Recs Am–64 D White
Pro–68 H Boyle, J Martin, D Jones
V'tors WD–U exc Tues (Ladies Day) Sat–M 12.30–3pm Sun–NA SOC
Fees £12 (£15)
Loc 2½ miles S of Tullamore, off Birr road
Arch James Braid

Co Roscommon

Athlone (1892)
Hodson Bay, Athlone
Tel **(0902) 92073/92235**
Fax **(0902) 94080**
Mem 900
Sec D Fagan (Hon)
Pro M Quinn
Holes 18 L 5922 metres SSS 71
V'tors U SOC
Fees D–£12 (£15)
Loc 3 miles N of Athlone on Roscommon road
Arch F Hawtree

Ballaghaderreen (1937)
Aughalustia, Ballaghaderreen
Tel **(0907) 60295**
Mem 150
Sec B Clancy (Hon)
Holes 9 L 5663 yds SSS 66
V'tors U SOC
Fees £6
Loc Ballaghaderreen 3 miles
Arch P Skerritt

Boyle (1911)
Knockadoobrusna, Roscommon Road, Boyle
Tel **(079) 62594**
Mem 150
Sec P Nangle (Hon)
Holes 9 L 4957 metres SSS 66
Recs Am–65 A Wynne (1987)
V'tors U SOC
Fees £5
Loc 1½ miles S of Boyle

Castlerea (1905)
Clonallis, Castlerea
Tel **(0907) 20068**
Mem 200
Sec W Gannon (Hon)
Holes 9 L 5466 yds SSS 66
Recs Am–63 R de Lacy Staunton
V'tors WD/Sat–U Sun–by arrangement
Fees £8 (£10)
Loc Knock Road, Castlerea

Roscommon (1904)
Moate Park, Roscommon
Tel **(0903) 26382**
Mem 500
Sec C McConn (Hon)
Holes 9 L 5784 metres Par 72 SSS 70
Recs Am–64 K Kearney (1992)
V'tors WD–U WE/BH–restricted SOC
Fees £10 SOC–£6
Loc 1 mile S of Roscommon
Mis Extension to 18 holes in 1995
Arch Eddie Connaughton

Co Sligo

Ballymote (1940)
Carrigans, Ballymote
Tel **(071) 83460**
Mem 49
Sec P Mullen (Hon)
Holes 9 L 4601 metres SSS 65
Recs Am–67 P Mullen
V'tors U
Fees £5 (£5)
Loc 15 miles S of Sligo

County Sligo (1894)
Rosses Point
Tel **(071) 77134/77186**
Fax **(071) 77460**
Mem 932
Sec R Mullen
Pro L Robinson (071) 77171
Holes 18 L 6003 metres SSS 72
Recs Am–66 F Howley (1991)
Pro–67 C O'Connor Sr (1975)
V'tors U–booking required
Fees £16 (£22)
Loc 5 miles NW of Sligo
Arch Colt/Allison

Enniscrone (1931)
Ballina Road, Enniscrone
Tel **(096) 36297**
Fax **(096) 36657**
Mem 700
Sec JM Fleming
Holes 18 L 6682 yds SSS 72
Recs Am–69 D Basquil
Pro–71 C O'Connor Sr, J O'Leary
V'tors WD–U WE/BH–phone first SOC
Fees D–£15 (£18)
Loc S of Enniscrone. Ballina 13 km
Arch Eddie Hackett

Strandhill (1932)
Strandhill
Tel **(071) 68188**
Mem 375
Sec V Harte (Sec/Mgr)
Holes 18 L 5937 yds SSS 68
V'tors WD–U WE/BH–restricted SOC
Fees IR£10 (IR£12)
Loc 6 miles W of Sligo

Tubbercurry (1990)
Ballymote Road, Tubbercurry
Tel **(071) 85849**
Mem 250
Holes 9 L 5478 metres SSS 69
V'tors U
Fees £7
Loc 20 miles S of Sligo
Arch Eddie Hackett

Co Tipperary

Ballykisteen G & CC (1994)
Monard
Tel **(052) 51439**
Mem 260
Sec DB Begley
Holes 18 L 6765 yds Par 72 SSS 73
V'tors U SOC–book 1 month in advance
Fees £15 (£20)
Loc 3 miles W of Tipperary town
Mis Driving range
Arch Des Smyth

Cahir Park (1968)
Kilcommon, Cahir
Tel **(052) 41474**
Mem 187
Sec M Fitzgerald (Hon)
Pro D Foran
Holes 9 L 5690 yds SSS 69
Recs Am–68
V'tors U SOC–WD/Sat
Fees £10
Loc 1 mile S of Cahir
Arch Eddie Hackett

Carrick-on-Suir (1939)
Garravone, Carrick-on-Suir
Tel **(051) 40047**
Mem 200
Holes 9 L 5948 yds SSS 68
Recs Am–67 C Carleton (1987)
V'tors U SOC–WD/Sat
Fees £10
Loc 2 miles S of Carrick on Dungarvan road
Arch Eddie Hackett

Clonmel (1911)
Lyreanearla, Mountain Road, Clonmel
Tel **(052) 21138**
Mem 572
Sec A Myles-Keating (052) 24050
Pro R Hayes
Holes 18 L 6330 yds SSS 70
Recs Am–63 M O'Neill
V'tors WD–U WE–SOC
Fees £13 (£15)
Loc 2 miles SW of Clonmel
Arch Eddie Hackett

County Tipperary G & CC (1993)
Dundrum House Hotel, Dundrum, Cashel
Tel **(062) 71116**
Fax **(062) 71366**
Mem 120
Sec W Crowe (Mgr)
Holes 18 L 6682 yds SSS 73
V'tors U SOC
Fees £15 (£20)
Loc 6 miles W of Cashel
Arch Philip Walton

Nenagh (1929)
Beechwood, Nenagh
Tel **(067) 31476**
Mem 700
Sec PJ Hayes (Hon)
Pro J Coyle (067) 33242
Holes 18 L 5483 metres Par 69 SSS 68
Recs Am–64 P Lyons (1984)
V'tors U SOC
Fees £12 (£15)
Loc 3 miles NE of Nenagh on Limerick-Dublin road
Arch Dr A Mackenzie/Hackett

Roscrea (1892)
Derryvale, Roscrea
Tel **(0505) 21130**
Mem 350
Sec K McDonnell (Hon)
Holes 18 L 5706 metres SSS 70
V'tors U
Fees £12
Loc 2 miles E of Roscrea on Dublin road
Arch Arthur Spring

Templemore (1970)
Manna South, Templemore
Tel **(0504) 31400**
Mem 240
Sec JK Moloughney (Hon)
Holes 9 L 5442 yds SSS 67
Recs Am–68
V'tors U exc Sun SOC
Fees £5 (£10)
Loc 1/2 mile S of Templemore

Thurles (1909)
Turtulla, Thurles
Tel **(0504) 21983/22466**
Mem 700
Sec T Ryan (Hon)
Pro S Hunt
Holes 18 L 5904 metres SSS 71
Recs Am–66 DF O'Sullivan
Pro–70 H Bradshaw
V'tors U
Fees £13 (£15)
Loc 1 mile S of Thurles

For list of abbreviations see page 435

Tipperary (1896)
Rathanny, Tipperary
Tel **(062) 51119**
Mem 460
Sec J Considine (Hon)
Holes 9 L 5805 metres SSS 70
Recs Am–69
V'tors U SOC
Fees D–£10
Loc Tipperary 1 mile

Co Tyrone

Dungannon (1890)
34 Springfield Lane, Mullaghmore, Dungannon BT70 1QX
Tel **(018687) 22098/27338**
Mem 585
Sec LRP Agnew
Holes 18 L 5818 yds SSS 68
Recs Am–68 D Fitzpatrick (1993)
Pro–62 D Clarke
V'tors U
Fees £10 (£13)
Loc 1 mile NW of Dungannon on Donaghmore road

Fintona (1896)
Eccleville, Demesne, Fintona
Tel **(01662) 841480**
Mem 235
Sec G McNulty (Hon)
Holes 9 L 5716 yds SSS 70
Recs Am–68 E Donnell
Pro–69 L Higgins, J Kinsilla L Robinson
V'tors U exc comp days SOC–WD
Fees £10
Loc 8 miles S of Omagh

Killymoon (1889)
200 Killymoon Road, Cookstown BT80 8TW
Tel **(016487) 63762/62254**
Mem 700
Sec L Hodgett (016487) 63762
Pro (016487) 63460
Holes 18 L 5488 metres SSS 69
Recs Am–64 A O'Neill
Pro–65 D Smyth
V'tors U H SOC
Fees £14 (£18)
Loc 1 mile S of Cookstown, off A29

Newtownstewart (1914)
38 Golf Course Road, Newtownstewart BT78 4HU
Tel **(016626) 61466**
Mem 700
Sec JE Mackin (016626) 71487
Pro None
Holes 18 L 5341 metres Par 70 SSS 69
Recs Am–66 G Forbes (1989)
Pro–66 J Fisher (1978)
V'tors WD–U WE–NA after noon SOC
Fees £10 (£15)
Loc 2 miles SW of Newtownstewart on B84

Omagh (1910)
83A Dublin Road, Omagh BT78 1HQ
Tel **(01662) 243160/241442**
Mem 860
Sec JA McElholm (Hon)
Holes 18 L 5429 metres SSS 69
Recs Am–WR Barton (1993)
Ladies–61 BM Taylor (1992)
V'tors U SOC
Fees £10 (£15)
Loc 1/2 mile from Omagh on A5

Strabane (1908)
Ballycolman, Strabane BT82 9PH
Tel **(01504) 382271/382007**
Fax **(01504) 382007**
Mem 600
Sec E McPhilemy (01504) 883098
Holes 18 L 5552 metres SSS 69
Recs Am–63 E Kennedy
Pro–69
V'tors WD–U WE–by arrangement SOC
Fees £8 (£12)
Loc 1/2 mile from Strabane, nr Fir Trees Hotel

Co Waterford

Dungarvan (1924)
Knocknagranagh, Dungarvan
Tel **(058) 43310/41605**
Fax **(058) 44113**
Mem 760
Sec N Hayes (Hon), T Whelan (Admin)
Pro D Kiely (058) 44707
Holes 18 L 6134 metres Par 72 SSS 73
V'tors U SOC
Fees £12 (£15)
Loc 2 miles E of Dungarvan on N25. 25 miles W of Waterford
Arch Maurice Fives

Faithlegg (1993)
Faithlegg House, Faithlegg
Tel **(051) 82241**
Fax **(051) 82664**
Mem 60
Sec V McGreevy (Golf Admin)
Pro T Higgins
Holes 18 L 6057 metres SSS 72
V'tors U SOC
Fees £20
Loc 6 miles E of Waterford City on Dunmore East road
Arch Patrick Merrigan

Lismore (1965)
Ballyin, Lismore
Tel **(058) 54026**
Mem 250
Sec P Norris
Holes 9 L 5291 metres SSS 67
V'tors WD–U before 5pm –M after 5pm WE–phone first SOC–exc Sun
Fees £8 (£10)
Loc 1 mile N of Lismore, off N72

Tramore (1894)
Newtown Hill, Tramore
Tel **(051) 386170/381247**
Fax **(051) 386170**
Mem 1396
Sec J Cox (Sec/Mgr)
Pro P McDaid
Holes 18 L 6055 metres SSS 73
Recs Am–66 E Power
Pro–66 H Boyle
V'tors U
Fees £17 (£20)
Loc 7 miles S of Waterford

Waterford (1912)
Newrath, Waterford
Tel **(051) 74182**
Fax **(051) 53405**
Mem 750
Sec J Condon (Sec/Mgr) (051) 76748
Pro E Condon (051) 54256
Holes 18 L 5722 metres SSS 70
Recs Am–65 J Morris (1992)
V'tors U
Fees £15 (£18)
Loc 1 mile N of Waterford (N25)
Arch Willie Park/James Braid

West Waterford (1993)
Aglish Road, Coolcormack, Dungarvan
Tel **(058) 43216**
Fax **(058) 44343**
Mem 150
Sec Mrs N Spratt
Pro To be appointed
Holes 18 L 6771 yds Par 72
V'tors U SOC
Fees £15 (£20)
Loc 2 miles W of Dungarvan, off N25
Arch Eddie Hackett

Co Westmeath

Moate (1901)
Ballinagarby, Moate
Tel **(0902) 81271/81270**
Mem 600
Sec J Creggy (Hon)
Holes 18 L 6294 yds SSS 70
V'tors U SOC–WD
Fees £7 (£10)
Loc 1 mile N of Moate
Arch Bobby Browne

Mount Temple (1991)
Mount Temple, Moate
Tel **(0902) 81841/81545**
Fax **(0902) 81957**
Mem 85
Sec M & M Dolan (Props)
Holes 18 L 6500 yds SSS 71
Recs Am–72 L Hogan (1994)
V'tors U H SOC
Fees £10 (£12)
Loc 3 miles N of N6, between Athlone and Moate
Arch Michael Dolan

For list of abbreviations see page 435

Mullingar (1894)
Belvedere, Mullingar
Tel **(044) 48366/48629**
Fax **(044) 41499**
Mem 586
Sec C Mulligan (Sec/Mgr)
Pro J Burns
Holes 18 L 6370 yds SSS 71
Recs Am–63 P Walton
Pro–64
V'tors U SOC
Fees £16 (£23)
Loc 3 miles S of Mullingar (M52)
Arch James Braid

Co Wexford

Courtown (1936)
Kiltennel, Gorey
Tel **(055) 25166/25432**
Fax **(055) 25553**
Mem 800
Sec J Finn (Sec/Mgr)
Pro J Coone (055) 25558
Holes 18 L 6398 yds SSS 70
Recs Am–67 J McGill (1987)
Pro–68 M Murphy (1976)
V'tors U SOC
Fees £12–£17 (£15–£20)
Loc 2 miles SE of Gorey
Arch Harris

Enniscorthy (1908)
Knockmarshal, Enniscorthy
Tel **(054) 33191**
Mem 600
Sec Ann Byrne
Holes 18 L 5697 metres SSS 70
Recs Am–69 C Morris (1990)
V'tors U exc Tues & Sun–phone first SOC
Fees £10 (£12)
Loc 1½ miles SW of Enniscorthy on New Ross road

New Ross (1905)
Tinneranny, New Ross
Tel **(051) 21433**
Mem 550
Sec Kathleen Daly (Sec/Mgr)
Holes 9 L 5172 metres SSS 69
Recs Am–66 M O'Brien
Pro–65 C O'Connor
V'tors U exc Sun SOC
Fees £8 (£12)
Loc 1 mile W of New Ross

Rosslare (1905)
Rosslare Strand, Rosslare
Tel **(053) 32113 (Clubhouse)**
Fax **(053) 32203**
Mem 1000
Sec JF Hall (Sec/Mgr) (053) 32203
Pro A Skerritt (053) 32238
Holes 18 L 6560 yds Par 72 SSS 71
9 L 3153 yds SSS 70
Recs Am–68 W Davis (1993)
V'tors U SOC
Fees 18 hole:£15–£18 (£20–£23)
9 hole:£8–£12
Loc 10 miles S of Wexford. Rosslare Ferry 6 miles
Arch Hawtree/Taylor/O'Connor Jr

St Helen's Bay (1993)
St Helen's, Kilrane, Rosslare Harbour
Tel **(053) 33234/33669**
Fax **(053) 33803**
Mem 200
Sec L Byrne
Holes 18 L 6091 metres SSS 72
V'tors U SOC
Fees £15
Loc Nr Rosslare Ferry terminal
Arch Philip Walton

Wexford (1960)
Mulgannon, Wexford
Tel **(053) 42238**
Mem 586
Sec P Daly (Hon)
Pro P Roche (053) 46300
Holes 18 L 6338 yds Par 72 SSS 70
V'tors U SOC
Fees £14 (£15)
Loc Wexford ½ mile

Co Wicklow

Arklow (1927)
Abbeylands, Arklow
Tel **(0402) 32492**
Fax **(0402) 31147**
Mem 500
Sec B Timmons (Hon)
Holes 18 L 5770 yds SSS 67
V'tors WD–U Sat–U after 5pm Sun–NA SOC–Mon–Sat
Fees £13 (£18)
Loc 1 mile from Arklow

Baltinglass (1928)
Baltinglass
Tel **(0508) 81350**
Mem 399
Sec M Byrne (Hon)
Pro M Murphy
Holes 9 L 6070 yds SSS 69
Recs Am–70 B Kilcoyne
Pro–70 S Hunt
V'tors U SOC
Fees £10 (£12)
Loc 38 miles S of Dublin (N81)

Blainroe (1978)
Blainroe
Tel **(0404) 68168**
Fax **(0404) 69369**
Mem 830
Sec W O'Sullivan (Sec/Mgr)
Pro J McDonald
Holes 18 L 6171 metres SSS 72
Recs Am–72
Pro–69
V'tors U
Fees £18 (£25)
Loc 3 miles S of Wicklow on coast
Arch CW Hawtree

Bray (1897)
Ravenswell Road, Bray
Tel **(01) 286 2484**
Mem 272
Sec T Brennan (Sec/Mgr)
Pro M Walby
Holes 9 L 5230 metres SSS 70
V'tors U before 6pm SOC–WD
Fees £17
Loc 12 miles S of Dublin

Charlesland G & CC (1993)
Greystones
Tel **(01) 287 6764**
Fax **(01) 287 3882**
Sec M Doherty (Golf Admin)
Pro P Heeney
Holes 18 L 6739 yds Par 72
V'tors U SOC
Fees IR£23 (IR£28)
Loc 18 miles SE of Dublin
Arch Eddie Hackett

Coollattin (1950)
Coollattin, Shillelagh
Tel **(055) 29125**
Mem 355
Sec R McCrea (Hon)
Holes 9 L 6203 yds SSS 70
Fees £10 (£12)
Loc 50 miles S of Dublin in Wicklow Mountains

Delgany (1908)
Delgany
Tel **(01) 287 4645/287 4536**
Fax **(01) 287 3977**
Mem 800
Sec RJ Kelly (Sec/Mgr)
(01) 287 4536
Pro E Darcy (01) 287 4697
Holes 18 L 5249 yds SSS 68
Recs Am–63
V'tors U exc comp days SOC–Mon/Thurs/Fri
Fees £17 (£20)
Loc 18 miles S of Dublin, nr Greystones

The European Club (1989)
Brittas Bay, Wicklow
Tel **(0404) 47415**
Fax **(01) 280 8457**
Mem 120
Sec P Ruddy
Holes 18 L 6800 yds SSS 71
V'tors U SOC
Fees £25 (£30)
Loc 30 miles S of Dublin on coast
Arch Pat Ruddy

Glenmalure (1993)
Greenane, Rathdrum
Tel **(0404) 46679**
Fax **(0404) 46783**
Mem 65
Sec C Morris (Mgr)
Holes 18 L 5237 metres SSS 66
V'tors U SOC
Fees IR£12 (IR£15)

For list of abbreviations see page 435

Loc 2 miles SW of Rathdrum on Glenmalure road
Arch Pat Suttle

Greystones (1895)
Greystones
Tel **(01) 287 6624**
Fax **(01) 287 3749**
Mem 850
Sec O Walsh (01) 287 4136
Pro K Daly (01) 287 5308
Holes 18 L 5401 metres SSS 68
Recs Am–67
Pro–66
V'tors WD–U
Fees £20 (£24)
Loc Greystones, 18 miles S of Dublin

Kilcoole (1992)
Kilcoole
Tel **(01) 287 2066**
Mem 250
Sec P McEntaggert
Holes 9 L 5506 metres Par 70 SSS 69
Recs Am–71 R Mullen (1993)
V'tors WD–U WE–NA before noon SOC–WD
Fees £10 (£12)
Loc S of Kilcoole on Newcastle road, off N11
Arch Brian Williams

Tulfarris (1987)
Blessington
Tel **(045) 64574**
Fax **(045) 64423**
Mem 150
Sec A Williams (Mgr)
Holes 9 L 2806 metres SSS 69
V'tors U SOC
Fees £12 (£15)
Loc 30 miles S of Dublin, off N81

Wicklow (1904)
Dunbur Road, Wicklow
Tel **(0404) 67379**
Mem 450
Sec J Kelly (Hon)
Pro D Daly (0404) 66122
Holes 18 L 5695 metres SSS 70
V'tors SOC–WD/Sat
Fees £15
Loc 32 miles S of Dublin, nr Wicklow town
Arch Craddock/Ruddy

Woodenbridge (1884)
Woodenbridge, Arklow
Tel **(0402) 35202**
Fax **(0402) 31402**
Mem 485
Sec D Healy
Holes 18 L 6316 yds Par 71 SSS 70
Recs Am–71 RJ Moran (1994)
V'tors U exc Sat & Thurs
Fees £20 (£25)
Loc 4 miles W of Arklow. 45 miles S of Dublin
Arch Patrick Merrigan

Scotland

BORDER REGION

Berwickshire

Duns (1894)
Hardens Road, Duns TD11 3NR
Mem 300
Sec A Campbell (01361) 882717
Holes 9 L 5826 yds SSS 68
Recs Am–65 I Angus
V'tors U SOC
Fees £10 (£10)
Loc 1 mile W of Duns, off A6105

Eyemouth (1880)
Gunsgreen House, Eyemouth TD14 5DX
Tel **(018907) 50551**
Mem 310
Sec M Hope (018907) 50432
Pro C Maltman
Holes 9 L 4608 metres SSS 65
Recs Am–61 J Patterson (1991)
V'tors U exc WE am–NA
Fees D–£9
Loc 4 miles N of border, off A1

The Hirsel (1948)
Kelso Road, Coldstream TD12 4NJ
Tel **(01890) 882678**
Mem 700
Sec JC Balfour (01890) 883052
Holes 18 L 6092 yds SSS 69
Recs Am–64 M Ledgerwood (1990)
V'tors U SOC
Fees £15 (£20)
Loc 1/2 mile W of Coldstream (A697)

Lauder (1896)
Galashiels Road, Lauder
Tel **(01578) 722526**
Mem 180
Sec D Dickson
Holes 9 L 6002 yds SSS 70
Recs Am–70 JFC Jefferies
Pro–70 W Park Jr (1905)
V'tors U SOC
Fees £6 (£7)
Loc 1/2 mile W of Lauder

Peeblesshire

Innerleithen (1886)
Leithen Water, Leithen Road, Innerleithen EH44 6NL
Tel **(01896) 830951**
Mem 175
Sec S Wyse (01896) 830071
Holes 9 L 5984 yds SSS 69
Recs Am–67 WN Smith
V'tors U
Fees D–£10 (D–£12) W–£40
Loc 1 mile N of Innerleithen on Heriot road
Arch Willie Park

Peebles (1892)
Kirkland Street, Peebles
Tel **(01721) 720197**
Mem 600
Sec H Gilmore
Holes 18 L 6137 yds SSS 69
Recs Am–64 D Campbell, JK Wells
Pro–70 RDBM Shade
V'tors H SOC
Fees £16 D–£22 (£22 D–£30)
Loc 23 miles S of Edinburgh, via A703
Arch James Braid/HS Colt

West Linton (1890)
West Linton EH46 7HN
Tel **(01968) 660463**
Mem 615
Sec G Scott (01968) 660970
Pro R Forrest (01968) 660256
Holes 18 L 6132 yds SSS 70
Recs Am–63 S Walker (1992)
Pro–71 B Gallacher
V'tors WD–U WE–NA before 1pm
Fees £15 D–£22 (£25) W–£75
Loc NW of Peebles on A702. 18 miles S of Edinburgh

Roxburghshire

Hawick (1877)
Vertish Hill, Hawick
Tel **(01450) 72293**
Mem 700
Sec J Reilly
Holes 18 L 5929 yds SSS 69
Recs Am–63 AJ Ballantyne
Pro–64 N Faldo
V'tors H SOC
Fees £18 D–£25
Loc 1/2 mile S of Hawick

Jedburgh (1892)
Dunion Road, Jedburgh
Tel **(01835) 863587**
Mem 300
Sec R Strachan
Holes 9 L 5492 yds SSS 67
Recs Am–62 E Redpath (1990)
Pro–66 C Montgomerie (1992)
V'tors U
Fees £12
Loc Jedburgh 1 mile
Arch Willie Park

Kelso (1887)
Berrymoss Racecourse Road, Kelso
Tel **(01573) 23009**
Mem 350
Sec JP Payne (01573) 23259

Holes 18 L 6066 yds SSS 69
Recs Am–64 JF Thomas
V'tors U SOC
Fees On application
Loc 1 mile N of Kelso, inside racecourse

Melrose (1880)
Dingleton, Melrose
Tel **(0189) 682 2855**
Fax **(0189) 682 2960**
Mem 310
Sec W MacRae (0189) 682 2391
Holes 9 L 5579 yds SSS 68
Recs Am–62 G Matthew (1989)
V'tors WD–U before 4pm
Fees D–£14
Loc S boundary of Melrose, off A68

Minto (1928)
Denholm, Hawick
Tel **(01450) 870220**
Mem 600
Sec I Todd
Holes 18 L 5460 yds SSS 68
Recs Am–65 C Kerr (1994)
V'tors U SOC
Fees £12 (£18)
Loc Denholm, 6 miles E of Hawick

Newcastleton
Holm Hill, Newcastleton TD9 0QD
Tel **(013873) 75257**
Sec FJ Ewart
Holes 9 L 5748 yds Par 70 SSS 68
V'tors U SOC
Fees D–£7 (£8) W–£35
Loc E of Newcastleton, off B6357
Arch J Shade

St Boswells (1899)
St Boswells TD6 0AT
Tel **(01835) 823858/823527**
Mem 330
Holes 9 L 5250 yds SSS 65
Recs Am–61 CI Ovens (1989)
V'tors U SOC
Fees £10 D–£15 (£15)
Loc Off A68 at St Boswells Green, by River Tweed
Arch Willie Park/J Shade

Selkirkshire

Galashiels (1884)
Ladhope Recreation Ground, Galashiels TD1 2NJ
Tel **(01896) 753724**
Mem 366
Sec R Gass (01896) 755307
Holes 18 L 5309 yds SSS 67
Recs Am–61 I Frizzel
Pro–70 J Braid
V'tors U SOC
Fees £10 D–£14 (£12 D–£16)
Loc 1/4 mile NE of Galashiels, off A7

Selkirk (1883)
The Hill, Selkirk
Tel **(01750) 20621**
Mem 363
Sec R Davies (01750) 20427
Holes 9 L 5560 yds SSS 67
Recs Am–60 MD Cleghorn
V'tors WD–U exc Mon pm SOC
Fees D–£11
Loc 1 mile S of Selkirk on A7
Arch Willie Park

Torwoodlee (1895)
Galashiels
Tel **(01896) 2260**
Mem 400
Sec A Wilson
Holes 9 L 5800 yds SSS 68
Recs Am–64 RV Rutherford, A Wilson
V'tors WD–U exc Thurs–NA after 1pm Sat–by application SOC
Fees £14 (£18)
Loc 1 mile N of Galashiels on A7
Mis Extension to 18 holes 1995
Arch Willie Park

CENTRAL REGION

Clackmannanshire

Alloa (1891)
Schawpark, Sauchie, Alloa FK10 3AX
Tel **(01259) 722745**
Mem 535 80(L) 130(J)
Sec AM Frame (01259) 50100
Pro W Bennett (01259) 724476
Holes 18 L 6240 yds SSS 70
Recs Am–63 AJ Liddle
Pro–66 R Weir, G Harvey
V'tors U WE–no parties
Fees £14 D–£22 (£26) (1994)
Loc Sauchie, N of Alloa
Arch James Braid

Alva
Beauclerc Street, Alva FK12 5LE
Tel **(01259) 760431**
Mem 320
Holes 9 L 2423 yds SSS 64
Recs Am–63 R Lyon, G Kennedy, N Chalmers (1990)
V'tors U
Fees On application
Loc Back Road, Alva, on A91 Stirling-St Andrews road

Braehead (1891)
Cambus, Alloa FK10 2NT
Tel **(01259) 722078**
Mem 800
Sec P MacMichael
Pro P Brookes
Holes 18 L 6013 yds SSS 68
Recs Am–64 D Mackison
V'tors U–booking necessary SOC
Fees £12 D–£20 (£20 D–£28)
Loc 2 miles W of Alloa (A907)

Dollar (1890)
Brewlands House, Dollar FK14 7EA
Tel **(01259) 742400**
Mem 480
Sec JC Brown
Holes 18 L 5242 yds SSS 66
Recs Am–64 D Ross
V'tors U SOC
Fees £8 D–£12 (£16)
Loc Dollar, off A91

Muckhart (1908)
Muckhart, Dollar FK14 7JH
Tel **(01259) 781423**
Mem 550 125(L) 100(J)
Sec J Muston (Mgr)
Pro K Salmoni
Holes 18 L 6034 yds SSS 70
Recs Am–66 E Carnegie (1983)
V'tors U SOC
Fees £12.50 (£18)
Loc A91, 3 miles E of Dollar, towards Rumbling Bridge

Tillicoultry (1899)
Alva Road, Tillicoultry FK13 6BL
Tel **(01259) 50124**
Mem 400
Sec R Whitehead
Holes 9 L 2528 yds SSS 66
Recs Am–63 P Morris
V'tors WD/WE–U SOC
Fees £9 (£15)
Loc 9 miles E of Stirling

Tulliallan (1902)
Kincardine, Alloa
Tel **(01259) 30396**
Mem 525 53(L) 100(J)
Sec JS McDowall (01324) 485420
Pro S Kelly (01259) 30798
Holes 18 L 5982 yds SSS 69
Recs Am–65 A Pickles, D Johnson
Pro–70 D Huish, S Walker, G Gray
V'tors U exc comp days
Fees On application
Loc 5 miles SE of Alloa

Perthshire

Callander (1890)
Aveland Road, Callander FK17 8EN
Tel **(01877) 330090**
Mem 700
Sec I Scott
Pro W Kelly (01877) 330975
Holes 18 L 5125 yds SSS 66
Recs Am–61 B Collier
Pro–59 D Matthew
V'tors U SOC
Fees On application
Loc Off A84, E end of Callander
Arch Tom Morris

Dunblane New (1923)
Perth Road, Dunblane FK15 0LJ
Tel **(01786) 823711**
Fax **(01786) 825946**
Mem 600
Sec RS MacRae
Pro RM Jamieson
Holes 18 L 5878 yds SSS 68
Recs Am–64 GK McDonald, AY Wilson, S Morrison
Pro–64 RM Jamieson
V'tors WD–Mon/Tues/Thurs/Fri am WE–M SOC
Fees £16 (£23)
Loc E side of Dunblane. 6 miles N of Stirling

Killin (1913)
Killin FK21 8TX
Tel **(01567) 820312**
Mem 298
Sec A Chisholm
Holes 9 L 2410 yds SSS 65
Recs Am–61 G Smith
V'tors U SOC–Apr–Oct
Fees £9 (£12)
Loc Killin, W end of Loch Tay
Arch John Duncan

Stirlingshire

Aberfoyle (1890)
Braeval, Aberfoyle FK8 3UY
Tel **(018772) 382493**
Mem 600
Sec RD Steele (018772) 382638
Holes 18 L 5204 yds SSS 66
Recs Am–64 EJ Barnard
V'tors WD–U WE–NA before 10.30am
Fees D–£12 (£16)
Loc Braeval, 18 miles NW of Stirling (A81)

Balmore (1906)
Balmore, Torrance
Tel **(01360) 2120240**
Mem 700
Sec GP Woolard (0141) 332 0392
Holes 18 L 5735 yds SSS 67
Recs Am–63 A Brodie
V'tors M SOC
Fees On application
Loc 4 miles N of Glasgow, off A807

Bonnybridge (1924)
Larbert Road, Bonnybridge
Tel **(01324) 812822**
Mem 425
Sec C Munn
Holes 9 L 6058 yds SSS 69
Recs Am–66 D Riddell, S Hunter
Pro–66 J McTear
V'tors WD–I
Fees On application
Loc 3 miles W of Falkirk

Bridge of Allan (1895)
Sunnylaw, Bridge of Allan
Tel **(01786) 832332**
Mem 300
Sec S Green, M Watson
Holes 9 L 4932 yds SSS 65
Recs Am–62 ID McFarlane
V'tors U exc Sat
Fees £8 (£12)
Loc 4 miles N of Stirling, off A9
Arch Tom Morris Sr

Buchanan Castle (1936)
Drymen G63 0HY
Tel **(01360) 660369**
Mem 830
Sec R Kinsella (01360) 660307
Pro K Baxter (01360) 660330
Holes 18 L 6015 yds SSS 69
Recs Am–64 C Dunan
Pro–66 D Huish, W Milne
V'tors M or by arrangement with Sec
Fees On application
Loc 18 miles NW of Glasgow. 25 miles W of Stirling, off A811
Arch James Braid

Campsie (1897)
Crow Road, Lennoxtown
Tel **(01360) 310244**
Mem 600
Pro D Baxter
Holes 18 L 5517 yds SSS 67
Recs Am–70 J Hope
Pro–73 K Stevely
V'tors WD–U before 4.30pm
Fees £10
Loc N of Lennoxtown on B822 Fintry road

Falkirk (1922)
Stirling Road, Camelon, Falkirk FK2 7YP
Tel **(01324) 611061/612219**
Mem 700
Sec J Elliott
Pro C Gillies
Holes 18 L 6282 yds SSS 69
Recs Am–66
Pro–66
V'tors WD–U until 4pm Sat–NA SOC–exc Sat
Fees £12 D–£20 (£25 D–£30)
Loc 1½ miles W of Falkirk on A9

Falkirk Tryst (1885)
86 Burnhead Road, Larbert FK5 4BD
Tel **(01324) 562415**
Mem 800
Sec RD Wallace (01324) 562054
Pro S Dunsmore (01324) 562091
Holes 18 L 6053 yds SSS 69
Recs Am–64 J Rankin
Pro–65 J Chillas
V'tors WD–U WE–M SOC–exc BH
Fees £13 D–£18
Loc 3 miles NW of Falkirk

Glenbervie (1932)
Stirling Road, Larbert FK5 4SJ
Tel **(01324) 562605**
Mem 600
Sec Mrs M Purves
Pro J Chillas (01324) 562725
Holes 18 L 6469 yds SSS 70
Recs Am–64 KW Goodwin (1989)
Pro–63 C Innes
V'tors WD–I WE–M SOC–Tues & Thurs
Fees £25 D–£35
Loc 1 mile N of Larbert on Stirling road

Grangemouth (1973)
Public
Polmonthill, Grangemouth FK2 0YA
Tel **(01324) 711500**
Mem 700
Sec I Hutton
Pro SJ Campbell (01324) 714355
Holes 18 L 6527 yds SSS 71
Recs Am–67 N Scaife (1990)
V'tors U–book with Pro SOC
Fees £5.50 D–£8.30 (£7.40 D–£10.20)
Loc 3 miles NE of Falkirk. M9 Junction 4

Kilsyth Lennox (1900)
Tak-Ma-Doon Road, Kilsyth G65 0RS
Tel **(01236) 823525 (Bookings)**
Mem 250
Sec AG Stevenson (01236) 823213
Holes 18 L 5930 yds Par 70
Recs Am–66 R Irvine (1986), W Erskine (1987)
V'tors WD–U until 5pm –M after 5pm Sat–NA before 4pm Sun–NA before 2pm SOC
Fees On application
Loc N of Kilsyth and A803. 12 miles NE of Glasgow

Polmont (1901)
Manuel Rigg, Maddiston, Falkirk FK2 0LS
Tel **(01324) 711277 (Clubhouse)**
Mem 300
Sec P Lees (01324) 713811
Holes 9 L 3044 yds SSS 69
Recs Am–69 W Shanks
V'tors U exc Sat–NA
Fees £7 Sun–£12
Loc 4 miles SE of Falkirk

Stirling (1869)
Queen's Road, Stirling FK8 2AA
Tel **(01786) 473801**
Fax **(01786) 450748**
Mem 1000
Sec WC McArthur (01786) 464098
Pro I Collins (01786) 471490
Holes 18 L 6409 yds SSS 71
Recs Am–66 KA Brunton (1993)
Pro–66 G Everitt (1993)
V'tors WD–U WE–NA SOC
Fees On application
Loc King's Park, Stirling
Arch James Braid

For list of abbreviations see page 435

Strathendrick (1901)
Glasgow Road, Drymen G63
Tel **(01360) 660695**
Mem 480
Sec R Smith (01360) 440582
Holes 9 L 5116 yds SSS 64
Recs Am–60 P Haggarty
Pro–64 C Dernie
V'tors M
Loc 25 miles W of Stirling, off A811

DUMFRIES & GALLOWAY

Dumfriesshire

Crichton Royal (1884)
Bankend Road, Dumfries DG1 4TH
Tel **(01387) 41122**
Fax **(01387) 66939**
Mem 400
Sec AB McKay
Holes 9 L 3084 yds SSS 69
Recs Am–67 RB Shearman
Pro–67 D Gemmell
V'tors WD–U before 3pm SOC
Fees £6 (£12)
Loc 1 mile from Dumfries, nr Hospital

Dumfries & County (1912)
Nunfield, Edinburgh Road, Dumfries DG1 1JX
Tel **(01387) 53585**
Mem 600 150(L) 100(J)
Sec EC Pringle
Pro GD Gray (01387) 68918
Holes 18 L 5928 yds SSS 68
Recs Am–64 D James, IR Brotherston, W Blayney, M Townsley
Pro–63 A Thomson, F Mann, J McAlister
V'tors WD–U exc 12.30–2pm–NA Sat–NA Sun–NA before 10am
Fees £21 (£25)
Loc 1 mile NE of Dumfries, on A701

Dumfries & Galloway (1880)
Laurieston Avenue, Maxwelltown, Dumfries
Tel **(01387) 253582**
Mem 450
Sec J Donnachie (01387) 263848
Pro J Fergusson (01387) 256902
Holes 18 L 5782 yds SSS 68
Recs Am–62 A Miller
Pro–63 K Baxter
V'tors U
Fees £20 (£24)

Gretna (1991)
Kirtle View, Gretna DG16 5HD
Tel **(01461) 338464**
Sec G & E Birnie (Props)
Holes 9 L 6430 yds SSS 71
V'tors U SOC
Fees £8 (£10)
Loc 1 mile W of Gretna, off A75
Mis Driving range

Hoddom Castle (1973)
Pay and play
Hoddom, Lockerbie DG11 1AS
Tel **(01576) 300251**
Sec D Laycock
Holes 9 L 2274 yds SSS 33
V'tors U
Fees £5 (£6)
Loc 2 miles SW of Ecclefechan on B725. M74 Junction 6

Langholm (1892)
Langholm
Tel **(013873) 80559**
Mem 150
Sec WJ Brown (013873) 80395
Holes 9 L 2872 yds SSS 68
Recs Am–66 C Hislop
V'tors U
Fees £10 (£10)
Loc 18 miles E of Lockerbie

Lochmaben (1926)
Castlehill Gate, Lochmaben DG11 1NT
Tel **(01387) 810552**
Mem 650
Sec JM Dickie
Holes 9 L 5304 yds SSS 66
Recs Am–62 D Hutchison
Pro–64 G Gray
V'tors WD–U before 5pm WE–U exc comp days
Fees £12 (£15)
Loc 4 miles W of Lockerbie on A709. 8 miles NE of Dumfries
Mis Extension to 18 holes 1995

Lockerbie (1889)
Corrie Road, Lockerbie DG11 2ND
Tel **(01576) 203363**
Mem 620
Sec J Thomson (01576) 202462
Holes 18 L 5418 yds SSS 66
Recs Am–65 R Nairn (1988)
Ladies–69 M Wright (1991)
V'tors U exc Sun–NA before 11.30am
Fees £14 Sat–£18 Sun–£16
Loc 1/2 mile NE of Lockerbie, on Corrie road
Arch James Braid

Moffat (1884)
Coatshill, Moffat DG10 9SB
Tel **(01683) 20020**
Mem 350
Sec TA Rankin
Pro None
Holes 18 L 5218 yds SSS 66
Recs Am–60 GJ Rodaks (1979)
V'tors WD–restricted Wed after 12 noon
Fees D–£17 (D–£25)
Loc Signposted on A701 from Beattock (A74)
Arch Ben Sayers

Powfoot (1903)
Cummertrees, Annan DG12 5QE
Tel **(01461) 700227**
Mem 820
Sec RG Anderson (01461) 202866
Pro G Dick (01461) 700327
Holes 18 L 6266 yds SSS 70
Recs Am–64 B Scott
Pro–67 J Stevens
V'tors WD–U Sat–NA Sun–NA before 2pm
Fees Winter £11 5D–£44
Summer D–£25 5D–£72
Loc 4 miles W of Annan. 15 miles SE of Dumfries, off B724

Sanquhar (1894)
Blackaddie Road, Sanquhar
Tel **(01659) 50577**
Mem 180
Sec Mrs J Murray (01659) 58181
Holes 9 L 5630 yds SSS 68
Recs Am–66 I Brotherston (1982)
J Copeland
V'tors U SOC
Fees On application
Loc 1/2 mile W of Sanquhar (A76). 30 miles N of Dumfries

Southerness (1947)
Southerness, Dumfries DG2 8AZ
Tel **(01387) 88677**
Fax **(01387) 88644**
Mem 800
Sec WD Ramage
Holes 18 L 6566 yds SSS 73
Recs Am–65 M Gronberg (1990)
V'tors H–phone first SOC
Fees D–£24 (D–£32)
Loc 16 miles S of Dumfries, off A710
Arch Mackenzie Ross

Thornhill (1893)
Black Nest, Thornhill DG3
Tel **(01848) 330546**
Mem 700
Sec JFK Crichton
Holes 18 L 6011 yds SSS 69
Recs Am–63 AJ Coltart (1990)
V'tors U
Fees On application
Loc 14 miles NW of Dumfries (A76)

For list of abbreviations see page 435

Kirkcudbrightshire

Castle Douglas (1905)
Abercromby Road, Castle Douglas
Tel **(01556) 502801/502099**
Mem 450
Sec AD Millar
Holes 9 L 5400 yds SSS 66
Recs Am–62 W Blayney, J Shepherd (1989)
V'tors U
Fees £12 (£15)
Loc Off A75/A713, NE of Castle Douglas

Colvend (1908)
Sandyhills, Dalbeattie DG5 4PY
Tel **(0155) 663 398**
Mem 400
Sec JB Henderson
Holes 9 L 2322 yds SSS 62
Recs Am–63 W Blayney (1990)
V'tors WD–U before 5pm –NA after 5pm (May–July) SOC
Fees £12
Loc 6 miles S of Dalbeattie on A710

Dalbeattie (1897)
Dalbeattie
Tel **(01556) 611421**
Mem 280
Sec T Moffat
Holes 9 L 4200 yds SSS 60
V'tors U
Fees On application
Loc 14 miles SW of Dumfries

Gatehouse (1921)
Gatehouse of Fleet
Mem 290
Sec P Colville (01557) 814734
Holes 9 L 2398 yds SSS 64
Recs Am–60 S Martin
V'tors U
Fees On application
Loc 3/4 mile N of Gatehouse. 9 miles NW of Kirkcudbright

Kirkcudbright (1893)
Stirling Crescent, Kirkcudbright DG6 4EZ
Tel **(01557) 330314**
Mem 500
Sec JH Sommerville
Holes 18 L 5598 yds SSS 67
Recs Am–62 S Calladine (1983), I Brotherston (1986) Ladies–70 F Rennie (1994)
V'tors U
Fees £15 W–£50
Loc Kirkcudbright

New Galloway (1902)
New Galloway
Tel **(016442) 737**
Mem 266
Sec AR Brown
Holes 9 L 5006 yds SSS 65
Recs Am–65 C White (1991), B Swanston (1993)
V'tors U
Fees D–£10
Loc S of New Galloway on A762. 20 miles N of Kirkcudbright
Arch Baillie

Wigtownshire

Newton Stewart (1981)
Kirroughtree Avenue, Minnigaff, Newton Stewart DG8 6PF
Tel **(01671) 402172**
Mem 300
Sec DC Matthewson
Holes 18 L 5970 yds SSS 69
Recs Am–64 IS Thomson (1990)
V'tors U H
Fees £14 D–£17 (£17 D–£20)
Loc N of Newton Stewart, off A75

Portpatrick Dunskey (1903)
Golf Course Road, Portpatrick DG9 8TB
Tel **(01776) 810273**
Fax **(01776) 810811**
Mem 480
Sec JA Horberry
Holes Dunskey 18 L 5882 yds SSS 68 Dinvin 9 hole Par 3 course
Recs Am–R Shaw Pro–64 B Dunbar, B Deas (1993) Ladies–71 M Wilson
V'tors U H SOC
Fees £15 D–£22 (£18 D–£27) W–£70 Dinvin £6 D–£12
Loc 8 miles SW of Stranraer

St Medan (1905)
Monreith, Newton Stewart DG8 8NJ
Tel **(01988) 700358**
Mem 300
Sec D O'Neill (01988) 500555
Holes 9 L 2277 yds SSS 63
Recs Am–60 J Grundy (1990)
V'tors U SOC
Fees £12
Loc 3 miles S of Port William, off A747

Stranraer (1906)
Creachmore, Leswalt, Stranraer DQ9 0LF
Tel **(01776) 870245**
Mem 547
Sec WI Wilson CA (01776) 703539
Holes 18 L 6308 yds SSS 72
Recs Am–66 CG Findlay Pro–72 J Panton
V'tors WE–NA before 9.30am and 11.45am–1.30pm
Fees £16 (£21)
Loc 2 miles N of Stranraer on A718
Arch James Braid

Wigtown & Bladnoch (1960)
Lightlands Terrace, Wigtown DG8 9EF
Tel **(01988) 403354**
Mem 150
Sec JI Alexander
Holes 9 L 2731 yds SSS 67
Recs Am–62 R Shaw
V'tors U SOC
Fees £10 (£10)
Loc Between Wigtown and Bladnoch, off A714

Wigtownshire County (1894)
Mains of Park, Glenluce, Newton Stewart DG8 0NN
Tel **(01581) 300420**
Mem 412
Sec R McKnight
Pro None
Holes 18 L 5823 yds SSS 68
Recs Am–64 A Lightbody (1993)
V'tors U exc Wed–NA after 6pm
Fees £16 D–£20 (£18 D–£22)
Loc 8 miles E of Stranraer on A75
Arch W Gordon Cunningham

FIFE REGION

Fife

Aberdour (1896)
Seaside Place, Aberdour KY3 0TX
Tel **(01383) 860256**
Fax **(01383) 860080**
Mem 420 160(L)
Sec JJ Train (01383) 860080
Pro G McCallum (01383) 860256
Holes 18 L 5460 yds SSS 67
Recs Am–63 S Meiklejohn (1990)
V'tors WD–book with Pro Sat–NA SOC
Fees £17 D–£28
Loc 8 miles SE of Dunfermline, on coast
Arch Robertson/Anderson

Anstruther (1890)
Marsfield Shore Road, Anstruther KY10 3DZ
Tel **(01333) 310956**
Fax **(01333) 312283**
Mem 500
Sec JF MacLeod
Holes 9 L 4504 yds SSS 63
Recs Am–62 G Taylor (1992) Pro–61 I Collins (1990)
V'tors U SOC
Fees £11 (£15) (1994)
Loc 9 miles S of St Andrews

Auchterderran (1904)

Public
Woodend Road, Cardenden KY5 0NH
Tel **(01592) 721579**
Mem 100
Sec W Nicolson
Holes 9 L 5400 yds SSS 66
Recs Am–66 C McRae
V'tors U
Fees On application
Loc 1 mile N of Cardenden. 6 miles W of Kirkcaldy, off A910

Balbirnie Park (1983)

Balbirnie Park, Markinch, Glenrothes KY7 6DD
Tel **(01592) 752006**
Mem 800
Sec AD Gordon
Holes 18 L 6210 yds SSS 70
Recs Am–66 G Birnie
Pro–69 C Gillies, S Walker
V'tors U–booking recommended
Fees £20 D–£27 (£28 D–£36)
Loc 2 miles E of Glenrothes

Ballingry (1908)

Public
Lochore Meadows Country Park, Crosshill, Lochgelly
Tel **(01592) 860086**
Mem 150
Sec W Glencross (01592) 861316
Holes 9 L 6482 yds SSS 71
Recs Am–68 S Meiklejohn (1990)
V'tors U
Fees On application
Loc 2 miles N of Lochgelly (B920)

Burntisland (1797)

51 Craigkennochie Terrace, Burntisland KY3 9EN
Tel **(01592) 872728**
Mem 100
Sec AD McPherson
Holes Play over Dodhead Course, Burntisland

Burntisland Golf House Club (1898)

Dodhead, Burntisland KY3 9EY
Tel **(01592) 873247**
Mem 780
Sec I McLean (Mgr)
(01592) 874093
Pro J Montgomery
Holes 18 L 5908 yds SSS 69
Recs Am–65 DA Paton
Pro–64 C Fraser
V'tors U
Fees £15 D–£21 (£25 D–£35)
Loc 1 mile E of Burntisland on B923
Arch Willie Park Jr/James Braid

Canmore (1898)

Venturefair, Dunfermline
Tel **(01383) 724969**
Mem 580 90(L) 80(J)
Sec JC Duncan (01383) 726098
Pro (01383) 728416
Holes 18 L 5437 yds SSS 66
Recs Am–61 R Wallace
V'tors WD–U WE–restricted
Fees £12 D–£18
Loc 1 mile N of Dunfermline on A823

Cowdenbeath (1991)

Public
Seco Place, Cowdenbeath
Tel **(01383) 511918**
Sec J Martin
Holes 9 L 6552 yds SSS 71
V'tors U
Fees £5.50 (£8.05)
Loc In Cowdenbeath, signposted from A909

Crail Golfing Society (1786)

Balcomie Clubhouse, Fifeness, Crail KY10 3XN
Tel **(01333) 450278**
Mem 750 200(L)
Sec Mrs M Hunter
(01333) 450686
Pro G Lennie (01333) 450960
Holes 18 L 5720 yds SSS 68
Recs Am–64 RW Malcolm
Pro–63 G Lennie
V'tors U
Fees On application
Loc 11 miles SE of St Andrews

Cupar (1855)

Hilltarvit, Cupar KY15 5JT
Tel **(01334) 653549**
Mem 475
Sec CJ McCulloch
(01334) 652176
Holes 9 L 5074 yds SSS 65
Recs Am–61 TR Spence
V'tors WD–U Sat–NA
SOC–WD/Sun
Fees £10 (£12)
Loc 10 miles W of St Andrews

Dunfermline (1887)

Pitfirrane, Crossford, Dunfermline KY12 8QV
Tel **(01383) 723534**
Mem 520
Sec R De Rose
Pro S Craig
Holes 18 L 6243 yds SSS 70
Recs Am–65 RW Malcolm
Pro–65 A Brooks
V'tors WD–U before 5pm –M after 5pm SOC
Fees £18 D–£28 (£25 D–£35)
Loc 2 miles W of Dunfermline on A994
Arch JR Stutt

Dunnikier Park (1963)

Public
Dunnikier Way, Kirkcaldy KY1 3LP
Tel **(01592) 261599**
Mem 600 35(L) 75(J)
Sec RA Waddell (01592) 200627
Pro G Whyte
Holes 18 L 6601 yds SSS 72
Recs Am–65 S Duthie (1988)
Pro–65 A Hunter (1988)
V'tors U SOC
Fees £10 (£14)
Loc N boundary of Kirkcaldy

Earlsferry Thistle (1875)

Melon Park, Elie KY9 1AS
Mem 60
Sec J Fyall
Holes Play over Golf House Club Course

Falkland (1976)

Public
The Myre, Falkland KY7 7AA
Tel **(01337) 857404**
Mem 350
Sec Mrs H Horsburgh
Holes 9 L 2384 metres SSS 66
Recs Am–62 AD Morrison (1993)
V'tors U SOC
Fees On application
Loc 5 miles N of Glenrothes on A912

Glenrothes (1958)

Public
Golf Course Road, Glenrothes KY6 2LA
Tel **(01592) 754561/758686**
Mem 800 35(L) 95(J)
Sec Mrs PV Landells
(01592) 756941
Holes 18 L 6444 yds SSS 71
Recs Am–65 C Birrell, NM Urquhart
Pro–69 R Craig, B Lawson
Ladies–70 L McKinlay (1989)
V'tors U
Fees £9 (£11)
Loc Glenrothes West, off A92. M90 Junction 3
Arch JR Stutt

Golf House Club (1875)

Elie, Leven KY9 1AS
Tel **(01333) 330327**
Fax **(01333) 330895**
Sec A Sneddon (01333) 330301
Pro R Wilson (01333) 330955
Holes 18 L 6261 yds SSS 70
9 L 2277 yds SSS 32
Recs Am–63 AW Mathers
Pro–62 K Nagle
V'tors July–Sept ballot. WE–no party bookings. WE–NA before 3pm (May–Sept)
Fees £24 D–£32 (£36 D–£48)
Loc 12 miles S of St Andrews

Kinghorn Ladies (1905)

Golf Clubhouse, McDuff Crescent, Kinghorn KY3 9RE
Tel **(01592) 890345**
Mem 38
Sec Miss E Douglas
(01592) 890512
Holes Play over Kinghorn Municipal

Kinghorn Municipal (1887)

Public
McDuff Crescent, Kinghorn KY3 9RE
Tel **(01592) 890345**
Fax **(01592) 55761**
Sec JP Robertson (01592) 203397
Pro None
Holes 18 L 5629 yds SSS 67
Recs Am–64 G Wilkinson (1991)
V'tors U SOC
Fees £7.60 (£10)
Loc 3 miles S of Kirkcaldy (A921)
Mis Kinghorn and Kinghorn Thistle Clubs play here
Arch Tom Morris

Kirkcaldy (1904)

Balwearie Road, Kirkcaldy KY2 5LT
Tel **(01592) 260370**
Mem 450 100(L)
Sec AC Thomson (01592) 205240
Pro S McKay (01592) 203258
Holes 18 L 6007 yds SSS 70
Recs Am–66 G Ridsdale, S Swan
V'tors U
Fees On application
Loc S end of Kirkcaldy

Ladybank (1879)

Annsmuir, Ladybank KY7 7RA
Tel **(01337) 830320 (Clubhouse), (01337) 830725 (Starter)**
Fax **(01337) 831505**
Mem 800
Sec AM Dick (01337) 830814
Pro MJ Gray (01337) 830725
Holes 18 L 6641 yds SSS 72
Recs Am–66 B Williams (1992), S Meiklejohn (1993) Pro–66 W Reilly, P Stewart (1984), K Knox (1990)
V'tors WD–U 9.30am–4.30pm M–after 4.30pm WE–NA 10.15am–5pm
Fees £26 (£28) W–£100
Loc 6 miles SW of Cupar

Leslie (1898)

Balsillie Laws, Leslie, Glenrothes KY6 3EZ
Tel **(01592) 620040**
Mem 300
Sec M Burns
Holes 9 L 4940 yds SSS 64
Recs Am–59 R Bremer Pro–64 J Chillas
V'tors U
Fees £5 (£8)
Loc 3 miles W of Glenrothes. M90 Junction 5/7, 11 miles

Leven Golfing Society (1820)

Links Road, Leven KY8 4HS
Tel **(01333) 426096/424229**
Mem 676
Sec J Bennett (01333) 423898
Holes Play over Leven Links

Leven Links (1846)

The Promenade, Leven KY8 4HS
Tel **(01333) 421390 (Starter)**
Fax **(01333) 428859**
Mem 1200
Sec (01333) 428859 (Links Joint Committee)
Pro G Finlayson (01333) 426381
Holes 18 L 6434 yds SSS 71
Recs Am–64 J Hawkesworth (1984), K Goodwin (1986), B McDermott (1991) Pro–63 P Hoad (1984)
V'tors WD–U before 5pm Sat–no parties Sun–NA before 10.30am SOC
Fees £20 (£24)
Loc E of Leven, on promenade. 12 miles SW of St Andrews

Leven Thistle (1867)

3 Balfour Street, Leven KY8 4JF
Tel **(01333) 426397**
Mem 500
Sec J Scott (01333) 426333
Holes Play over Leven Links

Lochgelly (1910)

Cartmore Road, Lochgelly
Tel **(01592) 780174**
Mem 450
Sec RF Stuart (01383) 512238
Holes 18 L 5491 yds SSS 67
Recs Am–64 D Walker (1988)
V'tors U
Fees £10 (£16)
Loc NW edge of Lochgelly. 5 miles W of Kirkcaldy

Lundin (1869)

Golf Road, Lundin Links KY8 6BA
Tel **(01333) 320202**
Mem 700
Sec AC McBride
Pro DK Webster (01333) 320051
Holes 18 L 6377 yds SSS 71
Recs Am–65 KWS Gray, S Machin Pro–63 AD Hare
V'tors WD–U H Sat–NA before 2.30pm Sun–M H
Fees £20 D–£30 Sat–£30
Loc 3 miles E of Leven

Lundin Ladies (1891)

Woodielea Road, Lundin Links KY8 6AR
Tel **(01333) 320022/320832**
Mem 350
Sec Mrs E Davidson (01333) 320490
Holes 9 L 4730 yds SSS 67
Recs Am–67 Miss L Bennett
V'tors U
Fees On application
Loc 3 miles E of Leven

Methil (1892)

Links House, Links Road, Leven KY8 4HS
Tel **(01333) 425535**
Mem 50
Sec ATJ Traill
Holes Play over Leven Links

Pitreavie (1922)

Queensferry Road, Dunfermline KY11 5PR
Tel **(01383) 722591**
Mem 700
Sec D Carter
Pro J Forrester (01383) 723151
Holes 18 L 6005 yds SSS 69
Recs Am–65 D Manson (1990) Pro–67 D Rees
V'tors U–phone Pro SOC (Parties–max 36–must be booked in advance)
Fees £14 D–£19 (£25) (1994)
Loc 2 miles off M90 Junction 2, between Rosyth and Dunfermline
Arch Dr A Mackenzie

St Michael's (1903)

Leuchars
Tel **(01334) 839365**
Fax **(01334) 838666**
Mem 300
Sec LM McIntosh
Holes 9 L 5578 yds SSS 68
Recs Am–65 N Manzie (1991)
V'tors Sun am–NA (Mar–Oct) SOC
Fees D–£12
Loc 5 miles N of St Andrews on Dundee road (A919)

Saline (1912)

Kinneddar Hill, Saline
Tel **(01383) 852591**
Mem 400
Sec R Hutchison (01383) 852344
Holes 9 L 5302 yds SSS 66
Recs Am–A Brown
V'tors U exc medal Sat
Fees £8 (£10)
Loc 5 miles NW of Dunfermline

Scoonie (1952)

Public
North Links, Leven KY8 1DH
Tel **(01333) 27057**
Sec KD Houston
Holes 18 L 5600 yds SSS 66
Recs Am–63 P Lamont
V'tors U SOC
Fees On application
Loc Adjoins Leven Links

Scotscraig (1817)

Golf Road, Tayport DD6 9DZ
Tel **(01382) 552515**
Mem 600
Sec K Gourlay
Pro J Farmer (Hon)
Holes 18 L 6496 yds SSS 71
Recs Am–69 D Landsborough Pro–69 C Maltman, D Thomson
V'tors WD–U WE–by prior arrangement SOC
Fees On application
Loc 10 miles N of St Andrews

Thornton (1921)
Station Road, Thornton KY1 4DW
Tel (01592) 771111
Mem 630
Sec BSL Main
Holes 18 L 6175 yds SSS 69
Recs Am–64 A McDonaugh (1994)
V'tors U
Fees £14 D–£20 (£20 D–£30)
Loc 5 miles N of Kirkcaldy, off A92

St Andrews Clubs

New Golf Club (1902)
3-6 Gibson Place, St Andrews KY16 9JE
Tel (01334) 473426
Mem 1500
Sec AJ Dochard (Sec/Mgr)
Holes Play over St Andrews Links

Royal & Ancient (1754)
St Andrews KY16 9JD
Tel (01334) 472112
Fax (01334) 477580
Mem 1800
Sec MF Bonallack OBE
Holes Play over St Andrews Links

St Andrews (1843)
Links House, The Links, St Andrews KY16 9JB
Tel (01334) 474637
Fax (01334) 479577
Mem 1600
Sec K Barber (Sec/Mgr) (0334) 73017
Holes Play over St Andrews Links

St Andrews Thistle (1817)
St Andrews KY16 9JB
Mem 190
Sec DL Joy (01334) 473749
Holes Play over St Andrews Links

St Regulus Ladies'
9 Pilmour Links, St Andrews KY16 9JG
Mem 186
Sec Mrs N Davidson (01382) 543183
Holes Play over St Andrews Links

The St Rule Club (1898)
12 The Links, St Andrews KY16 9JB
Tel (01334) 472988
Mem 200
Sec Mrs JA Sanderson (Golf), Mrs S Bishop (Club)
Holes Play over St Andrews Links

St Andrews Courses

Balgove (1972)
Public
St Andrews KY16 9JA
Tel (01334) 475757
Fax (01334) 477036
Holes 9 L 1520 yds (Beginners course)
V'tors U
Fees £5
Loc St Andrews Links
Mis Driving range
Arch Donald Steel

Eden Course (1913)
Public
St Andrews KY16 9JA
Tel (01334) 475757 (Bookings)/ 474296
Fax (01334) 477036
Holes 18 L 6112 yds SSS 70
Recs Am–72 RW Guy, A Clark
V'tors U SOC
Fees £15–£18
Loc St Andrews Links
Mis 3D–£60 W–£120 (unlimited play over Jubilee, New, Eden, Strathtyrum and Balgove courses)

Jubilee Course (1897)
Public
St Andrews
Tel (01334) 475757 (Bookings)/ 473938 (Starter)
Fax (01334) 477036
Holes 18 L 6805 yds SSS 73
V'tors U SOC
Fees £20–£25
Loc St Andrews Links
Mis 3D–£60 W–£120 (unlimited play over Jubilee, Eden & New courses)

New Course (1896)
Public
St Andrews KY16 9JA
Tel (01334) 475757 (Bookings)/ 473938 (Starter)
Fax (01334) 477036
Holes 18 L 6604 yds SSS 72
Recs Am–67 GM Mitchell Pro–63 F Jowie
V'tors U
Fees £20–£25
Loc St Andrews Links
Mis 3D–£60 W–£120 (unlimited play over Jubilee, New, Eden, Strathtyrum and Balgove courses)

Old Course (15th)
Public
St Andrews KY16 9JA
Tel (01334) 475757 (Bookings)/ 473393 (Starter)
Fax (01334) 477036
Holes 18 L 6566 yds SSS 72
Recs Am–66 C McLachlan Pro–62 C Strange (1987) Ladies–67 M McKay (1993)
V'tors H I No Sun play SOC
Fees £40–£50
Loc St Andrews Links
Mis Driving range

Strathtyrum Course (1993)
Public
St Andrews KY16 9JA
Tel (01334) 474296
Fax (01334) 477036
Holes 18 L 5094 yds
V'tors U SOC
Fees £12–£14
Loc St Andrews Links
Mis 3D–£60 W–£120 (unlimited play over Jubilee, New, Eden, Strathtyrum and Balgove courses)
Arch Donald Steel

GRAMPIAN REGION

Aberdeenshire

Aboyne (1883)
Formaston Park, Aboyne
Tel (013398) 86328
Mem 725 180(J)
Sec Mrs M MacLean (013398) 87078
Pro I Wright (013398) 86469
Holes 18 L 5910 yds SSS 68
Recs Am–62 G Forbes, C Forbes Pro–63 S Walker
V'tors U
Fees On application
Loc E end of Aboyne. 30 miles W of Aberdeen (A93)

Alford
Montgarrie Road, Alford AB33 8AE
Tel (019755) 62178
Mem 558
Sec Mrs M Ball
Holes 18 L 5290 yds SSS 66
V'tors WD–U WE–restricted on comp days SOC
Fees £9 (£15)
Loc 25 miles W of Aberdeen on A944

Auchmill (1975)
Public
Provost Rust Drive, Aberdeen
Tel (01224) 714577
Pro None
Holes 18 L 5439 metres SSS 69
V'tors U
Fees On application
Loc 3 miles NW of Aberdeen

Ballater (1892)
Victoria Road, Ballater AB35 5QX
Tel **(013397) 55567**
Fax **(013397) 55057**
Mem 670
Sec G Bryce (Mgr)
Pro F Smith (013397) 55658
Holes 18 L 6094 yds SSS 69
Recs Am–61 R Damron
Pro–62 K Stables
V'tors U
Fees On application
Loc 42 miles W of Aberdeen on A93

Balnagask
Public
St Fitticks Road, Aberdeen
Tel **(01224) 876407**
Pro I Smith
Holes 18 L 5472 metres SSS 69
V'tors U
Fees On application
Loc 1½ miles SE of Aberdeen

Bon Accord (1872)
19 Golf Road, Aberdeen AB2 1QB
Tel **(01224) 633464**
Mem 950
Sec JB Miller
Holes Play over King's Links

Braemar (1902)
Cluniebank Road, Braemar AB35 5XX
Tel **(013397) 41618**
Mem 287
Sec J Pennet (01224) 704471
Holes 18 L 4916 yds SSS 64
Recs Am–61 W Main (1989),
JF Hardie (1992),
C Forbes (1993)
Pro–64 L Vannett (1988)
V'tors U SOC
Fees £10 D–£14 (£14 D–£20) W–£50
Loc Braemar ½ mile. 17 miles W of Ballater
Arch J Anderson

Caledonian (1899)
20 Golf Road, Aberdeen AB2 1QB
Tel **(01224) 632443**
Mem 850
Sec GWK Mackie
Holes Play over King's Links

Cruden Bay (1899)
Cruden Bay AB42 7NN
Tel **(01779) 812285**
Fax **(01779) 812945**
Mem 1050
Sec RG Stewart
Pro RG Stewart (01779) 812414
Holes 18 L 6370 yds SSS 71
9 L 4710 yds SSS 62
Recs Am–66 PJ Macleod (1987),
D Jamieson (1989),
AJ Kerr (1993)
Pro–63 D Thomson (1989)
V'tors WD–U WE–H exc comp days SOC–WD
Fees £20 (£28)
Loc 22 miles NE of Aberdeen (A975)
Arch Thomas Simpson

Deeside (1903)
Bieldside, Aberdeen AB1 9DL
Tel **(01224) 869457**
Mem 600
Sec AG Macdonald (01224) 869457
Pro FJ Coutts (01224) 861041
Holes 18 L 5972 yds SSS 69
9 L 3316 yds SSS 36
Recs Am–64 AK Pirie, RH Willox, DA Rennie
Pro–64 S Torrance
V'tors I
Fees £20 (£25)
Loc 3 miles SW of Aberdeen on A93

Dunecht House (1925)
Dunecht, Skene AB3 7AX
Mem 360
Sec SRG Young (013306) 404
Holes 9 L 3135 yds SSS 70
Recs Am–72 A Angus (1987)
V'tors M
Loc 12 miles W of Aberdeen on A944

Fraserburgh (1881)
Philorth, Fraserburgh AB4 5TL
Tel **(01346) 516616**
Mem 610 72(L) 40(J)
Sec AD Stewart
Holes 18 L 6217 yds SSS 70
Recs Am–66 A Ritchie,
C McDonald,
A Ironside
Pro–67 I Smith
V'tors U SOC
Fees On application
Loc 1 mile SE of Fraserburgh

Hazlehead (1927)
Public
Hazlehead, Aberdeen
Tel **(01224) 321830**
Pro I Smith
Holes 18 L 5673 metres SSS 70
18 L 5303 metres SSS 68
9 L 2531 metres SSS 34
Recs Am–65 D Jamieson
Pro–67 P Oosterhuis
V'tors U
Fees On application
Loc 3 miles W of Aberdeen

Huntly (1892)
Cooper Park, Huntly AB54 4SH
Tel **(01466) 792643**
Mem 790
Sec G Alexander
Holes 18 L 5399 yds SSS 66
Recs Am–61 N Masson
V'tors U SOC
Fees D–£12 (D–£18) W–£60
Loc N side of Huntly. 38 miles NW of Aberdeen, off A96

Insch
Golf Terrace, Insch
Tel **(01464) 20363**
Mem 200
Sec Mrs A Sutherland (01464) 4315
Holes 9 L 5488 yds SSS 67
Recs Am–66 H McKenzie (1990)
V'tors U
Fees On application
Loc 28 miles NW of Aberdeen, off A96

Inverallochy
Public
Inverallochy, Fraserburgh AB43 5XX
Tel **(01346) 582000**
Mem 280
Sec GM Young (01346) 52324
Pro None
Holes 18 L 5137 yds SSS 65
Recs Am–60
V'tors U
Fees D–£10
Loc 4 miles E of Fraserburgh, off A92

Inverurie (1923)
Blackhall Road, Inverurie AB51 5JE
Tel **(01467) 620207**
Fax **(01467) 621051**
Mem 475 110(L)
Sec DL Taylor (01467) 624080
Pro H Ferguson (01467) 620193
Holes 18 L 5711 yds SSS 68
Recs Am–66 P Lovie,
B Cunningham
V'tors U SOC–WD
Fees D–£12 (£18) (1994)
Loc 1 mile W of Inverurie. 16 miles NW of Aberdeen

Kemnay (1908)
Monymusk Road, Kemnay AB51 5RA
Tel **(01467) 642225**
Mem 550
Sec D Imrie (01467) 643047
Holes 18 L 5903 yds SSS 69
Recs Am–70 (1994)
V'tors U
Fees £12 D–£17 (£14 D–£20)
Loc 15 miles W of Aberdeen (B993)

King's Links
Public
Golf Road, Aberdeen AB2 1QB
Tel **(01224) 632269**
Pro B Davidson (01224) 641577
Holes 18 L 5838 metres SSS 71
V'tors U
Fees On application
Loc 1 mile E of Aberdeen
Mis Driving range. Bon Accord, Caledonian and Northern Clubs play here

For list of abbreviations see page 435

Kintore (1911)

Kintore AB51 0UT

Tel **(01467) 32631**
Mem 460 66(L) 60(J)
Sec JA Smith
Holes 18 L 5985 yds SSS 69
Recs Am–65 K Bennet
Pro–66 K Walker
V'tors U
Fees On application
Loc 12 miles NW of Aberdeen on A96

McDonald (1927)

Ellon AB41 9AW

Tel **(01358) 720576**
Mem 650
Sec G Ironside
Pro R Urquhart (01358) 722891
Holes 18 L 5986 yds SSS 69
Recs Am–63
Pro–67
V'tors U
Fees On application
Loc 15 miles N of Aberdeen, off A92

Murcar (1909)

Bridge of Don, Aberdeen AB23 8BD

Tel **(01224) 704345**
Mem 830
Sec R Matthews (01224) 704354
Pro A White (01224) 704370
Holes 18 L 6226 yds SSS 71
9 hole course
Recs Am–65 R Grant, J Savege, E Morrison
Pro–65 PA Smith
V'tors WD–H before noon WE–H Sat–NA before 4pm Sun–NA before noon
Fees £18 D–£25 (D–£30)
Loc 5 miles N of Aberdeen. 9 hole course at Strabathie
Arch A Simpson

Newburgh-on-Ythan (1888)

Newburgh, Ellon AB41 0FB

Tel **(01358) 789438**
Mem 250 60(L) 80(J)
Sec AC Stevenson
Holes 9 L 6348 yds SSS 70
Recs Am–70
Pro–69 F Coutts
V'tors U exc Tues after 3pm–NA
Fees £10 (£12)
Loc 12 miles N of Aberdeen (A975)

Newmachar (1989)

Swailend, Newmachar, Aberdeen AB2 0UU

Tel **(01651) 863002**
Mem 800
Sec G McIntosh
Pro G Taylor (01651) 862127
Holes 18 L 6623 yds SSS 74
Recs Am–68 AJA Crombie (1992)
Pro–67 R Weir (1994)
V'tors H SOC
Fees £16 D–£24 (£20 D–£30)
Loc 12 miles N of Aberdeen on A947
Mis Driving range
Arch Dave Thomas

Oldmeldrum (1885)

Kirkbrae, Oldmeldrum AB51 0DJ

Tel **(01651) 872648**
Mem 800
Sec D Petrie (01651) 872383
Pro (01651) 873555
Holes 18 L 5988 yds Par 70 SSS 69
Recs Am–67 G Whyte (1994)
V'tors WD–U before 5pm
WE–phone first
Fees £10 (£15)
Loc 17 miles N of Aberdeen on A947

Peterculter (1989)

Oldtown, Burnside Road, Peterculter AB1 0LN

Tel **(01224) 734644**
Fax **(01224) 734644**
Mem 889
Sec RC Burnett (01224) 734994
Pro D Vannet (01224) 734994
Holes 18 L 5924 yds SSS 69
Recs Am–65 P Robb (1994)
V'tors WD–U before 4pm WE–U SOC–WD exc Mon
Fees £11–16 (£15–21)
Loc 8 miles W of Aberdeen on A93

Peterhead (1841)

Craigewan Links, Peterhead AB42 6LT

Tel **(01779) 472149**
Mem 620 55(L)
Sec W Bradford
Holes 18 L 6173 yds SSS 70
9 L 2237 yds SSS 62
Recs Am–64 K Buchan (1988)
Pro–64 J Farmer (1980)
V'tors U exc Sat–restricted
Fees D–£14 (D–£18)
Loc 2 miles N of Peterhead, on coast
Arch Willie Park Jr/James Braid

Portlethen (1983)

Badentoy Road, Portlethen, Aberdeen AB1 4YA

Tel **(01224) 781090**
Mem 1250
Sec D Black
Pro Muriel Thomson (01224) 782571
Holes 18 L 6735 yds SSS 72
Recs Am–68 G Esson (1993)
Pro–66 P Smith (1990)
V'tors WD–U WE–NA before 11am SOC
Fees £12 (£18)
Loc 6 miles S of Aberdeen on A92

Rosehearty

c/o Mason's Arms, Rosehearty, Fraserburgh

Tel **(01346) 571250 (Mem Sec)**
Mem 220
Sec A Downie
Holes 9 L 1684 yds SSS 58
Recs Am–59 R Ritchie Jr (1994)
V'tors U
Fees D–£6 (D–£10)
Loc 4 miles W of Fraserburgh (B9031)
Mis Extension to course 1995

Royal Aberdeen (1780)

Balgownie, Links Road, Bridge of Don, Aberdeen AB2 8AT

Tel **(01224) 702571**
Fax **(01224) 826591**
Mem 350 100(J)
Sec GF Webster
Pro R MacAskill (Gen Mgr) (01224) 702221
Holes 18 L 6372 yds SSS 71
18 L 4066 yds SSS 60
Recs Am–64 J Fought
Pro–64 F Mann
V'tors I H SOC
Fees £37 D–£48 (£48)
Loc 2 miles N of Aberdeen, off A92 Ellon road
Arch Simpson/Braid

Tarland (1908)

Tarland AB3 4YN

Tel **(013398) 81413**
Mem 260
Sec JH Honeyman
Holes 9 L 5812 yds SSS 68
Recs Am–67 J Cramond (1992)
V'tors WD–U WE–enquiry advisable SOC–WD only
Fees £12 (£15)
Loc 5 miles NW of Aboyne. 30 miles W of Aberdeen
Arch Tom Morris

Turriff (1896)

Rosehall, Turriff

Tel **(01888) 62982**
Fax **(01888) 62982**
Mem 811
Sec JD Stott (01888) 62982
Pro R Smith (01888) 63025
Holes 18 L 6145 yds SSS 69
Recs Am–63 G Wallace (1990)
Pro–64 S Aird, P Lawrie (1989)
V'tors H WE–NA before 10am SOC
Fees £12 D–£15 (£15 D–£20)
Loc 46 miles N of Aberdeen (A947)
Arch GM Fraser

Westhill (1977)

Westhill Heights, Skene

Tel **(01224) 740159 (Bookings), (01224) 743361 (Clubhouse)**
Mem 500
Sec JL Webster
Pro R McDonald
Holes 18 L 5921 yds SSS 69
Recs Am–64 A Reith
Pro–65 R McDonald
V'tors WD–U before 4.30pm & after 7pm –M 4.30–7pm Sat–M Sun–U after 10am
Fees £12 D–£16 (£15 D–£20)
Loc 6 miles W of Aberdeen, off A944

For list of abbreviations see page 435

Banffshire

Buckpool (1933)
Barhill Road, Buckie AB56 1DU
Tel **(01542) 832236**
Mem 500
Sec Miss M Coull (01542) 834322
Holes 18 L 6257 yds SSS 70
Recs Am–65 K Buchan (1991)
Pro–64 L Vannet (1989)
Ladies–68 L Smith (1989)
V'tors U
Fees D–£12 (D–£18) W–£40
Loc W end of Buckpool, 1/2 mile off A98

Cullen (1879)
The Links, Cullen, Buckie AB56 2UU
Tel **(01542) 840685**
Mem 625
Sec LIG Findlay (01542) 840174
Holes 18 L 4610 yds SSS 62
Recs Am–58 B Main (1979)
Ladies–62 M Seivwright (1993)
V'tors WD–U WE–restricted Jul/Aug SOC
Fees D–£11 (D–£15)
Loc 5 miles E of Buckie,off A98 between Aberdeen and Inverness
Arch Tom Morris

Duff House Royal (1909)
The Barnyards, Banff AB45 3SX
Tel **(01261) 812062**
Fax **(01261) 812224**
Mem 547 167(L) 132(J)
Sec H Liebnitz
Pro RS Strachan (01261) 812075
Holes 18 L 6161 yds SSS 69
Recs Am–63 DC Clark
V'tors WD–U H WE–H 8.30–11am and 12.30–3pm
Fees £16 (£24)
Loc Moray Firth coast, between Buckie and Fraserburgh
Arch Dr A & Maj CA Mackenzie

Dufftown (1896)
Dufftown AB55 4BX
Tel **(01340) 820325**
Fax **(01340) 820325**
Mem 310
Sec DM Smith
Holes 18 L 5308 yds SSS 67
Recs Am–67 D Smith, C Duncan (1993)
Pro–68 A Aird (1990)
V'tors U
Fees £10 D–£12
Loc 1 mile SW of Dufftown on Tomintoul road

Keith (1963)
Fife Park, Keith
Tel **(01542) 882469**
Mem 400
Sec A Stronach (01542) 882831
Holes 18 L 5614 yds SSS 68
Recs Am–65 Pro–64
V'tors U
Fees £8 (£10)
Loc Fife Park, W side of Keith

Rothes (1990)
Blackhall, Rothes, Aberlour AB38 7AN
Tel **(01340) 831443**
Mem 286
Sec JP Tilley (01340) 831277
Holes 9 L 2478 yds SSS 65
V'tors U
Fees £6 (£8)
Loc 1/2 mile SW of Rothes. 10 miles S of Elgin on A941
Arch John Souter

Royal Tarlair (1926)
Buchan Street, Macduff AB4 1TA
Tel **(01261) 832548/832897**
Mem 556
Sec Mrs T Watt
Holes 18 L 5866 yds SSS 68
Recs Am–64 A Morrison
V'tors U
Fees £10 D–£15 (£12.50 D–£19)
Loc Macduff, 4 miles E of Banff

Strathlene (1877)
Buckie AB5 2DJ
Tel **(01542) 31798**
Mem 300
Sec GML Clark
Holes 18 L 5957 yds SSS 69
Recs Am–65 AG Ross, J Geddes
V'tors U SOC
Fees £10 (£15) W–£40
Loc 1/2 mile E of Buckie
Arch G Smith

Kincardineshire

Auchenblae (1894)
Public
Auchenblae
Tel **(01561) 320331 (Bookings)**
Mem 85
Sec AI Robertson (01561) 378869
Holes 9 L 2208 yds SSS 63
Recs Am–62 AI Robertson, J McNicoll
Pro–60 A Locke
V'tors U exc Wed & Fri 5.30–9pm
Fees £6 Sat–£7 Sun–£8
Loc 11 miles SW of Stonehaven. 3 miles W of Fordoun

Banchory (1905)
Kinneskie, Banchory AB31 3TA
Tel **(01330) 822365**
Mem 800
Sec Mrs A Smith (Admin)
Pro C Dernie (01330) 822447
Holes 18 L 5245 yds SSS 65
Recs Am–60 D Reith (1990)
Pro–61 A Thomson, D Matthew
V'tors U
Fees £19 (£21)
Loc W of Banchory, off A93

Stonehaven (1888)
Cowie, Stonehaven AB3 2RH
Tel **(01569) 762124**
Mem 500
Sec RO Blair
Holes 18 L 5128 yds SSS 65
Recs Am–61 RG Forbes (1987)
V'tors Sat–NA before 3.45pm
Sun–NA before 10.45am
Fees £13 (£18)
Loc 1 mile N of Stonehaven

Torphins (1896)
Torphins
Tel **(013398) 82115**
Mem 370
Sec Sue Mortimer (013398) 82563
Holes 9 L 2342 yds SSS 63
Recs Am–63 J Cramond
V'tors U SOC
Fees £10 (£12)
Loc W of Torphins via Wester Beltie. 6 miles NW of Banchory

Morayshire

Elgin (1906)
Hardhillock, Birnie Road, Elgin IV30 3SX
Tel **(01343) 542338**
Fax **(01343) 542341**
Mem 854 113(L) 150(J)
Sec DJ Chambers
Pro I Rodger (01343) 542884
Holes 18 L 6401 yds SSS 71
Recs Am–64 NS Grant (1972)
Pro–66 H Bannerman (1973)
V'tors WD–U after 9.30am WE–U after 10am SOC
Fees £18 D–£24 (£24 D–£30)
Loc 1 mile S of Elgin

Forres (1889)
Muiryshade, Forres IV36 0RD
Tel **(01309) 672949**
Mem 716 130(J)
Sec DF Black
Pro S Aird (01309) 672250
Holes 18 L 6141 yds SSS 69
Recs Am–64 A Moir
V'tors U SOC
Fees £12 (£16)
Loc 1 mile SE of Forres, off B9010

Garmouth & Kingston (1932)
Garmouth, Fochabers IV32 7LU
Tel **(01343) 87388**
Mem 400
Sec A Robertson (01343) 87231
Holes 18 L 5616 yds SSS 67
Recs Am–62 G Hendry (1994)
Pro–70

For list of abbreviations see page 435

V'tors U SOC
Fees £10 D–£15 (£15 D–£20)
Loc 8 miles NE of Elgin

Grantown (1890)
Grantown-on-Spey PH26 3HY
Tel **(01479) 872079**
Mem 420
Sec D Elms (01479) 872715
Pro B Mitchell (01479) 872398
Holes 18 L 5672 yds SSS 67
Recs Am–60 G Bain
Pro–62 D Webster
V'tors WD–U WE–U after 10am SOC
Fees D–£13 (D–£18)
Loc E side of Grantown (A95)
Arch Willie Park

Hopeman (1923)
Hopeman, Moray IV30 2YA
Tel **(01343) 830578**
Mem 600
Sec WH Dunbar (01343) 830687
Holes 18 L 5531 yds SSS 67
Recs Am–66 K McKenzie (1987)
V'tors WD–U Sat–NA before 10.30am and 12.30–2pm Sun–NA before 9.30am SOC
Fees £12 (£17)
Loc 7 miles NW of Elgin on B9012
Arch J McKenzie

Moray (1889)
Stotfield Road, Lossiemouth IV31 6QS
Tel **(01343) 812018**
Fax **(01343) 815102**
Mem 1300
Sec J Hamilton
Pro A Thomson (01343) 813330
Holes Old 18 L 6643 yds SSS 72
New 18 L 6005 yds SSS 69
Recs Old Am–67 MM MacLeman (1987), NS Grant (1984) RJ Sheils (1992)
Pro–66 T Minshall (1981), D Huish (1988), F Coutts (1991)
New Am–66 I McGarva (1993)
Pro–67 AT MacKenzie (1984), DW Armor (1988)
V'tors U H SOC
Fees On application
Loc 6 miles N of Elgin

Spey Bay (1907)
Spey Bay Hotel, Spey Bay, Fochabers IV32 7PJ
Tel **(01343) 820424**
Mem 180
Holes 18 L 6059 yds SSS 69
Recs Am–66 M Cameron
V'tors U
Fees £10 (£13)
Loc 2 miles W of Buckie, off B9104
Mis Driving range

HIGHLAND REGION

Caithness

Lybster (1926)
Main Street, Lybster KW1 6BL
Mem 86
Sec M Bowman
Holes 9 L 1896 yds SSS 62
Recs Am–60 E Larnach (1982)
V'tors U SOC
Fees On application
Loc 13 miles S of Wick on A9

Reay (1893)
Reay, Thurso KW14 7RE
Tel **(01847) 81288**
Mem 363 64(L) 46(J)
Sec Miss P Peebles (01847) 81537
Pro None
Holes 18 L 5865 yds SSS 68
Recs Am–64 GA Dunnett (1990)
Ladies–71 E Manson (1988)
V'tors U exc comp days
Fees D–£10 W–£30
Loc 11 miles W of Thurso

Thurso (1893)
Newlands of Geise, Thurso KW14 7XD
Tel **(01847) 63807**
Mem 300
Sec Wendy Meiklejohn (01847) 65024
Holes 18 L 5818 yds SSS 69
Recs Am–63 G Dunnett (1989)
V'tors U
Fees £10
Loc 2 miles SW of Thurso

Wick (1870)
Reiss, Wick KW1 5LJ
Tel **(01955) 2726**
Mem 265
Sec Mrs MSW Abernethy (01955) 2702
Holes 18 L 5976 yds SSS 69
Recs Am–63 R Taylor (1988)
Pro–68 Dai Rees
V'tors U
Fees On application
Loc 3 miles N of Wick on A9

Inverness-shire

Abernethy (1893)
Nethy Bridge PH25 3EB
Tel **(01479) 821305**
Mem 320
Sec Mrs EJ Knight (01479) 873558
Holes 9 L 2484 yds SSS 66
Recs Am–61 I Murray
V'tors U SOC
Fees D–£9 (£12)
Loc 5 miles S of Grantown (B970)

Boat-of-Garten (1898)
Boat-of-Garten PH24 3BQ
Tel **(01479) 831282**
Fax **(01479) 831523**
Mem 396
Sec JR Ingram
Holes 18 L 5837 yds SSS 69
Recs Am–67 DF Sharp
Pro–64 G Harvey
V'tors U–booking advisable
Fees On application
Loc 27 miles SE of Inverness (A95)
Arch James Braid

Carrbridge (1980)
Carrbridge PH23 3AU
Tel **(01479) 841623 (Clubhouse)**
Mem 600
Sec Mrs AT Baird
Holes 9 L 2623 yds Par 71 SSS 68
Recs Am–64 G Hay (1992)
V'tors U exc comp days–NA
Fees D–£10 (D–£11) (1994)
Loc 23 miles SE of Inverness, off A9

Fort Augustus (1930)
Markethill, Fort Augustus PH32 4AU
Mem 110
Sec ID Aitchison (01320) 6460
Holes 9 L 5454 yds SSS 68
Recs Am–69 F Boyd (1985)
V'tors U
Fees On application
Loc W end of Fort Augustus

Fort William (1974)
North Road, Fort William PH33 6SW
Tel **(01397) 704464**
Mem 300
Sec J Allan
Holes 18 L 5686 metres SSS 71
V'tors U
Fees On application
Loc 3 miles N of Fort William (A82)
Arch JR Stutt

Inverness (1883)
Culcabock Road, Inverness IV2 3XQ
Tel **(01463) 239882**
Mem 1100
Sec G Thomson
Pro AP Thomson (01463) 231989
Holes 18 L 6226 yds SSS 70
Pro–63 J Farmer
V'tors WE/BH–restricted SOC
Fees £16 D–£22 (£20 D–£24)
Loc 1 mile S of Inverness

Kingussie (1891)
Gynack Road, Kingussie PH21 1LR
Tel **(01540) 661374** (Clubhouse)
Mem 700
Sec ND MacWilliam (01540) 661600

Pro None
Holes 18 L 5555 yds SSS 68
Recs Am–63 ND MacWilliam (1994)
Pro–66 K Hutton (1991)
V'tors U
Fees £12 D–£15 (£14 D–£18)
Loc 1/2 mile N of Kingussie, off A9
Arch H Vardon

Newtonmore (1893)
Newtonmore PH20 1AT
Tel **(01540) 673328**
Fax **(01540) 673878**
Mem 420
Sec RJ Cheyne (01540) 673878
Pro R Henderson (01540) 673611
Holes 18 L 5880 yds SSS 68
Recs Am–64 I Barclay
Pro–68 F Couttes (1993)
V'tors U SOC
Fees D–£18 (£20)
Loc 4 miles W of Kingussie. 46 miles S of Inverness

Spean Bridge
Spean Bridge, Fort William
Mem 65
Sec AJ McLaren (Pres) (01397) 704954
Holes 9 hole course SSS 62
V'tors U
Fees On application
Loc 9 miles N of Fort William on A82

Torvean (1962)
Public
Glenurquhart Road, Inverness
Tel **(01463) 711434** (Starter)
Mem 417
Sec Mrs KM Gray (01463) 225651
Holes 18 L 5784 yds SSS 68
Recs Am–65 DC Walker (1994)
Pro–70 R Weir (1988)
Ladies–75 C MacLeod (1989)
V'tors U
Fees £9 (£11)
Loc SW of Inverness on A82

Traigh
Traigh, Arisaig
Tel **(01687) 450645**
Mem 90
Sec W Henderson
Pro None
Holes 9 L 2405 yds SSS 64
V'tors U
Fees D–£9 W–£40
Loc 3 miles N of Arisaig on A830 Fort William-Mallaig road
Mis Redesigned course open May 1995
Arch John Salveson

Isle of Skye

Isle of Skye (1964)
Sconser
Mem 180
Sec A Mackenzie (01478) 613059/612341
Holes 9 L 4796 yds SSS 63
Recs Am–62 M Whatley
V'tors U
Fees D–£8
Loc Between Broadford and Sligachan

Skeabost (1982)
Skeabost Bridge, Skye IV5 9NP
Mem 80
Sec DJ Matheson (01470) 32202 (Skeabost House Hotel)
Holes 9 L 3224 yds SSS 59
V'tors U
Fees D–£6
Loc 6 miles NW of Portree on Dunvegan road

Nairnshire

Nairn (1887)
Seabank Road, Nairn IV12 4HB
Tel **(01667) 452103**
Fax **(01667) 456328**
Mem 938
Sec J Somerville (01667) 453208
Pro R Fyfe (01667) 452787
Holes 18 L 6722 yds SSS 72
9 hole course
Recs Am–66 S Tomisson
Pro–65 D Small
V'tors U SOC
Fees On application
Loc Nairn West Shore (A96)
Arch Old Tom Morris/Braid/Simpson

Nairn Dunbar (1899)
Lochloy Road, Nairn IV12 5AE
Tel **(01667) 452741**
Fax **(01667) 456897**
Mem 500
Sec Mrs SJ McLennan
Pro BR Mason (01667) 453964
Holes 18 L 6712 yds SSS 72
Recs Am–69 CJ Taylor
Pro–63 RM Collinson
V'tors U
Fees £18.50 D–£25 (£25 D–£30)
Loc In Nairn

Ross & Cromarty

Alness (1904)
Ardross Rd, Alness
Tel **(01349) 883877**
Mem 300
Sec JG Miller
Holes 9 L 2436 yds SSS 63
Recs Am–62 C MacIver (1983)
C Taylor (1989)
V'tors U exc Mon–NA 5–7pm SOC
Fees On application
Loc 1/4 mile N of Alness. 10 miles N of Dingwall

Fortrose & Rosemarkie (1888)
Ness Road East, Fortrose IV10 8SE
Tel **(01381) 620529**
Mem 800
Sec Mrs M Collier
Holes 18 L 5858 yds SSS 69
Recs Am–64 G Paterson
V'tors U SOC
Fees £13 D–£18 (£18) (1994)
Loc Black Isle, 12 miles N of Inverness
Arch James Braid

Gairloch (1898)
Gairloch IV21 2BQ
Tel **(01445) 712407**
Mem 285
Sec A Shinkins
Holes 9 L 2281 yds SSS 64
V'tors U
Fees D–£10 W–£45
Loc 60 miles W of Dingwall in Wester Ross

Invergordon (1954)
King George Street, Invergordon IV18 0UA
Tel **(01349) 852116**
Mem 110 30(L) 60(J)
Sec J Dinwoodie
Holes 9 L 6028 yds SSS 69
Recs Am–65 D Ross (1980), AJ Mackenzie (1990)
V'tors U SOC
Fees £7
Loc 15 miles NE of Dingwall (B817)

Lochcarron (1911)
Lochcarron, Strathcarron
Mem 124
Sec G Weighill (015202) 257
Holes 9 L 3578 yds SSS 60
V'tors U
Fees £5
Loc 1/2 mile E of Lochcarron in Wester Ross

Muir of Ord (1875)
Great North Road, Muir of Ord IV6 7SX
Tel **(01463) 870825**
Fax **(01463) 870825**
Mem 700
Sec D Noble
Pro G Vivers (01463) 871311
Holes 18 L 5202 yds SSS 66
Recs Am–62 S McIntosh (1989)
V'tors U SOC
Fees D–£12 (£15) W–£45
Loc 15 miles N of Inverness (A862)

Strathpeffer Spa (1888)
Strathpeffer IV14 9AS
Tel **(01997) 421219**
Mem 350 60(L) 80(J)
Sec N Roxburgh (01997) 421396
Holes 18 L 4792 yds SSS 65
Recs Am–60 D Krzyzanowski
Pro–66 A Herd
V'tors U SOC
Fees £10 D–£15 (£15)
Loc 1/4 mile N of Strathpeffer. 5 miles W of Dingwall

Tain (1890)
Tain
Tel **(01862) 892314**
Mem 500
Sec Mrs KD Ross
Holes 18 L 6238 yds SSS 70/69
Recs Am–66 JA Urquhart (1994)
V'tors U
Fees £12 D–£18 (£18 D–£24)
Loc 35 miles N of Inverness (A9). 8 miles S of Dornoch

Tarbat (1909)
Portmahomack, Tain IV20 1YB
Tel **(01862) 87236**
Fax **(01349) 853715**
Mem 200
Sec D Wilson
Holes 9 L 2568 yds SSS 66
Recs Am–63 D Mackay
V'tors U H SOC
Fees D–£5 (D–£6)
Loc 10 miles E of Tain
Arch J Sutherland

Sutherland

Bonar-Bridge & Ardgay (1901)
Bonar-Bridge, Ardgay IV24 3EJ
Mem 200
Sec A Turner (01549) 421248
Holes 9 L 4626 yds SSS 63
Recs Am–63 M Munro (1994)
V'tors U
Fees D–£8 (£8)
Loc 1/2 mile N of Bonar-Bridge on A9. 15 miles W of Dornoch

Brora (1891)
Golf Road, Brora KW9 6QS
Tel **(01408) 621417**
Sec J Fraser
Holes 18 L 6110 yds SSS 69
Recs Am–61 J Miller
Pro–67 D Huish
V'tors U exc comp days –H for open comps SOC
Fees D–£16 W–£70
Loc 18 miles N of Dornoch (A9)
Arch James Braid

Durness (1988)
Balnakeil, Durness IV27 4PN
Mem 100
Sec Mrs L Mackay (01971) 511364
Holes 9 L 5545 yds SSS 68
Recs Am–72 L Ross (1991)
V'tors U
Fees D–£9 W–£36
Loc 57 miles NW of Lairg on A838

Golspie (1889)
Ferry Road, Golspie KW10 6ST
Tel **(01408) 633266**
Mem 420
Sec Mrs M MacLeod
Holes 18 L 5836 yds SSS 68
Recs Am–65 J Miller
Pro–65 D Huish
V'tors U SOC
Fees D–£15
Loc 11 miles N of Dornoch

Helmsdale (1895)
Golf Road, Helmsdale KW8 6JA
Tel **(014312) 339**
Sec D Bishop
Holes 9 L 3720 yds SSS 60
V'tors U
Fees £5 D–£10 W–£25
Loc 30 miles N of Dornoch (A9)

Royal Dornoch (1877)
Golf Road, Dornoch IV25 3LW
Tel **(01862) 810219**
Fax **(01862) 810792**
Mem 820 252(L) 47(J)
Sec JS Duncan (Sec/Mgr)
Pro WE Skinner (01862) 810902
Holes C'ship 18 L 6581 yds SSS 72
Struie 18 L 5242 yds SSS 66
Recs Am–66 DWR Chalmers
Pro–65 K Stables
V'tors H
Fees On application
Loc 45 miles N of Inverness, off A9, N of Dornoch
Mis Helipad by clubhouse. Airstrip nearby

LOTHIAN REGION

East Lothian

Aberlady (1912)
Aberlady EH32 0QD
Mem 35
Sec K Hope (01875) 7374
Holes Play over Kilspindie course

Bass Rock (1873)
6 Harperdean Cottages, Harperdean, Haddington EH41 3SQ
Mem 104
Sec SH Butterworth (01620) 822082
Holes Play over North Berwick

Dirleton Castle (1854)
Gullane
Tel **(01620) 843496**
Mem 100
Sec RH Atkinson
Holes Play over Gullane courses

Dunbar (1794)
East Links, Dunbar EH42 1LP
Tel **(01368) 862317**
Fax **(01368) 865202**
Mem 750
Sec D Thompson
Pro D Small (01368) 862086
Holes 18 L 6426 yds SSS 71
Recs Am–66 J Grant (1989)
Pro–64 R Weir (1989)
V'tors U SOC–exc Thurs
Fees D–£28 (D–£40)
Loc 1/2 mile E of Dunbar. 30 miles E of Edinburgh, off A1

Gifford (1904)
Edinburgh Road, Gifford EH41 4QN
Tel **(01620) 810591**
Mem 450
Sec DA Fantom (01620) 810267
Holes 9 L 6243 yds SSS 70
Recs Am–65 M McEwan (1980), D Shearer (1993)
Ladies–67 D Martin
V'tors Tues & Wed–NA after 4pm
WE–NA after noon
Fees D–£10 (£10)
Loc 4 miles S of Haddington. 20 miles SE of Edinburgh (B6355)
Arch Willie Wood

Glen (1906)
East Links, North Berwick EH39 4LE
Tel **(01620) 892221**
Fax **(01620) 895288**
Mem 550
Sec DR Montgomery
Holes 18 L 6079 yds SSS 69
Recs Am–64 A Imlah (1992)
V'tors U–advance booking required
Fees £13.50 D–£19 (£15 D–£21)
Loc 25 miles E of Edinburgh, off A198
Arch Mackenzie Ross

Gullane (1882)
Gullane EH31 2BB
Tel **(01620) 843115 (Starter)**
Fax **(01620) 842327**
Mem 716 300(L) 60(J)
Sec AJB Taylor (01620) 842255
Pro J Hume (01620) 843111
Holes No 1 18 L 6466 yds SSS 71
No 2 18 L 6244 yds SSS 70
No 3 18 L 5166 yds SSS 65
6 hole children's course
Recs No 1 Am–65 ME Lewis
Pro–65 J Hobday (1992)
No 2 Am–64 RCH Robertson
Pro–66 H Bannerman
V'tors No 1–H Nos 2/3–U

For list of abbreviations see page 435

Fees No 1 £40 D–£60 (£50); No 2 £20 D–£30 (£25 D–£37.50); No 3 £12 D–£18 (£15 D–£22.50); Children's course free
Loc 18 miles E of Edinburgh on A198
Mis Advance booking advised

Haddington (1865)
Public
Amisfield Park, Haddington EH41 4PT
Tel **(01620) 823627**
Mem 610
Sec T Spiers
Pro J Sandilands (01620) 822727
Holes 18 L 6280 yds SSS 70
Recs Am–65 S Stephens
V'tors WD–U WE–U exc 10–12 and 2–4pm
Fees £10 (£13)
Loc 17 miles E of Edinburgh on A1. 3/4 mile E of Haddington

The Honourable Company of Edinburgh Golfers (1744)
Muirfield, Gullane EH31 2EG
Tel **(01620) 842123**
Fax **(01620) 842977**
Mem 625
Sec Gp Capt JA Prideaux
Holes 18 L 6601 yds SSS 73 (Championship 6963 yds)
Recs Am–69 PA Burt (1993) Pro–63 R Davis (1987)
V'tors WD–Tues & Thurs I H WE/BH–NA SOC
Fees £55 D–£75
Loc NE outskirts of Gullane, opposite sign for Greywalls Hotel on A198

Kilspindie (1867)
Aberlady, Longniddry EH32 0QD
Tel **(018757) 216/358**
Mem 460 150(L) 60(J)
Sec HF Brown (018757) 358
Pro GJ Sked (018757) 695
Holes 18 L 4957 metres SSS 66
Recs Am–62 RJ Humble (1990) Pro–60 L Vannet (1988)
V'tors Restricted–phone Sec in advance SOC–WD
Fees On application

Longniddry (1921)
Links Road, Longniddry EH32 0NL
Tel **(01875) 852141**
Mem 950
Sec N Robertson
Pro WJ Gray (01875) 852228
Holes 18 L 6219 yds SSS 70
Recs Am–63 C Hardin (1987) Pro–63 P Harrison (1987)
V'tors WD–U H SOC–Mon–Thurs after 9.18am and 2pm
Fees £25 D–£35
Loc 13 miles E of Edinburgh, off A1
Arch HS Colt

Luffness New (1894)
Aberlady EH32 0QA
Tel **(01620) 843114**
Fax **(01620) 842933**
Mem 700
Sec Lt Col JG Tedford (01620) 843336
Holes 18 L 6122 yds SSS 69
Recs Am–63 R Winchester Pro–62 C O'Connor
V'tors H or I XL before 10am WE/BH–NA SOC
Fees £27 D–£40
Loc 1 mile W of Gullane (A198)
Arch Tom Morris

Musselburgh (1938)
Monktonhall, Musselburgh
Tel **(0131) 665 2005**
Mem 800
Sec S Sullivan, G Finlay (Admin)
Pro F Mann (0131) 665 7055
Holes 18 L 6614 yds SSS 72
Recs Am–65 JM Noon Pro–67 EC Brown, B Devlin G Cunningham, A Jacklin Ladies–69 J Connachan
V'tors U
Fees £17 (£25)
Loc 1 mile S of Musselburgh on B6415
Arch James Braid

Musselburgh Old Course
Public
Silver Ring Clubhouse, Millhill, Musselburgh EH21 7RG
Tel **(0131) 665 6981**
Mem 150
Holes 9 L 5380 yds SSS 67
Recs Am–67 P Hosie
V'tors WD/BH–U WE–U after 1pm
Fees On application
Loc 7 miles E of Edinburgh on A1

North Berwick (1832)
West Links, Beach Road, North Berwick EH39 4BB
Tel **(01620) 892135**
Fax **(01620) 893274**
Mem 324
Sec W Gray
Pro D Huish (01620) 893233
Holes 18 L 6420 yds SSS 71
Recs Am–66 G Sherry (1994) Pro–64 N Job (1994)
V'tors U H
Fees £25 D–£35 (£35 D–£45) Winter–£15 (£20)
Loc 1/2 mile W of North Berwick (A198). 24 miles E of Edinburgh

Royal Musselburgh (1774)
Prestongrange House, Prestonpans EH32 9RP
Tel **(01875) 810276**
Fax **(01875) 810276**
Mem 800
Sec TH Hardie (Sec/Mgr) RS Gordon (Golf Sec)
Pro J Henderson (01875) 810139
Holes 18 L 6237 yds SSS 70
Recs Am–65 A Roy (1993)
V'tors U SOC
Fees 208 D–£35 (£35)
Loc 8 miles E of Edinburgh on A198 North Berwick road
Arch James Braid

Tantallon (1853)
32 Westgate, North Berwick EH39 4AH
Tel **(01620) 2114**
Mem 300
Sec T Hill
Holes Play over North Berwick West Links

Thorntree (1856)
Prestongrange House, Prestonpans EH32 9RP
Mem 100
Sec J Hanratty
Holes Play over Royal Musselburgh course

Winterfield (1935)
Public
St Margarets, North Road, Dunbar EH42 1AU
Tel **(01368) 862280**
Mem 400
Sec M O'Donnell (01368) 862564
Pro K Phillips (01368) 863562
Holes 18 L 5053 yds SSS 65
Recs Am–61 R Walkinshaw, J Huggan Pro–65 SWT Murray
V'tors U
Fees On application–phone Pro
Loc W side of Dunbar. 28 miles E of Edinburgh

Midlothian

Baberton (1893)
Baberton Avenue, Juniper Green, Edinburgh EH14 5DU
Tel **(0131) 453 3361**
Mem 800
Sec EW Horberry (0131) 453 4911
Pro K Kelly (0131) 453 3555
Holes 18 L 6098 yds SSS 69
Recs Am–64 RW Bradly (1989), D Beveridge Jr, BJH Tait (1991) Pro–62 B Barnes
V'tors I SOC–WD
Fees £17 D–£25
Loc 5 miles SW of Edinburgh (A70)

Braid Hills (1893)
Public
Braid Hills Road, Edinburgh EH10 6JY EH10 6JY
Tel **(0131) 447 6666 (Starter)**
Holes No 1 18 L 5239 yds SSS 68 No 2 18 L 4832 yds SSS 63
Recs Am–65

V'tors U–no phone bookings. No 2 course closed Sun
Fees £7
Loc 3 miles S of Edinburgh (A702)
Mis No 2 course open Apr-Oct

Braids United (1897)
22 Braid Hills Approach, Edinburgh EH10 6JY
Tel **(0131) 452 9408**
Mem 100
Sec G Hind (0131) 445 2044
Holes Play over Braids 1 and 2

Broomieknowe (1906)
36 Golf Course Road, Bonnyrigg EH19 2HZ
Tel **(0131) 663 9317**
Mem 500
Sec JG White
Pro M Patchett (0131) 660 2035
Holes 18 L 6200 yds Par 70
Recs Am–65 K Hastings (1990) Pro–64 SJ Knowles (1994)
V'tors WD–U WE/BH–NA
Fees £15 D–£25 (£20)
Loc 7 miles SE of Edinburgh
Arch Braid/Hawtree

Bruntsfield Links Golfing Society (1761)
The Clubhouse, 32 Barnton Avenue, Edinburgh EH4 6JH
Tel **(0131) 336 2006**
Mem 1000
Sec Lt Col MB Hext (031) 336 1479
Pro B Mackenzie (0131) 336 4050
Holes 18 L 6407 yds SSS 71
Recs Am–67 AW Ritchie
V'tors On application to Sec
Fees On application
Loc 3 miles W of Edinburgh
Arch Willie Park

Carrick Knowe (1930)
Public
Glendevon Park, Edinburgh EH12 5VZ
Tel **(0131) 337 1096 (Starter)**
Holes 18 L 6299 yds SSS 70
Recs Am–64 R Bradley
V'tors U–phone bookings not accepted
Fees £6.50 (1993)
Loc 5 miles W of Edinburgh

Craigentinny (1891)
Public
Craigentinny Avenue, Edinburgh EH7
Tel **(0131) 554 7501 (Starter), (0131) 661 5351 Ext 209**
Holes 18 L 5418 yds SSS 66
Recs Am–64
V'tors U–phone bookings not accepted
Fees £7
Loc 2½ miles E of Edinburgh

Craigmillar Park (1895)
1 Observatory Road, Edinburgh EH9 3HG
Tel **(0131) 667 2837**
Mem 425 100(L) 70(J)
Sec T Lawson (0131) 667 0047
Pro B McGhee (0131) 667 0047
Holes 18 L 5859 yds SSS 69
Recs Am–64 A Mail (1992) Ladies–66 M Pollock (1993)
V'tors WD–I or H before 3.30pm WE/BH–NA
Fees On application
Loc Blackford, S of Edinburgh
Arch James Braid

Dalmahoy Hotel CC
Dalmahoy, Kirknewton EH27 8EB
Tel **(0131) 333 4105/1845**
Fax **(0131) 335 3203**
Sec B Anderson (Dir), J Wilson (Sec)
Holes East 18 L 6677 yds SSS 72 West 18 L 5185 yds SSS 66
Recs East Am–65 M Backhausen, F Jacobsen Pro–62 B Barnes West Am–66 DC Brown Pro–62 I Young
V'tors WD–U H SOC–WD
Fees East–£39 West–£27
Loc 7 miles W of Edinburgh on A71
Arch James Braid

Duddingston (1895)
Duddingston Road West, Edinburgh EH15 3QD
Tel **(0131) 661 1005**
Mem 580
Sec JC Small (0131) 661 7688
Pro A McLean (0131) 661 4301
Holes 18 L 6438 yds SSS 71
Recs Am–64 G Macgregor Pro–65 S Torrance, C Maltman
V'tors WD–U SOC–Tues & Thurs
Fees £22 Soc–£19
Loc SE Edinburgh

Glencorse (1890)
Milton Bridge, Penicuik EH26 0RD
Tel **(01968) 677177**
Fax **(01968) 674399**
Mem 700
Sec W Oliver (01968) 677189
Pro C Jones (01968) 676481
Holes 18 L 5217 yds Par 64 SSS 66
Recs Am–62 N Shillinglaw (1992) Pro–62 C Ronald (1992)
V'tors WD–U SOC–Mon–Thurs
Fees £18 (£24)
Loc 8 miles S of Edinburgh (A701)

Kingsknowe (1908)
326 Lanark Road, Edinburgh EH14 2JD
Tel **(0131) 441 1144**
Mem 728
Sec R Wallace (0131) 441 1145
Pro A Marshall (0131) 441 4030
Holes 18 L 5966 yds SSS 69
Recs Am–63 JJ Little Pro–64 WB Murray
V'tors WD–U before 4.30pm WE–phone Pro SOC–WD
Fees On application
Loc SW Edinburgh

Liberton (1920)
297 Gilmerton Road, Edinburgh EH16 5UJ
Tel **(0131) 664 8580**
Mem 815
Sec AJR Poole (0131) 664 3009
Pro I Seath (0131) 664 1056
Holes 18 L 5299 yds SSS 66
Recs Am–61 RMF Jack, D Rennie Pro–63 JL Brash
V'tors Tues–Thurs–NA after 5pm WE/BH–No visiting clubs
Fees £15 (£25)
Loc 3 miles S of Edinburgh

Lothianburn (1893)
Biggar Road, Edinburgh EH20 7DU
Tel **(0131) 445 2206**
Mem 600 75(L) 100(J)
Sec WFA Jardine (0131) 445 5067
Pro K Mungall (0131) 445 2288
Holes 18 L 5750 yds SSS 69
Recs Am–63 PW Lamb (1983)
V'tors WD–U before 5pm –M after 5pm WE–NA SOC–H
Fees £12 D–£18 (£18 D–£23)
Loc S of Edinburgh, on A702. Lothianburn exit from Edinburgh by-pass
Arch James Braid (1928)

Merchants of Edinburgh (1907)
Craighill Gardens, Morningside, Edinburgh EH10 5PY
Tel **(0131) 447 1219**
Mem 730
Sec AM Montgomery
Pro NEM Colquhoun (0131) 447 8709
Holes 18 L 4889 yds SSS 64
Recs Am–61 WJ Jeffrey Jr (1974), PB Wilson (1993), BW Erskine (1994) Ladies–66 LM Caine (1991)
V'tors WD–U before 4pm –M after 4pm WE–M SOC–WD
Fees £15
Loc SW of Edinburgh, off A701

Mortonhall (1892)
231 Braid Road, Edinburgh EH10 6PB
Tel **(0131) 447 2411**
Mem 500
Sec Mrs CD Morrison (0131) 447 6974
Pro DB Horn (0131) 447 5185
Holes 18 L 6557 yds SSS 71
Recs Am–66 C Cassells Pro–68 G Cunningham
V'tors H SOC
Fees £20 (£25)
Loc 2 miles S of Edinburgh on A702
Arch James Braid/FW Hawtree

Murrayfield (1896)

43 Murrayfield Road, Edinburgh EH12 6EU

Tel **(0131) 337 1009**
Fax **(0131) 313 0721**
Mem 775
Sec Mrs MK Hermiston (0131) 337 3478
Pro J Fisher (0131) 337 3479
Holes 18 L 5727 yds SSS 68
Recs Am–64 DED Neave
Pro–63 WB Murray
V'tors WD–I WE–M
Fees £22 D–£28
Loc 2 miles W of Edinburgh centre

Newbattle (1896)

Abbey Road, Eskbank, Dalkeith EH22 3AD

Tel **(0131) 663 2123**
Mem 600
Sec HG Stanners (0131) 663 1819
Pro D Torrance (0131) 660 1631
Holes 18 L 6012 yds SSS 69
Recs Am–64 P Hardwick, DJ Henderson, K Goodwin
Pro–61 A Oldcorn
V'tors WD–U before 4pm WE–M
Fees £16 D–£24
Loc 6 miles S of Edinburgh on A7 and A68

Portobello (1853)

Public

Stanley Street, Portobello, Edinburgh EH15 1JJ

Tel **(0131) 669 4361 (Starter), (0131) 661 5351 Ext 209**
Mem 60
Holes 9 L 2419 yds SSS 32
Recs Am–27
V'tors U–phone bookings not accepted
Fees On application
Loc 4 miles E of Edinburgh on A1

Prestonfield (1920)

6 Priestfield Road North, Edinburgh EH16 5HS

Tel **(0131) 667 1273**
Mem 700
Sec MDAG Dillon
Pro B Commins (0131) 667 8597
Holes 18 L 6216 yds SSS 70
Recs Am–62 AM Dun (1976)
V'tors Sat–NA 8–10.30am and 12–1.30pm Sun–NA before 11.30am SOC
Fees £17 D–£25 (£25 D–£35)
Loc 2 miles SE of Edinburgh, off A68 Dalkeith road

Ratho Park (1928)

Ratho, Newbridge, Midlothian EH28 8NX

Tel **(0131) 333 1252/1752**
Fax **(0131) 333 1752**
Mem 550 98(L) 65(J)
Sec JC McLafferty (0131) 333 1752
Pro A Pate (0131) 333 1406
Holes 18 L 5900 yds SSS 68
Recs Am–61 DM Summers (1991)
Pro–64 WG Stowe
V'tors U SOC–Tues–Thurs
Fees £22 D–£33 (£33)
Loc 8 miles W of Edinburgh (A71)

Ravelston (1912)

24 Ravelston Dykes Road, Edinburgh EH4 5NZ

Tel **(0131) 315 2486**
Mem 610
Sec F Philip
Holes 9 L 5332 yds SSS 66
Recs Am–64 JW Fraser (1994)
Pro–67 W Murray (1987)
V'tors WD–H
Fees £15
Loc Off Queensferry Road (A90). Turn S at Blackhall
Arch James Braid

Royal Burgess Golfing Society of Edinburgh (1735)

181 Whitehouse Road, Barnton, Edinburgh EH4 6BY

Tel **(0131) 339 2075**
Fax **(0131) 339 3712**
Mem 620 50(J)
Sec JP Audis (0131) 339 2075
Pro G Yuille (0131) 339 6474
Holes 18 L 6494 yds SSS 71
Recs Am–66 J Yuille (1992)
Pro–63
V'tors I SOC
Fees On application
Loc Queensferry Road (A90)
Arch Tom Morris

Silverknowes (1947)

Public

Silverknowes, Parkway, Edinburgh EH4 5ET

Tel **(0131) 336 3843 (Starter), (0131) 661 5351 Ext 209**
Holes 18 L 6210 yds SSS 70
Recs Am–66
V'tors U–phone bookings not accepted
Fees £7
Loc 4 miles W of Edinburgh

Swanston (1927)

111 Swanston Road, Fairmilehead, Edinburgh EH10 7DS

Tel **(0131) 445 2239**
Mem 500
Sec J Allan
Pro J Scott Maxwell (0131) 445 4002
Holes 18 L 5024 yds SSS 65
Recs Am–63 G Millar
V'tors U exc comp days–NA WE–NA after 1pm
Fees £8 D–£12 (£10 D–£15)
Loc S of Edinburgh, off Biggar road (A702)

Torphin Hill (1895)

Torphin Road, Edinburgh EH13 0PG

Tel **(0131) 441 1100**
Mem 450
Sec RM Brannan
Holes 18 L 5025 yds SSS 66
Recs Am–65 G Campbell
V'tors WD–U WE–U exc comp days SOC
Fees D–£12 (D–£20)
Loc SW boundary of Edinburgh

Turnhouse (1897)

154 Turnhouse Road, Corstorphine, Edinburgh EH12 0AD

Tel **(0131) 339 1014**
Mem 500
Sec AB Hay (0131) 539 5937
Pro J Murray (0131) 339 7701
Holes 18 L 6171 yds SSS 69
Recs Am–65 E McIntosh (1990)
Pro–64 D Huish
V'tors M or by arrangement
Fees On application
Loc W of Edinburgh (A9080)

West Lothian

Bathgate (1892)

Edinburgh Road, Bathgate EH48 1BA

Tel **(01506) 652232**
Fax **(01506) 636775**
Mem 580
Sec W Gray (01506) 630505
Pro S Strachan (01506) 630553
Holes 18 L 6326 yds SSS 70
Recs Am–64 J McLean
Pro–58 S Torrance (1992)
V'tors U
Fees £15 (£25)
Loc 15 miles W of Edinburgh. M8 Junction 4

Deer Park CC (1978)

Knightsridge, Livingston EH54 9PG

Tel **(01506) 38843**
Fax **(01506) 35608**
Mem 500
Sec I Thomson
Pro W Yule
Holes 18 L 6636 yds SSS 72
Recs Am–67 D Thomson (1994)
Pro–66
V'tors U SOC
Fees £15 D–£19 (£25 D–£35)
Loc N of Livingston. M8 Junction 3

Dundas Park (1957)

(Sec) Hope Cottage, Loch Road, South Queensferry EH30 9LS

Mem 450
Sec KD Love (0131) 331 1416
Holes 9 L 5510 metres SSS 69
Recs Am–66 J McLaren
V'tors M I SOC
Fees On application
Loc Dundas Estate (Private). 1 mile S of Queencferry (A8000)

For list of abbreviations see page 435

Greenburn (1953)
6 Greenburn Road, Fauldhouse EH47 9HG
Tel **(01501) 770292**
Mem 500
Sec A Stein (01501) 741967
Pro M Leighton (01501) 771187
Holes 18 L 6210 yds SSS 71
Recs Am–65 B Watson
V'tors U
Fees On application
Loc 4 miles S of M8 Junction 4 (East)/Junction 5 (West)

Harburn (1921)
West Calder EH55 8RS
Tel **(01506) 871256**
Mem 470 80(L) 100(J)
Sec F Vinter (01506) 871131
Pro T Stangoe (01506) 871582
Holes 18 L 5921 yds SSS 69
Recs Am–62 M Kirk
Pro–64 A Alcorn
V'tors U
Fees £15 (£21)
Loc 2 miles S of W Calder on B7008, via A70 or A71

Linlithgow (1913)
Braehead, Linlithgow EH49 6QF
Tel **(01506) 842585**
Mem 430
Sec TB Thomson
Pro D Smith (01506) 844356
Holes 18 L 5729 yds SSS 68
Recs Am–64 J Cuddihy (1975)
Pro–65 J White (1988)
V'tors U exc Sat–NA SOC
Fees £12 D–£18 Sun–£18 D–£25
Loc SW of Linlithgow, off M9

Niddry Castle (1983)
Castle Road, Winchburgh EH52 2RQ
Tel **(01506) 891097**
Mem 375
Sec A Brockbank (01506) 891134
Holes 9 L 5476 yds SSS 67
Recs Am–69 S Cook,
J Wardrop (1992)
V'tors U
Fees £7.50 (£10) (1994)
Loc 10 miles W of Edinburgh (B9080)

Polkemmet (1981)
Public
Whitburn, Bathgate EH47 0AD
Tel **(01501) 743905**
Holes 9 L 2967 metres SSS 37
V'tors U
Fees £1.30–£2.80
Sun–£1.80–£3.50
Loc Between Whitburn and Harthill on B7066. M8 Junctions 4/5
Mis Driving range

Pumpherston (1895)
Drumshoreland Road, Pumpherston EH53 0LF
Tel **(01506) 432869**
Mem 326 13(L) 57(J)
Sec AH Docharty (01506) 854652
Holes 9 L 5434 yds SSS 66
V'tors M
Loc 14 miles W of Edinburgh. M8 Junction 3

Uphall (1895)
Houston Mains, Uphall EH52 6JT
Tel **(01506) 856404**
Mem 500
Sec AG Flood (Mgr)
Pro G Law (01506) 855553
Holes 18 L 5567 yds SSS 67
Recs Am–62 AJ Hogg (1992)
Pro–64 CJ Brooks,
A Oldcorn (1992)
V'tors U
Fees £13 D–£16 (£17 D–£25)
Loc 7 miles W of Edinburgh Airport (A8). M8 Junction 3

West Lothian (1892)
Airngath Hill, Linlithgow EH49 7RH
Tel **(01506) 826030**
Mem 500
Sec TB Fraser (01506) 825476
Holes 18 L 6578 yds SSS 71
Recs Am–64 AG O'Neill (1990)
Pro–68 J Farmer (1980)
V'tors WD–NA after 4pm WE–by arrangement
Fees On application
Loc 1 mile N of Linlithgow, towards Bo'ness

ORKNEY & SHETLAND

Orkney (1889)
Grainbank, Kirkwall, Orkney KW15 1RD
Tel **(01856) 872457**
Mem 415
Sec LF Howard (01856) 874165
Holes 18 L 5411 yds SSS 68
Recs Am–65 KD Peace
Pro–71 I Smith
V'tors U
Fees D–£10 W–£35
Loc 1 mile W of Kirkwall

Shetland (1891)
PO Box 18, Lerwick, Shetland
Tel **(01595) 84369**
Mem 400
Sec LE Groat (Mgr) (01595) 3065
Holes 18 L 5776 yds SSS 70
Recs Am–68 D Hutcheon (1992)
V'tors U
Fees £8
Loc 3 miles N of Lerwick
Arch Fraser Middleton

Stromness (1890)
Stromness, Orkney KW16 3DU
Tel **(01856) 850772**
Mem 250
Sec FJ Groundwater (01856) 850622
Holes 18 L 4672 yds SSS 64
Recs Am–61 G Dunnet
Pro–66 R Macaskill
V'tors U
Fees D–£10
Loc Stromness, 16 miles W of Kirkwall on Hoy Sound

Whalsay (1976)
Skaw Taing, Whalsay, Shetland
Mem 100
Sec HA Sandison
Pro None
Holes 18 L 6116 yds SSS 70
Recs Am–65 IG Sandison (1993)
V'tors U SOC
Fees D–£5 W–£15
Loc 5 miles N of Symbister Ferry

STRATHCLYDE

Argyll

Blairmore & Strone (1896)
High Road, Strone, Dunoon PA23 8JJ
Tel **(01369) 840676**
Mem 130
Sec JK Clark (01369) 840467
Holes 9 L 2122 yds SSS 62
Recs Am–63 JA Kirby (1987)
V'tors Mon–NA after 6pm Sat–NA 12–4pm
Fees D–£8 (D–£10) W–£30
Loc Strone, 8 miles N of Dunoon
Arch James Braid

Carradale (1906)
Carradale, Campbeltown PA28 6SA
Tel **(01583) 431643**
Mem 335
Sec JR Ogilvie
Pro None
Holes 9 L 2387 yds SSS 64
Recs Am–62 JW Campbell (1994)
Pro–68 R Weir (1994)
V'tors U
Fees D–£6
Loc Carradale, 15 miles N of Campbeltown (B842)

Colonsay
Isle of Colonsay PA61 7YP
Tel **(019512) 316**
Mem 100
Sec K Byrne
Holes 18 L 4775 yds Par 72
V'tors U
Fees On application
Loc W coast of Colonsay, at Machrins

For list of abbreviations see page 435

Cowal (1891)
Ardenslate Road, Dunoon PA23 8LT
Tel **(01369) 702216**
Fax **(01369) 705673**
Mem 509
Sec BR Chatham (01369) 705673
Pro RD Weir (01369) 702395
Holes 18 L 6251 yds SSS 70
Recs Am–64 A Brodie (1964)
Pro–63 RD Weir (1991)
V'tors WD–U H WE–restricted SOC
Fees On application
Loc NE boundary of Dunoon
Arch James Braid (1928)

Craignure (1981)
Scallastle, Craignure, Isle of Mull PA64 5AP
Tel **(01680) 812370**
Mem 57
Sec Mrs S Weir
Holes 9 L 4436 metres SSS 64
V'tors U
Fees D–£8
Loc 1 mile N of Craignure

Dalmally (1986)
Old Saw Mill, Dalmally PA33 1AS
Tel **(01838) 200373**
Mem 80
Sec AJ Burke (01838) 200370
Holes 9 L 2277 yds SSS 62
Recs Am–64 K MacIntyre (1994)
V'tors U
Fees £7
Loc 1 mile W of Dalmally on A85

Dunaverty (1889)
Southend, Campbeltown PA28 6RF
Tel **(01586) 830677**
Mem 350
Sec JB Galbraith (01586) 830698
Holes 18 L 4799 yds SSS 64
V'tors U
Fees £10
Loc 10 miles S of Campbeltown

Gigha (1992)
Isle of Gigha, Kintyre PA41 7AA
Mem 26
Sec M Tart (015835) 287
Holes 9 L 5026 yds SSS 66
V'tors U
Fees D–£5
Loc Off W coast of Kintyre

Glencruitten (1905)
Glencruitten Road, Oban PA34 4PU
Tel **(01631) 62868/64115**
Mem 350 105(L) 115(J)
Sec AG Brown
Holes 18 L 4452 yds SSS 63
Recs Am–55 JM Wilson
Pro–60 H Bannerman, G Cunningham
V'tors U
Fees On application
Loc Oban 1 mile
Arch James Braid

Innellan (1891)
Knockamillie Road, Innellan
Tel **(01369) 3546**
Mem 200
Sec JG Arden
Holes 9 L 4878 yds SSS 63
Recs Am–63
V'tors U SOC
Fees £6 (£7)
Loc 4 miles S of Dunoon (A815)

Inveraray (1893)
c/o 2 Dalmally Road, Inveraray PA32 8XD
Tel **(01499) 302079**
Mem 160
Sec D McNeil, A Bannister
Holes 9 L 5600 yds SSS 67
V'tors U SOC
Fees D–£6 (£8)
Loc 1 mile S of Inveraray on A83
Mis New course opened 1993

Kyles of Bute (1907)
Tighnabruaich PA21 2EE
Tel **(01700) 811603**
Mem 160
Sec J Thomson
Holes 9 L 2389 yds SSS 32
Recs Am–64 T Whyte (1985)
V'tors U
Fees D–£6 W–£20
Loc 26 miles W of Dunoon

Lochgilphead (1963)
Blarbuie Road, Lochgilphead PA31 8LD
Tel **(01546) 602340**
Mem 210
Sec AR Law (01546) 86302
Holes 9 L 4484 yds SSS 63
Recs Am–59 R Willan
Pro–62 R Weir (1991)
V'tors U SOC
Fees D–£7 (D–£10)
Loc 1/2 mile N of Lochgilphead by Hospital

Machrie Hotel (1891)
Port Ellen, Isle of Islay PA42 7AN
Tel **(01496) 2310**
Fax **(01496) 2404**
Mem 35
Sec M Macpherson
Holes 18 L 6226 yds SSS 70
Recs Am–66 I Middleton
Pro–67 M Seymour
V'tors H SOC
Fees £25 D–£40
Loc Machrie, 5 miles N of Port Ellen
Mis Driving range
Arch Willie Campbell

Machrihanish (1876)
Machrihanish, Campbeltown PA28 6PT
Tel **(01586) 810213**
Mem 525 135(L) 80(J)
Sec Mrs A Anderson
Pro K Campbell (01586) 810277
Holes 18 L 6228 yds SSS 70
9 hole course
Recs Am–66 SJ Campbell
Pro–64 B Lockie
V'tors U
Fees £18 D–£28 (D–£32)
Loc 5 miles W of Campbeltown

Tarbert (1910)
Kilberry Road, Tarbert PA29 6XX
Tel **(01880) 820565**
Mem 101
Sec P Cupples (01880) 820536
Holes 9 L 4460 yds SSS 64
Recs Am–62 D Lamont (1990)
Pro–63
V'tors U SOC
Fees £5 D–£8 W–£30
Loc 1 mile W of Tarbert on B8024, off A83

Tobermory (1896)
Erray Road, Tobermory, Isle of Mull PA75 6PS
Mem 120
Sec Dr WH Clegg (01688) 2020
Holes 9 L 2460 yds SSS 64
Recs Am–65 G Davidson (1994)
Ladies 72 J Jack (1993)
V'tors U
Fees D–£10 W–£35
Loc Tobermory, Isle of Mull
Mis Tickets from Western Isles Hotel
Arch David Adams

Vaul (1920)
Scarinish, Isle of Tiree PA77 6XH
Mem 100
Sec N McArthur (018792) 339
Holes 9 L 2911 yds SSS 70
V'tors U exc Sun–NA
Fees On application
Loc 3 miles N of Scarinish, E coast of Tiree. 40 min flight from Glasgow

Ayrshire

Annanhill (1957)
Public
Irvine Road, Kilmarnock KA3 2RT
Tel **(01563) 21512 (Starter)**
Mem 350
Sec D McKie
Holes 18 L 6270 yds SSS 70
Recs Am–65 I McKenzie
Pro–65 J Farmer
V'tors WD/Sun–U Sat–NA
SOC–exc Sat
Fees D–£8 (D–£12)
Loc 1 mile W of Kilmarnock
Arch J McLean

Ardeer (1880)
Greenhead Avenue, Stevenston KA20 4JX
Tel **(01294) 64542/601327**
Mem 500
Sec WF Hand (01294) 63538

Holes 18 L 6630 yds SSS 72
Recs Am–66 R Lauder (1992)
Pro–68 A Brooks, I Stanley, R Walker (1971)
V'tors U exc Sat–NA
Fees £10 D–£18 Sun–£14 D–£24
Loc ½ mile N of Stevenston, off A78

Auchenharvie (1981)

Public
Moor Park Road, West Brewery Park, Saltcoats KA20 3HU
Mem 80
Sec A Breslin (01294) 69361
Pro R Rodgers (01292) 603103
Holes 9 L 5300 yds SSS 66
Recs Am–67 R Galloway, J Murphy, P Rodgers, A Wylie
V'tors WD–U WE–U after 9.30am
Fees On application
Loc Low road between Saltcoats and Stevenston
Mis Driving range

Ballochmyle (1937)

Ballochmyle, Mauchline KA5 6LE
Tel **(01290) 550469**
Fax **(01290) 553150**
Mem 860
Sec DG Munro
Pro None
Holes 18 L 5952 yds SSS 69
Recs Am–65 J Howson (1991)
Pro–65 A Hunter (1987)
V'tors WD/WE–U BH–M SOC exc Wed/Sat/BH
Fees £18 D–£25 (D–£30)
Loc 1 mile S of Mauchline on B705, off A76

Beith (1896)

Bigholm Road, Beith KA15 2JQ
Tel **(01505) 503166**
Mem 380
Sec EJ Armstrong
Holes 9 L 5580 yds SSS 68
Recs Am–64 K Ross
V'tors U before 5pm exc Sat & Sun pm
Fees £10 (£15)
Loc 1 mile NE of Beith. 12 miles NE of Paisley

Belleisle (1927)

Public
Bellisle Park, Doonfoot Road, Ayr
Tel **(01292) 441258**
Fax **(01292) 442632**
Pro D Gemmell (Golf Mgr) (01292) 441314
Holes 18 L 6477 yds SSS 72
Recs Am–63 K Gimson
Pro–64 J Farmer
Ladies–71 B Robinson
V'tors WD–U WE–H
Fees £16 D–£23
Loc S of Ayr in Belleisle Park
Arch James Braid

Brunston Castle (1992)

Dailly, Girvan KA26 9RM
Tel **(01465) 81471**
Fax **(01465) 81545**
Mem 150
Sec I Tennant (Hon)
Holes 18 L 6792 yds SSS 72
V'tors U–booking necessary SOC
Fees £20 D–£30 (£25 D–£35)
Loc 4 miles E of Girvan
Arch Donald Steel

Caprington

Public
Ayr Road, Caprington, Kilmarnock KA1 4UW
Tel **(01563) 21915 (Starter)**
Mem 400
Sec F McCulloch
Holes 18 L 5460 yds SSS 69
9 hole course
Recs Am–63 S Fraser
Pro–66 E Brown
V'tors U
Fees On application
Loc 1 mile S of Kilmarnock (B7038)

Dalmilling (1961)

Public
Westwood Avenue, Ayr KA8 0QY
Tel **(01292) 263893**
Fax **(01292) 610543**
Pro P Cheyney (Golf Mgr)
Holes 18 L 5724 yds SSS 68
Recs Am–61 G McKay
V'tors U
Fees £10 D–£18
Loc NE boundary of Ayr, nr Ayr racecourse

Doon Valley (1927)

Hillside, Patna
Tel **(01292) 531607**
Mem 90
Sec J Green
Holes 9 L 5654 yds SSS 68
V'tors U
Fees £5 (£5)
Loc 8 miles SE of Ayr (A713)

Girvan (1900)

Public
Golf Course Road, Girvan KA26 9HW
Tel **(01465) 714272/ 714346** (Starter)
Fax **(01465) 714346**
Holes 18 L 5095 SSS 64
Recs Am–61 J Cannon
Pro–61 K Stevely
V'tors U
Fees £10 D–£18
Loc N side of Girvan (A77). 22 miles S of Ayr

Glasgow Gailes (1892)

Gailes, Irvine KA11 5AE
Tel **(01294) 311347**
Fax **(0141) 942 0770 (Sec)**
Mem 1100
Sec DW Deas (0141) 942 2011
Pro J Steven (0141) 942 8507
Holes 18 L 6510 yds Par 71 SSS 72
Recs Am–65 GC Sherry
Pro–64 C Gillies
V'tors WD–I WE/BH–NA before 2.30pm SOC
Fees £30 D–£37 (£33)
Loc 1 mile S of Irvine, off A78
Arch Willie Park Jr

Irvine (1887)

Bogside, Irvine KA12 8SN
Tel **(01294) 78139**
Mem 450
Sec A Morton (01294) 75979
Pro K Erskine (01294) 75626
Holes 18 L 6408 yds SSS 71
Recs Am–65 DA Roxburgh (1981)
Pro–66 R Weir (1987)
V'tors U SOC–WD
Fees £23 D–£28 (1993)
Loc 1 mile N of Irvine towards Kilwinning

Irvine Ravenspark (1907)

Public
Kidsneuk Lane, Irvine KA12 8SR
Tel **(01294) 271293**
Mem 400
Sec G Robertson
Pro P Bond (01294) 276467
Holes 18 L 6429 yds SSS 71
Recs Am–65 GJ Robertson
V'tors U
Fees £4 (£14)
Loc N side of Irvine, off A737. 7 miles N of Troon

Kilbirnie Place (1922)

Largs Road, Kilbirnie KA25 7AT
Tel **(01505) 683398**
Mem 300
Sec A Rice
Holes 18 L 5411 yds SSS 67
Recs Am–64 G McLean
V'tors U exc Sat
Fees On application
Loc ½ mile W of Kilbirnie, S of A760. 15 miles SW of Paisley

Kilmarnock (Barassie) (1887)

29 Hillhouse Road, Barassie, Troon KA10 6SY
Tel **(01292) 311077**
Fax **(01292) 313920**
Mem 450
Sec RL Bryce (01292) 313920
Pro WR Lockie (01292) 311322
Holes 18 L 6473 yds SSS 72
Recs Am–66 JW Milligan (1988)
Pro–63 GP Emmerson, C Van der Velde (1989), D Feherty (1994)
V'tors WE/Wed–NA SOC–Tues & Thurs
Fees £30 D–£40
Loc Opp Barassie Railway Station
Arch Theodore Moone

Largs (1891)
Irvine Road, Largs KA30 8EU
Tel **(01475) 674681**
Fax **(01475) 673594**
Mem 800
Sec B Godfrey (01475) 673594
Pro R Collinson (01475) 686192
Holes 18 L 6257 yds SSS 70
Recs Am–64 C White (1989)
Pro–65 M McLaren (1991)
V'tors U
Fees £20 D–£27
Loc 1 mile S of Largs

Loudoun Gowf (1909)
Galston KA4 8PA
Tel **(01563) 820551**
Mem 475
Sec TR Richmond
(01563) 821993
Holes 18 L 5854 yds SSS 68
Recs Am–61 AG Todd
V'tors WD–U WE–M
Fees £15 D–£25 (1994)
Loc 5 miles E of Kilmarnock (A71)

Maybole (1970)
Public
Memorial Park, Maybole KA19
Holes 9 L 2635 yds SSS 65
Recs Am–64 WW McCulloch
V'tors U
Fees £7 D–£11
Loc S of Maybole, off A77. 8 miles S of Ayr

Millport (1888)
Millport, Isle of Cumbrae KA28 0BA
Tel **(01475) 530311**
Mem 288 120(L) 78(J)
Sec WD Patrick (01475) 530306
Pro G McQueen (01475) 530305
Holes 18 L 5831 yds SSS 68
Recs Am–64 AD Harrington (1981)
V'tors U SOC
Fees £11 D–£15 (£15 D–£20)
W–£46 M–£106
Loc W of Millport (Largs car ferry)

New Cumnock (1901)
Lochil, Cumnock Road, New Cumnock KA18 4BQ
Tel **(01290) 32037**
Mem 250
Sec J Bryce
Holes 9 L 2588 yds SSS 65
Recs Am–62 R Hodge (1992)
V'tors U
Fees D–£6 (D–£6)

Prestwick (1851)
2 Links Road, Prestwick KA9 1QG
Tel **(01292) 77404**
Fax **(01292) 77255**
Mem 580
Sec DE Donaldson
Pro FC Rennie (01292) 79483
Holes 18 L 6668 yds SSS 73
Recs Am–68 PM Mayo, P Deeble, B Andrade (1987)
Pro–67 EC Brown, C O'Connor
V'tors WD–I on application only
Fees On application
Loc Prestwick Airport 1 mile, nr Railway Station

Prestwick St Cuthbert (1899)
East Road, Prestwick KA9 2SX
Tel **(01292) 77101**
Mem 865
Sec JC Rutherford
Holes 18 L 6470 yds SSS 71
Recs Am–66 G Hogg (1984), R McLellan (1992)
Ladies–67 CA Gibson (1992)
V'tors WD–U WE/BH–M SOC–WD
Fees £18 D–£24
Loc 1/2 mile E of Prestwick

Prestwick St Nicholas (1851)
Grangemuir Road, Prestwick KA9 1SN
Tel **(01292) 77608**
Mem 600 125(L) 62(J)
Sec JR Leishman
Pro S Smith (01292) 79755
Holes 18 L 5952 yds SSS 69
Recs Am–63 P Girvan
Pro–63 A Johnstone
V'tors WD–I WE/BH–NA
Fees On application
Loc Prestwick
Arch C Hunter

Routenburn (1914)
Greenock Road, Largs KA30 9AH
Tel **(01475) 673230**
Mem 400
Sec J Thomson (Mgr)
Pro G McQueen (01475) 687240
Holes 18 L 5650 yds SSS 68
Recs Am–63 C White
Pro–65 S Torrance
V'tors U SOC–WD
Fees £5.50 (£8)
Loc N of Largs, off A78
Arch James Braid

Royal Troon (1878)
Craigend Road, Troon KA10 6EP
Tel **(01292) 311555**
Fax **(01292) 318204**
Mem 500
Sec JD Montgomerie
Pro RB Anderson (01292) 313281
Holes Old 18 L 7097 yds SSS 74; Portland 18 L 6274 yds SSS 71
Recs Old Am–70 CW Green, J Harkis, R Claydon, DW Hawthorn
Pro–64 G Norman
Portland Am–65 GS Reynolds
Pro–65 WG Cunningham
V'tors Booking required. Mon/Tues/Thurs only–I H (max 18) XL WE–NA
Fees Old + Portland D–£85. Portland only D–£55 (inc lunch etc)
Loc SE side of Troon (B749). Prestwick Airport 3 miles
Arch W Fernie

Seafield (1930)
Public
Belleisle Park, Doonfoot Road, Ayr
Tel **(01292) 441258**
Fax **(01292) 442632**
Pro D Gemmell (Golf Mgr) (01292) 441314
Holes 18 L 5498 yds SSS 66
Recs Am–65 R Gibson
V'tors U
Fees £10 D–£18
Loc S of Ayr in Belleisle Park

Skelmorlie (1891)
Skelmorlie PA17 5ES
Tel **(01475) 520152**
Mem 390
Sec Mrs A Fahey (Hon)
Holes 13 L 5056 yds SSS 65
Recs Am–61 J McCreadie (1992)
Pro–69 J Braid, G Duncan
V'tors U exc Sat (Apr–Oct)
Fees D–£15 Sun–£18
Loc Wemyss Bay Station 1 1/2 miles

Troon Municipal
Public
Harling Drive, Troon KA10 6NF
Tel **(01292) 312464**
Fax **(01292) 312578**
Pro G McKInlay
Holes Lochgreen 18 L 6785 yds SSS 73; Darley 18 L 6501 yds SSS 72; Fullarton 18 L 4822 yds SSS 63
Recs Lochgreen Am–66 R Milligan
Pro–65 J Chillas
Darley Am–66 M Rossi
Pro–66 J White
Fullarton Am–58 A McQueen
V'tors U SOC
Fees Lochgreen £16
Darley £13 D–£23
Fullarton £10 D–£18
Loc 4 miles N of Prestwick at Station Brae

Troon Portland (1894)
1 Crosbie Road, Troon KA10
Tel **(01292) 313488**
Mem 120
Sec J Irving
Holes Play over Portland at Royal Troon

Troon St Meddans (1907)
Harling Drive, Troon KA10 6NF
Mem 200
Sec DG Baxter (01292) 313291
Holes Play over Troon Municipal courses Lochgreen and Darley

Turnberry Hotel (1906)

Turnberry KA26 9LT

Tel **(01655) 331000**
Fax **(01655) 331706**
Sec CJ Rouse (Gen Mgr)
Pro B Gunson
Holes Ailsa 18 L 6957 yds SSS 72
Arran 18 L 6014 yds SSS 69
Recs Ailsa Am–70 GK MacDonald
Pro–63 M Hayes, G Norman (1986)
Arran Am–66 AP Parkin
Pro–65 E McIntosh, C Ronald, S McGregor
V'tors On application
Fees On application
Loc 5 miles N of Girvan on A77
Arch Hutchison/Mackenzie Ross

West Kilbride (1893)

Fullerton Drive, Seamill, West Kilbride KA23 9HT

Tel **(01294) 823128**
Mem 900
Sec RJ Whittingham (01294) 823911
Pro G Howie (01294) 823042
Holes 18 L 6452 yds SSS 71
Recs Am–65 G Rankin (1993)
Pro–67 J Panton
V'tors WD–U WE–M BH–NA SOC
Fees On application
Loc West Kilbride
Arch Tom Morris

Western Gailes (1897)

Gailes, Irvine KA11 5AE

Tel **(01294) 311649**
Fax **(01294) 312312**
Mem 450
Sec AM McBean
Holes 18 L 6639 yds SSS 72
Recs Am–67 RA Muscroft (1986)
Pro–65 B Gallacher (1986)
V'tors WD–H exc Thurs (booking necessary)
Fees £40 D–£55
Loc 3 miles N of Troon (A78)

Dunbartonshire

Bearsden (1891)

Thorn Road, Bearsden, Glasgow G61 4BP

Tel **(0141) 942 2351**
Mem 500
Sec JR Mercer
Holes 9 L 6014 yds SSS 69
Recs Am–67 S Hardie (1991)
Pro–65 R Craig (1991)
V'tors M
Loc 6 miles NW of Glasgow

Cardross (1895)

Main Street, Cardross, Dumbarton G82 5LB

Tel **(01389) 841213**
Mem 850
Sec PA Laing (01389) 841754
Pro R Farrell (01389) 841350
Holes 18 L 6469 yds SSS 71
Recs Am–65 JLS Kinloch (1981)
Pro–65 J White (1990)
V'tors WD–U WE–M SOC
Fees £18 D–£30
Loc 4 miles W of Dumbarton on A814
Arch Fernie (1904)/Braid(1921)

Clober (1951)

Craigton Road, Milngavie, Glasgow G62 7HP

Tel **(0141) 956 1685**
Mem 575
Holes 18 L 5068 yds SSS 65
Recs Am–61 PW Smith, J Graham
V'tors WD–U before 4pm WE–M BH–NA SOC–WD
Fees £10
Loc 7 miles NW of Glasgow

Clydebank & District (1905)

Hardgate, Clydebank G81 5QY

Tel **(01389) 873289**
Mem 780
Sec W Manson (01389) 872832
Pro D Pirie (01389) 878686
Holes 18 L 5823 yds SSS 68
Recs Am–64 D Galbraith (1965), C Barrowman Jr (1993)
Pro–64 KW Walker (1994)
Ladies–68 V Melvin (1994)
V'tors WD–H
Fees On application
Loc 2 miles N of Clydebank

Clydebank Municipal (1927)

Public

Overtoun Road, Dalmuir, Clydebank G81 3RE

Tel **(0141) 952 8698 (Starter)**
Fax **(0141) 952 6372**
Pro R Bowman (0141) 952 6372
Holes 18 L 5349 yds SSS 66
Recs Am–63 J Semple, P Semple
Pro–63 G Weir
V'tors U exc Sat–NA 11am–2.30pm
Fees On application
Loc 8 miles W of Glasgow

Cumbernauld (1975)

Public

Palacerigg Country Park, Cumbernauld G67 3HU

Tel **(01236) 734969**
Mem 360
Sec DSA Cooper
Holes 18 L 6412 yds SSS 71
Recs Am–67 G Wilson
Pro–66 J Farmer
V'tors U SOC–WD only
Fees £7.50
Loc 3 miles SE of Cumbernauld
Arch Henry Cotton

Dougalston (1977)

Strathblane Road, Milngavie, Glasgow G62

Tel **(0141) 956 5750**
Fax **(0141) 956 6480**
Mem 440
Sec Grace Wilson (Mgr)
Holes 18 L 6269 yds SSS 71
Recs Am–71 J Carnegie, J McLaren (1987)
Pro–73 B Barnes
V'tors WD–U SOC
Fees £12 D–£18
Loc 7 miles N of Glasgow on A81

Douglas Park (1897)

Hillfoot, Bearsden, Glasgow G61 2TJ

Tel **(0141) 942 2220**
Mem 450 250(L) 100(J)
Sec DN Nicolson
Pro D Scott (0141) 942 1482
Holes 18 L 5982 yds SSS 69
Recs Am–64 F Giovannetti, AR Docherty
Pro–63 C Innes
V'tors M SOC
Loc 6 miles NW of Glasgow, nr Hillfoot Station

Dullatur (1896)

Dullatur, Glasgow G68 0AR G68 0AR

Tel **(01236) 723230**
Mem 420 60(L)
Sec W Laing (01236) 727847
Pro D Sinclair
Holes 18 L 6253 yds SSS 70
Recs Am–62 D Kane Jr (1989)
Pro–68 J Farmer
V'tors WD–U WE–M SOC
Fees £18
Loc 3 miles N of Cumbernauld

Dumbarton (1888)

Broadmeadow, Dumbarton G82 2BQ

Tel **(01389) 32830**
Mem 500
Sec R Turnbull
Holes 18 L 5981 yds SSS 69
Recs Am–64 CW Green
V'tors WD–U WE/BH–M
Fees On application
Loc 1 mile N of Dumbarton

Glasgow (1787)

Killermont, Bearsden, Glasgow G61 2TW

Tel **(0141) 942 2340**
Fax **(0141) 942 0770**
Mem 800
Sec DW Deas (0141) 942 2011
Pro J Steven (0141) 942 8507
Holes 18 L 5968 yds Par 70 SSS 69
Recs Am–63 JS Cochran
Pro–65 H Weetman
V'tors M
Loc 4 miles NW of Glasgow
Arch Tom Morris Sr

For list of abbreviations see page 435

Hayston (1926)
Campsie Road, Kirkintilloch, Glasgow G66 1RN
Tel **(0141) 776 1244**
Mem 440 70(L) 60(J)
Sec JV Carmichael (0141) 775 0723
Pro S Barnett (041) 775 0882
Holes 18 L 6042 yds SSS 69
Recs Am–62 LS Mann
Pro–65 W Milne
V'tors WD–I before 4.30pm –M after 4.30pm WE–M
Fees £15
Loc 1 mile N of Kirkintilloch
Arch James Braid

Helensburgh (1893)
25 East Abercromby Street, Helensburgh G84 9JD
Tel **(01436) 674173**
Fax **(01436) 671170**
Mem 825
Sec D Loch
Pro D Fotheringham (01436) 675505
Holes 18 L 6058 yds SSS 69
Recs Am–64 A Scott
Pro–65 RT Drummond, D Chillas, B Marchbank
V'tors WD–U WE–NA
Fees On application
Loc N of Helensburgh and A814. 8 miles W of Dumbarton
Arch Tom Morris

Hilton Park (1927)
Auldmarroch Estate, Stockiemuir Road, Milngavie G62 7HB
Tel **(0141) 956 5124/1215**
Mem 1200
Sec Mrs JA Warnock (0141) 956 4657
Pro W McCondichie (0141) 956 5125
Holes Hilton 18 L 6054 yds SSS 70
Allander 18 L 5374 yds SSS 67
Recs Hilton Am–66 AP McDonald
Pro–64 AF Anderson
Allander Am–66 I Weir
Pro–63 F Morris, N Wood
V'tors WD–U before 4pm
Fees On application
Loc 8 miles NW of Glasgow on A809
Arch James Braid

Kirkintilloch (1894)
Todhill, Campsie Road, Kirkintilloch G66 1RN
Tel **(0141) 776 1256**
Mem 420 92(L) 104(J)
Sec IM Gray (0141) 775 2387
Holes 18 L 5269 yds SSS 66
Recs Am–61 S Shaw
Pro–68 R Weir
V'tors M SOC
Fees SOC–On application
Loc 7 miles N of Glasgow

Lenzie (1889)
19 Crosshill Road, Lenzie G66 5DA
Tel **(0141) 776 1535**
Mem 501 125(L) 125(J)
Sec JA Chisholm (0141) 776 6020
Pro J McCallum (0141) 777 7748
Holes 18 L 5984 yds SSS 69
Recs Am–64 S Lindsay
Pro–65 J McCallum (1992)
V'tors M SOC
Fees On application
Loc 6 miles NE of Glasgow

Loch Lomond
Rossdhu House, Luss, Alexandria G83 8NT
Tel **(01436) 860223**
Fax **(01436) 860265**
Sec P Dellanzo (Golf Dir)
Pro C Campbell
Holes 18 L 7053 yds Par 71
V'tors M
Loc 20 miles NE of Glasgow on A82
Arch Weiskopf/Morrish

Milngavie (1895)
Laighpark, Milngavie, Glasgow G62 8EP
Tel **(0141) 956 1619**
Mem 390
Sec Mrs AJW Ness
Holes 18 L 5818 yds SSS 68
Recs Am–64 RGB McCallum, R Blair, AS McGarvie
V'tors M SOC
Fees On application
Loc 7 miles NW of Glasgow

Vale of Leven (1907)
Northfield Road, Bonhill, Alexandria G83 9ET
Tel **(01389) 752351**
Mem 600
Sec W McKinlay (01389) 752508
Holes 18 L 5156 yds SSS 66
Recs Am–60 G Brown (1988)
Pro–63 EC Brown (1959)
V'tors U exc Sat (Apr–Sept) SOC (max 36 members)
Fees £12 D–£16 (£16 D–£20)
Loc Bonhill, 3 miles N of Dumbarton, off A82

Westerwood Hotel G & CC (1989)
St Andrews Drive, Cumbernauld G68 0EW
Tel **(01236) 725281 (Pro)**
Pro S Killin
Holes 18 L 6735 yds SSS 73
V'tors U
Fees £22.50 (£27.50)
Loc 13 miles NE of Glasgow off A80
Arch Dave Thomas

Windyhill (1908)
Windyhill, Bearsden G61 4QQ
Tel **(0141) 942 2349**
Mem 650
Sec AJ Miller
Pro G Collinson (0141) 942 7157
Holes 18 L 6254 yds SSS 70
Recs Am–64 K Smyth (1994)
V'tors WD–I Sun–M SOC–WD
Fees £20
Loc 8 miles NW of Glasgow
Arch James Braid

Isle of Arran

Brodick (1897)
Brodick, Arran
Tel **(01770) 302349**
Mem 550
Sec HM Macrae
Pro PS McCalla (01770) 302513
Holes 18 L 4404 yds SSS 62
Recs Am–61 D Bell, A Neilson
V'tors U SOC
Fees £8 D–£12 (£9 D–£14)
Loc Brodick Pier 1 mile

Corrie (1892)
Corrie, Arran
Tel **(0177081) 223**
Mem 220
Sec R Stevenson
Holes 9 L 1948 yds SSS 61
Recs Am–60 S Bunyan
V'tors U exc Sat pm
Fees D–£6 W–£20
Loc 6 miles N of Brodick

Lamlash (1889)
Lamlash, Arran KA27 8LE
Tel **(01770) 600296** (Clubhouse), **(01770) 600196** (Starter)
Mem 450
Sec J Henderson
Holes 18 L 4611 yds SSS 63
Recs Am–62 B Morrison (1968)
Pro–64 R Burke (1972)
Ladies–66 B Livingston (1992)
V'tors U SOC
Fees D–£10 (D–£12)
W–£50 (1994)
Loc 3 miles S of Brodick on A841

Lochranza (1991)
Pay and play
Lochranza, Arran KA27 8HL
Tel **(0177083) 0273**
Fax **(0177083) 0273**
Sec IM Robertson
Holes 9 L 5600 yds SSS 70
Recs Am–74 D McAllister (1993)
V'tors U SOC–May–Oct
Fees 18 holes–£8
Loc 14 miles N of Brodick
Mis 9 double greens – 18 flags/tees
Arch IM Robertson

Machrie Bay (1900)
Machrie Bay, Brodick, Arran KA27 8DZ
Tel **(01770) 850261**
Mem 260
Sec AM Blair
Holes 9 L 2143 yds SSS 32

For list of abbreviations see page 435

Recs Am–62 A Kelso
Pro–59 W Hagen
V'tors U
Fees D–£5 W–£15
Loc 9 miles W of Brodick
Arch William Fernie

Shiskine (1896)

Shiskine, Blackwaterfoot, Arran KA27
Tel **(01770) 860226**
Mem 350 96(L) 34(J)
Sec Mrs F Crawford
(01770) 860293
J Faulkner (01770) 860392
Holes 12 L 2990 yds SSS 42
Recs Am–39 J Melvin, J Brown
Pro–36 DH McGillivray
V'tors U SOC
Fees £10 W–£30
Loc 11 miles SW of Brodick

Whiting Bay (1895)

Golf Course Road, Whiting Bay, Arran KA27 8PR
Tel **(017707) 487**
Mem 290
Sec Mrs I I'Anson
Holes 18 L 4405 yds SSS 63
Recs Am–58 N Auld
V'tors U
Fees On application
Loc 8 miles S of Brodick

Isle of Bute

Bute (1888)

Kingarth, Bute
Mem 115
Sec J Burnside (01700) 83648
Holes 9 L 2497 yds SSS 64
Recs Am–65 G McArthur (1990)
V'tors U Sat–U after 12.30pm
Fees D–£6
Loc Stravanan Bay, 6 miles S of Rothesay, off A845

Port Bannatyne (1968)

Mains Road, Port Bannatyne, Bute
Mem 180
Sec IL MacLeod (01700) 502009
Holes 13 L 4730 yds SSS 63
Recs Am–61 J Ewing
Pro–64 W Watson
V'tors U
Fees £7.50 (£7.50)
Loc 2 miles N of Rothesay

Rothesay (1892)

Canada Hill, Rothesay, Bute PA20 7HN
Tel **(01700) 502244**
Mem 350
Sec J Barker (01700) 503744
Pro J Dougal (01700) 503554
Holes 18 L 5358 yds SSS 67
Recs Am–62 G Reynolds (1993)
Pro–72 RDBM Shade (1968)
V'tors WD–U WE–book with Pro SOC
Fees £12 (£18) W–£60
Loc 2 miles E of Rothesay

Lanarkshire

Airdrie (1877)

Rochsoles, Airdrie ML6 0PQ
Tel **(01236) 762195**
Mem 450
Sec DM Hardie
Pro A McCloskey (01236) 754360
Holes 18 L 6004 yds SSS 69
Recs Am–64 G Russo, R Marshall
V'tors M I WE/BH–NA SOC
Fees £12 D–£20
Loc Airdrie 1 mile

Alexandra Park (1880)

Public
Alexandra Park, Dennistoun, Glasgow G31 8SE
Tel **(0141) 556 3991**
Mem 250
Sec G Campbell
Holes 9 L 4562 yds Par 62
V'tors U
Fees On application
Loc 1/2 mile E of Glasgow, nr M8
Arch Graham McArthur

Bellshill (1905)

Orbiston, Bellshill ML4 2RZ
Tel **(01698) 745124**
Mem 680
Sec JS Sloan
Holes 18 L 6494 yds SSS 71
Recs Am–68 J Simpson, A Megan, M Brown, D Cardwell
Pro–70 J McCallum
V'tors U exc WD 5–6.30pm
Fees £18 (£25)
Loc 10 miles SE of Glasgow between Bellshill and Motherwell

Biggar (1895)

Public
The Park, Broughton Road, Biggar ML12 6AH
Tel **(01899) 20618** (Clubhouse), **(01899) 20319** (Bookings)
Mem 250
Sec WS Turnbull (01899) 20566
Holes 18 L 5416 yds SSS 66
Recs Am–62 B Kerr (1987)
Pro–63 P Lawrie (1993)
V'tors U
Fees £9 (£14)
Loc 12 miles SE of Lanark (A702)
Arch Willie Park

Bishopbriggs (1906)

Brackenbrae Road, Bishopbriggs, Glasgow G64 2DX
Tel **(0141) 772 1810**
Mem 400 100(L) 100(J)
Sec J Magin (0141) 772 8938
Holes 18 L 6041 yds SSS 69
Recs Am–64 AF Dunsmore, S Finlayson, I Gillan
Pro–63 M Miller
V'tors M or I H
Fees On application
Loc 6 miles N of Glasgow on A803
Arch James Braid

Blairbeth (1910)

Burnside, Rutherglen, Glasgow G73
Tel **(0141) 634 3355**
Mem 450
Sec FT Henderson
(0141) 632 0604
Holes 18 L 5448 yds SSS 68
Recs Am–64 D Orr
Pro–69 WG Cunningham
V'tors SOC–WD
Fees On application
Loc 1 mile S of Rutherglen

Bothwell Castle (1922)

Blantyre Road, Bothwell G71 8PJ
Tel **(01698) 853177**
Mem 1137
Sec ADC Watson (01698) 852395
Pro JG Niven (01698) 852052
Holes 18 L 6243 yds SSS 70
Recs Am–64 S Gallacher (1994)
Pro–61 A Crerar (1994)
V'tors WD–U 9.30am–3.30pm
Fees £20 D–£28
Loc 3 miles N of Hamilton. M74 Junction 5

Calderbraes (1891)

57 Roundknowe Road, Uddingston G71 7TS
Tel **(01698) 813425**
Mem 300
Sec S McGuigan (0141) 773 2287
Holes 9 L 5046 yds Par 66 SSS 67
Recs Am–65 D Gilchrist (1986)
V'tors WD only
Fees D–£12
Loc Start of M74

Cambuslang (1892)

Westburn Drive, Cambuslang G72 7AN
Tel **(0141) 641 3130**
Mem 200 100(L) 75(J)
Sec W Lilly
Holes 9 L 6072 yds SSS 69
Recs Am–64 C Everett (1991)
V'tors I
Fees On application
Loc Cambuslang Station 3/4 mile

Carluke (1894)

Hallcraig, Mauldslie Road, Carluke ML8 5HG
Tel **(01555) 771070**
Mem 460 100(L)
Sec JH Muir (01555) 770620
Pro A Brooks (01555) 751053
Holes 18 L 5805 yds SSS 68
Recs Am–64 K Harrison
Pro–64 G Cunningham, R Davis, W Milne
V'tors WD–U before 4pm WE/BH–NA
Fees £15 D–£20
Loc 20 miles SE of Glasgow

Carnwath (1907)

Main Street, Carnwath ML11 8JX

Tel **(01555) 840251**
Mem 380
Sec To be appointed
Pro None
Holes 18 L 5955 yds SSS 69
Recs Am–65 B Holbrook
V'tors WD–U before 4pm Sat–NA Sun–restricted
Fees WD/Sat–D–£18 Sun/BH–D–£22
Loc 7 miles E of Lanark

Cathkin Braes (1888)

Cathkin Road, Rutherglen, Glasgow G73 4SE

Tel **(0141) 634 6605**
Fax **(0141) 634 6605**
Mem 880
Sec GL Stevenson
Pro S Bree (0141) 634 0650
Holes 18 L 6208 yds SSS 71
Recs Am–65 L McLaughlin (1994) Pro–66 C Maltman (1992)
V'tors WD–I
Fees £20
Loc 5 miles S of Glasgow (B759)
Arch James Braid

Cawder (1933)

Cadder Road, Bishopbriggs, Glasgow G64 3QD

Tel **(0141) 772 7101**
Fax **(0141) 772 4463**
Mem 1200
Sec GT Stoddart (0141) 772 5167
Pro K Stevely (0141) 772 7102
Holes Cawder 18 L 6295 yds SSS 71; Keir 18 L 5877 yds SSS 68
Recs Cawder Am–68 CW Green Pro–61 I Spencer Keir Am–63 G Rodaks, GH Murr
V'tors WD–U WE–NA SOC–WD
Fees £25
Loc N of Glasgow, off A803 Kirkintilloch road
Arch Braid/Steel

Coatbridge (1971)

Public
Townhead Road, Coatbridge ML52 2HX

Tel **(01236) 28975**
Mem 300
Sec O Dolan (01236) 26811
Pro G Weir (01236) 21492
Holes 18 L 6020 yds SSS 69
Recs Am–69 A Webster (1989)
V'tors U
Fees On application
Loc Townhead, E of Glasgow. ½ mile E of M73
Mis Driving range

Colville Park (1922)

Jerviston Estate, Motherwell ML1 4UG

Tel **(01698) 263017**
Mem 800 64(L) 140(J)
Sec S Connacher (01698) 265378
Pro Golf Shop (01698) 265779
Holes 18 L 6265 yds SSS 70
Recs Am–65 G King Pro–66 SD Brown
V'tors M SOC–WD only
Fees D–£20
Loc 1 mile NE of Motherwell on A723

Cowglen (1906)

301 Barrhead Road, Glasgow G43

Tel **(0141) 632 0556**
Mem 450
Sec RJG Jamieson (01292) 266600
Pro J McTear (0141) 649 9401
Holes 18 L 6006 yds SSS 69
Recs Am–63 D Barclay Howard Pro–63 S Torrance
V'tors M
Fees £18 D–£25
Loc 3 miles SW of Glasgow (B762)

Crow Wood (1925)

Cumbernauld Road, Muirhead, Glasgow G69 9JF

Tel **(0141) 799 2011**
Mem 700
Sec I McInnes (0141) 779 4954
Pro A Kershaw (0141) 779 1943
Holes 18 L 6249 yds SSS 71
Recs Am–62 D Robertson Pro–66 J McTear, A Oldcorn
V'tors WD–H (prior notice required) SOC
Fees £17 D–£25
Loc 5 miles NE of Glasgow, off A80
Arch James Braid

Deaconsbank (1922)

Public
Rouken Glen Park, Stewarton Road, Eastwood, Glasgow G46

Tel **(0141) 638 7044**
Sec C Cosh
Holes 18 L 4800 yds SSS 63
V'tors U
Fees On application
Loc 5 miles S of Glasgow, W of A77
Mis Driving range

Douglas Water (1922)

Douglas Water, Lanark ML11 9NB

Tel **(01555) 880361**
Mem 190
Sec R McMillan
Holes 9 L 2916 yds SSS 69
Recs Am–63 D Peat
V'tors U exc Sat–restricted
Fees £5 (£8)
Loc 7 miles S of Lanark

Drumpellier (1894)

Drumpellier Ave, Coatbridge ML5 1RX

Tel **(01236) 24139/28723**
Mem 500
Sec W Brownlie (01236) 23065/28538
Pro K Hutton (01236) 32971
Holes 18 L 6227 yds SSS 70
Recs Am–64 WS Bryson Pro–62 C Maltman
V'tors I
Fees £18 D–£25
Loc 8 miles E of Glasgow

East Kilbride (1900)

Chapelside Road, Nerston, East Kilbride G74 4PF

Tel **(013552) 20913**
Mem 800
Sec WG Gray
Pro A Taylor (013552) 22192
Holes 18 L 6419 yds SSS 71
Recs Am–65 WF Bryce Pro–64 D Ingram
V'tors M SOC
Fees £14 D–£20
Loc 8 miles S of Glasgow

Easter Moffat (1922)

Mansion House, Plains, Airdrie ML6 8NP

Tel **(01236) 842289/842878**
Mem 450
Sec JG Timmons (01236) 761440
Pro B Dunbar (01236) 843015
Holes 18 L 6221 yds SSS 70
Recs Am–67 Pro–66 R Shade
V'tors WD only BH–NA
Fees On application
Loc 3 miles E of Airdrie

Haggs Castle (1910)

70 Dumbreck Road, Dumbreck, Glasgow G41 4SN

Tel **(0141) 427 0480**
Fax **(0141) 427 1157**
Mem 970
Sec I Harvey (0141) 427 1157
Pro J McAlister (0141) 427 3355
Holes 18 L 6464 yds SSS 71
Recs Am–65 K Gallacher (1991) Pro–62 S Torrance (1984)
V'tors M SOC–Weds only
Fees SOC–£24 D–£36
Loc SW Glasgow (B768)

Hamilton (1892)

Riccarton, Ferniegair, by Hamilton

Tel **(01698) 282872**
Mem 480
Sec PE Soutter (01698) 286131
Pro MJ Moir (01698) 282324
Holes 18 L 6255 yds SSS 71
Recs Am–62 G Hogg
V'tors M or by arrangement
Fees On application
Loc 1½ miles S of Hamilton
Arch James Braid

Hollandbush (1954)

Public
Acre Tophead, Lesmahagow, Coalburn

Tel **(01555) 893484**
Mem 600
Sec J Hamilton
Pro I Rae (01555) 893646
Holes 18 L 6110 yds SSS 70

For list of abbreviations see page 435

Recs Am–63 G Brown, R Lynch
V'tors U
Fees £10
Loc 10 miles SW of Lanark, off A74

King's Park (1934)
Public
150A Croftpark Avenue, Croftfoot, Glasgow G54
Tel **(0141) 634 4745**
Sec P King
Holes 9 L 4236 yds Par 64 SSS 61
Recs Am–27 I Simpson
V'tors U
Fees On application
Loc 3½ miles S of Glasgow

Kirkhill (1910)
Greenlees Road, Cambuslang, Glasgow G72 8YN
Tel **(0141) 641 3083 (Clubhouse)**
Mem 570
Sec HG Marshall (013552) 31131
Holes 18 L 5889 yds SSS 69
Recs Am–63 D Martin
Pro–68 R Weir
V'tors WD–by prior arrangement WE/BH–NA SOC
Fees On application
Loc Cambuslang, SE Glasgow

Knightswood (1929)
Public
Knightswood Park, Lincoln Avenue, Glasgow G13
Tel **(0141) 959 2131**
Mem 76
Sec M Kelly
Holes 9 L 2736 yds SSS 33
V'tors U
Fees On application
Loc 4 miles NW of Glasgow, S of A82

Lanark (1851)
The Moor, Lanark ML11 2RX
Tel **(01555) 663219**
Fax **(01555) 663219**
Mem 500 130(L) 150(J)
Sec GH Cuthill
Pro R Wallace (01555) 661456
Holes 18 L 6426 yds SSS 71
9 hole course
Recs Am–64 CV McInally
Pro–62 C Maltman
V'tors WD–U until 4pm WE–M
Fees 18 hole:£22 D–£34 9 hole:£4
Loc 30 miles S of Glasgow, off A74
Arch Tom Morris

Larkhall
Public
Burnhead Road, Larkhall
Tel **(01698) 881113**
Mem 400
Sec I Gilmour
Holes 9 L 6754 yds SSS 72
Recs Am–67 S Crolla
V'tors U exc Tues 5–8pm & Sat 7am–5pm
Fees On application
Loc SW of Larkhall on B7109. 10 miles SE of Glasgow

Leadhills (1935)
Leadhills, Biggar ML12 6XR
Tel **(01659) 74222**
Mem 100
Sec H Shaw
Holes 9 L 2031 yds SSS 62
V'tors U
Fees On application
Loc 6 miles S of Abington, off A74

Lethamhill (1933)
Public
Cumbernauld Road, Glasgow G33 1AH
Tel **(0141) 770 6220**
Fax **(0141) 770 0520**
Holes 18 L 5946 yds SSS 68
Recs Am–70 R Harker
V'tors U
Fees £4.10
Loc 3 miles NE of Glasgow (A80)

Linn Park (1924)
Public
Simshill Road, Glasgow G44 5TA
Tel **(0141) 637 5871**
Mem 90
Sec R Flanagan
Holes 18 L 4592 yds SSS 65
Recs Am–62 J Cassidy (1989)
V'tors U
Fees £3.25 (£3.80)
Loc 4 miles S of Glasgow, W of B766

Littlehill (1926)
Public
Auchinairn Road, Glasgow G64 1UT
Tel **(0141) 772 1916**
Holes 18 L 6228 yds SSS 70
Recs Am–69
V'tors U
Fees £3.25 (£3.80)
Loc 3 miles NE of Glasgow, E of A803

Mount Ellen (1905)
Lochend Road, Gartcosh, Glasgow G69 9EY
Tel **(01236) 872277**
Mem 480
Sec WJ Dickson
Pro G Reilly
Holes 18 L 5525 yds SSS 68
V'tors WD–U from 9am–4pm WE–NA
Fees On application
Loc 8 miles NE of Glasgow, W of M73

Pollok (1893)
90 Barrhead Road, Glasgow G43 1BG
Tel **(0141) 632 1080**
Mem 500
Sec A Mathison Boyd (0141) 632 4351
Pro None
Holes 18 L 6257 yds SSS 70
Recs Am–62 G Shaw
Pro–62 G Cunningham
V'tors WD–I XL WE–NA SOC–WD
Fees £26 D–£33
Loc 3 miles SW of Glasgow (B762)

Ruchill (1928)
Public
Ruchil Park, Brassey Street, Maryhill, Glasgow G20
Mem 60
Sec DF Campbell (0141) 946 7676
Holes 9 L 2240 yds SSS 31
V'tors U
Fees On application
Loc 2 miles N of Glasgow, W of A879

Sandyhills (1905)
223 Sandyhills Road, Glasgow G32 9NA
Tel **(0141) 778 1179**
Mem 460
Sec P Ward
Holes 18 L 6253 yds SSS 70
Recs Am–65 J Hay
V'tors WE–M SOC
Fees On application
Loc 4 miles SE of Glasgow, N of A74

Shotts (1895)
Blairhead, Benhar Road, Shotts ML7 5BJ
Tel **(01501) 820431**
Mem 700
Sec J McDermott
Pro S Strachan (01501) 822658
Holes 18 L 6205 yds SSS 70
Recs Am–65 AJ Ferguson
Pro–65 B Gunson
V'tors WD–U Sat–NA before 4.30pm
Fees D–£17 (D–£20)
Loc 18 miles E of Glasgow on B7057. M8 Junction 5, 1½ miles
Arch James Braid

Strathaven (1908)
Glasgow Road, Strathaven ML10 6NL
Tel **(01357) 20421**
Mem 950
Sec AW Wallace (01357) 20421
Pro M McCrorie (01357) 21812
Holes 18 L 6226 yds SSS 70
Recs Am–66 RJC Milton, S Kirkland, AW Wallace, IA Ferguson, E McEwan
Pro–63 D Huish
V'tors WD–I before 4pm WE–NA
Fees On request
Loc N of Strathaven, off Glasgow road (A726)

Strathclyde Park

Public
Mote Hill, Hamilton
Tel **(01698) 266155**
Mem 180
Sec K Will
Pro W Walker (01698) 285511
Holes 9 L 6350 yds SSS 70
Recs Am–64 JJ Smith (1993)
V'tors U exc medal days (phone booking)
Fees £2.40
Mis Driving range

Torrance House (1969)

Public
Strathaven Road, East Kilbride, Glasgow G75 0QZ
Tel **(013552) 48638**
Mem 650
Sec JB Asher (013552) 49720
Pro J Dunlop (013552) 33451
Holes 18 L 6415 yds SSS 71
Recs Am–67 A Pitt
Pro–66 I Collins
V'tors U
Fees On application
Loc S of East Kilbride, off Strathaven road (A726)

Wishaw (1897)

55 Cleland Road, Wishaw ML2 7PH
Tel **(01698) 372869**
Mem 475 100(L)
Sec JM Mitchell
Pro JG Campbell (01698) 358247
Holes 18 L 6134 yds SSS 69
Recs Am–64 W Denholm (1983)
Pro–63 A Hunter (1989)
V'tors WD after 4pm–NA Sat–NA
Fees £12 D–£20 Sun–£25
Loc N of Wishaw town centre

Renfrewshire

Barshaw Municipal (1920)

Public
Barshaw Park, Glasgow Road, Paisley
Tel **(0141) 889 2908**
Mem 103
Sec W Collins (0141) 884 2533
Holes 18 L 5703 yds SSS 67
V'tors U
Fees £6
Loc 1 mile E of Paisley Cross, off A737

Bonnyton (1957)

Eaglesham, Glasgow G76 0QA
Tel **(013553) 2781**
Mem 950
Sec M Wise
Pro K McWade (013553) 2256
Holes 18 L 6252 yds SSS 71
Recs Am–67 S Black
Pro–68 J Wilson
V'tors I SOC–WD
Fees £25
Loc 2 miles W of Eaglesham. 6 miles S of Glasgow

Caldwell (1903)

Caldwell, Uplawmoor
Tel **(01505) 850329**
Fax **(01505) 850366**
Mem 450
Sec HIF Harper (01505) 850366
Pro S Forbes (01505) 850616
Holes 18 L 6228 yds SSS 70
Recs Am–64 JM Sharp (1974)
Pro–63 C Innes (1987), G Collinson (1988), C Gillies (1989)
V'tors WD–booking before 4pm–M after 4pm WE–M
Fees On application
Loc 5 miles SW of Barrhead on A736 Glasgow-Irvine road

Cathcart Castle (1895)

Mearns Road, Clarkston G76 7YL
Tel **(0141) 638 0082**
Mem 900
Sec IG Sutherland (0141) 638 9449
Pro D Naylor (0141) 638 3436
Holes 18 L 5832 yds SSS 68
Recs Am–62 S Black (1985)
Pro–64 A White (1983)
V'tors M SOC
Fees £17 D–£25
Loc 1 mile from Clarkston on B767

Cochrane Castle (1895)

Scott Avenue, Craigston, Johnstone PA5 0HF
Tel **(01505) 320146**
Mem 400
Sec JC Cowan
Pro S Campbell (01505) 328465
Holes 18 L 6226 yds SSS 70
Recs Am–65 R Davidson
Pro–71 S Kelly
V'tors WD–U WE–M
Fees £16 D–£22
Loc 1/2 mile S of A737. 1 mile S of Johnstone

East Renfrewshire (1922)

Loganswell, Pilmuir, Newton Mearns G77 6RT
Tel **(013555) 500256**
Mem 450
Sec AL Gillespie (0141) 226 4311
Pro GD Clarke (013555) 500206
Holes 18 L 6097 yds SSS 70
Recs Am–65 GK McGregor (1976)
Pro–64 CR Brooks (1989)
V'tors On application
Fees £25 D–£30
Loc 2 miles SW of Newton Mearns
Arch James Braid

Eastwood (1893)

Muirshield, Loganswell, Newton Mearns, Glasgow G77 6RX
Tel **(013555) 500261**
Mem 650
Sec VE Jones (013555) 500280
Pro A McGuinness (013555) 500285
Holes 18 L 5864 yds SSS 69
Recs Am–62 IA Carslaw (1975)
Pro–66 JC Farmer (1981)
V'tors M SOC
Fees £18 D–£26
Loc 9 miles SW of Glasgow

Elderslie (1909)

63 Main Road, Elderslie PA5 9AZ
Tel **(01505) 323956**
Mem 432
Sec Mrs A Anderson
Pro R Bowman (01505) 320032
Holes 18 L 6165 yds SSS 70
Recs Am–63 G MacKenzie (1994)
Pro–61 D Robertson (1994)
V'tors M SOC–WD
Fees £17.10 D–£23.50
Loc 2 miles SW of Paisley

Erskine (1904)

Bishopton PA7 5PH
Tel **(01505) 862302**
Mem 400 200(L)
Sec TA McKillop
Pro P Thomson (01505) 862108
Holes 18 L 6287 yds SSS 70
Recs Am–66 IG Riddell
Pro–63 G Collinson
V'tors WD–I WE–M
Fees £22
Loc 5 miles N of Paisley

Fereneze (1904)

Fereneze Avenue, Barrhead G78 1HJ
Tel **(0141) 881 1519**
Mem 700
Sec AD Gourley (0141) 221 6394
Pro (0141) 880 7058
Holes 18 L 5962 yds SSS 70
Recs Am–64 EH McMillan
Pro–64 C Elliot
V'tors M SOC–WD
Fees SOC–£20
Loc 9 miles SW of Glasgow

Gleddoch (1974)

Langbank PA14 6YE
Tel **(01475) 540304**
Fax **(01475) 540459**
Mem 600
Sec DW Tierney
Pro K Campbell (01475) 540704
Holes 18 L 6375 yds SSS 71
Recs Am–64 M O'Hare
Pro–67 J Chillas, C Gillies
V'tors WD–U WE–restricted SOC
Fees £25
Loc 16 miles W of Glasgow (M8/A8)
Arch J Hamilton Stutt

Gourock (1896)

Cowal View, Gourock PA19 6HD
Tel **(01475) 631001**
Mem 540 106(L) 100(J)
Sec MJ Walker
Pro AT Green (01475) 636834

Holes 18 L 6492 yds SSS 71
Recs Am–64 N Skinner
Pro–69 D Graham
V'tors WD–I SOC
Fees On application
Loc 3 miles SW of Greenock, off A770. 7 miles W of Port Glasgow

Greenock (1890)
Forsyth Street, Greenock PA16 8RE
Tel **(01475) 720793**
Mem 500 111(L) 110(J)
Sec EJ Black
Pro G Ross (01475) 787236
Holes 18 L 5888 yds SSS 68
9 L 2149 yds SSS 32
Recs Am–64 MC Mazzoni
Pro–66 H Thomson, J Panton, H Boyle
V'tors WD–U WE/BH–M
Fees D–£15 (£20)
Loc 1 mile SW of Greenock on A8
Arch James Braid

Kilmacolm (1891)
Porterfield Road, Kilmacolm PA13 3PD
Tel **(01505) 872139**
Mem 776
Sec RF McDonald
Pro D Stewart (01505) 872695
Holes 18 L 5890 yds SSS 68
Recs Am–64 M Stevenson
Pro–63 R Weir, J White
V'tors WD–U WE–M
Fees £20
Loc 10 miles W of Paisley (A761)

Lochwinnoch (1897)
Burnfoot Road, Lochwinnoch PA12 4AN
Tel **(01505) 842153**
Mem 500
Sec Mrs E McBride
Pro G Reilly (01505) 843029
Holes 18 L 6243 yds SSS 70
Recs Am–58 M Beattie (1994)
Pro–63 M Miller (1987)
V'tors WD–U before 4.30pm SOC–WD
Fees £15 D–£20
Loc 9 miles SW of Paisley

Old Ranfurly (1905)
Ranfurly Place, Bridge of Weir PA11 3DE
Tel **(01505) 613612** (Clubhouse)
Mem 375
Sec R Mitchell (01505) 613214
Holes 18 L 6089 yds SSS 69
Recs Am–62 A Hunter (1983)
Pro–66 C Elliot (1984)
V'tors WD–I WE–M SOC
Fees On application
Loc 7 miles W of Paisley, off A761

Paisley (1895)
Braehead, Paisley PA2 8TZ
Tel **(0141) 884 2292**
Mem 750
Sec WJ Cunningham (0141) 884 3903
Pro G Gilmour (0141) 884 4114
Holes 18 L 6466 yds SSS 72
Recs Am–66 DB Walker (1991)
V'tors WD–H SOC
Fees £16 D–£24 (1994)
Loc Braehead, S of Paisley

Port Glasgow (1895)
Devol Farm, Port Glasgow PA14 5XE
Tel **(01475) 704181**
Mem 375
Sec NL Mitchell (01475) 706273
Holes 18 L 5712 yds SSS 68
Recs Am–62 M Carmichael
V'tors WD–U before 5pm –M after 5pm WE–NA SOC
Fees On application
Loc 1 mile S of Port Glasgow

Ralston (1904)
Strathmore Avenue, Ralston, Paisley PA1 3DT
Tel **(0141) 882 1349**
Mem 440 165(L) 100(J)
Sec JW Horne (0141) 883 7045
Pro J Scott (0141) 810 4925
Holes 18 L 6100 yds SSS 69
Recs Am–63 J Armstrong
V'tors M
Loc 2 miles E of Paisley (A737)

Ranfurly Castle (1889)
Golf Road, Bridge of Weir PA11 3HN
Tel **(01505) 612609**
Mem 360 160(L) 100(J)
Sec J Walker
Pro T Eckford (01505) 614795
Holes 18 L 6284 yds SSS 70
Recs Am–65 WMB Brown
Pro–65 W Lockie (1989)
V'tors WD–H WE–M SOC–Tues
Fees £22 D–£27
Loc 7 miles W of Paisley (A761)
Arch Kirkcaldy/Auchterlonie

Renfrew (1894)
Blythswood Estate, Inchinnan Road, Renfrew PA4 9EG
Tel **(0141) 886 6692**
Mem 465 110(L) 80(J)
Sec AD Brockie
Pro D Grant (0141) 885 1754
Holes 18 L 6818 yds SSS 73
Recs Am–67 R Coultart (1991)
Pro–65 J Farmer (1991)
V'tors M SOC
Fees On application
Loc 3 miles N of Paisley, nr Airport

Whinhill (1911)
Beith Road, Greenock
Tel **(01475) 24694**
Mem 350
Sec D McConnell
Holes 18 L 5504 yds SSS 68
Recs Am–65 A Boffey (1987)
V'tors U
Fees On application
Loc Upper Greenock - Largs road

Whitecraigs (1905)
72 Ayr Road, Giffnock, Glasgow G46 6SW
Tel **(0141) 639 1681**
Mem 1150
Sec HJ Fairley (0141) 639 4530
Pro A Forrow (0141) 639 2140
Holes 18 L 6230 yds SSS 70
V'tors WD–I WE–M SOC–WD
Fees On application
Loc 6 miles S of Glasgow (A77), nr Whitecraigs Station

Williamwood (1906)
Clarkston Road, Netherlee, Glasgow G64
Tel **(0141) 637 1783**
Mem 680
Sec RG Cuthbert (0141) 226 4311
Pro J Gardner (0141) 637 2715
Holes 18 L 5878 yds SSS 69
Recs Am–61 H Kemp (1990)
Pro–61 BJ Gallacher (1974)
V'tors M
Loc 5 miles S of Glasgow
Arch James Braid

TAYSIDE

Angus

Arbroath (1903)
Public
Elliot, Arbroath DD11 2PE
Tel **(01241) 872069** (Clubhouse), **(01241) 875837** (Bookings)
Mem 500
Sec L Robb
Pro L Ewart (01241) 875837
Holes 18 L 6090 yds SSS 69
Recs Am–63 B Grieve (1992)
V'tors WD–U WE–NA before 10am
Fees £10 D–£16 (£15 D–£24)
Loc 1 mile S of Arbroath
Arch James Braid

Brechin (1893)
Trinity, Brechin DD9 7PD
Tel **(01356) 622383**
Mem 650
Sec AB May (01356) 622326
Pro S Rennie (01356) 625270
Holes 18 L 6200 yds SSS 70
Recs Am–65 G Tough
V'tors U ex Wed SOC
Fees £13 D–£18 (£17 D–£26)
Loc 1 mile N of Brechin on B90

Caird Park (1926)
Public
Mains Loan, Caird Park, Dundee DD4 9BX
Tel **(01382) 453606**
Mem 350
Sec G Martin (01382) 504064

Pro J Black (01382) 459438
Holes 18 L 6303 yds SSS 70
Yellow 9 L 1692 yds SSS 29
Red 9 L 1983 yds SSS 29
Recs Am–66 W Thompson (1987)
V'tors U SOC
Fees On application
Loc Off Kingsway by-pass, N of Dundee

Camperdown (1960)

Public
Camperdown Park, Dundee
Tel **(01382) 623398**
Mem 600
Sec R Gordon (01382) 814445
Pro R Brown
Holes 18 L 6561 yds SSS 72
Recs Am–68 A Morgan
V'tors U
Fees On application
Loc 2 miles NW of Dundee (A923)

Downfield (1932)

Turnberry Ave, Dundee DD2 3QP
Tel **(01382) 825595**
Fax **(01382) 813111**
Mem 750
Sec BF Mole
Pro KS Hutton (01382) 889246
Holes 18 L 6804 yds SSS 73
Recs Am–67 A Lionella (1967)
Pro–67 R Weir (1982)
V'tors WD–U 9.30–noon and 2.15–4pm Sun–limited access after 2pm
Fees £25 D–£36 (£30)
Loc N of Dundee, off A923

Edzell (1895)

High St, Edzell DD9 7TF
Tel **(01356) 648235**
Fax **(01356) 648094**
Mem 650
Sec JM Hutchison (01356) 647283
Pro AJ Webster (01356) 648462
Holes 18 L 6348 yds SSS 71
Recs Am–65 W Taylor, G Tough (1992)
Pro–67 I Young (1992)
V'tors WD–NA 4.45–6.15pm
WE–NA 7.30–10.30am & 12–2pm SOC
Fees £18 D–£27 (£24 D–£36)
Loc 6 miles N of Brechin

Forfar (1871)

Cunninghill, Arbroath Road, Forfar DD8 2RL
Tel **(01307) 462120**
Mem 500 140(L) 100(J)
Sec W Baird (01307) 463773
Pro P McNiven (01307) 465683
Holes 18 L 6033 yds Par 69 SSS 70
Recs Am–63 KG Law (1994)
Pro–65 E Brown
V'tors U exc Sat SOC
Fees £16 (£30)
Loc 1½ miles E of Forfar
Arch James Braid

Kirriemuir (1908)

Northmuir, Kirriemuir DD8 4PN
Tel **(01575) 72144 (Clubhouse), (01575) 73317 (Starter)**
Fax **(01575) 74608**
Mem 600
Sec A Caira (Mgr)
Pro A Caira (01575) 73317
Holes 18 L 5510 yds SSS 67
Recs Am–62 JL Adamson
Pro–63 D Huish
V'tors WD–U WE–NA SOC
Fees £15 D–£20
Loc NE outskirts of Kirriemuir. 17 miles N of Dundee
Arch James Braid

Letham Grange (1987)

Letham Grange, Colliston, Arbroath DD11 4RL
Tel **(01241) 890373**
Fax **(01241) 890414**
Mem 719
Sec Miss P Ogilvie
Pro D Scott (01241) 890377
Holes Old 18 L 6968 yds SSS 73
New 18 L 5528 yds SSS 68
Recs Old Am–69 D Downie (1994)
New Am–62 L McLaughlin (1994)
Old Pro–67 J Metcalfe, J Bickerton (1994)
V'tors WD–U exc Tues before 10am WE–M before 10.30am & 12.30–2pm (Old) –M before 9am & 1–2pm (New) BH–U SOC
Fees Old £20 D–£30 (£25)
New £12 D–£18 (£15)
Loc 4 miles NW of Arbroath on A993
Arch Old: Steel/Smith
New: T MacAuley

Monifieth Golf Links

Medal Starter's Box, Princes Street, Monifieth, Dundee DD5 4AW
Tel **(01382) 532767**
Mem 1600
Sec HR Nicoll (01382) 535553
Pro I McLeod (01382) 532945
Holes Medal 18 L 6650 yds SSS 72
Ashludie 18 L 5123 SSS 66
Recs Am–63 JL Adamson
Pro–64 S Sewgolum
V'tors WD–U Sat–NA before 2pm Sun–NA before 10am SOC
Fees Medal £22 D–£32 (£24 D–£36) Ashludie £14 D–£20 (£15 D–£22)
Loc 6 miles E of Dundee
Mis Abertay, Broughty, Grange/Dundee and Monifieth clubs play here

Montrose (1556)

Public
Traill Drive, Montrose DD10 8SW
Tel **(01674) 672932**
Fax **(01674) 671800**
Sec Mrs M Stewart
Pro K Stables (01674) 672634
Holes Medal 18 L 6443 yds SSS 71
Broomfield 18 L 4815 yds SSS 63
Recs Medal Am–64 G Tough (1991)
Pro–63 G Cunningham, D Huish
V'tors WD–U Sat–NA Sun–NA before 10am
Fees Medal £15 (£21) Broomfield £10 (£14)
Loc 1 mile from Montrose, off A90
Mis Royal Montrose, Caledonia and Mercantile clubs play here

Montrose Caledonia (1896)

Dorward Road, Montrose DD10 8SW
Tel **(01674) 72313**
Sec J Tasker (01674) 674498
Holes Play over Montrose courses

Montrose Mercantile (1879)

East Links, Montrose DD10 8SW
Tel **(01674) 72408**
Mem 930
Sec IH Spence (01674) 73070
Holes Play over Montrose courses

Panmure (1845)

Barry, Carnoustie DD7 7RT
Tel **(01241) 853120**
Fax **(01241) 859737**
Mem 500
Sec Maj (Retd) GW Paton (01241) 855120
Pro A Cullen (01241) 852460
Holes 18 L 6317 yds SSS 70
Recs Am–66 I Frame (1984)
Pro–62 C Moody (1990)
V'tors WD/Sun–U Sat–NA
Fees £25 D–£36
Loc 2 miles W of Carnoustie, off A930

Royal Montrose (1810)

Dorward Road, Montrose DD10 8SW
Tel **(01674) 72376**
Mem 650
Sec JD Sykes (01674) 73528
Holes Play over Montrose courses

Carnoustie Clubs

Carnoustie (1842)

3 Links Parade, Carnoustie DD7 7JE
Tel **(01241) 852480**
Fax **(01241) 856459**
Mem 900
Sec DW Curtis
Holes Play over Carnoustie courses

Carnoustie Caledonia (1887)

Links Parade, Carnoustie DD7 7JF
Tel **(01241) 852115**
Mem 618
Sec DC Thomson
Holes Play over Carnoustie courses

Carnoustie Ladies (1873)
12 Links Parade, Carnoustie DD7 6AZ
Tel **(01241) 855252**
Mem 106
Sec Mrs J Clark (01241) 859457
Holes Play over Carnoustie courses

Carnoustie Mercantile (1896)
Links Parade, Carnoustie DD7 7JE
Mem 50
Sec DG Ogilvie (01356) 647304 Police House, Dunlappie Road, Edzell DD9 7UB
Holes Play over Carnoustie courses

Dalhousie (1868)
Links Parade, Carnoustie DD7 7JE
Tel **(01241) 56322**
Mem 330
Sec PA Caie
Holes Play over Carnoustie courses

Carnoustie Courses

Buddon Links (1981)
Public
Links Parade, Carnoustie DD7 7JE
Tel **(01241) 853249** (Starter) **(01241) 853789** (Bookings)
Fax **(01241) 852720**
Sec EJC Smith
Holes 18 L 5300 yds SSS 66
V'tors WD–U WE–U after 10.30am
Fees £12
Loc 12 miles E of Dundee, by A92 or A930

Burnside (1914)
Public
Links Parade, Carnoustie DD7 7JE
Tel **(01241) 855344** (Starter) **(01241) 853789** (Bookings)
Fax **(01241) 852720**
Sec EJC Smith
Holes 18 L 6020 yds SSS 69 Pro–62 A Tait
V'tors WD–U Sat–U after 2pm Sun–U after 11am
Fees £16
Loc 12 miles E of Dundee, by A92 or A930

Carnoustie Championship (16th)
Public
Links Parade, Carnoustie DD7 7JE
Tel **(01241) 853249** (Starter) **(01241) 853789** (Bookings)
Fax **(01241) 852720**
Sec EJC Smith
Holes 18 L 6936 yds SSS 74 Pro–64 A Tait
V'tors WD–H Sat–H after 1.30pm Sun–H after 11am
Fees £40
Loc 12 miles E of Dundee, by A92 or A930

Kinross-shire

Bishopshire (1903)
Pay and play
Kinnesswood, Kinross
Mem 200
Sec J Proudfoot (01592) 780203
Holes 10 L 4700 metres SSS 64
Recs Am–63 J Morris
V'tors U
Fees £5 (£6)
Loc 3 miles E of Kinross (A911). M90 Junction 7
Arch W Park

Green Hotel (1900)
2 The Muirs, Kinross KY13 7AS
Tel **(01577) 863407**
Fax **(01577) 863180**
Mem 450
Sec Mrs M Smith
Holes Red 18 L 6257 yds SSS 70 Blue 18 L 6456 yds SSS 71
V'tors U
Fees £14 D–£20 (£20 D–£30)
Loc 17 miles S of Perth. M90 Junction 6/7

Milnathort (1910)
South Street, Milnathort KY13 2AW
Tel **(01577) 864069**
Mem 400
Holes 9 L 5969 yds SSS 69
Recs Am–65 D Reid (1992)
V'tors U SOC
Fees D–£10 (£15)
Loc 1 mile N of Kinross. M90 Junction 6/7

Perthshire

Aberfeldy (1895)
Taybridge Road, Aberfeldy PH15 2BH
Tel **(01887) 820535**
Mem 260
Sec AM Stewart (01887) 820117
Holes 9 L 2733 yds SSS 67
Recs Am–66 A McNeill (1987), JM Munro (1988)
V'tors U
Fees £10 D–£14 W–£40
Loc 10 miles W of Ballinluig, off A9

Alyth (1894)
Pitcrocknie, Alyth PH11 8HF
Tel **(01828) 632268**
Mem 850
Sec R Davidson
Pro T Melville (01828) 632411
Holes 18 L 6226 yds SSS 70
Recs Am–66 CR Brough, J Cochrane Jr, D Murison, DP Robertson Pro–64 I Young
V'tors U
Fees On application
Loc 16 miles NW of Dundee (A91)

Auchterarder (1892)
Ochil Road, Auchterarder PH3 1LS
Tel **(01764) 662804**
Mem 650
Sec WM Campbell (01764) 664669
Pro (01764) 663711
Holes 18 L 5757 yds SSS 68
Recs Am–65 C Long (1992) Pro–65 W Guy (1988)
V'tors U SOC
Fees £14 D–£20 Sat–£21 D–£28 Sun–£30
Loc 1 mile SW of Auchterarder

Blair Atholl (1896)
Blair Atholl PH18 5TG
Tel **(0179) 681407**
Mem 390
Sec JA McGregor (0179) 681274
Holes 9 L 2855 yds SSS 68
Recs Am–66
V'tors U
Fees £11 (£14)
Loc 35 miles N of Perth, off A9

Blairgowrie (1889)
Rosemount, Blairgowrie PH10 6LG
Tel **(01250) 872594**
Fax **(01250) 875451**
Mem 1200
Sec JN Simpson (Sec/Mgr) (01250) 872622
Pro GW Kinnoch (01250) 873116
Holes Rosemount 18 L 6588 yds SSS 72; Landsdowne 18 L 6895 yds SSS 73; Wee 9 L 4614 yds SSS 63
Recs Rosemount Am–64 E Giraud, W Taylor Pro–66 G Norman Lansdowne Am–68 BRN Grieve, EJ Lindsay, T McLevy Jr, RM Taylor Pro–69 J McAlister
V'tors Mon/Tues/Thurs–U H 8am–12 & 2–3.30pm Wed/Fri/WE–restricted
Fees £35 D–£48 (£40)
Loc 1 mile S of Blairgowrie, off A93. 15 miles N of Perth

Comrie (1891)
Comrie PH6 2HJ
Tel **(01764) 70055**
Mem 270
Sec DG McGlashan (01764) 70544
Holes 9 L 2983 yds SSS 69
Recs Am–65 A Philp
V'tors U
Fees £10 (£10)
Loc 7 miles W of Crieff (A85)

Craigie Hill (1909)
Cherrybank, Perth PH2 0NE
Tel **(01738) 624377**
Mem 625
Sec WA Miller (01738) 620829
Pro S Harrier (01738) 622644
Holes 18 L 5379 yds SSS 66
Recs Am–60 G Still (1988)
Pro–63 W Murray (1986)
V'tors U exc Sat
Fees £10 (£20)
Loc W boundary of Perth
Arch Fernie/Anderson

Crieff (1891)
Perth Road, Crieff PH7 3LR
Tel **(01764) 652909** (Bookings)
Mem 670
Sec JS Miller (01764) 652397
Pro DJW Murchie, JM Stark
Holes Ferntower 18 L 6402 yds SSS 71; Dornock 9 L 4772 yds SSS 63
Recs Ferntower Am–66
Pro–66
V'tors U H NA–12–2pm or after 5pm SOC
Fees Ferntower £17 (£22)
Dornock £11 (£14)
Loc 1 mile NE of Crieff (A85). 17 miles W of Perth

Dalmunzie (1948)
Glenshee, Blairgowrie PH10 7QG
Tel **(01250) 885226**
Mem 52
Sec S Winton (Mgr)
Holes 9 L 2035 yds SSS 60
V'tors U
Fees On application
Loc 22 miles N of Blairgowrie on A93. (Dalmunzie Hotel sign)

Dunkeld & Birnam (1892)
Fungarth, Dunkeld PH8 0HU
Tel **(01350) 727524**
Mem 300
Sec Mrs W Sinclair (01350) 727564
Holes 9 L 5240 yds SSS 66
Recs Am–66 P Lambie
V'tors WD–U WE–phone first
Fees On application
Loc Dunkeld 1 mile, off A923. 15 miles N of Perth

Dunning (1953)
Rollo Park, Dunning PH2 0QX
Tel **(01764) 684747**
Mem 580
Sec J Slater (01764) 684372
Holes 9 L 4836 yds SSS 64
V'tors WD–U before 5pm –M after 5pm Sat–NA before 4pm Sun–NA before 1pm SOC
Fees D–£8 (£8) W–£30
Loc 9 miles SW of Perth, off A9

Glenalmond
Trinity College, Glenalmond
Sec The Bursar (01738) 880275
Holes 9 L 5812 yds SSS 68
Recs Am–70 CMW Robertson
Pro–72 M Dennis
V'tors NA
Loc 10 miles NW of Perth
Arch James Braid

The Gleneagles Hotel
Auchterarder PH4 1QG
Tel **(01764) 663543** (Golf), **(01764) 662231** (Hotel)
Pro I Marchbank
Holes King's 18 L 6471 yds SSS 71
Queen's 18 L 5965 yds SSS 69
Monarch 18 L 7081 SSS 74
9 hole Par 3 course
Recs King's Am–65 GM Rutherford
Pro–60 P Curry (1994)
Queen's Pro–63 C Stadler
V'tors On application
Fees £50 (1994)
Loc 16 miles SW of Perth on A9
Mis Driving range. Pitch & putt. Dun Ochil, Dun Whinny and Glenearn clubs play here

Kenmore (1992)
Pay and play
Mains of Taymouth, Kenmore, Aberfeldy PH15 2HN
Tel **(01887) 830226**
Fax **(01887) 830211**
Mem 120
Sec R Menzies (Mgr)
Pro None
Holes 9 L 6052 yds SSS 69
Recs Am–71 F Menzies (1992)
V'tors U SOC
Fees 9 holes–£7 (£8)
18 holes–£10 (£12)
Loc 6 miles W of Aberfeldy on A827
Arch D Menzies & Partners

King James VI (1858)
Moncreiffe Island, Perth PH2 8NR
Tel **(01738) 25170, (01738) 32460** (Starter)
Mem 600
Sec D Barraclough (01738) 32460
Pro A Coles (01738) 32460
Holes 18 L 5664 yds SSS 68
Recs Am–63 G Clark (1976)
Pro–62 W Guy (1991)
V'tors U exc Sat Sun–by reservation
Fees £13 D–£20 Sun D–£27
Loc Island in River Tay, Perth

Murrayshall (1981)
Murrayshall, New Scone, Perth PH2 7PH
Tel **(01738) 51171**
Fax **(01738) 52595**
Mem 300
Sec A Euan Rodger (Mgr)
Pro N Mackintosh (01738) 52784
Holes 18 L 5877 metres SSS 71
Recs Am–67 G Redford
Pro–67 J Farmer
V'tors U SOC–WD/WE
Fees On application
Loc 3 miles NE of Perth, off A94
Mis Driving range

Muthill (1935)
Peat Road, Muthill PH5 2AD
Tel **(01764) 681523**
Mem 400
Sec WH Gordon (01764) 653319
Holes 9 L 2371 yds SSS 63
Recs Am–61 C MacGregor (1991)
Pro–68 RM Jamieson, W Milne (1985)
V'tors U
Fees On application
Loc 3 miles S of Crieff on A822

North Inch
Public
c/o Perth & Kinross Council, 3 High Street, Perth PH1 5JU
Tel **(01738) 36481** (Starter)
Sec N Taylor (01738) 39911
Holes 18 L 4340 metres SSS 65
V'tors U SOC
Fees On application
Loc Nr Perth and A9, by River Tay. Signs to Bell's Sports Centre

Pitlochry (1909)
Golf Course Road, Pitlochry PH16 5AU
Tel **(01796) 472792** (Starter)
Fax **(01796) 473599**
Mem 400
Sec DCM McKenzie JP (01796) 472114
Pro G Hampton
Holes 18 L 5811 yds SSS 68
Recs Am–63 CP Christy, MM Niven
Pro–64
V'tors U SOC
Fees D–£15 (D–£18)
Loc N side of Pitlochry (A9). 28 miles NW of Perth
Arch Fernie/Hutchison

Royal Perth Golfing Society (1833)
1/2 Atholl Crescent, Perth PH1 5NG
Tel **(01738) 622265**
Fax **(01738) 441131**
Mem 250
Sec RPJ Blake (Gen Sec) (01738) 440088, AH Anderson (Golf Sec) (01738) 637311
Holes Play over North Inch course

St Fillans (1903)
South Lochearn Rd, St Fillans PH26 2NG
Tel **(01764) 85312**
Mem 400
Sec J Allison (01764) 70951

Holes 9 L 5668 yds SSS 68
Recs Am–66 W Gemmell (1989)
V'tors U SOC
Fees On application
Loc 12 miles W of Crieff, on A85
Arch W Auchterlonie

Strathtay (1909)

Lorne Cottage, Dalguise, Dunkeld PH8 0JX
Tel **(01350) 727797**
Mem 184
Sec TD Lind
Holes 9 L 4082 yds SSS 63
Recs Am–61 AM Deboys
V'tors U exc Mon–NA after 5pm Sun–NA 2–4pm SOC
Fees D–£8 (£10)
Loc 4 miles W of Ballinluig (A827), towards Aberfeldy

Taymouth Castle (1923)

Kenmore, Aberfeldy PH15 2NT
Tel **(01887) 830228**
Fax **(01887) 830765**
Mem 200
Sec AA MacTaggart (Golf Dir)
Pro A Marshall
Holes 18 L 6066 yds SSS 69
Recs Am–63 MM Niven
Pro–A Learmonth (1962)
V'tors U WE–booking essential SOC
Fees £16 D–£26 (£20 D–£36)
Loc 6 miles W of Aberfeldy (A827)
Arch James Braid

WESTERN ISLES REGION

Askernish (1891)

Lochboisdale, Askernish, South Uist
Mem 30
Sec AL Macdonald (018784) 541
Holes 9 L 5114 yds SSS 67
Recs Am–66 K Robertson
V'tors U
Fees £2 (£2) W–£10
Loc 5 miles NW of Lochboisdale
Arch Tom Morris Sr

Stornoway (1890)

Lady Lever Park, Stornoway, Isle of Lewis PA87 0XP
Tel **(01851) 702240**
Mem 400
Sec G Davies (01851) 706764
Holes 18 L 5119 yds SSS 66
Recs Am–62 KW Galloway
Pro–65 JC Farmer
V'tors U exc Sun–NA SOC
Fees D–£12 W–£35
Loc Grounds of Lews Castle, Isle of Lewis

Wales

Clwyd

Abergele & Pensarn (1910)

Tan-y-Goppa Road, Abergele LL22 8DS
Tel **(01745) 824034**
Mem 1250
Sec HE Richards
Pro I Runcie (01745) 823813
Holes 18 L 6520 yds SSS 71
Recs Am–69 N Daniel (1991)
Pro–65 D Vaughan (1987)
V'tors U SOC
Fees £22 (£28)
Loc Abergele Castle Grounds
Arch Hawtree

Bryn Morfydd Hotel (1982)

Llanrhaeadr, Denbigh LL16 4NP
Tel **(01745) 890280**
Fax **(01745) 890488**
Mem 400
Sec CS Henderson (Golf Dir)
Holes 18 L 5660 yds SSS 67
9 hole Par 3 course
V'tors U SOC
Fees On application
Loc 2½ miles SE of Denbigh on A525
Arch Duchess-Alliss/Thomas. Dukes-Muirhead/Henderson

Caerwys (1989)

Pay and play
Caerwys, Mold CH7 5AQ
Tel **(01352) 720692**
Mem 150
Sec E Barlow
Pro N Lloyd
Holes 9 L 3080 yds SSS 60
Recs Am–61 T Adamson (1989)
V'tors U SOC
Fees £4.50 (£5.50)
Loc SW of Caerwys. 1½ miles S of A55 Express Way, between Holywell and St Asaph
Arch Eleanor Barlow

Chirk G & CC (1990)

Chirk, Wrexham
Tel **(01691) 774407**
Fax **(01691) 774407**
Mem 475
Sec JF Waugh
Pro JF Waugh
Holes 18 L 7300 yds SSS 75
9 hole Par 3 course
V'tors U after 9.30am SOC
Fees £18 D–£22 (£22 D–£30)
Loc 8 miles S of Wrexham on A483
Mis Driving range

Denbigh (1922)

Henllan Road, Denbigh LL16
Tel **(01745) 814159**
Mem 550
Sec GC Parry (01745) 816669
Pro M Jones (01745) 814159
Holes 18 L 5582 yds SSS 67
Recs Am–64 H Parry (1989)
Pro–69 C Defoy (1986)
V'tors U SOC
Fees £15 (£20)
Loc 2 miles NW of Denbigh (B5382)

Flint (1966)

Cornist Park, Flint CH6 5HJ
Tel **(01352) 732327/733461**
Mem 390
Sec TE Owens
Holes 9 L 5953 yds SSS 69
Recs Am–65 O O'Neil, G Houston
V'tors WD–U before 5pm SOC–WD
Fees D–£10 (£10)
Loc 1 mile SW of Flint. End of M56, 8 miles

Hawarden (1911)

Groomsdale Lane, Hawarden, Deeside CH5 3EH
Tel **(01244) 531447**
Mem 480
Sec T Hinks-Edwards (01352) 757955
Pro I Wright
Holes 18 L 5564 yds SSS 67
Recs Am–64 L Hinks-Edwards
V'tors WD–H SOC
Fees £20
Loc 6 miles W of Chester, off A55

Holywell (1906)

Brynford, Holywell CH8 8LQ
Tel **(01352) 710040**
Fax **(01352) 713937**
Mem 350 60(L)
Sec EK Carney (01352) 713937
Pro J Law (01352) 710040
Holes 18 L 6100 yds SSS 70
Recs Am–69 DP Hardie (1994)
V'tors WD–U WE–SOC
Fees £14 (£20)
Loc 2 miles S of Holywell, off A5026

Kinmel Park (1989)

Pay and play
Bodelwyddan LL18 5SR
Tel **(01745) 833548**
Pro P Stebbings
Holes 9 L 1550 yds Par 29
V'tors U
Fees £3
Loc Off A55, between Abergele and St Asaph

For list of abbreviations see page 435

Mold (1909)
Pantmywyn, Mold CH7 1IW
Tel **(01352) 740318/741513**
Fax **(01352) 741517**
Mem 350 85(L) 90(J)
Sec A Newall
Pro M Carty
Holes 18 L 5521 yds SSS 67
Recs Am–65 P Jones
Pro–64 D Wills
V'tors U SOC
Fees £16 (£21)
Loc 4 miles W of Mold
Arch Hawtree

Northop Country Park (1994)
Northop, Chester CH7 6WA
Tel **(01352) 840440**
Fax **(01352) 840445**
Pro D Llewellyn
Holes 18 L 6735 yds Par 72
V'tors U–phone first
Fees £25 (£35)
Loc 3 miles S of Flint, off A55
Mis Driving range
Arch John Jacobs

Old Colwyn (1907)
Woodland Avenue, Old Colwyn LL29 9NL
Tel **(01492) 515581**
Mem 350
Sec RG Tudor
Holes 9 L 5268 yds SSS 66
Recs Am–63 C Oldham, JD Jones Roberts
Pro–67 DJ Rees
V'tors WD–U WE–by arrangement SOC
Fees £10 (£15)
Loc 2 miles E of Colwyn Bay

Old Padeswood (1978)
Station Road, Padeswood, Mold CH7 4JL
Tel **(01244) 547401**
Mem 500
Sec BV Hellen (01352) 770506
Pro A Davies
Holes 18 L 6728 yds SSS 72
9 hole Par 3 course
Recs Am–66 L Lockett (1991)
Pro–65 I Higsby
Ladies–72 S Lovat (1994)
V'tors U exc comp days SOC–WD
Fees £16 D–£25 (£20 D–£30)
Loc 2 miles from Mold on A5118

Padeswood & Buckley (1933)
The Caia, Station Lane, Padeswood, Mold CH7 4JD
Tel **(01244) 550537**
Mem 592
Sec JG Peters
Pro D Ashton (01244) 543636
Holes 18 L 6001 yds Par 70 SSS 69
Recs Am–66 S Hurstfield
V'tors WD–U 9am–4pm –M after 4pm Sat–U Sun–NA SOC–WD Ladies Day–Wed
Fees £20 (£25)
Loc 8 miles W of Chester, off A5118. 2nd golf club on right
Arch D Williams

Prestatyn (1905)
Marine Road East, Prestatyn LL19 7HS
Tel **(01745) 854320**
Mem 650
Sec R Woodruff (Mgr) (01745) 888353
Pro M Staton (01745) 852083
Holes 18 L 6792 yds SSS 73
Recs Am–66 RJ Edwards (1993)
V'tors H SOC
Fees £18 (£25)
Loc 1 mile E of Prestatyn
Arch S Collins

Rhuddlan (1930)
Meliden Road, Rhuddlan, Rhyl LL18 6LB
Tel **(01745) 590217**
Fax **(01745) 590898**
Mem 515 155(L) 80(J)
Sec D Morris
Pro I Worsley (01745) 590898
Holes 18 L 6482 yds SSS 71
Recs Am–67 G Marsden (1991)
V'tors H or I Sun–M SOC–WD
Fees £22 (£27)
Loc 2 miles N of St Asaph, off A55
Arch F Hawtree

Rhyl (1890)
Coast Road, Rhyl LL18 3RE
Tel **(01745) 353171**
Mem 380
Sec F Bass
Pro T Leah
Holes 9 L 6153 yds SSS 70
Recs Am–66 T Leah (1993)
Pro–67 H Cotton, C Ward, N von Nida
V'tors U SOC
Fees £12 (£15)
Loc On A548 between Rhyl and Prestatyn
Arch James Braid

Ruthin-Pwllglas (1920)
Pwllglas, Ruthin
Tel **(01824) 702296**
Mem 360
Sec WK Roberts (01824) 703427
Holes 10 L 5362 yds SSS 66
Recs Am–66 H Roberts
V'tors U SOC
Fees £10 (£15)
Loc 2½ miles S of Ruthin

St Melyd (1922)
The Paddock, Meliden Road, Prestatyn LL19 9NB
Tel **(01745) 854405**
Mem 400
Sec PM Storey (01745) 853574
Pro R Bradbury (01745) 888858
Holes 9 L 5857 yds SSS 68
Recs Am–65 AR Grace (1990)
Pro–66 S Wilkinson
V'tors U SOC
Fees £15 (£19)
Loc S of Prestatyn on A547

Vale of Llangollen (1908)
Holyhead Road, Llangollen LL20 7PR
Tel **(01978) 860613**
Mem 600
Sec TF Ellis (01978) 860906
Pro DI Vaughan (01978) 860040
Holes 18 L 6661 yds SSS 72
Recs Am–67 DE Hart (1991)
Pro–68
V'tors U
Fees £20 (£25)
Loc 1½ miles E of Llangollen on A5

Wrexham (1906)
Holt Road, Wrexham LL13 9SB
Tel **(01978) 261033**
Mem 650
Sec KB Fisher (01978) 364268
Pro DA Larvin (01978) 351476
Holes 18 L 6078 yds SSS 69
Recs Am–65 SJ Edwards (1991), K Evans (1994)
Pro–66 SJ Edwards (1993)
V'tors H SOC–WD
Fees On application
Loc 2 miles NE of Wrexham on A534

Dyfed

Aberystwyth (1911)
Bryn-y-Mor, Aberystwyth SY23 2HY
Tel **(01970) 615104**
Mem 390
Sec B Thomas
Pro K Bayliss (01970) 625301
Holes 18 L 6109 yds SSS 71
Recs Am–69 RE Jones
Pro–67 P Parkin, G Emerson
V'tors U SOC
Fees On application
Loc Aberystwyth ½ mile

Ashburnham (1894)
Cliffe Terrace, Burry Port SA16 0HN
Tel **(01554) 832466**
Mem 725
Sec DK Williams (01554) 832269
Pro RA Ryder (01554) 833846
Holes 18 L 6916 yds SSS 72
Recs Am–70 J Grundy
Pro–71 C Evans, N Roderick
V'tors H
Fees £22.50 D–£30 (£30 D–£35)
Loc 5 miles W of Llanelli (A484)

Borth & Ynyslas (1885)
Borth SY24 5JS
Tel **(01970) 871202**
Mem 447
Sec S Wilson
Pro JG Lewis (01970) 871557

Holes 18 L 6100 yds SSS 70
Recs Am–65 M Stimson (1989), C Evans (1993)
Pro–68 JG Lewis
V'tors WD–U WE/BH–by prior arrangement SOC
Fees £18 (£25)
Loc 8 miles N of Aberystwyth (B4353), off A487

Cardigan (1928)
Gwbert-on-Sea, Cardigan SA43 1PR
Tel **(01239) 612035**
Mem 400
Sec J Rhapps
Pro C Parsons
Holes 18 L 6687 yds SSS 73
Recs Am–68 R Emanuel
V'tors U
Fees D–£15 (£20) W–£60
Loc 3 miles N of Cardigan

Carmarthen (1907)
Blaenycoed Road, Carmarthen SA33 6EH
Tel **(01267) 281214**
Mem 700
Sec J Coe (01267) 2817588
Pro P Gillis (01267) 281493
Holes 18 L 6212 yds SSS 71
Recs Am–68 M Thomas (1987)
Pro–69 B Barnes
V'tors H SOC
Fees £18 (£25)
Loc 4 miles NW of Carmarthen

Cilgwyn (1977)
Llangybi, Lampeter SA48 8NN
Tel **(01570) 45286**
Mem 290
Sec N Hill
Holes 9 L 5327 yds SSS 67
Recs Am–67 EL Jones (1991)
V'tors U SOC
Fees £10 (£15) W–£60
Loc 5 miles NE of Lampeter, off A485 at Llangybi

Glynhir (1909)
Glynhir Road, Llandybie, Ammanford SA18 2TF
Tel **(01269) 850472**
Mem 700
Sec EP Rees, DB Jones
Pro I Roberts (01269) 851010
Holes 18 L 5952 yds SSS 69
Recs Am–66 R Collins
V'tors WD/Sat–H Sun–NA SOC–WD
Fees Winter £10 (£12) 5D–£45
Summer £15 (£20) 5D–£65
Loc 3½ miles N of Ammanford
Arch Hawtree

Haverfordwest (1904)
Arnolds Down, Haverfordwest SA61 2XQ
Tel **(01437) 763565**
Mem 700
Sec MA Harding (01437) 764523
Pro A Pile (01437) 768409
Holes 18 L 6005 yds SSS 69
Recs Am–65 P Hunt (1994)
Pro–67 AJ Pile
Ladies–72 F Jones (1994)
V'tors U SOC
Fees £16 (£23)
Loc 1 mile E of Haverfordwest on A40

Milford Haven (1913)
Hubberston, Milford Haven SA72 2HQ
Tel **(01646) 692368**
Mem 315 60(L) 90(J)
Sec LM Meckimmon
Pro S Laidler (01646) 697762
Holes 18 L 6071 yds SSS 71
Recs Am–66 L Rees
Pro–71 B Huggett
V'tors U SOC
Fees £13 (£18)
Loc W boundary of Milford Haven

Newport (Pembs) (1925)
Newport SA42 0NR
Tel **(01239) 820244**
Mem 350
Sec R Dietrich
Pro C Parsons (01239) 615359
Holes 9 L 3089 yds SSS 68
Recs Am–67 A Evans
V'tors U SOC
Fees £12.50
Loc 2½ miles NW of Newport, towards Newport Beach
Arch James Braid

Penrhos G & CC (1991)
Llanrhystud, Aberystwyth SY23 5AY
Tel **(01974) 202999**
Fax **(01974) 202999**
Mem 300
Sec R Rees-Evans
Pro P Diamond
Holes 18 L 6641 yds SSS 72
9 hole Par 3 course
V'tors U SOC
Fees £15 (£18)
Loc 9 miles S of Aberystwyth, off A487
Mis Driving range
Arch Jim Walters

South Pembrokeshire (1970)
Defensible Barracks, Pembroke Dock SA72 6NY
Tel **(01646) 683817**
Mem 300
Sec WD Owen (01646) 682650
Holes 9 L 5804 yds SSS 69
Recs Am–65 A Jones
V'tors U before 4.30pm SOC
Fees On application
Loc Pembroke Dock

St Davids City (1902)
Whitesands Bay, St Davids
Tel **(01437) 721751** (Clubhouse)
Mem 200
Sec CWJ Snushall (01437) 720312
Holes 9 L 6121 yds SSS 70
Recs Am–67 KB Walsh (1989)
V'tors U SOC
Fees D–£13
Loc 2 miles W of St Davids. 15 miles NW of Haverfordwest

Tenby (1888)
The Burrows, Tenby SA70 7NP
Tel **(01834) 842787/842978**
Mem 800
Sec JA Pearson (01834) 842978
Pro T Mountford (01834) 844447
Holes 18 L 6450 yds SSS 71
Recs Am–66 S Wilkinson
V'tors H SOC
Fees £18 (£22.50)
Loc Tenby, South Beach
Arch James Braid

Gwent

Alice Springs (1989)
Bettws Newydd, Usk NP5 1JY
Tel **(01873) 880772 (Queens), (01873) 880708 (Kings)**
Fax **(01873) 880838**
Mem 350
Sec K Morgan
Pro J Howard (01873) 880914
Holes Queens 18 L 5870 yds SSS 69
Kings 18 L 6438 yds SSS 72
V'tors U SOC
Fees £12.50 (£15)
Loc 3 miles N of Usk on B4598
Mis Driving range
Arch Keith Morgan

Blackwood (1914)
Cwmgelli, Blackwood NP2 1EL
Tel **(01495) 223152**
Mem 300
Sec AM Reed-Gibbs
Pro None
Holes 9 L 5304 yds SSS 66
Recs Am–64 S Erasmus
Pro–64 F Hill
V'tors I SOC
Fees £12 (£15)
Loc ¼ mile N of Blackwood

Caerleon (1974)
Public
Broadway, Caerleon NP6 1AY
Tel **(01633) 420342**
Mem 150
Sec R Morgan
Pro A Campbell
Holes 9 L 3092 yds SSS
Pro–66 A Campbell
V'tors U
Fees 18 holes–£4.75 9 holes–£3.20
Loc M4 Junction 25, 3 miles
Mis Driving range
Arch Donald Steel

Dewstow (1988)

Caerwent, Newport NP6 4AH
Tel **(01291) 430444**
Fax **(01291) 425816**
Mem 650
Sec E Tose
Pro M Kedward
Holes Valley 18 L 6123 yds Par 72 SSS 70;
Park 18 L 6147 yds SSS 69
Recs Valley Am–73 P Collins (1994)
V'tors WD–U WE–by arrangement SOC
Fees £11 (£15)
Loc Caerwent, 5 miles W of Severn Bridge, off A48
Mis Driving range

Greenmeadow (1980)

Treherbert Road, Croesyceiliog, Cwmbran NP44 2BZ
Tel **(01633) 369321**
Mem 430
Sec PJ Richardson
Pro C Coombs (01633) 362626
Holes 15 L 5593 yds SSS 68
Recs Am–66 M Challinger (1989)
Pro–66 C Jenkins (1987)
V'tors U SOC
Fees On application
Loc 4 miles N of Newport on B4042. M4 Junction 26

Llanwern (1928)

Golf House, Tennyson Ave, Llanwern NP6 2DY
Tel **(01633) 412380**
Mem 829
Sec DJ Peak (01633) 412029
Pro S Price (01633) 413233
Holes 18 L 6139 yds SSS 69
9 L 5686 yds SSS 69
Recs Am–63 B Dredge (1994)
Pro–64 S Dodd (1992)
V'tors WD–U WE–restricted I H SOC
Fees WD–£20
Loc 1 mile S of M4 Junction 24

Monmouth (1921)

Leasebrook Lane, Monmouth
Tel **(01600) 712212**
Mem 500
Sec PC Harris (01600) 712941
Pro None
Holes 18 L 5698 yds SSS 69
Recs Am–65 DJ Wills (1979)
Pro–68 DR Hemming (1978)
V'tors U
Fees £15 5D–£60
Loc Signposted 1 mile along A40 Monmouth-Ross road

Monmouthshire (1892)

Llanfoist, Abergavenny NP7 9HE
Tel **(01873) 853171**
Fax **(01873) 852606**
Mem 480 106(L) 90(J)
Sec B Jackson (01873) 852606
Pro P Worthing (10873) 852532
Holes 18 L 6045 yds SSS 70
Recs Am–64 B Dredge (1990)
Pro–62 D Thomas (1962)
V'tors U H SOC
Fees £21 (£26)
Loc 2 miles SW of Abergavenny
Arch James Braid

Newport (1903)

Great Oak, Rogerstone, Newport NP1 9FX
Tel **(01633) 892683/894496**
Fax **(01633) 896676**
Mem 800
Sec JM Seatter (01633) 892643
Pro R Skuse (01633) 893271
Holes 18 L 6314 yds SSS 71
Recs Am–64 C Mayo (1993)
Pro–62 L Bond (1994)
V'tors WD–U H exc Tues Sat–M H 1–4pm SOC–WD exc Tues
Fees £30 (£40)
Loc 3 miles W of Newport on B4591. M4 Junction 27, 1 mile

Oakdale (1990)

Pay and play
Llwynon Lane, Oakdale NP2 0NF
Tel **(01495) 220044**
Sec M Lewis (Dir)
Pro None
Holes 9 L 1235 yds Par 28
V'tors U SOC
Fees £3.50
Loc 15 miles NW of Newport via A467/B4251. M4 Junction 28
Mis Driving range

Parc (1990)

Pay and play
Church Lane, Coedkernew, Newport NP1 9TU
Tel **(01633) 680933**
Fax **(01633) 681011**
Mem 450
Sec C Hicks (Mgr), M Cleary (Sec)
Pro B Edwards (01633) 680955
Holes 18 L 5512 yds SSS 70
Recs Am–71 C Hicks
V'tors U SOC
Fees £10 (£12)
Loc 2 miles W of Newport on A48. M4 Junction 28
Mis Floodlit driving range
Arch B Thomas

Pontnewydd (1875)

West Pontnewydd, Cwmbran NP44 1AB
Tel **(01633) 482170**
Mem 250
Sec HR Gabe (01633) 867185
Holes 10 L 5353 yds SSS 67
Recs Am–62 M Hayward
V'tors WD–U WE–M SOC
Fees £16
Loc W outskirts of Cwmbran

Pontypool (1903)

Lasgarn Lane, Trevethin, Pontypool NP4 8TR
Tel **(01495) 763655**
Mem 566 71(L) 72(J)
Sec Mrs E Wilce (01495) 764794
Pro J Howard (01495) 755544
Holes 18 L 6046 yds SSS 69
Recs Am–64 M Hayward (1982)
NR Davies (1985)
Pro–A Sherborne
V'tors U H SOC
Fees £16.50 (£22.50)
Loc 1 mile N of Pontypool (A4042)

The Rolls of Monmouth (1982)

The Hendre, Monmouth NP5 4HG
Tel **(01600) 715353**
Fax **(01600) 713115**
Mem 200
Sec Mrs SJ Orton
Pro None
Holes 18 L 6723 yds SSS 72
Recs Am–71 D Wills
Pro–68 M Thomas (1983)
V'tors U SOC
Fees £30 (£35)
Loc 3½ miles W of Monmouth on B4233

St Pierre (1962)

St Pierre Park, Chepstow NP6 6YA
Tel **(01291) 625261**
Fax **(01291) 629975**
Sec TJ Cleary
Pro R Doig (01291) 621400
Holes 18 L 6785 yds SSS 73
18 L 5732 yds SSS 68
Recs Old Am–69 AM Williams
Pro–63 H Henning
New Am–63 M Bearcroft
V'tors H SOC–WD
Fees On application
Loc 2 miles W of Chepstow (A48)

Tredegar & Rhymney (1921)

Tredegar, Rhymney
Tel **(01685) 840743**
Mem 204
Sec V Davies
Holes 9 L 5564 yds SSS 67
Recs Am–64 CL Jones
Pro–33 WS Phillips
V'tors U
Fees £10 (£12.50)
Loc 1½ miles W of Tredegar

Tredegar Park (1923)

Bassaleg Road, Newport NP9 3PX
Tel **(01633) 895219**
Fax **(01633) 897152**
Mem 800
Sec RT Howell (01633) 894433
Pro ML Morgan (01633) 894517
Holes 18 L 6097 yds SSS 70
Recs Am–67 A Wesson
V'tors H

For list of abbreviations see page 435

Fees D–£25 (D–£30)
Loc W of Newport, off M4 Junction 27

West Monmouthshire (1906)
Golf Road, Pond Road, Nantyglo, Brynmawr NP3 4QT
Tel **(01495) 310233/311361**
Fax **(01495) 311361**
Mem 600
Sec SE Williams
Holes 18 L 6118 yds SSS 69
Recs Am–66 D Phillips (1994)
V'tors WD/Sat–U Sun–M SOC–WD
Fees £15
Loc Nr Dunlop Semtex, off Brynmawr Bypass, towards Winchestown
Arch Ben Sayers

Woodlake Park (1993)
Glascoed, Pontypool NP4 0TE
Tel **(01291) 673933**
Mem 300
Sec MJ Wood
Pro CL Coombs
Holes 18 L 6300 yds SSS 70
Recs Am–68 M Skinner (1994)
Pro–67 M Wootton (1994)
V'tors H SOC
Fees Summer–£20 (£20)
Winter–£15 (£20)
Loc 3 miles W of Usk, nr Llandegfedd reservoir

Gwynedd

Aberdovey (1892)
Aberdovey LL35 0RT
Tel **(01654) 767210**
Fax **(01654) 767027**
Mem 800
Sec JM Griffiths (01654) 767493
Pro J Davies (01654) 767602
Holes 18 L 6445 yds SSS 71
Recs Am–66 BT Bell (1993)
Pro–67 J Smith
V'tors NA–8–9.30am & 1–2pm
Fees On application
Loc 3 miles W of Aberdovey (A493)

Abersoch (1907)
Golf Road, Abersoch LL53 7EY
Tel **(01758) 712622**
Mem 700
Sec B Guest
Holes 18 L 5819 yds SSS 69
V'tors U H SOC
Fees £15 (£18)
Loc 1/2 mile S of Abersoch. 7 miles S of Pwllheli

Bala (1973)
Penlan, Bala LL23 7YD
Tel **(01678) 520359**
Mem 320
Sec Dianne Davies
Holes 10 L 4962 yds SSS 64
Recs Am–64 DB Aykroyd
V'tors WD–U WE–NA pm SOC
Fees £12 (£15) W–£40
Loc 1 mile SW of Bala, off A494 to Dolgellau

Bala Lake Hotel
Bala LL23 7YF
Tel **(01678) 520344/520111**
Fax **(01678) 521193**
Mem 50
Sec D Pickering
Holes 9 L 4280 yds SSS 61
V'tors U
Fees On application
Loc 1 1/2 miles S of Bala on B4403

Betws-y-Coed (1977)
Clubhouse, Betws-y-Coed LL24
Tel **(01690) 710556**
Mem 400
Sec FR Slater
Holes 9 L 4996 yds SSS 64
Recs Am–63 DWP Hughes (1990)
V'tors U SOC
Fees £12.50 (£17.50)
Loc 1/2 mile off A5, in Betws-y-Coed

Caernarfon (1907)
Aberforeshore, LLanfaglan, Caernarfon LL54 5RP
Tel **(01286) 673783/678359**
Mem 650
Sec RE Jones
Holes 18 L 5870 yds SSS 68
Recs Am–67
Pro–64
V'tors U SOC
Fees £18 (£22)
Loc 2 1/2 miles SW of Caernarfon

Conwy (Caernarvonshire) (1890)
Morfa, Conwy LL32 8ER
Tel **(01492) 593400**
Mem 700
Sec EC Roberts (01492) 592423
Pro JP Lees (01492) 593225
Holes 18 L 6936 yds SSS 74
V'tors H WE–restricted SOC
Fees £22 (£27)
Loc 1/2 mile W of Conway, off A55

Criccieth (1905)
Ednyfed Hill, Criccieth
Tel **(01766) 522154**
Mem 200
Sec MG Hamilton (01766) 522697
Holes 18 L 5755 yds SSS 68
Recs Am–63 NJ Gore (1982)
Ladies–60 F Prole (1979)
V'tors U
Fees £12 Sun–£15
Loc 4 miles W of Portmadoc

Dolgellau (1911)
Pencefn Road, Dolgellau LL40 1SL
Tel **(01341) 422603**
Mem 300
Sec HM Edwards
Pro None
Holes 9 L 4671 yds SSS 63
Recs Am–63 AL Williams (1991)
Pro–61 L James (1937)
V'tors U SOC
Fees £12 (£15)
Loc 1/2 mile N of Dolgellau

Ffestiniog (1893)
Y Cefn, Ffestiniog
Tel **(01766) 762637 (Clubhouse)**
Mem 138
Sec A Roberts (01766) 831829
Holes 9 L 5032 metres Par 68 SSS 65
V'tors U
Fees On application
Loc 1 mile E of Ffestiniog on Bala road (B4391)

Llandudno (Maesdu) (1915)
Hospital Road, Llandudno LL30 1HU
Tel **(01492) 876450**
Fax **(01492) 871570**
Mem 1109
Sec G Dean
Pro S Boulden (01492) 875195
Holes 18 L 6513 yds SSS 72
Recs Am–67 G Jones, CT Brown, M Macara
Pro–66 PJ Butler
V'tors U H–recognised GC members SOC
Fees £22 (£30)
Loc 1 mile S of Llandudno Station, nr Hospital

Llandudno (North Wales) (1894)
72 Bryniau Road, West Shore, Llandudno LL30 2DZ
Tel **(01492) 875325**
Fax **(01492) 872420**
Mem 750
Sec GD Harwood
Pro RA Bradbury (0492) 876878
Holes 18 L 6247 yds SSS 70
Recs Am–66 JHM Williams, S Goldspink
Pro–63 WS Collins
V'tors U SOC–phone Sec
Fees £22 (£28)
Loc 3/4mile from Llandudno on West Shore

Llanfairfechan (1971)
Llannerch Road, Llanfairfechan LL33 0EB
Tel **(01248) 680144**
Mem 352
Sec MJ Charlesworth (01248) 680524
Holes 9 L 3119 yds SSS 57
Recs Am–53 MJ Charlesworth (1983)

V'tors U
Fees £10 (£15)
Loc 7 miles E of Bangor on A55

Nefyn & District (1907)
Morfa Nefyn, Pwllheli LL53 6DA
Tel **(01758) 720218 (Clubhouse)**
Fax **(01758) 720476**
Mem 750
Sec TG Owen (01758) 720966
Pro J Froom (01758) 720102
Holes 18 L 6548 yds SSS 71
Recs Am–68 TG Gruffydd
Pro–67 I Woosnam
V'tors U SOC
Fees £20 D–£25 (£25 D–£35)
Loc 1½ miles W of Nefyn. 20 miles W of Caernarfon

Penmaenmawr (1910)
Conway Old Road, Penmaenmawr LL34 6RD
Tel **(01492) 623330**
Mem 600
Sec Mrs JE Jones
Holes 9 L 5143 yds SSS 66
Recs Am–63 S Wilkinson
V'tors U SOC
Fees £15 (£18)
Loc 4 miles W of Conway

Portmadoc (1900)
Morfa Bychan, Porthmadog LL49 9UU
Tel **(01766) 512037**
Fax **(01766) 514638**
Mem 960
Sec L McDonough (01766) 514124
Pro P Bright (01766) 513828
Holes 18 L 6308 yds SSS 70
Recs Am–63 J Morrow
V'tors U H SOC
Fees D–£15 (D–£18)
Loc 2 miles S of Porthmadog, towards Black Rock Sands

Pwllheli (1900)
Golf Road, Pwllheli LL53 5PS
Tel **(01758) 701644**
Mem 820
Sec RE Williams
Pro GD Verity (01758) 612520
Holes 18 L 6091 yds SSS 69
Recs Am–66 MG Hughes (1988)
Pro–67 D Screeton
V'tors U
Fees D–£18 (D–£25)
Loc ½ mile SW of Pwllheli
Arch James Braid

Rhos-on-Sea (1899)
Penrhyn Bay, Llandudno LL30 3PU
Tel **(01492) 549641**
Mem 600
Sec IH Taylor
Pro M Jones
Holes 18 L 6064 yds SSS 69
Recs Am–69 P Knowles
Pro–66 M Greenough
V'tors U
Fees On application
Loc On coast at Rhos-on-Sea. 4 miles E of Llandudno

Royal St David's (1894)
Harlech LL46 2UB
Tel **(01766) 780203**
Fax **(01766) 781110**
Mem 700
Sec RI Jones (01766) 780361
Pro J Barnett (01766) 780857
Holes 18 L 6427 yds SSS 72
Recs Am–64 C Platt (1992)
Pro–64 K Stables (1988)
V'tors U H–booking necessary SOC
Fees D–£25 (D–£30)
Loc W of Harlech on A496

St Deiniol (1905)
Penybryn, Bangor LL57 1PX
Tel **(01248) 353098**
Mem 500
Sec EW Jones
Holes 18 L 5048 metres SSS 67
Recs Am–63 GA Roberts (1979)
V'tors U
Fees £12 (£16)
Loc Off A5/A55 Junction, 1 mile E of Bangor on A5122
Arch James Braid

Isle of Anglesey

Anglesey (1914)
Station Road, Rhosneigr LL64 5QX
Tel **(01407) 810219**
Mem 450
Sec A Jones (Sec/Mgr) (01407) 810930
Pro B Rimmer (01407) 811202
Holes 18 L 6204 yds SSS 70
Recs Am–66 M Robinson (1990)
V'tors U H SOC
Fees £15 (£20)
Loc 8 miles SE of Holyhead, off A4080

Baron Hill (1895)
Beaumaris LL58 8YW
Tel **(01248) 810231**
Mem 360
Sec A Plemming
Holes 9 L 5062 metres SSS 67
Recs Am–65 AW Jones
V'tors U exc comp days SOC–WD & Sat (apply Sec)
Fees £12 W–£45
Loc 1 mile SW of Beaumaris

Bull Bay (1913)
Bull Bay Road, Amlwch LL68 9RY
Tel **(01407) 830960**
Fax **(01407) 832612**
Mem 850
Sec DW Lewis OBE (Sec/Mgr)
Pro N Dunroe (01407) 831188
Holes 18 L 6217 yds SSS 70
Recs Am–65 MS Ellis (1994)
Pro–66 B Rimmer (1994)
V'tors H SOC
Fees £15 (£20)
Loc ½ mile W of Amlwch on A5025
Arch WH Fowler

Holyhead (1912)
Trearddur Bay, Holyhead LL65 2YG
Tel **(01407) 763279/762119**
Fax **(01407) 763279**
Mem 484 225(L) 109(J)
Sec JA Williams
Pro S Elliott (01407) 762022
Holes 18 L 5540 metres SSS 70
Recs Am–64 D McLean
Pro–69 H Gould
V'tors H SOC
Fees £20 (£25)
Loc 2 miles S of Holyhead
Arch James Braid

Llangefni (1983)
Public
Llangefni
Tel **(01248) 722193**
Pro P Lovell
Holes 9 L 1467 yds Par 28
V'tors U
Fees On application
Loc Llangefni ½ mile on B5111

Mid Glamorgan

Aberdare (1921)
Abernant, Aberdare CF44 0RY
Tel **(01685) 871188 (Clubhouse)**
Mem 600
Sec L Adler (01685) 872797
Pro AW Palmer (01685) 878735
Holes 18 L 5875 yds SSS 69
Recs Am–63 S Dodd (1988)
Pro–67 AW Palmer
V'tors I or H Sat–M SOC
Fees £14 (£18)
Loc ½ mile E of Aberdare. 12 miles NW of Pontypridd

Bargoed (1912)
Heolddu, Bargoed
Tel **(01443) 830143**
Mem 531
Sec WR Coleman (01443) 822377
Holes 18 L 6233 yds SSS 69
Recs Am–65 B Dredge
V'tors WD–U WE–M SOC–WD
Fees £10 (£15)
Loc NW boundary of Bargoed. 8 miles N of Caerphilly (A469)

Bryn Meadows Golf Hotel (1973)
The Bryn, Hengoed CF8 7SM
Tel **(01495) 225590/224103**
Fax **(01495) 228272**
Mem 550
Sec B Mayo
Pro B Hunter (01495) 221905
Holes 18 L 6156 yds SSS 69

For list of abbreviations see page 435

Recs Am–69 B Dredge
Pro–68 S Price
V'tors U
Fees £17.50 (£22.50)
Loc 6 miles N of Caerphilly (A469)
Arch Mayo/Jefferies

Caerphilly (1905)

Pencapel, Mountain Road, Caerphilly CF8 1HJ
Tel **(01222) 883481**
Mem 765
Sec (01222) 863441
Pro R Barter (01222) 869104
Holes 14 L 6063 yds SSS 71
Recs Am–65 L Absalom
Pro–68 B Huggett
V'tors WD–U H WE/BH–M
Fees £20 W–£40
Loc 7 miles N of Cardiff, off A469

Castell Heights (1982)

Pay and play
Blaengwynlais, Caerphilly CF8 1NG
Tel **(01222) 886666** (Bookings)
Fax **(01222) 869030**
Mem 600
Pro S Bebb
Holes 9 L 2688 yds SSS 66
Recs Am–32 P Page (1990)
V'tors U
Fees 9 holes–£4.50 (£5.50)
Loc 4 miles from M4 Junction 32
Mis Driving range
Arch J Page

Creigiau (1921)

Creigiau, Cardiff CF4 8NN
Tel **(01222) 890263**
Fax **(01222) 890263**
Mem 700
Sec MJ O'Dowd
Pro M Maddison (01222) 891909
Holes 18 L 5980 yds SSS 69
Recs Am–67 D Samuel
V'tors WD–U WE/BH–M SOC–WD
Fees £21
Loc 5 miles NW of Cardiff

Llantrisant & Pontyclun (1927)

Lanlay Road, Talbot Green, Llantrisant CF7 8HZ
Tel **(01443) 222148**
Mem 500
Sec JM Williams (01443) 224601
Pro N Watson (01443) 228169
Holes 12 L 5712 yds SSS 68
Recs Am–65 TJ Lewis (1974)
Pro–65 JJ Hastings (1982)
V'tors WD–U WE/BH–M SOC–WD
Fees On application
Loc 10 miles NW of Cardiff. 2 miles N of M4 Junction 34

Maesteg (1912)

Mount Pleasant, Neath Road, Maesteg CF34 9PR
Tel **(01656) 732037**
Mem 720
Sec WH Hanford (01656) 734106
Pro JR Black (01656) 735742
Holes 18 L 5900 yds SSS 69
Recs Am–69 R Jenkins (1991), M Donoghue (1992), N Hedley (1993)
Pro–64 G Ryall (1989)
V'tors WD–H SOC
Fees £15 (£20)
Loc 1 mile W of Maesteg on B4282. M4 Junctions 36 or 40

Merthyr Tydfil (1908)

Cilsanws Mountain, Cefn Coed, Merthyr Tydfil CF48 2NU
Tel **(01685) 723308**
Mem 200
Sec V Price
Holes 11 L 5951 yds SSS 69
Recs Am–66 N Evans
Pro–70 J Howard
V'tors U SOC–WD
Fees £12 (£16)
Loc 2 miles NW of Merthyr Tydfil, off A470 at Cefn Coed
Mis Extension to 18 holes 1996

Morlais Castle (1900)

Pant, Dowlais, Merthyr Tydfil CF28 2UY
Tel **(01685) 722822**
Mem 400
Sec N Powell
Pro P Worthing
Holes 18 L 6320 yds SSS 71
Recs Am–67 JP Davies (1993)
V'tors WD–U Sat–NA 12–4pm Sun–NA 8am–12noon SOC–WD
Fees £14 (£16)
Loc 3 miles N of Merthyr Tydfil, nr Mountain Railway

Mountain Ash (1908)

Cefnpennar, Mountain Ash CF45 4DT
Tel **(01443) 472265**
Mem 555
Sec G Matthews (01443) 479459
Pro C Hiscox (01443) 478770
Holes 18 L 5535 yds SSS 68
Recs Am–63 SJ Lewis
Pro–66 R Evans
V'tors WD–U H WE–M
Fees £18
Loc 9 miles NW of Pontypridd

Mountain Lakes (1988)

Blaengwynlais, Caerphilly CF8 1NG
Tel **(01222) 861128**
Fax **(01222) 869030**
Mem 480
Sec DC Rooney (Hon)
Pro S Bebb
Holes 18 L 5700 yds SSS 73
Pro–69 S Little (1990)
V'tors H SOC
Fees £15 (£15)
Loc 4 miles from M4 Junction 32
Mis Driving range
Arch R Sandow

Pontypridd (1905)

Ty Gwyn Road, Pontypridd CF37 4DJ
Tel **(01443) 402359**
Fax **(01443) 491622**
Mem 850
Sec JG Graham (01443) 409904
Pro W Walters (01443) 491210
Holes 18 L 5725 yds SSS 68
Recs Am–66 MC Sallam, PL Jenkins (1989)
V'tors WD–U H WE/BH–M H SOC–WD H
Fees On application
Loc E of Pontypridd, off A470. 12 miles NW of Cardiff

Pyle & Kenfig (1922)

Waun-y-Mer, Kenfig CF33 4PU
Tel **(01656) 783093/771613**
Fax **(01656) 772822**
Mem 860
Sec RC Thomas
Pro R Evans (01656) 772446
Holes 18 L 6655 yds SSS 73
Recs Am–68 S Reid
Pro–67 M Wootton
V'tors WD–U H WE–M SOC
Fees D–£35
Loc 2 miles NW of Porthcawl
Arch HS Colt

Rhondda (1910)

Penrhys, Ferndale, Rhondda CF43 3PW
Tel **(01443) 433204**
Fax **(01443) 433204**
Mem 500
Sec G Rees (01443) 441384
Pro R Davies (01443) 441385
Holes 18 L 6428 yds SSS 71
Recs Am–69 P Derham (1988)
Pro–67 D Ray (1991)
V'tors U H SOC
Fees £15 (£20)
Loc 6 miles W of Pontypridd

Royal Porthcawl (1891)

Rest Bay, Porthcawl CF36 3UW
Tel **(01656) 782251**
Fax **(01656) 771687**
Mem 800
Sec AW Woolcott
Pro P Evans (01656) 773702
Holes 18 L 6691 yds SSS 74
Recs Am–68 S Dodds
Pro–65 B Barnes
V'tors WD–I or H WE/BH–M SOC–H
Fees On application
Loc 22 miles W of Cardiff. M4 Junction 37

Southerndown (1905)

Ewenny, Bridgend CF32 0QP
Tel **(01656) 880326**
Mem 700
Sec KR Wilcox (01656) 880476
Pro DG McMonagle
Holes 18 L 6417 yds SSS 72
Recs Am–66 H Stott
Pro–64 G Hunt

For list of abbreviations see page 435

V'tors WD–U WE/BH–M SOC–Tues & Thurs–H
Fees £30 (£36)
Loc Ewenny, 3 miles S of Bridgend, nr Ogmore Castle ruins

Virginia Park (1993)
Pay and play
Virginia Park, Caerphilly CF8 3SW
Tel **(01222) 863919**
Mem 300
Sec R Howells
Holes 9 L 2566 yds Par 66 SSS 65
V'tors U SOC
Fees 18 holes–£11 9 holes–£6
Loc Caerphilly, 7 miles N of Cardiff
Mis Driving range

Whitehall (1922)
The Pavilion, Nelson, Treharris CF46 6ST
Tel **(01443) 740245**
Mem 300
Sec VE Davies
Holes 9 L 5666 yds SSS 68
Recs Am–66 M Heames (1985)
Pro–62 I Woosnam (1980)
V'tors WD–U WE–M
Fees £15
Loc 15 miles NW of Cardiff

Powys

Brecon (1902)
Newton Park, LLanfaes, Brecon LD3 8PA
Tel **(01874) 622004**
Mem 210
Sec DHE Roderick (01874) 625547
Holes 9 L 5218 yds SSS 66
Recs Am–61 R Dixon
Pro–66 WO Moses
V'tors U SOC
Fees £10
Loc ½ mile W of Brecon on A40

Builth Wells (1923)
Golf Club Road, Builth Wells LD2 3NF
Tel **(01982) 553296**
Fax **(01982) 551064**
Mem 425
Sec A Jones
Pro R Truman
Holes 18 L 5376 yds SSS 67
V'tors U H SOC
Fees £15 (£20)
Loc W of Builth Wells on Llandovery road (A483)

Cradoc (1967)
Penoyre Park, Cradoc, Brecon LD3 9LP
Tel **(01874) 623658**
Fax **(01874) 623658**
Mem 750
Sec GSW Davies
Pro D Beattie (01874) 625524
Holes 18 L 6301 yds SSS 71
Recs Am–65 DK Wood (1982)
V'tors U Sun–M SOC
Fees £18 (£20)
Loc 2 miles NW of Brecon, off B4520
Arch CK Cotton

Knighton (1913)
Little Ffrydd Wood, Knighton LD7 1EF
Tel **(01547) 528646**
Mem 200
Sec PJ Isherwood (Hon)
Holes 9 L 5320 yds SSS 66
Recs Am–66 M Caine, A Williams
Pro–71 H Vardon
V'tors U SOC
Fees £8 (£10)
Loc SW of Knighton. 20 miles NE of Llandrindod Wells
Arch H Vardon

Llandrindod (1905)
Llandrindod Wells LD1 5NY
Tel **(01597) 823873/822010**
Mem 530
Sec GR Harris
Pro None
Holes 18 L 5759 yds SSS 68
Recs Am–65 CJ Davies (1988)
V'tors U SOC
Fees £12 (£20)
Loc 1 mile E of Llandrindod Wells
Arch Harry Vardon

Machynlleth (1905)
Ffordd Drenewydd, Machynlleth SY20 8UH
Tel **(01654) 702000**
Mem 231
Holes 9 L 5726 yds SSS 67
Recs Am–65
Pro–65
V'tors U Sun–NA before 11.30am SOC
Fees £12 (£15)
Loc 1 mile E of Machynlleth, off A489

Rhosgoch (1991)
Rhosgoch, Builth Wells LD2 3JY
Tel **(01497) 851251**
Mem 150
Sec R Meredith
Holes 9 L 4842 yds SSS 64
V'tors U SOC
Fees £7 (£10)
Loc 5 miles N of Hay-on-Wye

St Giles Newtown (1919)
Pool Road, Newtown SY16 3AJ
Tel **(01686) 625844**
Mem 350
Sec TA Hall
Pro DP Owen
Holes 9 L 6006 yds SSS 69
Recs Am–64 A Jones
Pro–64 AP Parkin
V'tors WD/BH–I WE–H restricted
Fees £12.50 (£15)
Loc 1 mile E of Newtown (A483). 14 miles SW of Welshpool

St Idloes (1920)
Penrhallt, Llanidloes SY18 6LG
Tel **(015512) 2559**
Mem 292
Sec JC Green
Holes 9 L 5428 yds SSS 66
Recs Am–63 J Davies
V'tors U H Sun–restricted SOC
Fees £10 (£12) W–£45
Loc ½ mile from Llanidloes on Trefeglwys road (B4569)

Welsh Border Golf Complex (1991)
Bulthy Farm, Bulthy, Middletown SY21 8ER
Tel **(01743) 884247**
Mem 200
Pro DO Jones
Holes 9 L 3250 yds SSS
V'tors U SOC
Fees On application
Loc Between Shrewsbury and Welshpool on A458
Mis Driving range
Arch A Griffiths

Welshpool (1929)
Golfa Hill, Welshpool SY21 9AQ
Tel **(01938) 83249**
Mem 500
Sec DB Pritchard (01938) 552215
Pro None
Holes 18 L 5708 yds SSS 69
Recs Am–65 DH Ryan
Pro–69 S Bowen
V'tors U H
Fees £10 (£20)
Loc 4½ miles W of Welshpool, on Dolgellau road (A458)
Arch James Braid

South Glamorgan

Brynhill (1921)
Port Road, Colcot, Barry CF62 8PN
Tel **(01446) 735061**
Mem 700
Sec K Atkinson (01446) 720277
Pro P Fountain (01446) 733660
Holes 18 L 6021 yds SSS 69
Recs Am–65 C O'Carroll, N Caulfield
Ladies–62 A Phillips (1990)
V'tors WD/Sat–H Sun–NA SOC–WD
Fees £20 Sat–£25 SOC–£17
Loc A4050, 8 miles SW of Cardiff

Cardiff (1921)
Sherborne Avenue, Cyncoed, Cardiff CF2 6SJ
Tel **(01222) 753067**
Mem 930
Sec K Lloyd (01222) 753320

For list of abbreviations see page 435

Pro T Hanson (01222) 754772
Holes 18 L 6015 yds SSS 70
Recs Am–66 R Johnson
V'tors WD–H WE–M SOC–Thurs
Fees £28
Loc 3 miles N of Cardiff. 2 miles W of Pentwyn exit of A48(M). M4 Junction 29

Dinas Powis (1914)
Old Highwalls, Dinas Powis CF6 4AJ
Tel **(01222) 512727**
Mem 650
Sec WJ Hough
Pro G Bennett
Holes 18 L 5486 yds SSS 67
Recs Am–65 P Davidson
Pro–67 P Fountain
V'tors U
Fees D–£20 (D–£24)
Loc 3 miles SW of Cardiff (A4055)

Glamorganshire (1890)
Lavernock Road, Penarth CF64 5UP
Tel **(01222) 707048**
Sec AM Reed-Gibbs (01222) 701185
Pro A Kerr-Smith (01222) 707401
Holes 18 L 6181 yds SSS 70
Recs Am–65 MG Mouland (1979), N Grimmitt (1989)
Pro–65 A Jacklin (1969)
V'tors WD/WE–H SOC
Fees £24 (£30)
Loc 5 miles SW of Cardiff

Llanishen (1905)
Cwm, Lisvane, Cardiff CF4 5UD
Tel **(01222) 752205**
Mem 900
Sec PH Plumb (Sec/Mgr) (01222) 755078
Pro RA Jones (01222) 755076
Holes 18 L 5296 yds SSS 66
Recs Am–63 B Townley (1994)
Pro–63 JT Taylor
V'tors WD–U WE–M H SOC–Mon & Thurs
Fees £22
Loc 5 miles N of Cardiff

Peterstone
Peterstone, Wentloog, Cardiff CF3 8TN
Tel **(01633) 680009**
Fax **(01633) 680563**
Mem 750
Sec R Williams
Pro M Pycroft
Holes 18 L 6555 yds Par 72 SSS 71
Recs Am–68 C O'Carroll
V'tors U SOC–WD
Fees £15 (£17.50)
Loc 3 miles S of Castleton, off A48. M4 Junction 28
Arch Robert Sandon

Radyr (1902)
Drysgol Road, Radyr, Cardiff CF4 8BS
Tel **(01222) 842408**
Fax **(01222) 842408**
Mem 880
Sec S Gough (Mgr)
Pro S Gough (01222) 842476
Holes 18 L 6031 yds SSS 70
Recs Am–62 C Evans
Pro–63 PW Evans, JD Grundy
V'tors WD–H WE–M SOC–Wed–Fri
Fees D–£28
Loc 5 miles NW of Cardiff, off A4119

RAF St Athan (1977)
St Athan, Barry CF62 4WA
Tel **(01446) 751043**
Mem 450
Sec PF Woodhouse (01446) 797186
Pro N Gillette (01222) 373923
Holes 9 L 6452 yds SSS 71
V'tors U exc Sun am–NA
Fees £10 (£15)
Loc 2 miles E of Llantwit Major. 10 miles S of Bridgend

St Andrews Major (1993)
Coldbrook Road, Cadoxton, Barry CF6 3BB
Tel **(01446) 722227**
Holes 9 L 2931 yds
V'tors U
Fees 9 holes–£7. 18 holes–£12
Loc Barry Docks Link road. M4 Junction 33
Arch MRM Leisure

St Mary's Hotel G & CC (1990)
Pay and play
St Mary's Hill, Pencoed CF35 5EA
Tel **(01656) 860280/861100**
Fax **(01656) 863400**
Mem 1000
Sec C Milligan (Mgr) (01656) 861100
Pro J Harris
Holes 18 L 5123 yds SSS 66
9 L 2426 yds SSS 34
Recs Am–67 L Janes (1991)
Pro–64 R Troake
V'tors H SOC–WD
Fees 18 hole: £14 (£17)
9 hole: £3 (£4.50)
Loc Off M4 Junction 35
Mis Floodlit driving range

St Mellons (1937)
St Mellons, Cardiff CF3 8XS
Tel **(01633) 680401**
Mem 500 93(L) 70(J)
Sec Mrs K Newling (01633) 680408
Pro B Thomas (01633) 680101
Holes 18 L 6225 yds SSS 70
Recs Am–67 S Hopkins
Pro–66 E Foster
V'tors WD–U WE–M
Fees £20
Loc 4 miles E of Cardiff on A48

Wenvoe Castle (1936)
Wenvoe, Cardiff CF5 6BE
Tel **(01222) 591094**
Mem 540 100(L) 66(J)
Sec M Burke (01222) 594371
Pro R Day (01222) 593649
Holes 18 L 6422 yds SSS 71
Recs Am–68 N Jones (1989)
Pro–66 PW Evans (1990)
V'tors WD–H WE/BH–M SOC–WD
Fees £25
Loc 4 miles W of Cardiff, off A4050

Whitchurch (1915)
Pantmawr Road, Whitchurch, Cardiff CF4 6XD
Tel **(01222) 620125**
Fax **(01222) 529860**
Mem 438 111(L) 90(J)
Sec RG Burley (Mgr) (01222) 620985
Pro E Clark (01222) 614660
Holes 18 L 6319 yds SSS 70
Recs Am–62 J Povall (1964)
Pro–62 I Woosnam (1986)
V'tors WD–U WE/BH–M H SOC–Thurs
Fees £26 (£30)
Loc 3 miles NW of Cardiff on A470. M4 Junction 32

West Glamorgan

Clyne (1920)
120 Owls Lodge Lane, Mayals, Swansea SA3 5DP
Tel **(01792) 401989**
Mem 950
Sec KC Crawford
Pro M Bevan (01792) 402094
Holes 18 L 6312 yds SSS 71
Recs Am–66 C Dickens(1982)
Pro–64 M Bevan (1990)
V'tors U H SOC
Fees £18 (£25)
Loc SW of Swansea

Earlswood (1993)
Public
Jersey Marine, Neath SA10 6JP
Tel **(01792) 321578**
Sec Mrs D Goatcher (01792) 812198
Pro M Day
Holes 18 L 5174 yds SSS 68
V'tors U SOC
Fees £8
Loc 5 miles E of Swansea (B4290)

Fairwood Park (1969)
Blackhills Lane, Upper Killay, Swansea SA2 7JN
Tel **(01792) 203648**
Mem 650
Sec J Beer, J Pettifer (Mgr)
Pro M Evans (01792) 299194
Holes 18 L 6741 yds SSS 72

For list of abbreviations see page 435

Recs Am–69 R Maliphant, I Roberts (1989) Pro–67 J Lomas (1989), A Griffiths, M Wooton (1990)
V'tors U SOC
Fees £25 (£30)
Loc 4 miles W of Swansea (A4118)

Glynneath (1931)
Penycraig, Pontneathvaughan, Glynneath SA11 5UH
Tel **(01639) 720452**
Mem 580
Sec RM Ellis (01639) 720679
Holes 18 L 5456 yds SSS 67
Recs Am–66 JL Davies Pro–66 P Mayo
V'tors WD–U H WE–M SOC
Fees £15 (£18)
Loc 2 miles NW of Glynneath on B4242. 15 miles NE of Swansea

Inco (1965)
Clydach, Swansea
Tel **(01792) 844216**
Mem 260
Sec DGS Murdoch (01792) 843336
Holes 12 L 6273 yds SSS 70
Recs Am–68 V Smith, N O'Sullivan
V'tors U
Fees On application
Loc N of Swansea (A4067)

Langland Bay (1904)
Langland, Swansea SA3 4QR
Tel **(01792) 366023**
Mem 700
Sec TJ Jenkins (01792) 361721
Pro TJ Lynch (01792) 366186
Holes 18 L 5830 yds SSS 69
Recs Am–63 K Jones, S Dodd (1989) Pro–69 D Ridley
V'tors U SOC
Fees £24 (£26)
Loc 6 miles S of Swansea (A4067)

Morriston (1919)
160 Clasemont Road, Morriston, Swansea SA6 6AJ
Tel **(01792) 771079**
Fax **(01792) 796528**
Mem 400
Sec MR Jefford (Sec/Mgr) (01792) 796528
Pro DA Rees (01792) 772335
Holes 18 L 5785 yds SSS 68
Recs Am–61 M Gorvett (1994) Pro–64 DA Rees
V'tors U H SOC–WD
Fees £18 (£25)
Loc 4 miles N of Swansea on A48. M4 Junction 46, 1 mile

Neath (1934)
Cadoxton, Neath SA10 8AH
Tel **(01639) 643615**
Mem 520
Sec DM Hughes (01639) 632759
Pro EM Bennett (01639) 633693
Holes 18 L 6500 yds SSS 72
Recs Am–66 AL Cooper (1993) Pro–66 F Hill
V'tors WD–U WE–M SOC
Fees £17
Loc 2 miles NE of Neath (B4434)
Arch James Braid

Palleg (1930)
Palleg Road, Lower Cwmtwrch, Swansea Valley SA9 1QT
Tel **(01639) 842193**
Mem 200
Sec DW Moses
Holes 9 L 3209 yds SSS 72
Recs Am–71 C Williams, N Turner (1990)
V'tors WD–U WE–NA
Fees £10
Loc Ystalyfera 1 mile. 15 miles NE of Swansea (A4067)

Pennard (1896)
2 Southgate Road, Southgate, Swansea SA3 2BT
Tel **(01792) 233131**
Mem 775
Sec EM Howell (01792) 233131/873335
Pro MV Bennett (01792) 233451
Holes 18 L 6289 yds SSS 71
Recs Am–69 C Edwards Pro–64 G Emmerson (1994)
V'tors U H SOC–WD only
Fees £24 (£30) W–£80
Loc 8 miles W of Swansea, by A4067 and B4436

Pontardawe (1924)
Cefn Llan, Pontardawe, Swansea SA8 4SH
Tel **(01792) 863118**
Mem 610
Sec L Jones (01792) 830041
Pro G Hopkins (01792) 830977
Holes 18 L 6097 yds SSS 70
Recs Am–64 B Fisher (1993) Pro–71 D Thomas, R Brook
V'tors H SOC–WD
Fees £18
Loc 5 miles N of M4 Junction 45, off A4067

Swansea Bay (1892)
Jersey Marine, Neath SA10 6JP
Tel **(01792) 812198/814153**
Mem 400
Sec Mrs D Goatcher
Pro M Day
Holes 18 L 6605 yds SSS 72
Recs Am–71 C Smith
V'tors U SOC
Fees £16 (£22)
Loc 5 miles E of Swansea, off A483

For list of abbreviations see page 435

Driving Ranges in the British Isles

England

Avon

Clevedon Golf Centre
Lower Strode Road, Clevedon, Bristol
Tel **(01275) 340085**
Golf Par 3 course
Loc Clevedon, W of Bristol

Combe Grove Manor
Brassknocker Hill, Monkton Combe, Bath BA2 7HS
Tel **(01225) 835533**
Fax **(01225) 834961**
Golf 5 hole Par 3 course
Loc 2 miles SE of Bath, off A36.

Farrington
Marsh Lane, Farrington Gurney, Bristol BS18 5TS
Tel **(01761) 241274**
Golf 9 hole course. 18 hole course open Sept 1995
Loc 10 miles S of Bath (A39)

Mendip Spring
Honey Hall Lane, Congresbury BS19 5JT
Tel **(01934) 853337**
Fax **(01934) 853465**
Golf 18 & 9 hole courses
Loc Congresbury. M5 Junction 21

Poplars
Pilning Street, Pilning, Bristol
Tel **(01454) 632535**
Loc 8 miles N of Bristol, off A403

Stockwood Vale
Stockwood Lane, Keynsham, Bristol BS18 2ER
Tel **(0117) 986 6505**
Golf 9 hole course
Loc 1 mile SE of Bristol, off A174

Thornbury Golf Centre
Bristol Road, Thornbury
Tel **(01454) 281144**
Fax **(01454) 281177**
Golf 18 hole & 18 hole Par 3 courses
Loc 10 miles N of Bristol, off A38

Tickenham Golf Centre
Clevedon Road, Tickenham, Bristol BS21 6SB
Tel **(01275) 856626**
Golf 9 hole course
Loc 2 miles E of Clevedon (B3130)

Bedfordshire

Aylesbury Vale
Wing, Leighton Buzzard LU7 0UJ
Tel **(01525) 240196**
Golf 18 hole course
Loc 3 miles W of Leighton Buzzard on A418

Mowsbury
Kimbolton Road, Bedford MK41 8DQ
Tel **(01234) 216374**
Golf 18 hole course
Loc 3 miles N of Bedford on B660

Stockwood Park Golf Centre
Stockwood Park, London Road, Luton LU1 4LX
Tel **(01582) 413704**
Golf 18 hole course
Loc 1 mile S of Luton on A6

Tilsworth Golf Centre
Dunstable Road, Tilsworth, Leighton Buzzard
Tel **(01525) 210721/2**
Golf 18 hole course
Loc 2 miles N of Dunstable, off A5

Wyboston Lakes
Wyboston Lakes, Wyboston MK44 3AL
Tel **(01480) 212501**
Golf 18 hole course
Loc S of St Neots by A1/A45 junction

Berkshire

Bird Hills
Drift Road, Hawthorn Hill, Maidenhead SL6 3ST
Tel **(01628) 771030/75588/26035**
Golf 18 hole course
Loc 4 miles S of Maidenhead on A330

Blue Mountain Golf Centre
Wood Lane, Binfield RG12 5EY
Tel **(01344) 300200**
Golf 18 hole course
Loc 1 mile W of Bracknell on B3408

Downshire
Easthampstead Park, Wokingham RG11 3DH
Tel **(01344) 424066**
Golf 18 hole course. 9 hole pitch & putt course
Loc Off Nine Mile Ride, between Bracknell and Wokingham

Hennerton
Crazies Hill Road, Wargrave RG10 8LT
Tel **(01734) 401000/404778**
Fax **(01734) 401042**
Golf 9 hole course
Loc 2 miles E of Henley

Lavender Park Golf Centre
Swinley Road, Ascot SO5 1BD
Tel **(01344) 890940**
Golf 9 hole Par 3 course
Loc W of Ascot on B3017

Sindlesham
Mole Road, Wokingham RG11 5DJ
Tel **(01734) 788494**
Loc W of Wokingham, off A329.

Buckinghamshire

Aylesbury Golf Centre
Hulcott Lane, Bierton, Aylesbury HP22 5GA
Tel **(01296) 393644**
Golf 9 hole course
Loc 1 mile N of Aylesbury on A418

Colnbrook
Galleymead Road, Colnbrook, Slough SL3 0EN
Tel **(01753) 682670**
Loc 5 miles from M4 Junction 5

For list of abbreviations see page 435

Ivinghoe
Cheddington Road, Ivinghoe, Leighton Buzzard LU7 9DY
Tel (01296) 662720
Holes 28 closed, 5 open floodlit
Loc 1 mile N of Ivinghoe on B488

Silverstone
Silverstone Road, Stowe, Buckingham MK18 5LH
Tel (01280) 850005
Fax (01280) 850080
Golf 18 hole course
Loc By Silverstone Race Circuit

Wavendon Golf Centre
Lower End Road, Wavendon, Milton Keynes MK17 8DA
Tel (01908) 281811
Golf 18 hole course. 9 hole Par 3 course
Loc 2 miles W of M1 Junction 13

Wexham Park
Wexham Street, Wexham, Slough SL3 6NB
Tel (01753) 663271
Golf 18 hole course. 2 x 9 hole courses
Loc 2 miles N of Slough

Windmill Hill Golf Complex
Tattenhoe Lane, Bletchley, Milton Keynes MK3 7RB
Tel (01908) 378623
Fax (01908) 271478
Golf 18 hole course
Loc 4 miles from M1 Junction 14, on A421

Wycombe Heights
Rayners Avenue, Loudwater, High Wycombe
Tel (01494) 816686
Fax (01494) 816728
Golf 18 hole & 18 hole Par 3 courses
Loc 1/2 mile from M40 Junction 3, on A40 to Wycombe

Cambridgeshire

Abbotsley
Eynesbury Hardwicke, St Neots PE19 4XN
Tel (01480) 215153
Golf 18 hole course
Loc 2 miles S of St Neots (B1046)

Hemingford Golf Centre
Rideaway, Hemingford Abbots, Huntingdon PE18 9HQ
Tel (01480) 495000
Golf 9 hole course
Loc 10 miles W of Cambridge on A604

Lakeside Lodge
Fen Road, Pidley, Huntingdon PE17 3DD
Tel (01487) 741541
Golf 18 hole course. 9 hole Par 3 course
Loc 4 miles N of St Ives on B1040

Old Nene
Muchwood Lane, Bodsey, Ramsey PE17 1RB
Tel (01487) 813519
Golf 9 hole course
Loc 1 mile N of Ramsey towards Ramsey Mereside

Thorney Golf Centre
English Drove, Thorney, Peterborough PE6 0TJ
Tel (01733) 270570
Golf 18 hole & 9 hole Par 3 courses
Loc 8 miles E of Peterborough, off A47

Whaddon Golf Centre
Whaddon, Royston SG8 5RX
Tel (01223) 207325
Golf 9 hole Par 3 course
Loc 4 miles N of Royston, off A1198.

Channel Islands

Les Mielles
St Ouens Bay, Jersey
Tel (01534) 482787
Golf 9 hole Par 3 course
Loc Five Mile Road

St Pierre Park
Rohais, St Peter Port, Guernsey
Tel (01481) 727039
Golf 9 hole Par 3 course
Loc 1 mile W of St Peter Port

Cheshire

Alvaston Hall Golf Centre
Alvaston Hall, Middlewich Road, Nantwich CW5 6PD
Tel (01270) 610019
Golf 9 hole Par 3 course

Carden Park
Carden Park, Chester CH3 9DQ
Tel (01829) 250325
Golf 18 hole course. 9 hole Par 3 course
Loc 10 miles S of Chester on A534

Cranford Golf Centre
Harwood Road, Heaton Mersey, Stockport SK4 3AW
Tel (0161) 432 8242
Loc M63 Junction 12, 2 miles

Croft Golf Centre
Cross Lane, Croft WA3 7AW
Tel (01925) 763741
Loc 4 miles NE of Warrington

Drive Time
Centre Park, Warrington WA1 1QL
Tel (01925) 234800
Fax (01925) 240053
Loc Warrington town centre

Hartford
Burrows Hill, Hartford, Northwich CW8 3AA
Tel (01606) 871162
Loc Off A556 at Hartford

Sandfield
Ince Lane, Bridge Trafford, Chester CH2 4JR
Tel (01244) 301752
Golf 9 hole Par 3 course
Loc 5 miles NE of Chester (A56), nr M6/M62 Junction

The Tytherington
Macclesfield SK10 2JP
Tel (01625) 434562
Fax (01625) 430882
Loc N of Macclesfield (A523)
Golf 18 hole course

Cleveland

Hunley Hall
Brotton, Saltburn TS12 2QQ
Tel (01287)676216
Fax (01287) 678250
Golf 18 hole course
Loc 15 miles SE of Middlesbrough on A174

Knotty Hill Golf Centre
Sedgefield, Stockton-on-Tees TS21 2BB
Tel (01740) 620320
Fax (01740) 620320
Golf 18 hole course
Loc 1 mile N of Sedgefield on A177. A1(M) Junction 60

Middlesbrough
Ladgate Lane, Middlesbrough TS5 7YZ
Tel (01642) 300720
Fax (01642) 300726
Golf 18 hole course
Loc 2 miles S of Middlesbrough, nr A174

Cornwall

China Fleet
Saltash PL12 6LJ
Tel (01752) 848668
Golf 18 hole course
Loc 1 mile from Tamar Bridge, off A38

For list of abbreviations see page 435

Cornwall Golf Centre
Clifton Park, Carminow Cross, Bodmin
Tel **(01208) 77588**
Loc E of Bodmin towards Liskeard

Lanhydrock
Lostwithiel Road, Bodmin PL30 5AQ
Tel **(01208) 73600**
Fax **(01208) 77325**
Golf 18 hole course
Loc 1 mile S of Bodmin, off B3268

Lostwithiel
Lower Polscoe, Lostwithiel PL22 0HQ
Tel **(01208) 873550**
Golf 18 hole course
Loc 1 mile E of Lostwithiel, off A390

Radnor Golf Centre
Radnor Road, Treleigh, Redruth TR16 5EL
Tel **(01209) 211059**
Golf 9 hole Par 3 course
Loc 2 miles NE of Redruth

Cumbria

Brayton Park
Brayton, Aspatria, Carlisle CA5 3TD
Tel **(016973) 20840**
Golf 9 hole course
Loc 8 miles NE of Maryport, off A596

Eden
Crosby-on-Eden, Carlisle CA6 4RA
Tel **(01228) 573003**
Fax **(01228) 818435**
Golf 18 hole course
Loc 5 miles NE of Carlisle, off A689

Solway Village Golf Centre
Solway Village, Silloth-on-Solway CA5 4QQ
Tel **(016973) 31236**
Fax **(016973) 32553**
Golf 9 hole Par 3 course
Loc Silloth

Derbyshire

Bondhay G & CC
Bondhay Lane, Whitwell, Worksop S80 3EH
Tel **(01909) 723608**
Golf 18 hole course. 9 hole short course
Loc 5 miles W of Worksop, off A619

Grassmoor
North Wingfield Road, Grassmoor, Chesterfield S42 5EA
Tel **(01246) 856044**
Golf 18 hole course
Loc 2 miles S of Chesterfield on B6038

Horsley Lodge
Smalley Mill Road, Horsley DE2 5BL
Tel **(01332) 780838**
Golf 18 hole course
Loc 4 miles NE of Derby, off A38

Devon

Dainton Park
Totnes Road, Ipplepen, Newton Abbot TQ12 5TN
Tel **(01803) 813872**
Golf 18 hole course
Loc 2 miles S of Newton Abbot on A381

Dartmouth
Blackawton, Totnes TQ9 7DG
Tel **(01803) 712686/712650**
Fax **(01803) 712628**
Golf 18 & 9 hole courses
Loc 4 miles NE of Dartmouth on A3122

Dinnaton
Ivybridge PL21 9HU
Tel **(01752) 892512/892452**
Golf 2 x 9 hole courses
Loc 12 miles SE of Plymouth, off A38/B3213

Fingle Glen
Tedburn St Mary, Exeter EX6 6AF
Tel **(01647) 61817**
Golf 9 hole course
Loc 5 miles W of Exeter on A30

Hele Park Golf Centre
Ashburton Road, Newton Abbot TQ12 6JN
Tel **(01626) 336060**
Golf 9 hole course
Loc W of Newton Abbot on A383

Ilfracombe & Woolacombe
Woolacombe Road, Ilfracombe EX34 7HF
Tel **(01271) 866222**
Loc 1 mile from Mullacott Cross on B3343

Libbaton
High Bickington, Umberleigh EX37 9BS
Tel **(01769) 60269**
Golf 18 hole course
Loc 1 mile S of High Bickington on B3217, nr A377

Manor House
Moretonhampstead TQ13 8RE
Tel **(01647) 40355**
Golf 18 hole course
Loc 15 miles SW of Exeter on B3212

Newton Abbot
The Racecourse, Newton Abbot TQ12 3AF
Tel **(01626) 64885**
Loc NE of Newton Abbot (B3197)

Otter Valley Golf Centre
Upottery, Honiton EX14 9QP
Tel **(01404) 86266**
Loc 5 miles NE of Honiton, off A30

Thorn Park Golf Range
Salcombe Regis, Sidmouth EX10 0JH
Tel **(01395) 579564**
Loc 2 miles NE of Sidmouth

Torbay Golf Centre
Clennan Valley, Goodrington, Paignton TQ4 7JY
Tel **(01803) 528728**
Loc 2 miles S of Paignton

Woodbury Park
Woodbury, Exeter EX5 1JJ
Tel **(01395) 233382**
Golf 18 hole & 9 hole courses
Loc 6 miles SE of Exeter

Dorset

Bournemouth
Parley Green Lane, Hurn, Christchurch BH23 6BB
Tel **(01202) 593131**
Golf 6 hole course
Loc Hurn, NE Bournemouth

Crane Valley
West Farm, Romford, Verwood BH31 6LE
Tel **(01202) 814088**
Golf 18 & 9 hole courses
Loc Off B3038 Cranbourne road

Dudsbury
Christchurch Road, Ferndown BH22 8ST
Tel **(01202) 593499**
Fax **(01202) 594555**
Golf 18 hole course
Loc 3 miles N of Bournemouth

East Dorset Golf Centre
Hyde, Wareham BH20 7NT
Tel **(01929) 472272**
Golf 18 & 9 hole courses
Loc 5 miles W of Wareham nr Bere Regis

Halstock
Common Lane, Halstock BA22 9SF
Tel **(01935) 891689**
Golf 18 hole course
Loc 6 miles S of Yeovil, off A37

Iford Bridge
Barrack Road, Christchurch BH23 2BA
Tel **(01202) 473817**
Golf 9 hole course
Loc Bournemouth/Christchurch boundary

Moors Valley
Horton Road, Ringwood, Hants BH24 2ET
Tel **(01425) 479776**
Golf 18 hole course
Loc 4 miles S of Ringwood, off A31

Solent Meads
Rolls Drive, Hengistbury Head, Bournemouth
Tel **(01202) 420795**
Golf 18 hole Par 3 course
Loc S of Christchurch

Wessex Golf Centre
Radipole Lane, Weymouth
Tel **(01305) 784737**
Golf 9 hole Par 3 course
Loc 1 mile N of Weymouth, behind Football Club

Durham

Oakleaf Golf Complex
School Aycliffe Lane, Newton Aycliffe DL5 6QZ
Tel **(01325) 310820**
Golf 18 hole course
Loc 1 mile W of Newton Aycliffe on A6072

Roseberry Grange
Grange Villa, Chester-le-Street DH2 3NF
Tel **((0191) 370 0660**
Golf 18 hole course
Loc 3 miles W of Chester-le-Street on A693

Stressholme
Snipe Lane, Darlington DL2 2SA
Tel **(01325) 461002**
Fax **(01325) 351826**
Golf 18 hole course
Loc 2 miles S of Darlington on A66

Essex

Belhus Park Leisure Complex
South Ockenden, Thurrock RM15 4PX
Tel **(01708) 852248**
Golf 18 hole course
Loc 1 mile N of A13/M25

Belvedere
Hardings Elms Road, Crays Hill, Billericay CM11 2UH
Tel **(01268) 286612**
Loc 2 miles SE of Billericay (A129)

Benton Hall
Wickham Hill, Witham CM8 3LH
Tel **(01376) 502454**
Fax **(01376) 521050**
Golf 18 hole course. 9 hole Par 3 course
Loc Witham, off A12

Brentwood Park
Warley Gap, Brentwood CM13 3LE
Tel **(01277) 211994**
Fax **(01227) 220734**
Loc Warley, 1 mile S of Brentwood

Bunsay Downs
Little Baddow Road, Woodham Walter CM9 6RW
Tel **(01245) 412648/412369**
Golf 9 hole course. 9 hole Par 3 course
Loc 1½ miles N of Danbury, off A414 towards Woodham Walter

Castle Point
Somnes Avenue, Canvey Island SS8 9FG
Tel **(01268) 511758**
Golf 18 hole course
Loc On A130 to Canvey Island, off A13

Colchester
Old Ipswich Road, Ardleigh, Colchester
Tel **(01206) 230974**
Loc 1 mile NE of Colchester, off A12

Earls Colne Golf Centre
Earls Colne, Colchester CO6 2NS
Tel **(01787) 224466**
Fax **(01787) 224410**
Golf 18 & 9 hole courses
Loc 2 miles N of A120 on B1024

Epping Forest G&CC
Woolston Manor, Abridge Road, Chigwell IG7 6BX
Tel **(0181) 500 2549**
Fax **(0181) 501 5452**
Golf 18 hole course
Loc Nr M11 Junction 5

The Essex Golf Complex
Eastern Avenue, Southend-on-Sea SS2 4PT
Tel **(01702) 601701**
Fax **(01702) 601033**
Golf 18 hole course. 9 hole Par 3 course
Loc E side of Southend-on-Sea

Fairlop Waters
Forest Road, Barkingside, Ilford IG6 3JA
Tel **(0181) 500 9911**
Golf 18 hole course. 9 hole Par 3 course
Loc 2 miles from S end of M11, by Fairlop Tube Station

Hockley
Aldermans Hill, Hockley, Southend-on-Sea
Tel **(01702) 207218/201008**
Loc 3 miles NW of Southend (B1013)

Langdon Hills
Lower Dunton Road, Bulphan RM14 3TY
Tel **(01268) 548444/544300**
Fax **(01268) 490084**
Golf 18 & 9 hole courses
Loc SW of Basildon between A127 and A13. M25 Junction 29/30

Leigh
Leigh Marshes, Leigh-on-Sea SS9 2EU
Tel **(01702) 710586**
Loc Between Station and Two Tree Island

Mardyke Valley Golf Centre
South Road, South Ockendon RM15 6RR
Tel **(01708) 855011**
Fax **(01708) 855011**
Golf 3 hole course + practice centre
Loc 3 miles NE of M25 Junction 31

Pipps Hill
Cranes Farm Road, Basildon SS14 3DG
Tel **(01268) 523990**
Loc 1 mile N of Basildon on A1235

Tiptree
Newbridge Road, Tiptree CO5 0HS
Tel **(01621) 819374**
Loc 8 miles SW of Colchester (B1022)

Towerlands
Panfield Road, Braintree CM7 5BJ
Tel **(01376) 26802**
Golf 9 hole course
Loc 1 mile NW of Braintree

Warren Park Golf Centre
Whalebone Lane North, Chadwell Heath RM6 6SB
Tel **(0181) 597 1120**
Fax **(0181) 590 5457**
Loc A12 between Gants Hill and Romford

For list of abbreviations see page 435

Woodham Mortimer
Burnham Road, Woodham Mortimer, Maldon CM9 6SR
Tel **(01245) 222276**
Golf 18 hole pitch & putt course
Loc E of Danbury on B1010, off A414

Gloucestershire

Gloucester Hotel & CC
Robinswood Hill, Matson Lane, Gloucester GL4 9EA
Tel **(01452) 411311**
Golf 18 hole course. 9 hole Par 3 course
Loc 2 miles S of Gloucester

Sherdons Golf Centre
Manor Farm, Tredington, Tewkesbury
Tel **(01684) 274782**
Golf 9 hole course
Loc 2 miles S of Tewkesbury, off A38

Hampshire

Basingstoke Golf Centre
Worting Road, West Ham, Basingstoke RG23 0TY
Tel **(01256) 50054**
Golf 9 hole Par 3 course
Loc Basingstoke Leisure Park

Blacknest
Frith End, Binsted GU34 4QL
Tel **(01420) 22888**
Fax **(01420) 22001**
Golf 9 hole course. 9 hole Par 3 course
Loc 7 miles SW of Franham, off A325

Botley Park
Winchester Road, Boorley Green, Botley SO3 2UA
Tel **(01489) 780888**
Fax **(01489) 789242**
Golf 18 hole course
Loc 6 miles E of Southampton on B3354

Chilworth Golf Centre
Main Road, Chilworth SO16 7JP
Tel **(01703) 740544**
Fax **(01703) 733166**
Golf 2 x 9 hole courses
Loc Between Romsey and Southampton on A27

Dibden Golf Centre
Main Road, Dibden, Southampton SO4 5TB
Tel **(01703) 845596**
Golf 18 & 9 hole courses
Loc 10 miles W of Southampton on A326

Old Thorns
Longmoor Road, Griggs Green, Liphook GU30 7PE
Tel **(01428) 724555**
Golf 18 hole course
Loc Griggs Green exit off A3

Paultons Golf Centre
Old Salisbury Road, Ower, Romsey SO51 6AN
Tel **(01703) 813345**
Fax **(01703) 813993**
Golf 18 & 9 hole courses
Loc Nr M27 Junction 2

Portsmouth Golf Centre
Burrfields Road, Portsmouth PO3 5HH
Tel **(01705) 664549/699519**
Fax **(01705) 650525**
Golf 18 hole course
Loc 1 mile off M27 on A2030

Tadley
Bishopswood Lane, Tadley, Basingstoke RG26 6AT
Tel **(01734) 815213**
Golf 9 hole course
Loc 6 miles N of Basingstoke, off A340

Tournerbury Golf Centre
Tournerbury Road, Hayling Island PO11 9DL
Tel **(01705) 462266**
Golf 9 hole course
Loc E coast of Hayling Island. 3 miles S of Havant

Hereford & Worcester

Abbey Park
Dagnell End Road, Redditch B98 7BD
Tel **(01527) 63918/68006**
Golf 18 hole course
Loc On B4101, off A441 Redditch-Birmingham road

Bransford
Bransford, Worcester WR6 5JD
Tel **(01886) 833551**
Fax **(01886) 832461**
Golf 18 hole course
Loc 3 miles SW of Worcester on A4103

The Grove
Ford Bridge, Leominster HR6 0LE
Tel **(01568) 610602**
Loc 3 miles S of Leominster on By-pass

Ombersley
Bishops Wood Road, Lineholt, Ombersley WR9 0LE
Tel **(01905) 620747**
Fax **(01905) 620047**
Golf 18 hole course
Loc 7 miles N of Worcester, off A4025

Sapey
Upper Sapey, Worcester WR6 6XT
Tel **(01886) 853288**
Fax **(01886) 853485**
Golf 18 hole course
Loc 6 miles N of Bromyard on B4203

South Herefordshire
Twin Lakes, Hartleton, Ross-on-Wye HR9 7UA
Tel **(01989) 780535**
Fax **(01989) 740611**
Golf 18 hole course. 9 hole Par 3 course
Loc 3 miles NE of Ross-on-Wye

The Vale
Hill Furze Road, Bishampton, Pershore WR10 2LZ
Tel **(0138682) 520**
Golf 18 & 9 hole courses
Loc 6 miles NW of Evesham, off B4084

Wharton Park
Long Bank, Bewdley DY12 2QW
Tel **(01299) 405222/405163**
Fax **(01299) 405121**
Golf 18 hole course
Loc Bewdley By-pass (A456)

Worcester
Weir Lane, Lower Wick, Worcester WR2 4AY
Tel **(01905) 421213**
Loc Nr Worcester town centre
Golf 9 hole pitch & putt course

Wyre Forest Golf Centre
Birchen Coppice Farm, Zortech Avenue, Kidderminster DY11 7EX
Tel **(01299) 822682**
Golf 18 hole course
Loc Between Kidderminster and Stourport on A451

Hertfordshire

A 1
Rowley Lane, Arkley, Barnet
Tel **(0181) 447 1411**
Fax **(0181) 449 5033**
Loc 2 miles S of M25 Junction 23, off A1. Opposite Elstree Moat House

Bushey
High Street, Bushey WD2 1BJ
Tel **(0181) 950 2215**
Golf 9 hole course
Loc 1½ miles S of Watford.

For list of abbreviations see page 435

Chesfield Downs
Jack's Hill, Graveley, Stevenage SG4 7EQ
Tel (01462) 482929
Golf 18 hole course. 9 hole Par 3 course
Loc 2 miles N of Stevenage (B197)

Elstree
Watling Street, Elstree WD6 3AA
Tel (0181) 953 6115
Golf 18 hole course
Loc 2 miles from A41 along A5183.

Gosling Sports Park
Stanborough Road, Welwyn Garden City
Tel (01707) 331056
Loc S of Welwyn Garden City, nr A1(M).

Little Hay Golf Complex
Box Lane, Bovingdon, Hemel Hempstead HP3 0DQ
Tel (01442) 833798
Golf 18 hole course
Loc 2 miles W of Hemel on B4505 to Chesham

Oxhey
Prestwick Road, South Oxhey, Watford
Tel (01923) 248312
Golf 9 hole course
Loc 2 miles SW of Watford

Redbourn
Redbourn Golf Club, Kinsbourne Green Lane, Redbourn, St Albans AL3 7QA
Tel (01582) 793493
Fax (01582) 794362
Golf 18 hole course. 9 hole Par 3 course
Loc 4 miles N of St Albans, off A5. M1 Junction 9

Shooters Golf Centre
Shooters Way, Berkhamsted HP4 3UL
Tel (01442) 872048
Loc SW of Berkhamsted towards Wigginton

Stevenage
Aston Lane, Stevenage SG2 7EL
Tel (01438) 880424
Golf 18 hole course. 9 hole Par 3 course
Loc Off A602 Hertford road

Whitehill Golf Centre
Dane End, Ware SG12 0JS
Tel (01920) 438495
Golf 18 hole course
Loc 6 miles N of Ware, off A10

Humberside

Grange Park
Butterwick Road, Messingham, Scunthorpe DN17 3PP
Tel (01724) 764478
Golf 9 hole course
Loc 5 miles SE of Messingham

Hull Golf Centre
National Avenue, Hull HU5 4JB
Tel (01482) 492720
Golf 9 hole pitch & putt
Loc 2 miles NW of Hull, nr Outer Ring road

Isle of Man

Mount Murray
Santon
Tel (01624) 661111
Golf 18 hole course
Loc 3 miles S of Douglas

Kent

Birchwood Park
Birchwood Road, Wilmington, Dartford DA2 7HJ
Tel (01322) 660554
Golf 18 + 9 hole courses
Loc 2 miles S of A2

Boughton
Brickfield Lane, Boughton, Faversham ME13 9AJ
Tel (01227) 752277
Golf 18 hole course
Loc NE of Boughton, nr M2/A2 Junction

Chatham Golf Centre
Street-End Road, Chatham ME5 0BG
Tel (01634) 848925
Loc Chatham

Chelsfield Lakes Golf Centre
Chelsfield, Orpington BR6 7QR
Tel (01689) 896266
Golf 18 hole course. 9 hole Par 3 course
Loc 1 mile from M25 Junction 4 on A224

Edenbridge G & CC
Crouch House Road, Edenbridge TN8 5LQ
Tel (01732) 865097
Golf 2 x 18 + 9 hole courses
Loc 15 mins from Sevenoaks, Tonbridge and M25

Herne Bay
Bullockstone Road, Herne Bay CT6 7TL
Tel (01227) 742742
Loc 1/2 mile S of Herne Bay, off A299

JLS Golf Centre
Thong Lane, Gravesend DA12 4LG
Tel (01474) 335002
Golf 9 hole Par 3 course
Loc N of A2

Langley Park
Sutton Road, Maidstone ME17 3NQ
Tel (01622) 863163
Loc 4 miles S of Maidstone on A274

Oast Golf Centre
Church Road, Tonge, Sittingbourne ME9 9AR
Tel (01795) 473527
Golf 9 hole Par 3 course
Loc Off A2, between Bapchild and Teynham

Prince's
Prince's Golf Club, Sandwich Bay, Sandwich CT13 9QB
Tel (01304) 613797
Golf 3 x 9 hole courses
Loc Sandwich Bay

Ruxley Park Golf Centre
Sandy Lane, St Paul's Cray, Orpington BR5 3HY
Tel (01689) 871490
Fax (01689) 891428
Golf 18 hole course. 9 hole par 3 course
Loc Nr Ruxley roundabout (A20)

Sandwich
Ash Road, Sandwich CT13 9XX
Tel (01304) 612812
Loc Sandwich

Upchurch River Valley
Oak Lane, Upchurch, Sittingbourne ME9 7AY
Tel (01634) 379592
Fax (01634) 387784
Golf 18 hole course. 9 hole Par 3 course
Loc 3 miles NE of Rainham, off A2

Lancashire

Blackburn
Queens Park Playing Fields, Haslingden Road, Blackburn BB2 3HJ
Tel (01254) 581996
Loc 3/4 mile SE of Blackburn

Euxton Park Golf Centre
Euxton Lane, Chorley, Preston PR7 6DL
Tel **(012572) 61601**
Golf 9 hole Par 3 course
Loc 2 miles W of M61 Junction 8

Herons Reach
Village Hotel Leisure Club, East Park Drive, Blackpool FY3 8LL
Tel **(01253) 838866/766156**
Golf 18 hole course
Loc Follow signs to Blackpool Zoo

Hurlston Hall
Hurlston Lane, Southport Road, Scarisbrick L40 8JD
Tel **(01704) 840400**
Fax **(01704) 841404**
Golf 18 hole course
Loc 2 miles N of Ormskirk on A570

Kearsley
Moss Lane, Kearsley, Bolton BL4 8SF
Tel **(01204) 75726**
Loc 4 miles S of Bolton on A666
Golf 9 hole pitch & putt

Leisure Lakes
Tabby Nook, Mere Brow, Tarleton PR4 6LA
Tel **(01772) 815842**
Loc A565 between Southport and Preston

Phoenix
Fleetwood Road, Norbreck, Blackpool
Tel **(01253) 854846**
Golf 9 hole par 3 course
Loc North Blackpool

Poulton-le-Fylde
Myrtle Farm, Breck Road, Poulton-le-Fylde FY6 7HJ
Tel **(01253) 892444**
Golf 9 hole course
Loc 3 miles NE of Blackpool

Preston
Lightfoot Lane, Fulwood, Preston PR4 0AE
Tel **(01772) 861827**
Loc 1 mile W of M6 Junction 32, nr Rugby Club

Leicestershire

Blaby
Lutterworth Road, Blaby LE8 3DP
Tel **(0116) 278 4804**
Golf 9 hole course
Loc S of Blaby village

Charnwood Golf Centre
Derby Road Sports Ground, Loughborough LE11 0SS
Tel **(01509) 610022**
Golf 9 hole pitch & putt
Loc N Loughborough (A6)

Golf Link
Snibston Discovery Park, Ashby Road, Coalville LE6 2LN
Tel **(01530) 836591**
Golf 9 hole Par 3 course
Loc 4 miles from M1 Junction 22

Greetham Valley
Wood Lane, Greetham, Oakham LE15 7RG
Tel **(01780) 460444**
Fax **(01780) 460623**
Golf 18 hole course. 9 hole Par 3 course
Loc 5 miles NE of Oakham (B668)

Kingstand
Beggars Lane, Leicester Forest East, Leicester LE3 3NQ
Tel **(0116) 238 7908**
Golf 18 hole course
Loc W of Leicester, off A47

Langton Golf Academy
Langton Hall, Leicester LE16 7TY
Tel **(01858) 84374**
Golf 18 hole course
Loc 2 miles N of Market Harborough

Leicestershire Forest Golf Centre
Markfield Lane, Botcheston, Leicester LE6 9FJ
Tel **(01455) 824800**
Golf 18 hole course
Loc 6 miles W of Leicester

Western Park
Scudamore Road, Leicester LE3 1UQ
Tel **(0116) 287 2339**
Golf 18 hole course
Loc 4 miles W of Leicester

Whetstone
Cambridge Road, Cosby, Leicester LE9 5SH
Tel **(0116) 286 1424**
Fax **(0116) 286 1424**
Golf 18 hole course
Loc S of Leicester

Lincolnshire

Belton Woods
Belton, Grantham NG32 2LN
Tel **(01476) 593200**
Fax **(01476) 74547**
Golf 2 x 18 hole + 9 hole courses
Loc 2 miles N of Grantham on A607

The Elms Golf Centre
Croft, Wainfleet, Skegness PE24 4AW
Tel **(01754) 881230**
Fax **(01754) 880949**
Golf 9 hole Par 3 course
Loc 4 miles SW of Skegness (A52), off Wainfleet by-pass

Gainsborough
Thonock, Gainsborough DN21 1PZ
Tel **(01427) 613088**
Fax **(01427) 810172**
Golf 18 hole course
Loc 1 mile N of Gainsborough

Gedney Hill
West Drove, Gedney Hill, Holbeach PE12 0NT
Tel **(01406) 330922**
Golf 18 hole course
Loc 6 miles E of Crowland on B1166

Horncastle
West Ashby, Horncastle LN9 5PP
Tel **(01507) 526800**
Golf 18 hole course
Loc 1 mile N of Horncastle, off A158

Kenwick Park
Kenwick Hall, Louth LN11 8NR
Tel **(01507) 605134**
Golf 18 hole course
Loc 1 mile SE of Louth

Lincoln
Washingborough Road, Washingborough, Lincoln
Tel **(01522) 522059**
Golf 9 hole Par 3 course
Loc 1 mile SE of Lincoln

Millfield
Laughterton, Lincoln LN1 2LB
Tel **(01427) 718255**
Golf 18 hole course. 9 hole Par 3 course
Loc 9 miles W of Lincoln (A113)

London

Chingford
Waltham Way, Chingford, London E4 8AQ
Tel **(0181) 529 2409**
Loc 1 mile N of North Circular Road

Chiswick Bridge
Dukes Meadows, Great Chertsey Road, London W4 2SH
Tel **(0181) 995 0537**
Golf 9 hole Par 3 course open 1995
Loc SE of Chiswick (A316), by Chiswick Bridge

Docklands
Brunswick Wharf Road, Leamouth Road, London E14
Tel **(0171) 712 9944**

Fairways
Walthamstowe Avenue, Chingford, London E4 8TA
Tel (0181) 531 5126
Loc By Walthamstowe Dog Track on North Circular Road

Lee Valley Leisure
Picketts Lock Lane, Edmonton, London N9 0AS
Tel (0181) 803 3611
Golf 18 hole course
Loc 1 mile N of North Circular Rd

Richmond Park
Roehampton Gate, Richmond Park, London SW15 5JR
Tel (0181) 876 3205
Golf 2 x 18 hole courses
Loc In Richmond Park

Riverside
Summerton Way, Thamesmead, London SE28 8PP
Tel (0181) 310 7975
Golf 9 hole course
Loc E of Woolwich, off A2016

Manchester (Greater)

Bardsley Park Golf Centre
Knott Lanes, Bardsley, Oldham OL8 3JD
Tel (0161) 627 2463
Loc 3 miles E of Manchester on A627

Beacon Park
Beacon Lane, Up Holland WN8 7RU
Tel (01695) 622700
Golf 18 hole course
Loc Nr Up Holland. M6 Junction 26

Bolton Golf
Longsight Park, Longsight Lane, Harwood, Bolton
Tel (01204) 597779
Loc 1 mile NE of Bolton

Castle Hawk
Chadwick Lane, Castleton, Rochdale OL11 3BY
Tel (01706) 59995
Loc Castleton Station 1 mile

Merseyside

Formby Golf Centre
Moss Side, Formby L37 0AF
Tel (017048) 75952 (Pro), (017048) 34469 (Sec)
Golf 9 hole Par 3 course
Loc Formby By-Pass (A565)

Sherdley Park
Marshalls Cross Road, St Helens
Tel (01744) 813149
Golf 18 hole course
Loc 2 miles E of St Helens (A570)

Wirral Golf & Drive Centre
Tarran Way, Moreton, Wirral L46 4TP
Tel (0151) 677 6606
Fax (0151) 678 4359
Loc 1 mile W of M53 Junction 2

Middlesex

Airlinks
Southall Lane, Hounslow TW5 9PE
Tel (0181) 561 1418
Golf 18 hole course
Loc Off M4 Junction 3

Ealing
Rowdell Road, Northolt UB5 6AG
Tel (0181) 845 4967
Loc A40 Target roundabout

London Golf Centre
Ruislip Road, Northolt UB5 6QZ
Tel (0181) 845 3180
Golf 9 hole course
Loc Off A40, nr Polish War Memorial

Ruislip
Ickenham Road, Ruislip HA4 7DQ
Tel (01895) 638081
Fax (01895) 622172
Golf 18 hole course
Loc West Ruislip

Sunbury
Charlton Lane, Shepperton TW17 8QA
Tel (01932) 772898
Golf 9 hole course
Loc 1 mile from M3 Junction 1

Twickenham Park
Staines Road, Twickenham TW2 5JD
Tel (0181) 783 1698
Golf 9 hole course
Loc Nr end of M3

Norfolk

Albatross
Burnham Market Road, Fakenham
Tel (01328) 856614
Golf Par 3 course

Browston Hall
Browston Green, Great Yarmouth NR31 9DW
Tel (01493) 603511
Golf 9 hole pitch & putt
Loc 2 miles SW of Great Yarmouth, off A143

Eagles
School Road, Tylney All Saints, Kings Lynn PE34 4RS
Tel (01553) 827147
Golf 9 hole & Par 3 courses
Loc 5 miles W of Kings Lynn on A47

Middleton Hall
Hall Orchards, Middleton, Kings Lynn PE32 1RH
Tel (01553) 841800
Golf 9 hole course
Loc 2 miles SE of Kings Lynn on A47

Norwich Golf Centre
Long Lane, Bawburgh, Norwich NR9 3LX
Tel (01603) 746390
Golf 18 hole course
Loc 3 miles S of Norwich on B1108

Sprowston Park
Wroxham Road, Sprowston, Norwich NR7 8RP
Tel (01603) 410657
Golf 18 hole course
Loc 2 miles NE of Norwich on A1151

Wensum Valley
Beech Avenue, Taverham, Norwich NR8 6HP
Tel (01603) 261012
Golf 18 & 9 hole courses
Loc 4 miles NW of Norwich on A1067

Northamptonshire

Collingtree Park
Windingbrook Lane, Northampton NN4 0XN
Tel (01604) 700000
Fax (01604) 702600
Golf 18 hole course
Loc ½ mile E of M1 Junction 15

Delapre Golf Complex
Eagle Drive, Nene Valley Way, Northampton NN4 0DV
Tel (01604) 764036/763957
Fax (01604) 763957
Golf 18 & 9 hole courses. 2 x 9 hole Par 3 courses
Loc 3 miles from M1 Junction 15, on A508/A45

Hellidon Lakes
Hellidon, Daventry NN11 6LN
Tel (01327) 62550
Golf 18 hole course
Loc 7 miles SW of Daventry (A361)

West Park
Whittlebury, Towcester, NN12 8XW
Tel (01327) 858092
Fax (01327) 858009
Golf 2 x 18 hole courses
Loc 4 miles S of Towcester on A413

Northumberland

Belford
South Road, Belford NE70 7HY
Tel (01668) 213433
Golf 9 hole course
Loc 15 miles N of Alnwick, off A1

Slaley Hall
Slaley, Hexham NE47 0BY
Tel (01434) 673350
Golf 18 hole course
Loc S of Corbridge, off A68

Nottinghamshire

Cotgrave Place
Stragglethorpe, Nottingham NG12 3HB
Tel (0115) 933 4686
Loc 4 miles SE of Nottingham
Golf 18 hole & 9 hole courses

Edwalton
Edwalton, Nottingham
Tel (0115) 923 4775
Golf 9 hole course. 9 hole Par 3 course
Loc 2 miles S of Nottingham (A606)

John Reay Golf Centre
The Showground, Winthorpe, Newark
Tel (01636) 702161
Golf 9 hole Par 3 course
Loc 1 mile N of Newark on A46

Lenton Lane Golf Centre
Trent Side, Lenton Lane, Nottingham NG7 2SA
Tel (0115) 986 2179
Golf 9 hole pitch & putt course
Loc 1 mile from Nottingham (A52), under Clifton flyover

Oakmere Park
Oaks Lane, Oxton NG25 0RH
Tel (0115) 965 3545
Fax (0115) 965 5628
Golf 18 & 9 hole courses
Loc 8 miles NE of Nottingham on A614

Ramsdale Park Golf Centre
Oxton Road, Calverton, Nottingham NG14 6NU
Tel (0115) 965 5600
Fax (0115) 965 4105
Golf 18 hole & Par 3 courses
Loc 5 miles N of Nottingham on B6386

Springwater
Moor Lane, Calverton NG14 6FZ
Tel (0115) 965 2129
Golf 9 hole course
Loc NE of Nottingham, off A6097

Trent Lock Golf Centre
Lock Lane, Sawley, Long Eaton NG10 3DD
Tel (0115) 946 4398
Golf 18 hole course
Loc S of Long Eaton

Oxfordshire

Carswell
Carswell, Faringdon SN7 8PU
Tel (01367) 87422
Golf 18 hole course
Loc 12 miles W of Oxford on A420

Drayton Park
Steventon Road, Drayton, Abingdon OX14 2RR
Tel (01235) 550607
Golf 18 hole course. 9 hole pitch & putt course
Loc 5 miles S of Oxford on A34

Hadden Hill
Wallingford Road, Didcot OX11 9BJ
Tel (01235) 510410
Fax (01235) 510410
Golf 18 hole course
Loc E of Didcot on A4130

Hillside Farm
Bloxham, Banbury OX15 4PF
Tel (01295) 720361
Loc 5 miles S of Banbury (A361)

Lyneham
Lyneham, Chipping Norton OX7 6QQ
Tel (01993) 831841
Golf 18 hole course
Loc 4 miles W of Chipping Norton, off A361

Oxford Golf Centre
Binsey Lane, Oxford OX2 0EX
Tel (01865) 721592
Loc Off Botley road, W of Oxford

Witney Golf Centre
Downs Road, Witney OX8 5SY
Tel (01993) 779000
Fax (01993) 778866
Golf 18 hole course
Loc 2 miles W of Witney on B4047

Waterstock
Thame Road, Waterstock, Oxford OX33 1HT
Tel (01844) 338093
Fax (01844) 338036
Golf 18 hole course
Loc E of Oxford on A418

Woodcote
Reading Road, Woodcote RG8 0RB
Tel (01491) 681188
Loc 7 miles NW of Reading, off A4074

Shropshire

Ketley Golf Centre
Holyhead Road, Ketley, Telford TF3 1ED
Tel (01952) 251618
Golf 6 hole Par 3 course
Loc Between Wellington and Hadley

Mile End
Mile End, Oswestry SY11 4JE
Tel (01691) 670580
Golf 18 hole course open mid 1995
Loc 1 mile from Oswestry, off A5

The Shropshire
Muxton Grange, Telford TF2 8PQ
Tel (01952) 677866
Golf 3 x 9 hole courses. Pitch & putt course
Loc 4 miles NW of Telford (B5060)

Somerset

Cheddar Valley
Lyppiatt Lane, Cheddar BS27 3QT
Tel (01934) 742727
Loc 8 miles NW of Wells

Frome Golf Centre
Critchill Manor, Frome BA11 4LJ
Tel (01373) 453410
Golf 18 hole course
Loc 12 miles S of Bath

Long Sutton
Long Load, Langport TA10 9JU
Tel (01458) 241017
Golf 18 hole course
Loc 3 miles E of Langport

Swingrite Golf Centre
Haydon Lane, Holway, Taunton TA3 5AB
Tel (01823) 442600
Loc 1 mile SE of M5 Junction 25, off A358

Taunton Vale
Creech Heathfield, Taunton TA3 5EY
Tel (01823) 412220
Fax (01823) 413583
Golf 18 & 9 hole courses
Loc 3 miles N of Taunton, off A361

For list of abbreviations see page 435

Staffordshire

Craythorne

Craythorne Road, Stretton, Burton-on-Trent DE13 0AZ

Tel (01283) 564329
Fax (01283) 511908
Golf 18 hole course. 9 hole pitch & putt course
Loc 2 miles N of Burton. A5121/A38 Junction

Keele Golf Centre

Keele Road, Newcastle-under-Lyme ST5 5AB

Tel (01782) 717417
Golf 18 hole course
Loc 2 miles W of Newcastle on A525, opp University

Manor

Leese Hill, Kingstone, Uttoxeter ST14 8QT

Tel (01889) 563234
Golf 9 hole course
Loc 4 miles W of Uttoxeter

Seedy Mill

Elmhurst, Lichfield WS13 8HE

Tel (01543) 417333
Golf 18 hole course
Loc 2 miles N of Lichfield

Suffolk

Fynn Valley

Witnesham, Ipswich IP6 9JA

Tel (01473) 785463
Fax (01473) 785632
Golf 18 hole course. 9 hole Par 3 course
Loc 2 miles N of Ipswich on B1077

Ipswich Golf Centre

Bucklesham Road, Ipswich IP3 8TZ

Tel (01473) 726821
Loc 2 miles E of Ipswich

St Helena

Bramfield Road, Halesworth IP19 9XA

Tel (01986) 875567
Fax (01986) 874565
Golf 18 & 9 hole courses
Loc 1 mile S of Halesworth, off A144

Stoke-by-Nayland

Keepers Lane, Leavenheath, Colchester CO6 4PZ

Tel (01206) 262836
Fax (01206) 263356
Golf 2 x 18 hole courses
Loc 8 miles N of Colchester on B1068

Surrey

Beverley Park

Beverley Way, A3-Kingston By-pass, New Malden KT3 4PH

Tel (0181) 949 9200
Fax (0181) 949 2357
Loc 1½ miles S of Robin Hood r't on A3 Kingston by-pass

Broadwater Park

Guildford Road, Farncombe, Godalming GU7 3BU

Tel (01483) 429955
Golf 9 hole Par 3 course
Loc 4 miles SW of Guildford on A3100

Chessington Golf Centre

Garrison Lane, Chessington KT9 2LW

Tel (0181) 391 0948
Golf 9 hole Par 3 course
Loc Off A243, opp Chessington South Station

Croydon

175 Long Lane, Addiscombe CR0 7TE

Tel (0181) 656 1690
Fax (0181) 654 7859
Loc 3 miles E of Croydon

Fairmile

Portsmouth Road, Fairmile, Cobham KT11 1BW

Tel (0132) 864419
Loc 12 miles SW of London, on A307 between Esher and Cobham

Foxhills

Stonehill Road, Ottershaw KT16 0EL

Tel (01932) 872050
Fax (01932) 874762
Golf 2 x 18 hole courses
Loc 2 miles SW of Chertsey

Gatton Manor

Standon Lane, Ockley, Dorking RH5 5PQ

Tel (01306) 627555
Golf 18 hole course
Loc 1½ miles SW of Ockley, off A29

Hazelwood Golf Centre

Croysdale Avenue, Sunbury-on-Thames TW16 6QU

Tel (01932) 770932
Golf 9 hole course. Golf Academy
Loc Sunbury-on-Thames

Hoebridge Golf Centre

Old Woking Road, Old Woking GU22 8JH

Tel (01483) 722611
Fax (01483) 740369
Golf 18 hole & Par 3 courses. 9 hole Intermediate course
Loc 2 miles off A3 on B382, between Old Woking and West Byfleet

Horton Park

Hook Road, Epsom KT19 8QG

Tel (0181) 393 8400
Golf 18 hole course
Loc W of Ewell

Lingfield Park

Racecourse Road, Lingfield RH7 6PQ

Tel (01342) 834602
Golf 18 hole course
Loc By Lingfield racecourse

Oak Park Golf Complex

Heath Lane, Crondall, Farnham GU10 5PB

Tel (01252) 850880
Fax (01252) 850851
Golf 18 hole course
Loc Off A287, Farnham–Odiham road. M3 Junction 4A/5

Oaks Sports Centre

Woodmansterne Road, Carshalton SM5 4AN

Tel (0181) 643 8363
Golf 18 & 9 hole courses
Loc 2 miles from Sutton on B278

Pachesham Golf Centre

Oaklawn Road, Leatherhead KT22 0BT

Tel (01372) 843453
Golf 9 hole course
Loc NW of Leatherhead, off A244

Pine Ridge Golf Centre

Old Bisley Road, Frimley GU16 5NX

Tel (01276) 20770
Fax (01276) 678837
Golf 18 hole course
Loc Between Lightwater and Frimley

Richmond

Twickenham Road, Richmond TW9 2SS

Tel (0181) 940 5570
Loc By Royal Mid-Surrey GC, off A316 Chertsey Road

Sandown Golf Centre

More Lane, Esher KT10 8AN

Tel (01372) 463340
Golf 9 hole course. 9 hole Par 3 course
Loc Sandown Park racecourse

Silvermere

Redhill Road, Cobham KT11 1EF

Tel (01932) 867275
Golf 18 hole course
Loc Between Cobham and Byfleet

For list of abbreviations see page 435

Windlemere
Windlesham Road, West End, Woking GU24 9QL
Tel (01276) 858727
Golf 9 hole course
Loc A319 at Lightwater, nr Bagshot

Sussex (East)

Aldershaw
Kent Street, Sedlescombe TN33 0SD
Tel (01424) 870898
Golf 18 hole course
Loc 5 miles N of Hastings

Eastbourne Golfing Park
Lottbridge Drove, Eastbourne BN23 6QJ
Tel (0123) 520400
Golf 9 hole course
Loc S of Hampden Park

Hastings Golf Centre
Beauport Park, Battle Road, St Leonards-on-Sea TN38 0TA
Tel (01424) 852981
Golf 18 hole course
Loc 3 miles N of Hastings, off A2100

Horam Park
Chiddingly Road, Horam TN21 0JJ
Tel (014353) 3477
Golf 9 hole course
Loc 1/2 mile S of Horam

Wellshurst
North Street, Hellingly BN27 4EE
Tel (01435) 813636
Fax (01435) 812444
Golf 18 hole course
Loc 2 miles N of Hailsham on A267

Sussex (West)

Brookfield
Winterpit Lane, Plummers Plain, Horsham RH13 6LU
Tel (01403) 891568
Golf 6 hole course
Loc Horsham

Burgess Hill
Cuckfield Road, Burgess Hill
Tel (01444) 870615
Golf 9 hole course
Loc Burgess Hill

Chichester Golf Centre
Hunston Village, Chichester PO20 6AX
Tel (01243) 528999
Fax (01243) 539922
Golf 2 x 18 hole courses. 9 hole Par 3 course
Loc 3 miles S of A27 on B2145 to Selsey

Pease Pottage
Horsham Road, Pease Pottage, Crawley RH11 9HP
Tel (01293) 521706
Golf 9 hole course
Loc S of Crawley, off A23

Rustington Golf Centre
Golfers Lane, Littlehampton Road, Rustington BN16 4NB
Tel (01903) 850790
Fax (01903) 850982
Golf 9 hole Par 3 course
Loc 8 miles W of Worthing on A259

Singing Hills
Albourne, Brighton BN6 9EB
Tel (01273) 835353
Golf 3 x 9 hole courses
Loc 6 miles N of Brighton, off B2117

Slinfold Park G & CC
Stane Street, Slinfold, Horsham RH13 7RE
Tel (01403) 791154
Golf 18 hole course
Loc 2 miles W of Horsham

Tilgate Forest Golf Centre
Titmus Drive, Tilgate, Crawley RH10 5EU
Tel (01293) 530103
Fax (01293) 523478
Golf 18 hole course. 9 hole Par 3 course
Loc 2 miles SE of Crawley

West Chiltington
Broadford Bridge Road, West Chiltington RH20 2YA
Tel (01798) 813574
Fax (01798) 812631
Golf 18 hole course. 9 hole Par 3 course
Loc 2 miles E of Pulborough

Tyne & Wear

Gosforth Park Golfing Complex
High Gosforth Park, Newcastle-upon-Tyne NE3 5HQ
Tel (0191) 236 4480
Golf 18 hole course. 9 hole pitch & putt course
Loc 5 miles N of Newcastle on A1

Wallsend
Bigges Main, Wallsend NE28 8XF
Tel (0191) 262 1973
Golf 18 hole course
Loc Wallsend

Washington Moat House
Stone Cellar Road, Washington NE37 1PH
Tel (0191) 417 2626
Fax (0191) 415 1166
Golf 18 hole course. 9 hole pitch & putt course
Loc A194 to Washington

Warwickshire

Ansty Golf Centre
Brinklow Road, Ansty, Coventry CV7 9JH
Tel (01203) 621341
Golf 18 hole course
Loc 4 miles E of Coventry (B4029)

Brandon Wood
Brandon Lane, Wolston, Coventry CV8 3GQ
Tel (01203) 543141
Golf 18 hole course
Loc 6 miles SE of Coventry, off A45 Southbound

Lea Marston Golf Complex
Haunch Lane, Lea Marston B76 0BY
Tel (01675) 470707
Golf 9 hole Par 3 course
Loc 1 mile E of M42 Junction 9 on A4027

Purley Chase G & CC
Ridge Lane, Nuneaton CV10 0RB
Tel (01203) 393118/395348
Golf 18 hole course
Loc 2 miles S of Mancetter (A5)

Stratford Oaks
Bearley Road, Snitterfield, Stratford-on-Avon CV37 0EZ
Tel (01789) 731571
Golf 18 hole course
Loc 4 miles NE of Stratford

Warwick Golf Centre
Racecourse, Warwick CV34 5RX
Tel (01926) 494316
Golf 9 hole course
Loc Inside Warwick racecourse

West Midlands

The Belfry
Lichfield Road, Wishaw B76 9PR
Tel (01675) 470301
Golf 2 x 18 hole courses
Loc 4 miles N of M6 Junction 4

Bromsgrove Golf Centre
Stratford Road, Bromsgrove B60 1LD
Tel (01527) 575886
Fax (01527) 576090
Golf 9 hole course
Loc Junction of A38/A448

For list of abbreviations see page 435

Calderfields
Aldridge Rd, Walsall WS4 2JS
Tel (01922) 32243
Fax (01922) 38787
Golf 18 hole course
Loc 1 mile N of Walsall (A454)

Fishley Park
Fishley Lane, Pelsall, Walsall WS3 5AE
Tel (01922) 685279
Golf 9 hole pitch & putt

Four Ashes Golf Centre
Four Ashes Road, Dorridge, Solihull B93 8NQ
Tel (01564) 779055
Loc 3 miles S of Solihull

Halesowen
Quarry Lane, Halesowen B63 4PB
Tel (0121) 550 2920
Loc On A456 Halesowen By-pass

John Reay Golf Centre
Sandpits Lane, Keresley, Coventry
Tel (01203) 333920/333405
Fax (01203) 338002
Loc 2 miles NE of Coventry off A51

Perton Park
Wrottesley Park Road, Perton, Wolverhampton WV6 7HL
Tel (01902) 380103
Fax (01902) 326219
Golf 18 hole course
Loc 6 miles W of Wolverhampton, off A454

Sedgley
Sandyfields Road, Sedgley, Dudley DY3 3DL
Tel (01902) 880503
Golf 9 hole course
Loc 1/2 mile from Sedgley, off A463

Swindon
Bridgnorth Road, Swindon, Dudley DY3 4PU
Tel (01902) 896191
Golf 18 hole course. 9 hole Par 3 course
Loc 5 miles S of Wolverhampton

Three Hammers Golf Complex
Old Stafford Road, Coven, Wolverhampton WV10 7PP
Tel (01902) 790428
Fax (01902) 791349
Golf 18 hole Par 3 course
Loc 5 miles N of Wolverhampton on A449

Whitelakes Golf Centre
Tilehouse Lane, Wythall, Solihull
Tel (01564) 824460
Golf 9 hole Par 3 course
Loc 3 miles SDW of Solihull, off A435

Wiltshire

Bowood
Derry Hill, Calne SN11 9PQ
Tel (01249) 822228
Golf 18 hole course. 3 Academy holes
Loc 3 miles SE of Chippenham

Broome Manor
Pipers Way, Swindon SN3 1RG
Tel (01793) 532403
Golf 18 & 9 hole courses
Loc Swindon 2 miles

Thoulstone Park
Chapmanslade, Westbury BA13 4AQ
Tel (01373) 832825
Golf 18 hole course
Loc 1 mile from Warminster off A36

Twyford
Brach Farm, Twyford SP7 0JN
Tel (01747) 811356
Loc 3 miles S of Shaftesbury

Wingfield
Wingfield Road, Trowbridge BA14 9LW
Tel (01225) 776365
Loc 2 miles W of Trowbridge

Wrag Barn
Shrivenham Road, Highworth, Swindon SN6 7QQ
Tel (01793) 766027
Golf 18 hole course
Loc 6 miles NE of Swindon (B4000)

Yorkshire (North)

Forest Park
Stockton-on-Forest YO3 9UW
Tel (01904) 400425
Golf 18 & 9 hole courses
Loc 3 miles E of York (A64)

Romanby
Yafforth Road, Northallerton DL7 0PE
Tel (01609) 779988
Golf 18 hole course
Loc 1 mile W of Northallerton

Scalm Park
Thorpe Willoughby, Selby
Tel (01757) 210846
Loc 2 miles W of Selby on A63

Swallow Hall
Swallow Hall, Crockey Hill, York YO1 4SG
Tel (01904) 448889
Golf 18 hole Par 3 course
Loc 5 miles SE of York, off A19

York
Wiggington Road, York YO3 3RJ
Tel (01904) 690421
Loc 1 mile N of York on B1363

Yorkshire (South)

Arnold Palmer
Bradway Road, Bradway, Sheffield S17 4QU
Tel (0114) 236 1195

Austerfield Park
Cross Lane, Austerfield, Bawtry DN10 6RF
Tel (01302) 710841 (and fax)
Golf 18 hole course. 9 hole pitch & putt course
Loc 2 miles NE of Bawtry on A614

Sandhill
Chapel Lane, Little Houghton, Barnsley
Tel (01226) 751775
Golf 18 hole course
Loc Between Barnsley and Doncaster, off A635

Yorkshire (West)

Bradley Park
Bradley Road, Huddersfield HD2 1PZ
Tel (01484) 539988
Golf 18 hole course. 9 hole Par 3 course
Loc M62 Junction 25, 1 1/2 miles

Calverley
Woodhall Lane, Pudsey LS28 5JX
Tel (0113) 256 9244
Golf 18 & 9 hole courses
Loc 4 miles NE of Bradford

Garforth
Garforth, Leeds
Tel (0113) 287 1111
Loc E of Leeds, between Garforth and Barwick

Leeds Golf Centre
Wike Ridge Lane, Shadwell, Leeds LS17 9JW
Tel (0113) 288 6000
Fax (0113) 288 6185
Golf 18 & 9 hole courses
Loc NE of Leeds, off A58

Mid-Yorkshire
Havercroft Lane, Darrington, Pontefract WF8 3BP
Tel (01977) 600844
Golf 18 hole course
Loc Nr A1/M62 Junction

Oulton Park
Oulton, Rothwell, Leeds LS26 8EX
Tel (013) 282 3152
Fax (013) 282 6290
Golf 18 & 9 hole courses
Loc 5 miles SE of Leeds, off A642

Scotton
Low Moor Lane, Scotton, Knaresborough HG5 9HZ
Tel (01423) 868943
Loc 1 mile N of Knaresborough

Ireland

Ashfield
Freeduff, Cullyhanna, Newry, Co Armagh
Tel **(01693) 868180**
Golf 18 hole course

Ballyearl Golf Centre
585 Doagh Road, Newtonabbey, Belfast BT36 8RZ
Tel **(01232) 848287**
Golf 9 hole Par 3 course
Loc 1 mile N of Mossley, off B59

Ballymena
Warden Street, Ballymena, Co Antrim
Tel **(01266) 40654**

Banbridge
Ballykeel Road, Banbridge, Co Down
Tel **(018206) 62010**
Loc 2 miles NW of Banbridge

Blackwood
Crawfordsburn Road, Clandeboye, Bangor BT19 1GB
Tel **(01247) 853581**
Golf 18 hole course. 18 hole Par 3 course
Loc SW of Bangor, off A2

Celbridge
Dublin Road, Celbridge, Co Kildare
Tel **(01) 628 8833**
Loc 10 miles W of Dublin, nr Lucan
Golf 18 hole pitch & putt course

Clanabogan
85 Clanabogan Road, Omagh, Co Tyrone B BT78 5EB
Tel **(01662) 245409**
Loc 3 miles From Omagh

Craigavon Golf Centre
Turmoyra Lane, Silverwood, Lurgan, Co Armagh
Tel **(01762) 326606**
Golf 18 hole course. Pitch & putt
Loc 1½ miles from Lurgan

Downpatrick
86 Ardglass Road, Downpatrick, Co DownX BT30 7DX
Tel **(01396) 613558**
Loc ½ mile SE of Downpatrick on B1

Galway
Knocknacarra, Salt Hill, Galway, Co Galway
Tel **(091) 26737/26753**
Loc 2 miles W of Galway Town

Gold Coast
Ballynacourty, Dungarvan, Co Waterford
Tel **(058) 42416**
Golf 9 hole course
Loc E of Dungarvan, off R675

Harbour Point
Clash, Little Island, Co Cork
Tel **(021) 353094**
Golf 18 hole course
Loc 5 miles E of Cork

The Heath
The Heath, Portlaoise, Co Laois
Tel **(0502) 46533**
Golf 18 hole course
Loc 4 miles NE of Portlaoise

Kildare Hotel
Straffan, Co Kildare
Tel **(01) 627 3987**
Golf 18 hole course
Loc 18 miles SW of Dublin (N7)

Knockbracken Golf Centre
Ballymaconaghy Road, Knockbracken, Belfast BT8 4SB
Tel **(01232) 792108**
Golf 18 hole course
Loc 2 miles SW of Belfast

Lee Valley
Clashanure, Ovens, Co Cork
Tel **(021) 331721**
Fax **(021) 331695**
Golf 18 hole course
Loc 7 miles W of Cork (N22)

Leopardstown Golf Centre
Foxrock, Dublin 18
Tel **(01) 289 5341**
Golf 9 hole course. 18 hole pitch & putt course
Loc 5 miles S of Dublin

Limerick County G & CC
Ballyneety, Co Limerick
Tel **(061) 351881**
Golf 18 hole course
Loc 5 miles S of Limerick (R512)

Lochgeorge
Lochgeorge, Claregalway, Co Galway
Tel **(091) 98202**
Loc 7 miles N of Galway on Tuam road

Newry & Mourne Golf Centre
Milltown Street, Warrenpoint, Burren, Co Down
Tel **(016937) 73247**
Loc 1 mile N of Warrenpoint

Tralee
West Barrow, Ardfert, Co Kerry
Tel **(066) 21984**
Loc Ballyard, 2 miles S of Tralee

The Ward
Ashbourne Road, Dublin, Co Dublin
Tel **(01) 348711**
Loc 2 miles N of Dublin on N2

Scotland

Auchenharvie
Moorpark Road West, Stevenston KA20 3HU
Tel **(01294) 603103**
Golf 9 hole course
Loc 1 mile W of Stevenston

Bishopbriggs
Crosshill Road, Bishopbriggs, Glasgow G64 2PZ
Tel **(0141) 762 4883**
Loc 6 miles N of Glasgow, off A803

Braid Hills
Braid Hills Road, Edinburgh EH10
Tel **(0131) 417 6666**
Golf 2 x 18 hole courses
Loc 3 miles S of Edinburgh

Brunston Castle
Dailly, Girvan, Ayrshire KA26 9RM
Tel **(01465) 81471**
Golf 18 hole course
Loc 4 miles E of Girvan

Clydeway Golf Centre
Blantyre Farm Road, Uddingston, Lanarkshire
Tel **(0141) 641 8899**
Loc Uddingston, SE of Glasgow

Coatbridge
Townhead Road, Coatbridge ML52 2HX, Lanarkshire
Tel **(01236) 28975**
Golf 18 hole course
Loc Townhead, E of Glasgow

Cumbernauld
Cumbernauld, Dumbartonshire
Tel **(01236) 737000**
Loc 1 mile S of Cumbernauld

Deaconsbank
Rouken Glen Park, Stewarton Road, Eastwood, Glasgow
Tel **(0141) 638 7044**
Golf 18 hole course
Loc 5 miles S of Glasgow centre

Fairways
Fairways Leisure Park, Castle Heather, Inverness IV1 2AA
Tel **(01463) 713335**
Golf 18 hole course opening 1996
Loc Nr Inverness town centre

Glenrothes
Stenton Road, Glenrothes, Fife
Tel **(01592) 775374**
Loc SW of Glenrothes, by Technical College

Gretna
Kirtle View, Gretna, Dumfriesshire DG16 5HD
Tel **(01461) 338464**
Golf 9 hole course
Loc 1 mile W of Gretna, off A75

Kings Links Golf Centre
Golf Road, Aberdeen AB2 1RZ
Tel **(01224) 632269**
Golf 18 hole course
Loc 1 mile E of Aberdeen

Melville
South Melville, Lasswade, Midlothian EH18 1AN
Tel **(0131) 663 8038**
Fax **(0131) 654 0814**
Golf 9 hole course open mid 1995
Loc Nr Edinburgh City Bypass, exit A7

Middlebank
Middlebank, Errol, Tayside PH2 7SX
Tel **(01821) 670320**
Loc 8 miles E of Perth on A85

Murrayshall
Murrayshall, New Scone, Perth PH2 7PH
Tel **(01738) 51171**
Golf 18 hole course
Loc 3 miles NE of Perth, off A94

Normandy
Inchinnan Road, Renfrew PA4 9ES
Tel **(0141) 886 7477**
Fax **(0141) 885 0786**
Loc 1 mile W of Glasgow Airport

Polkemmet
Whitburn, Bathgate, W Lothian EH47 0AD
Tel **(01501) 743905**
Golf 9 hole course
Loc Between Whitburn and Harthill on B7066

Port Royal
Eastfield Road, Ingliston, Edinburgh EH28 8NQ
Tel **(0131) 333 4377**
Golf 9 hole Par 3 course
Loc By Edinburgh Airport

Prestwick
Monkton Road, Prestwick, Ayrshire KA9
Tel **(01292) 79849**

Spey Bay
Spey Bay, Fochabers, Moray IV32 7JP
Tel **(01343) 820424**
Golf 18 hole course
Loc 2 miles W of Buckie, off B9104

St Andrews
St Andrews Links, St Andrews, Fife
Tel **(01334) 474489**
Golf 5 x 18 hole courses
Loc 1/2 mile from St Andrews, off A91

Strathclyde Park
Mote Hill, Hamilton, Lanarkshire
Tel **(01698) 266155**
Golf 9 hole course
Loc A723, just off M74

Tayside
The Downs, Barry, Carnoustie DD7 7SA
Tel **(01382) 534226**
Loc 7 miles E of Dundee, off A930

Wales

Alice Springs
Bettws Newydd, Usk, Gwent NP5 1JY
Tel **(01873) 880772/880708**
Golf 2 x 18 hole courses
Loc 3 miles N of Usk on B4598

Bannel
Mold Road, Penymynydd, Clwyd CH4 0EN
Tel **(01244) 544639**
Loc 8 miles SW of Chester, off A55

Caerleon
Broadway, Caerleon, Gwent NP6 1AY
Tel **(01633) 420342**
Golf 9 hole course
Loc 3 miles from M4 Junction 25

Chirk
Chirk, Wrexham, Clwyd
Tel **(01691) 774407**
Golf 18 hole course. 9 hole Par 3 course
Loc 8 miles S of Wrexham on A483

Kinmel Park Golf Complex
Bodelwyddan, Clwyd LL18 5SR
Tel **(01745) 833548**
Golf 9 hole course
Loc Off A55, between Abergele and St Asaph

Mayfield
Clareston Hill, Freystrop, Haverfordwest, Dyfed
Tel **(01437) 890308**
Loc 1 mile SE of Haverfordwest on Burton road

Mountain Lakes
Blaengwynlais, Caerphilly, Mid Glamorgan CF8 1NG
Tel **(01222) 861128**
Fax **(01222) 869030**
Golf 18 & 9 hole courses
Loc 4 miles N of M4 Junction 32

North Wales
Llanerch Park, St Asaph, Clwyd LL17 0BD
Tel **(01745) 730805**
Golf 9 hole short course
Loc Off A525, between Trefnant and St Asaph

Oakdale
Llwynon Lane, Oakdale, Gwent NP2 0NF
Tel **(01495) 220044**
Golf 9 hole course
Loc 15 miles NW of Newport via A467/B4251

Parc Golf Centre
Church Lane, Coedkernew, Newport, Gwent NP1 9TU
Tel **(01633) 680933**
Fax **(01633) 681011**
Golf 18 hole course
Loc 2 miles W of Newport on A48

Penrhos G & CC
Llanrhystud, Aberyswyth SY23 5AY
Tel **(01974) 202999**
Golf 18 hole course
Loc 9 miles S of Aberystwyth, off A487

South Wales
Port Road East, Barry, South Glamorgan CF6 7PX
Tel **(01446) 742434**
Golf 9 hole Par 3 course
Loc 8 miles SW of Cardiff on A4050

St Mary's
Pencoed, Bridgend, Mid Glamorgan CF35 5EA
Tel **(01656) 860280/861100**
Golf 18 & 9 hole courses
Loc By M4 Junction 35

Talywain
Old Bucks Level, Talywain, Pontypool, Gwent NP4 7UQ
Tel **(01495) 774960**
Loc 3 miles N of Pontypool

Tregroes
Fishguard, Dyfed SA65 9QF
Tel **(01348) 872316**
Loc 1 mile S of Fishguard on A40

Virginia Park
Virginia Park, Caerphilly CF8 3SW, Mid Glamorgan
Tel **(01222) 863919**
Golf 9 hole course

Welsh Border Golf Complex
Bulthy Farm, Bulthy, Middletown, Powys SY21 8ER
Tel **(01743) 884247**
Golf 9 hole course
Loc Between Shrewsbury and Welshpool on A458

Wernddu Golf Centre
Wernddu Farm, Abergavenny, Gwent NP7 8NG
Tel **(01873) 856223**
Golf 2 x 9 hole courses
Loc 1 mile NE of Abergavenny on B4521, off A465

For list of abbreviations see page 435

Clubs and Courses in Continental Europe

For list of abbreviations see page 435

Austria

Innsbruck & Tirol

Achensee (1934)
6213 Pertisau/Achensee
Tel **(05243) 5377**
Fax **(05243) 6202**
Holes 9 L 3876 m SSS 62
V'tors U H
Fees 300s (420s)
Loc Pertisau, 50km NE of Innsbruck

Innsbruck-Igls (1956)
6074 Rinn, Oberdorf 11
Tel **(05223) 8177**
Fax **(05223) 8343**
Holes Rinn 18 L 5935 m SSS 71
Lans 9 L 4657 m SSS 66
V'tors H–booking necessary
Fees 460s (580s)
Loc Rinn, 10km E of Innsbruck. Lans, 8km from Innsbruck

Kaiserwinkl GC Kössen (1988)
6345 Kössen, Mühlau 1
Tel **(05375) 2122**
Fax **(05375) 2122-13**
Holes 18 L 5927 m SSS 72
V'tors H
Fees 550s (600s)
Loc 30km N of Kitzbühel, nr German border
Arch Donald Harradine

Kitzbühel (1955)
Schloss Kaps, 6370 Kitzbühel/Tirol
Tel **(05356) 3007**
Fax **(05356) 73018**
Holes 9 L 6085 m SSS 72
V'tors H
Fees 450s (550s)
Loc Kitzbühel
Arch J Morrison

Kitzbühel-Schwarzsee (1988)
6370 Kitzbühel, Golfweg Schwarzsee 35
Tel **(05356) 71645**
Fax **(05356) 72785**
Holes 18 L 6247 m SSS 72
V'tors H–booking necessary
Fees 500–600s (600–700s)
Loc 4km from Kitzbühel
Arch G Hauser

Seefeld-Wildmoos (1968)
6100 Seefeld, Postfach 22
Tel **(05212) 3003-0**
Fax **(05212) 3722-22**
Holes 18 L 5967 m SSS 72
V'tors H–booking necessary
Fees 490–730s
Loc 7km W of Seefeld. 24km W of Innsbruck
Arch Donald Harradine

Klagenfurt & South

Austria-Wörther See
9062 Moosburg, Golfstr 2
Tel **(04272) 83486, (04272) 82302 (Golf academy)**
Fax **(04272) 82055**
Holes 18 L 6216 m SSS 72
Fees 550s
Loc 6km N of Wörther See
Arch G Hauser

Bad Kleinkirchheim-Reichenau (1984)
9546 Bad Kleinkirchheim, Postfach 9
Tel **(04275) 594**
Fax **(04240) 8282-18**
Holes 18 L 6084 m SSS 72
V'tors H
Fees 550s
Loc Kleinkirchheim, 50km NW of Klagenfurt, via Route 95
Arch Donald Harradine

Kärntner (1927)
9082 Maria Wörth, Dellach 16
Tel **(04273) 2515**
Fax **(04273) 2606**
Holes 18 L 5744 m SSS 71
Fees D–600s
Loc Dellach, S side of Wörther See. 15km W of Klagenfurt

Klopeiner See-Turnersee (1988)
9122 St Kanzian, Klopeinerstr 5
Tel **(04239) 3800**
Fax **(04239) 3800-18**
Holes 18 L 6114 m SSS 72
V'tors U
Fees 550s
Loc 25km E of Klagenfurt
Arch Donald Harradine

Wörther See/Velden (1988)
9231 Köstenberg, Oberdorf 70
Tel **(04274) 7045/7087**
Fax **(04274) 708715**
Holes 18 L 6152 m SSS 72
V'tors H
Fees 600s
Loc 30km W of Klagenfurt. 12km from Velden
Arch Erhardt/Rossknecht

Linz & North

Amstetten-Ferschnitz (1972)
3325 Ferschnitz, Gut Edla 18
Holes 9 L 5948 m SSS 70
V'tors U H
Fees 350s (450s)
Loc 70km E of Linz
Arch McIntosh

Böhmerwald GC Ulrichsberg (1990)
4161 Ulrichsberg, Seitelschlag 50
Tel **(07288) 8200**
Fax **(07288) 8422**
Holes 18 L 6240 m SSS 73
9 hole Par 3 course
V'tors U H
Fees 450s (550s)
Loc 65km NW of Linz
Arch Rossknecht/Erhardt

Herzog Tassilo (1991)
Blankenbergerstr 30, 4540 Bad Hall
Tel **(07258) 5480**
Fax **(07258) 5480**
Holes 18 L 5756 m SSS 70
V'tors U
Fees 450s (550s)
Loc 30km SW of Linz
Arch Peter Mayerhofer

Linz-St Florian (1960)
4490 St Florian, Tillysburg 28
Tel **(07223) 2873**
Fax **(07223) 5467**
Holes 18 L 6091 m SSS 72
V'tors H
Fees 450s (580s)
Loc St Florian, 15km SE of Linz
Arch Donald Harradine

Mühlviertel (1990)
4222 St Georgen, Am Luftenberg 1
Tel **(07237) 3893**
Fax **(07237) 3893**
Holes 18 L 6041 m SSS 72
V'tors U H
Fees 450s (550s)
Loc 15km NE of Linz
Arch Keith Preston

Ottenstein (1988)
3532 Niedergrünbach 1
Tel **(02826) 7476**
Fax **(02826) 7476**
Holes 18 L 6048 m SSS 72
V'tors U
Fees 450s (550s)
Loc 90km NE of Linz
Arch Preston/Zinterl/Erhardt

Schloss Ernegg (1973)
3261 Steinakirchen, Schlosshotel Ernegg
Tel **(07488) 6770/214 (May-Oct)**
Fax **(07488) 6771/71171**
Holes 18 L 5699 m SSS 70
9 L 2076 m SSS 62
V'tors U
Fees 450s (600s)
Loc Steinakirchen, 60km SE of Linz
Arch Tucker/Day

St Pölten Schloss Goldegg (1989)
3100 St Pölten Schloss Goldegg
Tel **(02741) 7360**
Fax **(02741) 73608**
Holes 18 L 6249 m SSS 73
V'tors M or I
Fees 500s (600s)
Loc 8km NW of St Pölten. 60km W of Vienna

Traunsee-Kircham
4656 Kircham, Kampesberg 38
Tel **(07619) 2576**
Fax **(07619) 2576-11**
Holes 18 L 5818 m SSS 70
V'tors U
Fees 450s (550s)
Loc 10km E of Gmunden. 50km SW of Linz
Arch Matthias Hitzenberger

Waldviertel
3874 Haugschlag 160
Tel **(02865) 8441**
Fax **(02865) 8441-22**
Holes 18 L 6140 m SSS 72
18 hole Par 3 course
V'tors H
Fees 450s (600s)
Loc 25km N of Gmund. 120km NE of Linz

Weitra (1989)
3970 Weitra, Hausschachen
Tel **(02856) 2058**
Fax **(02856) 20584**
Holes 9 L 5726 m SSS 70-73
V'tors WD–U WE–H
Fees 250s (400s)
Loc 75km NE of Linz, nr Czech border
Arch M Gansdorfer

Wels (1981)
4616 Weisskirchen, Weyerbach 37
Tel **(07243) 56038**
Fax **(07243) 56685**
Holes 18 L 6100 m SSS 72
V'tors H
Fees 500s (600s)
Loc 5km from Salzburg-Vienna highway. 8km SE of Wels
Arch Hauser/Hunt Hastings

Salzburg Region

Badgastein (1960)
5640 Badgastein, Golfstrasse 6
Tel **(06434) 2775**
Fax **(06434) 2775-4**
Holes 9 L 5946 m SSS 71
V'tors H
Fees 390s (500s)
Loc Badgastein 2km
Arch B von Limburger

Goldegg
5622 Goldegg, Postfach 6
Tel **(06415) 8585**
Fax **(06415) 8580**
Holes 9 L 4456 m SSS 64
Fees 380s (440s)
Loc 75km SW of Salzburg

Gut Altentann (1989)
Hof 54, 5302 Henndorf am Wallersee
Tel **(06214) 6026-0**
Fax **(06214) 6105-81**
Holes 18 L 6223 m SSS 72
V'tors H–booking necessary
Fees 700s (850s)
Loc Henndorf, 16km N of Salzburg
Arch Jack Nicklaus

Gut Brandlhof G & CC (1983)
5760 Saalfelden am Steinernen Meer, Hohlwegen 3
Tel **(06582) 2176-555**
Fax **(06582) 2176-529**
Holes 18 L 6218 m SSS 72
6 hole short course
V'tors I H
Fees 550s (650s)
Loc Saalfelden, 70km SW of Salzburg towards Zell am See
Arch Kofler

Kobernausserwald
5242 St Johann a. Walde, Strass 1
Tel **(07743) 2719**
Fax **(07743) 2719**
Holes 9 L 5764 m SSS 70 Par 72
V'tors U
Fees 200s (350s)
Loc 30km E of Salzburg
Arch Heinz Schmidbauer

Lungau/Katschberg (1991)
5582 St Michael, Postfach 44
Tel **(06477) 7448**
Fax **(06477) 7448-4**
Holes 18 L 6372 m SSS 72
9 L 2502 m Par 56
V'tors U
Fees 520s (620s)
Loc St Michael, 120km S of Salzburg
Arch Keith Preston

Salzburg Klesheim (1955)
5071 Wals bei Salzburg, Schloss Klesheim
Tel **(0662) 850851**
Holes 9 L 5700 m SSS 70
V'tors U H
Fees 450s (450s)
Loc 5km N of Salzburg

Salzkammergut (1933)
4820 Bad Ischl, Postfach 506
Tel **(06132) 26340**
Fax **(06132) 26708**
Holes 18 L 5900 m SSS 71
V'tors U
Fees 500 (600s)
Loc 6km W of Bad Ischl, nr Strobl. 50km E of Salzburg

Schloss Fuschl (1964)
5322 Hof/Salzburg
Tel **(06229) 390**
Holes 9 L 3694 m SSS 61
Fees 250–300s
Loc Hof, 12km E of Salzburg

St Lorenz (1993)
Keuschen 166, 5310 Mondsee
Tel **(06232) 5656**
Fax **(06232) 5656**
Holes 9 L 5228 m SSS 68
V'tors H
Fees 400s (500s)
Loc 25km E of Salzburg
Arch Marc Miller

Tauerngolf (1990)
Römerstrasse 18, 5550 Radstadt
Tel **(06452) 51110**
Fax **(06452) 7336**
Holes 18 L 6124 m SSS 72
9 hole Par 3 course
V'tors U
Fees 520s (620s)
Loc 70km NW of Salzburg

Urslautal (1991)
Schinking 1, 5760 Saalfelden
Tel **(06584) 2000**
Fax **(06584) 7475-10**
Holes 18 L 6030 m SSS 71
V'tors U H
Fees 560s (660s)
Loc 80km SW of Salzburg
Arch Keith Preston

Zell am See-Kaprun (1983)
5700 Zell am See, Golfstr 25
Tel **(06542) 56161**
Fax **(06542) 56035**
Holes 18 L 6218 m SSS 72
18 L 6190 m SSS 72
V'tors M H
Fees 590s (690s)
Loc Zell am See, 95km SW of Salzburg
Arch Donald Harradine

For list of abbreviations see page 435

Steiermark

Dachstein Tauern (1990)
8967 Haus/Ennstal, Oberhaus 59
Tel **(03686) 2630**
Fax **(03686) 2630-15**
Holes 18 L 5910 m SSS 71
V'tors U
Fees 525s (625s)
Loc 2km from Schladming. 100km SE of Salzburg
Arch Bernhard Langer

Ennstal-Weissenbach G & LC (1978)
8940 Liezen, Postfach 193
Tel **(03612) 24821**
Fax **(03612) 24821-4**
Holes 9 L 5604 m SSS 70
V'tors U H
Fees 350s (450s)
Loc 3km SW of Liezen. 100km SE of Salzburg
Arch Gert Aigner

Erzherzog Johann (1992)
Puchbacherstr 109, 8591 Maria Lankowitz
Tel **(03144) 6970**
Fax **(03144) 69704**
Holes 18 L 6234 m SSS 72
V'tors U
Fees 500s (600s)
Loc 40km W of Graz
Arch Herwig Zisser

Furstenfeld (1984)
8282 Loipersdorf, Gillersdorf 50
Tel **(03382) 8533**
Fax **(03382) 8633**
Holes 18 L 6192 m SSS 72
V'tors U
Fees 450s (550s)
Loc 50km E of Graz
Arch Herwig Zisser

Graz (1989)
8051 Graz, Windhof 137
Tel **(0316) 572867**
Fax **(0316) 572867**
Holes 9 L 5090 m SSS 70
V'tors U
Fees 350–450s (500s)
Loc 10km W of Graz
Arch Herwig Zisser

Gut Murstätten (1989)
8403 Lebring, Oedt 4
Tel **(03182) 3555**
Fax **(03182) 3688**
Holes 18 L 6398 m SSS 74
9 L 3034 m SSS 72
V'tors H
Fees 550s (650s)
Loc 25km S of Graz
Arch J Dudok van Heel

Murhof (1963)
8130 Frohnleiten, Adriach 53
Tel **(03126) 3010**
Fax **(03126) 3000-29**
Holes 18 L 6381 m SSS 73
V'tors U H
Fees 620s (800s)
Loc Frohnleiten, 25km N of Graz. 150km S of Vienna
Arch B von Limburger

Reiting
8772 Traboch, Schulweg 7
Tel **(0663) 833308**
Fax **(03847) 5682**
Holes 9 L 6300 m SSS 72
V'tors U
Fees 350s (390s)
Loc 60km N of Graz

Schloss Frauenthal (1988)
8530 Deutschlandberg, Ulrichsberg
Tel **(03462) 5717**
Fax **(03462) 57175**
Holes 9 L 5856 m SSS 71
V'tors U H
Fees 350s (450s)
Loc 45km SW of Graz
Arch Stephan Breisach

Schloss Pichlarn (1972)
8952 Irdning, Ennstal Steiermark
Tel **(03682) 24393**
Fax **(03682) 24393**
Holes 18 L 6158 m SSS 72
V'tors U
Fees 500s (650s)
Loc 2km E of Irdning, off Salzburg-Graz road. 120km SE of Salzburg
Arch Donald Harradine

St Lorenzen
8642 St Lorenzen, Gassing 22
Tel **(03864) 3961**
Holes 9 L 5082 m SSS 67
V'tors U
Fees 150s (350s)
Loc 60km N of Graz, nr Kapfenberg
Arch Manfred Flasch

Vienna & East

Bad Tatzmannsdorf (1991)
Am Golfplatz 2, 7431 Bad Tatzmannsdorf
Tel **(03353) 8282**
Fax **(03353) 8282-705**
Holes 18 L 6304 m SSS 73
9 L 3660 m SSS 60
V'tors U H
Fees 18 hole:500s (600s)
9 hole:330s (380s)
Loc 120km SE of Vienna
Arch Rossknecht/Erhardt

Brunn G & CC (1988)
2345 Brunn/Gebirge, Rennweg 50
Tel **(02236) 31572/33711**
Fax **(02236) 33863**
Holes 18 L 6138 m SSS 72
V'tors H
Fees 500s (600s)
Loc 10km S of Vienna
Arch G Hauser

Colony Club Gutenhof (1988)
2325 Himberg, Gutenhof
Tel **(02235) 88055-0**
Fax **(02235) 88055-14**
Holes East 18 L 6335 m SSS 73
West 18 L 6397 m SSS 73
V'tors H
Fees 500s (650s)
Loc 22km SE of Vienna
Arch Rossknecht/Erhardt

Enzesfeld (1970)
2551 Enzesfeld
Tel **(02256) 81272**
Fax **(02256) 81272-4**
Holes 18 L 6176 m SSS 72
V'tors H
Fees 500s (750s)
Loc 32km S of Vienna. A2 Junction 29 (Leobersdorf)
Arch John Harris

Föhrenwald (1968)
2700 Wiener Neustadt, Postfach 105
Tel **(02622) 29171**
Fax **(02622) 25334**
Holes 18 L 6043 m SSS 72
Fees 400s (500s)
Loc 5km S of Wiener Neustadt on Route B54

Hainburg/Donau (1977)
2410 Hainburg, Auf der Heide 762
Tel **(02165) 2628**
Fax **(02165) 5331**
Holes 9 L 5950 m SSS 71
V'tors H
Fees 300s (500s)
Loc 55km E of Vienna
Arch G Hauser

Lechner
2871 Zöbern, Pichl 1
Tel **(02642) 8451**
Fax **(02642) 8451**
Holes 9 L 4088m Par 64 SSS 62
V'tors H
Fees 250s (350s)
Loc 90km S of Vienna via A2

Neusiedlersee-Donnerskirchen (1988)
7082 Donnerskirchen
Tel **(02683) 8110/8171**
Fax **(02683) 817231**
Holes 18 L 5937 m SSS 72
V'tors H

Fees 500s (700s)
Loc 45km SE of Vienna
Arch Rossknecht-Erhardt

Schloss Ebreichsdorf (1988)
2483 Ebreichsdorf, Schlossallee 1
Tel **(02254)73888**
Fax **(02254) 73888-13**
Holes 18 L 6246 m SSS 72
V'tors WD–H WE–on request
Fees 500s (700s)
Loc 28km S of Vienna
Arch Keith Preston

Schloss Schönborn
2013 Schönborn
Tel **(02267) 2863/2879**
Fax **(02267) 2879-19**
Holes 27 L 6265-6474 m SSS 73
V'tors U H
Fees 500s (750s)
Loc 40km N of Vienna

Schönfeld (1989)
2291 Schönfeld, Am Golfplatz 1
Tel **(02213) 2063**
Fax **(02213) 20631**
Holes 18 L 6175 m SSS 72
9 hole Par 3 course
V'tors 18 hole:WD–I WE–H
Fees 18 hole:400s (500s)
9 hole:300s (400s)
Loc 35km E of Vienna
Arch G Hauser

Semmering (1926)
2680 Semmering
Tel **(02664) 8154**
Holes 9 L 3786 m SSS 60
Fees 200s (300s)
Loc 30km SW of Vienna Neustadt

Wien (1901)
1020 Wien, Freudenau 65a
Tel **(0222) 728 9564 (Clubhouse), 728 9667 (Caddymaster)**
Fax **(0222) 728 9564-20**
Holes 18 L 5861 m SSS 71
V'tors WE–NA
Fees D–700s
Loc 10 mins SE of Vienna

Wienerberg (1989)
1100 Wien, Gutheil Schoder 9
Tel **(0222) 66123-7000**
Fax **(0222) 66123-7789**
Holes 9 L 5710 m SSS 70
V'tors H
Fees 500s
Loc Vienna District 10
Arch G Hauser

Wienerwald (1981)
3053 Laaben, Forsthof 211
Tel **(0222) 877 3111 (Sec)**
Holes 9 L 4652 m SSS 65
V'tors H
Fees 300s (500s)
Loc Laaben, 35km W of Vienna
Arch Herbert Illo Holy

Belgium

Antwerp Region

Bossenstein (1989)
Moor 16, Bossenstein Kasteel, 2520 Broechem
Tel **(03) 485 64 46**
Fax **(03) 485 78 41**
Holes 18 L 6203 m SSS 72
9 hole course
V'tors H
Fees 1000fr (1500fr)
Loc 15km E of Antwerp. 5km N of Lier
Arch Paul Rolin

Cleydael (1988)
Kasteel Cleydael, 2630 Aartselaar
Tel **(03) 887 00 79/887 18 74**
Fax **(03) 887 00 15**
Holes 18 L 6059 m SSS 72
V'tors H WE–NA before 2pm
Fees 1500fr (2000fr)
Loc 8km S of Antwerp. 40km N of Brussels
Arch Paul Rolin

Inter-Mol (1984)
Goorstraat, 2400 Mol
Tel **(014) 41 08 28/57 13 28**
Fax **(014) 58 42 73**
Holes 9 L 1493 m Par 28
V'tors H
Fees 400fr (600fr)
Loc Mol, 60km E of Antwerp

Kempense (1986)
Kiezelweg 78, 2400 Mol
Tel **(014) 81 46 41 (Clubhouse), (014) 81 62 34 (Caddymaster)**
Fax **(014) 81 62 78**
Holes 18 L 5904 m SSS 72
V'tors H
Fees 1000fr (1500fr)
Loc 60km E of Antwerp
Arch Marc de Keyser

Lilse (1988)
Haarlebeek 3, 2418 Lille
Tel **(014) 55 19 30**
Fax **(014) 55 19 31**
Holes 9 L 4582 m SSS 65
V'tors U
Fees 600fr (800fr)
Loc Lille, 10km SW of Turnhout, nr E7. 25km E of Antwerp

Rinkven G & CC (1980)
Sint Jobsteenweg 120, 2970 Schilde
Tel **(03) 384 07 84**
Fax **(03) 384 29 23**
Holes 27 holes:
6093-6220 m SSS 72-3
V'tors H–phone before visit
Fees 1250fr (2500fr)
Loc 17km NE of Antwerp, off E19

Royal Antwerp (1888)
Georges Capiaulei 2, 2950 Kapellen
Tel **(03) 666 84 56**
Fax **(03) 666 44 37**
Holes 18 L 6140 m SSS 73
9 L 2264 m SSS 33
V'tors WD–H (phone first)
Fees 1500–2000fr
Loc Kapellen, 20km N of Antwerp
Arch Willie Park/T Simpson (1920)

Steenhoven (1985)
Eerselseweg 40, 2400 Postel-Mol
Tel **(014) 37 72 50**
Fax **(016) 65 69 09**
Holes 18 L 5950 m SSS 71
V'tors H–booking necessary
Fees 1500fr (2500fr)
Loc 30 mins W of Antwerp
Arch Pierre de Broqueville

Ternesse G & CC (1976)
Uilenbaan 15, 2160 Wommelgem
Tel **(03) 353 02 92**
Fax **(03) 354 02 30**
Holes 18 L 5876 m SSS 72
V'tors H
Fees 1500fr (2500fr)
Loc 5km E of Antwerp on E313
Arch HJ Baker

Ardennes & South

Andenne (1988)
Ferme du Moulin 52, Stud, 5300 Andenne
Tel **(085) 84 34 04**
Fax **(085) 84 34 04**
Holes 9 L 2447 m SSS 66
V'tors U
Fees 500fr (700fr)
Loc Andenne, 20km E of Namur
Arch C Bertier

Château Royal d'Ardenne
5560 Houyet Dinant
Tel **(082) 66 62 28**
Fax **(082) 66 74 53**
Holes 18 L 5363 m SSS 71
V'tors H
Fees 1000fr (1500fr)
Loc 9km SE of Dinant on Rochefort road

For list of abbreviations see page 435

Falnuée (1987)
Rue E Pirson 55, 5032 Mazy
Tel **(081) 63 30 90**
Fax **(081) 63 37 64**
Holes 18 L 5700 m SSS 70
V'tors H
Fees 850fr (1400fr)
Loc 18km NW of Namur. Mons–Liège highway Junction 13
Arch J Jottrand

Five Nations C C
Ferme du Grand Scley, 5372 Méan
Tel **(086) 32 32 32**
Fax **(086) 32 30 11**
Holes 18 L 6066 m Par 72
V'tors U
Fees 1500fr (2000fr)
Loc 30km S of Liège
Arch Gary Player

Mont Garni (1989)
Rue du Mont Garni 3, 7331 Saint Ghislain
Tel **(065) 62 27 19**
Fax **(065) 62 34 10**
Holes 18 L 6353 m SSS 73
V'tors H
Fees 1000fr (1500fr)
Loc St Ghislain, 15km W of Mons. 65km SW of Brussels
Arch T Macauley

Rougemont
Chemin du Beau Vallon 45, 5170 Profondeville
Tel **(081) 41 14 18**
Fax **(081) 41 21 42**
Holes 18 L 5645 m SSS 72
V'tors U
Fees 950fr (1200fr)
Loc 10km S of Namur

Royal GC du Hainaut (1933)
Rue de la Verrerie 2, 7050 Erbisoeul
Tel **(065) 22 96 10 (Clubhouse), (065) 22 94 74 (Sec)**
Fax **(065) 22 51 54**
Holes 18 L 6108 m SSS 72
9 L 3233 m Par 36
V'tors U H
Fees 1000fr (1500fr)
Loc 6km NW of Mons towards Ath on N56. Paris-Brussels motorway Junction 23
Arch Martin Hawtree

Brussels & Brabant

Bercuit (1965)
Les Gottes 3, 1390 Grez-Doiceau
Tel **(010) 84 15 01**
Fax **(010) 84 55 95**
Holes 18 L 5986 m SSS 72
V'tors U
Fees D–1450fr (2500fr)
Loc 27km SE of Brussels. Brussels–Namur highway exit 8
Arch Robert Trent Jones Sr

Brabantse (1982)
Steenwagenstraat 11, 1820 Melsbroek
Tel **(02) 751 82 05**
Fax **(02) 751 84 25**
Holes 18 L 4618 m SSS 65
V'tors H
Fees 800fr (1500fr)
Loc 10km NE of Brussels, nr airport
Arch Paul Rolin

La Bruyère
Rue Jumerée 1, 1495 Sart-Dames-Avelines
Tel **(071) 87 72 67**
Fax **(071) 87 72 67**
Holes 18 L 5937 m SSS 71
Loc 40km S of Brussels towards Charleroi

Château de la Bawette (1988)
Chaussée du Chateau 5, 1300 Wavre
Tel **(010) 22 33 32**
Fax **(010) 22 90 04**
Holes 18 L 6076 m SSS 72
9 L 2146 m SSS 63
Fees 1500fr (2000fr)
Loc 1km N of Wavre. 20km SE of Brussels

Château de la Tournette
Chemin de Baudemont 23, 1400 Nivelles
Tel **(067) 21 95 25/22 02 30**
Fax **(067) 21 95 17**
Holes 18 L 6050 m Par 72
18 L 6024 m Par 71
V'tors U H
Fees 1000fr (1600fr)
Loc 29km S of Brussels (E19)
Arch Alliss/Clark

L'Empéreur
Rue Emile François 9, 1474 Ways (Genappe)
Tel **(067) 77 15 71**
Fax **(067) 77 18 33**
Holes 18 L 6037 m SSS 72
9 L 1600 m Par 31
V'tors U H
Fees 950fr (1550fr)
Loc 25km S of Brussels

Hulencourt
Bruyère d'Hulencourt 15, 1472 Vieux Genappe
Tel **(067) 79 40 40**
Fax **(067) 79 40 41**
Holes 18 L 6215 m SSS 72
9 hole Par 3 course
V'tors H–(max 28)
Fees 1400fr (2100fr)
Loc 30km S of Brussels
Arch JM Rossi

Kampenhout
Wildersedreef 56, 1910 Kampenhout
Tel **(016) 65 12 16**
Fax **(016) 65 16 80**
Holes 18 L 6142 m SSS 72
Fees 1000fr (1500fr)
Loc 15km NE of Brussels (E19)

Keerbergen (1965)
Vlieghavenlaan 50, 3140 Keerbergen
Tel **(015) 23 49 61**
Fax **(015) 23 57 37**
Holes 18 L 5530 m SSS 70
V'tors H
Fees 1000fr (1400fr)
Loc 30km NE of Brussels
Arch Cotton/Pennink/Lawrie

Louvain-la-Neuve
Dreve de Lauzelle, 1348 Ottignies
Tel **(010) 45 28 01**
Fax **(010) 45 44 17**
Holes 18 L 6226 m SSS 73
V'tors U
Fees 1200fr (2000fr)
Loc 20km SE of Brussels, off E411
Arch J Dudok van Heel

Overijse
Genslaan 55, 3090 Overijse
Tel **(02) 687 50 30**
Fax **(02) 687 37 68**
Holes 9 L 5782 m SSS 71
V'tors H
Fees 800fr (1500fr)
Loc 10km S of Brussels

Rigenée (1981)
Rue de Châtelet 62, 1495 Villers-la-Ville
Tel **(071) 87 77 65**
Fax **(071) 87 77 83**
Holes 18 L 6150 m SSS 72
V'tors H
Fees 900fr (1500fr)
Loc 35km S of Brussels towards Charleroi
Arch Paul Rolin

Royal Amicale Anderlecht (1987)
Rue Scholle 1, 1070 Bruxelles
Tel **(02) 521 16 87**
Fax **(02) 521 51 56**
Holes 18 L 5320 m SSS 69 Par 72
V'tors U
Fees 1000fr (1500fr)
Loc SW Brussels

Royal Golf Club de Belgique (1906)
Château de Ravenstein, 3080 Tervueren
Tel **(02) 767 58 01**
Fax **(02) 767 28 41**
Holes 18 L 6075 m SSS 72
9 L 1960 m Par 32
V'tors H–(max: 20men; 24 ladies) –phone first
Fees 1550fr (2550fr)
Loc 10km E of Brussels

For list of abbreviations see page 435

Royal Waterloo (1923)
Vieux Chemin de Wavre 50, 1380 Ohain
Tel (02) 633 18 50/633 15 97
Fax (02) 633 28 66
Holes 18 L 6211 m SSS 72
18 L 6224 m SSS 73
9 L 2143 m SSS 33
V'tors H
Fees D–1800fr (D–3000fr)
Loc 22km SE of Brussels
Arch Hawtree/Rolin

Sept Fontaines (1987)
1021, Chaussée d'Alsemberg, 1420 Braine l'Alleud
Tel (02) 353 02 46/353 03 46
Fax (02) 354 68 75
Holes 18 L 6047 m SSS 72
18 L 4870 m SSS 66
9 hole short course
V'tors U H
Fees 1200fr (2100fr)
Loc Braine, 15km S of Brussels. Motorway exit 15 (Huizingen)
Arch Rossi

Steenpoel (1986)
JM Vanlierdelaan 28B, 1701 Itterbeek
Tel (02) 569 69 81
Fax (02) 567 02 23
Holes 9 L 1050 m
V'tors H
Fees 500fr
Loc 8km W of Brussels
Arch Bertier/Vial

Winge G & CC (1988)
Leuvense Steenweg 206, 3390 Sint Joris Winge
Tel (016) 63 40 53
Fax (016) 63 21 40
Holes 18 L 6149 m SSS 73
V'tors H
Fees 1300–1800fr
Loc 35km E of Brussels via Leuven
Arch P Townsend

East

Avernas
Route de Grand Hallet 19A, 4280 Hannut
Tel (019) 51 30 66
Fax (019) 51 30 66
Holes 9 L 2674 m SSS 68
V'tors H
Fees 600fr (800fr)
Loc 40km W of Liège
Arch Hawtree/Cappart

Durbuy (1991)
Route d'Oppagne 34, 6940 Barvaux-su-Ourthe
Tel (086) 21 44 54, (086) 21 44 49
Holes 18 L 5963 m SSS 72
9 hole Par 3 course
V'tors U
Fees 1200fr (1500fr)
Loc 45km S of Liège
Arch Martin Hawtree

Flanders-Nippon (1988)
Vissenbroekstraat 15, 3500 Hasselt
Tel (011) 22 37 93/22 79 55
Fax (011) 24 32 05
Holes 18 L 5922 m SSS 72
9 L 1726 m SSS 32
V'tors U
Fees 1000fr (1500fr)
Loc Hasselt, 85km E of Brussels
Arch Rolin/Wirtz

Henri-Chapelle (1988)
Rue du Vivier 3, 4841 Henri-Chapelle
Tel (087) 88 19 91
Fax (087) 88 36 55
Holes 18 L 5931 m SSS 71
9 L 2255 m SSS 34
6 hole Par 3 course
V'tors 18 holes–H
Fees 18 hole:1200–1800fr
9 hole:900–1200fr
Loc 15km NE of Liège. 25km N of Maastricht
Arch Steensels/Dudok van Heel

International Gomze (1986)
Sur Counachamps, 4140 Gomze Andoumont
Tel (041) 60 92 07
Fax (041) 60 92 06
Holes 18 L 5918 m SSS 72
V'tors U H
Loc 15km S of Liège. Spa 20km

Limburg G & CC (1966)
Golfstraat 1, 3530 Houthalen
Tel (089) 38 35 43
Fax (089) 84 12 08
Holes 18 L 6118 m SSS 72
V'tors H
Fees 1300fr (1800fr)
Loc Houthalen, 15km N of Hasselt
Arch Hawtree

Royal GC du Sart Tilman (1939)
Route du Condroz 541, 4031 Liège
Tel (041) 36 20 21
Fax (041) 37 20 26
Holes 18 L 6002 m SSS 72
V'tors H–booking required
Fees D–1250fr (2000fr)
Loc 10km S of Liège on Route 620 (N35), towards Marche
Arch T Simpson

Royal Golf des Fagnes (1930)
1 Ave de l'Hippodrome, 4900 Spa
Tel (087) 77 16 13
Fax (087) 77 23 36
Holes 18 L 5948 m SSS 72
V'tors H–booking required
Fees 1300–1600fr (200–3300fr)
Loc 5km N of Spa. 35km SE of Liège
Arch T Simpson

Spiegelven GC Genk (1988)
Wiemesmeerstraat 109, 3600 Genk
Tel (0897) 35 96 16
Fax (0897) 36 41 84
Holes 18 L 6198 m SSS 72
V'tors H
Fees 1000fr (1500fr)
Loc Genk, 18km E of Hasselt. 20km N of Maastricht
Arch Ron Kirby

West & Oost Vlanderen

Damme G & CC (1987)
Doornstraat 16, 8340 Damme-Sijsele
Tel (050) 35 35 72
Fax (050) 35 89 25
Holes 18 L 6046 m SSS 72
9 hole short course
V'tors H
Fees 1300fr (1700fr)
Loc 7km E of Bruges. Knokke 15km
Arch J Dudok van Heel

Oudenaarde G & CC (1975)
Kasteel Petegem, Kortrykstraat 52, 9790 Wortegem-Petegem
Tel (055) 31 54 81
Fax (055) 31 98 49
Holes 18 L 6172 m SSS 72
9 L 2536 m Par 34
V'tors H
Fees 1000fr (1500fr)
Loc 3km SW of Oudenaarde
Arch HJ Baker

Royal Latem (1909)
9830 St Martens-Latem
Tel (09) 282 54 11
Fax (09) 282 90 19
Holes 18 L 5767 m SSS 70
V'tors H
Fees 1350fr (1800fr)
Loc 10km SW of Ghent on route N43 Ghent-Deinze

Royal Ostend (1903)
Koninklijke Baan 2, 8420 De Haan
Tel (059) 23 32 83
Fax (059) 23 37 49
Holes 18 L 5517 m SSS 70
V'tors H
Fees 1200–1500fr (1900–2200fr)
Loc 8km N of Ostend towards De Haan

Royal Zoute (1909)
Caddiespad 14, 8300 Knokke-le-Zoute
Tel **(050) 60 16 17 (Clubhouse), (050) 60 37 81 (Starter)**
Fax **(050) 62 30 29**
Holes No 1 18 L 6172 m SSS 73
No 2 18 L 3607 m SSS 60
V'tors H No 1 course–max 20 WE–restricted
Fees 1500–1700fr (1900–2500fr)
Loc Knokke-Heist

Waregem
Bergstraat 41, 8790 Waregem
Tel **(056) 60 88 08**
Fax **(056) 61 08 40**
Holes 18 L 6038 m SSS 72
V'tors H Sun–NA before 1pm
Fees 1000fr (1600fr)
Loc 30km SW of Ghent (E17)
Arch Paul Rolin

Czech Republic

Karlovy Vary (1930)
PO Box 60, 360 01 Karlovy Vary
Tel **(017) 24011**
Fax **(017) 24011**
Holes 18 L 6063 m SSS 72
V'tors H
Fees 600kcs
Loc 8km from Karlovy Vary (Road 6)
Arch Noskowski/Varin

Lísnice (1928)
252 03 Lísnice
Tel **(0305) 92660**
Holes 9 L 4414 m SSS 64
V'tors H
Fees 300kcs
Loc 30km from Prague towards Dobrís

Lokomotiva-Brno (1967)
c/o Chlupova 7, 602 00 Brno
Tel **(05) 744615**
Fax **(05) 759309**
Holes 9 L 4632 m SSS 68
V'tors H
Fees 100kcs (180kcs)
Loc Svratka, 80km NW of Brno. 100km SE of Prague
Arch Chocholac

Mariánské Lázne (1905)
PO Box 49/C, 353 01 Mariánské Lázne
Tel **(0165) 4300/3071/2623**
Fax **(0165) 5195**
Holes 18 L 6195 m SSS 72
V'tors H
Fees D–900kcs
Loc 2km NE of Mariánské Lázne, opposite Golf Hotel

Park GC Ostrava (1968)
747 15 Silherovice
Tel **(069) 97449**
Fax **(069) 97449**
Holes 18 L 5838 m SSS 71
V'tors H
Fees D–600kcs
Loc 15km N of Ostrava

Podebrady (1964)
PO Box 7, 29001 Podebrady
Tel **(0324) 3483**
Fax **(0324) 3483**
Holes 9 L 6240 m SSS 72
V'tors U
Fees 300kcs (400kcs)
Loc E side of Podebrady
Arch Wagner/Havelka

Praha (1926)
Na Morani 4, 128 00 Praha 2
Tel **(02) 292828/644 3828**
Fax (02) 292828
Holes 9 L 5960 m SSS 72
Fees 200kcs (400kcs)
Loc Prague-Motol, towards Plzen

Semily (1960)
c/o Najmanova 110, 513 01 Semily
Tel **(0431) 2705**
Fax **(0431) 2705**
Holes 8 L 4107 m SSS 64 Par 65
V'tors WD–U WE–NA before noon
Fees 300kcs
Loc 2km from Semily. 100km NW of Prague
Arch Schovánek/Janata

Denmark

Bornholm Island

Bornholms (1972)
Plantagevej 3B, 3700 Rønne
Tel **56 95 68 54**
Fax **56 95 68 54 (Apr-Oct)**
Holes 18 L 4815 m Par 68
9 hole Par 3 course
V'tors H
Fees D–160kr
Loc 4km E of Rønne, off Route 38 towards Aakirkeby

Nexø
Dueodde Golfbane, Strandmarksvejen 14, 3730 Nexø
Tel **56 48 89 87**
Fax **56 48 89 69**
Holes 18 L 5715 m SSS 70
V'tors H
Fees 150kr
Loc 12km S of Nexø, nr Dueodde beach
Arch Frederik Dreyer

Nordbornholm-Rø (1987)
Spellingevej 3, Rø, 3760 Gudhjem
Tel **56 48 40 50**
Fax **56 48 40 52**
Holes 18 L 5512 m SSS 71
V'tors WD–U WE–H booking required 8am–3pm
Fees D–150kr
Loc Rø, 8km W of Gudhjem. 22km NE of Rønne
Arch Anders Amilon

Funen

Faaborg (1989)
Dalkildegards Allee, 5600 Faaborg
Tel **62 61 77 43**
Holes 9 L 5710 m SSS 70
V'tors U H
Fees D–120kr
Loc 35km S of Odense
Arch JC Andersen

Lillebaelt
O.Hougvej 130, 5500 Middelfart
Tel **64 41 80 11**
Holes 18 L 5720 m SSS 72
V'tors U
Fees 150kr
Loc 45km W of Odense
Arch Malling Petersen

Odense (1927)
Hestehaven 200, 5220 Odense SØ
Tel **65 95 90 00**
Fax **65 95 90 88**
Holes 18 L 6156 m SSS 71
9 L 4154 m SSS 60
V'tors U
Fees 180kr
Loc SE outskirts of Odense
Arch Jan Sederholm

Odense Eventyr (1993)
Falen 227, 5250 Odense SV
Tel **66 17 11 44**
Fax **66 17 11 37**
Holes 27 L 8580 m SSS 72
V'tors H
Fees 180kr (200kr)
Loc 5km SW of Odense
Arch Michael Møller

SCT Knuds (1954)
Slipshavnsvej 16, 5800 Nyborg
Tel **65 31 12 12**
Fax **65 30 28 04**
Holes 18 L 6027 m SSS 72
V'tors H
Fees 170kr D–220kr (380kr)
Loc 3km SE of Nyborg

Svendborg (1970)
Tordensgaardevej 5, Sørup, 5700 Svendborg
Tel 62 22 40 77
Holes 18 L 5692 m SSS 70
V'tors U
Fees 150kr (180kr)
Loc 4km NW of Svendborg
Arch Frederik Dreyer

Vestfyns (1974)
Rønnemosegård, Krengerupvej 27, 5620 Glamsbjerg
Tel 64 72 15 77
Holes 18 L 5680 m SSS 71
Fees 150kr (180kr)
Loc Glamsbjerg, 40km SW of Odense

Greenland

Sondie Arctic Desert (1990)
Box 58, 3910 Kangerlussuaq, Greenland
Tel 29 91 14 13
Fax 29 91 11 74
Holes 18 L 5521 m SSS 72
V'tors U
Fees 50kr
Loc 2km E of Kangerlussuaq airport
Arch Ulf Larson

Jutland

Aalborg (1908)
Jaegersprisvej 35, Restup Enge, 9000 Aalborg
Tel 98 34 14 76
Fax 98 34 15 85
Holes 18 L 5800 m SSS 71
Fees D–180kr (200 kr)
Loc 7km SW of Aalborg

Aarhus (1931)
Ny Moesgaardvej 50, 8270 Hojbjerg
Tel 86 27 63 22
Fax 86 27 63 21
Holes 18 L 5725 m SSS 70
V'tors U
Fees D–180kr (D–220kr)
Loc 6km S of Aarhus, Route 451
Arch Brian Huggett

Blokhus Klit (1993)
Hunetorpvej 115, Box 230, 9490 Pandrup
Tel 98 20 95 00
Fax 98 20 95 01
Holes 18 L 5489 m SSS 70
V'tors U H
Fees 200kr
Loc 35km NW of Aalborg
Arch Frederik Dreyer

Breinholtgård (1992)
Koksspangvej 17-19, 6710 Esbjerg
Tel 75 11 57 00
Fax 75 11 57 00
Holes 18 L 6091 m SSS 73
9 hole course
V'tors U
Fees 180kr
Loc 11km N of Esbjerg
Arch Gaunt/Trådsdahl

Brønderslev (1971)
PO Box 94, 9700 Brønderslev
Tel 98 82 32 81
Fax 98 82 45 25
Holes 18 L 5783 m SSS 71
9 hole short course
V'tors H WE–booking necessary
Fees 170kr
Loc 3km W of Brønderslev
Arch Erik Schnack

Dejbjerg (1966)
Public
Letagervej 1, Dejbjerg, 6900 Skjern
Tel 97 35 09 59
Holes 18 L 5275 m SSS 69
V'tors U H–max 36
Fees D–130kr (D–160kr)
Loc 6km N of Skjern. 25km from W coast on Skjern-Ringkøbing road (Route 28)
Arch Schnack/Dreyer

Ebeltoft (1966)
Strandgårdshøj 8a, 8400 Ebeltoft
Tel 86 34 47 87/86 36 10 64
Holes 18 L 4925 m Par 68 SSS 67
V'tors U
Fees D–150kr
Loc 1km N of Ebeltoft
Arch Frederik Dreyer

Esbjerg (1921)
Sønderhedevej 11, Marbaek, 6710 Esbjerg
Tel 75 26 92 19
Fax 75 26 94 19
Holes 18 L 6434 m SSS 74
9 L 5520 m SSS 69
V'tors U H
Fees 180kr
Loc 15km N of Esbjerg
Arch Frederik Dreyer

Fanø Vesterhavsbad (1900)
Nordby, 6720 Fanø
Tel 75 16 22 36
Holes 18 L 4450 m SSS 64
Fees D–150kr
Loc W side of Fanø Island. Take ferry from Esbjerg

Grenaa (1981)
Vestermarken 1, 8500 Grenaa
Tel (86) 32 79 29/30 95 99
Holes 18 L 5773 m SSS 70
V'tors U
Fees 150kr
Loc 1km W of Grenaa. 60km NE of Aarhus
Arch Dreyer/Sommer

Gyttegård (1978)
Billundvej 43, 7250 Hejnsvig
Tel 75 33 56 49
Fax 75 33 63 82
Holes 18 L 5673 m SSS 70
V'tors U
Fees 150kr
Loc 2km NE of Hejnsvig. 10km S of Grindsted
Arch Amilon/Bossen

Haderslev (1971)
Simmerstedvej 151, 6100 Haderslev
Tel 74 52 83 01
Fax 74 53 36 01
Holes 18 L 5236 m SSS 68
V'tors H
Fees 150kr (180kr)
Loc 2km NW of Haderslev

Han Herreds
Starkaervej 20, 9690 Fjerritslev
Tel 98 21 26 66
Fax 98 21 26 77
Holes 18 L 5600 m SSS 69
V'tors H
Fees 140kr
Loc 1km N of Fjerritslev. 40km W of Aalborg

Henne (1989)
Hennebysvej 30, 6854 Henne
Tel 75 25 56 10
Fax 75 25 56 61
Holes 18 L 6193 m SSS 72
9 hole Par 3 course
V'tors U
Fees D–160kr
Loc 19km NW of Varde. 35km N of Esbjerg
Arch Frederik Dreyer

Herning
Golfvej 2, 7400 Herning
Tel 97 21 00 33
Fax 97 21 00 34
Holes 18 L 5571 m SSS 70
V'tors H
Fees 150kr (200kr)
Loc 2km E of Herning on Route 15
Arch Frederik Dreyer

Himmerland G & CC (1979)
Centervej 1, Gatten, 9670 Løgstør
Tel 98 66 16 00
Fax 98 66 14 56
Holes Old 18 L 5392 m SSS 69 Par 70; New 18 L 6102 m SSS 74 Par 73; 9 hole Par 3 course
V'tors U

Fees 170kr D–220kr (230kr D–280kr)
Loc Gatten, 35km NW of Hobro towards Løgstør (Route 29)
Arch Jan Sederström

Hjarbaek Fjord (1992)
Lynderup, 8832 Skals
Tel **86 69 62 88**
Fax **86 69 62 68**
Holes 27 L 8595 m SSS 72
V'tors H
Fees 190kr (220kr)
Loc 17km NW of Viborg
Arch Michael Møller

Hjorring (1985)
Vinstrupvej, PO Box 215, 9800 Hjorring
Tel **98 90 03 99**
Fax **98 90 31 00**
Holes 18 L 5886 m SSS 71
V'tors H WE–NA 9–11am
Fees 160kr
Loc N of Hjorring. 50km N of Aalborg
Arch Erik Schnack

Holmsland Klit
Klevevej 19, Søndervig, 6950 Ringkøbing
Tel **97 33 88 00**
Fax **97 33 86 80**
Holes 18 L 5611 m SSS 69
V'tors U
Fees 160kr
Loc 10km W of Ringkøbing
Arch Leif Baekgaard

Holstebro (1970)
Råsted, 7570 Vemb
Tel **97 48 51 55**
Holes 18 L 5853 m SSS 72
9 L 2510 m
V'tors H
Fees D–180kr (200kr)
Loc 13km W of Holstebro
Arch Schnack/Hingebjerg

Horsens (1972)
Silkeborgvej 44, 8700 Horsens
Tel **75 61 51 51**
Holes 18 L 6020 m SSS 72
6 hole short course
Fees 160kr
Loc 1km W of Horsens towards Silkeborg
Arch Jan Sederholm

Hvide Klit (1972)
Hvideklitvej 28, 9982 Aalbaek
Tel **98 48 90 21/48 84 26**
Fax **98 48 91 12**
Holes 18 L 5875 m SSS 72
V'tors H
Fees 180kr (180kr)
Loc 3km N of Aalbaek. 24km N of Frederikshavn
Arch Anders Amilon

Juelsminde (1973)
Bobroholtvej 11a, 7130 Juelsminde
Tel **75 69 34 92/30 70 69 70**
Holes 18 L 5680 m SSS 72
V'tors U H
Fees 150kr
Loc 20km S of Horsens on coast. 2km N of Juelsminde
Arch Mehlsen/Jacobsen/Møller

Kaj Lykke
Porsholtsvej 13, 6740 Bramming
Tel **75 10 22 46**
Holes 18 L 6050 m SSS 72
Par 3 course
Fees 140kr (160kr)
Loc 18km E of Esbjerg
Arch Bent Nielsen

Kalo (1992)
Aarhusvej 32, 8410 Rønde
Tel **86 37 36 00**
Fax **86 37 36 46**
Holes 18 L 6200 m SSS 72
V'tors U
Fees 200kr
Loc 20km E of Aarhus
Arch Frederik Dreyer

Kolding (1933)
Emerholtsvej, 6000 Kolding
Tel **75 52 37 93**
Holes 18 L 5376 m SSS 69
Fees 140kr (200kr)
Loc 3km N of Kolding

Lemvig (1986)
Søgårdevejen 6, 7620 Lemvig
Tel **97 81 09 20**
Holes 18 L 6069 m SSS 72
V'tors U
Fees 150kr (175kr)
Loc 2km N of Lemvig. 35km NE of Holsterbro
Arch Frederik Dreyer

Løkken (1990)
Vrenstedvej 226, PO Box 33, 9480 Løkken
Tel **98 99 26 57/98 99 10 33**
Fax **98 99 22 21**
Holes 18 L 5896 m Par 72
9 L 2964 m Par 29
V'tors U
Fees D–160kr
Loc 45km NW of Aalborg
Arch Kaj Andersen

Nordvestjysk (1971)
Nystrupvej 19, 7700 Thisted
Tel **97 97 41 41**
Fax **97 91 07 80**
Holes 18 L 5713 m SSS 70
V'tors H
Fees 150kr (150kr)
Loc 17km NW of Thisted
Arch Erik Schnack

Randers (1958)
Himmelbovej, Fladbro, 8900 Randers
Tel **86 42 88 69**
Holes 18 L 5453 m SSS 70
9 hole Par 3 course
Fees 150kr (180kr)
Loc 5km W of Randers towards Silkeborg

Ribe (1979)
Rønnehave, Snepsgårdevej 14, Postboks 37, 6760 Ribe
Tel **75 44 12 30**
Holes 18 L 5430 m SSS 68
V'tors U
Fees 100kr (120kr)
Loc 8km SE of Ribe on Haderslev road
Arch Frederik Dreyer

Rold Skov
Golfvej 1, 9520 Skørping
Tel **98 39 26 99**
Fax **98 39 26 52**
Holes 18 L 5850 m SSS 72
V'tors U
Fees 150kr
Loc 30km S of Aalborg
Arch Henrik Jacobsen

Saeby
Vandløsvej 50, 9300 Saeby
Tel **98 46 76 77**
Fax **98 46 11 24**
Holes 18 L 5944 m SSS 72
V'tors U
Fees 160kr
Loc 12km S of Fredrikshavn
Arch Anders Amilon

Silkeborg (1966)
Sensommervej 15C, 8600 Silkeborg
Tel **86 85 33 99**
Fax **86 85 35 22**
Holes 18 L 5975 m SSS 72
V'tors U
Fees 200kr (250kr)
Loc 5km E of Silkeborg
Arch Frederik Dreyer

Skanderborg
Hylke Møllevej, 8660 Skanderborg
Tel **86 53 86 88**
Fax **86 51 14 15**
Holes 9 L 2668 m SSS 68
6 hole Par 3 course
V'tors U
Fees 100kr (150kr)
Loc 20km S of Aarhus by Lake Skanderborg

Skive (1973)
Frugtparken 5, 7800 Skive
Tel **97 52 44 09**
Holes 9 L 5682 m SSS 70
V'tors U
Fees 100kr
Loc 3km NW of Skive. 32km NW of Viborg
Arch Erik Schnack

For list of abbreviations see page 435

Sønderjyllands (1968)
Uge Hedegård, 6360 Tinglev
Tel **74 68 75 25**
Holes 18 L 5771 m SSS 70
V'tors H
Fees 180kr (220kr)
Loc 3km NE of Tinglev. 15km S of Abenraa
Arch Erik Schnack

Varde (1991)
Gellerupvej 111b, 6800 Varde
Tel **75 22 49 44**
Holes 18 L 5809 m SSS 70
V'tors H
Fees 150kr
Loc 20km N of Esbjerg
Arch Erik Fauerholt

Vejle (1970)
Faellessletgard, Ibaekvej, 7100 Vejle
Tel **75 85 81 85**
Fax **75 85 83 01**
Holes 27 holes: 5685-6226 m SSS 70-73
9 hole Par 3 course
V'tors H
Fees 200kr
Loc 5km SE of Vejle
Arch J Malling Pedersen

Viborg (1973)
Møllevej 26, Overlund, 8800 Viborg
Tel **86 67 30 10**
Fax **86 67 34 15**
Holes 18 L 5902 m SSS 71
V'tors U H–booking necessary
Fees 150kr (150kr)
Loc 2km E of Viborg
Arch Frederik Dreyer

Zealand

Asserbo (1946)
Bødkergaardsvej, 3300 Frederiksvaerk
Tel **42 12 14 90**
Holes 18 L 5874 m SSS 71
V'tors H
Fees 160kr (220kr)
Loc 3km from Frederiksvaerk towards Liseleje
Arch Ross/Samuelsen

Copenhagen (1898)
Dyrehaven 2, 2800 Lyngby
Tel **31 63 04 83**
Fax **31 63 46 83**
Holes 18 L 5761 m SSS 71
V'tors WD–U WE–NA before noon
Fees 180kr (240kr)
Loc 13km N of Copenhagen, in deer park

Dragør
Kalvebodvej 100, 2791 Dragør
Tel **32 53 89 75**
Fax **32 53 88 09**
Holes 18 L 5864 m SSS 71
6 hole Par 3 course
V'tors WD–U WE–U H
Fees 170kr (220kr)
Loc 15km SE of Copenhagen centre, nr Airport
Arch Henning Jensen/Kierkegaard

Frederikssund (1974)
Egelundsgården, Skovnaesvej 9, 3630 Jaegerspris
Tel **42 31 08 77**
Holes 18 L 5912 m SSS 70
V'tors U H
Fees 150kr (200kr)
Loc 3km S of Frederikssund towards Skibby (Route 53)
Arch Dreyer/Samuelsen

Furesø (1974)
Hestkøbgård, Hestkøb Vaenge 4, 3460 Birkerød
Tel **42 81 74 44**
Fax **45 82 02 24**
Holes 18 L 5679 m SSS 71
V'tors H WD–NA before 9am
WE–NA before 11am
Fees 180kr (250kr)
Loc 25km N of Copenhagen
Arch Jan Sederholm

Gilleleje (1970)
Ferlevej 52, 3250 Gilleleje
Tel **49 71 80 56**
Fax **49 71 80 86**
Holes 18 L 6641 yds SSS 72
V'tors H WE–NA before 10am
Fees 170–200kr (220kr)
Loc 62km N of Copenhagen
Arch Jan Sederholm

Hedeland (1980)
Staerkendevej 232A, 2640 Hedehusene
Tel **42 13 61 88/42 13 61 69**
Fax **42 13 62 78**
Holes 18 L 6040 m SSS 72
9 hole Par 3 course
V'tors H
Fees 160kr (200kr)
Loc 7km SE of Roskilde. 20km SW of Copenhagen
Arch Jan Sederholm

Helsingør
G1 Hellebaekvej, 3000 Helsingør
Tel **49 21 29 70**
Fax **49 21 09 70**
Holes 18 L 5705 m SSS 71
V'tors U
Fees 180kr (260kr)
Loc 2km N of Helsingør

Hillerød (1966)
Nysogårdsvej, Hammersholt, 3400 Hillerød
Tel **42 26 50 46/42 25 40 30 (Pro)**
Fax **42 25 29 87**
Holes 18 L 5453 m SSS 70
V'tors H WE–NA before noon
Fees 190kr (250kr)
Loc 3km S of Hillerød
Arch Jan Sederholm

Holbaek (1964)
Dragerupvej 50, 4300 Holbaek
Tel **53 43 45 79**
Holes 18 L 5290 m Par 72
V'tors H
Fees 120kr (150kr)
Loc Kirsebaerholmen, 2km E of Holbaek
Arch Dreyer/Sederholm

Kalundborg (1974)
Kildekaergård, Rosnaesvej 225, 4400 Kalundborg
Tel **53 50 13 85**
Holes 9 L 5064 m SSS 68
V'tors U
Fees 100kr (120kr)
Loc Rosnaes, 8km W of Kalundborg
Arch Jan Sederholm

Køge (1970)
Gl.Hastrupvej12, 4600 Køge
Tel **53 65 10 00**
Fax **53 65 13 45**
Holes 18 L 6042 m SSS 71
V'tors WE–H max 24
Fees 150kr (200kr)
Loc 3km S of Køge. Copenhagen 38km

Kokkedal (1971)
Kokkedal Alle 9, 2970 Horsholm
Tel **42 86 99 59**
Fax **42 86 99 03**
Holes 18 L 5958 m SSS 72
V'tors H–WE pm only
Fees 180kr (270kr)
Loc Hørsholm, 30km N of Copenhagen
Arch Frank Pennink

Korsør (1964)
Tårnborgparken, Postbox 53, 4220 Korsør
Tel **53 57 18 36**
Fax **53 57 18 39**
Holes 18 L 5998 m SSS 73
6 hole Par 3 course
V'tors H WE–NA before 10am
Fees 150 (200kr)
Loc 1km E of Korsør, on Korsør Bay

Mølleåens (1970)
Stenbaekgård, Rosenlundvej 3, 3450 Lynge
Tel **42 18 86 31/42 18 86 36 (Pro)**
Fax **42 18 86 43**
Holes 18 L 5730 m SSS 70
V'tors H
Fees 160kr (230kr)
Loc 32km NW of Copenhagen
Arch Jan Sederholm

For list of abbreviations see page 435

Odsherred (1967)
4573 Hojby
Tel **59 30 20 76**
Holes 18 L 5710 m Par 71
V'tors H
Fees 160kr (190kr)
Loc 5km SW of Nykøbing
Arch Amilon/Dreyer

Roskilde (1973)
Gedevad, Kongemarken 30, 4000 Roskilde
Tel **42 37 01 80/46 32 61 00 (Pro)**
Holes 18 L 5700 m SSS 72
Loc 5km W of Roskilde

Rungsted (1937)
Vestre Stationsvej 16, 2960 Rungsted Kyst
Tel **42 86 34 44**
Fax **42 86 57 70**
Holes 18 L 6058 m SSS 73
V'tors H WE–NA before 1pm
Fees 300kr
Loc 24km N of Copenhagen
Arch Maj CA Mackenzie

Simon's Golf (1993)
Nybovej 5, 3490 Kvistgaard
Tel **42 19 14 78**
Fax **42 19 14 70**
Holes 18 L 6200 m SSS 74
V'tors H–max 36
Fees 250kr (350kr)
Loc 10km S of Helsingør. 35km N of Copenhagen
Arch Martin Hawtree

Skjoldenaesholm (1992)
4174 Jystrup
Tel **53 62 82 93**
Fax **53 62 85 82**
Holes 18 L 5974 m SSS 71
V'tors H–max 36
Fees 200kr (250kr)
Loc 10km N of Ringsted. 60km SW of Copenhagen
Arch Otto Bojesen

Skovlunde Herlev (1980)
Syvendehusvej 111, 2730 Herlev
Tel **44 68 90 09**
Fax **44 68 90 04**
Holes 18 L 4814 m SSS 68
9 hole Par 3 course
V'tors U
Fees 180kr (240kr)
Loc Herlev/Ballerup, 15km NW of Copenhagen
Arch TS Hansen

Søllerød
Brillerne 9, 2840 Holte
Tel **42 80 17 84/ 42 80 18 77 (Pro)**
Fax **42 80 70 08**
Holes 18 L 5872 m SSS 72
Fees 200kr (280kr)
Loc 19km N of Copenhagen

Sorø (1979)
Suserupvej 7, 4180 Sorø
Tel **53 64 93 95**
Fax **53 63 35 38**
Holes 18 L 5693 m Par 71
V'tors U
Fees 150kr (180kr)
Loc 6km S of Sorø. 10km W of Ringsted
Arch Jan Sederholm

Sydsjaellands (1974)
Borupgården, Mogenstrup, 4700 Naestved
Tel **53 76 15 55**
Fax **53 76 15 88**
Holes 18 L 5675 m SSS 70
V'tors H
Fees 160kr (200kr)
Loc 10km SE of Naestved towards Praestø
Arch Dreyer/Amilon

Vallensbaek
Golfsvinget 16-20, 2625 Vallensbaek
Tel **43 62 18 99**
Fax **43 62 18 33**
Holes 18 L 6119 m Par 71
9 L 3130 m
V'tors H
Fees 180kr (240kr)
Loc 15km W of Copenhagen
Arch Frederik Dreyer

Finland

Central

Botnia (1988)
Pl 87, 61801 Kauhajoki
Tel **(963) 24663**
Fax **(963) 231 3089**
Holes 9 L 2969 m SSS 72
Fees 100fmk
Loc 8km S of Kauhajoki. 300km NW of Helsinki
Arch Kosti Kuronen

Etelä Pojhanmaan (1986)
Isokoskentie 533, 60550 Nurmo
Tel **(964) 423 4545**
Fax **(964) 423 4547**
Holes 18 L 6210 m SSS 74
Fees 160fmk
Loc 5km E of Seinäjoki. 300km NW of Helsinki

Jyväs Golf (1978)
PL 411, 40101 Jyväskylä
Tel **(941) 244008**
Fax **(941) 244008**
Holes 9 L 5636 m SSS 72
V'tors U
Fees 120fmk
Loc 2km S of Jyväskylä
Arch T Valtakari

Karelia Golf (1987)
Vaskiportintie, 80780 Kontioniemi
Tel **(973) 732411**
Fax **(973) 732472**
Holes 18 L 6223 m SSS 74
V'tors U
Fees 150fmk D–200fmk
Loc 18km N of Joensuu. 460km NE of Helsinki
Arch Kosti Kuronen

Kokkolan (1957)
P O Box 164, 67101 Kokkola
Tel **(968) 822 1636**
Fax **(968) 822 1630**
Holes 18 L 5572 m SSS 71
V'tors U
Fees 120fmk
Loc 3km S of Kokkola. 500km N of Helsinki
Arch KJ Indola

Laukaan Golf (1989)
41530 Laukaa
Tel **(941) 832801**
Fax **(941) 832705**
Holes 18 L 6200 m SSS 75
Fees 120fmk (150fmk)
Loc 28km NE of Jyväskylä. 300km N of Helsinki

Pirilö Golf (1989)
Vanha Pirilontie, 68600 Pietarsaari
Tel **(967) 230262**
Fax **(967) 786 7299**
Holes 9 L 2930m SSS 72
Fees 70fmk
Loc 4km N of Pietarsaari. 471km NW of Helsinki

Tarina Golf Puijo (1988)
Golftie 135, 71800 Siilinjärvi
Tel **(971) 462 5299**
Fax **(971) 462 5269**
Holes 18 L 5779 m SSS 73
V'tors U H
Fees D–168fmk
Loc 21km N of Kuopio (Route 5)
Arch Kosti Kuronen

Vaasan (1969)
Golfkenttätie 61, 65380 Vaasa
Tel **(961) 356 9989**
Fax **(961) 356 9091**
Holes 18 L 5630 m Par 72 SSS 71
V'tors H or Green card
Fees 120fmk
Loc Kraklund, 6km SE of Vaasa on Route 724. 417km NW of Helsinki
Arch Björn Eriksson

Helsinki & South

Alands (1978)
P O Box 111, 22101 Mariehamn
Tel (928) 43883
Fax (928) 19034
Holes 27 L 5565 m SSS 71
Fees 160fmk (180fmk)
Loc 25km N of Mariehamn, Aland (off SW coast of Finland)

Aura Golf (1958)
Ruissalo 85, 20100 Turku
Tel (921) 258 9201
Fax (921) 258 9121
Holes 18 L 5823 m SSS 71
V'tors H
Fees 180fmk
Loc Ruissalo Island, 9km W of Turku
Arch Pekka Sivula

Espoo Ringside Golf (1990)
Niipperintie 20, 02920 Espoo
Tel (90) 841814
Fax (90) 841814
Holes 18 L 5855 m SSS 72
V'tors H
Fees 160fmk
Loc 20km NW of Helsinki
Arch Kosti Kuronen

Espoon Golfseura (1982)
P O Box 26, 02781 Espoo
Tel (90) 811212
Fax (90) 811153
Holes 18 L 5930 m SSS 73
V'tors H
Fees 130fmk
Loc Espoo, 24km W of Helsinki
Arch Jan Sederholm

Helsingin Golfklubi (1932)
Talin Kartano, 00350 Helsinki
Tel (90) 550235/557899
Fax (90) 565 3596
Holes 18 L 5870 m SSS 72
V'tors H–max 24
Fees 180fmk (200fmk)
Loc 7km W of Helsinki

Hyvinkään (1989)
Golftie 63, 05880 Hyvinkää
Tel (914) 489390
Fax (914) 489392
Holes 18 L 5890 m SSS 73
V'tors U
Fees 100fmk (150fmk)
Loc 3km N of Hyvinkää. 50km N of Helsinki
Arch Kosti Kuronen

Keimola Golf Oy (1988)
Kirkantie 32, 01750 Vantaa
Tel (90) 896991
Fax (90) 896790
Holes 27 L 5870-5924 m SSS 71-74
V'tors WD–U before 3pm –M after 3pm WE–M H
Fees 150fmk
Loc 15km N of Helsinki
Arch Pekka Wesamaa

Kurk Golf (1985)
02550 Evitskog
Tel (90) 263456
Fax (90) 263829
Holes 18 L 5871 m Par 73
V'tors H
Fees 135fmk (180fmk)
Loc 40km W of Helsinki
Arch Reijo Hillberg

Master Golf (1988)
Bodomintie 4, 02940 Espoo
Tel (90) 853 7002
Fax (90) 853 7027
Holes 27 L 5866-6109 m SSS 73-4
V'tors U
Fees 180fmk (220fmk)
Loc 25km NW of Helsinki
Arch Kuronen/Persson

Meri-Teijo (1990)
Mathildedalin Kartano, 25660 Mathildedal
Tel (924) 363801
Fax (924) 363890
Holes 18 L 6163 m SSS 75
Fees 100fmk (150fmk)
Loc 20km S of Salo. 70km E of Turku

Messilä (1988)
15980 Messilä
Tel (918) 860371
Fax (918) 860370
Holes 18 L 6013 m SSS 73
V'tors WD–U before 3pm
Fees D–160fmk
Loc 8km W of Lahti. 103km N of Helsinki

Nevas Golf (1988)
01190 Box
Tel (90) 272 6313
Fax (90) 272 6345
Holes 18 L 5267 m SSS 71
V'tors U
Fees 110fmk (150fmk)
Loc 30km E of Helsinki
Arch Kosti Kuronen

Nordcenter G & CC (1988)
10410 Aminnefors
Tel (911) 238850
Fax (911) 238871
Holes 18 L 6375 m SSS 74
18 L 6069 m SSS 71
V'tors Mon/Tues am–H
Fees 250fmk
Loc 80km W of Helsinki
Arch Fream/Benz

Nurmijärven (1990)
Ratasillantie, 05100 Röykkä
Tel (90) 276 8890
Holes 27 L 6002-6214 m SSS 73–5
V'tors U
Fees 150fmk
Loc 23km W of Klaukkala. 50km NW of Helsinki

Pickala Golf (1986)
Pickala Village, 02580 Siuntio
Tel (90) 296 6251
Fax (90) 296 6190
Holes Seaside 18 L 5820 m SSS 72
Park 18 L 5897 m SSS 72
V'tors H
Fees 170fmk (200fmk)
Loc 42km W of Helsinki, on South coast
Arch Reijo Hillberg

Ruukkigolf (1986)
Brödtorp, 10420 Skuru
Tel (911) 54485
Fax (911) 54285
Holes 18 L 6165 m SSS 74
Fees 100fmk (150fmk)
Loc 85km W of Helsinki

St Laurence (1989)
Kaivurinkatu, 08200 Lohja
Tel (912) 386603
Fax (912) 386666
Holes 18 L 6369 m SSS 75
V'tors WD–U H before 3pm WE–U H after 1pm
Fees 160fmk (180fmk)
Loc 50km W of Helsinki
Arch Kosti Kuronen

Sarfvik Golf (1984)
P O Box 27, 02321 Espoo
Tel (90) 297 7122
Fax (90) 297 7134
Holes 18 L 5885 m SSS 72
18 L 5938 m SSS 74
V'tors Old course WD–U H 10am–2pm
Fees 250fmk
Loc 20km W of Helsinki
Arch Jan Sederholm

Sea Golf Rönnäs (1989)
Rönnäs, 07750 Isnäs
Tel (915) 34434
Fax (915) 34458
Holes 18 L 6035 m SSS 74
Fees 150fmk
Loc 27km SE of Porvoo. 80km E of Helsinki

Seaside Golf (1989)
Harjattulantie 84, 20960 Turku
Tel (921) 587100
Fax (921) 34458
Holes 18 L 6348 m SSS 75
Fees 150fmk
Loc 22km S of Turku

Suur-Helsingin (1965)
Rinnekodintie 29, 02980 Espoo
Tel **(90) 855 8687**
Fax **(90) 855 0648**
Holes Lakisto 18 L 5551 m SSS 71
Luukki 18 L 5085 m SSS 70
Fees 150fmk
Loc 25km N of Helsinki

Golf Talma (1989)
Nygårdintie, 04240 Talma
Tel **(90) 236166**
Fax **(90) 236131**
Holes 18 L 5855 m SSS 72
9 L 2895 m SSS 36
9 hole Par 3 course
V'tors H
Fees 135fmk (180fmk)
Loc 35km N of Helsinki
Arch Henrik Wartiainen

Tuusula (1983)
P O Box 178, 04301 Tuusula
Tel **(90) 259466**
Fax **(90) 254660**
Holes 18 L 6363 m SSS 72
V'tors H
Fees 120–160fmk
Loc 30km N of Helsinki, nr airport

Virvik Golf (1981)
Virvik, 06100 Porvoo
Tel **(915) 579292**
Fax **(915) 579292**
Holes 18 L 5786 m SSS 72
V'tors H
Fees 100fmk (120fmk)
Loc 18km SE of Porvoo. 66km E of Helsinki
Arch Reijo Louhimo

North

Green Zone Golf (1987)
Näräntie, 95400 Tornio
Tel **(9698) 431711**
Fax **(9698) 431710**
Holes 18 L 5870 m SSS 73
V'tors U
Fees 120fmk
Loc 2km N of Tornio. 140km N of Oulu, on Finnish/Swedish border
Arch Ake Persson

Katinkulta (1990)
88610 Vuokatti
Tel **(986) 669 7393**
Fax **(986) 664 0710**
Holes 18 L 5975 m SSS 74
V'tors WD–U before 2pm WE–NA unless resident
Fees 180fmk
Loc 36km E of Kajaani. 600km N of Helsinki
Arch Jan Sederholm

Oulu (1964)
Hallituskatu 25 B11, 90100 Oulu
Tel **(981) 371666/395222 (Summer)**
Fax **(981) 379728/395129 (Summer)**
Holes 18 L 6160 m SSS 73
9 L 2990 m SSS 73
V'tors U
Fees 130–150fmk
Loc Sanginsuu, 18km E of Oulu
Arch Ronald Fream

Pielis Golf (1988)
Lomatie 1, 75500 Nurmes
Tel **(976) 480734**
Fax **(976) 480743**
Holes 9 L 5730 SSS 72
V'tors U
Fees 120fmk
Loc 4km E of Nurmes. 500km N of Helsinki
Arch Kosti Kuronen

Raahentienoon Golf (1990)
Kastellintie 44, 92320 Siikajoki
Tel **(982) 241060**
Holes 9 L 6190m SSS 73
Fees 100fmk
Loc 20km N of Raahe. 540km NW of Helsinki

St Lake Golf (1993)
86800 Pyhäsalmi
Tel **(984) 882001**
Fax **(984) 882001**
Holes 9 L 2670 m SSS 72
Fees 100fmk
Loc Pyhäsalmi, 500km N of Helsinki

South East

Hartolan Kunikkaalinen (1992)
Pl 4, 19601 Hartola
Tel **(918) 144310**
Fax **(918) 144319**
Holes 9 L 2845 m SSS 72
V'tors H
Fees 120fmk
Loc 1km S of Hartola. 80km N of Lahti
Arch Kosti Kuronen

Imatran Golf (1986)
Immanlanhovi, 55800 Imatra
Tel **(954) 473 4954**
Fax **(954) 473 4953**
Holes 18 L 6141 m SSS 74
V'tors U
Fees 130fmk (160fmk)
Loc 6km N of Imatra. 270km E of Helsinki
Arch Kosti Kuronen

Kartano Golf (1988)
P O Box 60, 79601 Joroinen
Tel **(972) 72257**
Fax **(972) 72263**
Holes 18 L 5714 m SSS 73
V'tors U
Fees 120fmk (150fmk)
Loc 20km S of Varkaus. 330km NE of Helsinki

Kerigolf (1990)
Hotellikylä Kerimaa, 58200 Kerimäki
Tel **(957) 252496**
Fax **(957) 252124**
Holes 18 L 6208 m SSS 75
V'tors H
Fees 150fmk
Loc 15km E of Savonlinna. 350km NE of Helsinki
Arch Ronald Fream

Koski Golf (1987)
Eerolan Golfkeskus, 45700 Kuusankoski
Tel **(951) 47622**
Fax **(951) 47820**
Holes 18 L 6375 m SSS 75
Fees D–100fmk (D–150fmk)
Loc 1km W of Kuusankoski. 70km E of Lahti

Kymen Golf (1964)
Mussalo Golfcourse, 48310 Kotka
Tel **(952) 605333**
Fax **(952) 605073**
Holes 18 L 6004 m SSS 74
V'tors U
Fees 100fmk (120fmk)
Loc 5km W of Kotka, Mussalo Island. 130km E of Helsinki
Arch Kosti Kuronen

Lahden Golf (1959)
P O Box 67, 15141 Lahti
Tel **(918) 784 1311**
Fax **(918) 784 1311**
Holes 18 L 5823 m SSS 73
V'tors U H
Fees 120fmk
Loc 6km NE of Lahti. 110km NE of Helsinki

Mikkelin Golf (1967)
Kalervonkatu 5, 50130 Mikkeli
Tel **(955) 151759**
Fax **(955) 151771**
Holes 9 L 2845 m SSS 71
Fees 80fmk
Loc 2km SW of Mikkeli. 240km NE of Helsinki
Arch E Inoranta

Porrassalmi (1989)
Annila, 50100 Mikkeli
Tel **(955) 335518/335446**
Fax **(955) 335446**
Holes 18 L 5140 m SSS 68
V'tors H
Fees 120–150fmk
Loc 5km S of Mikkeli

For list of abbreviations see page 435

Vierumäen Golfseura (1988)
Suomen Urheiluopisto, 19120 Vierumäki
Tel **(918) 124501**
Fax **(918) 124630**
Holes 18 L 5755 m SSS 73
Fees 150fmk
Loc 25km NE of Lahti

Viipurin Golf (1938)
Kahilanniemi, 53130 Lapeenranta
Tel **(952) 16840**
Holes 9 L 2708 m SSS 70
Loc 2km E of Lappeenranta, behind Etelä-Saimaa Hospital

South West

Aulangon (1959)
13600 Hämeenlinna
Tel **(917) 74070**
Holes 9 L 2450 m SSS 67
Fees 100fmk
Loc 5km NW of Hämeenlinna. 100km NW of Helsinki

Porin Golfkerho (1939)
P O Box 25, 28601 Pori
Tel **(939) 633 7294**
Fax **(939) 632 6559**
Holes 18 L 6160 m SSS 74
V'tors H
Fees 120fmk
Loc 5km NW of Pori, at Kalafornia
Arch Reijo Louhimo

Rauman Golf (1989)
Pomppuistentie, 26510 Uotila
Tel **(938) 823 0450**
Fax **(938) 823 0941**
Holes 9 L 3095 m SSS 72
Fees 100fmk
Loc 3km E of Rauma. 192km NW of Helsinki

River Golf (1988)
Taivalkunta, 37120 Nokia
Tel **(931) 340 0234**
Fax **(931) 3400 235**
Holes 18 L 5810 m SSS 72
V'tors U
Fees 150fmk (170fmk)
Loc Nokia, 20km W of Tampere
Arch Kosti Kuronen

Salo Golf (1988)
Liikuntapuisto 8, 24100 Salo
Tel **(924) 317321**
Holes 18 L 5824 m SSS 73
Fees 100fmk (120fmk)
Loc 110km W of Helsinki

Skärgården (1980)
Finbyvägen 87, PO Box 110, 21601 Pargas
Tel **(921) 882001**
Fax **(921) 882001**
Holes 9 L 5740 m SSS 72
V'tors U
Fees 100fmk
Loc 25km S of Turku
Arch Kosti Kuronen

Tammer Golf (1965)
P O Box 269, 33101 Tampere
Tel **(931) 613316**
Fax **(931) 613130**
Holes 18 L 5870 m SSS 72
Fees 150fmk
Loc Ruotula, 5km NE of Tampere

Tawast G & CC (1987)
Tawastintie 48, 13270 Hämeenlinna
Tel **(917) 619 7502**
Fax **(917) 619 7503**
Holes 18 L 6063 m SSS 73
18 L 5741 m SSS 72
V'tors U
Fees 160fmk
Loc 5km E of Hämeenlinna
Arch Reijo Hillberg

Vammala (1991)
38100 Karkku
Tel **(932) 34070**
Fax **(932) 34070**
Holes 18 L 5701 m SSS 71
V'tors H
Fees 130fmk
Loc 11km N of Vammala. 210km NW of Helsinki
Arch Kosti Kuronen

Wiurila G & CC (1990)
Viurilantie 126, 24910 Halikko
Tel **(924) 371400**
Fax **(924) 371404**
Holes 18 L 6160 m SSS 74
Fees 100fmk (150fmk)
Loc 5km W of Salo. 115km W of Helsinki

Yyteri Golf (1988)
P O Box 230, 28101 Pori
Tel **(939) 340340**
Fax **(939) 340345**
Holes 18 L 5738 m SSS 72
Fees 150fmk
Loc 20km W of Pori
Arch Reijo Louhimo

France

Bordeaux & South West

Albret (1986)
Le Pusocq, 47230 Barbaste
Tel **53 65 53 69**
Holes 18 L 5911 m SSS 71
Fees On application
Loc Barbaste, 30km W of Agen

Arcachon (1955)
35 Bd d'Arcachon, 33260 La Teste de Buch
Tel **56 54 44 00**
Fax **56 66 86 32**
Holes 18 L 5930 m SSS 71
V'tors U H
Fees D–160–250fr
Loc 60km SW of Bordeaux
Arch CR Blandford

Arcangues (1991)
64200 Arcangues
Tel **59 43 10 56**
Fax **59 43 12 60**
Holes 18 L 6142 m Par 72
V'tors U
Fees 230–300fr
Loc 3km SE of Biarritz
Arch Ronald Fream

Ardilouse (1980)
Domaine de l'Ardilouse, 33680 Lacanau-Océan
Tel **56 03 25 60**
Fax **56 26 30 57**
Holes 18 L 5932 m SSS 72
V'tors H
Fees 160–190fr (240fr)
Loc 45km W of Bordeaux
Arch John Harris

Biarritz (1888)
Ave Edith Cavell, 64200 Biarritz
Tel **59 03 71 80**
Fax **59 03 26 74**
Holes 18 L 5376 m SSS 68
V'tors U
Fees 220–300fr
Loc Biarritz
Arch Willie Dunn

Biscarrosse (1989)
Route d'Ispe, 40600 Biscarrosse
Tel **58 09 84 93**
Fax **58 09 84 50**
Holes Lake 9 L 2172 m SSS 32
Forest 9 L 3030 m SSS 36
V'tors U
Fees 160–250fr
Loc 80km SW of Bordeaux
Arch Brizon/Veyssieres

For list of abbreviations see page 435

Bordeaux-Lac (1977)
Avenue de Pernon, 33300 Bordeaux
Tel **56 50 92 72**
Fax **56 29 01 84**
Holes 18 L 6156 m SSS 72
18 L 6159 m SSS 72
Fees 170fr (190fr)
Loc 2km N of Bordeaux
Arch Jean Bourret

Bordelais (1900)
Domaine de Kater, Rue de Kater, 33200 Bordeaux-Caudéran
Tel **56 28 56 04/56 28 68 94**
Holes 18 L 4833 m SSS 67
V'tors H–restricted Tues
Fees 170fr (220fr)
Loc 3km NW of Bordeaux

Casteljaloux (1989)
Avenue du Lac, 47700 Casteljaloux
Tel **53 93 51 60**
Fax **53 93 04 10**
Holes 18 L 5916 m SSS 72
V'tors U
Fees 150–200fr (180–220fr)
Loc 60km NW of Agen
Arch Michel Gayon

Castelnaud (1987)
'La Menuisière', 47290 Castelnaud de Gratecambe
Tel **53 01 74 64**
Fax **53 01 78 99**
Holes 18 L 6322 m SSS 73
9 L 2184 m SSS 27
Loc 10km N of Villeneuve on N21. 40km N of Agen

Chantaco (1928)
Route d'Ascain, 64500 St Jean-de-Luz
Tel **59 26 14 22/59 26 19 22**
Fax **59 26 48 37**
Holes 18 L 5722 m SSS 70
V'tors U
Fees 250fr (400fr)
Loc 2km S of St Jean-de-Luz, on Route d'Ascain
Arch HS Colt

Château des Vigiers (1990)
24240 Monestier
Tel **53 61 50 00**
Fax **53 61 50 20**
Holes 18 L 6568 m Par 72
V'tors H
Fees 220–280fr (280fr)
Loc 15km SW of Bergerac. 75km E of Bordeaux
Arch Donald Steel

Chiberta (1926)
Boulevard des Plages, 64600 Anglet
Tel **59 63 83 20**
Fax **59 63 30 56**
Holes 18 L 5650 m SSS 70
V'tors H–booking required
Fees 200–240fr
Loc 3km N of Biarritz. Airport 5km
Arch T Simpson

Croix de Mortemart (1987)
St Felix de Reillac, 24260 Le Bugue
Tel **53 03 27 55**
Holes 18 L 6222 m Par 72
9 hole pitch & putt
V'tors U
Fees 150–180fr W–900fr
Loc 30km S of Perigueux, between La Douze and Le Bugue (D710)
Arch Martine Lacroix

Graves et Sauternais (1989)
St Pardon de Conques, 33210 Langon
Tel **56 62 25 43**
Holes 18 L 5810 m SSS 71
Loc 5km from Langon. 45km SW of Bordeaux via A62

Gujan (1990)
Route de Souguinet, 33470 Gujan Mestras
Tel **56 66 86 36**
Fax **56 66 10 93**
Holes 18 L 6300 m SSS 72
9 L 2520 m SSS 35
Fees 18 hole:200–250fr 9 hole:140–170fr
Loc 12km E of Arcachon on RN 250. 40km W of Bordeaux
Arch Alain Prat

Hossegor (1930)
Ave du Golf, BP 95, 40150 Hossegor
Tel **58 43 56 99**
Fax **58 43 98 52**
Holes 18 L 6001 m SSS 71
V'tors H
Fees 210–330fr (240–330fr)
Loc 15km N of Bayonne, on coast
Arch J Morrison

Makila
Route de Cambo, 64200 Bassussarry
Tel **59 58 42 42**
Fax **59 58 42 48**
Holes 18 L 6176 m SSS 72
V'tors H
Fees 200–300fr
Loc 5km SE of Biarritz. Airport 2km
Arch R Roquemore

Médoc
Chemin de Courmateau, Louens, 33290 Le Piam Médoc
Tel **56 70 21 10**
Fax **56 70 23 44**
Holes Chateaux 18 L 6316 m SSS 74
Vignes 18 L 6220 m SSS 73
V'tors H
Fees 200fr (270fr)
Loc 20km NW of Bordeaux
Arch Coore/Whitman

Moliets (1989)
40660 Moliets
Tel **58 48 54 65**
Fax **58 48 54 88**
Holes 18 L 6172 m SSS 73
9 hole course
V'tors U
Fees 230–300fr
Loc Moliets, 30km N of Bayonne. 40km N of Dax
Arch Robert Trent Jones

La Nivelle (1907)
Place William Sharp, 64500 Ciboure
Tel **59 47 18 99/59 47 19 72**
Holes 18 L 5570 m SSS 69
Fees 220–320fr (1991)
Loc 2km S of St Jean-de-Luz

Pau (1856)
Rue de Golf, 64140 Pau-Billère
Tel **59 32 02 33**
Fax **59 62 42 57**
Holes 18 L 5312 m SSS 69
V'tors U
Fees 200fr (250fr)
Loc 2km S of Pau. Bordeaux 200km
Arch Willie Dunn

Périgueux (1980)
Domaine de Saltgourde, 24430 Marsac
Tel **53 53 02 35**
Fax **53 09 46 29**
Holes 18 L 6120 m SSS 72
Fees D–180fr
Loc 3km W of Périgueux, via Angoulême–Riberac road
Arch Robert Berthet

Pessac (1989)
Rue de la Princesse, 33600 Pessac
Tel **56 36 24 47**
Fax **56 36 52 89**
Holes 27 L 6123-6242 m SSS 72
9 hole course
V'tors U
Fees 200fr (250fr)
Loc 4km W of Bordeaux
Arch Olivier Brizon

Royal Artiguelouve (1986)
Domaine St Michel, 64230 Artiguelouve
Tel **59 83 09 29**
Holes 18 L 6063 m Par 71
Loc 8km NW of Pau, off Bayonne road

Scottish Golf d'Aubertin (1987)
64290 Aubertin
Tel **59 82 73 73**
Holes 18 L 4806 m Par 66
Loc 20km S of Pau

Seignosse Golf Hotel (1989)
Avenue du Belvedère, 40510 Seignosse
Tel **58 43 17 32**
Fax **58 43 16 67**
Holes 18 L 6124 m Par 72
V'tors U
Fees 240–310fr
Loc 30km N of Biarritz, nr airport
Arch Robert von Hagge

Sporting Club de Cameyrac (1972)
Cameyrac, 33450 Saint-Loubes
Tel **56 72 96 79**
Holes 18 L 5927 m SSS 72
9 L 1188 m SSS 28
Fees 160fr (310fr)
Loc 15km E of Bordeaux

Brittany

Ajoncs d'Or (1976)
Kergrain Lantic, 22410 Saint-Quay Portrieux
Tel **96 71 90 74**
Fax **96 71 40 83**
Holes 18 L 6125 m SSS 72
V'tors U
Fees 170–190fr
Loc 17km N of Saint-Brieuc. 6km W of Étables-sur-Mer

Baden
Kernic, 56870 Baden
Tel **97 57 18 96**
Fax **97 57 22 05**
Holes 18 L 6145 m SSS 73
V'tors U
Fees 150–230fr
Loc 12km SW of Vannes
Arch Yves Bureau

Boisgelin (1987)
Pléhédel, 22290 Lanvollon
Tel **96 22 31 24**
Holes 18 hole course
V'tors U
Fees 100fr (150fr)
Loc 10km S of Paimpol on D7. 35km from Saint-Brieuc

Brest-Iroise (1976)
Parc de Lann-Rohou, Saint-Urbain, 29800 Landerneau
Tel **98 85 16 17**
Holes 18 L 5672 m Par 71
9 L 3329 m Par 37
V'tors U H
Fees 210fr (230fr)
Loc 25km E of Brest
Arch M Fenn

Cicé-Blossac (1992)
Domaine de Cicé-Blossac, 35170 Bruz
Tel **99 52 79 79**
Fax **99 57 93 60**
Holes 18 L 6343 m SSS 72
V'tors U
Fees 150–250fr
Loc Bruz, SW of Rennes (N177)
Arch Macauley/Quenouille

Dinard (1887)
35800 St-Briac-sur-Mer
Tel **99 88 32 07**
Fax **99 88 04 53**
Holes 18 L 5137 m Par 68
Fees 190fr (220fr)
Loc 8km W of Dinard. 15km W of Saint-Malo

La Freslonnière (1989)
Le Bois Briand, 35650 Le Rheu
Tel **99 14 84 09**
Fax **99 14 94 98**
Holes 18 L 5671 m SSS 71
V'tors U
Fees 200fr (230fr)
Loc 4km SW of Rennes, off N24
Arch A du Bouexic

L'Odet (1987)
Clohars-Fouesnant, 29950 Benodet
Tel **98 54 87 88**
Fax **98 54 61 40**
Holes 18 L 6235 m SSS 73
9 hole Par 3 course
V'tors U H
Fees 150–230fr
Loc 6km S of Benodet. 15km SE of Quimper
Arch Robert Berthet

Les Ormes (1988)
Château des Ormes, Epiniac, 35120 Dol-de-Bretagne
Tel **99 73 49 60**
Fax **99 73 49 55**
Holes 18 L 6070 m SSS 72
V'tors U
Fees 185–240fr
Loc 8km S of Dol, off D795
Arch A d'Ormesson

Pen Guen (1926)
22380 Saint-Cast-le-Guildo
Tel **96 41 91 20**
Holes 18 L 4940 m SSS 67
V'tors U
Fees 180–220fr
Loc 25km W of Dinard. 30km W of Saint-Malo

Pléneuf-Val André
Rue de la Plage des Vallées, 22370 Pléneuf-Val André
Tel **96 63 01 12**
Fax **96 63 01 06**
Holes 18 hole course
V'tors U
Fees 150fr (200fr)
Loc 30km E of St Brieuc on coast. 60km W of St Malo
Arch MA Prat

Ploemeur Océan
Saint-Jude, Kerham, 56270 Ploemeur
Tel **97 32 81 82**
Fax **97 32 80 90**
Holes 18 L 5957 m SSS 72
V'tors U H
Fees 140–230fr
Loc 10km from Lorient-Brest road, exit Ploemeur
Arch Macauley/Quenouille

Quimper-Cornouaille (1959)
Manoir du Mesmeur, 29940 La Forêt-Fouesnant
Tel **98 56 97 09**
Holes 18 L 5657 m SSS 71
Fees D–150fr
Loc 15km SE of Quimper
Arch F Hawtree

Rennes Saint Jacques
B P 1117, 37136 St-Jacques-de-la-Lande
Tel **99 64 24 18**
Holes 18 L 6135 m Par 72
9 L 2100 m Par 32
9 hole short course
V'tors H
Fees 150–230fr
Loc 5km SW of Rennes
Arch Robert Berthet

Rhuys-Kerver (1988)
Formule Golf, Domaine de Kerver, 56730 St-Gildas-de-Rhuys
Tel **97 45 30 09**
Fax **97 45 36 58**
Holes 18 L 6197 m SSS 73
V'tors U
Fees 150–230fr
Loc 30km S of Vannes
Arch Olivier Brizon

Les Rochers
Route d'Argentré du Plessis, 35500 Vitré
Tel **99 96 52 52**
Holes 18 L 5986 m SSS 72
V'tors U
Fees 160fr (220fr)
Loc Vitré, 30km E of Rennes
Arch JC Varro

Sables-d'Or-les-Pins (1925)
22240 Fréhel
Tel **96 41 42 57**
Fax **96 41 51 44**
Holes 18 L 5586 m SSS 71
V'tors H
Fees 170–210fr
Loc 6km SW of Fréhel. 30km W of Dinard

St Laurent (1975)
Ploemel, 56400 Auray
Tel **97 56 85 18**
Fax **97 56 89 99**
Holes 18 L 6212 m SSS 72
9 L 2705 m SSS 35

V'tors U
Fees 150–250fr
Loc Ploemel, 16km SW of Auray
Arch Fenn/Bureau

St Malo-Le Tronchet (1986)

Le Tronchet, 35540 Miniac-Morvan
Tel **99 58 96 69**
Holes 18 L 6049 m SSS 72
9 L 2684 m SSS 36
V'tors U
Fees D–220fr
Loc 23km S of St Malo, off RN 137
Arch Hubert Chesneau

St Samson (1964)

Route de Kérénoc, 22560 Pleumeur-Bodou
Tel **96 23 87 34**
Fax **96 23 84 59**
Holes 18 L 5682 m SSS 71
V'tors U
Fees D–180–200fr
Loc 7km N of Lannion on Tregastel road
Arch Donald Harradine

Sauzon (1987)

Les Poulins, 56360 Belle-Ile-en-Mer
Tel **97 31 64 65**
Holes 18 L 5820 m SSS 72
V'tors U
Fees 180fr
Loc Island off S coast of Brittany, near Quiberon
Arch Yves Bureau

Val Queven (1990)

Kerrousseau, 56530 Queven
Tel **97 05 17 96**
Fax **97 05 19 18**
Holes 18 L 6127 m SSS 72
V'tors U Sun–restricted
Fees 150–220fr
Loc 10km W of Lorient
Arch Yves Bureau

Burgundy & Auvergne

Beaune-Levernois (1990)

21200 Levernois
Tel **80 24 10 29**
Fax **80 24 03 78**
Holes 18 L 6484 m SSS 72
9 hole short course
V'tors U
Fees 140fr (220fr)
Loc 5km SE of Beaune (D470/D111)
Arch Ch Piot

Chalon-sur-Saône (1976)

Parc de Saint Nicholas, 71380 Chatenoy-en-Bresse
Tel **85 48 61 64/85 93 49 65**
Fax **85 93 56 95**
Holes 18 L 5859 m SSS 71
V'tors U
Fees D–135fr
Loc 3km SE of Chalon. 125km N of Lyon
Arch Michel Rio

Château d'Avoise (1992)

9 Rue de Mâcon, 71210 Montchanin
Tel **85 78 19 19**
Fax **85 78 15 16**
Holes 18 L 6210 m SSS 73
V'tors U
Fees 140fr (200fr)
Loc 25km W of Chalon
Arch Martin Hawtree

Château de Chailly

Chailly-sur-Armançon, 21320 Pouilly-en-Auxois
Tel **80 90 30 40**
Fax **80 90 30 00**
Holes 18 L 6146 m SSS 72
V'tors U
Fees 200fr (300fr)
Loc 45km SW of Dijon
Arch Sprecher/Watine

Château de la Salle (1989)

71260 La Salle-Mâcon Nord
Tel **85 36 09 71**
Fax **85 36 06 70**
Holes 18 L 6024 m SSS 71
V'tors U
Fees 150fr (200fr)
Loc 12km NW of Mâcon. Lyon 70km
Arch Robert Berthet

Le Coiroux (1977)

19190 Aubazine
Tel **55 27 25 66**
Fax **55 27 29 33**
Holes 18 L 5400 m Par 70
V'tors U
Fees 170fr (190fr)
Loc 15km E of Brive
Arch Hubert Chesneau

Dijon-Bourgogne (1972)

Bois des Norges, 21490 Ruffey-les-Echirey
Tel **80 35 71 10**
Fax **80 35 79 27**
Holes 18 L 6179 m SSS 72
V'tors U
Fees 190fr (250fr)
Loc 10km N of Dijon towards Langres
Arch Michael Fenn

La Fredière (1988)

La Fredière, Céron, 71110 Marcigny
Tel **85 25 27 40**
Fax **85 25 35 01**
Holes 18 L 4529 m SSS 68
V'tors U
Fees 150–180fr
Loc 35km NW of Roanne
Arch Gilles Charmat

La Jonchère

Montgrenier, 23230 Gouzon
Tel **55 62 23 05**
Holes 18 L 5858 m SSS 71
V'tors U
Fees 140fr (180fr)
Loc 30km SW of Montluçon. 100km NE of Limoges
Arch J-L Pega

Limoges-St Lazare (1976)

Avenue du Golf, 87000 Limoges
Tel **55 28 30 02**
Holes 18 L 6238 m SSS 73
V'tors U
Fees 90fr
Loc 2km S of Limoges on RN20
Arch Hubert Chesneau

Le Nivernais

Le Bardonnay, 58470 Magny Cours
Tel **86 58 18 30**
Fax **86 58 04 04**
Holes 18 L 5670 m Par 71
Fees 130fr (180fr)
Loc 12km S of Nevers on N7. 50km N of Moulins
Arch Alain Prat

La Porcelaine

Célicroux, 87350 Panazol
Tel **55 31 10 69**
Fax **56 06 23 97**
Holes 18 L 6035 m SSS 72
V'tors U
Fees 150fr (200fr)
Loc 6km NE of Limoges
Arch Jean Garaialde

Roncemay (1989)

89110 Aillant-sur-Tholon
Tel **86 73 69 87**
Holes 18 L 6401 m SSS 73
V'tors WE–M
Loc 25km NW of Auxerre
Arch Jeremy Pern

Sporting Club de Vichy (1907)

Allée Baugnies, 03700 Bellerive/Allier
Tel **70 32 39 11**
Fax **70 32 00 54**
Holes 18 L 5463 m SSS 70
V'tors H
Fees 250–300fr
Loc In Vichy
Arch Arnaud Massy

Val-de-Cher (1975)
03190 Nassigny
Tel **70 06 71 15**
Holes 18 L 5450 m SSS 70
V'tors U
Fees 170fr (220fr)
Loc 20km N of Montluçon on N144
Arch Gerard Vigand

Les Volcans (1984)
La Bruyère des Moines, 63870 Orcines
Tel **73 62 15 51**
Fax **73 62 26 52**
Holes 18 L 6286 m SSS 73
9 L 1377 m SSS 29
V'tors U H
Fees 200fr (250fr)
Loc 12km W of Clermont-Ferrand on RN 141
Arch Lucien Roux

Centre

Les Aisses (1992)
RN20 Sud, 45240 La Ferté St Aubin
Tel **38 64 80 87**
Fax **38 64 80 85**
Holes 27 L 6200 m SSS 72
V'tors U
Fees 180fr (250fr)
Loc 30km S of Orléans
Arch Olivier Brizon

Ardrée (1988)
37360 St Antoine-du-Rocher
Tel **47 56 77 38**
Fax **47 56 79 96**
Holes 18 L 5758 m Par 70
V'tors U
Fees 200–260fr
Loc 10km N of Tours
Arch Olivier Brizon

Les Bordes (1987)
41220 Saint Laurent-Nouan
Tel **54 87 72 13**
Fax **54 87 78 61**
Holes 18 L 6412 m Par 72
V'tors U
Fees 350fr (550fr)
Loc 30km SW of Orléans
Arch Robert van Hagge

Château de Cheverny
La Rousselière, 41700 Cheverny
Tel **54 79 24 70**
Fax **54 79 25 52**
Holes 18 L 6276 m Par 71
V'tors H
Fees 180fr (250fr)
Loc 15km S of Blois. 200km SW of Paris, via A10
Arch O Van der Vinckt

Château de Maintenon (1988)
Route de Gallardon, 28130 Maintenon
Tel **37 27 18 09**
Fax **37 27 10 12**
Holes 18 L 6393 m SSS 74
9 L 1541 m SSS 30
V'tors WD–U WE–restricted
Fees 250fr (450fr)
Loc 20km W of Rambouillet (D906). 70km SW of Paris
Arch Michel Gayon

Château des Forges (1991)
Domaine des Forges, 79340 Menigoute
Tel **49 69 91 77**
Holes 18 L 6400 m Par 74
9 L 3200 m Par 37
V'tors U
Fees 200fr (250fr)
Loc 30km W of Poitiers
Arch Bjorn Eriksson

Château des Sept Tours (1989)
37330 Courcelles-de-Touraine
Tel **47 24 69 75**
Fax **47 24 23 74**
Holes 18 L 6194 m SSS 73
V'tors U
Fees 180fr (240fr)
Loc 35km NW of Tours
Arch Donald Harradine

Châtellerault (1987)
Parc Thermal, 86270 La Roche Posay
Tel **49 86 25 10**
Fax **49 86 18 72**
Holes 18 L 5840 m SSS 72
V'tors U
Fees 150fr (200fr)
Loc La Roche-Posay, 20km E of Châtellerault. 40km NE of Poitiers
Arch JP Fourès

Cognac (1987)
Saint-Brice, 16100 Cognac
Tel **45 32 18 17**
Holes 18 L 6142 m SSS 72
V'tors H
Fees 180fr (250fr)
Loc 5km E of Cognac
Arch Jean Garaialde

Les Dryades
36160 Pouligny-Notre-Dame
Tel **54 30 28 00**
Holes 18 L 6120 m SSS 72
V'tors U
Fees 200fr (250fr)
Loc 10km S of La Châtre (D940). 60km SW of Bourges
Arch Michel Gayon

Haut-Poitou (1987)
86130 Saint-Cyr
Tel **49 62 53 62**
Fax **49 60 28 58**
Holes 18 L 6590 m SSS 75
9 L 1800 m Par 30
V'tors U
Fees 170fr Sun–200fr
Loc 20km N of Poitiers. 70km S of Tours
Arch HG Baker

Loudun (1985)
Domaine St Hilaire, 86120 Roiffe
Tel **49 98 78 06**
Fax **49 98 72 57**
Holes 18 L 6280 m Par 72
V'tors U
Fees 170–190fr (210–230fr)
Loc 15km NW of Loudun. 15km SE of Saumur
Arch Hubert Chesneau

Marcilly (1986)
Domaine de la Plaine, 45240 Marcilly-en-Villette
Tel **38 76 11 73**
Fax **38 76 18 73**
Holes 18 L 6324 m SSS 73
9 hole course
V'tors U
Fees 120fr (170fr)
Loc 20km SE of Orléans
Arch Olivier Brizon

Mazières (1987)
Le Petit Chêne, 79310 Mazières-en-Gâtine
Tel **49 63 20 95**
Holes 18 L 6060 m SSS 72
Loc 15km SW of Parthenay. 25km NE of Niort
Arch Robert Berthet

Mignaloux Beauvoir
Domaine de Beauvoir, 86800 Mignaloux Beauvoir
Tel **49 46 70 27**
Fax **49 55 31 95**
Holes 18 L 6032 m SSS 71
V'tors WD–M WE–NA
Fees 150–180fr
Loc 6km SE of Poitiers (RN147)
Arch Olivier Brizon

Oleron
La Vieille Perrotine, 17310 St Pierre d'Oleron
Tel **46 47 11 59**
Fax **46 47 49 59**
Holes 9 L 3000 m SSS 36
6 hole short course
V'tors U
Fees D–100fr (D–140fr)
Loc Island S of La Rochelle. A10 Junction 25 (Saintes)
Arch Olivier Brizon

For list of abbreviations see page 435

Orléans Val de Loire

Château de la Touche, 45450 Donnery
Tel **38 59 25 15/38 59 20 48**
Fax **38 57 01 98**
Holes 18 L 5771 m SSS 71
V'tors U
Fees 180fr (250fr)
Loc 16km E of Orléans
Arch Trent Jones/Van der Vinckt

Le Perche (1987)

La Vallée des Aulnes, 28400 Souancé au Perche
Tel **37 29 17 33**
Fax **37 29 12 88**
Holes 18 L 6073 m SSS 71
V'tors U
Fees 170fr (280fr)
Loc 60km SW of Chartres (D9). 130km SW of Paris
Arch Laurent Hechly

La Prée-La Rochelle (1990)

La Richardière, 17137 Marsilly
Tel **46 01 24 42**
Fax **46 01 25 84**
Holes 18 L 6012 m SSS 72
V'tors U
Fees 160–200fr (190–220fr)
Loc 6km N of La Rochelle
Arch Olivier Brizon

Royan (1977)

Maine-Gaudin, 17420 Saint-Palais
Tel **46 23 16 24**
Fax **46 23 23 38**
Holes 18 L 5970 m SSS 71
V'tors U H
Fees 165–230fr
Loc Saint-Palais, 7km W of Royan
Arch Robert Berthet

Sancerrois (1989)

St Thibault, 18300 Sancerre
Tel **48 54 11 22**
Fax **48 54 28 03**
Holes 18 L 5828 m SSS 72
V'tors U
Fees 120–170fr (180–220fr)
Loc 35km NE of Bourges
Arch Didier Fruchet

Sologne (1955)

Route de Jouy-le-Potier, 45240 Ardon
Tel **38 76 57 33**
Holes 18 L 6400 yds SSS 72
V'tors U
Fees 140fr (200fr)
Loc 25km S of Orléans on RN20

Sully-sur-Loire (1965)

L'Ousseau, 45600 Viglain
Tel **38 36 52 08**
Holes 18 L 6154 m SSS 72
9 L 3155 m SSS 36
Loc 3km SW of Sully-sur-Loire

Touraine (1971)

Château de la Touche, 37510 Ballan-Miré
Tel **47 53 20 28**
Fax **47 53 31 54**
Holes 18 L 5671 m SSS 71
V'tors WE–H
Fees D–230fr (D–280fr)
Loc Villandry, 8km SW of Tours
Arch Michael Fenn

Val de l'Indre (1989)

Villedieu-sur-Indre, 36320 Tregonce
Tel **54 26 59 44**
Holes 18 L 6250 m SSS 72
Fees 140–190fr
Loc 12km NW of Chateauroux. 80km SE of Tours on RN 143
Arch Yves Bureau

Vaugouard (1987)

Chemin des Bois, Fontenay-sur-Loing, 45210 Ferrières
Tel **38 95 81 52**
Fax **38 95 79 78**
Holes 18 L 5914 m SSS 72
V'tors U
Fees 150fr (250fr)
Loc 10km N of Montargis. Paris 100km
Arch Fromanger/Macadam

Channel Coast & North

Aa-Saint-Omer

Chemin des Bois, Acquin-Westbécourt, 62380 Lumbres
Tel **21 38 59 90**
Fax **21 38 59 90**
Holes 18 L 6313 m SSS 73
9 L 2003 m SSS 31
V'tors U H
Fees 230fr (270fr)
Loc 10km W of Saint-Omer. 40km S of Calais
Arch J Dudok van Heel

Abbeville (1989)

Route du Val, 80132 Grand Laviers
Tel **22 24 98 58**
Fax **22 24 49 61**
Holes 18 L 6045 m Par 72
V'tors U
Fees 150fr (180fr)
Loc 3km NW of Abbeville
Arch Didier Fruchet

L'Ailette

02000 Laon
Tel **23 24 83 99**
Fax **23 24 84 66**
Holes 18 L 6127 m Par 72
9 hole short course
V'tors WD–H WE–H restricted
Fees 185fr (240fr)
Loc 13km S of Laon. 45km NW of Reims
Arch Michel Gayon

Amiens (1951)

80115 Querrieu
Tel **22 93 04 26**
Fax **22 93 04 61**
Holes 18 L 6114 m SSS 72
V'tors U
Fees 150fr (250fr)
Loc 7km NE of Amiens (D929)
Arch Ross/Pennink

L'Amiraute (1992)

Departementale 278, Tourgéville, 14800 Deauville
Tel **31 14 42 00**
Fax **31 88 32 00**
Holes 18 L 6017 m Par 73
V'tors U
Fees 220–250fr (330–350fr)
Loc 4km S of Deauville
Arch Bill Baker

Apremont (1992)

60300 Apremont
Tel **44 25 61 11**
Fax **44 25 11 72**
Holes 18 L 6434 m SSS 72
V'tors H
Fees 250fr (500fr)
Loc 55km N of Paris
Arch John Jacobs

Arras (1989)

Rue Briquet Taillandier, 62223 Anzin-St-Aubin
Tel **21 50 24 24**
Fax **21 50 29 71**
Holes 18 L 6201 m SSS 72
V'tors U
Fees 170fr (220fr)
Loc 50km S of Lille. 110km SE of Calais
Arch JC Cornillot

Bois de Ruminghem (1991)

1613 Rue St Antoine, 62370 Ruminghem
Tel **21 85 30 33**
Fax **21 36 38 38**
Holes 18 L 6115 m Par 73
V'tors U
Fees 140fr (160fr)
Loc 30km SE of Calais
Arch Bill Baker

Bondues (1968)

Château de la Vigne, BP 54, 59587 Bondues Cedex
Tel **20 23 20 62**
Fax **20 23 24 11**
Holes 18 L 6223 m SSS 73
18 L 6000 m SSS 72
V'tors H–max 30
Fees D–200fr (D–300fr)
Loc 10km NE of Lille
Arch Hawtree/Trent Jones

For list of abbreviations see page 435

Brigode (1970)
36 Avenue de Golf,
59650 Villeneuve D'Ascq
Tel **20 91 17 86**
Fax **20 05 96 36**
Holes 18 L 6182 m SSS 72
V'tors WD–H (High season)
Fees 200fr (300fr)
Loc 8km NE of Lille
Arch HJ Baker

Les Bruyères (1991)
Chemin de l'Enfer, 62118 Pelves
Tel **21 58 95 42**
Fax **21 24 00 04**
Holes 18 L 5958 m SSS 72
V'tors U
Fees 130fr (150fr)
Loc 40km S of Lille. 180km N of Paris
Arch Ogama

Champagne (1986)
02130 Villers-Agron
Tel **23 71 62 08**
Fax **23 71 62 08**
Holes 18 L 5626 m SSS 72
V'tors U
Fees 150fr (220fr)
Loc 25km SW of Reims, via E50
Arch JC Cornillot

Chantilly (1909)
Vineuil Saint Firmin, 60500 Chantilly
Tel **44 57 04 43**
Fax **44 57 26 54**
Holes Vineuil 18 L 6597 m SSS 71
Longères 18 L 6378 m SSS 72
V'tors WE–NA
Fees WD–350fr
Loc 45km N of Paris
Arch Tom Simpson

Chaumont-en-Vexin (1963)
Château de Bertichère,
60240 Chaumont-en-Vexin
Tel **44 49 00 81/44 49 14 76**
Holes 18 L 6195 m SSS 72
V'tors H
Fees 200fr (400fr)
Loc 65km NW of Paris
Arch Donald Harradine

Compiègne (1896)
Ave Royale, 60200 Compiègne
Tel **44 40 15 73**
Fax **44 40 23 59**
Holes 18 L 6017 m SSS 71
V'tors U H
Fees 200fr (300fr)
Loc Compiègne, 80km NE of Paris

Domaine de Chantilly Golf Hotel
Route d'Apremont,
60500 Vineuil St-Firmin
Tel **44 58 47 74**
Fax **44 58 50 11**
Holes 18 L 6161 m SSS 73
V'tors U
Fees 150–170fr (250–270fr)
Loc 40km N of Paris (RN17)
Arch Huau/Nelson

Domaine du Tilleul (1984)
Landouzy-la-Ville, 02140 Vervins
Tel **23 98 48 00**
Fax **23 98 46 46**
Holes 18 L 5203 m SSS 71
V'tors Groups 10+ welcome
Fees 100–150fr
Loc 7km S of Hirson. 65km N of Reims

Dunkerque (1983)
Fort Vallières, Coudekerque-Village,
59380 Bergues
Tel **28 61 07 43**
Holes 18 L 6300 m SSS 71
Fees 160fr (200fr)
Loc 5km E of Dunkerque
Arch Robert Berthet

Hardelot Dunes Course (1991)
Ave Edouard VII, 62152 Neufchâtel Hardelot
Tel **21 91 90 90**
Fax **21 33 26 40**
Holes 18 L 6038 m SSS 73
V'tors U H
Fees 270–320fr
Loc Hardelot, 15km S of Boulogne
Arch Rolin/Cornillot

Hardelot Pins Course
Ave du Golf, 62152 Neufchâtel Hardelot
Tel **21 83 73 10**
Fax **21 83 24 33**
Holes 18 L 5870 m SSS 72
V'tors U H
Fees 270–300fr
Loc Hardelot, 15km S of Boulogne
Arch Tom Simpson

International Club du Lys
Rond-Point du Grand Cerf,
60260 Lamorlaye
Tel **44 21 26 00**
Fax **44 21 35 52**
Holes 18 L 6022 m SSS 70
18 L 4798 m SSS 66
V'tors WD–H WE–M H
Fees 250–270fr (450–470fr)
Loc 5km S of Chantilly
Arch Tom Simpson

Masako Ohya (1990)
Château d'Humières, 60113 Monchy-Humières
Tel **44 42 39 51**
Fax **44 42 48 92**
Holes 18 L 6176 m SSS 73
V'tors U
Fees 180fr (270fr)
Loc 80km N of Paris. A1 Junction 11

Morfontaine (1926)
60128 Mortefontaine
Tel **44 54 68 27**
Holes 18 L 6063 m SSS 72
9 L 2550 m SSS 35
V'tors Members' guests only
Fees NA
Loc 10km S of Senlis. N of Paris
Arch Tom Simpson

Mormal (1991)
Bois St Pierre, 59144 Preux-au-Sart
Tel **27 63 07 00**
Fax **27 39 93 62**
Holes 18 L 6022 m Par 72
V'tors H
Fees 150fr (200fr)
Loc 15km E of Valenciennes, off RN49
Arch JC Cornillot

Nampont-St-Martin (1978)
Maison Forte,
80120 Nampont-St-Martin
Tel **22 29 92 90/22 29 89 87**
Fax **22 29 97 54**
Holes Cygnes 18 L 5649 m SSS 70
Belvedère 18 L 5078 m SSS 70
V'tors U
Fees 130–150fr (150–180fr)
Loc 12km S of Montreuil-sur-Mer. 50km S of Boulogne
Arch Thomas Chatterton

Rebetz
Route de Noailles,
60240 Chaumont-en-Vexin
Tel **44 49 15 54**
Holes 18 L 6434 m SSS 73
V'tors U
Fees 200fr (400fr)
Loc Chaumont-en-Vexin, 65km NW of Paris, via D43
Arch J-P Fourès

Le Sart (1910)
5 Rue Jean-Jaurès,
59650 Villeneuve D'Ascq
Tel **20 72 02 51**
Fax **20 98 73 28**
Holes 18 L 5721 m SSS 71
V'tors H
Fees 200fr (300fr 2D–480fr)
Loc 5km E of Lille. Motorway Lille-Gand Junction 9 (Breucq–Le Sart)
Arch Allan Macbeth

Thumeries (1935)
Bois Lenglart, 59239 Thumeries
Tel **20 86 58 98**
Holes 18 L 5675 m SSS 70
Fees 160fr (210fr)
Loc 10km N of Douai
Arch Boomer/Rossi

For list of abbreviations see page 435

Le Touquet 'La Forêt' (1904)
Avenue du Golf, BP 41, 62520 Le Touquet
Tel 21 05 68 47
Fax 21 05 40 19
Holes 18 L 5773 m SSS 71
V'tors U H
Fees 250fr (320fr)
Loc 2km S of Le Touquet. 30km S of Boulogne
Arch HS Colt

Le Touquet 'La Mer' (1930)
Avenue du Golf, BP 41, 62520 Le Touquet
Tel 21 05 68 47
Fax 21 05 40 19
Holes 18 L 6330 m SSS 74
V'tors U H
Fees 250fr (320fr)
Loc As 'La Forêt'
Arch HS Colt

Le Touquet 'Le Manoir' (1994)
Ave du Golf, BP 41, 62520 Le Touquet
Tel 21 05 68 47
Fax 21 05 40 19
Holes 9 L 2800 m Par 35
V'tors U
Fees 130fr (180fr)
Loc As 'La Forêt'
Arch HJ Baker

Vert Parc (1991)
3 Route d'Ecuelles, 59480 Illies
Tel 20 29 37 87
Fax 20 29 37 87
Holes 18 L 6328 m SSS 73
V'tors U
Fees 140fr (220fr)
Loc 18km SW of Lille
Arch Patrice Simon

Wimereux (1906)
Route d'Ambleteuse, 62930 Wimereux
Tel 21 32 43 20
Holes 18 L 6150 m Par 72
V'tors H
Fees 185–210fr (200–250fr)
Loc 6km N of Boulogne on D940. 30km S of Calais
Arch Campbell/Hutchinson

Corsica

Spano
Cocody Village, Commune de Lumio, 20260 Calvi
Tel 95 60 75 52
Fax 95 60 70 73
Holes 9 L 2200 m SSS 64
V'tors U
Fees 120fr (140fr)
Arch Olivier Brizon

Spérone (1990)
Domaine de Spérone, 20169 Bonifacio
Tel 95 73 17 13
Fax 95 73 17 85
Holes 18 L 6130 m SSS 73
V'tors H–max 28
Fees 330fr W–1400fr
Loc S point of Corsica, SE of Bonifacio. 25km S of Airport
Arch Robert Trent Jones Sr

Ile de France

Ableiges (1989)
95450 Ableiges
Tel 34 66 06 05
Fax 34 66 04 20
Holes 18 L 6261 m SSS 73
9 L 2137 m Par 33
V'tors U H
Fees 200fr (350fr)
Loc 40km NW of Paris, nr Cergy Pontoise
Arch Pern/Garaialde

Belesbat
Courdimanche sur Essonne, 91820 Boutigny sur Essonne
Tel 69 23 19 00
Fax 69 23 19 01
Holes 18 L 6047 m SSS 72
V'tors Booking required
Fees 300fr (450fr)
Loc 40km S of Paris, between Etampes and Fontainebleau

Bondoufle (1990)
Departmentale 31, 91070 Bondoufle
Tel 60 86 41 71
Fax 60 86 41 56
Holes 18 L 6161 m SSS 73
V'tors U H
Fees 100–200fr (250–300fr)
Loc 30km S of Paris
Arch Michel Gayon

Bussy-St-Georges
Promenade des Golfeurs, 77600 Bussy-St-Georges
Tel 64 66 00 00
Fax 64 66 22 92
Holes 18 L 5924 m SSS 72
V'tors U
Fees 120–150fr (250–280fr)
Loc 20km E of Paris. Motorway A4 Junction 12
Arch Rolin/Cornillot

Cély (1990)
Le Château, Route de Saint-Germain, 77930 Cély-en-Bière
Tel 64 38 03 07
Fax 64 38 08 78
Holes 18 L 6026 m SSS 72
V'tors H
Fees 300fr (400fr)
Loc Fontainebleau 15km
Arch Adam/Fromanger

Cergy Pontoise (1988)
2 Allee de l'Obstacle d'Eau, 95490 Vaureal
Tel 34 21 03 48
Fax 34 21 03 34
Holes 18 6100 m SSS 72
V'tors WD–U WE–U H
Fees 160fr (260fr)
Loc 30km NW of Paris. A15 Junction 12
Arch Michel Gayon

Coudray (1960)
Ave du Coudray, 91830 Le Coudray-Montceaux
Tel 64 93 81 76/64 93 93 97 (Pro)
Fax 64 93 99 95
Holes 18 L 5637 m Par 71
9 L 1500 m Par 30
V'tors H
Fees 230fr (500fr)
Loc 35km S of Paris on A6 (Junction 11)
Arch CK Cotton

Courson Monteloup (1991)
91680 Bruyères-le-Chatel
Tel 64 58 80 80
Fax 64 58 83 06
Holes 36 hole course: 6171-6520 m SSS 72-75
V'tors WD–U WE–M exc Jul/Aug
Fees 230fr (400fr)
Loc 35km SW of Paris, off Route D3
Arch Robert von Hagge

Crécy-la-Chapelle (1987)
Ferme de Monpichet, 77580 Crécy-la-Chapelle
Tel 64 04 70 75
Holes 18 L 6211 m SSS 72
V'tors U
Fees 80fr (200fr)
Loc 20km E of Paris by A4

Domont-Montmorency
Route de Montmorency, 95330 Domont
Tel 39 91 07 50
Fax 39 91 25 70
Holes 18 L 5775 m SSS 71
V'tors H
Fees 260fr (480fr)
Loc 18km N of Paris
Arch Hawtree

Étiolles
Vieux Chemin de Paris, 91450 Étiolles
Tel 60 75 49 49
Fax 60 75 64 20
Holes 18 L 6239 m SSS 73
9 L 2665 m SSS 36
V'tors U
Fees 18 hole:250fr (380fr) 9 hole:220fr (310fr)
Loc 30km S of Paris
Arch Michel Gayon

For list of abbreviations see page 435

Fontainebleau (1909)
Route d'Orleans, 77300 Fontainebleau
Tel **64 22 22 95**
Fax **64 22 63 76**
Holes 18 L 6074 m SSS 72
V'tors WD–U WE–Jul/Aug only
Fees 350fr (500fr)
Loc 1km SW of Fontainebleau. SE of Paris
Arch Simpson/M Hawtree

Fontenailles (1991)
Domaine de Bois Boudran, 77370 Fontenailles
Tel **64 60 51 00**
Fax **60 67 52 12**
Holes 18 L 6263 m SSS 73
9 L 2870 m
V'tors WD–U WE–H
Fees 180–200fr (320–450fr)
Loc 60km SE of Paris
Arch Michel Gayon

Forges-les-Bains
Rue du Général Leclerc, 91470 Forges-les-Bains
Tel **64 91 48 18**
Fax **64 91 40 52**
Holes 18 L 6207 m SSS 72
V'tors U
Fees 200fr (300fr)
Loc 35km S of Paris, off A10
Arch Manuel Rossi

La Forteresse (1989)
77940 Thoury Ferrottes
Tel **60 96 95 10**
Fax **60 96 01 41**
Holes 18 L 6025 m SSS 72
V'tors WD–U WE–H
Fees 180fr (350fr)
Loc 25km SE of Fontainebleau
Arch Fromanger/Adam

Green Parc (1993)
Route de Villepech, 91280 St Pierre-du-Perray
Tel **60 75 40 60**
Fax **60 75 40 04**
Holes 18 L 5839 m SSS 71
V'tors U
Fees 100fr (220fr)
Loc 30km SW of Paris
Arch Robin Nelson

Meaux-Boutigny (1985)
Le Bordet, Rue de Barrois, 77470 Trilport
Tel **60 25 63 98**
Holes 18 L 5981 m SSS 71
9 hole course
V'tors U
Fees 180fr (300fr)
Loc 45km E of Paris-Highway 4
Arch Michel Gayon

Mont Griffon
BP 7, 95270 Luzarches
Tel **34 68 10 10**
Fax **34 68 04 10**
Holes 18 L 5905 m SSS 70
V'tors U
Fees 200fr (350fr)
Loc 27km N of Paris
Arch Nelson/Huau/Dongradi

Ormesson (1969)
Chemin du Belvedère, 94490 Ormesson-sur-Marne
Tel **45 76 20 71**
Fax **45 94 86 85**
Holes 18 L 6130 m SSS 72
V'tors H
Fees 210fr (350fr)
Loc 21km SE of Paris
Arch Harris/CK Cotton

Ozoir-la-Ferrière (1926)
Château des Agneaux, 77330 Ozoir-la-Ferrière
Tel **60 02 60 79**
Fax **64 40 28 20**
Holes 18 L 6105 m SSS 72
9 L 2700 m Par 35
Fees 18 hole:250fr (400fr)
9 hole:130fr (200fr)
Loc 25km SE of Paris via A4 (Porte de Bercy)

Paris International (1991)
18 Route du Golf, 95560 Baillet-en-France
Tel **34 69 90 00**
Fax **34 69 97 15**
Holes 18 L 6319 m SSS 72
V'tors I or M
Fees 450fr (700fr)
Loc 24km NW of Paris
Arch Jack Nicklaus

Seraincourt (1964)
Gaillonnet-Seraincourt, 95450 Vigny
Tel **34 75 47 28**
Fax **34 75 75 47**
Holes 18 L 5760 m SSS 70
V'tors WD–U WE–H
Fees 150fr (300fr)
Loc 35km NW of Paris

St Aubin (1976)
Route du Golf, 91190 St Aubin
Tel **69 41 25 19**
Fax **69 41 02 25**
Holes 18 L 5971 m SSS 71
9 L 1918 m SSS 31
V'tors U
Fees 100fr (200fr)
Loc 30km SW of Paris
Arch Berthet/Rio

St Germain-les-Corbeil
6 Ave du Golf, 91250 St Germain-les-Corbeil
Tel **60 75 81 54**
Fax **60 75 52 89**
Holes 18 L 5800 m SSS 71
Loc 30km S of Paris

St Pierre du Perray (1974)
Melun-Sénart, St Pierre du Perray, 91100 Corbeil
Tel **60 75 17 47**
Holes 18 L 6169 m SSS 72
Loc 30km SE of Paris, off N6
Arch Hubert Chesneau

Villarceaux (1971)
Château du Couvent, 95710 Chaussy
Tel **34 67 73 83**
Fax **34 67 72 66**
Holes 18 L 6175 m SSS 72
V'tors H
Fees 170fr (375fr)
Loc 60km NW of Paris
Arch M Backer

Languedoc-Roussillon

Cap d'Agde (1989)
4 Ave des Alizés, 34300 Cap d'Agde
Tel **67 26 54 40**
Fax **67 26 97 00**
Holes 18 L 6160 m SSS 72
V'tors U
Fees 190fr (230fr)
Loc 25km E of Béziers
Arch Ronald Fream

Coulondres (1984)
4 Rue des Erables, 34980 Saint-Gely-du-Fesc
Tel **67 84 13 75**
Fax **67 84 06 33**
Holes 18 L 6175 m SSS 73
V'tors U
Fees 150fr (200fr)
Loc 10km N of Montpellier towards Ganges
Arch Donald Harradine

Falgos (1992)
BP 9, 66260 St Laurent-de-Cerdans
Tel **68 39 51 42**
Fax **68 39 52 30**
Holes 18 L 5671 m SSS 70
V'tors U
Fees 160fr (200fr)
Loc 60km S of Perpignan, nr Spanish border (D115)

Fontcaude
Domaine de Fontcaude, 34990 Juvignac
Tel **67 03 34 30**
Fax **67 03 34 51**
Holes 18 L 6992 m SSS 72
9 hole short course
V'tors U
Fees 160fr (210fr)
Loc 2km W of Montpellier
Arch C Pitman

For list of abbreviations see page 435

La Grande-Motte
(1987)
BP 16, 34280 La Grande-Motte
Tel **67 56 05 00**
Fax **67 29 18 84**
Holes 18 L 6200 m SSS 72
18 L 4000 m Par 58
Fees 180fr (220fr)
Loc 18km E of Montpellier
Arch Robert Trent Jones

Massane
Domaine de Massane, 34670 Baillargues
Tel **67 87 87 87**
Fax **67 87 87 90**
Holes 18 L 6375 m SSS 74
9 hole course
V'tors H
Fees 195fr (270fr)
Loc 9km E of Montpellier
Arch Ronald Fream

Nîmes Campagne
(1968)
Route de Saint Gilles, 30900 Nîmes
Tel **66 70 17 37**
Fax **66 70 03 14**
Holes 18 L 6135 m SSS 72
V'tors H
Fees 200fr (250fr)
Loc 7km S of Nîmes, by Airport
Arch Morandi/Harradine

Nîmes-Vacquerolles
(1990)
Route de Sauve, 30900 Nîmes
Tel **66 23 33 33**
Fax **66 23 94 94**
Holes 18 L 6300 m SSS 73
V'tors U
Fees 160fr (220fr)
Loc W of Nîmes centre (D999)
Arch W Baker

St Cyprien (1974)
Le Mas D'Huston, 66750 St Cyprien Plage
Tel **68 21 01 71/68 21 05 46**
Fax **68 21 11 33**
Holes 18 L 6480 m SSS 73
9 L 2724 m SSS 35
Loc 15km SE of Perpignan
Arch Wright/Tomlinson

St Thomas (1992)
Route de Pézenas, 34500 Béziers
Tel **67 98 62 01**
Fax **67 98 61 01**
Holes 18 hole course
V'tors U
Fees 180–200fr (220–240fr)
Loc 7km NE of Béziers (RN 113)
Arch Patrice Lambert

Loire Valley

Angers (1963)
Moulin de Pistrait, 49320 St Jean des Mauvrets
Tel **41 91 96 56**
Holes 18 L 5460 m Par 70
Fees 170fr (220fr)
Loc 14km SE of Angers. Right bank of Loire.

Anjou G & CC (1990)
Route de Cheffes, 49330 Champigné
Tel **41 42 01 01**
Fax **41 42 04 37**
Holes 18 L 6227 m SSS 72
6 hole short course
V'tors U H
Fees 160fr (200fr)
Loc 23km N of Angers
Arch F Hawtree

Avrillé (1988)
Château de la Perrière, 49240 Avrillé
Tel **41 69 22 50**
Fax **41 34 44 60**
Holes 18 L 6116 m SSS 71
9 hole Par 3 course
V'tors U
Fees 195fr (230fr)
Loc 5km N of Angers
Arch Robert Berthet

La Baule (1976)
Domaine de Saint-Denac, 44117 Saint-André-des-Eaux
Tel **40 60 46 18/40 60 34 04**
Holes 18 L 6157 m SSS 72
V'tors H
Fees 170–320fr
Loc Avrillac, 3km NE of La Baule
Arch Alliss/Thomas

La Bretesche (1968)
Domaine de la Bretesche, 44780 Missillac
Tel **40 88 30 03**
Fax **40 88 36 28**
Holes 18 L 6080 m SSS 72
V'tors U
Fees 170–290fr
Loc 8km NW of Pontchâteau. 50km NW of Nantes
Arch Bill Baker

Cholet (1989)
Allée du Chêne Landry, 49300 Cholet
Tel **41 71 05 01**
Fax **41 56 06 94**
Holes 18 L 5999 m Par 71
V'tors WD–U WE–H
Fees 170fr (190fr)
Loc 2km N of Cholet. 52km SE of Nantes
Arch Olivier Brizon

La Domangère
La Roche-sur-Yon, Route de la Rochelle, 85310 Nesmy
Tel **51 07 60 15**
Fax **51 07 64 09**
Holes 18 L 6480 m SSS 72
V'tors U
Fees 140–230fr (180–230fr)
Loc 6km S of La Roche-sur-Yon. 70km S of Nantes
Arch Michel Gayon

Fontenelles
Saint-Gilles-Croix-de-Vie, 85220 Aiguillon-sur-Vie
Tel **51 54 13 94**
Fax **51 55 45 77**
Holes 18 L 6185 m Par 72
V'tors U
Fees 100–220fr
Loc 6km E of St-Gilles-Croix-de-Vie. 75km SW of Nantes
Arch Yves Bureau

Ile d'Or (1988)
BP 10, 49270 La Varenne
Tel **40 98 58 00**
Fax **40 98 51 62**
Holes 18 L 6292 m Par 72
9 L 1217 m Par 27
V'tors U H
Fees 140fr (220fr)
Loc 30km NE of Nantes
Arch Michel Gayon

Laval-Changé
Le Jariel, 53000 Changé-les-Laval
Tel **43 53 16 03**
Holes 18 L 6095 m Par 72
9 L 2100 m
V'tors Green card or H
Fees 180fr (220fr)
Loc 5km N of Laval. 60km E of Rennes
Arch JP Foures

Le Mans Mulsanne (1961)
Route de Tours, 72230 Mulsanne
Tel **43 42 00 36**
Fax **43 42 21 31**
Holes 18 L 5821 m SSS 71
V'tors H
Fees D–170–290fr (D–240–400fr)
Loc 12km S of Le Mans

Nantes
44360 Vigneux de Bretagne
Tel **40 63 25 82**
Holes 18 L 5940 m SSS 72
V'tors H
Fees 170fr (250fr)
Loc 12km NW of Nantes
Arch Frank Pennink

Nantes Erdre (1990)
Chemin du Bout des Landes, 44300 Nantes
Tel **40 59 21 21**
Fax **40 73 44 19**
Holes 18 L 6003 m SSS 71
V'tors U
Fees 170fr (220fr)
Loc Nantes
Arch Yves Bureau

Les Olonnes
Gaze, 85340 Olonne-sur-Mer
Tel **51 33 16 16**
Fax **51 30 10 45**
Holes 18 L 6127 m Par 72
V'tors U
Fees 120–250fr
Loc 3km N of Les Sables d'Olonne
Arch Bruno Parpoil

Pornic (1912)
49 Boulevard de l'Océan, Sainte-Marie/Mer, 44210 Pornic
Tel **40 82 06 69**
Holes 18 L 6119 m SSS 72
V'tors U
Fees 150–230fr (170–230fr)
Loc 1km E of Pornic. 40km S of La Baule
Arch Michel Gayon

Port Bourgenay (1990)
Avenue de la Mine, Port Bourgenay, 85440 Talmont-St-Hilaire
Tel **51 23 35 45**
Fax **51 23 35 48**
Holes 18 L 5800 m SSS 72
V'tors U
Fees 100–250fr
Loc 10km SE of Sables d'Olonne. 100km S of Nantes
Arch Pierre Thevenin

Sable-Solesmes
Domaine de l'Outinière, Route de Pincé, 72300 Sablé-sur-Sarthe
Tel **43 95 28 78**
Fax **43 92 39 05**
Holes 27 holes SSS 72:
Forêt 9 L 3197 m
Rivière 9 L 3010 m
Cascade 9 L 3069 m
V'tors U
Fees 280fr
Loc 40km SW of Le Mans
Arch Michel Gayon

Sarge (1990)
Rue du Golf, 72190 Sarge-le-Mans
Tel **43 76 25 07**
Fax **43 76 45 25**
Holes 18 L 6036 m SSS 72
V'tors U
Fees 120fr (180fr)
Loc 6km E of Le Mans
Arch Antoine d'Ormesson

Savenay (1990)
44260 Savenay
Tel **40 56 88 05**
Fax **40 56 89 04**
Holes 18 L 6335 m Par 73
9 L 1122 m Par 30
V'tors U
Fees 150–230fr
Loc 36km W of Nantes. 30km E of La Baule
Arch Michel Gayon

St Jean-de-Monts (1988)
Ave des Pays de Monts, 85160 Saint Jean-de-Monts
Tel **51 58 82 73**
Fax **51 59 18 32**
Holes 18 L 5962 m SSS 72
Loc 60km SW of Nantes on coast

Normandy

Bagnoles-de-l'Orne (1988)
Route de Domfront, 61140 Bagnoles-de-l'Orne
Tel **33 37 81 42**
Holes 9 L 2400 m SSS 66
Fees 120fr (150fr)
Loc Bagnoles, 80km S of Caen

Bellême-St-Martin (1988)
Les Sablons, 61130 Bellême
Tel **33 73 00 07**
Fax **33 73 00 17**
Holes 18 L 6011 m SSS 72
V'tors U
Fees 150fr (220fr)
Loc 40km NE of Le Mans
Arch Vialatel

Beuzeval-Houlgate (1980)
Route de Gonneville, 14510 Houlgate
Tel **31 24 80 49**
Fax **31 28 04 48**
Holes 18 L 5769 m SSS 73
V'tors U
Fees 140–160fr (170–200fr)
Loc 2km S of Houlgate towards Gonneville
Arch Alliss/Stockton

Brotonne (1990)
Jumièges, 76480 Duclair
Tel **35 05 32 97**
Fax **35 37 99 97**
Holes 18 L 6040 m SSS 72
V'tors U
Fees 110fr (150fr)
Loc 20km W of Rouen
Arch JP Fourès

Cabourg-Le Home (1955)
38 Av Président Réné Coty, Le Home Varaville, 14390 Cabourg
Tel **31 91 25 56**
Holes 18 L 5122 m SSS 68
V'tors H
Fees 160–260fr
Loc 4km W of Cabourg
Arch Olivier Brizon

Caen (1990)
Le Vallon, 14112 Bieville-Beuville
Tel **31 94 72 09**
Fax **31 47 45 30**
Holes 18 holes SSS 72 Par 72
9 hole course
V'tors U
Fees 160fr (200fr)
Loc 5km N of Caen (D60)
Arch F Hawtree

Champ de Bataille
Château du Champ de Bataille, 27110 Le Neubourg
Tel **32 35 03 72**
Fax **32 35 83 10**
Holes 18 L 5983 m SSS 72
Fees 220fr (330fr)
Loc 28km NW of Evreux. 38km SW of Rouen
Arch Nelson/Huau

Cherbourg (1973)
Domaine des Roches, 50470 La Glacerie
Tel **33 44 45 48**
Holes 9 L 2791 m SSS 35
V'tors H
Fees 120fr
Loc 6km S of Cherbourg

Clécy (1988)
Manoir de Cantelou, 14570 Clécy
Tel **31 69 72 72**
Fax **31 69 70 22**
Holes 18 L 5975 m SSS 72
V'tors U
Fees 150–210fr (190–210fr)
Loc 30km S of Caen, via D562
Arch W Baker

Coutainville (1925)
Ave du Golf, 50230 Agon-Coutainville
Tel **33 47 03 31**
Holes 9 L 5210 m SSS 68
V'tors H
Fees 150fr
Loc 12km W of Coutances. 75km S of Cherbourg

Dieppe-Pourville (1897)
Route de Pourville, 76200 Dieppe
Tel **35 84 25 05**
Fax **35 84 97 11**
Holes 18 L 5763 m SSS 70
V'tors U
Fees 160–200fr (230–270fr)
Loc 2km W of Dieppe towards Pourville
Arch Willie Park

Étretat (1908)
BP No 7, Route du Havre, 76790 Étretat
Tel **35 27 04 89**
Holes 18 L 5994 m SSS 72
V'tors H
Fees 250–310fr
Loc 25km N of Le Havre. Étretat 1km
Arch Chantepie/Fruchet

Fontenay-en-Cotentin (1975)
Fontenay-sur-Mer, 50310 Montebourg
Tel **33 21 44 27**
Holes 9 L 2954 m Par 36
V'tors U

Fees 110fr (140fr)
Loc 32km SE of Cherbourg, via RN13/D42

Forêt Verte

Bosc Guerard, 76710 Montville
Tel **35 33 62 94**
Holes 18 L 7000 yds SSS 72
V'tors U
Fees 120fr (180fr)
Loc 10km N of Rouen
Arch Thierry Huau

Granville (1912)

Bréville, 50290 Bréhal
Tel **33 50 23 06**
Holes 18 L 5854 m Par 72
9 L 2323 m Par 33
Fees 18 hole:140fr (220fr)
9 hole:100fr (130fr)
Loc 5km N of Granville

Le Havre (1933)

Hameau Saint-Supplix, 76930 Octeville-sur-Mer
Tel **35 46 36 50**
Holes 18 L 5830 m SSS 70
Fees 180fr
Loc 10km N of Le Havre

Léry Poses (1989)

BP 7, 27740 Poses
Tel **32 59 47 42**
Holes 18 L 6242 m SSS 73
9 hole Par 3 course
V'tors U
Fees 150fr (200fr)
Loc 25km SE of Rouen
Arch J Baker

New Golf Deauville (1929)

14 Saint Arnoult, 14800 Deauville
Tel **31 88 20 53**
Fax **31 88 06 00**
Holes 18 L 5933 m SSS 71
9 L 3033 m SSS 72
V'tors U–booking required
Fees 250–350fr
Loc 3km S of Deauville
Arch Simpson/Cotton

Omaha Beach (1986)

Ferme St Sauveur, 14520 Port-en-Bessin
Tel **31 21 72 94**
Fax **31 51 79 61**
Holes 18 L 6229 m SSS 72
9 L 2875 m SSS 35
V'tors U H
Fees 180–260fr (220–260fr)
Loc 8km N of Bayeux
Arch Yves Bureau

Rouen-Mont St Aignan (1911)

Rue Francis Poulenc, 76130 Mont St Aignan
Tel **35 76 38 65**
Fax **35 75 13 86**
Holes 18 L 5522 m SSS 70
V'tors H WE–H after 4pm
Fees 160fr (250fr)
Loc 4km N of Rouen

St Gatien Deauville (1987)

14130 St Gatien-des-Bois
Tel **31 65 19 99**
Fax **31 65 11 24**
Holes 18 L 6200 m SSS 72
9 L 3000 m SSS 36
V'tors U
Fees 180–200fr (270–300fr)
Loc 8km E of Deauville
Arch Olivier Brizon

St Julien

St Julien-sur-Calonne, 14130 Pont-l'Évêque
Tel **31 64 30 30**
Fax **31 64 12 43**
Holes 18 L 6290 m SSS 73
9 L 2133 m SSS 33
V'tors U
Fees 200–230fr (230–290fr)
Loc 3km SE of Pont l'Évêque
Arch Alain Prat

St Saëns (1987)

76680 St Saëns
Tel **35 34 25 24**
Fax **35 34 43 33**
Holes 18 L 6004 m SSS 71
V'tors U
Fees D–125fr (D–250fr)
Loc 30km NE of Rouen
Arch D Robinson

Le Vaudreuil (1962)

27100 Le Vaudreuil
Tel **32 59 02 60**
Fax **32 59 43 88**
Holes 18 L 6411 m SSS 73
V'tors H
Fees 170fr (250fr)
Loc 6km NE of Louviers. 25km SE of Rouen
Arch F Hawtree

North East

Ammerschwihr

BP 19, Route des Trois Épis, 68770 Ammerschwihr
Tel **89 47 17 30**
Fax **89 47 17 77**
Holes 18 L 6235 m Par 72
9 hole short course
V'tors U
Fees 160fr (190fr)
Loc 8km W of Colmar. 60km N of Mulhouse
Arch Robert Berthet

Bâle G & CC (1928)

Rue de Wentzwiller, 68220 Hagenthal-le-Bas
Tel **89 68 50 91**
Fax **89 68 55 66**
Holes 18 L 6255 m SSS 73 Par 72
V'tors H
Fees 280fr (360fr)
Loc 15km SW of Basle
Arch B von Limburger

Besançon (1968)

La Chevillote, 25620 Mamirolle
Tel **81 55 73 54**
Fax **81 55 88 64**
Holes 18 L 6070 m SSS 72
V'tors H
Fees 180fr (240fr)
Loc 12km E of Besançon
Arch Michael Fenn

Bitche (1988)

Rue des Prés, 57230 Bitche
Tel **87 96 15 30**
Fax **87 96 08 04**
Holes 18 L 6082 m SSS 72
9 L 2293 m SSS 34
V'tors U
Fees 18 hole:170fr (250fr)
9 hole:120fr (150fr)
Loc 75km NW of Strasbourg. 55km SE of Saarbrücken
Arch Fromanger

Châlons-en-Champagne (1988)

La Grande Romanie, 51460 Courtisols
Tel **26 66 65 97**
Fax **26 66 66 81**
Holes 18 L 6578 m SSS 76
V'tors U
Fees D–200fr (D–250fr)
Loc 6km from A4/A26 Junction, nr Châlons-sur-Marne
Arch Alain Tribout

Château de Bournel (1990)

25680 Cubry
Tel **81 86 00 10**
Fax **81 86 01 06**
Holes 18 L 5985 m SSS 72
Fees 180fr (270fr)
Loc 50km NE of Besançon
Arch Robert Berthet

Épinal (1985)

Rue du Merle-Blanc, 88001 Épinal
Tel **29 34 65 97**
Holes 18 L 5700 m SSS 70
V'tors H
Fees 100fr
Loc Épinal, 70km S of Nancy
Arch Michel Gayon

Faulquemont-Pontpierre (1993)

Rue du Golf, 57380 Faulquemont
Tel **87 29 21 21**
Fax **87 90 76 25**
Holes 18 L 6000 m SSS 72
9 hole par 3 course
V'tors U
Fees 140fr (200fr)
Loc 30km E of Metz
Arch Flipo/Fourès

Forêt d'Orient
BP13 Rouilly-Sacey, 10220 Piney
Tel **25 46 37 78**
Holes 18 L 6120 m Par 72
V'tors U
Fees 150fr (200fr)
Loc 20km E of Troyes
Arch E Rossi

La Grange aux Ormes
La Grange aux Ormes, 57157 Marly
Tel **87 63 10 62**
Fax **87 55 01 77**
Holes 18 L 5051 m Par 67
V'tors U
Fees 230fr
Loc Metz 2km
Arch Philippe Gourdon

Kempferhof (1988)
Rue du Moulin, 67115 Plobsheim
Tel **88 98 72 72**
Fax **88 98 74 76**
Holes 18 L 6020 m SSS 72
V'tors H
Fees 300fr (400fr)
Loc 10km S of Strasbourg
Arch Robert von Hagge

La Largue G & CC (1988)
Chemin du Largweg, 68580 Mooslargue
Tel **89 07 67 67**
Fax **89 25 62 83**
Holes 18 L 6150 m SSS 72
V'tors WD–H WE–NA before noon H
Fees 220fr (320fr)
Loc 25km W of Basle
Arch Jean Garaialde

Metz-Cherisey (1963)
Château de Cherisey, 57420 Cherisey
Tel **87 52 70 18**
Fax **87 52 42 44**
Holes 18 L 6172 m SSS 73
V'tors H
Fees 170fr (240fr)
Loc 15km SE of Metz
Arch Donald Harradine

Nancy-Pulnoy (1993)
10 Rue du Golf, 54425 Pulnoy
Tel **83 18 10 18**
Fax **83 18 10 19**
Holes 18 L 6000 m SSS 72
9 hole Par 3 course
V'tors WD–U WE–H
Fees 140fr (200fr)
Loc 10km E of Nancy
Arch Hawtree/Flipo

Nancy-Aingeray (1962)
Aingeray, 54460 Liverdun
Tel **83 24 53 87**
Holes 18 L 5577 m SSS 69
V'tors H
Fees 200fr (250fr)
Loc 17km NW of Nancy
Arch Michael Fenn

Prunevelle (1930)
Ferme des Petits-Bans,
25420 Dampierre-sur-le-Doubs
Tel **81 98 11 77**
Fax **81 90 28 65**
Holes 18 L 6281 m SSS 73
Fees 200fr (250fr)
Loc 10km S of Montbéliard, on D126

Reims-Champagne (1928)
Château des Dames de France,
51390 Gueux
Tel **26 05 46 10**
Fax **26 05 46 19**
Holes 18 L 6026 m SSS 72
V'tors H
Fees 200fr (300fr)
Loc 10km W of Reims
Arch Michael Fenn

Rhin Mulhouse (1969)
Ile du Rhin, 68490 Chalampe
Tel **89 26 07 86**
Fax **89 26 27 80**
Holes 18 L 5991 m SSS 72
V'tors WE–M
Fees 220fr (330fr)
Loc 20km E of Mulhouse
Arch Donald Harradine

Rougemont-le-Château
Route de Masevaux, 90110 Rougemont-le-Château
Tel **84 23 74 74**
Fax **84 23 03 15**
Holes 18 L 6002 m SSS 72
V'tors U H
Fees 180fr (300fr)
Loc 18km NE of Belfort.
25km NW of Mulhouse
Arch Robert Berthet

Strasbourg (1934)
Route du Rhin, 67400 Illkirch
Tel **88 66 17 22**
Fax **88 65 05 67**
Holes 27 holes:
5983-6171 m SSS 71-73
V'tors WD–H
Fees WD only–220fr
Loc 10km S of Strasbourg
Arch Donald Harradine

Technopole de Metz
Rue Félix Savart, 57070 Metz
Tel **87 20 33 11**
Fax **87 76 34 05**
Holes 18 L 5774 m SSS 71
6 hole Par 3 course
V'tors H or Green card
Fees 170fr (190fr)
Loc SE of Metz centre
Arch Robert Berthet

Troyes-Cordelière (1957)
Château de la Cordelière,
10210 Chaource
Tel **25 40 18 76**
Fax **25 40 13 66**
Holes 18 L 6154 m SSS 72
V'tors H
Fees 180fr (250fr)
Loc NE of Chaource on N443.
30km SE of Troyes
Arch P Hirigoyen

Val de Sorne
Vernantois, 39570 Lons-le-Saunier
Tel **84 43 04 80**
Fax **84 47 31 21**
Holes 18 L 6000 m SSS 72
V'tors U
Fees 170–190fr (200–250fr)
Loc 4kms SE of Lons-le Saunier, between Geneva and Lyon
Arch Hugues Lambert

La Vitarderie (1986)
Chemin de Bourdonnerie, BP 41,
51700 Dormans
Tel **26 58 25 09**
Fax **26 59 33 88**
Holes 18 L 5969 m SSS 72
V'tors U
Fees 100fr (150fr)
Loc Dormans, 20km SW of Reims
Arch Olivier Brizon

Vittel
BP 122, 88804 Vittel-Cedex
Tel **29 08 18 80 (1 May–31 Oct)**
Holes St Jean 18 L 6326 m SSS 72
Peulin 18 L 6100 m SSS 72
9 hole course
Fees 200fr Sat–250fr Sun–200fr
Loc Vittel, 70km S of Nancy
Arch Allison/Morrison/Begin

La Wantzenau
C D 302, 67610 La Wantzenau
Tel **88 96 37 73**
Holes 18 L 6340 m SSS 73
V'tors H
Fees 220fr (300fr)
Loc 12km N of Strasbourg
Arch Pern/Garaialde

Paris Region

Béthemont-Chisan CC
12 Rue du Parc de Béthemont,
78300 Poissy
Tel **39 75 51 13**
Fax **39 75 49 90**
Holes 18 L 6035 m SSS 72
V'tors U
Fees 300fr (500fr)
Loc 30km W of Paris
Arch Bernhard Langer

La Boulie
La Boulie, 78000 Versailles
Tel **39 50 59 41**
Holes 18 L 6055 m SSS 71
18 L 6206 m SSS 72
9 hole course
V'tors H WE–M
Fees 430fr
Loc 15km SW of Paris

Eurodisney (1992)
1 Allee de la Mare Houleuse, 77400 Magny-le-Hongre
Tel **60 45 68 04**
Holes 18 L 6221 m Par 72
9 L 2905 m Par 36
V'tors U
Fees 295fr (325fr)
Loc 32km E of Paris via A4
Arch Ronald Fream

Fourqueux (1963)
Rue Saint Nom 36, 78112 Fourqueux
Tel **34 51 41 47**
Fax **39 21 00 70**
Holes 27 holes:
5615-6025 m Par 73-74
V'tors WD–U WE–M
Fees 350fr (390fr)
Loc 4km SW of St Germain-en-Laye, W of Paris

Isabella (1969)
RN12, Sainte-Appoline, 78370 Plaisir
Tel **30 54 10 62**
Fax **30 54 67 58**
Holes 18 L 5629 m SSS 71
V'tors WD–H WE–NA
Fees 250fr
Loc 28km W of Paris (RN12)
Arch Paul Rolin

Joyenval (1992)
Chemin de la Tuilerie, 78240 Chambourcy
Tel **39 22 27 50**
Fax **39 79 12 90**
Holes 36 hole course
V'tors M
Loc 12km N of Paris, nr St Germain-en-Laye
Arch Robert Trent Jones Sr

National Golf Club (1990)
2 Avenue du Golf, 78280 Guyancourt
Tel **30 43 36 00**
Fax **30 43 85 58**
Holes Albatros 18 L 6515 m Par 72
Aigle 18 L 5936 m Par 71
Oiselet 9 L 2100 m
V'tors Albatros–H
Fees 140–200fr (200–300fr)
Loc St Quentin-en-Yvelines, SW of Paris, beyond Versailles (D36)
Arch Hubert Chesneau

Le Prieuré (1965)
78440 Sailly
Tel **34 76 70 12**
Fax **34 76 71 62**
Holes Ouest 18 L 6274 m SSS 72
Est 18 L 6157 m SSS 72
V'tors WD–H
Fees 260fr
Loc Sailly, 10km NW of Meulan (D130). 45km NW of Paris
Arch F Hawtree

Rochefort
78730 Rochefort-en-Yvelines
Tel **30 41 31 81**
Fax **30 41 94 01**
Holes 18 L 5735 m SSS 71
Fees D–300fr (D–500fr)
Loc 45km SW of Paris
Arch Hawtree

St Cloud (1911)
60 Rue du 19 Janvier, Garches 92380
Tel **47 01 01 85**
Fax **47 01 19 57**
Holes 18 L 5980 m SSS 71
18 L 4857 m SSS 67
V'tors H
Fees 400fr Sat–500fr Sun–600fr
Loc Porte Dauphine, 9km W of Paris
Arch HS Colt

St Germain (1922)
Route de Poissy, 78100 St Germain-en-Laye
Tel **34 51 75 90**
Fax **34 51 23 42**
Holes 18 L 6117 m SSS 72
9 L 2030 m SSS 33
V'tors WD–H WE–M
Fees 400fr
Loc 20km W of Paris
Arch HS Colt

St Nom-La-Bretêche (1959)
Hameau Tuilerie-Bignon, 78860 St Nom-La-Bretèche
Tel **30 80 04 40**
Fax **34 62 60 44**
Holes 18 L 6685 yds SSS 72
18 L 6712 yds SSS 72
V'tors H
Fees WD only–485fr
Loc 24km W of Paris on A-13
Arch F Hawtree

St Quentin-en-Yvelines
RD 912, 78190 Trappes
Tel **30 50 86 40**
Holes 18 L 5900 m SSS 71
18 L 5753 m SSS 70
V'tors H
Fees 150fr (210fr)
Loc 20km SW of Paris
Arch Hubert Chesneau

Tremblay Golf Academy (1991)
78490 Le Tremblay-sur-Mauldre
Tel **34 87 81 09**
Fax **34 87 87 38**
Holes 9 L 3100 m SSS 72
9 hole short course
V'tors H
Fees 140fr (180fr)
Loc 35km W of Paris
Arch Robert Berthet

La Vaucouleurs (1987)
78910 Civry-la-Forêt
Tel **34 87 62 29**
Fax **34 87 70 09**
Holes Rivière 18 L 6298 m SSS 74
Vallons 18 L 5700 m SSS 70
V'tors U
Fees 200fr (350fr)
Loc 50km W of Paris, between Mantes and Houdan
Arch Michel Gayon

Les Yvelines
Château de la Couharde, 78940 La-Queue-les-Yvelines
Tel **34 86 48 89**
Holes 27 holes
V'tors U
Loc Montfort-l'Amaury, 45km W of Paris

Provence & Côte d'Azur

Aix Marseille (1935)
13290 Les Milles
Tel **42 24 40 41/42 24 23 01**
Holes 18 L 6291 m SSS 73
V'tors H
Fees D–220fr (D–300fr)
Loc 7km SW of Aix-en-Provence. 15km N of Marseille

Barbaroux (1989)
Route de Cabasse, 83170 Brignoles
Tel **94 59 07 43**
Fax **94 59 00 93**
Holes 18 L 6367 m SSS 72
V'tors U
Fees 260fr (290fr)
Loc Brignoles, 50km E of Aix. 40km N of Toulon
Arch PB Dye/PD Dye

Les Baux de Provence (1987)
Domaine de Manville, 13520 Les Baux-de-Provence
Tel **90 54 37 02**
Fax **90 54 40 93**
Holes 9 L 2812 m SSS 36
V'tors U H
Fees D–160fr (D–210fr)
9 holes–100fr (150fr)

Loc 15km NE of Arles. 15km S of Avignon. 80km W of Marseilles
Arch Martin Hawtree

Beauvallon-Grimaud

Boulevard des Collines, 83120 Sainte-Maxime
Tel **94 96 16 98**
Holes 9 L 2503 m SSS 34
V'tors H
Fees 200–240fr
Loc 3km SW of Sainte Maxime

Biot (1930)

La Bastide du Roi, 06410 Biot
Tel **93 65 08 48**
Holes 18 L 5064 m SSS 70
V'tors U
Fees 230fr (250fr)
Loc Antibes 5km. Nice 15km

Cannes-Mandelieu (1891)

Route de Golf, 06210 Mandelieu
Tel **93 49 55 39**
Fax **93 49 92 90**
Holes 18 L 5871 m SSS 71
9 L 2852 m SSS 34
V'tors U
Fees 260fr (300fr)
Loc Mandelieu, 7km W of Cannes

Cannes-Mougins (1925)

175 Route d'Antibes, 06250 Mougins
Tel **93 75 79 13**
Fax **93 75 27 60**
Holes 18 L 6304 m SSS 72
V'tors H
Fees 320fr (360fr)
Loc 8km NE of Cannes (D35)
Arch Colt/Simpson (1925). Alliss/Thomas (1977)

Château L'Arc (1985)

Domaine de Château L'Arc, 13710 Fuveau
Tel **42 53 28 38**
Fax **42 29 08 41**
Holes 18 L 6300 m SSS 72
V'tors H
Fees 210fr (240fr)
Loc 15km SE of Aix-en-Provence
Arch Michel Gayon

Châteaublanc

Les Plans, 84310 Morières-les-Avignon
Tel **90 33 39 08**
Fax **90 33 43 24**
Holes 18 L 6141 m SSS 72
9 hole Par 3 course
V'tors H
Fees 170fr (200fr)
Loc 5km SE of Avignon, nr Airport
Arch Sprecher/Watine

Digne-les-Bains (1990)

St Pierre de Gaubert, 0400 Digne-les-Bains
Tel **92 30 58 00**
Fax **92 30 58 39**
Holes 18 L 5861 m SSS 72
V'tors U
Fees 140–200fr
Loc 100km NE of Aix-en-Provence
Arch Robert Berthet

Estérel Latitudes (1989)

Ave du Golf, 83700 St Raphaël
Tel **94 82 47 88**
Fax **94 44 64 61**
Holes 18 L 5921 m SSS 71
9 L 1392 m Par 29
Fees 260fr (290fr)
Loc 2km N of St-Raphaël
Arch Robert Trent Jones

Frégate (1992)

Domaine de Frégate, RD 559, 83270 St Cyr-sur-Mer
Tel **94 32 50 50**
Fax **94 29 96 94**
Holes 18 L 6210 m SSS 72
9 hole short course
V'tors U H
Fees 240fr (270fr)
Loc 25km W of Toulon on coast
Arch Ronald Fream

Gap-Bayard (1988)

Centre d'Oxygénation, 05000 Gap
Tel **92 50 16 83**
Fax **92 50 17 05**
Holes 18 L 6023 m SSS 72
V'tors U
Fees 160fr (190fr)
Loc 7km N of Gap. 80km S of Grenoble
Arch Hugues Lambert

Grand Avignon (1989)

BP 121, Les Chênes Verts, 84270 Vedene
Tel **90 31 49 94**
Fax **90 31 01 21**
Holes 18 L 6046 m SSS 69
9 hole short course
V'tors U
Fees 200–230fr
Loc Vedene, 5km NE of Avignon
Arch G Roumeas

La Grande Bastide (1990)

Chemin des Picholines, 06740 Châteauneuf de Grasse
Tel **93 77 70 08**
Fax **93 77 72 36**
Holes 18 L 6105 m SSS 72
V'tors U H
Fees 240fr (270fr)
Loc Grasse, 17km N of Cannes
Arch Cabell Robinson

Grasse CC (1992)

1 Route des Trois Ponts, 06130 Grasse
Tel **93 60 55 44**
Fax **93 60 55 19**
Holes 18 L 6021 m SSS 72
V'tors U
Fees 220fr (260fr)
Loc 18km N of Cannes
Arch JP Fourès

Le Lavandou

2 Ave du Cap Nègre, Cavalière, 83980 Le Lavandou
Tel **94 05 75 80**
Holes 18 L 5649 m Par 72
V'tors U
Fees 250–350fr
Loc 50km E of Toulon, between Hyères and St Tropez
Arch Yves Bureau

Monte Carlo (1910)

Route du Mont-Agel, 06320 La Turbie
Tel **93 41 09 11**
Fax **93 41 09 55**
Holes 18 L 5679 m SSS 71
V'tors H
Fees 350fr (450fr)
Loc Mont Agel, La Turbie, 10km N of Monte Carlo

Opio-Valbonne (1966)

Château de la Begude, 06560 Valbonne
Tel **93 12 00 08**
Fax **93 12 26 00**
Holes 18 L 5892 m SSS 72
V'tors H
Fees 300fr (330fr)
Loc 10km N of Cannes
Arch Donald Harradine

Pierrevert (1986)

Domaine de la Grande-Gardette, 04860 Pierrevert
Tel **92 72 17 19**
Fax **92 72 59 12**
Holes 18 L 6040 m SSS 72
V'tors U
Fees 160fr (220fr)
Loc 4km NW of Manosque. 45km NE of Aix

Pont Royal (1992)

Pont Royal, 13370 Mallemort
Tel **90 57 40 79**
Fax **90 59 45 83**
Holes 18 L 6307 m SSS 74
V'tors H
Fees 220–260fr
Loc 40km SE of Avignon on N7
Arch Severiano Ballesteros

Provence G & CC (1991)

Route de Fontaine de Vaucluse, L'Isle sur la Sorgue, 84800 Saumane
Tel **90 20 20 65**
Fax **90 20 32 01**
Holes 18 L 6045 m SSS 72
9 hole short course

For list of abbreviations see page 435

V'tors U
Fees 200fr (240fr)
Loc 20km E of Avignon
Arch Jean Garaialde

Riviera Golf
Avenue des Amazones, 06210 Mandelieu
Tel **92 97 67 67**
Holes 18 L 5736 m SSS 72
V'tors H–max 24 (men) 28 (ladies)
Fees 250fr (350fr)
Loc 10km SW of Cannes, off A8
Arch Robert Trent Jones

Roquebrune (1989)
CD 7, 83520 Roquebrune-sur-Argens
Tel **94 82 92 91**
Fax **94 82 94 74**
Holes 18 L 6031 m SSS 71
V'tors H
Fees 220fr (240fr)
Loc 35km N of Saint-Tropez. 40km SW of Cannes
Arch Udo Barth

Royal Mougins (1993)
424 Avenue du Roi, 06250 Mougins
Tel **92 92 49 69**
Fax **92 92 49 70**
Holes 18 L 6004 m SSS 72
V'tors H or I
Fees 320fr (400fr)
Loc 5km N of Cannes
Arch Robert von Hagge

La Sainte-Baume (1988)
83860 Nans-les-Pins
Tel **94 78 60 12**
Fax **94 78 63 52**
Holes 18 L 6134 m SSS 72
V'tors WD–U WE–H
Fees 180fr (250fr)
Loc 30km S of Aix-en-Provence, via A7 (exit Saint Maximin)
Arch Robert Berthet

Sainte-Maxime
Route de Débarquement, 83120 Sainte-Maxime
Tel **94 49 26 60**
Fax **94 49 00 39**
Holes 18 L 6200 m SSS 71
V'tors H
Fees 240fr
Loc 80km W of Nice (RN98)
Arch Donald Harradine

La Salette (1989)
Impasse des Vaudrans, 13011 Marseille
Tel **91 27 12 16**
Fax **91 27 21 33**
Holes 18 L 5824 m SSS 71
V'tors U
Fees 220fr (280fr)
Loc Nr centre of Marseilles
Arch Michel Gayon

Servanes (1989)
Domaine de Servanes, 13890 Mouriès
Tel **90 47 59 95**
Fax **90 47 52 58**
Holes 18 L 6100m SSS 72
V'tors H
Fees 180fr (250fr)
Loc 35km S of Avignon
Arch Sprecher/Watine

St Endreol (1992)
Route de Bagnols-en-Fôret, 83920 La Motte
Tel **94 99 22 99**
Fax **94 99 23 99**
Holes 18 L 6219 m SSS 73
V'tors U
Fees 270fr (290fr)
Loc 30km N of St Tropez. 30km W of Cannes
Arch Michel Gayon

Taulane
Domaine du Château de Taulane, RN 85, 83840 La Martre
Tel **93 60 31 30**
Fax **93 60 33 23**
Holes 18 L 6250 m Par 72
V'tors H
Fees 250–400fr (350–500fr)
Loc 55km N of Cannes on N85
Arch Gary Player

Valcros (1964)
Domaine de Valcros, 83250 La Lande-les-Maures
Tel **94 66 81 02**
Holes 18 L 5184 m SSS 68
V'tors H
Fees 200fr (250fr)
Loc 10km W of Le Lavandou
Arch F Hawtree

Valescure (1895)
BP 451, 83704 St-Raphaël Cedex
Tel **94 82 40 46**
Fax **94 82 41 42**
Holes 18 L 5067 m Par 68
V'tors U H
Fees 240fr (270fr)
Loc 5km E of St-Raphaël
Arch Lord Ashcombe

Vievola (1978)
06430 Tende
Tel **93 04 61 02**
Fax **93 04 73 89**
Holes 9 L 2004 m SSS 62
V'tors U
Fees 120fr (150fr)
Loc 4km from Italian border (RN 204). 40km N of Monte Carlo

Rhône-Alps

Aix-les-Bains (1913)
Avenue du Golf, 73100 Aix-les-Bains
Tel **79 61 23 35**
Fax **79 34 06 01**
Holes 18 L 5597 m SSS 71
V'tors H
Fees 200fr (300fr)
Loc 3km S of Aix

Albon (1989)
Domaine de Senaud, Albon, 26140 St Rambert d'Albon
Tel **75 03 18 76/75 03 03 90**
Fax **75 03 11 01**
Holes 18 L 6108 m Par 72
V'tors U
Fees 150fr
Loc 60km S of Lyon, motorway exit Chanas
Arch Antoine d'Ormesson

Annecy (1953)
Echarvines, 74290 Talloires
Tel **50 60 12 89**
Fax **50 60 08 80**
Holes 18 L 5017 m SSS 68
V'tors H
Fees 200–250fr
Loc 13km E of Annecy
Arch Cecil Blandford

Annonay-Gourdan (1988)
Domaine de Gourdan, 07430 Saint Clair
Tel **75 67 03 84**
Fax **75 67 79 50**
Holes 18 L 5900 m SSS 71
V'tors U
Fees 180fr (250fr)
Loc 35km SE of St Etienne. 50km SW of Lyon
Arch Sprecher/Watine

Les Arcs
Arc 1800, 73700 Bourg-St-Maurice
Tel **79 07 43 95**
Fax **79 07 47 65**
Holes 18 L 5513 m SSS 69
V'tors H
Fees 150–200fr
Loc 90km E of Chambery on N90

Le Beaujolais (1991)
69480 Lucenay-Anse
Tel **74 67 04 44**
Fax **74 67 09 60**
Holes 18 L 6137 m SSS 72
V'tors U H
Fees 190fr (260fr)
Loc 25km N of Lyon

Bossey G & CC (1985)
Château de Crevin, 74160 Bossey
Tel **50 43 75 25**
Fax **50 95 32 57**
Holes 18 L 6022 m Par 71

V'tors WD–U WE–NA
Fees 300fr
Loc 6km S of Geneva
Arch Robert Trent Jones Jr

La Bresse

Domaine de Mary, 01400 Condessiat
Tel **74 51 42 09**
Fax **74 51 40 09**
Holes 18 L 6217 m Par 72
V'tors WD–U WE–H
Fees 200fr (250fr)
Loc 15km SW of Bourg-en-Bresse, via RN83
Arch Jeremy Pern

Chamonix (1934)

BP 31, 74402 Chamonix Cedex
Tel **50 53 06 28**
Fax **50 53 38 69**
Holes 18 L 6087 m SSS 72
V'tors H
Fees 200–300fr
Loc 3km N of Chamonix (RN 506). Geneva 80km
Arch Robert Trent Jones Sr

Le Clou (1985)

01330 Villars-les-Dombes
Tel **74 98 19 65**
Fax **74 98 15 15**
Holes 18 L 5000 m SSS 67
V'tors WD–U WE–H
Fees D–160fr (D–200fr)
Loc 30km NE of Lyon

La Commanderie (1964)

L'Aumusse-Crottet, 01290 Pont-de-Veyle
Tel **85 30 44 12**
Fax **85 30 55 02**
Holes 18 L 5560 m SSS 69
V'tors H
Fees 150fr (200fr)
Loc 7km E of Mâcon on RN 79

Corrençon-en-Vercors (1987)

Les Ritons, 38250 Corrençon-en-Vercors
Tel **76 95 80 42**
Fax **76 95 84 63**
Holes 18 L 5550 m Par 71
V'tors U
Fees 150–200fr (180–250fr)
Loc 35km S of Grenoble, off D531
Arch Hugues Lambert

Divonne (1931)

01220 Divonne-les-Bains
Tel **50 40 34 11**
Fax **50 40 34 25**
Holes 18 L 6035 m SSS 72
V'tors H–max 35
Fees 250fr (500fr)
Loc Divonne ½km. 18km N of Geneva
Arch Nakowsky

La Dombes (1986)

01390 Mionnay
Tel **78 91 84 84**
Fax **78 91 02 73**
Holes 18 L 6060 m SSS 71
V'tors U
Fees 180fr (250fr)
Loc 20km N of Lyon towards Bourg

Esery (1990)

Esery, 74930 Reignier
Tel **50 36 58 70**
Fax **50 36 57 62**
Holes 18 L 6350 m SSS 73
9 L 2024 m SSS 31
V'tors WD–H WE–NA
Fees 280fr
Loc 10km S of Geneva
Arch Michel Gayon

Flaine-Les-Carroz (1984)

74300 Flaine
Tel **50 90 85 44**
Fax **50 90 88 21**
Holes 18 L 3693 m Par 63
V'tors U
Fees 140fr
Loc 4km N of Flaine. 60km SE of Geneva Airport
Arch Robert Berthet

Giez (1991)

Lac d'Annecy, 74210 Giez
Tel **50 44 48 41**
Fax **50 32 55 93**
Holes 18 holes SSS 71
9 holes SSS 66
V'tors U
Fees 190–240fr (240fr)
Loc 20km SE of Annecy
Arch Didier Fruchet

Le Gouverneur

Château du Breuil, 01390 Monthieux
Tel **72 26 40 34**
Holes 18 L 6477 m Par 72
18 L 5959 m Par 72
9 L 2365 m Par 34
Loc NE of Lyon, off A46

Grenoble-Bresson (1990)

Route de Montavie, 38320 Eybens
Tel **76 73 65 00**
Fax **76 73 65 51**
Holes 18 L 6343 m SSS 72
V'tors U
Fees 220fr (250–320fr)
Loc 10km SE of Grenoble
Arch Robert Trent Jones Jr

Grenoble-Uriage (1983)

Les Alberges, 38410 Uriage
Tel **76 89 03 47**
Holes 9 L 2500 m SSS 32
V'tors U
Fees 140fr (170–180fr)
Loc 15km E of Grenoble
Arch Watine/Sprecher

Lyon (1921)

38280 Villette-d'Anthon
Tel **78 31 11 33**
Fax **72 02 48 27**
Holes 18 L 6415 m SSS 72
18 L 6570 m SSS 72
V'tors U H
Fees 200fr (300fr)
Loc 20km E of Lyon
Arch Fenn/Lambert

Lyon-Chassieu

Route de Lyon, 69680 Chassieu
Tel **78 90 84 77**
Fax **78 90 88 85**
Holes 18 L 5941 m Par 70
V'tors H
Fees 160fr (220fr)
Loc 10km E of Lyon
Arch Chris Pittman

Lyon-Verger (1977)

69360 Saint-Symphorien D'Ozon
Tel **78 02 84 20**
Fax **78 02 08 12**
Holes 18 L 5800 m SSS 69
Fees 180fr (250fr)
Loc 14km S of Lyon on A7, or RN7 2km S of Feyzin

Maison Blanche G & CC (1991)

01170 Echenevex
Tel **50 42 44 42**
Fax **50 42 44 43**
Holes 18 L 6246 m SSS 72
9 L 1757 m Par 31
V'tors WD–U H
Fees 300fr (1994)
Loc 15km from Geneva
Arch Harradine/Dongradi

Méribel (1973)

BP 54, 73553 Méribel Cedex
Tel **79 00 52 67**
Holes 18 L 5319 m SSS 70
V'tors H
Fees 150–270fr
Loc 15km S of Moutiers. 35km S of Albertville
Arch Sprecher/Watine

Mont-d'Arbois (1964)

74120 Megève
Tel **50 21 29 79**
Fax **50 93 02 63**
Holes 18 L 6130 m SSS 72
V'tors WE–restricted. Booking required Jul/Aug
Fees 200–300fr
Loc 3km SE of Megève
Arch Henry Cotton

Royal Golf Club (1904)

Rive Sud du lac de Genève, 74500 Évian
Tel **50 26 85 00**
Fax **50 75 65 54**
Holes 18 L 6006 m SSS 72

V'tors U
Fees D–190–310fr (D–290–380fr)
Loc 2km W of Évian. 40km NE of Geneva Airport
Arch Cabell Robinson

Salvagny
100 Rue des Granges, 69890 La Tour de Salvagny
Tel **78 48 83 60**
Fax **78 48 00 16**
Holes 18 L 6300 m SSS 73 Par 72
V'tors U
Fees 200fr (290fr)
Loc Lyon 20km
Arch Drancourt

La Sorelle (1991)
Domaine de Gravagnieux, 01320 Villette-sur-Ain
Tel **74 35 47 27**
Fax **74 35 44 51**
Holes 18 L 6100 m SSS 72
V'tors U
Fees 140fr (190fr)
Loc 50km NE of Lyon
Arch Patrick Jacquier

St Quentin-Charmeil
38210 St Quentin-sur-Isère
Tel **76 93 67 28**
Fax **76 93 62 04**
Holes 18 L 6200 m Par 73
V'tors U
Fees 180fr (240fr)
Loc 30km NW of Grenoble, off A49
Arch Perl/Garaialde

Tignes (1968)
Val Claret, 73320 Tignes
Tel **79 06 37 42 (Summer)**
Fax **79 06 35 64**
Holes 18 L 4785 m SSS 68
V'tors H–max 35
Fees 200fr
Loc 50km E of Moutiers, off D902, nr Italian border. 70km S of Chamonix

Valdaine (1989)
Domaine de la Valdaine, Montboucher/Jabron, 26740 Montelimar-Montboucher
Tel **75 01 86 66**
Fax **75 01 24 49**
Holes 18 L 5631 m SSS 71
V'tors U
Fees 180fr (260fr)
Loc 4km E of Montelimar. 50km S of Valence
Arch TJ Macauley

Valence St Didier (1983)
26300 St Didier de Charpey
Tel **75 59 67 01**
Fax **75 59 68 19**
Holes 18 L 5807 m SSS 71
V'tors U
Fees 180fr (250fr)
Loc 12km E of Valence
Arch T Sprecher

Toulouse & Pyrenees

Albi Lasbordes (1989)
Château de Lasbordes, 81000 Albi
Tel **63 54 98 07**
Fax **63 47 21 55**
Holes 18 L 6200 m SSS 72
V'tors U
Fees 160fr (220fr)
Loc 80km NE of Toulouse
Arch Garaialde/Pern

Ariège (1986)
09240 La Bastide-de-Serou
Tel **61 64 56 78**
Fax **61 64 57 99**
Holes 18 L 6000 m SSS 71
V'tors H
Fees 120fr (170fr)
Loc Unjat, 17km NW of Foix
Arch Michel Gayon

La Bigorre (1992)
Pouzac, 65200 Bagnères de Bigorre
Tel **62 91 06 20**
Holes 18 L 5909 m SSS 72
V'tors U
Fees 150fr
Loc 18km S of Tarbes. 150km W of Toulouse
Arch Olivier Brizon

Château de Terrides (1986)
Domaine de Terrides, 82100 Labourgade
Tel **63 95 61 07**
Fax **63 95 64 97**
Holes 18 L 6420 m SSS 71
V'tors U
Fees 150fr (200fr)
Loc 45km NW of Toulouse
Arch J-P Foures

Embats
Route de Montesquiou, 32000 Auch
Tel **62 05 20 80**
Fax **62 05 92 55**
Holes 18 L 4751 m SSS 65
V'tors U
Fees 130fr (150fr)
Loc 4km W of Auch. 80km W of Toulouse

Étangs de Fiac (1989)
Brazis, 81500 Fiac
Tel **63 70 64 70**
Holes 18 L 5800 m SSS 71
V'tors U
Fees 150fr (200fr)
Loc 40km NE of Toulouse
Arch M Hawtree

Guinlet (1986)
32800 Eauze
Tel **62 09 80 84**
Fax **62 09 84 50**
Holes 18 L 5565 m Par 71
V'tors U
Fees 150fr (180fr)
Loc 60km SW of Agen. 150km SE of Bordeaux
Arch M Thevenin

Lannemezan
La Demi-Lune, 65300 Lannemezan
Tel **62 98 01 01**
Holes 18 L 5872 m Par 70
V'tors H
Fees 150–190fr (180–210fr)
Loc 38km SE of Tarbes
Arch Hirigoyen/Laserre

Lourdes
Lac de Lourdes, 65100 Lourdes
Tel **62 42 02 06**
Holes 18 L 5675 m SSS 72
V'tors U
Fees 160fr (180fr)
Loc 4km W of Lourdes
Arch Olivier Brizon

Luchon (1908)
BP 40, 31110 Bagnères de Luchon
Tel **61 79 03 27**
Holes 9 L 2375 m SSS 66
V'tors H
Fees 130fr (170fr)
Loc Luchon, 90km SE of Tarbes. 145km S of Toulouse
Arch Fenn/Hawtree

Mazamet-La Barouge (1956)
81660 Pont de l'Arn
Tel **63 61 08 00/63 67 06 72**
Fax **63 61 13 03**
Holes 18 L 5623 m SSS 70
V'tors U
Fees 160fr (220fr)
Loc 2km N of Mazamet. 80km E of Toulouse. 80km W of Béziers
Arch Mackenzie Ross/Hawtree

Tilbury (1990)
Le Bosc, Florentin, 81150 Marssac-sur-Tarn
Tel **63 55 20 50**
Holes 18 L 6100 m SSS 71
V'tors U
Fees 150fr (200fr)
Loc 10km W of Albi. 70km NE of Toulouse
Arch Robert Berthet

Toulouse (1951)
31320 Vieille-Toulouse
Tel **61 73 45 48**
Holes 18 L 5602 m SSS 69
V'tors U

Fees 180fr (250fr)
Loc 8km S of Toulouse
Arch Hawtree

Toulouse-La Ramée
Ferme Cousturier, 31170 Tournefeuille
Tel **61 07 09 09**
Fax **61 07 15 93**
Holes 18 L 5605 m SSS 69
9 hole short course
V'tors H
Fees 120fr (150fr)
Loc SW of Toulouse
Arch Hawtree

Toulouse-Palmola (1974)
Route d'Albi, 31660 Buzet-sur-Tarn
Tel **61 84 20 50**
Fax **61 84 48 92**
Holes 18 L 6156 m SSS 73
Fees 210fr (250–350fr)
Loc 20km NE of Toulouse. A68 Junction 4
Arch Michael Fenn

Toulouse-Seilh
Route de Grenade, 31840 Seilh
Tel **61 42 59 30**
Fax **61 42 34 17**
Holes Red 18 L 6122 m SSS 72
Yellow 18 L 4202 m SSS 64
V'tors H
Fees 150–200fr (200–250fr)
Loc 15km N of Toulouse. Blagnac Airport 5km
Arch Jean Garaialde

Toulouse-Teoula
71 Avenue des Landes, 31830 Plaisance du Touch
Tel **61 91 98 80**
Fax **61 91 49 66**
Holes 18 L 5500 m Par 69
V'tors U
Fees 150fr (200fr)
Loc 15km W of Toulouse
Arch Hawtree

Les Tumulus
1 Rue du Bois, 65310 Laloubère
Tel **62 45 14 50**
Holes 18 L 5050 m Par 70
V'tors U
Fees 150fr (200fr)
Loc 5km S of Tarbes, towards Bagnères
Arch Charles de Ginestet

Germany

Aachen & Saar

Aachen (1927)
Schürzelter Str 300, 52074 Aachen
Tel **(0241) 12501**
Fax **(0241) 171075**
Holes 18 L 6063 m Par 72
V'tors H
Fees D–50DM (D–70DM)
Loc Seffent, 5km NW of Aachen
Arch Murray/Morrison/Pennink

Eifel (1977)
Kölner Str, 54576 Hillesheim
Tel **(06593) 1241**
Fax **(06593) 9421**
Holes 18 L 6017 m Par 72
V'tors H–phone before play
Fees 60DM (80DM)
Loc 70km S of Cologne
Arch Grohs/Preismann

Haus Kambach (1989)
Kambachstrasse 9-15, 52249 Eschweiler-kinzweiler
Tel **(02403) 37615**
Fax **(02403) 21270**
Holes 18 L 6178 m SSS 72
V'tors U
Fees 40DM (50DM)
Loc 20km NE of Aachen

Nahetal (1970)
Drei Buchen, 55583 Bad Münster am Stein
Tel **(06708) 2145/3755**
Fax **(06708) 1731**
Holes 18 L 6065 m SSS 72
V'tors H
Fees 60DM (80DM)
Loc 6km S of Bad Kreuznach. 70km SW of Frankfurt
Arch Armin Keller

Pfalz Neustadt (1971)
Weinstrasse, 67435 Neustadt
Tel **(06327) 97420**
Fax **(06327) 974218**
Holes 18 L 6180 m SSS 72
V'tors U H WE–NA before 3pm
Fees 60DM (90DM)
Loc Geinsheim, 15km SE of Neustadt towards Speyer

Saarbrücken (1961)
Oberlimbergerweg, 66798 Wallerfangen-Gisingen
Tel **(06837) 401**
Fax **(06837) 1584**
Holes 18 L 6231 m SSS 73
V'tors H
Fees 65DM (90DM)
Loc B406 towards Wallerfangen. 8km N of Saarlouis
Arch Donald Harradine

Websweiler Hof (1991)
Websweiler Hof, 66424 Homburg
Tel **(06841) 71111**
Fax **(06841) 755555**
Holes 18 L 6425 m SSS 74
V'tors U
Fees 55DM (65DM)
Loc 35km E of Saarbrücken

Westpfalz Schwarzbachtal
Gartenstr 2, 66509 Rieschweiler-Mühlbach
Tel **(06336) 1666**
Fax **(06336) 5644**
Holes 18 L 5740 m SSS 70
Fees 50DM (70DM)
Loc 40km E of Saarbrücken

Woodlawn
6792 Ramstein Flugplatz
Tel **(06371) 476240**
Fax **(06371) 42158**
Holes 18 L 6225 yds Par 70
V'tors Military GC–visitors restricted
Fees $12 ($15)
Loc Ramstein 3km. Kaiserlautern 10km

Berlin

Berlin am Schäferberg
Am Wildgatter 47, 14109 Berlin
Tel **(030) 805 2328**
Fax **(030) 805 2328**
Holes 18 L 5689 m SSS 70
V'tors WE–M H–booking required
Fees $60
Loc SW Berlin. Motorway exit Wannsee , towards Glienicker Brücke

Berlin G & CC (1924)
Golfweg 22, 14109 Berlin, US Forces Europe
Tel **819 6533**
Fax **805 5534**
Holes 18 L 6350 yds Par 70
V'tors WD–H WE–M
Fees $40 ($50)
Loc Wannsee District (Berlin)
Arch Percy Alliss

Berlin Wannsee (1895)
Am Stölpchenweg, 14109 Berlin
Tel **805 5075**
Fax **805 5631**
Holes 9 L 5690 m SSS 70
V'tors WD–U H WE–M
Fees 60DM (80DM)
Loc 17km SW of Berlin

Berliner GC Gatow (1990)
Kladower Damm 182-288, Flugplatz Gatow, 14089 Berlin
Tel **(030) 365 76 60**
Fax **(030) 365 76 60**
Holes 9 L 5687 m SSS 70

V'tors H
Fees 40DM (50DM)
Loc 16km from Berlin

Motzener See G & CC (1991)

Bestenseer Strasse, 15741 Motzen
Tel **(033769) 50130**
Fax **(033769) 50134**
Holes 18 L 6330 m SSS 73
9 L 2756 m SSS 54
V'tors H–booking required
Fees 80DM
Loc 30km S of Berlin
Arch Kurt Rossknecht

Semlin am See (1992)

Ferchesarerstrasse, 14715 Semlin
Tel **(03385) 503685**
Fax **(03385) 503680**
Holes 18 L 6348 M SSS 73
V'tors H
Fees 50DM (70DM)
Loc 80km W of Berlin (B5/B188)
Arch Christoph Städler

Bremen & North West

Club Zur Vahr (1905)

Bgm-Spitta-Allee 34, 28329 Bremen
Tel **Bremen (0421) 230041, Garlstedt (04795) 417**
Fax **(0421) 244 9248**
Holes Garlstedt 18 L 6430 m SSS 75;
Bremen 9 L 5862 m SSS 71
V'tors WD–H WE–M
Fees Garlstedt–60DM (70DM)
Bremen–40DM (50DM)
Loc Garlstedt-15km N of Bremen. Vahr-E Bremen

Küsten GC Hohe Klint (1978)

Hohe Klint, 27478 Cuxhaven
Tel **(04723) 2737**
Fax **(04723) 5022**
Holes 18 L 6150 m SSS 72
V'tors U H
Fees 40DM (60DM)
Loc 12km SW of Cuxhaven on Route 6, nr Oxstedt

Münster-Wilkinghege (1963)

Steinfurterstr 448, 48159 Münster
Tel **(0251) 211201**
Fax **(0251) 261518**
Holes 18 L 5955 m SSS 71
V'tors WD–H WE–I
Fees 50DM (70DM)
Loc 2km N of Münster

Oldenburgischer (1964)

Am Golfplatz 1, 26180 Rastede
Tel **(04402) 7240**
Fax **(04402) 70417**
Holes 18 L 6087 m SSS 72
Fees 50DM (60DM)
Loc 10km N of Oldenburg, nr Rastede

Osnabrück (1955)

Karmannstr 1, 49084 Osnabrück
Tel **(05402) 5636**
Fax **(05402) 5257**
Holes 18 L 5881 m Par 71
V'tors U
Fees 60DM (70DM)
Loc 13km SE of Osnabrück

Ostfriesland (1980)

Postbox 1220, 26634 Wiesmoor
Tel **(04944) 3040**
Fax **(04944) 30477**
Holes 18 L 6256 m SSS 73
V'tors U
Fees 50DM (60DM)
Loc 25km SW of Wilhelmshaven
Arch Frank Pennink

RAF Gütersloh

RAF Gütersloh, BFPO 47
Tel **(05241) 842409**
Holes 9 L 5761 yds SSS 68
Loc 5km W of Gütersloh

Senne GC Gut Welschof

Augustdorferstr 70, 33758 Schloss Holte-Stukenbrock
Tel **(05207) 88738**
Fax **(05207) 88788**
Holes 18 L 6246 m SSS 72
V'tors U H
Fees 50DM (70DM)
Loc 25km N of Paderborn
Arch Christoph Städler

Soltau (1982)

Hof Loh, 29614 Soltau
Tel **(05191) 14077**
Fax **(05191) 2593**
Holes 18 L 6274 m SSS 73
9 L 2340 m SSS 54
V'tors H
Fees 50DM (60DM)
Loc Tetendorf, S of Soltau

Syke (1989)

Schultenweg 1, 28857 Syke-Okel
Tel **(04242) 8230**
Fax **(04242) 8255**
Holes 18 L 6287 m Par 73
V'tors U H
Fees 50DM (60DM)
Loc 20km S of Bremen

Westfälischer Gütersloh

Gütersloher Str 127, 33397 Rietberg
Tel **(05244) 2340/10528**
Fax **(05244) 1388**
Holes 18 L 6135 m SSS 72
Fees 50DM (70DM)
Loc 8km SE of Gütersloh, nr Neuenkirchen

Central

Bad Kissingen (1911)

Euerdorferstr 11, 97688 Bad Kissingen
Tel **(0971) 3608**
Fax **(0971) 60140**
Holes 18 L 5675 m SSS 70
V'tors U H
Fees 50DM (60DM)
Loc Bad Kissingen 2km. 65km N of Würzburg

Dillenburg

Am Altscheid, 35687 Dillenburg
Tel **(02771) 5001**
Fax **(02771) 5002**
Holes 18 hole course Par 72
V'tors U H
Fees 50DM (70DM)
Loc 30km S ofSiegen

Frankfurter (1913)

Golfstrasse 41, 60528 Frankfurt/Main
Tel **(069) 666 2318**
Fax **(069) 666 7018**
Holes 18 L 6455 yds SSS 71
Fees D–75DM (95DM)
Loc 6km SW of Frankfurt, nr Airport

Hanau-Wilhelmsbad (1959)

Wilhelmsbader Allee 32, 63454 Hanau
Tel **(06181) 82071**
Fax **(06181) 86967**
Holes 18 L 6192 m Par 72
V'tors WD–H WE–M H
Fees 80DM (100DM)
Loc 4km NW of Hanau on B8-40/AB66. Frankfurt 15km
Arch Ernst Kothe

Heidelberg-Lobenfeld (1968)

Biddersbacherhof, 74931 Lobbach-Lobenfeld
Tel **(06226) 40490/41615**
Fax **(06226) 42464**
Holes 18 L 6215 m SSS 72
V'tors WD–H WE–M H
Fees 50DM (70DM)
Loc 30km E of Heidelberg
Arch Donald Harradine

Hofgut Kolnhausen (1992)

35423 Lich
Tel **(06404) 91071**
Fax **(06404) 91072**
Holes 18 L 6065m SSS 72
V'tors H–booking necessary

Fees 80DM (100DM)
Loc 45km N of Frankfurt
Arch Heinz Fehring

Homburg (1899)

Saalburgchaussee 2, 61350 Bad Homburg
Tel **(06172) 38808**
Fax **(06172) 32648**
Holes 10 holes SSS 69
V'tors H
Fees 50DM (70DM)
Loc On B456 to Usingen

Idstein-Wörsdorf (1989)

Gut Henriettehntal, 65510 Idstein-Wörsdorf
Tel **(06126) 9322-0**
Fax **(06126) 9322-22**
Holes 18 L 6165 m SSS 72
V'tors I H
Fees 60DM (80DM)
Loc 25km N of Wiesbaden
Arch Kurt Rossknecht

Kronberg G & LC (1954)

Schloss Friedrichshof, Hainstr 25, 61476 Kronberg/Taunus
Tel **(06173) 1426**
Fax **(06173) 5953**
Holes 18 L 5183 m SSS 68
V'tors WD–U H WE–M H
Fees 70DM (90DM)
Loc 16km NW of Frankfurt
Arch Ernst Kothe

Kurhessischer GC Oberaula (1987)

Postfach 31, 36278 Oberaula
Tel **(06628) 1573**
Fax **(06628) 1573**
Holes 18 L 6050 m SSS 72
V'tors U H
Fees D–50DM (D–70DM)
Loc 50km S of Kassel, nr Kircheim
Arch Deutsche Golf Consult

Main-Taunus (1979)

Lange Seegewann 2, 65205 Wiesbaden
Tel **(06122) 52550/52208(Sec)**
Holes 18 L 6045 m SSS 72
V'tors H
Loc 15km NW of Frankfurt Airport

Mannheim-Viernheim (1930)

Alte Mannheimer Str 3, 68519 Viernheim
Tel **(06204) 71313 (Clubhouse), (06204) 78737 (Sec)**
Fax **(06204) 740181**
Holes 9 L 6060 m SSS 72
V'tors WD–H WE–M H (Summer)
Fees 50DM (60DM)
Loc 10km NE of Mannheim

Mittelrheinischer (1938)

Denzerheide, 56130 Bad Ems
Tel **(02603) 6541**
Fax **(02603) 13995**
Holes 18 L 6050 m SSS 72
V'tors WD–H (max 36) WE–H (max 28)
Fees 80DM (110DM)
Loc 13km E of Koblenz, nr Bad Ems (6km)
Arch Karl Hoffmann

Neuhof

Hofgut Neuhof, 63303 Dreieich
Tel **(06102) 37927**
Fax **(06102) 37012**
Holes 18 L 6151 m SSS 72
V'tors H
Fees 80DM (100DM)
Loc Hofgut Neuhof, S of Frankfurt, off A3
Arch Patrick Merrigan

Oberhessischer Marburg (1973)

Maximilianenhof, 35091 Cölbe-Bernsdorf
Tel **(06427) 2728/2824 (Pro)**
Fax **(06427) 3090**
Holes 9 L 6098 m SSS 72
V'tors I H
Fees 50DM (70DM)
Loc 8km N of Marburg, off B3 towards Reddehausen

Paderborner Land (1983)

Wilseder Weg 25, 33102 Paderborn
Tel **(05251) 4377**
Holes 18 L 5670 m SSS 68
Fees 20DM (30DM)
Loc Salzkotten/Thule, between B-1 and B-64

Rhein Main (1977)

Steubenstrasse 9, 65189 Wiesbaden
Tel **(0611) 373014**
Holes 18 L 6116 m SSS 71
V'tors M
Fees $50
Loc Wiesbaden 6km

Rheinblick

Weisser Weg, 65201 Wiesbaden-Frauenstein
Tel **(0611) 420675**
Fax **(0611) 941 0434**
Holes 18 L 6604 yds SSS 70
V'tors Limited to Monday play only
Fees $50
Loc 2km from Wiesbaden at Hessen

Rheintal (1971)

An der Bundesstrr 291, 68723 Oftersheim
Tel **(06202) 56390**
Holes 18 L 5840 m SSS 71
Fees On application
Loc Oftersheim, SE of Mannheim

Rhoen (1971)

Am Golfplatz, 36145 Hofbieber
Tel **(06657) 7077/1334**
Fax **(06657) 1754**
Holes 18 L 5676 m SSS 70
V'tors U
Fees 50DM (70DM)
Loc Hofbieber, 11km E of Fulda
Arch Kurt Peters

Schloss Braunfels (1970)

Homburger Hof, 35619 Braunfels
Tel **(06442) 4530**
Fax **(06442) 6683**
Holes 18 L 6288 m SSS 73
V'tors WD–U H WE–H NA after 10am
Fees 60DM (80DM)
Loc 70km N of Frankfurt

Schloss Sickendorf (1990)

Schloss Sickendorf, 36341 Lauterbach
Tel **(06641) 96130**
Fax **(06641) 961335**
Holes 18 L 6124 m SSS 72
V'tors H
Fees 40DM (60DM)
Loc 30km W of Fulda. 120km E of Frankfurt
Arch Spangemacher

Sennelager (British Army) (1963)

Bad Lippspringe, BFPO 16
Tel **(05252) 53794**
Fax **(05252) 53811**
Holes Old 18 L 5754 m SSS 72
New 9 L 5214 m SSS 68
V'tors WD–U H WE–M before 2pm
Fees (Forces) 30DM (40DM)
(Civilians) 50DM (60DM)
Loc 9km E of Paderborn, off Route 1

Spessart (1972)

Golfplatz Alsberg, 63628 Bad Soden-Salmünster
Tel **(06056) 3594**
Fax **(06056) 5365**
Holes 18 L 6039 m SSS 72
V'tors H
Fees 50DM (70DM) W–250DM
Loc 70km NE of Frankfurt, via A66 towards Fulda
Arch Elliot Rowan

Taunus G & LC (1979)

Merzhauser Landstr, 61276 Weilrod-Altweilnau
Tel **(06083) 1883**
Fax **(06083) 2745**
Holes 18 holes SSS 72
V'tors H
Fees 50DM (75DM)
Loc 25km NW of Bad Homburg

Wiesbaden (1893)
Chauseehaus 17, 65199 Wiesbaden
Tel **(0611) 460238**
Fax **(0611) 463251**
Holes 9 L 5320 m SSS 68
V'tors WD–H (max 36) WE–H (max 28)
Fees 55DM (75DM)
Loc 8km NW of Wiesbaden, towards Schlangenbad

Wiesloch-Hohenhardter Hof G & LC (1983)
Hohenhardter Hof, 69168 Wiesloch-Baiertal
Tel **(06222) 72081**
Fax **(06222) 71718**
Holes 18 L 6080 m SSS 72
V'tors WD–H WE–M
Fees 50DM (70DM)
Loc 17km S of Heidelberg
Arch Harradine/Weishaupt

Hamburg & North

Altenhof (1971)
Eckernförde, 24340 Altenhof
Tel **(04351) 41227, (04351) 45800 (Pro)**
Fax **(04351) 41227**
Holes 18 L 6071 m SSS 72
V'tors Mon–NA WE–H
Fees 50DM (60DM)
Loc 3km S of Eckernförde. 25km NW of Kiel
Arch Donald Harradine

Bucholz-Nordheide
An der Rehm 25, 21444 Bucholz
Tel **(04181) 36200**
Fax **(04181) 97294**
Holes 18 L 6130 m SSS 72
V'tors WD–U H WE–H NA after 10am
Fees 50DM (60DM)
Loc 30km S of Hamburg

Buxtehude (1982)
Zum Lehmfeld 1, 21614 Buxtehude
Tel **(04161) 81333**
Fax **(04161) 87268**
Holes 18 L 6505 m SSS 74
V'tors U
Fees 50–60DM (60–80DM)
Loc 30km SW of Hamburg on Route 73 from Harburg
Arch Wolfgang Siegmann

Föhr (1966)
25938 Nieblum
Tel **(04681) 3277**
Fax **(04681) 50465**
Holes 18 L 6089 m SSS 72
V'tors H
Fees 55DM (65DM)
Loc 3km SW of Wyk, by airport

Gut Grambek (1981)
Schlosstr 21, 23883 Grambek
Tel **(04542) 4627**
Fax **(04542) 88618**
Holes 18 L 6029 m SSS 71
V'tors H
Fees 50DM (70DM)
Loc 30km S of Lübeck. 50km E of Hamburg

Gut Kaden (1984)
Kadenerstrasse 9, 25486 Alveslohe
Tel **(04193) 92021/2/3**
Holes 18 L 6076 m SSS 72
V'tors WD–U WE–M only
Loc 30km N of Hamburg

Gut Waldhof (1969)
Am Waldhof, 24629 Kisdorferwohld
Tel **(04194) 383**
Fax **(04194) 1251**
Holes 18 L 6044 m Par 72
V'tors WD–H WE–M
Fees 50DM (60DM)
Loc 34km N of Hamburg via Autobahn A7 to Kaltenkirchen, or via route B432

Hamburg (1906)
In de Bargen 59, 22587 Hamburg
Tel **(040) 812177**
Fax **(040) 817315**
Holes 18 L 5925 m SSS 71
V'tors H WE–M
Fees 75DM (80DM)
Loc Blankenese, 14km W of Hamburg
Arch Colt/Allison/Morrison

Hamburg-Ahrensburg (1964)
Am Haidschlag 39-45, 22926 Ahrensburg
Tel **(04102) 51309**
Fax **(04102) 81410**
Holes 18 L 5782 m SSS 71
V'tors WE–M only
Fees 60DM (70DM)
Loc 20km NE of Hamburg. Motorway exit Ahrensburg

Hamburg-Waldorfer (1960)
Schevenbarg, 22949 Ammersbek
Tel **(040) 605 1337**
Fax **(040) 605 4879**
Holes 18 L 6154 m SSS 73
18 hole pitch & putt course
V'tors WD–U H WE–M H
Fees 70DM (85DM)
Loc 20km N of Hamburg
Arch B von Limburger

Hamburger GC In der Lüneburger Heide (1957)
Am Golfplatz 24, 21218 Seevetal
Tel **(04105) 2331**
Fax **(04105) 52571**
Holes 18 L 5903 m SSS 71
V'tors WD–U WE–M
Fees 60DM (75DM)
Loc 25km S of Hamburg
Arch Morrison/Gärtner

Hoisdorf (1977)
Hof Bornbek/Hoisdorf, 22952 Lütjensee
Tel **(04107) 7831**
Fax **(04107) 9934**
Holes 18 L 6010 m Par 71
V'tors WD–U WE–M only
Fees 60DM (70M)
Loc 25km NE of Hamburg

Jersbek
Oberteicher Weg, 22941 Jersbek
Tel **(04532) 23555**
Fax **(04532) 24779**
Holes 18 L 5867 m SSS 71
V'tors WD–H or I WE–M
Fees 50DM (60DM)
Loc 20km N of Hamburg
Arch Von Schinkel

Kieler GC Havighorst (1988)
Havighorster Weg 20, 24211 Havighorst
Tel **(04302) 742**
Fax **(04302) 742**
Holes 18 L 6242 m SSS 73
V'tors WD–U H WE–H
Fees 50DM (60DM)
Loc 10km S of Kiel. 85km N of Hamburg
Arch Udo Barth

Lübeck-Travemünder (1921)
Kowitzberg 41, 23570 Lübeck-Travemünde
Tel **(04502) 74018**
Holes 18 L 6071 m SSS 72
Loc NE of Lübeck

Maritim Timmendorfer Strand (1973)
Am Golfplatz 3, 23669 Timmendorfer Strand
Tel **(04503) 5152**
Fax **(04503) 86344**
Holes North 18 L 6095 m SSS 72
South 18 L 3755 m SSS 60
V'tors WE–booking required
Fees North D–60DM (D–80DM)
South D–45DM (D–70DM)
Loc 15km N of Lübeck
Arch B von Limburger

Mittelholsteinischer Aukrug (1969)
Zum Glasberg 9, 24613 Aukrug-Bargfeld
Tel **(04873) 595**
Fax **(04873) 1698**
Holes 18 L 6140 m SSS 72
V'tors WD–H WE–H booking necessary

Fees 45DM (60DM)
Loc 10km W of Neumunster. Mitte exit on Route 430

An der Pinnau (1982)
Pinnerbergerstr 81a, 25451 Quickborn
Tel **(04106) 81800**
Fax **(04106) 82003**
Holes 18 L 6490 m SSS 74
18 L 6115 m SSS 72
V'tors H or I
Fees 60DM (80DM)
Loc 25km NW of Hamburg, nr Renzel

Am Sachsenwald (1985)
Am Riesenbett, 21521 Dassendorf
Tel **(04104) 6120**
Fax **(04104) 6551**
Holes 18 L 6118 m SSS 72
V'tors H
Fees 50DM (60DM)
Loc 20km SE of Hamburg
Arch Deutsche Golf Consult

Schloss Breitenberg
25524 Breitenberg
Tel **(04828) 8188**
Fax **(04828) 8100**
Holes 18 hole course
V'tors H
Fees 50DM (60DM)
Loc 50km N of Hamburg
Arch Gerd Osterkamp

Schloss Lüdersburg (1985)
21379 Lüdersburg bei Lüneburg
Tel **(04139) 6970-0**
Fax **(04139) 6970 70**
Holes 18 L 6091 m SSS 73
6 hole Par 3 course
V'tors U H
Fees 60DM (80DM)
Loc 18km E of Lüneburg. 55km SE of Hamburg
Arch Wolfgang Siegmann

St Dionys (1972)
Widukindweg, 21357 St Dionys
Tel **(04133) 6277**
Fax **(04133) 6281**
Holes 18 L 6225 m SSS 73
V'tors By appointment only
Fees 60DM (80DM)
Loc 10km N of Lüneburg

Sylt
Am Golfplatz, 25996 Wenningstedt
Tel **(04651) 45311**
Fax **(04651) 45692**
Holes 18 L 6200 m SSS 72
V'tors H
Fees 50–100DM
Loc Sylt Island, 75km W of Flensburg

Treudelberg G & CC (1990)
Lemsahler Landstr 45, 22397 Hamburg
Tel **(040) 608 22500**
Fax **(040) 608 22444**
Holes 18 L 6182 m SSS 72
9 hole pitch & putt
V'tors U H
Fees 60DM (90DM)
Loc N of Hamburg centre
Arch Donald Steel

Uhlenhorst (1989)
24229 Uhlenhorst
Tel **(04349) 539**
Fax **(04349) 1434**
Holes 18 L 6195 m SSS 72
V'tors U
Fees 50DM (60DM)
Loc 8km N of Kiel
Arch Donald Harradine

Auf der Wendlohe
Oldesloerstr 251, 22457 Hamburg
Tel **(040) 550 5014/5**
Fax **(040) 550 3668**
Holes 27 holes:
5675-6050 m SSS 72
V'tors WE–M
Fees WD–60DM
Loc 15km N of Hamburg
Arch Ernst-Dietmar Hess

Wentorf-Reinbeker (1901)
Golfstrasse 2, 21465 Wentorf
Tel **(040) 720 2141**
Fax **(040) 720 2141**
Holes 18 L 5686 m SSS 70
V'tors WD–U H WE–M
Fees 60DM (70DM)
Loc 20km SE of Hamburg
Arch Ernst Hess

Worpswede (1974)
Giehlermühlen, 27729 Vollersode
Tel **(0421) 621425**
Holes 18 L 6200 m SSS 72
Loc Giehlermuhlen, 20km N of Bremen, off B74

Hanover & Weserbergland

Bad Salzuflen G & LC
Am Schwaghof, 32108 Bad Salzuflen
Tel **(05222) 10773**
Fax **(05222) 13954**
Holes 18 L 6138 m Par 72
V'tors H
Fees 60DM (70DM)
Loc 3km NE of Bad Salzuflen
Arch B von Limburger

Braunschweig (1926)
Schwartzkopffstr 10, 38126 Braunschweig
Tel **(0531) 691369**
Holes 18 L 5893 m SSS 71
Loc Braunschweig 5km

Burgdorf (1970)
Waldstr 15, 31303 Burgdorf-Ehlershausen
Tel **(05085) 7628**
Fax **(05085) 6617**
Holes 18 L 6426 m SSS 74
V'tors H
Fees 40DM (60DM)
Loc Burgdorf-Ehlershausen, 20km NE of Hanover

Gifhorn (1982)
Wilscher Weg 56, 38503 Gifhorn
Tel **(05371) 16737**
Fax **(05371) 51092**
Holes 18 L 6200 m SSS 71
V'tors H
Fees 40DM (60DM)
Loc 30km N of Braunschweig

Göttingen (1969)
Levershausen, 37154 Northeim
Tel **(05551) 61915**
Fax **(05551) 61863**
Holes 18 L 6050 m SSS 72
V'tors H
Fees 40DM (50DM)
Loc 20km N of Göttingen, towards Northeim

Hannover (1923)
Am Blauen See, 30823 Garbsen
Tel **(05137) 73235**
Holes 18 L 5855 m SSS 71
Loc 15km NW of Hanover

Herzogstadt Celle (1985)
Beukenbusch 1, 29229 Celle
Tel **(05086) 395**
Fax **(05086) 8288**
Holes 18 L 5915 m SSS 71
V'tors H
Fees 50DM (60DM)
Loc 6km NE of Celle, towards Lüneburg. 40km NE of Hanover
Arch Wolfgang Siegmann

Isernhagen (1983)
Auf Gut Lohne, 30916 Isernhagen
Tel **(05139) 2998**
Fax **(05139) 27033**
Holes 18 L 6379 m SSS 73
V'tors H–(max 34)
Fees 50DM (70DM)
Loc Gut Lohne, 12km NE of Hanover

Kassel-Wilhelmshöhe
Habichtswald, 34131 Kassel
Tel **(0561) 33509**
Fax **(0561) 37729**
Holes 18 L 5705 m SSS 70
Fees 40DM (60DM)
Loc 5km W of Kassel

Lipperland zu Lage
Ottenhauserstr 100, 32791 Lage/Lippe
Tel **(05232) 66829**
Fax **(05232) 18165**
Holes 18 L 6260 m SSS 73
V'tors H
Fees 30DM (40DM)
Loc 22km E of Bielefeld
Arch Heinz Wolters

Lippischer (1980)
Huxollweg 21A, 32825 Blomberg-Cappel
Tel **(05231) 459**
Fax **(05236) 8102**
Holes 18 L 6110 m SSS 72
Fees 50DM (60DM)
Loc 12km E of Detmold

Pyrmonter (1961)
Postfach 100 828, 31758 Hameln
Tel **(05281) 8196**
Fax **(05281) 8196**
Holes 18 L 5775 m SSS 70
V'tors H
Fees 50DM (60DM)
Loc 4km S of Bad Pyrmont. 20km SW of Hameln
Arch Donald Harradine

Ravensberger Land
Sudstrasse 96, 32130 Enger-Pödinghausen
Tel **(09224) 7308**
Fax **(09224) 79682**
Holes 18 hole course SSS 72
V'tors WD–H WE–M
Fees 30DM (40DM)
Loc 25km NE of Bielefeld towards Herford
Arch Heinz Wolters

Schloss Schwöbber (1985)
Wirtschaftshof, 31855 Aerzen
Tel **(05154) 2004**
Holes 18 L 6222 m SSS 73
18 hole short course
Loc 10km SW of Hameln. 60km SW of Hanover

Sieben-Berge (1965)
Postfach 1152, 31021 Gronau
Tel **(05182) 58212**
Holes 18 L 6126 m SSS 72
Fees 30DM (40DM)
Loc 35km S of Hanover

Weserbergland (1982)
Weissenfelder Mühle, Polle
Tel **(05535) 8842**
Fax **(05535) 1225**
Holes 18 holes SSS 72
V'tors H
Fees 50DM (60DM)
Loc 35km S of Hameln

Munich & South Bavaria

Altötting-Burghausen Schloss Piesing (1986)
Piesing 2, 84533 Haiming
Tel **(08678) 7001/3**
Fax **(08678) 7007**
Holes 18 L 6206 m SSS 72
9 L 3730 m SSS 60
V'tors U
Fees 60DM (80DM)
Loc Schloss Piesing, 4km N of Burghausen towards Haiming
Arch G von Mecklenberg

Augsburg (1959)
Engelshofer Str 2, 86399 Bobingen-Burgwalden
Tel **(08234) 5621**
Fax **(08234) 7855**
Holes 18 L 5833 m SSS 71
V'tors U
Fees 60DM (80DM)
Loc 18km SW of Augsburg

Bad Tölz (1973)
83646 Wackersberg
Tel **(08041) 9994**
Fax **(08041) 2116**
Holes 9 L 2942 m SSS 71
V'tors WD–H WE–M
Fees 50DM (60DM)
Loc 5km W of Bad Tölz. 55km S of Munich

Bad Wörishofen
Schlingenerstr 27, 87668 Rieden
Tel **(08346) 777**
Holes 18 L 6318 m SSS 71
Loc 10km S of Bad Wö]rishofen

Beuerberg (1982)
Gut Sterz, 82547 Beuerberg
Tel **(08179) 671/728**
Fax **(08179) 5234**
Holes 18 L 6518 m SSS 74
V'tors WD–H WE–M H
Fees 80DM (100DM)
Loc Beuerberg, 45km SW of Munich
Arch Donald Harradine

Im Chiemgau (1982)
Kötzing 1, 83339 Chieming-Hart
Tel **(08669) 7557**
Fax **(08669) 78153**
Holes 18 L 6200 m SSS 73
9 hole Par 3 course
Fees 70DM (100DM)
Loc 40km W of Salzburg

Erding-Grunbach (1973)
Am Kellerberg, 85461 Grünbach
Tel **(08122) 6465**
Fax **(08122) 49684**
Holes 18 L 6140 m SSS 72
V'tors WD–H (max 35)
WE–H (max 28)
Fees 60DM (80DM)
Loc 30km NE of Munich

Eschenried (1983)
Kurfürstenweg 10, 85232 Eschenried
Tel **(08131) 87238/79650**
Fax **(08131) 567418**
Holes 18 L 6088 m SSS 73 Par 72
V'tors U
Fees 70DM (90DM)
Loc 8km NW of Munich
Arch G von Mecklenburg

Falkenhof G & LC (1983)
PO Box 1560, 84483 Burghausen
Tel **(08678) 8996**
Fax **(08677) 65146**
Holes 9 L 3030 m SSS 72
Fees 30DM (60DM)
Loc Falkenhof-Marktl, 48km N of Salzburg. 100km E of Munich
Arch Kurt Rossknecht

Feldafing (1926)
Tutzingerstr 15, 82340 Feldafing
Tel **(08157) 7005**
Fax **(08157) 4603**
Holes 18 L 5708 m SSS 71
V'tors H WE–M
Fees 60DM (85DM)
Loc 32km S of Munich
Arch B von Limburger

Garmisch-Partenkirchen (1928)
Postfach 1345, 82453 Garmisch-Partenkirchen
Tel **(08824) 8344**
Fax **(08824) 325**
Holes 18 L 6190 m SSS 72
Fees 65DM (85DM)
Loc 11km N of Garmisch

Hohenpähl (1988)
82396 Pähl
Tel **(08808) 1330**
Fax **(08808) 775**
Holes 18 L 6073 m SSS 73
V'tors WD–H WE–M H
Fees 90DM (120DM)
Loc 40km S of Munich on B2

Holledau
Weihern 3, 84104 Rudelzhausen
Tel **(08756) 96010**
Fax **(08756) 815**
Holes 18 L 6085 m SSS 72
9 hole course
V'tors U H
Fees 50DM (70DM)
Loc 55km N of Munich

Iffeldorf
Gut Rettenberg, 82393 Iffeldorf
Tel **(08856) 81809**
Fax **(08856) 1759**
Holes 18 L 5904 m SSS 71
V'tors U
Fees 80DM (100DM)
Loc 45km S of Munich
Arch Hery Beer

Landshut (1989)
Oberlippach 2, 84095 Furth-Landshut
Tel **(08704) 8378**
Fax **(08704) 8379**
Holes 18 L 6081 m SSS 72
V'tors H
Fees 70DM (90DM)
Loc 65km E of Munich
Arch Kurt Rossknecht

Leutstetten
Gut Rieden, 82319 Starnberg
Tel **(08151) 15678**
Fax **(08151) 8811**
Holes 18 L 6046 yds SSS 72
V'tors U H
Fees 60DM (80DM)
Loc 25km S of Munich

Mangfalltal G & LC
Oed 1, 83620 Feldkirchen-Westerham
Tel **(08063) 6300**
Holes 18 L 5740 m SSS 72
Fees 40DM (55DM)
Loc 40km SE of Munich

Margarethenhof am Tegernsee (1982)
Gut Steinberg, PF 1101, 83701 Gmund am Tegernsee
Tel **(08022) 7506-0**
Fax **(08022) 74818**
Holes 18 L 6056 m SSS 72
V'tors WD–H WE–before 10am
Fees 100DM (120DM)
Loc Tegernsee, 45km S of Munich
Arch Frank Pennink

München Nord-Eichenried (1989)
Münchenstr 57, 85452 Eichenried
Tel **(08123) 1004**
Fax **(08123) 4491**
Holes 18 L 6318 m Par 73
Fees 70DM (90DM)
Loc 19km NE of Munich
Arch Kurt Rossknecht

München West-Odelzhausen
Gut Todtenried, 85235 Odelzhausen
Tel **(08134) 1618**
Fax **(08134) 7623**
Holes 18 L 6169 m SSS 72
V'tors WD–I before 10am
Fees 60DM (80DM)
Loc 35km NW of Munich

München-Riedhof
82544 Egling-Riedhof
Tel **(08171) 7065**
Fax **(08171) 72452**
Holes 18 L 6216 m SSS 72
V'tors WD–U H
Loc 25km S of Münich
Arch Heinz Fehring

Münchener (1910)
Tölzerstrasse, 82064 Strasslach
Tel **(08170) 450**
Fax **(08170) 611**
Holes Strasslach 18 L 6177 m SSS 72; Thalkirchen 9 L 2528 m SSS 69
V'tors WD–H WE–M
Fees 100DM
Loc Strasslach: 10km from Munich. Thalkirchen: Munich

Olching (1979)
Feursstrasse 89, 82140 Olching
Tel **(08142) 3240**
Holes 18 L 6262 m SSS 73
V'tors H WE–NA 10.30–2.30pm
Fees 70DM (100DM)
Loc 15km W of Munich
Arch J Dudok van Heel

Pfaffing Wasserburger
München Ost, Köckmühle, 83539 Pfaffing
Tel **(08076) 1718**
Fax **(08076) 8594**
Holes 18 L 6082 m SSS 73
9 hole course
V'tors U H
Fees 60DM (80DM)
Loc 50km E of Münich
Arch Kurt Rossknecht

Schloss Klingenburg-Günzburg (1978)
Schloss Klingenburg, 89341 Jettingen-Scheppach
Tel **(08225) 3030**
Fax **(08225) 30350**
Holes 18 L 6218 m SSS 72
V'tors WD–U WE–H
Fees 70DM (90DM)
Loc 40km W of Augsburg. 5km from Stuttgart–Munich motorway, exit Burgau
Arch Harradine/Sziedat

Schloss Maxlrain
Freitung 14, 83104 Tuntenhausen
Tel **(08061) 1403**
Fax **(08061) 30146**
Holes 18 L 6357 m SSS 73
9 hole Par 3 course
V'tors U H
Fees 70DM (90DM)
Loc 40km S of Munich
Arch Paul Krings

St Eurach G & LC (1973)
Eurach 8, 82393 Iffeldorf
Tel **(08801) 1332**
Fax **(08801) 2523**
Holes 18 L 6509 m SSS 74
V'tors H exc Wed & Fri pm–NA WE–NA
Fees 100DM
Loc 40km S of Munich
Arch Donald Harradine

Starnberg (1986)
Uneringerstr, 82319 Starnberg/Hadorf
Tel **(08151) 12157**
Holes 18 L 6344 m SSS 73
V'tors WE–booking required
Fees 70DM (90DM)
Loc 30km S of Munich

Tegernseer GC Bad Wiessee (1958)
Robognerhof 1, 83707 Bad Wiessee
Tel **(08022) 8769**
Fax **(08022) 82747**
Holes 18 L 5501 m SSS 69
V'tors WD–H
Fees 90DM
Loc Tegernsee, 50km S of Munich

Tutzing (1983)
82327 Tutzing-Deixlfurt
Tel **(08158) 3600**
Fax **(08158) 7234**
Holes 18 L 6159 m SSS 72
V'tors U H
Fees 70DM (90DM)
Loc Starnberger See, 30km SW of Munich

Wittelsbacher GC Rohrenfeld-Neuburg (1988)
Gut Rohrenfeld, 86633 Neuburg/Donau
Tel **(08431) 44118**
Fax **(08431) 41301**
Holes 18 L 6317 m SSS 73
V'tors U H
Fees 70DM (90DM)
Loc 7km E of Neuburg. 70km NW of Munich
Arch J Dudok van Heel

Wörthsee (1982)
Gut Schluifeld, 82237 Wörthsee
Tel **(08153) 3872**
Fax **(08153) 4280**
Holes 18 L 6270 m SSS 73
V'tors WD–H WE–NA
Fees 80DM (100DM)
Loc Wörthsee, 20km W of Munich

For list of abbreviations see page 435

Nuremberg & North Bavaria

Bad Griesbach

Holzhäuser 8, 94086 Bad Griesbach

Tel **(08532) 790-0**
Fax **(08532) 790-45**
Holes Uttlau 18 L 6115 m SSS 72
Lederbach 18 L 5998 m SSS 71
3 x 9 hole courses
V'tors I
Fees 70DM (70DM)
Loc 28km SW of Passau
Arch Kurt Rossknecht

Bamberg (1973)

Postfach 1525, 96006 Bamberg

Tel **(09547) 7212/7109**
Fax **(09547) 25130**
Holes 18 L 6175 m SSS 72
V'tors H
Fees 50DM (70DM)
Loc Gut Leimershof, 16km N of Bamberg
Arch Dieter Sziedat

Donau Rassbach (1986)

Rassbach 8, 94136 Thyrnau-Passau

Tel **(08501) 1313**
Fax **(08501) 8100**
Holes 18 L 6400 m SSS 73
V'tors U
Fees 60DM (70DM)
Loc 10km E of Passau
Arch Götz Mecklenburg

Fränkische Schweiz (1974)

Kanndorf 8, 91316 Ebermannstadt

Tel **(09194) 4827**
Fax **(09194) 5410**
Holes 18 L 6050 m SSS 72
V'tors H
Fees 60DM (80DM)
Loc 5km E of Ebermannstadt. 40km N of Nuremberg

Fürth (1992)

Vacherstrasse 261, 90768 Fürth

Tel **(0911) 757522**
Fax **(0911) 757522**
Holes 18 L 6478 yds SSS 71
V'tors H
Fees 50DM (75DM)
Loc 20km W of Nuremburg

Hof (1985)

Postfach 1324, 95012 Hof

Tel **(09281) 43749**
Fax **(09821) 60318/9035**
Holes 18 L 6040 m SSS 72
V'tors H
Fees 50DM (60DM)
Loc 2km NE of Hof (B173)
Arch Dieter Sziedat

Ingolstadt (1977)

Spitzlmühle, Gerolfingerstr, 85049 Ingolstadt

Tel **(0841) 85778**
Holes 18 L 5500 m SSS 69
Fees On application
Loc 3km from Ingolstadt towards Gerolfing

Lichtenau-Weickershof (1980)

Weickershof 1, 91586 Lichtenau

Tel **(09827) 6907**
Fax **(09827) 7242**
Holes 18 L 6070 m SSS 72
V'tors WD–H (max 35) WE–M
Fees 60DM (80DM)
Loc 10km E of Ansbach
Arch Dieter Sziedat

Neumarkt (1987)

Ruppertslohe 18, 92283 Lauterhofen

Tel **(09186) 1574**
Fax **(09186) 1527**
Holes 18 L 6054 m SSS 72
V'tors H
Fees 60DM (80DM)
Loc 25km SE of Nuremberg

Oberfranken Thurnau (1965)

Postfach 1349, 95304 Kulmbach

Tel **(09228) 319**
Fax **(09228) 7219**
Holes 18 L 6152 m SSS 72
V'tors U H
Fees 70DM (90DM)
Loc Thurnau, 18km NW of Bayreuth. 14km SW of Kulmbach
Arch Donald Harradine

Oberpfälzer Wald G & LC (1977)

Waldgasse 3B, 92421 Schwandorf

Tel **(09439) 466**
Fax **(09439) 1247**
Holes 18 L 6108 m SSS 73
V'tors U
Fees 50DM (60DM)
Loc Kemnath bei Fuhrn. 10km E of Schwarzenfeld, towards Neunburg
Arch Max Haseneder

Oberzwieselau (1990)

94227 Lindberg

Tel **(01049) 9922/2367**
Fax **(01049) 9922/60440**
Holes 18 L 6214 yds SSS 72
V'tors H (max 36)
Fees 60DM (80DM)
Loc 170km NW of Munich

Regensburg G & LC (1966)

Jagdschloss Thiergarten, 93177 Altenthann

Tel **(09403) 505**
Fax **(09403) 4391**
Holes 18 L 5785 m SSS 71
Fees 60DM (90DM)
Loc 14km E of Regensburg, nr Walhalla

Regensburg-Sinzing

Minoritenhof 1, 93161 Sinzing

Tel **(0941) 32504**
Fax **(0941) 36299**
Holes 18 L 5984 m SSS 72
6 hole short course
V'tors U H
Fees 60DM (70DM)
Loc 7km SW of Regensburg

Am Reichswald

Postfach 140101, 90117 Nürnberg

Tel **(0911) 305730**
Holes 18 L 6345 m SSS 73
V'tors H
Fees 70DM (100DM)
Loc 10km N of Nuremberg

Rottaler G & CC (1972)

Am Fischgartl 2, 84332 Herbertsfelden

Tel **(08561) 5969**
Fax **(08561) 2646**
Holes 18 L 6105 m SSS 72
Fees 50DM (60DM)
Loc 5km W of Pfarrkirchen on B388. 120km E of Munich

Sagmühle (1984)

Schwaim 52, 94086 Bad Griesbach

Tel **(08532) 2038**
Fax **(08532) 3165**
Holes 18 L 6168 m SSS 72
V'tors H
Fees 70DM (80DM)
Loc 25km SW of Passau
Arch Kurt Rossknecht

Schloss Fahrenbach (1993)

95709 Tröstau

Tel **(09232) 8820-256**
Fax **(09232) 882-345**
Holes 18 L 5858 m SSS 71
V'tors U
Fees £15 (£25)
Loc 15km W of Marktredwitz. 40km E of Bayreuth
Arch Deutsche Golf Consult

Schlossberg (1985)

Grünbach 8, 94419 Reisbach

Tel **(08734) 7035**
Holes 18 L 6070 m SSS 72
Fees 50DM (60DM)
Loc Somershausen, 15km from Dingolfing. 100km NE of Munich, off Route 11

Schmidmühlen G & CC (1968)

Am Theilberg, 92287 Schmidmühlen

Holes 18 L 5946 m SSS 72
Loc 35km NW of Regensburg

Schwanhof (1994)
Klaus Conrad Allee 1, 92706 Luhe-Wildenau
Tel **(09607) 92020**
Fax **(09607) 920248**
Holes 18 hole course SSS 72
V'tors U H
Fees 60DM (80DM)
Loc 80km N of Regensburg
Arch Jerry Pate

Rhineland

Ahaus
Schmäinghook 36, 48683 Ahaus-Alstätte
Tel **(02567) 405**
Fax **(02567) 3524**
Holes 18 hole course SSS 72
6 hole Par 3 course
V'tors U H
Fees 60DM (80DM)
Loc 60km W of Münster
Arch Deutsche Golf Consult

Bad Neuenahr G & LC (1979)
Remagener Weg, 53474 Bad Neuenahr-Ahrweiler
Tel **(02641) 2325**
Fax **(02641) 29750**
Holes 18 L 6060 m SSS 72
Fees 70DM (90DM)
Loc Bad Neuenahr, 40km S of Bonn

Bergisch-Land
Siebeneickerst 386, 42111 Wuppertal
Tel **(02053) 7177**
Fax **(02053) 7303**
Holes 18 L 5920 m SSS 71
V'tors WD–H WE–M
Fees 80DM
Loc Elberfeld, 8km W of Wuppertal

Bochum (1982)
Im Mailand 127, 44797 Bochum
Tel **(0234) 799832**
Fax **(0234) 795775**
Holes 18 L 5300 m SSS 68
V'tors WD–H
Fees 60DM (80DM)
Loc Bochum-Stiepel, 7km S of Bochum

Bonn-Godesberg in Wachtberg (1960)
Landgrabenweg, 53343 Wachtberg-Niederbachen
Tel **(0228) 344003**
Fax **(0228) 340820**
Holes 18 L 5900 m Par 71
V'tors WD–H WE–M
Fees 60DM (80DM)
Loc Niederbachem, 4km from Bad Godesberg

Burg Overbach (1984)
Postfach 1213, 53799 Much
Tel **(02245) 5550**
Holes 18 L 6056 m SSS 72
V'tors H
Fees 60DM (80DM)
Loc Much, 45km E of Cologne, off A4

Castrop-Rauxel
Dortmunder Str 383, 44577 Castrop-Rauxel
Tel **(02305) 62027**
Fax **(02305) 61410**
Holes 18 L 6181 m SSS 72
Fees 55DM (80DM)
Loc 10km W of Dortmund

Dortmund (1956)
Reichmarkstr 12, 44265 Dortmund
Tel **(0231) 774133/774609**
Fax **(0231) 774403**
Holes 18 L 6174 m SSS 72
V'tors WE–M
Fees 60DM (80DM)
Loc 8km S of Dortmund

Düsseldorf (1961)
Rommerljansweg 12, 40882 Ratingen
Tel **(02102) 81092**
Fax **(02102) 81782**
Holes 18 L 5905 m SSS 71
V'tors WD–U WE–M
Loc 11km N of Düsseldorf

Düsseldorf Hösel
In den Höfen 32, 40883 Ratingen
Tel **(02102) 68629**
Holes 18 L 6160 m SSS 72
Loc Hösel, 15km NE of Düsseldorf

Essen Haus Oefte (1959)
Laupendahler Landstr, 45239 Essen
Tel **(02054) 83911**
Holes 18 L 6100 m SSS 72
Fees 80DM (100DM)
Loc 14km SW of Essen

Essen-Heidhausen (1970)
Preutenborbeckstr 36, 45239 Essen
Tel **(0201) 404111**
Holes 18 L 5937 m SSS 71
Loc 10km S of Essen on B224, nr Werden

Gut Heckenhof (1993)
53783 Eitorf
Tel **(02243) 83137**
Fax **(02243) 83426**
Holes 18 L 6214 m SSS 72
V'tors H
Fees On request
Loc 40km SE of Cologne
Arch William Amick

Haus Bey (1992)
41334 Nettetal
Tel **(02153) 9197-0**
Fax **(02153) 919750**
Holes 18 L 6116 m SSS 72
V'tors WD–U H WE–M H
Fees 50DM (70DM)
Loc 40km SE of Düsseldorf
Arch Paul Krings

Hubbelrath (1961)
Bergische Landstr 700, 40629 Düsseldorf
Tel **(02104) 72178/71848**
Fax **(02104) 75685**
Holes East 18 L 6208 m SSS 72
West 18 L 4325 m SSS 62
V'tors WD–U exc 12–3 pm WE–M
Fees 100DM (120DM)
Loc Hubbelrath, 13km E of Düsseldorf, on Route B7
Arch B von Limburger

Issum-Niederrhein (1973)
Pauenweg 68, 47661 Issum 1
Tel **(02835) 3626**
Fax **(02835) 4267**
Holes 18 L 5728 m SSS 70
V'tors H
Fees 50DM (60DM)
Loc 10km E of Geldern

Juliana (1979)
Frielinghausen 1, 45549 Sprockhövel
Tel **(0202) 647070/648220**
Fax **(0202) 649891**
Holes 18 L 6100 m SSS 71
V'tors H
Fees 50DM (80DM)
Loc 30km E of Düsseldorf
Arch De Buer

Köln G & LC
Golfplatz 2, 51429 Bergisch Gladbach
Tel **(02204) 63114/63138**
Fax **(02204) 68192**
Holes 18 L 6045 m Par 72
V'tors H
Fees 70DM (90DM)
Loc 15km E of Cologne

Krefeld (1930)
Eltweg 2, 47809 Krefeld
Tel **(02151) 570071/72**
Holes 18 L 6060 m SSS 72
V'tors WD–U H
Fees 80DM (100DM)
Loc 7km SE of Krefeld. Düsseldorf 16km
Arch B von Limburger

Nordkirchen
Golfplatz 6, 59394 Nordkirchen
Tel **(02596) 3005**
Fax **(02596) 3006**
Holes 18 L 6200 m SSS 72
V'tors M
Fees 50DM (70DM)
Loc 30km S of Münster
Arch Christoph Städtler

RAF Germany (1956)
RAF Brüggen, BFPO 25
Tel **(02163) 80049/5207**
Fax **(02163) 80934**
Holes 18 L 6522 yds SSS 71
V'tors WD–U
Fees 30DM
Loc On B230, 1km from Dutch/ German border. 25km W of Mönchengladbach

Rhein Sieg (1971)
Postfach 1216, 53759 Hennef
Tel **(02242) 6501**
Holes 18 L 6081 m Par 72
Loc Hennef, 30km SE of Cologne

Royal Artillery (Dortmund) (1969)
Napier Barracks, Dortmund BFPO 20
Tel **(0231) 202551**
Holes 18 L 5967 m SSS 73
V'tors H–by prior arrangement
Fees Military–20DM (25DM) Civilians–on application
Loc Dortmund Brackel
Arch Brig Jones/Maj Coleman

Schloss Georghausen (1962)
Georghausen 8, 51789 Lindlar-Hommerich
Tel **(02207) 4938**
Fax **(02207) 81230**
Holes 18 L 6045 m SSS 72
V'tors H
Fees 60DM (80DM)
Loc 30km E of Cologne

Schloss Myllendonk (1965)
Myllendonkerstr 113, 41352 Korschenbroich 1
Tel **(02161) 641049**
Fax **(02161) 648806**
Holes 18 L 6120 m SSS 72
V'tors WD–H exc Mon & Fri pm WE–H
Fees 80DM (100DM)
Loc Korschenbroich, 5km E of Mönchengladbach

Schmitzhof (1975)
Arsbeckerstr 160, 41844 Wegberg
Tel **(02436) 479**
Fax **(02436) 2650**
Holes 18 L 6310 m SSS 73
V'tors H
Fees 50DM (70DM)
Loc Wegberg-Merbeck, 20km SW of Mönchengladbach

Schwarze Heide
Gahlenerstrasse 44, 46244 Bottrop-Kirchellen
Tel **(02045) 82488**
Fax **(02045) 83077**
Holes 18 L 6051 m SSS 72
V'tors I H
Fees 50DM (70DM)
Loc 55km N of Düsseldorf
Arch Peter Drecker

Unna-Fröndenberg
Schwarzer Weg 1, 58730 Fröndenberg .
Tel **(02373) 70068**
Fax **(02373) 70069**
Holes 18 L 6177 m SSS 72
V'tors H
Fees 50DM (60DM)
Loc 25km W of Dortmund
Arch Karl Grohs

Vestischer GC Recklinghausen (1974)
Bockholterstr 475, 45659 Recklinghausen
Tel **(02361) 26520**
Fax **(02361) 16887**
Holes 18 L 6111 m SSS 72
V'tors WD–H exc Mon–NA WE–M
Fees 50DM (70DM)
Loc Nr Loemühle Airport, N of Recklinghausen
Arch Donald Harradine

Wasserburg Anholt (1972)
Am Schloss 3, 46419 Isselburg Anholt
Tel **(02874) 3444**
Fax **(02874) 29164**
Holes 18 L 6115 m SSS 72
Loc Parkhotel, Wasserburg Anholt. 15km W of Bocholt

Westerwald (1979)
Postfach 1231, 57621 Hachenburg
Tel **(02666) 8220**
Holes 18 holes SSS 72
Fees 35M (45DM)
Loc Hachenburg, 60km E of Bonn

Stuttgart & South West

Algäuer G & LC (1984)
Hofgut Boschach, 87724 Ottobeuren
Tel **(08332) 1310**
Fax **(08332) 5161**
Holes 18 L 6215 m SSS 72 6 hole short course
V'tors H
Fees 50DM (70DM)
Loc 2km S of Ottobeuren. 20km N of Kempten

Bad Liebenzell
Golfplatz 9, 75378 Bad Liebenzell
Tel **(07052) 1574**
Fax **(07052) 5302**
Holes 18 L 6121 m SSS 72
V'tors H (max 33) WE–M
Fees 60DM (80DM)
Loc 35km W of Stuttgart
Arch Felix Elger

Bad Rappenau (1989)
Ehrenbergstrasse 25a, 74906 Bad Rappenau
Tel **(07264) 3666**
Fax **(07264) 3838**
Holes 18 L 6103 m SSS 72
V'tors U H
Fees 60DM (80DM)
Loc 10km NW of Heilbronn
Arch Karl Gross

Baden Hills GC Rastatt (1982)
Postfach 2, 76549 Hügelsheim
Tel **(07229) 5346**
Fax **(07229) 5347**
Holes 18 L 5906 m Par 71
V'tors H–booking necessary WD–U before 5pm WE–M before 3pm
Fees D–50DM (D–70DM)
Loc 10km W of Badeb-Baden. 50km N of Strasbourg

Baden-Baden (1901)
Fremersbergstr 127, 76530 Baden-Baden
Tel **(07221) 23579**
Fax **(07221) 23528**
Holes 18 L 4413 m Par 64
Fees 65DM (90DM)
Loc 1km S of Baden-Baden

Bodensee (1986)
Lampertsweiler 51, 88138 Weissensberg
Tel **(08389) 89190**
Fax **(08389) 89191**
Holes 18 L 6112 m SSS 72
V'tors H
Fees 70DM (90DM)
Loc 5km NE of Lindau/Bodensee
Arch Robert Trent Jones Sr

Freiburg (1970)
Krüttweg 1, 79199 Kirchzarten
Tel **(07661) 5569**
Fax **(07661) 62374**
Holes 18 L 6068 m SSS 72
V'tors H
Fees 60DM (70DM)
Loc Freiburg-Kappel/Kirchzarten

Hechingen Hohenzollern (1955)
Postfach 1124, 72379 Hechingen
Tel **(07471) 6478**
Holes 18 holes SSS 72
V'tors WE–M
Fees On application
Loc Hechingen, 50km S of Stuttgart

Heilbronn-Hohenlohe (1964)
Hofgasse, 74639 Zweiflingen-Friedrichsruhe
Tel **(07941) 38943**
Fax **(07941) 34541**
Holes 18 L 6082 m SSS 72
V'tors H

For list of abbreviations see page 435

Fees 60DM (80DM)
Loc 25km W of Heilbronn, nr Öhringen

Hohenstaufen (1959)
Unter den Ramsberg, 73072 Donzdorf-Reichenbach
Tel **(07162) 27171/20050**
Holes 18 L 6540 yds SSS 72
Loc 15km E of Goppingen. 45km E of Stuttgart

Konstanz (1965)
Langenrain, Kargegg, 78476 Allensbach
Tel **(07533) 5124**
Fax **(07533) 4897**
Holes 18 L 6058 m SSS 72
V'tors WD–I WE–H max 28
Fees 70DM (90DM)
Loc 15km NW of Konstanz, nr Langenrain

Lindau-Bad Schachen (1954)
Am Schönbühl 5, 88131 Lindau
Tel **(08382) 78090**
Fax **(08382) 78998**
Holes 18 L 5690 m SSS 70
Fees 60DM (80DM)
Loc Nr Lindau, Bodensee

Markgräflerland Kandern (1984)
Feuerbacher Str 29, 79400 Kandern
Tel **(07626) 1043**
Fax **(07626) 1433**
Holes 9 L 6100 m SSS 72
V'tors WD–U WE–M
Fees 40DM (60DM)
Loc Kandern, 10km N of Lörrach. 14km NW of Basle
Arch Karl Grohs

Neckartal (1974)
Aldingerstr, Gebäude 975, 71638 Ludwigsburg-Pattonville
Tel **(07141) 871319**
Fax **(07141) 81716**
Holes 18 L 6310 m SSS 73
V'tors WD–U WE–M
Fees 70DM (75DM)
Loc 5km NE of Stuttgart, nr Kornwestheim
Arch B von Limburger

Obere Alp (1989)
Am Golfplatz 1-3, 79780 Stühlingen
Tel **(07703) 7102**
Fax **(07703) 1799**
Holes 18 L 6216 m SSS 72
9 L 3664 m SSS 60
V'tors H
Fees 18 hole:70DM (90DM)
9 hole:45DM (55DM)
Loc 40km N of Zürich, nr Swiss border

Oberschwaben-Bad Waldsee (1968)
Hofgut Hopfenweiler, 88339 Bad Waldsee
Tel **(07524) 5900**
Fax **(07524) 6106**
Holes 18 L 6148 m SSS 72
V'tors H (max 34)
Fees 65DM (90DM)
Loc Bad Waldsee, 60km SW of Ulm
Arch Donald Harradine

Oeschberghof L & GC (1976)
Golfplatz 1, 78166 Donaueschingen
Tel **(0771) 84525**
Fax **(0771) 84540**
Holes 18 L 6580 m SSS 74
V'tors H
Fees 80DM (120DM)
Loc Donaueschingen, 60km E of Freiburg

Owingen-Überlingen
Alte Owinger Str, 88696 Owingen
Tel **(07551) 3979**
Fax **(07551) 3360**
Holes 18 L 6148 m SSS 72
V'tors H
Fees 60DM (80DM)
Loc 5km N of Überlingen, nr Lake Konstanz

Pforzheim Karlshäuser Hof
Karlshäuser Weg, 75248 Ölbronn-Dürrn
Tel **(07237) 9100**
Fax **(07237) 5161**
Holes 18 hole course SSS 72
V'tors H
Fees 60DM (80DM)
Loc 6km N of Pforzheim. 30km E of Karlsruhe
Arch Reinholf Weishaupt

Reutlingen-Sonnenbühl (1987)
Im Zerg, 72820 Sonnenbühl
Tel **(07128) 3532**
Fax **(07128) 3576**
Holes 18 L 6085 m SSS 72
V'tors H
Fees 60DM (80DM)
Loc 40km S of Stuttgart

Rhein Badenweiler (1971)
79401 Badenweiler
Tel **(07632) 7970**
Fax **(07632) 797150**
Holes 18 L 6134 m SSS 72
V'tors WD–H WE–M
Fees 60DM (90DM)
Loc 16km W of Badenweiler. 30km SW of Freiburg
Arch Donald Harradine

Schloss Langenstein (1991)
Schloss Langenstein, 78359 Orsingen-Neuzingen
Tel **(07774) 50651**
Fax **(07774) 50699**
Holes 18 L 6389 m SSS 73
9 hole course
V'tors WD–H WE–H (restricted)
Fees On request
Loc 120km S of Stuttgart
Arch Rod Whitman

Schloss Liebenstein (1982)
Postfach 27, 74380 Neckarwestheim
Tel **(07133) 16019**
Fax **(07133) 17585**
Holes 27 L 5890-6361 m SSS 71-73
V'tors U
Fees 60DM (80DM)
Loc 35km N of Stuttgart

Schloss Weitenburg (1984)
Sommerhalde 11, 72181 Starzach-Sulzau
Tel **(07472) 8061**
Fax **(07472) 8062**
Holes 18 L 6069 m SSS 72/73
9 hole course
V'tors I
Fees 18 hole:70DM (90DM)
9 hole:30DM (40DM)
Loc 50km SW of Stuttgart in Neckar Valley
Arch Heinz Fehring

Sonnenalp (1976)
Hotel Sonnenalp, 87527 Ofterschwang
Tel **(08321) 27276 (Sec)**
Fax **(08321) 272242**
Holes 18 L 5938 m SSS 71
Fees 95DM
Loc 4km W of Sonthofen
Arch Donald Harradine

Stuttgarter Solitude (1927)
71297 Mönsheim
Tel **(07044) 5852**
Fax **(07044) 5357**
Holes 18 L 6045 m SSS 72
V'tors WD–H max 28 WE–M (phone first)
Fees 70DM (100DM)
Loc 15km W of Stuttgart
Arch K von Limburger

Ulm/Neu-Ulm (1963)
Wochenauer Hof 2, 89186 Illerrieden
Tel **(07306) 2102**
Fax **(07306) 34413**
Holes 18 L 6055 m SSS 72
V'tors H
Fees 50DM (70DM)
Loc 15km S of Ulm
Arch Deutsche Golf Consult

For list of abbreviations see page 435

Waldegg-Wiggensbach (1988)

Hof Waldegg, 87487 Wiggensbach

Tel **(08370) 733**
Fax **(08370) 505**
Holes 18 L 5462 m SSS 69
V'tors H (max 36)
Fees 60DM (80DM)
Loc 10km W of Kempten, nr Swiss/Austrian border

Greece

Afandou (1973)

Afandou, Rhodes

Tel **(0241) 51255**
Holes 18 L 6060 m Par 72
V'tors U
Fees 4000–4500dra
Loc Afandou, 20km S of Rhodes town

Corfu (1972)

PO Box 71, Ropa Valley, 49100 Corfu

Tel **(0661) 94220/1**
Fax **(0661) 94220**
Holes 18 L 6300 m SSS 72
Fees 6000–10.000dra
Loc Ermones Bay, 16km W of Corfu town

Glyfada (1962)

PO Box 70116 Glyfada, Athens

Tel **(0894) 6820**
Fax **(0894) 3721**
Holes 18 L 6189 m SSS 72
V'tors H
Fees 9500dra (13.000dra)
Loc 12km S of Athens
Arch Donald Harradine

Porto Carras G & CC (1979)

Porto Carras, Halkidiki

Tel **(0375) 71381/71221**
Holes 18 L 6086 m SSS 72
Loc Sithonia Peninsula, 100km SE of Thessaloniki

Iceland

Akureyri (1935)

PO Box 896, 602 Akureyri

Tel **(6) 22974**
Fax **(6) 11755**
Holes 18 L 5783 m SSS 73
V'tors U H
Fees £20 (£25)
Loc 1km from Akureyri (N coast)

Borgarness (1973)

PO Box 112, 310 Borgarnes

Tel **(3) 71663**
Fax **(3) 71041**
Holes 9 L 5260 m SSS 71
9 L 2630 m SSS 70
V'tors U
Fees 1200Ikr
Loc 5km from Borgarnes. 100km N of Reykjavik (W coast)

Éskifjardar (1976)

735 Éskifirdi

Holes 9 L 4412 m SSS 66
Fees D–1000 Ikr
Loc 3km W of Éskifjördur (E coast)

Hornafjardar

Hornafirdi

Tel **(7) 8030**
Holes 9 L 3610 m SSS 63
Loc Hofn (SE coast)

Húsavík (1967)

PO Box 23, Kötlum, 640 Húsavík

Tel **(6) 41000**
Holes 9 L 2686 m SSS 70
V'tors U
Fees 1000Ikr
Loc 2km from Húsavík (N coast)
Arch Nils Skjöld

Isafjardar (1978)

PO Box 367, Isafjördur

Tel **(4) 3696 (Captain)**
Holes 9 L 4860 m SSS 68
Fees 1000Ikr
Loc 3km W of Isafjördur (NW coast)

Jökull (1973)

Vallholt 15, 355 Olafsvík

Tel **(3) 61198/61666**
Holes 9 L 4530 m SSS 65
Fees D–1000 Ikr
Loc 5km SE of Olafsvík (W coast)

Keilir (1967)

Box 148, 222 Hafnarfjördur

Tel **(1) 653360**
Fax **(1) 652560**
Holes 18 L 5110 m SSS 68
V'tors U
Fees £17 (£20)
Loc Hafnarfjördur, 10km S of Reykjavik (SW coast)

Leynir (1965)

PO Box 9, Akranes

Tel **(3) 12711**
Holes 9 L 2640 m SSS 70
Loc 2km from Akranes (SW coast)

Ness-Nesklúbburinn (1964)

PO Box 66, 172 Seltjarnes

Tel **(1) 611930**
Holes 9 L 4986 m SSS 68
V'tors U
Fees 2000 Ikr
Loc 3km W of Reykjavík

Olafsfjordur (1968)

Vesturgata 12, 625 Olafsfjordur

Tel **(6) 62364**
Fax **(6) 62374**
Holes 9 L 4570 m SSS 67
Fees £8
Loc 60km NW of Akureyri (N coast)

Reykjavíkur (1934)

Grafarholti, Box 12068, 132 Reykjavík

Tel **(1) 682211, (1) 682215 (Pro)**
Fax **(1) 682212**
Holes 18 L 5962 m SSS 73
Fees 2500 Ikr
Loc 8km E of Reykjavík

Saudárkróks (1970)

Saudárkrókur

Tel **(5) 35075**
Holes 9 L 5708 m SSS 71
Loc 2km W of Saudárkrókur (N coast)

Sudurnesja (1964)

PO Box 112, 230 Keflavik

Tel **(2) 14100**
Holes 18 L 5961 m SSS 73
Loc N of Keflavik (SW coast). Airport 5km

Vestmannaeyja (1938)

Vestmannaeyja Island

Tel **(8) 12363**
Holes 18 L 5601 m SSS 70
V'tors U
Fees D–1500Ikr
Loc 2km W of town centre. Large island off S coast. 20 min flight from Reykjavík.

Italy

Como/Milan/ Bergamo

Barlassina CC (1956)

Via Privata Golf 42, 20030 Birago di Camnago (MI)

Tel **(0362) 560621/2/3**
Fax **(0362) 560934**
Holes 18 L 6184 m SSS 72
V'tors U
Fees 80.000L (120.000L)
Loc 22km N of Milan
Arch J Morrison

Bergamo L'Albenza (1960)

Via Longoni 12, 24030 Almenno San Bartolomeo

Tel **(035) 640028/640707**
Fax **(035) 640028**
Holes 18 L 6198 m SSS 72
9 L 2962 m SSS 36

V'tors WD–U
Fees 70.000L (120.000L)
Loc 13km NW of Bergamo. Milan 45km
Arch Cotton/Sutton

Carimate (1962)

Via Airoldi, 22060 Carimate
Tel **(031) 790226**
Fax **(031) 790226**
Holes 18 L 5982 m SSS 71
V'tors H
Fees 60.000L (90.000L)
Loc 15km S of Como. 27km N of Milan
Arch Pier Mancinelli

Castelconturbia (1984)

Via Suno, 28010 Agrate Conturbia
Tel **(0322) 832093**
Fax **(0322) 832428**
Holes Red 9 L 3330 m Par 36
Yellow 9 L 3070 m Par 36
Blue 9 L 3210 m Par 36
V'tors WD–H WE–M H
Fees 80.000L (120.000L)
Loc 23km N of Novara. Milan 60km
Arch Robert Trent Jones Sr

Franciacorta (1987)

Loc Castagnola, 25040 Nigoline di Corte Franca, (Brescia)
Tel **(030) 984167**
Fax **(030) 984393**
Holes 18 L 6065 m SSS 72
9 hole Par 3 course
V'tors U
Fees 70.000L (90.000L)
Loc Nigoline, 25km E of Bergamo. Autostrada A4 exit Rovato
Arch Dye/Croze

Lanzo Intelvi (1962)

22024 Lanzo Intelvi (CO)
Tel **(031) 840169**
Holes 9 L 2438 m SSS 66
Loc 32km NW of Como

Menaggio & Cadenabbia (1907)

Via Golf 12, 22010 Grandola E Uniti
Tel **(0344) 32103/31564**
Fax **(0344) 32103**
Holes 18 L 5277 m SSS 69
V'tors WD–U H WE–H restricted
Fees 70.000L (100.000L)
Loc 5km W of Menaggio. 40km N of Como
Arch John Harris

Milano (1928)

20052 Parco di Monza (MI)
Tel **(039) 303081/2/3**
Fax **(039) 304427**
Holes 18 L 6414 m SSS 73
9 L 2976 m SSS 36
V'tors WD–H WE–by appointment
Fees 95.000L (143.000L)
Loc 6km N of Monza. 18km NE of Milan
Arch Gannon/Blandford

Molinetto CC (1982)

SS Padana Superiore 11, 20063 Cernusco S/N (MI)
Tel **(02) 9210 5128/9210 5983**
Fax **(02) 9210 6635**
Holes 18 L 6010 m Par 71
V'tors WD–H WE–restricted
Fees 80.000L (100.000L)
Loc Cernusco, 10km E of Milan

Monticello (1975)

Via Volta 4, 22070 Cassina Rizzardi
Tel **(031) 928055**
Fax **(031) 880207**
Holes 18 L 6413 m SSS 72
18 L 6056 m SSS 72
V'tors WD–H WE–NA
Fees 80.000L (100.000L)
Loc 10km SE of Como
Arch Jim Fazio

La Pinetina (1971)

Via al Golf 4, 22070 Appiano Gentile
Tel **(031) 933202**
Fax **(031) 890342**
Holes 18 L 6001 m SSS 71
V'tors WD–U WE–booking necessary
Fees 70.000L (110.000L)
Loc 12km SW of Como. Milan 25km

La Rossera (1970)

Via Montebello 4, 24060 Chiuduno
Tel **(035) 838600**
Fax **(035) 442 7047**
Holes 9 L 2510 m SSS 68
V'tors U
Fees 40.000L (60.000L)
Loc 18km SE of Bergamo

Le Rovedine (1978)

Via Carlo Marx, 20090 Noverasco di Opera (MI)
Tel **(02) 5760 6420/5760 2730**
Fax **(02) 5760 6405**
Holes 18 L 6307 m SSS 72
V'tors U
Fees 50.000L (75.000L)
Loc 4km S of Milan

Royal Sant'Anna (1978)

22040 Annone di Brianza (CO)
Tel **(0341) 577551**
Fax **(0341) 260143**
Holes 18 L 4500 m SSS 64
Loc 15km SE of Como. Milan 40km

Varese (1934)

Via Vittorio Veneto 32, 21020 Luvinate (VA)
Tel **(0332) 227394/229302**
Holes 18 L 5936 m SSS 72
V'tors WD–U H
Fees 80.000L (110.000L)
Loc 5km NW of Varese
Arch Gannon/Blandford

Vigevano (1974)

Via Chitola 49, 27029 Vigevano (PV)
Tel **(0381) 346628/346077**
Fax **(0381) 346091**
Holes 9 L 2978 m SSS 71
Loc 25km SE of Novara. 35km SW of Milan

Villa D'Este (1926)

Via Cantù 13, 22030 Montorfano (CO)
Tel **(031) 200200**
Fax **(031) 200786**
Holes 18 L 5787 m SSS 71
V'tors I H
Fees 80.000L (120.000L)
Loc 7km SE of Como
Arch Peter Gannon

Zoate

20067 Zoate di Tribiano (MI)
Tel **(02) 9063 2183/9063 1861**
Fax **(02) 9063 1861**
Holes 18 L 6122 m Par 72
V'tors WD–U H
Fees 70.000L (100.000L)
Loc Zoate, 17km SE of Milan
Arch Marmori

Elba

Acquabona

57037 Portoferraio, Isola di Elba (LI)
Tel **(0565) 940066**
Fax **(0565) 933410**
Holes 9 L 5144 m SSS 67
V'tors U
Loc 5km NW of Porto Azzurro. 6km NW of Porto Ferraio

Emilia Romagna

Adriatic GC Cervia (1985)

Via Jelenia Gora No 6, 48016 Cervia-Milano Marittima
Tel **(0544) 992786/992370 (Sec)**
Fax **(0544) 993410**
Holes 18 L 6246 m SSS 72
V'tors U H
Fees D–75.000L (D–90.000L)
Loc 20km SE of Ravenna
Arch Marco Croze

Bologna (1959)

Via Sabattini 69, 40050 Monte San Pietro (BO)
Tel **(051) 969100**
Fax **(051) 672 0017**
Holes 18 L 6171 m SSS 72
V'tors U
Fees 60.000L (90.000L)
Loc 20km W of Bologna
Arch Harris/Cotton

Croara (1976)
29010 Croara di Gazzola
Tel **(0523) 977105/977148**
Fax **(0523) 977100**
Holes 18 L 6065 m SSS 72
V'tors H
Fees 50.000L (70.000L)
Loc 16km SW of Piacenza. 84km SE of Milan
Arch Buratti/Croze

Matilde di Canossa
Via Casinazzo 1, 42100 San Bartolomeo
Tel **(0522) 371295**
Fax **(0522) 371204**
Holes 18 L 6231 m SSS 71
V'tors U
Fees 60.000L (85.000L)
Loc 50km NW of Bologna
Arch Marco Croze

La Rocca (1985)
Via Campi 8, 43038 Sala Baganza
Tel **(0521) 834037**
Fax **(0521) 834575**
Holes 18 L 6157 m SSS 72
Fees 50.000L (70.000L)
Loc 8km S of Parma

Gulf of Genoa

Degli Ulivi (1932)
Via Campo Golf 59, 18038 Sanremo
Tel **(0184) 557093**
Fax **(0184) 557388**
Holes 18 L 5203 m SSS 67
V'tors H
Fees 50.000L (80.000L)
Loc 5km N of Sanremo
Arch Peter Gannon

Garlenda (1965)
Via Golf 7, 17030 Garlenda
Tel **(0182) 580012**
Fax **(0182) 580561**
Holes 18 L 5973 m SSS 71
V'tors WE–H
Fees 80.000L (110.000L)
Loc 15km N of Alassio
Arch John Harris

Marigola (1975)
Via Vallata 5, 19032 Lerici (SP)
Tel **(0187) 970193**
Fax **(0187) 970193**
Holes 9 L 2116 m Par 49
V'tors U
Fees 30.000L (35.000L)
Loc 6km SE of La Spezia
Arch Franco Marmori

Pineta di Arenzano (1959)
Piazza del Golf 3, 16011 Arenzano (GE)
Tel **(010) 911 1817**
Fax **(010) 911 1270**
Holes 9 L 5527 m SSS 70
V'tors H
Fees 60.000L (85.000L)
Loc Arenzano Pineta, 20km W of Genoa
Arch Donald Harradine

Rapallo (1930)
Via Mameli 377, 16035 Rapallo (GE)
Tel **(0185) 261777/8**
Fax **(0185) 261779**
Holes 18 L 5694 m SSS 70
Fees 80.000L (Sat–125.000L)
Loc 25km SE of Genoa. Nr A12 motorway exit Rapallo

Lake Garda & Dolomites

Asiago (1967)
Via Meltar 2, 36012 Asiago (VI)
Tel **(0424) 462721**
Holes 9 L 2948 m SSS 71
Loc 3km N of Asiago. 50km N of Vicenza

Bogliaco (1912)
Via Golf 11, 25088 Toscolano Maderno
Tel **(0365) 643006**
Fax **(0365) 643006**
Holes 9 L 2572 m SSS 67
V'tors H
Fees 40.000L (60.000L)
Loc Lake Garda, 40km NE of Brescia

Ca' degli Ulivi (1988)
Via Ghiandare 2, 37010 Marciaga di Costermano (VR)
Tel **(045) 725 6463/725 6485**
Fax **(045) 725 6876**
Holes 18 L 6000m SSS 72
9 hole course
Loc Above village of Garda. Verona Airport 35km

Campo Carlo Magno (1922)
Golf Hotel, 38084 Madonna di Campiglio (TN)
Tel **(0465) 41003**
Fax **(0465) 40298**
Holes 9 L 5148 m SSS 67
V'tors U
Fees 70.000–95.000L
Loc Madonna di Campiglio 1km. 74km NW of Trento
Arch Henry Cotton

Gardagolf CC (1985)
Via Angelo Omodeo 2, 25080 Soiano Del Lago (BS)
Tel **(0365) 674707 (Sec)**
Fax **(0365) 674788**
Holes 18 L 6505 m SSS 74
9 L 2635 m Par 35
V'tors H
Fees 80.000L (110.000L)
Loc Lake Garda, 30km NE of Brescia.
Arch Cotton/Pennink/Steel

Karersee-Carezza
Loc Carezza 171, 39056 Welschofen-Nova Levante
Tel **(0471) 612200**
Holes 9 L 5340 m SSS 68
V'tors H
Fees 60.000L (70.000L)
Loc 30km S of Bolzano
Arch Marco Croze

Petersberg (1987)
Unterwinkel 5, 39040 Petersberg (BZ)
Tel **(0471) 615122**
Fax **(0471) 615229**
Holes 18 L 5100 m SSS 66
V'tors U
Fees 65.000L (80.000L)
Loc 35km SE of Bolzano, nr Nova Ponente
Arch Marco Croze

Ponte di Legno (1980)
Corso Milano 36, 25056 Ponte di Legno (BS)
Tel **(0364) 900306**
Fax **(0364) 91110**
Holes 9 L 4803 m SSS 66
V'tors WD–U WE–NA before 2pm
Fees 40.000L (60.000L)
Loc 15km N of Trento, nr San Michele
Arch Caremoli

Trentino Folgaria (1987)
Loc Costa di Folgaria, 38064 Folgaria (TN)
Tel **(0464) 720480**
Fax **(0461) 981682**
Holes 9 L 2582 m SSS 70
V'tors H
Fees 60.000L (70.000L)
Loc 30km S of Trento, off A22
Arch Marco Croze

Verona (1963)
Ca' del Sale 15, 37066 Sommacampagna
Tel **(045) 510060**
Fax **(045) 510242**
Holes 18 L 6037 m SSS 72
V'tors H WE–M
Fees 80.000L (100.000L)
Loc 7km W of Verona
Arch John Harris

Naples & South

Napoli (1983)
Via Campiglione 11, 80072 Arco Felice (NA)
Tel **(081) 526 4296**
Holes 9 L 4776 m SSS 68
V'tors M
Fees 30.000L (35.000L)
Loc Pozzuoli, 10km W of Naples

For list of abbreviations see page 435

Porto d'Orra (1977)
PB 102, 88063 Catanzaro Lido
Tel **(0961) 791045**
Fax **(0961) 791444**
Holes 9 L 5686 m SSS 70
Fees 35.000L (35.000L)
Loc 9km N of Catanzaro Lido on coast

Riva Dei Tessali (1971)
74011 Castellaneta
Tel **(099) 643 9251**
Fax **(099) 643 9255**
Holes 18 L 5960 m SSS 71
V'tors U
Fees 42.000L
Loc 34km SW of Taranto
Arch Marco Croze

San Michele
Loc Bosco 8/9, 87022 Cetraro (CS)
Tel **(0982) 91012**
Fax **(0982) 91430**
Holes 9 L 2760 m SSS 70
V'tors U H
Fees 30.000L (35.000L)
Loc Cetraro, 50km N of Cosenza. 250km SE of Naples
Arch Piero Mancinelli

Rome

Castelgandolfo (1987)
Via Santo Spirito 13, 00040 Castelgandolfo
Tel **(06) 931 2301/931 3084**
Fax **(06) 931 2244**
Holes 18 L 6025 m SSS 71
V'tors U H Sun–restricted
Fees 60.000L (120.000L)
Loc 22km SE of Rome
Arch Robert Trent Jones

Eucalyptus (1988)
Via Cogna 5, 04011 Aprilia (LT)
Tel **(06) 926252/926 8120**
Fax **(06) 926 8502**
Holes 18 L 6375 m SSS 72
V'tors WD–U WE–U H
Fees 30.000L (50.000L)
Loc 20km S of Rome on Aprilia-Anzio road
Arch Toni D'Onofrio

Fioranello
CP 96, 00040 Santa Maria delle Mole (RM)
Tel **(06) 713 8058**
Fax **(06) 713 8212**
Holes 18 L 5417 m Par 70
Fees 40.000L (50.000L)
Loc 17km SE of Rome

Fiuggi (1928)
Superstrada Anticolana 1, 03015 Fiuggi (FR)
Tel **(0775) 55250**
Fax **(0775) 506742**
Holes 9 L 5697 m SSS 70
V'tors U
Loc 60km SE of Rome

Marco Simone (1989)
Via di Marco Simone, 00012 Guidonia (RM)
Tel **(0774) 366469**
Fax **(0774) 366476**
Holes 18 L 6317 m SSS 73
18 hole course Par 64
V'tors U
Fees 80.000L (100.000L)
Loc 17km NE of Rome
Arch Fazio/Mezzacane

Nettuno
Via della Campana 18, 00048 Nettuno (RM)
Tel **(06) 981 9419**
Fax **(06) 981 9419**
Holes 18 L 6260 m SSS 72
V'tors U H
Fees 40.000L (50.000L)
Loc 60km S of Rome on coast
Arch Marco Croze

Olgiata (1961)
Largo Olgiata 15, 00123 Roma
Tel **(06) 378 9141**
Fax **(06) 378 9968**
Holes 18 L 6396 m SSS 72
9 L 2968 m SSS 71
Fees 50.000L (100.000L)
Loc 19km NW of Rome, nr La Storta

Parco de' Medici (1989)
Viale Parco de' Medici 20, 00149 Roma
Tel **(06) 655 3477**
Fax **(06) 655 3344**
Holes 18 L 6318 m SSS 73
V'tors U
Fees 90.000L
Loc 15km SW of Rome, nr Airport
Arch P Fazio

Le Querce
San Martino, 01015 Sutri (VT)
Tel **(0761) 68789**
Fax **(0761) 68142**
Holes 18 L 6433 m SSS 72
V'tors U
Fees 50.000L (70.000L)
Loc 42km N of Rome
Arch Fazio/Mezzacane

Roma (1903)
Via Appia Nuova 716A, 00178 Roma
Tel **(06) 780 3407**
Fax **(06) 783 46219**
Holes 18 L 5825 m SSS 71
V'tors WD–H WE–M H
Fees 65.000L (90.000L)
Loc 7km SE of Rome towards Ciampino

Tarquinia
Loc Pian di Spille, Via degli Alina 271, 01016 Marina Velca/Tarquinia (VT)
Tel **(0766) 812109**
Holes 9 L 5442 m SSS 69
Loc 80km N of Rome on coast

Torvaianica
Via Enna 30, 00040 Marina di Ardea
Tel **(06) 913 3250**
Fax **(06) 913 3592**
Holes 9 L 4416 m SSS 64
V'tors H
Fees 20.000L
Loc 30km S of Rome
Arch Leonardo Basili

Sardinia

Is Molas (1975)
CP 49, 09010 Pula
Tel **(070) 924 1013/4**
Fax **(070) 924 1015**
Holes 18 L 6383 m SSS 72
Fees 80.000L (100.000L)
Loc Pula, 32km S of Cagliari
Arch Cotton/Pennink/Lurie

Pevero GC Costa Smeralda (1972)
07020 Porto Cervo
Tel **(0789) 96072/96210/96211**
Fax **(0789) 96572**
Holes 18 L 6186 m SSS 72
V'tors U
Fees 60.000–130.000L
Loc Porto Cervo, 30km N of Olbia, on Costa Smeralda
Arch Robert Trent Jones

Turin & Piemonte

Alpino Di Stresa (1924)
Viale Golf Panorama 49, 28040 Vezzo (NO)
Tel **(0323) 20101**
Fax **(0323) 20642**
Holes 9 L 5359 m SSS 67
V'tors WE–U WE–restricted
Fees 50.000L (70.000L)
Loc 7km W of Stresa. Milan 80km
Arch Peter Gannon

Biella Le Betulle (1958)
Valcarozza, 13050 Magnano (VC)
Tel **(015) 679151**
Fax **(015) 679276**
Holes 18 L 6427 m SSS 72
V'tors U
Fees 90.000L (110.000L)
Loc 17km SW of Biella
Arch John Morrison

Cervino (1955)
11021 Cervinia-Breuil (AO)
Tel **(0166) 949131**
Fax **(011) 581 8432**
Holes 9 L 4796 m SSS 66
V'tors U
Fees 65.000L–85.000L
Loc 53km NE of Aosta
Arch Donald Harradine

Cherasco CC (1983)
Loc Fraschetta, Cascina Roma, 12062 Cherasco (CN)
Tel **(0172) 489772/488489**
Fax **(0172) 488304**
Holes 18 L 5863 m SSS 71
V'tors H
Fees 50.000L (80.000L)
Loc Cherasco, 45km S of Turin
Arch Gianmarco Croze

Claviere (1923)
Strada Nazionale 45, 10050 Claviere (TO)
Tel **(0122) 878917**
Holes 9 L 4650 m SSS 65
V'tors U
Fees 70.000L
Loc 96km W of Turin
Arch Luzi

Courmayeur
11013 Courmayeur (AO)
Tel **(0165) 89103**
Holes 9 L 2650 m SSS 67
Loc 5km NE of Courmayeur

Le Fronde (1973)
Via Sant-Agostino 68, 10051 Avigliana (TO)
Tel **(011) 938053/930540**
Fax **(011) 930928**
Holes 18 L 5976 m SSS 71
V'tors WD–U WE–H max 26 (men) 30 (ladies)
Fees 60.000L (80.000L)
Loc Avigliana, 20km W of Turin
Arch John Harris

Iles Borromees
Via de Martini 15, 28049 Stresa (NO)
Tel **(0323) 29285/30243**
Fax **(0323) 31075**
Holes 18 L 6445 m SSS 72
V'tors U
Fees 60.000L (80.000L)
Loc 5km S of Stresa. 80km NW of Milan
Arch Marco Croze

Margara (1975)
Via Tenuta Margara 5, 15043 Fubine (AL)
Tel **(0131) 778555**
Fax **(0131) 778772**
Holes 18 L 6045 m SSS 72
Loc 15km NW of Alessandria

La Margherita
Strada Pralormo 29, Carmagnola (TO)
Tel **(011) 979 5113**
Fax **(011) 979 5204**
Holes 18 L 6339 m SSS 73
V'tors U
Fees 50.000L (80.000L)
Loc 20km S of Turin
Arch Croze/Ferraris

Piandisole (1964)
Via Pineta 1, 28057 Premeno (NO)
Tel **(0323) 587100**
Holes 9 L 2830 m SSS 67
Fees 40.000L (60.000L)
Loc Premeno, 30km N of Stresa

I Roveri (1971)
Rotta Cerbiatta 24, 10070 Fiano (TO)
Tel **(011) 923 5719/923 5667**
Fax **(011) 923 5668**
Holes 18 L 6218 m SSS 72
9 L 3107 m SSS 36
V'tors WE–NA
Fees 80.000L (100.000L)
Loc 16km NW of Turin. Caselle Airport 10km
Arch Robert Trent Jones

Santa Croce
Fraz Mellana, 12012 Bóves (CN)
Tel **(0171) 387041**
Fax **(0171) 387512**
Holes 18 L 6000 m SSS 72
V'tors U
Fees 50.000L (70.000L)
Loc 80km S of Turin, nr Cúneo
Arch Graham Cooke

La Serra (1970)
Via Astigliano 42, 15048 Valenza (AL)
Tel **(0131) 954778**
Fax **(0131) 954778**
Holes 9 L 2820 m SSS 70
V'tors H
Fees 25.000L (40.000L)
Loc 4km W of Valenza. 7km N of Alessandria
Arch Migliorini

Sestrieres (1932)
Piazza Agnelli 4, 10058 Sestrieres (TO)
Tel **(0122) 755170/76243**
Fax **(0122) 76294**
Holes 18 L 4598 m Par 67 SSS 65
V'tors U H
Fees 50.000L (80.000L)
Loc Sestrieres, 96km W of Turin

Stupinigi (1972)
Corso Unione Sovietica 506, 10135 Torino
Tel **(011) 347 2640**
Fax **(011) 397 8038**
Holes 9 L 2175 m SSS 63
Loc Mirafiore, Turin

Torino (1924)
Via Grange 137, 10070 Fiano Torinese
Tel **(011) 923 5440/923 5670**
Fax **(011) 923 5886**
Holes 18 L 6216 m SSS 72
18 L 6214 m SSS 72
Fees 70.000L (90.000L)
Loc 23km NW of Turin
Arch John Morrison

Villa La Motta
Via Martiri della Libertà 2, 21028 Travedona Monate (VA)
Tel **(0332) 978101**
Fax **(0332) 977532**
Holes 18 L 6400 m SSS 73 Par 72
V'tors H
Fees 50.000L (90.000L)
Loc 30km SW of Varese. 50km NW of Milan
Arch Piero Mancinelli

Vinovo (1984)
Via Debouche, 10048 Vinovo (TO)
Tel **(011) 965 3880**
Fax **(011) 962 3748**
Holes 9 L 4164 m SSS 62
V'tors U
Fees 30.000L (40.000L)
Loc 3km SW of Turin
Arch AP Croce

Tuscany & Umbria

Casentino (1985)
Loc Il Palazzo, 52014 Poppi (Arezzo)
Tel **(0575) 52810**
Fax **(0575) 520167**
Holes 9 L 5550 m SSS 69
V'tors WD–U WE–H
Fees 30.000L W–150.000L
Loc Poppi, 50km SE of Florence

Castelfalfi G & CC
50050 Montaione (FI)
Tel **(0571) 698093/4**
Fax **(0571) 698098**
Holes 18 L 6095 m SSS 73
V'tors H
Fees 50.000L
Loc 45km SW of Florence
Arch Pier Mancinelli

Conero GC Sirolo (1987)
Via Betellico 6, 60020 Sirolo (AN)
Tel **(071) 736 0613**
Fax **(071) 736 0380**
Holes 18 L 6185 m Par 72
9 hole course Par 29
V'tors H
Fees 60.000L (75.000L)
Loc Sirolo, 20km SE of Ancona. Falconara Airport 25km
Arch Marco Croze

Cosmopolitan G & CC (1992)
Viale Pisorno 60, 56018 Tirrenia
Tel **(050) 33633**
Fax **(050) 33085**
Holes 18 L 6291 m SSS 73
V'tors U
Fees 60.000L
Loc 15km SW of Pisa
Arch David Mezzacane

Firenze Ugolino
Strada Chiantigiana 3, 50015 Grassina
Tel **(055) 205 1009/203 1085**
Fax **(055) 230 1141**
Holes 18 L 5785 m SSS 70
V'tors U
Fees 50.000L (70.000L)
Loc Grassina, 9km S of Florence

Lamborghini-Panicale (1992)
Loc Soderi 1, 06064 Panicale (PG)
Tel **(075) 837582**
Fax **(075) 837582**
Holes 9 L 2860 m SSS 36
V'tors H
Fees 25.000L (35.000L)
Loc 30km W of Perugia, nr Lake Trasimeno
Arch Lamborghini Ferruccio

Montecatini (1985)
Via Dei Brogi 5, Loc Pievaccia, 51015 Monsummano Terme
Tel **(0572) 62218**
Fax **(0572) 617435**
Holes 18 L 5932 m SSS 71
V'tors WD–U
Loc 8km SE of Montecatini Terme. 50km SW of Florence (A11)

Perugia (1960)
06074 Santa Sabina-Ellera
Tel **(075) 517 2204**
Fax **(075) 517 2370**
Holes 18 L 5650 m SSS 71
V'tors U
Fees 50.000L (60.000L)
Loc 6km NW of Perugia
Arch David Mezzacane

Punta Ala (1964)
Via del Golf 1, 58040 Punta Ala (GR)
Tel **(0564) 922121/922719**
Fax **(0564) 920182**
Holes 18 L 6213 m SSS 72
V'tors U
Fees 50.000–80.000L
Loc 40km NW of Grosseto. Siena 90km. Florence 150km

Tirrenia (1968)
Viale San Guido, 56018 Tirrenia (PI)
Tel **(050) 37518**
Fax **(050) 33286**
Holes 9 L 3065 m SSS 72
Loc 15km SW of Pisa on coast

Venice & North East

Albarella
Isola de Albarella, 45010 Rosolina (RO)
Tel **(0426) 330124**
Fax **(0426) 330628**
Holes 18 L 6040 m SSS 72
V'tors H
Fees 70.000L (90.000L)
Loc 64km S of Venice
Arch Harris/Croze

Ca' della Nave (1986)
Piazza Vittoria 14, 30030 Martellago
Tel **(041) 540 1555**
Fax **(041) 540 1926**
Holes 18 L 6380 m SSS 73
9 L 1240 m Par 28
V'tors H
Fees 80.000L (100.000L)
Loc Martellago, 12km NW of Venice
Arch Arnold Palmer

Cansiglio (1956)
CP 152, 31029 Vittorio Veneto
Tel **(0438) 585398**
Holes 9 L 5726 m SSS 70
V'tors WD–U WE–H
Fees 50.000L (65.000L)
Loc 21km NE of Vittorio Veneto
Arch Robert Trent Jones

Colli Berici
Strada Monti Comunali, 36040 Brendola (VI)
Tel **(0444) 601780**
Holes 9 L 2859 m SSS 35
Loc Vicenza 10km. Venice 100km

Frassanelle (1990)
35030 Frassanelle di Rovolon (PD)
Tel **(049) 991 0722**
Fax **(049) 991 0722**
Holes 18 L 6180 m SSS 72
V'tors H
Fees 70.000L (90.000L)
Loc 20km S of Padova, by Via dei Colli
Arch Marco Croze

Lignano
Via Bonifica 3, 33054 Lignano Sabbiadoro
Tel **(0431) 428025**
Fax **(0431) 423230**
Holes 18 L 6280 m SSS 72
V'tors H
Fees 60.000L (80.000L)
Loc 90km E of Venice on coast
Arch Marco Croze

La Montecchia (1989)
Via Montecchia 16, 35030 Selvazzano (PD)
Tel **(049) 805 5550**
Fax **(049) 805 5737**
Holes 18 L 6255 m SSS 72
9 L 3012 m Par 36
V'tors U H
Fees 60.000L
Loc 8km W of Padova. 40km W of Venice
Arch T Macauley

Padova (1966)
35050 Valsanzibio di Galzigano
Tel **(049) 913 0078**
Fax **(049) 913 1193**
Holes 18 L 6053 m SSS 72
Loc Valsanzibio, 20km S of Padua

San Floriano-Gorizia (1987)
Castello di San Floriano, 34070 San Floriano del Collio (GO)
Tel **(0481) 884252**
Fax **(0481) 884252**
Holes 9 L 2600 m Par 55
V'tors U
Fees 25.000L (30.000L)
Loc 6km NW of Gorizia. 50km SE of Udine, nr Slovenian border
Arch Pellicciari

Trieste (1954)
Via Padriciano 80, 34012 Trieste
Tel **(040) 226159/227062**
Fax **(040) 226159**
Holes 9 L 5826 m SSS 71
Loc Padriciano, 7km E of Trieste

Udine (1971)
Via dei Fagi 1, 33034 Fagagna-Villaverde (UD)
Tel **(0432) 800418**
Fax **(0432) 800418**
Holes 9 L 2944 m SSS 71
Loc 15km NW of Udine

Venezia (1928)
Via del Forte, 30011 Alberoni
Tel **(041) 731015/731333**
Fax **(041) 731339**
Holes 18 L 6199 m SSS 72
V'tors U H
Fees 80.000L (90.000L)
Loc Venice Lido
Arch Cruickshank/Cotton

Villa Condulmer (1960)
Via della Croce 3, 31021 Zerman di Mogliano Veneto
Tel **(041) 457062**
Fax **(041) 457202**
Holes 18 L 5995 m SSS 71
9 hole short course
Fees 60.000L (Sun–80.000L)
Loc 17km N of Venice
Arch Harris/Croze

Luxembourg

Clervaux (1990)
B P 5, 9701 Clervaux
Tel **92 93 95**
Fax **92 94 51**
Holes 18 holes SSS 72
V'tors H
Fees 900fl (1200fl)
Loc North Luxembourg

Gaichel
Rue de Eischen, 8469 La Gaichel
Tel **39 71 08**
Fax **39037**
Holes 9 L 5170 m SSS 70
V'tors U H
Fees 700fr (900fr)
Loc 10km W of Mersch on Belgian border. Arlon 3km
Arch Pierre Petry

Grand-Ducal de Luxembourg (1936)
1 Route de Trèves, 2633 Senneringberg
Tel **34 00 90**
Fax **34 83 91**
Holes 18 L 5765 m SSS 71
Fees 1500fr (2000fr)
Loc 7km N of Luxembourg

Kikuoka CC Chant Val (1991)
Scheierhaff, 5412 Canach
Tel **35 61 35**
Fax **35 74 50**
Holes 18 L 6404 m SSS 74
V'tors H
Fees 2060fr (2575fr)
Loc 20km E of Luxembourg City
Arch Iwao Uematsu

Malta

Royal Malta (1888)
Marsa HMR 15, Malta
Tel **23 38 51**
Fax **23 18 09**
Holes 18 L 5020 m SSS 68
V'tors U H exc Thurs–NA before 10am Sat–NA before noon
Fees £M10 W–£M50
Loc Marsa, 3 miles from Valetta

Netherlands

Amsterdam & Noord Holland

Amsterdam Old Course (1990)
Zwarte Laantje 4, 1099 CE Amsterdam
Tel **(020) 694 3650**
Fax **(020) 663 4621**
Holes 9 L 5264 m SSS 68
V'tors WE–H
Fees 75fl (90fl)
Loc 5km SE of Amsterdam

Amsterdamse (1934)
Baudinlaan 35, 1165 NE Halfweg
Tel **(02907) 7866**
Fax **(02907) 5966**
Holes 18 L 6124 m SSS 72
V'tors H
Fees 75fl (100fl)
Loc 10km W of Amsterdam
Arch Rolin/Jol

Haarlemmermeersche
Spieringweg, Cruquiusdijk 122, 2141 EV Vijfhuizen
Tel **(02508) 1706**
Fax **(02508) 3515**
Holes 9 L 6087 m SSS 72
9 hole short course
V'tors H
Fees 50fl
Loc Haarlemmermeer, W of Amsterdam
Arch C O'Connor Jr

Kennemer G & CC (1910)
PO Box 85, 2040 AB Zandvoort
Tel **(02507) 12836/18456**
Fax **(02507) 19520**
Holes 27 holes SSS 72:
Van Hengel 9 L 2951 m
Pennink 9 L 2916 m
Colt 9 L 2942 m
V'tors H WE–NA before 3pm
Fees 100fl
Loc Zandvoort, 6km W of Haarlem
Arch Colt/Pennink

De Noordhollandse (1982)
Sluispolderweg 6, 1817 BM Alkmaar
Tel **(072) 201143**
Fax **(072) 156179**
Holes 18 L 6084 m SSS 72
V'tors H or proficiency card
Fees 50–75fl (75–100fl)
Loc 2km N of Alkmaar
Arch Ryks/Dudok van Heel

Olympus (1973)
Abcouderstraatweg 46, 1105 AA Amsterdam Zuid-Oost
Tel **(02946) 5373/1241**
Fax **(02946) 5373**
Holes 18 L 5926 m SSS 71
V'tors U–phone first
Fees 50fl (60fl)
Loc SE of Amsterdam, nr A2 and AMC Hospital
Arch Dudok van Heel/Jol

Purmer (1989)
Westerweg 60, Postbus 587, 1440 AN Purmerend
Tel **(02990) 62143**
Fax **(02990) 62143..8888**
Holes 18 L 6079 m SSS 70
9 hole course
V'tors H
Fees 45–80fl
Loc 16km N of Amsterdam
Arch Huxley

Spaarnwoude (1977)
Het Hoge Land 3, 1981 LT Velsen
Tel **(023) 382708**
Fax **(023) 387274**
Holes 18 L 5676 m SSS 70
9 L 2981 m SSS 36
18 hole short course
V'tors H
Fees 38fl
Loc 14km W of Amsterdam. 10km NE of Haarlem
Arch Pennink/Jol

Zaanse (1988)
Zuiderweg 68, 1456 NH Wijdewormer
Tel **(02990) 38199**
Holes 9 L 5282 m SSS 68
V'tors WD–H WE–H before noon and after 3pm
Fees 40fl (50fl)
Loc 15km NE of Amsterdam
Arch Gerard Jol

Breda & South West

Brugse Vaart (1993)
Brugse Vaart 10, 4501 NE Oostburg
Tel **(01170) 53410**
Fax **(01170) 55511**
Holes 18 L 6195 m SSS 72
V'tors U
Fees 40fl (50fl)
Loc 15km N of Bruges, nr Knokke
Arch Devos/Bauwens

Domburgsche (1914)
Schelpweg 26, 4357 BP Domburg
Tel **(01188) 1573**
Fax **(01188) 2728**
Holes 9 L 5082 m SSS 67
V'tors H
Fees 50fl (60fl)
Loc 15km NW of Middelburg

Grevelingenhout (1988)
Oudendijk 2, 4311 NA Bruinisse
Tel **(01113) 2650**
Holes 18 L 5951 m SSS 71
9 hole Par 3 course
V'tors WD–U H WE–NA
Fees 73fl
Loc 55km SW of Rotterdam
Arch Donald Harradine

Oosterhoutse (1985)
Dukaatstraat 21, 4903 RN Oosterhout
Tel **(01620) 58759**
Fax **(01620) 33285**
Holes 18 L 6066 m SSS 72
V'tors WD–U H WE–M
Fees 60fl (65fl)
Loc 10km NE of Breda
Arch J Dudok van Heel

Reymerswael (1986)
Grensweg 21, 4411 St Rilland Bath
Tel **(01135) 1265**
Fax **(01135) 1264**
Holes 9 L 5986 m SSS 72
V'tors H
Fees 40fl (50fl)
Loc 20km W of Bergen op Zoom. 50km W of Breda, off A58

Toxandria (1928)
Veenstraat 89, 5124 NC Molenschot
Tel **(01611) 2347**
Fax **(01611) 1715**
Holes 18 L 5974 m SSS 71
V'tors WD–I Phone first
Fees 75fl (100fl)
Loc 8km E of Breda
Arch Morrison/Dudok van Heel

De Woeste Kop (1986)
Justasweg 4, 4571 NB Axel
Tel **(01155) 64467/64831 (Pro)**
Holes 9 L 5496 m SSS 69
V'tors U
Fees 30fl (50fl)
Loc 45km W of Antwerp
Arch Paneels/Bosch

Wouwse Plantage (1981)
Zoomvlietweg 66, 4725 TD Wouwse Plantage
Tel **(01657) 9593**
Holes 18 L 5909 m SSS 71
V'tors H WE–M
Fees 60fl (70fl)
Loc 10km E of Bergen-op-Zoom, nr Roosendaal
Arch Pennink/Rolin

East Central

Breuninkhof
Breuninkhof Weg, Bussloo
Tel **(05716) 1955**
Holes 9 L 6178 m SSS 72
V'tors H
Fees 55fl (65fl)
Loc 100km E of Amsterdam
Arch Eschauzier

Edese (1978)
Papendalaan 22, 6816 VD Arnhem
Tel **(08308) 21985**
Fax **(08308) 21348**
Holes 18 L 5740 m SSS 70
V'tors H
Fees 60fl (80fl)
Loc National Sportcentrum Pappendal. NW of Arnhem, towards Ede
Arch Pennink/Dudok van Heel

Hattemse G & CC (1930)
Veenwal 11, 8051 AS Hattem
Tel **(05206) 41909**
Holes 9 L 5808 yds SSS 68
V'tors WD–H WE–M+H
Fees 50fl
Loc Hattem, 5km S of Zwolle

Keppelse (1926)
Oude Zutphenseweg 15, Hoog-Keppel
Tel **(08348) 1416**
Holes 9 L 5360 m SSS 68
Fees 55fl (65fl)
Loc Laag-Keppel, 25km E of Arnhem

De Koepel (1983)
Postbox 88, 7640 AB Wierden
Tel **(0546) 576150/574070**
Fax **(0546) 574070**
Holes 9 L 2863 m SSS 70
V'tors WE–H
Fees 60fl (80fl)
Loc 7km W of Almelo

Nunspeetse G & CC (1987)
Plesmanlaan 30, Nunspeet
Tel **(03412) 61758**
Fax **(03412) 61149**
Holes 27 L 6100 m SSS 71
Fees 70fl (85fl)
Loc Nunspeet, 25km SW of Zwolle
Arch Paul Rolin

Rosendaelsche (1895)
Apeldoornseweg 450, 6816 SN Arnhem
Tel **(085) 421438**
Holes 18 L 6057 m SSS 72
V'tors WD–H WE–NA
Fees 75fl
Loc 5km N of Arnhem on Route N50
Arch Frank Pennink

Sallandsche De Hoek (1934)
PO Box 24, 7430 AA Diepenveen
Tel **(05709) 3269**
Fax **(05709) 3269**
Holes 18 L 5889 m SSS 71
V'tors H
Fees 75fl (90fl)
Loc 6km N of Deventer
Arch Pennink/Steel

Twentsche (1926)
Enschedesestraat 381, 7552 CV Hengelo
Tel **(074) 912773**
Holes 9 L 5444 m SSS 68
V'tors WD–H WE–M
Fees 50fl
Loc 3km SE of Hengelo

Veluwse (1957)
Nr 57, 7346 AC Hoog Soeren
Tel **(05769) 1275**
Holes 9 L 6264 yds SSS 70
V'tors WD–U WD–H
Fees 60fl (70fl)
Loc 5km W of Apeldoorn

Eindhoven & South East

Berendonck (1987)
Weg Door de Berendonck 40, 6603 LP Wijchen
Tel **(08894) 20039**
Fax **(08894) 11254**
Holes 18 L 5671 m SSS 70
V'tors WE–restricted
Fees 40fl (50fl)
Loc 5km SW of Nijmegen
Arch J Dudok van Heel

Best G & CC
Golflaan 1, 5683 RZ Best
Tel **(04998) 91443**
Fax **(04998) 93221**
Holes 18 L 6079 m SSS 71
V'tors U
Fees 60fl (80fl)
Loc Best, 15km NW of Eindhoven
Arch J Dudok van Heel

Crossmoor G & CC (1986)
Laurabosweg 8, 6006 VR Weert
Tel **(04950) 18438**
Holes 18 L 6052 m SSS 72
9 hole Par 3 course
V'tors H
Fees 60fl (80fl)
Loc Weert/Altweertheide, 30km SE of Eindhoven
Arch J Dudok van Heel

De Dommel (1928)
Zegenwerp 12, 5271 NC St Michielsgestel
Tel **(04105) 12316**
Holes 18 L 5565 m SSS 69
V'tors WD–H WE–NA
Fees 75fl (90fl)
Loc 10km S of Hertogenbosch
Arch Colt/Steel

Eindhovensche (1930)
Eindhovenseweg 300, 5553 VB Valkenswaard
Tel **(04902) 14816**
Fax **(04902) 44038**
Holes 18 L 5918 m SSS 71

V'tors H
Fees 75fl (100fl)
Loc 8km S of Eindhoven
Arch HS Colt

Geysteren G & CC (1974)
Het Spekt 2, 5862 AZ Geysteren
Tel **(04784) 1809/2592**
Fax **(04784) 2963**
Holes 18 L 6063 m SSS 72
V'tors WD–H WE–M
Fees 80fl (100fl)
Loc Off N271, nr Wanssum. 25km N of Venlo

Haviksoord (1976)
Maarheezerweg Nrd 11, 5595 XG Leende (NB)
Tel **(04906) 1818**
Fax **(040) 813306**
Holes 9 L 5880 m SSS 71
V'tors H
Fees 35fl (45fl)
Loc 10km S of Eindhoven

Het Rijk van Nijmegen (1985)
Postweg 17, 6561 KJ Groesbeek
Tel **(08891) 76644**
Fax **(08891) 76942**
Holes 18 L 6037 m SSS 72
18 L 5869 m SSS 70
V'tors H
Fees 60fl (80fl)
Loc 5km E of Nijmegen
Arch Paul Rolin

De Schoot (1973)
Schootsedijk 18, 5491 TD Sint Oedenrode
Tel **(04138) 73011**
Holes 9 L 2630 m SSS 68
V'tors U
Fees 40fl (45fl)
Loc 20km N of Eindhoven

Tongelreep G & CC (1984)
Charles Roelslaan 15, 5644 ZX Eindhoven
Tel **(040) 520962**
Holes 9 L 5260 m SSS 69
V'tors WD–H WE–H by introduction only
Fees 30fl (40fl)
Loc 3km S of Eindhoven
Arch J van Rooy

Limburg Province

Brunssummerheide (1985)
Rimburgerweg 50, Brunssum
Tel **(045) 270968**
Fax **(045) 273939**
Holes 27 L 5933 m SSS 71
9 hole Par 3 course
V'tors U H
Fees 60fl (75fl)
Loc 25km NE of Maastricht

Hoenshuis G & CC (1987)
Hoensweg 17, 6367 GN Voerendaal
Tel **(045) 753300/754488**
Fax **(045) 750900**
Holes 18 L 6074 m SSS 72
V'tors WE–NA 10am–2pm
Fees 60fl (90fl)
Loc Limburg, 10km NE of Maastricht
Arch Paul Rolin

De Zuid Limburgse G & CC (1956)
Dalbissenweg 22, 6281 NC Mechelen
Tel **(04455) 1397 (Clubhouse), (04455) 1254 (Sec)**
Fax **(04455) 1576**
Holes 18 L 5924 m SSS 71
V'tors WD–U WE–H
Fees 60fl (90fl)
Loc Mechelen, 23km SE of Maastricht
Arch Hawtree/Snelder/Rolin

North

Gelpenberg (1970)
Gebbeveenweg 1, 7854 TD Aalden
Tel **(05917) 1784**
Fax **(05917) 2174**
Holes 18 L 6031 m SSS 71
V'tors H
Fees 50fl (60fl)
Loc 16km W of Emmen
Arch Pennink/Steel

Holthuizen (1985)
Oosteinde 7a, 9301 ZP Roden
Tel **(05908) 15103**
Holes 9 L 5486 m SSS 69
V'tors H
Fees 52.50fl (62.50fl)
Loc 10km S of Groningen

Lauswolt G & CC (1964)
Van Harinxmaweg 8A, PO Box 36, 9244 ZN Beetsterzwaag
Tel **(05126) 2594/3590**
Fax **(05126) 3739**
Holes 9 L 4985 m SSS 67
V'tors H
Fees 80fl (100fl)
Loc Beetsterzwaag, 5km S of Drachten
Arch Pennink/Steel

Noord Nederlandse G & CC (1950)
Pollselaan 5, 9756 CJ Glimmen
Tel **(05906) 2004**
Fax **(05906) 1922**
Holes 18 L 4891 m SSS 70
V'tors H
Fees 60fl (90fl)
Loc 12km S of Groningen, off A28

De Semslanden (1989)
Nieuwe Dijk 1, 9514 BX Gasselternijveen
Tel **(05999) 65353/64661**
Holes 9 L 6058 m SSS 72
V'tors H
Fees 40fl (50fl)
Loc 20km W of Assen
Arch Eschauzier/Thate

Vegilinbosschen
Legemeersterweg 18, 8527 DS Legemeer
Tel **(05138) 96111**
Fax **(05138) 99777**
Holes 18 L 5765 m SSS 70
V'tors H
Fees 60fl (80fl)
Loc 100km N of Amsterdam
Arch Allen Rijks

Rotterdam & The Hague

Broekpolder (1981)
Watersportweg 100, 3138 HD Vlaardingen
Tel **(010) 475 0011/474 8140/ 474 8142**
Fax **(010) 474 4094**
Holes 18 L 6048 m SSS 72
V'tors H
Fees 50–80fl (75–100fl)
Loc 15km W of Rotterdam, off A20
Arch Frank Pennink

Capelle a/d Ijssel (1977)
Gravenweg 311, 2905 LB Capelle a/d Ijssel
Tel **(010) 442 2485**
Holes 18 L 5217 m SSS 68
V'tors WD–U WE–M
Fees 40fl (60fl)
Loc 5km S of Rotterdam
Arch Donald Harradine

Cromstrijen (1989)
Veerweg 26, 3281 LX Numansdorp
Tel **(01865) 4455**
Fax **(01865) 4681**
Holes 18 L 6128 m SSS 72
9 hole course
V'tors WD–I H WE–M H
Fees 65fl (85fl)
Loc 30km S of Rotterdam (A29)
Arch Tom McAuley

De Hooge Bergsche (1989)
Rottebandreef 40, 2661 JK Bergschenhoek
Tel **(01892) 20052/20703**
Fax **(01892) 19350**
Holes 18 L 5370 m SSS 68
V'tors U
Fees 45fl (60fl)
Loc Bergschenhoek, 2km NE of Rotterdam
Arch Gerard Jol

Kleiburg (1974)
Krabbeweg 9, 3231 NB Brielle
Tel **(01810) 17809/13330**
Fax **(01810) 10026**
Holes 18 L 5652 m SSS 69
V'tors U
Fees 40–55fl
Loc 25km W of Rotterdam
Arch Pennink/Jol

Koninklijke Haagsche G & CC (1893)
Groot Haesebroekeseweg 22, 2242 EC Wassenaar
Tel **(01751) 79607**
Fax **(01751) 40171**
Holes 18 L 5674 m SSS 71
V'tors I–phone first
Fees 120fl
Loc 6km N of The Hague
Arch Allison

Kralingen (1933)
Kralingseweg 200, 3062 CG Rotterdam
Tel **(010) 452 2283**
Holes 9 L 5277 yds SSS 66
V'tors H
Fees 30fl (40fl)
Loc 5km from centre of Rotterdam
Arch Copijn/Cotton

De Merwelanden (1985)
Golfbaan Crayestein, Baanhoekweg 50, 3313 LP Dordrecht
Tel **(078) 211221**
Fax **(078) 161036**
Holes 18 holes SSS 70
V'tors U
Fees 40fl (47.50fl)
Loc 20km SE of Rotterdam
Arch H & C Kuijsters

Noordwijkse (1915)
Randweg 25, PO Box 70, 2200 AB Noordwijk
Tel **(0252) 373763**
Fax **(0252) 370044**
Holes 18 L 5879 m SSS 72
V'tors WD–H before noon and after 3pm WE–H before 8am. Phone for reservations
Fees 100fl
Loc 5km N of Noordwyk. 15km NW of Leiden
Arch Frank Pennink

Rijswijkse (1987)
Delftweg 58, 2289 AL Rijswijk
Tel **(070) 319 24 24**
Fax **(070) 319 13 17**
Holes 18 L 6159 m Par 72 SSS 71
V'tors U H
Fees 70fl (90fl)
Loc 5km SE of The Hague
Arch Donald Steel

Rozenstein (1984)
Hoge Klei 1, 2242 XZ Wassenaar
Tel **(01751) 17846**
Holes 18 L 5820 m SSS 70
V'tors H
Fees 60fl (90fl)
Loc 14km NE of The Hague
Arch Dudok van Heel/Jol

Zeegersloot (1984)
Kromme Aarweg 5, PO Box 190, 2400 AD Alphen a/d Rijn
Tel **(01720) 74567/44670**
Fax **(01720) 94660**
Holes 18 L 5872 m SSS 71
9 hole Par 3 course
V'tors U H
Fees 18 hole:45fl (60fl)
9 hole:25fl (35fl)
Loc Alphen, 15km N of Gouda. 20km S of Amsterdam
Arch Gerard Jol

Utrecht & Hilversum

Almeerderhout (1986)
Watersnipweg 19-21, 1341 AA Almere
Tel **(036) 532 1818**
Fax **(036) 532 6645**
Holes 27 L 5896 m Par 72 SSS 71
9 hole Par 3 course
V'tors WD–U WE–M (Max h'cap 28)
Fees 55fl (75fl)
Loc 30km N of Hilversum
Arch J Dudok van Heel

Anderstein
Woudenbergseweg 13a, 3953 ME Maarsbergen
Tel **(03433) 1330/1560**
Fax **(03433) 2062**
Holes 18 L 6015 m SSS 71
V'tors WE–M only
Fees 60–75fl
Loc 20km E of Utrecht
Arch Jol/Dudok van Heel

De Batouwe (1990)
Oost Kanaalweg 1, 4011 LA Zoelen
Tel **(03440) 24370**
Fax **(03440) 13096**
Holes 18 L 5717 m Par 72 SSS 70
9 hole Par 3 course
V'tors U H–booking necessary
Fees 60fl (80fl)
Loc Tiel, 25km SE of Utrecht
Arch Alan Rijks

Flevoland
Bosweg 98, 8231 DZ Lelystad
Tel **(03200) 30077**
Holes 9 L 5888 m SSS 71
V'tors WD–U H WE–M+H
Fees D–45fl (D–55fl)
Loc Island of Flevoland. 1km NW of Lelystad. 45km N of Hilversum
Arch JS Eschauzier

De Haar (1974)
PO Box 104, Parkweg 5, 3450 AC Vleuten
Tel **(03407) 72860**
Fax **(03407) 73903**
Holes 9 L 6650 yds SSS 72
V'tors H
Fees 100fl (150fl)
Loc 10km NW of Utrecht
Arch F Pennink

Hilversumsche (1910)
Soestdijkerstraatweg 172, 1213 XJ Hilversum
Tel **(035) 857060**
Fax **(035) 853813**
Holes 18 L 5856 m SSS 71
V'tors Phone booking necessary
Fees 75fl (100fl)
Loc 3km E of Hilversum, nr Baarn
Arch H Burrows

De Hoge Kleij (1985)
Appelweg 4, 3832 RK Leusden
Tel **(033) 616944**
Fax **(033) 652921**
Holes 18 L 6046 m SSS 72
V'tors WE–H
Fees 60fl (90fl)
Loc 1km SE of Amersfoort 20km NE of Utrecht via A28
Arch Donald Steel

Nieuwegeinse (1985)
Postbus 486, 3437 AL Nieuwegein
Tel **(03402) 40769/42192**
Holes 9 L 2348 m SSS 65
V'tors U
Fees 35fl (50fl)
Loc 7km S of Utrecht
Arch Paul Rolin

Utrechtse De Pan (1894)
Amersfoortseweg 1, 3735 LJ Bosch en Duin
Tel **(03404) 55223 (Sec), (03404) 56427 (Pro)**
Fax **(03404) 63769**
Holes 18 L 6070 m SSS 72
V'tors WD–H (phone first) WE–NA
Fees 60fl (90fl)
Loc 10km E of Utrecht, off A28
Arch HS Colt

Zeewolde
Golflaan 1, 3896 LL Zeewolde
Tel **(03242) 2103**
Fax **(03242) 4100**
Holes 18 L 5954 m SSS 70
V'tors WE–H
Fees 45fl (65fl)
Loc 20km N of Hilversum. 60km NE of Amsterdam

For list of abbreviations see page 435

Norway

Arendal og Omegn (1986)
Postboks 158, 4901 Tvedestrand
Tel **37 16 29 33**
Fax **37 16 21 12**
Holes 9 L 2970 m SSS 36
Fees D–130kr
Loc Nes Verk, 95km NE of Kristiansand (E18)

Baerum
P O Box 31, 1355 Baerum
Tel **67 56 30 85**
Fax **67 56 03 87**
Holes 18 L 5300 m SSS 71
9 hole short course
V'tors WD–U H WE–M H between 11am–4pm. Booking advisable
Fees 200kr (250kr)
Loc 10km W of Oslo. 10km N of Sandvika

Bergen (1937)
PO Box 470, 5001 Bergen
Tel **05 18 20 77**
Holes 9 L 4461 m SSS 66
Fees D–150kr
Loc 8km N of Bergen

Borre
Semb Hovedgaard, 3186 Horten
Tel **33 07 32 40**
Fax **33 07 32 41**
Holes 18 L 6120 m SSS 73
V'tors H
Fees D–200kr
Loc Horten, 50km S of Drammen. 100km SW of Oslo
Arch T Nordström

Borregaard (1927)
PO Box 348, 1701 Sarpsborg
Tel **69 12 15 00**
Fax **69 15 74 11**
Holes 9 L 4500 m SSS 65
V'tors H
Fees 120kr
Loc Opsund, 1km N of Sarpsborg

Drobak
Belsjøun 50, 1440 Drobak
Tel **64 93 16 80**
Fax **64 93 39 80**
Holes 18 L 5340 m SSS 71
V'tors U
Fees 200kr
Loc 40km SE of Oslo

Groruddalen (1988)
Postboks 4 Vestli, 0911 Oslo
Tel **22 21 67 18**
Holes 9 L 2520 m SSS 54
V'tors U–before 2pm
Fees 100kr (150kr)
Loc 15km N of Oslo
Arch Leif Nilsson

Hedmark (1980)
PO Box 71, 2401 Elverum
Tel **62 41 35 88**
Holes 18 L 6319 m SSS 73
Fees 150kr
Loc Starmoen Fritidspark, 10km E of Elverum. 35km E of Hamar. 150km N of Oslo

Kjekstad (1976)
PO Box 201, 3440 Royken
Tel **31 28 58 50/31 28 53 53**
Fax **31 28 58 50**
Holes 18 L 5100 m SSS 67
V'tors H
Fees 150kr
Loc 12km SE of Drammen on Route 282. 40km SW of Oslo
Arch Jan Sederholm

Kristiansand (1973)
PO Box 6090, Søm, 4602 Kristiansand
Tel **38 04 35 85**
Fax **38 04 34 15**
Holes 9 L 2485 m SSS 70
V'tors U
Fees D–150kr
Loc 8km E of Kristiansand (E18)

Nes (1988)
Rommen Golfpark, 2160 Vormsund
Tel **63 90 29 29**
Holes 9 L 2649 m SSS 70
V'tors H or Green card
Fees 150kr (180kr)
Loc 50km NE of Oslo, via E6/RV2
Arch Hauser/Ritson

Onsoy
Postboks 458, 1601 Fredrikstad
Tel **69 33 35 90/69 33 35 55**
Holes 18 L 5600 m SSS 72
V'tors H
Fees 160–200kr
Loc 10km W of Fredrikstad. Oslo 80km
Arch Terje Andersen

Oppdal (1987)
PO Box 19, 7340 Oppdal
Holes 9 L 2621 m Par 68
V'tors U
Fees 150kr
Loc 120km S of Trondheim
Arch Jan Sederholm

Oppegård
P O Box 137, 1412 Sofiemyr
Tel **66 99 18 75**
Fax **66 99 18 95**
Holes 9 L 6315 m SSS 72
V'tors U
Fees 100kr (150kr)
Loc 22km S of Oslo

Oslo (1924)
Bogstad, 0757 Oslo
Tel **22 50 44 02**
Fax **22 73 09 12**
Holes 18 L 6719 yds SSS 72
V'tors H–(max: 24 men; 32 ladies) WD–restricted before 2pm WE–restricted after 2pm
Fees 250kr (300kr)
Loc 8km NW of Oslo. Signs to 'Bogstad Camping'

Oustoen CC (1965)
PO Box 82-Ljan, 1113 Oslo
Tel **67 53 52 95/22 29 62 02**
Fax **67 53 95 44**
Holes 18 L 5400m SSS 71
V'tors M
Fees 300kr
Loc Small island in Oslofjord, 10km W of Oslo

Skjeberg (1986)
PO Box 3014, Kurland, 1701 Sarpsborg
Tel **69 16 63 10**
Holes 18 L 5500 m SSS 72
V'tors U
Fees 130kr (150kr)
Loc Hevingen, 2km N of Sarpsborg
Arch Jan Sederholm

Sorknes
Sorknes Gaard, 2450 Rena
Tel **62 44 00 41**
Fax **62 44 00 27**
Holes 9 L 2850 m SSS 36
V'tors U
Fees 125kr (150kr)
Loc 170km N of Oslo
Arch Juul Soegaard

Stavanger (1956)
Longebakke 45, 4042 Hafrsfjord
Tel **51 55 54 31**
Fax **51 55 73 11**
Holes 18 L 5316 m SSS 70
V'tors H
Fees 200kr
Loc 6km SW of Stavanger
Arch F Smith

Trondheim (1950)
PO Box 169, 7001 Trondheim
Tel **73 53 18 85/92 01 74 47**
Fax **73 52 75 05**
Holes 9 L 5632 m SSS 72
V'tors H or Green Card
Fees 150kr
Loc Trondheim 3km

Vestfold (1958)
PO Box 64, 3173 Vear
Tel **33 36 56 55 (Sec)**
Fax **33 36 60 25**
Holes 18 L 5851 m SSS 73
V'tors H
Fees 200kr
Loc Tønsberg 8km
Arch F Smith

Portugal

Algarve

Alto Golf (1991)
P O Box 1, Alvor, 8500 Portimão
Tel **(082) 416913/401045-7**
Fax **(082) 401046**
Holes 18 L 6125 m SSS 73
V'tors H
Fees 7900esc
Loc 2km W of Portimão
Arch Cotton/Dobereiner

Carvoeiro (1991)
Vale Currais, Praia do Carvoeiro, Apartado 24, 8400 Lagoa Codex
Tel **(082) 342168**
Fax **(082) 342189**
Holes Gramacho 18 L 5919 m SSS 71; Vale da Pinta 18 L 5861 m SSS 71
V'tors U
Fees 8500esc
Loc 10km E of Portimao. 60km W of Faro, nr Lagoa
Arch Ronald Fream

Palmares (1975)
Meia Praia, 8600 Lagos
Tel **(082) 762953**
Fax **(082) 762534**
Holes 18 L 5961 m SSS 72
V'tors U
Fees 7000esc
Loc Meia Praia, 5km E of Lagos
Arch Frank Pennink

Parque da Floresta (1987)
Vale do Poço, Budens, 8650 Vila do Bispo
Tel **(082) 65333**
Fax **(082) 65157**
Holes 18 L 5787 m SSS 72
V'tors U
Fees D–6000esc
Loc 16km W of Lagos, nr Salema
Arch Pepe Gancedo

Penina (1966)
PO Box 146, Penina, 8502 Portimão
Tel **(082) 415415**
Fax **(082) 415000**
Holes Ch'ship 18 L 6439 m SSS 73; Monchique 9 L 3987 m SSS 71; Quinta 9 L 1851 m Par 30
V'tors H
Fees 5000–9500esc
Loc 5km W of Portimão. 12km E of Lagos
Arch Henry Cotton

Pine Cliffs G & CC (1991)
Sheraton Algarve Hotel, Praia da Falesia, 8200 Albufeira
Tel **(089) 501090/501999**
Fax **(089) 501950**
Holes 9 L 2324 m SSS 67
V'tors U H
Fees 9 holes–4000esc
Loc 7km W of Vilamoura
Arch Martin Hawtree

Pinheiros Altos (1992)
Quinta do Lago, 8135 Almancil
Tel **(089) 394340**
Holes 18 hole course
Fees 7000esc
Arch Ronald Fream

Quinta do Lago (1974)
Quinta Do Lago, 8135 Almancil
Tel **(089) 394782/394529/396002/3**
Fax **(089) 394013**
Holes Quinta do Lago 18 L 6488 m SSS 72; Ria Formosa 18 L 6205 m SSS 72
V'tors H–by prior arrangement
Fees 11.000esc
Loc 15km W of Faro. Airport 20km
Arch Mitchell/Lee

San Lorenzo (1988)
Quinta do Lago, 8135 Almancil
Tel **(089) 396522**
Fax **(089) 396908**
Holes 18 L 6238 m SSS 73
V'tors H–restricted
Fees 12.500esc
Loc 16km W of Faro
Arch Joseph Lee

Vale de Milho (1992)
Rua do Barranco, Praia do Carvoeiro, 8400 Lagoa
Tel **(082) 358502**
Fax **(082) 358497**
Holes 9 hole Par 3 course
Loc Jorge de Lagos Village. Carvoeiro 2km
Arch Dave Thomas

Vale do Lobo (1968)
8137 Vale Do Lobo
Tel **(089) 393939**
Fax **(089) 394713**
Holes 27 holes SSS 70-72
Green 9 L 2813 m Par 35
Orange 9 L 2975 m Par 36
Yellow 9 L 3036 m Par 36
Fees 10.000esc
Loc 19km W of Faro. Airport 19km
Arch Henry Cotton

Vila Sol (1991)
Alto do Semino, Vilamoura, 8125 Quarteira
Tel **(089) 302144/5/6**
Fax **(089) 302147**
Holes 18 L 6189 m SSS 72
V'tors U H
Fees 11.000 esc
Loc 5km E of Vilamoura. Faro Airport 10km
Arch Donald Steel

Vilamoura 1 (1969)
Vilamoura, 8125 Quarteira
Tel **(089) 321652**
Fax **(089) 380726**
Holes 18 L 6331 m SSS 72
V'tors H–booking necessary
Fees 8500esc
Loc Quarteira, 25km W of Faro
Arch Frank Pennink

Vilamoura 2 (1976)
Vilamoura, 8125 Quarteira
Tel **(089) 321562**
Fax **(089) 380726**
Holes 18 L 6256 m SSS 71
V'tors H–booking necessary
Fees 8500esc
Arch Pennink/Trent Jones

Vilamoura 3 (1990)
Vilamoura, 8125 Quarteira
Tel **(089) 380724**
Fax **(089) 380726**
Holes Pinhal 9 L 2935 m
Lago 9 L 2953 m
Marina 9 L 3180 m SSS 71/2
V'tors H–booking necessary
Fees 18 holes–6500esc
Arch Joseph Lee

Azores

Terceira Island (1954)
C P 15, 9760 Praia da Victória
Fax **(095) 92445**
Holes 18 L 5695 m SSS 70
V'tors U H
Fees US$ 30
Loc 13km NE of Angra do Heroismo

VerdeGolf CC (1990)
Av D João 111, Lote 4, 9500 Ponta Delgada (Açores)
Tel **(096) 34951**
Fax **(096) 34951**
Holes 18 L 6229 m SSS 72
V'tors U
Fees D–4000esc
Loc São Miguel Island. Furnas Villa 5km
Arch Mackenzie Ross/Cameron/Powell

Lisbon & Central Portugal

Aroeira (1972)
Herdade da Aroeira, Fonte da Telha, 2825 Monte da Caparica
Tel **(01) 297 1314/296 1802**
Fax **(01) 297 1283**
Holes 18 L 6040 m SSS 72
V'tors U H
Fees 6000esc (10.000esc)
Loc 20km S of Lisbon, off Setúbal/Costa da Caparica road
Arch Frank Pennink

Estoril (1945)

Avenida República, 2765 Estoril

Tel (01) 468 0176/468 1376
Fax (01) 468 2796
Holes 18 L 5210 m SSS 68
9 L 2350 m SSS 65
V'tors WD–U WE–M
Fees WD–7000–7350esc
Loc N of Estoril on Sintra road. 30km W of Lisbon
Arch Mackenzie Ross

Estoril-Sol Golf Academy (1976)

Quinta do Outeira, Linhó, 2710 Sintra

Tel (01) 923 2461
Fax (01) 923 2461
Holes 9 L 4228 m Par 62
V'tors U
Fees 3900esc
Loc 7km N of Estoril. Lisbon 35km
Arch Harris/Fream

Lisbon Sports Club (1922)

Casal da Carragueira, Belas, 2475 Queluz

Tel (01) 431 0077
Fax (01) 431 2482
Holes 18 L 5278 m SSS 69
V'tors U
Fees D–6000esc (8000esc)
Loc Belas-Queluz, 20km NW of Lisbon
Arch Hawtree

Montado

Algeruz, 2950 Palmela

Tel (01) 347 3381
Holes 18 L 6060 m SSS 72
Fees 6000P
Loc 5km E of Setúbal. 40km S of Lisbon

Penha Longa (1992)

Lagoa Azul, Linhó, 2710 Sintra

Tel (01) 924 9022
Fax (01) 924 9024
Holes 18 L 6228 m SSS 73
9 hole course (1995)
V'tors M H
Fees 8000esc (12.000esc)
Loc 8km N of Estoril. 17km W of Lisbon
Arch Robert Trent Jones Jr

Quinta da Marinha (1984)

Quinta da Marinha, 2750 Cascais

Tel (01) 486 9881
Holes 18 L 5606 m SSS 71
V'tors U
Fees 6000esc (7000esc)
Loc 2km W of Cascais. 32km W of Lisbon
Arch Robert Trent Jones

Tróia Golf

Torralta, Tróia, 2900 Setúbal

Tel (065) 44112
Fax (065) 44315
Holes 18 L 6338 m SSS 74
Loc S of Setúbal on Tróia peninsula. 50km S of Lisbon
Arch Robert Trent Jones

Vimeiro

Praia do Porto Novo, Vimeiro, 2560 Torres Vedras

Tel (061) 984157
Fax (061) 984621
Holes 9 L 4781 m SSS 67
Loc Vimeiro, 20km N of Torres Vedras. 65km N of Lisbon
Arch Frank Pennink

Madeira

Madeira (1991)

Sto Antonio da Serra, 9200 Machico

Tel (091) 552345/552356
Fax (091) 552367
Holes 18 L 6040 m Par 72
9 hole course
V'tors U
Fees 8000esc
Loc 25km E of Funchal. Airport 3km
Arch Robert Trent Jones

Palheiro (1993)

Palheiro Ferreiro, Sao Gonçalo, 9000 Funchal

Tel (091) 792116
Fax (091) 792456
Holes 18 L 6022 m SSS 71
V'tors U
Fees £30
Loc 5km from Funchal, off Airport road to Camacha
Arch Cabell Robinson

North

Estela (1989)

Rio Alto, Estela, 4490 Póvoa de Varzim

Tel (052) 612400
Fax (052) 612701
Holes 18 L 6188 m SSS 73
V'tors H
Fees 7000esc
Loc 7km N of Póvoa de Varzim. 40km N of Oporto (Route 13)
Arch Duarte Sottomayor

Miramar (1962)

Av Sacadura Cabral, Miramar, 4405 Valadares

Tel (02) 762 2067
Fax (02) 762 7859
Holes 9 L 2573 m SSS 67
V'tors H WE–NA after 10am
Fees 7500esc (9000esc)
Loc 12km S of Oporto

Oporto (1890)

Sisto-Paramos, 4500 Espinho

Tel (02) 722008
Fax (02) 726895
Holes 18 L 5780 m SSS 70
V'tors H WE–restricted
Fees 10.000esc
Loc Espinho, 15km S of Oporto

Vidago

Pavilhão do Golfe, 5425 Vidago

Tel (076) 97356
Fax (076) 996622
Holes 9 L 2256m SSS 64
Loc 50km N of Vila Real. 130km NE of Oporto
Arch Mackenzie Ross

Slovenia

Bled (1938)

Cesta Svobode 13, 64260 Bled

Tel (064) 718 230
Fax (064) 718 225
Holes 18 L 6320 m SSS 73
9 L 6614 m SSS 72
V'tors H
Fees £24
Loc 3km W of Bled. 50km NW of Ljubljana, nr Austro-Italian border
Arch Donald Harradine

Castle Mokrice (1992)

Terme Catez, Topliska Cesta 35, 68250 Brezice

Tel (0608) 57000/1
Fax (0608) 57007
Holes 18 holes SSS 70
V'tors U
Fees £20
Loc 100km SE of Ljubljana
Arch Donald Harradine

Lipica (1988)

Lipica 5, 66210 Sezana

Tel (067) 72930
Fax (067) 72818
Holes 9 L 6240 m SSS 71
V'tors U
Fees £12.50
Loc 11km NE of Trieste. 85km SW of Ljubljana
Arch Donald Harradine

Spain

Alicante & Murcia

Don Cayo (1974)
Conde de Altea 49, Altea (Alicante)
Tel **(96) 584 80 46**
Fax **(96) 584 11 88**
Holes 9 L 6156 m SSS 72
V'tors U H
Fees D–3800P
Loc 4km N of Altea, nr Callosa
Arch Barber/Sanz

Ifach (1974)
Crta Moraira-Calpe Km 3, Apdo 28, 03720 Benisa (Alicante)
Tel **(96) 649 71 14**
Fax **(96) 573 07 00**
Holes 9 L 3408 m SSS 59
V'tors U
Fees D–3300P
Loc 9km N of Calpe, towards Moraira
Arch Javier Arana

Jávea (1981)
Apartado 148, 03730 Jávea, Alicante
Tel **(96) 579 25 84**
Fax **(96) 646 05 54**
Holes 9 L 6070 m SSS 72
V'tors H
Fees D–4000P
Loc Lluca, Jávea. 90km NE of Alicante
Arch Francisco Moreno

La Manga (1971)
30385 Los Belones, Cartagena
Tel **(968) 13 72 34**
Fax **(968) 15 72 72**
Holes North 18 L 5780 m SSS 70
South 18 L 6259 m SSS 73
Princesa 18 L 5971 m SSS 72
V'tors U
Fees D–5250P
Loc 30km NE of Cartagena, nr Murcia airport
Arch RD Putman

La Marquesa (1989)
Ciudad Quesada II, 03170 Rojales, (Alicante)
Tel **(96) 671 42 58/671 95 34**
Fax **(96) 671 91 74**
Holes 18 L 5840 m Par 72 SSS 70
V'tors U
Fees D–3900P
Loc Rojales, 40km S of Alicante
Arch Justo Quesada

Las Ramblas (1991)
Crta Alicante-Cartagena Km50, 03189 Urb Villamartin, Orihuela (Alicante)
Tel **(96) 532 20 11**
Fax **(96) 676 51 58**
Holes 18 L 5770 m SSS 71
V'tors U H
Fees 4000P
Loc 9km S of Torrevieja
Arch José Gancedo

La Sella (1991)
Ptda Alqueria de Ferrando, 03749 Jesus Pobre (Alicante)
Tel **(96) 645 42 52/645 41 10**
Fax **(96) 645 42 01**
Holes 18 L 6028 m SSS 71
V'tors U H
Fees 5000–6000P
Loc Denia 5km
Arch Juan de la Cuadra

Villamartin (1972)
Crta Alicante-Cartagena Km50, 03189 Urb Villamartin, Orihuela (Alicante)
Tel **(96) 676 51 27/676 51 60**
Fax **(96) 676 51 58**
Holes 18 L 6132 m SSS 72
V'tors U H
Fees 5000P
Loc 8km S of Torrevieja
Arch Paul Putman

Almería

Almerimar (1976)
Urb Almerimar, 04700 El Ejido
Tel **(950) 48 02 34**
Fax **(950) 49 72 33**
Holes 18 L 6111 m SSS 72
V'tors U
Fees 4500P W–20.000P
Loc 35km W of Almería
Arch Gary Player

Cortijo Grande (1976)
Apdo 2, Cortijo Grande, 04630 Turre
Tel **(951) 47 91 76**
Holes 9 holes course SSS 36
Loc 20km W of Turre. 85km N of Almería, nr Mojácar

Playa Serena (1979)
Urb Playa Serena, 04740 Roquetas de Mar
Tel **(950) 33 30 55**
Fax **(950) 33 30 55**
Holes 18 L 6301 m SSS 72
V'tors H
Fees 3500P
Loc 20km S of Almerí]a
Arch Gallardo/Alliss

Balearic Islands

Canyamel
Urb Canyamel, Crta de Cuevas, 07580 Capdepera, Mallorca
Tel **(971) 56 44 57**
Holes 18 L 6115 m SSS 72
Loc 70km NE of Palma, nr Cala Ratjada

Capdepera GC Roca Viva (1989)
Apdo 6, 07580 Capdepera, Mallorca
Tel **(971) 56 58 75/56 58 57**
Fax **(971) 56 58 74**
Holes 18 L 6284 m SSS 72
V'tors U H
Fees D–6900P
Loc 71km E of Palma, between Artá and Capdepera
Arch Maples/Pape

Club Son Parc (1977)
Apdo 634, Mahón, Menorca
Tel **(971) 37 98 14**
Fax **(971) 36 88 06**
Holes 9 L 2791 m SSS 69
V'tors U H
Fees D–5000P
Loc Mercadel, 18km N of Mahón
Arch JF Martínez

Ibiza (1990)
Apdo 1270, 07840 Santa Eulalia
Tel **(071) 19 61 18**
Fax **(071) 19 60 51**
Holes 18 L 6083 m SSS 72
9 L 5867 m SSS 70
V'tors H
Fees 6000P
Loc 7km N of Ibiza town
Arch Thomas/Rivero

Pollensa (1986)
Ctra Palma-Pollensa Km 49, Apdo No 15, 07460 Pollensa, Mallorca
Tel **(971) 53 32 16**
Fax **(971) 53 32 65**
Holes 9 L 5304 m SSS 70
V'tors U
Fees 5700P
Loc Pollensa, 45km N of Palma
Arch José Gancedo

Poniente (1978)
Costa de Calvia, Mallorca
Tel **(971) 13 01 48**
Fax **(971) 13 01 76**
Holes 18 L 6430 m SSS 72
V'tors U
Fees 6200P
Loc 12km SW of Palma towards Cala Figuera
Arch John Harris

Real Menorca (1976)
Apartado 97, 07780 Mahón, Menorca
Tel **(971) 36 39 00**
Holes 9 L 5724 m SSS 72
Loc 7km N of Mahó]n
Arch John Harris

Royal Bendinat (1986)
C. Campoamor, 07015 Calviá, Mallorca
Tel **(971) 40 52 00**
Fax **(971) 70 07 86**
Holes 9 L 4988 m SSS 68

V'tors U H
Fees 5300P
Loc 7km W of Palma
Arch Martin Hawtree

Santa Ponsa (1976)

Santa Ponsa, 07180 Calvia (Mallorca)
Tel **(971) 69 02 11/69 08 00**
Fax **(971) 69 33 64**
Holes No 1 18 L 6520 m SSS 74
No 2 18 L 6053 m SSS 73
V'tors No 1–U H No 2–NA
Fees 6900P
Loc 18km W of Palma
Arch Folco Nardi

Son Servera (1967)

Costa de Los Pinos, 07759 Son Servera, Mallorca
Tel **(971) 56 78 02**
Fax **(971) 56 81 46**
Holes 9 L 5956 m SSS 72
V'tors H
Fees D–6000P
Loc Son Servera, 64km E of Palma
Arch John Harris

Son Vida (1964)

Plaza Son Vida, 07013 Palma de Mallorca
Tel **(971) 79 12 10**
Fax **(971) 79 11 27**
Holes 18 L 5740 m SSS 71
V'tors U H
Fees 7200P
Loc 5km NW of Palma
Arch Hawtree

Vall d'Or (1986)

Apdo 23, 07660 Cala D'Or, Mallorca
Tel **(971) 83 70 68/83 70 01**
Fax **(971) 83 72 99**
Holes 18 L 5799 m SSS 71
V'tors H
Fees 6900P
Loc 60km E of Palma, between Cala d'Or and Porto Colóm
Arch Benz/Bendly

Barcelona & Cataluña

Bonmont-Terres Noves (1990)

Urb Terres Noves, 43330 Montroig (Tarragona)
Tel (977) 81 81 40
Fax (977) 81 81 46
Holes 18 L 6202 m SSS 72
V'tors I or H
Fees 4500–5800P (5500–7000P)
Loc S of Tarragona. 130km S of Barcelona
Arch Robert Trent Jones Jr

Can Bosch (1984)

Trav de les Corts 322, 08029 Barcelona
Tel **(93) 405 04 22/866 25 71**
Fax **(93) 419 9659**
Holes 9 L 3027 m SSS 71
V'tors U H
Fees 3000P (6000P)
Loc 35km NE of Barcelona
Arch Ramon Espinosa

Costa Brava (1962)

La Masia, 17246 Sta Cristina d'Aro (Gerona)
Tel **(972) 83 71 50**
Fax **(972) 83 72 72**
Holes 18 L 5573 m SSS 70
V'tors H
Fees 4500–6500P
Loc Playa de Aro 5km. 30km SE of Gerona
Arch J Hamilton Stutt

Costa Dorada (1983)

Apartado 600, 43080 Tarragona
Tel **(977) 65 33 61**
Holes 18 L 6223 m SSS 73
Loc Tarragona
Arch José Gancedo

Empordà (1990)

Crta Torroella de Montgri, 17257 Gualta (Gerona)
Tel **(972) 760450/760136**
Fax **(972) 108206**
Holes 27 L 5855-6112 m SSS 70-71
V'tors U H
Fees 4500P (6000P)
Loc 35km E of Gerona, nr Pals. 130km N of Barcelona
Arch Robert von Hagge

Girona (1992)

Apartat de Correus 601, Travessia del Carril, 17001 Girona
Tel **(972) 17 16 41/17 18 09**
Fax **(972) 17 16 82**
Holes 18 L 6058 m SSS 72
V'tors H–booking required
Fees 4500P (5500P)
Loc Sant Julià de Ramis, 4km from Gerona
Arch Hawtree

Llavaneras (1945)

Camino del Golf, 08392 San Andres de Llavaneras, (Barcelona)
Tel **(93) 792 60 50**
Fax **(93) 795 25 58**
Holes 18 L 4644 m SSS 66
V'tors U H
Fees 5000P (7000P)
Loc 4km N of Mataró. 34km N of Barcelona.
Arch Hawtree/Espinosa

Mas Nou (1987)

Urb Mas Nou, 17250 Playa de Aro
Tel **(972) 82 60 84/82 61 18**
Fax **(972) 82 61 17**
Holes 18 L 6218 m SSS 72
9 hole Par 3 course
Fees 4000P (6000P)
Loc 35km SE of Gerona on Costa Brava. 100km N of Barcelona

Masia Bach (1990)

Ctra Martorell-Capellades, 08781 Sant Esteve Sesrovires
Tel **(93) 772 6310**
Fax **(93) 772 6356**
Holes 18 L 6039 m SSS 72
9 L 3780 m SSS 60
V'tors H
Fees 5750P (17.250P)
Loc 30km NW of Barcelona
Arch JM Olazábal

Osona Montanya (1988)

Masia L'Estanyol, 08553 El Brull (Barcelona)
Tel **(93) 884 01 70**
Fax **(93) 884 04 07**
Holes 18 L 6036 m Par 72
V'tors U H
Loc 60km NE of Barcelona
Arch Dave Thomas

Pals

Ctra de la Platja de Pals, 17526 Gerona
Tel **(972) 63 60 06**
Fax **(972) 63 70 09**
Holes 18 L 6222 m SSS 72
Fees D–4500–8500P
Loc 40km E of Gerona. 135km NE of Barcelona
Arch FW Hawtree

Peralada (1993)

La Garriga, 17491 Peralada, Gerona
Tel **(972) 53 82 87/53 82 88**
Fax **(972) 53 82 36**
Holes 18 L 6128 m SSS 72
V'tors H
Fees 5000P (6000P)
Loc Costa Brava, on French border. 40km S of Perpignan Airport, nr Llansá

Real Cerdaña (1929)

Apdo 63, Puigcerdá, (Gerona)
Tel **(972) 88 13 38**
Holes 18 L 5735 m SSS 70
Loc Cerdaña, 1km from Puigcerdá
Arch Javier Arana

Real Golf El Prat (1956)

Apdo 10, 8820 El Prat de Llobregat, (Barcelona)
Tel **(93) 379 02 78**
Fax **(93) 370 51 02**
Holes 4 x 9 holes:
6070-6266 m SSS 73-74
V'tors WD–H WE–M H
Fees 9500P (19.090P)
Loc El Prat, Airport 3km. 15km S of Barcelona
Arch Arana/Thomas

Reus Aiguesverds (1989)
Crta Cambrils, Mas Guardiá, 43206 Reus
Tel (977) 75 27 25
Fax (977) 75 19 38
Holes 18 L 6905 yds SSS 72
V'tors U
Fees 5000–6000P
Loc 10km W of Tarragona. 100km S of Barcelona

Sant Cugat (1914)
08190 Sant Cugat del Valles
Tel (93) 674 39 08/674 39 58
Holes 18 L 5209 m SSS 68
Loc 20km NW of Barcelona

Sant Jordi
Urb Sant Jordi d'Alfama, 43860 Ametlla de Mar, (Tarragona)
Tel (977) 49 34 57
Fax (977) 49 32 77
Holes 9 L 5696 m SSS 70
V'tors U H
Fees 3500P
Loc 50km S of Tarragona
Arch Lauresno Nomen

Terramar (1922)
Apdo 6, 08870 Sitges
Tel (93) 894 05 80/894 20 43
Fax (93) 894 70 51
Holes 18 L 5878 m SSS 71 Par 72
V'tors H
Fees 4500–7000P
Loc Sitges, 37km S of Barcelona
Arch Simpson/Hawtree/Piñero/Fazio

Vallromanes (1969)
C/Afveras, 08188 Vallromanes
Tel (93) 572 90 64
Fax (93) 572 93 30
Holes 18 L 6038 m SSS 72
V'tors H
Fees D–5750P (11.500P)
Loc 23km N of Barcelona between Alella and Granollers. A7 Junction 13/A19 Junction 5
Arch FW Hawtree

Burgos

Lerma (1991)
Ctra Madrid-Burgos Km195, 09340 Lerma (Burgos)
Tel (947) 17 12 14/17 12 16
Fax (947) 17 12 16
Holes 18 L 6235 m SSS 72
V'tors H
Fees 3500P (5500P)
Loc 30km S of Burgos, nr Villa Ducal de Lerma
Arch Pepe Gancedo

Canary Islands

Costa Teguise (1978)
Apdo 170, 35080 Arrecife de Lanzarote
Tel (928) 59 05 12
Fax (928) 59 04 90
Holes 18 L 5853 m SSS 72
V'tors U
Fees 6000P Residents–4800P
Loc 4km N of Arrecife
Arch John Harris

Maspalomas (1968)
Av de Africa, Maspalomas, 35100 Las Palmas de Gran Canaria
Tel (928) 76 25 81/76 73 43
Fax (928) 76 82 45
Holes 18 L 6216 m SSS 72
V'tors U
Fees 6000P
Loc S coast of Gran Canaria
Arch Mackenzie Ross

Real Golf Las Palmas (1891)
PO Box 93, Santa Brigida, 35310 Las Palmas, Gran Canaria
Tel (928) 35 10 50/35 01 04
Fax (928) 35 01 10
Holes 18 L 5690 m SSS 71
V'tors WE–NA
Fees WD–4500P
Loc Bandama, Las Palmas 14km
Arch Mackenzie Ross

Real Tenerife (1932)
El Peñón, Tacoronte, Tenerife
Tel (922) 63 66 07
Fax (922) 63 64 80
Holes 18 L 5670 m SSS 71
V'tors WD–H
Fees 5500P
Loc 10km N of Santa Cruz

Golf del Sur (1987)
San Miguel de Abona, 38620 Tenerife (Canarias)
Tel (922) 73 10 70
Fax (922) 78 52 72
Holes North 9 L 2913 m SSS 36
Links 9 L 2469 m SSS 34
South 9 L 2957 m SSS 36
V'tors H
Fees 5500–7700P
Loc Airport 3km. Playa de las Américas 12km
Arch Pepe Gancedo

Córdoba

Pozoblanco (1984)
Jacinto Benavente 8, 14400 Pozoblanco, (Córdoba)
Tel (957) 10 02 39/10 00 06
Holes 9 L 3020 m SSS 62
Loc Pozoblanco 3km
Arch Carlos Luca

Los Villares (1976)
Avda del Generalismo 1-2, PO Box 463, 14080 Córdoba
Tel (957) 35 02 08
Holes 18 L 5964 m SSS 73
Loc 9km N of Córdoba, towards Obejo

Galicia

Aero Club de Santiago (1976)
General Pardiñas 34, Santiago de Compostela (La Coruña)
Tel (981) 59 24 00
Holes 9 L 5816 m SSS 70
Loc Santiago Airport

Aero Club de Vigo (1951)
Reconquista 7, 36201 Vigo
Tel (986) 48 66 45/48 75 09
Holes 9 L 5622 m SSS 60
Loc Peinador Airport, 8km from Vigo

La Coruña (1962)
Apartado 737, 15080 La Coruña
Tel (981) 28 52 00
Holes 18 L 5782 m SSS 72
Loc Arteijo, 7km SW of La Coruña
Arch Antonio Lucena

La Toja (1970)
Isla de La Toja, El Grove, Pontevedra
Tel (986) 73 01 58/73 08 18
Holes 9 L 5178 m SSS 72
Loc La Toja island. 30km W of Pontevedra
Arch Ramón Espinosa

Madrid Region

Barberán (1967)
Apartado 150.239, Cuatro Vientos, 28080 Madrid
Tel (91) 509 12 58/509 11 40
Holes 11 L 6202 m SSS 72
V'tors U
Loc 10km SW of Madrid
Arch Ramón Espinosa

La Dehesa (1991)
Calle Real 19, 28691 Villanueva La Canada
Tel (91) 815 70 22/815 70 37
Fax (91) 815 54 68
Holes 18 L 6456 m SSS 72
V'tors M+H only
Fees 2500P (8500P)
Loc 35km NW of Madrid
Arch Manuel Piñero

Las Encinas de Boadilla (1984)
Crta Boadilla-Pozuelo Km 1400, Boadilla del Monte, Madrid
Tel (91) 633 11 00
Holes 9 L 1464 m SSS 50
Loc Pozuelo, 12km W of Madrid
Arch Francisco Moreno

Herreria (1966)
PO Box 28200, San Lorenzo del Escorial, (Madrid)
Tel (91) 890 51 11
Holes 18 L 6050 m SSS 72
Loc Escorial, 50km W of Madrid
Arch Antonio Lucena

Lomas-Bosque (1973)
Urb El Bosque, 28670 Villaviciosa de Odón, (Madrid)
Tel (91) 616 75 00
Fax (91) 616 73 93
Holes 18 L 6075 m SSS 72
9 hole Par 3 course
V'tors WD–U WE–M
Fees 5000P (10.000P)
Loc Madrid 20km
Arch RD Putman

La Moraleja (1976)
La Moraleja, Alcobendas (Madrid)
Tel (91) 650 07 00
Holes 18 L 6016 m SSS 72
V'tors M
Loc 9km N of Madrid on Burgos road
Arch Jack Nicklaus

Nuevo De Madrid (1972)
Las Matas (Madrid)
Tel (91) 630 08 20
Holes 18 L 5647 m SSS 70
Loc 25km NW of Madrid on La Coruña road

Puerta de Hierro (1904)
Avda de Miraflores, 28035 Madrid
Tel (91) 216 1745
Fax (91) 373 8111
Holes 18 L 6347 m SSS 73
18 L 5273 m SSS 68
V'tors M only
Fees 6900P (14.950P)
Loc 4km N of Madrid on Route VI
Arch Harris/Simpson

RAC de España (1967)
José Abascal 10, 28003 Madrid
Tel (91) 657 00 01
Holes 18 L 6505 m SSS 72
9 hole Par 3 course
Loc San Sebastián de los Reyes, 28km N of Madrid on Burgos road
Arch Javier Arana

Somosaguas (1971)
Somosaguas, 28011 Madrid
Tel (91) 352 16 47
Holes 9 L 6054 m SSS 72
Loc Somosaguas
Arch John Harris

Valdeláguila (1975)
Urb Valdeláguila, Villalbilla, (Madrid)
Tel (91) 885 96 59
Fax (91) 885 96 59
Holes 9 L 5714 m SSS 70
V'tors WD–U WE–NA
Fees 3000P
Loc 8km S of Alcalá de Henares

Villa de Madrid CC (1932)
Crta Castilla, 28040 Madrid
Tel (91) 357 21 32
Fax (91) 549 07 97
Holes 27 L 5900-6321 m SSS 73-74
V'tors U H
Fees 1950P (2900P)
Loc 4km NW of Madrid, in the Casa del Campo
Arch Javier Arana

Málaga Region

Añoreta (1989)
Avenida del Golf, 29730 Rincón de la Victoria, (Málaga)
Tel (952) 40 40 00
Fax (952) 40 40 50
Holes 18 L 5976 m SSS 71
V'tors U
Fees 2500P (3000P)
Loc 12km E of Málaga
Arch JM Canizares

La Cala (1991)
La Cala de Mijas, 29647 Mijas-Costa (Málaga)
Tel (952) 58 91 01/58 91 00 (Pro)
Fax (952) 58 91 05
Holes North 18 L 6160 m SSS 72
South 18 L 5960 m SSS 71
6 hole Par 3 course
V'tors U H
Fees 4500P
Loc 6km from Cala de Mijas, between Fuengirola and Marbella
Arch Cabell Robinson

El Candado (1965)
Urb El Candado, El Palo, 29018 Málaga
Tel (952) 29 93 40/1
Holes 9 L 4676 m SSS 66
Fees 3500P
Loc El Palo, 5km E of Málaga on Route N340
Arch Carlos Fernández

El Chaparral
Urb El Chaparral, Mijas-Costa
Tel (952) 49 38 00
Fax (952) 49 40 51
Holes 18 L 5700 m SSS 71
V'tors U H
Fees 4000P
Loc 5km W of Fuengirola on N340
Arch Pepe Gancedo

Guadalhorce (1990)
Crtra de Cártama, Apartado 48, 29590 Campanillas (Málaga)
Tel (952) 24 36 82
Fax (952) 24 16 78
Holes 18 L 6178 m SSS 72
9 hole Par 3 course
V'tors U
Fees 2500–3500P
Loc 8km W of Málaga
Arch Kosti Kuronen

Lauro (1992)
Los Caracolillos, 29130 Alaurín de la Torre (Málaga)
Tel (952) 41 27 67
Fax (952) 46 88 38
Holes 18 L 5971 m SSS 71
V'tors U
Fees D–3500P
Loc 20km SW of Málaga airport on Route C-344 towards Alhaurín El Grande
Arch Folco Nardi

Málaga Club de Campo (1925)
Parador de Golf, Apdo 324, 29080 Málaga
Tel (952) 38 12 55
Fax (952) 38 21 41
Holes 18 L 6249 m SSS 72
V'tors U
Fees 4400P
Loc Torremolinos 4km. 12km S of Málaga, nr Airport
Arch Tom Simpson

Mijas (1976)
Apartado 145, Fuengirola, Má]laga
Tel (952) 47 68 43
Fax (952) 46 79 43
Holes Los Lagos 18 L 6348 m SSS 73; Los Olivos 18 L 5896 m SSS 71
V'tors H–booking required Oct–Apr
Fees D–5800P
Loc 4km NW of Fuengirola (Mijas Valley)
Arch Robert Trent Jones

Miraflores (1990)
Urb Riviera del Sol, 29647 Mijas-Costa
Tel (952) 83 36 47
Holes 18 L 5845 m SSS 72
Fees 4500P
Loc 8km E of Marbella
Arch Folco Nardi

Los Moriscos (1974)
Costa Granada, Motril (Granada)
Tel (958) 82 55 27
Fax (958) 25 52 51
Holes 9 L 5689 m SSS 72 Par 70
V'tors U
Fees 2800P
Loc 8km W of Motril, nr Salobrena. 80km E of Málaga
Arch Ibergolf

La Siesta (1990)
Sitio de Calahonda, Mijas-Costa (Málaga)
Tel (952) 83 63 70
Holes 9 hole Par 3 course
Loc 20km E of Málaga

Torrequebrada (1976)
Public
Apdo 120, 29630 Benalmadena-Costa
Tel (952) 44 27 42/56 11 02
Fax (952) 56 11 29
Holes 18 L 5806 m SSS 71
V'tors H
Fees 6800P
Loc Benalmadena, 22km S of Málaga
Arch Pepe Gancedo

Marbella & Estepona

Alcaidesa Links
Cortijo las Aguzaderas, Apdo 125, San Roque (Cádiz)
Tel (956) 79 10 40
Fax (956) 79 10 41
Holes 18 L 5671 SSS 70
V'tors U H–booking advised
Fees D–4000P
Loc 15km E of Gibraltar
Arch Alliss/Clark

Aloha (1975)
29660 Nueva Andalucía (Málaga)
Tel (952) 81 08 76/81 37 50/ 81 23 88 (Caddymaster)
Fax (952) 81 23 89
Holes 18 L 6261 m SSS 72
9 hole short course
V'tors H–booking necessary
Fees 6000–8000P
Loc 8km W of Marbella, nr Puerto Banus
Arch Javier Arana

Los Arqueros (1991)
Aloha Pueblo, Nueva Andalucía, 29660 Marbella (Málaga)
Tel (952) 78 81 32
Holes 18 L 6130 m SSS 72
Fees 3500P
Loc 5km N of San Pedro de Alcántara
Arch Severiano Ballesteros

Atalaya G & CC (1968)
Crta Benahavis 7, Estepona, Marbella
Tel (952) 88 28 12
Fax (952) 88 78 97
Holes 18 L 6118 m SSS 71
18 L 5600 m SSS 67
V'tors U H
Fees Winter–£25 Summer–£15
Loc 12km S of Marbella. 60km SW of Málaga
Arch Von Limburger/Krings

Las Brisas (1968)
Apdo 147, 29660 Nueva Andalucía, (Málaga)
Tel (952) 81 08 75/81 30 21
Fax (952) 81 55 18
Holes 18 L 6094 m SSS 72
V'tors H
Fees 5000–9000P
Loc 8km S of Marbella, nr Puerto Banus
Arch Robert Trent Jones

La Cañada (1982)
Ctra Guadiaro Km 1, 11311 Guadiaro (Cádiz)
Tel (956) 79 41 00/79 44 11
Fax (956) 79 42 41
Holes 9 L 2873 m SSS 72
V'tors U
Fees 1200P
Loc Guadiaro, 2km from Sotogrande
Arch Robert Trent Jones

La Duquesa G & CC (1987)
Urb El Hacho, 29691 Manilva (Málaga)
Tel (952) 89 04 25/89 04 26
Fax (952) 89 00 57
Holes 18 L 6142 m SSS 72
Fees 5000P
Loc 10km S of Estepona
Arch Robert Trent Jones

Estepona (1989)
Paraje Arroyo Vaquero, Apartado 274, 29680 Estepona (Málaga)
Tel (952) 65 14 99
Holes 18 L 6001 m SSS 71
Loc 5km W of Estepona
Arch Luis López

Guadalmina (1959)
Guadalmina Alta, San Pedro de Alcántara, 29678 Marbella (Málaga)
Tel (952) 88 33 75
Fax (952) 88 34 83
Holes 18 L 6060 m SSS 72
18 L 6200 m SSS 72
9 hole Par 3 course
V'tors H
Fees 5000P
Loc San Pedro, 12km S of Marbella
Arch Arana/Nardi

Monte Mayor (1992)
Urb Los Naranjos, 29660 Marbella (Málaga)
Tel (952) 81 08 05, (908) 75 83 37
Fax (952) 81 48 54
Holes 18 L 5593 m SSS 71
V'tors U
Fees 4000P
Loc Benahavis, Crta N340 Km165
Arch Pepe Gancedo

Los Naranjos (1977)
Apdo 64, 29660 Nueva Andalucía, Marbella
Tel (952) 81 52 06/81 24 28
Fax (952) 81 14 28
Holes 18 L 6484 m SSS 72
V'tors U H
Fees 6800P
Loc 8km S of Marbella, nr Puerto Banus
Arch Robert Trent Jones Sr

El Paraiso (1974)
Ctra Cádiz-Málaga Km 167, 29680 Estepona (Málaga)
Tel (95) 288 38 35/288 38 46
Fax (95) 288 58 27
Holes 18 L 6116 m SSS 72
V'tors U
Fees D–5000P
Loc 14km S of Marbella
Arch Player/Kirby

La Quinta (1989)
Crta de Ronda, Benahavis, Marbella (Málaga)
Tel (952) 78 34 62/ 78 98 87
Fax (952) 78 34 66
Holes 27 L 5797-5945 m SSS 71-72
V'tors U H
Fees 6500P
Loc 4km N of San Pedro de Alcántara
Arch Piñero/García

Rio Real (1965)
Urb Rio Real, PO Box 82, 29600 Marbella (Málaga)
Tel (95) 277 95 09
Fax (95) 277 21 40
Holes 18 L 6130 m SSS 72
V'tors U
Fees 5500P
Loc 5km E of Marbella. Málaga Airport 50km
Arch Javier Arana

San Roque (1990)
CN 340 Km 126, San Roque, 11360 Cádiz
Tel (956) 61 30 30
Fax (956) 61 30 12/61 30 13
Holes 18 L 6440 m SSS 74
V'tors U H
Fees 6000P
Loc 3km W of Sotogrande. 15km E of Gibraltar
Arch Dave Thomas

Santa María G & CC

Coto de los Dolores, Urb Elviria, Crta N340 Km 192, 29600 Marbella (Málaga)

Tel (952) 83 03 86/83 03 88/ 83 10 36
Fax (952) 83 08 70
Holes 9 L 5792 m SSS 71
V'tors U
Fees 4500P
Loc 10km E of Marbella, opp Hotel Don Carlos
Arch A García Garrido

Sotogrande (1964)

Paseo del Parque, Apartado 14, Sotogrande (Cádiz)

Tel (956) 79 50 50/79 50 51
Fax (956) 79 50 29
Holes 18 L 6224 m SSS 74
9 L 1299 m Par 29
Fees 8000P
Loc 30km N of Gibraltar, nr Guadiaro
Arch Robert Trent Jones

Valderrama (1985)

Apartado 1, 11310 Sotogrande (Cádiz)

Tel (956) 79 57 75
Fax (956) 79 60 28
Holes 18 L 6326 m SSS 71
9 L 1100 m SSS 27
V'tors H–12–2pm
Fees 12.000P
Loc 18km N of Gibraltar
Arch Robert Trent Jones Sr

North Coast

Barganiza (1982)

Apartado 277, 33080 Oviedo, Asturias

Tel (985) 74 24 68
Holes 18 L 5549 m SSS 70
Fees 5000P
Loc 12km N of Oviedo on Gijon old road
Arch Victor García

Castiello (1958)

Apartado de Correos 161, Gijón

Tel (985) 36 63 13
Holes 18 L 4817 m SSS 67
V'tors WE–restricted in summer
Fees 3000P
Loc 5km S of Gijón on Oviedo old road

La Cuesta

Apdo 40, 33500 Llanes

Tel (98) 541 7084
Fax (98) 540 1973
Holes 9 L 5456 m SSS 69
V'tors U
Fees 2500P
Loc 3km from Llanes (N-634)

Laukariz (1976)

Laukariz-Munguia, (Viscaya)

Tel (94) 674 08 58/674 04 62
Holes 18 L 6112 m SSS 72
Loc 15km N of Bilbao towards Mungía
Arch RD Putman

Real Golf Neguri (1911)

Apdo Correos 9, 48990 Algorta

Tel (94) 469 02 00/04/08
Holes 18 L 6319 m SSS 72
6 hole Par 3 course
Fees 6000P
Loc La Galea, 20km N of Bilbao
Arch Javier Arana

Real Golf Pedreña (1928)

Apartado 233, Santander

Tel (942) 50 00 01/50 02 66
Fax (942) 50 04 21
Holes 18 L 5745 m SSS 70
9 L 2740 m SSS 36
V'tors H
Fees 5600P (9000P)
Loc 20km from Santander, on Bay of Santander
Arch Colt/Ballesteros

Real San Sebastián (1910)

PO Box 6, Fuenterrabia, (Guipúzcoa)

Tel (943) 61 68 45/61 68 46
Fax (943) 61 14 91
Holes 18 L 6020 m SSS 71
V'tors WD–U H(9am–noon) WE–NA
Fees 6000P
Loc Jaizubia Valley, 14km NE of San Sebastián
Arch P Hirigoyen

Real Zarauz (1916)

Apartado 82, Zarauz, (Guipúzcoa)

Tel (943) 83 01 45
Holes 9 L 5184 m SSS 68
Loc 25km W of San Sebastián

Pamplona

Ulzama (1965)

31779 Guerendiain (Navarra)

Tel (948) 30 51 62
Holes 18 L 6246 m SSS 73
Loc 12km N of Pamplona
Arch Javier Arana

Seville & Gulf of Cádiz

Bellavista (1976)

Crta Huelva-Punta Umbría, Apdo 335, Huelva

Tel (955) 31 90 17
Fax (955) 31 90 25
Holes 9 L 6270 m SSS 73
Fees 3500–5000P
Loc Aljaraque, 6km SW of Huelva, towards Punta Umbria

Islantilla (1993)

Urb Islantilla, Apdo 52, 21410 Isla Cristina (Huelva)

Tel (955) 48 60 39/48 60 49
Fax (955) 48 61 04
Holes 27 L 5926-6142 m SSS 72
V'tors U H
Fees 5000P
Loc 30km W of Huelva, nr Portuguese border
Arch Enrique Canales

Montecastillo (1993)

Carretera de Arcos, 11406 Jérez

Tel (956) 15 12 00
Fax (956) 15 12 09
Holes 18 L 6494 m SSS 72
V'tors H
Fees 4500P
Loc 10km NE of Jérez. 75km S of Seville
Arch Jack Nicklaus

Novo Sancti Petri (1990)

Urb Novo Sancti Petri, Playa de la Barrosa, 11139 Chiclana de la Frontera

Tel (956) 49 40 05/49 44 50
Fax (956) 49 43 50
Holes 27 L 5197-6466 m SSS 72
V'tors U H
Fees 7000P
Loc La Barrosa, 24km SE of Cádiz. Jérez Airport 50km
Arch Severiano Ballesteros

Pineda De Sevilla (1939)

Apartado 1049, 41080 Sevilla

Tel (954) 61 14 00/61 33 99
Holes 18 L 6120 m SSS 72
Loc 3km S of Seville on Cádiz road
Arch R & F Medina

Real Golf Sevilla (1992)

Autovia Sevilla-Utrera, 41089 Montequinto (Sevilla)

Tel (954) 12 43 01
Fax (954) 12 42 29
Holes 18 L 6321 m SSS 73
V'tors U H WE–booking necessary
Fees 6000P
Loc 3km S of Seville
Arch José María Olazabal

Sevilla Golf (1989)

Hacienda Las Minas, Ctra de Isla Mayor, Aznalcazar (Sevilla)

Tel (955) 75 04 14
Holes 9 L 5910 m SSS 71
Fees 3500P (5000P)
Loc 15km W of Seville
Arch A García Garrido

Vista Hermosa (1975)

Apartado 77, Urb Vista Hermosa, 11500 Puerto de Santa María, Cádiz

Tel (956) 87 56 05
Holes 9 L 5614 m SSS 70
Loc 25km W of Cádiz

For list of abbreviations see page 435

Valencia & Castellón

El Bosque (1989)
Crta Godelleta, 46370 Chiva-Valencia
Tel **(96) 180 41 42**
Fax **(96) 180 40 09**
Holes 18 L 6384 m SSS 74
V'tors U
Fees 5000P
Loc Nr Chiva, 24km W of Valencia, off Madrid road
Arch Robert Trent Jones Sr

Costa de Azahar (1960)
Ctra Grao-Benicasim, Castellón de la Plana
Tel **(964) 22 70 64**
Holes 9 L 2724 m SSS 70
Loc 5km NE of Castellón, on coast
Arch Angel Pérez

Escorpión (1975)
Apartado Correos 1, Betera (Valencia)
Tel **(96) 160 12 11**
Holes 18 L 6345 m SSS 73
Loc Betera, 20km N of Valencia
Arch Ron Kirby

Manises (1964)
Apartado 22.029, Manises (Valencia)
Tel **(96) 152 18 71**
Holes 9 L 6094 m Par 73
Loc 8km W of Valencia
Arch Javier Arana

Mediterraneo CC (1978)
Urb La Coma, Borriol (Castellón)
Tel **(964) 32 12 27**
Fax **(964) 32 13 57**
Holes 18 L 6239 m SSS 73
V'tors H
Fees 3500–4500P (4500–5000P)
Loc Borriol, 4km NW of Castellón
Arch Ramón Espinosa

Oliva Nova (1992)
Carretera Las Marinas, 03700 Denia
Tel **(096) 285 40 00**
Holes 18 L 6445m SSS 72
V'tors U
Loc 15km N of Denia, off A7
Arch Severiano Ballesteros

El Saler (1968)
Parador Luis Vives, 46012 El Saler (Valencia)
Tel **(96) 161 11 86**
Fax **(96) 162 70 16**
Holes 18 L 6485 m SSS 75
Fees D–4500P
Loc Oliva, 18km S of Valencia, towards Cullera
Arch Javier Arana

Zaragoza

Aero Club de Zaragoza (1966)
Coso 34, 50004 Zaragoza
Tel **(976) 21 43 78**
Holes 9 L 5042 m SSS 67
Loc 12km SW of Zaragoza, by airbase

La Penaza (1973)
Apartado 3039, Zaragoza
Tel **(976) 34 28 00/34 22 48**
Fax **(976) 34 28 00**
Holes 18 L 6161 m SSS 72
V'tors H
Fees D–5600P (6720P)
Loc 15km SW of Zaragoza on Madrid road, nr airbase
Arch FW Hawtree

Sweden

East Central

Ängsö (1979)
Björnövägen 2, 721 30 Västerås
Tel **(0171) 41012**
Fax **(0171) 41049**
Holes 18 hole course SSS 72
V'tors H
Fees 160kr (210kr)
Loc 15km E of Västerås
Arch Åke Hultström

Arboga
Åkervägen 5, 732 32 Arboga
Tel **(0589) 70100**
Holes 18 L 5890 m SSS 73
V'tors U
Fees 140kr
Loc 5km S of Arboga
Arch Sune Linde

Ärila (1951)
Nicolai, 611 92 Nyköping
Tel **(0155) 214967**
Fax **(0155) 267657**
Holes 18 L 5735 m SSS 72
V'tors H
Fees 200kr
Loc 5km SE of Nyköping
Arch Sköld/Linde

Arlandastad
Norslunda Gård, 195 95 Rosersberg
Tel **(08) 761 7034**
Fax **(08) 590 355 18**
Holes 18 L 5830 m SSS 72
9 L 1495 m SSS 29
V'tors H
Fees 150kr (200kr)
Loc 35km N of Stockholm, nr airport
Arch Sune Linde

Askersund (1980)
Box 3002, 696 03 Ammeberg
Tel **(0583) 34442**
Fax **(0583) 34369**
Holes 18 L 5800 m SSS 72
V'tors U
Fees 160kr
Loc 10km SE of Askersund towards Ammeberg. 1km on road to Kärra
Arch Ronald Fream

Burvik
Burvik, 740 12 Knutby
Tel **(0174) 43060**
Fax **(0174) 43062**
Holes 18 L 5785 m SSS 72
V'tors U
Loc 45km E of Uppsala. 70km N of Stockholm
Arch Bengt Lorichs

Edenhof (1991)
740 22 Bälinge
Tel **(018) 334185**
Fax **(018) 334186**
Holes 18 L 5898 m SSS 72
V'tors H
Fees 160kr (220kr)
Loc 17km NW of Uppsala
Arch Sune Linde

Enköping (1970)
Box 2006, 745 02 Enköping
Tel **(0171) 20830**
Fax **(0171) 20830**
Holes 18 L 5660 m SSS 71
V'tors H
Fees 160kr (200kr)
Loc 1km E of Enköping, off E18

Eskilstuna (1951)
Strängnäsvägen, 633 49 Eskilstuna
Tel **(016) 142629**
Fax **(016) 148729**
Holes 18 L 5610 m SSS 70
V'tors H
Fees 150kr
Loc 20km E of Örebro
Arch Douglas Brasier

Fagersta (1970)
Box 2051, 737 02 Fagersta
Tel **(0223) 54060**
Holes 18 L 5775 m SSS 71
Fees 100kr
Loc 7km W of Fagersta (Route 65). 70km N of Västerås

Frösåker (1989)
Frösåker Gård, 725 97 Västerås
Tel **(021) 25401**
Fax **(021) 25485**
Holes 18 L 5820 m SSS 72
V'tors U H

For list of abbreviations see page 435

Fees 150kr (200kr)
Loc Västerås 15km
Arch Sune Linde

Fullerö (1988)
Jotsberga, 725 91 Västerås
Tel **(021) 50132**
Fax **(021) 50431**
Holes 18 L 5707 m SSS 72
V'tors H
Fees 140kr (180kr)
Loc 6km SW of Västerås
Arch Hultström/Sjöberg

Grönlund (1989)
740 10 Almunge
Tel **(0174) 20670**
Fax **(0174) 20670**
Holes 18 L 5865 m SSS 71
V'tors H
Fees 150kr (200kr)
Loc 20km E of Uppsala. 25km NE of Arlanda Airport
Arch Åke Persson

Gustavsvik
Box 22033, 702 02 Örebro
Tel **(019) 244486**
Fax **(019) 246490**
Holes 18 holes SSS 72
V'tors H
Fees 170kr
Loc 1km S of Örebro
Arch Turner/Wirhed

Katrineholm (1959)
Box 74, 641 21 Katrineholm
Tel **(0150) 39270**
Fax **(0150) 39011**
Holes 18 L 5850 m SSS 72
V'tors U
Fees 160kr (180kr)
Loc 7km E of Katrineholm
Arch Nils Skjöld

Korslöt (1963)
Box 278, 731 26 Köping
Tel **(0221) 81090**
Fax **(0221) 81277**
Holes 18 L 5636 m SSS 71
V'tors 140kr (190kr)
Loc 5km N of Köping (Route 250)

Kumla (1987)
Box 46, 692 21 Kumla
Tel **(019) 577370**
Fax **(019) 577373**
Holes 18 L 5845 m SSS 72
V'tors U
Fees 180kr
Loc 8km E of Kumla. 20km SE of Örebro
Arch Jan Sederholm

Linde (1984)
Dalkarlshyttan, 711 31 Lindesberg
Tel **(0581) 13960**
Fax **(0581) 12936**
Holes 18 L 5539 m SSS 71
V'tors H
Fees 150kr (180kr)
Loc 42km N of Örebro on R60. Lindesberg 2km

Mosjö
Mosjö Gård, 705 94 Örebrö
Tel **(019) 225780**
Fax **(019) 225045**
Holes 18 L 6160 m SSS 74
V'tors WE–H
Fees 120kr (180kr)
Loc 10km S of Örebrö
Arch Åke Persson

Nora (1988)
Box 108, 713 23 Nora
Tel **(0587) 311660**
Fax **(0587) 15050**
Holes 18 L 5865 m SSS 72
V'tors U
Fees 120kr (150kr)
Loc 33km N of Örebro

Örebro (1939)
Lanna, 719 93 Vintrosa
Tel **(019) 291065**
Fax **(019) 291055**
Holes 18 L 5870 m SSS 72
V'tors H–(max 36)
Fees 220kr
Loc 18km W of Örebro on Route E18

Roslagen
Box 110, 761 22 Norrtälje
Tel **(0176) 37194**
Fax **(0176) 37103**
Holes 18 L 5512 m SSS 71
9 hole course
V'tors H
Fees 150kr (200kr)
Loc 7km N of Norrtälje

Sala (1970)
Fallet, Isätra, 733 92 Sala
Tel **(0224) 53077/53055/53064**
Holes 18 L 5570 m SSS 71
Fees 100kr
Loc 8km E of Sala towards Uppsala, Route 67/72

Sigtunabygden (1961)
Box 89, 193 22 Sigtuna
Tel **(08) 592 54012**
Fax **(08) 592 54167**
Holes 18 L 5740 m SSS 72
Fees 180kr (240kr)
Loc Sigtuna, 50km N of Stockholm
Arch Nils Sköld

Södertälje (1952)
Box 91, 151 21 Södertälje
Tel **(08) 550 38240**
Fax **(08) 550 62549**
Holes 18 L 5875 m SSS 72
V'tors H
Fees 180kr (230kr)
Loc 4km W of Södertälje

Strängnäs (1968)
Box 21, 645 21 Strängnäs
Tel **(0152) 14731**
Fax **(0152) 14716**
Holes 18 L 5790 m SSS 72
V'tors H
Fees 150kr (200kr)
Loc 3km S of Strängnäs
Arch Anders Amilon

Tortuna
Nicktuna, Tortuna, 725 96 Västeräs
Tel **(021) 65300**
Fax **(021) 65302**
Holes 18 L 5750 m SSS 72
V'tors U
Fees 150kr
Loc 6km N of Västeräs
Arch Husell/Hultström

Trosa (1972)
Box 80, 619 00 Trosa
Tel **(0156) 22458**
Fax **(0156) 22454**
Holes 18 L 5727 m SSS 72
V'tors U
Fees 180kr
Loc 5km W of Trosa, towards Uttervik

Upsala (1937)
Håmö Gård, Läby, 755 92 Uppsala
Tel **(018) 460120**
Holes 18 L 6176 m SSS 74
9 L 1643 m SSS 56
Fees 180kr (250kr)
Loc 10km W of Uppsala

Vassunda
Smedsby Gård, 741 91 Knivsta
Tel **(018) 381230**
Fax **(018) 381416**
Holes 18 L 6141 m SSS 72
V'tors H
Fees 150kr (180kr) (1994)
Loc 45km N of Stockholm
Arch Sune Linde

Västerås (1931)
Bjärby, 724 81 Västerås
Tel **(021) 357543**
Fax **(021) 357573**
Holes 18 L 5380 m SSS 69
V'tors U
Fees 150kr (200kr)
Loc 2km N of Västerås
Arch Nils Sköld

Far North

Boden (1946)
Box 107, 961 21 Boden
Tel **(0921) 72051**
Holes 18 L 5495 m SSS 72
9 hole course
V'tors H
Fees 150kr
Loc 7km S of Boden

Funäsdalsfjällen (1972)

Box 66, 840 95 Funäsdalen

Tel **(0684) 21100**
Fax **(0684) 21100**
Holes 18 L 5300 m SSS 72
V'tors U
Fees 130kr
Loc Funäsdalen, nr Norwegian border
Arch Sköld/Linde

Gällivare-Malmberget (1973)

Box 35, 983 21 Malmberget

Tel **(0970) 20770/20782**
Holes 18 L 5620 m SSS 71
Fees 100kr
Loc 4km N of Gällivare, towards Malmberget

Haparanda (1989)

Pl 2041, 953 35 Haparanda

Tel **(0922) 10660**
Holes 18 L 6230 m SSS 73
V'tors I
Fees 160kr
Loc 125km E of Luleå
Arch Peter Chamberlain

Härnösand (1957)

Box 52, 871 22 Härnösand

Tel **(0611) 66169**
Fax **(0611) 66169**
Holes 18 L 5410 m SSS 70
V'tors H
Fees D–160kr
Loc Vägnön, 16km N of Härnösand on E4, towards Hemsö Island
Arch Nils Sköld

Kalix (1990)

Box 32, 952 21 Kalix

Tel **(0923) 15945**
Fax **(0923) 16560**
Holes 18 L 5700m SSS 71
V'tors U
Fees 150kr
Loc 80km N of Luleå
Arch Jan Sederholm

Klövsjö-Vemdalen

Box 147, 840 32 Klövsjö

Tel **(0682) 23494**
Holes 18 L 5732 m SSS 72
9 hole course
V'tors H or Green Card
Fees 150kr (150kr)
Loc 100km S of Östersund
Arch Sune Linde

Luleå (1955)

Box 314, 951 25 Luleå

Tel **(0920) 56300/1/2**
Fax **(0920) 56303**
Holes 18 L 5675 m SSS 72
V'tors U
Fees 150kr
Loc Rutvik, 12km E of Luleå

Östersund-Frösö (1947)

Box 40, 832 01 Frösön

Tel **(063) 43001**
Fax **(063) 43765**
Holes 18 L 6000 m SSS 73
Fees 150kr
Loc Island of Frösö

Öviks GC Puttom (1967)

Ovansjö 1970, 891 95 Arnäsvall

Tel **(0660) 64091**
Fax **(0660) 64040**
Holes 18 L 5795 m SSS 72
Fees 160kr
Loc 15km N of Örnsköldsvik on E4
Arch Nils Sköld

Piteå (1960)

NöJtöJn, 941 90 Piteå

Tel **(0911) 14990**
Fax **(0911) 14960**
Holes 18 L 5325 m SSS 69
V'tors H
Fees 150kr
Loc 2km NE of Piteå
Arch Jan Sederholm

Skellefteå (1967)

Box 152, 931 22 Skellefteå

Tel **(0910) 79333/79866 (Pro)**
Fax **(0910) 79777**
Holes 18 L 6135 m SSS 73
V'tors U H
Fees 150kr
Loc Skellefteå 5km
Arch Sköld/Carlsson

Sollefteå-Långsele (1970)

Box 213, 881 25 Sollefteå

Tel **(0620) 21477/12670**
Fax **(0620) 21477/12670**
Holes 18 L 5765 m SSS 72
V'tors H
Fees 150kr (150kr)
Loc Österforse, 15km SW of Sollefteå (Route 89)
Arch Nils Sköld

Sundsvall (1952)

Golfvägen 5, 862 00 Kvissleby

Tel **(060) 561056**
Fax **(060) 561909**
Holes 18 L 5885 m SSS 72
V'tors WD–H before noon WE–H after 10am
Fees 180kr (200r)
Loc Skottsund, 15km S of Sundsvall

Timrå

Golfbanevägen 2, 860 32 Fagervik

Tel **(060) 570153**
Fax **(060) 578136**
Holes 18 L 5715 m SSS 72
V'tors H
Fees 160kr (200kr)
Loc 1km S of Sundsvall airport
Arch Sune Linde

Umeå (1954)

Lövön, 913 35 Holmsund

Tel **(090) 41071/23313**
Fax **(090) 149120**
Holes 18 L 5751 m SSS 72
9 L 2688 m SSS 70
V'tors U
Fees 200kr
Loc 16km SE of Umeå
Arch Bo Engdahl

Gothenburg

Albatross (1973)

Lillhagsvägen, 422 50 Hisings-Backa

Tel **(031) 551901/550500**
Fax **(031) 555900**
Holes 18 L 6020 m SSS 72
Fees 200kr
Loc 10km N of Gothenburg on Hising Island

Chalmers

Pl 1115, 438 00 Landvetter

Tel **(031) 918430**
Fax **(031) 916338**
Holes 18 L 5560 m SSS 71
V'tors WD–U H before 4pm –M H after 4pm WE–M H before 1pm –U H after 1pm
Fees D–150kr (D–200kr)
Loc 20km E of Gothenburg. 2km from Landvetter airport
Arch Gyllenhammar/Henrikson

Delsjö (1962)

Kallebäck, 412 76 Göteborg

Tel **(031) 406959**
Fax **(031) 407130**
Holes 18 L 5703 m SSS 71
V'tors H WE–NA before 1pm
Fees 200kr
Loc 5km E of Gothenburg (Route 40)
Arch Douglas Brasier

Forsgårdens (1982)

Gamla Forsv 1, 434 47 Kungsbacka

Tel **(0300) 13649**
Fax **(0300) 71987**
Holes 18 L 6110 m SSS 72
V'tors WD–NA after 4pm WE–NA before 1pm
Fees 200kr (200kr)
Loc 1km SE of Kungsbacka. 20km S of Gothenburg
Arch Sune linde

Göteborg (1902)

Box 2056, 436 02 Hovås

Tel **(031) 282444**
Fax **(031) 685333**
Holes 18 L 5935 yds SSS 70
V'tors WD–U WE–M before 2pm
Fees 220kr (250kr)
Loc 11km S of Gothenburg (Route 158)

Gullbringa (1967)
442 95 Kungälv
Tel (0303) 227161
Fax (0303) 227778
Holes 18 L 5775 m Par 70
9 L 2777 m
V'tors U
Fees 200kr
Loc 14km W of Kungälv, towards Marstrand

Kungälv-Kode
Pl 13013, 442 97 Kode
Tel (0303) 51300
Fax (0303) 50205
Holes 18 L 6000 m SSS 72
V'tors WD–U WE–M before noon
Fees 200kr
Loc 30km N of Gothenburg
Arch Lars Andreasson

Kungsbacka (1971)
Hamra Gård 515, 43040 Särö
Tel (031) 936277
Fax (031) 935085
Holes 18 L 5855 m SSS 72
9 L 2880 m SSS 36
V'tors WE–NA before 1pm
Fees 200kr
Loc 7km N of Kungsbacka on Route 158
Arch Pennink/Nordström

Lysegården (1966)
Box 82, 442 21 Kungälv
Tel (0303) 223426
Fax (0303) 223075
Holes 18 L 5670 m SSS 71
9 L 5444 m SSS 70
V'tors H
Fees 160kr
Loc 10km N of Kungälv
Arch Röhss/Engström

Mölndals (1979)
Box 77, 437 21 Mölndal
Tel (031) 993030
Holes 18 L 5625 m SSS 73
V'tors U
Fees 120kr (180kr)
Loc Lindome, 20km S of Gothenburg

Öijared (1958)
PI 1082, 448 92 Floda
Tel (0302) 30604
Fax (0302) 35370
Holes 18 L 5875 m SSS 72
18 L 5655 m SSS 71
V'tors H WE–NA before 1pm
Fees 160kr (200kr)
Loc 35km NE of Gothenburg (E20), nr Nääs
Arch Brasier/Amilon

Partille (1986)
Box 234, 433 24 Partille
Tel (031) 987043/987019 **(Pro)**
Fax (031) 987757
Holes 18 L 5475 m SSS 71
V'tors WD–H before 3pm WE–NA before 1pm
Fees D–160kr (200kr)
Loc Öjersjö, 10km E of Gothenburg

Särö (1899)
Box 74, 430 40 Särö
Tel (031) 936317
Fax (031) 936572
Holes 9 holes Par 27
9 holes Par 34
V'tors H
Fees 100kr (150kr)
Loc 10km W of Kungsbacka. Gothenburg 18km (Route 158)

Sjögärde
430 30 Frillesås
Tel (0340) 652230
Fax (0340) 652577
Holes 18 L 5639 m SSS 72
6 hole short course
V'tors H
Fees 180kr (200kr)
Loc 20km S of Kungsbacka
Arch Lars Andreasson

Stora Lundby (1983)
PI 4035, 440 06 Grabo
Tel (0302) 44200
Fax (0302) 44125
Holes 18 L 6040 m Par 72
9 hole Par 3 course
V'tors H
Fees 100–140kr (140–210kr)
Loc 25km NE of Gothenburg
Arch R Pennink

Malmö & South Coast

Barsebäck G & CC (1969)
246 55 Löddeköpinge
Tel (046) 776230
Fax (046) 775898
Holes Old 18 L 5910 m Par 72
New 18 L 6025 m Par 72
V'tors WD–H booking necessary
Fees D–260kr
Loc 35km N of Malmö
Arch Bruce/Steel

Bokskogen (1963)
Torups Nygård, 230 40 Bara
Tel (040) 481004
Fax (040) 481081
Holes Old 18 L 5992 m SSS 73
New 18 L 5499 m SSS 71
V'tors H WE–after 1pm Old course
Fees Old 180kr (220kr)
New 150kr (180kr)
Loc 15km SE of Malmö, off E65
Arch Amilon/Sederholm/Lorichs

Falsterbo (1909)
Fyrvägen, 230 11 Falsterbo
Tel (040) 470078/475078
Fax (040) 473579
Holes 18 L 6400 yds SSS 72
Fees 150–270kr
Loc 30km SW of Malmö

Flommens (1935)
239 40 Falsterbo
Tel (040) 475019
Fax (040) 473157
Holes 18 L 5735 m SSS 72
V'tors H WE–NA before 1pm
Fees 200kr
Loc 35km SW of Malmö

Kävlinge (1991)
Box 138, 244 22 Kävlinge
Tel (046) 736270
Fax (046) 736271
Holes 18 L 5700 m SSS 72
V'tors H
Fees 120kr (160kr)
Loc 12km N of Lund
Arch Rolf Collijn

Ljunghusen (1932)
Kinellsvag, Ljunghusen, 236 42 Höllviken
Tel (040) 450384
Fax (040) 454265
Holes 3 x 9 holes:
1-18 L 5895 m SSS 73
10-27 L 5670 m SSS 71
19-9 L 5455 m SSS 70
V'tors WD–U H WE–M before noon
Fees 200kr (220kr)
Loc Falsterbo Peninsula. 30km SW of Malmö
Arch Douglas Brasier

Lunds Akademiska (1936)
Kungsmarken, 225 92 Lund
Tel (046) 99005
Fax (046) 99146
Holes 18 L 5780 m SSS 72
V'tors H
Fees 150kr (200kr)
Loc 5km E of Lund
Arch Boström/Morrison

Malmö
Segesvängen, 212 27 Malmö
Tel (040) 292535
Holes 18 L 5720 m SSS 71
Fees 140kr (170kr)
Loc NE of Malmö

Örestad
Box 71, 234 00 Lomma
Tel (040) 410580
Fax (040) 416320
Holes 27 L 5986-6217 m SSS 73-74
18 hole short course
V'tors U
Fees 160kr (180kr)
Loc 15km N of Malmö
Arch Åke Persson

Österlen (1945)
Lilla Vik, 272 95 Simrishamn
Tel **(0414) 24230**
Holes 18 L 5855 m SSS 72
Fees 170–200kr
Loc Vik, 8km N of Simrishamn

Romeleåsen (1969)
Kvarnbrodda, 240 14 Veberöd
Tel **(046) 82012/82014**
Fax **(046) 82113**
Holes 18 L 5783 m SSS 72
Fees 150kr (200kr)
Loc 6km S of Veberöd. 25km E of Malmö

Söderslätts
Västra Grevie 19, 235 94 Vellinge
Tel **(040) 443039**
Fax **(040) 443469**
Holes 18 L 5700 m SSS 72
9 hole Par 3 course
V'tors WD–H WE–M
H before noon
Fees 150kr
Loc 15km SE of Malmö
Arch Sune Linde

Tegelberga
Alstad Pl 140, 231 96 Trelleborg
Tel **(040) 485690**
Fax **(040) 485691**
Holes 18 L 5700 m SSS 72
V'tors U
Fees 100–150kr (150–200kr)
Loc 11km N of Trelleborg. 25km E of Malmö
Arch Peter Chamberlain

Tomelilla
Ullstorp, 273 94 Tomelilla
Tel **(0417) 13420**
Fax **(0417) 14455**
Holes 18 L 6455 m SSS 75
9 hole course
Fees 120–160kr
Loc 15km N of Ystad. 60km E of Malmö

Trelleborg (1963)
Maglarp, Pl 401, 231 93 Trelleborg
Tel **(0410) 30460**
Fax **(0410) 30281**
Holes 18 L 5160 m SSS 69
V'tors U H
Fees 180kr
Loc 5km W of Trelleborg

Vellinge (1991)
Toftadalsgård, 235 41 Vellinge
Tel **(040) 443255**
Fax **(040) 443179**
Holes 18 L 5766 m SSS 72
9 hole short course
V'tors WD–U WE–NA before noon
Fees 150kr (180kr)
Loc 16km SE of Malmö
Arch Tommy Nordström

Ystad (1930)
Box 162, 271 24 Ystad
Tel **(0411) 50350**
Fax **(0411) 50392**
Holes 18 L 5800 m SSS 72
V'tors U
Fees 150kr
Loc 7km E of Ystad, towards Simrishamn
Arch Bruce/Lachmann

North

Avesta (1963)
Åsbo, 774 01 Avesta
Tel **(0226) 10363/10866/12766**
Fax **(0226) 12578**
Holes 18 L 5560 m SSS 71
V'tors U
Fees 150kr
Loc 3km NE of Avesta
Arch Sune Linde

Bollnäs
Box 1072, 821 12 Bollnäs
Tel **(0278) 50540/51310 (Shop)**
Holes 18 L 5870 m Par 72
Fees 150kr
Loc 15km S of Bollnäs on Route 83

Dalsjö
Box 2046, 781 02 Borlänge
Tel **(0243) 82800**
Fax **(0243) 220140**
Holes 18 L 5835 m SSS 72
V'tors U
Fees 160kr (180kr)
Loc 5km NE of Borlänge
Arch Jeremy Turner

Falun-Borlänge (1956)
Storgarden 10, 791 93 Falun
Tel **(023) 31015**
Fax **(023) 31072**
Holes 18 L 6085 m SSS 72
Fees 150kr
Loc Aspeboda, 8km N of Borlänge

Gävle (1949)
Bönavägen 23, 805 95 Gävle
Tel **(026) 120333**
Fax **(026) 516468**
Holes 18 L 5735 m SSS 73
9 L 2910 m SSS 36
Fees 160kr
Loc 3km N of Gävle

Hagge (1963)
Hagge, 771 90 Ludvika
Tel **(0240) 28087/28513**
Fax **(0240) 28515**
Holes 18 L 5519 m SSS 71
V'tors H
Fees D–150kr
Loc 7km S of Ludvika
Arch Sune Linde

Hofors (1965)
Box 117, 813 22 Hofors
Tel **(0290) 85125**
Fax **(0290) 85101**
Holes 18 L 5400 m SSS 70
V'tors U
Fees 120kr (150kr)
Loc 5km SE of Hofors

Högbo (1962)
Daniel Tilas Väg 4, 811 92 Sandviken
Tel **(026) 215015**
Fax **(026) 215322**
Holes 18 L 5810 m SSS 72
9 L 2600 m SSS 34
V'tors H
Fees 150kr
Loc 6km N of Sandviken (Route 272)
Arch Sköld/Linde

Hudiksvall (1964)
Tjuvskär, 824 01 Hudiksvall
Tel **(0650) 15930**
Fax **(0650) 18630**
Holes 18 L 5665 m SSS 72
V'tors U
Fees 150kr
Loc 4km SE of Hudiksvall
Arch Linde/Sköld

Leksand (1977)
Box 25, 793 21 Leksand
Tel **(0247) 14640**
Fax **(0247) 14157**
Holes 18 L 5263 m SSS 70
Fees 150kr (150kr)
Loc 2km N of Leksand

Ljusdal (1973)
Box 151, 827 23 Ljusdal
Tel **(0651) 16883**
Fax **(0651) 16883**
Holes 18 L 5920 m SSS 72
V'tors U
Fees 120kr
Loc 2km E of Ljusdal
Arch Eriksson/Skjöld

Mora (1980)
Box 264, 792 24 Mora
Tel **(0250) 10182**
Fax **(0250) 10306**
Holes 18 L 5600 m Par 72
Fees 150kr
Loc 1km N of Mora. 40km NW of Rättvik
Arch Sune Linde

Rättvik (1954)
Box 29, 795 21 Rättvik
Tel **(0248) 51030**
Fax **(0248) 12081**
Holes 18 L 5350 m SSS 70
V'tors U
Fees 130–200kr
Loc 2km N of Rättvik

Sälen (1983)
Box 20, 780 67 Sälen
Tel **(0280) 20670/20671**
Holes 18 L 5035 m SSS 72
V'tors U
Fees 120kr
Loc 230km NW of Borlänge. 400km NW of Stockholm

Säter (1984)
Box 89, 783 22 Säter
Tel **(0225) 50030**
Fax **(0225) 51424**
Holes 18 L 5781 m SSS 73
V'tors U
Fees 150kr
Loc 25km SE of Borlänge. 180km NW of Stockholm
Arch Sune Linde

Snöå (1990)
Snöå Bruk, 780 51 Dala-Järna
Tel **(0281) 24009/24072**
Holes 18 L 5738 m SSS 72
V'tors U
Fees 140kr
Loc 80km W of Borlänge, nr Dala-Järna (Route 71)
Arch Åke Persson

Söderhamn (1961)
Oxtorget 1C, 826 00 Söderhamn
Tel **(0270) 51300**
Fax **(0270) 51002**
Holes 18 L 5770 m SSS 72
V'tors H
Fees 130–150kr
Loc 8km N of Söderhamn

Skane & South

Ängelholm (1973)
Box 1117, 262 22 Ängelholm
Tel **(0431) 30260/31460**
Fax **(0431) 31568**
Holes 18 L 5760 m Par 72
V'tors U
Fees 120–180kr
Loc 10km E of Ängelholm on route 114
Arch Jan Sederholm

Araslöv
Starvägen 1, 291 75 Färlöv
Tel **(044) 71600**
Fax **(044) 71575**
Holes 18 L 5650 m SSS 71
V'tors H or Green card
Fees 150kr (150kr)
Loc 9km NW of Kristianstad (Route 19)
Arch Sune Linde

Båstad (1929)
Box 1037, 269 21 Båstad
Tel **(0431) 73136**
Fax **(0431) 73331**
Holes 18 L 5760 m Par 71
18 L 6325 m Par 73
V'tors H
Fees 250kr
Loc 4km W of Båstad (Route 115)
Arch Hawtree/Taylor/Nordström

Bedinge (1931)
Golfbanevägen, 230 21 Beddingestrand
Tel **(0410) 25514**
Fax **(0410) 25411**
Holes 18 L 5430 m SSS 70
V'tors H
Fees D–100–150kr
Loc Beddingestrand, 20km E of Trelleborg
Arch Åke Persson

Bjäre
Salomonhög 3086, 269 00 Båstad
Tel **(0431) 61053**
Fax **(0431) 61764**
Holes 18 L 5550 m SSS 71
V'tors H
Fees D–150–200kr
Loc 2km E of Båstad. 60km N of Helsingborg
Arch Svante Dahlgren

Bosjökloster (1974)
243 95 Höör
Tel **(0413) 25858**
Fax **(0413) 25895**
Holes 18 L 5890 m SSS 72
V'tors H
Fees 150kr
Loc 7km S of Höör. 40km NE of Malmö
Arch Douglas Brasier

Carlskrona (1949)
PO Almö, 370 24 Nättraby
Tel **(0457) 35123**
Fax **(0457) 35090**
Holes 18 L 5525 m Par 70
V'tors U
Fees D–160kr
Loc 18km SW of Karlskrona
Arch Jan Sederholm

Degeberga-Widtsköfle
Box 71, 297 21 Degeberga
Tel **(044) 355035**
Fax **(044) 355035**
Holes 18 L 6129 m SSS 72
9 hole Par 3 course
Fees 100–170kr
Loc 20km S of Kristianstad

Eslöv (1966)
Box 150, 241 22 Eslöv
Tel **(0413) 18610**
Fax **(0413) 18610**
Holes 18 L 5630 m SSS 71
V'tors H
Fees 150kr (180kr)
Loc 4km S of Eslöv (Route 113)
Arch Thure Bruce

Hässleholm (1978)
Skyrup, 282 00 Tyringe
Tel **(0451) 53111**
Fax **(0451) 53138**
Holes 18 L 5830 m SSS 72
V'tors U
Fees 120kr (140kr)
Loc 15km NW of Hässleholm

Helsingborg (1924)
260 40 Viken
Tel **(042) 236147**
Holes 9 L 4578 m SSS 65
Fees 100kr (120kr)
Loc 15km NW of Helsingborg

Karlshamn (1962)
Box 188, 374 23 Karlshamn
Tel **(0454) 50085**
Fax **(0454) 50160**
Holes 18 L 5861 m SSS 72
9 holes SSS 36
V'tors H
Fees D–160kr
Loc Morrum, 10km W of Karlshamn
Arch Douglas Brasier

Kristianstad (1924)
Box 41, 296 21 Åhus
Tel **(044) 247656**
Fax **(044) 247635**
Holes 18 L 5810 m SSS 72
9 L 2945 m SSS 36
V'tors H
Fees D–150kr (D–200kr)
Loc 18km SE of Kristianstad. Airport 20km
Arch Brasier/Nordström

Landskrona (1960)
Erikstorp, 261 61 Landskrona
Tel **(0418) 26010**
Fax **(0418) 36868**
Holes Old 18 L 5700 m SSS 71
New 18 L 4000 m SSS 62
V'tors U
Fees 160kr (200kr)
Loc 4km N of Landskrona, towards Borstahusen

Mölle (1943)
260 42 Mölle
Tel **(042) 347520**
Fax **(042) 347523**
Holes 18 L 5640 m SSS 70
V'tors H WE–restricted May–Aug
Fees 200kr
Loc Mölle, 35km NW of Helsingborg
Arch Thure Bruce

Örkelljunga
Box 149, 286 22 Örkelljunga
Tel **(0435) 54654/53640**
Fax **(0435) 53670**
Holes 18 L 5755 m SSS 72
V'tors H

Fees 150kr (200kr)
Loc 8km S of Örkelljunga. 40km NE of Helsingborg (E4)
Arch Hans Fock

Östra Göinge (1981)
Box 114, 289 00 Knislinge
Tel **(044) 60060**
Holes 18 L 5898 m Par 72
V'tors U
Fees 140kr
Loc 20km N of Kristianstad

Perstorp (1964)
PO Box 87, 284 00 Perstorp
Tel **(0435) 35411**
Fax **(0435) 35959**
Holes 18 L 5675 m SSS 71
6 hole short course
V'tors H
Fees 140kr (180kr)
Loc 1km S of Perstorp. 45km E of Helsingborg

Ronneby (1963)
Box 26, 372 21 Ronneby
Tel **(0457) 10315**
Holes 18 L 5323 m SSS 70
Fees 160kr
Loc 3km S of Ronneby

Rya (1934)
Rya 5500, 255 92 Helsingborg
Tel **(042) 220182**
Fax **(042) 220394**
Holes 18 L 5599 m SSS 71
Fees 180kr (200kr)
Loc 10km S of Helsingborg

Skepparslov (1984)
Udarpssäteri, 291 69 Kristianstad
Tel **(044) 229508**
Holes 18 L 5900 m SSS 72
V'tors U
Fees 100kr (150kr)
Loc 7km W of Kristianstad
Arch Rolf Collijn

Söderåsen (1966)
Box 41, 260 50 Billesholm
Tel **(042) 73337**
Fax **(042) 73963**
Holes 18 L 5780 m Par 73
V'tors U
Fees 160kr (200kr)
Loc 20km E of Helsingborg
Arch Thure Bruce

Sölvesborg
Box 63, 294 22 Sölvesborg
Tel **(0456) 70650**
Fax **(0456) 70650**
Holes 18 L 5900 m SSS 72
V'tors U
Fees 120kr (150kr)
Loc 30km E of Kristianstad
Arch Sune Linde

St Arild (1987)
Pl 1726 Fjälastorp, 260 41 Nyhamnsläge
Tel **(042) 346860**
Fax **(042) 346042**
Holes 18 L 5805 m SSS 72
V'tors H
Fees 120kr (200kr)
Loc 50km N of Helsingborg
Arch Jan Sederholm

Svalöv
Månstorp Pl 1365, 268 00 Svalöv
Tel **(0418) 62462**
Holes 18 L 5860 m SSS 73
Fees 130kr (160kr)
Loc 20km E of Landskrona

Torekov (1924)
Box 81, 260 93 Torekov
Tel **(0431) 63355**
Fax **(0431) 64916**
Holes 18 L 5701 m Par 72
V'tors Jun–Aug–H WE–M before noon
Fees 160–220kr
Loc 3km N of Torekov
Arch Nils Sköld

Trummenas
373 02 Ramdala
Tel **(0455) 60505**
Holes 18 L 5600 m SSS 72
9 hole course
V'tors H
Fees D–140kr W–590kr
Loc 15km NE of Karlskrona
Arch Ingemar Ericsson

Vasatorp (1973)
Box 13035, 250 13 Helsingborg
Tel **(042) 235058**
Fax **(042) 235135**
Holes 18 L 5875 m SSS 72
9 L 2940 m
V'tors H
Fees 200kr
Loc 8km E of Helsingborg
Arch Thure Bruce

Wittsjö (1962)
Ubbaltsgården, 280 22 Vittsjö
Tel **(0451) 22635**
Holes 18 L 5461 m SSS 71
V'tors U
Fees 130kr (170kr)
Loc 2km E of Vittsjö

South East

A 6 Golfklubb
Centralvägen, 553 05 Jönköping
Tel **(036) 308130**
Fax **(036) 308140**
Holes 27 hole course:
9 L 3185 m Par 38
9 L 3115 m Par 37
9 L 2935 m Par 36
V'tors U H
Fees 180kr
Loc 2km SE of Jönköping
Arch Peter Nordwall

Älmhult (1975)
Box 152, 343 22 Älmhult
Tel **(0476) 14135**
Holes 18 L 5407 m SSS 71
V'tors U H
Fees D–140kr
Loc 2km E of Älmhult on Route 120
Arch Persson/Söderberg

Åtvidaberg (1954)
Box 180, 597 24 Åtvidaberg
Tel **(0120) 35425**
Fax **(0120) 13502**
Holes 18 L 5856 m SSS 72
V'tors H
Fees 150kr (170kr)
Loc 30km SE of Linköping
Arch Douglas Brasier

Ekerum
387 92 Borgholm, Öland
Tel **(0485) 80000**
Fax **(0485) 80010**
Holes 18 L 6045 m SSS 73
9 L 2875 m SSS 36
V'tors U H
Fees 140–240kr (170–240kr)
Loc 12km S of Borgholm. 25km N of Öland bridge
Arch Peter Nordwall

Eksjö (1938)
Skedhult, 575 91 Eksjö
Tel **(0381) 13525**
Holes 18 L 5930 m SSS 72
V'tors U
Fees 160kr
Loc 6km W of Eksjö on Nässjö road

Emmaboda (1976)
Kyrkogatan, 360 60 Vissefjärda
Tel **(0471) 20505/20540**
Fax **(0471) 20440**
Holes 18 L 6165 m SSS 72
V'tors U
Fees 140kr
Loc 12km S of Emmaboda. 50km N of Karlskrona

Finspång (1965)
Viberga Gård, 612 92 Finspång
Tel **(0122) 13940**
Fax **(0122) 18888**
Holes 18 L 5800 m SSS 72
V'tors U
Fees 150kr
Loc 2km E of Finspång, Route 51. Norrköping 25km.
Arch Sköld/Linde

Gumbalde
Box 35, 620 13 Ståga, Gotland
Tel (0498) 482880
Fax (0498) 482884
Holes 18 L 5600 m SSS 71
V'tors U
Fees 160kr (180kr)
Loc 50km SE of Visby
Arch Lars Lagergren

Hook (1942)
560 13 Hok
Tel (0393) 21420
Holes 18 L 5758 m SSS 72
9 hole Par 3
Fees 180kr
Loc 30km SE of Jönköping

Isaberg (1968)
Nissafors Bruk, 330 27 Hestra
Tel (0370) 336330
Fax (0370) 336325
Holes East 18 L 5823 m SSS 72
West 18 L 5716 m SSS 72
V'tors H
Fees D–200kr W–1000kr
Loc 18km N of Gislaved, nr Nissafors. 60km S of Jönköping
Arch Amilon/Bruce/Persson

Jönköping (1936)
Kettilstorp, 556 27 Jönköping
Tel (036) 76567
Fax (036) 76511
Holes 18 L 6370 m SSS 70
V'tors WD–U H–phone in advance WE–H
Fees 200kr
Loc 3km S of Jönköping
Arch Nils Sköld

Kalmar (1947)
Box 278, 391 23 Kalmar 1
Tel (0480) 72111
Fax (0480) 72314
Holes Blue 18 L 5700 m SSS 72
Red 18 L 5634 m SSS 72
V'tors H
Fees 200kr
Loc 9km N of Kalmar

Lagan (1966)
Box 63, 340 14 Lagan
Tel (0372) 30450/35460
Fax (0372) 35307
Holes 18 L 5600 m SSS 71
V'tors U
Fees 150kr
Loc 10km N of Ljungby on Route E4
Arch Amilon/Persson

Landeryd (1987)
Bogestad Gård, 585 93 Linköping
Tel (013) 162520
Fax (013) 150493
Holes North 18 L 5675 m SSS 72
South 18 L 5085 m SSS 68
V'tors U
Fees 200kr
Loc 7km SE of Linköping

Linköping (1945)
Box 10054, 580 10 Linköping
Tel (013) 120646
Fax (013) 140769
Holes 18 L 5675 m SSS 71
V'tors H
Fees 160kr (180kr)
Loc 3km SW of Linköping

Mjölby (1983)
Blixberg, Miskarp, 595 92 Mjölby
Tel (0142) 12570
Fax (0142) 16553
Holes 18 L 5485 m SSS 71
V'tors H
Fees 130kr
Loc 35km WSW of Linköping (E4)
Arch Åke Persson

Motala (1956)
PO Box 264, 591 23 Motala
Tel (0141) 50840 (Sec)
Holes 18 L 5905 m SSS 72
Fees 140kr (140kr)
Loc 3km S of Motala (Route 50 or 32)

Norrköping (1928)
Klinga Golfbana, 605 97 Norrköping
Tel (011) 335235/183654
Holes 18 L 5860 m SSS 73
V'tors U
Fees 150kr
Loc 2km S of Norrköping on E4
Arch Nils Sköld

Nybro (1971)
Box 235, 382 00 Nybro
Tel (0480) 55044
Fax (0480) 55125
Holes 18 L 5829 m SSS 72
V'tors U
Fees 140kr
Loc 10km E of Nybro, towards Kalmar

Oskarshamn (1972)
Box 148, 572 23 Oskarshamn
Tel (0491) 94033
Fax (0491) 84140
Holes 18 L 5545 m SSS 71
V'tors H
Fees 160kr
Loc 10km SW of Oskarshamn, nr Forshult
Arch Nils Sköld

Skinnarebo
Skinnarebo, 555 93 Jönköping
Tel (036) 69075
Fax (036) 69075
Holes 18 L 5686 m SSS 71
9 hole Par 3 course
V'tors U
Fees 160kr
Loc 14km SW of Jönköping
Arch Björn Magnusson

Söderköping (1983)
Hylinge, 605 96 Norrköping
Tel (011) 70579
Holes 18 L 5730 m SSS 72
V'tors U
Fees 160kr
Loc Västra Husby, 9km W of Söderköping
Arch Ronald Fream

Tobo (1971)
Box 101, 598 22 Vimmerby
Tel (0492) 30346
Fax (0492) 30870
Holes 18 L 5720 m SSS 73
V'tors U
Fees 160kr
Loc 10km S of Vimmerby, nr Storebro. 60km SW of Västervik
Arch Brasier/Jensen

Tranås (1952)
N Storgatan 130, 573 00 Tranås
Tel (0140) 11661
Holes 18 L 5830 m SSS 72
Fees 120kr (150kr)
Loc 2km N of Tranås

Vadstena (1957)
Hagalund 3, 592 94 Vadstena
Tel (0143) 12440
Holes 18 L 5486 m SSS 71
Fees 150kr
Loc 3km S of Vadstena, towards Vaderstad

Värnamo (1962)
Box 146, 331 01 Värnamo
Tel (0370) 23123
Holes 18 L 6253 m SSS 72
Fees 180kr
Loc 8km E of Värnamo (Route 127)

Västervik (1959)
Box 62, 593 22 Västervik
Tel (0490) 32420
Holes 18 L 5760 m SSS 72
Fees 150kr
Loc 1km SE of Västervik

Växjö (1959)
Box 227, 351 05 Växjö
Tel (0470) 21515
Fax (0470) 21557
Holes 18 L 5860 m Par 72
V'tors H
Fees 160kr
Loc 5km NW of Växjö
Arch Douglas Brasier

Vetlanda (1983)
Box 249, 574 23 Vetlanda
Tel (0383) 18310
Fax (0383) 19278
Holes 18 L 5698 m SSS 72
V'tors U
Fees 140kr
Loc Östanå, 3km W of Vetlanda. 80km SE of Jönköping
Arch Jan Sederholm

For list of abbreviations see page 435

Visby
Box 1038, 621 21 Visby, Gotland
Tel **(0498) 245058**
Fax **(0498) 246240**
Holes 18 L 5765 m SSS 72
9 hole course
V'tors Jun–Sept–H
Fees 200kr
Loc Kronholmen, 25km S of Visby, Gotland island
Arch Nordwall/Sköld

Vreta Kloster
Box 144, 590 60 Ljungsbro
Tel **(013) 63680**
Fax **(013) 66545**
Holes 18 L 5720 m SSS 72
V'tors H
Fees 140kr
Loc 15km N of Linköping
Arch Sune Linde

South West

Alingsås (1985)
Hjälmared 4050, 441 95 Alingsås
Tel **(0322) 52421**
Holes 18 L 5600 m SSS 72
V'tors U
Fees 120–150kr (200kr)
Loc 5km SE of Alingsås towards Borås

Bäckavattnet (1977)
Marbäck, 305 94 Halmstad
Tel **(035) 44271**
Fax **(035) 44275**
Holes 18 L 5740 m SSS 72
V'tors H
Fees 180kr
Loc 13km E of Halmstad (RD25)

Billingen (1949)
St Kulhult, 540 17 Lerdala
Tel **(0511) 80291**
Fax **(0511) 80244**
Holes 18 L 5470 m Par 71
V'tors H
Fees 140kr (170kr)
Loc 20km NW of Skövde
Arch Douglas Brasier

Borås (1933)
Östra Vik, Kråkered, 505 95 Borås
Tel **(033) 250250**
Fax **(033) 250176**
Holes North 18 L 6005 m SSS 72
South 18 L 5085 m SSS 70
V'tors H–booking necessary
Fees 160kr (180kr)
Loc 6km S of Borås, on Route 41 towards Varberg
Arch Brasier/Persson

Ekarnas (1970)
Balders Väg 12, 467 00 Grästorp
Tel **(0514) 51450**
Fax **(0514) 51450**
Holes 18 L 5501 m SSS 71
V'tors H
Fees 120kr (150kr)
Loc 25km E of Trollhätten. Lidköping 35km
Arch Jan Andersson

Falkenberg (1949)
Golfvägen, 311 72 Falkenberg
Tel **(0346) 50287**
Fax **(0346) 50996**
Holes 27 L 5575-5680 m SSS 71
V'tors H
Fees 120–200kr
Loc 5km S of Falkenberg

Falköping
Box 99, 521 02 Falköping
Tel **(0515) 31270**
Fax **(0515) 31389**
Holes 18 L 5835 m SSS 73
V'tors U
Fees 120kr (150kr)
Loc 7km E of Falköping on Route 46 towards Skovde

Halmstad (1930)
302 73 Halmstad
Tel **(035) 30077/30280 (Starter)**
Fax **(035) 32308**
Holes 18 L 6259 m SSS 74
18 L 5787 m SSS 72
V'tors H WE–M before 1pm
Fees 210–260kr
Loc Tylosand, 9km W of Halmstad
Arch Sundblom/Sköld

Hökensås (1962)
PO Box 116, 544 00 Hjo
Tel **(0503) 16059**
Holes 18 L 5540 m SSS 72
9 hole course
V'tors U
Fees 150kr (170kr)
Loc 8km S of Hjo on Route 195

Hulta (1972)
Box 54, 517 00 Bollebygd
Tel **(033) 88180**
Holes 18 L 6000 m SSS 73
Fees 170kr (200kr)
Loc Bollebygd, 25km W of Borås

Knistad
541 92 Skövde
Tel **(0500) 463170**
Fax **(0500) 463075**
Holes 18 L 5790 m SSS 72
V'tors H
Fees 180kr
Loc 10km NE of Skövde
Arch Jeremy Turner

Laholm (1964)
Box 101, 312 22 Laholm
Tel **(0430) 30601**
Fax **(0430) 30891**
Holes 18 L 5430 m SSS 70
V'tors U H
Fees 150kr (180kr)
Loc 5 miles E of Laholm (Route 24)
Arch Jan Sederholm

Lidköping (1967)
Box 2029, 531 02 Lidköping
Tel **(0510) 46122/46144**
Holes 18 L 5540 m SSS 71
V'tors H
Fees 130kr (150kr)
Loc 5km E of Lidköping
Arch Douglas Brasier

Mariestad (1975)
PO Box 299, 542 23 Mariestad
Tel **(0501) 17383**
Fax **(0501) 78117**
Holes 18 L 5890 m SSS 72
V'tors H
Fees 150kr
Loc 4km W of Mariestad, at Lake Vänern

Marks (1962)
Brättingstorpsvägen 28, 511 58 Kinna
Tel **(0320) 14220**
Fax **(0320) 12516**
Holes 18 L 5530 m SSS 69
V'tors H
Fees 140kr (180kr)
Loc Kinna, 30km S of Borås

Onsjö (1974)
Box 6331 A, 462 42 Vänersborg
Tel **(0521) 68870**
Fax **(0521) 68871**
Holes 18 L 5730 m SSS 72
V'tors U
Fees 140kr (170kr)
Loc 3km S of Vänersborg. 80km N of Gothenburg

Ringenäs
Strandlida, 305 90 Halmstad
Tel **(035) 59050**
Fax **(035) 59135**
Holes 27 L 5395-5615 m SSS 71
V'tors H
Fees D–150–200kr (D–200kr)
Loc 10km NW of Halmstad on coast
Arch Sune Linde

Skogaby (1988)
312 93 Laholm
Tel **(0430) 60190**
Holes 18 L 5555 m SSS 71
V'tors U H
Fees 120kr (160kr)
Loc 10km E of Laholm. 30km SE of Halmstad
Arch J Rosengren

Töreboda (1965)
Box 18, 545 21 Töreboda
Tel **(0506) 16240**
Holes 18 L 5355 m SSS 70
V'tors U
Fees 140kr
Loc 7km E of Töreboda

Trollhättan (1963)
Box 254, 461 26 Trollhättan
Tel **(0520) 441000**
Fax **(0520) 441049**

For list of abbreviations see page 435

Holes 18 L 6200 m SSS 73
V'tors U
Fees 150kr
Loc Koberg, 20km SE of Trollhättan
Arch Nils Sköld

Ulricehamn (1947)
Box 179, 523 33 Ulricehamn
Tel **(0321) 10021**
Holes 18 L 5509 m SSS 71
Fees 140kr (180kr)
Loc Backasen, 2km E of Ulricehamn

Vara-Bjertorp
Bjertorp, 535 00 Kvänum
Tel **(0512) 20260**
Holes 18 L 6005 m SSS 73
V'tors H
Fees 140kr (180kr)
Loc 10km N of Vara. 110km NE of Gothenburg (E20)
Arch Jan Sederholm

Varberg (1950)
Himle, 430 10 Tvååker
Tel **(0340) 43446/37496**
Fax **(0340) 37440/43447**
Holes East 18 L 5700 m SSS 72
West 18 L 6640 m SSS 76
V'tors H
Fees 150–200kr
Loc East 15km E of Varberg. West 8km S of Varberg, nr E6
Arch Sköld/Nordström

Vinberg (1992)
Sannagård, 311 95 Falkenberg
Tel **(0346) 19020**
Holes 18 L 3556 m SSS 60
V'tors U
Fees 100kr (140kr)
Loc 5km E of Falkenberg on coast
Arch Nilsson/Haglund

Stockholm

Ågesta (1958)
123 52 Farsta
Tel **(08) 604 5641**
Holes 18 L 5705 m SSS 72
9 L 3660 m SSS 59
V'tors U
Fees 300kr
Loc Farsta, 15km S of Stockholm

Botkyrka
Malmbro Gård, 147 91 Grödinge
Tel **(08) 530 29650**
Fax **(08) 530 29409**
Holes 18 holes SSS 73
9 hole Par 3 course
V'tors WD–U H WE–H NA before noon
Fees 200kr (250kr)
Loc 45km S of Stockholm
Arch Bill Södenberg

Bro-Bålsta (1978)
Box 96, 197 22 Bro
Tel **(08) 582 41310**
Fax **(08) 582 40006**
Holes 18 L 6420 m SSS 75
9 L 1435 m SSS 56
V'tors H WE–NA before noon
Fees 240kr (280kr)
Loc 40km NW of Stockholm
Arch Peter Nordwall

Djursholm (1931)
Hagbardsvägen 1, 182 63 Djursholm
Tel **(08) 755 1477**
Fax **(08) 755 5932**
Holes 18 L 5595 m SSS 71
9 L 4400 m SSS 64
V'tors WD–U H before 3pm –M after 3pm WE–M before 3pm –U H after 3pm
Fees 260kr
Loc 12km N of Stockholm

Drottningholm (1958)
PO Box 183, 178 93 Drottningholm
Tel **(08) 759 0085**
Fax **(08) 759 0851**
Holes 18 L 5825 m SSS 72
V'tors WD–U H before 3pm –M after 3pm WE–M before 3pm –U H after 3pm
Fees 280kr
Loc 16km W of Stockholm
Arch Sundblom/Sköld

Fågelbro
Fågelbro Säteri, 139 60 Värmdö
Tel **(08) 571 40130/40115**
Fax **(08) 571 40671**
Holes 18 L 5635 m SSS 72
V'tors H
Fees 250kr (350kr)
Loc 35km E of Stockholm
Arch Eriksson/Oredsson

Haninge (1983)
Årsta Slott, 136 91 Haninge
Tel **(08) 500 32240/32270**
Fax **(08) 500 32340**
Holes 27 L 5930 m SSS 73
V'tors WD–U before 1pm –M after 1pm WE–M before 1pm –U after 1pm
Fees 250kr
Loc 30km S of Stockholm towards Nynäshamn
Arch Jan Sederholm

Ingarö (1962)
Fogelvik, 130 35 Ingarö
Tel **(08) 570 28244**
Fax **(08) 570 28379**
Holes 18 L 5603 m SSS 71
18 L 5618 m SSS 72
V'tors U H
Fees 200kr (250kr)
Loc 30km E of Stockholm via Route 222
Arch Sköld/Eriksson

Johannesberg G & CC (1990)
762 95 Rimbo
Tel **(08) 512 92480**
Fax **(08) 512 92390**
Holes 18 L 6328 m SSS 74
9 hole course
V'tors H
Fees 180kr (200kr)
Loc 55km N of Stockholm
Arch Donald Steel

Lidingö (1933)
Box 1035, 181 21 Lidingö
Tel **(08) 765 7911**
Fax **(08) 765 5479**
Holes 18 L 5770 m SSS 71
V'tors H
Fees 250kr
Loc 6km NE of Stockholm

Lindö (1978)
186 92 Vallentuna
Tel **(08) 511 72260**
Holes 18 L 2850 m SSS 71
Fees 200kr (250kr)
Loc 20km N of Stockholm

Nynäshamn (1977)
Box 4, 148 21 Ösmo
Tel **(08) 520 27190/520 38666**
Fax **(08) 520 38613**
Holes 27 L 5690 m SSS 72
V'tors H–phone first
Fees 200kr (250kr)
Loc Ösmo, 50km S of Stockholm
Arch Sune Linde

Österakers
Hagby 1, 184 92 Akersberga
Tel **(08) 540 85165**
Fax **(08) 540 66832**
Holes 18 L 5792 m SSS 72
18 L 5780 m SSS 72
V'tors WD–H before 3pm –M after 3pm WE–M before 2pm –H after 2pm
Fees 175–250kr
Loc 30km NE of Stockholm
Arch Jan Sederholm

Österhaninge (1992)
Box 82, 130 54 Dalarö
Tel **(08) 500 32285**
Fax **(08) 501 51835**
Holes 18 L 5141 m SSS 69
V'tors H
Fees 150kr (190kr)
Loc 35km S of Stockholm
Arch B Lorichs

Parkens
Stockholm Lindö Park, 186 92 Vallentuna
Tel **(08) 511 70055 (Bookings)**
Fax **(08) 511 70613**
Holes 18 L 5800 m SSS 72
V'tors U H–book day before play
Fees 200kr (250kr)
Loc 30km N of Stockholm
Arch Persson/Bruce

For list of abbreviations see page 435

Saltsjöbaden (1929)
Box 51, 133 21 Saltsjöbaden
Tel (08) 717 0125
Fax (08) 717 9713
Holes 18 L 5685 m SSS 72
9 L 3640 m SSS 60
V'tors WD–U WE–M before 2pm
Fees D–250kr
Loc 15km E of Stockholm (Route 228)

Sollentuna (1967)
Skillingegården, 191 77 Sollentuna
Tel (08) 754 3625
Fax (08) 754 1823
Holes 18 L 5910 m SSS 72
V'tors WD–H before 3pm WE–H after 1pm
Fees 230kr
Loc 19km N of Stockholm. 1km W of E4 (Rotebro)
Arch Nils Sköld

Stockholm (1904)
Kevingestrand 20, 182 31 Danderyd
Tel (08) 755 0031
Fax (08) 622 6447
Holes 18 L 5180 m SSS 69
V'tors WD–M after 4pm WE–M before 3pm
Fees 300kr
Loc 7km NE of Stockholm via Route E18

Täby (1968)
Skålhamra Gård, 183 43 Täby
Tel (08) 510 23261
Fax (08) 510 23441
Holes 18 L 5776 m SSS 73
V'tors WD–H
Fees 200–260kr
Loc 15km N of Stockholm

Ullna (1981)
Rosenkälla, 184 92 Åkersberga
Tel (08) 510 26075
Fax (08) 510 26068
Holes 18 L 5825 m SSS 72
V'tors H
Fees 350kr
Loc 20km N of Stockholm via Route E18
Arch Sven Tumba

Ulriksdal
Box 8033, 171 08 Solna
Tel (08) 857931
Holes 18 L 3900 m SSS 61
V'tors H
Fees 130kr (180kr)
Loc 8km N of Stockholm
Arch Alec Backhurst

Vallentuna
Box 266, 186 24 Vallentuna
Tel (08) 511 77000/77083
Fax (08) 511 72370
Holes 18 L 5700 m SSS 72
V'tors WD–U WE–U after 3pm
Fees 200kr (250kr)
Loc 35km N of Stockholm
Arch Sune Linde

Viksjö (1969)
Fjällens Gård, 175 45 Järfälla
Tel (08) 580 31300/31310
Fax (08) 580 31340
Holes 18 L 5930 m SSS 73
Fees 220kr (220kr)
Loc 18km NW of Stockholm

Wäsby
Box 2017, 194 02 Upplands Väsby
Tel (08) 510 23345/23177
Fax (08) 510 23364
Holes 18 L 6170 m SSS 72
9 hole course
V'tors WD–U WE–H
Fees 170kr (220kr)
Loc 20km N of Stockholm. 20km S of Airport
Arch Björn Eriksson

Wermdö G & CC (1966)
Torpa, 139 60 Värmdö
Tel (08) 570 20849
Fax (08) 570 20840
Holes 18 L 5630 m SSS 72
V'tors H WE–NA before noon
Fees D–300kr (D–350kr)
Loc 25km E of Stockholm via Route 222
Arch Nils Sköld

West Central

Arvika
Box 197, 671 25 Arvika 1
Tel (0570) 54133
Holes 18 L 5815 m SSS 72
V'tors U
Fees 160kr
Loc 11km E of Arvika (Route 61)
Arch Nils Sköld

Billerud (1961)
Valnäs, 660 40 Segmon
Tel (0555) 91313
Holes 18 L 5874 m SSS 72
V'tors H
Fees 160kr
Loc Valnäs, 15km N of Säffle
Arch Brasier/Sköld

Färgelanda
Box 23, 458 21 Färgelanda
Tel (0528) 20385
Holes 18 L 6000 m SSS 71
V'tors U
Fees 120kr (150kr)
Loc 23km N of Uddevalla. 100km N of Gothenburg
Arch Åke Persson

Fjällbacka (1965)
450 71 Fjällbacka
Tel (0525) 31150
Fax (0525) 32122
Holes 18 L 5850 m SSS 72
V'tors H
Fees D–160kr
Loc 2km N of Fjällbacka (Route 163)

Forsbacka (1969)
Box 136, 662 00 Åmål
Tel (0532) 43055
Holes 18 L 5860 m SSS 72
Fees 160kr
Loc 6km W of Åmål (Route 164)

Hammarö
Box 2080, 663 02 Hammarö
Tel (054) 521621
Holes 18 L 6200 m SSS 75
Fees 160kr
Loc 11km S of Karlstad

Karlskoga (1975)
Bricketorp 647, 691 94 Karlskoga
Tel (0586) 28190
Holes 18 L 5705 m Par 72
Fees 150kr
Loc Valåsen, 5km E of Karlskoga via Route E18

Karlstad (1957)
PO Box 294, 651 07 Karlstad
Tel (054) 866353
Fax (054) 866478
Holes 18 L 5970 m SSS 73
9 L 2875 m SSS 36
V'tors H
Fees 180kr
Loc 12km E of Karlstad (Route 63)

Kristinehamn (1974)
Box 337, 681 26 Kristinehamn
Tel (0550) 82310
Fax (0550) 19535
Holes 18 L 5800 m SSS 72
V'tors H
Fees 150kr
Loc 3km N of Kristinehamn
Arch Sune Linde

Lyckorna (1967)
Box 66, 459 22 Ljungskile
Tel (0522) 20176
Fax (0522) 22304
Holes 18 L 5820 m SSS 72
V'tors H
Fees 160kr
Loc 20km S of Uddevalla
Arch Anders Amilon

Orust (1981)
Pl 8290, 440 80 Ellös
Tel (0304) 053170
Holes 18 L 5770 m SSS 72
Fees 160kr (160kr)
Loc Ellös, 10km from Henän. 80km N of Gothenburg

Saxå (1964)
Centrumhuset, 712 30 Hällefors
Tel (0590) 24070
Fax (0591) 10503
Holes 18 L 5680 m SSS 73
V'tors U
Fees 150kr
Loc 15km E of Filipstad (Route 63)

Skaftö (1963)
Röd PL 4476, 450 34 Fiskebäckskil
Tel **(0523) 23211**
Fax **(0523) 23215**
Holes 18 L 4748 m SSS 68
V'tors WD–H
Fees 100–160kr
Loc 40km W of Uddevalla, through Fiskebäckskil
Arch Sköld/Sederholm

Strömstad (1967)
Box 129, 452 00 Strömstad 1
Tel **(0526) 11788**
Fax **(0526) 14766**
Holes 18 L 5615 m SSS 71
Fees 150kr (170kr)
Loc 6km N of Strömstad

Sunne (1970)
Box 108, 686 00 Sunne
Tel **(0565) 14100/14210**
Fax **(0565) 14855**
Holes 18 hole course SSS 72
V'tors H
Fees 160kr
Loc 2km S of Sunne. 60km N of Karlstad on Route 45
Arch Jan Sederholm

Torreby (1961)
Torreby Slott, 455 00 Munkedal
Tel **(0524) 21365/21109**
Fax **(0524) 21365**
Holes 18 L 5885 m SSS 72
V'tors H
Fees D–120–160kr
Loc Munkedal 8km. Uddevalla 30km.
Arch Douglas Brasier

Uddeholm (1965)
Risäter 20, 683 93 Råda
Tel **(0563) 60564**
Fax **(0563) 60017**
Holes 18 L 5830 m SSS 72
V'tors U H
Fees D–140kr
Loc Lake Råda, 80km N of Karlstad, via RD62

Switzerland

Bern

Blumisberg (1959)
3184 Wünnewil
Tel **(037) 36 34 38**
Fax **(037) 36 35 23**
Holes 18 L 6048 m SSS 73
V'tors WD–U H WE–M
Fees 80fr (80fr)
Loc Wünnewil, 16km SW of Bern
Arch B von Limburger

Neuchâtel (1928)
2072 Saint-Blaise
Tel **(038) 33 55 50**
Fax **(038) 33 29 40**
Holes 18 L 5823 m SSS 70
V'tors H
Fees 60fr (80fr)
Loc Voens/Saint-Blaise, 5km E of Neuchâtel. 30km W of Bern

Pont-la Ville
Le Château, 1649 Pont-la-Ville
Tel **(037) 33 91 11**
Fax **(037) 33 92 20**
Holes 18 L 5500 yds Par 68
V'tors U H
Fees 60–80fr (80–100fr)
Loc 12km S of Fribourg
Arch Jeremy Pern

Wallenried (1992)
1784 Wallenried
Tel **(037) 34 36 06**
Fax **(037) 34 36 10**
Holes 18 L 6000 m SSS 72
V'tors WD–U H
Fees 70fr (90fr)
Loc 6km W of Fribourg
Arch Ruzzo Reuss

Bernese Oberland

Gstaad-Saanenland (1962)
3780 Gstaad
Tel **(030) 435 81/433 70**
Holes 9 L 5580 m SSS 69
Loc Saanenmöser, 15km N of Gstaad

Interlaken-Unterseen (1964)
Postfach 110, 3800 Interlaken
Tel **(036) 22 60 22**
Fax **(036) 23 42 03**
Holes 18 L 5980 m SSS 72
V'tors H
Fees 70fr (80fr)
Loc Interlaken 3km
Arch Donald Harradine

Riederalp (1986)
3987 Riederalp
Tel **(028) 27 29 32/27 14 63**
Holes 9 L 3016 m SSS 54
Loc 10km NE of Brig

Lake Geneva & South West

Bonmont (1983)
Château de Bonmont, 1261 Chéserex
Tel **(022) 369 23 45**
Fax **(022) 369 24 17**
Holes 18 L 6120 m SSS 72
V'tors WD–restricted WE–M
Fees WD–80fr
Loc 3km from Nyon. 30km NE of Geneva
Arch Donald Harradine

Crans-sur-Sierre (1906)
3963 Crans-sur-Sierre-Montana
Tel **(027) 41 21 68/41 27 03**
Fax **(027) 41 46 71/41 95 68**
Holes 18 L 6260 m SSS 72
9 L 2667 m SSS 35
9 hole Par 3 course
V'tors H
Fees 18 hole:80fr W–420–500fr
9 hole:40fr
Loc 20km E of Sion. Geneva 2 hrs

Domaine Impérial (1987)
Villa Prangins, 1196 Gland
Tel **(0221) 364 45 45**
Fax **(0221) 364 43 32**
Holes 18 L 6297 m SSS 74
V'tors H–am only
Fees WD–90fr
Loc Nyon, 20km N of Geneva
Arch Pete Dye

Geneva (1923)
70 Route de la Capite, 1223 Cologny
Tel **(022) 735 75 40**
Fax **(022) 735 71 05**
Holes 18 L 6250 m Par 72
V'tors WD–am only Tues–Fri WE–M
Fees 80fr
Loc 4km from centre of Geneva
Arch Robert Trent Jones Sr

Lausanne (1921)
Route du Golf 3, 1000 Lausanne 25
Tel **(021) 784 13 15**
Fax **(021) 784 13 31**
Holes 18 L 6295 m SSS 74
V'tors H
Fees 80fr (100fr)
Loc 7km N of Lausanne towards Le Mont

Montreux (1898)
54 Route d'Evian, 1860 Aigle
Tel **(025) 26 46 16**
Fax **(025) 27 10 47**
Holes 18 L 6143 m SSS 72
V'tors H
Fees 70fr (90fr)
Loc Aigle, 15km S of Montreux
Arch Donald Harradine

Verbier (1970)
1936 Verbier
Tel **(026) 31 62 55/31 53 14**
Fax **(026) 31 60 93/35 21 22**
Holes 18 L 5300 m Par 70
18 hole Par 3 course
V'tors U
Fees 25fr (50fr)
Arch Donald Harradine

Villars (1922)
C P 152, 1884 Villars
Tel **(025) 35 42 14**
Fax **(025) 35 18 40**

For list of abbreviations see page 435

Holes 18 L 4093 m SSS 61
V'tors U
Fees 50fr (60fr)
Loc 7km E of Villars towards Les Diablerets
Arch Thierry Sprecher

Lugano & Ticino

Lugano (1923)
6983 Magliaso
Tel **(091) 71 15 57/71 58 01**
Fax **(091) 71 65 58**
Holes 18 L 5775 m SSS 71
V'tors H–(max 30)
Fees 80fr (100fr)
Loc 8km W of Lugano towards Ponte Tresa
Arch Harradine/Robinson

Patriziale Ascona (1928)
Via al Lido 81, 6612 Ascona
Tel **(093) 35 21 32**
Fax **(093) 35 07 96**
Holes 18 L 5893 m SSS 71
V'tors H–(max 30)
Fees 60fr (80fr)
Loc 5km W of Locarno
Arch CK Cotton

St Mortiz & Engadine

Arosa (1946)
Postfach 95, 7050 Arosa
Tel **(081) 31 22 15**
Fax **(081) 31 46 77**
Holes 9 L 4450 m Par 66 SSS 64
V'tors U
Fees 50fr
Loc 30km S of Chur
Arch P Harradine Sr

Bad Ragaz (1957)
Hans Albrecht Strasse, 7310 Bad Ragaz
Tel **(081) 303 37 17**
Fax **(081) 303 37 27**
Holes 18 L 5750 m SSS 71
V'tors H
Fees 100fr (120fr)
Loc 20km N of Chur. 100km SE of Zürich
Arch Donald Harradine

Davos (1929)
Postfach, 7260 Davos Dorf
Tel **(081) 46 56 34**
Fax **(081) 46 25 55**
Holes 18 L 5715 yds SSS 68
V'tors WD–U
Fees 70fr (90fr)
Loc 1km outside Davos
Arch Donald Harradine

Engadin (1893)
7503 Samedan
Tel **(082) 6 52 26**
Fax **(082) 6 46 82**
Holes 18 L 6350 m SSS 73
V'tors H
Fees 90fr
Loc 6km NE of St Moritz
Arch M Verdieri

Lenzerheide Valbella (1950)
7078 Lenzerheide
Tel **(081) 34 13 16**
Fax **(081) 34 52 22**
Holes 18 L 5274 m SSS 69
V'tors H
Fees 60–80fr
Loc 20km S of Chur towards St Moritz
Arch Donald Harradine

Vulpera (1923)
7552 Vulpera Spa
Tel **(081) 864 96 88**
Fax **(081) 864 96 88**
Holes 9 L 1982 m SSS 62
V'tors H
Fees 50fr (60fr) W–250fr
Loc Tarasp, nr Vulpera. 60km NE of St Moritz
Arch Dell/Spencer

Zürich & North

Breitenloo (1964)
8309 Oberwil b. Bassersdorf
Tel **(01) 836 40 80/836 64 86**
Fax **(01) 837 10 85**
Holes 18 L 6125 m SSS 72
V'tors WD–H by appointment WE–M H
Fees 100fr
Loc 10km NE of Zürich Airport
Arch Harradine/Pennink

Bürgenstock (1928)
6366 Bürgenstock
Tel **(041) 61 24 34**
Holes 9 L 1935 m Par 32
Loc 15km S of Lucerne
Mis Open May-Sept

Dolder (1907)
Kurhausstrasse 66, 8032 Zürich
Tel **(01) 261 50 45**
Fax **(01) 261 53 02**
Holes 9 L 1735 m SSS 58
V'tors WD–H WE–M
Fees WD–60fr
Loc Zürich

Erlen (1988)
Schlossgut Eppishausen, Schlossstr 7, 8586 Erlen
Tel **(072) 48 29 30**
Fax **(072) 48 29 40**
Holes 18 L 5913 m SSS 72
V'tors H
Loc 30km NW of St Gallen. 60km W of Zürich
Arch Rainer Preissmann

Hittnau-Zürich G & CC (1964)
8335 Hittnau
Tel **(01) 950 24 42**
Fax **(01) 951 01 66**
Holes 18 L 5773 m SSS 71
V'tors WE–M
Fees WD–80fr
Loc Hittnau, 30km E of Zürich

Lucerne (1903)
6006 Dietschiberg
Tel **(041) 36 97 87**
Fax **(041) 36 82 48**
Holes 18 L 6000 m SSS 72
V'tors H
Fees 80fr (100fr)
Loc Lucerne 2km

Mitteland (1988)
Postfach 87, Muhenstrasse 52, 5036 Oberentfelden
Tel **(064) 43 89 84**
Fax **(064) 43 84 36**
Holes 9 L 3960 m SSS 60
V'tors U
Fees 50fr (70fr)
Loc 50km W of Zürich
Arch Donald Harradine

Ostschweizischer (1948)
9246 Niederbüren
Tel **(071) 81 18 56**
Fax **(071) 81 18 25**
Holes 18 L 5920 m SSS 71
V'tors WD–H
Fees D–70fr (90fr)
Loc 25km NW of St Gallen
Arch Donald Harradine

Schinznach-Bad (1929)
5116 Schinznach-Bad
Tel **(056) 43 12 26**
Fax **(056) 43 34 83**
Holes 9 L 5670 m Par 71
V'tors WD–U
Fees 60fr
Loc 6km S of Brugg. 35km W of Zürich

Schönenberg (1967)
8824 Schönenberg
Tel **(01) 788 16 24**
Fax **(01) 788 20 10**
Holes 18 L 6340 m SSS 74
V'tors WD–H–by appointment WE–M H
Fees 100fr
Loc 20km S of Zürich
Arch Donald Harradine

Zürich-Zumikon (1931)
8126 Zumikon
Tel **(01) 918 00 50**
Fax **(01) 918 00 37**
Holes 18 L 6360 m SSS 74
V'tors WD–by appointment WE–M
Fees WD–100fr
Loc Zürich 10km
Arch Donald Harradine

PART VI

Government of the Game

Introduction

The Royal & Ancient Golf Club

In Britain it is not unusual for the Governing Body of a Sport to have its origins in a private club, which later comes to be recognised as the authority through which the game is administered. The Royal & Ancient Golf Club of St Andrews is a prime example and enjoys a similar status to the Marylebone Cricket Club. With the world-wide spread of golf and cricket this century, both have emerged as the international body to which most other countries look for rulings and guidance.

The Royal & Ancient Club's records date back to 1754 when the Society of St Andrews Golfers adopted the rules which had been formulated in 1744 by the Gentlemen Golfers of Leith, later to become the Honourable Company of Edinburgh Golfers; the older club located across the Forth at Muirfield.

When in 1834 King William IV granted the St Andrews Gentlemen Golfers the right and privilege of using the title *Royal & Ancient*, the Honourable Company had temporarily lost cohesion and the R&A gradually acquired the status of the premier club. During the latter half of the Victorian age, in the 1880s and 1890s when, following the spread of the railway system, many new clubs were founded, they looked to the R&A for leadership and advice.

With the appointment of the first Rules of Golf Committee in 1897, the R&A became recognised as the Governing Authority in all countries except the United States and Mexico where the United States Golf Association controls the game. Golf federations of many countries are affiliated to the R&A. This is made clear in the *Statement of Functions* of the R&A, reproduced with the permission of the General Committee. The work of the Championship Committee is expanded in a note below, with particular reference to The Open Championship.

The success of The Open in recent years, both as a spectacle and financially, has meant that the R&A can now support fully the development of the game, while remaining the guardian of its traditions. Its encouragement of young players, especially through the Boys and Youths Championships and the Golf Foundation, has helped produce the higher standards of play and younger champions now so apparent to all followers of the game.

Statement of Functions of the Royal & Ancient Golf Club throughout the world

With the ever continuing interest and developments in golf and the increasing complexity of the administration of the game, the Royal & Ancient Golf Club feels that a statement of its activities in this field would be of interest.

The functions for which the Club is responsible fall into three clearly defined categories. First, functions of an international nature, secondly functions of a national nature, and finally, the running of a Club with wide national and international Membership.

International Functions

In 1897 the Royal & Ancient became the Governing Authority on the Rules of Golf at the suggestion of the leading Golf Clubs in the United Kingdom at the time. Since then an ever increasing number of countries have sought affiliation to it, until today they number over 80, including several other Unions or Associations (eg the Ladies' Golf Union, European Golf Association, South American Golf Federation and Asia-Pacific Golf Confederation).

The Club in its negotiations with the United States Golf Association on matters pertaining to the Rules of Golf is not merely representing Great Britain and Ireland, but these many countries as well.

In 1919, when it took over the running of the Open and Amateur Championships, the Royal & Ancient became responsible for the Rules of Amateur Status and in matters pertaining thereto, likewise represents these many countries.

The Royal & Ancient also supplies one of each of the two Joint Chairmen and Joint Secretaries of the World Amateur Golf Council which is responsible for the organisation of all World Amateur Team Championships.

There is a close liaison at all times with the Professional Golfers' Association and the PGA European Tour.

National Functions

Prior to the First World War, a group of Clubs had been responsible for the running of the Open and Amateur Championships. In 1919 a meeting of these Clubs confirmed that the Royal & Ancient should be the Governing Authority for the game and agreed it should assume responsibility for the two Championships.

The decision that the Royal & Ancient should be the Governing Authority was endorsed at a Meeting of the English, Scottish, Irish and Welsh Unions in 1924, at which Meeting what is now the Council of National Golf Unions was formed with the object amongst others of directing the system of Standard Scratch Scores and Handicaps.

In 1948 the Royal & Ancient took over the Boys and in 1963 the Youths Championship from the private interests which had previously run them; this was done at the request of the individuals concerned. In 1969 the Royal & Ancient itself inaugurated the British Seniors Amateur Championship and in 1991 it agreed to become involved in the organisation and running of the Senior British Open Championship in conjunction with the PGA European Tour.

In addition to the organisation of five Championships, the Royal & Ancient is also responsible for the selection of Teams to represent Great Britain & Ireland in the Walker Cup, the Eisenhower Trophy, the St Andrews Trophy, and other International Tournaments. It is responsible for the organisation of such events when they are held in Great Britain and Ireland. In its World Amateur Golf Council role it takes it in turns with the USGA to organise the World Amateur Team Championships.

Club Functions

The Membership of the Club is limited to a total of 1,800, of which 1,050 may be resident in Great Britain and Ireland and 750 elsewhere: this Overseas Membership is spread over countries throughout the world.

The Membership both at home and abroad is representative and includes many who have given and are giving great services to golf in this country and abroad to many different Unions and Associations. This permits broad and effective representation on all the Club Committees concerned with international and national functions.

Exercise of International Functions

1. Rules of Golf

(a) Committee:

The Rules of Golf Committee exists for the purpose of reviewing the Rules of Golf from time to time and of making decisions on their interpretation and publishing these decisions where necessary.

The Committee consists of twelve Members elected by the Club, of whom three retire each year and are not eligible for re-election for one year, except in the case of the Chairman and Deputy Chairman, and of up to twelve additional persons invited annually to join the Committee from Golf Authorities at home and abroad.

At present the bodies represented are:

Council of National Golf Unions
United States Golf Association
European Golf Association
Australian Golf Union
New Zealand Golf Association
Royal Canadian Golf Association
South African Golf Union
Asia-Pacific Golf Confederation
South American Golf Federation
Japan Golf Association
Ladies' Golf Union

(b) Revision of the Rules of Golf:

As the only other Governing Authority for the Rules of Golf is the USGA, the R&A works closely with this body when amendments to the Rules are under consideration for the purpose of maintaining uniformity in the Rules and their interpretation. Every four years a Conference takes place with the USGA for the purpose of discussing the proposals for changes to be made. The Rules were amended in January 1992. Although the Conference takes place quadrennially, the Rules are under constant review and investigations as to possible improvements start not long after a revision has taken place, so that ample time can be given to consult with interested parties.

Two years after a revision has taken place an important meeting is held with the USGA in the United States at the time of the Walker Cup to discuss progress and to start clearing the ground for the next Conference.

(c) Decisions:
The Rules of Golf Committee has a Decisions Sub-Committee which answers queries from Clubs and from all the Unions and Associations affiliated to the R&A. Those Decisions which seem to establish important or interesting points of interpretation are published annually jointly by the R&A and the USGA and issued world-wide. The Decisions Book can be purchased directly from the R&A.

2. Implements and Ball

The Committee consists of four Members elected by the Club, one Member of the Rules of Golf Committee and one Member of the Championship Committee, together with Consultant Members invited by the Committee to advise on technical matters. One of the elected Members retires each year but the Chairman may be re-elected immediately for the sake of continuity.

The Committee works in close co-operation with the USGA I & B Committee in interpreting the Rules and Appendices relating to the control of the form and make of golf clubs and the specifications of the golf ball to ensure that the game and established golf courses are not harmed by technical developments.

3. Rules of Amateur Status

(a) Committee:
The Committee consists of five members, of which four are elected by the Club and one provided by the Council of National Golf Unions. There are also Advisory Members to the Committee, representing the same Golfing Authorities as on the Rules of Golf Committee.

(b) Revision of Rules of Amateur Status:
A procedure, similar to that for the Rules of Golf, is adopted for revision of the Rules of Amateur Status and no policy changes are made without full consultation with all the affiliated Unions, the USGA and the PGA.

(c) Decisions:
The work of the Committee consists of (a) dealing with Applications for reinstatement to Amateur Status, (b) answering inquiries about the nature of prizes, conditions for Tournaments, etc, arising out of the increased impact of commercial sponsors on Amateur golf and the issue of guidelines and Decisions, (c) answering queries from individuals regarding their own position under the Rules and (d) controlling Scholarships and other Grants-in-aid.

Exercise of National Functions

Championship Committee

The Championship Committee is responsible for the control of the five Championships and of the International Matches and Tournaments mentioned above.

The Committee consists of twelve elected Members elected by the Club, of whom three retire annually and are not eligible for re-election for one year. Two additional Members may also be invited to join the Committee annually together with the Chairmen of the two Sub-Committees, Rules and Business.

For the organisation of any particular event, others may be co-opted, if required.

The work of this Committee has greatly increased in recent years, as is clearly evident from the staging of the Open Championship, for which prize money in 1992 totalled £950,000. At the same time, more substantial reserve funds have been built up to ensure the continuance of the Open Championship as a premier world event.

The External Funds Committee make annual donations to a number of golfing bodies, especially those concerned with the training and development of junior golf and for research on greenkeeping matters. They also make grants and loans to assist with the development of new facilities both in the UK and abroad.

Selection Committee

The Selection Committee consists of a Chairman, who is a Member of the Club, and other Members, who need not to be Members of the Club, appointed by the General Committee. These other Members have for some years now been representative of each of the four Home Unions. Normally they hold their appointments for four years.

Exercise of Club Functions

The domestic affairs of the Club are run by Committees which it is not necessary to describe in this statement.

It is appropriate, however, to mention that the Club does not own a Golf Course. It is, nevertheless, much concerned with the maintenance and improvements of all four Golf Courses in St Andrews. These Courses are controlled by the St Andrews Links Trust and are run by the Links Management Committee. Three of the Trustees and four Members of the Management Committee are appointed by the Club and equal numbers are appointed by the North-East Fife District Council. One member of the Trust is appointed by the Secretary of State for Scotland and the current MP is also a Trustee. The Club contributes an annually negotiated sum to the Trust in return for Members' playing privileges.

Finance

International Functions

After taking into account income derived from subscriptions to the Rules of Golf Decisions Service and the sale of official Rules publications, the net expenses of the Rules of Golf, Rules of Amateur Status and Rules for Implements and Ball are borne by External Activities.

National Functions

Income and expenditure of all Championships run by the R&A and the expenses of Teams representing Great Britain & Ireland are accounted for in separate divisions of one Account.

Surpluses of all income over expenditure in the External Activities Account are held in reserve to ensure the continuance of the running of the various events at a high standard.

The Royal & Ancient Golf Club as a private Members' Club does not in any way benefit from the External Activities Account.

General Committee

Responsibility for directing and co-ordinating the three functions of the R&A – as a private club, as a governing authority for golf and as the body responsible for organising and running the championships and international matches – rests with the Club's General Committee, which controls all matters of policy. The Committee consists of fifteen R&A Members, eight of whom are elected by the Club; the other seven *ex-officio* members are the Captain and Chairmen of the Finance, Membership, Club, Rules of Golf, Championship and Amateur Status Committees.

The execution of the decisions of the Club Committees and of the decisions taken by the Members at Business Meetings is in the hands of the Secretary of the R&A, who is assisted by several senior officers and the appropriate infrastructure of secretaries and clerical staff.

Contacts with Affiliated Golfing Authorities

The R&A endeavours to consult with all those Golfing Authorities concerned whenever an issue of importance arises. This covers, in particular, matters relating to Rules of Golf, Rules of Amateur Status, and the Championships.

Meetings are held when appropriate with representatives of Golfing Authorities in Great Britain & Ireland and the European Golf Association. Consultations with other Golfing Authorities abroad are regularly conducted by correspondence.

In January 1970, a Conference attended by Golfing Unions and Associations in this country and representatives of the European Golf Association was held under the auspices of the R&A to discuss all matters of mutual interest, and in particular to establish the best means of communication in the future between the Unions and Associations concerned. This was followed by a similar Conference at Chantilly, Paris in 1976.

In May 1980 the first ever International Golf Conference was held in St Andrews at which 33 countries affiliated to the R&A were represented and to which the USGA, PGA and other golfing bodies in this country sent observers. Owing to the great success of this Conference the R&A held further ones in 1985 and 1989 at which 38 countries were represented.

The R&A is represented at Meetings of the World Amateur Golf Council, the Council of National Golf Unions and on the CCPR.

October 1991 (revised)

MF Bonallack OBE
Secretary
Royal & Ancient Golf Club
of St Andrews
Fife KY16 9JD

The Championship Committee

Until 1919 the Open and Amateur Championships of Great Britain were organised by a group of leading Clubs in Scotland and England. The Club where the Championship was to be played was charged with running it for that year. In 1919, the Royal & Ancient, by then the recognised governing authority of the game, was invited to take over the responsibility for both Championships and ever since its Championship Committee has controlled both. Once the course on which a Championship is to be played has been decided, usually several years ahead, the Committee works closely with the Club concerned.

The Amateur, which is nearly as old as The Open, may have lost some of its public appeal with the growth of Professional golf and the defection of so many able young amateurs to its lucrative tour. However, the Amateur Championship is still considered the most prestigious event in the amateur game and is always played on one of the best courses.

The Championship Committee today controls several more events besides the two oldest Championships. The Boys, started privately in 1921, and the Youths, in 1954, both now come under its wing, as does the Seniors which was inaugurated by the R&A in 1969. In addition, the biennial amateur matches against the United States and the Continent of Europe for the Walker Cup and the St Andrews Trophy respectively, are run by the Committee when played in Great Britain, as also are Boys' and Youths' Internationals against the Continent of Europe. The R&A Selection Committee chooses the team for all these amateur matches, as well as the team which competes for the Eisenhower Trophy, the World Amateur Team Championship. This was first played at St Andrews in 1958 and has since been held every two years in different parts of the world.

The remarkable development of The Open to the great occasion it is today has meant heavily increased responsibilities for the Championship Committee. TV and the media have given it an audience in millions compared with the few thousand interested in the past. The R&A's determination to match the growing interest with a new attitude and astute promotion has given the event the stature and following it now enjoys. The last 22 years has seen the winner's cheque grow from £1200 to £100,000, the total prize money from £15,000 to £1,100,000 in 1994. The financial success of The Open has provided considerable sums of money for the development of junior golf, and other worthy causes connected to golf.

The R&A works closely with the Club of the course where the Championship is to be played, whose members take on many of the essential duties necessary if it is to run smoothly. These include spectator control where local Clubs take charge of a hole each, usually providing three-hour shifts of up to 16 members at a time. This can involve as many as 800 men daily. Local volunteer stewards also cover such diverse duties as course controllers, supervision of litter collection and spectator stand control. Security, courtesy transport, car park supervision and public catering, to name a few of the mass of services necessary, are provided under contract by companies expert in these fields. Close liaison with the area police authority is vital. Facilities for the Press, Television and the vast tented village, each involving several hundred people, occupy large areas and are a major limiting factor when considering possible venues for future championships.

Important for both competitors and spectators and appreciated by both is the radio network which provides up-to-the-minute scores and positions of the leading players which appear very quickly on the leader boards erected at strategic points round the course. The system developed over many years is as quick, informative and accurate as any in existence.

The Committee consists of twelve Royal & Ancient members, who devote much time to their tasks. It has a full-time secretary who, together with the Secretary of the Club and some of his staff, is involved in the planning of The Open and other events throughout the year. Members of the Committee work long hours during Open week. From first light at about 5am, when the Head Greenkeeper and a nominated member of the Committee tour the course deciding the pin positions on each green for the day, to dusk when the last competitor comes in, all are occupied, mostly out on the course at selected points, in two-way radio contact with the centre, ready to give a ruling when required. In the final rounds the leading players are accompanied by a member of the committee for the whole round.

The many stands erected around the course, providing seats for sometimes 18,000 spectators, often quite close to greens, make for special problems. A loose shot which ends under a stand will probably mean the ball may be dropped without penalty in an area nearby, which has been predesignated by the committee; this shot should be of equal difficulty as it would have been if the stand had not been there. In these cases often an official decision is required.

At the end of every round each competitor's card must be immediately checked and recorded following which, in the case of a leader, he will meet the press in the interview room.

It is the Championship Committee too which decides if any round has to be halted, postponed or cancelled due to storm and tempest. Such decisions, so difficult with so many factors, consequent on a postponement, to be considered, have been eased a little with improved weather forecasting and continuous contact with the local weather bureau.

It will be seen that the work of the Committee is never ending with the myriad tasks necessary to ensure the even flow to a Championship. The success of The Open is due to sound planning, moving with the times and the expertise of the R&A staff which is the executive arm of the Committee. The Open may be the Championship with which all are familiar; however, it must be remembered that the many other events under the R&A's control also require planning and organisation. The work for these events goes on largely unnoticed, but must not be forgotten.

Rules of Golf

As Approved by
The Royal & Ancient Golf Club
of St Andrews, Scotland
and the
United States Golf Association

27th EDITION
EFFECTIVE 1st JANUARY 1992

Contents

Relief Situations and Procedure

Other Forms of Play

Administration

Foreword

to the 1992 Edition of the Rules of Golf

The Royal & Ancient Golf Club of St Andrews and the United States Golf Association have carried out their customary quadrennial review of the Rules of Golf and have agreed upon certain amendments which will become effective on 1st January 1992.

The changes in the Rules are intended to provide clarification and are part of the continuing policy of simplification. The principal changes are summarised on page 715.

The Royal & Ancient and United States Golf Association continue to enjoy the valuable assistance of golfing bodies throughout the world and will maintain their close liaison in all matters concerning the Rules and their interpretation.

We would like to take this opportunity to express our sincere thanks to our respective Committees and all those who have in so many ways helped us in our endeavours.

We dedicate this edition of the Rules to the late PJ Boatwright Jr.

John S Scrivener
Chairman
Rules of Golf Committee
Royal & Ancient Golf Club
of St Andrews

MJ Mastalir, Jr
Chairman
Rules of Golf Committee
United States Golf Association

Principal Changes introduced in the 1992 Code

DEFINITIONS

The terms "line of putt" and "line of play" are defined.

RULES

Rule 4.1e. Club Face
The restriction with regard to insets or attachments on metal clubs is eliminated.

Rule 4-4a. Selection and Replacement of Clubs
The addition or replacement of a club or clubs may not be made by borrowing any club selected for play by any other person playing on the course.

Rule 5-3. Ball Unfit for Play
Rule 12-2. Identifying Ball
If the player fails to carry out a part or parts of the procedure he is penalised only one stroke.

Rule 13-4. Ball Lying in or Touching Hazard
Expanded to state that if a ball lies in a hazard there is no penalty (provided nothing is done which constitutes testing the condition of the hazard or improves the lie of the ball) if the player touches the ground or water in a water hazard as a result of or to prevent falling, in removing an obstruction, in measuring or in retrieving or lifting a ball under any Rule.

Rule 24-2c. Ball Lost
There is an addition to the Rule to make provision for a ball lost in an immovable obstruction.

APPENDIX II

Rule 4.1a. General
Limited adjustability is permitted in the design of putters.

Rule 4.1c. Grip
If a putter has two grips, both of the grips must be circular in cross-section. However, putters which do not conform with this Rule may continue to be used until 31st December 1992.

The Rules of Golf

Section I Etiquette

Courtesy on the Course

Safety

Prior to playing a stroke or making a practice swing, the player should ensure that no one is standing close by or in a position to be hit by the club, the ball or any stones, pebbles, twigs or the like which may be moved by the stroke or swing.

Consideration for Other Players

The player who has the honour should be allowed to play before his opponent or fellow-competitor tees his ball.

No one should move, talk or stand close to or directly behind the ball or the hole when a player is addressing the ball or making a stroke.

In the interest of all, players should play without delay.

No player should play until the players in front are out of range.

Players searching for a ball should signal the players behind them to pass as soon as it becomes apparent that the ball will not easily be found. They should not search for five minutes before doing so. They should not continue play until the players following them have passed and are out of range.

When the play of a hole has been completed, players should immediately leave the putting green.

Priority on the Course

In the absence of special rules, two-ball matches should have precedence over and be entitled to pass any three- or four-ball match, which should invite them through.

A single player has no standing and should give way to a match of any kind.

Any match playing a whole round is entitled to pass a match playing a shorter round.

If a match fails to keep its place on the course and loses more than one clear hole on the players in front, it should invite the match following to pass.

Care of the Course

Holes in Bunkers

Before leaving a bunker, a player should carefully fill up and smooth over all holes and footprints made by him.

Replace Divots; Repair Ball-Marks and Damage by Spikes

Through the green, a player should ensure that any turf cut or displaced by him is replaced at once and pressed down and that any damage to the putting green made by a ball is carefully repaired. Damage to the putting green caused by golf shoe spikes should be repaired *on completion of the hole.*

Damage to Greens – Flagsticks, Bags, etc.

Players should ensure that, when putting down bags or the flagstick, no damage is done to the putting green and that neither they nor their caddies damage the hole by standing close to it, in handling the flagstick or in removing the ball from the hole. The flagstick should be properly replaced in the hole before the players leave the putting green. Players should not damage the putting green by leaning on their putters, particularly when removing the ball from the hole.

Golf Carts

Local notices regulating the movement of golf carts should be strictly observed.

Damage Through Practice Swings

In taking practice swings, players should avoid causing damage to the course, particularly the tees, by removing divots.

Section II Definitions

The Definitions are placed in alphabetical order and some are also repeated at the beginning of their relevant Rule. In the Rules themselves, defined terms which may be important to the application of a Rule are underlined the first time they appear.

Addressing the Ball

A player has "addressed the ball" when he has taken his stance and has also grounded his club, except that in a hazard a player has addressed the ball when he has taken his stance.

Advice

"Advice" is any counsel or suggestion which could influence a player in determining his play, the choice of a club or the method of making a stroke.

Information on the Rules or on matters of public information, such as the position of hazards or the flagstick on the putting green, is not advice.

Ball Deemed to Move
See "Move or Moved".

Ball Holed
See "Holed".

Ball Lost
See "Lost Ball".

Ball in Play
A ball is "in play" as soon as the player has made a stroke on the teeing ground. It remains in play until holed out, except when it is lost, out of bounds or lifted, or another ball has been substituted under an applicable Rule, whether or not such Rule permits substitution; a ball so substituted becomes the ball in play.

Bunker
A "bunker" is a hazard consisting of a prepared area of ground, often a hollow, from which turf or soil has been removed and replaced with sand or the like. Grass-covered ground bordering or within a bunker is not part of the bunker. The margin of a bunker extends vertically downwards, but not upwards.

Caddie
A "caddie" is one who carries or handles a player's clubs during play and otherwise assists him in accordance with the Rules.

When one caddie is employed by more than one player, he is always deemed to be the caddie of the player whose ball is involved, and equipment carried by him is deemed to be that player's equipment, except when the caddie acts upon specific directions of another player, in which case he is considered to be that other player's caddie.

Casual Water
"Casual water" is any temporary accumulation of water on the course which is visible before or after the player takes his stance and is not in a water hazard. Snow and natural ice, other than frost, are either casual water or loose impediments, at the option of the player. Manufactured ice is an obstruction. Dew and frost are not casual water.

Committee
The "Committee" is the committee in charge of the competition or, if the matter does not arise in a competition, the committee in charge of the course.

Competitor
A "competitor" is a player in a stroke competition. A "fellow-competitor" is any person with whom the competitor plays. Neither is partner of the other.

In stroke play foursome and four-ball competitions, where the context so admits, the word "competitor" or "fellow-competitor" includes his partner.

Course
The "course" is the whole area within which play is permitted (see Rule 33-2).

Equipment
"Equipment" is anything used, worn or carried by or for the player except any ball he has played at the hole being played and any small object, such as a coin or a tee, when used to mark the position of a ball or the extent of an area in which a ball is to be dropped. Equipment includes a golf cart, whether or not motorised. If such a cart is shared by two or more players, the cart and everything in it are deemed to be the equipment of the player whose ball is involved except that, when the cart is being moved by one of the players sharing it, the cart and everything in it are deemed to be that player's equipment.

Note: A ball played at the hole being played is equipment when it has been lifted and not put back into play.

Fellow Competitor
See "Competitor".

Flagstick
The "flagstick" is a movable straight indicator, with or without bunting or other material attached, centred in the hole to show its position. It shall be circular in cross-section.

Forecaddie
A "forecaddie" is one who is employed by the Committee to indicate to players the position of balls during play. He is an outside agency.

Ground Under Repair
"Ground under repair" is any portion of the course so marked by order of the Committee or so declared by its authorised representative. It includes material piled for removal and a hole made by a greenkeeper, even if not so marked. Stakes and lines defining ground under repair are in such ground. The margin of ground under repair extends vertically downwards, but not upwards.

Note 1: Grass cuttings and other material left on the course which have been abandoned and are not intended to be removed are not ground under repair unless so marked.

Note 2: The Committee may make a Local Rule prohibiting play from ground under repair.

Hazards
A "hazard" is any bunker or water hazard.

Hole
The "hole" shall be 4¼ inches (108mm) in

diameter and at least 4 inches (100mm) deep. If a lining is used, it shall be sunk at least 1 inch (25mm) below the putting green surface unless the nature of the soil makes it impracticable to do so; its outer diameter shall not exceed 4¼ inches (108mm).

Holed

A ball is "holed" when it is at rest within the circumference of the hole and all of it is below the level of the lip of the hole.

Honour

The side entitled to play first from the teeing ground is said to have the "honour".

Lateral Water Hazard

A "lateral water hazard" is a water hazard or that part of a water hazard so situated that it is not possible or is deemed by the Committee to be impracticable to drop a ball behind the water hazard in accordance with Rule 26-1b.

That part of a water hazard to be played as a lateral water hazard should be distinctively marked.

Note: Lateral water hazards should be defined by red stakes or lines.

Line of Play

The "line of play" is the direction which the player wishes his ball to take after a stroke, plus a reasonable distance on either side of the intended direction. The line of play extends vertically upwards from the ground, but does not extend beyond the hole.

Line of Putt

The "line of putt" is the line which the player wishes his ball to take after a stroke on the putting green. Except with respect to Rule 16-1e, the line of putt includes a reasonable distance on either side of the intended line. The line of putt does not extend beyond the hole.

Loose Impediments

"Loose impediments" are natural objects such as stones, leaves, twigs, branches and the like, dung, worms and insects and casts or heaps made by them, provided they are not fixed or growing, are not solidly embedded and do not adhere to the ball.

Sand and loose soil are loose impediments on the putting green, but not elsewhere.

Snow and natural ice, other than frost, are either casual water or loose impediments, at the option of the player. Manufactured ice is an obstruction.

Dew and frost are not loose impediments.

Lost Ball

A ball is "lost" if:

a. It is not found or identified as his by the player within five minutes after the player's side or his or their caddies have begun to search for it; or

b. The player has put another ball into play under the Rules, even though he may not have searched for the original ball; or

c. The player has played any stroke with a provisional ball from the place where the original ball is likely to be or from a point nearer the hole than that place, whereupon the provisional ball becomes the ball in play.

Time spent in playing a wrong ball is not counted in the five-minute period allowed for search.

Marker

A "marker" is one who is appointed by the Committee to record a competitor's score in stroke play. He may be a fellow-competitor. He is not a referee.

Matches

See "Sides and Matches".

Move or Moved

A ball is deemed to have "moved" if it leaves its position and comes to rest in any other place.

Observer

An "observer" is one who is appointed by the Committee to assist a referee to decide questions of fact and to report to him any breach of a Rule. An observer should not attend the flagstick, stand at or mark the position of the hole, or lift the ball or mark its position.

Obstructions

An "obstruction" is anything artificial, including the artificial surfaces and sides of roads and paths and manufactured ice, except:

a. Objects defining out of bounds, such as walls, fences, stakes and railings;

b. Any part of an immovable artificial object which is out of bounds; and

c. Any construction declared by the Committee to be an integral part of the course.

Out of Bounds

"Out of bounds" is ground on which play is prohibited.

When out of bounds is defined by reference to stakes or a fence or as being beyond stakes or a fence, the out of bounds line is determined by the nearest inside points of the stakes or fence posts at ground level excluding angled supports.

When out of bounds is defined by a line on the ground, the line itself is out of bounds.

The out of bounds line extends vertically upwards and downwards.

A ball is out of bounds when all of it lies out of bounds.

A player may stand out of bounds to play a ball lying within bounds.

Outside Agency

An "outside agency" is any agency not part of the match or, in stroke play, not part of the competitor's side, and includes a referee, a marker, an observer or a forecaddie. Neither wind nor water is an outside agency.

Partner

A "partner" is a player associated with another player on the same side.

In a threesome, foursome, best-ball or four-ball match, where the context so admits, the word "player" includes his partner or partners.

Penalty Stroke

A "penalty stroke" is one added to the score of a player or side under certain Rules. In a threesome or foursome, penalty strokes do not affect the order of play.

Provisional Ball

A "provisional ball" is a ball played under Rule 27-2 for a ball which may be lost outside a water hazard or may be out of bounds.

Putting Green

The "putting green" is all ground of the hole being played which is specially prepared for putting or otherwise defined as such by the Committee. A ball is on the putting green when any part of it touches the putting green.

Referee

A "referee" is one who is appointed by the Committee to accompany players to decide questions of fact and apply the Rules of Golf. He shall act on any breach of a Rule which he observes or is reported to him.

A referee should not attend the flagstick, stand at or mark the position of the hole, or lift the ball or mark its position.

Rub of the Green

A "rub of the green" occurs when a ball in motion is accidentally deflected or stopped by any outside agency (see Rule 19-1).

Rule

The term "Rule" includes Local Rules made by the Committee under Rule 33-8a.

Sides and Matches

Side: A player, or two or more players who are partners.

Single: A match in which one plays against another.

Threesome: A match in which one plays against two, and each side plays one ball.

Foursome: A match in which two play against two, and each side plays one ball.

Three-ball: A match play competition in which three play against one another, each playing his own ball. Each player is playing two distinct matches.

Best ball: A match in which one plays against the better ball of two or the best ball of three players.

Four-ball: A match in which two play their better ball against the better ball of two other players.

Stance

Taking the "stance" consists in a player placing his feet in position for and preparatory to making a stroke.

Stipulated Round

The "stipulated round" consists of playing the holes of the course in their correct sequence unless otherwise authorised by the Committee. The number of holes in a stipulated round is 18 unless a smaller number is authorised by the Committee. As to extension of stipulated round in match play, see Rule 2-3.

Stroke

A "stroke" is the forward movement of the club made with the intention of fairly striking at and moving the ball, but if a player checks his downswing voluntarily before the clubhead reaches the ball he is deemed not to have made a stroke.

Teeing Ground

The "teeing ground" is the starting place for the hole to be played. It is a rectangular area two club-lengths in depth, the front and the sides of which are defined by the outside limits of two tee-markers. A ball is outside the teeing ground when all of it lies outside the teeing ground.

Through the Green

"Through the green" is the whole area of the course except

a. The teeing ground and putting green of the hole being played; and

b. All hazards on the course.

Water Hazard

A "water hazard" is any sea, lake, pond, river, ditch, surface drainage ditch or other open water course (whether or not containing water) and anything of a similar nature.

All ground or water within the margin of a water hazard is part of the water hazard. The margin of a water hazard extends vertically upwards and downwards. Stakes and lines defining the margins of water hazards are in the hazards.

Note: Water hazards (other than lateral water hazards) should be defined by yellow stakes or lines.

Wrong Ball

A "wrong ball" is any ball other than:

a. The ball in play,
b. A provisional ball or
c. In stroke play, a second ball played under Rule 3-3 or Rule 20-7b.

Note: Ball in play includes a ball substituted for the ball in play when the player is proceeding under an applicable Rule which does not permit substitution.

Section III
The Rules of Play

THE GAME

Rule 1. The Game

1-1. General

The Game of Golf consists in playing a ball from the teeing ground into the hole by a stroke or successive strokes in accordance with the Rules.

1-2. Exerting Influence on Ball

No player or caddie shall take any action to influence the position or the movement of a ball except in accordance with the Rules.

PENALTY FOR BREACH OF RULE 1-2:
Match play – Loss of hole; Stroke play – Two strokes.

Note: In the case of a serious breach of Rule 1-2, the Committee may impose a penalty of disqualification.

1-3. Agreement to Waive Rules

Players shall not agree to exclude the operation of any Rule or to waive any penalty incurred.

PENALTY FOR BREACH OF RULE 1-3:
Match play – Disqualification of both sides;
Stroke play – Disqualification of competitors concerned.

(Agreeing to play out of turn in stroke play – see Rule 10-2c.)

1-4. Points Not Covered by Rules

If any point in dispute is not covered by the Rules, the decision shall be made in accordance with equity.

Rule 2. Match Play

2-1. Winner of Hole; Reckoning of Holes

In match play the game is played by holes.

Except as otherwise provided in the Rules, a hole is won by the side which holes its ball in the fewer strokes. In a handicap match the lower net score wins the hole.

The reckoning of holes is kept by the terms: so many "holes up" or "all square", and so many "to play".

A side is "dormie" when it is as many holes up as there are holes remaining to be played.

2-2. Halved Hole

A hole is halved if each side holes out in the same number of strokes.

When a player has holed out and his opponent has been left with a stroke for the half, if the player thereafter incurs a penalty, the hole is halved.

2-3. Winner of Match

A match (which consists of a stipulated round, unless otherwise decreed by the Committee) is won by the side which is leading by a number of holes greater than the number of holes remaining to be played.

The Committee may, for the purpose of settling a tie, extend the stipulated round to as many holes as are required for a match to be won.

2-4. Concession of Next Stroke, Hole or Match

When the opponent's ball is at rest or is deemed to be at rest under Rule 16-2, the player may concede the opponent to have holed out with his next stroke and the ball may be removed by either side with a club or otherwise.

A player may concede a hole or a match at any time prior to the conclusion of the hole or the match.

Concession of a stroke, hole or match may not be declined or withdrawn.

2-5. Claims

In match play, if a doubt or dispute arises between the players and no duly authorised representative of the Committee is available within a reasonable time, the players shall continue the match without delay. Any claim, if it is to be considered by the Committee, must be made before any player in the match plays from the next teeing ground or, in the case of the last hole of the match, before all players in the match leave the putting green.

No later claim shall be considered unless it is based on facts previously unknown to the player making the claim and the player making the claim had been given wrong information (Rules 6-2a and 9) by an opponent. In any case, no later claim shall be considered after the result of the match has been officially announced, unless the Committee is satisfied that the opponent knew he was giving wrong information.

2-6. General Penalty

The penalty for a breach of a Rule in match play is loss of hole except when otherwise provided.

Rule 3. Stroke Play

3-1. Winner

The competitor who plays the stipulated round or rounds in the fewest strokes is the winner.

3-2. Failure to Hole Out

If a competitor fails to hole out at any hole and does not correct his mistake before he plays a stroke from the next teeing ground or, in the case of the last hole of the round, before he leaves the putting green, *he shall be disqualified.*

3-3. Doubt as to Procedure

a. Procedure

In stroke play only, when during play of a hole a competitor is doubtful of his rights or procedure, he may, without penalty, play a second ball. After the situation which has caused the doubt has arisen, the competitor should, before taking further action, announce to his marker or a fellow-competitor his decision to invoke this Rule and the ball with which he will score if the Rules permit.

The competitor shall report the facts to the Committee before returning his score card unless he scores the same with both balls; if he fails to do so, *he shall be disqualified.*

b. Determination of Score for Hole

If the Rules allow the procedure selected in advance by the competitor, the score with the ball selected shall be his score for the hole.

If the competitor fails to announce in advance his decision to invoke this Rule or his selection, the score with the original ball or, if the original ball is not one of the balls being played, the first ball put into play shall count if the Rules allow the procedure adopted for such ball.

Note: A second ball played under Rule 3-3 is not a provisional ball under Rule 27-2.

3-4. Refusal to Comply with a Rule

If a competitor refuses to comply with a Rule affecting the rights of another competitor, *he shall be disqualified.*

3-5. General Penalty

The penalty for a breach of a Rule in stroke play is two strokes except when otherwise provided.

CLUBS AND THE BALL

The Royal & Ancient Golf Club of St Andrews and the United States Golf Association reserve the right to change the Rules and make and change the interpretations relating to clubs, balls and other implements at any time.

Rule 4. Clubs

If there may be any reasonable basis for doubt as to whether a club which is to be manufactured conforms with Rule 4 and Appendix II, the manufacturer should submit a sample to the Royal & Ancient Golf Club of St Andrews for a ruling, such sample to become its property for reference purposes. If a manufacturer fails to do so, he assumes the risk of a ruling that the club does not conform with the Rules of Golf.

A player in doubt as to the conformity of a club should consult the Royal & Ancient Golf Club of St Andrews.

4-1. Form and Make of Clubs

A club is an implement designed to be used for striking the ball.

A putter is a club designed primarily for use on the putting green.

The player's clubs shall conform with the provisions of this Rule and with the specifications and interpretations set forth in Appendix II.

a. General

The club shall be composed of a shaft and a head. All parts of the club shall be fixed so that the club is one unit. The club shall not be designed to be adjustable except for weight (see also Appendix II). The club shall not be substantially different from the traditional and customary form and make.

b. Shaft

The shaft shall be generally straight, with the same bending and twisting properties in any direction, and shall be attached to the clubhead at the heel either directly or through a single plain neck or socket. A putter shaft may be attached to any point in the head.

c. Grip

The grip consists of that part of the shaft designed to be held by the player and any material added to it for the purpose of obtaining a firm hold. The grip shall be substantially straight and plain in form and shall not be moulded for any part of the hands.

d. Clubhead

The distance from the heel to the toe of the clubhead shall be greater than the distance from the face to the back. The clubhead shall be generally plain in shape.

The clubhead shall have only one face designed for striking the ball, except that a putter may have two such faces if their characteristics are the same, they are opposite each other and the loft of each is the same and does not exceed ten degrees.

e. Club Face

The face shall not have any degree of concavity and, in relation to the ball, shall be hard and rigid. It shall be generally smooth except for such markings as are permitted by Appendix II.

f. Wear

A club which conforms with Rule 4-1 when new is deemed to conform after wear through normal use. Any part of a club which has been purposely altered is regarded as new and must conform, in the altered state, with the Rules.

g. Damage

If a player's club ceases to conform with Rule 4-1 because of damage sustained in the normal course of play, the player may:

(i) use the club in its damaged state, but only for the remainder of the stipulated round during which such damage was sustained; or

(ii) without unduly delaying play, repair it.

A club which ceases to conform because of damage sustained other than in the normal course of play shall not subsequently be used during the round.

(Damage changing playing characteristics of club – see Rule 4-2.)

(Damage rendering club unfit for play – see Rule 4-4a.)

4-2. Playing Characteristics Changed

During a stipulated round, the playing characteristics of a club shall not be purposely changed by adjustment or by any other means.

If the playing characteristics of a player's club are changed during a round because of damage sustained in the normal course of play, the player may:

(i) use the club in its altered state; or

(ii) without unduly delaying play, repair it.

If the playing characteristics of a player's club are changed because of damage sustained other than in the normal course of play, the club shall not subsequently be used during the round.

Damage to a club which occurred prior to a round may be repaired during the round, provided the playing characteristics are not changed and play is not unduly delayed.

4-3. Foreign Material

No foreign material shall be applied to the club face for the purpose of influencing the movement of the ball.

PENALTY FOR BREACH OF RULE 4-1, -2 or -3: *Disqualification.*

4-4. Maximum of Fourteen Clubs

a. Selection and Replacement of Clubs

The player shall start a stipulated round with not more than fourteen clubs. He is limited to the clubs thus selected for that round except that, without unduly delaying play, he may:

(i) if he started with fewer than fourteen, add as many as will bring his total to that number; and

(ii) replace, with any club, a club which becomes unfit for play in the normal course of play.

The addition or replacement of a club or clubs may not be made by borrowing any club selected for play by any other person playing on the course.

b. Partners May Share Clubs

Partners may share clubs, provided that the total number of clubs carried by the partners so sharing does not exceed fourteen.

PENALTY FOR BREACH OF RULE 4-4a or b, REGARDLESS OF NUMBER OF EXCESS CLUBS CARRIED:

Match play – At the conclusion of the hole at which the breach is discovered, the state of the match shall be adjusted by deducting one hole for each hole at which a breach occurred. Maximum deduction per round: two holes.

Stroke play – Two strokes for each hole at which any breach occurred; maximum penalty per round: four strokes.

Bogey and par competitions – Penalties as in match play.

Stableford competitions – see Note to Rule 32-1b.

c. Excess Club Declared Out of Play

Any club carried or used in breach of this Rule shall be declared out of play by the player immediately upon discovery that a breach has occurred and thereafter shall not be used by the player during the round.

PENALTY FOR BREACH OF RULE 4-4c: *Disqualification.*

Rule 5. The Ball

5-1. General

The ball the player uses shall conform to specifications set forth in Appendix III on maximum weight, minimum size, spherical symmetry, initial velocity and overall distance when tested under specified conditions.

Note: In laying down the conditions under which a competition is to be played (Rule 33-1), the Committee may stipulate that the ball to be used shall be of certain specifications, provided these specifications are within the limits prescribed by Appendix III, and that it be of a brand and marking as detailed on the current List of Conforming Golf Balls issued by the Royal & Ancient Golf Club of St Andrews.

5-2. Foreign Material

No foreign material shall be applied to a ball for the purpose of changing its playing characteristics.

PENALTY FOR BREACH OF RULES 5-1 or 5-2: *Disqualification.*

5-3. Ball Unfit for Play

A ball is unfit for play if it is visibly cut, cracked or out of shape. A ball is not unfit for play solely because mud or other materials adhere to it, its surface is scratched or scraped or its paint is damaged or discoloured.

If a player has reason to believe his ball has become unfit for play during the play of the hole being played, he may during the play of such hole lift his ball without penalty to determine whether it is unfit.

Before lifting the ball, the player must announce his intention to his opponent in match play or his marker or a fellow-competitor in stroke play and mark the position of the ball. He may then lift and examine the ball without cleaning it and must give his opponent, marker or fellow-competitor an opportunity to examine the ball.

If he fails to comply with this procedure *he shall incur a penalty of one stroke.*

If it is determined that the ball has become unfit for play during play of the hole being played, the player may substitute another ball, placing it on the spot where the original ball lay. Otherwise, the original ball shall be replaced.

If a ball breaks into pieces as a result of a stroke, the stroke shall be cancelled and the player shall play a ball without a penalty as nearly as possible at the spot from which the original ball was played (see Rule 20-5).

*PENALTY FOR BREACH OF RULE 5-3:
Match play – Loss of hole; Stroke play – Two strokes.
**If a player incurs the general penalty for breach of Rule 5-3, no additional penalty under the Rule shall be applied.*

Note: If the opponent, marker or fellow-competitor wishes to dispute a claim of unfitness, he must do so before the player plays another ball.

(Cleaning ball lifted from putting green or under any other Rule – see Rule 21.)

PLAYER'S RESPONSIBILITIES

Rule 6. The Player

Definition

A "marker" is one who is appointed by the Committee to record a competitor's score in stroke play. He may be a fellow-competitor. He is not a referee.

6-1. Conditions of Competition

The player is responsible for knowing the conditions under which the competition is to be played (Rule 33-1).

6-2. Handicap

a. Match Play

Before starting a match in a handicap competition, the players should determine from one another their respective handicaps. If a player begins the match having declared a higher handicap which would affect the number of strokes given or received, *he shall be disqualified;* otherwise, the player shall play off the declared handicap.

b. Stroke Play

In any round of a handicap competition, the competitor shall ensure that his handicap is recorded on his score card before it is returned to the Committee. If no handicap is recorded on his score card before it is returned, or if the recorded handicap is higher than that to which he is entitled and this affects the number of strokes received, *he shall be disqualified* from that round of the handicap competition; otherwise, the score shall stand.

Note: It is the player's responsibility to know the holes at which handicap strokes are to be given or received.

6-3. Time of Starting and Groups

a. Time of Starting

The player shall start at the time laid down by the Committee.

b. Groups

In stroke play, the competitor shall remain throughout the round in the group arranged by the Committee unless the Committee authorises or ratifies a change.

PENALTY FOR BREACH OF RULE 6-3:
Disqualification.
(Best-ball and four-ball play – see Rules 30-3a and 31-2.)

Note: The Committee may provide in the conditions of a competition (Rule 33-1) that, if the player arrives at his starting point, ready to play, within five minutes after his starting time, in the absence of circumstances which warrant waiving the penalty of disqualification as provided in Rule 33-7, the penalty for failure to start on time is loss of the first hole in match play or two strokes at the first hole in stroke play instead of disqualification.

6-4. Caddie

The player may have only one caddie at any one time, *under penalty of disqualification.*

For any breach of a Rule by his caddie, the player incurs the applicable penalty.

6-5. Ball

The responsibility for playing the proper ball rests with the player. Each player should put an identification mark on his ball.

6-6. Scoring in Stroke Play

a. Recording Scores

After each hole the marker should check the

score with the competitor and record it. On completion of the round the marker shall sign the card and hand it to the competitor. If more than one marker records the scores, each shall sign for the part for which he is responsible.

b. Signing and Returning Card

After completion of the round, the competitor should check his score for each hole and settle any doubtful points with the Committee. He shall ensure that the marker has signed the card, countersign the card himself and return it to the Committee as soon as possible.

PENALTY FOR BREACH OF RULE 6-6b:
Disqualification.

c. Alteration of Card

No alteration may be made on a card after the competitor has returned it to the Committee.

d. Wrong Score for Hole

The competitor is responsible for the correctness of the score recorded for each hole. If he returns a score for any hole lower than actually taken, *he shall be disqualified.* If he returns a score for any hole higher than actually taken, the score as returned shall stand.

Note 1: The Committee is responsible for the addition of scores and application of the handicap recorded on the card – see Rule 33-5.

Note 2: In four-ball stroke play, see also Rule 31-4 and -7a.

6-7. Undue Delay

The player shall play without undue delay. Between completion of a hole and playing from the next teeing ground, the player shall not unduly delay play.

PENALTY FOR BREACH OF RULE 6-7:
Match play – Loss of hole; Stroke play – Two strokes.
For repeated offence – Disqualification.
If the player unduly delays play between holes, he is delaying the play of the next hole and the penalty applies to that hole.

6-8. Discontinuance of Play

a. When Permitted

The player shall not discontinue play unless:
(i) the Committee has suspended play;
(ii) he believes there is danger from lightning;
(iii) he is seeking a decision from the Committee on a doubtful or disputed point (see Rules 2-5 and 34-3); or
(iv) there is some other good reason such as sudden illness.

Bad weather is not of itself a good reason for discontinuing play.

If the player discontinues play without specific permission from the Committee, he shall report to the Committee as soon as practicable. If he does so and the Committee considers his reason satisfactory, the player incurs no penalty. Otherwise, *the player shall be disqualified.*

Exception in match play: Players discontinuing match play by agreement are not subject to disqualification unless by so doing the competition is delayed.

Note: Leaving the course does not of itself constitute discontinuance of play.

b. Procedure When Play Suspended by Committee

When play is suspended by the Committee, if the players in a match or group are between the play of two holes, they shall not resume play until the Committee has ordered a resumption of play. If they are in the process of playing a hole, they may continue provided they do so without delay. If they choose to continue, they shall discontinue either before or immediately after completing the hole, and shall not thereafter resume play until the Committee has ordered a resumption of play.

When play has been suspended by the Committee, the player shall resume play when the Committee has ordered a resumption of play.

PENALTY FOR BREACH OF RULE 6-8b:
Disqualification.

c. Lifting Ball When Play Discontinued

When during the play of a hole a player discontinues play under Rule 6-8a, he may lift his ball. A ball may be cleaned when so lifted. If a ball has been so lifted, the player shall, when play is resumed, place a ball on the spot from which the original ball was lifted.

PENALTY FOR BREACH OF RULE 6-8c:
Match Play – Loss of hole; Stroke play – Two strokes.

Rule 7. Practice

7-1. Before or Between Rounds

a. Match Play

On any day of a match play competition, a player may practise on the competition course before a round.

b. Stroke Play

On any day of a stroke competition or play-off, a competitor shall not practise on the competition course or test the surface of any putting green on the course before a round or play-off. When two or more rounds of a stroke competition are to be played over consecutive days, practice between those rounds on any competition course remaining to be played is prohibited.

Exception: Practice putting or chipping on or near the first teeing ground before starting a round or play-off is permitted.

PENALTY FOR BREACH OF RULE 7-1b:
Disqualification.

Note: The Committee may in the conditions of a competition (Rule 33-1) prohibit practice on the competition course on any day of a match play competition or permit practice on the competition course or part of the course (Rule 33-2c) on any day of or between rounds of a stroke competition.

7-2. During Round

A player shall not play a practice stroke either during the play of a hole or between the play of two holes except that, between the play of two holes, the player may practise putting or chipping on or near the putting green of the hole last played, any practice putting green or the teeing ground of the next hole to be played in the round, provided such practice stroke is not played from a hazard and does not unduly delay play (Rule 6-7).

Exception: When play has been suspended by the Committee, a player may, prior to resumption of play, practise (a) as provided in this Rule, (b) anywhere other than on the competition course and (c) as otherwise permitted by the Committee.

PENALTY FOR BREACH OF RULE 7-2:
Match play – Loss of hole; Stroke play – Two strokes.

In the event of a breach between the play of two holes, the penalty applies to the next hole.

Note 1: A practice swing is not a practice stroke and may be taken at any place, provided the player does not breach the Rules.

Note 2: The Committee may prohibit practice on or near the putting green of the hole last played.

Rule 8. Advice; Indicating Line of Play

Definitions

"Advice" is any counsel or suggestion which could influence a player in determining his play, the choice of a club or the method of making a stroke.

Information on the Rules or on matters of public information, such as the position of hazards or the flagstick on the putting green, is not advice.

The "line of play" is the direction which the player wishes his ball to take after a stroke, plus a reasonable distance on either side of the intended direction. The line of play extends vertically upwards from the ground, but does not extend beyond the hole.

8-1. Advice

A player shall not give advice to anyone in the competition except his partner. A player may ask for advice from only his partner or either of their caddies.

8-2. Indicating Line of Play

a. Other Than on Putting Green

Except on the putting green, a player may have the line of play indicated to him by anyone, but no one shall stand on or close to the line while the stroke is being played. Any mark placed during the play of a hole by the player or with his knowledge to indicate the line shall be removed before the stroke is played.

Exception: Flagstick attended or held up – see Rule 17-1.

b. On the Putting Green

When the player's ball is on the putting green, the player, his partner or either of their caddies may, before but not during the stroke, point out a line for putting, but in so doing the putting green shall not be touched. No mark shall be placed anywhere to indicate a line for putting.

PENALTY FOR BREACH OF RULE: *Match play – Loss of hole; Stroke play – Two strokes.*

Note: In a team competition with or without concurrent individual competition, the Committee may in the conditions of the competition (Rule 33-1) permit each team to appoint one person, e.g. team captain or coach, who may give advice (including pointing out a line for putting) to members of that team. Such person shall be identified to the Committee prior to the start of the competition.

Rule 9. Information as to Strokes Taken

9-1. General

The number of strokes a player has taken shall include any penalty strokes incurred.

9.2 Match Play

A player who has incurred a penalty shall inform his opponent as soon as practicable, unless he is obviously proceeding under a Rule involving a penalty and this has been observed by his opponent. If he fails so to inform his opponent he shall be deemed to have given wrong information even if he was not aware that he had incurred a penalty.

An opponent is entitled to ascertain from the player, during the play of a hole, the number of strokes he has taken and, after play of a hole, the number of strokes taken on the hole just completed.

If during the play of a hole the player gives or is deemed to give wrong information as to the number of strokes taken, he shall incur no penalty if he corrects the mistake before his opponent has played his next stroke. If the player fails so to correct the wrong information, *he shall lose the hole.*

If after play of a hole the player gives or is

deemed to give wrong information as to the number of strokes taken on the hole just completed and this affects the opponent's understanding of the result of the hole, he shall incur no penalty if he corrects his mistake before any player plays from the next teeing ground or, in the case of the last hole of the match, before all players leave the putting green. If the player fails so to correct the wrong information, *he shall lose the hole.*

9-3. Stroke Play

A competitor who has incurred a penalty should inform his marker as soon as practicable.

ORDER OF PLAY

Rule 10. Order of Play

10-1. Match Play

a. Teeing Ground

The side entitled to play first from the teeing ground is said to have the "honour".

The side which shall have the honour at the first teeing ground shall be determined by the order of the draw. In the absence of a draw, the honour should be decided by lot.

The side which wins a hole shall take the honour at the next teeing ground. If a hole has been halved, the side which had the honour at the previous teeing ground shall retain it.

b. Other Than on Teeing Ground

When the balls are in play, the ball farther from the hole shall be played first. If the balls are equidistant from the hole, the ball to be played first should be decided by lot.

Exception: Rule 30-3c (best-ball and four-ball match play).

c. Playing Out of Turn

If a player plays when his opponent should have played, the opponent may immediately require the player to cancel the stroke so played and, in correct order, play a ball without penalty as nearly as possible at the spot from which the original ball was last played (see Rule 20-5).

10-2. Stroke Play

a. Teeing Ground

The competitor entitled to play first from the teeing ground is said to have the "honour".

The competitor who shall have the honour at the first teeing ground shall be determined by the order of the draw. In the absence of a draw, the honour should be decided by lot.

The competitor with the lowest score at a hole shall take the honour at the next teeing ground. The competitor with the second lowest score shall play next and so on. If two or more competitors have the same score at a hole, they shall play from the next teeing ground in the same order as at the previous teeing ground.

b. Other Than on Teeing Ground

When the balls are in play, the ball farthest from the hole shall be played first. If two or more balls are equidistant from the hole, the ball to be played first should be decided by lot.

Exceptions: Rules 22 (ball interfering with or assisting play) and 31-5 (four-ball stroke play).

c. Playing Out of Turn

If a competitor plays out of turn, no penalty is incurred and the ball shall be played as it lies. If, however, the Committee determines that competitors have agreed to play in an order other than that set forth in Clauses 2a and 2b of this Rule to give one of them an advantage, *they shall be disqualified.*

(Incorrect order of play in threesomes and foursomes stroke play – see Rule 29-3.)

10-3. Provisional Ball or Second Ball from Teeing Ground

If a player plays a provisional ball or a second ball from a teeing ground, he should do so after his opponent or fellow-competitor has played his first stroke. If a player plays a provisional ball or a second ball out of turn, Clauses 1c and 2c of this Rule shall apply.

10-4. Ball Moved in Measuring

If a ball is moved in measuring to determine which ball is farther from the hole, no penalty is incurred and the ball shall be replaced.

TEEING GROUND

Rule 11. Teeing Ground

Definition

The "teeing ground" is the starting place for the hole to be played. It is a rectangular area two club-lengths in depth, the front and the sides of which are defined by the outside limits of two tee-markers. A ball is outside the teeing ground when all of it lies outside the teeing ground.

11-1. Teeing

In teeing, the ball may be placed on the ground, on an irregularity of surface created by the player on the ground or on a tee, sand or other substance in order to raise it off the ground.

A player may stand outside the teeing ground to play a ball within it.

11-2. Tee-Markers

Before a player plays his first stroke with any ball from the teeing ground of the hole being played, the tee-markers are deemed to be fixed.

In such circumstances, if the player moves or allows to be moved a tee-marker for the purpose of avoiding interference with his stance, the area of his intended swing or his line of play, *he shall incur the penalty for a breach of Rule 13-2.*

11-3. Ball Falling Off Tee

If a ball, when not in play, falls off a tee or is knocked off a tee by the player in addressing it, it may be re-teed without penalty, but if a stroke is made at the ball in these circumstances, whether the ball is moving or not, the stroke counts but no penalty is incurred.

11-4. Playing from Outside Teeing Ground

a. Match Play

If a player, when starting a hole, plays a ball from outside the teeing ground, the opponent may immediately require the player to cancel the stroke so played and play a ball from within the teeing ground, without penalty.

b. Stroke Play

If a competitor, when starting a hole, plays a ball from outside the teeing ground, *he shall incur a penalty of two strokes* and shall then play a ball from within the teeing ground.

If the competitor plays a stroke from the next teeing ground without first correcting his mistake or, in the case of the last hole of the round, leaves the putting green, without first declaring his intention to correct his mistake, *he shall be disqualified.*

Strokes played by a competitor from outside the teeing ground do not count in his score.

11-5. Playing from Wrong Teeing Ground

The provisions of Rule 11-4 apply.

PLAYING THE BALL

Rule 12. Searching for and Identifying Ball

Definitions

A "hazard" is any bunker or water hazard.

A "bunker" is a hazard consisting of a prepared area of ground, often a hollow, from which turf or soil has been removed and replaced with sand or the like. Grass-covered ground bordering or within a bunker is not part of the bunker. The margin of a bunker extends vertically downwards, but not upwards.

A "water hazard" is any sea, lake, pond, river, ditch, surface drainage ditch or other open water course (whether or not containing water) and anything of a similar nature.

All ground or water within the margin of a water hazard is part of the water hazard. The margin of a water hazard extends vertically upwards and downwards. Stakes and lines defining the margins of water hazards are in the hazards.

12-1. Searching for Ball; Seeing Ball

In searching for his ball anywhere on the course, the player may touch or bend long grass, rushes, bushes, whins, heather or the like, but only to the extent necessary to find and identify it, provided that this does not improve the lie of the ball, the area of his intended swing or his line of play.

A player is not necessarily entitled to see his ball when playing a stroke.

In a hazard, if the ball is covered by loose impediments or sand, the player may remove by probing, raking or other means as much thereof as will enable him to see a part of the ball. If an excess is removed, no penalty is incurred and the ball shall be re-covered so that only a part of the ball is visible. If the ball is moved in such removal, no penalty is incurred; the ball shall be replaced and, if necessary, re-covered. As to removal of loose impediments outside a hazard, see Rule 23.

If a ball lying in casual water, ground under repair or a hole, cast or runway made by a burrowing animal, a reptile or a bird is accidentally moved during search, no penalty is incurred; the ball shall be replaced, unless the player elects to proceed under Rule 25-1b.

If a ball is believed to be lying in water in a water hazard, the player may probe for it with a club or otherwise. If the ball is moved in so doing, no penalty is incurred; the ball shall be replaced, unless the player elects to proceed under Rule 26-1.

PENALTY FOR BREACH OF RULE 12-1:
Match play – Loss of hole; Stroke play – Two strokes.

12-2. Identifying Ball

The responsibility for playing the proper ball rests with the player. Each player should put an identification mark on his ball.

Except in a hazard, the player may, without penalty, lift a ball he believes to be his own for the purpose of identification and clean it to the extent necessary for identification. If the ball is the player's ball, he shall replace it. Before lifting the ball, the player must announce his intention to his opponent in match play or his marker or a fellow-competitor in stroke play and mark the position of the ball. He must then give his opponent, marker or fellow-competitor an opportunity to observe the lifting and replacement. If he lifts his ball without announcing his intention in advance, marking the position of the ball or giving his opponent, marker or fellow-competitor an opportunity to observe, or if he lifts his ball for identification in a hazard, or cleans it more than necessary for identification, *he shall incur a penalty of one stroke* and the ball shall be replaced.

If a player who is required to replace a ball fails to do so, *he shall incur the penalty* for a breach of

Rule 20-3a, but no additional penalty under Rule 12-2 shall be applied.

Rule 13. Ball Played As It Lies; Lie, Area of Intended Swing and Line of Play; Stance

Definitions

A "hazard" is any bunker or water hazard.

A "bunker" is a hazard consisting of a prepared area of ground, often a hollow, from which turf or soil has been removed and replaced with sand or the like. Grass-covered ground bordering or within a bunker is not part of the bunker. The margin of a bunker extends vertically downwards, but not upwards.

A "water hazard" is any sea, lake, pond, river, ditch, surface drainage ditch or other open water course (whether or not containing water) and anything of a similar nature.

All ground or water within the margin of a water hazard is part of the water hazard. The margin of a water hazard extends vertically upwards and downwards. Stakes and lines defining the margins of water hazards are in the hazards.

The "line of play" is the direction which the player wishes his ball to take after a stroke, plus a reasonable distance on either side of the intended direction. The line of play extends vertically upwards from the ground, but does not extend beyond the hole.

13-1. Ball Played As It Lies

The ball shall be played as it lies, except as otherwise provided in the Rules. (Ball at rest moved – see Rule 18.)

13-2. Improving Lie, Area of Intended Swing or Line of Play

Except as provided in the Rules, a player shall not improve or allow to be improved:

the position or lie of his ball,

the area of his intended swing,

his line of play or a reasonable extension of that line beyond the hole or

the area in which he is to drop or place a ball

by any of the following actions:

moving, bending or breaking anything growing or fixed (including immovable obstructions and objects defining out of bounds) or removing or pressing down sand, loose soil, replaced divots, other cut turf placed in position or other irregularities of surface

except as follows:

as may occur in fairly taking his stance,

in making a stroke or the backward movement of his club for a stroke,

on the teeing ground in creating or eliminating irregularities of surface, or

on the putting green in removing sand and loose soil as provided in Rule 16-1a or in repairing damage as provided in Rule 16-1c.

The club may be grounded only lightly and shall not be pressed on the ground.

Exception: Ball lying in or touching hazard – see Rule 13-4.

13-3. Building Stance

A player is entitled to place his feet firmly in taking his stance, but he shall not build a stance.

13-4. Ball Lying in or Touching Hazard

Except as provided in the Rules, before making a stroke at a ball which lies in or touches a hazard (whether a bunker or a water hazard), the player shall not:

a. Test the condition of the hazard or any similar hazard,

b. Touch the ground in the hazard or water in the water hazard with a club or otherwise, or

c. Touch or move a loose impediment lying in or touching the hazard.

Exceptions:

1. Provided nothing is done which constitutes testing the condition of the hazard or improves the lie of the ball, there is no penalty if the player (a) touches the ground in any hazard or water in a water hazard as a result of or to prevent falling, in removing an obstruction, in measuring or in retrieving or lifting a ball under any Rule or (b) places his clubs in a hazard.

2. The player after playing the stroke, or his caddie at any time without the authority of the player, may smooth sand or soil in the hazard, provided that, if the ball still lies in the hazard, nothing is done which improves the lie of the ball or assists the player in his subsequent play of the hole.

Note: At any time, including at address or in the backward movement for the stroke, the player may touch with a club or otherwise any obstruction, any construction declared by the Committee to be an integral part of the course or any grass, bush, tree or other growing thing.

PENALTY FOR BREACH OF RULE: *Match play – Loss of hole; Stroke play – Two strokes.*

(Searching for ball – see Rule 12-1.)

Rule 14. Striking the Ball

Definition

A "stroke" is the forward movement of the club made with the intention of fairly striking at and moving the ball, but if a player checks his downswing voluntarily before the clubhead reaches the ball he is deemed not to have made a stroke.

14-1. Ball to be Fairly Struck At

The ball shall be fairly struck at with the head

of the club and must not be pushed, scraped or spooned.

14-2. Assistance

In making a stroke, a player shall not accept physical assistance or protection from the elements.

PENALTY FOR BREACH OF RULE 14-1 or -2;
Match play – Loss of hole; Stroke play – Two strokes.

14-3. Artificial Devices and Unusual Equipment

If there may be any reasonable basis for doubt as to whether an item which is to be manufactured would, if used by a player during a round, cause the player to be in breach of Rule 14-3, the manufacturer should submit a sample to the Royal & Ancient Golf Club of St Andrews for a ruling, such sample to become its property for reference purposes. If a manufacturer fails to do so, he assumes the risk of an unfavourable ruling.

A player in doubt as to whether use of an item would constitute a breach of Rule 14-3 should consult the Royal & Ancient Golf Club of St Andrews.

Except as provided in the Rules, during a stipulated round the player shall not use any artificial device or unusual equipment:

a. Which might assist him in making a stroke or in his play; or

b. For the purpose of gauging or measuring distance or conditions which might affect his play; or

c. Which might assist him in gripping the club, except that plain gloves may be worn, resin, tape or gauze may be applied to the grip (provided such application does not render the grip non-conforming under Rule 4-1c) and a towel or handkerchief may be wrapped around the grip.

PENALTY FOR BREACH OF RULE 14-3:
Disqualification.

14-4. Striking the Ball More than Once

If a player's club strikes the ball more than once in the course of a stroke, the player shall count the stroke and *add a penalty stroke*, making two strokes in all.

14-5. Playing Moving Ball

A player shall not play while his ball is moving.

Exceptions:

Ball falling off tee – Rule 11-3.
Striking the ball more than once – Rule 14-4.
Ball moving in water – Rule 14-6.

When the ball begins to move only after the player has begun the stroke or the backward movement of his club for the stroke, he shall incur no penalty under this Rule for playing a moving ball, but he is not exempt from any penalty incurred under the following Rules

Ball at rest moved by player – Rule 18-2a.
Ball at rest moving after address – Rule 18-2b.
Ball at rest moving after loose impediment touched – Rule 18-2c.

14-6. Ball Moving in Water

When a ball is moving in water in a water hazard, the player may, without penalty, make a stroke, but he must not delay making his stroke in order to allow the wind or current to improve the position of the ball. A ball moving in water in a water hazard may be lifted if the player elects to invoke Rule 26.

PENALTY FOR BREACH OF RULE 14-5 or -6:
Match play – Loss of hole; Stroke play – Two strokes.

Rule 15. Playing a Wrong Ball

Definition

A "wrong ball" is any ball other than:

a. The ball in play,

b. A provisional ball or

c. In stroke play, a second ball played under Rule 3-3 or Rule 20-7b.

Note: Ball in play includes a ball substituted for the ball in play when the player is proceeding under an applicable Rule which does not permit substitution.

15-1. General

A player must hole out with the ball played from the teeing ground unless a Rule permits him to substitute another ball. If a player substitutes another ball when proceeding under an applicable Rule which does not permit substitution, that ball is not a wrong ball; it becomes the ball in play and, if the error is not corrected as provided in Rule 20-6, *the player shall incur a penalty of loss of hole in match play or two strokes in stroke play.*

15-2. Match Play

If a player plays a stroke with a wrong ball except in a hazard, *he shall lose the hole.*

If a player plays any strokes in a hazard with a wrong ball, there is no penalty. Strokes played in a hazard with a wrong ball do not count in the player's score. If the wrong ball belongs to another player, its owner shall place a ball on the spot from which the wrong ball was first played.

If the player and opponent exchange balls during the play of a hole, the first to play the wrong ball other than from a hazard shall lose the hole; when this cannot be determined, the hole shall be played out with the balls exchanged.

15-3. Stroke Play

If a competitor plays a stroke or strokes with a wrong ball, *he shall incur a penalty of two strokes,* unless the only stroke or strokes played with such ball were played when it was lying in a hazard, in which case no penalty is incurred.

The competitor must correct his mistake by playing the correct ball. If he fails to correct his mistake before he plays a stroke from the next teeing ground or, in the case of the last hole of the round, fails to declare his intention to correct his mistake before leaving the putting green, *he shall be disqualified.*

Strokes played by a competitor with a wrong ball do not count in his score.

If the wrong ball belongs to another competitor, its owner shall place a ball on the spot from which the wrong ball was first played.

(Lie of ball to be placed or replaced altered – see Rule 20-3b.)

THE PUTTING GREEN

Rule 16. The Putting Green

Definitions

The "putting green" is all ground of the hole being played which is specially prepared for putting or otherwise defined as such by the Committee. A ball is on the putting green when any part of it touches the putting green.

The "line of putt" is the line which the player wishes his ball to take after a stroke on the putting green. Except with respect to Rule 16-1e, the line of putt includes a reasonable distance on either side of the intended line. The line of putt does not extend beyond the hole.

A ball is "holed" when it is at rest within the circumference of the hole and all of it is below the level of the lip of the hole.

16-1. General

a. Touching Line of Putt

The line of putt must not be touched except:

(i) the player may move sand and loose soil on the putting green and other loose impediments by picking them up or by brushing them aside with his hand or a club without pressing anything down;

(ii) in addressing the ball, the player may place the club in front of the ball without pressing anything down;

(iii) in measuring – Rule 10-4;

(iv) in lifting the ball – Rule 16-1b;

(v) in pressing down a ball-marker;

(vi) in repairing old hole plugs or ball marks on the putting green – Rule 16-1c; and

(vii) in removing movable obstructions – Rule 24-1.

(Indicating line for putting on putting green – see Rule 8-2b.)

b. Lifting Ball

A ball on the putting green may be lifted and, if desired, cleaned. A ball so lifted shall be replaced on the spot from which it was lifted.

c. Repair of Hole Plugs, Ball Marks and Other Damage

The player may repair an old hole plug or damage to the putting green caused by the impact of a ball, whether or not the player's ball lies on the putting green. If the ball is moved in the process of such repair, it shall be replaced, without penalty. Any other damage to the putting green shall not be repaired if it might assist the player in his subsequent play of the hole.

d. Testing Surface

During the play of a hole, a player shall not test the surface of the putting green by rolling a ball or roughening or scraping the surface.

e. Standing Astride or on Line of Putt

The player shall not make a stroke on the putting green from a stance astride, or with either foot touching, the line of putt or an extension of that line behind the ball.

f. Position of Caddie or Partner

While making a stroke on the putting green, the player shall not allow his caddie, his partner or his partner's caddie to position himself on or close to an extension of the line of putt behind the ball.

g. Playing Stroke While Another Ball in Motion

The player shall not play a stroke while another ball is in motion after a stroke from the putting green, except that, if a player does so, he incurs no penalty if it was his turn to play.

(Lifting ball interfering with or assisting play while another ball in motion – see Rule 22.)

PENALTY FOR BREACH OF RULE 16-1:
Match play – Loss of hole; Stroke play – Two strokes.

16-2. Ball Overhanging Hole

When any part of the ball overhangs the lip of the hole, the player is allowed enough time to reach the hole without unreasonable delay and an additional ten seconds to determine whether the ball is at rest. If by then the ball has not fallen into the hole, it is deemed to be at rest. If the ball subsequently falls into the hole, the player is deemed to have holed out with his last stroke, and *he shall add a penalty stroke to his score* for the hole; otherwise there is no penalty under this Rule.

(Undue delay – see Rule 6-7.)

Rule 17. The Flagstick

17-1. Flagstick Attended, Removed or Held Up

Before and during the stroke, the player may have the flagstick attended, removed or held up to indicate the position of the hole. This may be done only on the authority of the player before he plays his stroke.

If, prior to the stroke, the flagstick is attended, removed or held up by anyone with the player's knowledge and no objection is made, the player shall be deemed to have authorised it. If anyone attends or holds up the flagstick or stands near the hole while a stroke is being played, he shall be deemed to be attending the flagstick until the ball comes to rest.

17-2. Unauthorised Attendance

a. Match Play

In match play, an opponent or his caddie shall not, without the authority or prior knowledge of the player, attend, remove or hold up the flagstick while the player is making a stroke or his ball is in motion.

b. Stroke Play

In stroke play, if a fellow-competitor or his caddie attends, removes or holds up the flagstick without the competitor's authority or prior knowledge while the competitor is making a stroke or his ball is in motion, *the fellow-competitor shall incur the penalty* for breach of this Rule. In such circumstances, if the competitor's ball strikes the flagstick, the person attending it, or anything carried by him, the competitor incurs no penalty and the ball shall be played as it lies, except that, if the stroke was played from the putting green, the stroke shall be cancelled, the ball replaced and the stroke replayed.

PENALTY FOR BREACH OF RULE 17-1 or -2: *Match play – Loss of hole; Stroke play – Two strokes.*

17-3. Ball Striking Flagstick or Attendant

The player's ball shall not strike:

a. The flagstick when attended, removed or held up by the player, his partner or either of their caddies, or by another person with the player's authority or prior knowledge; or

b. The player's caddie, his partner or his partner's caddie when attending the flagstick, or another person attending the flagstick with the player's authority or prior knowledge, or anything carried by any such person; or

c. The flagstick in the hole, unattended, when the ball has been played from the putting green.

PENALTY FOR BREACH OF RULE 17-3; *Match play – Loss of hole; Stroke play – Two strokes, and the ball shall be played as it lies.*

17-4. Ball Resting Against Flagstick

If the ball rests against the flagstick when it is in the hole, the player or another person authorised by him may move or remove the flagstick and if the ball falls into the hole, the player shall be deemed to have holed out with his last stroke; otherwise the ball, if moved, shall be placed on the lip of the hole, without penalty.

BALL MOVED, DEFLECTED OR STOPPED

Rule 18. Ball At Rest Moved

Definitions

A ball is deemed to have "moved" if it leaves its position and comes to rest in any other place.

An "outside agency" is any agency not part of the match or, in stroke play, not part of the competitor's side, and includes a referee, a marker, an observer or a forecaddie. Neither wind nor water is an outside agency.

"Equipment" is anything used, worn or carried by or for the player except any ball he has played at the hole being played and any small object, such as a coin or a tee, when used to mark the position of a ball or the extent of an area in which a ball is to be dropped. Equipment includes a golf cart, whether or not motorised. If such a cart is shared by two or more players, the cart and everything in it are deemed to be the equipment of the player whose ball is involved except that, when the cart is being moved by one of the players sharing it, the cart and everything in it are deemed to be that player's equipment.

Note: A ball played at the hole being played is equipment when it has been lifted and not put back into play.

A player has "addressed the ball" when he has taken his stance and has also grounded his club, except that in a hazard a player has addressed the ball when he has taken his stance.

Taking the "stance" consists in a player placing his feet in position for and preparatory to making a stroke.

18-1. By Outside Agency

If a ball at rest is moved by an outside agency, the player shall incur no penalty and the ball shall be replaced before the player plays another stroke.

(Player's ball at rest moved by another ball – see Rule 18-5.)

18-2. By Player, Partner, Caddie or Equipment

a. General

When a player's ball is in play, if:

(i) the player, his partner or either of their

caddies lifts or moves it, touches it purposely (except with a club in the act of addressing it) or causes it to move except as permitted by a Rule, or

(ii) equipment of the player or his partner causes the ball to move,

the player shall incur a penalty stroke. The ball shall be replaced unless the movement of the ball occurs after the player has begun his swing and he does not discontinue his swing.

Under the Rules no penalty is incurred if a player accidentally causes his ball to move in the following circumstances:

In measuring to determine which ball farther from hole – Rule 10-4

In searching for covered ball in hazard or for ball in casual water, ground under repair, etc. – Rule 12-1

In the process of repairing hole plug or ball mark – Rule 16-1c

In the process of removing loose impediment on putting green – Rule 18-2c

In the process of lifting ball under a Rule – Rule 20-1

In the process of placing or replacing ball under a Rule – Rule 20-3a

In complying with Rule 22 relating to lifting ball interfering with or assisting play

In removal of movable obstruction – Rule 24-1.

b. Ball Moving After Address

If a player's ball in play moves after he has addressed it (other than as a result of a stroke), the player shall be deemed to have moved the ball and *shall incur a penalty stroke.* The player shall replace the ball unless the movement of the ball occurs after he has begun his swing and he does not discontinue his swing.

c. Ball Moving After Loose Impediment Touched

Through the green, if the ball moves after any loose impediment lying within a club-length of it has been touched by the player, his partner or either of their caddies and before the player has addressed it, the player shall be deemed to have moved the ball and *shall incur a penalty stroke.* The player shall replace the ball unless the movement of the ball occurs after he has begun his swing and he does not discontinue his swing.

On the putting green, if the ball or the ball-marker moves in the process of removing any loose impediment, the ball or the ball-marker shall be replaced. There is no penalty provided the movement of the ball or the ball-marker is directly attributable to the removal of the loose impediment. Otherwise, *the player shall incur a penalty stroke* under Rule 18-2a or 20-1.

18-3. By Opponent, Caddie or Equipment in Match Play

a. During Search

If, during search for a player's ball, it is moved by an opponent, his caddie or his equipment, no penalty is incurred and the player shall replace the ball.

b. Other Than During Search

If, other than during search for a ball, the ball is touched or moved by an opponent, his caddie or his equipment, except as otherwise provided in the Rules, *the opponent shall incur a penalty stroke.* The player shall replace the ball.

(Ball moved in measuring to determine which ball farther from the hole – see Rule 10-4.)

(Playing a wrong ball – see Rule 15-2.)

(Ball moved in complying with Rule 22 relating to lifting ball interfering with or assisting play.)

18-4. By Fellow-Competitor, Caddie or Equipment in Stroke Play

If a competitor's ball is moved by a fellow-competitor, his caddie or his equipment, no penalty is incurred. The competitor shall replace his ball.

(Playing a wrong ball – see Rule 15-3.)

18-5. By Another Ball

If a ball in play and at rest is moved by another ball in motion after a stroke, the moved ball shall be replaced.

*PENALTY FOR BREACH OF RULE:
Match play – Loss of hole. Stroke play – Two strokes.

**If a player who is required to replace a ball fails to do so, he shall incur the general penalty for breach of Rule 18 but no additional penalty under Rule 18 shall be applied.*

Note 1: If a ball to be replaced under this Rule is not immediately recoverable, another ball may be substituted.

Note 2: If it is impossible to determine the spot on which a ball is to be placed, see Rule 20-3c.

Rule 19. Ball in Motion Deflected or Stopped

Definitions

An "outside agency" is any agency not part of the match or, in stroke play, not part of the competitor's side, and includes a referee, a marker, an observer or a forecaddie. Neither wind nor water is an outside agency.

"Equipment" is anything used, worn or carried by or for the player except any ball he has played at the hole being played and any small object, such as a coin or a tee, when used to mark the position of a ball or the extent of an area in which a ball is to be dropped. Equipment includes a golf cart, whether or not motorised. If such a cart is shared by two or more players, the cart and everything in it are deemed to be the equipment of the player whose ball is involved except that, when the cart is being moved by one of the players sharing it, the cart and everything in it are deemed to be that player's equipment.

Note: A ball played at the hole being played is equipment when it has been lifted and not put back into play.

19-1. By Outside Agency

If a ball in motion is accidentally deflected or stopped by any outside agency, it is a rub of the green, no penalty is incurred and the ball shall be played as it lies except:

a. If a ball in motion after a stroke other than on the putting green comes to rest in or on any moving or animate outside agency, the player shall, through the green or in a hazard, drop the ball, or on the putting green place the ball, as near as possible to the spot where the outside agency was when the ball came to rest in or on it, and

b. If a ball in motion after a stroke on the putting green is deflected or stopped by, or comes to rest in or on any moving or animate outside agency except a worm or an insect, the stroke shall be cancelled, the ball replaced and the stroke replayed.

If the ball is not immediately recoverable, another ball may be substituted.

(Player's ball deflected or stopped by another ball – see Rule 19-5.)

Note: If the referee or the Committee determines that a player's ball has been purposely deflected or stopped by an outside agency, Rule 1-4 applies to the player. If the outside agency is a fellow-competitor or his caddie, Rule 1-2 applies to the fellow-competitor.

19-2. By Player, Partner, Caddie or Equipment

a. Match Play

If a player's ball is accidentally deflected or stopped by himself, his partner or either of their caddies or equipment, *he shall lose the hole.*

b. Stroke Play

If a competitor's ball is accidentally deflected or stopped by himself, his partner or either of their caddies or equipment, *the competitor shall incur a penalty of two strokes.* The ball shall be played as it lies, except when it comes to rest in or on the competitor's, his partner's or either of their caddies' clothes or equipment, in which case the competitor shall, through the green or in a hazard, drop the ball, or on the putting green place the ball, as near as possible to where the article was when the ball came to rest in or on it.

Exception: Dropped Ball – see Rule 20-2a.

(Ball purposely deflected or stopped by player, partner or caddie – see Rule 1-2.)

19-3. By Opponent, Caddie or Equipment in Match Play

If a player's ball is accidentally deflected or stopped by an opponent, his caddie or his equipment, no penalty is incurred. The player may play the ball as it lies or, before another stroke is played by either side, cancel the stroke and play a ball without penalty as nearly as possible at the spot from which the original ball was last played (see Rule 20-5).

If the ball has come to rest in or on the opponent's or his caddie's clothes or equipment, the player may through the green or in a hazard drop the ball, or on the putting green place the ball, as near as possible to where the article was when the ball came to rest in or on it.

Exception: Ball striking person attending flagstick – see Rule 17-3b.

(Ball purposely deflected or stopped by opponent or caddie – see Rule 1-2.)

19-4. By Fellow-Competitor, Caddie or Equipment in Stroke Play

See Rule 19-1 regarding ball deflected by outside agency.

19-5. By Another Ball

If a player's ball in motion after a stroke is deflected or stopped by a ball at rest, the player shall play his ball as it lies. In stroke play, if both balls lay on the putting green prior to the stroke, *the player incurs a penalty of two strokes.* Otherwise, no penalty is incurred.

If a player's ball in motion after a stroke is deflected or stopped by another ball in motion, the player shall play his ball as it lies. There is no penalty unless the player was in breach of Rule 16-1g, in which case *he shall incur the penalty for breach of that Rule.*

Exception: Ball in motion after a stroke on the putting green deflected or stopped by moving or animate outside agency – see Rule 19-1b.

PENALTY FOR BREACH OF RULE:
Match play – Loss of hole;
Stroke play – Two strokes.

RELIEF SITUATIONS AND PROCEDURE

Rule 20. Lifting, Dropping and Placing: Playing from Wrong Place

20.1 Lifting

A ball to be lifted under the Rules may be lifted by the player, his partner or another person authorised by the player. In any such case, the player shall be responsible for any breach of the Rules.

The position of the ball shall be marked before it is lifted under a Rule which requires it to be replaced. If it is not marked, the player *shall incur a penalty of one stroke* and the ball shall be replaced. If it is not replaced, *the player shall incur the general penalty* for breach of this Rule but no additional penalty under Rule 20-1 shall be applied.

If a ball or a ball-marker is accidentally moved in the process of lifting the ball under a Rule or marking its position, the ball or the ball-marker shall be replaced. There is no penalty provided the movement of the ball or the ball-marker is directly attributable to the specific act of marking the position of, or lifting the ball. Otherwise *the player shall incur a penalty stroke* under this Rule or Rule 18-2a.

Exception: If a player incurs a penalty for failing to act in accordance with Rule 5-3 or 12-2 no additional penalty under Rule 20-1 shall be applied.

Note: The position of a ball to be lifted should be marked by placing a ball-marker, a small coin or other similar object immediately behind the ball. If the ball-marker interferes with the play, stance or stroke of another player, it should be placed one or more clubhead-lengths to one side.

20-2. Dropping and Re-dropping

a. By Whom and How

A ball to be dropped under the Rules shall be dropped by the player himself. He shall stand erect, hold the ball at shoulder height and arm's length and drop it. If a ball is dropped by any other person or in any other manner and the error is not corrected as provided in Rule 20-6, *the player shall incur a penalty stroke.*

If the ball touches the player, his partner, either of their caddies or their equipment before or after it strikes a part of the course, the ball shall be re-dropped, without penalty. There is no limit to the number of times a ball shall be re-dropped in such circumstances.

(Taking action to influence position or movement of ball – see Rule 1-2.)

b. Where to Drop

When a ball is to be dropped as near as possible to a specific spot, it shall be dropped not nearer the hole than the specific spot which, if it is not precisely known to the player, shall be estimated.

A ball when dropped must first strike a part of the course where the applicable Rule requires it to be dropped. If it is not so dropped, Rules 20-6 and -7 apply.

c. When to Re-drop

A dropped ball shall be re-dropped without penalty if it:

(i) rolls into a hazard;
(ii) rolls out of a hazard;
(iii) rolls onto a putting green;
(iv) rolls out of bounds;
(v) rolls to a position where there is interference by the condition from which relief was taken under Rule 24-2 (immovable obstruction) or Rule 25-1 (abnormal ground condition);
(vi) rolls and comes to rest more than two club-lengths from where it first struck a part of the course; or
(vii) rolls and comes to rest nearer the hole than its original position or estimated position (see Rule 20-2b) unless otherwise permitted by the Rules.

If the ball when re-dropped rolls into any position listed above, it shall be placed as near as possible to the spot where it first struck a part of the course when re-dropped.

If a ball to be re-dropped or placed under this Rule is not immediately recoverable, another ball may be substituted.

20-3. Placing and Replacing

a. By Whom and Where

A ball to be placed under the Rules shall be placed by the player or his partner. If a ball is to be replaced, the player, his partner or the person who lifted or moved it shall place it on the spot from which it was lifted or moved. In any such case, the player shall be responsible for any breach of the Rules.

If a ball or the ball-marker is accidentally moved in the process of placing or replacing the ball, the ball or the ball-marker shall be replaced. There is no penalty provided the movement of the ball or the ball-marker is directly attributable to the specific act of placing or replacing the ball or removing the ball-marker. Otherwise, *the player shall incur a penalty stroke* under Rule 18-2a or 20-1.

b. Lie of Ball to Be Placed or Replaced Altered

If the original lie of a ball to be placed or replaced has been altered:

(i) except in a hazard, the ball shall be placed in the nearest lie most similar to the original lie which is not more than one club-length from the original lie, not nearer the hole and not in a hazard;
(ii) in a water hazard, the ball shall be placed in accordance with Clause (i) above, except that the ball must be placed in the water hazard;
(iii) in a bunker, the original lie shall be recreated as nearly as possible and the ball shall be placed in that lie.

c. Spot Not Determinable

If it is impossible to determine the spot where the ball is to be placed or replaced:

(i) through the green, the ball shall be dropped as near as possible to the place where it lay but not in a hazard
(ii) in a hazard, the ball shall be dropped in the hazard as near as possible to the place where it lay;
(iii) on the putting green, the ball shall be placed as near as possible to the place where it lay but not in a hazard.

d. Ball Fails to Remain on Spot

If a ball when placed fails to remain on the spot on which it was placed, it shall be replaced without penalty. If it still fails to remain on that spot:
(i) except in a hazard, it shall be placed at the nearest spot not nearer the hole or in a hazard where it can be placed at rest;
(ii) in a hazard, it shall be placed in the hazard at the nearest spot not nearer the hole where it can be placed at rest.

PENALTY FOR BREACH OF RULE 20-1,-2 or -3; *Match play – Loss of hole; Stroke play – Two strokes.*

20-4. When Ball Dropped or Placed is in Play

If the player's ball in play has been lifted, it is again in play when dropped or placed.

A substituted ball becomes the ball in play if it is dropped or placed under an applicable Rule, whether or not such Rule permits substitution. A ball substituted under an inapplicable Rule is a wrong ball.

20-5. Playing Next Stroke from Where Previous Stroke Played

When, under the Rules, a player elects or is required to play his next stroke from where a previous stroke was played, he shall proceed as follows: if the stroke is to be played from the teeing ground, the ball to be played shall be played from anywhere within the teeing ground and may be teed; if the stroke is to be played from through the green or a hazard, it shall be dropped; if the stroke is to be played on the putting green, it shall be placed.

PENALTY FOR BREACH OF RULE 20-5; *Match play – Loss of hole; Stroke play – Two strokes.*

20-6. Lifting Ball Wrongly Dropped or Placed

A ball dropped or placed in a wrong place or otherwise not in accordance with the Rules but not played may be lifted, without penalty, and the player shall then proceed correctly.

20-7. Playing from Wrong Place

For a ball played from outside the teeing ground or from a wrong teeing ground – see Rule 11-4 and 11-5.

a. Match Play

If a player plays a stroke with a ball which has been dropped or placed in a wrong place, *he shall lose the hole.*

b. Stroke Play

If a competitor plays a stroke with (i) his original ball which has been dropped or placed in a wrong place, (ii) a substituted ball which has been dropped or placed under an applicable Rule but in a wrong place or (iii) his ball in play when it has been moved and not replaced in a case where the Rules require replacement, *he shall,* provided a serious breach has not occurred, *incur the penalty prescribed by the applicable Rule* and play out the hole with the ball.

If, after playing from a wrong place, a competitor becomes aware of that fact and believes that a serious breach may be involved, he may, provided he has not played a stroke from the next teeing ground or, in the case of the last hole of the round, left the putting green, declare that he will play out the hole with a second ball dropped or placed in accordance with the Rules. The competitor shall report the facts to the Committee before returning his score card; if he fails to do so, *he shall be disqualified.* The Committee shall determine whether a serious breach of the Rule occurred. If so, the score with the second ball shall count and *the competitor shall add two penalty strokes to his score with that ball.*

If a serious breach has occurred and the competitor has failed to correct it as prescribed above, *he shall be disqualified.*

Note: If a competitor plays a second ball, penalty strokes incurred by playing the ball ruled not to count and strokes subsequently taken with that ball shall be disregarded.

Rule 21. Cleaning Ball

A ball on the putting green may be cleaned when lifted under Rule 16-1b. Elsewhere, a ball may be cleaned when lifted except when it has been lifted:

a. To determine if it is unfit for play (Rule 5-3)

b. For identification (Rule 12-2), in which case it may be cleaned only to the extent necessary for identification: or

c. Because it is interfering with or assisting play (Rule 22).

If a player cleans his ball during play of a hole except as provided in this Rule, *he shall incur a penalty of one stroke* and the ball, if lifted, shall be replaced.

If a player who is required to replace a ball fails to do so, *he shall incur the penalty* for breach of Rule 20-3a, but no additional penalty under Rule 21 shall be applied.

Exception: If a player incurs a penalty for failing to act in accordance with Rule 5-3, 12-2 or 22, no additional penalty under Rule 21 shall be applied.

Rule 22. Ball Interfering with or Assisting Play

Any player may:

a. Lift his ball if he considers that the ball might assist any other player or

b. Have any other ball lifted if he considers that the ball might interfere with his play or assist the play of any other player, but this may not be done while another ball is in motion. In stroke play, a player required to lift his ball may play first rather than lift. A ball lifted under this Rule shall be replaced.

If a ball is accidentally moved in complying with this Rule, no penalty is incurred and the ball shall be replaced.

PENALTY FOR BREACH OF RULE:
Match play – Loss of hole;
Stroke play – Two strokes.

Note: Except on the putting green, the ball may not be cleaned when lifted under this Rule – see Rule 21.

Rule 23. Loose Impediments

Definition

"Loose impediments" are natural objects such as stones, leaves, twigs, branches and the like, dung, worms and insects and casts or heaps made by them, provided they are not fixed or growing, are not solidly embedded and do not adhere to the ball.

Sand and loose soil are loose impediments on the putting green but not elsewhere.

Snow and natural ice, other than frost, are either casual water or loose impediments, at the option of the player. Manufactured ice is an obstruction.

Dew and frost are not loose impediments.

23-1. Relief

Except when both the loose impediment and the ball lie in or touch a hazard, any loose impediment may be removed without penalty. If the ball moves, see Rule 18-2c.

When a player's ball is in motion, a loose impediment which might influence the movement of the ball shall not be removed.

PENALTY FOR BREACH OF RULE:
Match play – Loss of hole;
Stroke play – Two strokes.

(Searching for ball in hazard – see Rule 12-1.)
(Touching line of putt – see Rule 16-1a.)

Rule 24. Obstructions

Definition

An "obstruction" is anything artificial, including the artificial surfaces and sides of roads and paths and manufactured ice, except:

a. Objects defining out of bounds, such as walls, fences, stakes and railings;

b. Any part of an immovable artificial object which is out of bounds; and

c. Any construction declared by the Committee to be an integral part of the course.

24-1. Movable Obstruction

A player may obtain relief from a movable obstruction as follows:

a. If the ball does not lie in or on the obstruction, the obstruction may be removed. If the ball moves, it shall be replaced, and there is no penalty provided that the movement of the ball is directly attributable to the removal of the obstruction. Otherwise, Rule 18-2a applies.

b. If the ball lies in or on the obstruction, the ball may be lifted, without penalty, and the obstruction removed. The ball shall through the green or in a hazard be dropped, or on the putting green be placed, as near as possible to the spot directly under the place where the ball lay in or on the obstruction, but not nearer the hole.

The ball may be cleaned when lifted under Rule 24-1.

When a ball is in motion, an obstruction which might influence the movement of the ball, other than an attended flagstick or equipment of the players, shall not be removed.

24-2. Immovable Obstruction

a. Interference

Interference by an immovable obstruction occurs when a ball lies in or on the obstruction, or so close to the obstruction that the obstruction interferes with the player's stance or the area of his intended swing. If the player's ball lies on the putting green, interference also occurs if an immovable obstruction on the putting green intervenes on his line of putt. Otherwise, intervention on the line of play is not, of itself, interference under this Rule.

b. Relief

Except when the ball lies in or touches a water hazard or a lateral water hazard, a player may obtain relief from interference by an immovable obstruction, without penalty, as follows:

(i) Through the Green: If the ball lies through the green, the point on the course nearest to where the ball lies shall be determined (without crossing over, through or under the obstruction) which (a) is not nearer the hole, (b) avoids interference (as defined) and (c) is not a hazard or on a putting green. The player shall lift the ball and drop it within one club-length of the point thus determined on ground which fulfils (a), (b) and (c) above.

Note: The prohibition against crossing over,

through or under the obstruction does not apply to the artificial surfaces and sides of roads and paths or when the ball lies in or on the obstruction.

(ii) In a Bunker: If the ball lies in or touches a bunker, the player shall lift and drop the ball in accordance with Clause (i) above, except that the ball must be dropped in the bunker.

(iii) On the Putting Green: If the ball lies on the putting green, the player shall lift the ball and place it in the nearest position to where it lay which affords relief from interference, but not nearer the hole nor in a hazard.

The ball may be cleaned when lifted under Rule 24-2b.

(Ball rolling to a position where there is interference by the condition from which relief was taken – see Rule 20-2c(v).)

Exception: A player may not obtain relief under Rule 24-2b if (a) it is clearly unreasonable for him to play a stroke because of interference by anything other than an immovable obstruction or (b) interference by an immovable obstruction would occur only through use of an unnecessarily abnormal stance, swing or direction of play.

Note: If a ball lies in or touches a water hazard (including a lateral water hazard), the player is not entitled to relief without penalty from interference by an immovable obstruction. The player shall play the ball as it lies or proceed under Rule 26-1.

c. Ball Lost

Except in a water hazard or a lateral water hazard, if there is reasonable evidence that a ball is lost in an immovable obstruction, the player may, without penalty, substitute another ball and follow the procedure prescribed in Rule 24-2b. For the purpose of applying this Rule, the ball shall be deemed to lie at the spot where it entered the obstruction. If the ball is lost in an underground drain pipe or culvert the entrance to which is in a hazard, a ball must be dropped in that hazard or the player may proceed under Rule 26-1, if applicable.

PENALTY FOR BREACH OF RULE: *Match play – Loss of hole; Stroke play – Two strokes.*

Rule 25. Abnormal Ground Conditions and Wrong Putting Green

Definitions

"Casual water" is any temporary accumulation of water on the course which is visible before or after the player takes his stance and is not in a water hazard. Snow and natural ice, other than frost, are casual water or loose impediments, at the option of the player. Manufactured ice is an obstruction. Dew and frost are not casual water.

"Ground under repair" is any portion of the course so marked by order of the Committee or so declared by its authorised representative. It includes material piled for removal and a hole made by a greenkeeper, even if not so marked. Stakes and lines defining ground under repair are in such ground. The margin of ground under repair extends vertically downwards, but not upwards.

Note 1: Grass cuttings and other material left on the course which have been abandoned and are not intended to be removed are not ground under repair unless so marked.

Note 2: The Committee may make a Local Rule prohibiting play from ground under repair.

25-1. Casual Water, Ground Under Repair and Certain Damage to Course

a. Interference

Interference by casual water, ground under repair or a hole, cast or runway made by a burrowing animal, a reptile or a bird occurs when a ball lies in or touches any of these conditions or when such a condition on the course interferes with the player's stance or the area of his intended swing.

If the player's ball lies on the putting green, interference also occurs if such condition on the putting green intervenes on his line of putt.

If interference exists, the player may either play the ball as it lies (unless prohibited by Local Rule) or take relief as provided in Clause b.

b. Relief

If the player elects to take relief, he shall proceed as follows:

(i) Through the Green: If the ball lies through the green, the point on the course nearest to where the ball lies shall be determined which (a) is not nearer the hole, (b) avoids interference by the condition, and (c) is not in a hazard or on a putting green. The player shall lift the ball and drop it without penalty within one club-length of the point thus determined on ground which fulfils (a), (b) and (c) above.

(ii) In a Hazard: If the ball lies in or touches a hazard, the player shall lift and drop the ball either:

(a) Without penalty, in the hazard, as near as possible to the spot where the ball lay, but not nearer the hole, on ground which affords maximum available relief from the condition; or

(b) *Under penalty of one stroke*, outside the hazard, keeping the point where the ball lay directly between the hole and the spot on which the ball is dropped.

Exception: If a ball lies in or touches a water hazard (including a lateral water hazard), the player is not entitled to relief without penalty from a hole, cast or runway made by a burrowing animal, a reptile or a bird. The player shall play the ball as it lies or proceed under Rule 26-1.

(iii) On the Putting Green: If the ball lies on the putting green, the player shall lift the ball and place it without penalty in the nearest position to where it lay which affords maximum available relief from the condition, but not nearer the hole nor in a hazard.

The ball may be cleaned when lifted under Rule 25-1b.

(Ball rolling to a position where there is interference by the condition from which relief was taken – see Rule 20-2c(v).)

Exception: A player may not obtain relief under Rule 25-1b if (a) it is clearly unreasonable for him to play a stroke because of interference by anything other than a condition covered by Rule 25-1a or (b) interference by such a condition would occur only through use of an unnecessarily abnormal stance, swing or direction of play.

c. Ball Lost Under Condition Covered by Rule 25-1

It is a question of fact whether a ball lost after having been struck toward a condition covered by Rule 25-1 is lost under such condition. In order to treat the ball as lost under such condition, there must be reasonable evidence to that effect. In the absence of such evidence, the ball must be treated as a lost ball and Rule 27 applies.

(i) Outside a Hazard: If a ball is lost outside a hazard under a condition covered by Rule 25-1, the player may take relief as follows: the point on the course nearest to where the ball last crossed the margin of the area shall be determined which (a) is not nearer the hole than where the ball last crossed the margin, (b) avoids interference by the condition and (c) is not in a hazard or on a putting green. He shall drop a ball without penalty within one club-length of the point thus determined on ground which fulfils (a), (b) and (c) above.

(ii) In a Hazard: If a ball is lost in a hazard under a condition covered by Rule 25-1, the player may drop a ball either:

(a) Without penalty, in the hazard, as near as possible to the point at which the original ball last crossed the margin of the area, but not nearer the hole, on ground, which affords maximum available relief from the condition; or

(b) *Under penalty of one stroke*, outside the hazard, keeping the point at which the original ball last crossed the margin of the hazard directly between the hole and the spot on which the ball is dropped.

Exception: If a ball lies in a water hazard (including a lateral water hazard), the player is not entitled to relief without penalty for a ball lost in a hole, cast or runway made by a burrowing animal, a reptile or a bird. The player shall proceed under Rule 26-1.

25-2. Embedded Ball

A ball embedded in its own pitch-mark in the ground in any closely mown area through the green may be lifted, cleaned and dropped, without penalty, as near as possible to the spot where it lay but not nearer the hole. "Closely mown area" means any area of the course, including paths through the rough, cut to fairway height or less.

25-3. Wrong Putting Green

A player must not play a ball which lies on a putting green other than that of the hole being played. The ball must be lifted and the player must proceed as follows: the point on the course nearest to where the ball lies shall be determined which (a) is not nearer the hole and (b) is not in a hazard or on a putting green. The player shall lift the ball and drop it without penalty within one club-length of the point thus determined on ground which fulfils (a) and (b) above. The ball may be cleaned when so lifted.

Note: Unless otherwise prescribed by the Committee, the term "a putting green other than that of the hole being played" includes a practice putting green or pitching green on the course.

PENALTY FOR BREACH OF RULE: *Match play – Loss of hole; Stroke play – Two strokes.*

Rule 26. Water Hazards (Including Lateral Water Hazards)

Definitions

A "water hazard" is any sea, lake, pond, river, ditch, surface drainage ditch or other open water course (whether or not containing water) and anything of a similar nature.

All ground or water within the margin of a water hazard is part of the water hazard. The margin of a water hazard extends vertically upwards and downwards. Stakes and lines defining the margins of water hazards are in the hazards.

Note: Water hazards (other than lateral water hazards) should be defined by yellow stakes or lines.

A "lateral water hazard" is a water hazard or that part of a water hazard so situated that it is not possible or is deemed by the Committee to be impracticable to drop a ball behind the water hazard in accordance with Rule 26-1b.

That part of a water hazard to be played as a lateral water hazard should be distinctively marked.

Note: Lateral water hazards should be defined by red stakes or lines.

26-1. Ball in Water Hazard

It is a question of fact whether a ball lost after having been struck toward a water hazard is lost inside or outside the hazard. In order to treat the ball as lost in the hazard, there must be reasonable evidence that the ball lodged in it. In the absence of such evidence, the ball must be treated as a lost ball and Rule 27 applies.

If a ball lies in, touches or is lost in a water hazard (whether the ball lies in water or not), the player may *under penalty of one stroke:*

a. Play a ball as nearly as possible at the spot from which the original ball was last played (see Rule 20-5); or

b. Drop a ball behind the water hazard, keeping the point at which the original ball last crossed the margin of the water hazard directly between the hole and the spot on which the ball is dropped, with no limit to how far behind the water hazard the ball may be dropped; or

c. *As additional options available only if the ball lies in, touches or is lost in a lateral water hazard,* drop a ball outside the water hazard within two club-lengths of (i) the point where the original ball last crossed the margin of the water hazard or (ii) a point on the opposite margin of the water hazard equidistant from the hole. The ball must be dropped and come to rest not nearer the hole than the point where the original ball last crossed the margin of the water hazard.

The ball may be cleaned when lifted under this Rule.

(Ball moving in water in a water hazard – see Rule 14-6.)

26-2. Ball Played Within Water Hazard

a. Ball Comes to Rest in Hazard

If a ball played from within a water hazard comes to rest in the hazard after the stroke, the player may:

(i) proceed under Rule 26-1; or
(ii) *under penalty of one stroke,* play a ball as nearly as possible at the spot from which the last stroke from outside the hazard was played (see Rule 20-5).

If the player proceeds under Rule 26-1a, he may elect not to play the dropped ball. If he so elects, he may:

(a) proceed under Rule 26-1b, *adding the additional penalty of one stroke* prescribed by that Rule; or

(b) proceed under Rule 26-1c, if applicable, *adding the additional penalty of one stroke* prescribed by that Rule; or

(c) *add an additional penalty of one stroke* and play a ball as nearly as possible at the spot from which the last stroke from outside the hazard was played (see Rule 20-5).

b. Ball Lost or Unplayable Outside Hazard or Out of Bounds

If a ball played from within a water hazard is lost or declared unplayable outside the hazard or is out of bounds, the player, after taking *a penalty of one stroke* under Rule 27-1 or 28a, may:

(i) play a ball as nearly as possible at the spot in the hazard from which the original ball was last played (see Rule 20-5); or
(ii) proceed under Rule 26-1b, or if applicable Rule 26-1c, *adding the additional penalty of one stroke* prescribed by the Rule and using as the reference point the point where the original ball last crossed the margin of the hazard before it came to rest in the hazard; or
(iii) *add an additional penalty of one stroke* and play a ball as nearly as possible at the spot from which the last stroke from outside the hazard was played (see Rule 20-5).

Note 1: When proceeding under Rule 26-2b, the player is not required to drop a ball under Rule 27-1 or 28a. If he does drop a ball, he is not required to play it. He may alternatively proceed under clause (ii) or (iii).

Note 2: If a ball played from within a water hazard is declared unplayable outside the hazard, nothing in Rule 26-2b precludes the player from proceeding under Rule 28b or c.

PENALTY FOR BREACH OF RULE: *Match play – Loss of hole; Stroke play – Two strokes.*

Rule 27. Ball Lost or Out of Bounds; Provisional Ball

If the original ball is lost in an immovable obstruction (Rule 24-2) or under a condition covered by Rule 25-1 (Casual water, ground under repair and certain damage to the course), the player may proceed under the applicable Rule. If the original ball is lost in a water hazard, the player shall proceed under Rule 26.

Such Rules may not be used unless there is reasonable evidence that the ball is lost in an immovable obstruction, under a condition covered by Rule 25-1 or in a water hazard.

Definitions

A ball is "lost" if:

a. It is not found or identified as his by the player within five minutes after the player's side or his or their caddies have begun to search for it; or

b. The player has put another ball into play under the Rules, even though he may not have searched for the original ball; or

c. The player has played any stroke with a provisional ball from the place where the original ball is likely to be or from a point nearer the hole than that place, whereupon the provisional ball becomes the ball in play.

Time spent in playing a wrong ball is not counted in the five-minute period allowed for search.

"Out of bounds" is ground on which play is prohibited.

When out of bounds is defined by reference to stakes or a fence, or as being beyond stakes or a fence, the out of bounds line is determined by the nearest inside points of the stakes or fence posts at ground level excluding angled supports.

When out of bounds is defined by a line on the ground, the line itself is out of bounds.

The out of bounds line extends vertically upwards and downwards.

A ball is out of bounds when all of it lies out of bounds.

A player may stand out of bounds to play a ball lying within bounds.

A "provisional ball" is a ball played under Rule 27-2 for a ball which may be lost outside a water hazard or may be out of bounds.

27-1. Ball Lost or Out of Bounds

If a ball is lost outside a water hazard or is out of bounds, the player shall play a ball, *under penalty of one stroke*, as nearly as possible at the spot from which the original ball was last played (see Rule 20-5).

PENALTY FOR BREACH OF RULE 27-1:
Match play – Loss of hole;
Stroke play – Two strokes.

27-2. Provisional Ball

a. Procedure

If a ball may be lost outside a water hazard or may be out of bounds, to save time the player may play another ball provisionally as nearly as possible at the spot from which the original ball was played (see Rule 20-5). The player shall inform his opponent in match play or his marker or a fellow-competitor in stroke play that he intends to play a provisional ball, and he shall play it before he or his partner goes forward to search for the original ball. If he fails to do so and plays another ball, such ball is not a provisional ball and becomes the ball in play *under penalty of stroke and distance* (Rule 27-1); the original ball is deemed to be lost.

b. When Provisional Ball Becomes Ball in Play

The player may play a provisional ball until he reaches the place where the original ball is likely to be. If he plays a stroke with the provisional ball from the place where the original ball is likely to be or from a point nearer the hole than that place, the original ball is deemed to be lost and the provisional ball becomes the ball in play *under penalty of stroke and distance* (Rule 27-1).

If the original ball is lost outside a water hazard or is out of bounds, the provisional ball becomes the ball in play, *under penalty of stroke and distance* (Rule 27-1).

c. When Provisional Ball to Be Abandoned

If the original ball is neither lost outside a water hazard nor out of bounds, the player shall abandon the provisional ball and continue play with the original ball. If he fails to do so, any further strokes played with the provisional ball shall constitute playing a wrong ball and the provisions of Rule 15 shall apply.

Note: If the original ball lies in a water hazard, the player shall play the ball as it lies or proceed under Rule 26. If it is lost in a water hazard or unplayable, the player shall proceed under Rule 26 or 28, whichever is applicable.

Rule 28. Ball Unplayable

The player may declare his ball unplayable at any place on the course except when the ball lies in or touches a water hazard. The player is the sole judge as to whether his ball is unplayable.

If the player deems his ball to be unplayable, he shall, *under penalty of one stroke*:

a. Play a ball as nearly as possible at the spot from which the original ball was last played (see Rule 20-5); or

b. Drop a ball within two club-lengths of the spot where the ball lay, but not nearer the hole; or

c. Drop a ball behind the point where the ball lay, keeping that point directly between the hole and the spot on which the ball is dropped, with no limit to how far behind that point the ball may be dropped.

If the unplayable ball lies in a bunker the player may proceed under Clause a, b or c. If he elects to proceed under Clause b or c, a ball must be dropped in the bunker.

The ball may be cleaned when lifted under this Rule.

PENALTY FOR BREACH OF RULE:
Match play – Loss of hole;
Stroke play – Two strokes.

OTHER FORMS OF PLAY

Rule 29. Threesomes and Foursomes

Definitions

Threesome: A match in which one plays against two, and each side plays one ball.

Foursome: A match in which two play against two, and each side plays one ball.

29-1. General

In a threesome or a foursome, during any stipulated round the partners shall play alternately from the teeing grounds and alternately during the play of each hole. Penalty strokes do not affect the order of play.

29-2. Match Play

If a player plays when his partner should have played, *his side shall lose the hole.*

29-3. Stroke Play

If the partners play a stroke or strokes in incorrect order, such stroke or strokes shall be cancelled and *the side shall incur a penalty of two strokes.* The side shall correct the error by playing a ball in correct order as nearly as possible at the spot from which it first played in incorrect order (see Rule 20-5). If the side plays a stroke from the next teeing ground without first correcting the error or, in the case of the last hole of the round, leaves the putting green without declaring its intention to correct the error, *the side shall be disqualified.*

Rule 30. Three-Ball, Best-Ball and Four-Ball Match Play

Definitions

Three-Ball: A match play competition in which three play against one another, each playing his own ball. Each player is playing two distinct matches.

Best-Ball: A match in which one plays against the better ball of two or the best ball of three players.

Four-Ball: A match in which two play their better ball against the better ball of two other players.

30-1. Rules of Golf Apply

The Rules of Golf, so far as they are not at variance with the following special Rules, shall apply to three-ball, best-ball and four-ball matches.

30-2. Three-Ball Match Play

a. Ball at Rest Moved by an Opponent

Except as otherwise provided in the Rules, if the player's ball is touched or moved by an opponent, his caddie or equipment other than during search, Rule 18-3b applies. *That opponent shall incur a penalty stroke in his match with the player,* but not in his match with the other opponent.

b. Ball Deflected or Stopped by an Opponent Accidentally

If a player's ball is accidentally deflected or stopped by an opponent, his caddie or equipment, no penalty shall be incurred. In his match with that opponent the player may play the ball as it lies or, before another stroke is played by either side, he may cancel the stroke and play a ball without penalty as nearly as possible at the spot from which the original ball was last played (see Rule 20-5). In his match with the other opponent, the ball shall be played as it lies.

Exception: Ball striking person attending flagstick – see Rule 17-3b.

(Ball purposely deflected or stopped by opponent – see Rule 1-2.)

30-3. Best-Ball and Four-Ball Match Play

a. Representation of Side

A side may be represented by one partner for all or any part of a match; all partners need not be present. An absent partner may join a match between holes, but not during play of a hole.

b. Maximum of Fourteen Clubs

The side shall be penalised for a breach of Rule 4-4 by any partner.

c. Order of Play

Balls belonging to the same side may be played in the order the side considers best.

d. Wrong Ball

If a player plays a stroke with a wrong ball except in a hazard, *he shall be disqualified for that hole*, but his partner incurs no penalty even if the wrong ball belongs to him. If the wrong ball belongs to another player, its owner shall place a ball on the spot from which the wrong ball was first played.

e. Disqualification of Side

(i) *A side shall be disqualified* for a breach of any of the following by any partner:

Rule 1-3 – Agreement to Waive Rules.
Rule 4-1, -2 or -3 – Clubs.
Rule 5-1 or -2 – The Ball
Rule 6-2a – Handicap (playing off higher handicap).
Rule 6-4 – Caddie.
Rule 6-7 – Undue Delay (repeated offence)
Rule 14-3 – Artificial Devices and Unusual Equipment.

(ii) *A side shall be disqualified* for a breach of any of the following by all partners:

Rule 6-3 – Time of Starting and Groups.
Rule 6-8 – Discontinuance of Play.

f. Effect of Other Penalties

If a player's breach of a Rule assists his partner's play or adversely affects an opponent's play, *the partner incurs the applicable penalty in addition to any penalty incurred by the player.*

In all other cases where a player incurs a penalty for breach of a Rule, the penalty shall not apply to his partner. Where the penalty is stated to be loss of hole, the effect shall be to disqualify the player for that hole.

g. Another Form of Match Played Concurrently

In a best-ball or four-ball match when another form of match is played concurrently, the above special Rules shall apply.

Rule 31. Four-Ball Stroke Play

In four-ball stroke play two competitors play as partners, each playing his own ball. The lower score of the partners is the score for the hole. If one partner fails to complete the play of a hole, there is no penalty.

31-1. Rules of Golf Apply

The Rules of Golf, so far as they are not at variance with the following special Rules, shall apply to four-ball stroke play.

31-2. Representation of Side

A side may be represented by either partner for all or any part of a stipulated round; both partners need not be present. An absent competitor may join his partner between holes, but not during play of a hole.

31-3. Maximum of Fourteen Clubs

The side shall be penalised for a breach of Rule 4-4 by either partner.

31-4. Scoring

The marker is required to record for each hole only the gross score of whichever partner's score is to count. The gross scores to count must be individually identifiable; otherwise *the side shall be disqualified.* Only one of the partners need be responsible for complying with Rule 6-6b.

(Wrong score – see Rule 31-7a.)

31-5. Order of Play

Balls belonging to the same side may be played in the order the side considers best.

31-6. Wrong Ball

If a competitor plays a stroke with a wrong ball except in a hazard, *he shall add two penalty strokes to his score for the hole* and shall then play the correct ball. His partner incurs no penalty even if the wrong ball belongs to him.

If the wrong ball belongs to another competitor, its owner shall place a ball on the spot from which the wrong ball was first played.

31-7. Disqualification Penalties

a. Breach by One Partner

A side shall be disqualified from the competition for a breach of any of the following by either partner:

Rule 1-3 – Agreement to Waive Rules.
Rule 3-4 – Refusal to Comply with Rule.
Rule 4-1, -2 or -3 Clubs.
Rule 5-1 -2 – The Ball.
Rule 6-2b – Handicap (playing off higher handicap; failure to record handicap).
Rule 6-4 – Caddie.
Rule 6-6b – Signing and Returning Card.
Rule 6-6d – Wrong Score for Hole, i.e. when the recorded score of the partner whose score is to count is lower than actually taken. If the recorded score of the partner whose score is to count is higher than actually taken, it must stand as returned.
Rule 6-7 – Undue Delay (repeated offence).
Rule 7-1 – Practice Before or Between Rounds.
Rule 14-3 – Artificial Devices and Unusual Equipment.
Rule 31-4 – Gross Scores to count Not Individually Identifiable.

b. Breach by Both Partners

A side shall be disqualified:

(i) for a breach by both partners of Rule 6-3 (Time of Starting and Groups) or Rule 6-8 (Discontinuance of Play), or

(ii) if, at the same hole, each partner is in breach of a Rule the penalty for which is disqualification from the competition or for a hole.

c. For the Hole Only

In all other cases where a breach of a Rule would entail disqualification, *the competitor shall be disqualified only for the hole at which the breach occurred.*

31-8. Effect of Other Penalties

If a competitor's breach of a Rule assists his partner's play, *the partner incurs the applicable penalty in addition to any penalty incurred by the competitor.*

In all other cases where a competitor incurs a penalty for breach of a Rule, the penalty shall not apply to his partner.

Rule 32. Bogey, Par and Stableford Competitions

32-1. Conditions

Bogey, par and Stableford competitions are forms of stroke competition in which play is against a fixed score at each hole. The Rules for stroke play, so far as they are not at variance with the following special Rules, apply.

a. Bogey and Par Competitions

The reckoning for bogey and par competitions is made as in match play. Any hole for which a competitor makes no return shall be regarded as a loss. The winner is the competitor who is most successful in the aggregate of holes.

The marker is responsible for marking only the gross number of strokes for each hole where the competitor makes a net score equal to or less than the fixed score.

Note: Maximum of 14 Clubs – Penalties as in match play – see Rule 4-4.

b. Stableford Competitions

The reckoning in Stableford competitions is made by points awarded in relation to a fixed score at each hole as follows:

Hole Played in	Points
More than one over fixed score or no score returned	0
One over fixed score	1
Fixed score	2
One under fixed score	3
Two under fixed score	4
Three under fixed score	5
Four under fixed score	6

The winner is the competitor who scores the highest number of points.

The marker shall be responsible for marking only the gross number of strokes at each hole where the competitor's net score earns one or more points.

Note: Maximum of 14 Clubs (Rule 4-4) – Penalties applied as follows: From total points scored for the round, deduction of two points for each hole at which any breach occurred; maximum deduction per round: four points.

32-2. Disqualification Penalties

a. From the Competition

A competitor shall be disqualified from the competition for a breach of any of the following:

Rule 1-3 – Agreement to Waive Rules.
Rule 3-4 – Refusal to Comply with Rule.
Rule 4-1, -2 or -3 – Clubs.
Rule 5-1 or -2 – The Ball.
Rule 6-2b – Handicap (playing off higher handicap; failure to record handicap).
Rule 6-3 – Time of Starting and Groups.
Rule 6-4 – Caddie.
Rule 6-6b – Signing and Returning Card.
Rule 6-6d – Wrong Score for Hole, except that no penalty shall be incurred when a breach of this Rule does not affect the result of the hole.
Rule 6-7 – Undue Delay (repeated offence).
Rule 6-8 – Discontinuance of Play.
Rule 7-1 – Practice Before or Between Rounds.
Rule 14-3 – Artificial Devices and Unusual Equipment.

b. For a Hole

In all other cases where a breach of a Rule would entail disqualification, *the competitor shall be disqualified only for the hole at which the breach occurred.*

ADMINISTRATION

Rule 33. The Committee

33-1. Conditions; Waiving Rule

The Committee shall lay down the conditions under which a competition is to be played.

The Committee has no power to waive a Rule of Golf.

Certain special rules governing stroke play are so substantially different from those governing match play that combining the two forms of play is not practicable and is not permitted. The results of matches played and the scores returned in these circumstances shall not be accepted.

In stroke play the Committee may limit a referee's duties.

33-2. The Course

a. Defining Bounds and Margins

The Committee shall define accurately:

(i) the course and out of bounds,
(ii) the margins of water hazards and lateral water hazards,
(iii) ground under repair, and
(iv) obstructions and integral parts of the course.

b. New Holes

New holes should be made on the day on which a stroke competition begins and at such other times as the Committee considers necessary, provided all competitors in a single round play with each hole cut in the same position.

Exception: When it is impossible for a damaged hole to be repaired so that it conforms with the Definition, the Committee may make a new hole in a nearby similar position.

c. Practice Ground

Where there is no practice ground available outside the area of a competition course, the Committee should lay down the area on which players may practise on any day of a competition, if it is practicable to do so. On any day of a stroke competition, the Committee should not normally permit practice on or to a putting green or from a hazard of the competition course.

d. Course Unplayable

If the Committee or its authorised representative considers that for any reason the course is not in a playable condition or that there are circumstances which render the proper playing of the game impossible, it may, in match play or stroke play, order a temporary suspension of play or, in stroke play, declare play null and void and cancel all scores for the round in question. When play has been temporarily suspended, it shall be resumed from where it was discontinued, even though resumption occurs on a subsequent day. When a round is cancelled, all penalties incurred in that round are cancelled.

(Procedure in discontinuing play – see Rule 6-8.)

33-3. Times of Starting and Groups

The Committee shall lay down the times of starting and, in stroke play, arrange the groups in which competitors shall play.

When a match play competition is played over an extended period, the Committee shall lay down the limit of time within which each round shall be completed. When players are allowed to arrange the date of their match within these limits, the Committee should announce that the match must be played at a stated time on the last day of the period unless the players agree to a prior date.

33-4. Handicap Stroke Table

The Committee shall publish a table indicating the order of holes at which handicap strokes are to be given or received.

33-5. Score Card

In stroke play, the Committee shall issue for each competitor a score card containing the date and the competitor's name, or in foursome, or four-ball stroke play, the competitors' names.

In stroke play, the Committee is responsible for the addition of scores and application of the handicap recorded on the card.

In four-ball stroke play, the Committee is responsible for recording the better-ball score for each hole and in the process applying the handicaps recorded on the card, and adding the better-ball scores.

In bogey, par and Stableford competitions, the Committee is responsible for applying the handicap recorded on the card and determining the result of each hole and the overall result or points total.

33-6. Decision of Ties

The Committee shall announce the manner, day and time for the decision of a halved match or of a tie, whether played on level terms or under handicap.

A halved match shall not be decided by stroke play. A tie in stroke play shall not be decided by a match.

33-7. Disqualification Penalty; Committee Discretion

A penalty of disqualification may in exceptional individual cases be waived, modified or imposed if the Committee considers such action warranted. Any penalty less than disqualification shall not be waived or modified.

33-8. Local Rules

a. Policy

The Committee may make and publish Local Rules for abnormal conditions if they are consistent with the policy of the Governing Authority for the country concerned as set forth in Appendix I to these Rules.

b. Waiving Penalty

A penalty imposed by a Rule of Golf shall not be waived by a Local Rule.

Rule 34. Disputes and Decisions

34-1. Claims and Penalties

a. Match Play

In match play if a claim is lodged with the Committee under Rule 2-5, a decision should be given as soon as possible so that the state of the match may, if necessary, be adjusted.

If a claim is not made within the time limit provided by Rule 2-5, it shall not be considered unless it is based on facts previously unknown to the player making the claim and the player making the claim had been given wrong information (Rules 6-2a and 9) by an opponent. In any case, no later claim shall be considered after the result of the match has been officially announced, unless the Committee is satisfied that the opponent knew he was giving wrong information.

b. Stroke Play

In stroke play no penalty shall be rescinded, modified or imposed after the competition has closed, except that a penalty of disqualification shall be imposed at any time after the competition has closed if a competitor:

(i) returned a score for any hole lower than actually taken (Rule 6-6d) for any reason other than failure to include a penalty which he did not know he had incurred; or

(ii) returned a score card on which he had recorded a handicap which he knew was higher than that to which he was entitled, and this affected the number of strokes received (Rule 6-2b); or

(iii) was in breach of Rule 1-3

A competition is deemed to have closed when the result has been officially announced or, in stroke play qualifying followed by match play, when the player has teed off in his first match.

34-2. Referee's Decision

If a referee has been appointed by the Committee, his decision shall be final.

34-3. Committee's Decision

In the absence of a referee, any dispute or doubtful point on the Rules shall be referred to the Committee, whose decision shall be final.

If the Committee cannot come to a decision, it shall refer the dispute or doubtful point to the Rules of Golf Committee of the Royal & Ancient Golf Club of St Andrews, whose decision shall be final.

If the dispute or doubtful point has not been referred to the Rules of Golf Committee, the player or players have the right to refer an agreed statement through the Secretary of the Club to the Rules of Golf Committee for an opinion as to the correctness of the decision given. The reply will be sent to the Secretary of the Club or Clubs concerned.

If play is conducted other than in accordance with the Rules of Golf, the Rules of Golf Committee will not give a decision on any question.

APPENDIX I

LOCAL RULES (RULE 33-8) AND CONDITIONS OF THE COMPETITION (RULE 33-1)

Part A Local Rules

The Committee may make and publish Local Rules (for Specimen Local Rules see Part B) for such abnormal conditions as:

1. Obstructions

a. General
Clarifying the status of objects which may be obstructions (Rule 24).

Declaring any construction to be an integral part of the course and, accordingly, not an obstruction, e.g. built-up sides of teeing grounds, putting greens and bunkers (Rules 24 and 33-2a).

b. Stones in Bunkers
Allowing the removal of stones in bunkers by declaring them to be "movable obstructions" (Rule 24).

c. Roads and Paths
(i) Declaring artificial surfaces and sides of roads and paths to be integral parts of the course, or
(ii) Providing relief of the type afforded under Rule 24-2b from roads and paths not having artificial surfaces and sides if they could unfairly affect play.

d. Fixed Sprinkler Heads
Providing relief from intervention by fixed sprinkler heads within two club-lengths of the putting green when the ball lies within two club-lengths of the sprinkler head.

e. Protection of Young Trees
Providing relief for the protection of young trees.

f. Temporary Immovable Obstructions
Specimen Local Rules for application in Tournament Play are available from the Royal & Ancient Golf Club of St Andrews.

2. Areas of the Course Requiring Preservation

Assisting preservation of the course by defining areas, including turf nurseries, young plantations and other parts of the course under cultivation, as "ground under repair" from which play is prohibited.

3. Unusual Damage to the Course or Accumulation of Leaves (or the like)

Declaring such areas to be "ground under repair" (Rule 25).

Note: For relief from aeration holes see Specimen Local Rule 8 in part B of this Appendix.

4. Extreme Wetness, Mud, Poor Conditions and Protection of Course

(a.) Lifting an Embedded Ball, Cleaning
Where the ground is unusually soft, the Committee may, by temporary Local Rule, allow the lifting of a ball which is embedded in its own pitch-mark in the ground in an area "through the green" which is not "closely mown" (Rule 25-2) if it is satisfied that the proper playing of the game would otherwise be prevented. The Local Rule shall be for that day only or for a short period, and if practicable shall be confined to specified areas. The Committee shall withdraw the Local Rule as soon as conditions warrant and should not print it on the score card.

In similarly adverse conditions, the Committee may, by temporary Local Rule, permit the cleaning of a ball "through the green".

(b.) "Preferred Lies" and "Winter Rules"
Adverse conditions, including the poor condition of the course or the existence of mud, are sometimes so general, particularly during winter months, that the Committee may decide to grant relief by Local Rule either to protect the course or to promote fair and pleasant play. Such Local Rule shall be withdrawn as soon as conditions warrant.

5. Other Local Conditions which Interfere with the Proper Playing of the Game

If this necessitates modification of a Rule of Golf the approval of the Governing Authority must be obtained.

Other matters which the Committee could cover by Local Rule include:

6. Water Hazards

a. Lateral Water Hazards
Clarifying the status of sections of water hazards which may be lateral water hazards (Rule 26).

b. Provisional Ball
Permitting play of a provisional ball for a ball which may be in a water hazard of such character that it would be impracticable to determine whether the ball is in the hazard or to do so would unduly delay play. In such a case, if a provisional ball is played and the original ball is in a water hazard, the player may play the original ball as it lies or continue the provisional ball in play, but he may not proceed under Rule 26-1.

7. Defining Bounds and Margins

Specifying means used to define out of bounds, hazards, water hazards, lateral water hazards and ground under repair.

8. Dropping Zones

Establishing special areas in which balls may or shall be dropped when it is not feasible or practicable to proceed exactly in conformity with Rule 24-2b (Immovable Obstruction), Rule 25-1b or Rule 25-1c (Ground Under Repair), Rule 26-1 (Water Hazards and Lateral Water Hazards) or Rule 28 (Ball Unplayable).

9. Priority on the Course

The Committee may make regulations governing Priority on the Course (see Etiquette).

Part B Specimen Local Rules

Within the policy set out in Part A of this Appendix the Committee may adopt a Specimen Local Rule by referring, on a score card or notice board, to the examples given below. However Specimen Local Rules 5, 6 or 7 should not be printed or referred to on a score card as they are all of limited duration.

1. Fixed Sprinkler Heads

All fixed sprinkler heads are immovable obstructions and relief from interference by them may be obtained under Rule 24-2. In addition, if such an obstruction on or within two club-lengths of the putting green of the hole being played intervenes on the line of play between the ball and the hole, the player may obtain relief, without penalty, as follows:

If the ball lies off the putting green but not in a hazard and is within two club-lengths of the intervening obstruction, it may be lifted, cleaned and dropped at the nearest point to where the ball lay which (a) is not nearer the hole, (b) avoids such intervention and (c) is not in a hazard or on a putting green.

PENALTY FOR BREACH OF LOCAL RULE:
Match play – Loss of hole; Stroke play – Two strokes.

2. Stones in Bunkers

Stones in bunkers are movable obstructions (Rule 24-1 applies).

3. Protection of Young Trees

Protection of young trees identified by ______. If such a tree interferes with a player's stance or the area of his intended swing, the ball must be lifted, without penalty, and dropped in accordance with the procedure prescribed in Rule 24-2b(i) (Immovable Obstruction). The ball may be cleaned when so lifted.

PENALTY FOR BREACH OF LOCAL RULE:
Match play – Loss of hole; Stroke play – Two strokes.

4. Ground Under Repair: Play Prohibited

If a player's ball lies in an area of "ground under repair" from which play is prohibited, or if such an area of "ground under repair" interferes with the player's stance or the area of his intended swing the player must take relief under Rule 25-1.

PENALTY FOR BREACH OF LOCAL RULE:
Match play – Loss of hole; Stroke play – Two strokes.

5. Lifting an Embedded Ball

(Specify the area if practicable) . . . through the green, a ball embedded in its own pitch-mark in ground other than sand may be lifted, cleaned and dropped, without penalty, as near as possible to the spot where it lay but not nearer the hole.

PENALTY FOR BREACH OF LOCAL RULE:
Match play – Loss of hole; Stroke play – Two strokes.

6. Cleaning Ball

(Specify the area if practicable) . . . through the green a ball may be lifted, cleaned and replaced without penalty.

Note: The position of the ball shall be marked before it is lifted under this Local Rule – see Rule 20-1.

7. "Preferred Lies" and "Winter Rules"

A ball lying on any "closely mown area" through the green may, without penalty, be moved or may be lifted, cleaned and placed within six inches of where it originally lay, but not nearer the hole. After the ball has been so moved or placed, it is in play.

PENALTY FOR BREACH OF LOCAL RULE:
Match play – Loss of hole; Stroke play – Two strokes.

8. Aeration Holes

If a ball comes to rest in an aeration hole, the player may, without penalty, lift the ball and clean it. Through the green, the player shall drop the ball as near as possible to where it lay, but not nearer the hole. On the putting green, the player shall place the ball at the nearest spot not nearer the hole which avoids such situation.

PENALTY FOR BREACH OF LOCAL RULE:
Match play – Loss of hole; Stroke play – Two strokes.

Part C Conditions of the Competition

Rule 33-1 provides, "The Committee shall lay down the conditions under which a competition is to be played". Such conditions should include many matters such as method of entry, eligibility, number of rounds to be played, settling ties, etc. which is not appropriate to deal with in the Rules of Golf or this Appendix.

However there are four matters which might be covered in the Conditions of Competition to which the Committee's attention is specifically drawn by way of a Note to the appropriate Rule. These are:

1. Specification of the Ball (Note to Rule 5-1)

Arising from the regulations for ball-testing

under Rule 5-1, Lists of Conforming Golf Balls will be issued from time to time.

It is recommended that the Lists should be applied to all National and County (or equivalent) Championships and to all top class events when restricted to low handicap players. In order to apply the Lists to a particular competition the Committee must lay this down in the Conditions of the Competition This should be referred to in the Entry Form, and also a notice should be displayed on the Club notice board and at the 1st Tee along the following lines:

.... (Name of Event) ....

.... (Date and Club) ....

The ball the player uses shall be named on the current List of Conforming Golf Balls issued by the Royal & Ancient Golf Club of St. Andrews.

Note 1: A penalty statement will be required and must be either:

(a) "PENALTY FOR BREACH OF CONDITION: *Disqualification*"

or

b) "PENALTY FOR BREACH OF CONDITION: *Match play – Loss of each hole at which a breach occurred: Stroke play – Two strokes for each hole at which a breach occurred.*"

If option (b) is adopted this only applies to use of a ball which, whilst not on the List of Conforming Golf Balls, does conform to the specifications set forth in Rule 5 and Appendix III. The penalty for use of a ball which does not so conform is disqualification.

Note 2: In Club events it is recommended that no such condition be applied.

2. Time of Starting (Note to Rule 6-3a)

If the Committee wishes to act in accordance with the Note, the following wording is recommended:

"If, in the absence of circumstances which warrant waiving the penalty of disqualification as provided in Rule 33-7, the player arrives at his starting point, ready to play, within five minutes after his starting time, the penalty for failure to start on time is loss of the first hole in match play or two strokes at the first hole in stroke play."

3. Practice

The Committee may make regulations governing practice in accordance with the Note to Rule 7-1. Exception (c) to Rule 7-2, Note 2 to Rule 7 and Rule 33-2c.

4. Advice in Team Competitions

If the Committee wishes to act in accordance with the Note, the following wording is recommended:

"In accordance with the Note to Rule 8 of the Rules of Golf each team may appoint one person (in addition to the persons from whom advice may be asked under that Rule) who may give advice to members of that team. Such person [*if it is desired to insert any restriction on who may be nominated insert such restriction here*] shall be identified to the Committee prior to the start of the competition."

APPENDICES II AND III

Any design in a club or ball which is not covered by Rules 4 and 5 and Appendices II and III, or which might significantly change the nature of the game, will be ruled on by the Royal & Ancient Golf Club of St Andrews and the United States Golf Association.

Note: Equipment approved for use or marketed prior to 1st January 1988 which conformed to the Rules in effect in 1987 but does not conform to the 1988 and subsequent Rules may be used until 31st December 1995; thereafter all equipment must conform to the current Rules.

Appendix II

Design of Clubs

Rule 4-1 prescribes general regulations for the design of clubs. The following paragraphs, which provide some detailed specifications and clarify how Rule 4-1 is interpreted, should be read in conjunction with this Rule.

4-1a. General

Adjustability – Exception for Putters. Clubs other than putters shall not be designed to be adjustable except for weight.

Some other forms of adjustability are permitted in the design of a putter provided that:

(i) the adjustment cannot be readily made;

(ii) all adjustable parts are firmly fixed and there is no reasonable likelihood of them working loose during a round; and

(iii) all configurations of adjustment conform with the Rules.

The disqualification penalty for purposely changing the playing characteristics of a club during a stipulated round (Rule 4-2) applies to all clubs including a putter.

Note: It is recommended that all putters with adjustable parts be submitted to the Royal & Ancient Golf Club of St Andrews for a ruling.

4-1b. Shaft

Generally Straight. The shaft shall be at least 18 inches (457mm) in length. It shall be straight from the top of the grip to a point not more than 5 inches (127mm) above the sole, measured along the axis of the shaft and the neck or socket.

Bending and Twisting Properties. The shaft must be so designed and manufactured that at any point along its length:

(i) it bends in such a way that the deflection is the same regardless of how the shaft is rotated about its longitudinal axis; and

(ii) it twists the same amount in both directions.

Attachment to Clubhead. The neck or socket must not be more than 5 inches (127mm) in length, measured from the top of the neck or socket to the sole along its axis. The shaft and the neck or socket must remain in line with the heel, or with a point to the right or left of the heel, when the club is viewed in the address position. The distance between the axis of the shaft or the neck or socket and the back of the heel must not exceed 0.625 inches (16mm).

Exception for Putters: The shaft or neck or socket of a putter may be fixed at any point in the head and need not remain in line with the heel. The axis of the shaft from the top to a point not more than 5 inches (127mm) above the sole must diverge from the vertical in the toe-heel plane by at least 10 degrees when the club is in its normal address position.

4-1c. Grip

(i) For clubs other than putters, the grip must be generally circular in cross-section, except that a continuous, straight, slightly raised rib may be incorporated along the full length of the grip.

(ii) A putter grip may have a non-circular cross-section, provided the cross-section has no concavity and remains generally similar throughout the length of the grip.

(iii) The grip may be tapered but must not have any bulge or waist.

(iv) For clubs other than putters the axis of the grip must coincide with the axis of the shaft.

(v) The cross-sectional dimension of a grip measured in any direction shall not exceed 1.75 inches (45mm).

(vi) A putter may have more than one grip, provided each is circular in cross-section and the axis of each coincides with the axis of the shaft

Note: Putters approved for use or marketed prior to 1st January 1992 which are in breach of clause (vi), but otherwise conform, may be used until 31st December 1992.

4-1d. Clubhead

Dimensions. The dimensions of a clubhead (see diagram) are measured, with the clubhead in its normal address position, on horizontal lines between vertical projections of the outermost points of (i) the heel and the toe and (ii) the face and the back. If the outermost point of the heel is not clearly defined, it is deemed to be 0.625 inches (16mm) above the horizontal plane on which the club is resting in its normal address position.

Plain in Shape. The clubhead shall be generally plain in shape. All parts shall be rigid, structural in nature and functional.

Features such as holes through the head, windows or transparencies, or appendages to the main body of the head such as plates, rods or fins for the purpose of meeting dimensional specifications, for aiming or for any other purpose are not permitted. Exceptions may be made for putters.

Any furrows in or runners on the sole shall not extend into the face.

4-1e. Club Face

General. Except for specified markings, the surface roughness must not exceed that of decorative sandblasting. Markings must not have sharp edges or raised lips, as determined by a finger test. The material and construction of the face shall not be designed or manufactured to have the effect at impact of a spring, or to impart significantly more spin to the ball than a standard steel face, or to have any other effect which would unduly influence the movement of the ball.

"Impact Area" Markings. Markings within the area where impact is intended (the 'impact area') are governed by the following:

(i) **Grooves.** A series of straight grooves with diverging sides and a symmetrical cross-section may be used. (See diagram). The width and cross-section must be generally consistent across the face of the club and along the length of the grooves. Any rounding of groove edges shall be in the form of a radius which does not exceed 0.020 inches (0.5mm). The width of the grooves shall not exceed 0.035 inches (0.9mm), using the 30 degree method of measurement on file with the Royal & Ancient Golf Club of St Andrews. The distance between edges of adjacent grooves must not be less than three times the width of a groove, and not less than 0.075 inches (1.9mm). The depth of a groove must not exceed 0.020 inches (0.5mm).

Note: Until 31st December 1995, a Committee is authorised to waive the above requirements for width and separation of grooves for clubs manufactured before 31st March 1990, provided the width of the grooves does not exceed 0.040 inches (1.00mm) and the distance between edges of adjacent grooves is not less than 2.3 times the width.

It is recommended that the granting of this waiver be the normal practice for amateur competition and, in that case, the Committee need not give written intimation that the waiver is being applied.

CLUBS

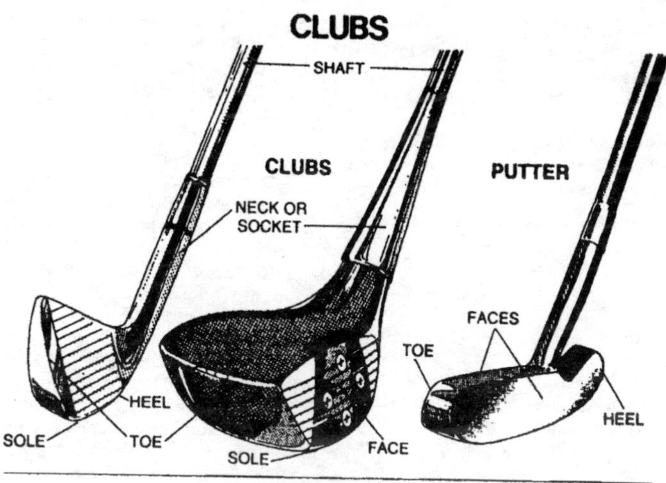

GRIPS

GROOVES

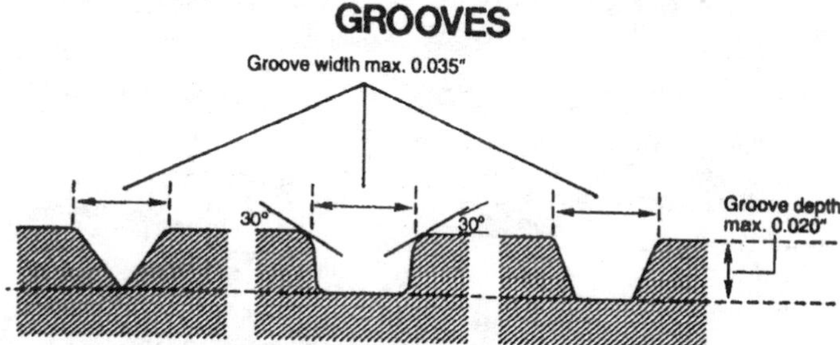

EXAMPLES OF PERMISSIBLE GROOVE CROSS-SECTIONS

Where a Committee opts not to grant the waiver and to apply the Rule strictly (as it is entitled to do), this should be clearly stated in the Conditions of the Competition and the Entry Form.

From 1st January 1996, the Rule may no longer be waived and markings on clubs must meet all the specifications of the Rule.

(ii) **Punch Marks.** Punch marks may be used. The area of any such mark must not exceed 0.0044 square inches (2.8 sq mm). A mark must not be closer to an adjacent mark than 0.168 inches (4.3mm) measured from centre to centre. The depth of a punch mark must not exceed 0.040 inches (1.0mm). If punch marks are used in combination with grooves, a punch mark may not be closer to a groove than 0.168 inches (4.3mm), measured from centre to centre.

Decorative Markings. The centre of the impact area may be indicated by a design within the boundary of a square whose sides are 0.375 inches (9.5mm) in length. Such a design must not unduly influence the movement of the ball. Decorative markings are permitted outside the impact area.

Non-metallic Club Face Markings. The above specifications do not apply to clubs on which the impact area of the face is non-metallic and whose loft angle is 24 degrees or less, but markings which could unduly influence the movement of the ball are prohibited. Clubs with this type of face and a loft angle exceeding 24 degrees may have grooves of maximum width 0.040 inches (1.0mm) and maximum depth of 1½ times the groove width, but must otherwise conform to the markings specifications above.

Putter Face Markings. The specifications above with regard to club face markings do not apply to putters.

Appendix III

The Ball

a. Weight

The weight of the ball shall not be greater than 1.620 ounces avoirdupois (45.93gm).

b. Size

The diameter of the ball shall not be less than 1.680 inches (42.67mm). This specification will be satisfied if, under its own weight, a ball falls through a 1.680 inches diameter ring gauge in fewer than 25 out of 100 randomly selected positions, the test being carried out at a temperature of 23±1°C.

c. Spherical Symmetry

The ball must not be designed, manufactured or intentionally modified to have flight properties which differ from those of a spherically symmetrical ball.

Furthermore the ball will not conform to the Rules of Golf if it fails to satisfy the performance specifications outlined below:

As described in procedures on file at the Royal & Ancient Golf Club of St Andrews, each ball type will be tested using 40 balls of that type, in 20 pairs. One ball of each pair will be launched spinning about one specified axis; the other ball of each pair will be launched spinning about a different, but also specified axis. Differences in carry and time of flight between the two balls of each pair will be recorded. If the mean of the differences in carry is greater than 3.0 yards, and that value is significant at the 5% level, OR if the mean of the differences in time of flight is greater than 0.20 seconds, and that value is significant at the 5% level, the ball type will not conform to the Rules of Golf.

Note: Methods of determining whether a ball performs as if it were generally spherically symmetrical may be subject to change as instrumentation becomes available to measure other properties accurately, such as the aerodynamic coefficient of lift, coefficient of drag and moment of inertia.

d. Initial Velocity

The velocity of the ball shall not be greater than 250 feet (76.2m) per second when measured on apparatus approved by the Royal & Ancient Golf Club of St. Andrews. A maximum tolerance of 2% will be allowed. The temperature of the ball when tested shall be 23±1°C.

e. Overall Distance Standard

A brand of golf ball, when tested on apparatus approved by the Royal & Ancient Golf Club of St. Andrews under the conditions set forth in the Overall Distance Standard for golf balls on file with the Royal & Ancient Golf Club of St. Andrews, shall not cover an average distance in carry and roll exceeding 280 yards (256 metres) plus a tolerance of 6%.

Note: The 6% tolerance will be reduced to a minimum of 4% as test techniques are improved.

HANDICAPS

The Rules of Golf do not legislate for the allocation and adjustment of handicaps or their playing differentials. Such matters are within the jurisdiction and control of the National Union concerned and queries should be directed accordingly.

Rules of Amateur Status

As approved by the Royal & Ancient Golf Club of St. Andrews

(Effective from 1st January 1992)

Definition of an Amateur Golfer
An Amateur Golfer is one who plays the game as a non-remunerative or non-profit-making sport.

The Governing Body
The Governing Body of golf for the Rules of Amateur Status in any country is the National Union of the country concerned except in Great Britain and Ireland where the Governing Body is the Royal & Ancient Golf Club of St. Andrews.

Any person who considers that any action he is proposing to take might endanger his Amateur Status should submit particulars to the appropriate Committee of the Governing Body for consideration.

RULE 1

Forfeiture of Amateur Status at any age

The following are examples of acts which are contrary to the Definition of an Amateur Golfer and cause forfeiture of Amateur Status:

1. Professionalism.

a. Receiving payment or compensation for serving as a Professional golfer or a teaching or playing assistant to a Professional golfer.

b. Taking any action for the purpose of becoming a Professional golfer except applying unsuccessfully for the position of a teaching or playing assistant to a Professional golfer.

Note 1. Such actions include filing application to a *final or sole qualifying* school or competition conducted to qualify persons to play as Professionals in tournaments; receiving services from or entering into an agreement, written or oral, with a sponsor or Professional agent; agreement to accept payment or compensation for allowing one's name or likeness as a skilled golfer to be used for any commercial purpose; and holding or retaining membership in any organisation of Professional golfers.

Note 2. Receiving payment or compensation as a shop assistant is not itself a breach of the Rules, provided duties do not include playing or giving instruction.

2. Playing for Prize Money.
Playing for prize money or its equivalent in a match, tournament or exhibition.

3. Instruction.
Receiving payment or compensation for giving instruction in playing golf, either orally, in writing, by pictures or by other demonstrations, to either individuals or groups.

Exceptions:

1. Golf instruction may be given by an employee of an educational institution or system to students of the institution or system and by camp counsellors to those in their charge, provided that the total time devoted to golf instruction during a year comprises less than 50 per cent of the time spent during the year in the performance of all duties as such employee or counsellor.

2. Payment or compensation may be accepted for instruction in writing, provided one's ability or reputation as a golfer was not a major factor in one's employment or in the commission or sale of one's work.

4. Prizes and Testimonials.

(a) Acceptance of a prize or prize voucher of retail value exceeding as follows:

	In Europe		Elsewhere
For an event of more than 2 rounds	£300	or the equivalent	$500 US
For an event of 2 rounds or less	£200	or the equivalent	$350 US

or such lesser figure, if any, as may be decided by the Governing Body of golf in any country, or

(b) Acceptance of a testimonial in Europe of retail value exceeding £300 or the equivalent, elsewhere of retail value exceeding $500 US or the equivalent, or such lesser figure as may be decided by the Governing Body of golf in any country, or

(c) For a junior golfer, of such age as may be determined by the Governing Body of golf in any country, taking part in an event limited exclusively to juniors, acceptance of a prize or prize voucher in Europe of retail value exceeding £100 or the equivalent;

elsewhere of retail value exceeding $200 US or the equivalent, or such lesser figure, if any, as may be decided by the Governing Body of golf in any country, or
(d) Conversion of a prize or prize voucher into money, or
(e) Accepting a gratuity in connection with a golfing event.

Exceptions:

1. Prizes of only symbolic value, provided that their symbolic nature is distinguished by distinctive permanent marking.

2. More than one testimonial award may be accepted from different donors even though their total retail value exceeds £300 or $500 US, provided they are not presented so as to evade such value limit for a single award.

Note 1: Events covered. The limits referred to in Clauses (a) or (c) above apply to total prize or prize vouchers received by any one person for any event or series of events in any one tournament or exhibition, including hole-in-one or other events in which golf skill is a factor.

Note 2: 'Retail value' is the price at which merchandise is available to anyone at a retail source, and the onus of proving the value of a particular prize rests with the donor.

Note 3: Purpose of prize vouchers. A prize voucher may be issued and redeemed only by the Committee in charge of a competition for the purchase of goods from a Professional's shop or other retail source, which may be specified by the Committee. It may not be used for such items as travel or hotel expenses, a bar bill, or a Club Subscription.

Note 4: Maximum Value of Prizes in any event for individuals. It is recommended that the total value of scratch or each division of handicap prizes should not exceed twice the maximum retail value of prize permitted in Rule 1-4(a) and (c) in an 18-hole competition, three times in a 36-hole competition, four times in a 54-hole competition and five times in a 72-hole competition.

Note 5: Testimonial Awards. Such awards relate to notable performances or contributions to golf as distinguished from tournament prizes.

5. Lending Name or Likeness.

Because of golf skill or golf reputation receiving or contracting to receive payment, compensation or personal benefit, directly or indirectly, for allowing one's name or likeness to be used in any way for the advertisement or sale of anything, whether or not used in or appertaining to golf except as a golf author or broadcaster as permitted by Rule 1-7.

Note: A player may accept equipment from anyone dealing in such equipment provided no advertising is involved.

6. Personal Appearance.

Because of golf skill or golf reputation, receiving payment or compensation, directly or indirectly, for a personal appearance.

Exception: Actual expenses in connection with personal appearances may be paid or reimbursed provided no golf competition or exhibition is involved.

7. Broadcasting or Writing.

Because of golf skill or golf reputation, receiving payment or compensation, directly or indirectly, for broadcasting concerning golf, a golf event or golf events, writing golf articles or books, or allowing one's name to be advertised or published as the author of golf articles or books of which one is not actually the author.

Exceptions:

1. Broadcasting or writing as part of one's primary occupation or career, provided instruction in playing golf is not included (Rule 1-3).

2. Part-time broadcasting or writing, provided (a) the player is actually the author of the commentary, articles or books, (b) instruction in playing golf is not included and (c) the payment or compensation does not have the purpose or effect, directly or indirectly, of financing participation in a golf competition or golf competitions.

8. Expenses.

Accepting expenses, in money or otherwise, from any source to engage in a golf competition or exhibition.

Exceptions:

A player may receive expenses, not exceeding the actual expenses incurred, as follows:

1. From a member of the family or legal guardian;

or

2. As a player in a golf competition or exhibition limited exclusively to players who have not reached their 18th birthday prior to the year of the event;

or

3. As a representative of his Country, County, Club or similar body in team competitions or team training camps at home or abroad, or as a representative of his Country taking part in a National Championship abroad immediately preceding or following directly upon an international team competition, where such expenses are paid by the body he represents, or by the body controlling golf in the territory he is visiting;

or

4. As an individual nominated by a National or County Union or a Club to engage in an event at home or abroad provided that:

(a) The player nominated has not reached such age as may be determined by the Governing Body of Golf in the country from which the nomination is made.

(b) The expenses shall be paid only by the National Union or County Union responsible in the area from which the nomination is made or, subject to the approval of the nominating body, by the body controlling golf in the territory he is visiting. The expenses shall be limited to a *specified number of* competitive days in any one calendar year *as may be determined by the Governing Body of Golf in the country from which the nomination is made.* The expenses are deemed to include reasonable travelling time and practice days in connection with the competitive days.

(c) Where the event is to take place abroad, the approval of the National Union of the country in which the event is to be staged and, if the nominating body is not the National Union of the country from which the nomination is made, the approval of the National Union shall first be obtained by the nominating body.

(d) Where the event is to take place at home, and where the nomination is made by a County Union or Club, the approval of the National Union or the County Union in the area in which the event is to be staged shall first be obtained.

(*Note:* The Term 'County Union' covers any Province, State or equivalent Union or Association); *or*

5. As a player invited for reasons unrelated to golf skill, e.g. celebrities, business associates, etc. to take part in golfing events; *or*

6. As a player in an exhibition in aid of a recognised Charity provided the exhibition is not run in connection with another golfing event; *or*

7. As a player in a handicap individual or handicap team sponsored golfing event where expenses are paid by the sponsor on behalf of the player to take part in the event provided the event has been approved as follows:

(a) where the event is to take place at home the approval of the Governing Body (see Definition) shall first be obtained in advance by the sponsor, and

(b) where the event is to take place both at home and abroad the approval of the two or more Governing Bodies shall first be obtained in advance by the sponsor. The application for this approval should be sent to the Governing Body of golf in the country where the competition commences.

(c) where the event is to take place abroad the approval of two or more Governing Bodies shall first be obtained by the sponsor. The application for this approval should be sent to the Governing Body of golf in the country whose players shall be taking part in the event abroad

(*Note 1:* Business Expenses. It is permissible to play in a golf competition while on a business trip with expenses paid provided that the golf part of the expenses is borne personally and is not charged to business. Further, the business involved must be actual and substantial, and not merely a subterfuge for legitimising expenses when the primary purpose is a golf competition.)

(*Note 2:* Private Transport. Acceptance of private transport furnished or arranged for by a tournament sponsor, directly or indirectly, as an inducement for a player to engage in a golf competition or exhibition shall be considered accepting expenses under Rule 1-8.)

9. Scholarships.

Because of golf skill or golf reputation, accepting the benefits of a scholarship or grant-in-aid other than ones whose terms and conditions have been approved by the Amateur Status Committee of the Royal & Ancient Golf Club of St. Andrews.

10. Membership.

Because of golf skill accepting membership in a Golf Club without full payment for the class of membership for the purpose of playing for that Club.

11. Conduct Detrimental to Golf.

Any conduct, including activities in connection with golf gambling, which is considered detrimental to the best interests of the game.

Rule 2

Procedure for Enforcement and Reinstatement

1. Decision on a Breach.

Whenever information of a possible breach of the Definition of an Amateur Golfer by a player claiming to be an Amateur shall come to the attention of the appropriate Committee of the Governing Body, the Committee, after such investigation as it may deem desirable, shall decide whether a breach has occurred. Each case shall be considered on its merits. The decision of the committee shall be final.

2. Enforcement.

Upon a decision that a player has acted contrary to the Definition of an Amateur Golfer, the Committee may declare the Amateur Status of the player forfeited or require the player to refrain or desist from specified actions as a condition of retaining his Amateur Status.

The Committee shall use its best endeavours to ensure that the player is notified and may notify any interested Golf Association of any action taken under this paragraph.

3. Reinstatement.

The Committee shall have sole power to reinstate a player to Amateur Status or to deny reinstatement. Each application for reinstatement shall be decided on its merits. In considering an application for reinstatement, the Committee shall normally be guided by the following principles:

a. Awaiting Reinstatement.

The professional holds an advantage over the Amateur by reason of having devoted himself to the game as his profession; other persons infringing the Rules of Amateur Status also obtain advantages not available to the Amateur. They do not necessarily lose such advantage merely by deciding to cease infringing the Rules. Therefore, an applicant for reinstatement to Amateur Status shall undergo a period awaiting reinstatement as prescribed by the Committee.

The period awaiting reinstatement shall start from the date of the player's last breach of the Definition of an Amateur Golfer unless the Committee decides that it shall start from the date when the player's last breach became known to the Committee.

b. Period Awaiting Reinstatement.

The period awaiting reinstatement shall normally be related to the period the player was in breach. However, no applicant shall normally be eligible for reinstatement until he has conducted himself in accordance with the Definition of an Amateur Golfer for a period of at least two consecutive years. The Committee, however, reserves the right to extend or to shorten such a period. A longer period will normally be required of applicants who have been in breach for more than five years. Players of national prominence who have been in breach for more than five years shall not normally be eligible for reinstatement.

c. One Reinstatement.

A player shall not normally be reinstated more than once.

d. Status While Awaiting Reinstatement.

During the period awaiting reinstatement an applicant for reinstatement shall conform with the Definition of an Amateur Golfer.

He shall not be eligible to enter competitions as an Amateur. He may, however, enter competitions, and win a prize, solely among members of a Club of which he is a member, subject to the approval of the Club; but he may not represent such Club against other Clubs.

Forms of Application for Countries under the Jurisdiction of the Royal & Ancient Golf Club

(a) Each application for reinstatement shall be submitted on the approved form to the County Union where the applicant wishes to play as an Amateur. Such Union shall, after making all necessary enquiries, forward it through the National Union (and in the case of lady applicants, the Ladies' Golf Union) and the appropriate Professional Golfers' Association, with comments endorsed thereon, to the Governing Body of golf in that country. Forms of application for reinstatement may be obtained from the Royal & Ancient Golf Club or from the National or County Unions. The application shall include such information as the Royal & Ancient Golf Club may require from time to time and it shall be signed and certified by the applicant.

(b) Any application made in countries under the jurisdiction of the Royal & Ancient Golf Club of St. Andrews which the Governing Body of golf in that country considers to be doubtful or not to be covered by the above regulations may be submitted to the Royal & Ancient Golf Club of St. Andrews whose decision shall be final.

R. & A. POLICY ON GAMBLING

The Definition of an Amateur Golfer provides that an Amateur golfer is one who plays the game as a non-remunerative or non-profit-making sport. When gambling motives are introduced evils can arise which threaten the integrity both of the game and of the individual players.

The R&A does not object to participation in wagering among individual golfers or teams of golfers when participation in the wagering is limited to the players, the players may only wager on themselves or their teams, the sole source of all money won by players is advanced by the players and the primary purpose is the playing of the game for enjoyment.

The distinction between playing for prize money and gambling is essential to the validity of the Rules of Amateur Status. The following constitute golf wagering and not playing for prize money:

1. Participation in wagering among individual golfers.

2. Participation in wagering among teams.

Organised Amateur events open to the general golfing public and designed and promoted to create cash prizes are not approved by the R&A. Golfers participating in such events without irrevocably waiving their right to cash prizes are deemed by the R&A to be playing for prize money.

The R&A is opposed to and urges Unions and Clubs and all other sponsors of golf competitions to prohibit types of gambling such as: Calcuttas, auction sweepstakes and any other forms of gambling organised for general participation or permitting participants to bet on someone other than themselves or their teams.

Attention is drawn to Rule 1-11 relating to conduct detrimental to the game, under which players can forfeit their Amateur Status. It is the Club which, by permitting competitions where excessive gambling is involved, or illegal prizes are offered, bears the responsibility for which the individual is penalised and Unions have the power to invoke severe sanctions against a Club or individual for consistently ignoring this policy.

INDEX

INDEX **Rule**

INDEX **Rule**

INDEX

INDEX | **Rule**

INDEX

INDEX **Rule**

INDEX	**Rule**

INDEX **Rule**

INDEX — Rule

INDEX **Rule**

INDEX

The Standard Scratch Score and Handicapping Scheme

Implemented 1983, since revised

This scheme does not apply to ladies' clubs under the jurisdiction of the Ladies' Golf Union.

Published and administered by the Council of National Golf Unions and adopted by the Unions affiliated to the European Golf Association

Foreword

The Standard Scratch Score and Handicapping Scheme was prepared by the British Golf Unions' Joint Advisory Council in 1925 at the request of the Royal & Ancient Golf Club of St Andrews and has been in operation throughout Great Britain and Ireland since 1st March, 1926.

The Scheme incorporated in this book, known as the Standard Scratch Score and Handicapping Scheme 1983, introduced a new concept in handicapping based on the system presently in use by the Australian Golf Union and which takes account of all scores returned by players under Medal Play conditions.

No change has been made in the present method of fixing the Standard Scratch Scores of courses but, on the principle that uniformity and equity in handicapping can be more effectively achieved if there is uniformity and equity in the fixing of Standard Scratch Scores, the Council of National Golf Unions has examined the Course Rating System of the United States Golf Association and has agreed that the Scratch Rating calculated by that procedure may be progressively adopted by National Unions as the Standard Scratch Score pursuant to clause 1.

Unions may now direct that the Standard Scratch Score be calculated in accordance with the Scratch Score Rating Procedure of the United States Golf Association.

Amended editions of this Scheme were published on 1st January 1966 and 1st January 1989. Further amendments since made are incorporated in this revised edition of the Scheme.

The principal changes are:

(a) The definition of a "Member" in relation to the scheme (Definition E).

(b) The introduction of a different "Buffer Zone" depending on Categories of Handicap (Definition T and Clause 16).

(c) The restriction of allocating a Standard Scratch Score to courses measuring between 3000 and 4000 yards (Clause 1(6)).

(d) The use of the Scratch Score Rating Procedure of the United States Golf Association (Clause 1(7)).

(e) The permitted adjustment to a Measured Course to include the use of a temporary tee (Clause 7(a)).

(f) The use of preferred lies is permitted between 1st October and 30th April (Clause 6).

(g) Unions are now required to establish a procedure to adjudicate upon Suspension of Handicaps (Clause 9(9)). This requirement imposes subsequent obligations on Area Authorities (Clause 10(3)) and Affiliated Clubs (Clause 11(5)).

(h) Handicap Committees will in future report to Union and Area Authority reductions of members' playing handicaps to below scratch (Clause 12(6)(d)).

(i) Alteration of Handicaps. With the introduction of different Buffer Zones there are adjustments to Procedure and Tables (Clause 16).

(j) Discretion is given to Unions to impose a maximum handicap increase under Clause 16(6) in a calendar year (Clause 16(10)(b)).

(k) Suspension, lapsing and loss of Handicaps. This clause has been amended (Clause 17).

(l) The procedure for Restoration of Handicaps following suspension, lapse or loss, has been changed (Clause 18).

(m) The Procedure & Tables for calculating the Competition Scratch Score (including the omission of Category 4 scores) have been altered.

(n) Handicap Allowances recommended by the Council of National Golf Unions (Appendix G).

(o) Decisions 1, 7 & 8 have been amended (Appendix I).

(p) Specific requirements relating to Computer Software (Appendix H).

Part One
Definitions

Definition

A. UNION.
B. AREA AUTHORITY.
C. AFFILIATED CLUB.
D. HOME CLUB.
E. MEMBER.
F. HANDICAPPING AUTHORITY.
G. HANDICAP COMMITTEE.
H. HANDICAPS.
I. CATEGORIES OF HANDICAP.
J. MEASURED COURSE.
K. DISTANCE POINT.
L. MEDAL TEE.
M. MEDAL PLAY CONDITIONS.
N. QUALIFYING COMPETITION.
O. QUALIFYING SCORE.
P. AGGREGATE FOURBALL COMPETITION.
Q. STANDARD SCRATCH SCORE.
R. COMPETITION SCRATCH SCORE.
S. NETT DIFFERENTIAL.
T. BUFFER ZONE.

Part Two
The Golf Course and the Standard Scratch Score

Clause

1. The STANDARD SCRATCH SCORE.
2. Course measurement.
3. Alterations to courses.
4. Tees.
5. Par.
6. Preferred lies.
7. Permitted adjustments to a MEASURED COURSE.

Part Three
Handicapping

8. Introduction.
9. Rights and obligations of the UNION.
10. Rights and obligations of the AREA AUTHORITY.
11. Rights and obligations of the AFFILIATED CLUB.
12. Rights and obligations of the HANDICAP COMMITTEE.
13. Rights and obligations of the player.
14. QUALIFYING SCORES.
15. Allotment of handicaps.
16. Alteration of handicaps.
17. Suspension, lapsing and loss of handicaps.
18. Restoration of handicaps.
19. Powers of the HANDICAP COMMITTEE relating to general play.
20. COMPETITION SCRATCH SCORE.

APPENDIX A – Handicap record sheet.
APPENDIX B – Handicap adjustment table.
APPENDIX C – Stableford and par conversion table.
APPENDIX D – COMPETITION SCRATCH SCORE pro forma
APPENDIX E – COMPETITION SCRATCH SCORE Table A
APPENDIX F – COMPETITION SCRATCH SCORE Table B
APPENDIX G – Handicap Allowances
APPENDIX H – Computer Software Requirements
APPENDIX I – Decisions

Part One
Definitions

Throughout the Scheme whenever a word or expression is used which is defined within the following definitions the word or expression is printed in capital letters.

A – Union

A UNION is any national organisation in control of amateur golf in any country.

B – Area Authority

An AREA AUTHORITY is any authority appointed by a UNION to act on behalf of that UNION for the purposes of the Scheme within a specified area.

C – Affiliated Club

An AFFILIATED CLUB is a club affiliated to a UNION or AREA AUTHORITY which pays to the UNION and AREA AUTHORITY a specified annual per capita fee in respect of each eligible MEMBER.

D – Home Club

A player's HOME CLUB is an AFFILIATED CLUB of which the player is a MEMBER. If the player is a MEMBER of more than one AFFILIATED CLUB he shall nominate one as his HOME CLUB.

E – Member

A MEMBER is an amateur golfer who is eligible to compete in all QUALIFYING COMPETITIONS arranged by an AFFILIATED CLUB subject only to exclusion by virtue of one or more of the following:

(a) Restrictions imposed relating solely to the handicap of the players who may compete; or

(b) Restrictions imposed relating solely to the age of the players who may compete; or

(c) Such other restrictions as may be permitted by the UNION provided that any restrictions so permitted shall stipulate a minimum number of QUALIFYING COMPETITIONS in a calendar year in which the MEMBER shall have a reasonable opportunity to compete.

Note: Under this definition a MEMBER need not necessarily be a member as defined by the constitution or rules of his AFFILIATED CLUB or CLUBS.

F – Handicapping Authority

The HANDICAPPING AUTHORITY for a player is his HOME CLUB subject to the overall jurisdiction of the UNION.

G – Handicap Committee

The HANDICAP COMMITTEE is the body appointed by an AFFILIATED CLUB to administer the Scheme within the CLUB.

H – Handicaps

(1) EXACT HANDICAP – a player's EXACT HANDICAP is his handicap calculated in accordance with the provisions of the Scheme to one decimal place.
(2) PLAYING HANDICAP – a player's PLAYING HANDICAP is his EXACT HANDICAP calculated to the nearest whole number (0.5 is rounded upwards).

I – Categories of Handicap

Handicaps are divided into the following CATEGORIES:
CATEGORY 1: Handicaps of 5 or less.
CATEGORY 2: Handicaps of 6 to 12 inclusive.
CATEGORY 3: Handicaps of 13 to 20 inclusive.
CATEGORY 4: Handicaps of 21 to 28 inclusive.

J – Measured Course

Any course played over by an AFFILIATED CLUB the measured length of which has been certified in accordance with the requirements of clause 2.

K – Distance Point

The DISTANCE POINT is the position of a permanent marker indicating the point from which the length of a hole is measured.

L – Medal Tee

A MEDAL TEE is a rectangular area the front of which shall not be more than 10 yards (9 metres) in front of the relevant DISTANCE POINT and the rear of which shall not be less than 2 yards (2 metres) behind the DISTANCE POINT.
Note: Special rules apply when the length of a MEASURED COURSE has been temporarily reduced – see clause 7.

M – Medal Play Conditions

MEDAL PLAY CONDITIONS prevail during stroke, par and Stableford competitions played with full handicap allowance over 18 holes under the Rules of Golf from MEDAL TEES. MEDAL PLAY CONDITIONS shall not prevail when the length of the course played varies by more than 100 yards (91 metres) from the length of the MEASURED COURSE.
Note: Special rules apply when the length of a MEASURED COURSE has been temporarily reduced – see clause 7.

N – Qualifying Competition

A QUALIFYING COMPETITION is any competition in which MEDAL PLAY CONDITIONS prevail and for which a COMPETITION SCRATCH SCORE is calculated subject to restrictions and limitations contained in the Scheme or imposed by UNIONS.

O – Qualifying Score

A QUALIFYING SCORE is any score including a "no return" returned in a QUALIFYING COMPETITION.

P – Aggregate Fourball Competition

An AGGREGATE FOURBALL COMPETITION is a QUALIFYING COMPETITION in which the completed scores at each hole of a team of not more than two amateur players are aggregated.

Q – Standard Scratch Score

The STANDARD SCRATCH SCORE is the score allotted to an 18 hole golf course after the application of clause 1.

R – Competition Scratch Score

The COMPETITION SCRATCH SCORE is the score determined by clause 20.

S – Nett Differential

The NETT DIFFERENTIAL is the difference (+ or –) between the nett score returned by a player in a QUALIFYING COMPETITION and the COMPETITION SCRATCH SCORE.

T – Buffer Zone

A score is within a player's BUFFER ZONE when a NETT DIFFERENTIAL is within the following bands for his HANDICAP CATEGORY.

CATEGORY 1	0 to +1
CATEGORY 2	0 to +2
CATEGORY 3	0 to +3
CATEGORY 4	0 to +4

Note: When a player's score is within his BUFFER ZONE his EXACT HANDICAP remains unchanged.

Part Two
The Golf Course and the Standard Scratch Score

1. The Standard Scratch Score

1.(1) The STANDARD SCRATCH SCORE is the score which a scratch player is expected to return in ideal conditions over a MEASURED COURSE. In the case of a nine-hole course it represents two rounds.
1.(2) The allocation of STANDARD SCRATCH SCORES shall be the responsibility of the UNION.
1.(3) The Table below will provide a guide to officials in making their assessments.
1.(4) In assessing the STANDARD SCRATCH SCORE of a course, officials will take as the starting point the Provisional Standard Scratch Score from the Table. They will then consider the following points:

Table of Provisional Standard Scratch Scores

Standard length of Course	Lengths included in Standard Length		Provisional Standard Scratch Score
Yards	*Yards*	*Metres*	
7100	7001-7200	6402-6584	74
6900	6801-7000	6219-6401	73
6700	6601-6800	6036-6218	72
6500	6401-6600	5853-6035	71
6300	6201-6400	5670-5852	70
6100	5951-6200	5442-5669	69
5800	5701-5950	5213-5441	68
5500	5451-5700	4984-5212	67
5300	5201-5450	4756-4983	66
5100	5001-5200	4573-4755	65
4900	4801-5000	4390-4572	64
4700	4601-4800	4207-4389	63
4500	4401-4600	4024-4206	62
4300	4201-4400	3841-4023	61
4100	4001-4200	3659-3840	60

1 yard = 0.91440 metres
1 metre = 1.09361 yards

(a) The terrain and general layout of the course.
(b) Normal ground conditions – Is run average, above average or below average?
(c) Sizes of greens and whether watered or unwatered.
(d) Hazards – Are greens well guarded or open?
(e) Width of fairways, the effect of trees and nature of rough.
(f) Nearness of "out of bounds" to fairways and greens.
(g) Average weather conditions throughout the playing year. Is the course exposed and subject to high winds for most of the year? Is it sheltered from the full effects of adverse weather?
(h) The distance by which the length of the course varies from the standard length shown in column one of the Table.

1.(5) Having considered all these points, officials will fix the STANDARD SCRATCH SCORE of the course by:
(a) Confirming the Provisional Standard Scratch Score as the STANDARD SCRATCH SCORE.
(b) Adding a stroke or strokes to the Provisional Standard Scratch Score.
(c) Deducting a stroke or strokes from the Provisional Standard Scratch Score.

1.(6) With effect from 1st January 1993 no course of less than 3,000 yards shall be allocated a STANDARD SCRATCH SCORE. At the discretion of a UNION courses between 3,000 and 4,000 yards may be allocated such STANDARD SCRATCH SCORE as the UNION shall determine.

1.(7) A UNION may direct that the STANDARD SCRATCH SCORE shall be in accordance with the Scratch Score Rating Procedure of The United States Golf Association.

2. Course Measurement

Measurement shall be by plan or projection along the horizontal plane from the DISTANCE POINT on the MEDAL TEE to the centre of the green of each hole.

In the case of a dog-leg hole, measurement shall be along the centre line of the fairway to the axis and then to the centre of the green. Measurement shall be carried out by a qualified surveyor, or someone competent and experienced in the handling of surveying instruments, who shall grant a certificate showing details of the length of each hole and the total playing length of the course. Subsequent alterations to the length of the course will require a certificate only for the altered hole or holes which shall be measured in the manner prescribed above.

3. Alterations to Courses

When alterations have been carried out to a course increasing or decreasing its length, the club shall submit a "Form of Application" through its AREA AUTHORITY to the UNION. In the case of a new course, a "Form of Application" shall be submitted by the club through its AREA AUTHORITY to the UNION who will fix the STANDARD SCRATCH SCORE. The UNION is responsible for all STANDARD SCRATCH SCORES in the country over which it has jurisdiction.

4. Tees

All clubs with the requisite facilities should have back and forward MEDAL TEES with a yardage measurement from each tee and a separate STANDARD SCRATCH SCORE as measured from back and forward MEDAL TEES permanently marked.

Wherever possible when courses are being remeasured the DISTANCE POINT on each MEDAL TEE should be so positioned that the tee markers when placed adjacent to the DISTANCE POINT provide a teeing area which satisfies the following recommendation of the Royal & Ancient Golf Club of St Andrews:

"Committees should bear in mind the definition of 'Teeing Ground' (Rules of Golf) which states; 'It is a rectangular area two club-lengths in depth'. The Tee Markers should be placed in such a position that the player has the benefit of the full depth to which the definition entitles him."

To facilitate the use of the correct tees the Royal & Ancient Golf Club of St Andrews recommends that tee boxes or other objects in use to mark the teeing ground shall be painted as follows:

Ladies' Standard MEDAL TEES	Red
Men's Forward MEDAL TEES	Yellow
Men's Back MEDAL TEES	White

When a National Championship is being played over a course the tee markers may be coloured Blue.

5. Par

The STANDARD SCRATCH SCORE must not be allocated amongst the individual holes, but should be printed as a total on the card. The par figure for each hole should be printed alongside each hole on the card. Par for each hole shall be fixed by the club in relation to the length and playing difficulty of each hole and shall be fixed within the following ranges:

	Yards	*Metres*
Par 3	0–250	0–229
Par 4	220–500	201–457
Par 5	440+	402+

e.g. if a hole is 460 yards (421 metres) it may be allotted par 4 or 5 depending upon its average playing difficulty.

The total of the Par figures for each hole of a course will not necessarily coincide with the STANDARD SCRATCH SCORE of that course. Par figures should be used for Stableford, Par, and similar competitions.

6. Preferred Lies

When preferred lies are in operation the following points shall be taken into consideration: MEDAL PLAY CONDITIONS will apply notwithstanding the application of a Local Rule for preferred lies as a result of adverse conditions during the period from 1st October to 30th April. Preferred lies may be used during that period but are not mandatory upon clubs during any part thereof. The Local Rule may apply to specified holes only. Outside that period MEDAL PLAY CONDITIONS will not apply if preferred lies are in operation unless the consent of the UNION or AREA AUTHORITY has been first obtained.

It is emphasised that preferred lies shall apply only when a Local Rule has been made and published in accordance with Appendix 1 of the Rules of Golf as follows:

"A ball lying on any 'closely mown area' through the green may, without penalty, be moved or may be lifted, cleaned and placed within six inches of where it originally lay, but not nearer the hole. After the ball has been so moved or placed, it is in play."

Penalty for breach of Local Rule: Match Play – Loss of hole; Stroke play – Two strokes.

Note: "closely mown area" means any area of the course, including paths through the rough, cut to fairway height or less. (Rule 25-2).

7. Permitted Adjustment to a Measured Course

Whilst each AFFILIATED CLUB must endeavour to maintain the length of its MEASURED COURSE at all times MEDAL PLAY CONDITIONS nevertheless prevail when the length of a course has been reduced in the following circumstances:

(a) When, to allow movement of the playing position on the MEDAL TEE or the use of a temporary green or tee, the length of the course being played has been reduced by not more than 100 yards (91 metres) from the length of the MEASURED COURSE.

(b) When, to allow work to proceed on course alterations or for reasons other than weather conditions, it is necessary to reduce the playing length of the MEASURED COURSE by between 100 and 300 yards (91 and 274 metres). In these circumstances, the club shall reduce the STANDARD SCRATCH SCORE of the MEASURED COURSE temporarily by 1 stroke and report to the UNION, or to such other body nominated by the UNION, the reduction in the STANDARD SCRATCH SCORE, and the reason for it. The club must also notify the UNION or other body when the course has been restored to its measured length and the official STANDARD SCRATCH SCORE reinstated.

Part Three Handicapping

8. Introduction

8.(1) The Council of National Golf Unions Standard Scratch Score and Handicapping Scheme has been revised to achieve a uniformity and equity in handicapping throughout Great Britain and Ireland and those member countries of the European Golf Association adopting the Scheme. The nature of the game of golf, with its varying playing conditions, makes handicapping a relatively inexact operation. Nevertheless, if the same principles are sensibly and universally applied by HANDICAP COMMITTEES, a high degree of uniformity in handicapping can be achieved. It is therefore of paramount importance that all parties to the Scheme fulfil their obligations to it and these are set out below.

8.(2) Handicapping within the Scheme is delegated to AFFILIATED CLUBS subject to the overall jurisdiction of the UNION.

9. Rights and Obligations of the Union

The UNION:

9.(1) Shall have overall jurisdiction for the administration of the Scheme.

9.(2) May delegate any part of that jurisdiction to an AREA AUTHORITY.

9.(3) Shall ratify all PLAYING HANDICAPS reduced to below scratch on the first occasion in any calendar year, immediately after the reduction.

9.(4) Shall have the right to obtain information upon handicaps from AFFILIATED CLUBS at any time.

9.(5) Shall establish within the UNION conditions, restrictions and limitations to be imposed in respect of competitions deemed to be QUALIFYING COMPETITIONS.

9.(6) Shall settle any dispute referred to it. Its decision shall be final.

9.(7) May at its discretion authorise HOME CLUBS to increase the handicaps of players in any of the CATEGORIES 2, 3, and 4 pursuant to clause 19. When such authority has been given the requirements of clause 19.(2) and (3) that the increase shall be effected by the UNION or AREA AUTHORITY shall not apply. Notwithstanding the foregoing, the UNION may, if it considers that handicaps have been unjustifiably increased by a HOME CLUB, require that club to comply with all of the provisions of clause 19.

9.(8) May at its discretion direct that scores returned by a player in CATEGORIES 3 and/or 4 at a club which is not his HOME CLUB or alternatively at a club of which he is not a MEMBER shall be disregarded for handicap increase pursuant to clause 16.(3).

9.(9) Establish a procedure to adjudicate upon the suspension of handicaps pursuant to clause 17(1) and appoint a committee to perform duties referred to in that clause.

10. Rights and Obligations of the Area Authority

The AREA AUTHORITY shall:

10.(1) Administer the responsibilities delegated to it by the UNION.

10.(2) Have the right to obtain information upon handicaps from AFFILIATED CLUBS at any time.

10.(3) Appoint a committee to perform the duties referred to in clause 17(1).

11. Rights and Obligations of the Affiliated Club

The AFFILIATED CLUB shall:
11.(1) Act as the HANDICAPPING AUTHORITY for all members for whom it is the HOME CLUB subject to the overall jurisdiction of the UNION.
11.(2) Ensure that the Scheme is properly applied in the club.
11.(3) Ensure that with effect from 1st January 1994 any computer software used for the calculation of handicaps shall satisfy the requirements set out in Appendix H.
11.(4) Ensure that all handicaps are calculated in accordance with the Scheme.
11.(5) Appoint a HANDICAP COMMITTEE of which the majority shall be MEMBERS to perform the obligations set out in clause 12 below.
11.(6) Appoint a committee of which the majority shall be MEMBERS to perform the duties referred to in clause 17(1).

12. Rights and Obligations of the Handicap Committee

The HANDICAP COMMITTEE shall:
12.(1) Maintain a list in which the names of competitors must be entered prior to competing in a QUALIFYING COMPETITION at the club.
12.(2) Ensure, so far as possible, that all cards taken out in QUALIFYING COMPETITIONS are returned to the committee including incomplete cards.
12.(3) At the conclusion of each round of a QUALIFYING COMPETITION calculate the COMPETITION SCRATCH SCORE as required by clause 20.
12.(4) Post on the club's notice board all changes of MEMBERS' PLAYING HANDICAPS immediately they are made.
12.(5) Ensure that a record of MEMBERS' current PLAYING HANDICAPS is available in a prominent position in the club house.
12.(6) When the club is a player's HOME CLUB:

- (a) Maintain on his behalf a handicap record sheet which shall include all the information shown in Appendix A.
- (b) Ensure his scores are recorded immediately after completion of each QUALIFYING COMPETITION at the HOME CLUB or the reporting of a QUALIFYING SCORE returned elsewhere, and that all EXACT HANDICAPS are calculated in relation to scores recorded in chronological order.
- (c) Keep his EXACT HANDICAP up to date at all times.
- (d) Notify the UNION and AREA AUTHORITY immediately the committee reduces a MEMBER'S PLAYING HANDICAP to below scratch on the first occasion in any calendar year and obtain ratification from the UNION or, if so delegated, from the AREA AUTHORITY.
  Note: The reduction is effective before ratification.
- (e) Unless some other body has been appointed by the HOME CLUB for this purpose, exercise the power to suspend handicaps contained in clause 17.
- (f) When a MEMBER changes his HOME CLUB send to the new HOME CLUB a copy of the player's current handicap record sheet.
- (g) Specify the conditions which apply when a player wishes to obtain a handicap under the provisions of clause 15.
- (h) Exercise the powers to adjust players' handicaps contained in clause 19.
- (i) As required by clause 19.(5) advise players of changes made to their handicaps under the provisions of clause 19.

13. Rights and Obligations of the Player

The player shall:
13.(1) Have one handicap only which shall be allotted and adjusted by his HOME CLUB. That handicap shall apply elsewhere including other clubs of which the player is a MEMBER.
13.(2) If he is a MEMBER of more than one AFFILIATED CLUB select one as his HOME CLUB and notify that club and the others of his choice.
13.(3) Not change his HOME CLUB except by giving advance notice of the change which can take effect only at the end of a calendar year unless he has ceased to be a member of his HOME CLUB or both clubs agree to the change taking place at an earlier date.
13.(4) Report to his HOME CLUB the names of all other AFFILIATED CLUBS of which he is, becomes, or ceases to be, a MEMBER and report to all other AFFILIATED CLUBS of which he is a MEMBER:

- (a) The name of his HOME CLUB and any changes of his HOME CLUB and
- (b) Alterations to his PLAYING HANDICAP made by his HOME CLUB.

13.(5) Ensure that before competing in a QUALIFYING COMPETITION his entry has been inserted in the competition entry list.
13.(6) Ensure that all competition cards in QUALIFYING COMPETITIONS, whether or not complete, are returned to the organising committee.
13.(7) Subject to the provisions of clause 9.(8) report to his HOME CLUB immediately all QUALIFYING SCORES (including no returns) returned away from his HOME CLUB advising the HOME CLUB of the date of the QUALIFYING COMPETITION, the venue and the COMPETITION SCRATCH SCORE together with the following:

- (a) After a stroke play QUALIFYING COMPETITION the gross score returned.

(b) After a Stableford QUALIFYING COMPETITION the par of the course and the number of points scored.

(c) After a par QUALIFYING COMPETITION the par of the course and the score versus par.

Note 1: Players are reminded that failure to report scores returned away from their HOME CLUBS (including no returns) when so required by the scheme is likely to lead to the suspension of offending players' handicaps under the provisions of clause 17.

Note 2: In the event of a QUALIFYING COMPETITION being declared abandoned or scores returned being deemed by clause 20 not to be QUALIFYING SCORES the player is required to report the above information only if he has returned a NETT DIFFERENTIAL of less than zero.

13.(8) Prior to playing in any competition at a club other than his HOME CLUB ensure that any appropriate reductions to his PLAYING HANDICAP have been made or alternatively comply with the obligations set out in clause 16.(11).

13.(9) Enter his current PLAYING HANDICAP on all cards returned in a QUALIFYING COMPETITION even though the event may not be a handicap competition.

13.(10) Provide to his HOME CLUB such information regarding scores in non-qualifying competitions if so directed by a UNION.

14. Qualifying Scores

14.(1) The only scores to be recorded on a player's handicap record sheet are:

(a) QUALIFYING SCORES as defined.

(b) NETT DIFFERENTIALS of less than zero returned in any abandoned round of a QUALIFYING COMPETITION or in any round of a QUALIFYING COMPETITION when that round has been deemed under the provisions of clause 20 not to be a QUALIFYING SCORE.

(c) Correct scores in a QUALIFYING COMPETITION which are disqualified for any reason.

(d) Scores returned in a QUALIFYING COMPETITION played over 18 holes on a course reduced in length under the provisions of clause 7.

(e) Scores returned in a QUALIFYING COMPETITION played over a MEASURED COURSE when Local Rules are in operation for preferred lies (as permitted by clause 6) or for any other purpose provided the rules are authorised by Appendix 1 of the Rules of Golf or associated guidance notes or have been approved by the Rules of Golf Committee of the Royal & Ancient Golf Club of St Andrews.

(f) The individual scores and no returns returned by players in AGGREGATE FOURBALL COMPETITIONS.

Note 1: The competition must be a QUALIFYING COMPETITION.

Note 2: QUALIFYING SCORES returned in Stableford and par competitions shall be converted into NETT DIFFERENTIALS by using the tables in Appendix C.

14.(2) The following returns shall not be accepted as QUALIFYING SCORES in any circumstances:

(a) Scores returned in any better ball fourball competition.

(b) Scores returned in competitions over less than 18 holes.

(c) Scores returned in any competition which is not played in accordance with the Rules of Golf and authorised Local Rules. e.g. A competition which limits the number of clubs permitted to less than 14.

(d) Scores returned in an extended competition in which the player has the option of selecting the day or days on which he shall compete and/or how many returns he shall make except the following competitions in which only one return is permitted:

(i) A competition over no more than two days which need not be consecutive, or

(ii) A competition extended over three or more days solely to accommodate the number of players entered.

(e) Subject to clause 14.(1)(b) scores returned in any round of a QUALIFYING COMPETITION deemed under the provisions of clause 20 not to be QUALIFYING SCORES.

(f) Any competition other than an AGGREGATE FOURBALL COMPETITION in which competitors play in partnership with another competitor.

(g) Stableford and par competitions played with less than full handicap allowance.

(h) Scores returned in events run by organisations which are not HANDICAPPING AUTHORITIES unless such events have been previously approved by a UNION as a QUALIFYING COMPETITION.

15. Allotment of Handicaps

15.(1) The maximum handicap is 28. (Maximum EXACT HANDICAP 28.0.)

15.(2) A handicap can be allotted only to a MEMBER of an AFFILIATED CLUB.

15.(3) To obtain a handicap a player shall submit three cards preferably marked over a MEASURED COURSE which shall be adjusted by the HANDICAP COMMITTEE so that any score of more than 2 over par at any hole shall be amended to 2 over par.

After these adjustments have been made an EXACT HANDICAP shall be allotted equivalent to the number of strokes by which the best of the three rounds differs from the STANDARD SCRATCH SCORE. The HANDICAP COMMITTEE may allot a player an initial whole number EXACT HANDICAP less than the best score if it has reason to consider that a lower handicap is more appropriate to the player's ability. In exceptional circumstances a higher handicap may be allotted than that indicated by the best score.

When a player fails to return cards justifying an EXACT HANDICAP of 28.0 he may, at the discretion of the HANDICAP COMMITTEE, be given an EXACT HANDICAP of 28.0. The player's PLAYING HANDICAP shall equal the EXACT HANDICAP allotted. AFFILIATED CLUBS may at their absolute discretion refuse to allot a handicap until a specified standard has been attained.

15.(4) A player without a handicap shall not be allotted a CATEGORY 1 HANDICAP without the written authority of the UNION, or AREA AUTHORITY if so delegated.

16. Alteration of Handicaps

16.(1) Definition I divides handicaps into the following four CATEGORIES:
CATEGORY 1: Handicaps of 5 or less.
CATEGORY 2: Handicaps of 6 to 12 inclusive.
CATEGORY 3: Handicaps of 13 to 20 inclusive.
CATEGORY 4: Handicaps of 21 to 28 inclusive.

16.(2) If a player returns a NETT DIFFERENTIAL within his BUFFER ZONE his EXACT HANDICAP is not changed.

16.(3) Subject to the provisions of clauses 9.(8), 20.(3) and 20.(4), if a player returns a score with a NETT DIFFERENTIAL above his BUFFER ZONE or records a "no return" his EXACT HANDICAP is increased by 0.1.

16.(4) If a player returns a NETT DIFFERENTIAL of less than zero his EXACT HANDICAP is reduced by an amount *per stroke that the* NETT DIFFERENTIAL *is below zero*, the amount per stroke being determined by his HANDICAP CATEGORY.

16.(5) The recording of scores shall be kept by NETT DIFFERENTIAL i.e. the difference (+ or –) between the player's nett score and the COMPETITION SCRATCH SCORE. The date, NETT DIFFERENTIAL, EXACT HANDICAP and PLAYING HANDICAP must be recorded on the player's handicap record sheet.

16.(6) EXACT HANDICAPS shall be adjusted as follows, with reference to the handicap adjustment table, Appendix B opposite.

For example:

If a player on 11.2 returns a score with a NETT DIFFERENTIAL of 4 his EXACT HANDICAP becomes 11.3. If he then returns a score with a NETT DIFFERENTIAL of –7 his EXACT HANDICAP is reduced by 7 times 0.2 = 1.4, i.e. to an EXACT HANDICAP of 9.9 and his PLAYING HANDICAP is 10 which is immediately his new handicap.

Appendix B: Handicap Adjustment Table

CATEGORY	PLAYING HANDICAP	If NETT DIFFERENTIAL is: Above BUFFER ZONE. Add *only*	Below CSS. Subtract for *each* Stroke below
1	Up to 5	0.1	0.1
2	6 to 12	0.1	0.2
3	13 to 20	0.1	0.3
4	21 to 28	0.1	0.4

16.(7) When a player's handicap is to be reduced so that it goes from a higher CATEGORY to a lower CATEGORY, it shall be reduced at the rate appropriate to the higher CATEGORY only so far as brings his PLAYING HANDICAP into the lower CATEGORY and the balance of the reduction shall be at the rate appropriate to the lower CATEGORY.

For example:

If a player on 21.2 returns a score with a NETT DIFFERENTIAL of –6, i.e. 6 strokes below his PLAYING HANDICAP of 21, his handicap is reduced as follows:

21.2–(2 times 0.4) (i.e. –0.8)=20.4
20.4–(4 times 0.3) (i.e. –1.2)=19.2

16.(8) A player whose EXACT HANDICAP contains 0.5 or over shall be given the next higher handicap, e.g. 12.5 exact would be 13 PLAYING HANDICAP. This applies when handicaps are to be increased or reduced.

Note: EXACT HANDICAP –0.5 rounded upwards is PLAYING HANDICAP scratch and not plus one.

16.(9) Reductions of PLAYING HANDICAPS shall be made on the day the score becomes known to the HOME CLUB.

16.(10)
(a) Increases of PLAYING HANDICAPS shall be made at the end of each calendar month or at such shorter intervals as the HOME CLUB may decide.
(a) A UNION may at its discretion restrict an increase of EXACT HANDICAPS to 2.0 strokes in a calendar year except increases granted under clause 19.

16.(11) If, for any reason, a player is unable to report to his HOME CLUB a QUALIFYING SCORE or SCORES which may have a NETT DIFFERENTIAL of less than zero or has been unable to ascertain, after reporting such scores, whether or not his PLAYING HANDICAP has been reduced, he shall then, before competing in a further competition at a club other than his HOME CLUB, either:

(a) For that competition only, make such reduction to his PLAYING HANDICAP as shall be appropriate under the Scheme by applying the COMPETITION SCRATCH SCORE if known, other-

wise the STANDARD SCRATCH SCORE to his gross score, or
(b) Report to the committee organising the competition any relevant score returned which after deduction of his PLAYING HANDICAP is two above the STANDARD SCRATCH SCORE or less. The committee may, for that competition only, reduce the player's PLAYING HANDICAP.
Note: Increases to PLAYING HANDICAPS may not be made under the provisions of this sub clause.
16.(12) The procedure for the restoration of handicaps which have been lost is contained in clause 18.

17. Suspension, Lapsing and Loss of Handicaps

17.(1) Subject to the provisions of Clause 17(2) the UNION, AREA AUTHORITY or a player's HOME CLUB shall suspend the handicap of any player who in its opinion has:

(a) Constantly or blatantly failed to comply with the obligations and responsibilities imposed by this Scheme, or
(b) Conducted himself in a manner prejudicial to the interests of his UNION, AREA AUTHORITY or HOME CLUB or to the game of Golf.

The player must be notified of the period of suspension and of any other conditions imposed. No player's handicap shall be suspended without first affording him the opportunity of appearing before the committee or other body.
17.(2) Subject to any directions to the contrary issued by a UNION no proceedings pursuant to Clause 17(1) shall be considered by an AREA AUTHORITY or HOME CLUB without the written authority of the UNION. Following the receipt of a request for such an authority, UNIONS shall direct whether the UNION, the AREA AUTHORITY or HOME CLUB shall hear and determine the issue. UNIONS shall direct the appeal procedure to be made available to a player should he be dissatisfied with the determination. Subject to any directions made by a UNION this restriction shall not apply to proceedings brought against a MEMBER by his HOME CLUB in respect of an alleged offence committed at that club.
17.(3) If a player is suspended from membership of his HOME CLUB his handicap shall lapse automatically until his membership is reinstated.
17.(4) A player's handicap is lost immediately he ceases to be a MEMBER of an AFFILIATED CLUB or loses his amateur status.
17.(5) Whilst a player's handicap is suspended, lapsed or has been lost he shall not enter or compete in any competition which requires a competitor to be the holder of a C.O.N.G.U. handicap as designated by this scheme for either entering or competing in the competition.
17.(6) The suspension of a player's handicap shall apply at all AFFILIATED CLUBS of which the player is or becomes a MEMBER during the period of suspension.

18. Restoration of Handicaps

18.(1) If the handicap of a player is to be reinstated within 6 months of the date on which his handicap was lost, or suspended or lapsed upon his suspension from membership of his HOME CLUB it shall be reinstated at the same handicap the player last held. In all other cases the player shall be allotted a new handicap after he has complied with the requirements of Clause 15.
18.(2) When allotting a new handicap to a player the HANDICAP COMMITTEE shall give due consideration to the handicap he last held and a CATEGORY 1 HANDICAP shall not be allotted without the written approval of the UNION or AREA AUTHORITY if so delegated.

19. Powers of the Handicap Committee Relating to General Play

19.(1) Whenever the HANDICAP COMMITTEE of a player's HOME CLUB considers that a player's EXACT HANDICAP is too high and does not reflect his current playing ability the HANDICAP COMMITTEE must, subject to the provisions of sub clause (3) of this clause, reduce his EXACT HANDICAP to the figure it considers appropriate.
19.(2)

(a) Whenever the HANDICAP COMMITTEE of a player's HOME CLUB considers that a player's EXACT HANDICAP is too low and does not reflect his current playing ability the HANDICAP COMMITTEE must, subject to the provisions of sub clause (3) of this clause, recommend to the UNION, or AREA AUTHORITY if so delegated, that his EXACT HANDICAP should be increased to the figure it considers appropriate.
(b) In the event of a UNION delegating to HOME CLUBS the unconditional authority to increase the handicaps of players in any of the CATEGORIES 2, 3 and 4 HOME CLUBS need not submit to the UNION or AREA AUTHORITY proposals in respect of any changes of handicaps of players in the nominated CATEGORIES.

19.(3) When the HANDICAP COMMITTEE has decided

(a) That the EXACT HANDICAP of a CATEGORY 1 player shall be reduced, or
(b) That the EXACT HANDICAP of a CATEGORY 2 player shall be reduced into CATEGORY 1, or
(c) That the EXACT HANDICAP of any player shall be increased (Subject to the provision of clause 9(7))

Then the HANDICAP COMMITTEE must refer the

matter to the UNION, or AREA AUTHORITY if so delegated, with its recommended adjustment. The UNION or AREA AUTHORITY shall then authorise the recommended variation, reject the recommendation or refer the matter back to the HANDICAP COMMITTEE for further consideration. The UNION or AREA AUTHORITY shall be supplied with all the information upon which the recommendation is based and with any further information required.

19.(4) When deciding whether to effect or recommend an adjustment of handicap the HANDICAP COMMITTEE of the player's HOME CLUB shall consider all available information regarding the player's golfing ability.

It shall consider in particular:

(a) The frequency of QUALIFYING SCORES recently returned by the player to and below his PLAYING HANDICAP.
(b) The player's achievements in match play, four-ball better-ball competitions and other non-qualifying events.
(c) QUALIFYING SCORES returned by the player in stroke play competitions which are adversely affected by one or more particularly bad holes. It may prove helpful to take into account the number of points the player would have scored if these QUALIFYING SCORES had been in Stableford competitions played with full handicap allowance.

19.(5) The HANDICAP COMMITTEE shall advise a player of any change of handicap under this clause and the change will become effective when the player becomes aware of the adjustment.

19.(6) The HANDICAP COMMITTEE or other body organising a competition at a club which is not the player's HOME CLUB may, if it considers that his handicap is too high because of scores reported pursuant to sub clause 16.(11)(b) or for any other reason, reduce that handicap. Any reduction made under this clause shall apply only to the competition for which it is made.

19.(7) An AFFILIATED CLUB may not apply a formula by which handicaps shall be adjusted under this clause. Any handicap so adjusted shall not be a C.O.N.G.U. handicap designated under this scheme.

19.(8) Decisions made by a HANDICAP COMMITTEE, UNION or AREA AUTHORITY under this clause shall be final.

Note 1: In the interests of equitable handicapping it is essential that all HANDICAP COMMITTEES keep the handicaps of the MEMBERS for whom they act as the HOME CLUB under review and that adjustments of handicaps are considered as soon as it comes to the committee's notice that a player's handicap may no longer correctly reflect his current general golfing ability.

Note 2: The HANDICAP COMMITTEE should consider dealing more severely with a player whose general standard of play is known to be improving than it should with a player who it is believed has returned scores below his general ability but whose general playing ability is not considered to be improving.

20. Competition Scratch Score

20.(1) At the conclusion of each round of a QUALIFYING COMPETITION the COMPETITION SCRATCH SCORE shall be calculated by following the procedure set out in Appendix D and applying the relevant Table in either Appendix E or F.

20.(2) In the event of one round of a QUALIFYING COMPETITION extending over more than one day the COMPETITION SCRATCH SCORE shall be calculated for each day.

20.(3) The relevant Table dictates any adjustment to be made to the STANDARD SCRATCH SCORE to provide the COMPETITION SCRATCH SCORE or to direct that the scores returned shall not count as QUALIFYING SCORES (indicated by "N/C" in the Table column heading). When the COMPETITION SCRATCH SCORE has been established all NETT DIFFERENTIALS shall be calculated in relation thereto and handicap adjustments made and entered in the player's Handicap Record Sheets. (See Definition T – BUFFER ZONE.)

20.(4) If the Table indicates that the scores returned shall not count as QUALIFYING SCORES then the COMPETITION SCRATCH SCORE shall be deemed to be three strokes more than the STANDARD SCRATCH SCORE. All players who after the application of the COMPETITION SCRATCH SCORE to their scores have returned a NETT DIFFERENTIAL of less than zero shall have their EXACT HANDICAPS reduced to the extent dictated by the NETT DIFFERENTIAL so calculated. A NETT DIFFERENTIAL of zero or above shall not result in a handicap increase.

20.(5) If a QUALIFYING COMPETITION is abandoned for any reason the COMPETITION SCRATCH SCORE shall be regarded as equal to the STANDARD SCRATCH SCORE and players returning NETT DIFFERENTIALS of less than zero shall have their EXACT HANDICAPS reduced to the extent dictated by the NETT DIFFERENTIAL. A NETT DIFFERENTIAL of zero or above shall not result in a handicap increase.

Note: UNIONS, AREA AUTHORITIES and any organisations so authorised by a UNION shall establish the COMPETITION SCRATCH SCORES for events they organise.

20.(6) Where a player is a MEMBER of two or more AFFILIATED CLUBS and competes in a QUALIFYING COMPETITION organised by two or more of those clubs and played over the same course and the score in one round is used in all the competitions then the COMPETITION SCRATCH SCORE applicable shall be that applied by his HOME CLUB or if none of the clubs is his HOME CLUB the highest COMPETITION SCRATCH SCORE shall be applied.

Appendix A
Handicap Record Sheet

NAME ____________________________________

HOME CLUB ________________________________

OTHER CLUBS ______________________________

Date	Nett differential	Handicap		Date	Nett differential	Handicap	
		Exact	Playing			Exact	Playing
May 1	B/F	21.0	21	June 30	B/F	19.4	19
6	4	21.0	21	July			
7	5	21.1	21	8 (a.m.)	7	19.5	19
20	N/R	21.2	21	8 (p.m.)	6	19.6	19
21	–6	19.2	19	29	8	19.7	19 *Note 2*
				30	4	19.8	20
June 4	1	19.2	19	Aug 6	2	19.8	20
5	4	19.3	19	7	–6	18.0	18
25	7	19.4	19	20	0	18.0	18
26	2	19.4	19	21	7	18.1	18

Notes to Appendix A

1 The sheet above shows the PLAYING HANDICAPS when increases are made on the last day of each calendar month.

2 If the increases had been made immediately the PLAYING HANDICAP would have been increased to 20 on the 8th July a.m. and the NETT DIFFERENTIALS of 6, 8 and 4 respectively on the 8th p.m., 29th and 30th July would each have been reduced by 1. Thus, with the operation of the BUFFER ZONE, the EXACT HANDICAP would have remained at 19.7 on 31st July and been 0.1 less than those shown thereafter.

3 NETT DIFFERENTIAL is the difference (+ or –) between the Nett Score returned by a player in a QUALIFYING COMPETITION and the COMPETITION SCRATCH SCORE.

4 Scores returned on courses other than that of the player's HOME CLUB should be distinguished by marking the NETT DIFFERENTIAL thus: □

5 Reductions of PLAYING HANDICAPS are effected immediately.

6 Increases of PLAYING HANDICAPS shall be made at the end of each calendar month or at such shorter intervals as the HOME CLUB may decide.

7 When scores are received by the HOME CLUB out of chronological order the player's EXACT HANDICAP shall be recorded so that it relates to chronological order.

Appendix B
Table of Handicap Adjustments

Nett Differentials	−1	−2	−3	−4	−5	−6	−7	−8	−9	−10	−11	−12	Over Buffer Zone
Exact Handicaps Up to 5.4	−0.1	−0.2	−0.3	−0.4	−0.5	−0.6	−0.7	−0.8	−0.9	−1.0	−1.1	−1.2	+0.1
5.5–5.6	−0.2	−0.3	−0.4	−0.5	−0.6	−0.7	−0.8	−0.9	−1.0	−1.1	−1.2	−1.3	+0.1
5.7–5.8	−0.2	−0.4	−0.5	−0.6	−0.7	−0.8	−0.9	−1.0	−1.1	−1.2	−1.3	−1.4	+0.1
5.9–6.0	−0.2	−0.4	−0.6	−0.7	−0.8	−0.9	−1.0	−1.1	−1.2	−1.3	−1.4	−1.5	+0.1
6.1–6.2	−0.2	−0.4	−0.6	−0.8	−0.9	−1.0	−1.1	−1.2	−1.3	−1.4	−1.5	−1.6	+0.1
6.3–6.4	−0.2	−0.4	−0.6	−0.8	−1.0	−1.1	−1.2	−1.3	−1.4	−1.5	−1.6	−1.7	+0.1
6.5–6.6	−0.2	−0.4	−0.6	−0.8	−1.0	−1.2	−1.3	−1.4	−1.5	−1.6	−1.7	−1.8	+0.1
6.7–6.8	−0.2	−0.4	−0.6	−0.8	−1.0	−1.2	−1.4	−1.5	−1.6	−1.7	−1.8	−1.9	+0.1
6.9–7.0	−0.2	−0.4	−0.6	−0.8	−1.0	−1.2	−1.4	−1.6	−1.7	−1.8	−1.9	−2.0	+0.1
7.1–7.2	−0.2	−0.4	−0.6	−0.8	−1.0	−1.2	−1.4	−1.6	−1.8	−1.9	−2.0	−2.1	+0.1
7.3–7.4	−0.2	−0.4	−0.6	−0.8	−1.0	−1.2	−1.4	−1.6	−1.8	−2.0	−2.1	−2.2	+0.1
7.5–7.6	−0.2	−0.4	−0.6	−0.8	−1.0	−1.2	−1.4	−1.6	−1.8	−2.0	−2.2	−2.3	+0.1
7.7–12.4	−0.2	−0.4	−0.6	−0.8	−1.0	−1.2	−1.4	−1.6	−1.8	−2.0	−2.2	−2.4	+0.1
12.5–12.7	−0.3	−0.5	−0.7	−0.9	−1.1	−1.3	−1.5	−1.7	−1.9	−2.1	−2.3	−2.5	+0.1
12.8–13.0	−0.3	−0.6	−0.8	−1.0	−1.2	−1.4	−1.6	−1.8	−2.0	−2.2	−2.4	−2.6	+0.1
13.1–13.3	−0.3	−0.6	−0.9	−1.1	−1.3	−1.5	−1.7	−1.9	−2.1	−2.3	−2.5	−2.7	+0.1
13.4–13.6	−0.3	−0.6	−0.9	−1.2	−1.4	−1.6	−1.8	−2.0	−2.2	−2.4	−2.6	−2.8	+0.1
13.7–13.9	−0.3	−0.6	−0.9	−1.2	−1.5	−1.7	−1.9	−2.1	−2.3	−2.5	−2.7	−2.9	+0.1
14.0–14.2	−0.3	−0.6	−0.9	−1.2	−1.5	−1.8	−2.0	−2.2	−2.4	−2.6	−2.8	−3.0	+0.1
14.3–14.5	−0.3	−0.6	−0.9	−1.2	−1.5	−1.8	−2.1	−2.3	−2.5	−2.7	−2.9	−3.1	+0.1
14.6–14.8	−0.3	−0.6	−0.9	−1.2	−1.5	−1.8	−2.1	−2.4	−2.6	−2.8	−3.0	−3.2	+0.1
14.9–15.1	−0.3	−0.6	−0.9	−1.2	−1.5	−1.8	−2.1	−2.4	−2.7	−2.9	−3.1	−3.3	+0.1
15.2–15.4	−0.3	−0.6	−0.9	−1.2	−1.5	−1.8	−2.1	−2.4	−2.7	−3.0	−3.2	−3.4	+0.1
15.5–15.7	−0.3	−0.6	−0.9	−1.2	−1.5	−1.8	−2.1	−2.4	−2.7	−3.0	−3.3	−3.5	+0.1
15.8–20.4	−0.3	−0.6	−0.9	−1.2	−1.5	−1.8	−2.1	−2.4	−2.7	−3.0	−3.3	−3.6	+0.1
20.5–20.8	−0.4	−0.7	−1.0	−1.3	−1.6	−1.9	−2.2	−2.5	−2.8	−3.1	−3.4	−3.7	+0.1
20.9–21.2	−0.4	−0.8	−1.1	−1.4	−1.7	−2.0	−2.3	−2.6	−2.9	−3.2	−3.5	−3.8	+0.1
21.3–21.6	−0.4	−0.8	−1.2	−1.5	−1.8	−2.1	−2.4	−2.7	−3.0	−3.3	−3.6	−3.9	+0.1
21.7–22.0	−0.4	−0.8	−1.2	−1.6	−1.9	−2.2	−2.5	−2.8	−3.1	−3.4	−3.7	−4.0	+0.1
22.1–22.4	−0.4	−0.8	−1.2	−1.6	−2.0	−2.3	−2.6	−2.9	−3.2	−3.5	−3.8	−4.1	+0.1
22.5–22.8	−0.4	−0.8	−1.2	−1.6	−2.0	−2.4	−2.7	−3.0	−3.3	−3.6	−3.9	−4.2	+0.1
22.9–23.2	−0.4	−0.8	−1.2	−1.6	−2.0	−2.4	−2.8	−3.1	−3.4	−3.7	−4.0	−4.3	+0.1
23.3–23.6	−0.4	−0.8	−1.2	−1.6	−2.0	−2.4	−2.8	−3.2	−3.5	−3.8	−4.1	−4.4	+0.1
23.7–24.0	−0.4	−0.8	−1.2	−1.6	−2.0	−2.4	−2.8	−3.2	−3.6	−3.9	−4.2	−4.5	+0.1
24.1–24.4	−0.4	−0.8	−1.2	−1.6	−2.0	−2.4	−2.8	−3.2	−3.6	−4.0	−4.3	−4.6	+0.1
24.5–24.8	−0.4	−0.8	−1.2	−1.6	−2.0	−2.4	−2.8	−3.2	−3.6	−4.0	−4.4	−4.7	+0.1
24.9–28.0	−0.4	−0.8	−1.2	−1.6	−2.0	−2.4	−2.8	−3.2	−3.6	−4.0	−4.4	−4.8	+0.1

Appendix C

Table for converting Par and Stableford scores to nett differentials
(Note – the Table is based on full handicap allowance)

Score versus PAR	7 down	6 down	5 down	4 down	3 down	2 down	1 down	All Square	1 up	2 up	3 up	4 up	5 up	6 up	7 up
STABLEFORD points scored	29	30	31	32	33	34	35	36	37	38	39	40	41	42	43
Par 7 less than CSS	0	–1	–2	–3	–4	–5	–6	–7	–8	–9	–10	–11	–12	–13	–14
Par 6 less than CSS	+1	0	–1	–2	–3	–4	–5	–6	–7	–8	–9	–10	–11	–12	–13
Par 5 less than CSS	+2	+1	0	–1	–2	–3	–4	–5	–6	–7	–8	–9	–10	–11	–12
Par 4 less than CSS	+3	+2	+1	0	–1	–2	–3	–4	–5	–6	–7	–8	–9	–10	–11
Par 3 less than CSS	+4	+3	+2	+1	0	–1	–2	–3	–4	–5	–6	–7	–8	–9	–10
Par 2 less than CSS	+5	+4	+3	+2	+1	0	–1	–2	–3	–4	–5	–6	–7	–8	–9
Par 1 less than CSS	+6	+5	+4	+3	+2	+1	0	–1	–2	–3	–4	–5	–6	–7	–8
Par equal to CSS	+7	+6	+5	+4	+3	+2	+1	0	–1	–2	–3	–4	–5	–6	–7
Par 1 more than CSS	+8	+7	+6	+5	+4	+3	+2	+1	0	–1	–2	–3	–4	–5	–6
Par 2 more than CSS	+9	+8	+7	+6	+5	+4	+3	+2	+1	0	–1	–2	–3	–4	–5
Par 3 more than CSS	+10	+9	+8	+7	+6	+5	+4	+3	+2	+1	0	–1	–2	–3	–4
Par 4 more than CSS	+11	+10	+9	+8	+7	+6	+5	+4	+3	+2	+1	0	–1	–2	–3
Par 5 more than CSS	+12	+11	+10	+9	+8	+7	+6	+5	+4	+3	+2	+1	0	–1	–2
Par 6 more than CSS	+13	+12	+11	+10	+9	+8	+7	+6	+5	+4	+3	+2	+1	0	–1

Example:–
(a) 3 up on a Par 72 course with a CSS of 70. Par is 2 more than CSS so Nett Differential = –1.
(b) 37 Stableford points on a course with Par 68 & CSS 69. Par is 1 less than CSS so Nett Differential = –2.

Appendix D
Standard Scratch Score and Handicapping Scheme

The Competition Scratch Score

Number of Competitors Including No Returns			PERCENTAGES	ROUNDED %
Category 1	A	A x 100 / D	F	I
Category 2	B	B x 100 / D	G	J
Category 3	C	100 minus boxes I & J		K
Total	D	Total:		100
Number of Nett Scores in Categories 1, 2 & 3 at 2 over SSS and better	E	E x 100 / D	H	L

Procedure

1. Enter in Boxes A, B and C the number of competitors, including no returns, from each of the Categories 1, 2 & 3.
2. Enter the total number of competitors in Categories 1, 2 & 3, **including no returns**, in Box D.
3. Enter in Box E the number of competitors in Categories 1, 2 and 3 who have returned nett scores two over SSS and better. For Par and Stableford competitions use the converted equivalent.

Note: To establish the converted equivalent of a score Two over SSS calculate as follows:
(a) Stableford Competitions = Par less SSS plus 36 less 2
(b) Par Competitions = Par less SSS less 2

4. In Boxes F, G and H enter the percentages of the adjacent boxes in relation to Box D as indicated.
5. Round the number in Box F to the nearest 10% and enter the result in Box I (5% upwards).
6. Round the number in Box G to the nearest 10% and enter the result in Box J (5% upwards).

Note: Occasionally the rounding of Boxes F and G will produce a total of Boxes I and J in excess of 100. When this occurs round the number in Box G downwards and insert the amended number in Box J.

7. Enter in Box K the total of Boxes I and J deducted from 100. (The percentage in Box K may not coincide with the rounded percentage Box C would give if calculated.)
8. Round the number in Box H to the nearest whole number (0.5 upwards) and enter the result in Box L.
9. Select the relevant Table – Table A when the total number of competitors exceeds 30, otherwise Table B. Select the row which contains the percentage shown in Boxes I, J and K.
10. In the row selected find the column which includes the number in Box L. The SSS adjustment is shown in the heading of that column and that number is added to or deducted from the SSS to provide the COMPETITION SCRATCH SCORE ("CSS"). For each QUALIFYING COMPETITION the CSS replaces the SSS for all handicapping purposes. The BUFFER ZONES are applied to the CSS and not the SSS.
11. The heading N/C at the top of a column in the Tables indicates that scores returned shall not result in handicap increases. Reductions of handicap will be made on the basis that the CSS is three strokes higher than the SSS.
12. When a competition has been abandoned for any reason reductions of handicaps shall be on the basis that the CSS is equal to the SSS but no handicaps shall be increased.
13. In the event of all the competitors in a QUALIFYING COMPETITION holding handicaps in CATEGORY 4 the COMPETITION SCRATCH SCORE shall be the STANDARD SCRATCH SCORE.
14. HANDICAP COMMITTEES are reminded that they no longer have a discretion to determine that a QUALIFYING COMPETITION shall or shall not be "non-counting".

Appendix E

Table A More than 30 competitors

Categories			Adjustments to SSS to determine the CSS					
1	2	3	N/C	+3	+2	+1	0	−1
0%	0%	100%	0-4	5-7	8-10	11-15	16-30	31+
0%	10%	90%	0-4	5-7	8-11	12-15	16-32	33+
0%	20%	80%	0-5	6-7	8-11	12-16	17-34	35+
0%	30%	70%	0-5	6-8	9-12	13-17	18-36	37+
0%	40%	60%	0-5	6-8	9-12	13-18	19-38	39+
0%	50%	50%	0-5	6-8	9-13	14-19	20-40	41+
0%	60%	40%	0-5	6-9	10-14	15-20	21-41	42+
0%	70%	30%	0-5	6-9	10-14	15-21	22-43	44+
0%	80%	20%	0-5	6-9	10-15	16-22	23-45	46+
0%	90%	10%	0-6	7-10	11-15	16-23	24-47	48+
0%	100%	0%	0-6	7-10	11-16	17-24	25-49	50+
10%	0%	90%	0-5	6-8	9-12	13-17	18-34	35+
10%	10%	80%	0-5	6-8	9-12	13-18	19-36	37+
10%	20%	70%	0-5	6-8	9-13	14-18	19-38	39+
10%	30%	60%	0-5	6-9	10-13	14-19	20-39	40+
10%	40%	50%	0-5	6-9	10-14	15-20	21-41	42+
10%	50%	40%	0-5	6-9	10-14	15-21	22-43	44+
10%	60%	30%	0-6	7-9	10-15	16-22	23-45	46+
10%	70%	20%	0-6	7-10	11-16	17-23	24-47	48+
10%	80%	10%	0-6	7-10	11-16	17-24	25-49	50+
10%	90%	0%	0-6	7-10	11-17	8-25	26-51	52+
20%	0%	80%	0-5	6-8	9-13	14-19	20-38	39+
20%	10%	70%	0-5	6-9	10-14	15-20	21-39	40+
20%	20%	60%	0-5	6-9	10-14	15-21	22-41	42+
20%	30%	50%	0-6	7-9	10-15	16-22	23-43	44+
20%	40%	40%	0-6	7-10	11-15	16-22	23-45	46+
20%	50%	30%	0-6	7-10	11-16	17-23	24-47	48+
20%	60%	20%	0-6	7-10	11-16	17-24	25-49	50+
20%	70%	10%	0-6	7-11	12-17	18-25	26-51	52+
20%	80%	0%	0-6	7-11	12-18	19-26	27-53	54+
30%	0%	70%	0-6	7-9	10-14	15-21	22-41	42+
30%	10%	60%	0-6	7-10	11-15	16-22	23-43	44+
30%	20%	50%	0-6	7-10	11-16	17-23	24-45	46+
I	J	K	VALUES OF L (Percentages)					

Categories			Adjustments to SSS to determine the CSS					
1	2	3	N/C	+3	+2	+1	0	−1
30%	30%	40%	0-6	7-10	11-16	17-24	25-47	48+
30%	40%	30%	0-6	7-11	12-17	18-25	26-49	50+
30%	50%	20%	0-6	7-11	12-17	18-26	27-51	52+
30%	60%	10%	0-6	7-11	12-18	19-26	27-53	54+
30%	70%	0%	0-7	8-11	12-18	19-27	28-55	56+
40%	0%	60%	0-6	7-10	11-16	17-23	24-45	46+
40%	10%	50%	0-6	7-10	11-16	17-24	25-47	48+
40%	20%	40%	0-6	7-11	12-17	18-25	26-49	50+
40%	30%	30%	0-6	7-11	12-18	19-26	27-51	52+
40%	40%	20%	0-7	8-11	12-18	19-27	28-53	54+
40%	50%	10%	0-7	8-12	13-19	20-28	29-55	56+
40%	60%	0%	0-7	8-12	13-19	20-29	30-57	58+
50%	0%	50%	0-6	7-11	12-17	18-25	26-49	50+
50%	10%	40%	0-7	8-11	12-18	19-26	27-51	52+
50%	20%	30%	0-7	8-12	13-18	19-27	28-53	54+
50%	30%	20%	0-7	8-12	13-19	20-28	29-55	56+
50%	40%	10%	0-7	8-12	13-20	21-29	30-57	58+
50%	50%	0%	0-7	8-13	14-20	21-30	31-59	60+
60%	0%	40%	0-7	8-12	13-19	20-27	28-53	54+
60%	10%	30%	0-7	8-12	13-19	20-28	29-55	56+
60%	20%	20%	0-7	8-12	13-20	21-29	30-57	58+
60%	30%	10%	0-7	8-13	14-20	21-30	31-59	60+
60%	40%	0%	0-7	8-13	14-21	22-31	32-61	62+
70%	0%	30%	0-7	8-13	14-20	21-30	31-57	58+
70%	10%	20%	0-7	8-13	14-21	22-31	32-59	60+
70%	20%	10%	0-8	9-13	14-21	22-31	32-60	61+
70%	30%	0%	0-8	9-14	15-22	23-32	33-62	63+
80%	0%	20%	0-8	9-13	14-22	23-32	33-60	61+
80%	10%	10%	0-8	9-14	15-22	23-33	34-62	63+
80%	20%	0%	0-8	9-14	15-23	24-34	35-64	65+
90%	0%	10%	0-8	9-14	15-23	24-34	35-64	65+
90%	10%	0%	0-8	9-15	16-24	25-35	36-66	67+
100%	0%	0%	0-9	10-15	16-24	25-36	37-68	69+
I	J	K	VALUES OF L (Percentages)					

Appendix F

Table B Less than 31 competitors

Categories			Adjustments to SSS to determine the CSS					
1	2	3	N/C	+3	+2	+1	0	−1
0%	0%	100%	0-3	4-5	6-8	9-12	13-30	31+
0%	10%	90%	0-3	4-6	7-9	10-13	14-32	33+
0%	20%	80%	0-3	4-6	7-9	10-14	15-34	35+
0%	30%	70%	0-4	5-6	7-10	11-14	15-36	37+
0%	40%	60%	0-4	5-6	7-10	11-15	16-38	39+
0%	50%	50%	0-4	5-7	8-10	11-16	17-40	41+
0%	60%	40%	0-4	5-7	8-11	12-17	18-41	42+
0%	70%	30%	0-4	5-7	8-11	12-17	18-43	44+
0%	80%	20%	0-4	5-7	8-12	13-18	19-45	46+
0%	90%	10%	0-4	5-7	8-12	13-19	20-47	48+
0%	100%	0%	0-4	5-8	9-13	14-19	20-49	50+
10%	0%	90%	0-4	5-6	7-9	10-14	15-34	35+
10%	10%	80%	0-4	5-6	7-10	11-15	16-36	37+
10%	20%	70%	0-4	5-6	7-10	11-15	16-38	39+
10%	30%	60%	0-4	5-7	8-11	12-16	17-39	40+
10%	40%	50%	0-4	5-7	8-11	12-17	18-41	42+
10%	50%	40%	0-4	5-7	8-12	13-18	19-43	44+
10%	60%	30%	0-4	5-7	8-12	13-18	19-45	46+
10%	70%	20%	0-4	5-8	9-12	13-19	20-47	48+
10%	80%	10%	0-4	5-8	9-13	14-20	21-49	50+
10%	90%	0%	0-4	5-8	9-13	14-20	21-51	52+
20%	0%	80%	0-4	5-7	8-11	12-16	17-38	39+
20%	10%	70%	0-4	5-7	8-11	12-16	17-39	40+
20%	20%	60%	0-4	5-7	8-11	12-17	18-41	42+
20%	30%	50%	0-4	5-7	8-12	13-18	19-43	44+
20%	40%	40%	0-4	5-7	8-12	13-19	20-45	46+
20%	50%	30%	0-4	5-8	9-13	14-19	20-47	48+
20%	60%	20%	0-4	5-8	9-13	14-20	21-49	50+
20%	70%	10%	0-4	5-8	9-13	14-21	22-51	52+
20%	80%	0%	0-5	6-8	9-14	15-22	23-53	54+
30%	0%	70%	0-4	5-7	8-12	13-18	19-41	42+
30%	10%	60%	0-4	5-7	8-12	13-18	19-43	44+
30%	20%	50%	0-4	5-8	9-12	13-19	20-45	46+
30%	30%	40%	0-4	5-8	9-13	14-20	21-47	48+
30%	40%	30%	0-4	5-8	9-13	14-20	21-49	50+
30%	50%	20%	0-5	6-8	9-14	15-21	22-51	52+
30%	60%	10%	0-5	6-9	10-14	15-22	23-53	54+
30%	70%	0%	0-5	6-9	10-15	16-23	24-55	56+
40%	0%	60%	0-4	5-8	9-13	14-19	20-45	46+
40%	10%	50%	0-4	5-8	9-13	14-20	21-47	48+
40%	20%	40%	0-5	6-8	9-14	15-21	22-49	50+
40%	30%	30%	0-5	6-8	9-14	15-21	22-51	52+
40%	40%	20%	0-5	6-9	10-14	15-22	23-53	54+
40%	50%	10%	0-5	6-9	10-15	16-23	24-55	56+
40%	60%	0%	0-5	6-9	10-15	16-24	24-57	58+
50%	0%	50%	0-5	6-8	9-14	15-21	22-49	50+
50%	10%	40%	0-5	6-9	10-14	15-22	23-51	52+
50%	20%	30%	0-5	6-9	10-15	16-22	23-53	54+
50%	30%	20%	0-5	6-9	10-15	16-23	24-55	56+
50%	40%	10%	0-5	6-9	10-16	17-24	25-57	58+
50%	50%	0%	0-5	6-10	11-16	17-25	26-59	60+
60%	0%	40%	0-5	6-9	10-15	16-23	24-53	54+
60%	10%	30%	0-5	6-9	10-15	16-24	25-55	56+
60%	20%	20%	0-5	6-9	10-16	17-24	25-57	58+
60%	30%	10%	0-5	6-10	11-16	17-25	26-59	60+
60%	40%	0%	0-5	6-10	11-17	18-26	27-61	62+
70%	0%	30%	0-5	6-10	11-16	17-25	26-57	58+
70%	10%	20%	0-5	6-10	11-16	17-25	26-59	60+
70%	20%	10%	0-5	6-10	11-17	18-26	27-60	61+
70%	30%	0%	0-5	6-10	11-17	18-27	28-62	63+
80%	0%	20%	0-5	6-10	11-17	18-26	27-60	61+
80%	10%	10%	0-6	7-10	11-18	19-27	28-62	63+
80%	20%	0%	0-6	7-11	12-18	19-28	29-64	65+
90%	0%	10%	0-6	7-11	12-18	19-28	29-64	65+
90%	10%	0%	0-6	7-11	12-19	20-29	30-66	67+
100%	0%	0%	0-6	7-11	12-19	20-30	31-68	69+
I	J	K	VALUES OF L (Percentages)					

Appendix G

Handicap Allowances

as recommended by Council of National Golf Unions

The Council of National Golf Unions recommends that the following handicap allowances shall apply in the following forms of play. The reference to handicaps in all cases refers to PLAYING HANDICAPS.

Match Play

Singles The full difference between the HANDICAPS of the two players.

Foursomes 1/2 of the full difference between the aggregate HANDICAP of either side.

Four-ball (better ball) Back marker to concede strokes to the other three players based on 3/4 of the difference between the full handicap.

Strokes to be taken according to the Stroke Table.

Bogey or Par Competitions

Singles Full handicap

Foursomes 1/2 of the aggregate HANDICAP of the partners.

Four-ball (better ball) Each partner receives 3/4 of full handicap.

Strokes to be taken according to the Stroke Table.

Stroke Play

Singles Full handicap

Foursomes 1/2 of aggregate HANDICAPS of the partners.

Four-ball (better ball) Each partner receives 3/4 of the full handicap and strokes to be taken according to the Stroke Table.

Stableford Competitions

Singles Full handicap

Foursomes 1/2 of aggregate HANDICAPS of the partners.

Four-ball (better ball) Each partner receives 3/4 of full handicap.

Strokes to be taken according to the Stroke Table and not added to the points scored.

Note 1: Half Strokes. Half strokes or over to be counted as one; smaller fractions to be disregarded.

Note 2: Handicap allowances in a handicap competition must be laid down by the Committee in the Conditions of the Competition (Rules of Golf 33-1).

Note 3: 36-hole competitions. In handicap competitions over 36 holes, strokes should be given or taken in accordance with the 18 hole Stroke Table unless the Committee introduces a special Stroke Table.

Note 4: Sudden death play-off. When extra holes are played in handicap competitions, strokes should be taken in accordance with the Stroke Table.

Appendix H

Computer Software relating to the Standard Scratch and Handicapping Scheme

With effect from 1st January 1994 any software used by Affiliated Clubs shall provide a printed record for submission, when required, to Area Authorities or National Unions which contain all of the following information:

1. The name of the Affiliated Club.
2. The name of the Player.
3. The Player's Home Club.
4. The name of any other Clubs of which the Player is a member.
5. The Player's Exact handicap held immediately before the entry for the first Qualifying Competition shown in the records.
6. The date of each Qualifying Competition.
7. The Nett Differential in each Qualifying Competition or an entry identifying a "No Return".
8. All entries must be displayed and handicap adjustments made in chronological order.
9. The Exact Handicap and the Playing Handicap must be shown after each Qualifying Competition.
10 An identification of Nett Differentials returned elsewhere than the Player's Home Club.
11. Identification of any handicap adjustments made pursuant to Clause 19.
12. A Statement of the frequency of upward revisions of Playing Handicaps (Clause 16(10)).

Appendix I

Decisions

1. Scores in Extended Competitions

If from a series of any number of scores special prizes are awarded for the best eclectic score or the best nett or gross aggregate of a prescribed number of scores, the individual scores in the series will be QUALIFYING COMPETITIONS provided each score is returned under MEDAL PLAY CONDITIONS in a QUALIFYING COMPETITION, as defined in the Scheme, and not returned solely for the purpose of the eclectic, nett or gross aggregate awards.

2. Qualifying Scores

(a) If a club with a large number of QUALIFYING COMPETITIONS in the calendar year wishes to deprive certain of the competitions of their status as QUALIFYING COMPETITIONS it may do so provided competitors are so advised before play commences.

(b) It would be outside the spirit of the Handicapping Scheme to declare that all Club Medal Competitions during a specified period would not be regarded as QUALIFYING COMPETITIONS, although played under full MEDAL PLAY CONDITIONS.

(c) In both (a) and (b) above it would be more appropriate to play unofficial MEDAL COMPETITIONS under conditions which would not give them the status of QUALIFYING COMPETITIONS.

Note: A declaration that a competition is not a QUALIFYING COMPETITION disqualifies all scores returned in that competition for handicapping purposes. Thus a player returning a score below his handicap will not have his EXACT HANDICAP reduced nor will a score above a player's BUFFER ZONE increase his EXACT HANDICAP. Clause 19(4)(b) does however allow scores in non qualifying competitions to be one of a number of considerations when deciding to effect or recommend a handicap adjustment.

(d) A competition will not lose the status of QUALIFYING COMPETITION when played under conditions when, because of work proceeding or ground conditions in the area, pegging-up has been made obligatory by the club on a restricted area of the course, provided the playing of QUALIFYING COMPETITIONS under such conditions has the prior approval of the UNION or AREA AUTHORITY.

3. Upwards adjustment of Handicaps

(a) Clubs may elect to adjust PLAYING HANDICAPS upwards at the end of each calendar month or at shorter intervals, including immediate adjustment after completion of each QUALIFYING COMPETITION at the club.

(b) There could be slight differences in EXACT HANDICAPS produced by each method when comparison is made at the end of a calendar month.

(c) The procedure for recording NETT DIFFERENTIALS set out in the Scheme should be adhered to whatever method is used.

(d) There is no objection to clubs electing to adjust PLAYING HANDICAPS upwards at the end of each calendar month, or at more frequent intervals, taking steps to adjust and record EXACT and PLAYING HANDICAPS so that at the end of each month they correspond with those derived by adjusting handicaps after the playing of each QUALIFYING COMPETITION.

4. Limitation of Handicaps

Clubs have inquired whether they may impose a limit of handicap to some of their competitions e.g. insist that a 24 handicap player competes from a handicap of 18. This is permitted by Rule of Golf 33-1. However, when recording the players' scores for handicapping purposes, adjustments must be made to ensure that the NETT DIFFERENTIAL is recorded from his current PLAYING HANDICAP i.e. in the example quoted 24 instead of 18.

This is comparatively simple for MEDAL COMPETITION, but is impractical for Stableford and Par competitions as it is unlikely for example that a player would record a score at a hole where a stroke allowance of one from an 18 handicap gave him no points, whereas from a handicap of 24 with a stroke allowance of two at that particular hole he might have registered one point.

5. Incomplete Cards and No Returns

(a) All cards must be returned, whether complete or not.

(b) It is expected that every player who enters for an 18-hole QUALIFYING COMPETITION intends to complete the round.

(c) Since an Incomplete Card and a No Return have the effect of increasing a player's handicap, the club would be justified in refusing to accept a card or record a 'N.R.' when the player has walked in after playing only a few holes.

(d) Cards should not be issued to players when there is obviously insufficient light for them to complete the round.

(e) Sympathetic consideration should be given to players who have had to discontinue play for any cause considered to be reasonable by the organising committee.

(f) Clauses 17 and 19 of the Scheme give clubs the discretion to deal with players who persistently submit Incomplete Cards or make No Returns if they consider they are attempting to 'build a handicap'.

6. Reduction of Handicaps during a Competition

Where the conditions of a competition do not provide otherwise the handicap of a player applying at the beginning of a competition shall apply throughout that competition. This provision shall apply to a competition in which supplementary prizes are awarded for the best scores returned in an individual round or in combinations of individual rounds of the competition. The provisions shall not apply in circumstances where the winner is the player returning the lowest aggregate score in two or more separate competitions.

Where a player's handicap has been reduced during the course of a competition in which the original handicap continues to apply the player shall play from his reduced handicap in all other competitions commencing after the handicap reduction.

7. Overseas Scores

Scores returned in tournaments organised by the European Golf Association are QUALIFYING SCORES for handicapping purposes and must be returned to the HOME CLUB pursuant to clause 13.(7) provided COMPETITION SCRATCH SCORES have been calculated. Other scores returned in overseas tournaments may be returned and used, if considered appropriate, under the terms of clause 19.

8. Clause 19

Reductions pursuant to Clause 19 can be made only when the HANDICAP COMMITTEE has reason to believe that the handicap of a player may be too high. The Committee must consider all available information regarding the player's ability. A low score in a single event is not sufficient evidence alone to justify a Clause 19 reduction.

If the handicap of any player is reduced other than to the extent required by Clause 16 or by the correct application of Clause 19, the player's handicap will not be a C.O.N.G.U. handicap and cannot be used in any competition for which a C.O.N.G.U. handicap is required.

Stationery

Enquiries regarding storage binders and handicap record sheets suitable for use in connection with the Standard Scratch Score and Handicapping Scheme 1983 to be directed to Hon. Secretary of the Council of National Golf Unions: A. Thirlwell, 19 Birch Green, Formby, Liverpool L37 1NG.

Forms of application for:

An alteration to the Basic Standard Scratch Score.

An addition for course value to the Provisional Standard Scratch Score.

The above forms may be obtained from the Secretaries of:

(a) County Golf Unions or District Committees.
(b) Area Authorities.
(c) National Golf Unions.
(d) Council of National Golf Unions.

Draws for Match Play Competitions

Cold Draw

When the number of entries is not a whole power of 2, i.e. 4, 8, 16, 32, 64 etc, a number of first round byes are necessary. Subtract the number of entries from the nearest of these numbers above the number of entries to give the number of byes. *Example:* (a) 28 entries – subtracting from 32 gives 4 first round byes; (b) 33 entries – subtracting from 64 gives 31 first round byes.

All names (or numbers representing names) are put in a hat and the requisite number of byes drawn out singly and placed in pairs in the second round of the draw, alternately at the top and bottom, i.e. the first two names go at the top of the draw, the next two at the bottom and so on until all the byes have been drawn. If there is an odd number of byes, the last drawn is bracketed to play against the winner of either the first or last first round match. Having drawn all the byes, the remaining names are then drawn and placed in pairs in the first round in the order drawn in the middle of the draw.

Automatic Draw

When a stroke play qualifying round(s) is used to determine the qualifiers for the ensuing match play, the automatic draw is used, based on the qualifying position of each qualifier, i.e. the leading qualifier is number 1 in the draw, the second qualifier is number 2 and so on.

The following table gives the automatic draw for up to 64 qualifiers. Use the first column for 64 qualifiers, the second column for 32 qualifiers, and so on.

1 64	1	1	1	1	1
33 32	32				
17 48	17	16			
49 16	16				
9 56	9	9	8		
41 24	24				
25 40	25	8			
57 8	8				
5 60	5	5	5	4	
37 28	28				
21 44	21	12			
53 12	12				
13 52	13	13	4		
45 20	20				
29 36	29	4			
61 4	4				
3 62	3	3	3	3	2
35 30	30				
19 46	19	14			
51 14	14				
11 54	11	11	6		
43 22	22				
27 38	27	6			
59 6	6				
7 58	7	7	7	2	
39 26	26				
23 42	23	10			
55 10	10				
15 50	15	15	2		
47 18	18				
31 34	31	2			
63 2	2				

The LGU System of Handicapping

Effective from 1 February 1994

CONTENTS

Section I Definitions

Average differential
The sum of the differentials divided by their number.

***Bona fide* Society**
A society which meets the following LGU criteria, and is thereby permitted to organise Qualifying Competitions for its members:
a. The society must have a committee with annually elected officers including a Secretary conversant with LGU handicapping regulations.
b. Members must have an authentic golfing bond such as in Girls', Past Lady Captains' and Seniors' Golfing Societies, or a common bond through the members' professions or businesses, such as the National Westminster Bank Golfing Society for Bank employees.

Completed Gross Score
The term used to distinguish a total 18 hole gross score when a gross score has been recorded for each hole, from a Converted Gross Score. The card must be checked, signed by the marker and countersigned by the player. The card should also show the player's name and the date.

Converted Gross Score
The total 18 hole gross score converted from the points scored in Stableford Qualifying Competition, or the result against par in Par Qualifying Competition. The card must be checked, signed by the marker and countersigned by the player. The card should also show the player's name and the date.

Committee
The term "Committee" is deemed to refer to the Committee of the Ladies' Section. The term

"Club Committee" refers to the Committee in charge of the course. Where the management of the club and/or course is entirely in the hands of the Ladies' Committee the term "Club Committee" shall be deemed to refer to such.

Differential
The difference between the total gross score and the Scratch Score of the course on which it is returned.

Extra Day Score
A Completed Gross Score which is returned other than in Qualifying Competition. The card should be marked "EDS" (even when returning in a non-qualifying event).

Handicap Advisers
Handicap Advisers and their Deputies are persons appointed by the National Organisation to assist Handicap Secretaries in dealing with problems and exceptional cases, and to keep records of all players with handicaps under 4.

Handicap Secretary
A player's Handicap Secretary is the Handicap Secretary of her Home Club. The Handicap Secretary of an Individual Member of the LGU, or of a National Organisation, is the Administrator of the LGU or the Secretary of the National Organisation respectively. The Handicap Secretary of a visitor from overseas, unless she joins an affiliated club as an annual member, is the Administrator of the LGU.

Home Club
The Home Club is the club which a member of more than one club has chosen to be that where her handicap records shall be maintained and of which the Handicap Secretary shall be her Handicap Secretary.

Home/Away Courses
Home Course Any course situated at, and associated with, a club at which the player has club membership. (Except at her Home Club a course at which a player holds Honorary club membership shall count as an Away Course in a Qualifying Competition open to non-members.)
Away Course A course at which a player has no club membership.

Individual Members
(a) *of the LGU:* Players temporarily resident overseas, for a period of not less than one year, are entitled to apply for individual membership of the LGU.
(b) *of the National Organisations:* Players unable to become an annual playing member of an affiliated club may apply to their National Organisation for individual membership.

Lapsed Handicap
A handicap has lapsed if four scores have not been returned in an LGU year by Category C, D and E players, six scores in Qualifying Competitions by Category B players (unless increasing to Category C) and ten scores in Qualifying Competitions by Category A players (unless increasing to Category B).

LGU Medal Competition
LGU Medal Competitions are designated Stroke Play Competitions. Any number to a maximum of sixteen may be held and may be played in conjunction with club stroke play competitions authorised by the Committee. A minimum of four cards must be returned to qualify for the annual Silver and Bronze Medals.

LGU Tees and Teeing Grounds
The LGU tees, indicated by a Permanent Marker on the right hand side of the tee, are those from which the Scratch Score has been fixed. The actual teeing ground in play (see Rules of Golf Definition) is indicated by red tee markers which, for the convenience of the greenkeeper, may be moved in any direction from the Permanent Marker provided the hole is not altered in length by more than ten yards.
Note: In the event of the teeing ground having been accidentally or otherwise moved beyond the permitted limit the score cannot count for handicap or for LGU Competitions unless a special Scratch Score is allotted by the National Organisation.

Live Score
A score returned (in accordance with Regulation III.4) in the current LGU year (1 February to 31 January) or in the preceding LGU year.

National Organisation
The National Organisations are: the English Ladies' Golf Association, the Irish Ladies' Golf Union, the Scottish Ladies' Golfing Association and the Welsh Ladies' Golf Union.

In the case of overseas affiliated clubs, for "National Organisation" read "LGU".

Qualifying Competition
A stroke competition held on a specified day arranged with Club Committee permission.

Qualifying Competition Score
A gross score returned in a Qualifying Competition which counts as a competition score for LGU handicap purposes.

Scratch Score
The Scratch Score of a course is the score expected of a Scratch player in normal Spring and Autumn conditions of wind and weather.

Symbols

@ – marks a regained handicap in Categories A and B only, which has had to be assessed rather than calculated because the required types of score have not been returned.

* – asterisk – marks a handicap when the result of the calculation has been limited by the regulations.

P – marks a handicap when the player is not eligible to play in LGU Medal Competitions.

Section II Introduction

1. Basis of the System

The chief features of the LGU System of Handicapping are: that all handicaps shall be fixed on the basis of the LGU Scratch Score; that handicaps shall be assessed on actual scores returned and not on general form; and that the player's LGU handicap shall be the same in every club.

2. Overseas Unions and Clubs

Overseas affiliated Unions and Clubs shall be permitted to make such adjustments to these regulations as may be deemed by their Executive Committee to be necessary on account of climatic or other conditions peculiar to the territory administered by them, so long as these adjustments do not depart from the fundamental principles of the LGU System of Handicapping as stated in the paragraph above or contravene the Rules of Golf as laid down by the Royal & Ancient Golf Club of St Andrews. The LGU must be informed as and when such adjustments are made.

3. Queries

Queries on LGU Regulations shall be, and on the Rules of Golf may be, submitted in accordance with the following procedures:–

(a) **SECRETARIES and COMMITTEES of Affiliated Clubs** should submit queries to their Handicap Adviser and National Organisation in that order. Handicap queries should be referred to the Club Handicap Secretary, the Handicap Adviser and the National Organisation in that order.

(b) **MEMBERS OF AFFILIATED CLUBS** may submit queries to their National Organisation and must have their statements signed as read on behalf of the Ladies' Committee. If there is any difference of opinion the Committee or opposing party should submit their own statement in writing.

(c) **OVERSEAS UNIONS and CLUBS.** In the case of clubs affiliated to the Ladies' Golf Union outside Great Britain and Ireland or directly affiliated to the LGU, queries should be submitted to the LGU. Statements should be signed as read on behalf of such Union or Club Committee.

Correspondence of this nature sent to the LGU and the National Organisations is filed for reference and cannot be returned.

Section III The Player's Responsibilities and Rights

1. General

Playing off the Correct Handicap. It is the player's responsibility to know and to apply the Handicapping Regulations and to play off the correct handicap at all times. The card of any score which might affect the handicap must be returned to the player's Handicap Secretary as soon as possible. She should be able to produce a current Handicap Certificate when required to do so. In case of doubt or disagreement between the player and her Handicap Secretary as to what is the player's correct handicap, she should play off the lower until an official decision can be obtained from the Handicap Adviser or the National Organisation.

Handicap Reduction. Any reduction in handicap is automatic and comes into force immediately, except:–

(i) in the event of a tie in a competition which has been completed in one day or on consecutive days, where this is resolved by a replay or a play-off; and

(ii) in a 36-, 54- or 72-hole competition played on the same day or on consecutive days.

Playing away from Home. A player must notify her Handicap Secretary of any score (which might affect her handicap) returned by her on any course other than at her Home Club.

2. Eligibility to Hold an LGU Handicap

An LGU handicap may be obtained and held by an amateur lady golfer who is either:–

(a) an annual playing member, including a five day, country, junior or life member (whether honorary or paying) of a club affiliated to the LGU either directly or through its National Organisation; or

(b) an Individual Member of either the LGU or one of the four National Organisations; or

(c) a temporary member of an affiliated club, provided her membership is to last for a period of not less than twelve months.

Note: Should membership cease or expire the player's LGU handicap is no longer valid, but her scores remain **LIVE** if returned before such cessation or expiry.

3. How to Gain an LGU Handicap

Four Extra Day Scores must be returned on the course or courses of an LGU affiliated club or clubs, the Scratch Score of which must be not less than 60. Play must be in twos (threes and fours are not acceptable), no more than one player per marker, and must be in accordance with Regulations III4.(a), (b), (c), (d) and (e).

Overseas players joining an LGU affiliated club who hold or have held a recognised handicap. Four live scores returned on an LGU affiliated course must be submitted to the LGU Administrator with the current overseas handicap certificate or information of the handicap last held and the year of lapse. Live scores from non-LGU-affiliated courses overseas which might affect the handicap should be enclosed with course particulars as detailed in the Note to Regulation III4.(b) below. In any event the LGU handicap shall be no higher than a current CONGU or USGA handicap, or the equivalent figure in the case of a lapsed handicap after application of Table II, the Table of Permitted Increases for Lapsed Handicaps.

4. Scores Acceptable for LGU Handicap

To be acceptable for handicap:–

(a) Scores must be returned in accordance with the Rules of Golf as approved by the Royal & Ancient Golf Club of St Andrews and with the Club's Local Rules and Bye-Laws, which must not contravene any R.&A. Rule or LGU Regulation.

Only scores returned in Qualifying Competitions are acceptable as competition scores for LGU Handicap purposes.

(b) Scores must be returned on the course of an LGU affiliated club with an LGU Scratch Score of not less than 60. Play must be from **LGU TEES.** Extra Day Scores returned on a course of which the player is not a member must be countersigned by a local official to certify that the Scratch Score is correctly stated. Completed cards should either be returned in person by the player to her Handicap Secretary without delay or left in the card box of the club visited, with the name and address of the home club and the cost of postage. Qualifying Competition Scores returned on a course of which a player has no membership must be signed by an official of the Competition Committee who must have confirmed the Scratch Score of the day with the Secretary of the host club.

Note: Scores returned on non-LGU-affiliated courses overseas (see lists in the Lady Golfers' Handbook) may count for handicap at the discretion of the LGU. Such cards, duly countersigned by a local official as showing the correct Scratch Score and accompanied by relevant information about local condition, type of soil, terrain, course difficulties, etc. should be forwarded to the Administrator, LGU, The Scores, St Andrews, Fife, KY16 9AT, with a stamped, addressed envelope to the Handicap Secretary of the player's Home Club.

(c) Scores must be marked by an annual playing member of a recognised golf club or an Individual Member (see Definitions) who has or has had a handicap. A marker should not mark the card of more than one player.

(d) A score must be that of the first round of the day on any one course, except in the case of a Qualifying Competition consisting of 36 holes played on one day, when both scores shall count.

(e) **ADVERSE CONDITIONS** – (See Rules of Golf Appendix 1–4) **Local Rules for the Preservation of the Course**

Scores may be returned when the following conditions apply:–

(i) Where the Club Committee has made a local rule that the ball may be placed without penalty through the green.

(ii) Where the Club Committee has made a local rule that tee pegs must be used on any closely mown area or through the green:

(1) A deduction from the Scratch Score of two strokes must be made where more than nine holes are affected.

(2) A deduction from the Scratch Score of one stroke must be made where nine holes are affected.

(3) A deduction from the Scratch Score of one stroke will be at the discretion of the area Scratch Score Assessor where fewer than three holes are affected.

In the case of (ii)(1), (2) and (3) the area Scratch Score Assessor **MUST** be notified.

(iii) **The Green.** Where, for the preservation of the green, a temporary hole (see Rules of Golf Definitions) is off but adjacent to the green, provided this does not alter the length of the hole by more than ten yards.

Note: **LGU TEES.** Where, for the preservation of the course, the teeing ground has been moved beyond the permitted ten yards, scores may count for handicap only if a special Scratch Score is allotted by the National Organisation.

(f) Completed Gross Scores, returned in a stroke competition from which a player has been disqualified under R&A Rule 6–2b on her nett score, shall count for handicap.

In Stableford and Par Qualifying Competitions, if no handicap is recorded on the card before it is returned, or if the recorded handicap is higher than that to which a competitor is entitled and this affects the number of strokes received, the player shall be disqualified under R&A Rule 6–2b. The results shall be adjusted according to the player's correct handicap and, on being converted, the Converted Gross Score shall count for handicap.

(g) **SOCIETY DAY COMPETITIONS.** Handicap Secretaries must accept a score returned from a Society Day competition as a Qualifying Competition Score if they are satisfied the society is *bona fide* (see LGU definition of a Bona fide Society).

(h) All scores returned in Stroke Competitions, even if the competition is declared null and void, count for LGU handicap purposes, subject to Regulations III4.(a) to (g) above and provided competitors play from **LGU Tees** (see Definition and Note) and the SS of the course is not less than 60. Scores may be returned in twos, threes or fours, as arranged by the Committee.

Note: The exception to this is in a competition where the best-ball or better-ball score (see Rules of Golf Definitions) is to count, and in Pro-Am and Am-Am team events.

(i) **EXTRA DAY SCORES** must be returned in accordance with Regulations III4.(a) to (e) and should normally be marked in twos, but at the discretion of the Committee may be marked in threes or fours, in which case a notice to this effect must be posted on the Notice Board (but see Regulation III3. for gaining a first handicap). The player's name and the date must be recorded on the scorecard.

5. Calculation of LGU Handicap

(a) General

Handicaps are divided into five categories: Silver Division – A, B, C and Bronze Division – D and E. Handicaps are calculated as follows, on the basis of live scores returned in accordance with Regulation III4. above:

Note 1: For all handicaps, scores must be returned on courses with a Scratch Score of not less than 60.

Note 2: In all calculations above Scratch 1/2, 2/3 and 3/4 count as 1 and 1/3, 1/4 count as 0. In all calculations below scratch, fractions of 1/2 and less count as 0, fractions greater than 1/2 count as 1.

(i) Bronze Division

Category E, 36*–30. The handicap is the difference between the player's best live score and the Scratch Score of the course on which it was played, i.e. the handicap is her best **DIFFERENTIAL.** If the differential is more than 36 the handicap is 36* (*Example E¹*) or 36*P (see Regulation IV2.(a)). If the differential is 36–30 then that is the handicap (*Example E²*). If the best differential is less than 30, the handicap is 30 until the average of the two best differentials is less than 29 1/2 (*Example E³*).

EXAMPLES

E¹ Best gross score 115 SS 72 Differential 43
Handicap 36*

E² Best gross score 102 SS 69 Differential 33
Handicap 33

E³ Best gross score 101 SS 74 Differential 27
106 SS 70 Previous best differential 36

AVERAGE DIFFERENTIAL 31 1/2
Handicap 30

Category D, 29–19. The handicap is the average of the two best differentials (*Examples D¹, D²*), but if the average is less than 18 1/2 the handicap is 19 until the average of the **four** best differentials is less than 18 1/2 (*Example D³*).

EXAMPLES

D¹ Gross score 99 SS 73 Best differential 26
Gross score 104 SS 73 Previous best differential 31
Average differential 28 1/2
Handicap 29

D² Gross score 95 SS 71 Best differential 24
Gross score 98 SS 70 Previous best differential 28
Average differential 26
Handicap 26

D³ Gross scores Best differentials
87 SS 72 15
92 SS 72 20
Average differential 17 1/2
but . . . Handicap 19
96 SS 73 23
94 SS 71 23
Average differential (of four) 20 1/4
Handicap 19

(ii) Silver Division

Category C, 18–10. The handicap is the average of the four best differentials (*Example C¹*), but if this average is less than 9 1/2, the handicap is 10 until the conditions for Category B are fulfilled (Example C²).

EXAMPLES

C¹ Best differentials:
10
11
13
17 Average 12 3/4 Handicap 13

C^2 EDS = Extra Day Scores;
QCS = Qualifying Competition Scores.
Best differentials:
10 (EDS)
9 (QCS)
7 (EDS)
6 (QCS) Average 8 but . . . Handicap 10

11 (QCS)
13 (QCS)
12 (QCS)
14 (QCS)
Average differential of six Qualifying Competition Scores = $10^5/_6$

Handicap 10

Category B, 9–4. The handicap is the average of the six best differentials of scores returned in Qualifying Competitions (*Example* B^1), but if this average is less than $3^1/_2$, the handicap is 4 until the conditions for Category A are fulfilled (*Example* B^2).

EXAMPLES

B^1 Best differentials from Qualifying Competition Scores:
7
5
5
6
4
4 Average differential $5^1/_6$ Handicap 5

B^2 Best differentials from Qualifying Competition Scores:
H1, H2 = HOME COURSES, A1, A2 etc = Away Courses:
3 (H1)
5 (H2)
4 (H1)
2 (H1)
2 (H1)
3 (A1) Average differential $3^1/_6$ but . . . Handicap 4

6 (A1)
7 (A2)
6 (H2)
8 (A1) Average differential 4.6 Handicap 4

Category A, 3 and under. To obtain a handicap of 3 or under, a player must return at least ten scores in Qualifying Competitions. Only six of these scores may be from a Home Course, and the remaining four must be from at least two different Away Courses. The handicap is the average of the ten best differentials so obtained (*Examples* A^1 *and* A^2).

EXAMPLE: (*Abbreviations as in* B^2)

A^1 Best differentials from Qualifying Competition Scores:
0 (H)
–1 (H)
–1 (H)
0 (H)
3 (H)
0 (H)
1 (A1)
0 (A1)
1 (A2)
3 (A2) Average differential 0.6 Handicap 1

A^2 Best differentials from Qualifying Competition Scores:
–1 (H)
–1 (H)
–2 (H)
1 (A1)
–2 (H)
–1 (A2)
0 (H)
–1 (H)
2 (A3)
0 (A1) Average differential –0.5
Handicap Scratch (–0.5 = 0)

(b) Stableford and Par Qualifying Competitions

(It is recommended that at least 50% of stroke competitions should be Stroke Play competitions. i.e. those where a Completed Gross Score must be returned.)

Where no point is recorded for any hole in a Stableford Qualifying Competition, or a loss is recorded for any hole in a Par Qualifying Competition, the Conversion Chart/formulae MUST be used in arriving at a Converted Gross Score.

Note: Conversion Charts specific to the total PAR of a course (not the SSS) are obtainable from the National Organisation.

Conversion of Stableford Qualifying Scores to Converted Gross Scores

Formula:

Par + 36 – Stableford points scored + Full Handicap = Converted Gross Score

Example:

73 + 36 – 38 + 20 = 91

Conversion of Par Qualifying Scores to Converted Gross Scores

(1) Holes Up
Formula:

Par – Holes Up + Full Handicap = Converted Gross Score

Example:

73 – 1 + 20 = 92

(2) All Square
Formula:

Par + Full Handicap = Converted Gross Score

Example:

73 + 20 = 93

(3) Holes Down
Formula:

Par + Holes Down + Full Handicap = Converted Gross Score

Example:

73 + 1 + 20 = 94

The above formulae may be applied ONLY to 18 hole Qualifying Competitions and multiples thereof.

Stableford and Par Qualifying Competitions must be played off full handicap.

Stableford and Par Qualifying Competitions must not be combined with Stroke Play Qualifying Competitions.

Where an overall handicap limit is in force, such handicap, if lower than the player's handicap, is that which must be recorded on the card. In Stableford and Par Qualifying Competitions, such handicap must be used when converting to the Converted Gross Score.

6. Annual Revision of Handicaps and LAPSED HANDICAPS

(a) General

On 31 January each year all handicaps shall be recalculated on the basis of scores returned during the preceding twelve months and in accordance with the Regulations in force during that period. Any increase in handicap resulting from such recalculation shall be limited by Table I – Table of Permitted Increases for Revised Handicaps set out below. At no other time during the year may a player's handicap be increased (except in accordance with Regulation III7.(b) or (c)).

TABLE I – TABLE OF PERMITTED INCREASES FOR REVISED HANDICAPS

Handicaps plus to 34 may go up 2 strokes.
Handicap 35 may go up 1 stroke.

A handicap limited by the Table of Permitted Increases for Revised Handicaps shall be marked with an asterisk until the calculation of live scores results in a handicap equal to or less than that held.

(b) Minimum Number of Scores to be Returned

Handicap Categories E, D, C. To retain a handicap, a player with handicap 36*–10 must have returned at least four scores.

Handicap Category B. To retain a handicap, a player with handicap 9–4 must have returned at least six scores in Qualifying Competitions.

Exception: If a player with handicap 8 or 9 prior to Revision has returned at least four scores (not necessarily in Qualifying Competitions) the handicap shall not lapse, but shall be calculated in accordance with the Regulations governing handicaps 18–10 and Table I – the Table of Permitted Increases for Revised Handicaps.

Handicap Category A. To retain a handicap a player with handicap 3 or under must have returned at least ten scores in Qualifying Competitions. Only six of these may be from a Home Course, and the remaining four must be from at least two different Away Courses.

Exceptions: (a) If a player with handicap 2 or 3 prior to Revision has returned at least six scores in Qualifying Competitions, the handicap shall not lapse, but shall be calculated in accordance with Regulations governing handicaps 9–4 and the Table I – Table of Permitted Increases for Revised Handicaps.

(b) If a player with handicap 1 or under prior to Revision has returned ten scores in Qualifying Competitions, but not the necessary Away Scores, the handicap shall not lapse, but shall be increased by two strokes and marked with an @ until the necessary Away Scores have been returned.

(c) Lapsed Handicaps

A handicap lapses if a player has not returned the minimum number and types of scores necessary to retain a handicap (see (b) above). When a player's handicap has lapsed she does not have a valid handicap until the conditions have been fulfilled to regain it (see (d) below) and is ineligible to enter competitions.

(d) To Regain a Handicap which has Lapsed

Handicap Categories E, D, C. To regain a handicap which has lapsed, a player whose most recent handicap was in Category E, D or C, (36*–10) must return the number of Extra Day Scores necessary to increase the number of "live" scores to four. The handicap shall then be calculated in accordance with Regulations, but it shall be limited by Table II – Table of Permitted Increases for Lapsed Handicaps set out below and must be confirmed, before use, by the player's Handicap Secretary.

Handicap Category B. To regain a handicap which has lapsed, a player whose most recent handicap was in Category B (9–4) must return the necessary Extra Day Scores which together with the "live" Qualifying Competition Scores make a total of six, except that a player with fewer than two "live" Qualifying Competition Scores is only required to return four Extra Day Scores. The handicap shall be increased in accordance with Table II – Table of Permitted Increases for Lapsed Handicaps, by the maximum permitted increase and must be confirmed, before use, by the player's Handicap Secretary. If the regained handicap is in Category B the handicap shall be marked with an @ until scores returned fulfil all the conditions necessary for this category of player.

Handicap Category A. To regain a handicap which has lapsed, a player whose most recent handicap was in Category A (3 and under) must return the necessary Extra Day Scores which together with the "live" Qualifying Competition Scores make a total of ten, except that a player with fewer than six "live" Qualifying Competition Scores is only required to return four Extra Day Scores. The handicap shall be increased in accordance with Table II – Table of Permitted Increases for Lapsed Handicaps by the maximum permitted

TABLE II – TABLE OF PERMITTED INCREASES FOR LAPSED HANDICAPS

(i) If lapsed for less than one year the handicap shall be limited to two strokes higher than that last held.
(ii) For each year in excess of one the handicap may be increased by a further stroke. (The part year in which the handicap is regained counts as a whole year.)

EXAMPLES:

Handicap Lapsed on	Handicap regained during	Period Handicap lapsed	Max Inc over previous Handicap
(i) 31 January 1989	1993–1994 (LGU year)	5 years	6 strokes
(ii) " " 1990	"	4 years	5 strokes
(iii) " " 1991	"	3 years	4 strokes
(iv) " " 1992	"	2 years	3 strokes
(v) " " 1993	"	less than 1 year	2 strokes

A handicap limited by the Table of Permitted Increases for Lapsed Handicaps shall be marked with an asterisk.

increase and must be confirmed before use, by the player's Handicap Secretary. If the regained handicap is in Category A or B the handicap shall be marked with an @ until scores returned fulfil all the conditions necessary for the player's category.

Note: Any Extra Day Scores used to regain a lapsed handicap, Category A or B, may only be used.

Transition to a Higher Category. The number of Extra Day Scores required to regain a handicap by a player in Category A or B shall be determined after taking into account the "live" Qualifying Competition Scores and Table II – Table of Permitted Increases for Lapsed Handicaps. Players are only required to return a maximum of four Extra Day Scores before regaining a handicap. If the regained handicap is in Category A or B it shall be marked with an @ until scores returned fulfil all the conditions necessary for the player's category. When the appropriate scores have been returned, the handicap shall be calculated in accordance with Regulations and shall be marked with an asterisk until the calculation results in a handicap equal to or less than the regained handicap.

Note: A player whose most recent handicap was in Category A or B and permitted by Table II – Table of Permitted Increases for Lapsed Handicaps to be increased to Category C, D or E, is required to return the necessary Extra Day Scores to increase the number of "live" scores to four.

7. Special Categories of Handicap

(a) **Juniors**. An LGU Junior handicap (limit 45) may be obtained and held by any girl who is a junior, i.e. who has not reached her twelfth birthday on 1 January, by returning two scores over nine specified holes. Any nine holes on the course may be chosen to make up the round, at the discretion of the club, and a special SS for those holes must be obtained from the National Organisation. Each score returned, and the special SS for the nine holes, shall be doubled in order to arrive at the number of strokes above SS. Handicaps will be reduced in accordance with Regulations (one card 45–30, etc.). Juniors may hold a standard LGU handicap but may not hold both.

To retain a Junior LGU handicap two scores over nine holes must be returned annually. An LGU Junior handicap shall be acceptable for all junior competitions, and these Regulations shall apply to all players with Junior handicaps. Handicap Certificates for LGU Junior handicaps will be issued by the Handicap Secretary and *the date and year when the player will attain her twelfth birthday must be entered on the Handicap Certificate.*

(b) **Former Professional Golfers.** On reinstatement as an amateur a player who has been a professional golfer must apply for a handicap to the Administrator, LGU. The Executive Council shall, at their discretion, allot a handicap of not more than Scratch on the basis of live scores returned during the player's period of probation in accordance with the Regulations governing handicaps of 3 and under. For the first two years after reinstatement the player's Handicap Secretary must submit all scores returned twice yearly on 1 January and 1 July to the Administrator, LGU, The Scores, St. Andrews, Fife, KY16 9AT. Handicaps will be reviewed by the Executive Council and revised at their discretion.

(c) **After Serious Illness and Disablement.** A person wishing to regain a handicap or have her handicap reassessed after serious illness or disablement may apply through her Club Committee to the National Organisation with all relevant details, including a minimum of four live scores returned, so that consideration may be given to the circumstances and the player may obtain a realistic handicap.

Handicaps shall be adjusted in accordance with Regulations.

(d) **Individual Members and Visitors from Overseas.** The handicaps of Individual Members of the LGU or of the National Organisations shall be managed by the Administrator of the LGU or the Secretary of the appropriate National Organisation. All scores returned must be countersigned by the Handicap Secretary of the club at which they were returned and forwarded to the appropriate Secretary, who will act as Handicap Secretary for these players.

Handicaps of visitors from overseas who are not annual playing members of an affiliated club in Great Britain or Ireland shall be managed by the Administrator of the LGU, to whom scores should be forwarded after countersignature as above.

(e) **Senior Veterans and Disabled Players.** Where a club has members who do not normally play 18 holes but who wish to play competitive golf informally, it is suggested that special handicaps be allotted by the Committee on the basis of nine-hole scores doubled. The Committee should specify which nine holes are to be played and allot for those holes a 'scratch score', which should also be doubled to arrive at the handicap. *Handicaps so obtained are not LGU handicaps and are not valid for any purpose for which an LGU handicap is required.*

8. Membership of More than One Club

(a) A member belonging to more than one affiliated club must inform the Ladies' Secretary and Handicap Secretary of each club of the other affiliated clubs to which she belongs and also of any scores (together with Scratch Score) which may affect her handicap.

(b) Handicap Secretary. If a player is a member of more than one club she must decide which club she wishes to be her Home Club for handicap purposes and notify the Ladies' Secretary of that club accordingly. A player's Handicap Secretary shall be the Handicap Secretary of her Home Club.

(c) A member changing her Home Club must ask for a copy of her Handicap Register Form and take it with her Handicap Certificate to the Handicap Secretary of her new Home Club.

(d) A member joining an additional club must inform the Ladies' Secretary and the Handicap Secretary of such club of her existing or lapsed handicap, and of the scores, with relative dates, on which it was gained, and also the names of all clubs of which she is or has been a member.

(e) An annual playing member of a club affiliated to the LGU, who also has membership of a club under the jurisdiction of a different handicapping system, must return all scores which might affect her LGU handicap to her LGU Handicap Secretary, or in accordance with the Note to Regulation III 4.(b) in the case of scores from non-LGU-affiliated courses overseas. Her handicap at her non-LGU-affiliated club, is NOT an LGU handicap and may be different from her LGU handicap. The use of her LGU handicap is mandatory only in competitions run by an organisation affiliated to the LGU. It is up to the competition committee of the host club to state which handicap must be used in a competition run under the jurisdiction of a different Handicapping System.

For details of the following, please refer to the Lady Golfers' Handbook:

- Responsibilities of Affiliated Clubs and of the National Organisations in relation to Handicapping, Competitions and Other Matters
- Scratch Scores
- LGU Tees and Teeing Grounds in Play
- Starting Places
- Handicap Records and Certificates
- LGU Silver and Bronze Medal Competitions
- LGU Gold and Silver Medal Competitions
- LGU Challenge Bowl Competitions
- Coronation Foursomes Competition
- LGU Pendant Competition
- Australian Spoons Competitions

INDEX

Governing Bodies

Home Unions

The English Golf Union

The English Golf Union was founded in 1924 and embraces 34 County Unions with over 1,550 affiliated clubs, 23 clubs overseas, and 447 Golfing Societies and Associations. Its objects are:

(1) To further the interests of Amateur Golf in England.
(2) To assist in maintaining a uniform system of handicapping.
(3) To arrange an English Championship; an English Stroke Play Championship; an English County Championship, International and other Matches and Competitions.
(4) To co-operate with the Royal & Ancient Golf Club of St Andrews and the Council of National Golf Unions.
(5) To co-operate with other National Golf Unions and Associations in such manner as may be decided.

The Scottish Golf Union

The Scottish Golf Union was founded in 1920 and embraces 661 clubs. Subject to the stipulation and declaration that the Union recognises the Royal & Ancient Golf Club of St Andrews as the Ruling Authority in the game of golf, the objects of the Union are:

(a) To foster and maintain a high standard of Amateur Golf in Scotland and to administer and organise and generally act as the governing body of amateur golf in Scotland.
(b) To institute and thereafter carry through annually a Scottish Amateur Championship, a Scottish Open Amateur Stroke Play Championship and other such competitions and matches as they consider appropriate.
(c) To administer and apply the rules of the Standard Scratch Score and Handicapping Scheme as approved by the Council of National Golf Unions from time to time.
(d) To deal with other matters of general or local interest to amateur golfers in Scotland.

The Union's organisation consists of Area Committees covering the whole of Scotland. There are 16 Areas, each having its own Association or Committee elected by the Clubs in that particular area and each Area Association or Committee elects one delegate to serve on the Executive of the Union.

Golfing Union of Ireland

The Golfing Union of Ireland, founded in 1891, embraces 275 Clubs. Its objects are:

(1) Securing the federation of the various Clubs.
(2) Arranging Amateur Championships, Inter-Provincial and Inter-Club Competitions, and International Matches.
(3) Securing a uniform standard of handicapping.
(4) Providing for advice and assistance, other than financial, to affiliated Clubs in all matters appertaining to Golf, and generally to promote the game in every way, in which this can be better done by the Union than by individual Clubs.

Its functions include the holding of the *Close* Championship for Amateur Golfers and Tournaments for Team Matches.

Its organisation consists of Provincial Councils in each of the four Provinces elected by the Clubs in the Province – each province electing a limited number of delegates to the Central Council which meets annually.

Welsh Golfing Union

The Welsh Golfing Union was founded in 1895 and is the second oldest of the four National Unions. Unlike the other Unions it is an association of Golf Clubs and Golfing Organisations. The present membership is 127. For the purpose of electing the Executive Council, Wales is divided into ten districts which between them return 22 members.

The objects of the Union are:

(a) To take any steps which may be deemed necessary to further the interests of the amateur game in Wales.
(b) To hold a Championship Meeting or Meetings each year.
(c) To encourage, financially and/or otherwise,

Inter-Club, Inter-County, and International Matches, and such other events as may be authorised by the Council.
(d) To assist in setting up and maintaining a uniform system of Handicapping.
(e) To assist in the establishment and maintenance of high standards of greenkeeping.

Note: The union recognises the Royal & Ancient Golf Club of St Andrews as the ruling authority.

The Council of National Golf Unions

At a meeting of Representatives of Golf Unions and Associations in Great Britain and Ireland, called at the special request of the Scottish Golf Union, and held in York, on 14th February, 1924, resolutions were adopted from which the Council of National Golf Unions was constituted.

The Council holds an Annual Meeting in March, and such other meetings as may be necessary. Two representatives are elected from each national Home Union – England, Scotland, Ireland and Wales – and hold office until the next Annual meeting when they are eligible for re-election.

The principal function of the Council, as laid down by the York Conference, was to formulate a system of Standard Scratch Scores and Handicapping, and to co-operate with the Royal & Ancient Championship Committee in matters coming under their jurisdiction. The responsibilities undertaken by the Council at the instance of the Royal & Ancient Golf Club or the National Unions are as follows:

1 The Standard Scratch Score and Handicapping Scheme, formulated in March, 1926, approved by the Royal & Ancient, and last revised in 1989.
2 The nomination of two members on the Board of Management of The Sports Turf Research Institute, with an experimental station at St Ives, Bingley, Yorkshire.
3 The management of the Annual Amateur International Matches between the four countries – England, Scotland, Ireland and Wales.

United States Golf Association

The USGA is the national governing body of golf. Its single most important goal is preserving the integrity and values of the game.

Formed on 22nd December, 1894, a year when two clubs proclaimed different US Amateur Champions, representatives of five clubs met at a dinner at the Calumet Club in New York City. They created a central governing body to establish uniform rules, to conduct national championships and to nurture the virtues of sportsmanship in golf.

The names of the standing committees give an idea of what the USGA does: Rules of Golf, Championship, Amateur Status and Conduct, Implements and Ball, Handicap, Women's, Sectional Affairs, Green Section, Public Links, Women's Public Links, Junior Championship, Girls' Junior, Senior Championship, Senior Women's Championship, Bob Jones Award, Museum, Green Section Award, Finance, Public Information, Membership, Regional Association, Associates, Intercollegiate Relations, Mid-Amateur Championship, International Team Selection, Development, Turfgrass Research, Nominating.

The USGA, as the governing body of the game in the United States, makes and interprets the Rules of Golf in co-operation with the Royal & Ancient Golf Club of St Andrews, Scotland; developed and maintains the national system of handicapping; controls the standards of the ball and the implements of the game; works in turfgrass and turf management; and, generally speaking, preserves and promotes the game.

The Professional Golfers' Association

The Professional Golfers' Association was founded in 1901 to promote interest in the game of golf; to protect and advance the mutual and trade interests of its members; to arrange and hold meetings and tournaments periodically for the members; to institute and operate funds for the benefit of the members; to assist the members to obtain employment; and effect any other objects of a like nature as may be determined from time to time by the Association.

Classes of Membership

There shall be nine (9) classes of membership:

(i) **Class A** Members engaged as the nominated professional on a full-time basis at a PGA Club, PGA Course or PGA Driving Range in one of the seven Regions; and members engaged as the nominated professional on a full-time basis, at an establishment in one of the seven Regions at which the public can play and/or practise which, in the opinion of the Executive Committee does not qualify as a PGA Club, Course or Driving Range but does warrant Class A status.
Note: Class A(T) – Class A members currently engaged at an establishment which has been inspected and approved as a PGA Training Establishment and currently holds that status will be identified where appropriate by the suffix (T) after their classification.
(ii) **Class B** Members engaged by a Class A or D member to assist the nominated professional at any PGA Establishment in one of the seven Regions on a full-time basis.

(iii) **Class C** Tournament playing members (men and women).

(iv) **Class D** Members engaged as the nominated professional on a full-time basis at a PGA Establishment within the seven Regions which does not qualify as a 'Class A' establishment, or engaged on a full-time basis within the seven Regions by any other Company or any other individual designated by the Executive Committee for this purpose. (Former Class G.)

(v) **Class E** Honorary Associate Members (HAM). Those who in the opinion of the Executive Committee through their past or continuing membership justify retaining the full privileges of membership as Honorary Associate Members (HAM).

(vi) **Class F** Associate Members (AM).
(a) Those who have ceased to be eligible for other categories of membership who in the opinion of the Executive Committee through their past membership justify retaining limited privileges of membership as Associate Members; and (b) Members of the PGA European Tour or WPGET who do not qualify for Class C membership but who in the opinion of the Executive Committee justify limited privileges of membership as Associate Members.

(vii) **Class G** Honorary Life Members (HLM) Those recommended by the Board to a Special General Meeting of the Association for election as Honorary Life Members. No form of application is needed nor need reference be made to the Regional Committee concerned.

(viii) **Class H** Members who are qualified members of the Association, and ineligible for any other class of membership, engaged on a full-time basis at an establishment acceptable to the Association outside the jurisdiction of the seven Regions. (Overseas.)

(ix) **Class O** Members who have not qualified at the official training centre of the Association, who are ineligible for any other class of membership, and who are current members of another PGA approved by the Association and have held such membership for not less than two years.

The Management of the Association is under the overall direction and control of a Board. The Association is divided into seven Regions each of which employs a full-time secretary and runs tournaments for the benefit of members within its Region.

The Association is responsible for arranging and obtaining sponsorship of the Ryder Cup, Club Professionals' Championship, PGA Cup matches, Seniors' Championship, PGA Assistants' Championship, Assistants' Match Play Championship and other National Championships.

Anyone who intends to become a club professional must serve a minimum of three years in registration and qualify at the PGA Training School before election as a full Member.

PGA European Tour

To be eligible to become a member of the PGA European Tour a player must possess certain minimum standards which shall be determined by the Tournament Committee. In 1976 a Qualifying School for potential new members was introduced to be held annually. The leading players are awarded cards allowing them to compete in PGA European Tour tournaments.

In 1985 the PGA European Tour became ALL EXEMPT with no more Monday pre-qualifying. Full details can be obtained from the Wentworth Headquarters.

Women Professional Golfers' European Tour

The Women Professional Golfers' European Tour (WPG European Tour) was founded in 1988 to further the development of women's professional golf throughout Europe and its membership is open to all nationalities. An amateur wishing to join the Tour must be 18 years of age, have a handicap of 1 or less and is on probation for eight rounds in tournaments, during which she must attain certain playing standards as determined by the Tournament Committee.

Government of the Amateur and Open Golf Championship

In December 1919 on the invitation of the clubs who had hitherto controlled the amateur and Open Golf Championships, the Royal & Ancient took over the government of those events. These two championships are controlled by a committee appointed by the Royal & Ancient Golf Club of St Andrews. The Committee shall be called the Royal and Ancient Golf Club Championship Committee and shall consist of twelve members (who shall be members of the Club) to be elected by the Club, and additional members not exceeding two (who shall not necessarily be members of the Club) from Golf Authorities both at home and abroad, who shall be invited annually to join the Committee by the twelve members elected by the Club. Such invited members shall, irrespective of the date of their invitation to become members of the Committee, remain members only until the date of the first Autumn Meeting occurring after the date of their invitation to become members. During their term of office, such invited members (who are not already members of the Club) shall be admitted as honorary temporary members of the Club. Two Business Members, who shall be members of the Club, shall be co-opted on the nomination of the Chairman of the Championship Committee after consultation with the Chairman of the General Committee.

LGU

The Ladies' Golf Union was founded in 1893 with the following objects:

(1) To promote the interests of the game of Golf.
(2) To obtain a uniformity of the rules of the game by establishing a representative legislative authority.
(3) To establish a uniform system of handicapping.
(4) To act as a tribunal and court of reference on points of uncertainty.
(5) To arrange the Annual Championship Competition and obtain the funds necessary for that purpose.

After 100 years, only the language has changed, the present Constitution defining the objects as:

(1) To uphold the rules of the game, to advance and safeguard the interests of women's golf and to decide all doubtful and disputed points in connection therewith.
(2) To maintain, regulate and enforce the LGU System of Handicapping.
(3) To employ the funds of The Union in such a manner as shall be deemed best for the interests of women's golf, with power to borrow or raise money to use for the same purpose.
(4) To maintain and regulate International events, Championships and Competitions held under the LGU regulations and to promote the interests of Great Britain and Ireland in Ladies International Golf.
(5) To make, maintain and publish such regulations as may be considered necessary for the above purposes.

The constituents of the LGU are:

Home Countries. The English Ladies' Golf Association (founded 1952), the Irish Ladies' Golf Union (founded 1893), the Scottish Ladies' Golfing Association (founded 1904), the Welsh Ladies' Golf Union (founded 1904), plus ladies' societies, girls' schools and ladies' clubs affiliated to these organisations. *Overseas.* Affiliated ladies' golf unions and golf clubs in the Commonwealth and any other overseas ladies' golfing organisation affiliated to the LGU.

Individual lady members of clubs within the above categories are regarded as *members of the LGU.*

The Rules of the Game and of Amateur Status, which the LGU is bound to uphold, are those published by the Royal & Ancient Golf Club of St Andrews.

In endeavouring to fulfil its responsibilities towards advancing and safeguarding women's golf, the LGU maintains contact with other golfing organisations – the Royal & Ancient Golf Club of St Andrews, the Council of National Golf Unions, the Golf Foundation, the Central Council of Physical Recreation, the Sports Council, the Women Professional Golfers' European Tour and the Women's Committee of the United States Golf Association. This contact ensures that the LGU is informed of developments and projected developments and has an opportunity to comment upon and to influence the future of the game for women.

Either directly or through its constituent national organisations the LGU advises and is the ultimate authority on doubts or disputes which may arise in connection with the handicapping system and regulations governing competitions played under LGU conditions.

The handicapping system, together with the system for assessment of Scratch Scores, is formulated and published by the LGU. The handicapping system undergoes detailed revision and is republished every four years, in the year following the revision of the Rules of Golf. Handicap Certificates are provided by the LGU and distributed through the National Organisations and appointed club officials to every member of every affiliated club which has fulfilled the requisite conditions for obtaining an LGU handicap. Computer handicap certificates from LGU approved computer systems are also acceptable provided they contain all the necessary relevant details.

The funds of the LGU are administered by the Hon. Treasurer on the authority of the Executive Council, and the accounts are submitted annually for adoption in General Meeting.

All ladies' British Open Championships and the Home International matches, at both senior and junior level, are organised annually by the LGU. International events involving a British or a combined British and Irish team are organised and controlled by the LGU when held in this country and the LGU acts as the co-ordinating body for the Commonwealth Tournament in whichever of the four participating countries it is held, four-yearly, by rotation. The LGU selects and trains the teams, provides the uniforms and pays all the expenses of participation, whether held in this country or overseas. The LGU also maintains and regulates certain competitions played under handicap, such as Medal Competitions, Coronation Foursomes, Challenge Bowls, Australian Spoons and the LGU Pendant Competition.

The day-to-day administration of certain of the LGU responsibilities in the home countries is undertaken by the National Organisations, such as that concerned with handicapping regulations, Scratch Scores, and the organisation of Challenge Bowls and Australian Spoons Competitions.

Membership subscriptions to the LGU are assessed on a per capita basis of the club membership. To save unnecessary expense and duplication of administrative work in the home countries LGU subscriptions are collected by the National Organisations along with their own, and transmitted in bulk to the LGU.

Policy is determined and control over all the LGU's activities is exercised by an Executive Council of eight members – two each elected by the English, Irish, Scottish and Welsh national organisations. The Chairman is elected annually by the Councillors and may hold office for one year only, during which term her place on the Council is taken by her Deputy and she has no vote other than a casting vote. The President and the Hon. Treasurer of the Union also attend and take part in Council meetings but with no vote. The Council meets five times a year.

The Annual General Meeting is held in January. The formal business includes presentation of the Report of the Executive Council for the previous year and of the Accounts for the last completed financial year, the election or re-election of President, Vice-Presidents, Hon. Treasurer and Auditors, and a report of the election of Councillors and their Deputies for the ensuing year and of the European Technical Committee representative. Voting is on the following basis: Executive Council, one each (8); members in the four home countries, one per national organisation (4) and in addition one per 100 affiliated clubs or part thereof (at present 22); one per overseas Commonwealth Union with a membership of 50 or more clubs (at present 3), and one per 100 individually affiliated clubs (1).

The Lady Golfer's Handbook is published annually by the LGU and is distributed free to all affiliated clubs and organisations and to appointed Handicap Advisers. It is also available for sale to anyone interested. It contains the regulations for handicapping and Scratch Score assessment, for British Championships and international matches (with results for the past twenty years) and for LGU competitions, and sets out the Rules of the Union. It also lists every affiliated organisation, with names and addresses of officials, and every affiliated club, with Scratch Score, county of affiliation, number of members, and other useful information.

Miscellaneous Rulings

Limitation of the Golf Ball

At the Autumn Business Meeting, 1920, of the Royal & Ancient Club the following resolution was adopted: *On and after 1st May, 1921, the weight of the ball shall not be greater than 1.62 ounces avoirdupois, and the size not less than 1.62 inches in diameter. The Rules of Golf Committee and the Executive Committee of the United States Golf Association will take whatever steps they think necessary to limit the powers of the ball with regard to distance, should any ball of greater power be introduced.* The United States Golf Association intimated, May, 1929, that they had resolved to adopt *an easier and pleasanter ball for the average golfer*, and from 1st January, 1931, to 31st December, 1932, the standards of specification of the ball in competitions under their jurisdiction was not less than 1.68 inches in diameter, and not greater than 1.55 ounces in weight. In January, 1932, another alteration was made in the specification of the ball, the weight being increased to 1.62 and the size remaining the same, viz, not less than 1.68.

The Royal Canadian Golf Association adopted the USGA specification as from 1st January, 1948. The effect of this difference between the legislation of the Royal & Ancient, the Royal Canadian Golf Association, and the USGA is that golfers competing in the United States and Canada must use a ball that is larger, but no heavier, than the ball which is legal in other parts of the world.

In May, 1951, a special committee was set up by the Royal & Ancient Golf Club and the United States Golf Association to discuss the desirability of uniformity in the Rules of Golf and the form and make of clubs and balls. The committee recommended that both sizes of ball (1.62 inches and 1.68 inches in diameter both having the same weight, 1.62 ounces) be legal in all countries. At their autumn meeting the United States Golfers' Association rejected this proposal but agreed that in international team competition in the United States, the size of the ball be not less than 1.62 inches in diameter.

The matter of a uniform ball worldwide was investigated by a special committee from the R&A and the USGA but was dropped in 1974 when the two bodies could not reach agreement.

In 1987, however, the Royal & Ancient Golf Club of St Andrews proposed and adopted an amendment which decreed that the diameter of the golf ball should be not less than 1.68 inches (42.67 mm) instead of 1.62 inches (41.15 mm). The change of rule was introduced on 1st January 1990. An official statement declared: 'With the steady and, in most countries, rapid decline in the use of the 1.62 inch ("small") ball, the R&A has been considering changing to the 1.68 inch ("large") ball for some time, but has held off from doing so mainly because of the large number of Japanese golfers still using the small ball. With the use of the small ball in Japan now dropping steadily and in most other countries now being at 10% or less, it seems an appropriate time to make this change.' A maximum initial velocity standard of not greater than 250 feet per second on special apparatus was introduced by the R&A in 1976.

The R&A issues lists of conforming golf balls annually.

Limitation of Number of Clubs

At the Business Meeting of the Royal & Ancient Golf Club, May, 1937, the Rules of Golf Committee submitted a recommendation that on and after 1st January, 1938, the preamble to the Rules of Golf shall read: *The game of golf consists of a ball being played from a teeing ground to a hole by successive strokes with clubs (not exceeding fourteen in number) and balls made in conformity with the directions laid down in the clause on 'Form and make of golf clubs and balls'.* The recommendation was not approved by the members.

In September, 1938, at the Business Meeting of the Royal & Ancient, a similar recommendation was approved by the members, and the limitation of the number of clubs to fourteen became operative as from 1st May, 1939.

The United States Golf Association decided to limit the number of clubs to fourteen as from 1st January, 1938.

Steel-Shafted Clubs

The Royal & Ancient Golf Club authorised steel shafts, November, 1929, in the following announcement: *The Rules of Golf Committee have decided that steel shafts, as approved by the Rules of Golf Committee are declared to conform with the requirements of the clause in the Rules of Golf on the form and make of golf clubs.*

Laminated Shafts

The Rules of Golf Committee on 5th December, 1932, announced that clubs with laminated shafts built entirely of wood are permissible.

Recognised Golf Clubs

The Rules of Golf Committee, in answering a query, gave the opinion that a recognised Golf Club is one which has regularly appointed office-bearers.

The English Golf Union decided that a recognised Golf Club for the purpose of competitive golf in England is a golf club affiliated to the English Golf Union through its County Union, or where there is no County Union direct to the English Golf Union as an Associate Member.

Championship Conditions

Men

The Amateur Championship

The Championship, until 1982, was decided entirely by match play over 18 holes except for the final which was over 36 holes. Since 1983 the Championship has comprised two stroke-play rounds of 18 holes each from which the top 64 scores over the 36 holes qualify for the match-play stages. Matches are over 18 holes except for the final which is over 36 holes.

Full particulars of conditions of entry and method of play can be obtained from the Championship Entries Department, Royal & Ancient Golf Club, St Andrews, Fife KY16 9JD.

The Seniors' Open Amateur

The Championship consists of 18 holes on each of two days, the lowest 50 scores over the 36 holes and any tying for 50th place then playing a further 18 holes the following day.

Conditions for entry include:

Entrants must have attained the age of 55 years prior to the first day on which the Championship is played.

Entries are limited to 252 competitors.

Full particulars of conditions of entry and method of play can be obtained from Championship Entries Department, Royal & Ancient Golf Club, St Andrews, Fife KY16 9JD.

National Championships

The English, Scottish, Irish and Welsh Amateur Championships are played by holes, each match consisting of one round of 18 holes except the final which is contested over 36 holes.

Full particulars of conditions of entry and method of play can be obtained from the secretaries of the respective national Unions.

English Open Amateur Stroke Play Championship

The Championship consists of one round of 18 holes on each of two days after which the leading 40 and those tying for 40th place play a further two rounds. The remainder are eliminated.

Conditions for entry include:

Entrants must have a handicap not exceeding three.

Where the entries exceed 130, an 18-hole qualifying round is held the day before the Championship. Certain players are exempt from qualifying.

Full particulars of conditions of entry and method of play can be obtained from the Secretary, English Golf Union.

British Mid-Amateur Championship

The Championship was introduced in 1995 and replaces the Youths Championship. Entrants must have reached the age of 25 by the day before the competition starts. The handicap limit is three. The field will be limited to 144 players.

There is a 36-hole strokeplay qualifying competition on the first two days with the leading 64 players advancing to the matchplay stages, each round being over 18 holes.

Full particulars can be obtained from the Championship Entries Department, Royal & Ancient Golf Club, St Andrews, Fife KY16 9JD.

Boys

Boys' Amateur Championship

The Championship is played by match play, each match consisting of one round of 18 holes except for the final which is over 36 holes.

Conditions of entry include:

Entrants must be under 18 years of age at 00.00 hours on 1st January in the year of the Championship.

Entries are limited to 192 competitors, the higher handicaps being balloted out if necessary.

Full particulars of conditions of entry and method of play can be obtained from the Championship Entries Department, Royal & Ancient Golf Club, St Andrews, Fife KY16 9JD.

Ladies

Ladies' British Open Amateur Championship

The Championship consists of one 18-hole qualifying round on each of two days. The players returning the 64 lowest scores over 36 holes shall qualify for match play. Ties for 64th place shall be decided by hole-by-hole play-off.

Ladies' British Open Amateur Stroke Play Championship

The Championship consists of 72 holes stroke play; 18 holes are played on each of two days after which the first 32 and all ties for 32nd place qualify for a further 36 holes on the third day. Handicap limit is 4.

Ladies' British Open Championship

The Championship consists of 72 holes stroke play. 18 holes are played on each of four days, the field being reduced after the first 36 holes.

Entries accepted from lady amateurs with a handicap not exceeding scratch and from lady professionals.

Full particulars of conditions of entry and method of play for all three Championships can be obtained from the Administrator, LGU, The Scores, St Andrews, Fife KY16 9AT.

National Championships

Conditions of entry and method of play for the English, Scottish, Welsh and Irish Ladies' Close Championships can be obtained from the Secretaries of the respective associations.

Other championships organised by the respective national associations, from whom full particulars can be obtained, include English Ladies', Intermediate, English Ladies' Stroke-Play, Scottish Girls' Open Amateur Stroke Play (under 21) and Welsh Ladies' Open Amateur Stroke Play.

Girls

Girls' British Open Amateur Championship

The Championship consists of two 18-hole qualifying rounds, followed by match play in two flights each of sixteen players.

Conditions of entry include:

Entrants must be under 18 years of age on the 1st January in the year of the Championship.

Competitors are required to hold a certified LGU international handicap not exceeding 15, or to be members of their National Junior Team for the current year.

Full particulars of conditions of entry and method of play can be obtained from the Administrator, LGU, The Scores, St Andrews, Fife KY16 9AT.

National Championships

The English, Scottish, Irish and Welsh Girls' Close Championships are open to all girls of relevant nationality and appropriate age which may vary from country to country. A handicap limit may be set by some countries.

Full particulars of conditions of entry and method of play can be obtained via the secretaries of the respective associations.

International Match Conditions

Men – Amateur

Walker Cup – Great Britain and Ireland *v* United States
Deed of Gift to United States Golf Association International Challenge Trophy

Mr GH Walker of the United States presented a Cup for international competition to be known as *The United States Golf Association International Challenge Trophy*, popularly described as *The Walker Cup*.

The Cup shall be played for by teams of amateur golfers selected from Clubs under the jurisdiction of the United States Golf Association on the one side and from England, Scotland, Wales, Northern Ireland and Eire on the other.

The International Walker Cup Match shall be held every two years in the United States of America and Great Britain and Ireland alternately.

The teams shall consist of not more than ten players and a captain.

The contest consists of four foursomes and eight singles matches over 18 holes on each of two days.

St Andrews Trophy

First staged in 1956, the St Andrews Trophy is a biennial match played between two teams of Amateur golfers representing Great Britain and Ireland and the Continent of Europe. The match is played over two consecutive days with four morning foursomes being followed each afternoon by eight singles.

Team selection for the Great Britain and Ireland team is carried out by the Selection Committee of the Royal & Ancient Golf Club; that for the Continent of Europe team, a much harder task in view of the geographical and multi-national problems, by a committee of the European Golf Association.

Eisenhower Trophy

Founded in 1958 in recognition of the need for an official team championship for amateurs. Each country enters a team of four players who play stroke play over 72 holes, the total of the three best individual scores to be counted each day. (One score to be discarded.) The winner to be the team with the lowest aggregate for the 72 holes. The first event was played at St Andrews in 1958 and the trophy has been played for every second year.

European Team Championship

Founded in 1959 by the European Golf Association for competition among member countries of the Association. The Championship is held biennially and played in rotation round the countries which are grouped in four geographical zones.

Each team consists of six players who play two qualifying rounds of 18 holes, the five best scores of each round constituting the team aggregate. Flights for match play are then arranged according to qualifying round rankings. For the match play, teams consist of five players, playing two foursomes in the morning and five singles in the afternoon.

A similar championship is held every year for junior teams.

From 1990, the European Golf Association began organising the International European Championships – formally known as the European Individual Amateur Championships – on an annual basis.

Home Internationals *(Raymond Trophy)*

The first official International Match recorded was in 1902 at Hoylake between England and Scotland who won 32 to 25 on a holes up basis.

In 1932 International Week was inaugurated under the auspices of the British Golf Unions' Joint Advisory Council with the full approval of the four National Golf Unions. The Council of National Golf Unions is now responsible for running the matches.

Teams of 11 players from England, Scotland, Ireland and Wales engage in matches consisting of 5 foursomes and 10 singles over 18 holes, the foursomes being in the morning and the singles in the afternoon. Each team plays every other team.

The eligibility of players to play for their country shall be their eligibility to play in the Amateur Championship of their country.

Men – Professional

Ryder Cup

This Cup was presented by Mr Samuel Ryder, St Albans, England (who died 2nd January, 1936), for competition between a team of British professionals and a team of American professionals. The trophy was first competed for in 1927. In 1929 the original conditions were varied to confine the British team to British-born professionals resident in Great Britain, and the American team to American-born professionals resident in the United States, in the year of the match. In 1977 the British team was extended to include European players. The matches are played biennially, in alternate continents, in accordance with the conditions as agreed between the respective PGAs.

World Cup *(formerly Canada Cup)*

Founded in America in 1953 as an International Team event for professional golfers with the intention of spreading international goodwill.

Each country is represented by two players, the best team score over 72 holes being the winners of the World Cup and the best individual score the International Trophy. It is played annually, but not in 1986.

Ladies

Great Britain and Ireland *v* United States (Curtis Cup)

For a trophy presented by the late Misses Margaret and Harriot Curtis of Boston, USA, for biennial competition between teams from the United States of America and Great Britain and Ireland.

The match is sponsored jointly by the United States Golf Association and the Ladies' Golf Union who may select teams of not more than 8 players.

The match consists of 3 foursomes and 6 singles of 18 holes on each of two days, the foursomes being played each morning.

Europe *v* United States (Solheim Cup)

The Solheim Cup, named after Karsten Solheim who heads the sponsoring Ping company, is the women's equivalent of the Ryder Cup. In 1990 the inaugural competition between the top women professional golfers from Europe and America took place in Florida. The matches are played biennially in alternate continents. The format is foursomes and four-ball matches on the first two days, followed by singles on the third in accordance with the conditions as agreed between the WPG European Tour and the LPGA.

Great Britain and Ireland *v* Continent of Europe (Vagliano Trophy)

For a trophy presented to the Comité des Dames de la Fédération Française de Golf and the Ladies' Golf Union by Monsieur AA Vagliano, originally for annual competition between teams of women amateur golfers from France and Great Britain and Ireland but, since 1959, by mutual agreement, for competition between teams from the Continent of Europe and Great Britain and Ireland.

The match is played biennially, alternately in Great Britain and Ireland and on the Continent of Europe, with teams of not more than 9 players plus a non-playing captain.

The match consists of 4 foursomes and 8 singles, of 18 holes on each of two days. The foursomes are played each morning.

Women's World Amateur Team Championship (Espirito Santo Trophy)

For the Espirito Santo Trophy presented by Mrs Ricardo Santo of Portugal for biennial competition between teams of not more than three women amateur golfers who represent a national association affiliated to the World Amateur Golf Council. First competed for in 1964.

The tournament consists of 72 holes stroke play, 18 holes on each of four days, the two best scores in each round each day constituting the team aggregate.

Commonwealth Tournament (Lady Astor Trophy)

For a trophy presented by the late Viscountess Astor CH, and the Ladies' Golf Union for competition once in every four years between teams of women amateur golfers from Commonwealth countries.

The inaugural Commonwealth Tournament was played at St Andrews in 1959 between teams from Australia, Canada, New Zealand, South Africa and Great Britain and was won by the British team. The tournament is played in rotation in the competing countries, for the present Great Britain, Australia, Canada, and New Zealand, each country being entitled to nominate 6 players including a playing or non-playing captain.

Each team plays every other team and each team match consists of 2 foursomes and 4 singles over 18 holes. The foursomes are played in the morning and the singles in the afternoon.

European Ladies' Amateur Team Championship

The Championship is held biennially between teams of amateur women golfers from the European countries. Each team consists of not more than 6 players who play two qualifying rounds, the five best scores in each round constituting the team aggregate. The match play draw is made in flights according to the position in the qualifying rounds. The match play consists of 2 foursomes and 5 singles on each of three days.

A similar championship is held in alternate years for junior ladies' teams, under 21 years of age.

Home Internationals

Teams from England, Scotland, Ireland and Wales compete annually for a trophy presented to the LGU by the late Mr TH Miller. The qualifications for a player being eligible to play for her country are the same as those laid down by each country for its Close Championship.

Each team plays each other team. The matches consist of 6 singles and 3 foursomes, each of 18 holes. Each country may nominate teams of not more than 8 players.

Boys

England *v* Scotland; Wales *v* Ireland

The International Matches between England and Scotland (10 players a side) and Wales and Ireland (10 players a side) are played on the Thursday preceding the Boys' Championship. The following day the winners of these two matches play against each other, as do the losers. To be eligible to play in these matches a boy must qualify by age to be eligible to play in the Boys' Championship.

Great Britain and Ireland *v* Continent of Europe

The International Match between Great Britain and Ireland and the Continent of Europe for the Jacques Leglise Trophy is played on the Saturday preceding the Boys' Championship. This match consists of 4 foursomes followed by 8 singles.

Girls

Home Internationals

Teams from England, Scotland, Ireland and Wales compete annually for the Stroyan Cup. The qualifications for a player for the Girls' International Matches shall be the same as those laid down by each country for its Girls' Close Championship except that a player shall be under 18 years on the 1st January in the year of the Championship.

Each team, consisting of not more than 8 players, plays each other team, a draw taking place to decide the order of play between the teams. The matches consist of 6 singles and 3 foursomes, each of 18 holes.

Golf Associations

The National Association of Public Golf Courses (Affiliated to English Golf Union)

1927 saw the foundation of the Association by the late FG Hawtree (Golf Course Architect) and the late JH Taylor (five times Open Champion). They were both farsighted enough to see the need for cohesion between *Private* golf, *Public* golf and the Local Councils. Up to the outbreak of World War II the Association struggled on, sustained by a small amount of very welcome financial support from the *News of the World.* This enabled the *unofficial* Championship to be staged.

After the War, the Association was revitalised and the Championship was recognised by the National Union, and so from a shaky start of 240 qualifiers, there are now some 3500 Public Course golfers trying to qualify, from a total estimated membership of 50,000. The success and importance of the *Public Courses Championship of England* prompted the commencement of the Championship for Ladies and then the Championship for Juniors – which share equal importance. Soon after the establishment of Individual Championships there came the introduction of various Club Team events, and these have now progressed to National Level with a vast following from Club members. Thus the Association now organises some 14 national events annually for the membership.

Some years ago it was realised that the Local Councils (Course Management Authorities) could not enjoy official recognition and membership of the County Unions or National Unions except through the Association. This has now been remedied and many CMA are full subscribing members of the Association, and many others permit the *Courtesy of the Course* for all our National and Zonal Tournaments. Advice is offered to CMA – when requested – on such matters as Course Construction, Club formation and integration, establishment of Standard Scratch Score and Par Values, and many other topics concerned with the management of the game of golf.

Some overseas organisations and Councils have already sought our advice and help in recent years, when forming their own Courses, Clubs and Associations.

The Constitutional aims have not changed over the years, and the Association is proud to have maintained these Aims through the activities provided by the National Executive of the Association. The aims are:

1. To unite the Clubs formed on Public Courses in England and Wales, and their Course Managements in the furtherance of the interests of Amateur Golf.
2. To promote Annual Public Courses Championships and such other matches, competitions and tournaments as shall be authorised by the executive of the Association.
3. To afford direct representation of Public Course Interests in the National Union.

The total organisation of the Association is wholly voluntary and honorary, from the President down through Vice-Presidents, Chairmen, Secretary, Treasurer and Zone Secretaries. It is quite fantastic for an unpaid Organisation to cover such an exacting *field* of work, but most gratifying to the National Executive who have secured the progress of recent years.

Association of Golf Club Secretaries

Membership is 1500, consisting of Secretaries and retired Secretaries of Clubs largely situated in Great Britain but also from Clubs in other parts of the World. The Association offers from the Headquarters at Weston-super-Mare, Avon advice on all aspects of Golf Club Management, and a training course for new and intending Secretaries. Apart from national events, including a Conference, the Association organises golfing and business meetings for its members at regional level. There are 11 regions within Great Britain.

The Association of Golf Writers

A group of 30 newspapermen attending the Walker Cup Match at St Andrews on 2 June 1938 decided there was a need for an organisation to 'protect the interests of golf writers'. Their main objective was to establish a close liaison with the governing bodies and promoters of golf.

Thus was born The Association of Golf Writers, now solidly established and rightly respected as the official negotiating body of the golfing press. The Association owes much to a membership which has included many internationally recognised names who have contributed to elevating the Association to a unique level among British sports writers' associations.

Secretary: Renton Laidlaw, *Evening Standard*, 2 Derry Street, London W8 5EE.

The Sports Turf Research Institute
(Bingley, West Yorkshire)

The Institute is officially recognised as the national centre for sports and amenity turf. Non-commercial and non-profit making, its affairs are administered by a Board, whose members are nominated by the sport controlling bodies in membership of the Institute. Golf is represented by nominees of the Royal & Ancient Golf Club of St Andrews, four individual National Golf Unions, and the Councils of National Golf Unions.

The institute's aim is to raise the standard of turf used for all sports. Valuable data is accumulated from research activities and is disseminated to subscribing clubs and organisations.

The British Association of Golf Course Architects

Objects of the Association: to encourage the highest standards of Golf Course Design and Construction; to have the fullest regard to the best interests of Members' Clients; to maintain a Register of Members fully qualified by training and experience in the design and construction of Golf Courses; to promote the interests of its members and the game of golf; to support research and development in golf course Design, Construction and Maintenance; to enable members to meet together, share knowledge and experience, and discuss matters affecting their work; to follow the best accepted principles of golf course architecture with the object of providing the maximum enjoyment of the game for all players.

The British Association of Golf Course Constructors

Objects: To promote the development of the golf course construction industry, to promote the adoption of policies to ensure a high quality of workmanship and working practices, to collect and disseminate information of value regarding the construction of golf courses to other members of the association, to members of the allied industries and to the public to promote the training and education of personnel within the industry and to maintain agreed standards of golf course construction by adherence to contractual procedures and codes of practice.

British and International Golf Greenkeepers' Association

The Association was formed in 1987 resulting from an amalgamation of the British, English and Scottish Associations. The Association has an official magazine, *Greenkeeping International,* which is issued free to all members.

The objects are to promote and advance all aspects of greenkeeping; to assist and encourage the proficiency of members; to arrange an International Annual Conference, educational seminars, functions and competitions; to maintain a Benevolent Fund; to act as an employment agency; to provide a magazine; to collaborate with any body or organisation which may benefit the Association or its members or with which there may be a common interest; to carry out and perform any other duties which shall be in the general interests of the Association or its members.

National Golf Clubs' Advisory Association

The National Golf Clubs' Advisory Association was founded in 1922. The objects are to protect the interests of Golf Clubs in general and to give legal advice and direction, under the opinion of Counsel, on the administrative and legal responsibilities of Golf Clubs. In cases taken to the Courts for decisions on any points which in the opinion of the Executive Committee involve principles affecting the general interests of affiliated clubs financial assistance may sometimes be given.

European Golf Association
Association Européenne de Golf

Formed at a meeting held at Luxembourg, 20th November, 1937, membership shall be restricted to European National Amateur Golf Associations or Unions. The Association shall concern itself solely with matters of an international character. The Association shall have as its prime objects:

(a) To encourage international development of golf and strengthen bonds of friendship between the national organisations and to encourage the formation of new ones.
(b) To co-ordinate dates of the Open and Amateur Championships of its members.
(c) To arrange when such have been decided upon, European Team Championships and Matches of international character.
(d) To decide and publish the Calendar dates of the Open and Amateur Championships and Matches.

Golf Club Stewards' Association

The Golf Club Stewards' Association was founded as early as 1912. Its members are Stewards in Golf Clubs throughout the UK and Eire. It has a National Committee and Regional Branches in the South, North-West, Midlands, East Anglia, Yorkshire, Wales and the West, North-East Scotland and Ireland. The objects of the Association are to promote the interests of members; to administer a Benevolent Fund for members in need and to arrange golf competitions and matches. It also serves as an Agency for the employment of Stewards in Golf Clubs.

Addresses of Golfing Organisations – Worldwide

National Associations

Great Britain & Ireland

Royal and Ancient Golf Club
Sec, MF Bonallack, St Andrews, Fife KY16 9JD. *Tel* (01334) 472112 *Fax* (01334) 477580.

Council of National Golf Unions
Hon Sec, A Thirlwell, 19 Birch Green, Formby, Liverpool L37 1NG. *Tel/Fax* (01704) 831800.

Ladies' Golf Union
Administrator, Mrs EA Mackie, The Scores, St Andrews, Fife KY16 9AT. *Tel* (01334) 475811 *Fax* (01334) 472818.

The Professional Golfers' Association
Sec, DKC Wright, Apollo House, The Belfry, Sutton Coldfield, West Midlands B76 9PT. *Tel* (01675) 470333 *Fax* (01675) 470674.

East Region *Sec,* M Crane, John O'Gaunt Golf Club, Sutton Park, Sandy, Biggleswade, Beds SG19 2LY. *Tel* (01767) 261888 *Fax* (01767) 261381.

Midland Region *Sec,* J Grant, King's Norton Golf Club, Brockhill Lane, Weatheroak, Nr Alvechurch, Worcs B48 7ED. *Tel* (01564) 824909 *Fax* (01564) 822805.

North Region *Sec,* D Nutter, No 2 Cottage, Bolton Golf Club, Lostock Park, Chorley New Road, Bolton, Lancs BL6 4AJ. *Tel* (01204) 496137 *Fax* (01204) 847959.

South Region *Sec* S Christie, Clandon Regis Golf Club, Epsom Road, West Clandon, Guildford, Surrey GU4 7TT. *Tel* (01483) 224200 *Fax* (01483) 223224.

West Region *Sec,* R Ellis, Exeter Golf and Country Club, Topsham Road, Countess Wear, Exeter, Devon EX2 7AE. *Tel* (01392) 877657 *Fax* (01392) 876382.

Irish Region *Sec,* M McCumiskey, Dundalk Golf Club, Blackrock, Dundalk, Co Louth, Eire. *Tel* (00 353) 422 1193 *Fax* (00 353) 422 1899.

Scottish Region *Sec,* N Simpson, Glenbervie Golf Club, Stirling Road, Larbert FK5 4SJ. *Tel* (01324) 562451 *Fax* (01324) 562190.

PGA European Tour
Executive Director, KD Schofield, PGA European Tour, Wentworth Drive, Virginia Water, Surrey GU25 4LX. *Tel* (01344) 842881 *Fax* (01344) 842929.

Women Professional Golfers' European Tour
Chief Exec, T Coates, The Tytherington Club, Macclesfield, Cheshire SK10 2JP. *Tel* (01625) 611444 *Fax* (01625) 610406.

Artisan Golfers' Association
Hon Sec, A Everett, 51 Rose Hill Park West, Sutton, Surrey SM1 3LA. *Tel* 0181-644 7037.

Association of Golf Club Secretaries
Sec, R Burniston, 7a Beaconsfield Road, Weston-super-Mare, BS23 1YE. *Tel* (01934) 641166 *Fax* (01934) 644254.

Association of Golf Writers
Sec, R Laidlaw, 17 Cheniston Court, Ridgemount Road, Sunningdale, Berks SL5 9SF. *Tel* (01344) 25957 *Fax* (01344) 24977.

British Association of Golf Course Constructors
Hon Sec, TJ Banks, 2 Angel Court, Dairy Yard, off High Street, Market Harborough, Leics LE16 7NL. *Tel* (01858) 464346 *Fax* (01858) 434734.

British Golf Collectors Society
Sec, CH Ibbetson, 9 Vicars Moor Lane, Winchmore Hill, London N21 2QN. *Tel* (0181) 360 2978.

The British Golf Museum
Bruce Embankment, St Andrews, Fife KY16 9AB. *Tel* (01334) 78880 *Fax* (01334) 73306.

The British Institute of Golf Course Architects
Sec, Mrs S Furnival, Godstone Road, Oxted, Surrey RH8 9NQ. *Tel* (01883) 712072 *Fax* (01883) 730376.

British & International Golf Greenkeepers' Association
Exec Dir, N Thomas BA, Aldwark Manor, Aldwark, Alne, York Y06 2NF.
Tel (01347) 838581/2 *Fax* (01347) 838864.

British Left-Handed Golfers' Society
Hon Sec, AC Kirkland, 7 Ingersley Road, Bollington, Cheshire SK10 5RE.
Tel (01625) 575516.

British Turf & Landscape Irrigation Association
3 Ferrands Park Way, Harden, Bingley, W Yorks BD16 1HZ. *Tel* (01535) 273188.

Golf Club Stewards' Association
Sec, G Shaw, 50 The Park, St Albans, Herts AL1 4RY. *Tel* (01727) 857334.

Golf Foundation
Exec Dir, Miss L Attwood, MBE, Foundation House, Hanbury Manor, Ware, Herts SG12 0UH.
Tel (01920) 484044 *Fax* (01920) 484055.

Golf Society of Great Britain
Mrs EJ Drummond, Southview, Warren Road, Thurlestone, Devon TQ7 3NT.
Tel (01548) 560630.

Hole in One Golf Society
Sec, B Dickinson, PO Box 109, New Lane, Greengates, Bradford, Yorkshire BD10 9UY.
Tel (01474) 534298.

National Association of Public Golf Courses
Hon Sec, AK Witte, 35 Sinclair Grove, Golders Green, London NW11 9JH. *Tel* 0181-458 5433.

National Golf Clubs' Advisory Association
Sec, J Crowther, Suite 2, Angel House, Portland Square, Bakewell, Derbyshire DE45 1HB
Tel (01629) 813844 *Fax* (01629) 812614.

National Turfgrass Council
Chief Exec, PH Helm,Hunters Lodge, Dr Browns Road, Minchinhampton, Glos GL6 9BT.
Tel (01453) 883588 *Fax* (01453) 731449.

Public Schools' Old Boys' Golf Association
Jt Secs: P de Pinna, Bruins, Wythwood, Haywards Heath, West Sussex RH16 4RD.
Tel 0171-265 0071. JBM Urry, Dormers, 232 Dickens Heath Road, Shirley, Solihull, West Midlands B90 1QQ. *Tel* 0121-328 5665.

Public Schools' Golfing Society
Hon Sec, JNS Lowe, Flushing House, Church Road, Great Bookham, Surrey KT23 3JT.
Tel (01372) 458651.

Senior Golfers' Society
Sec, Brigadier D Ross, CBE, Milland Farmhouse, Liphook, Hants GU30 7JP. *Tel* (01428) 76200.

The Society of One-Armed Golfers
Hon Sec, D Reid, 11 Coldwell Lane, Felling, Tyne & Wear NE10 9EX. *Tel* 0191-469 4742.

Sports Turf Research Institute
Bingley, West Yorks BD16 1AU.
Tel (01274) 565131 *Fax* (01274) 561891.

Regional Associations

England

English Golf Union
Sec, PM Baxter, 1–3 Upper King Street, Leicester LE1 6XF. *Tel* (0116) 255 3042
Fax (0116) 247 1322.

Midland Group *Sec,* RJW Baldwin, Chantry Cottage, Friar Street, Droitwich, Worcs WR9 8EQ. *Tel* (01905) 778560.

Northern Group *Hon Sec,* EG Bunting, 7 Northbrook Court, Hartlepool, Cleveland TS26 0DJ. *Tel* (01429) 274828.

South Eastern Group *Hon Sec,* MA Hobson, 22 Wye Court, Malvern Way, Ealing, London W13 8EA. *Tel* 081-997 7466.

South Western Group *Sec,* JT Lumley, Hartland, Potterne, Devizes, Wilts SN10 5PA.
Tel (01380) 723935.

English Ladies' Golf Association
Sec, Mrs MJ Carr, Edgbaston Golf Club, Church Road, Birmingham B15 3TB.
Tel 0121-456 2088. *Fax* 0121-454 5542

Northern Division *Hon Sec,* Mrs L Young, 10 Cleehill Drive, North Shields, Tyne & Wear NE29 9EW. *Tel* 0191-257 6925.

Midlands Division *Hon Sec,* Mrs C Stevenson, 3 Leaholme Gardens, Pedmore, Stourbridge, West Midlands DY9 0XX. *Tel* (01562) 884582.

South-Eastern Division *Hon Sec,* Mrs B Mortimer, 6 Beck River Park, Rectory Road, Beckenham, Kent BR3 1HT. *Tel* 0181–658 7424.

South-Western Division *Hon Sec,* Mrs VJ Wilde, 19 Ferndown Close, Kingsweston, Bristol BS11 0UP. *Tel* (0117) 968 3543.

English Schools' Golf Association
Hon Sec, R Snell, 20 Dykenook Close, Whickham, Newcastle-upon-Tyne NE16 5TD.
Tel 0191-488 3538.

Bedfordshire County Golf Union
Hon Sec, CLE Spurr, 8 Gainsborough Avenue, St Albans, Herts AL1 4NL. *Tel/Fax* (01727) 857834.

Bedfordshire Ladies' County Golf Association
Hon Sec, Mrs H Molloy, Keepers Cottage, Beadlow, Shefford, Beds. *Tel* (01525) 861202.

Bedfordshire & Cambridgeshire PGA
Sec, L Scarbrow, 22 Hillcrest Road, Luton LU2 7AB. *Tel* (01582) 240197.

Berks, Bucks & Oxon PGA
Hon Sec, Mrs M Green, Wayside, Aylesbury Road, Monks Risborough, Aylesbury, Bucks HP27 0JS. *Tel* (01884) 343012.

Berks, Bucks & Oxon Union of Golf Clubs
Sec, R Stewart, Leyacre, Lodersfield, Lechlade, Glos GL7 3DJ. *Tel* (01367) 252926 *Fax* (01367) 253403.

Berkshire Ladies' County Golf Association
Hon Sec, Mrs J West, 4 Mansfield Place, Ascot, Berks SL5 8ND. *Tel* (01344) 883682.

Buckinghamshire Ladies' County Golf Association
Hon Sec, Mrs S Munn, 'Garah', 21 Clifton Lawns, Chesham Bois, Bucks HP6 5PT. *Tel* (01494) 433860.

Cambridgeshire Area Golf Union
Sec, RAC Blows, 2A Dukes Meadow, Stapleford, Cambridge CB2 5BH. *Tel* (01223) 842062.

Cambs & Hunts Ladies' County Golf Association
Hon Sec, Mrs A Guy, The Paddock, 14 Mingle Lane, Stapleford, Cambs. CB2 5BG. *Tel* (01223) 843267.

Channel Islands Ladies' Golf Association
Hon Sec, Mrs AGR Willis, Oakenbirch, Park Estate, St Brelade, Jersey JE3 8EQ. *Tel* (01534) 842072.

Cheshire County Ladies' Golf Association
Hon Sec, Mrs B Walker, 12 Higher Downs, Knutsford, Cheshire WA16 8AW. *Tel* (01565) 634124.

Cheshire PGA
Sec, D Nutter, No 2 Cottage, Bolton Golf Club, Lostock Park, Chorley New Road, Bolton BL6 4AJ. *Tel* (01204) 496137.

Cheshire Union of Golf Clubs
Hon Sec, BH Nattrass, 48 Hockenhull Lane, Tarvin, Chester CH3 8LD. *Tel/Fax* (01829) 741898.

Cornwall Golf Union
Hon Sec, JG Rowe, 8 Lydcott Crescent, Widegates, Looe, Cornwall PL13 1QG. *Tel* (015034) 240492.

Cornwall Ladies' County Golf Association
Hon Sec, Mrs A Eddy, Penmester, Hain Walk, St Ives, Cornwall. *Tel* (01736) 795392.

Cumbria Ladies' County Golf Association
Hon Sec, Mrs V Hetherington, The Patch, Lowmoor Road, Wiston CA7 9QR. *Tel* (016973) 42403.

Cumbria Union of Golf Clubs
Hon Sec, T Edmondson, Thorn Lea, Lazonby, Penrith, Cumbria CA10 1AT. *Tel* (01768) 83231.

Derbyshire Ladies' County Golf Association
Hon Sec, Mrs G Mountain, Highland Cottage, Old Brampton, Chesterfield, Derbyshire S42 7SG. *Tel* (01246) 566484.

Derbyshire PGA
Sec, F McCabe, Hillside, Lower Hall Close, Holbrook, Derby. *Tel* (01332) 880411.

Derbyshire Union of Golf Clubs
Sec, R Rose, 104 Alexandra Road, Burton on Trent DE15 0JB *Tel* (01283) 565513.

Devon County Golf Union
Hon Sec, TC Reynolds, 'Broadlands', Boundary Park, Stony Cross, Bideford, N Devon EX39 4DZ. *Tel* (01271) 858470 *Fax* (01271) 858695.

Devon County Ladies' Golf Association
Hon Sec, Mrs V Irish, Homefield, Aveton Gifford, Kingsbridge, Devon TQ7 4LF. *Tel* (01548) 550369.

Dorset County Golf Union
Hon Sec, Lt Col MD Hutchins, 38 Carlton Road, Bournemouth BH1 3TG. *Tel* (01202) 290821 *Fax* (01202) 311288.

Dorset Ladies' County Golf Association
Hon Sec, Mrs AG Bell, 3 Onslow Gardens, Wimborne, Dorset BH21 2QG. *Tel* (01202) 889904.

Durham County Golf Union
Hon Sec, L Inskip, 5 Silverdale Way, Whickham, Tyne & Wear NE16 5SL. *Tel* 0191-488 1680.

Durham County Ladies' Golf Association
Sec, Mrs R Foy, Jolby Manor, Stapleton, Darlington DL2 2QS. *Tel* (01325) 377500.

Essex County Amateur Golf Union
Sec, EV Sadler, 9 Willow Walk, Hadleigh, Benfleet, Essex SS7 2RW. *Tel/Fax* (01702) 559871.

Essex Ladies' County Golf Association
Hon Sec, Mrs C Davies, 26 Theydon Park Road, Theydon Bois, Essex CM16 7LP. *Tel* (01992) 813491.

Essex PGA
Sec, A Birch, 27 Curlew Crescent, Basildon, Essex SX16 5HR. *Tel* (01268) 533849.

Gloucestershire & Somerset PGA
Sec, N Boland, Cotswold Hills GC, Ullenwood, Cheltenham GL53 9QT. *Tel* (01242) 515263.

Gloucestershire Golf Union
Hon Sec, RF Crisp, 2 Hartley Close, Sandy Lane, Charlton Kings, Cheltenham GL53 9DN. *Tel* (01242) 514024.

Gloucestershire Ladies' County Golf Association
Hon Sec, Mrs EA Bates, 128 Claverham Road, Claverham, Avon BS19 4LQ. *Tel* (01934) 833470.

Hampshire, Isle of Wight & Channel Islands Golf Union
Sec, K Maplesden, 5 Coldharbour Wood, Rake, Liss, Hants GU33 7JJ. *Tel* (01730) 895102.

Hampshire Ladies' County Golf Association
Sec, Mrs P Bodkin, Highwood Farm, Ringwood, Hants BH24 3LG. *Tel* (01425) 473809

Hampshire PGA
Sec, C Maltby, 3 Lily Close, Kempshott Down, Basingstoke, Hants RG22 5NT. *Tel* (01256) 466070.

Hertfordshire County Ladies' Golf Association
Hon Sec, Mrs A Green, Rathgar Lodge, 40a Woodside Avenue, Beaconsfield, Bucks HP9 1JH. *Tel* (01494) 674791.

Hertfordshire Golf Union
Hon Sec, JC Harkett, 5 Willow Way, Harpenden, Herts AL5 5JF. *Tel* (01582) 760841 *Fax* (01582) 462608.

Hertfordshire PGA
Hon Sec, RA Gurney, 1 Field Lane, Letchworth, Herts SG6 3LF. *Tel* (01462) 682256.

Isle of Man Golf Union
Hon Sec, AD Horne, 27 Ballahane Close, Port Erin, Isle of Man. *Tel* (01624) 834389.

Isle of Wight Ladies' Golf Association
Hon Sec, Mrs ED Train, 15 Rectory Drive, Wooton, IOW PO33 4QQ. *Tel* (01983) 883169.

Kent County Golf Union
Hon Sec, BM Evans, 52 Queens Road, Littlestone, New Romney, Kent TN28 8LY. *Tel* (01679) 63613.

Kent County Ladies' Golf Association
Hon Sec, Mrs E Tappin, Brooklands, Larchdene, Farnborough Park, Kent BR6 8PL. *Tel* (01689) 859394.

Kent PGA
Joint Secs, E Impett, 20 The Grove, Barham, Kent. *Tel* (01227) 831655. R Burkin, 35 Valley Walk, Shirley, Croydon, Surrey CR0 8SR. *Tel* 0181–656 3935.

Lancashire Ladies' County Golf Association
Hon Sec, Mrs SA Hampson, Highmoor Farm, Highmoor Lane, Wrightington, Wigan WN6 9PS. *Tel* (01257) 252140.

Lancashire PGA
Sec, L Massey, Bolton Golf Club, Lostock Park, Chorley New Road, Bolton BL6 4AJ. *Tel* (01204) 496137

Lancashire Union of Golf Clubs
Sec, N Hardman, 5 Dicconson Terrace, Lytham St Annes, Lancs FY8 5JY. *Tel* (01253) 733323 *Fax* (01253) 795721.

Leicestershire & Rutland Golf Union
Hon Sec, C Chamberlain, 10 Shipton Close, The Meadows, Wigston Magna, Leicester LE18 3WL. *Tel* (0116) 288 9862.

Leicestershire & Rutland Ladies' County Golf Association
Hon Sec, Mrs DL Sabey, 4 Bailey's Lane, Burton Overy, Leics LE8 0DD. *Tel* (0116) 259 2697.

Leicestershire PGA
Sec, D Freeman, 218 Hamilton Lane, Scraptoft, Leics. *Tel* (0116) 241 4735.

Lincolnshire Ladies' County Association
Hon Sec, Mrs S Gee, 17 Parksgate Avenue, Lincoln LN6 7HP. *Tel* (01522) 688778.

Lincolnshire PGA
Sec, JK Britten, Gainsborough GC, Thonock, Gainsborough DN21 1PZ. *Tel* (01427) 612278.

Lincolnshire Union of Golf Clubs
Hon Sec, DC Hanson, 'Cotswell', Burton, Lincoln LN1 2RD. *Tel* (01522) 520646.

Middlesex County Golf Union
Hon Sec, PSV Cooke, 36 Grants Close, Mill Hill, London NW7 1DD. *Tel* 0181-349 0414.

Middlesex Ladies' County Golf Association
Hon Sec, Mrs B Bullivant, 18 St Leonards Close, Bushey, Herts WD2 2RD. *Tel* (01923) 228749.

Middlesex PGA
Sec, B Eady, 8 Woodbank Drive, Chalfont St Giles, Bucks HP8 4RP. *Tel* (01494) 874487.

Norfolk County Golf Union
Hon Sec/Treas, RJ Trower, 12a Stanley Avenue, Thorpe, Norwich, Norfolk NR7 0BE. *Tel* (01603) 31026.

Norfolk Ladies' County Association
Hon Sec, Mrs J Foad, 28 St Leonard's Close, Wymondham, Norfolk NR18 0JF. *Tel* (01953) 602692.

Norfolk PGA
Hon Sec, DM Bray, 4 Bluebell Drive, Sheringham, Norfolk NR26 8XE. *Tel* (01263) 821905.

North East & North West PGA
Sec, R Sentance, 7 Larch Lea, Ponteland, Newcastle-upon-Tyne NE20 9LG. *Tel* (01661) 825151.

Northamptonshire Golf Union
Joint Hon Secs, RG Halliday and TCA Knight, c/o 12 Edge Hill Road, Duston, Northampton NN5 6BY. *Tel* (01604) 751031.

Northamptonshire Ladies' County Golf Association
Hon Sec, Mrs J Ray, The Dairy, 12 Cotterstock Road, Oundle PE8 5HA. *Tel* (01832) 273573.

Northamptonshire PGA
Sec, G Mobbs, Ivycroft, Back Lane, Chapel Brampton, Northants. *Tel* (01604) 843305.

Northumberland Ladies' County Golf Association
Hon Sec, Mrs M Canning, 23 Mast Lane, Cullercoats, North Shields NE30 3DF. *Tel* 0191-252 5382.

Northumberland Union of Golf Clubs
Hon Sec, WE Procter, 5 Oakhurst Drive, Kenton Park, Gosforth, Newcastle-upon-Tyne NE3 4JS. *Tel* 0191-274 5310 *office*; 0191–285 4981.

Nottinghamshire County Ladies' Golf Association
Hon Sec, Mrs B Jackson, Cranmer Lodge, Main Street, Kinoulton, Notts, NG12 3EL. *Tel* (01949) 81201.

Nottinghamshire PGA
Sec, RW Futer, 52 Barden Road, Mapperley, Nottingham NG3 5QD. *Tel* (0115) 952 0956.

Nottinghamshire Union of Golf Clubs
Hon Sec, E Peters, 48 Weaverthorpe Road, Woodthorpe, Notts NG5 4NB. *Tel* (0115) 926 6560.

Oxfordshire Ladies' County Golf Association
Hon Sec, Mrs BM Notton, 29 Home Close, Wootton, Abingdon, Oxon 0X13 6DD. *Tel* (01865) 739547.

Sheffield PGA
Sec, G Walker, Hillsborough GC, Worrall Road, Sheffield S6 4BE. *Tel* (01742) 332666.

Shropshire & Herefordshire Union of Golf Clubs
Hon Sec, JR Davies, 23 Poplar Crescent, Bayston Hill, Shrewsbury SY3 0QB. *Tel* (01743) 872655.

Shropshire & Hereford PGA
Sec, P Hinton, 1 Stanley Lane Cottages, Bridgnorth, Shropshire. *Tel* (01746) 752045.

Shropshire Ladies' County Golf Association
Hon Sec, Mrs HF Davies, Brooklands, Oldwoods, Bowmere Heath, Shrewsbury SY4 3AX. *Tel* (01939) 290427.

Somerset Golf Union
Hon Sec, CF Carr, 21 Greenacre Road, Bridgwater, Somerset TA6 7RD. *Tel* (01823) 272842.

Somerset Ladies' County Golf Association
Hon Sec, Mrs D Bowerman, Ridgedown, Blagdon Hill, Taunton TA3 7SL. *Tel* (01823) 42256.

South-Western Counties Golf Association
Hon Sec/Treas, JT Lumley, Hartland, Potterne, Devizes, Wilts SN10 5PA. *Tel* (01380) 723935.

Staffordshire Ladies' County Golf Association
Hon Sec, Mrs A Adams, 'Tanglewood', 19 Beacon Road, Walsall, West Midlands WS5 3LF. *Tel* 0121–357 6217.

Staffordshire PGA
Sec, E Griffiths, 22 Wynn Road, Penn, Wolverhampton. *Tel* (01902) 332180.

Staffordshire Union of Golf Clubs
Hon Sec, BA Cox, 34 Lordswood Square, Harborne, Birmingham B17 9BS. *Tel* 021-427 4962.

Suffolk County Golf Union
Hon Sec, SC Goodman, Taybank, 2 Brices Way, Glemsford, Sudbury, Suffolk CO10 7UP. *Tel* (01787) 280178.

Suffolk Ladies' County Golf Association
Hon Sec, Mrs J Dunnett, Springlea, Church Lane, Playford, Ipswich IP6 9DR. *Tel* (01473) 624077.

Suffolk PGA
Sec, M Jillings, Bury St Edmunds GC, Tut Hill, Bury St Edmunds, Suffolk IP28 2LG. *Tel* (01284) 755978.

Surrey County Golf Union
Hon Sec, MW Ashton, Clearglen House, 151 Frimley Road, Camberley, Surrey GU15 2PS. *Tel* (01276) 677959 *Fax* (01276) 63334.

Surrey Ladies' County Golf Association
Hon Sec, Mrs D Marchant, Larchfield, Hunts Hill, Normandy, Guildford, Surrey GU3 2AH. *Tel* (01483) 810873.

Surrey PGA
Sec, P Bowles, 27 Lower Wood Road, Claygate, Surrey KT10 0EU. *Tel* (01372) 463882.

Sussex County Golf Union
Sec, DG Pulford, Suite 1, 216 South Coast Road, Peacehaven, East Sussex BN10 8JR. *Tel/Fax* (01273) 589791.

Sussex County Ladies' Golf Association
Hon Sec, Mrs BJ Page, Ewerby, 7 Denmans Close, Lindfield, West Sussex RH16 2JX. *Tel* (01444) 482454.

Sussex PGA
Sec, C Pluck, 96 Cranston Avenue, Bexhill, East Sussex TN39 3NL. *Tel* (01424) 221298.

Warwickshire Ladies' County Golf Association
Hon Sec, Miss P Lazenby, Cawston Old Farm, Lawford Lane, Bilton, Rugby CV22 7QS. *Tel* (01788) 522907.

Warwickshire PGA
Sec, J Tunnicliff, 80 Wychwood Ave, Knowle, Solihull B93 9DZ. *Tel* (01675) 470809.

Warwickshire Union of Golf Clubs
Hon Sec, J Stubbings, Quaker Cottage, Wiggins Hill Road, Wishaw, Sutton Coldfield B76 9QE. *Tel* (01675) 470809.

Wiltshire County Golf Union
Hon Sec/Treas, RF Buthlay, 10 Priory Park, Bradford-on-Avon, Wilts. BA15 1QU. *Tel/Fax* (01225) 866401.

Wiltshire Ladies' County Golf Association
Hon Sec, Mrs E Bentall, 7 Fairview Road, Salisbury, Wilts SP1 1JX. *Tel* (01722) 335026.

Wiltshire PGA
Sec, L Ross, Marlborough GC, The Common, Marlborough, Wilts. *Tel* (01672) 512493.

Worcestershire County Ladies' Golf Association
Hon Sec, Mrs JW O'Donnell, 25 Riverview Close, Worcester WR2 6DB. *Tel* (01905) 422825.

Worcestershire PGA
Sec, J Sanders, 2 Hawford House, Claines, Worcester WR3 7SQ. *Tel* (01905) 454048.

Worcestershire Union of Golf Clubs
Hon Sec, WR Painter, 70 Cardinal Drive, Kidderminster, Worcs DY10 4RY. *Tel* (01562) 823109.

Yorkshire Ladies' County Golf Association
Hon Sec, Mrs M Elliott, Ingle Court, Lepton, Huddersfield, Yorks HD8 0NN. *Tel* (01484) 602011.

Yorkshire PGA
Sec, J Pape, 1 Summerhill Gardens, Leeds, Yorks LS8 2EL. *Tel* (0113) 266 4746.

Yorkshire Union of Golf Clubs
Hon Sec, K Dowswell, 33 George Street, Wakefield, W Yorks WF1 1LX. *Tel* (01924) 383869 *Fax* (01924) 383634.

Ireland

Irish Golf Union
Sec, IER Dickson, Glencar House, 81 Eglington Road, Donnybrook, Dublin 4.
Tel (00 353) 1 269 4111
Fax (00 353) 1 269 5368

Connacht Branch *Hon Sec,* S Hosty, 14 Rockbarton Green, Salthill, Galway. *Tel/Fax* (00 353) 91 27072.

Leinster Branch *Sec,* P Smyth, 1 Clonskeagh Square, Clonskeagh Road, Dublin 14.
Tel (00 353) 1 269 6977
Fax (00 353) 1 269 3602.

Munster Branch *Hon Sec,* R Barry, Sunville, Dromsligo, Mallow, Co Cork. *Tel* (00 353) 22 21026 *Fax* (00 353) 22 42373

Ulster Branch *Sec,* BG Edwards, 58a High Street, Holywood, Co Down, BT18 9AE. *Tel* (01232) 423708 *Fax* (01232) 426766.

Irish Ladies' Golf Union
Sec, Miss MP Turvey, 1 Clonskeagh Square, Clonskeagh Road, Dublin 14. *Tel* (00 353) 1 269 6244 *Fax* (00 353) 1 283 8670.

Eastern District *Hon Sec,* Mrs G Gregory, 62 Knocknashee, Dublin 14. *Tel* (00 353) 1 298 5813.

Midland District *Hon Sec,* Mrs O Langan, 4 Braganza, Athy Road, Carlow. *Tel* (00 353) 503 42383

Northern District *Hon Sec,* Mrs B McCaw, The Rock, Drumbo, Co. Down BT27 5LB. *Tel* (01232) 826576.

Southern District *Hon Sec,* Mrs J Bouchier-Hayes, Stella Mariae, Gortbey, Newcastle West, Co Limerick. *Tel* (00 353) 69 62178.

Western District *Hon Sec,* Mrs H Sweeney, Galway Road, Roscommon. *Tel* (00 353) 903 26229.

Scotland

Scottish Golf Union
Sec, JW Hume, The Cottage, 181a Whitehouse Road, Barnton, Edinburgh EH4 6BY. *Tel* 0131-339 7546 *Fax* 0131-339 1169.

Area Associations:

Angus T Logan, 31 Woodlands Drive, Coatbridge, Lanarkshire. *Tel* (01236) 428799.

Argyll & Bute DG Smith, 120 Auchamore Rd, Dunoon, Argyll PA23 7JJ. *Tel* (01369) 3114.

Ayrshire RL Crawford, 14 Maxwell Gardens, Hurlford, Kilmarnock, Ayrshire KA1 5BY. *Tel* (01563) 21190.

Borders RG Scott, Buckholmburn, Edinburgh Road, Galashiels TD1 2EY. *Tel* (01896) 752697.

Clackmannanshire T Johnson, 75 Dewar Avenue, Kincardine FK10 4RR. *Tel* (01259) 731168.

Dunbartonshire AW Jones, 107 Larkfield Road, Lenzie, Glasgow G66 3AS. *Tel* 0141-776 7430.

Fife BR Wright, 26 East Fergus Place, Kirkcaldy, Fife KY1 1XT. *Tel* (01592) 206605 *(office)*.

Glasgow RGJ Jamieson, 9 Miller Road, Ayr KA7 2AX. *Tel* (01292) 266600 *(office)*.

Lanarkshire JT Durrant, 30 Woodlands Crescent, Bothwell, Glasgow G71 8PP. *Tel* (01698) 852331.

Lothians J Wood, 28 Stoneyhill Avenue, Musselburgh EH21 6SB. *Tel* 0131-665 4813.

North GB Thomson, Leys View, Culduthel Road, Inverness IV2 4BH. *Tel* (01463) 235861.

North-East IAD McPherson, Rana, Aulton Road, Cruden Bay, Peterhead AB42 7NJ. *Tel* (01779) 812395.

Perth & Kinross DY Rae, 18 Carlownie Place, Auchterarder PH3 1BT. *Tel* (017646) 628837.

Renfrewshire JI McCosh, 'Muirfield', 20 Williamson Place, Johnstone, Renfrewshire PA5 9DW. *Tel* (01505) 327974.

South JH Sommerville, Cherry Cottage, Kirkcudbright DG6 4EU. *Tel* (01557) 330445.

Stirlingshire I Hutton, 18 Turret Drive, Polmont FK2 0QW. *Tel* (01324) 712585.

West N Lancaster, 8 Park Road, Muirhead, Chryston G69. *Tel* 0141–779 2427.

Scottish Ladies' Golfing Association
Sec, Mrs LH Park, Room 1007 Terminal Blding, Prestwick Airport, Prestwick, Ayrshire KA9 2PL. *Tel* (01292) 79582 *Fax* (01292) 671279.

Scottish Ladies' Golfing Association – County Golf
Hon Sec, Miss MJ Greig, 10 Nelson Street, Dumfries DG2 9AY. *Tel* (01387) 54429.

Aberdeen Ladies' County Golf Association
Hon Sec, Mrs M Robinson, 7 Carnegie Gardens, Aberdeen AB2 4AW. *Tel* (01224) 313582.

Angus Ladies' County Golf Association
Hon Sec, Mrs J Lettice, 104 Spey Drive, Menzieshill, Dundee DD2 4AR. *Tel* (01382) 60588.

Ayrshire Ladies' County Golf Association
Hon Sec, Mrs M Mowat, 9 Southpark Road, Ayr. *Tel* (01292) 268773.

Border Counties' Ladies Golf Association
Hon Sec, Mrs E Wanless, Fullarton, Darnick, Melrose, Roxburghshire. *Tel* (01896) 822962.

Dumfriesshire Ladies' County Golf Association
Hon Sec, Miss MJ Greig, 10 Nelson Street, Dumfries DG2 9AY. *Tel* (01387) 54429.

Dunbartonshire & Argyll Ladies' County Association
Hon Sec, Mrs WA Cochran, 5 Mosspark Avenue, Milngavie, Glasgow G62 8NL. *Tel* 0141-956 1565.

East Lothian Ladies' County Association
Hon Sec, Mrs IG Campbell, Glenlair, Main Street, Gullane. *Tel* (01620) 842534.

Fife County Ladies' Golf Association
Hon Sec, Mrs MJ Tulloch, 2 Beldorney Place, Dunfermline KY12 0XN. *Tel* (01383) 737798.

Galloway Ladies' County Golf Association
Hon Sec, Mrs M Gemmell, Priory Croft, Whithorn. *Tel* (01988) 500559.

Lanarkshire Ladies' County Golf Association
Hon Sec, M Allen, 11 Sheepburn Road, Uddingston, Glasgow G71 7DT. *Tel* (01698) 81219.

Midlothian County Ladies' Golf Association
Hon Sec, Mrs E Hay, 5 Baird Grove, Edinburgh EH12 5RP. *Tel* 0131-337 6917.

Northern Counties' Ladies Golf Association
Hon Sec, K Caithness, 4 Drummond Place, Inverness. *Tel* (01463) 222662.

Perth & Kinross Ladies' County Golf Association
Hon Sec, Miss W Garland, 42 Smithfield Crescent, Blairgowrie. *Tel* (01250) 873018.

Renfrewshire Ladies' County Golf Association
Hon Sec, Mrs PS McKenzie, Holly Lodge, Hazelwood Road, Bridge of Weir PA11 3DB. *Tel* (01505) 612920.

Stirling & Clackmannan Ladies' Golf Association
Sec, Mrs JC Williamson, 7 Craighorn Drive, Falkirk FK1 5NX. *Tel* (01324) 29672.

Scottish Golfer's Alliance
Sec/Treas, Mrs MA Caldwell, 5 Deveron Avenue, Giffnock, Glasgow G46 6NH.

Scottish Schools' Golf Association
Sec, JB MacLeod, Leith Academy, 20 Academy Park, Edinburgh. *Tel* 0131-554 0606.

Wales

Welsh Golfing Union
Sec, R Dixon, Powys House, Cwmbran, Gwent NP44 1PB. *Tel* (01633) 870261 *Fax* (01633) 871837.

Welsh Ladies' Golf Union
Hon Sec, Mrs S Webster, Powys House, South Walk, Cwmbran, Gwent NP44 1PB. *Tel/Fax* (01633) 871622.

Anglesey Golf Union
Hon Sec, GP Jones, 20 Gwelfor Estate, Cemaes, Anglesey. *Tel* (01407) 710755.

Brecon & Radnor Golf Union
Hon Sec, DJ Davies, Garden House, Howey, Llandrindod Wells, Powys. *Tel* (01597) 824316.

Caernarvonshire & Anglesey Ladies' County Golf Association
Hon Sec, Mrs BR Williams, Deunant, Rhostrehwfa Road, Llangefni, Anglesey LL77 7YP. *Tel* (01248) 722338.

Caernarvonshire & District Golfing Union
Hon Sec, RE Jones, 23 Bryn Rhos, Rhosbodrual, Caernarfon, Gwynedd LL55 2BT. *Tel* (01286) 673486.

Denbighshire Golfing Union
Hon Sec, EG Howells, 10 Lon Howell, Myddleton Park, Dinbych, Clwyd CH7 3NH.

Denbighshire & Flintshire Ladies' County Golf Association
Sec, Mrs BR Fisher, Hyperion, Tram Road, Buckley, Clwyd CH7 3NH. *Tel* (01244) 543499.

Dyfed Golfing Union
Hon Sec, J Pearson, Tenby Golf Club, The Burrows, Tenby, Dyfed. *Tel* (01834) 842978.

Flintshire Golfing Union
Hon Sec, H Griffith, Cornist Lodge, Cornist Park, Flint, Clwyd CH6 5HJ. *Tel* (01352) 732186.

Glamorgan County Golf Union
Hon Sec, GB Hughes, 46 Gelli Fawr Road, Morriston, Swansea SA6 7PW. *Tel* (01792) 773043.

Glamorgan Ladies' County Golf Association
Sec, Mrs S Williams, 19 Trem-y-Don, Barry, South Glamorgan CF62 6QJ. *Tel* (01446) 734865.

Gwent Golf Union
Sec, CM Buckley, 3 Oak Court, Woodfield Park, Blackwood, Gwent NP2 0BY. *Tel* (01495) 223520.

Mid Wales Ladies' County Golf Association
Sec, Miss A James, Ael-y-Bryn, Pontfaen Road, Lampeter, Dyfed SA48 7JW. *Tel* (01570) 422463.

Monmouthshire Ladies' County Golf Association
Hon Sec, Mrs R Morris, 405 Chepstow Road, Newport, Gwent NP9 8JH. *Tel* (01633) 279368.

Europe

European Golf Association
Place de la Croix Blanche 19, CH-1066 Epalinges, Switzerland. *Tel* +41 21 784 35 32. *Fax* +41 21 784 35 36.

Austrian Golf Federation
Haus des Sports, Prinz-Eugen-Strasse 12, A-1040 Vienna. *Tel* +43 1 505 32 45 *Fax* +43 1 505 49 62.

Austrian PGA
Rögergasse 34, A-1090 Wien. *Tel* +43 1 222 310 7804.

Royal Belgian Golf Federation
Chausée de la Hulpe 110, 1050 Brussels. *Tel* +32 2 672 23 89 *Fax* +32 2 672 08 97.

Czech Golf Federation
Strakonicka 510, 150 00 Prague 5 – Smichov, Czech Republic. *Tel/Fax* +42 2 54 45 86

Danish Golf Union
Idrattens Hus, 2605 Brondby. *Tel* +45 42 45 55 55 *Fax* +45 42 45 35 85.

Finnish Golf Union
Radiokatu 20, SF-00240 Helsinki. *Tel* +358 0 158 2244 *Fax* +358 0 147 145.

French Golf Federation
69 Avenue Victor Hugo, 75783 Paris, Cedex 16. *Tel* +33 1 44 17 63 00 *Fax* +33 1 44 17 63 63.

French PGA
176 Rue Jean Jaures, 92800 Puteaux. *Tel* +33 1 47 72 78 23.

German Golf Association
Postfach 2106, 65011 Wiesbaden. *Tel* +49 611 990200 *Fax* +49 611 990 2040.

German PGA
Hauptstrasse 6, 8902 Neusaess. *Tel* +49 821 465048.

Hellenic Golf Federation
PO Box 70003, GR 16610, Glyfada, Athens. *Tel* +30 1 894 1933/5727 *Fax* +30 1 894 3721.

Golf Union of Iceland
Sport Center, 104 Reykjavik. *Tel* +354 568 6686 *Fax* +354 568 6086.

Italian Golf Federation
Viale Tiziano 74, 00196 Rome. *Tel* +39 6 323 1825 *Fax* +39 6 322 0250.

Luxembourg Golf Union
C/o GC Grand Ducal, 1 Route de Treves, 2633 Senningerberg. *Tel* +352 34 00 90 *Fax* +352 34 83 91.

Netherlands Golf Federation
Burg. van der Borchlaan 1, 3722 GZ Bilthoven. *Tel* +31 30 287018 *Fax* +31 3406 21177.

Netherlands PGA
PO Box 221, 3454 ZL De Meern. *Tel* +31 3406 21888.

Norwegian Golf Union
Hauger Skolevei 1, 1351 Rud. *Tel* +47 67 154600 *Fax* +47 67 13 86 40.

Portuguese Golf Federation
Rua Almeida Brandao 39, 1200 Lisbon.
Tel Lisbon +351 1 397 0245
Fax +351 1 397 4658.

Slovenian Golf Association
GC Bled, C. Svobede 13, 64260 Bled.
Tel +38 64 78282 *Fax* +38 64 78281.

Spanish Golf Association
Capitan Haya 9-5, 28020 Madrid.
Tel +34 1 555 26 82 / 555 27 57
Fax +34 1 556 32 90.

Swedish Golf Federation
PO Box 84, S-182 11 Danderyd.
Tel +46 8 622 1500 *Fax* +46 8 755 8439.

Swedish PGA
PO Box 35, S-181 21 Lidingo. *Tel* +46 8 731 5650.

Swiss Golf Association
Place de la Croix Blanche 19, 1066 Epalinges.
Tel +41 21 784 3531 *Fax* +41 21 784 3536.

Swiss PGA
Chemin des Salines, 1860 Aigle.
Tel +41 25 26 50 21.

America: USA & Canada

Canadian Ladies' Golf Association
1600 James Naismith Drive, Gloucester, Ontario K1B 5N4. *Tel* +1 613 748 5642.
Fax +1 613 748 5720.

Canadian PGA
13450 Dublin Line, Acton, Ontario L7J 2W7.
Tel +1 519 853 5450 *Fax* +1 519 853 5449.

Ladies Professional Golf Association
2570 West International Speedway Blvd, Suite B, Daytona Beach, Florida 32114. *Tel* +1 904 254 8800
Fax +1 904 254 4755.

National Golf Foundation
1150 South US Highway One, Jupiter, Florida 33477. *Tel* +1 407 744 6006.

PGA of America
Box 109601, 100 Avenue of the Champions, Palm Beach Gardens, Florida 33418.
Tel +1 407 624 8400 *Fax* +1 407 624 8448.

PGA Tour
Sawgrass, Ponte Vedra, Florida 32082.
Tel +1 904 285 3700 *Fax* +1 904 285 7913.

Royal Canadian Golf Association
1333 Dorval Drive, Oakville, Ontario L6J 4Z3.
Tel +1 905 849 9700 *Fax* +1 905 845 7040.

United States Golf Association
Golf House, PO Box 708, Far Hills, New Jersey 07931. *Tel* +1 908 234 2300 *Fax* +1 908 234 2179.

Central America

Bahamas Golf Federation
PO Box N4568, Nassau.

Barbados Golf Association
C/o Sandy Lane Golf Club, PO Box 743, Kingston 8.

Bermuda Golf Association
PO Box HM 433, Hamilton HM BX.
Tel +1 809 298 1367

El Salvador Golf Federation
Apartado Postal 631, San Salvador.

Jamaica Golf Association
Constant Spring GC, PO Box 743, Kingston 8.
Tel +1 809 925 2325.

Mexican Golf Association
Cincinnati, No. 40-104, Mexico 18, DF.

South America

Argentine Golf Association
Corrientes 538, Piso 11, 1043 Buenos Aires.
Tel +54 1 325 7498.

Bolivian Golf Federation
Casilla de Correo 6130, La Paz.

Brazilian Golf Federation
Rua 7 de Abril, 01044 São Paulo.

Chilean Golf Federation
Casilla 13307, Correo 21, Santiago.

Colombian Golf Union
Carrer 7A, 72-64 of Int 26 Apartado Aereo 90985, Bogotà.

Ecuador Golf Federation
Casilla 521, Guayaquil.

Paraguay Golf Association
Casilla de Correo 302, Asunción.

Peru Golf Federation
Casilla 5637, Lima.

South American Golf Federation
Casilla de Correo No. 53826, Punta Del Este, CP 21000 – Maldonado.
Tel +598 42 70691.

Uruguay Golf Association
Casilla 1484, Montevideo.

Venezuela Golf Federation
Local 5, Avda. Avila, La Florida, Caracas 1050.

Africa

Botswana Golf Union
PO Box 1368, Gaborone.

Ghana Golf Association
PO Box 8, Achimola.

Kenya Golf Union
PO Box 49609, Nairobi.
Tel +254 2 720074

Kenya Ladies' Golf Union
PO Box 45615, Nairobi.

Malawi Golf Union
PO Box 1198, Blantyre.

Malawi Ladies' Golf Union
PO Box 5319, Limbe.

Namibian Golf Union
PO Box 2989, Windhoek 9000.

Nigeria Golf Union
National Sports Commission, Surulere,
PO Box 145, Lagos.

Sierra Leone Golf Federation
Freetown Golf Club, PO Box 237, Lumley Beach, Freetown.

South African Golf Federation
PO Box 391994, Bramley, South Africa 2018.
Tel +27 11 442 3723
Fax +27 11 442 3753

South African Ladies' Golf Union
PO Box 135, 1930 Vereenigning, Transvaal.
Tel /Fax +27 16 231936.

South African PGA
PO Box 79432, Senderwood 2145.
Tel +27 11 485 2327
Fax +27 11 485 1799.

South African Women's PGA
PO Box 781547, Sandton 2146.
Tel +27 11 783 3213
Fax +27 11 789 1367.

Swaziland Golf Union
PO Box 1739, Mbabane.

Tanzania Golf Union
PO Box 2569, Dar es Salaam.
Tel +255 51 36415/6.

Tanzania Ladies' Golf Union
PO Box 286, Dar es Salaam.

Uganda Golf Union
Kitante Road, PO Box 2574, Kampala.

Zaire Golf Federation
BP 1648, Lubumbashi.

Zambian Golf Union
PO Box 31943, Lusaka.

Zambia Ladies' Golf Union
PO Box 90554, Luanshya.

Zimbabwe Golf Association
PO Box 3327, Harare.

Zimbabwe Ladies' Golf Union
PO Box 3814, Harare.

Asia and Far East

Asia-Pacific Golf Confederation
52, 1st Floor, Jalan Hang, Lekiu 50100,
Kuala Lumpur.

Asia Professional Golf Circuit
230 East Foothill Drive, Phoenix, AZ85020.
Tel +1 602 395 9384
Fax +1 602 395 9370.

China Golf Association
75 Lane 187, Tunhau S Road, Taipei,
Taiwan 10647.

PGA Republic of China
No 196 Pei Ling 5th Road, Taipei, Taiwan.
Tel +886 2 8220318 *Fax* +886 2 8229684.

Hong Kong Golf Association
Suite 1420, Princes Building, 10 Chater Road,
Hong Kong. *Tel* +852 2522 8804
Fax +852 2845 1553.

Hong Kong PGA
110 Yu To Sang Building, 37 Queens Road,
Central, Hong Kong HX7 3751.
Tel +852 523 3171.

Indian Golf Union
Tata Centre (3rd Floor), 43 Chowringhee Road,
Calcutta 700071.

Indonesian Golf Association
C/o bank Bumi Daya,
Jln Imam Bonjol 61-PO Box 106, Jakarta Pusat.

Japan Golf Association
606-6th Floor, Palace Building, Marunouchi,
Chiyoda-ku, Tokyo. *Tel* +81 3 3215 0003
Fax +81 3 3214 2831.

Japan Ladies PGA
7–16–3 Ginza, Chuo-ku, Tokyo 104.
Tel +81 3 3546 7801 *Fax* +81 3 3546 7805.

Japan PGA
Tomin-Ueno Building, 4F, 1-7-15,
Higashi-Ueno, Taito-Ku, Tokyo 110.
Tel +81 3 3546 7801 *Fax* +81 3 3546 7805.

Korean Golf Association
13th Floor, Manhattan Bldg, 36-2,
Yeo-Eui-Do-Dowg, Yeong Deung Po-Ku, Seoul.
Tel +82 2 783 4748.

Malaysian Golf Association
12a Persiaran Ampang, 55000 Kuala Lumpur.
Tel +60 3 4577931 *Fax* +60 3 4565596.

Pakistan Golf Federation
PO Box No. 1295, Rawalpindi.

Philippines Golf Association
209 Administration Building, Rizal Memorial
Sports Complex, Vito Cruz, Manila.
Tel +63 2 588845 *Fax* +63 2 521 1587.

Singapore Golf Association
Thomson Road, PO Box 0172, Singapore 9157. *Tel* +65 466 4892 *Fax* +65 466 4897.

Sri Lanka Golf Union
2 Gower Street, Colombo 5, Sri Lanka.

Thailand Golf Association
Railway Training Centre, Vibhavadee Rangsit Road, Bangkok 10900. *Tel* +66 251 34988/9.

Australasia

Australian Golf Union
Golf Australia House, 153–155 Cecil Street, South Melbourne, Victoria 3205. *Tel* +61 3 699 7944 *Fax* +61 3 690 8510.

Australian Ladies' Golf Union
355 Moray Street, South Melbourne, Victoria 3205. *Tel* +61 3 690 9344 *Fax* +61 3 696 2060.

Australian PGA
4/140 George Street, Hornsby 2077 New South Wales. *Tel* +61 2 476333 *Fax* +61 2 477 7625.

New Zealand Golf Association
PO Box 11842, Wellington Library, 65 Victoria Street, Wellington. *Tel* +64 4 4722 967 *Fax* +64 4 4997 330.

New Zealand Ladies' Golf Union
PO Box 11187, 65 Victoria Street, Wellington. *Tel* +64 4 4726 733 *Fax* +64 4 4726 732.

New Zealand PGA
PO Box 11-934, Wellington. *Tel* +64 4 4722 687 *Fax* +64 4 4712 152.

PART VII

Golf History

The Championships of Great Britain

The Open Championship

The Open Championship was initiated by Prestwick Golf Club in 1860 and was played there until 1870. The Club presented the Championship Belt which was to be held for a year by the winner and which would become the absolute property of any player who won three years in succession. The competition consisted of three rounds of the 12 holes Prestwick then had, to be played on one day. The Open did not become a four-round contest until 1892. There were few entrants in the early years and nearly all were professionals, who were sometimes also greenkeepers and clubmakers, with a few amateurs.

Young Tom Morris won the Belt outright in 1870. There was no contest the following year, but in 1872 Prestwick, the Royal and Ancient and the Honourable Company, who were still playing at Musselburgh, subscribed to provide the present trophy, which was not to be won outright. Since then only three winners would have so earned it: Jamie Anderson and Bob Ferguson during the following ten years and Peter Thomson since in 1954-56. The Championship was to be held on the courses of the three subscribing Clubs in turn. Young Tom won the first for the new cup in 1872 at St Andrews, but died tragically at the age of 24 in 1875.

The three courses continued to be used until 1892 when it was first played at Muirfield to where the Honourable Company had moved. That year was also the first in which the Championship became a 72-hole contest over two days. In 1890, at Prestwick, John Ball had become the first amateur to win. Only two others have followed his success, Harold Hilton in 1892 and 1897, and Bobby Jones in 1926, 1927 and 1930. Roger Wethered tied with Jock Hutchison at St Andrews in 1920, but lost the play-off; if he had not incurred a penalty stroke through treading on his ball in the third round, he may well have won.

The Triumvirate

The year 1894 saw the first occasion the Open was played in England at Sandwich and the first English professional to win, JH Taylor. He won again the next year and for the fifth time in 1913. Harry Vardon and James Braid were the two others of the *great triumvirate* who together won sixteen Opens between 1894 and 1914. Taylor's five wins were spread over twenty years and Vardon's six over nineteen. Braid's wins were concentrated into ten years from 1901 to 1910, all of them in Scotland. Vardon won three times at Prestwick but never at St Andrews where Taylor and Braid both won twice. Only Taylor managed a win at Hoylake. No other player won more than once during their supremacy. The winning scores at the time were very high by today's standards, for although the courses were marginally shorter, the equipment and clothing were primitive compared with those in use now. At Sandwich Taylor's score was 326, or 38 over an average of 4s. His 304 at Hoylake in 1913 was played in appalling weather, wearing a tweed jacket, cap and boots, and using wooden shafts and leather grips. He had no protective clothing or umbrella and won by 8 strokes from Ted Ray. The last winning total over 300 was Hagen's 301 at Hoylake in 1924.

Better Standards

That improved equipment has helped combat the greater length and heavier rough of today's Championship courses is suggested by comparing the average winning scores for decades of this century.

Decade	*Average winning score*	*Decade*	*Average winning score*
1905–14	302	1956–65	280
1920–29	295	1966–75	280
1930–39	289	1976–85	277
1946–55	284		

Of the 123 Opens held so far, twenty Scots have won, eighteen Americans, sixteen English, four Australians, two South Africans and one each from France, Ireland, New Zealand, Argentina, Spain and Zimbabwe. The Scots have won thirty-nine times but only twice since Braid in 1910 (Duncan in 1920 and Lyle in 1985), the USA thirty-one times, England twenty-nine, Australia nine times, South Africa seven times, Spain three times and each of the others once. Since the triumvirate's day ended, the only Englishmen to win more than once have been Sir Henry Cotton and Nick Faldo both with three victories. The Americans have won thirty out of the last sixty-four Opens played.

It will be seen that certain nationalities tend to dominate for a decade or so; the Scots until 1893, then the English until 1914, the USA in the 1920s and until 1933 when the English had a short resuscitation. The Commonwealth were to the fore from 1949 to 1965 (Locke, Thomson, Nagle and Charles) with the Americans coming back again to win in 13 out of 18 years between 1966 and 1983. Equally dominating in their periods were Hagen and Jones in the twenties, Cotton in the thirties, Locke and Thomson the fifties, and thereafter Palmer, Nicklaus, Player, Trevino, Watson and Ballesteros.

Open Courses

Only fourteen courses have accommodated the Open. Prestwick, discarded after 1925 as unsuitable for large crowds, and St Andrews share the lead, each having staged the championship on 24 occasions. The second group comprises Muirfield with fourteen, Royal St George's, Sandwich twelve and Hoylake with ten. Hoylake's last Open was in 1967; that it is not used now is due not to any lack of quality of the course but to lack of space. Deal appeared in 1909 and 1920, and was due again in 1949 but the sea broke across the course, and Sandwich came in for the last time until 1981. Troon and Royal Lytham and St Annes each held an Open between the wars, Carnoustie two and Princes, Sandwich, when Sarazen won in 1932, one; this course, which was used as a tank training ground during the Second World War, has not been asked again. In 1951, Portrush, the only Irish course to stage an Open, also provided the only English winner between Cotton and Jacklin in Max Faulkner. Birkdale and Turnberry are firmly established in the rota which appears to have settled at four Scottish courses, St Andrews, Muirfield, Troon and Turnberry, and three in England, Royal Lytham and St Annes, Birkdale and Royal St George's, Sandwich.

Traditionally the Open is only played on Links courses. While there may yet be new venues by the sea capable of being stretched and groomed to be worthy of holding an Open, the many other considerations to be weighed, such as an adequate road system to carry vast crowds and nearly as many acres as the course covers to accommodate the tented village and services, it is not easy to see where the Championship Committee will turn.

Qualifying

How does one qualify to play in an Open? Since qualifying was first introduced in 1914, there have been numerous changes. Regional qualifying was tried for a year in 1926. At one of the courses used, Sunningdale, Bobby Jones (and even he had to qualify!) played what many consider the classic round of golf: a 66, all 4s and 3s, never over par, 8 birdies, 33 putts and 33 other shots.

Until 1963 all competitors, even the holder, had to play two qualifying rounds on the Open course on the Monday and Tuesday of the Open week. The qualifiers then had one round on Wednesday, one on Thursday and the leading group of between 40 and 60 players finished with two rounds on Friday. In 1963 certain exemptions from qualifying were introduced. The two rounds on the Friday were dropped in 1966 in favour of one round each on Friday and Saturday; not until 1980 was the first round played on Thursday and the last on Sunday. As the entry continued to increase, in 1970 nearby courses were used for qualifying and in 1977 regional qualifying was reintroduced in the previous week with final qualifying on nearby courses later.

There have been surprisingly few ties involving a play-off, only twelve in 119 Championships. The first should have been in 1876 involving David Strath and Bob Martin. However, Strath took umbrage over a complaint against him and refused to play again, Martin being declared the winner. Until 1963 ties were decided over 36 holes; the last two, between Nicklaus and Sanders at St Andrews in 1971 and Watson and Newton at Carnoustie in 1975, were played over 18. Later it was decided that in the event of a tie, the winner would be found immediately by a play-off over specified holes, followed by 'sudden death' if necessary. This happened in 1989 when Calcavecchia beat Norman and Grady over 4 holes after finishing level on 275.

Prize Money

In 1863 the total prize money was £10, its distribution among the fourteen entrants, six of whom were amateurs, is unknown. A year later it had risen by over 50% to £16; the winner taking £6. By 1993 the total prize fund reached £1,000,000 of which the winner received £100,000. Until about 1955, the winner's and leaders' rewards were very modest; even in 1939 the cheque for the first man was £100 out of a total of £500. With some justification the prestige of winning the Open then was adjudged to be of much more value than any monetary award. The growth since the 1950s has been astonishing and is evidence that, while it is still a tremendous asset for any man to have won the Open, the authorities have recognised that it will not maintain its leading place without substantial reward.

The rapid advance of the Open to the major spectacle it has become is due to a combination of factors. Not least of these is the TV presentation of the BBC, acknowledged as the world's best in golf, the interest and enthusiasm of thousands of spectators keen to watch on the spot rather than on the box, and the Royal & Ancient's promotion of this world showpiece of golf that it has become. Behind it all has been the foresight of successive Championship Committees and, in the late 1960s and 1970s, the masterly spreading of the gospel by Keith Mackenzie, Secretary of the R&A in 1966-82, that is so ably continued by his successor, Michael Bonallack.

Laurence Viney

The Amateur Championship

Early History

Golf has always been a competitive game and club medals have been keenly contested since the nineteenth century. Many of the leading amateurs were members of several clubs and, aided by an excellent railway system, they competed against each other at such venues as St Andrews, Prestwick, Hoylake and Musselburgh. An embryonic *open amateur competition* was held in the late 1850s (the first being won by Robert Chambers, the publisher, in 1858) but there seems to have been little enthusiasm for such an event and it died around the time of the first Open Championship (1860). The best amateurs began to enter the Open from 1861. By the 1870s, there was renewed interest in organising a tournament for amateurs only but nothing happened, probably because no one club took a strong enough lead. A proposal in 1877 to the membership of the R&A that it sponsor a sort of Amateur Championship (involving club members and others nominated by members) was defeated.

It fell to the Hoylake golfers to set in motion the championship we now know as *The Amateur*. In 1884 the Secretary of Royal Liverpool, Thomas Potter, proposed that an event – open to all amateurs – should be organised. This original intention was not carried out until 1886 and so the winner of 1885 (AF Macfie) triumphed over a strong but limited, field drawn from certain clubs. The clubs which were responsible for the running of the championship until the R&A took over in 1920 – and who made contributions for the purchase of the trophy – were:

Royal & Ancient
Royal Burgess Golfing Society of Edinburgh
Royal Liverpool
Royal St George's
Royal Albert, Montrose
Royal North Devon
Royal Aberdeen
Royal Blackheath
Royal Wimbledon
Royal Dublin
Alnmouth
North Berwick, New Club
Panmure, Dundee
Prestwick
Bruntsfield Links Golfing Society, Edinburgh
Dalhousie
Gullane
Formby
Honourable Company of Edinburgh Golfers
Innerleven
King James VI, Perth
Kilspindie
Luffness
Tantallon
Troon
West Lancashire

The first championship was not without its teething troubles. The format which was adopted allowed both golfers to proceed to the next round if their match was halved, so the first championship had three semi-finalists – and Macfie got a bye into the final. From 1886, the usual format was adopted.

More serious than the problem of an idiosyncratic draw, however, was the question of amateur status, raised for the first time in 1886.

The committee had to decide if it should accept the entries of John Ball III and Douglas Rolland. As a 15-year-old, Ball had finished fourth in the 1878 Open at Prestwick and on the advice of Jack Morris he accepted the prize money of 10s (50p). Rolland, a stonemason, had accepted second prize in the 1884 Open. Rolland's entry to the Amateur was refused while Ball's was accepted. Ball went on to win the championship a record eight times and the Open Championship of 1890.

The Format

After such a difficult start, the format of 18-hole matches with a 36-hole final remained until 1956. This arrangement made for many closely fought matches, as shown in 1930, the year of RT Jones' Grand Slam triumph. Jones' only victory in the event came in the right year and it is worth pointing out that, in making his way to the final, he won in the fourth round at the 19th (by laying a stymie) against Cyril Tolley, the holder, and his victories in the sixth round and in the semi-final were by the narrowest of margins. In addition, the fact that the draw was not seeded sometimes meant early meetings between top golfers; for example, in 1926 the visiting American Walker Cup Team members, von Elm and Ouimet, met in the second round and von Elm went on to meet Jesse Sweetser in the third.

As a result of such events, there was some pressure for the introduction of seeding the draw but it was not until 1958 that the practice was officially adopted. In the fifties and sixties there were other changes in format in an attempt to satisfy large numbers of golfers who wished to play and to ensure a worthy winner.

The popularity of the championship has posed difficulties for the R&A. The mathematically ideal number of entrants to be fitted into a convenient format is 256. In 1950, 324 entered the championship causing golf to be played on the Old Course for 14 hours a day. In order to restrict the numbers turning up to the championship proper, an experiment in regional qualifying was held in 1958 (again a St Andrews year) and 488 players with handicaps of 5 and under played 36 holes of stroke play on 14 courses. This system was quickly replaced and in 1961 the handicap limit was lowered (to 3) and a balloting-out of higher handicaps was introduced so that 256 were left to play for the trophy. This method was followed until 1983 with the introduction of 36 holes of stroke play to find 64 players for match play, from which to find the eventual winner. The handicap limit in 1992 was 2.

There was also pressure for the introduction of 36-hole matches. As early as 1922 the R&A's championship committee canvassed the opinion of the 252 men who played that year. Nineteen of these voted in favour of 36-hole matches, seven for district qualification, fifty-two voted for a stroke play qualification followed by 18-hole matches and the others who replied wanted no change to the system. In 1956 and 1957 the last 3 rounds were played over 36 holes, in 1958 and 1959 the semi-final and final were over 36 holes and then the old format returned.

There is constant pressure on the organisers to find a format to satisfy the needs of large numbers of home and foreign players, to take into account differences in national handicapping systems, to preserve the atmosphere of the championship, to maintain match play as a central feature of top-level amateur golf and even to take into account the vagaries of the weather. The task is almost impossible.

The Winners

Any man who wins the Amateur is a considerable golfer but there are certain outstanding champions. John Ball of Royal Liverpool won the title eight times between 1888 and 1912. It is interesting to note that he never successfully defended his title. Michael Bonallack triumphed five times between 1961 and 1970, including an incredible hat-trick of victories in which he successively beat Joe Carr and Bill Hyndman twice.

Several golfers have successfully defended their title: Horace Hutchinson, Harold Hilton, Lawson Little and Peter McEvoy, while others have won twice or more – Johnny Laidlay, Freddie Tait, Bob Maxwell, Cyril Tolley, Edward Holderness, Frank Stranahan, Joe Carr and Trevor Homer.

The oldest man to win was the Hon Michael Scott, at the age of 54 in 1933. The youngest winners – John Beharrell and Bobby Cole – were both 18 years and 1 month old. Cole's victory over Ronnie Shade was achieved over 18 holes – play being affected by poor visibility. The first overseas winner was Walter Travis who won in 1904 – one consequence of his victory was the banning of the use of centre-shafted putters. The first Continental winner was the Frenchman, Philippe Ploujoux, who won in 1981. A visiting Walker Cup team always makes for an exciting championship and from fifteen visits to Great Britain the title has crossed the Atlantic twelve times.

No doubt there have been hundreds of thrilling matches played in the championship but few can have been as pulsating as the 1899 final at Prestwick where Johnny Ball beat Freddie Tait at the 37th hole. The victory must have been a sweet one for Ball, since Tait, the hero of Scotland, had won the previous year over Ball's home links of Hoylake. Tait was killed the following year in the Boer War. *The great battle* as Jones described his 4th round tie against Tolley in 1930 rivals the Ball-Tait final for tense excitement and for sheer brilliance of scoring Michael Bonallack's 1st round in the final of 1968 must take pride of place.

The Amateur Championship was 100 years old in 1985 and in essence it has changed remarkably little. How will the Championship react to changes such as the increasing popularity of the game at home and abroad, the lure of the professional ranks with its dependence on stroke play and the increasing commercialism of all sport? There is every reason to believe that it will continue to stand for all that is great in golf.

David Christie

Famous Players of the Past

In making the difficult choice of the names to be included, effort has been made to acknowledge the outstanding players and personalities of each successive era from the early pioneers to the stars of recent times.

Anderson, Jamie (1842–1912)

Winner of three consecutive Open Championships (1877-78-79). Born at St Andrews, he was the son of *Old Daw*, a St Andrews caddie and character. Jamie began golf when 10 years old, and rapidly developed into a fine player, noted for straight hitting and good putting. Anderson's method was to play steadily and on one occasion at St Andrews he remarked that he had played 90 consecutive holes without a bad shot or one stroke made otherwise than he had intended. He was for a period professional to Ardeer Club, but returned to St Andrews to follow his vocation of playing professional.

Anderson, Willie (1878–1910)

One of the Scottish emigrants to America, his flat swing won him the US Open in 1901, 1903, 1904 and 1905. He shares the record of four Open titles with Jones, Hogan and Nicklaus, and remains the only man to win three in a row.

Armour, Thomas D (1896–1968)

Open Champion, 1931. US Open Champion, 1927. USPGA 1930. He had a distinguished amateur career – including the French Open Amateur and tied first place in the Canadian Open. He had the unique distinction of playing in 1921 for Britain against the US as an amateur and in 1925 as a professional for the US against Britain in the unofficial international matches that preceded the inception of the Walker Cup and Ryder Cup events. When he came to the end of his tournament career he quickly gained an outstanding reputation as a coach, and books he wrote on the technique of the game were best-sellers

Auchterlonie, William (1872–1963)

Won the Open title at Prestwick at the age of 21 with a set of seven clubs which he had made himself and shortly afterwards founded the famous club-making firm in St Andrews. He never played with more than his seven clubs and was a great believer that a golfer had to be master of the half, three-quarter and full shots with each club. As professional to the Royal & Ancient Golf Club from 1935 to his death he saw one of his ambitions fulfilled – the Centenary Open at St Andrews in 1960.

Ball, John (1862–1940)

One of the greatest amateur golfers of all time. His father owned the Royal Hotel, Hoylake, prior to the formation of the golf links and when there was a small racecourse on the land later formed into the Royal Liverpool Links. The links became John Ball's playground. In 1878, when fifteen years old, he competed in the Open Championship, finished fourth, eight strokes behind the winner and ahead of many famous Scottish professionals of that time. Between 1888 and 1912 he won the Amateur Championship eight times. In 1890 he was the first amateur to win the Open Championship. He played for England against Scotland continuously from 1902 to 1911, captaining the side each year. He was Amateur Champion in 1899 when war with South Africa broke out and Ball served in that campaign with the Cheshire Yeomanry and did not compete in the Championships of 1900-01-02. In the First World War he served in the Home Forces. He played in his last Amateur Championship in 1921, the year of the first American invasion, and he reached the fifth round although in his fifty-eighth year. Modest and retiring, he rarely spoke about his golf. On the morning of his last round in the Championship he remarked to a friend in the clubhouse, *If only a storm of wind and rain would sweep across the links from the Welsh hills I feel I could beat all of them once again.* But it was a week of torrid heat and he failed. He retired to his farm in North Wales, where he died in December 1940.

Barton, Miss Pamela (1917–43)

At the age of twenty-two when the Second World War broke out, Miss Pamela Barton had already achieved great fame in the golfing world. She won the Ladies' Championship, 1936-39, runner-up,

Pam Barton

1934-35, the American Ladies' Championship, 1936 and the French Ladies' Championship, 1934. In 1936, at the age of nineteen, she held both the British and American Ladies' Championships, the first person to do so since 1909. Miss Barton played for England in the home internationals in 1935-36-37-38-39; for Great Britain *v* United States in 1934-36; *v* France, 1934-36-37-38-39. She was a member of the Ladies' Golf Union teams which toured Canada and America, 1934, and Australia and New Zealand in 1935. Of a charming and cheerful disposition, Miss Barton, who became a Flight-Officer in the WAAF, was killed in a plane crash at an RAF airfield in Kent.

Boros, Julius (1920–94)

Of Hungarian extraction he is remembered for his long, lazy swing and quiet personality. He won two US Open Championships, the first in 1952 and the second 11 years later, at the age of 43, in a play-off against Arnold Palmer and Jackie Cupit. It made him the oldest winner of the title until overtaken by Hale Irwin (45) in 1990. He became the oldest US PGA champion at 48 in 1968, while his best finish in the US Masters was third in 1963 and his best in the Open Championship 15th at Muirfield in 1966.

Braid, James (1870–1950)

One of the greatest figures in golf of all times, James Braid, with Harry Vardon and JH Taylor, made up the Triumvirate which dominated British professional golf for twenty years before the First World War. He was the first person to win the Open Championship five times. This record was later equalled by Taylor and beaten by Vardon. Braid's achievements were remarkable for the short time in which they were accomplished. In ten years he won five times and was second on three occasions. His victories were in 1901, 1905, 1906, 1908, 1910. He won the Match Play Tournament four times, 1903-5-7-11, a record which was unequalled till 1950, and the French Open Championship in 1910. He played for Scotland *v* England in 1903-4-5-6-7-9-10-12 and for Great Britain against America, 1921. A joiner by trade, Braid played as an amateur in Fife and Edinburgh and in 1893 went to London and worked as a club-maker. Taylor and Vardon were well established in the golfing world before Braid turned professional in 1896 and he quickly came into prominence by finishing level with Taylor, who by that time had been Champion twice, in a challenge match. In a historic international foursomes, Braid partnered by Alex Herd lost to Vardon and Taylor in a match for £400 over four courses. A tall powerful player who lashed the ball with *divine* fury, he was famous for his imperturbability; no matter how the game was progressing he always appeared outwardly calm and it was this serenity of temperament which assisted him to his Championship victories on two occasions. A man of few words, it was once said that *Nobody could be as wise as James Braid looked.* One of the founder members of the Professional Golfers' Association, Braid did much to elevate the status of the professional golfer. Braid made a major contribution to golf architecture; Gleneagles, Rosemount, Carnoustie and Dalmahoy all bear his stamp. He was admired and respected by all who knew him, as much for his modest and kindly nature as for his prowess as a golfer. He was professional at Romford for eight years and at Walton Heath for forty-five, and was for twenty-five years an honorary member of the latter club, becoming one of its directors. He was made an honorary member of the Royal & Ancient Golf Club in the last years of his life and had the distinction of being the only honorary member of the Parliamentary Golfing Society.

Campbell, Miss Dorothy Iona (1883–1946)

Won British Ladies' Championship, 1909-11; Scottish Ladies' Championship, 1905-6-8; American Ladies' Championship, 1909-10; Canadian Ladies' Championship 1910-11-12. One of only two women golfers to win the British, American and Canadian Championships, the other being Marlene Stewart (Mrs M Stewart Streit). Played for Scotland in international matches and for British Ladies *v* American Ladies.

Compston, Archie (1893–1962)

One of the outstanding personalities of British golf in the years between the two World Wars who fought hard to resist the developing dominance of the American invasion. He played in three Ryder Cup matches – in 1927, 1929 and 1931. In a 72 hole challenge match he beat Hagen by 18 and 17 in 1928 at Moor Park and in the Open which followed he finished third to Hagen. He tied for second place in the Open of 1925.

Cotton, Sir Henry (1907–87)

Sir Henry Cotton bestrode the British professional golf scene as player, teacher, writer, course architect and encourager of youth from 1930 until his death in December 1987, a few days before his well-deserved knighthood was announced.

He was the only Briton to win the Open more than once in a period of 75 years, between 1914 and 1989; his three victories at Sandwich in 1934, Carnoustie in 1937 and Muirfield in 1948 were pinnacles in a dedicated, sometimes controversial, but highly successful career. All three victories contained at least one memorable round. His 65 at Sandwich (after which a golf ball was named), his last round 71 at Carnoustie in a downpour and his record 66 at Muirfield, with King George VI among the spectators, showed a style both of play and of life admired by all.

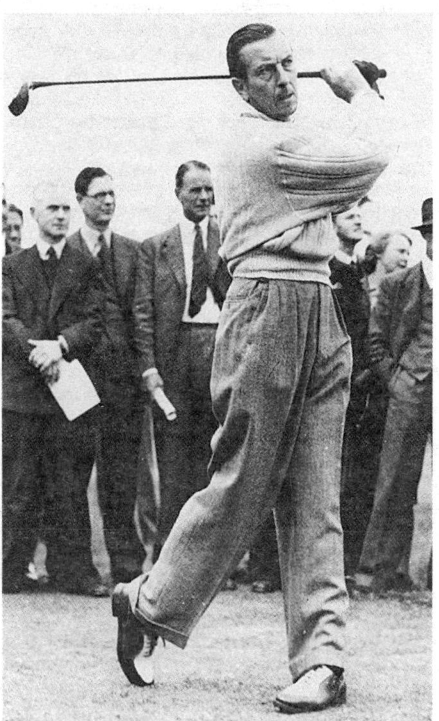

Henry Cotton

No man did more to raise the status of the professional golfer. His insistence on having Honorary Membership of clubs to which he was attached – Waterloo Brussels, Ashridge, Royal Mid-Surrey and Temple near Maidenhead – began a practice now followed by many clubs with their professionals. As Ryder Cup player and Captain, founder-member of the Golf Foundation, and his Rookie of the Year award, he led by example. His reward, which many would say came too late, was the first knighthood given for service to golf.

His many playing successes included winning 11 Continental Opens and five finals in the *News of the World* Match Play Tournament, which at the time was second only in prestige to the Open which he won twice. He was four times selected for the Ryder Cup team, being Captain in 1937 and non-playing Captain in 1953. Captain of the PGA in 1934 and 1954, he also had many other lesser tournament wins.

During the war, in which he served in the RAF, he played exhibition matches in aid of the Red Cross and encouraged his fellow professionals to do likewise. After he retired from Championship play, he devoted his time to writing articles for the golf press and several books. He was also a great supporter of the Golf Foundation and for the development of his beloved Penina in Portugal where he spent much of his last years.

He was elected to Honorary Membership of the Royal & Ancient Club in 1968 and was aware of his coming knighthood when he died a few days before it was announced.

The Curtis Sisters:
Harriet (1878–1944)
Margaret (1880–1965)

The names of Harriet Curtis and her sister Margaret will always be remembered in golf because in 1932 they donated the Curtis Cup for biennial competition between women golfers of the United States and Great Britain and Ireland. Harriet won the US Women's Amateur championship in 1906 and played her sister Margaret in the final the following year, when Margaret won the first of her three titles. Margaret competed in the event for the last time in 1947 at the age of 65, more than 50 years after her first appearance.

Darwin, Bernard (1876–1961)

One of the most respected and widely known personalities in the game. As a graceful and authoritative writer on golf and golfers he had no equal. He knew intimately every player and every course of note throughout the world, and his phenomenal memory, fluent pen and gentle humour established him as the top historian of the game over many years. In 1937 he was awarded the CBE for his services to literature, which included journalism, books of children's stories and other sports besides golf. He was captain of the Royal & Ancient Club in 1934-35, and played internationally for England from 1902 until 1924 and in the first Walker Cup match (1922). He had travelled to the US to report the match for *The Times* and had been called in to play and captain the side when Robert Harris fell ill. During his playing career he won many amateur titles and trophies. He was a grandson of Charles Darwin.

Demaret, Jimmy (1910–83)

One of the game's most colourful characters, stemming no doubt from the fact that he was still a nightclub singer in 1940 when he won six consecutive tournaments against very strong opposition. It culminated with the Masters which he also won in 1947 and 1950, making him the first man to collect three green jackets. It was a remarkable victory because Demaret made up seven strokes on Jim Ferrier over the last six holes, winning by two after being five behind. Demaret was a co-owner of the Champions club in Houston, where the 1967 Ryder Cup and 1969 US Open were played. His record in the Ryder Cup in the years 1947-49-51 is without parallel. He won all his six matches, two of the three foursomes being in partnership with Ben Hogan.

Duncan, George (1884–1964)

He was the last Scottish-born winner of the Open title domiciled in Britain. He won the title in 1920 and his victory was achieved after two opening rounds of 80 which left him 13 strokes behind the leader. Two years later, at Sandwich, he finished second to Hagen after one of the most exciting finishes up to that time. Hagen had finished and was already being hailed as the winner when Duncan, a very late starter, reached the 18th hole needing a 4 to tie. He failed but his round was notable as the only one under 70 in that Open and the first to break 70 in the Open since 1904. Prior to the first war, Duncan was a prominent challenger to the established Triumvirate and would probably have achieved greater fame but for the war years during which he would have been at his prime. One of the fastest players of all time, he wasted no time especially on the greens and his book *Golf at a Gallop* was appropriately titled.

The Dunns

The twin brothers Dunn, born at Musselburgh in 1821, were prominent in golf between 1840 and 1860. In 1849, old Willie Dunn and Jamie Dunn played their great match against Allan Robertson and old Tom Morris. Willie Dunn became custodian in the Blackheath Links until 1864, and he then returned to Leith, and later to North Berwick, where he died at the age of 59. Willie Dunn was celebrated for the peculiar grace of his style and, as the longest driver of his day, he was a doughty match fighter, and one of his famous games was with Allan Robertson in 1843, when he played the St Andrews champion 20 rounds, and lost by 2 rounds and 1 to play. Another famous match was in 1852, when, partnered by Sir Robert Hay, he played Allan Robertson and Old Tom. Jamie Dunn, his twin brother, was also a fine player.

Willie's son went to America, and won the first Championship of America in 1894. He was among the first to experiment with the idea of steel shafts. About 1900 he inserted thin steel rods in split cane and lancewood shafts. He invented a coneshaped paper tee, the forerunner of the wooden tee, and was a pioneer of indoor golf schools. He died in London in 1952.

Ferguson, Bob (1848–1915)

Started to caddie on Musselburgh when aged eight. In 1866, when 18, he won the first prize in the Leith Tournament, in which all the great professionals of the day took part. The late Sir Charles Tennant put up the money for young Ferguson, who, in 1868 and 1869, beat Tom Morris six times. In 1875, at Hoylake, with young Tom Morris representing Scotland in a foursome, he beat Bob Kirk, Blackheath, and John Allan, Westward Ho! representing England. He won the Open Championship in 1880, 1881, and 1882. In 1883 he tied with Willie Fernie, losing the 36-hole play-off by one stroke. After this Championship he became ill with typhoid, and was never able to reproduce his great form. He became the custodian of the Musselburgh links, taught the young and was widely respected in the community.

Fernie, Willie (1851–1924)

Born in St Andrews, he went to Dumfries in 1880 as greenkeeper. In 1882 he was second to Bob Ferguson in the Open Championship and after a tie with the same player he won the Open Championship in 1883 at Musselburgh after a 36-hole play-off. He became professional to Felixstowe and Ardeer and in 1887 to Troon, and was there as professional until February, 1924. He was a very stylish player and in great demand as a teacher. He played in many important stake matches, the two biggest being against Andrew Kirkaldy over Troon, Prestwick and St Andrews which he won by 4 and 3, and against Willie Park over Musselburgh and Troon which he lost by 13 and 12. He played for Scotland against England in 1904.

Hagen, Walter (1892–1969)

The first of the great golfers with star quality. People flocked to see him as much because he was a *character* as for his outstanding skill and many achievements. He did not want to be a millionaire, but merely to live like one, and this he did in dramatic style as when he used a hired Rolls-Royce as a changing room at the Open because professionals were not admitted to the clubhouse, and when he gave the whole of his first prize in the Open to his caddie. He also pioneered stylish dressing on the course. As a player he had great mastery of the recovery shot, nerves of steel beneath his debonair exterior and a fine putting touch. His best achievement was probably his four consecutive wins in the USPGA championship when the event was decided by matchplay over 36 holes. He won the US Open in 1914 and 1919 and the Open in 1922-24-28-29 and represented the US against Britain on seven occasions. His world tours with Kirkwood, his extrovert approach and the entertainment he provided on and off the course were the forerunners of the spectacular development of golf as a spectator sport. In spite of his being a contemporary of the immortal Bobby Jones, his personality was such that he was never overshadowed.

Walter Hagen

Herd, Alexander 'Sandy' (1868–1944)

His life in the forefront of the game was more prolonged than his contemporaries of the Victorian era, and when he took part in his last Open at St Andrews in 1939 he was 71 and his appearances in the Championship covered a span of 54 years. A brilliant shot player, success often eluded him as he was prone to leave his putts short and to indecision. On his first appearance in the Open, at the age of 17, he possessed only four clubs and although he was frequently in contention it was not until 1902 that he won the Championship. He was the first player to win the Open using a rubber-cored ball. In 1920 at Deal and again the following year at St Andrews he was joint leader in the Open after three rounds. In 1926, aged 58, he won the PGA match-play tournament at Royal Mid-Surrey in a 36-hole final, having played five rounds in the previous three days to reach it. Those three achievements when he was in his fifties are convincing proof of the longevity of his game. His life in golf brought him into competition with all the great Victorians – Taylor, Vardon, Kirkaldy, Braid and Park – and continued through the Jones and Hagen era up to the days of Locke, Cotton, Rees and Sarazen and others who, over 100 years after Herd's birth, were still playing Open Championship golf.

Hilton, Harold (1869–1942)

Born at West Kirby, a few miles from Hoylake, he was one of the most scientific of golfers. He learned his game at Royal Liverpool, where he won success in boys' competitions. In 1892, the year the Open Championship was extended to 72 holes, he won, and again in 1897. He won the Amateur Championship and the Irish Open Championship four times each, the St George's Cup twice, the American Amateur Championship once and became the first player, and the only Britisher, to hold both the US and British Amateur titles at the same time. He was small, 5 feet 7 inches, but immensely powerful in build. Hilton made a major contribution to golf literature as the first editor of *Golf Monthly*.

Hunter, Charles (1836–1921)

A caddie and club-maker under old Tom Morris at Prestwick, he was for three years professional at the Blackheath Club, London, and succeeded old Tom as the Prestwick Club professional in 1864. He played in the first Open Championship at Prestwick in 1860, and he was a conspicuous figure at every championship and tournament held at Prestwick, acting as starter and in charge of the house flag up till the time of his death. He did not take much part in professional competitions, preferring to attend to his club-making and his members. In fact, during one championship round, while playing a niblick shot, he received word that the Lord Ailsa wished him to come at once and pick him out a set of clubs. He put his niblick back in his bag, pocketed his ball and returned to his workshop. In 1919 he was presented with his portrait in oils by the Prestwick Club, and a replica hangs in the Club. At the Open Championship of 1914 at Prestwick, he was the recipient of a presentation from his brother professionals. As a man of fine integrity, his friendship was valued by all golfers of his time.

Hutchinson, Horace (1859–1932)

An eminent golfer from the early eighties until 1907. He was a stylish and attractive player. Won the Amateur Championship in 1886 and 1887, runner-up 1885 (the first year of the Championship), and he was in the final in 1903. He was a semi-finalist in 1896, 1901, and 1904. He represented England *v* Scotland 1902-3-4-6-7, and was chosen in 1905 but illness prevented him taking his place. His career in the front rank of the game extended over twenty years. He was a voluminous and pleasant writer on golf and out-door life. He was the first Englishman to captain the Royal & Ancient. In other years he was also Captain of Royal Liverpool, Royal St George's and President of Royal North Devon.

Jones, Bobby (1902–1971)

By the time he retired from competitive golf in 1930 at the age of 28, Jones had established himself as one of the greatest golfers of all time, if not the greatest. He represented America in the Walker Cup from its inauguration in 1922 until 1930 and played in the match against Great Britain in 1921. His victories included the US Open in 1923-26-29-30 (tied in 1925 and 1928 but lost the play-off; second in 1922 and 1924); US Amateur 1924-25-27-28-30 (runner-up in 1919 and 1926); Open Championship 1926-27-30; Amateur Championship 1930. In 1930, Jones reached a pinnacle which will probably never be equalled when he achieved the Grand Slam – winning in one year the Open and Amateur Championships of America and Britain. He then retired from championship golf. His stylish swing was the subject of admiration wherever he went – full, flowing, smooth, graceful and rhythmical. Yet he was of such a nervous disposition that he was frequently physically sick and unable to eat during a championship. During his championship winning years, Jones was also a keen scholar and gained first-class honours degrees in law, English literature and mechanical engineering at three different universities. He finally settled on a legal career with his own practice in Atlanta. It was there that he and his friend Clifford Roberts conceived and developed the idea of the great Augusta National course and the Masters tournament, now a fitting memorial to the *Master Golfer* himself. In recognition of his great skill and courage, and the esteem in which he was held in Britain and St Andrews, he was made an honorary member of the Royal & Ancient in 1956 and two years later, when in St Andrews as captain of the US team in the inaugural competition for the Eisenhower Trophy, he was given the Freedom of the Burgh of St Andrews. He died on 18th December, 1971 after many years of suffering from a crippling spinal disease. As a final tribute a memorial service was held at St Andrews.

Bobby Jones

Kirkaldy, Andrew (1860–1934)

A rugged type of the old school of Scottish professionals, he was the last survivor of that race. After army service in Egypt and India he was appointed professional at Winchester. He had no liking for the steady sedate life of an English professional and after six weeks returned to his native St Andrews, where he lived the rest of his days acting as a playing professional until he was appointed professional to the Royal and Ancient Golf Club. He was a man of powerful physique. He was a beautiful golfer to watch, particularly his iron shots. In the Open Championship, 1889, he tied with Willie Park at Musselburgh, but lost on the replay. He played in many money matches and the most notable was in 1895. JH Taylor had won the Open Championship in 1894, the first English professional to do so, and prior to the Open Championship, at St Andrews in 1895, the young English champion challenged the world for £50 a-side. Kirkaldy accepted and won by a hole. Candid, outspoken, sometimes uncouth Kirkaldy in his old age was respected by princes and peers.

Laidlay, John Ernest (1860–1940)

Johnny Laidlay played high-quality golf for fifty years – a testimony to his technique and temperament. In all, he won more than 130 medals. At a time when golf was booming and the opposition tough, he won the Amateur Championship twice (1889, 1891) was runner-up three times and beaten semi-finalist three times. He was second in the 1893 Open Championship when his characteristically good putting failed. He played for Scotland every year from 1902 until 1911, when he was fifty-one. The longevity of his very individual swing was perhaps due to his early golfing experiences at Musselburgh where he saw Young Tom Morris, knew Willie Park well and played a lot with Bob Ferguson (including a famous round by moonlight). His contribution to the game was the overlapping grip – known erroneously as the Vardon grip. Laidlay played cricket for Scotland (vs Yorkshire – taking 6 wickets for 18 runs); he was a pioneer of wildlife photography and carved beautiful furniture.

Leitch, 'Cecil' (1891–1977)

Although she had reached the semi-final of the British Ladies' Championship in 1908 at the age of 17 and had won the French Ladies' Championship in 1912, it was in 1914 that she really established herself as Britain's dominant woman golfer when she won the English Ladies', the French Ladies' and the British Ladies'. She retained each of these titles when they were next held after the First World War (the English in 1919 and the British and French in 1920) and who can say how many times she might have won them in the intervening years. In all she won the French Ladies' in 1912-14-20-21-24, the English Ladies' in 1914-19, the British Ladies' in 1914-20-21-26 and the Canadian Ladies' in 1921. Her total of four victories in the British Ladies' has never been bettered and has been equalled only by her great rival Joyce Wethered, against whom in the 1920s she had many memorable matches. Miss Leitch was an outspoken person who occasionally battled with the golfing authorities. Her strong attacking play mirrored her personality. Aged 19, in 1910 she accepted the challenge from Harold Hilton, at his peak, to take on any woman golfer over 72 holes giving half a stroke (a stroke at every second hole). Miss Leitch won this famous challenge match by 2 and 1 and later also beat John Ball, eight times Amateur Champion. Right to the end of her life, Cecil Leitch took an active interest in golf, attending major events whenever possible.

Lema, Tony (1934–66)

'Champagne Tony', as he was called because of his habit of treating the golf writers after his victories, had much in common with Walter Hagen. He loved the 'high life' but behind it was steely resolve as well. A beautiful swinger of the club, he was a golfer of grace rather than power. His victory in the Open Championship of St Andrews in 1964 was remarkable because he had never played golf in Europe before. He had just won three American tournaments in quick succession but arrived late and had only 27 holes of practice. Aided by that famous local caddie, Tip Anderson, he quickly mastered these most revered of links and won by five strokes from Jack Nicklaus. A player who did nothing by halves – such as losing to Gary Player in the world matchplay championship after being seven up with 17 to play – he was killed when the private aeroplane in which he was travelling crashed on a golf course in Illinois. He was only 32.

Little, Lawson (1910–68)

As an amateur he established two records in that he won both the Amateur and American Amateur Championships in 1934 and again in 1935. In the final of the 1934 Amateur he won by the margin of 14 and 13 and for the 23 holes played he was ten under 4's. He turned professional in 1936 and won the Canadian Open in the same year and in 1940, won the US Open after a play-off.

Locke, Bobby (1917–87)

The son of Northern Irish emigrants, Artur D'Arcy Locke turned professional in 1938 after a very successful amateur career, in which he won the South African Boys' Championship, the South African Amateur (twice) and Open Championship (twice) as well as finishing leading amateur in the Open Championships of 1936 and 1937. As a result of his visits to Britain, he developed a characteristic hook to increase his length and although never a long hitter, his deadly short game made him a formidable competitor. In his first year as a professional he won the Irish,

Bobby Locke

Transvaal, South African and New Zealand Open Championships as well as the South African Professional title.

During the war, Locke flew Liberator bombers for nearly 2000 hours. He left the South African Air Force weighing four stones heavier and immediately resumed his winning way. Second to Snead at St Andrews in the 1946 Open, he was encouraged to visit America where he was greatly successful. He beat Snead 12–2 in a series of matches and won five tournaments in 1947, two in 1948, three in 1949 and one in 1950. Locke had bad relations with the USPGA who disliked his success and they banned him from their tournaments. Locke concentrated his efforts on Europe. He won the Open Championship four times – 1949-50-52-59 – as well as the Open Championships of Canada (1947), France (1952-53), Germany (1954), Switzerland (1954), Egypt (1954) and South Africa (six times as a professional). He also won a number of British titles including the Dunlop Masters, Spalding, the Lotus, Daks and Bowmaker Tournaments. The 1957 Open Championship was the first to be shown on television and the first in which the leaders went out last. Locke won by 3 strokes and his score of 279 was the first time 280 had been beaten at St Andrews. Locke had to mark his ball on the 72nd hole and in front of the cameras replaced it on the wrong spot. The R & A decided to let his score stand as he had derived no advantage from his technical error and disqualification would have been inequitable and against the spirit of the game.

Bobby Locke will be remembered as a beautifully dressed golfer – plus fours, white shirt and tie – with a superb temperament, especially after a disastrous hole, great self discipline, the highest standards of behaviour and a wonderful short game. He was virtually in retirement when he had a serious car crash. On recovery he continued to play golf but his competitive career was at an end. He was made an honorary member of the R & A in 1976.

Longhurst, Henry (1909–78)

After leaving Cambridge University, he acquired a job as a golf writer in which he could indulge his love of the game and be paid for it. He never ceased to be amazed at his own good fortune. His regular weekly article in the *Sunday Times* became compulsory reading for the golfing cognoscenti. From writing he became involved in radio and, later, television, through which he became world famous as a commentator. Television was the perfect medium for his talents. His humour, easy manner, gifted observation and perception, mellow voice, calm delivery and economy of word were all perfectly suited to a slow-moving sport, and from his vast knowledge and understanding of the game, he was always able to fill in any gaps in the action with an apt story or two. Longhurst also wrote several amusing books about different periods of his life, including a brief spell as an MP. He was awarded the CBE for his services to golf and was one of only a handful of people to be made an honorary member of the Royal & Ancient Golf Club. His own golf was good enough to have won the German Open Amateur in 1936 and to be runner-up in the French Open Amateur in 1937.

Mackenzie, Alister (1870–1934)

A prolific designer of golf courses all over the world, Dr Alexander 'Alister' Mackenzie was a family doctor and surgeon before abandoning medicine to work full time in golf. An early design, in conjunction with Harry S. Colt, was in 1907 for Alwoodley GC, Leeds, where he was a founder member and honorary secretary until 1912. He designed and redesigned dozens of courses in Britain and did outstanding work in Australia and New Zealand. But he is best remembered for designing Cypress Point in California and, with Bobby Jones, the Augusta National in Georgia, home of the US Masters.

Massy, Arnaud (1877–1958)

Born in Biarritz, France, he became, in 1907, the first overseas player to win the Open Championship. He won at Hoylake beating JH Taylor by two strokes. He also tied with Harry Vardon at St George's in 1911 but conceded the title at the 35th hole of the play-off.

Micklem, Gerald (1911–88)

Gerald Micklem devoted so much of his life to the benefit of golf, both as player and administrator, that he will always be remembered for his dedication to the cause of amateurs and professionals alike. He was one of the last true Corinthians, an almost forgotten appellation, who gave his time unsparingly to the game's development, whether locally at his favourite Sunningdale, at the Royal & Ancient or on the international scene. After a pre-war Oxford Blue, he was English Champion in 1947 and 1953, four times in the Walker Cup side between 1947 and 1955 and non-playing Captain in 1957 and 1959, and 12 years a Home International from 1947. He was second in the Brabazon and also won the St George's Challenge Cup, the Berkshire Trophy, the President's Putter and several Royal & Ancient Members' medals.

When he ceased to play in tournaments, his administrative responsibilities were legion. Captain of many English and British teams in European and International events, he took a leading part in the development of the Open, being Chairman of the Championship Committee of the Royal & Ancient during a key period. It was in this appointment that he made his greatest contribution to the future of the game. It was his vision and enterprise which led to the spectacle that the Open is today, as the most prestigious and best organised Championship anywhere in the world. He was Captain of the Royal & Ancient Club in 1968.

To the end of his life he lent his support to most golf ventures and many were the amateurs and professionals whom he helped and who were made welcome at his home, close to Sunningdale, and who remember his generosity and advice given, based on his wide knowledge of the game.

Mitchell, Abe (1897–1947)

The finest player who never won an Open Championship was the tribute paid by JH Taylor. He finished in the first six five times in the Open and was three times winner of the Match Play Championship. Along with Duncan and later Compston, he was one of the few British hopes against the American invasion of the twenties.

The Morrises:
Old Tom (1821–1908)
Young Tom (1851–75)

Old Tom Morris and his son, young Tom Morris, played a prominent part in golf in the period from 1850 to 1875. The father was born at St Andrews on 16th June, 1821. At the age of eighteen, he was apprenticed to Allan Robertson in the ball-making trade. When Morris was thirty years of age, Colonel Fairlie of Coodham took him to Prestwick, and he remained there until 1865, when he returned to St Andrews and became greenkeeper to the Royal & Ancient Golf Club, a position he held until 1904.

Young Tom was born at St Andrews in 1851, and exhibited early remarkable powers as a golfer. At the age of sixteen he won the Open Professional Tournament at Montrose against the best players in the country, and he won the Championship Belt outright by scoring three successive victories in 1868-69-70. The Championship lapsed for a year, but when it was resumed in 1872, young Tom scored his fourth successive victory.

There is no doubt that young Tom was the finest golfer of his time, but the tragic death of his wife, while he was engaged playing with his father in a great golf match at North Berwick against the brothers Willie and Mungo Park, had a most depressing effect on him, and he survived his wife by only a few months. Near the finish of this match, a telegram reached North Berwick intimating that, following her confinement, young Tom's wife was dangerously ill. The telegram was held over by Provost Brodie and not handed to young Tom until the end of the match. The yacht of John Lewis, an Edinburgh golfer, was put at the service of the Morrises but before the party embarked, a second telegram brought the sad news to young Tom that his wife had died. It was a mournful party that made the voyage across the Forth to St Andrews. The brilliant young golfer never recovered from the shock, and he died on Christmas Day of the same year, 1875, at the age of twenty-four.

There was a second son, JOF Morris, who played in professional tournaments, but, although a fine golfer, he never approached the brilliant execution of his elder brother.

Old Tom competed in every Open Golf Championship up to and including 1896, the year Harry Vardon scored his first victory in the Open Championship. Old Tom died at St Andrews in 1908. He was respected throughout the golfing world for his honest, sturdy qualities. His portrait hangs in the R & A Clubhouse, and the home green at St Andrews is named in his memory. A monument, a sculpted figure of Young Tom in golfing pose, was erected by public subscription in St Andrews Cathedral Churchyard and a smaller memorial stone was placed on the grave when Old Tom died.

Ouimet, Francis (1893–1967)

He is often described as the player who started the golf boom in the US when, as a young amateur, he tied with Harry Vardon and Ted Ray for the 1913 US Open and went on to win the play-off. In an illustrious career he won the US Amateur twice and was a member of every Walker Cup team from 1922 to 1934 and was non-playing Captain from then until 1949. Ouimet was the first non-British national, to be elected Captain of the R & A Golf Club in 1951. He was prominent in golf legislation and administration in America and a committee member of the USGA for many years.

The Parks

Brothers Willie and Mungo Park of Musselburgh are famous in the annals of golf for the numerous money matches they played.

Willie had the distinction of winning the very first Open Championship in 1860 and repeated his victory in 1863, 1866 and 1875. For twenty years Willie had a standing challenge in *Bell's Life*, London, to play any man in the world for £100 a side. Willie took part in numerous matches against Tom Morris for very large stakes and in the last of these at Musselburgh in 1882, the match came to an abrupt end when Park was two up with six to play. The referee stopped play because spectators were interfering with the balls. Morris and the referee retired to Foreman's public house. Park sent a message saying if Morris did not come out and finish the match he would play the remaining holes alone and claim the stakes. This he did.

Mungo followed in his brother's footsteps by winning the Open Championship in 1874. He was for many years greenkeeper and professional at Alnmouth.

Willie's son, Willie Junior, kept up the golfing tradition of the family by winning the Open in 1887 and 1889. He designed many golf courses in Europe and America, sometimes in conjunction with property development as at Sunningdale, and was the pioneer of the modern ideas of golf course construction. Like his forebears he took part in many private challenge matches, the one against Harry Vardon at North Berwick in 1899 being watched by the greatest crowd ever for that time and for many years afterwards. Willie Junior died in 1925 aged 61.

The third generation of this golfing family sustained a prominent golf association through Miss Doris Park (Mrs Aylmer Porter), daughter of Willie Junior, who established a distinguished record in ladies' international and championship golf.

Philp, Hugh

The master craftsman among the half-dozen club-makers located in St Andrews in the early days of the nineteenth century. He was especially skilled in making a wooden putter with a long head of pear shaped design. He is believed to have made not many more than one hundred putters. The wooden putter was for centuries a favoured club at St Andrews for long approach putting. The creations of Hugh Philp are highly prized by golf club collectors. After his death in 1856 his business was carried on by Robert Forgan.

Ray, Ted (1877–1943)

Born Jersey, his early days coincided with the famous Triumvirate and it was not until 1912 that he won the Open and was runner-up the following year to Taylor. He was again runner-up in 1925 at the age of 48. In 1913 he tied for the US Open with Ouimet and Vardon, but lost the play-off. After the war he returned to America and won the US Open title in 1920 and was the last British player to hold the title until Tony Jacklin, in 1970. He and Vardon were the only British players to win both the US Open and the Open until they were joined by Jacklin. Noted for his long driving and powers of recovery, he was invariably to be seen playing with a pipe clenched between his teeth.

Rees, Dai (1913–83)

One of Britain's outstanding golfers from the 1930s to the 1960s. He played in nine Ryder Cup matches between 1937 and 1961, and was also non-playing captain in 1967. In 1957, he captained the only British team to win the Ryder Cup since 1933. He was three times a runner-up in the Open Championship and once third, and won the PGA Match-Play Championship four times, and the Dunlop Masters twice, in addition to numerous other tournament successes in Britain, on the

Dai Rees

Continent of Europe, and in Australasia. At the age of 60, he finished third in the Martini tournament. He was made an honorary member of the Royal & Ancient Golf Club in 1976.

Robertson, Allan (1815–58)

According to tradition, he was never beaten in an individual stake match on level terms. A short, thick-set man, he had a beautiful well-timed swing, and several golfers who could recall Robertson, and who saw Harry Vardon at his best, were of the opinion that there was considerable similarity in the elegance and grace of the two players. Tom Morris, senior, worked in Allan Robertson's shop, where the principal trade was making feather balls. A disagreement occurred between Robertson and Morris on the advent of the gutta ball, because Old Tom decided to play with the invention, and Allan considered the gutta might damage his trade in featheries. Allan, through agents, endeavoured to buy up all gutta balls in order to protect his industry of feather balls. Allan Robertson and Tom Morris never seem to have come together in any single match for large stakes, but it is recorded that they never lost a foursome in which they were partners.

Ryder, Samuel (1858–1936)

Sam Ryder was a prosperous seed merchant and the Mayor of St Albans. He did not take up golf until the age of 52 but became one of the most famous names in golf as donor of the Ryder Cup, played for in biennial competition between teams of professionals from Great Britain and Ireland (now Europe) and the United States. Ryder attended an unofficial international match between British and American professionals at Wentworth in 1926 and was greatly impressed by the chivalry and camaraderie of the two sides. He declared afterwards, 'We must do this again'.The first Ryder Cup match was played the following year at Worcester, Massachusetts, and the first in Britain in 1929 at Moortown, Yorkshire.

Sayers, Bernard (1857–1924)

Of very small stature, one of the smallest Scottish professionals, and light of build, he nevertheless took a leading position in the game for over 40 years with his outstanding skill and rigid physical training. He engaged in numerous stake matches and played for Scotland against England in every match from 1903 to 1913, except 1911. He played in every Open Championship from 1880 to 1923. Of a bright and sunny disposition, he contributed much to the merriment of championship and professional gatherings. He taught princes and nobles to play the game, was presented to King Edward, and received a presentation from King George, when Duke of York.

Smith, Mrs Frances (*née* Bunty Stephens) (1925–78)

Dominated post-war women's golf by winning the British Ladies' Championship in 1949 and 1954 (runner-up 1951-52), the English Ladies' in 1948-54-55 (runner-up 1959) and the French Ladies' in 1949. She represented Great Britain in the Curtis Cup on six consecutive occasions from 1950 to 1960. A pronounced pause at the top of her swing made her style most distinctive. She was awarded the OBE for her services to golf and was president of the English Ladies' Golf Association at the time of her death.

Smith, Horton (1908–63)

Came to notice first from Joplin, Missouri, when 20 years old, and brilliantly embarked on the professional circuit in the winter of 1929 when he won all but one of the open tournaments in which he played. He was promoted to that year's Ryder Cup team and also played in 1933 and 1935. He won the first US Masters Tournament in 1934 and again in 1936 as well as more than thirty other major events. On his 21st birthday he won the French Open. He was President of the American PGA, 1952-54 and received two national distinctions: the Ben Hogan Award for overcoming illness or injury, and the Bobby Jones Award for distinguished sportsmanship in golf. The day after the Ryder Cup match which he attended in Atlanta in 1963 he collapsed and died in a Detroit hospital.

Smith, Macdonald (1890–1949)

Born at Carnoustie, he was one of the great golfers who never won the Open Championship, in which he consistently finished in a high place, coming second in 1930 and 1932, third in 1923 and 1924, fourth in 1925 and 1934 and fifth in 1931. He went to America before he was 20. In the Open Championship at Prestwick in 1925 he entered the last round with a lead of five strokes over the field, but a wildly enthusiastic Scottish crowd of 20,000 engulfed and overwhelmed him. The sequel to these unruly scenes was the introduction of gate money the following year and Prestwick was dropped from the rota for the Open. He died in Los Angeles.

Tait, Freddie (1870–1900)

Born at 17 Drummond Place, in Edinburgh (his father PG Tait was a Professor at Edinburgh University). He joined the R & A in 1890, and that year beat all previous St Andrews' amateur records by holing the course in 77, and in 1894 he reduced the record to 72. He was first amateur in the Open Championship in 1894, 1896 and 1899 and third in 1896 and 1897. He won the Amateur Championship in 1896 at Sandwich, beating in successive rounds GC Broadwood, Charles Hutchings, JE Laidlay, John Ball, Horace Hutchinson, and HH Hilton, the strongest amateurs of the day. He repeated his victory in 1898 at Hoylake, and in 1899 he fought and lost at the 37th the historic final with John Ball at Prestwick. There is a Freddie Tait Cup given annually to the best amateur in the South African Open Championship. This cup was purchased from the surplus of the fund collected during the visit of the British amateur golfers to South Africa in 1928. He was killed in the South African War at Koodoosberg Drift, aged 30.

Taylor, John Henry (1871–1963)

Last survivor of the famous Triumvirate – Taylor, Braid and Vardon – died at his Devonshire home in February, 1963, within a month of his 92nd birthday. Born at Northam, Devon, he had been professional at Burnham, Winchester and Royal Mid-Surrey. JH won the Open Championship five times – 1894-95-1900-09-13 – and also tied with Harry Vardon in 1896, but lost the replay. He was runner-up in 1904-05-06-14. His brilliant career included the French and German Open Championships and he was second in the US Open in 1900. Among the many honours he received were honorary membership of the R& A Golf Club in 1949. He was regarded as the pioneer of British professionalism and helped to start the Professional Golfers' Association. He did much to raise the whole status of the professional and, in the words of Bernard Darwin, *turned a feckless company into a self-respecting and respected body of men.* On his retirement in 1957 the Royal North Devon Golf Club paid him their greatest compliment by electing him President.

Tolley, Cyril (1896–1978)

A dominant figure in amateur golf in the inter-war period. He won the first of two Amateur Championships in 1920 while still a student at Oxford and continued to win championships and represent England and Britain until 1938. Among other titles he won the Welsh Open (1921 and 1923) and remains the only amateur to have won the French Open (1924 and 1929). A powerful hitter with a delicate touch, Tolley was a crowd pleaser. He is remembered as much for a match he lost as for some of his victories. Having won the Amateur Championship in 1929, Tolley was a favourite to win at St Andrews in 1930. The draw was unseeded and he met Bobby Jones in the fourth round. A huge crowd turned out to watch a very exciting match which Jones won on the 19th with a stymie. Tolley was elected Captain of the R & A in 1948.

Travis, Walter (1862–1925)

Born in Australia, Travis was the first overseas golfer to win the British Amateur, at Sandwich in 1904. He won the title using a centre-shafted putter, which was subsequently banned for many years. He won the US Amateur Championship in 1900, having taken up the game four years previously at the age of 35. He repeated his victory in 1901 and 1903 and was a semi-finalist five times between 1898 and 1914, winning also the stroke competition six times between 1900 and 1908. The *Old Man* as he was known is reckoned to have been one of the finest judges of distance who ever played golf. He died in New York.

Vardon, Harry (1870–1937)

Born Grouville, Jersey, Vardon created a record by winning the Open Championship six times, his wins being in 1896, 1898, 1899, 1903, 1911 and 1914. He also won the American Open in 1900 and tied in 1913, subsequently losing the play-off. He had a serious illness in 1903 and it was said that he never quite regained his former dominance, particularly on the putting green.

That he was the foremost golfer of his time cannot be disputed and he innovated the modern upright swing and popularised the overlapping grip invented by JE Laidlay.

Had it not been for ill-health and the intervention of the First World War, his outstanding records both in the UK and America would almost certainly have been added to in later years. But in any event his profound influence on the game lives on. More than 100 years after his birth

Harry Vardon

his achievements are still the standard of comparison with the latter-day giants of the game.

Vare, Glenna (*née* Collett) (1903–89)

A natural all-rounder at games, her six American Amateur championships set new standards. It was only achieved however by intense study of the mechanics of the swing and concentrated practice. She attacked the ball, with both irons and woods, with uncommon verve. Sadly, perhaps, a British Amateur title eluded her, despite being in successive finals in 1929 and 1930. In the first against Joyce Wethered at St Andrews she was three under fours for the first 11 holes and five up but became victim of an outstanding counter-attack by the finest woman golfer of her time. A year later she lost again, this time unexpectedly to a little-known 19-year-old, Diana (Fishwick) Critchley, at Formby. She played in five Curtis Cup matches and was also captain, proving as popular with foe as with friend.

Walker, George (1874–1953)

President of the United States Golf Association in 1920 and one of the instigators of the biennial Walker Cup matches between the leading amateurs of Great Britain and Ireland and the United States. He donated the trophy for the first match, played at Long Island, New York, on 29th August 1922, and won by the host country. Educated partly in England, at Stoneyhurst, Walker was an all-round sportsman and a good golfer, though not of international standard. His grandson, George Bush, became President of the United States.

Wethered, Roger (1899–1983)

One of the outstanding amateurs of the period between the two World Wars, winning the Amateur Championship in 1923, and being runner-up in 1928 and 1930. He won the President's Putter of the Oxford and Cambridge GS five times (once a tie) between 1926 and 1936, played in the Walker Cup against the United States six times between 1921 and 1934, and for England against Scotland every year from 1922 to 1930. He was captain of the Royal & Ancient in 1946. But he will probably be best remembered for the fact that he tied with Jock Hutchison, a Scot who had settled in the United States, in the 1921 Open Championship at St Andrews, despite having incurred a penalty stroke by inadvertently treading on his ball. Wethered was reluctant to stay on for the 36-hole play-off the following day because of a cricket engagement in England, but was persuaded to do so, only to be beaten by nine strokes, 150 to 159. No British amateur has come so close to winning the Open Championship since.

The Whitcombe Brothers: Ernest (1890–1971) Charles (1895–1978) Reginald (1898–1957)

The story of the Whitcombes is told in a limited edition publication, *The Whitcombe Brothers – A Golfing Legend*, and what a remarkable story it is. They were born in Burnham, Somerset, and won many titles between them. All three played in the 1935 Ryder Cup contest at Ridgewood, New Jersey, but only Reg, the youngest, won the Open Championship (at Sandwich in 1938). Ernest finished second to Walter Hagen in 1924 at Hoylake after leading by three strokes at one time and Charles took 76 in the final round at Muirfield in 1935 to lose by five strokes and finish third.

Wood, Craig (1901–68)

Born at Lake Placid, New York, Wood was a player of 'near misses'. Like Greg Norman many years later, Wood lost play-offs for what are known now as all the major championships even if they were not then. They were the 1933 Open Championship to Densmore Shute at St Andrews, the 1934 PGA Championship to Paul Runyan at Buffalo, the 1935 Masters to Gene Sarazen at Augusta and the 1939 US Open to Byron Nelson at Philadelphia. However, success did finally come for Wood in 1941 when he won both the Masters and US Open. He was also a member of three American Ryder Cup teams.

Zaharias, Mrs George (Mildred Babe Didrikson) (1915–56)

In the 1932 Olympic Games she established three world records for women: 80 metres hurdles, javelin, and high jump. On giving up athletics she took up golf and won the Texas Women's Open in 1940-45-46; the Western Open, 1940-44-45-50; and the US National Women's Amateur, 1946. In 1947 she won the Ladies' Championship, the first American to do so.

In August 1947 she turned professional and went on to win the US National Women's Open, 1948-50. In winning the Tampa Open, 1951, she set up a women's world record aggregate, for the time, of 288 for 72 holes.

She was voted Woman Athlete of the year five times in 1932-45-46-47-50, and in 1949 was voted Greatest Female Athlete of the Half-Century.

The first woman to hold the post of head professional to a golf club, the *Babe* was a courageous and fighting character who left her mark in the world of sport.

Interesting Facts and Unusual Incidents

Royal Golf Clubs

● The right to the designation *Royal* is bestowed by the favour of the Sovereign or a member of the Royal House. In most cases the title is granted along with the bestowal of royal patronage on the club. The Perth Golfing Society was the first to receive the designation *Royal.* That was accorded in June 1833. King William IV bestowed the honour on the Royal & Ancient Club in 1834. The most recent Club to be so designated is the Royal Troon in 1978.

Royal and Presidential Golfers

● In the long history of the Royal and Ancient game no reigning British monarch has played in an open competition. The Duke of Windsor, when Prince of Wales in 1922, competed in the Royal & Ancient Autumn Medal at St Andrews. He also took part in competitions at Mid-Surrey, Sunningdale, Royal St George's and in the Parliamentary Handicap. He also occasionally competed in American events, sometimes partnered by a professional, and on a private visit to London in 1952 he competed in the Autumn competition of Royal St George's at Sandwich scoring 97. As Prince of Wales he had played on courses all over the world and, after his abdication, as Duke of Windsor he continued to enjoy the game for many years.

● King George VI (when Duke of York) in 1930 and the Duke of Kent in 1937 also competed in the Autumn Meeting of the Royal & Ancient, these occasions being after they had formally played themselves into the Captaincy of the Club and each returned his card in the medal round.

● King Leopold of Belgium played in the Belgian Amateur Championship at Le Zoute, the only reigning monarch ever to have played in a national championship. The Belgian King played in many competitions subsequent to his abdication. In 1949 he reached the quarter-finals of the French Amateur Championship at St Cloud, playing as Count de Rethy.

● King Baudouin of Belgium in 1958 played in the triangular match Belgium-France-Holland and won his match against a Dutch player. He also took part in the Gleneagles Hotel tournament (playing as Mr B de Rethy), partnered by Dai Rees in 1959.

● United States President George Bush accepted an invitation in 1990 to become an Honorary Member of the Royal & Ancient Golf Club of St Andrews. The honour recognised his long connection and that of his family with golf and the R&A. Both President Bush's father, Prescott Bush Sr, and his grandfather, George Herbert Walker – who donated the Walker Cup – were presidents of the United States Golf Association. Other Honorary Members of the R&A include Kel Nagle, Jack Nicklaus, Arnold Palmer, Gene Sarazen, Peter Thomson, Roberto De Vicenzo and Gary Player.

● In September 1992, the Royal & Ancient Golf Club of St Andrews announced that His Royal Highness The Duke of York had accepted the Club's invitation of Honorary Membership. The Duke of York is the third member of the Royal Family to accept membership and joins Their Royal Highnesses The Duke of Edinburgh and The Duke of Kent. In August The Duke of York visited the Club and played his first round on the Old Course, impressing the locals and caddies with his considerable skill and in particular with the length of many of his drives, said the official announcement.

First Lady Golfer

● Mary Queen of Scots, who was beheaded on 8th February, 1587, was probably the first lady golfer so mentioned by name. As evidence of her indifference to the fate of Darnley, her husband who was murdered at Kirk o' Field, Edinburgh, she was charged at her trial with having played at golf in the fields beside Seton a few days after his death.

Record Championship Victories

● In the Amateur Championship at Muirfield, 1920, Captain Carter, an Irish golfer, defeated an American entrant by 10 and 8. This is the only known instance where a player has won every hole in an Amateur Championship tie.

● In the final of the Canadian Ladies' Championship at Rivermead, Ottawa, 1921, Cecil Leitch defeated Mollie McBride by 17 and 15. Miss Leitch only lost 1 hole in the match, the ninth. She was 14 up at the end of the first round, and only 3 holes were necessary in the second round, Miss Leitch winning them all. She won 18 holes out of 21 played, lost 1, and halved 2.

● In the final of the French Ladies' Open Championship at Le Touquet in 1927, Mlle de la Chaume (St Cloud) defeated Mrs Alex Johnston (Moor Park) by 15 and 14, the largest victory in a European golf championship.

● At Prestwick in 1934, W Lawson Little, Presidio, San Francisco, defeated James Wallace, Troon Portland, by 14 and 13 in the final of the Amateur Championship, the record victory in the Amateur Championship. Wallace failed to win a single hole.

Players who have won Two or More Major Championships in the Same Year since 1916

● (The first Masters Tournament was played in 1934.)

1922 Gene Sarazen – USPGA, US Open
1924 Walter Hagen – USPGA, Open
1926 Bobby Jones – US Open, Open
1930 Bobby Jones – US Open, Open (Bobby Jones also won the US Amateur and British Amateur in this year.)
1932 Gene Sarazen – US Open, Open
1941 Craig Wood – Masters, US Open
1948 Ben Hogan – USPGA, US Open
1949 Sam Snead – USPGA, Masters
1951 Ben Hogan – Masters, US Open
1953 Ben Hogan – Masters, US Open, Open
1956 Jack Burke – USPGA, Masters
1960 Arnold Palmer – Masters, US Open
1962 Arnold Palmer – Masters, Open
1963 Jack Nicklaus – USPGA, Masters
1966 Jack Nicklaus – Masters, Open
1971 Lee Trevino – US Open, Open
1972 Jack Nicklaus – Masters, Open
1974 Gary Player – Masters, Open
1975 Jack Nicklaus – USPGA, Masters
1977 Tom Watson – Masters, Open
1980 Jack Nicklaus – USPGA, US Open
1982 Tom Watson – US Open, Open
1990 Nick Faldo – Masters, Open
1994 Nick Price – Open, US PGA

Outstanding Records in Championships, International Matches and on the Professional Circuit

● The record number of victories in the Open Championship is six, held by Harry Vardon who won in 1896-98-99-1903-11-14.

● Five-time winners of the Championship are JH Taylor in 1894-95-1900-09-13; James Braid in 1901-05-06-08-10; Peter Thomson in 1954-55-56-58-65 and Tom Watson in 1975-77-80-82-83. Thomson's 1965 win was achieved when the Championship had become a truly international event. In 1957 he finished second behind Bobby Locke. By winning again in 1958 Thomson was prevented only by Bobby Locke from winning five consecutive Open Championships.

● Four successive victories in the Open by *Young* Tom Morris is a record so far never equalled. He won in 1868-69-70-72. (The Championship was not played in 1871.) Other four-time winners are Bobby Locke in 1949-50-52-57, Walter Hagen in 1922-24-28-29, Willie Park 1860-63-66-75, and *Old* Tom Morris 1861-62-64-67.

● Since the Championship began in 1860, players who have won three times in succession are Jamie Anderson, Bob Ferguson, and Peter Thomson.

● Robert Tyre Jones won the Open three times in 1926-27-30; the Amateur in 1930; the American Open in 1923-26-29-30; and the American Amateur in 1924-25-27-28-30. In winning the four major golf titles of the world in one year (1930) he achieved a feat unlikely ever to be equalled. Jones retired from competitive golf after winning the 1930 American Open, the last of these Championships, at the age of 28.

● Jack Nicklaus has had the most wins (six) in the US Masters Tournament, followed by Arnold Palmer with four.

● In modern times there are four championships generally regarded as standing above all others – the Open, US Open, US Masters, and USPGA. Four players have held all these titles, Gene Sarazen, Ben Hogan, Gary Player, and Jack Nicklaus, who in 1978 became the first player to have held each of them at least three times. His record in these events is – Open 1966-70-78; US Open 1962-67-72-80; US Masters 1963-65-66-72-75-86; USPGA 1963-71-73-75-80. His total of major championships is now 18.

The nearest approach to achieving the Grand Slam of the Open, US Open, US Masters and USPGA in one year was by Ben Hogan in 1953 when he won the first three and could not compete in the USPGA as it then overlapped with the Open Championship.

● In 1975 Jack Nicklaus came very near to winning the Grand Slam, winning the Masters and the USPGA and finishing only two shots and one shot behind the winning scores in the US Open and the Open Championship respectively.

● The record number of victories in the US Open is four, held by W Anderson, Bobby Jones, Ben Hogan and Jack Nicklaus.

● Bobby Jones (amateur), Gene Sarazen, Ben Hogan, Lee Trevino and Tom Watson are the only players to have won the Open and US Open Championships in the same year. Tony Jacklin won the Open in 1969 and the US Open in 1970 and for a few weeks was the holder of both.

● In winning the Amateur Championship in 1970 Michael Bonallack became the first player to win in three consecutive years.
● The English Amateur record number of victories is held by Michael Bonallack, who won the title five times.
● John Ball holds the record number of victories in the Amateur Championship, which he won eight times. Next comes Michael Bonallack (who was internationally known as *The Duke*) with five wins.
● Cecil Leitch and Joyce Wethered each won the British Ladies' title four times.
● The Scottish Amateur record was held by Ronnie Shade, who won five titles in successive years – 1963-64-65-66-67. His long reign as Champion ended when he was beaten in the fourth round of the 1968 Championship after winning 44 consecutive matches.
● Joyce Wethered established an unbeaten record by winning the English Ladies' in five successive years from 1920 to 1924 inclusive.
● In winning the Amateur Championships of Britain and America in 1934 and 1935 Lawson Little won 31 consecutive matches. Other dual winners of these championships in the same year are RT Jones (1930) and Bob Dickson (1967).
● Peter Thomson's victory in the 1971 New Zealand Open Championship was his ninth in that championship.
● In a four-week spell in 1971, Lee Trevino won in succession the US Open, the Canadian Open and the Open Championships.
● The finalists in the 1970 Amateur Championship, Michael Bonallack and Bill Hyndman, were the same as in 1969. This was the first time the same two players reached the final in successive years.
● On the US professional circuit the greatest number of consecutive victories is 11, achieved by Byron Nelson in 1945. Nelson also holds the record for most victories in one calendar year, again in 1945 when he won a total of 18 tournaments.
● Raymond Floyd, by winning the Doral Classic in March 1992, joined Sam Snead as the only winners of US Tour events in four different decades.
● Jack Nicklaus and the late Walter Hagen have had five wins each in the USPGA Championship. All Hagen's wins were in successive years and at match play; all Nicklaus's at stroke play.
● In 1953 Flori van Donck of Belgium had seven major victories in Europe, including the Open Championships of Switzerland, Italy, Holland, Germany and Belgium.
● Mrs Anne Sander won four major amateur titles each under a different name. She won the US Ladies' in 1958 as Miss Quast, in 1961 as Mrs Decker, in 1963 as Mrs Welts and the British Ladies' in 1980 as Mrs Sander.
● The highest number of appearances in the Ryder Cup matches is held by Christy O'Connor who made his tenth appearance in 1973.
● The greatest number of appearances in the Walker Cup matches is held by Irishman Joe Carr who made his tenth appearance in 1967.
● In the Curtis Cup Mary McKenna made her ninth consecutive appearance in 1986.
● Players who have represented their country in both Walker and Ryder Cup matches are, for the United States, Fred Haas, Ken Venturi, Gene Littler, Jack Nicklaus, Tommy Aaron, Mason Rudolph, Bob Murphy, Lanny Wadkins, Tom Kite, Jerry Pate, Craig Stadler, Jay Haas, Bill Rodgers, Hal Sutton, Curtis Strange and Davis Love III; and for Great Britain and Ireland, Norman Drew, Peter Townsend, Clive Clark, Peter Oosterhuis, Howard Clark, Mark James, Michael King, Paul Way, Ronan Rafferty, Sandy Lyle, David Gilford, Colin Montgomerie and Peter Baker.

Remarkable Recoveries in Match Play

● There have been two remarkable recoveries in the Walker Cup Matches. In 1930 at Sandwich, JA Stout, Great Britain, round in 68, was 4 up at the end of the first round against Donald Moe. Stout started in the second round, 3, 3, 3, and was 7 up. He was still 7 up with 13 to play. Moe, who went round in 67, won back the 7 holes to draw level at the 17th green. At the 18th or 36th of the match, Moe, after a long drive placed his iron shot within three feet of the hole and won the match by 1 hole.
● In 1936 at Pine Valley, George Voigt and Harry Girvan for America were 7 up with 11 to play against Alec Hill and Cecil Ewing. The British pair drew level at the 17th hole, or the 35th of the match, and the last hole was halved.
● In the 1965 Piccadilly Match-Play Championship Gary Player beat Tony Lema after being 7 down with 17 to play.
● Bobby Cruickshank, the old Edinburgh player, had an extraordinary recovery in a 36-hole match in a USPGA Championship for he defeated Al Watrous after being 11 down with 12 to play.
● In a match at the Army GC, Aldershot, on 5th July, 1974, for the Gradoville Bowl, MC Smart was 8 down with 8 to play against Mike Cook. Smart succeeded in winning all the remaining holes and the 19th for victory.

Oldest Champions

Open Championship

Belt: 46 years. Tom Morris in 1867.
Cup: 44 years 93 days. Roberto De Vicenzo in 1967.
44 years 42 days. Harry Vardon in 1914.
42 years 97 days. JH Taylor in 1913.
Amateur Championship: Hon Michael Scott, 54 years, Hoylake 1933.

British Ladies Amateur: Mrs Jessie Valentine, 43 years, Hunstanton 1958.
Scottish Amateur: JM Cannon, 53 years, Troon 1969.
English Amateur: Terry Shingler, 41 years 11 months, Walton Heath 1977. Gerald Micklem, 41 years 8 months, Royal Birkdale 1947.
US Open: Hale Irwin, 45 years, Medinah, Illinois, 1990.
US Amateur: Jack Westland, 47 years, Seattle 1952. Westland was defeated in the 1931 final, 21 years previously, by Francis Ouimet at Beverley, Chicago, Illinois.
US Masters: Jack Nicklaus, 46 years, in 1986.
USPGA: Julius Boros, 48 years, in 1968. Lee Trevino, 43 years, in 1984.
USPGA Tour: Sam Snead, 52 years, Greensborough Open in 1965. Julius Boros lost play-off in Westchester Classic 1975. Sam Snead, 61 years, equal second in Glen Campbell Open 1974.

Youngest Champions

Open Championship

Belt: 17 years 5 months. Tom Morris, Jr in 1868.
Cup: 21 years 25 days. Willie Auchterlonie in 1893.
21 years 5 months. Tom Morris, Jr in 1872.
22 years 103 days. Severiano Ballesteros in 1979.
Amateur Championship: JC Beharrell, 18 years 1 month, Troon 1956. R Cole (S Africa) 18 years 1 month, Carnoustie 1966.
British Ladies Amateur: May Hezlett, 17 years, Newcastle Co Down 1899. Michelle Walker, 18 years, Alwoodley 1971.
English Amateur: Nick Faldo, 18 years, Lytham St Annes 1975. Paul Downes, 18 years, Birkdale 1978.
English Amateur Stroke Play: Ronan Rafferty, 16 years, Hunstanton 1980.
British Ladies Open Stroke Play: Helen Dobson, 18 years, Southerness, 1989.

Disqualifications

Disqualifications are now numerous, usually for some irregularity over signing a scorecard or for late arrival at the first tee. We therefore show here only incidents in major events involving famous players or players who were in a winning position or, alternatively, incidents which were in themselves unusual.

● JJ McDermott, the American Open Champion 1911-12, arrived for the Open Championship at Prestwick in 1914 to discover that he had made a mistake of a week in the date the championship began. The American could not play as the qualifying rounds were completed on the day he arrived.

● In the Amateur Championship at Sandwich in 1937, Brigadier-General Critchley, arriving from New York at Southampton on the *Queen Mary*, which had been delayed by fog, flew by specially chartered aeroplane to Sandwich. He circled over the clubhouse, so that the officials knew he was nearly there, but he arrived six minutes late, and his name had been struck out. At the same championship a player, entered from Burma, who had travelled across the Pacific and the American Continent, and also was on the *Queen Mary*, travelled from Southampton by motor car and arrived four hours after his starting time to find after journeying more than halfway round the world he was *struck out*.

● An unprecedented disqualification was that of A Murray in the New Zealand Open Championship, 1937. Murray, who was New Zealand Champion in 1935, was playing with JP Hornabrook, New Zealand Amateur Champion, and at the 8th hole in the last round, while waiting for his partner to putt, Murray dropped a ball on the edge of the green and made a practice putt along the edge. Murray returned the lowest score in the championship, but he was disqualified for taking the practice putt.

● At the Open Championship at St Andrews in 1946, John Panton, Glenbervie, in the evening practised putting on a green on the New Course, which was one of the qualifying courses. He himself reported his inadvertence to the Royal & Ancient and he was disqualified.

● At the Open Championship, Sandwich, 1949, C Rotar, an American, qualified by four strokes to compete in the championship but he was disqualified because he had used a putter which did not conform to the accepted form and make of a golf club, the socket being bent over the centre of the club head. This is the only case where a player has been disqualified in the Open Championship for using an illegal club.

● In the 1957 American Women's Open Championship, Mrs Jackie Pung had the lowest score, 298 over four rounds, but lost the championship. The card she signed for the final round read *five* at the 4th hole instead of the correct *six*. Her total of 72 was correct but the error, under rigid rules, resulted in her disqualification. Betty Jameson, who partnered Mrs Pung and also returned a wrong score, was also disqualified.

Longest Match

● WR Chamberlain, a retired farmer, and George New, a postmaster at Chilton Foliat, on 1st August, 1922, met at Littlecote, the 9-hole course of Sir Ernest Wills, and they agreed to play every Thursday afternoon over the course. This they did until New's sudden death on 13th January,

1938. An accurate record of the matches was kept giving details of each round including wind direction and playing conditions. In the elaborate system nearly two million facts were recorded. They played 814 rounds, and aggregated 86,397 strokes, of which Chamberlain took 44,008 and New 42,371. New, therefore, was 1,637 strokes up. The last round of all was halved, a suitable end to such an unusual contest.

Longest Ties

● The longest known ties in 18-hole match play rounds in major events were in an early round of the News of the World Match Play Championship at Turnberry in 1960, when WS Collins beat WJ Branch at the 31st hole and in the third round of the same tournament at Walton Heath in 1961 when Harold Henning beat Peter Alliss also at the 31st hole.

● In the 1970 Scottish Amateur Championship at Balgownie, Aberdeen, E Hammond beat J McIvor at the 29th hole in their second round tie.

● CA Palmer beat Lionel Munn at the 28th hole at Sandwich in 1908. This is the record tie of the British Amateur Championship. Munn has also been engaged in two other extended ties in the Amateur Championship. At Muirfield, in 1932, in the semi-final, he was defeated by John de Forest, the ultimate winner, at the 26th hole, and at St Andrews, in 1936, in the second round he was defeated by JL Mitchell, again at the 26th hole.

The following examples of long ties are in a different category for they occurred in competitions, either stroke play or match play, where the conditions stipulated that in the event of a tie, a further stated number of holes had to be played – in some cases 36 holes, but mostly 18. With this method a vast number of extra holes was sometimes necessary to settle ties.

● The longest known was between two American women in a tournament at Peterson (New Jersey) when 88 extra holes were required before Mrs Edwin Labaugh emerged as winner.

● In a match on the Queensland course, Australia, in October, 1933, HB Bonney and Col HCH Robertson versus BJ Canniffe and Dr Wallis Hoare required to play a further four 18-hole matches after being level at the end of the original 18 holes. In the fourth replay Hoare and Caniffe won by 3 and 2 which meant that 70 extra holes had been necessary to decide the tie.

● After finishing all square in the final of the Dudley GC's foursomes competition in 1950, FW Mannell and AG Walker played a further three 18-hole replays against T Poole and E Jones, each time finishing all square. A further 9 holes were then arranged when Mannell and Walker won by 3 and 2 making a total of 61 extra holes to decide the tie.

● RA Whitcombe and Mark Seymour tied for first prize in the Penfold £750 Tournament at St Annes-on-Sea, in 1934. They had to play off over 36 holes and tied again. They were then required to play another 9 holes when Whitcombe won with 34 against 36. The tournament was over 72 holes. The first tie added 36 holes and the extra 9 holes made an aggregate of 117 holes to decide the winner. This is a record in first-class British golf but in no way compares with other long ties as it involved only two replays – one of 36 holes and one of 9.

● In the American Open Championship at Toledo, Ohio, in 1931, G Von Elm and Billy Burke tied for the title. Each returned aggregates of 292. On the first replay both finished in 149 for 36 holes but on the second replay Burke won with a score of 148 against 149. This is a record tie in a national open championship.

● Paul Downes was beaten by Robin Davenport at the 9th extra hole in the 4th round of the 1981 English Amateur Championship, a record marathon match for the championship.

● Severiano Ballesteros was beaten by Johnny Miller at the 9th extra hole of a sudden-death play-off at the 1982 million dollar Sun City Challenge, a record for any 72-hole professional event.

● José Maria Olazabal beat Ronan Rafferty at the 9th extra hole to win the 1989 Dutch Open on the Kennemer Golf and Country Club course.

Long Drives

It is impossible to state with any certainty what is the longest ever drive. Many long drives have never been measured and many others have most likely never been brought to our attention. Then there are several outside factors which can produce freakishly long drives, such as a strong following wind, downhill terrain or bonehard ground. Where all three of these favourable conditions prevail outstandingly long drives can be achieved. Another consideration is that a long drive made during a tournament is a different proposition from one made for length alone, either on the practice ground, a long driving competition or in a game of no consequence. All this should be borne in mind when considering the long drives shown here.

● When professional Carl Hooper hit a wayward drive on the 3rd hole (456 yards) at the Oak Hills Country Club, San Antonio, during the 1992 Texas Open, he wrote himself into the record books but out of the tournament. The ball kept bouncing and rolling on a tarmac cart path until it was stopped by a fence – 787 yards away. It took Hooper two recovery shots with a 4-iron and then an 8-iron to return to the fairway. He eventually holed out for a double bogey six and failed to survive the half-way qualifying cut.

● Tommie Campbell of Portmarnock hit a drive of 392 yards at Dun Laoghaire GC in July 1964.

● Playing in Australia, American George Bayer is reported to have driven to within chipping distance of a 589 yards hole. *It was certainly a drive of over 500 yards,* said Bayer acknowledging the strong following wind, sharp downslope where his ball landed and the bonehard ground.

● In September, 1934, over the East Devon course, THV Haydon, Wimbledon, drove to the edge of the 9th green which was a hole of 465 yards, giving a drive of not less than 450 yards.

● EC Bliss drove 445 yards at Herne Bay in August, 1913. The drive was measured by a Government Surveyor who also measured the drop in height from tee to resting place of the ball at 57 feet.

Long Carries

● At Sitwell Park, Rotherham, in 1935, W Smithson, the home professional, drove a ball which carried a dyke at 380 yards from the 2nd tee.

● George Bell, of Penrith GC, New South Wales, Australia, using a number 2 wood drove across the Nepean River, a certified carry of 309 yards in a driving contest in 1964.

● After the 1986 Irish Professional Championship at Waterville, Co. Kerry, four long-hitting professionals tried for the longest-carry record over water, across a lake in the Waterville Hotel grounds. Liam Higgins, the local professional, carried 310 yards and Paul Leonard 311, beating the previous record by 2 yards.

● In the 1972 Algarve Open at Penina, Henry Cotton vouched for a carry of 305 yards over a ditch at the 18th hole by long-hitting Spanish professional Francisco Abreu. There was virtually no wind assistance.

● At the Home International matches at Portmarnock in 1949 a driving competition was held in which all the players in the English, Scottish, Welsh and Irish teams competed. The actual carry was measured. The longest was 280 yards by Jimmy Bruen.

● On 6th April, 1976, Tony Jacklin hit a number of balls into Vancouver harbour, Canada, from the 495-foot high roof of a new building complex. The longest carry was measured at 389 yards.

Long Hitting

There have been numerous long hits, not on golf courses, where an outside agency has assisted the length of the shot. Such an example was a 'drive' by Liam Higgins in 1986, on the Airport runway at Baldonal, near Dublin, of 632 yards.

Longest Albatrosses

● The longest-known albatrosses (three under par) recorded at par 5 holes are:

● 609 yards-15th hole at Mahaka Inn West Course, Hawaii, by John Eakin of California on 12th November, 1972.

● 602 yards-16th hole at Whiting Field Golf Course, Milton, Florida, by 27-year-old Bill Graham with a drive and a 3-wood, aided by a 25 mph tail wind.

● The longest-known albatrosses in Open Championships are:

580 yards-14th hole at Crans-sur-Sierre, by American Billy Casper in the 1971 Swiss Open.

558 yards-5th hole at Muirfield by American Johnny Miller in the 1972 Open Championship.

● In the 1994 German Amateur Championship at Wittelsbacher GC, Rohrenfield, Graham Rankin, a member of the visiting Scottish national team, had a two at the 592-yard 18th.

Eagles (Multiple and Consecutive)

● Wilf Jones scored three consecutive eagles at the first three holes at Moor Hall GC when playing in a competition there on August Bank Holiday Monday 1968. He scored 3, 1, 2 at holes measuring 529 yards, 176 yards and 302 yards.

● In a round of the 1980 Jubilee Cup, a mixed foursomes match play event of Colchester GC, Mrs Nora Booth and her son Brendan scored three consecutive gross eagles of 1, 3, 2 at the 8th, 9th and 10th holes.

● Three players in a four-ball match at Kington GC, Herefordshire, on 22nd July, 1948, all had eagle 2s at the 18th hole (272 yards). They were RN Bird, R Morgan and V Timson.

● Four Americans from Wisconsin on holiday at Gleneagles in 1977 scored three eagles and a birdie at the 300-yard par-4 14th hole on the King's course. The birdie was by Dr Kim Lulloff and the eagles by Dr Gordon Meiklejohn, Richard Johnson and Jack Kubitz.

● In an open competition at Glen Innes GC, Australia on 13th November, 1977, three players in a four-ball scored eagle 3s at the 9th hole (442 metres). They were Terry Marshall, Roy McHarg and Jack Rohleder.

● David McCarthy, a member of Moortown Golf Club, Leeds, had three consecutive eagles (3,3,2) on the 4th, 5th and 6th holes during a Pro-Am competition at Lucerne, Switzerland, on 7th August, 1992.

Speed of Golf Ball and Club Head and Effect of Wind and Temperature

● In *The Search for the Perfect Swing*, a scientific study of the golf swing, a first class golfer is said to have the club head travelling at 100 mph at impact. This will cause the ball to leave the club at 135 mph. An outstandingly long hitter might manage to have the club head travelling at 130 mph which would produce a ball send-off speed of 175 mph. The resultant shot would carry 280 yards.

● According to Thomas Hardman, Wilson's director of research and development, wind will reduce or increase the flight of a golf ball by approximately 1½ yards for every mile per hour of wind. Every two degrees of temperature will make a yard difference in a ball's flight.

Most Northerly Course

● The most northerly course is the Akureyri Golf Club in Iceland which is situated 65°40' North of the equator. Not far south is the Luleò course in Sweden, at 65°35' North.

Most Southerly Course

● Golf's most southerly course is Scott Base Country Club, 13° north of the South Pole. The course is run by the New Zealand Antarctic Programme and players must be kitted in full survival gear. The most difficult aspect is finding the orange golf balls which tend to get buried in the snow. Other obstacles include penguins, seals and skuas. If the ball is stolen by a skua then a penalty of one shot is incurred; but if the ball hits a skua it counts as a birdie.

Highest Golf Courses

● The highest golf course in the world is thought to be the Tuctu GC in Peru which is 14,335 feet above sea-level. High courses are also found in Bolivia with the La Paz GC being about 13,500 feet. In the Himalayas, near the border with Tibet, a 9-hole course at 12,800 feet has been laid out by keen golfers in the Indian Army.

● The highest known course in Europe is at Sestriere in the Italian Alps, 6,500 feet above sea-level.

● The highest courses in Great Britain are Leadhills in Scotland at 1,500 feet, Tredegar in Wales rising to 1,300 feet and Church Stretton in England at 1,250 feet.

Longest Courses

● The longest course in the world is Dub's Dread GC, Piper, Kansas, USA measuring 8,101 yards (par 78).

● The longest course for the Open Championship was 7,252 yards at Carnoustie in 1968.

Longest Holes

● The longest hole in the world, as far as is known, is the 6th hole measuring 782 metres (860 yards) at Koolan Island GC, Western Australia. The par of the hole is 7. There are several holes over 700 yards throughout the world. At Teyateyaneng, South Africa, one hole measures 619 yards.

● The longest hole for the Open Championship is 577 yards (6th hole) at Royal Troon.

Longest Tournaments

● The longest tournament held was over 144 holes in the World Open at Pinehurst, N Carolina, USA, first held in 1973. Play was over two weeks with a cut imposed at the halfway mark.

● An annual tournament is played in Germany on the longest day of the year, comprising 100 holes' medal play. The best return, in 1968, was 417 strokes.

Largest Entries

The Open – 1,827, Sandwich, 1993.
The Amateur – 488, St Andrews, 1958.

● US Open – The US Open of 1990 received a record 6,198 entries.

● The largest entry for a PGA European Tour event was 398 for the 1978 Colgate PGA Championship. Since 1985, when the all-exempt ruling was introduced, all PGA tournaments have had 144 competitors, slightly more or less.

● In 1952, Bobby Locke, the Open Champion, played a round at Wentworth, against any golfer in Britain. Cards costing 2s. 6d. each (12½p), were taken out by 24,000 golfers. The challenge was to beat the local par by more than Locke beat the par at Wentworth; 1,641 competitors, including women, succeeded in *beating* the Champion and each received a certificate signed by him. As a result of this challenge the British Golf Foundation benefited to the extent of £3,026, the proceeds from the sale of cards. A similar tournament was held in the United States and Canada when 87,094 golfers participated; 14,667 players bettered Ben Hogan's score under handicap. The fund benefited by $80,024.

Largest Prize Money

● The Machrie Tournament of 1901 was the first tournament with a first prize of £100. It was won by JH Taylor, then Open Champion, who beat James Braid in the final.

● The richest event in the world is currently the American Tour Championship. It was played at San Francisco's Olympic Club in 1993 with prize money of $3 million.

● (For prize money in the Open Championship see under Conditions and History of Open Championship.)

Holing-in-One

Odds Against

● At the Wanderers Club, Johannesburg in January, 1951, forty-nine amateurs and professionals each played three balls at a hole 146 yards long. Of the 147 balls hit, the nearest was by Koos de Beer, professional at Reading Country Club, which finished 10½ inches from the hole. Harry Bradshaw, the Irish professional who was touring with the British team in South Africa, touched the pin with his second shot, but the ball rolled on and stopped 3 feet 2 inches from the cup.

● A competition on similar lines was held in 1951 in New York when 1,409 players who had done a hole-in-one held a competition over several days at short holes on three New York golf courses. Each player was allowed a total of five shots, giving an aggregate of 7,045 shots. No player holed-in-one, and the nearest ball finished 3½ inches from the hole.

● A further illustration of the element of luck in holing-in-one is derived from an effort by Harry Gonder, an American professional, who in 1940 stood for 16 hours 25 minutes and hit 1,817 balls trying to do a 160 yard hole-in-one. He had two official witnesses and caddies to tee and retrieve the balls and count the strokes. His 1,756th shot struck the hole but stopped an inch from the hole. This was his nearest effort.

● From this and other similar information an estimate of the odds against holing-in-one at any particular hole within the range of one shot was made at somewhere between 1,500 and 2,000 to 1 by a proficient player. Subsequently, however, statistical analysis in America has come up with the following odds: a male professional or top amateur 3,708 to 1; a female professional or top amateur 4,648 to 1; an average golfer 42,952 to 1.

Hole-in-One First Recorded

● Earliest recorded hole-in-one was in 1868 at the Open Championship when Tom Morris (Young Tom) did the 8th hole 145 yards Prestwick in one stroke. This was the first of four Open Championships won successively by Young Tom.

● The first hole-in-one recorded with the 1.66 in ball was in 1972 by John G Salvesen, a member of the R & A Championship Committee. At the time this size of ball was only experimental. Salvesen used a 7-iron for his historical feat at the 11th hole on the Old Course, St Andrews.

Holing-in-One in Important Events

Since the day of the first known hole-in-one by Tom Morris jun, at the 8th hole (145 yards) at Prestwick in the 1868 Open Championship, holes-in-one, even in championships, have become too numerous for each to be recorded. Only where other unusual or interesting circumstances prevailed are the instances shown here.

● All hole-in-one achievements are remarkable. Many are extraordinary. Among the more amazing was that of 2-handicap Leicestershire golfer Bob Taylor, a member of the Scraptoft Club. During the final practice day for the 1974 Eastern Counties Foursomes Championship on the Hunstanton Links, he holed his tee shot with a 1-iron at the 188-yards 16th. The next day, in the first round of the competition, he repeated the feat, the only difference being that because of a change of wind he used a 6-iron. When he stepped on to the 16th tee the following day his partner jokingly offered him odds of 1,000,000 to one against holing-in-one for a third successive time. Taylor again used his 6-iron – and holed in one!

● 1878–Jamie Anderson, competing in the Open Championship at Prestwick, holed the 17th hole in one. Anderson was playing the next to last hole, and though it seemed then that he was winning easily, it turned out afterwards that if he had not taken this hole in one stroke he would very likely have lost. Anderson was just about to make his tee shot when Andy Stuart (winner of the first Irish Open Championship in 1892), who was acting as marker to Anderson, remarked he was standing outside the teeing ground, and that if he played the stroke from there he would be disqualified. Anderson picked up his ball and teed it in a proper place. Then he holed-in-one. He won the Championship by one stroke.

● On a Friday the 13th in 1990, Richard Allen holed-in-one at the 13th at the Barwon Heads Golf Club, Victoria, Australia, and then lost the hole. He was giving a handicap stroke to his opponent, brother-in-law Jason Ennels, who also holed-in-one.

● 1906–R Johnston, North Berwick, competing in the Open Championship, did the 14th hole at Muirfield in one. Johnston played with only one club throughout – an adjustable head club.

● 1959–The first hole-in-one in the US Women's Open Championship was recorded. It was by Patty Berg on the 7th hole (170 yards) at Churchill Valley CC, Pittsburgh.

● 1962–On 6th April, playing in the second round of the Schweppes Close Championship at Little Aston, H Middleton of Shandon Park, Belfast, holed his tee shot at the 159 yards 5th hole, winning a prize of £1,000. Ten minutes later, playing two matches ahead of Middleton, RA Jowle, son of the professional, Frank Jowle, holed his tee shot at the 179 yards 9th hole. As an amateur he was rewarded by the sponsors with a £30 voucher.

● 1963–By holing out in one stroke at the 18th hole (156 yards) at Moor Park on the first day of the Esso Golden round-robin tournament, HR Henning, South Africa, won the £10,000 prize offered for this feat.

● 1967–Tony Jacklin in winning the Masters tournament at St George's, Sandwich, did the 16th hole in one. His ace has an exceptional place in the records for it was seen by millions on TV, the ball in view in its flight till it went into the hole in his final round of 64.

● 1971–John Hudson, 25-year-old professional at Hendon, achieved a near miracle when he holed two consecutive holes-in-one in the Martini Tournament at Norwich. They were at the 11th and 12th holes (195 yards and 311 yards respectively) in the second round.

● 1971–In the Open Championship at Birkdale, Lionel Platts holed-in-one at the 212-yard 4th hole in the second round. This was the first instance of an Open Championship hole-in-one being recorded by television. It was incidentally Platts' seventh ace of his career.

● Nick Faldo's hole-in-one at the 14th in the 1993 Ryder Cup at The Belfry was only the second to be recorded in the history of the match. The other was by Peter Butler at Muirfield's 16th hole in 1973.

● 1973–In the 1973 Open Championship at Troon, two holes-in-one were recorded, both at the 8th hole, known as the Postage Stamp, in the first round. They were achieved by Gene Sarazen and amateur David Russell, who were by coincidence respectively the oldest and youngest competitors.

● Mrs Argea Tissies, whose husband Hermann took 15 at Royal Troon's Postage Stamp 8th hole in the 1950 Open, scored a hole-in-one at the 2nd hole at Punta Ala in the second round of the Italian Ladies Senior Open of 1978. Exactly five years later on the same date, at the same time of day, in the same round of the same tournament at the same hole, she did it again with the same club.

● In less than two hours play in the second round of the 1989 US Open at Oak Hill Country Club, Rochester, New York, four competitors – Doug Weaver, Mark Wiebe, Jerry Pate and Nick Price – each holed the 167 yards 6th hole in one. The odds against four professionals achieving such a record in a field of 156 are reckoned at 332,000 to 1.

Holing-in-One – Longest Holes

● Bob Mitera, when a 21-year-old American student, standing 5 feet 6 inches and weighing under 12 stones, claimed the world record for the longest hole-in-one. Playing over the appropriately named Miracle Hill course at Omaha, on 7th October, 1965, Bob holed his drive at the 10th hole, 447 yards long. The ground sloped sharply downhill.

● Two longer holes-in-one have been achieved, but because they were at dog-leg holes they are not generally accepted as being the longest holes-in-one. They were 480 yards (5th hole, Hope CC, Arkansas) by L Bruce on 15th November, 1962 and 477 yards (14th hole, Martin County CC, Stuart, Florida) by Billy Newman on 13th August, 1972. The estimated length by cutting the corner was around 360 yards.

● In March, 1961, Lou Kretlow holed his tee shot at the 427 yards 16th hole at Lake Hefner course, Oklahoma City, USA.

● The longest known hole-in-one in Great Britain was the 393-yard 7th hole at West Lancashire GC, where in 1972 the assistant professional Peter Parkinson holed his tee shot.

● Other long holes-in-one recorded in Great Britain have been 380 yards (5th hole at Tankersley Park) by David Hulley in 1961; 380 yards (12th hole at White Webbs) by Danny Dunne on 30th July, 1976; 370 yards (17th hole at Chilwell Manor, distance from the forward tee) by Ray Newton in 1977; 365 yards (10th hole at Harewood Downs) by K Saunders in 1965; 365 yards (7th hole at Catterick Garrison GC) by Leslie Bruckner on 18th July, 1980.

● The longest-recorded hole-in-one by a woman was that accomplished in September, 1949 by Marie Robie – the 393-yard hole at Furnace Brook course, Wollaston, Mass, USA.

● In April 1988, Mary Anderson, a bio-chemistry student at Trinity College, Dublin, holed-in-one at the 290-yard 6th hole at the Island GC, Co Dublin.

Holing-in-One – Greatest Number by One Person

47–Amateur Norman Manley of Long Beach, California.

42–US professional Art Wall between 1936 and April 1979.

35–Mancil Davis, professional at the Trophy Club, Forth Worth, Texas. Davis achieved his last in 1979 at the age of 25.

31–British professional CT le Chevalier who died in 1973.

21–British amateur, Jim Hay of Kirkintilloch GC.

10–Mrs Olga Penman, formerly of Harewood Downs GC.

At One Hole

10–Joe Vitullo at 16th hole of Hubbard GC, Ohio.

5–Left-hander, the late Fred Francis at 7th (now 16th) hole of Cardigan GC.

Holing-in-One – Greatest Frequency

● The greatest number of holes-in-one in a calendar year is 11, by JO Boydstone of California in 1962.

● John Putt of Frilford Heath GC had six holes-in-one in 1970, followed by three in 1971.

● Douglas Porteous, of Ruchill GC, Glasgow, achieved seven holes-in-one in the space of eight months. Four of them were scored in a five-day period from 26th to 30th September, 1974, in three consecutive rounds of golf. The first two were achieved at Ruchill GC in one round, the third there two days later, and the fourth at Clydebank and District GC after another two days. The following May, Porteous had three holes-in-one, the first at Linn Park GC incredibly followed by two more in the one round at Clober GC.

● Mrs Kathleen Hetherington of West Essex has holed-in-one five times, four being at the 15th hole at West Essex. Four of her five aces were within seven months in 1966.

● Mrs Dorothy Hill of Dumfries and Galloway GC holed-in-one three times in 11 days in 1977.

● James C Reid of Brodick, aged 59 and 8 handicap in 1987, achieved 14 holes-in-one, all but one on Isle of Arran courses. His success was in spite of severe physical handicaps of a stiff left knee, a damaged right ankle, two discs removed from his back and a hip replacement.

Holing Successive Holes-in-One

● Successive holes-in-one are rare; successive par 4 holes-in-one may be classed as near miracles. NL Manley performed the most incredible feat in September, 1964, at Del Valle Country Club, Saugus, California, USA. The par 4 7th (330 yards) and 8th (290 yards) are both slightly downhill, dog-leg holes. Manley had *aces* at both, en route to a course record of 61 (par 71).

● The first recorded example in Britain of a player holing-in-one stroke at each of two successive holes was achieved on 6th February, 1964, at the Walmer and Kingsdown course, Kent. The young assistant professional at that club, Roger Game (aged 17) holed out with a No. 4 wood at the 244-yard 7th hole, and repeated the feat at the 256-yard 8th hole, using a No. 5 iron.

● The first occasion of holing-in-one at consecutive holes in a major professional event occurred when John Hudson, 25-year-old professional at Hendon, holed-in-one at the 11th and 12th holes at Norwich during the second round of the 1971 Martini tournament. Hudson used a 4-iron at the 195-yard 11th and a driver at the 311-yard downhill 12th hole.

● Assistant professional Tom Doty (23 years), playing in a friendly match on a course near Chicago in October, 1971, had a remarkable four hole score which included two consecutive holes-in-one, sandwiched either side by an albatross and an eagle: 4th hole (500 yards)-2; 5th hole (360 yards dog-leg)-1; 6th hole (175 yards)-1; 7th hole (375 yards)-2. Thus he was 10 under par for four consecutive holes.

Holing-in-One Twice (or More) in the Same Round by the Same Person

What might be thought to be a very rare feat indeed – that of holing-in-one twice in the same round – has in fact happened on many occasions as the following instances show. It is, nevertheless, compared to the number of golfers in the world, still something of an outstanding achievement. The first known occasion was in 1907 when J Ireland playing in a three-ball match at Worlington holed the 5th and 18th holes in one stroke and two years later in 1909 HC Josecelyne holed the 3rd (175 yards) and the 14th (115 yards) at Acton on 24th November.

● The first mention of two holes-in-one in a round by a woman is of special note in that it was followed later by a similar feat by another lady at the same club. On 19th May, 1942, Mrs W Driver, of Balgowlah Golf Club, New South Wales, holed out in one at the 3rd and 8th holes in the same round, while on 29th July, 1948, Mrs F Burke at the same club holed out in one at the 2nd and 8th holes.

● The Rev Harold Snider, aged 75, scored his first hole-in-one on 9th June, 1976 at the 8th hole of the Ironwood course, near Phoenix. By the end of his round he had scored three holes-in-one, the other two being at the 13th (110 yards) and 14th (135 yards). Ironwood is a par-3 course, giving more opportunity of scoring holes-in-one, but, nevertheless, three holes-in-one in one round on any type of course is an outstanding achievement.

● The youngest-known person to have had two holes-in-one in one round was a 14-year-old American, Peter Townsend.

● The youngest British player to achieve two holes-in-one in the same round is Ross Martin on 17th June, 1993, at Newquay GC, Cornwall, seven days after his 15th birthday. The holes were the 163-yard 7th and the 125-yard 16th.

● The youngest woman to have performed the feat was a 17-year-old, Marjorie Merchant, playing at the Lomas Athletic GC, Argentina, at the 4th (170 yards) and 8th (130 yards) holes.

● Tony Hannam, left-handed, handicap 16 and age 71, followed a hole-in-one at the 142 yards 4th of the Bude and North Cornwall Golf Club course with another at the 143 yards 10th on Friday, 18th September, 1992.

Holes-in-One on the Same Day

● In July 1987, at the Skerries Club, Co Dublin, Rank Xerox sponsored two tournaments, a men's 18-hole four-ball with 134 pairs competing and a 9-hole mixed foursomes with 33. During the day each of the four par-3 holes on the course were holed-in-one, the 2nd by Noel Bollard, 5th by Bart Reynolds, 12th by Jackie Carr and 15th by Gerry Ellis.

Two Holes-in-One at the Same Hole in the Same Game

First in World

● George Stewart and Fred Spellmeyer at the 18th hole, Forest Hills, New Jersey, USA in October 1919.

First in Great Britain

● Miss G Clutterbuck and Mrs HM Robinson at the 15th hole (120 yards), St Augustine GC, Ramsgate, on 8th May, 1925.

First in Denmark

● In a Club match in August 1987 at Himmerland, Steffan Jacobsen of Aalborg and Peter Forsberg of Himmerland halved the 15th hole in one shot, the first known occasion in Denmark.

First in Australia

● Dr & Mrs B Rankine, playing in a mixed 'Canadian foursome' event at the Osmond Club near Adelaide, South Australia in April 1987, holed-in-one in consecutive shots at the 2nd hole (162 metres), he from the men's tee with a 3-iron and his wife from the ladies' tee with a 1½ wood.

Holing-in-One – Miscellaneous Incidents

● Chemistry student Jason Bohn, aged 19, of State College, Pennsylvania, supported a charity golf event at Tuscaloosa, Alabama, in 1992 when twelve competitors were invited to try and hole in one at the 135-yard 2nd hole for a special prize covered by insurance. One attempt only was allowed. Bohn succeeded and was offered US$1m (paid at the rate of $5,000 a month for the next 20 years) at the cost of losing his amateur status. He took the money.

● The late Harry Vardon, who scored the greatest number of victories in the Open Championship, only once did a hole-in-one. That was in 1903 at Mundesley, Norfolk, where Vardon was convalescing from a long illness.

● Bob Hope had a hole-in-one at Palm Springs, California, at the age of 90.

● In April 1984 Joseph McCaffrey and his son, Gordon, each holed-in-one in the Spring Medal at the 164-yard 12th hole at Vale of Leven Club, Dunbartonshire.

● In a guest day at Rochford Hundred, Essex, in 1994, there were holes-in-one at all the par threes. First Paul Cairns, of Langdon Hills, holed a 4-iron at the 205-yard 15th, next Paul Francis, a member of the home club, sank a 7-iron at the 156-yard seventh and finally Jim Crabb, of Three Rivers, holed a 9-iron at the 136-yard 11th.

● In 1977, 14-year-old Gillian Field after a series of lessons holed-in-one at the 10th hole at Moor Place GC in her first round of golf.

● By holing-in-one at the 2nd hole in a match against D Graham in the 1979 Suntory World Match Play at Wentworth, Japanese professional Isao Aoki won himself a Bovis home at Gleneagles worth, inclusive of furnishings, £55,000.

● On the morning after being elected captain for 1973 of the Norwich GC, JS Murray hit his first shot as captain straight into the hole at the 169 yards first hole.

● Using the same club and ball, 11-handicap left-hander Christopher Smyth holed-in-one at the 2nd hole (170 yards) in two consecutive medal competitions at Headfort GC, Co Meath, in January, 1976.

● Playing over Rickmansworth course at Easter, 1960, Mrs AE (Paddy) Martin achieved a remarkable sequence of *aces*. On Good Friday she sank her tee shot at the third hole (125 yards). The next day, using the same ball and the same No. 8 iron, at the same hole, she scored another *one*. And on the Monday (same ball, same club, same hole) she again holed out from the tee.

● Alex Evans, aged eight, holed-in-one with a 4-wood at the 136-yard fourth hole at Bromborough, Merseyside, in 1994.

● In January 1985 Otto Bucher of Switzerland, aged 99, holed-in-one at the 130-yard 12th hole at the La Manga Championship South course in Spain.

● At Barton-on-Sea in February 1989 Mrs Dorothy Huntley-Flindt, aged 91, holed in one at the par 3 13th. The following day Mr John Chape, a fellow member in his 80s, holed the par 3 5th in one.

● In 1988 senior citizen Mrs Joan Hall twice holed in one in 19 days at the 12th at Immingham and the 5th at Market Rasen. Three months later she achieved a third ace at Immingham's 17th.

● Michael Monk, age 82, a member of Tandridge Golf Club, Surrey, waited until 1992 to record his first hole-in-one. It continued a run of rare successes for his family. In the previous 12 months, Mr Monk's daughter, Elizabeth, 52, daughter-in-law, Celia, 48, and grandson, Jeremy, 16, had all holed in one on the same course.

● Lou Holloway, a left-hander, recorded his second hole-in-one at the Mount Derby course in New Zealand 13 years after acing the same hole while playing right-handed.

● Ryan Procop, an American schoolboy, holed-in-one at a 168-yard par 3 at Glen Eagles GC, Ohio, with a putter. He confessed that he was so disgusted with himself after a 12 on the previous hole that he just grabbed his putter and hit from the tee.

● Ernie and Shirley Marsden, of Warwick Golf Club, are believed in 1993 to have equalled the record for holes-in-one by a married couple. Each has had three, as have another English couple, Mr and Mrs BE Simmonds.

Challenge Matches

One of the first recorded professional challenge matches was in 1843 when Allan Robertson beat Willie Dunn in a 20-round match at St Andrews over 360 holes by 2 rounds and 1 to play. Thereafter until about 1905 many matches are recorded, some for up to £200 a side – a considerable sum for the time. The Morrises, the Dunns and the Parks were the main protagonists until Vardon, Braid and Taylor took over in the 1890s. Often matches were on a home-and-away basis over 72 holes or more, with many spectators; Vardon and Willie Park Jr attracted over 10,000 at North Berwick in 1899.

Between the wars Walter Hagen, Archie Compston, Henry Cotton and Bobby Locke all played several such matches. Compston surprisingly beat Hagen by 18 up and 17 to play at Moor Park in 1928; yet typically Hagen went on to win the Open the following week at Sandwich. Cotton played classic golf at Walton Heath in 1937 when he beat Densmore Shute for £500 a side at Walton Heath by 6 and 5 over 72 holes.

Curious and Large Wagers

(See also bets recorded under Cross-Country Matches, and in Challenge Matches)

● In the Royal and Ancient Club minutes an entry on 3rd November, 1870 was made in the following terms:

> *Sir David Moncrieffe, Bart, of Moncrieffe, backs his life against the life of John Whyte-Melville, Esq, of Strathkinnes, for a new silver club as a present to the St Andrews Golf Club, the price of the club to be paid by the survivor and the arms of the parties to be engraved on the club, and the present bet inscribed on it. No balls to be attached to it. In testimony of which this bet is subscribed by the parties thereto.*

Thirteen years later, Mr Whyte-Melville, in a feeling and appropriate speech, expressed his deep regret at the lamented death of Sir Robert Moncrieffe, one of the most distinguished and zealous supporters of the club. Whyte-Melville, while lamenting the cause that led to it, had pleasure in fulfilling the duty imposed upon him by the bet, and accordingly delivered to the captain the silver putter. Whyte-Melville in 1883 was elected captain of the club a second time; he died in his eighty-sixth year in July, 1883, before he could take office and the captaincy remained vacant for a year. His portrait hangs in the Royal & Ancient clubhouse and is one of the finest and most distinguished pictures in the smoking room.

● In 1914 Francis Ouimet, who in the previous autumn had won the American Open Championship after a triangular tie with Harry Vardon and Ted Ray, came to Great Britain with Jerome D Travers, the holder of the American amateur title, to compete in the British Amateur Championship at Sandwich. An American syndicate took a bet of £30,000 to £10,000 that one or other of the two United States champions would be the winner. It only took two rounds to decide the bet against the Americans. Ouimet was beaten by a then quite unknown player, HS Tubbs, while Travers was defeated by Charles Palmer, who was fifty-six years of age at the time.

● 1907 John Ball for a wager undertook to go round Hoylake during a dense fog in under 90, in not more than two and a quarter hours and without losing a ball. Ball played with a black ball, went round in 81, and also beat the time.

● The late Ben Sayers, for a wager, played the eighteen holes of the Burgess Society course scoring a four at every hole. Sayers was about to start against an American, when his opponent asked him what he could do the course in. *Fours* replied Sayers, meaning 72, or an average of 4s for the round. A bet was made, then the American added, *Remember a three or a five is not a four.* There were eight bogey 5s and two 3s on the Burgess course at the time Old Ben achieved his feat.

Feats of Endurance

Although golf is not a game where endurance, in the ordinary sense in which the term is employed in sport, is required, there are several instances of feats on the links which demanded great physical exertion.

● Four British golfers, Simon Gard, Nick Harley, Patrick Maxwell and his brother Alastair Maxwell, completed 14 rounds in one day at Iceland's Akureyri Golf Club, the most northern 18-hole course in the world, during June, 1991 when there was 24-hour daylight. It was claimed a record and £10,000 was raised for charity.

● In 1971 during a 24-hour period from 6 pm on 27th November until 5.15 pm on 28th November, Ian Colston completed 401 holes over the 6,061 yards Bendigo course, Victoria, Australia. Colston was a top marathon athlete but was not a golfer. However prior to his golfing marathon he took some lessons and became adept with a 6-iron, the only club he used throughout the 401 holes. The only assistance Colston had was a team of harriers to carry his 6-iron and look for his ball, and a band of motor-cyclists who provided light during the night. This is, as far as is known, the greatest number of holes played in 24 hours on foot on a full-size course.

● In 1934 Col Bill Farnham played 376 holes in 24 hours 10 minutes at the Guildford Lake Course, Guildford, Connecticut, using only a mashie and a putter.

● To raise funds for extending the Skipton GC course from 12 to 18 holes, the club professional, 24-year-old Graham Webster, played 277 holes in the hours of daylight on Monday 20th June,

1977. Playing with nothing longer than a 5-iron he averaged 81 per 18-hole round. Included in his marathon was a hole-in-one.

- Michael Moore, a 7 handicap 26-year-old member of Okehampton GC, completed on foot 15 rounds 6 holes (276 holes) there on Sunday, 25th June, 1972, in the hours of daylight. He started at 4.15 am and stopped at 9.15 pm. The distance covered was estimated at 56 miles.
- On 21st June, 1976, 5-handicapper Sandy Small played 15 rounds (270 holes) over his home course Cosby GC, length 6,128 yards, to raise money for the Society of Physically Handicapped Children. Using only a 5-iron, 9-iron and putter, Small started at 4.10 am and completed his 270th hole at 10.39 pm with the aid of car headlights. His fastest round was his first (40 minutes) and slowest his last (82 minutes). His best round of 76 was achieved in the second round.
- During the weekend of 20th-21st June, 1970, Peter Chambers of Yorkshire completed over 14 rounds of golf over the Scarborough South Cliff course. In a non-stop marathon lasting just under 24 hours, Chambers played 257 holes in 1,168 strokes, an average of 84.4 strokes per round.
- Bruce Sutherland, on the Craiglockhart Links, Edinburgh, started at 8.15 pm on 21st June, 1927, and played almost continuously until 7.30 pm on 22nd June, 1927. During the night four caddies with acetylene lamps lit the way, and lost balls were reduced to a minimum. He completed fourteen rounds. Mr Sutherland, who was a physical culture teacher, never recovered from the physical strain and died a few years later.
- Sidney Gleave, motor-cycle racer, and Ernest Smith, golf professional, Davyhulme Club, Manchester, on 12th June, 1939, played five rounds of golf in five different countries – Scotland, Ireland, Isle of Man, England and Wales. Smith had to play the five rounds under 80 in one day to win the £100 wager. They travelled by plane, and the following was their programme with time taken and Smith's score:

  Start – Prestwick St Nicholas (Scotland), 3.40 am. Score 70. Time taken, 1 hour 35 minutes.

  2nd Course – Bangor (Ireland), 7.15 am. Score 76. Time taken, 1 hour 30 minutes.

  3rd Course – Castletown (Isle of Man), 10.15 am. Score 76. Time taken, 1 hour 40 minutes.

  4th Course – Blackpool, Stanley Park (England), 1.30 pm. Score 72. Time taken, 1 hour 55 minutes.

  5th Course – Hawarden (Wales), 6 pm. Score 68 (record). Time taken, 2 hours 15 minutes.
- On Wednesday, 3rd July, 1974, ES Wilson, Whitehead, Co Antrim and Dr GW Donaldson, Newry, Co Down, played a nine-hole match in each of seven countries in the one day. The first 9 holes was at La Moye (Channel Islands) followed by Hawarden (Wales), Chester (England), Turnberry (Scotland), Castletown (Isle of Man), Dundalk (Eire) and Warrenpoint (N Ireland). They started their first round at 4.25 am and their last round at 9.25 pm. Wilson piloted his own plane throughout.
- In June 1986 to raise money for the upkeep of his medieval church, the Rector of Mark with Allerton, Somerset, the Rev Michael Pavey, played a sponsored 18 holes on 18 different courses in the Bath & Wells Diocese. With his partner, the well-known broadcaster on music, Antony Hopkins, they played the 1st at Minehead at 5.55 am and finished playing the 18th at Burnham and Berrow at 6.05 pm. They covered 240 miles in the 'round' including the distances to reach the correct tee for the 'next' hole on each course. Par for the 'round' was 70. Together the pair raised £10,500 for the church.
- To raise funds for the Marlborough Club's centenary year (1988), Laurence Ross, the Club professional, in June 1987, played 8 rounds in 12 hours. Against a par of 72, he completed the 576 holes in 3 under par, playing from back tees and walking all the way.
- As part of the 1992 Centenary Celebrations of the Royal Cinque Ports Golf Club at Deal, Kent, and to support charity, a six-handicap member, John Brazell, played all 37 royal courses in Britain and Ireland in 17 days. He won 22 matches, halved three, lost 12; hit 2,834 shots for an average score of 76.6; lost 11 balls and made 62 birdies. The aim was to raise £30,000 for Leukaemia Research and the Spastics Society.
- To raise more than £500 for the Guide Dogs for the Blind charity in the summer of 1992, Mrs Cheryle Power, a member of the Langley Park Golf Club, Beckenham, Kent, played 100 holes in a day – starting at 5 am and finishing at 8.45 pm.
- David Steele, a former European Tour player, completed 17½ rounds, 315 holes, between 6 am and 9.45 pm in 1993 at the San Roque club near Gibraltar in a total of 1,291 shots. Steele was assisted by a caddie cart and raised £15,000 for charity.

Fastest Rounds

- Dick Kimbrough, 41, completed a round on foot on 8th August, 1972, at North Platte CC, Nebraska (6,068 yards) in 30 minutes 10 seconds. He carried only a 3-iron.
- At Mowbray Course, Cape Town, November 1931, Len Richardson, who had represented South Africa in the Olympic Games, played a round which measured 6,248 yards in 31 minutes 22 seconds.
- The women's all-time record for the fastest round played on a course of at least 5,600 yards is held by Sue Ledger, 20, who completed the East Berks course in 38 minutes 8 seconds, beating the previous record by 17 minutes.
- In April, 1934, after attending a wedding in

Bournemouth, Hants, Captain Gerald Moxom hurried to his club, West Hill in Surrey, to play in the captain's prize competition. With daylight fading and still dressed in his morning suit, he went round in 65 minutes and won the competition with a net 71 into the bargain.

● On 14th June, 1922, Jock Hutchison and Joe Kirkwood (Australia) played round the Old Course at St Andrews in 1 hour 20 minutes. Hutchison, out in 37, led by three holes at the ninth and won by 4 and 3.

● Fastest rounds can also take another form – the time taken for a ball to be propelled round 18 holes. The fastest known round of this type is 8 minutes 53.8 seconds on 25th August, 1979 by 42 members at Ridgemount CC Rochester, New York, a course measuring 6,161 yards. The Rules of Golf were observed but a ball was available on each tee; to be driven off the instant the ball had been holed at the preceding hole.

● The fastest round with the same ball took place in January 1992 at the Paradise Golf Club, Arizona. It took only 11 minutes 24 seconds; 91 golfers being positioned around the course ready to hit the ball as soon as it came to rest and then throwing the ball from green to tee.

Curious Scoring

● In a Stableford Competition at the Knighton Heath Golf Club, Bournemouth, on 5th May, 1991, Nigel Tanswell equalled the 6,120 yards course record with a gross score of 64 by playing the back nine holes in an eight under par 26 with one eagle and six birdies.

● In the third round of the 1994 Volvo PGA Championship at Wentworth, Des Smyth, of Ireland, made birdie twos at each of the four short holes, the second, fifth, 10th and 14th. He also had a two at the second hole in the fourth round.

● RH Corbett, playing in the semi-final of the Tangye Cup at Mullion in 1916, did a score of 27. The remarkable part of Corbett's score was that it was made up of nine successive 3s, bogey being 5, 3, 4, 4, 5, 3, 4, 4, 3.

● At Little Chalfont in June 1985 Adrian Donkersley played six successive holes in 6, 5, 4, 3, 2, 1 from the 9th to the 14th holes against a par of 4, 4, 3, 4, 3, 3.

● On 2nd September, 1920, playing over Torphin, near Edinburgh, William Ingle did the first five holes in 1, 2, 3, 4, 5.

● In the summer of 1970, Keith McMillan, on holiday at Cullen, had a remarkable series of 1, 2, 3, 4, 5 at the 11th to 15th holes.

● Marc Osborne was only 14 years of age when he equalled the Betchworth Park amateur course record with a 66 in July, 1993. He was playing in the Mortimer Cup, a 36-hole medal competition, and had at the time a handicap of 6.8.

● Playing at Addington Palace, July, 1934, Ronald Jones, a member of Hendon Club, holed five consecutive holes in 5, 4, 3, 2, 1.

● Harry Dunderdale of Lincoln GC scored 5, 4, 3, 2, 1 in five consecutive holes during the first round of his club championship in 1978. The hole-in-one was the 7th, measuring 294 yards.

● At Westerhope near Newcastle in January 1986 Alan Crosby, the Club professional, played the first four holes in 4, 3, 2, 1 against the par of 4, 4, 3, 4.

● At the Open Amateur Tournament of the Royal Ashdown Forest in 1936 Bobby Locke in his morning round had a score of 72, accomplishing every hole in 4.

● Severiano Ballesteros in winning the 1978 Swiss Open scored four rounds of 68.

● Henry Cotton told of one of the most extraordinary scoring feats ever. With some other professionals he was at Sestrieres in the thirties for the Italian Open Championship and Joe Ezar, a colourful character in those days on both sides of the Atlantic, accepted a wager from a club official – 1,000 lira for a 66 to break the course record; 2,000 for a 65; and 4,000 for a 64. *I'll do 64,* said Ezar, and proceeded to jot down the hole-by-hole score figures he would do next day for that total. With the exception of the ninth and tenth holes where his predicted score was 3, 4 and the actual score was 4, 3, he accomplished this amazing feat exactly as nominated.

● Nick Faldo scored par figures at all 18 holes in the final round of the 1987 Open Championship at Muirfield to win the title.

● During the Colts Championship at Knowle Golf Club, Bristol, Chris Newman (Cotswold Hills) scored eight consecutive 3s with birdies at four of the holes.

High Scores

● In the qualifying competition at Formby for the 1976 Open Championship, Maurice Flitcroft, a 46-year-old crane driver from Barrow-in-Furness, took 121 strokes for the first round and then withdrew saying, *I have no chance of qualifying.* Flitcroft entered as a professional but had never before played 18 holes. He had taken the game up 18 months previously but, as he was not a member of a club, had been limited to practising on a local beach. His round was made up thus: 7, 5, 6, 6, 6, 6, 12, 6, 7-61; 11, 5, 6, 8, 4, 9, 5, 7, 5-60, total 121. After his round Flitcroft said, *I've made a lot of progress in the last few months and I'm sorry I did not do better. I was trying too hard at the beginning but began to put things together at the end of the round.* R & A officials who were not amused by the bogus professional's efforts, refunded the £30 entry money to Flitcroft's two fellow-competitors.

● Playing in the qualifying rounds of the 1965 Open Championship at Southport, an American self-styled professional entrant from Milwaukee,

Walter Danecki, achieved the inglorious feat of scoring a total of 221 strokes for 36 holes, 81 over par. His first round over the Hillside course was 108, followed by a second round of 113. Walter, who afterwards admitted he felt *a little discouraged and sad*, declared that he entered because he was *after the money*.

- The highest individual scoring ever known in the rounds connected with the Open Championship occurred at Muirfield, 1935, when a Scottish professional started 7, 10, 5, 10, and took 65 to reach the 9th hole. Another 10 came at the 11th and the player decided to retire at the 12th hole. There he was in a bunker, and after playing four shots he had not regained the fairway.
- In 1883 in the Open Championship at Musselburgh, Willie Fernie, the winner, had a 10, the only time double figures appeared on the card of the Open Champion of the year. Fernie won after a tie with Bob Ferguson, and his score for the last hole in the tie was 2. He holed from just off the green to win by one stroke.
- In the first Open Championship at Prestwick in 1860 a competitor took 21, the highest score for one hole ever recorded in this event. The record is preserved in the archives of the Prestwick Golf Club, where the championship was founded.
- In the first round of the 1980 US Masters, Tom Weiskopf hit his ball into the water hazard in front of the par-3 12th hole five times and scored 13 for the hole.
- In the French Open at St Cloud, in 1968, Brian Barnes took 15 for the short 8th hole in the second round. After missing putts at which he hurriedly snatched while the ball was moving he penalised himself further by standing astride the line of a putt. The amazing result was that he actually took 12 strokes from about three feet from the hole.
- US professional Dave Hill 6-putted the fifth green at Oakmont in the 1962 US Open Championship.
- Many high scores have been made at the Road Hole at St Andrews. Davie Ayton, on one occasion, was coming in a certain winner of the Open Championship when he got on the road and took 11. In 1921, at the Open Championship, one professional took 13. In 1923, competing for the Autumn Medal of the Royal & Ancient, JB Anderson required a five and a four to win the second award, but he took 13 at the Road Hole. Anderson was close to the green in two, was twice in the bunkers in the face of the green, and once on the road. In 1935, RH Oppenheimer tied for the Royal Medal (the first award) in the Autumn Meeting of the Royal & Ancient. On the play-off he was one stroke behind Captain Aitken when they stood on the 17th tee. Oppenheimer drove three balls out of bounds and eventually took 11 to the Road Hole.
- British professional Mark James scored 111 in the second round of the 1978 Italian Open. He played the closing holes with only his right hand due to an injury to his left hand.
- In the 1927 Shawnee Open, Tommy Armour took 23 strokes to the 17th hole. Armour had won the American Open Championship a week earlier. In an effort to play the hole in a particular way, Armour hooked ball after ball out of bounds and finished with a 21 on the card. There was some doubt about the accuracy of this figure and on reaching the clubhouse Armour stated that it should be 23. This is the highest score by a professional in a tournament.

Freak Matches

- In 1912, the late Harry Dearth, an eminent vocalist, attired in a complete suit of heavy armour, played a match at Bushey Hall. He was beaten 2 and 1.
- In 1914, at the start of the First World War, JN Farrar, a native of Hoylake, was stationed at Royston, Herts. A bet was made of 10-1 that he would not go round Royston under 100 strokes, equipped in full infantry marching order, water bottle, full field kit and haversack. Farrar went round in 94. At the camp were several golfers, including professionals, who tried the same feat but failed.
- Captain Pennington, who was killed in an air crash in 1933, took part in a match *from the air* against AJ Young, the professional at Sonning. Captain Pennington, with 80 golf balls in the locker of his machine, had to find the Sonning greens by dropping the balls as he circled over the course. The balls were covered in white cloth to ensure that they did not bounce once they struck the ground. The airman completed the course in 40 minutes, taking 29 *strokes*, while Young occupied two hours for his round of 68.
- In April 1924, at Littlehampton, Harry Rowntree, an amateur golfer, played the better ball of Edward Ray and George Duncan, receiving an allowance of 150 yards to use as he required during the round. Rowntree won by 6 and 5 and had used only 50 yards 2 feet of his handicap. At one hole Duncan had a two – Rowntree, who was 25 yards from the hole, took this distance from his handicap and won the hole in one. Ray (died 1945) afterwards declared that, conceded a handicap of one yard per round, he could win every championship in the world. And he might, when reckoning is taken of the number of times a putt just stops an inch or two or how much difference to a shot three inches will make for the lie of the ball, either in a bunker or on the fairway. Many single matches on the same system have been played. An 18 handicap player opposed to a scratch player should make a close match with an allowance of 50 yards.
- The first known instance of a golf match by telephone occurred in 1957, when the Cotswold

Hills Golf Club, Cheltenham, England, won a golf tournament against the Cheltenham Golf Club, Melbourne, Australia, by six strokes. A large crowd assembled at the English club to wait for the 12,000 miles telephone call from Australia. The match had been played at the suggestion of a former member of the Cotswold Hills Club, Harry Davies, and was open to every member of the two clubs. The result of the match was decided on the aggregate of the eight best scores on each side and the English club won by 564 strokes to 570.

Golf Matches Against Other Sports

● HH Hilton and Percy Ashworth, many times racket champion, contested a driving match, the former driving a golf ball with a driver, and the latter a racket ball with a racket. Best distances: Against breeze – Golfer 182 yards; Racket player 125 yards. Down wind – Golfer 230 yards; Racket player 140 yards. Afterwards Ashworth hit a golf ball with the racket and got a greater distance than with the racket ball, but was still a long way behind the ball driven by Hilton.

● In 1913, at Wellington, Shropshire, a match between a golfer and a fisherman casting a 2½ oz weight was played. The golfer, Rupert May, took 87; the fisherman JJD Mackinlay, in difficulty because of his short casts, 102. His longest cast, 105 yards, was within 12 yards of the world record at the time, held by French angler, Decautelle. When within a rod's length of a hole he ran the weight to the rod end and dropped into the hole. Five times he broke his line, and was allowed another shot without penalty.

● In December, 1913, FMA Webster, of the London Athletic Club, and Dora Roberts, with javelins, played a match with the late Harry Vardon and Mrs Gordon Robertson, who used the regulation clubs and golf balls. The golfers conceded two-thirds in the matter of distance, and they won by 5 up and 4 to play in a contest of 18 holes. The javelin throwers had a mark of two feet square in which to *hole out* while the golfers had to get their ball into the ordinary golf hole. Mr Webster's best throw was one of 160 feet.

● Several matches have taken place between a golfer on the one side and an archer on the other. The wielder of the bow and arrow has nearly always proved the victor. In 1953 at Kirkhill Golf Course, Lanarkshire, five archers beat six golfers by two games to one. There were two special rules for the match; when an archer's arrow landed six feet from the hole or the golfer's ball three feet from the hole, they were counted as holed. When the arrows landed in bunkers or in the rough, archers lifted their arrow and added a stroke. The sixth archer in this match called off and one archer shot two arrows from each of the 18 tees.

● In 1954, at the Southbroom Club, South Africa, a match over 9 holes was played between an archer and a fisherman against two golfers. The participants were all champions of their own sphere and consisted of Vernon Adams (archer), Dennis Burd (fisherman), Jeanette Wahl (champion of Southbroom and Port Shepstone), and Ron Burd (professional at Southbroom). The conditions were that the archer had holed out when his arrows struck a small leather bag placed on the green beside the hole and in the event of his placing his approach shot within a bow's length of the pin he was deemed to have 1-putted. The fisherman, to achieve a 1-putt, had to land his sinker within a rod's length of the pin. The two golfers were ahead for brief spells, but it was the opposition who led at the deciding 9th hole where *Robin Hood* played a perfect approach for a birdie.

● An *Across England* combined match was begun on 11th October, 1965, by four golfers and two archers from Crowborough Beacon Golf Club, Sussex, accompanied by *Penny*, a white Alsatian dog, whose duty it was to find lost balls. They teed *off* from Carlisle Castle via Hadrian's Wall, the Pennine Way, finally holing out in the 18th hole at Newcastle United Golf Club in 612 teed shots. Casualties included 110 lost golf balls and 19 lost or broken arrows. The match took five-and-a-half days, and the distance travelled was about 60 miles. The golfers were Miss P Ward, K Meaney, K Ashdown and CA Macey; the archers were WH Hulme and T Scott. The first arrow was fired from the battlements of Carlisle Castle, a distance of nearly 300 yards, by Cumberland Champion R Willis, who also fired the second arrow right across the River Eden. R Clough, president of Newcastle United GC, holed the last two putts. The match was in aid of *Guide Dogs for the Blind* and *Friends of Crowborough Hospital.*

Cross-country Matches

● Taking 1 year, 114 days, Floyd Rood golfed his way from coast to coast across the United States. He took 114,737 shots including 3,511 penalty shots for the 3,397 mile *course.*

● Two Californian teenagers, Bob Aube (17) and Phil Marrone (18) went on a golfing safari in 1974 from San Francisco to Los Angeles, a trip of over 500 miles lasting 16 days. The first six days they played alongside motorways. Over 1,000 balls were used.

● In 1830, the Gold Medal winner of the Royal & Ancient backed himself for 10 sovereigns to drive from the 1st hole at St Andrews to the toll bar at Cupar, distance nine miles, in 200 teed shots. He won easily.

● In 1848, two Edinburgh golfers played a match from Bruntsfield Links to the top of Arthur's Seat – an eminence overlooking the Scottish capital, 822 feet above sea level.

● On a winter's day in 1898, Freddie Tait backed himself to play a gutta ball in 40 teed shots from Royal St George's Clubhouse, Sandwich, to the Cinque Ports Club, Deal. He was to hole out by hitting any part of the Deal Clubhouse. The distance as the crow flies was three miles. The redoubtable Tait holed out with his 32nd shot, so effectively that the ball went through a window.

● In 1900 three members of the Hackensack (NJ) Club played a game of four-and-a-half hours over an extemporised course six miles long, which stretched from Hackensack to Paterson. Despite rain, cornfields, and wide streams, the three golfers – JW Hauleebeek, Dr ER Pfaare, and Eugene Crassons – completed the round, the first and the last named taking 305 strokes each, and Dr Pfaare 327 strokes. The players used only two clubs, the mashie and the cleek.

● On 3rd December, 1920, P Rupert Phillips and W Raymond Thomas teed up on the first tee of the Radyr Golf Club and played to the last hole at Southerndown. The distance as the crow flies was 15½ miles, but circumventing swamps, woods, and plough, they covered, approximately, 20 miles. The wager was that they would not do the *hole* in 1,000 strokes, but they holed out at their 608th stroke two days later. They carried large ordnance maps.

● On 12th March, 1921, A Stanley Turner, Macclesfield, played from his house to the Cat and Fiddle Inn, five miles distance, in 64 strokes. The route was broken and hilly with a rise of nearly 1,000 feet. Turner was allowed to tee up within two club lengths after each shot and the wagering was 6-4 against his doing the distance in 170 strokes.

● In 1919, a golfer drove a ball from Piccadilly Circus and, proceeding via the Strand, Fleet Street and Ludgate Hill, *holed out* at the Royal Exchange, London. The player drove off at 8 am on a Sunday, a time when the usually thronged thoroughfares were deserted.

● On 23rd April, 1939, Richard Sutton, a London stockbroker, played from Tower Bridge, London, to White's Club, St James's Street, in 142 strokes. The bet was he would not do *the course* in under 200 shots. Sutton used a putter, crossed the Thames at Southwark Bridge, and hit the ball short distances to keep out of trouble.

● Golfers produced the most original event in Ireland's three-week national festival of An Tostal, in 1953 – a cross-country competition with an advertised £1,000,000 for the man who could hole out in one. The 150 golfers drove off from the first tee at Kildare Club to hole out eventually on the 18th green, five miles away, on the nearby Curragh course, a distance of 8,800 yards. The unusual hazards to be negotiated included the main Dublin-Cork railway line and highway, the Curragh Racecourse, hoofprints left by Irish thoroughbred racehorses out exercising on the plains from nearby stables, army tank tracks and about 150 telephone lines. The Golden Ball Trophy, which is played for annually – a standard size golf ball in gold, mounted on a black marble pillar beside the silver figure of a golfer on a green marble base, designed by Captain Maurice Cogan, Army GHQ, Dublin — was for the best gross. And it went to one of the longest hitters in international golf – Amateur Champion, Irish internationalist and British Walker Cup player Joe Carr, with the remarkable score of 52.

● In 1961, as a University Charities Week stunt, four Aberdeen University students set out to golf their way up Ben Nevis (4,406 feet). About halfway up, after losing 63 balls and expending 659 strokes, the quartet conceded victory to Britain's highest mountain.

● Among several cross-country golfing exploits, one of the most arduous was faced by Iain Williamson and Tony Kent, who teed off from Cained Point on the summit of Fairfield in the Lake District. With the hole cut in the lawn of the Bishop of Carlisle's home at Rydal Park, it measured 7,200 yards and passed through the summits of Great Rigg Mann, Heron Pike and Nab Scar, descending altogether 1,900 feet. Eight balls were lost and the two golfers holed out in a combined total of 303 strokes.

Long-lived Golfers

● James Priddy, aged 80, played in the Seniors' Open at his home club, Weston-super-Mare, Avon, on 27th June, 1990, and scored a gross 70 to beat his age by 10 shots.

● The oldest golfer who ever lived is believed to have been Arthur Thompson of British Columbia, Canada. He equalled his age when 103 at Uplands GC, a course of over 6,000 yards. He died two years later.

● Nathaniel Vickers celebrated his 103rd birthday on Sunday, 9th October, 1949, and died the following day. He was the oldest member of the United States Senior Golf Association and until 1942 he competed regularly in their events and won many trophies in the various age divisions. When 100 years old, he apologised for being able to play only 9 holes a day. Vickers predicted he would live until 103 and he died a few hours after he had celebrated his birthday.

● American George Miller, who died in 1979 aged 102, played regularly when 100 years old.

● In his 93rd year, the Rev Harcourt Just had a daily round of six to 10 holes at St Andrews. In 1950, the Town Council gave him the *Courtesy of the Course*, which excused the venerable minister paying the yearly charge.

● George Swanwick, a member of Wallasey, celebrated his 90th birthday with a luncheon at the club on 1st April, 1971. He played golf several times a week, carrying his own clubs and had holed-in-one at the ages of 75 and 85. His ambition was to complete the sequence aged 95 . . . but he died in 1973 aged 92.

● The 10th Earl of Wemyss played a round on his 92nd birthday, in 1910, at Craigielaw. At the age of 87 the Earl was partnered by Harry Vardon in a match at Kilspindie, the golf course on his East Lothian estate at Gosford. After playing his ball the venerable earl mounted a pony and rode to the next shot. He died on 30th June, 1914.

● FL Callender, aged 78, in September 1932, played nine consecutive rounds in the Jubilee Vase, St Andrews. He was defeated in the ninth, the final round, by 4 and 2. Callender's handicap was 12. This is the best known achievement of a septuagenarian in golf.

● Mr Bernard Matthews, aged 82, of Banstead Downs Club, handicap 6, holed the course in 72 gross in August 1988. A week later he holed it in 70, twelve shots below his age. He came back in 31, finishing 4, 3, 3, 2, 3, against a par of 5, 4, 3, 3, 4. Mr Matthews's eclectic score at his Club is 37, or one over 2's.

Playing in the Dark

On numerous occasions it has been necessary to hold lamps, lighted candles, or torches at holes in order that players might finish a competition. Large entries, slow play, early darkness and an eclipse of the sun have all been causes of playing in darkness.

● Since 1972, the Whitburn Golf Club at South Shields, Tyne and Wear, has held an annual Summer Solstice Competition. All competitors, who draw lots for starting tees, must begin before 4.24 and 13 seconds am, the time the sun rises over the first hole on the longest day of the year.

● At the Open Championship in Musselburgh in November 1889 many players finished when the light had so far gone that the adjacent street lamps were lit. The cards were checked by candlelight. Several players who had no chance of the championship were paid small sums to withdraw in order to permit others who had a chance to finish in daylight. This was the last championship at Musselburgh.

● At the Southern Section of the PGA tournament on 25th September, 1907, at Burnham Beeches, several players concluded the round by the aid of torch lights placed near the holes.

● In the Irish Open Championship at Portmarnock in September, 1907, a tie in the third round between WC Pickeman and A Jeffcott was postponed owing to darkness, at the 22nd hole. The next morning Pickeman won at the 24th.

● The qualifying round of the American Amateur Championship in 1910 could not be finished in one day, and several competitors had to stop their round on account of darkness, and complete it early in the morning of the following day.

● On 10th January, 1926, in the final of the President's Putter, at Rye, EF Storey and RH Wethered were all square at the 24th hole. It was 5 pm and so dark that, although a fair crowd was present, the balls could not be followed. The tie was abandoned and the Putter held jointly for the year. Each winner of the Putter affixes the ball he played; for 1926 there are two balls, respectively engraved with the names of the finalists.

● In the 1932 Walker Cup contest at Brooklyn, a total eclipse of the sun occurred.

● At Perth, on 14th September, 1932, a competition was in progress under good clear evening light, and a full bright moon. The moon rose at 7.10 and an hour later came under eclipse to the earth's surface. The light then became so bad that on the last three greens competitors holed out by the aid of the light from matches.

● At Carnoustie, 1932, in the competition for the *Craw's Nest* the large entry necessitated competitors being sent off in 3-ball matches. The late players had to be assisted by electric torches flashed on the greens.

● In February, 1950, Max Faulkner and his partner, R Dolman, in a Guildford Alliance event finished their round in complete darkness. A photographer's flash bulbs were used at the last hole to direct Faulkner's approach. Several of the other competitors also finished in darkness. At the last hole they had only the light from the clubhouse to aim at and one played his approach so boldly that he put his ball through the hall doorway and almost into the dressing room.

● On the second day of the 1969 Ryder Cup contest, the last 4-ball match ended in near total darkness on the 18th green at Royal Birkdale. With the help of the clubhouse lights the two American players, Lee Trevino and Miller Barber, and Tony Jacklin for Britain each faced putts of around five feet to win their match. All missed and their game was halved.

The occasions mentioned above all occurred in competitions where it was not intended to play in the dark. There are, however, numerous instances where players set out to play in the dark either for bets or for novelty.

● On 29th November, 1878, RW Brown backed himself to go round the Hoylake links in 150 strokes, starting at 11 pm. The conditions of the match were that Mr Brown was only to be penalised *loss of distance* for a lost ball, and that no one was to help him to find it. He went round in 147 strokes, and won his bet by the narrow margin of three strokes.

● In 1876 David Strath backed himself to go round St Andrews under 100, in moonlight. He took 95, and did not lose a ball.

● In September 1928, at St Andrews, the first and last holes were illuminated by lanterns, and at 11 pm four members of the Royal and Ancient set out to play a foursome over the 2 holes. Electric lights, lanterns, and rockets were used to brighten the fairway, and the headlights of motor cars parked on Links Place formed a helpful battery. The 1st hole was won in four, and each side got a five at the 18th. About 1,000 spectators followed the freak match, which was played to celebrate the appointment of Angus Hambro to the captaincy of the club.

● In 1931, Rufus Stewart, professional, Kooyonga Club, South Australia, and former Australian Open Champion, played 18 holes of exhibition golf at night without losing a single ball over the Kooyonga course, and completed the round in 77.

● At Ashley Wood Golf Club, Blandford, Dorset, a night-time golf tournament was arranged annually with up to 180 golfers taking part over four nights. Over £6000 has been raised in four years for the Muscular Dystrophy Charity.

● At Pannal, 3rd July, 1937, RH Locke, playing in bright moonlight, holed his tee shot at the 15th hole, distance 220 yards, the only known case of holing-in-one under such conditions.

Fatal and Other Accidents on the Links

The history of golf is, unfortunately, marred by a great number of fatal accidents on or near the course. In the vast majority of such cases they have been caused either by careless swinging of the club or by an uncontrolled shot when the ball has struck a spectator or bystander. In addition to the fatal accidents there is an even larger number on record which have resulted in serious injury or blindness. We do not propose to list these accidents except where they have some unusual feature. We would remind all golfers of the tragic consequences which have so often been caused by momentary carelessness. The fatal accidents which follow have an unusual cause and other accidents given may have their humorous aspect.

● English tournament professional Richard Boxall was three shots off the lead in the third round of the 1991 Open Championship when he fractured his left leg driving from the 9th tee at Royal Birkdale. He was taken from the course to hospital by ambulance and was listed in the official results as 'retired' which entitled him to a consolation prize of £3000.

A month later, Russell Weir of Scotland, was competing in the European Teaching Professionals' Championship near Rotterdam when he also fractured his left leg driving from the 7th tee in the first round.

● In July, 1971, Rudolph Roy, aged 43, was killed at a Montreal course; in playing out of woods, the shaft of his club snapped, rebounded off a tree and the jagged edge plunged into his body.

● Harold Wallace, aged 75, playing at Lundin Links with two friends in 1950, was crossing the railway line which separates the fifth green and sixth tee, when a light engine knocked him down and he was killed instantly.

● In the summer of 1963, Harold Kalles, of Toronto, Canada, died six days after his throat had been cut by a golf club shaft, which broke against a tree as he was trying to play out of a bunker.

● At Jacksonville, Florida, on 18th March, 1952, two women golfers were instantly killed when hit simultaneously by the whirling propeller of a navy fighter plane. They were playing together when the plane with a dead engine coming in out of control, hit them from behind.

● In May, 1993, at Ponoka Community GC, Alberta, Canada, Richard McCulough hit a poor tee shot on the 13th hole and promptly smashed his driver angrily against a golf cart. The head of the driver and six inches of shaft flew through the air, piercing McCulough's throat and severing his carotoid artery. He died in hospital.

● Britain's first national open event for competitors aged over 80, at Moortown, Leeds in September, 1992, was marred when 81-year-old Frank Hart collapsed on the fourth tee and died. Play continued and Charles Mitchell, aged 80, won the Stableford competition with a gross score of 81 for 39 points.

● Playing in the 1993 Carlesburg-Tetley Cornish Festival at Tehidy Park, Ian Cornwell was struck on the leg by a wayward shot from a player two groups behind. Later, as he was leaving the 16th green, he was hit again, this time below the ear, by the same player, knocking him unconscious. This may be the first time that a player has been hit twice in the same round by the same player.

Lightning on the Links

There have been a considerable number of fatal and serious accidents through players and caddies having been struck by lightning on the course. The Royal & Ancient and the USGA have, since 1952, provided for discontinuance of play during lightning storms under the Rules of Golf (Rule 37, 6) and the United States Golf Association have given the following guide for personal safety during thunderstorms:

(a) Do not go out of doors or remain out during thunderstorms unless it is necessary. Stay inside of a building where it is dry, preferably away from fireplaces, stoves, and other metal objects.

(b) If there is any choice of shelter, choose in the following order:
   1. Large metal or metal-frame buildings.
   2. Dwellings or other buildings which are protected against lightning.
   3. Large unprotected buildings.
   4. Small unprotected buildings.

(c) If remaining out of doors is unavoidable, keep away from:
   1. Small sheds and shelters if in an exposed location.
   2. Isolated trees.

3. Wire fences.
4. Hilltops and wide open spaces.

(d) Seek shelter in:
1. A cave.
2. A depression in the ground.
3. A deep valley or canyon.
4. The foot of a steep or overhanging cliff.
5. Dense woods.
6. A grove of trees.

Note – Raising golf clubs or umbrellas above the head is dangerous.

● A serious incident with lightning involving well-known golfers was at the 1975 Western Open in Chicago when Lee Trevino, Jerry Heard and Bobby Nichols were all struck and had to be taken to hospital. At the same time Tony Jacklin had a club thrown 15 feet out of his hands.

● Two well-known competitors were struck by lightning in European events in 1977. They were Mark James of Britain in the Swiss Open and Severiano Ballesteros of Spain in the Scandinavian Open. Fortunately neither appeared to be badly injured.

● Two spectators were killed by lightning at the US Open and US PGA Championships in 1991.

Spectators Interfering with Balls

● Deliberate interference by spectators with balls in play during important money matches was not unknown in the old days when there was intense rivalry between the *schools* of Musselburgh, St Andrews, and North Berwick, and disputes arose in stake matches caused by the action of spectators in kicking the ball into either a favourable or an unfavourable position.

● Tom Morris, in his last match with Willie Park at Musselburgh, refused to go on because of interference by the spectators, and in the match on the same course about 40 years later, in 1895, between Willie Park junior and JH Taylor, the barracking of the crowd and interference with play was so bad that when the Park-Vardon match came to be arranged in 1899, Vardon refused to accept Musselburgh as a venue.

● Even in modern times spectators have been known to interfere deliberately with players' balls, though it is usually by children. In the 1972 Penfold Tournament at Queen's Park, Bournemouth, Christy O'Connor jun had his ball stolen by a young boy, but not being told of this at the time had to take the penalty for a lost ball. O'Connor finished in a tie for first place, but lost the play-off.

● In 1912 in the last round of the final of the Amateur Championship at Westward Ho! between Abe Mitchell and John Ball, the drive of the former to the short 14th hit an open umbrella held by a lady protecting herself from the heavy rain, and instead of landing on the green the ball was diverted into a bunker. Mitchell, who was leading at the time by 2 holes, lost the hole and Ball won the Championship at the 38th hole.

● In the match between the professionals of Great Britain and America at Southport in 1937 a dense crowd collected round the 15th green waiting for the Sarazen-Alliss match. The American's ball landed in the lap of a woman, who picked it up and threw it so close to the hole that Sarazen got a two against Alliss' three.

● In a memorable tie between Bobby Jones and Cyril Tolley in the 1930 Amateur Championship at St Andrews, Jones' approach to the 17th green struck spectators massed at the left end of the green and led to controversy as to whether it would otherwise have gone on to the famous road. Jones himself had deliberately played for that part of the green and had requested stewards to get the crowd back. Had the ball gone on to the road, the historic Jones Quadrilateral of the year – the Open and Amateur Championships of Britain and the United States – might not have gone into the records.

● In the 1983 Suntory World Match Play Championship at Wentworth Nick Faldo hit his second shot over the green at the 16th hole into a group of spectators. To everyone's astonishment and discomfiture the ball reappeared on the green about 30 ft from the hole, propelled there by a thoroughly misguided and anonymous spectator. The referee ruled that Faldo play the ball where it lay on the green. Faldo's opponent, Graham Marsh, understandably upset by the incident, took three putts against Faldo's two, thus losing a hole he might well otherwise have won. Faldo won the match 2 and 1, but lost in the final to Marsh's fellow Australian Greg Norman by 3 and 2.

Golf Balls Killing Animals and Fish, and Incidents with Animals

● An astounding fatality to an animal through being hit by a golf ball occurred at St Margaret's-at-Cliffe Golf Club, Kent on 13th June, 1934, when WJ Robinson, the professional, killed a cow with his tee shot to the 18th hole. The cow was standing in the fairway about 100 yards from the tee, and the ball struck her on the back of the head. She fell like a log, but staggered to her feet and walked about 50 yards before dropping again. When the players reached her she was dead.

● JW Perret, of Ystrad Mynach, playing with Chas R Halliday, of Ralston, in the qualifying rounds of the Society of One Armed Golfers' Championship over the Darley course, Troon, on 27th August, 1935, killed two gulls at successive holes with his second shots. The *deadly* shots were at the 1st and 2nd holes.

● On the first day of grouse shooting of the 1975 season (12th August), 11-year-old schoolboy, Willie Fraser, of Kingussie, beat all the guns when he killed a grouse with his tee shot on the local course.

● On 10th June, 1904, while playing in the Edinburgh High Constables' Competition at Kilspindie, Captain Ferguson sent a long ball into the rough at the Target hole, and on searching for it found that it had struck and killed a young hare.
● Playing in a mixed open tournament at the Waimairi Beach Golf Club in Christchurch, New Zealand, in the summer of 1961, Mrs RT Challis found her ball in fairly long spongy grass where a placing rule applied. She picked up, placed the ball and played her stroke. A young hare leaped into the air and fell dead at her feet. She had placed the ball on the leveret without seeing it and without disturbing it.
● In 1906 in the Border Championship at Hawick, a gull and a weasel were killed by balls during the afternoon's play.
● A golfer at Newark, in May, 1907, drove his ball into the river. The ball struck a trout 2lb in weight and killed it.
● On 24th April, 1975, at Scunthorpe GC, Jim Tollan's drive at the 14th hole, called *The Mallard*, struck and killed a female mallard duck in flight. The duck was stuffed and is displayed in the Scunthorpe Clubhouse.
● A Samuel, Melbourne Club, at Sandringham, was driving with an iron club from the 17th tee, when a kitten, which had been playing in the long grass, sprang suddenly at the ball. Kitten and club arrived at the objective simultaneously, with the result that the kitten took an unexpected flight through the air, landing some 20 yards away.
● As Susan Rowlands was lining up a vital putt in the closing stages of the final of the 1978 Welsh Girls' Championship at Abergele, a tiny mouse scampered up her trouser leg. After holing the putt, the mouse ran down again. Susan, who won the final admitted that she fortunately had not known it was there.

Interference by Birds and Animals

● Crows, ravens, hawks and seagulls frequently carry off golf balls, sometimes dropping the ball actually on the green, and it is a common incident for a cow to swallow a golf ball. A plague of crows on the Liverpool course at Hoylake are addicted to golf balls – they stole 26 in one day – selecting only new balls. It was suggested that members should carry shotguns as a 15th club!
● A match was approaching a hole in a rather low-lying course, when one of the players made a crisp chip from about 30 yards from the hole. The ball trickled slowly across the green and eventually disappeared into the hole. After a momentary pause, the ball was suddenly ejected on to the green, and out jumped a large frog.
● A large black crow named Jasper which frequented the Lithgow GC in New South Wales, Australia, stole 30 golf balls in the club's 1972 Easter Tournament.
● As Mrs Molly Whitaker was playing from a bunker at Beachwood course, Natal, South Africa, a large monkey leaped from a bush and clutched her round the neck. A caddie drove it off by clipping it with an iron club.
● In Massachusetts a goose, having been hit rather hard by a golf ball which then came to rest by the side of a water hazard, took revenge by waddling over to the ball and kicking it into the water.
● In the summer of 1963, SC King had a good drive to the 10th hole at the Guernsey Club. His partner, RW Clark, was in the rough, and King helped him to search. Returning to his ball, he found a cow eating it. Next day, at the same hole, the positions were reversed, and King was in the rough. Clark placed his woollen hat over his ball, remarking, *I'll make sure the cow doesn't eat mine.* On his return he found the cow thoroughly enjoying his hat; nothing was left but the pom-pom.

Armless, One-armed, Legless and Ambidextrous Players

● In September, 1933, at Burgess Golfing Society of Edinburgh, the first championship for one-armed golfers was held. There were 43 entries and 37 of the competitors had lost an arm in the 1914-18 war. Play was over two rounds and the championship was won by WE Thomson, Eastwood, Glasgow, with a score of 169 (82 and 87) for two rounds. The Burgess course was 6,300 yards long. Thomson drove the last green, 260 yards. The championship and an international match are played annually.
● In the Boys' Amateur Championship 1923, at Dunbar and 1949 at St Andrews, there were competitors each with one arm. The competitor in 1949, RP Reid, Cupar, Fife, who lost his arm working a machine in a butcher's shop, got through to the third round.
● There have been cases of persons with no arms playing golf. One, Thomas McAuliffe, who held the club between his right shoulder and cheek, once went round Buffalo CC, USA, in 108.
● Group Captain Bader, who lost both legs in a flying accident prior to the World War 1939-45, took part in golf competitions and reached a single-figure handicap in spite of his disability.
● In 1909, Scott of Silloth, and John Haskins of Hoylake, both one-armed golfers, played a home and away match for £20 a side. Scott finished five up at Silloth. He was seven up and 14 to play at Hoylake but Haskins played so well that Scott eventually only won by 3 and 1. This was the first match between one-armed golfers. Haskins in 1919 was challenged by Mr Mycock, of Buxton, another one-armed player. The match was 36 holes, home and away. The first half was played over the Buxton and High Peak Links, and the

latter half over the Liverpool Links, and resulted in a win for Haskins by 11 and 10. Later in the same year Haskins received another challenge to play against Alexander Smart of Aberdeen. The match was 18 holes over the Balgownie Course, and ended in favour of Haskins.

● In a match, November, 1926, between the Geduld and Sub Nigel Clubs – two golf clubs connected with the South African gold mines of the same names – each club had two players minus an arm. The natural consequence was that the quartet were matched. The players were – AWP Charteris and E Mitchell, Sub Nigel; and EP Coles and J Kirby, Geduld. This is the first record of four one-armed players in a foursome.

● At Joliet Country Club, USA, a one-armed golfer named DR Anderson drove a ball 300 yards.

● Left-handedness, but playing golf right-handed, is prevalent and for a man to throw with his left hand and play golf right-handed is considered an advantage, for Bobby Jones, Jesse Sweetser, Walter Hagen, Jim Barnes, Joe Kirkwood and more recently Johnny Miller were eminent golfers who were left-handed and ambidextrous.

● In a practice round for the Open Championship in July, 1927, at St Andrews, Len Nettlefold and Joe Kirkwood changed sets of clubs at the 9th hole. Nettlefold was a left-handed golfer and Kirkwood right-handed. They played the last nine, Kirkwood with the left-handed clubs and Nettlefold with the right-handed clubs.

● The late Harry Vardon, when he was at Ganton, got tired of giving impossible odds to his members and beating them, so he collected a set of left-handed clubs, and rating himself at scratch, conceded the handicap odds to them. He won with the same monotonous regularity.

● Ernest Jones, who was professional at the Chislehurst Club, was badly wounded in the war in France in 1916 and his right leg had to be amputated below the knee. He persevered with the game, and before the end of the year he went round the Clacton course balanced on his one leg in 72. Jones later settled in the United States where he built fame and fortune as a golf teacher.

● Major Alexander McDonald Fraser of Edinburgh had the distinction of holding two handicaps simultaneously in the same club – one when he played left-handed and the other for his right-handed play. In medal competitions he had to state before teeing up which method he would use.

● Former England test cricketer Brian Close once held a handicap of 2 playing right-handed, but after retiring from cricket in 1977 decided to apply himself as a left-handed player. His left-handed handicap at the time of his retirement was 7. Close had the distinction of once beating Ted Dexter, another distinguished test cricketer and noted golfer twice in the one day, playing right-handed in the morning and left-handed in the afternoon.

Blind and Blindfolded Golf

● Major Towse, VC, whose eyes were shot out during the South African War, 1899, was probably the first blind man to play golf. His only stipulations when playing the game were that he should be allowed to touch the ball with his hands to ascertain its position, and that his caddie could ring a small bell to indicate the position of the hole. Major Towse, who played with considerable skill, was also an expert oarsman and bridge player. He died in 1945, aged 81.

● The United States Blind Golfers' Association in 1946 promoted an Invitational Golf Tournament for the blind at Country Club, Inglewood, California. This competition is held annually and in 1953 there were 24 competitors and 11 players completed the two rounds of 36 holes. The winner was Charley Boswell who lost his eyesight leading a tank unit in Germany in 1944.

● In July, 1954, at Lambton Golf and Country Club, Toronto, the first international championship for the blind was held. It resulted in a win for Joe Lazaro, of Waltham, Mass, with a score of 220 for the two rounds. He drove the 215-yard 16th hole and just missed an ace, his ball stopping 18 inches from the hole. Charley Boswell, who won the United States Blind Golfers' Association Tournament in 1953, was second. The same Charles Boswell, of Birmingham, Alabama holed the 141-yard 14th hole at the Vestavia CC in one in October, 1970.

● Another blind person to have holed-in-one was American Ben Thomas while on holiday in South Carolina in 1978.

● Rick Sorenson undertook a bet in which, playing 18 holes blindfolded at Meadowbrook Course, Minneapolis, on 25th May, 1973, he was to pay $10 for every hole over par and receive $100 for every hole in par or better. He went round in 86 losing $70 on the deal.

● Alfred Toogood played blindfolded in a match against Tindal Atkinson at Sunningdale in 1912. Toogood was beaten 8 and 7. Previously, in 1908, I Millar, Newcastle-upon-Tyne, played a match blindfolded against AT Broughton, Birkdale, at Newcastle, County Down. Blindfold putting matches have been frequently played.

● Wing-Commander *Laddie* Lucas, DSO, DFC, MP, played over Sandy Lodge golf course in Hertfordshire on 7th August, 1954, completely blindfolded and had a score of 87.

Trick Shots

● Joe Kirkwood, Australia, specialised in public exhibitions of trick and fancy shots. He played all kinds of strokes after nominating them, and among his ordinary strokes nothing was more impressive than those hit for low flight. He played a full drive from the face of a wristlet watch, and the toe of a spectator's shoe, full strokes at a suspended ball, and played for slice and pull at will, and exhibited his ambidexterity by playing left-handed strokes with right-handed clubs. Holing six balls, stymieing, a full shot at a ball catching it as it descended, and hitting 12 full shots in rapid succession, with his face turned away from the ball, were shots among his repertoire. In playing the last named Kirkwood placed the balls in a row, about six inches apart, and moved quickly along the line. Kirkwood, who was born in Australia lived for many years in America. He died in November, 1970 aged 73.

● On 2nd April, 1894, a 3-ball match was played over Musselburgh course between Messrs Grant, Bowden, and Waggot, the clubmaker, the latter teeing on the face of a watch at each tee. He finished the round in 41 the watch being undamaged in any way.

● In a match at Esher on 23rd November, 1931, George Ashdown, the professional, played his tee shot for each of the 18 holes from a rubber tee strapped to the forehead of Miss Ena Shaw.

● EA Forrest, a South African professional in a music hall turn of trick golf shots, played blindfolded shots, one being from the ball teed on the chin of his recumbent partner.

● The late Paul Hahn, an American trick specialist could hit four balls with two clubs Holding a club in each hand he hit two balls, hooking one and slicing the other with the same swing. Hahn had a repertoire of 30 trick shots. In 1955 he flew round the world, exhibiting in 14 countries and on all five continents.

Balls Colliding and Touching

● Competing in the 1980 Corfu International Championship, Sharon Peachey drove from one tee and her ball collided in mid-air with one from a competitor playing another hole. Her ball ended in a pond.

● Playing in the Cornish team championship in 1973 at West Cornwall GC Tom Scott-Brown, of West Cornwall GC, and Paddy Bradley, of Tehidy GC, saw their drives from the fourth and eighth tees collide in mid-air.

● Playing in a 4-ball match at Guernsey Club in June, 1966, all four players were near the 13th green from the tee. Two of them – DG Hare and S Machin – chipped up simultaneously; the balls collided in mid-air; Machin's ball hit the green, then the flagstick, and dropped into the hole for a birdie 2.

● In May, 1926, during the meeting of the Army Golfing Society at St Andrews, Colonel Howard and Lieutenant-Colonel Buchanan Dunlop, while playing in the foursomes against J Rodger and J Mackie, hit full iron shots for the seconds to the 16th green. Each thought he had to play his ball first, and hidden by a bunker the players struck their balls simultaneously. The balls, going towards the hole about 20 yards from the pin and five feet in the air, met with great force and dropped either side of the hole five yards apart.

● In 1972, before a luncheon celebrating the centenary year of the Ladies' Section of Royal Wimbledon GC, a 12-hole competition was held during which two competitors, Mrs L Champion and Mrs A McKendrick, driving from the eighth and ninth tees respectively, saw their balls collide in mid-air.

● In 1928, at Wentworth Falls, Australia, Dr Alcorn and EA Avery, of the Leura Club, were playing with the professional, E Barnes. The tee shots of Avery and Barnes at the 9th hole finished on opposite sides of the fairway. Unknown to each other, both players hit their seconds (chip shots) at the same time. Dr Alcorn, standing at the pin, suddenly saw two balls approaching the hole from different angles. They met in the air and then dropped into the hole.

● At Rugby, 1931, playing in a 4-ball match, H Fraser pulled his drive from the 10th tee in the direction of the ninth tee. Simultaneously a club member, driving from the ninth tee, pulled his drive. The tees were about 350 yards apart. The two balls collided in mid-air.

● Two golf balls, being played in opposite directions, collided in flight over Longniddry Golf Course on 27th June, 1953. Immediately after Stewart Elder, of Longniddry, had driven from the third tee, another ball, which had been pulled off line from the second fairway, which runs alongside the third, struck his ball about 20 feet above the ground. SJ Fleming, of Tranent, who was playing with Elder, heard a loud crack and thought Elder's ball had exploded. The balls were found undamaged about 70 yards apart.

Three and Two Balls Dislodged by One Shot

● In 1934 on the short 3rd hole (now the 13th) of Olton Course, Warwickshire, JR Horden, a scratch golfer of the club, sent his tee shot into long wet grass a few feet over the back of the green. When he played an *explosion* shot three balls dropped on to the putting green, his own and two others.

● AM Chevalier, playing at Hale, Cheshire, March, 1935, drove his ball into a grass bunker, and when he reached it there was only part of it showing. He played the shot with a niblick and to his amazement not one but three balls shot into the air. They all dropped back into the bunker and came to rest within a foot of each other. Then came another surprise. One of the *finds* was of the same manufacture and bore the same number as the ball he was playing with.

● Playing to the 9th hole, at Osborne House Club, Isle of Wight, George A Sherman lost his ball which had sunk out of sight on the sodden fairway. A few weeks later, playing from the same tee, his ball again was plugged, only the top showing. Under a local rule he lifted his ball to place it, and exactly under it lay the ball he had lost previously.

Balls in Strange Places

● Playing at the John O' Gaunt Club, Sutton, near Biggleswade (Beds), a member drove a ball which did not touch the ground until it reached London – over 40 miles away. The ball landed in a vegetable lorry which was passing the golf course and later fell out of a package of cabbages when they were unloaded at Covent Garden, London.

● In the English Open Amateur Stroke Play at Moortown in 1974, Nigel Denham, a Yorkshire County player, in the first round saw his overhit second shot to the 18th green bounce up some steps into the clubhouse. His ball went through an open door, ricocheted off a wall and came to rest in the men's bar, 20 feet from the windows. As the clubhouse was not out of bounds Denham decided to play the shot back to the green and opened a window 4 feet by 2 feet through which he pitched his ball to 12 feet from the flag. (Several weeks later the R&A declared that Denham should have been penalised two shots for opening the window. The clubhouse was an immovable obstruction and no part of it should have been moved.)

● In the Open Championship at Sandwich, 1949, Harry Bradshaw, Kilcroney, Dublin, at the 5th hole in his second round, drove into the rough and found his ball inside a beer bottle with the neck and shoulder broken off and four sharp points sticking up. Bradshaw, if he had treated the ball as in an unplayable lie might have been involved in a disqualification, so he decided to play it where it lay. With his blaster he smashed the bottle and sent the ball about 30 yards. The hole, a par 4, cost him 6.

● Kevin Sharman of Woodbridge GC hit a low, very straight drive at the club's 8th hole in 1979. After some minutes' searching, his ball was found embedded in a plastic sphere on top of the direction post.

● On the Dublin Course, 16th July, 1936, in the Irish Open Championship, AD Locke, the South African, played his tee shot at the 100-yard 12th hole, but the ball could not be found on arrival on the green. The marker removed the pin and it was discovered that the ball had been entangled in the flag. It dropped near the edge of the hole and Locke holed the short putt for a *birdie* two.

● While playing a round on the Geelong Golf Club Course, Australia, Easter, 1923, Captain Charteris topped his tee shot to the short 2nd hole, which lies over a creek with deep and steep clay banks. His ball came to rest on the near slope of the creek bank. He elected to play the ball as it lay, and took his niblick. After the shot, the ball was nowhere to be seen. It was found later embedded in a mass of gluey clay stuck fast to the face of the niblick. It could not be shaken off. Charteris did what was afterwards approved by the R&A, cleaned the ball and dropped it behind without penalty.

● In October, 1929, at Blackmoor Golf Club, Bordon, Hants, a player driving from the first tee holed out his ball in the chimney of a house some 120 yards distant and some 40 yards out of bounds on the right. The owner and his wife were sitting in front of the fire when they heard a rattle in the chimney and were astonished to see a golf ball drop into the fire.

● A similar incident occurred in an inter-club match between Musselburgh and Lothianburn at Prestongrange in 1938 when a member of the former team hooked his ball at the 2nd hole and gave it up for lost. To his amazement a woman emerged from one of the houses adjacent to this part of the course and handed back the ball which she said had come down the chimney and landed on a pot which was on the fire.

● In July, 1955, J Lowrie, starter at the Eden Course, St Andrews, witnessed a freak shot. A visitor drove from the first tee just as a north-bound train was passing. He sliced the shot and the ball disappeared through an open window of a passenger compartment. Almost immediately the ball emerged again, having been thrown back on to the fairway by a man in the compartment, who waved a greeting which presumably indicated that no one was hurt.

● At Coombe Wood Golf Club a player hit a ball towards the 16th green where it landed in the vertical exhaust of a tractor which was mowing the fairway. The greenkeeper was somewhat surprised to find a temporary loss of power in the tractor. When sufficient compression had built up in the exhaust system, the ball was forced out with tremendous velocity, hit the roof of a house nearby, bounced off and landed some three feet from the pin on the green.

● When carrying out an inspection of the air conditioning system at St John's Hospital, Chelmsford, in 1993, a golf ball was found in the ventilator immediately above the operating theatre. It was probably the result of a hooked drive from the first tee at Chelmsford Golf Club, which is close by, but the ball can only have entered the duct on a rebound through a three-inch gap under a ventilator hood and then descended through a series of sharp bends to its final resting place.

● There have been many occasions when misdirected shots have finished in strange places after an unusual line of flight and bounce. At Ashford, Middlesex, John Miller, aged 69, hit his tee shot out of bounds at the 12th hole (237 yards). It struck a parked car, passed through a copse, hit more cars, jumped a canopy, flew through the clubhouse kitchen window, finishing in a cooking stock-pot, without once touching the ground. Mr Miller had previously done the hole-in-one on four occasions.

Balls Hit To and From Great Heights

- In 1798 two Edinburgh golfers undertook to drive a ball over the spire of St Giles' Cathedral, Edinburgh, for a wager. Mr Sceales, of Leith, and Mr Smellie, a printer, were each allowed six shots and succeeded in sending the balls well over the weather-cock, a height of more than 160 feet from the ground.
- Some years later Donald McLean, an Edinburgh lawyer, won a substantial bet by driving a ball over the Melville Monument in St Andrew Square, Edinburgh – height, 154 feet.
- Tom Morris in 1860, at the famous bridge of Ballochmyle, stood in the quarry beneath and, from a stick elevated horizontally, attempted to send golf balls over the bridge. He could raise them only to the pathway, 400 feet high, which was in itself a great feat with the gutta ball.
- Captain Ernest Carter, on 28th September, 1922, drove a ball from the roadway at the 1st tee on Harlech Links against the wall of Harlech Castle. The embattlements are 200 feet over the level of the roadway, and the point where the ball struck the embattlements was 180 yards from the point where the ball was teed. Captain Carter, who was laid odds of £100 to £1, used a baffy.
- In 1896 Freddie Tait, then a subaltern in the Black Watch, drove a ball from the Rookery, the highest building on Edinburgh Castle, in a match against a brother officer to hole out in the fountain in Princes Street Gardens 350 feet below and about 300 yards distant.
- Prior to the 1977 Lancôme Tournament in Paris, Arnold Palmer hit three balls from the second stage of the Eiffel Tower, over 300 feet above ground. The longest was measured at 403 yards. One ball was hooked and hit a bus but no serious damage was done as all traffic had been stopped for safety reasons.
- Long drives have been made from mountain peaks, across the gorge at Victoria Falls, from the Pyramids, high buildings in New York, and from many other similar places. As an illustration of such freakish *drives* a member of the New York Rangers' Hockey Team from the top of Mount Edith Cavell, 11,033 feet high, drove a ball which struck the Ghost Glacier 5,000 feet below and bounced off the rocky ledge another 1,000 feet – a total drop of 2,000 yards. Later, in June, 1968, from Pikes Peak, Colorado (14,110 feet), Arthur Lynskey hit a ball which travelled 200 yards horizontally but 2 miles vertically.

Remarkable Shots

- Remarkable shots are as numerous as the grains of sand; around every 19th hole, legends are recalled of astounding shots. One shot is commemorated by a memorial tablet at the 17th hole at the Lytham and St Annes Club. It was made by Bobby Jones in the final round of the Open Championship in 1926. He was partnered by Al Watrous, another American player. They had been running neck and neck and at the end of the third round, Watrous was just leading Jones with 215 against 217. At the 16th Jones drew level then on the 17th he drove into a sandy lie in broken ground. Watrous reached the green with his second. Jones took a mashie-iron (the equivalent to a No. 4 iron today) and hit a magnificent shot to the green to get his 4. This remarkable recovery unnerved Watrous, who 3-putted, and Jones, getting another 4 at the last hole against 5, won his first Open Championship with 291 against Watrous' 293. The tablet is near the spot where Jones played his second shot.
- Arnold Palmer (USA), playing in the second round of the Australian Wills Masters tournament at Melbourne, in October, 1964, hooked his second shot at the 9th hole high into the fork of a gum tree. Climbing 20 feet up the tree, Palmer, with the head of his No. 1 iron reversed, played a *hammer* stroke and knocked the ball some 30 yards forward, followed by a brilliant chip to the green and a putt.
- In the foursome during the Ryder Cup at Moortown in 1929, Joe Turnesa hooked the American side's second shot at the last hole behind the marquee adjoining the clubhouse, Johnny Farrel then pitched the ball over the marquee on to the green only feet away from the pin and Turnesa holed out for a 4.

Miscellaneous Incidents and Strange Golfing Facts

- Gary Player of South Africa was honoured by his country by having his portrait on new postage stamps which were issued on 12th December, 1976. It was the first time a specific golfer had ever been depicted on any country's postage stamps. In 1981 the US Postal Service introduced stamps featuring Bobby Jones and Babe Zaharias. They are the first golfers to be thus honoured by the United States.
- Gary Harris, aged 18, became the first player to make five consecutive appearances for England in the European Boys Team Championship at Vilamoura, Portugal, in 1994.
- In February, 1971, the first ever golf shots on the moon's surface were played by Captain Alan Shepard, commander of the Apollo 14 spacecraft. Captain Shepard hit two balls with an iron head attached to a makeshift shaft. With a one-handed

swing he claimed he hit the first ball 200 yards aided by the reduced force of gravity on the moon. Subsequent findings put this distance in doubt. The second was a shank. Acknowledging the occasion the R&A sent Captain Shepard the following telegram: *Warmest congratulations to all of you on your great achievement and safe return. Please refer to Rules of Golf section on etiquette, paragraph 6, quote – before leaving a bunker a player should carefully fill up all holes made by him therein, unquote.* Shepard presented the club to the USGA Museum in 1974.

● Charles (Chick) Evans competed in every US Amateur Championship held between 1907 and 1962 by which time he was 72 years old. This amounted to 50 consecutive occasions discounting the six years of the two World Wars when the championship was not held.

● In winning the 1977 US Open at Southern Hills CC, Tulsa, Oklahoma, Hubert Green had to contend with a death threat. Coming off the 14th green in the final round, he was advised by USGA officials that a phone call had been received saying that he would be killed. Green decided that play should continue and happily he went on to win, unharmed.

● It was discovered at the 1977 USPGA Championship that the clubs with which Tom Watson had won the Open Championship and the US Masters earlier in the year were illegal, having grooves which exceeded the permitted specifications. The set he used in winning the 1975 Open Championship were then flown out to him and they too were found to be illegal. No retrospective action was taken.

● Mrs Fred Daly, wife of the former Open champion, saved the clubhouse of Balmoral GC, Belfast, from destruction when three men entered the professionals' shop on 5th August, 1976 and left a bag containing a bomb outside the shop beside the clubhouse when refused money. Mrs Daly carried the bag over to a hedge some distance away where the bomb exploded 15 minutes later. The only damage was broken windows. On the same day several hours afterwards, Dungannon GC in Co Tyrone suffered extensive damage to the clubhouse from terrorist bombs. Co Down GC, proposed venue of the 1979 home international matches suffered bomb damage in May that year and through fear for the safety of team members the 1979 matches were cancelled.

● The Army Golfing Society and St Andrews on 21st April, 1934, played a match 200-a-side, the largest golf match ever played. Play was by foursomes. The Army won 58, St Andrews 31 and 11 were halved.

● Jamie Ortiz-Patino, owner of the Valderrama Golf Club at Sotogrande, Spain, paid a record £84,000 (increased to £92,400 with 10 per cent buyers premium) for a late seventeenth- or early eighteenth-century rake iron offered at auction in Musselburgh in July, 1992. The iron, which had been kept in a garden shed, was bought to be exhibited in a museum being created in Valderrama.

● A Christie's golf auction during the week of the 1991 Open Championship created two world records. An American dealer bought a blacksmith-made iron club head dating from the seventeenth century for £44,000. It had been found 10 years before in a hedge near the North Berwick Golf Club in Scotland. Also, £165,000 was paid by a Japanese collector for an oil painting by Sir Francis Grant (1810–1878) of the 1823 Royal & Ancient captain, John Whyte-Melville, standing beside the Swilcan Burn at St Andrews. The same Japanese buyer successfully bid £35,200 for a rare gutty golf ball marking device from the workshops of Old Tom Morris in St Andrews, while an unused feathery golf ball by Allan Robertson fetched £11,000.

● In 1986 Alistair Risk and three colleagues on the 17th green at Brora, Sutherland, watched a cow giving birth to twin calves between the markers on the 18th tee, causing them to play their next tee shots from in front of the tee. Their application for a ruling from the R&A brought a Rules Committee reply that while technically a rule had been broken, their action was considered within the spirit of the game and there should be no penalty. The Secretary added that the Rules Committee hoped that mother and twins were doing well.

● In view of the increasing number of people crossing the road (known as Granny Clark's Wynd) which runs across the first and 18th fairways of the Old Course, St Andrews, as a right of way, the St Andrews Links committee decided in 1969 to control the flow by erecting traffic lights, with appropriate green for go, yellow for caution and red for stop. The lights are controlled from the starter's box on the first tee. Golfers on the first tee must wait until the lights turn to green before driving off and a notice has been erected at the Wynd warning pedestrians not to cross at yellow or stop.

● A traffic light for golfers was also installed in 1971 on one of Japan's most congested courses. After putting on the uphill 9th hole of the Fukuoka course in Southern Japan, players have to switch on a go-ahead signal for following golfers waiting to play their shots to the green.

● A 22-year-old professional at Brett Essex GC, Brentwood, David Moore, who was playing in the Mufulira Open in Zambia in 1976, was shot dead it is alleged by the man with whom he was staying for the duration of the tournament. It appeared his host then shot himself.

● Peggy Carrick and her daughter, Angela Uzielli, won the Mothers and Daughters Tournament at Royal Mid-Surrey in 1994 for the 21st time.

● Patricia Shepherd has won the ladies' club championship at Turriff GC Aberdeenshire 30 consecutive times from 1959 to 1988.

● Mrs Jackie Mercer won the South African

Ladies' Championship in 1979, 31 years after her first victory in the event as Miss Jacqueline Smith.

● During the Royal & Ancient medal meeting on 25th September, 1907, a member of the Royal & Ancient drove a ball which struck the sharp point of a hatpin in the hat of a lady who was crossing the course. The ball was so firmly impaled that it remained in position. The lady was not hurt.

● John Cook, former English Amateur champion, narrowly escaped death during an attempted coup against King Hassan of Morocco in July 1971. Cook had been playing in a tournament arranged by King Hassan, a keen golfer, and was at the King's birthday party in Rabat when rebels broke into the party demanding that the king give up his throne. Cook and many others present were taken hostage.

● When playing from the 9th tee at Lossiemouth golf course in June, 1971, Martin Robertson struck a Royal Navy jet aircraft which was coming in to land at the nearby airfield. The plane was not damaged.

● At a court in Inglewood, California, in 1978, Jim Brown was convicted of beating and choking an opponent during a dispute over where a ball should have been placed on the green.

● During the Northern Ireland troubles a home-made hand grenade was found in a bunker at Dungannon GC, Co Tyrone, on Sunday, 12th September, 1976.

● Tiger Woods, 18, became both the youngest and the first black golfer to win the United States Amateur Championship at Sawgrass in 1994.

● To mark the centenary of the Jersey Golf Club in 1978, the Jersey Post Office issued a set of four special stamps featuring Jersey's most famous golfer, Harry Vardon. The background of the 13p stamp was a brief biography of Vardon's career reproduced from the Golfer's Handbook.

● Forty-one-year-old John Mosley went for a round of golf at Delaware Park GC, Buffalo, New York, in July, 1972. He stepped on to the first tee and was challenged over a green fee by an official guard. A scuffle developed, a shot was fired and Mosley, a bullet in his chest, died on the way to hospital. His wife was awarded $131,250 in an action against the City of Buffalo and the guard. The guard was sentenced to 7½ years for second-degree manslaughter.

● When three competitors in a 1968 Pennsylvania pro-am event were about to drive from the 16th tee, two bandits (one with pistol) suddenly emerged from the bushes, struck one of the players and robbed them of wrist watches and $300.

● In the 1932 Walker Cup match at Brooklyn, Leonard Crawley succeeded in denting the cup. An errant iron shot to the 18th green hit the cup, which was on display outside the clubhouse.

● Three golf officials appeared in court in Johannesburg, South Africa, accused of violating a 75-year-old Sunday Observance Law by staging the final round of the South African PGA championship on Sunday, 28th February, 1971. The championship should have been completed on the Saturday but heavy rain prevented any play.

● In the Open Championship of 1876, at St Andrews, Bob Martin and David Strath tied at 176. A protest was lodged against Strath alleging he played his approach to the 17th green and struck a spectator. The Royal & Ancient ordered the replay, but Strath refused to play off the tie until a decision had been given on the protest. No decision was given and Bob Martin was declared the Champion.

● At Rose Bay, New South Wales, on 11th July, 1931, DJ Bayly MacArthur, on stepping into a bunker, began to sink. MacArthur, who weighed 14 stone, shouted for help. He was rescued when up to the armpits. He had stepped on a patch of quicksand, aggravated by excess of moisture.

● The late Bobby Cruickshank was the victim of his own jubilation in the 1934 US Open at Merion. In the 4th round while in with a chance of winning he half-topped his second shot at the 11th hole. The ball was heading for a pond in front of the green but instead of ending up in the water it hit a rock and bounced on to the green. In his delight Cruickshank threw his club into the air only to receive a resounding blow on the head as it returned to earth.

● A dog with an infallible nose for finding lost golf balls was, in 1971, given honorary membership of the Waihi GC, Hamilton, New Zealand. The dog, called Chico, was trained to search for lost balls, to be sold back to the members, the money being put into the club funds.

● By 1980 Waddy, an 11-year-old beagle belonging to Bob Inglis, the secretary of Brokenhurst Manor GC, had found over 35,000 golf balls.

● Herbert M Hepworth, Headingley, Leeds, Lord Mayor of Leeds in 1906, scored one thousand holes in 2, a feat which took him 30 years to accomplish. It was celebrated by a dinner in 1931 at the Leeds club. The first 2 of all was scored on 12th June, 1901, at Cobble Hall Course, Leeds, and the 1,000th in 1931 at Alwoodley, Leeds. Hepworth died in November, 1942.

● Fiona MacDonald was the first female to play in the Oxford and Cambridge University match at Ganton in 1986.

● Mrs Sara Gibbon won the Farnham (Surrey) Club's Grandmother's competition 48 hours after her first grand-child was born.

● At Carnoustie in the first qualifying round for the 1952 Scottish Amateur Championship a competitor drove three balls in succession out of bounds at the 1st hole and thereupon withdrew.

● In 1993, the Clark family from Hagley GC, Worcestershire, set a record for the county's three major professional events. The Worcestershire stroke play championship was won by Finlay Clark, the eldest son, who beat his father, Iain, and younger brother Cameron, who tied second.

In the county match play it was the turn of Iain, who beat his son, Finlay, by two and one in the final. Cameron won the play-off for third place. Then in the Worcestershire Annual Pro-Am it was the turn of Cameron, with his brother, Finlay, second and father, Iain, third. To add to the achievements of the family, Cameron also won the Midland Professional Match Play Championship.

● During a Captain–Pro foursomes challenge match at Chelmsford in 1993, Club Professional, Dennis Bailey, put the ball into a hole only once in all 18 holes – when he holed-in-one at the fourth.

Strange Local Rules

● The Duke of Windsor, who played on an extraordinary variety of the world's courses, once took advantage of a local rule at Jinja in Uganda and lifted his ball from a hippo's footprint without penalty.

● At the Glen Canyon course in Arizona a local rule provides that *If your ball lands within a club length of a rattlesnake you are allowed to move the ball.*

● Another local rule in Uganda read: *If a ball comes to rest in dangerous proximity to a crocodile, another ball may be dropped.*

● The 6th hole at Koolan Island GC, Western Australia also serves as a local air strip and a local rule reads *Aircraft and vehicular traffic have right of way at all times.*

● A local rule at the RAF Waddington GC reads *When teeing off from the 2nd, right of way must be given to taxi-ing aircraft.*

Record Scoring

The Open Championship

Most times champions

6 Harry Vardon, 1896-98-99-1903-11-14
5 James Braid, 1901-05-06-08-10; JH Taylor, 1984-95-1900-09-13; Peter Thomson, 1954-55-56-58-65; Tom Watson, 1975-77-80-82-83

Most times runner-up

7 Jack Nicklaus, 1964-67-68-72-76-77-79
6 JH Taylor, 1896-1904-05-06-07-14

Oldest winner

Old Tom Morris, 46 years 99 days, 1867
Roberto De Vicenzo, 44 years 93 days, 1967

Youngest winner

Young Tom Morris, 17 years 5 months 8 days, 1868
Willie Auchterlonie, 21 years 24 days, 1893
Severiano Ballesteros, 22 years 3 months 12 days, 1979

Youngest and oldest competitor

John Ball, 14 years, 1878
Gene Sarazen, 71 years 4 months 13 days, 1973

Widest margin of victory

13 strokes Old Tom Morris, 1862
12 strokes Young Tom Morris, 1870
8 strokes JH Taylor, 1900 and 1913; James Braid, 1908
6 strokes Bobby Jones, 1927; Walter Hagen, 1929; Arnold Palmer, 1962; Johnny Miller, 1976

Lowest winning aggregates

267 Greg Norman, 66-68-69-64, Sandwich, 1993
268 Tom Watson, 68-70-65-65, Turnberry, 1977; Nick Price, 69-66-67-66, Turnberry, 1994
270 Nick Faldo, 67-65-67-71, St Andrews, 1990

Lowest aggregate by runner-up

269 (68-70-65-66), Jack Nicklaus, Turnberry, 1977; (69-63-70-67) Nick Faldo, Sandwich, 1993; (68-66-68-67) Jesper Parnevik, Turnberry, 1994

Lowest aggregate by an amateur

281 (68-72-70-71), Iain Pyman, Sandwich, 1993

Lowest round

63 Mark Hayes, second round, Turnberry, 1977; Isao Aoki, third round, Muirfield, 1980; Greg Norman, second round, Turnberry, 1986; Jodie Mudd, fourth round, Royal Birkdale, 1991; Nick Faldo, second round, Sandwich, 1993; Payne Stewart, fourth round, Sandwich, 1993

Lowest round by an amateur

66 Frank Stranahan, fourth round, Troon, 1950

Lowest first round

64 Craig Stadler, Royal Birkdale, 1983; Christy O'Connor Jr, Royal St George's, 1985; Rodger Davis, Muirfield, 1987; Steve Pate, Ray Floyd, Muirfield, 1992

Lowest second round

63 Mark Hayes, Turnberry, 1977; Greg Norman, Turnberry, 1986; Nick Faldo, Sandwich, 1993

Lowest third round

63 Isao Aoki, Muirfield, 1980; Paul Broadhurst, St Andrews, 1990

Lowest fourth round

63 Jodie Mudd, Royal Birkdale, 1991; Payne Stewart, Sandwich, 1993

Lowest first 36 holes

130 (66-64), Nick Faldo, Muirfield, 1992
132 (67-65), Henry Cotton, Sandwich, 1934; Nick Faldo (67-65) and Greg Norman (66-66), St Andrews, 1990; Nick Faldo (69-63), Sandwich, 1993

Lowest second 36 holes

130 (65-65), Tom Watson, Turnberry, 1977 (64-66) Ian Baker-Finch, R. Birkdale, 1991; (66-64) Anders Forsbrand, Turnberry, 1994

Lowest first 54 holes

199 (67-65-67), Nick Faldo, St Andrews, 1990; (66-64-69) Nick Faldo, Muirfield, 1992

Lowest final 54 holes

199 (66-67-66) Nick Price, Turnberry, 1994
200 (70-65-65), Tom Watson, Turnberry, 1977; (63-70-67), Nick Faldo, Sandwich, 1993 (66-64-70), Fuzzy Zoeller, Turnberry, 1994

Lowest 9 holes

28 Denis Durnian, first 9, Royal Birkdale, 1983

Champions in three decades

Harry Vardon, 1986, 1903, 1911
JH Taylor, 1894, 1900, 1913
Gary Player, 1959, 1968, 1974

Biggest span between first and last victories

19 years, JH Taylor, 1894-1913
18 years, Harry Vardon, 1896-1914
15 years, Willie Park, 1860–75
15 years, Gary Player, 1959-74
14 years, Henry Cotton, 1934-48

Successive victories

4 Young Tom Morris, 1868-72 (no championship in 1871)
3 Jamie Anderson, 1877-79; Bob Ferguson, 1880-82, Peter Thomson, 1954-56
2 Old Tom Morris, 1861-62; JH Taylor, 1894-95; Harry Vardon, 1898-99; James Braid, 1905-06; Bobby Jones, 1926-27; Walter Hagen, 1928-29; Bobby Locke, 1949-50; Arnold Palmer, 1961-62; Lee Trevino, 1971-72; Tom Watson, 1982-83

Victories by amateurs

3 Bobby Jones, 1926-27-30
2 Harold Hilton, 1892-97
1 John Ball, 1890
Roger Wethered lost a play-off in 1921

Highest number of top five finishes

16 JH Taylor and Jack Nicklaus
15 Harry Vardon and James Braid

Players with four rounds under 70

Greg Norman (66-68-69-64), Sandwich, 1993; Ernie Els (68-69-69-68), Sandwich, 1993; Nick Price (69-66-67-66), Turnberry, 1994; Jesper Parnevik (68-66-68-67), Turnberry, 1994

Highest number of rounds under 70

31 Jack Nicklaus
29 Nick Faldo
26 Tom Watson
21 Lee Trevino
20 Greg Norman
19 Severiano Ballesteros
18 Nick Price

Outright leader after every round

Willie Auchterlonie, 1893; JH Taylor, 1894 and 1900; James Braid, 1908; Ted Ray, 1912; Bobby Jones, 1927; Gene Sarazen, 1932; Henry Cotton, 1934; Tom Weiskopf, 1973

Record leads (since 1892)

After 18 holes
4 strokes, James Braid, 1908; Bobby Jones, 1927; Henry Cotton, 1934; Christy O'Connor Jr, 1985

After 36 holes:
9 strokes, Henry Cotton, 1934

After 54 holes:
10 strokes, Henry Cotton, 1934
7 strokes, Tony Lema, 1964
6 strokes, James Braid, 1908
5 strokes, Arnold Palmer, 1962; Bill Rogers, 1981; Nick Faldo, 1990

Champions with each round lower than previous one

Jack White, 1904, Sandwich, 80-75-72-69
James Braid, 1906, Muirfield, 77-76-74-73
Ben Hogan, 1953, Carnoustie, 73-71-70-68
Gary Player, 1959, Muirfield, 75-71-70-68

Champion with four rounds the same

Densmore Shute, 1933, St Andrews, 73-73-73-73 (excluding the play-off)

Biggest Variation between rounds of a champion

14 strokes, Henry Cotton, 1934, second round 65, fourth round 79
11 strokes, Jack White, 1904, first round 80, fourth round 69; Greg Norman, 1986, first round 74, second round 63, third round 74

Biggest variation between two rounds

17 strokes, Jack Nicklaus, 1981, first round 83, second round 66; Ian Baker-Finch, 1986, first round 86, second round 69

Best comeback by champions

After 18 holes:
Harry Vardon, 1896, 11 strokes behind the leader

After 36 holes:
George Duncan, 1920, 13 strokes behind leader

After 54 holes:
Jim Barnes, 1925, 5 strokes behind the leader
Of non-champions, Greg Norman, 1989, seven strokes behind the leader and lost in a play-off

Best finishing round by a champion

64 Greg Norman, Sandwich, 1993
65 Tom Watson, Turnberry, 1977; Severiano Ballesteros, Royal Lytham, 1988

Worst finishing round by a champion since 1920

79 Henry Cotton, Sandwich, 1934
78 Reg Whitcombe, Sandwich, 1938
77 Walter Hagen, Hoylake, 1924

Best opening round by a champion

66 Peter Thomson, Royal Lytham, 1958; Nick Faldo, Muirfield, 1992; Greg Norman, Sandwich, 1993
67 Henry Cotton, Sandwich, 1934; Tom Watson, Royal Birkdale, 1983; Severiano Ballesteros, Royal Lytham, 1988; Nick Faldo, St Andrews, 1990

Worst opening round by a champion since 1919

80 George Duncan, Deal, 1920 (he also had a second round of 80)
77 Walter Hagen, Hoylake, 1924

Biggest Recovery in 18 Holes by a champion

George Duncan, Deal, 1920, was 13 strokes behind the leader, Abe Mitchell, after 36 holes and level after 54

Most consecutive appearances

40 Gary Player, 1955–94

Championship since 1946 with the fewest rounds under 70

St Andrews, 1946; Hoylake, 1947; Portrush, 1951; Hoylake, 1956; Carnoustie, 1968. All had only two rounds under 70

Longest course

Carnoustie, 1968, 7,252 yd (6,631m)

Largest entries

1,827 in 1993, Sandwich
1,707 in 1990, St Andrews

Courses most often used

Prestwick, 24 (but not since 1925); St Andrews, 24; Muirfield, 14; Sandwich, 12; Hoylake, 10; Royal Lytham, 8; Royal Birkdale, 7; Royal Troon and Musselburgh, 6; Carnoustie, 5; Turnberry, 3; Deal, 2; Royal Portrush and Prince's, 1

Attendances

Year	*Attendance*	*Year*	*Attendance*
1962	37,098	1979	134,501
1963	24,585	1980	131,610
1964	35,954	1981	111,987
1965	32,927	1982	133,299
1966	40,182	1983	142,892
1967	29,880	1984	193,126
1968	51,819	1985	141,619
1969	46,001	1986	134,261
1970	82,593	1987	139,189
1971	70,076	1988	191,334
1972	84,746	1989	160,639
1973	78,810	1990	207,000
1974	92,796	1991	192,154
1975	85,258	1992	150,100
1976	92,021	1993	140,100
1977	87,615	1994	128,000
1978	125,271		

Prize money

Year	*Total*	*First Prize £*	*Year*	*Total*	*First Prize £*	*Year*	*Total*	*First Prize £*
1860	nil	nil	1954	3,500	750	1978	125,000	12,500
1863	10	nil	1955	3,750	1,000	1979	155,000	15,500
1864	16	6	1958	4,850	1,000	1980	200,000	25,000
1876	20	20	1959	5,000	1,000	1982	250,000	32,000
1889	22	8	1960	7,000	1,250	1983	300,000	40,000
1891	28.50	10	1961	8,500	1,400	1984	451,000	55,000
1892	110	(Am)	1963	8,500	1,500	1985	530,000	65,000
1893	100	30	1965	10,000	1,750	1986	600,000	70,000
1910	125	50	1966	15,000	2,100	1987	650,000	75,000
1920	225	75	1968	20,000	3,000	1988	700,000	80,000
1927	275	100	1969	30,000	4,250	1989	750,000	80,000
1930	400	100	1970	40,000	5,250	1990	815,000	85,000
1931	500	100	1971	45,000	5,500	1991	900,000	90,000
1946	1,000	150	1972	50,000	5,500	1992	950,000	95,000
1949	1,700	300	1975	75,000	7,500	1993	1,000,000	100,000
1953	2,450	500	1977	100,000	10,000	1994	1,100,000	110,000

US Open

Most times champion

4 Willie Anderson, 1901-03-04-05; Bobby Jones, 1923-26-29-30; Ben Hogan, 1948-50-51-53; Jack Nicklaus, 1962-67-72-80

Most times runner-up

4 Bobby Jones, 1922-24-25-28; Sam Snead, 1937-47-49-53; Arnold Palmer, 1962-63-66-67

Oldest winner

Hale Irwin, 45 years, Medinah, 1990

Youngest winner

Johnny McDermott, 19 years, Chicago, 1911

Biggest winning margin

11 strokes Willie Smith, Baltimore, 1899

Lowest winning aggregate

272 Jack Nicklaus, Baltusrol, 1980; Lee Janzen, Baltusrol, 1993

Lowest round

63 Johnny Miller, Oakmont, 1973; Jack Nicklaus, Baltusrol, 1980; Tom Weiskopf, Baltusrol, 1980

Successive victories

3 Willie Anderson, 1903-04-05

Players with four rounds under 70

Lee Trevino, 69-68-69-69, Oak Hill, 1968; Lee Janzen, 67-67-69-69, Baltusrol, 1993

Wire to wire winners

Walter Hagen, Midlothian, 1914; Jim Barnes, Columbia, 1921; Ben Hogan, Oakmont, 1953; Tony Jacklin, Hazeltine, 1970

Best opening round by a champion

63 Jack Nicklaus, Baltusrol, 1980

Worst opening round by a champion

91 Horace Rawlins, Newport, RI, 1895
Since World War II: **76** Ben Hogan, Oakland Hills, 1951

US Masters

Most times champion

6 Jack Nicklaus, 1963-65-66-72-75-86
4 Arnold Palmer, 1958-60-62-64

Most times runner-up

4 Ben Hogan, 1942-46-54-55; Jack Nicklaus, 1964-71-77-81

Oldest winner

Jack Nicklaus, 46 years, 1986

Youngest winner

Severiano Ballesteros, 23 years, 4 days, 1980

Biggest winning margin

9 strokes Jack Nicklaus, 1965

Lowest winning aggregate

271 Jack Nicklaus, 1965; Raymond Floyd, 1976

Lowest aggregate by an amateur

281 Charles Coe, 1961 (joint second)

Lowest round

63 Nick Price, 1986

Successive victories

2 Jack Nicklaus, 1965-66; Nick Faldo, 1989-90

Players with four rounds under 70

None

Wire to wire winners

Craig Wood, 1941; Arnold Palmer, 1960; Jack Nicklaus, 1972; Raymond Floyd, 1976

Best opening round by a champion

65 Raymond Floyd, 1976

Worst opening round by a champion

75 Craig Stadler, 1982

Albatrosses

There have been three albatross twos in the Masters at Augusta National: by Gene Sarazen at the 15th in 1935, by Bruce Devlin at the eighth in 1967 and by Jeff Maggert at the 13th in 1994.

US PGA Championship

Note: The PGA was a match play event from 1916 to 1957. Since 1958 it has been played as stroke play

Most times champion

5 Walter Hagen, 1921-24-25-26-27; Jack Nicklaus 1963-71-73-75-80

Most times runner-up

4 Jack Nicklaus, 1964-65-74-83

Oldest winner

Julius Boros, 48 years 4 months 18 days, Pecan Valley, 1968

Youngest winner

Gene Sarazen, 20 years 6 months 9 days, Oakmont, 1922

Biggest winning margin

7 strokes Jack Nicklaus, Oak Hill, 1980

Lowest winning aggregate

271 Bobby Nichols, Columbus, 1964

Lowest round

63 Bruce Crampton, Firestone, 1975; Raymond Floyd, Southern Hills, 1982; Gary Player, Shoal Creek, 1984

Most successive victories

4 Walter Hagen, 1924-25-26-27

Players with four rounds under 70

Arnold Palmer, 68-69-69-69, Columbus, 1964 (tied 2nd); Ben Crenshaw, 69-67-69-67, Oakland Hills, 1979 (tied 2nd); Lee Trevino, 69-68-67-69, Shoal Creek, 1984 (1st)

Wire to wire winners

Bobby Nichols, Columbus, 1964; Raymond Floyd, Dayton, 1969; Jack Nicklaus, PGA National, 1971; Raymond Floyd, Southern Hills, 1982; Hal Sutton, Riviera, 1983

Best opening round by a champion

65 David Graham, Oakland Hills, 1979

Worst opening round by a champion

75 John Mahaffey, Oakmont, 1978

European PGA Tour

Lowest 72-hole aggregate

258 (14 under par) David Llewellyn (Wales), AGF Biarritz Open, 1988; (18 under par) Ian Woosnam (Wales), Monte Carlo Open, 1990.

259 (25 under par) Mark McNulty (Zimbabwe), German Open at Frankfurt, 1987.

Lowest 9 holes

27 (9 under par) José María Canizares (Spain), Swiss Open at Crans-sur-Sierre, 1978; (7 under par) Robert Lee (England), Johnnie Walker Monte Carlo Open at Mont Agel, 1985; (6 under par) Robert Lee, Portuguese Open at Estoril, 1987.

Lowest 18 holes

60 (11 under par) Baldovino Dassu (Italy), Swiss Open at Crans-sur-Sierre, 1971; David Llewellyn (Wales), AGF Biarritz Open, 1988; (9 under par) Ian Woosnam (Wales), Torras Monte Carlo Open at Mont Agel, 1990; (12 under par) Jamie Spence, Canon European Masters at Crans-sur-Sierre, Switzerland, 1992; (10 under par) Paul Curry, Bell's Scottish Open at Gleneagles, 1992; (9 under par) both Darren Clarke and Johan Rystrom, Monte Carlo Open at Mont Agel, 1992.

Lowest 36 holes

125 (13 under par) Sam Torrance (Scotland), Johnnie Walker Monte Carlo Open at Mont Agel, 1985; (13 under par) Lu Liang Huan (Taiwan), French Open at Biarritz, 1971; (11 under par) David Llewellyn, AGF Biarritz Open, 1988; (13 under par) Ian Woosnam, Torras Monte Carlo Open at Mont Agel, 1990.

Lowest 54 holes

192 (24 under par) Anders Forbrand (Sweden), Ebel European Masters Swiss Open at Crans-sur-Sierre, 1987.

Largest winning margin

17 strokes Bernhard Langer, Cacharel Under-25s' Championship in Nîmes, 1979.

Highest winning score

306 Peter Butler (England), Schweppes PGA Close Championship at Royal Birkdale, 1963.

US Tour

Lowest 72-hole aggregate

257 (27 under par) Mike Souchak, 60-68-64-65, Texas Open, 1955.

Lowest 18 holes

59 Sam Snead, third round, Greenbrier Open (Sam Snead Festival), White Sulphur Springs, West Virginia, 1959; Al Geiberger, second round, Danny Thomas Memphis Classic, Colonial CC, 1977 (when preferred lies were in operation); (13 under par) Chip Beck on the 6,914-yards Sunrise GC course, Las Vegas, in the third round of the Las Vegas Invitational – he finished third but won a bonus prize of $500,000 and another $500,000 for charities.

Lowest 9 holes

27 Mike Souchak, Texas Open, 1955; Andy North, BC Open, 1975.

Lowest first 36 holes

126 Tommy Bolt, 1954; Paul Azinger, 1989. (On the US mini-tour a 36-hole score of 123 was achieved by Bob Risch in the 1978 Mesa Centennial Open.)

Lowest 54 holes

189 Chandler Harper, Texas Open (last three rounds), 1954.

Largest winning margin

16 strokes J Douglas Edgar, Canadian Open Championship, 1919; Bobby Locke, Chicago Victory National Championship, 1948.

National opens – excluding Europe and USA

Lowest 72-hole aggregate

255 Peter Tupling, Nigerian Open, Lagos, 1981.

Lowest 36-hole aggregate

124 (18 under par) Sandy Lyle, Nigerian Open, Ikoyi GC, Lagos, 1978. (Lyle was in his first year as a professional.)

Lowest 18 holes

59 Gary Player, second round, Brazilian Open, Gavea GC (6,185 yards), Rio de Janeiro, 1974.

Professional events–excluding Europe and USA

Lowest 72-hole aggregate

260 Bob Charles, 66-62-69-63, Spalding Masters at Tauranga, New Zealand, 1969.

Lowest 18-hole aggregate

60 Billy Dunk (Australia), Merewether, NSW, 1970.

Lowest 9-hole aggregate

27 Bill Brask (US) at Tauranga in the New Zealand PGA in 1976.

Miscellaneous British

Women's world record

The Professional Golfers' Association in Britain claimed a women's world record for the score of 62 by Janice Arnold during a WPGA tournament in September 1990. Miss Arnold, a New Zealand professional, won the 36-hole event by 12 shots with a 17 under par total of 131 on a course of 5,815 yards at the Coventry Golf Club. The record first-round 62 with 31 out and back included seven birdies, one eagle 3 and holing of a five-iron shot for an albatross 2.

72-hole aggregate

Andrew Brooks recorded a 72-hole aggregate of 259 in winning the Skol (Scotland) tournament at Williamwood in 1974.

Lowest rounds

Playing on the ladies' course (4,020 yards) at Sunningdale on 26th September, 1961, Arthur Lees, the professional there, went round in 52, 10 under par. He went out in 26 (2, 3, 3, 4, 3, 3, 3, 3, 2) and came back in 26 (2, 3, 3, 3, 2, 3, 4, 3, 3).

AE Smith, the Woolacombe Bay professional, recorded a score of 55 in a game there with a club member on 1st January, 1936. The course measured 4,248 yards. Smith went out in 29 and came back in 26 finishing with a hole-in-one at the 18th hole.

Other low scores recorded in Britain are by CC Aylmer, an English International who went round Ranelagh in 56; George Duncan, Axenfels in 56; Harry Bannerman, Banchory in 56 in 1971; Ian Connelly, Welwyn Garden City in 56 in 1972; James Braid, Hedderwick near Dunbar in 57; H Hardman, Wirral in 58; Norman Quigley, Windermere in 58 in 1937; Robert Webster, Eaglescliffe in 58, in 1970. Harry Weetman scored 58 in a round at the 6,171 yards Croham Hurst on 30th January, 1956.

D Sewell had a round of 60 in an Alliance Meeting at Ferndown, Bournemouth, a full-size course. He scored 30 for each half and had a total of 26 putts. In September 1986, Jeffrey Burn, handicap 1 of Shrewsbury GC scored 60 in a club competition, made up of 8 birdies, an eagle and 9 pars. He was 30 out and 30 home and no 5 on his card. Andrew Sherborne, as a 20-year-old amateur, went round Cirencester in 60 strokes. Dennis Gray completed a round at Broome Manor, Swindon (6,906 yards, SSS 73) in the summer of 1976 in 60 (28 out, 32 in).

Playing over Aberdour on 13th June, 1936, Hector Thomson, British Amateur champion, 1936, and Jack McLean, former Scottish Amateur champion, each did 61 in the second round of an exhibition. McLean in his first round had a 63, which gave him an aggregate 124 for 36 holes.

Steve Tredinnick in a friendly match against business tycoon Joe Hyman scored a 61 over West Sussex (6,211 yards) in 1970. It included a hole-in-one at the 12th (198 yards) and a 2 at the 17th (445 yards).

Another round of 61 on a full-size course was achieved by 18-year-old Michael Jones on his home course, Worthing GC (6,274 yards) in the first round of the President's Cup in May, 1974.

In the Second City Pro-Am tournament in 1970, at Handsworth, Simon Fogarty did the second 9 holes in 27 against the par of 36.

Miscellaneous USA

Lowest rounds

The lowest known scores recorded for 18 holes in America are 55 by EF Staugaard in 1935 over the 6,419 yards Montebello Park, California, and 55 by Homero Blancas in 1962 over the 5,002 yards Premier course in Longview, Texas. Staugaard in his round had 2 eagles, 13 birdies and 3 pars.

Equally outstanding is a round of 58 (13 under par) achieved by a 13-year-old boy, Douglas Beecher, on 6th July, 1976 at Pitman CC, New Jersey. The course measured 6,180 yards from the back tees, and the middle tees, off which Douglas played, were estimated by the club professional to reduce the yardage by under 180 yards.

In 1941 at a course in Portsmouth, Virginia, measuring 6,100 yards, Chandler Harper scored 58.

Jack Nicklaus in an exhibition match at Breakers Club, Palm Beach, California, in 1973 scored 59 over the 6,200 yards course.

Ben Hogan, practising on a 7,006-yard course at Palm Beach, Florida, went round in 61 – 11 under par.

The lowest 9-hole score in America is 25, held jointly by Bill Burke over the second half of the 6,384 yards Normandie CC, St Louis in May, 1970 at the age of 29; by Daniel Cavin who had seven 3s and two 2s on the par 36 Bill Brewer Course, Texas in September, 1959; and by Douglas Beecher over the second half of Pitman CC, New Jersey on 6th July, 1976 at the amazingly young age of 13. The back 9 holes of the Pitman course measured 3,150 yards (par 35) from the back tees, but even though Douglas played off the middle tees, the yardage was still over 3,000 yards for the 9 holes. He scored 8 birdies and 1 eagle.

Horton Smith scored 119 for two consecutive rounds in winning the Catalina Open in California in December, 1928. The course, however, measured only 4,700 yards.

Miscellaneous – excluding GB and USA

Tony Jacklin won the 1973 Los Lagartos Open with an aggregate of 261, 27 under par.

Henry Cotton in 1950 had a round of 56 at Monte Carlo (29 out, 27 in).

In a Pro-Am tournament prior to the 1973 Nigerian Open, British professional David Jagger went round in 59.

Max Banbury recorded a 9-hole score of 26 at Woodstock, Ontario, playing in a competition in 1952.

Women's

The lowest score recorded on a full-size course by a woman is 62 by Mary (Mickey) Wright of Dallas, Texas. This was achieved on the Hogan Park course (6,286 yards) at Midland, Texas, in November, 1964. It was equalled by 16-year-old Rae Rothfelder on 9th July, 1978 at Diamond Oak G&CC, Fort Worth, Texas, a course measuring 6,124 yards.

The lowest 72-hole score on the US Ladies' PGA circuit is 271 by Hollis Stacy in the 1977 Rail Muscular Dystrophy.

The lowest 9-hole score on the US Ladies' PGA circuit is 29, first achieved by Marlene Bauer Hagge in 1971 and equalled by Carol Mann (1975), Pat Bradley (1978 and again in 1979), Alexandra Reinhardt (1978), and Silvia Bertolaccini (1979).

The lowest score for 36 holes on the USLPGA circuit is 131 achieved by Kathy Martin in the 1976 Birmingham Classic and by Silvia Bertolaccini in the 1977 Lady Keystone Open.

The lowest 9-hole score on the WPGA circuit is 30 by Susan Moon at Valbonne in 1979.

In the Women's World Team Championship in Mexico in 1966, Mrs Belle Robertson, playing for the British team, was the only player to break 70. She scored 69 in the third round.

At Westgate-on-Sea GC (measuring 5,002 yards), Wanda Morgan scored 60 in an open tournament in 1929.

Since scores cannot properly be taken in match play no stroke records can be made in match play events. Nevertheless we record here two outstanding examples of low scoring in the finals of national championships. Mrs Catherine Lacoste de Prado is credited with a score of 62 in the first round of the 36-hole final of the 1972 French Ladies' Open Championship at Morfontaine. She went out in 29 and came back in 33 on a course measuring 5,933 yards. In the final of the English Ladies' Championship at Woodhall Spa in 1954, Frances Stephens (later Mrs Smith) did the first nine holes against Elizabeth Price (later Mrs Fisher) in 30. It included a hole-in-one at the 5th. The nine holes measured 3,280 yards.

Amateurs

National championships

The following examples of low scoring cannot be regarded as genuine stroke play records since they took place in match play. Nevertheless they are recorded here as being worthy of note.

Michael Bonallack in beating David Kelley in the final of the English championship in 1968 at Ganton did the first 18 holes in 61 with only one putt under two feet conceded. He was out in 32 and home in 29. The par of the course was 71.

Charles McFarlane, playing in the fourth round of the Amateur Championship at Sandwich in 1914 against Charles Evans did the first nine holes in 31, winning by 6 and 5.

This score of 31 at Sandwich was equalled on several occasions in later years there. Then, in 1948, Richard Chapman of America went out in 29 in the fourth round eventually beating Hamilton McInally, Scottish Champion in 1937, 1939 and 1947, by 9 and 7.

In the fourth round of the Amateur Championship at Hoylake in 1953, Harvie Ward, the holder, did the first nine holes against Frank Stranahan in 32. The total yardage for the holes was 3,474 yards and included one hole of 527 yards and five holes over 400 yards. Ward won by one hole.

Francis Ouimet in the first round of the American Amateur Championship in 1932 against George Voigt did the first nine holes in 30. Ouimet won by 6 and 5.

Open competitions

The 1970 South African Dunlop Masters Tournament was won by an amateur, John Fourie, with a score of 266, 14 under par. He led from start to finish with rounds of 65, 68, 65, 68, finally winning by six shots from Gary Player.

Jim Ferrier, Manly, won the New South Wales championship at Sydney in 1935 with 266. His rounds were: 67, 65, 70, 64, giving an aggregate 16 strokes better than that of the runner-up. At the time he did this amazing score Ferrier was 20 years old and an amateur.

Holes below par

Most holes below par

EF Staugaard in a round of 55 over the 6,419 yards Montbello Park, California, in 1935, had 2 eagles, 13 birdies and 3 pars.

American Jim Clouette scored 14 birdies in a round at Longhills GC, Arkansas, in 1974. The course measured 6,257 yards.

Jimmy Martin in his round of 63 in the Swallow-Penfold at Stoneham in 1961 had 1 eagle and 11 birdies.

In the Ricarton Rose Bowl at Hamilton, Scotland, in August, 1981, Wilma Aitken, a women's amateur internationalist, had 11 birdies in a round of 64, including 9 consecutive birdies from the 3rd to the 11th.

Mrs Donna Young scored 9 birdies and 1 eagle in one round in the 1975 Colgate European Women's Open.

Consecutive holes below par

Lionel Platts had 10 consecutive birdies from the 8th to 17th holes at Blairgowrie GC during a practice round for the 1973 Sumrie Better-Ball tournament.

Roberto De Vicenzo in the Argentine Centre of the Republic Championship in April, 1974 at the Cordoba GC, Villa Allende, broke par at each of the first 9 holes. (By starting his round at the 10th hole they were in fact the second 9 holes played by Vicenzo.) He had 1 eagle (at the 7th hole) and 8 birdies. The par for the 3,602 yards half was 37, completed by Vicenzo in 27.

Nine consecutive holes under par have been recorded by Claude Harmon in a friendly match over Winged Foot GC, Mamaroneck, NY, in 1931; by Les Hardie at Eastern GC, Melbourne, in April, 1934; by Jimmy Smith at McCabe GC, Nashville, Tenn, in 1969; by 13-year-old Douglas Beecher, in 1976, at Pitman CC, New Jersey; by Rick Sigda at Greenfield CC, Mass, in 1979; and by Ian Jelley at Brookman Park in 1994.

TW Egan in winning the East of Ireland Championship in 1962 at Baltray had 8 consecutive birdies (2nd to 9th) in the third round.

On the United States PGA tour, 8 consecutive holes below par have been achieved by three players – Bob Goalby in the 1961 St Petersburg Open, Fuzzy Zoeller in the 1976 Quad Cities Open and Dewey Arnette in the 1987 Buick Open.

Fred Couples set a PGA European Tour record with 12 birdies in a round of 61 during the 1991 Scandinavian Masters on the 72-par Drottningholm course. Ian Woosnam, Tony Johnstone and Severiano Ballesteros share another record with 8 successive birdies.

The United States Ladies' PGA record is 7 consecutive holes below par achieved by Carol Mann in the Borden Classic at Columbus, Ohio in 1975.

Miss Wilma Aitken recorded 9 successive birdies (from the 3rd to the 11th) in the 1981 Ricarton Rose Bowl.

Low scoring rarities

At Standerton GC, South Africa, in May 1937, FF Bennett, playing for Standerton against Witwatersrand University, did the second hole, 110 yards, in three 2s and a 1. Standerton is a 9-hole course, and in the match Bennett had to play four rounds.

In 1957 a four-ball comprising HJ Marr, E Stevenson, C Bennett and WS May completed the 2nd hole (160 yards) in the grand total of 6 strokes. Marr and Stevenson both holed in 1 while Bennett and May both made 2.

The old Meadow Brook Club of Long Island, USA, had five par 3 holes and George Low in a round there in the 1950s scored 2 at each of them.

In a friendly match on a course near Chicago in 1971, assistant professional Tom Doty (23 years) had a remarkable low run over four consecutive holes: 4th (500 yards) 2; 5th (360 yards, dogleg) 1; 6th (175 yards) 1; 7th (375 yards) 2.

RW Bishop, playing in the Oxley Park, July medal competition in 1966, scored three consecutive 2s. They occurred at the 12th, 13th and 14th holes which measured 151, 500 and 136 yards respectively.

In the 1959 PGA Close Championship at Ashburnham, Bob Boobyer scored five 2s in one of the rounds.

American Art Wall scored three consecutive 2s in the first round of the US Masters in 1974. They were at the 4th, 5th and 6th holes, the par of which was 3, 4 and 3.

Nine consecutive 3s have been recorded by RH Corbett in 1916 in the semi-final of the Tangye Cup; by Dr James Stothers of Ralston GC over the 2,056 yards 9-hole course at Carradale, Argyll during the summer of 1971; by Irish internationalist Brian Kissock in the Homebright Open at Carnalea GC, Bangor in June, 1975; and by American club professional Ben Toski.

The most consecutive 3s in a British PGA event is seven by Eric Brown in the Dunlop at Gleneagles (Queen's Course) in 1960.

Hubert Green scored eight consecutive 3s in a round in the 1980 US Open.

The greatest number of 3s in one round in a British PGA event is 11 by Brian Barnes in the 1977 Skol Lager tournament at Gleneagles.

Fewest putts

The lowest known number of putts in one round is 14, achieved by Colin Collen-Smith in a round at Betchworth Park, Dorking in June, 1947. He single-putted 14 greens and chipped into the hole on four occasions. Professional Richard Stanwood in a round at Riverside GC, Pocatello, Idaho on 17th May, 1976 took 15 putts, chipping into the hole on five occasions. Several instances of 16 putts in one round have been recorded in friendly games.

For 9 holes, the fewest putts is 5 by Ron Stutesman for the first 9 holes at Orchard Hills G&CC, Washington, USA in 1978.

Walter Hagen in nine consecutive holes on one occasion took only seven putts. He holed long putts on seven greens and chips at the other two holes.

In competitive stroke rounds in Britain and Ireland, the lowest known number of putts in one round is 18, in a medal round at Portpatrick Dunskey GC, Wilmslow GC professional Fred Taggart is reported to have taken 20 putts in one round of the 1934 Open Championship. Padraigh Hogan (Elm Park), when competing in the Junior Scratch Cup at Carlow in 1976, took only 20 putts in a round of 67.

The fewest putts in a British PGA event is believed to be 22 by Bill Large in a qualifying round over Moor Park High Course for the 1972 Benson and Hedges Match Play.

Overseas, outside the United States of America, the fewest putts is 19 achieved by Robert Wynn (GB) in a round in the 1973 Nigerian Open and by Mary Bohen (US) in the final round of the 1977 South Australian Open at Adelaide.

The USPGA record for fewest putts in one round is 18, achieved by Andy North (1990); Kenny Knox (1989); Mike McGee (1987) and Sam Trehan (1979). For 9 holes the record is 8 putts by Kenny Knox (1989); Jim Colbert (1987) and Sam Trehan (1979).

The fewest putts recorded for a 72-hole US PGA Tour event is 93 by Kenny Knox in the 1989 Heritage Classic at Harbour Town Golf Links.

The fewest putts recorded by a woman is 17, by Joan Joyce in the Lady Michelob tournament, Georgia in May, 1982.

Index